Part of the four-volume Microsoft® .NET Framework 1.1 Class Library Reference: System

M000191340

MICROSOFT®
.NET
FRAMEWORK 1.1
CLASS LIBRARY REFERENCE

VOLUME 3: SYSTEM.IO.ISOLATEDSTORAGE THROUGH SYSTEM.RUNTIME. INTEROPSERVICES.EXPANDO

Microsoft®
.net

PUBLISHED BY
Microsoft Press
A Division of Microsoft Corporation
One Microsoft Way
Redmond, Washington 98052-6399

Library of Congress Cataloging-in-Publication Data
Microsoft .NET Framework 1.1 Class Library Reference Volumes 1-4: System / Microsoft Corporation.
    p. cm.
  Includes index.
  ISBN 0-7356-1555-1
  1. Microsoft .NET framework.   2. Internet programming.   3. Computer
software--Development.   I. Microsoft Corporation.

  QA76.76.M52 M53   2002
  005.2'76--dc21   2002071763

Printed and bound in the United States of America.

1 2 3 4 5 6 7 8 9   QWT   8 7 6 5 4 3

Distributed in Canada by H.B. Fenn and Company Ltd.

A CIP catalogue record for this book is available from the British Library.

Microsoft Press books are available through booksellers and distributors worldwide. For further information about international editions, contact your local Microsoft Corporation office or contact Microsoft Press International directly at fax (425) 936-7329. Visit our Web site at www.microsoft.com/mspress. Send comments to *mspinput@microsoft.com*.

For Microsoft: **For mediaService, Siegen, Germany:**
Acquisitions Editor: Juliana Aldous   **Project Manager:** Gerhard Alfes
Project Editor: Dick Brown

SubAssy Part No. X08-72929
Body Part No. X08-72930

Contents

Document Conventions

The following table shows the typographic conventions used in this book.

Convention	Description	Example
Monospace	Indicates source code, code examples, input to the command line, application output, code lines embedded in text, and variables and code elements.	`Public Class`
Bold	Indicates most predefined programming elements, including namespaces, classes, delegates, objects, interfaces, methods, functions, macros, structures, constructors, properties, events, enumerations, fields, operators, statements, directives, data types, keywords, exceptions, non-HTML attributes, and configuration t ags, as well as registry keys, subkeys, and values. Also indicates the following HTML elements: attributes, directives, keywords, values, and headers.	**Path** class **Resolve** method
	In addition, indicates required user input, including command-line options, that must be entered exactly as shown.	
Italic	Indicates placeholders, most often method or function parameters and HTML placeholders; these placeholders represent information that must be supplied by the implementation or the user.	*context* parameter
	For command-line input, indicates parameter values.	
Capital letters	Indicates the names of keys and key sequences.	ENTER CTRL+R
Plus sign	Indicates a combination of keys. For example, ALT+F1 means to h old down the ALT key while pressing the F1 key.	ALT+F1
↵	The "rundown" is a line-continuation character this book uses in code samples for Visual Basic, C#, C++, and JScript. It indicates that a code statement is too long to fit on one line in the book, and so has been continued on the next line.	`string strSource ="We will` ↵ `search on this string";`
	All code samples are available in the .NET Framework 1.1 online documentation, which is also included in the Visual Studio .NET 2003 Help.	

System.IO.Isolated-Storage Namespace

The **System.IO.IsolatedStorage** namespace contains types that allow the creation and use of isolated stores. With these stores, you can read and write data that less trusted code cannot access and prevent the exposure of sensitive information that can be saved elsewhere on the file system. Data is stored in compartments that are isolated by the current user and by the assembly in which the code exists. Additionally, data can be isolated by domain. Roaming profiles can be used in conjunction with isolated storage so isolated stores will travel with the user's profile. The **IsolatedStorageScope** enumeration indicates different types of isolation. For more information about when to use isolated storage, see the **Performing Isolated Storage Tasks** topic.

The **System.IO.IsolatedStorage.IsolatedStorageFileClassTopic** class provides most of the necessary functionality for isolated storage. Use this class to obtain, delete and manage isolated storage. **System.IO.IsolatedStorage.IsolatedStorageFileStreamClassTopic** handles reading and writing files to a store. This is similar to reading and writing in standard File I/O classes. For more information about I/O, see the **System.IO** namespace.

INormalizeForIsolatedStorage Interface

Enables comparisons between an isolated store and an application domain and assembly's evidence.

```
[Visual Basic]
Public Interface INormalizeForIsolatedStorage
[C#]
public interface INormalizeForIsolatedStorage
[C++]
public __gc __interface INormalizeForIsolatedStorage
[JScript]
public interface INormalizeForIsolatedStorage
```

Remarks

Isolated storage uses evidence about an assembly in order to identify it and provide it with a unique file storage location. When an assembly requests a store, its evidence (as presented by the host that loaded it) is processed and compared with the evidence used to create the existing stores. This determines if you need to create a new store or if one already exists for the assembly in question. Due to the comparison technique used, pieces of evidence that are functionally equivalent might not result in a true comparison if the serialized forms are not identical. When implementing custom evidence, consider whether this is the case for your evidence class and, if so, implement **INormalizeForIsolatedStorage**. For evidence that implements this interface, the **Normalize** method is called and comparisons are based on the normalized copy of the object returned by that method.

Notes to Implementers: Implement this interface when you are implementing custom evidence and need to determine if a store already exists. Serialized objects should not be used for comparisons in some instances, such as that of case sensitive strings. For example,

www.MSN.com is equal to WWW.msn.com and will return a **true** when compared. To create an **INormalizeForIsolatedStorage** object, you need to implement the **Normalize** method.

Notes to Callers: Call the methods of this interface to normalize the instance before making comparisons between an assembly's evidence and currently existing isolated stores.

Requirements

Namespace: System.IO.IsolatedStorage

Platforms: Windows 98, Windows NT 4.0, Windows Millennium Edition, Windows 2000, Windows XP Home Edition, Windows XP Professional, Windows .NET Server family

Assembly: Mscorlib (in Mscorlib.dll)

INormalizeForIsolatedStorage.Normalize Method

When overridden in a derived class, returns a normalized copy of the object on which it is called.

```
[Visual Basic]
Function Normalize() As Object
[C#]
object Normalize();
[C++]
Object* Normalize();
[JScript]
function Normalize() : Object;
```

Return Value

A normalized object that represents the instance on which this method was called. This instance can be a string, stream, or any serializable object.

Remarks

Notes to Implementers: When you override this method and the object returned is a stream, it is assumed to be serialized and is compared directly to the serialized form of the evidence used to create existing stores. If the object returned is a string, it is considered the name of an isolated store and compared to the names of the existing stores.

Notes to Callers: You typically call this method if you are writing a class derived from isolated storage and you need to check to see if isolated storage already exists for the current assembly.

Requirements

Platforms: Windows 98, Windows NT 4.0, Windows Millennium Edition, Windows 2000, Windows XP Home Edition, Windows XP Professional, Windows .NET Server family

IsolatedStorage Class

Represents the abstract base class from which all isolated storage implementations must derive.

System.Object
  System.MarshalByRefObject
    System.IO.IsolatedStorage.IsolatedStorage
      System.IO.IsolatedStorage.IsolatedStorageFile

```
[Visual Basic]
MustInherit Public Class IsolatedStorage
   Inherits MarshalByRefObject
[C#]
public abstract class IsolatedStorage : MarshalByRefObject
[C++]
public __gc __abstract class IsolatedStorage : public
   MarshalByRefObject
[JScript]
public abstract class IsolatedStorage extends MarshalByRefObject
```

Thread Safety

Any public static (**Shared** in Visual Basic) members of this type are safe for multithreaded operations. Any instance members are not guaranteed to be thread safe.

Requirements

Namespace: System.IO.IsolatedStorage

Platforms: Windows 98, Windows NT 4.0, Windows Millennium Edition, Windows 2000, Windows XP Home Edition, Windows XP Professional, Windows .NET Server family

Assembly: Mscorlib (in Mscorlib.dll)

IsolatedStorage Constructor

Initializes a new instance of the **IsolatedStorage** class.

```
[Visual Basic]
Protected Sub New()
[C#]
protected IsolatedStorage();
[C++]
protected: IsolatedStorage();
[JScript]
protected function IsolatedStorage();
```

Remarks

This constructor is called by derived class constructors to initialize state in this type.

Requirements

Platforms: Windows 98, Windows NT 4.0, Windows Millennium Edition, Windows 2000, Windows XP Home Edition, Windows XP Professional, Windows .NET Server family

IsolatedStorage.AssemblyIdentity Property

Gets an assembly identity used to scope isolated storage.

```
[Visual Basic]
Public ReadOnly Property AssemblyIdentity As Object
```

```
[C#]
public object AssemblyIdentity {get;}
[C++]
public: __property Object* get_AssemblyIdentity();
[JScript]
public function get AssemblyIdentity() : Object;
```

Property Value

An **Object** that represents the **Assembly** identity.

Exceptions

Exception Type	Condition
SecurityException	The code lacks the required **SecurityPermission** to access this object.

Requirements

Platforms: Windows 98, Windows NT 4.0, Windows Millennium Edition, Windows 2000, Windows XP Home Edition, Windows XP Professional, Windows .NET Server family

.NET Framework Security:
- **SecurityPermission** for the ability to access evidence. Associated enumeration: **SecurityPermissionFlag.ControlPolicy**

IsolatedStorage.CurrentSize Property

Gets a value representing the current size of isolated storage.

```
[Visual Basic]
<CLSCompliant(False)>
Public Overridable ReadOnly Property CurrentSize As UInt64
[C#]
[CLSCompliant(false)]
public virtual ulong CurrentSize {get;}
[C++]
[CLSCompliant(false)]
public: __property virtual unsigned __int64 get_CurrentSize();
[JScript]
public
   CLSCompliant(false)
function get CurrentSize() : UInt64;
```

Property Value

The number of storage units currently used within the isolated storage scope.

Exceptions

Exception Type	Condition
InvalidOperationException	The current size of the isolated store is undefined.

Remarks

Represents the total usage of all storage resources within the isolated storage scope. **IsolatedStorageFile.CurrentSize** implements this property. In the case of **IsolatedStorageFile** objects this value is in bytes. In the case of implementations of other storage objects such as a database, this value might be in other units of storage.

Requirements

Platforms: Windows 98, Windows NT 4.0,
Windows Millennium Edition, Windows 2000,
Windows XP Home Edition, Windows XP Professional,
Windows .NET Server family

IsolatedStorage.DomainIdentity Property

Gets a domain identity that scopes isolated storage.

```
[Visual Basic]
Public ReadOnly Property DomainIdentity As Object
[C#]
public object DomainIdentity {get;}
[C++]
public: _property Object* get_DomainIdentity();
[JScript]
public function get DomainIdentity() : Object;
```

Property Value

An **Object** that represents the **Domain** identity.

Exceptions

Exception Type	Condition
SecurityException	The code lacks the required **SecurityPermission** to access this object. These permissions are granted by the runtime based on security policy.
InvalidOperationException	The **IsolatedStorage** is not isolated by the domain **IsolatedStorageScope**.

Requirements

Platforms: Windows 98, Windows NT 4.0,
Windows Millennium Edition, Windows 2000,
Windows XP Home Edition, Windows XP Professional,
Windows .NET Server family

.NET Framework Security:

- **SecurityPermission** for the ability to access evidence.
  Associated enumeration:
  SecurityPermissionFlag.ControlPolicy

IsolatedStorage.MaximumSize Property

Gets a value representing the maximum amount of space available for isolated storage. When overridden in a derived class, this value can take on different units of measure.

```
[Visual Basic]
<CLSCompliant(False)>
Public Overridable ReadOnly Property MaximumSize As UInt64
[C#]
[CLSCompliant(false)]
public virtual ulong MaximumSize {get;}
[C++]
[CLSCompliant(false)]
public: _property virtual unsigned _int64 get_MaximumSize();
[JScript]
public
   CLSCompliant(false)
function get MaximumSize() : UInt64;
```

Property Value

The maximum amount of isolated storage space in bytes. Derived classes can return different units of value.

Exceptions

Exception Type	Condition
InvalidOperationException	The quota has not been defined.

Remarks

The default implementation of **MaximumSize** returns the value of **IsolatedStoragePermission.UserQuota**, which is expressed in bytes. Derived classes can express the value in other units of measure. A potential example of such an implementation is an isolated storage database.

You cannot set **MaximumSize**, but the quota is configured in the security policy, and can be set. Code receives a quota of space on the basis of its evidence, so the same code can receive a different quota if it is run with different evidence (for example, the same application run locally and from a share on an intranet can receive different quotas). **IsolatedStorageFile.MaximumSize** implements this property.

Requirements

Platforms: Windows 98, Windows NT 4.0,
Windows Millennium Edition, Windows 2000,
Windows XP Home Edition, Windows XP Professional,
Windows .NET Server family

IsolatedStorage.Scope Property

Gets an **IsolatedStorageScope** enumeration value specifying the scope used to isolate the store.

```
[Visual Basic]
Public ReadOnly Property Scope As IsolatedStorageScope
[C#]
public IsolatedStorageScope Scope {get;}
[C++]
public: _property IsolatedStorageScope get_Scope();
[JScript]
public function get Scope() : IsolatedStorageScope;
```

Property Value

A bitwise combination of **IsolatedStorageScope** values specifying the scope used to isolate the store.

Remarks

Stores are isolated by a combination of factors (user, assembly, domain, and so on).

Requirements

Platforms: Windows 98, Windows NT 4.0,
Windows Millennium Edition, Windows 2000,
Windows XP Home Edition, Windows XP Professional,
Windows .NET Server family

IsolatedStorage.SeparatorExternal Property

Gets a backslash character that can be used in a directory string. When overridden in a derived class, another character might be returned.

```
[Visual Basic]
Protected Overridable ReadOnly Property SeparatorExternal As Char
[C#]
protected virtual char SeparatorExternal {get;}
[C++]
protected: __property virtual __wchar_t get_SeparatorExternal();
[JScript]
protected function get SeparatorExternal() : Char;
```

Property Value

The default implementation returns the '\' character.

Remarks

Notes to Inheritors: When you inherit from **IsolatedStorage**, you can override **SeparatorExternal** and return a character other than the '\' to control the naming syntax of the store. In a Windows **IsolatedStorageFile** this separator is a '\'.

Requirements

Platforms: Windows 98, Windows NT 4.0, Windows Millennium Edition, Windows 2000, Windows XP Home Edition, Windows XP Professional, Windows .NET Server family

IsolatedStorage.SeparatorInternal Property

Gets a period character that can be used in a directory string. When overridden in a derived class, another character might be returned.

```
[Visual Basic]
Protected Overridable ReadOnly Property SeparatorInternal As Char
[C#]
protected virtual char SeparatorInternal {get;}
[C++]
protected: __property virtual __wchar_t get_SeparatorInternal();
[JScript]
protected function get SeparatorInternal() : Char;
```

Property Value

The default implementation returns the '.' (period) character.

Remarks

Notes to Inheritors: When you inherit from **IsolatedStorage**, you can override **SeparatorInternal** and return a character other than the '.' to control the naming syntax of the store. In a Windows **IsolatedStorageFile** this separator is a '.'.

Requirements

Platforms: Windows 98, Windows NT 4.0, Windows Millennium Edition, Windows 2000, Windows XP Home Edition, Windows XP Professional, Windows .NET Server family

IsolatedStorage.GetPermission Method

When implemented by a derived class, returns a permission that represents access to isolated storage from within a permission set.

```
[Visual Basic]
Protected MustOverride Function GetPermission( _
    ByVal ps As PermissionSet _
) As IsolatedStoragePermission
```

```
[C#]
protected abstract IsolatedStoragePermission GetPermission(
    PermissionSet ps
);
[C++]
protected: virtual IsolatedStoragePermission* GetPermission(
    PermissionSet* ps
) = 0;
[JScript]
protected abstract function GetPermission(
    ps : PermissionSet
) : IsolatedStoragePermission;
```

Parameters

ps

The **PermissionSet** that contains the set of permissions granted to code attempting to use isolated storage.

Return Value

An **IsolatedStoragePermission** object.

Remarks

You call this method on derived classes to determine what permission type governs their use, and to return the permission of the type that has been granted. Use this information to determine the allowable quota and any other derived class-specific isolated storage settings.

Requirements

Platforms: Windows 98, Windows NT 4.0, Windows Millennium Edition, Windows 2000, Windows XP Home Edition, Windows XP Professional, Windows .NET Server family

IsolatedStorage.InitStore Method

Initializes a new instance of the **IsolatedStorage** object.

```
[Visual Basic]
Protected Sub InitStore( _
    ByVal scope As IsolatedStorageScope, _
    ByVal domainEvidenceType As Type, _
    ByVal assemblyEvidenceType As Type _
)
[C#]
protected void InitStore(
    IsolatedStorageScope scope,
    Type domainEvidenceType,
    Type assemblyEvidenceType
);
[C++]
protected: void InitStore(
    IsolatedStorageScope scope,
    Type* domainEvidenceType,
    Type* assemblyEvidenceType
);
[JScript]
protected function InitStore(
    scope : IsolatedStorageScope,
    domainEvidenceType : Type,
    assemblyEvidenceType : Type
);
```

Parameters

scope

A bitwise combination of the **IsolatedStorageScope** values.

domainEvidenceType

The type of the **Evidence** that you can chose from the list of **Evidence** present in the domain of the calling application. A null reference (**Nothing** in Visual Basic) lets the **IsolatedStorage** choose the evidence.

assemblyEvidenceType

The type of the **Evidence** that you can chose from the list of **Evidence** present in the domain of the calling application. A null reference (**Nothing** in Visual Basic) lets the **IsolatedStorage** choose the evidence.

Exceptions

Exception Type	Condition
IsolatedStorageException	The assembly specified has insufficient permissions to create isolated stores.

Remarks

Derived classes use this method to initialize a new instance.

Requirements

Platforms: Windows 98, Windows NT 4.0, Windows Millennium Edition, Windows 2000, Windows XP Home Edition, Windows XP Professional, Windows .NET Server family

.NET Framework Security:

- **IsolatedStorageFilePermission** for permission to use isolated storage. Associated enumeration: **IsolatedStorageContainment.DomainIsolationByUser**

  -or-

- **IsolatedStorageContainment.AssemblyIsolationByUser**

  -or-

- **IsolatedStorageContainment.DomainIsolationByRoamingUser**

  -or-

- **IsolatedStorageContainment.AssemblyIsolationByRoamingUser**

Requirements

Platforms: Windows 98, Windows NT 4.0, Windows Millennium Edition, Windows 2000, Windows XP Home Edition, Windows XP Professional, Windows .NET Server family

IsolatedStorage.Remove Method

When overridden in a derived class, removes the individual isolated store and all contained data.

```
[Visual Basic]
Public MustOverride Sub Remove()
[C#]
public abstract void Remove();
[C++]
public: virtual void Remove() = 0;
[JScript]
public abstract function Remove();
```

Return Value

This is an abstract method in this base class; it must be implemented by derived classes.

IsolatedStorageException Class

The exception that is thrown when an operation in isolated storage fails.

System.Object
  System.Exception
    System.IO.IsolatedStorage.IsolatedStorageException

```
[Visual Basic]
<Serializable>
Public Class IsolatedStorageException
   Inherits Exception
[C#]
[Serializable]
public class IsolatedStorageException : Exception
[C++]
[Serializable]
public __gc class IsolatedStorageException : public Exception
[JScript]
public
   Serializable
class IsolatedStorageException extends Exception
```

Thread Safety

Any public static (**Shared** in Visual Basic) members of this type are safe for multithreaded operations. Any instance members are not guaranteed to be thread safe.

Remarks

IsolatedStorageException uses the ISS_E_ISOSTORE, which has the value 0x80131450.

The most common examples of isolated storage exceptions are as follows.

- Missing evidence. Isolated storage requires evidence (information about the assembly and its origin) in order to determine the identity of the code and connect it to the correct associated file space. Without this information, isolated storage cannot be used.
- Invalid operations. Some **FileStream** operations are not supported for isolated storage.

Requirements

Namespace: System.IO.IsolatedStorage

Platforms: Windows 98, Windows NT 4.0, Windows Millennium Edition, Windows 2000, Windows XP Home Edition, Windows XP Professional, Windows .NET Server family

Assembly: Mscorlib (in Mscorlib.dll)

IsolatedStorageException Constructor

Initializes a new instance of the **IsolatedStorageException** class.

Overload List

Initializes a new instance of the **IsolatedStorageException** class with default properties.

  [Visual Basic] **Public Sub New()**
  [C#] **public IsolatedStorageException();**
  [C++] **public: IsolatedStorageException();**
  [JScript] **public function IsolatedStorageException();**

Initializes a new instance of the **IsolatedStorageException** class with a specified error message.

  [Visual Basic] **Public Sub New(String)**
  [C#] **public IsolatedStorageException(string);**
  [C++] **public: IsolatedStorageException(String*);**
  [JScript] **public function IsolatedStorageException(String);**

Initializes a new instance of the **IsolatedStorageException** class with serialized data.

  [Visual Basic] **Protected Sub New(SerializationInfo, StreamingContext)**
  [C#] **protected IsolatedStorageException(SerializationInfo, StreamingContext);**
  [C++] **protected: IsolatedStorageException(SerializationInfo*, StreamingContext);**
  [JScript] **protected function IsolatedStorageException(SerializationInfo, StreamingContext);**

Initializes a new instance of the **IsolatedStorageException** class with a specified error message and a reference to the inner exception that is the cause of this exception.

  [Visual Basic] **Public Sub New(String, Exception)**
  [C#] **public IsolatedStorageException(string, Exception);**
  [C++] **public: IsolatedStorageException(String*, Exception*);**
  [JScript] **public function IsolatedStorageException(String, Exception);**

IsolatedStorageException Constructor ()

Initializes a new instance of the **IsolatedStorageException** class with default properties.

```
[Visual Basic]
Public Sub New()
[C#]
public IsolatedStorageException();
[C++]
public: IsolatedStorageException();
[JScript]
public function IsolatedStorageException();
```

Remarks

The following table shows the initial property values for an instance of **IsolatedStorageException**.

Property	Value
InnerException	A null reference (**Nothing** in Visual Basic).
Message	The localized error message string.

Requirements

Platforms: Windows 98, Windows NT 4.0, Windows Millennium Edition, Windows 2000, Windows XP Home Edition, Windows XP Professional, Windows .NET Server family

IsolatedStorageException Constructor (String)

Initializes a new instance of the **IsolatedStorageException** class with a specified error message.

```
[Visual Basic]
Public Sub New( _
    ByVal message As String _
)
[C#]
public IsolatedStorageException(
    string message
);
[C++]
public: IsolatedStorageException(
    String* message
);
[JScript]
public function IsolatedStorageException(
    message : String
);
```

Parameters
message
> The error message that explains the reason for the exception.

Remarks
The following table shows the initial property values for an instance of **IsolatedStorageException**.

Property	Value
InnerException	A null reference (**Nothing** in Visual Basic).
Message	The error message string.

Requirements
Platforms: Windows 98, Windows NT 4.0, Windows Millennium Edition, Windows 2000, Windows XP Home Edition, Windows XP Professional, Windows .NET Server family

IsolatedStorageException Constructor (SerializationInfo, StreamingContext)

Initializes a new instance of the **IsolatedStorageException** class with serialized data.

```
[Visual Basic]
Protected Sub New( _
    ByVal info As SerializationInfo, _
    ByVal context As StreamingContext _
)
[C#]
protected IsolatedStorageException(
    SerializationInfo info,
    StreamingContext context
);
[C++]
protected: IsolatedStorageException(
    SerializationInfo* info,
    StreamingContext context
);
```

```
[JScript]
protected function IsolatedStorageException(
    info : SerializationInfo,
    context : StreamingContext
);
```

Parameters
info
> The object that holds the serialized object data.

context
> The contextual information about the source or destination.

Remarks
This constructor is called during deserialization to reconstitute the exception object transmitted over a stream.

Requirements
Platforms: Windows 98, Windows NT 4.0, Windows Millennium Edition, Windows 2000, Windows XP Home Edition, Windows XP Professional, Windows .NET Server family

IsolatedStorageException Constructor (String, Exception)

Initializes a new instance of the **IsolatedStorageException** class with a specified error message and a reference to the inner exception that is the cause of this exception.

```
[Visual Basic]
Public Sub New( _
    ByVal message As String, _
    ByVal inner As Exception _
)
[C#]
public IsolatedStorageException(
    string message,
    Exception inner
);
[C++]
public: IsolatedStorageException(
    String* message,
    Exception* inner
);
[JScript]
public function IsolatedStorageException(
    message : String,
    inner : Exception
);
```

Parameters
message
> The error message that explains the reason for the exception.

inner
> The exception that is the cause of the current exception. If the *inner* parameter is not a null reference (**Nothing** in Visual Basic), the current exception is raised in a **catch** block that handles the inner exception.

Remarks

An exception that is thrown as a direct result of a previous exception should include a reference to the previous exception in the **InnerException** property. The **InnerException** property returns the same value that is passed into the constructor, or a null reference (**Nothing** in Visual Basic) if the **InnerException** property does not supply the inner exception value to the constructor.

The following table shows the initial property values for an instance of **IsolatedStorageException**.

Property	Value
InnerException	The inner exception reference.
Message	The error message string.

Requirements

Platforms: Windows 98, Windows NT 4.0, Windows Millennium Edition, Windows 2000, Windows XP Home Edition, Windows XP Professional, Windows .NET Server family

IsolatedStorageFile Class

Represents an isolated storage area containing files and directories.

System.Object
  System.MarshalByRefObject
    System.IO.IsolatedStorage.IsolatedStorage
      System.IO.IsolatedStorage.IsolatedStorageFile

```
[Visual Basic]
NotInheritable Public Class IsolatedStorageFile
    Inherits IsolatedStorage
    Implements IDisposable
[C#]
public sealed class IsolatedStorageFile : IsolatedStorage,
    IDisposable
[C++]
public _gc _sealed class IsolatedStorageFile : public
    IsolatedStorage, IDisposable
[JScript]
public class IsolatedStorageFile extends IsolatedStorage implements
    IDisposable
```

Thread Safety

Any public static (**Shared** in Visual Basic) members of this type are
safe for multithreaded operations. Any instance members are not
guaranteed to be thread safe.

Remarks

This object corresponds to a specific isolated storage scope, where
files represented by **IsolatedStorageFileStream** objects exist.
Applications can use isolated storage to save data in their own
isolated portion of the file system, without having to specify a
particular path within the file system. Since isolated stores are
scoped to particular assemblies, most other managed code will not
be able to access your code's data (highly trusted managed code and
administration tools can access stores from other assemblies).
Unmanaged code can access any isolated stores.

Example

[Visual Basic, C#, C++] The following console application
demonstrates how you can use **IsolatedStorageFile** and
IsolatedStorageFileStream to write data to an Isolated Storage file.
The user is requested to log in. If the user is a new user, a News URL
and a Sports URL are recorded as personal preferences in Isolated
Storage. If the user is a returning user, the user's current preferences
are displayed. The code examples used throughout this namespace
are presented in the context of this sample application.

[Visual Basic, C#, C++] You can use the **Isolated Storage Tool
(Storeadm.exe)** utility to list and remove the Isolated Storage files
that are created with this console application.

```
[Visual Basic]
Imports System
Imports System.IO
Imports System.IO.IsolatedStorage
Imports System.Security.Policy
Imports Microsoft.VisualBasic

Namespace ISOCS
    _
    Class ConsoleApp

        <STAThread()> Overloads Shared _
        Sub Main(ByVal args() As String)
```

```
            ' Prompt the user for their username.
            Console.WriteLine("Enter your login ID:")

            ' Does no error checking.
            Dim lp As New LoginPrefs(Console.ReadLine())

            If lp.NewPrefs Then
                Console.WriteLine("Please set preferences for a    ↵
new user.")
                GatherInfoFromUser(lp)

                ' Write the new preferences to storage.
                Dim percentUsed As Double = lp.SetPrefsForUser()
                Console.WriteLine(("Your preferences have been    ↵
written. Current space used is " & percentUsed.ToString() & " %"))
            Else
                Console.WriteLine("Welcome back.")

                Console.WriteLine("Your preferences have    ↵
expired, please reset them.")
                GatherInfoFromUser(lp)
                lp.SetNewPrefsForUser()

                Console.WriteLine("Your news site has been set    ↵
to {0}" & ControlChars.Cr & " and your sports site has been set    ↵
to {1}.", lp.NewsUrl, lp.SportsUrl)
            End If
            lp.GetIsoStoreInfo()
            Console.WriteLine("Enter 'd' to delete the    ↵
IsolatedStorage files and exit, or press any other key to exit    ↵
without deleting files.")
            Dim consoleInput As String = Console.ReadLine()
            If consoleInput.ToLower() = "d" Then
                lp.DeleteFiles()
                lp.DeleteDirectories()
            End If
        End Sub 'Main

        Shared Sub GatherInfoFromUser(ByVal lp As LoginPrefs)
            Console.WriteLine("Please enter the URL of your    ↵
news site.")
            lp.NewsUrl = Console.ReadLine()
            Console.WriteLine("Please enter the URL of your    ↵
sports site.")
            lp.SportsUrl = Console.ReadLine()
        End Sub 'GatherInfoFromUser
    End Class 'ConsoleApp
    _

    Public Class LoginPrefs

        Public Sub New(ByVal myUserName As String)
            userName = myUserName
            myNewPrefs = GetPrefsForUser()
        End Sub 'New
        Private userName As String

        Private myNewsUrl As String

        Public Property NewsUrl() As String
            Get
                Return myNewsUrl
            End Get
            Set(ByVal Value As String)
                myNewsUrl = value
            End Set
        End Property
        Private mySportsUrl As String

        Public Property SportsUrl() As String
            Get
                Return mySportsUrl
            End Get
            Set(ByVal Value As String)
                mySportsUrl = value
```

```vb
            End Set
        End Property
        Private myNewPrefs As Boolean

        Public ReadOnly Property NewPrefs() As Boolean
            Get
                Return myNewPrefs
            End Get
        End Property

        Private Function GetPrefsForUser() As Boolean
            Try

                ' Retrieve an IsolatedStorageFile for the
current Domain and Assembly.
                Dim isoFile As IsolatedStorageFile = _
                    IsolatedStorageFile.GetStore(IsolatedStorageScope.
User _
                    Or IsolatedStorageScope.Assembly _
                    Or IsolatedStorageScope.Domain, Nothing, Nothing)

                Dim isoStream As New
IsolatedStorageFileStream(Me.userName, FileMode.Open, _
                    FileAccess.Read, FileShare.Read)

                ' We only get this far if a file corresponding
to the username exists.
                ' Though you can perform operations on the
stream, you cannot get a handle to the file.
                Try

                    Dim aFileHandle As IntPtr = isoStream.Handle
                    Console.WriteLine(("A pointer to a file
handle has been obtained. " & aFileHandle.ToString() & " " &
aFileHandle.GetHashCode()))

                Catch ex As Exception
                    ' Handle the exception.
                    Console.WriteLine("Expected exception")
                    Console.WriteLine(ex.ToString())
                End Try

                Dim reader As New StreamReader(isoStream)
                ' Read the data.
                Me.NewsUrl = reader.ReadLine()
                Me.SportsUrl = reader.ReadLine()
                reader.Close()
                isoFile.Close()
                Return False
            Catch ex As System.IO.FileNotFoundException
                ' Expected exception if a file cannot be not
found. This indicates that we have a new user.
                Return True
            End Try
        End Function 'GetPrefsForUser

        Public Function GetIsoStoreInfo() As Boolean
            Try
                'Get a User store with type evidence for the
current Domain and the Assembly.
                Dim isoFile As IsolatedStorageFile =
IsolatedStorageFile.GetStore(IsolatedStorageScope.User Or
IsolatedStorageScope.Assembly Or IsolatedStorageScope.Domain,
GetType(System.Security.Policy.Url),
GetType(System.Security.Policy.Url))

                Dim dirNames As [String]() =
isoFile.GetDirectoryNames("*")
                Dim fileNames As [String]() = isoFile.GetFileNames("*")
                Dim name As String

                ' List directories currently in this Isolated Storage.
                If dirNames.Length > 0 Then
```

```vb
                    For Each name In dirNames
                        Console.WriteLine("Directory Name: " & name)
                    Next name
                End If

                ' List the files currently in this Isolated Storage.
                ' The list represents all users who have
personal preferences stored for this application.
                If fileNames.Length > 0 Then

                    For Each name In fileNames
                        Console.WriteLine("File Name: " & name)
                    Next name
                End If

                isoFile.Close()
                Return True
            Catch ex As Exception
                Console.WriteLine(ex.ToString())
            End Try
        End Function 'GetIsoStoreInfo

        Public Function SetPrefsForUser() As Double
            Try
                Dim isoFile As IsolatedStorageFile
                isoFile = IsolatedStorageFile.GetUserStoreForDomain()

                ' Open or create a writable file.
                Dim isoStream As New
IsolatedStorageFileStream(Me.userName, FileMode.OpenOrCreate,
FileAccess.Write, isoFile)

                Dim writer As New StreamWriter(isoStream)
                writer.WriteLine(Me.NewsUrl)
                writer.WriteLine(Me.SportsUrl)
                ' Calculate the amount of space used to record
the user's preferences.
                Dim d As Double = Convert.ToDouble
(isoFile.CurrentSize) / Convert.ToDouble(isoFile.MaximumSize)
                Console.WriteLine(("CurrentSize = " &
isoFile.CurrentSize.ToString()))
                Console.WriteLine(("MaximumSize = " &
isoFile.MaximumSize.ToString()))
                ' StreamWriter.Close implicitly closes isoStream.
                writer.Close()
                isoFile.Dispose()
                isoFile.Close()
                Return d
            Catch ex As Exception
                Console.WriteLine(ex.ToString())
            End Try
        End Function 'SetPrefsForUser
        'ToDo:  Handle the exception.

        Public Sub DeleteFiles()
            Try
                Dim isoFile As IsolatedStorageFile =
IsolatedStorageFile.GetStore(IsolatedStorageScope.User Or
IsolatedStorageScope.Assembly Or
IsolatedStorageScope.Domain, GetType
(System.Security.Policy.Url), GetType(System.Security.Policy.Url))
                Dim name As String
                Dim dirNames As [String]() =
isoFile.GetDirectoryNames("*")
                Dim fileNames As [String]() = isoFile.GetFileNames("*")
                ' List the files currently in this Isolated Storage.
                ' The list represents all users who have personal
                ' preferences stored for this application.
                If fileNames.Length > 0 Then
                    For Each name In fileNames
                        ' Delete the files.
                        isoFile.DeleteFile(name)
                    Next name
                    'Confirm no files are left.
                    fileNames = isoFile.GetFileNames("*")
```

```vb
            End If
        Catch ex As Exception
            Console.WriteLine(ex.ToString())
        End Try
    End Sub 'DeleteFiles

    Public Sub DeleteDirectories()
        Try
            Dim isoFile As IsolatedStorageFile =
IsolatedStorageFile.GetStore(IsolatedStorageScope.User Or
IsolatedStorageScope.Assembly Or
solatedStorageScope.Domain, GetType
(System.Security.Policy.Url), GetType(System.Security.Policy.Url))
            Dim name As String
            Dim dirNames As [String]() =
isoFile.GetDirectoryNames("*")
            Dim fileNames As [String]() =
isoFile.GetFileNames("Archive\*")
            ' Delete all the files currently in the
Archive directory.
            If fileNames.Length > 0 Then
                For Each name In fileNames
                    isoFile.DeleteFile(("Archive\" & name))
                Next name
                'Confirm no files are left.
                fileNames = isoFile.GetFileNames("Archive\*")
            End If
            If dirNames.Length > 0 Then
                For Each name In dirNames
                    ' Delete the the directories in the
Isolated Storage.
                    ' This deletes the Archive directory,
there should not be any others.
                    isoFile.DeleteDirectory(name)
                Next name
            End If
            dirNames = isoFile.GetDirectoryNames("*")
            isoFile.Remove()
        Catch ex As Exception
            Console.WriteLine(ex.ToString())
        End Try
    End Sub 'DeleteDirectories

    Public Function SetNewPrefsForUser() As Double
        Try
            Dim inputChar As Byte
            Dim isoFile As IsolatedStorageFile =
IsolatedStorageFile.GetStore(IsolatedStorageScope.User
Or IsolatedStorageScope.Assembly Or
IsolatedStorageScope.Domain, GetType
(System.Security.Policy.Url), GetType(System.Security.Policy.Url))

            ' If this is not a new user, archive the
old preferences and
            ' overwrite them using the new preferences.
            If Not Me.myNewPrefs Then
                If isoFile.GetDirectoryNames("Archive")
.Length = 0 Then
                    isoFile.CreateDirectory("Archive")
                Else

                    Dim source As New
IsolatedStorageFileStream(Me.userName, FileMode.OpenOrCreate, isoFile)
                    Dim canWrite, canRead As Boolean
                    ' This is the stream from which data
will be read.
                    If source.CanRead Then canRead =
True Else canRead = False
                    Console.WriteLine("Is the source file
readable? " & canRead)
                    Console.WriteLine("Creating new
IsolatedStorageFileStream for Archive.")

                    ' Open or create a writable file with
a maximum size of 10K.
                    Dim target As New
IsolatedStorageFileStream("Archive\ " & Me.userName,
FileMode.OpenOrCreate, FileAccess.Write, FileShare.Write,
10240, isoFile)

                    ' This is the stream to which data
will be written.
                    If target.CanWrite Then canWrite = True
Else canWrite = False
                    Console.WriteLine("Is the target file
writable? " & canWrite)
                    target.SetLength(0)  'rewind the target file

                    ' Stream the old file to a new file
in the Archive directory.
                    If source.IsAsync And target.IsAsync Then
                        ' IsolatedStorageFileStreams cannot
be asynchronous.  However, you
                        ' can use the asynchronous BeginRead
and BeginWrite functions
                        ' with some possible performance penalty.
                        Console.WriteLine("IsolatedStorageFileStreams
can not be
asynchronous.")
                    Else
                        Console.WriteLine("Writing data to
the new file.")

                        While source.Position < source.Length
                            inputChar = CByte(source.ReadByte())
                            target.WriteByte(inputChar)
                        End While

                        ' Determine the size of the
IsolatedStorageFileStream
                        ' by checking its Length property.
                        Console.WriteLine
(("Total Bytes Read: " & source.Length))
                    End If

                    ' After you have read and written
to the streams, close them.
                    target.Close()
                    source.Close()
                End If
            End If

            ' Open or create a writable file with a maximum
size of 10K.
            Dim isoStream As New
IsolatedStorageFileStream(Me.userName, FileMode.OpenOrCreate,
FileAccess.Write, FileShare.Write, 10240, isoFile)
            isoStream.SetLength(0) 'Position to overwrite
the old data.
            Dim writer As New StreamWriter(isoStream)
            ' Update the data based on the new inputs.
            writer.WriteLine(Me.NewsUrl)
            writer.WriteLine(Me.SportsUrl)

            ' Calculate the amount of space used to record
this user's preferences.
            Dim d As Double = Convert.ToDouble
(isoFile.CurrentSize) / Convert.ToDouble(isoFile.MaximumSize)
            Console.WriteLine(("CurrentSize = " &
isoFile.CurrentSize.ToString()))
            Console.WriteLine(("MaximumSize = " &
isoFile.MaximumSize.ToString()))
            ' StreamWriter.Close implicitly closes isoStream.
            writer.Close()
            isoFile.Close()

            Return d
        Catch ex As Exception
            Console.WriteLine(ex.ToString())
            Return 0.0
        End Try
```

```
        End Function 'SetNewPrefsForUser
    End Class 'LoginPrefs
End Namespace 'ISOCS

[C#]
using System;
using System.IO;
using System.IO.IsolatedStorage;
using System.Security.Policy;

[assembly: CLSCompliantAttribute(true)]

    class ConsoleApp
    {
        [STAThread]
        static void Main(string[] args)
        {

            // Prompt the user for their username.

            Console.WriteLine("Login:");

            // Does no error checking.
            LoginPrefs lp = new LoginPrefs(Console.ReadLine());

            if (lp.NewPrefs)
            {
                Console.WriteLine("Please set preferences        ⏎
for a new user.");
                GatherInfoFromUser(lp);

                // Write the new preferences to storage.
                double percentUsed = lp.SetPrefsForUser();
                Console.WriteLine("Your preferences have been    ⏎
written. Current space used is " + percentUsed.ToString() + " %");
            }
            else
            {
                Console.WriteLine("Welcome back.");

                Console.WriteLine("Your preferences have         ⏎
expired, please reset them.");
                GatherInfoFromUser(lp);
                lp.SetNewPrefsForUser();

                Console.WriteLine("Your news site has been       ⏎
set to {0}\n and your sports site has been set to {1}.",          ⏎
lp.NewsUrl, lp.SportsUrl);
            }
            lp.GetIsoStoreInfo ();
            Console.WriteLine("Enter 'd' to delete the           ⏎
IsolatedStorage files and exit, or press any other key           ⏎
to exit without deleting files.");
            string consoleInput = Console.ReadLine();
            if (consoleInput.ToLower() == "d")
            {
                lp.DeleteFiles();
                lp.DeleteDirectories();
            }

        }

        static void GatherInfoFromUser (LoginPrefs lp )
        {
            Console.WriteLine("Please enter the URL of your      ⏎
news site.");
            lp.NewsUrl = Console.ReadLine();
            Console.WriteLine("Please enter the URL of your      ⏎
sports site.");
            lp.SportsUrl = Console.ReadLine();
        }
    }

    public class LoginPrefs
    {
        public LoginPrefs(string myUserName)
        {
            userName = myUserName;
            myNewPrefs = GetPrefsForUser();
        }
        string userName;

        string myNewsUrl;
        public string NewsUrl
        {
            get { return myNewsUrl; }
            set { myNewsUrl = value; }
        }

        string mySportsUrl;
        public string SportsUrl
        {
            get { return mySportsUrl; }
            set { mySportsUrl = value; }
        }
        bool myNewPrefs;
        public bool NewPrefs
        {
            get { return myNewPrefs; }
        }

        private bool GetPrefsForUser()
        {
            try
            {
                // Retrieve an IsolatedStorageFile for the       ⏎
current Domain and Assembly.
                IsolatedStorageFile isoFile =
                    IsolatedStorageFile.GetStore(Isolated        ⏎
StorageScope.User |
                    IsolatedStorageScope.Assembly |
                    IsolatedStorageScope.Domain ,
                    null,
                    null);

                IsolatedStorageFileStream isoStream =
                    new IsolatedStorageFileStream( this.userName,
                    FileMode.Open,
                    FileAccess.Read,
                    FileShare.Read);

                // We only get this far if a file corresponding  ⏎
to the username exists.
                // Though you can perform operations on the      ⏎
stream, you cannot get a handle to the file.

                try
                {

                    IntPtr aFileHandle = isoStream.Handle;
                    Console.WriteLine("A pointer to a file handle ⏎
has been obtained. "
                        + aFileHandle.ToString() + " "
                        + aFileHandle.GetHashCode());
                }

                catch (Exception e)
                {
                    // Handle the exception.
                    Console.WriteLine("Expected exception");
                    Console.WriteLine(e);
                }

                StreamReader reader = new StreamReader(isoStream);
                // Read the data.
                this.NewsUrl = reader.ReadLine();
                this.SportsUrl = reader.ReadLine();
                reader.Close();
                isoFile.Close();
```

```
                return false;
            }
            catch (System.IO.FileNotFoundException)
            {
                // Expected exception if a file cannot be not        ⌋
found. This indicates that we have a new user.
                return true;
            }
        }
        public bool GetIsoStoreInfo ()
        {
            // Get a User store with type evidence for the          ⌋
current Domain and the Assembly.
            IsolatedStorageFile isoFile = IsolatedStorageFile.      ⌋
GetStore( IsolatedStorageScope.User |
                IsolatedStorageScope.Assembly |
                IsolatedStorageScope.Domain,
                typeof(System.Security.Policy.Url),
                typeof(System.Security.Policy.Url));

            String [] dirNames  = isoFile.GetDirectoryNames("*");
            String [] fileNames = isoFile.GetFileNames("*");

            // List directories currently in this Isolated Storage.
            if (dirNames.Length>0)
            {
                for (int i=0;i<dirNames.Length;++i)
                {
                    Console.WriteLine("Directory Name: " +          ⌋
dirNames[i]);
                }
            }

            // List the files currently in this Isolated Storage.
            // The list represents all users who have personal      ⌋
preferences stored for this application.
            if (fileNames.Length>0)
            {
                for (int i=0;i<fileNames.Length;++i)
                {
                    Console.WriteLine("File Name: " + fileNames[i]);
                }
            }

            isoFile.Close();
            return true;
        }

        public double SetPrefsForUser ()
        {
            try
            {
                IsolatedStorageFile isoFile;
                isoFile = IsolatedStorageFile.GetUserStoreForDomain();

                // Open or create a writable file.
                IsolatedStorageFileStream isoStream =
                    new IsolatedStorageFileStream( this.userName,
                    FileMode.OpenOrCreate,
                    FileAccess.Write,
                    isoFile);

                StreamWriter writer = new StreamWriter(isoStream);
                writer.WriteLine(this.NewsUrl);
                writer.WriteLine(this.SportsUrl);
                // Calculate the amount of space used to            ⌋
record the user's preferences.
                double d = isoFile.CurrentSize/isoFile.MaximumSize;
                Console.WriteLine("CurrentSize = " +                ⌋
isoFile.CurrentSize.ToString());
                Console.WriteLine("MaximumSize = " +                ⌋
isoFile.MaximumSize.ToString());
                // StreamWriter.Close implicitly closes isoStream.
                writer.Close();
                isoFile.Dispose();
```

```
                isoFile.Close();
                return d;
            }
            catch (IsolatedStorageException)
            {
                //ToDo:  Handle the exception.
                return 0.0;
            }
        }

        public void DeleteFiles ()
        {
            try
            {
                IsolatedStorageFile isoFile =                       ⌋
IsolatedStorageFile.GetStore( IsolatedStorageScope.User |
                    IsolatedStorageScope.Assembly |
                    IsolatedStorageScope.Domain,
                    typeof(System.Security.Policy.Url),
                    typeof(System.Security.Policy.Url));

                String [] dirNames  = isoFile.GetDirectoryNames("*");
                String [] fileNames = isoFile.GetFileNames("*");

                // List the files currently in this Isolated Storage.
                // The list represents all users who have personal
                // preferences stored for this application.
                if (fileNames.Length>0)
                {
                    for (int i=0;i<fileNames.Length;++i)
                    {
                        // Delete the files.
                        isoFile.DeleteFile(fileNames[i]);
                    }
                    // Confirm that no files remain.
                    fileNames = isoFile.GetFileNames("*");
                }
            }
            catch (Exception e)
            {
                Console.WriteLine(e.ToString());
            }

        }
        public void DeleteDirectories()
        {
            try
            {
                IsolatedStorageFile isoFile =                       ⌋
IsolatedStorageFile.GetStore( IsolatedStorageScope.User |
                    IsolatedStorageScope.Assembly |
                    IsolatedStorageScope.Domain,
                    typeof(System.Security.Policy.Url),
                    typeof(System.Security.Policy.Url));

                String [] dirNames  = isoFile.GetDirectoryNames("*");
                String [] fileNames =                               ⌋
isoFile.GetFileNames("Archive\\*");

                // Delete all the files currently in the            ⌋
Archive directory.

                if (fileNames.Length>0)
                {
                    for (int i=0;i<fileNames.Length;++i)
                    {
                        // Delete the files.
                        isoFile.DeleteFile("Archive\\" + fileNames[i]);
                    }
                    // Confirm that no files remain.
                    fileNames = isoFile.GetFileNames("Archive\\*");
                }

                if (dirNames.Length>0)
                {
```

```
                    for (int i=0; i<dirNames.Length; ++i)
                    {
                            // Delete the the directories in the
Isolated Storage.
                            // This deletes the Archive directory,
there should not be any others.
                            isoFile.DeleteDirectory(dirNames[i]);
                    }
                }
                dirNames = isoFile.GetDirectoryNames("*");
                isoFile.Remove();
            }
            catch (Exception e)
            {
                Console.WriteLine(e.ToString());
            }
        }
        public double SetNewPrefsForUser ()
        {
            try
            {
                byte inputChar;
                IsolatedStorageFile isoFile =
IsolatedStorageFile.GetStore( IsolatedStorageScope.User |
                    IsolatedStorageScope.Assembly |
                    IsolatedStorageScope.Domain,
                    typeof(System.Security.Policy.Url),
                    typeof(System.Security.Policy.Url));

                // If this is not a new user, archive the old preferences
                // and overwrite them using the new preferences.
                if (! this.myNewPrefs)
                {
                    if ( isoFile.GetDirectoryNames("Archive").
Length == 0 )
                        isoFile.CreateDirectory("Archive");
                    else
                    {
                        IsolatedStorageFileStream source =
                            new
IsolatedStorageFileStream(this.userName,FileMode.OpenOrCreate,
                            isoFile);
                        // This is the stream from which data
will be read.
                        Console.WriteLine("Is the source file
readable? " + (source.CanRead?"true":"false"));
                        Console.WriteLine("Creating new
IsolatedStorageFileStream for Archive.");

                        // Open or create a writable file
with a maximum size of 10K.
                        IsolatedStorageFileStream target =
                            new IsolatedStorageFileStream
("Archive\\ " + this.userName,
                            FileMode.OpenOrCreate,
                            FileAccess.Write,
                            FileShare.Write,
                            10240,
                            isoFile);

                        Console.WriteLine("Is the target file
writable? " + (target.CanWrite?"true":"false"));

                        // Stream the old file to a new file
in the Archive directory.
                        if (source.IsAsync && target.IsAsync)
                        {
                            // IsolatedStorageFileStreams
cannot be asynchronous.  However, you
                            // can use the asynchronous
BeginRead and BeginWrite functions
                            // with some possible performance penalty.
                            Console.WriteLine
("IsolatedStorageFileStreams can not be asynchronous.");
                        }
                        else
                        {
                            Console.WriteLine("Writing data
to the new file.");

                            while (source.Position < source.Length)
                            {
                                inputChar = (byte)source.ReadByte();
                                target.WriteByte(inputChar);
                            }

                            // Determine the size of the
IsolatedStorageFileStream
                            // by checking its Length property.
                            Console.WriteLine("Total Bytes
Read: " + source.Length);

                        }

                        // After you have read and written
to the streams, close them.
                        target.Close();
                        source.Close();
                    }
                }

                // Open or create a writable file with a
maximum size of 10K.
                IsolatedStorageFileStream isoStream =
                    new IsolatedStorageFileStream(this.userName,
                    FileMode.OpenOrCreate,
                    FileAccess.Write,
                    FileShare.Write,
                    10240,
                    isoFile);
                isoStream.Position = 0;  // Position to overwrite
the old data.

                StreamWriter writer = new StreamWriter(isoStream);
                // Update the data based on the new inputs.
                writer.WriteLine(this.NewsUrl);
                writer.WriteLine(this.SportsUrl);

                // Calculate the amount of space used to record
this user's preferences.
                double d = isoFile.CurrentSize/isoFile.MaximumSize;
                Console.WriteLine("CurrentSize = " +
isoFile.CurrentSize.ToString());
                Console.WriteLine("MaximumSize = " +
isoFile.MaximumSize.ToString());
                // StreamWriter.Close implicitly closes isoStream.
                writer.Close();
                isoFile.Close();

                return d;
            }
            catch (Exception e)
            {
                Console.WriteLine(e.ToString());
                return 0.0;
            }
        }
    }

[C++]
#using <mscorlib.dll>
using namespace System;
using namespace System::IO;
using namespace System::IO::IsolatedStorage;
using namespace System::Security::Policy;

//namespace ISOCS
//{
```

```cpp
//class ConsoleApp
//{

__gc public class LoginPrefs
{
private:
    String* userName;
    String* newsUrl;
    String* sportsUrl;
    bool newPrefs;

public:
    bool GetPrefsForUser()
    {
        try
        {

            // Retrieve an IsolatedStorageFile for
the current Domain and Assembly.
            IsolatedStorageFile* isoFile =
                IsolatedStorageFile::GetStore(

static_cast<IsolatedStorageScope>(IsolatedStorageScope::User |
                IsolatedStorageScope::Assembly |
                IsolatedStorageScope::Domain),
                (Type*)0, 0);
            IsolatedStorageFileStream* isoStream = new
IsolatedStorageFileStream(this->userName,
                FileMode::Open,
                FileAccess::ReadWrite,
                isoFile);

            // We only get this far if a file corresponding
to the username exists.
            // Though you can perform operations on the
stream, you cannot get a handle to the file.
            try
            {

                IntPtr aFileHandle = isoStream->Handle;
                Console::WriteLine(S"A pointer to a file
handle has been obtained. {0} {1}",
                    __box(aFileHandle),
__box(aFileHandle.GetHashCode()));
            }

            catch (Exception* e)
            {
                // Handle the exception.
                Console::WriteLine("Expected exception");
                Console::WriteLine(e->ToString());
            }

            StreamReader* reader = new StreamReader(isoStream);
            // Read the data.
            this->NewsUrl = reader->ReadLine();
            this->SportsUrl = reader->ReadLine();
            reader->Close();
            isoFile->Close();
            isoStream->Close();
            return false;

        }
        catch (System::IO::FileNotFoundException* e)
        {
            // Expected exception if a file cannot be
not found. This indicates that we have a new user.
            return true;
        }
    }
    bool GetIsoStoreInfo ()
    {
        // Get a User store with type evidence for
the current Domain and the Assembly.
        IsolatedStorageFile* isoFile =
IsolatedStorageFile::GetStore(

static_cast<IsolatedStorageScope>(IsolatedStorageScope::User |
                IsolatedStorageScope::Assembly |
                IsolatedStorageScope::Domain),
                __typeof(System::Security::Policy::Url),
                __typeof(System::Security::Policy::Url));

        String* dirNames[] = isoFile->GetDirectoryNames("*");
        String* fileNames[] = isoFile->GetFileNames("*");

        // List directories currently in this Isolated Storage.
        if (dirNames->Length>0)
        {
            for (int i=0;i<dirNames->Length;++i)
            {
                Console::WriteLine(S"Directory Name:
{0}", dirNames[i]);
            }
        }

        // List the files currently in this Isolated Storage.
        // The list represents all users who have
personal preferences stored for this application.
        if (fileNames->Length>0)
        {
            for (int i=0;i<fileNames->Length;++i)
            {
                Console::WriteLine(S"File Name: {0}",
fileNames[i]);
            }
        }

        isoFile->Close();
        return true;
    }

    double SetPrefsForUser ()
    {
        try
        {
            IsolatedStorageFile* isoFile;
            isoFile = IsolatedStorageFile::GetUserStoreForDomain();

            // Open or create a writable file.
            IsolatedStorageFileStream* isoStream =
                new IsolatedStorageFileStream( this->userName,
                FileMode::OpenOrCreate,
                FileAccess::Write,
                isoFile);

            StreamWriter* writer = new StreamWriter(isoStream);
            writer->WriteLine(this->NewsUrl);
            writer->WriteLine(this->SportsUrl);
            // Calculate the amount of space used to
record the user's preferences.
            double d = isoFile->CurrentSize/isoFile->MaximumSize;
            Console::WriteLine(S"CurrentSize = {0}",
isoFile->CurrentSize.ToString());
            Console::WriteLine(S"MaximumSize = {0}",
isoFile->MaximumSize.ToString());
            writer->Close();
            isoFile->Close();
            isoStream->Close();
            return d;

        }
        catch (Exception* e) //(IsolatedStorageException*)
        {
            //ToDo:  Handle the exception.
            Console::WriteLine(e->ToString());
            return 0.0;
        }
    }

    void DeleteFiles ()
    {
```

```
            try
            {
                IsolatedStorageFile* isoFile =
IsolatedStorageFile::GetStore(

static_cast<IsolatedStorageScope>(IsolatedStorageScope::User |
                    IsolatedStorageScope::Assembly |
                    IsolatedStorageScope::Domain),
                    __typeof(System::Security::Policy::Url),
                    __typeof(System::Security::Policy::Url));

                String* dirNames[]  = isoFile->GetDirectoryNames("*");
                String* fileNames[] = isoFile->GetFileNames("*");

                // List the files currently in this Isolated Storage.
                // The list represents all users who have personal
                // preferences stored for this application.
                if (fileNames->Length>0)
                {
                    for (int i=0;i<fileNames->Length;++i)
                    {
                        //Delete the files.
                        isoFile->DeleteFile(fileNames[i]);
                    }
                    // Confirm that no files remain.
                    fileNames = isoFile->GetFileNames("*");
                }
            isoFile->Close();
            }
            catch (Exception* e)
            {
                Console::WriteLine(e->ToString());
            }

        }
        void DeleteDirectories()
        {
            try
            {
                IsolatedStorageFile* isoFile =
IsolatedStorageFile::GetStore(

static_cast<IsolatedStorageScope>(IsolatedStorageScope::User |
                    IsolatedStorageScope::Assembly |
                    IsolatedStorageScope::Domain),
                    __typeof(System::Security::Policy::Url),
                    __typeof(System::Security::Policy::Url));

                String* dirNames[]  = isoFile-
>GetDirectoryNames("*");
                String* fileNames[] = isoFile-
>GetFileNames("Archive\\*");

                // Delete the current files within the
Archive directory.

                if (fileNames->Length>0)
                {
                    for (int i=0;i<fileNames->Length;++i)
                    {
                        //delete files
                        isoFile->DeleteFile
((S"Archive\\{0}", fileNames[i]));
                    }
                    //Confirm no files are left.
                    fileNames = isoFile->GetFileNames("Archive\\*");
                }

                if (dirNames->Length>0)
                {
                    for (int i=0; i<dirNames->Length; ++i)
                    {
                        // Delete the the directories in the
Isolated Storage.
                        // This deletes the Archive directory,
```

```
there should not be any others.
                        isoFile->DeleteDirectory(dirNames[i]);
                    }
                }
                dirNames = isoFile->GetDirectoryNames("*");
                isoFile->Remove();
            }
            catch (Exception* e)
            {
                Console::WriteLine(e->ToString());
            }

        }
        double SetNewPrefsForUser ()
        {
            try
            {
                Byte inputChar;
                IsolatedStorageFile* isoFile =
IsolatedStorageFile::GetStore(

static_cast<IsolatedStorageScope>(IsolatedStorageScope::User |
                    IsolatedStorageScope::Assembly |
                    IsolatedStorageScope::Domain),
                    __typeof(System::Security::Policy::Url),
                    __typeof(System::Security::Policy::Url));

                // If this is not a new user, archive the
old preferences and
                // overwrite them using the new preferences.
                if (! this->NewPrefs)
                {
                    if ( isoFile->GetDirectoryNames
("Archive")->Length == 0 )
                        isoFile->CreateDirectory("Archive");
                    else
                    {
                        // This is the stream to which data
will be written.
                        IsolatedStorageFileStream* source =
                            new IsolatedStorageFileStream
(this->userName,FileMode::OpenOrCreate,
                            isoFile);
                        // This is the stream from which
data will be read.
                        Console::WriteLine(S"Is the source
file readable?  {0}", (source->CanRead ? S"true" : S"false"));
                        Console::WriteLine("Creating new
IsolatedStorageFileStream for Archive.");

                        // Open or create a writable file
with a maximum size of 10K.
                        IsolatedStorageFileStream* target =
                            new IsolatedStorageFileStream
(("Archive\\ {0}", this->userName),
                            FileMode::OpenOrCreate,
                            FileAccess::Write,
                            FileShare::Write,
                            10240,
                            isoFile);

                        Console::WriteLine("Is the target
file writable? {0}", (target->CanWrite ? S"true" : S"false"));

                        // Stream the old file to a new file
in the Archive directory.
                        if (source->IsAsync && target->IsAsync)
                        {
                            // IsolatedStorageFileStreams
cannot be asynchronous.  However, you
                            // can use the asynchronous
BeginRead and BeginWrite functions
                            // with some possible performance penalty.
```

```
                    Console::WriteLine("Isolated                    ↵
StorageFileStreams can not be asynchronous.");
                }
                else
                {
                    Console::WriteLine("Writing data to            ↵
the new file.");

                    while (source->Position < source->Length)
                    {
                        inputChar = (Byte)source->ReadByte();
                        target->WriteByte((Byte)source           ↵
>ReadByte());
                    }

                    // Determine the size of the                 ↵
IsolatedStorageFileStream
                    // by checking its Length property.
                    Console::WriteLine                           ↵
(S"Total Bytes Read: {0}", source->Length.ToString());

                }

                // After you have read and written              ↵
to the streams, close them.
                target->Close();
                source->Close();
            }
        }

        // Open or create a writable file, no larger than 10k
        IsolatedStorageFileStream* isoStream =
            new IsolatedStorageFileStream(this->userName,
            FileMode::OpenOrCreate,
            FileAccess::Write,
            FileShare::Write,
            10240,
            isoFile);
        isoStream->Position = 0;  // Position to                 ↵
overwrite the old data.
        StreamWriter* writer = new StreamWriter(isoStream);
        // Update the data based on the new inputs.
        writer->WriteLine(this->NewsUrl);
        writer->WriteLine(this->SportsUrl);

        // Calculate the amount of space used to                 ↵
record this user's preferences.
        double d = isoFile->CurrentSize/isoFile->MaximumSize;
        Console::WriteLine(S"CurrentSize = {0}",                 ↵
isoFile->CurrentSize.ToString());
        Console::WriteLine(S"MaximumSize = {0}",                 ↵
isoFile->MaximumSize.ToString());
        // StreamWriter.Close implicitly closes isoStream.
        writer->Close();
        isoFile->Close();

        return d;
    }
    catch (Exception* e)
    {
        Console::WriteLine(e->ToString());
        return 0.0;
    }
}

        LoginPrefs(String* aUserName)
{
    userName = aUserName;
    newPrefs = GetPrefsForUser();
}

__property String* get_NewsUrl()
{
return newsUrl;
}

__property void set_NewsUrl(String* value)
{
```

```
    newsUrl = value;
    }
    __property String* get_SportsUrl() {
        return sportsUrl;
    }

    __property void set_SportsUrl(String* value)
    {
        sportsUrl = value;
    }

    __property bool get_NewPrefs()
    {
        return newPrefs;
    }
};
void GatherInfoFromUser (LoginPrefs* lp )
{
    Console::WriteLine("Please enter the URL of your news site.");
    lp->NewsUrl = Console::ReadLine();
    Console::WriteLine("Please enter the URL of your sports    ↵
site.");
    lp->SportsUrl = Console::ReadLine();
}

void main()
{

    // Prompt the user for their username.

    Console::WriteLine("Enter your login ID:");

    // Does no error checking.
    LoginPrefs* lp = new LoginPrefs(Console::ReadLine());

    if (lp->NewPrefs)
    {
        Console::WriteLine("Please set preferences for          ↵
a new user.");
        GatherInfoFromUser(lp);

        // Write the new preferences to storage.
        double percentUsed = lp->SetPrefsForUser();
        Console::WriteLine(S"Your preferences have              ↵
been written. Current space used is {0}%", __box(percentUsed));
    }
    else
    {
        Console::WriteLine("Welcome back.");

        Console::WriteLine("Your preferences have expired       ↵
please reset them.");
        GatherInfoFromUser(lp);
        lp->SetNewPrefsForUser();

        Console::WriteLine("Your news site has been             ↵
set to {0}\n and your sports site has been set to {1}.", lp->    ↵
NewsUrl, lp->SportsUrl);
    }
        lp->GetIsoStoreInfo ();
        Console::WriteLine("Enter 'd' to delete the             ↵
solatedStorage files and exit, or press any other key to        ↵
exit without deleting files.");
        String* consoleInput = Console::ReadLine();

        if (consoleInput->Equals("d"))
        {
            lp->DeleteFiles();
            lp->DeleteDirectories();
        }

    }
//}
```

Requirements

Namespace: System.IO.IsolatedStorage

Platforms: Windows 98, Windows NT 4.0, Windows Millennium Edition, Windows 2000, Windows XP Home Edition, Windows XP Professional, Windows .NET Server family

Assembly: Mscorlib (in Mscorlib.dll)

IsolatedStorageFile.CurrentSize Property

Gets the current size of the isolated storage.

```
[Visual Basic]
<CLSCompliant(False)>
Overrides Public ReadOnly Property CurrentSize As UInt64
[C#]
[CLSCompliant(false)]
public override ulong CurrentSize {get;}
[C++]
[CLSCompliant(false)]
public: __property unsigned __int64 get_CurrentSize();
[JScript]
public
    CLSCompliant(false)
override function get CurrentSize() : UInt64;
```

Property Value

The total number of bytes of storage currently in use within the isolated storage scope.

Exceptions

Exception Type	Condition
InvalidOperationException	The property is unavailable. The current store has a roaming scope or is not open.

Remarks

Represents the total usage of all files and directories within the isolated storage scope.

The current size cannot be accurately determined for stores that are participating in a roaming user profile. Because roaming profiles are often cached on multiple client machines and later synchronized with a server, quotas cannot be enforced for such stores and the current size is not reported.

The **Anticipating Out of Space Conditions** example demonstrates the use of the **CurrentSize** property.

Example

[Visual Basic, C#, C++] The following code example demonstrates the **CurrentSize** property. For the complete context of this example, see the **IsolatedStorageFile** overview.

```
[Visual Basic]
Dim writer As New StreamWriter(isoStream)
' Update the data based on the new inputs.
writer.WriteLine(Me.NewsUrl)
writer.WriteLine(Me.SportsUrl)

' Calculate the amount of space used to record this      ⌐
user's preferences.
Dim d As Double = Convert.ToDouble(isoFile.CurrentSize) /  ⌐
Convert.ToDouble(isoFile.MaximumSize)
Console.WriteLine(("CurrentSize = " & isoFile.CurrentSize.ToString()))
Console.WriteLine(("MaximumSize = " & isoFile.MaximumSize.ToString()))
```

```
[C#]
StreamWriter writer = new StreamWriter(isoStream);
// Update the data based on the new inputs.
writer.WriteLine(this.NewsUrl);
writer.WriteLine(this.SportsUrl);

// Calculate the amount of space used to record this user's    ⌐
preferences.
double d = isoFile.CurrentSize/isoFile.MaximumSize;
Console.WriteLine("CurrentSize = " + isoFile.CurrentSize.ToString());
Console.WriteLine("MaximumSize = " + isoFile.MaximumSize.ToString());
```

```
[C++]
StreamWriter* writer = new StreamWriter(isoStream);
// Update the data based on the new inputs.
writer->WriteLine(this->NewsUrl);
writer->WriteLine(this->SportsUrl);

// Calculate the amount of space used to record this user's    ⌐
preferences.
double d = isoFile->CurrentSize/isoFile->MaximumSize;
Console::WriteLine(S"CurrentSize = {0}", isoFile-     ⌐
>CurrentSize.ToString());
Console::WriteLine(S"MaximumSize = {0}", isoFile-     ⌐
>MaximumSize.ToString());
```

Requirements

Platforms: Windows 98, Windows NT 4.0, Windows Millennium Edition, Windows 2000, Windows XP Home Edition, Windows XP Professional, Windows .NET Server family

IsolatedStorageFile.MaximumSize Property

Gets a value representing the maximum amount of space available for isolated storage within the limits established by the quota.

```
[Visual Basic]
<CLSCompliant(False)>
Overrides Public ReadOnly Property MaximumSize As UInt64
[C#]
[CLSCompliant(false)]
public override ulong MaximumSize {get;}
[C++]
[CLSCompliant(false)]
public: __property unsigned __int64 get_MaximumSize();
[JScript]
public
    CLSCompliant(false)
override function get MaximumSize() : UInt64;
```

Property Value

The limit of isolated storage space in bytes.

Exceptions

Exception Type	Condition
InvalidOperationException	The property is unavailable. **MaximumSize** cannot be determined without evidence from the assembly's creation. The evidence could not be determined when the object was created.

Remarks

The number of bytes available is constrained by the isolated storage quota set by the administrator. Quota is configured in security policy on the basis of evidence, so the same code can receive a different quota if it is run with different evidence. For example, an application that is run locally and also from a share on an intranet would likely receive different quotas.

The **Anticipating Out of Space Conditions** example demonstrates the use of the **MaximumSize** property.

Example

[Visual Basic, C#, C++] The following code example demonstrates the **MaximumSize** property. For the complete context of this example, see the **IsolatedStorageFile** overview.

```
[Visual Basic]
Dim writer As New StreamWriter(isoStream)
' Update the data based on the new inputs.
writer.WriteLine(Me.NewsUrl)
writer.WriteLine(Me.SportsUrl)
' Calculate the amount of space used to record this user's
preferences.
Dim d As Double = Convert.ToDouble(isoFile.CurrentSize) /
Convert.ToDouble(isoFile.MaximumSize)
Console.WriteLine(("CurrentSize = " & isoFile.CurrentSize.ToString()))
Console.WriteLine(("MaximumSize = " & isoFile.MaximumSize.ToString()))
```

```
[C#]
StreamWriter writer = new StreamWriter(isoStream);
// Update the data based on the new inputs.
writer.WriteLine(this.NewsUrl);
writer.WriteLine(this.SportsUrl);

// Calculate the amount of space used to record this user's
preferences.
double d = isoFile.CurrentSize/isoFile.MaximumSize;
Console.WriteLine("CurrentSize = " + isoFile.CurrentSize.ToString());
Console.WriteLine("MaximumSize = " + isoFile.MaximumSize.ToString());
```

```
[C++]
StreamWriter* writer = new StreamWriter(isoStream);
// Update the data based on the new inputs.
writer->WriteLine(this->NewsUrl);
writer->WriteLine(this->SportsUrl);

// Calculate the amount of space used to record this user's
preferences.
double d = isoFile->CurrentSize/isoFile->MaximumSize;
Console::WriteLine(S"CurrentSize = {0}", isoFile-
>CurrentSize.ToString());
Console::WriteLine(S"MaximumSize = {0}", isoFile-
>MaximumSize.ToString());
```

Requirements

Platforms: Windows 98, Windows NT 4.0, Windows Millennium Edition, Windows 2000, Windows XP Home Edition, Windows XP Professional, Windows .NET Server family

IsolatedStorageFile.Close Method

Closes a store previously opened with **GetStore**, **GetUserStoreForAssembly**, or **GetUserStoreForDomain**.

```
[Visual Basic]
Public Sub Close()
[C#]
public void Close();
[C++]
public: void Close();
[JScript]
public function Close();
```

Example

[Visual Basic, C#, C++] The following code example demonstrates how you can use the **Close** method. For the complete context of this example, see the **IsolatedStorageFile** overview.

```
[Visual Basic]
Dim isoFile As IsolatedStorageFile
isoFile = IsolatedStorageFile.GetUserStoreForDomain()

' Open or create a writable file.
Dim isoStream As New IsolatedStorageFileStream(Me.userName,
FileMode.OpenOrCreate, _
    FileAccess.Write, isoFile)

Dim writer As New StreamWriter(isoStream)
writer.WriteLine(Me.NewsUrl)
writer.WriteLine(Me.SportsUrl)
' Calculate the amount of space used to record the user's preferences.
Dim d As Double = Convert.ToDouble(isoFile.CurrentSize) /
Convert.ToDouble(isoFile.MaximumSize)
Console.WriteLine(("CurrentSize = " & isoFile.CurrentSize.ToString()))
Console.WriteLine(("MaximumSize = " & isoFile.MaximumSize.ToString()))
' StreamWriter.Close implicitly closes isoStream.
writer.Close()
isoFile.Dispose()
isoFile.Close()
Return d
```

```
[C#]
IsolatedStorageFile isoFile;
isoFile = IsolatedStorageFile.GetUserStoreForDomain();

// Open or create a writable file.
IsolatedStorageFileStream isoStream =
    new IsolatedStorageFileStream( this.userName,
    FileMode.OpenOrCreate,
    FileAccess.Write,
    isoFile);

StreamWriter writer = new StreamWriter(isoStream);
writer.WriteLine(this.NewsUrl);
writer.WriteLine(this.SportsUrl);
// Calculate the amount of space used to record the user's preferences.
double d = isoFile.CurrentSize/isoFile.MaximumSize;
Console.WriteLine("CurrentSize = " + isoFile.CurrentSize.ToString());
Console.WriteLine("MaximumSize = " + isoFile.MaximumSize.ToString());
// StreamWriter.Close implicitly closes isoStream.
writer.Close();
isoFile.Dispose();
isoFile.Close();
return d;
```

```
[C++]
IsolatedStorageFile* isoFile;
isoFile = IsolatedStorageFile::GetUserStoreForDomain();

// Open or create a writable file.
IsolatedStorageFileStream* isoStream =
    new IsolatedStorageFileStream( this->userName,
    FileMode::OpenOrCreate,
    FileAccess::Write,
    isoFile);

StreamWriter* writer = new StreamWriter(isoStream);
writer->WriteLine(this->NewsUrl);
writer->WriteLine(this->SportsUrl);
// Calculate the amount of space used to record the user's preferences.
double d = isoFile->CurrentSize/isoFile->MaximumSize;
Console::WriteLine(S"CurrentSize = {0}", isoFile-
>CurrentSize.ToString());
Console::WriteLine(S"MaximumSize = {0}", isoFile-
>MaximumSize.ToString());
writer->Close();
isoFile->Close();
isoStream->Close();
return d;
```

[Visual Basic, C#, C++]

Requirements

Platforms: Windows 98, Windows NT 4.0, Windows Millennium Edition, Windows 2000, Windows XP Home Edition, Windows XP Professional, Windows .NET Server family

.NET Framework Security:

- **ReflectionPermission** for enhancing security and performance when invoked late-bound through mechanisms such as **Type.InvokeMember**. Associated enumeration: **ReflectionPermissionFlag.MemberAccess**.

IsolatedStorageFile.CreateDirectory Method

Creates a directory in the isolated storage scope.

```
[Visual Basic]
Public Sub CreateDirectory( _
   ByVal dir As String _
)
[C#]
public void CreateDirectory(
   string dir
);
[C++]
public: void CreateDirectory(
   String* dir
);
[JScript]
public function CreateDirectory(
   dir : String
);
```

Parameters

dir

   The relative path of the directory to create within the isolated storage scope.

Exceptions

Exception Type	Condition
IsolatedStorageException	The current code has insufficient permissions to create isolated storage directory.
ArgumentNullException	The directory path is a null reference (**Nothing** in Visual Basic).

Remarks

The created directory initially contains no files. The **Creating Files and Directories** example demonstrates the use of the **CreateDirectory** method

Example

See related example in the **System.IO.IsolatedStorage.File** class topic.

Requirements

Platforms: Windows 98, Windows NT 4.0, Windows Millennium Edition, Windows 2000, Windows XP Home Edition, Windows XP Professional, Windows .NET Server family

.NET Framework Security:

- **IsolatedStorageFilePermission** for accessing the isolated storage scope.
- **ReflectionPermission** for enhancing security and performance when invoked late-bound through mechanisms such as **Type.InvokeMember**. Associated enumeration: **ReflectionPermissionFlag.MemberAccess**.

IsolatedStorageFile.DeleteDirectory Method

Deletes a directory in the isolated storage scope.

```
[Visual Basic]
Public Sub DeleteDirectory( _
   ByVal dir As String _
)
[C#]
public void DeleteDirectory(
   string dir
);
[C++]
public: void DeleteDirectory(
   String* dir
);
[JScript]
public function DeleteDirectory(
   dir : String
);
```

Parameters

dir

   The relative path of the directory to delete within the isolated storage scope.

Exceptions

Exception Type	Condition
IsolatedStorageException	The directory could not be deleted.
ArgumentNullException	The directory path was a null reference (**Nothing** in Visual Basic).

Remarks

A directory must be empty before it is deleted. The deleted directory cannot be recovered once deleted.

The **Deleting Files and Directories** example demonstrates the use of the **DeleteDirectory** method.

Example

See related example in the **System.IO.IsolatedStorage.File** class topic.

Requirements

Platforms: Windows 98, Windows NT 4.0, Windows Millennium Edition, Windows 2000, Windows XP Home Edition, Windows XP Professional, Windows .NET Server family

.NET Framework Security:

- **IsolatedStorageFilePermission** for accessing the isolated storage scope
- **ReflectionPermission** for enhancing security and performance when invoked late-bound through mechanisms such as **Type.InvokeMember**. Associated enumeration: **ReflectionPermissionFlag.MemberAccess**.

IsolatedStorageFile.DeleteFile Method

Deletes a file in the isolated storage scope.

```
[Visual Basic]
Public Sub DeleteFile( _
    ByVal file As String _
)
[C#]
public void DeleteFile(
    string file
);
[C++]
public: void DeleteFile(
    String* file
);
[JScript]
public function DeleteFile(
    file : String
);
```

Parameters

file
> The relative path of the file to delete within the isolated storage scope.

Exceptions

Exception Type	Condition
IsolatedStorageException	The target file is open or the path is incorrect.
ArgumentNullException	The file path is a null reference (**Nothing** in Visual Basic).

Remarks

The deleted file cannot be recovered once deleted.

The **Deleting Files and Directories** example demonstrates the use of the **DeleteFile** method.

Example

See related example in the **System.IO.IsolatedStorage.File** class topic.

Requirements

Platforms: Windows 98, Windows NT 4.0, Windows Millennium Edition, Windows 2000, Windows XP Home Edition, Windows XP Professional, Windows .NET Server family

.NET Framework Security:
- **IsolatedStorageFilePermission** for accessing files in the isolated storage scope.
- **ReflectionPermission** for enhancing security and performance when invoked late-bound through mechanisms such as **Type.InvokeMember**. Associated enumeration: **ReflectionPermissionFlag.MemberAccess**.

IsolatedStorageFile.Dispose Method

Closes a store previously opened with **GetStore**, **GetUserStoreForAssembly**, or **GetUserStoreForDomain**.

```
[Visual Basic]
Public Overridable Sub Dispose() Implements IDisposable.Dispose
```

```
[C#]
public virtual void Dispose();
[C++]
public: virtual void Dispose();
[JScript]
public function Dispose();
```

Implements

IDisposable.Dispose

Remarks

Call **Dispose** when you are finished using the **IsolatedStorageFile**. The **Dispose** method leaves the **IsolatedStorageFile** in an unusable state. After calling **Dispose**, you must release all references to the **IsolatedStorageFile** so the memory it was occupying can be reclaimed by garbage collection.

> **Note** Always call Dispose before you release your last reference to the **IsolatedStorageFile**. Otherwise, the resources the **IsolatedStorageFileStream** is using will not be freed until garbage collection calls the **IsolatedStorageFileStream** object's destructor.

Example

See related example in the **System.IO.IsolatedStorage.File** class topic.

Requirements

Platforms: Windows 98, Windows NT 4.0, Windows Millennium Edition, Windows 2000, Windows XP Home Edition, Windows XP Professional, Windows .NET Server family

.NET Framework Security:
- **ReflectionPermission** for enhancing security and performance when invoked late-bound through mechanisms such as **Type.InvokeMember**. Associated enumeration: **ReflectionPermissionFlag.MemberAccess**.

IsolatedStorageFile.Finalize Method

Closes an isolated store. This method will run even if an exception is thrown or the program crashes.

[C#] In C#, finalizers are expressed using destructor syntax.

[C++] In C++, finalizers are expressed using destructor syntax.

```
[Visual Basic]
Overrides Protected Sub Finalize()
[C#]
~IsolatedStorageFile();
[C++]
~IsolatedStorageFile();
[JScript]
protected override function Finalize();
```

Requirements

Platforms: Windows 98, Windows NT 4.0, Windows Millennium Edition, Windows 2000, Windows XP Home Edition, Windows XP Professional, Windows .NET Server family

IsolatedStorageFile.GetDirectoryNames Method

Enumerates directories in an isolated storage scope that match a
given pattern.

```
[Visual Basic]
Public Function GetDirectoryNames( _
   ByVal searchPattern As String _
) As String()
[C#]
public string[] GetDirectoryNames(
   string searchPattern
);
[C++]
public: String* GetDirectoryNames(
   String* searchPattern
) __gc[];
[JScript]
public function GetDirectoryNames(
   searchPattern : String
) : String[];
```

Parameters

searchPattern
> A search pattern. Both single-character ("?") and multi-character
> ("*") wildcards are supported.

Return Value

An **Array** of the relative paths of directories in the isolated storage
scope that match *searchPattern*. A zero-length array specifies that
there are no directories that match.

Exceptions

Exception Type	Condition
ArgumentNullException	The *searchPattern* was a null reference (**Nothing** in Visual Basic).

Remarks

Wildcard characters must only be in the final element of a
searchPattern. For instance, "directory1/*etc*" is a valid search
string, but "*etc*/directory" is not.

The *searchPattern* "Project\Data*" will give all subdirectories of
Project beginning with Data in the isolated storage scope. The
searchPattern "*" will return all directories located in the root. For
complete description of search string criteria, see the **Directory** class.

For information on getting file names, see the **GetFileNames** method.

The **Finding Existing Files and Directories** example demonstrates
the use of the **GetDirectoryNames** method.

Example

See related example in the **System.IO.IsolatedStorage.File** class
topic.

Requirements

Platforms: Windows 98, Windows NT 4.0,
Windows Millennium Edition, Windows 2000,
Windows XP Home Edition, Windows XP Professional,
Windows .NET Server family

.NET Framework Security:
- **ReflectionPermission** for enhancing security and performance
  when invoked late-bound through mechanisms such as
  Type.InvokeMember. Associated enumeration:
  ReflectionPermissionFlag.MemberAccess.

IsolatedStorageFile.GetEnumerator Method

Gets the enumerator for the **IsolatedStorageFile** stores within an
isolated storage scope.

```
[Visual Basic]
Public Shared Function GetEnumerator( _
   ByVal scope As IsolatedStorageScope _
) As IEnumerator
[C#]
public static IEnumerator GetEnumerator(
   IsolatedStorageScope scope
);
[C++]
public: static IEnumerator* GetEnumerator(
   IsolatedStorageScope scope
);
[JScript]
public static function GetEnumerator(
   scope : IsolatedStorageScope
) : IEnumerator;
```

Parameters

scope
> Represents the **IsolatedStorageScope** for which to return
> isolated stores. **User** and **User|Roaming** are the only
> **IsolatedStorageScope** combinations supported.

Return Value

Enumerator for the **IsolatedStorageFile** stores within the specified
isolated storage scope.

Remarks

The **Enumerating Stores** example demonstrates the use of the
GetEnumerator method.

Requirements

Platforms: Windows 98, Windows NT 4.0,
Windows Millennium Edition, Windows 2000,
Windows XP Home Edition, Windows XP Professional,
Windows .NET Server family

.NET Framework Security:
- **IsolatedStorageFilePermission** for using isolated storage.
  Associated Enumeration: **AdministerIsolatedStorageByUser**
- **ReflectionPermission** for enhancing security and performance
  when invoked late-bound through mechanisms such as
  Type.InvokeMember. Associated enumeration:
  ReflectionPermissionFlag.MemberAccess.

IsolatedStorageFile.GetFileNames Method

Enumerates files in isolated storage scope that match a given pattern.

```
[Visual Basic]
Public Function GetFileNames( _
   ByVal searchPattern As String _
) As String()
[C#]
public string[] GetFileNames(
   string searchPattern
);
[C++]
public: String* GetFileNames(
   String* searchPattern
) __gc[];
```

```
[JScript]
public function GetFileNames(
    searchPattern : String
) : String[];
```

Parameters

searchPattern

A search pattern. Both single-character ("?") and multi-character ("*") wildcards are supported.

Return Value

An **Array** of relative paths of files in the isolated storage scope that match *searchPattern*. A zero-length array specifies that there are no files that match.

Exceptions

Exception Type	Condition
ArgumentNullException	The *searchPattern* was a null reference (**Nothing** in Visual Basic).

Remarks

The *searchPattern* "Project\Data*.txt" will give all ".txt" files beginning with Data in the Project directory of the isolated storage scope.

The **Finding Existing Files and Directories** example demonstrates the use of the **GetFileNames** method.

Example

See related example in the **System.IO.IsolatedStorage.File** class topic.

Requirements

Platforms: Windows 98, Windows NT 4.0, Windows Millennium Edition, Windows 2000, Windows XP Home Edition, Windows XP Professional, Windows .NET Server family

.NET Framework Security:

- **ReflectionPermission** for enhancing security and performance when invoked late-bound through mechanisms such as **Type.InvokeMember**. Associated enumeration: **ReflectionPermissionFlag.MemberAccess**.

IsolatedStorageFile.GetPermission Method

Returns the **IsolatedStoragePermission** from within a given permission set that represents access to isolated storage.

```
[Visual Basic]
Overrides Protected Function GetPermission( _
    ByVal ps As PermissionSet _
) As IsolatedStoragePermission
[C#]
protected override IsolatedStoragePermission GetPermission(
    PermissionSet ps
);
[C++]
protected: IsolatedStoragePermission* GetPermission(
    PermissionSet* ps
);
[JScript]
protected override function GetPermission(
    ps : PermissionSet
) : IsolatedStoragePermission;
```

Parameters

ps

The **PermissionSet** that contains the set of permissions granted to code that is attempting to use isolated storage.

Return Value

An **IsolatedStoragePermission** object that represents the **IsolatedStorageFile** object in the supplied permission set. The value is a null reference (**Nothing** in Visual Basic) if there is no permission of type **IsolatedStorageFilePermission** in the supplied set.

Remarks

This method is called during a store's initialization to determine the isolated storage file permissions that are granted to an assembly. The **IsolatedStorage** base class uses these permissions to determine the quota.

Requirements

Platforms: Windows 98, Windows NT 4.0, Windows Millennium Edition, Windows 2000, Windows XP Home Edition, Windows XP Professional, Windows .NET Server family

.NET Framework Security:

- **ReflectionPermission** for enhancing security and performance when invoked late-bound through mechanisms such as **Type.InvokeMember**. Associated enumeration: **ReflectionPermissionFlag.MemberAccess**.

IsolatedStorageFile.GetStore Method

Obtains isolated storage corresponding to the given application domain and assembly evidence objects and isolated storage scope.

Overload List

Obtains the isolated storage corresponding to the given application domain and assembly evidence objects.

[Visual Basic] **Overloads Public Shared Function GetStore(IsolatedStorageScope, Object, Object) As IsolatedStorageFile**

[C#] **public static IsolatedStorageFile GetStore(IsolatedStorageScope, object, object);**

[C++] **public: static IsolatedStorageFile* GetStore(IsolatedStorageScope, Object*, Object*);**

[JScript] **public static function GetStore(IsolatedStorageScope, Object, Object) : IsolatedStorageFile;**

Obtains isolated storage corresponding to the isolated storage scope given the application domain and assembly evidence types.

[Visual Basic] **Overloads Public Shared Function GetStore(IsolatedStorageScope, Type, Type) As IsolatedStorageFile**

[C#] **public static IsolatedStorageFile GetStore(IsolatedStorageScope, Type, Type);**

[C++] **public: static IsolatedStorageFile* GetStore(IsolatedStorageScope, Type*, Type*);**

[JScript] **public static function GetStore(IsolatedStorageScope, Type, Type) : IsolatedStorageFile;**

Obtains isolated storage corresponding to the given application domain and the assembly evidence objects and types.

[Visual Basic] **Overloads Public Shared Function GetStore(IsolatedStorageScope, Evidence, Type, Evidence, Type) As IsolatedStorageFile**

[C#] **public static IsolatedStorageFile GetStore(IsolatedStorageScope, Evidence, Type, Evidence, Type);**

[C++] **public: static IsolatedStorageFile* GetStore(IsolatedStorageScope, Evidence*, Type*, Evidence*, Type*);**

[JScript] **public static function GetStore(IsolatedStorageScope, Evidence, Type, Evidence, Type) : IsolatedStorageFile;**

Example

See related example in the **System.IO.IsolatedStorage.File** class topic.

IsolatedStorageFile.GetStore Method (IsolatedStorageScope, Object, Object)

Obtains the isolated storage corresponding to the given application domain and assembly evidence objects.

```
[Visual Basic]
Overloads Public Shared Function GetStore( _
   ByVal scope As IsolatedStorageScope, _
   ByVal domainIdentity As Object, _
   ByVal assemblyIdentity As Object _
) As IsolatedStorageFile
[C#]
public static IsolatedStorageFile GetStore(
   IsolatedStorageScope scope,
   object domainIdentity,
   object assemblyIdentity
);
[C++]
public: static IsolatedStorageFile* GetStore(
   IsolatedStorageScope scope,
   Object* domainIdentity,
   Object* assemblyIdentity
);
[JScript]
public static function GetStore(
   scope : IsolatedStorageScope,
   domainIdentity : Object,
   assemblyIdentity : Object
) : IsolatedStorageFile;
```

Parameters

scope
  A bitwise combination of the **IsolatedStorageScope** values.
domainIdentity
  An **Object** that contains evidence for the application domain identity.
assemblyIdentity
  An **Object** that contains evidence for the code assembly identity.

Return Value

An **IsolatedStorageFile** representing the parameters.

Exceptions

Exception Type	Condition
SecurityException	Sufficient isolated storage permissions have not been granted.

Exception Type	Condition
ArgumentNullException	Neither the *domainIdentity* nor *assemblyIdentity* have been passed in. This verifies that the correct constructor is being used. -or- Either *domainIdentity* or *assemblyIdentity* are a null reference (**Nothing** in Visual Basic).
ArgumentException	The *scope* is invalid.

Remarks

This form of **GetStore** is most useful for administrative code that needs to open a store as if it were another assembly. The store is opened for the evidence provided and not for the currently executing assembly.

For example, to open a store for your assembly that is capable of roaming and is the same across applications, you can use the following code:

```
[Visual Basic]
Dim scope AS IsolatedStorageScope
scope = (IsolatedStorageScope.User Or
IsolatedStorageScope.Assembly Or IsolatedStorageScope.Roaming)
Dim isoStore As IsolatedStorageFile
isoStore = IsolatedStorageFile.GetStore(scope, Nothing, Nothing)

[C#]
IsolatedStorageScope scope = IsolatedStorageScope.User |
IsolatedStorageScope.Assembly | IsolatedStorageScope.Roaming;
IsolatedStorageFile store = IsolatedStorageFile.GetStore
  (scope, null, null);
```

Alternatively, to open a store that is capable of roaming and is unique to an application for the same assembly, you can use the following code:

```
[Visual Basic]
Dim scope AS IsolatedStorageScope
scope = (IsolatedStorageScope.User Or
IsolatedStorageScope.Assembly Or IsolatedStorageScope.Domain
Or IsolatedStorageScope.Roaming)
Dim isoStore As IsolatedStorageFile
isoStore = IsolatedStorageFile.GetStore(scope, Nothing, Nothing)

[C#]
IsolatedStorageScope scope = IsolatedStorageScope.User |
IsolatedStorageScope.Assembly | IsolatedStorageScope.Domain |
IsolatedStorageScope.Roaming;
IsolatedStorageFile store = IsolatedStorageFile.GetStore
  (scope, null, null);
```

Note[note] If *scope* is **Domain** and the application domain the assembly is installed in does not have **IsolatedStorageFilePermission**, **GetStore** will return an **IsolatedStorageFile** without a quota. Later attempts to create an **IsolatedStorageFile** object using the **IsolatedStorageFile** that does not have a quota will fail with an **IsolatedStorageException**.

Requirements

Platforms: Windows 98, Windows NT 4.0, Windows Millennium Edition, Windows 2000, Windows XP Home Edition, Windows XP Professional, Windows .NET Server family

.NET Framework Security:

- **IsolatedStorageFilePermission** for using isolated storage. Associated Enumeration: **AdministerIsolatedStorageByUser**

- **ReflectionPermission** for enhancing security and performance when invoked late-bound through mechanisms such as **Type.InvokeMember**. Associated enumeration: **ReflectionPermissionFlag.MemberAccess**.

IsolatedStorageFile.GetStore Method (IsolatedStorageScope, Type, Type)

Obtains isolated storage corresponding to the isolated storage scope given the application domain and assembly evidence types.

```
[Visual Basic]
Overloads Public Shared Function GetStore( _
    ByVal scope As IsolatedStorageScope, _
    ByVal domainEvidenceType As Type, _
    ByVal assemblyEvidenceType As Type _
) As IsolatedStorageFile
[C#]
public static IsolatedStorageFile GetStore(
    IsolatedStorageScope scope,
    Type domainEvidenceType,
    Type assemblyEvidenceType
);
[C++]
public: static IsolatedStorageFile* GetStore(
    IsolatedStorageScope scope,
    Type* domainEvidenceType,
    Type* assemblyEvidenceType
);
[JScript]
public static function GetStore(
    scope : IsolatedStorageScope,
    domainEvidenceType : Type,
    assemblyEvidenceType : Type
) : IsolatedStorageFile;
```

Parameters

scope
    A bitwise combination of the **IsolatedStorageScope** values.

domainEvidenceType
    The type of the **Evidence** that you can chose from the list of **Evidence** present in the domain of the calling application. A null reference (**Nothing** in Visual Basic) lets the **IsolatedStorage** choose the evidence.

assemblyEvidenceType
    The type of the **Evidence** that you can chose from the list of **Evidence** present in the domain of the calling application. A null reference (**Nothing** in Visual Basic) lets the **IsolatedStorage** choose the evidence.

Return Value

An **IsolatedStorageFile** representing the parameters.

Exceptions

Exception Type	Condition
SecurityException	Sufficient isolated storage permissions have not been granted.
ArgumentException	The *scope* is invalid.

Exception Type	Condition
IsolatedStorageException	The evidenceType provided is missing in the assembly Evidence list.

Remarks

This is the overload of **GetStore** most likely to be called from application code.

This overload of **GetStore** opens an isolated store for the evidence types that are passed in.

> **Note** If *scope* is **Domain** and the application domain the assembly is installed in does not have **IsolatedStorageFilePermission**, **GetStore** will return an **IsolatedStorageFile** without a quota. Later attempts to create an **IsolatedStorageFile** object using the **IsolatedStorageFile** that does not have a quota will fail with an **IsolatedStorageException**.

Example

See related example in the **System.IO.IsolatedStorage.File** class topic.

Requirements

Platforms: Windows 98, Windows NT 4.0, Windows Millennium Edition, Windows 2000, Windows XP Home Edition, Windows XP Professional, Windows .NET Server family

.NET Framework Security:

- **IsolatedStorageFilePermission** for using isolated storage. Associated Enumeration: **AdministerIsolatedStorageByUser**

- **ReflectionPermission** for enhancing security and performance when invoked late-bound through mechanisms such as **Type.InvokeMember**. Associated enumeration: **ReflectionPermissionFlag.MemberAccess**.

IsolatedStorageFile.GetStore Method (IsolatedStorageScope, Evidence, Type, Evidence, Type)

Obtains isolated storage corresponding to the given application domain and the assembly evidence objects and types.

```
[Visual Basic]
Overloads Public Shared Function GetStore( _
    ByVal scope As IsolatedStorageScope, _
    ByVal domainEvidence As Evidence, _
    ByVal domainEvidenceType As Type, _
    ByVal assemblyEvidence As Evidence, _
    ByVal assemblyEvidenceType As Type _
) As IsolatedStorageFile
[C#]
public static IsolatedStorageFile GetStore(
    IsolatedStorageScope scope,
    Evidence domainEvidence,
    Type domainEvidenceType,
    Evidence assemblyEvidence,
    Type assemblyEvidenceType
);
[C++]
public: static IsolatedStorageFile* GetStore(
    IsolatedStorageScope scope,
    Evidence* domainEvidence,
    Type* domainEvidenceType,
```

```
    Evidence* assemblyEvidence,
    Type* assemblyEvidenceType
);
[JScript]
public static function GetStore(
    scope : IsolatedStorageScope,
    domainEvidence : Evidence,
    domainEvidenceType : Type,
    assemblyEvidence : Evidence,
    assemblyEvidenceType : Type
) : IsolatedStorageFile;
```

Parameters

scope

A bitwise combination of the **IsolatedStorageScope** values.

domainEvidence

An **Evidence** object containing the application domain identity.

domainEvidenceType

The identity **Type** to choose from the application domain evidence.

assemblyEvidence

An **Evidence** object containing the code assembly identity.

assemblyEvidenceType

The identity **Type** to choose from the application code assembly evidence.

Return Value

An **IsolatedStorageFile** representing the parameters.

Exceptions

Exception Type	Condition
SecurityException	Sufficient isolated storage permissions have not been granted.
ArgumentNullException	The *domainEvidence* or *assemblyEvidence* identity has not been passed in.
ArgumentException	The *scope* is invalid.

Remarks

Note[note] If *scope* is **Domain** and the application domain the assembly is installed in does not have **IsolatedStorageFilePermission**, **GetStore** will return an **IsolatedStorageFile** without a quota. Later attempts to create an **IsolatedStorageFile** object using the **IsolatedStorageFile** that does not have a quota will fail with an **IsolatedStorageException**.

Requirements

Platforms: Windows 98, Windows NT 4.0, Windows Millennium Edition, Windows 2000, Windows XP Home Edition, Windows XP Professional, Windows .NET Server family

.NET Framework Security:

* **IsolatedStorageFilePermission** for using isolated storage. Associated Enumeration: **AdministerIsolatedStorageByUser**
* **ReflectionPermission** for enhancing security and performance when invoked late-bound through mechanisms such as **Type.InvokeMember**. Associated enumeration: **ReflectionPermissionFlag.MemberAccess**.

IsolatedStorageFile.GetUserStoreForAssembly Method

Obtains isolated storage corresponding to the calling code's assembly identity.

```
[Visual Basic]
Public Shared Function GetUserStoreForAssembly() As _
    IsolatedStorageFile
[C#]
public static IsolatedStorageFile GetUserStoreForAssembly();
[C++]
public: static IsolatedStorageFile* GetUserStoreForAssembly();
[JScript]
public static function GetUserStoreForAssembly() :
    IsolatedStorageFile;
```

Return Value

An **IsolatedStorageFile** corresponding to the isolated storage scope based on the calling code's assembly identity.

Exceptions

Exception Type	Condition
SecurityException	Sufficient isolated storage permissions have not been granted.

Remarks

The same assembly within different applications always use the same isolated store when using this method.

GetUserStoreForAssembly is functionally equivalent to:

```
[Visual Basic]
GetStore(IsolatedStorageScope.Assembly Or                    ⌐
IsolatedStorageScope.User, Nothing, Nothing)

[C#]
GetStore(IsolatedStorageScope.Assembly |                     ⌐
IsolatedStorageScope.User, null, null);
```

> **Note** Different assemblies running within the same application domain always have distinct isolated stores.

Requirements

Platforms: Windows 98, Windows NT 4.0, Windows Millennium Edition, Windows 2000, Windows XP Home Edition, Windows XP Professional, Windows .NET Server family

.NET Framework Security:

* **IsolatedStorageFilePermission** for using isolated storage. Associated Enumeration: **AssemblyIsolationByUser**
* **ReflectionPermission** for enhancing security and performance when invoked late-bound through mechanisms such as **Type.InvokeMember**. Associated enumeration: **ReflectionPermissionFlag.MemberAccess**.

IsolatedStorageFile.GetUserStoreForDomain Method

Obtains isolated storage corresponding to the application domain identity and assembly identity.

```
[Visual Basic]
Public Shared Function GetUserStoreForDomain() As _
    IsolatedStorageFile
```

```
[C#]
public static IsolatedStorageFile GetUserStoreForDomain();
[C++]
public: static IsolatedStorageFile* GetUserStoreForDomain();
[JScript]
public static function GetUserStoreForDomain() :
    IsolatedStorageFile;
```

Return Value

An **IsolatedStorageFile** corresponding to the
IsolatedStorageScope, based on a combination of the application
domain identity and the assembly identity.

Exceptions

Exception Type	Condition
SecurityException	Sufficient isolated storage permissions have not been granted.
IsolatedStorageException	The store failed to open.
	-or-
	The assembly specified has insufficient permissions to create isolated stores.

Remarks

The same assembly code will use different isolated stores when used
in the context of different applications.

GetUserStoreForDomain is functionally equivalent to:

[Visual Basic]
```
GetStore(IsolatedStorageScope.User Or
IsolatedStorageScope.Assembly Or IsolatedStorageScope.Domain,
    Nothing, Nothing)
```

[C#]
```
GetStore(IsolatedStorageScope.Assembly |
IsolatedStorageScope.Domain | IsolatedStorageScope.User, null, null);
```

Different assemblies running within the same application domain
always have distinct isolated stores.

> **Note** **GetUserStoreForDomain** will return an **IsolatedStorageFile** without a quota if the application domain into which
> the assembly is installed does not have **IsolatedStorageFilePermission**. Later attempts to create an **IsolatedStorageFile**
> object using the **IsolatedStorageFile** that does not have a
> quota will fail with an **IsolatedStorageException**.

Example

See related example in the **System.IO.IsolatedStorage.File** class
topic.

Requirements

Platforms: Windows 98, Windows NT 4.0,
Windows Millennium Edition, Windows 2000,
Windows XP Home Edition, Windows XP Professional,
Windows .NET Server family

.NET Framework Security:

- **IsolatedStorageFilePermission** for using isolated storage.
  Associated Enumeration: **DomainIsolationByUser**

- **ReflectionPermission** for enhancing security and performance
  when invoked late-bound through mechanisms such as
  Type.InvokeMember. Associated enumeration:
  ReflectionPermissionFlag.MemberAccess.

IsolatedStorageFile.Remove Method

Removes the isolated storage scope and all its contents.

Overload List

Removes the isolated storage scope and all its contents.

> [Visual Basic] **Overloads Overrides Public Sub Remove()**
> [C#] **public override void Remove();**
> [C++] **public: void Remove();**
> [JScript] **public override function Remove();**

Removes the specified isolated storage scope for all identities.

> [Visual Basic] **Overloads Public Shared Sub Remove
> (IsolatedStorageScope)**
> [C#] **public static void Remove(IsolatedStorageScope);**
> [C++] **public: static void Remove(IsolatedStorageScope);**
> [JScript] **public static function Remove
> (IsolatedStorageScope);**

IsolatedStorageFile.Remove Method ()

Removes the isolated storage scope and all its contents.

```
[Visual Basic]
Overrides Overloads Public Sub Remove()
[C#]
public override void Remove();
[C++]
public: void Remove();
[JScript]
public override function Remove();
```

Exceptions

Exception Type	Condition
IsolatedStorageException	The isolated store cannot be deleted.

Remarks

> **CAUTION** This method irrevocably removes the entire scope
> and all contained directories and files.

The **Deleting Stores** example demonstrates the use of the **Remove**
method.

Example

See related example in the **System.IO.IsolatedStorage.File** class
topic.

Requirements

Platforms: Windows 98, Windows NT 4.0,
Windows Millennium Edition, Windows 2000,
Windows XP Home Edition, Windows XP Professional,
Windows .NET Server family

.NET Framework Security:

- **ReflectionPermission** for enhancing security and performance
  when invoked late-bound through mechanisms such as
  Type.InvokeMember. Associated enumeration:
  ReflectionPermissionFlag.MemberAccess.

IsolatedStorageFile.Remove Method (IsolatedStorageScope)

Removes the specified isolated storage scope for all identities.

```
[Visual Basic]
Overloads Public Shared Sub Remove( _
   ByVal scope As IsolatedStorageScope _
)
[C#]
public static void Remove(
   IsolatedStorageScope scope
);
[C++]
public: static void Remove(
   IsolatedStorageScope scope
);
[JScript]
public static function Remove(
   scope : IsolatedStorageScope
);
```

Parameters

scope

A bitwise combination of the **IsolatedStorageScope** values.

Exceptions

Exception Type	Condition
IsolatedStorageException	The isolated store cannot be removed.

Remarks

CAUTION   This method irrevocably removes the entire scope and all contained directories and files.

The **Deleting Stores** example demonstrates the use of the **Remove** method.

Example

Requirements

Platforms: Windows 98, Windows NT 4.0, Windows Millennium Edition, Windows 2000, Windows XP Home Edition, Windows XP Professional, Windows .NET Server family

.NET Framework Security:

- **IsolatedStorageFilePermission** for using isolated storage. Associated Enumeration: **AdministerIsolatedStorageByUser**
- **ReflectionPermission** for enhancing security and performance when invoked late-bound through mechanisms such as **Type.InvokeMember**. Associated enumeration: **ReflectionPermissionFlag.MemberAccess**.

IsolatedStorageFileStream Class

Exposes a file within isolated storage.

System.Object
  System.MarshalByRefObject
    System.IO.Stream
      System.IO.FileStream
        System.IO.IsolatedStorage.IsolatedStorageFileStream

```
[Visual Basic]
Public Class IsolatedStorageFileStream
   Inherits FileStream
[C#]
public class IsolatedStorageFileStream : FileStream
[C++]
public __gc class IsolatedStorageFileStream : public FileStream
[JScript]
public class IsolatedStorageFileStream extends FileStream
```

Thread Safety

Any public static (**Shared** in Visual Basic) members of this type are safe for multithreaded operations. Any instance members are not guaranteed to be thread safe.

Remarks

Use this class to read, write and create files in isolated storage.

Since this class extends **FileStream**, you can use an instance of **IsolatedStorageFileStream** in most situations where a **FileStream** might otherwise be used, such as to construct a **StreamReader** or **StreamWriter**.

Example

[Visual Basic, C#, C++] The following console application demonstrates how you can use **IsolatedStorageFile** and **IsolatedStorageFileStream** to write data to an Isolated Storage file. The user is requested to log in. If the user is a new user, a News URL and a Sports URL are recorded as personal preferences in Isolated Storage. If the user is a returning user, the user's current preferences are displayed. The code examples used throughout this namespace are presented in the context of this sample application.

[Visual Basic, C#, C++] You can use the **Isolated Storage Tool (Storeadm.exe)** utility to list and remove the Isolated Storage files that are created with this console application.

```
[Visual Basic]
'This sample demonstrates methods of classes found in the        ⏎
System.IO IsolatedStorage namespace.
Imports System
Imports System.IO
Imports System.IO.IsolatedStorage
Imports System.Security.Policy
Imports Microsoft.VisualBasic

Namespace ISOCS
_
    Class ConsoleApp

        <STAThread()> Overloads Shared _
        Sub Main(ByVal args() As String)

            ' Prompt the user for their username.
            Console.WriteLine("Enter your login ID:")
```

```
            ' Does no error checking.
            Dim lp As New LoginPrefs(Console.ReadLine())

            If lp.NewPrefs Then
                Console.WriteLine("Please set preferences for     ⏎
a new user.")
                GatherInfoFromUser(lp)

                ' Write the new preferences to storage.
                Dim percentUsed As Double = lp.SetPrefsForUser()
                Console.WriteLine(("Your preferences have been    ⏎
written. Current space used is " & percentUsed.ToString() & " %"))
            Else
                Console.WriteLine("Welcome back.")

                Console.WriteLine("Your preferences have          ⏎
expired, please reset them.")
                GatherInfoFromUser(lp)
                lp.SetNewPrefsForUser()

                Console.WriteLine("Your news site has been set    ⏎
to {0}" & ControlChars.Cr & " and your sports site has been set   ⏎
to {1}.", lp.NewsUrl, lp.SportsUrl)
            End If
            lp.GetIsoStoreInfo()
            Console.WriteLine("Enter 'd' to delete the           ⏎
IsolatedStorage files and exit, or press any other key to exit    ⏎
without deleting files.")
            Dim consoleInput As String = Console.ReadLine()
            If consoleInput.ToLower() = "d" Then
                lp.DeleteFiles()
                lp.DeleteDirectories()
            End If
        End Sub 'Main

        Shared Sub GatherInfoFromUser(ByVal lp As LoginPrefs)
            Console.WriteLine("Please enter the URL of your       ⏎
news site.")
            lp.NewsUrl = Console.ReadLine()
            Console.WriteLine("Please enter the URL of your       ⏎
sports site.")
            lp.SportsUrl = Console.ReadLine()
        End Sub 'GatherInfoFromUser
    End Class 'ConsoleApp
    _
    Public Class LoginPrefs

        Public Sub New(ByVal myUserName As String)
            userName = myUserName
            myNewPrefs = GetPrefsForUser()
        End Sub 'New
        Private userName As String

        Private myNewsUrl As String

        Public Property NewsUrl() As String
            Get
                Return myNewsUrl
            End Get
            Set(ByVal Value As String)
                myNewsUrl = value
            End Set
        End Property
        Private mySportsUrl As String

        Public Property SportsUrl() As String
            Get
                Return mySportsUrl
            End Get
            Set(ByVal Value As String)
                mySportsUrl = value
            End Set
        End Property
        Private myNewPrefs As Boolean
```

```vb
        Public ReadOnly Property NewPrefs() As Boolean
            Get
                Return myNewPrefs
            End Get
        End Property

        Private Function GetPrefsForUser() As Boolean
            Try
                ' Retrieve an IsolatedStorageFile for the          ↵
current Domain and Assembly.
                Dim isoFile As IsolatedStorageFile = _
                    IsolatedStorageFile.GetStore(IsolatedStorageScope.User _
                    Or IsolatedStorageScope.Assembly _
                    Or IsolatedStorageScope.Domain, Nothing, Nothing)

                Dim isoStream As New
IsolatedStorageFileStream(Me.userName, FileMode.Open, _
                    FileAccess.Read, FileShare.Read)
                ' farThe code executes to this point only           ↵
if a file corresponding to the username exists.
                ' Though you can perform operations on the          ↵
stream, you cannot get a handle to the file.
                Try

                    Dim aFileHandle As IntPtr = isoStream.Handle
                    Console.WriteLine(("A pointer to a file          ↵
handle has been obtained. " & aFileHandle.ToString() & " " &        ↵
aFileHandle.GetHashCode()))

                Catch ex As Exception
                    ' Handle the exception.
                    Console.WriteLine("Expected exception")
                    Console.WriteLine(ex.ToString())
                End Try

                Dim reader As New StreamReader(isoStream)
                ' Read the data.
                Me.NewsUrl = reader.ReadLine()
                Me.SportsUrl = reader.ReadLine()
                reader.Close()
                isoFile.Close()
                Return False
            Catch ex As System.IO.FileNotFoundException
                ' Expected exception if a file cannot be found.      ↵
This indicates that we have a new user.
                Return True
            End Try
        End Function 'GetPrefsForUser

        Public Function GetIsoStoreInfo() As Boolean
            Try
                'Get a User store with type evidence for the        ↵
current Domain and the Assembly.
                Dim isoFile As IsolatedStorageFile = _
                    IsolatedStorageFile.GetStore(IsolatedStorageScope.  ↵
User Or _
                    IsolatedStorageScope.Assembly Or                 ↵
IsolatedStorageScope.Domain, _
                    GetType(System.Security.Policy.Url),             ↵
GetType(System.Security.Policy.Url))
                Dim dirNames As [String]() =                         ↵
isoFile.GetDirectoryNames("*")
                Dim fileNames As [String]() = isoFile.GetFileNames("*")
                Dim name As String

                ' List directories currently in this Isolated Storage.
                If dirNames.Length > 0 Then

                    For Each name In dirNames
                        Console.WriteLine("Directory Name: " & name)
                    Next name
                End If

                ' List the files currently in this Isolated Storage.
                ' The list represents all users who have             ↵
```

personal preferences stored for this application.

```vb
                If fileNames.Length > 0 Then

                    For Each name In fileNames
                        Console.WriteLine("File Name: " & name)
                    Next name
                End If
                isoFile.Close()
                Return True
            Catch ex As Exception
                Console.WriteLine(ex.ToString())
            End Try
        End Function 'GetIsoStoreInfo

        Public Function SetPrefsForUser() As Double
            Try
                Dim isoFile As IsolatedStorageFile
                isoFile = IsolatedStorageFile.GetUserStoreForDomain()

                ' Open or create a writable file.
                Dim isoStream As New                                 ↵
IsolatedStorageFileStream(Me.userName, FileMode.OpenOrCreate, _
                    FileAccess.Write, isoFile)

                Dim writer As New StreamWriter(isoStream)
                writer.WriteLine(Me.NewsUrl)
                writer.WriteLine(Me.SportsUrl)
                ' Calculate the amount of space used to record       ↵
the user's preferences.
                Dim d As Double = Convert.ToDouble                   ↵
(isoFile.CurrentSize) / Convert.ToDouble(isoFile.MaximumSize)
                Console.WriteLine(("CurrentSize = " &                ↵
isoFile.CurrentSize.ToString()))
                Console.WriteLine(("MaximumSize = " &                ↵
isoFile.MaximumSize.ToString()))
                ' StreamWriter.Close implicitly closes isoStream.
                writer.Close()
                isoFile.Dispose()
                isoFile.Close()
                Return d
            Catch ex As Exception
                Console.WriteLine(ex.ToString())
            End Try
        End Function 'SetPrefsForUser
        'ToDo:  Handle the exception.

        Public Sub DeleteFiles()
            Try
                Dim isoFile As IsolatedStorageFile =                 ↵
IsolatedStorageFile.GetStore(IsolatedStorageScope.User Or            ↵
IsolatedStorageScope.Assembly Or IsolatedStorageScope.Domain,        ↵
GetType(System.Security.Policy.Url),                                 ↵
GetType(System.Security.Policy.Url))
                Dim name As String
                Dim dirNames As [String]() =                         ↵
isoFile.GetDirectoryNames("*")
                Dim fileNames As [String]() = isoFile.GetFileNames("*")
                ' List the files currently in this Isolated Storage.
                ' The list represents all users who have personal
                ' preferences stored for this application.
                If fileNames.Length > 0 Then
                    For Each name In fileNames
                        ' Delete the files.
                        isoFile.DeleteFile(name)
                    Next name
                    'Confirm no files are left.
                    fileNames = isoFile.GetFileNames("*")
                End If
            Catch ex As Exception
                Console.WriteLine(ex.ToString())
            End Try
        End Sub 'DeleteFiles

        ' This method deletes directories in the specified          ↵
Isolated Storage, after first
```

```
            ' deleting the files they contain. In this example,              ↵
      the Archive directory is deleted.
            ' There should be no other directories in this                   ↵
      Isolated Storage.
            Public Sub DeleteDirectories()
                Try
                    Dim isoFile As IsolatedStorageFile =                     ↵
      IsolatedStorageFile.GetStore(IsolatedStorageScope.User _
                        Or IsolatedStorageScope.Assembly Or                  ↵
      IsolatedStorageScope.Domain, _
                        GetType(System.Security.Policy.Url),                 ↵
      GetType(System.Security.Policy.Url))
                    Dim name As String
                    Dim dirNames As [String]() =                            ↵
      isoFile.GetDirectoryNames("*")
                    Dim fileNames As [String]() =                            ↵
      isoFile.GetFileNames("Archive\*")
                    ' Delete all the files currently in the                  ↵
      Archive directory.
                    If fileNames.Length > 0 Then
                        For Each name In fileNames
                            isoFile.DeleteFile(("Archive\" & name))
                        Next name
                        'Confirm no files are left.
                        fileNames = isoFile.GetFileNames("Archive\*")
                    End If
                    If dirNames.Length > 0 Then
                        For Each name In dirNames
                            ' Delete the Archive directory.
                            isoFile.DeleteDirectory(name)
                        Next name
                    End If
                    dirNames = isoFile.GetDirectoryNames("*")
                    isoFile.Remove()
                Catch ex As Exception
                    Console.WriteLine(ex.ToString())
                End Try
            End Sub 'DeleteDirectories

            Public Function SetNewPrefsForUser() As Double
                Try
                    Dim inputChar As Byte
                    Dim isoFile As IsolatedStorageFile =                     ↵
      IsolatedStorageFile.GetStore(IsolatedStorageScope.User Or              ↵
      IsolatedStorageScope.Assembly Or IsolatedStorageScope.Domain,          ↵
      GetType(System.Security.Policy.Url),
      GetType(System.Security.Policy.Url))

                    ' If this is not a new user, archive the old             ↵
      preferences and
                    ' overwrite them using the new preferences.
                    If Not Me.myNewPrefs Then
                        If isoFile.GetDirectoryNames("Archive").             ↵
      Length = 0 Then
                            isoFile.CreateDirectory("Archive")
                        Else

                            Dim source As New
      IsolatedStorageFileStream(Me.userName, FileMode.OpenOrCreate, isoFile)
                            Dim canWrite, canRead As Boolean
                            ' This is the stream from which                  ↵
      data will be read.
                            If source.CanRead Then canRead =                 ↵
      True Else canRead = False
                            Console.WriteLine("Is the source file            ↵
      readable? " & canRead)
                            Console.WriteLine("Creating new                  ↵
      IsolatedStorageFileStream for Archive.")
                            ' Open or create a writable file.
                            Dim target As New                                ↵
      IsolatedStorageFileStream("Archive\ " & Me.userName, _
                                FileMode.OpenOrCreate,
      FileAccess.Write, FileShare.Write, isoFile)
                            ' This is the stream to which data               ↵
      will be written.
```

```
                            If target.CanWrite Then canWrite =               ↵
      True Else canWrite = False
                            Console.WriteLine("Is the target file writable? "
      & canWrite)
                            target.SetLength(0)  'rewind the target file

                            ' Stream the old file to a new file              ↵
      in the Archive directory.
                            If source.IsAsync And target.IsAsync Then
                                ' IsolatedStorageFileStreams               ↵
      cannot be asynchronous.  However, you
                                ' can use the asynchronous                   ↵
      BeginRead and BeginWrite functions
                                ' with some possible performance penalty.
                                Console.WriteLine("IsolatedStorageFileStreams
      cannot be asynchronous.")
                            Else
                                Console.WriteLine("Writing data              ↵
      to the new file.")
                                While source.Position < source.Length
                                    inputChar = CByte(source.ReadByte())
                                    target.WriteByte(inputChar)
                                End While

                                ' Determine the size of the                  ↵
      IsolatedStorageFileStream
                                ' by checking its Length property.
                                Console.WriteLine                            ↵
      (("Total Bytes Read: " & source.Length))
                            End If

                            ' After you have read and written                ↵
      to the streams, close them.
                            target.Close()
                            source.Close()
                        End If
                    End If
                    ' Open or create a writable file with a maximum          ↵
      size of 10K.
                    Dim isoStream As New
      IsolatedStorageFileStream(Me.userName, FileMode.OpenOrCreate, _
                        FileAccess.Write, FileShare.Write, 10240, isoFile)
                    isoStream.SetLength(0) 'Position to overwrite            ↵
      the old data.
                    Dim writer As New StreamWriter(isoStream)
                    ' Update the data based on the new inputs.
                    writer.WriteLine(Me.NewsUrl)
                    writer.WriteLine(Me.SportsUrl)

                    ' Calculate the amount of space used to record           ↵
      this user's preferences.
                    Dim d As Double = Convert.ToDouble                       ↵
      (isoFile.CurrentSize) / Convert.ToDouble(isoFile.MaximumSize)
                    Console.WriteLine(("CurrentSize = " &                    ↵
      isoFile.CurrentSize.ToString()))
                    Console.WriteLine(("MaximumSize = " &                    ↵
      isoFile.MaximumSize.ToString()))
                    ' StreamWriter.Close implicitly closes isoStream.
                    writer.Close()
                    isoFile.Close()

                    Return d
                Catch ex As Exception
                    Console.WriteLine(ex.ToString())
                    Return 0.0
                End Try
            End Function 'SetNewPrefsForUser
        End Class 'LoginPrefs
    End Namespace 'ISOCS

    [C#]
    // This sample demonstrates methods of classes found in                  ↵
    the System.IO IsolatedStorage namespace.
    using System;
    using System.IO;
```

```csharp
using System.IO.IsolatedStorage;
using System.Security.Policy;

[assembly: CLSCompliantAttribute(true)]

    class ConsoleApp
    {
        [STAThread]
        static void Main(string[] args)
        {

            // Prompt the user for their username.

            Console.WriteLine("Login:");

            // Does no error checking.
            LoginPrefs lp = new LoginPrefs(Console.ReadLine());

            if (lp.NewPrefs)
            {
                Console.WriteLine("Please set preferences
for a new user.");
                GatherInfoFromUser(lp);

                // Write the new preferences to storage.
                double percentUsed = lp.SetPrefsForUser();
                Console.WriteLine("Your preferences have
been written. Current space used is " + percentUsed.ToString() + " %");
            }
            else
            {
                Console.WriteLine("Welcome back.");

                Console.WriteLine("Your preferences have
expired, please reset them.");
                GatherInfoFromUser(lp);
                lp.SetNewPrefsForUser();

                Console.WriteLine("Your news site has been set
to {0}\n and your sports site has been set to {1}.",
lp.NewsUrl, lp.SportsUrl);
            }
            lp.GetIsoStoreInfo ();
            Console.WriteLine("Enter 'd' to delete the
IsolatedStorage files and exit, or press any other key to
exit without deleting files.");
            string consoleInput = Console.ReadLine();
            if (consoleInput.ToLower() == "d")
            {
                lp.DeleteFiles();
                lp.DeleteDirectories();
            }

        }

        static void GatherInfoFromUser (LoginPrefs lp )
        {
            Console.WriteLine("Please enter the URL of your
news site.");
            lp.NewsUrl = Console.ReadLine();
            Console.WriteLine("Please enter the URL of your
sports site.");
            lp.SportsUrl = Console.ReadLine();
        }
    }

    public class LoginPrefs
    {
        public LoginPrefs(string myUserName)
        {
            userName = myUserName;
            myNewPrefs = GetPrefsForUser();
        }
        string userName;

        string myNewsUrl;
        public string NewsUrl
        {
            get { return myNewsUrl; }
            set { myNewsUrl = value; }
        }

        string mySportsUrl;
        public string SportsUrl
        {
            get { return mySportsUrl; }
            set { mySportsUrl = value; }
        }
        bool myNewPrefs;
        public bool NewPrefs
        {
            get { return myNewPrefs; }
        }

        private bool GetPrefsForUser()
        {
            try
            {

                // Retrieve an IsolatedStorageFile for the
current Domain and Assembly.
                IsolatedStorageFile isoFile =
                    IsolatedStorageFile.GetStore(IsolatedStorage
Scope.User |

                    IsolatedStorageScope.Assembly |
                    IsolatedStorageScope.Domain ,
                    null,
                    null);

                IsolatedStorageFileStream isoStream =
                    new IsolatedStorageFileStream( this.userName,
                    FileMode.Open,
                    FileAccess.Read,
                    FileShare.Read);

                // The code executes to this point only if a
file corresponding to the username exists.
                // Though you can perform operations on the
stream, you cannot get a handle to the file.

                try
                {

                    IntPtr aFileHandle = isoStream.Handle;
                    Console.WriteLine("A pointer to a file
handle has been obtained. "
                        + aFileHandle.ToString() + " "
                        + aFileHandle.GetHashCode());
                }

                catch (Exception e)
                {
                    // Handle the exception.
                    Console.WriteLine("Expected exception");
                    Console.WriteLine(e);
                }

                StreamReader reader = new StreamReader(isoStream);
                // Read the data.
                this.NewsUrl = reader.ReadLine();
                this.SportsUrl = reader.ReadLine();
                reader.Close();
                isoFile.Close();
                return false;
            }
            catch (System.IO.FileNotFoundException)
            {
                // Expected exception if a file cannot
be found. This indicates that we have a new user.
                return true;
```

```
        }
    }
    public bool GetIsoStoreInfo ()
    {
        // Get a User store with type evidence for the
current Domain and the Assembly.
        IsolatedStorageFile isoFile =
IsolatedStorageFile.GetStore( IsolatedStorageScope.User |
            IsolatedStorageScope.Assembly |
            IsolatedStorageScope.Domain,
            typeof(System.Security.Policy.Url),
            typeof(System.Security.Policy.Url));

        String [] dirNames  = isoFile.GetDirectoryNames("*");
        String [] fileNames = isoFile.GetFileNames("*");

        // List directories currently in this Isolated Storage.
        if (dirNames.Length>0)
        {
            for (int i=0;i<dirNames.Length;++i)
            {
                Console.WriteLine("Directory Name: " +
dirNames[i]);
            }
        }

        // List the files currently in this Isolated Storage.
        // The list represents all users who have
personal preferences stored for this application.
        if (fileNames.Length>0)
        {
            for (int i=0;i<fileNames.Length;++i)
            {
                Console.WriteLine("File Name: " + fileNames[i]);
            }
        }

        isoFile.Close();
        return true;
    }

    public double SetPrefsForUser ()
    {
        try
        {
            IsolatedStorageFile isoFile;
            isoFile = IsolatedStorageFile.GetUserStoreForDomain();

            // Open or create a writable file.
            IsolatedStorageFileStream isoStream =
                new IsolatedStorageFileStream( this.userName,
                FileMode.OpenOrCreate,
                FileAccess.Write,
                isoFile);

            StreamWriter writer = new StreamWriter(isoStream);
            writer.WriteLine(this.NewsUrl);
            writer.WriteLine(this.SportsUrl);
            // Calculate the amount of space used to record the user's
preferences.
            double d = isoFile.CurrentSize/isoFile.MaximumSize;
            Console.WriteLine("CurrentSize = " +
isoFile.CurrentSize.ToString());
            Console.WriteLine("MaximumSize = " +
isoFile.MaximumSize.ToString());
            // StreamWriter.Close implicitly closes isoStream.
            writer.Close();
            isoFile.Dispose();
            isoFile.Close();
            return d;
        }
        catch (IsolatedStorageException)
        {
            //ToDo:  Handle the exception.
            return 0.0;
```

```
        }
    }

    public void DeleteFiles ()
    {
        try
        {
            IsolatedStorageFile isoFile =
IsolatedStorageFile.GetStore( IsolatedStorageScope.User |
                IsolatedStorageScope.Assembly |
                IsolatedStorageScope.Domain,
                typeof(System.Security.Policy.Url),
                typeof(System.Security.Policy.Url));

            String [] dirNames  = isoFile.GetDirectoryNames("*");
            String [] fileNames = isoFile.GetFileNames("*");

            // List the files currently in this Isolated Storage.
            // The list represents all users who have personal
            // preferences stored for this application.
            if (fileNames.Length>0)
            {
                for (int i=0;i<fileNames.Length;++i)
                {
                    // Delete the files.
                    isoFile.DeleteFile(fileNames[i]);
                }
                // Confirm that no files remain.
                fileNames = isoFile.GetFileNames("*");
            }
        }
        catch (Exception e)
        {
            Console.WriteLine(e.ToString());
        }

    }
    // This method deletes directories in the specified
Isolated Storage, after first
    // deleting the files they contain. In this example,
the Archive directory is deleted.
    // There should be no other directories in this Isolated Storage.
    public void DeleteDirectories()
    {
        try
        {
            IsolatedStorageFile isoFile =
IsolatedStorageFile.GetStore( IsolatedStorageScope.User |
                IsolatedStorageScope.Assembly |
                IsolatedStorageScope.Domain,
                typeof(System.Security.Policy.Url),
                typeof(System.Security.Policy.Url));
            String [] dirNames  = isoFile.GetDirectoryNames("*");
            String [] fileNames =
isoFile.GetFileNames("Archive\\*");

            // Delete all the files currently in the
Archive directory.

            if (fileNames.Length>0)
            {
                for (int i=0;i<fileNames.Length;++i)
                {
                    // Delete the files.
                    isoFile.DeleteFile("Archive\\" + fileNames[i]);
                }
                // Confirm that no files remain.
                fileNames = isoFile.GetFileNames("Archive\\*");
            }

            if (dirNames.Length>0)
            {
                for (int i=0; i<dirNames.Length; ++i)
                {
                    // Delete the Archive directory.
```

```
                }
            }
            dirNames = isoFile.GetDirectoryNames("*");
            isoFile.Remove();
        }
        catch (Exception e)
        {
            Console.WriteLine(e.ToString());
        }
    }
    public double SetNewPrefsForUser ()
    {
        try
        {
            byte inputChar;
            IsolatedStorageFile isoFile =
IsolatedStorageFile.GetStore( IsolatedStorageScope.User |
                IsolatedStorageScope.Assembly |
                IsolatedStorageScope.Domain,
                typeof(System.Security.Policy.Url),
                typeof(System.Security.Policy.Url));

            // If this is not a new user, archive the
old preferences and
            // overwrite them using the new preferences.
            if (! this.myNewPrefs)
            {
                if ( isoFile.GetDirectoryNames("Archive")
.Length == 0 )
                    isoFile.CreateDirectory("Archive");
                else
                {
                    IsolatedStorageFileStream source =
                        new
IsolatedStorageFileStream(this.userName,FileMode.OpenOrCreate,
                        isoFile);
                    // This is the stream from which data
will be read.
                    Console.WriteLine("Is the source file
readable? " + (source.CanRead?"true":"false"));
                    Console.WriteLine("Creating new
IsolatedStorageFileStream for Archive.");

                    // Open or create a writable file.
                    IsolatedStorageFileStream target =
                        new IsolatedStorageFileStream
("Archive\\ " + this.userName,
                        FileMode.OpenOrCreate,
                        FileAccess.Write,
                        FileShare.Write,
                        isoFile);
                    Console.WriteLine("Is the target file
writable? " + (target.CanWrite?"true":"false"));
                    // Stream the old file to a new file
in the Archive directory.
                    if (source.IsAsync && target.IsAsync)
                    {
                        // IsolatedStorageFileStreams
cannot be asynchronous.  However, you
                        // can use the asynchronous
BeginRead and BeginWrite functions
                        // with some possible performance penalty.

                        Console.WriteLine("IsolatedStorageFileStreams
cannot be asynchronous.");
                    }

                    else
                    {
                        Console.WriteLine
("Writing data to the new file.");
                        while (source.Position < source.Length)
                        {
                            inputChar = (byte)source.ReadByte();
                            target.WriteByte(inputChar);
                        }

                        // Determine the size of the
IsolatedStorageFileStream
                        // by checking its Length property.
                        Console.WriteLine("Total Bytes Read:
" + source.Length);

                    }

                    // After you have read and written to
the streams, close them.
                    target.Close();
                    source.Close();
                }
            }

            // Open or create a writable file with a
maximum size of 10K.
            IsolatedStorageFileStream isoStream =
                new IsolatedStorageFileStream(this.userName,
                FileMode.OpenOrCreate,
                FileAccess.Write,
                FileShare.Write,
                10240,
                isoFile);
            isoStream.Position = 0;  // Position to
overwrite the old data.
            StreamWriter writer = new StreamWriter(isoStream);
            // Update the data based on the new inputs.
            writer.WriteLine(this.NewsUrl);
            writer.WriteLine(this.SportsUrl);

            // Calculate the amount of space used to
record this user's preferences.
            double d = isoFile.CurrentSize/isoFile.MaximumSize;
            Console.WriteLine("CurrentSize = " +
isoFile.CurrentSize.ToString());
            Console.WriteLine("MaximumSize = " +
isoFile.MaximumSize.ToString());
            // StreamWriter.Close implicitly closes isoStream.
            writer.Close();
            isoFile.Close();

            return d;
        }
        catch (Exception e)
        {
            Console.WriteLine(e.ToString());
            return 0.0;
        }
    }
}

[C++]
// This sample demonstrates methods of classes found in
the System.IO IsolatedStorage namespace.
#using <mscorlib.dll>
using namespace System;
using namespace System::IO;
using namespace System::IO::IsolatedStorage;
using namespace System::Security::Policy;

//namespace ISOCS
//{
    //class ConsoleApp
    //{

    __gc public class LoginPrefs
    {
    private:
        String* userName;
        String* newsUrl;
```

```
        String* sportsUrl;
        bool newPrefs;

    public:
        bool GetPrefsForUser()
        {
            try
            {
                // Retrieve an IsolatedStorageFile for the       ↵
current Domain and Assembly.
                IsolatedStorageFile* isoFile =
                    IsolatedStorageFile::GetStore(

static_cast<IsolatedStorageScope>(IsolatedStorageScope::User |
                    IsolatedStorageScope::Assembly |
                    IsolatedStorageScope::Domain),
                    (Type*)0, 0);
                IsolatedStorageFileStream* isoStream = new     ↵
IsolatedStorageFileStream(this->userName,
                    FileMode::Open,
                    FileAccess::ReadWrite,
                    isoFile);
                // farThe code executes to this point only if a  ↵
file corresponding to the username exists.
                // Though you can perform operations on the      ↵
stream,                                                          ↵
you cannot get a handle to the file.
                try
                {
                    IntPtr aFileHandle = isoStream->Handle;
                    Console::WriteLine(S"A pointer to a file     ↵
handle has been obtained. {0} {1}",
                        __box(aFileHandle), __box(aFileHandle.GetHashCode()));
                }

                catch (Exception* e)
                {
                    // Handle the exception.
                    Console::WriteLine("Expected exception");
                    Console::WriteLine(e->ToString());
                }

                StreamReader* reader = new StreamReader(isoStream);
                // Read the data.
                this->NewsUrl = reader->ReadLine();
                this->SportsUrl = reader->ReadLine();
                reader->Close();
                isoFile->Close();
                isoStream->Close();
                return false;
            }
            catch (Exception* e)
            {
                // Expected exception if a file cannot be found.  ↵
This indicates that we have a new user.
                String* errorMessage = e->ToString();
                return true;
            }
        }
        bool GetIsoStoreInfo ()
        {
            // Get a User store with type evidence for the        ↵
current Domain and the Assembly.
            IsolatedStorageFile* isoFile =                        ↵
IsolatedStorageFile::GetStore(

static_cast<IsolatedStorageScope>(IsolatedStorageScope::User |
                IsolatedStorageScope::Assembly |
                IsolatedStorageScope::Domain),
                __typeof(System::Security::Policy::Url),
                __typeof(System::Security::Policy::Url));
            String* dirNames[]  = isoFile->GetDirectoryNames("*");
            String* fileNames[] = isoFile->GetFileNames("*");
```

```
            // List directories currently in this Isolated Storage.
            if (dirNames->Length>0)
            {
                for (int i=0;i<dirNames->Length;++i)
                {
                    Console::WriteLine(S"Directory Name:          ↵
{0}", dirNames[i]);
                }
            }

            // List the files currently in this Isolated Storage.
            // The list represents all users who have            ↵
personal preferences stored for this application.
            if (fileNames->Length>0)
            {
                for (int i=0;i<fileNames->Length;++i)
                {
                    Console::WriteLine(S"File Name: {0}",          ↵
fileNames[i]);
                }
            }
            isoFile->Close();
            return true;
        }

        double SetPrefsForUser ()
        {
            try
            {
                IsolatedStorageFile* isoFile;
                isoFile = IsolatedStorageFile::GetUserStoreForDomain();

                // Open or create a writable file.
                IsolatedStorageFileStream* isoStream =
                    new IsolatedStorageFileStream( this->userName,
                    FileMode::OpenOrCreate,
                    FileAccess::Write,
                    isoFile);

                StreamWriter* writer = new StreamWriter(isoStream);
                writer->WriteLine(this->NewsUrl);
                writer->WriteLine(this->SportsUrl);
                // Calculate the amount of space used to          ↵
record the user's preferences.
                double d = isoFile->CurrentSize/isoFile->MaximumSize;
                Console::WriteLine(S"CurrentSize = {0}",          ↵
isoFile->CurrentSize.ToString());
                Console::WriteLine(S"MaximumSize = {0}",          ↵
isoFile->MaximumSize.ToString());
                writer->Close();
                isoFile->Close();
                isoStream->Close();
                return d;
            }
            catch (Exception* e)
            {
                //ToDo:  Handle the exception.
                Console::WriteLine(e->ToString());
                return 0.0;
            }
        }

        void DeleteFiles ()
        {
            try
            {
                IsolatedStorageFile* isoFile =                    ↵
IsolatedStorageFile::GetStore(

static_cast<IsolatedStorageScope>(IsolatedStorageScope::User |
                IsolatedStorageScope::Assembly |
                IsolatedStorageScope::Domain),
                __typeof(System::Security::Policy::Url),
                __typeof(System::Security::Policy::Url));
```

```cpp
        String* dirNames[]  = isoFile->GetDirectoryNames("*");
        String* fileNames[] = isoFile->GetFileNames("*");

        // List the files currently in this Isolated Storage.
        // The list represents all users who have personal
        // preferences stored for this application.
        if (fileNames->Length>0)
        {
            for (int i=0;i<fileNames->Length;++i)
            {
                //Delete the files.
                isoFile->DeleteFile(fileNames[i]);
            }
            // Confirm that no files remain.
            fileNames = isoFile->GetFileNames("*");
        }
        isoFile->Close();
    }
    catch (Exception* e)
    {
        Console::WriteLine(e->ToString());
    }

}
// This method deletes directories in the specified
Isolated Storage, after first
// deleting the files they contain. In this example,
the Archive directory is deleted.
// There should be no other directories in this Isolated Storage.
    void DeleteDirectories()
    {
        try
        {
            IsolatedStorageFile* isoFile =
IsolatedStorageFile::GetStore(

static_cast<IsolatedStorageScope>(IsolatedStorageScope::User |
                IsolatedStorageScope::Assembly |
                IsolatedStorageScope::Domain),
                __typeof(System::Security::Policy::Url),
                __typeof(System::Security::Policy::Url));

            String* dirNames[]  = isoFile-
>GetDirectoryNames("*");
            String* fileNames[] = isoFile-
>GetFileNames("Archive\\*");

            // Delete the current files within
the Archive directory.

            if (fileNames->Length>0)
            {
                for (int i=0;i<fileNames->Length;++i)
                {
                    //delete files
                    isoFile->DeleteFile((S"Archive\\
{0}", fileNames[i]));
                }
                //Confirm no files are left.
                fileNames = isoFile->GetFileNames("Archive\\*");
            }

            if (dirNames->Length>0)
            {
                for (int i=0; i<dirNames->Length; ++i)
                {
                    // Delete the Archive directory.
                    isoFile->DeleteDirectory(dirNames[i]);
                }
            }
            dirNames = isoFile->GetDirectoryNames("*");
            isoFile->Remove();
        }
        catch (Exception* e)
        {
```

```cpp
            Console::WriteLine(e->ToString());
        }

    }
    double SetNewPrefsForUser ()
    {
        try
        {
            Byte inputChar;
            IsolatedStorageFile* isoFile =
IsolatedStorageFile::GetStore(

static_cast<IsolatedStorageScope>(IsolatedStorageScope::User |
                IsolatedStorageScope::Assembly |
                IsolatedStorageScope::Domain),
                __typeof(System::Security::Policy::Url),
                __typeof(System::Security::Policy::Url));

            // If this is not a new user, archive
the old preferences and
            // overwrite them using the new preferences.
            if (! this->NewPrefs)
            {
                if ( isoFile->GetDirectoryNames
("Archive")->Length == 0 )
                    isoFile->CreateDirectory("Archive");
                else
                {
                    // This is the stream to which
data will be written.
                    IsolatedStorageFileStream* source =
                        new IsolatedStorageFileStream
(this->userName,FileMode::OpenOrCreate,
                        isoFile);
                    // This is the stream from which
data will be read.
                    Console::WriteLine(S"Is the source
file readable? {0}", (source->CanRead ? S"true" : S"false"));
                    Console::WriteLine("Creating new
IsolatedStorageFileStream for Archive.");
                    // Open or create a writable file.
                    IsolatedStorageFileStream* target =
                        new IsolatedStorageFileStream
(("Archive\\ {0}", this->userName),
                        FileMode::OpenOrCreate,
                        FileAccess::Write,
                        FileShare::Write,
                        isoFile);
                    Console::WriteLine("Is the target
file writable? {0}", (target->CanWrite ? S"true" : S"false"));
                    // Stream the old file to a new
file in the Archive directory.
                    if (source->IsAsync && target->IsAsync)
                    {
                        // IsolatedStorageFileStreams
cannot be asynchronous. However, you
                        // can use the asynchronous
BeginRead and BeginWrite functions
                        // with some possible performance penalty.

                        Console::WriteLine("IsolatedStorageFileStreams
cannot be
asynchronous.");
                    }
                    else
                    {
                        Console::WriteLine("Writing data
to the new file.");

                        while (source->Position < source->Length)
                        {
                            inputChar = (Byte)source->ReadByte();
                            target->WriteByte((Byte)source-
>ReadByte());
                        }
```

```
                    // Determine the size of the
                    // IsolatedStorageFileStream
                    // by checking its Length property.
                    Console::WriteLine(S"Total Bytes              ⅃
Read: {0}", source->Length.ToString());
                }

                    // After you have read and written          ⅃
to the streams, close them.
                    target->Close();
                    source->Close();
                }
            }
            // Open or create a writable file, no larger than 10k
            IsolatedStorageFileStream* isoStream =
                new IsolatedStorageFileStream(this->userName,
                FileMode::OpenOrCreate,
                FileAccess::Write,
                FileShare::Write,
                10240,
                isoFile);
            isoStream->Position = 0;  // Position to           ⅃
overwrite the old data.
            StreamWriter* writer = new StreamWriter(isoStream);
            // Update the data based on the new inputs.
            writer->WriteLine(this->NewsUrl);
            writer->WriteLine(this->SportsUrl);

            // Calculate the amount of space used to           ⅃
record this user's preferences.
            double d = isoFile->CurrentSize/isoFile->MaximumSize;
            Console::WriteLine(S"CurrentSize = {0}",           ⅃
isoFile->CurrentSize.ToString());
            Console::WriteLine(S"MaximumSize = {0}",           ⅃
isoFile->MaximumSize.ToString());
            // StreamWriter.Close implicitly closes isoStream.
            writer->Close();
            isoFile->Close();

            return d;
        }
        catch (Exception* e)
        {
            Console::WriteLine(e->ToString());
            return 0.0;
        }
    }

        LoginPrefs(String* aUserName)
    {
        userName = aUserName;
        newPrefs = GetPrefsForUser();
    }

    __property String* get_NewsUrl()
    {
    return newsUrl;
    }

    __property void set_NewsUrl(String* value)
    {
    newsUrl = value;
    }
    __property String* get_SportsUrl() {
        return sportsUrl;
    }

    __property void set_SportsUrl(String* value)
    {
        sportsUrl = value;
    }

    __property bool get_NewPrefs()
    {
        return newPrefs;
    }
```

```
    };
    void GatherInfoFromUser (LoginPrefs* lp )
    {
        Console::WriteLine("Please enter the URL of your news site.");
        lp->NewsUrl = Console::ReadLine();
        Console::WriteLine("Please enter the URL of your        ⅃
sports site.");
        lp->SportsUrl = Console::ReadLine();
    }

    void main()
    {

        // Prompt the user for their username.

        Console::WriteLine("Enter your login ID:");

        // Does no error checking.
        LoginPrefs* lp = new LoginPrefs(Console::ReadLine());

        if (lp->NewPrefs)
        {
            Console::WriteLine("Please set preferences for      ⅃
a new user.");
            GatherInfoFromUser(lp);

            // Write the new preferences to storage.
            double percentUsed = lp->SetPrefsForUser();
            Console::WriteLine(S"Your preferences have been     ⅃
written. Current space used is {0}%", __box(percentUsed));
        }
        else
        {
            Console::WriteLine("Welcome back.");

            Console::WriteLine("Your preferences have expired,  ⅃
please reset them.");
            GatherInfoFromUser(lp);
            lp->SetNewPrefsForUser();

            Console::WriteLine("Your news site has been set     ⅃
to {0}\n and your sports site has been set to {1}.",           ⅃
lp->NewsUrl, lp->SportsUrl);
        }
        lp->GetIsoStoreInfo ();
        Console::WriteLine("Enter 'd' to delete the            ⅃
IsolatedStorage files and exit, or press any other key to     ⅃
exit without deleting files.");
        String* consoleInput = Console::ReadLine();

        if (consoleInput->Equals("d"))
        {
            lp->DeleteFiles();
            lp->DeleteDirectories();
        }

    }

//}
```

Requirements

Namespace: System.IO.IsolatedStorage

Platforms: Windows 98, Windows NT 4.0,
Windows Millennium Edition, Windows 2000,
Windows XP Home Edition, Windows XP Professional,
Windows .NET Server family

Assembly: Mscorlib (in Mscorlib.dll)

IsolatedStorageFileStream Constructor

Initializes a new instance of the **IsolatedStorageFileStream** class. The only way to open an **IsolatedStorageFileStream** is by one of its constructors.

Overload List

Initializes a new instance of an **IsolatedStorageFileStream** object giving access to the file designated by *path* in the specified *mode*.

[Visual Basic] **Public Sub New(String, FileMode)**

[C#] **public IsolatedStorageFileStream(string, FileMode);**

[C++] **public: IsolatedStorageFileStream(String*, FileMode);**

[JScript] **public function IsolatedStorageFileStream(String, FileMode);**

Initializes a new instance of an **IsolatedStorageFileStream** object giving access to the file designated by *path* in the specified *mode*, with the kind of *access* requested.

[Visual Basic] **Public Sub New(String, FileMode, FileAccess)**

[C#] **public IsolatedStorageFileStream(string, FileMode, FileAccess);**

[C++] **public: IsolatedStorageFileStream(String*, FileMode, FileAccess);**

[JScript] **public function IsolatedStorageFileStream(String, FileMode, FileAccess);**

Initializes a new instance of an **IsolatedStorageFileStream** object giving access to the file designated by *path,* in the specified *mode,* and in the context of the **IsolatedStorageFile** specified by *isf.*

[Visual Basic] **Public Sub New(String, FileMode, IsolatedStorageFile)**

[C#] **public IsolatedStorageFileStream(string, FileMode, IsolatedStorageFile);**

[C++] **public: IsolatedStorageFileStream(String*, FileMode, IsolatedStorageFile*);**

[JScript] **public function IsolatedStorageFileStream(String, FileMode, IsolatedStorageFile);**

Initializes a new instance of an **IsolatedStorageFileStream** object giving access to the file designated by *path,* in the specified *mode,* with the specified file *access,*using the file sharing mode specified by *share.*

[Visual Basic] **Public Sub New(String, FileMode, FileAccess, FileShare)**

[C#] **public IsolatedStorageFileStream(string, FileMode, FileAccess, FileShare);**

[C++] **public: IsolatedStorageFileStream(String*, FileMode, FileAccess, FileShare);**

[JScript] **public function IsolatedStorageFileStream(String, FileMode, FileAccess, FileShare);**

Initializes a new instance of an **IsolatedStorageFileStream** object giving access to the file designated by *path* in the specified *mode*, with the specified file *access*, and in the context of the **IsolatedStorageFile** specified by *isf.*

[Visual Basic] **Public Sub New(String, FileMode, FileAccess, IsolatedStorageFile)**

[C#] **public IsolatedStorageFileStream(string, FileMode, FileAccess, IsolatedStorageFile);**

[C++] **public: IsolatedStorageFileStream(String*, FileMode, FileAccess, IsolatedStorageFile*);**

[JScript] **public function IsolatedStorageFileStream(String, FileMode, FileAccess, IsolatedStorageFile);**

Initializes a new instance of an **IsolatedStorageFileStream** object giving access to the file designated by *path,* in the specified *mode,* with the specified file *access,* using the file sharing mode specified by *share,* with the *buffersize* specified.

[Visual Basic] **Public Sub New(String, FileMode, FileAccess, FileShare, Integer)**

[C#] **public IsolatedStorageFileStream(string, FileMode, FileAccess, FileShare, int);**

[C++] **public: IsolatedStorageFileStream(String*, FileMode, FileAccess, FileShare, int);**

[JScript] **public function IsolatedStorageFileStream(String, FileMode, FileAccess, FileShare, int);**

Initializes a new instance of an **IsolatedStorageFileStream** object giving access to the file designated by *path,* in the specified *mode,* with the specified file *access,* using the file sharing mode specified by *share,* and in the context of the **IsolatedStorageFile** specified by *isf.*

[Visual Basic] **Public Sub New(String, FileMode, FileAccess, FileShare, IsolatedStorageFile)**

[C#] **public IsolatedStorageFileStream(string, FileMode, FileAccess, FileShare, IsolatedStorageFile);**

[C++] **public: IsolatedStorageFileStream(String*, FileMode, FileAccess, FileShare, IsolatedStorageFile*);**

[JScript] **public function IsolatedStorageFileStream(String, FileMode, FileAccess, FileShare, IsolatedStorageFile);**

Initializes a new instance of an **IsolatedStorageFileStream** object giving access to the file designated by *path,* in the specified *mode,* with the specified file *access,* using the file sharing mode specified by *share,* with the *buffersize* specified, and in the context of the **IsolatedStorageFile** specified by *isf.*

[Visual Basic] **Public Sub New(String, FileMode, FileAccess, FileShare, Integer, IsolatedStorageFile)**

[C#] **public IsolatedStorageFileStream(string, FileMode, FileAccess, FileShare, int, IsolatedStorageFile);**

[C++] **public: IsolatedStorageFileStream(String*, FileMode, FileAccess, FileShare, int, IsolatedStorageFile*);**

[JScript] **public function IsolatedStorageFileStream(String, FileMode, FileAccess, FileShare, int, IsolatedStorageFile);**

Example

See related example in the **System.IO.IsolatedStorage.FileStream** class topic.

IsolatedStorageFileStream Constructor (String, FileMode)

Initializes a new instance of an **IsolatedStorageFileStream** object giving access to the file designated by *path* in the specified *mode*.

```
[Visual Basic]
Public Sub New( _
   ByVal path As String, _
   ByVal mode As FileMode _
)
```

```
[C#]
public IsolatedStorageFileStream(
    string path,
    FileMode mode
);
[C++]
public: IsolatedStorageFileStream(
    String* path,
    FileMode mode
);
[JScript]
public function IsolatedStorageFileStream(
    path : String,
    mode : FileMode
);
```

Parameters

path
    The relative path of the file within isolated storage.
mode
    One of the **FileMode** values.

Exceptions

Exception Type	Condition
ArgumentException	The *path* is badly formed.
ArgumentNullException	The *path* is a null reference (**Nothing** in Visual Basic).
DirectoryNotFoundException	The *path* is badly formed.
FileNotFoundException	No file was found and the *mode* is set to **Open**

Remarks

The isolated store that is used is scoped by the current executing assembly's identity and that of the application domain in which it is running. This store will remain open only for the lifetime of the **IsolatedStorageFileStream** object. To specify a different isolated storage scope, or to allow the store to remain open (so multiple **IsolatedStorageFileStream** objects can be opened from it), use the form of the constructor that accepts an **IsolatedStorageFile** object.

The *mode* parameter indicates whether a new file should be created, an existing one used, and so on.

> **CAUTION** When you compile a set of characters with a particular cultural setting and retrieve those same characters with a different cultural setting, the characters might not be interpretable and can cause an exception to be thrown.

Requirements

Platforms: Windows 98, Windows NT 4.0, Windows Millennium Edition, Windows 2000, Windows XP Home Edition, Windows XP Professional, Windows .NET Server family

.NET Framework Security:
- **IsolatedStorageFilePermission** code must have isolated storage access

IsolatedStorageFileStream Constructor (String, FileMode, FileAccess)

Initializes a new instance of an **IsolatedStorageFileStream** object giving access to the file designated by *path* in the specified *mode*, with the kind of *access* requested.

```
[Visual Basic]
Public Sub New( _
    ByVal path As String, _
    ByVal mode As FileMode, _
    ByVal access As FileAccess _
)
[C#]
public IsolatedStorageFileStream(
    string path,
    FileMode mode,
    FileAccess access
);
[C++]
public: IsolatedStorageFileStream(
    String* path,
    FileMode mode,
    FileAccess access
);
[JScript]
public function IsolatedStorageFileStream(
    path : String,
    mode : FileMode,
    access : FileAccess
);
```

Parameters

path
    The relative path of the file within isolated storage.
mode
    One of the **FileMode** values.
access
    A bitwise combination of the **FileAccess** values.

Exceptions

Exception Type	Condition
ArgumentException	The *path* is badly formed.
ArgumentNullException	The *path* is a null reference (**Nothing** in Visual Basic).
FileNotFoundException	No file was found and the *mode* is set to **Open**.

Remarks

The isolated store that is used is scoped by the current executing assembly's identity and that of the application domain in which it is running. This store will remain open only for the lifetime of the **IsolatedStorageFileStream** object. To specify a different isolated storage scope, or to allow the store to remain open (so multiple **IsolatedStorageFileStream** objects can be opened from it), use the form of the constructor that accepts an **IsolatedStorageFile** object.

The *mode* parameter indicates whether a new file should be created or an existing one used. The *access* parameter includes read-only, read/write, and write-only.

CAUTION When you compile a set of characters with a particular cultural setting and retrieve those same characters with a different cultural setting, the characters might not be interpretable, and can cause an exception to be thrown.

Requirements

Platforms: Windows 98, Windows NT 4.0, Windows Millennium Edition, Windows 2000, Windows XP Home Edition, Windows XP Professional, Windows .NET Server family

.NET Framework Security:

*   **IsolatedStorageFilePermission** code must have isolated storage access

IsolatedStorageFileStream Constructor (String, FileMode, IsolatedStorageFile)

Initializes a new instance of an **IsolatedStorageFileStream** object giving access to the file designated by *path*, in the specified *mode*, and in the context of the **IsolatedStorageFile** specified by *isf*.

```
[Visual Basic]
Public Sub New( _
   ByVal path As String, _
   ByVal mode As FileMode, _
   ByVal isf As IsolatedStorageFile _
)
[C#]
public IsolatedStorageFileStream(
   string path,
   FileMode mode,
   IsolatedStorageFile isf
);
[C++]
public: IsolatedStorageFileStream(
   String* path,
   FileMode mode,
   IsolatedStorageFile* isf
);
[JScript]
public function IsolatedStorageFileStream(
   path : String,
   mode : FileMode,
   isf : IsolatedStorageFile
);
```

Parameters

path
   The relative path of the file within isolated storage.
mode
   One of the **FileMode** values.
isf
   The **IsolatedStorageFile** in which to open the **IsolatedStorageFileStream**.

Exceptions

Exception Type	Condition
ArgumentException	The *path* is badly formed.

Exception Type	Condition
ArgumentNullException	The *path* is a null reference (**Nothing** in Visual Basic).
FileNotFoundException	No file was found and the *mode* is set to **Open**.
IsolatedStorageException	*isf* does not have a quota.

Remarks

The *mode* parameter indicates whether a new file should be created, an existing one used, and so on.

CAUTION When you compile a set of characters with a particular cultural setting and retrieve those same characters with a different cultural setting, the characters might not be interpretable, and can cause an exception to be thrown.

Example

See related example in the **System.IO.IsolatedStorage.FileStream** class topic.

Requirements

Platforms: Windows 98, Windows NT 4.0, Windows Millennium Edition, Windows 2000, Windows XP Home Edition, Windows XP Professional, Windows .NET Server family

.NET Framework Security:

*   **IsolatedStorageFilePermission** code must have isolated storage access

IsolatedStorageFileStream Constructor (String, FileMode, FileAccess, FileShare)

Initializes a new instance of an **IsolatedStorageFileStream** object giving access to the file designated by *path*, in the specified *mode*, with the specified file *access*,using the file sharing mode specified by *share*.

```
[Visual Basic]
Public Sub New( _
   ByVal path As String, _
   ByVal mode As FileMode, _
   ByVal access As FileAccess, _
   ByVal share As FileShare _
)
[C#]
public IsolatedStorageFileStream(
   string path,
   FileMode mode,
   FileAccess access,
   FileShare share
);
[C++]
public: IsolatedStorageFileStream(
   String* path,
   FileMode mode,
   FileAccess access,
   FileShare share
);
```

```
[JScript]
public function IsolatedStorageFileStream(
    path : String,
    mode : FileMode,
    access : FileAccess,
    share : FileShare
);
```

Parameters

path
> The relative path of the file within isolated storage.

mode
> One of the **FileMode** values.

access
> A bitwise combination of the **FileAccess** values.

share
> A bitwise combination of the **FileShare** values.

Exceptions

Exception Type	Condition
ArgumentException	The *path* is badly formed.
ArgumentNullException	The *path* is a null reference (**Nothing** in Visual Basic).
FileNotFoundException	No file was found and the *mode* is set to **Open**.

Remarks

The isolated store that is used is scoped by the current executing assembly's identity and that of the application domain in which it is running. This store will remain open only for the lifetime of the **IsolatedStorageFileStream** object. To specify a different isolated storage scope, or to allow the store to remain open (so multiple **IsolatedStorageFileStream** objects can be opened from it), use the form of the constructor that accepts an **IsolatedStorageFile** object.

> **CAUTION** When you compile a set of characters with a particular cultural setting and retrieve those same characters with a different cultural setting, the characters might not be interpretable and can cause an exception to be thrown.

Example

See related example in the **System.IO.IsolatedStorage.FileStream** class topic.

Requirements

Platforms: Windows 98, Windows NT 4.0, Windows Millennium Edition, Windows 2000, Windows XP Home Edition, Windows XP Professional, Windows .NET Server family

.NET Framework Security:

- **IsolatedStorageFilePermission** code must have isolated storage access

IsolatedStorageFileStream Constructor (String, FileMode, FileAccess, IsolatedStorageFile)

Initializes a new instance of an **IsolatedStorageFileStream** object giving access to the file designated by *path* in the specified *mode*, with the specified file *access*, and in the context of the **IsolatedStorageFile** specified by *isf*.

```
[Visual Basic]
Public Sub New( _
    ByVal path As String, _
    ByVal mode As FileMode, _
    ByVal access As FileAccess, _
    ByVal isf As IsolatedStorageFile _
)
```

```
[C#]
public IsolatedStorageFileStream(
    string path,
    FileMode mode,
    FileAccess access,
    IsolatedStorageFile isf
);
```

```
[C++]
public: IsolatedStorageFileStream(
    String* path,
    FileMode mode,
    FileAccess access,
    IsolatedStorageFile* isf
);
```

```
[JScript]
public function IsolatedStorageFileStream(
    path : String,
    mode : FileMode,
    access : FileAccess,
    isf : IsolatedStorageFile
);
```

Parameters

path
> The relative path of the file within isolated storage.

mode
> One of the **FileMode** values.

access
> A bitwise combination of the **FileAccess** values.

isf
> The **IsolatedStorageFile** in which to open the **IsolatedStorageFileStream**.

Exceptions

Exception Type	Condition
ArgumentException	The *path* is badly formed.
ArgumentNullException	The *path* is a null reference (**Nothing** in Visual Basic).
FileNotFoundException	No file was found and the *mode* is set to **Open**.
IsolatedStorageException	*isf* does not have a quota.

Remarks

The *mode* parameter indicates whether a new file should be created or an existing one used. The *access* parameter includes read-only, read/write, and write-only.

> **CAUTION** When you compile a set of characters with a particular cultural setting and retrieve those same characters with a different cultural setting, the characters might not be interpretable, and can cause an exception to be thrown.

Example

See related example in the **System.IO.IsolatedStorage.FileStream** class topic.

Requirements

Platforms: Windows 98, Windows NT 4.0, Windows Millennium Edition, Windows 2000, Windows XP Home Edition, Windows XP Professional, Windows .NET Server family

.NET Framework Security:

- **IsolatedStorageFilePermission** code must have isolated storage access

IsolatedStorageFileStream Constructor (String, FileMode, FileAccess, FileShare, Int32)

Initializes a new instance of an **IsolatedStorageFileStream** object giving access to the file designated by *path,* in the specified *mode,* with the specified file *access,* using the file sharing mode specified by *share,* with the *buffersize* specified.

```
[Visual Basic]
Public Sub New( _
    ByVal path As String, _
    ByVal mode As FileMode, _
    ByVal access As FileAccess, _
    ByVal share As FileShare, _
    ByVal bufferSize As Integer _
)
[C#]
public IsolatedStorageFileStream(
    string path,
    FileMode mode,
    FileAccess access,
    FileShare share,
    int bufferSize
);
[C++]
public: IsolatedStorageFileStream(
    String* path,
    FileMode mode,
    FileAccess access,
    FileShare share,
    int bufferSize
);
[JScript]
public function IsolatedStorageFileStream(
    path : String,
    mode : FileMode,
    access : FileAccess,
    share : FileShare,
    bufferSize : int
);
```

Parameters

path
    The relative path of the file within isolated storage.
mode
    One of the **FileMode** values.
access
    A bitwise combination of the **FileAccess** values.

share
    A bitwise combination of the **FileShare** values.
bufferSize
    The FileStream buffer size.

Exceptions

Exception Type	Condition
ArgumentException	The *path* is badly formed.
ArgumentNullException	The *path* is a null reference (**Nothing** in Visual Basic).
FileNotFoundException	No file was found and the *mode* is set to **Open**.

Remarks

The isolated store that is used is scoped by the current executing assembly's identity and that of the application domain in which it is running. This store will remain open only for the lifetime of the **IsolatedStorageFileStream** object. To specify a different isolated storage scope, or to allow the store to remain open (so multiple **IsolatedStorageFileStream** objects can be opened from it), use the form of the constructor that accepts an **IsolatedStorageFile** object.

The *mode* parameter indicates whether a new file should be created or an existing one used. The *access* parameter includes read-only, read/write, and write-only.

> **CAUTION** When you compile a set of characters with a particular cultural setting and retrieve those same characters with a different cultural setting, the characters might not be interpretable, and can cause an exception to be thrown.

Requirements

Platforms: Windows 98, Windows NT 4.0, Windows Millennium Edition, Windows 2000, Windows XP Home Edition, Windows XP Professional, Windows .NET Server family

.NET Framework Security:

- **IsolatedStorageFilePermission** code must have isolated storage access

IsolatedStorageFileStream Constructor (String, FileMode, FileAccess, FileShare, IsolatedStorageFile)

Initializes a new instance of an **IsolatedStorageFileStream** object giving access to the file designated by *path,* in the specified *mode,* with the specified file *access,* using the file sharing mode specified by *share,* and in the context of the **IsolatedStorageFile** specified by *isf.*

```
[Visual Basic]
Public Sub New( _
    ByVal path As String, _
    ByVal mode As FileMode, _
    ByVal access As FileAccess, _
    ByVal share As FileShare, _
    ByVal isf As IsolatedStorageFile _
)
```

```
[C#]
public IsolatedStorageFileStream(
    string path,
    FileMode mode,
    FileAccess access,
    FileShare share,
    IsolatedStorageFile isf
);
[C++]
public: IsolatedStorageFileStream(
    String* path,
    FileMode mode,
    FileAccess access,
    FileShare share,
    IsolatedStorageFile* isf
);
[JScript]
public function IsolatedStorageFileStream(
    path : String,
    mode : FileMode,
    access : FileAccess,
    share : FileShare,
    isf : IsolatedStorageFile
);
```

Parameters

path
  The relative path of the file within isolated storage.
mode
  One of the **FileMode** values.
access
  A bitwise combination of the **FileAccess** values.
share
  A bitwise combination of the **FileShare** values.
isf
  The **IsolatedStorageFile** in which to open the
  IsolatedStorageFileStream.

Exceptions

Exception Type	Condition
ArgumentException	The *path* is badly formed.
ArgumentNullException	The *path* is a null reference (**Nothing** in Visual Basic).
FileNotFoundException	No file was found and the *mode* is set to **Open**.
IsolatedStorageException	*isf* does not have a quota.

Remarks

The *mode* parameter indicates whether a new file should be created or an existing one used. The *access* parameter includes read-only, read/write, and write-only.

> **CAUTION** When you compile a set of characters with a particular cultural setting and retrieve those same characters with a different cultural setting, the characters might not be interpretable, and can cause an exception to be thrown.

Example

See related example in the **System.IO.IsolatedStorage.FileStream** class topic.

Requirements

Platforms: Windows 98, Windows NT 4.0, Windows Millennium Edition, Windows 2000, Windows XP Home Edition, Windows XP Professional, Windows .NET Server family

.NET Framework Security:

- **IsolatedStorageFilePermission** code must have isolated storage access

IsolatedStorageFileStream Constructor (String, FileMode, FileAccess, FileShare, Int32, IsolatedStorageFile)

Initializes a new instance of an **IsolatedStorageFileStream** object giving access to the file designated by *path,* in the specified *mode,* with the specified file *access,* using the file sharing mode specified by *share,* with the *buffersize* specified, and in the context of the **IsolatedStorageFile** specified by *isf.*

```
[Visual Basic]
Public Sub New( _
    ByVal path As String, _
    ByVal mode As FileMode, _
    ByVal access As FileAccess, _
    ByVal share As FileShare, _
    ByVal bufferSize As Integer, _
    ByVal isf As IsolatedStorageFile _
)
[C#]
public IsolatedStorageFileStream(
    string path,
    FileMode mode,
    FileAccess access,
    FileShare share,
    int bufferSize,
    IsolatedStorageFile isf
);
[C++]
public: IsolatedStorageFileStream(
    String* path,
    FileMode mode,
    FileAccess access,
    FileShare share,
    int bufferSize,
    IsolatedStorageFile* isf
);
[JScript]
public function IsolatedStorageFileStream(
    path : String,
    mode : FileMode,
    access : FileAccess,
    share : FileShare,
    bufferSize : int,
    isf : IsolatedStorageFile
);
```

Parameters

path
  The relative path of the file within isolated storage.

mode
>One of the **FileMode** values.

access
>A bitwise combination of the **FileAccess** values.

share
>A bitwise combination of the **FileShare** values

bufferSize
>The FileStream buffer size.

isf
>The **IsolatedStorageFile** in which to open the **IsolatedStorageFileStream**.

Exceptions

Exception Type	Condition
ArgumentException	The *path* is badly formed.
ArgumentNullException	The *path* is a null reference (**Nothing** in Visual Basic).
FileNotFoundException	No file was found and the *mode* is set to **Open**.
IsolatedStorageException	*isf* does not have a quota.

Remarks

The *mode* parameter indicates whether a new file should be created or an existing one used. The *access* parameter includes read-only, read/write, and write-only.

> **CAUTION** When you compile a set of characters with a particular cultural setting and retrieve those same characters with a different cultural setting, the characters might not be interpretable, and can cause an exception to be thrown.

Example

See related example in the **System.IO.IsolatedStorage.FileStream** class topic.

Requirements

Platforms: Windows 98, Windows NT 4.0, Windows Millennium Edition, Windows 2000, Windows XP Home Edition, Windows XP Professional, Windows .NET Server family

.NET Framework Security:

- **IsolatedStorageFilePermission** code must have isolated storage access

IsolatedStorageFileStream.CanRead Property

Gets a Boolean value indicating whether the file can be read.

```
[Visual Basic]
Overrides Public ReadOnly Property CanRead As Boolean
[C#]
public override bool CanRead {get;}
[C++]
public: __property bool get_CanRead();
[JScript]
public override function get CanRead() : Boolean;
```

Property Value

true if an **IsolatedStorageFileStream** can be read; otherwise, **false**.

Remarks

Use this property to determine whether the **IsolatedStorageFileStream** can be read.

Example

See related example in the **System.IO.IsolatedStorage.FileStream** class topic.

Requirements

Platforms: Windows 98, Windows NT 4.0, Windows Millennium Edition, Windows 2000, Windows XP Home Edition, Windows XP Professional, Windows .NET Server family

IsolatedStorageFileStream.CanSeek Property

Gets a Boolean value indicating whether seek operations are supported.

```
[Visual Basic]
Overrides Public ReadOnly Property CanSeek As Boolean
[C#]
public override bool CanSeek {get;}
[C++]
public: __property bool get_CanSeek();
[JScript]
public override function get CanSeek() : Boolean;
```

Property Value

true if an **IsolatedStorageFileStream** supports seek operations; otherwise, **false**.

Remarks

Use this property to determine whether the **IsolatedStorageFileStream** supports seek operations.

Requirements

Platforms: Windows 98, Windows NT 4.0, Windows Millennium Edition, Windows 2000, Windows XP Home Edition, Windows XP Professional, Windows .NET Server family

IsolatedStorageFileStream.CanWrite Property

Gets a Boolean value indicating whether you can write to the file.

```
[Visual Basic]
Overrides Public ReadOnly Property CanWrite As Boolean
[C#]
public override bool CanWrite {get;}
[C++]
public: __property bool get_CanWrite();
[JScript]
public override function get CanWrite() : Boolean;
```

Property Value

true if an **IsolatedStorageFileStream** can be written; otherwise, **false**.

Remarks

Use this property to determine whether the **IsolatedStorageFileStream** can be written.

Example

See related example in the **System.IO.IsolatedStorage.FileStream** class topic.

Requirements

Platforms: Windows 98, Windows NT 4.0, Windows Millennium Edition, Windows 2000, Windows XP Home Edition, Windows XP Professional, Windows .NET Server family

IsolatedStorageFileStream.Handle Property

Gets the file handle for the file that the current **IsolatedStorageFileStream** object encapsulates. Accessing this property is not permitted on an **IsolatedStorageFileStream**, and throws an **IsolatedStorageException**.

```
[Visual Basic]
Overrides Public ReadOnly Property Handle As IntPtr
[C#]
public override IntPtr Handle {get;}
[C++]
public: __property IntPtr get_Handle();
[JScript]
public override function get Handle() : IntPtr;
```

Property Value

The file handle for the file that the current **IsolatedStorageFileStream** object encapsulates.

Exceptions

Exception Type	Condition
IsolatedStorageException	The property is accessed.

Example

[Visual Basic, C#, C++] The following code example demonstrates the **Handle** property.

```
[Visual Basic]
Private Function GetPrefsForUser() As Boolean
    Try
        ' Retrieve an IsolatedStorageFile for the current Domain
and Assembly.
        Dim isoFile As IsolatedStorageFile = _
            IsolatedStorageFile.GetStore(IsolatedStorageScope.User _
            Or IsolatedStorageScope.Assembly _
            Or IsolatedStorageScope.Domain, Nothing, Nothing)

        Dim isoStream As New IsolatedStorageFileStream _
(Me.userName, FileMode.Open, _
            FileAccess.Read, FileShare.Read)
        ' farThe code executes to this point only if a file
corresponding to the username exists.
        ' Though you can perform operations on the stream,
you cannot get a handle to the file.
        Try

            Dim aFileHandle As IntPtr = isoStream.Handle
            Console.WriteLine(("A pointer to a file handle has
been obtained. " & aFileHandle.ToString() & " " &
aFileHandle.GetHashCode()))

        Catch ex As Exception
            ' Handle the exception.
            Console.WriteLine("Expected exception")
            Console.WriteLine(ex.ToString())
        End Try
```

```
        Dim reader As New StreamReader(isoStream)
        ' Read the data.
        Me.NewsUrl = reader.ReadLine()
        Me.SportsUrl = reader.ReadLine()
        reader.Close()
        isoFile.Close()
        Return False
    Catch ex As System.IO.FileNotFoundException
        ' Expected exception if a file cannot be found. This
indicates that we have a new user.
        Return True
    End Try
End Function 'GetPrefsForUser
```

```
[C#]
private bool GetPrefsForUser()
{
    try
    {

        // Retrieve an IsolatedStorageFile for the current
Domain and Assembly.
        IsolatedStorageFile isoFile =
            IsolatedStorageFile.GetStore(IsolatedStorageScope.User |
            IsolatedStorageScope.Assembly |
            IsolatedStorageScope.Domain ,
            null,
            null);

        IsolatedStorageFileStream isoStream =
            new IsolatedStorageFileStream( this.userName,
            FileMode.Open,
            FileAccess.Read,
            FileShare.Read);

        // The code executes to this point only if a file
corresponding to the username exists.
        // Though you can perform operations on the stream,
you cannot get a handle to the file.

        try
        {

            IntPtr aFileHandle = isoStream.Handle;
            Console.WriteLine("A pointer to a file handle
has been obtained. "
                + aFileHandle.ToString() + " "
                + aFileHandle.GetHashCode());
        }

        catch (Exception e)
        {
            // Handle the exception.
            Console.WriteLine("Expected exception");
            Console.WriteLine(e);
        }

        StreamReader reader = new StreamReader(isoStream);
        // Read the data.
        this.NewsUrl = reader.ReadLine();
        this.SportsUrl = reader.ReadLine();
        reader.Close();
        isoFile.Close();
        return false;
    }
    catch (System.IO.FileNotFoundException)
    {
        // Expected exception if a file cannot be found.
This indicates that we have a new user.
        return true;
    }
}
```

```
[C++]
bool GetPrefsForUser()
        {
    try
    {
        // Retrieve an IsolatedStorageFile for the current
Domain and Assembly.
        IsolatedStorageFile* isoFile =
            IsolatedStorageFile::GetStore(
            static_cast<IsolatedStorageScope>
(IsolatedStorageScope::User |
            IsolatedStorageScope::Assembly |
            IsolatedStorageScope::Domain),
            (Type*)0, 0);
        IsolatedStorageFileStream* isoStream = new
IsolatedStorageFileStream(this->userName,
            FileMode::Open,
            FileAccess::ReadWrite,
            isoFile);
        // farThe code executes to this point only if a file
corresponding to the username exists.
        // Though you can perform operations on the stream,
you cannot get a handle to the file.
        try
        {

            IntPtr aFileHandle = isoStream->Handle;
            Console::WriteLine(S"A pointer to a file handle has
been obtained. {0} {1}",
                __box(aFileHandle), __box(aFileHandle.GetHashCode()));
        }

        catch (Exception* e)
        {
            // Handle the exception.
            Console::WriteLine("Expected exception");
            Console::WriteLine(e->ToString());
        }

        StreamReader* reader = new StreamReader(isoStream);
        // Read the data.
        this->NewsUrl = reader->ReadLine();
        this->SportsUrl = reader->ReadLine();
        reader->Close();
        isoFile->Close();
        isoStream->Close();
        return false;
    }
    catch (Exception* e)
    {
        // Expected exception if a file cannot be found. This
indicates that we have a new user.
        String* errorMessage = e->ToString();
        return true;
    }
        }
```

Requirements

Platforms: Windows 98, Windows NT 4.0,
Windows Millennium Edition, Windows 2000,
Windows XP Home Edition, Windows XP Professional,
Windows .NET Server family

.NET Framework Security:

- **SecurityPermission** for the ability to access unmanaged code. Associated enumeration: **SecurityPermissionFlag.UnmanagedCode**

IsolatedStorageFileStream.IsAsync Property

Gets a Boolean value indicating whether the **IsolatedStorageFileStream** was opened asynchronously or synchronously.

```
[Visual Basic]
Overrides Public ReadOnly Property IsAsync As Boolean
[C#]
public override bool IsAsync {get;}
[C++]
public: __property bool get_IsAsync();
[JScript]
public override function get IsAsync() : Boolean;
```

Property Value

true if the **IsolatedStorageFileStream** supports asynchronous access; otherwise, **false**.

Remarks

Asynchronous **IsolatedStorageFileStream** objects cannot be created, unlike **FileStream**. However, the **BeginWrite**, **BeginRead**, **EndWrite**, and **EndRead** methods are supported on synchronous instances, with some performance penalties.

Example

See related example in the **System.IO.IsolatedStorage.FileStream** class topic.

Requirements

Platforms: Windows 98, Windows NT 4.0,
Windows Millennium Edition, Windows 2000,
Windows XP Home Edition, Windows XP Professional,
Windows .NET Server family

IsolatedStorageFileStream.Length Property

Gets the length of the **IsolatedStorageFileStream**.

```
[Visual Basic]
Overrides Public ReadOnly Property Length As Long
[C#]
public override long Length {get;}
[C++]
public: __property __int64 get_Length();
[JScript]
public override function get Length() : long;
```

Property Value

The length of the **IsolatedStorageFileStream** in bytes.

Remarks

Length represents the number of bytes currently in the file. It is not affected by isolated storage quota.

Example

[Visual Basic, C#, C++] The following code example demonstrates the **Length** property.

```
[Visual Basic]
Console.WriteLine("Writing data to the new file.")
While source.Position < source.Length
    inputChar = CByte(source.ReadByte())
    target.WriteByte(inputChar)
End While

' Determine the size of the IsolatedStorageFileStream
' by checking its Length property.
Console.WriteLine(("Total Bytes Read: " & source.Length))
```

```
[C#]
Console.WriteLine("Writing data to the new file.");
while (source.Position < source.Length)
{
    inputChar = (byte)source.ReadByte();
    target.WriteByte(inputChar);
}

// Determine the size of the IsolatedStorageFileStream
// by checking its Length property.
Console.WriteLine("Total Bytes Read: " + source.Length);

[C++]
Console::WriteLine("Writing data to the new file.");
while (source->Position < source->Length)
{
    inputChar = (Byte)source->ReadByte();
    target->WriteByte((Byte)source->ReadByte());
}

// Determine the size of the IsolatedStorageFileStream
// by checking its Length property.
Console::WriteLine(S"Total Bytes Read: {0}", source-
>Length.ToString());
```

Requirements

Platforms: Windows 98, Windows NT 4.0,
Windows Millennium Edition, Windows 2000,
Windows XP Home Edition, Windows XP Professional,
Windows .NET Server family

IsolatedStorageFileStream.Position Property

Gets or sets the current position of this **IsolatedStorageFileStream**
to the specified value.

```
[Visual Basic]
Overrides Public Property Position As Long
[C#]
public override long Position {get; set;}
[C++]
public: __property __int64 get_Position();
public: __property void set_Position(__int64);
[JScript]
public override function get Position() : long;
public override function set Position(long);
```

Property Value

The current position of this **IsolatedStorageFileStream**.

Exceptions

Exception Type	Condition
ArgumentOutOfRangeException	The position cannot be set to a negative number.

Remarks

Setting this property works when the **CanSeek** property is **true**.

Example

See related example in the **System.IO.IsolatedStorage.FileStream**
class topic.

```
[Visual Basic]
Console.WriteLine("Writing data to the new file.")
While source.Position < source.Length
    inputChar = CByte(source.ReadByte())
    target.WriteByte(inputChar)
End While
```

```
' Determine the size of the IsolatedStorageFileStream
' by checking its Length property.
Console.WriteLine(("Total Bytes Read: " & source.Length))

[C#]
Console.WriteLine("Writing data to the new file.");
while (source.Position < source.Length)
{
    inputChar = (byte)source.ReadByte();
    target.WriteByte(inputChar);
}

// Determine the size of the IsolatedStorageFileStream
// by checking its Length property.
Console.WriteLine("Total Bytes Read: " + source.Length);

[C++]
Console::WriteLine("Writing data to the new file.");
while (source->Position < source->Length)
{
    inputChar = (Byte)source->ReadByte();
    target->WriteByte((Byte)source->ReadByte());
}

// Determine the size of the IsolatedStorageFileStream
// by checking its Length property.
Console::WriteLine(S"Total Bytes Read: {0}", source-
>Length.ToString());
```

Requirements

Platforms: Windows 98, Windows NT 4.0,
Windows Millennium Edition, Windows 2000,
Windows XP Home Edition, Windows XP Professional,
Windows .NET Server family

IsolatedStorageFileStream.BeginRead Method

Begins an asynchronous read.

```
[Visual Basic]
Overrides Public Function BeginRead( _
    ByVal buffer() As Byte, _
    ByVal offset As Integer, _
    ByVal numBytes As Integer, _
    ByVal userCallback As AsyncCallback, _
    ByVal stateObject As Object _
) As IAsyncResult
[C#]
public override IAsyncResult BeginRead(
    byte[] buffer,
    int offset,
    int numBytes,
    AsyncCallback userCallback,
    object stateObject
);
[C++]
public: IAsyncResult* BeginRead(
    unsigned char buffer __gc[],
    int offset,
    int numBytes,
    AsyncCallback* userCallback,
    Object* stateObject
);
```

```
[JScript]
public override function BeginRead(
   buffer : Byte[],
   offset : int,
   numBytes : int,
   userCallback : AsyncCallback,
   stateObject : Object
) : IAsyncResult;
```

Parameters
buffer
  The buffer into which to read data.
offset
  The byte offset in *array* at which to begin reading.
numBytes
  The maximum number of bytes to read.
userCallback
  The method to be called when the asynchronous read operation is completed. This parameter is optional.
stateObject
  The status of the asynchronous read.

Return Value
An **IAsyncResult** that represents the asynchronous read, which is possibly still pending. This **IAsyncResult** must be passed to this stream's **EndRead** method to determine how many bytes were read. This can be done either by the same code that called **BeginRead** or in a callback passed to **BeginRead**.

Exceptions

Exception Type	Condition
IOException	An asynchronous read was attempted past the end of the file.

Remarks
The current position in the stream is updated when you issue the asynchronous read or write, not when the I/O operation completes.

You must call **EndRead** with this **IAsyncResult** to find out how many bytes were read.

Requirements
Platforms: Windows 98, Windows NT 4.0, Windows Millennium Edition, Windows 2000, Windows XP Home Edition, Windows XP Professional, Windows .NET Server family

IsolatedStorageFileStream.BeginWrite Method

Begins an asynchronous write.

```
[Visual Basic]
Overrides Public Function BeginWrite( _
   ByVal buffer() As Byte, _
   ByVal offset As Integer, _
   ByVal numBytes As Integer, _
   ByVal userCallback As AsyncCallback, _
   ByVal stateObject As Object _
) As IAsyncResult
```

```
[C#]
public override IAsyncResult BeginWrite(
   byte[] buffer,
   int offset,
   int numBytes,
   AsyncCallback userCallback,
   object stateObject
);
```

```
[C++]
public: IAsyncResult* BeginWrite(
   unsigned char buffer __gc[],
   int offset,
   int numBytes,
   AsyncCallback* userCallback,
   Object* stateObject
);
```

```
[JScript]
public override function BeginWrite(
   buffer : Byte[],
   offset : int,
   numBytes : int,
   userCallback : AsyncCallback,
   stateObject : Object
) : IAsyncResult;
```

Parameters
buffer
  The buffer to which to write data.
offset
  The byte offset in *array* at which to begin writing.
numBytes
  The maximum number of bytes to write.
userCallback
  The method to be called when the asynchronous write operation is completed. This parameter is optional.
stateObject
  The status of the asynchronous write.

Return Value
An **IAsyncResult** that represents the asynchronous write, which is possibly still pending. This **IAsyncResult** must be passed to this stream's **EndWrite** method to ensure that the write is complete, then frees resources appropriately. This can be done either by the same code that called **BeginWrite** or in a callback passed to **BeginWrite**.

Exceptions

Exception Type	Condition
IOException	An asynchronous write was attempted past the end of the file.

Remarks
If a **IsolatedStorageFileStream** is writable, writing at the end of the stream expands the stream.

The current position in the stream is updated when you issue the asynchronous read or write, not when the I/O operation completes.

You must call **EndWrite** with the **IAsyncResult** that this method returns to find out how many bytes were written.

Requirements
Platforms: Windows 98, Windows NT 4.0, Windows Millennium Edition, Windows 2000, Windows XP Home Edition, Windows XP Professional, Windows .NET Server family

IsolatedStorageFileStream.Close Method

Releases resources associated with the **IsolatedStorageFileStream**.

```
[Visual Basic]
Overrides Public Sub Close()
[C#]
public override void Close();
[C++]
public: void Close();
[JScript]
public override function Close();
```

Remarks

Any data previously written to the buffer is copied to the file before the file stream is closed, so it is not necessary to call **Flush** before invoking **Close**.

Following a call to **Close**, any operations on the file stream might raise exceptions. After **Close** has been called once, it does nothing if called again. The **Finalize** method invokes **Close** so the file stream is closed before the garbage collector finalizes the object.

IsolatedStorageFileStream objects require an **IsolatedStorageFile** that determines the storage context for the files accessed. For streams opened without passing an **IsolatedStorageFile** object, a default **IsolatedStorageFile** is created for the executing assembly and then closed during the call to **Close**.

> **Note** The **Close** method calls **Dispose** with *disposing* set to **true** to release its resources, then calls **SuppressFinalize** to suppress finalization of this object by the garbage collector.

Example

[Visual Basic, C#] The following code example demonstrates the **Close** method.

```
[C#]
IsolatedStorageFileStream source =
    new IsolatedStorageFileStream(this.userName,FileMode.Open,isoFile);
// This stream is the one that data will be read from
Console.WriteLine("Source can be read?" +
(source.CanRead?"true":"false"));
IsolatedStorageFileStream target =
    new IsolatedStorageFileStream("Archive\\ " +
this.userName,FileMode.OpenOrCreate,isoFile);
// This stream is the one that data will be written to
Console.WriteLine("Target is writable?" +
(target.CanWrite?"true":"false"));
// Do work ...
// After you have read and written to the streams, close them
source.Close();
target.Close();

[Visual Basic]
Dim source As New
IsolatedStorageFileStream(UserName,FileMode.Open,isoFile)
' This stream is the one that data will be read from
If source.CanRead Then
    Console.WriteLine("Source can read ? true")
Else
    Console.WriteLine("Source can read ? false")
End If
Dim target As New IsolatedStorageFileStream("Archive\\ " & UserName, _
                                   FileMode.OpenOrCreate, _
                                   isoFile)
' This stream is the one that data will be written to
If target.CanWrite Then
    Console.WriteLine("Target is writable? true")
Else
    Console.WriteLine("Target is writable? false")
```

```
End If
' After you have read and written to the streams, close them
source.Close()
target.Close()
```

Requirements

Platforms: Windows 98, Windows NT 4.0, Windows Millennium Edition, Windows 2000, Windows XP Home Edition, Windows XP Professional, Windows .NET Server family

IsolatedStorageFileStream.Dispose Method

Releases resources associated with the **IsolatedStorageFileStream**.

```
[Visual Basic]
Overrides Protected Sub Dispose( _
    ByVal disposing As Boolean _
)
[C#]
protected override void Dispose(
    bool disposing
);
[C++]
protected: void Dispose(
    bool disposing
);
[JScript]
protected override function Dispose(
    disposing : Boolean
);
```

Parameters

disposing
    A value that indicates all associated resources should be closed.

Remarks

Call **Dispose** when you are finished using the **IsolatedStorageFile-Stream**. The **Dispose** method leaves the **IsolatedStorageFileStream** in an unusable state. After calling **Dispose**, you must release all references to the **IsolatedStorageFileStream** so the memory it was occupying can be reclaimed by garbage collection.

> **Note** Always call **Dispose** before you release your last reference to the **IsolatedStorageFileStream**. Otherwise, the resources the **IsolatedStorageFileStream** is using will not be freed until garbage collection calls the **IsolatedSto-rageFileStream** object's destructor.

Requirements

Platforms: Windows 98, Windows NT 4.0, Windows Millennium Edition, Windows 2000, Windows XP Home Edition, Windows XP Professional, Windows .NET Server family

IsolatedStorageFileStream.EndRead Method

Ends a pending asynchronous read request.

```
[Visual Basic]
Overrides Public Function EndRead( _
    ByVal asyncResult As IAsyncResult _
) As Integer
```

```
[C#]
public override int EndRead(
    IAsyncResult asyncResult
);
[C++]
public: int EndRead(
    IAsyncResult* asyncResult
);
[JScript]
public override function EndRead(
    asyncResult : IAsyncResult
) : int;
```

Parameters

asyncResult

 The pending asynchronous request.

Return Value

The number of bytes read from the stream, between zero and the number of requested bytes. Streams will only return zero at the end of the stream. Otherwise, they will block until at least one byte is available.

Exceptions

Exception Type	Condition
ArgumentNullException	The *asyncResult* is a null reference (**Nothing** in Visual Basic).

Remarks

EndRead must be called exactly once on every **IAsyncResult** from **BeginRead**, and calling **EndRead** is the only way to know how many bytes were read from the **Stream**. **EndRead** will block until the I/O operation has completed.

Requirements

Platforms: Windows 98, Windows NT 4.0, Windows Millennium Edition, Windows 2000, Windows XP Home Edition, Windows XP Professional, Windows .NET Server family

IsolatedStorageFileStream.EndWrite Method

Ends an asynchronous write.

```
[Visual Basic]
Overrides Public Sub EndWrite( _
    ByVal asyncResult As IAsyncResult _
)
[C#]
public override void EndWrite(
    IAsyncResult asyncResult
);
[C++]
public: void EndWrite(
    IAsyncResult* asyncResult
);
[JScript]
public override function EndWrite(
    asyncResult : IAsyncResult
);
```

Parameters

asyncResult

 The pending asynchronous I/O request to end.

Exceptions

Exception Type	Condition
ArgumentNullException	The *asyncResult* parameter is a null reference (**Nothing** in Visual Basic).

Remarks

EndWrite must be called exactly once on every **IAsyncResult** from **BeginWrite**.

EndWrite will block until the I/O operation has completed.

Requirements

Platforms: Windows 98, Windows NT 4.0, Windows Millennium Edition, Windows 2000, Windows XP Home Edition, Windows XP Professional, Windows .NET Server family

IsolatedStorageFileStream.Flush Method

Updates the file with the current state of the buffer then clears the buffer.

```
[Visual Basic]
Overrides Public Sub Flush()
[C#]
public override void Flush();
[C++]
public: void Flush();
[JScript]
public override function Flush();
```

Remarks

Since a buffer can be used for either reading or writing, but not both simultaneously, **Flush** performs two functions. First, any data previously written to the buffer is copied to the file and the buffer is cleared. Second, if **CanSeek** is **true** and data was previously copied from the file to the buffer for reading, the current position within the file is decremented by the number of unread bytes in the buffer. The buffer is then cleared.

Requirements

Platforms: Windows 98, Windows NT 4.0, Windows Millennium Edition, Windows 2000, Windows XP Home Edition, Windows XP Professional, Windows .NET Server family

IsolatedStorageFileStream.Read Method

Copies bytes from the current buffered **IsolatedStorageFileStream** to an array.

```
[Visual Basic]
Overrides Public Function Read( _
    ByVal buffer() As Byte, _
    ByVal offset As Integer, _
    ByVal count As Integer _
) As Integer
[C#]
public override int Read(
    byte[] buffer,
    int offset,
    int count
);
```

```
[C++]
public: int Read(
    unsigned char buffer __gc[],
    int offset,
    int count
);
[JScript]
public override function Read(
    buffer : Byte[],
    offset : int,
    count : int
) : int;
```

Parameters

buffer

The buffer to read.

offset

The offset in the buffer at which to begin writing.

count

The maximum number of bytes to read.

Return Value

The total number of bytes read into the *buffer*. This can be less than the number of bytes requested if that many bytes are not currently available, or zero if the end of the stream is reached.

Remarks

The *buffer* parameter can be an instance of the **Buffer** class, or an array of one of the following types: **Byte**, **SByte**, **Char**, **Int16**, **Int32**, **Int64**, **UInt16**, **UInt32**, **UInt64**, **Single**, or **Double**. The *offset* parameter gives the offset of the byte in buffer at which to begin writing (index in the buffer), and the *count* parameter gives the maximum number of bytes that will be read from this stream. The returned value is the actual number of bytes read, or zero if the end of the stream is reached. If the read operation is successful, the current position of the stream is advanced by the number of bytes read. If an exception occurs, the current position of the stream is unchanged.

The **Read** method treats the *buffer* parameter as a block of bytes, regardless of its actual type. Likewise, the *offset* and *count* parameters are always specified in bytes. For *buffer* parameters other than byte arrays, this means that an element index must be multiplied by the element size in bytes to form a correct value for *offset* or *count*.

The **Read** method will return zero only if the end of the stream is reached. In all other cases, **Read** always reads at least one byte from the stream before returning. If no data is available from the **IsolatedStorageFileStream** upon a call to **Read**, the method will block until at least one byte of data can be returned.

Requirements

Platforms: Windows 98, Windows NT 4.0, Windows Millennium Edition, Windows 2000, Windows XP Home Edition, Windows XP Professional, Windows .NET Server family

IsolatedStorageFileStream.ReadByte Method

Reads a single byte from the **IsolatedStorageFileStream** in isolated storage.

```
[Visual Basic]
Overrides Public Function ReadByte() As Integer
[C#]
public override int ReadByte();
```

```
[C++]
public: int ReadByte();
[JScript]
public override function ReadByte() : int;
```

Return Value

The 8-bit unsigned integer value read from the isolated storage file.

Example

[Visual Basic, C#, C++] The following code example demonstrates how the **ReadByte** method can be used to read data from an **IsolatedStorageFileStream**. For the complete context of this example, see the **IsolatedStorageFileStream** overview.

```
[Visual Basic]
Console.WriteLine("Writing data to the new file.")
While source.Position < source.Length
    inputChar = CByte(source.ReadByte())
    target.WriteByte(inputChar)
End While

' Determine the size of the IsolatedStorageFileStream
' by checking its Length property.
Console.WriteLine(("Total Bytes Read: " & source.Length))
```

```
[C#]
Console.WriteLine("Writing data to the new file.");
while (source.Position < source.Length)
{
    inputChar = (byte)source.ReadByte();
    target.WriteByte(inputChar);
}

// Determine the size of the IsolatedStorageFileStream
// by checking its Length property.
Console.WriteLine("Total Bytes Read: " + source.Length);
```

```
[C++]
Console::WriteLine("Writing data to the new file.");
while (source->Position < source->Length)
{
    inputChar = (Byte)source->ReadByte();
    target->WriteByte((Byte)source->ReadByte());
}

// Determine the size of the IsolatedStorageFileStream
// by checking its Length property.
Console::WriteLine(S"Total Bytes Read: {0}", source-
>Length.ToString());
```

Requirements

Platforms: Windows 98, Windows NT 4.0, Windows Millennium Edition, Windows 2000, Windows XP Home Edition, Windows XP Professional, Windows .NET Server family

IsolatedStorageFileStream.Seek Method

Sets the current position of this **IsolatedStorageFileStream** to the specified value.

```
[Visual Basic]
Overrides Public Function Seek( _
    ByVal offset As Long, _
    ByVal origin As SeekOrigin _
) As Long
[C#]
public override long Seek(
    long offset,
    SeekOrigin origin
);
```

```
[C++]
public: __int64 Seek(
    __int64 offset,
    SeekOrigin origin
);
[JScript]
public override function Seek(
    offset : long,
    origin : SeekOrigin
) : long;
```

Parameters

offset
> The new position of the **IsolatedStorageFileStream**.

origin
> One of the **SeekOrigin** values.

Return Value

The new position in the **IsolatedStorageFileStream**.

Exceptions

Exception Type	Condition
ArgumentException	The *origin* must be one of the **SeekOrigin** values.

Remarks

Some **IsolatedStorageFileStream** objects support positioning beyond the length of the stream, others will throw an exception in this case.

Requirements

Platforms: Windows 98, Windows NT 4.0, Windows Millennium Edition, Windows 2000, Windows XP Home Edition, Windows XP Professional, Windows .NET Server family

IsolatedStorageFileStream.SetLength Method

Sets the length of this **IsolatedStorageFileStream** to the specified *value*.

```
[Visual Basic]
Overrides Public Sub SetLength( _
    ByVal value As Long _
)
[C#]
public override void SetLength(
    long value
);
[C++]
public: void SetLength(
    __int64 value
);
[JScript]
public override function SetLength(
    value : long
);
```

Parameters

value
> The new length of the **IsolatedStorageFileStream**.

Remarks

If the specified *value* is less than the current length of the **IsolatedStorageFileStream**, the stream is truncated. If the specified *value* is larger than the current length of the stream, the stream is expanded. If the stream is expanded, the contents of the stream between the old and the new length are undefined. In order to use this method, an **IsolatedStorageFileStream** must support both writing and seeking.

Requirements

Platforms: Windows 98, Windows NT 4.0, Windows Millennium Edition, Windows 2000, Windows XP Home Edition, Windows XP Professional, Windows .NET Server family

IsolatedStorageFileStream.Write Method

Writes a block of bytes to the **IsolatedStorageFileStream** using data read from a byte array.

```
[Visual Basic]
Overrides Public Sub Write( _
    ByVal buffer() As Byte, _
    ByVal offset As Integer, _
    ByVal count As Integer _
)
[C#]
public override void Write(
    byte[] buffer,
    int offset,
    int count
);
[C++]
public: void Write(
    unsigned char buffer __gc[],
    int offset,
    int count
);
[JScript]
public override function Write(
    buffer : Byte[],
    offset : int,
    count : int
);
```

Parameters

buffer
> The buffer to write.

offset
> The byte offset in buffer from which to begin.

count
> The maximum number of bytes to write.

Exceptions

Exception Type	Condition
IsolatedStorageException	The write attempt exceeds the quota for the **IsolatedStorageFileStream**.

Remarks

The *offset* parameter gives the offset of the byte in the *buffer* at which to begin reading, and the *count* parameter gives the number of bytes that will be written to this **IsolatedStorageFileStream**. If the write operation is successful, the current position of the **IsolatedStorageFileStream** is advanced by the number of bytes written. If an exception occurs, the current position of the **IsolatedStorageFileStream** is unchanged.

Requirements

Platforms: Windows 98, Windows NT 4.0, Windows Millennium Edition, Windows 2000, Windows XP Home Edition, Windows XP Professional, Windows .NET Server family

IsolatedStorageFileStream.WriteByte Method

Writes a single byte to the **IsolatedStorageFileStream**.

```
[Visual Basic]
Overrides Public Sub WriteByte( _
   ByVal value As Byte _
)
[C#]
public override void WriteByte(
   byte value
);
[C++]
public: void WriteByte(
   unsigned char value
);
[JScript]
public override function WriteByte(
   value : Byte
);
```

Parameters

value
    The byte value to write to the isolated storage file.

Exceptions

Exception Type	Condition
IsolatedStorageException	The write attempt exceeds the quota for the **IsolatedStorageFileStream**.

Example

See related example in the **System.IO.IsolatedStorage.FileStream** class topic.

Requirements

Platforms: Windows 98, Windows NT 4.0, Windows Millennium Edition, Windows 2000, Windows XP Home Edition, Windows XP Professional, Windows .NET Server family

IsolatedStorageScope Enumeration

Enumerates the levels of isolated storage scope that are supported by **IsolatedStorage**.

This enumeration has a **FlagsAttribute** attribute that allows a bitwise combination of its member values.

```
[Visual Basic]
<Flags>
<Serializable>
Public Enum IsolatedStorageScope
[C#]
[Flags]
[Serializable]
public enum IsolatedStorageScope
[C++]
[Flags]
[Serializable]
__value public enum IsolatedStorageScope
[JScript]
public
   Flags
   Serializable
enum IsolatedStorageScope
```

Remarks

Use **IsolatedStorageScope** to specify a degree of scope for an isolated store. You can specify combinations of these levels that are supported by **IsolatedStorage**.

Members

Member name	Description	Value
Assembly	Isolated storage scoped to the identity of the assembly.	4
Domain	Isolated storage scoped to the application domain identity.	2
None	No isolated storage usage.	0
Roaming	The isolated store can be placed in a location on the file system that might roam (if roaming user data is enabled on the underlying operating system).	8
User	Isolated storage scoped by user identity.	1

Example

[Visual Basic, C#, C++] The following code example demonstrates how the **IsolatedStorageScope** enumeration is used in the **GetStore** methods.

```
[Visual Basic]
' Retrieve an IsolatedStorageFile for the current Domain and Assembly.
Dim isoFile As IsolatedStorageFile = _
    IsolatedStorageFile.GetStore(IsolatedStorageScope.User _
    Or IsolatedStorageScope.Assembly _
    Or IsolatedStorageScope.Domain, Nothing, Nothing)

Dim isoStream As New IsolatedStorageFileStream(Me.userName, _
FileMode.Open, _
    FileAccess.Read, FileShare.Read)
```

```
[C#]
        // Retrieve an IsolatedStorageFile for the
current Domain and Assembly.
        IsolatedStorageFile isoFile =
            IsolatedStorageFile.GetStore(IsolatedStorageScope.User

            IsolatedStorageScope.Assembly |
            IsolatedStorageScope.Domain ,
            null,
            null);

        IsolatedStorageFileStream isoStream =
            new IsolatedStorageFileStream( this.userName,
            FileMode.Open,
            FileAccess.Read,
            FileShare.Read);
```

```
[C++]
// Retrieve an IsolatedStorageFile for the current Domain and Assembly.
IsolatedStorageFile* isoFile =
    IsolatedStorageFile::GetStore(
    static_cast<IsolatedStorageScope>(IsolatedStorageScope::User |
    IsolatedStorageScope::Assembly |
    IsolatedStorageScope::Domain),
    (Type*)0, 0);
IsolatedStorageFileStream* isoStream = new
IsolatedStorageFileStream(this->userName,
    FileMode::Open,
    FileAccess::ReadWrite,
    isoFile);
```

Requirements

Namespace: System.IO.IsolatedStorage

Platforms: Windows 98, Windows NT 4.0, Windows Millennium Edition, Windows 2000, Windows XP Home Edition, Windows XP Professional, Windows .NET Server family

Assembly: Mscorlib (in Mscorlib.dll)

System.Management Namespace

Provides access to a rich set of management information and management events about the system, devices, and applications instrumented to the Windows Management Instrumentation (WMI) infrastructure. Applications and services can query for interesting management information (such as how much free space is left on the disk, what is the current CPU utilization, which database a certain application is connected to, and much more), using classes derived from **ManagementObjectSearcher** and **ManagementQuery**, or subscribe to a variety of management events using the **ManagementEventWatcher** class. The accessible data can be from both managed and unmanaged components in the distributed environment.

AuthenticationLevel Enumeration

Describes the authentication level to be used to connect to WMI. This is used for the COM connection to WMI.

```
[Visual Basic]
<Serializable>
Public Enum AuthenticationLevel
[C#]
[Serializable]
public enum AuthenticationLevel
[C++]
[Serializable]
__value public enum AuthenticationLevel
[JScript]
public
    Serializable
enum AuthenticationLevel
```

Members

Member name	Description
Call	Call-level COM authentication.
Connect	Connect-level COM authentication.
Default	The default COM authentication level. WMI uses the default Windows Authentication setting.
None	No COM authentication.
Packet	Packet-level COM authentication.
PacketIntegrity	Packet Integrity-level COM authentication.
PacketPrivacy	Packet Privacy-level COM authentication.
Unchanged	Authentication level should remain as it was before.

Requirements

Namespace: System.Management

Platforms: Windows 98, Windows NT 4.0, Windows Millennium Edition, Windows 2000, Windows XP Home Edition, Windows XP Professional, Windows .NET Server family

Assembly: System.Management (in System.Management.dll)

CimType Enumeration

Describes the possible CIM types for properties, qualifiers, or method parameters.

```
[Visual Basic]
<Serializable>
Public Enum CimType
[C#]
[Serializable]
public enum CimType
[C++]
[Serializable]
_value public enum CimType
[JScript]
public
   Serializable
enum CimType
```

Members

Member name	Description
Boolean	A boolean.
Char16	A 16-bit character.
DateTime	A date or time value, represented in a string in DMTF date/time format: yyyymmddHHMMSS.mmmmmmsUUU
	where:
	yyyymmdd - is the date in year/month/day
	HHMMSS - is the time in hours/minutes/seconds
	mmmmmm - is the number of microseconds in 6 digits
	sUUU - is a sign (+ or -) and a 3-digit UTC offset
Object	An embedded object.
	Note that embedded objects differ from references in that the embedded object doesn't have a path and its lifetime is identical to the lifetime of the containing object.
Real32	A floating-point 32-bit number.
Real64	A floating point 64-bit number.
Reference	A reference to another object. This is represented by a string containing the path to the referenced object
SInt16	A signed 16-bit integer.
SInt32	A signed 32-bit integer.
SInt64	A signed 64-bit integer.
SInt8	A signed 8-bit integer.
String	A string.
UInt16	An unsigned 16-bit integer.
UInt32	An unsigned 32-bit integer.
UInt64	An unsigned 64-bit integer.
UInt8	An unsigned 8-bit integer.

Requirements

Namespace: System.Management

Platforms: Windows 98, Windows NT 4.0, Windows Millennium Edition, Windows 2000, Windows XP Home Edition, Windows XP Professional, Windows .NET Server family

Assembly: System.Management (in System.Management.dll)

CodeLanguage Enumeration

Defines the languages supported by the code generator.

```
[Visual Basic]
<Serializable>
Public Enum CodeLanguage
[C#]
[Serializable]
public enum CodeLanguage
[C++]
[Serializable]
__value public enum CodeLanguage
[JScript]
public
    Serializable
enum CodeLanguage
```

Members

Member name	Description
CSharp	A value for generating C# code.
JScript	A value for generating JScript code.
VB	A value for generating Visual Basic code.

Requirements

Namespace: System.Management

Platforms: Windows 98, Windows NT 4.0,
Windows Millennium Edition, Windows 2000,
Windows XP Home Edition, Windows XP Professional,
Windows .NET Server family

Assembly: System.Management (in System.Management.dll)

ComparisonSettings Enumeration

Describes the object comparison modes that can be used with **CompareTo**. Note that these values may be combined.

This enumeration has a **FlagsAttribute** attribute that allows a bitwise combination of its member values.

```
[Visual Basic]
<Flags>
<Serializable>
Public Enum ComparisonSettings
[C#]
[Flags]
[Serializable]
public enum ComparisonSettings
[C++]
[Flags]
[Serializable]
__value public enum ComparisonSettings
[JScript]
public
    Flags
   Serializable
enum ComparisonSettings
```

Requirements

Namespace: System.Management

Platforms: Windows 98, Windows NT 4.0, Windows Millennium Edition, Windows 2000, Windows XP Home Edition, Windows XP Professional, Windows .NET Server family

Assembly: System.Management (in System.Management.dll)

Members

Member name	Description	Value
IgnoreCase	A mode that compares string values in a case-insensitive manner. This applies to strings and to qualifier values. Property and qualifier names are always compared in a case-insensitive manner whether this flag is specified or not.	16
IgnoreClass	A mode that assumes that the objects being compared are instances of the same class. Consequently, this value causes comparison of instance-related information only. Use this flag to optimize performance. If the objects are not of the same class, the results are undefined.	8
IgnoreDefault-Values	A mode that ignores the default values of properties. This value is only meaningful when comparing classes.	4
IgnoreFlavor	A mode that ignores qualifier flavors. This flag still takes qualifier values into account, but ignores flavor distinctions such as propagation rules and override restrictions.	32
IgnoreObject-Source	A mode that ignores the source of the objects, namely the server and the namespace they came from, in comparison to other objects.	2
IgnoreQualifiers	A mode that compares the objects, ignoring qualifiers.	1
IncludeAll	A mode that compares all elements of the compared objects.	0

CompletedEventArgs Class

Holds event data for the **Completed** event.

System.Object
  System.EventArgs
    System.Management.ManagementEventArgs
      System.Management.CompletedEventArgs

```
[Visual Basic]
Public Class CompletedEventArgs
   Inherits ManagementEventArgs
[C#]
public class CompletedEventArgs : ManagementEventArgs
[C++]
public __gc class CompletedEventArgs : public ManagementEventArgs
[JScript]
public class CompletedEventArgs extends ManagementEventArgs
```

Thread Safety

Any public static (**Shared** in Visual Basic) members of this type are
safe for multithreaded operations. Any instance members are not
guaranteed to be thread safe.

Requirements

Namespace: System.Management

Platforms: Windows 98, Windows NT 4.0,
Windows Millennium Edition, Windows 2000,
Windows XP Home Edition, Windows XP Professional,
Windows .NET Server family

Assembly: System.Management (in System.Management.dll)

CompletedEventArgs.Status Property

Gets the completion status of the operation.

```
[Visual Basic]
Public ReadOnly Property Status As ManagementStatus
[C#]
public ManagementStatus Status {get;}
[C++]
public: __property ManagementStatus get_Status();
[JScript]
public function get Status() : ManagementStatus;
```

Property Value

A **ManagementStatus** value indicating the return code of the
operation.

Requirements

Platforms: Windows 98, Windows NT 4.0,
Windows Millennium Edition, Windows 2000,
Windows XP Home Edition, Windows XP Professional,
Windows .NET Server family

.NET Framework Security:

- Full trust for the immediate caller. This member cannot be used
  by partially trusted code.

CompletedEventArgs.StatusObject Property

Gets or sets additional status information within a WMI object. This
may be null.

```
[Visual Basic]
Public ReadOnly Property StatusObject As ManagementBaseObject
[C#]
public ManagementBaseObject StatusObject {get;}
[C++]
public: __property ManagementBaseObject* get_StatusObject();
[JScript]
public function get StatusObject() : ManagementBaseObject;
```

Property Value

A null reference (**Nothing** in Visual Basic) if an error did not occur.
Otherwise, may be non-null if the provider supports extended error
information.

Requirements

Platforms: Windows 98, Windows NT 4.0,
Windows Millennium Edition, Windows 2000,
Windows XP Home Edition, Windows XP Professional,
Windows .NET Server family

.NET Framework Security:

- Full trust for the immediate caller. This member cannot be used
  by partially trusted code.

CompletedEventHandler Delegate

Represents the method that will handle the **Completed** event.

```
[Visual Basic]
<Serializable>
Public Delegate Sub CompletedEventHandler( _
   ByVal sender As Object, _
   ByVal e As CompletedEventArgs _
)
[C#]
[Serializable]
public delegate void CompletedEventHandler(
   object sender,
   CompletedEventArgs e
);
[C++]
[Serializable]
public __gc __delegate void CompletedEventHandler(
   Object* sender,
   CompletedEventArgs* e
);
```

[JScript] In JScript, you can use the delegates in the .NET
Framework, but you cannot define your own.

Parameters [Visual Basic, C#, C++]

The declaration of your event handler must have the same
parameters as the **CompletedEventHandler** delegate declaration.

Requirements

Namespace: System.Management

Platforms: Windows 98, Windows NT 4.0,
Windows Millennium Edition, Windows 2000,
Windows XP Home Edition, Windows XP Professional,
Windows .NET Server family

Assembly: System.Management (in System.Management.dll)

ConnectionOptions Class

Specifies all settings required to make a WMI connection.

System.Object
  System.Management.ManagementOptions
    System.Management.ConnectionOptions

[Visual Basic]
```
Public Class ConnectionOptions
    Inherits ManagementOptions
```
[C#]
```
public class ConnectionOptions : ManagementOptions
```
[C++]
```
public __gc class ConnectionOptions : public ManagementOptions
```
[JScript]
```
public class ConnectionOptions extends ManagementOptions
```

Thread Safety

Any public static (**Shared** in Visual Basic) members of this type are safe for multithreaded operations. Any instance members are not guaranteed to be thread safe.

Example

[C#]
```
using System;
using System.Management;

// This example demonstrates how to connect to remote machine
// using supplied credentials.
class Sample_ConnectionOptions
{
    public static int Main(string[] args) {
        ConnectionOptions options = new ConnectionOptions();
        options.Username = UserName; //could be in domain\user format
        options.Password = SecurelyStoredPassword;
        ManagementScope scope = new ManagementScope(
            "\\\\servername\\root\\cimv2",
            options);
        try {
            scope.Connect();
            ManagementObject disk = new ManagementObject(
                scope,
                new ManagementPath("Win32_logicaldisk='c:'"),
                null);
            disk.Get();
        }
        catch (Exception e) {
            Console.WriteLine("Failed to connect: " + e.Message);
        }
        return 0;
    }
}
```

[Visual Basic]
```
Imports System
Imports System.Management

' This example demonstrates how to connect to remote machine
' using supplied credentials.
Class Sample_ConnectionOptions
    Overloads Public Shared Function Main(args() As String) As Integer
        Dim options As New ConnectionOptions()
        options.Username = UserName
        options.Password = SecurelyStoredPassword
        Dim scope As New ManagementScope
("\\servername\root\cimv2", options)
        Try
            scope.Connect()
            Dim disk As New ManagementObject(scope, _
```

```
            New ManagementPath("Win32_logicaldisk='c:'"), Nothing)
            disk.Get()
        Catch e As UnauthorizedAccessException
            Console.WriteLine(("Failed to connect: " + e.Message))
        End Try
        Return 0
    End Function
End Class
```

Requirements

Namespace: System.Management

Platforms: Windows 98, Windows NT 4.0, Windows Millennium Edition, Windows 2000, Windows XP Home Edition, Windows XP Professional, Windows .NET Server family

Assembly: System.Management (in System.Management.dll)

ConnectionOptions Constructor

Initializes a new instance of the **ConnectionOptions** class.

Overload List

Initializes a new instance of the **ConnectionOptions** class for the connection operation, using default values. This is the default constructor.

  [Visual Basic] **Public Sub New()**

  [C#] **public ConnectionOptions();**

  [C++] **public: ConnectionOptions();**

  [JScript] **public function ConnectionOptions();**

Initializes a new instance of the **ConnectionOptions** class to be used for a WMI connection, using the specified values.

  [Visual Basic] **Public Sub New(String, String, String, String, ImpersonationLevel, AuthenticationLevel, Boolean, ManagementNamedValueCollection, TimeSpan)**

  [C#] **public ConnectionOptions(string, string, string, string, ImpersonationLevel, AuthenticationLevel, bool, ManagementNamedValueCollection, TimeSpan);**

  [C++] **public: ConnectionOptions(String*, String*, String*, String*, ImpersonationLevel, AuthenticationLevel, bool, ManagementNamedValueCollection*, TimeSpan);**

  [JScript] **public function ConnectionOptions(String, String, String, String, ImpersonationLevel, AuthenticationLevel, Boolean, ManagementNamedValueCollection, TimeSpan);**

ConnectionOptions Constructor ( )

Initializes a new instance of the **ConnectionOptions** class for the connection operation, using default values. This is the default constructor.

```
[Visual Basic]
Public Sub New()
[C#]
public ConnectionOptions();
[C++]
public: ConnectionOptions();
[JScript]
public function ConnectionOptions();
```

Requirements

Platforms: Windows 98, Windows NT 4.0,
Windows Millennium Edition, Windows 2000,
Windows XP Home Edition, Windows XP Professional,
Windows .NET Server family

.NET Framework Security:

• Full trust for the immediate caller. This member cannot be used
  by partially trusted code.

ConnectionOptions Constructor (String, String, String, String, ImpersonationLevel, AuthenticationLevel, Boolean, ManagementNamedValueCollection, TimeSpan)

Initializes a new instance of the **ConnectionOptions** class to be
used for a WMI connection, using the specified values.

```
[Visual Basic]
Public Sub New( _
   ByVal locale As String, _
   ByVal username As String, _
   ByVal password As String, _
   ByVal authority As String, _
   ByVal impersonation As ImpersonationLevel, _
   ByVal authentication As AuthenticationLevel, _
   ByVal enablePrivileges As Boolean, _
   ByVal context As ManagementNamedValueCollection, _
   ByVal timeout As TimeSpan _
)
[C#]
public ConnectionOptions(
   string locale,
   string username,
   string password,
   string authority,
   ImpersonationLevel impersonation,
   AuthenticationLevel authentication,
   bool enablePrivileges,
   ManagementNamedValueCollection context,
   TimeSpan timeout
);
[C++]
public: ConnectionOptions(
   String* locale,
   String* username,
   String* password,
   String* authority,
   ImpersonationLevel impersonation,
   AuthenticationLevel authentication,
   bool enablePrivileges,
   ManagementNamedValueCollection* context,
   TimeSpan timeout
);
[JScript]
public function ConnectionOptions(
   locale : String,
   username : String,
   password : String,
   authority : String,
   impersonation : ImpersonationLevel,
   authentication : AuthenticationLevel,
```

```
   enablePrivileges : Boolean,
   context : ManagementNamedValueCollection,
   timeout : TimeSpan
);
```

Parameters

locale
   The locale to be used for the connection.
username
   The user name to be used for the connection. If null, the
   credentials of the currently logged-on user are used.
password
   The password for the given user name. If the user name is also
   null, the credentials used will be those of the currently logged-on
   user.
authority
   The authority to be used to authenticate the specified user.
impersonation
   The COM impersonation level to be used for the connection.
authentication
   The COM authentication level to be used for the connection.
enablePrivileges
   true to enable special user privileges; otherwise, **false**. This
   parameter should only be used when performing an operation
   that requires special Windows NT user privileges.
context
   A provider-specific, named value pairs object to be passed
   through to the provider.
timeout
   Reserved for future use.

Requirements

Platforms: Windows 98, Windows NT 4.0,
Windows Millennium Edition, Windows 2000,
Windows XP Home Edition, Windows XP Professional,
Windows .NET Server family

.NET Framework Security:

• Full trust for the immediate caller. This member cannot be used
  by partially trusted code.

ConnectionOptions.Authentication Property

Gets or sets the COM authentication level to be used for operations
in this connection.

```
[Visual Basic]
Public Property Authentication As AuthenticationLevel
[C#]
public AuthenticationLevel Authentication {get; set;}
[C++]
public: __property AuthenticationLevel get_Authentication();
public: __property void set_Authentication(AuthenticationLevel);
[JScript]
public function get Authentication() : AuthenticationLevel;
public function set Authentication(AuthenticationLevel);
```

Property Value

The COM authentication level to be used for operations in this
connection. The default value is **AuthenticationLevel.Unchanged**,
which indicates that the client will use the authentication level
requested by the server, according to the standard DCOM
negotiation process.

Remarks

On Windows 2000 and below, the WMI service will request Connect level authentication, while on Windows XP and higher it will request Packet level authentication. If the client requires a specific authentication setting, this property can be used to control the authentication level on this particular connection. For example, the property can be set to **AuthenticationLevel.PacketPrivacy** if the client requires all communication to be encrypted.

Requirements

Platforms: Windows 98, Windows NT 4.0,
Windows Millennium Edition, Windows 2000,
Windows XP Home Edition, Windows XP Professional,
Windows .NET Server family

.NET Framework Security:

*   Full trust for the immediate caller. This member cannot be used by partially trusted code.

ConnectionOptions.Authority Property

Gets or sets the authority to be used to authenticate the specified user.

```
[Visual Basic]
Public Property Authority As String
[C#]
public string Authority {get; set;}
[C++]
public: __property String* get_Authority();
public: __property void set_Authority(String*);
[JScript]
public function get Authority() : String;
public function set Authority(String);
```

Property Value

If not null, this property can contain the name of the Windows NT/ Windows 2000 domain in which to obtain the user to authenticate.

Remarks

The property must be passed as follows: If it begins with the string "Kerberos:", Kerberos authentication will be used and this property should contain a Kerberos principal name. For example, Kerberos:<principal name>.

If the property value begins with the string "NTLMDOMAIN:", NTLM authentication will be used and the property should contain a NTLM domain name. For example, NTLMDOMAIN:<domain name>.

If the property is null, NTLM authentication will be used and the NTLM domain of the current user will be used.

Requirements

Platforms: Windows 98, Windows NT 4.0,
Windows Millennium Edition, Windows 2000,
Windows XP Home Edition, Windows XP Professional,
Windows .NET Server family

.NET Framework Security:

*   Full trust for the immediate caller. This member cannot be used by partially trusted code.

ConnectionOptions.EnablePrivileges Property

Gets or sets a value indicating whether user privileges need to be enabled for the connection operation. This property should only be used when the operation performed requires a certain user privilege to be enabled (for example, a machine reboot).

```
[Visual Basic]
Public Property EnablePrivileges As Boolean
[C#]
public bool EnablePrivileges {get; set;}
[C++]
public: __property bool get_EnablePrivileges();
public: __property void set_EnablePrivileges(bool);
[JScript]
public function get EnablePrivileges() : Boolean;
public function set EnablePrivileges(Boolean);
```

Property Value

true if user privileges need to be enabled for the connection operation; otherwise, **false**. The default value is **false**.

Requirements

Platforms: Windows 98, Windows NT 4.0,
Windows Millennium Edition, Windows 2000,
Windows XP Home Edition, Windows XP Professional,
Windows .NET Server family

.NET Framework Security:

*   Full trust for the immediate caller. This member cannot be used by partially trusted code.

ConnectionOptions.Impersonation Property

Gets or sets the COM impersonation level to be used for operations in this connection.

```
[Visual Basic]
Public Property Impersonation As ImpersonationLevel
[C#]
public ImpersonationLevel Impersonation {get; set;}
[C++]
public: __property ImpersonationLevel get_Impersonation();
public: __property void set_Impersonation(ImpersonationLevel);
[JScript]
public function get Impersonation() : ImpersonationLevel;
public function set Impersonation(ImpersonationLevel);
```

Property Value

The COM impersonation level to be used for operations in this connection. The default value is **ImpersonationLevel.Impersonate**, which indicates that the WMI provider can impersonate the client when performing the requested operations in this connection.

Remarks

The **ImpersonationLevel.Impersonate** setting is advantageous when the provider is a trusted application or service. It eliminates the need for the provider to perform client identity and access checks for the requested operations. However, note that if for some reason the provider cannot be trusted, allowing it to impersonate the client may constitute a security threat. In such cases, it is recommended that this property be set by the client to a lower value, such as **ImpersonationLevel.Identify**. Note that this may cause failure of the provider to perform the requested operations, for lack of sufficient permissions or inability to perform access checks.

Requirements

Platforms: Windows 98, Windows NT 4.0,
Windows Millennium Edition, Windows 2000,
Windows XP Home Edition, Windows XP Professional,
Windows .NET Server family

.NET Framework Security:
* Full trust for the immediate caller. This member cannot be used by partially trusted code.

ConnectionOptions.Locale Property

Gets or sets the locale to be used for the connection operation.

```
[Visual Basic]
Public Property Locale As String
[C#]
public string Locale {get; set;}
[C++]
public: __property String* get_Locale();
public: __property void set_Locale(String*);
[JScript]
public function get Locale() : String;
public function set Locale(String);
```

Property Value

The default value is DEFAULTLOCALE.

Requirements

Platforms: Windows 98, Windows NT 4.0, Windows Millennium Edition, Windows 2000, Windows XP Home Edition, Windows XP Professional, Windows .NET Server family

.NET Framework Security:
* Full trust for the immediate caller. This member cannot be used by partially trusted code.

ConnectionOptions.Password Property

Gets or sets the password for the specified user.

```
[Visual Basic]
Property Password As String
[C#]
string Password {set;}
[C++]
public: __property void set_Password(String*);
[JScript]
public function set Password(String);
```

Property Value

The default value is null. If the user name is also null, the credentials used will be those of the currently logged-on user.

Remarks

A blank string ("") specifies a valid zero-length password.

Requirements

Platforms: Windows 98, Windows NT 4.0, Windows Millennium Edition, Windows 2000, Windows XP Home Edition, Windows XP Professional, Windows .NET Server family

.NET Framework Security:
* Full trust for the immediate caller. This member cannot be used by partially trusted code.

ConnectionOptions.Username Property

Gets or sets the user name to be used for the connection operation.

```
[Visual Basic]
Public Property Username As String
[C#]
public string Username {get; set;}
[C++]
public: __property String* get_Username();
public: __property void set_Username(String*);
[JScript]
public function get Username() : String;
public function set Username(String);
```

Property Value

Null if the connection will use the currently logged-on user; otherwise, a string representing the user name. The default value is null.

Remarks

If the user name is from a domain other than the current domain, the string may contain the domain name and user name, separated by a backslash: `string username = "EnterDomainHere\\EnterUsernameHere";`

The *strUser* parameter cannot be an empty string.

Requirements

Platforms: Windows 98, Windows NT 4.0, Windows Millennium Edition, Windows 2000, Windows XP Home Edition, Windows XP Professional, Windows .NET Server family

.NET Framework Security:
* Full trust for the immediate caller. This member cannot be used by partially trusted code.

ConnectionOptions.Clone Method

Returns a copy of the object.

```
[Visual Basic]
Overrides Public Function Clone() As Object Implements _
   ICloneable.Clone
[C#]
public override object Clone();
[C++]
public: Object* Clone();
[JScript]
public override function Clone() : Object;
```

Return Value

The cloned object.

Implements

ICloneable.Clone

Requirements

Platforms: Windows 98, Windows NT 4.0, Windows Millennium Edition, Windows 2000, Windows XP Home Edition, Windows XP Professional, Windows .NET Server family

.NET Framework Security:
* Full trust for the immediate caller. This member cannot be used by partially trusted code.

DeleteOptions Class

Specifies options for deleting a management object.

System.Object
  System.Management.ManagementOptions
    System.Management.DeleteOptions

```
[Visual Basic]
Public Class DeleteOptions
   Inherits ManagementOptions
[C#]
public class DeleteOptions : ManagementOptions
[C++]
public __gc class DeleteOptions : public ManagementOptions
[JScript]
public class DeleteOptions extends ManagementOptions
```

Thread Safety

Any public static (**Shared** in Visual Basic) members of this type are safe for multithreaded operations. Any instance members are not guaranteed to be thread safe.

Example

```
[C#]
using System;
using System.Management;

// This example demonstrates how to specify a timeout value
// when deleting a ManagementClass object.
class Sample_DeleteOptions
{
    public static int Main(string[] args) {
        ManagementClass newClass = new ManagementClass();
        newClass["__CLASS"] = "ClassToDelete";
        newClass.Put();

        // Set deletion options: delete operation timeout value
        DeleteOptions opt = new DeleteOptions(null, new
TimeSpan(0,0,0,5));

        ManagementClass dummyClassToDelete =
            new ManagementClass("ClassToDelete");
        dummyClassToDelete.Delete(opt);

        return 0;
    }
}

[Visual Basic]
Imports System
Imports System.Management

' This sample demonstrates how to specify a timeout value
' when deleting a ManagementClass object.
Class Sample_DeleteOptions
    Overloads Public Shared Function Main(args() As String) As Integer
        Dim newClass As New ManagementClass()
        newClass("__CLASS") = "ClassToDelete"
        newClass.Put()

        ' Set deletion options: delete operation timeout value
        Dim opt As New DeleteOptions(Nothing, New TimeSpan(0, 0, 0, 5))

        Dim dummyClassToDelete As New ManagementClass("ClassToDelete")
        dummyClassToDelete.Delete(opt)
        Return 0
    End Function
End Class
```

Requirements

Namespace: System.Management

Platforms: Windows 98, Windows NT 4.0, Windows Millennium Edition, Windows 2000, Windows XP Home Edition, Windows XP Professional, Windows .NET Server family

Assembly: System.Management (in System.Management.dll)

DeleteOptions Constructor

Initializes a new instance of the **DeleteOptions** class.

Overload List

Initializes a new instance of the **DeleteOptions** class for the delete operation, using default values. This is the default constructor.

  [Visual Basic] **Public Sub New()**
  [C#] **public DeleteOptions();**
  [C++] **public: DeleteOptions();**
  [JScript] **public function DeleteOptions();**

Initializes a new instance of the **DeleteOptions** class for a delete operation, using the specified values.

  [Visual Basic] **Public Sub New(ManagementNamedValueCollection, TimeSpan)**
  [C#] **public DeleteOptions(ManagementNamedValueCollection, TimeSpan);**
  [C++] **public: DeleteOptions(ManagementNamedValueCollection*, TimeSpan);**
  [JScript] **public function DeleteOptions(ManagementNamedValueCollection, TimeSpan);**

DeleteOptions Constructor ()

Initializes a new instance of the **DeleteOptions** class for the delete operation, using default values. This is the default constructor.

```
[Visual Basic]
Public Sub New()
[C#]
public DeleteOptions();
[C++]
public: DeleteOptions();
[JScript]
public function DeleteOptions();
```

Requirements

Platforms: Windows 98, Windows NT 4.0, Windows Millennium Edition, Windows 2000, Windows XP Home Edition, Windows XP Professional, Windows .NET Server family

.NET Framework Security:

- Full trust for the immediate caller. This member cannot be used by partially trusted code.

DeleteOptions Constructor (ManagementNamedValueCollection, TimeSpan)

Initializes a new instance of the **DeleteOptions** class for a delete operation, using the specified values.

```
[Visual Basic]
Public Sub New( _
   ByVal context As ManagementNamedValueCollection, _
   ByVal timeout As TimeSpan _
)
[C#]
public DeleteOptions(
   ManagementNamedValueCollection context,
   TimeSpan timeout
);
[C++]
public: DeleteOptions(
   ManagementNamedValueCollection* context,
   TimeSpan timeout
);
[JScript]
public function DeleteOptions(
   context : ManagementNamedValueCollection,
   timeout : TimeSpan
);
```

Parameters

context
   A provider-specific, named-value pairs object to be passed through to the provider.

timeout
   The length of time to let the operation perform before it times out. The default value is **InfiniteTimeout**. Setting this parameter will invoke the operation semisynchronously.

Requirements

Platforms: Windows 98, Windows NT 4.0, Windows Millennium Edition, Windows 2000, Windows XP Home Edition, Windows XP Professional, Windows .NET Server family

.NET Framework Security:

• Full trust for the immediate caller. This member cannot be used by partially trusted code.

DeleteOptions.Clone Method

Returns a copy of the object.

```
[Visual Basic]
Overrides Public Function Clone() As Object Implements _
   ICloneable.Clone
[C#]
public override object Clone();
[C++]
public: Object* Clone();
[JScript]
public override function Clone() : Object;
```

Return Value

A cloned object.

Implements

ICloneable.Clone

Requirements

Platforms: Windows 98, Windows NT 4.0, Windows Millennium Edition, Windows 2000, Windows XP Home Edition, Windows XP Professional, Windows .NET Server family

.NET Framework Security:

• Full trust for the immediate caller. This member cannot be used by partially trusted code.

EnumerationOptions Class

Provides a base class for query and enumeration-related options objects.

System.Object
  System.Management.ManagementOptions
    System.Management.EnumerationOptions

```
[Visual Basic]
Public Class EnumerationOptions
   Inherits ManagementOptions
[C#]
public class EnumerationOptions : ManagementOptions
[C++]
public __gc class EnumerationOptions : public ManagementOptions
[JScript]
public class EnumerationOptions extends ManagementOptions
```

Thread Safety

Any public static (**Shared** in Visual Basic) members of this type are safe for multithreaded operations. Any instance members are not guaranteed to be thread safe.

Example

```
[C#]
using System;
using System.Management;

// This example demonstrates how to enumerate all top-level WMI classes
// and subclasses in root/cimv2 namespace.
class Sample_EnumerationOptions
{
    public static int Main(string[] args) {
        ManagementClass newClass = new ManagementClass();
        EnumerationOptions options = new EnumerationOptions();
        options.EnumerateDeep = false;
        foreach(ManagementObject o in
newClass.GetSubclasses(options)) {
            Console.WriteLine(o["__Class"]);
        }
        return 0;
    }
}
```

```
[Visual Basic]
Imports System
Imports System.Management

' This example demonstrates how to enumerate all top-level WMI classes
' and subclasses in root/cimv2 namespace.
Class Sample_EnumerationOptions
    Overloads Public Shared Function Main(args() As String) As Integer
        Dim newClass As New ManagementClass()
        Dim options As New EnumerationOptions()
        options.EnumerateDeep = False
        Dim o As ManagementObject
        For Each o In newClass.GetSubclasses(options)
            Console.WriteLine(o("__Class"))
        Next o
        Return 0
    End Function
End Class
```

Requirements

Namespace: System.Management

Platforms: Windows 98, Windows NT 4.0, Windows Millennium Edition, Windows 2000, Windows XP Home Edition, Windows XP Professional, Windows .NET Server family

Assembly: System.Management (in System.Management.dll)

EnumerationOptions Constructor

Initializes a new instance of the **EnumerationOptions** class.

Overload List

Initializes a new instance of the **EnumerationOptions** class with default values (see the individual property descriptions for what the default values are). This is the default constructor.

> [Visual Basic] **Public Sub New()**
> [C#] **public EnumerationOptions();**
> [C++] **public: EnumerationOptions();**
> [JScript] **public function EnumerationOptions();**

Initializes a new instance of the **EnumerationOptions** class to be used for queries or enumerations, allowing the user to specify values for the different options.

> [Visual Basic] **Public Sub New(ManagementNamedValue-Collection, TimeSpan, Integer, Boolean, Boolean, Boolean, Boolean, Boolean, Boolean, Boolean)**
> [C#] **public EnumerationOptions(ManagementNamed-ValueCollection, TimeSpan, int, bool, bool, bool, bool, bool, bool, bool);**
> [C++] **public: EnumerationOptions(ManagementNamed-ValueCollection*, TimeSpan, int, bool, bool, bool, bool, bool, bool, bool);**
> [JScript] **public function EnumerationOptions(Management-NamedValueCollection, TimeSpan, int, Boolean, Boolean, Boolean, Boolean, Boolean, Boolean, Boolean);**

EnumerationOptions Constructor ( )

Initializes a new instance of the **EnumerationOptions** class with default values (see the individual property descriptions for what the default values are). This is the default constructor.

```
[Visual Basic]
Public Sub New()
[C#]
public EnumerationOptions();
[C++]
public: EnumerationOptions();
[JScript]
public function EnumerationOptions();
```

Requirements

Platforms: Windows 98, Windows NT 4.0, Windows Millennium Edition, Windows 2000, Windows XP Home Edition, Windows XP Professional, Windows .NET Server family

.NET Framework Security:
- Full trust for the immediate caller. This member cannot be used by partially trusted code.

EnumerationOptions Constructor (ManagementNamedValueCollection, TimeSpan, Int32, Boolean, Boolean, Boolean, Boolean, Boolean, Boolean, Boolean)

Initializes a new instance of the **EnumerationOptions** class to be used for queries or enumerations, allowing the user to specify values for the different options.

```
[Visual Basic]
Public Sub New( _
   ByVal context As ManagementNamedValueCollection, _
   ByVal timeout As TimeSpan, _
   ByVal blockSize As Integer, _
   ByVal rewindable As Boolean, _
   ByVal returnImmediatley As Boolean, _
   ByVal useAmendedQualifiers As Boolean, _
   ByVal ensureLocatable As Boolean, _
   ByVal prototypeOnly As Boolean, _
   ByVal directRead As Boolean, _
   ByVal enumerateDeep As Boolean _
)
[C#]
public EnumerationOptions(
   ManagementNamedValueCollection context,
   TimeSpan timeout,
   int blockSize,
   bool rewindable,
   bool returnImmediatley,
   bool useAmendedQualifiers,
   bool ensureLocatable,
   bool prototypeOnly,
   bool directRead,
   bool enumerateDeep
);
[C++]
public: EnumerationOptions(
   ManagementNamedValueCollection* context,
   TimeSpan timeout,
   int blockSize,
   bool rewindable,
   bool returnImmediatley,
   bool useAmendedQualifiers,
   bool ensureLocatable,
   bool prototypeOnly,
   bool directRead,
   bool enumerateDeep
);
[JScript]
public function EnumerationOptions(
   context : ManagementNamedValueCollection,
   timeout : TimeSpan,
   blockSize : int,
   rewindable : Boolean,
   returnImmediatley : Boolean,
   useAmendedQualifiers : Boolean,
   ensureLocatable : Boolean,
   prototypeOnly : Boolean,
   directRead : Boolean,
   enumerateDeep : Boolean
);
```

Parameters

context
   The options context object containing provider-specific information that can be passed through to the provider.
timeout
   The timeout value for enumerating through the results.
blockSize
   The number of items to retrieve at one time from WMI.
rewindable
   true to specify whether the result set is rewindable (=allows multiple traversal or one-time); otherwise, **false**.
returnImmediatley
   true to specify whether the operation should return immediately (semi-sync) or block until all results are available; otherwise, **false**.
useAmendedQualifiers
   true to specify whether the returned objects should contain amended (locale-aware) qualifiers; otherwise, **false**.
ensureLocatable
   true to specify to WMI that it should ensure all returned objects have valid paths; otherwise, **false**.
prototypeOnly
   true to return a prototype of the result set instead of the actual results; otherwise, **false**.
directRead
   true to to retrieve objects of only the specified class only or from derived classes as well; otherwise, **false**.
enumerateDeep
   true to specify recursive enumeration in subclasses; otherwise, **false**.

Requirements

Platforms: Windows 98, Windows NT 4.0, Windows Millennium Edition, Windows 2000, Windows XP Home Edition, Windows XP Professional, Windows .NET Server family

.NET Framework Security:
- Full trust for the immediate caller. This member cannot be used by partially trusted code.

EnumerationOptions.BlockSize Property

Gets or sets the block size for block operations. When enumerating through a collection, WMI will return results in groups of the specified size.

```
[Visual Basic]
Public Property BlockSize As Integer
[C#]
public int BlockSize {get; set;}
[C++]
public: __property int get_BlockSize();
public: __property void set_BlockSize(int);
[JScript]
public function get BlockSize() : int;
public function set BlockSize(int);
```

Property Value

The default value is 1.

Requirements

Platforms: Windows 98, Windows NT 4.0,
Windows Millennium Edition, Windows 2000,
Windows XP Home Edition, Windows XP Professional,
Windows .NET Server family

.NET Framework Security:

• Full trust for the immediate caller. This member cannot be used
  by partially trusted code.

EnumerationOptions.DirectRead Property

Gets or sets a value indicating whether direct access to the WMI
provider is requested for the specified class, without any regard to its
superclass or derived classes.

```
[Visual Basic]
Public Property DirectRead As Boolean
[C#]
public bool DirectRead {get; set;}
[C++]
public: __property bool get_DirectRead();
public: __property void set_DirectRead(bool);
[JScript]
public function get DirectRead() : Boolean;
public function set DirectRead(Boolean);
```

Property Value

true if only objects of the specified class should be received, without
regard to derivation or inheritance; otherwise, **false**. The default
value is **false**.

Requirements

Platforms: Windows 98, Windows NT 4.0,
Windows Millennium Edition, Windows 2000,
Windows XP Home Edition, Windows XP Professional,
Windows .NET Server family

.NET Framework Security:

• Full trust for the immediate caller. This member cannot be used
  by partially trusted code.

EnumerationOptions.EnsureLocatable Property

Gets or sets a value indicating whether to the objects returned should
have locatable information in them. This ensures that the system
properties, such as **__PATH**, **__RELPATH**, and **__SERVER**, are
non-NULL. This flag can only be used in queries, and is ignored in
enumerations.

```
[Visual Basic]
Public Property EnsureLocatable As Boolean
[C#]
public bool EnsureLocatable {get; set;}
[C++]
public: __property bool get_EnsureLocatable();
public: __property void set_EnsureLocatable(bool);
[JScript]
public function get EnsureLocatable() : Boolean;
public function set EnsureLocatable(Boolean);
```

Property Value

true if WMI should ensure all returned objects have valid paths;
otherwise, **false**. The default value is **false**.

Requirements

Platforms: Windows 98, Windows NT 4.0,
Windows Millennium Edition, Windows 2000,
Windows XP Home Edition, Windows XP Professional,
Windows .NET Server family

.NET Framework Security:

• Full trust for the immediate caller. This member cannot be used
  by partially trusted code.

EnumerationOptions.EnumerateDeep Property

Gets or sets a value indicating whether recursive enumeration is
requested into all classes derived from the specified superclass. If
false, only immediate derived class members are returned.

```
[Visual Basic]
Public Property EnumerateDeep As Boolean
[C#]
public bool EnumerateDeep {get; set;}
[C++]
public: __property bool get_EnumerateDeep();
public: __property void set_EnumerateDeep(bool);
[JScript]
public function get EnumerateDeep() : Boolean;
public function set EnumerateDeep(Boolean);
```

Property Value

true if recursive enumeration is requested into all classes derived
from the specified superclass; otherwise, **false**. The default value is
false.

Requirements

Platforms: Windows 98, Windows NT 4.0,
Windows Millennium Edition, Windows 2000,
Windows XP Home Edition, Windows XP Professional,
Windows .NET Server family

.NET Framework Security:

• Full trust for the immediate caller. This member cannot be used
  by partially trusted code.

EnumerationOptions.PrototypeOnly Property

Gets or sets a value indicating whether the query should return a
prototype of the result set instead of the actual results. This flag is
used for prototyping.

```
[Visual Basic]
Public Property PrototypeOnly As Boolean
[C#]
public bool PrototypeOnly {get; set;}
[C++]
public: __property bool get_PrototypeOnly();
public: __property void set_PrototypeOnly(bool);
[JScript]
public function get PrototypeOnly() : Boolean;
public function set PrototypeOnly(Boolean);
```

Property Value

true if the query should return a prototype of the result set instead of
the actual results; otherwise, **false**. The default value is **false**.

Requirements

Platforms: Windows 98, Windows NT 4.0,
Windows Millennium Edition, Windows 2000,
Windows XP Home Edition, Windows XP Professional,
Windows .NET Server family

.NET Framework Security:

- Full trust for the immediate caller. This member cannot be used by partially trusted code.

EnumerationOptions.ReturnImmediately Property

Gets or sets a value indicating whether the invoked operation should be performed in a synchronous or semisynchronous fashion. If this property is set to **true**, the enumeration is invoked and the call returns immediately. The actual retrieval of the results will occur when the resulting collection is walked.

```
[Visual Basic]
Public Property ReturnImmediately As Boolean
[C#]
public bool ReturnImmediately {get; set;}
[C++]
public: __property bool get_ReturnImmediately();
public: __property void set_ReturnImmediately(bool);
[JScript]
public function get ReturnImmediately() : Boolean;
public function set ReturnImmediately(Boolean);
```

Property Value

true if the invoked operation should be performed in a synchronous or semisynchronous fashion; otherwise, **false**. The default value is **true**.

Requirements

Platforms: Windows 98, Windows NT 4.0,
Windows Millennium Edition, Windows 2000,
Windows XP Home Edition, Windows XP Professional,
Windows .NET Server family

.NET Framework Security:

- Full trust for the immediate caller. This member cannot be used by partially trusted code.

EnumerationOptions.Rewindable Property

Gets or sets a value indicating whether the collection is assumed to be rewindable. If **true**, the objects in the collection will be kept available for multiple enumerations. If **false**, the collection can only be enumerated one time.

```
[Visual Basic]
Public Property Rewindable As Boolean
[C#]
public bool Rewindable {get; set;}
[C++]
public: __property bool get_Rewindable();
public: __property void set_Rewindable(bool);
[JScript]
public function get Rewindable() : Boolean;
public function set Rewindable(Boolean);
```

Property Value

true if the collection is assumed to be rewindable; otherwise, **false**. The default value is **true**.

Remarks

A rewindable collection is more costly in memory consumption as all the objects need to be kept available at the same time. In a collection defined as non-rewindable, the objects are discarded after being returned in the enumeration.

Requirements

Platforms: Windows 98, Windows NT 4.0,
Windows Millennium Edition, Windows 2000,
Windows XP Home Edition, Windows XP Professional,
Windows .NET Server family

.NET Framework Security:

- Full trust for the immediate caller. This member cannot be used by partially trusted code.

EnumerationOptions.UseAmendedQualifiers Property

Gets or sets a value indicating whether the objects returned from WMI should contain amended information. Typically, amended information is localizable information attached to the WMI object, such as object and property descriptions.

```
[Visual Basic]
Public Property UseAmendedQualifiers As Boolean
[C#]
public bool UseAmendedQualifiers {get; set;}
[C++]
public: __property bool get_UseAmendedQualifiers();
public: __property void set_UseAmendedQualifiers(bool);
[JScript]
public function get UseAmendedQualifiers() : Boolean;
public function set UseAmendedQualifiers(Boolean);
```

Property Value

true if the objects returned from WMI should contain amended information; otherwise, **false**. The default value is **false**.

Remarks

If descriptions and other amended information are not of interest, setting this property to **false** is more efficient.

Requirements

Platforms: Windows 98, Windows NT 4.0,
Windows Millennium Edition, Windows 2000,
Windows XP Home Edition, Windows XP Professional,
Windows .NET Server family

.NET Framework Security:

- Full trust for the immediate caller. This member cannot be used by partially trusted code.

EnumerationOptions.Clone Method

Returns a copy of the object.

```
[Visual Basic]
Overrides Public Function Clone() As Object Implements _
    ICloneable.Clone
[C#]
public override object Clone();
[C++]
public: Object* Clone();
[JScript]
public override function Clone() : Object;
```

Return Value

The cloned object.

Implements

ICloneable.Clone

Requirements

Platforms: Windows 98, Windows NT 4.0,
Windows Millennium Edition, Windows 2000,
Windows XP Home Edition, Windows XP Professional,
Windows .NET Server family

.NET Framework Security:

- Full trust for the immediate caller. This member cannot be used by partially trusted code.

EventArrivedEventArgs Class

Holds event data for the **EventArrived** event.

System.Object
  System.EventArgs
    System.Management.ManagementEventArgs
      System.Management.EventArrivedEventArgs

```
[Visual Basic]
Public Class EventArrivedEventArgs
   Inherits ManagementEventArgs
[C#]
public class EventArrivedEventArgs : ManagementEventArgs
[C++]
public __gc class EventArrivedEventArgs : public
   ManagementEventArgs
[JScript]
public class EventArrivedEventArgs extends ManagementEventArgs
```

Thread Safety

Any public static (**Shared** in Visual Basic) members of this type are safe for multithreaded operations. Any instance members are not guaranteed to be thread safe.

Requirements

Namespace: System.Management

Platforms: Windows 98, Windows NT 4.0, Windows Millennium Edition, Windows 2000, Windows XP Home Edition, Windows XP Professional, Windows .NET Server family

Assembly: System.Management (in System.Management.dll)

EventArrivedEventArgs.NewEvent Property

Gets the WMI event that was delivered.

```
[Visual Basic]
Public ReadOnly Property NewEvent As ManagementBaseObject
[C#]
public ManagementBaseObject NewEvent {get;}
[C++]
public: __property ManagementBaseObject* get_NewEvent();
[JScript]
public function get NewEvent() : ManagementBaseObject;
```

Property Value

The object representing the WMI event.

Requirements

Platforms: Windows 98, Windows NT 4.0, Windows Millennium Edition, Windows 2000, Windows XP Home Edition, Windows XP Professional, Windows .NET Server family

.NET Framework Security:

- Full trust for the immediate caller. This member cannot be used by partially trusted code.

EventArrivedEventHandler Delegate

Represents the method that will handle the **EventArrived** event.

```
[Visual Basic]
<Serializable>
Public Delegate Sub EventArrivedEventHandler( _
   ByVal sender As Object, _
   ByVal e As EventArrivedEventArgs _
)
[C#]
[Serializable]
public delegate void EventArrivedEventHandler(
   object sender,
   EventArrivedEventArgs e
);
[C++]
[Serializable]
public __gc __delegate void EventArrivedEventHandler(
   Object* sender,
   EventArrivedEventArgs* e
);
```

[JScript] In JScript, you can use the delegates in the .NET Framework, but you cannot define your own.

Parameters [Visual Basic, C#, C++]

The declaration of your event handler must have the same parameters as the **EventArrivedEventHandler** delegate declaration.

Requirements

Namespace: System.Management

Platforms: Windows 98, Windows NT 4.0, Windows Millennium Edition, Windows 2000, Windows XP Home Edition, Windows XP Professional, Windows .NET Server family

Assembly: System.Management (in System.Management.dll)

EventQuery Class

Represents a WMI event query.

System.Object
  System.Management.ManagementQuery
    System.Management.EventQuery
      System.Management.WqlEventQuery

```
[Visual Basic]
Public Class EventQuery
   Inherits ManagementQuery
[C#]
public class EventQuery : ManagementQuery
[C++]
public __gc class EventQuery : public ManagementQuery
[JScript]
public class EventQuery extends ManagementQuery
```

Thread Safety

Any public static (**Shared** in Visual Basic) members of this type are safe for multithreaded operations. Any instance members are not guaranteed to be thread safe.

Remarks

Objects of this class or its derivatives are used in **ManagementEventWatcher** to subscribe to WMI events. Use more specific derivatives of this class whenever possible.

Example

```
[C#]
using System;
using System.Management;

// This sample demonstrates how to subscribe to an event
// using the EventQuery object.

class Sample_EventQuery
{
    public static int Main(string[] args)
    {
        //For this example, we make sure we have an arbitrary
        //class on root\default
        ManagementClass newClass = new ManagementClass(
            "root\\default",
            String.Empty,
            null);
        newClass["__Class"] = "TestWql";
        newClass.Put();

        //Create a query object for watching for class deletion events
        EventQuery eventQuery = new EventQuery("select * from
__classdeletionevent");

        //Initialize an event watcher object with this query
        ManagementEventWatcher watcher = new ManagementEventWatcher(
            new ManagementScope("root/default"),
            eventQuery);

        //Set up a handler for incoming events
        MyHandler handler = new MyHandler();
        watcher.EventArrived += new
EventArrivedEventHandler(handler.Arrived);

        //Start watching for events
        watcher.Start();

        //For this example, we delete the class to trigger an event
        newClass.Delete();
```

```
        //Nothing better to do - we loop to wait for an event
        //to arrive.
        while (!handler.IsArrived) {
            System.Threading.Thread.Sleep(1000);
        }

        //In this example we only want to wait for one event,
        //so we can stop watching
        watcher.Stop();

        //Get some values from the event.
        //Note: this can also be done in the event handler.
        ManagementBaseObject eventArg =
(ManagementBaseObject)(handler.ReturnedArgs.NewEvent["TargetClass"]);
        Console.WriteLine("Class Deleted = " + eventArg["__CLASS"]);

        return 0;
    }

    public class MyHandler
    {
        private bool isArrived = false;
        private EventArrivedEventArgs args;

        //Handles the event when it arrives
        public void Arrived(object sender, EventArrivedEventArgs e) {
            args = e;
            isArrived = true;
        }

        //Public property to get at the event information stored
        //in the handler
        public EventArrivedEventArgs ReturnedArgs {
            get {
                return args;
            }
        }

        //Used to determine whether the event has arrived or not.
        public bool IsArrived {
            get {
                return isArrived;
            }
        }
    }
}
```

```
[Visual Basic]
Imports System
Imports System.Management

' This sample demonstrates how to subscribe an event
' using the EventQuery object.

Class Sample_EventQuery
    Public Shared Sub Main()

        'For this example, we make sure we have an arbitrary
        'class on root\default
        Dim newClass As New ManagementClass( _
            "root\default", _
            String.Empty, Nothing)
            newClass("__Class") = "TestWql"
            newClass.Put()

        'Create a query object for watching for class deletion events
        Dim eventQuery As New EventQuery("select * from
__classdeletionevent")

        'Initialize an event watcher object with this query
        Dim watcher As New ManagementEventWatcher( _
            New ManagementScope("root/default"), _
            eventQuery)
```

```
'Set up a handler for incoming events
Dim handler As New MyHandler()
AddHandler watcher.EventArrived, AddressOf handler.Arrived

'Start watching for events
watcher.Start()

'For this example, we delete the class to trigger an event
newClass.Delete()

'Nothing better to do - we loop to wait for an event to arrive.
While Not handler.IsArrived
    Console.Write("0")
    System.Threading.Thread.Sleep(1000)
End While

'In this example we only want to wait for one event, so
we can stop watching
    watcher.Stop()

'Get some values from the event
'Note: this can also be done in the event handler.
Dim eventArg As ManagementBaseObject = CType( _
    handler.ReturnedArgs.NewEvent("TargetClass"), _
    ManagementBaseObject)
Console.WriteLine(("Class Deleted = " + eventArg("__CLASS")))

End Sub

Public Class MyHandler
    Private _isArrived As Boolean = False
    Private args As EventArrivedEventArgs

    'Handles the event when it arrives
    Public Sub Arrived(sender As Object, e As
EventArrivedEventArgs)
        args = e
        _isArrived = True
    End Sub

    'Public property to get at the event information stored
in the handler
    Public ReadOnly Property ReturnedArgs() As
EventArrivedEventArgs
        Get
            Return args
        End Get
    End Property

    'Used to determine whether the event has arrived or not.
    Public ReadOnly Property IsArrived() As Boolean
        Get
            Return _isArrived
        End Get
    End Property
End Class
End Class
```

Requirements

Namespace: System.Management

Platforms: Windows 98, Windows NT 4.0,
Windows Millennium Edition, Windows 2000,
Windows XP Home Edition, Windows XP Professional,
Windows .NET Server family

Assembly: System.Management (in System.Management.dll)

EventQuery Constructor

Initializes a new instance of the **EventQuery** class.

Overload List

Initializes a new instance of the **EventQuery** class. This is the default constructor.

> [Visual Basic] **Public Sub New()**
>
> [C#] **public EventQuery();**
>
> [C++] **public: EventQuery();**
>
> [JScript] **public function EventQuery();**

Initializes a new instance of the **EventQuery** class for the specified query.

> [Visual Basic] **Public Sub New(String)**
>
> [C#] **public EventQuery(string);**
>
> [C++] **public: EventQuery(String*);**
>
> [JScript] **public function EventQuery(String);**

Initializes a new instance of the **EventQuery** class for the specified language and query.

> [Visual Basic] **Public Sub New(String, String)**
>
> [C#] **public EventQuery(string, string);**
>
> [C++] **public: EventQuery(String*, String*);**
>
> [JScript] **public function EventQuery(String, String);**

EventQuery Constructor ( )

Initializes a new instance of the **EventQuery** class. This is the default constructor.

```
[Visual Basic]
Public Sub New()
[C#]
public EventQuery();
[C++]
public: EventQuery();
[JScript]
public function EventQuery();
```

Requirements

Platforms: Windows 98, Windows NT 4.0,
Windows Millennium Edition, Windows 2000,
Windows XP Home Edition, Windows XP Professional,
Windows .NET Server family

.NET Framework Security:

- Full trust for the immediate caller. This member cannot be used by partially trusted code.

EventQuery Constructor (String)

Initializes a new instance of the **EventQuery** class for the specified query.

```
[Visual Basic]
Public Sub New( _
    ByVal query As String _
)
[C#]
public EventQuery(
    string query
);
```

```
[C++]
public: EventQuery(
    String* query
);
[JScript]
public function EventQuery(
    query : String
);
```

Parameters

query

A textual representation of the event query.

Requirements

Platforms: Windows 98, Windows NT 4.0,
Windows Millennium Edition, Windows 2000,
Windows XP Home Edition, Windows XP Professional,
Windows .NET Server family

.NET Framework Security:

- Full trust for the immediate caller. This member cannot be used by partially trusted code.

EventQuery Constructor (String, String)

Initializes a new instance of the **EventQuery** class for the specified language and query.

```
[Visual Basic]
Public Sub New( _
    ByVal language As String, _
    ByVal query As String _
)
[C#]
public EventQuery(
    string language,
    string query
);
[C++]
public: EventQuery(
    String* language,
    String* query
);
[JScript]
public function EventQuery(
    language : String,
    query : String
);
```

Parameters

language

The language in which the query string is specified.

query

The string representation of the query.

Requirements

Platforms: Windows 98, Windows NT 4.0,
Windows Millennium Edition, Windows 2000,
Windows XP Home Edition, Windows XP Professional,
Windows .NET Server family

.NET Framework Security:

- Full trust for the immediate caller. This member cannot be used by partially trusted code.

EventQuery.Clone Method

Returns a copy of the object.

```
[Visual Basic]
Overrides Public Function Clone() As Object Implements _
    ICloneable.Clone
[C#]
public override object Clone();
[C++]
public: Object* Clone();
[JScript]
public override function Clone() : Object;
```

Return Value

The cloned object.

Implements

ICloneable.Clone

Requirements

Platforms: Windows 98, Windows NT 4.0,
Windows Millennium Edition, Windows 2000,
Windows XP Home Edition, Windows XP Professional,
Windows .NET Server family

.NET Framework Security:

- Full trust for the immediate caller. This member cannot be used by partially trusted code.

EventWatcherOptions Class

Specifies options for management event watching.

System.Object
  System.Management.ManagementOptions
    System.Management.EventWatcherOptions

```
[Visual Basic]
Public Class EventWatcherOptions
    Inherits ManagementOptions
[C#]
public class EventWatcherOptions : ManagementOptions
[C++]
public __gc class EventWatcherOptions : public ManagementOptions
[JScript]
public class EventWatcherOptions extends ManagementOptions
```

Thread Safety

Any public static (**Shared** in Visual Basic) members of this type are safe for multithreaded operations. Any instance members are not guaranteed to be thread safe.

Example

```csharp
[C#]
using System;
using System.Management;

// This example demonstrates how to specify a timeout and a batch count
// when listening to an event using ManagementEventWatcher object.
class Sample_EventWatcherOptions
{
    public static int Main(string[] args) {
        ManagementClass newClass = new ManagementClass();
        newClass["__CLASS"] = "TestDeletionClass";
        newClass.Put();

        EventWatcherOptions options = new EventWatcherOptions(null,
                           new TimeSpan(0,0,0,5),
                                                 1);
        ManagementEventWatcher watcher = new
ManagementEventWatcher(null,
                       new WqlEventQuery("__classdeletionevent"),
                                      options);
        MyHandler handler = new MyHandler();
        watcher.EventArrived += new
EventArrivedEventHandler(handler.Arrived);
        watcher.Start();

        // Delete class to trigger event
        newClass.Delete();

        //For the purpose of this example, we will wait
        // two seconds before main thread terminates.
        System.Threading.Thread.Sleep(2000);

        watcher.Stop();

        return 0;
    }

    public class MyHandler
    {
        public void Arrived(object sender, EventArrivedEventArgs e) {
            Console.WriteLine("Class Deleted= " +

((ManagementBaseObject)e.NewEvent["TargetClass"])["__CLASS"]);
        }
    }
}
```

```vbnet
[Visual Basic]
Imports System
Imports System.Management

' This example demonstrates how to specify a timeout and a batch count
' when listening to an event using the ManagementEventWatcher object.
Class Sample_EventWatcherOptions
    Public Shared Sub Main()
        Dim newClass As New ManagementClass()
        newClass("__CLASS") = "TestDeletionClass"
        newClass.Put()

        Dim options As _
            New EventWatcherOptions(Nothing, New TimeSpan _
(0, 0, 0, 5), 1)
        Dim watcher As New ManagementEventWatcher( _
            Nothing, _
            New WqlEventQuery("__classdeletionevent"), _
            options)
        Dim handler As New MyHandler()
        AddHandler watcher.EventArrived, AddressOf handler.Arrived
        watcher.Start()

        ' Delete class to trigger event
        newClass.Delete()

        ' For the purpose of this example, we will wait
        ' two seconds before main thread terminates.
        System.Threading.Thread.Sleep(2000)
        watcher.Stop()
    End Sub

    Public Class MyHandler
        Public Sub Arrived(sender As Object, e As _
EventArrivedEventArgs)
            Console.WriteLine("Class Deleted = " & _
                CType(e.NewEvent("TargetClass"), _
ManagementBaseObject)("__CLASS"))
        End Sub
    End Class
End Class
```

Requirements

Namespace: System.Management

Platforms: Windows 98, Windows NT 4.0, Windows Millennium Edition, Windows 2000, Windows XP Home Edition, Windows XP Professional, Windows .NET Server family

Assembly: System.Management (in System.Management.dll)

EventWatcherOptions Constructor

Initializes a new instance of the **EventWatcherOptions** class.

Overload List

Initializes a new instance of the **EventWatcherOptions** class for event watching, using default values. This is the default constructor.

  [Visual Basic] **Public Sub New()**

  [C#] **public EventWatcherOptions();**

  [C++] **public: EventWatcherOptions();**

  [JScript] **public function EventWatcherOptions();**

Initializes a new instance of the **EventWatcherOptions** class with the given values.

  [Visual Basic] **Public Sub New(ManagementNamedValue-Collection, TimeSpan, Integer)**

```
[C#] public EventWatcherOptions(Management-
NamedValueCollection, TimeSpan, int);
```

```
[C++] public: EventWatcherOptions(ManagementNamed-
ValueCollection*, TimeSpan, int);
```

```
[JScript] public function EventWatcherOptions(Manage-
mentNamedValueCollection, TimeSpan, int);
```

EventWatcherOptions Constructor ( )

Initializes a new instance of the **EventWatcherOptions** class for event watching, using default values. This is the default constructor.

```
[Visual Basic]
Public Sub New()
[C#]
public EventWatcherOptions();
[C++]
public: EventWatcherOptions();
[JScript]
public function EventWatcherOptions();
```

Requirements

Platforms: Windows 98, Windows NT 4.0, Windows Millennium Edition, Windows 2000, Windows XP Home Edition, Windows XP Professional, Windows .NET Server family

.NET Framework Security:

- Full trust for the immediate caller. This member cannot be used by partially trusted code.

EventWatcherOptions Constructor (ManagementNamedValueCollection, TimeSpan, Int32)

Initializes a new instance of the **EventWatcherOptions** class with the given values.

```
[Visual Basic]
Public Sub New( _
   ByVal context As ManagementNamedValueCollection, _
   ByVal timeout As TimeSpan, _
   ByVal blockSize As Integer _
)
[C#]
public EventWatcherOptions(
   ManagementNamedValueCollection context,
   TimeSpan timeout,
   int blockSize
);
[C++]
public: EventWatcherOptions(
   ManagementNamedValueCollection* context,
   TimeSpan timeout,
   int blockSize
);
[JScript]
public function EventWatcherOptions(
   context : ManagementNamedValueCollection,
   timeout : TimeSpan,
   blockSize : int
);
```

Parameters

context
   The options context object containing provider-specific information to be passed through to the provider.
timeout
   The timeout to wait for the next events.
blockSize
   The number of events to wait for in each block.

Requirements

Platforms: Windows 98, Windows NT 4.0, Windows Millennium Edition, Windows 2000, Windows XP Home Edition, Windows XP Professional, Windows .NET Server family

.NET Framework Security:

- Full trust for the immediate caller. This member cannot be used by partially trusted code.

EventWatcherOptions.BlockSize Property

Gets or sets the block size for block operations. When waiting for events, this value specifies how many events to wait for before returning.

```
[Visual Basic]
Public Property BlockSize As Integer
[C#]
public int BlockSize {get; set;}
[C++]
public: __property int get_BlockSize();
public: __property void set_BlockSize(int);
[JScript]
public function get BlockSize() : int;
public function set BlockSize(int);
```

Property Value

The default value is 1.

Requirements

Platforms: Windows 98, Windows NT 4.0, Windows Millennium Edition, Windows 2000, Windows XP Home Edition, Windows XP Professional, Windows .NET Server family

.NET Framework Security:

- Full trust for the immediate caller. This member cannot be used by partially trusted code.

EventWatcherOptions.Clone Method

Returns a copy of the object.

```
[Visual Basic]
Overrides Public Function Clone() As Object Implements _
   ICloneable.Clone
[C#]
public override object Clone();
[C++]
public: Object* Clone();
[JScript]
public override function Clone() : Object;
```

Return Value

The cloned object.

Implements

ICloneable.Clone

Requirements

Platforms: Windows 98, Windows NT 4.0,
Windows Millennium Edition, Windows 2000,
Windows XP Home Edition, Windows XP Professional,
Windows .NET Server family

.NET Framework Security:

- Full trust for the immediate caller. This member cannot be used
  by partially trusted code.

ImpersonationLevel Enumeration

Describes the impersonation level to be used to connect to WMI.

```
[Visual Basic]
<Serializable>
Public Enum ImpersonationLevel
[C#]
[Serializable]
public enum ImpersonationLevel
[C++]
[Serializable]
__value public enum ImpersonationLevel
[JScript]
public
   Serializable
enum ImpersonationLevel
```

Members

Member name	Description
Anonymous	Anonymous COM impersonation level that hides the identity of the caller. Calls to WMI may fail with this impersonation level.
Default	Default impersonation.
Delegate	Delegate-level COM impersonation level that allows objects to permit other objects to use the credentials of the caller. This level, which will work with WMI calls but may constitute an unnecessary security risk, is supported only under Windows 2000.
Identify	Identify-level COM impersonation level that allows objects to query the credentials of the caller. Calls to WMI may fail with this impersonation level.
Impersonate	Impersonate-level COM impersonation level that allows objects to use the credentials of the caller. This is the recommended impersonation level for WMI calls.

Requirements

Namespace: System.Management

Platforms: Windows 98, Windows NT 4.0, Windows Millennium Edition, Windows 2000, Windows XP Home Edition, Windows XP Professional, Windows .NET Server family

Assembly: System.Management (in System.Management.dll)

InvokeMethodOptions Class

Specifies options for invoking a management method.

System.Object
  System.Management.ManagementOptions
    System.Management.InvokeMethodOptions

```
[Visual Basic]
Public Class InvokeMethodOptions
    Inherits ManagementOptions
[C#]
public class InvokeMethodOptions : ManagementOptions
[C++]
public __gc class InvokeMethodOptions : public ManagementOptions
[JScript]
public class InvokeMethodOptions extends ManagementOptions
```

Thread Safety

Any public static (**Shared** in Visual Basic) members of this type are safe for multithreaded operations. Any instance members are not guaranteed to be thread safe.

Example

```
[C#]
using System;
using System.Management;

// This example demonstrates how to stop a system service.
class Sample_InvokeMethodOptions
{
    public static int Main(string[] args) {
        ManagementObject service =
            new ManagementObject("win32_service=\"winmgmt\"");
        InvokeMethodOptions options = new InvokeMethodOptions();
        options.Timeout = new TimeSpan(0,0,5);

        ManagementBaseObject outParams =
service.InvokeMethod("StopService", null, options);

        Console.WriteLine("Return Status = " +
outParams["ReturnValue"]);

        return 0;
    }
}

[Visual Basic]
Imports System
Imports System.Management

' This sample demonstrates how to stop a system service.
Class Sample_InvokeMethodOptions
    Overloads Public Shared Function Main(args() As String) As Integer
        Dim service As New ManagementObject("win32_service=""winmgmt""")
        Dim options As New InvokeMethodOptions()
        options.Timeout = New TimeSpan(0, 0, 0, 5)

        Dim outParams As ManagementBaseObject = service.InvokeMethod( _
            "StopService", _
            Nothing, _
            options)

        Console.WriteLine("Return Status = " & _
            outParams("ReturnValue").ToString())

        Return 0
    End Function
End Class
```

Requirements

Namespace: System.Management

Platforms: Windows 98, Windows NT 4.0, Windows Millennium Edition, Windows 2000, Windows XP Home Edition, Windows XP Professional, Windows .NET Server family

Assembly: System.Management (in System.Management.dll)

InvokeMethodOptions Constructor

Initializes a new instance of the **InvokeMethodOptions** class.

Overload List

Initializes a new instance of the **InvokeMethodOptions** class for the **InvokeMethod** operation, using default values. This is the default constructor.

> [Visual Basic] **Public Sub New()**
> [C#] **public InvokeMethodOptions();**
> [C++] **public: InvokeMethodOptions();**
> [JScript] **public function InvokeMethodOptions();**

Initializes a new instance of the **InvokeMethodOptions** class for an invoke operation using the specified values.

> [Visual Basic] **Public Sub New(ManagementNamed-ValueCollection, TimeSpan)**
> [C#] **public InvokeMethodOptions(Management-NamedValueCollection, TimeSpan);**
> [C++] **public: InvokeMethodOptions(Management-NamedValueCollection*, TimeSpan);**
> [JScript] **public function InvokeMethod-Options(ManagementNamedValueCollection, TimeSpan);**

InvokeMethodOptions Constructor ( )

Initializes a new instance of the **InvokeMethodOptions** class for the **InvokeMethod** operation, using default values. This is the default constructor.

```
[Visual Basic]
Public Sub New()
[C#]
public InvokeMethodOptions();
[C++]
public: InvokeMethodOptions();
[JScript]
public function InvokeMethodOptions();
```

Requirements

Platforms: Windows 98, Windows NT 4.0, Windows Millennium Edition, Windows 2000, Windows XP Home Edition, Windows XP Professional, Windows .NET Server family

.NET Framework Security:

- Full trust for the immediate caller. This member cannot be used by partially trusted code.

InvokeMethodOptions Constructor (ManagementNamedValueCollection, TimeSpan)

Initializes a new instance of the **InvokeMethodOptions** class for an invoke operation using the specified values.

```
[Visual Basic]
Public Sub New( _
    ByVal context As ManagementNamedValueCollection, _
    ByVal timeout As TimeSpan _
)
[C#]
public InvokeMethodOptions(
    ManagementNamedValueCollection context,
    TimeSpan timeout
);
[C++]
public: InvokeMethodOptions(
    ManagementNamedValueCollection* context,
    TimeSpan timeout
);
[JScript]
public function InvokeMethodOptions(
    context : ManagementNamedValueCollection,
    timeout : TimeSpan
);
```

Parameters

context

A provider-specific, named-value pairs object to be passed through to the provider.

timeout

The length of time to let the operation perform before it times out. The default value is **InfiniteTimeout**. Setting this parameter will invoke the operation semisynchronously.

Requirements

Platforms: Windows 98, Windows NT 4.0, Windows Millennium Edition, Windows 2000, Windows XP Home Edition, Windows XP Professional, Windows .NET Server family

.NET Framework Security:

- Full trust for the immediate caller. This member cannot be used by partially trusted code.

InvokeMethodOptions.Clone Method

Returns a copy of the object.

```
[Visual Basic]
Overrides Public Function Clone() As Object Implements _
    ICloneable.Clone
[C#]
public override object Clone();
[C++]
public: Object* Clone();
[JScript]
public override function Clone() : Object;
```

Return Value

The cloned object.

Implements

ICloneable.Clone

Requirements

Platforms: Windows 98, Windows NT 4.0, Windows Millennium Edition, Windows 2000, Windows XP Home Edition, Windows XP Professional, Windows .NET Server family

.NET Framework Security:

- Full trust for the immediate caller. This member cannot be used by partially trusted code.

ManagementBaseObject Class

Contains the basic elements of a management object. It serves as a base class to more specific management object classes.

System.Object
  System.MarshalByRefObject
    System.ComponentModel.Component
      System.Management.ManagementBaseObject
        System.Management.ManagementObject

```
[Visual Basic]
<Serializable>
Public Class ManagementBaseObject
   Inherits Component
   Implements ICloneable, ISerializable
[C#]
[Serializable]
public class ManagementBaseObject : Component, ICloneable,
   ISerializable
[C++]
[Serializable]
public __gc class ManagementBaseObject : public Component,
   ICloneable, ISerializable
[JScript]
public
   Serializable
class ManagementBaseObject extends Component implements
   ICloneable, ISerializable
```

Thread Safety

Any public static (**Shared** in Visual Basic) members of this type are safe for multithreaded operations. Any instance members are not guaranteed to be thread safe.

Requirements

Namespace: System.Management

Platforms: Windows 98, Windows NT 4.0, Windows Millennium Edition, Windows 2000, Windows XP Home Edition, Windows XP Professional, Windows .NET Server family

Assembly: System.Management (in System.Management.dll)

ManagementBaseObject Constructor

Initializes a new instance of the **ManagementBaseObject** class that is serializable.

```
[Visual Basic]
Protected Sub New( _
   ByVal info As SerializationInfo, _
   ByVal context As StreamingContext _
)
[C#]
protected ManagementBaseObject(
   SerializationInfo info,
   StreamingContext context
);
```

```
[C++]
protected: ManagementBaseObject(
   SerializationInfo* info,
   StreamingContext context
);
[JScript]
protected function ManagementBaseObject(
   info : SerializationInfo,
   context : StreamingContext
);
```

Parameters

info
    The **SerializationInfo** to populate with data.
context
    The destination (see **StreamingContext**) for this serialization.

Requirements

Platforms: Windows 98, Windows NT 4.0, Windows Millennium Edition, Windows 2000, Windows XP Home Edition, Windows XP Professional, Windows .NET Server family

.NET Framework Security:
- Full trust for the immediate caller. This member cannot be used by partially trusted code.

ManagementBaseObject.ClassPath Property

Gets or sets the path to the management object's class.

```
[Visual Basic]
Public Overridable ReadOnly Property ClassPath As ManagementPath
[C#]
public virtual ManagementPath ClassPath {get;}
[C++]
public: __property virtual ManagementPath* get_ClassPath();
[JScript]
public function get ClassPath() : ManagementPath;
```

Property Value

A **ManagementPath** that represents the path to the management object's class.

Example

For example, for the \\MyBox\root\cimv2:Win32_LogicalDisk= 'C:' object, the class path is \\MyBox\root\cimv2:Win32_LogicalDisk .

Requirements

Platforms: Windows 98, Windows NT 4.0, Windows Millennium Edition, Windows 2000, Windows XP Home Edition, Windows XP Professional, Windows .NET Server family

.NET Framework Security:
- Full trust for the immediate caller. This member cannot be used by partially trusted code.

ManagementBaseObject.Item Property

Gets access to property values through [] notation.

[C#] In C#, this property is the indexer for the **ManagementBaseObject** class.

```
[Visual Basic]
Public Default Property Item( _
   ByVal propertyName As String _
) As Object
[C#]
public object this[
   string propertyName
] {get; set;}
[C++]
public: __property Object* get_Item(
   String* propertyName
);
public: __property void set_Item(
   String* propertyName,
   Object*
);
[JScript]
returnValue = ManagementBaseObjectObject.Item(propertyName);
ManagementBaseObjectObject.Item(propertyName) = returnValue;
-or-
returnValue = ManagementBaseObjectObject(propertyName);
ManagementBaseObjectObject(propertyName) = returnValue;
```

[JScript] In JScript, you can use the default indexed properties defined by a type, but you cannot explicitly define your own. However, specifying the **expando** attribute on a class automatically provides a default indexed property whose type is **Object** and whose index type is **String**.

Arguments [JScript]

propertyName

The name of the property of interest.

Parameters [Visual Basic, C#, C++]

propertyName

The name of the property of interest.

Property Value

An **Object** containing the value of the requested property.

Requirements

Platforms: Windows 98, Windows NT 4.0, Windows Millennium Edition, Windows 2000, Windows XP Home Edition, Windows XP Professional, Windows .NET Server family

.NET Framework Security:

- Full trust for the immediate caller. This member cannot be used by partially trusted code.

ManagementBaseObject.Properties Property

Gets or sets a collection of **PropertyData** objects describing the properties of the management object.

```
[Visual Basic]
Public Overridable ReadOnly Property Properties As _
   PropertyDataCollection
[C#]
public virtual PropertyDataCollection Properties {get;}
[C++]
public: __property virtual PropertyDataCollection* get_Properties();
[JScript]
public function get Properties() : PropertyDataCollection;
```

Property Value

A **PropertyDataCollection** that represents the properties of the management object.

Requirements

Platforms: Windows 98, Windows NT 4.0, Windows Millennium Edition, Windows 2000, Windows XP Home Edition, Windows XP Professional, Windows .NET Server family

.NET Framework Security:

- Full trust for the immediate caller. This member cannot be used by partially trusted code.

ManagementBaseObject.Qualifiers Property

Gets or sets the collection of **QualifierData** objects defined on the management object. Each element in the collection holds information such as the qualifier name, value, and flavor.

```
[Visual Basic]
Public Overridable ReadOnly Property Qualifiers As _
   QualifierDataCollection
[C#]
public virtual QualifierDataCollection Qualifiers {get;}
[C++]
public: __property virtual QualifierDataCollection* get_Qualifiers();
[JScript]
public function get Qualifiers() : QualifierDataCollection;
```

Property Value

A **QualifierDataCollection** that represents the qualifiers defined on the management object.

Requirements

Platforms: Windows 98, Windows NT 4.0, Windows Millennium Edition, Windows 2000, Windows XP Home Edition, Windows XP Professional, Windows .NET Server family

.NET Framework Security:

- Full trust for the immediate caller. This member cannot be used by partially trusted code.

ManagementBaseObject.SystemProperties Property

Gets or sets the collection of WMI system properties of the management object (for example, the class name, server, and namespace). WMI system property names begin with "__".

```
[Visual Basic]
Public Overridable ReadOnly Property SystemProperties As _
   PropertyDataCollection
[C#]
public virtual PropertyDataCollection SystemProperties {get;}
[C++]
public: __property virtual PropertyDataCollection* get_SystemProperties();
[JScript]
public function get SystemProperties() : PropertyDataCollection;
```

Property Value

A **PropertyDataCollection** that represents the system properties of the management object.

Requirements

Platforms: Windows 98, Windows NT 4.0, Windows Millennium Edition, Windows 2000, Windows XP Home Edition, Windows XP Professional, Windows .NET Server family

.NET Framework Security:
- Full trust for the immediate caller. This member cannot be used by partially trusted code.

ManagementBaseObject.Clone Method

Returns a copy of the object.

```
[Visual Basic]
Public Overridable Function Clone() As Object Implements _
    ICloneable.Clone
[C#]
public virtual object Clone();
[C++]
public: virtual Object* Clone();
[JScript]
public function Clone() : Object;
```

Return Value

The new cloned object.

Implements

ICloneable.Clone

Requirements

Platforms: Windows 98, Windows NT 4.0, Windows Millennium Edition, Windows 2000, Windows XP Home Edition, Windows XP Professional, Windows .NET Server family

.NET Framework Security:
- Full trust for the immediate caller. This member cannot be used by partially trusted code.

ManagementBaseObject.CompareTo Method

Compares this object to another, based on specified options.

```
[Visual Basic]
Public Function CompareTo( _
    ByVal otherObject As ManagementBaseObject, _
    ByVal settings As ComparisonSettings _
) As Boolean
[C#]
public bool CompareTo(
    ManagementBaseObject otherObject,
    ComparisonSettings settings
);
[C++]
public: bool CompareTo(
    ManagementBaseObject* otherObject,
    ComparisonSettings settings
);
```

```
[JScript]
public function CompareTo(
    otherObject : ManagementBaseObject,
    settings : ComparisonSettings
) : Boolean;
```

Parameters

otherObject
> The object to which to compare this object.

settings
> Options on how to compare the objects.

Return Value

true if the objects compared are equal according to the given options; otherwise, **false**.

Requirements

Platforms: Windows 98, Windows NT 4.0, Windows Millennium Edition, Windows 2000, Windows XP Home Edition, Windows XP Professional, Windows .NET Server family

.NET Framework Security:
- Full trust for the immediate caller. This member cannot be used by partially trusted code.

ManagementBaseObject.Equals Method

Compares two management objects.

```
[Visual Basic]
Overrides Public Function Equals( _
    ByVal obj As Object _
) As Boolean
[C#]
public override bool Equals(
    object obj
);
[C++]
public: bool Equals(
    Object* obj
);
[JScript]
public override function Equals(
    obj : Object
) : Boolean;
```

Parameters

obj
> An object to compare with this instance.

Return Value

true if *obj* is an instance of **ManagementBaseObject** and represents the same object as this instance; otherwise, **false**.

Requirements

Platforms: Windows 98, Windows NT 4.0, Windows Millennium Edition, Windows 2000, Windows XP Home Edition, Windows XP Professional, Windows .NET Server family

.NET Framework Security:
- Full trust for the immediate caller. This member cannot be used by partially trusted code.

ManagementBaseObject.GetHashCode Method

Serves as a hash function for a particular type, suitable for use in hashing algorithms and data structures like a hash table.

```
[Visual Basic]
Overrides Public Function GetHashCode() As Integer
[C#]
public override int GetHashCode();
[C++]
public: int GetHashCode();
[JScript]
public override function GetHashCode() : int;
```

Return Value

A hash code for the current object.

Requirements

Platforms: Windows 98, Windows NT 4.0, Windows Millennium Edition, Windows 2000, Windows XP Home Edition, Windows XP Professional, Windows .NET Server family

.NET Framework Security:
- Full trust for the immediate caller. This member cannot be used by partially trusted code.

ManagementBaseObject.GetPropertyQualifier-Value Method

Returns the value of the specified property qualifier.

```
[Visual Basic]
Public Function GetPropertyQualifierValue( _
    ByVal propertyName As String, _
    ByVal qualifierName As String _
) As Object
[C#]
public object GetPropertyQualifierValue(
    string propertyName,
    string qualifierName
);
[C++]
public: Object* GetPropertyQualifierValue(
    String* propertyName,
    String* qualifierName
);
[JScript]
public function GetPropertyQualifierValue(
    propertyName : String,
    qualifierName : String
) : Object;
```

Parameters

propertyName
    The name of the property to which the qualifier belongs.
qualifierName
    The name of the property qualifier of interest.

Return Value

The value of the specified qualifier.

Requirements

Platforms: Windows 98, Windows NT 4.0, Windows Millennium Edition, Windows 2000, Windows XP Home Edition, Windows XP Professional, Windows .NET Server family

.NET Framework Security:
- Full trust for the immediate caller. This member cannot be used by partially trusted code.

ManagementBaseObject.GetPropertyValue Method

Gets an equivalent accessor to a property's value.

```
[Visual Basic]
Public Function GetPropertyValue( _
    ByVal propertyName As String _
) As Object
[C#]
public object GetPropertyValue(
    string propertyName
);
[C++]
public: Object* GetPropertyValue(
    String* propertyName
);
[JScript]
public function GetPropertyValue(
    propertyName : String
) : Object;
```

Parameters

propertyName
    The name of the property of interest.

Return Value

The value of the specified property.

Requirements

Platforms: Windows 98, Windows NT 4.0, Windows Millennium Edition, Windows 2000, Windows XP Home Edition, Windows XP Professional, Windows .NET Server family

.NET Framework Security:
- Full trust for the immediate caller. This member cannot be used by partially trusted code.

ManagementBaseObject.GetQualifierValue Method

Gets the value of the specified qualifier.

```
[Visual Basic]
Public Function GetQualifierValue( _
    ByVal qualifierName As String _
) As Object
[C#]
public object GetQualifierValue(
    string qualifierName
);
```

```
[C++]
public: Object* GetQualifierValue(
    String* qualifierName
);
[JScript]
public function GetQualifierValue(
    qualifierName : String
) : Object;
```

Parameters

qualifierName
    The name of the qualifier of interest.

Return Value

The value of the specified qualifier.

Requirements

Platforms: Windows 98, Windows NT 4.0,
Windows Millennium Edition, Windows 2000,
Windows XP Home Edition, Windows XP Professional,
Windows .NET Server family

.NET Framework Security:

- Full trust for the immediate caller. This member cannot be used by partially trusted code.

ManagementBaseObject.GetText Method

Returns a textual representation of the object in the specified format.

```
[Visual Basic]
Public Function GetText( _
    ByVal format As TextFormat _
) As String
[C#]
public string GetText(
    TextFormat format
);
[C++]
public: String* GetText(
    TextFormat format
);
[JScript]
public function GetText(
    format : TextFormat
) : String;
```

Parameters

format
    The requested textual format.

Return Value

The textual representation of the object in the specified format.

Remarks

Currently, the only format that WMI supports is Managed Object Format (MOF). In the future, other formats will be supported, such as Extensible Markup Language (XML).

Requirements

Platforms: Windows 98, Windows NT 4.0,
Windows Millennium Edition, Windows 2000,
Windows XP Home Edition, Windows XP Professional,
Windows .NET Server family

.NET Framework Security:

- Full trust for the immediate caller. This member cannot be used by partially trusted code.

ManagementBaseObject.ISerializable.Get-ObjectData Method

This member supports the .NET Framework infrastructure and is not intended to be used directly from your code.

```
[Visual Basic]
Private Sub GetObjectData( _
    ByVal info As SerializationInfo, _
    ByVal context As StreamingContext _
) Implements ISerializable.GetObjectData
[C#]
void ISerializable.GetObjectData(
    SerializationInfo info,
    StreamingContext context
);
[C++]
private: void ISerializable::GetObjectData(
    SerializationInfo* info,
    StreamingContext context
);
[JScript]
private function ISerializable.GetObjectData(
    info : SerializationInfo,
    context : StreamingContext
);
```

ManagementBaseObject.SetProperty-QualifierValue Method

Sets the value of the specified property qualifier.

```
[Visual Basic]
Public Sub SetPropertyQualifierValue( _
    ByVal propertyName As String, _
    ByVal qualifierName As String, _
    ByVal qualifierValue As Object _
)
[C#]
public void SetPropertyQualifierValue(
    string propertyName,
    string qualifierName,
    object qualifierValue
);
[C++]
public: void SetPropertyQualifierValue(
    String* propertyName,
    String* qualifierName,
    Object* qualifierValue
);
[JScript]
public function SetPropertyQualifierValue(
    propertyName : String,
    qualifierName : String,
    qualifierValue : Object
);
```

Parameters

propertyName
> The name of the property to which the qualifier belongs.

qualifierName
> The name of the property qualifier of interest.

qualifierValue
> The new value for the qualifier.

Requirements

Platforms: Windows 98, Windows NT 4.0,
Windows Millennium Edition, Windows 2000,
Windows XP Home Edition, Windows XP Professional,
Windows .NET Server family

.NET Framework Security:
- Full trust for the immediate caller. This member cannot be used by partially trusted code.

ManagementBaseObject.SetPropertyValue Method

Sets the value of the named property.

```
[Visual Basic]
Public Sub SetPropertyValue( _
   ByVal propertyName As String, _
   ByVal propertyValue As Object _
)
[C#]
public void SetPropertyValue(
   string propertyName,
   object propertyValue
);
[C++]
public: void SetPropertyValue(
   String* propertyName,
   Object* propertyValue
);
[JScript]
public function SetPropertyValue(
   propertyName : String,
   propertyValue : Object
);
```

Parameters

propertyName
> The name of the property to be changed.

propertyValue
> The new value for this property.

Requirements

Platforms: Windows 98, Windows NT 4.0,
Windows Millennium Edition, Windows 2000,
Windows XP Home Edition, Windows XP Professional,
Windows .NET Server family

.NET Framework Security:
- Full trust for the immediate caller. This member cannot be used by partially trusted code.

ManagementBaseObject.SetQualifierValue Method

Sets the value of the named qualifier.

```
[Visual Basic]
Public Sub SetQualifierValue( _
   ByVal qualifierName As String, _
   ByVal qualifierValue As Object _
)
[C#]
public void SetQualifierValue(
   string qualifierName,
   object qualifierValue
);
[C++]
public: void SetQualifierValue(
   String* qualifierName,
   Object* qualifierValue
);
[JScript]
public function SetQualifierValue(
   qualifierName : String,
   qualifierValue : Object
);
```

Parameters

qualifierName
> The name of the qualifier to set. This parameter cannot be null.

qualifierValue
> The value to set.

Requirements

Platforms: Windows 98, Windows NT 4.0,
Windows Millennium Edition, Windows 2000,
Windows XP Home Edition, Windows XP Professional,
Windows .NET Server family

.NET Framework Security:
- Full trust for the immediate caller. This member cannot be used by partially trusted code.

ManagementBaseObject to IntPtr Conversion

Provides the internal WMI object represented by a ManagementObject.

See remarks with regard to usage.

```
[Visual Basic]
returnValue = ManagementBaseObject.op_Explicit(managementObject)
[C#]
public static explicit operator IntPtr(
   ManagementBaseObject managementObject
);
[C++]
public: static IntPtr op_Explicit();
[JScript]
returnValue = IntPtr(managementObject);
```

[Visual Basic] In Visual Basic, you can use the conversion operators defined by a type, but you cannot define your own.

[JScript] In JScript, you can use the conversion operators defined by a type, but you cannot define your own.

Arguments [Visual Basic, JScript]

managementObject

The **ManagementBaseObject** that references the requested WMI object.

Parameters [C#]

managementObject

The **ManagementBaseObject** that references the requested WMI object.

Return Value

An **IntPtr** representing the internal WMI object.

Remarks

This operator is used internally by instrumentation code. It is not intended for direct use by regular client or instrumented applications.

Requirements

Platforms: Windows 98, Windows NT 4.0, Windows Millennium Edition, Windows 2000, Windows XP Home Edition, Windows XP Professional, Windows .NET Server family

.NET Framework Security:

- Full trust for the immediate caller. This member cannot be used by partially trusted code.

ManagementClass Class

Represents a management class.

System.Object
  System.MarshalByRefObject
    System.ComponentModel.Component
      System.Management.ManagementBaseObject
        System.Management.ManagementObject
          System.Management.ManagementClass

```
[Visual Basic]
<Serializable>
Public Class ManagementClass
   Inherits ManagementObject
[C#]
[Serializable]
public class ManagementClass : ManagementObject
[C++]
[Serializable]
public __gc class ManagementClass : public ManagementObject
[JScript]
public
   Serializable
class ManagementClass extends ManagementObject
```

Thread Safety

Any public static (**Shared** in Visual Basic) members of this type are
safe for multithreaded operations. Any instance members are not
guaranteed to be thread safe.

Example

```
[C#]
using System;
using System.Management;

// This example demonstrates getting information about a class
 using the ManagementClass object
class Sample_ManagementClass
{
    public static int Main(string[] args) {
        ManagementClass diskClass = new
ManagementClass("Win32_LogicalDisk");
        diskClass.Get();
        Console.WriteLine("Logical Disk class has " +
diskClass.Properties.Count + " properties");
        return 0;
    }
}
```

```
[Visual Basic]
Imports System
Imports System.Management

' This example demonstrates getting information about a class
using the ManagementClass object
Class Sample_ManagementClass
    Overloads Public Shared Function Main(args() As String) As Integer
        Dim diskClass As New ManagementClass("Win32_LogicalDisk")
        diskClass.Get()
        Console.WriteLine(("Logical Disk class has " & _
                        diskClass.Properties.Count.ToString() & _
                        " properties"))
        Return 0
    End Function
End Class
```

Requirements

Namespace: System.Management

Platforms: Windows 98, Windows NT 4.0,
Windows Millennium Edition, Windows 2000,
Windows XP Home Edition, Windows XP Professional,
Windows .NET Server family

Assembly: System.Management (in System.Management.dll)

ManagementClass Constructor

Initializes a new instance of the **ManagementClass** class.

Overload List

Initializes a new instance of the **ManagementClass** class. This is the
default constructor.

  [Visual Basic] **Public Sub New()**
  [C#] **public ManagementClass();**
  [C++] **public: ManagementClass();**
  [JScript] **public function ManagementClass();**

Initializes a new instance of the **ManagementClass** class initialized
to the given path.

  [Visual Basic] **Public Sub New(ManagementPath)**
  [C#] **public ManagementClass(ManagementPath);**
  [C++] **public: ManagementClass(ManagementPath*);**
  [JScript] **public function ManagementClass(Manage-mentPath);**

Initializes a new instance of the **ManagementClass** class initialized
to the given path.

  [Visual Basic] **Public Sub New(String)**
  [C#] **public ManagementClass(string);**
  [C++] **public: ManagementClass(String*);**
  [JScript] **public function ManagementClass(String);**

Initializes a new instance of the **ManagementClass** class initialized
to the given WMI class path using the specified options.

  [Visual Basic] **Public Sub New(ManagementPath, ObjectGetOptions)**
  [C#] **public ManagementClass(ManagementPath, ObjectGetOptions);**
  [C++] **public: ManagementClass(ManagementPath*, ObjectGetOptions*);**
  [JScript] **public function ManagementClass(Management-Path, ObjectGetOptions);**

Initializes a new instance of the **ManagementClass** class initialized
to the given WMI class path using the specified options.

  [Visual Basic] **Public Sub New(String, ObjectGetOptions)**
  [C#] **public ManagementClass(string, ObjectGetOptions);**
  [C++] **public: ManagementClass(String*, ObjectGetOptions*);**
  [JScript] **public function ManagementClass(String, ObjectGetOptions);**

Initializes a new instance of the **ManagementClass** class for the
specified WMI class in the specified scope and with the specified
options.

  [Visual Basic] **Public Sub New(ManagementScope, ManagementPath, ObjectGetOptions)**

[C#] **public ManagementClass(ManagementScope, ManagementPath, ObjectGetOptions);**

[C++] **public: ManagementClass(ManagementScope*, ManagementPath*, ObjectGetOptions*);**

[JScript] **public function ManagementClass(Management-Scope, ManagementPath, ObjectGetOptions);**

Initializes a new instance of the **ManagementClass** class for the specified WMI class, in the specified scope, and with the specified options.

[Visual Basic] **Public Sub New(String, String, ObjectGetOptions)**

[C#] **public ManagementClass(string, string, ObjectGetOptions);**

[C++] **public: ManagementClass(String*, String*, ObjectGetOptions*);**

[JScript] **public function ManagementClass(String, String, ObjectGetOptions);**

Example

[Visual Basic, C#] **Note** This example shows how to use one of the overloaded versions of the **ManagementClass** constructor. For other examples that might be available, see the individual overload topics.

```
[C#]
ManagementClass c = new ManagementClass("\\\\MyBox\\root\\cimv2",
                        "Win32_Environment",
                   new ObjectGetOptions(null, true));
```

```
[Visual Basic]
Dim c As New ManagementClass("\\MyBox\root\cimv2", _
                             "Win32_Environment", _
                   new ObjectGetOptions(Null, True))
```

ManagementClass Constructor ( )

Initializes a new instance of the **ManagementClass** class. This is the default constructor.

```
[Visual Basic]
Public Sub New()
[C#]
public ManagementClass();
[C++]
public: ManagementClass();
[JScript]
public function ManagementClass();
```

Example

```
[C#]
ManagementClass c = new ManagementClass();
```

```
[Visual Basic]
Dim c As New ManagementClass()
```

Requirements

Platforms: Windows 98, Windows NT 4.0, Windows Millennium Edition, Windows 2000, Windows XP Home Edition, Windows XP Professional, Windows .NET Server family

.NET Framework Security:
- Full trust for the immediate caller. This member cannot be used by partially trusted code.

ManagementClass Constructor (ManagementPath)

Initializes a new instance of the **ManagementClass** class initialized to the given path.

```
[Visual Basic]
Public Sub New( _
    ByVal path As ManagementPath _
)
[C#]
public ManagementClass(
    ManagementPath path
);
[C++]
public: ManagementClass(
    ManagementPath* path
);
[JScript]
public function ManagementClass(
    path : ManagementPath
);
```

Parameters

path
    A **ManagementPath** specifying which WMI class to bind to.

Remarks

The *path* parameter must specify a WMI class path.

Example

```
[C#]
ManagementClass c = new ManagementClass(
    new ManagementPath("Win32_LogicalDisk"));
```

```
[Visual Basic]
Dim c As New ManagementClass( _
    New ManagementPath("Win32_LogicalDisk"))
```

Requirements

Platforms: Windows 98, Windows NT 4.0, Windows Millennium Edition, Windows 2000, Windows XP Home Edition, Windows XP Professional, Windows .NET Server family

.NET Framework Security:
- Full trust for the immediate caller. This member cannot be used by partially trusted code.

ManagementClass Constructor (String)

Initializes a new instance of the **ManagementClass** class initialized to the given path.

```
[Visual Basic]
Public Sub New( _
    ByVal path As String _
)
[C#]
public ManagementClass(
    string path
);
[C++]
public: ManagementClass(
    String* path
);
```

```
[JScript]
public function ManagementClass(
    path : String
);
```

Parameters

path

The path to the WMI class.

Example

```
[C#]
ManagementClass c = new
                ManagementClass("Win32_LogicalDisk");
```

```
[Visual Basic]
Dim c As New ManagementClass("Win32_LogicalDisk")
```

Requirements

Platforms: Windows 98, Windows NT 4.0,
Windows Millennium Edition, Windows 2000,
Windows XP Home Edition, Windows XP Professional,
Windows .NET Server family

.NET Framework Security:

- Full trust for the immediate caller. This member cannot be used
  by partially trusted code.

ManagementClass Constructor (ManagementPath, ObjectGetOptions)

Initializes a new instance of the **ManagementClass** class initialized
to the given WMI class path using the specified options.

```
[Visual Basic]
Public Sub New( _
    ByVal path As ManagementPath, _
    ByVal options As ObjectGetOptions _
)
[C#]
public ManagementClass(
    ManagementPath path,
    ObjectGetOptions options
);
[C++]
public: ManagementClass(
    ManagementPath* path,
    ObjectGetOptions* options
);
[JScript]
public function ManagementClass(
    path : ManagementPath,
    options : ObjectGetOptions
);
```

Parameters

path

A **ManagementPath** representing the WMI class path.

options

An **ObjectGetOptions** representing the options to use when
retrieving this class.

Example

```
[C#]
ManagementPath p = new ManagementPath("Win32_Process");
//Options specify that amended qualifiers are to be retrieved
  along with the class
ObjectGetOptions o = new ObjectGetOptions(null, true);
ManagementClass c = new ManagementClass(p,o);
```

```
[Visual Basic]
Dim p As New ManagementPath("Win32_Process")
' Options specify that amended qualifiers are to be retrieved
along with the class
Dim o As New ObjectGetOptions(Null, True)
Dim c As New ManagementClass(p,o)
```

Requirements

Platforms: Windows 98, Windows NT 4.0,
Windows Millennium Edition, Windows 2000,
Windows XP Home Edition, Windows XP Professional,
Windows .NET Server family

.NET Framework Security:

- Full trust for the immediate caller. This member cannot be used
  by partially trusted code.

ManagementClass Constructor (String, ObjectGetOptions)

Initializes a new instance of the **ManagementClass** class initialized
to the given WMI class path using the specified options.

```
[Visual Basic]
Public Sub New( _
    ByVal path As String, _
    ByVal options As ObjectGetOptions _
)
[C#]
public ManagementClass(
    string path,
    ObjectGetOptions options
);
[C++]
public: ManagementClass(
    String* path,
    ObjectGetOptions* options
);
[JScript]
public function ManagementClass(
    path : String,
    options : ObjectGetOptions
);
```

Parameters

path

The path to the WMI class.

options

An **ObjectGetOptions** representing the options to use when
retrieving the WMI class.

Example

[C#]
```
//Options specify that amended qualifiers should be retrieved    ↵
    along with the class
ObjectGetOptions o = new ObjectGetOptions(null, true);
ManagementClass c = new ManagementClass("Win32_ComputerSystem",o);
```

[Visual Basic]
```
' Options specify that amended qualifiers should be retrieved    ↵
    along with the class
Dim o As New ObjectGetOptions(Null, True)
Dim c As New ManagementClass("Win32_ComputerSystem",o)
```

Requirements

Platforms: Windows 98, Windows NT 4.0,
Windows Millennium Edition, Windows 2000,
Windows XP Home Edition, Windows XP Professional,
Windows .NET Server family

.NET Framework Security:

- Full trust for the immediate caller. This member cannot be used
  by partially trusted code.

ManagementClass Constructor (ManagementScope, ManagementPath, ObjectGetOptions)

Initializes a new instance of the **ManagementClass** class for the
specified WMI class in the specified scope and with the specified
options.

[Visual Basic]
```
Public Sub New( _
    ByVal scope As ManagementScope, _
    ByVal path As ManagementPath, _
    ByVal options As ObjectGetOptions _
)
```
[C#]
```
public ManagementClass(
    ManagementScope scope,
    ManagementPath path,
    ObjectGetOptions options
);
```
[C++]
```
public: ManagementClass(
    ManagementScope* scope,
    ManagementPath* path,
    ObjectGetOptions* options
);
```
[JScript]
```
public function ManagementClass(
    scope : ManagementScope,
    path : ManagementPath,
    options : ObjectGetOptions
);
```

Parameters

scope
> A **ManagementScope** that specifies the scope (server and
> namespace) where the WMI class resides.

path
> A **ManagementPath** that represents the path to the WMI class in
> the specified scope.

options
> An **ObjectGetOptions** that specifies the options to use when
> retrieving the WMI class.

Remarks

The path can be specified as a full path (including server and
namespace). However, if a scope is specified, it will override the first
portion of the full path.

Example

[C#]
```
ManagementScope s = new ManagementScope("\\\\MyBox\\root\\cimv2");
ManagementPath p = new ManagementPath("Win32_Environment");
ObjectGetOptions o = new ObjectGetOptions(null, true);
ManagementClass c = new ManagementClass(s, p, o);
```

[Visual Basic]
```
Dim s As New ManagementScope("\\MyBox\root\cimv2")
Dim p As New ManagementPath("Win32_Environment")
Dim o As New ObjectGetOptions(Null, True)
Dim c As New ManagementClass(s, p, o)
```

Requirements

Platforms: Windows 98, Windows NT 4.0,
Windows Millennium Edition, Windows 2000,
Windows XP Home Edition, Windows XP Professional,
Windows .NET Server family

.NET Framework Security:

- Full trust for the immediate caller. This member cannot be used
  by partially trusted code.

ManagementClass Constructor (String, String, ObjectGetOptions)

Initializes a new instance of the **ManagementClass** class for the
specified WMI class, in the specified scope, and with the specified
options.

[Visual Basic]
```
Public Sub New( _
    ByVal scope As String, _
    ByVal path As String, _
    ByVal options As ObjectGetOptions _
)
```
[C#]
```
public ManagementClass(
    string scope,
    string path,
    ObjectGetOptions options
);
```
[C++]
```
public: ManagementClass(
    String* scope,
    String* path,
    ObjectGetOptions* options
);
```
[JScript]
```
public function ManagementClass(
    scope : String,
    path : String,
    options : ObjectGetOptions
);
```

Parameters

scope

The scope in which the WMI class resides.

path

The path to the WMI class within the specified scope.

options

An **ObjectGetOptions** that specifies the options to use when retrieving the WMI class.

Remarks

The path can be specified as a full path (including server and namespace). However, if a scope is specified, it will override the first portion of the full path.

Example

```
[C#]
ManagementClass c = new ManagementClass("\\\\MyBox\\root\\cimv2",
                    "Win32_Environment",
                        new ObjectGetOptions(null, true));
```

```
[Visual Basic]
Dim c As New ManagementClass("\\MyBox\root\cimv2", _
                                "Win32_Environment", _
                new ObjectGetOptions(Null, True))
```

Requirements

Platforms: Windows 98, Windows NT 4.0, Windows Millennium Edition, Windows 2000, Windows XP Home Edition, Windows XP Professional, Windows .NET Server family

.NET Framework Security:

- Full trust for the immediate caller. This member cannot be used by partially trusted code.

ManagementClass.Derivation Property

Gets or sets an array containing all WMI classes in the inheritance hierarchy from this class to the top.

```
[Visual Basic]
Public ReadOnly Property Derivation As StringCollection
[C#]
public StringCollection Derivation {get;}
[C++]
public: __property StringCollection* get_Derivation();
[JScript]
public function get Derivation() : StringCollection;
```

Property Value

A string collection containing the names of all WMI classes in the inheritance hierarchy of this class.

Remarks

This property is read-only.

Example

```
[C#]
ManagementClass c = new ManagementClass("Win32_LogicalDisk");
foreach (string s in c.Derivation)
    Console.WriteLine("Further derived from : ", s);
```

```
[Visual Basic]
Dim c As New ManagementClass("Win32_LogicalDisk")
Dim s As String
For Each s In c.Derivation
    Console.WriteLine("Further derived from : " & s)
Next s
```

Requirements

Platforms: Windows 98, Windows NT 4.0, Windows Millennium Edition, Windows 2000, Windows XP Home Edition, Windows XP Professional, Windows .NET Server family

.NET Framework Security:

- Full trust for the immediate caller. This member cannot be used by partially trusted code.

ManagementClass.Methods Property

Gets or sets a collection of **MethodData** objects that represent the methods defined in the WMI class.

```
[Visual Basic]
Public ReadOnly Property Methods As MethodDataCollection
[C#]
public MethodDataCollection Methods {get;}
[C++]
public: __property MethodDataCollection* get_Methods();
[JScript]
public function get Methods() : MethodDataCollection;
```

Property Value

A **MethodDataCollection** representing the methods defined in the WMI class.

Example

```
[C#]
ManagementClass c = new ManagementClass("Win32_Process");
foreach (Method m in c.Methods)
    Console.WriteLine("This class contains this method : ", m.Name);
```

```
[Visual Basic]
Dim c As New ManagementClass("Win32_Process")
Dim m As Method
For Each m in c.Methods
    Console.WriteLine("This class contains this method : " & m.Name)
```

Requirements

Platforms: Windows 98, Windows NT 4.0, Windows Millennium Edition, Windows 2000, Windows XP Home Edition, Windows XP Professional, Windows .NET Server family

.NET Framework Security:

- Full trust for the immediate caller. This member cannot be used by partially trusted code.

ManagementClass.Path Property

Gets or sets the path of the WMI class to which the **ManagementClass** object is bound.

```
[Visual Basic]
Overrides Public Property Path As ManagementPath
[C#]
public override ManagementPath Path {get; set;}
[C++]
public: __property ManagementPath* get_Path();
public: __property void set_Path(ManagementPath*);
[JScript]
public override function get Path() : ManagementPath;
public override function set Path(ManagementPath);
```

Property Value

The path of the object's class.

Remarks

When the property is set to a new value, the **ManagementClass** object will be disconnected from any previously-bound WMI class. Reconnect to the new WMI class path.

Example

```
[C#]
ManagementClass c = new ManagementClass();
c.Path = "Win32_Environment";
```

```
[Visual Basic]
Dim c As New ManagementClass()
c.Path = "Win32_Environment"
```

Requirements

Platforms: Windows 98, Windows NT 4.0, Windows Millennium Edition, Windows 2000, Windows XP Home Edition, Windows XP Professional, Windows .NET Server family

.NET Framework Security:

• Full trust for the immediate caller. This member cannot be used by partially trusted code.

ManagementClass.Clone Method

Returns a copy of the object.

```
[Visual Basic]
Overrides Public Function Clone() As Object Implements _
    ICloneable.Clone
[C#]
public override object Clone();
[C++]
public: Object* Clone();
[JScript]
public override function Clone() : Object;
```

Return Value

The cloned object.

Implements

ICloneable.Clone

Remarks

Note that this does not create a copy of the WMI class; only an additional representation is created.

Requirements

Platforms: Windows 98, Windows NT 4.0, Windows Millennium Edition, Windows 2000, Windows XP Home Edition, Windows XP Professional, Windows .NET Server family

.NET Framework Security:

• Full trust for the immediate caller. This member cannot be used by partially trusted code.

ManagementClass.CreateInstance Method

Creates a new instance of the WMI class.

```
[Visual Basic]
Public Function CreateInstance() As ManagementObject
```

```
[C#]
public ManagementObject CreateInstance();
[C++]
public: ManagementObject* CreateInstance();
[JScript]
public function CreateInstance() : ManagementObject;
```

Return Value

A **ManagementObject** that represents a new instance of the WMI class.

Remarks

Note that the new instance is not committed until the **Put** () method is called. Before committing it, the key properties must be specified.

Example

```
[C#]
ManagementClass envClass = new ManagementClass("Win32_Environment");
        ManagementObject newInstance =
            existingClass.CreateInstance("My_Service");
        newInstance["Name"] = "Cori";
        newInstance.Put(); //to commit the new instance.
```

```
[Visual Basic]
Dim envClass As New ManagementClass("Win32_Environment")
Dim newInstance As ManagementObject

newInstance = existingClass.CreateInstance("My_Service")
newInstance("Name") = "Cori"
newInstance.Put() 'to commit the new instance.
```

Requirements

Platforms: Windows 98, Windows NT 4.0, Windows Millennium Edition, Windows 2000, Windows XP Home Edition, Windows XP Professional, Windows .NET Server family

.NET Framework Security:

• Full trust for the immediate caller. This member cannot be used by partially trusted code.

ManagementClass.Derive Method

Derives a new class from this class.

```
[Visual Basic]
Public Function Derive( _
    ByVal newClassName As String _
) As ManagementClass
[C#]
public ManagementClass Derive(
    string newClassName
);
[C++]
public: ManagementClass* Derive(
    String* newClassName
);
[JScript]
public function Derive(
    newClassName : String
) : ManagementClass;
```

Parameters

newClassName
    The name of the new class to be derived.

Return Value

A new **ManagementClass** that represents a new WMI class derived from the original class.

Remarks

Note that the newly returned class has not been committed until the **Put** () method is explicitly called.

Example

```
[C#]
ManagementClass existingClass = new ManagementClass("CIM_Service");
         ManagementClass newClass =
existingClass.Derive("My_Service");
             newClass.Put(); //to commit the new class to the WMI
repository.
```

```
[Visual Basic]
Dim existingClass As New ManagementClass("CIM_Service")
Dim newClass As ManagementClass

newClass = existingClass.Derive("My_Service")
newClass.Put()  'to commit the new class to the WMI repository.
```

Requirements

Platforms: Windows 98, Windows NT 4.0, Windows Millennium Edition, Windows 2000, Windows XP Home Edition, Windows XP Professional, Windows .NET Server family

.NET Framework Security:

- Full trust for the immediate caller. This member cannot be used by partially trusted code.

ManagementClass.GetInstances Method

Returns the collection of all instances of the class.

Overload List

Returns the collection of all instances of the class.

[Visual Basic] **Overloads Public Function GetInstances() As ManagementObjectCollection**

[C#] **public ManagementObjectCollection GetInstances();**

[C++] **public: ManagementObjectCollection* GetInstances();**

[JScript] **public function GetInstances() : ManagementObjectCollection;**

Returns the collection of all instances of the class using the specified options.

[Visual Basic] **Overloads Public Function GetInstances(EnumerationOptions) As ManagementObjectCollection**

[C#] **public ManagementObjectCollection GetInstances(EnumerationOptions);**

[C++] **public: ManagementObjectCollection* GetInstances(EnumerationOptions*);**

[JScript] **public function GetInstances(EnumerationOptions) : ManagementObjectCollection;**

Returns the collection of all instances of the class, asynchronously.

[Visual Basic] **Overloads Public Sub GetInstances(ManagementOperationObserver)**

[C#] **public void GetInstances(Management-OperationObserver);**

[C++] **public: void GetInstances(Management-OperationObserver*);**

[JScript] **public function GetInstances(Management-OperationObserver);**

Returns the collection of all instances of the class, asynchronously, using the specified options.

[Visual Basic] **Overloads Public Sub GetInstances(ManagementOperationObserver, EnumerationOptions)**

[C#] **public void GetInstances(Management-OperationObserver, EnumerationOptions);**

[C++] **public: void GetInstances(ManagementOperation-Observer*, EnumerationOptions*);**

[JScript] **public function GetInstances(Management-OperationObserver, EnumerationOptions);**

Example

[Visual Basic, C#] **Note** This example shows how to use one of the overloaded versions of **GetInstances**. For other examples that might be available, see the individual overload topics.

```
[C#]
ManagementClass c = new ManagementClass("Win32_Share");
MyHandler h = new MyHandler();
ManagementOperationObserver ob = new ManagementOperationObserver();
ob.ObjectReady += new ObjectReadyEventHandler (h.NewObject);
ob.Completed += new CompletedEventHandler (h.Done);

c.GetInstances(ob);

while (!h.Completed)
    System.Threading.Thread.Sleep (1000);

//Here you can use the object
Console.WriteLine(o["SomeProperty"]);

public class MyHandler
{
    private bool completed = false;

    public void NewObject(object sender, ObjectReadyEventArgs e) {
        Console.WriteLine("New result arrived !",
((ManagementObject)(e.NewObject))["Name"]);
    }

    public void Done(object sender, CompletedEventArgs e) {
        Console.WriteLine("async Get completed !");
        completed = true;
    }

    public bool Completed {
        get {
            return completed;
        }
    }
}
```

```
[Visual Basic]
Dim c As New ManagementClass("Win32_Share")
Dim h As New MyHandler()
Dim ob As New ManagementOperationObserver()
ob.ObjectReady += New ObjectReadyEventHandler(h.NewObject)
ob.Completed += New CompletedEventHandler(h.Done)

c.GetInstances(ob)

While Not h.Completed
    System.Threading.Thread.Sleep(1000)
End While
```

```
'Here you can use the object
'Console.WriteLine(o("SomeProperty"))

Public Class MyHandler
    Private completed As Boolean = false

    Public Sub Done(sender As Object, e As EventArrivedEventArgs)
        Console.WriteLine("async Get completed !")
    completed = True
    End Sub

    Public ReadOnly Property Completed() As Boolean
        Get
            Return completed
    End Get
    End Property
End Class
```

ManagementClass.GetInstances Method ()

Returns the collection of all instances of the class.

```
[Visual Basic]
Overloads Public Function GetInstances() As ManagementObjectCollection
[C#]
public ManagementObjectCollection GetInstances();
[C++]
public: ManagementObjectCollection* GetInstances();
[JScript]
public function GetInstances() : ManagementObjectCollection;
```

Return Value

A collection of the **ManagementObject** objects representing the instances of the class.

Example

```
[C#]
ManagementClass c = new ManagementClass("Win32_Process");
foreach (ManagementObject o in c.GetInstances())
    Console.WriteLine("Next instance of Win32_Process : ", o.Path);

[Visual Basic]
Dim c As New ManagementClass("Win32_Process")
Dim o As ManagementObject
For Each o In c.GetInstances()
    Console.WriteLine("Next instance of Win32_Process : " & o.Path)
Next o
```

Requirements

Platforms: Windows 98, Windows NT 4.0,
Windows Millennium Edition, Windows 2000,
Windows XP Home Edition, Windows XP Professional,
Windows .NET Server family

.NET Framework Security:
- Full trust for the immediate caller. This member cannot be used by partially trusted code.

ManagementClass.GetInstances Method (EnumerationOptions)

Returns the collection of all instances of the class using the specified options.

```
[Visual Basic]
Overloads Public Function GetInstances( _
    ByVal options As EnumerationOptions _
) As ManagementObjectCollection
```

```
[C#]
public ManagementObjectCollection GetInstances(
    EnumerationOptions options
);
[C++]
public: ManagementObjectCollection* GetInstances(
    EnumerationOptions* options
);
[JScript]
public function GetInstances(
    options : EnumerationOptions
) : ManagementObjectCollection;
```

Parameters

options
    The additional operation options.

Return Value

A collection of the **ManagementObject** objects representing the instances of the class, according to the specified options.

Example

```
[C#]
EnumerationOptions opt = new EnumerationOptions();
//Will enumerate instances of the given class and any subclasses.
o.enumerateDeep = true;
ManagementClass c = new ManagementClass("CIM_Service");
foreach (ManagementObject o in c.GetInstances(opt))
    Console.WriteLine(o["Name"]);

[Visual Basic]
Dim opt As New EnumerationOptions()
'Will enumerate instances of the given class and any subclasses.
o.enumerateDeep = True
Dim c As New ManagementClass("CIM_Service")
Dim o As ManagementObject
For Each o In c.GetInstances(opt)
    Console.WriteLine(o["Name"])
Next o
```

Requirements

Platforms: Windows 98, Windows NT 4.0,
Windows Millennium Edition, Windows 2000,
Windows XP Home Edition, Windows XP Professional,
Windows .NET Server family

.NET Framework Security:
- Full trust for the immediate caller. This member cannot be used by partially trusted code.

ManagementClass.GetInstances Method (ManagementOperationObserver)

Returns the collection of all instances of the class, asynchronously.

```
[Visual Basic]
Overloads Public Sub GetInstances( _
    ByVal watcher As ManagementOperationObserver _
)
[C#]
public void GetInstances(
    ManagementOperationObserver watcher
);
[C++]
public: void GetInstances(
    ManagementOperationObserver* watcher
);
```

```
[JScript]
public function GetInstances(
    watcher : ManagementOperationObserver
);
```

Parameters

watcher

The object to handle the asynchronous operation's progress.

Example

```
[C#]
ManagementClass c = new ManagementClass("Win32_Share");
MyHandler h = new MyHandler();
ManagementOperationObserver ob = new ManagementOperationObserver();
ob.ObjectReady += new ObjectReadyEventHandler (h.NewObject);
ob.Completed += new CompletedEventHandler (h.Done);

c.GetInstances(ob);

while (!h.Completed)
    System.Threading.Thread.Sleep (1000);

//Here you can use the object
Console.WriteLine(o["SomeProperty"]);

public class MyHandler
{
    private bool completed = false;

    public void NewObject(object sender, ObjectReadyEventArgs e) {
        Console.WriteLine("New result arrived !",
((ManagementObject)(e.NewObject))["Name"]);
    }

    public void Done(object sender, CompletedEventArgs e) {
        Console.WriteLine("async Get completed !");
        completed = true;
    }

    public bool Completed {
        get {
            return completed;
        }
    }
}
```

```
[Visual Basic]
Dim c As New ManagementClass("Win32_Share")
Dim h As New MyHandler()
Dim ob As New ManagementOperationObserver()
ob.ObjectReady += New ObjectReadyEventHandler(h.NewObject)
ob.Completed += New CompletedEventHandler(h.Done)

c.GetInstances(ob)

While Not h.Completed
    System.Threading.Thread.Sleep(1000)
End While

'Here you can use the object
Console.WriteLine(o["SomeProperty"))

Public Class MyHandler
    Private completed As Boolean = false

    Public Sub Done(sender As Object, e As EventArrivedEventArgs)
        Console.WriteLine("async Get completed !")
        completed = True
    End Sub

    Public ReadOnly Property Completed() As Boolean
        Get
            Return completed
        End Get
    End Property
End Class
```

Requirements

Platforms: Windows 98, Windows NT 4.0, Windows Millennium Edition, Windows 2000, Windows XP Home Edition, Windows XP Professional, Windows .NET Server family

.NET Framework Security:

- Full trust for the immediate caller. This member cannot be used by partially trusted code.

ManagementClass.GetInstances Method (ManagementOperationObserver, EnumerationOptions)

Returns the collection of all instances of the class, asynchronously, using the specified options.

```
[Visual Basic]
Overloads Public Sub GetInstances( _
    ByVal watcher As ManagementOperationObserver, _
    ByVal options As EnumerationOptions _
)
[C#]
public void GetInstances(
    ManagementOperationObserver watcher,
    EnumerationOptions options
);
[C++]
public: void GetInstances(
    ManagementOperationObserver* watcher,
    EnumerationOptions* options
);
[JScript]
public function GetInstances(
    watcher : ManagementOperationObserver,
    options : EnumerationOptions
);
```

Parameters

watcher

The object to handle the asynchronous operation's progress.

options

The specified additional options for getting the instances.

Requirements

Platforms: Windows 98, Windows NT 4.0, Windows Millennium Edition, Windows 2000, Windows XP Home Edition, Windows XP Professional, Windows .NET Server family

.NET Framework Security:

- Full trust for the immediate caller. This member cannot be used by partially trusted code.

ManagementClass.GetRelatedClasses Method

Retrieves classes related to the WMI class.

Overload List

Retrieves classes related to the WMI class.

[Visual Basic] **Overloads Public Function GetRelatedClasses() As ManagementObjectCollection**

[C#] **public ManagementObjectCollection GetRelatedClasses();**

[C++] **public: ManagementObjectCollection* GetRelatedClasses();**

[JScript] **public function GetRelatedClasses() : ManagementObjectCollection;**

Retrieves classes related to the WMI class, asynchronously.

[Visual Basic] **Overloads Public Sub GetRelatedClasses(ManagementOperationObserver)**

[C#] **public void GetRelatedClasses(Management-OperationObserver);**

[C++] **public: void GetRelatedClasses(Management-OperationObserver*);**

[JScript] **public function GetRelatedClasses(Management-OperationObserver);**

Retrieves classes related to the WMI class.

[Visual Basic] **Overloads Public Function GetRelatedClasses(String) As ManagementObjectCollection**

[C#] **public ManagementObjectCollection GetRelated-Classes(string);**

[C++] **public: ManagementObjectCollection* GetRelated-Classes(String*);**

[JScript] **public function GetRelatedClasses(String) : ManagementObjectCollection;**

Retrieves classes related to the WMI class, asynchronously, given the related class name.

[Visual Basic] **Overloads Public Sub GetRelated-Classes(ManagementOperationObserver, String)**

[C#] **public void GetRelatedClasses(Management-OperationObserver, string);**

[C++] **public: void GetRelatedClasses(Management-OperationObserver*, String*);**

[JScript] **public function GetRelatedClasses(Management-OperationObserver, String);**

Retrieves classes related to the WMI class based on the specified options.

[Visual Basic] **Overloads Public Function GetRelated-Classes(String, String, String, String, String, String, EnumerationOptions) As ManagementObjectCollection**

[C#] **public ManagementObjectCollection GetRelated-Classes(string, string, string, string, string, string, EnumerationOptions);**

[C++] **public: ManagementObjectCollection* GetRelated-Classes(String*, String*, String*, String*, String*, String*, EnumerationOptions*);**

[JScript] **public function GetRelatedClasses(String, String, String, String, String, String, EnumerationOptions) : ManagementObjectCollection;**

Retrieves classes related to the WMI class, asynchronously, using the specified options.

[Visual Basic] **Overloads Public Sub GetRelated-Classes(ManagementOperationObserver, String, String, String, String, String, String, EnumerationOptions)**

[C#] **public void GetRelatedClasses(ManagementOperation-Observer, string, string, string, string, string, string, EnumerationOptions);**

[C++] **public: void GetRelatedClasses(Management-OperationObserver*, String*, String*, String*, String*, String*, String*, EnumerationOptions*);**

[JScript] **public function GetRelatedClasses(Management-OperationObserver, String, String, String, String, String, String, EnumerationOptions);**

Example

[Visual Basic, C#] **Note** This example shows how to use one of the overloaded versions of **GetRelatedClasses**. For other examples that might be available, see the individual overload topics.

[C#]
```
ManagementClass c = new ManagementClass("Win32_LogicalDisk");

foreach (ManagementClass r in c.GetRelatedClasses())
    Console.WriteLine("Instances of {0} may have
                       relationships to this class", r["__CLASS"]);
```

[Visual Basic]
```
Dim c As New ManagementClass("Win32_LogicalDisk")
Dim r As ManagementClass

For Each r In c.GetRelatedClasses()
    Console.WriteLine("Instances of {0} may have relationships _
                       to this class", r("__CLASS"))
Next r
```

ManagementClass.GetRelatedClasses Method ()

Retrieves classes related to the WMI class.

[Visual Basic]
```
Overloads Public Function GetRelatedClasses() As
ManagementObjectCollection
```
[C#]
```
public ManagementObjectCollection GetRelatedClasses();
```
[C++]
```
public: ManagementObjectCollection* GetRelatedClasses();
```
[JScript]
```
public function GetRelatedClasses() : ManagementObjectCollection;
```

Return Value

A collection of the **ManagementClass** or **ManagementObject** objects that represents WMI classes or instances related to the WMI class.

Remarks

The method queries the WMI schema for all possible associations that the WMI class may have with other classes, or in rare cases, to instances.

Example

[C#]
```
ManagementClass c = new ManagementClass("Win32_LogicalDisk");

foreach (ManagementClass r in c.GetRelatedClasses())
    Console.WriteLine("Instances of {0} may have
                       relationships to this class", r["__CLASS"]);
```

[Visual Basic]
```
Dim c As New ManagementClass("Win32_LogicalDisk")
Dim r As ManagementClass

For Each r In c.GetRelatedClasses()
    Console.WriteLine("Instances of {0} may have relationships _
                       to this class", r("__CLASS"))
Next r
```

Requirements

Platforms: Windows 98, Windows NT 4.0,
Windows Millennium Edition, Windows 2000,
Windows XP Home Edition, Windows XP Professional,
Windows .NET Server family

.NET Framework Security:

- Full trust for the immediate caller. This member cannot be used
  by partially trusted code.

ManagementClass.GetRelatedClasses Method (ManagementOperationObserver)

Retrieves classes related to the WMI class, asynchronously.

```
[Visual Basic]
Overloads Public Sub GetRelatedClasses( _
   ByVal watcher As ManagementOperationObserver _
)
[C#]
public void GetRelatedClasses(
   ManagementOperationObserver watcher
);
[C++]
public: void GetRelatedClasses(
   ManagementOperationObserver* watcher
);
[JScript]
public function GetRelatedClasses(
   watcher : ManagementOperationObserver
);
```

Parameters

watcher
   The object to handle the asynchronous operation's progress.

Requirements

Platforms: Windows 98, Windows NT 4.0,
Windows Millennium Edition, Windows 2000,
Windows XP Home Edition, Windows XP Professional,
Windows .NET Server family

.NET Framework Security:

- Full trust for the immediate caller. This member cannot be used
  by partially trusted code.

ManagementClass.GetRelatedClasses Method (String)

Retrieves classes related to the WMI class.

```
[Visual Basic]
Overloads Public Function GetRelatedClasses( _
   ByVal relatedClass As String _
) As ManagementObjectCollection
[C#]
public ManagementObjectCollection GetRelatedClasses(
   string relatedClass
);
[C++]
public: ManagementObjectCollection* GetRelatedClasses(
   String* relatedClass
);
```

```
[JScript]
public function GetRelatedClasses(
   relatedClass : String
) : ManagementObjectCollection;
```

Parameters

relatedClass
   The class from which resulting classes have to be derived.

Return Value

A collection of classes related to this class.

Requirements

Platforms: Windows 98, Windows NT 4.0,
Windows Millennium Edition, Windows 2000,
Windows XP Home Edition, Windows XP Professional,
Windows .NET Server family

.NET Framework Security:

- Full trust for the immediate caller. This member cannot be used
  by partially trusted code.

ManagementClass.GetRelatedClasses Method (ManagementOperationObserver, String)

Retrieves classes related to the WMI class, asynchronously, given
the related class name.

```
[Visual Basic]
Overloads Public Sub GetRelatedClasses( _
   ByVal watcher As ManagementOperationObserver, _
   ByVal relatedClass As String _
)
[C#]
public void GetRelatedClasses(
   ManagementOperationObserver watcher,
   string relatedClass
);
[C++]
public: void GetRelatedClasses(
   ManagementOperationObserver* watcher,
   String* relatedClass
);
[JScript]
public function GetRelatedClasses(
   watcher : ManagementOperationObserver,
   relatedClass : String
);
```

Parameters

watcher
   The object to handle the asynchronous operation's progress.
relatedClass
   The name of the related class.

Requirements

Platforms: Windows 98, Windows NT 4.0,
Windows Millennium Edition, Windows 2000,
Windows XP Home Edition, Windows XP Professional,
Windows .NET Server family

.NET Framework Security:

- Full trust for the immediate caller. This member cannot be used
  by partially trusted code.

ManagementClass.GetRelatedClasses Method (String, String, String, String, String, String, EnumerationOptions)

Retrieves classes related to the WMI class based on the specified options.

```
[Visual Basic]
Overloads Public Function GetRelatedClasses( _
    ByVal relatedClass As String, _
    ByVal relationshipClass As String, _
    ByVal relationshipQualifier As String, _
    ByVal relatedQualifier As String, _
    ByVal relatedRole As String, _
    ByVal thisRole As String, _
    ByVal options As EnumerationOptions _
) As ManagementObjectCollection
[C#]
public ManagementObjectCollection GetRelatedClasses(
    string relatedClass,
    string relationshipClass,
    string relationshipQualifier,
    string relatedQualifier,
    string relatedRole,
    string thisRole,
    EnumerationOptions options
);
[C++]
public: ManagementObjectCollection* GetRelatedClasses(
    String* relatedClass,
    String* relationshipClass,
    String* relationshipQualifier,
    String* relatedQualifier,
    String* relatedRole,
    String* thisRole,
    EnumerationOptions* options
);
[JScript]
public function GetRelatedClasses(
    relatedClass : String,
    relationshipClass : String,
    relationshipQualifier : String,
    relatedQualifier : String,
    relatedRole : String,
    thisRole : String,
    options : EnumerationOptions
) : ManagementObjectCollection;
```

Parameters

relatedClass
    The class from which resulting classes have to be derived.

relationshipClass
    The relationship type which resulting classes must have with the source class.

relationshipQualifier
    This qualifier must be present on the relationship.

relatedQualifier
    This qualifier must be present on the resulting classes.

relatedRole
    The resulting classes must have this role in the relationship.

thisRole
    The source class must have this role in the relationship.

options
    The options for retrieving the resulting classes.

Return Value

A collection of classes related to this class.

Requirements

Platforms: Windows 98, Windows NT 4.0, Windows Millennium Edition, Windows 2000, Windows XP Home Edition, Windows XP Professional, Windows .NET Server family

.NET Framework Security:

- Full trust for the immediate caller. This member cannot be used by partially trusted code.

ManagementClass.GetRelatedClasses Method (ManagementOperationObserver, String, String, String, String, String, String, EnumerationOptions)

Retrieves classes related to the WMI class, asynchronously, using the specified options.

```
[Visual Basic]
Overloads Public Sub GetRelatedClasses( _
    ByVal watcher As ManagementOperationObserver, _
    ByVal relatedClass As String, _
    ByVal relationshipClass As String, _
    ByVal relationshipQualifier As String, _
    ByVal relatedQualifier As String, _
    ByVal relatedRole As String, _
    ByVal thisRole As String, _
    ByVal options As EnumerationOptions _
)
[C#]
public void GetRelatedClasses(
    ManagementOperationObserver watcher,
    string relatedClass,
    string relationshipClass,
    string relationshipQualifier,
    string relatedQualifier,
    string relatedRole,
    string thisRole,
    EnumerationOptions options
);
[C++]
public: void GetRelatedClasses(
    ManagementOperationObserver* watcher,
    String* relatedClass,
    String* relationshipClass,
    String* relationshipQualifier,
    String* relatedQualifier,
    String* relatedRole,
    String* thisRole,
    EnumerationOptions* options
);
[JScript]
public function GetRelatedClasses(
    watcher : ManagementOperationObserver,
    relatedClass : String,
    relationshipClass : String,
    relationshipQualifier : String,
    relatedQualifier : String,
    relatedRole : String,
    thisRole : String,
    options : EnumerationOptions
);
```

Parameters

watcher
  Handler for progress and results of the asynchronous operation.

relatedClass
  The class from which resulting classes have to be derived.

relationshipClass
  The relationship type which resulting classes must have with the source class.

relationshipQualifier
  This qualifier must be present on the relationship.

relatedQualifier
  This qualifier must be present on the resulting classes.

relatedRole
  The resulting classes must have this role in the relationship.

thisRole
  The source class must have this role in the relationship.

options
  The options for retrieving the resulting classes.

Requirements

Platforms: Windows 98, Windows NT 4.0, Windows Millennium Edition, Windows 2000, Windows XP Home Edition, Windows XP Professional, Windows .NET Server family

.NET Framework Security:

• Full trust for the immediate caller. This member cannot be used by partially trusted code.

ManagementClass.GetRelationshipClasses Method

Retrieves relationship classes that relate the class to others.

Overload List

Retrieves relationship classes that relate the class to others.

[Visual Basic] **Overloads Public Function GetRelationshipClasses() As ManagementObjectCollection**

[C#] **public ManagementObjectCollection GetRelationshipClasses();**

[C++] **public: ManagementObjectCollection* GetRelationshipClasses();**

[JScript] **public function GetRelationshipClasses() : ManagementObjectCollection;**

Retrieves relationship classes that relate the class to others, asynchronously.

[Visual Basic] **Overloads Public Sub GetRelationshipClasses(ManagementOperationObserver)**

[C#] **public void GetRelationshipClasses(ManagementOperationObserver);**

[C++] **public: void GetRelationshipClasses(ManagementOperationObserver*);**

[JScript] **public function GetRelationshipClasses(ManagementOperationObserver);**

Retrieves relationship classes that relate the class to others, where the endpoint class is the specified class.

[Visual Basic] **Overloads Public Function GetRelationshipClasses(String) As ManagementObjectCollection**

[C#] **public ManagementObjectCollection GetRelationshipClasses(string);**

[C++] **public: ManagementObjectCollection* GetRelationshipClasses(String*);**

[JScript] **public function GetRelationshipClasses(String) : ManagementObjectCollection;**

Retrieves relationship classes that relate the class to the specified WMI class, asynchronously.

[Visual Basic] **Overloads Public Sub GetRelationshipClasses(ManagementOperationObserver, String)**

[C#] **public void GetRelationshipClasses(ManagementOperationObserver, string);**

[C++] **public: void GetRelationshipClasses(ManagementOperationObserver*, String*);**

[JScript] **public function GetRelationshipClasses(ManagementOperationObserver, String);**

Retrieves relationship classes that relate this class to others, according to specified options.

[Visual Basic] **Overloads Public Function GetRelationshipClasses(String, String, String, EnumerationOptions) As ManagementObjectCollection**

[C#] **public ManagementObjectCollection GetRelationshipClasses(string, string, string, EnumerationOptions);**

[C++] **public: ManagementObjectCollection* GetRelationshipClasses(String*, String*, String*, EnumerationOptions*);**

[JScript] **public function GetRelationshipClasses(String, String, String, EnumerationOptions) : ManagementObjectCollection;**

Retrieves relationship classes that relate the class according to the specified options, asynchronously.

[Visual Basic] **Overloads Public Sub GetRelationshipClasses(ManagementOperationObserver, String, String, String, EnumerationOptions)**

[C#] **public void GetRelationshipClasses(ManagementOperationObserver, string, string, string, EnumerationOptions);**

[C++] **public: void GetRelationshipClasses(ManagementOperationObserver*, String*, String*, String*, EnumerationOptions*);**

[JScript] **public function GetRelationshipClasses(ManagementOperationObserver, String, String, String, EnumerationOptions);**

ManagementClass.GetRelationshipClasses Method ()

Retrieves relationship classes that relate the class to others.

```
[Visual Basic]
Overloads Public Function GetRelationshipClasses() As _
    ManagementObjectCollection
[C#]
public ManagementObjectCollection GetRelationshipClasses();
[C++]
public: ManagementObjectCollection* GetRelationshipClasses();
[JScript]
public function GetRelationshipClasses() :
    ManagementObjectCollection;
```

Return Value

A collection of association classes that relate the class to any other class.

Requirements

Platforms: Windows 98, Windows NT 4.0, Windows Millennium Edition, Windows 2000, Windows XP Home Edition, Windows XP Professional, Windows .NET Server family

.NET Framework Security:

- Full trust for the immediate caller. This member cannot be used by partially trusted code.

ManagementClass.GetRelationshipClasses Method (ManagementOperationObserver)

Retrieves relationship classes that relate the class to others, asynchronously.

```
[Visual Basic]
Overloads Public Sub GetRelationshipClasses( _
    ByVal watcher As ManagementOperationObserver _
)
[C#]
public void GetRelationshipClasses(
    ManagementOperationObserver watcher
);
[C++]
public: void GetRelationshipClasses(
    ManagementOperationObserver* watcher
);
[JScript]
public function GetRelationshipClasses(
    watcher : ManagementOperationObserver
);
```

Parameters

watcher
    The object to handle the asynchronous operation's progress.

Requirements

Platforms: Windows 98, Windows NT 4.0, Windows Millennium Edition, Windows 2000, Windows XP Home Edition, Windows XP Professional, Windows .NET Server family

.NET Framework Security:

- Full trust for the immediate caller. This member cannot be used by partially trusted code.

ManagementClass.GetRelationshipClasses Method (String)

Retrieves relationship classes that relate the class to others, where the endpoint class is the specified class.

```
[Visual Basic]
Overloads Public Function GetRelationshipClasses( _
    ByVal relationshipClass As String _
) As ManagementObjectCollection
[C#]
public ManagementObjectCollection GetRelationshipClasses(
    string relationshipClass
);
```

```
[C++]
public: ManagementObjectCollection* GetRelationshipClasses(
    String* relationshipClass
);
[JScript]
public function GetRelationshipClasses(
    relationshipClass : String
) : ManagementObjectCollection;
```

Parameters

relationshipClass
    The endpoint class for all relationship classes returned.

Return Value

A collection of association classes that relate the class to the specified class.

Requirements

Platforms: Windows 98, Windows NT 4.0, Windows Millennium Edition, Windows 2000, Windows XP Home Edition, Windows XP Professional, Windows .NET Server family

.NET Framework Security:

- Full trust for the immediate caller. This member cannot be used by partially trusted code.

ManagementClass.GetRelationshipClasses Method (ManagementOperationObserver, String)

Retrieves relationship classes that relate the class to the specified WMI class, asynchronously.

```
[Visual Basic]
Overloads Public Sub GetRelationshipClasses( _
    ByVal watcher As ManagementOperationObserver, _
    ByVal relationshipClass As String _
)
[C#]
public void GetRelationshipClasses(
    ManagementOperationObserver watcher,
    string relationshipClass
);
[C++]
public: void GetRelationshipClasses(
    ManagementOperationObserver* watcher,
    String* relationshipClass
);
[JScript]
public function GetRelationshipClasses(
    watcher : ManagementOperationObserver,
    relationshipClass : String
);
```

Parameters

watcher
    The object to handle the asynchronous operation's progress.
relationshipClass
    The WMI class to which all returned relationships should point.

Requirements

Platforms: Windows 98, Windows NT 4.0, Windows Millennium Edition, Windows 2000, Windows XP Home Edition, Windows XP Professional, Windows .NET Server family

.NET Framework Security:

- Full trust for the immediate caller. This member cannot be used by partially trusted code.

ManagementClass.GetRelationshipClasses Method (String, String, String, EnumerationOptions)

Retrieves relationship classes that relate this class to others, according to specified options.

```
[Visual Basic]
Overloads Public Function GetRelationshipClasses( _
   ByVal relationshipClass As String, _
   ByVal relationshipQualifier As String, _
   ByVal thisRole As String, _
   ByVal options As EnumerationOptions _
) As ManagementObjectCollection
[C#]
public ManagementObjectCollection GetRelationshipClasses(
   string relationshipClass,
   string relationshipQualifier,
   string thisRole,
   EnumerationOptions options
);
[C++]
public: ManagementObjectCollection* GetRelationshipClasses(
   String* relationshipClass,
   String* relationshipQualifier,
   String* thisRole,
   EnumerationOptions* options
);
[JScript]
public function GetRelationshipClasses(
   relationshipClass : String,
   relationshipQualifier : String,
   thisRole : String,
   options : EnumerationOptions
) : ManagementObjectCollection;
```

Parameters

relationshipClass
   All resulting relationship classes must derive from this class.
relationshipQualifier
   Resulting relationship classes must have this qualifier.
thisRole
   The source class must have this role in the resulting relationship classes.
options
   Specifies options for retrieving the results.

Return Value

A collection of association classes that relate this class to others, according to the specified options.

Requirements

Platforms: Windows 98, Windows NT 4.0, Windows Millennium Edition, Windows 2000, Windows XP Home Edition, Windows XP Professional, Windows .NET Server family

.NET Framework Security:

- Full trust for the immediate caller. This member cannot be used by partially trusted code.

ManagementClass.GetRelationshipClasses Method (ManagementOperationObserver, String, String, String, EnumerationOptions)

Retrieves relationship classes that relate the class according to the specified options, asynchronously.

```
[Visual Basic]
Overloads Public Sub GetRelationshipClasses( _
   ByVal watcher As ManagementOperationObserver, _
   ByVal relationshipClass As String, _
   ByVal relationshipQualifier As String, _
   ByVal thisRole As String, _
   ByVal options As EnumerationOptions _
)
[C#]
public void GetRelationshipClasses(
   ManagementOperationObserver watcher,
   string relationshipClass,
   string relationshipQualifier,
   string thisRole,
   EnumerationOptions options
);
[C++]
public: void GetRelationshipClasses(
   ManagementOperationObserver* watcher,
   String* relationshipClass,
   String* relationshipQualifier,
   String* thisRole,
   EnumerationOptions* options
);
[JScript]
public function GetRelationshipClasses(
   watcher : ManagementOperationObserver,
   relationshipClass : String,
   relationshipQualifier : String,
   thisRole : String,
   options : EnumerationOptions
);
```

Parameters

watcher
   The handler for progress and results of the asynchronous operation.
relationshipClass
   The class from which all resulting relationship classes must derive.
relationshipQualifier
   The qualifier which the resulting relationship classes must have.
thisRole
   The role which the source class must have in the resulting relationship classes.
options
   The options for retrieving the results.

Return Value

A collection of association classes relating this class to others, according to the given options.

Requirements

Platforms: Windows 98, Windows NT 4.0, Windows Millennium Edition, Windows 2000, Windows XP Home Edition, Windows XP Professional, Windows .NET Server family

NET Framework Security:

- Full trust for the immediate caller. This member cannot be used by partially trusted code.

ManagementClass.GetStronglyTypedClassCode Method

Generates a strongly-typed class for a given WMI class.

Overload List

Generates a strongly-typed class for a given WMI class.

[Visual Basic] **Overloads Public Function GetStronglyTypedClassCode(Boolean, Boolean) As CodeTypeDeclaration**

[C#] **public CodeTypeDeclaration GetStronglyTypedClassCode(bool, bool);**

[C++] **public: CodeTypeDeclaration* GetStronglyTypedClassCode(bool, bool);**

[JScript] **public function GetStronglyTypedClassCode(Boolean, Boolean) : CodeTypeDeclaration;**

Generates a strongly-typed class for a given WMI class. This function generates code for Visual Basic, C#, or JScript, depending on the input parameters.

[Visual Basic] **Overloads Public Function GetStronglyTypedClassCode(CodeLanguage, String, String) As Boolean**

[C#] **public bool GetStronglyTypedClassCode(CodeLanguage, string, string);**

[C++] **public: bool GetStronglyTypedClassCode(CodeLanguage, String*, String*);**

[JScript] **public function GetStronglyTypedClassCode(CodeLanguage, String, String) : Boolean;**

Example

> [C#] **Note** This example shows how to use one of the overloaded versions of **GetStronglyTypedClassCode**. For other examples that might be available, see the individual overload topics.

```
[C#]
using System;
using System.Management;

ManagementClass cls = new
ManagementClass(null,"Win32_LogicalDisk",null,"");
cls.GetStronglyTypedClassCode(CodeLanguage.CSharp,
"C:\temp\Logicaldisk.cs",String.Empty);
```

ManagementClass.GetStronglyTypedClassCode Method (Boolean, Boolean)

Generates a strongly-typed class for a given WMI class.

```
[Visual Basic]
Overloads Public Function GetStronglyTypedClassCode( _
    ByVal includeSystemClassInClassDef As Boolean, _
    ByVal systemPropertyClass As Boolean _
) As CodeTypeDeclaration
```

```
[C#]
public CodeTypeDeclaration GetStronglyTypedClassCode(
    bool includeSystemClassInClassDef,
    bool systemPropertyClass
);
[C++]
public: CodeTypeDeclaration* GetStronglyTypedClassCode(
    bool includeSystemClassInClassDef,
    bool systemPropertyClass
);
[JScript]
public function GetStronglyTypedClassCode(
    includeSystemClassInClassDef : Boolean,
    systemPropertyClass : Boolean
) : CodeTypeDeclaration;
```

Parameters

includeSystemClassInClassDef
> **true** if the class for managing system properties must be included; otherwise, **false**.

systemPropertyClass
> **true** if the generated class will manage system properties; otherwise, **false**.

Return Value

A **CodeTypeDeclaration** instance representing the declaration for the strongly-typed class.

Example

```
[C#]
using System;
using System.Management;
using System.CodeDom;
using System.IO;
using System.CodeDom.Compiler;
using Microsoft.CSharp;

void GenerateCSharpCode()
{
    string strFilePath = "C:\\temp\\LogicalDisk.cs";
    CodeTypeDeclaration ClsDom;

    ManagementClass cls1 = new
ManagementClass(null,"Win32_LogicalDisk",null);
    ClsDom = cls1.GetStronglyTypedClassCode(false,false);

    ICodeGenerator cg = (new CSharpCodeProvider())
.CreateGenerator ();
    CodeNamespace cn = new CodeNamespace("TestNamespace");

    // Add any imports to the code
    cn.Imports.Add (new CodeNamespaceImport("System"));
    cn.Imports.Add (new CodeNamespaceImport("System.ComponentModel"));
    cn.Imports.Add (new CodeNamespaceImport("System.Management"));
    cn.Imports.Add(new CodeNamespaceImport("System.Collections"));

    // Add class to the namespace
    cn.Types.Add (ClsDom);

    //Now create the filestream (output file)
    TextWriter tw = new StreamWriter(new
FileStream (strFilePath,FileMode.Create));

    // And write it to the file
    cg.GenerateCodeFromNamespace (cn, tw, new
CodeGeneratorOptions());

    tw.Close();
}
```

Requirements

Platforms: Windows 98, Windows NT 4.0,
Windows Millennium Edition, Windows 2000,
Windows XP Home Edition, Windows XP Professional,
Windows .NET Server family

.NET Framework Security:

• Full trust for the immediate caller. This member cannot be used
  by partially trusted code.

ManagementClass.GetStronglyTypedClassCode Method (CodeLanguage, String, String)

Generates a strongly-typed class for a given WMI class. This
function generates code for Visual Basic, C#, or JScript, depending
on the input parameters.

```
[Visual Basic]
Overloads Public Function GetStronglyTypedClassCode( _
   ByVal lang As CodeLanguage, _
   ByVal filePath As String, _
   ByVal classNamespace As String _
) As Boolean
[C#]
public bool GetStronglyTypedClassCode(
   CodeLanguage lang,
   string filePath,
   string classNamespace
);
[C++]
public: bool GetStronglyTypedClassCode(
   CodeLanguage lang,
   String* filePath,
   String* classNamespace
);
[JScript]
public function GetStronglyTypedClassCode(
   lang : CodeLanguage,
   filePath : String,
   classNamespace : String
) : Boolean;
```

Parameters

lang
   The language of the code to be generated.
filePath
   The path of the file where the code is to be written.
classNamespace
   The .NET namespace into which the class should be generated. If
   this is empty, the namespace will be generated from the WMI
   namespace.

Return Value

true, if the method succeeded; otherwise, **false**.

Example

```
[C#]
using System;
using System.Management;

ManagementClass cls = new
ManagementClass(null,"Win32_LogicalDisk",null,"");
cls.GetStronglyTypedClassCode(CodeLanguage.CSharp,"C:\temp\Logicaldisk.c
s",String.Empty);
```

Requirements

Platforms: Windows 98, Windows NT 4.0,
Windows Millennium Edition, Windows 2000,
Windows XP Home Edition, Windows XP Professional,
Windows .NET Server family

.NET Framework Security:

• Full trust for the immediate caller. This member cannot be used
  by partially trusted code.

ManagementClass.GetSubclasses Method

Returns the collection of all subclasses for the class.

Overload List

Returns the collection of all subclasses for the class.

> [Visual Basic] **Overloads Public Function GetSubclasses() As ManagementObjectCollection**
>
> [C#] **public ManagementObjectCollection GetSubclasses();**
>
> [C++] **public: ManagementObjectCollection* GetSubclasses();**
>
> [JScript] **public function GetSubclasses() : ManagementObjectCollection;**

Retrieves the subclasses of the class using the specified options.

> [Visual Basic] **Overloads Public Function GetSubclasses (EnumerationOptions) As ManagementObjectCollection**
>
> [C#] **public ManagementObjectCollection GetSubclasses(EnumerationOptions);**
>
> [C++] **public: ManagementObjectCollection* GetSubclasses(EnumerationOptions*);**
>
> [JScript] **public function GetSubclasses(Enumeration-Options) : ManagementObjectCollection;**

Returns the collection of all subclasses of the class, asynchronously.

> [Visual Basic] **Overloads Public Sub GetSubclasses(ManagementOperationObserver)**
>
> [C#] **public void GetSubclasses(Management-OperationObserver);**
>
> [C++] **public: void GetSubclasses(Management-OperationObserver*);**
>
> [JScript] **public function GetSubclasses(Management-OperationObserver);**

Retrieves the subclasses of the class, asynchronously, using the
specified options.

> [Visual Basic] **Overloads Public Sub GetSubclasses(ManagementOperationObserver, EnumerationOptions)**
>
> [C#] **public void GetSubclasses(Management-OperationObserver, EnumerationOptions);**
>
> [C++] **public: void GetSubclasses(Management-OperationObserver*, EnumerationOptions*);**
>
> [JScript] **public function GetSubclasses(Management-OperationObserver, EnumerationOptions);**

Example

[Visual Basic, C#] **Note** This example shows how to use one of
the overloaded versions of **GetSubclasses**. For other examples
that might be available, see the individual overload topics.

```
[C#]
EnumerationOptions opt = new EnumerationOptions();

//Causes return of deep subclasses as opposed to only immediate ones.
opt.enumerateDeep = true;

ManagementObjectCollection c = (new
    ManagementClass("Win32_Share")).GetSubclasses(opt);
```

```
[Visual Basic]
Dim opt As New EnumerationOptions()

'Causes return of deep subclasses as opposed to only immediate ones.
opt.enumerateDeep = true

Dim cls As New ManagementClass("Win32_Share")
Dim c As ManagementObjectCollection

c = cls.GetSubClasses(opt)
```

ManagementClass.GetSubclasses Method ()

Returns the collection of all subclasses for the class.

```
[Visual Basic]
Overloads Public Function GetSubclasses() As
ManagementObjectCollection
[C#]
public ManagementObjectCollection GetSubclasses();
[C++]
public: ManagementObjectCollection* GetSubclasses();
[JScript]
public function GetSubclasses() : ManagementObjectCollection;
```

Return Value

A collection of the **ManagementObject** objects that represent the subclasses of the WMI class.

Requirements

Platforms: Windows 98, Windows NT 4.0, Windows Millennium Edition, Windows 2000, Windows XP Home Edition, Windows XP Professional, Windows .NET Server family

.NET Framework Security:
- Full trust for the immediate caller. This member cannot be used by partially trusted code.

ManagementClass.GetSubclasses Method (EnumerationOptions)

Retrieves the subclasses of the class using the specified options.

```
[Visual Basic]
Overloads Public Function GetSubclasses( _
   ByVal options As EnumerationOptions _
) As ManagementObjectCollection
[C#]
public ManagementObjectCollection GetSubclasses(
   EnumerationOptions options
);
[C++]
public: ManagementObjectCollection* GetSubclasses(
   EnumerationOptions* options
);
```

```
[JScript]
public function GetSubclasses(
   options : EnumerationOptions
) : ManagementObjectCollection;
```

Parameters

options
   The specified additional options for retrieving subclasses of the class.

Return Value

A collection of the **ManagementObject** objects representing the subclasses of the WMI class, according to the specified options.

Example

```
[C#]
EnumerationOptions opt = new EnumerationOptions();

//Causes return of deep subclasses as opposed to only immediate ones.
opt.enumerateDeep = true;

ManagementObjectCollection c = (new
    ManagementClass("Win32_Share")).GetSubclasses(opt);
```

```
[Visual Basic]
Dim opt As New EnumerationOptions()

'Causes return of deep subclasses as opposed to only immediate ones.
opt.enumerateDeep = true

Dim cls As New ManagementClass("Win32_Share")
Dim c As ManagementObjectCollection

c = cls.GetSubClasses(opt)
```

Requirements

Platforms: Windows 98, Windows NT 4.0, Windows Millennium Edition, Windows 2000, Windows XP Home Edition, Windows XP Professional, Windows .NET Server family

.NET Framework Security:
- Full trust for the immediate caller. This member cannot be used by partially trusted code.

ManagementClass.GetSubclasses Method (ManagementOperationObserver)

Returns the collection of all subclasses of the class, asynchronously.

```
[Visual Basic]
Overloads Public Sub GetSubclasses( _
   ByVal watcher As ManagementOperationObserver _
)
[C#]
public void GetSubclasses(
   ManagementOperationObserver watcher
);
[C++]
public: void GetSubclasses(
   ManagementOperationObserver* watcher
);
[JScript]
public function GetSubclasses(
   watcher : ManagementOperationObserver
);
```

Parameters

watcher

> The object to handle the asynchronous operation's progress.

Requirements

Platforms: Windows 98, Windows NT 4.0,
Windows Millennium Edition, Windows 2000,
Windows XP Home Edition, Windows XP Professional,
Windows .NET Server family

.NET Framework Security:

- Full trust for the immediate caller. This member cannot be used
  by partially trusted code.

ManagementClass.GetSubclasses Method
(ManagementOperationObserver, EnumerationOptions)

Retrieves the subclasses of the class, asynchronously, using the
specified options.

```
[Visual Basic]
Overloads Public Sub GetSubclasses( _
   ByVal watcher As ManagementOperationObserver, _
   ByVal options As EnumerationOptions _
)
[C#]
public void GetSubclasses(
   ManagementOperationObserver watcher,
   EnumerationOptions options
);
[C++]
public: void GetSubclasses(
   ManagementOperationObserver* watcher,
   EnumerationOptions* options
);
[JScript]
public function GetSubclasses(
   watcher : ManagementOperationObserver,
   options : EnumerationOptions
);
```

Parameters

watcher

> The object to handle the asynchronous operation's progress.

options

> The specified additional options to use in subclass retrieval.

Requirements

Platforms: Windows 98, Windows NT 4.0,
Windows Millennium Edition, Windows 2000,
Windows XP Home Edition, Windows XP Professional,
Windows .NET Server family

.NET Framework Security:

- Full trust for the immediate caller. This member cannot be used
  by partially trusted code.

ManagementDateTime-Converter Class

Note: This namespace, class, or member is supported only in version 1.1 of the .NET Framework.

Provides methods to convert DMTF datetime and time interval to CLR compliant **DateTime** and **TimeSpan** format and vice versa.

System.Object
  System.Management.ManagementDateTimeConverter

```
[Visual Basic]
NotInheritable Public Class ManagementDateTimeConverter
[C#]
public sealed class ManagementDateTimeConverter
[C++]
public __gc __sealed class ManagementDateTimeConverter
[JScript]
public class ManagementDateTimeConverter
```

Thread Safety

Any public static (**Shared** in Visual Basic) members of this type are safe for multithreaded operations. Any instance members are not guaranteed to be thread safe.

Example

```
[C#]
using System;
using System.Management;

// The sample below demonstrates the various conversions
that can be done using ManagementDateTimeConverter class
class Sample_ManagementDateTimeConverterClass
{
    public static int Main(string[] args)
    {
        string dmtfDate = "20020408141835.999999-420";
        string dmtfTimeInterval = "00000010122532:123456:000";

        // Converting DMTF datetime to System.DateTime
        DateTime dt = ManagementDateTimeConverter.ToDateTime(dmtfDate);

        // Converting System.DateTime to DMTF datetime
        string dmtfDate =
ManagementDateTimeConverter.ToDateTime(DateTime.Now);

        // Converting DMTF timeinterval to System.TimeSpan
        System.TimeSpan tsRet = ManagementDateTimeConverter.
ToTimeSpan(dmtfTimeInterval);

        //Converting System.TimeSpan to DMTF time interval format
        System.TimeSpan ts = new System.TimeSpan(10,12,25,32,456);
        string dmtfTimeInt =
ManagementDateTimeConverter.ToDmtfTimeInterval(ts);

        return 0;

    }
}

[Visual Basic]
Imports System
Imports System.Management

'The sample below demonstrates the various conversions that
 can be done using ManagementDateTimeConverter class
Class Sample_ManagementClass
    Overloads Public Shared Function Main(args() As String) As Integer
```

```
        Dim dmtfDate As String = "20020408141835.999999-420"
        Dim dmtfTimeInterval As String = "00000010122532:123456:000"

        'Converting DMTF datetime and intervals to System.DateTime
        Dim dt As DateTime =
ManagementDateTimeConverter.ToDateTime(dmtfDate)

        'Converting System.DateTime to DMTF datetime
        dmtfDate = ManagementDateTimeConverter.ToDateTime(DateTime.Now)

        ' Converting DMTF timeinterval to System.TimeSpan
        Dim tsRet As System.TimeSpan =
ManagementDateTimeConverter.ToTimeSpan(dmtfTimeInterval)

        'Converting System.TimeSpan to DMTF time interval format
        Dim ts As System.TimeSpan = New System.TimeSpan
(10, 12, 25, 32, 456)
        String dmtfTimeInt =
ManagementDateTimeConverter.ToDmtfTimeInterval(ts)

        Return 0
    End Function
End Class
```

Requirements

Namespace: System.Management

Platforms: Windows 98, Windows NT 4.0, Windows Millennium Edition, Windows 2000, Windows XP Home Edition, Windows XP Professional, Windows .NET Server family

Assembly: System.Management (in System.Management.dll)

ManagementDateTimeConverter.ToDateTime Method

Note: This namespace, class, or member is supported only in version 1.1 of the .NET Framework.

Converts a given DMTF datetime to **DateTime** object. The returned DateTime will be in the current TimeZone of the system.

```
[Visual Basic]
Public Shared Function ToDateTime( _
    ByVal dmtfDate As String _
) As DateTime
[C#]
public static DateTime ToDateTime(
    string dmtfDate
);
[C++]
public: static DateTime ToDateTime(
    String* dmtfDate
);
[JScript]
public static function ToDateTime(
    dmtfDate : String
) : DateTime;
```

Parameters

dmtfDate
  A string representing the datetime in DMTF format.

Return Value

A **DateTime** object that represents the given DMTF datetime.

Remarks

Date and time in WMI is represented in DMTF datetime format. This format is explained in WMI SDK documentation. DMTF datetime string has an UTC offset which this datetime string represents. During conversion to **DateTime**, UTC offset is used to convert the date to the current timezone. According to DMTF format a particular field can be represented by the character '*'. This will be converted to the MinValue of this field that can be represented in **DateTime**.

Example

```
[C#]
// Convert a DMTF datetime to System.DateTime
DateTime date =
ManagementDateTimeConverter.ToDateTime("20020408141835.999999-420");
```

```
[Visual Basic]
' Convert a DMTF datetime to System.DateTime
Dim date as DateTime =
ManagementDateTimeConverter.ToDateTime("20020408141835.999999-420")
```

Requirements

Platforms: Windows 98, Windows NT 4.0, Windows Millennium Edition, Windows 2000, Windows XP Home Edition, Windows XP Professional, Windows .NET Server family

.NET Framework Security:

- Full trust for the immediate caller. This member cannot be used by partially trusted code.

ManagementDateTimeConverter.ToDmtf-DateTime Method

Note: This namespace, class, or member is supported only in version 1.1 of the .NET Framework.

Converts a given **DateTime** object to DMTF format.

```
[Visual Basic]
Public Shared Function ToDmtfDateTime( _
   ByVal date As DateTime _
) As String
[C#]
public static string ToDmtfDateTime(
   DateTime date
);
[C++]
public: static String* ToDmtfDateTime(
   DateTime date
);
[JScript]
public static function ToDmtfDateTime(
   date : DateTime
) : String;
```

Parameters

date

A **DateTime** object representing the datetime to be converted to DMTF datetime.

Return Value

A string that represents the DMTF datetime for the given DateTime object.

Remarks

Date and time in WMI is represented in DMTF datetime format. This format is explained in WMI SDK documentation. The DMTF datetime string represented will be with respect to the UTC offset of the current timezone. The lowest precision in DMTF is microseconds and in **DateTime** is Ticks, which is equivalent to 100 of nanoseconds. During conversion these Ticks are converted to microseconds and rounded off to the the nearest microsecond.

Example

```
[C#]
// Convert the current time in System.DateTime to DMTF format
string dmtfDateTime =
ManagementDateTimeConverter.ToDmtfDateTime(DateTime.Now);
```

```
[Visual Basic]
' Convert the current time in System.DateTime to DMTF format
Dim dmtfDateTime as String =
ManagementDateTimeConverter.ToDmtfDateTime(DateTime.Now)
```

Requirements

Platforms: Windows 98, Windows NT 4.0, Windows Millennium Edition, Windows 2000, Windows XP Home Edition, Windows XP Professional, Windows .NET Server family

.NET Framework Security:

- Full trust for the immediate caller. This member cannot be used by partially trusted code.

ManagementDateTimeConverter.ToDmtfTime-Interval Method

Note: This namespace, class, or member is supported only in version 1.1 of the .NET Framework.

Converts a given **TimeSpan** object to DMTF time interval.

```
[Visual Basic]
Public Shared Function ToDmtfTimeInterval( _
   ByVal timespan As TimeSpan _
) As String
[C#]
public static string ToDmtfTimeInterval(
   TimeSpan timespan
);
[C++]
public: static String* ToDmtfTimeInterval(
   TimeSpan timespan
);
[JScript]
public static function ToDmtfTimeInterval(
   timespan : TimeSpan
) : String;
```

Parameters

timespan

A **TimeSpan** object representing the datetime to be converted to DMTF time interval.

Return Value

A string that represents the DMTF time interval for the given TimeSpan object.

Remarks

Time interval in WMI is represented in DMTF datetime format. This format is explained in WMI SDK documentation. The lowest precision in DMTF is microseconds and in **TimeSpan** is Ticks, which is equivalent to 100 of nanoseconds.During conversion these Ticks are converted to microseconds and rounded off to the the nearest microsecond.

Example

[C#]
```
// Construct a Timespan object and convert it to DMTF format
System.TimeSpan ts = new System.TimeSpan(10,12,25,32,456);
String dmtfTimeInterval =
ManagementDateTimeConverter.ToDmtfTimeInterval(ts);
```

[Visual Basic]
```
// Construct a Timespan object and convert it to DMTF format
Dim ts as System.TimeSpan = new System.TimeSpan(10,12,25,32,456)
Dim dmtfTimeInterval as String =
ManagementDateTimeConverter.ToDmtfTimeInterval(ts)
```

Requirements

Platforms: Windows 98, Windows NT 4.0, Windows Millennium Edition, Windows 2000, Windows XP Home Edition, Windows XP Professional, Windows .NET Server family

.NET Framework Security:
- Full trust for the immediate caller. This member cannot be used by partially trusted code.

ManagementDateTimeConverter.ToTimeSpan Method

Note: This namespace, class, or member is supported only in version 1.1 of the .NET Framework.

Converts a given DMTF time interval to **TimeSpan** object.

```
[Visual Basic]
Public Shared Function ToTimeSpan( _
    ByVal dmtfTimespan As String _
) As TimeSpan
[C#]
public static TimeSpan ToTimeSpan(
    string dmtfTimespan
);
[C++]
public: static TimeSpan ToTimeSpan(
    String* dmtfTimespan
);
[JScript]
public static function ToTimeSpan(
    dmtfTimespan : String
) : TimeSpan;
```

Parameters

dmtfTimespan
   A string represesentation of the DMTF time interval.

Return Value

A **TimeSpan** object that represents the given DMTF time interval.

Remarks

Time interval in WMI is represented in DMTF format. This format is explained in WMI SDK documentation. If the DMTF time interval value is more than that of **MaxValue** then **ArgumentOutOfRangeException** is thrown.

Example

[C#]
```
// Convert a DMTF time interval to System.TimeSpan
TimeSpan dmtfTimeInterval =
ManagementDateTimeConverter.ToTimeSpan("00000010122532:123456:000");
```

[Visual Basic]
```
' Convert a DMTF time interval to System.TimeSpan
Dim ts as TimeSpan =
ManagementDateTimeConverter.ToTimeSpan("00000010122532:123456:000")
```

Requirements

Platforms: Windows 98, Windows NT 4.0, Windows Millennium Edition, Windows 2000, Windows XP Home Edition, Windows XP Professional, Windows .NET Server family

.NET Framework Security:
- Full trust for the immediate caller. This member cannot be used by partially trusted code.

ManagementEventArgs Class

Represents the virtual base class to hold event data for WMI events.

System.Object
  System.EventArgs
    System.Management.ManagementEventArgs
      Derived classes

```
[Visual Basic]
MustInherit Public Class ManagementEventArgs
   Inherits EventArgs
[C#]
public abstract class ManagementEventArgs : EventArgs
[C++]
public __gc __abstract class ManagementEventArgs : public EventArgs
[JScript]
public abstract class ManagementEventArgs extends EventArgs
```

Thread Safety

Any public static (**Shared** in Visual Basic) members of this type are safe for multithreaded operations. Any instance members are not guaranteed to be thread safe.

Requirements

Namespace: System.Management

Platforms: Windows 98, Windows NT 4.0, Windows Millennium Edition, Windows 2000, Windows XP Home Edition, Windows XP Professional, Windows .NET Server family

Assembly: System.Management (in System.Management.dll)

ManagementEventArgs.Context Property

Gets the operation context echoed back from the operation that triggered the event.

```
[Visual Basic]
Public ReadOnly Property Context As Object
[C#]
public object Context {get;}
[C++]
public: __property Object* get_Context();
[JScript]
public function get Context() : Object;
```

Property Value

A WMI context object containing context information provided by the operation that triggered the event.

Requirements

Platforms: Windows 98, Windows NT 4.0, Windows Millennium Edition, Windows 2000, Windows XP Home Edition, Windows XP Professional, Windows .NET Server family

.NET Framework Security:

- Full trust for the immediate caller. This member cannot be used by partially trusted code.

ManagementEventWatcher Class

Subscribes to temporary event notifications based on a specified event query.

System.Object
  System.MarshalByRefObject
    System.ComponentModel.Component
      System.Management.ManagementEventWatcher

```
[Visual Basic]
Public Class ManagementEventWatcher
   Inherits Component
[C#]
public class ManagementEventWatcher : Component
[C++]
public __gc class ManagementEventWatcher : public Component
[JScript]
public class ManagementEventWatcher extends Component
```

Thread Safety

Any public static (**Shared** in Visual Basic) members of this type are safe for multithreaded operations. Any instance members are not guaranteed to be thread safe.

Example

```csharp
[C#]
using System;
using System.Management;

// This example demonstrates how to subscribe to an event
using the ManagementEventWatcher object.
class Sample_ManagementEventWatcher
{
    public static int Main(string[] args) {

        //For the example, we'll put a class into the
repository, and watch
        //for class deletion events when the class is deleted.
        ManagementClass newClass = new ManagementClass();
        newClass["__CLASS"] = "TestDeletionClass";
        newClass.Put();

        //Set up an event watcher and a handler for the event
        ManagementEventWatcher watcher = new ManagementEventWatcher(
            new WqlEventQuery("__ClassDeletionEvent"));
        MyHandler handler = new MyHandler();
        watcher.EventArrived += new
EventArrivedEventHandler(handler.Arrived);

        //Start watching for events
        watcher.Start();

        // For the purpose of this sample, we delete the
class to trigger the event
        // and wait for two seconds before terminating the consumer
        newClass.Delete();

        System.Threading.Thread.Sleep(2000);

        //Stop watching
        watcher.Stop();

        return 0;
    }

    public class MyHandler {
        public void Arrived(object sender, EventArrivedEventArgs e) {
```

```
            Console.WriteLine("Class Deleted = " +
((ManagementBaseObject)e.NewEvent["TargetClass"])["__CLASS"]);
        }
    }
}
```

```vbnet
[Visual Basic]
Imports System
Imports System.Management

' This example demonstrates how to subscribe an event using
 the ManagementEventWatcher object.
Class Sample_ManagementEventWatcher
    Public Shared Sub Main()

        ' For the example, we'll put a class into the
repository, and watch
        ' for class deletion events when the class is deleted.
        Dim newClass As New ManagementClass()
        newClass("__CLASS") = "TestDeletionClass"
        newClass.Put()

        ' Set up an event watcher and a handler for the event
        Dim watcher As _
            New ManagementEventWatcher(New
WqlEventQuery("__ClassDeletionEvent"))
        Dim handler As New MyHandler()
        AddHandler watcher.EventArrived, AddressOf handler.Arrived

        ' Start watching for events
        watcher.Start()

        ' For the purpose of this sample, we delete the
class to trigger the event
        ' and wait for two seconds before terminating the consumer
        newClass.Delete()

        System.Threading.Thread.Sleep(2000)

        ' Stop watching
        watcher.Stop()

    End Sub

    Public Class MyHandler
        Public Sub Arrived(sender As Object, e As
EventArrivedEventArgs)
            Console.WriteLine("Class Deleted = " & _
                CType(e.NewEvent("TargetClass"),
ManagementBaseObject)("__CLASS"))
        End Sub
    End Class
End Class
```

Requirements

Namespace: System.Management

Platforms: Windows 98, Windows NT 4.0, Windows Millennium Edition, Windows 2000, Windows XP Home Edition, Windows XP Professional, Windows .NET Server family

Assembly: System.Management (in System.Management.dll)

ManagementEventWatcher Constructor

Initializes a new instance of the **ManagementEventWatcher** class.

Overload List

Initializes a new instance of the **ManagementEventWatcher** class. For further initialization, set the properties on the object. This is the default constructor.

[Visual Basic] **Public Sub New()**

[C#] **public ManagementEventWatcher();**

[C++] **public: ManagementEventWatcher();**

[JScript] **public function ManagementEventWatcher();**

Initializes a new instance of the **ManagementEventWatcher** class when given a WMI event query.

[Visual Basic] **Public Sub New(EventQuery)**

[C#] **public ManagementEventWatcher(EventQuery);**

[C++] **public: ManagementEventWatcher(EventQuery*);**

[JScript] **public function ManagementEventWatcher(EventQuery);**

Initializes a new instance of the **ManagementEventWatcher** class when given a WMI event query in the form of a string.

[Visual Basic] **Public Sub New(String)**

[C#] **public ManagementEventWatcher(string);**

[C++] **public: ManagementEventWatcher(String*);**

[JScript] **public function ManagementEventWatcher(String);**

Initializes a new instance of the **ManagementEventWatcher** class that listens for events conforming to the given WMI event query.

[Visual Basic] **Public Sub New(ManagementScope, EventQuery)**

[C#] **public ManagementEventWatcher(ManagementScope, EventQuery);**

[C++] **public: ManagementEventWatcher(Management-Scope*, EventQuery*);**

[JScript] **public function ManagementEventWatcher(ManagementScope, EventQuery);**

Initializes a new instance of the **ManagementEventWatcher** class that listens for events conforming to the given WMI event query. For this variant, the query and the scope are specified as strings.

[Visual Basic] **Public Sub New(String, String)**

[C#] **public ManagementEventWatcher(string, string);**

[C++] **public: ManagementEventWatcher(String*, String*);**

[JScript] **public function ManagementEventWatcher(String, String);**

Initializes a new instance of the **ManagementEventWatcher** class that listens for events conforming to the given WMI event query, according to the specified options. For this variant, the query and the scope are specified objects. The options object can specify options such as timeout and context information.

[Visual Basic] **Public Sub New(ManagementScope, EventQuery, EventWatcherOptions)**

[C#] **public ManagementEventWatcher(ManagementScope, EventQuery, EventWatcherOptions);**

[C++] **public: ManagementEventWatcher(Management-Scope*, EventQuery*, EventWatcherOptions*);**

[JScript] **public function ManagementEventWatcher(ManagementScope, EventQuery, EventWatcherOptions);**

Initializes a new instance of the **ManagementEventWatcher** class that listens for events conforming to the given WMI event query, according to the specified options. For this variant, the query and the scope are specified as strings. The options object can specify options such as a timeout and context information.

[Visual Basic] **Public Sub New(String, String, EventWatcherOptions)**

[C#] **public ManagementEventWatcher(string, string, EventWatcherOptions);**

[C++] **public: ManagementEventWatcher(String*, String*, EventWatcherOptions*);**

[JScript] **public function ManagementEventWatcher(String, String, EventWatcherOptions);**

ManagementEventWatcher Constructor ()

Initializes a new instance of the **ManagementEventWatcher** class. For further initialization, set the properties on the object. This is the default constructor.

```
[Visual Basic]
Public Sub New()
[C#]
public ManagementEventWatcher();
[C++]
public: ManagementEventWatcher();
[JScript]
public function ManagementEventWatcher();
```

Requirements

Platforms: Windows 98, Windows NT 4.0, Windows Millennium Edition, Windows 2000, Windows XP Home Edition, Windows XP Professional, Windows .NET Server family

.NET Framework Security:

- Full trust for the immediate caller. This member cannot be used by partially trusted code.

ManagementEventWatcher Constructor (EventQuery)

Initializes a new instance of the **ManagementEventWatcher** class when given a WMI event query.

```
[Visual Basic]
Public Sub New( _
    ByVal query As EventQuery _
)
[C#]
public ManagementEventWatcher(
    EventQuery query
);
[C++]
public: ManagementEventWatcher(
    EventQuery* query
);
[JScript]
public function ManagementEventWatcher(
    query : EventQuery
);
```

Parameters

query

> An **EventQuery** object representing a WMI event query, which determines the events for which the watcher will listen.

Remarks

The namespace in which the watcher will be listening for events is the default namespace that is currently set.

Requirements

Platforms: Windows 98, Windows NT 4.0, Windows Millennium Edition, Windows 2000, Windows XP Home Edition, Windows XP Professional, Windows .NET Server family

.NET Framework Security:

- Full trust for the immediate caller. This member cannot be used by partially trusted code.

ManagementEventWatcher Constructor (String)

Initializes a new instance of the **ManagementEventWatcher** class when given a WMI event query in the form of a string.

```
[Visual Basic]
Public Sub New( _
    ByVal query As String _
)
[C#]
public ManagementEventWatcher(
    string query
);
[C++]
public: ManagementEventWatcher(
    String* query
);
[JScript]
public function ManagementEventWatcher(
    query : String
);
```

Parameters

query

> A WMI event query, which defines the events for which the watcher will listen.

Remarks

The namespace in which the watcher will be listening for events is the default namespace that is currently set.

Requirements

Platforms: Windows 98, Windows NT 4.0, Windows Millennium Edition, Windows 2000, Windows XP Home Edition, Windows XP Professional, Windows .NET Server family

.NET Framework Security:

- Full trust for the immediate caller. This member cannot be used by partially trusted code.

ManagementEventWatcher Constructor (ManagementScope, EventQuery)

Initializes a new instance of the **ManagementEventWatcher** class that listens for events conforming to the given WMI event query.

```
[Visual Basic]
Public Sub New( _
    ByVal scope As ManagementScope, _
    ByVal query As EventQuery _
)
[C#]
public ManagementEventWatcher(
    ManagementScope scope,
    EventQuery query
);
[C++]
public: ManagementEventWatcher(
    ManagementScope* scope,
    EventQuery* query
);
[JScript]
public function ManagementEventWatcher(
    scope : ManagementScope,
    query : EventQuery
);
```

Parameters

scope

> A **ManagementScope** object representing the scope (namespace) in which the watcher will listen for events.

query

> An **EventQuery** object representing a WMI event query, which determines the events for which the watcher will listen.

Requirements

Platforms: Windows 98, Windows NT 4.0, Windows Millennium Edition, Windows 2000, Windows XP Home Edition, Windows XP Professional, Windows .NET Server family

.NET Framework Security:

- Full trust for the immediate caller. This member cannot be used by partially trusted code.

ManagementEventWatcher Constructor (String, String)

Initializes a new instance of the **ManagementEventWatcher** class that listens for events conforming to the given WMI event query. For this variant, the query and the scope are specified as strings.

```
[Visual Basic]
Public Sub New( _
    ByVal scope As String, _
    ByVal query As String _
)
[C#]
public ManagementEventWatcher(
    string scope,
    string query
);
```

```
[C++]
public: ManagementEventWatcher(
    String* scope,
    String* query
);
[JScript]
public function ManagementEventWatcher(
    scope : String,
    query : String
);
```

Parameters

scope

The management scope (namespace) in which the watcher will listen for events.

query

The query that defines the events for which the watcher will listen.

Requirements

Platforms: Windows 98, Windows NT 4.0, Windows Millennium Edition, Windows 2000, Windows XP Home Edition, Windows XP Professional, Windows .NET Server family

.NET Framework Security:

• Full trust for the immediate caller. This member cannot be used by partially trusted code.

ManagementEventWatcher Constructor (ManagementScope, EventQuery, EventWatcherOptions)

Initializes a new instance of the **ManagementEventWatcher** class that listens for events conforming to the given WMI event query, according to the specified options. For this variant, the query and the scope are specified objects. The options object can specify options such as timeout and context information.

```
[Visual Basic]
Public Sub New( _
    ByVal scope As ManagementScope, _
    ByVal query As EventQuery, _
    ByVal options As EventWatcherOptions _
)
[C#]
public ManagementEventWatcher(
    ManagementScope scope,
    EventQuery query,
    EventWatcherOptions options
);
[C++]
public: ManagementEventWatcher(
    ManagementScope* scope,
    EventQuery* query,
    EventWatcherOptions* options
);
[JScript]
public function ManagementEventWatcher(
    scope : ManagementScope,
    query : EventQuery,
    options : EventWatcherOptions
);
```

Parameters

scope

A **ManagementScope** object representing the scope (namespace) in which the watcher will listen for events.

query

An **EventQuery** object representing a WMI event query, which determines the events for which the watcher will listen.

options

An **EventWatcherOptions** object representing additional options used to watch for events.

Requirements

Platforms: Windows 98, Windows NT 4.0, Windows Millennium Edition, Windows 2000, Windows XP Home Edition, Windows XP Professional, Windows .NET Server family

.NET Framework Security:

• Full trust for the immediate caller. This member cannot be used by partially trusted code.

ManagementEventWatcher Constructor (String, String, EventWatcherOptions)

Initializes a new instance of the **ManagementEventWatcher** class that listens for events conforming to the given WMI event query, according to the specified options. For this variant, the query and the scope are specified as strings. The options object can specify options such as a timeout and context information.

```
[Visual Basic]
Public Sub New( _
    ByVal scope As String, _
    ByVal query As String, _
    ByVal options As EventWatcherOptions _
)
[C#]
public ManagementEventWatcher(
    string scope,
    string query,
    EventWatcherOptions options
);
[C++]
public: ManagementEventWatcher(
    String* scope,
    String* query,
    EventWatcherOptions* options
);
[JScript]
public function ManagementEventWatcher(
    scope : String,
    query : String,
    options : EventWatcherOptions
);
```

Parameters

scope

The management scope (namespace) in which the watcher will listen for events.

query

The query that defines the events for which the watcher will listen.

options

An **EventWatcherOptions** object representing additional options used to watch for events.

Requirements

Platforms: Windows 98, Windows NT 4.0, Windows Millennium Edition, Windows 2000, Windows XP Home Edition, Windows XP Professional, Windows .NET Server family

.NET Framework Security:

- Full trust for the immediate caller. This member cannot be used by partially trusted code.

ManagementEventWatcher.Options Property

Gets or sets the options used to watch for events.

```
[Visual Basic]
Public Property Options As EventWatcherOptions
[C#]
public EventWatcherOptions Options {get; set;}
[C++]
public: __property EventWatcherOptions* get_Options();
public: __property void set_Options(EventWatcherOptions*);
[JScript]
public function get Options() : EventWatcherOptions;
public function set Options(EventWatcherOptions);
```

Property Value

The options used to watch for events.

Requirements

Platforms: Windows 98, Windows NT 4.0, Windows Millennium Edition, Windows 2000, Windows XP Home Edition, Windows XP Professional, Windows .NET Server family

.NET Framework Security:

- Full trust for the immediate caller. This member cannot be used by partially trusted code.

ManagementEventWatcher.Query Property

Gets or sets the criteria to apply to events.

```
[Visual Basic]
Public Property Query As EventQuery
[C#]
public EventQuery Query {get; set;}
[C++]
public: __property EventQuery* get_Query();
public: __property void set_Query(EventQuery*);
[JScript]
public function get Query() : EventQuery;
public function set Query(EventQuery);
```

Property Value

The criteria to apply to the events, which is equal to the event query.

Requirements

Platforms: Windows 98, Windows NT 4.0, Windows Millennium Edition, Windows 2000, Windows XP Home Edition, Windows XP Professional, Windows .NET Server family

.NET Framework Security:

- Full trust for the immediate caller. This member cannot be used by partially trusted code.

ManagementEventWatcher.Scope Property

Gets or sets the scope in which to watch for events (namespace or scope).

```
[Visual Basic]
Public Property Scope As ManagementScope
[C#]
public ManagementScope Scope {get; set;}
[C++]
public: __property ManagementScope* get_Scope();
public: __property void set_Scope(ManagementScope*);
[JScript]
public function get Scope() : ManagementScope;
public function set Scope(ManagementScope);
```

Property Value

The scope in which to watch for events (namespace or scope).

Requirements

Platforms: Windows 98, Windows NT 4.0, Windows Millennium Edition, Windows 2000, Windows XP Home Edition, Windows XP Professional, Windows .NET Server family

.NET Framework Security:

- Full trust for the immediate caller. This member cannot be used by partially trusted code.

ManagementEventWatcher.Finalize Method

Ensures that outstanding calls are cleared. This is the destructor for the object.

[C#] In C#, finalizers are expressed using destructor syntax.

[C++] In C++, finalizers are expressed using destructor syntax.

```
[Visual Basic]
Overrides Protected Sub Finalize()
[C#]
~ManagementEventWatcher();
[C++]
~ManagementEventWatcher();
[JScript]
protected override function Finalize();
```

Requirements

Platforms: Windows 98, Windows NT 4.0, Windows Millennium Edition, Windows 2000, Windows XP Home Edition, Windows XP Professional, Windows .NET Server family

.NET Framework Security:

- Full trust for the immediate caller. This member cannot be used by partially trusted code.

ManagementEventWatcher.Start Method

Subscribes to events with the given query and delivers them, asynchronously, through the **EventArrived** event.

```
[Visual Basic]
Public Sub Start()
[C#]
public void Start();
[C++]
public: void Start();
[JScript]
public function Start();
```

Requirements

Platforms: Windows 98, Windows NT 4.0, Windows Millennium Edition, Windows 2000, Windows XP Home Edition, Windows XP Professional, Windows .NET Server family

.NET Framework Security:

- Full trust for the immediate caller. This member cannot be used by partially trusted code.

ManagementEventWatcher.Stop Method

Cancels the subscription whether it is synchronous or asynchronous.

```
[Visual Basic]
Public Sub Stop()
[C#]
public void Stop();
[C++]
public: void Stop();
[JScript]
public function Stop();
```

Requirements

Platforms: Windows 98, Windows NT 4.0, Windows Millennium Edition, Windows 2000, Windows XP Home Edition, Windows XP Professional, Windows .NET Server family

.NET Framework Security:

- Full trust for the immediate caller. This member cannot be used by partially trusted code.

ManagementEventWatcher.WaitForNextEvent Method

Waits for the next event that matches the specified query to arrive, and then returns it.

```
[Visual Basic]
Public Function WaitForNextEvent() As ManagementBaseObject
[C#]
public ManagementBaseObject WaitForNextEvent();
[C++]
public: ManagementBaseObject* WaitForNextEvent();
[JScript]
public function WaitForNextEvent() : ManagementBaseObject;
```

Return Value

A **ManagementBaseObject** representing the newly arrived event.

Remarks

If the event watcher object contains options with a specified timeout, the API will wait for the next event only for the specified amount of time; otherwise, the API will be blocked until the next event occurs.

Requirements

Platforms: Windows 98, Windows NT 4.0, Windows Millennium Edition, Windows 2000, Windows XP Home Edition, Windows XP Professional, Windows .NET Server family

.NET Framework Security:

- Full trust for the immediate caller. This member cannot be used by partially trusted code.

ManagementEventWatcher.EventArrived Event

Occurs when a new event arrives.

```
[Visual Basic]
Public Event EventArrived As EventArrivedEventHandler
[C#]
public event EventArrivedEventHandler EventArrived;
[C++]
public: __event EventArrivedEventHandler* EventArrived;
```

[JScript] In JScript, you can handle the events defined by a class, but you cannot define your own.

Event Data

The event handler receives an argument of type **EventArrivedEventArgs** containing data related to this event. The following **EventArrivedEventArgs** properties provide information specific to this event.

Property	Description
Context (inherited from **ManagementEvent-Args**)	Gets the operation context echoed back from the operation that triggered the event.
NewEvent	Gets the WMI event that was delivered.

Requirements

Platforms: Windows 98, Windows NT 4.0, Windows Millennium Edition, Windows 2000, Windows XP Home Edition, Windows XP Professional, Windows .NET Server family

.NET Framework Security:

- Full trust for the immediate caller. This member cannot be used by partially trusted code.

ManagementEventWatcher.Stopped Event

Occurs when a subscription is canceled.

```
[Visual Basic]
Public Event Stopped As StoppedEventHandler
[C#]
public event StoppedEventHandler Stopped;
[C++]
public: __event StoppedEventHandler* Stopped;
```

[JScript] In JScript, you can handle the events defined by a class, but you cannot define your own.

Event Data

The event handler receives an argument of type **StoppedEventArgs** containing data related to this event. The following **StoppedEventArgs** properties provide information specific to this event.

Property	Description
Context (inherited from **ManagementEventArgs**)	Gets the operation context echoed back from the operation that triggered the event.
Status	Gets the completion status of the operation.

Requirements

Platforms: Windows 98, Windows NT 4.0, Windows Millennium Edition, Windows 2000, Windows XP Home Edition, Windows XP Professional, Windows .NET Server family

.NET Framework Security:

- Full trust for the immediate caller. This member cannot be used by partially trusted code.

ManagementException Class

Represents management exceptions.

System.Object
  System.Exception
    System.SystemException
      System.Management.ManagementException

```
[Visual Basic]
<Serializable>
Public Class ManagementException
  Inherits SystemException
[C#]
[Serializable]
public class ManagementException : SystemException
[C++]
[Serializable]
public __gc class ManagementException : public SystemException
[JScript]
public
  Serializable
class ManagementException extends SystemException
```

Thread Safety

Any public static (**Shared** in Visual Basic) members of this type are safe for multithreaded operations. Any instance members are not guaranteed to be thread safe.

Example

```
[C#]
using System;
using System.Management;

// This sample demonstrates how to display error
// information stored in a ManagementException object.
class Sample_ManagementException
{
    public static int Main(string[] args)
    {
        try
        {
            ManagementObject disk =
                new
ManagementObject("Win32_LogicalDisk.DeviceID='BAD:'");
            disk.Get(); // throws ManagementException
            Console.WriteLine("This shouldn't be displayed.");
        }
        catch (ManagementException e)
        {
            Console.WriteLine("ErrorCode " + e.ErrorCode);
            Console.WriteLine("Message " + e.Message);
            Console.WriteLine("Source " + e.Source);
            if (e.ErrorInformation) //extended error object
                Console.WriteLine("Extended Description
: " + e.ErrorInformation["Description"]);
        }
        return 0;
    }
}
```

```
[Visual Basic]
Imports System
Imports System.Management

' This sample demonstrates how to display error
' information stored in a ManagementException object.
Class Sample_ManagementException
    Overloads Public Shared Function Main(args() As String) As Integer
        Try
            Dim disk As New
ManagementObject("Win32_LogicalDisk.DeviceID='BAD:'")
            disk.Get() ' throws ManagementException
            Console.WriteLine("This shouldn't be displayed.")
        Catch e As ManagementException
            Console.WriteLine("ErrorCode " & e.ErrorCode)
            Console.WriteLine("Message " & e.Message)
            Console.WriteLine("Source " & e.Source)
            If e.ErrorInformation != Nothing Then 'extended error object
                Console.WriteLine("Extended Description
: " & e.ErrorInformation("Description"))
            End If
        End Try
        Return 0
    End Function
End Class
```

Requirements

Namespace: System.Management

Platforms: Windows 98, Windows NT 4.0, Windows Millennium Edition, Windows 2000, Windows XP Home Edition, Windows XP Professional, Windows .NET Server family

Assembly: System.Management (in System.Management.dll)

ManagementException Constructor

Note: This namespace, class, or member is supported only in version 1.1 of the .NET Framework.

Overload List

Initializes a new instance of the **ManagementException** class

  [Visual Basic] **Public Sub New()**

  [C#] **public ManagementException();**

  [C++] **public: ManagementException();**

  [JScript] **public function ManagementException();**

Initializes a new instance of the **ManagementException** class with a specified error message.

  [Visual Basic] **Public Sub New(String)**

  [C#] **public ManagementException(string);**

  [C++] **public: ManagementException(String*);**

  [JScript] **public function ManagementException(String);**

Initializes a new instance of the **ManagementException** class that is serializable.

  [Visual Basic] **Protected Sub New(SerializationInfo, StreamingContext)**

  [C#] **protected ManagementException(SerializationInfo, StreamingContext);**

  [C++] **protected: ManagementException(SerializationInfo*, StreamingContext);**

  [JScript] **protected function Management-Exception(SerializationInfo, StreamingContext);**

Initializes a empty new instance of the **ManagementException** class

  [Visual Basic] **Public Sub New(String, Exception)**

  [C#] **public ManagementException(string, Exception);**

  [C++] **public: ManagementException(String*, Exception*);**

  [JScript] **public function ManagementException(String, Exception);**

ManagementException Constructor ( )

Note: This namespace, class, or member is supported only in version 1.1 of the .NET Framework.

Initializes a new instance of the **ManagementException** class

```
[Visual Basic]
Public Sub New()
[C#]
public ManagementException();
[C++]
public: ManagementException();
[JScript]
public function ManagementException();
```

Requirements

Platforms: Windows 98, Windows NT 4.0, Windows Millennium Edition, Windows 2000, Windows XP Home Edition, Windows XP Professional, Windows .NET Server family

.NET Framework Security:

- Full trust for the immediate caller. This member cannot be used by partially trusted code.

ManagementException Constructor (String)

Note: This namespace, class, or member is supported only in version 1.1 of the .NET Framework.

Initializes a new instance of the **ManagementException** class with a specified error message.

```
[Visual Basic]
Public Sub New( _
   ByVal message As String _
)
[C#]
public ManagementException(
   string message
);
[C++]
public: ManagementException(
   String* message
);
[JScript]
public function ManagementException(
   message : String
);
```

Parameters

message
   The message that describes the error.

Requirements

Platforms: Windows 98, Windows NT 4.0, Windows Millennium Edition, Windows 2000, Windows XP Home Edition, Windows XP Professional, Windows .NET Server family

.NET Framework Security:

- Full trust for the immediate caller. This member cannot be used by partially trusted code.

ManagementException Constructor (SerializationInfo, StreamingContext)

Initializes a new instance of the **ManagementException** class that is serializable.

```
[Visual Basic]
Protected Sub New( _
   ByVal info As SerializationInfo, _
   ByVal context As StreamingContext _
)
[C#]
protected ManagementException(
   SerializationInfo info,
   StreamingContext context
);
[C++]
protected: ManagementException(
   SerializationInfo* info,
   StreamingContext context
);
[JScript]
protected function ManagementException(
   info : SerializationInfo,
   context : StreamingContext
);
```

Parameters

info
   The **SerializationInfo** to populate with data.
context
   The destination (see **StreamingContext**) for this serialization.

Requirements

Platforms: Windows 98, Windows NT 4.0, Windows Millennium Edition, Windows 2000, Windows XP Home Edition, Windows XP Professional, Windows .NET Server family

.NET Framework Security:

- Full trust for the immediate caller. This member cannot be used by partially trusted code.

ManagementException Constructor (String, Exception)

Note: This namespace, class, or member is supported only in version 1.1 of the .NET Framework.

Initializes a empty new instance of the **ManagementException** class

```
[Visual Basic]
Public Sub New( _
   ByVal message As String, _
   ByVal innerException As Exception _
)
[C#]
public ManagementException(
   string message,
   Exception innerException
);
```

```
[C++]
public: ManagementException(
    String* message,
    Exception* innerException
);
[JScript]
public function ManagementException(
    message : String,
    innerException : Exception
);
```

Parameters

message

The message that describes the error.

innerException

Requirements

Platforms: Windows 98, Windows NT 4.0,
Windows Millennium Edition, Windows 2000,
Windows XP Home Edition, Windows XP Professional,
Windows .NET Server family

.NET Framework Security:

- Full trust for the immediate caller. This member cannot be used by partially trusted code.

ManagementException.ErrorCode Property

Gets the error code reported by WMI, which caused this exception.

```
[Visual Basic]
Public ReadOnly Property ErrorCode As ManagementStatus
[C#]
public ManagementStatus ErrorCode {get;}
[C++]
public: __property ManagementStatus get_ErrorCode();
[JScript]
public function get ErrorCode() : ManagementStatus;
```

Property Value

A **ManagementStatus** value representing the error code returned by the WMI operation.

Requirements

Platforms: Windows 98, Windows NT 4.0,
Windows Millennium Edition, Windows 2000,
Windows XP Home Edition, Windows XP Professional,
Windows .NET Server family

.NET Framework Security:

- Full trust for the immediate caller. This member cannot be used by partially trusted code.

ManagementException.ErrorInformation Property

Gets the extended error object provided by WMI.

```
[Visual Basic]
Public ReadOnly Property ErrorInformation As ManagementBaseObject
[C#]
public ManagementBaseObject ErrorInformation {get;}
```

```
[C++]
public: __property ManagementBaseObject* get_ErrorInformation();
[JScript]
public function get ErrorInformation() : ManagementBaseObject;
```

Property Value

A **ManagementBaseObject** representing the extended error object provided by WMI, if available; a null reference (**Nothing** in Visual Basic) otherwise.

Requirements

Platforms: Windows 98, Windows NT 4.0,
Windows Millennium Edition, Windows 2000,
Windows XP Home Edition, Windows XP Professional,
Windows .NET Server family

.NET Framework Security:

- Full trust for the immediate caller. This member cannot be used by partially trusted code.

ManagementException.GetObjectData Method

Populates the **SerializationInfo** object with the data needed to serialize the **ManagementException** object.

```
[Visual Basic]
Overrides Public Sub GetObjectData( _
    ByVal info As SerializationInfo, _
    ByVal context As StreamingContext _
) Implements ISerializable.GetObjectData
[C#]
public override void GetObjectData(
    SerializationInfo info,
    StreamingContext context
);
[C++]
public: void GetObjectData(
    SerializationInfo* info,
    StreamingContext context
);
[JScript]
public override function GetObjectData(
    info : SerializationInfo,
    context : StreamingContext
);
```

Parameters

info

The **SerializationInfo** to populate with data.

context

The destination (see **StreamingContext**) for this serialization.

Implements

ISerializable.GetObjectData

Requirements

Platforms: Windows 98, Windows NT 4.0,
Windows Millennium Edition, Windows 2000,
Windows XP Home Edition, Windows XP Professional,
Windows .NET Server family

.NET Framework Security:

- Full trust for the immediate caller. This member cannot be used by partially trusted code.

ManagementNamedValue-
Collection Class

Represents a collection of named values suitable for use as context information to WMI operations. The names are case-insensitive.

System.Object
 System.Collections.Specialized.NameObjectCollectionBase
  System.Management.ManagementNamedValueCollection

[Visual Basic]
```
Public Class ManagementNamedValueCollection
   Inherits NameObjectCollectionBase
```
[C#]
```
public class ManagementNamedValueCollection :
   NameObjectCollectionBase
```
[C++]
```
public __gc class ManagementNamedValueCollection : public
   NameObjectCollectionBase
```
[JScript]
```
public class ManagementNamedValueCollection extends
   NameObjectCollectionBase
```

Thread Safety

Any public static (**Shared** in Visual Basic) members of this type are safe for multithreaded operations. Any instance members are not guaranteed to be thread safe.

Requirements

Namespace: System.Management

Platforms: Windows 98, Windows NT 4.0, Windows Millennium Edition, Windows 2000, Windows XP Home Edition, Windows XP Professional, Windows .NET Server family

Assembly: System.Management (in System.Management.dll)

ManagementNamedValueCollection
Constructor

Initializes a new instance of the **ManagementNamedValueCollection** class.

Overload List

Initializes a new instance of the **ManagementNamedValueCollection** class, which is empty. This is the default constructor.

[Visual Basic] **Public Sub New()**
[C#] **public ManagementNamedValueCollection();**
[C++] **public: ManagementNamedValueCollection();**
[JScript] **public function ManagementNamed-
ValueCollection();**

Initializes a new instance of the **ManagementNamedValueCollection** class that is serializable and uses the specified **SerializationInfo** and **StreamingContext**.

[Visual Basic] **Public Sub New(SerializationInfo, StreamingContext)**
[C#] **public ManagementNamedValue-
Collection(SerializationInfo, StreamingContext);**
[C++] **public: ManagementNamedValue-
Collection(SerializationInfo*, StreamingContext);**
[JScript] **public function ManagementNamedValue-
Collection(SerializationInfo, StreamingContext);**

ManagementNamedValueCollection
Constructor ()

Initializes a new instance of the **ManagementNamedValueCollection** class, which is empty. This is the default constructor.

[Visual Basic]
```
Public Sub New()
```
[C#]
```
public ManagementNamedValueCollection();
```
[C++]
```
public: ManagementNamedValueCollection();
```
[JScript]
```
public function ManagementNamedValueCollection();
```

Requirements

Platforms: Windows 98, Windows NT 4.0, Windows Millennium Edition, Windows 2000, Windows XP Home Edition, Windows XP Professional, Windows .NET Server family

.NET Framework Security:
- Full trust for the immediate caller. This member cannot be used by partially trusted code.

ManagementNamedValueCollection
Constructor (SerializationInfo,
StreamingContext)

Initializes a new instance of the **ManagementNamedValueCollection** class that is serializable and uses the specified **SerializationInfo** and **StreamingContext**.

[Visual Basic]
```
Public Sub New( _
   ByVal info As SerializationInfo, _
   ByVal context As StreamingContext _
)
```
[C#]
```
public ManagementNamedValueCollection(
   SerializationInfo info,
   StreamingContext context
);
```
[C++]
```
public: ManagementNamedValueCollection(
   SerializationInfo* info,
   StreamingContext context
);
```
[JScript]
```
public function ManagementNamedValueCollection(
   info : SerializationInfo,
   context : StreamingContext
);
```

Parameters

info

The **SerializationInfo** to populate with data.

context

The destination (see **StreamingContext**) for this serialization.

Requirements

Platforms: Windows 98, Windows NT 4.0,
Windows Millennium Edition, Windows 2000,
Windows XP Home Edition, Windows XP Professional,
Windows .NET Server family

.NET Framework Security:

- Full trust for the immediate caller. This member cannot be used by partially trusted code.

ManagementNamedValueCollection.Item Property

Returns the value associated with the specified name from this collection.

[C#] In C#, this property is the indexer for the **ManagementNamedValueCollection** class.

```
[Visual Basic]
Public Default ReadOnly Property Item( _
   ByVal name As String _
) As Object
[C#]
public object this[
   string name
] {get;}
[C++]
public: __property Object* get_Item(
   String* name
);
[JScript]
returnValue = ManagementNamedValueCollectionObject.Item(name);
-or-
returnValue = ManagementNamedValueCollectionObject(name);
```

[JScript] In JScript, you can use the default indexed properties defined by a type, but you cannot explicitly define your own. However, specifying the **expando** attribute on a class automatically provides a default indexed property whose type is **Object** and whose index type is **String**.

Arguments [JScript]

name

The name of the value to be returned.

Parameters [Visual Basic, C#, C++]

name

The name of the value to be returned.

Property Value

An **Object** containing the value of the specified item in this collection.

Requirements

Platforms: Windows 98, Windows NT 4.0,
Windows Millennium Edition, Windows 2000,
Windows XP Home Edition, Windows XP Professional,
Windows .NET Server family

.NET Framework Security:

- Full trust for the immediate caller. This member cannot be used by partially trusted code.

ManagementNamedValueCollection.Add Method

Adds a single-named value to the collection.

```
[Visual Basic]
Public Sub Add( _
   ByVal name As String, _
   ByVal value As Object _
)
[C#]
public void Add(
   string name,
   object value
);
[C++]
public: void Add(
   String* name,
   Object* value
);
[JScript]
public function Add(
   name : String,
   value : Object
);
```

Parameters

name

The name of the new value.

value

The value to be associated with the name.

Requirements

Platforms: Windows 98, Windows NT 4.0,
Windows Millennium Edition, Windows 2000,
Windows XP Home Edition, Windows XP Professional,
Windows .NET Server family

.NET Framework Security:

- Full trust for the immediate caller. This member cannot be used by partially trusted code.

ManagementNamedValueCollection.Clone Method

Creates a clone of the collection. Individual values are cloned. If a value does not support cloning, then a **NotSupportedException** is thrown.

```
[Visual Basic]
Public Function Clone() As ManagementNamedValueCollection
[C#]
public ManagementNamedValueCollection Clone();
[C++]
public: ManagementNamedValueCollection* Clone();
[JScript]
public function Clone() : ManagementNamedValueCollection;
```

Return Value

The new copy of the collection.

Requirements

Platforms: Windows 98, Windows NT 4.0,
Windows Millennium Edition, Windows 2000,
Windows XP Home Edition, Windows XP Professional,
Windows .NET Server family

.NET Framework Security:

- Full trust for the immediate caller. This member cannot be used by partially trusted code.

Requirements

Platforms: Windows 98, Windows NT 4.0,
Windows Millennium Edition, Windows 2000,
Windows XP Home Edition, Windows XP Professional,
Windows .NET Server family

.NET Framework Security:

- Full trust for the immediate caller. This member cannot be used by partially trusted code.

ManagementNamedValueCollection.Remove Method

Removes a single-named value from the collection. If the collection does not contain an element with the specified name, the collection remains unchanged and no exception is thrown.

```
[Visual Basic]
Public Sub Remove( _
   ByVal name As String _
)
[C#]
public void Remove(
   string name
);
[C++]
public: void Remove(
   String* name
);
[JScript]
public function Remove(
   name : String
);
```

Parameters

name
>   The name of the value to be removed.

Requirements

Platforms: Windows 98, Windows NT 4.0,
Windows Millennium Edition, Windows 2000,
Windows XP Home Edition, Windows XP Professional,
Windows .NET Server family

.NET Framework Security:

- Full trust for the immediate caller. This member cannot be used by partially trusted code.

ManagementNamedValueCollection.RemoveAll Method

Removes all entries from the collection.

```
[Visual Basic]
Public Sub RemoveAll()
[C#]
public void RemoveAll();
[C++]
public: void RemoveAll();
[JScript]
public function RemoveAll();
```

ManagementObject Class

Represents a data management object.

System.Object
 System.MarshalByRefObject
  System.ComponentModel.Component
   System.Management.ManagementBaseObject
    System.Management.ManagementObject
     System.Management.ManagementClass

```
[Visual Basic]
<Serializable>
Public Class ManagementObject
   Inherits ManagementBaseObject
[C#]
[Serializable]
public class ManagementObject : ManagementBaseObject
[C++]
[Serializable]
public __gc class ManagementObject : public ManagementBaseObject
[JScript]
public
   Serializable
class ManagementObject extends ManagementBaseObject
```

Thread Safety

Any public static (**Shared** in Visual Basic) members of this type are safe for multithreaded operations. Any instance members are not guaranteed to be thread safe.

Example

```
[C#]
using System;
using System.Management;

// This example demonstrates reading a property of a ManagementObject.
class Sample_ManagementObject
{
    public static int Main(string[] args) {
        ManagementObject disk = new ManagementObject(
            "win32_logicaldisk.deviceid=\"c:\"");
        disk.Get();
        Console.WriteLine("Logical Disk Size = " + disk
["Size"] + " bytes");
        return 0;
    }
}
```

```
[Visual Basic]
Imports System
Imports System.Management

' This example demonstrates reading a property of a ManagementObject.
Class Sample_ManagementObject
    Overloads Public Shared Function Main(args() As String) As Integer
        Dim disk As New
ManagementObject("win32_logicaldisk.deviceid=""c:""")
        disk.Get()
        Console.WriteLine(("Logical Disk Size = " &
disk("Size").ToString() _
            & " bytes"))
        Return 0
    End Function
End Class
```

Requirements

Namespace: System.Management

Platforms: Windows 98, Windows NT 4.0, Windows Millennium Edition, Windows 2000, Windows XP Home Edition, Windows XP Professional, Windows .NET Server family

Assembly: System.Management (in System.Management.dll)

ManagementObject Constructor

Initializes a new instance of the **ManagementObject** class.

Overload List

Initializes a new instance of the **ManagementObject** class. This is the default constructor.

 [Visual Basic] **Public Sub New()**

 [C#] **public ManagementObject();**

 [C++] **public: ManagementObject();**

 [JScript] **public function ManagementObject();**

Initializes a new instance of the **ManagementObject** class for the specified WMI object path. The path is provided as a **ManagementPath**.

 [Visual Basic] **Public Sub New(ManagementPath)**

 [C#] **public ManagementObject(ManagementPath);**

 [C++] **public: ManagementObject(ManagementPath*);**

 [JScript] **public function Management-Object(ManagementPath);**

Initializes a new instance of the **ManagementObject** class for the specified WMI object path. The path is provided as a string.

 [Visual Basic] **Public Sub New(String)**

 [C#] **public ManagementObject(string);**

 [C++] **public: ManagementObject(String*);**

 [JScript] **public function ManagementObject(String);**

Initializes a new instance of the **ManagementObject** class bound to the specified WMI path, including the specified additional options.

 [Visual Basic] **Public Sub New(ManagementPath, ObjectGetOptions)**

 [C#] **public ManagementObject(ManagementPath, ObjectGetOptions);**

 [C++] **public: ManagementObject(ManagementPath*, ObjectGetOptions*);**

 [JScript] **public function ManagementObject(Management-Path, ObjectGetOptions);**

Initializes a new instance of the **ManagementObject** class that is serializable.

 [Visual Basic] **Public Sub New(SerializationInfo, StreamingContext)**

 [C#] **public ManagementObject(SerializationInfo, StreamingContext);**

 [C++] **public: ManagementObject(SerializationInfo*, StreamingContext*);**

 [JScript] **public function ManagementObject(Serialization-Info, StreamingContext);**

Initializes a new instance of the **ManagementObject** class bound to the specified WMI path, including the specified additional options. In this variant, the path can be specified as a string.

> [Visual Basic] **Public Sub New(String, ObjectGetOptions)**
>
> [C#] **public ManagementObject(string, ObjectGetOptions);**
>
> [C++] **public: ManagementObject(String*, ObjectGetOptions*);**
>
> [JScript] **public function ManagementObject(String, ObjectGetOptions);**

Initializes a new instance of the **ManagementObject** class bound to the specified WMI path that includes the specified options.

> [Visual Basic] **Public Sub New(ManagementScope, ManagementPath, ObjectGetOptions)**
>
> [C#] **public ManagementObject(ManagementScope, ManagementPath, ObjectGetOptions);**
>
> [C++] **public: ManagementObject(ManagementScope*, ManagementPath*, ObjectGetOptions*);**
>
> [JScript] **public function ManagementObject(Management-Scope, ManagementPath, ObjectGetOptions);**

Initializes a new instance of the **ManagementObject** class bound to the specified WMI path, and includes the specified options. The scope and the path are specified as strings.

> [Visual Basic] **Public Sub New(String, String, ObjectGetOptions)**
>
> [C#] **public ManagementObject(string, string, ObjectGetOptions);**
>
> [C++] **public: ManagementObject(String*, String*, ObjectGetOptions*);**
>
> [JScript] **public function ManagementObject(String, String, ObjectGetOptions);**

Example

[Visual Basic, C#] **Note** This example shows how to use one of the overloaded versions of the **ManagementObject** constructor. For other examples that might be available, see the individual overload topics.

```
[C#]
GetObjectOptions opt = new GetObjectOptions(null, true);
ManagementObject o = new ManagementObject
("root\\MyNamespace", "MyClass.Name='abc'", opt);
```

```
[Visual Basic]
Dim opt As New GetObjectOptions(null, true)
Dim o As New ManagementObject("root\MyNamespace",
"MyClass.Name=""abc""", opt);
```

ManagementObject Constructor ()

Initializes a new instance of the **ManagementObject** class. This is the default constructor.

```
[Visual Basic]
Public Sub New()
[C#]
public ManagementObject();
[C++]
public: ManagementObject();
[JScript]
public function ManagementObject();
```

Example

```
[C#]
ManagementObject o = new ManagementObject();

//Now set the path on this object to bind it to a 'real'
 manageable entity
o.Path = "Win32_LogicalDisk='c:'";

//Now it can be used
Console.WriteLine(o["FreeSpace"]);
```

```
[Visual Basic]
Dim o As New ManagementObject()

'Now set the path on this object to bind it to a 'real'
manageable entity
o.Path = "Win32_LogicalDisk=""c:"""

'Now it can be used
Console.WriteLine(o("FreeSpace"))
```

Requirements

Platforms: Windows 98, Windows NT 4.0, Windows Millennium Edition, Windows 2000, Windows XP Home Edition, Windows XP Professional, Windows .NET Server family

.NET Framework Security:

- Full trust for the immediate caller. This member cannot be used by partially trusted code.

ManagementObject Constructor (ManagementPath)

Initializes a new instance of the **ManagementObject** class for the specified WMI object path. The path is provided as a **ManagementPath**.

```
[Visual Basic]
Public Sub New( _
   ByVal path As ManagementPath _
)
[C#]
public ManagementObject(
   ManagementPath path
);
[C++]
public: ManagementObject(
   ManagementPath* path
);
[JScript]
public function ManagementObject(
   path : ManagementPath
);
```

Parameters

path
>   A **ManagementPath** that contains a path to a WMI object.

Example

```
[C#]
ManagementPath p = new ManagementPath("Win32_Service.Name='Alerter'");
ManagementObject o = new ManagementObject(p);
```

```
[Visual Basic]
Dim p As New ManagementPath("Win32_Service.Name=""Alerter""")
Dim o As New ManagementObject(p)
```

Requirements

Platforms: Windows 98, Windows NT 4.0,
Windows Millennium Edition, Windows 2000,
Windows XP Home Edition, Windows XP Professional,
Windows .NET Server family

.NET Framework Security:

- Full trust for the immediate caller. This member cannot be used
  by partially trusted code.

ManagementObject Constructor (String)

Initializes a new instance of the **ManagementObject** class for the
specified WMI object path. The path is provided as a string.

```
[Visual Basic]
Public Sub New( _
   ByVal path As String _
)
[C#]
public ManagementObject(
   string path
);
[C++]
public: ManagementObject(
   String* path
);
[JScript]
public function ManagementObject(
   path : String
);
```

Parameters

path
   A WMI path.

Remarks

If the specified path is a relative path only (a server or namespace is
not specified), the default path is the local machine, and the default
namespace is the **DefaultPath** path (by default, root\cimv2). If the
user specifies a full path, the default settings are overridden.

Example

```
[C#]
ManagementObject o = new
ManagementObject("Win32_Service.Name='Alerter'");

//or with a full path :

ManagementObject o = new
ManagementObject("\\\\MyServer\\root\\MyApp:MyClass.Key='abc'");

[Visual Basic]
Dim o As New ManagementObject("Win32_Service.Name=""Alerter""")

//or with a full path :

Dim o As New
ManagementObject("\\\\MyServer\\root\\MyApp:MyClass.Key=""abc""");
```

Requirements

Platforms: Windows 98, Windows NT 4.0,
Windows Millennium Edition, Windows 2000,
Windows XP Home Edition, Windows XP Professional,
Windows .NET Server family

.NET Framework Security:

- Full trust for the immediate caller. This member cannot be used
  by partially trusted code.

ManagementObject Constructor (ManagementPath, ObjectGetOptions)

Initializes a new instance of the **ManagementObject** class bound to
the specified WMI path, including the specified additional options.

```
[Visual Basic]
Public Sub New( _
   ByVal path As ManagementPath, _
   ByVal options As ObjectGetOptions _
)
[C#]
public ManagementObject(
   ManagementPath path,
   ObjectGetOptions options
);
[C++]
public: ManagementObject(
   ManagementPath* path,
   ObjectGetOptions* options
);
[JScript]
public function ManagementObject(
   path : ManagementPath,
   options : ObjectGetOptions
);
```

Parameters

path
   A **ManagementPath** containing the WMI path.

options
   An **ObjectGetOptions** containing additional options for binding
   to the WMI object. This parameter could be null if default
   options are to be used.

Example

```
[C#]
ManagementPath p = new
ManagementPath("Win32_ComputerSystem.Name='MyMachine'");

//Set options for no context info, but requests amended qualifiers
//to be contained in the object
ObjectGetOptions opt = new ObjectGetOptions(null, true);

ManagementObject o = new ManagementObject(p, opt);

Console.WriteLine(o.GetQualifierValue("Description"));

[Visual Basic]
Dim p As New ManagementPath("Win32_ComputerSystem.Name=""MyMachine""")

'Set options for no context info, but requests amended qualifiers
'to be contained in the object
Dim opt As New ObjectGetOptions(null, true)

Dim o As New ManagementObject(p, opt)

Console.WriteLine(o.GetQualifierValue("Description"));
```

Requirements

Platforms: Windows 98, Windows NT 4.0, Windows Millennium Edition, Windows 2000, Windows XP Home Edition, Windows XP Professional, Windows .NET Server family

.NET Framework Security:

Full trust for the immediate caller. This member cannot be used by partially trusted code.

ManagementObject Constructor (SerializationInfo, StreamingContext)

Initializes a new instance of the **ManagementObject** class that is serializable.

```
[Visual Basic]
Public Sub New( _
    ByVal info As SerializationInfo, _
    ByVal context As StreamingContext _
)
[C#]
public ManagementObject(
    SerializationInfo info,
    StreamingContext context
);
[C++]
public: ManagementObject(
    SerializationInfo* info,
    StreamingContext context
);
[JScript]
public function ManagementObject(
    info : SerializationInfo,
    context : StreamingContext
);
```

Parameters

info

The **SerializationInfo** to populate with data.

context

The destination (see **StreamingContext**) for this serialization.

Requirements

Platforms: Windows 98, Windows NT 4.0, Windows Millennium Edition, Windows 2000, Windows XP Home Edition, Windows XP Professional, Windows .NET Server family

.NET Framework Security:

- Full trust for the immediate caller. This member cannot be used by partially trusted code.

ManagementObject Constructor (String, ObjectGetOptions)

Initializes a new instance of the **ManagementObject** class bound to the specified WMI path, including the specified additional options. In this variant, the path can be specified as a string.

```
[Visual Basic]
Public Sub New( _
    ByVal path As String, _
    ByVal options As ObjectGetOptions _
)
[C#]
public ManagementObject(
    string path,
    ObjectGetOptions options
);
[C++]
public: ManagementObject(
    String* path,
    ObjectGetOptions* options
);
[JScript]
public function ManagementObject(
    path : String,
    options : ObjectGetOptions
);
```

Parameters

path

The WMI path to the object.

options

An **ObjectGetOptions** representing options to get the specified WMI object.

Example

```
[C#]
//Set options for no context info,
//but requests amended qualifiers to be contained in the object
ObjectGetOptions opt = new ObjectGetOptions(null, true);

ManagementObject o = new
ManagementObject("Win32_ComputerSystem.Name='MyMachine'", opt);

Console.WriteLine(o.GetQualifierValue("Description"));
```

```
[Visual Basic]
'Set options for no context info,
'but requests amended qualifiers to be contained in the object
Dim opt As New ObjectGetOptions(null, true)

Dim o As New ManagementObject("Win32_ComputerSystem.Name=""MyMachine""",
opt);

Console.WriteLine(o.GetQualifierValue("Description"))
```

Requirements

Platforms: Windows 98, Windows NT 4.0, Windows Millennium Edition, Windows 2000, Windows XP Home Edition, Windows XP Professional, Windows .NET Server family

.NET Framework Security:

- Full trust for the immediate caller. This member cannot be used by partially trusted code.

ManagementObject Constructor (ManagementScope, ManagementPath, ObjectGetOptions)

Initializes a new instance of the **ManagementObject** class bound to the specified WMI path that includes the specified options.

```
[Visual Basic]
Public Sub New( _
   ByVal scope As ManagementScope, _
   ByVal path As ManagementPath, _
   ByVal options As ObjectGetOptions _
)
[C#]
public ManagementObject(
   ManagementScope scope,
   ManagementPath path,
   ObjectGetOptions options
);
[C++]
public: ManagementObject(
   ManagementScope* scope,
   ManagementPath* path,
   ObjectGetOptions* options
);
[JScript]
public function ManagementObject(
   scope : ManagementScope,
   path : ManagementPath,
   options : ObjectGetOptions
);
```

Parameters

scope

A **ManagementScope** representing the scope in which the WMI object resides. In this version, scopes can only be WMI namespaces.

path

A **ManagementPath** representing the WMI path to the manageable object.

options

An **ObjectGetOptions** specifying additional options for getting the object.

Remarks

Because WMI paths can be relative or full, a conflict between the scope and the path specified may arise. However, if a scope is specified and a relative WMI path is specified, then there is no conflict. The following are some possible conflicts:

If a scope is not specified and a relative WMI path is specified, then the scope will default to the local machine's **DefaultPath**.

If a scope is not specified and a full WMI path is specified, then the scope will be inferred from the scope portion of the full path. For example, the full WMI path: \\MyMachine\root\MyNamespace:MyClass.Name ='abc' will represent the WMI object 'MyClass.Name='abc'" in the scope '\\MyMachine\root\MyNamespace'.If a scope is specified and a full WMI path is specified, then the scope will override the scope portion of the full path. For example, if the following scope was specified: \\MyMachine\root\MyScope, and the following full path was specified: \\MyMachine\root\MyNamespace:MyClass.Name ='abc', then look for the following object:

```
\\MyMachine\root\MyScope:MyClass.Name=
'abc' (the scope part of the full path is ignored).
```

Example

```
[C#]
ManagementScope s = new ManagementScope("\\\\MyMachine\\root\\cimv2");
ManagementPath p = new ManagementPath("Win32_LogicalDisk.Name='c:'");
ManagementObject o = new ManagementObject(s,p);

[Visual Basic]
Dim s As New ManagementScope("\\MyMachine\root\cimv2");
Dim p As New ManagementPath("Win32_LogicalDisk.Name=""c:""");
Dim o As New ManagementObject(s,p);
```

Requirements

Platforms: Windows 98, Windows NT 4.0, Windows Millennium Edition, Windows 2000, Windows XP Home Edition, Windows XP Professional, Windows .NET Server family

.NET Framework Security:

- Full trust for the immediate caller. This member cannot be used by partially trusted code.

ManagementObject Constructor (String, String, ObjectGetOptions)

Initializes a new instance of the **ManagementObject** class bound to the specified WMI path, and includes the specified options. The scope and the path are specified as strings.

```
[Visual Basic]
Public Sub New( _
   ByVal scopeString As String, _
   ByVal pathString As String, _
   ByVal options As ObjectGetOptions _
)
[C#]
public ManagementObject(
   string scopeString,
   string pathString,
   ObjectGetOptions options
);
[C++]
public: ManagementObject(
   String* scopeString,
   String* pathString,
   ObjectGetOptions* options
);
[JScript]
public function ManagementObject(
   scopeString : String,
   pathString : String,
   options : ObjectGetOptions
);
```

Parameters

scopeString

The scope for the WMI object.

pathString

The WMI object path.

options

An **ObjectGetOptions** representing additional options for getting the WMI object.

Remarks

See the equivalent overload for details.

Example

```
[C#]
GetObjectOptions opt = new GetObjectOptions(null, true);
ManagementObject o = new ManagementObject
("root\\MyNamespace", "MyClass.Name='abc'", opt);
```

```
[Visual Basic]
Dim opt As New GetObjectOptions(null, true)
Dim o As New ManagementObject("root\MyNamespace",
"MyClass.Name=""abc""", opt);
```

Requirements

Platforms: Windows 98, Windows NT 4.0,
Windows Millennium Edition, Windows 2000,
Windows XP Home Edition, Windows XP Professional,
Windows .NET Server family

.NET Framework Security:

• Full trust for the immediate caller. This member cannot be used by partially trusted code.

ManagementObject.ClassPath Property

Gets or sets the path to the object's class.

```
[Visual Basic]
Overrides Public ReadOnly Property ClassPath As ManagementPath
[C#]
public override ManagementPath ClassPath {get;}
[C++]
public: __property ManagementPath* get_ClassPath();
[JScript]
public override function get ClassPath() : ManagementPath;
```

Property Value

A **ManagementPath** representing the path to the object's class.

Remarks

This property is read-only.

Example

```
[C#]
ManagementObject o = new ManagementObject("MyClass.Name='abc'");

//Get the class definition for the object above.
ManagementClass c = new ManagementClass(o.ClassPath);
```

```
[Visual Basic]
Dim o As New ManagementObject("MyClass.Name=""abc""")

'Get the class definition for the object above.
Dim c As New ManagementClass(o.ClassPath);
```

Requirements

Platforms: Windows 98, Windows NT 4.0,
Windows Millennium Edition, Windows 2000,
Windows XP Home Edition, Windows XP Professional,
Windows .NET Server family

.NET Framework Security:

• Full trust for the immediate caller. This member cannot be used by partially trusted code.

ManagementObject.Options Property

Gets or sets additional information to use when retrieving the object.

```
[Visual Basic]
Public Property Options As ObjectGetOptions
[C#]
public ObjectGetOptions Options {get; set;}
[C++]
public: __property ObjectGetOptions* get_Options();
public: __property void set_Options(ObjectGetOptions*);
[JScript]
public function get Options() : ObjectGetOptions;
public function set Options(ObjectGetOptions);
```

Property Value

An **ObjectGetOptions** to use when retrieving the object.

Remarks

When the property is changed after the management object has been bound to a WMI object, the management object is disconnected from the original WMI object and later rebound using the new options.

Example

```
[C#]
//Contains default options
ManagementObject o = new ManagementObject("MyClass.Name='abc'");

//Replace default options, in this case requesting retrieval of
//amended qualifiers along with the WMI object.
o.Options = new ObjectGetOptions(null, true);
```

```
[Visual Basic]
'Contains default options
Dim o As New ManagementObject("MyClass.Name=""abc""")

'Replace default options, in this case requesting retrieval of
'amended qualifiers along with the WMI object.
o.Options = New ObjectGetOptions(null, true)
```

Requirements

Platforms: Windows 98, Windows NT 4.0,
Windows Millennium Edition, Windows 2000,
Windows XP Home Edition, Windows XP Professional,
Windows .NET Server family

.NET Framework Security:

• Full trust for the immediate caller. This member cannot be used by partially trusted code.

ManagementObject.Path Property

Gets or sets the object's WMI path.

```
[Visual Basic]
Public Overridable Property Path As ManagementPath
[C#]
public virtual ManagementPath Path {get; set;}
[C++]
public: __property virtual ManagementPath* get_Path();
public: __property virtual void set_Path(ManagementPath*);
[JScript]
public function get Path() : ManagementPath;
public function set Path(ManagementPath);
```

Property Value

A **ManagementPath** representing the object's path.

Remarks

Changing the property after the management object has been bound to a WMI object in a particular namespace results in releasing the original WMI object. This causes the management object to be rebound to the new object specified by the new path properties and scope values.

The rebinding is performed in a "lazy" manner, that is, only when a requested value requires the management object to be bound to the WMI object. Changes can be made to more than just the property before attempting to rebind (for example, modifying the scope and path properties simultaneously).

Example

```
[C#]
ManagementObject o = new ManagementObject();

//Specify the WMI path to which this object should be bound to
o.Path = new ManagementPath("MyClass.Name='foo'");

[Visual Basic]
Dim o As New ManagementObject()

'Specify the WMI path to which this object should be bound to
o.Path = New ManagementPath("MyClass.Name=""foo""");
```

Requirements

Platforms: Windows 98, Windows NT 4.0, Windows Millennium Edition, Windows 2000, Windows XP Home Edition, Windows XP Professional, Windows .NET Server family

.NET Framework Security:

- Full trust for the immediate caller. This member cannot be used by partially trusted code.

ManagementObject.Scope Property

Gets or sets the scope in which this object resides.

```
[Visual Basic]
Public Property Scope As ManagementScope
[C#]
public ManagementScope Scope {get; set;}
[C++]
public: __property ManagementScope* get_Scope();
public: __property void set_Scope(ManagementScope*);
[JScript]
public function get Scope() : ManagementScope;
public function set Scope(ManagementScope);
```

Property Value

A **ManagementScope**.

Remarks

Changing this property after the management object has been bound to a WMI object in a particular namespace results in releasing the original WMI object. This causes the management object to be rebound to the new object specified by the new path properties and scope values.

The rebinding is performed in a "lazy" manner, that is, only when a requested value requires the management object to be bound to the

WMI object. Changes can be made to more than just this property before attempting to rebind (for example, modifying the scope and path properties simultaneously).

Example

```
[C#]
//Create the object with the default namespace (root\cimv2)
ManagementObject o = new ManagementObject();

//Change the scope (=namespace) of this object to the one specified.
o.Scope = new ManagementScope("root\\MyAppNamespace");

[Visual Basic]
'Create the object with the default namespace (root\cimv2)
Dim o As New ManagementObject()

'Change the scope (=namespace) of this object to the one specified.
o.Scope = New ManagementScope("root\MyAppNamespace")
```

Requirements

Platforms: Windows 98, Windows NT 4.0, Windows Millennium Edition, Windows 2000, Windows XP Home Edition, Windows XP Professional, Windows .NET Server family

.NET Framework Security:

- Full trust for the immediate caller. This member cannot be used by partially trusted code.

ManagementObject.Clone Method

Creates a copy of the object.

```
[Visual Basic]
Overrides Public Function Clone() As Object Implements _
    ICloneable.Clone
[C#]
public override object Clone();
[C++]
public: Object* Clone();
[JScript]
public override function Clone() : Object;
```

Return Value

The copied object.

Implements

ICloneable.Clone

Requirements

Platforms: Windows 98, Windows NT 4.0, Windows Millennium Edition, Windows 2000, Windows XP Home Edition, Windows XP Professional, Windows .NET Server family

.NET Framework Security:

- Full trust for the immediate caller. This member cannot be used by partially trusted code.

ManagementObject.CopyTo Method

Copies the object to a different location.

Overload List

Copies the object to a different location.

[Visual Basic] **Overloads Public Function CopyTo(ManagementPath) As ManagementPath**

[C#] **public ManagementPath CopyTo(ManagementPath);**

[C++] **public: ManagementPath* CopyTo(ManagementPath*);**

[JScript] **public function CopyTo(ManagementPath) : ManagementPath;**

Copies the object to a different location.

[Visual Basic] **Overloads Public Function CopyTo(String) As ManagementPath**

[C#] **public ManagementPath CopyTo(string);**

[C++] **public: ManagementPath* CopyTo(String*);**

[JScript] **public function CopyTo(String) : ManagementPath;**

Copies the object to a different location, asynchronously.

[Visual Basic] **Overloads Public Sub CopyTo(ManagementOperationObserver, ManagementPath)**

[C#] **public void CopyTo(ManagementOperationObserver, ManagementPath);**

[C++] **public: void CopyTo(ManagementOperationObserver*, ManagementPath*);**

[JScript] **public function CopyTo(ManagementOperationObserver, ManagementPath);**

Copies the object to a different location, asynchronously.

[Visual Basic] **Overloads Public Sub CopyTo(ManagementOperationObserver, String)**

[C#] **public void CopyTo(ManagementOperationObserver, string);**

[C++] **public: void CopyTo(ManagementOperationObserver*, String*);**

[JScript] **public function CopyTo(ManagementOperationObserver, String);**

Copies the object to a different location.

[Visual Basic] **Overloads Public Function CopyTo(ManagementPath, PutOptions) As ManagementPath**

[C#] **public ManagementPath CopyTo(ManagementPath, PutOptions);**

[C++] **public: ManagementPath* CopyTo(ManagementPath*, PutOptions*);**

[JScript] **public function CopyTo(ManagementPath, PutOptions) : ManagementPath;**

Copies the object to a different location.

[Visual Basic] **Overloads Public Function CopyTo(String, PutOptions) As ManagementPath**

[C#] **public ManagementPath CopyTo(string, PutOptions);**

[C++] **public: ManagementPath* CopyTo(String*, PutOptions*);**

[JScript] **public function CopyTo(String, PutOptions) : ManagementPath;**

Copies the object to a different location, asynchronously.

[Visual Basic] **Overloads Public Sub CopyTo(ManagementOperationObserver, ManagementPath, PutOptions)**

[C#] **public void CopyTo(ManagementOperationObserver, ManagementPath, PutOptions);**

[C++] **public: void CopyTo(ManagementOperationObserver*, ManagementPath*, PutOptions*);**

[JScript] **public function CopyTo(ManagementOperationObserver, ManagementPath, PutOptions);**

Copies the object to a different location, asynchronously.

[Visual Basic] **Overloads Public Sub CopyTo(ManagementOperationObserver, String, PutOptions)**

[C#] **public void CopyTo(ManagementOperationObserver, string, PutOptions);**

[C++] **public: void CopyTo(ManagementOperationObserver*, String*, PutOptions*);**

[JScript] **public function CopyTo(ManagementOperationObserver, String, PutOptions);**

ManagementObject.CopyTo Method (ManagementPath)

Copies the object to a different location.

```
[Visual Basic]
Overloads Public Function CopyTo( _
   ByVal path As ManagementPath _
) As ManagementPath
[C#]
public ManagementPath CopyTo(
   ManagementPath path
);
[C++]
public: ManagementPath* CopyTo(
   ManagementPath* path
);
[JScript]
public function CopyTo(
   path : ManagementPath
) : ManagementPath;
```

Parameters
path
  The **ManagementPath** to which the object should be copied.

Return Value
The new path of the copied object.

Requirements
Platforms: Windows 98, Windows NT 4.0, Windows Millennium Edition, Windows 2000, Windows XP Home Edition, Windows XP Professional, Windows .NET Server family

.NET Framework Security:
• Full trust for the immediate caller. This member cannot be used by partially trusted code.

ManagementObject.CopyTo Method (String)

Copies the object to a different location.

```
[Visual Basic]
Overloads Public Function CopyTo( _
   ByVal path As String _
) As ManagementPath
[C#]
public ManagementPath CopyTo(
   string path
);
```

```
[C++]
public: ManagementPath* CopyTo(
   String* path
);
[JScript]
public function CopyTo(
   path : String
) : ManagementPath;
```

Parameters
path
> The path to which the object should be copied.

Return Value
The new path of the copied object.

Requirements

Platforms: Windows 98, Windows NT 4.0,
Windows Millennium Edition, Windows 2000,
Windows XP Home Edition, Windows XP Professional,
Windows .NET Server family

.NET Framework Security:
• Full trust for the immediate caller. This member cannot be used
  by partially trusted code.

ManagementObject.CopyTo Method (ManagementOperationObserver, ManagementPath)

Copies the object to a different location, asynchronously.

```
[Visual Basic]
Overloads Public Sub CopyTo( _
   ByVal watcher As ManagementOperationObserver, _
   ByVal path As ManagementPath _
)
[C#]
public void CopyTo(
   ManagementOperationObserver watcher,
   ManagementPath path
);
[C++]
public: void CopyTo(
   ManagementOperationObserver* watcher,
   ManagementPath* path
);
[JScript]
public function CopyTo(
   watcher : ManagementOperationObserver,
   path : ManagementPath
);
```

Parameters
watcher
> The object that will receive the results of the operation.
path
> A **ManagementPath** specifying the path to which the object
> should be copied.

Requirements

Platforms: Windows 98, Windows NT 4.0,
Windows Millennium Edition, Windows 2000,
Windows XP Home Edition, Windows XP Professional,
Windows .NET Server family

.NET Framework Security:
• Full trust for the immediate caller. This member cannot be used
  by partially trusted code.

ManagementObject.CopyTo Method (ManagementOperationObserver, String)

Copies the object to a different location, asynchronously.

```
[Visual Basic]
Overloads Public Sub CopyTo( _
   ByVal watcher As ManagementOperationObserver, _
   ByVal path As String _
)
[C#]
public void CopyTo(
   ManagementOperationObserver watcher,
   string path
);
[C++]
public: void CopyTo(
   ManagementOperationObserver* watcher,
   String* path
);
[JScript]
public function CopyTo(
   watcher : ManagementOperationObserver,
   path : String
);
```

Parameters
watcher
> The object that will receive the results of the operation.
path
> The path to which the object should be copied.

Requirements

Platforms: Windows 98, Windows NT 4.0,
Windows Millennium Edition, Windows 2000,
Windows XP Home Edition, Windows XP Professional,
Windows .NET Server family

.NET Framework Security:
• Full trust for the immediate caller. This member cannot be used
  by partially trusted code.

ManagementObject.CopyTo Method (ManagementPath, PutOptions)

Copies the object to a different location.

```
[Visual Basic]
Overloads Public Function CopyTo( _
   ByVal path As ManagementPath, _
   ByVal options As PutOptions _
) As ManagementPath
[C#]
public ManagementPath CopyTo(
   ManagementPath path,
   PutOptions options
);
```

```
[C++]
public: ManagementPath* CopyTo(
    ManagementPath* path,
    PutOptions* options
);
[JScript]
public function CopyTo(
    path : ManagementPath,
    options : PutOptions
) : ManagementPath;
```

Parameters
path
> The **ManagementPath** to which the object should be copied.

options
> The options for how the object should be put.

Return Value
The new path of the copied object.

Requirements
Platforms: Windows 98, Windows NT 4.0,
Windows Millennium Edition, Windows 2000,
Windows XP Home Edition, Windows XP Professional,
Windows .NET Server family

.NET Framework Security:
- Full trust for the immediate caller. This member cannot be used by partially trusted code.

ManagementObject.CopyTo Method (String, PutOptions)

Copies the object to a different location.

```
[Visual Basic]
Overloads Public Function CopyTo( _
    ByVal path As String, _
    ByVal options As PutOptions _
) As ManagementPath
[C#]
public ManagementPath CopyTo(
    string path,
    PutOptions options
);
[C++]
public: ManagementPath* CopyTo(
    String* path,
    PutOptions* options
);
[JScript]
public function CopyTo(
    path : String,
    options : PutOptions
) : ManagementPath;
```

Parameters
path
> The path to which the object should be copied.

options
> The options for how the object should be put.

Return Value
The new path of the copied object.

Requirements
Platforms: Windows 98, Windows NT 4.0,
Windows Millennium Edition, Windows 2000,
Windows XP Home Edition, Windows XP Professional,
Windows .NET Server family

.NET Framework Security:
- Full trust for the immediate caller. This member cannot be used by partially trusted code.

ManagementObject.CopyTo Method (ManagementOperationObserver, ManagementPath, PutOptions)

Copies the object to a different location, asynchronously.

```
[Visual Basic]
Overloads Public Sub CopyTo( _
    ByVal watcher As ManagementOperationObserver, _
    ByVal path As ManagementPath, _
    ByVal options As PutOptions _
)
[C#]
public void CopyTo(
    ManagementOperationObserver watcher,
    ManagementPath path,
    PutOptions options
);
[C++]
public: void CopyTo(
    ManagementOperationObserver* watcher,
    ManagementPath* path,
    PutOptions* options
);
[JScript]
public function CopyTo(
    watcher : ManagementOperationObserver,
    path : ManagementPath,
    options : PutOptions
);
```

Parameters
watcher
> The object that will receive the results of the operation.

path
> The path to which the object should be copied.

options
> The options for how the object should be put.

Requirements
Platforms: Windows 98, Windows NT 4.0,
Windows Millennium Edition, Windows 2000,
Windows XP Home Edition, Windows XP Professional,
Windows .NET Server family

.NET Framework Security:
- Full trust for the immediate caller. This member cannot be used by partially trusted code.

ManagementObject.CopyTo Method (ManagementOperationObserver, String, PutOptions)

Copies the object to a different location, asynchronously.

```
[Visual Basic]
Overloads Public Sub CopyTo( _
   ByVal watcher As ManagementOperationObserver, _
   ByVal path As String, _
   ByVal options As PutOptions _
)
[C#]
public void CopyTo(
   ManagementOperationObserver watcher,
   string path,
   PutOptions options
);
[C++]
public: void CopyTo(
   ManagementOperationObserver* watcher,
   String* path,
   PutOptions* options
);
[JScript]
public function CopyTo(
   watcher : ManagementOperationObserver,
   path : String,
   options : PutOptions
);
```

Parameters

watcher
   The object that will receive the results of the operation.

path
   The path to which the object should be copied.

options
   The options for how the object should be put.

Requirements

Platforms: Windows 98, Windows NT 4.0, Windows Millennium Edition, Windows 2000, Windows XP Home Edition, Windows XP Professional, Windows .NET Server family

.NET Framework Security:

• Full trust for the immediate caller. This member cannot be used by partially trusted code.

ManagementObject.Delete Method

Deletes the object.

Overload List

Deletes the object.

   [Visual Basic] **Overloads Public Sub Delete()**
   [C#] **public void Delete();**
   [C++] **public: void Delete();**
   [JScript] **public function Delete();**

Deletes the object.

   [Visual Basic] **Overloads Public Sub Delete(DeleteOptions)**
   [C#] **public void Delete(DeleteOptions);**
   [C++] **public: void Delete(DeleteOptions*);**

   [JScript] **public function Delete(DeleteOptions);**

Deletes the object.

   [Visual Basic] **Overloads Public Sub Delete(ManagementOperationObserver)**
   [C#] **public void Delete(ManagementOperationObserver);**
   [C++] **public: void Delete(ManagementOperation-Observer*);**
   [JScript] **public function Delete(ManagementOperation-Observer);**

Deletes the object.

   [Visual Basic] **Overloads Public Sub Delete(ManagementOperationObserver, DeleteOptions)**
   [C#] **public void Delete(ManagementOperationObserver, DeleteOptions);**
   [C++] **public: void Delete(ManagementOperationObserver*, DeleteOptions*);**
   [JScript] **public function Delete(ManagementOperation-Observer, DeleteOptions);**

ManagementObject.Delete Method ()

Deletes the object.

```
[Visual Basic]
Overloads Public Sub Delete()
[C#]
public void Delete();
[C++]
public: void Delete();
[JScript]
public function Delete();
```

Requirements

Platforms: Windows 98, Windows NT 4.0, Windows Millennium Edition, Windows 2000, Windows XP Home Edition, Windows XP Professional, Windows .NET Server family

.NET Framework Security:

• Full trust for the immediate caller. This member cannot be used by partially trusted code.

ManagementObject.Delete Method (DeleteOptions)

Deletes the object.

```
[Visual Basic]
Overloads Public Sub Delete( _
   ByVal options As DeleteOptions _
)
[C#]
public void Delete(
   DeleteOptions options
);
[C++]
public: void Delete(
   DeleteOptions* options
);
[JScript]
public function Delete(
   options : DeleteOptions
);
```

Parameters

options

The options for how to delete the object.

Requirements

Platforms: Windows 98, Windows NT 4.0,
Windows Millennium Edition, Windows 2000,
Windows XP Home Edition, Windows XP Professional,
Windows .NET Server family

.NET Framework Security:

• Full trust for the immediate caller. This member cannot be used
  by partially trusted code.

ManagementObject.Delete Method
(ManagementOperationObserver)

Deletes the object.

```
[Visual Basic]
Overloads Public Sub Delete( _
   ByVal watcher As ManagementOperationObserver _
)
[C#]
public void Delete(
   ManagementOperationObserver watcher
);
[C++]
public: void Delete(
   ManagementOperationObserver* watcher
);
[JScript]
public function Delete(
   watcher : ManagementOperationObserver
);
```

Parameters

watcher

The object that will receive the results of the operation.

Requirements

Platforms: Windows 98, Windows NT 4.0,
Windows Millennium Edition, Windows 2000,
Windows XP Home Edition, Windows XP Professional,
Windows .NET Server family

.NET Framework Security:

• Full trust for the immediate caller. This member cannot be used
  by partially trusted code.

ManagementObject.Delete Method
(ManagementOperationObserver, DeleteOptions)

Deletes the object.

```
[Visual Basic]
Overloads Public Sub Delete( _
   ByVal watcher As ManagementOperationObserver, _
   ByVal options As DeleteOptions _
)
[C#]
public void Delete(
   ManagementOperationObserver watcher,
   DeleteOptions options
);
```

```
[C++]
public: void Delete(
   ManagementOperationObserver* watcher,
   DeleteOptions* options
);
[JScript]
public function Delete(
   watcher : ManagementOperationObserver,
   options : DeleteOptions
);
```

Parameters

watcher

The object that will receive the results of the operation.

options

The options for how to delete the object.

Requirements

Platforms: Windows 98, Windows NT 4.0,
Windows Millennium Edition, Windows 2000,
Windows XP Home Edition, Windows XP Professional,
Windows .NET Server family

.NET Framework Security:

• Full trust for the immediate caller. This member cannot be used
  by partially trusted code.

ManagementObject.Get Method

Binds to the management object.

Overload List

Binds to the management object.

[Visual Basic] **Overloads Public Sub Get()**

[C#] **public void Get();**

[C++] **public: void Get();**

[JScript] **public function Get();**

Binds to the management object asynchronously.

[Visual Basic] **Overloads Public Sub
Get(ManagementOperationObserver)**

[C#] **public void Get(ManagementOperationObserver);**

[C++] **public: void Get(ManagementOperationObserver*);**

[JScript] **public function
Get(ManagementOperationObserver);**

Example

[Visual Basic, C#] **Note** This example shows how to use one of
the overloaded versions of **Get**. For other examples that might
be available, see the individual overload topics.

```
[C#]
ManagementObject o = new ManagementObject("MyClass.Name='abc'");

//Set up handlers for asynchronous get
MyHandler h = new MyHandler();
ManagementOperationObserver ob = new ManagementOperationObserver();
ob.Completed += new CompletedEventHandler(h.Done);

//Get the object asynchronously
o.Get(ob);
```

```
//Wait until operation is completed
while (!h.Completed)
    System.Threading.Thread.Sleep (1000);

//Here we can use the object
Console.WriteLine(o["SomeProperty"]);

public class MyHandler
{
    private bool completed = false;

    public void Done(object sender, CompletedEventArgs e) {
        Console.WriteLine("async Get completed !");
        completed = true;
    }

    public bool Completed {
        get {
            return completed;
        }
    }
}
```

```
[Visual Basic]
Dim o As New ManagementObject("MyClass.Name=""abc""")

'Set up handlers for asynchronous get
Dim h As New MyHandler()
Dim ob As New ManagementOperationObserver()
ob.Completed += New CompletedEventHandler(h.Done)

'Get the object asynchronously
o.Get(ob)

'Wait until operation is completed
While Not h.Completed
    System.Threading.Thread.Sleep(1000)
End While

'Here we can use the object
Console.WriteLine(o("SomeProperty"))

Public Class MyHandler
    Private _completed As Boolean = false;

    Public Sub Done(sender As Object, e As EventArrivedEventArgs)
        Console.WriteLine("async Get completed !")
        _completed = True
    End Sub

    Public ReadOnly Property Completed() As Boolean
        Get
            Return _completed
        End Get
    End Property
End Class
```

ManagementObject.Get Method ()

Binds to the management object.

```
[Visual Basic]
Overloads Public Sub Get()
[C#]
public void Get();
[C++]
public: void Get();
[JScript]
public function Get();
```

Remarks

The method is implicitly invoked at the first attempt to get or set information to the WMI object. It can also be explicitly invoked at the user's discretion, to better control the timing and manner of retrieval.

Example

```
[C#]
ManagementObject o = new ManagementObject("MyClass.Name='abc'");
string s = o["SomeProperty"]; //this causes an implicit Get().

//or :

ManagementObject o= new ManagementObject("MyClass.Name= 'abc'");
o.Get(); //explicitly
//Now it's faster because the object has already been retrieved.
string s = o["SomeProperty"];
```

```
[Visual Basic]
Dim o As New ManagementObject("MyClass.Name=""abc""")
string s = o("SomeProperty") 'this causes an implicit Get().

'or :

Dim o As New ManagementObject("MyClass.Name= ""abc""")
o.Get() 'explicitly
'Now it's faster because the object has already been retrieved.
string s = o("SomeProperty");
```

Requirements

Platforms: Windows 98, Windows NT 4.0, Windows Millennium Edition, Windows 2000, Windows XP Home Edition, Windows XP Professional, Windows .NET Server family

.NET Framework Security:
- Full trust for the immediate caller. This member cannot be used by partially trusted code.

ManagementObject.Get Method (ManagementOperationObserver)

Binds to the management object asynchronously.

```
[Visual Basic]
Overloads Public Sub Get( _
    ByVal watcher As ManagementOperationObserver _
)
[C#]
public void Get(
    ManagementOperationObserver watcher
);
[C++]
public: void Get(
    ManagementOperationObserver* watcher
);
[JScript]
public function Get(
    watcher : ManagementOperationObserver
);
```

Parameters

watcher

The object to receive the results of the operation as events.

Remarks

The method will issue the request to get the object and then will immediately return. The results of the operation will then be delivered through events being fired on the watcher object provided.

Example

[C#]
```
ManagementObject o = new ManagementObject("MyClass.Name='abc'");

//Set up handlers for asynchronous get
MyHandler h = new MyHandler();
ManagementOperationObserver ob = new ManagementOperationObserver();
ob.Completed += new CompletedEventHandler(h.Done);

//Get the object asynchronously
o.Get(ob);

//Wait until operation is completed
while (!h.Completed)
    System.Threading.Thread.Sleep (1000);

//Here we can use the object
Console.WriteLine(o["SomeProperty"]);

public class MyHandler
{
    private bool completed = false;

    public void Done(object sender, CompletedEventArgs e) {
        Console.WriteLine("async Get completed !");
        completed = true;
    }

    public bool Completed {
        get {
            return completed;
        }
    }
}
```

[Visual Basic]
```
Dim o As New ManagementObject("MyClass.Name=""abc""")

'Set up handlers for asynchronous get
Dim h As New MyHandler()
Dim ob As New ManagementOperationObserver()
ob.Completed += New CompletedEventHandler(h.Done)

'Get the object asynchronously
o.Get(ob)

'Wait until operation is completed
While Not h.Completed
    System.Threading.Thread.Sleep(1000)
End While

'Here we can use the object
Console.WriteLine(o("SomeProperty"))

Public Class MyHandler
    Private _completed As Boolean = false;

    Public Sub Done(sender As Object, e As EventArrivedEventArgs)
        Console.WriteLine("async Get completed !")
        _completed = True
    End Sub

    Public ReadOnly Property Completed() As Boolean
        Get
            Return _completed
        End Get
    End Property
End Class
```

Requirements

Platforms: Windows 98, Windows NT 4.0, Windows Millennium Edition, Windows 2000, Windows XP Home Edition, Windows XP Professional, Windows .NET Server family

.NET Framework Security:
- Full trust for the immediate caller. This member cannot be used by partially trusted code.

ManagementObject.GetMethodParameters Method

Returns a **ManagementBaseObject** representing the list of input parameters for a method.

```
[Visual Basic]
Public Function GetMethodParameters( _
    ByVal methodName As String _
) As ManagementBaseObject
[C#]
public ManagementBaseObject GetMethodParameters(
    string methodName
);
[C++]
public: ManagementBaseObject* GetMethodParameters(
    String* methodName
);
[JScript]
public function GetMethodParameters(
    methodName : String
) : ManagementBaseObject;
```

Parameters

methodName
    The name of the method.

Return Value

A **ManagementBaseObject** containing the input parameters to the method.

Remarks

Gets the object containing the input parameters to a method, and then fills in the values and passes the object to the **InvokeMethod** () call.

Requirements

Platforms: Windows 98, Windows NT 4.0, Windows Millennium Edition, Windows 2000, Windows XP Home Edition, Windows XP Professional, Windows .NET Server family

.NET Framework Security:
- Full trust for the immediate caller. This member cannot be used by partially trusted code.

ManagementObject.GetRelated Method

Gets a collection of objects related to the object (associators).

Overload List

Gets a collection of objects related to the object (associators).

[Visual Basic] **Overloads Public Function GetRelated() As ManagementObjectCollection**

[C#] **public ManagementObjectCollection GetRelated();**

[C++] **public: ManagementObjectCollection* GetRelated();**

[JScript] **public function GetRelated() : ManagementObjectCollection;**

Gets a collection of objects related to the object (associators) asynchronously. This call returns immediately, and a delegate is called when the results are available.

[Visual Basic] **Overloads Public Sub GetRelated(ManagementOperationObserver)**

[C#] **public void GetRelated(Management-OperationObserver);**

[C++] **public: void GetRelated(Management-OperationObserver*);**

[JScript] **public function GetRelated(ManagementOperationObserver);**

Gets a collection of objects related to the object (associators).

[Visual Basic] **Overloads Public Function GetRelated(String) As ManagementObjectCollection**

[C#] **public ManagementObjectCollection GetRelated(string);**

[C++] **public: ManagementObjectCollection* GetRelated(String*);**

[JScript] **public function GetRelated(String) : ManagementObjectCollection;**

Gets a collection of objects related to the object (associators).

[Visual Basic] **Overloads Public Sub GetRelated(ManagementOperationObserver, String)**

[C#] **public void GetRelated(ManagementOperationObserver, string);**

[C++] **public: void GetRelated(ManagementOperationObserver*, String*);**

[JScript] **public function GetRelated(ManagementOperationObserver, String);**

Gets a collection of objects related to the object (associators).

[Visual Basic] **Overloads Public Function GetRelated(String, String, String, String, String, String, Boolean, EnumerationOptions) As ManagementObjectCollection**

[C#] **public ManagementObjectCollection GetRelated(string, string, string, string, string, string, bool, EnumerationOptions);**

[C++] **public: ManagementObjectCollection* GetRelated(String*, String*, String*, String*, String*, String*, bool, EnumerationOptions*);**

[JScript] **public function GetRelated(String, String, String, String, String, Boolean, EnumerationOptions) : ManagementObjectCollection;**

Gets a collection of objects related to the object (associators).

[Visual Basic] **Overloads Public Sub GetRelated(ManagementOperationObserver, String, String, String, String, String, String, Boolean, EnumerationOptions)**

[C#] **public void GetRelated(ManagementOperationObserver, string, string, string, string, string, string, bool, EnumerationOptions);**

[C++] **public: void GetRelated(ManagementOperationObserver*, String*, String*, String*, String*, String*, String*, bool, EnumerationOptions*);**

[JScript] **public function GetRelated(ManagementOperationObserver, String, String, String, String, String, String, Boolean, EnumerationOptions);**

Example

> [Visual Basic, C#] **Note** This example shows how to use one of the overloaded versions of **GetRelated**. For other examples that might be available, see the individual overload topics.

```
[C#]
ManagementObject o = new ManagementObject("Win32_Service='Alerter'");
foreach (ManagementBaseObject b in o.GetRelated("Win32_Service")
    Console.WriteLine("Service related to the Alerter service {0} ↵
is {1}", b["Name"], b["State"]);
```

```
[Visual Basic]
Dim o As New ManagementObject("Win32_Service=""Alerter""")
Dim b As ManagementBaseObject
For Each b in o.GetRelated("Win32_Service")
    Console.WriteLine("Service related to the Alerter service ↵
{0} is {1}", b("Name"), b("State"))
Next b
```

ManagementObject.GetRelated Method ()

Gets a collection of objects related to the object (associators).

```
[Visual Basic]
Overloads Public Function GetRelated() As ManagementObjectCollection
[C#]
public ManagementObjectCollection GetRelated();
[C++]
public: ManagementObjectCollection* GetRelated();
[JScript]
public function GetRelated() : ManagementObjectCollection;
```

Return Value

A **ManagementObjectCollection** containing the related objects.

Remarks

The operation is equivalent to an ASSOCIATORS OF query where ResultClass = relatedClass.

Example

```
[C#]
ManagementObject o = new ManagementObject("Win32_Service='Alerter'");
foreach(ManagementBaseObject b in o.GetRelated())
    Console.WriteLine("Object related to Alerter service : ", b.Path);
```

```
[Visual Basic]
Dim o As New ManagementObject("Win32_Service=""Alerter""")
Dim b As ManagementBaseObject
For Each b In o.GetRelated()
    Console.WriteLine("Object related to Alerter service : ", b.Path)
Next b
```

Requirements

Platforms: Windows 98, Windows NT 4.0, Windows Millennium Edition, Windows 2000, Windows XP Home Edition, Windows XP Professional, Windows .NET Server family

.NET Framework Security:

- Full trust for the immediate caller. This member cannot be used by partially trusted code.

ManagementObject.GetRelated Method (ManagementOperationObserver)

Gets a collection of objects related to the object (associators) asynchronously. This call returns immediately, and a delegate is called when the results are available.

```
[Visual Basic]
Overloads Public Sub GetRelated( _
    ByVal watcher As ManagementOperationObserver _
)
[C#]
public void GetRelated(
    ManagementOperationObserver watcher
);
[C++]
public: void GetRelated(
    ManagementOperationObserver* watcher
);
[JScript]
public function GetRelated(
    watcher : ManagementOperationObserver
);
```

Parameters

watcher
   The object to use to return results.

Requirements

Platforms: Windows 98, Windows NT 4.0, Windows Millennium Edition, Windows 2000, Windows XP Home Edition, Windows XP Professional, Windows .NET Server family

.NET Framework Security:
- Full trust for the immediate caller. This member cannot be used by partially trusted code.

ManagementObject.GetRelated Method (String)

Gets a collection of objects related to the object (associators).

```
[Visual Basic]
Overloads Public Function GetRelated( _
    ByVal relatedClass As String _
) As ManagementObjectCollection
[C#]
public ManagementObjectCollection GetRelated(
    string relatedClass
);
[C++]
public: ManagementObjectCollection* GetRelated(
    String* relatedClass
);
[JScript]
public function GetRelated(
    relatedClass : String
) : ManagementObjectCollection;
```

Parameters

relatedClass
   A class of related objects.

Return Value

A **ManagementObjectCollection** containing the related objects.

Example

```
[C#]
ManagementObject o = new ManagementObject("Win32_Service='Alerter'");
foreach (ManagementBaseObject b in o.GetRelated("Win32_Service")
    Console.WriteLine("Service related to the Alerter service    ⏎
{0} is {1}", b["Name"], b["State"]);

[Visual Basic]
Dim o As New ManagementObject("Win32_Service=""Alerter""");
Dim b As ManagementBaseObject
For Each b in o.GetRelated("Win32_Service")
    Console.WriteLine("Service related to the Alerter service    ⏎
{0} is {1}", b("Name"), b("State"))
Next b
```

Requirements

Platforms: Windows 98, Windows NT 4.0, Windows Millennium Edition, Windows 2000, Windows XP Home Edition, Windows XP Professional, Windows .NET Server family

.NET Framework Security:
- Full trust for the immediate caller. This member cannot be used by partially trusted code.

ManagementObject.GetRelated Method (ManagementOperationObserver, String)

Gets a collection of objects related to the object (associators).

```
[Visual Basic]
Overloads Public Sub GetRelated( _
    ByVal watcher As ManagementOperationObserver, _
    ByVal relatedClass As String _
)
[C#]
public void GetRelated(
    ManagementOperationObserver watcher,
    string relatedClass
);
[C++]
public: void GetRelated(
    ManagementOperationObserver* watcher,
    String* relatedClass
);
[JScript]
public function GetRelated(
    watcher : ManagementOperationObserver,
    relatedClass : String
);
```

Parameters

watcher
   The object to use to return results.
relatedClass
   The class of related objects.

Remarks

This operation is equivalent to an ASSOCIATORS OF query where ResultClass = <relatedClass>.

Requirements

Platforms: Windows 98, Windows NT 4.0, Windows Millennium Edition, Windows 2000, Windows XP Home Edition, Windows XP Professional, Windows .NET Server family

.NET Framework Security:

• Full trust for the immediate caller. This member cannot be used by partially trusted code.

ManagementObject.GetRelated Method (String, String, String, String, String, String, Boolean, EnumerationOptions)

Gets a collection of objects related to the object (associators).

```
[Visual Basic]
Overloads Public Function GetRelated( _
   ByVal relatedClass As String, _
   ByVal relationshipClass As String, _
   ByVal relationshipQualifier As String, _
   ByVal relatedQualifier As String, _
   ByVal relatedRole As String, _
   ByVal thisRole As String, _
   ByVal classDefinitionsOnly As Boolean, _
   ByVal options As EnumerationOptions _
) As ManagementObjectCollection
[C#]
public ManagementObjectCollection GetRelated(
   string relatedClass,
   string relationshipClass,
   string relationshipQualifier,
   string relatedQualifier,
   string relatedRole,
   string thisRole,
   bool classDefinitionsOnly,
   EnumerationOptions options
);
[C++]
public: ManagementObjectCollection* GetRelated(
   String* relatedClass,
   String* relationshipClass,
   String* relationshipQualifier,
   String* relatedQualifier,
   String* relatedRole,
   String* thisRole,
   bool classDefinitionsOnly,
   EnumerationOptions* options
);
[JScript]
public function GetRelated(
   relatedClass : String,
   relationshipClass : String,
   relationshipQualifier : String,
   relatedQualifier : String,
   relatedRole : String,
   thisRole : String,
   classDefinitionsOnly : Boolean,
   options : EnumerationOptions
) : ManagementObjectCollection;
```

Parameters

relatedClass
   The class of the related objects.
relationshipClass
   The relationship class of interest.
relationshipQualifier
   The qualifier required to be present on the relationship class.

relatedQualifier
   The qualifier required to be present on the related class.
relatedRole
   The role that the related class is playing in the relationship.
thisRole
   The role that this class is playing in the relationship.
classDefinitionsOnly
   When this method returns, it contains only class definitions for the instances that match the query.
options
   Extended options for how to execute the query.

Return Value

A **ManagementObjectCollection** containing the related objects.

Remarks

This operation is equivalent to an ASSOCIATORS OF query where ResultClass = <relatedClass>.

Requirements

Platforms: Windows 98, Windows NT 4.0, Windows Millennium Edition, Windows 2000, Windows XP Home Edition, Windows XP Professional, Windows .NET Server family

.NET Framework Security:

• Full trust for the immediate caller. This member cannot be used by partially trusted code.

ManagementObject.GetRelated Method (ManagementOperationObserver, String, String, String, String, String, String, Boolean, EnumerationOptions)

Gets a collection of objects related to the object (associators).

```
[Visual Basic]
Overloads Public Sub GetRelated( _
   ByVal watcher As ManagementOperationObserver, _
   ByVal relatedClass As String, _
   ByVal relationshipClass As String, _
   ByVal relationshipQualifier As String, _
   ByVal relatedQualifier As String, _
   ByVal relatedRole As String, _
   ByVal thisRole As String, _
   ByVal classDefinitionsOnly As Boolean, _
   ByVal options As EnumerationOptions _
)
[C#]
public void GetRelated(
   ManagementOperationObserver watcher,
   string relatedClass,
   string relationshipClass,
   string relationshipQualifier,
   string relatedQualifier,
   string relatedRole,
   string thisRole,
   bool classDefinitionsOnly,
   EnumerationOptions options
);
```

```
[C++]
public: void GetRelated(
   ManagementOperationObserver* watcher,
   String* relatedClass,
   String* relationshipClass,
   String* relationshipQualifier,
   String* relatedQualifier,
   String* relatedRole,
   String* thisRole,
   bool classDefinitionsOnly,
   EnumerationOptions* options
);
[JScript]
public function GetRelated(
   watcher : ManagementOperationObserver,
   relatedClass : String,
   relationshipClass : String,
   relationshipQualifier : String,
   relatedQualifier : String,
   relatedRole : String,
   thisRole : String,
   classDefinitionsOnly : Boolean,
   options : EnumerationOptions
);
```

Parameters

watcher
   The object to use to return results.
relatedClass
   The class of the related objects.
relationshipClass
   The relationship class of interest.
relationshipQualifier
   The qualifier required to be present on the relationship class.
relatedQualifier
   The qualifier required to be present on the related class.
relatedRole
   The role that the related class is playing in the relationship.
thisRole
   The role that this class is playing in the relationship.
classDefinitionsOnly
   Return only class definitions for the instances that match the query.
options
   Extended options for how to execute the query.

Remarks

This operation is equivalent to an ASSOCIATORS OF query where ResultClass = <relatedClass>.

Requirements

Platforms: Windows 98, Windows NT 4.0, Windows Millennium Edition, Windows 2000, Windows XP Home Edition, Windows XP Professional, Windows .NET Server family

.NET Framework Security:
• Full trust for the immediate caller. This member cannot be used by partially trusted code.

ManagementObject.GetRelationships Method

Gets a collection of associations to the object.

Overload List

Gets a collection of associations to the object.

   [Visual Basic] **Overloads Public Function GetRelationships() As ManagementObjectCollection**
   [C#] **public ManagementObjectCollection GetRelationships();**
   [C++] **public: ManagementObjectCollection* GetRelationships();**
   [JScript] **public function GetRelationships() : ManagementObjectCollection;**

Gets a collection of associations to the object.

   [Visual Basic] **Overloads Public Sub GetRelationships(ManagementOperationObserver)**
   [C#] **public void GetRelationships(ManagementOperationObserver);**
   [C++] **public: void GetRelationships(ManagementOperationObserver*);**
   [JScript] **public function GetRelationships(ManagementOperationObserver);**

Gets a collection of associations to the object.

   [Visual Basic] **Overloads Public Function GetRelationships(String) As ManagementObjectCollection**
   [C#] **public ManagementObjectCollection GetRelationships(string);**
   [C++] **public: ManagementObjectCollection* GetRelationships(String*);**
   [JScript] **public function GetRelationships(String) : ManagementObjectCollection;**

Gets a collection of associations to the object.

   [Visual Basic] **Overloads Public Sub GetRelationships(ManagementOperationObserver, String)**
   [C#] **public void GetRelationships(ManagementOperationObserver, string);**
   [C++] **public: void GetRelationships(ManagementOperationObserver*, String*);**
   [JScript] **public function GetRelationships(ManagementOperationObserver, String);**

Gets a collection of associations to the object.

   [Visual Basic] **Overloads Public Function GetRelationships(String, String, String, Boolean, EnumerationOptions) As ManagementObjectCollection**
   [C#] **public ManagementObjectCollection GetRelationships(string, string, string, bool, EnumerationOptions);**
   [C++] **public: ManagementObjectCollection* GetRelationships(String*, String*, String*, bool, EnumerationOptions*);**
   [JScript] **public function GetRelationships(String, String, String, Boolean, EnumerationOptions) : ManagementObjectCollection;**

Gets a collection of associations to the object.

   [Visual Basic] **Overloads Public Sub GetRelationships(ManagementOperationObserver, String, String, String, Boolean, EnumerationOptions)**

[C#] public void GetRelationships(ManagementOperation-Observer, string, string, string, bool, EnumerationOptions);

[C++] public: void GetRelationships(ManagementOperation-Observer*, String*, String*, String*, bool, EnumerationOptions*);

[JScript] public function GetRelationships(Management-OperationObserver, String, String, String, Boolean, EnumerationOptions);

ManagementObject.GetRelationships Method ()

Gets a collection of associations to the object.

```
[Visual Basic]
Overloads Public Function GetRelationships() As
ManagementObjectCollection
[C#]
public ManagementObjectCollection GetRelationships();
[C++]
public: ManagementObjectCollection* GetRelationships();
[JScript]
public function GetRelationships() : ManagementObjectCollection;
```

Return Value

A **ManagementObjectCollection** containing the association objects.

Remarks

The operation is equivalent to a REFERENCES OF query.

Requirements

Platforms: Windows 98, Windows NT 4.0, Windows Millennium Edition, Windows 2000, Windows XP Home Edition, Windows XP Professional, Windows .NET Server family

.NET Framework Security:

- Full trust for the immediate caller. This member cannot be used by partially trusted code.

ManagementObject.GetRelationships Method (ManagementOperationObserver)

Gets a collection of associations to the object.

```
[Visual Basic]
Overloads Public Sub GetRelationships( _
   ByVal watcher As ManagementOperationObserver _
)
[C#]
public void GetRelationships(
   ManagementOperationObserver watcher
);
[C++]
public: void GetRelationships(
   ManagementOperationObserver* watcher
);
[JScript]
public function GetRelationships(
   watcher : ManagementOperationObserver
);
```

Parameters

watcher
    The object to use to return results.

Remarks

This operation is equivalent to a REFERENCES OF query

Requirements

Platforms: Windows 98, Windows NT 4.0, Windows Millennium Edition, Windows 2000, Windows XP Home Edition, Windows XP Professional, Windows .NET Server family

.NET Framework Security:

- Full trust for the immediate caller. This member cannot be used by partially trusted code.

ManagementObject.GetRelationships Method (String)

Gets a collection of associations to the object.

```
[Visual Basic]
Overloads Public Function GetRelationships( _
   ByVal relationshipClass As String _
) As ManagementObjectCollection
[C#]
public ManagementObjectCollection GetRelationships(
   string relationshipClass
);
[C++]
public: ManagementObjectCollection* GetRelationships(
   String* relationshipClass
);
[JScript]
public function GetRelationships(
   relationshipClass : String
) : ManagementObjectCollection;
```

Parameters

relationshipClass
    The associations to include.

Return Value

A **ManagementObjectCollection** containing the association objects.

Remarks

This operation is equivalent to a REFERENCES OF query where the AssocClass = <relationshipClass>.

Requirements

Platforms: Windows 98, Windows NT 4.0, Windows Millennium Edition, Windows 2000, Windows XP Home Edition, Windows XP Professional, Windows .NET Server family

.NET Framework Security:

- Full trust for the immediate caller. This member cannot be used by partially trusted code.

ManagementObject.GetRelationships Method (ManagementOperationObserver, String)

Gets a collection of associations to the object.

```
[Visual Basic]
Overloads Public Sub GetRelationships( _
   ByVal watcher As ManagementOperationObserver, _
   ByVal relationshipClass As String _
)
[C#]
public void GetRelationships(
   ManagementOperationObserver watcher,
   string relationshipClass
);
[C++]
public: void GetRelationships(
   ManagementOperationObserver* watcher,
   String* relationshipClass
);
[JScript]
public function GetRelationships(
   watcher : ManagementOperationObserver,
   relationshipClass : String
);
```

Parameters

watcher
   The object to use to return results.
relationshipClass
   The associations to include.

Remarks

This operation is equivalent to a REFERENCES OF query where the AssocClass = <relationshipClass>.

Requirements

Platforms: Windows 98, Windows NT 4.0, Windows Millennium Edition, Windows 2000, Windows XP Home Edition, Windows XP Professional, Windows .NET Server family

.NET Framework Security:
- Full trust for the immediate caller. This member cannot be used by partially trusted code.

ManagementObject.GetRelationships Method (String, String, String, Boolean, EnumerationOptions)

Gets a collection of associations to the object.

```
[Visual Basic]
Overloads Public Function GetRelationships( _
   ByVal relationshipClass As String, _
   ByVal relationshipQualifier As String, _
   ByVal thisRole As String, _
   ByVal classDefinitionsOnly As Boolean, _
   ByVal options As EnumerationOptions _
) As ManagementObjectCollection
[C#]
public ManagementObjectCollection GetRelationships(
   string relationshipClass,
   string relationshipQualifier,
   string thisRole,
   bool classDefinitionsOnly,
   EnumerationOptions options
);
```

```
[C++]
public: ManagementObjectCollection* GetRelationships(
   String* relationshipClass,
   String* relationshipQualifier,
   String* thisRole,
   bool classDefinitionsOnly,
   EnumerationOptions* options
);
[JScript]
public function GetRelationships(
   relationshipClass : String,
   relationshipQualifier : String,
   thisRole : String,
   classDefinitionsOnly : Boolean,
   options : EnumerationOptions
) : ManagementObjectCollection;
```

Parameters

relationshipClass
   The type of relationship of interest.
relationshipQualifier
   The qualifier to be present on the relationship.
thisRole
   The role of this object in the relationship.
classDefinitionsOnly
   When this method returns, it contains only the class definitions for the result set.
options
   The extended options for the query execution.

Return Value

A **ManagementObjectCollection** containing the association objects.

Remarks

This operation is equivalent to a REFERENCES OF query with possibly all the extensions.

Requirements

Platforms: Windows 98, Windows NT 4.0, Windows Millennium Edition, Windows 2000, Windows XP Home Edition, Windows XP Professional, Windows .NET Server family

.NET Framework Security:
- Full trust for the immediate caller. This member cannot be used by partially trusted code.

ManagementObject.GetRelationships Method (ManagementOperationObserver, String, String, String, Boolean, EnumerationOptions)

Gets a collection of associations to the object.

```
[Visual Basic]
Overloads Public Sub GetRelationships( _
   ByVal watcher As ManagementOperationObserver, _
   ByVal relationshipClass As String, _
   ByVal relationshipQualifier As String, _
   ByVal thisRole As String, _
   ByVal classDefinitionsOnly As Boolean, _
   ByVal options As EnumerationOptions _
)
```

```
[C#]
public void GetRelationships(
    ManagementOperationObserver watcher,
    string relationshipClass,
    string relationshipQualifier,
    string thisRole,
    bool classDefinitionsOnly,
    EnumerationOptions options
);
[C++]
public: void GetRelationships(
    ManagementOperationObserver* watcher,
    String* relationshipClass,
    String* relationshipQualifier,
    String* thisRole,
    bool classDefinitionsOnly,
    EnumerationOptions* options
);
[JScript]
public function GetRelationships(
    watcher : ManagementOperationObserver,
    relationshipClass : String,
    relationshipQualifier : String,
    thisRole : String,
    classDefinitionsOnly : Boolean,
    options : EnumerationOptions
);
```

Parameters

watcher
The object to use to return results.

relationshipClass
The type of relationship of interest.

relationshipQualifier
The qualifier to be present on the relationship.

thisRole
The role of this object in the relationship.

classDefinitionsOnly
When this method returns, it contains only the class definitions for the result set.

options
The extended options for the query execution.

Remarks

This operation is equivalent to a REFERENCES OF query with possibly all the extensions.

Requirements

Platforms: Windows 98, Windows NT 4.0, Windows Millennium Edition, Windows 2000, Windows XP Home Edition, Windows XP Professional, Windows .NET Server family

.NET Framework Security:

* Full trust for the immediate caller. This member cannot be used by partially trusted code.

ManagementObject.InvokeMethod Method

Invokes a method on the object.

Overload List

Invokes a method on the object.

> [Visual Basic] **Overloads Public Function InvokeMethod(String, Object()) As Object**
>
> [C#] **public object InvokeMethod(string, object[]);**
>
> [C++] **public: Object* InvokeMethod(String*, Object[]);**
>
> [JScript] **public function InvokeMethod(String, Object[]) : Object;**

Invokes a method on the object, asynchronously.

> [Visual Basic] **Overloads Public Sub InvokeMethod(ManagementOperationObserver, String, Object())**
>
> [C#] **public void InvokeMethod(ManagementOperationObserver, string, object[]);**
>
> [C++] **public: void InvokeMethod(ManagementOperationObserver*, String*, Object[]);**
>
> [JScript] **public function InvokeMethod(ManagementOperationObserver, String, Object[]);**

Invokes a method on the WMI object. The input and output parameters are represented as **ManagementBaseObject** objects.

> [Visual Basic] **Overloads Public Function InvokeMethod(String, ManagementBaseObject, InvokeMethodOptions) As ManagementBaseObject**
>
> [C#] **public ManagementBaseObject InvokeMethod(string, ManagementBaseObject, InvokeMethodOptions);**
>
> [C++] **public: ManagementBaseObject* InvokeMethod(String*, ManagementBaseObject*, InvokeMethodOptions*);**
>
> [JScript] **public function InvokeMethod(String, ManagementBaseObject, InvokeMethodOptions) : ManagementBaseObject;**

Invokes a method on the object, asynchronously.

> [Visual Basic] **Overloads Public Sub InvokeMethod(ManagementOperationObserver, String, ManagementBaseObject, InvokeMethodOptions)**
>
> [C#] **public void InvokeMethod(ManagementOperationObserver, string, ManagementBaseObject, InvokeMethodOptions);**
>
> [C++] **public: void InvokeMethod(ManagementOperationObserver*, String*, ManagementBaseObject*, InvokeMethodOptions*);**
>
> [JScript] **public function InvokeMethod(ManagementOperationObserver, String, ManagementBaseObject, InvokeMethodOptions);**

Example

> [Visual Basic, C#] **Note** This example shows how to use one of the overloaded versions of **InvokeMethod**. For other examples that might be available, see the individual overload topics.

```
[C#]
using System;
using System.Management;

// This sample demonstrates invoking a WMI method using
  parameter objects
public class InvokeMethod
{
    public static void Main()
    {
```

```
        //Get the object on which the method will be invoked
        ManagementClass processClass = new
ManagementClass("Win32_Process");

        //Get an input parameters object for this method
        ManagementBaseObject inParams =
processClass.GetMethodParameters("Create");

        //Fill in input parameter values
        inParams["CommandLine"] = "calc.exe";

        //Execute the method
        ManagementBaseObject outParams =
processClass.InvokeMethod ("Create", inParams, null);

        //Display results
        //Note: The return code of the method is provided in the
"returnValue" property of the outParams object
        Console.WriteLine("Creation of calculator process
returned: " + outParams["returnValue"]);
        Console.WriteLine("Process ID: " + outParams["processId"]);
    }
}
```

[Visual Basic]
```
Imports System
Imports System.Management

' This sample demonstrates invoking a WMI method using parameter
objects
Class InvokeMethod
    Public Overloads Shared Function Main(ByVal args()
As String) As Integer

        ' Get the object on which the method will be invoked
        Dim processClass As New ManagementClass("Win32_Process")

        ' Get an input parameters object for this method
        Dim inParams As ManagementBaseObject =
processClass.GetMethodParameters("Create")

        ' Fill in input parameter values
        inParams("CommandLine") = "calc.exe"

        ' Execute the method
        Dim outParams As ManagementBaseObject =
processClass.InvokeMethod("Create", inParams, Nothing)

        ' Display results
        ' Note: The return code of the method is provided
in the "returnValue" property of the outParams object
        Console.WriteLine("Creation of calculator process
returned: {0}", outParams("returnValue"))
        Console.WriteLine("Process ID: {0}", outParams("processId"))

        Return 0
    End Function
End Class
```

ManagementObject.InvokeMethod Method (String, Object[])

Invokes a method on the object.

[Visual Basic]
```
Overloads Public Function InvokeMethod( _
    ByVal methodName As String, _
    ByVal args() As Object _
) As Object
```
[C#]
```
public object InvokeMethod(
    string methodName,
    object[] args
);
```

[C++]
```
public: Object* InvokeMethod(
    String* methodName,
    Object* args __gc[]
);
```
[JScript]
```
public function InvokeMethod(
    methodName : String,
    args : Object[]
) : Object;
```

Parameters

methodName
    The name of the method to execute.

args
    An array containing parameter values.

Return Value

The value returned by the method.

Remarks

If the method is static, the execution should still succeed.

Example

[C#]
```
using System;
using System.Management;

// This sample demonstrates invoking a WMI method using an
array of arguments.
public class InvokeMethod
{
    public static void Main()
    {

        //Get the object on which the method will be invoked
        ManagementClass processClass = new
ManagementClass("Win32_Process");

        //Create an array containing all arguments for the method
        object[] methodArgs = {"notepad.exe", null, null, 0};

        //Execute the method
        object result = processClass.InvokeMethod ("Create",
methodArgs);

        //Display results
        Console.WriteLine ("Creation of process returned: " + result);
        Console.WriteLine ("Process id: " + methodArgs[3]);
    }

}
```

[Visual Basic]
```
Imports System
Imports System.Management

' This sample demonstrates invoking a WMI method using an
array of arguments.
Class InvokeMethod
    Public Overloads Shared Function Main(ByVal args()
As String) As Integer

        ' Get the object on which the method will be invoked
        Dim processClass As New ManagementClass("Win32_Process")

        ' Create an array containing all arguments for the method
        Dim methodArgs() As Object = {"notepad.exe",
Nothing, Nothing, 0}
```

```
      ' Execute the method
      Dim result As Object = processClass.InvokeMethod    ⌐
("Create", methodArgs)

      'Display results
      Console.WriteLine("Creation of process returned: {0}",  ⌐
result)
      Console.WriteLine("Process id: {0}", methodArgs(3))
      Return 0
   End Function
End Class
```

Requirements

Platforms: Windows 98, Windows NT 4.0,
Windows Millennium Edition, Windows 2000,
Windows XP Home Edition, Windows XP Professional,
Windows .NET Server family

.NET Framework Security:

- Full trust for the immediate caller. This member cannot be used
  by partially trusted code.

ManagementObject.InvokeMethod Method (ManagementOperationObserver, String, Object[])

Invokes a method on the object, asynchronously.

```
[Visual Basic]
Overloads Public Sub InvokeMethod( _
   ByVal watcher As ManagementOperationObserver, _
   ByVal methodName As String, _
   ByVal args() As Object _
)
[C#]
public void InvokeMethod(
   ManagementOperationObserver watcher,
   string methodName,
   object[] args
);
[C++]
public: void InvokeMethod(
   ManagementOperationObserver* watcher,
   String* methodName,
   Object* args __gc[]
);
[JScript]
public function InvokeMethod(
   watcher : ManagementOperationObserver,
   methodName : String,
   args : Object[]
);
```

Parameters

watcher
   The object to receive the results of the operation.
methodName
   The name of the method to execute.
args
   An array containing parameter values.

Remarks

If the method is static, the execution should still succeed.

Requirements

Platforms: Windows 98, Windows NT 4.0,
Windows Millennium Edition, Windows 2000,
Windows XP Home Edition, Windows XP Professional,
Windows .NET Server family

.NET Framework Security:

- Full trust for the immediate caller. This member cannot be used
  by partially trusted code.

ManagementObject.InvokeMethod Method (String, ManagementBaseObject, InvokeMethodOptions)

Invokes a method on the WMI object. The input and output
parameters are represented as **ManagementBaseObject** objects.

```
[Visual Basic]
Overloads Public Function InvokeMethod( _
   ByVal methodName As String, _
   ByVal inParameters As ManagementBaseObject, _
   ByVal options As InvokeMethodOptions _
) As ManagementBaseObject
[C#]
public ManagementBaseObject InvokeMethod(
   string methodName,
   ManagementBaseObject inParameters,
   InvokeMethodOptions options
);
[C++]
public: ManagementBaseObject* InvokeMethod(
   String* methodName,
   ManagementBaseObject* inParameters,
   InvokeMethodOptions* options
);
[JScript]
public function InvokeMethod(
   methodName : String,
   inParameters : ManagementBaseObject,
   options : InvokeMethodOptions
) : ManagementBaseObject;
```

Parameters

methodName
   The name of the method to execute.
inParameters
   A **ManagementBaseObject** holding the input parameters to the
   method.
options
   An **InvokeMethodOptions** containing additional options for the
   execution of the method.

Return Value

A **ManagementBaseObject** containing the output parameters and
return value of the executed method.

Example

```
[C#]
using System;
using System.Management;

// This sample demonstrates invoking a WMI method using    ⌐
 parameter objects
public class InvokeMethod
{
```

```
public static void Main()
{
    //Get the object on which the method will be invoked
    ManagementClass processClass = new
ManagementClass("Win32_Process");

    //Get an input parameters object for this method
    ManagementBaseObject inParams =
processClass.GetMethodParameters("Create");

    //Fill in input parameter values
    inParams["CommandLine"] = "calc.exe";

    //Execute the method
    ManagementBaseObject outParams = processClass.InvokeMethod
("Create", inParams, null);

    //Display results
    //Note: The return code of the method is provided in the
"returnValue" property of the outParams object
    Console.WriteLine("Creation of calculator process
returned: " + outParams["returnValue"]);
    Console.WriteLine("Process ID: " + outParams["processId"]);
}
}
```

[Visual Basic]
```
Imports System
Imports System.Management

' This sample demonstrates invoking a WMI method using
 parameter objects
Class InvokeMethod
    Public Overloads Shared Function Main(ByVal args()
As String) As Integer

        ' Get the object on which the method will be invoked
        Dim processClass As New ManagementClass("Win32_Process")

        ' Get an input parameters object for this method
        Dim inParams As ManagementBaseObject =
processClass.GetMethodParameters("Create")

        ' Fill in input parameter values
        inParams("CommandLine") = "calc.exe"

        ' Execute the method
        Dim outParams As ManagementBaseObject =
processClass.InvokeMethod("Create", inParams, Nothing)

        ' Display results
        ' Note: The return code of the method is provided
in the "returnValue" property of the outParams object
        Console.WriteLine("Creation of calculator process
returned: {0}", outParams("returnValue"))
        Console.WriteLine("Process ID: {0}", outParams("processId"))

        Return 0
    End Function
End Class
```

Requirements

Platforms: Windows 98, Windows NT 4.0,
Windows Millennium Edition, Windows 2000,
Windows XP Home Edition, Windows XP Professional,
Windows .NET Server family

.NET Framework Security:
- Full trust for the immediate caller. This member cannot be used
by partially trusted code.

ManagementObject.InvokeMethod Method (ManagementOperationObserver, String, ManagementBaseObject, InvokeMethodOptions)

Invokes a method on the object, asynchronously.

```
[Visual Basic]
Overloads Public Sub InvokeMethod( _
    ByVal watcher As ManagementOperationObserver, _
    ByVal methodName As String, _
    ByVal inParameters As ManagementBaseObject, _
    ByVal options As InvokeMethodOptions _
)
[C#]
public void InvokeMethod(
    ManagementOperationObserver watcher,
    string methodName,
    ManagementBaseObject inParameters,
    InvokeMethodOptions options
);
[C++]
public: void InvokeMethod(
    ManagementOperationObserver* watcher,
    String* methodName,
    ManagementBaseObject* inParameters,
    InvokeMethodOptions* options
);
[JScript]
public function InvokeMethod(
    watcher : ManagementOperationObserver,
    methodName : String,
    inParameters : ManagementBaseObject,
    options : InvokeMethodOptions
);
```

Parameters

watcher
A **ManagementOperationObserver** used to handle the
asynchronous execution's progress and results.
methodName
The name of the method to be executed.
inParameters
A **ManagementBaseObject** containing the input parameters for
the method.
options
An **InvokeMethodOptions** containing additional options used to
execute the method.

Remarks

The method invokes the specified method execution and then
returns. Progress and results are reported through events on the
ManagementOperationObserver.

Requirements

Platforms: Windows 98, Windows NT 4.0,
Windows Millennium Edition, Windows 2000,
Windows XP Home Edition, Windows XP Professional,
Windows .NET Server family

.NET Framework Security:
- Full trust for the immediate caller. This member cannot be used
by partially trusted code.

ManagementObject.Put Method

Commits the changes to the object.

Overload List

Commits the changes to the object.

[Visual Basic] **Overloads Public Function Put() As ManagementPath**

[C#] **public ManagementPath Put();**

[C++] **public: ManagementPath* Put();**

[JScript] **public function Put() : ManagementPath;**

Commits the changes to the object, asynchronously.

[Visual Basic] **Overloads Public Sub Put(ManagementOperationObserver)**

[C#] **public void Put(ManagementOperationObserver);**

[C++] **public: void Put(ManagementOperationObserver*);**

[JScript] **public function Put(Management-OperationObserver);**

Commits the changes to the object.

[Visual Basic] **Overloads Public Function Put(PutOptions) As ManagementPath**

[C#] **public ManagementPath Put(PutOptions);**

[C++] **public: ManagementPath* Put(PutOptions*);**

[JScript] **public function Put(PutOptions) : ManagementPath;**

Commits the changes to the object asynchronously and using the specified options.

[Visual Basic] **Overloads Public Sub Put(Management-OperationObserver, PutOptions)**

[C#] **public void Put(ManagementOperationObserver, PutOptions);**

[C++] **public: void Put(ManagementOperationObserver*, PutOptions*);**

[JScript] **public function Put(ManagementOperation-Observer, PutOptions);**

ManagementObject.Put Method ()

Commits the changes to the object.

```
[Visual Basic]
Overloads Public Function Put() As ManagementPath
[C#]
public ManagementPath Put();
[C++]
public: ManagementPath* Put();
[JScript]
public function Put() : ManagementPath;
```

Return Value

A **ManagementPath** containing the path to the committed object.

Requirements

Platforms: Windows 98, Windows NT 4.0, Windows Millennium Edition, Windows 2000, Windows XP Home Edition, Windows XP Professional, Windows .NET Server family

.NET Framework Security:
- Full trust for the immediate caller. This member cannot be used by partially trusted code.

ManagementObject.Put Method (ManagementOperationObserver)

Commits the changes to the object, asynchronously.

```
[Visual Basic]
Overloads Public Sub Put( _
   ByVal watcher As ManagementOperationObserver _
)
[C#]
public void Put(
   ManagementOperationObserver watcher
);
[C++]
public: void Put(
   ManagementOperationObserver* watcher
);
[JScript]
public function Put(
   watcher : ManagementOperationObserver
);
```

Parameters

watcher

A **ManagementOperationObserver** used to handle the progress and results of the asynchronous operation.

Requirements

Platforms: Windows 98, Windows NT 4.0, Windows Millennium Edition, Windows 2000, Windows XP Home Edition, Windows XP Professional, Windows .NET Server family

.NET Framework Security:
- Full trust for the immediate caller. This member cannot be used by partially trusted code.

ManagementObject.Put Method (PutOptions)

Commits the changes to the object.

```
[Visual Basic]
Overloads Public Function Put( _
   ByVal options As PutOptions _
) As ManagementPath
[C#]
public ManagementPath Put(
   PutOptions options
);
[C++]
public: ManagementPath* Put(
   PutOptions* options
);
[JScript]
public function Put(
   options : PutOptions
) : ManagementPath;
```

Parameters

options

The options for how to commit the changes.

Return Value

A **ManagementPath** containing the path to the committed object.

Requirements

Platforms: Windows 98, Windows NT 4.0,
Windows Millennium Edition, Windows 2000,
Windows XP Home Edition, Windows XP Professional,
Windows .NET Server family

.NET Framework Security:

- Full trust for the immediate caller. This member cannot be used by partially trusted code.

ManagementObject.Put Method (ManagementOperationObserver, PutOptions)

Commits the changes to the object asynchronously and using the specified options.

```
[Visual Basic]
Overloads Public Sub Put( _
   ByVal watcher As ManagementOperationObserver, _
   ByVal options As PutOptions _
)
[C#]
public void Put(
   ManagementOperationObserver watcher,
   PutOptions options
);
[C++]
public: void Put(
   ManagementOperationObserver* watcher,
   PutOptions* options
);
[JScript]
public function Put(
   watcher : ManagementOperationObserver,
   options : PutOptions
);
```

Parameters

watcher
> A **ManagementOperationObserver** used to handle the progress and results of the asynchronous operation.

options
> A **PutOptions** used to specify additional options for the commit operation.

Requirements

Platforms: Windows 98, Windows NT 4.0,
Windows Millennium Edition, Windows 2000,
Windows XP Home Edition, Windows XP Professional,
Windows .NET Server family

.NET Framework Security:

- Full trust for the immediate caller. This member cannot be used by partially trusted code.

ManagementObject.ToString Method

Returns the full path of the object. This is an override of the default object implementation.

```
[Visual Basic]
Overrides Public Function ToString() As String
[C#]
public override string ToString();
[C++]
public: String* ToString();
[JScript]
public override function ToString() : String;
```

Return Value

The full path of the object.

Requirements

Platforms: Windows 98, Windows NT 4.0,
Windows Millennium Edition, Windows 2000,
Windows XP Home Edition, Windows XP Professional,
Windows .NET Server family

.NET Framework Security:

- Full trust for the immediate caller. This member cannot be used by partially trusted code.

ManagementObjectCollection Class

Represents different collections of management objects retrieved through WMI. The objects in this collection are of **ManagementBaseObject**-derived types, including **ManagementObject** and **ManagementClass**.

The collection can be the result of a WMI query executed through a **ManagementObjectSearcher** object, or an enumeration of management objects of a specified type retrieved through a **ManagementClass** representing that type. In addition, this can be a collection of management objects related in a specified way to a specific management object - in this case the collection would be retrieved through a method such as **GetRelated**.

The collection can be walked using the **ManagementObjectCollection.ManagementObjectEnumerator** and objects in it can be inspected or manipulated for various management tasks.

System.Object
  System.Management.ManagementObjectCollection

```
[Visual Basic]
Public Class ManagementObjectCollection
    Implements ICollection, IEnumerable, IDisposable
[C#]
public class ManagementObjectCollection : ICollection, IEnumerable,
    IDisposable
[C++]
public __gc class ManagementObjectCollection : public ICollection,
    IEnumerable, IDisposable
[JScript]
public class ManagementObjectCollection implements ICollection,
    IEnumerable, IDisposable
```

Thread Safety

Any public static (**Shared** in Visual Basic) members of this type are safe for multithreaded operations. Any instance members are not guaranteed to be thread safe.

Example

```
[C#]
using System;
using System.Management;

// This example demonstrates how to enumerate instances
 of a ManagementClass object.
class Sample_ManagementObjectCollection
{
    public static int Main(string[] args) {
        ManagementClass diskClass = new
ManagementClass("Win32_LogicalDisk");
        ManagementObjectCollection disks = diskClass.GetInstances();
        foreach (ManagementObject disk in disks) {
            Console.WriteLine("Disk = " + disk["deviceid"]);
        }
        return 0;
    }
}

[Visual Basic]
Imports System
Imports System.Management
```

```
' This example demonstrates how to enumerate instances
 of a ManagementClass object.
Class Sample_ManagementObjectCollection
    Overloads Public Shared Function Main(args() As String) As Integer
        Dim diskClass As New ManagementClass("Win32_LogicalDisk")
        Dim disks As ManagementObjectCollection =
diskClass.GetInstances()
        Dim disk As ManagementObject
        For Each disk In disks
            Console.WriteLine("Disk = " & disk("deviceid").ToString())
        Next disk
        Return 0
    End Function
End Class
```

Requirements

Namespace: System.Management

Platforms: Windows 98, Windows NT 4.0, Windows Millennium Edition, Windows 2000, Windows XP Home Edition, Windows XP Professional, Windows .NET Server family

Assembly: System.Management (in System.Management.dll)

ManagementObjectCollection.Count Property

Represents the number of objects in the collection.

```
[Visual Basic]
Public Overridable ReadOnly Property Count As Integer  Implements _
    ICollection.Count
[C#]
public virtual int Count {get;}
[C++]
public: __property virtual int get_Count();
[JScript]
public function get Count() : int;
```

Property Value

The number of objects in the collection.

Implements

ICollection.Count

Remarks

This property is very expensive - it requires that all members of the collection be enumerated.

Requirements

Platforms: Windows 98, Windows NT 4.0, Windows Millennium Edition, Windows 2000, Windows XP Home Edition, Windows XP Professional, Windows .NET Server family

.NET Framework Security:

- Full trust for the immediate caller. This member cannot be used by partially trusted code.

ManagementObjectCollection.IsSynchronized Property

Represents whether the object is synchronized.

```
[Visual Basic]
Public Overridable ReadOnly Property IsSynchronized As Boolean  _
    Implements ICollection.IsSynchronized
```

```
[C#]
public virtual bool IsSynchronized {get;}
[C++]
public: __property virtual bool get_IsSynchronized();
[JScript]
public function get IsSynchronized() : Boolean;
```

Property Value

true, if the object is synchronized; otherwise, **false**.

Implements

ICollection.IsSynchronized

Requirements

Platforms: Windows 98, Windows NT 4.0,
Windows Millennium Edition, Windows 2000,
Windows XP Home Edition, Windows XP Professional,
Windows .NET Server family

.NET Framework Security:

- Full trust for the immediate caller. This member cannot be used
  by partially trusted code.

ManagementObjectCollection.SyncRoot Property

Represents the object to be used for synchronization.

```
[Visual Basic]
Public Overridable ReadOnly Property SyncRoot As Object  Implements _
    ICollection.SyncRoot
[C#]
public virtual object SyncRoot {get;}
[C++]
public: __property virtual Object* get_SyncRoot();
[JScript]
public function get SyncRoot() : Object;
```

Property Value

The object to be used for synchronization.

Implements

ICollection.SyncRoot

Requirements

Platforms: Windows 98, Windows NT 4.0,
Windows Millennium Edition, Windows 2000,
Windows XP Home Edition, Windows XP Professional,
Windows .NET Server family

.NET Framework Security:

- Full trust for the immediate caller. This member cannot be used
  by partially trusted code.

ManagementObjectCollection.CopyTo Method

Copies the collection to an array.

Overload List

Copies the collection to an array.

[Visual Basic] **Overloads Public Overridable Sub
CopyTo(Array, Integer) Implements ICollection.CopyTo**

[C#] **public virtual void CopyTo(Array, int);**

[C++] **public: virtual void CopyTo(Array*, int);**

[JScript] **public function CopyTo(Array, int);**

Copies the items in the collection to a **ManagementBaseObject**
array.

[Visual Basic] **Overloads Public Sub
CopyTo(ManagementBaseObject(), Integer)**

[C#] **public void CopyTo(ManagementBaseObject[], int);**

[C++] **public: void CopyTo(ManagementBaseObject*[], int);**

[JScript] **public function CopyTo(ManagementBaseObject[],
int);**

ManagementObjectCollection.CopyTo Method (Array, Int32)

Copies the collection to an array.

```
[Visual Basic]
Overloads Public Overridable Sub CopyTo( _
    ByVal array As Array, _
    ByVal index As Integer _
) Implements ICollection.CopyTo
[C#]
public virtual void CopyTo(
    Array array,
    int index
);
[C++]
public: virtual void CopyTo(
    Array* array,
    int index
);
[JScript]
public function CopyTo(
    array : Array,
    index : int
);
```

Parameters

array
    An array to copy to.
index
    The index to start from.

Implements

ICollection.CopyTo

Requirements

Platforms: Windows 98, Windows NT 4.0,
Windows Millennium Edition, Windows 2000,
Windows XP Home Edition, Windows XP Professional,
Windows .NET Server family

.NET Framework Security:

- Full trust for the immediate caller. This member cannot be used
  by partially trusted code.

ManagementObjectCollection.CopyTo Method (ManagementBaseObject[], Int32)

Copies the items in the collection to a **ManagementBaseObject**
array.

```
[Visual Basic]
Overloads Public Sub CopyTo( _
    ByVal objectCollection() As ManagementBaseObject, _
    ByVal index As Integer _
)
```

```
[C#]
public void CopyTo(
   ManagementBaseObject[] objectCollection,
   int index
);
[C++]
public: void CopyTo(
   ManagementBaseObject* objectCollection[],
   int index
);
[JScript]
public function CopyTo(
   objectCollection : ManagementBaseObject[],
   index : int
);
```

Parameters

objectCollection
   The target array.
index
   The index to start from.

Requirements

Platforms: Windows 98, Windows NT 4.0,
Windows Millennium Edition, Windows 2000,
Windows XP Home Edition, Windows XP Professional,
Windows .NET Server family

.NET Framework Security:

- Full trust for the immediate caller. This member cannot be used
  by partially trusted code.

ManagementObjectCollection.Dispose Method

Releases resources associated with this object. After this method has
been called, an attempt to use this object will result in an
ObjectDisposedException being thrown.

```
[Visual Basic]
Public Overridable Sub Dispose() Implements IDisposable.Dispose
[C#]
public virtual void Dispose();
[C++]
public: virtual void Dispose();
[JScript]
public function Dispose();
```

Implements

IDisposable.Dispose

Requirements

Platforms: Windows 98, Windows NT 4.0,
Windows Millennium Edition, Windows 2000,
Windows XP Home Edition, Windows XP Professional,
Windows .NET Server family

.NET Framework Security:

- Full trust for the immediate caller. This member cannot be used
  by partially trusted code.

ManagementObjectCollection.Finalize Method

Disposes of resources the object is holding. This is the destructor for
the object.

[C#] In C#, finalizers are expressed using destructor syntax.

[C++] In C++, finalizers are expressed using destructor syntax.

```
[Visual Basic]
Overrides Protected Sub Finalize()
[C#]
~ManagementObjectCollection();
[C++]
~ManagementObjectCollection();
[JScript]
protected override function Finalize();
```

Requirements

Platforms: Windows 98, Windows NT 4.0,
Windows Millennium Edition, Windows 2000,
Windows XP Home Edition, Windows XP Professional,
Windows .NET Server family

.NET Framework Security:

- Full trust for the immediate caller. This member cannot be used
  by partially trusted code.

ManagementObjectCollection.GetEnumerator Method

Returns the enumerator for the collection.

```
[Visual Basic]
Public Function GetEnumerator() As ManagementObjectEnumerator
[C#]
public ManagementObjectEnumerator GetEnumerator();
[C++]
public: ManagementObjectEnumerator* GetEnumerator();
[JScript]
public function GetEnumerator() : ManagementObjectEnumerator;
```

Return Value

An **IEnumerator** that can be used to iterate through the collection.

Requirements

Platforms: Windows 98, Windows NT 4.0,
Windows Millennium Edition, Windows 2000,
Windows XP Home Edition, Windows XP Professional,
Windows .NET Server family

.NET Framework Security:

- Full trust for the immediate caller. This member cannot be used
  by partially trusted code.

ManagementObjectCollection.IEnumerable.GetEnumerator Method

This member supports the .NET Framework infrastructure and is not
intended to be used directly from your code.

```
[Visual Basic]
Private Function GetEnumerator() As IEnumerator Implements _
   IEnumerable.GetEnumerator
[C#]
IEnumerator IEnumerable.GetEnumerator();
[C++]
private: IEnumerator* IEnumerable::GetEnumerator();
[JScript]
private function IEnumerable.GetEnumerator() : IEnumerator;
```

ManagementObject-Collection.Management-ObjectEnumerator Class

Represents the enumerator on the collection.

System.Object
  System.Management.ManagementObjectCollection.Managem entObjectEnumerator

[Visual Basic]
```
Public Class ManagementObjectCollection.ManagementObjectEnumerator
   Implements IEnumerator, IDisposable
```
[C#]
```
public class ManagementObjectCollection.ManagementObjectEnumerator
   : IEnumerator, IDisposable
```
[C++]
```
public __gc class
   ManagementObjectCollection.ManagementObjectEnumerator : public
   IEnumerator, IDisposable
```
[JScript]
```
public class ManagementObjectCollection.ManagementObjectEnumerator
   implements IEnumerator, IDisposable
```

Thread Safety

Any public static (**Shared** in Visual Basic) members of this type are safe for multithreaded operations. Any instance members are not guaranteed to be thread safe.

Example

[C#]
```
using System;
using System.Management;

// This example demonstrates how to enumerate all logical disks
// using the ManagementObjectEnumerator object.
class Sample_ManagementObjectEnumerator
{
    public static int Main(string[] args) {
        ManagementClass diskClass = new
ManagementClass("Win32_LogicalDisk");
        ManagementObjectCollection disks = diskClass.GetInstances();
        ManagementObjectCollection.ManagementObjectEnumerator
disksEnumerator =
            disks.GetEnumerator();
        while(disksEnumerator.MoveNext()) {
            ManagementObject disk =
(ManagementObject)disksEnumerator.Current;
            Console.WriteLine("Disk found: " + disk["deviceid"]);
        }
        return 0;
    }
}
```

[Visual Basic]
```
Imports System
            Imports System.Management
            ' This sample demonstrates how to
enumerate all logical disks
            ' using ManagementObjectEnumerator object.
            Class Sample_ManagementObjectEnumerator
            Overloads Public Shared Function Main
(args() As String) As Integer
                Dim diskClass As New
ManagementClass("Win32_LogicalDisk")
                Dim disks As ManagementObjectCollection =
diskClass.GetInstances()
                Dim disksEnumerator As _
```

```
ManagementObjectCollection.ManagementObjectEnumerator =
            disks.GetEnumerator()
            While disksEnumerator.MoveNext()
            Dim disk As ManagementObject = _
            CType(disksEnumerator.Current, ManagementObject)
            Console.WriteLine("Disk found: " & disk("deviceid"))
            End While
            Return 0
            End Function
            End Class
```

Requirements

Namespace: System.Management

Platforms: Windows 98, Windows NT 4.0, Windows Millennium Edition, Windows 2000, Windows XP Home Edition, Windows XP Professional, Windows .NET Server family

Assembly: System.Management (in System.Management.dll)

ManagementObjectCollection.Management-ObjectEnumerator.Current Property

Returns the current object in the enumeration.

[Visual Basic]
```
Public ReadOnly Property Current As ManagementBaseObject
```
[C#]
```
public ManagementBaseObject Current {get;}
```
[C++]
```
public: __property ManagementBaseObject* get_Current();
```
[JScript]
```
public function get Current() : ManagementBaseObject;
```

Property Value

The current object in the enumeration.

Requirements

Platforms: Windows 98, Windows NT 4.0, Windows Millennium Edition, Windows 2000, Windows XP Home Edition, Windows XP Professional, Windows .NET Server family

.NET Framework Security:

- Full trust for the immediate caller. This member cannot be used by partially trusted code.

ManagementObjectCollection.Management-ObjectEnumerator.System.Collections.IEnumerator.Current Property

Note: This namespace, class, or member is supported only in version 1.1 of the .NET Framework.

[Visual Basic]
```
Private ReadOnly Property Current As Object Implements _
   IEnumerator.Current
```
[C#]
```
object IEnumerator.Current {get;}
```
[C++]
```
private: __property Object*
   System::Collections::IEnumerator::get_Current();
```
[JScript]
```
private function get IEnumerator.Current() : Object;
```

Implements

IEnumerator.Current

Requirements

Platforms: Windows 98, Windows NT 4.0,
Windows Millennium Edition, Windows 2000,
Windows XP Home Edition, Windows XP Professional,
Windows .NET Server family

.NET Framework Security:

- Full trust for the immediate caller. This member cannot be used by partially trusted code.

ManagementObjectCollection.Management-ObjectEnumerator.Dispose Method

Releases resources associated with this object. After this method has been called, an attempt to use this object will result in an ObjectDisposedException being thrown.

```
[Visual Basic]
Public Overridable Sub Dispose() Implements IDisposable.Dispose
[C#]
public virtual void Dispose();
[C++]
public: virtual void Dispose();
[JScript]
public function Dispose();
```

Implements

IDisposable.Dispose

Requirements

Platforms: Windows 98, Windows NT 4.0,
Windows Millennium Edition, Windows 2000,
Windows XP Home Edition, Windows XP Professional,
Windows .NET Server family

.NET Framework Security:

- Full trust for the immediate caller. This member cannot be used by partially trusted code.

ManagementObjectCollection.Management-ObjectEnumerator.Finalize Method

Disposes of resources the object is holding. This is the destructor for the object.

[C#] In C#, finalizers are expressed using destructor syntax.

[C++] In C++, finalizers are expressed using destructor syntax.

```
[Visual Basic]
Overrides Protected Sub Finalize()
[C#]
~ManagementObjectEnumerator();
[C++]
~ManagementObjectEnumerator();
[JScript]
protected override function Finalize();
```

Requirements

Platforms: Windows 98, Windows NT 4.0,
Windows Millennium Edition, Windows 2000,
Windows XP Home Edition, Windows XP Professional,
Windows .NET Server family

.NET Framework Security:

- Full trust for the immediate caller. This member cannot be used by partially trusted code.

ManagementObjectCollection.Management-ObjectEnumerator.MoveNext Method

Indicates whether the enumerator has moved to the next object in the enumeration.

```
[Visual Basic]
Public Overridable Function MoveNext() As Boolean Implements _
   IEnumerator.MoveNext
[C#]
public virtual bool MoveNext();
[C++]
public: virtual bool MoveNext();
[JScript]
public function MoveNext() : Boolean;
```

Return Value

true, if the enumerator was successfully advanced to the next element; **false** if the enumerator has passed the end of the collection.

Implements

IEnumerator.MoveNext

Requirements

Platforms: Windows 98, Windows NT 4.0,
Windows Millennium Edition, Windows 2000,
Windows XP Home Edition, Windows XP Professional,
Windows .NET Server family

.NET Framework Security:

- Full trust for the immediate caller. This member cannot be used by partially trusted code.

ManagementObjectCollection.Management-ObjectEnumerator.Reset Method

Resets the enumerator to the beginning of the collection.

```
[Visual Basic]
Public Overridable Sub Reset() Implements IEnumerator.Reset
[C#]
public virtual void Reset();
[C++]
public: virtual void Reset();
[JScript]
public function Reset();
```

Implements

IEnumerator.Reset

Requirements

Platforms: Windows 98, Windows NT 4.0,
Windows Millennium Edition, Windows 2000,
Windows XP Home Edition, Windows XP Professional,
Windows .NET Server family

.NET Framework Security:

- Full trust for the immediate caller. This member cannot be used by partially trusted code.

ManagementObjectSearcher Class

Retrieves a collection of management objects based on a specified query.

This class is one of the more commonly used entry points to retrieving management information. For example, it can be used to enumerate all disk drives, network adapters, processes and many more management objects on a system, or to query for all network connections that are up, services that are paused etc.

When instantiated, an instance of this class takes as input a WMI query represented in an **ObjectQuery** or it's derivatives, and optionally a **ManagementScope** representing the WMI namespace to execute the query in. It can also take additional advanced options in an **EnumerationOptions** object. When the Get() method on this object is invoked, the ManagementObjectSearcher executes the given query in the specified scope and returns a collection of management objects that match the query in a **ManagementObjectCollection**.

System.Object
  System.MarshalByRefObject
    System.ComponentModel.Component
      System.Management.ManagementObjectSearcher

```
[Visual Basic]
Public Class ManagementObjectSearcher
    Inherits Component
[C#]
public class ManagementObjectSearcher : Component
[C++]
public __gc class ManagementObjectSearcher : public Component
[JScript]
public class ManagementObjectSearcher extends Component
```

Thread Safety

Any public static (**Shared** in Visual Basic) members of this type are safe for multithreaded operations. Any instance members are not guaranteed to be thread safe.

Example

```
[C#]
using System;
using System.Management;

// This sample demonstrates perform a query using
// ManagementObjectSearcher object.
class Sample_ManagementObjectSearcher
{
    public static int Main(string[] args) {
        ManagementObjectSearcher searcher = new
            ManagementObjectSearcher("select * from win32_share");
        foreach (ManagementObject share in searcher.Get()) {
            Console.WriteLine("Share = " + share["Name"]);
        }
        return 0;
    }
}
```

```
[Visual Basic]
Imports System
Imports System.Management

' This sample demonstrates perform a query using
' ManagementObjectSearcher object.
```

```
Class Sample_ManagementObjectSearcher
    Overloads Public Shared Function Main(args() As String) As Integer
        Dim searcher As New ManagementObjectSearcher          ⌐
("SELECT * FROM Win32_Share")
        Dim share As ManagementObject
        For Each share In searcher.Get()
            Console.WriteLine("Share = " & share("Name").ToString())
        Next share
        Return 0
    End Function
End Class
```

Requirements

Namespace: System.Management

Platforms: Windows 98, Windows NT 4.0, Windows Millennium Edition, Windows 2000, Windows XP Home Edition, Windows XP Professional, Windows .NET Server family

Assembly: System.Management (in System.Management.dll)

ManagementObjectSearcher Constructor

Initializes a new instance of the **ManagementObjectSearcher** class.

Overload List

Initializes a new instance of the **ManagementObjectSearcher** class. After some properties on this object are set, the object can be used to invoke a query for management information. This is the default constructor.

  [Visual Basic] **Public Sub New()**

  [C#] **public ManagementObjectSearcher();**

  [C++] **public: ManagementObjectSearcher();**

  [JScript] **public function ManagementObjectSearcher();**

Initializes a new instance of the **ManagementObjectSearcher** class used to invoke the specified query for management information.

  [Visual Basic] **Public Sub New(ObjectQuery)**

  [C#] **public ManagementObjectSearcher(ObjectQuery);**

  [C++] **public: ManagementObjectSearcher(ObjectQuery*);**

  [JScript] **public function ManagementObject-Searcher(ObjectQuery);**

Initializes a new instance of the **ManagementObjectSearcher** class used to invoke the specified query for management information.

  [Visual Basic] **Public Sub New(String)**

  [C#] **public ManagementObjectSearcher(string);**

  [C++] **public: ManagementObjectSearcher(String*);**

  [JScript] **public function ManagementObject-Searcher(String);**

Initializes a new instance of the **ManagementObjectSearcher** class used to invoke the specified query in the specified scope.

  [Visual Basic] **Public Sub New(ManagementScope, ObjectQuery)**

  [C#] **public ManagementObjectSearcher(ManagementScope, ObjectQuery);**

  [C++] **public: ManagementObject-Searcher(ManagementScope*, ObjectQuery*);**

  [JScript] **public function ManagementObject-Searcher(ManagementScope, ObjectQuery);**

Initializes a new instance of the **ManagementObjectSearcher** class used to invoke the specified query in the specified scope.

> [Visual Basic] **Public Sub New(String, String)**
>
> [C#] **public ManagementObjectSearcher(string, string);**
>
> [C++] **public: ManagementObjectSearcher(String*, String*);**
>
> [JScript] **public function ManagementObjectSearcher(String, String);**

Initializes a new instance of the **ManagementObjectSearcher** class to be used to invoke the specified query in the specified scope, with the specified options.

> [Visual Basic] **Public Sub New(ManagementScope, ObjectQuery, EnumerationOptions)**
>
> [C#] **public ManagementObjectSearcher(ManagementScope, ObjectQuery, EnumerationOptions);**
>
> [C++] **public: ManagementObjectSearcher(ManagementScope*, ObjectQuery*, EnumerationOptions*);**
>
> [JScript] **public function ManagementObjectSearcher(ManagementScope, ObjectQuery, EnumerationOptions);**

Initializes a new instance of the **ManagementObjectSearcher** class used to invoke the specified query, in the specified scope, and with the specified options.

> [Visual Basic] **Public Sub New(String, String, EnumerationOptions)**
>
> [C#] **public ManagementObjectSearcher(string, string, EnumerationOptions);**
>
> [C++] **public: ManagementObjectSearcher(String*, String*, EnumerationOptions*);**
>
> [JScript] **public function ManagementObjectSearcher(String, String, EnumerationOptions);**

Example

> [Visual Basic, C#] **Note** This example shows how to use one of the overloaded versions of the **ManagementObjectSearcher** constructor. For other examples that might be available, see the individual overload topics.

```
[C#]
ManagementObjectSearcher s = new ManagementObjectSearcher(
    "root\\MyApp",
    "SELECT * FROM MyClass",
    new EnumerationOptions(null, InfiniteTimeout, 1, true,
false, true);
```

```
[Visual Basic]
Dim s As New ManagementObjectSearcher( _
    "root\MyApp", _
    "SELECT * FROM MyClass", _
    New EnumerationOptions(Null, InfiniteTimeout, 1, True, False, True)
```

ManagementObjectSearcher Constructor ( )

Initializes a new instance of the **ManagementObjectSearcher** class. After some properties on this object are set, the object can be used to invoke a query for management information. This is the default constructor.

```
[Visual Basic]
Public Sub New()
[C#]
public ManagementObjectSearcher();
```

```
[C++]
public: ManagementObjectSearcher();
[JScript]
public function ManagementObjectSearcher();
```

Example

```
[C#]
ManagementObjectSearcher s = new ManagementObjectSearcher();
```

```
[Visual Basic]
Dim s As New ManagementObjectSearcher()
```

Requirements

Platforms: Windows 98, Windows NT 4.0, Windows Millennium Edition, Windows 2000, Windows XP Home Edition, Windows XP Professional, Windows .NET Server family

.NET Framework Security:

* Full trust for the immediate caller. This member cannot be used by partially trusted code.

ManagementObjectSearcher Constructor (ObjectQuery)

Initializes a new instance of the **ManagementObjectSearcher** class used to invoke the specified query for management information.

```
[Visual Basic]
Public Sub New( _
    ByVal query As ObjectQuery _
)
[C#]
public ManagementObjectSearcher(
    ObjectQuery query
);
[C++]
public: ManagementObjectSearcher(
    ObjectQuery* query
);
[JScript]
public function ManagementObjectSearcher(
    query : ObjectQuery
);
```

Parameters

query
> An **ObjectQuery** representing the query to be invoked by the searcher.

Example

```
[C#]
SelectQuery q = new SelectQuery("Win32_Service", "State='Running'");
ManagementObjectSearcher s = new ManagementObjectSearcher(q);
```

```
[Visual Basic]
Dim q As New SelectQuery("Win32_Service", "State=""Running""")
Dim s As New ManagementObjectSearcher(q)
```

Requirements

Platforms: Windows 98, Windows NT 4.0, Windows Millennium Edition, Windows 2000, Windows XP Home Edition, Windows XP Professional, Windows .NET Server family

.NET Framework Security:

- Full trust for the immediate caller. This member cannot be used by partially trusted code.

ManagementObjectSearcher Constructor (String)

Initializes a new instance of the **ManagementObjectSearcher** class used to invoke the specified query for management information.

```
[Visual Basic]
Public Sub New( _
   ByVal queryString As String _
)
[C#]
public ManagementObjectSearcher(
   string queryString
);
[C++]
public: ManagementObjectSearcher(
   String* queryString
);
[JScript]
public function ManagementObjectSearcher(
   queryString : String
);
```

Parameters

queryString
   The WMI query to be invoked by the object.

Example

```
[C#]
ManagementObjectSearcher s =
   new ManagementObjectSearcher("SELECT * FROM Win32_Service");
```

```
[Visual Basic]
Dim s As New ManagementObjectSearcher("SELECT * FROM Win32_Service")
```

Requirements

Platforms: Windows 98, Windows NT 4.0, Windows Millennium Edition, Windows 2000, Windows XP Home Edition, Windows XP Professional, Windows .NET Server family

.NET Framework Security:

- Full trust for the immediate caller. This member cannot be used by partially trusted code.

ManagementObjectSearcher Constructor (ManagementScope, ObjectQuery)

Initializes a new instance of the **ManagementObjectSearcher** class used to invoke the specified query in the specified scope.

```
[Visual Basic]
Public Sub New( _
   ByVal scope As ManagementScope, _
   ByVal query As ObjectQuery _
)
[C#]
public ManagementObjectSearcher(
   ManagementScope scope,
   ObjectQuery query
);
```

```
[C++]
public: ManagementObjectSearcher(
   ManagementScope* scope,
   ObjectQuery* query
);
[JScript]
public function ManagementObjectSearcher(
   scope : ManagementScope,
   query : ObjectQuery
);
```

Parameters

scope
   A **ManagementScope** representing the scope in which to invoke the query.
query
   An **ObjectQuery** representing the query to be invoked.

Remarks

If no scope is specified, the default scope (**DefaultPath**) is used.

Example

```
[C#]
ManagementScope myScope = new ManagementScope("root\\MyApp");
SelectQuery q = new SelectQuery("Win32_Environment", "User=<system>");
ManagementObjectSearcher s = new ManagementObjectSearcher(myScope,q);
```

```
[Visual Basic]
Dim myScope As New ManagementScope("root\MyApp")
Dim q As New SelectQuery("Win32_Environment", "User=<system>")
Dim s As New ManagementObjectSearcher(myScope,q)
```

Requirements

Platforms: Windows 98, Windows NT 4.0, Windows Millennium Edition, Windows 2000, Windows XP Home Edition, Windows XP Professional, Windows .NET Server family

.NET Framework Security:

- Full trust for the immediate caller. This member cannot be used by partially trusted code.

ManagementObjectSearcher Constructor (String, String)

Initializes a new instance of the **ManagementObjectSearcher** class used to invoke the specified query in the specified scope.

```
[Visual Basic]
Public Sub New( _
   ByVal scope As String, _
   ByVal queryString As String _
)
[C#]
public ManagementObjectSearcher(
   string scope,
   string queryString
);
[C++]
public: ManagementObjectSearcher(
   String* scope,
   String* queryString
);
```

```
[JScript]
public function ManagementObjectSearcher(
    scope : String,
    queryString : String
);
```

Parameters

scope
    The scope in which to query.
queryString
    The query to be invoked.

Remarks

If no scope is specified, the default scope (**DefaultPath**) is used.

Example

```
[C#]
ManagementObjectSearcher s = new ManagementObjectSearcher(
                               "root\\MyApp",
                               "SELECT * FROM
MyClass WHERE MyProp=5");

[Visual Basic]
Dim s As New ManagementObjectSearcher( _
                               "root\MyApp", _
                               "SELECT *
FROM MyClass WHERE MyProp=5")
```

Requirements

Platforms: Windows 98, Windows NT 4.0,
Windows Millennium Edition, Windows 2000,
Windows XP Home Edition, Windows XP Professional,
Windows .NET Server family

.NET Framework Security:
•   Full trust for the immediate caller. This member cannot be used
    by partially trusted code.

ManagementObjectSearcher Constructor (ManagementScope, ObjectQuery, EnumerationOptions)

Initializes a new instance of the **ManagementObjectSearcher** class
to be used to invoke the specified query in the specified scope, with
the specified options.

```
[Visual Basic]
Public Sub New( _
    ByVal scope As ManagementScope, _
    ByVal query As ObjectQuery, _
    ByVal options As EnumerationOptions _
)
[C#]
public ManagementObjectSearcher(
    ManagementScope scope,
    ObjectQuery query,
    EnumerationOptions options
);
[C++]
public: ManagementObjectSearcher(
    ManagementScope* scope,
    ObjectQuery* query,
    EnumerationOptions* options
);
```

```
[JScript]
public function ManagementObjectSearcher(
    scope : ManagementScope,
    query : ObjectQuery,
    options : EnumerationOptions
);
```

Parameters

scope
    A **ManagementScope** specifying the scope of the query
query
    An **ObjectQuery** specifying the query to be invoked
options
    An **EnumerationOptions** specifying additional options to be
    used for the query.

Example

```
[C#]
ManagementScope scope = new ManagementScope("root\\MyApp");
SelectQuery q = new SelectQuery("SELECT * FROM MyClass");
EnumerationOptions o = new EnumerationOptions(null,
InfiniteTimeout, 1, true, false, true);
ManagementObjectSearcher s = new ManagementObjectSearcher(scope, q, o);

[Visual Basic]
Dim scope As New ManagementScope("root\MyApp")
Dim q As New SelectQuery("SELECT * FROM MyClass")
Dim o As New EnumerationOptions(Null, InfiniteTimeout, 1,
True, False, True)
Dim s As New ManagementObjectSearcher(scope, q, o)
```

Requirements

Platforms: Windows 98, Windows NT 4.0,
Windows Millennium Edition, Windows 2000,
Windows XP Home Edition, Windows XP Professional,
Windows .NET Server family

.NET Framework Security:
•   Full trust for the immediate caller. This member cannot be used
    by partially trusted code.

ManagementObjectSearcher Constructor (String, String, EnumerationOptions)

Initializes a new instance of the **ManagementObjectSearcher** class
used to invoke the specified query, in the specified scope, and with
the specified options.

```
[Visual Basic]
Public Sub New( _
    ByVal scope As String, _
    ByVal queryString As String, _
    ByVal options As EnumerationOptions _
)
[C#]
public ManagementObjectSearcher(
    string scope,
    string queryString,
    EnumerationOptions options
);
```

```
[C++]
public: ManagementObjectSearcher(
    String* scope,
    String* queryString,
    EnumerationOptions* options
);
[JScript]
public function ManagementObjectSearcher(
    scope : String,
    queryString : String,
    options : EnumerationOptions
);
```

Parameters

scope

The scope in which the query should be invoked.

queryString

The query to be invoked.

options

An **EnumerationOptions** specifying additional options for the query.

Example

```
[C#]
ManagementObjectSearcher s = new ManagementObjectSearcher(
    "root\\MyApp",
    "SELECT * FROM MyClass",
    new EnumerationOptions(null, InfiniteTimeout, 1,
true, false, true);
```

```
[Visual Basic]
Dim s As New ManagementObjectSearcher( _
    "root\MyApp", _
    "SELECT * FROM MyClass", _
    New EnumerationOptions(Null, InfiniteTimeout, 1,
True, False, True)
```

Requirements

Platforms: Windows 98, Windows NT 4.0,
Windows Millennium Edition, Windows 2000,
Windows XP Home Edition, Windows XP Professional,
Windows .NET Server family

.NET Framework Security:

- Full trust for the immediate caller. This member cannot be used by partially trusted code.

ManagementObjectSearcher.Options Property

Gets or sets the options for how to search for objects.

```
[Visual Basic]
Public Property Options As EnumerationOptions
[C#]
public EnumerationOptions Options {get; set;}
[C++]
public: __property EnumerationOptions* get_Options();
public: __property void set_Options(EnumerationOptions*);
[JScript]
public function get Options() : EnumerationOptions;
public function set Options(EnumerationOptions);
```

Property Value

The options for how to search for objects.

Requirements

Platforms: Windows 98, Windows NT 4.0,
Windows Millennium Edition, Windows 2000,
Windows XP Home Edition, Windows XP Professional,
Windows .NET Server family

.NET Framework Security:

- Full trust for the immediate caller. This member cannot be used by partially trusted code.

ManagementObjectSearcher.Query Property

Gets or sets the query to be invoked in the searcher (that is, the criteria to be applied to the search for management objects).

```
[Visual Basic]
Public Property Query As ObjectQuery
[C#]
public ObjectQuery Query {get; set;}
[C++]
public: __property ObjectQuery* get_Query();
public: __property void set_Query(ObjectQuery*);
[JScript]
public function get Query() : ObjectQuery;
public function set Query(ObjectQuery);
```

Property Value

The criteria to apply to the query.

Remarks

When the value of this property is changed, the **ManagementObjectSearcher** is reset to use the new query.

Requirements

Platforms: Windows 98, Windows NT 4.0,
Windows Millennium Edition, Windows 2000,
Windows XP Home Edition, Windows XP Professional,
Windows .NET Server family

.NET Framework Security:

- Full trust for the immediate caller. This member cannot be used by partially trusted code.

ManagementObjectSearcher.Scope Property

Gets or sets the scope in which to look for objects (the scope represents a WMI namespace).

```
[Visual Basic]
Public Property Scope As ManagementScope
[C#]
public ManagementScope Scope {get; set;}
[C++]
public: __property ManagementScope* get_Scope();
public: __property void set_Scope(ManagementScope*);
[JScript]
public function get Scope() : ManagementScope;
public function set Scope(ManagementScope);
```

Property Value

The scope (namespace) in which to look for objects.

Remarks

When the value of this property is changed, the **ManagementObjectSearcher** is re-bound to the new scope.

Example

[C#]
```
ManagementObjectSearcher s = new ManagementObjectSearcher();
s.Scope = "root\\MyApp";
```

[Visual Basic]
```
Dim s As New ManagementObjectSearcher()
s.Scope = "root\MyApp"
```

Requirements

Platforms: Windows 98, Windows NT 4.0,
Windows Millennium Edition, Windows 2000,
Windows XP Home Edition, Windows XP Professional,
Windows .NET Server family

.NET Framework Security:

- Full trust for the immediate caller. This member cannot be used by partially trusted code.

ManagementObjectSearcher.Get Method

Invokes the specified WMI query and returns the resulting collection.

Overload List

Invokes the specified WMI query and returns the resulting collection.

> [Visual Basic] **Overloads Public Function Get() As ManagementObjectCollection**
>
> [C#] **public ManagementObjectCollection Get();**
>
> [C++] **public: ManagementObjectCollection* Get();**
>
> [JScript] **public function Get() : Management-ObjectCollection;**

Invokes the WMI query, asynchronously, and binds to a watcher to deliver the results.

> [Visual Basic] **Overloads Public Sub Get(Management-OperationObserver)**
>
> [C#] **public void Get(ManagementOperationObserver);**
>
> [C++] **public: void Get(ManagementOperationObserver*);**
>
> [JScript] **public function Get(Management-OperationObserver);**

ManagementObjectSearcher.Get Method ()

Invokes the specified WMI query and returns the resulting collection.

```
[Visual Basic]
Overloads Public Function Get() As ManagementObjectCollection
[C#]
public ManagementObjectCollection Get();
[C++]
public: ManagementObjectCollection* Get();
[JScript]
public function Get() : ManagementObjectCollection;
```

Return Value

A **ManagementObjectCollection** containing the objects that match the specified query.

Requirements

Platforms: Windows 98, Windows NT 4.0,
Windows Millennium Edition, Windows 2000,
Windows XP Home Edition, Windows XP Professional,
Windows .NET Server family

.NET Framework Security:

- Full trust for the immediate caller. This member cannot be used by partially trusted code.

ManagementObjectSearcher.Get Method (ManagementOperationObserver)

Invokes the WMI query, asynchronously, and binds to a watcher to deliver the results.

```
[Visual Basic]
Overloads Public Sub Get( _
   ByVal watcher As ManagementOperationObserver _
)
[C#]
public void Get(
   ManagementOperationObserver watcher
);
[C++]
public: void Get(
   ManagementOperationObserver* watcher
);
[JScript]
public function Get(
   watcher : ManagementOperationObserver
);
```

Parameters

watcher
> The watcher that raises events triggered by the operation.

Requirements

Platforms: Windows 98, Windows NT 4.0,
Windows Millennium Edition, Windows 2000,
Windows XP Home Edition, Windows XP Professional,
Windows .NET Server family

.NET Framework Security:

- Full trust for the immediate caller. This member cannot be used by partially trusted code.

ManagementOperation-Observer Class

Used to manage asynchronous operations and handle management information and events received asynchronously.

System.Object
  System.Management.ManagementOperationObserver

```
[Visual Basic]
Public Class ManagementOperationObserver
[C#]
public class ManagementOperationObserver
[C++]
public __gc class ManagementOperationObserver
[JScript]
public class ManagementOperationObserver
```

Thread Safety

Any public static (**Shared** in Visual Basic) members of this type are safe for multithreaded operations. Any instance members are not guaranteed to be thread safe.

Example

```csharp
[C#]
using System;
using System.Management;

// This sample demonstrates how to read a
ManagementObject asychronously
// using the ManagementOperationObserver object.

class Sample_ManagementOperationObserver {
    public static int Main(string[] args) {

        //Set up a handler for the asynchronous callback
        ManagementOperationObserver observer = new
ManagementOperationObserver();
        MyHandler completionHandler = new MyHandler();
        observer.Completed += new
CompletedEventHandler(completionHandler.Done);

        //Invoke the asynchronous read of the object
        ManagementObject disk = new
ManagementObject("Win32_logicaldisk='C:'");
        disk.Get(observer);

        //For the purpose of this sample, we keep the main
        // thread alive until the asynchronous operation is completed.

        while (!completionHandler.IsComplete) {
            System.Threading.Thread.Sleep(500);
        }

        Console.WriteLine("Size= " + disk["Size"] + " bytes.");

        return 0;
    }

    public class MyHandler
    {
        private bool isComplete = false;

        public void Done(object sender, CompletedEventArgs e) {
            isComplete = true;
        }

        public bool IsComplete {
            get {
                return isComplete;
```

```vbnet
                }
            }
        }
}

[Visual Basic]
Imports System
Imports System.Management

' This sample demonstrates how to read a ManagementObject asychronously
' using the ManagementOperationObserver object.

Class Sample_ManagementOperationObserver
    Overloads Public Shared Function Main(args() As String) As Integer

        'Set up a handler for the asynchronous callback
        Dim observer As New ManagementOperationObserver()
        Dim completionHandler As New MyHandler()
        AddHandler observer.Completed, AddressOf completionHandler.Done

        ' Invoke the object read asynchronously
        Dim disk As New ManagementObject("Win32_logicaldisk='C:'")
        disk.Get(observer)

        ' For the purpose of this sample, we keep the main
        ' thread alive until the asynchronous operation is finished.
        While Not completionHandler.IsComplete Then
            System.Threading.Thread.Sleep(500)
        End While

        Console.WriteLine("Size = " + disk("Size").ToString()
& " bytes")

        Return 0
    End Function

    Public Class MyHandler
        Private _isComplete As Boolean = False

        Public Sub Done(sender As Object, e As CompletedEventArgs)
            _isComplete = True
        End Sub 'Done

        Public ReadOnly Property IsComplete() As Boolean
            Get
                Return _isComplete
            End Get
        End Property
    End Class
End Class
```

Requirements

Namespace: System.Management

Platforms: Windows 98, Windows NT 4.0, Windows Millennium Edition, Windows 2000, Windows XP Home Edition, Windows XP Professional, Windows .NET Server family

Assembly: System.Management (in System.Management.dll)

ManagementOperationObserver Constructor

Initializes a new instance of the **ManagementOperationObserver** class. This is the default constructor.

```
[Visual Basic]
Public Sub New()
[C#]
public ManagementOperationObserver();
```

```
[C++]
public: ManagementOperationObserver();
[JScript]
public function ManagementOperationObserver();
```

Requirements

Platforms: Windows 98, Windows NT 4.0,
Windows Millennium Edition, Windows 2000,
Windows XP Home Edition, Windows XP Professional,
Windows .NET Server family

.NET Framework Security:
- Full trust for the immediate caller. This member cannot be used by partially trusted code.

ManagementOperationObserver.Cancel Method

Cancels all outstanding operations.

```
[Visual Basic]
Public Sub Cancel()
[C#]
public void Cancel();
[C++]
public: void Cancel();
[JScript]
public function Cancel();
```

Requirements

Platforms: Windows 98, Windows NT 4.0,
Windows Millennium Edition, Windows 2000,
Windows XP Home Edition, Windows XP Professional,
Windows .NET Server family

.NET Framework Security:
- Full trust for the immediate caller. This member cannot be used by partially trusted code.

ManagementOperationObserver.Completed Event

Occurs when an operation has completed.

```
[Visual Basic]
Public Event Completed As CompletedEventHandler
[C#]
public event CompletedEventHandler Completed;
[C++]
public: _event CompletedEventHandler* Completed;
```

[JScript] In JScript, you can handle the events defined by a class, but you cannot define your own.

Event Data

The event handler receives an argument of type **CompletedEventArgs** containing data related to this event. The following **CompletedEventArgs** properties provide information specific to this event.

Property	Description
Context (inherited from **ManagementEvent-Args**)	Gets the operation context echoed back from the operation that triggered the event.

Property	Description
Status	Gets the completion status of the operation.
StatusObject	Gets or sets additional status information within a WMI object. This may be null.

Requirements

Platforms: Windows 98, Windows NT 4.0,
Windows Millennium Edition, Windows 2000,
Windows XP Home Edition, Windows XP Professional,
Windows .NET Server family

.NET Framework Security:
- Full trust for the immediate caller. This member cannot be used by partially trusted code.

ManagementOperationObserver.ObjectPut Event

Occurs when an object has been successfully committed.

```
[Visual Basic]
Public Event ObjectPut As ObjectPutEventHandler
[C#]
public event ObjectPutEventHandler ObjectPut;
[C++]
public: _event ObjectPutEventHandler* ObjectPut;
```

[JScript] In JScript, you can handle the events defined by a class, but you cannot define your own.

Event Data

The event handler receives an argument of type **ObjectPutEventArgs** containing data related to this event. The following **ObjectPutEventArgs** properties provide information specific to this event.

Property	Description
Context (inherited from **ManagementEvent-Args**)	Gets the operation context echoed back from the operation that triggered the event.
Path	Gets the identity of the object that has been put.

Requirements

Platforms: Windows 98, Windows NT 4.0,
Windows Millennium Edition, Windows 2000,
Windows XP Home Edition, Windows XP Professional,
Windows .NET Server family

.NET Framework Security:
- Full trust for the immediate caller. This member cannot be used by partially trusted code.

ManagementOperationObserver.ObjectReady Event

Occurs when a new object is available.

```
[Visual Basic]
Public Event ObjectReady As ObjectReadyEventHandler
[C#]
public event ObjectReadyEventHandler ObjectReady;
```

```
[C++]
public: _event ObjectReadyEventHandler* ObjectReady;
```

[JScript] In JScript, you can handle the events defined by a class, but you cannot define your own.

Event Data

The event handler receives an argument of type **ObjectReadyEventArgs** containing data related to this event. The following **ObjectReadyEventArgs** properties provide information specific to this event.

Property	Description
Context (inherited from **ManagementEvent-Args**)	Gets the operation context echoed back from the operation that triggered the event.
NewObject	Gets the newly-returned object.

Requirements

Platforms: Windows 98, Windows NT 4.0, Windows Millennium Edition, Windows 2000, Windows XP Home Edition, Windows XP Professional, Windows .NET Server family

.NET Framework Security:
* Full trust for the immediate caller. This member cannot be used by partially trusted code.

ManagementOperationObserver.Progress Event

Occurs to indicate the progress of an ongoing operation.

```
[Visual Basic]
Public Event Progress As ProgressEventHandler
[C#]
public event ProgressEventHandler Progress;
[C++]
public: _event ProgressEventHandler* Progress;
```

[JScript] In JScript, you can handle the events defined by a class, but you cannot define your own.

Event Data

The event handler receives an argument of type **ProgressEventArgs** containing data related to this event. The following **ProgressEventArgs** properties provide information specific to this event.

Property	Description
Context (inherited from **ManagementEvent-Args**)	Gets the operation context echoed back from the operation that triggered the event.
Current	Gets the current amount of work done by the operation. This is always less than or equal to **UpperBound**.
Message	Gets or sets optional additional information regarding the operation's progress.
UpperBound	Gets the total amount of work required to be done by the operation.

Requirements

Platforms: Windows 98, Windows NT 4.0, Windows Millennium Edition, Windows 2000, Windows XP Home Edition, Windows XP Professional, Windows .NET Server family

.NET Framework Security:
* Full trust for the immediate caller. This member cannot be used by partially trusted code.

ManagementOptions Class

Provides an abstract base class for all options objects.

System.Object
  System.Management.ManagementOptions
    Derived classes

[Visual Basic]
```
MustInherit Public Class ManagementOptions
    Implements ICloneable
```
[C#]
```
public abstract class ManagementOptions : ICloneable
```
[C++]
```
public __gc __abstract class ManagementOptions : public ICloneable
```
[JScript]
```
public abstract class ManagementOptions implements ICloneable
```

Thread Safety

Any public static (**Shared** in Visual Basic) members of this type are safe for multithreaded operations. Any instance members are not guaranteed to be thread safe.

Requirements

Namespace: System.Management

Platforms: Windows 98, Windows NT 4.0, Windows Millennium Edition, Windows 2000, Windows XP Home Edition, Windows XP Professional, Windows .NET Server family

Assembly: System.Management (in System.Management.dll)

ManagementOptions.InfiniteTimeout Field

Specifies an infinite timeout.

[Visual Basic]
```
Public Shared ReadOnly InfiniteTimeout As TimeSpan
```
[C#]
```
public static readonly TimeSpan InfiniteTimeout;
```
[C++]
```
public: static TimeSpan InfiniteTimeout;
```
[JScript]
```
public static var InfiniteTimeout : TimeSpan;
```

Requirements

Platforms: Windows 98, Windows NT 4.0, Windows Millennium Edition, Windows 2000, Windows XP Home Edition, Windows XP Professional, Windows .NET Server family

ManagementOptions.Context Property

Gets or sets a WMI context object. This is a name-value pairs list to be passed through to a WMI provider that supports context information for customized operation.

[Visual Basic]
```
Public Property Context As ManagementNamedValueCollection
```
[C#]
```
public ManagementNamedValueCollection Context {get; set;}
```
[C++]
```
public: __property ManagementNamedValueCollection* get_Context();
public: __property void set_Context(ManagementNamedValueCollection*);
```
[JScript]
```
public function get Context() : ManagementNamedValueCollection;
public function set Context(ManagementNamedValueCollection);
```

Property Value

A name-value pairs list to be passed through to a WMI provider that supports context information for customized operation.

Requirements

Platforms: Windows 98, Windows NT 4.0, Windows Millennium Edition, Windows 2000, Windows XP Home Edition, Windows XP Professional, Windows .NET Server family

.NET Framework Security:

• Full trust for the immediate caller. This member cannot be used by partially trusted code.

ManagementOptions.Timeout Property

Gets or sets the timeout to apply to the operation. Note that for operations that return collections, this timeout applies to the enumeration through the resulting collection, not the operation itself (the **ReturnImmediately** property is used for the latter). This property is used to indicate that the operation should be performed semisynchronously.

[Visual Basic]
```
Public Property Timeout As TimeSpan
```
[C#]
```
public TimeSpan Timeout {get; set;}
```
[C++]
```
public: __property TimeSpan get_Timeout();
public: __property void set_Timeout(TimeSpan);
```
[JScript]
```
public function get Timeout() : TimeSpan;
public function set Timeout(TimeSpan);
```

Property Value

The default value for this property is **InfiniteTimeout**, which means the operation will block. The value specified must be positive.

Requirements

Platforms: Windows 98, Windows NT 4.0, Windows Millennium Edition, Windows 2000, Windows XP Home Edition, Windows XP Professional, Windows .NET Server family

.NET Framework Security:

• Full trust for the immediate caller. This member cannot be used by partially trusted code.

ManagementOptions.Clone Method

Returns a copy of the object.

[Visual Basic]
```
Public MustOverride Function Clone() As Object Implements _
    ICloneable.Clone
```
[C#]
```
public abstract object Clone();
```
[C++]
```
public: virtual Object* Clone() = 0;
```
[JScript]
```
public abstract function Clone() : Object;
```

Return Value

The cloned object.

Implements

ICloneable.Clone

Requirements

Platforms: Windows 98, Windows NT 4.0,
Windows Millennium Edition, Windows 2000,
Windows XP Home Edition, Windows XP Professional,
Windows .NET Server family

.NET Framework Security:

- Full trust for the immediate caller. This member cannot be used
  by partially trusted code.

ManagementPath Class

Provides a wrapper for parsing and building paths to WMI objects.

System.Object
   System.Management.ManagementPath

```
[Visual Basic]
Public Class ManagementPath
   Implements ICloneable
[C#]
public class ManagementPath : ICloneable
[C++]
public __gc class ManagementPath : public ICloneable
[JScript]
public class ManagementPath implements ICloneable
```

Thread Safety

Any public static (**Shared** in Visual Basic) members of this type are safe for multithreaded operations. Any instance members are not guaranteed to be thread safe.

Example

```csharp
[C#]
using System;
using System.Management;

// This sample displays all properties in a ManagementPath object.

class Sample_ManagementPath
{
    public static int Main(string[] args) {
        ManagementPath path = new ManagementPath(
"\\\\MyServer\\MyNamespace:Win32_logicaldisk='c:'");

        // Results of full path parsing
        Console.WriteLine("Path: " + path.Path);
        Console.WriteLine("RelativePath: " + path.RelativePath);
        Console.WriteLine("Server: " + path.Server);
        Console.WriteLine("NamespacePath: " + path.NamespacePath);
        Console.WriteLine("ClassName: " + path.ClassName);
        Console.WriteLine("IsClass: " + path.IsClass);
        Console.WriteLine("IsInstance: " + path.IsInstance);
        Console.WriteLine("IsSingleton: " + path.IsSingleton);

        // Change a portion of the full path
        path.Server = "AnotherServer";
        Console.WriteLine("New Path: " + path.Path);
        return 0;
    }
}
```

```vbnet
[Visual Basic]
Imports System
Imports System.Management

'This sample displays all properties in a ManagementPath object.
Class Sample_ManagementPath Overloads
    Public Shared Function Main(args() As String) As Integer
        Dim path As _ New
        ManagementPath("\\MyServer\MyNamespace:Win32_LogicalDisk='c:'")

        ' Results of full path parsing
        Console.WriteLine("Path: " & path.Path)
        Console.WriteLine("RelativePath: " & path.RelativePath)
        Console.WriteLine("Server: " & path.Server)
        Console.WriteLine("NamespacePath: " & path.NamespacePath)
        Console.WriteLine("ClassName: " & path.ClassName)
        Console.WriteLine("IsClass: " & path.IsClass)
        Console.WriteLine("IsInstance: " & path.IsInstance)
        Console.WriteLine("IsSingleton: " & path.IsSingleton)
```

```vbnet
        ' Change a portion of the full path
        path.Server= "AnotherServer"
        Console.WriteLine("New Path: " & path.Path)
        Return 0
    End Function
End Class
```

Requirements

Namespace: System.Management

Platforms: Windows 98, Windows NT 4.0, Windows Millennium Edition, Windows 2000, Windows XP Home Edition, Windows XP Professional, Windows .NET Server family

Assembly: System.Management (in System.Management.dll)

ManagementPath Constructor

Initializes a new instance of the **ManagementPath** class.

Overload List

Initializes a new instance of the **ManagementPath** class that is empty. This is the default constructor.

   [Visual Basic] **Public Sub New()**

   [C#] **public ManagementPath();**

   [C++] **public: ManagementPath();**

   [JScript] **public function ManagementPath();**

Initializes a new instance of the **ManagementPath** class for the given path.

   [Visual Basic] **Public Sub New(String)**

   [C#] **public ManagementPath(string);**

   [C++] **public: ManagementPath(String*);**

   [JScript] **public function ManagementPath(String);**

ManagementPath Constructor ()

Initializes a new instance of the **ManagementPath** class that is empty. This is the default constructor.

```
[Visual Basic]
Public Sub New()
[C#]
public ManagementPath();
[C++]
public: ManagementPath();
[JScript]
public function ManagementPath();
```

Requirements

Platforms: Windows 98, Windows NT 4.0, Windows Millennium Edition, Windows 2000, Windows XP Home Edition, Windows XP Professional, Windows .NET Server family

.NET Framework Security:

- Full trust for the immediate caller. This member cannot be used by partially trusted code.

ManagementPath Constructor (String)

Initializes a new instance of the **ManagementPath** class for the given path.

```
[Visual Basic]
Public Sub New( _
   ByVal path As String _
)
[C#]
public ManagementPath(
   string path
);
[C++]
public: ManagementPath(
   String* path
);
[JScript]
public function ManagementPath(
   path : String
);
```

Parameters

path
> The object path.

Requirements

Platforms: Windows 98, Windows NT 4.0, Windows Millennium Edition, Windows 2000, Windows XP Home Edition, Windows XP Professional, Windows .NET Server family

.NET Framework Security:

- Full trust for the immediate caller. This member cannot be used by partially trusted code.

ManagementPath.ClassName Property

Gets or sets the class portion of the path.

```
[Visual Basic]
Public Property ClassName As String
[C#]
public string ClassName {get; set;}
[C++]
public: __property String* get_ClassName();
public: __property void set_ClassName(String*);
[JScript]
public function get ClassName() : String;
public function set ClassName(String);
```

Property Value

A string containing the name of the class.

Requirements

Platforms: Windows 98, Windows NT 4.0, Windows Millennium Edition, Windows 2000, Windows XP Home Edition, Windows XP Professional, Windows .NET Server family

.NET Framework Security:

- Full trust for the immediate caller. This member cannot be used by partially trusted code.

ManagementPath.DefaultPath Property

Gets or sets the default scope path used when no scope is specified. The default scope is \\.\root\cimv2, and can be changed by setting this property.

```
[Visual Basic]
Public Shared Property DefaultPath As ManagementPath
[C#]
public static ManagementPath DefaultPath {get; set;}
[C++]
public: __property static ManagementPath* get_DefaultPath();
public: __property static void set_DefaultPath(ManagementPath*);
[JScript]
public static function get DefaultPath() : ManagementPath;
public static function set DefaultPath(ManagementPath);
```

Property Value

By default the scope value is \\.\root\cimv2, or a different scope path if the default was changed.

Requirements

Platforms: Windows 98, Windows NT 4.0, Windows Millennium Edition, Windows 2000, Windows XP Home Edition, Windows XP Professional, Windows .NET Server family

.NET Framework Security:

- Full trust for the immediate caller. This member cannot be used by partially trusted code.

ManagementPath.IsClass Property

Gets or sets a value indicating whether this is a class path.

```
[Visual Basic]
Public ReadOnly Property IsClass As Boolean
[C#]
public bool IsClass {get;}
[C++]
public: __property bool get_IsClass();
[JScript]
public function get IsClass() : Boolean;
```

Property Value

true if this is a class path; otherwise, **false**.

Requirements

Platforms: Windows 98, Windows NT 4.0, Windows Millennium Edition, Windows 2000, Windows XP Home Edition, Windows XP Professional, Windows .NET Server family

.NET Framework Security:

- Full trust for the immediate caller. This member cannot be used by partially trusted code.

ManagementPath.IsInstance Property

Gets or sets a value indicating whether this is an instance path.

```
[Visual Basic]
Public ReadOnly Property IsInstance As Boolean
[C#]
public bool IsInstance {get;}
```

```
[C++]
public: __property bool get_IsInstance();
[JScript]
public function get IsInstance() : Boolean;
```

Property Value

true if this is an instance path; otherwise, **false**.

Requirements

Platforms: Windows 98, Windows NT 4.0,
Windows Millennium Edition, Windows 2000,
Windows XP Home Edition, Windows XP Professional,
Windows .NET Server family

.NET Framework Security:

• Full trust for the immediate caller. This member cannot be used
by partially trusted code.

ManagementPath.IsSingleton Property

Gets or sets a value indicating whether this is a singleton instance
path.

```
[Visual Basic]
Public ReadOnly Property IsSingleton As Boolean
[C#]
public bool IsSingleton {get;}
[C++]
public: __property bool get_IsSingleton();
[JScript]
public function get IsSingleton() : Boolean;
```

Property Value

true if this is a singleton instance path; otherwise, **false**.

Requirements

Platforms: Windows 98, Windows NT 4.0,
Windows Millennium Edition, Windows 2000,
Windows XP Home Edition, Windows XP Professional,
Windows .NET Server family

.NET Framework Security:

• Full trust for the immediate caller. This member cannot be used
by partially trusted code.

ManagementPath.NamespacePath Property

Gets or sets the namespace part of the path. Note that this does not
include the server name, which can be retrieved separately.

```
[Visual Basic]
Public Property NamespacePath As String
[C#]
public string NamespacePath {get; set;}
[C++]
public: __property String* get_NamespacePath();
public: __property void set_NamespacePath(String*);
[JScript]
public function get NamespacePath() : String;
public function set NamespacePath(String);
```

Property Value

A string containing the namespace portion of the path represented in
this object.

Requirements

Platforms: Windows 98, Windows NT 4.0,
Windows Millennium Edition, Windows 2000,
Windows XP Home Edition, Windows XP Professional,
Windows .NET Server family

.NET Framework Security:

• Full trust for the immediate caller. This member cannot be used
by partially trusted code.

ManagementPath.Path Property

Gets or sets the string representation of the full path in the object.

```
[Visual Basic]
Public Property Path As String
[C#]
public string Path {get; set;}
[C++]
public: __property String* get_Path();
public: __property void set_Path(String*);
[JScript]
public function get Path() : String;
public function set Path(String);
```

Property Value

A string containing the full path represented in this object.

Requirements

Platforms: Windows 98, Windows NT 4.0,
Windows Millennium Edition, Windows 2000,
Windows XP Home Edition, Windows XP Professional,
Windows .NET Server family

.NET Framework Security:

• Full trust for the immediate caller. This member cannot be used
by partially trusted code.

ManagementPath.RelativePath Property

Gets or sets the relative path: class name and keys only.

```
[Visual Basic]
Public Property RelativePath As String
[C#]
public string RelativePath {get; set;}
[C++]
public: __property String* get_RelativePath();
public: __property void set_RelativePath(String*);
[JScript]
public function get RelativePath() : String;
public function set RelativePath(String);
```

Property Value

A string containing the relative path (not including the server and
namespace portions) represented in this object.

Requirements

Platforms: Windows 98, Windows NT 4.0,
Windows Millennium Edition, Windows 2000,
Windows XP Home Edition, Windows XP Professional,
Windows .NET Server family

.NET Framework Security:

- Full trust for the immediate caller. This member cannot be used by partially trusted code.

ManagementPath.Server Property

Gets or sets the server part of the path.

```
[Visual Basic]
Public Property Server As String
[C#]
public string Server {get; set;}
[C++]
public: __property String* get_Server();
public: __property void set_Server(String*);
[JScript]
public function get Server() : String;
public function set Server(String);
```

Property Value

A string containing the server name from the path represented in this object.

Requirements

Platforms: Windows 98, Windows NT 4.0, Windows Millennium Edition, Windows 2000, Windows XP Home Edition, Windows XP Professional, Windows .NET Server family

.NET Framework Security:

- Full trust for the immediate caller. This member cannot be used by partially trusted code.

ManagementPath.Clone Method

Returns a copy of the **ManagementPath**.

```
[Visual Basic]
Public Function Clone() As ManagementPath
[C#]
public ManagementPath Clone();
[C++]
public: ManagementPath* Clone();
[JScript]
public function Clone() : ManagementPath;
```

Return Value

The cloned object.

Requirements

Platforms: Windows 98, Windows NT 4.0, Windows Millennium Edition, Windows 2000, Windows XP Home Edition, Windows XP Professional, Windows .NET Server family

.NET Framework Security:

- Full trust for the immediate caller. This member cannot be used by partially trusted code.

ManagementPath.ICloneable.Clone Method

Standard Clone returns a copy of this ManagementPath as a generic "Object" type

```
[Visual Basic]
Private Function Clone() As Object Implements ICloneable.Clone
[C#]
object ICloneable.Clone();
[C++]
private: Object* ICloneable::Clone();
[JScript]
private function ICloneable.Clone() : Object;
```

Return Value

The cloned object.

Implements

ICloneable.Clone

Requirements

Platforms: Windows 98, Windows NT 4.0, Windows Millennium Edition, Windows 2000, Windows XP Home Edition, Windows XP Professional, Windows .NET Server family

.NET Framework Security:

- Full trust for the immediate caller. This member cannot be used by partially trusted code.

ManagementPath.SetAsClass Method

Sets the path as a new class path. This means that the path must have a class name but not key values.

```
[Visual Basic]
Public Sub SetAsClass()
[C#]
public void SetAsClass();
[C++]
public: void SetAsClass();
[JScript]
public function SetAsClass();
```

Requirements

Platforms: Windows 98, Windows NT 4.0, Windows Millennium Edition, Windows 2000, Windows XP Home Edition, Windows XP Professional, Windows .NET Server family

.NET Framework Security:

- Full trust for the immediate caller. This member cannot be used by partially trusted code.

ManagementPath.SetAsSingleton Method

Sets the path as a new singleton object path. This means that it is a path to an instance but there are no key values.

```
[Visual Basic]
Public Sub SetAsSingleton()
[C#]
public void SetAsSingleton();
[C++]
public: void SetAsSingleton();
```

```
[JScript]
public function SetAsSingleton();
```

Requirements

Platforms: Windows 98, Windows NT 4.0,
Windows Millennium Edition, Windows 2000,
Windows XP Home Edition, Windows XP Professional,
Windows .NET Server family

.NET Framework Security:

- Full trust for the immediate caller. This member cannot be used by partially trusted code.

ManagementPath.ToString Method

Returns the full object path as the string representation.

```
[Visual Basic]
Overrides Public Function ToString() As String
[C#]
public override string ToString();
[C++]
public: String* ToString();
[JScript]
public override function ToString() : String;
```

Return Value

A string containing the full object path represented by this object. This value is equivalent to the value of the **Path** property.

Requirements

Platforms: Windows 98, Windows NT 4.0,
Windows Millennium Edition, Windows 2000,
Windows XP Home Edition, Windows XP Professional,
Windows .NET Server family

.NET Framework Security:

- Full trust for the immediate caller. This member cannot be used by partially trusted code.

ManagementQuery Class

Provides an abstract base class for all management query objects.

System.Object
  System.Management.ManagementQuery
    System.Management.EventQuery
    System.Management.ObjectQuery

```
[Visual Basic]
MustInherit Public Class ManagementQuery
    Implements ICloneable
[C#]
public abstract class ManagementQuery : ICloneable
[C++]
public __gc __abstract class ManagementQuery : public ICloneable
[JScript]
public abstract class ManagementQuery implements ICloneable
```

Thread Safety

Any public static (**Shared** in Visual Basic) members of this type are safe for multithreaded operations. Any instance members are not guaranteed to be thread safe.

Remarks

This class is abstract; only derivatives of it are actually used in the API.

Requirements

Namespace: System.Management

Platforms: Windows 98, Windows NT 4.0, Windows Millennium Edition, Windows 2000, Windows XP Home Edition, Windows XP Professional, Windows .NET Server family

Assembly: System.Management (in System.Management.dll)

ManagementQuery.QueryLanguage Property

Gets or sets the query language used in the query string, defining the format of the query string.

```
[Visual Basic]
Public Overridable Property QueryLanguage As String
[C#]
public virtual string QueryLanguage {get; set;}
[C++]
public: __property virtual String* get_QueryLanguage();
public: __property virtual void set_QueryLanguage(String*);
[JScript]
public function get QueryLanguage() : String;
public function set QueryLanguage(String);
```

Property Value

Can be set to any supported query language. "WQL" is the only value supported intrinsically by WMI.

Requirements

Platforms: Windows 98, Windows NT 4.0, Windows Millennium Edition, Windows 2000, Windows XP Home Edition, Windows XP Professional, Windows .NET Server family

.NET Framework Security:

- Full trust for the immediate caller. This member cannot be used by partially trusted code.

ManagementQuery.QueryString Property

Gets or sets the query in text format.

```
[Visual Basic]
Public Overridable Property QueryString As String
[C#]
public virtual string QueryString {get; set;}
[C++]
public: __property virtual String* get_QueryString();
public: __property virtual void set_QueryString(String*);
[JScript]
public function get QueryString() : String;
public function set QueryString(String);
```

Property Value

If the query object is constructed with no parameters, the property is null until specifically set. If the object was constructed with a specified query, the property returns the specified query string.

Requirements

Platforms: Windows 98, Windows NT 4.0, Windows Millennium Edition, Windows 2000, Windows XP Home Edition, Windows XP Professional, Windows .NET Server family

.NET Framework Security:

- Full trust for the immediate caller. This member cannot be used by partially trusted code.

ManagementQuery.Clone Method

Returns a copy of the object.

```
[Visual Basic]
Public MustOverride Function Clone() As Object Implements _
    ICloneable.Clone
[C#]
public abstract object Clone();
[C++]
public: virtual Object* Clone() = 0;
[JScript]
public abstract function Clone() : Object;
```

Return Value

The cloned object.

Implements

ICloneable.Clone

Requirements

Platforms: Windows 98, Windows NT 4.0, Windows Millennium Edition, Windows 2000, Windows XP Home Edition, Windows XP Professional, Windows .NET Server family

.NET Framework Security:

- Full trust for the immediate caller. This member cannot be used by partially trusted code.

ManagementQuery.ParseQuery Method

Parses the query string and sets the property values accordingly.

```
[Visual Basic]
Protected Friend Overridable Sub ParseQuery( _
   ByVal query As String _
)
[C#]
protected internal virtual void ParseQuery(
   string query
);
[C++]
protected public: virtual void ParseQuery(
   String* query
);
[JScript]
protected internal function ParseQuery(
   query : String
);
```

Parameters

query

    The query string to be parsed.

Requirements

Platforms: Windows 98, Windows NT 4.0,
Windows Millennium Edition, Windows 2000,
Windows XP Home Edition, Windows XP Professional,
Windows .NET Server family

.NET Framework Security:

- Full trust for the immediate caller. This member cannot be used by partially trusted code.

ManagementScope Class

Represents a scope for management operations. In v1.0 the scope defines the WMI namespace in which management operations are performed.

System.Object
  System.Management.ManagementScope

```
[Visual Basic]
Public Class ManagementScope
   Implements ICloneable
[C#]
public class ManagementScope : ICloneable
[C++]
public __gc class ManagementScope : public ICloneable
[JScript]
public class ManagementScope implements ICloneable
```

Thread Safety

Any public static (**Shared** in Visual Basic) members of this type are safe for multithreaded operations. Any instance members are not guaranteed to be thread safe.

Example

```
[C#]
using System;
using System.Management;

// This sample demonstrates how to connect to root/default namespace
// using ManagementScope object.
class Sample_ManagementScope
{
    public static int Main(string[] args)
    {
        ManagementScope scope = new ManagementScope("root\\default");
        scope.Connect();
        ManagementClass newClass = new ManagementClass(
            scope,
            new ManagementPath(),
            null);
        return 0;
    }
}
```

```
[Visual Basic]
Imports System
Imports System.Management

' This sample demonstrates how to connect to root/default namespace
' using ManagmentScope object.
Class Sample_ManagementScope
    Overloads Public Shared Function Main(args() As String) As Integer
        Dim scope As New ManagementScope("root\default")
        scope.Connect()
        Dim newClass As New ManagementClass(scope, _
            New ManagementPath(), _
            Nothing)
        Return 0
    End Function
End Class
```

Requirements

Namespace: System.Management

Platforms: Windows 98, Windows NT 4.0, Windows Millennium Edition, Windows 2000, Windows XP Home Edition, Windows XP Professional, Windows .NET Server family

Assembly: System.Management (in System.Management.dll)

ManagementScope Constructor

Initializes a new instance of the **ManagementScope** class.

Overload List

Initializes a new instance of the **ManagementScope** class, with default values. This is the default constructor.

[Visual Basic] **Public Sub New()**
[C#] **public ManagementScope();**
[C++] **public: ManagementScope();**
[JScript] **public function ManagementScope();**

Initializes a new instance of the **ManagementScope** class representing the specified scope path.

[Visual Basic] **Public Sub New(ManagementPath)**
[C#] **public ManagementScope(ManagementPath);**
[C++] **public: ManagementScope(ManagementPath*);**
[JScript] **public function Management-Scope(ManagementPath);**

Initializes a new instance of the **ManagementScope** class representing the specified scope path.

[Visual Basic] **Public Sub New(String)**
[C#] **public ManagementScope(string);**
[C++] **public: ManagementScope(String*);**
[JScript] **public function ManagementScope(String);**

Initializes a new instance of the **ManagementScope** class representing the specified scope path, with the specified options.

[Visual Basic] **Public Sub New(ManagementPath, ConnectionOptions)**
[C#] **public ManagementScope(ManagementPath, ConnectionOptions);**
[C++] **public: ManagementScope(ManagementPath*, ConnectionOptions*);**
[JScript] **public function ManagementScope(Management-Path, ConnectionOptions);**

Initializes a new instance of the **ManagementScope** class representing the specified scope path, with the specified options.

[Visual Basic] **Public Sub New(String, ConnectionOptions)**
[C#] **public ManagementScope(string, ConnectionOptions);**
[C++] **public: ManagementScope(String*, ConnectionOptions*);**
[JScript] **public function ManagementScope(String, ConnectionOptions);**

Example

[Visual Basic, C#] **Note** This example shows how to use one of the overloaded versions of the **ManagementScope** constructor. For other examples that might be available, see the individual overload topics.

```
[C#]
ConnectionOptions opt = new ConnectionOptions();
opt.Username = UserName;
opt.Password = SecurelyStoredPassword;
ManagementScope s = new ManagementScope
("\\\\MyServer\\root\\default", opt);
```

```
[Visual Basic]
Dim opt As New ConnectionOptions()
opt.Username = UserName
opt.Password = SecurelyStoredPassword
Dim s As New ManagementScope("\\MyServer\root\default", opt);
```

ManagementScope Constructor ()

Initializes a new instance of the **ManagementScope** class, with default values. This is the default constructor.

```
[Visual Basic]
Public Sub New()
[C#]
public ManagementScope();
[C++]
public: ManagementScope();
[JScript]
public function ManagementScope();
```

Remarks

If the object doesn't have any properties set before connection, it will be initialized with default values (for example, the local machine and the root\cimv2 namespace).

Example

```
[C#]
ManagementScope s = new ManagementScope();
```

```
[Visual Basic]
Dim s As New ManagementScope()
```

Requirements

Platforms: Windows 98, Windows NT 4.0, Windows Millennium Edition, Windows 2000, Windows XP Home Edition, Windows XP Professional, Windows .NET Server family

.NET Framework Security:

- Full trust for the immediate caller. This member cannot be used by partially trusted code.

ManagementScope Constructor (ManagementPath)

Initializes a new instance of the **ManagementScope** class representing the specified scope path.

```
[Visual Basic]
Public Sub New( _
   ByVal path As ManagementPath _
)
[C#]
public ManagementScope(
   ManagementPath path
);
[C++]
public: ManagementScope(
   ManagementPath* path
);
[JScript]
public function ManagementScope(
   path : ManagementPath
);
```

Parameters

path
   A **ManagementPath** containing the path to a server and namespace for the **ManagementScope**.

Example

```
[C#]
ManagementScope s = new ManagementScope(new
ManagementPath("\\\\MyServer\\root\\default"));
```

```
[Visual Basic]
Dim p As New ManagementPath("\\MyServer\root\default")
Dim s As New ManagementScope(p)
```

Requirements

Platforms: Windows 98, Windows NT 4.0, Windows Millennium Edition, Windows 2000, Windows XP Home Edition, Windows XP Professional, Windows .NET Server family

.NET Framework Security:

- Full trust for the immediate caller. This member cannot be used by partially trusted code.

ManagementScope Constructor (String)

Initializes a new instance of the **ManagementScope** class representing the specified scope path.

```
[Visual Basic]
Public Sub New( _
   ByVal path As String _
)
[C#]
public ManagementScope(
   string path
);
[C++]
public: ManagementScope(
   String* path
);
[JScript]
public function ManagementScope(
   path : String
);
```

Parameters

path
   The server and namespace path for the **ManagementScope**.

Example

```
[C#]
ManagementScope s = new ManagementScope("\\\\MyServer\\root\\default");
```

```
[Visual Basic]
Dim s As New ManagementScope("\\MyServer\root\default")
```

Requirements

Platforms: Windows 98, Windows NT 4.0, Windows Millennium Edition, Windows 2000, Windows XP Home Edition, Windows XP Professional, Windows .NET Server family

.NET Framework Security:

- Full trust for the immediate caller. This member cannot be used by partially trusted code.

ManagementScope Constructor (ManagementPath, ConnectionOptions)

Initializes a new instance of the **ManagementScope** class representing the specified scope path, with the specified options.

```
[Visual Basic]
Public Sub New( _
    ByVal path As ManagementPath, _
    ByVal options As ConnectionOptions _
)
[C#]
public ManagementScope(
    ManagementPath path,
    ConnectionOptions options
);
[C++]
public: ManagementScope(
    ManagementPath* path,
    ConnectionOptions* options
);
[JScript]
public function ManagementScope(
    path : ManagementPath,
    options : ConnectionOptions
);
```

Parameters

path

A **ManagementPath** containing the path to the server and namespace for the **ManagementScope**.

options

The **ConnectionOptions** containing options for the connection.

Example

```
[C#]
ConnectionOptions opt = new ConnectionOptions();
opt.Username = UserName;
opt.Password = SecurelyStoredPassword;

ManagementPath p = new ManagementPath("\\\\MyServer\\root\\default");
ManagementScope = new ManagementScope(p, opt);

[Visual Basic]
Dim opt As New ConnectionOptions()
opt.UserName = UserName
opt.Password = SecurelyStoredPassword

Dim p As New ManagementPath("\\MyServer\root\default")
Dim s As New ManagementScope(p, opt)
```

Requirements

Platforms: Windows 98, Windows NT 4.0, Windows Millennium Edition, Windows 2000, Windows XP Home Edition, Windows XP Professional, Windows .NET Server family

.NET Framework Security:

- Full trust for the immediate caller. This member cannot be used by partially trusted code.

ManagementScope Constructor (String, ConnectionOptions)

Initializes a new instance of the **ManagementScope** class representing the specified scope path, with the specified options.

```
[Visual Basic]
Public Sub New( _
    ByVal path As String, _
    ByVal options As ConnectionOptions _
)
[C#]
public ManagementScope(
    string path,
    ConnectionOptions options
);
[C++]
public: ManagementScope(
    String* path,
    ConnectionOptions* options
);
[JScript]
public function ManagementScope(
    path : String,
    options : ConnectionOptions
);
```

Parameters

path

The server and namespace for the **ManagementScope**.

options

A **ConnectionOptions** containing options for the connection.

Example

```
[C#]
ConnectionOptions opt = new ConnectionOptions();
opt.Username = UserName;
opt.Password = SecurelyStoredPassword;
ManagementScope s = new ManagementScope
    ("\\\\MyServer\\root\\default", opt);

[Visual Basic]
Dim opt As New ConnectionOptions()
opt.Username = UserName
opt.Password = SecurelyStoredPassword
Dim s As New ManagementScope("\\MyServer\root\default", opt);
```

Requirements

Platforms: Windows 98, Windows NT 4.0, Windows Millennium Edition, Windows 2000, Windows XP Home Edition, Windows XP Professional, Windows .NET Server family

.NET Framework Security:

- Full trust for the immediate caller. This member cannot be used by partially trusted code.

ManagementScope.IsConnected Property

Gets or sets a value indicating whether the **ManagementScope** is currently bound to a WMI server and namespace.

```
[Visual Basic]
Public ReadOnly Property IsConnected As Boolean
[C#]
public bool IsConnected {get;}
```

```
[C++]
public: __property bool get_IsConnected();
[JScript]
public function get IsConnected() : Boolean;
```

Property Value

true if a connection is alive (bound to a server and namespace); otherwise, **false**.

Remarks

A scope is disconnected after creation until someone explicitly calls **Connect** (), or uses the scope for any operation that requires a live connection. Also, the scope is disconnected from the previous connection whenever the identifying properties of the scope are changed.

Requirements

Platforms: Windows 98, Windows NT 4.0, Windows Millennium Edition, Windows 2000, Windows XP Home Edition, Windows XP Professional, Windows .NET Server family

.NET Framework Security:

- Full trust for the immediate caller. This member cannot be used by partially trusted code.

ManagementScope.Options Property

Gets or sets options for making the WMI connection.

```
[Visual Basic]
Public Property Options As ConnectionOptions
[C#]
public ConnectionOptions Options {get; set;}
[C++]
public: __property ConnectionOptions* get_Options();
public: __property void set_Options(ConnectionOptions*);
[JScript]
public function get Options() : ConnectionOptions;
public function set Options(ConnectionOptions);
```

Property Value

The valid **ConnectionOptions** containing options for the WMI connection.

Example

```
[C#]
//This constructor creates a scope object with default options
ManagementScope s = new ManagementScope("root\\MyApp");

//Change default connection options -
//In this example, set the system privileges to enabled for
 operations that require system privileges.
s.Options.EnablePrivileges = true;
```

```
[Visual Basic]
'This constructor creates a scope object with default options
Dim s As New ManagementScope("root\\MyApp")

'Change default connection options -
'In this example, set the system privileges to enabled for
operations that require system privileges.
s.Options.EnablePrivileges = True
```

Requirements

Platforms: Windows 98, Windows NT 4.0, Windows Millennium Edition, Windows 2000, Windows XP Home Edition, Windows XP Professional, Windows .NET Server family

.NET Framework Security:

- Full trust for the immediate caller. This member cannot be used by partially trusted code.

ManagementScope.Path Property

Gets or sets the path for the **ManagementScope**.

```
[Visual Basic]
Public Property Path As ManagementPath
[C#]
public ManagementPath Path {get; set;}
[C++]
public: __property ManagementPath* get_Path();
public: __property void set_Path(ManagementPath*);
[JScript]
public function get Path() : ManagementPath;
public function set Path(ManagementPath);
```

Property Value

A **ManagementPath** containing the path to a server and namespace.

Example

```
[C#]
ManagementScope s = new ManagementScope();
s.Path = new ManagementPath("root\\MyApp");
```

```
[Visual Basic]
Dim s As New ManagementScope()
s.Path = New ManagementPath("root\MyApp")
```

Requirements

Platforms: Windows 98, Windows NT 4.0, Windows Millennium Edition, Windows 2000, Windows XP Home Edition, Windows XP Professional, Windows .NET Server family

.NET Framework Security:

- Full trust for the immediate caller. This member cannot be used by partially trusted code.

ManagementScope.Clone Method

Returns a copy of the object.

```
[Visual Basic]
Public Function Clone() As ManagementScope
[C#]
public ManagementScope Clone();
[C++]
public: ManagementScope* Clone();
[JScript]
public function Clone() : ManagementScope;
```

Return Value

A new copy of the **ManagementScope**.

Requirements

Platforms: Windows 98, Windows NT 4.0, Windows Millennium Edition, Windows 2000, Windows XP Home Edition, Windows XP Professional, Windows .NET Server family

.NET Framework Security:

- Full trust for the immediate caller. This member cannot be used by partially trusted code.

ManagementScope.Connect Method

Connects this **ManagementScope** to the actual WMI scope.

```
[Visual Basic]
Public Sub Connect()
[C#]
public void Connect();
[C++]
public: void Connect();
[JScript]
public function Connect();
```

Remarks

This method is called implicitly when the scope is used in an operation that requires it to be connected. Calling it explicitly allows the user to control the time of connection.

Example

```
[C#]
ManagementScope s = new ManagementScope("root\\MyApp");

//Explicit call to connect the scope object to the WMI namespace
s.Connect();

//The following doesn't do any implicit scope connections      ⏎
because s is already connected.
ManagementObject o = new ManagementObject(s,                   ⏎
"Win32_LogicalDisk='C:'", null);

[Visual Basic]
Dim s As New ManagementScope("root\\MyApp")

'Explicit call to connect the scope object to the WMI namespace
s.Connect()

'The following doesn't do any implicit scope connections because ⏎
s is already connected.
Dim o As New ManagementObject(s, "Win32_LogicalDisk=""C:""", null)
```

Requirements

Platforms: Windows 98, Windows NT 4.0, Windows Millennium Edition, Windows 2000, Windows XP Home Edition, Windows XP Professional, Windows .NET Server family

.NET Framework Security:

- Full trust for the immediate caller. This member cannot be used by partially trusted code.

ManagementScope.ICloneable.Clone Method

Clone a copy of this object.

```
[Visual Basic]
Private Function Clone() As Object Implements ICloneable.Clone
[C#]
object ICloneable.Clone();
[C++]
private: Object* ICloneable::Clone();
[JScript]
private function ICloneable.Clone() : Object;
```

Return Value

A new copy of this object. object.

Implements

ICloneable.Clone

Requirements

Platforms: Windows 98, Windows NT 4.0, Windows Millennium Edition, Windows 2000, Windows XP Home Edition, Windows XP Professional, Windows .NET Server family

.NET Framework Security:

- Full trust for the immediate caller. This member cannot be used by partially trusted code.

ManagementStatus Enumeration

Represents the enumeration of all WMI error codes that are currently defined.

```
[Visual Basic]
<Serializable>
Public Enum ManagementStatus
[C#]
[Serializable]
public enum ManagementStatus
[C++]
[Serializable]
__value public enum ManagementStatus
[JScript]
public
   Serializable
enum ManagementStatus
```

Members

Member name	Description
AccessDenied	The current user does not have permission to perform the action.
AggregatingByObject	A GROUP BY clause references a property that is an embedded object without using dot notation.
AlreadyExists	In a put operation, the **wbemChangeFlagCreateOnly** flag was specified, but the instance already exists.
AmendedObject	An amended object was used in a put operation without the WBEM_FLAG_USE_AMENDED_QUALIFIERS flag being specified.
BackupRestore-WinmgmtRunning	An request was made to back up or restore the repository while WinMgmt.exe was using it.
BufferTooSmall	The supplied buffer was too small to hold all the objects in the enumerator or to read a string property.
CallCanceled	An asynchronous process has been canceled internally or by the user. Note that because of the timing and nature of the asynchronous operation, the operation may not have been truly canceled.
CannotBeAbstract	The class was made abstract when its superclass is not abstract.
CannotBeKey	There was an illegal attempt to specify a key qualifier on a property that cannot be a key. The keys are specified in the class definition for an object and cannot be altered on a per-instance basis.
CannotBeSingleton	An illegal attempt was made to make a class singleton, such as when the class is derived from a non-singleton class.

Member name	Description
CannotChangeIndex-Inheritance	An attempt was made to change an index when instances or derived classes are already using the index.
CannotChangeKey-Inheritance	An attempt was made to change a key when instances or derived classes are already using the key.
CircularReference	An attempt has been made to create a reference that is circular (for example, deriving a class from itself).
ClassHasChildren	An attempt was made to make a change that would invalidate a derived class.
ClassHasInstances	An attempt has been made to delete or modify a class that has instances.
ClientTooSlow	The client was not retrieving objects quickly enough from an enumeration.
CriticalError	An internal, critical, and unexpected error occurred. Report this error to Microsoft Technical Support.
Different	The compared items (such as objects and classes) are not identical.
DuplicateObjects	More than one copy of the same object was detected in the result set of an enumeration.
Failed	The call failed.
False	This value is returned when no more objects are available, the number of objects returned is less than the number requested, or at the end of an enumeration. It is also returned when the method is called with a value of 0 for the *uCount* parameter.
IllegalNull	A value of null was specified for a property that may not be null, such as one that is marked by a **Key**, **Indexed**, or **Not_Null** qualifier.
IllegalOperation	The user requested an illegal operation, such as spawning a class from an instance.
IncompleteClass	The current object is not a valid class definition. Either it is incomplete, or it has not been registered with WMI using **Put** ().
InitializationFailure	A component, such as a provider, failed to initialize for internal reasons.
InvalidCimType	The CIM type specified is not valid.
InvalidClass	The specified class is not valid.
InvalidContext	The context object is not valid.
InvalidDuplicate-Parameter	A duplicate parameter has been declared in a CIM method.
InvalidFlavor	The specified flavor was invalid.
InvalidMethod	The requested method is not available.
InvalidMethod-Parameters	The parameters provided for the method are not valid.
InvalidNamespace	The specified namespace could not be found.
InvalidObject	The specified instance is not valid.

Member name	Description
InvalidObjectPath	The specified object path was invalid.
InvalidOperation	The requested operation is not valid. This error usually applies to invalid attempts to delete classes or properties.
InvalidOperator	The operator is not valid for this property type.
InvalidParameter	One of the parameters to the call is not correct.
InvalidParameterID	A method parameter has an invalid **ID** qualifier.
InvalidProperty	The property type is not recognized.
InvalidPropertyType	The CIM type specified for a property is not valid.
InvalidProvider-Registration	A provider referenced in the schema has an incorrect or incomplete registration.
InvalidQualifier	An attempt has been made to mismatch qualifiers, such as putting [key] on an object instead of a property.
InvalidQualifierType	The value provided for a qualifier was not a legal qualifier type.
InvalidQuery	The query was not syntactically valid.
InvalidQueryType	The requested query language is not supported.
InvalidStream	One or more network packets were corrupted during a remote session.
InvalidSuperclass	The specified superclass is not valid.
InvalidSyntax	Reserved for future use.
LocalCredentials	The user specified a username, password, or authority on a local connection. The user must use an empty user name and password and rely on default security.
MarshalInvalid-Signature	The packet is corrupted.
MarshalVersion-Mismatch	The packet has an unsupported version.
MethodDisabled	An attempt was made to execute a method marked with [disabled].
MethodNotImple-mented	An attempt was made to execute a method not marked with [implemented] in any relevant class.
MissingAggregation-List	A GROUP BY clause was used. Aggregation on all properties is not supported.
MissingGroupWithin	A GROUP BY clause was used without the corresponding GROUP WITHIN clause.
MissingParameterID	A parameter was missing from the method call.
NoError	The operation was successful.
NoMoreData	No more data is available from the enumeration; the user should terminate the enumeration.

Member name	Description
Nonconsecutive-ParameterIDs	One or more of the method parameters have **ID** qualifiers that are out of sequence.
NondecoratedObject	Reserved for future use.
NotAvailable	The resource, typically a remote server, is not currently available.
NotEventClass	The FROM clause of a filtering query references a class that is not an event class.
NotFound	The object could not be found.
NotSupported	The feature or operation is not supported.
OperationCanceled	The operation was canceled.
OutOfDiskSpace	There is not enough free disk space to continue the operation.
OutOfMemory	There was not enough memory for the operation.
OverrideNotAllowed	The add operation cannot be performed on the qualifier because the owning object does not permit overrides.
ParameterIDOnRetval	The return value for a method has an **ID** qualifier.
PartialResults	The user did not receive all of the requested objects because of inaccessible resources (other than security violations).
Pending	A request is still in progress; however, the results are not yet available.
PrivilegeNotHeld	The operation failed because the client did not have the necessary security privilege.
PropagatedMethod	An attempt was made to reuse an existing method name from a superclass, and the signatures did not match.
PropagatedProperty	The user attempted to delete a property that was not owned. The property was inherited from a parent class.
PropagatedQualifier	The user attempted to delete a qualifier that was not owned. The qualifier was inherited from a parent class.
PropertyNotAnObject	Dot notation was used on a property that is not an embedded object.
ProviderFailure	The provider failed after initialization.
ProviderLoadFailure	COM cannot locate a provider referenced in the schema.
ProviderNotCapable	The provider cannot perform the requested operation, such as requesting a query that is too complex, retrieving an instance, creating or updating a class, deleting a class, or enumerating a class.
ProviderNotFound	A provider referenced in the schema does not have a corresponding registration.
QueryNotImplemented	Reserved for future use.

Member name	Description
QueueOverflow	The asynchronous delivery queue overflowed from the event consumer being too slow.
ReadOnly	The property that you are attempting to modify is read-only.
RefresherBusy	The refresher is busy with another operation.
RegistrationTooBroad	The provider registration overlaps with the system event domain.
RegistrationTooPrecise	A WITHIN clause was not used in this query.
ResetToDefault	An overridden property was deleted. This value is returned to signal that the original, non-overridden value has been restored as a result of the deletion.
ServerTooBusy	The delivery of an event has failed. The provider may choose to re-raise the event.
ShuttingDown	The user has requested an operation while WMI is in the process of quitting.
SystemProperty	There was an attempt to get qualifiers on a system property.
Timedout	A call timed out. This is not an error condition; therefore, some results may have been returned.
TooManyProperties	An attempt was made to create more properties than the current version of the class supports.
TooMuchData	Reserved for future use.
TransportFailure	A networking error that prevents normal operation has occurred.
TypeMismatch	A type mismatch occurred.
Unexpected	The client made an unexpected and illegal sequence of calls.
Uninterpretable-ProviderQuery	An event provider registration query (__EventProviderRegistration) did not specify the classes for which events were provided.
UnknownObjectType	An object with an incorrect type or version was encountered during marshaling.
UnknownPacketType	A packet with an incorrect type or version was encountered during marshaling.
UnparsableQuery	The filtering query is syntactically invalid.
UnsupportedClass-Update	The specified class is not supported.
Unsupported-Parameter	One or more parameter values, such as a query text, is too complex or unsupported. WMI is requested to retry the operation with simpler parameters.
UnsupportedPut-Extension	The provider does not support the requested put operation.
UpdateOverrideNot-Allowed	An attempt was made in a derived class to override a non-overrideable qualifier.

Member name	Description
UpdatePropagated-Method	A method was redeclared with a conflicting signature in a derived class.
UpdateTypeMismatch	A property was redefined with a conflicting type in a derived class.
ValueOutOfRange	The request was made with an out-of-range value, or is incompatible with the type.

Requirements

Namespace: System.Management

Platforms: Windows 98, Windows NT 4.0, Windows Millennium Edition, Windows 2000, Windows XP Home Edition, Windows XP Professional, Windows .NET Server family

Assembly: System.Management (in System.Management.dll)

MethodData Class

Contains information about a WMI method.

System.Object
   System.Management.MethodData

```
[Visual Basic]
Public Class MethodData
[C#]
public class MethodData
[C++]
public __gc class MethodData
[JScript]
public class MethodData
```

Thread Safety

Any public static (**Shared** in Visual Basic) members of this type are safe for multithreaded operations. Any instance members are not guaranteed to be thread safe.

Example

```
[C#]
using System;
using System.Management;

// This example shows how to obtain meta data
// about a WMI method with a given name in a given WMI class

class Sample_MethodData
{
    public static int Main(string[] args) {

        // Get the "SetPowerState" method in
the Win32_LogicalDisk class
        ManagementClass diskClass = new
ManagementClass("win32_logicaldisk");
        MethodData m = diskClass.Methods["SetPowerState"];

        // Get method name (albeit we already know it)
        Console.WriteLine("Name: " + m.Name);

        // Get the name of the top-most class where this
specific method was defined
        Console.WriteLine("Origin: " + m.Origin);

        // List names and types of input parameters
        ManagementBaseObject inParams = m.InParameters;
        foreach(PropertyData pdata in inParams.Properties) {
            Console.WriteLine();
            Console.WriteLine("InParam_Name: " + pdata.Name);
            Console.WriteLine("InParam_Type: " + pdata.Type);
        }

        // List names and types of output parameters
        ManagementBaseObject outParams = m.OutParameters;
        foreach(PropertyData pdata in outParams.Properties) {
            Console.WriteLine();
            Console.WriteLine("OutParam_Name: " + pdata.Name);
            Console.WriteLine("OutParam_Type: " + pdata.Type);
        }

        return 0;
    }
}

[Visual Basic]
Imports System
Imports System.Management
```

```
' This example shows how to obtain meta data
' about a WMI method with a given name in a given WMI class

Class Sample_ManagementClass
    Overloads Public Shared Function Main(args() As String) As Integer

        ' Get the "SetPowerState" method in the Win32_LogicalDisk class
        Dim diskClass As New ManagementClass("Win32_LogicalDisk")
        Dim m As MethodData = diskClass.Methods("SetPowerState")

        ' Get method name (albeit we already know it)
        Console.WriteLine("Name: " & m.Name)

        ' Get the name of the top-most class where
        ' this specific method was defined
        Console.WriteLine("Origin: " & m.Origin)

        ' List names and types of input parameters
        Dim inParams As ManagementBaseObject
        inParams = m.InParameters
        Dim pdata As PropertyData
        For Each pdata In inParams.Properties
            Console.WriteLine()
            Console.WriteLine("InParam_Name: " & pdata.Name)
            Console.WriteLine("InParam_Type: " & pdata.Type)
        Next pdata

        ' List names and types of output parameters
        Dim outParams As ManagementBaseObject
        outParams = m.OutParameters
        For Each pdata in outParams.Properties
            Console.WriteLine()
            Console.WriteLine("OutParam_Name: " & pdata.Name)
            Console.WriteLine("OutParam_Type: " & pdata.Type)
        Next pdata

        Return 0
    End Function
End Class
```

Requirements

Namespace: System.Management

Platforms: Windows 98, Windows NT 4.0, Windows Millennium Edition, Windows 2000, Windows XP Home Edition, Windows XP Professional, Windows .NET Server family

Assembly: System.Management (in System.Management.dll)

MethodData.InParameters Property

Gets or sets the input parameters to the method. Each parameter is described as a property in the object. If a parameter is both in and out, it appears in both the **InParameters** and **OutParameters** properties.

```
[Visual Basic]
Public ReadOnly Property InParameters As ManagementBaseObject
[C#]
public ManagementBaseObject InParameters {get;}
[C++]
public: __property ManagementBaseObject* get_InParameters();
[JScript]
public function get InParameters() : ManagementBaseObject;
```

Property Value

A **ManagementBaseObject** containing all the input parameters to the method.

Remarks

Each parameter in the object should have an **ID** qualifier, identifying the order of the parameters in the method call.

Requirements

Platforms: Windows 98, Windows NT 4.0, Windows Millennium Edition, Windows 2000, Windows XP Home Edition, Windows XP Professional, Windows .NET Server family

.NET Framework Security:

- Full trust for the immediate caller. This member cannot be used by partially trusted code.

MethodData.Name Property

Gets or sets the name of the method.

```
[Visual Basic]
Public ReadOnly Property Name As String
[C#]
public string Name {get;}
[C++]
public: __property String* get_Name();
[JScript]
public function get Name() : String;
```

Property Value

The name of the method.

Requirements

Platforms: Windows 98, Windows NT 4.0, Windows Millennium Edition, Windows 2000, Windows XP Home Edition, Windows XP Professional, Windows .NET Server family

.NET Framework Security:

- Full trust for the immediate caller. This member cannot be used by partially trusted code.

MethodData.Origin Property

Gets the name of the management class in which the method was first introduced in the class inheritance hierarchy.

```
[Visual Basic]
Public ReadOnly Property Origin As String
[C#]
public string Origin {get;}
[C++]
public: __property String* get_Origin();
[JScript]
public function get Origin() : String;
```

Property Value

A string representing the originating management class name.

Requirements

Platforms: Windows 98, Windows NT 4.0, Windows Millennium Edition, Windows 2000, Windows XP Home Edition, Windows XP Professional, Windows .NET Server family

.NET Framework Security:

- Full trust for the immediate caller. This member cannot be used by partially trusted code.

MethodData.OutParameters Property

Gets or sets the output parameters to the method. Each parameter is described as a property in the object. If a parameter is both in and out, it will appear in both the **InParameters** and **OutParameters** properties.

```
[Visual Basic]
Public ReadOnly Property OutParameters As ManagementBaseObject
[C#]
public ManagementBaseObject OutParameters {get;}
[C++]
public: __property ManagementBaseObject* get_OutParameters();
[JScript]
public function get OutParameters() : ManagementBaseObject;
```

Property Value

A **ManagementBaseObject** containing all the output parameters to the method.

Remarks

Each parameter in this object should have an **ID** qualifier to identify the order of the parameters in the method call.

The ReturnValue property is a special property of the **OutParameters** object and holds the return value of the method.

Requirements

Platforms: Windows 98, Windows NT 4.0, Windows Millennium Edition, Windows 2000, Windows XP Home Edition, Windows XP Professional, Windows .NET Server family

.NET Framework Security:

- Full trust for the immediate caller. This member cannot be used by partially trusted code.

MethodData.Qualifiers Property

Gets a collection of qualifiers defined in the method. Each element is of type **QualifierData** and contains information such as the qualifier name, value, and flavor.

```
[Visual Basic]
Public ReadOnly Property Qualifiers As QualifierDataCollection
[C#]
public QualifierDataCollection Qualifiers {get;}
[C++]
public: __property QualifierDataCollection* get_Qualifiers();
[JScript]
public function get Qualifiers() : QualifierDataCollection;
```

Property Value

A **QualifierDataCollection** containing the qualifiers for this method.

Requirements

Platforms: Windows 98, Windows NT 4.0, Windows Millennium Edition, Windows 2000, Windows XP Home Edition, Windows XP Professional, Windows .NET Server family

.NET Framework Security:

- Full trust for the immediate caller. This member cannot be used by partially trusted code.

MethodDataCollection Class

Represents the set of methods available in the collection.

System.Object
    System.Management.MethodDataCollection

```
[Visual Basic]
Public Class MethodDataCollection
    Implements ICollection, IEnumerable
[C#]
public class MethodDataCollection : ICollection, IEnumerable
[C++]
public __gc class MethodDataCollection : public ICollection,
    IEnumerable
[JScript]
public class MethodDataCollection implements ICollection,
    IEnumerable
```

Thread Safety

Any public static (**Shared** in Visual Basic) members of this type are
safe for multithreaded operations. Any instance members are not
guaranteed to be thread safe.

Example

```
[C#]
using System;
using System.Management;

// This sample demonstrates enumerate all methods in a
  ManagementClass object.
class Sample_MethodDataCollection
{
    public static int Main(string[] args) {
        ManagementClass diskClass = new
ManagementClass("win32_logicaldisk");
        MethodDataCollection diskMethods = diskClass.Methods;
        foreach (MethodData method in diskMethods) {
            Console.WriteLine("Method = " + method.Name);
        }
        return 0;
    }
}

[Visual Basic]
Imports System
Imports System.Management

' This sample demonstrates enumerate all methods in a
ManagementClass object.
Class Sample_MethodDataCollection
    Overloads Public Shared Function Main(args() As String) As Integer
        Dim diskClass As New ManagementClass("win32_logicaldisk")
        Dim diskMethods As MethodDataCollection = diskClass.Methods
        Dim method As MethodData
        For Each method In diskMethods
            Console.WriteLine("Method = " & method.Name)
        Next method
        Return 0
    End Function
End Class
```

Requirements

Namespace: System.Management

Platforms: Windows 98, Windows NT 4.0,
Windows Millennium Edition, Windows 2000,
Windows XP Home Edition, Windows XP Professional,
Windows .NET Server family

Assembly: System.Management (in System.Management.dll)

MethodDataCollection.Count Property

Represents the number of objects in the **MethodDataCollection**.

```
[Visual Basic]
Public Overridable ReadOnly Property Count As Integer  Implements _
    ICollection.Count
[C#]
public virtual int Count {get;}
[C++]
public: __property virtual int get_Count();
[JScript]
public function get Count() : int;
```

Property Value

The number of objects in the **MethodDataCollection**.

Implements

ICollection.Count

Requirements

Platforms: Windows 98, Windows NT 4.0,
Windows Millennium Edition, Windows 2000,
Windows XP Home Edition, Windows XP Professional,
Windows .NET Server family

.NET Framework Security:
- Full trust for the immediate caller. This member cannot be used
  by partially trusted code.

MethodDataCollection.IsSynchronized Property

Indicates whether the object is synchronized.

```
[Visual Basic]
Public Overridable ReadOnly Property IsSynchronized As Boolean _
    Implements ICollection.IsSynchronized
[C#]
public virtual bool IsSynchronized {get;}
[C++]
public: __property virtual bool get_IsSynchronized();
[JScript]
public function get IsSynchronized() : Boolean;
```

Property Value

true if the object is synchronized; otherwise, **false**.

Implements

ICollection.IsSynchronized

Requirements

Platforms: Windows 98, Windows NT 4.0,
Windows Millennium Edition, Windows 2000,
Windows XP Home Edition, Windows XP Professional,
Windows .NET Server family

.NET Framework Security:
- Full trust for the immediate caller. This member cannot be used
  by partially trusted code.

MethodDataCollection.Item Property

Returns the specified **MethodData** from the
MethodDataCollection.

[C#] In C#, this property is the indexer for the
MethodDataCollection class.

```
[Visual Basic]
Public Overridable Default ReadOnly Property Item( _
   ByVal methodName As String _
) As MethodData
[C#]
public virtual MethodData this[
   string methodName
] {get;}
[C++]
public: __property virtual MethodData* get_Item(
   String* methodName
);
[JScript]
returnValue = MethodDataCollectionObject.Item(methodName);
-or-
returnValue = MethodDataCollectionObject(methodName);
```

[JScript] In JScript, you can use the default indexed properties defined by a type, but you cannot explicitly define your own. However, specifying the **expando** attribute on a class automatically provides a default indexed property whose type is **Object** and whose index type is **String**.

Arguments [JScript]
methodName
   The name of the method requested.

Parameters [Visual Basic, C#, C++]
methodName
   The name of the method requested.

Property Value

A **MethodData** instance containing all information about the specified method.

Requirements

Platforms: Windows 98, Windows NT 4.0, Windows Millennium Edition, Windows 2000, Windows XP Home Edition, Windows XP Professional, Windows .NET Server family

.NET Framework Security:

- Full trust for the immediate caller. This member cannot be used by partially trusted code.

MethodDataCollection.SyncRoot Property

Represents the object to be used for synchronization.

```
[Visual Basic]
Public Overridable ReadOnly Property SyncRoot As Object  Implements _
   ICollection.SyncRoot
[C#]
public virtual object SyncRoot {get;}
[C++]
public: __property virtual Object* get_SyncRoot();
[JScript]
public function get SyncRoot() : Object;
```

Property Value

The object to be used for synchronization.

Implements

ICollection.SyncRoot

Requirements

Platforms: Windows 98, Windows NT 4.0, Windows Millennium Edition, Windows 2000, Windows XP Home Edition, Windows XP Professional, Windows .NET Server family

.NET Framework Security:

- Full trust for the immediate caller. This member cannot be used by partially trusted code.

MethodDataCollection.Add Method

Adds a **MethodData** to the **MethodDataCollection**.

Overload List

Adds a **MethodData** to the **MethodDataCollection**. This overload will add a new method with no parameters to the collection.

> [Visual Basic] **Overloads Public Overridable Sub Add(String)**
>
> [C#] **public virtual void Add(string);**
>
> [C++] **public: virtual void Add(String*);**
>
> [JScript] **public function Add(String);**

Adds a **MethodData** to the **MethodDataCollection**. This overload will add a new method with the specified parameter objects to the collection.

> [Visual Basic] **Overloads Public Overridable Sub Add(String, ManagementBaseObject, ManagementBaseObject)**
>
> [C#] **public virtual void Add(string, ManagementBaseObject, ManagementBaseObject);**
>
> [C++] **public: virtual void Add(String*, ManagementBaseObject*, ManagementBaseObject*);**
>
> [JScript] **public function Add(String, ManagementBaseObject, ManagementBaseObject);**

MethodDataCollection.Add Method (String)

Adds a **MethodData** to the **MethodDataCollection**. This overload will add a new method with no parameters to the collection.

```
[Visual Basic]
Overloads Public Overridable Sub Add( _
   ByVal methodName As String _
)
[C#]
public virtual void Add(
   string methodName
);
[C++]
public: virtual void Add(
   String* methodName
);
[JScript]
public function Add(
   methodName : String
);
```

Parameters
methodName
   The name of the method to add.

Remarks

Adding **MethodData** objects to the **MethodDataCollection** can only be done when the class has no instances. Any other case will result in an exception.

Requirements

Platforms: Windows 98, Windows NT 4.0, Windows Millennium Edition, Windows 2000, Windows XP Home Edition, Windows XP Professional, Windows .NET Server family

.NET Framework Security:

- Full trust for the immediate caller. This member cannot be used by partially trusted code.

MethodDataCollection.Add Method (String, ManagementBaseObject, ManagementBaseObject)

Adds a **MethodData** to the **MethodDataCollection**. This overload will add a new method with the specified parameter objects to the collection.

```
[Visual Basic]
Overloads Public Overridable Sub Add( _
    ByVal methodName As String, _
    ByVal inParams As ManagementBaseObject, _
    ByVal outParams As ManagementBaseObject _
)
[C#]
public virtual void Add(
    string methodName,
    ManagementBaseObject inParams,
    ManagementBaseObject outParams
);
[C++]
public: virtual void Add(
    String* methodName,
    ManagementBaseObject* inParams,
    ManagementBaseObject* outParams
);
[JScript]
public function Add(
    methodName : String,
    inParams : ManagementBaseObject,
    outParams : ManagementBaseObject
);
```

Parameters

methodName
    The name of the method to add.
inParams
    The **ManagementBaseObject** holding the input parameters to the method.
outParams
    The **ManagementBaseObject** holding the output parameters to the method.

Remarks

Adding **MethodData** objects to the **MethodDataCollection** can only be done when the class has no instances. Any other case will result in an exception.

Requirements

Platforms: Windows 98, Windows NT 4.0, Windows Millennium Edition, Windows 2000, Windows XP Home Edition, Windows XP Professional, Windows .NET Server family

.NET Framework Security:

- Full trust for the immediate caller. This member cannot be used by partially trusted code.

MethodDataCollection.CopyTo Method

Copies the **MethodDataCollection** into an array.

Overload List

Copies the **MethodDataCollection** into an array.

> [Visual Basic] **Overloads Public Overridable Sub CopyTo(Array, Integer) Implements ICollection.CopyTo**
> [C#] **public virtual void CopyTo(Array, int);**
> [C++] **public: virtual void CopyTo(Array*, int);**
> [JScript] **public function CopyTo(Array, int);**

Copies the **MethodDataCollection** to a specialized **MethodData** array.

> [Visual Basic] **Overloads Public Sub CopyTo(MethodData(), Integer)**
> [C#] **public void CopyTo(MethodData[], int);**
> [C++] **public: void CopyTo(MethodData*[], int);**
> [JScript] **public function CopyTo(MethodData[], int);**

MethodDataCollection.CopyTo Method (Array, Int32)

Copies the **MethodDataCollection** into an array.

```
[Visual Basic]
Overloads Public Overridable Sub CopyTo( _
    ByVal array As Array, _
    ByVal index As Integer _
) Implements ICollection.CopyTo
[C#]
public virtual void CopyTo(
    Array array,
    int index
);
[C++]
public: virtual void CopyTo(
    Array* array,
    int index
);
[JScript]
public function CopyTo(
    array : Array,
    index : int
);
```

Parameters

array
    The array to which to copy the collection.
index
    The index from which to start.

Implements

ICollection.CopyTo

Requirements

Platforms: Windows 98, Windows NT 4.0,
Windows Millennium Edition, Windows 2000,
Windows XP Home Edition, Windows XP Professional,
Windows .NET Server family

.NET Framework Security:

- Full trust for the immediate caller. This member cannot be used by partially trusted code.

MethodDataCollection.CopyTo Method (MethodData[], Int32)

Copies the **MethodDataCollection** to a specialized **MethodData** array.

```
[Visual Basic]
Overloads Public Sub CopyTo( _
   ByVal methodArray() As MethodData, _
   ByVal index As Integer _
)
[C#]
public void CopyTo(
   MethodData[] methodArray,
   int index
);
[C++]
public: void CopyTo(
   MethodData* methodArray[],
   int index
);
[JScript]
public function CopyTo(
   methodArray : MethodData[],
   index : int
);
```

Parameters

methodArray
   The destination array to which to copy the **MethodData** objects.
index
   The index in the destination array from which to start the copy.

Requirements

Platforms: Windows 98, Windows NT 4.0,
Windows Millennium Edition, Windows 2000,
Windows XP Home Edition, Windows XP Professional,
Windows .NET Server family

.NET Framework Security:

- Full trust for the immediate caller. This member cannot be used by partially trusted code.

MethodDataCollection.GetEnumerator Method

Returns an enumerator for the **MethodDataCollection**.

```
[Visual Basic]
Public Function GetEnumerator() As MethodDataEnumerator
[C#]
public MethodDataEnumerator GetEnumerator();
```

```
[C++]
public: MethodDataEnumerator* GetEnumerator();
[JScript]
public function GetEnumerator() : MethodDataEnumerator;
```

Return Value

An **IEnumerator** to enumerate through the collection.

Remarks

Each call to this method returns a new enumerator on the collection. Multiple enumerators can be obtained for the same method collection. However, each enumerator takes a snapshot of the collection, so changes made to the collection after the enumerator was obtained are not reflected.

Requirements

Platforms: Windows 98, Windows NT 4.0,
Windows Millennium Edition, Windows 2000,
Windows XP Home Edition, Windows XP Professional,
Windows .NET Server family

.NET Framework Security:

- Full trust for the immediate caller. This member cannot be used by partially trusted code.

MethodDataCollection.IEnumerable.Get-Enumerator Method

This member supports the .NET Framework infrastructure and is not intended to be used directly from your code.

```
[Visual Basic]
Private Function GetEnumerator() As IEnumerator Implements _
   IEnumerable.GetEnumerator
[C#]
IEnumerator IEnumerable.GetEnumerator();
[C++]
private: IEnumerator* IEnumerable::GetEnumerator();
[JScript]
private function IEnumerable.GetEnumerator() : IEnumerator;
```

MethodDataCollection.Remove Method

Removes a **MethodData** from the **MethodDataCollection**.

```
[Visual Basic]
Public Overridable Sub Remove( _
   ByVal methodName As String _
)
[C#]
public virtual void Remove(
   string methodName
);
[C++]
public: virtual void Remove(
   String* methodName
);
[JScript]
public function Remove(
   methodName : String
);
```

Parameters

methodName

  The name of the method to remove from the collection.

Remarks

Removing **MethodData** objects from the **MethodDataCollection** can only be done when the class has no instances. Any other case will result in an exception.

Requirements

Platforms: Windows 98, Windows NT 4.0, Windows Millennium Edition, Windows 2000, Windows XP Home Edition, Windows XP Professional, Windows .NET Server family

.NET Framework Security:

- Full trust for the immediate caller. This member cannot be used by partially trusted code.

MethodDataCollection.Method DataEnumerator Class

Represents the enumerator for **MethodData** objects in the **MethodDataCollection**.

System.Object
  System.Management.MethodDataCollection.MethodDataEnu merator

```
[Visual Basic]
Public Class MethodDataCollection.MethodDataEnumerator
   Implements IEnumerator
[C#]
public class MethodDataCollection.MethodDataEnumerator :
   IEnumerator
[C++]
public __gc class MethodDataCollection.MethodDataEnumerator :
   public IEnumerator
[JScript]
public class MethodDataCollection.MethodDataEnumerator implements
   IEnumerator
```

Thread Safety

Any public static (**Shared** in Visual Basic) members of this type are safe for multithreaded operations. Any instance members are not guaranteed to be thread safe.

Example

```
[C#]
using System;
using System.Management;

// This sample demonstrates how to enumerate all methods in
// Win32_LogicalDisk class using MethodDataEnumerator object.

class Sample_MethodDataEnumerator
{
 public static int Main(string[] args)
 {
  ManagementClass diskClass = new ManagementClass("win32_logicaldisk");
  MethodDataCollection.MethodDataEnumerator diskEnumerator =
   diskClass.Methods.GetEnumerator();
  while(diskEnumerator.MoveNext())
  {
   MethodData method = diskEnumerator.Current;
   Console.WriteLine("Method = " + method.Name);
  }
  return 0;
 }
}
```

```
[Visual Basic]
Imports System
Imports System.Management

' This sample demonstrates how to enumerate all methods in
'Win32_LogicalDisk class using MethodDataEnumerator object.

Class Sample_MethodDataEnumerator
 Overloads Public Shared Function Main(args() As String) As Integer
  Dim diskClass As New ManagementClass("win32_logicaldisk")
  Dim diskEnumerator As _
      MethodDataCollection.MethodDataEnumerator = _
      diskClass.Methods.GetEnumerator()
  While diskEnumerator.MoveNext()
   Dim method As MethodData = diskEnumerator.Current
   Console.WriteLine("Method = " & method.Name)
```

```
End While
Return 0
End Function
End Class
```

Requirements

Namespace: System.Management

Platforms: Windows 98, Windows NT 4.0, Windows Millennium Edition, Windows 2000, Windows XP Home Edition, Windows XP Professional, Windows .NET Server family

Assembly: System.Management (in System.Management.dll)

MethodDataCollection.MethodDataEnumerator. Current Property

Returns the current **MethodData** in the **MethodDataCollection** enumeration.

```
[Visual Basic]
Public ReadOnly Property Current As MethodData
[C#]
public MethodData Current {get;}
[C++]
public: __property MethodData* get_Current();
[JScript]
public function get Current() : MethodData;
```

Property Value

The current **MethodData** item in the collection.

Requirements

Platforms: Windows 98, Windows NT 4.0, Windows Millennium Edition, Windows 2000, Windows XP Home Edition, Windows XP Professional, Windows .NET Server family

.NET Framework Security:

- Full trust for the immediate caller. This member cannot be used by partially trusted code.
-

MethodDataCollection.MethodDataEnumerator. System.Collections.IEnumerator.Current Property

Note: This namespace, class, or member is supported only in version 1.1 of the .NET Framework.

```
[Visual Basic]
Private ReadOnly Property Current As Object Implements _
   IEnumerator.Current
[C#]
object IEnumerator.Current {get;}
[C++]
private: __property Object*
   System::Collections::IEnumerator::get_Current();
[JScript]
private function get IEnumerator.Current() : Object;
```

Implements

IEnumerator.Current

Requirements

Platforms: Windows 98, Windows NT 4.0, Windows Millennium Edition, Windows 2000, Windows XP Home Edition, Windows XP Professional, Windows .NET Server family

.NET Framework Security:

- Full trust for the immediate caller. This member cannot be used by partially trusted code.

MethodDataCollection.MethodDataEnumerator. MoveNext Method

Moves to the next element in the **MethodDataCollection** enumeration.

```
[Visual Basic]
Public Overridable Function MoveNext() As Boolean Implements _
    IEnumerator.MoveNext
[C#]
public virtual bool MoveNext();
[C++]
public: virtual bool MoveNext();
[JScript]
public function MoveNext() : Boolean;
```

Return Value

true if the enumerator was successfully advanced to the next method; **false** if the enumerator has passed the end of the collection.

Implements

IEnumerator.MoveNext

Requirements

Platforms: Windows 98, Windows NT 4.0, Windows Millennium Edition, Windows 2000, Windows XP Home Edition, Windows XP Professional, Windows .NET Server family

.NET Framework Security:

- Full trust for the immediate caller. This member cannot be used by partially trusted code.

MethodDataCollection.MethodDataEnumerator. Reset Method

Resets the enumerator to the beginning of the **MethodDataCollection** enumeration.

```
[Visual Basic]
Public Overridable Sub Reset() Implements IEnumerator.Reset
[C#]
public virtual void Reset();
[C++]
public: virtual void Reset();
[JScript]
public function Reset();
```

Implements

IEnumerator.Reset

Requirements

Platforms: Windows 98, Windows NT 4.0, Windows Millennium Edition, Windows 2000, Windows XP Home Edition, Windows XP Professional, Windows .NET Server family

.NET Framework Security:

- Full trust for the immediate caller. This member cannot be used by partially trusted code.

ObjectGetOptions Class

Specifies options for getting a management object.

System.Object
　System.Management.ManagementOptions
　　System.Management.ObjectGetOptions

```
[Visual Basic]
Public Class ObjectGetOptions
   Inherits ManagementOptions
[C#]
public class ObjectGetOptions : ManagementOptions
[C++]
public __gc class ObjectGetOptions : public ManagementOptions
[JScript]
public class ObjectGetOptions extends ManagementOptions
```

Thread Safety

Any public static (**Shared** in Visual Basic) members of this type are safe for multithreaded operations. Any instance members are not guaranteed to be thread safe.

Example

```
[C#]
using System;
using System.Management;

// This example demonstrates how to set a timeout value and list
// all amended qualifiers in a ManagementClass object.
class Sample_ObjectGetOptions
{
    public static int Main(string[] args) {
        // Request amended qualifiers
        ObjectGetOptions options =
            new ObjectGetOptions(null, new TimeSpan(0,0,0,5), true);
        ManagementClass diskClass =
            new ManagementClass("root/cimv2", "Win32_Process",
options);
        foreach(QualifierData qualifier in diskClass.Qualifiers) {
            Console.WriteLine(qualifier.Name + ":" + qualifier.Value);
        }
        return 0;
    }
}
```

```
[Visual Basic]
Imports System
Imports System.Management

' This example demonstrates how to set a timeout value and list
' all amended qualifiers in a ManagementClass object.
Class Sample_ObjectGetOptions
    Overloads Public Shared Function Main(args() As String) As Integer
        ' Request amended qualifiers
        Dim options As _
            New ObjectGetOptions(Nothing, New TimeSpan
(0, 0, 0, 5), True)
        Dim diskClass As New ManagementClass( _
            "root/cimv2", _
            "Win32_Process", _
            options)
        Dim qualifier As QualifierData
        For Each qualifier In diskClass.Qualifiers
            Console.WriteLine(qualifier.Name & ":" & qualifier.Value)
        Next qualifier
        Return 0
    End Function
End Class
```

Requirements

Namespace: System.Management

Platforms: Windows 98, Windows NT 4.0, Windows Millennium Edition, Windows 2000, Windows XP Home Edition, Windows XP Professional, Windows .NET Server family

Assembly: System.Management (in System.Management.dll)

ObjectGetOptions Constructor

Initializes a new instance of the **ObjectGetOptions** class.

Overload List

Initializes a new instance of the **ObjectGetOptions** class for getting a WMI object, using default values. This is the default constructor.

　[Visual Basic] **Public Sub New()**

　[C#] **public ObjectGetOptions();**

　[C++] **public: ObjectGetOptions();**

　[JScript] **public function ObjectGetOptions();**

Initializes a new instance of the **ObjectGetOptions** class for getting a WMI object, using the specified provider-specific context.

　[Visual Basic] **Public Sub New(Management-NamedValueCollection)**

　[C#] **public ObjectGetOptions(Management-NamedValueCollection);**

　[C++] **public: ObjectGetOptions(Management-NamedValueCollection*);**

　[JScript] **public function ObjectGetOptions(Management-NamedValueCollection);**

Initializes a new instance of the **ObjectGetOptions** class for getting a WMI object, using the given options values.

　[Visual Basic] **Public Sub New(ManagementNamedValueCollection, TimeSpan, Boolean)**

　[C#] **public ObjectGetOptions(Management-NamedValueCollection, TimeSpan, bool);**

　[C++] **public: ObjectGetOptions(Management-NamedValueCollection*, TimeSpan, bool);**

　[JScript] **public function ObjectGetOptions(Management-NamedValueCollection, TimeSpan, Boolean);**

ObjectGetOptions Constructor ()

Initializes a new instance of the **ObjectGetOptions** class for getting a WMI object, using default values. This is the default constructor.

```
[Visual Basic]
Public Sub New()
[C#]
public ObjectGetOptions();
[C++]
public: ObjectGetOptions();
[JScript]
public function ObjectGetOptions();
```

Requirements

Platforms: Windows 98, Windows NT 4.0,
Windows Millennium Edition, Windows 2000,
Windows XP Home Edition, Windows XP Professional,
Windows .NET Server family

.NET Framework Security:

• Full trust for the immediate caller. This member cannot be used
  by partially trusted code. For more information, see **Using
  Libraries From Partially Trusted Code**

ObjectGetOptions Constructor (ManagementNamedValueCollection)

Initializes a new instance of the **ObjectGetOptions** class for getting
a WMI object, using the specified provider-specific context.

```
[Visual Basic]
Public Sub New( _
   ByVal context As ManagementNamedValueCollection _
)
[C#]
public ObjectGetOptions(
   ManagementNamedValueCollection context
);
[C++]
public: ObjectGetOptions(
   ManagementNamedValueCollection* context
);
[JScript]
public function ObjectGetOptions(
   context : ManagementNamedValueCollection
);
```

Parameters

context

A provider-specific, named-value pairs context object to be
passed through to the provider.

Requirements

Platforms: Windows 98, Windows NT 4.0,
Windows Millennium Edition, Windows 2000,
Windows XP Home Edition, Windows XP Professional,
Windows .NET Server family

.NET Framework Security:

• Full trust for the immediate caller. This member cannot be used
  by partially trusted code. For more information, see **Using
  Libraries From Partially Trusted Code**

ObjectGetOptions Constructor (ManagementNamedValueCollection, TimeSpan, Boolean)

Initializes a new instance of the **ObjectGetOptions** class for getting
a WMI object, using the given options values.

```
[Visual Basic]
Public Sub New( _
   ByVal context As ManagementNamedValueCollection, _
   ByVal timeout As TimeSpan, _
   ByVal useAmendedQualifiers As Boolean _
)
```

```
[C#]
public ObjectGetOptions(
   ManagementNamedValueCollection context,
   TimeSpan timeout,
   bool useAmendedQualifiers
);
[C++]
public: ObjectGetOptions(
   ManagementNamedValueCollection* context,
   TimeSpan timeout,
   bool useAmendedQualifiers
);
[JScript]
public function ObjectGetOptions(
   context : ManagementNamedValueCollection,
   timeout : TimeSpan,
   useAmendedQualifiers : Boolean
);
```

Parameters

context

A provider-specific, named-value pairs context object to be
passed through to the provider.

timeout

The length of time to let the operation perform before it times
out. The default is **InfiniteTimeout**.

useAmendedQualifiers

true if the returned objects should contain amended (locale-
aware) qualifiers; otherwise, **false**.

Requirements

Platforms: Windows 98, Windows NT 4.0,
Windows Millennium Edition, Windows 2000,
Windows XP Home Edition, Windows XP Professional,
Windows .NET Server family

.NET Framework Security:

• Full trust for the immediate caller. This member cannot be used
  by partially trusted code.

ObjectGetOptions.UseAmendedQualifiers Property

Gets or sets a value indicating whether the objects returned from
WMI should contain amended information. Typically, amended
information is localizable information attached to the WMI object,
such as object and property descriptions.

```
[Visual Basic]
Public Property UseAmendedQualifiers As Boolean
[C#]
public bool UseAmendedQualifiers {get; set;}
[C++]
public: __property bool get_UseAmendedQualifiers();
public: __property void set_UseAmendedQualifiers(bool);
[JScript]
public function get UseAmendedQualifiers() : Boolean;
public function set UseAmendedQualifiers(Boolean);
```

Property Value

true if the objects returned from WMI should contain amended
information; otherwise, **false**. The default value is **false**.

Requirements

Platforms: Windows 98, Windows NT 4.0,
Windows Millennium Edition, Windows 2000,
Windows XP Home Edition, Windows XP Professional,
Windows .NET Server family

.NET Framework Security:
- Full trust for the immediate caller. This member cannot be used by partially trusted code.

ObjectGetOptions.Clone Method

Returns a copy of the object.

```
[Visual Basic]
Overrides Public Function Clone() As Object Implements _
   ICloneable.Clone
[C#]
public override object Clone();
[C++]
public: Object* Clone();
[JScript]
public override function Clone() : Object;
```

Return Value

The cloned object.

Implements

ICloneable.Clone

Requirements

Platforms: Windows 98, Windows NT 4.0,
Windows Millennium Edition, Windows 2000,
Windows XP Home Edition, Windows XP Professional,
Windows .NET Server family

.NET Framework Security:
- Full trust for the immediate caller. This member cannot be used by partially trusted code.

ObjectPutEventArgs Class

Holds event data for the **ObjectPut** event.

System.Object
  System.EventArgs
    System.Management.ManagementEventArgs
      System.Management.ObjectPutEventArgs

```
[Visual Basic]
Public Class ObjectPutEventArgs
   Inherits ManagementEventArgs
[C#]
public class ObjectPutEventArgs : ManagementEventArgs
[C++]
public __gc class ObjectPutEventArgs : public ManagementEventArgs
[JScript]
public class ObjectPutEventArgs extends ManagementEventArgs
```

Thread Safety

Any public static (**Shared** in Visual Basic) members of this type are safe for multithreaded operations. Any instance members are not guaranteed to be thread safe.

Requirements

Namespace: System.Management

Platforms: Windows 98, Windows NT 4.0, Windows Millennium Edition, Windows 2000, Windows XP Home Edition, Windows XP Professional, Windows .NET Server family

Assembly: System.Management (in System.Management.dll)

ObjectPutEventArgs.Path Property

Gets the identity of the object that has been put.

```
[Visual Basic]
Public ReadOnly Property Path As ManagementPath
[C#]
public ManagementPath Path {get;}
[C++]
public: __property ManagementPath* get_Path();
[JScript]
public function get Path() : ManagementPath;
```

Property Value

A **ManagementPath** containing the path of the object that has been put.

Requirements

Platforms: Windows 98, Windows NT 4.0, Windows Millennium Edition, Windows 2000, Windows XP Home Edition, Windows XP Professional, Windows .NET Server family

.NET Framework Security:

- Full trust for the immediate caller. This member cannot be used by partially trusted code.

ObjectPutEventHandler Delegate

Represents the method that will handle the **ObjectPut** event.

```
[Visual Basic]
<Serializable>
Public Delegate Sub ObjectPutEventHandler( _
   ByVal sender As Object, _
   ByVal e As ObjectPutEventArgs _
)
[C#]
[Serializable]
public delegate void ObjectPutEventHandler(
   object sender,
   ObjectPutEventArgs e
);
[C++]
[Serializable]
public __gc __delegate void ObjectPutEventHandler(
   Object* sender,
   ObjectPutEventArgs* e
);
```

[JScript] In JScript, you can use the delegates in the .NET Framework, but you cannot define your own.

Parameters [Visual Basic, C#, C++]

The declaration of your event handler must have the same parameters as the **ObjectPutEventHandler** delegate declaration.

Requirements

Namespace: System.Management

Platforms: Windows 98, Windows NT 4.0, Windows Millennium Edition, Windows 2000, Windows XP Home Edition, Windows XP Professional, Windows .NET Server family

Assembly: System.Management (in System.Management.dll)

ObjectQuery Class

Represents a management query that returns instances or classes.

System.Object
  System.Management.ManagementQuery
    System.Management.ObjectQuery
      System.Management.WqlObjectQuery

```
[Visual Basic]
Public Class ObjectQuery
   Inherits ManagementQuery
[C#]
public class ObjectQuery : ManagementQuery
[C++]
public __gc class ObjectQuery : public ManagementQuery
[JScript]
public class ObjectQuery extends ManagementQuery
```

Thread Safety

Any public static (**Shared** in Visual Basic) members of this type are safe for multithreaded operations. Any instance members are not guaranteed to be thread safe.

Remarks

This class or its derivatives are used to specify a query in the **ManagementObjectSearcher**. Use a more specific query class whenever possible.

Example

```
[C#]
using System;
using System.Management;

// This sample demonstrates creating a query.

class Sample_ObjectQuery
{
    public static int Main(string[] args)
    {
        ObjectQuery objectQuery = new ObjectQuery
("select * from Win32_Share");
        ManagementObjectSearcher searcher =
            new ManagementObjectSearcher(objectQuery);
        foreach (ManagementObject share in searcher.Get())
        {
            Console.WriteLine("Share = " + share["Name"]);
        }
        return 0;
    }
}

[Visual Basic]
Imports System
Imports System.Management

' This sample demonstrates creating a query.

Class Sample_ObjectQuery
    Overloads Public Shared Function Main(args() As String) As Integer
        Dim objectQuery As New ObjectQuery("select * from Win32_Share")
        Dim searcher As New ManagementObjectSearcher(objectQuery)
        Dim share As ManagementObject
        For Each share In searcher.Get()
            Console.WriteLine("Share = " & share("Name"))
        Next share
        Return 0
    End Function
End Class
```

Requirements

Namespace: System.Management

Platforms: Windows 98, Windows NT 4.0, Windows Millennium Edition, Windows 2000, Windows XP Home Edition, Windows XP Professional, Windows .NET Server family

Assembly: System.Management (in System.Management.dll)

ObjectQuery Constructor

Initializes a new instance of the **ObjectQuery** class.

Overload List

Initializes a new instance of the **ObjectQuery** class with no initialized values. This is the default constructor.

> [Visual Basic] **Public Sub New()**
> [C#] **public ObjectQuery();**
> [C++] **public: ObjectQuery();**
> [JScript] **public function ObjectQuery();**

Initializes a new instance of the **ObjectQuery** class for a specific query string.

> [Visual Basic] **Public Sub New(String)**
> [C#] **public ObjectQuery(string);**
> [C++] **public: ObjectQuery(String*);**
> [JScript] **public function ObjectQuery(String);**

Initializes a new instance of the **ObjectQuery** class for a specific query string and language.

> [Visual Basic] **Public Sub New(String, String)**
> [C#] **public ObjectQuery(string, string);**
> [C++] **public: ObjectQuery(String*, String*);**
> [JScript] **public function ObjectQuery(String, String);**

ObjectQuery Constructor ()

Initializes a new instance of the **ObjectQuery** class with no initialized values. This is the default constructor.

```
[Visual Basic]
Public Sub New()
[C#]
public ObjectQuery();
[C++]
public: ObjectQuery();
[JScript]
public function ObjectQuery();
```

Requirements

Platforms: Windows 98, Windows NT 4.0, Windows Millennium Edition, Windows 2000, Windows XP Home Edition, Windows XP Professional, Windows .NET Server family

.NET Framework Security:

- Full trust for the immediate caller. This member cannot be used by partially trusted code. For more information, see **Using Libraries From Partially Trusted Code**

ObjectQuery Constructor (String)

Initializes a new instance of the **ObjectQuery** class for a specific query string.

```
[Visual Basic]
Public Sub New( _
   ByVal query As String _
)
[C#]
public ObjectQuery(
   string query
);
[C++]
public: ObjectQuery(
   String* query
);
[JScript]
public function ObjectQuery(
   query : String
);
```

Parameters

query

   The string representation of the query.

Requirements

Platforms: Windows 98, Windows NT 4.0, Windows Millennium Edition, Windows 2000, Windows XP Home Edition, Windows XP Professional, Windows .NET Server family

.NET Framework Security:

• Full trust for the immediate caller. This member cannot be used by partially trusted code.

ObjectQuery Constructor (String, String)

Initializes a new instance of the **ObjectQuery** class for a specific query string and language.

```
[Visual Basic]
Public Sub New( _
   ByVal language As String, _
   ByVal query As String _
)
[C#]
public ObjectQuery(
   string language,
   string query
);
[C++]
public: ObjectQuery(
   String* language,
   String* query
);
[JScript]
public function ObjectQuery(
   language : String,
   query : String
);
```

Parameters

language

   The query language in which this query is specified.

query

   The string representation of the query.

Requirements

Platforms: Windows 98, Windows NT 4.0, Windows Millennium Edition, Windows 2000, Windows XP Home Edition, Windows XP Professional, Windows .NET Server family

.NET Framework Security:

• Full trust for the immediate caller. This member cannot be used by partially trusted code.

ObjectQuery.Clone Method

Returns a copy of the object.

```
[Visual Basic]
Overrides Public Function Clone() As Object Implements _
   ICloneable.Clone
[C#]
public override object Clone();
[C++]
public: Object* Clone();
[JScript]
public override function Clone() : Object;
```

Return Value

The cloned object.

Implements

ICloneable.Clone

Requirements

Platforms: Windows 98, Windows NT 4.0, Windows Millennium Edition, Windows 2000, Windows XP Home Edition, Windows XP Professional, Windows .NET Server family

.NET Framework Security:

• Full trust for the immediate caller. This member cannot be used by partially trusted code.

ObjectReadyEventArgs Class

Holds event data for the **ObjectReady** event.

System.Object
  System.EventArgs
    System.Management.ManagementEventArgs
      System.Management.ObjectReadyEventArgs

```
[Visual Basic]
Public Class ObjectReadyEventArgs
    Inherits ManagementEventArgs
[C#]
public class ObjectReadyEventArgs : ManagementEventArgs
[C++]
public __gc class ObjectReadyEventArgs : public ManagementEventArgs
[JScript]
public class ObjectReadyEventArgs extends ManagementEventArgs
```

Thread Safety

Any public static (**Shared** in Visual Basic) members of this type are
safe for multithreaded operations. Any instance members are not
guaranteed to be thread safe.

Requirements

Namespace: System.Management

Platforms: Windows 98, Windows NT 4.0,
Windows Millennium Edition, Windows 2000,
Windows XP Home Edition, Windows XP Professional,
Windows .NET Server family

Assembly: System.Management (in System.Management.dll)

ObjectReadyEventArgs.NewObject Property

Gets the newly-returned object.

```
[Visual Basic]
Public ReadOnly Property NewObject As ManagementBaseObject
[C#]
public ManagementBaseObject NewObject {get;}
[C++]
public: __property ManagementBaseObject* get_NewObject();
[JScript]
public function get NewObject() : ManagementBaseObject;
```

Property Value

A **ManagementBaseObject** representing the newly-returned object.

Requirements

Platforms: Windows 98, Windows NT 4.0,
Windows Millennium Edition, Windows 2000,
Windows XP Home Edition, Windows XP Professional,
Windows .NET Server family

.NET Framework Security:

- Full trust for the immediate caller. This member cannot be used
  by partially trusted code.

ObjectReadyEventHandler Delegate

Represents the method that will handle the **ObjectReady** event.

```
[Visual Basic]
<Serializable>
Public Delegate Sub ObjectReadyEventHandler( _
   ByVal sender As Object, _
   ByVal e As ObjectReadyEventArgs _
)
[C#]
[Serializable]
public delegate void ObjectReadyEventHandler(
   object sender,
   ObjectReadyEventArgs e
);
[C++]
[Serializable]
public __gc __delegate void ObjectReadyEventHandler(
   Object* sender,
   ObjectReadyEventArgs* e
);
```

[JScript] In JScript, you can use the delegates in the .NET Framework, but you cannot define your own.

Parameters [Visual Basic, C#, C++]

The declaration of your event handler must have the same parameters as the **ObjectReadyEventHandler** delegate declaration.

Requirements

Namespace: System.Management

Platforms: Windows 98, Windows NT 4.0, Windows Millennium Edition, Windows 2000, Windows XP Home Edition, Windows XP Professional, Windows .NET Server family

Assembly: System.Management (in System.Management.dll)

ProgressEventArgs Class

Holds event data for the **Progress** event.

System.Object
  System.EventArgs
    System.Management.ManagementEventArgs
     System.Management.ProgressEventArgs

```
[Visual Basic]
Public Class ProgressEventArgs
   Inherits ManagementEventArgs
[C#]
public class ProgressEventArgs : ManagementEventArgs
[C++]
public __gc class ProgressEventArgs : public ManagementEventArgs
[JScript]
public class ProgressEventArgs extends ManagementEventArgs
```

Thread Safety

Any public static (**Shared** in Visual Basic) members of this type are
safe for multithreaded operations. Any instance members are not
guaranteed to be thread safe.

Requirements

Namespace: System.Management

Platforms: Windows 98, Windows NT 4.0,
Windows Millennium Edition, Windows 2000,
Windows XP Home Edition, Windows XP Professional,
Windows .NET Server family

Assembly: System.Management (in System.Management.dll)

ProgressEventArgs.Current Property

Gets the current amount of work done by the operation. This is
always less than or equal to **UpperBound**.

```
[Visual Basic]
Public ReadOnly Property Current As Integer
[C#]
public int Current {get;}
[C++]
public: __property int get_Current();
[JScript]
public function get Current() : int;
```

Property Value

An integer representing the current amount of work already
completed by the operation.

Requirements

Platforms: Windows 98, Windows NT 4.0,
Windows Millennium Edition, Windows 2000,
Windows XP Home Edition, Windows XP Professional,
Windows .NET Server family

.NET Framework Security:

- Full trust for the immediate caller. This member cannot be used
  by partially trusted code.

ProgressEventArgs.Message Property

Gets or sets optional additional information regarding the operation's
progress.

```
[Visual Basic]
Public ReadOnly Property Message As String
[C#]
public string Message {get;}
[C++]
public: __property String* get_Message();
[JScript]
public function get Message() : String;
```

Property Value

A string containing additional information regarding the operation's
progress.

Requirements

Platforms: Windows 98, Windows NT 4.0,
Windows Millennium Edition, Windows 2000,
Windows XP Home Edition, Windows XP Professional,
Windows .NET Server family

.NET Framework Security:

- Full trust for the immediate caller. This member cannot be used
  by partially trusted code.

ProgressEventArgs.UpperBound Property

Gets the total amount of work required to be done by the operation.

```
[Visual Basic]
Public ReadOnly Property UpperBound As Integer
[C#]
public int UpperBound {get;}
[C++]
public: __property int get_UpperBound();
[JScript]
public function get UpperBound() : int;
```

Property Value

An integer representing the total amount of work for the operation.

Requirements

Platforms: Windows 98, Windows NT 4.0,
Windows Millennium Edition, Windows 2000,
Windows XP Home Edition, Windows XP Professional,
Windows .NET Server family

.NET Framework Security:

- Full trust for the immediate caller. This member cannot be used
  by partially trusted code.

ProgressEventHandler Delegate

Represents the method that will handle the **Progress** event.

```
[Visual Basic]
<Serializable>
Public Delegate Sub ProgressEventHandler( _
   ByVal sender As Object, _
   ByVal e As ProgressEventArgs _
)
[C#]
[Serializable]
public delegate void ProgressEventHandler(
   object sender,
   ProgressEventArgs e
);
[C++]
[Serializable]
public __gc __delegate void ProgressEventHandler(
   Object* sender,
   ProgressEventArgs* e
);
```

[JScript] In JScript, you can use the delegates in the .NET Framework, but you cannot define your own.

Parameters [Visual Basic, C#, C++]

The declaration of your event handler must have the same parameters as the **ProgressEventHandler** delegate declaration.

Requirements

Namespace: System.Management

Platforms: Windows 98, Windows NT 4.0, Windows Millennium Edition, Windows 2000, Windows XP Home Edition, Windows XP Professional, Windows .NET Server family

Assembly: System.Management (in System.Management.dll)

PropertyData Class

Represents information about a WMI property.

For a list of all members of this type, see **PropertyData Members**.

System.Object
   System.Management.PropertyData

```
[Visual Basic]
Public Class PropertyData
[C#]
public class PropertyData
[C++]
public __gc class PropertyData
[JScript]
public class PropertyData
```

Thread Safety

Any public static (**Shared** in Visual Basic) members of this type are safe for multithreaded operations. Any instance members are not guaranteed to be thread safe.

Example

```
[C#]
using System;
using System.Management;

// This sample displays all properties that qualifies the
"DeviceID" property
// in Win32_LogicalDisk.DeviceID='C' instance.
class Sample_PropertyData
{
    public static int Main(string[] args) {
        ManagementObject disk =
            new ManagementObject("Win32_LogicalDisk.DeviceID=\"C:\"");
        PropertyData diskProperty = disk.Properties["DeviceID"];
        Console.WriteLine("Name: " + diskProperty.Name);
        Console.WriteLine("Type: " + diskProperty.Type);
        Console.WriteLine("Value: " + diskProperty.Value);
        Console.WriteLine("IsArray: " + diskProperty.IsArray);
        Console.WriteLine("IsLocal: " + diskProperty.IsLocal);
        Console.WriteLine("Origin: " + diskProperty.Origin);
        return 0;
    }
}
```

```
[Visual Basic]
Imports System
Imports System.Management

' This sample displays all properties that qualifies the
"DeviceID" property
' in Win32_LogicalDisk.DeviceID='C' instance.
Class Sample_PropertyData
    Overloads Public Shared Function Main(args() As String) As Integer
        Dim disk As New
ManagementObject("Win32_LogicalDisk.DeviceID=""C:""")
        Dim diskProperty As PropertyData = disk.Properties("DeviceID")
        Console.WriteLine("Name: " & diskProperty.Name)
        Console.WriteLine("Type: " & diskProperty.Type)
        Console.WriteLine("Value: " & diskProperty.Value)
        Console.WriteLine("IsArray: " & diskProperty.IsArray)
        Console.WriteLine("IsLocal: " & diskProperty.IsLocal)
        Console.WriteLine("Origin: " & diskProperty.Origin)
        Return 0
    End Function
End Class
```

Requirements

Namespace: System.Management

Platforms: Windows 98, Windows NT 4.0, Windows Millennium Edition, Windows 2000, Windows XP Home Edition, Windows XP Professional, Windows .NET Server family

Assembly: System.Management (in System.Management.dll)

PropertyData.IsArray Property

Gets or sets a value indicating whether the property is an array.

```
[Visual Basic]
Public ReadOnly Property IsArray As Boolean
[C#]
public bool IsArray {get;}
[C++]
public: __property bool get_IsArray();
[JScript]
public function get IsArray() : Boolean;
```

Property Value

true if the property is an array; otherwise, **false**.

Requirements

Platforms: Windows 98, Windows NT 4.0, Windows Millennium Edition, Windows 2000, Windows XP Home Edition, Windows XP Professional, Windows .NET Server family

.NET Framework Security:

- Full trust for the immediate caller. This member cannot be used by partially trusted code.

PropertyData.IsLocal Property

Gets or sets a value indicating whether the property has been defined in the current WMI class.

```
[Visual Basic]
Public ReadOnly Property IsLocal As Boolean
[C#]
public bool IsLocal {get;}
[C++]
public: __property bool get_IsLocal();
[JScript]
public function get IsLocal() : Boolean;
```

Property Value

true if the property has been defined in the current WMI class; otherwise, **false**.

Requirements

Platforms: Windows 98, Windows NT 4.0, Windows Millennium Edition, Windows 2000, Windows XP Home Edition, Windows XP Professional, Windows .NET Server family

.NET Framework Security:

- Full trust for the immediate caller. This member cannot be used by partially trusted code.

PropertyData.Name Property

Gets or sets the name of the property.

```
[Visual Basic]
Public ReadOnly Property Name As String
```

```
[C#]
public string Name {get;}
[C++]
public: __property String* get_Name();
[JScript]
public function get Name() : String;
```

Property Value

A string containing the name of the property.

Requirements

Platforms: Windows 98, Windows NT 4.0,
Windows Millennium Edition, Windows 2000,
Windows XP Home Edition, Windows XP Professional,
Windows .NET Server family

.NET Framework Security:

- Full trust for the immediate caller. This member cannot be used by partially trusted code.

PropertyData.Origin Property

Gets or sets the name of the WMI class in the hierarchy in which the property was introduced.

```
[Visual Basic]
Public ReadOnly Property Origin As String
[C#]
public string Origin {get;}
[C++]
public: __property String* get_Origin();
[JScript]
public function get Origin() : String;
```

Property Value

A string containing the name of the originating WMI class.

Requirements

Platforms: Windows 98, Windows NT 4.0,
Windows Millennium Edition, Windows 2000,
Windows XP Home Edition, Windows XP Professional,
Windows .NET Server family

.NET Framework Security:

- Full trust for the immediate caller. This member cannot be used by partially trusted code.

PropertyData.Qualifiers Property

Gets or sets the set of qualifiers defined on the property.

```
[Visual Basic]
Public ReadOnly Property Qualifiers As QualifierDataCollection
[C#]
public QualifierDataCollection Qualifiers {get;}
[C++]
public: __property QualifierDataCollection* get_Qualifiers();
[JScript]
public function get Qualifiers() : QualifierDataCollection;
```

Property Value

A **QualifierDataCollection** that represents the set of qualifiers defined on the property.

Requirements

Platforms: Windows 98, Windows NT 4.0,
Windows Millennium Edition, Windows 2000,
Windows XP Home Edition, Windows XP Professional,
Windows .NET Server family

.NET Framework Security:

- Full trust for the immediate caller. This member cannot be used by partially trusted code.

PropertyData.Type Property

Gets or sets the CIM type of the property.

```
[Visual Basic]
Public ReadOnly Property Type As CimType
[C#]
public CimType Type {get;}
[C++]
public: __property CimType get_Type();
[JScript]
public function get Type() : CimType;
```

Property Value

A **CimType** value representing the CIM type of the property.

Requirements

Platforms: Windows 98, Windows NT 4.0,
Windows Millennium Edition, Windows 2000,
Windows XP Home Edition, Windows XP Professional,
Windows .NET Server family

.NET Framework Security:

- Full trust for the immediate caller. This member cannot be used by partially trusted code.

PropertyData.Value Property

Gets or sets the current value of the property.

```
[Visual Basic]
Public Property Value As Object
[C#]
public object Value {get; set;}
[C++]
public: __property Object* get_Value();
public: __property void set_Value(Object*);
[JScript]
public function get Value() : Object;
public function set Value(Object);
```

Property Value

An object containing the value of the property.

Requirements

Platforms: Windows 98, Windows NT 4.0,
Windows Millennium Edition, Windows 2000,
Windows XP Home Edition, Windows XP Professional,
Windows .NET Server family

.NET Framework Security:

- Full trust for the immediate caller. This member cannot be used by partially trusted code.

PropertyDataCollection Class

Represents the set of properties of a WMI object.

System.Object
  System.Management.PropertyDataCollection

[Visual Basic]
Public Class PropertyDataCollection
    Implements ICollection, IEnumerable
[C#]
public class PropertyDataCollection : ICollection, IEnumerable
[C++]
public __gc class PropertyDataCollection : public ICollection,
   IEnumerable
[JScript]
public class PropertyDataCollection implements ICollection,
   IEnumerable

Thread Safety

Any public static (**Shared** in Visual Basic) members of this type are safe for multithreaded operations. Any instance members are not guaranteed to be thread safe.

Example

```
[C#]
using System;
using System.Management;

// This sample demonstrates how to enumerate properties
// in a ManagementObject object.
class Sample_PropertyDataCollection
{
    public static int Main(string[] args) {
        ManagementObject disk = new
ManagementObject("win32_logicaldisk.deviceid = \"c:\"");
        PropertyDataCollection diskProperties = disk.Properties;
        foreach (PropertyData diskProperty in diskProperties) {
            Console.WriteLine("Property = " + diskProperty.Name);
        }
        return 0;
    }
}

[Visual Basic]
Imports System
Imports System.Management

' This sample demonstrates how to enumerate properties
' in a ManagementObject object.
Class Sample_PropertyDataCollection
    Overloads Public Shared Function Main(args() As String) As Integer
        Dim disk As New
ManagementObject("win32_logicaldisk.deviceid=""c:""")
        Dim diskProperties As PropertyDataCollection = disk.Properties
        Dim diskProperty As PropertyData
        For Each diskProperty In diskProperties
            Console.WriteLine("Property = " & diskProperty.Name)
        Next diskProperty
        Return 0
    End Function
End Class
```

Requirements

Namespace: System.Management

Platforms: Windows 98, Windows NT 4.0, Windows Millennium Edition, Windows 2000, Windows XP Home Edition, Windows XP Professional, Windows .NET Server family

Assembly: System.Management (in System.Management.dll)

PropertyDataCollection.Count Property

Gets or sets the number of objects in the **PropertyDataCollection**.

[Visual Basic]
Public Overridable ReadOnly Property Count As Integer Implements _
  ICollection.Count
[C#]
public virtual int Count {get;}
[C++]
public: __property virtual int get_Count();
[JScript]
public function get Count() : int;

Property Value

The number of objects in the collection.

Implements

ICollection.Count

Requirements

Platforms: Windows 98, Windows NT 4.0, Windows Millennium Edition, Windows 2000, Windows XP Home Edition, Windows XP Professional, Windows .NET Server family

.NET Framework Security:

- Full trust for the immediate caller. This member cannot be used by partially trusted code

PropertyDataCollection.IsSynchronized Property

Gets or sets a value indicating whether the object is synchronized.

[Visual Basic]
Public Overridable ReadOnly Property IsSynchronized As Boolean _
  Implements ICollection.IsSynchronized
[C#]
public virtual bool IsSynchronized {get;}
[C++]
public: __property virtual bool get_IsSynchronized();
[JScript]
public function get IsSynchronized() : Boolean;

Property Value

true if the object is synchronized; otherwise, **false**.

Implements

ICollection.IsSynchronized

Requirements

Platforms: Windows 98, Windows NT 4.0, Windows Millennium Edition, Windows 2000, Windows XP Home Edition, Windows XP Professional, Windows .NET Server family

.NET Framework Security:

- Full trust for the immediate caller. This member cannot be used by partially trusted code

PropertyDataCollection.Item Property

Returns the specified property from the **PropertyDataCollection**, using [] syntax.

[C#] In C#, this property is the indexer for the
PropertyDataCollection class.

```
[Visual Basic]
Public Overridable Default ReadOnly Property Item( _
  ByVal propertyName As String _
) As PropertyData
[C#]
public virtual PropertyData this[
  string propertyName
] {get;}
[C++]
public: __property virtual PropertyData* get_Item(
  String* propertyName
);
[JScript]
returnValue = PropertyDataCollectionObject.Item(propertyName);
-or-
returnValue = PropertyDataCollectionObject(propertyName);
```

[JScript] In JScript, you can use the default indexed properties
defined by a type, but you cannot explicitly define your own.
However, specifying the **expando** attribute on a class automatically
provides a default indexed property whose type is **Object** and whose
index type is **String**.

Arguments [JScript]

propertyName

The name of the property to retrieve.

Parameters [Visual Basic, C#, C++]

propertyName

The name of the property to retrieve.

Property Value

A **PropertyData**, based on the name specified.

Example

```
[C#]
ManagementObject o = new ManagementObject
("Win32_LogicalDisk.Name = 'C:'");
Console.WriteLine("Free space on C: drive is: ",
c.Properties["FreeSpace"].Value);

[Visual Basic]
Dim o As New ManagementObject("Win32_LogicalDisk.Name=""C:""")
Console.WriteLine("Free space on C: drive is: " &
c.Properties("FreeSpace").Value)
```

Requirements

Platforms: Windows 98, Windows NT 4.0,
Windows Millennium Edition, Windows 2000,
Windows XP Home Edition, Windows XP Professional,
Windows .NET Server family

.NET Framework Security:

- Full trust for the immediate caller. This member cannot be used
  by partially trusted code

PropertyDataCollection.SyncRoot Property

Gets or sets the object to be used for synchronization.

```
[Visual Basic]
Public Overridable ReadOnly Property SyncRoot As Object  Implements _
  ICollection.SyncRoot
[C#]
public virtual object SyncRoot {get;}
```

```
[C++]
public: __property virtual Object* get_SyncRoot();
[JScript]
public function get SyncRoot() : Object;
```

Property Value

The object to be used for synchronization.

Implements

ICollection.SyncRoot

Requirements

Platforms: Windows 98, Windows NT 4.0,
Windows Millennium Edition, Windows 2000,
Windows XP Home Edition, Windows XP Professional,
Windows .NET Server family

.NET Framework Security:

- Full trust for the immediate caller. This member cannot be used
  by partially trusted code

PropertyDataCollection.Add Method

Adds a new **PropertyData** with the specified value.

Overload List

Adds a new **PropertyData** with the specified value. The value
cannot be null and must be convertable to a CIM type.

> [Visual Basic] **Overloads Public Overridable Sub Add(String, Object)**
>
> [C#] **public virtual void Add(string, object);**
>
> [C++] **public: virtual void Add(String*, Object*);**
>
> [JScript] **public function Add(String, Object);**

Adds a new **PropertyData** with no assigned value.

> [Visual Basic] **Overloads Public Sub Add(String, CimType, Boolean)**
>
> [C#] **public void Add(string, CimType, bool);**
>
> [C++] **public: void Add(String*, CimType, bool);**
>
> [JScript] **public function Add(String, CimType, Boolean);**

Adds a new **PropertyData** with the specified value and CIM type.

> [Visual Basic] **Overloads Public Sub Add(String, Object, CimType)**
>
> [C#] **public void Add(string, object, CimType);**
>
> [C++] **public: void Add(String*, Object*, CimType);**
>
> [JScript] **public function Add(String, Object, CimType);**

PropertyDataCollection.Add Method (String, Object)

Adds a new **PropertyData** with the specified value. The value
cannot be null and must be convertable to a CIM type.

```
[Visual Basic]
Overloads Public Overridable Sub Add( _
  ByVal propertyName As String, _
  ByVal propertyValue As Object _
)
[C#]
public virtual void Add(
  string propertyName,
  object propertyValue
);
```

```
[C++]
public: virtual void Add(
   String* propertyName,
   Object* propertyValue
);
[JScript]
public function Add(
   propertyName : String,
   propertyValue : Object
);
```

Parameters

propertyName
>The name of the new property.

propertyValue
>The value of the property (cannot be null).

Remarks

Properties can only be added to class definitions, not to instances. This method is only valid when invoked on a **PropertyDataCollection** in a **ManagementClass**.

Requirements

Platforms: Windows 98, Windows NT 4.0, Windows Millennium Edition, Windows 2000, Windows XP Home Edition, Windows XP Professional, Windows .NET Server family

.NET Framework Security:

• Full trust for the immediate caller. This member cannot be used by partially trusted code

PropertyDataCollection.Add Method (String, CimType, Boolean)

Adds a new **PropertyData** with no assigned value.

```
[Visual Basic]
Overloads Public Sub Add( _
   ByVal propertyName As String, _
   ByVal propertyType As CimType, _
   ByVal isArray As Boolean _
)
[C#]
public void Add(
   string propertyName,
   CimType propertyType,
   bool isArray
);
[C++]
public: void Add(
   String* propertyName,
   CimType propertyType,
   bool isArray
);
[JScript]
public function Add(
   propertyName : String,
   propertyType : CimType,
   isArray : Boolean
);
```

Parameters

propertyName
>The name of the property.

propertyType
>The CIM type of the property.

isArray
>**true** to specify that the property is an array type; otherwise, **false**.

Remarks

Properties can only be added to class definitions, not to instances. This method is only valid when invoked on a **PropertyDataCollection** in a **ManagementClass**.

Requirements

Platforms: Windows 98, Windows NT 4.0, Windows Millennium Edition, Windows 2000, Windows XP Home Edition, Windows XP Professional, Windows .NET Server family

.NET Framework Security:

• Full trust for the immediate caller. This member cannot be used by partially trusted code

PropertyDataCollection.Add Method (String, Object, CimType)

Adds a new **PropertyData** with the specified value and CIM type.

```
[Visual Basic]
Overloads Public Sub Add( _
   ByVal propertyName As String, _
   ByVal propertyValue As Object, _
   ByVal propertyType As CimType _
)
[C#]
public void Add(
   string propertyName,
   object propertyValue,
   CimType propertyType
);
[C++]
public: void Add(
   String* propertyName,
   Object* propertyValue,
   CimType propertyType
);
[JScript]
public function Add(
   propertyName : String,
   propertyValue : Object,
   propertyType : CimType
);
```

Parameters

propertyName
>The name of the property.

propertyValue
>The value of the property (which can be null).

propertyType
>The CIM type of the property.

Remarks

Properties can only be added to class definitions, not to instances. This method is only valid when invoked on a **PropertyDataCollection** in a **ManagementClass**.

Requirements

Platforms: Windows 98, Windows NT 4.0, Windows Millennium Edition, Windows 2000, Windows XP Home Edition, Windows XP Professional, Windows .NET Server family

.NET Framework Security:

*   Full trust for the immediate caller. This member cannot be used by partially trusted code

PropertyDataCollection.CopyTo Method

Copies the **PropertyDataCollection** into an array.

Overload List

Copies the **PropertyDataCollection** into an array.

> [Visual Basic] **Overloads Public Overridable Sub CopyTo(Array, Integer) Implements ICollection.CopyTo**
>
> [C#] **public virtual void CopyTo(Array, int);**
>
> [C++] **public: virtual void CopyTo(Array*, int);**
>
> [JScript] **public function CopyTo(Array, int);**

Copies the **PropertyDataCollection** to a specialized **PropertyData** object array.

> [Visual Basic] **Overloads Public Sub CopyTo(PropertyData(), Integer)**
>
> [C#] **public void CopyTo(PropertyData[], int);**
>
> [C++] **public: void CopyTo(PropertyData*[], int);**
>
> [JScript] **public function CopyTo(PropertyData[], int);**

PropertyDataCollection.CopyTo Method (Array, Int32)

Copies the **PropertyDataCollection** into an array.

```
[Visual Basic]
Overloads Public Overridable Sub CopyTo( _
    ByVal array As Array, _
    ByVal index As Integer _
) Implements ICollection.CopyTo
[C#]
public virtual void CopyTo(
    Array array,
    int index
);
[C++]
public: virtual void CopyTo(
    Array* array,
    int index
);
[JScript]
public function CopyTo(
    array : Array,
    index : int
);
```

Parameters

array
> The array to which to copy the **PropertyDataCollection**.

index
> The index from which to start copying.

Implements

ICollection.CopyTo

Requirements

Platforms: Windows 98, Windows NT 4.0, Windows Millennium Edition, Windows 2000, Windows XP Home Edition, Windows XP Professional, Windows .NET Server family

.NET Framework Security:

*   Full trust for the immediate caller. This member cannot be used by partially trusted code

PropertyDataCollection.CopyTo Method (PropertyData[], Int32)

Copies the **PropertyDataCollection** to a specialized **PropertyData** object array.

```
[Visual Basic]
Overloads Public Sub CopyTo( _
    ByVal propertyArray() As PropertyData, _
    ByVal index As Integer _
)
[C#]
public void CopyTo(
    PropertyData[] propertyArray,
    int index
);
[C++]
public: void CopyTo(
    PropertyData* propertyArray[],
    int index
);
[JScript]
public function CopyTo(
    propertyArray : PropertyData[],
    index : int
);
```

Parameters

propertyArray
> The destination array to contain the copied **PropertyDataCollection**.

index
> The index in the destination array from which to start copying.

Requirements

Platforms: Windows 98, Windows NT 4.0, Windows Millennium Edition, Windows 2000, Windows XP Home Edition, Windows XP Professional, Windows .NET Server family

.NET Framework Security:

*   Full trust for the immediate caller. This member cannot be used by partially trusted code

PropertyDataCollection.GetEnumerator Method

Returns the enumerator for this **PropertyDataCollection**.

```
[Visual Basic]
Public Function GetEnumerator() As PropertyDataEnumerator
[C#]
public PropertyDataEnumerator GetEnumerator();
[C++]
public: PropertyDataEnumerator* GetEnumerator();
[JScript]
public function GetEnumerator() : PropertyDataEnumerator;
```

Return Value

An **IEnumerator** that can be used to iterate through the collection.

Requirements

Platforms: Windows 98, Windows NT 4.0,
Windows Millennium Edition, Windows 2000,
Windows XP Home Edition, Windows XP Professional,
Windows .NET Server family

.NET Framework Security:

- Full trust for the immediate caller. This member cannot be used by partially trusted code

PropertyDataCollection.IEnumerable.Get-Enumerator Method

This member supports the .NET Framework infrastructure and is not intended to be used directly from your code.

```
[Visual Basic]
Private Function GetEnumerator() As IEnumerator Implements _
   IEnumerable.GetEnumerator
[C#]
IEnumerator IEnumerable.GetEnumerator();
[C++]
private: IEnumerator* IEnumerable::GetEnumerator();
[JScript]
private function IEnumerable.GetEnumerator() : IEnumerator;
```

PropertyDataCollection.Remove Method

Removes a **PropertyData** from the **PropertyDataCollection**.

```
[Visual Basic]
Public Overridable Sub Remove( _
   ByVal propertyName As String _
)
[C#]
public virtual void Remove(
   string propertyName
);
[C++]
public: virtual void Remove(
   String* propertyName
);
[JScript]
public function Remove(
   propertyName : String
);
```

Parameters

propertyName
   The name of the property to be removed.

Remarks

Properties can only be removed from class definitions, not from instances. This method is only valid when invoked on a property collection in a **ManagementClass**.

Example

```
[C#]
ManagementClass c = new ManagementClass("MyClass");
c.Properties.Remove("PropThatIDontWantOnThisClass");
```

```
[Visual Basic]
Dim c As New ManagementClass("MyClass")
c.Properties.Remove("PropThatIDontWantOnThisClass")
```

Requirements

Platforms: Windows 98, Windows NT 4.0,
Windows Millennium Edition, Windows 2000,
Windows XP Home Edition, Windows XP Professional,
Windows .NET Server family

.NET Framework Security:

- Full trust for the immediate caller. This member cannot be used by partially trusted code

PropertyDataCollection.Pro-pertyDataEnumerator Class

Represents the enumerator for **PropertyData** objects in the **PropertyDataCollection**.

System.Object
   System.Management.PropertyDataCollection.PropertyDataE
numerator

```
[Visual Basic]
Public Class PropertyDataCollection.PropertyDataEnumerator
   Implements IEnumerator
[C#]
public class PropertyDataCollection.PropertyDataEnumerator :
   IEnumerator
[C++]
public __gc class PropertyDataCollection.PropertyDataEnumerator :
   public IEnumerator
[JScript]
public class PropertyDataCollection.PropertyDataEnumerator
   implements IEnumerator
```

Thread Safety

Any public static (**Shared** in Visual Basic) members of this type are safe for multithreaded operations. Any instance members are not guaranteed to be thread safe.

Example

```
[C#]
using System;
using System.Management;

// This sample demonstrates how to enumerate all properties in a
// ManagementObject using the PropertyDataEnumerator object.
class Sample_PropertyDataEnumerator
{
    public static int Main(string[] args) {
        ManagementObject disk = new
ManagementObject("Win32_LogicalDisk.DeviceID='C:'");
        PropertyDataCollection.PropertyDataEnumerator
propertyEnumerator = disk.Properties.GetEnumerator();
        while(propertyEnumerator.MoveNext()) {
            PropertyData p = (PropertyData)propertyEnumerator.Current;
            Console.WriteLine("Property found: " + p.Name);
        }
        return 0;
    }
}
```

```
[Visual Basic]
Imports System
Imports System.Management

' This sample demonstrates how to enumerate all properties in a
' ManagementObject using PropertyDataEnumerator object.
Class Sample_PropertyDataEnumerator
    Overloads Public Shared Function Main(args() As String) As Integer
        Dim disk As New
ManagementObject("Win32_LogicalDisk.DeviceID='C:'")
        Dim propertyEnumerator As _
            PropertyDataCollection.PropertyDataEnumerator =
disk.Properties.GetEnumerator()
        While propertyEnumerator.MoveNext()
            Dim p As PropertyData = _
                CType(propertyEnumerator.Current, PropertyData)
            Console.WriteLine("Property found: " & p.Name)
        End While
        Return 0
```

```
        End Function
End Class
```

Requirements

Namespace: System.Management

Platforms: Windows 98, Windows NT 4.0, Windows Millennium Edition, Windows 2000, Windows XP Home Edition, Windows XP Professional, Windows .NET Server family

Assembly: System.Management (in System.Management.dll)

PropertyDataCollection.PropertyData-Enumerator.Current Property

Gets the current **PropertyData** in the **PropertyDataCollection** enumeration.

```
[Visual Basic]
Public ReadOnly Property Current As PropertyData
[C#]
public PropertyData Current {get;}
[C++]
public: __property PropertyData* get_Current();
[JScript]
public function get Current() : PropertyData;
```

Property Value

The current **PropertyData** element in the collection.

Requirements

Platforms: Windows 98, Windows NT 4.0, Windows Millennium Edition, Windows 2000, Windows XP Home Edition, Windows XP Professional, Windows .NET Server family

.NET Framework Security:

- Full trust for the immediate caller. This member cannot be used by partially trusted code.

PropertyDataCollection.PropertyData-Enumerator.System.Collections.IEnumerator.Current Property

Note: This namespace, class, or member is supported only in version 1.1 of the .NET Framework.

```
[Visual Basic]
Private ReadOnly Property Current As Object Implements _
   IEnumerator.Current
[C#]
object IEnumerator.Current {get;}
[C++]
private: __property Object*
   System::Collections::IEnumerator::get_Current();
[JScript]
private function get IEnumerator.Current() : Object;
```

Implements

IEnumerator.Current

Requirements

Platforms: Windows 98, Windows NT 4.0,
Windows Millennium Edition, Windows 2000,
Windows XP Home Edition, Windows XP Professional,
Windows .NET Server family

.NET Framework Security:

- Full trust for the immediate caller. This member cannot be used
  by partially trusted code.

Requirements

Platforms: Windows 98, Windows NT 4.0,
Windows Millennium Edition, Windows 2000,
Windows XP Home Edition, Windows XP Professional,
Windows .NET Server family

.NET Framework Security:

- Full trust for the immediate caller. This member cannot be used
  by partially trusted code.

PropertyDataCollection.PropertyData-Enumerator.MoveNext Method

Moves to the next element in the **PropertyDataCollection**
enumeration.

```
[Visual Basic]
Public Overridable Function MoveNext() As Boolean Implements _
    IEnumerator.MoveNext
[C#]
public virtual bool MoveNext();
[C++]
public: virtual bool MoveNext();
[JScript]
public function MoveNext() : Boolean;
```

Return Value

true if the enumerator was successfully advanced to the next
element; **false** if the enumerator has passed the end of the collection.

Implements

IEnumerator.MoveNext

Requirements

Platforms: Windows 98, Windows NT 4.0,
Windows Millennium Edition, Windows 2000,
Windows XP Home Edition, Windows XP Professional,
Windows .NET Server family

.NET Framework Security:

- Full trust for the immediate caller. This member cannot be used
  by partially trusted code.

PropertyDataCollection.PropertyData-Enumerator.Reset Method

Resets the enumerator to the beginning of the
PropertyDataCollection enumeration.

```
[Visual Basic]
Public Overridable Sub Reset() Implements IEnumerator.Reset
[C#]
public virtual void Reset();
[C++]
public: virtual void Reset();
[JScript]
public function Reset();
```

Implements

IEnumerator.Reset

PutOptions Class

Specifies options for committing management object changes.

System.Object
  System.Management.ManagementOptions
    System.Management.PutOptions

```
[Visual Basic]
Public Class PutOptions
   Inherits ManagementOptions
[C#]
public class PutOptions : ManagementOptions
[C++]
public __gc class PutOptions : public ManagementOptions
[JScript]
public class PutOptions extends ManagementOptions
```

Thread Safety

Any public static (**Shared** in Visual Basic) members of this type are safe for multithreaded operations. Any instance members are not guaranteed to be thread safe.

Example

```
[C#]
using System;
using System.Management;

// This example demonstrates how to specify a PutOptions using
// PutOptions object when saving a ManagementClass object to
// the WMI respository.
class Sample_PutOptions
{
    public static int Main(string[] args) {
        ManagementClass newClass = new ManagementClass("root/default",
                                                       String.Empty,
                                                       null);
        newClass["__Class"] = "class999xc";

        PutOptions options = new PutOptions();
        options.Type = PutType.UpdateOnly;

        try
        {
            newClass.Put(options); //will fail if the class
doesn't already exist
        }
        catch (ManagementException e)
        {
            Console.WriteLine("Couldn't update class: " + e.ErrorCode);
        }
        return 0;
    }
}
```

```
[Visual Basic]
Imports System
Imports System.Management

' This example demonstrates how to specify a PutOptions using
' PutOptions object when saving a ManagementClass object to
' WMI respository.
Class Sample_PutOptions
    Overloads Public Shared Function Main(args() As String) As Integer
        Dim newClass As New ManagementClass( _
            "root/default", _
            String.Empty, _
            Nothing)
        newClass("__Class") = "class999xc"
```

```
        Dim options As New PutOptions()
        options.Type = PutType.UpdateOnly 'will fail if the
class doesn't already exist

        Try
            newClass.Put(options)
        Catch e As ManagementException
            Console.WriteLine("Couldn't update class: " & e.ErrorCode)
        End Try
        Return 0
    End Function
End Class
```

Requirements

Namespace: System.Management

Platforms: Windows 98, Windows NT 4.0, Windows Millennium Edition, Windows 2000, Windows XP Home Edition, Windows XP Professional, Windows .NET Server family

Assembly: System.Management (in System.Management.dll)

PutOptions Constructor

Initializes a new instance of the **PutOptions** class.

Overload List

Initializes a new instance of the **PutOptions** class for put operations, using default values. This is the default constructor.

  [Visual Basic] **Public Sub New()**

  [C#] **public PutOptions();**

  [C++] **public: PutOptions();**

  [JScript] **public function PutOptions();**

Initializes a new instance of the **PutOptions** class for committing a WMI object, using the specified provider-specific context.

  [Visual Basic] **Public Sub New(ManagementNamed-ValueCollection)**

  [C#] **public PutOptions(ManagementNamed-ValueCollection);**

  [C++] **public: PutOptions(ManagementNamed-ValueCollection*);**

  [JScript] **public function PutOptions(ManagementNamed-ValueCollection);**

Initializes a new instance of the **PutOptions** class for committing a WMI object, using the specified option values.

  [Visual Basic] **Public Sub New(ManagementNamedValue-Collection, TimeSpan, Boolean, PutType)**

  [C#] **public PutOptions(ManagementNamedValueCollection, TimeSpan, bool, PutType);**

  [C++] **public: PutOptions(ManagementNamed-ValueCollection*, TimeSpan, bool, PutType);**

  [JScript] **public function PutOptions(ManagementNamed-ValueCollection, TimeSpan, Boolean, PutType);**

PutOptions Constructor ()

Initializes a new instance of the **PutOptions** class for put operations, using default values. This is the default constructor.

```
[Visual Basic]
Public Sub New()
```

```
[C#]
public PutOptions();
[C++]
public: PutOptions();
[JScript]
public function PutOptions();
```

Requirements

Platforms: Windows 98, Windows NT 4.0,
Windows Millennium Edition, Windows 2000,
Windows XP Home Edition, Windows XP Professional,
Windows .NET Server family

.NET Framework Security:
*   Full trust for the immediate caller. This member cannot be used
    by partially trusted code.

PutOptions Constructor (ManagementNamedValueCollection)

Initializes a new instance of the **PutOptions** class for committing a
WMI object, using the specified provider-specific context.

```
[Visual Basic]
Public Sub New( _
    ByVal context As ManagementNamedValueCollection _
)
[C#]
public PutOptions(
    ManagementNamedValueCollection context
);
[C++]
public: PutOptions(
    ManagementNamedValueCollection* context
);
[JScript]
public function PutOptions(
    context : ManagementNamedValueCollection
);
```

Parameters

context
    A provider-specific, named-value pairs context object to be
    passed through to the provider.

Requirements

Platforms: Windows 98, Windows NT 4.0,
Windows Millennium Edition, Windows 2000,
Windows XP Home Edition, Windows XP Professional,
Windows .NET Server family

.NET Framework Security:
*   Full trust for the immediate caller. This member cannot be used
    by partially trusted code.

PutOptions Constructor (ManagementNamedValueCollection, TimeSpan, Boolean, PutType)

Initializes a new instance of the **PutOptions** class for committing a
WMI object, using the specified option values.

```
[Visual Basic]
Public Sub New( _
    ByVal context As ManagementNamedValueCollection, _
    ByVal timeout As TimeSpan, _
    ByVal useAmendedQualifiers As Boolean, _
    ByVal putType As PutType _
)
[C#]
public PutOptions(
    ManagementNamedValueCollection context,
    TimeSpan timeout,
    bool useAmendedQualifiers,
    PutType putType
);
[C++]
public: PutOptions(
    ManagementNamedValueCollection* context,
    TimeSpan timeout,
    bool useAmendedQualifiers,
    PutType putType
);
[JScript]
public function PutOptions(
    context : ManagementNamedValueCollection,
    timeout : TimeSpan,
    useAmendedQualifiers : Boolean,
    putType : PutType
);
```

Parameters

context
    A provider-specific, named-value pairs object to be passed
    through to the provider.
timeout
    The length of time to let the operation perform before it times
    out. The default is **InfiniteTimeout**.
useAmendedQualifiers
    true if the returned objects should contain amended (locale-
    aware) qualifiers; otherwise, **false**.
putType
    The type of commit to be performed (update or create).

Requirements

Platforms: Windows 98, Windows NT 4.0,
Windows Millennium Edition, Windows 2000,
Windows XP Home Edition, Windows XP Professional,
Windows .NET Server family

.NET Framework Security:
*   Full trust for the immediate caller. This member cannot be used
    by partially trusted code.

PutOptions.Type Property

Gets or sets the type of commit to be performed for the object.

```
[Visual Basic]
Public Property Type As PutType
[C#]
public PutType Type {get; set;}
[C++]
public: __property PutType get_Type();
public: __property void set_Type(PutType);
```

```
[JScript]
public function get Type() : PutType;
public function set Type(PutType);
```

Property Value

The default value is **UpdateOrCreate**.

Requirements

Platforms: Windows 98, Windows NT 4.0,
Windows Millennium Edition, Windows 2000,
Windows XP Home Edition, Windows XP Professional,
Windows .NET Server family

.NET Framework Security:

• Full trust for the immediate caller. This member cannot be used
  by partially trusted code.

PutOptions.UseAmendedQualifiers Property

Gets or sets a value indicating whether the objects returned from
WMI should contain amended information. Typically, amended
information is localizable information attached to the WMI object,
such as object and property descriptions.

```
[Visual Basic]
Public Property UseAmendedQualifiers As Boolean
[C#]
public bool UseAmendedQualifiers {get; set;}
[C++]
public: __property bool get_UseAmendedQualifiers();
public: __property void set_UseAmendedQualifiers(bool);
[JScript]
public function get UseAmendedQualifiers() : Boolean;
public function set UseAmendedQualifiers(Boolean);
```

Property Value

true if the objects returned from WMI should contain amended
information; otherwise, **false**. The default value is **false**.

Requirements

Platforms: Windows 98, Windows NT 4.0,
Windows Millennium Edition, Windows 2000,
Windows XP Home Edition, Windows XP Professional,
Windows .NET Server family

.NET Framework Security:

• Full trust for the immediate caller. This member cannot be used
  by partially trusted code.

PutOptions.Clone Method

Returns a copy of the object.

```
[Visual Basic]
Overrides Public Function Clone() As Object Implements _
    ICloneable.Clone
[C#]
public override object Clone();
[C++]
public: Object* Clone();
[JScript]
public override function Clone() : Object;
```

Return Value

The cloned object.

Implements

ICloneable.Clone

Requirements

Platforms: Windows 98, Windows NT 4.0,
Windows Millennium Edition, Windows 2000,
Windows XP Home Edition, Windows XP Professional,
Windows .NET Server family

.NET Framework Security:

• Full trust for the immediate caller. This member cannot be used
  by partially trusted code.

PutType Enumeration

Describes the possible effects of saving an object to WMI when using **Put**.

```
[Visual Basic]
<Serializable>
Public Enum PutType
[C#]
[Serializable]
public enum PutType
[C++]
[Serializable]
__value public enum PutType
[JScript]
public
    Serializable
enum PutType
```

Members

Member name	Description
CreateOnly	Creates an object only; does not update an existing object.
UpdateOnly	Updates an existing object only; does not create a new object.
UpdateOrCreate	Saves the object, whether updating an existing object or creating a new object.

Requirements

Namespace: System.Management

Platforms: Windows 98, Windows NT 4.0, Windows Millennium Edition, Windows 2000, Windows XP Home Edition, Windows XP Professional, Windows .NET Server family

Assembly: System.Management (in System.Management.dll)

QualifierData Class

Contains information about a WMI qualifier.

System.Object
   System.Management.QualifierData

```
[Visual Basic]
Public Class QualifierData
[C#]
public class QualifierData
[C++]
public __gc class QualifierData
[JScript]
public class QualifierData
```

Thread Safety

Any public static (**Shared** in Visual Basic) members of this type are safe for multithreaded operations. Any instance members are not guaranteed to be thread safe.

Example

```
[C#]
using System;
using System.Management;

// This sample demonstrates how to enumerate qualifiers
// of a ManagementClass object.
class Sample_QualifierData
{
    public static int Main(string[] args) {
        ManagementClass diskClass = new
ManagementClass("Win32_LogicalDisk");
        diskClass.Options.UseAmendedQualifiers = true;
        QualifierData diskQualifier =
diskClass.Qualifiers["Description"];
        Console.WriteLine(diskQualifier.Name +
" = " + diskQualifier.Value);
        return 0;
    }
}

[Visual Basic]
Imports System
Imports System.Management

' This sample demonstrates how to enumerate qualifiers
' of a ManagementClass object.
Class Sample_QualifierData
    Overloads Public Shared Function Main(args() As String) As Integer
        Dim diskClass As New ManagementClass("win32_logicaldisk")
        diskClass.Options.UseAmendedQualifiers = True
        Dim diskQualifier As QualifierData =
diskClass.Qualifiers("Description")
        Console.WriteLine(diskQualifier.Name + " = " +
diskQualifier.Value)
        Return 0
    End Function
End Class
```

Requirements

Namespace: System.Management

Platforms: Windows 98, Windows NT 4.0, Windows Millennium Edition, Windows 2000, Windows XP Home Edition, Windows XP Professional, Windows .NET Server family

Assembly: System.Management (in System.Management.dll)

QualifierData.IsAmended Property

Gets or sets a value indicating whether the qualifier is amended.

```
[Visual Basic]
Public Property IsAmended As Boolean
[C#]
public bool IsAmended {get; set;}
[C++]
public: __property bool get_IsAmended();
public: __property void set_IsAmended(bool);
[JScript]
public function get IsAmended() : Boolean;
public function set IsAmended(Boolean);
```

Property Value

true if this qualifier is amended; otherwise, **false**.

Remarks

Amended qualifiers are qualifiers whose value can be localized through WMI. Localized qualifiers reside in separate namespaces in WMI and can be merged into the basic class definition when retrieved.

Requirements

Platforms: Windows 98, Windows NT 4.0, Windows Millennium Edition, Windows 2000, Windows XP Home Edition, Windows XP Professional, Windows .NET Server family

.NET Framework Security:
- Full trust for the immediate caller. This member cannot be used by partially trusted code.

QualifierData.IsLocal Property

Gets or sets a value indicating whether the qualifier has been defined locally on this class or has been propagated from a base class.

```
[Visual Basic]
Public ReadOnly Property IsLocal As Boolean
[C#]
public bool IsLocal {get;}
[C++]
public: __property bool get_IsLocal();
[JScript]
public function get IsLocal() : Boolean;
```

Property Value

true if the qualifier has been defined locally on this class; otherwise, **false**.

Requirements

Platforms: Windows 98, Windows NT 4.0, Windows Millennium Edition, Windows 2000, Windows XP Home Edition, Windows XP Professional, Windows .NET Server family

.NET Framework Security:
- Full trust for the immediate caller. This member cannot be used by partially trusted code.

QualifierData.IsOverridable Property

Gets or sets a value indicating whether the value of the qualifier can be overridden when propagated.

```
[Visual Basic]
Public Property IsOverridable As Boolean
[C#]
public bool IsOverridable {get; set;}
[C++]
public: __property bool get_IsOverridable();
public: __property void set_IsOverridable(bool);
[JScript]
public function get IsOverridable() : Boolean;
public function set IsOverridable(Boolean);
```

Property Value

true if the value of the qualifier can be overridden when propagated; otherwise, **false**.

Requirements

Platforms: Windows 98, Windows NT 4.0, Windows Millennium Edition, Windows 2000, Windows XP Home Edition, Windows XP Professional, Windows .NET Server family

.NET Framework Security:
- Full trust for the immediate caller. This member cannot be used by partially trusted code.

QualifierData.Name Property

Represents the name of the qualifier.

```
[Visual Basic]
Public ReadOnly Property Name As String
[C#]
public string Name {get;}
[C++]
public: __property String* get_Name();
[JScript]
public function get Name() : String;
```

Property Value

The name of the qualifier.

Requirements

Platforms: Windows 98, Windows NT 4.0, Windows Millennium Edition, Windows 2000, Windows XP Home Edition, Windows XP Professional, Windows .NET Server family

.NET Framework Security:
- Full trust for the immediate caller. This member cannot be used by partially trusted code.

QualifierData.PropagatesToInstance Property

Gets or sets a value indicating whether the qualifier should be propagated to instances of the class.

```
[Visual Basic]
Public Property PropagatesToInstance As Boolean
[C#]
public bool PropagatesToInstance {get; set;}
[C++]
public: __property bool get_PropagatesToInstance();
public: __property void set_PropagatesToInstance(bool);
[JScript]
public function get PropagatesToInstance() : Boolean;
public function set PropagatesToInstance(Boolean);
```

Property Value

true if this qualifier should be propagated to instances of the class; otherwise, **false**.

Requirements

Platforms: Windows 98, Windows NT 4.0, Windows Millennium Edition, Windows 2000, Windows XP Home Edition, Windows XP Professional, Windows .NET Server family

.NET Framework Security:
- Full trust for the immediate caller. This member cannot be used by partially trusted code.

QualifierData.PropagatesToSubclass Property

Gets or sets a value indicating whether the qualifier should be propagated to subclasses of the class.

```
[Visual Basic]
Public Property PropagatesToSubclass As Boolean
[C#]
public bool PropagatesToSubclass {get; set;}
[C++]
public: __property bool get_PropagatesToSubclass();
public: __property void set_PropagatesToSubclass(bool);
[JScript]
public function get PropagatesToSubclass() : Boolean;
public function set PropagatesToSubclass(Boolean);
```

Property Value

true if the qualifier should be propagated to subclasses of this class; otherwise, **false**.

Requirements

Platforms: Windows 98, Windows NT 4.0, Windows Millennium Edition, Windows 2000, Windows XP Home Edition, Windows XP Professional, Windows .NET Server family

.NET Framework Security:
- Full trust for the immediate caller. This member cannot be used by partially trusted code.

QualifierData.Value Property

Gets or sets the value of the qualifier.

```
[Visual Basic]
Public Property Value As Object
[C#]
public object Value {get; set;}
[C++]
public: __property Object* get_Value();
public: __property void set_Value(Object*);
[JScript]
public function get Value() : Object;
public function set Value(Object);
```

Property Value

The value of the qualifier.

Remarks

Qualifiers can only be of the following subset of CIM types: **string, uint16, uint32, sint32, uint64, sint64, real32, real64, bool**.

Requirements

Platforms: Windows 98, Windows NT 4.0, Windows Millennium Edition, Windows 2000, Windows XP Home Edition, Windows XP Professional, Windows .NET Server family

.NET Framework Security:
- Full trust for the immediate caller. This member cannot be used by partially trusted code.

QualifierDataCollection Class

Represents a collection of **QualifierData** objects.

System.Object
  System.Management.QualifierDataCollection

```
[Visual Basic]
Public Class QualifierDataCollection
   Implements ICollection, IEnumerable
[C#]
public class QualifierDataCollection : ICollection, IEnumerable
[C++]
public __gc class QualifierDataCollection : public ICollection,
   IEnumerable
[JScript]
public class QualifierDataCollection implements ICollection,
   IEnumerable
```

Thread Safety

Any public static (**Shared** in Visual Basic) members of this type are safe for multithreaded operations. Any instance members are not guaranteed to be thread safe.

Example

```
[C#]
using System;
using System.Management;

// This sample demonstrates how to list all qualifiers
including amended
// qualifiers of a ManagementClass object.
class Sample_QualifierDataCollection
{
    public static int Main(string[] args) {
        ManagementClass diskClass = new
ManagementClass("Win32_LogicalDisk");
        diskClass.Options.UseAmendedQualifiers = true;
        QualifierDataCollection qualifierCollection =
diskClass.Qualifiers;
        foreach (QualifierData q in qualifierCollection) {
            Console.WriteLine(q.Name + " = " + q.Value);
        }
        return 0;
    }
}

[Visual Basic]
Imports System
            Imports System.Management
            ' This sample demonstrates how to list
all qualifiers including amended
            ' qualifiers of a ManagementClass object.
            Class Sample_QualifierDataCollection
            Overloads Public Shared Function Main
 (args() As String) As Integer
            Dim diskClass As New
ManagementClass("Win32_LogicalDisk")
            diskClass.Options.UseAmendedQualifiers = true
            Dim qualifierCollection As
QualifierDataCollection = diskClass.Qualifiers
            Dim q As QualifierData
            For Each q In qualifierCollection
            Console.WriteLine(q.Name & " = " & q.Value)
            Next q
            Return 0
            End Function
            End Class
```

Requirements

Namespace: System.Management

Platforms: Windows 98, Windows NT 4.0, Windows Millennium Edition, Windows 2000, Windows XP Home Edition, Windows XP Professional, Windows .NET Server family

Assembly: System.Management (in System.Management.dll)

QualifierDataCollection.Count Property

Gets or sets the number of **QualifierData** objects in the **QualifierDataCollection**.

```
[Visual Basic]
Public Overridable ReadOnly Property Count As Integer  Implements _
   ICollection.Count
[C#]
public virtual int Count {get;}
[C++]
public: __property virtual int get_Count();
[JScript]
public function get Count() : int;
```

Property Value

The number of objects in the collection.

Implements

ICollection.Count

Requirements

Platforms: Windows 98, Windows NT 4.0, Windows Millennium Edition, Windows 2000, Windows XP Home Edition, Windows XP Professional, Windows .NET Server family

.NET Framework Security:

- Full trust for the immediate caller. This member cannot be used by partially trusted code.

QualifierDataCollection.IsSynchronized Property

Gets or sets a value indicating whether the object is synchronized.

```
[Visual Basic]
Public Overridable ReadOnly Property IsSynchronized As Boolean _
   Implements ICollection.IsSynchronized
[C#]
public virtual bool IsSynchronized {get;}
[C++]
public: __property virtual bool get_IsSynchronized();
[JScript]
public function get IsSynchronized() : Boolean;
```

Property Value

true if the object is synchronized; otherwise, **false**.

Implements

ICollection.IsSynchronized

Requirements

Platforms: Windows 98, Windows NT 4.0,
Windows Millennium Edition, Windows 2000,
Windows XP Home Edition, Windows XP Professional,
Windows .NET Server family

.NET Framework Security:

- Full trust for the immediate caller. This member cannot be used by partially trusted code.

QualifierDataCollection.Item Property

Gets the specified **QualifierData** from the
QualifierDataCollection.

[C#] In C#, this property is the indexer for the
QualifierDataCollection class.

```
[Visual Basic]
Public Overridable Default ReadOnly Property Item( _
   ByVal qualifierName As String _
) As QualifierData
[C#]
public virtual QualifierData this[
   string qualifierName
] {get;}
[C++]
public: __property virtual QualifierData* get_Item(
   String* qualifierName
);
[JScript]
returnValue = QualifierDataCollectionObject.Item(qualifierName);
-or-
returnValue = QualifierDataCollectionObject(qualifierName);
```

[JScript] In JScript, you can use the default indexed properties
defined by a type, but you cannot explicitly define your own.
However, specifying the **expando** attribute on a class automatically
provides a default indexed property whose type is **Object** and whose
index type is **String**.

Arguments [JScript]

qualifierName
   The name of the **QualifierData** to access in the
   QualifierDataCollection.

Parameters [Visual Basic, C#, C++]

qualifierName
   The name of the **QualifierData** to access in the
   QualifierDataCollection.

Property Value

A **QualifierData**, based on the name specified.

Requirements

Platforms: Windows 98, Windows NT 4.0,
Windows Millennium Edition, Windows 2000,
Windows XP Home Edition, Windows XP Professional,
Windows .NET Server family

.NET Framework Security:

- Full trust for the immediate caller. This member cannot be used by partially trusted code.

QualifierDataCollection.SyncRoot Property

Gets or sets the object to be used for synchronization.

```
[Visual Basic]
Public Overridable ReadOnly Property SyncRoot As Object  Implements _
   ICollection.SyncRoot
[C#]
public virtual object SyncRoot {get;}
[C++]
public: __property virtual Object* get_SyncRoot();
[JScript]
public function get SyncRoot() : Object;
```

Property Value

The object to be used for synchronization.

Implements

ICollection.SyncRoot

Requirements

Platforms: Windows 98, Windows NT 4.0,
Windows Millennium Edition, Windows 2000,
Windows XP Home Edition, Windows XP Professional,
Windows .NET Server family

.NET Framework Security:

- Full trust for the immediate caller. This member cannot be used by partially trusted code.

QualifierDataCollection.Add Method

Adds a **QualifierData** to the **QualifierDataCollection**.

Overload List

Adds a **QualifierData** to the **QualifierDataCollection**. This
overload specifies the qualifier name and value.

   [Visual Basic] **Overloads Public Overridable Sub Add(String, Object)**

   [C#] **public virtual void Add(string, object);**

   [C++] **public: virtual void Add(String*, Object*);**

   [JScript] **public function Add(String, Object);**

Adds a **QualifierData** to the **QualifierDataCollection**. This
overload specifies all property values for a **QualifierData** object.

   [Visual Basic] **Overloads Public Overridable Sub Add(String, Object, Boolean, Boolean, Boolean, Boolean)**

   [C#] **public virtual void Add(string, object, bool, bool, bool, bool);**

   [C++] **public: virtual void Add(String*, Object*, bool, bool, bool, bool);**

   [JScript] **public function Add(String, Object, Boolean, Boolean, Boolean, Boolean);**

QualifierDataCollection.Add Method (String, Object)

Adds a **QualifierData** to the **QualifierDataCollection**. This
overload specifies the qualifier name and value.

```
[Visual Basic]
Overloads Public Overridable Sub Add( _
   ByVal qualifierName As String, _
   ByVal qualifierValue As Object _
)
```

```
[C#]
public virtual void Add(
    string qualifierName,
    object qualifierValue
);
[C++]
public: virtual void Add(
    String* qualifierName,
    Object* qualifierValue
);
[JScript]
public function Add(
    qualifierName : String,
    qualifierValue : Object
);
```

Parameters

qualifierName
> The name of the **QualifierData** to be added to the
> **QualifierDataCollection**.

qualifierValue
> The value for the new qualifier.

Requirements

Platforms: Windows 98, Windows NT 4.0,
Windows Millennium Edition, Windows 2000,
Windows XP Home Edition, Windows XP Professional,
Windows .NET Server family

.NET Framework Security:

- Full trust for the immediate caller. This member cannot be used
  by partially trusted code.

QualifierDataCollection.Add Method (String, Object, Boolean, Boolean, Boolean, Boolean)

Adds a **QualifierData** to the **QualifierDataCollection**. This
overload specifies all property values for a **QualifierData** object.

```
[Visual Basic]
Overloads Public Overridable Sub Add( _
    ByVal qualifierName As String, _
    ByVal qualifierValue As Object, _
    ByVal isAmended As Boolean, _
    ByVal propagatesToInstance As Boolean, _
    ByVal propagatesToSubclass As Boolean, _
    ByVal isOverridable As Boolean _
)
[C#]
public virtual void Add(
    string qualifierName,
    object qualifierValue,
    bool isAmended,
    bool propagatesToInstance,
    bool propagatesToSubclass,
    bool isOverridable
);
[C++]
public: virtual void Add(
    String* qualifierName,
    Object* qualifierValue,
    bool isAmended,
    bool propagatesToInstance,
```

```
    bool propagatesToSubclass,
    bool isOverridable
);
[JScript]
public function Add(
    qualifierName : String,
    qualifierValue : Object,
    isAmended : Boolean,
    propagatesToInstance : Boolean,
    propagatesToSubclass : Boolean,
    isOverridable : Boolean
);
```

Parameters

qualifierName
> The qualifier name.

qualifierValue
> The qualifier value.

isAmended
> **true** to specify that this qualifier is amended (flavor); otherwise,
> **false**.

propagatesToInstance
> **true** to propagate this qualifier to instances; otherwise, **false**.

propagatesToSubclass
> **true** to propagate this qualifier to subclasses; otherwise, **false**.

isOverridable
> **true** to specify that this qualifier's value is overridable in
> instances of subclasses; otherwise, **false**.

Requirements

Platforms: Windows 98, Windows NT 4.0,
Windows Millennium Edition, Windows 2000,
Windows XP Home Edition, Windows XP Professional,
Windows .NET Server family

.NET Framework Security:

- Full trust for the immediate caller. This member cannot be used
  by partially trusted code.

QualifierDataCollection.CopyTo Method

Copies the **QualifierDataCollection** into an array.

Overload List

Copies the **QualifierDataCollection** into an array.

> [Visual Basic] **Overloads Public Overridable Sub
> CopyTo(Array, Integer) Implements ICollection.CopyTo**
>
> [C#] **public virtual void CopyTo(Array, int);**
>
> [C++] **public: virtual void CopyTo(Array*, int);**
>
> [JScript] **public function CopyTo(Array, int);**

Copies the **QualifierDataCollection** into a specialized
QualifierData array.

> [Visual Basic] **Overloads Public Sub CopyTo(QualifierData(),
> Integer)**
>
> [C#] **public void CopyTo(QualifierData[], int);**
>
> [C++] **public: void CopyTo(QualifierData*[], int);**
>
> [JScript] **public function CopyTo(QualifierData[], int);**

QualifierDataCollection.CopyTo Method (Array, Int32)

Copies the **QualifierDataCollection** into an array.

```
[Visual Basic]
Overloads Public Overridable Sub CopyTo( _
   ByVal array As Array, _
   ByVal index As Integer _
) Implements ICollection.CopyTo
[C#]
public virtual void CopyTo(
   Array array,
   int index
);
[C++]
public: virtual void CopyTo(
   Array* array,
   int index
);
[JScript]
public function CopyTo(
   array : Array,
   index : int
);
```

Parameters

array

The array to which to copy the **QualifierDataCollection**.

index

The index from which to start copying.

Implements

ICollection.CopyTo

Requirements

Platforms: Windows 98, Windows NT 4.0, Windows Millennium Edition, Windows 2000, Windows XP Home Edition, Windows XP Professional, Windows .NET Server family

.NET Framework Security:

- Full trust for the immediate caller. This member cannot be used by partially trusted code.

QualifierDataCollection.CopyTo Method (QualifierData[], Int32)

Copies the **QualifierDataCollection** into a specialized **QualifierData** array.

```
[Visual Basic]
Overloads Public Sub CopyTo( _
   ByVal qualifierArray() As QualifierData, _
   ByVal index As Integer _
)
[C#]
public void CopyTo(
   QualifierData[] qualifierArray,
   int index
);
[C++]
public: void CopyTo(
   QualifierData* qualifierArray[],
   int index
);
```

```
[JScript]
public function CopyTo(
   qualifierArray : QualifierData[],
   index : int
);
```

Parameters

qualifierArray

The specialized array of **QualifierData** objects to which to copy the **QualifierDataCollection**.

index

The index from which to start copying.

Requirements

Platforms: Windows 98, Windows NT 4.0, Windows Millennium Edition, Windows 2000, Windows XP Home Edition, Windows XP Professional, Windows .NET Server family

.NET Framework Security:

- Full trust for the immediate caller. This member cannot be used by partially trusted code.

QualifierDataCollection.GetEnumerator Method

Returns an enumerator for the **QualifierDataCollection**. This method is strongly typed.

```
[Visual Basic]
Public Function GetEnumerator() As QualifierDataEnumerator
[C#]
public QualifierDataEnumerator GetEnumerator();
[C++]
public: QualifierDataEnumerator* GetEnumerator();
[JScript]
public function GetEnumerator() : QualifierDataEnumerator;
```

Return Value

An **IEnumerator** that can be used to iterate through the collection.

Requirements

Platforms: Windows 98, Windows NT 4.0, Windows Millennium Edition, Windows 2000, Windows XP Home Edition, Windows XP Professional, Windows .NET Server family

.NET Framework Security:

- Full trust for the immediate caller. This member cannot be used by partially trusted code.

QualifierDataCollection.IEnumerable.Get-Enumerator Method

This member supports the .NET Framework infrastructure and is not intended to be used directly from your code.

```
[Visual Basic]
Private Function GetEnumerator() As IEnumerator Implements _
   IEnumerable.GetEnumerator
[C#]
IEnumerator IEnumerable.GetEnumerator();
[C++]
private: IEnumerator* IEnumerable::GetEnumerator();
[JScript]
private function IEnumerable.GetEnumerator() : IEnumerator;
```

QualifierDataCollection.Remove Method

Removes a **QualifierData** from the **QualifierDataCollection** by name.

```
[Visual Basic]
Public Overridable Sub Remove( _
    ByVal qualifierName As String _
)
[C#]
public virtual void Remove(
    string qualifierName
);
[C++]
public: virtual void Remove(
    String* qualifierName
);
[JScript]
public function Remove(
    qualifierName : String
);
```

Parameters

qualifierName

The name of the **QualifierData** to remove.

Requirements

Platforms: Windows 98, Windows NT 4.0,
Windows Millennium Edition, Windows 2000,
Windows XP Home Edition, Windows XP Professional,
Windows .NET Server family

.NET Framework Security:

- Full trust for the immediate caller. This member cannot be used
  by partially trusted code.

QualifierDataCollection.QualifierDataEnumerator Class

Represents the enumerator for **QualifierData** objects in the **QualifierDataCollection**.

System.Object
  System.Management.QualifierDataCollection.QualifierDataE
numerator

```
[Visual Basic]
Public Class QualifierDataCollection.QualifierDataEnumerator
   Implements IEnumerator
[C#]
public class QualifierDataCollection.QualifierDataEnumerator :
   IEnumerator
[C++]
public __gc class QualifierDataCollection.QualifierDataEnumerator :
   public IEnumerator
[JScript]
public class QualifierDataCollection.QualifierDataEnumerator
   implements IEnumerator
```

Thread Safety

Any public static (**Shared** in Visual Basic) members of this type are safe for multithreaded operations. Any instance members are not guaranteed to be thread safe.

Example

```
[C#]
using System;
using System.Management;

// This sample demonstrates how to enumerate qualifiers
 of a ManagementClass
// using QualifierDataEnumerator object.
class Sample_QualifierDataEnumerator
{
    public static int Main(string[] args) {
        ManagementClass diskClass = new
ManagementClass("Win32_LogicalDisk");
        diskClass.Options.UseAmendedQualifiers = true;
        QualifierDataCollection diskQualifier = diskClass.Qualifiers;
        QualifierDataCollection.QualifierDataEnumerator
            qualifierEnumerator = diskQualifier.GetEnumerator();
        while(qualifierEnumerator.MoveNext()) {
            Console.WriteLine(qualifierEnumerator.Current.Name +
" = " +
                qualifierEnumerator.Current.Value);
        }
        return 0;
    }
}
```

```
[Visual Basic]
Imports System
Imports System.Management

' This sample demonstrates how to enumerate qualifiers of a
ManagementClass
' using QualifierDataEnumerator object.
Class Sample_QualifierDataEnumerator
    Overloads Public Shared Function Main(args() As String) As Integer
        Dim diskClass As New ManagementClass("win32_logicaldisk")
        diskClass.Options.UseAmendedQualifiers = True
        Dim diskQualifier As QualifierDataCollection =
diskClass.Qualifiers
        Dim qualifierEnumerator As _
            QualifierDataCollection.QualifierDataEnumerator = _
                diskQualifier.GetEnumerator()
        While qualifierEnumerator.MoveNext()
            Console.WriteLine(qualifierEnumerator.Current.Name & _
                " = " & qualifierEnumerator.Current.Value)
        End While
        Return 0
    End Function
End Class
```

Requirements

Namespace: System.Management

Platforms: Windows 98, Windows NT 4.0, Windows Millennium Edition, Windows 2000, Windows XP Home Edition, Windows XP Professional, Windows .NET Server family

Assembly: System.Management (in System.Management.dll)

QualifierDataCollection.QualifierDataEnumerator.Current Property

Gets or sets the current **QualifierData** in the **QualifierDataCollection** enumeration.

```
[Visual Basic]
Public ReadOnly Property Current As QualifierData
[C#]
public QualifierData Current {get;}
[C++]
public: __property QualifierData* get_Current();
[JScript]
public function get Current() : QualifierData;
```

Property Value

The current **QualifierData** element in the collection.

Requirements

Platforms: Windows 98, Windows NT 4.0, Windows Millennium Edition, Windows 2000, Windows XP Home Edition, Windows XP Professional, Windows .NET Server family

.NET Framework Security:

- Full trust for the immediate caller. This member cannot be used by partially trusted code.

QualifierDataCollection.QualifierDataEnumerator.System.Collections.IEnumerator.Current Property

Note: This namespace, class, or member is supported only in version 1.1 of the .NET Framework.

```
[Visual Basic]
Private ReadOnly Property Current As Object Implements _
    IEnumerator.Current
[C#]
object IEnumerator.Current {get;}
[C++]
private: __property Object*
    System::Collections::IEnumerator::get_Current();
[JScript]
private function get IEnumerator.Current() : Object;
```

Implements

IEnumerator.Current

Requirements

Platforms: Windows 98, Windows NT 4.0, Windows Millennium Edition, Windows 2000, Windows XP Home Edition, Windows XP Professional, Windows .NET Server family

.NET Framework Security:

- Full trust for the immediate caller. This member cannot be used by partially trusted code.

QualifierDataCollection.QualifierData-Enumerator.MoveNext Method

Moves to the next element in the **QualifierDataCollection** enumeration.

```
[Visual Basic]
Public Overridable Function MoveNext() As Boolean Implements _
    IEnumerator.MoveNext
[C#]
public virtual bool MoveNext();
[C++]
public: virtual bool MoveNext();
[JScript]
public function MoveNext() : Boolean;
```

Return Value

true if the enumerator was successfully advanced to the next element; **false** if the enumerator has passed the end of the collection.

Implements

IEnumerator.MoveNext

Requirements

Platforms: Windows 98, Windows NT 4.0, Windows Millennium Edition, Windows 2000, Windows XP Home Edition, Windows XP Professional, Windows .NET Server family

.NET Framework Security:

- Full trust for the immediate caller. This member cannot be used by partially trusted code.

QualifierDataCollection.QualifierData-Enumerator.Reset Method

Resets the enumerator to the beginning of the **QualifierDataCollection** enumeration.

```
[Visual Basic]
Public Overridable Sub Reset() Implements IEnumerator.Reset
[C#]
public virtual void Reset();
[C++]
public: virtual void Reset();
[JScript]
public function Reset();
```

Implements

IEnumerator.Reset

Requirements

Platforms: Windows 98, Windows NT 4.0, Windows Millennium Edition, Windows 2000, Windows XP Home Edition, Windows XP Professional, Windows .NET Server family

.NET Framework Security:

- Full trust for the immediate caller. This member cannot be used by partially trusted code.

RelatedObjectQuery Class

Represents a WQL ASSOCIATORS OF data query. It can be used for both instances and schema queries.

System.Object
　System.Management.ManagementQuery
　　System.Management.ObjectQuery
　　　System.Management.WqlObjectQuery
　　　　System.Management.RelatedObjectQuery

```
[Visual Basic]
Public Class RelatedObjectQuery
   Inherits WqlObjectQuery
[C#]
public class RelatedObjectQuery : WqlObjectQuery
[C++]
public __gc class RelatedObjectQuery : public WqlObjectQuery
[JScript]
public class RelatedObjectQuery extends WqlObjectQuery
```

Thread Safety

Any public static (**Shared** in Visual Basic) members of this type are safe for multithreaded operations. Any instance members are not guaranteed to be thread safe.

Example

```
[C#]
using System;
using System.Management;

// This sample demonstrates how to query all instances associated
// with Win32_LogicalDisk='C:'.

class Sample_RelatedObjectQuery
{
    public static int Main(string[] args) {

        //This query requests all objects related to the 'C:' drive.
        RelatedObjectQuery relatedQuery =
            new RelatedObjectQuery("win32_logicaldisk='c:'");
        ManagementObjectSearcher searcher =
            new ManagementObjectSearcher(relatedQuery);

        foreach (ManagementObject relatedObject in searcher.Get()) {
            Console.WriteLine(relatedObject.ToString());
        }

        return 0;
    }
}
```

```
[Visual Basic]
Imports System
Imports System.Management

' This sample demonstrates how to query all instances associated
' with Win32_LogicalDisk='C:'.

Class Sample_RelatedObjectQuery
    Overloads Public Shared Function Main(args() As String) As Integer

        'This query requests all objects related to the 'C:' drive.
        Dim relatedQuery As New
RelatedObjectQuery("win32_logicaldisk='c:'")
        Dim searcher As New ManagementObjectSearcher(relatedQuery)

        Dim relatedObject As ManagementObject
        For Each relatedObject In searcher.Get()
```

```
        Console.WriteLine(relatedObject.ToString())
        Next relatedObject

        Return 0
    End Function
End Class
```

Requirements

Namespace: System.Management

Platforms: Windows 98, Windows NT 4.0, Windows Millennium Edition, Windows 2000, Windows XP Home Edition, Windows XP Professional, Windows .NET Server family

Assembly: System.Management (in System.Management.dll)

RelatedObjectQuery Constructor

Initializes a new instance of the **RelatedObjectQuery** class.

Overload List

Initializes a new instance of the **RelatedObjectQuery** class. This is the default constructor.

　[Visual Basic] **Public Sub New()**
　[C#] **public RelatedObjectQuery();**
　[C++] **public: RelatedObjectQuery();**
　[JScript] **public function RelatedObjectQuery();**

Initializes a new instance of the **RelatedObjectQuery** class. If the specified string can be succesfully parsed as a WQL query, it is considered to be the query string; otherwise, it is assumed to be the path of the source object for the query. In this case, the query is assumed to be an instance query.

　[Visual Basic] **Public Sub New(String)**
　[C#] **public RelatedObjectQuery(string);**
　[C++] **public: RelatedObjectQuery(String*);**
　[JScript] **public function RelatedObjectQuery(String);**

Initializes a new instance of the **RelatedObjectQuery** class for the given source object and related class. The query is assumed to be an instance query (as opposed to a schema query).

　[Visual Basic] **Public Sub New(String, String)**
　[C#] **public RelatedObjectQuery(string, string);**
　[C++] **public: RelatedObjectQuery(String*, String*);**
　[JScript] **public function RelatedObjectQuery(String, String);**

Initializes a new instance of the **RelatedObjectQuery** class for a schema query using the given set of parameters. This constructor is used for schema queries only: the first parameter must be set to **true**.

　[Visual Basic] **Public Sub New(Boolean, String, String, String, String, String, String)**
　[C#] **public RelatedObjectQuery(bool, string, string, string, string, string, string, string);**
　[C++] **public: RelatedObjectQuery(bool, String*, String*, String*, String*, String*, String*, String*);**
　[JScript] **public function RelatedObjectQuery(Boolean, String, String, String, String, String, String, String);**

Initializes a new instance of the **RelatedObjectQuery** class for the given set of parameters. The query is assumed to be an instance query (as opposed to a schema query).

[Visual Basic] **Public Sub New(String, String, String, String, String, String, String, Boolean)**

[C#] **public RelatedObjectQuery(string, string, string, string, string, string, string, bool);**

[C++] **public: RelatedObjectQuery(String*, String*, String*, String*, String*, String*, String*, bool);**

[JScript] **public function RelatedObjectQuery(String, String, String, String, String, String, String, Boolean);**

Example

[Visual Basic, C#] **Note** This example shows how to use one of the overloaded versions of the **RelatedObjectQuery** constructor. For other examples that might be available, see the individual overload topics.

```
[C#]
//This query retrieves all objects related to the 'mymachine'
computer system
//It specifies the full query string in the constructor
RelatedObjectQuery q =
    new RelatedObjectQuery("associators of
{Win32_ComputerSystem.Name='mymachine'}");

//or

//This query retrieves all objects related to the 'Alerter' service
//It specifies only the object of interest in the constructor
RelatedObjectQuery q =
    new RelatedObjectQuery("Win32_Service.Name='Alerter'");
```

```
[Visual Basic]
'This query retrieves all objects related to the 'mymachine'
 computer system
'It specifies the full query string in the constructor
Dim q As New RelatedObjectQuery("associators of
{Win32_ComputerSystem.Name='mymachine'}")

'or

'This query retrieves all objects related to the 'Alerter' service
'It specifies only the object of interest in the constructor
Dim q As New RelatedObjectQuery("Win32_Service.Name='Alerter'")
```

RelatedObjectQuery Constructor ()

Initializes a new instance of the **RelatedObjectQuery** class. This is the default constructor.

```
[Visual Basic]
Public Sub New()
[C#]
public RelatedObjectQuery();
[C++]
public: RelatedObjectQuery();
[JScript]
public function RelatedObjectQuery();
```

Requirements

Platforms: Windows 98, Windows NT 4.0, Windows Millennium Edition, Windows 2000, Windows XP Home Edition, Windows XP Professional, Windows .NET Server family

.NET Framework Security:

- Full trust for the immediate caller. This member cannot be used by partially trusted code.

RelatedObjectQuery Constructor (String)

Initializes a new instance of the **RelatedObjectQuery** class. If the specified string can be succesfully parsed as a WQL query, it is considered to be the query string; otherwise, it is assumed to be the path of the source object for the query. In this case, the query is assumed to be an instance query.

```
[Visual Basic]
Public Sub New( _
    ByVal queryOrSourceObject As String _
)
[C#]
public RelatedObjectQuery(
    string queryOrSourceObject
);
[C++]
public: RelatedObjectQuery(
    String* queryOrSourceObject
);
[JScript]
public function RelatedObjectQuery(
    queryOrSourceObject : String
);
```

Parameters

queryOrSourceObject
    The query string or the path of the source object.

Example

```
[C#]
//This query retrieves all objects related to the 'mymachine'
 computer system
//It specifies the full query string in the constructor
RelatedObjectQuery q =
    new RelatedObjectQuery("associators of
{Win32_ComputerSystem.Name='mymachine'}");

//or

//This query retrieves all objects related to the 'Alerter' service
//It specifies only the object of interest in the constructor
RelatedObjectQuery q =
    new RelatedObjectQuery("Win32_Service.Name='Alerter'");
```

```
[Visual Basic]
'This query retrieves all objects related to the 'mymachine'
computer system
'It specifies the full query string in the constructor
Dim q As New RelatedObjectQuery("associators of
{Win32_ComputerSystem.Name='mymachine'}")

'or

'This query retrieves all objects related to the 'Alerter' service
'It specifies only the object of interest in the constructor
Dim q As New RelatedObjectQuery("Win32_Service.Name='Alerter'")
```

Requirements

Platforms: Windows 98, Windows NT 4.0, Windows Millennium Edition, Windows 2000, Windows XP Home Edition, Windows XP Professional, Windows .NET Server family

.NET Framework Security:

- Full trust for the immediate caller. This member cannot be used by partially trusted code.

RelatedObjectQuery Constructor (String, String)

Initializes a new instance of the **RelatedObjectQuery** class for the given source object and related class. The query is assumed to be an instance query (as opposed to a schema query).

```
[Visual Basic]
Public Sub New( _
   ByVal sourceObject As String, _
   ByVal relatedClass As String _
)
[C#]
public RelatedObjectQuery(
   string sourceObject,
   string relatedClass
);
[C++]
public: RelatedObjectQuery(
   String* sourceObject,
   String* relatedClass
);
[JScript]
public function RelatedObjectQuery(
   sourceObject : String,
   relatedClass : String
);
```

Parameters

sourceObject
    The path of the source object for this query.
relatedClass
    The related objects class.

Requirements

Platforms: Windows 98, Windows NT 4.0, Windows Millennium Edition, Windows 2000, Windows XP Home Edition, Windows XP Professional, Windows .NET Server family

.NET Framework Security:

• Full trust for the immediate caller. This member cannot be used by partially trusted code.

RelatedObjectQuery Constructor (Boolean, String, String, String, String, String, String, String)

Initializes a new instance of the **RelatedObjectQuery** class for a schema query using the given set of parameters. This constructor is used for schema queries only: the first parameter must be set to **true**.

```
[Visual Basic]
Public Sub New( _
   ByVal isSchemaQuery As Boolean, _
   ByVal sourceObject As String, _
   ByVal relatedClass As String, _
   ByVal relationshipClass As String, _
   ByVal relatedQualifier As String, _
   ByVal relationshipQualifier As String, _
   ByVal relatedRole As String, _
   ByVal thisRole As String _
)
```

```
[C#]
public RelatedObjectQuery(
   bool isSchemaQuery,
   string sourceObject,
   string relatedClass,
   string relationshipClass,
   string relatedQualifier,
   string relationshipQualifier,
   string relatedRole,
   string thisRole
);
[C++]
public: RelatedObjectQuery(
   bool isSchemaQuery,
   String* sourceObject,
   String* relatedClass,
   String* relationshipClass,
   String* relatedQualifier,
   String* relationshipQualifier,
   String* relatedRole,
   String* thisRole
);
[JScript]
public function RelatedObjectQuery(
   isSchemaQuery : Boolean,
   sourceObject : String,
   relatedClass : String,
   relationshipClass : String,
   relatedQualifier : String,
   relationshipQualifier : String,
   relatedRole : String,
   thisRole : String
);
```

Parameters

isSchemaQuery
    true to indicate that this is a schema query; otherwise, **false**.
sourceObject
    The path of the source class.
relatedClass
    The related objects' required base class.
relationshipClass
    The relationship type.
relatedQualifier
    The qualifier required to be present on the related objects.
relationshipQualifier
    The qualifier required to be present on the relationships.
relatedRole
    The role that the related objects are required to play in the relationship.
thisRole
    The role that the source class is required to play in the relationship.

Requirements

Platforms: Windows 98, Windows NT 4.0, Windows Millennium Edition, Windows 2000, Windows XP Home Edition, Windows XP Professional, Windows .NET Server family

.NET Framework Security:

• Full trust for the immediate caller. This member cannot be used by partially trusted code.

RelatedObjectQuery Constructor (String, String, String, String, String, String, String, Boolean)

Initializes a new instance of the **RelatedObjectQuery** class for the given set of parameters. The query is assumed to be an instance query (as opposed to a schema query).

```
[Visual Basic]
Public Sub New( _
   ByVal sourceObject As String, _
   ByVal relatedClass As String, _
   ByVal relationshipClass As String, _
   ByVal relatedQualifier As String, _
   ByVal relationshipQualifier As String, _
   ByVal relatedRole As String, _
   ByVal thisRole As String, _
   ByVal classDefinitionsOnly As Boolean _
)
[C#]
public RelatedObjectQuery(
   string sourceObject,
   string relatedClass,
   string relationshipClass,
   string relatedQualifier,
   string relationshipQualifier,
   string relatedRole,
   string thisRole,
   bool classDefinitionsOnly
);
[C++]
public: RelatedObjectQuery(
   String* sourceObject,
   String* relatedClass,
   String* relationshipClass,
   String* relatedQualifier,
   String* relationshipQualifier,
   String* relatedRole,
   String* thisRole,
   bool classDefinitionsOnly
);
[JScript]
public function RelatedObjectQuery(
   sourceObject : String,
   relatedClass : String,
   relationshipClass : String,
   relatedQualifier : String,
   relationshipQualifier : String,
   relatedRole : String,
   thisRole : String,
   classDefinitionsOnly : Boolean
);
```

Parameters

sourceObject
   The path of the source object.
relatedClass
   The related objects required class.
relationshipClass
   The relationship type.
relatedQualifier
   The qualifier required to be present on the related objects.

relationshipQualifier
   The qualifier required to be present on the relationships.
relatedRole
   The role that the related objects are required to play in the relationship.
thisRole
   The role that the source object is required to play in the relationship.
classDefinitionsOnly
   true to return only the class definitions of the related objects; otherwise, **false**.

Requirements

Platforms: Windows 98, Windows NT 4.0, Windows Millennium Edition, Windows 2000, Windows XP Home Edition, Windows XP Professional, Windows .NET Server family

.NET Framework Security:
- Full trust for the immediate caller. This member cannot be used by partially trusted code.

RelatedObjectQuery.ClassDefinitionsOnly Property

Gets or sets a value indicating that for all instances that adhere to the query, only their class definitions be returned. This parameter is only valid for instance queries.

```
[Visual Basic]
Public Property ClassDefinitionsOnly As Boolean
[C#]
public bool ClassDefinitionsOnly {get; set;}
[C++]
public: __property bool get_ClassDefinitionsOnly();
public: __property void set_ClassDefinitionsOnly(bool);
[JScript]
public function get ClassDefinitionsOnly() : Boolean;
public function set ClassDefinitionsOnly(Boolean);
```

Property Value

true if the query requests only class definitions of the result set; otherwise, **false**.

Remarks

Setting this property value overrides any previous value stored in the object. The query string is rebuilt to reflect the new flag.

Requirements

Platforms: Windows 98, Windows NT 4.0, Windows Millennium Edition, Windows 2000, Windows XP Home Edition, Windows XP Professional, Windows .NET Server family

.NET Framework Security:
- Full trust for the immediate caller. This member cannot be used by partially trusted code.

RelatedObjectQuery.IsSchemaQuery Property

Gets or sets a value indicating whether this is a schema query or an instance query.

```
[Visual Basic]
Public Property IsSchemaQuery As Boolean
[C#]
public bool IsSchemaQuery {get; set;}
[C++]
public: __property bool get_IsSchemaQuery();
public: __property void set_IsSchemaQuery(bool);
[JScript]
public function get IsSchemaQuery() : Boolean;
public function set IsSchemaQuery(Boolean);
```

Property Value

true if this query should be evaluated over the schema; **false** if the query should be evaluated over instances.

Remarks

Setting this property value overrides any previous value stored in the object. The query string is rebuilt to reflect the new query type.

Requirements

Platforms: Windows 98, Windows NT 4.0, Windows Millennium Edition, Windows 2000, Windows XP Home Edition, Windows XP Professional, Windows .NET Server family

.NET Framework Security:

- Full trust for the immediate caller. This member cannot be used by partially trusted code.

RelatedObjectQuery.RelatedClass Property

Gets or sets the class of the endpoint objects.

```
[Visual Basic]
Public Property RelatedClass As String
[C#]
public string RelatedClass {get; set;}
[C++]
public: __property String* get_RelatedClass();
public: __property void set_RelatedClass(String*);
[JScript]
public function get RelatedClass() : String;
public function set RelatedClass(String);
```

Property Value

A string containing the related class name.

Remarks

Setting this property value overrides any previous value stored in the object. The query string is rebuilt to reflect the new related class.

Example

[Visual Basic, C#] To find all the Win32 services available on a computer, this property is set to "Win32_Service":

```
[C#]
RelatedObjectQuery q = new
RelatedObjectQuery("Win32_ComputerSystem='MySystem'");
q.RelatedClass = "Win32_Service";
```

```
[Visual Basic]
Dim q As New RelatedObjectQuery("Win32_ComputerSystem=""MySystem""")
q.RelatedClass = "Win32_Service"
```

Requirements

Platforms: Windows 98, Windows NT 4.0, Windows Millennium Edition, Windows 2000, Windows XP Home Edition, Windows XP Professional, Windows .NET Server family

.NET Framework Security:

- Full trust for the immediate caller. This member cannot be used by partially trusted code.

RelatedObjectQuery.RelatedQualifier Property

Gets or sets a qualifier required to be defined on the related objects.

```
[Visual Basic]
Public Property RelatedQualifier As String
[C#]
public string RelatedQualifier {get; set;}
[C++]
public: __property String* get_RelatedQualifier();
public: __property void set_RelatedQualifier(String*);
[JScript]
public function get RelatedQualifier() : String;
public function set RelatedQualifier(String);
```

Property Value

A string containing the name of the qualifier required on the related objects.

Remarks

Setting this property value overrides any previous value stored in the object. The query string is rebuilt to reflect the new qualifier.

Requirements

Platforms: Windows 98, Windows NT 4.0, Windows Millennium Edition, Windows 2000, Windows XP Home Edition, Windows XP Professional, Windows .NET Server family

.NET Framework Security:

- Full trust for the immediate caller. This member cannot be used by partially trusted code.

RelatedObjectQuery.RelatedRole Property

Gets or sets the role that the related objects returned should be playing in the relationship.

```
[Visual Basic]
Public Property RelatedRole As String
[C#]
public string RelatedRole {get; set;}
[C++]
public: __property String* get_RelatedRole();
public: __property void set_RelatedRole(String*);
[JScript]
public function get RelatedRole() : String;
public function set RelatedRole(String);
```

Property Value

A string containing the role of the related objects.

Remarks

Setting this property value overrides any previous value stored in the object. The query string is rebuilt to reflect the new role.

Requirements

Platforms: Windows 98, Windows NT 4.0,
Windows Millennium Edition, Windows 2000,
Windows XP Home Edition, Windows XP Professional,
Windows .NET Server family

.NET Framework Security:

- Full trust for the immediate caller. This member cannot be used
  by partially trusted code.

RelatedObjectQuery.RelationshipClass Property

Gets or sets the type of relationship (association).

```
[Visual Basic]
Public Property RelationshipClass As String
[C#]
public string RelationshipClass {get; set;}
[C++]
public: __property String* get_RelationshipClass();
public: __property void set_RelationshipClass(String*);
[JScript]
public function get RelationshipClass() : String;
public function set RelationshipClass(String);
```

Property Value

A string containing the relationship class name.

Remarks

Setting this property value overrides any previous value stored in the
object. The query string is rebuilt to reflect the new relationship
class.

Example

[Visual Basic, C#] For example, for finding all the Win32 services
dependent on a service, this property should be set to the
"Win32_DependentService" association class:

```
[C#]
RelatedObjectQuery q = new RelatedObjectQuery("Win32_Service='TCP/IP'");
q.RelationshipClass = "Win32_DependentService";

[Visual Basic]
Dim q As New RelatedObjectQuery("Win32_Service=""TCP/IP""")
q.RelationshipClass = "Win32_DependentService"
```

Requirements

Platforms: Windows 98, Windows NT 4.0,
Windows Millennium Edition, Windows 2000,
Windows XP Home Edition, Windows XP Professional,
Windows .NET Server family

.NET Framework Security:

- Full trust for the immediate caller. This member cannot be used
  by partially trusted code.

RelatedObjectQuery.RelationshipQualifier Property

Gets or sets a qualifier required to be defined on the relationship
objects.

```
[Visual Basic]
Public Property RelationshipQualifier As String
[C#]
public string RelationshipQualifier {get; set;}
```

```
[C++]
public: __property String* get_RelationshipQualifier();
public: __property void set_RelationshipQualifier(String*);
[JScript]
public function get RelationshipQualifier() : String;
public function set RelationshipQualifier(String);
```

Property Value

A string containing the name of the qualifier required on the
relationship objects.

Remarks

Setting this property value overrides any previous value stored in the
object. The query string is rebuilt to reflect the new qualifier.

Requirements

Platforms: Windows 98, Windows NT 4.0,
Windows Millennium Edition, Windows 2000,
Windows XP Home Edition, Windows XP Professional,
Windows .NET Server family

.NET Framework Security:

- Full trust for the immediate caller. This member cannot be used
  by partially trusted code.

RelatedObjectQuery.SourceObject Property

Gets or sets the source object to be used for the query. For instance
queries, this is typically an instance path. For schema queries, this is
typically a class name.

```
[Visual Basic]
Public Property SourceObject As String
[C#]
public string SourceObject {get; set;}
[C++]
public: __property String* get_SourceObject();
public: __property void set_SourceObject(String*);
[JScript]
public function get SourceObject() : String;
public function set SourceObject(String);
```

Property Value

A string representing the path of the object to be used for the query.

Remarks

Setting this property value overrides any previous value stored in the
object. The query string is rebuilt to reflect the new source object.

Requirements

Platforms: Windows 98, Windows NT 4.0,
Windows Millennium Edition, Windows 2000,
Windows XP Home Edition, Windows XP Professional,
Windows .NET Server family

.NET Framework Security:

- Full trust for the immediate caller. This member cannot be used
  by partially trusted code.

RelatedObjectQuery.ThisRole Property

Gets or sets the role that the source object should be playing in the
relationship.

```
[Visual Basic]
Public Property ThisRole As String
[C#]
public string ThisRole {get; set;}
[C++]
public: __property String* get_ThisRole();
public: __property void set_ThisRole(String*);
[JScript]
public function get ThisRole() : String;
public function set ThisRole(String);
```

Property Value

A string containing the role of this object.

Remarks

Setting this property value overrides any previous value stored in the object. The query string is rebuilt to reflect the new role.

Requirements

Platforms: Windows 98, Windows NT 4.0, Windows Millennium Edition, Windows 2000, Windows XP Home Edition, Windows XP Professional, Windows .NET Server family

.NET Framework Security:

- Full trust for the immediate caller. This member cannot be used by partially trusted code.

RelatedObjectQuery.BuildQuery Method

Builds the query string according to the current property values.

```
[Visual Basic]
Protected Friend Sub BuildQuery()
[C#]
protected internal void BuildQuery();
[C++]
protected public: void BuildQuery();
[JScript]
protected internal function BuildQuery();
```

Requirements

Platforms: Windows 98, Windows NT 4.0, Windows Millennium Edition, Windows 2000, Windows XP Home Edition, Windows XP Professional, Windows .NET Server family

.NET Framework Security:

- Full trust for the immediate caller. This member cannot be used by partially trusted code.

RelatedObjectQuery.Clone Method

Creates a copy of the object.

```
[Visual Basic]
Overrides Public Function Clone() As Object Implements _
   ICloneable.Clone
[C#]
public override object Clone();
[C++]
public: Object* Clone();
[JScript]
public override function Clone() : Object;
```

Return Value

The copied object.

Implements

ICloneable.Clone

Requirements

Platforms: Windows 98, Windows NT 4.0, Windows Millennium Edition, Windows 2000, Windows XP Home Edition, Windows XP Professional, Windows .NET Server family

.NET Framework Security:

- Full trust for the immediate caller. This member cannot be used by partially trusted code.

RelatedObjectQuery.ParseQuery Method

Parses the query string and sets the property values accordingly.

```
[Visual Basic]
Protected Friend Overrides Sub ParseQuery( _
   ByVal query As String _
)
[C#]
protected internal override void ParseQuery(
   string query
);
[C++]
protected public: void ParseQuery(
   String* query
);
[JScript]
protected internal override function ParseQuery(
   query : String
);
```

Parameters

query
   The query string to be parsed.

Requirements

Platforms: Windows 98, Windows NT 4.0, Windows Millennium Edition, Windows 2000, Windows XP Home Edition, Windows XP Professional, Windows .NET Server family

.NET Framework Security:

- Full trust for the immediate caller. This member cannot be used by partially trusted code.

RelationshipQuery Class

Represents a WQL REFERENCES OF data query.

System.Object
   System.Management.ManagementQuery
      System.Management.ObjectQuery
         System.Management.WqlObjectQuery
            System.Management.RelationshipQuery

```
[Visual Basic]
Public Class RelationshipQuery
   Inherits WqlObjectQuery
[C#]
public class RelationshipQuery : WqlObjectQuery
[C++]
public __gc class RelationshipQuery : public WqlObjectQuery
[JScript]
public class RelationshipQuery extends WqlObjectQuery
```

Thread Safety

Any public static (**Shared** in Visual Basic) members of this type are safe for multithreaded operations. Any instance members are not guaranteed to be thread safe.

Example

[Visual Basic, C#] The following example searches for all objects related to the 'C:' drive object:

```
[C#]
using System;
using System.Management;

class Sample_RelationshipQuery
{
    public static int Main(string[] args) {
        RelationshipQuery query =
            new RelationshipQuery("references of    ⏎
{Win32_LogicalDisk.DeviceID='C:'}");
        ManagementObjectSearcher searcher =
            new ManagementObjectSearcher(query);

        foreach (ManagementObject assoc in searcher.Get()) {
            Console.WriteLine("Association class = " +    ⏎
assoc["__CLASS"]);
        }

        return 0;
    }
}

[Visual Basic]
Imports System
Imports System.Management

Class Sample_RelatedObjectQuery
    Overloads Public Shared Function Main(args() As String) As Integer
        Dim query As New RelationshipQuery("references of    ⏎
{Win32_LogicalDisk.DeviceID='C:'}")
        Dim searcher As New ManagementObjectSearcher(query)
        Dim assoc As ManagementObject

        For Each assoc In searcher.Get()
            Console.WriteLine("Association class = " &    ⏎
assoc("__CLASS"))
        Next assoc

        Return 0
    End Function
End Class
```

Requirements

Namespace: System.Management

Platforms: Windows 98, Windows NT 4.0, Windows Millennium Edition, Windows 2000, Windows XP Home Edition, Windows XP Professional, Windows .NET Server family

Assembly: System.Management (in System.Management.dll)

RelationshipQuery Constructor

Initializes a new instance of the **RelationshipQuery** class.

Overload List

Initializes a new instance of the **RelationshipQuery** class. This is the default constructor.

   [Visual Basic] **Public Sub New()**

   [C#] **public RelationshipQuery();**

   [C++] **public: RelationshipQuery();**

   [JScript] **public function RelationshipQuery();**

Initializes a new instance of the **RelationshipQuery** class. If the specified string can be succesfully parsed as a WQL query, it is considered to be the query string; otherwise, it is assumed to be the path of the source object for the query. In this case, the query is assumed to be an instances query.

   [Visual Basic] **Public Sub New(String)**

   [C#] **public RelationshipQuery(string);**

   [C++] **public: RelationshipQuery(String*);**

   [JScript] **public function RelationshipQuery(String);**

Initializes a new instance of the **RelationshipQuery** class for the given source object and relationship class. The query is assumed to be an instance query (as opposed to a schema query).

   [Visual Basic] **Public Sub New(String, String)**

   [C#] **public RelationshipQuery(string, string);**

   [C++] **public: RelationshipQuery(String*, String*);**

   [JScript] **public function RelationshipQuery(String, String);**

Initializes a new instance of the **RelationshipQuery** class for a schema query using the given set of parameters. This constructor is used for schema queries only, so the first parameter must be **true**.

   [Visual Basic] **Public Sub New(Boolean, String, String, String, String)**

   [C#] **public RelationshipQuery(bool, string, string, string, string);**

   [C++] **public: RelationshipQuery(bool, String*, String*, String*, String*);**

   [JScript] **public function RelationshipQuery(Boolean, String, String, String, String);**

Initializes a new instance of the **RelationshipQuery** class for the given set of parameters. The query is assumed to be an instance query (as opposed to a schema query).

   [Visual Basic] **Public Sub New(String, String, String, String, Boolean)**

   [C#] **public RelationshipQuery(string, string, string, string, bool);**

   [C++] **public: RelationshipQuery(String*, String*, String*, String*, bool);**

[JScript] **public function RelationshipQuery(String, String, String, String, Boolean);**

Example

[Visual Basic, C#] This example shows the two different ways to use this constructor:

> [Visual Basic, C#] **Note** This example shows how to use one of the overloaded versions of the **RelationshipQuery** constructor. For other examples that might be available, see the individual overload topics.

```
[C#]
//Full query string is specified to the constructor
RelationshipQuery q = new RelationshipQuery
("references of {Win32_ComputerSystem.Name='mymachine'}");

//Only the object of interest is specified to the constructor
RelationshipQuery q = new
RelationshipQuery("Win32_Service.Name='Alerter'");
```

```
[Visual Basic]
'Full query string is specified to the constructor
Dim q As New RelationshipQuery("references of
{Win32_ComputerSystem.Name='mymachine'}")

'Only the object of interest is specified to the constructor
Dim q As New RelationshipQuery("Win32_Service.Name='Alerter'")
```

RelationshipQuery Constructor ()

Initializes a new instance of the **RelationshipQuery** class. This is the default constructor.

```
[Visual Basic]
Public Sub New()
[C#]
public RelationshipQuery();
[C++]
public: RelationshipQuery();
[JScript]
public function RelationshipQuery();
```

Requirements

Platforms: Windows 98, Windows NT 4.0, Windows Millennium Edition, Windows 2000, Windows XP Home Edition, Windows XP Professional, Windows .NET Server family

.NET Framework Security:
- Full trust for the immediate caller. This member cannot be used by partially trusted code.

RelationshipQuery Constructor (String)

Initializes a new instance of the **RelationshipQuery** class. If the specified string can be succesfully parsed as a WQL query, it is considered to be the query string; otherwise, it is assumed to be the path of the source object for the query. In this case, the query is assumed to be an instances query.

```
[Visual Basic]
Public Sub New( _
   ByVal queryOrSourceObject As String _
)
```

```
[C#]
public RelationshipQuery(
   string queryOrSourceObject
);
[C++]
public: RelationshipQuery(
   String* queryOrSourceObject
);
[JScript]
public function RelationshipQuery(
   queryOrSourceObject : String
);
```

Parameters

queryOrSourceObject
> The query string or the class name for this query.

Example

[Visual Basic, C#] This example shows the two different ways to use this constructor:

```
[C#]
//Full query string is specified to the constructor
RelationshipQuery q = new RelationshipQuery("references
 of {Win32_ComputerSystem.Name='mymachine'}");

//Only the object of interest is specified to the constructor
RelationshipQuery q = new
RelationshipQuery("Win32_Service.Name='Alerter'");
```

```
[Visual Basic]
'Full query string is specified to the constructor
Dim q As New RelationshipQuery("references of
{Win32_ComputerSystem.Name='mymachine'}")

'Only the object of interest is specified to the constructor
Dim q As New RelationshipQuery("Win32_Service.Name='Alerter'")
```

Requirements

Platforms: Windows 98, Windows NT 4.0, Windows Millennium Edition, Windows 2000, Windows XP Home Edition, Windows XP Professional, Windows .NET Server family

.NET Framework Security:
- Full trust for the immediate caller. This member cannot be used by partially trusted code.

RelationshipQuery Constructor (String, String)

Initializes a new instance of the **RelationshipQuery** class for the given source object and relationship class. The query is assumed to be an instance query (as opposed to a schema query).

```
[Visual Basic]
Public Sub New( _
   ByVal sourceObject As String, _
   ByVal relationshipClass As String _
)
[C#]
public RelationshipQuery(
   string sourceObject,
   string relationshipClass
);
```

```
[C++]
public: RelationshipQuery(
   String* sourceObject,
   String* relationshipClass
);
[JScript]
public function RelationshipQuery(
   sourceObject : String,
   relationshipClass : String
);
```

Parameters

sourceObject
   The path of the source object for this query.
relationshipClass
   The type of relationship for which to query.

Requirements

Platforms: Windows 98, Windows NT 4.0,
Windows Millennium Edition, Windows 2000,
Windows XP Home Edition, Windows XP Professional,
Windows .NET Server family

.NET Framework Security:

- Full trust for the immediate caller. This member cannot be used by partially trusted code.

RelationshipQuery Constructor (Boolean, String, String, String, String)

Initializes a new instance of the **RelationshipQuery** class for a schema query using the given set of parameters. This constructor is used for schema queries only, so the first parameter must be **true**.

```
[Visual Basic]
Public Sub New( _
   ByVal isSchemaQuery As Boolean, _
   ByVal sourceObject As String, _
   ByVal relationshipClass As String, _
   ByVal relationshipQualifier As String, _
   ByVal thisRole As String _
)
[C#]
public RelationshipQuery(
   bool isSchemaQuery,
   string sourceObject,
   string relationshipClass,
   string relationshipQualifier,
   string thisRole
);
[C++]
public: RelationshipQuery(
   bool isSchemaQuery,
   String* sourceObject,
   String* relationshipClass,
   String* relationshipQualifier,
   String* thisRole
);
```

```
[JScript]
public function RelationshipQuery(
   isSchemaQuery : Boolean,
   sourceObject : String,
   relationshipClass : String,
   relationshipQualifier : String,
   thisRole : String
);
```

Parameters

isSchemaQuery
   true to indicate that this is a schema query; otherwise, **false**.
sourceObject
   The path of the source class for this query.
relationshipClass
   The type of relationship for which to query.
relationshipQualifier
   A qualifier required to be present on the relationship class.
thisRole
   The role that the source class is required to play in the relationship.

Requirements

Platforms: Windows 98, Windows NT 4.0,
Windows Millennium Edition, Windows 2000,
Windows XP Home Edition, Windows XP Professional,
Windows .NET Server family

.NET Framework Security:

- Full trust for the immediate caller. This member cannot be used by partially trusted code.

RelationshipQuery Constructor (String, String, String, String, Boolean)

Initializes a new instance of the **RelationshipQuery** class for the given set of parameters. The query is assumed to be an instance query (as opposed to a schema query).

```
[Visual Basic]
Public Sub New( _
   ByVal sourceObject As String, _
   ByVal relationshipClass As String, _
   ByVal relationshipQualifier As String, _
   ByVal thisRole As String, _
   ByVal classDefinitionsOnly As Boolean _
)
[C#]
public RelationshipQuery(
   string sourceObject,
   string relationshipClass,
   string relationshipQualifier,
   string thisRole,
   bool classDefinitionsOnly
);
[C++]
public: RelationshipQuery(
   String* sourceObject,
   String* relationshipClass,
   String* relationshipQualifier,
   String* thisRole,
   bool classDefinitionsOnly
);
```

```
[JScript]
public function RelationshipQuery(
   sourceObject : String,
   relationshipClass : String,
   relationshipQualifier : String,
   thisRole : String,
   classDefinitionsOnly : Boolean
);
```

Parameters

sourceObject
　　The path of the source object for this query.

relationshipClass
　　The type of relationship for which to query.

relationshipQualifier
　　A qualifier required to be present on the relationship object.

thisRole
　　The role that the source object is required to play in the relationship.

classDefinitionsOnly
　　When this method returns, it contains a boolean that indicates that only class definitions for the resulting objects are returned.

Requirements

Platforms: Windows 98, Windows NT 4.0, Windows Millennium Edition, Windows 2000, Windows XP Home Edition, Windows XP Professional, Windows .NET Server family

.NET Framework Security:

- Full trust for the immediate caller. This member cannot be used by partially trusted code.

RelationshipQuery.ClassDefinitionsOnly Property

Gets or sets a value indicating that only the class definitions of the relevant relationship objects be returned.

```
[Visual Basic]
Public Property ClassDefinitionsOnly As Boolean
[C#]
public bool ClassDefinitionsOnly {get; set;}
[C++]
public: __property bool get_ClassDefinitionsOnly();
public: __property void set_ClassDefinitionsOnly(bool);
[JScript]
public function get ClassDefinitionsOnly() : Boolean;
public function set ClassDefinitionsOnly(Boolean);
```

Property Value

true if the query requests only class definitions of the result set; otherwise, **false**.

Remarks

Setting this property value overrides any previous value stored in the object. As a side-effect, the query string is rebuilt to reflect the new flag.

Requirements

Platforms: Windows 98, Windows NT 4.0, Windows Millennium Edition, Windows 2000, Windows XP Home Edition, Windows XP Professional, Windows .NET Server family

.NET Framework Security:

- Full trust for the immediate caller. This member cannot be used by partially trusted code.

RelationshipQuery.IsSchemaQuery Property

Gets or sets a value indicating whether this query is a schema query or an instance query.

```
[Visual Basic]
Public Property IsSchemaQuery As Boolean
[C#]
public bool IsSchemaQuery {get; set;}
[C++]
public: __property bool get_IsSchemaQuery();
public: __property void set_IsSchemaQuery(bool);
[JScript]
public function get IsSchemaQuery() : Boolean;
public function set IsSchemaQuery(Boolean);
```

Property Value

true if this query should be evaluated over the schema; **false** if the query should be evaluated over instances.

Remarks

Setting this property value overrides any previous value stored in the object. The query string is rebuilt to reflect the new query type.

Requirements

Platforms: Windows 98, Windows NT 4.0, Windows Millennium Edition, Windows 2000, Windows XP Home Edition, Windows XP Professional, Windows .NET Server family

.NET Framework Security:

- Full trust for the immediate caller. This member cannot be used by partially trusted code.

RelationshipQuery.RelationshipClass Property

Gets or sets the class of the relationship objects wanted in the query.

```
[Visual Basic]
Public Property RelationshipClass As String
[C#]
public string RelationshipClass {get; set;}
[C++]
public: __property String* get_RelationshipClass();
public: __property void set_RelationshipClass(String*);
[JScript]
public function get RelationshipClass() : String;
public function set RelationshipClass(String);
```

Property Value

A string containing the relationship class name.

Remarks

Setting this property value overrides any previous value stored in the object. The query string is rebuilt to reflect the new class.

Requirements

Platforms: Windows 98, Windows NT 4.0, Windows Millennium Edition, Windows 2000, Windows XP Home Edition, Windows XP Professional, Windows .NET Server family

RelationshipQuery.RelationshipQualifier Property

Gets or sets a qualifier required on the relationship objects.

```
[Visual Basic]
Public Property RelationshipQualifier As String
[C#]
public string RelationshipQualifier {get; set;}
[C++]
public: __property String* get_RelationshipQualifier();
public: __property void set_RelationshipQualifier(String*);
[JScript]
public function get RelationshipQualifier() : String;
public function set RelationshipQualifier(String);
```

Property Value

A string containing the name of the qualifier required on the relationship objects.

Remarks

Setting this property value overrides any previous value stored in the object. The query string is rebuilt to reflect the new qualifier.

Requirements

Platforms: Windows 98, Windows NT 4.0, Windows Millennium Edition, Windows 2000, Windows XP Home Edition, Windows XP Professional, Windows .NET Server family

RelationshipQuery.SourceObject Property

Gets or sets the source object for this query.

```
[Visual Basic]
Public Property SourceObject As String
[C#]
public string SourceObject {get; set;}
[C++]
public: __property String* get_SourceObject();
public: __property void set_SourceObject(String*);
[JScript]
public function get SourceObject() : String;
public function set SourceObject(String);
```

Property Value

A string representing the path of the object to be used for the query.

Remarks

Setting this property value overrides any previous value stored in the object. The query string is rebuilt to reflect the new source object.

Requirements

Platforms: Windows 98, Windows NT 4.0, Windows Millennium Edition, Windows 2000, Windows XP Home Edition, Windows XP Professional, Windows .NET Server family

RelationshipQuery.ThisRole Property

Gets or sets the role of the source object in the relationship.

```
[Visual Basic]
Public Property ThisRole As String
[C#]
public string ThisRole {get; set;}
[C++]
public: __property String* get_ThisRole();
public: __property void set_ThisRole(String*);
[JScript]
public function get ThisRole() : String;
public function set ThisRole(String);
```

Property Value

A string containing the role of this object.

Remarks

Setting this property value overrides any previous value stored in the object. The query string is rebuilt to reflect the new role.

Requirements

Platforms: Windows 98, Windows NT 4.0, Windows Millennium Edition, Windows 2000, Windows XP Home Edition, Windows XP Professional, Windows .NET Server family

RelationshipQuery.BuildQuery Method

Builds the query string according to the current property values.

```
[Visual Basic]
Protected Friend Sub BuildQuery()
[C#]
protected internal void BuildQuery();
[C++]
protected public: void BuildQuery();
[JScript]
protected internal function BuildQuery();
```

Requirements

Platforms: Windows 98, Windows NT 4.0, Windows Millennium Edition, Windows 2000, Windows XP Home Edition, Windows XP Professional, Windows .NET Server family

RelationshipQuery.Clone Method

Creates a copy of the object.

```
[Visual Basic]
Overrides Public Function Clone() As Object Implements _
   ICloneable.Clone
[C#]
public override object Clone();
[C++]
public: Object* Clone();
[JScript]
public override function Clone() : Object;
```

Return Value

The copied object.

Implements

ICloneable.Clone

Requirements

Platforms: Windows 98, Windows NT 4.0,
Windows Millennium Edition, Windows 2000,
Windows XP Home Edition, Windows XP Professional,
Windows .NET Server family

.NET Framework Security:

- Full trust for the immediate caller. This member cannot be used by partially trusted code.

RelationshipQuery.ParseQuery Method

Parses the query string and sets the property values accordingly.

```
[Visual Basic]
Protected Friend Overrides Sub ParseQuery( _
   ByVal query As String _
)
[C#]
protected internal override void ParseQuery(
   string query
);
[C++]
protected public: void ParseQuery(
   String* query
);
[JScript]
protected internal override function ParseQuery(
   query : String
);
```

Parameters

query
   The query string to be parsed.

Requirements

Platforms: Windows 98, Windows NT 4.0,
Windows Millennium Edition, Windows 2000,
Windows XP Home Edition, Windows XP Professional,
Windows .NET Server family

.NET Framework Security:

- Full trust for the immediate caller. This member cannot be used by partially trusted code.

SelectQuery Class

Represents a WQL SELECT data query.

System.Object
   System.Management.ManagementQuery
     System.Management.ObjectQuery
       System.Management.WqlObjectQuery
         System.Management.SelectQuery

```
[Visual Basic]
Public Class SelectQuery
   Inherits WqlObjectQuery
[C#]
public class SelectQuery : WqlObjectQuery
[C++]
public __gc class SelectQuery : public WqlObjectQuery
[JScript]
public class SelectQuery extends WqlObjectQuery
```

Thread Safety

Any public static (**Shared** in Visual Basic) members of this type are safe for multithreaded operations. Any instance members are not guaranteed to be thread safe.

Example

```
[C#]
using System;
using System.Management;

// This sample demonstrates how to perform a WQL select query.

class Sample_SelectQuery
{
    public static int Main(string[] args) {
        SelectQuery selectQuery = new SelectQuery("win32_logicaldisk");
        ManagementObjectSearcher searcher =
            new ManagementObjectSearcher(selectQuery);

        foreach (ManagementObject disk in searcher.Get()) {
            Console.WriteLine(disk.ToString());
        }
        return 0;
    }
}

[Visual Basic]
Imports System
Imports System.Management

' This sample demonstrates how to perform a WQL select query.

Class Sample_SelectQuery
    Overloads Public Shared Function Main(args() As String) As Integer
        Dim selectQuery As New SelectQuery("win32_logicaldisk")
        Dim searcher As New ManagementObjectSearcher(selectQuery)

        Dim disk As ManagementObject
        For Each disk In  searcher.Get()
            Console.WriteLine(disk.ToString())
        Next disk

        Return 0
    End Function
End Class
```

Requirements

Namespace: System.Management

Platforms: Windows 98, Windows NT 4.0, Windows Millennium Edition, Windows 2000, Windows XP Home Edition, Windows XP Professional, Windows .NET Server family

Assembly: System.Management (in System.Management.dll)

SelectQuery Constructor

Initializes a new instance of the **SelectQuery** class.

Overload List

Initializes a new instance of the **SelectQuery** class. This is the default constructor.

> [Visual Basic] **Public Sub New()**
>
> [C#] **public SelectQuery();**
>
> [C++] **public: SelectQuery();**
>
> [JScript] **public function SelectQuery();**

Initializes a new instance of the **SelectQuery** class for the specified query or the specified class name.

> [Visual Basic] **Public Sub New(String)**
>
> [C#] **public SelectQuery(string);**
>
> [C++] **public: SelectQuery(String*);**
>
> [JScript] **public function SelectQuery(String);**

Initializes a new instance of the **SelectQuery** class for a schema query, optionally specifying a condition. For schema queries, only the *condition* parameter is valid: *className* and *selectedProperties* are not supported and are ignored.

> [Visual Basic] **Public Sub New(Boolean, String)**
>
> [C#] **public SelectQuery(bool, string);**
>
> [C++] **public: SelectQuery(bool, String*);**
>
> [JScript] **public function SelectQuery(Boolean, String);**

Initializes a new instance of the **SelectQuery** class with the specified class name and condition.

> [Visual Basic] **Public Sub New(String, String)**
>
> [C#] **public SelectQuery(string, string);**
>
> [C++] **public: SelectQuery(String*, String*);**
>
> [JScript] **public function SelectQuery(String, String);**

Initializes a new instance of the **SelectQuery** class with the specified class name and condition, selecting only the specified properties.

> [Visual Basic] **Public Sub New(String, String, String())**
>
> [C#] **public SelectQuery(string, string, string[]);**
>
> [C++] **public: SelectQuery(String*, String*, String*[]);**
>
> [JScript] **public function SelectQuery(String, String, String[]);**

Example

> [Visual Basic, C#] **Note** This example shows how to use one of the overloaded versions of the **SelectQuery** constructor. For other examples that might be available, see the individual overload topics.

```
[C#]
String[] properties = {"VariableName", "VariableValue"};

SelectQuery s = new SelectQuery("Win32_Environment",
                                "User='<system>'",
                                properties);
```

```
[Visual Basic]
Dim properties As String[] = {"VariableName", "VariableValue"}

Dim s As New SelectQuery("Win32_Environment", _
                         "User=""<system>""", _
                         properties)
```

SelectQuery Constructor ()

Initializes a new instance of the **SelectQuery** class. This is the default constructor.

```
[Visual Basic]
Public Sub New()
[C#]
public SelectQuery();
[C++]
public: SelectQuery();
[JScript]
public function SelectQuery();
```

Requirements

Platforms: Windows 98, Windows NT 4.0, Windows Millennium Edition, Windows 2000, Windows XP Home Edition, Windows XP Professional, Windows .NET Server family

.NET Framework Security:

- Full trust for the immediate caller. This member cannot be used by partially trusted code.

SelectQuery Constructor (String)

Initializes a new instance of the **SelectQuery** class for the specified query or the specified class name.

```
[Visual Basic]
Public Sub New( _
    ByVal queryOrClassName As String _
)
[C#]
public SelectQuery(
    string queryOrClassName
);
[C++]
public: SelectQuery(
    String* queryOrClassName
);
[JScript]
public function SelectQuery(
    queryOrClassName : String
);
```

Parameters

queryOrClassName

The entire query or the class name to use in the query. The parser in this class attempts to parse the string as a valid WQL SELECT query. If the parser is unsuccessful, it assumes the string is a class name.

Example

```
[C#]
SelectQuery s = new SelectQuery("SELECT * FROM Win32_Service
WHERE State='Stopped');
```

or

```
//This is equivalent to "SELECT * FROM Win32_Service"
SelectQuery s = new SelectQuery("Win32_Service");
```

```
[Visual Basic]
Dim s As New SelectQuery("SELECT * FROM Win32_Service WHERE
State='Stopped')
```

or

```
//This is equivalent to "SELECT * FROM Win32_Service"
Dim s As New SelectQuery("Win32_Service")
```

Requirements

Platforms: Windows 98, Windows NT 4.0, Windows Millennium Edition, Windows 2000, Windows XP Home Edition, Windows XP Professional, Windows .NET Server family

.NET Framework Security:

- Full trust for the immediate caller. This member cannot be used by partially trusted code.

SelectQuery Constructor (Boolean, String)

Initializes a new instance of the **SelectQuery** class for a schema query, optionally specifying a condition. For schema queries, only the *condition* parameter is valid: *className* and *selectedProperties* are not supported and are ignored.

```
[Visual Basic]
Public Sub New( _
    ByVal isSchemaQuery As Boolean, _
    ByVal condition As String _
)
[C#]
public SelectQuery(
    bool isSchemaQuery,
    string condition
);
[C++]
public: SelectQuery(
    bool isSchemaQuery,
    String* condition
);
[JScript]
public function SelectQuery(
    isSchemaQuery : Boolean,
    condition : String
);
```

Parameters

isSchemaQuery

true to indicate that this is a schema query; otherwise, **false**. A **false** value is invalid in this constructor.

condition

The condition to be applied to form the result set of classes.

Example

[C#]
```
SelectQuery s = new SelectQuery(true, "__CLASS = 'Win32_Service'");
```

[Visual Basic]
```
Dim s As New SelectQuery(true, "__CLASS = ""Win32_Service""")
```

Requirements

Platforms: Windows 98, Windows NT 4.0,
Windows Millennium Edition, Windows 2000,
Windows XP Home Edition, Windows XP Professional,
Windows .NET Server family

.NET Framework Security:

- Full trust for the immediate caller. This member cannot be used
  by partially trusted code.

SelectQuery Constructor (String, String)

Initializes a new instance of the **SelectQuery** class with the specified
class name and condition.

[Visual Basic]
```
Public Sub New( _
    ByVal className As String, _
    ByVal condition As String _
)
```
[C#]
```
public SelectQuery(
    string className,
    string condition
);
```
[C++]
```
public: SelectQuery(
    String* className,
    String* condition
);
```
[JScript]
```
public function SelectQuery(
    className : String,
    condition : String
);
```

Parameters

className
    The name of the class to select in the query.
condition
    The condition to be applied in the query.

Example

[C#]
```
SelectQuery s = new SelectQuery("Win32_Process", "HandleID=1234");
```

[Visual Basic]
```
Dim s As New SelectQuery("Win32_Process", "HandleID=1234")
```

Requirements

Platforms: Windows 98, Windows NT 4.0,
Windows Millennium Edition, Windows 2000,
Windows XP Home Edition, Windows XP Professional,
Windows .NET Server family

.NET Framework Security:

- Full trust for the immediate caller. This member cannot be used
  by partially trusted code.

SelectQuery Constructor (String, String, String[])

Initializes a new instance of the **SelectQuery** class with the specified
class name and condition, selecting only the specified properties.

[Visual Basic]
```
Public Sub New( _
    ByVal className As String, _
    ByVal condition As String, _
    ByVal selectedProperties() As String _
)
```
[C#]
```
public SelectQuery(
    string className,
    string condition,
    string[] selectedProperties
);
```
[C++]
```
public: SelectQuery(
    String* className,
    String* condition,
    String* selectedProperties __gc[]
);
```
[JScript]
```
public function SelectQuery(
    className : String,
    condition : String,
    selectedProperties : String[]
);
```

Parameters

className
    The name of the class from which to select.
condition
    The condition to be applied to instances of the selected class.
selectedProperties
    An array of property names to be returned in the query results.

Example

[C#]
```
String[] properties = {"VariableName", "VariableValue"};

SelectQuery s = new SelectQuery("Win32_Environment",
                                "User='<system>'",
                                properties);
```

[Visual Basic]
```
Dim properties As String[] = {"VariableName", "VariableValue"}

Dim s As New SelectQuery("Win32_Environment", _
                         "User=""<system>""", _
                         properties)
```

Requirements

Platforms: Windows 98, Windows NT 4.0,
Windows Millennium Edition, Windows 2000,
Windows XP Home Edition, Windows XP Professional,
Windows .NET Server family

.NET Framework Security:

- Full trust for the immediate caller. This member cannot be used
  by partially trusted code.

SelectQuery.ClassName Property

Gets or sets the class name to be selected from in the query.

```
[Visual Basic]
Public Property ClassName As String
[C#]
public string ClassName {get; set;}
[C++]
public: __property String* get_ClassName();
public: __property void set_ClassName(String*);
[JScript]
public function get ClassName() : String;
public function set ClassName(String);
```

Property Value

A string representing the name of the class.

Remarks

Setting this property value overrides any previous value stored in the object. The query string is rebuilt to reflect the new class name.

Example

```
[C#]
SelectQuery s = new SelectQuery("SELECT * FROM Win32_LogicalDisk");
Console.WriteLine(s.QueryString); //output is : SELECT * FROM     ↵
Win32_LogicalDisk

s.ClassName = "Win32_Process";
Console.WriteLine(s.QueryString); //output is : SELECT * FROM     ↵
Win32_Process

[Visual Basic]
Dim s As New SelectQuery("SELECT * FROM Win32_LogicalDisk")
Console.WriteLine(s.QueryString)  'output is : SELECT * FROM     ↵
Win32_LogicalDisk

s.ClassName = "Win32_Process"
Console.WriteLine(s.QueryString)  'output is : SELECT * FROM     ↵
Win32_Process
```

Requirements

Platforms: Windows 98, Windows NT 4.0, Windows Millennium Edition, Windows 2000, Windows XP Home Edition, Windows XP Professional, Windows .NET Server family

.NET Framework Security:

- Full trust for the immediate caller. This member cannot be used by partially trusted code.

SelectQuery.Condition Property

Gets or sets the condition to be applied in the SELECT query.

```
[Visual Basic]
Public Property Condition As String
[C#]
public string Condition {get; set;}
[C++]
public: __property String* get_Condition();
public: __property void set_Condition(String*);
[JScript]
public function get Condition() : String;
public function set Condition(String);
```

Property Value

A string containing the condition to be applied in the SELECT query.

Remarks

Setting this property value overrides any previous value stored in the object. The query string is rebuilt to reflect the new condition.

Requirements

Platforms: Windows 98, Windows NT 4.0, Windows Millennium Edition, Windows 2000, Windows XP Home Edition, Windows XP Professional, Windows .NET Server family

.NET Framework Security:

- Full trust for the immediate caller. This member cannot be used by partially trusted code.

SelectQuery.IsSchemaQuery Property

Gets or sets a value indicating whether this query is a schema query or an instances query.

```
[Visual Basic]
Public Property IsSchemaQuery As Boolean
[C#]
public bool IsSchemaQuery {get; set;}
[C++]
public: __property bool get_IsSchemaQuery();
public: __property void set_IsSchemaQuery(bool);
[JScript]
public function get IsSchemaQuery() : Boolean;
public function set IsSchemaQuery(Boolean);
```

Property Value

true if this query should be evaluated over the schema; **false** if the query should be evaluated over instances.

Remarks

Setting this property value overrides any previous value stored in the object. The query string is rebuilt to reflect the new query type.

Requirements

Platforms: Windows 98, Windows NT 4.0, Windows Millennium Edition, Windows 2000, Windows XP Home Edition, Windows XP Professional, Windows .NET Server family

.NET Framework Security:

- Full trust for the immediate caller. This member cannot be used by partially trusted code.

SelectQuery.QueryString Property

Gets or sets the query in the **SelectQuery**, in string form.

```
[Visual Basic]
Overrides Public Property QueryString As String
[C#]
public override string QueryString {get; set;}
[C++]
public: __property String* get_QueryString();
public: __property void set_QueryString(String*);
[JScript]
public override function get QueryString() : String;
public override function set QueryString(String);
```

Property Value

A string representing the query.

Remarks

Setting this property value overrides any previous value stored in the object. In addition, setting this property causes the other members of the object to be updated when the string is reparsed.

Example

```
[C#]
SelectQuery s = new SelectQuery();
s.QueryString = "SELECT * FROM Win32_LogicalDisk";
```

```
[Visual Basic]
Dim s As New SelectQuery()
s.QueryString = "SELECT * FROM Win32_LogicalDisk"
```

Requirements

Platforms: Windows 98, Windows NT 4.0, Windows Millennium Edition, Windows 2000, Windows XP Home Edition, Windows XP Professional, Windows .NET Server family

.NET Framework Security:

- Full trust for the immediate caller. This member cannot be used by partially trusted code.

SelectQuery.SelectedProperties Property

Gets or sets an array of property names to be selected in the query.

```
[Visual Basic]
Public Property SelectedProperties As StringCollection
[C#]
public StringCollection SelectedProperties {get; set;}
[C++]
public: __property StringCollection* get_SelectedProperties();
public: __property void set_SelectedProperties(StringCollection*);
[JScript]
public function get SelectedProperties() : StringCollection;
public function set SelectedProperties(StringCollection);
```

Property Value

A **StringCollection** containing the names of the properties to be selected in the query.

Remarks

Setting this property value overrides any previous value stored in the object. The query string is rebuilt to reflect the new properties.

Requirements

Platforms: Windows 98, Windows NT 4.0, Windows Millennium Edition, Windows 2000, Windows XP Home Edition, Windows XP Professional, Windows .NET Server family

.NET Framework Security:

- Full trust for the immediate caller. This member cannot be used by partially trusted code.

SelectQuery.BuildQuery Method

Builds the query string according to the current property values.

```
[Visual Basic]
Protected Friend Sub BuildQuery()
```

```
[C#]
protected internal void BuildQuery();
[C++]
protected public: void BuildQuery();
[JScript]
protected internal function BuildQuery();
```

Requirements

Platforms: Windows 98, Windows NT 4.0, Windows Millennium Edition, Windows 2000, Windows XP Home Edition, Windows XP Professional, Windows .NET Server family

.NET Framework Security:

- Full trust for the immediate caller. This member cannot be used by partially trusted code.

SelectQuery.Clone Method

Creates a copy of the object.

```
[Visual Basic]
Overrides Public Function Clone() As Object Implements _
   ICloneable.Clone
[C#]
public override object Clone();
[C++]
public: Object* Clone();
[JScript]
public override function Clone() : Object;
```

Return Value

The copied object.

Implements

ICloneable.Clone

Requirements

Platforms: Windows 98, Windows NT 4.0, Windows Millennium Edition, Windows 2000, Windows XP Home Edition, Windows XP Professional, Windows .NET Server family

.NET Framework Security:

- Full trust for the immediate caller. This member cannot be used by partially trusted code.

SelectQuery.ParseQuery Method

Parses the query string and sets the property values accordingly.

```
[Visual Basic]
Protected Friend Overrides Sub ParseQuery( _
   ByVal query As String _
)
[C#]
protected internal override void ParseQuery(
   string query
);
[C++]
protected public: void ParseQuery(
   String* query
);
```

```
[JScript]
protected internal override function ParseQuery(
   query : String
);
```

Parameters

query

   The query string to be parsed.

Requirements

Platforms: Windows 98, Windows NT 4.0,
Windows Millennium Edition, Windows 2000,
Windows XP Home Edition, Windows XP Professional,
Windows .NET Server family

.NET Framework Security:

• Full trust for the immediate caller. This member cannot be used
  by partially trusted code.

StoppedEventArgs Class

Holds event data for the **Stopped** event.

System.Object
  System.EventArgs
    System.Management.ManagementEventArgs
      System.Management.StoppedEventArgs

```
[Visual Basic]
Public Class StoppedEventArgs
    Inherits ManagementEventArgs
[C#]
public class StoppedEventArgs : ManagementEventArgs
[C++]
public __gc class StoppedEventArgs : public ManagementEventArgs
[JScript]
public class StoppedEventArgs extends ManagementEventArgs
```

Thread Safety

Any public static (**Shared** in Visual Basic) members of this type are
safe for multithreaded operations. Any instance members are not
guaranteed to be thread safe.

Requirements

Namespace: System.Management

Platforms: Windows 98, Windows NT 4.0,
Windows Millennium Edition, Windows 2000,
Windows XP Home Edition, Windows XP Professional,
Windows .NET Server family

Assembly: System.Management (in System.Management.dll)

StoppedEventArgs.Status Property

Gets the completion status of the operation.

```
[Visual Basic]
Public ReadOnly Property Status As ManagementStatus
[C#]
public ManagementStatus Status {get;}
[C++]
public: __property ManagementStatus get_Status();
[JScript]
public function get Status() : ManagementStatus;
```

Property Value

A **ManagementStatus** value representing the status of the
operation.

Requirements

Platforms: Windows 98, Windows NT 4.0,
Windows Millennium Edition, Windows 2000,
Windows XP Home Edition, Windows XP Professional,
Windows .NET Server family

.NET Framework Security:

- Full trust for the immediate caller. This member cannot be used
  by partially trusted code.

StoppedEventHandler Delegate

Represents the method that will handle the **Stopped** event.

```
[Visual Basic]
<Serializable>
Public Delegate Sub StoppedEventHandler( _
   ByVal sender As Object, _
   ByVal e As StoppedEventArgs _
)
[C#]
[Serializable]
public delegate void StoppedEventHandler(
   object sender,
   StoppedEventArgs e
);
[C++]
[Serializable]
public __gc __delegate void StoppedEventHandler(
   Object* sender,
   StoppedEventArgs* e
);
```

[JScript] In JScript, you can use the delegates in the .NET Framework, but you cannot define your own.

Parameters [Visual Basic, C#, C++]

The declaration of your event handler must have the same parameters as the **StoppedEventHandler** delegate declaration.

Requirements

Namespace: System.Management

Platforms: Windows 98, Windows NT 4.0, Windows Millennium Edition, Windows 2000, Windows XP Home Edition, Windows XP Professional, Windows .NET Server family

Assembly: System.Management (in System.Management.dll)

TextFormat Enumeration

Describes the possible text formats that can be used with **GetText**.

```
[Visual Basic]
<Serializable>
Public Enum TextFormat
[C#]
[Serializable]
public enum TextFormat
[C++]
[Serializable]
__value public enum TextFormat
[JScript]
public
    Serializable
enum TextFormat
```

Members

Member name	Description
CimDtd20	XML DTD that corresponds to CIM DTD version 2.0
Mof	Managed Object Format
WmiDtd20	XML WMI DTD that corresponds to CIM DTD version 2.0. Using this value enables a few WMI-specific extensions, like embedded objects.

Requirements

Namespace: System.Management

Platforms: Windows 98, Windows NT 4.0, Windows Millennium Edition, Windows 2000, Windows XP Home Edition, Windows XP Professional, Windows .NET Server family

Assembly: System.Management (in System.Management.dll)

WqlEventQuery Class

Represents a WMI event query in WQL format.

System.Object
    System.Management.ManagementQuery
        System.Management.EventQuery
            System.Management.WqlEventQuery

```
[Visual Basic]
Public Class WqlEventQuery
    Inherits EventQuery
[C#]
public class WqlEventQuery : EventQuery
[C++]
public __gc class WqlEventQuery : public EventQuery
[JScript]
public class WqlEventQuery extends EventQuery
```

Thread Safety

Any public static (**Shared** in Visual Basic) members of this type are safe for multithreaded operations. Any instance members are not guaranteed to be thread safe.

Example

```csharp
[C#]
using System;
using System.Management;

// This sample demonstrates how to subscribe to an event
// using a WQL event query.

class Sample_EventQuery
{
    public static int Main(string[] args)
    {
        //For this example, we make sure we have an arbitrary
        //class on root\default
        ManagementClass newClass = new ManagementClass(
            "root\\default",
            String.Empty,
            null);
        newClass["__Class"] = "TestWql";
        newClass.Put();

        //Create a query object for watching for class deletion events
        WqlEventQuery eventQuery = new WqlEventQuery("select *
from __classdeletionevent");

        //Initialize an event watcher object with this query
        ManagementEventWatcher watcher = new ManagementEventWatcher(
            new ManagementScope("root/default"),
            eventQuery);

        //Set up a handler for incoming events
        MyHandler handler = new MyHandler();
        watcher.EventArrived += new
EventArrivedEventHandler(handler.Arrived);

        //Start watching for events
        watcher.Start();

        //For this example, we delete the class to trigger an event
        newClass.Delete();

        //Nothing better to do - we loop to wait for an event
to arrive.
        while (!handler.IsArrived) {
            System.Threading.Thread.Sleep(1000);
        }
```

```csharp
        //In this example we only want to wait for one event, so
we can stop watching
        watcher.Stop();

        return 0;
    }
}

public class MyHandler
{
    private bool isArrived = false;

    //Handles the event when it arrives
    public void Arrived(object sender, EventArrivedEventArgs e) {
        ManagementBaseObject eventArg =
(ManagementBaseObject)(e.NewEvent["TargetClass"]);
        Console.WriteLine("Class Deleted = " +
eventArg["__CLASS"]);
        isArrived = true;
    }

    //Used to determine whether the event has arrived or not.
    public bool IsArrived {
        get {
            return isArrived;
        }
    }
}
```

```vbnet
[Visual Basic]
Imports System
Imports System.Management

' This sample demonstrates how to subscribe an event
' using a WQL event query.

Class Sample_EventQuery
    Public Shared Sub Main()

        'For this example, we make sure we have an arbitrary
'class on root\default
        Dim newClass As New ManagementClass( _
            "root\default", _
            String.Empty, Nothing)
        newClass("__Class") = "TestWql"
        newClass.Put()

        'Create a query object for watching for class deletion events
        Dim eventQuery As New WqlEventQuery("select * from
__classdeletionevent")

        'Initialize an event watcher object with this query
        Dim watcher As New ManagementEventWatcher( _
            New ManagementScope("root/default"), _
            eventQuery)

        'Set up a handler for incoming events
        Dim handler As New MyHandler()
        AddHandler watcher.EventArrived, AddressOf handler.Arrived

        'Start watching for events
        watcher.Start()

        'For this example, we delete the class to trigger an event
        newClass.Delete()

        'Nothing better to do - we loop to wait for an event to arrive.
        While Not handler.IsArrived
            Console.Write("0")
            System.Threading.Thread.Sleep(1000)
        End While

        'In this example we only want to wait for one event, so
we can stop watching
        watcher.Stop()
```

```
    End Sub

    Public Class MyHandler
        Private _isArrived As Boolean = False

        'Handles the event when it arrives
        Public Sub Arrived(sender As Object, e As      ⏎
EventArrivedEventArgs)
            Dim eventArg As ManagementBaseObject = CType( _
                e.NewEvent("TargetClass"), _
                ManagementBaseObject)
            Console.WriteLine(("Class Deleted = " +     ⏎
eventArg("__CLASS")))
            _isArrived = True
        End Sub

        'Used to determine whether the event has arrived or not.
        Public ReadOnly Property IsArrived() As Boolean
            Get
                Return _isArrived
            End Get
        End Property
    End Class
End Class
```

Requirements

Namespace: System.Management

Platforms: Windows 98, Windows NT 4.0,
Windows Millennium Edition, Windows 2000,
Windows XP Home Edition, Windows XP Professional,
Windows .NET Server family

Assembly: System.Management (in System.Management.dll)

WqlEventQuery Constructor

Initializes a new instance of the **WqlEventQuery** class.

Overload List

Initializes a new instance of the **WqlEventQuery** class. This is the default constructor.

[Visual Basic] **Public Sub New()**
[C#] **public WqlEventQuery();**
[C++] **public: WqlEventQuery();**
[JScript] **public function WqlEventQuery();**

Initializes a new instance of the **WqlEventQuery** class based on the given query string or event class name.

[Visual Basic] **Public Sub New(String)**
[C#] **public WqlEventQuery(string);**
[C++] **public: WqlEventQuery(String*);**
[JScript] **public function WqlEventQuery(String);**

Initializes a new instance of the **WqlEventQuery** class for the specified event class name, with the specified condition.

[Visual Basic] **Public Sub New(String, String)**
[C#] **public WqlEventQuery(string, string);**
[C++] **public: WqlEventQuery(String*, String*);**
[JScript] **public function WqlEventQuery(String, String);**

Initializes a new instance of the **WqlEventQuery** class for the specified event class, with the specified latency time.

[Visual Basic] **Public Sub New(String, TimeSpan)**
[C#] **public WqlEventQuery(string, TimeSpan);**
[C++] **public: WqlEventQuery(String*, TimeSpan);**
[JScript] **public function WqlEventQuery(String, TimeSpan);**

Initializes a new instance of the **WqlEventQuery** class with the specified event class name, condition, and grouping interval.

[Visual Basic] **Public Sub New(String, String, TimeSpan)**
[C#] **public WqlEventQuery(string, string, TimeSpan);**
[C++] **public: WqlEventQuery(String*, String*, TimeSpan);**
[JScript] **public function WqlEventQuery(String, String, TimeSpan);**

Initializes a new instance of the **WqlEventQuery** class with the specified event class name, polling interval, and condition.

[Visual Basic] **Public Sub New(String, TimeSpan, String)**
[C#] **public WqlEventQuery(string, TimeSpan, string);**
[C++] **public: WqlEventQuery(String*, TimeSpan, String*);**
[JScript] **public function WqlEventQuery(String, TimeSpan, String);**

Initializes a new instance of the **WqlEventQuery** class with the specified event class name, condition, grouping interval, and grouping properties.

[Visual Basic] **Public Sub New(String, String, TimeSpan, String())**
[C#] **public WqlEventQuery(string, string, TimeSpan, string[]);**
[C++] **public: WqlEventQuery(String*, String*, TimeSpan, String*[]);**
[JScript] **public function WqlEventQuery(String, String, TimeSpan, String[]);**

Initializes a new instance of the **WqlEventQuery** class with the specified event class name, condition, grouping interval, grouping properties, and specified number of events.

[Visual Basic] **Public Sub New(String, TimeSpan, String, TimeSpan, String(), String)**
[C#] **public WqlEventQuery(string, TimeSpan, string, TimeSpan, string[], string);**
[C++] **public: WqlEventQuery(String*, TimeSpan, String*, TimeSpan, String*[], String*);**
[JScript] **public function WqlEventQuery(String, TimeSpan, String, TimeSpan, String[], String);**

Example

[Visual Basic, C#] This example creates the event query: "SELECT * FROM __InstanceCreationEvent WHERE **TargetInstance** ISA **Win32_NTLogEvent** GROUP WITHIN 300 BY **TargetInstance. SourceName** HAVING **NumberOfEvents** > 15" which means "deliver aggregate events only if the number of **Win32_NT-LogEvent** events received from the same source exceeds 15."

> [Visual Basic, C#] **Note** This example shows how to use one of the overloaded versions of the **WqlEventQuery** constructor. For other examples that might be available, see the individual overload topics.

```
[C#]
//Requests sending aggregated events if the number of events   ⏎
exceeds 15.
String[] props = {"TargetInstance.SourceName"};
WqlEventQuery q = new WqlEventQuery("__InstanceCreationEvent",
                        "TargetInstance isa       ⏎
'Win32_NTLogEvent'",
                        new TimeSpan(0,10,0),
                        props,
                        "NumberOfEvents >15");
```

```
[Visual Basic]
'Requests sending aggregated events if the number of events exceeds 15.
Dim props() As String = {"TargetInstance.SourceName"};
Dim t As New TimeSpan(0,10,0)
Dim q As WqlEventQuery("__InstanceCreationEvent", _
                        "TargetInstance isa ""Win32_NTLogEvent""", _
                        t, _
                        props, _
                        "NumberOfEvents >15")
```

WqlEventQuery Constructor ()

Initializes a new instance of the **WqlEventQuery** class. This is the default constructor.

```
[Visual Basic]
Public Sub New()
[C#]
public WqlEventQuery();
[C++]
public: WqlEventQuery();
[JScript]
public function WqlEventQuery();
```

Requirements

Platforms: Windows 98, Windows NT 4.0, Windows Millennium Edition, Windows 2000, Windows XP Home Edition, Windows XP Professional, Windows .NET Server family

.NET Framework Security:

- Full trust for the immediate caller. This member cannot be used by partially trusted code.

WqlEventQuery Constructor (String)

Initializes a new instance of the **WqlEventQuery** class based on the given query string or event class name.

```
[Visual Basic]
Public Sub New( _
   ByVal queryOrEventClassName As String _
)
[C#]
public WqlEventQuery(
   string queryOrEventClassName
);
[C++]
public: WqlEventQuery(
   String* queryOrEventClassName
);
[JScript]
public function WqlEventQuery(
   queryOrEventClassName : String
);
```

Parameters

queryOrEventClassName
   The string representing either the entire event query or the name of the event class to query. The object will try to parse the string as a valid event query. If unsuccessful, the parser will assume that the parameter represents an event class name.

Example

[Visual Basic, C#] The two options below are equivalent:

```
[C#]
//Full query string specified to the constructor
WqlEventQuery q = new WqlEventQuery("SELECT * FROM MyEvent");

//Only relevant event class name specified to the constructor
WqlEventQuery q = new WqlEventQuery("MyEvent"); //results
in the same query as above.
```

```
[Visual Basic]
'Full query string specified to the constructor
Dim q As New WqlEventQuery("SELECT * FROM MyEvent")

'Only relevant event class name specified to the constructor
Dim q As New WqlEventQuery("MyEvent") 'results in the same
   query as above
```

Requirements

Platforms: Windows 98, Windows NT 4.0, Windows Millennium Edition, Windows 2000, Windows XP Home Edition, Windows XP Professional, Windows .NET Server family

.NET Framework Security:

- Full trust for the immediate caller. This member cannot be used by partially trusted code.

WqlEventQuery Constructor (String, String)

Initializes a new instance of the **WqlEventQuery** class for the specified event class name, with the specified condition.

```
[Visual Basic]
Public Sub New( _
   ByVal eventClassName As String, _
   ByVal condition As String _
)
[C#]
public WqlEventQuery(
   string eventClassName,
   string condition
);
[C++]
public: WqlEventQuery(
   String* eventClassName,
   String* condition
);
[JScript]
public function WqlEventQuery(
   eventClassName : String,
   condition : String
);
```

Parameters

eventClassName
   The name of the event class to query.
condition
   The condition to apply to events of the specified class.

Example

[Visual Basic, C#] This example shows how to create an event query that contains a condition in addition to the event class:

```
[C#]
//Requests all "MyEvent" events where the event's properties
//match the specified condition
WqlEventQuery q = new WqlEventQuery("MyEvent", "FirstProp
< 20 and SecondProp = 'red'");
```

```
[Visual Basic]
'Requests all "MyEvent" events where the event's properties
'match the specified condition
Dim q As New WqlEventQuery("MyEvent", "FirstProp
< 20 and SecondProp = 'red'")
```

Requirements

Platforms: Windows 98, Windows NT 4.0,
Windows Millennium Edition, Windows 2000,
Windows XP Home Edition, Windows XP Professional,
Windows .NET Server family

.NET Framework Security:

- Full trust for the immediate caller. This member cannot be used by partially trusted code.

WqlEventQuery Constructor (String, TimeSpan)

Initializes a new instance of the **WqlEventQuery** class for the specified event class, with the specified latency time.

```
[Visual Basic]
Public Sub New( _
    ByVal eventClassName As String, _
    ByVal withinInterval As TimeSpan _
)
[C#]
public WqlEventQuery(
    string eventClassName,
    TimeSpan withinInterval
);
[C++]
public: WqlEventQuery(
    String* eventClassName,
    TimeSpan withinInterval
);
[JScript]
public function WqlEventQuery(
    eventClassName : String,
    withinInterval : TimeSpan
);
```

Parameters

eventClassName
    The name of the event class to query.

withinInterval
    A timespan value specifying the latency acceptable for receiving this event. This value is used in cases where there is no explicit event provider for the query requested, and WMI is required to poll for the condition. This interval is the maximum amount of time that can pass before notification of an event must be delivered.

Example

[Visual Basic, C#] This example shows creating an event query that contains a time interval.

```
[C#]
//Requests all instance creation events, with a specified latency of
//10 seconds. The query created is "SELECT * FROM
_InstanceCreationEvent WITHIN 10"
WqlEventQuery q = new WqlEventQuery("_InstanceCreationEvent",
                              new TimeSpan(0,0,10));
```

```
[Visual Basic]
'Requests all instance creation events, with a specified latency of
'10 seconds. The query created is "SELECT * FROM
_InstanceCreationEvent WITHIN 10"
Dim t As New TimeSpan(0,0,10)
Dim q As New WqlEventQuery("_InstanceCreationEvent", t)
```

Requirements

Platforms: Windows 98, Windows NT 4.0,
Windows Millennium Edition, Windows 2000,
Windows XP Home Edition, Windows XP Professional,
Windows .NET Server family

.NET Framework Security:

- Full trust for the immediate caller. This member cannot be used by partially trusted code.

WqlEventQuery Constructor (String, String, TimeSpan)

Initializes a new instance of the **WqlEventQuery** class with the specified event class name, condition, and grouping interval.

```
[Visual Basic]
Public Sub New( _
    ByVal eventClassName As String, _
    ByVal condition As String, _
    ByVal groupWithinInterval As TimeSpan _
)
[C#]
public WqlEventQuery(
    string eventClassName,
    string condition,
    TimeSpan groupWithinInterval
);
[C++]
public: WqlEventQuery(
    String* eventClassName,
    String* condition,
    TimeSpan groupWithinInterval
);
[JScript]
public function WqlEventQuery(
    eventClassName : String,
    condition : String,
    groupWithinInterval : TimeSpan
);
```

Parameters

eventClassName
    The name of the event class to query.

condition
    The condition to apply to events of the specified class.

groupWithinInterval
    The specified interval at which WMI sends one aggregate event, rather than many events.

Example

[Visual Basic, C#] This example creates the event query: "SELECT * FROM **FrequentEvent** WHERE **InterestingProperty** = 5 GROUP WITHIN 10", which means "send notification of events of type **FrequentEvent**, in which the **InterestingProperty** is equal to 5, but send an aggregate event in a 10-second interval."

```
[C#]
//Sends an aggregate of the requested events every 10 seconds
WqlEventQuery q = new WqlEventQuery("FrequentEvent",
                                    "InterestingProperty = 5",
                                    new TimeSpan(0,0,10));
```

```
[Visual Basic]
'Sends an aggregate of the requested events every 10 seconds
Dim t As New TimeSpan(0,0,10)
Dim q As New WqlEventQuery("FrequentEvent", _
                           "InterestingProperty = 5", _
                           t)
```

Requirements

Platforms: Windows 98, Windows NT 4.0,
Windows Millennium Edition, Windows 2000,
Windows XP Home Edition, Windows XP Professional,
Windows .NET Server family

.NET Framework Security:
- Full trust for the immediate caller. This member cannot be used
  by partially trusted code.

WqlEventQuery Constructor (String, TimeSpan, String)

Initializes a new instance of the **WqlEventQuery** class with the
specified event class name, polling interval, and condition.

```
[Visual Basic]
Public Sub New( _
   ByVal eventClassName As String, _
   ByVal withinInterval As TimeSpan, _
   ByVal condition As String _
)
[C#]
public WqlEventQuery(
   string eventClassName,
   TimeSpan withinInterval,
   string condition
);
[C++]
public: WqlEventQuery(
   String* eventClassName,
   TimeSpan withinInterval,
   String* condition
);
[JScript]
public function WqlEventQuery(
   eventClassName : String,
   withinInterval : TimeSpan,
   condition : String
);
```

Parameters

eventClassName
   The name of the event class to query.

withinInterval
   A timespan value specifying the latency acceptable for receiving
   this event. This value is used in cases where there is no explicit
   event provider for the query requested and WMI is required to
   poll for the condition. This interval is the maximum amount of
   time that can pass before notification of an event must be
   delivered.

condition
   The condition to apply to events of the specified class.

Example

[Visual Basic, C#] This example creates the event query: "SELECT
* FROM __InstanceCreationEvent WITHIN 10 WHERE
TargetInstance ISA Win32_Service ", which means "send
notification of the creation of **Win32_Service** instances, with a 10-
second polling interval."

```
[C#]
//Requests notification of the creation of Win32_Service
instances with a 10 second
//allowed latency.
WqlEventQuery q = new WqlEventQuery("__InstanceCreationEvent",
                                    new TimeSpan(0,0,10),
                                    "TargetInstance isa 'Win32_Service'");
```

```
[Visual Basic]
'Requests notification of the creation of Win32_Service
 instances with a 10 second
'allowed latency.
Dim t As New TimeSpan(0,0,10)
Dim q As New WqlEventQuery("__InstanceCreationEvent", _
                           t, _
                           "TargetInstance isa ""Win32_Service""")
```

Requirements

Platforms: Windows 98, Windows NT 4.0,
Windows Millennium Edition, Windows 2000,
Windows XP Home Edition, Windows XP Professional,
Windows .NET Server family

.NET Framework Security:
- Full trust for the immediate caller. This member cannot be used
  by partially trusted code.

WqlEventQuery Constructor (String, String, TimeSpan, String[])

Initializes a new instance of the **WqlEventQuery** class with the
specified event class name, condition, grouping interval, and
grouping properties.

```
[Visual Basic]
Public Sub New( _
   ByVal eventClassName As String, _
   ByVal condition As String, _
   ByVal groupWithinInterval As TimeSpan, _
   ByVal groupByPropertyList() As String _
)
[C#]
public WqlEventQuery(
   string eventClassName,
   string condition,
   TimeSpan groupWithinInterval,
   string[] groupByPropertyList
);
[C++]
public: WqlEventQuery(
   String* eventClassName,
   String* condition,
   TimeSpan groupWithinInterval,
   String* groupByPropertyList __gc[]
);
```

```
[JScript]
public function WqlEventQuery(
    eventClassName : String,
    condition : String,
    groupWithinInterval : TimeSpan,
    groupByPropertyList : String[]
);
```

Parameters

eventClassName
    The name of the event class to query.
condition
    The condition to apply to events of the specified class.
groupWithinInterval
    The specified interval at which WMI sends one aggregate event,
    rather than many events.
groupByPropertyList
    The properties in the event class by which the events should be
    grouped.

Example

[Visual Basic, C#] This example creates the event query: "SELECT
* FROM **EmailEvent** WHERE **Sender** = 'MyBoss' GROUP
WITHIN 300 BY **Importance** ", which means "send notification
when new email from a particular sender has arrived within the last
10 minutes, combined with other events that have the same value in
the **Importance** property."

```
[C#]
//Requests "EmailEvent" events where the Sender property
is "MyBoss", and
//groups them based on importance
String[] props = {"Importance"};
WqlEventQuery q = new WqlEventQuery("EmailEvent",
                                    "Sender = 'MyBoss'",
                                    new TimeSpan(0,10,0),
                                    props);
```

```
[Visual Basic]
'Requests "EmailEvent" events where the Sender property
is "MyBoss", and
'groups them based on importance
Dim props() As String = {"Importance"}
Dim t As New TimeSpan(0,10,0)
Dim q As New WqlEventQuery("EmailEvent", _
                           "Sender = ""MyBoss""", _
                           t, _
                           props)
```

Requirements

Platforms: Windows 98, Windows NT 4.0,
Windows Millennium Edition, Windows 2000,
Windows XP Home Edition, Windows XP Professional,
Windows .NET Server family

.NET Framework Security:
*   Full trust for the immediate caller. This member cannot be used
    by partially trusted code.

WqlEventQuery Constructor (String, TimeSpan, String, TimeSpan, String[], String)

Initializes a new instance of the **WqlEventQuery** class with the
specified event class name, condition, grouping interval, grouping
properties, and specified number of events.

```
[Visual Basic]
Public Sub New( _
    ByVal eventClassName As String, _
    ByVal withinInterval As TimeSpan, _
    ByVal condition As String, _
    ByVal groupWithinInterval As TimeSpan, _
    ByVal groupByPropertyList() As String, _
    ByVal havingCondition As String _
)
```

```
[C#]
public WqlEventQuery(
    string eventClassName,
    TimeSpan withinInterval,
    string condition,
    TimeSpan groupWithinInterval,
    string[] groupByPropertyList,
    string havingCondition
);
```

```
[C++]
public: WqlEventQuery(
    String* eventClassName,
    TimeSpan withinInterval,
    String* condition,
    TimeSpan groupWithinInterval,
    String* groupByPropertyList __gc[],
    String* havingCondition
);
```

```
[JScript]
public function WqlEventQuery(
    eventClassName : String,
    withinInterval : TimeSpan,
    condition : String,
    groupWithinInterval : TimeSpan,
    groupByPropertyList : String[],
    havingCondition : String
);
```

Parameters

eventClassName
    The name of the event class on which to be queried.
withinInterval
    A timespan value specifying the latency acceptable for receiving
    this event. This value is used in cases where there is no explicit
    event provider for the query requested, and WMI is required to
    poll for the condition. This interval is the maximum amount of
    time that can pass before notification of an event must be
    delivered.
condition
    The condition to apply to events of the specified class.
groupWithinInterval
    The specified interval at which WMI sends one aggregate event,
    rather than many events.
groupByPropertyList
    The properties in the event class by which the events should be
    grouped.
havingCondition
    The condition to apply to the number of events.

Example

[Visual Basic, C#] This example creates the event query: "SELECT
* FROM **__InstanceCreationEvent** WHERE **TargetInstance** ISA
Win32_NTLogEvent GROUP WITHIN 300 BY **Target-**

Instance.SourceName HAVING **NumberOfEvents** > 15" which means "deliver aggregate events only if the number of **Win32_NT-LogEvent** events received from the same source exceeds 15."

[C#]
```
//Requests sending aggregated events if the number of
events exceeds 15.
String[] props = {"TargetInstance.SourceName"};
WqlEventQuery q = new WqlEventQuery("__InstanceCreationEvent",
                                    "TargetInstance isa
'Win32_NTLogEvent'",
                                    new TimeSpan(0,10,0),
                                    props,
                                    "NumberOfEvents >15");
```

[Visual Basic]
```
'Requests sending aggregated events if the number of events exceeds 15.
Dim props() As String = {"TargetInstance.SourceName"};
Dim t As New TimeSpan(0,10,0)
Dim q As WqlEventQuery("__InstanceCreationEvent", _
                       "TargetInstance isa ""Win32_NTLogEvent""", _
                       t, _
                       props, _
                       "NumberOfEvents >15")
```

Requirements

Platforms: Windows 98, Windows NT 4.0, Windows Millennium Edition, Windows 2000, Windows XP Home Edition, Windows XP Professional, Windows .NET Server family

.NET Framework Security:

- Full trust for the immediate caller. This member cannot be used by partially trusted code.

WqlEventQuery.Condition Property

Gets or sets the condition to be applied to events of the specified class.

[Visual Basic]
```
Public Property Condition As String
```
[C#]
```
public string Condition {get; set;}
```
[C++]
```
public: __property String* get_Condition();
public: __property void set_Condition(String*);
```
[JScript]
```
public function get Condition() : String;
public function set Condition(String);
```

Property Value

The condition is represented as a string, containing one or more clauses of the form: <propName> <operator> <value> combined with and/or operators. <propName> must represent a property defined on the event class specified in this query.

Remarks

Setting this property value overrides any previous value stored in the object. The query string is rebuilt to reflect the new condition.

Example

[Visual Basic, C#] This example creates a new **WqlEventQuery** that represents the query: "SELECT * FROM **MyEvent** WHERE **PropVal** > 8".

[C#]
```
WqlEventQuery q = new WqlEventQuery();
q.EventClassName = "MyEvent";
q.Condition = "PropVal > 8";
```

[Visual Basic]
```
Dim q As New WqlEventQuery()
q.EventClassName = "MyEvent"
q.Condition = "PropVal > 8"
```

Requirements

Platforms: Windows 98, Windows NT 4.0, Windows Millennium Edition, Windows 2000, Windows XP Home Edition, Windows XP Professional, Windows .NET Server family

.NET Framework Security:

- Full trust for the immediate caller. This member cannot be used by partially trusted code.

WqlEventQuery.EventClassName Property

Gets or sets the event class to query.

[Visual Basic]
```
Public Property EventClassName As String
```
[C#]
```
public string EventClassName {get; set;}
```
[C++]
```
public: __property String* get_EventClassName();
public: __property void set_EventClassName(String*);
```
[JScript]
```
public function get EventClassName() : String;
public function set EventClassName(String);
```

Property Value

A string containing the name of the event class to query.

Remarks

Setting this property value overrides any previous value stored in the object. The query string is rebuilt to reflect the new class name.

Example

[Visual Basic, C#] This example creates a new **WqlEventQuery** that represents the query: "SELECT * FROM **MyEvent** ".

[C#]
```
WqlEventQuery q = new WqlEventQuery();
q.EventClassName = "MyEvent";
```

[Visual Basic]
```
Dim q As New WqlEventQuery()
q.EventClassName = "MyEvent"
```

Requirements

Platforms: Windows 98, Windows NT 4.0, Windows Millennium Edition, Windows 2000, Windows XP Home Edition, Windows XP Professional, Windows .NET Server family

.NET Framework Security:

- Full trust for the immediate caller. This member cannot be used by partially trusted code.

WqlEventQuery.GroupByPropertyList Property

Gets or sets properties in the event to be used for grouping events of the same type.

```
[Visual Basic]
Public Property GroupByPropertyList As StringCollection
[C#]
public StringCollection GroupByPropertyList {get; set;}
[C++]
public: __property StringCollection* get_GroupByPropertyList();
public: __property void set_GroupByPropertyList(StringCollection*);
[JScript]
public function get GroupByPropertyList() : StringCollection;
public function set GroupByPropertyList(StringCollection);
```

Property Value

Null, if no grouping is required; otherwise, a collection of event property names.

Remarks

Setting this property value overrides any previous value stored in the object. The query string is rebuilt to reflect the new grouping.

Example

[Visual Basic, C#] This example creates a new **WqlEventQuery** that represents the query: "SELECT * FROM **EmailEvent** GROUP WITHIN 300 BY **Sender** ", which means "send notification of all **EmailEvent** events, aggregated by the **Sender** property, within 10-minute intervals."

```
[C#]
WqlEventQuery q = new WqlEventQuery();
q.EventClassName = "EmailEvent";
q.GroupWithinInterval = new TimeSpan(0,10,0);
q.GroupByPropertyList = new StringCollection();
q.GroupByPropertyList.Add("Sender");
```

```
[Visual Basic]
Dim q As New WqlEventQuery()
q.EventClassName = "EmailEvent"
q.GroupWithinInterval = New TimeSpan(0,10,0)
q.GroupByPropertyList = New StringCollection()
q.GroupByPropertyList.Add("Sender")
```

Requirements

Platforms: Windows 98, Windows NT 4.0, Windows Millennium Edition, Windows 2000, Windows XP Home Edition, Windows XP Professional, Windows .NET Server family

.NET Framework Security:

- Full trust for the immediate caller. This member cannot be used by partially trusted code.

WqlEventQuery.GroupWithinInterval Property

Gets or sets the interval to be used for grouping events of the same type.

```
[Visual Basic]
Public Property GroupWithinInterval As TimeSpan
[C#]
public TimeSpan GroupWithinInterval {get; set;}
[C++]
public: __property TimeSpan get_GroupWithinInterval();
public: __property void set_GroupWithinInterval(TimeSpan);
[JScript]
public function get GroupWithinInterval() : TimeSpan;
public function set GroupWithinInterval(TimeSpan);
```

Property Value

Null, if there is no grouping involved; otherwise, the interval in which WMI should group events of the same type.

Remarks

Setting this property value overrides any previous value stored in the object. The query string is rebuilt to reflect the new interval.

Example

[Visual Basic, C#] This example creates a new **WqlEventQuery** that represents the query: "SELECT * FROM **MyEvent** WHERE **PropVal** > 8 GROUP WITHIN 10", which means "send notification of all **MyEvent** events where the **PropVal** property is greater than 8, and aggregate these events within 10-second intervals."

```
[C#]
WqlEventQuery q = new WqlEventQuery();
q.EventClassName = "MyEvent";
q.Condition = "PropVal > 8";
q.GroupWithinInterval = new TimeSpan(0,0,10);
```

```
[Visual Basic]
Dim q As New WqlEventQuery()
q.EventClassName = "MyEvent"
q.Condition = "PropVal > 8"
q.GroupWithinInterval = New TimeSpan(0,0,10)
```

Requirements

Platforms: Windows 98, Windows NT 4.0, Windows Millennium Edition, Windows 2000, Windows XP Home Edition, Windows XP Professional, Windows .NET Server family

.NET Framework Security:

- Full trust for the immediate caller. This member cannot be used by partially trusted code.

WqlEventQuery.HavingCondition Property

Gets or sets the condition to be applied to the aggregation of events, based on the number of events received.

```
[Visual Basic]
Public Property HavingCondition As String
[C#]
public string HavingCondition {get; set;}
[C++]
public: __property String* get_HavingCondition();
public: __property void set_HavingCondition(String*);
[JScript]
public function get HavingCondition() : String;
public function set HavingCondition(String);
```

Property Value

Null, if no aggregation or no condition should be applied; otherwise, a condition of the form "NumberOfEvents <operator> <value>".

Remarks

Setting this property value overrides any previous value stored in the object. The query string is rebuilt to reflect the new grouping condition.

Example

[Visual Basic, C#] This example creates a new **WqlEventQuery** that represents the query: "SELECT * FROM **EmailEvent** GROUP WITHIN 300 HAVING **NumberOfEvents** > 5", which means "send notification of all **EmailEvent** events, aggregated within 10-minute intervals, if there are more than 5 occurrences."

```
[C#]
WqlEventQuery q = new WqlEventQuery();
q.EventClassName = "EmailEvent";
q.GroupWithinInterval = new TimeSpan(0,10,0);
q.HavingCondition = "NumberOfEvents > 5";
```

```
[Visual Basic]
Dim q As New WqlEventQuery()
q.EventClassName = "EmailEvent"
q.GroupWithinInterval = new TimeSpan(0,10,0)
q.HavingCondition = "NumberOfEvents > 5"
```

Requirements

Platforms: Windows 98, Windows NT 4.0, Windows Millennium Edition, Windows 2000, Windows XP Home Edition, Windows XP Professional, Windows .NET Server family

.NET Framework Security:

- Full trust for the immediate caller. This member cannot be used by partially trusted code.

WqlEventQuery.QueryLanguage Property

Gets or sets the language of the query.

```
[Visual Basic]
Overrides Public ReadOnly Property QueryLanguage As String
[C#]
public override string QueryLanguage {get;}
[C++]
public: __property String* get_QueryLanguage();
[JScript]
public override function get QueryLanguage() : String;
```

Property Value

The value of this property in this object is always "WQL".

Requirements

Platforms: Windows 98, Windows NT 4.0, Windows Millennium Edition, Windows 2000, Windows XP Home Edition, Windows XP Professional, Windows .NET Server family

.NET Framework Security:

- Full trust for the immediate caller. This member cannot be used by partially trusted code.

WqlEventQuery.QueryString Property

Gets or sets the string representing the query.

```
[Visual Basic]
Overrides Public Property QueryString As String
[C#]
public override string QueryString {get; set;}
[C++]
public: __property String* get_QueryString();
public: __property void set_QueryString(String*);
```

```
[JScript]
public override function get QueryString() : String;
public override function set QueryString(String);
```

Property Value

A string representing the query.

Requirements

Platforms: Windows 98, Windows NT 4.0, Windows Millennium Edition, Windows 2000, Windows XP Home Edition, Windows XP Professional, Windows .NET Server family

.NET Framework Security:

- Full trust for the immediate caller. This member cannot be used by partially trusted code.

WqlEventQuery.WithinInterval Property

Gets or sets the polling interval to be used in this query.

```
[Visual Basic]
Public Property WithinInterval As TimeSpan
[C#]
public TimeSpan WithinInterval {get; set;}
[C++]
public: __property TimeSpan get_WithinInterval();
public: __property void set_WithinInterval(TimeSpan);
[JScript]
public function get WithinInterval() : TimeSpan;
public function set WithinInterval(TimeSpan);
```

Property Value

Null, if there is no polling involved; otherwise, a valid **TimeSpan** value if polling is required.

Remarks

This property should only be set in cases where there is no event provider for the event requested, and WMI is required to poll for the requested condition.

Setting this property value overrides any previous value stored in the object. The query string is rebuilt to reflect the new interval.

Example

[Visual Basic, C#] This example creates a new **WqlEventQuery** that represents the query: "SELECT * FROM **__InstanceModificationEvent** WITHIN 10 WHERE **PropVal** > 8".

```
[C#]
WqlEventQuery q = new WqlEventQuery();
q.EventClassName = "__InstanceModificationEvent";
q.Condition = "PropVal > 8";
q.WithinInterval = new TimeSpan(0,0,10);
```

```
[Visual Basic]
Dim q As New WqlEventQuery()
q.EventClassName = "__InstanceModificationEvent"
q.Condition = "PropVal > 8"
q.WithinInterval = New TimeSpan(0,0,10)
```

Requirements

Platforms: Windows 98, Windows NT 4.0, Windows Millennium Edition, Windows 2000, Windows XP Home Edition, Windows XP Professional, Windows .NET Server family

NET Framework Security:

- Full trust for the immediate caller. This member cannot be used by partially trusted code.

WqlEventQuery.BuildQuery Method

Builds the query string according to the current property values.

```
[Visual Basic]
Protected Friend Sub BuildQuery()
[C#]
protected internal void BuildQuery();
[C++]
protected public: void BuildQuery();
[JScript]
protected internal function BuildQuery();
```

Requirements

Platforms: Windows 98, Windows NT 4.0, Windows Millennium Edition, Windows 2000, Windows XP Home Edition, Windows XP Professional, Windows .NET Server family

.NET Framework Security:

- Full trust for the immediate caller. This member cannot be used by partially trusted code.

WqlEventQuery.Clone Method

Creates a copy of the object.

```
[Visual Basic]
Overrides Public Function Clone() As Object Implements _
    ICloneable.Clone
[C#]
public override object Clone();
[C++]
public: Object* Clone();
[JScript]
public override function Clone() : Object;
```

Return Value

The copied object.

Implements

ICloneable.Clone

Requirements

Platforms: Windows 98, Windows NT 4.0, Windows Millennium Edition, Windows 2000, Windows XP Home Edition, Windows XP Professional, Windows .NET Server family

.NET Framework Security:

- Full trust for the immediate caller. This member cannot be used by partially trusted code.

WqlEventQuery.ParseQuery Method

Parses the query string and sets the property values accordingly.

```
[Visual Basic]
Protected Friend Overrides Sub ParseQuery( _
    ByVal query As String _
)
```

```
[C#]
protected internal override void ParseQuery(
    string query
);
[C++]
protected public: void ParseQuery(
    String* query
);
[JScript]
protected internal override function ParseQuery(
    query : String
);
```

Parameters

query
    The query string to be parsed.

Requirements

Platforms: Windows 98, Windows NT 4.0, Windows Millennium Edition, Windows 2000, Windows XP Home Edition, Windows XP Professional, Windows .NET Server family

.NET Framework Security:

- Full trust for the immediate caller. This member cannot be used by partially trusted code.

WqlObjectQuery Class

Represents a WMI data query in WQL format.

System.Object
   System.Management.ManagementQuery
      System.Management.ObjectQuery
         System.Management.WqlObjectQuery
            System.Management.RelatedObjectQuery
            System.Management.RelationshipQuery
            System.Management.SelectQuery

```
[Visual Basic]
Public Class WqlObjectQuery
  Inherits ObjectQuery
[C#]
public class WqlObjectQuery : ObjectQuery
[C++]
public __gc class WqlObjectQuery : public ObjectQuery
[JScript]
public class WqlObjectQuery extends ObjectQuery
```

Thread Safety

Any public static (**Shared** in Visual Basic) members of this type are safe for multithreaded operations. Any instance members are not guaranteed to be thread safe.

Example

```
[C#]
using System;
using System.Management;

// This sample demonstrates how to use a WqlObjectQuery class to
// perform an object query.

class Sample_WqlObjectQuery
{
    public static int Main(string[] args) {
        WqlObjectQuery objectQuery = new WqlObjectQuery
("select * from Win32_Share");
        ManagementObjectSearcher searcher =
            new ManagementObjectSearcher(objectQuery);

        foreach (ManagementObject share in searcher.Get()) {
            Console.WriteLine("Share = " + share["Name"]);
        }

        return 0;
    }
}
```

```
[Visual Basic]
Imports System
Imports System.Management

' This sample demonstrate how to use a WqlObjectQuery class to
' perform an object query.

Class Sample_WqlObjectQuery
    Overloads Public Shared Function Main(args() As String) As Integer
        Dim objectQuery As New WqlObjectQuery("select * from
Win32_Share")
        Dim searcher As New ManagementObjectSearcher(objectQuery)

        Dim share As ManagementObject
        For Each share In searcher.Get()
            Console.WriteLine("Share = " & share("Name"))
        Next share

        Return 0
    End Function
End Class
```

Requirements

Namespace: System.Management

Platforms: Windows 98, Windows NT 4.0, Windows Millennium Edition, Windows 2000, Windows XP Home Edition, Windows XP Professional, Windows .NET Server family

Assembly: System.Management (in System.Management.dll)

WqlObjectQuery Constructor

Initializes a new instance of the **WqlObjectQuery** class.

Overload List

Initializes a new instance of the **WqlObjectQuery** class. This is the default constructor.

   [Visual Basic] **Public Sub New()**
   [C#] **public WqlObjectQuery();**
   [C++] **public: WqlObjectQuery();**
   [JScript] **public function WqlObjectQuery();**

Initializes a new instance of the **WqlObjectQuery** class initialized to the specified query.

   [Visual Basic] **Public Sub New(String)**
   [C#] **public WqlObjectQuery(string);**
   [C++] **public: WqlObjectQuery(String*);**
   [JScript] **public function WqlObjectQuery(String);**

WqlObjectQuery Constructor ()

Initializes a new instance of the **WqlObjectQuery** class. This is the default constructor.

```
[Visual Basic]
Public Sub New()
[C#]
public WqlObjectQuery();
[C++]
public: WqlObjectQuery();
[JScript]
public function WqlObjectQuery();
```

Requirements

Platforms: Windows 98, Windows NT 4.0, Windows Millennium Edition, Windows 2000, Windows XP Home Edition, Windows XP Professional, Windows .NET Server family

.NET Framework Security:

- Full trust for the immediate caller. This member cannot be used by partially trusted code.

WqlObjectQuery Constructor (String)

Initializes a new instance of the **WqlObjectQuery** class initialized to the specified query.

```
[Visual Basic]
Public Sub New( _
   ByVal query As String _
)
```

```
[C#]
public WqlObjectQuery(
    string query
);
[C++]
public: WqlObjectQuery(
    String* query
);
[JScript]
public function WqlObjectQuery(
    query : String
);
```

Parameters

query
    The representation of the data query.

Requirements

Platforms: Windows 98, Windows NT 4.0,
Windows Millennium Edition, Windows 2000,
Windows XP Home Edition, Windows XP Professional,
Windows .NET Server family

.NET Framework Security:

- Full trust for the immediate caller. This member cannot be used by partially trusted code.

WqlObjectQuery.QueryLanguage Property

Gets or sets the language of the query.

```
[Visual Basic]
Overrides Public ReadOnly Property QueryLanguage As String
[C#]
public override string QueryLanguage {get;}
[C++]
public: __property String* get_QueryLanguage();
[JScript]
public override function get QueryLanguage() : String;
```

Property Value

The value of this property is always "WQL".

Requirements

Platforms: Windows 98, Windows NT 4.0,
Windows Millennium Edition, Windows 2000,
Windows XP Home Edition, Windows XP Professional,
Windows .NET Server family

.NET Framework Security:

- Full trust for the immediate caller. This member cannot be used by partially trusted code.

WqlObjectQuery.Clone Method

Creates a copy of the object.

```
[Visual Basic]
Overrides Public Function Clone() As Object Implements _
    ICloneable.Clone
[C#]
public override object Clone();
[C++]
public: Object* Clone();
```

```
[JScript]
public override function Clone() : Object;
```

Return Value

The copied object.

Implements

ICloneable.Clone

Requirements

Platforms: Windows 98, Windows NT 4.0,
Windows Millennium Edition, Windows 2000,
Windows XP Home Edition, Windows XP Professional,
Windows .NET Server family

.NET Framework Security:

- Full trust for the immediate caller. This member cannot be used by partially trusted code.

System.Management. Instrumentation Namespace

Provides the classes necessary for instrumenting applications for management and exposing their management information and events through WMI to potential consumers. Consumers such as Microsoft Application Center or Microsoft Operations Manager can then manage your application easily, and monitoring and configuring of your application is available for administrator scripts or other applications, both managed as well as unmanaged. Instrumentation of your application is easy to achieve using the InstrumentationClass custom attribute on classes you wish to expose, or using the provided **BaseEvent** and **Instance** base classes and the **Instrumentation** helper class.

BaseEvent Class

Represents classes derived from **BaseEvent** that are known to be management event classes. These derived classes inherit an implementation of **IEvent** that allows events to be fired through the **Fire** method.

System.Object
   System.Management.Instrumentation.BaseEvent

[Visual Basic]
```
MustInherit Public Class BaseEvent
    Implements IEvent
```
[C#]
```
public abstract class BaseEvent : IEvent
```
[C++]
```
public __gc __abstract class BaseEvent : public IEvent
```
[JScript]
```
public abstract class BaseEvent implements IEvent
```

Thread Safety

Any public static (**Shared** in Visual Basic) members of this type are safe for multithreaded operations. Any instance members are not guaranteed to be thread safe.

Example

[C#]
```csharp
using System;
using System.Management;
using System.Configuration.Install;
using System.Management.Instrumentation;

// This example demonstrates how to create a Management
Event class by deriving
// from BaseEvent class and to fire a Management Event from
managed code.

// Specify which namespace the Manaegment Event class is created in
[assembly:Instrumented("Root/Default")]

// Let the system know you will run InstallUtil.exe utility against
// this assembly
[System.ComponentModel.RunInstaller(true)]
public class MyInstaller : DefaultManagementProjectInstaller {}
```

```csharp
// Create a Management Instrumentation Event class
public class MyEvent : BaseEvent
{
    public string EventName;
}

public class Sample_EventProvider
{
    public static int Main(string[] args) {
        MyEvent e = new MyEvent();
        e.EventName = "Hello";

        // Fire the Management Event
        e.Fire();

        return 0;
    }
}
```

[Visual Basic]
```vb
Imports System
Imports System.Management
Imports System.Configuration.Install
Imports System.Management.Instrumentation

' This sample demonstrates how to create a Management Event
class by deriving
' from BaseEvent class and to fire a Management Event from
managed code.

' Specify which namespace the Manaegment Event class is created in
<assembly: Instrumented("Root/Default")>

' Let the system know InstallUtil.exe utility will be run against
' this assembly
<System.ComponentModel.RunInstaller(True)> _
Public Class MyInstaller
    Inherits DefaultManagementProjectInstaller
End Class

' Create a Management Instrumentation Event class
<InstrumentationClass(InstrumentationType.Event)> _
Public Class MyEvent
    Inherits BaseEvent
    Public EventName As String
End Class

Public Class Sample_EventProvider
    Public Shared Function Main(args() As String) As Integer
        Dim e As New MyEvent()
        e.EventName = "Hello"

        ' Fire the Management Event
        e.Fire()

        Return 0
    End Function
End Class
```

Requirements

Namespace: System.Management.Instrumentation

Platforms: Windows 98, Windows NT 4.0, Windows Millennium Edition, Windows 2000, Windows XP Home Edition, Windows XP Professional, Windows .NET Server family

Assembly: System.Management (in System.Management.dll)

BaseEvent Constructor

Initializes a new instance of the **BaseEvent** class.

```
[Visual Basic]
Protected Sub New()
[C#]
protected BaseEvent();
[C++]
protected: BaseEvent();
[JScript]
protected function BaseEvent();
```

Remarks

This constructor is called by derived class constructors to initialize state in this type.

Requirements

Platforms: Windows 98, Windows NT 4.0, Windows Millennium Edition, Windows 2000, Windows XP Home Edition, Windows XP Professional, Windows .NET Server family

.NET Framework Security:

- Full trust for the immediate caller. This member cannot be used by partially trusted code.

BaseEvent.Fire Method

Raises a management event.

```
[Visual Basic]
Public Overridable Sub Fire() Implements IEvent.Fire
[C#]
public virtual void Fire();
[C++]
public: virtual void Fire();
[JScript]
public function Fire();
```

Implements

IEvent.Fire

Requirements

Platforms: Windows 98, Windows NT 4.0, Windows Millennium Edition, Windows 2000, Windows XP Home Edition, Windows XP Professional, Windows .NET Server family

.NET Framework Security:

- Full trust for the immediate caller. This member cannot be used by partially trusted code

DefaultManagementProject- Installer Class

Installs an instrumented assembly. This class is a default project installer for assemblies that contain management instrumentation and do not use other installers (such as services, or message queues). To use this default project installer, simply derive a class from **DefaultManagementProjectInstaller** inside the assembly. No methods need to be overridden.

System.Object
  System.MarshalByRefObject
    System.ComponentModel.Component
      System.Configuration.Install.Installer
        System.Management.Instrumentation.DefaultManagementProjectInstaller

[Visual Basic]
```
Public Class DefaultManagementProjectInstaller
   Inherits Installer
```
[C#]
```
public class DefaultManagementProjectInstaller : Installer
```
[C++]
```
public __gc class DefaultManagementProjectInstaller : public
   Installer
```
[JScript]
```
public class DefaultManagementProjectInstaller extends Installer
```

Thread Safety

Any public static (**Shared** in Visual Basic) members of this type are safe for multithreaded operations. Any instance members are not guaranteed to be thread safe.

Remarks

If your project has a master project installer, use the **ManagementInstaller** class instead.

Example

[Visual Basic, C#] Add the following code to your instrumented assembly to enable the installation step:

[C#]
```
[System.ComponentModel.RunInstaller(true)]
public class MyInstaller : DefaultManagementProjectInstaller {}
```

[Visual Basic]
```
<System.ComponentModel.RunInstaller(true)>
public class MyInstaller
    Inherits DefaultManagementProjectInstaller
```

Requirements

Namespace: System.Management.Instrumentation

Platforms: Windows 98, Windows NT 4.0, Windows Millennium Edition, Windows 2000, Windows XP Home Edition, Windows XP Professional, Windows .NET Server family

Assembly: System.Management (in System.Management.dll)

DefaultManagementProjectInstaller Constructor

Initializes a new instance of the **DefaultManagementProjectInstaller** class. This is the default constructor.

[Visual Basic]
```
Public Sub New()
```
[C#]
```
public DefaultManagementProjectInstaller();
```
[C++]
```
public: DefaultManagementProjectInstaller();
```
[JScript]
```
public function DefaultManagementProjectInstaller();
```

Requirements

Platforms: Windows 98, Windows NT 4.0, Windows Millennium Edition, Windows 2000, Windows XP Home Edition, Windows XP Professional, Windows .NET Server family

.NET Framework Security:

- Full trust for the immediate caller. This member cannot be used by partially trusted code.

IEvent Interface

Specifies a source of a management instrumentation event. Objects
that implement this interface are known to be sources of
management instrumentation events. Classes that do not derive from
BaseEvent should implement this interface instead.

```
[Visual Basic]
Public Interface IEvent
[C#]
public interface IEvent
[C++]
public __gc __interface IEvent
[JScript]
public interface IEvent
```

Classes that Implement IEvent

Class	Description
BaseEvent	Represents classes derived from **BaseEvent** that are known to be management event classes. These derived classes inherit an implementation of **IEvent** that allows events to be fired through the **Fire** method.

Requirements

Namespace: System.Management.Instrumentation

Platforms: Windows 98, Windows NT 4.0,
Windows Millennium Edition, Windows 2000,
Windows XP Home Edition, Windows XP Professional,
Windows .NET Server family

Assembly: System.Management (in System.Management.dll)

IEvent.Fire Method

Raises a management event.

```
[Visual Basic]
Sub Fire()
[C#]
void Fire();
[C++]
void Fire();
[JScript]
function Fire();
```

Requirements

Platforms: Windows 98, Windows NT 4.0,
Windows Millennium Edition, Windows 2000,
Windows XP Home Edition, Windows XP Professional,
Windows .NET Server family

.NET Framework Security:

- Full trust for the immediate caller. This member cannot be used
  by partially trusted code.

IgnoreMemberAttribute Class

Allows a particular member of an instrumented class to be ignored by management instrumentation

System.Object
  System.Attribute
    System.Management.Instrumentation.IgnoreMemberAttribute

```
[Visual Basic]
<AttributeUsage(AttributeTargets.Method Or _
   AttributeTargets.Property Or AttributeTargets.Field)>
Public Class IgnoreMemberAttribute
   Inherits Attribute
[C#]
[AttributeUsage(AttributeTargets.Method | AttributeTargets.Property
   | AttributeTargets.Field)]
public class IgnoreMemberAttribute : Attribute
[C++]
[AttributeUsage(AttributeTargets::Method |
   AttributeTargets::Property | AttributeTargets::Field)]
public __gc class IgnoreMemberAttribute : public Attribute
[JScript]
public
   AttributeUsage(AttributeTargets.Method | AttributeTargets.Property
   | AttributeTargets.Field)
class IgnoreMemberAttribute extends Attribute
```

Thread Safety

Any public static (**Shared** in Visual Basic) members of this type are safe for multithreaded operations. Any instance members are not guaranteed to be thread safe.

Requirements

Namespace: System.Management.Instrumentation

Platforms: Windows 98, Windows NT 4.0, Windows Millennium Edition, Windows 2000, Windows XP Home Edition, Windows XP Professional, Windows .NET Server family

Assembly: System.Management (in System.Management.dll)

IgnoreMemberAttribute Constructor

Initializes a new instance of the **IgnoreMemberAttribute** class.

```
[Visual Basic]
Public Sub New()
[C#]
public IgnoreMemberAttribute();
[C++]
public: IgnoreMemberAttribute();
[JScript]
public function IgnoreMemberAttribute();
```

Remarks

The default constructor initializes any fields to their default values.

Requirements

Platforms: Windows 98, Windows NT 4.0, Windows Millennium Edition, Windows 2000, Windows XP Home Edition, Windows XP Professional, Windows .NET Server family

.NET Framework Security:
- Full trust for the immediate caller. This member cannot be used by partially trusted code.

IInstance Interface

Specifies a source of a management instrumentation instance. Objects that implement this interface are known to be sources of management instrumentation instances. Classes that do not derive from **Instance** should implement this interface instead.

```
[Visual Basic]
Public Interface IInstance
[C#]
public interface IInstance
[C++]
public __gc __interface IInstance
[JScript]
public interface IInstance
```

Classes that Implement IInstance

Class	Description
Instance	Represents derived classes known to be management instrumentation instance classes. These derived classes inherit an implementation of **IInstance** that allows instances to be published through the **Published** property.

Requirements

Namespace: System.Management.Instrumentation

Platforms: Windows 98, Windows NT 4.0, Windows Millennium Edition, Windows 2000, Windows XP Home Edition, Windows XP Professional, Windows .NET Server family

Assembly: System.Management (in System.Management.dll)

IInstance.Published Property

Gets or sets a value indicating whether instances of classes that implement this interface are visible through management instrumentation.

```
[Visual Basic]
Property Published As Boolean
[C#]
bool Published {get; set;}
[C++]
__property bool get_Published();
__property void set_Published(bool);
[JScript]
function get Published() : Boolean;function set Published(Boolean);
```

Property Value

true, if the instance is visible through management instrumentation; otherwise, **false**.

Requirements

Platforms: Windows 98, Windows NT 4.0, Windows Millennium Edition, Windows 2000, Windows XP Home Edition, Windows XP Professional, Windows .NET Server family

.NET Framework Security:

- Full trust for the immediate caller. This member cannot be used by partially trusted code.

Instance Class

Represents derived classes known to be management instrumentation instance classes. These derived classes inherit an implementation of **IInstance** that allows instances to be published through the **Published** property.

System.Object
   System.Management.Instrumentation.Instance

```
[Visual Basic]
MustInherit Public Class Instance
    Implements IInstance
[C#]
public abstract class Instance : IInstance
[C++]
public __gc __abstract class Instance : public IInstance
[JScript]
public abstract class Instance implements IInstance
```

Thread Safety

Any public static (**Shared** in Visual Basic) members of this type are safe for multithreaded operations. Any instance members are not guaranteed to be thread safe.

Example

```
[C#]
using System;
using System.Management;
using System.Configuration.Install;
using System.Management.Instrumentation;

// This sample demonstrates how to create a Management
Instrumentation Instance
// class and how to publish an instance of this class to WMI.

// Specify which namespace the Instance class is created in
[assembly:Instrumented("Root/Default")]

// Let the system know InstallUtil.exe utility will be run against
// this assembly
[System.ComponentModel.RunInstaller(true)]
public class MyInstaller : DefaultManagementProjectInstaller {}

// Create a Management Instrumentation Instance class
[InstrumentationClass(InstrumentationType.Instance)]
public class InstanceClass : Instance
{
    public string SampleName;
    public int SampleNumber;
}

public class Sample_InstanceProvider
{
    public static int Main(string[] args) {
        InstanceClass instClass = new InstanceClass();
        instClass.SampleName = "Hello";
        instClass.SampleNumber = 888;

        // Publish this instance to WMI
        instClass.Published = true;

        return 0;
    }
}

[Visual Basic]
Imports System
Imports System.Management
Imports System.Configuration.Install
Imports System.Management.Instrumentation
```

```
' This sample demonstrate how to create a Management
Instrumentation Instance
' class and how to publish an instance of this class to WMI.
' Specify which namespace the Instance class is created in
<assembly: Instrumented("Root/Default")>

' Let the system know InstallUtil.exe utility will be run against
' this assembly
<System.ComponentModel.RunInstaller(True)> _
Public Class MyInstaller
    Inherits DefaultManagementProjectInstaller
End Class

' Create a Management Instrumentation Instance class
<InstrumentationClass(InstrumentationType.Instance)> _
Public Class InstanceClass
    Inherits Instance
    Public SampleName As String
    Public SampleNumber As Integer
End Class

Public Class Sample_InstanceProvider
    Overloads Public Shared Function Main(args() As String) As Integer
        Dim instClass As New InstanceClass()
        instClass.SampleName = "Hello"
        instClass.SampleNumber = 888

        ' Publish this instance to WMI
        instClass.Published = True

        Return 0
    End Function
End Class
```

Requirements

Namespace: System.Management.Instrumentation

Platforms: Windows 98, Windows NT 4.0, Windows Millennium Edition, Windows 2000, Windows XP Home Edition, Windows XP Professional, Windows .NET Server family

Assembly: System.Management (in System.Management.dll)

Instance Constructor

Initializes a new instance of the **Instance** class.

```
[Visual Basic]
Protected Sub New()
[C#]
protected Instance();
[C++]
protected: Instance();
[JScript]
protected function Instance();
```

Remarks

This constructor is called by derived class constructors to initialize state in this type.

Requirements

Platforms: Windows 98, Windows NT 4.0, Windows Millennium Edition, Windows 2000, Windows XP Home Edition, Windows XP Professional, Windows .NET Server family

.NET Framework Security:

- Full trust for the immediate caller. This member cannot be used by partially trusted code.

Instance.Published Property

Gets or sets a value indicating whether instances of classes that
implement this interface are visible through management
instrumentation.

```
[Visual Basic]
Public Overridable Property Published As Boolean  Implements _
    IInstance.Published
[C#]
public virtual bool Published {get; set;}
[C++]
public: __property virtual bool get_Published();
public: __property virtual void set_Published(bool);
[JScript]
public function get Published() : Boolean;
public function set Published(Boolean);
```

Property Value

true, if the instance is visible through management instrumentation;
otherwise, **false**.

Implements

IInstance.Published

Requirements

Platforms: Windows 98, Windows NT 4.0,
Windows Millennium Edition, Windows 2000,
Windows XP Home Edition, Windows XP Professional,
Windows .NET Server family

.NET Framework Security:

• Full trust for the immediate caller. This member cannot be used
  by partially trusted code.

Instrumentation Class

Provides helper functions for exposing events and data for management. There is a single instance of this class per application domain.

System.Object
   System.Management.Instrumentation.Instrumentation

```
[Visual Basic]
Public Class Instrumentation
[C#]
public class Instrumentation
[C++]
public __gc class Instrumentation
[JScript]
public class Instrumentation
```

Thread Safety

Any public static (**Shared** in Visual Basic) members of this type are safe for multithreaded operations. Any instance members are not guaranteed to be thread safe.

Requirements

Namespace: System.Management.Instrumentation

Platforms: Windows 98, Windows NT 4.0, Windows Millennium Edition, Windows 2000, Windows XP Home Edition, Windows XP Professional, Windows .NET Server family

Assembly: System.Management (in System.Management.dll)

Instrumentation Constructor

Initializes a new instance of the **Instrumentation** class.

```
[Visual Basic]
Public Sub New()
[C#]
public Instrumentation();
[C++]
public: Instrumentation();
[JScript]
public function Instrumentation();
```

Remarks

The default constructor initializes any fields to their default values.

Requirements

Platforms: Windows 98, Windows NT 4.0, Windows Millennium Edition, Windows 2000, Windows XP Home Edition, Windows XP Professional, Windows .NET Server family

.NET Framework Security:

- Full trust for the immediate caller. This member cannot be used by partially trusted code.

Instrumentation.Fire Method

Raises a management event.

```
[Visual Basic]
Public Shared Sub Fire( _
   ByVal eventData As Object _
)
```

```
[C#]
public static void Fire(
   object eventData
);
[C++]
public: static void Fire(
   Object* eventData
);
[JScript]
public static function Fire(
   eventData : Object
);
```

Parameters

eventData
   The object that determines the class, properties, and values of the event.

Requirements

Platforms: Windows 98, Windows NT 4.0, Windows Millennium Edition, Windows 2000, Windows XP Home Edition, Windows XP Professional, Windows .NET Server family

.NET Framework Security:

- Full trust for the immediate caller. This member cannot be used by partially trusted code.

Instrumentation.IsAssemblyRegistered Method

Determines if the instrumentation schema of the specified assembly has already been correctly registered with WMI.

```
[Visual Basic]
Public Shared Function IsAssemblyRegistered( _
   ByVal assemblyToRegister As Assembly _
) As Boolean
[C#]
public static bool IsAssemblyRegistered(
   Assembly assemblyToRegister
);
[C++]
public: static bool IsAssemblyRegistered(
   Assembly* assemblyToRegister
);
[JScript]
public static function IsAssemblyRegistered(
   assemblyToRegister : Assembly
) : Boolean;
```

Parameters

assemblyToRegister
   The assembly containing instrumentation instance or event types.

Return Value

true if the instrumentation schema in the specified assembly is registered with WMI; otherwise, false.

Requirements

Platforms: Windows 98, Windows NT 4.0, Windows Millennium Edition, Windows 2000, Windows XP Home Edition, Windows XP Professional, Windows .NET Server family

.NET Framework Security:
- Full trust for the immediate caller. This member cannot be used by partially trusted code.

Instrumentation.Publish Method

Makes an instance visible through management instrumentation.

```
[Visual Basic]
Public Shared Sub Publish( _
   ByVal instanceData As Object _
)
[C#]
public static void Publish(
   object instanceData
);
[C++]
public: static void Publish(
   Object* instanceData
);
[JScript]
public static function Publish(
   instanceData : Object
);
```

Parameters

instanceData
> The instance that is to be visible through management instrumentation.

Requirements

Platforms: Windows 98, Windows NT 4.0, Windows Millennium Edition, Windows 2000, Windows XP Home Edition, Windows XP Professional, Windows .NET Server family

.NET Framework Security:
- Full trust for the immediate caller. This member cannot be used by partially trusted code.

Instrumentation.RegisterAssembly Method

Registers the management instance or event classes in the specified assembly with WMI. This ensures that the instrumentation schema is accessible to System.Management client applications.

```
[Visual Basic]
Public Shared Sub RegisterAssembly( _
   ByVal assemblyToRegister As Assembly _
)
[C#]
public static void RegisterAssembly(
   Assembly assemblyToRegister
);
[C++]
public: static void RegisterAssembly(
   Assembly* assemblyToRegister
);
[JScript]
public static function RegisterAssembly(
   assemblyToRegister : Assembly
);
```

Parameters

assemblyToRegister
> The assembly containing instrumentation instance or event types.

Requirements

Platforms: Windows 98, Windows NT 4.0, Windows Millennium Edition, Windows 2000, Windows XP Home Edition, Windows XP Professional, Windows .NET Server family

.NET Framework Security:
- Full trust for the immediate caller. This member cannot be used by partially trusted code.

Instrumentation.Revoke Method

Makes an instance that was previously published through the **Publish** method no longer visible through management instrumentation.

```
[Visual Basic]
Public Shared Sub Revoke( _
   ByVal instanceData As Object _
)
[C#]
public static void Revoke(
   object instanceData
);
[C++]
public: static void Revoke(
   Object* instanceData
);
[JScript]
public static function Revoke(
   instanceData : Object
);
```

Parameters

instanceData
> The object to remove from visibility for management instrumentation.

Requirements

Platforms: Windows 98, Windows NT 4.0, Windows Millennium Edition, Windows 2000, Windows XP Home Edition, Windows XP Professional, Windows .NET Server family

.NET Framework Security:
- Full trust for the immediate caller. This member cannot be used by partially trusted code.

Instrumentation.SetBatchSize Method

Specifies the maximum number of objects of the specified type to be provided at a time.

```
[Visual Basic]
Public Shared Sub SetBatchSize( _
   ByVal instrumentationClass As Type, _
   ByVal batchSize As Integer _
)
```

```
[C#]
public static void SetBatchSize(
   Type instrumentationClass,
   int batchSize
);
[C++]
public: static void SetBatchSize(
   Type* instrumentationClass,
   int batchSize
);
[JScript]
public static function SetBatchSize(
   instrumentationClass : Type,
   batchSize : int
);
```

Parameters

instrumentationClass
>   The class for which the batch size is being set.

batchSize
>   The maximum number of objects to be provided at a time.

Requirements

Platforms: Windows 98, Windows NT 4.0,
Windows Millennium Edition, Windows 2000,
Windows XP Home Edition, Windows XP Professional,
Windows .NET Server family

.NET Framework Security:

- Full trust for the immediate caller. This member cannot be used
  by partially trusted code.

InstrumentationClassAttribute Class

Specifies that a class provides event or instance instrumentation.

System.Object
  System.Attribute
    System.Management.Instrumentation.InstrumentationClass
Attribute

```
[Visual Basic]
<AttributeUsage(AttributeTargets.Class Or AttributeTargets.Struct)>
Public Class InstrumentationClassAttribute
   Inherits Attribute
[C#]
[AttributeUsage(AttributeTargets.Class | AttributeTargets.Struct)]
public class InstrumentationClassAttribute : Attribute
[C++]
[AttributeUsage(AttributeTargets::Class |
   AttributeTargets::Struct)]
public __gc class InstrumentationClassAttribute : public Attribute
[JScript]
public
   AttributeUsage(AttributeTargets.Class | AttributeTargets.Struct)
class InstrumentationClassAttribute extends Attribute
```

Thread Safety

Any public static (**Shared** in Visual Basic) members of this type are safe for multithreaded operations. Any instance members are not guaranteed to be thread safe.

Requirements

Namespace: System.Management.Instrumentation

Platforms: Windows 98, Windows NT 4.0, Windows Millennium Edition, Windows 2000, Windows XP Home Edition, Windows XP Professional, Windows .NET Server family

Assembly: System.Management (in System.Management.dll)

InstrumentationClassAttribute Constructor

Initializes a new instance of the **InstrumentationClassAttribute** class.

Overload List

Initializes a new instance of the **InstrumentationClassAttribute** class that is used if this type is derived from another type that has the **InstrumentationClassAttribute** attribute, or if this is a top-level instrumentation class (for example, an instance or abstract class without a base class, or an event derived from **__ExtrinsicEvent**).

[Visual Basic] **Public Sub New(InstrumentationType)**

[C#] **public InstrumentationClassAttribute(InstrumentationType);**

[C++] **public: InstrumentationClassAttribute(InstrumentationType);**

[JScript] **public function InstrumentationClassAttribute(InstrumentationType);**

Initializes a new instance of the **InstrumentationClassAttribute** class that has schema for an existing base class. The class must contain proper member definitions for the properties of the existing WMI base class.

[Visual Basic] **Public Sub New(InstrumentationType, String)**

[C#] **public InstrumentationClassAttribute(InstrumentationType, string);**

[C++] **public: InstrumentationClassAttribute(InstrumentationType, String*);**

[JScript] **public function InstrumentationClassAttribute(InstrumentationType, String);**

InstrumentationClassAttribute Constructor (InstrumentationType)

Initializes a new instance of the **InstrumentationClassAttribute** class that is used if this type is derived from another type that has the **InstrumentationClassAttribute** attribute, or if this is a top-level instrumentation class (for example, an instance or abstract class without a base class, or an event derived from **__ExtrinsicEvent**).

```
[Visual Basic]
Public Sub New( _
   ByVal instrumentationType As InstrumentationType _
)
[C#]
public InstrumentationClassAttribute(
   InstrumentationType instrumentationType
);
[C++]
public: InstrumentationClassAttribute(
   InstrumentationType instrumentationType
);
[JScript]
public function InstrumentationClassAttribute(
   instrumentationType : InstrumentationType
);
```

Parameters

instrumentationType
  The type of instrumentation provided by this class.

Requirements

Platforms: Windows 98, Windows NT 4.0, Windows Millennium Edition, Windows 2000, Windows XP Home Edition, Windows XP Professional, Windows .NET Server family

.NET Framework Security:

- Full trust for the immediate caller. This member cannot be used by partially trusted code.

InstrumentationClassAttribute Constructor (InstrumentationType, String)

Initializes a new instance of the **InstrumentationClassAttribute** class that has schema for an existing base class. The class must contain proper member definitions for the properties of the existing WMI base class.

```
[Visual Basic]
Public Sub New( _
   ByVal instrumentationType As InstrumentationType, _
   ByVal managedBaseClassName As String _
)
[C#]
public InstrumentationClassAttribute(
   InstrumentationType instrumentationType,
   string managedBaseClassName
);
[C++]
public: InstrumentationClassAttribute(
   InstrumentationType instrumentationType,
   String* managedBaseClassName
);
[JScript]
public function InstrumentationClassAttribute(
   instrumentationType : InstrumentationType,
   managedBaseClassName : String
);
```

Parameters

instrumentationType
   The type of instrumentation provided by this class.
managedBaseClassName
   The name of the base class.

Requirements

Platforms: Windows 98, Windows NT 4.0,
Windows Millennium Edition, Windows 2000,
Windows XP Home Edition, Windows XP Professional,
Windows .NET Server family

.NET Framework Security:
- Full trust for the immediate caller. This member cannot be used by partially trusted code.

InstrumentationClassAttribute.Instrumentation Type Property

Gets or sets the type of instrumentation provided by this class.

```
[Visual Basic]
Public ReadOnly Property InstrumentationType As InstrumentationType
[C#]
public InstrumentationType InstrumentationType {get;}
[C++]
public: __property InstrumentationType get_InstrumentationType();
[JScript]
public function get InstrumentationType() : InstrumentationType;
```

Property Value

Contains an **InstrumentationType** value that indicates whether this is an instrumented event, instance or abstract class.

Requirements

Platforms: Windows 98, Windows NT 4.0,
Windows Millennium Edition, Windows 2000,
Windows XP Home Edition, Windows XP Professional,
Windows .NET Server family

.NET Framework Security:
- Full trust for the immediate caller. This member cannot be used by partially trusted code.

InstrumentationClassAttribute.ManagedBase-ClassName Property

Gets or sets the name of the base class of this instrumentation class.

```
[Visual Basic]
Public ReadOnly Property ManagedBaseClassName As String
[C#]
public string ManagedBaseClassName {get;}
[C++]
public: __property String* get_ManagedBaseClassName();
[JScript]
public function get ManagedBaseClassName() : String;
```

Property Value

If not null, this string indicates the WMI baseclass that this class inherits from in the CIM schema.

Requirements

Platforms: Windows 98, Windows NT 4.0,
Windows Millennium Edition, Windows 2000,
Windows XP Home Edition, Windows XP Professional,
Windows .NET Server family

.NET Framework Security:
- Full trust for the immediate caller. This member cannot be used by partially trusted code.

InstrumentationType Enumeration

Specifies the type of instrumentation provided by a class.

```
[Visual Basic]
<Serializable>
Public Enum InstrumentationType
[C#]
[Serializable]
public enum InstrumentationType
[C++]
[Serializable]
__value public enum InstrumentationType
[JScript]
public
    Serializable
enum InstrumentationType
```

Members

Member name	Description
Abstract	Specifies that the class defines an abstract class for management instrumentation.
Event	Specifies that the class provides events for management instrumentation.
Instance	Specifies that the class provides instances for management instrumentation.

Example

```csharp
[C#]
using System;
using System.Management;
using System.Configuration.Install;
using System.Management.Instrumentation;

// This example demonstrates how to create a Management Event
class by using
// the InstrumentationClass attribute and to fire a Management
Event from
// managed code.

// Specify which namespace the Management Event class is created in
[assembly:Instrumented("Root/Default")]

// Let the system know you will run InstallUtil.exe utility against
// this assembly
[System.ComponentModel.RunInstaller(true)]
public class MyInstaller : DefaultManagementProjectInstaller {}

// Create a Management Instrumentation Event class
[InstrumentationClass(InstrumentationType.Event)]
public class MyEvent
{
    public string EventName;
}

public class WMI_InstrumentedEvent_Example
{
    public static void Main() {
        MyEvent e = new MyEvent();
        e.EventName = "Hello";

        // Fire a Management Event
        Instrumentation.Fire(e);

        return;
    }
}
```

```vbnet
[Visual Basic]
Imports System
Imports System.Management
Imports System.Configuration.Install
Imports System.Management.Instrumentation

' This sample demonstrates how to create a Management Event
class by using
' the InstrumentationClass attribute and to fire a Management
Event from
' managed code.

' Specify which namespace the Manaegment Event class is created in
<assembly: Instrumented("Root/Default")>

' Let the system know InstallUtil.exe utility will be run against
' this assembly
<System.ComponentModel.RunInstaller(True)> _
Public Class MyInstaller
    Inherits DefaultManagementProjectInstaller
End Class 'MyInstaller

' Create a Management Instrumentation Event class
<InstrumentationClass(InstrumentationType.Event)> _
Public Class MyEvent
    Public EventName As String
End Class

Public Class Sample_EventProvider
    Public Shared Function Main(args() As String) As Integer
        Dim e As New MyEvent()
        e.EventName = "Hello"

        ' Fire a Management Event
        Instrumentation.Fire(e)

        Return 0
    End Function
End Class
```

Requirements

Namespace: System.Management.Instrumentation

Platforms: Windows 98, Windows NT 4.0, Windows Millennium Edition, Windows 2000, Windows XP Home Edition, Windows XP Professional, Windows .NET Server family

Assembly: System.Management (in System.Management.dll)

InstrumentedAttribute Class

Specifies that this assembly provides management instrumentation. This attribute should appear one time per assembly.

System.Object
  System.Attribute
    System.Management.Instrumentation.InstrumentedAttribute

```
[Visual Basic]
<AttributeUsage(AttributeTargets.Assembly)>
Public Class InstrumentedAttribute
    Inherits Attribute
[C#]
[AttributeUsage(AttributeTargets.Assembly)]
public class InstrumentedAttribute : Attribute
[C++]
[AttributeUsage(AttributeTargets::Assembly)]
public __gc class InstrumentedAttribute : public Attribute
[JScript]
public
    AttributeUsage(AttributeTargets.Assembly)
class InstrumentedAttribute extends Attribute
```

Thread Safety

Any public static (**Shared** in Visual Basic) members of this type are safe for multithreaded operations. Any instance members are not guaranteed to be thread safe.

Requirements

Namespace: System.Management.Instrumentation

Platforms: Windows 98, Windows NT 4.0, Windows Millennium Edition, Windows 2000, Windows XP Home Edition, Windows XP Professional, Windows .NET Server family

Assembly: System.Management (in System.Management.dll)

InstrumentedAttribute Constructor

Initializes a new instance of the **InstrumentedAttribute** class.

Overload List

Initializes a new instance of the **InstrumentedAttribute** class that is set for the root\default namespace. This is the default constructor.

[Visual Basic] **Public Sub New()**

[C#] **public InstrumentedAttribute();**

[C++] **public: InstrumentedAttribute();**

[JScript] **public function InstrumentedAttribute();**

Initializes a new instance of the **InstrumentedAttribute** class that is set to the specified namespace for instrumentation within this assembly.

[Visual Basic] **Public Sub New(String)**

[C#] **public InstrumentedAttribute(string);**

[C++] **public: InstrumentedAttribute(String*);**

[JScript] **public function InstrumentedAttribute(String);**

Initializes a new instance of the **InstrumentedAttribute** class that is set to the specified namespace and security settings for instrumentation within this assembly.

[Visual Basic] **Public Sub New(String, String)**

[C#] **public InstrumentedAttribute(string, string);**

[C++] **public: InstrumentedAttribute(String*, String*);**

[JScript] **public function InstrumentedAttribute(String, String);**

InstrumentedAttribute Constructor ( )

Initializes a new instance of the **InstrumentedAttribute** class that is set for the root\default namespace. This is the default constructor.

```
[Visual Basic]
Public Sub New()
[C#]
public InstrumentedAttribute();
[C++]
public: InstrumentedAttribute();
[JScript]
public function InstrumentedAttribute();
```

Requirements

Platforms: Windows 98, Windows NT 4.0, Windows Millennium Edition, Windows 2000, Windows XP Home Edition, Windows XP Professional, Windows .NET Server family

.NET Framework Security:

- Full trust for the immediate caller. This member cannot be used by partially trusted code.
- InstrumentedAttribute Constructor (String)

Initializes a new instance of the **InstrumentedAttribute** class that is set to the specified namespace for instrumentation within this assembly.

```
[Visual Basic]
Public Sub New( _
    ByVal namespaceName As String _
)
[C#]
public InstrumentedAttribute(
    string namespaceName
);
[C++]
public: InstrumentedAttribute(
    String* namespaceName
);
[JScript]
public function InstrumentedAttribute(
    namespaceName : String
);
```

Parameters

namespaceName
    The namespace for instrumentation instances and events.

Requirements

Platforms: Windows 98, Windows NT 4.0, Windows Millennium Edition, Windows 2000, Windows XP Home Edition, Windows XP Professional, Windows .NET Server family

.NET Framework Security:

- Full trust for the immediate caller. This member cannot be used by partially trusted code.

InstrumentedAttribute Constructor (String, String)

Initializes a new instance of the **InstrumentedAttribute** class that is set to the specified namespace and security settings for instrumentation within this assembly.

```
[Visual Basic]
Public Sub New( _
   ByVal namespaceName As String, _
   ByVal securityDescriptor As String _
)
[C#]
public InstrumentedAttribute(
   string namespaceName,
   string securityDescriptor
);
[C++]
public: InstrumentedAttribute(
   String* namespaceName,
   String* securityDescriptor
);
[JScript]
public function InstrumentedAttribute(
   namespaceName : String,
   securityDescriptor : String
);
```

Parameters

namespaceName
   The namespace for instrumentation instances and events.
securityDescriptor
   A security descriptor that allows only the specified users or groups to run applications that provide the instrumentation supported by this assembly.

Requirements

Platforms: Windows 98, Windows NT 4.0, Windows Millennium Edition, Windows 2000, Windows XP Home Edition, Windows XP Professional, Windows .NET Server family

.NET Framework Security:

- Full trust for the immediate caller. This member cannot be used by partially trusted code.

InstrumentedAttribute.NamespaceName Property

Gets or sets the namespace for instrumentation instances and events in this assembly.

```
[Visual Basic]
Public ReadOnly Property NamespaceName As String
[C#]
public string NamespaceName {get;}
[C++]
public: __property String* get_NamespaceName();
[JScript]
public function get NamespaceName() : String;
```

Property Value

If not specified, the default namespace will be set as "\\.\root\default". Otherwise, a string indicating the name of the namespace for instrumentation instances and events in this assembly.

Remarks

It is highly recommended that the namespace name be specified by the assembly, and that it should be a unique namespace per assembly, or per application. Having a specific namespace for each assembly or application instrumentation allows more granularity for securing access to instrumentation provided by different assemblies or applications.

Requirements

Platforms: Windows 98, Windows NT 4.0, Windows Millennium Edition, Windows 2000, Windows XP Home Edition, Windows XP Professional, Windows .NET Server family

.NET Framework Security:

- Full trust for the immediate caller. This member cannot be used by partially trusted code.

InstrumentedAttribute.SecurityDescriptor Property

Gets or sets a security descriptor that allows only the specified users or groups to run applications that provide the instrumentation supported by this assembly.

```
[Visual Basic]
Public ReadOnly Property SecurityDescriptor As String
[C#]
public string SecurityDescriptor {get;}
[C++]
public: __property String* get_SecurityDescriptor();
[JScript]
public function get SecurityDescriptor() : String;
```

Property Value

If null, the default value is defined as the Local Administrators Group. This will only allow members of the local administrators group to publish data and fire events from this assembly. Otherwise, this is a string in SDDL format representing the security descriptor that defines which users and groups can provide instrumentation data and events from this application.

Remarks

Users or groups not specified in this security descriptor may still run the application, but cannot provide instrumentation from this assembly.

Requirements

Platforms: Windows 98, Windows NT 4.0, Windows Millennium Edition, Windows 2000, Windows XP Home Edition, Windows XP Professional, Windows .NET Server family

.NET Framework Security:

- Full trust for the immediate caller. This member cannot be used by partially trusted code.

ManagedNameAttribute Class

Allows an instrumented class, or member of an instrumented class, to present an alternate name through management instrumentation.

System.Object
  System.Attribute
    System.Management.Instrumentation.ManagedName
    Attribute

```
[Visual Basic]
<AttributeUsage(AttributeTargets.Class Or AttributeTargets.Struct _
    Or AttributeTargets.Method Or AttributeTargets.Property Or _
    AttributeTargets.Field)>
Public Class ManagedNameAttribute
    Inherits Attribute
[C#]
[AttributeUsage(AttributeTargets.Class | AttributeTargets.Struct |
    AttributeTargets.Method | AttributeTargets.Property |
    AttributeTargets.Field)]
public class ManagedNameAttribute : Attribute
[C++]
[AttributeUsage(AttributeTargets::Class | AttributeTargets::Struct
    | AttributeTargets::Method | AttributeTargets::Property |
    AttributeTargets::Field)]
public __gc class ManagedNameAttribute : public Attribute
[JScript]
public
    AttributeUsage(AttributeTargets.Class | AttributeTargets.Struct |
    AttributeTargets.Method | AttributeTargets.Property |
    AttributeTargets.Field)
class ManagedNameAttribute extends Attribute
```

Thread Safety

Any public static (**Shared** in Visual Basic) members of this type are safe for multithreaded operations. Any instance members are not guaranteed to be thread safe.

Requirements

Namespace: System.Management.Instrumentation

Platforms: Windows 98, Windows NT 4.0, Windows Millennium Edition, Windows 2000, Windows XP Home Edition, Windows XP Professional, Windows .NET Server family

Assembly: System.Management (in System.Management.dll)

ManagedNameAttribute Constructor

Initializes a new instance of the **ManagedNameAttribute** class that allows the alternate name to be specified for the type, field, property, method, or parameter to which this attribute is applied.

```
[Visual Basic]
Public Sub New( _
    ByVal name As String _
)
[C#]
public ManagedNameAttribute(
    string name
);
```

```
[C++]
public: ManagedNameAttribute(
    String* name
);
[JScript]
public function ManagedNameAttribute(
    name : String
);
```

Parameters

name
  The alternate name for the type, field, property, method, or parameter to which this attribute is applied.

Requirements

Platforms: Windows 98, Windows NT 4.0, Windows Millennium Edition, Windows 2000, Windows XP Home Edition, Windows XP Professional, Windows .NET Server family

.NET Framework Security:
• Full trust for the immediate caller. This member cannot be used by partially trusted code.

ManagedNameAttribute.Name Property

Note: This namespace, class, or member is supported only in version 1.1 of the .NET Framework.

Gets the name of the managed entity.

```
[Visual Basic]
Public ReadOnly Property Name As String
[C#]
public string Name {get;}
[C++]
public: __property String* get_Name();
[JScript]
public function get Name() : String;
```

Property Value

Contains the name of the managed entity.

Requirements

Platforms: Windows 98, Windows NT 4.0, Windows Millennium Edition, Windows 2000, Windows XP Home Edition, Windows XP Professional, Windows .NET Server family

.NET Framework Security:
• Full trust for the immediate caller. This member cannot be used by partially trusted code.

ManagementInstaller Class

Installs instrumented assemblies. Include an instance of this installer class in the project installer for an assembly that includes instrumentation.

System.Object
   System.MarshalByRefObject
      System.ComponentModel.Component
         System.Configuration.Install.Installer
            System.Management.Instrumentation.Management Installer

```
[Visual Basic]
Public Class ManagementInstaller
   Inherits Installer
[C#]
public class ManagementInstaller : Installer
[C++]
public __gc class ManagementInstaller : public Installer
[JScript]
public class ManagementInstaller extends Installer
```

Thread Safety

Any public static (**Shared** in Visual Basic) members of this type are safe for multithreaded operations. Any instance members are not guaranteed to be thread safe.

Remarks

If this is the only installer for your application, you may use the helper class **DefaultManagementProjectInstaller** provided in this namespace.

Example

[Visual Basic, C#] If you have a master project installer for your project, add the following code to your project installer's constructor:

```
[C#]
// Instantiate installer for assembly.
ManagementInstaller managementInstaller = new ManagementInstaller();

// Add installer to collection.
Installers.Add(managementInstaller);

[Visual Basic]
'Instantiate installer for assembly.
Dim managementInstaller As New ManagementInstaller()

'Add installer to collection.
Installers.Add(managementInstaller)
```

Requirements

Namespace: System.Management.Instrumentation

Platforms: Windows 98, Windows NT 4.0, Windows Millennium Edition, Windows 2000, Windows XP Home Edition, Windows XP Professional, Windows .NET Server family

Assembly: System.Management (in System.Management.dll)

ManagementInstaller Constructor

Initializes a new instance of the **ManagementInstaller** class.

```
[Visual Basic]
Public Sub New()
[C#]
public ManagementInstaller();
[C++]
public: ManagementInstaller();
[JScript]
public function ManagementInstaller();
```

Remarks

The default constructor initializes any fields to their default values.

Requirements

Platforms: Windows 98, Windows NT 4.0, Windows Millennium Edition, Windows 2000, Windows XP Home Edition, Windows XP Professional, Windows .NET Server family

.NET Framework Security:

- Full trust for the immediate caller. This member cannot be used by partially trusted code.

ManagementInstaller.HelpText Property

Gets or sets installer options for this class.

```
[Visual Basic]
Overrides Public ReadOnly Property HelpText As String
[C#]
public override string HelpText {get;}
[C++]
public: __property String* get_HelpText();
[JScript]
public override function get HelpText() : String;
```

Property Value

The help text for all the installers in the installer collection, including the description of what each installer does and the command-line options (for the installation program) that can be passed to and understood by each installer.

Requirements

Platforms: Windows 98, Windows NT 4.0, Windows Millennium Edition, Windows 2000, Windows XP Home Edition, Windows XP Professional, Windows .NET Server family

.NET Framework Security:

- Full trust for the immediate caller. This member cannot be used by partially trusted code.

ManagementInstaller.Commit Method

Commits the assembly to the operation.

```
[Visual Basic]
Overrides Public Sub Commit( _
   ByVal savedState As IDictionary _
)
[C#]
public override void Commit(
   IDictionary savedState
);
```

```
[C++]
public: void Commit(
    IDictionary* savedState
);
[JScript]
public override function Commit(
    savedState : IDictionary
);
```

Parameters

savedState
    The state of the assembly.

Requirements

Platforms: Windows 98, Windows NT 4.0,
Windows Millennium Edition, Windows 2000,
Windows XP Home Edition, Windows XP Professional,
Windows .NET Server family

.NET Framework Security:
- Full trust for the immediate caller. This member cannot be used by partially trusted code.

ManagementInstaller.Install Method

Installs the assembly.

```
[Visual Basic]
Overrides Public Sub Install( _
    ByVal savedState As IDictionary _
)
[C#]
public override void Install(
    IDictionary savedState
);
[C++]
public: void Install(
    IDictionary* savedState
);
[JScript]
public override function Install(
    savedState : IDictionary
);
```

Parameters

savedState
    The state of the assembly.

Requirements

Platforms: Windows 98, Windows NT 4.0,
Windows Millennium Edition, Windows 2000,
Windows XP Home Edition, Windows XP Professional,
Windows .NET Server family

.NET Framework Security:
- Full trust for the immediate caller. This member cannot be used by partially trusted code.

ManagementInstaller.Rollback Method

Rolls back the state of the assembly.

```
[Visual Basic]
Overrides Public Sub Rollback( _
    ByVal savedState As IDictionary _
)
```

```
[C#]
public override void Rollback(
    IDictionary savedState
);
[C++]
public: void Rollback(
    IDictionary* savedState
);
[JScript]
public override function Rollback(
    savedState : IDictionary
);
```

Parameters

savedState
    The state of the assembly.

Requirements

Platforms: Windows 98, Windows NT 4.0,
Windows Millennium Edition, Windows 2000,
Windows XP Home Edition, Windows XP Professional,
Windows .NET Server family

.NET Framework Security:
- Full trust for the immediate caller. This member cannot be used by partially trusted code.

ManagementInstaller.Uninstall Method

Uninstalls the assembly.

```
[Visual Basic]
Overrides Public Sub Uninstall( _
    ByVal savedState As IDictionary _
)
[C#]
public override void Uninstall(
    IDictionary savedState
);
[C++]
public: void Uninstall(
    IDictionary* savedState
);
[JScript]
public override function Uninstall(
    savedState : IDictionary
);
```

Parameters

savedState
    The state of the assembly.

Requirements

Platforms: Windows 98, Windows NT 4.0,
Windows Millennium Edition, Windows 2000,
Windows XP Home Edition, Windows XP Professional,
Windows .NET Server family

.NET Framework Security:
- Full trust for the immediate caller. This member cannot be used by partially trusted code.

System.Messaging Namespace

The **System.Messaging** namespace provides classes that allow you to connect to, monitor, and administer message queues on the network and send, receive, or peek messages.

Members of the **MessageQueue** class include the following methods for reading and writing messages to the queue.

- The **Send** method enables your application to write messages to the queue. Overloads of the method enable you to specify whether to send your message using a **Message** (which provides detailed control over the information you send) or any other managed object, including application-specific classes. The method also supports sending messages as part of a transaction.

- The **Receive**, **ReceiveById**, and **ReceiveByCorrelationId** methods provide functionality for reading messages from a queue. Like the **Send** method, these methods provide overloads that support transactional queue processing. These methods also provide overloads with time-out parameters that enable processing to continue if the queue is empty. Because these methods are examples of synchronous processing, they interrupt the current thread until a message is available, unless you specify a time-out.

- The **Peek** method is similar to **Receive**, but it does not cause a message to be removed from the queue when it is read. Because **Peek** does not change the queue contents, there are no overloads to support transactional processing. However, because **Peek**, like **Receive**, reads messages synchronously from the queue, overloads of the method do support specifying a time-out in order to prevent the thread from waiting indefinitely.

- The **BeginPeek**, **EndPeek**, **BeginReceive**, and **EndReceive** methods provide ways to asynchronously read messages from the queue. They do not interrupt the current thread while waiting for a message to arrive in the queue.

Other methods of the **MessageQueue** class provide functionality for retrieving lists of queues by specified criteria and determining if specific queues exist.

- **GetPrivateQueuesByMachine** enables the retrieval of the private queues on a computer.

- **GetPublicQueuesByCategory**, **GetPublicQueuesByLabel**, and **GetPublicQueuesByMachine** provide ways to retrieve public queues by common criteria. An overload of **GetPublicQueues** provides even finer detail for selecting queues based on a number of search criteria.

Other methods of the **MessageQueue** class include those for creating and deleting Message Queueing queues, using a message enumerator to step through the messages in a queue, using a queue enumerator for iterating through the queues on the system, methods for setting ACL-based access rights, and methods for working with the connection cache.

The **Message** class provides detailed control over the information you send to a queue, and is the object used when receiving or peeking messages from a queue. Besides the message body, the properties of the **Message** class include acknowledgment settings, formatter selection, identification, authentication and encryption information, timestamps, indications about using tracing, server journaling, and dead-letter queues, and transaction data.

The **MessageQueue** component is associated with three formatters that enable you to serialize and deserialize messages sent and received from queues.

- The **XmlMessageFormatter** provides loosely coupled messaging, enabling independent versioning of serialized types on the client and server.
- The **ActiveXMessageFormatter** is compatible with the MSMQ COM control. It allows you to send types that can be received by the control and to receive types that were sent by the control.
- The **BinaryMessageFormatter** provides a faster alternative to the **XmlMessageFormatter**, but without the benefit of loosely coupled messaging..

Other classes in the Messaging namespace support code-access and ACL-based security, filtering **Message** properties when reading messages from a queue, and using transactions when sending and receiving messages.

AccessControlEntry Class

Specifies access rights for a trustee (user, group, or computer) to perform application-specific implementations of common tasks.

System.Object
  System.Messaging.AccessControlEntry
    System.Messaging.MessageQueueAccessControlEntry

```
[Visual Basic]
Public Class AccessControlEntry
[C#]
public class AccessControlEntry
[C++]
public __gc class AccessControlEntry
[JScript]
public class AccessControlEntry
```

Thread Safety

Any public static (**Shared** in Visual Basic) members of this type are safe for multithreaded operations. Any instance members are not guaranteed to be thread safe.

Remarks

Many applications have similar operations to which a trustee can be assigned rights, for example, reading, writing, and deleting objects. When you assign rights for these general operations, the application interprets them in a way specific to that application. For example, Message Queuing interprets the reading operation as receiving or peeking messages from a queue. The **AccessControlEntry** class provides access to these common rights.

When working with access control entries, you specify a trustee to whom you are assigning the rights. You must set at least one of the **GenericAccessRights**, **StandardAccessRights**, or **CustomAccessRights** properties to indicate which rights to assign to the trustee. You can set the **EntryType** property to specify whether the rights you indicate should be granted or denied. The default entry type is to allow rights.

Requirements

Namespace: System.Messaging

Platforms: Windows 98, Windows NT 4.0, Windows Millennium Edition, Windows 2000, Windows XP Home Edition, Windows XP Professional, Windows .NET Server family

Assembly: System.Messaging (in System.Messaging.dll)

AccessControlEntry Constructor

Initializes a new instance of the **AccessControlEntry** class.

Overload List

Initializes a new instance of the **AccessControlEntry** class that specifies neither a trustee nor set of rights to apply.

> [Visual Basic] **Public Sub New()**
>
> [C#] **public AccessControlEntry();**
>
> [C++] **public: AccessControlEntry();**
>
> [JScript] **public function AccessControlEntry();**

Initializes a new instance of the **AccessControlEntry** class that specifies a trustee to grant or deny rights to.

> [Visual Basic] **Public Sub New(Trustee)**
>
> [C#] **public AccessControlEntry(Trustee);**
>
> [C++] **public: AccessControlEntry(Trustee*);**
>
> [JScript] **public function AccessControlEntry(Trustee);**

Initializes a new instance of the **AccessControlEntry** class that specifies a trustee, rights to assign, and whether to grant or deny these rights.

> [Visual Basic] **Public Sub New(Trustee, GenericAccessRights, StandardAccessRights, AccessControlEntryType)**
>
> [C#] **public AccessControlEntry(Trustee, GenericAccess-Rights, StandardAccessRights, AccessControlEntryType);**
>
> [C++] **public: AccessControlEntry(Trustee*, GenericAccess-Rights, StandardAccessRights, AccessControlEntryType);**
>
> [JScript] **public function AccessControlEntry(Trustee, GenericAccessRights, StandardAccessRights, AccessControlEntryType);**

AccessControlEntry Constructor ()

Initializes a new instance of the **AccessControlEntry** class that specifies neither a trustee nor set of rights to apply.

```
[Visual Basic]
Public Sub New()
[C#]
public AccessControlEntry();
[C++]
public: AccessControlEntry();
[JScript]
public function AccessControlEntry();
```

Remarks

Set the **Trustee** property and at least one of the **GenericAccessRights**, **StandardAccessRights**, or **CustomAccessRights** properties before using this **AccessControlEntry** instance to set access rights for a trustee.

You can optionally set the **EntryType** property, though it defaults to **Allow** if you choose not to do so.

Requirements

Platforms: Windows 98, Windows NT 4.0, Windows Millennium Edition, Windows 2000, Windows XP Home Edition, Windows XP Professional, Windows .NET Server family

.NET Framework Security:

- Full trust for the immediate caller. This member cannot be used by partially trusted code.

AccessControlEntry Constructor (Trustee)

Initializes a new instance of the **AccessControlEntry** class that specifies a trustee to grant or deny rights to.

```
[Visual Basic]
Public Sub New( _
    ByVal trustee As Trustee _
)
[C#]
public AccessControlEntry(
    Trustee trustee
);
[C++]
public: AccessControlEntry(
    Trustee* trustee
);
[JScript]
public function AccessControlEntry(
    trustee : Trustee
);
```

Parameters

trustee
> A **Trustee** that specifies a user, group, computer, domain, or alias.

Exceptions

Exception Type	Condition
ArgumentNullException	The *trustee* parameter is a null reference (**Nothing** in Visual Basic).

Remarks

Set the **EntryType** property and at least one of the **GenericAccessRights**, **StandardAccessRights**, or **CustomAccessRights** properties before using this **AccessControlEntry** instance to set access rights for a trustee.

Requirements

Platforms: Windows 98, Windows NT 4.0, Windows Millennium Edition, Windows 2000, Windows XP Home Edition, Windows XP Professional, Windows .NET Server family

.NET Framework Security:

- Full trust for the immediate caller. This member cannot be used by partially trusted code.

AccessControlEntry Constructor (Trustee, GenericAccessRights, StandardAccessRights, AccessControlEntryType)

Initializes a new instance of the **AccessControlEntry** class that specifies a trustee, rights to assign, and whether to grant or deny these rights.

```
[Visual Basic]
Public Sub New( _
    ByVal trustee As Trustee, _
    ByVal genericAccessRights As GenericAccessRights, _
    ByVal standardAccessRights As StandardAccessRights, _
    ByVal entryType As AccessControlEntryType _
)
```

```
[C#]
public AccessControlEntry(
    Trustee trustee,
    GenericAccessRights genericAccessRights,
    StandardAccessRights standardAccessRights,
    AccessControlEntryType entryType
);
[C++]
public: AccessControlEntry(
    Trustee* trustee,
    GenericAccessRights genericAccessRights,
    StandardAccessRights standardAccessRights,
    AccessControlEntryType entryType
);
[JScript]
public function AccessControlEntry(
    trustee : Trustee,
    genericAccessRights : GenericAccessRights,
    standardAccessRights : StandardAccessRights,
    entryType : AccessControlEntryType
);
```

Parameters

trustee

A **Trustee** that specifies a user, group, computer, domain, or alias.

genericAccessRights

A bitwise combination of the **GenericAccessRights** values.

standardAccessRights

A bitwise combination of the **StandardAccessRights** values.

entryType

One of the **AccessControlEntryType** values, which specifies whether to allow, deny, set, or revoke the specified rights.

Exceptions

Exception Type	Condition
ArgumentNullException	The *trustee* parameter is a null reference (**Nothing** in Visual Basic).
InvalidEnumArgument-Exception	The *genericAccessRights* or *standardAccessRights*, or *entryType* parameters are not valid enumeration values.

Remarks

This overload of the constructor sets the **CustomAccessRights** property to a bitwise combination of the *genericAccessRights* and *standardAccessRights* parameters you specify.

Requirements

Platforms: Windows 98, Windows NT 4.0, Windows Millennium Edition, Windows 2000, Windows XP Home Edition, Windows XP Professional, Windows .NET Server family

.NET Framework Security:

- Full trust for the immediate caller. This member cannot be used by partially trusted code.

AccessControlEntry.CustomAccessRights Property

Gets or sets custom access rights.

```
[Visual Basic]
Protected Property CustomAccessRights As Integer
[C#]
protected int CustomAccessRights {get; set;}
[C++]
protected: __property int get_CustomAccessRights();
protected: __property void set_CustomAccessRights(int);
[JScript]
protected function get CustomAccessRights() : int;
protected function set CustomAccessRights(int);
```

Property Value

Application-specific access rights, usually defined as a bitflag.

Requirements

Platforms: Windows 98, Windows NT 4.0, Windows Millennium Edition, Windows 2000, Windows XP Home Edition, Windows XP Professional, Windows .NET Server family

.NET Framework Security:

- Full trust for the immediate caller. This member cannot be used by partially trusted code.

AccessControlEntry.EntryType Property

Gets or sets a value that indicates how the access rights apply to the trustee.

```
[Visual Basic]
Public Property EntryType As AccessControlEntryType
[C#]
public AccessControlEntryType EntryType {get; set;}
[C++]
public: __property AccessControlEntryType get_EntryType();
public: __property void set_EntryType(AccessControlEntryType);
[JScript]
public function get EntryType() : AccessControlEntryType;
public function set EntryType(AccessControlEntryType);
```

Property Value

One of the **AccessControlEntryType** values, which specifies whether to allow, deny, set, or revoke the specified rights. The default is **Allow**.

Exceptions

Exception Type	Condition
InvalidEnumArgument-Exception	The entry type is not a valid **AccessControlEntryType** enumeration value.

Requirements

Platforms: Windows 98, Windows NT 4.0, Windows Millennium Edition, Windows 2000, Windows XP Home Edition, Windows XP Professional, Windows .NET Server family

.NET Framework Security:

- Full trust for the immediate caller. This member cannot be used by partially trusted code.

AccessControlEntry.GenericAccessRights Property

Gets or sets a set of common access rights that map to both standard and object-specific access rights for reading, writing, and executing.

```
[Visual Basic]
Public Property GenericAccessRights As GenericAccessRights
[C#]
public GenericAccessRights GenericAccessRights {get; set;}
[C++]
public: __property GenericAccessRights get_GenericAccessRights();
public: __property void set_GenericAccessRights(GenericAccessRights);
[JScript]
public function get GenericAccessRights() : GenericAccessRights;
public function set GenericAccessRights(GenericAccessRights);
```

Property Value

A bitwise combination of the **GenericAccessRights** values.

Exceptions

Exception Type	Condition
InvalidEnumArgument-Exception	The value you set is not a valid combination of **GenericAccessRights** bitflag members.

Remarks

Securable objects use the four high-order bits of the Windows 2000/ Windows NT access mask format to specify the generic access rights. Each type of securable object maps these bits to a set of its standard and object-specific access rights. Applications that define private securable objects can also use the generic access rights.

Requirements

Platforms: Windows 98, Windows NT 4.0, Windows Millennium Edition, Windows 2000, Windows XP Home Edition, Windows XP Professional, Windows .NET Server family

.NET Framework Security:

- Full trust for the immediate caller. This member cannot be used by partially trusted code.

AccessControlEntry.StandardAccessRights Property

Gets or sets a set of standard access rights that correspond to operations common to most types of securable objects.

```
[Visual Basic]
Public Property StandardAccessRights As StandardAccessRights
[C#]
public StandardAccessRights StandardAccessRights {get; set;}
[C++]
public: __property StandardAccessRights get_StandardAccessRights();
public: __property void
set_StandardAccessRights(StandardAccessRights);
[JScript]
public function get StandardAccessRights() : StandardAccessRights;
public function set StandardAccessRights(StandardAccessRights);
```

Property Value

A bitwise combination of the **StandardAccessRights** values.

Exceptions

Exception Type	Condition
InvalidEnumArgu-mentException	The value you set is not a valid combination of **StandardAccessRights** bitflag members.

Remarks

The Windows 2000/Windows NT access mask format includes a set of bits for the standard access rights. Each type of securable object has a set of access rights that correspond to operations specific to that type of object. In addition to these object-specific access rights, there is a set of standard access rights that correspond to operations common to most types of securable objects.

Requirements

Platforms: Windows 98, Windows NT 4.0, Windows Millennium Edition, Windows 2000, Windows XP Home Edition, Windows XP Professional, Windows .NET Server family

.NET Framework Security:

- Full trust for the immediate caller. This member cannot be used by partially trusted code.

AccessControlEntry.Trustee Property

Gets or sets the user, group, domain, or alias to which you are assigning access rights.

```
[Visual Basic]
Public Property Trustee As Trustee
[C#]
public Trustee Trustee {get; set;}
[C++]
public: __property Trustee* get_Trustee();
public: __property void set_Trustee(Trustee*);
[JScript]
public function get Trustee() : Trustee;
public function set Trustee(Trustee);
```

Property Value

A **Trustee** that specifies a user account, group account, or logon session to which an **AccessControlEntry** applies.

Exceptions

Exception Type	Condition
ArgumentNullException	The **Trustee** property is a null reference (**Nothing** in Visual Basic).

Remarks

Both users and programs, such as Win32 services, use user accounts to log on to the local computer. Group accounts cannot be used to log on to a computer, but are useful in **AccessControlEntry** instances to allow or deny a set of access rights to one or more user accounts.

Requirements

Platforms: Windows 98, Windows NT 4.0, Windows Millennium Edition, Windows 2000, Windows XP Home Edition, Windows XP Professional, Windows .NET Server family

.NET Framework Security:

- Full trust for the immediate caller. This member cannot be used by partially trusted code.

AccessControlEntryType Enumeration

Specifies whether to allow, deny, or revoke access rights for a trustee.

```
[Visual Basic]
<Serializable>
Public Enum AccessControlEntryType
[C#]
[Serializable]
public enum AccessControlEntryType
[C++]
[Serializable]
__value public enum AccessControlEntryType
[JScript]
public
   Serializable
enum AccessControlEntryType
```

Remarks

When you use the **AccessControlEntry** class to specify a new access right for a trustee, you set its **EntryType** property to describe whether to grant the right or deny it. Furthermore, you can define whether the new right is appended to an existing list (if the trustee already exists in the context for which you are adding or removing access privileges) or if the new right overwrites and deletes any previously defined rights.

When creating a new **Allow** entry, there might be a preexisting **Deny** entry for the same trustee that takes precedence and must be addressed. Similary, when creating a new **Deny** entry, there might be an existing **Allow** entry that takes precedence. See the **AccessControlList** topic for information about the order in which access rights are applied.

Members

Member name	Description
Allow	An access-allowed entry that causes the new rights to be added to any existing rights the trustee has.
Deny	An access-denied entry that denies the specified rights in addition to any currently denied rights of the trustee.
Revoke	An entry that removes all existing allowed or denied rights for the specified trustee.
Set	An access-allowed entry that is similar to **Allow**, except that the new entry allows only the specified rights. Using it discards any existing rights, including all existing access-denied entries for the trustee.

Requirements

Namespace: System.Messaging

Platforms: Windows 98, Windows NT 4.0, Windows Millennium Edition, Windows 2000, Windows XP Home Edition, Windows XP Professional, Windows .NET Server family

Assembly: System.Messaging (in System.Messaging.dll)

AccessControlList Class

Contains a list of access control entries, specifying access rights for one or more trustees.

System.Object
  System.Collections.CollectionBase
    System.Messaging.AccessControlList

```
[Visual Basic]
Public Class AccessControlList
   Inherits CollectionBase
[C#]
public class AccessControlList : CollectionBase
[C++]
public __gc class AccessControlList : public CollectionBase
[JScript]
public class AccessControlList extends CollectionBase
```

Thread Safety

Any public static (**Shared** in Visual Basic) members of this type are safe for multithreaded operations. Any instance members are not guaranteed to be thread safe.

Remarks

Use the **AccessControlList** class to specify multiple trustees and access rights to add with a single call when setting permissions. Construct your access control list by adding an access control entry for each trustee and access rights combination.

An **AccessControlList** identifies the trustees that are allowed or denied access to a securable object. When a process tries to access a securable object, the system checks the access control entries in the object's access control list to determine whether to grant access to it. If the object does not have an access control list, the system grants full access to everyone. If the object's access control list has no entries, the system denies all attempts to access the object.

The system checks the access control entries in sequence until it finds one or more that allow all the requested access rights, or until any of the requested access rights are denied.

The system examines each **AccessControlEntry** in sequence until one of the following events occurs:

- An access-denied **AccessControlEntry** explicitly denies any of the requested access rights to one of the trustees listed in the thread's access token.
- One or more access-allowed **AccessControlEntry** items for trustees listed in the thread's access token explicitly grant all the requested access rights.
- All **AccessControlEntry** items have been checked and there is still at least one requested access right that has not been explicitly allowed, in which case, access is implicitly denied.

Requirements

Namespace: System.Messaging

Platforms: Windows 98, Windows NT 4.0, Windows Millennium Edition, Windows 2000, Windows XP Home Edition, Windows XP Professional, Windows .NET Server family

Assembly: System.Messaging (in System.Messaging.dll)

AccessControlList Constructor

Initializes a new instance of the **AccessControlList** class.

```
[Visual Basic]
Public Sub New()
[C#]
public AccessControlList();
[C++]
public: AccessControlList();
[JScript]
public function AccessControlList();
```

Requirements

Platforms: Windows 98, Windows NT 4.0, Windows Millennium Edition, Windows 2000, Windows XP Home Edition, Windows XP Professional, Windows .NET Server family

.NET Framework Security:

- Full trust for the immediate caller. This member cannot be used by partially trusted code.

AccessControlList.Add Method

Appends an access control entry to the access control list.

```
[Visual Basic]
Public Function Add( _
   ByVal entry As AccessControlEntry _
) As Integer
[C#]
public int Add(
   AccessControlEntry entry
);
[C++]
public: int Add(
   AccessControlEntry* entry
);
[JScript]
public function Add(
   entry : AccessControlEntry
) : int;
```

Parameters

entry
   An **AccessControlEntry** to append to the end of the access control list.

Return Value

The position into which the new access control entry was inserted.

Exceptions

Exception Type	Condition
ArgumentNullException	The *entry* parameter is a null reference (**Nothing** in Visual Basic).

Requirements

Platforms: Windows 98, Windows NT 4.0, Windows Millennium Edition, Windows 2000, Windows XP Home Edition, Windows XP Professional, Windows .NET Server family

.NET Framework Security:

- Full trust for the immediate caller. This member cannot be used by partially trusted code.

AccessControlList.Contains Method

Determines whether the access control list contains a specific access control entry.

```
[Visual Basic]
Public Function Contains( _
   ByVal entry As AccessControlEntry _
) As Boolean
[C#]
public bool Contains(
   AccessControlEntry entry
);
[C++]
public: bool Contains(
   AccessControlEntry* entry
);
[JScript]
public function Contains(
   entry : AccessControlEntry
) : Boolean;
```

Parameters

entry
> The **AccessControlEntry** to locate in the access control list.

Return Value

true if the access control entry is found in the access control list; otherwise, **false**.

Requirements

Platforms: Windows 98, Windows NT 4.0, Windows Millennium Edition, Windows 2000, Windows XP Home Edition, Windows XP Professional, Windows .NET Server family

.NET Framework Security:

- Full trust for the immediate caller. This member cannot be used by partially trusted code.

AccessControlList.CopyTo Method

Copies the entire access control list to a compatible one-dimensional array of access control entries, starting at the specified index of the target array.

```
[Visual Basic]
Public Sub CopyTo( _
   ByVal array() As AccessControlEntry, _
   ByVal index As Integer _
)
[C#]
public void CopyTo(
   AccessControlEntry[] array,
   int index
);
[C++]
public: void CopyTo(
   AccessControlEntry* array[],
   int index
);
[JScript]
public function CopyTo(
   array : AccessControlEntry[],
   index : int
);
```

Parameters

array
> An array of type **AccessControlEntry** to which the access control list entries will be copied. The array must have zero-based indexing.

index
> The index in the array at which to begin copying the access control list entries.

Exceptions

Exception Type	Condition
ArgumentNullException	The *array* parameter is a null reference (**Nothing** in Visual Basic).
ArgumentOutOfRange-Exception	The *index* parameter is less than zero.
ArgumentException	The *index* parameter is greater than or equal to the length of the *array* parameter.
	-or-
	The number of elements in the source access control list is greater than the available space from *index* to the end of the destination array of access control entries.

Requirements

Platforms: Windows 98, Windows NT 4.0, Windows Millennium Edition, Windows 2000, Windows XP Home Edition, Windows XP Professional, Windows .NET Server family

.NET Framework Security:

- Full trust for the immediate caller. This member cannot be used by partially trusted code.

AccessControlList.IndexOf Method

Determines the specific index of an access control entry in the access control list.

```
[Visual Basic]
Public Function IndexOf( _
   ByVal entry As AccessControlEntry _
) As Integer
[C#]
public int IndexOf(
   AccessControlEntry entry
);
[C++]
public: int IndexOf(
   AccessControlEntry* entry
);
[JScript]
public function IndexOf(
   entry : AccessControlEntry
) : int;
```

Parameters

entry
> The **AccessControlEntry** to locate in the access control list.

Return Value

The index of the entry if it was found in the list; otherwise, -1

Requirements

Platforms: Windows 98, Windows NT 4.0,
Windows Millennium Edition, Windows 2000,
Windows XP Home Edition, Windows XP Professional,
Windows .NET Server family

.NET Framework Security:

- Full trust for the immediate caller. This member cannot be used by partially trusted code.

AccessControlList.Insert Method

Inserts an access control entry into the access control list at the specified position.

```
[Visual Basic]
Public Sub Insert( _
   ByVal index As Integer, _
   ByVal entry As AccessControlEntry _
)
[C#]
public void Insert(
   int index,
   AccessControlEntry entry
);
[C++]
public: void Insert(
   int index,
   AccessControlEntry* entry
);
[JScript]
public function Insert(
   index : int,
   entry : AccessControlEntry
);
```

Parameters

index
   The zero-based index at which the access control entry should be inserted.
entry
   An **AccessControlEntry** to insert into the access control list.

Exceptions

Exception Type	Condition
ArgumentOutOfRange-Exception	The *index* parameter is not a valid index in this access control list.
ArgumentNullException	The *entry* parameter is a null reference (**Nothing** in Visual Basic).

Remarks

If the *index* parameter equals the number of items in the access control list, then the entry is appended to the end. Otherwise, the entries after the insertion point move down to accommodate the new item in the list.

Requirements

Platforms: Windows 98, Windows NT 4.0,
Windows Millennium Edition, Windows 2000,
Windows XP Home Edition, Windows XP Professional,
Windows .NET Server family

.NET Framework Security:

- Full trust for the immediate caller. This member cannot be used by partially trusted code.

AccessControlList.Remove Method

Removes the first occurrence of a specific access control entry from the access control list.

```
[Visual Basic]
Public Sub Remove( _
   ByVal entry As AccessControlEntry _
)
[C#]
public void Remove(
   AccessControlEntry entry
);
[C++]
public: void Remove(
   AccessControlEntry* entry
);
[JScript]
public function Remove(
   entry : AccessControlEntry
);
```

Parameters

entry
   The **AccessControlEntry** to remove from the access control list.

Exceptions

Exception Type	Condition
ArgumentNullException	The *entry* parameter is a null reference (**Nothing** in Visual Basic).

Remarks

The access control entries that follow the removed item move up to occupy the vacated spot.

Requirements

Platforms: Windows 98, Windows NT 4.0,
Windows Millennium Edition, Windows 2000,
Windows XP Home Edition, Windows XP Professional,
Windows .NET Server family

.NET Framework Security:

- Full trust for the immediate caller. This member cannot be used by partially trusted code.

AcknowledgeTypes Enumeration

Specifies the types of acknowledgment message Message Queuing returns to the sending application.

This enumeration has a **FlagsAttribute** attribute that allows a bitwise combination of its member values.

```
[Visual Basic]
<Flags>
<Serializable>
Public Enum AcknowledgeTypes
[C#]
[Flags]
[Serializable]
public enum AcknowledgeTypes
[C++]
[Flags]
[Serializable]
__value public enum AcknowledgeTypes
[JScript]
public
   Flags
   Serializable
enum AcknowledgeTypes
```

Remarks

The **AcknowledgeTypes** class provides a set of flags that you can combine to request one or more categories of acknowledgment messages.

When an application sends a message, it can request that Message Queuing return acknowledgment messages indicating the success or failure of the original message. Message Queuing sends these acknowledgment messages to the administration queue you specify. Acknowledgment types can be divided broadly into four groups: positive arrival acknowledgments, positive read acknowledgments, negative arrival acknowledgments, and negative read acknowledgments. Requesting acknowledgments enables your application to receive notification of certain occurrences--for example, a message reaching its destination queue, a message being retrieved, or a time-out preventing a message from reaching or being retrieved from the destination queue.

When you are using the **Message** class to send messages to a queue, you specify the types of acknowledgments your application should receive in the **AcknowledgeType** property, and you specify the administration queue that receives the acknowledgment messages in the **AdministrationQueue** property.

When you use the **Message** class to read acknowledgment messages in the administration queue, the instance's **Acknowledgment** property indicates the condition responsible for the acknowledgment message, for example, if a time-out expired before the original message was read from the queue.

Members

Member name	Description	Value
FullReachQueue	A mask used to request positive acknowledgment if the original message reaches the queue, or negative acknowledgment if the time-to-reach-queue timer expires or if the original message cannot be authenticated.	5

Member name	Description	Value
FullReceive	A mask used to request positive acknowledgment if the original message is received from the queue before its time-to-be-received timer expires, or negative acknowledgment otherwise.	14
NegativeReceive	A mask used to request a negative acknowledgment when the original message fails to be received from the queue.	8
	Note Using the **MessageQueue.Peek** method does not remove a message from the queue, so this acknowledgment type could be returned even if you did peek the message. Only the **MessageQueue.Receive** method (or the related asynchronous **MessageQueue.BeginReceive** method) removes a message from the queue.	
None	A mask used to request that no acknowledgment messages (positive or negative) be posted.	0
NotAcknowledgeReachQueue	A mask used to request a negative acknowledgment when the original message cannot reach the queue. This can happen when the time-to-reach-queue timer expires, or if a message cannot be authenticated.	4
NotAcknowledgeReceive	A mask used to request a negative acknowledgment when an error occurs that prevents the original message from being received from the queue before its time-to-be-received timer expires.	12
PositiveArrival	A mask used to request a positive acknowledgment when the original message reaches the queue.	1
PositiveReceive	A mask used to request a positive acknowledgment when the original message is successfully retrieved from the queue.	2

Example

[Visual Basic, C#, C++] The following example sends and receives a message containing an order to and from a queue. It specifically requests a positive acknowledgment when the original message reaches or is retrieved from the queue.

```
[Visual Basic]
Imports System
Imports System.Messaging

Namespace MyProject
   _

   '/ <summary>
   '/ Provides a container class for the example.
   '/ </summary>
   Public Class MyNewQueue
```

```vbnet
'***************************************************
' Provides an entry point into the application.
'
' This example sends and receives a message from
' a queue.
'***************************************************
Public Shared Sub Main()
    ' Create a new instance of the class.
    Dim myNewQueue As New MyNewQueue()

    ' Create new queues.
    CreateQueue(".\myQueue")
    CreateQueue(".\myAdministrationQueue")

    ' Send messages to a queue.
    myNewQueue.SendMessage()

    ' Receive messages from a queue.
    Dim messageId As String = myNewQueue.ReceiveMessage()

    ' Receive acknowledgment message.
    If Not (messageId Is Nothing) Then
        myNewQueue.ReceiveAcknowledgment
(messageId, ".\myAdministrationQueue")
    End If

    Return
End Sub 'Main

'***************************************************
' Creates a new queue.
'***************************************************
Public Shared Sub CreateQueue(queuePath As String)
    Try
        If Not MessageQueue.Exists(queuePath) Then
            MessageQueue.Create(queuePath)
        Else
            Console.WriteLine((queuePath + " already exists."))
        End If
    Catch e As MessageQueueException
        Console.WriteLine(e.Message)
    End Try
End Sub 'CreateQueue

'***************************************************
' Sends a string message to a queue.
'***************************************************
Public Sub SendMessage()

    ' Connect to a queue on the local computer.
    Dim myQueue As New MessageQueue(".\myQueue")

    ' Create a new message.
    Dim myMessage As New Message("Original Message")

    myMessage.AdministrationQueue = New
MessageQueue(".\myAdministrationQueue")
    myMessage.AcknowledgeType =
AcknowledgeTypes.PositiveReceive Or AcknowledgeTypes.PositiveArrival

    ' Send the Order to the queue.
    myQueue.Send(myMessage)

    Return
End Sub 'SendMessage

'***************************************************
' Receives a message containing an Order.
'***************************************************
Public Function ReceiveMessage() As String
    ' Connect to the a queue on the local computer.
    Dim myQueue As New MessageQueue(".\myQueue")

    myQueue.MessageReadPropertyFilter.CorrelationId = True
```

```vbnet
    ' Set the formatter to indicate body contains an Order.
    myQueue.Formatter = New XmlMessageFormatter
(New Type() {GetType(String)})

    Dim returnString As String = Nothing

    Try
        ' Receive and format the message.
        Dim myMessage As Message = myQueue.Receive()

        ' Display message information.
Console.WriteLine("_____")
        Console.WriteLine("Original message information--")
        Console.WriteLine(("Body: " + myMessage.Body.ToString()))
        Console.WriteLine(("Id: " + myMessage.Id.ToString()))

Console.WriteLine("_____")

        returnString = myMessage.Id

    Catch
    ' Handle Message Queuing exceptions.

    ' Handle invalid serialization format.
    Catch e As InvalidOperationException
        Console.WriteLine(e.Message)
    End Try

    ' Catch other exceptions as necessary.
    Return returnString
End Function 'ReceiveMessage

'***************************************************
' Receives a message containing an Order.
'***************************************************
Public Sub ReceiveAcknowledgment(messageId As String,
queuePath As String)
    Dim found As Boolean = False
    Dim queue As New MessageQueue(queuePath)
    queue.MessageReadPropertyFilter.CorrelationId = True
    queue.MessageReadPropertyFilter.Acknowledgment = True

    Try
        While Not (queue.PeekByCorrelationId(messageId) Is Nothing)
            Dim myAcknowledgmentMessage As Message =
queue.ReceiveByCorrelationId(messageId)

            ' Output acknowledgment message information.
    The correlation Id is identical
            ' to the id of the original message.
            Console.WriteLine("Acknowledgment Message
Information--")
            Console.WriteLine(("Correlation Id: " +
myAcknowledgmentMessage.CorrelationId.ToString()))
            Console.WriteLine(("Id: " +
myAcknowledgmentMessage.Id.ToString()))
            Console.WriteLine(("Acknowledgment Type: " +
myAcknowledgmentMessage.Acknowledgment.ToString()))

Console.WriteLine("_____")

            found = True
        End While
    Catch e As InvalidOperationException
        ' This exception would be thrown if there is no
(further) acknowledgment message
        ' with the specified correlation Id. Only output
a message if there are no messages;
        ' not if the loop has found at least one.
        If found = False Then
            Console.WriteLine(e.Message)
        End If
    End Try
End Sub 'ReceiveAcknowledgment ' Handle other causes of
```

```
invalid operation exception.
   End Class 'MyNewQueue
End Namespace 'MyProject

[C#]
using System;
using System.Messaging;

namespace MyProject
{

    /// <summary>
    /// Provides a container class for the example.
    /// </summary>
    public class MyNewQueue
    {

        //****************************************************
        // Provides an entry point into the application.
        //
        // This example sends and receives a message from
        // a queue.
        //****************************************************

        public static void Main()
        {
            // Create a new instance of the class.
            MyNewQueue myNewQueue = new MyNewQueue();

            // Create new queues.
            CreateQueue(".\\myQueue");
            CreateQueue(".\\myAdministrationQueue");

            // Send messages to a queue.
            myNewQueue.SendMessage();

            // Receive messages from a queue.
            string messageId = myNewQueue.ReceiveMessage();

            // Receive acknowledgment message.
            if(messageId != null)
            {
                myNewQueue.ReceiveAcknowledgment        ⌐
(messageId, ".\\myAdministrationQueue");
            }

            return;
        }

        //****************************************************
        // Creates a new queue.
        //****************************************************

        public static void CreateQueue(string queuePath)
        {
            try
            {
                if(!MessageQueue.Exists(queuePath))
                {
                    MessageQueue.Create(queuePath);
                }
                else
                {
                    Console.WriteLine(queuePath + " already exists.");
                }
            }
            catch (MessageQueueException e)
            {
                Console.WriteLine(e.Message);
            }

        }
```

```
//****************************************************
// Sends a string message to a queue.
//****************************************************

public void SendMessage()
{

    // Connect to a queue on the local computer.
    MessageQueue myQueue = new MessageQueue(".\\myQueue");

    // Create a new message.
    Message myMessage = new Message("Original Message");

    myMessage.AdministrationQueue = new            ⌐
MessageQueue(".\\myAdministrationQueue");
    myMessage.AcknowledgeType =                    ⌐
AcknowledgeTypes.PositiveReceive | AcknowledgeTypes.PositiveArrival;

    // Send the Order to the queue.
    myQueue.Send(myMessage);

    return;
}

//****************************************************
// Receives a message containing an Order.
//****************************************************

public  string ReceiveMessage()
{
    // Connect to the a queue on the local computer.
    MessageQueue myQueue = new MessageQueue(".\\myQueue");

    myQueue.MessageReadPropertyFilter.CorrelationId = true;

    // Set the formatter to indicate body contains an Order.
    myQueue.Formatter = new XmlMessageFormatter(new Type[]
        {typeof(string)});

    string returnString = null;

    try
    {
        // Receive and format the message.
        Message myMessage =    myQueue.Receive();

        // Display message information.

Console.WriteLine("_____");
        Console.WriteLine("Original message information--");
        Console.WriteLine("Body: " +myMessage.Body.ToString());
        Console.WriteLine("Id: " + myMessage.Id.ToString());
Console.WriteLine("_____");

        returnString =  myMessage.Id;

    }

    catch (MessageQueueException)
    {
        // Handle Message Queuing exceptions.
    }

    // Handle invalid serialization format.
    catch (InvalidOperationException e)
    {
        Console.WriteLine(e.Message);
    }

    // Catch other exceptions as necessary.

    return returnString;
}
```

```
//**************************************************
// Receives a message containing an Order.
//**************************************************

public void ReceiveAcknowledgment(string messageId, string      ↵
queuePath)
    {
        bool found = false;
        MessageQueue queue = new MessageQueue(queuePath);
        queue.MessageReadPropertyFilter.CorrelationId = true;
        queue.MessageReadPropertyFilter.Acknowledgment = true;

        try
        {
            while(queue.PeekByCorrelationId(messageId) != null)
            {
                Message myAcknowledgmentMessage =              ↵
queue.ReceiveByCorrelationId(messageId);

                // Output acknowledgment message information. The
correlation Id is identical
                // to the id of the original message.
                Console.WriteLine("Acknowledgment Message       ↵
Information--");
                Console.WriteLine("Correlation Id: " +          ↵
myAcknowledgmentMessage.CorrelationId.ToString());
                Console.WriteLine("Id: " +                      ↵
myAcknowledgmentMessage.Id.ToString());
                Console.WriteLine("Acknowledgment Type: " +     ↵
myAcknowledgmentMessage.Acknowledgment.ToString());

Console.WriteLine("_____");

                found = true;
            }
        }
        catch (InvalidOperationException e)
        {
            // This exception would be thrown if there          ↵
is no (further) acknowledgment message
            // with the specified correlation Id. Only           ↵
output a message if there are no messages;
            // not if the loop has found at least one.
            if(found == false)
            {
                Console.WriteLine(e.Message);
            }

            // Handle other causes of invalid operation exception.
        }
    }
}

[C++]
#using <mscorlib.dll>
#using <system.dll>
#using <system.messaging.dll>

using namespace System;
using namespace System::Messaging;

__gc class MyNewQueue
{
public:
    static void CreateQueue(String* queuePath)
    {
        try
        {
            if (!MessageQueue::Exists(queuePath))
            {
                MessageQueue::Create(queuePath);
            }
            else
```

```
            {
                Console::WriteLine("{0} already exists.", queuePath );
            }
        }
        catch (MessageQueueException* e)
        {
            Console::WriteLine(e->Message);
        }
    }

public:
    void SendMessage()
    {
        // Connect to a queue on the local computer.
        MessageQueue* myQueue = new MessageQueue(S".\\myQueue");

        // Create a new message.
        Message* myMessage = new Message(S"Original Message");
        myMessage->AdministrationQueue = new                    ↵
MessageQueue(S".\\myAdministrationQueue");
        myMessage->AcknowledgeType =                            ↵
(AcknowledgeTypes)(AcknowledgeTypes::PositiveReceive |          ↵
AcknowledgeTypes::PositiveArrival);                             ↵

        // Send the Order to the queue.
        myQueue->Send(myMessage);

        return;
    }

public:
    String* ReceiveMessage()
    {
        // Connect to the a queue on the local computer.
        MessageQueue* myQueue = new MessageQueue(S".\\myQueue");

        myQueue->MessageReadPropertyFilter->CorrelationId = true;

        Type* p __gc[] = new Type*[1];
        p[0] =   __typeof(String);
        myQueue->Formatter = new XmlMessageFormatter( p );

        String* returnString = 0;

        try
        {
            // Receive and format the message.
            Message* myMessage = myQueue->Receive();

            // Display message information.

Console::WriteLine(S"_____");
            Console::WriteLine(S"Original message information--");
            Console::WriteLine(S"Body: {0}", myMessage->Body);
            Console::WriteLine(S"Id: {0}", myMessage->Id);

Console::WriteLine(S"_____");

            returnString =  myMessage->Id;

        }
        catch (MessageQueueException*)
        {
            // Handle Message Queuing exceptions.
        }

        // Handle invalid serialization format.
        catch (InvalidOperationException* e)
        {
            Console::WriteLine(e->Message);
        }

        // Catch other exceptions as necessary.
```

```
        return returnString;
    }
public:
    void ReceiveAcknowledgment(String* messageId, String* queuePath)
    {
        bool found = false;
        MessageQueue* queue = new MessageQueue(queuePath);
        queue->MessageReadPropertyFilter->CorrelationId = true;
        queue->MessageReadPropertyFilter->Acknowledgment = true;

        try
        {
            while(queue->PeekByCorrelationId(messageId) != 0)
            {
                Message* myAcknowledgmentMessage = queue-        ⌐
    ReceiveByCorrelationId(messageId);

                // Output acknowledgment message               ⌐
    information. The correlation Id is identical
                // to the id of the original message.
                Console::WriteLine(S"Acknowledgment            ⌐
    Message Information--");
                Console::WriteLine(S"Correlation Id: {0}",     ⌐
    myAcknowledgmentMessage->CorrelationId);
                Console::WriteLine(S"Id: {0}",                 ⌐
    myAcknowledgmentMessage->Id);
                Console::WriteLine(S"Acknowledgment Type: {0}",⌐
    __box(myAcknowledgmentMessage->Acknowledgment));
    Console::WriteLine(S"_____");

                found = true;
            }
        }
        catch (InvalidOperationException* e)
        {
            // This exception would be thrown if there is no   ⌐
    (further) acknowledgment message
            // with the specified correlation Id. Only output  ⌐
    a message if there are no messages;
            // not if the loop has found at least one.
            if (found == false)
            {
                Console::WriteLine(e->Message);
            }

            // Handle other causes of invalid operation exception.
        }
    }
};

int main()
{
    // Create a new instance of the class.
    MyNewQueue* myNewQueue = new MyNewQueue();

    // Create new queues.
    MyNewQueue::CreateQueue(S".\\myQueue");
    MyNewQueue::CreateQueue(S".\\myAdministrationQueue");

    // Send messages to a queue.
    myNewQueue->SendMessage();

    // Receive messages from a queue.
    String* messageId = myNewQueue->ReceiveMessage();

    // Receive acknowledgment message.
    if (messageId != 0)
    {
        myNewQueue->ReceiveAcknowledgment(messageId,          ⌐
    S".\\myAdministrationQueue");
    }

    return 0;
```

Requirements

Namespace: System.Messaging

Platforms: Windows 98, Windows NT 4.0,
Windows Millennium Edition, Windows 2000,
Windows XP Home Edition, Windows XP Professional,
Windows .NET Server family

Assembly: System.Messaging (in System.Messaging.dll)

Acknowledgment Enumeration

Specifies the result of an attempted message delivery.

```
[Visual Basic]
<Serializable>
Public Enum Acknowledgment
[C#]
[Serializable]
public enum Acknowledgment
[C++]
[Serializable]
__value public enum Acknowledgment
[JScript]
public
   Serializable
enum Acknowledgment
```

Remarks

The **Acknowledgment** class defines the types of acknowledgment messages Message Queuing posts in the administration queue and the conditions that cause an acknowledgment message to be sent. Acknowledgment types can be divided broadly into four groups: positive arrival acknowledgments, positive read acknowledgments, negative arrival acknowledgments, and negative read acknowledgments.

Note The administration queue associated with message is specified in the **Message.AdministrationQueue** property.

Message Queuing sets the **Message.Acknowledgment** property to one of the **Acknowledgment** enumeration values when it creates an acknowledgment message. The **Message.Acknowledgment** property value is typically meaningful only when the instance refers to a system-sent acknowledgment message. Reading the **Message.Acknowledgment** property for a message other than an acknowledgment message throws an exception.

Message Queuing does not send an acknowledgment message unless the sending application requests that it do so. Your application makes this request by setting the appropriate value for the **Message.AcknowledgeType** property. Message Queuing sends all acknowledgment messages to the administration queue specified in the **AdministrationQueue** property of the original **Message**.

Members

Member name	Description
AccessDenied	A negative arrival acknowledgment indicating that the sending application does not have the necessary rights to send a message to the destination queue.
BadDestinationQueue	A negative arrival acknowledgment indicating that the destination queue is not available to the sending application.
BadEncryption	A negative arrival acknowledgment indicating that the destination queue manager could not decrypt a private message.

Member name	Description
BadSignature	A negative arrival acknowledgment indicating that the original message's digital signature is not valid and could not be authenticated by Message Queuing.
CouldNotEncrypt	A negative arrival acknowledgment indicating that the source queue manager could not encrypt a private message.
HopCountExceeded	A negative arrival acknowledgment indicating that the original message's hop count (which indicates the number of intermediate servers) was exceeded. **Note** The maximum hop count, 15, is set by Message Queuing and is immutable.
None	The message is not an acknowledgment message.
NotTransactional-Message	A negative arrival acknowledgment indicating that a nontransactional message was sent to a transactional queue.
NotTransactionalQueue	A negative arrival acknowledgment indicating that a transactional message was sent to a non-transactional queue.
Purged	A negative arrival acknowledgment indicating that the message was purged before reaching its destination queue.
QueueDeleted	A negative read acknowledgment indicating that the queue was deleted before the message could be read.
QueueExceed-MaximumSize	A negative arrival acknowledgment indicating that the original message was not delivered because its destination queue is full.
QueuePurged	A negative read acknowledgment indicating that the queue was purged before the message could be read.
ReachQueue	A positive arrival acknowledgment indicating that the original message reached its destination queue.
ReachQueueTimeout	A negative arrival acknowledgment indicating that the time-to-reach-queue or time-to-be-received timer expired before the original message could reach the destination queue.
Receive	A positive read acknowledgment indicating that the original message was received by the receiving application.
ReceiveTimeout	A negative read acknowledgment indicating that the original message was not received from the queue before its time-to-be-received timer expired.

Example

[Visual Basic, C#, C++] The following example sends and receives a message containing an order to and from a queue. It specifically requests a positive acknowledgment when the original message reaches or is retrieved from the queue.

```vbnet
[Visual Basic]
Imports System
Imports System.Messaging

Namespace MyProject

  '/ <summary>
  '/ Provides a container class for the example.
  '/ </summary>
  Public Class MyNewQueue

    '****************************************************
    ' Provides an entry point into the application.
    '
    ' This example sends and receives a message from
    ' a queue.
    '****************************************************
    Public Shared Sub Main()
      ' Create a new instance of the class.
      Dim myNewQueue As New MyNewQueue()

      ' Create new queues.
      CreateQueue(".\myQueue")
      CreateQueue(".\myAdministrationQueue")

      ' Send messages to a queue.
      myNewQueue.SendMessage()

      ' Receive messages from a queue.
      Dim messageId As String = myNewQueue.ReceiveMessage()

      ' Receive acknowledgment message.
      If Not (messageId Is Nothing) Then
        myNewQueue.ReceiveAcknowledgment(messageId, _
".\myAdministrationQueue")
      End If

      Return
    End Sub 'Main

    '****************************************************
    ' Creates a new queue.
    '****************************************************
    Public Shared Sub CreateQueue(queuePath As String)
      Try
        If Not MessageQueue.Exists(queuePath) Then
          MessageQueue.Create(queuePath)
        Else
          Console.WriteLine((queuePath + " already exists."))
        End If
      Catch e As MessageQueueException
        Console.WriteLine(e.Message)
      End Try
    End Sub 'CreateQueue

    '****************************************************
    ' Sends a string message to a queue.
    '****************************************************
    Public Sub SendMessage()

      ' Connect to a queue on the local computer.
      Dim myQueue As New MessageQueue(".\myQueue")

      ' Create a new message.
      Dim myMessage As New Message("Original Message")
      myMessage.AdministrationQueue = New _
MessageQueue(".\myAdministrationQueue")
      myMessage.AcknowledgeType = _
AcknowledgeTypes.PositiveReceive Or AcknowledgeTypes.PositiveArrival

      ' Send the Order to the queue.
      myQueue.Send(myMessage)

      Return
    End Sub 'SendMessage

    '****************************************************
    ' Receives a message containing an Order.
    '****************************************************
    Public Function ReceiveMessage() As String
      ' Connect to the a queue on the local computer.
      Dim myQueue As New MessageQueue(".\myQueue")

      myQueue.MessageReadPropertyFilter.CorrelationId = True

      ' Set the formatter to indicate body contains an Order.
      myQueue.Formatter = New XmlMessageFormatter _
(New Type() {GetType(String)})

      Dim returnString As String = Nothing

      Try
        ' Receive and format the message.
        Dim myMessage As Message = myQueue.Receive()

        ' Display message information.

Console.WriteLine("_____")
        Console.WriteLine("Original message information--")
        Console.WriteLine(("Body: " + myMessage.Body.ToString()))
        Console.WriteLine(("Id: " + myMessage.Id.ToString()))

Console.WriteLine("_____")

        returnString = myMessage.Id

      Catch
        ' Handle Message Queuing exceptions.

        ' Handle invalid serialization format.
      Catch e As InvalidOperationException
        Console.WriteLine(e.Message)
      End Try

        ' Catch other exceptions as necessary.
      Return returnString
    End Function 'ReceiveMessage


    '****************************************************
    ' Receives a message containing an Order.
    '****************************************************
    Public Sub ReceiveAcknowledgment(messageId As String, _
queuePath As String)
      Dim found As Boolean = False
      Dim queue As New MessageQueue(queuePath)
      queue.MessageReadPropertyFilter.CorrelationId = True
      queue.MessageReadPropertyFilter.Acknowledgment = True

      Try
        While Not (queue.PeekByCorrelationId(messageId) Is Nothing)
          Dim myAcknowledgmentMessage As Message = _
queue.ReceiveByCorrelationId(messageId)

          ' Output acknowledgment message information. The _
correlation Id is identical
          ' to the id of the original message.
          Console.WriteLine("Acknowledgment Message _
Information--")
          Console.WriteLine(("Correlation Id: " + _
```

```
myAcknowledgmentMessage.CorrelationId.ToString())))
            Console.WriteLine(("Id: " +
myAcknowledgmentMessage.Id.ToString())))
            Console.WriteLine(("Acknowledgment Type: " +
myAcknowledgmentMessage.Acknowledgment.ToString())))

Console.WriteLine("_____")

            found = True
          End While
       Catch e As InvalidOperationException
          ' This exception would be thrown if there is no
(further) acknowledgment message
          ' with the specified correlation Id. Only output
a message if there are no messages;
          ' not if the loop has found at least one.
          If found = False Then
             Console.WriteLine(e.Message)
          End If
       End Try
     End Sub 'ReceiveAcknowledgment ' Handle other causes of
invalid operation exception.
   End Class 'MyNewQueue
End Namespace 'MyProject

[C#]
using System;
using System.Messaging;

namespace MyProject
{

    /// <summary>
    /// Provides a container class for the example.
    /// </summary>
    public class MyNewQueue
    {

       //*************************************************
       // Provides an entry point into the application.
       //
       // This example sends and receives a message from
       // a queue.
       //*************************************************

       public static void Main()
       {
          // Create a new instance of the class.
          MyNewQueue myNewQueue = new MyNewQueue();

          // Create new queues.
          CreateQueue(".\\myQueue");
          CreateQueue(".\\myAdministrationQueue");

          // Send messages to a queue.
          myNewQueue.SendMessage();

          // Receive messages from a queue.
          string messageId = myNewQueue.ReceiveMessage();

          // Receive acknowledgment message.
          if(messageId != null)
          {
             myNewQueue.ReceiveAcknowledgment
(messageId, ".\\myAdministrationQueue");
          }

          return;
       }

       //*************************************************
       // Creates a new queue.
       //*************************************************
```

```
       public static void CreateQueue(string queuePath)
       {
          try
          {
             if(!MessageQueue.Exists(queuePath))
             {
                MessageQueue.Create(queuePath);
             }
             else
             {
                Console.WriteLine(queuePath + " already exists.");
             }
          }
          catch (MessageQueueException e)
          {
             Console.WriteLine(e.Message);
          }

       }

       //*************************************************
       // Sends a string message to a queue.
       //*************************************************

       public void SendMessage()
       {

          // Connect to a queue on the local computer.
          MessageQueue myQueue = new MessageQueue(".\\myQueue");

          // Create a new message.
          Message myMessage = new Message("Original Message");

          myMessage.AdministrationQueue = new
MessageQueue(".\\myAdministrationQueue");
          myMessage.AcknowledgeType =
AcknowledgeTypes.PositiveReceiveAcknowledgeTypes.PositiveArrival;

          // Send the Order to the queue.
          myQueue.Send(myMessage);

          return;
       }

       //*************************************************
       // Receives a message containing an Order.
       //*************************************************

       public  string ReceiveMessage()
       {
          // Connect to the a queue on the local computer.
          MessageQueue myQueue = new MessageQueue(".\\myQueue");

          myQueue.MessageReadPropertyFilter.CorrelationId = true;

          // Set the formatter to indicate body contains an Order.
          myQueue.Formatter = new XmlMessageFormatter(new Type[]
             {typeof(string)});

          string returnString = null;

          try
          {
             // Receive and format the message.
             Message myMessage =   myQueue.Receive();

             // Display message information.
Console.WriteLine("_____");
             Console.WriteLine("Original message information--");
             Console.WriteLine("Body: " +myMessage.Body.ToString());
             Console.WriteLine("Id: " + myMessage.Id.ToString());

Console.WriteLine("_____");
```

```
                returnString = myMessage.Id;

        }

        catch (MessageQueueException)
        {
            // Handle Message Queuing exceptions.
        }

        // Handle invalid serialization format.
        catch (InvalidOperationException e)
        {
            Console.WriteLine(e.Message);
        }

        // Catch other exceptions as necessary.

        return returnString;

    }

    //*************************************************
    // Receives a message containing an Order.
    //*************************************************

    public void ReceiveAcknowledgment(string messageId, string ↵
queuePath)
    {
        bool found = false;
        MessageQueue queue = new MessageQueue(queuePath);
        queue.MessageReadPropertyFilter.CorrelationId = true;
        queue.MessageReadPropertyFilter.Acknowledgment = true;

        try
        {
            while(queue.PeekByCorrelationId(messageId) != null)
            {
                Message myAcknowledgmentMessage =          ↵
queue.ReceiveByCorrelationId(messageId);

                // Output acknowledgment message            ↵
information. The correlation Id is identical
                // to the id of the original message.
                Console.WriteLine("Acknowledgment Message   ↵
Information--");
                Console.WriteLine("Correlation Id: " +
myAcknowledgmentMessage.CorrelationId.ToString());      ↵
                Console.WriteLine("Id: " +                 ↵
myAcknowledgmentMessage.Id.ToString());
                Console.WriteLine("Acknowledgment Type:     ↵
" + myAcknowledgmentMessage.Acknowledgment.ToString());
Console.WriteLine("_____");

                found = true;
            }
        }
        catch (InvalidOperationException e)
        {
            // This exception would be thrown if there     ↵
is no (further) acknowledgment message
            // with the specified correlation Id. Only     ↵
output a message if there are no messages;
            // not if the loop has found at least one.
            if(found == false)
            {
                Console.WriteLine(e.Message);
            }

            // Handle other causes of invalid operation exception.
        }
    }
  }
}
```

```
[C++]
#using <mscorlib.dll>
#using <system.dll>
#using <system.messaging.dll>

using namespace System;
using namespace System::Messaging;

__gc class MyNewQueue
{
public:
    static void CreateQueue(String* queuePath)
    {
        try
        {
            if (!MessageQueue::Exists(queuePath))
            {
                MessageQueue::Create(queuePath);
            }
            else
            {
                Console::WriteLine("{0} already exists.", queuePath );
            }
        }
        catch (MessageQueueException* e)
        {
            Console::WriteLine(e->Message);
        }

    }

public:
    void SendMessage()
    {

        // Connect to a queue on the local computer.
        MessageQueue* myQueue = new MessageQueue(S".\\myQueue");

        // Create a new message.
        Message* myMessage = new Message(S"Original Message");
        myMessage->AdministrationQueue = new                    ↵
MessageQueue(S".\\myAdministrationQueue");
        myMessage->AcknowledgeType =                            ↵
(AcknowledgeTypes)(AcknowledgeTypes::PositiveReceive |          ↵
AcknowledgeTypes::PositiveArrival);

        // Send the Order to the queue.
        myQueue->Send(myMessage);

        return;
    }

public:
    String* ReceiveMessage()
    {
        // Connect to the a queue on the local computer.
        MessageQueue* myQueue = new MessageQueue(S".\\myQueue");

        myQueue->MessageReadPropertyFilter->CorrelationId = true;

        Type* p __gc[] = new Type*[1];
        p[0] =   __typeof(String);
        myQueue->Formatter = new XmlMessageFormatter( p );

        String* returnString = 0;

        try
        {
            // Receive and format the message.
            Message* myMessage = myQueue->Receive();

            // Display message information.

Console::WriteLine(S"_____");
            Console::WriteLine(S"Original message information--");
```

```
            Console::WriteLine(S"Body: {0}", myMessage->Body);
            Console::WriteLine(S"Id: {0}", myMessage->Id);
Console::WriteLine(S"_____");

            returnString = myMessage->Id;

        }
        catch (MessageQueueException*)
        {
            // Handle Message Queuing exceptions.
        }

        // Handle invalid serialization format.
        catch (InvalidOperationException* e)
        {
            Console::WriteLine(e->Message);
        }

        // Catch other exceptions as necessary.

        return returnString;
    }

public:
    void ReceiveAcknowledgment(String* messageId, String* queuePath)
    {
        bool found = false;
        MessageQueue* queue = new MessageQueue(queuePath);
        queue->MessageReadPropertyFilter->CorrelationId = true;
        queue->MessageReadPropertyFilter->Acknowledgment = true;

        try
        {
            while(queue->PeekByCorrelationId(messageId) != 0)
            {
                Message* myAcknowledgmentMessage = queue-
>ReceiveByCorrelationId(messageId);

                // Output acknowledgment message
information. The correlation Id is identical
                // to the id of the original message.
                Console::WriteLine(S"Acknowledgment Message
Information--");
                Console::WriteLine(S"Correlation Id: {0}",
myAcknowledgmentMessage->CorrelationId);
                Console::WriteLine(S"Id: {0}",
myAcknowledgmentMessage->Id);
                Console::WriteLine(S"Acknowledgment Type: {0}",
__box(myAcknowledgmentMessage->Acknowledgment));
Console::WriteLine(S"_____");

                found = true;
            }
        }
        catch (InvalidOperationException* e)
        {
            // This exception would be thrown if there is no
(further) acknowledgment message
            // with the specified correlation Id. Only output
a message if there are no messages;
            // not if the loop has found at least one.
            if (found == false)
            {
                Console::WriteLine(e->Message);
            }

            // Handle other causes of invalid operation exception.
        }

    }
};
```

```
int main()
{
    // Create a new instance of the class.
    MyNewQueue* myNewQueue = new MyNewQueue();

    // Create new queues.
    MyNewQueue::CreateQueue(S".\\myQueue");
    MyNewQueue::CreateQueue(S".\\myAdministrationQueue");

    // Send messages to a queue.
    myNewQueue->SendMessage();

    // Receive messages from a queue.
    String* messageId = myNewQueue->ReceiveMessage();

    // Receive acknowledgment message.
    if (messageId != 0)
    {
        myNewQueue->ReceiveAcknowledgment(messageId,
S".\\myAdministrationQueue");
    }

    return 0;
}
```

Requirements

Namespace: System.Messaging

Platforms: Windows 98, Windows NT 4.0,
Windows Millennium Edition, Windows 2000,
Windows XP Home Edition, Windows XP Professional,
Windows .NET Server family

Assembly: System.Messaging (in System.Messaging.dll)

ActiveXMessageFormatter Class

Serializes or deserializes primitive data types and other objects to or from the body of a Message Queuing message, using a format that is compatible with the MSMQ ActiveX Component.

System.Object
   System.Messaging.ActiveXMessageFormatter

```
[Visual Basic]
Public Class ActiveXMessageFormatter
    Implements IMessageFormatter, ICloneable
[C#]
public class ActiveXMessageFormatter : IMessageFormatter,
    ICloneable
[C++]
public __gc class ActiveXMessageFormatter : public
    IMessageFormatter, ICloneable
[JScript]
public class ActiveXMessageFormatter implements IMessageFormatter,
    ICloneable
```

Thread Safety

Any public static (**Shared** in Visual Basic) members of this type are safe for multithreaded operations. Any instance members are not guaranteed to be thread safe.

Remarks

The **ActiveXMessageFormatter** is compatible with messages sent using Message Queuing COM components, allowing interoperability with applications that use the MSMQ COM control.

The **ActiveXMessageFormatter** can serialize most primitives, as well as objects that implement the IPersistStream OLE interface. It can deserialize the same set of primitives, but requires further effort when deserializing a COM object (for example, an object created using Visual Basic 6.0) that implements IPersistStream. The object to deserialize must be in memory by first importing the object into a .NET Framework application.

When an application sends a message to the queue using an instance of the **MessageQueue** class, the formatter serializes the object into a stream and inserts it into the message body. When reading from a queue using a **MessageQueue**, the formatter deserializes the message data into the **Body** property of a **Message**.

ActiveX serialization is very compact, which makes using the **ActiveXMessageFormatter** and MSMQ COM control a very fast method of serialization.

Requirements

Namespace: System.Messaging

Platforms: Windows 98, Windows NT 4.0, Windows Millennium Edition, Windows 2000, Windows XP Home Edition, Windows XP Professional, Windows .NET Server family

Assembly: System.Messaging (in System.Messaging.dll)

ActiveXMessageFormatter Constructor

Initializes a new instance of the **ActiveXMessageFormatter** class.

```
[Visual Basic]
Public Sub New()
[C#]
public ActiveXMessageFormatter();
[C++]
public: ActiveXMessageFormatter();
[JScript]
public function ActiveXMessageFormatter();
```

Remarks

The default constructor initializes any fields to their default values.

Requirements

Platforms: Windows 98, Windows NT 4.0, Windows Millennium Edition, Windows 2000, Windows XP Home Edition, Windows XP Professional, Windows .NET Server family

.NET Framework Security:
- Full trust for the immediate caller. This member cannot be used by partially trusted code.

ActiveXMessageFormatter.CanRead Method

Determine whether the formatter can deserialize the contents of the message.

```
[Visual Basic]
Public Overridable Function CanRead( _
    ByVal message As Message _
) As Boolean Implements IMessageFormatter.CanRead
[C#]
public virtual bool CanRead(
    Message message
);
[C++]
public: virtual bool CanRead(
    Message* message
);
[JScript]
public function CanRead(
    message : Message
) : Boolean;
```

Parameters

message
   The **Message** to inspect.

Return Value

true if the **ActiveXMessageFormatter** can deserialize the message; otherwise, **false**.

Implements

IMessageFormatter.CanRead

Exceptions

Exception Type	Condition
ArgumentNullException	The *message* parameter is a null reference (**Nothing** in Visual Basic).

Remarks

CanRead returns **false** if the message body is not a primitive that the Message Queuing ActiveX control can deserialize, or if it does not implement the IPersistStream interface.

Requirements

Platforms: Windows 98, Windows NT 4.0,
Windows Millennium Edition, Windows 2000,
Windows XP Home Edition, Windows XP Professional,
Windows .NET Server family

.NET Framework Security:

- Full trust for the immediate caller. This member cannot be used
  by partially trusted code.

ActiveXMessageFormatter.Clone Method

Creates an instance of the **ActiveXMessageFormatter** class that is
identical to the current **ActiveXMessageFormatter**.

```
[Visual Basic]
Public Overridable Function Clone() As Object Implements _
   ICloneable.Clone
[C#]
public virtual object Clone();
[C++]
public: virtual Object* Clone();
[JScript]
public function Clone() : Object;
```

Return Value

An object whose properties are identical to those of this
ActiveXMessageFormatter.

Implements

ICloneable.Clone

Remarks

This method is used by the **MessageQueue** class in order to receive
multiple messages at the same time (for example, if the application
is receiving asynchronously). You typically do not need to call this
method in your application code.

Requirements

Platforms: Windows 98, Windows NT 4.0,
Windows Millennium Edition, Windows 2000,
Windows XP Home Edition, Windows XP Professional,
Windows .NET Server family

.NET Framework Security:

- Full trust for the immediate caller. This member cannot be used
  by partially trusted code.

ActiveXMessageFormatter.InitStreamedObject Method

Provides a utility to help the serialize COM objects that implement
IPersistStream and require IPersistStreamInit to be called.

```
[Visual Basic]
Public Shared Sub InitStreamedObject( _
   ByVal streamedObject As Object _
)
[C#]
public static void InitStreamedObject(
   object streamedObject
);
[C++]
public: static void InitStreamedObject(
   Object* streamedObject
);
```

```
[JScript]
public static function InitStreamedObject(
   streamedObject : Object
);
```

Parameters

streamedObject
    An OLE object that implements IPersistStreamInit.

Requirements

Platforms: Windows 98, Windows NT 4.0,
Windows Millennium Edition, Windows 2000,
Windows XP Home Edition, Windows XP Professional,
Windows .NET Server family

.NET Framework Security:

- Full trust for the immediate caller. This member cannot be used
  by partially trusted code.

ActiveXMessageFormatter.Read Method

Reads the contents from the given message and creates an object
containing the deserialized message.

```
[Visual Basic]
Public Overridable Function Read( _
   ByVal message As Message _
) As Object Implements IMessageFormatter.Read
[C#]
public virtual object Read(
   Message message
);
[C++]
public: virtual Object* Read(
   Message* message
);
[JScript]
public function Read(
   message : Message
) : Object;
```

Parameters

message
    The **Message**, in MSMQ ActiveX control format, to deserialize.

Return Value

The deserialized message.

Implements

IMessageFormatter.Read

Exceptions

Exception Type	Condition
InvalidOperation-Exception	The **BodyType** property of the *message* passed as a parameter cannot be mapped to a primitive type, nor does it represent a streamed object.
NotSupportedException	The body represents a stored object. The **ActiveXMessageFormatter** does not support deserialization of stored objects.
ArgumentNullException	The *message* parameter is a null reference (**Nothing** in Visual Basic).

Remarks

If the body of the message represents a primitive type, the message's **BodyType** property must be one of the following managed types.

BodyType Value	Managed Type
VT_LPSTR	**Char** array (deserialized using ASCII encoding)
VT_BSTR, VT_LPWSTR	**String** (deserialized using Unicode encoding)
VT_VECTOR | VT_UI1	**Byte** array
VT_BOOL	**Boolean**
VT_CLSID	**Guid**
VT_CY	**Decimal**
VT_DATE	**DateTime**
VT_I1, VT_UI1	**Byte**
VT_I2	**Int16**
VT_UI2	**UInt16**
VT_I4	**Int32**
VT_UI4	**UInt32**
VT_I8	**Int64**
VT_UI8	**UInt64**
VT_R4	**Single**
VT_R8	**Double**
VT_NULL	A null reference (**Nothing** in Visual Basic)
VT_STREAMED_OBJECT	**Object**

Requirements

Platforms: Windows 98, Windows NT 4.0, Windows Millennium Edition, Windows 2000, Windows XP Home Edition, Windows XP Professional, Windows .NET Server family

.NET Framework Security:
- Full trust for the immediate caller. This member cannot be used by partially trusted code.

ActiveXMessageFormatter.Write Method

Serializes an object into the body of the message.

```
[Visual Basic]
Public Overridable Sub Write( _
   ByVal message As Message, _
   ByVal obj As Object _
) Implements IMessageFormatter.Write
[C#]
public virtual void Write(
   Message message,
   object obj
);
[C++]
public: virtual void Write(
   Message* message,
   Object* obj
);
```

```
[JScript]
public function Write(
   message : Message,
   obj : Object
);
```

Parameters

message
> The **Message** whose **Body** property will contain the serialized object.

obj
> The object to be serialized into the message body.

Implements

IMessageFormatter.Write

Exceptions

Exception Type	Condition
InvalidOperation-Exception	The object to serialize is not a primitive nor a streamed object that implements the OLE IPersistStream interface.
ArgumentNull-Exception	The *message* parameter is a null reference (**Nothing** in Visual Basic).

Remarks

The following table shows the relationship between managed types and the **BodyType** property. The object that you serialize must be one of these managed types or must implement the OLE IPersistStream interface.

BodyType Value	Managed Type
VT_LPSTR	**Char** []
VT_BSTR, VT_LPWSTR	**String**
VT_VECTOR | VT_UI1	**Byte** []
VT_BOOL	**Boolean**
VT_CLSID	**Guid**
VT_CY	**Decimal**
VT_DATE	**DateTime**
VT_I1, VT_UI1	**Byte**
VT_I2	**Int16**
VT_UI2	**UInt16**
VT_I4	**Int32**
VT_UI4	**UInt32**
VT_I8	**Int64**
VT_UI8	**UInt64**
VT_R4	**Single**
VT_R8	**Double**
VT_NULL	A null reference (**Nothing** in Visual Basic)
VT_STREAMED_OBJECT	IPersistStream (OLE) **Object**

Requirements

Platforms: Windows 98, Windows NT 4.0, Windows Millennium Edition, Windows 2000, Windows XP Home Edition, Windows XP Professional, Windows .NET Server family

.NET Framework Security:
- Full trust for the immediate caller. This member cannot be used by partially trusted code.

BinaryMessageFormatter Class

Serializes or deserializes an object, or an entire graph of connected objects, to or from the body of a Message Queuing message, using a binary format.

System.Object
  System.Messaging.BinaryMessageFormatter

```
[Visual Basic]
Public Class BinaryMessageFormatter
   Implements IMessageFormatter, ICloneable
[C#]
public class BinaryMessageFormatter : IMessageFormatter, ICloneable
[C++]
public __gc class BinaryMessageFormatter : public
   IMessageFormatter, ICloneable
[JScript]
public class BinaryMessageFormatter implements IMessageFormatter,
   ICloneable
```

Thread Safety

Any public static (**Shared** in Visual Basic) members of this type are safe for multithreaded operations. Any instance members are not guaranteed to be thread safe.

Remarks

The **BinaryMessageFormatter** is very efficient and can be used to serialize most objects. The result is very compact and fast to parse, but does not allow for loosely coupled messaging as the **XmlMessageFormatter** does.

> **Note** Loosely coupled means that the client and the server can independently version the type that is sent and received.

When the application sends a message to the queue using an instance of the **MessageQueue** class, the formatter serializes the object into a stream and inserts it into the message body. When reading from a queue using a **MessageQueue**, the formatter deserializes the message data into the **Body** property of a **Message**.

BinaryMessageFormatter provides faster throughput than the **XmlMessageFormatter**. Use the **BinaryMessageFormatter** when pure speed rather than loosely coupled messaging is desired.

Requirements

Namespace: System.Messaging

Platforms: Windows 98, Windows NT 4.0, Windows Millennium Edition, Windows 2000, Windows XP Home Edition, Windows XP Professional, Windows .NET Server family

Assembly: System.Messaging (in System.Messaging.dll)

BinaryMessageFormatter Constructor

Initializes a new instance of the **BinaryMessageFormatter** class.

Overload List

Initializes a new instance of the **BinaryMessageFormatter** class, without specifying a type style or top object assembly style.

  [Visual Basic] **Public Sub New()**

  [C#] **public BinaryMessageFormatter();**

  [C++] **public: BinaryMessageFormatter();**

  [JScript] **public function BinaryMessageFormatter();**

Initializes a new instance of the **BinaryMessageFormatter** class, specifying the formats of the root object and the type descriptions.

  [Visual Basic] **Public Sub New(FormatterAssemblyStyle, FormatterTypeStyle)**

  [C#] **public BinaryMessageFormatter(FormatterAssemblyStyle, FormatterTypeStyle);**

  [C++] **public: BinaryMessageFormatter(FormatterAssemblyStyle, FormatterTypeStyle);**

  [JScript] **public function BinaryMessageFormatter (FormatterAssemblyStyle, FormatterTypeStyle);**

BinaryMessageFormatter Constructor ()

Initializes a new instance of the **BinaryMessageFormatter** class, without specifying a type style or top object assembly style.

```
[Visual Basic]
Public Sub New()
[C#]
public BinaryMessageFormatter();
[C++]
public: BinaryMessageFormatter();
[JScript]
public function BinaryMessageFormatter();
```

Remarks

You must specify values for the **TopObjectFormat** property (which defines how the root object in a graph is laid out) and the **TypeFormat** property (which defines how object type descriptions are laid out) before using an instance of the **BinaryMessageFormatter** class to serialize and send a message.

Requirements

Platforms: Windows 98, Windows NT 4.0, Windows Millennium Edition, Windows 2000, Windows XP Home Edition, Windows XP Professional, Windows .NET Server family

.NET Framework Security:

- Full trust for the immediate caller. This member cannot be used by partially trusted code.

BinaryMessageFormatter Constructor (FormatterAssemblyStyle, FormatterTypeStyle)

Initializes a new instance of the **BinaryMessageFormatter** class, specifying the formats of the root object and the type descriptions.

```
[Visual Basic]
Public Sub New( _
   ByVal topObjectFormat As FormatterAssemblyStyle, _
   ByVal typeFormat As FormatterTypeStyle _
)
[C#]
public BinaryMessageFormatter(
   FormatterAssemblyStyle topObjectFormat,
   FormatterTypeStyle typeFormat
);
```

```
[C++]
public: BinaryMessageFormatter(
    FormatterAssemblyStyle topObjectFormat,
    FormatterTypeStyle typeFormat
);
[JScript]
public function BinaryMessageFormatter(
    topObjectFormat : FormatterAssemblyStyle,
    typeFormat : FormatterTypeStyle
);
```

Parameters

topObjectFormat
> Determines how the top (root) object of a graph is laid out in the serialized stream.

typeFormat
> Determines how type descriptions are laid out in the serialized stream.

Remarks

Requirements

Platforms: Windows 98, Windows NT 4.0, Windows Millennium Edition, Windows 2000, Windows XP Home Edition, Windows XP Professional, Windows .NET Server family

.NET Framework Security:

- Full trust for the immediate caller. This member cannot be used by partially trusted code.

BinaryMessageFormatter.TopObjectFormat Property

Gets or sets a value that defines how the top (root) object of a graph is laid out in the serialized stream.

```
[Visual Basic]
Public Property TopObjectFormat As FormatterAssemblyStyle
[C#]
public FormatterAssemblyStyle TopObjectFormat {get; set;}
[C++]
public: __property FormatterAssemblyStyle get_TopObjectFormat();
public: __property void set_TopObjectFormat(FormatterAssemblyStyle);
[JScript]
public function get TopObjectFormat() : FormatterAssemblyStyle;
public function set TopObjectFormat(FormatterAssemblyStyle);
```

Property Value

A **FormatterAssemblyStyle** that defines the root object format.

Remarks

Currently, you should accept the default value, **AssemblyStyle**.

Requirements

Platforms: Windows 98, Windows NT 4.0, Windows Millennium Edition, Windows 2000, Windows XP Home Edition, Windows XP Professional, Windows .NET Server family

.NET Framework Security:

- Full trust for the immediate caller. This member cannot be used by partially trusted code.

BinaryMessageFormatter.TypeFormat Property

Gets or sets a value that defines how type descriptions are laid out in the serialized stream.

```
[Visual Basic]
Public Property TypeFormat As FormatterTypeStyle
[C#]
public FormatterTypeStyle TypeFormat {get; set;}
[C++]
public: __property FormatterTypeStyle get_TypeFormat();
public: __property void set_TypeFormat(FormatterTypeStyle);
[JScript]
public function get TypeFormat() : FormatterTypeStyle;
public function set TypeFormat(FormatterTypeStyle);
```

Property Value

A **FormatterTypeStyle** that defines the type description format.

Remarks

Currently, you should accept the default value, **TypesWhenNeeded**.

Requirements

Platforms: Windows 98, Windows NT 4.0, Windows Millennium Edition, Windows 2000, Windows XP Home Edition, Windows XP Professional, Windows .NET Server family

.NET Framework Security:

- Full trust for the immediate caller. This member cannot be used by partially trusted code.

BinaryMessageFormatter.CanRead Method

Determines whether the formatter can deserialize the contents of the message.

```
[Visual Basic]
Public Overridable Function CanRead( _
    ByVal message As Message _
) As Boolean Implements IMessageFormatter.CanRead
[C#]
public virtual bool CanRead(
    Message message
);
[C++]
public: virtual bool CanRead(
    Message* message
);
[JScript]
public function CanRead(
    message : Message
) : Boolean;
```

Parameters

message
> The **Message** to inspect.

Return Value

true if the binary message formatter can deserialize the message; otherwise, **false**.

Implements

IMessageFormatter.CanRead

Exceptions

Exception Type	Condition
ArgumentNullException	The *message* parameter is a null reference (**Nothing** in Visual Basic).

Remarks

CanRead returns **false** if the message body is not a binary object.

On the receiving computer, **CanRead** returns true if the assembly for the class to be deserialized exists locally. The assembly must be found in the global assembly cache, or be linked to the application (for example, if the object represents a custom class).

Requirements

Platforms: Windows 98, Windows NT 4.0, Windows Millennium Edition, Windows 2000, Windows XP Home Edition, Windows XP Professional, Windows .NET Server family

.NET Framework Security:
- Full trust for the immediate caller. This member cannot be used by partially trusted code.

BinaryMessageFormatter.Clone Method

Creates an instance of the **BinaryMessageFormatter** class whose read/write properties (the root object and type description formats) are the same as the current **BinaryMessageFormatter**.

```
[Visual Basic]
Public Overridable Function Clone() As Object Implements _
   ICloneable.Clone
[C#]
public virtual object Clone();
[C++]
public: virtual Object* Clone();
[JScript]
public function Clone() : Object;
```

Return Value

An object whose properties are identical to those of this **BinaryMessageFormatter**, but whose metadata does not specify it to be a formatter class instance.

Implements

ICloneable.Clone

Remarks

This method creates a copy of the formatter and initializes all its properties to the values of this **BinaryMessageFormatter**. It is used for scalability, but does not guarantee read or write thread safety.

Requirements

Platforms: Windows 98, Windows NT 4.0, Windows Millennium Edition, Windows 2000, Windows XP Home Edition, Windows XP Professional, Windows .NET Server family

.NET Framework Security:
- Full trust for the immediate caller. This member cannot be used by partially trusted code.

BinaryMessageFormatter.Read Method

Reads the contents from the given message and creates an object containing the deserialized message.

```
[Visual Basic]
Public Overridable Function Read( _
   ByVal message As Message _
) As Object Implements IMessageFormatter.Read
[C#]
public virtual object Read(
   Message message
);
[C++]
public: virtual Object* Read(
   Message* message
);
[JScript]
public function Read(
   message : Message
) : Object;
```

Parameters

message
    The **Message**, in binary format, to deserialize.

Return Value

The deserialized message.

Implements

IMessageFormatter.Read

Exceptions

Exception Type	Condition
InvalidOperation-Exception	The message's **BodyType** property does not indicate a binary object.
ArgumentNullException	The *message* parameter is a null reference (**Nothing** in Visual Basic).

Remarks

The body of the message must be in binary format, and the same serializer must be used to deserialize the message as that which initially serialized it. If the body represents a custom class, the assembly for that class must exist locally.

Requirements

Platforms: Windows 98, Windows NT 4.0, Windows Millennium Edition, Windows 2000, Windows XP Home Edition, Windows XP Professional, Windows .NET Server family

.NET Framework Security:
- Full trust for the immediate caller. This member cannot be used by partially trusted code.

BinaryMessageFormatter.Write Method

Serializes an object into the body of the message.

```
[Visual Basic]
Public Overridable Sub Write( _
   ByVal message As Message, _
   ByVal obj As Object _
) Implements IMessageFormatter.Write
```

```
[C#]
public virtual void Write(
   Message message,
   object obj
);
[C++]
public: virtual void Write(
   Message* message,
   Object* obj
);
[JScript]
public function Write(
   message : Message,
   obj : Object
);
```

Parameters

message

> The **Message** whose **Body** property will contain the serialized object.

obj

> The object to be serialized into the message body.

Implements

IMessageFormatter.Write

Exceptions

Exception Type	Condition
ArgumentNullException	The *message* parameter is a null reference (**Nothing** in Visual Basic).

Remarks

The top object format and type format need not be specified to write to the queue as they must be when reading. The **TopObjectFormat** and **TypeFormat** properties are used by the formatter only when deserializing a message.

The **BinaryMessageFormatter** can serialize most objects, but the result is not loosely coupled. However, it is compact, so the formatter is efficient for large objects.

Requirements

Platforms: Windows 98, Windows NT 4.0, Windows Millennium Edition, Windows 2000, Windows XP Home Edition, Windows XP Professional, Windows .NET Server family

.NET Framework Security:

- Full trust for the immediate caller. This member cannot be used by partially trusted code.

CryptographicProviderType Enumeration

Specifies the cryptographic service providers available for validating digital signatures.

```
[Visual Basic]
<Serializable>
Public Enum CryptographicProviderType
[C#]
[Serializable]
public enum CryptographicProviderType
[C++]
[Serializable]
_value public enum CryptographicProviderType
[JScript]
public
   Serializable
enum CryptographicProviderType
```

Remarks

A cryptographic service provider contains implementations of cryptographic standards and algorithms. Applications can require the authentication provider name or authentication provider type of a cryptographic service provider to validate the digital signatures.

Members

Member name	Description
Dss	A provider type that, like **RsqSig**, only supports hashes and digital signatures. **Dss** specifies the DSA (Digital Signature Algorithm) signature algorithm.
Fortezza	A provider type that contains a set of cryptographic protocols and algorithms owned by the National Institute of Standards and Technology.
MicrosoftExchange	A provider type designed for the cryptographic needs of the Microsoft Exchange mail application and other applications compatible with Microsoft Mail.
	Note This provider type is preliminary.
None	No cryptographic provider type specified.
RsaFull	The full RSA provider type, which supports both digital signatures and data encryption. Considered a general purpose cryptographic services provider. The RSA public-key algorithm is used for all public-key operations.
	Note RSA Data Security, Inc., is a major developer and publisher of public-key cryptography standards. The "RSA" in the name stands for the names of the company's three developers and the owners: Rivest, Shamir, and Adelman

Member name	Description
RsqSig	A subset of the **RsaFull** provider type, which supports only those functions and algorithms required for hashes and digital signatures.
Ssl	A provider type that supports the Secure Sockets Layer (SSL) protocol.
SttAcq	Secure Transaction Technology Provider.
SttBrnd	Secure Transaction Technology Provider.
SttIss	Secure Transaction Technology Provider.
SttMer	Secure Transaction Technology Provider.
SttRoot	Secure Transaction Technology Provider.

Requirements

Namespace: System.Messaging

Platforms: Windows 98, Windows NT 4.0, Windows Millennium Edition, Windows 2000, Windows XP Home Edition, Windows XP Professional, Windows .NET Server family

Assembly: System.Messaging (in System.Messaging.dll)

DefaultPropertiesToSend Class

Specifies the default property values that will be used when sending objects other than **Message** instances to a message queue.

System.Object
  System.Messaging.DefaultPropertiesToSend

```
[Visual Basic]
Public Class DefaultPropertiesToSend
[C#]
public class DefaultPropertiesToSend
[C++]
public __gc class DefaultPropertiesToSend
[JScript]
public class DefaultPropertiesToSend
```

Thread Safety

Any public static (**Shared** in Visual Basic) members of this type are safe for multithreaded operations. Any instance members are not guaranteed to be thread safe.

Remarks

You can set default values on selected properties for messages sent to a **MessageQueue**. **DefaultPropertiesToSend** is used to specify default property values of the message being sent when objects other than **Message** instances are sent to a queue, for example the string argument passed into the **Send** method in the code fragment, `myMessageQueue.Send("hello")`. The **Message** class has corresponding, identically named properties to those in **DefaultPropertiesToSend** that provide the values when sending a **Message** instance specifically. Even if you have specified **MessageQueue.DefaultPropertiesToSend** for a queue, sending a **Message** object to that queue will cause the values for the identically-named **Message** properties to override the queue's **DefaultPropertiesToSend** values.

Properties that you do not set explicitly default to the values specified by the constructor, **DefaultPropertiesToSend**.

For a list of initial property values for an instance of **DefaultPropertiesToSend**, see the **DefaultPropertiesToSend** constructor.

Example

[Visual Basic, C#, C++] The following example uses the priority of a message to determine default properties to send for the message.

```
[Visual Basic]
Imports System
Imports System.Messaging

Namespace MyProject

    '/ <summary>
    '/ Provides a container class for the example.
    '/ </summary>
    Public Class MyNewQueue

        '***************************************************
        ' Provides an entry point into the application.
        '
        ' This example specifies different types of default
        ' properties for messages.
        '***************************************************
```

```
Public Shared Sub Main()

    ' Create a new instance of the class.
    Dim myNewQueue As New MyNewQueue()

    ' Send normal and high priority messages.
    myNewQueue.SendNormalPriorityMessages()
    myNewQueue.SendHighPriorityMessages()

    Return

End Sub 'Main

'***************************************************
' Associates selected message property values
' with high priority messages.
'***************************************************

Public Sub SendHighPriorityMessages()

    ' Connect to a message queue.
    Dim myQueue As New MessageQueue(".\myQueue")

    ' Associate selected default property values with high
    ' priority messages.
    myQueue.DefaultPropertiesToSend.Priority = _
        MessagePriority.High
    myQueue.DefaultPropertiesToSend.Label = _
        "High Priority Message"
    myQueue.DefaultPropertiesToSend.Recoverable = True
    myQueue.DefaultPropertiesToSend.TimeToReachQueue = _
        New TimeSpan(0, 0, 30)

    ' Send messages using these defaults.
    myQueue.Send("High priority message data 1.")
    myQueue.Send("High priority message data 2.")
    myQueue.Send("High priority message data 3.")

    Return

End Sub 'SendHighPriorityMessages

'***************************************************
' Associates selected message property values
' with normal priority messages.
'***************************************************

Public Sub SendNormalPriorityMessages()

    ' Connect to a message queue.
    Dim myQueue As New MessageQueue(".\myQueue")

    ' Associate selected default property values with normal
    ' priority messages.
    myQueue.DefaultPropertiesToSend.Priority = _
        MessagePriority.Normal
    myQueue.DefaultPropertiesToSend.Label = _
        "Normal Priority Message"
    myQueue.DefaultPropertiesToSend.Recoverable = False
    myQueue.DefaultPropertiesToSend.TimeToReachQueue = _
        New TimeSpan(0, 2, 0)

    ' Send messages using these defaults.
    myQueue.Send("Normal priority message data 1.")
    myQueue.Send("Normal priority message data 2.")
    myQueue.Send("Normal priority message data 3.")

    Return

    End Sub 'SendNormalPriorityMessages

    End Class 'MyNewQueue
End Namespace 'MyProject
```

```csharp
[C#]
using System;
using System.Messaging;

namespace MyProject
{
    /// <summary>
    /// Provides a container class for the example.
    /// </summary>
    public class MyNewQueue
    {

        //***************************************************
        // Provides an entry point into the application.
        //
        // This example specifies different types of default
        // properties for messages.
        //***************************************************

        public static void Main()
        {
            // Create a new instance of the class.
            MyNewQueue myNewQueue = new MyNewQueue();

            // Send normal and high priority messages.
            myNewQueue.SendNormalPriorityMessages();
            myNewQueue.SendHighPriorityMessages();

            return;
        }

        //***************************************************
        // Associates selected message property values
        // with high priority messages.
        //***************************************************

        public void SendHighPriorityMessages()
        {

            // Connect to a message queue.
            MessageQueue myQueue = new
                MessageQueue(".\\myQueue");

            // Associate selected default property values with high
            // priority messages.
            myQueue.DefaultPropertiesToSend.Priority =
                MessagePriority.High;
            myQueue.DefaultPropertiesToSend.Label =
                "High Priority Message";
            myQueue.DefaultPropertiesToSend.Recoverable = true;
            myQueue.DefaultPropertiesToSend.TimeToReachQueue =
                new TimeSpan(0,0,30);

            // Send messages using these defaults.
            myQueue.Send("High priority message data 1.");
            myQueue.Send("High priority message data 2.");
            myQueue.Send("High priority message data 3.");

            return;
        }

        //***************************************************
        // Associates selected message property values
        // with normal priority messages.
        //***************************************************

        public void SendNormalPriorityMessages()
        {

            // Connect to a message queue.
            MessageQueue myQueue = new MessageQueue(".\\myQueue");

            // Associate selected default property values with normal
            // priority messages.
            myQueue.DefaultPropertiesToSend.Priority =
                MessagePriority.Normal;
            myQueue.DefaultPropertiesToSend.Label =
                "Normal Priority Message";
            myQueue.DefaultPropertiesToSend.Recoverable = false;
            myQueue.DefaultPropertiesToSend.TimeToReachQueue =
                new TimeSpan(0,2,0);

            // Send messages using these defaults.
            myQueue.Send("Normal priority message data 1.");
            myQueue.Send("Normal priority message data 2.");
            myQueue.Send("Normal priority message data 3.");

            return;
        }
    }
}
```

```cpp
[C++]
#using <mscorlib.dll>
#using <system.dll>
#using <system.messaging.dll>

using namespace System;
using namespace System::Messaging;

__gc class MyNewQueue
{
public:
    // Associates selected message property values
    // with high priority messages.
    void SendHighPriorityMessages()
    {
        // Connect to a message queue.
        MessageQueue* myQueue = new MessageQueue(S".\\myQueue");

        // Associate selected default property values with high
        // priority messages.
        myQueue->DefaultPropertiesToSend->Priority =
    MessagePriority::High;
        myQueue->DefaultPropertiesToSend->Label = S"High
    Priority Message";
        myQueue->DefaultPropertiesToSend->Recoverable = true;
        myQueue->DefaultPropertiesToSend->TimeToReachQueue =
    TimeSpan(0, 0, 30);

        // Send messages using these defaults.
        myQueue->Send(S"High priority message data 1.");
        myQueue->Send(S"High priority message data 2.");
        myQueue->Send(S"High priority message data 3.");

        return;
    }

    // Associates selected message property values
    // with normal priority messages.
    void SendNormalPriorityMessages()
    {
        // Connect to a message queue.
        MessageQueue* myQueue = new MessageQueue(S".\\myQueue");

        // Associate selected default property values with normal
        // priority messages.
        myQueue->DefaultPropertiesToSend->Priority =
    MessagePriority::Normal;
        myQueue->DefaultPropertiesToSend->Label = S"Normal Priority
    Message";
        myQueue->DefaultPropertiesToSend->Recoverable = false;
        myQueue->DefaultPropertiesToSend->TimeToReachQueue =
    TimeSpan(0, 2, 0);

        // Send messages using these defaults.
        myQueue->Send(S"Normal priority message data 1.");
        myQueue->Send(S"Normal priority message data 2.");
        myQueue->Send(S"Normal priority message data 3.");
```

```
        return;
    }
};

// Provides an entry point into the application.
// This example specifies different types of default
// properties for messages.
int main()
{
    // Create a new instance of the class.
    MyNewQueue* myNewQueue = new MyNewQueue();

    // Send normal and high priority messages.
    myNewQueue->SendNormalPriorityMessages();
    myNewQueue->SendHighPriorityMessages();

    return 0;
}
```

Requirements

Namespace: System.Messaging

Platforms: Windows 98, Windows NT 4.0,
Windows Millennium Edition, Windows 2000,
Windows XP Home Edition, Windows XP Professional,
Windows .NET Server family

Assembly: System.Messaging (in System.Messaging.dll)

DefaultPropertiesToSend Constructor

Initializes a new instance of the **DefaultPropertiesToSend** class.

```
[Visual Basic]
Public Sub New()
[C#]
public DefaultPropertiesToSend();
[C++]
public: DefaultPropertiesToSend();
[JScript]
public function DefaultPropertiesToSend();
```

Remarks

You can create a new instance of **DefaultPropertiesToSend** to
define default property values to associate with objects sent to a
queue which are not of type **Message**. When working with
MessageQueue objects, a **DefaultPropertiesToSend** instance is
created for you and associated with the
MessageQueue.DefaultPropertiesToSend member of the
MessageQueue.

There are two ways to define a queue's default properties to send, as
shown in the following C# code. You can set values for this instance
of **DefaultPropertiesToSend** and associate it with the queue's
MessageQueue.DefaultPropertiesToSend property:

```
DefaultPropertiesToSend myDefaultProperties = new
DefaultPropertiesToSend();
// Set default values for the properties.
myDefaultProperties.Label = "myLabel";
myDefaultProperties.Recoverable = false;
...
myMessageQueue.DefaultPropertiesToSend = myDefaultProperties;
myMessageQueue.Send("hello");
```

Or, you can individually assign values to the **MessageQueue**
instance's **DefaultPropertiesToSend** property directly:

```
myMessageQueue.DefaultPropertiesToSend.Label = "myLabel";
myMessageQueue.DefaultPropertiesToSend.Recoverable = false;
...
myMessageQueue.Send("hello");
```

If you choose the second of these options, you do not need to call the
ctor constructor explicitly. You might want to create instances of
DefaultPropertiesToSend, for example, if the properties' default
values depend on some criterion of the message being sent. You can
create multiple **DefaultPropertiesToSend** instances and assign one
to the queue's **MessageQueue.DefaultPropertiesToSend** property
before sending the message to the queue.

The following table shows initial property values for an instance of
DefaultPropertiesToSend.

Property	Initial Value
AcknowledgeType	**AcknowledgeTypes.None**
AdministrationQueue	A null reference (**Nothing** in Visual Basic)
AppSpecific	0
AttachSenderId	**true**
EncryptionAlgorithm	**EncryptionAlgorithm.RC2**
Extension	A zero-length array of bytes
HashAlgorithm	**HashAlgorithm.MD5**
Label	An empty string ("")
Priority	**MessagePriority.Normal**
Recoverable	**false**
ResponseQueue	A null reference (**Nothing**)
TimeToBeReceived	**Message.InfiniteTimeout**
TimeToReachQueue	**Message.InfiniteTimeout**
TransactionStatusQueue	A null reference (**Nothing**)
UseAuthentication	**false**
UseDeadLetterQueue	**false**
UseEncryption	**false**
UseJournalQueue	**false**
UseTracing	**false**

Requirements

Platforms: Windows 98, Windows NT 4.0,
Windows Millennium Edition, Windows 2000,
Windows XP Home Edition, Windows XP Professional,
Windows .NET Server family

.NET Framework Security:

- Full trust for the immediate caller. This member cannot be used
  by partially trusted code.

DefaultPropertiesToSend.AcknowledgeType Property

Gets or sets the type of acknowledgement message to be returned to
the sending application.

```
[Visual Basic]
Public Property AcknowledgeType As AcknowledgeTypes
[C#]
public AcknowledgeTypes AcknowledgeType {get; set;}
[C++]
public: __property AcknowledgeTypes get_AcknowledgeType();
public: __property void set_AcknowledgeType(AcknowledgeTypes);
```

```
[JScript]
public function get AcknowledgeType() : AcknowledgeTypes;
public function set AcknowledgeType(AcknowledgeTypes);
```

Property Value

One of the **AcknowledgeTypes** enumeration values. This value is used to determine the type of acknowledgment messages the system posts in the administration queue and when acknowledgments are returned to the sending application. The default is **AcknowledgeTypes.None**.

Remarks

The **AcknowledgeType** property specifies the type of acknowledgment messages to return to the sending application. Set the **AcknowledgeType** property to request, for example, notification when a message reaches its destination, when it is retrieved, or whether a time-out has prevented the message from reaching or being retrieved from the destination queue.

Requirements

Platforms: Windows 98, Windows NT 4.0, Windows Millennium Edition, Windows 2000, Windows XP Home Edition, Windows XP Professional, Windows .NET Server family

.NET Framework Security:
- Full trust for the immediate caller. This member cannot be used by partially trusted code.

DefaultPropertiesToSend.AdministrationQueue Property

Gets or sets the queue that receives acknowledgement messages generated by Message Queuing.

```
[Visual Basic]
Public Property AdministrationQueue As MessageQueue
[C#]
public MessageQueue AdministrationQueue {get; set;}
[C++]
public: _property MessageQueue* get_AdministrationQueue();
public: _property void set_AdministrationQueue(MessageQueue*);
[JScript]
public function get AdministrationQueue() : MessageQueue;
public function set AdministrationQueue(MessageQueue);
```

Property Value

The **MessageQueue** that specifies the administration queue used for system-generated acknowledgment messages. The default is a null reference (**Nothing** in Visual Basic).

Remarks

The queue specified in the **AdministrationQueue** property can be any non-transactional queue. The acknowledgment messages sent to the administration queue can indicate whether or not the original message reached its destination queue, and whether or not it was removed from the queue.

When the **AcknowledgeType** property has any value other than **None**, the sending application must specify the queue to be used as the administration queue.

Requirements

Platforms: Windows 98, Windows NT 4.0, Windows Millennium Edition, Windows 2000,

Windows XP Home Edition, Windows XP Professional, Windows .NET Server family

.NET Framework Security:
- Full trust for the immediate caller. This member cannot be used by partially trusted code.

DefaultPropertiesToSend.AppSpecific Property

Gets or sets additional, application-specific information.

```
[Visual Basic]
Public Property AppSpecific As Integer
[C#]
public int AppSpecific {get; set;}
[C++]
public: _property int get_AppSpecific();
public: _property void set_AppSpecific(int);
[JScript]
public function get AppSpecific() : int;
public function set AppSpecific(int);
```

Property Value

Information specific to the application. The default is 0.

Remarks

The **AppSpecific** property contains additional, application-specific information that can be used to organize different types of messages, for example using application-specific indexes. It is the responsibility of the application to interpret **AppSpecific** information.

Where possible, message data should be included in the body of the message rather than in the **AppSpecific** property.

> **Note** When working with foreign queues, use the **Extension** property to specify non-Message Queuing message properties. As with **AppSpecific**, it is the responsibility of the application to understand the content of the **Extension** property.

Requirements

Platforms: Windows 98, Windows NT 4.0, Windows Millennium Edition, Windows 2000, Windows XP Home Edition, Windows XP Professional, Windows .NET Server family

.NET Framework Security:
- Full trust for the immediate caller. This member cannot be used by partially trusted code.

DefaultPropertiesToSend.AttachSenderId Property

Gets or sets a value indicating whether the sender ID should be attached to the message.

```
[Visual Basic]
Public Property AttachSenderId As Boolean
[C#]
public bool AttachSenderId {get; set;}
[C++]
public: _property bool get_AttachSenderId();
public: _property void set_AttachSenderId(bool);
[JScript]
public function get AttachSenderId() : Boolean;
public function set AttachSenderId(Boolean);
```

Property Value

true if sender ID should be attached to the message; otherwise, **false**. The default is **true**.

Remarks

The sender ID is an array of bytes that represents the identifier of the sending user. The sender ID is set by Message Queuing and is used by the receiving Queue Manager to verify whether the sender has access rights to a queue. The SenderId is only trustworthy if the message was authenticated when it reached the destination queue.

When the sender ID is not attached to the message, the sending application is indicating that Message Queuing should not validate the message's sender when the message is sent to the destination queue. If the destination queue only accepts authenticated messages, and either **UseAuthentication** or **AttachSenderId** is **false**, the message will be rejected when it reaches the queue.

Requirements

Platforms: Windows 98, Windows NT 4.0, Windows Millennium Edition, Windows 2000, Windows XP Home Edition, Windows XP Professional, Windows .NET Server family

.NET Framework Security:
- Full trust for the immediate caller. This member cannot be used by partially trusted code.

DefaultPropertiesToSend.EncryptionAlgorithm Property

Gets or sets the encryption algorithm used to encrypt the body of a private message.

```
[Visual Basic]
Public Property EncryptionAlgorithm As EncryptionAlgorithm
[C#]
public EncryptionAlgorithm EncryptionAlgorithm {get; set;}
[C++]
public: __property EncryptionAlgorithm get_EncryptionAlgorithm();
public: __property void set_EncryptionAlgorithm(EncryptionAlgorithm);
[JScript]
public function get EncryptionAlgorithm() : EncryptionAlgorithm;
public function set EncryptionAlgorithm(EncryptionAlgorithm);
```

Property Value

One of the **EncryptionAlgorithm** enumeration values. The default is **RC2**.

Remarks

If a message is private, it is encrypted before it is sent and is decrypted when it is received. The **EncryptionAlgorithm** property specifies the algorithm used to encrypt the message body of a private message.

A queue can require that incoming messages be encrypted. If a nonencrypted (non-private) message is sent to a queue that only accepts private messages, or if a private message is sent to a queue that only accepts non-private messages, the message is rejected by the queue. The sending application can request a negative acknowledgment message be returned to the sending application if a message was rejected.

Requirements

Platforms: Windows 98, Windows NT 4.0, Windows Millennium Edition, Windows 2000, Windows XP Home Edition, Windows XP Professional, Windows .NET Server family

.NET Framework Security:
- Full trust for the immediate caller. This member cannot be used by partially trusted code.

DefaultPropertiesToSend.Extension Property

Gets or sets additional information associated with the message.

```
[Visual Basic]
Public Property Extension As Byte ()
[C#]
public byte[] Extension {get; set;}
[C++]
public: __property unsigned char get_Extension();
public: __property void set_Extension(unsigned char __gc[]);
[JScript]
public function get Extension() : Byte[];
public function set Extension(Byte[]);
```

Property Value

An array of bytes that provides additional, application-defined information associated with the message. The default is a zero-length array.

Remarks

The **Extension** property provides for additional application-defined information that is associated with the message, such as a large binary object. It is the responsibility of the receiving application to interpret the contents of the **Extension**.

Where possible, message data should be included in the body of the message rather than in the extension.

When working with foreign queues, use the **Extension** property to specify non-Message Queuing message properties.

> **Note** A foreign queue exists in a queuing system other than Microsoft Message Queuing. Microsoft Message Queuing communicates with such queues through a connector application.

Requirements

Platforms: Windows 98, Windows NT 4.0, Windows Millennium Edition, Windows 2000, Windows XP Home Edition, Windows XP Professional, Windows .NET Server family

.NET Framework Security:
- Full trust for the immediate caller. This member cannot be used by partially trusted code.

DefaultPropertiesToSend.HashAlgorithm Property

Gets or sets the hashing algorithm used when authenticating messages or creating a digital signature for a message.

```
[Visual Basic]
Public Property HashAlgorithm As HashAlgorithm
```

```
[C#]
public HashAlgorithm HashAlgorithm {get; set;}
[C++]
public: __property HashAlgorithm get_HashAlgorithm();
public: __property void set_HashAlgorithm(HashAlgorithm);
[JScript]
public function get HashAlgorithm() : HashAlgorithm;
public function set HashAlgorithm(HashAlgorithm);
```

Property Value

One of the **HashAlgorithm** enumeration values. The default is **MD5**.

Remarks

The **HashAlgorithm** property identifies the hashing algorithm Message Queuing uses when authenticating messages or when creating a digital signature for a message.

Message Queuing on the source computer uses the hashing algorithm when creating a digital signature for a message. The target Queue Manager then uses the same hashing algorithm to authenticate the message when it is received.

Requirements

Platforms: Windows 98, Windows NT 4.0, Windows Millennium Edition, Windows 2000, Windows XP Home Edition, Windows XP Professional, Windows .NET Server family

.NET Framework Security:
- Full trust for the immediate caller. This member cannot be used by partially trusted code.

DefaultPropertiesToSend.Label Property

Gets or sets an application-defined string that describes the message.

```
[Visual Basic]
Public Property Label As String
[C#]
public string Label {get; set;}
[C++]
public: __property String* get_Label();
public: __property void set_Label(String*);
[JScript]
public function get Label() : String;
public function set Label(String);
```

Property Value

The label of the message. The default is an empty string ("").

Remarks

A message label can be used for display purposes, for example, or to selectively process messages based on the label value. The maximum length for a message label is 249 Unicode characters. The label does not need to be unique across messages.

Message queue and message labels represent an application-defined value that can help to identify the queue or message in human-readable terms. It is the responsibility of the application to interpret label contents; they have no intrinsic meaning to the Message Queuing application.

Requirements

Platforms: Windows 98, Windows NT 4.0, Windows Millennium Edition, Windows 2000, Windows XP Home Edition, Windows XP Professional, Windows .NET Server family

.NET Framework Security:
- Full trust for the immediate caller. This member cannot be used by partially trusted code.

DefaultPropertiesToSend.Priority Property

Gets or sets the message priority, used to determine where the message is placed in the queue.

```
[Visual Basic]
Public Property Priority As MessagePriority
[C#]
public MessagePriority Priority {get; set;}
[C++]
public: __property MessagePriority get_Priority();
public: __property void set_Priority(MessagePriority);
[JScript]
public function get Priority() : MessagePriority;
public function set Priority(MessagePriority);
```

Property Value

One of the **MessagePriority** enumeration values that represents the priority level of a non-transactional message. The default is **Normal**.

Remarks

The **Priority** property affects how Message Queuing handles the message while it is en route, as well as where the message is placed in the queue when it reaches its destination. Higher priority messages are given preference during routing and inserted toward the front of the queue. Messages with the same priority are placed in the queue according to their arrival time.

Message priority can only be set meaningfully for non-transactional messages. The priority for transactional messages is automatically set to **Lowest**, which causes transactional message priority to be ignored.

Requirements

Platforms: Windows 98, Windows NT 4.0, Windows Millennium Edition, Windows 2000, Windows XP Home Edition, Windows XP Professional, Windows .NET Server family

.NET Framework Security:
- Full trust for the immediate caller. This member cannot be used by partially trusted code.

DefaultPropertiesToSend.Recoverable Property

Gets or sets a value indicating whether the message is guaranteed to be delivered in the event of a computer failure or network problem.

```
[Visual Basic]
Public Property Recoverable As Boolean
[C#]
public bool Recoverable {get; set;}
[C++]
public: __property bool get_Recoverable();
public: __property void set_Recoverable(bool);
```

```
[JScript]
public function get Recoverable() : Boolean;
public function set Recoverable(Boolean);
```

Property Value

true if the message is guaranteed delivery by saving it to disk while en route; **false** if delivery is not assured. The default is **false**.

Remarks

The **Recoverable** property indicates whether delivery of a message is guaranteed, even if a computer crashes while the message is en route to the destination queue.

If delivery of a message is guaranteed, the message is stored locally at every step along the route until the message is successfully forwarded to the next computer. Setting **Recoverable** to **true** on **DefaultPropertiesToSend** could affect the throughput.

If the message is transactional, Message Queuing automatically treats the message as recoverable, regardless of whether **Recoverable** is set to **true**.

Requirements

Platforms: Windows 98, Windows NT 4.0, Windows Millennium Edition, Windows 2000, Windows XP Home Edition, Windows XP Professional, Windows .NET Server family

.NET Framework Security:
- Full trust for the immediate caller. This member cannot be used by partially trusted code.

DefaultPropertiesToSend.ResponseQueue Property

Gets or sets the queue that receives application-generated response messages.

```
[Visual Basic]
Public Property ResponseQueue As MessageQueue
[C#]
public MessageQueue ResponseQueue {get; set;}
[C++]
public: __property MessageQueue* get_ResponseQueue();
public: __property void set_ResponseQueue(MessageQueue*);
[JScript]
public function get ResponseQueue() : MessageQueue;
public function set ResponseQueue(MessageQueue);
```

Property Value

The **MessageQueue** to which application-generated response messages are returned. The default is a null reference (**Nothing** in Visual Basic).

Remarks

The **ResponseQueue** property identifies the queue that receives application-generated response messages that are returned to the sending application by the receiving application. Response queues are specified by the sending application when the application sends its messages. Any available queue can be specified as a response queue.

Messages returned to the response queue are application-specific. The application must define what is in the messages as well as what is to be done when a message is received.

Requirements

Platforms: Windows 98, Windows NT 4.0, Windows Millennium Edition, Windows 2000, Windows XP Home Edition, Windows XP Professional, Windows .NET Server family

.NET Framework Security:
- Full trust for the immediate caller. This member cannot be used by partially trusted code.

DefaultPropertiesToSend.TimeToBeReceived Property

Gets or sets the time limit for the message to be retrieved from the destination queue.

```
[Visual Basic]
Public Property TimeToBeReceived As TimeSpan
[C#]
public TimeSpan TimeToBeReceived {get; set;}
[C++]
public: __property TimeSpan get_TimeToBeReceived();
public: __property void set_TimeToBeReceived(TimeSpan);
[JScript]
public function get TimeToBeReceived() : TimeSpan;
public function set TimeToBeReceived(TimeSpan);
```

Property Value

The total time in seconds for a sent message to be received from the destination queue. The default is **InfiniteTimeout**.

Remarks

The **TimeToBeReceived** property specifies the total time in seconds for a sent message to be received from the destination queue. This time limit includes the time spent getting to the destination queue, plus the time spent waiting in the queue before the message is retrieved by an application.

> **CAUTION** When using dependent client computers, synchronize the clock on the client computer with the clock on the server running Message Queuing. If the two clocks are not synchronized, you might see unpredictable behavior when sending messages when **TimeToBeReceived** is not **InfiniteTimeout**.

If the **TimeToBeReceived** interval expires before the message is removed from the queue, the Message Queuing application discards the message. The message is either sent to the dead-letter queue, if the message's **UseDeadLetterQueue** property is set to **true**, or ignored, if **UseDeadLetterQueue** is **false**. If **TimeToBeReceived** is less than **TimeToReachQueue**, **TimeToBeReceived** takes precedence.

The message's **AcknowledgeType** property can be set to request that Message Queuing send a negative acknowledgment message back to the sending application if the message is not retrieved before the timer expires.

> **CAUTION** If you have specified to receive **TimeToReachQueue** negative acknowledgments, you will not receive them when **TimeToBeReceived** is less than **TimeToReachQueue**.

When several messages are sent in a transaction, Message Queuing uses the value of the first message's **TimeToBeReceived** property.

Requirements

Platforms: Windows 98, Windows NT 4.0,
Windows Millennium Edition, Windows 2000,
Windows XP Home Edition, Windows XP Professional,
Windows .NET Server family

.NET Framework Security:

- Full trust for the immediate caller. This member cannot be used by partially trusted code.

DefaultPropertiesToSend.TimeToReachQueue Property

Gets or sets the time limit for the message to reach the queue.

```
[Visual Basic]
Public Property TimeToReachQueue As TimeSpan
[C#]
public TimeSpan TimeToReachQueue {get; set;}
[C++]
public: __property TimeSpan get_TimeToReachQueue();
public: __property void set_TimeToReachQueue(TimeSpan);
[JScript]
public function get TimeToReachQueue() : TimeSpan;
public function set TimeToReachQueue(TimeSpan);
```

Property Value

The time limit in seconds for a message to reach the destination queue, from the time the message is sent. The default is **InfiniteTimeout**.

Remarks

If the **TimeToReachQueue** interval expires before the message reaches its destination, the Message Queuing application discards the message. The message is either sent to the dead-letter queue, if the message's **UseDeadLetterQueue** property is set to **true**, or ignored, if **UseDeadLetterQueue** is false. If **TimeToReachQueue** is greater than **TimeToBeReceived**, **TimeToBeReceived** takes precedence.

The message's **AcknowledgeType** property can be set to request that Message Queuing send a negative acknowledgment message back to the sending application if the message does not arrive before the timer expires.

If **TimeToReachQueue** is 0 seconds, Message Queuing tries once to send the message to its destination if the queue is waiting for the message. If the queue is local, the message always reaches the queue.

When several messages are sent in a transaction, Message Queuing uses the value of the first message's **TimeToReachQueue** property.

Requirements

Platforms: Windows 98, Windows NT 4.0,
Windows Millennium Edition, Windows 2000,
Windows XP Home Edition, Windows XP Professional,
Windows .NET Server family

.NET Framework Security:

- Full trust for the immediate caller. This member cannot be used by partially trusted code.

DefaultPropertiesToSend.TransactionStatusQueue Property

Gets the transaction status queue on the source computer.

```
[Visual Basic]
Public Property TransactionStatusQueue As MessageQueue
[C#]
public MessageQueue TransactionStatusQueue {get; set;}
[C++]
public: __property MessageQueue* get_TransactionStatusQueue();
public: __property void set_TransactionStatusQueue(MessageQueue*);
[JScript]
public function get TransactionStatusQueue() : MessageQueue;
public function set TransactionStatusQueue(MessageQueue);
```

Property Value

The transaction status queue on the source computer, used for sending acknowledgement messages back to the sending application. The default is a null reference (**Nothing** in Visual Basic).

Remarks

The **TransactionStatusQueue** property identifies the transaction status queue on the source computer. The property is set by Message Queuing, and is used by connector applications when retrieving transactional messages sent to a foreign queue.

> **Note** A foreign queue exists in a queuing system other than Microsoft Message Queuing. Microsoft Message Queuing communicates with such queues through a connector application.

The connector application can use the transaction status queue to send acknowledgment messages back to the sending application. The transaction status queue should receive these acknowledgments even if the sending application does not request other acknowledgments.

Requirements

Platforms: Windows 98, Windows NT 4.0,
Windows Millennium Edition, Windows 2000,
Windows XP Home Edition, Windows XP Professional,
Windows .NET Server family

.NET Framework Security:

- Full trust for the immediate caller. This member cannot be used by partially trusted code.

DefaultPropertiesToSend.UseAuthentication Property

Gets or sets a value indicating whether the message must be authenticated before being sent.

```
[Visual Basic]
Public Property UseAuthentication As Boolean
[C#]
public bool UseAuthentication {get; set;}
[C++]
public: __property bool get_UseAuthentication();
public: __property void set_UseAuthentication(bool);
[JScript]
public function get UseAuthentication() : Boolean;
public function set UseAuthentication(Boolean);
```

Property Value

true if the sending application requested authentication for the message; otherwise, **false**. The default is **false**.

Remarks

The **UseAuthentication** property specifies whether the message needs to be authenticated. If the sending application requests authentication, Message Queuing creates a digital signature and uses it to sign the message when it is sent and to authenticate the message when it is received.

If a message is sent to a queue that only accepts authenticated messages, the message will be rejected when it reaches the queue if **UseAuthentication** is set to **false**.

> **Note** It is not possible to look at the properties of a message and determine whether a message failed authentication. Messages that fail authentication are discarded and are not delivered to the queue.

Requirements

Platforms: Windows 98, Windows NT 4.0, Windows Millennium Edition, Windows 2000, Windows XP Home Edition, Windows XP Professional, Windows .NET Server family

.NET Framework Security:

- Full trust for the immediate caller. This member cannot be used by partially trusted code.

DefaultPropertiesToSend.UseDeadLetterQueue Property

Gets or sets a value indicating whether a copy of the message that could not be delivered should be sent to a dead-letter queue.

```
[Visual Basic]
Public Property UseDeadLetterQueue As Boolean
[C#]
public bool UseDeadLetterQueue {get; set;}
[C++]
public: __property bool get_UseDeadLetterQueue();
public: __property void set_UseDeadLetterQueue(bool);
[JScript]
public function get UseDeadLetterQueue() : Boolean;
public function set UseDeadLetterQueue(Boolean);
```

Property Value

true if message delivery failure should result in a copy of the message being sent to a dead-letter queue; otherwise, **false**. The default is **false**.

Remarks

UseJournalQueue and **UseDeadLetterQueue** specify how Message Queuing will track a message. If **UseDeadLetterQueue** is **true**, then in case of delivery failure (for non-transactional messages), the message is sent to the non-transactional dead-letter queue on the computer that could not deliver the message (for example, if a message timer expires).

In the case of delivery failure for transactional messages, the message is sent to the transactional dead-letter queue on the source computer in all negative and in-doubt cases.

When you store messages in a dead-letter queue, empty the queue periodically to remove messages that are no longer needed. Messages stored in dead-letter queues count against the size quota for the computer where the queue resides. The computer quota is set by the administrator and refers to the total size allocated for storing messages on a computer, not just in a single queue.

> **Note** You do not create a journal or dead-letter queue. These are both system queues that are generated by Message Queuing.

Requirements

Platforms: Windows 98, Windows NT 4.0, Windows Millennium Edition, Windows 2000, Windows XP Home Edition, Windows XP Professional, Windows .NET Server family

.NET Framework Security:

- Full trust for the immediate caller. This member cannot be used by partially trusted code.

DefaultPropertiesToSend.UseEncryption Property

Gets or sets a value indicating whether to make the message private.

```
[Visual Basic]
Public Property UseEncryption As Boolean
[C#]
public bool UseEncryption {get; set;}
[C++]
public: __property bool get_UseEncryption();
public: __property void set_UseEncryption(bool);
[JScript]
public function get UseEncryption() : Boolean;
public function set UseEncryption(Boolean);
```

Property Value

true to require Message Queuing to encrypt the message; otherwise, **false**. The default is **false**.

Remarks

If a message is private, its body is encrypted before it is sent and is decrypted when it is received. To send a private message, the sending application must specify that encryption be used and, optionally, which encryption algorithm to apply.

> **Note** When sending private messages, it is not necessary that your application perform the message encryption. Message Queuing can encrypt the message body for you when your application sends messages within a Microsoft Windows 2000 enterprise where there is access to the directory service. When receiving private messages, it is always the receiving Queue Manager that decrypts the message body.

Requirements

Platforms: Windows 98, Windows NT 4.0, Windows Millennium Edition, Windows 2000, Windows XP Home Edition, Windows XP Professional, Windows .NET Server family

.NET Framework Security:

- Full trust for the immediate caller. This member cannot be used by partially trusted code.

DefaultPropertiesToSend.UseJournalQueue Property

Gets or sets a value indicating whether a copy of the message should be kept in a machine journal on the originating computer.

```
[Visual Basic]
Public Property UseJournalQueue As Boolean
[C#]
public bool UseJournalQueue {get; set;}
[C++]
public: __property bool get_UseJournalQueue();
public: __property void set_UseJournalQueue(bool);
[JScript]
public function get UseJournalQueue() : Boolean;
public function set UseJournalQueue(Boolean);
```

Property Value

true to require that a copy of a message be kept in the originating computer's machine journal after it has been successfully transmitted from the originating computer to the next step; otherwise, **false**. The default is **false**.

Remarks

UseJournalQueue and **UseDeadLetterQueue** specify how Message Queuing will track a message. If **UseJournalQueue** is **true**, then at each step that a message is transmitted, a copy is kept in the computer journal on the originating computer.

> **Note** The sent message will only be copied to the journal queue if the destination queue is on a remote computer. If the destination is on the local computer, the message is sent directly to the queue; there are no intermiediate steps to require journaling.

When you store messages in a journal queue, empty the queue periodically to remove messages that are no longer needed. Messages stored in journal queues count against the quota for the computer where the queue resides (the computer quota is set by the administrator).

> **Note** You do not create a journal or dead-letter queue. These are both system queues that are generated by Message Queuing.

Journaling can be specified by both the message and the queue. When **DefaultPropertiesToSend.UseJournalQueue** is **true**, the message is journaled when it is sent. When **MessageQueue.UseJournalQueue** is **true**, the message is journaled when it is received.

Requirements

Platforms: Windows 98, Windows NT 4.0, Windows Millennium Edition, Windows 2000, Windows XP Home Edition, Windows XP Professional, Windows .NET Server family

.NET Framework Security:

- Full trust for the immediate caller. This member cannot be used by partially trusted code.

DefaultPropertiesToSend.UseTracing Property

Gets or sets a value indicating whether to trace a message as it moves toward its destination queue.

```
[Visual Basic]
Public Property UseTracing As Boolean
[C#]
public bool UseTracing {get; set;}
[C++]
public: __property bool get_UseTracing();
public: __property void set_UseTracing(bool);
[JScript]
public function get UseTracing() : Boolean;
public function set UseTracing(Boolean);
```

Property Value

true if each intermediate step made by the original message en route to the destination queue will generate a report to be sent to the system's report queue; otherwise, **false**. The default is **false**.

Remarks

The **UseTracing** property specifies whether to track the route of a message as it moves toward its destination queue. If **true**, a Message Queuing-generated report message is sent to a report queue each time the message passes through a Message Queuing routing server. The report queue is specified by the source Queue Manager. Report queues are not limited to Message Queuing-generated report messages. Your application-generated messages can be sent to report queues as well.

> **Note** Using tracing involves setting up Active Directory and specifying a report queue for the Message Queuing enterprise. These settings are configured by the administrator.

Requirements

Platforms: Windows 98, Windows NT 4.0, Windows Millennium Edition, Windows 2000, Windows XP Home Edition, Windows XP Professional, Windows .NET Server family

.NET Framework Security:

- Full trust for the immediate caller. This member cannot be used by partially trusted code.

EncryptionAlgorithm Enumeration

Specifies the encryption algorithm used to encrypt the message body of a private message.

```
[Visual Basic]
<Serializable>
Public Enum EncryptionAlgorithm
[C#]
[Serializable]
public enum EncryptionAlgorithm
[C++]
[Serializable]
__value public enum EncryptionAlgorithm
[JScript]
public
    Serializable
enum EncryptionAlgorithm
```

Remarks

Cipher modes define the method in which data is encrypted. The stream cipher mode encodes data one bit at a time. The block cipher mode encodes data one block at a time. Although it tends to execute more slowly than stream cipher, block cipher is more secure. The following table describes the cipher mode for each of the **EncryptionAlgorithm** values.

Encryption	Cipher Mode
RC2	64-bit block
RC4	stream

The Message Queuing message object's property ultimately provides access to operating system encryption levels.

Members

Member name	Description
None	No encryption.
Rc2	The value MQMSG_CALG_RC2. This is the default value for the encryption property of the Message Queuing application's message object.
Rc4	The value MQMSG_CALG_RC4. This corresponds to the less secure option for the encryption property of the Message Queuing application's message object.

Requirements

Namespace: System.Messaging

Platforms: Windows 98, Windows NT 4.0, Windows Millennium Edition, Windows 2000, Windows XP Home Edition, Windows XP Professional, Windows .NET Server family

Assembly: System.Messaging (in System.Messaging.dll)

EncryptionRequired Enumeration

Specifies the privacy level of messages received by the queue.

```
[Visual Basic]
<Serializable>
Public Enum EncryptionRequired
[C#]
[Serializable]
public enum EncryptionRequired
[C++]
[Serializable]
__value public enum EncryptionRequired
[JScript]
public
   Serializable
enum EncryptionRequired
```

Remarks

You can specify whether the queue accepts private (encrypted) messages, nonprivate (nonencrypted) messages, or both.

> **Note** Documentation often refers to nonencrypted messages as **clear**.

Members

Member name	Description
Body	Accepts only private (encrypted) messages.
None	Accepts only nonprivate (nonencrypted) messages.
Optional	Does not force privacy. Accepts private (encrypted) messages and nonprivate (nonencrypted) messages.

Requirements

Namespace: System.Messaging

Platforms: Windows 98, Windows NT 4.0, Windows Millennium Edition, Windows 2000, Windows XP Home Edition, Windows XP Professional, Windows .NET Server family

Assembly: System.Messaging (in System.Messaging.dll)

GenericAccessRights Enumeration

Uses the Windows 2000/Windows NT access format to specify a set of common access rights that Message Queuing maps to both standard and object-specific access rights for reading, writing, and executing.

This enumeration has a **FlagsAttribute** attribute that allows a bitwise combination of its member values.

```
[Visual Basic]
<Flags>
<Serializable>
Public Enum GenericAccessRights
[C#]
[Flags]
[Serializable]
public enum GenericAccessRights
[C++]
[Flags]
[Serializable]
__value public enum GenericAccessRights
[JScript]
public
    Flags
    Serializable
enum GenericAccessRights
```

Remarks

The **GenericAccessRights** enumeration provides less detail in what you can specify, but is typically simpler than specifying all the corresponding standard and specific rights. Each object type can map generic access rights to a set of standard (common to most types of securable objects) and object-specific rights.

For example, giving a user **GenericAccessRights.Read** and **GenericAccessRights.Write** access to a message queue enables sending, peeking, and receiving messages from a queue. However, for finer access rights control, you can use the **StandardAccessRights** and the **MessageQueueAccessRights** enumeration to specify, for example, that a user can peek but not receive messages, can delete queues or messages, or can set queue properties.

Members

Member name	Description	Value
All	Read, write, and execute access.	268435456
Execute	Execute access.	536870912
None	No access.	0
Read	Read access.	-2147483648
Write	Write access.	1073741824

Requirements

Namespace: System.Messaging

Platforms: Windows 98, Windows NT 4.0, Windows Millennium Edition, Windows 2000, Windows XP Home Edition, Windows XP Professional, Windows .NET Server family

Assembly: System.Messaging (in System.Messaging.dll)

HashAlgorithm Enumeration

Specifies the hash algorithm used by Message Queuing when authenticating messages.

```
[Visual Basic]
<Serializable>
Public Enum HashAlgorithm
[C#]
[Serializable]
public enum HashAlgorithm
[C++]
[Serializable]
__value public enum HashAlgorithm
[JScript]
public
   Serializable
enum HashAlgorithm
```

Remarks

Message authentication provides two services. It provides a way to ensure message integrity and a way to verify who sent the message. To request authentication, the sending application must set the authentication level of the message to be authenticated and attach a security certificate to the message.

To authenticate messages, the Message Queuing run-time DLL on the source computer uses a hashing algorithm when creating a digital signature for a message. The target Queue Manager then uses the same hashing algorithm to authenticate the message when it is received.

For more information about the authentication process, see the Message Queuing authentication topics in the MSDN Library at www.msdn.Microsoft.com.

Members

Member name	Description
Mac	MAC keyed hashing algorithm.
Md2	MD2 hashing algorithm.
Md4	MD4 hashing algorithm.
Md5	MD5 hashing algorithm.
None	No hashing algorithm.
Sha	SHA hashing algorithm.

Requirements

Namespace: System.Messaging

Platforms: Windows 98, Windows NT 4.0, Windows Millennium Edition, Windows 2000, Windows XP Home Edition, Windows XP Professional, Windows .NET Server family

Assembly: System.Messaging (in System.Messaging.dll)

IMessageFormatter Interface

Serializes or deserializes objects from the body of a Message Queuing message.

System.ICloneable
   System.Messaging.IMessageFormatter

[Visual Basic]
Public Interface IMessageFormatter
   Inherits ICloneable
[C#]
public interface IMessageFormatter : ICloneable
[C++]
public __gc __interface IMessageFormatter : public ICloneable
[JScript]
public interface IMessageFormatter implements ICloneable

Classes that Implement IMessageFormatter

Class	Description
ActiveXMessage-Formatter	Serializes or deserializes primitive data types and other objects to or from the body of a Message Queuing message, using a format that is compatible with the MSMQ ActiveX Component.
BinaryMessageFormatter	Serializes or deserializes an object, or an entire graph of connected objects, to or from the body of a Message Queuing message, using a binary format.
XmlMessageFormatter	Serializes and deserializes objects to or from the body of a message, using the XML format based on the XSD schema definition.

Remarks

When an application sends a message to the queue using an instance of the **MessageQueue** class, the formatter serializes the object (which can be a instance of any class) into a stream and inserts it into the message body. When reading from a queue using a **MessageQueue**, the formatter deserializes the message data into the **Body** property of a **Message**.

BinaryMessageFormatter and **ActiveXMessageFormatter** provide faster throughput than the **XmlMessageFormatter**. The **ActiveXMessageFormatter** allows interoperability with Visual Basic 6.0 Message Queuing applications. The **XmlMessageFormatter** is loosely coupled, which means that the server and client can version the type that is sent and received independently.

Requirements

Namespace: System.Messaging

Platforms: Windows 98, Windows NT 4.0, Windows Millennium Edition, Windows 2000, Windows XP Home Edition, Windows XP Professional, Windows .NET Server family

Assembly: System.Messaging (in System.Messaging.dll)

IMessageFormatter.CanRead Method

When implemented in a class, determines whether the formatter can deserialize the contents of the message.

[Visual Basic]
Function CanRead(_
   ByVal message As Message _
) As Boolean
[C#]
bool CanRead(
   Message message
);
[C++]
bool CanRead(
   Message* message
);
[JScript]
function CanRead(
   message : Message
) : Boolean;

Parameters

message
   The **Message** to inspect.

Return Value

true if the formatter can deserialize the message; otherwise, **false**.

Requirements

Platforms: Windows 98, Windows NT 4.0, Windows Millennium Edition, Windows 2000, Windows XP Home Edition, Windows XP Professional, Windows .NET Server family

.NET Framework Security:

- Full trust for the immediate caller. This member cannot be used by partially trusted code.

IMessageFormatter.Read Method

When implemented in a class, reads the contents from the given message and creates an object containing data from the message.

[Visual Basic]
Function Read(_
   ByVal message As Message _
) As Object
[C#]
object Read(
   Message message
);
[C++]
Object* Read(
   Message* message
);
[JScript]
function Read(
   message : Message
) : Object;

Parameters

message
   The **Message** to deserialize.

Return Value

The deserialized message.

Remarks

Requirements

Platforms: Windows 98, Windows NT 4.0,
Windows Millennium Edition, Windows 2000,
Windows XP Home Edition, Windows XP Professional,
Windows .NET Server family

.NET Framework Security:

- Full trust for the immediate caller. This member cannot be used
  by partially trusted code.

IMessageFormatter.Write Method

When implemented in a class, serializes an object into the body of
the message.

```
[Visual Basic]
Sub Write( _
   ByVal message As Message, _
   ByVal obj As Object _
)
[C#]
void Write(
   Message message,
   object obj
);
[C++]
void Write(
   Message* message,
   Object* obj
);
[JScript]
function Write(
   message : Message,
   obj : Object
);
```

Parameters

message

   The **Message** that will contain the serialized object.

obj

   The object to be serialized into the message.

Requirements

Platforms: Windows 98, Windows NT 4.0,
Windows Millennium Edition, Windows 2000,
Windows XP Home Edition, Windows XP Professional,
Windows .NET Server family

.NET Framework Security:

- Full trust for the immediate caller. This member cannot be used
  by partially trusted code.

Message Class

Provides access to the properties needed to define a Message Queuing message.

System.Object
  System.MarshalByRefObject
    System.ComponentModel.Component
      System.Messaging.Message

```
[Visual Basic]
Public Class Message
   Inherits Component
[C#]
public class Message : Component
[C++]
public __gc class Message : public Component
[JScript]
public class Message extends Component
```

Thread Safety

Any public static (**Shared** in Visual Basic) members of this type are safe for multithreaded operations. Any instance members are not guaranteed to be thread safe.

Remarks

Use the **Message** class to peek or receive messages from a queue, or to have fine control over message properties when sending a message to a queue.

MessageQueue uses the **Message** class when it peeks or receives messages from queues, because both the **MessageQueue.Peek** and **MessageQueue.Receive** methods create a new instance of the **Message** class and set the instance's properties. The **Message** class's read-only properties apply to retrieving messages from a queue, while the read/write properties apply to sending and retrieving messages.

The **MessageQueue** class's **Send** method allows you to specify any object type for a message being sent to that queue. You can use the **MessageQueue** instance's **DefaultPropertiesToSend** property to specify settings for generic messages sent to the queue. The types of settings include formatter, label, encryption, and authentication. You can also specify values for the appropriate **DefaultPropertiesToSend** members when you coordinate your messaging application to respond to acknowledgment and report messages. Using a **Message** instance to send a message to the queue gives you the flexibility to access and modify many of these properties--either for a single message or on a message-by-message basis. **Message** properties take precedence over **DefaultPropertiesToSend**.

Message data is stored in the **Body** property and to a lesser extent, the **AppSpecific** and **Extension** properties. When message data is encrypted, serialized, or deserialized, only the contents of the **Body** property are affected.

The contents of the **Body** property are serialized when the message is sent, using the **Formatter** property you specify. The serialized contents are found in the **BodyStream** property . You can also set the **BodyStream** property directly, for example, to send a file as the data content of a message. You can change the **Body** or **Formatter** properties at any time before sending the message, and the data will be serialized appropriately when you call **Send**.

The properties defined by the **MessageQueue.DefaultPropertiesToSend** property apply only to messages that are not of type **Message**. If you specify the **DefaultPropertiesToSend** property for a

MessageQueue, the identically-named properties in a **Message** instance sent to that queue cause these default properties to be ignored.

For a list of initial property values for an instance of **Message**, see the **Message** constructor.

Requirements

Namespace: System.Messaging

Platforms: Windows 98, Windows NT 4.0, Windows Millennium Edition, Windows 2000, Windows XP Home Edition, Windows XP Professional, Windows .NET Server family

Assembly: System.Messaging (in System.Messaging.dll)

Message Constructor

Initializes a new instance of the **Message** class.

Overload List

Initializes a new instance of the **Message** class with an empty body.

  [Visual Basic] **Public Sub New()**
  [C#] **public Message();**
  [C++] **public: Message();**
  [JScript] **public function Message();**

Initializes a new instance of the **Message** class, using the **XmlMessageFormatter** to serialize the specified object into the body of the message.

  [Visual Basic] **Public Sub New(Object)**
  [C#] **public Message(object);**
  [C++] **public: Message(Object*);**
  [JScript] **public function Message(Object);**

Initializes a new instance of the **Message** class, using the specified formatter to serialize the specified object into the body of the message.

  [Visual Basic] **Public Sub New(Object, IMessageFormatter)**
  [C#] **public Message(object, IMessageFormatter);**
  [C++] **public: Message(Object*, IMessageFormatter*);**
  [JScript] **public function Message(Object, IMessageFormatter);**

Example

[Visual Basic, C#, C++] The following example creates a new queue, sends a message containing an order to it and then retreives it.

[Visual Basic, C#, C++] **Note** This example shows how to use one of the overloaded versions of the **Message** constructor. For other examples that might be available, see the individual overload topics.

```
[Visual Basic]
Imports System
Imports System.Messaging
Imports System.Drawing
Imports System.IO

Namespace MyProject
    _

    ' The following example
    ' sends to a queue and receives from a queue.
    Public Class Order
        Public orderId As Integer
```

```vb
        Public orderTime As DateTime
End Class 'Order
_

'/ <summary>
'/ Provides a container class for the example.
'/ </summary>
Public Class MyNewQueue

    '**************************************************
    ' Provides an entry point into the application.
    '
    ' This example sends and receives a message from
    ' a queue.
    '**************************************************
    Public Shared Sub Main()
        ' Create a new instance of the class.
        Dim myNewQueue As New MyNewQueue()

        ' Create a queue on the local computer.
        CreateQueue(".\myQueue")

        ' Send a message to a queue.
        myNewQueue.SendMessage()

        ' Receive a message from a queue.
        myNewQueue.ReceiveMessage()

        Return
    End Sub 'Main

    '**************************************************
    ' Creates a new queue.
    '**************************************************
    Public Shared Sub CreateQueue(queuePath As String)
        Try
            If Not MessageQueue.Exists(queuePath) Then
                MessageQueue.Create(queuePath)
            Else
                Console.WriteLine((queuePath + " already exists."))
            End If
        Catch e As MessageQueueException
            Console.WriteLine(e.Message)
        End Try
    End Sub 'CreateQueue

    '**************************************************
    ' Sends an Order to a queue.
    '**************************************************
    Public Sub SendMessage()
        Try

            ' Create a new order and set values.
            Dim sentOrder As New Order()
            sentOrder.orderId = 3
            sentOrder.orderTime = DateTime.Now

            ' Connect to a queue on the local computer.
            Dim myQueue As New MessageQueue(".\myQueue")

            ' Create the new order.
            Dim myMessage As New Message(sentOrder)

            ' Send the order to the queue.
            myQueue.Send(myMessage)
        Catch e As ArgumentException
            Console.WriteLine(e.Message)
        End Try

        Return
    End Sub 'SendMessage

    '**************************************************
    ' Receives a message containing an order.
    '**************************************************
```

```vb
    Public Sub ReceiveMessage()
        ' Connect to the a queue on the local computer.
        Dim myQueue As New MessageQueue(".\myQueue")

        ' Set the formatter to indicate body contains an Order.
        myQueue.Formatter = New XmlMessageFormatter _
(New Type() {GetType(MyProject.Order)})

        Try
            ' Receive and format the message.
            Dim myMessage As Message = myQueue.Receive()
            Dim myOrder As Order = CType(myMessage.Body, Order)

            ' Display message information.
            Console.WriteLine(("Order ID: " + _
myOrder.orderId.ToString()))
            Console.WriteLine(("Sent: " + _
myOrder.orderTime.ToString()))

        Catch
        ' Handle Message Queuing exceptions.

        ' Handle invalid serialization format.
        Catch e As InvalidOperationException
            Console.WriteLine(e.Message)
        End Try

        ' Catch other exceptions as necessary.
        Return
    End Sub 'ReceiveMessage
End Class 'MyNewQueue
End Namespace 'MyProject
```

[C#]
```csharp
using System;
using System.Messaging;
using System.Drawing;
using System.IO;

namespace MyProject
{

    // The following example
    // sends to a queue and receives from a queue.
    public class Order
    {
        public int orderId;
        public DateTime orderTime;
    };

    /// <summary>
    /// Provides a container class for the example.
    /// </summary>
    public class MyNewQueue
    {

        //**************************************************
        // Provides an entry point into the application.
        //
        // This example sends and receives a message from
        // a queue.
        //**************************************************

        public static void Main()
        {
            // Create a new instance of the class.
            MyNewQueue myNewQueue = new MyNewQueue();

            // Create a queue on the local computer.
            CreateQueue(".\\myQueue");

            // Send a message to a queue.
            myNewQueue.SendMessage();
```

```
        // Receive a message from a queue.
        myNewQueue.ReceiveMessage();

        return;
    }

//**************************************************
// Creates a new queue.
//**************************************************

public static void CreateQueue(string queuePath)
{
    try
    {
        if(!MessageQueue.Exists(queuePath))
        {
            MessageQueue.Create(queuePath);
        }
        else
        {
            Console.WriteLine(queuePath + " already exists.");
        }
    }
    catch (MessageQueueException e)
    {
        Console.WriteLine(e.Message);
    }

}

//**************************************************
// Sends an Order to a queue.
//**************************************************

public void SendMessage()
{
    try
    {

        // Create a new order and set values.
        Order sentOrder = new Order();
        sentOrder.orderId = 3;
        sentOrder.orderTime = DateTime.Now;

        // Connect to a queue on the local computer.
        MessageQueue myQueue = new MessageQueue(".\\myQueue");

        // Create the new order.
        Message myMessage = new Message(sentOrder);

        // Send the order to the queue.
        myQueue.Send(myMessage);
    }
    catch(ArgumentException e)
    {
        Console.WriteLine(e.Message);

    }

    return;
}

//**************************************************
// Receives a message containing an order.
//**************************************************

public  void ReceiveMessage()
{
    // Connect to the a queue on the local computer.
    MessageQueue myQueue = new MessageQueue(".\\myQueue");

    // Set the formatter to indicate body contains an Order.
    myQueue.Formatter = new XmlMessageFormatter(new Type[]
        {typeof(MyProject.Order)});
```

```
    try
    {
        // Receive and format the message.
        Message myMessage =    myQueue.Receive();
        Order myOrder = (Order)myMessage.Body;

        // Display message information.
        Console.WriteLine("Order ID: " +
            myOrder.orderId.ToString());
        Console.WriteLine("Sent: " +
            myOrder.orderTime.ToString());
    }

    catch (MessageQueueException)
    {
        // Handle Message Queuing exceptions.
    }

        // Handle invalid serialization format.
    catch (InvalidOperationException e)
    {
        Console.WriteLine(e.Message);
    }

    // Catch other exceptions as necessary.

        return;
    }
  }
}

[C++]
#using <mscorlib.dll>
#using <system.dll>
#using <system.messaging.dll>
#using <system.drawing.dll>

using namespace System;
using namespace System::Messaging;
using namespace System::Drawing;
using namespace System::IO;

__gc class Order
{
public:
    int orderId;
public:
    DateTime orderTime;
};

__gc class MyNewQueue
{
public:
    static void CreateQueue(String* queuePath)
    {
        try
        {
            if (!MessageQueue::Exists(queuePath))
            {
                MessageQueue::Create(queuePath);
            }
            else
            {
                Console::WriteLine("{0} already exists.", queuePath );
            }
        }
        catch (MessageQueueException* e)
        {
            Console::WriteLine(e->Message);
        }
    }

public:
    void SendMessage()
    {
```

```
        try
        {
            // Create a new order and set values.
            Order* sentOrder = new Order();
            sentOrder->orderId = 3;
            sentOrder->orderTime = DateTime::Now;

            // Connect to a queue on the local computer.
            MessageQueue* myQueue = new MessageQueue(S".\\myQueue");

            // Create the new order.
            Message* myMessage = new Message(sentOrder);

            // Send the order to the queue.
            myQueue->Send(myMessage);
        }
        catch (ArgumentException* e)
        {
            Console::WriteLine(e->Message);

        }
        return;
    }
public:
    void ReceiveMessage()
    {
        // Connect to the a queue on the local computer.
        MessageQueue* myQueue = new MessageQueue(S".\\myQueue");

        // Set the formatter to indicate body contains an Order.
        Type* p __gc[] = new Type*[1];
        p[0] = __typeof(Order);
        myQueue->Formatter = new XmlMessageFormatter( p );

        try
        {
            // Receive and format the message.
            Message* myMessage = myQueue->Receive();
            Order* myOrder = dynamic_cast<Order*>(myMessage->Body);

            // Display message information.
            Console::WriteLine(S"Order ID: {0}", __box(myOrder-
>orderId));
            Console::WriteLine(S"Sent: {0}", __box(myOrder-
>orderTime));
        }
        catch (MessageQueueException*)
        {
            // Handle Message Queuing exceptions.
        }
        // Handle invalid serialization format.
        catch (InvalidOperationException* e)
        {
            Console::WriteLine(e->Message);
        }
        // Catch other exceptions as necessary.

        return;
    }
};

int main()
{
    // Create a new instance of the class.
    MyNewQueue* myNewQueue = new MyNewQueue();

    // Create a queue on the local computer.
    MyNewQueue::CreateQueue(S".\\myQueue");

    // Send a message to a queue.
    myNewQueue->SendMessage();

    // Receive a message from a queue.
    myNewQueue->ReceiveMessage();

    return 0;
}
```

Message Constructor ()

Initializes a new instance of the **Message** class with an empty body.

```
[Visual Basic]
Public Sub New()
[C#]
public Message();
[C++]
public: Message();
[JScript]
public function Message();
```

Remarks

Use this overload to create a new instance of the **Message** class that has an empty body.

Specify either the **Body** property or the **BodyStream** property before sending the **Message** object. The **Body** property can be any object that can be serialized, such as a text string, a structure object, a class instance, or an embedded object.

Unless you write the contents of the message directly to the **BodyStream** property, set the **Formatter** property before you send the message. The body is serialized using the **Formatter** property's value at the time the **Send** method is called on the **MessageQueue** instance.

The **XmlMessageFormatter** is loosely coupled, so it is not necessary to have the same object type on the sender and receiver when using this format. The **ActiveXMessageFormatter** and **BinaryMessageFormatter** serialize the data into binary representation. The **ActiveXMessageFormatter** is used when sending or receiving COM components.

The following table shows initial property values for an instance of **Message**.

Property	Initial Value
AcknowledgeType	**AcknowledgeType.None**
AdministrationQueue	A null reference (**Nothing** in Visual Basic)
AppSpecific	0
AttachSenderId	**true**
AuthenticationProviderName	Microsoft Base Cryptographic Provider, Ver. 1.0
AuthenticationProviderType	**CryptoProviderType.RSA_FULL**
Body	A null reference (**Nothing**)
BodyStream	**Stream.null**
BodyType	0
ConnectorType	**Guid.Empty**
CorrelationId	An empty string, ("")
DestinationSymmetricKey	A zero-length array of bytes
DigitalSignature	A zero-length array of bytes
EncryptionAlgorithm	**EncryptionAlgorithm.RC2**
Extension	A zero-length array of bytes
Formatter	**XmlMessageFormatter**
HashAlgorithm	**HashAlgorithm.MD5**
Label	An empty string, ("")
Priority	**MessagePriority.Normal**
Recoverable	**false**

Property	Initial Value
ResponseQueue	A null reference (**Nothing**)
SenderCertificate	A zero-length array of bytes
TimeToBeReceived	**Message.InfiniteTimeout**
TimeToReachQueue	**Message.InfiniteTimeout**
TransactionStatusQueue	A null reference (**Nothing**)
UseAuthentication	**false**
UseDeadLetterQueue	**false**
UseEncryption	**false**
UseJournalQueue	**false**
UseTracing	**false**

Example

[Visual Basic, C#, C++] The following example sends 2 messages of different priorities to the queue, and retrieves them subsequently.

[Visual Basic]

```vb
Imports System
Imports System.Messaging

Namespace MyProject

    '/ <summary>
    '/ Provides a container class for the example.
    '/ </summary>
    Public Class MyNewQueue

        '****************************************************
        ' Provides an entry point into the application.
        '
        ' This example sends and receives a message from
        ' a queue.
        '****************************************************
        Public Shared Sub Main()
            ' Create a new instance of the class.
            Dim myNewQueue As New MyNewQueue()

            ' Send messages to a queue.
            myNewQueue.SendMessage(MessagePriority.Normal, _
        "First Message Body.")
            myNewQueue.SendMessage(MessagePriority.Highest, _
        "Second Message Body.")

            ' Receive messages from a queue.
            myNewQueue.ReceiveMessage()
            myNewQueue.ReceiveMessage()

            Return
        End Sub 'Main

        '****************************************************
        ' Sends a string message to a queue.
        '****************************************************
        Public Sub SendMessage(priority As MessagePriority, _
        messageBody As String)

            ' Connect to a queue on the local computer.
            Dim myQueue As New MessageQueue(".\myQueue")

            ' Create a new message.
            Dim myMessage As New Message()

            If priority > MessagePriority.Normal Then
                myMessage.Body = "High Priority: " + messageBody
            Else
                myMessage.Body = messageBody
            End If
```

```vb
            ' Set the priority of the message.
            myMessage.Priority = priority

            ' Send the Order to the queue.
            myQueue.Send(myMessage)

            Return
        End Sub 'SendMessage

        '****************************************************
        ' Receives a message.
        '****************************************************
        Public Sub ReceiveMessage()
            ' Connect to a queue on the local computer.
            Dim myQueue As New MessageQueue(".\myQueue")

            ' Set the queue to read the priority. By default, it
            ' is not read.
            myQueue.MessageReadPropertyFilter.Priority = True

            ' Set the formatter to indicate body contains a string.
            myQueue.Formatter = New XmlMessageFormatter _
        (New Type() {GetType(String)})

            Try
                ' Receive and format the message.
                Dim myMessage As Message = myQueue.Receive()

                ' Display message information.
                Console.WriteLine(("Priority: " + _
        myMessage.Priority.ToString()))
                Console.WriteLine(("Body: " + myMessage.Body.ToString()))

            Catch
                ' Handle Message Queuing exceptions.

                ' Handle invalid serialization format.
            Catch e As InvalidOperationException
                Console.WriteLine(e.Message)
            End Try

                ' Catch other exceptions as necessary.
            Return
        End Sub 'ReceiveMessage
    End Class 'MyNewQueue
End Namespace 'MyProject
```

[C#]

```csharp
using System;
using System.Messaging;

namespace MyProject
{

    /// <summary>
    /// Provides a container class for the example.
    /// </summary>
    public class MyNewQueue
    {

        //****************************************************
        // Provides an entry point into the application.
        //
        // This example sends and receives a message from
        // a queue.
        //****************************************************

        public static void Main()
        {
            // Create a new instance of the class.
            MyNewQueue myNewQueue = new MyNewQueue();

            // Send messages to a queue.
            myNewQueue.SendMessage(MessagePriority.Normal,
```

```
"First Message Body.");
        myNewQueue.SendMessage(MessagePriority.Highest,      ⌐
"Second Message Body.");

        // Receive messages from a queue.
        myNewQueue.ReceiveMessage();
        myNewQueue.ReceiveMessage();

        return;
    }

    //**************************************************
    // Sends a string message to a queue.
    //**************************************************

    public void SendMessage(MessagePriority priority, string   ⌐
messageBody)
    {

        // Connect to a queue on the local computer.
        MessageQueue myQueue = new MessageQueue(".\\myQueue");

        // Create a new message.
        Message myMessage = new Message();

        if(priority > MessagePriority.Normal)
        {
            myMessage.Body = "High Priority: " + messageBody;
        }
        else myMessage.Body = messageBody;

        // Set the priority of the message.
        myMessage.Priority = priority;

        // Send the Order to the queue.
        myQueue.Send(myMessage);

        return;
    }

    //**************************************************
    // Receives a message.
    //**************************************************

    public  void ReceiveMessage()
    {
        // Connect to the a queue on the local computer.
        MessageQueue myQueue = new MessageQueue(".\\myQueue");

        // Set the queue to read the priority. By default, it
        // is not read.
        myQueue.MessageReadPropertyFilter.Priority = true;

        // Set the formatter to indicate body contains a string.
        myQueue.Formatter = new XmlMessageFormatter(new Type[]
            {typeof(string)});

        try
        {
            // Receive and format the message.
            Message myMessage =    myQueue.Receive();

            // Display message information.
            Console.WriteLine("Priority: " +
                myMessage.Priority.ToString());
            Console.WriteLine("Body: " +
                myMessage.Body.ToString());
        }

        catch (MessageQueueException)
        {
            // Handle Message Queuing exceptions.
        }
```

```
            // Handle invalid serialization format.
            catch (InvalidOperationException e)
            {
                Console.WriteLine(e.Message);
            }

            // Catch other exceptions as necessary.

            return;
        }
    }
}

[C++]
#using <mscorlib.dll>
#using <system.dll>
#using <system.messaging.dll>

using namespace System;
using namespace System::Messaging;

__gc class MyNewQueue
{
public:
    void SendMessage(MessagePriority priority, String* messageBody)
    {

        // Connect to a queue on the local computer.
        MessageQueue* myQueue = new MessageQueue(S".\\myQueue");

        // Create a new message.
        Message* myMessage = new Message();

        if (priority > MessagePriority::Normal)
        {
            myMessage->Body = S"High Priority: {0}", messageBody;
        }
        else myMessage->Body = messageBody;

        // Set the priority of the message.
        myMessage->Priority = priority;

        // Send the Order to the queue.
        myQueue->Send(myMessage);

        return;
    }

public:
    void ReceiveMessage()
    {
        // Connect to the a queue on the local computer.
        MessageQueue* myQueue = new MessageQueue(S".\\myQueue");

        // Set the queue to read the priority. By default, it
        // is not read.
        myQueue->MessageReadPropertyFilter->Priority = true;

        // Set the formatter to indicate body contains a String*.
        Type* p __gc[] = new Type* __gc[1];
        p[0] = __typeof(String);
        myQueue->Formatter = new XmlMessageFormatter( p );

        try
        {
            // Receive and format the message.
            Message* myMessage = myQueue->Receive();

            // Display message information.
            Console::WriteLine(S"Priority: {0}", __box    ⌐
(myMessage->Priority));
            Console::WriteLine(S"Body: {0}", myMessage->Body);
        }
        catch (MessageQueueException*)
        {
```

```
        // Handle Message Queuing exceptions.
    }

    // Handle invalid serialization format.
    catch (InvalidOperationException* e)
    {
        Console::WriteLine(e->Message);
    }
    // Catch other exceptions as necessary.

    return;
    }
};

int main()
{
    // Create a new instance of the class.
    MyNewQueue* myNewQueue = new MyNewQueue();

    // Send messages to a queue.
    myNewQueue->SendMessage(MessagePriority::Normal,
S"First Message Body.");
    myNewQueue->SendMessage(MessagePriority::Highest,
S"Second Message Body.");

    // Receive messages from a queue.
    myNewQueue->ReceiveMessage();
    myNewQueue->ReceiveMessage();

    return 0;
}
```

Requirements

Platforms: Windows 98, Windows NT 4.0,
Windows Millennium Edition, Windows 2000,
Windows XP Home Edition, Windows XP Professional,
Windows .NET Server family

.NET Framework Security:

• Full trust for the immediate caller. This member cannot be used
  by partially trusted code.

Message Constructor (Object)

Initializes a new instance of the **Message** class, using the
XmlMessageFormatter to serialize the specified object into the
body of the message.

```
[Visual Basic]
Public Sub New( _
    ByVal body As Object _
)
[C#]
public Message(
    object body
);
[C++]
public: Message(
    Object* body
);
[JScript]
public function Message(
    body : Object
);
```

Parameters

body
    The object to be serialized into the body of the message.

Remarks

Use this overload to create a new instance of the **Message** class that
contains the **Body** specified by the *body* parameter. The *body*
parameter can be any object that can be serialized, such as a text
string, a structure object, a class instance, or an embedded object.
The body is serialized using the **XmlMessageFormatter** unless you
change the **Formatter** property before the **Message** is sent. If you
change the **Body** or **Formatter** property at any time before calling
Send, the message will be serialized according to the new property
value.

The **XmlMessageFormatter** is loosely coupled, so it is not
necessary to have the same object type on the sender and receiver
when using this format. The **ActiveXMessageFormatter** and
BinaryMessageFormatter serialize the data into binary
representation. The **ActiveXMessageFormatter** is used when
sending or receiving COM components.

The following table shows initial property values for an instance of
Message.

Property	Initial Value
AcknowledgeType	**AcknowledgeType.None**
AdministrationQueue	A null reference (**Nothing** in Visual Basic)
AppSpecific	0
AttachSenderId	**true**
AuthenticationProviderName	Microsoft Base Cryptographic Provider, Ver. 1.0
AuthenticationProviderType	**CryptoProviderType.RSA_FULL**
Body	The *body* parameter.
BodyStream	**Stream.null**
BodyType	0
ConnectorType	**Guid.Empty**
CorrelationId	An empty string, ("")
DestinationSymmetricKey	A zero-length array of bytes
DigitalSignature	A zero-length array of bytes
EncryptionAlgorithm	**EncryptionAlgorithm.RC2**
Extension	A zero-length array of bytes
Formatter	**XmlMessageFormatter**
HashAlgorithm	**HashAlgorithm.MD5**
Label	An empty string, ("")
Priority	**MessagePriority.Normal**
Recoverable	**false**
ResponseQueue	A null reference (**Nothing**)
SenderCertificate	A zero-length array of bytes
TimeToBeReceived	**Message.InfiniteTimeout**
TimeToReachQueue	**Message.InfiniteTimeout**
TransactionStatusQueue	A null reference (**Nothing**)
UseAuthentication	**false**
UseDeadLetterQueue	**false**
UseEncryption	**false**
UseJournalQueue	**false**
UseTracing	**false**

Example

See related example in the **System.Messaging.Message** constructor topic.

Requirements

Platforms: Windows 98, Windows NT 4.0, Windows Millennium Edition, Windows 2000, Windows XP Home Edition, Windows XP Professional, Windows .NET Server family

.NET Framework Security:
- Full trust for the immediate caller. This member cannot be used by partially trusted code.

Message Constructor (Object, IMessageFormatter)

Initializes a new instance of the **Message** class, using the specified formatter to serialize the specified object into the body of the message.

```
[Visual Basic]
Public Sub New( _
    ByVal body As Object, _
    ByVal formatter As IMessageFormatter _
)
[C#]
public Message(
    object body,
    IMessageFormatter formatter
);
[C++]
public: Message(
    Object* body,
    IMessageFormatter* formatter
);
[JScript]
public function Message(
    body : Object,
    formatter : IMessageFormatter
);
```

Parameters

body
    The object to be serialized into the body of the message.
formatter
    An **IMessageFormatter** that specifies the formatter with which to serialize the message body.

Remarks

Use this overload to create a new instance of the **Message** class that contains the **Body** specified by the *body* parameter and that uses any valid formatter to serialize the body. The *body* parameter is any object that can be serialized, such as a text string, a structure object, a class instance, or an embedded object. If you change the **Body** or **Formatter** property at any time before calling **Send**, the message will be serialized according to the new property value.

The **XmlMessageFormatter** is loosely coupled, so it is not necessary to have the same object type on the sender and receiver when using this format. The **ActiveXMessageFormatter** and **BinaryMessageFormatter** serialize the data into binary representation. The **ActiveXMessageFormatter** is used when sending or receiving COM components.

The following table shows initial property values for an instance of **Message**.

Property	Initial Value
AcknowledgeType	AcknowledgeType.None
AdministrationQueue	A null reference (**Nothing** in Visual Basic)
AppSpecific	0
AttachSenderId	true
AuthenticationProviderName	Microsoft Base Cryptographic Provider, Ver. 1.0
AuthenticationProviderType	CryptoProviderType.RSA_FULL
Body	The *body* parameter.
BodyStream	Stream.null
BodyType	0
ConnectorType	Guid.Empty
CorrelationId	An empty string, ("")
DestinationSymmetricKey	A zero-length array of bytes
DigitalSignature	A zero-length array of bytes
EncryptionAlgorithm	EncryptionAlgorithm.RC2
Extension	A zero-length array of bytes
Formatter	The *formatter* parameter.
HashAlgorithm	HashAlgorithm.MD5
Label	An empty string, ("")
Priority	MessagePriority.Normal
Recoverable	false
ResponseQueue	A null reference (**Nothing**)
SenderCertificate	A zero-length array of bytes
TimeToBeReceived	Message.InfiniteTimeout
TimeToReachQueue	Message.InfiniteTimeout
TransactionStatusQueue	A null reference (**Nothing**)
UseAuthentication	false
UseDeadLetterQueue	false
UseEncryption	false
UseJournalQueue	false
UseTracing	false

Requirements

Platforms: Windows 98, Windows NT 4.0, Windows Millennium Edition, Windows 2000, Windows XP Home Edition, Windows XP Professional, Windows .NET Server family

.NET Framework Security:
- Full trust for the immediate caller. This member cannot be used by partially trusted code.

Message.InfiniteTimeout Field

Specifies that no timeout exists.

```
[Visual Basic]
Public Shared ReadOnly InfiniteTimeout As TimeSpan
[C#]
public static readonly TimeSpan InfiniteTimeout;
```

```
[C++]
public: static TimeSpan InfiniteTimeout;
[JScript]
public static var InfiniteTimeout : TimeSpan;
```

Remarks

TimeToBeReceived and **TimeToReachQueue** require a value that specifies a timeout. For the former, the timeout is the maximum time allowed for a message to be received from the queue. For the latter, the timeout is the time allowed for a message to to reach the queue. In both cases, you can specify the timeout as a number of seconds or use **InfiniteTimeout** to indicate that no timeout exists.

Requirements

Platforms: Windows 98, Windows NT 4.0, Windows Millennium Edition, Windows 2000, Windows XP Home Edition, Windows XP Professional, Windows .NET Server family

Message.AcknowledgeType Property

Gets or sets the type of acknowledgment message to be returned to the sending application.

```
[Visual Basic]
Public Property AcknowledgeType As AcknowledgeTypes
[C#]
public AcknowledgeTypes AcknowledgeType {get; set;}
[C++]
public: __property AcknowledgeTypes get_AcknowledgeType();
public: __property void set_AcknowledgeType(AcknowledgeTypes);
[JScript]
public function get AcknowledgeType() : AcknowledgeTypes;
public function set AcknowledgeType(AcknowledgeTypes);
```

Property Value

One of the **AcknowledgeTypes** values, which represent both the types of acknowledgment messages the system posts in the administration queue and the conditions under which acknowledgments are returned to the sending application. The default is **None**.

Exceptions

Exception Type	Condition
InvalidOperation-Exception	The message is filtered to ignore the **AcknowledgeType** property.

Remarks

The **AcknowledgeType** property specifies the type of acknowledgment messages requested by the sending application. Set the **AcknowledgeType** property before sending the message to request notification of certain occurrences--for example, a message reaching its destination queue, a message being retrieved, or a timeout preventing a message from reaching or being retrieved from the destination queue.

Message Queuing returns notification by sending acknowledgment messages to the **AdministrationQueue** property specified by the original message. An acknowledgment message's **Acknowledgment** property indicates the type of acknowledgment that it represents. For example, if an acknowledgment message was sent because a message did not reach the destination before the **TimeToReachQueue** interval expired, the **Acknowledgment** property of the acknowledgment message would contain the value **ReachQueueTimeout**.

Example

See related example in the **System.Messaging.Message** constructor topic.

Requirements

Platforms: Windows 98, Windows NT 4.0, Windows Millennium Edition, Windows 2000, Windows XP Home Edition, Windows XP Professional, Windows .NET Server family

.NET Framework Security:

- Full trust for the immediate caller. This member cannot be used by partially trusted code.

Message.Acknowledgment Property

Gets the classification of acknowledgment that this message represents.

```
[Visual Basic]
Public ReadOnly Property Acknowledgment As Acknowledgment
[C#]
public Acknowledgment Acknowledgment {get;}
[C++]
public: __property Acknowledgment get_Acknowledgment();
[JScript]
public function get Acknowledgment() : Acknowledgment;
```

Property Value

One of the **Acknowledgment** enumeration values.

Exceptions

Exception Type	Condition
InvalidOperation-Exception	The message has not been sent. This property can only be read on messages retrieved from a queue. -or- The message queue is filtered to ignore the **Acknowledgment** property.

Remarks

When you receive a message from an administration queue, read the **Acknowledgment** property to verify the status of the original message.

When a message is sent to its destination queue, Message Queuing can be requested to post an acknowledgment message. Such a message can indicate, for example, whether the message arrived and was retrieved within specified timeouts, or it can indicate what went wrong in the case of delivery failure. The destination queue returns acknowledgment messages and posts them to the administration queue specified in the original message's **AdministrationQueue** property. The **Id** property of an acknowledgment message identifies the acknowledgment message--not the original message. You can find the identifier of the original message in the acknowledgment **Message** instance's **CorrelationId** property.

If this **Message** instance represents an acknowledgment message, the **Acknowledgment** property specifies the type of acknowledgment. Otherwise, the **Acknowledgment** property contains the value **Normal**.

Use the **AcknowledgeType** property of the original message to specify the circumstances under which acknowledgments will be returned.

Requirements

Platforms: Windows 98, Windows NT 4.0,
Windows Millennium Edition, Windows 2000,
Windows XP Home Edition, Windows XP Professional,
Windows .NET Server family

.NET Framework Security:

- Full trust for the immediate caller. This member cannot be used by partially trusted code.

Message.AdministrationQueue Property

Gets or sets the queue that receives the acknowledgement messages that Message Queuing generates.

```
[Visual Basic]
Public Property AdministrationQueue As MessageQueue
[C#]
public MessageQueue AdministrationQueue {get; set;}
[C++]
public: __property MessageQueue* get_AdministrationQueue();
public: __property void set_AdministrationQueue(MessageQueue*);
[JScript]
public function get AdministrationQueue() : MessageQueue;
public function set AdministrationQueue(MessageQueue);
```

Property Value

The **MessageQueue** that specifies the administration queue used for system-generated acknowledgment messages. The default is a null reference (**Nothing** in Visual Basic).

Exceptions

Exception Type	Condition
InvalidOperation-Exception	The message queue is filtered to ignore the **AdministrationQueue** property.

Remarks

The queue specified in the **AdministrationQueue** property can be any non-transactional queue. The acknowledgment messages sent to the administration queue can indicate whether the original message reached its destination queue and whether it was removed from the queue.

When the **AcknowledgeType** property has any value other than **None**, the sending application must specify the queue to use as the administration queue.

Example

See related example in the **System.Messaging.Message** constructor topic.

Requirements

Platforms: Windows 98, Windows NT 4.0,
Windows Millennium Edition, Windows 2000,
Windows XP Home Edition, Windows XP Professional,
Windows .NET Server family

.NET Framework Security:

- Full trust for the immediate caller. This member cannot be used by partially trusted code.

Message.AppSpecific Property

Gets or sets additional, application-specific information.

```
[Visual Basic]
Public Property AppSpecific As Integer
[C#]
public int AppSpecific {get; set;}
[C++]
public: __property int get_AppSpecific();
public: __property void set_AppSpecific(int);
[JScript]
public function get AppSpecific() : int;
public function set AppSpecific(int);
```

Property Value

Information that is specific to the application. The default is zero.

Exceptions

Exception Type	Condition
InvalidOperation-Exception	The message queue is filtered to ignore the **AppSpecific** property.

Remarks

The **AppSpecific** property contains application-specific information that you can use to organize different types of messages. For example, you can use application-specific indexes. It is the responsibility of the application to interpret **AppSpecific** property information.

Whenever possible, you should include message data in the body of the message rather than the **AppSpecific** property.

> **Note** When working with foreign queues, use the **Extension** property to specify message properties that don't exist in Message Queuing. As with the **AppSpecific** property, it is the responsibility of the application to understand the content of the **Extension** property.

Requirements

Platforms: Windows 98, Windows NT 4.0,
Windows Millennium Edition, Windows 2000,
Windows XP Home Edition, Windows XP Professional,
Windows .NET Server family

.NET Framework Security:

- Full trust for the immediate caller. This member cannot be used by partially trusted code.

Message.ArrivedTime Property

Gets the time that the message arrived in the destination queue.

```
[Visual Basic]
Public ReadOnly Property ArrivedTime As DateTime
[C#]
public DateTime ArrivedTime {get;}
[C++]
public: __property DateTime get_ArrivedTime();
[JScript]
public function get ArrivedTime() : DateTime;
```

Property Value

A **DateTime** that represents the message's arrival time in the destination queue. The time is adjusted from GMT to the local time of the computer on which the destination queue resides.

Exceptions

Exception Type	Condition
InvalidOperationException	The message has not been sent. This property can only be read on messages retrieved from a queue.
	-or-
	The message queue is filtered to ignore the **ArrivedTime** property.

Remarks

The message's **TimeToBeReceived** property indicates how quickly the message must be received from the destination queue. The **TimeToBeReceived** property timer starts when the message is sent-- not when the message arrives in the queue.

Requirements

Platforms: Windows 98, Windows NT 4.0, Windows Millennium Edition, Windows 2000, Windows XP Home Edition, Windows XP Professional, Windows .NET Server family

.NET Framework Security:

- Full trust for the immediate caller. This member cannot be used by partially trusted code.

Message.AttachSenderId Property

Gets or sets a value indicating whether the sender identifier should be attached to the message.

```
[Visual Basic]
Public Property AttachSenderId As Boolean
[C#]
public bool AttachSenderId {get; set;}
[C++]
public: __property bool get_AttachSenderId();
public: __property void set_AttachSenderId(bool);
[JScript]
public function get AttachSenderId() : Boolean;
public function set AttachSenderId(Boolean);
```

Property Value

true if the **SenderId** should be attached to the message; otherwise, **false**. The default is **true**.

Exceptions

Exception Type	Condition
InvalidOperation-Exception	The message queue is filtered to ignore the **AttachSenderId** property.

Remarks

The **SenderId** property is an array of bytes that represents the identifier of the sending user. The sender identifier is set by Message Queuing and is used by the receiving Queue Manager to verify whether the sender has access rights to a queue.

The absence of the sender identifier is an indication by the sending application that Message Queuing should not validate the message's sender nor verify the sender's access rights to the receiving queue. The **SenderId** is trustworthy only if the message was authenticated when it reached the destination queue. The message is rejected when it reaches the destination queue if the queue accepts only authenticated messages and either the **UseAuthentication** or the **AttachSenderId** property is **false**.

> **CAUTION** If a message is rejected, it is either sent to the dead-letter queue (if **UseDeadLetterQueue** is **true**), or it is ignored. You can request acknowledgments when a message fails to reach a queue. Otherwise, when **UseDeadLetterQueue** is **false** the message might be lost without warning.

Requirements

Platforms: Windows 98, Windows NT 4.0, Windows Millennium Edition, Windows 2000, Windows XP Home Edition, Windows XP Professional, Windows .NET Server family

.NET Framework Security:

- Full trust for the immediate caller. This member cannot be used by partially trusted code.

Message.Authenticated Property

Gets a value indicating whether the message was authenticated.

```
[Visual Basic]
Public ReadOnly Property Authenticated As Boolean
[C#]
public bool Authenticated {get;}
[C++]
public: __property bool get_Authenticated();
[JScript]
public function get Authenticated() : Boolean;
```

Property Value

true if authentication was requested for the message when it entered the queue; otherwise, **false**.

Exceptions

Exception Type	Condition
InvalidOperation-Exception	The message has not been sent. This property can only be read on messages retrieved from a queue.
	-or-
	The message queue is filtered to ignore the **Authenticated** property.

Remarks

The **Authenticated** property is used only by the application while it is interacting with the message and trying to determine if authentication was requested. If the message is in the queue, the message was authenticated. Conversely, if the **Authenticated** property is **true**, the receiving Queue Manager authenticated the message when it received that message.

> **Note** You cannot determine if a message failed authentication by looking at its properties. Message Queuing discards messages that fail authentication before they are delivered to the queue. However, you can request that an acknowledgment message be sent if a delivery failure prevents the message from arriving in the queue.

Requirements

Platforms: Windows 98, Windows NT 4.0, Windows Millennium Edition, Windows 2000, Windows XP Home Edition, Windows XP Professional, Windows .NET Server family

.NET Framework Security:

- Full trust for the immediate caller. This member cannot be used by partially trusted code.

Message.AuthenticationProviderName Property

Gets or sets the name of the cryptographic provider used to generate the digital signature of the message.

```
[Visual Basic]
Public Property AuthenticationProviderName As String
[C#]
public string AuthenticationProviderName {get; set;}
[C++]
public: __property String* get_AuthenticationProviderName();
public: __property void set_AuthenticationProviderName(String*);
[JScript]
public function get AuthenticationProviderName() : String;
public function set AuthenticationProviderName(String);
```

Property Value

The name of the cryptographic provider used to generate the digital signature of the message. The default is Microsoft Base Cryptographic Provider, Ver. 1.0.

Exceptions

Exception Type	Condition
InvalidOperation- Exception	The **AuthenticationProviderName** property could not be set. -or- The message queue is filtered to ignore the **AuthenticationProviderName** property.
ArgumentException	The **AuthenticationProviderName** was set to a null reference (**Nothing** in Visual Basic).

Remarks

You typically use the **AuthenticationProviderName** when working with foreign queues. Message Queuing requires the authentication provider name and authentication provider type of the cryptographic provider (authentication provider) to validate the digital signatures of both messages sent to a foreign queue and messages passed to Message Queuing from a foreign queue.

When sending a message, always set the **AuthenticationProviderName** and **ConnectorType** properties

together. When the message is sent, Message Queuing ignores the authentication provider name if the connector type is not also set.

The **AuthenticationProviderName** property cannot be a null reference (**Nothing** in Visual Basic), but it can be an empty string ("").

Requirements

Platforms: Windows 98, Windows NT 4.0, Windows Millennium Edition, Windows 2000, Windows XP Home Edition, Windows XP Professional, Windows .NET Server family

.NET Framework Security:

- Full trust for the immediate caller. This member cannot be used by partially trusted code.

Message.AuthenticationProviderType Property

Gets or sets the type of cryptographic provider used to generate the digital signature of the message.

```
[Visual Basic]
Public Property AuthenticationProviderType As _
  CryptographicProviderType
[C#]
public CryptographicProviderType AuthenticationProviderType {get;
  set;}
[C++]
public: __property CryptographicProviderType
get_AuthenticationProviderType();
public: __property void
set_AuthenticationProviderType(CryptographicProviderType);
[JScript]
public function get AuthenticationProviderType() :
CryptographicProviderType;
public function set
AuthenticationProviderType(CryptographicProviderType);
```

Property Value

One of the **CryptographicProviderType** values. The default is **RSA_FULL**.

Exceptions

Exception Type	Condition
InvalidOperation- Exception	The **AuthenticationProviderType** property could not be set. -or- The message queue is filtered to ignore the **AuthenticationProviderType** property.

Remarks

You typically use the **AuthenticationProviderType** property when working with foreign queues to specify which cryptographic service provider is associated with a message. Message Queuing requires the authentication provider name and authentication provider type of the cryptographic provider (authentication provider) to validate the digital signatures of both messages sent to a foreign queue and messages passed to Message Queuing from a foreign queue.

> **Note** Only **RsaFull** is intended to be used with messaging.

When sending a message, always set the **AuthenticationProvider-Type** and **ConnectorType** properties together. When the message is sent, Message Queuing ignores the authentication provider type if the connector type is not also set.

Requirements

Platforms: Windows 98, Windows NT 4.0, Windows Millennium Edition, Windows 2000, Windows XP Home Edition, Windows XP Professional, Windows .NET Server family

.NET Framework Security:

- Full trust for the immediate caller. This member cannot be used by partially trusted code.

Message.Body Property

Gets or sets the content of the message.

```
[Visual Basic]
Public Property Body As Object
[C#]
public object Body {get; set;}
[C++]
public: __property Object* get_Body();
public: __property void set_Body(Object*);
[JScript]
public function get Body() : Object;
public function set Body(Object);
```

Property Value

An object that specifies the message contents. The object can be a string, a date, a currency, a number, an array of bytes, or any managed object.

Exceptions

Exception Type	Condition
InvalidOperation-Exception	The **Formatter** property is a null reference (**Nothing** in Visual Basic).
	-or-
	The message queue is filtered to ignore the **Body** property.

Remarks

The message's **Body** property usually contains the data associated with the message. Although you can also send application-specific data in the **AppSpecific** and **Extension** properties, you should include message data in the **Body** of the message whenever possible. Only the **Body** property contents are serialized or encrypted.

The **Body** property can contain any object whose size does not exceed 4 MB. If you use **MessageQueue.Send** to send any object that is not of type **Message** to the **MessageQueue**, that object will be located in the **Body** property of the **Message** instance returned by **Peek** or **Receive**.

> **Note** The string argument in MessageQueue.Send("hello.") is an example of such a generic object.

The **BodyType** property indicates the type of information that is stored in the message body. Message Queuing uses this information to identify the type of the **Body** property contents.

Specify either the **Body** property or the **BodyStream** property before sending the **Message** object. The **Body** property can be any serializable object, such as a text string, structure object, class instance, or embedded object.

Unless you write the contents of the message directly to the **BodyStream** property, set the **Formatter** property before you send the message. When the **Send** method is called on the **MessageQueue** instance, the body is serialized using the formatter contained in the **Formatter** property. If you send the message without specifying a value for the **Formatter** property, the formatter defaults to **XmlMessageFormatter**.

Example

See related example in the **System.Messaging.Message** constructor topic.

Requirements

Platforms: Windows 98, Windows NT 4.0, Windows Millennium Edition, Windows 2000, Windows XP Home Edition, Windows XP Professional, Windows .NET Server family

.NET Framework Security:

- Full trust for the immediate caller. This member cannot be used by partially trusted code.

Message.BodyStream Property

Gets or sets the information in the body of the message.

```
[Visual Basic]
Public Property BodyStream As Stream
[C#]
public Stream BodyStream {get; set;}
[C++]
public: __property Stream* get_BodyStream();
public: __property void set_BodyStream(Stream*);
[JScript]
public function get BodyStream() : Stream;
public function set BodyStream(Stream);
```

Property Value

A **Stream** that contains the serialized information included in the **Body** of the message.

Exceptions

Exception Type	Condition
InvalidOperation-Exception	The message queue is filtered to ignore the **Body** property.

Remarks

The body of a message can consist of any type of information--for example, a string, a date, a currency, a number, an array of bytes, or any managed object. This information is serialized into a **Stream** to be passed to the queue.

Specify either the **Body** property or the **BodyStream** property before sending the **Message** object. If you set the **Body** property, the contents are serialized into the **BodyStream** property. However, you can choose to write the **BodyStream** property directly. This is useful, for example, when you want to open a connection to a file and stream its contents as the body of your message.

Unless you write the contents of the message directly to the **BodyStream** property, set the **Formatter** property before you send the message. When the **Send** method is called on the **MessageQueue** instance, the body is serialized using the formatter contained in the **Formatter** property. If you send the message without specifying a value for the **Formatter** property, the formatter defaults to **XmlMessageFormatter**.

If you set the **UseEncryption** property to **true** for the body of this message, the message will be encrypted when it is sent--not when you set the **Body** property. Therefore, the **BodyStream** property is never encrypted.

Requirements

Platforms: Windows 98, Windows NT 4.0, Windows Millennium Edition, Windows 2000, Windows XP Home Edition, Windows XP Professional, Windows .NET Server family

.NET Framework Security:

*   Full trust for the immediate caller. This member cannot be used by partially trusted code.

Message.BodyType Property

Gets or sets the type of data that the message body contains.

```
[Visual Basic]
Public Property BodyType As Integer
[C#]
public int BodyType {get; set;}
[C++]
public: __property int get_BodyType();
public: __property void set_BodyType(int);
[JScript]
public function get BodyType() : int;
public function set BodyType(int);
```

Property Value

The message body's true type, such as a string, a date, a currency, or a number.

Exceptions

Exception Type	Condition
InvalidOperation-Exception	The message queue is filtered to ignore the **Body** property.

Remarks

Message Queuing recognizes the body contents as an object or as a serialized stream. The **BodyType** property indicates the type of the object within the **Body** property of the message.

The **XmlMessageFormatter** performs binding between native types and the object in a message body. If you use the **XmlMessageFormatter**, the formatter sets the **BodyType** property for you.

Other formatters can provide binding functionality also, as shown in the following C# code.

```
message.Formatter = new ActiveXMessageFormatter();
object myObject message.Body;
if (myObject is string) {
}
if (myObject is int) {
}
if (myObject is float) {
}
```

Requirements

Platforms: Windows 98, Windows NT 4.0, Windows Millennium Edition, Windows 2000, Windows XP Home Edition, Windows XP Professional, Windows .NET Server family

.NET Framework Security:

*   Full trust for the immediate caller. This member cannot be used by partially trusted code.

Message.ConnectorType Property

Gets or sets a value that indicates that some message properties typically set by Message Queuing were set by the sending application.

```
[Visual Basic]
Public Property ConnectorType As Guid
[C#]
public Guid ConnectorType {get; set;}
[C++]
public: __property Guid get_ConnectorType();
public: __property void set_ConnectorType(Guid);
[JScript]
public function get ConnectorType() : Guid;
public function set ConnectorType(Guid);
```

Property Value

A **Guid** defined by the application and used in conjunction with connector applications or message encryption. This **Guid** allows a receiving application to interpret message properties that were set by the sending application but that are normally set by Message Queuing.

Exceptions

Exception Type	Condition
InvalidOperation-Exception	The message queue is filtered to ignore the **ConnectorType** property.

Remarks

Message Queuing requires the **ConnectorType** property be set whenever an application sets a message property that is normally set by Message Queuing. An application typically uses a **ConnectorType** in the following two cases:

*   Whenever a connector application passes a message. The **ConnectorType** tells the sending and receiving applications how to interpret the security and acknowledgment properties of the message.
*   Whenever the sending application, rather than Message Queuing, encrypts a message. The **ConnectorType** tells Message Queuing to use the **DestinationSymmetricKey** property value to decrypt the message.

You must set the **ConnectorType** property if you set any of the following properties (otherwise, the queue ignores these properties when the message is sent):

*   **AuthenticationProviderName**
*   **AuthenticationProviderType**
*   **DestinationSymmetricKey**
*   **DigitalSignature**
*   **MessageType**
*   **SenderId**

Requirements

Platforms: Windows 98, Windows NT 4.0,
Windows Millennium Edition, Windows 2000,
Windows XP Home Edition, Windows XP Professional,
Windows .NET Server family

.NET Framework Security:
- Full trust for the immediate caller. This member cannot be used by partially trusted code.

Message.CorrelationId Property

Gets or sets the message identifier used by acknowledgment, report, and response messages to reference the original message.

```
[Visual Basic]
Public Property CorrelationId As String
[C#]
public string CorrelationId {get; set;}
[C++]
public: __property String* get_CorrelationId();
public: __property void set_CorrelationId(String*);
[JScript]
public function get CorrelationId() : String;
public function set CorrelationId(String);
```

Property Value

The message identifier specified by the **Id** property of the original message. The correlation identifier is used by Message Queuing when it generates an acknowledgment or report message, and by an application when it generates a response message.

Exceptions

Exception Type	Condition
InvalidOperation-Exception	The message queue is filtered to ignore the **CorrelationId** property.
ArgumentException	The **CorrelationId** is a null reference (**Nothing** in Visual Basic).

Remarks

When Message Queuing generates an acknowledgment or report message, it uses the correlation identifier property to specify the message identifier of the original message. In this manner, the correlation identifier ties the report or acknowledgment message to the original message.

The sending application can then match the acknowledgment or report with the original message by using the **CorrelationId** property to identify the original message's **Id** property.

> **Note** Connector applications also must set the **CorrelationId** property of the acknowledgment and report messages to the message identifier of the original message.

When your application sends a response message to the sending application, you can set the **CorrelationId** property of the response message to the message identifier of the original message. The sending application can then match your response message to the message that was sent.

Example

See related example in the **System.Messaging.Message** constructor topic.

Requirements

Platforms: Windows 98, Windows NT 4.0,
Windows Millennium Edition, Windows 2000,
Windows XP Home Edition, Windows XP Professional,
Windows .NET Server family

.NET Framework Security:
- Full trust for the immediate caller. This member cannot be used by partially trusted code.

Message.DestinationQueue Property

Gets the intended destination queue for a message.

```
[Visual Basic]
Public ReadOnly Property DestinationQueue As MessageQueue
[C#]
public MessageQueue DestinationQueue {get;}
[C++]
public: __property MessageQueue* get_DestinationQueue();
[JScript]
public function get DestinationQueue() : MessageQueue;
```

Property Value

A **MessageQueue** that specifies the intended destination queue for the message.

Exceptions

Exception Type	Condition
InvalidOperation-Exception	The message has not been sent. This property can only be read on messages retrieved from a queue. -or- The message queue is filtered to ignore the **DestinationQueue** property.

Remarks

The **DestinationQueue** property is most commonly used to determine the original destination of a message that arrived in a journal or dead-letter queue. Normally, you do not need to examine this property, because you typically retrieve the message from its destination queue.

Requirements

Platforms: Windows 98, Windows NT 4.0,
Windows Millennium Edition, Windows 2000,
Windows XP Home Edition, Windows XP Professional,
Windows .NET Server family

.NET Framework Security:
- Full trust for the immediate caller. This member cannot be used by partially trusted code.

Message.DestinationSymmetricKey Property

Gets or sets the symmetric key used to encrypt application-encrypted messages or messages sent to foreign queues.

```
[Visual Basic]
Public Property DestinationSymmetricKey As Byte ()
[C#]
public byte[] DestinationSymmetricKey {get; set;}
```

```
[C++]
public: _property unsigned char get_DestinationSymmetricKey();
public: _property void set_DestinationSymmetricKey(unsigned char
    _gc[]);
[JScript]
public function get DestinationSymmetricKey() : Byte[];
public function set DestinationSymmetricKey(Byte[]);
```

Property Value

An array of byte values that specifies the destination symmetric key used to encrypt the message. The default is a zero-length array.

Exceptions

Exception Type	Condition
InvalidOperation-Exception	The message queue is filtered to ignore the **DestinationSymmetricKey** property.
ArgumentException	The **DestinationSymmetricKey** is a null reference (**Nothing** in Visual Basic).

Remarks

Two scenarios require you to use the **DestinationSymmetricKey** property. The first is when your application, rather than Message Queuing, encrypts a message. The second is when you send an encrypted message to a queuing system other than Message Queuing.

Before you set this property, you must encrypt the symmetric key with the public key of the receiving queue manager. When you send an application-encrypted message, the receiving queue manager uses the symmetric key to decrypt the message before sending it to its destination queue.

If you send a message to a foreign queue, the message is first received by the appropriate connector application--which forwards the encrypted message with the attached symmetric key to the receiving application. It is then the responsibility of the receiving application to decrypt the message using the symmetric key.

When you set the **DestinationSymmetricKey** property, you must also set the **ConnectorType** property. When the message is sent, Message Queuing ignores the **DestinationSymmetricKey** property if the **ConnectorType** property is not also set.

The **DestinationSymmetricKey** property has a maximum array size of 256.

Requirements

Platforms: Windows 98, Windows NT 4.0, Windows Millennium Edition, Windows 2000, Windows XP Home Edition, Windows XP Professional, Windows .NET Server family

.NET Framework Security:
- Full trust for the immediate caller. This member cannot be used by partially trusted code.

Message.DigitalSignature Property

Gets or sets the digital signature that Message Queuing uses to authenticate the message.

```
[Visual Basic]
Public Property DigitalSignature As Byte ()
[C#]
public byte[] DigitalSignature {get; set;}
```

```
[C++]
public: _property unsigned char get_DigitalSignature();
public: _property void set_DigitalSignature(unsigned char _gc[]);
[JScript]
public function get DigitalSignature() : Byte[];
public function set DigitalSignature(Byte[]);
```

Property Value

An array of byte values that specifies the Message Queuing 1.0 digital signature used to authenticate the message. The default is a zero-length array.

Exceptions

Exception Type	Condition
InvalidOperation-Exception	The message queue is filtered to ignore the **DigitalSignature** property.
ArgumentException	The **DigitalSignature** property is a null reference (**Nothing** in Visual Basic).

Remarks

Message Queuing uses the digital signature when authenticating messages that were sent by Message Queuing version 1.0. In most cases, Message Queuing generates and sets the **DigitalSignature** property when the sending application requests authentication. The receiving application uses this property to retrieve the digital signature attached to the message.

> **Note** You can only use the **DigitalSignature** property when running Message Queuing version 2.0. The sending application must specify Message Queuing version 1.0 signatures when requesting authentication. If the sending application sends a Message Queuing version 2.0 signature, this property contains a buffer of four bytes, each containing zero.

The **DigitalSignature** property, together with the **SenderCertificate** property, is also used by connector applications when a message is sent. In this scenario, the connector application--rather than Message Queuing--generates the digital signature, which it bases on the certificate of the user sending the message.

The **DigitalSignature** property has a maximum array size of 256.

When you set the **DigitalSignature** property, you must also set the **ConnectorType** property. When a message is sent, Message Queuing ignores the **DigitalSignature** property if the **ConnectorType** property is not also set.

Requirements

Platforms: Windows 98, Windows NT 4.0, Windows Millennium Edition, Windows 2000, Windows XP Home Edition, Windows XP Professional, Windows .NET Server family

.NET Framework Security:
- Full trust for the immediate caller. This member cannot be used by partially trusted code.

Message.EncryptionAlgorithm Property

Gets or sets the encryption algorithm used to encrypt the body of a private message.

```
[Visual Basic]
Public Property EncryptionAlgorithm As EncryptionAlgorithm
```

```
[C#]
public EncryptionAlgorithm EncryptionAlgorithm {get; set;}
[C++]
public: __property EncryptionAlgorithm get_EncryptionAlgorithm();
public: __property void set_EncryptionAlgorithm(EncryptionAlgorithm);
[JScript]
public function get EncryptionAlgorithm() : EncryptionAlgorithm;
public function set EncryptionAlgorithm(EncryptionAlgorithm);
```

Property Value

One of the **EncryptionAlgorithm** enumeration values. The default is **RC2**.

Exceptions

Exception Type	Condition
InvalidOperation-Exception	The message queue is filtered to ignore the **EncryptionAlgorithm** property.

Remarks

If a message is private (encrypted), it is encrypted before it is sent and decrypted upon receipt. The **EncryptionAlgorithm** property specifies the algorithm used to encrypt the message body of a private message.

A queue can require that incoming messages be encrypted. If an application sends a non-encrypted (non-private) message to a queue that accepts only private messages, or if it sends a private message to a queue that accepts only non-private messages, the queue rejects the message. The sending application can request that a negative acknowledgment message be returned in such a case.

Requirements

Platforms: Windows 98, Windows NT 4.0, Windows Millennium Edition, Windows 2000, Windows XP Home Edition, Windows XP Professional, Windows .NET Server family

.NET Framework Security:
- Full trust for the immediate caller. This member cannot be used by partially trusted code.

Message.Extension Property

Gets or sets additional, application-defined information associated with the message.

```
[Visual Basic]
Public Property Extension As Byte ()
[C#]
public byte[] Extension {get; set;}
[C++]
public: __property unsigned char get_Extension();
public: __property void set_Extension(unsigned char __gc[]);
[JScript]
public function get Extension() : Byte[];
public function set Extension(Byte[]);
```

Property Value

An array of byte values that provides application-defined information associated with the message. The default is a zero-length array.

Exceptions

Exception Type	Condition
InvalidOperation-Exception	The message queue is filtered to ignore the **Extension** property.
ArgumentException	The **Extension** property is a null reference (**Nothing** in Visual Basic).

Remarks

The **Extension** property provides for application-defined information, like a large binary object, that is associated with the message. It is the responsibility of the receiving application to interpret the contents of the **Extension** property.

Where possible, you should include message data in the **Body** property of the message rather than the **Extension** property.

When working with foreign queues, use the **Extension** property to specify message properties that do not exist in Message Queuing.

> **Note** A foreign queue exists in a queuing system other than Microsoft Message Queuing. Message Queuing communicates with such queues through a connector application.

Requirements

Platforms: Windows 98, Windows NT 4.0, Windows Millennium Edition, Windows 2000, Windows XP Home Edition, Windows XP Professional, Windows .NET Server family

.NET Framework Security:
- Full trust for the immediate caller. This member cannot be used by partially trusted code.

Message.Formatter Property

Gets or sets the formatter used to serialize an object into or deserialize an object from the message body.

```
[Visual Basic]
Public Property Formatter As IMessageFormatter
[C#]
public IMessageFormatter Formatter {get; set;}
[C++]
public: __property IMessageFormatter* get_Formatter();
public: __property void set_Formatter(IMessageFormatter*);
[JScript]
public function get Formatter() : IMessageFormatter;
public function set Formatter(IMessageFormatter);
```

Property Value

The **IMessageFormatter** that produces a stream to be written to or read from the message body. The default is **XmlMessageFormatter**.

Exceptions

Exception Type	Condition
ArgumentException	The **Formatter** property is a null reference (**Nothing** in Visual Basic).

Remarks

Use the **Formatter** property when reading and writing a message. When a message is sent to the queue, the formatter serializes the **Body** property into a stream that can be sent to the message queue. When reading from a queue, the formatter deserializes the message data into the **Body** property.

Unless you write the contents of the message directly to the **BodyStream** property, set the **Formatter** property before you send the message. When the **Send** method is called on the **MessageQueue** instance, the body is serialized using the formatter contained in the **Formatter** property. If you send the message without specifying a value for the **Formatter** property, the formatter defaults to **XmlMessageFormatter**.

The **XmlMessageFormatter** is loosely coupled, so it is not necessary to have the same object type on the sender and receiver when using this format. The **ActiveXMessageFormatter** and **BinaryMessageFormatter** serialize the data into binary representation. The **ActiveXMessageFormatter** is used when sending or receiving COM components.

Requirements

Platforms: Windows 98, Windows NT 4.0, Windows Millennium Edition, Windows 2000, Windows XP Home Edition, Windows XP Professional, Windows .NET Server family

.NET Framework Security:

- Full trust for the immediate caller. This member cannot be used by partially trusted code.

Message.HashAlgorithm Property

Gets or sets the hashing algorithm that Message Queuing uses when authenticating a message or creating a digital signature for a message.

```
[Visual Basic]
Public Property HashAlgorithm As HashAlgorithm
[C#]
public HashAlgorithm HashAlgorithm {get; set;}
[C++]
public: __property HashAlgorithm get_HashAlgorithm();
public: __property void set_HashAlgorithm(HashAlgorithm);
[JScript]
public function get HashAlgorithm() : HashAlgorithm;
public function set HashAlgorithm(HashAlgorithm);
```

Property Value

One of the **HashAlgorithm** enumeration values. For Windows XP, the default is **SHA**. Otherwise, the default is **MD5**.

Exceptions

Exception Type	Condition
InvalidOperation-Exception	The message queue is filtered to ignore the **HashAlgorithm** property.

Remarks

On the source computer, Message Queuing uses the hashing algorithm when creating a digital signature for a message. The target Queue Manager then uses the same hashing algorithm to authenticate the message when it is received.

Requirements

Platforms: Windows 98, Windows NT 4.0, Windows Millennium Edition, Windows 2000, Windows XP Home Edition, Windows XP Professional, Windows .NET Server family

.NET Framework Security:

- Full trust for the immediate caller. This member cannot be used by partially trusted code.

Message.Id Property

Gets the message's identifier.

```
[Visual Basic]
Public ReadOnly Property Id As String
[C#]
public string Id {get;}
[C++]
public: __property String* get_Id();
[JScript]
public function get Id() : String;
```

Property Value

The message's unique identifier, which is generated by Message Queuing.

Exceptions

Exception Type	Condition
InvalidOperation-Exception	The message has not been sent. This property can only be read on messages retrieved from a queue. -or- The message queue is filtered to ignore the **Id** property.

Remarks

Message Queuing generates a message identifier when the message is sent. The identifier is composed of 20 bytes and includes two items: the machine **Guid** of the sending computer and a unique identifier for the message on the computer. The combination of the two items produces a message identifier that is unique on the network.

Message Queuing generates message identifiers for all messages-- including acknowledgment and report messages. An acknowledgment message is generally sent by Message Queuing in reaction to the arrival or failure of an original, sent message. You can find the **Id** property value of the original message in the **CorrelationId** property of an acknowledgment message.

You can also use the **Id** property when sending a response message to a response queue. To include the identifier of the original message in a response message, set the **CorrelationId** property of the response message to the **Id** property of the original message. The application reading the response message can then use the correlation identifier of the response message to identify the original message.

Example

See related example in the **System.Messaging.Message** constructor topic.

Requirements

Platforms: Windows 98, Windows NT 4.0, Windows Millennium Edition, Windows 2000, Windows XP Home Edition, Windows XP Professional, Windows .NET Server family

.NET Framework Security:

- Full trust for the immediate caller. This member cannot be used by partially trusted code.

Message.IsFirstInTransaction Property

Gets a value indicating whether the message was the first message sent in a transaction.

```
[Visual Basic]
Public ReadOnly Property IsFirstInTransaction As Boolean
[C#]
public bool IsFirstInTransaction {get;}
[C++]
public: __property bool get_IsFirstInTransaction();
[JScript]
public function get IsFirstInTransaction() : Boolean;
```

Property Value

true if the message was the first message sent in a transaction; otherwise, **false**.

Exceptions

Exception Type	Condition
InvalidOperationException	The message has not been sent. This property can only be read on messages retrieved from a queue. -or- The message queue is filtered to ignore the **IsFirstInTransaction** property.

Remarks

Receiving applications use the **IsFirstInTransaction** property to verify that a message was the first message sent in a single transaction to a single queue.

> **Note** This property is available only with Message Queuing 2.0 and later.

To verify transaction boundaries, you can use the **IsFirstInTransaction** property along with two other properties: **IsLastInTransaction** and **TransactionId**. Use the former to check whether a message was the last message sent in the transaction, and use the latter to retrieve the identifier of the transaction.

If only one message is sent in a transaction, the **IsFirstInTransaction** and **IsLastInTransaction** properties are both set to **true**.

Requirements

Platforms: Windows 98, Windows NT 4.0, Windows Millennium Edition, Windows 2000, Windows XP Home Edition, Windows XP Professional, Windows .NET Server family

.NET Framework Security:
- Full trust for the immediate caller. This member cannot be used by partially trusted code.

Message.IsLastInTransaction Property

Gets a value indicating whether the message was the last message sent in a transaction.

```
[Visual Basic]
Public ReadOnly Property IsLastInTransaction As Boolean
[C#]
public bool IsLastInTransaction {get;}
[C++]
public: __property bool get_IsLastInTransaction();
[JScript]
public function get IsLastInTransaction() : Boolean;
```

Property Value

true if the message was the last message sent in a single transaction; otherwise, **false**.

Exceptions

Exception Type	Condition
InvalidOperationException	The message has not been sent. This property can only be read on messages retrieved from a queue. -or- The message queue is filtered to ignore the **IsLastInTransaction** property.

Remarks

Receiving applications use the **IsLastInTransaction** property to verify that a message was the last message sent in a single transaction to a single queue.

> **Note** This property is available only with Message Queuing 2.0 and later.

To verify transaction boundaries, you can use the **IsLastInTransaction** property along with two other properties: **IsFirstInTransaction** and **TransactionId**. Use the former to check whether a message was the first message sent in the transaction, and use the latter to retrieve the identifier of the transaction.

If only one message is sent in a transaction, the **IsFirstInTransaction** and **IsLastInTransaction** properties are both set to **true**.

Requirements

Platforms: Windows 98, Windows NT 4.0, Windows Millennium Edition, Windows 2000, Windows XP Home Edition, Windows XP Professional, Windows .NET Server family

.NET Framework Security:
- Full trust for the immediate caller. This member cannot be used by partially trusted code.

Message.Label Property

Gets or sets an application-defined Unicode string that describes the message.

```
[Visual Basic]
Public Property Label As String
[C#]
public string Label {get; set;}
[C++]
public: __property String* get_Label();
public: __property void set_Label(String*);
[JScript]
public function get Label() : String;
public function set Label(String);
```

Property Value

The label of the message. The default is an empty string ("").

Exceptions

Exception Type	Condition
InvalidOperationException	The message queue is filtered to ignore the **Label** property.

Remarks

You can use a message label can be used for several purposes. For example, you can use it for display purposes or to selectively process messages based on the label value. The label does not need to be unique across messages.

Message queue and message labels represent an application-defined value that can help identify the queue or message in human-readable terms. It is the responsibility of the application to interpret the label contents, which have no intrinsic meaning to the Message Queuing application.

Requirements

Platforms: Windows 98, Windows NT 4.0, Windows Millennium Edition, Windows 2000, Windows XP Home Edition, Windows XP Professional, Windows .NET Server family

.NET Framework Security:

- Full trust for the immediate caller. This member cannot be used by partially trusted code.

Message.MessageType Property

Gets the message type: normal, acknowledgment, or report.

```
[Visual Basic]
Public ReadOnly Property MessageType As MessageType
[C#]
public MessageType MessageType {get;}
[C++]
public: __property MessageType get_MessageType();
[JScript]
public function get MessageType() : MessageType;
```

Property Value

One of the **MessageType** values.

Exceptions

Exception Type	Condition
InvalidOperationException	The message has not been sent. This property can only be read on messages retrieved from a queue. -or- The message queue is filtered to ignore the **MessageType** property.

Remarks

Message Queuing typically sets this property when it sends the message. A Message Queuing message can be one of the following types:

- Normal, which is either a typical message sent from an application to a queue, or a response message returned to the sending application.

- Acknowledgement, which Message Queuing generates whenever the sending application requests one. For example, Message Queuing can generate positive or negative messages to indicate that the original message arrived or was read. Message Queuing returns the appropriate acknowledgment message to the administration queue specified by the sending application.

- Report, which Message Queuing generates whenever a report queue is defined at the source Queue Manager. When tracing is enabled, Message Queuing sends a report message to the Message Queuing report queue each time the original message enters or leaves a Message Queuing server.

Requirements

Platforms: Windows 98, Windows NT 4.0, Windows Millennium Edition, Windows 2000, Windows XP Home Edition, Windows XP Professional, Windows .NET Server family

.NET Framework Security:

- Full trust for the immediate caller. This member cannot be used by partially trusted code.

Message.Priority Property

Gets or sets the message priority, which determines where in the queue the message is placed.

```
[Visual Basic]
Public Property Priority As MessagePriority
[C#]
public MessagePriority Priority {get; set;}
[C++]
public: __property MessagePriority get_Priority();
public: __property void set_Priority(MessagePriority);
[JScript]
public function get Priority() : MessagePriority;
public function set Priority(MessagePriority);
```

Property Value

One of the **MessagePriority** values, which represent the priority levels of non-transactional messages. The default is **Normal**.

Exceptions

Exception Type	Condition
InvalidOperationException	The message queue is filtered to ignore the **Priority** property.

Remarks

The **Priority** property affects how Message Queuing handles the message both while it is en route and once it reaches its destination. Higher-priority messages are given preference during routing and inserted toward the front of the destination queue. Messages with the same priority are placed in the queue according to their arrival time.

You can set a meaningful priority only for non-transactional messages. Message Queuing automatically sets the priority for transactional messages to **Lowest**, which causes transactional message priority to be ignored.

Example

See related topic in the **System.Messaging.Message** constructor topic.

Requirements

Platforms: Windows 98, Windows NT 4.0, Windows Millennium Edition, Windows 2000, Windows XP Home Edition, Windows XP Professional, Windows .NET Server family

.NET Framework Security:
- Full trust for the immediate caller. This member cannot be used by partially trusted code.

Message.Recoverable Property

Gets or sets a value indicating whether the message is guaranteed to be delivered in the event of a computer failure or network problem.

```
[Visual Basic]
Public Property Recoverable As Boolean
[C#]
public bool Recoverable {get; set;}
[C++]
public: __property bool get_Recoverable();
public: __property void set_Recoverable(bool);
[JScript]
public function get Recoverable() : Boolean;
public function set Recoverable(Boolean);
```

Property Value

true if delivery of the message is guaranteed (through saving the message to disk while en route); **false** if delivery is not assured. The default is **false**.

Exceptions

Exception Type	Condition
InvalidOperationException	The message queue is filtered to ignore the **Recoverable** property.

Remarks

The **Recoverable** property indicates whether the delivery of a message is guaranteed--even if a computer crashes while the message is en route to the destination queue.

If delivery of a message is guaranteed, the message is stored locally at every step along the route, until the message is successfully forwarded to the next computer. Setting the **Recoverable** property to **true** could affect throughput.

If the message is transactional, Message Queuing automatically treats the message as recoverable, regardless of the value of the **Recoverable** property.

Requirements

Platforms: Windows 98, Windows NT 4.0, Windows Millennium Edition, Windows 2000, Windows XP Home Edition, Windows XP Professional, Windows .NET Server family

.NET Framework Security:
- Full trust for the immediate caller. This member cannot be used by partially trusted code.

Message.ResponseQueue Property

Gets or sets the queue that receives application-generated response messages.

```
[Visual Basic]
Public Property ResponseQueue As MessageQueue
[C#]
public MessageQueue ResponseQueue {get; set;}
[C++]
public: __property MessageQueue* get_ResponseQueue();
public: __property void set_ResponseQueue(MessageQueue*);
[JScript]
public function get ResponseQueue() : MessageQueue;
public function set ResponseQueue(MessageQueue);
```

Property Value

The **MessageQueue** to which application-generated response messages are returned. The default is a null reference (**Nothing** in Visual Basic).

Exceptions

Exception Type	Condition
InvalidOperationException	The message queue is filtered to ignore the **ResponseQueue** property.

Remarks

The **ResponseQueue** property identifies the queue that receives application-generated response messages, which the receiving application returns to the sending application. The sending application specifies response queues when the application sends its messages. Any available queue can be specified as a response queue.

Messages returned to the response queue are application-specific. The application must define the contents of the messages as well as the action to take upon receipt of a message.

Requirements

Platforms: Windows 98, Windows NT 4.0, Windows Millennium Edition, Windows 2000, Windows XP Home Edition, Windows XP Professional, Windows .NET Server family

.NET Framework Security:
- Full trust for the immediate caller. This member cannot be used by partially trusted code.

Message.SenderCertificate Property

Gets or sets the security certificate used to authenticate messages.

```
[Visual Basic]
Public Property SenderCertificate As Byte ()
[C#]
public byte[] SenderCertificate {get; set;}
[C++]
public: __property unsigned char get_SenderCertificate();
public: __property void set_SenderCertificate(unsigned char
    __gc[]);
[JScript]
public function get SenderCertificate() : Byte[];
public function set SenderCertificate(Byte[]);
```

Property Value

An array of byte values that represents a security certificate, which Message Queuing uses to verify the sender of the message. The default is a zero-length array.

Exceptions

Exception Type	Condition
InvalidOperationException	The message queue is filtered to ignore the **SenderCertificate** property.

Remarks

The receiving application uses the **SenderCertificate** property when the message includes an external security certificate.

Message Queuing can authenticate a message using either an internal or external security certificate. Message Queuing provides internal certificates, which are used to verify message integrity. A certification authority provides an external certificate, which you can access through the **SenderCertificate** property of the message. In addition to allowing Message Queuing to authenticate the message, an external certificate allows the receiving application to further verify the sender. An internal certificate has no usable value to a receiving application.

An external certificate must be registered with the directory service of the Message Queuing system. An external certificate contains information about the certification authority, the certificate user, the validity period of the certificate, the public key of the certificate user, and the certification authority's signature.

Requirements

Platforms: Windows 98, Windows NT 4.0, Windows Millennium Edition, Windows 2000, Windows XP Home Edition, Windows XP Professional, Windows .NET Server family

.NET Framework Security:

- Full trust for the immediate caller. This member cannot be used by partially trusted code.

Message.SenderId Property

Gets the identifier of the sending user.

```
[Visual Basic]
Public ReadOnly Property SenderId As Byte ()
[C#]
public byte[] SenderId {get;}
[C++]
public: __property unsigned char get_SenderId();
[JScript]
public function get SenderId() : Byte[];
```

Property Value

An array of byte values that identifies the sender. The receiving Queue Manager uses the identifier when it authenticates the message--to verify the sender of the message and the sender's access rights to the queue.

Exceptions

Exception Type	Condition
InvalidOperationException	The message has not been sent. This property can only be read on messages retrieved from a queue. -or- The message queue is filtered to ignore the **SenderId** property.

Remarks

If the **AttachSenderId** property is **false**, the sender identifier specified in the **SenderId** property is not attached to the message when it is sent. This indicates to Message Queuing that the sender should not be validated when it sends the message to the destination queue. If the **AttachSenderId** property is **true**, the **SenderId** property value is trustworthy only if the message was authenticated. Use the **Authenticated** property in conjunction with the **SenderId** property to verify the sender's access rights.

A connector application is an application that uses a connector server to provide communication between Message Queuing and other queuing systems. Message Queuing requires connector applications to provide sender identification. You must set the **ConnectorType** property when sending a message through a connector application.

Requirements

Platforms: Windows 98, Windows NT 4.0, Windows Millennium Edition, Windows 2000, Windows XP Home Edition, Windows XP Professional, Windows .NET Server family

.NET Framework Security:

- Full trust for the immediate caller. This member cannot be used by partially trusted code.

Message.SenderVersion Property

Gets the version of Message Queuing used to send the message.

```
[Visual Basic]
Public ReadOnly Property SenderVersion As Long
[C#]
public long SenderVersion {get;}
[C++]
public: __property __int64 get_SenderVersion();
[JScript]
public function get SenderVersion() : long;
```

Property Value

The version of Message Queuing used to send the message.

Exceptions

Exception Type	Condition
InvalidOperationException	The message has not been sent. This property can only be read on messages retrieved from a queue. -or- The message queue is filtered to ignore the **SenderVersion** property.

Remarks

The **SenderVersion** property is important for certain features. For example, transaction processing is supported only by Message Queuing 2.0 and later, and digital signatures are used to authenticate messages sent by MSMQ 1.0.

The sending Queue Manager sets the **SenderVersion** property when the message is sent.

Requirements

Platforms: Windows 98, Windows NT 4.0, Windows Millennium Edition, Windows 2000, Windows XP Home Edition, Windows XP Professional, Windows .NET Server family

.NET Framework Security:

- Full trust for the immediate caller. This member cannot be used by partially trusted code.

Message.SentTime Property

Gets the date and time on the sending computer that the message was sent by the source queue manager.

```
[Visual Basic]
Public ReadOnly Property SentTime As DateTime
[C#]
public DateTime SentTime {get;}
[C++]
public: __property DateTime get_SentTime();
[JScript]
public function get SentTime() : DateTime;
```

Property Value

A **DateTime** that represents the time the message was sent.

Exceptions

Exception Type	Condition
InvalidOperationException	The message has not been sent. This property can only be read on messages retrieved from a queue.
	-or-
	The message queue is filtered to ignore the **SentTime** property.

Remarks

The **SentTime** property is adjusted to the local time of the computer on which this instance of the **Message** class was created. This time zone could be different from those of the source and destination queues.

Requirements

Platforms: Windows 98, Windows NT 4.0, Windows Millennium Edition, Windows 2000, Windows XP Home Edition, Windows XP Professional, Windows .NET Server family

.NET Framework Security:

- Full trust for the immediate caller. This member cannot be used by partially trusted code.

Message.SourceMachine Property

Gets the computer from which the message originated.

```
[Visual Basic]
Public ReadOnly Property SourceMachine As String
[C#]
public string SourceMachine {get;}
[C++]
public: __property String* get_SourceMachine();
[JScript]
public function get SourceMachine() : String;
```

Property Value

The name of the computer from which the message was sent.

Exceptions

Exception Type	Condition
InvalidOperationException	The message has not been sent. This property can only be read on messages retrieved from a queue.
	-or-
	The message queue is filtered to ignore the **SourceMachine** property.
MessageQueueException	The computer information or directory service could not be accessed.

Remarks

The format of the **SourceMachine** property does not include a preceding \\. For example, `myServer` is a valid **SourceMachine**.

Requirements

Platforms: Windows 98, Windows NT 4.0, Windows Millennium Edition, Windows 2000, Windows XP Home Edition, Windows XP Professional, Windows .NET Server family

.NET Framework Security:

- Full trust for the immediate caller. This member cannot be used by partially trusted code.

Message.TimeToBeReceived Property

Gets or sets the maximum amount of time for the message to be received from the destination queue.

```
[Visual Basic]
Public Property TimeToBeReceived As TimeSpan
[C#]
public TimeSpan TimeToBeReceived {get; set;}
[C++]
public: __property TimeSpan get_TimeToBeReceived();
public: __property void set_TimeToBeReceived(TimeSpan);
[JScript]
public function get TimeToBeReceived() : TimeSpan;
public function set TimeToBeReceived(TimeSpan);
```

Property Value

The total time for a sent message to be received from the destination queue. The default is **InfiniteTimeout**.

Exceptions

Exception Type	Condition
InvalidOperationException	The message queue is filtered to ignore the **TimeToBeReceived** property.
ArgumentException	The value specified for **TimeToBeReceived** is invalid.

Remarks

The **TimeToBeReceived** property specifies the total time for a sent message to be received from the destination queue. The time limit includes the time spent getting to the destination queue and the time spent waiting in the queue before the message is received.

CAUTION When using dependent client computers, be sure the clock on the client computer is synchronized with the clock on the server that is running Message Queuing. Otherwise, unpredictable behavior might result when sending a message whose **TimeToBeReceived** property is not **InfiniteTimeout**.

If the interval specified by the **TimeToBeReceived** property expires before the message is removed from the queue, Message Queuing discards the message in one of two ways. If the message's **UseDeadLetterQueue** property is **true**, the message is sent to the dead-letter queue. If **UseDeadLetterQueue** is **false**, the message is ignored.

You can set the message's **AcknowledgeType** property to request that Message Queuing send a negative acknowledgment message back to the sending application if the message is not retrieved before the timer expires.

If the value specified by the **TimeToBeReceived** property is less than the value specified by the **TimeToReachQueue** property, **TimeToBeReceived** takes precedence.

When several messages are sent in a single transaction, Message Queuing uses the **TimeToBeReceived** property of the first message.

Requirements

Platforms: Windows 98, Windows NT 4.0, Windows Millennium Edition, Windows 2000, Windows XP Home Edition, Windows XP Professional, Windows .NET Server family

.NET Framework Security:
- Full trust for the immediate caller. This member cannot be used by partially trusted code.

Message.TimeToReachQueue Property

Gets or sets the maximum amount of time for the message to reach the queue.

```
[Visual Basic]
Public Property TimeToReachQueue As TimeSpan
[C#]
public TimeSpan TimeToReachQueue {get; set;}
[C++]
public: __property TimeSpan get_TimeToReachQueue();
public: __property void set_TimeToReachQueue(TimeSpan);
[JScript]
public function get TimeToReachQueue() : TimeSpan;
public function set TimeToReachQueue(TimeSpan);
```

Property Value

The time limit for the message to reach the destination queue, beginning from the time the message is sent. The default is **InfiniteTimeout**.

Exceptions

Exception Type	Condition
InvalidOperationException	The message queue is filtered to ignore the **TimeToReachQueue** property.
ArgumentException	The value specified for **TimeToReachQueue** is invalid. It might represent a negative number.

Remarks

If the interval specified by the **TimeToReachQueue** property expires before the message reaches its destination, Message Queuing discards the message in one of two ways. If the message's **UseDeadLetterQueue** property is **true**, the message is sent to the dead-letter queue. If **UseDeadLetterQueue** is **false**, the message is ignored

You can set he message's **AcknowledgeType** property to request that Message Queuing send a negative acknowledgment message back to the sending application if the message does not arrive before the timer expires.

If the **TimeToReachQueue** property is set to 0 seconds, Message Queuing tries once to send the message to its destination--if the queue is waiting for the message. If the queue is local, the message always reaches it.

If the value specified by the **TimeToReachQueue** property is greater than the value specified by the **TimeToBeReceived** property, **TimeToBeReceived** takes precedence.

When several messages are sent in a single transaction, Message Queuing uses the **TimeToReachQueue** property of the first message.

Requirements

Platforms: Windows 98, Windows NT 4.0, Windows Millennium Edition, Windows 2000, Windows XP Home Edition, Windows XP Professional, Windows .NET Server family

.NET Framework Security:
- Full trust for the immediate caller. This member cannot be used by partially trusted code.

Message.TransactionId Property

Gets the identifier for the transaction of which the message was a part.

```
[Visual Basic]
Public ReadOnly Property TransactionId As String
[C#]
public string TransactionId {get;}
[C++]
public: __property String* get_TransactionId();
[JScript]
public function get TransactionId() : String;
```

Property Value

The identifier for the transaction associated with the message.

Exceptions

Exception Type	Condition
InvalidOperationException	The message has not been sent. This property can only be read on messages retrieved from a queue. -or- The message queue is filtered to ignore the **TransactionId** property.

Remarks

Receiving applications use the **TransactionId** property to verify that a message was sent as part of a specific transaction. The transaction dentifier contains the identifier of the sending computer (first 16 bits) followed by a 4-byte transaction sequence number.

Note This property is available only for Message Queuing 2.0 and later.

Transaction identifiers are not guaranteed to be unique, because transaction sequence numbers are not persistent, and they start over again at 2^{20}. Message Queuing guarantees only that subsequent transactions will have different transaction sequence numbers.

You can use the **TransactionId** property along with the **IsFirstInTransaction** and **IsLastInTransaction** properties to verify transaction boundaries.

Requirements

Platforms: Windows 98, Windows NT 4.0, Windows Millennium Edition, Windows 2000, Windows XP Home Edition, Windows XP Professional, Windows .NET Server family

.NET Framework Security:
- Full trust for the immediate caller. This member cannot be used by partially trusted code.

Message.TransactionStatusQueue Property

Gets the transaction status queue on the source computer.

```
[Visual Basic]
Public Property TransactionStatusQueue As MessageQueue
[C#]
public MessageQueue TransactionStatusQueue {get; set;}
[C++]
public: __property MessageQueue* get_TransactionStatusQueue();
public: __property void set_TransactionStatusQueue(MessageQueue*);
[JScript]
public function get TransactionStatusQueue() : MessageQueue;
public function set TransactionStatusQueue(MessageQueue);
```

Property Value

The transaction status queue on the source computer, which is used for sending acknowledgement messages back to the sending application. The default is a null reference (**Nothing** in Visual Basic).

Exceptions

Exception Type	Condition
InvalidOperationException	The message has not been sent. This property can only be read on messages retrieved from a queue. -or- The message queue is filtered to ignore the **TransactionStatusQueue** property.

Remarks

The **TransactionStatusQueue** property identifies the transactional queue on the source computer that receives read-receipt acknowledgments from connector applications. Message Queuing sets the property, and connector applications use the property when retrieving transactional messages sent to foreign queues.

Note A foreign queue exists in a queuing system other than Microsoft Message Queuing. Message Queuing communicates with such queues through a connector application.

The connector application can use the transaction status queue to send acknowledgment messages back to the sending application. The transaction status queue should receive these acknowledgments even if the sending application does not request other acknowledgments.

Requirements

Platforms: Windows 98, Windows NT 4.0, Windows Millennium Edition, Windows 2000, Windows XP Home Edition, Windows XP Professional, Windows .NET Server family

.NET Framework Security:
- Full trust for the immediate caller. This member cannot be used by partially trusted code.

Message.UseAuthentication Property

Gets or sets a value indicating whether the message was (or must be) authenticated before being sent.

```
[Visual Basic]
Public Property UseAuthentication As Boolean
[C#]
public bool UseAuthentication {get; set;}
[C++]
public: __property bool get_UseAuthentication();
public: __property void set_UseAuthentication(bool);
[JScript]
public function get UseAuthentication() : Boolean;
public function set UseAuthentication(Boolean);
```

Property Value

true if the sending application requested authentication for the message; otherwise, **false**. The default is **false**.

Exceptions

Exception Type	Condition
InvalidOperationException	The message queue is filtered to ignore the **UseAuthentication** property.

Remarks

The **UseAuthentication** property specifies whether the message needs to be authenticated. If the sending application requests authentication, Message Queuing creates a digital signature and uses it to sign the message when it is sent and authenticate the message when it is received.

If **UseAuthentication** is **false** and a message is sent to a queue that accepts only authenticated messages, the message will be rejected when it reaches the queue.

Note You cannot determine if a message failed authentication by looking at its properties. Message Queuing discards such messages before they are delivered to the queue. However, you can request that an acknowledgment message be sent if a delivery failure prevents a message from arriving in the queue.

Requirements

Platforms: Windows 98, Windows NT 4.0,
Windows Millennium Edition, Windows 2000,
Windows XP Home Edition, Windows XP Professional,
Windows .NET Server family

.NET Framework Security:

• Full trust for the immediate caller. This member cannot be used
by partially trusted code.

Message.UseDeadLetterQueue Property

Gets or sets a value indicating whether a copy of the message that
could not be delivered should be sent to a dead-letter queue.

```
[Visual Basic]
Public Property UseDeadLetterQueue As Boolean
[C#]
public bool UseDeadLetterQueue {get; set;}
[C++]
public: __property bool get_UseDeadLetterQueue();
public: __property void set_UseDeadLetterQueue(bool);
[JScript]
public function get UseDeadLetterQueue() : Boolean;
public function set UseDeadLetterQueue(Boolean);
```

Property Value

true if message-delivery failure should result in a copy of the
message being sent to a dead-letter queue; otherwise, **false**. The
default is **false**.

Exceptions

Exception Type	Condition
InvalidOperationException	The message queue is filtered to ignore the **UseDeadLetterQueue** property.

Remarks

The **UseJournalQueue** and **UseDeadLetterQueue** properties
specify how Message Queuing tracks a message. If
UseDeadLetterQueue is **true**, delivery failure (of a nontransactional message), causes the message to be sent to the nontransactional dead-letter queue on the computer that could not
deliver the message. (Deliver failure could be caused by a message
timer expiring, for example.)

In the case of delivery failure for a transactional message, Message
Queuing sends the message to the transactional dead-letter queue on
the source machine in all negative and in-doubt cases.

When you store messages in a dead-letter queue, you should clear
the queue periodically to remove messages that are no longer
needed. Messages stored in dead-letter queues count against the size
quota for the computer where the queue resides. The computer quota
is set by the administrator and refers to the size allocated for storing
messages on the whole computer, not just in a single queue.

> **Note** You do not create a journal or dead-letter queue. These
> are both system queues that Message Queuing generates.

Requirements

Platforms: Windows 98, Windows NT 4.0,
Windows Millennium Edition, Windows 2000,
Windows XP Home Edition, Windows XP Professional,
Windows .NET Server family

.NET Framework Security:

• Full trust for the immediate caller. This member cannot be used
by partially trusted code.

Message.UseEncryption Property

Gets or sets a value indicating whether to make the message private.

```
[Visual Basic]
Public Property UseEncryption As Boolean
[C#]
public bool UseEncryption {get; set;}
[C++]
public: __property bool get_UseEncryption();
public: __property void set_UseEncryption(bool);
[JScript]
public function get UseEncryption() : Boolean;
public function set UseEncryption(Boolean);
```

Property Value

true to require Message Queuing to encrypt the message; otherwise,
false. The default is **false**.

Exceptions

Exception Type	Condition
InvalidOperationException	The message queue is filtered to ignore the **UseEncryption** property.

Remarks

If a message is private, its body is encrypted before it is sent and
decrypted when it is received. To send a private message, the
sending application must specify that encryption be used and,
optionally, the encryption algorithm.

> **Note** When sending private messages, your application does
> not need to perform the message encryption. Message Queuing
> can encrypt the message body for you--if your application is
> sending messages within a Microsoft Windows 2000
> enterprise, which has access to the directory service. When
> receiving private messages, the receiving Queue Manager
> always decrypts the message body.

Requirements

Platforms: Windows 98, Windows NT 4.0,
Windows Millennium Edition, Windows 2000,
Windows XP Home Edition, Windows XP Professional,
Windows .NET Server family

.NET Framework Security:

• Full trust for the immediate caller. This member cannot be used
by partially trusted code.

Message.UseJournalQueue Property

Gets or sets a value indicating whether a copy of the message should
be kept in a machine journal on the originating computer.

```
[Visual Basic]
Public Property UseJournalQueue As Boolean
[C#]
public bool UseJournalQueue {get; set;}
[C++]
public: __property bool get_UseJournalQueue();
public: __property void set_UseJournalQueue(bool);
```

```
[JScript]
public function get UseJournalQueue() : Boolean;
public function set UseJournalQueue(Boolean);
```

Property Value

true to require that a copy of a message be kept in the originating computer's machine journal after the message has been successfully transmitted (from the originating computer to the next server); otherwise, **false**. The default is **false**.

Exceptions

Exception Type	Condition
InvalidOperationException	The message queue is filtered to ignore the **UseJournalQueue** property.

Remarks

The **UseJournalQueue** and **UseDeadLetterQueue** properties specify how Message Queuing tracks a message. If **UseJournalQueue** is **true**, then a copy is kept in the computer journal on the originating machine at each step that a message is transmitted.

> **Note** The sent message is only copied to the journal queue if the destination queue is on a remote computer. If the destination is on the local computer, the message is sent directly to the queue; there are no intermediate steps to require journaling.

When you store messages in a journal queue, clear the queue periodically to remove messages that are no longer needed. Messages stored in journal queues count against the quota for the computer where the queue resides. (The computer quota is set by the administrator.)

> **Note** You do not create a journal or dead-letter queue. These are both system queues that Message Queuing generates.

Requirements

Platforms: Windows 98, Windows NT 4.0, Windows Millennium Edition, Windows 2000, Windows XP Home Edition, Windows XP Professional, Windows .NET Server family

.NET Framework Security:

- Full trust for the immediate caller. This member cannot be used by partially trusted code.

Message.UseTracing Property

Gets or sets a value indicating whether to trace a message as it moves toward its destination queue.

```
[Visual Basic]
Public Property UseTracing As Boolean
[C#]
public bool UseTracing {get; set;}
[C++]
public: __property bool get_UseTracing();
public: __property void set_UseTracing(bool);
[JScript]
public function get UseTracing() : Boolean;
public function set UseTracing(Boolean);
```

Property Value

true if each intermediate step made by the original message en route to the destination queue generates a report to be sent to the system's report queue; otherwise, **false**. The default is **false**.

Exceptions

Exception Type	Condition
InvalidOperationException	The message queue is filtered to ignore the **UseTracing** property.

Remarks

The **UseTracing** property specifies whether to track the route of a message as it moves toward its destination queue. If **true**, a report message (generated by Message Queuing) is sent to a report queue each time the message passes through a Message Queuing routing server. The report queue is specified by the source Queue Manager. Report queues are not limited to report messages generated by Message Queuing; your application-generated messages can also be sent to report queues.

> **Note** Using tracing involves setting up Active Directory and specifying a report queue for the Message Queuing enterprise. The administrator configures these settings.

Requirements

Platforms: Windows 98, Windows NT 4.0, Windows Millennium Edition, Windows 2000, Windows XP Home Edition, Windows XP Professional, Windows .NET Server family

.NET Framework Security:

- Full trust for the immediate caller. This member cannot be used by partially trusted code.

MessageEnumerator Class

Provides a forward-only cursor to enumerate through messages in a message queue.

System.Object
  System.MarshalByRefObject
    System.Messaging.MessageEnumerator

```
[Visual Basic]
Public Class MessageEnumerator
   Inherits MarshalByRefObject
   Implements IEnumerator, IDisposable
[C#]
public class MessageEnumerator : MarshalByRefObject, IEnumerator,
   IDisposable
[C++]
public __gc class MessageEnumerator : public MarshalByRefObject,
   IEnumerator, IDisposable
[JScript]
public class MessageEnumerator extends MarshalByRefObject
   implements IEnumerator, IDisposable
```

Thread Safety

Any public static (**Shared** in Visual Basic) members of this type are safe for multithreaded operations. Any instance members are not guaranteed to be thread safe.

Remarks

Use **MessageEnumerator** for dynamic interaction with messages in a queue. Methods available through the **MessageQueue** class can return either a **MessageEnumerator** pointing to a dynamic list of messages in the queue, or an array that contains a copy at a given instant - a snapshot - of the queue at the time the specified method was called.

Unlike a static snapshot, an enumerator allows you to modify the collection. Using a **MessageEnumerator**, you can remove messages from the queue, and the change is immediately reflected in the queue.

An enumerator does not remove the messages from the queue when it queries the queue. It returns information about the message at the current cursor position, but it leaves the message in the queue.

A **MessageEnumerator** is a cursor, initialized to the head of a dynamic list. The list order is the same as the order of the messages in the queue, according to message priority. You can move the cursor to the first message in the queue by calling **MoveNext**. After the enumerator has been initialized, you can use **MoveNext** to step forward through the remaining messages. You can specify whether to wait for a message to become available by passing a timeout into the **MoveNext** method.

Because the enumerator is dynamic, a message that is appended beyond the cursor's current position (for example, due to low priority), can be accessed by the enumerator. A message that is inserted before the cursor's current position cannot be accessed. It is not possible to step backward with a **MessageEnumerator**. A cursor allows forward-only movement. The **Reset** method enables you to place the cursor back at the beginning of the queue.

Instances of **MessageEnumerator** for a given queue work independently. You can create two **MessageEnumerator** instances that apply to the same queue. The changes that one **MessageEnumerator** makes to the messages in the queue will be reflected immediately in a second enumerator if the second enumerator is positioned before the first.

However, if two enumerators have the same position and one of them removes the message at that position, an exception is thrown if the other enumerator attempts to get the value of the **Current** property on the now-deleted message.

> **Note** If you create an instance of **MessageQueue** with **MessageQueue.DenySharedReceive** set to **true**, no other application can modify the messages in your enumerator while you have the connection to the queue.

Example

[Visual Basic, C#, C++] The following example gets a dynamic list of messages in a queue and counts all messages with the **Priority** property set to **MessagePriority.Lowest**.

```
[Visual Basic]
Imports System
Imports System.Messaging

Namespace MyProject

   '/ <summary>
   '/ Provides a container class for the example.
   '/ </summary>
   Public Class MyNewQueue

      '****************************************************
      ' Provides an entry point into the application.
      '
      ' This example uses a cursor to step through the
      ' messages in a queue and counts the number of
      ' Lowest priority messages.
      '****************************************************

      Public Shared Sub Main()

         ' Create a new instance of the class.
         Dim myNewQueue As New MyNewQueue()

         ' Output the count of Lowest priority messages.
         myNewQueue.CountLowestPriority()

         Return

      End Sub 'Main

      '****************************************************
      ' Iterates through messages in a queue and examines
      ' their priority.
      '****************************************************

      Public Sub CountLowestPriority()

         ' Holds the count of Lowest priority messages.
         Dim numberItems As Int32 = 0

         ' Connect to a queue.
         Dim myQueue As New MessageQueue(".\myQueue")

         ' Get a cursor into the messages in the queue.
         Dim myEnumerator As MessageEnumerator = _
            myQueue.GetMessageEnumerator()

         ' Specify that the messages's priority should be read.
         myQueue.MessageReadPropertyFilter.Priority = True

         ' Move to the next message and examine its priority.
         While myEnumerator.MoveNext()

            ' Increase the count if the priority is Lowest.
            If myEnumerator.Current.Priority = _
               MessagePriority.Lowest Then
```

```
            numberItems += 1
        End If

    End While

    ' Display final count.
    Console.WriteLine(("Lowest priority messages: " + _
        numberItems.ToString()))

    Return

    End Sub 'CountLowestPriority

End Class 'MyNewQueue
End Namespace 'MyProject
```

[C#]
```
using System;
using System.Messaging;

namespace MyProject
{

    /// <summary>
    /// Provides a container class for the example.
    /// </summary>
    public class MyNewQueue
    {

        //*************************************************
        // Provides an entry point into the application.
        //
        // This example uses a cursor to step through the
        // messages in a queue and counts the number of
        // Lowest priority messages.
        //*************************************************

        public static void Main()
        {
            // Create a new instance of the class.
            MyNewQueue myNewQueue = new MyNewQueue();

            // Output the count of Lowest priority messages.
            myNewQueue.CountLowestPriority();

            return;
        }

        //*************************************************
        // Iterates through messages in a queue and examines
        // their priority.
        //*************************************************

        public void CountLowestPriority()
        {
            // Holds the count of Lowest priority messages.
            uint numberItems = 0;

            // Connect to a queue.
            MessageQueue myQueue = new MessageQueue(".\\myQueue");

            // Get a cursor into the messages in the queue.
            MessageEnumerator myEnumerator =
                myQueue.GetMessageEnumerator();

            // Specify that the messages's priority should be read.
            myQueue.MessageReadPropertyFilter.Priority = true;

            // Move to the next message and examine its priority.
            while(myEnumerator.MoveNext())
            {
                // Increase the count if priority is Lowest.
                if(myEnumerator.Current.Priority ==
                    MessagePriority.Lowest)

                    numberItems++;
            }
```

```
            // Display final count.
            Console.WriteLine("Lowest priority messages: " +
                numberItems.ToString());

            return;
        }
    }
}
```

[C++]
```
#using <mscorlib.dll>
#using <system.dll>
#using <system.messaging.dll>

using namespace System;
using namespace System::Messaging;

__gc class MyNewQueue
{
public:
    void CountLowestPriority()
    {
        // Holds the count of Lowest priority messages.
        UInt32 numberItems = 0;

        // Connect to a queue.
        MessageQueue* myQueue = new MessageQueue(S".\\myQueue");

        // Get a cursor into the messages in the queue.
        MessageEnumerator* myEnumerator =
            myQueue->GetMessageEnumerator();

        // Specify that the messages's priority should be read.
        myQueue->MessageReadPropertyFilter->Priority = true;

        // Move to the next message and examine its priority.
        while(myEnumerator->MoveNext())
        {
            // Increase the count if priority is Lowest.
            if (myEnumerator->Current->Priority ==
                MessagePriority::Lowest)

                numberItems++;
        }

        // Display final count.
        Console::WriteLine(S"Lowest priority messages:
{0}", __box(numberItems));

        return;
    }
};

int main()
{
    // Create a new instance of the class.
    MyNewQueue* myNewQueue = new MyNewQueue();

    // Output the count of Lowest priority messages.
    myNewQueue->CountLowestPriority();

    return 0;
}
```

Requirements

Namespace: System.Messaging

Platforms: Windows 98, Windows NT 4.0,
Windows Millennium Edition, Windows 2000,
Windows XP Home Edition, Windows XP Professional,
Windows .NET Server family

Assembly: System.Messaging (in System.Messaging.dll)

MessageEnumerator.Current Property

Gets the current **Message** that this enumerator points to.

```
[Visual Basic]
Public ReadOnly Property Current As Message
[C#]
public Message Current {get;}
[C++]
public: __property Message* get_Current();
[JScript]
public function get Current() : Message;
```

Property Value

The current message.

Exceptions

Exception Type	Condition
InvalidOperationException	You called **Current** before the first call to **MoveNext**. The cursor is located before the first element of the message enumeration. -or- You called **Current** after a call to **MoveNext** had returned **false** (indicating the cursor is located after the last element of the message enumeration.)
MessageQueueException	The message the enumerator is currently pointing to no longer exists. It might have been deleted.

Remarks

When the enumerator is created, it points to the head of the queue, at a location before the first message. In this case, **Current** is not valid and will throw an exception if it is accessed. You must call **MoveNext** to position the cursor at the first message in the queue.

Requirements

Platforms: Windows 98, Windows NT 4.0, Windows Millennium Edition, Windows 2000, Windows XP Home Edition, Windows XP Professional, Windows .NET Server family

.NET Framework Security:
- Full trust for the immediate caller. This member cannot be used by partially trusted code.

MessageEnumerator.CursorHandle Property

Gets the native Message Queuing cursor handle used to browse messages in the queue.

```
[Visual Basic]
Public ReadOnly Property CursorHandle As IntPtr
[C#]
public IntPtr CursorHandle {get;}
[C++]
public: __property IntPtr get_CursorHandle();
[JScript]
public function get CursorHandle() : IntPtr;
```

Property Value

The native cursor handle.

Exceptions

Exception Type	Condition
MessageQueueException	The handle does not exist.

Remarks

This property contains the native handle to the enumeration. When you have finished working with the enumerator, call **Close** to release this resource.

Requirements

Platforms: Windows 98, Windows NT 4.0, Windows Millennium Edition, Windows 2000, Windows XP Home Edition, Windows XP Professional, Windows .NET Server family

.NET Framework Security:
- Full trust for the immediate caller. This member cannot be used by partially trusted code.

MessageEnumerator.Close Method

Frees the resources associated with the enumerator.

```
[Visual Basic]
Public Sub Close()
[C#]
public void Close();
[C++]
public: void Close();
[JScript]
public function Close();
```

Remarks

The operating system retains an open handle to the queue during the lifetime of the cursor. When you have finished working with the enumerator, call **Close** to release the resources associated with the handle.

Requirements

Platforms: Windows 98, Windows NT 4.0, Windows Millennium Edition, Windows 2000, Windows XP Home Edition, Windows XP Professional, Windows .NET Server family

.NET Framework Security:
- Full trust for the immediate caller. This member cannot be used by partially trusted code.

MessageEnumerator.Dispose Method

Releases the resources used by the **MessageEnumerator**.

Overload List

Releases all resources used by the **MessageEnumerator**.

[Visual Basic] **Overloads Public Overridable Sub Dispose() Implements IDisposable.Dispose**

[C#] **public virtual void Dispose();**

[C++] **public: virtual void Dispose();**

[JScript] **public function Dispose();**

Releases the unmanaged resources used by the **MessageEnume-rator** and optionally releases the managed resources.

> [Visual Basic] **Overloads Protected Overridable Sub Dispose(Boolean)**
>
> [C#] **protected virtual void Dispose(bool);**
>
> [C++] **protected: virtual void Dispose(bool);**
>
> [JScript] **protected function Dispose(Boolean);**

MessageEnumerator.Dispose Method ()

Releases all resources used by the **MessageEnumerator**.

```
[Visual Basic]
Overloads Public Overridable Sub Dispose() Implements _
    IDisposable.Dispose
[C#]
public virtual void Dispose();
[C++]
public: virtual void Dispose();
[JScript]
public function Dispose();
```

Implements

IDisposable.Dispose

Remarks

Calling **Dispose** allows the resources used by the **MessageEnume-rator** to be reallocated for other purposes. For more information about **Dispose**, see **Cleaning Up Unmanaged Resources**.

Requirements

Platforms: Windows 98, Windows NT 4.0, Windows Millennium Edition, Windows 2000, Windows XP Home Edition, Windows XP Professional, Windows .NET Server family

.NET Framework Security:

- Full trust for the immediate caller. This member cannot be used by partially trusted code.

MessageEnumerator.Dispose Method (Boolean)

Releases the unmanaged resources used by the **MessageEnumerator** and optionally releases the managed resources.

```
[Visual Basic]
Overloads Protected Overridable Sub Dispose( _
    ByVal disposing As Boolean _
)
[C#]
protected virtual void Dispose(
    bool disposing
);
[C++]
protected: virtual void Dispose(
    bool disposing
);
[JScript]
protected function Dispose(
    disposing : Boolean
);
```

Parameters

disposing
> **true** to release both managed and unmanaged resources; **false** to release only unmanaged resources.

Remarks

This method is called by the public **Dispose()** method and the **Finalize** method. **Dispose()** invokes the protected **Dispose(Boolean)** method with the *disposing* parameter set to **true**. **Finalize** invokes **Dispose** with *disposing* set to **false**.

When the *disposing* parameter is **true**, this method releases all resources held by any managed objects that this **MessageEnume-rator** references. This method invokes the **Dispose()** method of each referenced object.

Notes to Inheritors: **Dispose** can be called multiple times by other objects. When overriding **Dispose(Boolean)**, be careful not to reference objects that have been previously disposed of in an earlier call to **Dispose**. For more information about how to implement **Dispose**, see **Implementing a Dispose Method**.

For more information about **Dispose** and **Finalize**, see **Cleaning Up Unmanaged Resources** and **Overriding the Finalize Method**.

Requirements

Platforms: Windows 98, Windows NT 4.0, Windows Millennium Edition, Windows 2000, Windows XP Home Edition, Windows XP Professional, Windows .NET Server family

.NET Framework Security:

- Full trust for the immediate caller. This member cannot be used by partially trusted code.

MessageEnumerator.Finalize Method

This member overrides **Object.Finalize**.

```
[Visual Basic]
Overrides Protected Sub Finalize()
[C#]
~MessageEnumerator();
[C++]
~MessageEnumerator();
[JScript]
protected override function Finalize();
```

Requirements

Platforms: Windows 98, Windows NT 4.0, Windows Millennium Edition, Windows 2000, Windows XP Home Edition, Windows XP Professional, Windows .NET Server family

.NET Framework Security:

- Full trust for the immediate caller. This member cannot be used by partially trusted code.

MessageEnumerator.MoveNext Method

Advances the enumerator to the next message in the queue.

Overload List

Advances the enumerator to the next message in the queue, if one is currently available.

[Visual Basic] **Overloads Public Overridable Function MoveNext() As Boolean Implements IEnumerator.MoveNext**

[C#] **public virtual bool MoveNext();**

[C++] **public: virtual bool MoveNext();**

[JScript] **public function MoveNext() : Boolean;**

Advances the enumerator to the next message in the queue. If the enumerator is positioned at the end of the queue, **MoveNext** waits until a message is available or the given timeout expires.

[Visual Basic] **Overloads Public Function MoveNext(TimeSpan) As Boolean**

[C#] **public bool MoveNext(TimeSpan);**

[C++] **public: bool MoveNext(TimeSpan);**

[JScript] **public function MoveNext(TimeSpan) : Boolean;**

MessageEnumerator.MoveNext Method ()

Advances the enumerator to the next message in the queue, if one is currently available.

```
[Visual Basic]
Overloads Public Overridable Function MoveNext() As Boolean Implements
_
    IEnumerator.MoveNext
[C#]
public virtual bool MoveNext();
[C++]
public: virtual bool MoveNext();
[JScript]
public function MoveNext() : Boolean;
```

Return Value

true if the enumerator was succesfully advanced to the next message; **false** if the enumerator has reached the end of the queue.

Implements

IEnumerator.MoveNext

Exceptions

Exception Type	Condition
MessageQueueException	An exception specific to Message Queuing was thrown.

Remarks

This overload returns immediately if there is no message in the queue. There is another overload that waits a specified **TimeSpan** for a message to arrive.

If a message is not currently available because the queue is empty or because you have moved beyond the last element in the collection, **MoveNext** returns **false** to the calling method.

Upon creation, an enumerator is conceptually positioned before the first message of the queue, and the first call to **MoveNext** brings the first message of the queue into view.

Requirements

Platforms: Windows 98, Windows NT 4.0, Windows Millennium Edition, Windows 2000, Windows XP Home Edition, Windows XP Professional, Windows .NET Server family

.NET Framework Security:

- Full trust for the immediate caller. This member cannot be used by partially trusted code.

MessageEnumerator.MoveNext Method (TimeSpan)

Advances the enumerator to the next message in the queue. If the enumerator is positioned at the end of the queue, **MoveNext** waits until a message is available or the given timeout expires.

```
[Visual Basic]
Overloads Public Function MoveNext( _
    ByVal timeout As TimeSpan _
) As Boolean
[C#]
public bool MoveNext(
    TimeSpan timeout
);
[C++]
public: bool MoveNext(
    TimeSpan timeout
);
[JScript]
public function MoveNext(
    timeout : TimeSpan
) : Boolean;
```

Parameters

timeout
> The **TimeSpan** to wait for a message to be available if the enumerator is positioned at the end of the queue.

Return Value

true if the enumerator successfully advanced to the next message; **false** if the enumerator has reached the end of the queue and a message does not become available within the time specified by the *timeout* parameter.

Exceptions

Exception Type	Condition
ArgumentException	The value specified for the timeout parameter is invalid. It might represent a negative number.
MessageQueueException	An exception specific to Message Queuing was thrown.
	-or-
	The timeout has expired.

Remarks

This overload waits if there is no message in the queue or if the cursor has reached the end of the queue. If a message is not currently available because the queue is empty or because you have moved beyond the last element in the collection, **MoveNext** waits the specified timeout.

If the cursor is already at the end of the queue, **MoveNext** only returns **true** if the new message arrives within the specified time interval, has lower priority than all messages currently in the queue and is placed at the end of the queue. An overload with no parameter returns immediately if no further messages are in the queue.

Upon creation, an enumerator is conceptually positioned before the first message of the enumeration, and the first call to **MoveNext** brings the first message of the enumeration into view.

Requirements

Platforms: Windows 98, Windows NT 4.0, Windows Millennium Edition, Windows 2000, Windows XP Home Edition, Windows XP Professional, Windows .NET Server family

.NET Framework Security:
* Full trust for the immediate caller. This member cannot be used by partially trusted code.

MessageEnumerator.RemoveCurrent Method

Removes the current message from the queue and returns the message to the calling application. Removing the message deletes it from the queue.

Overload List

Removes the current message from a transactional or non-transactional queue and returns the message to the calling application. There is no timeout specified for a message to arrive in the queue.

[Visual Basic] **Overloads Public Function RemoveCurrent() As Message**

[C#] **public Message RemoveCurrent();**

[C++] **public: Message* RemoveCurrent();**

[JScript] **public function RemoveCurrent() : Message;**

Removes the current message from a transactional queue and returns the message to the calling application. There is no timeout specified for a message to arrive in the queue.

[Visual Basic] **Overloads Public Function RemoveCurrent(MessageQueueTransaction) As Message**

[C#] **public Message RemoveCurrent(MessageQueueTransaction);**

[C++] **public: Message* RemoveCurrent(MessageQueueTransaction*);**

[JScript] **public function RemoveCurrent(MessageQueueTransaction) : Message;**

Removes the current message from a queue and returns the message to the calling application. There is no timeout specified for a message to arrive in the queue.

[Visual Basic] **Overloads Public Function RemoveCurrent(MessageQueueTransactionType) As Message**

[C#] **public Message RemoveCurrent(MessageQueueTransactionType);**

[C++] **public: Message* RemoveCurrent(MessageQueueTransactionType);**

[JScript] **public function RemoveCurrent(MessageQueueTransactionType) : Message;**

Removes the current message from the queue and returns the message to the calling application. If there is a message to remove, the method returns it immediately. Otherwise, the method waits the specified timeout for a new message to arrive.

[Visual Basic] **Overloads Public Function RemoveCurrent(TimeSpan) As Message**

[C#] **public Message RemoveCurrent(TimeSpan);**

[C++] **public: Message* RemoveCurrent(TimeSpan);**

[JScript] **public function RemoveCurrent(TimeSpan) : Message;**

Removes the current message from a transactional queue and returns the message to the calling application. If there is a message to remove, the method returns it immediately. Otherwise, the method waits the specified timeout for a new message to arrive.

[Visual Basic] **Overloads Public Function RemoveCurrent(TimeSpan, MessageQueueTransaction) As Message**

[C#] **public Message RemoveCurrent(TimeSpan, MessageQueueTransaction);**

[C++] **public: Message* RemoveCurrent(TimeSpan, MessageQueueTransaction*);**

[JScript] **public function RemoveCurrent(TimeSpan, MessageQueueTransaction) : Message;**

Removes the current message from a queue and returns the message to the calling application. If there is a message to remove, the method returns it immediately. Otherwise, the method waits the specified timeout for a new message to arrive.

[Visual Basic] **Overloads Public Function RemoveCurrent (TimeSpan, MessageQueueTransactionType) As Message**

[C#] **public Message RemoveCurrent(TimeSpan, MessageQueueTransactionType);**

[C++] **public: Message* RemoveCurrent(TimeSpan, MessageQueueTransactionType);**

[JScript] **public function RemoveCurrent(TimeSpan, MessageQueueTransactionType) : Message;**

MessageEnumerator.RemoveCurrent Method ()

Removes the current message from a transactional or non-transactional queue and returns the message to the calling application. There is no timeout specified for a message to arrive in the queue.

```
[Visual Basic]
Overloads Public Function RemoveCurrent() As Message
[C#]
public Message RemoveCurrent();
[C++]
public: Message* RemoveCurrent();
[JScript]
public function RemoveCurrent() : Message;
```

Return Value

A **Message** that references the first message available in the queue.

Remarks

RemoveCurrent removes and returns the message at the cursor's current location.

If you are using queue journaling, removing the message causes a copy to be kept in the journal queue, just as the **MessageQueue** class's **Receive** method does.

When you remove the current message, the cursor is moved to the next message. You do not have to call **MoveNext** after calling **RemoveCurrent**.

If you call this overload on a transactional queue, Message Queuing creates a single internal transaction.

Requirements

Platforms: Windows 98, Windows NT 4.0, Windows Millennium Edition, Windows 2000, Windows XP Home Edition, Windows XP Professional, Windows .NET Server family

.NET Framework Security:
* Full trust for the immediate caller. This member cannot be used by partially trusted code.

MessageEnumerator.RemoveCurrent Method (MessageQueueTransaction)

Removes the current message from a transactional queue and returns the message to the calling application. There is no timeout specified for a message to arrive in the queue.

```
[Visual Basic]
Overloads Public Function RemoveCurrent( _
   ByVal transaction As MessageQueueTransaction _
) As Message
[C#]
public Message RemoveCurrent(
   MessageQueueTransaction transaction
);
[C++]
public: Message* RemoveCurrent(
   MessageQueueTransaction* transaction
);
[JScript]
public function RemoveCurrent(
   transaction : MessageQueueTransaction
) : Message;
```

Parameters

transaction
> The **MessageQueueTransaction** object that specifies the transaction in which the message will be removed.

Return Value

A **Message** that references the first message available in the queue.

Exceptions

Exception Type	Condition
ArgumentNullException	The *transaction* parameter is a null reference (**Nothing** in Visual Basic).

Remarks

RemoveCurrent removes and returns the message at the cursor's current location, using the internal transaction context defined by the *transaction* parameter.

If you are using queue journaling, removing the message causes a copy to be kept in the journal queue, just as the **MessageQueue** class's **Receive** method does.

When working with transactional queues, a rollback of a transaction causes any messages removed by a call to **RemoveCurrent** to be returned to the queue. The removal is not irreversible until the transaction is committed.

When you remove the current message, the cursor is moved to the next message. You do not have to call **MoveNext** after calling **RemoveCurrent**.

Requirements

Platforms: Windows 98, Windows NT 4.0, Windows Millennium Edition, Windows 2000, Windows XP Home Edition, Windows XP Professional, Windows .NET Server family

.NET Framework Security:
- Full trust for the immediate caller. This member cannot be used by partially trusted code.

MessageEnumerator.RemoveCurrent Method (MessageQueueTransactionType)

Removes the current message from a queue and returns the message to the calling application. There is no timeout specified for a message to arrive in the queue.

```
[Visual Basic]
Overloads Public Function RemoveCurrent( _
   ByVal transactionType As MessageQueueTransactionType _
) As Message
[C#]
public Message RemoveCurrent(
   MessageQueueTransactionType transactionType
);
[C++]
public: Message* RemoveCurrent(
   MessageQueueTransactionType transactionType
);
[JScript]
public function RemoveCurrent(
   transactionType : MessageQueueTransactionType
) : Message;
```

Parameters

transactionType
> One of the **MessageQueueTransactionType** values, describing the type of transaction context to associate with the message.

Return Value

A **Message** that references the first message available in the queue.

Exceptions

Exception Type	Condition
InvalidEnumArgument-Exception	The *transactionType* parameter is not one of the **MessageQueueTransactionType** members.

Remarks

RemoveCurrent removes and returns the message at the cursor's current location, using a transaction context defined by the *transactionType* parameter.

Specify **Automatic** for the *transactionType* parameter if there is already an external transaction context attached to the thread that you want to use to receive the message. Specify **Single** if you want to receive the message as a single internal transaction. You can specify **None** if you want to receive a message from a transactional queue outside of a transaction context.

If you are using queue journaling, removing the message causes a copy to be kept in the journal queue, just as the **MessageQueue** class's **Receive** method does.

When working with transactional queues, a rollback of a transaction causes any messages removed by a call to **RemoveCurrent** to be returned to the queue. The removal is not irreversible until the transaction is committed.

When you remove the current message, the cursor is moved to the next message. You do not have to call **MoveNext** after calling **RemoveCurrent**.

Requirements

Platforms: Windows 98, Windows NT 4.0,
Windows Millennium Edition, Windows 2000,
Windows XP Home Edition, Windows XP Professional,
Windows .NET Server family

.NET Framework Security:

- Full trust for the immediate caller. This member cannot be used
  by partially trusted code.

MessageEnumerator.RemoveCurrent Method (TimeSpan)

Removes the current message from the queue and returns the
message to the calling application. If there is a message to remove,
the method returns it immediately. Otherwise, the method waits the
specified timeout for a new message to arrive.

```
[Visual Basic]
Overloads Public Function RemoveCurrent( _
    ByVal timeout As TimeSpan _
) As Message
[C#]
public Message RemoveCurrent(
    TimeSpan timeout
);
[C++]
public: Message* RemoveCurrent(
    TimeSpan timeout
);
[JScript]
public function RemoveCurrent(
    timeout : TimeSpan
) : Message;
```

Parameters

timeout
    The interval of time to wait for a message to arrive in the queue.

Return Value

A **Message** that references the first message available in the queue.

Exceptions

Exception Type	Condition
ArgumentException	The value specified for the *timeout* parameter is invalid.
MessageQueueException	The timeout has expired.

Remarks

RemoveCurrent removes and returns the message at the cursor's
current location. If the cursor is at the end of the queue, this overload
of the method waits until a message is available or the interval
specified by the *timeout* parameter has expired.

If you are using queue journaling, removing the message causes a
copy to be kept in the journal queue, just as the **MessageQueue**
class's **Receive** method does.

When you remove the current message, the cursor is moved to the
next message. You do not have to call **MoveNext** after calling
RemoveCurrent.

If you call this overload on a transactional queue, Message Queuing
creates a single internal transaction.

Requirements

Platforms: Windows 98, Windows NT 4.0,
Windows Millennium Edition, Windows 2000,
Windows XP Home Edition, Windows XP Professional,
Windows .NET Server family

.NET Framework Security:

- Full trust for the immediate caller. This member cannot be used
  by partially trusted code.

MessageEnumerator.RemoveCurrent Method (TimeSpan, MessageQueueTransaction)

Removes the current message from a transactional queue and returns
the message to the calling application. If there is a message to
remove, the method returns it immediately. Otherwise, the method
waits the specified timeout for a new message to arrive.

```
[Visual Basic]
Overloads Public Function RemoveCurrent( _
    ByVal timeout As TimeSpan, _
    ByVal transaction As MessageQueueTransaction _
) As Message
[C#]
public Message RemoveCurrent(
    TimeSpan timeout,
    MessageQueueTransaction transaction
);
[C++]
public: Message* RemoveCurrent(
    TimeSpan timeout,
    MessageQueueTransaction* transaction
);
[JScript]
public function RemoveCurrent(
    timeout : TimeSpan,
    transaction : MessageQueueTransaction
) : Message;
```

Parameters

timeout
    The interval of time to wait for the message to be removed.
transaction
    The **MessageQueueTransaction** object that specifies the
transaction context for the message.

Return Value

A **Message** that references the first message available in the queue.

Exceptions

Exception Type	Condition
ArgumentException	The value specified for the *timeout* parameter is invalid.
ArgumentNullException	The *transaction* parameter is a null reference (**Nothing** in Visual Basic).
MessageQueueException	The timeout has expired.

Remarks

RemoveCurrent removes and returns the message at the cursor's
current location. If the cursor is at the end of the queue, this overload
of the method waits until a message is available or the interval
specified by the *timeout* parameter has expired.

When working with transactional queues, a rollback of a transaction causes any messages removed by a call to **RemoveCurrent** to be returned to the queue. The removal is not irreversible until the transaction is committed.

If you are using queue journaling, removing the message causes a copy to be kept in the journal queue, just as the **MessageQueue** class's **Receive** method does.

When you remove the current message, the cursor is moved to the next message. You do not have to call **MoveNext** after calling **RemoveCurrent**.

Requirements

Platforms: Windows 98, Windows NT 4.0, Windows Millennium Edition, Windows 2000, Windows XP Home Edition, Windows XP Professional, Windows .NET Server family

.NET Framework Security:
- Full trust for the immediate caller. This member cannot be used by partially trusted code.

MessageEnumerator.RemoveCurrent Method (TimeSpan, MessageQueueTransactionType)

Removes the current message from a queue and returns the message to the calling application. If there is a message to remove, the method returns it immediately. Otherwise, the method waits the specified timeout for a new message to arrive.

```
[Visual Basic]
Overloads Public Function RemoveCurrent( _
   ByVal timeout As TimeSpan, _
   ByVal transactionType As MessageQueueTransactionType _
) As Message
[C#]
public Message RemoveCurrent(
   TimeSpan timeout,
   MessageQueueTransactionType transactionType
);
[C++]
public: Message* RemoveCurrent(
   TimeSpan timeout,
   MessageQueueTransactionType transactionType
);
[JScript]
public function RemoveCurrent(
   timeout : TimeSpan,
   transactionType : MessageQueueTransactionType
) : Message;
```

Parameters

timeout
   The interval of time to wait for the message to be removed.
transactionType
   One of the **MessageQueueTransactionType** values, describing the type of transaction context to associate with the message.

Return Value

A **Message** that references the first message available in the queue.

Exceptions

Exception Type	Condition
ArgumentException	The value specified for the *timeout* parameter is invalid.
MessageQueueException	The timeout has expired.
InvalidEnumArgumentException	The *transactionType* parameter is not one of the **MessageQueueTransactionType** members.

Remarks

RemoveCurrent removes and returns the message at the cursor's current location, using a transaction context defined by the *transactionType* parameter. If the cursor is at the end of the queue, this overload of the method waits until a message is available or the interval specified by the *timeout* parameter has expired.

Specify **Automatic** for the *transactionType* parameter if there is already an external transaction context attached to the thread that you want to use to receive the message. Specify **Single** if you want to receive the message as a single internal transaction. You can specify **None** if you want to receive a message from a transactional queue outside of a transaction context.

If you are using queue journaling, removing the message causes a copy to be kept in the journal queue, just as the **MessageQueue** class's **Receive** method does.

When working with transactional queues, a rollback of a transaction causes any messages removed by a call to **RemoveCurrent** to be returned to the queue. The removal is not irreversible until the transaction is committed.

When you remove the current message, the cursor is moved to the next message. You do not have to call **MoveNext** after calling **RemoveCurrent**.

Requirements

Platforms: Windows 98, Windows NT 4.0, Windows Millennium Edition, Windows 2000, Windows XP Home Edition, Windows XP Professional, Windows .NET Server family

.NET Framework Security:
- Full trust for the immediate caller. This member cannot be used by partially trusted code.

MessageEnumerator.Reset Method

Resets the current enumerator so it points to the head of the queue.

```
[Visual Basic]
Public Overridable Sub Reset() Implements IEnumerator.Reset
[C#]
public virtual void Reset();
[C++]
public: virtual void Reset();
[JScript]
public function Reset();
```

Implements

IEnumerator.Reset

Remarks

An enumerator can only move in a forward direction. Use this method to start over at the beginning of the queue.

After calling **Reset**, the cursor points to the first message. You do not need to call **MoveNext** after calling **Reset** to move the cursor forward to the first message in the queue.

Requirements

Platforms: Windows 98, Windows NT 4.0,
Windows Millennium Edition, Windows 2000,
Windows XP Home Edition, Windows XP Professional,
Windows .NET Server family

.NET Framework Security:

- Full trust for the immediate caller. This member cannot be used by partially trusted code.

MessagePriority Enumeration

Specifies the priority Message Queuing applies to a message while it is en route to a queue, and when inserting the message into the destination queue.

```
[Visual Basic]
<Serializable>
Public Enum MessagePriority
[C#]
[Serializable]
public enum MessagePriority
[C++]
[Serializable]
__value public enum MessagePriority
[JScript]
public
    Serializable
enum MessagePriority
```

Remarks

The **MessagePriority** enumeration is used by the **Message** class's **Priority** property. This property affects how Message Queuing handles the message both while it is en route and once it reaches its destination. Higher-priority messages are given preference during routing and inserted toward the front of the destination queue. Messages with the same priority are placed in the queue according to their arrival time.

When Message Queuing routes a message to a public queue, the priority level of the message is added to the priority level of the public queue (which you can access through the **MessageQueue** class's **BasePriority** property). The priority level of the queue has no effect on how messages are placed in the queue, only on how Message Queuing handles the message while en route.

> **Note** Base priority applies only to public queues. For a private queue, the base priority is always zero.

You can set a meaningful priority only for nontransactional messages. Message Queuing automatically sets the priority for transactional messages to **Lowest**, which causes transactional message priority to be ignored.

Members

Member name	Description
AboveNormal	Between **High** and **Normal** message priority.
High	High message priority.
Highest	Highest message priority.
Low	Low message priority.
Lowest	Lowest message priority.
Normal	Normal message priority.
VeryHigh	Between **Highest** and **High** message priority.
VeryLow	Between **Low** and **Lowest** message priority.

Example

[Visual Basic, C#, C++] The following example sends 2 messages of different priorities to the queue, and retrieves them subsequently.

```
[Visual Basic]
Imports System
Imports System.Messaging

Namespace MyProject
    _

    '/ <summary>
    '/ Provides a container class for the example.
    '/ </summary>
    Public Class MyNewQueue


        '****************************************************
        ' Provides an entry point into the application.
        '
        ' This example sends and receives a message from
        ' a queue.
        '****************************************************
        Public Shared Sub Main()
            ' Create a new instance of the class.
            Dim myNewQueue As New MyNewQueue()

            ' Send messages to a queue.
            myNewQueue.SendMessage(MessagePriority.Normal, _
        "First Message Body.")
            myNewQueue.SendMessage(MessagePriority.Highest, _
        "Second Message Body.")

            ' Receive messages from a queue.
            myNewQueue.ReceiveMessage()
            myNewQueue.ReceiveMessage()

            Return
        End Sub 'Main

        '****************************************************
        ' Sends a string message to a queue.
        '****************************************************
        Public Sub SendMessage(priority As MessagePriority, _
    messageBody As String)

            ' Connect to a queue on the local computer.
            Dim myQueue As New MessageQueue(".\myQueue")

            ' Create a new message.
            Dim myMessage As New Message()

            If priority > MessagePriority.Normal Then
                myMessage.Body = "High Priority: " + messageBody
            Else
                myMessage.Body = messageBody
            End If
            ' Set the priority of the message.
            myMessage.Priority = priority


            ' Send the Order to the queue.
            myQueue.Send(myMessage)

            Return
        End Sub 'SendMessage

        '****************************************************
        ' Receives a message.
        '****************************************************
        Public Sub ReceiveMessage()
            ' Connect to the a queue on the local computer.
            Dim myQueue As New MessageQueue(".\myQueue")

            ' Set the queue to read the priority. By default, it
            ' is not read.
            myQueue.MessageReadPropertyFilter.Priority = True
```

```vb
        ' Set the formatter to indicate body contains a string.
        myQueue.Formatter = New XmlMessageFormatter          ⌐
(New Type() {GetType(String)})

        Try
            ' Receive and format the message.
            Dim myMessage As Message = myQueue.Receive()

            ' Display message information.
            Console.WriteLine(("Priority: " +                ⌐
myMessage.Priority.ToString()))
            Console.WriteLine(("Body: " + myMessage.Body.ToString()))

        Catch
        ' Handle Message Queuing exceptions.

        ' Handle invalid serialization format.
        Catch e As InvalidOperationException
            Console.WriteLine(e.Message)
        End Try

        ' Catch other exceptions as necessary.
        Return
    End Sub 'ReceiveMessage
  End Class 'MyNewQueue
End Namespace 'MyProject
```

```csharp
[C#]
using System;
using System.Messaging;

namespace MyProject
{

    /// <summary>
    /// Provides a container class for the example.
    /// </summary>
    public class MyNewQueue
    {

        //*************************************************
        // Provides an entry point into the application.
        //
        // This example sends and receives a message from
        // a queue.
        //*************************************************

        public static void Main()
        {
            // Create a new instance of the class.
            MyNewQueue myNewQueue = new MyNewQueue();

            // Send messages to a queue.
            myNewQueue.SendMessage(MessagePriority.Normal,    ⌐
"First Message Body.");
            myNewQueue.SendMessage(MessagePriority.Highest,   ⌐
"Second Message Body.");

            // Receive messages from a queue.
            myNewQueue.ReceiveMessage();
            myNewQueue.ReceiveMessage();

            return;
        }

        //*************************************************
        // Sends a string message to a queue.
        //*************************************************

        public void SendMessage(MessagePriority priority,    ⌐
string messageBody)
        {

            // Connect to a queue on the local computer.
            MessageQueue myQueue = new MessageQueue(".\\myQueue");

            // Create a new message.
            Message myMessage = new Message();

            if(priority > MessagePriority.Normal)
            {
                myMessage.Body = "High Priority: " + messageBody;
            }
            else myMessage.Body = messageBody;

            // Set the priority of the message.
            myMessage.Priority = priority;

            // Send the Order to the queue.
            myQueue.Send(myMessage);

            return;
        }

        //*************************************************
        // Receives a message.
        //*************************************************

        public  void ReceiveMessage()
        {
            // Connect to the a queue on the local computer.
            MessageQueue myQueue = new MessageQueue(".\\myQueue");

            // Set the queue to read the priority. By default, it
            // is not read.
            myQueue.MessageReadPropertyFilter.Priority = true;

            // Set the formatter to indicate body contains a string.
            myQueue.Formatter = new XmlMessageFormatter(new Type[]
                {typeof(string)});

            try
            {
                // Receive and format the message.
                Message myMessage =    myQueue.Receive();

                // Display message information.
                Console.WriteLine("Priority: " +
                    myMessage.Priority.ToString());
                Console.WriteLine("Body: " +
                    myMessage.Body.ToString());
            }

            catch (MessageQueueException)
            {
                // Handle Message Queuing exceptions.
            }

            // Handle invalid serialization format.
            catch (InvalidOperationException e)
            {
                Console.WriteLine(e.Message);
            }

            // Catch other exceptions as necessary.

            return;
        }
    }
}
```

```cpp
[C++]
#using <mscorlib.dll>
#using <system.dll>
#using <system.messaging.dll>

using namespace System;
using namespace System::Messaging;

__gc class MyNewQueue
{
```

```
public:
    void SendMessage(MessagePriority priority, String* messageBody)
    {

        // Connect to a queue on the local computer.
        MessageQueue* myQueue = new MessageQueue(S".\\myQueue");

        // Create a new message.
        Message* myMessage = new Message();

        if (priority > MessagePriority::Normal)
        {
            myMessage->Body = S"High Priority: {0}", messageBody;
        }
        else myMessage->Body = messageBody;

        // Set the priority of the message.
        myMessage->Priority = priority;

        // Send the Order to the queue.
        myQueue->Send(myMessage);

        return;
    }

public:
    void ReceiveMessage()
    {
        // Connect to the a queue on the local computer.
        MessageQueue* myQueue = new MessageQueue(S".\\myQueue");

        // Set the queue to read the priority. By default, it
        // is not read.
        myQueue->MessageReadPropertyFilter->Priority = true;

        // Set the formatter to indicate body contains a String*.
        Type* p __gc[] = new Type* __gc[1];
        p[0] = __typeof(String);
        myQueue->Formatter = new XmlMessageFormatter( p );

        try
        {
            // Receive and format the message.
            Message* myMessage = myQueue->Receive();

            // Display message information.
            Console::WriteLine(S"Priority: {0}", __box
(myMessage->Priority));
            Console::WriteLine(S"Body: {0}", myMessage->Body);
        }
        catch (MessageQueueException*)
        {
            // Handle Message Queuing exceptions.
        }

        // Handle invalid serialization format.
        catch (InvalidOperationException* e)
        {
            Console::WriteLine(e->Message);
        }
        // Catch other exceptions as necessary.

        return;
    }
};

int main()
{
    // Create a new instance of the class.
    MyNewQueue* myNewQueue = new MyNewQueue();

    // Send messages to a queue.
    myNewQueue->SendMessage(MessagePriority::Normal,
S"First Message Body.");

    myNewQueue->SendMessage(MessagePriority::Highest,
S"Second Message Body.");

    // Receive messages from a queue.
    myNewQueue->ReceiveMessage();
    myNewQueue->ReceiveMessage();

    return 0;
```

Requirements

Namespace: System.Messaging

Platforms: Windows 98, Windows NT 4.0, Windows Millennium Edition, Windows 2000, Windows XP Home Edition, Windows XP Professional, Windows .NET Server family

Assembly: System.Messaging (in System.Messaging.dll)

MessagePropertyFilter Class

Controls and selects the properties that are retrieved when peeking or receiving messages from a message queue.

System.Object
   System.Messaging.MessagePropertyFilter

```
[Visual Basic]
Public Class MessagePropertyFilter
[C#]
public class MessagePropertyFilter
[C++]
public __gc class MessagePropertyFilter
[JScript]
public class MessagePropertyFilter
```

Thread Safety

Any public static (**Shared** in Visual Basic) members of this type are safe for multithreaded operations. Any instance members are not guaranteed to be thread safe.

Remarks

Setting the **MessagePropertyFilter** on a **MessageQueue** instance controls the set of properties that are retrieved when peeking or receiving a message. The filter is set on the instance of **MessageQueue** that retrieves the message information. When you set a **MessagePropertyFilter** Boolean-valued member to **false**, you prevent the information of the associated **Message** property from being retrieved by the **MessageQueue**.

There are several filter properties that are not Boolean values. They are integer values that get or set the default sizes of the **Message.Body**, **Message.Extension**, or **Message.Label**.

Retrieving a limited set of properties helps improve performance because smaller amounts of data are transferred from the queue.

> **Note** When setting a property on **MessagePropertyFilter**, you are only indicating whether that property is retrieved when a message is received or peeked. You are not changing the associated property value for the **Message**.

The **MessagePropertyFilter** constructor sets all filter properties to their default values, which for the Boolean values is **false**. See the constructor topic for the defaults assigned to the integer-valued properties.

Example

[Visual Basic, C#, C++] The following example sends 2 messages of different priorities to the queue, and retrieves them subsequently.

```
[Visual Basic]
Imports System
Imports System.Messaging

Namespace MyProject
    -

    '/ <summary>
    '/ Provides a container class for the example.
    '/ </summary>
    Public Class MyNewQueue

        '**************************************************
        ' Provides an entry point into the application.
        '
        ' This example sends and receives a message from
```

```
        ' a queue.
        '**************************************************
        Public Shared Sub Main()
            ' Create a new instance of the class.
            Dim myNewQueue As New MyNewQueue()

            ' Send messages to a queue.
            myNewQueue.SendMessage(MessagePriority.Normal, _
        "First Message Body.")
            myNewQueue.SendMessage(MessagePriority.Highest, _
        "Second Message Body.")

            ' Receive messages from a queue.
            myNewQueue.ReceiveMessage()
            myNewQueue.ReceiveMessage()

            Return
        End Sub 'Main

        '**************************************************
        ' Sends a string message to a queue.
        '**************************************************
        Public Sub SendMessage(priority As MessagePriority, _
        messageBody As String)

            ' Connect to a queue on the local computer.
            Dim myQueue As New MessageQueue(".\myQueue")

            ' Create a new message.
            Dim myMessage As New Message()

            If priority > MessagePriority.Normal Then
                myMessage.Body = "High Priority: " + messageBody
            Else
                myMessage.Body = messageBody
            End If
            ' Set the priority of the message.
            myMessage.Priority = priority

            ' Send the Order to the queue.
            myQueue.Send(myMessage)

            Return
        End Sub 'SendMessage

        '**************************************************
        ' Receives a message.
        '**************************************************
        Public Sub ReceiveMessage()
            ' Connect to the a queue on the local computer.
            Dim myQueue As New MessageQueue(".\myQueue")

            ' Set the queue to read the priority. By default, it
            ' is not read.
            myQueue.MessageReadPropertyFilter.Priority = True

            ' Set the formatter to indicate body contains a string.
            myQueue.Formatter = New XmlMessageFormatter _
        (New Type() {GetType(String)})

            Try
                ' Receive and format the message.
                Dim myMessage As Message = myQueue.Receive()

                ' Display message information.
                Console.WriteLine(("Priority: " + _
        myMessage.Priority.ToString()))
                Console.WriteLine(("Body: " + myMessage.Body.ToString()))

            Catch
            ' Handle Message Queuing exceptions.

            ' Handle invalid serialization format.
            Catch e As InvalidOperationException
```

```
            Console.WriteLine(e.Message)
        End Try

        ' Catch other exceptions as necessary.
        Return
    End Sub 'ReceiveMessage
    End Class 'MyNewQueue
End Namespace 'MyProject

[C#]
using System;
using System.Messaging;

namespace MyProject
{

    /// <summary>
    /// Provides a container class for the example.
    /// </summary>
    public class MyNewQueue
    {

        //*************************************************
        // Provides an entry point into the application.
        //
        // This example sends and receives a message from
        // a queue.
        //*************************************************

        public static void Main()
        {
            // Create a new instance of the class.
            MyNewQueue myNewQueue = new MyNewQueue();

            // Send messages to a queue.
            myNewQueue.SendMessage(MessagePriority.Normal,  ⌐
"First Message Body.");
            myNewQueue.SendMessage(MessagePriority.Highest, ⌐
"Second Message Body.");

            // Receive messages from a queue.
            myNewQueue.ReceiveMessage();
            myNewQueue.ReceiveMessage();

            return;
        }

        //*************************************************
        // Sends a string message to a queue.
        //*************************************************

        public void SendMessage(MessagePriority priority,  ⌐
string messageBody)
        {

            // Connect to a queue on the local computer.
            MessageQueue myQueue = new MessageQueue(".\\myQueue");

            // Create a new message.
            Message myMessage = new Message();

            if(priority > MessagePriority.Normal)
            {
                myMessage.Body = "High Priority: " + messageBody;
            }
            else myMessage.Body = messageBody;

            // Set the priority of the message.
            myMessage.Priority = priority;

            // Send the Order to the queue.
            myQueue.Send(myMessage);

            return;
        }
```

```
        //*************************************************
        // Receives a message.
        //*************************************************

        public void ReceiveMessage()
        {

            // Connect to the a queue on the local computer.
            MessageQueue myQueue = new MessageQueue(".\\myQueue");

            // Set the queue to read the priority. By default, it
            // is not read.
            myQueue.MessageReadPropertyFilter.Priority = true;

            // Set the formatter to indicate body contains a string.
            myQueue.Formatter = new XmlMessageFormatter(new Type[]
                {typeof(string)});

            try
            {
                // Receive and format the message.
                Message myMessage =   myQueue.Receive();

                // Display message information.
                Console.WriteLine("Priority: " +
                    myMessage.Priority.ToString());
                Console.WriteLine("Body: " +
                    myMessage.Body.ToString());
            }

            catch (MessageQueueException)
            {
                // Handle Message Queuing exceptions.
            }

            // Handle invalid serialization format.
            catch (InvalidOperationException e)
            {
                Console.WriteLine(e.Message);
            }

            // Catch other exceptions as necessary.

            return;
        }
    }
}

[C++]
#using <mscorlib.dll>
#using <system.dll>
#using <system.messaging.dll>

using namespace System;
using namespace System::Messaging;

__gc class MyNewQueue
{
public:
    void SendMessage(MessagePriority priority, String* messageBody)
    {

        // Connect to a queue on the local computer.
        MessageQueue* myQueue = new MessageQueue(S".\\myQueue");

        // Create a new message.
        Message* myMessage = new Message();

        if (priority > MessagePriority::Normal)
        {
            myMessage->Body = S"High Priority: {0}", messageBody;
        }
        else myMessage->Body = messageBody;

        // Set the priority of the message.
        myMessage->Priority = priority;
```

```
        // Send the Order to the queue.
        myQueue->Send(myMessage);

        return;
    }
public:
    void ReceiveMessage()
    {
        // Connect to the a queue on the local computer.
        MessageQueue* myQueue = new MessageQueue(S".\\myQueue");

        // Set the queue to read the priority. By default, it
        // is not read.
        myQueue->MessageReadPropertyFilter->Priority = true;

        // Set the formatter to indicate body contains a String*.
        Type* p __gc[] = new Type* __gc[1];
        p[0] = __typeof(String);
        myQueue->Formatter = new XmlMessageFormatter( p );

        try
        {
            // Receive and format the message.
            Message* myMessage = myQueue->Receive();

            // Display message information.
            Console::WriteLine(S"Priority: {0}", __box
(myMessage->Priority));
            Console::WriteLine(S"Body: {0}", myMessage->Body);
        }
        catch (MessageQueueException*)
        {
            // Handle Message Queuing exceptions.
        }

        // Handle invalid serialization format.
        catch (InvalidOperationException* e)
        {
            Console::WriteLine(e->Message);
        }
        // Catch other exceptions as necessary.

        return;
    }
};

int main()
{
    // Create a new instance of the class.
    MyNewQueue* myNewQueue = new MyNewQueue();

    // Send messages to a queue.
    myNewQueue->SendMessage(MessagePriority::Normal,
S"First Message Body.");
    myNewQueue->SendMessage(MessagePriority::Highest,
S"Second Message Body.");

    // Receive messages from a queue.
    myNewQueue->ReceiveMessage();
    myNewQueue->ReceiveMessage();

    return 0;
```

Requirements

Namespace: System.Messaging

Platforms: Windows 98, Windows NT 4.0, Windows Millennium Edition, Windows 2000, Windows XP Home Edition, Windows XP Professional, Windows .NET Server family

Assembly: System.Messaging (in System.Messaging.dll)

MessagePropertyFilter Constructor

Initializes a new instance of the **MessagePropertyFilter** class and sets default values for all properties.

```
[Visual Basic]
Public Sub New()
[C#]
public MessagePropertyFilter();
[C++]
public: MessagePropertyFilter();
[JScript]
public function MessagePropertyFilter();
```

Remarks

The **ctor** constructor sets all Boolean values to **false** and sets the integer-valued properties to the following default values.

Property	Default Value
DefaultBodySize	1024
DefaultExtensionSize	255
DefaultLabelSize	255

Requirements

Platforms: Windows 98, Windows NT 4.0, Windows Millennium Edition, Windows 2000, Windows XP Home Edition, Windows XP Professional, Windows .NET Server family

.NET Framework Security:
- Full trust for the immediate caller. This member cannot be used by partially trusted code.

MessagePropertyFilter.AcknowledgeType Property

Gets or sets a value indicating whether to retrieve **Message.AcknowledgeType** property information when receiving or peeking a message.

```
[Visual Basic]
Public Property AcknowledgeType As Boolean
[C#]
public bool AcknowledgeType {get; set;}
[C++]
public: __property bool get_AcknowledgeType();
public: __property void set_AcknowledgeType(bool);
[JScript]
public function get AcknowledgeType() : Boolean;
public function set AcknowledgeType(Boolean);
```

Property Value

true to receive **Message.AcknowledgeType** information; otherwise, **false**. The default is **false**.

Remarks

The **AcknowledgeType** property of the **Message** class specifies the type of acknowledgment messages requested by the sending application. The type of acknowledgment defines when acknowledgments are returned. Set the **Message.AcknowledgeType** property before sending the message to request a specific type of acknowledgment.

Requirements

Platforms: Windows 98, Windows NT 4.0,
Windows Millennium Edition, Windows 2000,
Windows XP Home Edition, Windows XP Professional,
Windows .NET Server family

.NET Framework Security:

- Full trust for the immediate caller. This member cannot be used by partially trusted code.

MessagePropertyFilter.Acknowledgment Property

Gets or sets a value indicating whether to retrieve
Message.Acknowledgment property information when receiving or peeking a message.

```
[Visual Basic]
Public Property Acknowledgment As Boolean
[C#]
public bool Acknowledgment {get; set;}
[C++]
public: __property bool get_Acknowledgment();
public: __property void set_Acknowledgment(bool);
[JScript]
public function get Acknowledgment() : Boolean;
public function set Acknowledgment(Boolean);
```

Property Value

true to receive **Message.Acknowledgment** information; otherwise,
false. The default is **false**.

Remarks

The **Message.Acknowledgment** property of the **Message** class
specifies the type of acknowledgment messages the system posts in
the administration queue, which determines when acknowledgments
are generated.

Acknowledgments are returned from the destination queue and
posted as messages to the **AdministrationQueue** specified by the
original message. The type of acknowledgment generated depends
on what was requested.

Read the **Message.Acknowledgment** property when receiving a
message from an administration queue to verify the status of the
message originally sent to the message queue.

Example

See related example in the
System.Messaging.MessagePropertyFilter class topic.

Requirements

Platforms: Windows 98, Windows NT 4.0,
Windows Millennium Edition, Windows 2000,
Windows XP Home Edition, Windows XP Professional,
Windows .NET Server family

.NET Framework Security:

- Full trust for the immediate caller. This member cannot be used by partially trusted code.

MessagePropertyFilter.AdministrationQueue Property

Gets or sets a value indicating whether to retrieve
Message.AdministrationQueue property information when
receiving or peeking a message.

```
[Visual Basic]
Public Property AdministrationQueue As Boolean
[C#]
public bool AdministrationQueue {get; set;}
[C++]
public: __property bool get_AdministrationQueue();
public: __property void set_AdministrationQueue(bool);
[JScript]
public function get AdministrationQueue() : Boolean;
public function set AdministrationQueue(Boolean);
```

Property Value

true to receive **Message.AdministrationQueue** information;
otherwise, **false**. The default is **false**.

Remarks

The **AdministrationQueue** property of the **Message** class specifies
the name of the queue that receives system-generated
acknowledgments.

Requirements

Platforms: Windows 98, Windows NT 4.0,
Windows Millennium Edition, Windows 2000,
Windows XP Home Edition, Windows XP Professional,
Windows .NET Server family

.NET Framework Security:

- Full trust for the immediate caller. This member cannot be used by partially trusted code.

MessagePropertyFilter.AppSpecific Property

Gets or sets a value indicating whether to retrieve
Message.AppSpecific property information when receiving or
peeking a message.

```
[Visual Basic]
Public Property AppSpecific As Boolean
[C#]
public bool AppSpecific {get; set;}
[C++]
public: __property bool get_AppSpecific();
public: __property void set_AppSpecific(bool);
[JScript]
public function get AppSpecific() : Boolean;
public function set AppSpecific(Boolean);
```

Property Value

true to receive **Message.AppSpecific** information; otherwise, **false**.
The default is **false**.

Remarks

The **AppSpecific** property of the **Message** class contains additional,
application-specific information.

Requirements

Platforms: Windows 98, Windows NT 4.0,
Windows Millennium Edition, Windows 2000,

Windows XP Home Edition, Windows XP Professional,
Windows .NET Server family

.NET Framework Security:

- Full trust for the immediate caller. This member cannot be used
  by partially trusted code.

MessagePropertyFilter.ArrivedTime Property

Gets or sets a value indicating whether to retrieve
Message.ArrivedTime property information when receiving or
peeking a message.

```
[Visual Basic]
Public Property ArrivedTime As Boolean
[C#]
public bool ArrivedTime {get; set;}
[C++]
public: __property bool get_ArrivedTime();
public: __property void set_ArrivedTime(bool);
[JScript]
public function get ArrivedTime() : Boolean;
public function set ArrivedTime(Boolean);
```

Property Value

true to receive **Message.ArrivedTime** information; otherwise,
false. The default is **false**.

Remarks

The **ArrivedTime** property of the **Message** class indicates when the
message arrived at the destination queue. This is local time, adjusted
from GMT, of the computer on which the message is retrieved.

Requirements

Platforms: Windows 98, Windows NT 4.0,
Windows Millennium Edition, Windows 2000,
Windows XP Home Edition, Windows XP Professional,
Windows .NET Server family

.NET Framework Security:

- Full trust for the immediate caller. This member cannot be used
  by partially trusted code.

MessagePropertyFilter.AttachSenderId Property

Gets or sets a value indicating whether to retrieve
Message.AttachSenderId property information when receiving or
peeking a message.

```
[Visual Basic]
Public Property AttachSenderId As Boolean
[C#]
public bool AttachSenderId {get; set;}
[C++]
public: __property bool get_AttachSenderId();
public: __property void set_AttachSenderId(bool);
[JScript]
public function get AttachSenderId() : Boolean;
public function set AttachSenderId(Boolean);
```

Property Value

true to receive **Message.AttachSenderId** information; otherwise,
false. The default is **false**.

Remarks

The **AttachSenderId** property of the **Message** class specifies
whether the **Message.SenderId** should be or has been attached to
the message. The **Message.SenderId** is set by Message Queuing
and is used by the receiving Queue Manager to verify whether the
sender has access rights to a queue.

Requirements

Platforms: Windows 98, Windows NT 4.0,
Windows Millennium Edition, Windows 2000,
Windows XP Home Edition, Windows XP Professional,
Windows .NET Server family

.NET Framework Security:

- Full trust for the immediate caller. This member cannot be used
  by partially trusted code.

MessagePropertyFilter.Authenticated Property

Gets or sets a value indicating whether to retrieve
Message.Authenticated property information when receiving or
peeking a message.

```
[Visual Basic]
Public Property Authenticated As Boolean
[C#]
public bool Authenticated {get; set;}
[C++]
public: __property bool get_Authenticated();
public: __property void set_Authenticated(bool);
[JScript]
public function get Authenticated() : Boolean;
public function set Authenticated(Boolean);
```

Property Value

true to receive **Message.Authenticated** information; otherwise,
false. The default is **false**.

Remarks

The **Authenticated** property of the **Message** class is used by the
receiving application to determine if authentication was requested. If
authentication was requested and the message is in the queue, then
the message is authenticated.

> **Note** It is not possible to look at the properties of a message
> and determine whether a message failed authentication.
> Messages that fail authentication are discarded and are not
> delivered to the queue.

Requirements

Platforms: Windows 98, Windows NT 4.0,
Windows Millennium Edition, Windows 2000,
Windows XP Home Edition, Windows XP Professional,
Windows .NET Server family

.NET Framework Security:

- Full trust for the immediate caller. This member cannot be used
  by partially trusted code.

MessagePropertyFilter.AuthenticationProvider-Name Property

Gets or sets a value indicating whether to retrieve **Message.AuthenticationProviderName** property information when receiving or peeking a message.

```
[Visual Basic]
Public Property AuthenticationProviderName As Boolean
[C#]
public bool AuthenticationProviderName {get; set;}
[C++]
public: __property bool get_AuthenticationProviderName();
public: __property void set_AuthenticationProviderName(bool);
[JScript]
public function get AuthenticationProviderName() : Boolean;
public function set AuthenticationProviderName(Boolean);
```

Property Value

true to receive **Message.AuthenticationProviderName** information; otherwise, **false**. The default is **false**.

Remarks

The **AuthenticationProviderName** property of the **Message** class specifies the name of the cryptographic provider used to generate the digital signature of the message.
Message.AuthenticationProviderName is typically used when working with foreign queues.

> **Note** A foreign queue exists in a queuing system other than Microsoft Message Queuing. Microsoft Message Queuing communicates with such queues through a connector application.

Requirements

Platforms: Windows 98, Windows NT 4.0, Windows Millennium Edition, Windows 2000, Windows XP Home Edition, Windows XP Professional, Windows .NET Server family

.NET Framework Security:
- Full trust for the immediate caller. This member cannot be used by partially trusted code.

MessagePropertyFilter.AuthenticationProvider-Type Property

Gets or sets a value indicating whether to retrieve **Message.AuthenticationProviderType** property information when receiving or peeking a message.

```
[Visual Basic]
Public Property AuthenticationProviderType As Boolean
[C#]
public bool AuthenticationProviderType {get; set;}
[C++]
public: __property bool get_AuthenticationProviderType();
public: __property void set_AuthenticationProviderType(bool);
[JScript]
public function get AuthenticationProviderType() : Boolean;
public function set AuthenticationProviderType(Boolean);
```

Property Value

true to receive **Message.AuthenticationProviderType** information; otherwise, **false**. The default is **false**.

Remarks

The **AuthenticationProviderType** property of the **Message** class specifies the type of cryptographic provider used to generate the digital signature of the message. **AuthenticationProviderType** is typically used when working with foreign queues.

> **Note** A foreign queue exists in a queuing system other than Microsoft Message Queuing. Microsoft Message Queuing communicates with such queues through a connector application.

Requirements

Platforms: Windows 98, Windows NT 4.0, Windows Millennium Edition, Windows 2000, Windows XP Home Edition, Windows XP Professional, Windows .NET Server family

.NET Framework Security:
- Full trust for the immediate caller. This member cannot be used by partially trusted code.

MessagePropertyFilter.Body Property

Gets or sets a value indicating whether to retrieve **Message.Body** property information when receiving or peeking a message.

```
[Visual Basic]
Public Property Body As Boolean
[C#]
public bool Body {get; set;}
[C++]
public: __property bool get_Body();
public: __property void set_Body(bool);
[JScript]
public function get Body() : Boolean;
public function set Body(Boolean);
```

Property Value

true to receive **Message.Body** information; otherwise, **false**. The default is **false**.

Remarks

The **Body** property of the **Message** class represents the serialized contents of the message. The body can contain up to 4 MB of data.

Requirements

Platforms: Windows 98, Windows NT 4.0, Windows Millennium Edition, Windows 2000, Windows XP Home Edition, Windows XP Professional, Windows .NET Server family

.NET Framework Security:
- Full trust for the immediate caller. This member cannot be used by partially trusted code.

MessagePropertyFilter.ConnectorType Property

Gets or sets a value indicating whether to retrieve **Message.ConnectorType** property information when receiving or peeking a message.

[Visual Basic]
```
Public Property ConnectorType As Boolean
```
[C#]
```
public bool ConnectorType {get; set;}
```
[C++]
```
public: __property bool get_ConnectorType();
public: __property void set_ConnectorType(bool);
```
[JScript]
```
public function get ConnectorType() : Boolean;
public function set ConnectorType(Boolean);
```

Property Value

true to receive **Message.ConnectorType** information; otherwise, **false**. The default is **false**.

Remarks

The **ConnectorType** property of the **Message** class is required when an application sets a message property that is typically set by Message Queuing. It is used in two instances.

- When a message is passed by a connector application, the **Message.ConnectorType** is required for the sending and receiving applications to interpret the security and acknowledgment properties of the message.
- When sending application-encrypted messages, the **Message.ConnectorType** property informs Message Queuing to use the symmetric key.

Requirements

Platforms: Windows 98, Windows NT 4.0, Windows Millennium Edition, Windows 2000, Windows XP Home Edition, Windows XP Professional, Windows .NET Server family

.NET Framework Security:
- Full trust for the immediate caller. This member cannot be used by partially trusted code.

MessagePropertyFilter.CorrelationId Property

Gets or sets a value indicating whether to retrieve **Message.CorrelationId** property information when receiving or peeking a message.

[Visual Basic]
```
Public Property CorrelationId As Boolean
```
[C#]
```
public bool CorrelationId {get; set;}
```
[C++]
```
public: __property bool get_CorrelationId();
public: __property void set_CorrelationId(bool);
```
[JScript]
```
public function get CorrelationId() : Boolean;
public function set CorrelationId(Boolean);
```

Property Value

true to receive **Message.CorrelationId** information; otherwise, **false**. The default is **false**.

Remarks

The **CorrelationId** property of the **Message** class specifies a message identifier that is used by acknowledgment and report messages to reference the original message. It provides an application-defined identifier that the receiving application can use to sort messages.

Example

See related example in the **System.Messaging.MessagePropertyFilter** class topic.

Requirements

Platforms: Windows 98, Windows NT 4.0, Windows Millennium Edition, Windows 2000, Windows XP Home Edition, Windows XP Professional, Windows .NET Server family

.NET Framework Security:
- Full trust for the immediate caller. This member cannot be used by partially trusted code.

MessagePropertyFilter.DefaultBodySize Property

Gets or sets the size, in bytes, of the default body buffer.

[Visual Basic]
```
Public Property DefaultBodySize As Integer
```
[C#]
```
public int DefaultBodySize {get; set;}
```
[C++]
```
public: __property int get_DefaultBodySize();
public: __property void set_DefaultBodySize(int);
```
[JScript]
```
public function get DefaultBodySize() : int;
public function set DefaultBodySize(int);
```

Property Value

The default body buffer size to create when the message is received. The default is 1024 bytes.

Exceptions

Exception Type	Condition
ArgumentException	The assigned value is negative.

Remarks

The default body size specifies the number of bytes to allocate for the message's body contents. The **Body** property of the **Message** class represents the serialized contents of the message. The body can contain up to 4 MB of data. Restricting the body size can improve performance.

Requirements

Platforms: Windows 98, Windows NT 4.0, Windows Millennium Edition, Windows 2000, Windows XP Home Edition, Windows XP Professional, Windows .NET Server family

.NET Framework Security:
- Full trust for the immediate caller. This member cannot be used by partially trusted code.

MessagePropertyFilter.DefaultExtensionSize Property

Gets or sets the size, in bytes, of the default extension buffer.

[Visual Basic]
```
Public Property DefaultExtensionSize As Integer
```
[C#]
```
public int DefaultExtensionSize {get; set;}
```

```
[C++]
public: _property int get_DefaultExtensionSize();
public: _property void set_DefaultExtensionSize(int);
[JScript]
public function get DefaultExtensionSize() : int;
public function set DefaultExtensionSize(int);
```

Property Value

The default extension buffer size to create when the message is received. The default is 255 bytes.

Exceptions

Exception Type	Condition
ArgumentException	The assigned value is negative.

Remarks

The default extension size specifies the number of bytes to allocate for the message's extension. The **Extension** property of the **Message** class represents the additional, application-defined information associated with the message, such as a binary large object. It is the responsibility of the application to interpret the contents of the **Extension**.

Requirements

Platforms: Windows 98, Windows NT 4.0, Windows Millennium Edition, Windows 2000, Windows XP Home Edition, Windows XP Professional, Windows .NET Server family

.NET Framework Security:

- Full trust for the immediate caller. This member cannot be used by partially trusted code.

MessagePropertyFilter.DefaultLabelSize Property

Gets or sets the size, in bytes, of the default label buffer.

```
[Visual Basic]
Public Property DefaultLabelSize As Integer
[C#]
public int DefaultLabelSize {get; set;}
[C++]
public: _property int get_DefaultLabelSize();
public: _property void set_DefaultLabelSize(int);
[JScript]
public function get DefaultLabelSize() : int;
public function set DefaultLabelSize(int);
```

Property Value

The default label buffer size to create when the message is received. The default is 255 bytes.

Exceptions

Exception Type	Condition
ArgumentException	The assigned value is negative.

Remarks

The default label size specifies the number of bytes to allocate for the message's label. The **Label** property of the **Message** class specifies the label of the message.

Requirements

Platforms: Windows 98, Windows NT 4.0, Windows Millennium Edition, Windows 2000, Windows XP Home Edition, Windows XP Professional, Windows .NET Server family

.NET Framework Security:

- Full trust for the immediate caller. This member cannot be used by partially trusted code.

MessagePropertyFilter.DestinationQueue Property

Gets or sets a value indicating whether to retrieve **Message.DestinationQueue** property information when receiving or peeking a message.

```
[Visual Basic]
Public Property DestinationQueue As Boolean
[C#]
public bool DestinationQueue {get; set;}
[C++]
public: _property bool get_DestinationQueue();
public: _property void set_DestinationQueue(bool);
[JScript]
public function get DestinationQueue() : Boolean;
public function set DestinationQueue(Boolean);
```

Property Value

true to receive **Message.DestinationQueue** information; otherwise, **false**. The default is **false**.

Remarks

The **DestinationQueue** property of the **Message** class identifies the original destination queue of the message. It is typically used to determine the original destination of a message that is in a journal or dead-letter queue. It can also be used when sending a response message back to a response queue.

Requirements

Platforms: Windows 98, Windows NT 4.0, Windows Millennium Edition, Windows 2000, Windows XP Home Edition, Windows XP Professional, Windows .NET Server family

.NET Framework Security:

- Full trust for the immediate caller. This member cannot be used by partially trusted code.

MessagePropertyFilter.DestinationSymmetric-Key Property

Gets or sets a value indicating whether to retrieve **Message.DestinationSymmetricKey** property information when receiving or peeking a message.

```
[Visual Basic]
Public Property DestinationSymmetricKey As Boolean
[C#]
public bool DestinationSymmetricKey {get; set;}
[C++]
public: _property bool get_DestinationSymmetricKey();
public: _property void set_DestinationSymmetricKey(bool);
```

```
[JScript]
public function get DestinationSymmetricKey() : Boolean;
public function set DestinationSymmetricKey(Boolean);
```

Property Value

true to receive **Message.DestinationSymmetricKey** information; otherwise, **false**. The default is **false**.

Remarks

The **DestinationSymmetricKey** property of the **Message** class specifies the symmetric key used to encrypt the message. It is required when you send application-encrypted messages, or when you send encrypted messages to a foreign queue.

> **Note** A foreign queue exists in a queuing system other than Microsoft Message Queuing. Microsoft Message Queuing communicates with such queues through a connector application.

Requirements

Platforms: Windows 98, Windows NT 4.0, Windows Millennium Edition, Windows 2000, Windows XP Home Edition, Windows XP Professional, Windows .NET Server family

.NET Framework Security:
- Full trust for the immediate caller. This member cannot be used by partially trusted code.

MessagePropertyFilter.DigitalSignature Property

Gets or sets a value indicating whether to retrieve **Message.DigitalSignature** property information when receiving or peeking a message.

```
[Visual Basic]
Public Property DigitalSignature As Boolean
[C#]
public bool DigitalSignature {get; set;}
[C++]
public: __property bool get_DigitalSignature();
public: __property void set_DigitalSignature(bool);
[JScript]
public function get DigitalSignature() : Boolean;
public function set DigitalSignature(Boolean);
```

Property Value

true to receive **Message.DigitalSignature** information; otherwise, **false**. The default is **false**.

Remarks

The **DigitalSignature** property of the **Message** class specifies the digital signature used to authenticate the message. In most cases, it is generated and set by Message Queuing when the sending application requests authentication.

Requirements

Platforms: Windows 98, Windows NT 4.0, Windows Millennium Edition, Windows 2000, Windows XP Home Edition, Windows XP Professional, Windows .NET Server family

.NET Framework Security:
- Full trust for the immediate caller. This member cannot be used by partially trusted code.

MessagePropertyFilter.EncryptionAlgorithm Property

Gets or sets a value indicating whether to retrieve **Message.EncryptionAlgorithm** property information when receiving or peeking a message.

```
[Visual Basic]
Public Property EncryptionAlgorithm As Boolean
[C#]
public bool EncryptionAlgorithm {get; set;}
[C++]
public: __property bool get_EncryptionAlgorithm();
public: __property void set_EncryptionAlgorithm(bool);
[JScript]
public function get EncryptionAlgorithm() : Boolean;
public function set EncryptionAlgorithm(Boolean);
```

Property Value

true to receive **Message.EncryptionAlgorithm** information; otherwise, **false**. The default is **false**.

Remarks

If a message is private, it is encrypted before it is sent and decrypted when it is received. The **EncryptionAlgorithm** property of the **Message** class specifies the algorithm used to encrypt the message body of a private message.

Requirements

Platforms: Windows 98, Windows NT 4.0, Windows Millennium Edition, Windows 2000, Windows XP Home Edition, Windows XP Professional, Windows .NET Server family

.NET Framework Security:
- Full trust for the immediate caller. This member cannot be used by partially trusted code.

MessagePropertyFilter.Extension Property

Gets or sets a value indicating whether to retrieve **Message.Extension** property information when receiving or peeking a message.

```
[Visual Basic]
Public Property Extension As Boolean
[C#]
public bool Extension {get; set;}
[C++]
public: __property bool get_Extension();
public: __property void set_Extension(bool);
[JScript]
public function get Extension() : Boolean;
public function set Extension(Boolean);
```

Property Value

true to receive **Message.Extension** information; otherwise, **false**. The default is **false**.

Remarks

The **Extension** property of the **Message** class provides for additional application-defined information that is associated with the message, like a large binary object. It is the responsibility of the receiving application to interpret the contents of the **Extension**.

Requirements

Platforms: Windows 98, Windows NT 4.0, Windows Millennium Edition, Windows 2000, Windows XP Home Edition, Windows XP Professional, Windows .NET Server family

.NET Framework Security:

- Full trust for the immediate caller. This member cannot be used by partially trusted code.

MessagePropertyFilter.HashAlgorithm Property

Gets or sets a value indicating whether to retrieve **Message.HashAlgorithm** property information when receiving or peeking a message.

```
[Visual Basic]
Public Property HashAlgorithm As Boolean
[C#]
public bool HashAlgorithm {get; set;}
[C++]
public: __property bool get_HashAlgorithm();
public: __property void set_HashAlgorithm(bool);
[JScript]
public function get HashAlgorithm() : Boolean;
public function set HashAlgorithm(Boolean);
```

Property Value

true to receive **Message.HashAlgorithm** information; otherwise, **false**. The default is **false**.

Remarks

The **HashAlgorithm** property of the **Message** class identifies the hashing algorithm Message Queuing uses when authenticating messages. The hashing algorithm is also used when creating a digital signature for a message.

Requirements

Platforms: Windows 98, Windows NT 4.0, Windows Millennium Edition, Windows 2000, Windows XP Home Edition, Windows XP Professional, Windows .NET Server family

.NET Framework Security:

- Full trust for the immediate caller. This member cannot be used by partially trusted code.

MessagePropertyFilter.Id Property

Gets or sets a value indicating whether to retrieve **Message.Id** property information when receiving or peeking a message.

```
[Visual Basic]
Public Property Id As Boolean
[C#]
public bool Id {get; set;}
[C++]
public: __property bool get_Id();
public: __property void set_Id(bool);
```

```
[JScript]
public function get Id() : Boolean;
public function set Id(Boolean);
```

Property Value

true to receive **Message.Id** information; otherwise, **false**. The default is **false**.

Remarks

The **Id** property of the **Message** class indicates the Message Queuing-generated unique identifier of the message. This identifier is generated when the message is sent.

Requirements

Platforms: Windows 98, Windows NT 4.0, Windows Millennium Edition, Windows 2000, Windows XP Home Edition, Windows XP Professional, Windows .NET Server family

.NET Framework Security:

- Full trust for the immediate caller. This member cannot be used by partially trusted code.

MessagePropertyFilter.IsFirstInTransaction Property

Gets or sets a value indicating whether to retrieve **Message.IsFirstInTransaction** property information when receiving or peeking a message.

```
[Visual Basic]
Public Property IsFirstInTransaction As Boolean
[C#]
public bool IsFirstInTransaction {get; set;}
[C++]
public: __property bool get_IsFirstInTransaction();
public: __property void set_IsFirstInTransaction(bool);
[JScript]
public function get IsFirstInTransaction() : Boolean;
public function set IsFirstInTransaction(Boolean);
```

Property Value

true to receive **Message.IsFirstInTransaction** information; otherwise, **false**. The default is **false**.

Remarks

The **IsFirstInTransaction** property of the **Message** class is used by receiving applications to verify whether a message is the first message sent in a single transaction to a single queue.

Requirements

Platforms: Windows 98, Windows NT 4.0, Windows Millennium Edition, Windows 2000, Windows XP Home Edition, Windows XP Professional, Windows .NET Server family

.NET Framework Security:

- Full trust for the immediate caller. This member cannot be used by partially trusted code.

MessagePropertyFilter.IsLastInTransaction Property

Gets or sets a value indicating whether to retrieve **Message.IsLastInTransaction** property information when receiving or peeking a message.

```
[Visual Basic]
Public Property IsLastInTransaction As Boolean
[C#]
public bool IsLastInTransaction {get; set;}
[C++]
public: __property bool get_IsLastInTransaction();
public: __property void set_IsLastInTransaction(bool);
[JScript]
public function get IsLastInTransaction() : Boolean;
public function set IsLastInTransaction(Boolean);
```

Property Value

true to receive **Message.IsLastInTransaction** information; otherwise, **false**. The default is **false**.

Remarks

The **IsLastInTransaction** property of the **Message** class is used by receiving applications to verify whether a message is the last message sent from a single transaction to a single queue.

Requirements

Platforms: Windows 98, Windows NT 4.0, Windows Millennium Edition, Windows 2000, Windows XP Home Edition, Windows XP Professional, Windows .NET Server family

.NET Framework Security:

- Full trust for the immediate caller. This member cannot be used by partially trusted code.

MessagePropertyFilter.Label Property

Gets or sets a value indicating whether to retrieve **Message.Label** property information when receiving or peeking a message.

```
[Visual Basic]
Public Property Label As Boolean
[C#]
public bool Label {get; set;}
[C++]
public: __property bool get_Label();
public: __property void set_Label(bool);
[JScript]
public function get Label() : Boolean;
public function set Label(Boolean);
```

Property Value

true to receive **Message.Label** information; otherwise, **false**. The default is **false**.

Remarks

The **Label** property of the **Message** class specifies the label of the message.

Requirements

Platforms: Windows 98, Windows NT 4.0, Windows Millennium Edition, Windows 2000,

Windows XP Home Edition, Windows XP Professional, Windows .NET Server family

.NET Framework Security:

- Full trust for the immediate caller. This member cannot be used by partially trusted code.

MessagePropertyFilter.MessageType Property

Gets or sets a value indicating whether to retrieve **Message.MessageType** property information when receiving or peeking a message.

```
[Visual Basic]
Public Property MessageType As Boolean
[C#]
public bool MessageType {get; set;}
[C++]
public: __property bool get_MessageType();
public: __property void set_MessageType(bool);
[JScript]
public function get MessageType() : Boolean;
public function set MessageType(Boolean);
```

Property Value

true to receive **Message.MessageType** information; otherwise, **false**. The default is **false**.

Remarks

The **MessageType** property of the **Message** class identifies the type of the message. A message can be a normal message, a positive or negative acknowledgment message, or a report message.

Requirements

Platforms: Windows 98, Windows NT 4.0, Windows Millennium Edition, Windows 2000, Windows XP Home Edition, Windows XP Professional, Windows .NET Server family

.NET Framework Security:

- Full trust for the immediate caller. This member cannot be used by partially trusted code.

MessagePropertyFilter.Priority Property

Gets or sets a value indicating whether to retrieve **Message.Priority** property information when receiving or peeking a message.

```
[Visual Basic]
Public Property Priority As Boolean
[C#]
public bool Priority {get; set;}
[C++]
public: __property bool get_Priority();
public: __property void set_Priority(bool);
[JScript]
public function get Priority() : Boolean;
public function set Priority(Boolean);
```

Property Value

true to receive **Message.Priority** information; otherwise, **false**. The default is **false**.

Remarks

The **Priority** property of the **Message** class affects how Message Queuing handles the message while it is en route, as well as where the message is placed in the queue when it reaches its destination.

Message priority can only be set meaningfully for non-transactional messages. The priority for transactional messages is automatically set to zero, which causes transactional message priority to be ignored.

Example

See related example in the **System.Messaging.MessagePropertyFilter** class topic.

Requirements

Platforms: Windows 98, Windows NT 4.0, Windows Millennium Edition, Windows 2000, Windows XP Home Edition, Windows XP Professional, Windows .NET Server family

.NET Framework Security:

- Full trust for the immediate caller. This member cannot be used by partially trusted code.

MessagePropertyFilter.Recoverable Property

Gets or sets a value indicating whether to retrieve **Message.Recoverable** property information when receiving or peeking a message.

```
[Visual Basic]
Public Property Recoverable As Boolean
[C#]
public bool Recoverable {get; set;}
[C++]
public: __property bool get_Recoverable();
public: __property void set_Recoverable(bool);
[JScript]
public function get Recoverable() : Boolean;
public function set Recoverable(Boolean);
```

Property Value

true to receive **Message.Recoverable** information; otherwise, **false**. The default is **false**.

Remarks

The **Recoverable** property of the **Message** class indicates whether delivery of a message is guaranteed, even if a computer crashes while the message is en route to the destination queue.

If delivery of a message is guaranteed, the message is stored locally at every step until the message is successfully forwarded to the next computer. Setting **Message.Recoverable** to **true** on the message could affect the throughput.

Requirements

Platforms: Windows 98, Windows NT 4.0, Windows Millennium Edition, Windows 2000, Windows XP Home Edition, Windows XP Professional, Windows .NET Server family

.NET Framework Security:

- Full trust for the immediate caller. This member cannot be used by partially trusted code.

MessagePropertyFilter.ResponseQueue Property

Gets or sets a value indicating whether to retrieve **Message.ResponseQueue** property information when receiving or peeking a message.

```
[Visual Basic]
Public Property ResponseQueue As Boolean
[C#]
public bool ResponseQueue {get; set;}
[C++]
public: __property bool get_ResponseQueue();
public: __property void set_ResponseQueue(bool);
[JScript]
public function get ResponseQueue() : Boolean;
public function set ResponseQueue(Boolean);
```

Property Value

true to receive **Message.ResponseQueue** information; otherwise, **false**. The default is **false**.

Remarks

The **ResponseQueue** property of the **Message** class identifies the queue that receives application-generated response messages that are sent back to the sending application by the receiving application. Response queues are specified by the sending application when the application sends its messages. Any available queue can be specified as a response queue.

Messages returned to the response queue are application-specific. The application must define what is in the messages as well as what is to be done when a message is received.

Requirements

Platforms: Windows 98, Windows NT 4.0, Windows Millennium Edition, Windows 2000, Windows XP Home Edition, Windows XP Professional, Windows .NET Server family

.NET Framework Security:

- Full trust for the immediate caller. This member cannot be used by partially trusted code.

MessagePropertyFilter.SenderCertificate Property

Gets or sets a value indicating whether to retrieve **Message.SenderCertificate** property information when receiving or peeking a message.

```
[Visual Basic]
Public Property SenderCertificate As Boolean
[C#]
public bool SenderCertificate {get; set;}
[C++]
public: __property bool get_SenderCertificate();
public: __property void set_SenderCertificate(bool);
[JScript]
public function get SenderCertificate() : Boolean;
public function set SenderCertificate(Boolean);
```

Property Value

true to receive **Message.SenderCertificate** information; otherwise, **false**. The default is **false**.

Remarks

The **SenderCertificate** property of the **Message** class specifies the security certificate used to authenticate messages.

Requirements

Platforms: Windows 98, Windows NT 4.0, Windows Millennium Edition, Windows 2000, Windows XP Home Edition, Windows XP Professional, Windows .NET Server family

.NET Framework Security:

- Full trust for the immediate caller. This member cannot be used by partially trusted code.

MessagePropertyFilter.SenderId Property

Gets or sets a value indicating whether to retrieve **Message.SenderId** property information when receiving or peeking a message.

```
[Visual Basic]
Public Property SenderId As Boolean
[C#]
public bool SenderId {get; set;}
[C++]
public: __property bool get_SenderId();
public: __property void set_SenderId(bool);
[JScript]
public function get SenderId() : Boolean;
public function set SenderId(Boolean);
```

Property Value

true to receive **Message.SenderId** information; otherwise, **false**. The default is **false**.

Remarks

The **SenderId** property of the **Message** class is used primarily by the receiving queue manager when authenticating a message. The property is set by Message Queuing and is used by the queue manager to verify who sent the message and that the sender has access rights to the receiving queue.

Requirements

Platforms: Windows 98, Windows NT 4.0, Windows Millennium Edition, Windows 2000, Windows XP Home Edition, Windows XP Professional, Windows .NET Server family

.NET Framework Security:

- Full trust for the immediate caller. This member cannot be used by partially trusted code.

MessagePropertyFilter.SenderVersion Property

Gets or sets a value indicating whether to retrieve **Message.SenderVersion** property information when receiving or peeking a message.

```
[Visual Basic]
Public Property SenderVersion As Boolean
[C#]
public bool SenderVersion {get; set;}
[C++]
public: __property bool get_SenderVersion();
public: __property void set_SenderVersion(bool);
```

```
[JScript]
public function get SenderVersion() : Boolean;
public function set SenderVersion(Boolean);
```

Property Value

true to receive **Message.SenderVersion** information; otherwise, **false**. The default is **false**.

Remarks

The **SenderVersion** property of the **Message** class specifies the version of Message Queuing used to send the message. The property is important to be aware of when using features like transaction processing, which is only supported by Message Queuing version 2.0 and later, or digital signatures, which are used to authenticate messages sent by version 1.0.

Message.SenderVersion is set by the sending queue manager when the message is sent.

Requirements

Platforms: Windows 98, Windows NT 4.0, Windows Millennium Edition, Windows 2000, Windows XP Home Edition, Windows XP Professional, Windows .NET Server family

.NET Framework Security:

- Full trust for the immediate caller. This member cannot be used by partially trusted code.

MessagePropertyFilter.SentTime Property

Gets or sets a value indicating whether to retrieve **Message.SentTime** property information when receiving or peeking a message.

```
[Visual Basic]
Public Property SentTime As Boolean
[C#]
public bool SentTime {get; set;}
[C++]
public: __property bool get_SentTime();
public: __property void set_SentTime(bool);
[JScript]
public function get SentTime() : Boolean;
public function set SentTime(Boolean);
```

Property Value

true to receive **Message.SentTime** information; otherwise, **false**. The default is **false**.

Remarks

The **SentTime** property of the **Message** class indicates the sending machine's date and time when the message was sent by the source Queue Manager.

Requirements

Platforms: Windows 98, Windows NT 4.0, Windows Millennium Edition, Windows 2000, Windows XP Home Edition, Windows XP Professional, Windows .NET Server family

.NET Framework Security:

- Full trust for the immediate caller. This member cannot be used by partially trusted code.

MessagePropertyFilter.SourceMachine Property

Gets or sets a value indicating whether to retrieve
Message.SourceMachine property information when receiving or
peeking a message.

```
[Visual Basic]
Public Property SourceMachine As Boolean
[C#]
public bool SourceMachine {get; set;}
[C++]
public: __property bool get_SourceMachine();
public: __property void set_SourceMachine(bool);
[JScript]
public function get SourceMachine() : Boolean;
public function set SourceMachine(Boolean);
```

Property Value

true to receive **Message.SourceMachine** information; otherwise,
false. The default is **false**.

Remarks

The **SourceMachine** property of the **Message** class specifies the
computer where the message originated.

Requirements

Platforms: Windows 98, Windows NT 4.0,
Windows Millennium Edition, Windows 2000,
Windows XP Home Edition, Windows XP Professional,
Windows .NET Server family

.NET Framework Security:

- Full trust for the immediate caller. This member cannot be used
  by partially trusted code.

MessagePropertyFilter.TimeToBeReceived Property

Gets or sets a value indicating whether to retrieve
Message.TimeToBeReceived property information when receiving
or peeking a message.

```
[Visual Basic]
Public Property TimeToBeReceived As Boolean
[C#]
public bool TimeToBeReceived {get; set;}
[C++]
public: __property bool get_TimeToBeReceived();
public: __property void set_TimeToBeReceived(bool);
[JScript]
public function get TimeToBeReceived() : Boolean;
public function set TimeToBeReceived(Boolean);
```

Property Value

true to receive **Message.TimeToBeReceived** information;
otherwise, **false**. The default is **false**.

Remarks

The **TimeToBeReceived** property of the **Message** class specifies the
total time in seconds for a sent message to be received from the
destination queue. The time limit for the message to be retrieved
from the target queue includes the time spent getting to the
destination queue, plus the time spent waiting in the queue before
the message is retrieved by an application.

Requirements

Platforms: Windows 98, Windows NT 4.0,
Windows Millennium Edition, Windows 2000,
Windows XP Home Edition, Windows XP Professional,
Windows .NET Server family

.NET Framework Security:

- Full trust for the immediate caller. This member cannot be used
  by partially trusted code.

MessagePropertyFilter.TimeToReachQueue Property

Gets or sets a value indicating whether to retrieve
Message.TimeToReachQueue property information when
receiving or peeking a message.

```
[Visual Basic]
Public Property TimeToReachQueue As Boolean
[C#]
public bool TimeToReachQueue {get; set;}
[C++]
public: __property bool get_TimeToReachQueue();
public: __property void set_TimeToReachQueue(bool);
[JScript]
public function get TimeToReachQueue() : Boolean;
public function set TimeToReachQueue(Boolean);
```

Property Value

true to receive **Message.TimeToReachQueue** information;
otherwise, **false**. The default is **false**.

Remarks

The **TimeToReachQueue** property of the **Message** class specifies a
time limit in seconds from the time the message is sent for it to reach
the destination queue.

Requirements

Platforms: Windows 98, Windows NT 4.0,
Windows Millennium Edition, Windows 2000,
Windows XP Home Edition, Windows XP Professional,
Windows .NET Server family

.NET Framework Security:

- Full trust for the immediate caller. This member cannot be used
  by partially trusted code.

MessagePropertyFilter.TransactionId Property

Gets or sets a value indicating whether to retrieve
Message.TransactionId property information when receiving or
peeking a message.

```
[Visual Basic]
Public Property TransactionId As Boolean
[C#]
public bool TransactionId {get; set;}
[C++]
public: __property bool get_TransactionId();
public: __property void set_TransactionId(bool);
[JScript]
public function get TransactionId() : Boolean;
public function set TransactionId(Boolean);
```

Property Value

true to receive **Message.TransactionId** information; otherwise, **false**. The default is **false**.

Remarks

The **TransactionId** property of the **Message** class identifies the transaction that sent the message. Use this property within a receiving application to verify that a message was sent as part of a specific transaction.

Requirements

Platforms: Windows 98, Windows NT 4.0, Windows Millennium Edition, Windows 2000, Windows XP Home Edition, Windows XP Professional, Windows .NET Server family

.NET Framework Security:

- Full trust for the immediate caller. This member cannot be used by partially trusted code.

MessagePropertyFilter.TransactionStatusQueue Property

Gets or sets a value indicating whether to retrieve **Message.TransactionStatusQueue** property information when receiving or peeking a message.

```
[Visual Basic]
Public Property TransactionStatusQueue As Boolean
[C#]
public bool TransactionStatusQueue {get; set;}
[C++]
public: __property bool get_TransactionStatusQueue();
public: __property void set_TransactionStatusQueue(bool);
[JScript]
public function get TransactionStatusQueue() : Boolean;
public function set TransactionStatusQueue(Boolean);
```

Property Value

true to receive **Message.TransactionStatusQueue** information; otherwise, **false**. The default is **false**.

Remarks

The **TransactionStatusQueue** property of the **Message** class identifies the transaction status queue on the source computer. The property is used for sending acknowledgment messages back to the sending application. The transaction status queue is used by connector applications when receiving transactional messages sent to a foreign queue.

> **Note** A foreign queue exists in a queuing system other than Microsoft Message Queuing. Microsoft Message Queuing communicates with such queues through a connector application.

Requirements

Platforms: Windows 98, Windows NT 4.0, Windows Millennium Edition, Windows 2000, Windows XP Home Edition, Windows XP Professional, Windows .NET Server family

.NET Framework Security:

- Full trust for the immediate caller. This member cannot be used by partially trusted code.

MessagePropertyFilter.UseAuthentication Property

Gets or sets a value indicating whether to retrieve **Message.UseAuthentication** property information when receiving or peeking a message.

```
[Visual Basic]
Public Property UseAuthentication As Boolean
[C#]
public bool UseAuthentication {get; set;}
[C++]
public: __property bool get_UseAuthentication();
public: __property void set_UseAuthentication(bool);
[JScript]
public function get UseAuthentication() : Boolean;
public function set UseAuthentication(Boolean);
```

Property Value

true to receive **Message.UseAuthentication** information; otherwise, **false**. The default is **false**.

Remarks

The **UseAuthentication** property of the **Message** class specifies whether the message needs to be authenticated.

> **Note** It is not possible to look at the properties of a message and determine whether a message failed authentication. Messages that fail authentication are discarded and are not delivered to the queue.

Requirements

Platforms: Windows 98, Windows NT 4.0, Windows Millennium Edition, Windows 2000, Windows XP Home Edition, Windows XP Professional, Windows .NET Server family

.NET Framework Security:

- Full trust for the immediate caller. This member cannot be used by partially trusted code.

MessagePropertyFilter.UseDeadLetterQueue Property

Gets or sets a value indicating whether to retrieve **Message.UseDeadLetterQueue** property information when receiving or peeking a message.

```
[Visual Basic]
Public Property UseDeadLetterQueue As Boolean
[C#]
public bool UseDeadLetterQueue {get; set;}
[C++]
public: __property bool get_UseDeadLetterQueue();
public: __property void set_UseDeadLetterQueue(bool);
[JScript]
public function get UseDeadLetterQueue() : Boolean;
public function set UseDeadLetterQueue(Boolean);
```

Property Value

true to receive **Message.UseDeadLetterQueue** information; otherwise, **false**. The default is **false**.

Remarks

The **UseDeadLetterQueue** property of the **Message** class specifies whether a copy of a message that could not be delivered should be sent to a dead-letter queue.

Requirements

Platforms: Windows 98, Windows NT 4.0, Windows Millennium Edition, Windows 2000, Windows XP Home Edition, Windows XP Professional, Windows .NET Server family

.NET Framework Security:

- Full trust for the immediate caller. This member cannot be used by partially trusted code.

MessagePropertyFilter.UseEncryption Property

Gets or sets a value indicating whether to retrieve **Message.UseEncryption** property information when receiving or peeking a message.

```
[Visual Basic]
Public Property UseEncryption As Boolean
[C#]
public bool UseEncryption {get; set;}
[C++]
public: __property bool get_UseEncryption();
public: __property void set_UseEncryption(bool);
[JScript]
public function get UseEncryption() : Boolean;
public function set UseEncryption(Boolean);
```

Property Value

true to receive **Message.UseEncryption** information; otherwise, **false**. The default is **false**.

Remarks

The **UseEncryption** property of the **Message** class specifies whether to encrypt a message.

Requirements

Platforms: Windows 98, Windows NT 4.0, Windows Millennium Edition, Windows 2000, Windows XP Home Edition, Windows XP Professional, Windows .NET Server family

.NET Framework Security:

- Full trust for the immediate caller. This member cannot be used by partially trusted code.

MessagePropertyFilter.UseJournalQueue Property

Gets or sets a value indicating whether to retrieve **Message.UseJournalQueue** property information when receiving or peeking a message.

```
[Visual Basic]
Public Property UseJournalQueue As Boolean
[C#]
public bool UseJournalQueue {get; set;}
[C++]
public: __property bool get_UseJournalQueue();
public: __property void set_UseJournalQueue(bool);
```

```
[JScript]
public function get UseJournalQueue() : Boolean;
public function set UseJournalQueue(Boolean);
```

Property Value

true to receive **Message.UseJournalQueue** information; otherwise, **false**. The default is **false**.

Remarks

The **UseJournalQueue** property of the **Message** class specifies whether a copy of the message should be kept in a machine journal on the originating computer.

Requirements

Platforms: Windows 98, Windows NT 4.0, Windows Millennium Edition, Windows 2000, Windows XP Home Edition, Windows XP Professional, Windows .NET Server family

.NET Framework Security:

- Full trust for the immediate caller. This member cannot be used by partially trusted code.

MessagePropertyFilter.UseTracing Property

Gets or sets a value indicating whether to retrieve **Message.UseTracing** property information when receiving or peeking a message.

```
[Visual Basic]
Public Property UseTracing As Boolean
[C#]
public bool UseTracing {get; set;}
[C++]
public: __property bool get_UseTracing();
public: __property void set_UseTracing(bool);
[JScript]
public function get UseTracing() : Boolean;
public function set UseTracing(Boolean);
```

Property Value

true to receive **Message.UseTracing** information; otherwise, **false**. The default is **false**.

Remarks

The **UseTracing** property of the **Message** class specifies whether to track the route of a message as it moves toward its destination queue. If **true**, each time the original message passes through a Message Queuing routing server, a Message Queuing-generated report message is sent to the system report queue.

> **Note** Using tracing involves setting up Active Directory and specifying a report queue for the Message Queuing enterprise. These settings are configured by the administrator.

Requirements

Platforms: Windows 98, Windows NT 4.0, Windows Millennium Edition, Windows 2000, Windows XP Home Edition, Windows XP Professional, Windows .NET Server family

.NET Framework Security:

- Full trust for the immediate caller. This member cannot be used by partially trusted code.

MessagePropertyFilter.ClearAll Method

Sets all Boolean filter values to **false**, so that no message properties are retrieved when receiving a message.

```
[Visual Basic]
Public Sub ClearAll()
[C#]
public void ClearAll();
[C++]
public: void ClearAll();
[JScript]
public function ClearAll();
```

Return Value

Use **ClearAll** to set all **MessagePropertyFilter** Boolean properties to **false**. This causes no message properties to be retrieved when receiving messages. **ClearAll** does not affect the values for **DefaultBodySize**, **DefaultExtensionSize**, or **DefaultLabelSize**.

After calling **ClearAll**, it is necessary to set at least one filter property to **true** in order to receive data related to a message. You can either set individual properties to **true**, or you can call **SetDefaults** or **SetAll**.

Requirements

Platforms: Windows 98, Windows NT 4.0, Windows Millennium Edition, Windows 2000, Windows XP Home Edition, Windows XP Professional, Windows .NET Server family

.NET Framework Security:

- Full trust for the immediate caller. This member cannot be used by partially trusted code.

MessagePropertyFilter.SetAll Method

Specifies to retrieve all message properties when receiving a message.

```
[Visual Basic]
Public Sub SetAll()
[C#]
public void SetAll();
[C++]
public: void SetAll();
[JScript]
public function SetAll();
```

Remarks

Use **SetAll** to set all Boolean **MessagePropertyFilter** properties to **true**. This causes all message properties to be retrieved when receiving messages. **SetAll** does not affect the values for **DefaultBodySize**, **DefaultExtensionSize**, or **DefaultLabelSize**.

After calling **SetAll**, you can set individual filter values to **false** in order to restrict the properties retrieved when the message is received.

Requirements

Platforms: Windows 98, Windows NT 4.0, Windows Millennium Edition, Windows 2000, Windows XP Home Edition, Windows XP Professional, Windows .NET Server family

.NET Framework Security:

- Full trust for the immediate caller. This member cannot be used by partially trusted code.

MessagePropertyFilter.SetDefaults Method

Sets the filter values of common Message Queuing properties to **true** and the integer-valued properties to their default values.

```
[Visual Basic]
Public Sub SetDefaults()
[C#]
public void SetDefaults();
[C++]
public: void SetDefaults();
[JScript]
public function SetDefaults();
```

Remarks

Use **SetDefaults** to set the following **MessagePropertyFilter** Boolean-valued properties to **true** and the rest to **false**. These are the most common properties a **MessageQueue** will typically interact with.

- **ArrivedTime**
- **AdministrationQueue**
- **Body**
- **CorrelationId**
- **Id**
- **Label**
- **ResponseQueue**
- **SentTime**

SetDefaults sets the following properties to their default values.

Property	Default Value
DefaultBodySize	1024
DefaultExtensionSize	255
DefaultLabelSize	255

The **MessageQueue.MessageReadPropertyFilter** property represents a **MessagePropertyFilter** on which **SetDefaults** has been called.

Requirements

Platforms: Windows 98, Windows NT 4.0, Windows Millennium Edition, Windows 2000, Windows XP Home Edition, Windows XP Professional, Windows .NET Server family

.NET Framework Security:

- Full trust for the immediate caller. This member cannot be used by partially trusted code.

MessageQueue Class

Provides access to a queue on a Message Queuing server.

System.Object
  System.MarshalByRefObject
    System.ComponentModel.Component
      System.Messaging.MessageQueue

```
[Visual Basic]
Public Class MessageQueue
   Inherits Component
   Implements IEnumerable
[C#]
public class MessageQueue : Component, IEnumerable
[C++]
public __gc class MessageQueue : public Component, IEnumerable
[JScript]
public class MessageQueue extends Component implements IEnumerable
```

Thread Safety

Only the following methods are safe for multithreaded operations: **BeginPeek**, **BeginReceive**, **EndPeek**, **EndReceive**, **GetAllMessages**, and **Peek**, **Receive**.

Remarks

Message Queuing technology allows applications running at different times to communicate across heterogeneous networks and systems, which might be temporarily offline. Applications send, receive, or peek (read without removing) messages from queues. Message Queuing is an optional component of Windows 2000 and Windows NT, and must be installed separately.

The **MessageQueue** class is a wrapper around Message Queuing. There are multiple versions of Message Queuing, and using the **MessageQueue** class can result in slightly different behavior, depending on the operating system you are using. For information about specific features of each version of Message Queuing, see the topic "What's New in Message Queuing" in the Platform SDK in MSDN.

The **MessageQueue** class provides a reference to a Message Queuing queue. You can specify a path in the **MessageQueue** constructor to connect to an existing resource, or you can create a new queue on the server. Before you can call **Send**, **Peek**, or **Receive**, you must associate the new instance of the **MessageQueue** class with an existing queue. At that point, you can manipulate the queue properties such as **Category** and **Label**.

MessageQueue supports two types of message retrieval: synchronous and asynchronous. The synchronous methods, **Peek** and **Receive**, cause the process thread to wait a specified time interval for a new message to arrive in the queue. The asynchronous methods, **BeginPeek** and **BeginReceive**, allow the main application tasks to continue in a separate thread until a message arrives in the queue. These methods work by using callback objects and state objects to communicate information between threads.

When you create a new instance of the **MessageQueue** class, you are not creating a new Message Queuing queue. Instead, you can use the **Create**, **Delete**, and **Purge** methods to manage queues on the server.

> **Note** Unlike **Purge**, **Create** and **Delete** are static (**Shared** in Visual Basic) members, so you can call them without creating a new instance of the **MessageQueue** class.

You can set the **MessageQueue** object's **Path** property with one of three names: the friendly name, the **FormatName**, or the **Label**. The friendly name, which is defined by the queue's **MachineName** and **QueueName** properties, is **MachineName\ QueueName** for a public queue, and **MachineName\ Private$\ QueueName** for a private queue. The **FormatName** property allows offline access to message queues. Lastly, you can use the queue's **Label** property to set the queue's **Path**.

For a list of initial property values for an instance of **MessageQueue**, see the **MessageQueue** constructor.

Example

[Visual Basic, C#, C++] The following example creates new **MessageQueue** objects using various path name syntax types. In each case, it sends a message to the queue whose path is defined in the constructor.

```
[Visual Basic]
Imports System
Imports System.Messaging

Namespace MyProject

   '/ <summary>
   '/ Provides a container class for the example.
   '/ </summary>
   Public Class MyNewQueue

      '****************************************************
      ' Provides an entry point into the application.
      '
      ' This example demonstrates several ways to set
      ' a queue's path.
      '****************************************************

      Public Shared Sub Main()

         ' Create a new instance of the class.
         Dim myNewQueue As New MyNewQueue()

         myNewQueue.SendPublic()
         myNewQueue.SendPrivate()
         myNewQueue.SendByLabel()
         myNewQueue.SendByFormatName()
         myNewQueue.MonitorComputerJournal()
         myNewQueue.MonitorQueueJournal()
         myNewQueue.MonitorDeadLetter()
         myNewQueue.MonitorTransactionalDeadLetter()

         Return

      End Sub 'Main

      ' References public queues.
      Public Sub SendPublic()

         Dim myQueue As New MessageQueue(".\myQueue")
         myQueue.Send("Public queue by path name.")

         Return

      End Sub 'SendPublic

      ' References private queues.
      Public Sub SendPrivate()

         Dim myQueue As New MessageQueue(".\Private$\myQueue")
         myQueue.Send("Private queue by path name.")

         Return

      End Sub 'SendPrivate
```

```vb
' References queues by label.
Public Sub SendByLabel()

    Dim myQueue As New MessageQueue("Label:TheLabel")
    myQueue.Send("Queue by label.")

    Return

End Sub 'SendByLabel

' References queues by format name.
Public Sub SendByFormatName()

    Dim myQueue As New _
        MessageQueue("FormatName:Public=" + _
        "5A5F7535-AE9A-41d4-935C-845C2AFF7112")
    myQueue.Send("Queue by format name.")

    Return

End Sub 'SendByFormatName

' References computer journal queues.
Public Sub MonitorComputerJournal()

    Dim computerJournal As New MessageQueue(".\Journal$")

    While True

        Dim journalMessage As Message = _
            computerJournal.Receive()

        ' Process the journal message.

    End While

    Return
End Sub 'MonitorComputerJournal

' References queue journal queues.
Public Sub MonitorQueueJournal()

    Dim queueJournal As New _
                MessageQueue(".\myQueue\Journal$")

    While True

        Dim journalMessage As Message = _
            queueJournal.Receive()

        ' Process the journal message.

    End While

    Return
End Sub 'MonitorQueueJournal

' References dead-letter queues.
Public Sub MonitorDeadLetter()
    Dim deadLetter As New MessageQueue(".\DeadLetter$")

    While True

        Dim deadMessage As Message = deadLetter.Receive()

        ' Process the dead-letter message.

    End While

    Return

End Sub 'MonitorDeadLetter

' References transactional dead-letter queues.
Public Sub MonitorTransactionalDeadLetter()
```

```vb
    Dim TxDeadLetter As New MessageQueue(".\XactDeadLetter$")

    While True

        Dim txDeadLetterMessage As Message = _
            TxDeadLetter.Receive()

        ' Process the transactional dead-letter message.

    End While

    Return

    End Sub 'MonitorTransactionalDeadLetter

End Class 'MyNewQueue
End Namespace 'MyProject
```

```csharp
[C#]
using System;
using System.Messaging;

namespace MyProject
{
    /// <summary>
    /// Provides a container class for the example.
    /// </summary>
    public class MyNewQueue
    {

        //***************************************************
        // Provides an entry point into the application.
        //
        // This example demonstrates several ways to set
        // a queue's path.
        //***************************************************

        public static void Main()
        {
            // Create a new instance of the class.
            MyNewQueue myNewQueue = new MyNewQueue();

            myNewQueue.SendPublic();
            myNewQueue.SendPrivate();
            myNewQueue.SendByLabel();
            myNewQueue.SendByFormatName();
            myNewQueue.MonitorComputerJournal();
            myNewQueue.MonitorQueueJournal();
            myNewQueue.MonitorDeadLetter();
            myNewQueue.MonitorTransactionalDeadLetter();

            return;
        }

        // References public queues.
        public void SendPublic()
        {
            MessageQueue myQueue = new MessageQueue(".\\myQueue");
            myQueue.Send("Public queue by path name.");

            return;
        }

        // References private queues.
        public void SendPrivate()
        {
            MessageQueue myQueue = new
                MessageQueue(".\\Private$\\myQueue");
            myQueue.Send("Private queue by path name.");

            return;
        }

        // References queues by label.
        public void SendByLabel()
```

```
    {
        MessageQueue myQueue = new MessageQueue("Label:TheLabel");
        myQueue.Send("Queue by label.");

        return;
    }

    // References queues by format name.
    public void SendByFormatName()
    {
        MessageQueue myQueue = new
            MessageQueue("FormatName:Public=5A5F7535-AE9A-41d4" +
            "-935C-845C2AFF7112");
        myQueue.Send("Queue by format name.");

        return;
    }

    // References computer journal queues.
    public void MonitorComputerJournal()
    {
        MessageQueue computerJournal = new
            MessageQueue(".\\Journal$");
        while(true)
        {
            Message journalMessage = computerJournal.Receive();
            // Process the journal message.
        }
    }

    // References queue journal queues.
    public void MonitorQueueJournal()
    {
        MessageQueue queueJournal = new
            MessageQueue(".\\myQueue\\Journal$");
        while(true)
        {
            Message journalMessage = queueJournal.Receive();
            // Process the journal message.
        }
    }

    // References dead-letter queues.
    public void MonitorDeadLetter()
    {
        MessageQueue deadLetter = new
            MessageQueue(".\\DeadLetter$");
        while(true)
        {
            Message deadMessage = deadLetter.Receive();
            // Process the dead-letter message.
        }
    }

    // References transactional dead-letter queues.
    public void MonitorTransactionalDeadLetter()
    {
        MessageQueue TxDeadLetter = new
            MessageQueue(".\\XactDeadLetter$");
        while(true)
        {
            Message txDeadLetter = TxDeadLetter.Receive();
            // Process the transactional dead-letter message.
        }
    }
}
}

[C++]
#using <mscorlib.dll>
#using <system.dll>
#using <system.messaging.dll>
```

```
using namespace System;
using namespace System::Messaging;

__gc class MyNewQueue
{
    // References public queues.
public:
    void SendPublic()
    {
        MessageQueue* myQueue = new MessageQueue(S".\\myQueue");
        myQueue->Send(S"Public queue by path name.");

        return;
    }

    // References private queues.
public:
    void SendPrivate()
    {
        MessageQueue* myQueue = new
MessageQueue(S".\\Private$\\myQueue");
        myQueue->Send(S"Private queue by path name.");

        return;
    }

    // References queues by label.
public:
    void SendByLabel()
    {
        MessageQueue* myQueue = new MessageQueue(S"Label:TheLabel");
        myQueue->Send(S"Queue by label.");

        return;
    }

    // References queues by format name.
public:
    void SendByFormatName()
    {
        MessageQueue* myQueue = new
MessageQueue(S"FormatName:Public=5A5F7535-AE9A-41d4 -935C-
845C2AFF7112");
        myQueue->Send(S"Queue by format name.");

        return;
    }

    // References computer journal queues.
public:
    void MonitorComputerJournal()
    {
        MessageQueue* computerJournal = new
MessageQueue(S".\\Journal$");
        while(true)
        {
            Message* journalMessage = computerJournal->Receive();
            // Process the journal message.
        }
    }

    // References queue journal queues.
public:
    void MonitorQueueJournal()
    {
        MessageQueue* queueJournal = new
MessageQueue(S".\\myQueue\\Journal$");
        while(true)
        {
            Message* journalMessage = queueJournal->Receive();
            // Process the journal message.
        }
    }
```

```cpp
    // References dead-letter queues.
public:
    void MonitorDeadLetter()
    {
        MessageQueue* deadLetter = new MessageQueue(S".\\DeadLetter$");
        while(true)
        {
            Message* deadMessage = deadLetter->Receive();
            // Process the dead-letter message.
        }
    }

    // References transactional dead-letter queues.
public:
    void MonitorTransactionalDeadLetter()
    {
        MessageQueue* TxDeadLetter = new
MessageQueue(S".\\XactDeadLetter$");
        while(true)
        {
            Message* txDeadLetter = TxDeadLetter->Receive();
            // Process the transactional dead-letter message.
        }
    }

};

//*************************************************
// Provides an entry point into the application.
//
// This example demonstrates several ways to set
// a queue's path.
//*************************************************
int main()
{
    // Create a new instance of the class.
    MyNewQueue* myNewQueue = new MyNewQueue();

    myNewQueue->SendPublic();
    myNewQueue->SendPrivate();
    myNewQueue->SendByLabel();
    myNewQueue->SendByFormatName();
    myNewQueue->MonitorComputerJournal();
    myNewQueue->MonitorQueueJournal();
    myNewQueue->MonitorDeadLetter();
    myNewQueue->MonitorTransactionalDeadLetter();

    return 0;
}
```

[Visual Basic, C#, C++] The following example sends a message to a queue, and receives a message from a queue, using an application-specific class called "Order".

[Visual Basic]
```vb
Imports System
Imports System.Messaging

Namespace MyProject

    ' This class represents an object the following example
    ' sends to a queue and receives from a queue.
    Public Class Order
        Public orderId As Integer
        Public orderTime As DateTime
    End Class 'Order

    '/ <summary>
    '/ Provides a container class for the example.
    '/ </summary>
    Public Class MyNewQueue

        '*************************************************
        ' Provides an entry point into the application.
        '
```

```vb
        ' This example sends and receives a message from
        ' a qeue.
        '*************************************************

        Public Shared Sub Main()

            ' Create a new instance of the class.
            Dim myNewQueue As New MyNewQueue()

            ' Send a message to a queue.
            myNewQueue.SendMessage()

            ' Receive a message from a queue.
            myNewQueue.ReceiveMessage()

            Return

        End Sub 'Main

        '*************************************************
        ' Sends an Order to a queue.
        '*************************************************

        Public Sub SendMessage()

            ' Create a new order and set values.
            Dim sentOrder As New Order()
            sentOrder.orderId = 3
            sentOrder.orderTime = DateTime.Now

            ' Connect to a queue on the local computer.
            Dim myQueue As New MessageQueue(".\myQueue")

            ' Send the Order to the queue.
            myQueue.Send(sentOrder)

            Return

        End Sub 'SendMessage

        '*************************************************
        ' Receives a message containing an Order.
        '*************************************************

        Public Sub ReceiveMessage()

            ' Connect to the a queue on the local computer.
            Dim myQueue As New MessageQueue(".\myQueue")

            ' Set the formatter to indicate the body contains an Order.
            myQueue.Formatter = New XmlMessageFormatter(New Type() _
                {GetType(MyProject.Order)})

            Try

                ' Receive and format the message.
                Dim myMessage As Message = myQueue.Receive()
                Dim myOrder As Order = CType(myMessage.Body, Order)

                ' Display message information.
                Console.WriteLine(("Order ID: " + _
                    myOrder.orderId.ToString()))
                Console.WriteLine(("Sent: " + _
                    myOrder.orderTime.ToString()))

            Catch m As MessageQueueException
                ' Handle Message Queuing exceptions.

            Catch e As InvalidOperationException
                ' Handle invalid serialization format.
                Console.WriteLine(e.Message)

                ' Catch other exceptions as necessary.

            End Try
```

```
            Return

        End Sub 'ReceiveMessage

    End Class 'MyNewQueue
End Namespace 'MyProject

[C#]
using System;
using System.Messaging;

namespace MyProject
{

    // This class represents an object the following example
    // sends to a queue and receives from a queue.
    public class Order
    {
        public int orderId;
        public DateTime orderTime;
    };

    /// <summary>
    /// Provides a container class for the example.
    /// </summary>
    public class MyNewQueue
    {

        //*************************************************
        // Provides an entry point into the application.
        //
        // This example sends and receives a message from
        // a queue.
        //*************************************************

        public static void Main()
        {
            // Create a new instance of the class.
            MyNewQueue myNewQueue = new MyNewQueue();

            // Send a message to a queue.
            myNewQueue.SendMessage();

            // Receive a message from a queue.
            myNewQueue.ReceiveMessage();

            return;
        }

        //*************************************************
        // Sends an Order to a queue.
        //*************************************************

        public void SendMessage()
        {

            // Create a new order and set values.
            Order sentOrder = new Order();
            sentOrder.orderId = 3;
            sentOrder.orderTime = DateTime.Now;

            // Connect to a queue on the local computer.
            MessageQueue myQueue = new MessageQueue(".\\myQueue");

            // Send the Order to the queue.
            myQueue.Send(sentOrder);

            return;
        }

        //*************************************************
        // Receives a message containing an Order.
        //*************************************************
```

```
        public void ReceiveMessage()
        {
            // Connect to the a queue on the local computer.
            MessageQueue myQueue = new MessageQueue(".\\myQueue");

            // Set the formatter to indicate body contains an Order.
            myQueue.Formatter = new XmlMessageFormatter(new Type[]
                {typeof(MyProject.Order)});

            try
            {
                // Receive and format the message.
                Message myMessage =    myQueue.Receive();
                Order myOrder = (Order)myMessage.Body;

                // Display message information.
                Console.WriteLine("Order ID: " +
                    myOrder.orderId.ToString());
                Console.WriteLine("Sent: " +
                    myOrder.orderTime.ToString());
            }

            catch (MessageQueueException)
            {
                // Handle Message Queuing exceptions.
            }

            // Handle invalid serialization format.
            catch (InvalidOperationException e)
            {
                Console.WriteLine(e.Message);
            }

            // Catch other exceptions as necessary.

            return;
        }
    }
}

[C++]
#using <mscorlib.dll>
#using <system.dll>
#using <system.messaging.dll>

using namespace System;
using namespace System::Messaging;

// This class represents an Object* the following example
// sends to a queue and receives from a queue.
__gc class Order
{
public:
    int orderId;
public:
    DateTime orderTime;
};

/// <summary>
/// Provides a container class for the example.
/// </summary>
__gc class MyNewQueue
{
    //*************************************************
    // Sends an Order to a queue.
    //*************************************************
public:
    void SendMessage()
    {

        // Create a new order and set values.
        Order* sentOrder = new Order();
        sentOrder->orderId = 3;
        sentOrder->orderTime = DateTime::Now;
```

```
    // Connect to a queue on the local computer.
    MessageQueue* myQueue = new MessageQueue(S".\\myQueue");

    // Send the Order to the queue.
    myQueue->Send(sentOrder);

    return;
}

//***************************************************
// Receives a message containing an Order.
//***************************************************
public:
    void ReceiveMessage()
    {
        // Connect to the a queue on the local computer.
        MessageQueue* myQueue = new MessageQueue(S".\\myQueue");

        // Set the formatter to indicate body contains an Order.
        Type* p __gc[] = new Type* __gc[1];
        p[0] = __typeof(Order);
        myQueue->Formatter = new XmlMessageFormatter( p );

        try
        {
            // Receive and format the message.
            Message* myMessage = myQueue->Receive();
            Order* myOrder = static_cast<Order*>(myMessage->Body);

            // Display message information.
            Console::WriteLine(S"Order ID: {0}", __box(myOrder-
>orderId));
            Console::WriteLine(S"Sent: {0}", __box(myOrder-
>orderTime));
        }
        catch (MessageQueueException*)
        {
            // Handle Message Queuing exceptions.
        }

        // Handle invalid serialization format.
        catch (InvalidOperationException* e)
        {
            Console::WriteLine(e->Message);
        }

        // Catch other exceptions as necessary.

        return;
    }
};

//***************************************************
// Provides an entry point into the application.
//
// This example sends and receives a message from
// a queue.
//***************************************************
int main()
{
    // Create a new instance of the class.
    MyNewQueue* myNewQueue = new MyNewQueue();

    // Send a message to a queue.
    myNewQueue->SendMessage();

    // Receive a message from a queue.
    myNewQueue->ReceiveMessage();

    return 0;
}
```

Requirements

Namespace: System.Messaging

Platforms: Windows 98, Windows NT 4.0, Windows Millennium Edition, Windows 2000, Windows XP Home Edition, Windows XP Professional, Windows .NET Server family

Assembly: System.Messaging (in System.Messaging.dll)

MessageQueue Constructor

Initializes a new instance of the **MessageQueue** class.

Overload List

Initializes a new instance of the **MessageQueue** class. After the default constructor initializes the new instance, you must set the instance's **Path** property before you can use the instance.

[Visual Basic] **Public Sub New()**
[C#] **public MessageQueue();**
[C++] **public: MessageQueue();**
[JScript] **public function MessageQueue();**

Initializes a new instance of the **MessageQueue** class that references the Message Queuing queue at the specified path.

[Visual Basic] **Public Sub New(String)**
[C#] **public MessageQueue(string);**
[C++] **public: MessageQueue(String*);**
[JScript] **public function MessageQueue(String);**

Initializes a new instance of the **MessageQueue** class that references the Message Queuing queue at the specified path and with the specified read-access restriction.

[Visual Basic] **Public Sub New(String, Boolean)**
[C#] **public MessageQueue(string, bool);**
[C++] **public: MessageQueue(String*, bool);**
[JScript] **public function MessageQueue(String, Boolean);**

Example

See related example in the **System.Messaging.MessageQueue** class topic.

MessageQueue Constructor ()

Initializes a new instance of the **MessageQueue** class. After the default constructor initializes the new instance, you must set the instance's **Path** property before you can use the instance.

```
[Visual Basic]
Public Sub New()
[C#]
public MessageQueue();
[C++]
public: MessageQueue();
[JScript]
public function MessageQueue();
```

Remarks

Use this overload to create a new instance of the **MessageQueue** class that is not immediately tied to a queue on the Message Queuing server. Before using this instance, you must connect it to an existing Message Queuing queue by setting the **Path** property. Alternatively, you can set the **MessageQueue** reference to the **Create** method's return value, thereby creating a new Message Queuing queue.

> **Note** The **ctor** constructor instantiates a new instance of the **MessageQueue** class; it does not create a new Message Queuing queue.

The following table shows initial property values for an instance of **MessageQueue**.

Property	Initial Value
DefaultPropertiesToSend	The values set by the default constructor of the **DefaultPropertiesToSend** class.
Formatter	**XmlMessageFormatter**
MessageReadProperty-Filter	The values set by the default constructor of the **MessagePropertyFilter** class. All the filter values are set to **true**.
DenySharedReceive	**false**

Requirements

Platforms: Windows 98, Windows NT 4.0, Windows Millennium Edition, Windows 2000, Windows XP Home Edition, Windows XP Professional, Windows .NET Server family

.NET Framework Security:
- Full trust for the immediate caller. This member cannot be used by partially trusted code.

MessageQueue Constructor (String)

Initializes a new instance of the **MessageQueue** class that references the Message Queuing queue at the specified path.

```
[Visual Basic]
Public Sub New( _
   ByVal path As String _
)
[C#]
public MessageQueue(
   string path
);
[C++]
public: MessageQueue(
   String* path
);
[JScript]
public function MessageQueue(
   path : String
);
```

Parameters

path
    The location of the queue referenced by this **MessageQueue**. For information on the proper syntax for this parameter, see the Remarks section.

Exceptions

Exception Type	Condition
ArgumentException	The **Path** property is invalid, possibly because it has not been set.

Remarks

Use this overload when you want to tie the new **MessageQueue** instance to a particular Message Queuing queue, for which you know the path, format name, or label. If you want to grant exclusive access to the first application that references the queue, you must set the **DenySharedReceive** property to **true** or use the constructor that passes a read-access restriction parameter.

> **Note** The **ctor** constructor instantiates a new instance of the **MessageQueue** class; it does not create a new Message Queuing queue. To create a new queue in Message Queuing, use **Create**.

The syntax of the *path* parameter depends on the type of queue it references.

Queue Type	Syntax
Public queue	*MachineName*\ *QueueName*
Private queue	*MachineName*\ **Private$**\ *QueueName*
Journal queue	*MachineName*\ *QueueName*\ **Journal$**
Machine journal queue	*MachineName*\ **Journal$**
Machine dead-letter queue	*MachineName*\ **Deadletter$**
Machine transactional dead-letter queue	*MachineName*\ **XactDeadletter$**

Alternatively, you can use the **FormatName** or **Label** to describe the queue path.

Reference	Syntax	Example
Format name	**FormatName:** [*format name*]	**FormatName:Public=** 5A5F7535-AE9A-41d4-935C-845C2AFF7112 **FormatName:DIRECT=SPX:** *NetworkNumber*; *HostNumber*\ *QueueName* **FormatName:DIRECT=TCP:** *IPAddress*\ *QueueName* **FormatName:DIRECT=OS:** *MachineName*\ *QueueName*
Label	**Label:** [*label*]	**Label:** TheLabel

To work offline, you must use the format name syntax, not the path name syntax for the constructor. Otherwise, an exception is thrown because the primary domain controller is not available to resolve the path to the format name.

The following table shows initial property values for an instance of **MessageQueue**. These values are based on the properties of the Message Queuing queue with the path specified by the *path* parameter.

Property	Initial Value
Authenticate	**false**
BasePriority	0
Category	**Empty**
DefaultPropertiesToSend	The values set by the default constructor of the **DefaultPropertiesToSend** class.

Property	Initial Value
EncryptionRequired	**true**, if the Message Queuing queue's PrivLevel setting is "Body"; otherwise, **false.**
Formatter	**XmlMessageFormatter**
Label	**Empty**
MachineName	The value of the Message Queuing queue's computer name property.
MaximumJournalSize	**InfiniteQueueSize**
MaximumQueueSize	**InfiniteQueueSize**
MessageReadProperty-Filter	The values set by the default constructor of the **MessagePropertyFilter** class.
Path	**Empty**, if not set by the constructor.
QueueName	**Empty**, if not set by the constructor.
DenySharedReceive	false
UseJournalQueue	**true**, if the Message Queuing object's journal setting is enabled; otherwise, **false**.

Example

See related example in the **System.Messaging.MessageQueue** class topic.

Requirements

Platforms: Windows 98, Windows NT 4.0, Windows Millennium Edition, Windows 2000, Windows XP Home Edition, Windows XP Professional, Windows .NET Server family

.NET Framework Security:

- Full trust for the immediate caller. This member cannot be used by partially trusted code.

MessageQueue Constructor (String, Boolean)

Initializes a new instance of the **MessageQueue** class that references the Message Queuing queue at the specified path and with the specified read-access restriction.

```
[Visual Basic]
Public Sub New( _
    ByVal path As String, _
    ByVal sharedModeDenyReceive As Boolean _
)
[C#]
public MessageQueue(
    string path,
    bool sharedModeDenyReceive
);
[C++]
public: MessageQueue(
    String* path,
    bool sharedModeDenyReceive
);
[JScript]
public function MessageQueue(
    path : String,
    sharedModeDenyReceive : Boolean
);
```

Parameters

path

The location of the queue referenced by this **MessageQueue**, which can be "." for the local computer. For information on the proper syntax for this parameter, see the Remarks section.

sharedModeDenyReceive

true to grant exclusive read access to the first application that accesses the queue; otherwise, **false.**

Exceptions

Exception Type	Condition
ArgumentException	The **Path** property is invalid, possibly because it has not been set.

Remarks

Use this overload when you want to tie the new **MessageQueue** to a particular Message Queuing queue, for which you know the path, format name, or label. If you want to grant exclusive access to the first application that references the queue, set the *sharedModeDenyReceive* parameter to **true**. Otherwise, set *sharedModeDenyReceive* to **false** or use the constructor that has only a *path* parameter.

Setting *sharedModeDenyReceive* to **true** affects all objects that access the Message Queuing queue, including other applications. The effects of the parameter are not restricted to this application.

> **Note** The **ctor** constructor creates a new instance of the **MessageQueue** class; it does not create a new Message Queuing queue. To create a new queue in Message Queuing, use **Create**.

The syntax of the *path* parameter depends on the type of queue.

Queue Type	Syntax
Public queue	*MachineName\ QueueName*
Private queue	*MachineName* **Private$** *QueueName*
Journal queue	*MachineName\ QueueName* **Journal$**
Machine journal queue	*MachineName* **Journal$**
Machine dead-letter queue	*MachineName* **Deadletter$**
Machine transactional dead-letter queue	*MachineName* **XactDeadletter$**

Alternatively, you can use the format name or label of a Message Queuing queue to describe the queue path.

Reference	Syntax	Example
Format name	**FormatName:** [*format name*]	**FormatName:Public=** 5A5F7535-AE9A-41d4-935C-845C2AFF7112
		FormatName:DIRECT=SPX: *NetworkNumber; HostNumber\ QueueName*
		FormatName:DIRECT=TCP: *IPAddress\ QueueName*
		FormatName:DIRECT=OS: *MachineName\ QueueName*
Label	**Label:** [*label*]	**Label:** TheLabel

To work offline, you must use the format name syntax, rather than the friendly name syntax. Otherwise, an exception is thrown because the primary domain controller (on which Active Directory resides) is not available to resolve the path to the format name.

If a **MessageQueue** opens a queue with the *sharedModeDenyReceive* parameter set to **true**, any **MessageQueue** that subsequently tries to read from the queue generates a **MessageQueueException** because of a sharing violation. A **MessageQueueException** is also thrown if a **MessageQueue** tries to access the queue in exclusive mode while another **MessageQueue** already has nonexclusive access to the queue.

The following table shows initial property values for an instance of **MessageQueue**. These values are based on the properties of the Message Queuing queue, with the path specified by the *path* parameter.

Property	Initial Value
Authenticate	**false**.
BasePriority	0.
Category	**Empty**.
DefaultPropertiesToSend	The values set by the default constructor of the **DefaultPropertiesToSend** class.
EncryptionRequired	**true**, if the Message Queuing queue's PrivLevel setting is "Body"; otherwise, **false**.
Formatter	**XmlMessageFormatter**.
Label	**Empty**.
MachineName	The value of the Message Queuing queue's computer name property.
MaximumJournalSize	**InfiniteQueueSize**.
MaximumQueueSize	**InfiniteQueueSize**.
MessageReadProperty-Filter	The values set by the default constructor of the **MessagePropertyFilter** class.
Path	**Empty**, if not set by the constructor.
QueueName	**Empty**, if not set by the constructor.
DenySharedReceive	The value of the *sharedModeDenyReceive* parameter.
UseJournalQueue	**true**, if the Message Queuing object's journal setting is enabled; otherwise, **false**.

Example

See related example in the **System.Messaging.MessageQueue** class topic.

Requirements

Platforms: Windows 98, Windows NT 4.0, Windows Millennium Edition, Windows 2000, Windows XP Home Edition, Windows XP Professional, Windows .NET Server family

.NET Framework Security:

- Full trust for the immediate caller. This member cannot be used by partially trusted code.

MessageQueue.InfiniteQueueSize Field

Specifies that no size restriction exists for a queue.

```
[Visual Basic]
Public Shared ReadOnly InfiniteQueueSize As Long
[C#]
public static readonly long InfiniteQueueSize;
[C++]
public: static __int64 InfiniteQueueSize;
[JScript]
public static var InfiniteQueueSize : long;
```

Remarks

This field is frequently used when setting **MaximumJournalSize** or **MaximumQueueSize**.

Requirements

Platforms: Windows 98, Windows NT 4.0, Windows Millennium Edition, Windows 2000, Windows XP Home Edition, Windows XP Professional, Windows .NET Server family

MessageQueue.InfiniteTimeout Field

Specifies that no time-out exists for methods that peek or receive messages.

```
[Visual Basic]
Public Shared ReadOnly InfiniteTimeout As TimeSpan
[C#]
public static readonly TimeSpan InfiniteTimeout;
[C++]
public: static TimeSpan InfiniteTimeout;
[JScript]
public static var InfiniteTimeout : TimeSpan;
```

Remarks

MessageQueue supports two types of message retrieval: synchronous and asynchronous. The synchronous methods, **Peek** and **Receive**, cause the process thread to wait a specified time interval for a new message to arrive in the queue. If the specified time interval is **InfiniteTimeout**, the process thread remains blocked until a new message is available. On the other hand, **BeginPeek** and **BeginReceive** (the asynchronous methods), allow the main application tasks to continue in a separate thread until a message arrives in the queue.

Requirements

Platforms: Windows 98, Windows NT 4.0, Windows Millennium Edition, Windows 2000, Windows XP Home Edition, Windows XP Professional, Windows .NET Server family

MessageQueue.Authenticate Property

Gets or sets a value indicating whether the queue accepts only authenticated messages.

```
[Visual Basic]
Public Property Authenticate As Boolean
[C#]
public bool Authenticate {get; set;}
```

```
[C++]
public: __property bool get_Authenticate();
public: __property void set_Authenticate(bool);
[JScript]
public function get Authenticate() : Boolean;
public function set Authenticate(Boolean);
```

Property Value

true if the queue accepts only authenticated messages; otherwise, **false**. The default is **false**.

Exceptions

Exception Type	Condition
MessageQueueException	An error occurred when accessing a Message Queuing API.

Remarks

Message authentication provides a way to ensure message integrity and to verify who sent the message. To request authentication, the sending application sets the message's authentication level.

> **Note** When you set **Authenticate** to **true**, you are restricting access to the queue on the server, not only to this **MessageQueue** instance. All clients working against the same Message Queuing queue will be affected.

A queue that accepts only authenticated messages will reject a nonauthenticated message. To request notification of message rejection, a sending application can set the **AcknowledgeType** property of the message. Because no other indication of message rejection exists, the sending application can lose the message unless you request that it be sent to the dead-letter queue.

The following table shows whether this property is available in various Workgroup modes.

Workgroup Mode	Available
Local computer	Yes
Local computer + direct format name	Yes
Remote computer	No
Remote computer + direct format name	No

Requirements

Platforms: Windows 98, Windows NT 4.0, Windows Millennium Edition, Windows 2000, Windows XP Home Edition, Windows XP Professional, Windows .NET Server family

.NET Framework Security:
* Full trust for the immediate caller. This member cannot be used by partially trusted code.

MessageQueue.BasePriority Property

Gets or sets the base priority Message Queuing uses to route a public queue's messages over the network.

```
[Visual Basic]
Public Property BasePriority As Short
[C#]
public short BasePriority {get; set;}
[C++]
public: __property short get_BasePriority();
public: __property void set_BasePriority(short);
```

```
[JScript]
public function get BasePriority() : Int16;
public function set BasePriority(Int16);
```

Property Value

The single base priority for all messages sent to the (public) queue. The default is zero (0).

Exceptions

Exception Type	Condition
ArgumentException	The base priority was set to an invalid value.
MessageQueueException	An error occurred when accessing a Message Queuing API.

Remarks

A message queue's base priority specifies how a message en route to that queue is treated as it travels through the network. You can set the **BasePriority** property to confer a higher or lower priority to all messages sent to the specified queue than those sent to other queues. Setting this property modifies the Message Queuing queue. Therefore, any other **MessageQueue** instances are affected by the change.

A message queue's **BasePriority** is not related to the **Priority** property of a message, which specifies the order in which an incoming message is placed in the queue.

BasePriority applies only to public queues whose paths are specified using the format name. The base priority of a private queue is always zero (0).

The following table shows whether this property is available in various Workgroup modes.

Workgroup Mode	Available
Local computer	Yes
Local computer + direct format name	Yes
Remote computer	No
Remote computer + direct format name	No

Requirements

Platforms: Windows 98, Windows NT 4.0, Windows Millennium Edition, Windows 2000, Windows XP Home Edition, Windows XP Professional, Windows .NET Server family

.NET Framework Security:
* Full trust for the immediate caller. This member cannot be used by partially trusted code.

MessageQueue.CanRead Property

Gets a value indicating whether the **MessageQueue** can be read.

```
[Visual Basic]
Public ReadOnly Property CanRead As Boolean
[C#]
public bool CanRead {get;}
[C++]
public: __property bool get_CanRead();
[JScript]
public function get CanRead() : Boolean;
```

Property Value

true if the **MessageQueue** exists and the application can read from it; otherwise, **false**.

Remarks

CanRead indicates whether the application is able to peek or receive messages from the queue. If **CanRead** is **true**, the **MessageQueue** can receive or peek messages from the queue. Otherwise, it cannot.

CanRead is **false** if a queue is already open with exclusive read access (or if it's open with nonexclusive access and this **MessageQueue** requests exclusive access), or if the application does not have sufficient rights to access it. If your application tries to read from a queue when **CanRead** is **false**, access is denied.

The following table shows whether this property is available in various Workgroup modes.

Workgroup Mode	Available
Local computer	Yes
Local computer + direct format name	Yes
Remote computer	No
Remote computer + direct format name	Yes

Requirements

Platforms: Windows 98, Windows NT 4.0, Windows Millennium Edition, Windows 2000, Windows XP Home Edition, Windows XP Professional, Windows .NET Server family

.NET Framework Security:
- Full trust for the immediate caller. This member cannot be used by partially trusted code.

MessageQueue.CanWrite Property

Gets a value indicating whether the **MessageQueue** can be written to.

```
[Visual Basic]
Public ReadOnly Property CanWrite As Boolean
[C#]
public bool CanWrite {get;}
[C++]
public: __property bool get_CanWrite();
[JScript]
public function get CanWrite() : Boolean;
```

Property Value

true if the **MessageQueue** exists and the application can write to it; otherwise, **false**.

Remarks

CanWrite indicates whether the application is able to send messages to the queue. If **CanWrite** is **true**, the **MessageQueue** can send messages to the queue. Otherwise, it cannot.

CanWrite is **false** if a queue is already open with exclusive write access (or if it's open with nonexclusive access and this **MessageQueue** requests exclusive access), or if the application does not have sufficient rights to access it. If your application tries to write to a queue when **CanWrite** is **false**, access is denied.

The following table shows whether this property is available in various Workgroup modes.

Workgroup Mode	Available
Local computer	Yes
Local computer + direct format name	Yes
Remote computer	No
Remote computer + direct format name	Yes

Requirements

Platforms: Windows 98, Windows NT 4.0, Windows Millennium Edition, Windows 2000, Windows XP Home Edition, Windows XP Professional, Windows .NET Server family

.NET Framework Security:
- Full trust for the immediate caller. This member cannot be used by partially trusted code.

MessageQueue.Category Property

Gets or sets the queue category.

```
[Visual Basic]
Public Property Category As Guid
[C#]
public Guid Category {get; set;}
[C++]
public: __property Guid get_Category();
public: __property void set_Category(Guid);
[JScript]
public function get Category() : Guid;
public function set Category(Guid);
```

Property Value

A **Guid** that represents the queue category (Message Queuing type identifier), which allows an application to categorize its queues. The default is **Guid.empty**.

Exceptions

Exception Type	Condition
ArgumentException	The queue category was set to an invalid value.
MessageQueueException	An error occurred when accessing a Message Queuing API.

Remarks

The queue category allows an application to categorize its queues. For example, you can place all Billing queues in one category and all Order queues in another.

The **Category** property provides access to the Message Queuing Type ID property (which is read/write), accessible through the **Queue Properties** dialog box on the Computer Management Console. You can define a new category. Although you can use **NewGuid** to create a category value that is unique across all **Guid** values, such an action is unnecessary. The category value needs to be distinct only from other categories, not from all other **Guid** values. For example, you can assign {00000000-0000-0000-0000-000000000001} as the **Category** for one set of queues and {00000000-0000-0000-0000-000000000002} as the **Category** for another set.

It is not necessary to set the **Category**. The value can be a null reference (**Nothing** in Visual Basic).

Setting this property modifies the Message Queuing queue. Therefore, any other **MessageQueue** instances are affected by the change.

The following table shows whether this property is available in various Workgroup modes.

Workgroup Mode	Available
Local computer	Yes
Local computer + direct format name	Yes
Remote computer	No
Remote computer + direct format name	No

Requirements

Platforms: Windows 98, Windows NT 4.0, Windows Millennium Edition, Windows 2000, Windows XP Home Edition, Windows XP Professional, Windows .NET Server family

.NET Framework Security:
- Full trust for the immediate caller. This member cannot be used by partially trusted code.

MessageQueue.CreateTime Property

Gets the time and date that the queue was created in Message Queuing.

```
[Visual Basic]
Public ReadOnly Property CreateTime As DateTime
[C#]
public DateTime CreateTime {get;}
[C++]
public: __property DateTime get_CreateTime();
[JScript]
public function get CreateTime() : DateTime;
```

Property Value

A **DateTime** representing the date and time at which the queue was created.

Exceptions

Exception Type	Condition
MessageQueueException	An error occurred when accessing a Message Queuing API.

Remarks

CreateTime refers to the queue on the Message Queuing server, not the **MessageQueue** instance.

If the queue exists, this property represents the time the queue was created, adjusted to the local time of the server on which the queue exists.

The following table shows whether this property is available in various Workgroup modes.

Workgroup Mode	Available
Local computer	Yes
Local computer + direct format name	Yes
Remote computer	No
Remote computer + direct format name	No

Requirements

Platforms: Windows 98, Windows NT 4.0, Windows Millennium Edition, Windows 2000, Windows XP Home Edition, Windows XP Professional, Windows .NET Server family

.NET Framework Security:
- Full trust for the immediate caller. This member cannot be used by partially trusted code.

MessageQueue.DefaultPropertiesToSend Property

Gets or sets the message property values to be used by default when the application sends messages to the queue.

```
[Visual Basic]
Public Property DefaultPropertiesToSend As DefaultPropertiesToSend
[C#]
public DefaultPropertiesToSend DefaultPropertiesToSend {get; set;}
[C++]
public: __property DefaultPropertiesToSend*
get_DefaultPropertiesToSend();
public: __property void
set_DefaultPropertiesToSend(DefaultPropertiesToSend*);
[JScript]
public function get DefaultPropertiesToSend() :
DefaultPropertiesToSend;
public function set DefaultPropertiesToSend(DefaultPropertiesToSend);
```

Property Value

A **DefaultPropertiesToSend** containing the default Message Queuing message property values used when the application sends objects other than **Message** instances to the queue.

Exceptions

Exception Type	Condition
ArgumentException	The default properties could not be set for the queue, possibly because one of the properties is invalid.

Remarks

When you send any object that is not of type **Message** to the queue, the **MessageQueue** inserts the object into a Message Queuing message. At that time, the **MessageQueue** applies to the message the property values you specify in the **DefaultPropertiesToSend** property. Conversely, if you send a **Message** to the queue, these properties are already specified for the instance itself, so **DefaultPropertiesToSend** is ignored for the **Message**.

Although you set the properties through the **MessageQueue** object, the **DefaultPropertiesToSend** refers to the properties of the messages that are sent to the queue, not the queue itself.

The default values for the properties are represented in the following table.

Property	Default Value
AcknowledgeType	**AcknowledgeType.None**.
AdministrationQueue	A null reference (**Nothing** in Visual Basic).
AppSpecific	Zero (0).
AttachSenderId	**true**.

Property	Default Value
EncryptionAlgorithm	EncryptionAlgorithm.RC2.
Extension	A zero-length array of bytes.
HashAlgorithm	HashAlgorithm.MD5.
Label	Empty string ("").
Priority	MessagePriority.Normal.
Recoverable	false.
ResponseQueue	A null reference (Nothing).
TimeToBeReceived	Message.InfiniteTimeout.
TimeToReachQueue	Message.InfiniteTimeout.
TransactionStatusQueue	A null reference (Nothing).
UseAuthentication	false.
UseDeadLetterQueue	false.
UseEncryption	false.
UseJournalQueue	false.
UseTracing	false.

The following table shows whether this property is available in various Workgroup modes.

Workgroup Mode	Available
Local computer	Yes
Local computer + direct format name	Yes
Remote computer	Yes
Remote computer + direct format name	Yes

Example

See related example in the **System.Messaging.MessageQueue** class topic.

Requirements

Platforms: Windows 98, Windows NT 4.0, Windows Millennium Edition, Windows 2000, Windows XP Home Edition, Windows XP Professional, Windows .NET Server family

.NET Framework Security:
- Full trust for the immediate caller. This member cannot be used by partially trusted code.

MessageQueue.DenySharedReceive Property

Gets or sets a value indicating whether this **MessageQueue** has exclusive access to receive messages from the Message Queuing queue.

```
[Visual Basic]
Public Property DenySharedReceive As Boolean
[C#]
public bool DenySharedReceive {get; set;}
[C++]
public: __property bool get_DenySharedReceive();
public: __property void set_DenySharedReceive(bool);
[JScript]
public function get DenySharedReceive() : Boolean;
public function set DenySharedReceive(Boolean);
```

Property Value

true if this **MessageQueue** has exclusive rights to receive messages from the queue; otherwise, **false**. The default is **false**.

Remarks

DenySharedReceive specifies the shared mode of the queue referenced by this **MessageQueue**. Set **DenySharedReceive** to **true** to indicate that only this **MessageQueue** should have access to peek or receive messages from the queue with the specified **Path**. If another **MessageQueue** or another application is associated with the same queue resource, that instance or application will not be able to peek or receive messages, but it can still send them.

If **DenySharedReceive** is **false**, the queue is available to multiple applications for sending, peeking, or receiving messages.

The following table shows whether this property is available in various Workgroup modes.

Workgroup Mode	Available
Local computer	Yes
Local computer + direct format name	Yes
Remote computer	Yes
Remote computer + direct format name	Yes

Requirements

Platforms: Windows 98, Windows NT 4.0, Windows Millennium Edition, Windows 2000, Windows XP Home Edition, Windows XP Professional, Windows .NET Server family

.NET Framework Security:
- Full trust for the immediate caller. This member cannot be used by partially trusted code.

MessageQueue.EnableConnectionCache Property

Gets or sets a value indicating whether a cache of connections will be maintained by the application.

```
[Visual Basic]
Public Shared Property EnableConnectionCache As Boolean
[C#]
public static bool EnableConnectionCache {get; set;}
[C++]
public: __property static bool get_EnableConnectionCache();
public: __property static void set_EnableConnectionCache(bool);
[JScript]
public static function get EnableConnectionCache() : Boolean;
public static function set EnableConnectionCache(Boolean);
```

Property Value

true to create and use a connection cache; otherwise, **false**.

Remarks

A connection cache is a list of references to structures that contain read or write handles to queues. When **EnableConnectionCache** is **true**, the **MessageQueue** borrows handles from the cache each time you call **Send**, **Peek**, or **Receive**, rather than open new handles. This can improve performance. Using a connection cache also insulates the **MessageQueue** from changes in the network topology.

If you create a new connection to a queue when the connection cache is full, the **MessageQueue** overwrites the least recently accessed structure with the new connection. You can clear the cache entirely by calling **ClearConnectionCache**, for example if the format names of the queues you are working with have changed so that the previous read and write handles are no longer valid.

The following table shows whether this property is available in various Workgroup modes.

Workgroup Mode	Available
Local computer	Yes
Local computer + direct format name	Yes
Remote computer	Yes
Remote computer + direct format name	Yes

Requirements

Platforms: Windows 98, Windows NT 4.0, Windows Millennium Edition, Windows 2000, Windows XP Home Edition, Windows XP Professional, Windows .NET Server family

.NET Framework Security:

- Full trust for the immediate caller. This member cannot be used by partially trusted code.

MessageQueue.EncryptionRequired Property

Gets or sets a value indicating whether the queue accepts only nonprivate (nonencrypted) messages.

```
[Visual Basic]
Public Property EncryptionRequired As EncryptionRequired
[C#]
public EncryptionRequired EncryptionRequired {get; set;}
[C++]
public: __property EncryptionRequired get_EncryptionRequired();
public: __property void set_EncryptionRequired(EncryptionRequired);
[JScript]
public function get EncryptionRequired() : EncryptionRequired;
public function set EncryptionRequired(EncryptionRequired);
```

Property Value

One of the **EncryptionRequired** values. The default is **None**.

Exceptions

Exception Type	Condition
MessageQueueException	An error occurred when accessing a Message Queuing API.

Remarks

When you specify that encryption is required for the messages sent to a queue, only the message bodies are encrypted. The other members (for example, the **Label** and **SenderId** properties) cannot be encrypted.

Setting this property modifies the Message Queuing queue. Therefore, any other **MessageQueue** instances are affected by the change.

Encrypting a message makes the message private. You can specify the queue's encryption requirement to be **None**, **Body**, or **Optional** by setting the **EncryptionRequired** property appropriately. The **UseEncryption** setting of the message must correspond to the encryption requirement of the queue. If the message is not encrypted but the queue specifies **Body**, or if the message is encrypted but the queue specifies **None**, the message is rejected by the queue. If the sending application requests a negative acknowledgment message in this event, Message Queuing indicates the message's rejection to the

sending application. If the **UseDeadLetterQueue** property is **true**, a message that fails encryption is sent to the dead-letter queue. Otherwise, the message is lost.

The following table shows whether this property is available in various Workgroup modes.

Workgroup Mode	Available
Local computer	Yes
Local computer + direct format name	Yes
Remote computer	No
Remote computer + direct format name	No

Requirements

Platforms: Windows 98, Windows NT 4.0, Windows Millennium Edition, Windows 2000, Windows XP Home Edition, Windows XP Professional, Windows .NET Server family

.NET Framework Security:

- Full trust for the immediate caller. This member cannot be used by partially trusted code.

MessageQueue.FormatName Property

Gets the unique queue name that Message Queuing generated at the time of the queue's creation.

```
[Visual Basic]
Public ReadOnly Property FormatName As String
[C#]
public string FormatName {get;}
[C++]
public: __property String* get_FormatName();
[JScript]
public function get FormatName() : String;
```

Property Value

The name for the queue, which is unique on the network.

Exceptions

Exception Type	Condition
MessageQueueException	The **Path** is not set.
	-or-
	An error occurred when accessing a Message Queuing API.

Remarks

The **FormatName** property contains the format name of the queue. Message Queuing uses the format name to identify which queue to open and how to access it. Unlike most of a queue's characteristics, the format name is not a Message Queuing application queue property, so you cannot access it through the Message Queuing management tool. The format name is simply a unique name for the queue, which Message Queuing generates when it creates the queue or which the application generates later.

If you specify a path using the path name syntax (such as myComputer\myQueue) rather than using the format name syntax when you read or write to the queue, the primary domain controller (which uses Active Directory) translates the **Path** into the associated **FormatName** before accessing the queue. If your application is working offline, you must use the format name syntax; otherwise, the primary domain controller will not be available to perform the path translation.

The following table shows whether this property is available in various Workgroup modes.

Workgroup Mode	Available
Local computer	Yes
Local computer + direct format name	Yes
Remote computer	Yes
Remote computer + direct format name	Yes

Requirements

Platforms: Windows 98, Windows NT 4.0, Windows Millennium Edition, Windows 2000, Windows XP Home Edition, Windows XP Professional, Windows .NET Server family

.NET Framework Security:
- Full trust for the immediate caller. This member cannot be used by partially trusted code.

MessageQueue.Formatter Property

Gets or sets the formatter used to serialize an object into or deserialize an object from the body of a message read from or written to the queue.

```
[Visual Basic]
Public Property Formatter As IMessageFormatter
[C#]
public IMessageFormatter Formatter {get; set;}
[C++]
public: __property IMessageFormatter* get_Formatter();
public: __property void set_Formatter(IMessageFormatter*);
[JScript]
public function get Formatter() : IMessageFormatter;
public function set Formatter(IMessageFormatter);
```

Property Value

The **IMessageFormatter** that produces a stream to be written to or read from the message body. The default is **XmlMessageFormatter**.

Remarks

The **Formatter** property contains an instance of a formatter object, which transforms messages when your application reads or writes to the queue.

When the application sends message to the queue, the formatter serializes the object into a stream and inserts it into the message body. When reading from a queue, the formatter deserializes the message data into the **Body** property of a **Message**.

The **XmlMessageFormatter** is loosely coupled, so it is not necessary to have the same object type on the sender and receiver when using this format. The **ActiveXMessageFormatter** and **BinaryMessageFormatter** serialize the data into binary representation. The **ActiveXMessageFormatter** is used when sending or receiving COM components.

BinaryMessageFormatter and **ActiveXMessageFormatter** provide faster throughput than the **XmlMessageFormatter**. The **ActiveXMessageFormatter** allows interoperability with Visual Basic 6.0 Message Queuing applications.

When your application sends messages to the queue, the **MessageQueue.Formatter** applies only to those messages that use

the default message properties, **DefaultPropertiesToSend**. If you send a **Message** to the queue, Message Queuing uses the formatter defined in the **Message.Formatter** property to serialize the body instead.

> **Note** The **MessageQueue** class will always use a **Message** to receive or peek a message from the queue. The message is deserialized using the **MessageQueue.Formatter** property.

The following table shows whether this property is available in various Workgroup modes.

Workgroup Mode	Available
Local computer	Yes
Local computer + direct format name	Yes
Remote computer	No
Remote computer + direct format name	Yes

Requirements

Platforms: Windows 98, Windows NT 4.0, Windows Millennium Edition, Windows 2000, Windows XP Home Edition, Windows XP Professional, Windows .NET Server family

.NET Framework Security:
- Full trust for the immediate caller. This member cannot be used by partially trusted code.

MessageQueue.Id Property

Gets the unique Message Queuing identifier of the queue.

```
[Visual Basic]
Public ReadOnly Property Id As Guid
[C#]
public Guid Id {get;}
[C++]
public: __property Guid get_Id();
[JScript]
public function get Id() : Guid;
```

Property Value

An **Id** that represents the message identifier generated by the Message Queuing application.

Exceptions

Exception Type	Condition
MessageQueueException	An error occurred when accessing a Message Queuing API.

Remarks

Message Queuing sets the **Id** property when it creates the queue.

The following table shows whether this property is available in various Workgroup modes.

Workgroup Mode	Available
Local computer	Yes
Local computer + direct format name	Yes
Remote computer	No
Remote computer + direct format name	No

Requirements

Platforms: Windows 98, Windows NT 4.0,
Windows Millennium Edition, Windows 2000,
Windows XP Home Edition, Windows XP Professional,
Windows .NET Server family

.NET Framework Security:
- Full trust for the immediate caller. This member cannot be used by partially trusted code.

MessageQueue.Label Property

Gets or sets the queue description.

```
[Visual Basic]
Public Property Label As String
[C#]
public string Label {get; set;}
[C++]
public: __property String* get_Label();
public: __property void set_Label(String*);
[JScript]
public function get Label() : String;
public function set Label(String);
```

Property Value

The label for the message queue. The default is an empty string ("").

Exceptions

Exception Type	Condition
ArgumentException	The label was set to an invalid value.
MessageQueueException	An error occurred when accessing a Message Queuing API.

Remarks

The maximum length of a message queue label is 124 characters.

The **Label** property does not need to be unique across all queues. However, if multiple queues share the same **Label**, you cannot use the **Send** method to broadcast a message to all of them. If you use the label syntax for the **Path** property when you send the message, an exception will be thrown if the **Label** is not unique.

The following table shows whether this property is available in various Workgroup modes.

Workgroup Mode	Available
Local computer	Yes
Local computer + direct format name	Yes
Remote computer	No
Remote computer + direct format name	No

Requirements

Platforms: Windows 98, Windows NT 4.0,
Windows Millennium Edition, Windows 2000,
Windows XP Home Edition, Windows XP Professional,
Windows .NET Server family

.NET Framework Security:
- Full trust for the immediate caller. This member cannot be used by partially trusted code.

MessageQueue.LastModifyTime Property

Gets the last time the properties of a queue were modified.

```
[Visual Basic]
Public ReadOnly Property LastModifyTime As DateTime
[C#]
public DateTime LastModifyTime {get;}
[C++]
public: __property DateTime get_LastModifyTime();
[JScript]
public function get LastModifyTime() : DateTime;
```

Property Value

A **DateTime** that indicates when the queue properties were last modified.

Exceptions

Exception Type	Condition
MessageQueueException	An error occurred when accessing a Message Queuing API.

Remarks

The last modification time includes when the queue was created and any **MessageQueue** property that modifies the Message Queuing queue, such as **BasePriority**. The value of the **LastModifyTime** property represents the system time of the local computer.

You must call **Refresh** before getting the **LastModifyTime** property; otherwise, the modification time associated with this **MessageQueue** might not be current.

The following table shows whether this property is available in various Workgroup modes.

Workgroup Mode	Available
Local computer	Yes
Local computer + direct format name	Yes
Remote computer	No
Remote computer + direct format name	No

Requirements

Platforms: Windows 98, Windows NT 4.0,
Windows Millennium Edition, Windows 2000,
Windows XP Home Edition, Windows XP Professional,
Windows .NET Server family

.NET Framework Security:
- Full trust for the immediate caller. This member cannot be used by partially trusted code.

MessageQueue.MachineName Property

Gets or sets the name of the computer where the Message Queuing queue is located.

```
[Visual Basic]
Public Property MachineName As String
[C#]
public string MachineName {get; set;}
[C++]
public: __property String* get_MachineName();
public: __property void set_MachineName(String*);
[JScript]
public function get MachineName() : String;
public function set MachineName(String);
```

Property Value

The name of the computer where the queue is located. The Message Queuing default is ".", the local computer.

Exceptions

Exception Type	Condition
ArgumentException	The MachineName is a null reference (Nothing in Visual Basic).
ArgumentException	The name of the computer is invalid, possibly because the syntax is incorrect.
MessageQueueException	An error occurred when accessing a Message Queuing API.

Remarks

The MachineName is an integral component of the friendly name syntax of the queue Path. The following table shows the syntax you should use for a queue of a specified type when you want to identify the queue path using its friendly name.

Queue Type	Syntax
Public queue	*MachineName\ QueueName*
Private queue	*MachineName* **Private$** *QueueName*
Journal queue	*MachineName\ QueueName* **Journal$**
Machine journal queue	*MachineName* **Journal$**
Machine dead-letter queue	*MachineName* **Deadletter$**
Machine transactional dead-letter queue	*MachineName* **XactDeadletter$**

Use "." for the local computer when specifying the MachineName. Only the computer name is recognized for this property, for example, Server0. The MachineName property does not support the IP address format.

If you define the Path in terms of the MachineName, the application throws an exception when working offline because the domain controller is required for path translation. Therefore, you must use the FormatName for the Path syntax when working offline.

> **Note** The MachineName, Path, and QueueName properties are related. Changing the MachineName property causes the Path property to change. It is built from the new MachineName and the QueueName. Changing the Path (for example, to use the format name syntax) resets the MachineName and QueueName properties to refer to the new queue. If the QueueName property is empty, the Path is set to the Journal queue of the computer you specify.

The following table shows whether this property is available in various Workgroup modes.

Workgroup Mode	Available
Local computer	Yes
Local computer + direct format name	Yes
Remote computer	Yes
Remote computer + direct format name	No

Requirements

Platforms: Windows 98, Windows NT 4.0, Windows Millennium Edition, Windows 2000, Windows XP Home Edition, Windows XP Professional, Windows .NET Server family

.NET Framework Security:

- Full trust for the immediate caller. This member cannot be used by partially trusted code.

MessageQueue.MaximumJournalSize Property

Gets or sets the maximum size of the journal queue.

```
[Visual Basic]
Public Property MaximumJournalSize As Long
[C#]
public long MaximumJournalSize {get; set;}
[C++]
public: __property __int64 get_MaximumJournalSize();
public: __property void set_MaximumJournalSize(__int64);
[JScript]
public function get MaximumJournalSize() : long;
public function set MaximumJournalSize(long);
```

Property Value

The maximum size, in kilobytes, of the journal queue. The Message Queuing default specifies that no limit exists.

Exceptions

Exception Type	Condition
ArgumentException	The maximum journal queue size was set to an invalid value.
MessageQueueException	An error occurred when accessing a Message Queuing API.

Remarks

MaximumJournalSize provides access to the Message Queuing journal storage limit. It is relevant only when **UseJournalQueue** is **true**. Setting this property modifies the Message Queuing queue. Therefore, any other **MessageQueue** instances are affected by the change

If you store messages in a journal or dead-letter queue, you should periodically clear the queue to remove messages that are no longer needed. Messages in such a queue count toward the message quota for the computer where the queue resides. (The administrator sets the computer quota.)

The following table shows whether this property is available in various Workgroup modes.

Workgroup Mode	Available
Local computer	Yes
Local computer + direct format name	Yes
Remote computer	No
Remote computer + direct format name	No

Requirements

Platforms: Windows 98, Windows NT 4.0, Windows Millennium Edition, Windows 2000, Windows XP Home Edition, Windows XP Professional, Windows .NET Server family

.NET Framework Security:
- Full trust for the immediate caller. This member cannot be used by partially trusted code.

MessageQueue.MaximumQueueSize Property

Gets or sets the maximum size of the queue.

```
[Visual Basic]
Public Property MaximumQueueSize As Long
[C#]
public long MaximumQueueSize {get; set;}
[C++]
public: __property __int64 get_MaximumQueueSize();
public: __property void set_MaximumQueueSize(__int64);
[JScript]
public function get MaximumQueueSize() : long;
public function set MaximumQueueSize(long);
```

Property Value

The maximum size, in kilobytes, of the queue. The Message Queuing default specifies that no limit exists.

Exceptions

Exception Type	Condition
ArgumentException	The maximum queue size contains a negative value.
MessageQueueException	An error occurred when accessing a Message Queuing API.

Remarks

The **MaximumQueueSize** provides access to the Message Queuing message storage limit, which is separate from the computer's message quota that the administrator defines. For more information on the message quota, see **MaximumJournalSize**.

Setting this property modifies the Message Queuing queue. Therefore, any other **MessageQueue** instances are affected by the change

If an attempt is made to exceed either the maximum queue size or the computer message quota, messages might be lost. When the queue quota is reached, Message Queuing notifies the administration queue of the sending application to indicate that the queue is full, by returning a negative acknowledgment message. Message Queuing continues to send negative acknowledgments until the total size of the messages in the queue drops below the limit.

The following table shows whether this property is available in various Workgroup modes.

Workgroup Mode	Available
Local computer	Yes
Local computer + direct format name	Yes
Remote computer	No
Remote computer + direct format name	No

Requirements

Platforms: Windows 98, Windows NT 4.0, Windows Millennium Edition, Windows 2000, Windows XP Home Edition, Windows XP Professional, Windows .NET Server family

.NET Framework Security:
- Full trust for the immediate caller. This member cannot be used by partially trusted code.

MessageQueue.MessageReadPropertyFilter Property

Gets or sets the property filter for receiving or peeking messages.

```
[Visual Basic]
Public Property MessageReadPropertyFilter As MessagePropertyFilter
[C#]
public MessagePropertyFilter MessageReadPropertyFilter {get; set;}
[C++]
public: __property MessagePropertyFilter*
get_MessageReadPropertyFilter();
public: __property void
set_MessageReadPropertyFilter(MessagePropertyFilter*);
[JScript]
public function get MessageReadPropertyFilter() :
MessagePropertyFilter;
public function set MessageReadPropertyFilter(MessagePropertyFilter);
```

Property Value

The **MessagePropertyFilter** used by the queue to filter the set of properties it receives or peeks for each message.

Exceptions

Exception Type	Condition
ArgumentException	The filter is a null reference (**Nothing** in Visual Basic).

Remarks

This filter is a set of Boolean values restricting the message properties that the **MessageQueue** receives or peeks. When the **MessageQueue** receives or peeks a message from the server queue, it retrieves only those properties for which the **MessageReadPropertyFilter** value is **true**.

The following shows initial property values for the **MessageReadPropertyFilter** property. These settings are identical to calling **SetDefaults** on a **MessagePropertyFilter**.

Property	Default Value
Acknowledgment	false
AcknowledgeType	false
AdministrationQueue	true
AppSpecific	false
ArrivedTime	true
AttachSenderId	false
Authenticated	false
AuthenticationProviderName	false
AuthenticationProviderType	false
Body	true
ConnectorType	false
CorrelationId	true
DefaultBodySize	1024 bytes
DefaultExtensionSize	255 bytes
DefaultLabelSize	255 bytes
DestinationQueue	false

Property	Default Value
DestinationSymmetricKey	false
DigitalSignature	false
EncryptionAlgorithm	false
Extension	false
HashAlgorithm	false
Id	true
IsFirstInTransaction	false
IsLastInTransaction	false
Label	true
MessageType	false
Priority	false
Recoverable	false
ResponseQueue	true
SenderCertificate	false
SenderId	false
SenderVersion	false
SentTime	true
SourceMachine	false
TimeToBeReceived	false
TimeToReachQueue	false
TransactionId	false
TransactionStatusQueue	false
UseAuthentication	false
UseDeadLetterQueue	false
UseEncryption	false
UseJournalQueue	false
UseTracing	false

The following table shows whether this property is available in various Workgroup modes.

Workgroup Mode	Available
Local computer	Yes
Local computer + direct format name	Yes
Remote computer	Yes
Remote computer + direct format name	Yes

Example

See related example in the **System.Messaging.MessageQueue** class topic.

Requirements

Platforms: Windows 98, Windows NT 4.0, Windows Millennium Edition, Windows 2000, Windows XP Home Edition, Windows XP Professional, Windows .NET Server family

.NET Framework Security:

- Full trust for the immediate caller. This member cannot be used by partially trusted code.

MessageQueue.Path Property

Gets or sets the queue's path. Setting the **Path** causes the **MessageQueue** to point to a new queue.

```
[Visual Basic]
Public Property Path As String
[C#]
public string Path {get; set;}
[C++]
public: __property String* get_Path();
public: __property void set_Path(String*);
[JScript]
public function get Path() : String;
public function set Path(String);
```

Property Value

The queue that is referenced by the **MessageQueue**. The default depends on which **MessageQueue** constructor you use; it is either a null reference (**Nothing** in Visual Basic) or is specified by the constructor's *path* parameter.

Exceptions

Exception Type	Condition
ArgumentException	The path is invalid, possibly because the syntax is invalid.

Remarks

The syntax for the **Path** property depends on the type of queue it points to.

Queue Type	Syntax
Public queue	*MachineName*\ *QueueName*
Private queue	*MachineName*\ **Private$**\ *QueueName*
Journal queue	*MachineName*\ *QueueName*\ **Journal$**
Machine journal queue	*MachineName*\ **Journal$**
Machine dead-letter queue	*MachineName*\ **Deadletter$**
Machine transactional dead-letter queue	*MachineName*\ **XactDeadletter$**

Use "." to represent the local computer.

> **Note** The **MachineName**, **Path**, and **QueueName** properties are related. Changing the **MachineName** property causes the **Path** property to change. It is built from the new **MachineName** and the **QueueName**. Changing the **Path** (for example, to use the format name syntax) resets the **MachineName** and **QueueName** properties to refer to the new queue.

Alternatively, you can use the **FormatName** or **Label** to describe the queue path.

Reference	Syntax	Example
Format name	**FormatName:** [*format name*]	**FormatName:Public=** 5A5F7535-AE9A-41d4-935C-845C2AFF7112
Label	**Label:** [*label*]	**Label:** TheLabel

If you use the label syntax for the **Path** property when you send the message, an exception will be thrown if the **Label** is not unique.

To work offline, you must use the format name syntax, rather than the friendly name syntax in the first table. Otherwise, an exception is thrown because the primary domain controller (on which Active

Directory resides) is not available to resolve the path to the format name.

Setting a new path closes the message queue and releases all handles.

The following table shows whether this property is available in various Workgroup modes.

Workgroup Mode	Available
Local computer	Yes
Local computer + direct format name	Yes
Remote computer	Yes
Remote computer + direct format name	Yes

Example

See related example in the **System.Messaging.MessageQueue** class topic.

Requirements

Platforms: Windows 98, Windows NT 4.0, Windows Millennium Edition, Windows 2000, Windows XP Home Edition, Windows XP Professional, Windows .NET Server family

.NET Framework Security:

- Full trust for the immediate caller. This member cannot be used by partially trusted code.

MessageQueue.QueueName Property

Gets or sets the friendly name that identifies the queue.

```
[Visual Basic]
Public Property QueueName As String
[C#]
public string QueueName {get; set;}
[C++]
public: __property String* get_QueueName();
public: __property void set_QueueName(String*);
[JScript]
public function get QueueName() : String;
public function set QueueName(String);
```

Property Value

The name that identifies the queue referenced by this **MessageQueue**. The value cannot be a null reference (**Nothing** in Visual Basic).

Exceptions

Exception Type	Condition
ArgumentException	The queue name is a null reference (**Nothing** in Visual Basic).

Remarks

You can combine the **QueueName** with the **MachineName** to create a friendly **Path** name for the queue. The syntax for the friendly-name variation of the **Path** property depends on the type of queue.

Queue Type	Syntax
Public queue	*MachineName\ QueueName*
Private queue	*MachineName\ **Private$** QueueName*
Journal queue	*MachineName\ QueueName* **Journal$**

Use "." to represent the local computer.

Changing the **QueueName** property affects the **Path** property. If you set the **QueueName** without setting the **MachineName** property, the **Path** property becomes *.\ QueueName*. Otherwise, the **Path** becomes *MachineName\ QueueName*.

The following table shows whether this property is available in various Workgroup modes.

Workgroup Mode	Available
Local computer	Yes
Local computer + direct format name	Yes
Remote computer	Yes
Remote computer + direct format name	No

Requirements

Platforms: Windows 98, Windows NT 4.0, Windows Millennium Edition, Windows 2000, Windows XP Home Edition, Windows XP Professional, Windows .NET Server family

.NET Framework Security:

- Full trust for the immediate caller. This member cannot be used by partially trusted code.

MessageQueue.ReadHandle Property

Gets the native handle used to read messages from the message queue.

```
[Visual Basic]
Public ReadOnly Property ReadHandle As IntPtr
[C#]
public IntPtr ReadHandle {get;}
[C++]
public: __property IntPtr get_ReadHandle();
[JScript]
public function get ReadHandle() : IntPtr;
```

Property Value

A handle to the native queue object that you use for peeking and receiving messages from the queue.

Exceptions

Exception Type	Condition
MessageQueueException	An error occurred when accessing a Message Queuing API.

Remarks

The **ReadHandle** provides a native Windows handle to the message queue object that is used for peeking and receiving messages from the queue. If you change the path of the queue, the handle is closed and reopened with a new value.

The following table shows whether this property is available in various Workgroup modes.

Workgroup Mode	Available
Local computer	Yes
Local computer + direct format name	Yes
Remote computer	No
Remote computer + direct format name	Yes

Requirements

Platforms: Windows 98, Windows NT 4.0,
Windows Millennium Edition, Windows 2000,
Windows XP Home Edition, Windows XP Professional,
Windows .NET Server family

.NET Framework Security:

• Full trust for the immediate caller. This member cannot be used
  by partially trusted code.

MessageQueue.SynchronizingObject Property

Gets or sets the object that marshals the event-handler call resulting
from a **ReceiveCompleted** or **PeekCompleted** event.

```
[Visual Basic]
Public Property SynchronizingObject As ISynchronizeInvoke
[C#]
public ISynchronizeInvoke SynchronizingObject {get; set;}
[C++]
public: __property ISynchronizeInvoke* get_SynchronizingObject();
public: __property void set_SynchronizingObject(ISynchronizeInvoke*);
[JScript]
public function get SynchronizingObject() : ISynchronizeInvoke;
public function set SynchronizingObject(ISynchronizeInvoke);
```

Property Value

An **ISynchronizeInvoke**, which represents the object that marshals
the event-handler call resulting from a **ReceiveCompleted** or
PeekCompleted event. The default is a null reference (**Nothing** in
Visual Basic).

Remarks

A **ReceiveCompleted** or **PeekCompleted** event results from a
BeginReceive or **BeginPeek** request, respectively, to a specific
thread. Typically, the **SynchronizingObject** is set when its related
component is placed inside a control or a form, because those
components are bound to a specific thread.

Typically, the synchronizing object marshals a method call into a
single thread.

Requirements

Platforms: Windows 98, Windows NT 4.0,
Windows Millennium Edition, Windows 2000,
Windows XP Home Edition, Windows XP Professional,
Windows .NET Server family

.NET Framework Security:

• Full trust for the immediate caller. This member cannot be used
  by partially trusted code.

MessageQueue.Transactional Property

Gets a value indicating whether the queue accepts only transactions.

```
[Visual Basic]
Public ReadOnly Property Transactional As Boolean
[C#]
public bool Transactional {get;}
[C++]
public: __property bool get_Transactional();
[JScript]
public function get Transactional() : Boolean;
```

Property Value

true if the queue accepts only messages sent as part of a transaction;
otherwise, **false**.

Exceptions

Exception Type	Condition
MessageQueueException	An error occurred when accessing a Message Queuing API.

Remarks

Transactional messaging refers to the coupling of several related
messages into a single transaction. Sending messages as part of a
transaction ensures that the messages are delivered in order,
delivered only once, and successfully retrieved from their
destination queue.

If a queue is transactional, it accepts only messages that are sent as
part of a transaction. However, a nontransactional message can be
sent or received from a local transaction queue without explicitly
using transactional **Begin**, **Commit**, and **Abort** syntax. If a
nontransactional message is sent to a transactional queue, this
component creates a single-message transaction for it, except in the
case of referencing a queue on a remote computer using a direct
format name. In this situation, if you do not specify a transaction
context when sending a message, one is not created for you and the
message will be sent to the dead-letter queue.

> **Note** If you send a nontransactional message to a transactional
> queue, you will not be able to roll back the message in the
> event of an exception.

> [Visual Basic] **Note** **MessageQueueTransaction** is threading
> apartment aware, so if your apartment state is **STA**, you cannot
> use the transaction in multiple threads. Visual Basic sets the
> state of the main thread to **STA**, so you must apply the
> **MTAThreadAttribute** in the Main subroutine. Otherwise,
> sending a transactional message using another thread throws a
> **MessageQueueException** exception. You apply the
> **MTAThreadAttribute** by using the following fragment.

```
[Visual Basic]
<System.MTAThreadAttribute>
public sub Main()
```

The following table shows whether this property is available in
various Workgroup modes.

Workgroup Mode	Available
Local computer	Yes
Local computer + direct format name	Yes
Remote computer	No
Remote computer + direct format name	No

Requirements

Platforms: Windows 98, Windows NT 4.0,
Windows Millennium Edition, Windows 2000,
Windows XP Home Edition, Windows XP Professional,
Windows .NET Server family

.NET Framework Security:

• Full trust for the immediate caller. This member cannot be used
  by partially trusted code.

MessageQueue.UseJournalQueue Property

Gets or sets a value indicating whether received messages are copied to the journal queue.

```
[Visual Basic]
Public Property UseJournalQueue As Boolean
[C#]
public bool UseJournalQueue {get; set;}
[C++]
public: __property bool get_UseJournalQueue();
public: __property void set_UseJournalQueue(bool);
[JScript]
public function get UseJournalQueue() : Boolean;
public function set UseJournalQueue(Boolean);
```

Property Value

true if messages received from the queue are copied to its journal queue; otherwise, **false**.

Exceptions

Exception Type	Condition
MessageQueueException	An error occurred when accessing a Message Queuing API.

Remarks

When the Message Queuing application creates a new application queue, it automatically creates an associated journal queue in the same location. The journal queue is used to track the messages removed from a queue. Setting this property modifies the Message Queuing queue. Therefore, any other **MessageQueue** instances are affected by the change.

> **Note** The journal queue does not track messages removed from the queue because their time-to-be-received timer expired, nor does it track messages purged from the queue by using a Message Queuing directory service (Information Store or Active Directory).

Applications cannot send messages to journal queues; they are limited to read-only access of these queues. Furthermore, Message Queuing never removes messages from journal queues. The application using the queue must clear these messages either by receiving them or by purging the queue.

The following table shows whether this property is available in various Workgroup modes.

Workgroup Mode	Available
Local computer	Yes
Local computer + direct format name	Yes
Remote computer	No
Remote computer + direct format name	No

Requirements

Platforms: Windows 98, Windows NT 4.0, Windows Millennium Edition, Windows 2000, Windows XP Home Edition, Windows XP Professional, Windows .NET Server family

.NET Framework Security:
- Full trust for the immediate caller. This member cannot be used by partially trusted code.

MessageQueue.WriteHandle Property

Gets the native handle used to send messages to the message queue.

```
[Visual Basic]
Public ReadOnly Property WriteHandle As IntPtr
[C#]
public IntPtr WriteHandle {get;}
[C++]
public: __property IntPtr get_WriteHandle();
[JScript]
public function get WriteHandle() : IntPtr;
```

Property Value

A handle to the native queue object that you use for sending messages to the queue.

Exceptions

Exception Type	Condition
MessageQueueException	The message queue is not available for writing.

Remarks

The **WriteHandle** provides a native Windows handle to the message queue object that is used for sending messages to the queue. If you change the path of the queue, the handle is closed and reopened with a new value.

The following table shows whether this property is available in various Workgroup modes.

Workgroup Mode	Available
Local computer	Yes
Local computer + direct format name	Yes
Remote computer	No
Remote computer + direct format name	Yes

Requirements

Platforms: Windows 98, Windows NT 4.0, Windows Millennium Edition, Windows 2000, Windows XP Home Edition, Windows XP Professional, Windows .NET Server family

.NET Framework Security:
- Full trust for the immediate caller. This member cannot be used by partially trusted code.

MessageQueue.BeginPeek Method

Initiates an asynchronous peek operation by telling Message Queuing to begin peeking a message and notify the event handler when finished.

Overload List

Initiates an asynchronous peek operation that has no time-out. The operation is not complete until a message becomes available in the queue.

[Visual Basic] **Overloads Public Function BeginPeek() As IAsyncResult**

[C#] **public IAsyncResult BeginPeek();**

[C++] **public: IAsyncResult* BeginPeek();**

[JScript] **public function BeginPeek() : IAsyncResult;**

Initiates an asynchronous peek operation that has a specified time-out. The operation is not complete until either a message becomes available in the queue or the time-out occurs.

[Visual Basic] **Overloads Public Function BeginPeek(TimeSpan) As IAsyncResult**

[C#] **public IAsyncResult BeginPeek(TimeSpan);**

[C++] **public: IAsyncResult* BeginPeek(TimeSpan);**

[JScript] **public function BeginPeek(TimeSpan) : IAsyncResult;**

Initiates an asynchronous peek operation that has a specified time-out and a specified state object, which provides associated information throughout the operation's lifetime. The operation is not complete until either a message becomes available in the queue or the time-out occurs.

[Visual Basic] **Overloads Public Function BeginPeek(TimeSpan, Object) As IAsyncResult**

[C#] **public IAsyncResult BeginPeek(TimeSpan, object);**

[C++] **public: IAsyncResult* BeginPeek(TimeSpan, Object*);**

[JScript] **public function BeginPeek(TimeSpan, Object) : IAsyncResult;**

Initiates an asynchronous peek operation that has a specified time-out and a specified state object, which provides associated information throughout the operation's lifetime. This overload receives notification, through a callback, of the identity of the event handler for the operation. The operation is not complete until either a message becomes available in the queue or the time-out occurs.

[Visual Basic] **Overloads Public Function BeginPeek(TimeSpan, Object, AsyncCallback) As IAsyncResult**

[C#] **public IAsyncResult BeginPeek(TimeSpan, object, AsyncCallback);**

[C++] **public: IAsyncResult* BeginPeek(TimeSpan, Object*, AsyncCallback*);**

[JScript] **public function BeginPeek(TimeSpan, Object, AsyncCallback) : IAsyncResult;**

Example

[Visual Basic, C#, C++] The following example creates an asynchronous peek operation, using the queue path ".\myQueue". It creates an event handler, MyPeekCompleted, and attaches it to the **PeekCompleted** event handler delegate. **BeginPeek** is called, with a time-out of one minute. Each call to **BeginPeek** has a unique associated integer that identifies that particular operation. When a **PeekCompleted** event is raised or the time-out expired, the message, if one exists, is retrieved and its body and the operation-specific integer identifier are written to the screen. Then **BeginPeek** is called again to initiate a new asynchronous peek operation with the same time-out and the associated integer of the just completed operation.

[Visual Basic, C#, C++] **Note**   This example shows how to use one of the overloaded versions of **BeginPeek**. For other examples that might be available, see the individual overload topics.

[Visual Basic]
```
Imports System
Imports System.Messaging
```

```
Namespace MyProject

    '/ <summary>
    '/ Provides a container class for the example.
    '/ </summary>
    Public Class MyNewQueue

        ' Represents a state object associated with each message.
        Private Shared messageNumber As Integer = 0

        '****************************************************
        ' Provides an entry point into the application.
        '
        ' This example performs asynchronous peek operation
        ' processing.
        '****************************************************

        Public Shared Sub Main()
            ' Create an instance of MessageQueue. Set its formatter.
            Dim myQueue As New MessageQueue(".\myQueue")
            myQueue.Formatter = New XmlMessageFormatter(New Type() _
                {GetType([String])})

            ' Add an event handler for the PeekCompleted event.
            AddHandler myQueue.PeekCompleted, AddressOf _
                MyPeekCompleted

            ' Begin the asynchronous peek operation with a time-out
            ' of one minute.
            myQueue.BeginPeek(New TimeSpan(0, 1, 0), messageNumber)
            messageNumber += 1

            ' Do other work on the current thread.
            Return
        End Sub 'Main

        '****************************************************
        ' Provides an event handler for the PeekCompleted
        ' event.
        '****************************************************

        Private Shared Sub MyPeekCompleted(ByVal [source] As _
            [Object], ByVal asyncResult As _
            PeekCompletedEventArgs)

            Try
                ' Connect to the queue.
                Dim mq As MessageQueue = _
                    CType([source], MessageQueue)

                ' End the asynchronous peek operation.
                Dim m As Message = _
                    mq.EndPeek(asyncResult.AsyncResult)

                ' Display message information on the screen,
                ' including(the) message number (state object).
                Console.WriteLine(("Message: " + _
                    CInt(asyncResult.AsyncResult.AsyncState) + _
                    " " + CStr(m.Body)))

                ' Restart the asynchronous peek operation, with the
                ' same time-out.
                mq.BeginPeek(New TimeSpan(0, 1, 0), messageNumber)
                messageNumber += 1

            Catch e As MessageQueueException

                If e.MessageQueueErrorCode = _
                    MessageQueueErrorCode.IOTimeout Then

                    Console.WriteLine(e.ToString())

                    ' Handle other sources of MessageQueueException.

                End If
```

```
            ' Handle other exceptions.

          End Try

          Return

        End Sub 'MyPeekCompleted

    End Class 'MyNewQueue
End Namespace 'MyProject
```

```
[C#]
using System;
using System.Messaging;

namespace MyProject
{
    /// <summary>
    /// Provides a container class for the example.
    /// </summary>
    public class MyNewQueue
    {
        // Represents a state object associated with each message.
        static int messageNumber = 0;

        //**************************************************
        // Provides an entry point into the application.
        //
        // This example performs asynchronous peek operation
        // processing.
        //**************************************************

        public static void Main()
        {
            // Create an instance of MessageQueue. Set its formatter.
            MessageQueue myQueue = new MessageQueue(".\\myQueue");
            myQueue.Formatter = new XmlMessageFormatter(new Type[]
                {typeof(String)});

            // Add an event handler for the PeekCompleted event.
            myQueue.PeekCompleted += new
                PeekCompletedEventHandler(MyPeekCompleted);

            // Begin the asynchronous peek operation with a time-out
            // of one minute.
            myQueue.BeginPeek(new TimeSpan(0,1,0), messageNumber++);

            // Do other work on the current thread.

            return;
        }

        //**************************************************
        // Provides an event handler for the PeekCompleted
        // event.
        //**************************************************

        private static void MyPeekCompleted(Object source,
            PeekCompletedEventArgs asyncResult)
        {
            try
            {
                // Connect to the queue.
                MessageQueue mq = (MessageQueue)source;

                // End the asynchronous peek operation.
                Message m = mq.EndPeek(asyncResult.AsyncResult);

                // Display message information on the screen,
                // including the message number (state object).
                Console.WriteLine("Message: " +
                    (int)asyncResult.AsyncResult.AsyncState + " "
                    +(string)m.Body);
```

```
                // Restart the asynchronous peek operation, with the
                // same time-out.
                mq.BeginPeek(new TimeSpan(0,1,0), messageNumber++);

            }

            catch(MessageQueueException e)
            {
                if (e.MessageQueueErrorCode ==
                    MessageQueueErrorCode.IOTimeout)
                {
                    Console.WriteLine(e.ToString());
                }

                // Handle other sources of MessageQueueException.

            }

            // Handle other exceptions.

            return;
        }
    }
}
```

```
[C++]
#using <mscorlib.dll>
#using <system.dll>
#using <system.messaging.dll>

using namespace System;
using namespace System::Messaging;

__gc class MyNewQueue
{
public:
    // Represents a state Object* associated with each message.
    static int messageNumber = 0;

    // Provides an event handler for the PeekCompleted
    // event.
    //

public:
    static void MyPeekCompleted(Object* source,
        PeekCompletedEventArgs* asyncResult)
    {
        try
        {
            // Connect to the queue.
            MessageQueue* mq = dynamic_cast<MessageQueue*>(source);

            // End the asynchronous peek operation.
            Message* m = mq->EndPeek(asyncResult->AsyncResult);

            // Display message information on the screen,
            // including the message number (state Object*).
            Console::WriteLine(S"Message: {0} {1}", asyncResult-
>AsyncResult->AsyncState , static_cast<String*>(m->Body));

//      Console.WriteLine("Message: " +
//          (int)asyncResult.AsyncResult.AsyncState + " "
//          +(string)m.Body);

            // Restart the asynchronous peek operation, with the
            // same time-out.
            mq->BeginPeek(TimeSpan(0, 1, 0), __box(messageNumber++));

        }
        catch (MessageQueueException* e)
        {
            if (e->MessageQueueErrorCode ==
                MessageQueueErrorCode::IOTimeout)
            {
                Console::WriteLine(e);
            }
```

```
        // Handle other sources of MessageQueueException.
    }

    // Handle other exceptions.

    return;
    }
};

// Provides an entry point into the application.
//
// This example performs asynchronous peek operation
// processing.
int main()
{
    // Create an instance of MessageQueue. Set its formatter.
    MessageQueue* myQueue = new MessageQueue(S".\\myQueue");

    Type* p __gc[] = new Type* __gc[1];
    p[0] = __typeof(String);
    myQueue->Formatter = new XmlMessageFormatter( p );

    // Add an event handler for the PeekCompleted event.
    myQueue->PeekCompleted += new PeekCompletedEventHandler(0,    ⌐
MyNewQueue::MyPeekCompleted);

    // Begin the asynchronous peek operation with a time-->Item[Out]
    // of one minute.
    myQueue->BeginPeek(TimeSpan(0, 1, 0),    ⌐
__box(MyNewQueue::messageNumber++));

    // Do other work on the current thread.

    return 0;
}
```

MessageQueue.BeginPeek Method ()

Initiates an asynchronous peek operation that has no time-out. The operation is not complete until a message becomes available in the queue.

```
[Visual Basic]
Overloads Public Function BeginPeek() As IAsyncResult
[C#]
public IAsyncResult BeginPeek();
[C++]
public: IAsyncResult* BeginPeek();
[JScript]
public function BeginPeek() : IAsyncResult;
```

Return Value

The **IAsyncResult** that identifies the posted asynchronous request.

Exceptions

Exception Type	Condition
MessageQueueException	An error occurred when accessing a Message Queuing API.

Remarks

In asynchronous processing, you use **BeginPeek** to raise the **PeekCompleted** event when a message becomes available in the queue.

> **Note** **PeekCompleted** is also raised if a message already exists in the queue.

To use **BeginPeek**, create an event handler that processes the results of the asynchronous operation, and associate it with your event delegate. **BeginPeek** initiates an asynchronous peek operation; the

MessageQueue is notified, through the raising of the **PeekCompleted** event, when a message arrives in the queue. The **MessageQueue** can then access the message by calling **EndPeek** or by retrieving the result using the **PeekCompletedEventArgs**.

> **Note** The **BeginPeek** method returns immediately, but the asynchronous operation is not completed until the event handler is called.

Because **BeginPeek** is asynchronous, you can call it to peek the queue without blocking the current thread of execution. To synchronously peek the queue, use the **Peek** method.

Once an asynchronous operation completes, you can call **BeginPeek** or **BeginReceive** again in the event handler to keep receiving notifications.

The **IAsyncResult** that **BeginPeek** returns identifies the asynchronous operation that the method started. You can use this **IAsyncResult** throughout the lifetime of the operation, although you generally do not use it until **EndPeek** is called. However, if you start several asynchronous operations, you can place their **IAsyncResult** values in an array and specify whether to wait for all operations or any operation to complete. In this case, you use the **AsyncWaitHandle** property of the **IAsyncResult** to identify the completed operation.

If **CanRead** is **false**, the completion event is raised, but an exception will be thrown when calling **EndPeek**.

The following table shows whether this method is available in various Workgroup modes.

Workgroup Mode	Available
Local computer	Yes
Local computer + direct format name	Yes
Remote computer	No
Remote computer + direct format name	Yes

Example

See related example in the **System.Messaging.MessageQueue.BeginPeek** method topic.

Requirements

Platforms: Windows 98, Windows NT 4.0, Windows Millennium Edition, Windows 2000, Windows XP Home Edition, Windows XP Professional, Windows .NET Server family

.NET Framework Security:

- Full trust for the immediate caller. This member cannot be used by partially trusted code.

MessageQueue.BeginPeek Method (TimeSpan)

Initiates an asynchronous peek operation that has a specified time-out. The operation is not complete until either a message becomes available in the queue or the time-out occurs.

```
[Visual Basic]
Overloads Public Function BeginPeek( _
    ByVal timeout As TimeSpan _
) As IAsyncResult
[C#]
public IAsyncResult BeginPeek(
    TimeSpan timeout
);
```

```
[C++]
public: IAsyncResult* BeginPeek(
    TimeSpan timeout
);
[JScript]
public function BeginPeek(
    timeout : TimeSpan
) : IAsyncResult;
```

Parameters
timeout
   A **TimeSpan** that indicates the interval of time to wait for a
   message to become available.

Return Value
The **IAsyncResult** that identifies the posted asynchronous request.

Exceptions

Exception Type	Condition
ArgumentException	The value specified for the *timeout* parameter is invalid.
MessageQueueException	An error occurred when accessing a Message Queuing API.

Remarks
In asynchronous processing, you use **BeginPeek** to raise the
PeekCompleted event when a message becomes available in the
queue or when the specified interval of time has expired.

> **Note**   **PeekCompleted** is also raised if a message already
> exists in the queue.

To use **BeginPeek**, create an event handler that processes the results
of the asynchronous operation, and associate it with your event
delegate. **BeginPeek** initiates an asynchronous peek operation; the
MessageQueue is notified, through the raising of the
PeekCompleted event, when a message arrives in the queue. The
MessageQueue can then access the message by calling **EndPeek** or
by retrieving the result using the **PeekCompletedEventArgs**.

> **Note**   The **BeginPeek** method returns immediately, but the
> asynchronous operation is not completed until the event
> handler is called.

Because **BeginPeek** is asynchronous, you can call it to peek the
queue without blocking the current thread of execution. To
synchronously peek the queue, use the **Peek** method.

Once an asynchronous operation completes, you can call **BeginPeek**
or **BeginReceive** again in the event handler to keep receiving
notifications.

The **IAsyncResult** that **BeginPeek** returns identifies the
asynchronous operation that the method started. You can use this
IAsyncResult throughout the lifetime of the operation, although you
generally do not use it until **EndPeek** is called. However, if you start
several asynchronous operations, you can place their **IAsyncResult**
values in an array and specify whether to wait for all operations or
any operation to complete. In this case, you use the
AsyncWaitHandle property of the **IAsyncResult** to identify the
completed operation.

This overload specifies a time-out. If the interval specified by the
timeout parameter expires, this component raises the
PeekCompleted event, and the **IsCompleted** property of the

operation's associated **IAsyncResult** is **true**. Because no message
exists, a subsequent call to **EndPeek** will throw an exception.

If **CanRead** is **false**, the completion event is raised, but an exception
will be thrown when calling **EndPeek**.

The following table shows whether this method is available in
various Workgroup modes.

Workgroup Mode	Available
Local computer	Yes
Local computer + direct format name	Yes
Remote computer	No
Remote computer + direct format name	Yes

Example
See related example in the
System.Messaging.MessageQueue.BeginPeek method topic.

Requirements
Platforms: Windows 98, Windows NT 4.0,
Windows Millennium Edition, Windows 2000,
Windows XP Home Edition, Windows XP Professional,
Windows .NET Server family

.NET Framework Security:
- Full trust for the immediate caller. This member cannot be used
  by partially trusted code.

MessageQueue.BeginPeek Method (TimeSpan, Object)
Initiates an asynchronous peek operation that has a specified time-
out and a specified state object, which provides associated
information throughout the operation's lifetime. The operation is not
complete until either a message becomes available in the queue or
the time-out occurs.

```
[Visual Basic]
Overloads Public Function BeginPeek( _
    ByVal timeout As TimeSpan, _
    ByVal stateObject As Object _
) As IAsyncResult
[C#]
public IAsyncResult BeginPeek(
    TimeSpan timeout,
    object stateObject
);
[C++]
public: IAsyncResult* BeginPeek(
    TimeSpan timeout,
    Object* stateObject
);
[JScript]
public function BeginPeek(
    timeout : TimeSpan,
    stateObject : Object
) : IAsyncResult;
```

Parameters
timeout
   A **TimeSpan** that indicates the interval of time to wait for a
   message to become available.
stateObject
   A state object, specified by the application, that contains
   information associated with the asynchronous operation.

Return Value

The **IAsyncResult** that identifies the posted asynchronous request.

Exceptions

Exception Type	Condition
ArgumentException	The value specified for the *timeout* parameter is invalid.
MessageQueueException	An error occurred when accessing a Message Queuing API.

Remarks

In asynchronous processing, you use **BeginPeek** to raise the **PeekCompleted** event when a message becomes available in the queue or when the specified interval of time has expired.

> **Note**   **PeekCompleted** is also raised if a message already exists in the queue.

Use this overload to associate information with the operation that will be preserved throughout the operation's lifetime. The event handler can access this information by looking at the **AsyncState** property of the **IAsyncResult** that is associated with the operation.

To use **BeginPeek**, create an event handler that processes the results of the asynchronous operation, and associate it with your event delegate. **BeginPeek** initiates an asynchronous peek operation; the **MessageQueue** is notified, through the raising of the **PeekCompleted** event, when a message arrives in the queue. The **MessageQueue** can then access the message by calling **EndPeek** or by retrieving the result using the **PeekCompletedEventArgs**.

> **Note**   The **BeginPeek** method returns immediately, but the asynchronous operation is not completed until the event handler is called.

Because **BeginPeek** is asynchronous, you can call it to peek the queue without blocking the current thread of execution. To synchronously peek the queue, use the **Peek** method.

Once an asynchronous operation completes, you can call **BeginPeek** or **BeginReceive** again in the event handler to keep receiving notifications.

BeginPeek returns an **IAsyncResult** that identifies the asynchronous operation that the method started. You can use this **IAsyncResult** throughout the lifetime of the operation, although you generally do not use it until **EndPeek** is called. However, if you start several asynchronous operations, you can place their **IAsyncResult** values in an array and specify whether to wait for all operations or any operation to complete. In this case, you use the **AsyncWaitHandle** property of the **IAsyncResult** to identify the completed operation.

This overload specifies a time-out and a state object. If the interval specified by the *timeout* parameter expires, this component raises the **PeekCompleted** event, and the **IsCompleted** property of the operation's associated **IAsyncResult** is **true**. Because no message exists, a subsequent call to **EndPeek** will throw an exception.

The state object associates state information with the operation. For example, if you call **BeginPeek** multiple times to initiate multiple operations, you can identify each operation through a separate state object that you define. For an illustration of this scenario, see the Example section.

You can also use the state object to pass information across process threads. If a thread is started but the callback is on a different thread

in an asynchronous scenario, the state object is marshaled and passed back along with information from the event.

If **CanRead** is **false**, the completion event is raised, but an exception will be thrown when calling **EndPeek**.

The following table shows whether this method is available in various Workgroup modes.

Workgroup Mode	Available
Local computer	Yes
Local computer + direct format name	Yes
Remote computer	No
Remote computer + direct format name	Yes

Example

See related example in the **System.Messaging.MessageQueue.BeginPeek** method topic.

Requirements

Platforms: Windows 98, Windows NT 4.0, Windows Millennium Edition, Windows 2000, Windows XP Home Edition, Windows XP Professional, Windows .NET Server family

.NET Framework Security:

- Full trust for the immediate caller. This member cannot be used by partially trusted code.

MessageQueue.BeginPeek Method (TimeSpan, Object, AsyncCallback)

Initiates an asynchronous peek operation that has a specified time-out and a specified state object, which provides associated information throughout the operation's lifetime. This overload receives notification, through a callback, of the identity of the event handler for the operation. The operation is not complete until either a message becomes available in the queue or the time-out occurs.

```
[Visual Basic]
Overloads Public Function BeginPeek( _
    ByVal timeout As TimeSpan, _
    ByVal stateObject As Object, _
    ByVal callback As AsyncCallback _
) As IAsyncResult
[C#]
public IAsyncResult BeginPeek(
    TimeSpan timeout,
    object stateObject,
    AsyncCallback callback
);
[C++]
public: IAsyncResult* BeginPeek(
    TimeSpan timeout,
    Object* stateObject,
    AsyncCallback* callback
);
[JScript]
public function BeginPeek(
    timeout : TimeSpan,
    stateObject : Object,
    callback : AsyncCallback
) : IAsyncResult;
```

Parameters

timeout
> A **TimeSpan** that indicates the interval of time to wait for a message to become available.

stateObject
> A state object, specified by the application, that contains information associated with the asynchronous operation.

callback
> The **AsyncCallback** that will receive the notification of the asynchronous operation completion.

Return Value

The **IAsyncResult** that identifies the posted asynchronous request.

Exceptions

Exception Type	Condition
ArgumentException	The value specified for the *timeout* parameter is invalid.
MessageQueueException	An error occurred when accessing a Message Queuing API.

Remarks

When you use this overload, the callback specified in the callback parameter is invoked directly when a message becomes available in the queue or when the specified interval of time has expired; the **PeekCompleted** event is not raised. The other overloads of **BeginPeek** rely on this component to raise the **PeekCompleted** event.

> **Note** **PeekCompleted** is also raised if a message already exists in the queue.

> **Note** The **BeginPeek** method returns immediately, but the asynchronous operation is not completed until the event handler is called.

Because **BeginPeek** is asynchronous, you can call it to peek the queue without blocking the current thread of execution. To synchronously peek the queue, use the **Peek** method.

Once an asynchronous operation completes, you can call **BeginPeek** or **BeginReceive** again in the event handler to keep receiving notifications.

BeginPeek returns an **IAsyncResult** that identifies the asynchronous operation that the method started. You can use this **IAsyncResult** throughout the lifetime of the operation, although you generally do not use it until **EndPeek** is called. However, if you start several asynchronous operations, you can place their **IAsyncResult** values in an array and specify whether to wait for all operations or any operation to complete. In this case, you use the **AsyncWaitHandle** property of the **IAsyncResult** to identify the completed operation.

The state object associates state information with the operation. For example, if you call **BeginPeek** multiple times to initiate multiple operations, you can identify each operation through a separate state object that you define.

The following table shows whether this method is available in various Workgroup modes.

Workgroup Mode	Available
Local computer	Yes
Local computer + direct format name	Yes

Workgroup Mode	Available
Remote computer	No
Remote computer + direct format name	Yes

Requirements

Platforms: Windows 98, Windows NT 4.0, Windows Millennium Edition, Windows 2000, Windows XP Home Edition, Windows XP Professional, Windows .NET Server family

.NET Framework Security:
- Full trust for the immediate caller. This member cannot be used by partially trusted code.

MessageQueue.BeginReceive Method

Initiates an asynchronous receive operation by telling Message Queuing to begin receiving a message and notify the event handler when finished.

Overload List

Initiates an asynchronous receive operation that has no time-out. The operation is not complete until a message becomes available in the queue.

> [Visual Basic] **Overloads Public Function BeginReceive() As IAsyncResult**
> [C#] **public IAsyncResult BeginReceive();**
> [C++] **public: IAsyncResult* BeginReceive();**
> [JScript] **public function BeginReceive() : IAsyncResult;**

Initiates an asynchronous receive operation that has a specified time-out. The operation is not complete until either a message becomes available in the queue or the time-out occurs.

> [Visual Basic] **Overloads Public Function BeginReceive(TimeSpan) As IAsyncResult**
> [C#] **public IAsyncResult BeginReceive(TimeSpan);**
> [C++] **public: IAsyncResult* BeginReceive(TimeSpan);**
> [JScript] **public function BeginReceive(TimeSpan) : IAsyncResult;**

Initiates an asynchronous receive operation that has a specified time-out and a specified state object, which provides associated information throughout the operation's lifetime. The operation is not complete until either a message becomes available in the queue or the time-out occurs.

> [Visual Basic] **Overloads Public Function BeginReceive(TimeSpan, Object) As IAsyncResult**
> [C#] **public IAsyncResult BeginReceive(TimeSpan, object);**
> [C++] **public: IAsyncResult* BeginReceive(TimeSpan, Object*);**
> [JScript] **public function BeginReceive(TimeSpan, Object) : IAsyncResult;**

Initiates an asynchronous receive operation that has a specified time-out and a specified state object, which provides associated information throughout the operation's lifetime. This overload receives notification, through a callback, of the identity of the event handler for the operation. The operation is not complete until either a message becomes available in the queue or the time-out occurs.

> [Visual Basic] **Overloads Public Function BeginReceive (TimeSpan, Object, AsyncCallback) As IAsyncResult**

[C#] public IAsyncResult BeginReceive(TimeSpan, object, AsyncCallback);

[C++] public: IAsyncResult* BeginReceive(TimeSpan, Object*, AsyncCallback*);

[JScript] public function BeginReceive(TimeSpan, Object, AsyncCallback) : IAsyncResult;

Example

[Visual Basic, C#, C++] The following example chains asynchronous requests. It assumes there is a queue on the local computer called "myQueue". The Main function begins the asynchronous operation that is handled by the MyReceiveCompleted routine. MyReceiveCompleted processes the current message and begins a new asynchronous receive operation.

[Visual Basic, C#, C++] **Note** This example shows how to use one of the overloaded versions of **BeginReceive**. For other examples that might be available, see the individual overload topics.

```
[Visual Basic]
Imports System
Imports System.Messaging
Imports System.Threading

Namespace MyProject

    '/ <summary>
    '/ Provides a container class for the example.
    '/ </summary>
    Public Class MyNewQueue

        ' Define static class members.
        Private Shared signal As New ManualResetEvent(False)
        Private Shared count As Integer = 0

        '***************************************************
        ' Provides an entry point into the application.
        '
        ' This example performs asynchronous receive
        ' operation processing.
        '***************************************************

        Public Shared Sub Main()
            ' Create an instance of MessageQueue. Set its formatter.
            Dim myQueue As New MessageQueue(".\myQueue")
            myQueue.Formatter = New XmlMessageFormatter(New Type() _
                {GetType([String])})

            ' Add an event handler for the ReceiveCompleted event.
            AddHandler myQueue.ReceiveCompleted, AddressOf _
                MyReceiveCompleted

            ' Begin the asynchronous receive operation.
            myQueue.BeginReceive()

            signal.WaitOne()

            ' Do other work on the current thread.

            Return

        End Sub 'Main

        '***************************************************
        ' Provides an event handler for the ReceiveCompleted
        ' event.
        '***************************************************

        Private Shared Sub MyReceiveCompleted(ByVal [source] As _
            [Object], ByVal asyncResult As ReceiveCompletedEventArgs)
```

```
            Try
                ' Connect to the queue.
                Dim mq As MessageQueue = CType([source], MessageQueue)

                ' End the asynchronous receive operation.
                Dim m As Message = _
                    mq.EndReceive(asyncResult.AsyncResult)

                count += 1
                If count = 10 Then
                    signal.Set()
                End If

                ' Restart the asynchronous receive operation.
                mq.BeginReceive()

            Catch
                ' Handle sources of MessageQueueException.

                ' Handle other exceptions.

            End Try

            Return

        End Sub 'MyReceiveCompleted

    End Class 'MyNewQueue
End Namespace 'MyProject
```

```
[C#]
using System;
using System.Messaging;
using System.Threading;

namespace MyProject
{
    /// <summary>
    /// Provides a container class for the example.
    /// </summary>
    public class MyNewQueue
    {
        // Define static class members.
        static ManualResetEvent signal = new ManualResetEvent(false);
        static int count = 0;

        //***************************************************
        // Provides an entry point into the application.
        //
        // This example performs asynchronous receive
        // operation processing.
        //***************************************************

        public static void Main()
        {
            // Create an instance of MessageQueue. Set its formatter.
            MessageQueue myQueue = new MessageQueue(".\\myQueue");
            myQueue.Formatter = new XmlMessageFormatter(new Type[]
                {typeof(String)});

            // Add an event handler for the ReceiveCompleted event.
            myQueue.ReceiveCompleted +=
                new ReceiveCompletedEventHandler(MyReceiveCompleted);

            // Begin the asynchronous receive operation.
            myQueue.BeginReceive();

            signal.WaitOne();

            // Do other work on the current thread.

            return;
        }
```

```
//*************************************************
// Provides an event handler for the ReceiveCompleted
// event.
//*************************************************
private static void MyReceiveCompleted(Object source,
    ReceiveCompletedEventArgs asyncResult)
{
    try
    {
        // Connect to the queue.
        MessageQueue mq = (MessageQueue)source;

        // End the asynchronous receive operation.
        Message m = mq.EndReceive(asyncResult.AsyncResult);

        count += 1;
        if (count == 10)
        {
            signal.Set();
        }

        // Restart the asynchronous receive operation.
        mq.BeginReceive();
    }
    catch(MessageQueueException)
    {
        // Handle sources of MessageQueueException.
    }

    // Handle other exceptions.

    return;
    }
  }
}

[C++]
#using <mscorlib.dll>
#using <system.dll>
#using <system.messaging.dll>

using namespace System;
using namespace System::Messaging;
using namespace System::Threading;

__gc class MyNewQueue
{
public:
    // Define static class members.
    static ManualResetEvent* signal = new ManualResetEvent(false);
    static int count = 0;

    // Provides an event handler for the ReceiveCompleted
    // event.

public:
    static void MyReceiveCompleted(Object* source,
        ReceiveCompletedEventArgs* asyncResult)
    {
        try
        {
            // Connect to the queue.
            MessageQueue* mq = dynamic_cast<MessageQueue*>(source);

            // End the asynchronous receive operation.
            mq->EndReceive(asyncResult->AsyncResult);

            count += 1;
            if (count == 10)
            {
                signal->Set();
            }
```

```
            // Restart the asynchronous receive operation.
            mq->BeginReceive();
        }
        catch (MessageQueueException*)
        {
            // Handle sources of MessageQueueException.
        }

        // Handle other exceptions.

        return;
    }
};

// Provides an entry point into the application.
//
// This example performs asynchronous receive
// operation processing.

int main()
{
    // Create an instance of MessageQueue. Set its formatter.
    MessageQueue* myQueue = new MessageQueue(S".\\myQueue");

    Type* p __gc[] = new Type* __gc[1];
    p[0] = __typeof(String);
    myQueue->Formatter = new XmlMessageFormatter( p );

    // Add an event handler for the ReceiveCompleted event.
    myQueue->ReceiveCompleted += new
ReceiveCompletedEventHandler(0, MyNewQueue::MyReceiveCompleted);

    // Begin the asynchronous receive operation.
    myQueue->BeginReceive();

    MyNewQueue::signal->WaitOne();

    // Do other work on the current thread.

    return 0;
}
```

[Visual Basic, C#, C++] The following example queues asynchronous requests. The call to **BeginReceive** uses the **AsyncWaitHandle** in its return value. The Main routine waits for all asynchronous operations to be completed before exiting.

```
[Visual Basic]
Imports System
Imports System.Messaging
Imports System.Threading

Namespace MyProject

    '/ <summary>
    '/ Provides a container class for the example.
    '/ </summary>
    Public Class MyNewQueue

        '*************************************************
        ' Provides an entry point into the application.
        '
        ' This example performs asynchronous receive
        ' operation processing.
        '*************************************************

        Public Shared Sub Main()

            ' Create an instance of MessageQueue. Set its formatter.
            Dim myQueue As New MessageQueue(".\myQueue")
            myQueue.Formatter = New XmlMessageFormatter(New Type() _
                {GetType([String])})
```

```vb
    ' Add an event handler for the ReceiveCompleted event.
    AddHandler myQueue.ReceiveCompleted, AddressOf _
        MyReceiveCompleted

    ' Define wait handles for multiple operations.
    Dim waitHandleArray(10) As WaitHandle

    Dim i As Integer
    For i = 0 To 9
        ' Begin asynchronous operations.
        waitHandleArray(i) = _
            myQueue.BeginReceive().AsyncWaitHandle
    Next i

    ' Specify to wait for all operations to return.
    WaitHandle.WaitAll(waitHandleArray)

    Return

End Sub 'Main

'****************************************************
' Provides an event handler for the ReceiveCompleted
' event.
'****************************************************

Private Shared Sub MyReceiveCompleted(ByVal [source] As _
    [Object], ByVal asyncResult As ReceiveCompletedEventArgs)

    Try
        ' Connect to the queue.
        Dim mq As MessageQueue = CType([source], MessageQueue)

        ' End the asynchronous receive operation.
        Dim m As Message = _
            mq.EndReceive(asyncResult.AsyncResult)

        ' Process the message here.
        Console.WriteLine("Message received.")

    Catch

        ' Handle sources of MessageQueueException.

        ' Handle other exceptions.

    End Try

    Return

End Sub 'MyReceiveCompleted

    End Class 'MyNewQueue
End Namespace 'MyProject
```

```csharp
[C#]
using System;
using System.Messaging;
using System.Threading;

namespace MyProject
{
    /// <summary>
    /// Provides a container class for the example.
    /// </summary>
    public class MyNewQueue
    {

        //****************************************************
        // Provides an entry point into the application.
        //
        // This example performs asynchronous receive
        // operation processing.
        //****************************************************

        public static void Main()
        {
            // Create an instance of MessageQueue. Set its formatter.
            MessageQueue myQueue = new MessageQueue(".\\myQueue");
            myQueue.Formatter = new XmlMessageFormatter(new Type[]
                {typeof(String)});

            // Add an event handler for the ReceiveCompleted event.
            myQueue.ReceiveCompleted +=
                new ReceiveCompletedEventHandler(MyReceiveCompleted);

            // Define wait handles for multiple operations.
            WaitHandle[] waitHandleArray = new WaitHandle[10];
            for(int i=0; i<10; i++)
            {
                // Begin asynchronous operations.
                waitHandleArray[i] =
                    myQueue.BeginReceive().AsyncWaitHandle;
            }

            // Specify to wait for all operations to return.
            WaitHandle.WaitAll(waitHandleArray);

            return;
        }

        //****************************************************
        // Provides an event handler for the ReceiveCompleted
        // event.
        //****************************************************

        private static void MyReceiveCompleted(Object source,
            ReceiveCompletedEventArgs asyncResult)
        {
            try
            {
                // Connect to the queue.
                MessageQueue mq = (MessageQueue)source;

                // End the asynchronous receive operation.
                Message m = mq.EndReceive(asyncResult.AsyncResult);

                // Process the message here.
                Console.WriteLine("Message received.");

            }
            catch(MessageQueueException)
            {
                // Handle sources of MessageQueueException.
            }

            // Handle other exceptions.

            return;
        }
    }
}
```

```cpp
[C++]
#using <mscorlib.dll>
#using <system.dll>
#using <system.messaging.dll>

using namespace System;
using namespace System::Messaging;
using namespace System::Threading;

__gc class MyNewQueue
{
    // Provides an event handler for the ReceiveCompleted
    // event.

public:
    static void MyReceiveCompleted(Object* source,
        ReceiveCompletedEventArgs* asyncResult)
```

```
{
    try
    {
        // Connect to the queue.
        MessageQueue* mq = dynamic_cast<MessageQueue*>(source);

        // End the asynchronous receive operation.
        mq->EndReceive(asyncResult->AsyncResult);

        // Process the message here.
        Console::WriteLine(S"Message received.");

    }
    catch (MessageQueueException*)
    {
        // Handle sources of MessageQueueException.
    }

    // Handle other exceptions.

    return;
    }
};

// Provides an entry point into the application.
//
// This example performs asynchronous receive
// operation processing.

int main()
{
    // Create an instance of MessageQueue. Set its formatter.
    MessageQueue* myQueue = new MessageQueue(S".\\myQueue");

    Type* p __gc[] = new Type* __gc[1];
    p[0] = __typeof(String);
    myQueue->Formatter = new XmlMessageFormatter( p );

    // Add an event handler for the ReceiveCompleted event.
    myQueue->ReceiveCompleted += new
ReceiveCompletedEventHandler(0, MyNewQueue::MyReceiveCompleted);

    // Define wait handles for multiple operations.
    WaitHandle* waitHandleArray[] = new WaitHandle*[10];
    for (int i=0; i<10; i++)
    {
        // Begin asynchronous operations.
        waitHandleArray->Item[i] = myQueue->
BeginReceive()->AsyncWaitHandle;
    }

    // Specify to wait for all operations to return.
    WaitHandle::WaitAll(waitHandleArray);

    return 0;
}
```

MessageQueue.BeginReceive Method ()

Initiates an asynchronous receive operation that has no time-out. The operation is not complete until a message becomes available in the queue.

```
[Visual Basic]
Overloads Public Function BeginReceive() As IAsyncResult
[C#]
public IAsyncResult BeginReceive();
[C++]
public: IAsyncResult* BeginReceive();
[JScript]
public function BeginReceive() : IAsyncResult;
```

Return Value

The **IAsyncResult** that identifies the posted asynchronous request.

Exceptions

Exception Type	Condition
MessageQueueException	An error occurred when accessing a Message Queuing API.

Remarks

In asynchronous processing, you use **BeginReceive** to raise the **ReceiveCompleted** event when a message has been removed from the queue.

> **Note** **ReceiveCompleted** is also raised if a message already exists in the queue.

To use **BeginReceive**, create an event handler that processes the results of the asynchronous operation and associate it with your event delegate. **BeginReceive** initiates an asynchronous receive operation; the **MessageQueue** is notified, through the raising of the **ReceiveCompleted** event, when a message arrives in the queue. The **MessageQueue** can then access the message by calling **EndReceive**.

> **Note** The **BeginReceive** method returns immediately, but the asynchronous operation is not completed until the event handler is called.

Because **BeginReceive** is asynchronous, you can call it to receive a message from the queue without blocking the current thread of execution. To synchronously receive a message, use the **Receive** method.

Once an asynchronous operation completes, you can call **BeginPeek** or **BeginReceive** again in the event handler to keep receiving notifications.

The **IAsyncResult** that **BeginReceive** returns identifies the asynchronous operation that the method started. You can use this **IAsyncResult** throughout the lifetime of the operation, although you generally do not use it until **EndReceive** is called. However, if you start several asynchronous operations, you can place their **IAsyncResult** values in an array and specify whether to wait for all operations or any operation to complete. In this case, you use the **AsyncWaitHandle** property of the **IAsyncResult** to identify the completed operation.

If **CanRead** is **false**, the completion event is raised, but an exception will be thrown when calling **EndReceive**.

> **Note** Do not use the asynchronous call **BeginReceive** with transactions. If you want to perform a transactional asynchronous operation, call **BeginPeek**, and put the transaction and the (synchronous) **Receive** method within the event handler you create for the peek operation. Your event handler might contain functionality as shown in the following C# code.

```
myMessageQueue.BeginTransaction();
myMessageQueue.Receive();
myMessageQueue.CommitTransaction();
```

The following table shows whether this method is available in various Workgroup modes.

Workgroup Mode	Available
Local computer	Yes
Local computer + direct format name	Yes
Remote computer	No
Remote computer + direct format name	Yes

Example

See related example in the
System.Messaging.MessageQueue.BeginReceive method topic.

Requirements

Platforms: Windows 98, Windows NT 4.0,
Windows Millennium Edition, Windows 2000,
Windows XP Home Edition, Windows XP Professional,
Windows .NET Server family

.NET Framework Security:

- Full trust for the immediate caller. This member cannot be used
  by partially trusted code.

MessageQueue.BeginReceive Method (TimeSpan)

Initiates an asynchronous receive operation that has a specified time-
out. The operation is not complete until either a message becomes
available in the queue or the time-out occurs.

```
[Visual Basic]
Overloads Public Function BeginReceive( _
    ByVal timeout As TimeSpan _
) As IAsyncResult
[C#]
public IAsyncResult BeginReceive(
    TimeSpan timeout
);
[C++]
public: IAsyncResult* BeginReceive(
    TimeSpan timeout
);
[JScript]
public function BeginReceive(
    timeout : TimeSpan
) : IAsyncResult;
```

Parameters

timeout
    A **TimeSpan** that indicates the interval of time to wait for a
    message to become available.

Return Value

The **IAsyncResult** that identifies the posted asynchronous request.

Exceptions

Exception Type	Condition
ArgumentException	The value specified for the *timeout* parameter is invalid, possibly because it represents a negative number.
MessageQueueException	An error occurred when accessing a Message Queuing API.

Remarks

In asynchronous processing, you use **BeginReceive** to raise the
ReceiveCompleted event when a message becomes available in the
queue or when the specified interval of time has expired.

> **Note** **ReceiveCompleted** is also raised if a message already
> exists in the queue.

To use **BeginReceive**, create an event handler that processes the
results of the asynchronous operation and associate it with your
event delegate. **BeginReceive** initiates an asynchronous receive
operation; the **MessageQueue** is notified, through the raising of the
ReceiveCompleted event, when a message arrives in the queue. The
MessageQueue can then access the message by calling **EndReceive**
or retrieving the result using the **ReceiveCompletedEventArgs**.

> **Note** The **BeginReceive** method returns immediately, but the
> asynchronous operation is not completed until the event
> handler is called.

Because **BeginReceive** is asynchronous, you can call it to receive a
message from the queue without blocking the current thread of
execution. To synchronously receive a message, use the **Receive**
method.

Once an asynchronous operation completes, you can call **BeginPeek**
or **BeginReceive** again in the event handler to keep receiving
notifications.

If **CanRead** is **false**, the completion event is raised, but an exception
will be thrown when calling **EndReceive**.

The **IAsyncResult** that **BeginReceive** returns identifies the
asynchronous operation that the method started. You can use this
IAsyncResult throughout the lifetime of the operation, although you
generally do not use it until **EndReceive** is called. However, if you
start several asynchronous operations, you can place their
IAsyncResult values in an array and specify whether to wait for all
operations or any operation to complete. In this case, you use the
AsyncWaitHandle property of the **IAsyncResult** to identify the
completed operation.

This overload specifies a time-out. If the interval specified by the
timeout parameter expires, this component raises the
ReceiveCompleted event, but the **IsCompleted** property of the
operation's associated **IAsyncResult** is **false**. Because no message
exists, a subsequent call to **EndReceive** will throw an exception.

> **Note** Do not use the asynchronous call **BeginReceive** with
> transactions. If you want to perform a transactional
> asynchronous operation, call **BeginPeek**, and put the
> transaction and the (synchronous) **Receive** method within the
> event handler you create for the peek operation. Your event
> handler might contain functionality as shown in the following
> C# code.

```
myMessageQueue.BeginTransaction();
myMessageQueue.Receive();
myMessageQueue.CommitTransaction();
```

The following table shows whether this method is available in
various Workgroup modes.

Workgroup Mode	Available
Local computer	Yes
Local computer + direct format name	Yes

Workgroup Mode	Available
Remote computer	No
Remote computer + direct format name	Yes

Requirements

Platforms: Windows 98, Windows NT 4.0, Windows Millennium Edition, Windows 2000, Windows XP Home Edition, Windows XP Professional, Windows .NET Server family

.NET Framework Security:
- Full trust for the immediate caller. This member cannot be used by partially trusted code.

MessageQueue.BeginReceive Method (TimeSpan, Object)

Initiates an asynchronous receive operation that has a specified time-out and a specified state object, which provides associated information throughout the operation's lifetime. The operation is not complete until either a message becomes available in the queue or the time-out occurs.

```
[Visual Basic]
Overloads Public Function BeginReceive( _
    ByVal timeout As TimeSpan, _
    ByVal stateObject As Object _
) As IAsyncResult
[C#]
public IAsyncResult BeginReceive(
    TimeSpan timeout,
    object stateObject
);
[C++]
public: IAsyncResult* BeginReceive(
    TimeSpan timeout,
    Object* stateObject
);
[JScript]
public function BeginReceive(
    timeout : TimeSpan,
    stateObject : Object
) : IAsyncResult;
```

Parameters

timeout
   A **TimeSpan** that indicates the interval of time to wait for a message to become available.
stateObject
   A state object, specified by the application, that contains information associated with the asynchronous operation.

Return Value

The **IAsyncResult** that identifies the posted asynchronous request.

Exceptions

Exception Type	Condition
ArgumentException	The value specified for the *timeout* parameter is invalid.
MessageQueueException	An error occurred when accessing a Message Queuing API.

Remarks

In asynchronous processing, you use **BeginReceive** to raise the **ReceiveCompleted** event when a message becomes available in the queue or when the specified interval of time has expired.

> **Note** **ReceiveCompleted** is also raised if a message already exists in the queue.

Use this overload to associate information with the operation that will be preserved throughout the operation's lifetime. The event handler can detect this information by looking at the **AsyncState** property of the **IAsyncResult** that is associated with the operation.

To use **BeginReceive**, create an event handler that processes the results of the asynchronous operation and associate it with your event delegate. **BeginReceive** initiates an asynchronous receive operation; the **MessageQueue** is notified, through the raising of the **ReceiveCompleted** event, when a message arrives in the queue. The **MessageQueue** can then access the message by calling **EndReceive** or retrieving the result using the **ReceiveCompletedEventArgs**.

> **Note** The **BeginReceive** method returns immediately, but the asynchronous operation is not completed until the event handler is called.

Because **BeginReceive** is asynchronous, you can call it to receive a message from the queue without blocking the current thread of execution. To synchronously receive a message, use the **Receive** method.

Once an asynchronous operation completes, you can call **BeginPeek** or **BeginReceive** again in the event handler to keep receiving notifications.

The **IAsyncResult** that **BeginReceive** returns identifies the asynchronous operation that the method started. You can use this **IAsyncResult** throughout the lifetime of the operation, although you generally do not use it until **EndReceive** is called. However, if you start several asynchronous operations, you can place their **IAsyncResult** values in an array and specify whether to wait for all operations or any operation to complete. In this case, you use the **AsyncWaitHandle** property of the **IAsyncResult** to identify the completed operation.

This overload specifies a time-out and a state object. If the interval specified by the *timeout* parameter expires, this component raises the **ReceiveCompleted** event, but the **IsCompleted** property of the operation's associated **IAsyncResult** is false. Because no message exists, a subsequent call to **EndReceive** will throw an exception.

The state object associates state information with the operation. For example, if you call **BeginReceive** multiple times to initiate multiple operations, you can identify each operation through a separate state object that you define.

You can also use the state object to pass information across process threads. If a thread is started but the callback is on a different thread in an asynchronous scenario, the state object is marshaled and passed back along with information from the event.

> **Note** Do not use the asynchronous call **BeginReceive** with transactions. If you want to perform a transactional asynchronous operation, call **BeginPeek**, and put the transaction and the (synchronous) **Receive** method within the event handler you create for the peek operation. Your event handler might contain functionality as shown in the following C# code.

```
myMessageQueue.BeginTransaction();
myMessageQueue.Receive();
myMessageQueue.CommitTransaction();
```

The following table shows whether this method is available in various Workgroup modes.

Workgroup Mode	Available
Local computer	Yes
Local computer + direct format name	Yes
Remote computer	No
Remote computer + direct format name	Yes

Requirements

Platforms: Windows 98, Windows NT 4.0, Windows Millennium Edition, Windows 2000, Windows XP Home Edition, Windows XP Professional, Windows .NET Server family

.NET Framework Security:

- Full trust for the immediate caller. This member cannot be used by partially trusted code.

MessageQueue.BeginReceive Method (TimeSpan, Object, AsyncCallback)

Initiates an asynchronous receive operation that has a specified time-out and a specified state object, which provides associated information throughout the operation's lifetime. This overload receives notification, through a callback, of the identity of the event handler for the operation. The operation is not complete until either a message becomes available in the queue or the time-out occurs.

```
[Visual Basic]
Overloads Public Function BeginReceive( _
   ByVal timeout As TimeSpan, _
   ByVal stateObject As Object, _
   ByVal callback As AsyncCallback _
) As IAsyncResult
[C#]
public IAsyncResult BeginReceive(
   TimeSpan timeout,
   object stateObject,
   AsyncCallback callback
);
[C++]
public: IAsyncResult* BeginReceive(
   TimeSpan timeout,
   Object* stateObject,
   AsyncCallback* callback
);
[JScript]
public function BeginReceive(
   timeout : TimeSpan,
   stateObject : Object,
   callback : AsyncCallback
) : IAsyncResult;
```

Parameters

timeout
   A **TimeSpan** that indicates the interval of time to wait for a message to become available.

stateObject
   A state object, specified by the application, that contains information associated with the asynchronous operation.
callback
   The **AsyncCallback** that will receive the notification of the asynchronous operation completion.

Return Value

The **IAsyncResult** that identifies the posted asynchronous request.

Exceptions

Exception Type	Condition
ArgumentException	The value specified for the *timeout* parameter is invalid.
MessageQueueException	An error occurred when accessing a Message Queuing API.

Remarks

When you use this overload, the callback specified in the callback parameter is invoked directly when a message becomes available in the queue or when the specified interval of time has expired; the **ReceiveCompleted** event is not raised. The other overloads of **BeginReceive** rely on this component to raise the **ReceiveCompleted** event.

> **Note** **ReceiveCompleted** is also raised if a message already exists in the queue.

To use **BeginReceive**, create an event handler that processes the results of the asynchronous operation and associate it with your event delegate. **BeginReceive** initiates an asynchronous receive operation; the **MessageQueue** is notified, through the raising of the **ReceiveCompleted** event, when a message arrives in the queue. The **MessageQueue** can then access the message by calling **EndReceive** or retrieving the result using the **ReceiveCompletedEventArgs**.

> **Note** The **BeginReceive** method returns immediately, but the asynchronous operation is not completed until the event handler is called.

Because **BeginReceive** is asynchronous, you can call it to receive a message from the queue without blocking the current thread of execution. To synchronously receive a message, use the **Receive** method.

Once an asynchronous operation completes, you can call **BeginPeek** or **BeginReceive** again in the event handler to keep receiving notifications.

The **IAsyncResult** that **BeginReceive** returns identifies the asynchronous operation that the method started. You can use this **IAsyncResult** throughout the lifetime of the operation, although you generally do not use it until **EndReceive** is called. However, if you start several asynchronous operations, you can place their **IAsyncResult** values in an array and specify whether to wait for all operations or any operation to complete. In this case, you use the **AsyncWaitHandle** property of the **IAsyncResult** to identify the completed operation.

The state object associates state information with the operation. For example, if you call **BeginReceive** multiple times to initiate multiple operations, you can identify each operation through a separate state object that you define.

You can also use the state object to pass information across process threads. If a thread is started but the callback is on a different thread in an asynchronous scenario, the state object is marshaled and passed back along with information from the event.

> **Note** Do not use the asynchronous call **BeginReceive** with transactions. If you want to perform a transactional asynchronous operation, call **BeginPeek**, and put the transaction and the (synchronous) **Receive** method within the event handler you create for the peek operation. Your event handler might contain functionality as shown in the following C# code.

```
myMessageQueue.BeginTransaction();
myMessageQueue.Receive();
myMessageQueue.CommitTransaction();
```

The following table shows whether this method is available in various Workgroup modes.

Workgroup Mode	Available
Local computer	Yes
Local computer + direct format name	Yes
Remote computer	No
Remote computer + direct format name	Yes

Requirements

Platforms: Windows 98, Windows NT 4.0, Windows Millennium Edition, Windows 2000, Windows XP Home Edition, Windows XP Professional, Windows .NET Server family

.NET Framework Security:

- Full trust for the immediate caller. This member cannot be used by partially trusted code.

MessageQueue.ClearConnectionCache Method

Clears the connection cache.

```
[Visual Basic]
Public Shared Sub ClearConnectionCache()
[C#]
public static void ClearConnectionCache();
[C++]
public: static void ClearConnectionCache();
[JScript]
public static function ClearConnectionCache();
```

Remarks

When you call **ClearConnectionCache**, the format names stored in the cache are removed and handles opened and stored in the cache are closed.

The following table shows whether this method is available in various Workgroup modes.

Workgroup Mode	Available
Local computer	Yes
Local computer + direct format name	Yes
Remote computer	Yes
Remote computer + direct format name	Yes

Requirements

Platforms: Windows 98, Windows NT 4.0, Windows Millennium Edition, Windows 2000, Windows XP Home Edition, Windows XP Professional, Windows .NET Server family

.NET Framework Security:

- Full trust for the immediate caller. This member cannot be used by partially trusted code.

MessageQueue.Close Method

Frees all resources allocated by the **MessageQueue**.

```
[Visual Basic]
Public Sub Close()
[C#]
public void Close();
[C++]
public: void Close();
[JScript]
public function Close();
```

Remarks

Close frees all resources associated with a **MessageQueue**, including shared resources if appropriate. The system re-acquires these resources automatically if they are still available, for example when you call the **Send** method, as in the following C# code.

```
myMessageQueue.Send("Text 1.");
myMessageQueue.Close();
myMessageQueue.Send("Text 2."); //Resources are reaquired.
```

When you call **Close**, all **MessageQueue** properties that directly access the Message Queuing queue are cleared out. The **Path**, **DefaultPropertiesToSend**, **Formatter**, and **MessageReadPropertyFilter** all remain as they were.

You should call **Close** for a queue before you delete queue on the Message Queuing server. Otherwise, messages sent to the queue could throw exceptions or appear in the dead-letter queue.

The following table shows whether this method is available in various Workgroup modes.

Workgroup Mode	Available
Local computer	Yes
Local computer + direct format name	Yes
Remote computer	Yes
Remote computer + direct format name	Yes

Example

See related example in the **System.Messaging.MessageQueue** class topic.

Requirements

Platforms: Windows 98, Windows NT 4.0, Windows Millennium Edition, Windows 2000, Windows XP Home Edition, Windows XP Professional, Windows .NET Server family

.NET Framework Security:

- Full trust for the immediate caller. This member cannot be used by partially trusted code.

MessageQueue.Create Method

Creates a new queue at the specified path on a Message Queuing server.

Overload List

Creates a nontransactional Message Queuing queue at the specified path.

> [Visual Basic] **Overloads Public Shared Function Create(String) As MessageQueue**
> [C#] **public static MessageQueue Create(string);**
> [C++] **public: static MessageQueue* Create(String*);**
> [JScript] **public static function Create(String) : MessageQueue;**

Creates a transactional or nontransactional Message Queuing queue at the specified path.

> [Visual Basic] **Overloads Public Shared Function Create(String, Boolean) As MessageQueue**
> [C#] **public static MessageQueue Create(string, bool);**
> [C++] **public: static MessageQueue* Create(String*, bool);**
> [JScript] **public static function Create(String, Boolean) : MessageQueue;**

Example

See related example in the **System.Messaging.MessageQueue** class topic.

MessageQueue.Create Method (String)

Creates a nontransactional Message Queuing queue at the specified path.

```
[Visual Basic]
Overloads Public Shared Function Create( _
   ByVal path As String _
) As MessageQueue
[C#]
public static MessageQueue Create(
   string path
);
[C++]
public: static MessageQueue* Create(
   String* path
);
[JScript]
public static function Create(
   path : String
) : MessageQueue;
```

Parameters

path
> The path of the queue to create.

Return Value

A **MessageQueue** that represents the new queue.

Exceptions

Exception Type	Condition
ArgumentException	The *path* parameter is a null reference (**Nothing** in Visual Basic) or is an empty string ("").

Exception Type	Condition
MessageQueueException	A queue already exists at the specified path. -or- An error occurred when accessing a Message Queuing API.

Remarks

Use this overload to create a nontransactional Message Queuing queue.

To create a new instance of the **MessageQueue** class in your application and bind it to an existing queue, use the **MessageQueue** constructor. To create a new queue in Message Queuing, call **Create**.

The syntax for the *path* parameter depends on the type of queue it references.

Queue Type	Syntax
Public queue	*MachineName\ QueueName*
Private queue	*MachineName\Private$\ QueueName*

Use "." for the local computer. For more syntax, see the **Path** property.

The following table shows whether this method is available in various Workgroup modes.

Workgroup Mode	Available
Local computer	No
Local computer + direct format name	No
Remote computer	No
Remote computer + direct format name	No

Example

See related example in the **System.Messaging.MessageQueue** class topic.

Requirements

Platforms: Windows 98, Windows NT 4.0, Windows Millennium Edition, Windows 2000, Windows XP Home Edition, Windows XP Professional, Windows .NET Server family

.NET Framework Security:
- Full trust for the immediate caller. This member cannot be used by partially trusted code.

MessageQueue.Create Method (String, Boolean)

Creates a transactional or nontransactional Message Queuing queue at the specified path.

```
[Visual Basic]
Overloads Public Shared Function Create( _
   ByVal path As String, _
   ByVal transactional As Boolean _
) As MessageQueue
[C#]
public static MessageQueue Create(
   string path,
   bool transactional
);
```

```
[C++]
public: static MessageQueue* Create(
    String* path,
    bool transactional
);
[JScript]
public static function Create(
    path : String,
    transactional : Boolean
) : MessageQueue;
```

Parameters

path
> The path of the queue to create.

transactional
> **true** to create a transactional queue; **false** to create a nontransactional queue.

Return Value

A **MessageQueue** that represents the new queue.

Exceptions

Exception Type	Condition
ArgumentException	The *path* parameter is a null reference (**Nothing** in Visual Basic) or is an empty string ("").
MessageQueueException	A queue already exists at the specified path. -or- An error occurred when accessing a Message Queuing API.

Remarks

You can use this overload to create a transactional queue in Message Queuing. You can create a nontransactional queue, by setting the *transactional* parameter to **false** or by calling the other overload of **Create**.

To create a new instance of the **MessageQueue** class in your application and bind it to an existing queue, use the **MessageQueue** constructor. To create a new queue in Message Queuing, call **Create**.

The syntax for the *path* parameter depends on the type of queue it references.

Queue Type	Syntax
Public queue	*MachineName\ QueueName*
Private queue	*MachineName*\Private$\ *QueueName*

Use "." for the local computer. For more syntax, see the **Path** property.

The following table shows whether this method is available in various Workgroup modes.

Workgroup Mode	Available
Local computer	No
Local computer + direct format name	No
Remote computer	No
Remote computer + direct format name	No

Example

See related example in the **System.Messaging.MessageQueue** class topic.

Requirements

Platforms: Windows 98, Windows NT 4.0, Windows Millennium Edition, Windows 2000, Windows XP Home Edition, Windows XP Professional, Windows .NET Server family

.NET Framework Security:
- Full trust for the immediate caller. This member cannot be used by partially trusted code.

MessageQueue.Delete Method

Deletes a queue on a Message Queuing server.

```
[Visual Basic]
Public Shared Sub Delete( _
    ByVal path As String _
)
[C#]
public static void Delete(
    string path
);
[C++]
public: static void Delete(
    String* path
);
[JScript]
public static function Delete(
    path : String
);
```

Parameters

path
> The location of the queue to be deleted.

Exceptions

Exception Type	Condition
ArgumentException	The *path* parameter is a null reference (**Nothing** in Visual Basic) or is an empty string ("").
MessageQueueException	The syntax for the *path* parameter is invalid. -or- An error occurred when accessing a Message Queuing API.

Remarks

The syntax for the *path* parameter depends on the type of queue.

Queue Type	Syntax
Public queue	*MachineName\ QueueName*
Private queue	*MachineName*\Private$\ *QueueName*

For more syntax, see the **Path** property.

Alternatively, you can use the **FormatName** or **Label** to describe the queue path.

Reference	Syntax
Format name	FormatName:[*format name*]
Label	Label:[*label*]

The following table shows whether this method is available in various Workgroup modes.

Workgroup Mode	Available
Local computer	No
Local computer + direct format name	No
Remote computer	No
Remote computer + direct format name	No

Example

See related example in the **System.Messaging.MessageQueue** class topic.

Requirements

Platforms: Windows 98, Windows NT 4.0, Windows Millennium Edition, Windows 2000, Windows XP Home Edition, Windows XP Professional, Windows .NET Server family

.NET Framework Security:
• Full trust for the immediate caller. This member cannot be used by partially trusted code.

MessageQueue.Dispose Method

Overload List

This member supports the .NET Framework infrastructure and is not intended to be used directly from your code.

[Visual Basic] **Overloads Overrides Protected Sub Dispose(Boolean)**

[C#] **protected override void Dispose(bool);**

[C++] **protected: void Dispose(bool);**

[JScript] **protected override function Dispose(Boolean);**

Inherited from **Component**.

[Visual Basic] **Overloads Public Overridable Sub Dispose() Implements IDisposable.Dispose**

[C#] **public virtual void Dispose();**

[C++] **public: virtual void Dispose();**

[JScript] **public function Dispose();**

MessageQueue.Dispose Method (Boolean)

This member overrides **Component.Dispose**.

```
[Visual Basic]
Overrides Overloads Protected Sub Dispose( _
   ByVal disposing As Boolean _
)
[C#]
protected override void Dispose(
   bool disposing
);
[C++]
protected: void Dispose(
   bool disposing
);
[JScript]
protected override function Dispose(
   disposing : Boolean
);
```

Requirements

Platforms: Windows 98, Windows NT 4.0, Windows Millennium Edition, Windows 2000, Windows XP Home Edition, Windows XP Professional, Windows .NET Server family

.NET Framework Security:
• Full trust for the immediate caller. This member cannot be used by partially trusted code.

MessageQueue.EndPeek Method

Completes the specified asynchronous peek operation.

```
[Visual Basic]
Public Function EndPeek( _
   ByVal asyncResult As IAsyncResult _
) As Message
[C#]
public Message EndPeek(
   IAsyncResult asyncResult
);
[C++]
public: Message* EndPeek(
   IAsyncResult* asyncResult
);
[JScript]
public function EndPeek(
   asyncResult : IAsyncResult
) : Message;
```

Parameters

asyncResult
> The **IAsyncResult** that identifies the asynchronous peek operation to finish, and from which to retrieve an end result.

Return Value

The **Message** associated with the completed asynchronous operation.

Exceptions

Exception Type	Condition
ArgumentNullException	The *asyncResult* parameter is a null reference (**Nothing** in Visual Basic).
ArgumentException	The syntax of the *asyncResult* parameter is invalid.
MessageQueueException	An error occurred when accessing a Message Queuing API.

Remarks

When the **PeekCompleted** event is raised, **EndPeek** completes the operation that was initiated by the **BeginPeek** call. To do so, **EndPeek** peeks the message.

BeginPeek can specify a time-out, which causes the **PeekCompleted** event to be raised if the time-out occurs before a message appears in the queue. In this case, the **IsCompleted** property of the *asyncResult* parameter is set to **true**, but no message is associated with the operation. When a time-out occurs without a message arriving in the queue, a subsequent call to **EndPeek** throws an exception.

EndPeek is used to read the message that caused the **PeekCompleted** event to be raised.

If you want to continue to asynchronously peek messages, you can again call **BeginPeek** after calling **EndPeek**.

The following table shows whether this method is available in various Workgroup modes.

Workgroup Mode	Available
Local computer	Yes
Local computer + direct format name	Yes
Remote computer	No
Remote computer + direct format name	Yes

Example

See related example in the **System.Messaging.MessageQueue.BeginPeek** method topic.

Requirements

Platforms: Windows 98, Windows NT 4.0, Windows Millennium Edition, Windows 2000, Windows XP Home Edition, Windows XP Professional, Windows .NET Server family

.NET Framework Security:

- Full trust for the immediate caller. This member cannot be used by partially trusted code.

MessageQueue.EndReceive Method

Completes the specified asynchronous receive operation.

```
[Visual Basic]
Public Function EndReceive( _
    ByVal asyncResult As IAsyncResult _
) As Message
[C#]
public Message EndReceive(
    IAsyncResult asyncResult
);
[C++]
public: Message* EndReceive(
    IAsyncResult* asyncResult
);
[JScript]
public function EndReceive(
    asyncResult : IAsyncResult
) : Message;
```

Parameters

asyncResult
    The **IAsyncResult** that identifies the asynchronous receive operation to finish, and from which to retrieve an end result.

Return Value

The **Message** associated with the completed asynchronous operation.

Exceptions

Exception Type	Condition
ArgumentNullException	The *asyncResult* parameter is a null reference (**Nothing** in Visual Basic).
ArgumentException	The syntax of the *asyncResult* parameter is invalid.
MessageQueueException	An error occurred when accessing a Message Queuing API.

Remarks

When the **ReceiveCompleted** event is raised, **EndReceive** completes the operation that was initiated by the **BeginReceive** call. To do so, **EndReceive** receives the message.

BeginReceive can specify a time-out, which causes the **ReceiveCompleted** event to be raised if the time-out occurs before a message appears in the queue. In this case, the **IsCompleted** property of the *asyncResult* parameter is set to **true**, but no message is associated with the operation. When a time-out occurs without a message arriving in the queue, a subsequent call to **EndReceive** throws an exception.

EndReceive is used to read (removing from the queue) the message that caused the **ReceiveCompleted** event to be raised.

If you want to continue to asynchronously receive messages, you can again call **BeginReceive** after calling **EndReceive**.

The following table shows whether this method is available in various Workgroup modes.

Workgroup Mode	Available
Local computer	Yes
Local computer + direct format name	Yes
Remote computer	No
Remote computer + direct format name	Yes

Example

See related example in the **System.Messaging.MessageQueue** class topic.

Requirements

Platforms: Windows 98, Windows NT 4.0, Windows Millennium Edition, Windows 2000, Windows XP Home Edition, Windows XP Professional, Windows .NET Server family

.NET Framework Security:

- Full trust for the immediate caller. This member cannot be used by partially trusted code.

MessageQueue.Exists Method

Determines whether a Message Queuing queue at the specified path exists.

```
[Visual Basic]
Public Shared Function Exists( _
    ByVal path As String _
) As Boolean
[C#]
public static bool Exists(
    string path
);
[C++]
public: static bool Exists(
    String* path
);
[JScript]
public static function Exists(
    path : String
) : Boolean;
```

Parameters

path
The location of the queue to find.

Return Value

true if a queue with the specified path exists; otherwise, **false**.

Exceptions

Exception Type	Condition
ArgumentException	The *path* syntax is invalid.
MessageQueueException	An error occurred when accessing a Message Queuing API.
	-or-
	The **Exists** method is being called on a remote private queue
InvalidOperationException	The application used a format name syntax when verifying queue existence.

Remarks

The **Exists** method determines whether a Message Queuing queue exists at a specified path. No method exists to determine whether a queue with a specified format name exists. For more information about the format name syntax and other path syntax forms, see the **Path** property.)

Exists is an expensive operation. Use it only when it is necessary within the application.

The syntax for the *path* parameter depends on the type of queue.

Queue Type	Syntax
Public queue	*MachineName\ QueueName*

> **Note** **Exists** cannot be called to verify the existence of a remote private queue.

Alternatively, you can use the **Label** to describe the queue path.

Reference	Syntax
Label	Label:[*label*]

The following table shows whether this method is available in various Workgroup modes.

Workgroup Mode	Available
Local computer	Yes
Local computer + direct format name	No
Remote computer	No
Remote computer + direct format name	No

Example

See related example in the **System.Messaging.MessageQueue** class topic.

Requirements

Platforms: Windows 98, Windows NT 4.0, Windows Millennium Edition, Windows 2000, Windows XP Home Edition, Windows XP Professional, Windows .NET Server family

.NET Framework Security:

- Full trust for the immediate caller. This member cannot be used by partially trusted code.

MessageQueue.GetAllMessages Method

Returns all the messages that are in the queue.

```
[Visual Basic]
Public Function GetAllMessages() As Message()
[C#]
public Message[] GetAllMessages();
[C++]
public: Message* GetAllMessages() [];
[JScript]
public function GetAllMessages() : Message[];
```

Return Value

An array of type **Message** that represents all the messages in the queue, in the same order as they appear in the Message Queuing queue.

Exceptions

Exception Type	Condition
MessageQueueException	An error occurred when accessing a Message Queuing API.

Remarks

GetAllMessages returns a static snapshot of the messages in the queue, not dynamic links to those messages. Therefore, you cannot use the array to modify the messages in the queue. If you want real-time, dynamic interaction with the queue (such as the ability to delete messages), call the **GetMessageEnumerator** method, which returns a dynamic list of the messages in the queue.

Because **GetAllMessages** returns a copy of the messages in the queue at the time the method was called, the array does not reflect new messages that arrive in the queue or messages that are removed from the queue.

> **Note** **GetAllMessages** retrieves only those properties not filtered out by the **MessageReadPropertyFilter** property.

The following table shows whether this method is available in various Workgroup modes.

Workgroup Mode	Available
Local computer	Yes
Local computer + direct format name	Yes
Remote computer	No
Remote computer + direct format name	Yes

Requirements

Platforms: Windows 98, Windows NT 4.0, Windows Millennium Edition, Windows 2000, Windows XP Home Edition, Windows XP Professional, Windows .NET Server family

.NET Framework Security:

- Full trust for the immediate caller. This member cannot be used by partially trusted code.

MessageQueue.GetEnumerator Method

Enumerates the messages in a queue.

```
[Visual Basic]
Public Overridable Function GetEnumerator() As IEnumerator _
    Implements IEnumerable.GetEnumerator
```

```
[C#]
public virtual IEnumerator GetEnumerator();
[C++]
public: virtual IEnumerator* GetEnumerator();
[JScript]
public function GetEnumerator() : IEnumerator;
```

Return Value

An **IEnumerator** that provides a dynamic connection to the messages in the queue.

Implements

IEnumerable.GetEnumerator

Remarks

The following table shows whether this method is available in various Workgroup modes.

Workgroup Mode	Available
Local computer	Yes
Local computer + direct format name	Yes
Remote computer	No
Remote computer + direct format name	Yes

Requirements

Platforms: Windows 98, Windows NT 4.0, Windows Millennium Edition, Windows 2000, Windows XP Home Edition, Windows XP Professional, Windows .NET Server family

.NET Framework Security:

- Full trust for the immediate caller. This member cannot be used by partially trusted code.

MessageQueue.GetMachineId Method

Gets the identifier of the computer on which the queue referenced by this **MessageQueue** is located.

```
[Visual Basic]
Public Shared Function GetMachineId( _
   ByVal machineName As String _
) As Guid
[C#]
public static Guid GetMachineId(
   string machineName
);
[C++]
public: static Guid GetMachineId(
   String* machineName
);
[JScript]
public static function GetMachineId(
   machineName : String
) : Guid;
```

Parameters

machineName
   The name of the computer that contains the queue, without the two preceding backslashes (\\).

Return Value

A **Guid** that represents a unique identifier for the computer on which the queue is located.

Exceptions

Exception Type	Condition
MessageQueueException	The computer identifier could not be retrieved, possibly because the directory service is not available; for example, if you are working offline. -or- An error occurred when accessing a Message Queuing API.

Remarks

You can use a computer's identifier for two purposes, among others: to read the computer journal and to set security certificates. However, you cannot call **GetMachineId** for a remote computer when you are working offline because the application must have access to the directory service on the domain controller.

The computer identifier (or "machine identifier") is a **Guid** that Message Queuing creates when a computer is added to the enterprise. Message Queuing combines the computer identifier with the Machine and Journal keywords to create the machine journal's format name, which has the syntax Machine=<computeridentifier>;Journal. The machine journal, which is also known as the journal queue, is a system queue that stores copies of application-generated messages when the **UseJournalQueue** property is **true**.

> **Note** This syntax for the journal is only valid when constructing the format name for the queue. The path name syntax is *MachineName*\Journal$.

The following table shows whether this method is available in various Workgroup modes.

Workgroup Mode	Available
Local computer	No
Local computer + direct format name	No
Remote computer	No
Remote computer + direct format name	No

Requirements

Platforms: Windows 98, Windows NT 4.0, Windows Millennium Edition, Windows 2000, Windows XP Home Edition, Windows XP Professional, Windows .NET Server family

.NET Framework Security:

- Full trust for the immediate caller. This member cannot be used by partially trusted code.

MessageQueue.GetMessageEnumerator Method

Creates an enumerator object for all the messages in the queue.

```
[Visual Basic]
Public Function GetMessageEnumerator() As MessageEnumerator
[C#]
public MessageEnumerator GetMessageEnumerator();
[C++]
public: MessageEnumerator* GetMessageEnumerator();
[JScript]
public function GetMessageEnumerator() : MessageEnumerator;
```

Return Value

The **MessageEnumerator** holding the messages that are contained in the queue.

Remarks

GetMessageEnumerator creates a dynamic list of all the messages in a queue. You can remove from the queue the message at the enumerator's current position by calling **RemoveCurrent** for the **MessageEnumerator** that **GetMessageEnumerator** returns.

Because the cursor is associated with the dynamic list of messages in the queue, the enumeration reflects any modification you make to the messages in the queue, if the message is beyond the current cursor position. For example, the enumerator can automatically access a lower-priority message placed beyond the cursor's current position, but not a higher-priority message inserted before that position. However, you can reset the enumeration, thereby moving the cursor back to the beginning of the list, by calling **Reset** for the **MessageEnumerator**.

> **Note** The order of the messages in the enumeration reflects their order in the queue, so higher-priority messages will appear before lower-priority ones.

If you want a static snapshot of the messages in the queue rather than a dynamic connection to them, call **GetAllMessages**. This method returns an array of **Message** objects, which represent the messages at the time the method was called.

The following table shows whether this method is available in various Workgroup modes.

Workgroup Mode	Available
Local computer	Yes
Local computer + direct format name	Yes
Remote computer	Yes
Remote computer + direct format name	Yes

Example

See related example in the **System.Messaging.MessageQueue** class topic.

Requirements

Platforms: Windows 98, Windows NT 4.0, Windows Millennium Edition, Windows 2000, Windows XP Home Edition, Windows XP Professional, Windows .NET Server family

.NET Framework Security:

- Full trust for the immediate caller. This member cannot be used by partially trusted code.

MessageQueue.GetMessageQueueEnumerator Method

Creates an enumerator object for a dynamic listing of the public queues on the network.

Overload List

Provides forward-only cursor semantics to enumerate through all public queues on the network.

[Visual Basic] **Overloads Public Shared Function GetMessageQueueEnumerator() As MessageQueueEnumerator**

[C#] **public static MessageQueueEnumerator GetMessageQueueEnumerator();**

[C++] **public: static MessageQueueEnumerator* GetMessageQueueEnumerator();**

[JScript] **public static function GetMessageQueueEnumerator() : MessageQueueEnumerator;**

Provides forward-only cursor semantics to enumerate through all public queues on the network that meet the specified criteria.

[Visual Basic] **Overloads Public Shared Function GetMessageQueueEnumerator(MessageQueueCriteria) As MessageQueueEnumerator**

[C#] **public static MessageQueueEnumerator GetMessageQueueEnumerator(MessageQueueCriteria);**

[C++] **public: static MessageQueueEnumerator* GetMessageQueueEnumerator(MessageQueueCriteria*);**

[JScript] **public static function GetMessageQueueEnumerator(MessageQueueCriteria) : MessageQueueEnumerator;**

Example

See related example in the **System.Messaging.MessageQueue** class topic.

MessageQueue.GetMessageQueueEnumerator Method ()

Provides forward-only cursor semantics to enumerate through all public queues on the network.

```
[Visual Basic]
Overloads Public Shared Function GetMessageQueueEnumerator() As _
    MessageQueueEnumerator
[C#]
public static MessageQueueEnumerator GetMessageQueueEnumerator();
[C++]
public: static MessageQueueEnumerator* GetMessageQueueEnumerator();
[JScript]
public static function GetMessageQueueEnumerator() :
    MessageQueueEnumerator;
```

Return Value

A **MessageQueueEnumerator** that provides a dynamic listing of all the public message queues on the network.

Remarks

This overload of **GetMessageQueueEnumerator** returns an enumeration of all the public queues that are on the network.

Because the cursor is associated with a dynamic listing, the enumeration reflects any modification you make to a queue list for queues deleted or added beyond the cursor's current position. Additions or deletion of queues located before the cursor's current position are not reflected. For example, the enumerator can automatically access a queue appended beyond the cursor position but not one inserted before that position. However, you can reset the enumeration, thereby moving the cursor back to the beginning of the list, by calling **Reset** for the **MessageQueueEnumerator**.

> **Note** There is no defined ordering of queues in a network. An enumerator does not order them, for example, by computer, label, public or private status, or any other accessible criteria.

If you want a static snapshot of the queues on the network rather than a dynamic connection to them, call **GetPublicQueues** or **GetPrivateQueuesByMachine**. Each of these two methods returns an array of **MessageQueue** objects, which represent the queues at the time the method was called.

The following table shows whether this method is available in various Workgroup modes.

Workgroup Mode	Available
Local computer	No
Local computer + direct format name	No
Remote computer	No
Remote computer + direct format name	No

Example

See related example in the **System.Messaging.MessageQueue** class topic.

Requirements

Platforms: Windows 98, Windows NT 4.0, Windows Millennium Edition, Windows 2000, Windows XP Home Edition, Windows XP Professional, Windows .NET Server family

.NET Framework Security:

- Full trust for the immediate caller. This member cannot be used by partially trusted code.

MessageQueue.GetMessageQueueEnumerator Method (MessageQueueCriteria)

Provides forward-only cursor semantics to enumerate through all public queues on the network that meet the specified criteria.

```
[Visual Basic]
Overloads Public Shared Function GetMessageQueueEnumerator( _
    ByVal criteria As MessageQueueCriteria _
) As MessageQueueEnumerator
[C#]
public static MessageQueueEnumerator GetMessageQueueEnumerator(
    MessageQueueCriteria criteria
);
[C++]
public: static MessageQueueEnumerator* GetMessageQueueEnumerator(
    MessageQueueCriteria* criteria
);
[JScript]
public static function GetMessageQueueEnumerator(
    criteria : MessageQueueCriteria
) : MessageQueueEnumerator;
```

Parameters

criteria

A **MessageQueueCriteria** that contains the criteria used to filter the available message queues.

Return Value

A **MessageQueueEnumerator** that provides a dynamic listing of the public message queues on the network that satisfy the restrictions specified by the *criteria* parameter.

Remarks

This overload of **GetMessageQueueEnumerator** returns a listing of all the public queues on the network that satisfy criteria defined in the application criteria. You can specify the criteria to include, for example, queue creation or modification time, computer name, label, category, or any combination of these.

Because the cursor is associated with a dynamic listing, the enumeration reflects any modification you make to a queue that occurs beyond the cursor's current position. Changes to queues located before the cursor's current position are not reflected. For example, the enumerator can automatically access a queue appended beyond the cursor position but not one inserted before that position. However, you can reset the enumeration, thereby moving the cursor back to the beginning of the list, by calling **Reset** for the **MessageQueueEnumerator**.

> **Note** There is no defined ordering of queues in a network. An enumerator does not order them, for example, by computer, label, public or private status, or any other accessible criteria.

If you want a static snapshot of the queues on the network rather than a dynamic connection to them, specify criteria for **GetPublicQueues** or call **GetPrivateQueuesByMachine**. Each of these two methods returns an array of **MessageQueue** objects, which represent the queues at the time the method was called. Calling **GetPublicQueuesByCategory**, **GetPublicQueuesByLabel**, or **GetPublicQueuesByMachine** provides the same results as calling **GetPublicQueues** with the filtering criteria of **Category**, **Label**, and **MachineName** respectively.

The following table shows whether this method is available in various Workgroup modes.

Workgroup Mode	Available
Local computer	No
Local computer + direct format name	No
Remote computer	No
Remote computer + direct format name	No

Example

See related example in the **System.Messaging.MessageQueue** class topic.

Requirements

Platforms: Windows 98, Windows NT 4.0, Windows Millennium Edition, Windows 2000, Windows XP Home Edition, Windows XP Professional, Windows .NET Server family

.NET Framework Security:

- Full trust for the immediate caller. This member cannot be used by partially trusted code.

MessageQueue.GetPrivateQueuesByMachine Method

Retrieves all the private queues on the specified computer.

```
[Visual Basic]
Public Shared Function GetPrivateQueuesByMachine( _
    ByVal machineName As String _
) As MessageQueue()
[C#]
public static MessageQueue[] GetPrivateQueuesByMachine(
    string machineName
);
[C++]
public: static MessageQueue* GetPrivateQueuesByMachine(
    String* machineName
) [];
```

```
[JScript]
public static function GetPrivateQueuesByMachine(
    machineName : String
) : MessageQueue[];
```

Parameters

machineName
The computer from which to retrieve the private queues.

Return Value

An array of **MessageQueue** objects that reference the retrieved private queues.

Exceptions

Exception Type	Condition
ArgumentException	The *machineName* parameter is a null reference (**Nothing** in Visual Basic) or an empty string ("").
MessageQueueException	An error occurred when accessing a Message Queuing API.

Remarks

GetPrivateQueuesByMachine retrieves a static snapshot of the queues on a specified computer.

The following table shows whether this method is available in various Workgroup modes.

Workgroup Mode	Available
Local computer	Yes
Local computer + direct format name	Yes
Remote computer	Yes
Remote computer + direct format name	Yes

Example

See related example in the **System.Messaging.MessageQueue** class topic.

Requirements

Platforms: Windows 98, Windows NT 4.0, Windows Millennium Edition, Windows 2000, Windows XP Home Edition, Windows XP Professional, Windows .NET Server family

.NET Framework Security:
- Full trust for the immediate caller. This member cannot be used by partially trusted code.

MessageQueue.GetPublicQueues Method

Retrieves all the public queues on the network.

Overload List

Retrieves all the public queues on the network.

[Visual Basic] **Overloads Public Shared Function GetPublicQueues() As MessageQueue()**

[C#] **public static MessageQueue[] GetPublicQueues();**

[C++] **public: static MessageQueue* GetPublicQueues() [];**

[JScript] **public static function GetPublicQueues() : MessageQueue[];**

Retrieves all the public queues on the network that meet the specified criteria.

[Visual Basic] **Overloads Public Shared Function GetPublicQueues(MessageQueueCriteria) As MessageQueue()**

[C#] **public static MessageQueue[] GetPublicQueues(MessageQueueCriteria);**

[C++] **public: static MessageQueue* GetPublicQueues(MessageQueueCriteria*) [];**

[JScript] **public static function GetPublicQueues(MessageQueueCriteria) : MessageQueue[];**

Example

See related example in the **System.Messaging.MessageQueue** class topic.

MessageQueue.GetPublicQueues Method ()

Retrieves all the public queues on the network.

```
[Visual Basic]
Overloads Public Shared Function GetOverloads PublicQueues() As
MessageQueue()
[C#]
public static MessageQueue[] GetPublicQueues();
[C++]
public: static MessageQueue* GetPublicQueues() [];
[JScript]
public static function GetPublicQueues() : MessageQueue[];
```

Return Value

An array of **MessageQueue** objects that reference the retrieved public queues.

Exceptions

Exception Type	Condition
MessageQueueException	An error occurred when accessing a Message Queuing API.

Remarks

Use this overload if you want a complete list of all the public queues on the network. If you want to restrict the list by certain criteria, such as **MachineName**, **Category**, or last modified time use another overload of this method. (Alternatively, you can use **GetPublicQueuesByMachine**, **GetPublicQueuesByCategory**, or **GetPublicQueuesByLabel**.)

GetPublicQueues retrieves a static snapshot of the queues. To interact with a dynamic list of the queues, use **GetMessageQueueEnumerator**.

The following table shows whether this method is available in various Workgroup modes.

Workgroup Mode	Available
Local computer	No
Local computer + direct format name	No
Remote computer	No
Remote computer + direct format name	No

Example

See related example in the **System.Messaging.MessageQueue** class topic.

Requirements

Platforms: Windows 98, Windows NT 4.0,
Windows Millennium Edition, Windows 2000,
Windows XP Home Edition, Windows XP Professional,
Windows .NET Server family

.NET Framework Security:

- Full trust for the immediate caller. This member cannot be used by partially trusted code.

MessageQueue.GetPublicQueues Method (MessageQueueCriteria)

Retrieves all the public queues on the network that meet the specified criteria.

```
[Visual Basic]
Overloads Public Shared Function GetOverloads PublicQueues( _
   ByVal criteria As MessageQueueCriteria _
) As MessageQueue()
[C#]
public static MessageQueue[] GetPublicQueues(
   MessageQueueCriteria criteria
);
[C++]
public: static MessageQueue* GetPublicQueues(
   MessageQueueCriteria* criteria
) [];
[JScript]
public static function GetPublicQueues(
   criteria : MessageQueueCriteria
) : MessageQueue[];
```

Parameters

criteria

A **MessageQueueCriteria** that contains the criteria used to filter the queues.

Return Value

An array of **MessageQueue** objects that reference the retrieved public queues.

Exceptions

Exception Type	Condition
MessageQueueException	An error occurred when accessing a Message Queuing API.

Remarks

If you want to filter all the public queues on the network by label, category, or computer name, the **MessageQueue** class contains specific methods that provide that functionality (**GetPublicQueuesByLabel**, **GetPublicQueuesByCategory**, and **GetPublicQueuesByMachine**, respectively). Use this overload to get a list of all the public queues on the network that meet more than one of these criteria (for example, if you want to specify both a label and a category). You can also filter by message criteria other than **Label**, **Category**, and **MachineName**. For example, you use this overload to filter by a queue's last-modified time. Simply create a new instance of the **MessageQueueCriteria** class, set the appropriate properties in the instance, and pass the instance as the *criteria* parameter.

GetPublicQueues retrieves a static snapshot of the queues. To interact with a dynamic list of the queues, use **GetMessageQueueEnumerator**.

The following table shows whether this method is available in various Workgroup modes.

Workgroup Mode	Available
Local computer	No
Local computer + direct format name	No
Remote computer	No
Remote computer + direct format name	No

Example

See related example in the **System.Messaging.MessageQueue** class topic.

Requirements

Platforms: Windows 98, Windows NT 4.0,
Windows Millennium Edition, Windows 2000,
Windows XP Home Edition, Windows XP Professional,
Windows .NET Server family

.NET Framework Security:

- Full trust for the immediate caller. This member cannot be used by partially trusted code.

MessageQueue.GetPublicQueuesByCategory Method

Retrieves all the public queues on the network that belong to the specified category.

```
[Visual Basic]
Public Shared Function GetPublicQueuesByCategory( _
   ByVal category As Guid _
) As MessageQueue()
[C#]
public static MessageQueue[] GetPublicQueuesByCategory(
   Guid category
);
[C++]
public: static MessageQueue* GetPublicQueuesByCategory(
   Guid category
) [];
[JScript]
public static function GetPublicQueuesByCategory(
   category : Guid
) : MessageQueue[];
```

Parameters

category

A **Guid** that groups the set of queues to be retrieved.

Return Value

An array of **MessageQueue** objects that reference the retrieved public queues.

Exceptions

Exception Type	Condition
MessageQueueException	An error occurred when accessing a Message Queuing API.

Remarks

Use this method to filter the public queues by category. The **Category** property provides access to the Message Queuing type ID property (which is read/write) of a particular queue. Although you can use **NewGuid** to create a category value that is unique across all **Guid** values, it is not necessary. The category value needs to be distinct only from other categories, not from all other **Guid** values. For example, you can assign {00000000-0000-0000-0000-000000000001} as the **Category** for one set of queues and {00000000-0000-0000-0000-000000000002} as the **Category** for another set.

GetPublicQueuesByCategory retrieves a static snapshot of the queues. To interact with a dynamic list of the queues, use **GetMessageQueueEnumerator**. You can specify the category as part of the **MessageQueueCriteria** you pass into the method.

The following table shows whether this method is available in various Workgroup modes.

Workgroup Mode	Available
Local computer	No
Local computer + direct format name	No
Remote computer	No
Remote computer + direct format name	No

Example

See related example in the **System.Messaging.MessageQueue** class topic.

Requirements

Platforms: Windows 98, Windows NT 4.0, Windows Millennium Edition, Windows 2000, Windows XP Home Edition, Windows XP Professional, Windows .NET Server family

.NET Framework Security:
- Full trust for the immediate caller. This member cannot be used by partially trusted code.

MessageQueue.GetPublicQueuesByLabel Method

Retrieves all the public queues on the network that carry the specified label.

```
[Visual Basic]
Public Shared Function GetPublicQueuesByLabel( _
    ByVal label As String _
) As MessageQueue()
[C#]
public static MessageQueue[] GetPublicQueuesByLabel(
    string label
);
[C++]
public: static MessageQueue* GetPublicQueuesByLabel(
    String* label
) [];
[JScript]
public static function GetPublicQueuesByLabel(
    label : String
) : MessageQueue[];
```

Parameters

label
    A label that groups the set of queues to be retrieved.

Return Value

An array of **MessageQueue** objects that reference the retrieved public queues.

Exceptions

Exception Type	Condition
MessageQueueException	An error occurred when accessing a Message Queuing API.
ArgumentNullException	The *label* parameter is a null reference (**Nothing** in Visual Basic).

Remarks

Use this method to filter the public queues by label.

GetPublicQueuesByLabel retrieves a static snapshot of the queues. To interact with a dynamic list of the queues, use **GetMessageQueueEnumerator**. You can specify the label as part of the **MessageQueueCriteria** you pass into the method.

The following table shows whether this method is available in various Workgroup modes.

Workgroup Mode	Available
Local computer	No
Local computer + direct format name	No
Remote computer	No
Remote computer + direct format name	No

Example

See related example in the **System.Messaging.MessageQueue** class topic.

Requirements

Platforms: Windows 98, Windows NT 4.0, Windows Millennium Edition, Windows 2000, Windows XP Home Edition, Windows XP Professional, Windows .NET Server family

.NET Framework Security:
- Full trust for the immediate caller. This member cannot be used by partially trusted code.

MessageQueue.GetPublicQueuesByMachine Method

Retrieves all the public queues that reside on the specified computer.

```
[Visual Basic]
Public Shared Function GetPublicQueuesByMachine( _
    ByVal machineName As String _
) As MessageQueue()
[C#]
public static MessageQueue[] GetPublicQueuesByMachine(
    string machineName
);
[C++]
public: static MessageQueue* GetPublicQueuesByMachine(
    String* machineName
) [];
```

```
[JScript]
public static function GetPublicQueuesByMachine(
    machineName : String
) : MessageQueue[];
```

Parameters

machineName
> The name of the computer that contains the set of public queues to be retrieved.

Return Value

An array of **MessageQueue** objects that reference the public queues on the computer.

Exceptions

Exception Type	Condition
ArgumentException	The *machineName* parameter has incorrect syntax.
MessageQueueException	An error occurred when accessing a Message Queuing API.

Remarks

Use this method to filter the public queues by computer.

GetPublicQueuesByMachine retrieves a static snapshot of the queues. To interact with a dynamic list of the queues, use **GetMessageQueueEnumerator**. You can specify the computer name as part of the **MessageQueueCriteria** you pass into the method.

The following table shows whether this method is available in various Workgroup modes.

Workgroup Mode	Available
Local computer	No
Local computer + direct format name	No
Remote computer	No
Remote computer + direct format name	No

Example

See related example in the **System.Messaging.MessageQueue** class topic.

Requirements

Platforms: Windows 98, Windows NT 4.0, Windows Millennium Edition, Windows 2000, Windows XP Home Edition, Windows XP Professional, Windows .NET Server family

.NET Framework Security:
- Full trust for the immediate caller. This member cannot be used by partially trusted code.

MessageQueue.Peek Method

Returns a copy of the first message in the queue, without removing the message from the queue.

Overload List

Returns without removing (peeks) the first message in the queue referenced by this **MessageQueue**. The **Peek** method is synchronous, so it blocks the current thread until a message becomes available.

> [Visual Basic] **Overloads Public Function Peek() As Message**

> [C#] **public Message Peek();**
> [C++] **public: Message* Peek();**
> [JScript] **public function Peek() : Message;**

Returns without removing (peeks) the first message in the queue referenced by this **MessageQueue**. The **Peek** method is synchronous, so it blocks the current thread until a message becomes available or the specified time-out occurs.

> [Visual Basic] **Overloads Public Function Peek(TimeSpan) As Message**
> [C#] **public Message Peek(TimeSpan);**
> [C++] **public: Message* Peek(TimeSpan);**
> [JScript] **public function Peek(TimeSpan) : Message;**

Example

See related example in the **System.Messaging.MessageQueue** class topic.

MessageQueue.Peek Method ()

Returns without removing (peeks) the first message in the queue referenced by this **MessageQueue**. The **Peek** method is synchronous, so it blocks the current thread until a message becomes available.

```
[Visual Basic]
Overloads Public Function Peek() As Message
[C#]
public Message Peek();
[C++]
public: Message* Peek();
[JScript]
public function Peek() : Message;
```

Return Value

The **Message** that represents the first message in the queue.

Exceptions

Exception Type	Condition
MessageQueueException	An error occurred when accessing a Message Queuing API.

Remarks

Use this overload to peek a queue, or to wait until a message exists in the queue.

The **Peek** method reads, but does not remove, the first message from the queue. Therefore, repeated calls to **Peek** return the same message, unless a higher priority message arrives in the queue. The **Receive** method, on the other hand, both reads and removes the first message from the queue. Repeated calls to **Receive**, therefore, return different messages.

> **Note** Message Queuing orders messages in the queue according to priority and arrival time. A newer message is placed before an older one only if it is of a higher priority.

Use **Peek** when it is acceptable for the current thread to be blocked while it waits for a message to arrive in the queue. Because this overload does not specify a time-out, the application might wait indefinitely. If you need the application processing to continue without waiting, use the asynchronous **BeginPeek** method. Alternatively, you can specify a time-out for a message to arrive in the queue by using the overload of **Peek** that specifies a time-out.

The following table shows whether this method is available in various Workgroup modes.

Workgroup Mode	Available
Local computer	Yes
Local computer + direct format name	Yes
Remote computer	No
Remote computer + direct format name	Yes

Example

See related example in the **System.Messaging.MessageQueue** class topic.

Requirements

Platforms: Windows 98, Windows NT 4.0, Windows Millennium Edition, Windows 2000, Windows XP Home Edition, Windows XP Professional, Windows .NET Server family

.NET Framework Security:
- Full trust for the immediate caller. This member cannot be used by partially trusted code.

MessageQueue.Peek Method (TimeSpan)

Returns without removing (peeks) the first message in the queue referenced by this **MessageQueue**. The **Peek** method is synchronous, so it blocks the current thread until a message becomes available or the specified time-out occurs.

```
[Visual Basic]
Overloads Public Function Peek( _
   ByVal timeout As TimeSpan _
) As Message
[C#]
public Message Peek(
   TimeSpan timeout
);
[C++]
public: Message* Peek(
   TimeSpan timeout
);
[JScript]
public function Peek(
   timeout : TimeSpan
) : Message;
```

Parameters

timeout
   A **TimeSpan** that indicates the maximum time to wait for the queue to contain a message.

Return Value

The **Message** that represents the first message in the queue.

Exceptions

Exception Type	Condition
ArgumentException	The value specified for the *timeout* parameter is invalid, possibly *timeout* is less than **TimeSpan.Zero** or greater than **TimeSpan.MaxValue**.
MessageQueueException	An error occurred when accessing a Message Queuing API.

Remarks

Use this overload to peek a queue, or to wait a specified period of time until a message exists in the queue. The method returns immediately if a message already exists in the queue.

The **Peek** method reads, but does not remove, the first message from the queue. Therefore, repeated calls to **Peek** return the same message, unless a higher priority message arrives in the queue. The **Receive** method, on the other hand, both reads and removes the first message from the queue. Repeated calls to **Receive**, therefore, return different messages.

> **Note** Message Queuing orders messages in the queue according to priority and arrival time. A newer message is placed before an older one only if it is of a higher priority.

Use **Peek** when it is acceptable for the current thread to be blocked while it waits for a message to arrive in the queue. The thread will be blocked up to the specified period of time, or indefinitely if you indicated **InfiniteTimeout**. If you need the application processing to continue without waiting, use the asynchronous **BeginPeek** method.

The following table shows whether this method is available in various Workgroup modes.

Workgroup Mode	Available
Local computer	Yes
Local computer + direct format name	Yes
Remote computer	No
Remote computer + direct format name	Yes

Example

See related example in the **System.Messaging.MessageQueue** class topic.

Requirements

Platforms: Windows 98, Windows NT 4.0, Windows Millennium Edition, Windows 2000, Windows XP Home Edition, Windows XP Professional, Windows .NET Server family

.NET Framework Security:
- Full trust for the immediate caller. This member cannot be used by partially trusted code.

MessageQueue.PeekByCorrelationId Method

Peeks a message that matches a given correlation identifier.

Overload List

Peeks the message that matches the given correlation identifier and immediately raises an exception if no message with the specified correlation identifier currently exists in the queue.

   [Visual Basic] **Overloads Public Function PeekByCorrelationId(String) As Message**

   [C#] **public Message PeekByCorrelationId(string);**

   [C++] **public: Message* PeekByCorrelationId(String*);**

   [JScript] **public function PeekByCorrelationId(String) : Message;**

Peeks the message that matches the given correlation identifier and waits until either a message with the specified correlation identifier is available in the queue, or the time-out expires.

> [Visual Basic] **Overloads Public Function PeekByCorrelationId(String, TimeSpan) As Message**
>
> [C#] **public Message PeekByCorrelationId(string, TimeSpan);**
>
> [C++] **public: Message* PeekByCorrelationId(String*, TimeSpan);**
>
> [JScript] **public function PeekByCorrelationId(String, TimeSpan) : Message;**

Example

See related example in the **System.Messaging.MessageQueue** class topic.

MessageQueue.PeekByCorrelationId Method (String)

Peeks the message that matches the given correlation identifier and immediately raises an exception if no message with the specified correlation identifier currently exists in the queue.

```
[Visual Basic]
Overloads Public Function PeekByCorrelationId( _
    ByVal correlationId As String _
) As Message
[C#]
public Message PeekByCorrelationId(
    string correlationId
);
[C++]
public: Message* PeekByCorrelationId(
    String* correlationId
);
[JScript]
public function PeekByCorrelationId(
    correlationId : String
) : Message;
```

Parameters

correlationId
> The **CorrelationId** of the message to peek.

Return Value

The **Message** whose **CorrelationId** matches the *correlationId* parameter passed in.

Exceptions

Exception Type	Condition
ArgumentNullException	The *correlationId* parameter is a null reference (**Nothing** in Visual Basic).
InvalidOperation-Exception	The message with the specified *correlationId* could not be found.
MessageQueueException	An error occurred when accessing a Message Queuing API.

Remarks

This method looks in the queue referenced by the **MessageQueue** for a message whose **CorrelationId** matches the specified *correlationId* parameter. If no message is found that matches the *correlationID* parameter, an exception is thrown.

The **CorrelationId** property is used to tie a message sent to the queue to associated response, report, or acknowledgment messages.

Two other methods allow you to peek messages in a queue. The **Peek** method returns the first message in the queue, and the **PeekById** method is used to retrieve a message by specifying its unique identifier.

The following table shows whether this method is available in various Workgroup modes.

Workgroup Mode	Available
Local computer	Yes
Local computer + direct format name	Yes
Remote computer	No
Remote computer + direct format name	Yes

Example

See related example in the **System.Messaging.MessageQueue** class topic.

Requirements

Platforms: Windows 98, Windows NT 4.0, Windows Millennium Edition, Windows 2000, Windows XP Home Edition, Windows XP Professional, Windows .NET Server family

.NET Framework Security:
- Full trust for the immediate caller. This member cannot be used by partially trusted code.

MessageQueue.PeekByCorrelationId Method (String, TimeSpan)

Peeks the message that matches the given correlation identifier and waits until either a message with the specified correlation identifier is available in the queue, or the time-out expires.

```
[Visual Basic]
Overloads Public Function PeekByCorrelationId( _
    ByVal correlationId As String, _
    ByVal timeout As TimeSpan _
) As Message
[C#]
public Message PeekByCorrelationId(
    string correlationId,
    TimeSpan timeout
);
[C++]
public: Message* PeekByCorrelationId(
    String* correlationId,
    TimeSpan timeout
);
[JScript]
public function PeekByCorrelationId(
    correlationId : String,
    timeout : TimeSpan
) : Message;
```

Parameters

correlationId
> The **CorrelationId** of the message to peek.

timeout
> A **TimeSpan** that indicates the time to wait until a new message is available for inspection .

Return Value

The **Message** whose **CorrelationId** matches the *correlationId* parameter passed in.

Exceptions

Exception Type	Condition
ArgumentNullException	The *correlationId* parameter is a null reference (**Nothing** in Visual Basic).
ArgumentException	The value specified for the *timeout* parameter is invalid, possibly *timeout* is less than **TimeSpan.Zero** or greater than **TimeSpan.MaxValue**.
InvalidOperation-Exception	The message with the specified *correlationId* does not exist in the queue and did not arrive before the time-out expired.
MessageQueueException	A message did not arrive before the time-out expired. -or- An error occurred when accessing a Message Queuing API.

Remarks

This method looks in the queue referenced by the **MessageQueue** for a message whose **CorrelationId** matches the specified *correlationId* parameter. If no message is found that matches the *correlationID* parameter within the period specified by the *timeout* parameter, an exception is thrown.

The **CorrelationId** property is used to tie a message sent to the queue to associated response, report, or acknowledgment messages.

Two other methods allow you to peek messages in a queue. The **Peek** method returns the first message in the queue, and the **PeekById** method is used to retrieve a message by specifying its unique identifier.

The following table shows whether this method is available in various Workgroup modes.

Workgroup Mode	Available
Local computer	Yes
Local computer + direct format name	Yes
Remote computer	No
Remote computer + direct format name	Yes

Requirements

Platforms: Windows 98, Windows NT 4.0, Windows Millennium Edition, Windows 2000, Windows XP Home Edition, Windows XP Professional, Windows .NET Server family

.NET Framework Security:

- Full trust for the immediate caller. This member cannot be used by partially trusted code.

MessageQueue.PeekById Method

Returns a copy of the message that has the specified message identifier, without removing the message from the queue.

Overload List

Peeks the message whose message identifier matches the *id* parameter.

> [Visual Basic] **Overloads Public Function PeekById(String) As Message**
>
> [C#] **public Message PeekById(string);**
>
> [C++] **public: Message* PeekById(String*);**
>
> [JScript] **public function PeekById(String) : Message;**

Peeks the message whose message identifier matches the *id* parameter. Waits until the message appears in the queue or a time-out occurs.

> [Visual Basic] **Overloads Public Function PeekById(String, TimeSpan) As Message**
>
> [C#] **public Message PeekById(string, TimeSpan);**
>
> [C++] **public: Message* PeekById(String*, TimeSpan);**
>
> [JScript] **public function PeekById(String, TimeSpan) : Message;**

MessageQueue.PeekById Method (String)

Peeks the message whose message identifier matches the *id* parameter.

```
[Visual Basic]
Overloads Public Function PeekById( _
   ByVal id As String _
) As Message
[C#]
public Message PeekById(
   string id
);
[C++]
public: Message* PeekById(
   String* id
);
[JScript]
public function PeekById(
   id : String
) : Message;
```

Parameters

id
    The **Id** of the message to peek.

Return Value

The **Message** whose **Id** property matches the *id* parameter.

Exceptions

Exception Type	Condition
ArgumentNullException	The *id* parameter is a null reference (**Nothing** in Visual Basic).
InvalidOperation-Exception	No message with the specified *id* exists.
MessageQueueException	An error occurred when accessing a Message Queuing API.

Remarks

Use **PeekById** to read, without removing from the queue, a message that has a known message identifier. The identifier of a message is unique across the Message Queuing enterprise, so there will be at most one message in the queue that matches the given *id* parameter.

This overload throws an exception if the queue does not currently contain the message.

Two additional methods allow you to peek messages in a queue: **Peek** and **PeekByCorrelationId**. The **Peek** method returns the first message in the queue; **PeekByCorrelationId** returns an acknowledgment, report, or application-generated response message that was created as a result of a message sent to the queue.

The following table shows whether this method is available in various Workgroup modes.

Workgroup Mode	Available
Local computer	Yes
Local computer + direct format name	Yes
Remote computer	No
Remote computer + direct format name	Yes

Requirements

Platforms: Windows 98, Windows NT 4.0, Windows Millennium Edition, Windows 2000, Windows XP Home Edition, Windows XP Professional, Windows .NET Server family

.NET Framework Security:
- Full trust for the immediate caller. This member cannot be used by partially trusted code.

MessageQueue.PeekById Method (String, TimeSpan)

Peeks the message whose message identifier matches the *id* parameter. Waits until the message appears in the queue or a time-out occurs.

```
[Visual Basic]
Overloads Public Function PeekById( _
    ByVal id As String, _
    ByVal timeout As TimeSpan _
) As Message
[C#]
public Message PeekById(
    string id,
    TimeSpan timeout
);
[C++]
public: Message* PeekById(
    String* id,
    TimeSpan timeout
);
[JScript]
public function PeekById(
    id : String,
    timeout : TimeSpan
) : Message;
```

Parameters

id
    The **Id** of the message to peek.

timeout
    A **TimeSpan** that indicates the maximum amount of time to wait for the message to appear in the queue.

Return Value

The **Message** whose **Id** property matches the *id* parameter.

Exceptions

Exception Type	Condition
ArgumentNullException	The *id* parameter is a null reference (**Nothing** in Visual Basic).
ArgumentException	The value specified for the *timeout* parameter is invalid, possibly *timeout* is less than **TimeSpan.Zero** or greater than **TimeSpan.MaxValue**.
InvalidOperation-Exception	The message with the specified *id* does not exist in the queue and did not arrive before the period specified by the *timeout* parameter expired.
MessageQueueException	An error occurred when accessing a Message Queuing API.

Remarks

Use **PeekById** to read, without removing from the queue, a message that has a known message identifier. The identifier of a message is unique across the Message Queuing enterprise, so there will be at most one message in the queue that matches the given *id* parameter. This overload throws an exception if the queue does not currently contain the message and the message does not arrive before the time-out occurs.

Two additional methods allow you to peek messages in a queue: **Peek** and **PeekByCorrelationId**. The **Peek** method returns the first message in the queue; **PeekByCorrelationId** returns an acknowledgment, report, or application-generated response message that was created as a result of a message sent to the queue.

The following table shows whether this method is available in various Workgroup modes.

Workgroup Mode	Available
Local computer	Yes
Local computer + direct format name	Yes
Remote computer	No
Remote computer + direct format name	Yes

Requirements

Platforms: Windows 98, Windows NT 4.0, Windows Millennium Edition, Windows 2000, Windows XP Home Edition, Windows XP Professional, Windows .NET Server family

.NET Framework Security:
- Full trust for the immediate caller. This member cannot be used by partially trusted code.

MessageQueue.Purge Method

Deletes all the messages contained in the queue.

```
[Visual Basic]
Public Sub Purge()
[C#]
public void Purge();
[C++]
public: void Purge();
[JScript]
public function Purge();
```

Exceptions

Exception Type	Condition
MessageQueueException	An error occurred when accessing a Message Queuing API.

Remarks

Purging the queue causes Message Queuing to set the queue modification flag, which affects the **LastModifyTime** property. Messages that are purged from the queue are lost; they are not sent to the dead-letter queue or the journal queue.

The following table shows whether this method is available in various Workgroup modes.

Workgroup Mode	Available
Local computer	Yes
Local computer + direct format name	Yes
Remote computer	No
Remote computer + direct format name	Yes

Requirements

Platforms: Windows 98, Windows NT 4.0, Windows Millennium Edition, Windows 2000, Windows XP Home Edition, Windows XP Professional, Windows .NET Server family

.NET Framework Security:

- Full trust for the immediate caller. This member cannot be used by partially trusted code.

MessageQueue.Receive Method

Receives the first message in the queue, removing it from the queue.

Overload List

Receives the first message available in the queue referenced by the **MessageQueue**. This call is synchronous, and blocks the current thread of execution until a message is available.

[Visual Basic] **Overloads Public Function Receive() As Message**

[C#] **public Message Receive();**

[C++] **public: Message* Receive();**

[JScript] **public function Receive() : Message;**

Receives the first message available in the transactional queue referenced by the **MessageQueue**. This call is synchronous, and blocks the current thread of execution until a message is available.

[Visual Basic] **Overloads Public Function Receive(MessageQueueTransaction) As Message**

[C#] **public Message Receive(MessageQueueTransaction);**

[C++] **public: Message* Receive(MessageQueueTransaction*);**

[JScript] **public function Receive(MessageQueueTransaction) : Message;**

Receives the first message available in the queue referenced by the **MessageQueue**. This call is synchronous, and blocks the current thread of execution until a message is available.

[Visual Basic] **Overloads Public Function Receive(MessageQueueTransactionType) As Message**

[C#] **public Message Receive(MessageQueueTransactionType);**

[C++] **public: Message* Receive(MessageQueueTransactionType);**

[JScript] **public function Receive(MessageQueueTransactionType) : Message;**

Receives the first message available in the queue referenced by the **MessageQueue** and waits until either a message is available in the queue, or the time-out expires.

[Visual Basic] **Overloads Public Function Receive(TimeSpan) As Message**

[C#] **public Message Receive(TimeSpan);**

[C++] **public: Message* Receive(TimeSpan);**

[JScript] **public function Receive(TimeSpan) : Message;**

Receives the first message available in the transactional queue referenced by the **MessageQueue** and waits until either a message is available in the queue, or the time-out expires.

[Visual Basic] **Overloads Public Function Receive(TimeSpan, MessageQueueTransaction) As Message**

[C#] **public Message Receive(TimeSpan, MessageQueueTransaction);**

[C++] **public: Message* Receive(TimeSpan, MessageQueueTransaction*);**

[JScript] **public function Receive(TimeSpan, MessageQueueTransaction) : Message;**

Receives the first message available in the queue referenced by the **MessageQueue**. This call is synchronous, and waits until either a message is available in the queue, or the time-out expires.

[Visual Basic] **Overloads Public Function Receive(TimeSpan, MessageQueueTransactionType) As Message**

[C#] **public Message Receive(TimeSpan, MessageQueueTransactionType);**

[C++] **public: Message* Receive(TimeSpan, MessageQueueTransactionType);**

[JScript] **public function Receive(TimeSpan, MessageQueueTransactionType) : Message;**

Example

See related example in the **System.Messaging.MessageQueue** class topic.

MessageQueue.Receive Method ()

Receives the first message available in the queue referenced by the **MessageQueue**. This call is synchronous, and blocks the current thread of execution until a message is available.

```
[Visual Basic]
Overloads Public Function Receive() As Message
[C#]
public Message Receive();
[C++]
public: Message* Receive();
[JScript]
public function Receive() : Message;
```

Return Value

A **Message** that references the first message available in the queue.

Exceptions

Exception Type	Condition
MessageQueueException	An error occurred when accessing a Message Queuing API.

Remarks

Use this overload to receive a message from a queue, or wait until there are messages in the queue.

The **Receive** method allows for the synchronous reading of a message, thereby removing it from the queue. Subsequent calls to **Receive** will return the messages that follow in the queue, or new, higher priority messages.

To read the first message in a queue without removing it from the queue, use the **Peek** method. The **Peek** method always returns the first message in the queue, so subsequent calls to the method return the same message unless a higher priority message arrives in the queue.

Use a call to **Receive** when it is acceptable for the current thread to be blocked while it waits for a message to arrive in the queue. Because this overload of the **Receive** method specifies an infinite time-out, the application might wait indefinitely. If the application processing should continue without waiting for the message, consider using the asynchronous method, **BeginReceive**.

The following table shows whether this method is available in various Workgroup modes.

Workgroup Mode	Available
Local computer	Yes
Local computer + direct format name	Yes
Remote computer	No
Remote computer + direct format name	Yes

Example

See related example in the **System.Messaging.MessageQueue** class topic.

Requirements

Platforms: Windows 98, Windows NT 4.0, Windows Millennium Edition, Windows 2000, Windows XP Home Edition, Windows XP Professional, Windows .NET Server family

.NET Framework Security:
- Full trust for the immediate caller. This member cannot be used by partially trusted code.

MessageQueue.Receive Method (MessageQueueTransaction)

Receives the first message available in the transactional queue referenced by the **MessageQueue**. This call is synchronous, and blocks the current thread of execution until a message is available.

```
[Visual Basic]
Overloads Public Function Receive( _
   ByVal transaction As MessageQueueTransaction _
) As Message
[C#]
public Message Receive(
   MessageQueueTransaction transaction
);
```

```
[C++]
public: Message* Receive(
   MessageQueueTransaction* transaction
);
[JScript]
public function Receive(
   transaction : MessageQueueTransaction
) : Message;
```

Parameters

transaction
   The **MessageQueueTransaction** object.

Return Value

A **Message** that references the first message available in the queue.

Exceptions

Exception Type	Condition
MessageQueueException	An error occurred when accessing a Message Queuing API. -or- The queue is non-transactional.

Remarks

Use this overload to receive a message from a transactional queue using the internal transaction context defined by the *transaction* parameter, or wait until there are messages in the queue.

The **Receive** method allows for the synchronous reading of a message, thereby removing it from the queue. Subsequent calls to **Receive** will return the messages that follow in the queue.

Because this method is called on a transactional queue, the message that is received would be returned to the queue if the transaction is aborted. The message is not permanently removed from the queue until the transaction is committed.

To read the first message in a queue without removing it from the queue, use the **Peek** method. The **Peek** method always returns the first message in the queue, so subsequent calls to the method return the same message unless a higher priority message arrives in the queue. There is no transaction context associated with a message returned by a call to **Peek**. Because **Peek** does not remove any messages in the queue, there would be nothing to roll back by a call to **Abort**.

Use a call to **Receive** when it is acceptable for the current thread to be blocked while it waits for a message to arrive in the queue. Because this overload of the **Receive** method specifies an infinite time-out, the application might wait indefinitely. If the application processing should continue without waiting for the message, consider using the asynchronous method, **BeginReceive**.

The following table shows whether this method is available in various Workgroup modes.

Workgroup Mode	Available
Local computer	Yes
Local computer + direct format name	Yes
Remote computer	No
Remote computer + direct format name	Yes

Example

See related example in the **System.Messaging.MessageQueue** class topic.

Requirements

Platforms: Windows 98, Windows NT 4.0,
Windows Millennium Edition, Windows 2000,
Windows XP Home Edition, Windows XP Professional,
Windows .NET Server family

.NET Framework Security:

- Full trust for the immediate caller. This member cannot be used
  by partially trusted code.

MessageQueue.Receive Method (MessageQueueTransactionType)

Receives the first message available in the queue referenced by the
MessageQueue. This call is synchronous, and blocks the current
thread of execution until a message is available.

```
[Visual Basic]
Overloads Public Function Receive( _
   ByVal transactionType As MessageQueueTransactionType _
) As Message
[C#]
public Message Receive(
   MessageQueueTransactionType transactionType
);
[C++]
public: Message* Receive(
   MessageQueueTransactionType transactionType
);
[JScript]
public function Receive(
   transactionType : MessageQueueTransactionType
) : Message;
```

Parameters

transactionType
> One of the **MessageQueueTransactionType** values, describing
> the type of transaction context to associate with the message.

Return Value

A **Message** that references the first message available in the queue.

Exceptions

Exception Type	Condition
MessageQueueException	An error occurred when accessing a Message Queuing API.
InvalidEnumArgument-Exception	The *transactionType* parameter is not one of the **MessageQueueTransactionType** members.

Remarks

Use this overload to receive a message from a queue using a
transaction context defined by the *transactionType* parameter, or
wait until there are messages in the queue.

Specify **Automatic** for the *transactionType* parameter if there is
already an external transaction context attached to the thread that
you want to use to receive the message. Specify **Single** if you want
to receive the message as a single internal transaction. You can
specify **None** if you want to receive a message from a transactional
queue outside of a transaction context.

The **Receive** method allows for the synchronous reading of a
message, thereby removing it from the queue. Subsequent calls to
Receive will return the messages that follow in the queue.

If this method is called to receive a message from a transactional
queue, the message that is received would be returned to the queue if
the transaction is aborted. The message is not permanently removed
from the queue until the transaction is committed.

To read the first message in a queue without removing it from the
queue, use the **Peek** method. The **Peek** method always returns the
first message in the queue, so subsequent calls to the method return
the same message unless a higher priority message arrives in the
queue. There is no transaction context associated with a message
returned by a call to **Peek**. Because **Peek** does not remove any
messages in the queue, there would be nothing to roll back by a call
to **Abort**.

Use a call to **Receive** when it is acceptable for the current thread to
be blocked while it waits for a message to arrive in the queue.
Because this overload of the **Receive** method specifies an infinite
time-out, the application might wait indefinitely. If the application
processing should continue without waiting for the message,
consider using the asynchronous method, **BeginReceive**.

The following table shows whether this method is available in
various Workgroup modes.

Workgroup Mode	Available
Local computer	Yes
Local computer + direct format name	Yes
Remote computer	No
Remote computer + direct format name	Yes

Requirements

Platforms: Windows 98, Windows NT 4.0,
Windows Millennium Edition, Windows 2000,
Windows XP Home Edition, Windows XP Professional,
Windows .NET Server family

.NET Framework Security:

- Full trust for the immediate caller. This member cannot be used
  by partially trusted code.

MessageQueue.Receive Method (TimeSpan)

Receives the first message available in the queue referenced by the
MessageQueue and waits until either a message is available in the
queue, or the time-out expires.

```
[Visual Basic]
Overloads Public Function Receive( _
   ByVal timeout As TimeSpan _
) As Message
[C#]
public Message Receive(
   TimeSpan timeout
);
[C++]
public: Message* Receive(
   TimeSpan timeout
);
[JScript]
public function Receive(
   timeout : TimeSpan
) : Message;
```

Parameters

timeout

A **TimeSpan** that indicates the time to wait until a new message is available for inspection.

Return Value

A **Message** that references the first message available in the queue.

Exceptions

Exception Type	Condition
ArgumentException	The value specified for the *timeout* parameter is invalid, possibly *timeout* is less than **TimeSpan.Zero** or greater than **TimeSpan.MaxValue**.
MessageQueueException	A message did not arrive in the queue before the time-out expired. -or- An error occurred when accessing a Message Queuing API

Remarks

Use this overload to receive a message and return in a specified period of time if there are no messages in the queue.

The **Receive** method allows for the synchronous reading of a message, removing it from the queue. Subsequent calls to **Receive** will return the messages that follow in the queue, or new, higher priority messages.

To read the first message in a queue without removing it from the queue, use the **Peek** method. The **Peek** method always returns the first message in the queue, so subsequent calls to the method return the same message unless a higher priority message arrives in the queue.

Use a call to **Receive** when it is acceptable for the current thread to be blocked while it waits for a message to arrive in the queue. The thread will be blocked for the given period of time, or indefinitely if you specified the value **InfiniteTimeout** for the *timeout* parameter. If the application processing should continue without waiting for a message, consider using the asynchronous method, **BeginReceive**.

The following table shows whether this method is available in various Workgroup modes.

Workgroup Mode	Available
Local computer	Yes
Local computer + direct format name	Yes
Remote computer	No
Remote computer + direct format name	Yes

Example

See related example in the **System.Messaging.MessageQueue** class topic.

Requirements

Platforms: Windows 98, Windows NT 4.0, Windows Millennium Edition, Windows 2000, Windows XP Home Edition, Windows XP Professional, Windows .NET Server family

.NET Framework Security:

• Full trust for the immediate caller. This member cannot be used by partially trusted code.

MessageQueue.Receive Method (TimeSpan, MessageQueueTransaction)

Receives the first message available in the transactional queue referenced by the **MessageQueue** and waits until either a message is available in the queue, or the time-out expires.

```
[Visual Basic]
Overloads Public Function Receive( _
    ByVal timeout As TimeSpan, _
    ByVal transaction As MessageQueueTransaction _
) As Message
[C#]
public Message Receive(
    TimeSpan timeout,
    MessageQueueTransaction transaction
);
[C++]
public: Message* Receive(
    TimeSpan timeout,
    MessageQueueTransaction* transaction
);
[JScript]
public function Receive(
    timeout : TimeSpan,
    transaction : MessageQueueTransaction
) : Message;
```

Parameters

timeout

A **TimeSpan** that indicates the time to wait until a new message is available for inspection.

transaction

The **MessageQueueTransaction** object.

Return Value

A **Message** that references the first message available in the queue.

Exceptions

Exception Type	Condition
ArgumentException	The value specified for the *timeout* parameter is invalid, possibly *timeout* is less than **TimeSpan.Zero** or greater than **TimeSpan.MaxValue**.
MessageQueueException	A message did not arrive in the queue before the time-out expired. -or- The queue is non-transactional. -or- An error occurred when accessing a Message Queuing API.

Remarks

Use this overload to receive a message from a transactional queue using the internal transaction context defined by the *transaction* parameter, and return within a specified period of time if there are no messages in the queue.

The **Receive** method allows for the synchronous reading of a message, thereby removing it from the queue. Subsequent calls to **Receive** will return the messages that follow in the queue.

Because this method is called on a transactional queue, the message that is received would be returned to the queue if the transaction is aborted. The message is not permanently removed from the queue until the transaction is committed.

To read the first message in a queue without removing it from the queue, use the **Peek** method. The **Peek** method always returns the first message in the queue, so subsequent calls to the method return the same message unless a higher priority message arrives in the queue. There is no transaction context associated with a message returned by a call to **Peek**. Because **Peek** does not remove any messages in the queue, there would be nothing to roll back by a call to **Abort**.

Use a call to **Receive** when it is acceptable for the current thread to be blocked while it waits for a message to arrive in the queue. The thread will be blocked for the given period of time, or indefinitely if you specified the value **InfiniteTimeout** for the *timeout* parameter. If the application processing should continue without waiting for a message, consider using the asynchronous method, **BeginReceive**.

The following table shows whether this method is available in various Workgroup modes.

Workgroup Mode	Available
Local computer	Yes
Local computer + direct format name	Yes
Remote computer	No
Remote computer + direct format name	Yes

Example

See related example in the **System.Messaging.MessageQueue** class topic.

Requirements

Platforms: Windows 98, Windows NT 4.0, Windows Millennium Edition, Windows 2000, Windows XP Home Edition, Windows XP Professional, Windows .NET Server family

.NET Framework Security:

- Full trust for the immediate caller. This member cannot be used by partially trusted code.

MessageQueue.Receive Method (TimeSpan, MessageQueueTransactionType)

Receives the first message available in the queue referenced by the **MessageQueue**. This call is synchronous, and waits until either a message is available in the queue, or the time-out expires.

```
[Visual Basic]
Overloads Public Function Receive( _
   ByVal timeout As TimeSpan, _
   ByVal transactionType As MessageQueueTransactionType _
) As Message
[C#]
public Message Receive(
   TimeSpan timeout,
   MessageQueueTransactionType transactionType
);
[C++]
public: Message* Receive(
   TimeSpan timeout,
   MessageQueueTransactionType transactionType
);
```

```
[JScript]
public function Receive(
   timeout : TimeSpan,
   transactionType : MessageQueueTransactionType
) : Message;
```

Parameters

timeout
> A **TimeSpan** that indicates the time to wait until a new message is available for inspection.

transactionType
> One of the **MessageQueueTransactionType** values, describing the type of transaction context to associate with the message.

Return Value

A **Message** that references the first message available in the queue.

Exceptions

Exception Type	Condition
ArgumentException	The value specified for the *timeout* parameter is invalid, possibly *timeout* is less than **TimeSpan.Zero** or greater than **TimeSpan.MaxValue**.
InvalidEnumArgument-Exception	The *transactionType* parameter is not one of the **MessageQueueTransactionType** members.
MessageQueueException	A message did not arrive in the queue before the time-out expired. -or- An error occurred when accessing a Message Queuing API.

Remarks

Use this overload to receive a message from a queue using a transaction context defined by the *transactionType* parameter, and return in a specified period of time if there are no messages in the queue.

Specify **Automatic** for the *transactionType* parameter if there is already an external transaction context attached to the thread that you want to use to receive the message. Specify **Single** if you want to receive the message as a single internal transaction. You can specify **None** if you want to receive a message from a transactional queue outside of a transaction context.

The **Receive** method allows for the synchronous reading of a message, thereby removing it from the queue. Subsequent calls to **Receive** will return the messages that follow in the queue.

If this method is called to receive a message from a transactional queue, the message that is received would be returned to the queue if the transaction is aborted. The message is not permanently removed from the queue until the transaction is committed.

To read the first message in a queue without removing it from the queue, use the **Peek** method. The **Peek** method always returns the first message in the queue, so subsequent calls to the method return the same message unless a higher priority message arrives in the queue. There is no transaction context associated with a message returned by a call to **Peek**. Because **Peek** does not remove any messages in the queue, there would be nothing to roll back by a call to **Abort**.

Use a call to **Receive** when it is acceptable for the current thread to be blocked while it waits for a message to arrive in the queue. The thread will be blocked for the given period of time, or indefinitely if you specified the value **InfiniteTimeout** for the *timeout* parameter. If the application processing should continue without waiting for a message, consider using the asynchronous method, **BeginReceive**.

The following table shows whether this method is available in various Workgroup modes.

Workgroup Mode	Available
Local computer	Yes
Local computer + direct format name	Yes
Remote computer	No
Remote computer + direct format name	Yes

Requirements

Platforms: Windows 98, Windows NT 4.0, Windows Millennium Edition, Windows 2000, Windows XP Home Edition, Windows XP Professional, Windows .NET Server family

.NET Framework Security:

- Full trust for the immediate caller. This member cannot be used by partially trusted code.

MessageQueue.ReceiveByCorrelationId Method

Receives a message that matches a given correlation identifier.

Overload List

Receives the message that matches the given correlation identifier, from a nontransactional queue, and immediately raises an exception if no message with the specified correlation identifier currently exists in the queue.

[Visual Basic] **Overloads Public Function ReceiveByCorrelationId(String) As Message**

[C#] **public Message ReceiveByCorrelationId(string);**

[C++] **public: Message* ReceiveByCorrelationId(String*);**

[JScript] **public function ReceiveByCorrelationId(String) : Message;**

Receives the message that matches the given correlation identifier, from a transactional queue, and immediately raises an exception if no message with the specified correlation identifier currently exists in the queue.

[Visual Basic] **Overloads Public Function ReceiveByCorrelationId(String, MessageQueueTransaction) As Message**

[C#] **public Message ReceiveByCorrelationId(string, MessageQueueTransaction);**

[C++] **public: Message* ReceiveByCorrelationId(String*, MessageQueueTransaction*);**

[JScript] **public function ReceiveByCorrelationId(String, MessageQueueTransaction) : Message;**

Receives the message that matches the given correlation identifier, and immediately raises an exception if no message with the specified correlation identifier currently exists in the queue.

[Visual Basic] **Overloads Public Function ReceiveByCorrelationId(String, MessageQueueTransactionType) As Message**

[C#] **public Message ReceiveByCorrelationId(string, MessageQueueTransactionType);**

[C++] **public: Message* ReceiveByCorrelationId(String*, MessageQueueTransactionType);**

[JScript] **public function ReceiveByCorrelationId(String, MessageQueueTransactionType) : Message;**

Receives the message that matches the given correlation identifier, from a nontransactional queue, and waits until either a message with the specified correlation identifier is available in the queue, or the time-out expires.

[Visual Basic] **Overloads Public Function ReceiveByCorrelationId(String, TimeSpan) As Message**

[C#] **public Message ReceiveByCorrelationId(string, TimeSpan);**

[C++] **public: Message* ReceiveByCorrelationId(String*, TimeSpan);**

[JScript] **public function ReceiveByCorrelationId(String, TimeSpan) : Message;**

Receives the message that matches the given correlation identifier, from a transactional queue, and waits until either a message with the specified correlation identifier is available in the queue, or the time-out expires.

[Visual Basic] **Overloads Public Function ReceiveByCorrelationId(String, TimeSpan, MessageQueueTransaction) As Message**

[C#] **public Message ReceiveByCorrelationId(string, TimeSpan, MessageQueueTransaction);**

[C++] **public: Message* ReceiveByCorrelationId(String*, TimeSpan, MessageQueueTransaction*);**

[JScript] **public function ReceiveByCorrelationId(String, TimeSpan, MessageQueueTransaction) : Message;**

Receives the message that matches the given correlation identifier, and waits until either a message with the specified correlation identifier is available in the queue, or the time-out expires.

[Visual Basic] **Overloads Public Function ReceiveByCorrelationId(String, TimeSpan, MessageQueueTransactionType) As Message**

[C#] **public Message ReceiveByCorrelationId(string, TimeSpan, MessageQueueTransactionType);**

[C++] **public: Message* ReceiveByCorrelationId(String*, TimeSpan, MessageQueueTransactionType);**

[JScript] **public function ReceiveByCorrelationId(String, TimeSpan, MessageQueueTransactionType) : Message;**

Example

See related example in the **System.Messaging.MessageQueue** class topic.

MessageQueue.ReceiveByCorrelationId Method (String)

Receives the message that matches the given correlation identifier, from a nontransactional queue, and immediately raises an exception if no message with the specified correlation identifier currently exists in the queue.

```
[Visual Basic]
Overloads Public Function ReceiveByCorrelationId( _
    ByVal correlationId As String _
) As Message
```

```
[C#]
public Message ReceiveByCorrelationId(
    string correlationId
);
[C++]
public: Message* ReceiveByCorrelationId(
    String* correlationId
);
[JScript]
public function ReceiveByCorrelationId(
    correlationId : String
) : Message;
```

Parameters

correlationId
    The **CorrelationId** of the message to receive.

Return Value

The **Message** whose **CorrelationId** matches the *correlationId*
parameter passed in.

Exceptions

Exception Type	Condition
ArgumentNullException	The *correlationId* parameter is a null reference (**Nothing** in Visual Basic).
InvalidOperation-Exception	The message with the specified *correlationId* could not be found.
MessageQueueException	An error occurred when accessing a Message Queuing API.

Remarks

This method looks in the nontransactional queue referenced by the
MessageQueue for a message whose **CorrelationId** matches the
specified *correlationId* parameter. If no message is found that
matches the *correlationID* parameter, an exception is thrown.
Otherwise, the message is removed from the queue and returned to
the application.

The **CorrelationId** property is used to tie a message sent to the
queue to associated response, report, or acknowledgment messages.

Two other methods allow you to receive messages from a queue. The
Receive method returns the first message in the queue, and the
ReceiveById method retrieves a message by specifying its unique
identifier.

To read a message with a specified correlation identifier without
removing it from the queue, use the **PeekByCorrelationId** method.
The **PeekByCorrelationId** method always returns the first message
in the queue, so subsequent calls to the method return the same
message unless a higher priority message arrives in the queue.

The following table shows whether this method is available in
various Workgroup modes.

Workgroup Mode	Available
Local computer	Yes
Local computer + direct format name	Yes
Remote computer	No
Remote computer + direct format name	Yes

Example

See related example in the **System.Messaging.MessageQueue** class
topic.

Requirements

Platforms: Windows 98, Windows NT 4.0,
Windows Millennium Edition, Windows 2000,
Windows XP Home Edition, Windows XP Professional,
Windows .NET Server family

.NET Framework Security:

- Full trust for the immediate caller. This member cannot be used
  by partially trusted code.

MessageQueue.ReceiveByCorrelationId Method (String, MessageQueueTransaction)

Receives the message that matches the given correlation identifier,
from a transactional queue, and immediately raises an exception if
no message with the specified correlation identifier currently exists
in the queue.

```
[Visual Basic]
Overloads Public Function ReceiveByCorrelationId( _
    ByVal correlationId As String, _
    ByVal transaction As MessageQueueTransaction _
) As Message
[C#]
public Message ReceiveByCorrelationId(
    string correlationId,
    MessageQueueTransaction transaction
);
[C++]
public: Message* ReceiveByCorrelationId(
    String* correlationId,
    MessageQueueTransaction* transaction
);
[JScript]
public function ReceiveByCorrelationId(
    correlationId : String,
    transaction : MessageQueueTransaction
) : Message;
```

Parameters

correlationId
    The **CorrelationId** of the message to receive.
transaction
    The **MessageQueueTransaction** object.

Return Value

The **Message** whose **CorrelationId** matches the *correlationId*
parameter passed in.

Exceptions

Exception Type	Condition
ArgumentNullException	The *correlationId* parameter is a null reference (**Nothing** in Visual Basic). -or- The *transaction* parameter is a null reference (**Nothing**).
InvalidOperation-Exception	The message with the specified *correlationId* could not be found.
MessageQueueException	The queue is non-transactional. -or- An error occurred when accessing a Messsage Queuing API.

Remarks

This method looks in the transactional queue referenced by the **MessageQueue** for a message whose **CorrelationId** matches the specified *correlationId* parameter. If no message is found that matches the *correlationID* parameter, an exception is thrown. Otherwise, the message is removed from the queue and returned to the application using the internal transaction context defined by the *transaction* parameter.

Because this method is called on a transactional queue, the message that is received would be returned to the queue if the transaction is aborted. The message is not permanently removed from the queue until the transaction is committed.

The **CorrelationId** property is used to tie a message sent to the queue to associated response, report, or acknowledgment messages.

Two other methods allow you to receive messages from a queue. The **Receive** method returns the first message in the queue, and the **ReceiveById** method is used to retrieve a message by specifying its unique identifier.

To read a message with a specified correlation identifier without removing it from the queue, use the **PeekByCorrelationId** method. The **PeekByCorrelationId** method always returns the first message in the queue, so subsequent calls to the method return the same message unless a higher priority message arrives in the queue. There is no transaction context associated with a message returned by a call to **PeekByCorrelationId**. Because **PeekByCorrelationId** does not remove any messages in the queue, there would be nothing to roll back if the transaction were aborted.

The following table shows whether this method is available in various Workgroup modes.

Workgroup Mode	Available
Local computer	Yes
Local computer + direct format name	Yes
Remote computer	No
Remote computer + direct format name	Yes

Requirements

Platforms: Windows 98, Windows NT 4.0, Windows Millennium Edition, Windows 2000, Windows XP Home Edition, Windows XP Professional, Windows .NET Server family

.NET Framework Security:
- Full trust for the immediate caller. This member cannot be used by partially trusted code.

MessageQueue.ReceiveByCorrelationId Method (String, MessageQueueTransactionType)

Receives the message that matches the given correlation identifier, and immediately raises an exception if no message with the specified correlation identifier currently exists in the queue.

```
[Visual Basic]
Overloads Public Function ReceiveByCorrelationId( _
    ByVal correlationId As String, _
    ByVal transactionType As MessageQueueTransactionType _
) As Message
```

```
[C#]
public Message ReceiveByCorrelationId(
    string correlationId,
    MessageQueueTransactionType transactionType
);
```

```
[C++]
public: Message* ReceiveByCorrelationId(
    String* correlationId,
    MessageQueueTransactionType transactionType
);
```

```
[JScript]
public function ReceiveByCorrelationId(
    correlationId : String,
    transactionType : MessageQueueTransactionType
) : Message;
```

Parameters

correlationId
    The **CorrelationId** of the message to receive.

transactionType
    One of the **MessageQueueTransactionType** values, describing the type of transaction context to associate with the message.

Return Value

The **Message** whose **CorrelationId** matches the *correlationId* parameter passed in.

Exceptions

Exception Type	Condition
ArgumentNullException	The *correlationId* parameter is a null reference (**Nothing** in Visual Basic).
InvalidOperation-Exception	The message with the specified *correlationId* could not be found.
InvalidEnumArgument-Exception	The *transactionType* parameter is not one of the **MessageQueue-TransactionType** members.
MessageQueueException	An error occurred when accessing a Message Queuing API.

Remarks

This method looks in the queue referenced by the **MessageQueue** for a message whose **CorrelationId** matches the specified *correlationId* parameter. If no message is found that matches the *correlationID* parameter, an exception is thrown. Otherwise, the message is removed from the queue and returned to the application using a transaction context defined by the *transactionType* parameter.

Specify **Automatic** for the *transactionType* parameter if there is already an external transaction context attached to the thread that you want to use to receive the message. Specify **Single** if you want to receive the message as a single internal transaction. You can specify **None** if you want to receive a message from a transactional queue outside of a transaction context.

If this method is called to receive a message from a transactional queue, the message that is received would be returned to the queue if the transaction is aborted. The message is not permanently removed from the queue until the transaction is committed.

The **CorrelationId** property is used to tie a message sent to the queue to associated response, report, or acknowledgment messages.

Two other methods allow you to receive messages from a queue. The **Receive** method returns the first message in the queue, and the

ReceiveById method is used to retrieve a message by specifying its unique identifier.

To read a message with a specified correlation identifier without removing it from the queue, use the **PeekByCorrelationId** method. The **PeekByCorrelationId** method always returns the first message in the queue, so subsequent calls to the method return the same message unless a higher priority message arrives in the queue. There is no transaction context associated with a message returned by a call to **PeekByCorrelationId**. Because **PeekByCorrelationId** does not remove any messages in the queue, there would be nothing to roll back if the transaction were aborted.

The following table shows whether this method is available in various Workgroup modes.

Workgroup Mode	Available
Local computer	Yes
Local computer + direct format name	Yes
Remote computer	No
Remote computer + direct format name	Yes

Requirements

Platforms: Windows 98, Windows NT 4.0, Windows Millennium Edition, Windows 2000, Windows XP Home Edition, Windows XP Professional, Windows .NET Server family

.NET Framework Security:

- Full trust for the immediate caller. This member cannot be used by partially trusted code.

MessageQueue.ReceiveByCorrelationId Method (String, TimeSpan)

Receives the message that matches the given correlation identifier, from a nontransactional queue, and waits until either a message with the specified correlation identifier is available in the queue, or the time-out expires.

```
[Visual Basic]
Overloads Public Function ReceiveByCorrelationId( _
    ByVal correlationId As String, _
    ByVal timeout As TimeSpan _
) As Message
[C#]
public Message ReceiveByCorrelationId(
    string correlationId,
    TimeSpan timeout
);
[C++]
public: Message* ReceiveByCorrelationId(
    String* correlationId,
    TimeSpan timeout
);
[JScript]
public function ReceiveByCorrelationId(
    correlationId : String,
    timeout : TimeSpan
) : Message;
```

Parameters

correlationId
    The **CorrelationId** of the message to receive.

timeout
    A **TimeSpan** that indicates the time to wait until a new message is available for inspection .

Return Value

The **Message** whose **CorrelationId** matches the *correlationId* parameter passed in.

Exceptions

Exception Type	Condition
ArgumentNullException	The *correlationId* parameter is a null reference (**Nothing** in Visual Basic).
ArgumentException	The value specified for the *timeout* parameter is invalid, possibly *timeout* is less than **TimeSpan.Zero** or greater than **TimeSpan.MaxValue**.
MessageQueueException	The message with the specified *correlationId* does not exist in the queue and did not arrive before the time-out expired. -or- An error occurred when accessing a Message Queuing API.

Remarks

This method looks in the nontransactional queue referenced by the **MessageQueue** for a message whose **CorrelationId** matches the specified *correlationId* parameter. This method returns immediately if the message with the correlation identifier specified by the *correlationId* parameter is in the queue. Otherwise, the method waits the given period of time for the message to arrive. If the message does not arrive before the time-out expires, an exception is thrown.

The **CorrelationId** property is used to tie a message sent to the queue to associated response, report, or acknowledgment messages.

Two other methods allow you to receive messages from a queue. The **Receive** method returns the first message in the queue, and the **ReceiveById** method is used to retrieve a message by specifying its unique identifier.

To read a message with a specified correlation identifier without removing it from the queue, use the **PeekByCorrelationId** method. The **PeekByCorrelationId** method always returns the first message in the queue, so subsequent calls to the method return the same message unless a higher priority message arrives in the queue.

The following table shows whether this method is available in various Workgroup modes.

Workgroup Mode	Available
Local computer	Yes
Local computer + direct format name	Yes
Remote computer	No
Remote computer + direct format name	Yes

Requirements

Platforms: Windows 98, Windows NT 4.0, Windows Millennium Edition, Windows 2000, Windows XP Home Edition, Windows XP Professional, Windows .NET Server family

.NET Framework Security:

- Full trust for the immediate caller. This member cannot be used by partially trusted code.

MessageQueue.ReceiveByCorrelationId Method (String, TimeSpan, MessageQueueTransaction)

Receives the message that matches the given correlation identifier, from a transactional queue, and waits until either a message with the specified correlation identifier is available in the queue, or the time-out expires.

```
[Visual Basic]
Overloads Public Function ReceiveByCorrelationId( _
   ByVal correlationId As String, _
   ByVal timeout As TimeSpan, _
   ByVal transaction As MessageQueueTransaction _
) As Message
[C#]
public Message ReceiveByCorrelationId(
   string correlationId,
   TimeSpan timeout,
   MessageQueueTransaction transaction
);
[C++]
public: Message* ReceiveByCorrelationId(
   String* correlationId,
   TimeSpan timeout,
   MessageQueueTransaction* transaction
);
[JScript]
public function ReceiveByCorrelationId(
   correlationId : String,
   timeout : TimeSpan,
   transaction : MessageQueueTransaction
) : Message;
```

Parameters

correlationId
  The **CorrelationId** of the message to receive.

timeout
  A **TimeSpan** that indicates the time to wait until a new message is available for inspection .

transaction
  The **MessageQueueTransaction** object.

Return Value

The **Message** whose **CorrelationId** matches the *correlationId* parameter passed in.

Exceptions

Exception Type	Condition
ArgumentNullException	The *correlationId* parameter is a null reference (**Nothing** in Visual Basic). -or- The *transaction* parameter is a null reference (**Nothing**).
ArgumentException	The value specified for the *timeout* parameter is invalid, possibly *timeout* is less than **TimeSpan.Zero** or greater than **TimeSpan.MaxValue**.

Exception Type	Condition
MessageQueueException	The message with the specified *correlationId* does not exist in the queue and did not arrive before the time-out expired. -or- The queue is non-transactional. -or- An error occurred when accessing a Message Queuing API.

Remarks

This method looks in the transactional queue referenced by the **MessageQueue** for a message whose **CorrelationId** matches the specified *correlationId* parameter. This method returns immediately if the message with the correlation identifier specified by the *correlationId* parameter is in the queue, using the internal transaction context defined by the *transaction* parameter. Otherwise, the method waits the given period of time for the message to arrive. If the message does not arrive before the time-out expires, an exception is thrown.

Because this method is called on a transactional queue, the message that is received would be returned to the queue if the transaction is aborted. The message is not permanently removed from the queue until the transaction is committed.

The **CorrelationId** property is used to tie a message sent to the queue to associated response, report, or acknowledgment messages.

Two other methods allow you to receive messages from a queue. The **Receive** method returns the first message in the queue, and the **ReceiveById** method is used to retrieve a message by specifying its unique identifier.

To read a message with a specified correlation identifier without removing it from the queue, use the **PeekByCorrelationId** method. The **PeekByCorrelationId** method always returns the first message in the queue, so subsequent calls to the method return the same message unless a higher priority message arrives in the queue. There is no transaction context associated with a message returned by a call to **PeekByCorrelationId**. Because **PeekByCorrelationId** does not remove any messages in the queue, there would be nothing to roll back if the transaction were aborted.

The following table shows whether this method is available in various Workgroup modes.

Workgroup Mode	Available
Local computer	Yes
Local computer + direct format name	Yes
Remote computer	No
Remote computer + direct format name	Yes

Requirements

Platforms: Windows 98, Windows NT 4.0, Windows Millennium Edition, Windows 2000, Windows XP Home Edition, Windows XP Professional, Windows .NET Server family

.NET Framework Security:

- Full trust for the immediate caller. This member cannot be used by partially trusted code.

MessageQueue.ReceiveByCorrelationId Method (String, TimeSpan, MessageQueueTransactionType)

Receives the message that matches the given correlation identifier, and waits until either a message with the specified correlation identifier is available in the queue, or the time-out expires.

```
[Visual Basic]
Overloads Public Function ReceiveByCorrelationId( _
   ByVal correlationId As String, _
   ByVal timeout As TimeSpan, _
   ByVal transactionType As MessageQueueTransactionType _
) As Message
[C#]
public Message ReceiveByCorrelationId(
   string correlationId,
   TimeSpan timeout,
   MessageQueueTransactionType transactionType
);
[C++]
public: Message* ReceiveByCorrelationId(
   String* correlationId,
   TimeSpan timeout,
   MessageQueueTransactionType transactionType
);
[JScript]
public function ReceiveByCorrelationId(
   correlationId : String,
   timeout : TimeSpan,
   transactionType : MessageQueueTransactionType
) : Message;
```

Parameters

correlationId
   The **CorrelationId** of the message to receive.
timeout
   A **TimeSpan** that indicates the time to wait until a new message is available for inspection .
transactionType
   One of the **MessageQueueTransactionType** values, describing the type of transaction context to associate with the message.

Return Value

The **Message** whose **CorrelationId** matches the *correlationId* parameter passed in.

Exceptions

Exception Type	Condition
ArgumentNullException	The *correlationId* parameter is a null reference (**Nothing** in Visual Basic).
InvalidOperation-Exception	The message with the specified *correlationId* could not be found.
ArgumentException	The value specified for the *timeout* parameter is invalid, possibly *timeout* is less than **TimeSpan.Zero** or greater than **TimeSpan.MaxValue**.
InvalidEnumArgument-Exception	The *transactionType* parameter is not one of the **MessageQueueTransactionType** members.

Exception Type	Condition
MessageQueueException	The message with the specified *correlationId* does not exist in the queue and did not arrive before the time-out expired. -or- An error occurred when accessing a Message Queuing API.

Remarks

This method looks in the queue referenced by the **MessageQueue** for a message whose **CorrelationId** matches the specified *correlationId* parameter. This method returns immediately if the message with the correlation identifier specified by the *correlationId* parameter is in the queue, using a transaction context defined by the *transactionType* parameter. Otherwise, the method waits the given period of time for the message to arrive. If the message does not arrive before the time-out expires, an exception is thrown.

Specify **Automatic** for the *transactionType* parameter if there is already an external transaction context attached to the thread that you want to use to receive the message. Specify **Single** if you want to receive the message as a single internal transaction. You can specify **None** if you want to receive a message from a transactional queue outside of a transaction context.

If this method is called to receive a message from a transactional queue, the message that is received would be returned to the queue if the transaction is aborted. The message is not permanently removed from the queue until the transaction is committed.

The **CorrelationId** property is used to tie a message sent to the queue to associated response, report, or acknowledgment messages.

Two other methods allow you to receive messages from a queue. The **Receive** method returns the first message in the queue, and the **ReceiveById** method is used to retrieve a message by specifying its unique identifier.

To read a message with a specified correlation identifier without removing it from the queue, use the **PeekByCorrelationId** method. The **PeekByCorrelationId** method always returns the first message in the queue, so subsequent calls to the method return the same message unless a higher priority message arrives in the queue. There is no transaction context associated with a message returned by a call to **PeekByCorrelationId**. Because **PeekByCorrelationId** does not remove any messages in the queue, there would be nothing to roll back if the transaction were aborted.

The following table shows whether this method is available in various Workgroup modes.

Workgroup Mode	Available
Local computer	Yes
Local computer + direct format name	Yes
Remote computer	No
Remote computer + direct format name	Yes

Requirements

Platforms: Windows 98, Windows NT 4.0, Windows Millennium Edition, Windows 2000, Windows XP Home Edition, Windows XP Professional, Windows .NET Server family

.NET Framework Security:

- Full trust for the immediate caller. This member cannot be used by partially trusted code.

MessageQueue.ReceiveById Method

Receives the message that matches the given identifier, removing it from the queue.

Overload List

Receives the message that matches the given identifier from a non-transactional queue, and immediately raises an exception if no message with the specified identifier currently exists in the queue.

[Visual Basic] **Overloads Public Function ReceiveById(String) As Message**

[C#] **public Message ReceiveById(string);**

[C++] **public: Message* ReceiveById(String*);**

[JScript] **public function ReceiveById(String) : Message;**

Receives the message that matches the given identifier, from a transactional queue, and immediately raises an exception if no message with the specified identifier currently exists in the queue.

[Visual Basic] **Overloads Public Function ReceiveById(String, MessageQueueTransaction) As Message**

[C#] **public Message ReceiveById(string, MessageQueueTransaction);**

[C++] **public: Message* ReceiveById(String*, MessageQueueTransaction*);**

[JScript] **public function ReceiveById(String, MessageQueueTransaction) : Message;**

Receives the message that matches the given identifier, and immediately raises an exception if no message with the specified identifier currently exists in the queue.

[Visual Basic] **Overloads Public Function ReceiveById(String, MessageQueueTransactionType) As Message**

[C#] **public Message ReceiveById(string, MessageQueueTransactionType);**

[C++] **public: Message* ReceiveById(String*, MessageQueueTransactionType);**

[JScript] **public function ReceiveById(String, MessageQueueTransactionType) : Message;**

Receives the message that matches the given identifier, from a nontransactional queue, and waits until either a message with the specified identifier is available in the queue or the time-out expires.

[Visual Basic] **Overloads Public Function ReceiveById(String, TimeSpan) As Message**

[C#] **public Message ReceiveById(string, TimeSpan);**

[C++] **public: Message* ReceiveById(String*, TimeSpan);**

[JScript] **public function ReceiveById(String, TimeSpan) : Message;**

Receives the message that matches the given identifier, from a transactional queue, and waits until either a message with the specified identifier is available in the queue or the time-out expires.

[Visual Basic] **Overloads Public Function ReceiveById(String, TimeSpan, MessageQueueTransaction) As Message**

[C#] **public Message ReceiveById(string, TimeSpan, MessageQueueTransaction);**

[C++] **public: Message* ReceiveById(String*, TimeSpan, MessageQueueTransaction*);**

[JScript] **public function ReceiveById(String, TimeSpan, MessageQueueTransaction) : Message;**

Receives the message that matches the given identifier, and waits until either a message with the specified identifier is available in the queue or the time-out expires.

[Visual Basic] **Overloads Public Function ReceiveById(String, TimeSpan, MessageQueueTransactionType) As Message**

[C#] **public Message ReceiveById(string, TimeSpan, MessageQueueTransactionType);**

[C++] **public: Message* ReceiveById(String*, TimeSpan, MessageQueueTransactionType);**

[JScript] **public function ReceiveById(String, TimeSpan, MessageQueueTransactionType) : Message;**

MessageQueue.ReceiveById Method (String)

Receives the message that matches the given identifier from a non-transactional queue, and immediately raises an exception if no message with the specified identifier currently exists in the queue.

```
[Visual Basic]
Overloads Public Function ReceiveById( _
   ByVal id As String _
) As Message
[C#]
public Message ReceiveById(
   string id
);
[C++]
public: Message* ReceiveById(
   String* id
);
[JScript]
public function ReceiveById(
   id : String
) : Message;
```

Parameters

id

    The **Id** of the message to receive.

Return Value

The **Message** whose **Id** property matches the *id* parameter passed in.

Exceptions

Exception Type	Condition
ArgumentNullException	The *id* parameter is a null reference (**Nothing** in Visual Basic).
InvalidOperation-Exception	The message with the specified *id* could not be found.
MessageQueueException	An error occurred when accessing a Message Queuing API.

Remarks

Use this method to read a message with a known identifier and remove it from the queue. This method throws an exception immediately if the message is not in the queue.

The **Id** property of a message is unique across the Message Queuing enterprise, so there will be at most one message in the queue that matches the given *id* parameter. .

Two other methods allow you to receive messages from a queue. The **Receive** method returns the first message in the queue, and the **ReceiveByCorrelationId** method is used to retrieve an acknowledgment, report, or application-generated response message that was created as a result of a message sent to the queue.

To read a message with a specified identifier without removing it from the queue, use the **PeekById** method. The **PeekById** method always returns the first message in the queue, so subsequent calls to the method return the same message unless a higher priority message arrives in the queue.

The following table shows whether this method is available in various Workgroup modes.

Workgroup Mode	Available
Local computer	Yes
Local computer + direct format name	Yes
Remote computer	No
Remote computer + direct format name	Yes

Requirements

Platforms: Windows 98, Windows NT 4.0, Windows Millennium Edition, Windows 2000, Windows XP Home Edition, Windows XP Professional, Windows .NET Server family

.NET Framework Security:

- Full trust for the immediate caller. This member cannot be used by partially trusted code.

MessageQueue.ReceiveById Method (String, MessageQueueTransaction)

Receives the message that matches the given identifier, from a transactional queue, and immediately raises an exception if no message with the specified identifier currently exists in the queue.

```
[Visual Basic]
Overloads Public Function ReceiveById( _
   ByVal id As String, _
   ByVal transaction As MessageQueueTransaction _
) As Message
[C#]
public Message ReceiveById(
   string id,
   MessageQueueTransaction transaction
);
[C++]
public: Message* ReceiveById(
   String* id,
   MessageQueueTransaction* transaction
);
[JScript]
public function ReceiveById(
   id : String,
   transaction : MessageQueueTransaction
) : Message;
```

Parameters

id

The **Id** of the message to receive.

transaction

The **MessageQueueTransaction** object .

Return Value

The **Message** whose **Id** property matches the *id* parameter passed in.

Exceptions

Exception Type	Condition
ArgumentNullException	The *id* parameter is a null reference (**Nothing** in Visual Basic).
	-or-
	The *transaction* parameter is a null reference (**Nothing**).
InvalidOperation-Exception	The message with the specified *id* could not be found.
MessageQueueException	The queue is non-transactional.
	-or-
	An error occurred when accessing a Message Queuing API.

Remarks

Use this method to read a message with a known identifier and remove it from the queue, using the internal transaction context defined by the *transaction* parameter. This method throws an exception immediately if the message is not in the queue

The **Id** property of a message is unique across the Message Queuing enterprise, so there will be at most one message in the queue that matches the given *id* parameter.

Because this method is called on a transactional queue, the message that is received would be returned to the queue if the transaction is aborted. The message is not permanently removed from the queue until the transaction is committed.

Two other methods allow you to receive messages from a queue. The **Receive** method returns the first message in the queue, and the **ReceiveByCorrelationId** method is used to retrieve an acknowledgment, report, or application-generated response message that was created as a result of a message sent to the queue.

To read a message with a specified identifier without removing it from the queue, use the **PeekById** method. The **PeekById** method always returns the first message in the queue, so subsequent calls to the method return the same message unless a higher priority message arrives in the queue. There is no transaction context associated with a message returned by a call to **PeekById**. Because **PeekById** does not remove any messages in the queue, there would be nothing to roll back if the transaction were aborted.

The following table shows whether this method is available in various Workgroup modes.

Workgroup Mode	Available
Local computer	Yes
Local computer + direct format name	Yes
Remote computer	No
Remote computer + direct format name	Yes

Requirements

Platforms: Windows 98, Windows NT 4.0, Windows Millennium Edition, Windows 2000, Windows XP Home Edition, Windows XP Professional, Windows .NET Server family

.NET Framework Security:

- Full trust for the immediate caller. This member cannot be used by partially trusted code.

MessageQueue.ReceiveById Method (String, MessageQueueTransactionType)

Receives the message that matches the given identifier, and immediately raises an exception if no message with the specified identifier currently exists in the queue.

```
[Visual Basic]
Overloads Public Function ReceiveById( _
   ByVal id As String, _
   ByVal transactionType As MessageQueueTransactionType _
) As Message
[C#]
public Message ReceiveById(
   string id,
   MessageQueueTransactionType transactionType
);
[C++]
public: Message* ReceiveById(
   String* id,
   MessageQueueTransactionType transactionType
);
[JScript]
public function ReceiveById(
   id : String,
   transactionType : MessageQueueTransactionType
) : Message;
```

Parameters

id

The **Id** of the message to receive.

transactionType

One of the **MessageQueueTransactionType** values, describing the type of transaction context to associate with the message.

Return Value

The **Message** whose **Id** property matches the *id* parameter passed in.

Exceptions

Exception Type	Condition
ArgumentNullException	The *id* parameter is a null reference (**Nothing** in Visual Basic).
InvalidOperation-Exception	The message with the specified *id* could not be found.
InvalidEnumArgument-Exception	The *transactionType* parameter is not one of the **MessageQueueTransactionType** members.
MessageQueueException	An error occurred when accessing a Message Queuing API.

Remarks

Use this method to read a message with a known identifier and remove it from the queue. This method throws an exception immediately if the message is not in the queue. Otherwise, the message is removed from the queue and returned to the application using a transaction context defined by the *transactionType* parameter.

Specify **Automatic** for the *transactionType* parameter if there is already an external transaction context attached to the thread that you want to use to receive the message. Specify **Single** if you want to receive the message as a single internal transaction. You can specify **None** if you want to receive a message from a transactional queue outside of a transaction context.

The **Id** property of a message is unique across the Message Queuing enterprise, so there will be at most one message in the queue that matches the given *id* parameter. If the message with the specified identifier is in a queue other than the one associated with this **MessageQueue** instance, the message will not be found.

If this method is called to receive a message from a transactional queue, the message that is received would be returned to the queue if the transaction is aborted. The message is not permanently removed from the queue until the transaction is committed.

Two other methods allow you to receive messages from a queue. The **Receive** method returns the first message in the queue, and the **ReceiveByCorrelationId** method is used to retrieve an acknowledgment, report, or application-generated response message that was created as a result of a message sent to the queue.

To read a message with a specified identifier without removing it from the queue, use the **PeekById** method. The **PeekById** method always returns the first message in the queue, so subsequent calls to the method return the same message unless a higher priority message arrives in the queue. There is no transaction context associated with a message returned by a call to **PeekById**. Because **PeekById** does not remove any messages from the queue, there would be nothing to roll back if the transaction were aborted.

The following table shows whether this method is available in various Workgroup modes.

Workgroup Mode	Available
Local computer	Yes
Local computer + direct format name	Yes
Remote computer	No
Remote computer + direct format name	Yes

Requirements

Platforms: Windows 98, Windows NT 4.0, Windows Millennium Edition, Windows 2000, Windows XP Home Edition, Windows XP Professional, Windows .NET Server family

.NET Framework Security:

- Full trust for the immediate caller. This member cannot be used by partially trusted code.

MessageQueue.ReceiveById Method (String, TimeSpan)

Receives the message that matches the given identifier, from a nontransactional queue, and waits until either a message with the specified identifier is available in the queue or the time-out expires.

```
[Visual Basic]
Overloads Public Function ReceiveById( _
   ByVal id As String, _
   ByVal timeout As TimeSpan _
) As Message
[C#]
public Message ReceiveById(
   string id,
   TimeSpan timeout
);
[C++]
public: Message* ReceiveById(
   String* id,
   TimeSpan timeout
);
[JScript]
public function ReceiveById(
   id : String,
   timeout : TimeSpan
) : Message;
```

Parameters

id

The **Id** of the message to receive.

timeout

A **TimeSpan** that indicates the time to wait until a new message is available for inspection.

Return Value

The **Message** whose **Id** property matches the *id* parameter passed in.

Exceptions

Exception Type	Condition
ArgumentNullException	The *id* parameter is a null reference (**Nothing** in Visual Basic).
ArgumentException	The value specified for the *timeout* parameter is invalid, possibly *timeout* is less than **TimeSpan.Zero** or greater than **TimeSpan.MaxValue**.
MessageQueueException	A message with the specified *id* did not arrive in the queue before the time-out expired. -or- An error occurred when accessing a Message Queuing API.

Remarks

Use this method to read a message with a known identifier and remove it from the queue. This method returns immediately if the message with the identifier specified by the *id* parameter is in the queue. Otherwise, the method waits the given period of time for the message to arrive. If the message does not arrive before the time-out expires, an exception is thrown.

The **Id** property of a message is unique across the Message Queuing enterprise, so there will be at most one message in the queue that matches the given *id* parameter.

Use this overload of **ReceiveById** when it is acceptable for the current thread to be blocked while it waits for a message to arrive in the queue. The thread will be blocked for the given period of time, or

indefinitely if you specified the value **InfiniteTimeout** for the *timeout* parameter.

Two other methods allow you to receive messages from a queue. The **Receive** method returns the first message in the queue, and the **ReceiveByCorrelationId** method is used to retrieve an acknowledgment, report, or application-generated response message that was created as a result of a message sent to the queue.

To read a message with a specified identifier without removing it from the queue, use the **PeekById** method. The **PeekById** method always returns the first message in the queue, so subsequent calls to the method return the same message unless a higher priority message arrives in the queue.

The following table shows whether this method is available in various Workgroup modes.

Workgroup Mode	Available
Local computer	Yes
Local computer + direct format name	Yes
Remote computer	No
Remote computer + direct format name	Yes

Requirements

Platforms: Windows 98, Windows NT 4.0, Windows Millennium Edition, Windows 2000, Windows XP Home Edition, Windows XP Professional, Windows .NET Server family

.NET Framework Security:

- Full trust for the immediate caller. This member cannot be used by partially trusted code.

MessageQueue.ReceiveById Method (String, TimeSpan, MessageQueueTransaction)

Receives the message that matches the given identifier, from a transactional queue, and waits until either a message with the specified identifier is available in the queue or the time-out expires.

```
[Visual Basic]
Overloads Public Function ReceiveById( _
   ByVal id As String, _
   ByVal timeout As TimeSpan, _
   ByVal transaction As MessageQueueTransaction _
) As Message
[C#]
public Message ReceiveById(
   string id,
   TimeSpan timeout,
   MessageQueueTransaction transaction
);
[C++]
public: Message* ReceiveById(
   String* id,
   TimeSpan timeout,
   MessageQueueTransaction* transaction
);
[JScript]
public function ReceiveById(
   id : String,
   timeout : TimeSpan,
   transaction : MessageQueueTransaction
) : Message;
```

Parameters

id

The **Id** of the message to receive.

timeout

A **TimeSpan** that indicates the time to wait until a new message is available for inspection.

transaction

The **MessageQueueTransaction** object .

Return Value

The **Message** whose **Id** property matches the *id* parameter passed in.

Exceptions

Exception Type	Condition
ArgumentNullException	The *id* parameter is a null reference (**Nothing** in Visual Basic). -or- The *transaction* parameter is a null reference (**Nothing**).
ArgumentException	The value specified for the *timeout* parameter is invalid, possibly *timeout* is less than **TimeSpan.Zero** or greater than **TimeSpan.MaxValue**.
MessageQueueException	A message with the specified *id* did not arrive in the queue before the time-out expired. -or- The queue is non-transactional. -or- An error occurred when accessing a Message Queuing API.

Remarks

Use this method to read a message with a known identifier and remove it from the queue, using the internal transaction context defined by the *transaction* parameter. This method returns immediately if the message with the identifier specified by the *id* parameter is in the queue. Otherwise, the method waits the given period of time for the message to arrive. If the message does not arrive before the time-out expires, an exception is thrown.

The **Id** property of a message is unique across the Message Queuing enterprise, so there will be at most one message in the queue that matches the given *id* parameter.

Use this overload of **ReceiveById** when it is acceptable for the current thread to be blocked while it waits for a message to arrive in the queue. The thread will be blocked for the given period of time, or indefinitely if you specified the value **InfiniteTimeout** for the *timeout* parameter.

Because this method is called on a transactional queue, the message that is received would be returned to the queue if the transaction is aborted. The message is not permanently removed from the queue until the transaction is committed.

Two other methods allow you to receive messages from a queue. The **Receive** method returns the first message in the queue, and the **ReceiveByCorrelationId** method is used to retrieve an acknowledgment, report, or application-generated response message that was created as a result of a message sent to the queue.

To read a message with a specified identifier without removing it from the queue, use the **PeekById** method. The **PeekById** method always returns the first message in the queue, so subsequent calls to the method return the same message, unless a higher priority message arrives in the queue. There is no transaction context associated with a message returned by a call to **PeekById**. Because **PeekById** does not remove any messages in the queue, there would be nothing to roll back if the transaction were aborted.

The following table shows whether this method is available in various Workgroup modes.

Workgroup Mode	Available
Local computer	Yes
Local computer + direct format name	Yes
Remote computer	No
Remote computer + direct format name	Yes

Requirements

Platforms: Windows 98, Windows NT 4.0, Windows Millennium Edition, Windows 2000, Windows XP Home Edition, Windows XP Professional, Windows .NET Server family

.NET Framework Security:

- Full trust for the immediate caller. This member cannot be used by partially trusted code.

MessageQueue.ReceiveById Method (String, TimeSpan, MessageQueueTransactionType)

Receives the message that matches the given identifier, and waits until either a message with the specified identifier is available in the queue or the time-out expires.

```
[Visual Basic]
Overloads Public Function ReceiveById( _
    ByVal id As String, _
    ByVal timeout As TimeSpan, _
    ByVal transactionType As MessageQueueTransactionType _
) As Message
[C#]
public Message ReceiveById(
    string id,
    TimeSpan timeout,
    MessageQueueTransactionType transactionType
);
[C++]
public: Message* ReceiveById(
    String* id,
    TimeSpan timeout,
    MessageQueueTransactionType transactionType
);
[JScript]
public function ReceiveById(
    id : String,
    timeout : TimeSpan,
    transactionType : MessageQueueTransactionType
) : Message;
```

Parameters

id

The **Id** of the message to receive.

timeout

A **TimeSpan** that indicates the time to wait until a new message is available for inspection.

transactionType

One of the **MessageQueueTransactionType** values, describing the type of transaction context to associate with the message.

Return Value

The **Message** whose **Id** property matches the *id* parameter passed in.

Exceptions

Exception Type	Condition
ArgumentNullException	The *id* parameter is a null reference (**Nothing** in Visual Basic).
ArgumentException	The value specified for the *timeout* parameter is invalid, possibly *timeout* is less than **TimeSpan.Zero** or greater than **TimeSpan.MaxValue**.
MessageQueueException	A message with the specified *id* did not arrive in the queue before the time-out expired. -or- An error occurred when accessing a Message Queuing API.
InvalidEnumArgument-Exception	The *transactionType* parameter is not one of the **MessageQueueTransactionType** members.

Remarks

Use this method to read a message with a known identifier and remove it from the queue. This method returns immediately if the message with the identifier specified by the *id* parameter is in the queue, using a transaction context defined by the *transactionType* parameter. Otherwise, the method waits the given period of time for the message to arrive. If the message does not arrive before the time-out expires, an exception is thrown.

Specify **Automatic** for the *transactionType* parameter if there is already an external transaction context attached to the thread that you want to use to receive the message. Specify **Single** if you want to receive the message as a single internal transaction. You can specify **None** if you want to receive a message from a transactional queue outside of a transaction context.

The **Id** property of a message is unique across the Message Queuing enterprise, so there will be at most one message in the queue that matches the given *id* parameter. If the message with the specified identifier is in a queue other than the one associated with this **MessageQueue** instance, the message will not be found.

Use this overload of **ReceiveById** when it is acceptable for the current thread to be blocked while it waits for a message to arrive in the queue. The thread will be blocked for the given period of time, or indefinitely if you specified the value **InfiniteTimeout** for the *timeout* parameter.

If this method is called to receive a message from a transactional queue, the message that is received would be returned to the queue if the transaction is aborted. The message is not permanently removed from the queue until the transaction is committed.

Two other methods allow you to receive messages from a queue. The **Receive** method returns the first message in the queue, and the

ReceiveByCorrelationId method is used to retrieve an acknowledgment, report, or application-generated response message that was created as a result of a message sent to the queue.

To read a message with a specified identifier without removing it from the queue, use the **PeekById** method. The **PeekById** method always returns the first message in the queue, so subsequent calls to the method return the same message unless a higher priority message arrives in the queue. There is no transaction context associated with a message returned by a call to **PeekById**. Because **PeekById** does not remove any messages in the queue, there would be nothing to roll back if the transaction were aborted.

The following table shows whether this method is available in various Workgroup modes.

Workgroup Mode	Available
Local computer	Yes
Local computer + direct format name	Yes
Remote computer	No
Remote computer + direct format name	Yes

Requirements

Platforms: Windows 98, Windows NT 4.0, Windows Millennium Edition, Windows 2000, Windows XP Home Edition, Windows XP Professional, Windows .NET Server family

.NET Framework Security:

• Full trust for the immediate caller. This member cannot be used by partially trusted code.

MessageQueue.Refresh Method

Refreshes the properties presented by the **MessageQueue** to reflect the current state of the resource.

```
[Visual Basic]
Public Sub Refresh()
[C#]
public void Refresh();
[C++]
public: void Refresh();
[JScript]
public function Refresh();
```

Remarks

Refresh synchronizes the properties of a **MessageQueue** with its associated Message Queuing server resource. If any property, such as **Label** or **Category**, has changed on the server since the time the **MessageQueue** was created, **Refresh** updates the **MessageQueue** with the new information.

The following table shows whether this method is available in various Workgroup modes.

Workgroup Mode	Available
Local computer	Yes
Local computer + direct format name	Yes
Remote computer	No
Remote computer + direct format name	Yes

Requirements

Platforms: Windows 98, Windows NT 4.0, Windows Millennium Edition, Windows 2000, Windows XP Home Edition, Windows XP Professional, Windows .NET Server family

.NET Framework Security:
- Full trust for the immediate caller. This member cannot be used by partially trusted code.

MessageQueue.ResetPermissions Method

Resets the permission list to the operating system's default values. Removes any queue permissions you have appended to the default list.

```
[Visual Basic]
Public Sub ResetPermissions()
[C#]
public void ResetPermissions();
[C++]
public: void ResetPermissions();
[JScript]
public function ResetPermissions();
```

Exceptions

Exception Type	Condition
MessageQueueException	An error occurred when accessing a Message Queuing API.

Remarks

When you call **ResetPermissions**, you return the permission list to its default values. Generally, this grants the queue creator all permissions, and gives the group Everyone the following rights:
- Get the properties of the queue.
- Get queue permissions.
- Write to the queue.

The following table shows whether this method is available in various Workgroup modes.

Workgroup Mode	Available
Local computer	Yes
Local computer + direct format name	Yes
Remote computer	No
Remote computer + direct format name	No

Requirements

Platforms: Windows 98, Windows NT 4.0, Windows Millennium Edition, Windows 2000, Windows XP Home Edition, Windows XP Professional, Windows .NET Server family

.NET Framework Security:
- Full trust for the immediate caller. This member cannot be used by partially trusted code.

MessageQueue.Send Method

Sends an object to a queue.

Overload List

Sends an object to nontransactional queue referenced by this **MessageQueue**.

[Visual Basic] **Overloads Public Sub Send(Object)**

[C#] **public void Send(object);**

[C++] **public: void Send(Object*);**

[JScript] **public function Send(Object);**

Sends an object to the transactional queue referenced by this **MessageQueue**.

[Visual Basic] **Overloads Public Sub Send(Object, MessageQueueTransaction)**

[C#] **public void Send(object, MessageQueueTransaction);**

[C++] **public: void Send(Object*, MessageQueueTransaction*);**

[JScript] **public function Send(Object, MessageQueueTransaction);**

Sends an object to the queue referenced by this **MessageQueue**.

[Visual Basic] **Overloads Public Sub Send(Object, MessageQueueTransactionType)**

[C#] **public void Send(object, MessageQueueTransactionType);**

[C++] **public: void Send(Object*, MessageQueueTransactionType);**

[JScript] **public function Send(Object, MessageQueueTransactionType);**

Sends an object to the nontransactional queue referenced by this **MessageQueue** and specifies a label for the message.

[Visual Basic] **Overloads Public Sub Send(Object, String)**

[C#] **public void Send(object, string);**

[C++] **public: void Send(Object*, String*);**

[JScript] **public function Send(Object, String);**

Sends an object to the transactional queue referenced by this **MessageQueue** and specifies a label for the message.

[Visual Basic] **Overloads Public Sub Send(Object, String, MessageQueueTransaction)**

[C#] **public void Send(object, string, MessageQueueTransaction);**

[C++] **public: void Send(Object*, String*, MessageQueueTransaction*);**

[JScript] **public function Send(Object, String, MessageQueueTransaction);**

Sends an object to the queue referenced by this **MessageQueue** and specifies a label for the message.

[Visual Basic] **Overloads Public Sub Send(Object, String, MessageQueueTransactionType)**

[C#] **public void Send(object, string, MessageQueueTransactionType);**

[C++] **public: void Send(Object*, String*, MessageQueueTransactionType);**

[JScript] **public function Send(Object, String, MessageQueueTransactionType);**

Example

See related example in the **System.Messaging.MessageQueue** class topic.

MessageQueue.Send Method (Object)

Sends an object to nontransactional queue referenced by this **MessageQueue**.

```
[Visual Basic]
Overloads Public Sub Send( _
   ByVal obj As Object _
)
[C#]
public void Send(
   object obj
);
[C++]
public: void Send(
   Object* obj
);
[JScript]
public function Send(
   obj : Object
);
```

Parameters

obj
   The object to send to the queue.

Exceptions

Exception Type	Condition
MessageQueueException	The **Path** property has not been set.
	-or-
	An error occurred when accessing a Message Queuing API.

Remarks

Use this overload to send a message containing the *obj* parameter to the queue referenced by the **MessageQueue**. The object you send to the queue can be a **Message** or any managed object. If you send any object other than a **Message**, the object is serialized and inserted into the body of the message.

If you use this overload to send a message to a transactional queue, the message will be sent to the dead-letter queue. If you want the message to be part of a transaction that contains other messages, use an overload that takes a **MessageQueueTransaction** or **MessageQueueTransactionType** as a parameter.

If you do not set the **Formatter** property before calling **Send**, the formatter defaults to the **XmlMessageFormatter**.

The **DefaultPropertiesToSend** property applies to any object other than a **Message**. If you specify, for example, a label or a priority using the **DefaultPropertiesToSend** member, these values apply to any message that contains an object that is not of type **Message** when your application sends it to the queue. When sending a **Message**, the property values set for the **Message** take precedence over **DefaultPropertiesToSend**, and the message's **Message.Formatter** property takes precedence over the queue's **MessageQueue.Formatter** property.

The following table shows whether this method is available in various Workgroup modes.

Workgroup Mode	Available
Local computer	Yes
Local computer + direct format name	Yes
Remote computer	No
Remote computer + direct format name	Yes

Example

See related example in the **System.Messaging.MessageQueue** class topic.

Requirements

Platforms: Windows 98, Windows NT 4.0, Windows Millennium Edition, Windows 2000, Windows XP Home Edition, Windows XP Professional, Windows .NET Server family

.NET Framework Security:
- Full trust for the immediate caller. This member cannot be used by partially trusted code.

MessageQueue.Send Method (Object, MessageQueueTransaction)

Sends an object to the transactional queue referenced by this **MessageQueue**.

```
[Visual Basic]
Overloads Public Sub Send( _
   ByVal obj As Object, _
   ByVal transaction As MessageQueueTransaction _
)
[C#]
public void Send(
   object obj,
   MessageQueueTransaction transaction
);
[C++]
public: void Send(
   Object* obj,
   MessageQueueTransaction* transaction
);
[JScript]
public function Send(
   obj : Object,
   transaction : MessageQueueTransaction
);
```

Parameters

obj
   The object to send to the queue.
transaction
   The **MessageQueueTransaction** object.

Exceptions

Exception Type	Condition
ArgumentNullException	The *transaction* parameter is a null reference (**Nothing** in Visual Basic).
MessageQueueException	The **Path** property has not been set.
	-or-
	The Message Queuing application indicated an incorrect transaction usage.
	-or-
	An error occurred when accessing a Message Queuing API.

Remarks

Use this overload to send a message containing the *obj* parameter to the transactional queue referenced by the **MessageQueue**, using an internal transaction context defined by the *transaction* parameter. The object you send to the queue can be a **Message** or any managed object. If you send any object other than a **Message**, the object is serialized and inserted into the body of the message.

If you use this overload to send a message to a nontransactional queue, the message might be sent to the dead-letter queue without throwing an exception.

If you do not set the **Formatter** property before calling **Send**, the formatter defaults to the **XmlMessageFormatter**.

The **DefaultPropertiesToSend** property applies to any object other than a **Message**. If you specify, for example, a label or a priority using the **DefaultPropertiesToSend** member, these values apply to any message that contains an object that is not of type **Message** when your application sends it to the queue. When sending a **Message**, the property values set for the **Message** take precedence over **DefaultPropertiesToSend**, and the message's **Message.Formatter** property takes precedence over the queue's **MessageQueue.Formatter** property.

[Visual Basic] **Note** **MessageQueueTransaction** is threading apartment aware, so if your apartment state is **STA**, you cannot use the transaction in multiple threads. Visual Basic sets the state of the main thread to **STA**, so you must apply the **MTAThreadAttribute** in the Main subroutine. Otherwise, sending a transactional message using another thread throws a **MessageQueueException** exception. You apply the **MTAThreadAttribute** by using the following fragment.

[Visual Basic]
```
<System.MTAThreadAttribute>
public sub Main()
```

The following table shows whether this method is available in various Workgroup modes.

Workgroup Mode	Available
Local computer	Yes
Local computer + direct format name	Yes
Remote computer	No
Remote computer + direct format name	Yes

Example

See related example in the **System.Messaging.MessageQueue** class topic.

Requirements

Platforms: Windows 98, Windows NT 4.0, Windows Millennium Edition, Windows 2000, Windows XP Home Edition, Windows XP Professional, Windows .NET Server family

.NET Framework Security:
• Full trust for the immediate caller. This member cannot be used by partially trusted code.

MessageQueue.Send Method (Object, MessageQueueTransactionType)

Sends an object to the queue referenced by this **MessageQueue**.

[Visual Basic]
```
Overloads Public Sub Send( _
   ByVal obj As Object, _
   ByVal transactionType As MessageQueueTransactionType _
)
```
[C#]
```
public void Send(
   object obj,
   MessageQueueTransactionType transactionType
);
```
[C++]
```
public: void Send(
   Object* obj,
   MessageQueueTransactionType transactionType
);
```
[JScript]
```
public function Send(
   obj : Object,
   transactionType : MessageQueueTransactionType
);
```

Parameters

obj
　The object to send to the queue.
transactionType
　One of the **MessageQueueTransactionType** values, describing the type of transaction context to associate with the message.

Exceptions

Exception Type	Condition
MessageQueueTrans-action	The Message Queuing application indicated an incorrect transaction usage.
InvalidEnumArgument-Exception	The *transactionType* parameter is not one of the **MessageQueue-TransactionType** members.
MessageQueueException	The **Path** property has not been set. -or- An error occurred when accessing a Message Queuing API.

Remarks

Use this overload to send a message containing the *obj* parameter to the queue referenced by the **MessageQueue**, using a transaction context defined by the *transactionType* parameter. Specify **Automatic** for the *transactionType* parameter if there is already an external transaction context attached to the thread that you want to use to send the message. Specify **Single** if you want to send the message as a single internal transaction. You can specify **None** if you want to send a transactional message to a nontransactional thread.

The object you send to the queue can be a **Message** or any managed object. If you send any object other than a **Message**, the object is serialized and inserted into the body of the message.

If you do not set the **Formatter** property before calling **Send**, the formatter defaults to the **XmlMessageFormatter**.

The **DefaultPropertiesToSend** property applies to any object other than a **Message**. If you specify, for example, a label or a priority using the **DefaultPropertiesToSend** member, these values apply to any message that contains an object that is not of type **Message** when your application sends it to the queue. When sending a **Message**, the property values set for the **Message** take precedence over **DefaultPropertiesToSend**, and the message's **Message.Formatter** property takes precedence over the queue's **MessageQueue.Formatter** property.

The following table shows whether this method is available in various Workgroup modes.

Workgroup Mode	Available
Local computer	Yes
Local computer + direct format name	Yes
Remote computer	No
Remote computer + direct format name	Yes

Requirements

Platforms: Windows 98, Windows NT 4.0, Windows Millennium Edition, Windows 2000, Windows XP Home Edition, Windows XP Professional, Windows .NET Server family

.NET Framework Security:
- Full trust for the immediate caller. This member cannot be used by partially trusted code.

MessageQueue.Send Method (Object, String)

Sends an object to the nontransactional queue referenced by this **MessageQueue** and specifies a label for the message.

```
[Visual Basic]
Overloads Public Sub Send( _
   ByVal obj As Object, _
   ByVal label As String _
)
[C#]
public void Send(
   object obj,
   string label
);
[C++]
public: void Send(
   Object* obj,
   String* label
);
[JScript]
public function Send(
   obj : Object,
   label : String
);
```

Parameters

obj
   The object to send to the queue.
label
   The label of the message.

Exceptions

Exception Type	Condition
ArgumentNullException	The *label* parameter is a null reference (**Nothing** in Visual Basic).

Exception Type	Condition
MessageQueueException	The **Path** property has not been set. -or- An error occurred when accessing a Message Queuing API.

Remarks

Use this overload to send a message containing the *obj* parameter to the queue referenced by the **MessageQueue**. With this overload, you can specify the string label that identifies the message. The object you send to the queue can be a **Message**, a structure, a data object, or any managed object. If you send any object other than a **Message**, the object is serialized and inserted into the body of the message.

> **Note** The message label is distinct from the message queue label, but both are application-dependent and have no inherit meaning to Message Queuing.

If you use this overload to send a message to a transactional queue, the message will be sent to the dead-letter queue. If you want the message to be part of a transaction that contains other messages, use an overload that takes a **MessageQueueTransaction** or **MessageQueueTransactionType** as a parameter.

The **Path** property for this **MessageQueue** instance must be specified before you send the message. If you do not set the **Formatter** property before calling **Send**, the formatter defaults to the **XmlMessageFormatter**.

The **DefaultPropertiesToSend** property applies to any object other than a **Message**. If you specify, for example, a label or a priority using the **DefaultPropertiesToSend** member, these values apply to any message that contains an object that is not of type **Message** when your application sends it to the queue. When sending a **Message**, the property values set for the **Message** take precedence over **DefaultPropertiesToSend**, and the message's **Message.Formatter** property takes precedence over the queue's **MessageQueue.Formatter** property.

The following table shows whether this method is available in various Workgroup modes.

Workgroup Mode	Available
Local computer	Yes
Local computer + direct format name	Yes
Remote computer	No
Remote computer + direct format name	Yes

Requirements

Platforms: Windows 98, Windows NT 4.0, Windows Millennium Edition, Windows 2000, Windows XP Home Edition, Windows XP Professional, Windows .NET Server family

.NET Framework Security:
- Full trust for the immediate caller. This member cannot be used by partially trusted code.

MessageQueue.Send Method (Object, String, MessageQueueTransaction)

Sends an object to the transactional queue referenced by this **MessageQueue** and specifies a label for the message.

[Visual Basic]
```
Overloads Public Sub Send( _
   ByVal obj As Object, _
   ByVal label As String, _
   ByVal transaction As MessageQueueTransaction _
)
```
[C#]
```
public void Send(
   object obj,
   string label,
   MessageQueueTransaction transaction
);
```
[C++]
```
public: void Send(
   Object* obj,
   String* label,
   MessageQueueTransaction* transaction
);
```
[JScript]
```
public function Send(
   obj : Object,
   label : String,
   transaction : MessageQueueTransaction
);
```

Parameters

obj
   The object to send to the queue.
label
   The label of the message.
transaction
   The **MessageQueueTransaction** object.

Exceptions

Exception Type	Condition
ArgumentNullException	The *label* parameter is a null reference (**Nothing** in Visual Basic). -or- The *transaction* parameter is a null reference (**Nothing**).
MessageQueueException	The **Path** property has not been set. -or- The Message Queuing application indicated an incorrect transaction usage. -or- An error occurred when accessing a Message Queuing API.

Remarks

Use this overload to send a message containing the *obj* parameter to the transactional queue referenced by the **MessageQueue**, using an internal transaction context defined by the *transaction* parameter. With this overload, you can specify the string label that identifies the message. The object you send to the queue can be a **Message**, a structure, a data object, or any managed object. If you send any object other than a **Message**, the object is serialized and inserted into the body of the message.

Note   The message label is distinct from the message queue label, but both are application-dependent and have no inherit meaning to Message Queuing.

If you use this overload to send a message to a nontransactional queue, the message might be sent to the dead-letter queue without throwing an exception.

If you do not set the **Formatter** property before calling **Send**, the formatter defaults to the **XmlMessageFormatter**.

The **DefaultPropertiesToSend** property applies to any object other than a **Message**. If you specify, for example, a label or a priority using the **DefaultPropertiesToSend** member, these values apply to any message that contains an object that is not of type **Message** when your application sends it to the queue. When sending a **Message**, the property values set for the **Message** take precedence over **DefaultPropertiesToSend**, and the message's **Message.Formatter** property takes precedence over the queue's **MessageQueue.Formatter** property

[Visual Basic] **Note**   **MessageQueueTransaction** is threading apartment aware, so if your apartment state is **STA**, you cannot use the transaction in multiple threads. Visual Basic sets the state of the main thread to **STA**, so you must apply the **MTAThreadAttribute** in the Main subroutine. Otherwise, sending a transactional message using another thread throws a **MessageQueueException** exception. You apply the **MTAThreadAttribute** by using the following fragment.

[Visual Basic]
```
<System.MTAThreadAttribute>
public sub Main()
```

The following table shows whether this method is available in various Workgroup modes.

Workgroup Mode	Available
Local computer	Yes
Local computer + direct format name	Yes
Remote computer	No
Remote computer + direct format name	Yes

Requirements

Platforms: Windows 98, Windows NT 4.0, Windows Millennium Edition, Windows 2000, Windows XP Home Edition, Windows XP Professional, Windows .NET Server family

.NET Framework Security:
• Full trust for the immediate caller. This member cannot be used by partially trusted code.

MessageQueue.Send Method (Object, String, MessageQueueTransactionType)

Sends an object to the queue referenced by this **MessageQueue** and specifies a label for the message.

[Visual Basic]
```
Overloads Public Sub Send( _
   ByVal obj As Object, _
   ByVal label As String, _
   ByVal transactionType As MessageQueueTransactionType _
)
```

```
[C#]
public void Send(
    object obj,
    string label,
    MessageQueueTransactionType transactionType
);
[C++]
public: void Send(
    Object* obj,
    String* label,
    MessageQueueTransactionType transactionType
);
[JScript]
public function Send(
    obj : Object,
    label : String,
    transactionType : MessageQueueTransactionType
);
```

Parameters

obj
> The object to send to the queue.

label
> The label of the message.

transactionType
> One of the **MessageQueueTransactionType** values, describing the type of transaction context to associate with the message.

Exceptions

Exception Type	Condition
ArgumentNullException	The *label* parameter is a null reference (**Nothing** in Visual Basic).
MessageQueue-Transaction	The Message Queuing application indicated an incorrect transaction usage.
InvalidEnumArgument-Exception	The *transactionType* parameter is not one of the **MessageQueueTransactionType** members.
MessageQueueException	The **Path** property has not been set. -or- An error occurred when accessing a Message Queuing API.

Remarks

Use this overload to send a message containing the *obj* parameter to the queue referenced by the **MessageQueue**, using a transaction context defined by the *transactionType* parameter. Specify **Automatic** for the *transactionType* parameter if there is already an external transaction context attached to the thread that you want to use to send the message. Specify **Single** if you want to send the message as a single internal transaction. You can specify **None** if you want to send a transactional message to a nontransactional thread.

The object you send to the queue can be a **Message** or any managed object. If you send any object other than a **Message**, the object is serialized and inserted into the body of the message. With this overload, you can specify the string label that identifies the message.

Note The message label is distinct from the message queue label, but both are application-dependent and have no inherit meaning to Message Queuing.

If you do not set the **Formatter** property before calling **Send**, the formatter defaults to the **XmlMessageFormatter**.

The **DefaultPropertiesToSend** property applies to any object other than a **Message**. If you specify, for example, a label or a priority using the **DefaultPropertiesToSend** member, these values apply to any message that contains an object that is not of type **Message** when your application sends it to the queue. When sending a **Message**, the property values set for the **Message** take precedence over **DefaultPropertiesToSend**, and the message's **Message.Formatter** property takes precedence over the queue's **MessageQueue.Formatter** property.

The following table shows whether this method is available in various Workgroup modes.

Workgroup Mode	Available
Local computer	Yes
Local computer + direct format name	Yes
Remote computer	No
Remote computer + direct format name	Yes

Requirements

Platforms: Windows 98, Windows NT 4.0, Windows Millennium Edition, Windows 2000, Windows XP Home Edition, Windows XP Professional, Windows .NET Server family

.NET Framework Security:
- Full trust for the immediate caller. This member cannot be used by partially trusted code.

MessageQueue.SetPermissions Method

Adds permissions to the current set. This controls who has access rights to queue properties and messages in the queue.

Overload List

Assigns access rights to the queue based on the contents of an access control list.

> [Visual Basic] **Overloads Public Sub SetPermissions(AccessControlList)**
>
> [C#] **public void SetPermissions(AccessControlList);**
>
> [C++] **public: void SetPermissions(AccessControlList*);**
>
> [JScript] **public function SetPermissions(AccessControlList);**

Assigns access rights to the queue based on the contents of an access control entry.

> [Visual Basic] **Overloads Public Sub SetPermissions(MessageQueueAccessControlEntry)**
>
> [C#] **public void SetPermissions(MessageQueue-AccessControlEntry);**
>
> [C++] **public: void SetPermissions(MessageQueue-AccessControlEntry*);**
>
> [JScript] **public function SetPermissions(MessageQueue-AccessControlEntry);**

Gives a computer, group, or user the specified access rights.

[Visual Basic] **Overloads Public Sub SetPermissions(String, MessageQueueAccessRights)**

[C#] **public void SetPermissions(string, MessageQueue-AccessRights);**

[C++] **public: void SetPermissions(String*, MessageQueue-AccessRights);**

[JScript] **public function SetPermissions(String, MessageQueueAccessRights);**

Gives a computer, group, or user the specified access rights, with the specified access control type (allow, deny, revoke, or set).

[Visual Basic] **Overloads Public Sub SetPermissions(String, MessageQueueAccessRights, AccessControlEntryType)**

[C#] **public void SetPermissions(string, MessageQueueAccessRights, AccessControlEntryType);**

[C++] **public: void SetPermissions(String*, MessageQueueAccessRights, AccessControlEntryType);**

[JScript] **public function SetPermissions(String, MessageQueueAccessRights, AccessControlEntryType);**

MessageQueue.SetPermissions Method (AccessControlList)

Assigns access rights to the queue based on the contents of an access control list.

```
[Visual Basic]
Overloads Public Sub SetPermissions( _
    ByVal dacl As AccessControlList _
)
[C#]
public void SetPermissions(
    AccessControlList dacl
);
[C++]
public: void SetPermissions(
    AccessControlList* dacl
);
[JScript]
public function SetPermissions(
    dacl : AccessControlList
);
```

Parameters

dacl

An **AccessControlList** that contains one or more access control entries that specify the trustees and the permissions to grant.

Exceptions

Exception Type	Condition
MessageQueueException	An error occurred when accessing a Message Queuing API.

Remarks

Use this overload to grant, deny, or revoke rights by using a collection of access control entries to specify trustee and permissions information. This is used, for example, to grant permissions to multiple users at the same time.

The trustee you specify when you construct the *ace* parameter can be an individual user, a group of users, or a computer. If the trustee is an individual, use the format **DOMAIN** *user*. You can specify "." for the trustee to indicate the local computer.

The permissions you assign through **SetPermissions** add rights to the existing list. By default, the creator of a public or private queue has full control, and the domain group Everyone has permission to get queue properties, get permissions, and write to the queue. When you call **SetPermissions**, the user and permissions information is appended to the bottom of the existing list.

The system examines each **AccessControlEntry** in sequence until one of the following events occurs:

- An access-denied **AccessControlEntry** explicitly denies any of the requested access rights to one of the trustees listed in the thread's access token.
- One or more access-allowed **AccessControlEntry** items for trustees listed in the thread's access token explicitly grant all the requested access rights.
- All **AccessControlEntry** items have been checked and there is still at least one requested access right that has not been explicitly allowed, in which case, access is implicitly denied.

When you construct the *dacl* parameter, you add **AccessControlEntry** instances to your **AccessControlList** collection. When you construct each access control entry, you can specify generic or standard access rights. The rights to a queue can be any combination of the following:

- Delete
- Read Security
- Write Security
- Synchronize
- Modify Owner
- Read
- Write
- Execute
- Required
- All
- None

These rights are a set of bit flags that you can combine using the OR bitwise operator.

- Full Control
- Delete Message
- Receive Message
- Peek Message
- Receive Journal Message
- Get Queue Properties
- Set Queue Properties
- Get Permissions
- Set Permissions
- Take Queue Ownership
- Write Message

The following table shows whether this method is available in various Workgroup modes.

Workgroup Mode	Available
Local computer	Yes
Local computer + direct format name	Yes
Remote computer	No
Remote computer + direct format name	No

Requirements

Platforms: Windows 98, Windows NT 4.0,
Windows Millennium Edition, Windows 2000,
Windows XP Home Edition, Windows XP Professional,
Windows .NET Server family

.NET Framework Security:

- Full trust for the immediate caller. This member cannot be used by partially trusted code.

MessageQueue.SetPermissions Method (MessageQueueAccessControlEntry)

Assigns access rights to the queue based on the contents of an access control entry.

```
[Visual Basic]
Overloads Public Sub SetPermissions( _
   ByVal ace As MessageQueueAccessControlEntry _
)
[C#]
public void SetPermissions(
   MessageQueueAccessControlEntry ace
);
[C++]
public: void SetPermissions(
   MessageQueueAccessControlEntry* ace
);
[JScript]
public function SetPermissions(
   ace : MessageQueueAccessControlEntry
);
```

Parameters

ace

A **MessageQueueAccessControlEntry** that specifies a user, an access type, and a permission type.

Exceptions

Exception Type	Condition
MessageQueueException	An error occurred when accessing a Message Queuing API.

Remarks

Use this overload to grant, deny, or revoke rights by using an access control entry to specify trustee and rights information.

The trustee you specify when you construct the *ace* parameter can be an individual user, a group of users, or a computer. If the trustee is an individual, use the format **DOMAIN** *user.* You can specify "." for the trustee to indicate the local computer.

The permissions you assign through **SetPermissions** add rights to the existing list. By default, the creator of a public or private queue has full control, and the domain group Everyone has permission to get queue properties, get permissions, and write to the queue. When you call **SetPermissions**, the user and permissions information is appended to the bottom of the existing list.

The system examines each **AccessControlEntry** in sequence until one of the following events occurs:

- An access-denied **AccessControlEntry** explicitly denies any of the requested access rights to one of the trustees listed in the thread's access token.

- One or more access-allowed **AccessControlEntry** items for trustees listed in the thread's access token explicitly grant all the requested access rights.

- All **AccessControlEntry** items have been checked and there is still at least one requested access right that has not been explicitly allowed, in which case, access is implicitly denied.

The rights to a queue, which you specify in the *rights* parameter when you construct your **MessageQueueAccessControlEntry**, can be any combination of the following:

- Full Control
- Delete Message
- Receive Message
- Peek Message
- Receive Journal Message
- Get Queue Properties
- Set Queue Properties
- Get Permissions
- Set Permissions
- Take Queue Ownership
- Write Message

The *rights* parameter you specify in the constructor for the *ace* parameter is a flag of the **MessageQueueAccessRights** enumeration. It represents a set of bit flags that you can combine using the bitwise operator OR when you build the *rights* parameter.

The following table shows whether this method is available in various Workgroup modes.

Workgroup Mode	Available
Local computer	Yes
Local computer + direct format name	Yes
Remote computer	No
Remote computer + direct format name	No

Requirements

Platforms: Windows 98, Windows NT 4.0,
Windows Millennium Edition, Windows 2000,
Windows XP Home Edition, Windows XP Professional,
Windows .NET Server family

.NET Framework Security:

- Full trust for the immediate caller. This member cannot be used by partially trusted code.

MessageQueue.SetPermissions Method (String, MessageQueueAccessRights)

Gives a computer, group, or user the specified access rights.

```
[Visual Basic]
Overloads Public Sub SetPermissions( _
   ByVal user As String, _
   ByVal rights As MessageQueueAccessRights _
)
[C#]
public void SetPermissions(
   string user,
   MessageQueueAccessRights rights
);
```

```
[C++]
public: void SetPermissions(
   String* user,
   MessageQueueAccessRights rights
);
[JScript]
public function SetPermissions(
   user : String,
   rights : MessageQueueAccessRights
);
```

Parameters

user
   The individual, group, or computer that gets additional rights to the queue.

rights
   A **MessageQueueAccessRights** that indicates the set of rights to the queue that Message Queuing assigns to the *user* passed in.

Exceptions

Exception Type	Condition
ArgumentException	The *user* is a null reference (**Nothing** in Visual Basic).
MessageQueueException	An error occurred when accessing a Message Queuing API.

Remarks

Use this overload to grant specified rights to an individual user. The user can be any valid trustee, which includes individual users, groups of users, or a computer. If the user is an individual, use the format **DOMAIN** *user* for the *user* parameter. You can specify "." for the *user* parameter to indicate the local computer.

The permissions you assign through **SetPermissions** add rights to the existing list. By default, the creator of a public or private queue has full control, and the domain group Everyone has permission to get queue properties, get permissions, and write to the queue. When you call **SetPermissions**, the user and permissions information is appended to the bottom of the existing list.

The system examines each **AccessControlEntry** in sequence until one of the following events occurs:

- An access-denied **AccessControlEntry** explicitly denies any of the requested access rights to one of the trustees listed in the thread's access token.
- One or more access-allowed **AccessControlEntry** items for trustees listed in the thread's access token explicitly grant all the requested access rights.
- All **AccessControlEntry** items have been checked and there is still at least one requested access right that has not been explicitly allowed, in which case, access is implicitly denied.

The rights to a queue, specified in the *rights* parameter, can be any combination of the following:

- Full Control
- Delete Message
- Receive Message
- Peek Message
- Receive Journal Message
- Get Queue Properties
- Set Queue Properties
- Get Permissions

- Set Permissions
- Take Queue Ownership
- Write Message

The **MessageQueueAccessRights** enumeration represents a set of bit flags that you can combine using the bitwise operator OR to build the *rights* parameter.

With this overload, you can only grant permissions; you cannot revoke or deny them. You must use a different overload to explicitly grant any **AccessControlEntryType** other than **Allow**.

The following table shows whether this method is available in various Workgroup modes.

Workgroup Mode	Available
Local computer	Yes
Local computer + direct format name	Yes
Remote computer	No
Remote computer + direct format name	No

Requirements

Platforms: Windows 98, Windows NT 4.0, Windows Millennium Edition, Windows 2000, Windows XP Home Edition, Windows XP Professional, Windows .NET Server family

.NET Framework Security:
- Full trust for the immediate caller. This member cannot be used by partially trusted code.

MessageQueue.SetPermissions Method (String, MessageQueueAccessRights, AccessControlEntryType)

Gives a computer, group, or user the specified access rights, with the specified access control type (allow, deny, revoke, or set).

```
[Visual Basic]
Overloads Public Sub SetPermissions( _
   ByVal user As String, _
   ByVal rights As MessageQueueAccessRights, _
   ByVal entryType As AccessControlEntryType _
)
[C#]
public void SetPermissions(
   string user,
   MessageQueueAccessRights rights,
   AccessControlEntryType entryType
);
[C++]
public: void SetPermissions(
   String* user,
   MessageQueueAccessRights rights,
   AccessControlEntryType entryType
);
[JScript]
public function SetPermissions(
   user : String,
   rights : MessageQueueAccessRights,
   entryType : AccessControlEntryType
);
```

Parameters

user
> The individual, group, or computer that gets additional rights to the queue.

rights
> A **MessageQueueAccessRights** that indicates the set of rights to the queue that Message Queuing assigns to the *user* passed in.

entryType
> An **AccessControlEntryType** that specifies whether to grant, deny, or revoke the permissions specified by the *rights* parameter.

Exceptions

Exception Type	Condition
MessageQueueException	An error occurred when accessing a Message Queuing API.

Remarks

Use this overload to grant, deny, or revoke specified rights for an individual user. The user can be any valid trustee, which includes individual users, groups of users, or a computer. If the user is an individual, use the format **DOMAIN** *user* for the *user* parameter. You can specify "." for the *user* parameter to indicate the local computer.

The permissions you assign through **SetPermissions** add rights to the existing list. By default, the creator of a public or private queue has full control, and the domain group Everyone has permission to get queue properties, get permissions, and write to the queue. When you call **SetPermissions**, the user and permissions information is appended to the bottom of the existing list.

The system examines each **AccessControlEntry** in sequence until one of the following events occurs:

- An access-denied **AccessControlEntry** explicitly denies any of the requested access rights to one of the trustees listed in the thread's access token.
- One or more access-allowed **AccessControlEntry** items for trustees listed in the thread's access token explicitly grant all the requested access rights.
- All **AccessControlEntry** items have been checked and there is still at least one requested access right that has not been explicitly allowed, in which case, access is implicitly denied.

The rights to a queue, specified in the *rights* parameter, can be any combination of the following:

- Full Control
- Delete Message
- Receive Message
- Peek Message
- Receive Journal Message
- Get Queue Properties
- Set Queue Properties
- Get Permissions
- Set Permissions
- Take Queue Ownership
- Write Message

The **MessageQueueAccessRights** enumeration represents a set of bit flags that you can combine using the bitwise operator OR to build the *rights* parameter.

The following table shows whether this method is available in various Workgroup modes.

Workgroup Mode	Available
Local computer	Yes
Local computer + direct format name	Yes
Remote computer	No
Remote computer + direct format name	No

Requirements

Platforms: Windows 98, Windows NT 4.0, Windows Millennium Edition, Windows 2000, Windows XP Home Edition, Windows XP Professional, Windows .NET Server family

.NET Framework Security:

- Full trust for the immediate caller. This member cannot be used by partially trusted code.

MessageQueue.PeekCompleted Event

Occurs when a message is read without being removed from the queue. This is a result of the asynchronous operation, **BeginPeek**.

```
[Visual Basic]
Public Event PeekCompleted As PeekCompletedEventHandler
[C#]
public event PeekCompletedEventHandler PeekCompleted;
[C++]
public: __event PeekCompletedEventHandler* PeekCompleted;
```

[JScript] In JScript, you can handle the events defined by a class, but you cannot define your own.

Event Data

The event handler receives an argument of type **PeekCompletedEventArgs** containing data related to this event. The following **PeekCompletedEventArgs** properties provide information specific to this event.

Property	Description
AsyncResult	Gets or sets the result of the asynchronous operation requested.
Message	Gets the message associated with the asynchronous peek operation.

Remarks

BeginPeek is used in asynchronous processing to raise the **PeekCompleted** event when a message is available in the queue.

EndPeek is used to complete the operation initiated by a call to **BeginPeek** and peek the message when the **PeekCompleted** event is raised.

When you create a **PeekCompletedEventHandler** delegate, you identify the method that will handle the event. To associate the event with your event handler, add an instance of the delegate to the event. The event handler is called whenever the event occurs, unless you remove the delegate. For more information about event handler delegates, see **Events and Delegates**.

Example

See related example in the **System.Messaging.MessageQueue** class topic.

Requirements

Platforms: Windows 98, Windows NT 4.0,
Windows Millennium Edition, Windows 2000,
Windows XP Home Edition, Windows XP Professional,
Windows .NET Server family

.NET Framework Security:

- Full trust for the immediate caller. This member cannot be used
  by partially trusted code.

MessageQueue.ReceiveCompleted Event

Occurs when a message has been removed from the queue. This
event is raised by the asynchronous operation, **BeginReceive**.

```
[Visual Basic]
Public Event ReceiveCompleted As ReceiveCompletedEventHandler
[C#]
public event ReceiveCompletedEventHandler ReceiveCompleted;
[C++]
public: __event ReceiveCompletedEventHandler* ReceiveCompleted;
```

[JScript] In JScript, you can handle the events defined by a class, but
you cannot define your own.

Event Data

The event handler receives an argument of type
ReceiveCompletedEventArgs containing data related to this event.
The following **ReceiveCompletedEventArgs** properties provide
information specific to this event.

Property	Description
AsyncResult	Gets or sets the result of the asynchronous operation requested.
Message	Gets the message associated with the asynchronous receive operation.

Remarks

BeginReceive is used in asynchronous processing to raise the
ReceiveCompleted event when a message is available in the queue.

EndReceive is used to complete the operation initiated by a call to
BeginReceive and peek the message when the **ReceiveCompleted**
event is raised.

When you create a **ReceiveCompletedEventHandler** delegate, you
identify the method that will handle the event. To associate the event
with your event handler, add an instance of the delegate to the event.
The event handler is called whenever the event occurs, unless you
remove the delegate. For more information about event handler
delegates, see **Events and Delegates**.

Example

See related example in the **System.Messaging.MessageQueue** class
topic.

Requirements

Platforms: Windows 98, Windows NT 4.0,
Windows Millennium Edition, Windows 2000,
Windows XP Home Edition, Windows XP Professional,
Windows .NET Server family

.NET Framework Security:

- Full trust for the immediate caller. This member cannot be used
  by partially trusted code.

MessageQueueAccessControl Entry Class

Specifies access rights for a trustee (user, group, or computer) to perform Message Queuing tasks.

System.Object
  System.Messaging.AccessControlEntry
    System.Messaging.MessageQueueAccessControlEntry

```
[Visual Basic]
Public Class MessageQueueAccessControlEntry
  Inherits AccessControlEntry
[C#]
public class MessageQueueAccessControlEntry : AccessControlEntry
[C++]
public __gc class MessageQueueAccessControlEntry : public
  AccessControlEntry
[JScript]
public class MessageQueueAccessControlEntry extends
  AccessControlEntry
```

Thread Safety

Any public static (**Shared** in Visual Basic) members of this type are safe for multithreaded operations. Any instance members are not guaranteed to be thread safe.

Remarks

Use the **MessageQueueAccessControlEntry** class to specify rights to apply to a trustee. These rights include peeking, receiving, or sending messages; viewing or modifying queue properties or permissions; and deleting queues. The **MessageQueue** class's **SetPermissions** method provides overloads for passing an instance of this class directly into the method, or adding it to an instance of **AccessControlList** so that you can add rights for more than one trustee at a time. The new access right is appended to the end of the queue's discretionary access control list (DACL), which identifies the users and groups that can access the queue.

> **Note** There are some exceptions to this generalization about where the new right is added and its effects. See the **AccessControlList** topic for more information.

An overload of the **MessageQueueAccessControlEntry** constructor allows you specify an **AccessControlEntryType** member to indicate whether to allow or deny rights to the trustee. The order in which rights are allowed or denied in the resource's DACL affects whether the trustee has the specified rights. For example, if rights have already been granted to the trustee and you later add an entry that denies them, the system finds the granted rights first, so the user is granted rights you might have intended they be denied. You can use two entry types to override this behavior: **Set** and **Revoke**. For more information about controlling the way in which access rights are determined, see the **AccessControlEntryType** enumeration topic.

The **MessageQueueAccessControlEntry** class is associated with security based on access control lists (ACLs), which you can use to give users access to the Message Queuing system itself. This is different from code access security, which is implemented through the **MessageQueuePermission** and related classes. Message Queuing code access security defines queue-specific operations or queue access that an application might require which is subject to security control; it does not represent a right for the application to perform these operations or receive access in and of itself. See the topic **Code Access Security** for more information about code access security.

To set message queue permissions for a trustee, create a new instance of the **Trustee** class and pass it into an overload of the **MessageQueueAccessControlEntry** constructor. Specify the message queue access rights either by passing an instance of **MessageQueueAccessRights** into the constructor or by setting the **MessageQueueAccessRights** property on an existing **MessageQueueAccessControlEntry** instance.

You can then pass the **MessageQueueAccessControlEntry** instance directly to the **MessageQueue.SetPermissions** method, or alternately add the entry to an instance of **AccessControlList** before calling **SetPermissions**.

Requirements

Namespace: System.Messaging

Platforms: Windows 98, Windows NT 4.0, Windows Millennium Edition, Windows 2000, Windows XP Home Edition, Windows XP Professional, Windows .NET Server family

Assembly: System.Messaging (in System.Messaging.dll)

MessageQueueAccessControlEntry Constructor

Initializes a new instance of the **MessageQueueAccessControlEntry** class with the specified trustee and Message Queuing access rights.

Overload List

Initializes a new instance of the **MessageQueueAccessControlEntry** class, granting the specified Message Queuing access rights to the specified trustee.

> [Visual Basic] **Public Sub New(Trustee, MessageQueueAccessRights)**
>
> [C#] **public MessageQueueAccessControlEntry(Trustee, MessageQueueAccessRights);**
>
> [C++] **public: MessageQueueAccessControlEntry(Trustee*, MessageQueueAccessRights);**
>
> [JScript] **public function MessageQueueAccessControlEntry(Trustee, MessageQueueAccessRights);**

Initializes a new instance of the **MessageQueueAccessControlEntry** class, with the specified trustee and Message Queuing access rights. The type of access (such as **Allow** or **Deny**) is defined by the entry type you pass in.

> [Visual Basic] **Public Sub New(Trustee, MessageQueueAccessRights, AccessControlEntryType)**
>
> [C#] **public MessageQueueAccessControlEntry(Trustee, MessageQueueAccessRights, AccessControlEntryType);**
>
> [C++] **public: MessageQueueAccessControlEntry(Trustee*, MessageQueueAccessRights, AccessControlEntryType);**
>
> [JScript] **public function MessageQueueAccessControlEntry(Trustee, MessageQueueAccessRights, AccessControlEntryType);**

MessageQueueAccessControlEntry Constructor (Trustee, MessageQueueAccessRights)

Initializes a new instance of the **MessageQueueAccessControlEntry** class, granting the specified Message Queuing access rights to the specified trustee.

```
[Visual Basic]
Public Sub New( _
    ByVal trustee As Trustee, _
    ByVal rights As MessageQueueAccessRights _
)
[C#]
public MessageQueueAccessControlEntry(
    Trustee trustee,
    MessageQueueAccessRights rights
);
[C++]
public: MessageQueueAccessControlEntry(
    Trustee* trustee,
    MessageQueueAccessRights rights
);
[JScript]
public function MessageQueueAccessControlEntry(
    trustee : Trustee,
    rights : MessageQueueAccessRights
);
```

Parameters

trustee
> A **Trustee** that specifies a user, group, computer, domain, or alias.

rights
> A bitwise combination of the **MessageQueueAccessRights** values which defines the combination of rights to grant to the trustee.

Remarks

Use this overload of the constructor to grant rights to the specified trustee. The rights you specify in the *rights* parameter are a bitwise combination of members of the **MessageQueueAccessRights** bitflag, which includes such rights as receiving messages, deleting queues, and setting queue properties. The constructor uses the rights you pass in to set this instance's **MessageQueueAccessRights** property.

Pass this instance of **MessageQueueAccessControlEntry** directly into an overload of the **SetPermissions** method to grant rights only to this trustee, or add this instance to an **AccessControlList** before calling **SetPermissions** to grant or deny rights to multiple trustees at once.

Requirements

Platforms: Windows 98, Windows NT 4.0, Windows Millennium Edition, Windows 2000, Windows XP Home Edition, Windows XP Professional, Windows .NET Server family

.NET Framework Security:
- Full trust for the immediate caller. This member cannot be used by partially trusted code.

MessageQueueAccessControlEntry Constructor (Trustee, MessageQueueAccessRights, AccessControlEntryType)

Initializes a new instance of the **MessageQueueAccessControlEntry** class, with the specified trustee and Message Queuing access rights. The type of access (such as **Allow** or **Deny**) is defined by the entry type you pass in.

```
[Visual Basic]
Public Sub New( _
    ByVal trustee As Trustee, _
    ByVal rights As MessageQueueAccessRights, _
    ByVal entryType As AccessControlEntryType _
)
[C#]
public MessageQueueAccessControlEntry(
    Trustee trustee,
    MessageQueueAccessRights rights,
    AccessControlEntryType entryType
);
[C++]
public: MessageQueueAccessControlEntry(
    Trustee* trustee,
    MessageQueueAccessRights rights,
    AccessControlEntryType entryType
);
[JScript]
public function MessageQueueAccessControlEntry(
    trustee : Trustee,
    rights : MessageQueueAccessRights,
    entryType : AccessControlEntryType
);
```

Parameters

trustee
> A **Trustee** that specifies a user, group, computer, domain, or alias.

rights
> A bitwise combination of the **MessageQueueAccessRights** values which defines the combination of rights to grant to the trustee.

entryType
> One of the **AccessControlEntryType** values, which specifies whether to allow, deny, set or revoke the specified rights.

Remarks

Use this overload of the constructor to grant or deny rights to the specified trustee. The rights you specify in the *rights* parameter are a bitwise combination of members of the **MessageQueueAccessRights** bitflag, which includes such rights as receiving messages, deleting queues, and setting queue properties. The constructor uses the rights you pass in to set this instance's **MessageQueueAccessRights** property.

For more information about granting or denying rights, see the **AccessControlEntryType** topic. For two members, **Allow** and **Deny**, there may be preexisting and possibly contradictory access rights, so the order in which the rights appear in the queue's discretionary access control list (DACL) affects whether the right is ultimately granted. Two other members, **Set** and **Revoke**, overwrite any existing rights. Use the member whose behavior is applicable to your application.

Pass this instance of **MessageQueueAccessControlEntry** directly into an overload of the **SetPermissions** method to grant or deny rights only to this trustee, or add this instance to an **AccessControlList** before calling **SetPermissions** to grant or deny rights to multiple trustees at once.

Requirements

Platforms: Windows 98, Windows NT 4.0, Windows Millennium Edition, Windows 2000, Windows XP Home Edition, Windows XP Professional, Windows .NET Server family

.NET Framework Security:

- Full trust for the immediate caller. This member cannot be used by partially trusted code.

MessageQueueAccessControlEntry.Message-QueueAccessRights Property

Gets or sets the set of Message Queuing-specific rights to apply to the trustee.

```
[Visual Basic]
Public Property MessageQueueAccessRights As _
   MessageQueueAccessRights
[C#]
public MessageQueueAccessRights MessageQueueAccessRights {get;
   set;}
[C++]
public: __property MessageQueueAccessRights
get_MessageQueueAccessRights();
public: __property void
set_MessageQueueAccessRights(MessageQueueAccessRights);
[JScript]
public function get MessageQueueAccessRights() :
MessageQueueAccessRights;
public function set
MessageQueueAccessRights(MessageQueueAccessRights);
```

Property Value

A bitwise combination of the **MessageQueueAccessRights** members. The default is defined by the *rights* parameter passed into the constructor.

Remarks

The **MessageQueueAccessRights** property enables you to specify Message Queuing object-specific rights such as receiving, peeking, or writing messages, or setting queue properties. The value of this property is set by the **MessageQueueAccessControlEntry** constructor, but you can change it at any time before using this instance of **MessageQueueAccessControlEntry** in a call to **MessageQueue.SetPermissions**.

Requirements

Platforms: Windows 98, Windows NT 4.0, Windows Millennium Edition, Windows 2000, Windows XP Home Edition, Windows XP Professional, Windows .NET Server family

.NET Framework Security:

- Full trust for the immediate caller. This member cannot be used by partially trusted code.

MessageQueueAccessRights Enumeration

Specifies a set of object-specific access rights for operations specific to Message Queuing.

This enumeration has a **FlagsAttribute** attribute that allows a bitwise combination of its member values.

```
[Visual Basic]
<Flags>
<Serializable>
Public Enum MessageQueueAccessRights
[C#]
[Flags]
[Serializable]
public enum MessageQueueAccessRights
[C++]
[Flags]
[Serializable]
_value public enum MessageQueueAccessRights
[JScript]
public
    Flags
    Serializable
enum MessageQueueAccessRights
```

Remarks

The **MessageQueueAccessRights** enumeration enables you to specify Message Queuing object-specific rights such as receiving, peeking, or writing messages, or setting queue properties. It is one of two enumerations to which the **GenericAccessRights** enumeration maps extensive read, write, or execute abilities. The other, **StandardAccessRights**, enables you to specify rights common to most objects, for example, deleting the object or reading a security descriptor.

> **Note** Both **StandardAccessRights** and **MessageQueueAccessRights** provide a member for deleting a queue. The needs of the application define which set of flags you use.

The access rights associated with the **MessageQueueAccessRights** enumeration are listed in the **Permissions** box of the queue properties window.

Members

Member name	Description	Value
ChangeQueuePermis-sions	The right to modify queue permissions.	262144
DeleteJournalMessage	The right to delete messages from the journal queue.	8
DeleteMessage	The right to delete messages from the queue.	1
DeleteQueue	The right to delete the queue.	65536
FullControl	Full rights to the queue. A union of all other rights in the enumeration.	983103

Member name	Description	Value
GenericRead	A combination of **GetQueueProperties**, **GetQueuePermissions**, **ReceiveMessage**, and **ReceiveJournalMessage**.	131115
GenericWrite	A combination of **GetQueueProperties**, **GetQueuePermissions**, and **WriteMessage**.	131108
GetQueuePermissions	The right to read queue permissions.	131072
GetQueueProperties	The right to read properties of the queue.	32
PeekMessage	The right to peek messages from the queue.	2
ReceiveJournalMessage	The right to receive messages from the journal queue. This includes the rights to delete and peek messages from the journal queue.	10
ReceiveMessage	The right to receive messages from the queue. This includes the rights to delete and peek messages.	3
SetQueueProperties	The right to modify properties of the queue.	16
TakeQueueOwnership	The right to take ownership of the queue.	524288
WriteMessage	The right to send messages to the queue.	4

Requirements

Namespace: System.Messaging

Platforms: Windows 98, Windows NT 4.0, Windows Millennium Edition, Windows 2000, Windows XP Home Edition, Windows XP Professional, Windows .NET Server family

Assembly: System.Messaging (in System.Messaging.dll)

MessageQueueCriteria Class

Filters message queues when performing a query using the
MessageQueue class's **GetPublicQueues** method.

System.Object
   System.Messaging.MessageQueueCriteria

[Visual Basic]
```
Public Class MessageQueueCriteria
```
[C#]
```
public class MessageQueueCriteria
```
[C++]
```
public __gc class MessageQueueCriteria
```
[JScript]
```
public class MessageQueueCriteria
```

Thread Safety

Any public static (**Shared** in Visual Basic) members of this type are
safe for multithreaded operations. Any instance members are not
guaranteed to be thread safe.

Remarks

The **MessageQueue** class provides a number of methods that enable
you to filter your search for public queues on the network. Specific
methods for filtering by queue label, category, or server location are
the **GetPublicQueuesByLabel**, **GetPublicQueuesByCategory**,
and **GetPublicQueuesByMachine**.

The **MessageQueueCriteria** class, when used with the
GetPublicQueues method, allows you to refine your filter. You can
specify search criteria not specifically addressed through one of the
GetPublicQueuesBy... methods, or by multiple criteria. You can
pass a **MessageQueueCriteria** instance into the **GetPublicQueues**
method in order to search, for example, by queue creation or
modification times, the computer the queue resides on, the queue
label or category, or any combination of these properties.

When filtering by multiple properties, the criteria are composed by
applying the AND operator to the set of properties. Thus, when you
specify a value for the **CreatedAfter** property together with the
MachineName property, you are asking for all queues that were
created after a specified time and that reside on a specific computer.

When you set any property, the method that sets the property also
sets a flag to indicate that it should be included in the filter you are
building. You cannot remove individual properties from the search
filter. Instead, you remove all properties from the filter by calling
ClearAll, and then set the properties that you do want to build into
the search filter. **ClearAll** resets all properties into a "not set" default
state.

> **Note** You must set a property before trying to read it. Reading
> a property the application has not yet set throws an exception.

Example

[Visual Basic, C#, C++] The following example iterates through
message queues and displays the path of each queue that was created
in the last day and that exists on the computer "MyComputer".

[Visual Basic]
```
Imports System
Imports System.Messaging

Namespace MyProject
```

```
'/ <summary>
'/ Provides a container class for the example.
'/ </summary>
Public Class MyNewQueue

    '****************************************************
    ' Provides an entry point into the application.
    '
    ' This example uses a cursor to step through the
    ' message queues and list the public queues on the
    ' network that specify certain criteria.
    '****************************************************

    Public Shared Sub Main()

        ' Create a new instance of the class.
        Dim myNewQueue As New MyNewQueue()

        ' Output the count of Lowest priority messages.
        myNewQueue.ListPublicQueuesByCriteria()

        Return

    End Sub 'Main

    '****************************************************
    ' Iterates through message queues and displays the
    ' path of each queue that was created in the last
    ' day and that exists on the computer "MyComputer".
    '****************************************************

    Public Sub ListPublicQueuesByCriteria()

        Dim numberQueues As Int32 = 0

        ' Specify the criteria to filter by.
        Dim myCriteria As New MessageQueueCriteria()
        myCriteria.MachineName = "MyComputer"
        myCriteria.CreatedAfter = DateTime.Now.Subtract(New _
            TimeSpan(1, 0, 0, 0))

        ' Get a cursor into the queues on the network.
        Dim myQueueEnumerator As MessageQueueEnumerator = _
            MessageQueue.GetMessageQueueEnumerator(myCriteria)

        ' Move to the next queue and read its path.
        While myQueueEnumerator.MoveNext()
            ' Increase the count if the priority is Lowest.
            Console.WriteLine(myQueueEnumerator.Current.Path)
            numberQueues += 1
        End While

        ' Handle no queues matching the criteria.
        If numberQueues = 0 Then
            Console.WriteLine("No queues match the criteria.")
        End If

        Return

    End Sub 'ListPublicQueuesByCriteria

End Class 'MyNewQueue
End Namespace 'MyProject
```

[C#]
```
using System;
using System.Messaging;

namespace MyProject
{
    /// <summary>
    /// Provides a container class for the example.
    /// </summary>
    public class MyNewQueue
    {
```

```
//************************************************
// Provides an entry point into the application.
//
// This example uses a cursor to step through the
// message queues and list the public queues on the
// network that specify certain criteria.
//************************************************

public static void Main()
{
    // Create a new instance of the class.
    MyNewQueue myNewQueue = new MyNewQueue();

    // Output the count of Lowest priority messages.
    myNewQueue.ListPublicQueuesByCriteria();

    return;
}


//************************************************
// Iterates through message queues and displays the
// path of each queue that was created in the last
// day and that exists on the computer "MyComputer".
//************************************************

public void ListPublicQueuesByCriteria()
{
    uint numberQueues = 0;

    // Specify the criteria to filter by.
    MessageQueueCriteria myCriteria = new
        MessageQueueCriteria();
    myCriteria.MachineName = "MyComputer";
    myCriteria.CreatedAfter = DateTime.Now.Subtract(new
        TimeSpan(1,0,0,0));

    // Get a cursor into the queues on the network.
    MessageQueueEnumerator myQueueEnumerator =
        MessageQueue.GetMessageQueueEnumerator(myCriteria);

    // Move to the next queue and read its path.
    while(myQueueEnumerator.MoveNext())
    {
        // Increase the count if priority is Lowest.
        Console.WriteLine(myQueueEnumerator.Current.Path);
        numberQueues++;
    }

    // Handle no queues matching the criteria.
    if (numberQueues == 0)
    {
        Console.WriteLine("No public queues match criteria.");
    }

    return;
    }
}
}

[C++]
#using <mscorlib.dll>
#using <system.dll>
#using <system.messaging.dll>

using namespace System;
using namespace System::Messaging;

__gc class MyNewQueue
{
    // Iterates through message queues and displays the
    // path of each queue that was created in the last
    // day and that exists on the computer S"MyComputer".

public:
    void ListPublicQueuesByCriteria()
```

```
    {
        UInt32 numberQueues = 0;

        // Specify the criteria to filter by.
        MessageQueueCriteria* myCriteria = new MessageQueueCriteria();
        myCriteria->MachineName = S"MyComputer";
        myCriteria->CreatedAfter = DateTime::Now.Subtract
(TimeSpan(1, 0, 0, 0));

        // Get a cursor into the queues on the network.
        MessageQueueEnumerator* myQueueEnumerator =
            MessageQueue::GetMessageQueueEnumerator(myCriteria);

        // Move to the next queue and read its path.
        while(myQueueEnumerator->MoveNext())
        {
            // Increase the count if priority is Lowest.
            Console::WriteLine(myQueueEnumerator->Current->Path);
            numberQueues++;
        }

        // Handle no queues matching the criteria.
        if (numberQueues == 0)
        {
            Console::WriteLine(S"No public queues match criteria.");
        }

        return;
    }
};

int main()
{
    // Create a new instance of the class.
    MyNewQueue* myNewQueue = new MyNewQueue();

    // Output the count of Lowest priority messages.
    myNewQueue->ListPublicQueuesByCriteria();

    return 0;
}
```

Requirements

Namespace: System.Messaging

Platforms: Windows 98, Windows NT 4.0,
Windows Millennium Edition, Windows 2000,
Windows XP Home Edition, Windows XP Professional,
Windows .NET Server family

Assembly: System.Messaging (in System.Messaging.dll)

MessageQueueCriteria Constructor

Initializes a new instance of the **MessageQueueCriteria** class.

```
[Visual Basic]
Public Sub New()
[C#]
public MessageQueueCriteria();
[C++]
public: MessageQueueCriteria();
[JScript]
public function MessageQueueCriteria();
```

Remarks

The default constructor initializes any fields to their default values.

Requirements

Platforms: Windows 98, Windows NT 4.0,
Windows Millennium Edition, Windows 2000,

Windows XP Home Edition, Windows XP Professional, Windows .NET Server family

.NET Framework Security:

- Full trust for the immediate caller. This member cannot be used by partially trusted code.

MessageQueueCriteria.Category Property

Gets or sets the category by which to filter queues in the network.

```
[Visual Basic]
Public Property Category As Guid
[C#]
public Guid Category {get; set;}
[C++]
public: __property Guid get_Category();
public: __property void set_Category(Guid);
[JScript]
public function get Category() : Guid;
public function set Category(Guid);
```

Property Value

The queues' category.

Exceptions

Exception Type	Condition
InvalidOperationException	The application did not set the **Category** property before reading it.

Remarks

The queue category allows an application to categorize its queues. For example, you can place all Billing queues in one category and all Order queues in another. The **Category** property is application-defined and has no intrinsic meaning to Message Queuing.

If you are filtering only by category when searching the queues on the network, you can use the method **GetPublicQueuesByCategory**, which is specifically designed for this purpose. If you are searching by multiple criteria that include the category, set this **Category** property and pass the parameter into **GetPublicQueues**.

Requirements

Platforms: Windows 98, Windows NT 4.0, Windows Millennium Edition, Windows 2000, Windows XP Home Edition, Windows XP Professional, Windows .NET Server family

.NET Framework Security:

- Full trust for the immediate caller. This member cannot be used by partially trusted code.

MessageQueueCriteria.CreatedAfter Property

Gets or sets the lower boundary of the queue creation date and time by which to filter queues on the network.

```
[Visual Basic]
Public Property CreatedAfter As DateTime
[C#]
public DateTime CreatedAfter {get; set;}
[C++]
public: __property DateTime get_CreatedAfter();
public: __property void set_CreatedAfter(DateTime);
```

```
[JScript]
public function get CreatedAfter() : DateTime;
public function set CreatedAfter(DateTime);
```

Property Value

A **DateTime** that specifies the lower boundary for a queue's creation date and time.

Exceptions

Exception Type	Condition
InvalidOperation-Exception	The application did not set the **CreatedAfter** property before reading it.

Remarks

The **MessageQueueCriteria** properties are combined using a logical AND, so setting both **CreatedAfter** and **CreatedBefore** bounds a time interval for the queues' creation. If you set only **CreatedAfter**, there is no upper boundary on the date.

If you try to set **CreatedAfter** to a later **DateTime** value than **CreatedBefore**, **CreatedBefore** is reset to the same (new) value as **CreatedAfter**.

Requirements

Platforms: Windows 98, Windows NT 4.0, Windows Millennium Edition, Windows 2000, Windows XP Home Edition, Windows XP Professional, Windows .NET Server family

.NET Framework Security:

- Full trust for the immediate caller. This member cannot be used by partially trusted code.

MessageQueueCriteria.CreatedBefore Property

Gets or sets the upper boundary of the queue creation date and time by which to filter queues on the network.

```
[Visual Basic]
Public Property CreatedBefore As DateTime
[C#]
public DateTime CreatedBefore {get; set;}
[C++]
public: __property DateTime get_CreatedBefore();
public: __property void set_CreatedBefore(DateTime);
[JScript]
public function get CreatedBefore() : DateTime;
public function set CreatedBefore(DateTime);
```

Property Value

A **DateTime** that specifies the upper boundary for a queue's creation date and time.

Exceptions

Exception Type	Condition
InvalidOperation-Exception	The application did not set the **CreatedBefore** property before reading it.

Remarks

The **MessageQueueCriteria** properties are combined using a logical AND, so setting both **CreatedAfter** and **CreatedBefore** bounds a time interval for the queues' creation. If you set only **CreatedBefore**, there is no lower boundary on the date.

If you try to set **CreatedBefore** to an earlier **DateTime** value than **CreatedAfter**, **CreatedAfter** is reset to the same (new) value as **CreatedBefore**.

Requirements

Platforms: Windows 98, Windows NT 4.0, Windows Millennium Edition, Windows 2000, Windows XP Home Edition, Windows XP Professional, Windows .NET Server family

.NET Framework Security:
- Full trust for the immediate caller. This member cannot be used by partially trusted code.

MessageQueueCriteria.Label Property

Gets or sets the label by which to filter queues in the network.

```
[Visual Basic]
Public Property Label As String
[C#]
public string Label {get; set;}
[C++]
public: __property String* get_Label();
public: __property void set_Label(String*);
[JScript]
public function get Label() : String;
public function set Label(String);
```

Property Value

The queues' label.

Exceptions

Exception Type	Condition
InvalidOperation-Exception	The application did not set the **Label** property before reading it.

Remarks

A message queue's label is an application-defined description of the queue. It does not have any intrinsic meaning to Message Queuing.

If you are filtering only by label when searching the queues on the network, you can use the method **GetPublicQueuesByLabel**, which is specifically designed for this purpose. If you are searching by multiple criteria that include the label, set this **Label** property and pass the parameter into **GetPublicQueues**.

Requirements

Platforms: Windows 98, Windows NT 4.0, Windows Millennium Edition, Windows 2000, Windows XP Home Edition, Windows XP Professional, Windows .NET Server family

.NET Framework Security:
- Full trust for the immediate caller. This member cannot be used by partially trusted code.

MessageQueueCriteria.MachineName Property

Gets or sets the computer name by which to filter queues in the network.

```
[Visual Basic]
Public Property MachineName As String
[C#]
public string MachineName {get; set;}
[C++]
public: __property String* get_MachineName();
public: __property void set_MachineName(String*);
[JScript]
public function get MachineName() : String;
public function set MachineName(String);
```

Property Value

The server name of the computer on which the queues reside.

Exceptions

Exception Type	Condition
InvalidOperation-Exception	The application did not set the **MachineName** property before reading it. -or- The computer name syntax is invalid.

Remarks

A message queue's **MachineName** reflects the name of the server on which the queue resides, without preceding backslashes (\\).

If you are filtering only by computer name when searching the queues on the network, you can use the method **GetPublicQueuesByMachine**, which is specifically designed for this purpose. If you are searching by multiple criteria that include the computer name, set this **MachineName** property and pass the parameter into **GetPublicQueues**.

You can also search for private queues on the network by specifying a computer name in the **GetPrivateQueuesByMachine** method.

Requirements

Platforms: Windows 98, Windows NT 4.0, Windows Millennium Edition, Windows 2000, Windows XP Home Edition, Windows XP Professional, Windows .NET Server family

.NET Framework Security:
- Full trust for the immediate caller. This member cannot be used by partially trusted code.

MessageQueueCriteria.ModifiedAfter Property

Gets or sets the lower boundary of the queue modification date and time by which to filter queues on the network.

```
[Visual Basic]
Public Property ModifiedAfter As DateTime
[C#]
public DateTime ModifiedAfter {get; set;}
[C++]
public: __property DateTime get_ModifiedAfter();
public: __property void set_ModifiedAfter(DateTime);
[JScript]
public function get ModifiedAfter() : DateTime;
public function set ModifiedAfter(DateTime);
```

Property Value

A **DateTime** that specifies the lower boundary for a queue's last modification date and time.

Exceptions

Exception Type	Condition
InvalidOperation-Exception	The application did not set the **ModifiedAfter** property before reading it.

Remarks

A queue's modification flag is set when you change the properties of a queue, but not when a message is read or written to the queue.

The **MessageQueueCriteria** properties are combined using a logical AND, so setting both **ModifiedAfter** and **ModifiedBefore** bounds a time interval for the queues' last modification. If you set only **ModifiedAfter**, there is no upper boundary on the date.

If you try to set **ModifiedAfter** to a later **DateTime** value than **ModifiedBefore**, **ModifiedBefore** is reset to the same (new) value as **ModifiedAfter**.

Requirements

Platforms: Windows 98, Windows NT 4.0, Windows Millennium Edition, Windows 2000, Windows XP Home Edition, Windows XP Professional, Windows .NET Server family

.NET Framework Security:

- Full trust for the immediate caller. This member cannot be used by partially trusted code.

MessageQueueCriteria.ModifiedBefore Property

Gets or sets the upper boundary of the queue modification date and time by which to filter queues on the network.

```
[Visual Basic]
Public Property ModifiedBefore As DateTime
[C#]
public DateTime ModifiedBefore {get; set;}
[C++]
public: __property DateTime get_ModifiedBefore();
public: __property void set_ModifiedBefore(DateTime);
[JScript]
public function get ModifiedBefore() : DateTime;
public function set ModifiedBefore(DateTime);
```

Property Value

A **DateTime** that specifies the upper boundary for a queue's last modification date and time.

Exceptions

Exception Type	Condition
InvalidOperation-Exception	The application did not set the **ModifiedBefore** property before reading it.

Remarks

A queue's modification flag is set when you change the properties of a queue, but not when a message is read or written to the queue.

The **MessageQueueCriteria** properties are combined using a logical AND, so setting both **ModifiedBefore** and **ModifiedAfter** bounds a time interval for the queues' last modification. If you set only **ModifiedBefore**, there is no lower boundary on the date.

If you try to set **ModifiedBefore** to an earlier **DateTime** value than **ModifiedAfter**, **ModifiedAfter** is reset to the same (new) value as **ModifiedBefore**.

Requirements

Platforms: Windows 98, Windows NT 4.0, Windows Millennium Edition, Windows 2000, Windows XP Home Edition, Windows XP Professional, Windows .NET Server family

.NET Framework Security:

- Full trust for the immediate caller. This member cannot be used by partially trusted code.

MessageQueueCriteria.ClearAll Method

Clears all properties from being built into a filter and puts all property values into a "not set" state.

```
[Visual Basic]
Public Sub ClearAll()
[C#]
public void ClearAll();
[C++]
public: void ClearAll();
[JScript]
public function ClearAll();
```

Remarks

When you call **ClearAll**, the method sets flags related to each of the **MessageQueueCriteria** properties, which indicate that no properties are to be included when the application creates the search filter. **ClearAll** resets all properties that currently have values into a "not set" default state. Any properties that you subsequently change are combined using the logical AND operator to define a new filter for the **GetPublicQueues** method. When you change the property, the method that sets the property also sets a flag to indicate that it should be included in the filter you are building.

You cannot remove individual properties from the search filter. Instead, you remove all properties from the filter by calling **ClearAll**, and then set the properties that you do want to build into the search filter.

Requirements

Platforms: Windows 98, Windows NT 4.0, Windows Millennium Edition, Windows 2000, Windows XP Home Edition, Windows XP Professional, Windows .NET Server family

.NET Framework Security:

- Full trust for the immediate caller. This member cannot be used by partially trusted code.

MessageQueueEnumerator Class

Provides a forward-only cursor to enumerate through messages in a message queue.

System.Object
  System.MarshalByRefObject
    System.Messaging.MessageQueueEnumerator

```
[Visual Basic]
Public Class MessageQueueEnumerator
    Inherits MarshalByRefObject
    Implements IEnumerator, IDisposable
[C#]
public class MessageQueueEnumerator : MarshalByRefObject,
    IEnumerator, IDisposable
[C++]
public __gc class MessageQueueEnumerator : public
    MarshalByRefObject, IEnumerator, IDisposable
[JScript]
public class MessageQueueEnumerator extends MarshalByRefObject
    implements IEnumerator, IDisposable
```

Thread Safety

Any public static (**Shared** in Visual Basic) members of this type are safe for multithreaded operations. Any instance members are not guaranteed to be thread safe.

Remarks

Use **MessageQueueEnumerator** for dynamic interaction with queues on the network. Methods available through the **MessageQueue** class can return either a **MessageQueueEnumerator** containing a dynamic list of queues, or an array that contains a snapshot of the queue collection at the time the specified method was called.

> **Note** There is no defined ordering of queues in a network. They are not ordered, for example, by computer, label, public/private status, or other user-accessible criteria. A **MessageQueueEnumerator** is a cursor, initialized to the head of a dynamic list. You can move the cursor to the first queue of the enumeration by calling **MoveNext**. After the enumerator has been initialized, you can use **MoveNext** to step forward through the remaining queues.

It is not possible to step backward with a **MessageQueueEnumerator**. A cursor only allows forward movement through the queue enumeration. However, you can call **Reset** to reset the enumeration and put the cursor at the beginning of the list again. Because the enumerator is dynamic, a queue that is appended beyond the cursor's current position can be accessed by the enumerator. A queue that is inserted before the cursor's current position cannot be accessed without first calling Reset.

Example

[Visual Basic, C#] The following example iterates through all the message queues in the network, and examines the path for each queue. Finally, it displays the number of public queues on the network.

```
[Visual Basic]
Imports System
Imports System.Messaging
```

```
Namespace MyProject

    '/ <summary>
    '/ Provides a container class for the example.
    '/ </summary>
    Public Class MyNewQueue

        '***************************************************
        ' Provides an entry point into the application.
        '
        ' This example uses a cursor to step through the
        ' message queues and list the public queues on the
        ' network.
        '***************************************************

        Public Shared Sub Main()

            ' Create a new instance of the class.
            Dim myNewQueue As New MyNewQueue()

            ' Output the count of Lowest priority messages.
            myNewQueue.ListPublicQueues()

            Return

        End Sub 'Main

        '***************************************************
        ' Iterates through message queues and examines the
        ' path for each queue. Also displays the number of
        ' public queues on the network.
        '***************************************************

        Public Sub ListPublicQueues()

            ' Holds the count of private queues.
            Dim numberQueues As Int32 = 0

            ' Get a cursor into the queues on the network.
            Dim myQueueEnumerator As MessageQueueEnumerator = _
                MessageQueue.GetMessageQueueEnumerator()

            ' Move to the next queue and read its path.
            While myQueueEnumerator.MoveNext()
                ' Increase the count if the priority is Lowest.
                Console.WriteLine(myQueueEnumerator.Current.Path)
                numberQueues += 1
            End While

            ' Display final count.
            Console.WriteLine(("Number of public queues: " + _
                numberQueues.ToString()))

            Return

        End Sub 'ListPublicQueues

    End Class 'MyNewQueue
End Namespace 'MyProject

[C#]
using System;
using System.Messaging;

namespace MyProject
{
    /// <summary>
    /// Provides a container class for the example.
    /// </summary>
    public class MyNewQueue
    {

        //***************************************************
        // Provides an entry point into the application.
        //
        // This example uses a cursor to step through the
        // message queues and list the public queues on the
```

```
// network.
//**************************************************

public static void Main()
{
    // Create a new instance of the class.
    MyNewQueue myNewQueue = new MyNewQueue();

    // Output the count of Lowest priority messages.
    myNewQueue.ListPublicQueues();

    return;
}

//**************************************************
// Iterates through message queues and examines the
// path for each queue. Also displays the number of
// public queues on the network.
//**************************************************

public void ListPublicQueues()
{
    // Holds the count of private queues.
    uint numberQueues = 0;

    // Get a cursor into the queues on the network.
    MessageQueueEnumerator myQueueEnumerator =
        MessageQueue.GetMessageQueueEnumerator();

    // Move to the next queue and read its path.
    while(myQueueEnumerator.MoveNext())
    {
        // Increase the count if priority is Lowest.
        Console.WriteLine(myQueueEnumerator.Current.Path);
        numberQueues++;
    }

    // Display final count.
    Console.WriteLine("Number of public queues: " +
        numberQueues.ToString());

    return;
}
}
}
```

Requirements

Namespace: System.Messaging

Platforms: Windows 98, Windows NT 4.0,
Windows Millennium Edition, Windows 2000,
Windows XP Home Edition, Windows XP Professional,
Windows .NET Server family

Assembly: System.Messaging (in System.Messaging.dll)

MessageQueueEnumerator.Current Property

Gets the current **MessageQueue** of the enumeration.

```
[Visual Basic]
Public ReadOnly Property Current As MessageQueue
[C#]
public MessageQueue Current {get;}
[C++]
public: __property MessageQueue* get_Current();
[JScript]
public function get Current() : MessageQueue;
```

Property Value

The queue at which the cursor is currently positioned.

Exceptions

Exception Type	Condition
InvalidOperation-Exception	You called **Current** before the first call to **MoveNext**. The cursor is located before the first queue in the enumeration. -or- You called **Current** after a call to **MoveNext** had returned false (indicating the cursor is located after the last queue in the enumeration).

Remarks

When the enumerator is created, it does not point to anything, so **Current** is not valid and will throw an exception if it is accessed. You must call **MoveNext** to position the cursor at the first queue in the enumeration.

Multiple calls to **Current** with no intervening calls to **MoveNext** will return the same **MessageQueue** object.

Requirements

Platforms: Windows 98, Windows NT 4.0,
Windows Millennium Edition, Windows 2000,
Windows XP Home Edition, Windows XP Professional,
Windows .NET Server family

.NET Framework Security:

- Full trust for the immediate caller. This member cannot be used by partially trusted code.

MessageQueueEnumerator.LocatorHandle Property

Gets the native Message Queuing handle used to locate queues in a network.

```
[Visual Basic]
Public ReadOnly Property LocatorHandle As IntPtr
[C#]
public IntPtr LocatorHandle {get;}
[C++]
public: __property IntPtr get_LocatorHandle();
[JScript]
public function get LocatorHandle() : IntPtr;
```

Property Value

The native handle to the current queue.

Exceptions

Exception Type	Condition
MessageQueueException	The handle does not exist.
SecurityException	The calling code does not have browse permissions.

Remarks

When you no longer need this **MessageQueueEnumerator** instance, call **Close** to free this handle to the resource.

Requirements

Platforms: Windows 98, Windows NT 4.0,
Windows Millennium Edition, Windows 2000,
Windows XP Home Edition, Windows XP Professional,
Windows .NET Server family

.NET Framework Security:
- Full trust for the immediate caller. This member cannot be used by partially trusted code.

MessageQueueEnumerator.Close Method

Frees the resources associated with the enumerator.

```
[Visual Basic]
Public Sub Close()
[C#]
public void Close();
[C++]
public: void Close();
[JScript]
public function Close();
```

Remarks

The operating system retains an open handle, **LocatorHandle**, to the queue enumerator during the lifetime of the cursor. When you finish working with the enumerator, call **Close** to release the resources associated with the handle.

Requirements

Platforms: Windows 98, Windows NT 4.0, Windows Millennium Edition, Windows 2000, Windows XP Home Edition, Windows XP Professional, Windows .NET Server family

.NET Framework Security:
- Full trust for the immediate caller. This member cannot be used by partially trusted code.

MessageQueueEnumerator.Dispose Method

Releases the resources used by the **MessageQueueEnumerator**.

Overload List

Releases all resources used by the **MessageQueueEnumerator**.

[Visual Basic] **Overloads Public Overridable Sub Dispose() Implements IDisposable.Dispose**
[C#] **public virtual void Dispose();**
[C++] **public: virtual void Dispose();**
[JScript] **public function Dispose();**

Releases the unmanaged resources used by the **MessageQueueEnumerator** and optionally releases the managed resources.

[Visual Basic] **Overloads Protected Overridable Sub Dispose(Boolean)**
[C#] **protected virtual void Dispose(bool);**
[C++] **protected: virtual void Dispose(bool);**
[JScript] **protected function Dispose(Boolean);**

MessageQueueEnumerator.Dispose Method ()

Releases all resources used by the **MessageQueueEnumerator**.

```
[Visual Basic]
Overloads Public Overridable Sub Dispose() Implements _
    IDisposable.Dispose
[C#]
public virtual void Dispose();
```

```
[C++]
public: virtual void Dispose();
[JScript]
public function Dispose();
```

Implements

IDisposable.Dispose

Remarks

Calling **Dispose** allows the resources used by the **MessageQueueEnumerator** to be reallocated for other purposes. For more information about **Dispose**, see **Cleaning Up Unmanaged Resources**.

Requirements

Platforms: Windows 98, Windows NT 4.0, Windows Millennium Edition, Windows 2000, Windows XP Home Edition, Windows XP Professional, Windows .NET Server family

.NET Framework Security:
- Full trust for the immediate caller. This member cannot be used by partially trusted code.

MessageQueueEnumerator.Dispose Method (Boolean)

Releases the unmanaged resources used by the **MessageQueueEnumerator** and optionally releases the managed resources.

```
[Visual Basic]
Overloads Protected Overridable Sub Dispose( _
    ByVal disposing As Boolean _
)
[C#]
protected virtual void Dispose(
    bool disposing
);
[C++]
protected: virtual void Dispose(
    bool disposing
);
[JScript]
protected function Dispose(
    disposing : Boolean
);
```

Parameters

disposing
   true to release both managed and unmanaged resources; **false** to release only unmanaged resources.

Remarks

This method is called by the public **Dispose()** method and the **Finalize** method. **Dispose()** invokes the protected **Dispose(Boolean)** method with the *disposing* parameter set to **true**. **Finalize** invokes **Dispose** with *disposing* set to **false**.

When the *disposing* parameter is **true**, this method releases all resources held by any managed objects that this **MessageQueueEnumerator** references. This method invokes the **Dispose()** method of each referenced object.

Notes to Inheritors: **Dispose** can be called multiple times by other objects. When overriding **Dispose(Boolean)**, be careful not to reference objects that have been previously disposed of in an earlier call to **Dispose**.

Requirements

Platforms: Windows 98, Windows NT 4.0,
Windows Millennium Edition, Windows 2000,
Windows XP Home Edition, Windows XP Professional,
Windows .NET Server family

.NET Framework Security:
- Full trust for the immediate caller. This member cannot be used by partially trusted code.

MessageQueueEnumerator.Finalize Method

Releases the resources held by the queue.

[C#] In C#, finalizers are expressed using destructor syntax.

[C++] In C++, finalizers are expressed using destructor syntax.

```
[Visual Basic]
Overrides Protected Sub Finalize()
[C#]
~MessageQueueEnumerator();
[C++]
~MessageQueueEnumerator();
[JScript]
protected override function Finalize();
```

Remarks

This method overrides **Object.Finalize**. Application code should not call this method; an object's **Finalize** method is automatically invoked during garbage collection, unless finalization by the garbage collector has been disabled by a call to the **GC.SuppressFinalize** method.

Requirements

Platforms: Windows 98, Windows NT 4.0,
Windows Millennium Edition, Windows 2000,
Windows XP Home Edition, Windows XP Professional,
Windows .NET Server family

.NET Framework Security:
- Full trust for the immediate caller. This member cannot be used by partially trusted code.

MessageQueueEnumerator.MoveNext Method

Advances the enumerator to the next queue of the enumeration, if one is currently available.

```
[Visual Basic]
Public Overridable Function MoveNext() As Boolean Implements _
    IEnumerator.MoveNext
[C#]
public virtual bool MoveNext();
[C++]
public: virtual bool MoveNext();
[JScript]
public function MoveNext() : Boolean;
```

Return Value

true, if the enumerator was succesfully advanced to the next queue;
false, if the enumerator has reached the end of the enumeration.

Implements

IEnumerator.MoveNext

Exceptions

Exception Type	Condition
SecurityException	The calling code does not have browse permissions.

Remarks

MoveNext returns **false** immediately if there are no queues associated with the enumeration.

MoveNext will return **true** until it has reached the end of the collection. It will then return **false** for each successive call. However once **MoveNext** has returned **false**, accessing the **Current** property will throw an exception.

Upon creation, an enumerator is conceptually positioned before the first **MessageQueue** of the enumeration, and the first call to **MoveNext** brings the first queue of the enumeration into view.

Requirements

Platforms: Windows 98, Windows NT 4.0,
Windows Millennium Edition, Windows 2000,
Windows XP Home Edition, Windows XP Professional,
Windows .NET Server family

.NET Framework Security:
- Full trust for the immediate caller. This member cannot be used by partially trusted code.

MessageQueueEnumerator.Reset Method

Resets the cursor, so it points to the beginning of the enumeration.

```
[Visual Basic]
Public Overridable Sub Reset() Implements IEnumerator.Reset
[C#]
public virtual void Reset();
[C++]
public: virtual void Reset();
[JScript]
public function Reset();
```

Implements

IEnumerator.Reset

Remarks

An enumerator moves in a forward-only direction. Use this method to return to the beginning of the enumeration of queues.

Reset positions the cursor at the first queue in the list. You do not need to call **MoveNext** after calling **Reset** to move the cursor forward to the first queue in the enumeration.

Requirements

Platforms: Windows 98, Windows NT 4.0,
Windows Millennium Edition, Windows 2000,
Windows XP Home Edition, Windows XP Professional,
Windows .NET Server family

.NET Framework Security:
- Full trust for the immediate caller. This member cannot be used by partially trusted code.

MessageQueueErrorCode Enumeration

Identifies the source of an error that occurred within the Message Queuing application and generated a **MessageQueueException** exception.

```
[Visual Basic]
<Serializable>
Public Enum MessageQueueErrorCode
[C#]
[Serializable]
public enum MessageQueueErrorCode
[C++]
[Serializable]
__value public enum MessageQueueErrorCode
[JScript]
public
    Serializable
enum MessageQueueErrorCode
```

Remarks

The **MessageQueueErrorCode** enumeration gives detailed information about an error condition during a messaging operation.

The **MessageQueueException** uses the **MessageQueueErrorCode** property to identify the nature of the Message Queuing error. The **MessageQueueErrorCode** value determines a text string to associate with the error.

Members

Member name	Description
AccessDenied	Message text: Access is denied.
	Message Queuing returns this error if access to the specified queue or computer is denied. If this error is returned, verify that you have access rights for the operation, such as creating, deleting, or setting properties for a queue. For information about changing access rights for a queue, see the **MessageQueueAccessRights** and **MessageQueue.SetPermissions** topics.
BadSecurityContext	This member supports the .NET Framework infrastructure and is not intended to be used directly from your code.
Base	This member supports the .NET Framework infrastructure and is not intended to be used directly from your code.
BufferOverflow	This member supports the .NET Framework infrastructure and is not intended to be used directly from your code.

Member name	Description
CannotCreateCertificate-Store	Message text: Unable to create a certificate store for the internal certificate.
	Message Queuing returns this error if you do not have permission to manipulate your own profile.
CannotCreateHashEx	Message text: Unable to create a hash object for an authenticated message.
	See the **Message** class's **HashAlgorithm** property for more information about hash algorithms.
CannotCreateOnGlobal-Catalog	Message text: Failed to create an object on a specified global catalog server.
CannotGetDistinguished Name	Message text: Failed to retrieve the distinguished name of local computer.
CannotGrantAddGuid	Message text: Failed to grant the "Add Guid" permission to current user.
CannotHashDataEx	Message text: Unable to hash data for an authenticated message.
CannotImpersonateClient	Message text: The RPC server cannot impersonate the client application, hence security credentials could not be verified.
	Message Queuing returns this error if the directory service server cannot impersonate the client application. This is necessary to verify the security credentials.
CannotJoinDomain	Message text: Failed to join Message Queuing enterprise on Windows 2000 domain.
CannotLoadMsmqOcm	Message text: Cannot load the MSMQOCM.DLL library.
CannotOpenCertificate-Store	Message text: Unable to open the certificates store for the internal certificate.
	Message Queuing returns this error if you do not have permission to manipulate your own profile.
CannotSetCryptographic SecurityDescriptor	Message text: Unable to set the security descriptor for the cryptographic keys.
	For information about cryptographic providers, see the **Cryptographic ProviderType** and **Message.AuthenticationProviderType** topics.
CannotSignDataEx	Message text: Unable to sign data before sending an authenticated message.
	See the **Message** class's **DigitalSignature** property for more information about signing data.

Member name	Description
CertificateNotProvided	Message text: A user attempted to send an authenticated message without a certificate.
	Message Queuing returns this error if the sending application attempts to use security context information to authenticate a message, and the security context does not include a certificate. For more information about certificates, see the **Message** class's **SenderCertificate** property.
ComputerDoesNot-SupportEncryption	Message text: The computer does not support encryption operations.
	Message Queuing returns this error when the application requests encryption and the computer (source or destination) does not support encryption operations. When this error is returned, the encryption operation fails. For more information about using encryption, see the **MessageQueue.Encryption-Required** and **Message.Encryption-Algorithm** topics.
CorruptedInternal-Certificate	Message text: The internal Message Queuing certificate is corrupted.
	This error applies only to Message Queuing 1.0.
CorruptedPersonalCert-Store	Message text: The personal certificate store is corrupted.
	Message Queuing returns this error when the Microsoft Internet Explorer personal certificate store is corrupted.
CorruptedQueueWas-Deleted	Message text: The .ini file for the queue in LQS was deleted because it was corrupted.
CorruptedSecurityData	Message text: A cryptographic function has failed.
CouldNotGetAccountInfo	Message text: Could not get the account information for the user.
CouldNotGetUserSid	Message text: Could not get the SID information out of the thread token.
	For more information about sender identifiers, see the **Message** class's **SenderId** property.
DeleteConnectedNetwork-InUse	Message text: The connected network cannot be deleted; it is in use.
	Message Queuing returns this error if it cannot delete the specified connected network because the network is defined in at least one other computer. Remove the connected network from all connected network lists and try again to delete it.

Member name	Description
DependentClientLicense-Overflow	Message text: The number of dependent clients served by this Message Queuing server reached its upper limit.
DsError	Message text: Internal directory service error.
DsIsFull	Message text: Directory service is full.
	Message Queuing returns this error if the information store is full. This error applies only to Message Queuing 1.0.
DtcConnect	Message text: Cannot connect to MS DTC.
	Message Queuing returns this error if it is unable to connect to the Microsoft Distributed Transaction Coordinator.
EncryptionProviderNot-Supported	Message text: The Cryptographic Service Provider is not supported by Message Queuing.
FailVerifySignatureEx	Message text: Signature of received message is not valid.
FormatNameBufferToo-Small	This member supports the .NET Framework infrastructure and is not intended to be used directly from your code.
Generic	Message text: Generic Error.
	Message Queuing returns this error if it cannot identify a more specific source.
GuidNotMatching	Message text: Failed to create Message Queuing configuration object with a GUID that matches the computer installation. You must uninstall Message Queuing and then reinstall it.
IllegalContext	Message text: Invalid context parameter.
IllegalCriteriaColumns	This member supports the .NET Framework infrastructure and is not intended to be used directly from your code.
IllegalCursorAction	This member supports the .NET Framework infrastructure and is not intended to be used directly from your code.
IllegalEnterprise-Operation	Message text: The operation is invalid for a Message Queuing services object.
IllegalFormatName	Message text: The given format name is invalid.
	For valid format name syntax options, see the **MessageQueue** class's **FormatName** property.

Member name	Description
IllegalMessageProperties	This member supports the .NET Framework infrastructure and is not intended to be used directly from your code.
IllegalOperation	Message text: The operation is invalid on foreign message queuing systems.
IllegalPrivateProperties	This member supports the .NET Framework infrastructure and is not intended to be used directly from your code.
IllegalPropertyId	This member supports the .NET Framework infrastructure and is not intended to be used directly from your code.
IllegalPropertySize	This member supports the .NET Framework infrastructure and is not intended to be used directly from your code.
IllegalPropertyValue	Message text: Invalid property value.
IllegalPropertyVt	This member supports the .NET Framework infrastructure and is not intended to be used directly from your code.
IllegalQueuePathName	Message text: Invalid queue path name.
	See the **MessageQueue** class's **Path** property for valid path syntax options.
IllegalQueueProperties	This member supports the .NET Framework infrastructure and is not intended to be used directly from your code.
IllegalRelation	This member supports the .NET Framework infrastructure and is not intended to be used directly from your code.
IllegalRestrictionProperty Id	This member supports the .NET Framework infrastructure and is not intended to be used directly from your code.
IllegalSecurityDescriptor	This member supports the .NET Framework infrastructure and is not intended to be used directly from your code.
IllegalSort	This member supports the .NET Framework infrastructure and is not intended to be used directly from your code.
IllegalSortPropertyId	This member supports the .NET Framework infrastructure and is not intended to be used directly from your code.

Member name	Description
IllegalUser	Message text: The user has an invalid user name.
	Message Queuing returns this error if your application is connecting to it through an invalid user name.
InsufficientProperties	Message text: Not all the required properties for the operation were specified in the input parameters.
InsufficientResources	Message text: Insufficient resources to perform operation.
	Message Queuing returns this error, for example, if there is not enough memory to complete the operation. When this error is returned, the operation fails.
InvalidCertificate	Message text: The user certificate is not valid.
	Message Queuing returns this error if the security certificate specified in the **Message** class's **SenderCertificate** property is invalid, or if the certificate is not correctly placed in the Microsoft Internet Explorer personal certificate store.
InvalidHandle	This member supports the .NET Framework infrastructure and is not intended to be used directly from your code.
InvalidOwner	Message text: Invalid object owner. For example CreateQueue failed because the Queue Manager object is invalid.
	Message Queuing returns this error, for example, if your application attempts to create a queue on a computer on which Message Queuing is not installed.
InvalidParameter	This member supports the .NET Framework infrastructure and is not intended to be used directly from your code.
IOTimeout	Message text: The receive or peek message time-out has expired.
	Message Queuing returns this error if the time-out specified in a call to **MessageQueue.Receive** or **MessageQueue.Peek** expires before a new message arrives in the queue. This can only happen if there was no message already in the queue; both methods would return immediately if a message exists.
LabelBufferTooSmall	This member supports the .NET Framework infrastructure and is not intended to be used directly from your code.

Member name	Description
MachineExists	Message text: Computer with the same name already exists in the site.
MachineNotFound	Message text: The specified computer could not be found.
	Message Queuing returns this error if it cannot find the queue's computer in the directory service.
MessageAlreadyReceived	Message text: A message that is currently pointed at by the cursor has been removed from the queue by another process or by another call to receive the message without the use of this cursor.
	Message Queuing returns this error when some other cursor, application, or the system administrator has already removed the message from the queue. This error is most likely to occur when using the **MessageEnumerator** class, such as the instance returned through a call to **MessageQueue.GetMessageEnumerator** or **MessageQueue.GetEnumerator**.
MessageStorageFailed	Message text: Could not store a recoverable or journal message. Message was not sent.
	Message Queuing returns this error if the local computer cannot store a recoverable message (one whose delivery is guaranteed in the case of a network problem) or a journal message. See the **Message** class's **Recoverable** and **UseJournalQueue** properties for more information about these message sending options.
MissingConnectorType	Message text: Connector Type is mandatory when sending an Acknowledgment or secure message.
	Message Queuing returns this error when the application sets a property typically set by Message Queuing, but doesn't specify the connector to use. For more information about connector types, see the **Message** class's **ConnectorType** property.
MqisReadOnlyMode	Message text: MQIS database is in read-only mode.
MqisServerEmpty	Message text: The list of MQIS servers (in registry) is empty.
	This error applies only to Message Queuing 1.0.

Member name	Description
NoDs	Message text: No connection with this site's controller(s).
	Message Queuing returns this error if the application cannot access the directory service. If this error is returned, verify permissions for accessing the directory service.
NoEntryPointMsmqOcm	Message text: Cannot locate an entry point in the MSMQOCM.DLL library.
NoGlobalCatalogInDomain	Message text: Unable to find Global Catalog servers in the specified domain.
NoInternalUserCertificate	Message text: The internal Message Queuing certificate for the user does not exist.
	Message Queuing returns this error if no internal certificate is registered or the registered certificate is corrupted.
NoMsmqServersOnDc	Message text: Failed to find Message Queuing servers on domain controllers.
NoMsmqServersOnGlobalCatalog	Message text: Failed to find Message Queuing servers on Global Catalog domain controllers.
NoResponseFromObjectServer	Message text: No response from object owner.
	Message Queuing returns this error if there is no response from the directory service server. When this error is returned, the status of the operation is unknown.
ObjectServerNotAvailable	Message text: Object owner is not reachable.
	Message Queuing returns this error if the directory service server for the object is not available. When this error is returned, the operation fails.
OperationCanceled	Message text: The operation was canceled before it could be completed.
PrivilegeNotHeld	Message text: Client does not have the required privileges to perform the operation.
Property	This member supports the .NET Framework infrastructure and is not intended to be used directly from your code.
PropertyNotAllowed	Message text: Invalid property for the requested operation
ProviderNameBufferTooSmall	This member supports the .NET Framework infrastructure and is not intended to be used directly from your code.

Member name	Description
PublicKeyDoesNotExist	Message text: The public key for the computer does not exist.
	Message Queuing returns this error if it was able to query the directory service, but the enhanced key was not found. This error applies only to Message Queuing 2.0.
PublicKeyNotFound	Message text: Unable to find the public key for computer.
	Message Queuing returns this error, for example, if you are trying to retrieve the computer properties of a computer running Message Queuing 1.0 or if you are trying to get remote computer properties while working offline. This error applies only to Message Queuing 2.0.
QDnsPropertyNot-Supported	This member supports the .NET Framework infrastructure and is not intended to be used directly from your code.
QueueDeleted	Message text: The queue was deleted. Messages cannot be received anymore using this queue instance. The queue should be closed.
QueueExists	Message text: A queue with the same pathname is already registered.
	Message Queuing registers public queues in the directory service, and registers private queues on the local computer.
QueueNotAvailable	Message text: Error while reading from a queue residing on a remote computer.
QueueNotFound	Message text: The queue is not registered in the directory service.
	Message Queuing returns this error if it cannot find the queue. This includes public queues not registered in the directory service and Internet queues that do not exist in the Message Queuing namespace.
RemoteMachineNot-Available	Message text: The remote machine is not available.
ResultBufferTooSmall	This member supports the .NET Framework infrastructure and is not intended to be used directly from your code.
SecurityDescriptor-BufferTooSmall	This member supports the .NET Framework infrastructure and is not intended to be used directly from your code.
SenderCertificateBuffer-TooSmall	This member supports the .NET Framework infrastructure and is not intended to be used directly from your code.

Member name	Description
SenderIdBufferTooSmall	This member supports the .NET Framework infrastructure and is not intended to be used directly from your code.
ServiceNotAvailable	Message text: The Message Queues service is not available.
	Message Queuing returns this error if the application is unable to connect to the Queue Manager.
SharingViolation	Message text: Sharing violation. The queue is already opened for exclusive receive.
	Message Queuing returns this error if an application is trying to open an already opened queue that has exclusive read rights. For more information about receiving messages exclusively from a queue, see the **MessageQueue** class's **DenySharedReceive** property.
SignatureBufferTooSmall	This member supports the .NET Framework infrastructure and is not intended to be used directly from your code.
StaleHandle	This member supports the .NET Framework infrastructure and is not intended to be used directly from your code.
SymmetricKeyBuffer-TooSmall	This member supports the .NET Framework infrastructure and is not intended to be used directly from your code.
TransactionEnlist	Message text: Cannot enlist the transaction.
TransactionImport	Message text: Cannot import the transaction.
TransactionSequence	Message text: Wrong transaction operations sequence.
TransactionUsage	Message text: Wrong transaction usage.
	Message Queuing returns this error if an attempt was made to open a remote queue for read access from within a transaction, or an attempt was made to read a message from a nontransactional queue from within a transaction.
UnsupportedAccessMode	Message text: The specified access mode is not supported.
	Message Queuing returns this error if the access mode specified when opening the queue is set to an invalid value, or the access mode and the share mode specified are not compatible.

Member name	Description
UnsupportedFormat-NameOperation	Message text: The requested operation for the specified format name is not supported.
	Message Queuing returns this error when the requested operation is not supported for the specified format name. Operations include trying to open a queue to receive messages by specifying a direct format name.
UnsupportedOperation	Message text: The operation is not supported for a WORKGROUP installation computer.
UserBufferTooSmall	This member supports the .NET Framework infrastructure and is not intended to be used directly from your code.
WksCantServeClient	Message text: Message Queuing-independent clients cannot serve Message Queuing-dependent clients.
WriteNotAllowed	Message text: Another MQIS server is being installed; write operations to the database are not allowed at this time.

Example

[Visual Basic, C#, C++] The following example verifies whether a Message Queuing queue exists, and then deletes it.

[Visual Basic]
```
Imports System
Imports System.Messaging

Namespace MyProject

    '/ <summary>
    '/ Provides a container class for the example.
    '/ </summary>
    Public Class MyNewQueue

        '***************************************************
        ' Provides an entry point into the application.
        '
        ' This example verifies existence and attempts to
        ' delete a queue.
        '***************************************************

        Public Shared Sub Main()

            ' Determine whether the queue exists.
            If MessageQueue.Exists(".\myQueue") Then

                Try

                    ' Delete the queue.
                    MessageQueue.Delete(".\myQueue")

                Catch e As MessageQueueException

                    If e.MessageQueueErrorCode = _
                        MessageQueueErrorCode.AccessDenied Then

                        Console.WriteLine("Access is denied. " _
                            + "Queue might be a system queue.")
                    End If

                    ' Handle other sources of exceptions as necessary.
```

```
                End Try

            End If

            Return

        End Sub 'Main

    End Class 'MyNewQueue
End Namespace 'MyProject
```

[C#]
```
using System;
using System.Messaging;

namespace MyProject
{
    /// <summary>
    /// Provides a container class for the example.
    /// </summary>
    public class MyNewQueue
    {

        //**************************************************
        // Provides an entry point into the application.
        //
        // This example verifies existence and attempts to
        // delete a queue.
        //**************************************************

        public static void Main()
        {

            // Determine whether the queue exists.
            if (MessageQueue.Exists(".\\myQueue"))
            {
                try
                {
                    // Delete the queue.
                    MessageQueue.Delete(".\\myQueue");
                }
                catch(MessageQueueException e)
                {
                    if(e.MessageQueueErrorCode ==
                        MessageQueueErrorCode.AccessDenied)
                    {
                        Console.WriteLine("Access is denied. " +
                            "Queue might be a system queue.");
                    }

                    // Handle other sources of MessageQueueException.
                }
            }

            return;
        }
    }
}
```

[C++]
```
#using <mscorlib.dll>
#using <system.dll>
#using <system.messaging.dll>

using namespace System;
using namespace System::Messaging;

int main()
{
    // Determine whether the queue exists.
    if (MessageQueue::Exists(S".\\myQueue"))
    {
        try
```

```
    {
        // Delete the queue.
        MessageQueue::Delete(S".\\myQueue");
    }
    catch (MessageQueueException* e)
    {
        if (e->MessageQueueErrorCode ==
            MessageQueueErrorCode::AccessDenied)
        {
            Console::WriteLine(S"Access is denied. Queue          ↵
might be a system queue.");
        }
        // Handle other sources of MessageQueueException.
    }

}

    return 0;
}
```

Requirements

Namespace: System.Messaging

Platforms: Windows 98, Windows NT 4.0,
Windows Millennium Edition, Windows 2000,
Windows XP Home Edition, Windows XP Professional,
Windows .NET Server family

Assembly: System.Messaging (in System.Messaging.dll)

MessageQueueException Class

The exception that is thrown if a Microsoft Message Queuing internal error occurs.

System.Object
  System.Exception
    System.SystemException
      System.Runtime.InteropServices.ExternalException
        System.Messaging.MessageQueueException

```
[Visual Basic]
<Serializable>
Public Class MessageQueueException
   Inherits ExternalException
[C#]
[Serializable]
public class MessageQueueException : ExternalException
[C++]
[Serializable]
public __gc class MessageQueueException : public ExternalException
[JScript]
public
   Serializable
class MessageQueueException extends ExternalException
```

Thread Safety

Any public static (**Shared** in Visual Basic) members of this type are safe for multithreaded operations. Any instance members are not guaranteed to be thread safe.

Remarks

Exceptions associated with the **MessageQueueException** class are generated by internal errors within Message Queuing that should be dealt with through your code.

Every exception consists of an error code and a text string that describes the source of the error. See the **MessageQueueErrorCode** class for a list of these error codes and their descriptions.

Example

```
[Visual Basic]
Imports System
Imports System.Messaging

Namespace MyProject

    '/ <summary>
    '/ Provides a container class for the example.
    '/ </summary>
    Public Class MyNewQueue

        '****************************************************
        ' Provides an entry point into the application.
        '
        ' This example verifies existence and attempts to
        ' delete a queue.
        '****************************************************

        Public Shared Sub Main()

            ' Determine whether the queue exists.
            If MessageQueue.Exists(".\myQueue") Then

                Try
```

```
                    ' Delete the queue.
                    MessageQueue.Delete(".\myQueue")

                Catch e As MessageQueueException

                    If e.MessageQueueErrorCode = _
                        MessageQueueErrorCode.AccessDenied Then

                        Console.WriteLine("Access is denied. " _
                            + "Queue might be a system queue.")
                    End If

                    ' Handle other sources of exceptions as necessary.

                End Try

            End If

            Return

        End Sub 'Main

    End Class 'MyNewQueue
End Namespace 'MyProject
```

```
[C#]
using System;
using System.Messaging;

namespace MyProject
{
    /// <summary>
    /// Provides a container class for the example.
    /// </summary>
    public class MyNewQueue
    {

        //****************************************************
        // Provides an entry point into the application.
        //
        // This example verifies existence and attempts to
        // delete a queue.
        //****************************************************

        public static void Main()
        {
            // Determine whether the queue exists.
            if (MessageQueue.Exists(".\\myQueue"))
            {
                try
                {
                    // Delete the queue.
                    MessageQueue.Delete(".\\myQueue");
                }
                catch(MessageQueueException e)
                {
                    if(e.MessageQueueErrorCode ==
                        MessageQueueErrorCode.AccessDenied)
                    {
                        Console.WriteLine("Access is denied. " +
                            "Queue might be a system queue.");
                    }

                    // Handle other sources of MessageQueueException.
                }
            }

            return;
        }
    }
}
```

```
[C++]
#using <mscorlib.dll>
#using <system.dll>
#using <system.messaging.dll>

using namespace System;
using namespace System::Messaging;

int main()
{
    // Determine whether the queue exists.
    if (MessageQueue::Exists(S".\\myQueue"))
    {
        try
        {
            // Delete the queue.
            MessageQueue::Delete(S".\\myQueue");
        }
        catch (MessageQueueException* e)
        {
            if (e->MessageQueueErrorCode ==
                MessageQueueErrorCode::AccessDenied)
            {
                Console::WriteLine(S"Access is denied. Queue
might be a system queue.");
            }
            // Handle other sources of MessageQueueException.
        }
    }

    return 0;
}
```

Requirements

Namespace: System.Messaging

Platforms: Windows 98, Windows NT 4.0,
Windows Millennium Edition, Windows 2000,
Windows XP Home Edition, Windows XP Professional,
Windows .NET Server family

Assembly: System.Messaging (in System.Messaging.dll)

MessageQueueException Constructor

This member supports the .NET Framework infrastructure and is not
intended to be used directly from your code.

```
[Visual Basic]
Protected Sub New( _
    ByVal info As SerializationInfo, _
    ByVal context As StreamingContext _
)
[C#]
protected MessageQueueException(
    SerializationInfo info,
    StreamingContext context
);
[C++]
protected: MessageQueueException(
    SerializationInfo* info,
    StreamingContext context
);
[JScript]
protected function MessageQueueException(
    info : SerializationInfo,
    context : StreamingContext
);
```

MessageQueueException.Message Property

Gets a value that describes the Message Queuing error.

```
[Visual Basic]
Overrides Public ReadOnly Property Message As String
[C#]
public override string Message {get;}
[C++]
public: __property String* get_Message();
[JScript]
public override function get Message() : String;
```

Property Value

The description of the Message Queuing internal error that
generated this **MessageQueueException**.

Remarks

When you get this property, the method attempts to retrieve the text
string associated with the **MessageQueueErrorCode** property. If
the method is unable to interpret the error code that Message
Queuing generated, the **Message** property gets the value
"UnknownError".

Requirements

Platforms: Windows 98, Windows NT 4.0,
Windows Millennium Edition, Windows 2000,
Windows XP Home Edition, Windows XP Professional,
Windows .NET Server family

.NET Framework Security:

- Full trust for the immediate caller. This member cannot be used
  by partially trusted code.

MessageQueueException.MessageQueueError-Code Property

Gets a value that indicates the error code associated with this
exception.

```
[Visual Basic]
Public ReadOnly Property MessageQueueErrorCode As _
    MessageQueueErrorCode
[C#]
public MessageQueueErrorCode MessageQueueErrorCode {get;}
[C++]
public: __property MessageQueueErrorCode
    get_MessageQueueErrorCode();
[JScript]
public function get MessageQueueErrorCode() : MessageQueueErrorCode;
```

Property Value

A **MessageQueueErrorCode** that identifies the type of error
Message Queuing generated.

Remarks

The **Message** property contains a string associated with this
MessageQueueErrorCode that more fully describes the source of
the error.

Requirements

Platforms: Windows 98, Windows NT 4.0,
Windows Millennium Edition, Windows 2000,
Windows XP Home Edition, Windows XP Professional,
Windows .NET Server family

.NET Framework Security:
- Full trust for the immediate caller. This member cannot be used by partially trusted code.

MessageQueueException.GetObjectData Method

Populates a serialization information object with the data needed to serialize the **MessageQueueException**.

```
[Visual Basic]
Overrides Public Sub GetObjectData( _
   ByVal info As SerializationInfo, _
   ByVal context As StreamingContext _
) Implements ISerializable.GetObjectData
[C#]
public override void GetObjectData(
   SerializationInfo info,
   StreamingContext context
);
[C++]
public: void GetObjectData(
   SerializationInfo* info,
   StreamingContext context
);
[JScript]
public override function GetObjectData(
   info : SerializationInfo,
   context : StreamingContext
);
```

Parameters

info
>   A **SerializationInfo** that holds the serialized data associated with the **MessageQueueException**.

context
>   A **StreamingContext** that contains the source and destination of the serialized stream associated with the **MessageQueueException**.

Implements

ISerializable.GetObjectData

Exceptions

Exception Type	Condition
ArgumentNullException	The *info* parameter is a null reference (**Nothing** in Visual Basic).

Requirements

Platforms: Windows 98, Windows NT 4.0, Windows Millennium Edition, Windows 2000, Windows XP Home Edition, Windows XP Professional, Windows .NET Server family

.NET Framework Security:
- Full trust for the immediate caller. This member cannot be used by partially trusted code.

MessageQueueInstaller Class

Allows you to install and configure a queue that your application needs in order to run. This class is called by the installation utility, for example InstallUtil.exe, when installing a **MessageQueue**.

System.Object
  System.MarshalByRefObject
    System.ComponentModel.Component
      System.Configuration.Install.Installer
        System.Configuration.Install.ComponentInstaller
          System.Messaging.MessageQueueInstaller

```
[Visual Basic]
Public Class MessageQueueInstaller
   Inherits ComponentInstaller
[C#]
public class MessageQueueInstaller : ComponentInstaller
[C++]
public __gc class MessageQueueInstaller : public ComponentInstaller
[JScript]
public class MessageQueueInstaller extends ComponentInstaller
```

Thread Safety

Any public static (**Shared** in Visual Basic) members of this type are safe for multithreaded operations. Any instance members are not guaranteed to be thread safe.

Remarks

The **MessageQueueInstaller** is used by the installation utility to write registry values that are associated with the queue. For more information on installation utilities, see **Installer Tool (Installutil.exe)**.

To install a queue, create a project installer class that inherits from the **Installer**, and set the **RunInstallerAttribute** for the class to **true**. Within your project, create a **MessageQueueInstaller** instance for each queue in the installation and add the instance to your project installer class.

When creating a **MessageQueueInstaller** instance, you can optionally pass an existing **MessageQueue** (for example, from a test server) to the **MessageQueueInstaller** constructor. This approach automatically provides the configuration settings for the new queue by mirroring the settings of the queue passed in. Alternatively, you can manually set the properties in the **MessageQueueInstaller** instance to the states you want and call the default constructor.

When the install utility is called, it looks for the **RunInstallerAttribute**. If it is **true**, the utility installs all the queues in the **Installers** collection associated with your project installer. If **RunInstallerAttribute** is **false**, the utility ignores the project installer.

You modify other properties of a **MessageQueueInstaller** instance either before or after adding the instance to the **Installers** collection of your project installer. For example, a queue's **Path** must be set before the install utility executes.

Typically, you do not call the methods of the **MessageQueueInstaller** from within your code; they are generally called only by the installutil.exe installation utility. The utility automatically calls the **Install** method during the installation process and calls **Commit** if the installation did not throw an exception. It backs out failures, if necessary, by calling **Rollback** for the object that generated the exception.

An application's install routine uses the project installer's **Installer.Context** to automatically maintain information about the components that have already been installed. This state information is continuously updated as each **MessageQueueInstaller** instance is installed by the utility. It is not usually necessary for your code to explicitly modify the state information.

Requirements

Namespace: System.Messaging

Platforms: Windows 98, Windows NT 4.0, Windows Millennium Edition, Windows 2000, Windows XP Home Edition, Windows XP Professional, Windows .NET Server family

Assembly: System.Messaging (in System.Messaging.dll)

MessageQueueInstaller Constructor

Initializes a new instance of the **MessageQueueInstaller** class.

Overload List

Initializes a new instance of the **MessageQueueInstaller** class. Does not set any instance properties.

 [Visual Basic] **Public Sub New()**
 [C#] **public MessageQueueInstaller();**
 [C++] **public: MessageQueueInstaller();**
 [JScript] **public function MessageQueueInstaller();**

Initializes a new instance of the **MessageQueueInstaller** class, initializing the installation settings to those of an existing **MessageQueue** instance.

 [Visual Basic] **Public Sub New(MessageQueue)**
 [C#] **public MessageQueueInstaller(MessageQueue);**
 [C++] **public: MessageQueueInstaller(MessageQueue*);**
 [JScript] **public function MessageQueueInstaller(MessageQueue);**

MessageQueueInstaller Constructor ()

Initializes a new instance of the **MessageQueueInstaller** class. Does not set any instance properties.

```
[Visual Basic]
Public Sub New()
[C#]
public MessageQueueInstaller();
[C++]
public: MessageQueueInstaller();
[JScript]
public function MessageQueueInstaller();
```

Requirements

Platforms: Windows 98, Windows NT 4.0, Windows Millennium Edition, Windows 2000, Windows XP Home Edition, Windows XP Professional, Windows .NET Server family

.NET Framework Security:
- Full trust for the immediate caller. This member cannot be used by partially trusted code.

MessageQueueInstaller Constructor (MessageQueue)

Initializes a new instance of the **MessageQueueInstaller** class, initializing the installation settings to those of an existing **MessageQueue** instance.

```
[Visual Basic]
Public Sub New( _
    ByVal componentToCopy As MessageQueue _
)
[C#]
public MessageQueueInstaller(
    MessageQueue componentToCopy
);
[C++]
public: MessageQueueInstaller(
    MessageQueue* componentToCopy
);
[JScript]
public function MessageQueueInstaller(
    componentToCopy : MessageQueue
);
```

Parameters

componentToCopy

> The **MessageQueue** component whose settings determine the property settings of the new queue installed.

Remarks

Requirements

Platforms: Windows 98, Windows NT 4.0, Windows Millennium Edition, Windows 2000, Windows XP Home Edition, Windows XP Professional, Windows .NET Server family

.NET Framework Security:

- Full trust for the immediate caller. This member cannot be used by partially trusted code.

MessageQueueInstaller.Authenticate Property

Gets or sets a value indicating whether the queue to be installed accepts only authenticated messages.

```
[Visual Basic]
Public Property Authenticate As Boolean
[C#]
public bool Authenticate {get; set;}
[C++]
public: __property bool get_Authenticate();
public: __property void set_Authenticate(bool);
[JScript]
public function get Authenticate() : Boolean;
public function set Authenticate(Boolean);
```

Property Value

true if the queue accepts only authenticated messages; otherwise, **false**. The default is **false**.

Remarks

When a nonauthenticated message is sent to a queue that accepts only authenticated messages, the message is rejected. The sending application can request notification of a message rejection by setting the **AcknowledgeType** for the message. Otherwise, there is no indication that the message was rejected, so the message can be lost unless you send it to the dead-letter queue.

Requirements

Platforms: Windows 98, Windows NT 4.0, Windows Millennium Edition, Windows 2000, Windows XP Home Edition, Windows XP Professional, Windows .NET Server family

.NET Framework Security:

- Full trust for the immediate caller. This member cannot be used by partially trusted code.

MessageQueueInstaller.BasePriority Property

Gets or sets the base priority that is used to route a public queue's messages over the network.

```
[Visual Basic]
Public Property BasePriority As Short
[C#]
public short BasePriority {get; set;}
[C++]
public: __property short get_BasePriority();
public: __property void set_BasePriority(short);
[JScript]
public function get BasePriority() : Int16;
public function set BasePriority(Int16);
```

Property Value

The single base priority for all messages sent to the public queue. The default is zero (0).

Remarks

The **BasePriority** is used for routing the queue's messages over the network. Use the **BasePriority** to give the messages sent to the queue a higher or lower priority than that for messages sent to other queues. When a queue's base priority is set, all the messages sent to it are given a higher priority than that of the messages sent to queues with a lower base priority. The queue's base priority has no effect on the order of the messages in the queue or on how messages are read from the queue.

The **BasePriority** applies only to public queues that are accessed through the domain controller (in other words, using the public format name). The base priority of private queues and of directly-accessed public queues is always zero.

Requirements

Platforms: Windows 98, Windows NT 4.0, Windows Millennium Edition, Windows 2000, Windows XP Home Edition, Windows XP Professional, Windows .NET Server family

.NET Framework Security:

- Full trust for the immediate caller. This member cannot be used by partially trusted code.

MessageQueueInstaller.Category Property

Gets or sets an implementation-specific queue type.

```
[Visual Basic]
Public Property Category As Guid
[C#]
public Guid Category {get; set;}
```

```
[C++]
public: __property Guid get_Category();
public: __property void set_Category(Guid);
[JScript]
public function get Category() : Guid;
public function set Category(Guid);
```

Property Value

A **Guid** that represents the queue category (or Message Queuing type identifier), which allows applications to categorize their queues according to how they are used. The default is **Guid.empty**.

Remarks

The queue category enables an application to categorize associated queues according to the way they are used. The **Category** can be a null reference. You can also define a new category.

The **Category** property provides access to the Message Queuing type identifier property, which is associated with a particular queue and is read/write. You can use the **NewGuid** method to create a category value that is guaranteed to be unique across all **Guid** values. However, it is necessary only for the category value to be distinct from other categories, not from all other **Guid** values. For example, you can set the **Category** for one group of queues to {00000000-0000-0000-0000-000000000001} and the **Category** for another group to {00000000-0000-0000-0000-000000000002}.

Requirements

Platforms: Windows 98, Windows NT 4.0, Windows Millennium Edition, Windows 2000, Windows XP Home Edition, Windows XP Professional, Windows .NET Server family

.NET Framework Security:

- Full trust for the immediate caller. This member cannot be used by partially trusted code.

MessageQueueInstaller.EncryptionRequired Property

Gets or sets a value indicating whether the queue accepts only private, or encrypted, messages.

```
[Visual Basic]
Public Property EncryptionRequired As EncryptionRequired
[C#]
public EncryptionRequired EncryptionRequired {get; set;}
[C++]
public: __property EncryptionRequired get_EncryptionRequired();
public: __property void set_EncryptionRequired(EncryptionRequired);
[JScript]
public function get EncryptionRequired() : EncryptionRequired;
public function set EncryptionRequired(EncryptionRequired);
```

Property Value

One of the **EncryptionRequired** values that indicates the encryption level required on messages sent to the queue. The default is **Optional**.

Remarks

When encryption is specified, only the **Body** of a message is encrypted. Other properties, such as the **Label**, are not encrypted.

Requirements

Platforms: Windows 98, Windows NT 4.0, Windows Millennium Edition, Windows 2000, Windows XP Home Edition, Windows XP Professional, Windows .NET Server family

.NET Framework Security:

- Full trust for the immediate caller. This member cannot be used by partially trusted code.

MessageQueueInstaller.Label Property

Gets or sets a description of the queue.

```
[Visual Basic]
Public Property Label As String
[C#]
public string Label {get; set;}
[C++]
public: __property String* get_Label();
public: __property void set_Label(String*);
[JScript]
public function get Label() : String;
public function set Label(String);
```

Property Value

The label that describes the message queue. The default is an empty string ("").

Exceptions

Exception Type	Condition
ArgumentException	The **Label** is a null reference (**Nothing** in Visual Basic).

Remarks

The **Label** property does not need to be unique across queues.

Requirements

Platforms: Windows 98, Windows NT 4.0, Windows Millennium Edition, Windows 2000, Windows XP Home Edition, Windows XP Professional, Windows .NET Server family

.NET Framework Security:

- Full trust for the immediate caller. This member cannot be used by partially trusted code.

MessageQueueInstaller.MaximumJournalSize Property

Gets or sets the maximum size of the journal that is associated with the queue.

```
[Visual Basic]
Public Property MaximumJournalSize As Long
[C#]
public long MaximumJournalSize {get; set;}
[C++]
public: __property __int64 get_MaximumJournalSize();
public: __property void set_MaximumJournalSize(__int64);
[JScript]
public function get MaximumJournalSize() : long;
public function set MaximumJournalSize(long);
```

Property Value

The maximum size, in kilobytes, of the journal queue, which records messages that are removed from the queue. The Message Queuing default is no limit.

Remarks

When a queue is created, Message Queuing automatically creates a queue journal in the same location as the new queue. The queue journal is used to track the messages that are removed from the queue.

> **Note** Two types of messages remain untracked: those that are removed from the queue because their time-to-be-received timer expired, and those that are purged from the queue.

Applications cannot send messages to the journal queue. However, you must periodically clear the queue to remove the messages that are no longer needed. Messages that are stored in journal queues count toward the quota for the computer where the queues reside. (The computer quota is set by the administrator.)

Requirements

Platforms: Windows 98, Windows NT 4.0, Windows Millennium Edition, Windows 2000, Windows XP Home Edition, Windows XP Professional, Windows .NET Server family

.NET Framework Security:

- Full trust for the immediate caller. This member cannot be used by partially trusted code.

MessageQueueInstaller.MaximumQueueSize Property

Gets or sets the maximum size of the queue.

```
[Visual Basic]
Public Property MaximumQueueSize As Long
[C#]
public long MaximumQueueSize {get; set;}
[C++]
public: __property __int64 get_MaximumQueueSize();
public: __property void set_MaximumQueueSize(__int64);
[JScript]
public function get MaximumQueueSize() : long;
public function set MaximumQueueSize(long);
```

Property Value

The maximum size, in kilobytes, of the queue. The Message Queuing default is no limit.

Remarks

The maximum queue size is typically set at the time of queue creation, although it can be reset later.

Requirements

Platforms: Windows 98, Windows NT 4.0, Windows Millennium Edition, Windows 2000, Windows XP Home Edition, Windows XP Professional, Windows .NET Server family

.NET Framework Security:

- Full trust for the immediate caller. This member cannot be used by partially trusted code.

MessageQueueInstaller.Path Property

Gets or sets the location of the queue that is referenced by this object.

```
[Visual Basic]
Public Property Path As String
[C#]
public string Path {get; set;}
[C++]
public: __property String* get_Path();
public: __property void set_Path(String*);
[JScript]
public function get Path() : String;
public function set Path(String);
```

Property Value

The path that represents the location of the queue in the network.

Exceptions

Exception Type	Condition
ArgumentException	The **Path** was set to an invalid value, possibly because the syntax is invalid. -or- The **Path** is a null reference (**Nothing** in Visual Basic).

Remarks

The syntax for the **Path** property depends on the type of queue it references. The following table shows the syntax you should use for queues of various types.

Queue type	Syntax
Public queue	*machineName*\ *queueName*
Private queue	*machineName*\Private$\ *queueName*
Journal queue	*machineName*\ *queueName*\Journal$
Machine journal queue	*machineName*\Journal$
Machine deadletter queue	*machineName*\Deadletter$
Machine transactional deadletter queue	*machineName*\XactDeadletter$

Use "." for the local computer.

You can also use the **FormatName** or **Label** of a Message Queuing application object to describe the queue path. The following table shows the proper syntax for each type of reference.

Reference	Syntax
Format name	FormatName:[*format name*]
Label	Label:[*label*]

If you are working offline, you must use the format name to define the queue **Path**. If you do not, the application will throw an exception, because the primary domain controller is unavailable to resolve the **Path** into the **FormatName**.

Requirements

Platforms: Windows 98, Windows NT 4.0, Windows Millennium Edition, Windows 2000, Windows XP Home Edition, Windows XP Professional, Windows .NET Server family

.NET Framework Security:

- Full trust for the immediate caller. This member cannot be used by partially trusted code.

MessageQueueInstaller.Permissions Property

Gets or sets permissions associated with the queue.

```
[Visual Basic]
Public Property Permissions As AccessControlList
[C#]
public AccessControlList Permissions {get; set;}
[C++]
public: __property AccessControlList* get_Permissions();
public: __property void set_Permissions(AccessControlList*);
[JScript]
public function get Permissions() : AccessControlList;
public function set Permissions(AccessControlList);
```

Property Value

An **AccessControlList** that contains one or more access control entries that specify the trustees and permissions to grant for the queue.

Remarks

By default, the creator of a public or private queue has full control, and the domain group Everyone has permission to get queue properties, get permissions, and write to the queue. Message Queuing accesses each permission list entry in turn until it finds one that applies to the current user and the current attempted action. As with the operating system permissions, the rights that you specifically deny to a user take precedence over those you allow.

When you construct the **Permissions** property, add **AccessControlEntry** instances to your **AccessControlList** collection. When you construct each access control entry, you can specify generic or standard access rights. The rights to a queue can be any combination of the following:

- Delete
- Read Security
- Write Security
- Synchronize
- Modify Owner
- Read
- Write
- Execute
- Required
- All
- None

These rights are a set of bit flags that you can combine using the bitwise OR.

- Full Control
- Delete Message
- Receive Message
- Peek Message
- Receive Journal Message
- Get Queue Properties
- Set Queue Properties
- Get Permissions
- Set Permissions
- Take Queue Ownership
- Write Message

Requirements

Platforms: Windows 98, Windows NT 4.0, Windows Millennium Edition, Windows 2000, Windows XP Home Edition, Windows XP Professional, Windows .NET Server family

.NET Framework Security:

- Full trust for the immediate caller. This member cannot be used by partially trusted code.

MessageQueueInstaller.Transactional Property

Gets or sets a value indicating whether the queue accepts only messages sent as part of a transaction.

```
[Visual Basic]
Public Property Transactional As Boolean
[C#]
public bool Transactional {get; set;}
[C++]
public: __property bool get_Transactional();
public: __property void set_Transactional(bool);
[JScript]
public function get Transactional() : Boolean;
public function set Transactional(Boolean);
```

Property Value

true if the queue can only accept messages sent as part of a transaction; otherwise, **false**. The default is **false**.

Remarks

Messages can be retrieved from a local transaction queue with or without using a transaction. If you do not specify a transaction context, Message Queuing creates a single internal transaction for you.

Requirements

Platforms: Windows 98, Windows NT 4.0, Windows Millennium Edition, Windows 2000, Windows XP Home Edition, Windows XP Professional, Windows .NET Server family

.NET Framework Security:

- Full trust for the immediate caller. This member cannot be used by partially trusted code.

MessageQueueInstaller.UninstallAction Property

Gets or sets a value indicating what the installer does with the queue at uninstall time: remove it, restore it to its pre-installation state, or leave it in its current installed state.

```
[Visual Basic]
Public Property UninstallAction As UninstallAction
[C#]
public UninstallAction UninstallAction {get; set;}
[C++]
public: __property UninstallAction get_UninstallAction();
public: __property void set_UninstallAction(UninstallAction);
[JScript]
public function get UninstallAction() : UninstallAction;
public function set UninstallAction(UninstallAction);
```

Property Value

One of the **UninstallAction** values that indicates what state to leave the queue in when the **MessageQueue** is uninstalled. The default is **Remove**.

Remarks

When you install a queue, you can optionally use an existing queue. If you do so, you must decide whether the queue should return to its pre-installation state, or remain in its current, post-installation state. If you elect to return the queue to its pre-installation state, messages that were deleted from the queue at install time are not restored. You can reset only queue properties that are associated with the **MessageQueueInstaller** to their pre-installation values.

Requirements

Platforms: Windows 98, Windows NT 4.0, Windows Millennium Edition, Windows 2000, Windows XP Home Edition, Windows XP Professional, Windows .NET Server family

.NET Framework Security:
- Full trust for the immediate caller. This member cannot be used by partially trusted code.

MessageQueueInstaller.UseJournalQueue Property

Gets or sets a value indicating whether messages that are retrieved from the queue are also copied to the associated journal queue.

```
[Visual Basic]
Public Property UseJournalQueue As Boolean
[C#]
public bool UseJournalQueue {get; set;}
[C++]
public: __property bool get_UseJournalQueue();
public: __property void set_UseJournalQueue(bool);
[JScript]
public function get UseJournalQueue() : Boolean;
public function set UseJournalQueue(Boolean);
```

Property Value

true to copy messages that are retrieved from the queue to the journal queue; otherwise, **false**. The default is **false**.

Remarks

A journal queue lets you keep track of messages even after they have been retrieved from the queue. However, two types of messages remain untracked: those that are removed from the queue when their time-to-be-received timer expires, and those that are purged from the queue.

A journal queue should be cleared periodically to remove messages that are no longer needed. Messages stored in the journal queue count toward the quota for the computer on which the journal is located.

Requirements

Platforms: Windows 98, Windows NT 4.0, Windows Millennium Edition, Windows 2000, Windows XP Home Edition, Windows XP Professional, Windows .NET Server family

.NET Framework Security:
- Full trust for the immediate caller. This member cannot be used by partially trusted code.

MessageQueueInstaller.Commit Method

Completes the installation process by committing the **MessageQueue** installation information that the **Install** method wrote to the registry. This method is meant to be used by installation tools, which automatically call the appropriate methods.

```
[Visual Basic]
Overrides Public Sub Commit( _
   ByVal savedState As IDictionary _
)
[C#]
public override void Commit(
   IDictionary savedState
);
[C++]
public: void Commit(
   IDictionary* savedState
);
[JScript]
public override function Commit(
   savedState : IDictionary
);
```

Parameters

savedState
> An **IDictionary** that contains the post-installation state of the computer.

Remarks

Typically, you do not call the methods of the **MessageQueueInstaller** from within your code; they are generally called only by the installutil.exe installation utility. The utility automatically calls the **Install** method during the installation process. Installation is transactional, so if there is a failure of any installation project component during the installation, all the previously-installed components are rolled back to their pre-installation states. This is accomplished by calling each component's **Rollback** method.

After a successful installation of all the components that are associated with the installation project has occurred, the installation utility commits the installations. **Commit** completes the installation of the **MessageQueue** by setting the queue to the appropriate initial state. If the queue specified by the **Path** property already exists and contains messages, **Commit** clears the messages. **Commit**, rather than **Install**, clears the messages because the act of purging the messages cannot be rolled back.

An application's install routine uses the project installer's **Installer.Context** to automatically maintain information about the components that have already been installed. This state information, which is passed to **Commit** as the *savedState* parameter, is continuously updated as the utility commits each **MessageQueueInstaller** instance. Usually, it is not necessary for your code to explicitly modify this state information. When the queue has been cleared, **Commit** posts a log entry to the *savedState* that is associated with the installation.

Requirements

Platforms: Windows 98, Windows NT 4.0, Windows Millennium Edition, Windows 2000, Windows XP Home Edition, Windows XP Professional, Windows .NET Server family

.NET Framework Security:
- Full trust for the immediate caller. This member cannot be used by partially trusted code.

MessageQueueInstaller.CopyFromComponent Method

Copies the property values of a **MessageQueue** component that are required at install time for a message queue.

```
[Visual Basic]
Overrides Public Sub CopyFromComponent( _
   ByVal component As IComponent _
)
[C#]
public override void CopyFromComponent(
   IComponent component
);
[C++]
public: void CopyFromComponent(
   IComponent* component
);
[JScript]
public override function CopyFromComponent(
   component : IComponent
);
```

Parameters

component
   An **IComponent** to use as a template for the **MessageQueueInstaller**.

Exceptions

Exception Type	Condition
ArgumentException	The component associated with this **MessageQueueInstaller** is not a **MessageQueue**.

Remarks

Typically, you do not call the methods of the **MessageQueueInstaller** from within your code; they are generally called only by the installutil.exe installation utility. **CopyFromComponent** is used by the installation utility to set the property values for the **MessageQueueInstaller** to the values of an existing **MessageQueue**.

If the **Path** of the **MessageQueue** that is passed in is an empty string (""), you must set the **Path** property to a nonempty value before the installer executes.

Requirements

Platforms: Windows 98, Windows NT 4.0, Windows Millennium Edition, Windows 2000, Windows XP Home Edition, Windows XP Professional, Windows .NET Server family

.NET Framework Security:
- Full trust for the immediate caller. This member cannot be used by partially trusted code.

MessageQueueInstaller.Install Method

Performs the installation and writes message queue information to the registry. This method is meant to be used by installation tools, which automatically call the appropriate methods.

```
[Visual Basic]
Overrides Public Sub Install( _
   ByVal stateSaver As IDictionary _
)
[C#]
public override void Install(
   IDictionary stateSaver
);
[C++]
public: void Install(
   IDictionary* stateSaver
);
[JScript]
public override function Install(
   stateSaver : IDictionary
);
```

Parameters

stateSaver
   An **IDictionary** used to save information needed to perform a commit, rollback, or uninstall operation.

Remarks

The **Install** method writes message queue information to the registry, and associates the **MessageQueue** instance with a queue that is located at the path specified by the **Path** property. If the queue does not already exist, **Install** creates a transactional queue. **Install** sets the new or existing queue properties to those that you have specified in the **MessageQueueInstaller**. If the queue already exists, its properties are reset to those of the **MessageQueueInstaller**. If the existing queue is not transactional, it is deleted and then recreated as a transactional queue.

> **CAUTION** If it is necessary to recreate the queue, messages in the queue will be lost.

Typically, you do not call the methods of the **MessageQueueInstaller** from within your code; they are generally called only by the installutil.exe installation utility. The utility automatically calls the **Install** method during the installation process to write registry information that is associated with the MessageQueue being installed. Installation is transactional, so if there is a failure of any installation project component during the installation, all the previously-installed components are rolled back to their pre-installation states. This is accomplished by calling each component's **Rollback** method.

After a successful installation of all the components that are associated with the installation project has occurred, the installation utility commits the installations. **Commit** completes the installation of the **MessageQueue** by setting the queue to the appropriate initial state. If the queue specified by the **Path** property already exists and contains messages, **Commit** clears the messages. **Commit**, rather than **Install**, clears the messages because the act of purging the messages cannot be rolled back.

An application's install routine uses the project installer's **Installer.Context** to automatically maintain information about the components that have already been installed. This state information, which is passed to **Install** as the *stateSaver* parameter, is continuously updated as the utility installs each **MessageQueueInstaller** instance. Usually, it is not necessary for your code to explicitly modify this state information.

Requirements

Platforms: Windows 98, Windows NT 4.0, Windows Millennium Edition, Windows 2000, Windows XP Home Edition, Windows XP Professional, Windows .NET Server family

.NET Framework Security:
- Full trust for the immediate caller. This member cannot be used by partially trusted code.

MessageQueueInstaller.IsEquivalentInstaller Method

Determines whether the specified installer can handle the same kind of installation as this installer.

```
[Visual Basic]
Overrides Public Function IsEquivalentInstaller( _
    ByVal otherInstaller As ComponentInstaller _
) As Boolean
[C#]
public override bool IsEquivalentInstaller(
    ComponentInstaller otherInstaller
);
[C++]
public: bool IsEquivalentInstaller(
    ComponentInstaller* otherInstaller
);
[JScript]
public override function IsEquivalentInstaller(
    otherInstaller : ComponentInstaller
) : Boolean;
```

Parameters
otherInstaller
> The installer to compare.

Return Value

true if this installer and the installer specified by the *otherInstaller* parameter can handle the same kind of installation; otherwise, **false**.

Remarks

Typically, **IsEquivalentInstaller** returns **true** only if this installer and the installer specified by the *otherInstaller* parameter are of the same type.

Requirements

Platforms: Windows 98, Windows NT 4.0, Windows Millennium Edition, Windows 2000, Windows XP Home Edition, Windows XP Professional, Windows .NET Server family

.NET Framework Security:
- Full trust for the immediate caller. This member cannot be used by partially trusted code.

MessageQueueInstaller.Rollback Method

Restores the computer to the state it was in before the installation, by rolling back the queue information that the installation procedure wrote to the registry. This method is meant to be used by installation tools, which automatically call the appropriate methods.

```
[Visual Basic]
Overrides Public Sub Rollback( _
    ByVal savedState As IDictionary _
)
[C#]
public override void Rollback(
    IDictionary savedState
);
[C++]
public: void Rollback(
    IDictionary* savedState
);
[JScript]
public override function Rollback(
    savedState : IDictionary
);
```

Parameters
savedState
> An **IDictionary** that contains the pre-installation state of the computer.

Remarks

The **Rollback** method undoes the effects of the **Install** method. **Rollback** is called if the installation of any component in the installation project fails. The **Install** method creates or sets the properties for a queue. **Rollback** either deletes the queue or resets the properties of a pre-existing queue to their pre-installation values.

Typically, you do not call the methods of the **MessageQueueInstaller** from within your code; they are generally called only by the InstallUtil.exe installation utility. The utility automatically calls the **Rollback** method after an installation failure to undo any changes that the installation process has already made.

An application's install routine uses the project installer's **Installer.Context** to automatically maintain information about the components that have already been installed. This state information, which is passed to **Rollback** as the *savedState* parameter, is continuously updated as the utility rolls back each **MessageQueueInstaller** instance. Usually, it is not necessary for your code to explicitly modify this state information.

Requirements

Platforms: Windows 98, Windows NT 4.0, Windows Millennium Edition, Windows 2000, Windows XP Home Edition, Windows XP Professional, Windows .NET Server family

.NET Framework Security:
- Full trust for the immediate caller. This member cannot be used by partially trusted code.

MessageQueueInstaller.Uninstall Method

Removes an installation by removing queue information from the registry. This method is meant to be used by uninstallation tools, which automatically call the appropriate methods.

```
[Visual Basic]
Overrides Public Sub Uninstall( _
    ByVal savedState As IDictionary _
)
```

```
[C#]
public override void Uninstall(
   IDictionary savedState
);
[C++]
public: void Uninstall(
   IDictionary* savedState
);
[JScript]
public override function Uninstall(
   savedState : IDictionary
);
```

Parameters

savedState

> An **IDictionary** that contains the post-installation state of the computer.

Remarks

If the **UninstallAction** is **Remove**, **Uninstall** also deletes the queue associated with the **MessageQueue**.

Typically, you do not call the methods of the **MessageQueueInstaller** from within your code; they are generally called only by the InstallUtil.exe installation utility (in uninstall mode). The utility automatically calls the **Uninstall** method to restore the parts of the system that were affected by the installation to their pre-installation states. This includes deleting registry information that is associated with the MessageQueue being uninstalled.

An application's uninstall routine uses the project installer's **Installer.Context** to automatically maintain information about the components that have already been uninstalled. This state information, which is passed to **Uninstall** as the *savedState* parameter, is continuously updated as the utility uninstalls each **MessageQueueInstaller** instance. Usually, it is not necessary for your code to explicitly modify this state information.

Requirements

Platforms: Windows 98, Windows NT 4.0, Windows Millennium Edition, Windows 2000, Windows XP Home Edition, Windows XP Professional, Windows .NET Server family

.NET Framework Security:

- Full trust for the immediate caller. This member cannot be used by partially trusted code.

MessageQueuePermission Class

Allows control of code access permissions for messaging.

System.Object
  System.Security.CodeAccessPermission
    System.Messaging.MessageQueuePermission

```
[Visual Basic]
<Serializable>
NotInheritable Public Class MessageQueuePermission
    Inherits CodeAccessPermission
    Implements IUnrestrictedPermission
[C#]
[Serializable]
public sealed class MessageQueuePermission : CodeAccessPermission,
    IUnrestrictedPermission
[C++]
[Serializable]
public __gc __sealed class MessageQueuePermission : public
    CodeAccessPermission, IUnrestrictedPermission
[JScript]
public
    Serializable
class MessageQueuePermission extends CodeAccessPermission
    implements IUnrestrictedPermission
```

Thread Safety

Any public static (**Shared** in Visual Basic) members of this type are safe for multithreaded operations. Any instance members are not guaranteed to be thread safe.

Requirements

Namespace: System.Messaging

Platforms: Windows 98, Windows NT 4.0, Windows Millennium Edition, Windows 2000, Windows XP Home Edition, Windows XP Professional, Windows .NET Server family

Assembly: System.Messaging (in System.Messaging.dll)

MessageQueuePermission Constructor

Initializes a new instance of the **MessageQueuePermission** class.

Overload List

Initializes a new instance of the **MessageQueuePermission** class.

  [Visual Basic] **Public Sub New()**

  [C#] **public MessageQueuePermission();**

  [C++] **public: MessageQueuePermission();**

  [JScript] **public function MessageQueuePermission();**

Initializes a new instance of the **MessageQueuePermission** class with the specified permission access level entries.

  [Visual Basic] **Public Sub New(MessageQueuePermissionEntry())**

  [C#] **public MessageQueuePermission (MessageQueuePermissionEntry[]);**

  [C++] **public: MessageQueuePermission (MessageQueuePermissionEntry*[]);**

  [JScript] **public function MessageQueuePermission (MessageQueuePermissionEntry[]);**

Initializes a new instance of the **MessageQueuePermission** class with the specified permission state.

  [Visual Basic] **Public Sub New(PermissionState)**

  [C#] **public MessageQueuePermission(PermissionState);**

  [C++] **public: MessageQueuePermission(PermissionState);**

  [JScript] **public function MessageQueuePermission(PermissionState);**

Initializes a new instance of the **MessageQueuePermission** class with the specified access levels and the path of the queue.

  [Visual Basic] **Public Sub New(MessageQueuePermissionAccess, String)**

  [C#] **public MessageQueuePermission (MessageQueuePermissionAccess, string);**

  [C++] **public: MessageQueuePermission (MessageQueuePermissionAccess, String*);**

  [JScript] **public function MessageQueuePermission (MessageQueuePermissionAccess, String);**

Initializes a new instance of the **MessageQueuePermission** class with the specified access levels, computer to use, queue description, and queue category.

  [Visual Basic] **Public Sub New(MessageQueuePermissionAccess, String, String, String)**

  [C#] **public MessageQueuePermission (MessageQueuePermissionAccess, string, string, string);**

  [C++] **public: MessageQueuePermission (MessageQueuePermissionAccess, String*, String*, String*);**

  [JScript] **public function MessageQueuePermission (MessageQueuePermissionAccess, String, String, String);**

MessageQueuePermission Constructor ()

Initializes a new instance of the **MessageQueuePermission** class.

```
[Visual Basic]
Public Sub New()
[C#]
public MessageQueuePermission();
[C++]
public: MessageQueuePermission();
[JScript]
public function MessageQueuePermission();
```

Requirements

Platforms: Windows 98, Windows NT 4.0, Windows Millennium Edition, Windows 2000, Windows XP Home Edition, Windows XP Professional, Windows .NET Server family

.NET Framework Security:

- Full trust for the immediate caller. This member cannot be used by partially trusted code.

MessageQueuePermission Constructor (MessageQueuePermissionEntry[ ])

Initializes a new instance of the **MessageQueuePermission** class with the specified permission access level entries.

```
[Visual Basic]
Public Sub New( _
    ByVal permissionAccessEntries() As MessageQueuePermissionEntry _
)
[C#]
public MessageQueuePermission(
    MessageQueuePermissionEntry[] permissionAccessEntries
);
[C++]
public: MessageQueuePermission(
    MessageQueuePermissionEntry* permissionAccessEntries[]
);
[JScript]
public function MessageQueuePermission(
    permissionAccessEntries : MessageQueuePermissionEntry[]
);
```

Parameters

permissionAccessEntries

An array of **MessageQueuePermissionEntry** objects. The **PermissionEntries** property is set to this value.

Requirements

Platforms: Windows 98, Windows NT 4.0, Windows Millennium Edition, Windows 2000, Windows XP Home Edition, Windows XP Professional, Windows .NET Server family

.NET Framework Security:

- Full trust for the immediate caller. This member cannot be used by partially trusted code.

MessageQueuePermission Constructor (PermissionState)

Initializes a new instance of the **MessageQueuePermission** class with the specified permission state.

```
[Visual Basic]
Public Sub New( _
    ByVal state As PermissionState _
)
[C#]
public MessageQueuePermission(
    PermissionState state
);
[C++]
public: MessageQueuePermission(
    PermissionState state
);
[JScript]
public function MessageQueuePermission(
    state : PermissionState
);
```

Parameters

state

One of the **PermissionState** values.

Requirements

Platforms: Windows 98, Windows NT 4.0, Windows Millennium Edition, Windows 2000, Windows XP Home Edition, Windows XP Professional, Windows .NET Server family

.NET Framework Security:

- Full trust for the immediate caller. This member cannot be used by partially trusted code.

MessageQueuePermission Constructor (MessageQueuePermissionAccess, String)

Initializes a new instance of the **MessageQueuePermission** class with the specified access levels and the path of the queue.

```
[Visual Basic]
Public Sub New( _
    ByVal permissionAccess As MessageQueuePermissionAccess, _
    ByVal path As String _
)
[C#]
public MessageQueuePermission(
    MessageQueuePermissionAccess permissionAccess,
    string path
);
[C++]
public: MessageQueuePermission(
    MessageQueuePermissionAccess permissionAccess,
    String* path
);
[JScript]
public function MessageQueuePermission(
    permissionAccess : MessageQueuePermissionAccess,
    path : String
);
```

Parameters

permissionAccess

One of the **MessageQueuePermissionAccess** values.

path

The path of the queue that is referenced by the **MessageQueue**.

Requirements

Platforms: Windows 98, Windows NT 4.0, Windows Millennium Edition, Windows 2000, Windows XP Home Edition, Windows XP Professional, Windows .NET Server family

.NET Framework Security:

- Full trust for the immediate caller. This member cannot be used by partially trusted code.

MessageQueuePermission Constructor (MessageQueuePermissionAccess, String, String, String)

Initializes a new instance of the **MessageQueuePermission** class with the specified access levels, computer to use, queue description, and queue category.

```
[Visual Basic]
Public Sub New( _
   ByVal permissionAccess As MessageQueuePermissionAccess, _
   ByVal machineName As String, _
   ByVal label As String, _
   ByVal category As String _
)
[C#]
public MessageQueuePermission(
   MessageQueuePermissionAccess permissionAccess,
   string machineName,
   string label,
   string category
);
[C++]
public: MessageQueuePermission(
   MessageQueuePermissionAccess permissionAccess,
   String* machineName,
   String* label,
   String* category
);
[JScript]
public function MessageQueuePermission(
   permissionAccess : MessageQueuePermissionAccess,
   machineName : String,
   label : String,
   category : String
);
```

Parameters

permissionAccess
> One of the **MessageQueuePermissionAccess** values.

machineName
> The name of the computer where the Message Queuing queue is located.

label
> The queue description.

category
> The queue category (Message Queuing type identifier).

Requirements

Platforms: Windows 98, Windows NT 4.0,
Windows Millennium Edition, Windows 2000,
Windows XP Home Edition, Windows XP Professional,
Windows .NET Server family

.NET Framework Security:

- Full trust for the immediate caller. This member cannot be used by partially trusted code.

MessageQueuePermission.PermissionEntries Property

Gets the collection of permission entries for this permissions request.

```
[Visual Basic]
Public ReadOnly Property PermissionEntries As _
   MessageQueuePermissionEntryCollection
[C#]
public MessageQueuePermissionEntryCollection PermissionEntries
   {get;}
```

```
[C++]
public: __property MessageQueuePermissionEntryCollection*
   get_PermissionEntries();
[JScript]
public function get PermissionEntries() :
   MessageQueuePermissionEntryCollection;
```

Property Value

A **MessageQueuePermissionEntryCollection** that contains the permission entries for this permissions request.

Requirements

Platforms: Windows 98, Windows NT 4.0,
Windows Millennium Edition, Windows 2000,
Windows XP Home Edition, Windows XP Professional,
Windows .NET Server family

.NET Framework Security:

- Full trust for the immediate caller. This member cannot be used by partially trusted code.

MessageQueuePermission.Copy Method

This member overrides **CodeAccessPermission.Copy**.

```
[Visual Basic]
Overrides Public Function Copy() As IPermission Implements _
   IPermission.Copy
[C#]
public override IPermission Copy();
[C++]
public: IPermission* Copy();
[JScript]
public override function Copy() : IPermission;
```

Requirements

Platforms: Windows 98, Windows NT 4.0,
Windows Millennium Edition, Windows 2000,
Windows XP Home Edition, Windows XP Professional,
Windows .NET Server family

.NET Framework Security:

- Full trust for the immediate caller. This member cannot be used by partially trusted code.

MessageQueuePermission.FromXml Method

This member overrides **CodeAccessPermission.FromXml**.

```
[Visual Basic]
Overrides Public Sub FromXml( _
   ByVal securityElement As SecurityElement _
) Implements ISecurityEncodable.FromXml
[C#]
public override void FromXml(
   SecurityElement securityElement
);
[C++]
public: void FromXml(
   SecurityElement* securityElement
);
[JScript]
public override function FromXml(
   securityElement : SecurityElement
);
```

Requirements

Platforms: Windows 98, Windows NT 4.0, Windows Millennium Edition, Windows 2000, Windows XP Home Edition, Windows XP Professional, Windows .NET Server family

.NET Framework Security:

- Full trust for the immediate caller. This member cannot be used by partially trusted code.

MessageQueuePermission.Intersect Method

This member overrides **CodeAccessPermission.Intersect**.

```
[Visual Basic]
Overrides Public Function Intersect( _
   ByVal target As IPermission _
) As IPermission Implements IPermission.Intersect
[C#]
public override IPermission Intersect(
   IPermission target
);
[C++]
public: IPermission* Intersect(
   IPermission* target
);
[JScript]
public override function Intersect(
   target : IPermission
) : IPermission;
```

Requirements

Platforms: Windows 98, Windows NT 4.0, Windows Millennium Edition, Windows 2000, Windows XP Home Edition, Windows XP Professional, Windows .NET Server family

.NET Framework Security:

- Full trust for the immediate caller. This member cannot be used by partially trusted code.

MessageQueuePermission.IsSubsetOf Method

This member overrides **CodeAccessPermission.IsSubsetOf**.

```
[Visual Basic]
Overrides Public Function IsSubsetOf( _
   ByVal target As IPermission _
) As Boolean Implements IPermission.IsSubsetOf
[C#]
public override bool IsSubsetOf(
   IPermission target
);
[C++]
public: bool IsSubsetOf(
   IPermission* target
);
[JScript]
public override function IsSubsetOf(
   target : IPermission
) : Boolean;
```

Requirements

Platforms: Windows 98, Windows NT 4.0, Windows Millennium Edition, Windows 2000, Windows XP Home Edition, Windows XP Professional, Windows .NET Server family

.NET Framework Security:

- Full trust for the immediate caller. This member cannot be used by partially trusted code.

MessageQueuePermission.IsUnrestricted Method

This member supports the .NET Framework infrastructure and is not intended to be used directly from your code.

```
[Visual Basic]
Public Overridable Function IsUnrestricted() As Boolean Implements _
   IUnrestrictedPermission.IsUnrestricted
[C#]
public virtual bool IsUnrestricted();
[C++]
public: virtual bool IsUnrestricted();
[JScript]
public function IsUnrestricted() : Boolean;
```

MessageQueuePermission.ToXml Method

This member overrides **CodeAccessPermission.ToXml**.

```
[Visual Basic]
Overrides Public Function ToXml() As SecurityElement Implements _
   ISecurityEncodable.ToXml
[C#]
public override SecurityElement ToXml();
[C++]
public: SecurityElement* ToXml();
[JScript]
public override function ToXml() : SecurityElement;
```

Requirements

Platforms: Windows 98, Windows NT 4.0, Windows Millennium Edition, Windows 2000, Windows XP Home Edition, Windows XP Professional, Windows .NET Server family

.NET Framework Security:

- Full trust for the immediate caller. This member cannot be used by partially trusted code.

MessageQueuePermission.Union Method

This member overrides **CodeAccessPermission.Union**.

```
[Visual Basic]
Overrides Public Function Union( _
   ByVal target As IPermission _
) As IPermission Implements IPermission.Union
[C#]
public override IPermission Union(
   IPermission target
);
```

```
[C++]
public: IPermission* Union(
   IPermission* target
);
[JScript]
public override function Union(
   target : IPermission
) : IPermission;
```

Requirements

Platforms: Windows 98, Windows NT 4.0,
Windows Millennium Edition, Windows 2000,
Windows XP Home Edition, Windows XP Professional,
Windows .NET Server family

.NET Framework Security:

- Full trust for the immediate caller. This member cannot be used
  by partially trusted code.

MessageQueuePermission-Access Enumeration

Defines access levels used by **System.Messaging** permission classes.

This enumeration has a **FlagsAttribute** attribute that allows a bitwise combination of its member values.

```
[Visual Basic]
<Flags>
<Serializable>
Public Enum MessageQueuePermissionAccess
[C#]
[Flags]
[Serializable]
public enum MessageQueuePermissionAccess
[C++]
[Flags]
[Serializable]
__value public enum MessageQueuePermissionAccess
[JScript]
public
    Flags
    Serializable
enum MessageQueuePermissionAccess
```

Members

Member name	Description	Value
Administer	The **MessageQueue** can look at the queues that are available, read the messages in the queue, and send and receive messages.	62
Browse	The **MessageQueue** can look at the queues that are available.	2
None	The **MessageQueue** has no permissions.	0
Peek	The **MessageQueue** can look at the queues that are available and read the messages in the queue.	10
Receive	The **MessageQueue** can look at the queues that are available, read the messages in the queue, and receive messages.	26
Send	The **MessageQueue** can look at the queues that are available and send messages.	6

Requirements

Namespace: System.Messaging

Platforms: Windows 98, Windows NT 4.0, Windows Millennium Edition, Windows 2000, Windows XP Home Edition, Windows XP Professional, Windows .NET Server family

Assembly: System.Messaging (in System.Messaging.dll)

MessageQueuePermission-Attribute Class

Allows declaritive **MessageQueue** permission checks.

System.Object
  System.Attribute
    System.Security.Permissions.SecurityAttribute
      System.Security.Permissions.CodeAccessSecurityAttribute
        System.Messaging.MessageQueuePermissionAttribute

```
[Visual Basic]
<AttributeUsage(AttributeTargets.Assembly Or AttributeTargets.Class _
  Or AttributeTargets.Struct Or AttributeTargets.Constructor Or _
  AttributeTargets.Method Or AttributeTargets.Event)>
<Serializable>
Public Class MessageQueuePermissionAttribute
  Inherits CodeAccessSecurityAttribute
[C#]
[AttributeUsage(AttributeTargets.Assembly | AttributeTargets.Class
  | AttributeTargets.Struct | AttributeTargets.Constructor |
  AttributeTargets.Method | AttributeTargets.Event)]
[Serializable]
public class MessageQueuePermissionAttribute :
  CodeAccessSecurityAttribute
[C++]
[AttributeUsage(AttributeTargets::Assembly |
  AttributeTargets::Class | AttributeTargets::Struct |
  AttributeTargets::Constructor | AttributeTargets::Method |
  AttributeTargets::Event)]
[Serializable]
public __gc class MessageQueuePermissionAttribute : public
  CodeAccessSecurityAttribute
[JScript]
public
  AttributeUsage(AttributeTargets.Assembly | AttributeTargets.Class |
  AttributeTargets.Struct | AttributeTargets.Constructor |
  AttributeTargets.Method | AttributeTargets.Event)
  Serializable
class MessageQueuePermissionAttribute extends
  CodeAccessSecurityAttribute
```

Thread Safety

Any public static (**Shared** in Visual Basic) members of this type are safe for multithreaded operations. Any instance members are not guaranteed to be thread safe.

Remarks

For more information about using attributes, see **Extending Metadata Using Attributes**.

Requirements

Namespace: System.Messaging

Platforms: Windows 98, Windows NT 4.0, Windows Millennium Edition, Windows 2000, Windows XP Home Edition, Windows XP Professional, Windows .NET Server family

Assembly: System.Messaging (in System.Messaging.dll)

MessageQueuePermissionAttribute Constructor

Initializes a new instance of the **MessageQueuePermissionAttribute** class.

```
[Visual Basic]
Public Sub New( _
  ByVal action As SecurityAction _
)
[C#]
public MessageQueuePermissionAttribute(
  SecurityAction action
);
[C++]
public: MessageQueuePermissionAttribute(
  SecurityAction action
);
[JScript]
public function MessageQueuePermissionAttribute(
  action : SecurityAction
);
```

Parameters

action
  One of the **SecurityAction** values.

Requirements

Platforms: Windows 98, Windows NT 4.0, Windows Millennium Edition, Windows 2000, Windows XP Home Edition, Windows XP Professional, Windows .NET Server family

.NET Framework Security:

- Full trust for the immediate caller. This member cannot be used by partially trusted code.

MessageQueuePermissionAttribute.Category Property

Gets or sets the queue category.

```
[Visual Basic]
Public Property Category As String
[C#]
public string Category {get; set;}
[C++]
public: __property String* get_Category();
public: __property void set_Category(String*);
[JScript]
public function get Category() : String;
public function set Category(String);
```

Property Value

The queue category (Message Queuing type identifier), which allows an application to categorize its queues.

Exceptions

Exception Type	Condition
InvalidOperation-Exception	The value is a null reference (**Nothing** in Visual Basic).

Requirements

Platforms: Windows 98, Windows NT 4.0,
Windows Millennium Edition, Windows 2000,
Windows XP Home Edition, Windows XP Professional,
Windows .NET Server family

.NET Framework Security:

• Full trust for the immediate caller. This member cannot be used
  by partially trusted code.

MessageQueuePermissionAttribute.Label Property

Gets or sets the queue description.

```
[Visual Basic]
Public Property Label As String
[C#]
public string Label {get; set;}
[C++]
public: __property String* get_Label();
public: __property void set_Label(String*);
[JScript]
public function get Label() : String;
public function set Label(String);
```

Property Value

The label for the message queue.

Exceptions

Exception Type	Condition
InvalidOperation-Exception	The value is a null reference (**Nothing** in Visual Basic).

Requirements

Platforms: Windows 98, Windows NT 4.0,
Windows Millennium Edition, Windows 2000,
Windows XP Home Edition, Windows XP Professional,
Windows .NET Server family

.NET Framework Security:

• Full trust for the immediate caller. This member cannot be used
  by partially trusted code.

MessageQueuePermissionAttribute.Machine-Name Property

Gets or sets the name of the computer where the Message Queuing
queue is located.

```
[Visual Basic]
Public Property MachineName As String
[C#]
public string MachineName {get; set;}
[C++]
public: __property String* get_MachineName();
public: __property void set_MachineName(String*);
[JScript]
public function get MachineName() : String;
public function set MachineName(String);
```

Property Value

The name of the computer where the queue is located.

Exceptions

Exception Type	Condition
InvalidOperation-Exception	The value is a null reference (**Nothing** in Visual Basic).

Requirements

Platforms: Windows 98, Windows NT 4.0,
Windows Millennium Edition, Windows 2000,
Windows XP Home Edition, Windows XP Professional,
Windows .NET Server family

.NET Framework Security:

• Full trust for the immediate caller. This member cannot be used
  by partially trusted code.

MessageQueuePermissionAttribute.Path Property

Gets or sets the queue's path.

```
[Visual Basic]
Public Property Path As String
[C#]
public string Path {get; set;}
[C++]
public: __property String* get_Path();
public: __property void set_Path(String*);
[JScript]
public function get Path() : String;
public function set Path(String);
```

Property Value

The queue that is referenced by the **MessageQueue**.

Exceptions

Exception Type	Condition
InvalidOperation-Exception	The value is a null reference (**Nothing** in Visual Basic).

Requirements

Platforms: Windows 98, Windows NT 4.0,
Windows Millennium Edition, Windows 2000,
Windows XP Home Edition, Windows XP Professional,
Windows .NET Server family

.NET Framework Security:

• Full trust for the immediate caller. This member cannot be used
  by partially trusted code.

MessageQueuePermissionAttribute.Permission Access Property

Gets or sets the permission access levels used in the permissions
request.

```
[Visual Basic]
Public Property PermissionAccess As MessageQueuePermissionAccess
[C#]
public MessageQueuePermissionAccess PermissionAccess {get; set;}
```

```
[C++]
public: __property MessageQueuePermissionAccess
get_PermissionAccess();
public: __property void
set_PermissionAccess(MessageQueuePermissionAccess);
[JScript]
public function get PermissionAccess() : MessageQueuePermissionAccess;
public function set PermissionAccess(MessageQueuePermissionAccess);
```

Property Value

A bitwise combination of the **MessageQueuePermissionAccess** values.

Requirements

Platforms: Windows 98, Windows NT 4.0, Windows Millennium Edition, Windows 2000, Windows XP Home Edition, Windows XP Professional, Windows .NET Server family

.NET Framework Security:

- Full trust for the immediate caller. This member cannot be used by partially trusted code.

MessageQueuePermissionAttribute.CreatePer mission Method

Creates the permission based on the requested access levels, category, label, computer name, and path that are set through the **PermissionAccess**, **Category**, **Label**, **MachineName**, and **Path** properties on the attribute.

```
[Visual Basic]
Overrides Public Function CreatePermission() As IPermission
[C#]
public override IPermission CreatePermission();
[C++]
public: IPermission* CreatePermission();
[JScript]
public override function CreatePermission() : IPermission;
```

Return Value

An **IPermission** that represents the created permission.

Requirements

Platforms: Windows 98, Windows NT 4.0, Windows Millennium Edition, Windows 2000, Windows XP Home Edition, Windows XP Professional, Windows .NET Server family

.NET Framework Security:

- Full trust for the immediate caller. This member cannot be used by partially trusted code.

MessageQueuePermission-Entry Class

Defines the smallest unit of a code access security permission set for messaging.

System.Object
  System.Messaging.MessageQueuePermissionEntry

```
[Visual Basic]
<Serializable>
Public Class MessageQueuePermissionEntry
[C#]
[Serializable]
public class MessageQueuePermissionEntry
[C++]
[Serializable]
public __gc class MessageQueuePermissionEntry
[JScript]
public
    Serializable
class MessageQueuePermissionEntry
```

Thread Safety

Any public static (**Shared** in Visual Basic) members of this type are safe for multithreaded operations. Any instance members are not guaranteed to be thread safe.

Requirements

Namespace: System.Messaging

Platforms: Windows 98, Windows NT 4.0, Windows Millennium Edition, Windows 2000, Windows XP Home Edition, Windows XP Professional, Windows .NET Server family

Assembly: System.Messaging (in System.Messaging.dll)

MessageQueuePermissionEntry Constructor

Initializes a new instance of the **MessageQueuePermissionEntry** class.

Overload List

Initializes a new instance of the **MessageQueuePermissionEntry** class with the specified permission access levels and the path of the queue.

  [Visual Basic] **Public Sub New(MessageQueuePermissionAccess, String)**

  [C#] **public MessageQueuePermissionEntry (MessageQueuePermissionAccess, string);**

  [C++] **public: MessageQueuePermissionEntry (MessageQueuePermissionAccess, String*);**

  [JScript] **public function MessageQueuePermissionEntry(MessageQueuePermissionAccess, String);**

Initializes a new instance of the **MessageQueuePermissionEntry** class with the specified permission access levels, the name of the computer where the queue is located, the queue description, and the queue category.

  [Visual Basic] **Public Sub New(MessageQueuePermissionAccess, String, String, String)**

  [C#] **public MessageQueuePermissionEntry (MessageQueuePermissionAccess, string, string, string);**

  [C++] **public: MessageQueuePermissionEntry (MessageQueuePermissionAccess, String*, String*, String*);**

  [JScript] **public function MessageQueuePermissionEntry (MessageQueuePermissionAccess, String, String, String);**

MessageQueuePermissionEntry Constructor (MessageQueuePermissionAccess, String)

Initializes a new instance of the **MessageQueuePermissionEntry** class with the specified permission access levels and the path of the queue.

```
[Visual Basic]
Public Sub New( _
    ByVal permissionAccess As MessageQueuePermissionAccess, _
    ByVal path As String _
)
[C#]
public MessageQueuePermissionEntry(
    MessageQueuePermissionAccess permissionAccess,
    string path
);
[C++]
public: MessageQueuePermissionEntry(
    MessageQueuePermissionAccess permissionAccess,
    String* path
);
[JScript]
public function MessageQueuePermissionEntry(
    permissionAccess : MessageQueuePermissionAccess,
    path : String
);
```

Parameters

permissionAccess
  A bitwise combination of the **MessageQueuePermissionAccess** values. The **PermissionAccess** property is set to this value.

path
  The path of the queue that is referenced by the **MessageQueue** object. The **Path** property is set to this value.

Requirements

Platforms: Windows 98, Windows NT 4.0, Windows Millennium Edition, Windows 2000, Windows XP Home Edition, Windows XP Professional, Windows .NET Server family

.NET Framework Security:

- Full trust for the immediate caller. This member cannot be used by partially trusted code.

MessageQueuePermissionEntry Constructor (MessageQueuePermissionAccess, String, String, String)

Initializes a new instance of the **MessageQueuePermissionEntry** class with the specified permission access levels, the name of the computer where the queue is located, the queue description, and the queue category.

```
[Visual Basic]
Public Sub New( _
    ByVal permissionAccess As MessageQueuePermissionAccess, _
    ByVal machineName As String, _
    ByVal label As String, _
    ByVal category As String _
)
[C#]
public MessageQueuePermissionEntry(
    MessageQueuePermissionAccess permissionAccess,
    string machineName,
    string label,
    string category
);
[C++]
public: MessageQueuePermissionEntry(
    MessageQueuePermissionAccess permissionAccess,
    String* machineName,
    String* label,
    String* category
);
[JScript]
public function MessageQueuePermissionEntry(
    permissionAccess : MessageQueuePermissionAccess,
    machineName : String,
    label : String,
    category : String
);
```

Parameters

permissionAccess

  A bitwise combination of the **MessageQueuePermissionAccess** values. The **PermissionAccess** property is set to this value.

machineName

  The name of the computer where the Message Queuing queue is located. The **MachineName** property is set to this value.

label

  The queue description. The **Label** property is set to this value.

category

  The queue category (Message Queuing type identifier). The **Category** property is set to this value.

Requirements

Platforms: Windows 98, Windows NT 4.0, Windows Millennium Edition, Windows 2000, Windows XP Home Edition, Windows XP Professional, Windows .NET Server family

.NET Framework Security:

• Full trust for the immediate caller. This member cannot be used by partially trusted code.

MessageQueuePermissionEntry.Category Property

Gets the queue category.

```
[Visual Basic]
Public ReadOnly Property Category As String
[C#]
public string Category {get;}
[C++]
public: __property String* get_Category();
[JScript]
public function get Category() : String;
```

Property Value

The queue category (Message Queuing type identifier), which allows an application to categorize its queues.

Requirements

Platforms: Windows 98, Windows NT 4.0, Windows Millennium Edition, Windows 2000, Windows XP Home Edition, Windows XP Professional, Windows .NET Server family

.NET Framework Security:

• Full trust for the immediate caller. This member cannot be used by partially trusted code.

MessageQueuePermissionEntry.Label Property

Gets the queue description.

```
[Visual Basic]
Public ReadOnly Property Label As String
[C#]
public string Label {get;}
[C++]
public: __property String* get_Label();
[JScript]
public function get Label() : String;
```

Property Value

The label for the message queue.

Requirements

Platforms: Windows 98, Windows NT 4.0, Windows Millennium Edition, Windows 2000, Windows XP Home Edition, Windows XP Professional, Windows .NET Server family

.NET Framework Security:

• Full trust for the immediate caller. This member cannot be used by partially trusted code.

MessageQueuePermissionEntry.MachineName Property

Gets the name of the computer where the Message Queuing queue is located.

```
[Visual Basic]
Public ReadOnly Property MachineName As String
[C#]
public string MachineName {get;}
```

```
[C++]
public: __property String* get_MachineName();
[JScript]
public function get MachineName() : String;
```

Property Value

The name of the computer where the queue is located.

Requirements

Platforms: Windows 98, Windows NT 4.0,
Windows Millennium Edition, Windows 2000,
Windows XP Home Edition, Windows XP Professional,
Windows .NET Server family

.NET Framework Security:

* Full trust for the immediate caller. This member cannot be used by partially trusted code.

MessageQueuePermissionEntry.Path Property

Gets the queue's path.

```
[Visual Basic]
Public ReadOnly Property Path As String
[C#]
public string Path {get;}
[C++]
public: __property String* get_Path();
[JScript]
public function get Path() : String;
```

Property Value

The queue that is referenced by the **MessageQueue**.

Requirements

Platforms: Windows 98, Windows NT 4.0,
Windows Millennium Edition, Windows 2000,
Windows XP Home Edition, Windows XP Professional,
Windows .NET Server family

.NET Framework Security:

* Full trust for the immediate caller. This member cannot be used by partially trusted code.

MessageQueuePermissionEntry.Permission-Access Property

Gets the permission access levels used in the permissions request.

```
[Visual Basic]
Public ReadOnly Property PermissionAccess As _
   MessageQueuePermissionAccess
[C#]
public MessageQueuePermissionAccess PermissionAccess {get;}
[C++]
public: __property MessageQueuePermissionAccess
   get_PermissionAccess();
[JScript]
public function get PermissionAccess() :
   MessageQueuePermissionAccess;
```

Property Value

A bitwise combination of the **MessageQueuePermissionAccess** values.

Requirements

Platforms: Windows 98, Windows NT 4.0,
Windows Millennium Edition, Windows 2000,
Windows XP Home Edition, Windows XP Professional,
Windows .NET Server family

.NET Framework Security:

* Full trust for the immediate caller. This member cannot be used by partially trusted code.

MessageQueuePermission-EntryCollection Class

Contains a strongly typed collection of **MessageQueuePermissionEntry** objects.

System.Object
    System.Collections.CollectionBase
        System.Messaging.MessageQueuePermissionEntryCollectio
n

```
[Visual Basic]
<Serializable>
Public Class MessageQueuePermissionEntryCollection
    Inherits CollectionBase
[C#]
[Serializable]
public class MessageQueuePermissionEntryCollection :
    CollectionBase
[C++]
[Serializable]
public __gc class MessageQueuePermissionEntryCollection : public
    CollectionBase
[JScript]
public
    Serializable
class MessageQueuePermissionEntryCollection extends
    CollectionBase
```

Thread Safety

Any public static (**Shared** in Visual Basic) members of this type are safe for multithreaded operations. Any instance members are not guaranteed to be thread safe.

Requirements

Namespace: System.Messaging

Platforms: Windows 98, Windows NT 4.0, Windows Millennium Edition, Windows 2000, Windows XP Home Edition, Windows XP Professional, Windows .NET Server family

Assembly: System.Messaging (in System.Messaging.dll)

MessageQueuePermissionEntryCollection.Item Property

Gets or sets the object at a specified index.

[C#] In C#, this property is the indexer for the **MessageQueuePermissionEntryCollection** class.

```
[Visual Basic]
Public Default Property Item( _
    ByVal index As Integer _
) As MessageQueuePermissionEntry
[C#]
public MessageQueuePermissionEntry this[
    int index
] {get; set;}
[C++]
public: __property MessageQueuePermissionEntry* get_Item(
    int index
);
```

```
public: __property void set_Item(
    int index,
    MessageQueuePermissionEntry*
);
[JScript]
returnValue = MessageQueuePermissionEntryCollectionObject.Item(index);
MessageQueuePermissionEntryCollectionObject.Item(index) = returnValue;
-or-
returnValue = MessageQueuePermissionEntryCollectionObject(index);
MessageQueuePermissionEntryCollectionObject(index) = returnValue;
```

[JScript] In JScript, you can use the default indexed properties defined by a type, but you cannot explicitly define your own. However, specifying the **expando** attribute on a class automatically provides a default indexed property whose type is **Object** and whose index type is **String**.

Arguments [JScript]

index
    The zero-based index into the collection.

Parameters [Visual Basic, C#, C++]

index
    The zero-based index into the collection.

Property Value

The **MessageQueuePermissionEntry** that exists at the specified index.

Requirements

Platforms: Windows 98, Windows NT 4.0, Windows Millennium Edition, Windows 2000, Windows XP Home Edition, Windows XP Professional, Windows .NET Server family

.NET Framework Security:

*   Full trust for the immediate caller. This member cannot be used by partially trusted code.

MessageQueuePermissionEntryCollection.Add Method

Adds a specified **MessageQueuePermissionEntry** to this collection.

```
[Visual Basic]
Public Function Add( _
    ByVal value As MessageQueuePermissionEntry _
) As Integer
[C#]
public int Add(
    MessageQueuePermissionEntry value
);
[C++]
public: int Add(
    MessageQueuePermissionEntry* value
);
[JScript]
public function Add(
    value : MessageQueuePermissionEntry
) : int;
```

Parameters

value
    The **MessageQueuePermissionEntry** to add.

Return Value

The zero-based index of the added **MessageQueuePermissionEntry**.

Requirements

Platforms: Windows 98, Windows NT 4.0, Windows Millennium Edition, Windows 2000, Windows XP Home Edition, Windows XP Professional, Windows .NET Server family

.NET Framework Security:

- Full trust for the immediate caller. This member cannot be used by partially trusted code.

MessageQueuePermissionEntryCollection. AddRange Method

Appends a set of specified permission entries to this collection.

Overload List

Appends a set of specified permission entries to this collection.

[Visual Basic] **Overloads Public Sub AddRange(MessageQueuePermissionEntry())**

[C#] **public void AddRange(MessageQueuePermissionEntry[]);**

[C++] **public: void AddRange(MessageQueuePermissionEntry*[]);**

[JScript] **public function AddRange(MessageQueuePermissionEntry[]);**

Appends a set of specified permission entries to this collection.

[Visual Basic] **Overloads Public Sub AddRange(MessageQueuePermissionEntryCollection)**

[C#] **public void AddRange(MessageQueuePermissionEntryCollection);**

[C++] **public: void AddRange(MessageQueuePermissionEntryCollection*);**

[JScript] **public function AddRange(MessageQueuePermissionEntryCollection);**

MessageQueuePermissionEntryCollection.AddRange Method (MessageQueuePermissionEntry[])

Appends a set of specified permission entries to this collection.

```
[Visual Basic]
Overloads Public Sub AddRange( _
   ByVal value() As MessageQueuePermissionEntry _
)
[C#]
public void AddRange(
   MessageQueuePermissionEntry[] value
);
[C++]
public: void AddRange(
   MessageQueuePermissionEntry* value[]
);
[JScript]
public function AddRange(
   value : MessageQueuePermissionEntry[]
);
```

Parameters

value

An array of type **MessageQueuePermissionEntry** objects that contains the permission entries to add.

Requirements

Platforms: Windows 98, Windows NT 4.0, Windows Millennium Edition, Windows 2000, Windows XP Home Edition, Windows XP Professional, Windows .NET Server family

.NET Framework Security:

- Full trust for the immediate caller. This member cannot be used by partially trusted code.

MessageQueuePermissionEntryCollection.AddRange Method (MessageQueuePermissionEntryCollection)

Appends a set of specified permission entries to this collection.

```
[Visual Basic]
Overloads Public Sub AddRange( _
   ByVal value As MessageQueuePermissionEntryCollection _
)
[C#]
public void AddRange(
   MessageQueuePermissionEntryCollection value
);
[C++]
public: void AddRange(
   MessageQueuePermissionEntryCollection* value
);
[JScript]
public function AddRange(
   value : MessageQueuePermissionEntryCollection
);
```

Parameters

value

A **MessageQueuePermissionEntryCollection** that contains the permission entries to add.

Requirements

Platforms: Windows 98, Windows NT 4.0, Windows Millennium Edition, Windows 2000, Windows XP Home Edition, Windows XP Professional, Windows .NET Server family

.NET Framework Security:

- Full trust for the immediate caller. This member cannot be used by partially trusted code.

MessageQueuePermissionEntryCollection. Contains Method

Determines whether this collection contains a specified **MessageQueuePermissionEntry**.

```
[Visual Basic]
Public Function Contains( _
   ByVal value As MessageQueuePermissionEntry _
) As Boolean
```

```csharp
[C#]
public bool Contains(
    MessageQueuePermissionEntry value
);
[C++]
public: bool Contains(
    MessageQueuePermissionEntry* value
);
[JScript]
public function Contains(
    value : MessageQueuePermissionEntry
) : Boolean;
```

Parameters

value

The **MessageQueuePermissionEntry** to find.

Return Value

true if the specified **MessageQueuePermissionEntry** belongs to this collection; otherwise, **false**.

Requirements

Platforms: Windows 98, Windows NT 4.0, Windows Millennium Edition, Windows 2000, Windows XP Home Edition, Windows XP Professional, Windows .NET Server family

.NET Framework Security:

- Full trust for the immediate caller. This member cannot be used by partially trusted code.

MessageQueuePermissionEntryCollection.Copy To Method

Copies the permission entries from this collection to an array, starting at a particular index of the array.

```vbnet
[Visual Basic]
Public Sub CopyTo( _
    ByVal array() As MessageQueuePermissionEntry, _
    ByVal index As Integer _
)
[C#]
public void CopyTo(
    MessageQueuePermissionEntry[] array,
    int index
);
[C++]
public: void CopyTo(
    MessageQueuePermissionEntry* array[],
    int index
);
[JScript]
public function CopyTo(
    array : MessageQueuePermissionEntry[],
    index : int
);
```

Parameters

array

An array of type **MessageQueuePermissionEntry** that receives this collection's permission entries.

index

The zero-based index at which to begin copying the permission entries.

Requirements

Platforms: Windows 98, Windows NT 4.0, Windows Millennium Edition, Windows 2000, Windows XP Home Edition, Windows XP Professional, Windows .NET Server family

.NET Framework Security:

- Full trust for the immediate caller. This member cannot be used by partially trusted code.

MessageQueuePermissionEntryCollection.Index Of Method

Determines the index of a specified permission entry in this collection.

```vbnet
[Visual Basic]
Public Function IndexOf( _
    ByVal value As MessageQueuePermissionEntry _
) As Integer
[C#]
public int IndexOf(
    MessageQueuePermissionEntry value
);
[C++]
public: int IndexOf(
    MessageQueuePermissionEntry* value
);
[JScript]
public function IndexOf(
    value : MessageQueuePermissionEntry
) : int;
```

Parameters

value

The permission entry to search for.

Return Value

The zero-based index of the specified permission entry, or -1 if the permission entry was not found in the collection.

Requirements

Platforms: Windows 98, Windows NT 4.0, Windows Millennium Edition, Windows 2000, Windows XP Home Edition, Windows XP Professional, Windows .NET Server family

.NET Framework Security:

- Full trust for the immediate caller. This member cannot be used by partially trusted code.

MessageQueuePermissionEntryCollection.Insert Method

Inserts a permission entry into this collection at a specified index.

```vbnet
[Visual Basic]
Public Sub Insert( _
    ByVal index As Integer, _
    ByVal value As MessageQueuePermissionEntry _
)
```

```
[C#]
public void Insert(
   int index,
   MessageQueuePermissionEntry value
);
[C++]
public: void Insert(
   int index,
   MessageQueuePermissionEntry* value
);
[JScript]
public function Insert(
   index : int,
   value : MessageQueuePermissionEntry
);
```

Parameters

index

   The zero-based index into the collection at which to insert the permission entry.

value

   The permission entry to insert into this collection.

Requirements

Platforms: Windows 98, Windows NT 4.0, Windows Millennium Edition, Windows 2000, Windows XP Home Edition, Windows XP Professional, Windows .NET Server family

.NET Framework Security:

• Full trust for the immediate caller. This member cannot be used by partially trusted code.

MessageQueuePermissionEntryCollection. OnClear Method

This member overrides **CollectionBase.OnClear**.

```
[Visual Basic]
Overrides Protected Sub OnClear()
[C#]
protected override void OnClear();
[C++]
protected: void OnClear();
[JScript]
protected override function OnClear();
```

Requirements

Platforms: Windows 98, Windows NT 4.0, Windows Millennium Edition, Windows 2000, Windows XP Home Edition, Windows XP Professional, Windows .NET Server family

.NET Framework Security:

• Full trust for the immediate caller. This member cannot be used by partially trusted code.

MessageQueuePermissionEntryCollection. OnInsert Method

This member overrides **CollectionBase.OnInsert**.

```
[Visual Basic]
Overrides Protected Sub OnInsert( _
   ByVal index As Integer, _
   ByVal value As Object _
)
[C#]
protected override void OnInsert(
   int index,
   object value
);
[C++]
protected: void OnInsert(
   int index,
   Object* value
);
[JScript]
protected override function OnInsert(
   index : int,
   value : Object
);
```

Requirements

Platforms: Windows 98, Windows NT 4.0, Windows Millennium Edition, Windows 2000, Windows XP Home Edition, Windows XP Professional, Windows .NET Server family

.NET Framework Security:

• Full trust for the immediate caller. This member cannot be used by partially trusted code.

MessageQueuePermissionEntryCollection. OnRemove Method

This member overrides **CollectionBase.OnRemove**.

```
[Visual Basic]
Overrides Protected Sub OnRemove( _
   ByVal index As Integer, _
   ByVal value As Object _
)
[C#]
protected override void OnRemove(
   int index,
   object value
);
[C++]
protected: void OnRemove(
   int index,
   Object* value
);
[JScript]
protected override function OnRemove(
   index : int,
   value : Object
);
```

Requirements

Platforms: Windows 98, Windows NT 4.0, Windows Millennium Edition, Windows 2000, Windows XP Home Edition, Windows XP Professional, Windows .NET Server family

.NET Framework Security:

- Full trust for the immediate caller. This member cannot be used by partially trusted code.

MessageQueuePermissionEntryCollection. OnSet Method

This member overrides **CollectionBase.OnSet**.

```
[Visual Basic]
Overrides Protected Sub OnSet( _
   ByVal index As Integer, _
   ByVal oldValue As Object, _
   ByVal newValue As Object _
)
[C#]
protected override void OnSet(
   int index,
   object oldValue,
   object newValue
);
[C++]
protected: void OnSet(
   int index,
   Object* oldValue,
   Object* newValue
);
[JScript]
protected override function OnSet(
   index : int,
   oldValue : Object,
   newValue : Object
);
```

Requirements

Platforms: Windows 98, Windows NT 4.0, Windows Millennium Edition, Windows 2000, Windows XP Home Edition, Windows XP Professional, Windows .NET Server family

.NET Framework Security:

- Full trust for the immediate caller. This member cannot be used by partially trusted code.

MessageQueuePermissionEntryCollection. Remove Method

Removes a specified permission entry from this collection.

```
[Visual Basic]
Public Sub Remove( _
   ByVal value As MessageQueuePermissionEntry _
)
[C#]
public void Remove(
   MessageQueuePermissionEntry value
);
[C++]
public: void Remove(
   MessageQueuePermissionEntry* value
);
```

```
[JScript]
public function Remove(
   value : MessageQueuePermissionEntry
);
```

Parameters

value

   The permission entry to remove.

Requirements

Platforms: Windows 98, Windows NT 4.0, Windows Millennium Edition, Windows 2000, Windows XP Home Edition, Windows XP Professional, Windows .NET Server family

.NET Framework Security:

- Full trust for the immediate caller. This member cannot be used by partially trusted code.

MessageQueueTransaction Class

Provides a Message Queuing internal transaction.

System.Object
  System.Messaging.MessageQueueTransaction

```
[Visual Basic]
Public Class MessageQueueTransaction
    Implements IDisposable
[C#]
public class MessageQueueTransaction : IDisposable
[C++]
public __gc class MessageQueueTransaction : public IDisposable
[JScript]
public class MessageQueueTransaction implements IDisposable
```

Thread Safety

This type is safe for multithreaded operations.

Remarks

To send or receive a message as part of a transaction, you can use the **MessageQueueTransaction** class to create a transaction and pass it to an overload of the **MessageQueue.Send** method or the **MessageQueue.Receive** method that takes a *transaction* parameter. Messages sent as part of a transaction must be sent to transactional queues. Messages received from transactional queues must be received using a specified transaction.

> **Note** In addition to the **Receive** method, you can receive messages with a specified identifier or specified correlation identifier. See the **ReceiveById** and **ReceiveByCorrelationId** methods for more information about selectively receiving messages from transactional queues.

Messages sent to transactional queues are removed if the transaction is rolled back. Similarly, messages received from transactional queues are returned to the queue if the transaction is rolled back.

If you instantiate a **MessageQueueTransaction** and pass it to an applicable overload of the **Send** method or **Receive** method to send a message to a nontransactional queue or receive a message from a nontransational queue, the method throws an exception indicating "Wrong Transaction Usage."

> [Visual Basic] **Note** **MessageQueueTransaction** is threading apartment aware, so if your apartment state is **STA**, you cannot use the transaction in multiple threads. Visual Basic sets the state of the main thread to **STA**, so you must apply the **MTAThreadAttribute** in the Main subroutine. Otherwise, sending a transactional message using another thread throws a **MessageQueueException** exception. You apply the **MTAThreadAttribute** by using the following fragment.

```
[Visual Basic]
<System.MTAThreadAttribute>
public sub Main()
```

Requirements

Namespace: System.Messaging

Platforms: Windows 98, Windows NT 4.0, Windows Millennium Edition, Windows 2000, Windows XP Home Edition, Windows XP Professional, Windows .NET Server family

Assembly: System.Messaging (in System.Messaging.dll)

MessageQueueTransaction Constructor

Initializes a new instance of the **MessageQueueTransaction** class.

```
[Visual Basic]
Public Sub New()
[C#]
public MessageQueueTransaction();
[C++]
public: MessageQueueTransaction();
[JScript]
public function MessageQueueTransaction();
```

Remarks

This constructor sets the **Status** property to **Initialized**.

Requirements

Platforms: Windows 98, Windows NT 4.0, Windows Millennium Edition, Windows 2000, Windows XP Home Edition, Windows XP Professional, Windows .NET Server family

.NET Framework Security:

- Full trust for the immediate caller. This member cannot be used by partially trusted code.

MessageQueueTransaction.Status Property

Gets the status of the transaction.

```
[Visual Basic]
Public ReadOnly Property Status As MessageQueueTransactionStatus
[C#]
public MessageQueueTransactionStatus Status {get;}
[C++]
public: __property MessageQueueTransactionStatus get_Status();
[JScript]
public function get Status() : MessageQueueTransactionStatus;
```

Property Value

One of the **MessageQueueTransactionStatus** values that indicates whether the transaction has been committed, aborted, initialized, or is pending.

Remarks

When an instance of the **MessageQueueTransaction** class has been created, the **Status** is set by the constructor to **Initialized**. After a call to **Begin** but before a call to **Commit** or **Abort**, the **Status** is **Pending**.

Requirements

Platforms: Windows 98, Windows NT 4.0, Windows Millennium Edition, Windows 2000, Windows XP Home Edition, Windows XP Professional, Windows .NET Server family

.NET Framework Security:

- Full trust for the immediate caller. This member cannot be used by partially trusted code.

MessageQueueTransaction.Abort Method

Rolls back the pending internal transaction.

```
[Visual Basic]
Public Sub Abort()
[C#]
public void Abort();
[C++]
public: void Abort();
[JScript]
public function Abort();
```

Exceptions

Exception Type	Condition
InvalidOperation-Exception	The internal transaction you are attempting to roll back has not started.
MessageQueueException	An internal Message Queuing error occurs.

Remarks

Abort marks the unsuccessful completion of a process begun at a call to **Begin**.

Typically, one makes a call to **Begin** within a Try...Catch exception-handling block, putting a call to **Commit** in the Try clause, and a call to **Abort** in the Catch clause.

Abort rolls back the entire transaction. This includes all messages sent or received after the call to **Begin**.

Requirements

Platforms: Windows 98, Windows NT 4.0, Windows Millennium Edition, Windows 2000, Windows XP Home Edition, Windows XP Professional, Windows .NET Server family

.NET Framework Security:

- Full trust for the immediate caller. This member cannot be used by partially trusted code.

MessageQueueTransaction.Begin Method

Begins a new Message Queuing internal transaction.

```
[Visual Basic]
Public Sub Begin()
[C#]
public void Begin();
[C++]
public: void Begin();
[JScript]
public function Begin();
```

Exceptions

Exception Type	Condition
InvalidOperation-Exception	The transaction has already been started.

Exception Type	Condition
MessageQueueException	An internal Message Queuing error occurs.

Remarks

Begin marks the start of processing that will be committed or rolled back, depending on the success of the transaction. If an exception occurs during processing, the entire transaction is rolled back. This includes all messages sent or received after the call to **Begin**.

Typically, one makes a call to **Begin** within a Try...Catch exception-handling block, putting a call to **Commit** in the Try clause, and a call to **Abort** in the Catch clause.

Requirements

Platforms: Windows 98, Windows NT 4.0, Windows Millennium Edition, Windows 2000, Windows XP Home Edition, Windows XP Professional, Windows .NET Server family

.NET Framework Security:

- Full trust for the immediate caller. This member cannot be used by partially trusted code.

MessageQueueTransaction.Commit Method

Commits a pending internal transaction.

```
[Visual Basic]
Public Sub Commit()
[C#]
public void Commit();
[C++]
public: void Commit();
[JScript]
public function Commit();
```

Exceptions

Exception Type	Condition
InvalidOperation-Exception	The transaction you are trying to commit has not started.
MessageQueueException	An internal Message Queuing error occurs.

Remarks

Commit marks the successful completion of processing begun at a call to **Begin**. If an exception occurs between the call the **Begin** and the call to **Commit**, the entire transaction is rolled back. This includes all messages sent or received after the call to **Begin**.

Typically, one makes a call to **Begin** within a Try...Catch exception-handling block, putting a call to **Commit** in the Try clause, and a call to **Abort** in the Catch clause.

Requirements

Platforms: Windows 98, Windows NT 4.0, Windows Millennium Edition, Windows 2000, Windows XP Home Edition, Windows XP Professional, Windows .NET Server family

.NET Framework Security:

- Full trust for the immediate caller. This member cannot be used by partially trusted code.

MessageQueueTransaction.Dispose Method

Releases the resources used by the **MessageQueueTransaction**.

Overload List

Releases all resources used by the **MessageQueueTransaction**.

[Visual Basic] **Overloads Public Overridable Sub Dispose()
Implements IDisposable.Dispose**
[C#] **public virtual void Dispose();**
[C++] **public: virtual void Dispose();**
[JScript] **public function Dispose();**

Releases the unmanaged resources used by the
MessageQueueTransaction and optionally releases the managed
resources.

[Visual Basic] **Overloads Protected Overridable Sub
Dispose(Boolean)**
[C#] **protected virtual void Dispose(bool);**
[C++] **protected: virtual void Dispose(bool);**
[JScript] **protected function Dispose(Boolean);**

MessageQueueTransaction.Dispose Method ()

Releases all resources used by the **MessageQueueTransaction**.

```
[Visual Basic]
Overloads Public Overridable Sub Dispose() Implements _
    IDisposable.Dispose
[C#]
public virtual void Dispose();
[C++]
public: virtual void Dispose();
[JScript]
public function Dispose();
```

Implements

IDisposable.Dispose

Remarks

Calling **Dispose** allows the resources used by the
MessageQueueTransaction to be reallocated for other purposes.
For more information about **Dispose**, see **Cleaning Up Unmanaged
Resources**.

Any pending internal transactions are rolled back by **Dispose**.

Requirements

Platforms: Windows 98, Windows NT 4.0,
Windows Millennium Edition, Windows 2000,
Windows XP Home Edition, Windows XP Professional,
Windows .NET Server family

.NET Framework Security:

- Full trust for the immediate caller. This member cannot be used
  by partially trusted code.

MessageQueueTransaction.Dispose Method (Boolean)

Releases the unmanaged resources used by the
MessageQueueTransaction and optionally releases the managed
resources.

```
[Visual Basic]
Overloads Protected Overridable Sub Dispose( _
    ByVal disposing As Boolean _
)
```

```
[C#]
protected virtual void Dispose(
    bool disposing
);
[C++]
protected: virtual void Dispose(
    bool disposing
);
[JScript]
protected function Dispose(
    disposing : Boolean
);
```

Parameters

disposing
> **true** to release both managed and unmanaged resources; **false** to
> release only unmanaged resources.

Remarks

This method is called by the public **Dispose()** method and the
Finalize method. **Dispose()** invokes the protected **Dispose(Boolean)**
method with the *disposing* parameter set to **true**. **Finalize** invokes
Dispose with *disposing* set to **false**.

When the *disposing* parameter is **true**, this method releases all
resources held by any managed objects that this
MessageQueueTransaction references. This method invokes the
Dispose() method of each referenced object.

Notes to Inheritors: **Dispose** can be called multiple times by other
objects. When overriding **Dispose(Boolean)**, be careful not to
reference objects that have been previously disposed of in an earlier
call to **Dispose**.

Requirements

Platforms: Windows 98, Windows NT 4.0,
Windows Millennium Edition, Windows 2000,
Windows XP Home Edition, Windows XP Professional,
Windows .NET Server family

.NET Framework Security:

- Full trust for the immediate caller. This member cannot be used
  by partially trusted code.

MessageQueueTransaction.Finalize Method

This member overrides **Object.Finalize**.

```
[Visual Basic]
Overrides Protected Sub Finalize()
[C#]
~MessageQueueTransaction();
[C++]
~MessageQueueTransaction();
[JScript]
protected override function Finalize();
```

Requirements

Platforms: Windows 98, Windows NT 4.0,
Windows Millennium Edition, Windows 2000,
Windows XP Home Edition, Windows XP Professional,
Windows .NET Server family

.NET Framework Security:

- Full trust for the immediate caller. This member cannot be used
  by partially trusted code.

MessageQueueTransaction-Status Enumeration

Specifies the state of an internal Message Queuing transaction.

```
[Visual Basic]
<Serializable>
Public Enum MessageQueueTransactionStatus
[C#]
[Serializable]
public enum MessageQueueTransactionStatus
[C++]
[Serializable]
__value public enum MessageQueueTransactionStatus
[JScript]
public
   Serializable
enum MessageQueueTransactionStatus
```

Remarks

When an instance of the **MessageQueueTransaction** class has been created, its **Status** property is set by the constructor to **Initialized**. After a transaction has begun, but before it is committed or rolled back, the **Status** is **Pending**.

Members

Member name	Description
Aborted	The transaction has been aborted and all participants have been notified.
Committed	The transaction has been committed and all participants have been notified.
Initialized	The transaction has been initialized. It has not yet been started.
Pending	The transaction has been started. It has not yet been either committed or rolled back.

Requirements

Namespace: System.Messaging

Platforms: Windows 98, Windows NT 4.0, Windows Millennium Edition, Windows 2000, Windows XP Home Edition, Windows XP Professional, Windows .NET Server family

Assembly: System.Messaging (in System.Messaging.dll)

MessageQueueTransactionType Enumeration

Specifies the type of a Message Queuing transaction.

```
[Visual Basic]
<Serializable>
Public Enum MessageQueueTransactionType
[C#]
[Serializable]
public enum MessageQueueTransactionType
[C++]
[Serializable]
__value public enum MessageQueueTransactionType
[JScript]
public
    Serializable
enum MessageQueueTransactionType
```

Remarks

When you read or write a message using an overload of the **MessageQueue** class's **Send** or **Receive** methods (including **ReceiveById** and **ReceiveByCorrelationId**) that takes a *transactionType* parameter, you can specify how you are interacting with the queue. **Automatic** enables you to send and receive from external transactions (such as when you are interacting with database applications), while **Single** is used for single internal Message Queuing transactions.

None enables you to receive a message from a transactional queue outside of a transaction or send a transactional message to a nontransactional queue. This is useful, for example, when routing several messages sent within a single transaction.

If you want to send or receive a message using an internal Message Queuing transaction but not a single internal transaction, create an instance of the **MessageQueueTransaction** class and pass it into an overload of the **Send** or **Receive** methods that takes a *transaction* parameter rather than one that takes a *transactionType* parameter.

Members

Member name	Description
Automatic	A transaction type used for Microsoft Transaction Server (MTS) or COM+ 1.0 Services. If there is already an MTS transaction context, it will be used when sending or receiving the message.
None	Operation will not be transactional.
Single	A transaction type used for single internal transactions.

Requirements

Namespace: System.Messaging

Platforms: Windows 98, Windows NT 4.0, Windows Millennium Edition, Windows 2000, Windows XP Home Edition, Windows XP Professional, Windows .NET Server family

Assembly: System.Messaging (in System.Messaging.dll)

MessageType Enumeration

Identifies the type of a message. A message can be a typical Message Queuing message, a positive (arrival and read) or negative (arrival and read) acknowledgment message, or a report message.

```
[Visual Basic]
<Serializable>
Public Enum MessageType
[C#]
[Serializable]
public enum MessageType
[C++]
[Serializable]
__value public enum MessageType
[JScript]
public
    Serializable
enum MessageType
```

Remarks

Typical (**Normal** type) messages are those that you send to a queue using either the **Message** class or any overload of the **MessageQueue.Send** method.

Message Queuing generates acknowledgment messages whenever the sending application requests one. If you send a message using the **Message** class, you can use its **AcknowledgeType** property to specify the types of acknowledgments to receive. For example, Message Queuing can generate positive or negative messages to indicate that the original message arrived or was read. Message Queuing returns the appropriate acknowledgment message to the administration queue specified by the sending application. When you receive or peek an acknowledgment message using a **Message**, its **Acknowledgment** property indicates the reason Message Queuing sent the acknowledgment.

Message Queuing generates report messages whenever a report queue is defined at the source queue manager. When tracing is enabled (by setting the **Message.UseTracing** property on the original message), Message Queuing sends a report message to the Message Queuing report queue each time the original message enters or leaves a Message Queuing server.

Members

Member name	Description
Acknowledgment	An acknowledgment message.
Normal	A normal Message Queuing message.
Report	A report message.

Requirements

Namespace: System.Messaging

Platforms: Windows 98, Windows NT 4.0, Windows Millennium Edition, Windows 2000, Windows XP Home Edition, Windows XP Professional, Windows .NET Server family

Assembly: System.Messaging (in System.Messaging.dll)

MessagingDescriptionAttribute Class

Specifies a description for a property or event.

System.Object
  System.Attribute
    System.ComponentModel.DescriptionAttribute
      System.Messaging.MessagingDescriptionAttribute

[Visual Basic]
```
<AttributeUsage(AttributeTargets.All)>
Public Class MessagingDescriptionAttribute
   Inherits DescriptionAttribute
```
[C#]
```
[AttributeUsage(AttributeTargets.All)]
public class MessagingDescriptionAttribute : DescriptionAttribute
```
[C++]
```
[AttributeUsage(AttributeTargets::All)]
public __gc class MessagingDescriptionAttribute : public
   DescriptionAttribute
```
[JScript]
```
public
   AttributeUsage(AttributeTargets.All)
class MessagingDescriptionAttribute extends
   DescriptionAttribute
```

Thread Safety

Any public static (**Shared** in Visual Basic) members of this type are safe for multithreaded operations. Any instance members are not guaranteed to be thread safe.

Remarks

A visual designer can display the description when referencing the component member, such as in a Properties window. Access the **Description** property to get or set the text associated with this attribute.

Requirements

Namespace: System.Messaging

Platforms: Windows 98, Windows NT 4.0, Windows Millennium Edition, Windows 2000, Windows XP Home Edition, Windows XP Professional, Windows .NET Server family

Assembly: System.Messaging (in System.Messaging.dll)

MessagingDescriptionAttribute Constructor

Initializes a new instance of the **MessagingDescriptionAttribute** class, using the specified description.

[Visual Basic]
```
Public Sub New( _
   ByVal description As String _
)
```
[C#]
```
public MessagingDescriptionAttribute(
   string description
);
```
[C++]
```
public: MessagingDescriptionAttribute(
   String* description
);
```
[JScript]
```
public function MessagingDescriptionAttribute(
   description : String
);
```

Parameters

description
  The application-defined description text.

Remarks

The description you specify in the **ctor** constructor is displayed by a visual designer when you access the property, event, or extender to which the attribute applies

Requirements

Platforms: Windows 98, Windows NT 4.0, Windows Millennium Edition, Windows 2000, Windows XP Home Edition, Windows XP Professional, Windows .NET Server family

.NET Framework Security:
- Full trust for the immediate caller. This member cannot be used by partially trusted code.

MessagingDescriptionAttribute.Description Property

Gets description text associated with the item monitored.

[Visual Basic]
```
Overrides Public ReadOnly Property Description As String
```
[C#]
```
public override string Description {get;}
```
[C++]
```
public: __property String* get_Description();
```
[JScript]
```
public override function get Description() : String;
```

Property Value

An application-defined description.

Requirements

Platforms: Windows 98, Windows NT 4.0, Windows Millennium Edition, Windows 2000, Windows XP Home Edition, Windows XP Professional, Windows .NET Server family

.NET Framework Security:
- Full trust for the immediate caller. This member cannot be used by partially trusted code.

PeekCompletedEventArgs Class

Provides data for the **PeekCompleted** event. When your asynchronous peek operation calls an event handler, an instance of this class is passed to the handler.

System.Object
  System.EventArgs
    System.Messaging.PeekCompletedEventArgs

```
[Visual Basic]
Public Class PeekCompletedEventArgs
   Inherits EventArgs
[C#]
public class PeekCompletedEventArgs : EventArgs
[C++]
public __gc class PeekCompletedEventArgs : public EventArgs
[JScript]
public class PeekCompletedEventArgs extends EventArgs
```

Thread Safety

Any public static (**Shared** in Visual Basic) members of this type are safe for multithreaded operations. Any instance members are not guaranteed to be thread safe.

Remarks

When you use event notification to peek (read without removing) messages asynchronously from the queue, you must create a method that handles your message processing. Your code must call **BeginPeek** to begin the asynchronous processing. When a message is peeked, your application is notified through the **PeekCompleted** event. An instance of **PeekCompletedEventArgs** is passed into the event delegate that calls your event handler. The data associated with the **PeekCompleted** event is contained in the delegate's **AsyncResult** parameter.

> **Note** There are two ways to provide notification of event completion: event notification and callbacks. **PeekCompletedEventArgs** is used only with event notification. For information comparing callbacks and event notification, see "Events vs. Callbacks" on MSDN.

PeekCompletedEventArgs provides access to the message that initiated the end of the asynchronous peek operation, through the **Message** member. This is an alternate access to the message, and behaves much the same as a call to **MessageQueue.EndPeek**.

Example

[Visual Basic, C#, C++] The following example creates an event handler for the **PeekCompleted** event and associates it with the event delegate by using the **PeekCompletedEventHandler**. The event handler, MyPeekCompleted, peeks a message and writes its label to the screen.

```
[Visual Basic]
Imports System
Imports System.Messaging

Namespace MyProject

   '/ <summary>
   '/ Provides a container class for the example.
   '/ </summary>
   Public Class MyNewQueue
```

```
'*************************************************
' Provides an entry point into the application.
'
' This example performs asynchronous peek operation
' processing.
'*************************************************

Public Shared Sub Main()
   ' Create an instance of MessageQueue. Set its formatter.
   Dim myQueue As New MessageQueue(".\myQueue")
   myQueue.Formatter = New XmlMessageFormatter(New Type() _
      {GetType([String])})

   ' Add an event handler for the PeekCompleted event.
   AddHandler myQueue.PeekCompleted, AddressOf _
      MyPeekCompleted

   ' Begin the asynchronous peek operation.
   myQueue.BeginPeek()

   ' Do other work on the current thread.
   Return
End Sub 'Main

'*************************************************
' Provides an event handler for the PeekCompleted
' event.
'*************************************************

Private Shared Sub MyPeekCompleted(ByVal [source] As _
   [Object], ByVal asyncResult As PeekCompletedEventArgs)

   ' Connect to the queue.
   Dim mq As MessageQueue = CType([source], MessageQueue)

   ' End the asynchronous peek operation.
   Dim m As Message = mq.EndPeek(asyncResult.AsyncResult)

   ' Display message information on the screen.
   Console.WriteLine(("Message: " + CStr(m.Body)))

   ' Restart the asynchronous peek operation.
   mq.BeginPeek()

   Return

End Sub 'MyPeekCompleted

   End Class 'MyNewQueue
End Namespace 'MyProject
```

```
[C#]
using System;
using System.Messaging;

namespace MyProject
{
   /// <summary>
   /// Provides a container class for the example.
   /// </summary>
   public class MyNewQueue
   {

      //*************************************************
      // Provides an entry point into the application.
      //
      // This example performs asynchronous peek operation
      // processing.
      //*************************************************

      public static void Main()
      {
         // Create an instance of MessageQueue. Set its formatter.
         MessageQueue myQueue = new MessageQueue(".\\myQueue");
```

```
myQueue.Formatter = new XmlMessageFormatter(new Type[]
    {typeof(String)});

// Add an event handler for the PeekCompleted event.
myQueue.PeekCompleted += new
    PeekCompletedEventHandler(MyPeekCompleted);

// Begin the asynchronous peek operation.
myQueue.BeginPeek();

// Do other work on the current thread.

return;
}

//**************************************************
// Provides an event handler for the PeekCompleted
// event.
//**************************************************

private static void MyPeekCompleted(Object source,
    PeekCompletedEventArgs asyncResult)
{
    // Connect to the queue.
    MessageQueue mq = (MessageQueue)source;

    // End the asynchronous peek operation.
    Message m = mq.EndPeek(asyncResult.AsyncResult);

    // Display message information on the screen.
    Console.WriteLine("Message: " + (string)m.Body);

    // Restart the asynchronous peek operation.
    mq.BeginPeek();

    return;
}
}
}

[C++]
#using <mscorlib.dll>
#using <system.dll>
#using <system.messaging.dll>

using namespace System;
using namespace System::Messaging;

__gc class MyNewQueue
{
public:
    static void MyPeekCompleted(Object* source,
PeekCompletedEventArgs* asyncResult)
    {
        // Connect to the queue.
        MessageQueue* mq = dynamic_cast<MessageQueue*>(source);

        // End the asynchronous peek operation.
        Message* m = mq->EndPeek(asyncResult->AsyncResult);

        // Display message information on the screen.
        Console::WriteLine(S"Message: {0}", static_cast
<String*>(m->Body));

        // Restart the asynchronous peek operation.
        mq->BeginPeek();

        return;
    }
};

// Provides an entry point into the application.
//
// This example performs asynchronous peek operation
// processing.
```

```
//**************************************************
// Provides an event handler for the PeekCompleted
// event.

int main()
{
    // Create an instance of MessageQueue. Set its formatter.
    MessageQueue* myQueue = new MessageQueue(S".\\myQueue");

    Type* p __gc[] = new Type* __gc[1];
    p[0] = __typeof(String);
    myQueue->Formatter = new XmlMessageFormatter( p );

    // Add an event handler for the PeekCompleted event.
    myQueue->PeekCompleted += new
PeekCompletedEventHandler(0, MyNewQueue::MyPeekCompleted);

    // Begin the asynchronous peek operation.
    myQueue->BeginPeek();

    // Do other work on the current thread.

    return 0;
}
```

Requirements

Namespace: System.Messaging

Platforms: Windows 98, Windows NT 4.0, Windows Millennium Edition, Windows 2000, Windows XP Home Edition, Windows XP Professional, Windows .NET Server family

Assembly: System.Messaging (in System.Messaging.dll)

PeekCompletedEventArgs.AsyncResult Property

Gets or sets the result of the asynchronous operation requested.

```
[Visual Basic]
Public Property AsyncResult As IAsyncResult
[C#]
public IAsyncResult AsyncResult {get; set;}
[C++]
public: __property IAsyncResult* get_AsyncResult();
public: __property void set_AsyncResult(IAsyncResult*);
[JScript]
public function get AsyncResult() : IAsyncResult;
public function set AsyncResult(IAsyncResult);
```

Property Value

An **IAsyncResult** that contains the data associated with the peek operation.

Remarks

AsyncResult identifies ongoing or completed asynchronous operations. The property contains data that helps determine which of several potential asynchronous operations to complete, and when passed to the event handler, enables **EndPeek** to access the message associated with the completed operation.

When you call **BeginPeek**, an **IAsyncResult** is returned immediately, even though a message, if one exists, has not yet been retrieved because the operation is not completed. The **AsyncResult** indicates the state of the asynchronous operation. **BeginPeek** creates the object, which is modified throughout the operation until **EndPeek** completes it.

Requirements

Platforms: Windows 98, Windows NT 4.0,
Windows Millennium Edition, Windows 2000,
Windows XP Home Edition, Windows XP Professional,
Windows .NET Server family

.NET Framework Security:

- Full trust for the immediate caller. This member cannot be used
  by partially trusted code.

PeekCompletedEventArgs.Message Property

Gets the message associated with the asynchronous peek operation.

```
[Visual Basic]
Public ReadOnly Property Message As Message
[C#]
public Message Message {get;}
[C++]
public: __property Message* get_Message();
[JScript]
public function get Message() : Message;
```

Property Value

A **Message** that represents the end result of the asynchronous peek
operation.

Exceptions

Exception Type	Condition
MessageQueueException	The **Message** could not be retrieved. The timeout on the asynchronous operation might have expired.

Remarks

The **Message** property provides a means for retrieving the message
that initiated the end of the asynchronous peek operation.

> **Note**   **MessageQueue.EndPeek** is called the first time the
> **Message** property is read, so it is not necessary to call
> **EndPeek** prior to getting the value of this property.

Requirements

Platforms: Windows 98, Windows NT 4.0,
Windows Millennium Edition, Windows 2000,
Windows XP Home Edition, Windows XP Professional,
Windows .NET Server family

.NET Framework Security:

- Full trust for the immediate caller. This member cannot be used
  by partially trusted code.

PeekCompletedEventHandler Delegate

Represents the method that will handle the **PeekCompleted** event of a **MessageQueue**.

```vbnet
[Visual Basic]
<Serializable>
Public Delegate Sub PeekCompletedEventHandler( _
   ByVal sender As Object, _
   ByVal e As PeekCompletedEventArgs _
)
```

```csharp
[C#]
[Serializable]
public delegate void PeekCompletedEventHandler(
   object sender,
   PeekCompletedEventArgs e
);
```

```cpp
[C++]
[Serializable]
public __gc __delegate void PeekCompletedEventHandler(
   Object* sender,
   PeekCompletedEventArgs* e
);
```

[JScript] In JScript, you can use the delegates in the .NET Framework, but you cannot define your own.

Parameters [Visual Basic, C#, C++]

The declaration of your event handler must have the same parameters as the **PeekCompletedEventHandler** delegate declaration.

sender
   The source of the event, the **MessageQueue**.

e
   A **PeekCompletedEventArgs** that contains the event data.

Remarks

When you create a **PeekCompletedEventHandler** delegate, you identify the method that will handle the event. To associate the event with your event handler, add an instance of the delegate to the event. The event handler is called whenever the event occurs, unless you remove the delegate. For more information about event-handler delegates, see **Events and Delegates**.

Example

[Visual Basic, C#, C++] The following example illustrates how to create an event delegate (**PeekCompletedEventHandler**) for the event handler (MyPeekCompleted) and associate it with the **MessageQueue.PeekCompleted** event. The event handler peeks a message and writes its label to the screen.

```vbnet
[Visual Basic]
Imports System
Imports System.Messaging

Namespace MyProject

   '/ <summary>
   '/ Provides a container class for the example.
   '/ </summary>
   Public Class MyNewQueue

      '****************************************************
      ' Provides an entry point into the application.
```

```vbnet
      ' This example performs asynchronous peek operation
      ' processing.
      '****************************************************

      Public Shared Sub Main()
         ' Create an instance of MessageQueue. Set its formatter.
         Dim myQueue As New MessageQueue(".\myQueue")
         myQueue.Formatter = New XmlMessageFormatter(New Type() _
            {GetType([String])})

         ' Add an event handler for the PeekCompleted event.
         AddHandler myQueue.PeekCompleted, AddressOf _
            MyPeekCompleted

         ' Begin the asynchronous peek operation.
         myQueue.BeginPeek()

         ' Do other work on the current thread.
         Return
      End Sub 'Main

      '****************************************************
      ' Provides an event handler for the PeekCompleted
      ' event.
      '****************************************************

      Private Shared Sub MyPeekCompleted(ByVal [source] As _
         [Object], ByVal asyncResult As PeekCompletedEventArgs)

         ' Connect to the queue.
         Dim mq As MessageQueue = CType([source], MessageQueue)

         ' End the asynchronous peek operation.
         Dim m As Message = mq.EndPeek(asyncResult.AsyncResult)

         ' Display message information on the screen.
         Console.WriteLine(("Message: " + CStr(m.Body)))

         ' Restart the asynchronous peek operation.
         mq.BeginPeek()

         Return

      End Sub 'MyPeekCompleted

   End Class 'MyNewQueue
End Namespace 'MyProject
```

```csharp
[C#]
using System;
using System.Messaging;

namespace MyProject
{
   /// <summary>
   /// Provides a container class for the example.
   /// </summary>
   public class MyNewQueue
   {

      //****************************************************
      // Provides an entry point into the application.
      //
      // This example performs asynchronous peek operation
      // processing.
      //****************************************************

      public static void Main()
      {
         // Create an instance of MessageQueue. Set its formatter.
         MessageQueue myQueue = new MessageQueue(".\\myQueue");
         myQueue.Formatter = new XmlMessageFormatter(new Type[]
            {typeof(String)});
```

```
        // Add an event handler for the PeekCompleted event.
        myQueue.PeekCompleted += new
            PeekCompletedEventHandler(MyPeekCompleted);

        // Begin the asynchronous peek operation.
        myQueue.BeginPeek();

        // Do other work on the current thread.

        return;
    }


    //*************************************************
    // Provides an event handler for the PeekCompleted
    // event.
    //*************************************************

    private static void MyPeekCompleted(Object source,
        PeekCompletedEventArgs asyncResult)
    {
        // Connect to the queue.
        MessageQueue mq = (MessageQueue)source;

        // End the asynchronous peek operation.
        Message m = mq.EndPeek(asyncResult.AsyncResult);

        // Display message information on the screen.
        Console.WriteLine("Message: " + (string)m.Body);

        // Restart the asynchronous peek operation.
        mq.BeginPeek();

        return;
    }
}
```

```
[C++]
#using <mscorlib.dll>
#using <system.dll>
#using <system.messaging.dll>

using namespace System;
using namespace System::Messaging;

__gc class MyNewQueue
{
public:
    static void MyPeekCompleted(Object* source,
PeekCompletedEventArgs* asyncResult)
    {
        // Connect to the queue.
        MessageQueue* mq = dynamic_cast<MessageQueue*>(source);

        // End the asynchronous peek operation.
        Message* m = mq->EndPeek(asyncResult->AsyncResult);

        // Display message information on the screen.
        Console::WriteLine(S"Message: {0}",
static_cast<String*>(m->Body));

        // Restart the asynchronous peek operation.
        mq->BeginPeek();

        return;
    }
};

// Provides an entry point into the application.
//
// This example performs asynchronous peek operation
// processing.
//*************************************************
// Provides an event handler for the PeekCompleted
// event.
```

```
int main()
{
    // Create an instance of MessageQueue. Set its formatter.
    MessageQueue* myQueue = new MessageQueue(S".\\myQueue");

    Type* p __gc[] = new Type* __gc[1];
    p[0] = __typeof(String);
    myQueue->Formatter = new XmlMessageFormatter( p );

    // Add an event handler for the PeekCompleted event.
    myQueue->PeekCompleted += new
PeekCompletedEventHandler(0, MyNewQueue::MyPeekCompleted);

    // Begin the asynchronous peek operation.
    myQueue->BeginPeek();

    // Do other work on the current thread.

    return 0;
}
```

Requirements

Namespace: System.Messaging

Platforms: Windows 98, Windows NT 4.0,
Windows Millennium Edition, Windows 2000,
Windows XP Home Edition, Windows XP Professional,
Windows .NET Server family

Assembly: System.Messaging (in System.Messaging.dll)

ReceiveCompletedEventArgs Class

Provides data for the **ReceiveCompleted** event. When your asynchronous receive operation calls an event handler, an instance of this class is passed to the handler.

System.Object
  System.EventArgs
    System.Messaging.ReceiveCompletedEventArgs

```
[Visual Basic]
Public Class ReceiveCompletedEventArgs
   Inherits EventArgs
[C#]
public class ReceiveCompletedEventArgs : EventArgs
[C++]
public __gc class ReceiveCompletedEventArgs : public EventArgs
[JScript]
public class ReceiveCompletedEventArgs extends EventArgs
```

Thread Safety

Any public static (**Shared** in Visual Basic) members of this type are safe for multithreaded operations. Any instance members are not guaranteed to be thread safe.

Remarks

When you use event notification to receive messages asynchronously from the queue, you must create a method that handles your message processing. Your code must call **BeginReceive** to begin the asynchronous processing. When a message is received, your application is notified through the **ReceiveCompleted** event. An instance of **ReceiveCompletedEventArgs** is passed into the event delegate that calls your event handler. The data associated with the **ReceiveCompleted** event is contained in the delegate's **AsyncResult** parameter.

Note There are two ways to provide notification of event completion: event notification and callbacks. **ReceiveCompletedEventArgs** is used only with event notification. For information comparing callbacks and event notification, see "Events vs. Callbacks" on MSDN.

ReceiveCompletedEventArgs provides access to the message that initiated the end of the asynchronous receive operation, through the **Message** member. This is an alternate access to the message, and behaves much the same as a call to **MessageQueue.EndReceive**.

Example

[Visual Basic, C#, C++] The following example creates an event handler for the **ReceiveCompleted** event and associates it with the event delegate by using the **ReceiveCompletedEventHandler**. The event handler, MyReceiveCompleted, receives a message from a queue and writes its body to the screen.

```vbnet
[Visual Basic]
Imports System
Imports System.Messaging

Namespace MyProject

    '/ <summary>
    '/ Provides a container class for the example.
```

```vbnet
    '/ </summary>
    Public Class MyNewQueue


        '****************************************************
        ' Provides an entry point into the application.

        ' This example performs asynchronous receive operation
        ' processing.
        '****************************************************

        Public Shared Sub Main()

            ' Create an instance of MessageQueue. Set its formatter.
            Dim myQueue As New MessageQueue(".\myQueue")
            myQueue.Formatter = New XmlMessageFormatter(New Type() _
                {GetType([String])})

            ' Add an event handler for the ReceiveCompleted event.
            AddHandler myQueue.ReceiveCompleted, AddressOf _
                MyReceiveCompleted

            ' Begin the asynchronous receive operation.
            myQueue.BeginReceive()

            ' Do other work on the current thread.

            Return

        End Sub 'Main


        '****************************************************
        ' Provides an event handler for the ReceiveCompleted
        ' event.
        '****************************************************

        Private Shared Sub MyReceiveCompleted(ByVal [source] As _
            [Object], ByVal asyncResult As ReceiveCompletedEventArgs)

            ' Connect to the queue.
            Dim mq As MessageQueue = CType([source], MessageQueue)

            ' End the asynchronous Receive operation.
            Dim m As Message = mq.EndReceive(asyncResult.AsyncResult)

            ' Display message information on the screen.
            Console.WriteLine(("Message: " + CStr(m.Body)))

            ' Restart the asynchronous Receive operation.
            mq.BeginReceive()

            Return

        End Sub 'MyReceiveCompleted

    End Class 'MyNewQueue
End Namespace 'MyProject
```

```csharp
[C#]
using System;
using System.Messaging;

namespace MyProject
{
    /// <summary>
    /// Provides a container class for the example.
    /// </summary>
    public class MyNewQueue
    {

        //****************************************************
        // Provides an entry point into the application.
        //
        // This example performs asynchronous receive operation
        // processing.
        //****************************************************
```

```
    public static void Main()
    {
        // Create an instance of MessageQueue. Set its formatter.
        MessageQueue myQueue = new MessageQueue(".\\myQueue");
        myQueue.Formatter = new XmlMessageFormatter(new Type[]
            {typeof(String)});

        // Add an event handler for the ReceiveCompleted event.
        myQueue.ReceiveCompleted += new
            ReceiveCompletedEventHandler(MyReceiveCompleted);

        // Begin the asynchronous receive operation.
        myQueue.BeginReceive();

        // Do other work on the current thread.

        return;
    }

    //**************************************************
    // Provides an event handler for the ReceiveCompleted
    // event.
    //**************************************************

    private static void MyReceiveCompleted(Object source,
        ReceiveCompletedEventArgs asyncResult)
    {
        // Connect to the queue.
        MessageQueue mq = (MessageQueue)source;

        // End the asynchronous Receive operation.
        Message m = mq.EndReceive(asyncResult.AsyncResult);

        // Display message information on the screen.
        Console.WriteLine("Message: " + (string)m.Body);

        // Restart the asynchronous Receive operation.
        mq.BeginReceive();

        return;
    }
}
}

[C++]
#using <mscorlib.dll>
#using <system.dll>
#using <system.messaging.dll>

using namespace System;
using namespace System::Messaging;

__gc class MyNewQueue
{
    //**************************************************
    // Provides an event handler for the ReceiveCompleted
    // event.
    //**************************************************
public:
    static void MyReceiveCompleted(Object* source,
        ReceiveCompletedEventArgs* asyncResult)
    {
        // Connect to the queue.
        MessageQueue* mq = dynamic_cast<MessageQueue*>(source);

        // End the asynchronous Receive operation.
        Message* m = mq->EndReceive(asyncResult->AsyncResult);

        // Display message information on the screen.
        Console::WriteLine(S"Message: {0}", m->Body);

        // Restart the asynchronous Receive operation.
        mq->BeginReceive();
```

```
        return;
    }
};

//**************************************************
// Provides an entry point into the application.
//
// This example performs asynchronous receive operation
// processing.
//**************************************************
int main()
{
    // Create an instance of MessageQueue. Set its formatter.
    MessageQueue* myQueue = new MessageQueue(S".\\myQueue");

    Type* p __gc[] = new Type* __gc[1];
    p[0] = __typeof(String);
    myQueue->Formatter = new XmlMessageFormatter( p );

    // Add an event handler for the ReceiveCompleted event.
    myQueue->ReceiveCompleted += new
ReceiveCompletedEventHandler(0, MyNewQueue::MyReceiveCompleted);

    // Begin the asynchronous receive operation.
    myQueue->BeginReceive();

    // Do other work on the current thread.
    return 0;
}
```

Requirements

Namespace: System.Messaging

Platforms: Windows 98, Windows NT 4.0,
Windows Millennium Edition, Windows 2000,
Windows XP Home Edition, Windows XP Professional,
Windows .NET Server family

Assembly: System.Messaging (in System.Messaging.dll)

ReceiveCompletedEventArgs.AsyncResult Property

Gets or sets the result of the asynchronous operation requested.

```
[Visual Basic]
Public Property AsyncResult As IAsyncResult
[C#]
public IAsyncResult AsyncResult {get; set;}
[C++]
public: __property IAsyncResult* get_AsyncResult();
public: __property void set_AsyncResult(IAsyncResult*);
[JScript]
public function get AsyncResult() : IAsyncResult;
public function set AsyncResult(IAsyncResult);
```

Property Value

An **IAsyncResult** that contains the data associated with the receive operation.

Remarks

AsyncResult identifies ongoing or completed asynchronous operations. The property contains data that helps determine which of several potential asynchronous operations to complete, and when passed to the event handler, enables **EndReceive** to access the message associated with the completed operation.

When you call **BeginReceive**, an **IAsyncResult** is returned immediately, even though a message, if one exists, has not yet been retrieved because the operation is not completed. The **AsyncResult** indicates the state of the asynchronous operation. **BeginReceive** creates the object, which is modified throughout the operation until **EndReceive** completes it.

Requirements

Platforms: Windows 98, Windows NT 4.0, Windows Millennium Edition, Windows 2000, Windows XP Home Edition, Windows XP Professional, Windows .NET Server family

.NET Framework Security:
- Full trust for the immediate caller. This member cannot be used by partially trusted code. For more information, see **Using Libraries From Partially Trusted Code**

ReceiveCompletedEventArgs.Message Property

Gets the message associated with the asynchronous receive operation.

```
[Visual Basic]
Public ReadOnly Property Message As Message
[C#]
public Message Message {get;}
[C++]
public: __property Message* get_Message();
[JScript]
public function get Message() : Message;
```

Property Value

A **Message** that represents the end result of the asynchronous receive operation.

Exceptions

Exception Type	Condition
MessageQueueException	The **Message** could not be retrieved. The timeout on the asynchronous operation might have expired.

Remarks

The **Message** property provides a means for retrieving the message that initiated the end of the asynchronous receive operation.

> **Note** **MessageQueue.EndReceive** is called the first time the **Message** property is read, so it is not necessary to call **EndReceive** prior to getting the value of this property.

Requirements

Platforms: Windows 98, Windows NT 4.0, Windows Millennium Edition, Windows 2000, Windows XP Home Edition, Windows XP Professional, Windows .NET Server family

.NET Framework Security:
- Full trust for the immediate caller. This member cannot be used by partially trusted code.

ReceiveCompletedEvent-Handler Delegate

Represents the method that will handle the **ReceiveCompleted** event of a **MessageQueue**.

```
[Visual Basic]
<Serializable>
Public Delegate Sub ReceiveCompletedEventHandler( _
   ByVal sender As Object, _
   ByVal e As ReceiveCompletedEventArgs _
)
[C#]
[Serializable]
public delegate void ReceiveCompletedEventHandler(
   object sender,
   ReceiveCompletedEventArgs e
);
[C++]
[Serializable]
public __gc __delegate void ReceiveCompletedEventHandler(
   Object* sender,
   ReceiveCompletedEventArgs* e
);
```

[JScript] In JScript, you can use the delegates in the .NET Framework, but you cannot define your own.

Parameters [Visual Basic, C#, C++]

The declaration of your event handler must have the same parameters as the **ReceiveCompletedEventHandler** delegate declaration.

sender

The source of the event, the **MessageQueue**.

e

A **ReceiveCompletedEventArgs** that contains the event data.

Remarks

When you create a **ReceiveCompletedEventHandler** delegate, you identify the method that will handle the event. To associate the event with your event handler, add an instance of the delegate to the event. The event handler is called whenever the event occurs, unless you remove the delegate. For more information about event-handler delegates, see **Events and Delegates**.

Example

[Visual Basic, C#, C++] The following example illustrates how to create an event delegate (**ReceiveCompletedEventHandler**) for the event handler (MyReceiveCompleted) and associate it with the **MessageQueue.ReceiveCompleted** event. The event handler receives a message from a queue, and writes its label to the screen.

```
[Visual Basic]
Imports System
Imports System.Messaging

Namespace MyProject

   '/ <summary>
   '/ Provides a container class for the example.
   '/ </summary>
   Public Class MyNewQueue

      '****************************************************
      ' Provides an entry point into the application.
```

```
' This example performs asynchronous receive operation
' processing.
'****************************************************
Public Shared Sub Main()

   ' Create an instance of MessageQueue. Set its formatter.
   Dim myQueue As New MessageQueue(".\myQueue")
   myQueue.Formatter = New XmlMessageFormatter(New Type() _
      {GetType([String])})

   ' Add an event handler for the ReceiveCompleted event.
   AddHandler myQueue.ReceiveCompleted, AddressOf _
      MyReceiveCompleted

   ' Begin the asynchronous receive operation.
   myQueue.BeginReceive()

   ' Do other work on the current thread.

   Return

End Sub 'Main

'****************************************************
' Provides an event handler for the ReceiveCompleted
' event.
'****************************************************
Private Shared Sub MyReceiveCompleted(ByVal [source] As _
   [Object], ByVal asyncResult As ReceiveCompletedEventArgs)

   ' Connect to the queue.
   Dim mq As MessageQueue = CType([source], MessageQueue)

   ' End the asynchronous Receive operation.
   Dim m As Message = mq.EndReceive(asyncResult.AsyncResult)

   ' Display message information on the screen.
   Console.WriteLine(("Message: " + CStr(m.Body)))

   ' Restart the asynchronous Receive operation.
   mq.BeginReceive()

   Return

End Sub 'MyReceiveCompleted

   End Class 'MyNewQueue
End Namespace 'MyProject

[C#]
using System;
using System.Messaging;

namespace MyProject
{
   /// <summary>
   /// Provides a container class for the example.
   /// </summary>
   public class MyNewQueue
   {

      //****************************************************
      // Provides an entry point into the application.
      //
      // This example performs asynchronous receive operation
      // processing.
      //****************************************************

      public static void Main()
      {
         // Create an instance of MessageQueue. Set its formatter.
         MessageQueue myQueue = new MessageQueue(".\\myQueue");
```

```
        myQueue.Formatter = new XmlMessageFormatter(new Type[]
            {typeof(String)});

        // Add an event handler for the ReceiveCompleted event.
        myQueue.ReceiveCompleted += new
            ReceiveCompletedEventHandler(MyReceiveCompleted);

        // Begin the asynchronous receive operation.
        myQueue.BeginReceive();

        // Do other work on the current thread.

        return;
    }

    //*************************************************
    // Provides an event handler for the ReceiveCompleted
    // event.
    //*************************************************

    private static void MyReceiveCompleted(Object source,
        ReceiveCompletedEventArgs asyncResult)
    {
        // Connect to the queue.
        MessageQueue mq = (MessageQueue)source;

        // End the asynchronous Receive operation.
        Message m = mq.EndReceive(asyncResult.AsyncResult);

        // Display message information on the screen.
        Console.WriteLine("Message: " + (string)m.Body);

        // Restart the asynchronous Receive operation.
        mq.BeginReceive();

        return;
    }
  }
}

[C++]
#using <mscorlib.dll>
#using <system.dll>
#using <system.messaging.dll>

using namespace System;
using namespace System::Messaging;

__gc class MyNewQueue
{
    //*************************************************
    // Provides an event handler for the ReceiveCompleted
    // event.
    //*************************************************
public:
    static void MyReceiveCompleted(Object* source,
        ReceiveCompletedEventArgs* asyncResult)
    {
        // Connect to the queue.
        MessageQueue* mq = dynamic_cast<MessageQueue*>(source);

        // End the asynchronous Receive operation.
        Message* m = mq->EndReceive(asyncResult->AsyncResult);

        // Display message information on the screen.
        Console::WriteLine(S"Message: {0}", m->Body);

        // Restart the asynchronous Receive operation.
        mq->BeginReceive();

        return;
    }
};
```

```
//*************************************************
// Provides an entry point into the application.
//
// This example performs asynchronous receive operation
// processing.
//*************************************************
int main()
{
    // Create an instance of MessageQueue. Set its formatter.
    MessageQueue* myQueue = new MessageQueue(S".\\myQueue");

    Type* p __gc[] = new Type* __gc[1];
    p[0] = __typeof(String);
    myQueue->Formatter = new XmlMessageFormatter( p );

    // Add an event handler for the ReceiveCompleted event.
    myQueue->ReceiveCompleted += new
ReceiveCompletedEventHandler(0, MyNewQueue::MyReceiveCompleted);

    // Begin the asynchronous receive operation.
    myQueue->BeginReceive();

    // Do other work on the current thread.
    return 0;
}
```

Requirements

Namespace: System.Messaging

Platforms: Windows 98, Windows NT 4.0,
Windows Millennium Edition, Windows 2000,
Windows XP Home Edition, Windows XP Professional,
Windows .NET Server family

Assembly: System.Messaging (in System.Messaging.dll)

StandardAccessRights Enumeration

Specifies a set of standard access rights that correspond to operations common to most types of securable objects.

This enumeration has a **FlagsAttribute** attribute that allows a bitwise combination of its member values.

```
[Visual Basic]
<Flags>
<Serializable>
Public Enum StandardAccessRights
[C#]
[Flags]
[Serializable]
public enum StandardAccessRights
[C++]
[Flags]
[Serializable]
__value public enum StandardAccessRights
[JScript]
public
   Flags
   Serializable
enum StandardAccessRights
```

Remarks

The **StandardAccessRights** class provides access rights for common operations, such as deleting, reading, and writing. The precise meaning of each member is specific to the object type to which it is applied.

StandardAccessRights is one of two enumerations to which the **GenericAccessRights** enumeration maps extensive read, write, or execute abilities. **StandardAccessRights** enables you to specify rights common to most objects, for example, deleting the object or reading a security descriptor.

> **Note** Both **StandardAccessRights** and **MessageQueueAccessRights** provide a member for deleting a queue. The needs of the application define which set of flags you use.

Members

Member name	Description	Value
All	Combines **Delete**, **ReadSecurity**, **WriteSecurity**, **ModifyOwner**, and **Synchronize** access.	2031616
Delete	The right to delete the object.	65536
Execute	The right to read the information in the object's security descriptor. On Windows 2000 and Windows NT, the security descriptor contains the security information for a securable object. It identifies the object's owner and primary group. **Execute** is currently defined to equal **ReadSecurity**.	131072
ModifyOwner	The right to change the owner in the object's security descriptor.	524288

Member name	Description	Value
None	No access.	0
Read	The right to read the information in the object's security descriptor. **Read** is currently defined to equal **ReadSecurity**.	131072
ReadSecurity	The right to read the information in the object's security descriptor.	131072
Required	Combines **Delete**, **ReadSecurity**, **WriteSecurity**, and **ModifyOwner** access.	851968
Synchronize	The right to use the object for synchronization. This enables a thread to wait until the object is in a specific state.	1048576
Write	The right to read the information in the object's security descriptor. **Write** is currently defined to equal **ReadSecurity**.	131072
WriteSecurity	The right to modify the discretionary access control list (DACL) in the security descriptor.	262144

> **Note** The DACL controls access to the object. Being able to write to the DACL gives the user the ability to set security for the object.

Requirements

Namespace: System.Messaging

Platforms: Windows 98, Windows NT 4.0, Windows Millennium Edition, Windows 2000, Windows XP Home Edition, Windows XP Professional, Windows .NET Server family

Assembly: System.Messaging (in System.Messaging.dll)

Trustee Class

Specifies a user account, group account, or logon session to which an access control entry applies.

System.Object
  System.Messaging.Trustee

```
[Visual Basic]
Public Class Trustee
[C#]
public class Trustee
[C++]
public __gc class Trustee
[JScript]
public class Trustee
```

Thread Safety

Any public static (**Shared** in Visual Basic) members of this type are safe for multithreaded operations. Any instance members are not guaranteed to be thread safe.

Remarks

The trustee is the entity to whom you are granting or denying access rights when you create an access control entry. Set the **TrusteeType** member (either directly or using the **Trustee** constructor) to specify whether the trustee is a user, computer, or other type. If you do not specify the trustee type before setting permissions for the trustee, the type defaults to **Unknown**.

You must specify a value for the **Name** property before using the **Trustee** to set permissions. The **Name** contains the name of the user, group, or computer account to which the new access rights will be assigned. Optionally, you can set the **SystemName** property to identify the name of the system on which the trustee account is looked up to resolve the name's security identifier. If you do not specify a value for **SystemName**, the local computer looks up the account name.

Requirements

Namespace: System.Messaging

Platforms: Windows 98, Windows NT 4.0, Windows Millennium Edition, Windows 2000, Windows XP Home Edition, Windows XP Professional, Windows .NET Server family

Assembly: System.Messaging (in System.Messaging.dll)

Trustee Constructor

Initializes a new instance of the **Trustee** class.

Overload List

Initializes a new instance of the **Trustee** class without setting any of its read/write properties.

  [Visual Basic] **Public Sub New()**
  [C#] **public Trustee();**
  [C++] **public: Trustee();**
  [JScript] **public function Trustee();**

Initializes a new instance of the **Trustee** class of type **Unknown**, setting the **Name** property to the value specified, and the **SystemName** to a null reference (**Nothing** in Visual Basic).

  [Visual Basic] **Public Sub New(String)**

  [C#] **public Trustee(string);**
  [C++] **public: Trustee(String*);**
  [JScript] **public function Trustee(String);**

Initializes a new instance of the **Trustee** class of type **Unknown**, setting the **Name** and the **SystemName** properties to the values specified.

  [Visual Basic] **Public Sub New(String, String)**
  [C#] **public Trustee(string, string);**
  [C++] **public: Trustee(String*, String*);**
  [JScript] **public function Trustee(String, String);**

Initializes a new instance of the **Trustee** class of the specified type, setting the **Name** and the **SystemName** properties to the values specified.

  [Visual Basic] **Public Sub New(String, String, TrusteeType)**
  [C#] **public Trustee(string, string, TrusteeType);**
  [C++] **public: Trustee(String*, String*, TrusteeType);**
  [JScript] **public function Trustee(String, String, TrusteeType);**

Trustee Constructor ( )

Initializes a new instance of the **Trustee** class without setting any of its read/write properties.

```
[Visual Basic]
Public Sub New()
[C#]
public Trustee();
[C++]
public: Trustee();
[JScript]
public function Trustee();
```

Remarks

You must specify a value for the **Name** property before using the **Trustee** instance to set permissions. Optionally, you can set the **SystemName** property to identify the name of the system on which the trustee account is looked up to resolve the name's security identifier. If you do not specify a value for **SystemName**, the local computer looks up the account name.

Requirements

Platforms: Windows 98, Windows NT 4.0, Windows Millennium Edition, Windows 2000, Windows XP Home Edition, Windows XP Professional, Windows .NET Server family

.NET Framework Security:

- Full trust for the immediate caller. This member cannot be used by partially trusted code.

Trustee Constructor (String)

Initializes a new instance of the **Trustee** class of type **Unknown**, setting the **Name** property to the value specified, and the **SystemName** to a null reference (**Nothing** in Visual Basic).

```
[Visual Basic]
Public Sub New( _
  ByVal name As String _
)
```

```
[C#]
public Trustee(
    string name
);
[C++]
public: Trustee(
    String* name
);
[JScript]
public function Trustee(
    name : String
);
```

Parameters

name
> The value to assign to the **Name** property.

Exceptions

Exception Type	Condition
ArgumentNullException	The *name* parameter is a null reference (**Nothing** in Visual Basic).

Remarks

Use this overload to set the trustee account and specify that the local computer be used to look up the account. The **TrusteeType** property is set to **Unknown**, but you can modify that value before using this instance of **Trustee** to set permissions.

Requirements

Platforms: Windows 98, Windows NT 4.0, Windows Millennium Edition, Windows 2000, Windows XP Home Edition, Windows XP Professional, Windows .NET Server family

.NET Framework Security:
- Full trust for the immediate caller. This member cannot be used by partially trusted code.

Trustee Constructor (String, String)

Initializes a new instance of the **Trustee** class of type **Unknown**, setting the **Name** and the **SystemName** properties to the values specified.

```
[Visual Basic]
Public Sub New( _
    ByVal name As String, _
    ByVal systemName As String _
)
[C#]
public Trustee(
    string name,
    string systemName
);
[C++]
public: Trustee(
    String* name,
    String* systemName
);
[JScript]
public function Trustee(
    name : String,
    systemName : String
);
```

Parameters

name
> The value to assign to the **Name** property.
systemName
> The value to assign to the **SystemName** property.

Exceptions

Exception Type	Condition
ArgumentNullException	The *name* parameter is a null reference (**Nothing** in Visual Basic).

Remarks

Use this overload to set the trustee account and specify that a network computer be used to look up the account. The **TrusteeType** property is set to **Unknown**, but you can modify that value before using this instance of **Trustee** to set permissions.

Requirements

Platforms: Windows 98, Windows NT 4.0, Windows Millennium Edition, Windows 2000, Windows XP Home Edition, Windows XP Professional, Windows .NET Server family

.NET Framework Security:
- Full trust for the immediate caller. This member cannot be used by partially trusted code.

Trustee Constructor (String, String, TrusteeType)

Initializes a new instance of the **Trustee** class of the specified type, setting the **Name** and the **SystemName** properties to the values specified.

```
[Visual Basic]
Public Sub New( _
    ByVal name As String, _
    ByVal systemName As String, _
    ByVal trusteeType As TrusteeType _
)
[C#]
public Trustee(
    string name,
    string systemName,
    TrusteeType trusteeType
);
[C++]
public: Trustee(
    String* name,
    String* systemName,
    TrusteeType trusteeType
);
[JScript]
public function Trustee(
    name : String,
    systemName : String,
    trusteeType : TrusteeType
);
```

Parameters

name
> The value to assign to the **Name** property.
systemName
> The value to assign to the **SystemName** property.

trusteeType
    A **TrusteeType** that indicates the account type of the trustee.

Exceptions

Exception Type	Condition
ArgumentNullException	The *name* parameter is a null reference (**Nothing** in Visual Basic).

Remarks

Use this overload when the trustee type is known to set the trustee account and specify a network computer to be used to look up the account.

This overload sets the **TrusteeType** property at construction, but you can modify that value before using this instance of **Trustee** to set permissions. The **Unknown** trustee type (which the other overloads of the constructor set by default) should be used only when you do not know the kind of trust that is being used, but know that it is valid.

Requirements

Platforms: Windows 98, Windows NT 4.0, Windows Millennium Edition, Windows 2000, Windows XP Home Edition, Windows XP Professional, Windows .NET Server family

.NET Framework Security:
* Full trust for the immediate caller. This member cannot be used by partially trusted code.

Trustee.Name Property

Gets or sets the name of the trustee.

```
[Visual Basic]
Public Property Name As String
[C#]
public string Name {get; set;}
[C++]
public: __property String* get_Name();
public: __property void set_Name(String*);
[JScript]
public function get Name() : String;
public function set Name(String);
```

Property Value

The name of the account to which the new rights will be assigned. The default is a null reference (**Nothing** in Visual Basic).

Exceptions

Exception Type	Condition
ArgumentNullException	The **Name** property is a null reference (**Nothing** in Visual Basic).

Remarks

You must specify a value for the **Name** property before using the **Trustee** to set permissions. The **Name** contains the name of the user, group, or computer account to which the new access rights will be assigned.

If you do not specify a value for the **SystemName** property, the account you identify in the **Name** property is looked up on the local computer. If you do specify a **SystemName**, the account is looked up on the computer you specify.

If you are not connected to the network (for example, if you are in workgroup mode), the **Name** property can be any local user or group. In this case, you should not specify any value for **SystemName**, as workgroup mode is local by definition.

Requirements

Platforms: Windows 98, Windows NT 4.0, Windows Millennium Edition, Windows 2000, Windows XP Home Edition, Windows XP Professional, Windows .NET Server family

.NET Framework Security:
* Full trust for the immediate caller. This member cannot be used by partially trusted code.

Trustee.SystemName Property

Gets or sets the computer on which to look up the trustee's account.

```
[Visual Basic]
Public Property SystemName As String
[C#]
public string SystemName {get; set;}
[C++]
public: __property String* get_SystemName();
public: __property void set_SystemName(String*);
[JScript]
public function get SystemName() : String;
public function set SystemName(String);
```

Property Value

The local or remote computer on which the account exists. The default is a null reference (**Nothing** in Visual Basic), which indicates that the name will be looked up on the local computer.

Remarks

You must specify a value for **Name** before you use this instance of **Trustee** to set permissions, but **SystemName** is optional. If you leave **SystemName** a null reference (**Nothing** in Visual Basic), the local computer is used to look up the account you specify in the **Name** property.

Requirements

Platforms: Windows 98, Windows NT 4.0, Windows Millennium Edition, Windows 2000, Windows XP Home Edition, Windows XP Professional, Windows .NET Server family

.NET Framework Security:
* Full trust for the immediate caller. This member cannot be used by partially trusted code.

Trustee.TrusteeType Property

Gets or sets the type of the trustee, which identifies whether the trustee is a user, group, computer, domain, or alias.

```
[Visual Basic]
Public Property TrusteeType As TrusteeType
[C#]
public TrusteeType TrusteeType {get; set;}
[C++]
public: __property TrusteeType get_TrusteeType();
public: __property void set_TrusteeType(TrusteeType);
```

```
[JScript]
public function get TrusteeType() : TrusteeType;
public function set TrusteeType(TrusteeType);
```

Property Value

A **TrusteeType** that indicates what type of account the trustee has on the system. The default is **Unknown**.

Exceptions

Exception Type	Condition
InvalidEnumArgument-Exception	The trustee type specified is not one of the **TrusteeType** enumeration members.

Remarks

The **TrusteeType** indicates what type of account the trustee is associated with on the domain controller or on the local computer. This can be, for example, a user account, a group account, or a computer account.

If you are specifying a predefined group name for the **Name** property, such as EVERYONE, the **TrusteeType** is **Group**, rather than **Alias**.

Requirements

Platforms: Windows 98, Windows NT 4.0, Windows Millennium Edition, Windows 2000, Windows XP Home Edition, Windows XP Professional, Windows .NET Server family

.NET Framework Security:

- Full trust for the immediate caller. This member cannot be used by partially trusted code.

TrusteeType Enumeration

Specifies the type of a trustee.

```
[Visual Basic]
<Serializable>
Public Enum TrusteeType
[C#]
[Serializable]
public enum TrusteeType
[C++]
[Serializable]
__value public enum TrusteeType
[JScript]
public
    Serializable
enum TrusteeType
```

Remarks

A trustee is often a user or group, but it might also be a computer on the network or a recognized domain. When you want to grant or set access rights, specify the trustee type in the **TrusteeType** member of a **Trustee**.

Members

Member name	Description
Alias	The trustee is an alias.
Computer	The trustee is a computer.
Domain	The trustee is a domain.
Group	The trustee is a group.
Unknown	The trustee type is unknown, but not necessarily invalid.
User	The trustee is a user.

Requirements

Namespace: System.Messaging

Platforms: Windows 98, Windows NT 4.0, Windows Millennium Edition, Windows 2000, Windows XP Home Edition, Windows XP Professional, Windows .NET Server family

Assembly: System.Messaging (in System.Messaging.dll)

XmlMessageFormatter Class

Serializes and deserializes objects to or from the body of a message, using the XML format based on the XSD schema definition.

System.Object
   System.Messaging.XmlMessageFormatter

```
[Visual Basic]
Public Class XmlMessageFormatter
   Implements IMessageFormatter, ICloneable
[C#]
public class XmlMessageFormatter : IMessageFormatter, ICloneable
[C++]
public __gc class XmlMessageFormatter : public IMessageFormatter,
   ICloneable
[JScript]
public class XmlMessageFormatter implements IMessageFormatter,
   ICloneable
```

Thread Safety

Any public static (**Shared** in Visual Basic) members of this type are safe for multithreaded operations. Any instance members are not guaranteed to be thread safe.

Remarks

The **XmlMessageFormatter** is the default formatter that an instance of **MessageQueue** uses to serialize messages written to the queue. When you create an instance of **MessageQueue**, an instance of **XmlMessageFormatter** is created for you and associated with the **MessageQueue**. You can specify a different formatter by creating it in your code and assigning it to the **Formatter** property of your **MessageQueue**.

A queue's default **XmlMessageFormatter** instance can be used to write to the queue, but it cannot be used to read from the queue until you set either the **TargetTypes** or **TargetTypeNames** property on the formatter. You can either set one or both of these values on the default formatter instance, or you can create a new instance of the formatter and set the values automatically by passing them as arguments into the appropriate **XmlMessageFormatter** constructor.

When specifying **TargetTypes** rather than **TargetTypeNames**, type existence is checked at compile time rather than read time, reducing possibility for error. **TargetTypeNames** requires every entry to be fully qualified, specifying its assembly name. Further, when working with multiple concurrent versions, the version number must also be appended to the target type name as well.

The **TargetTypeNames** and **TargetTypes** properties tell the formatter what schemas to attempt to match when deserializing a message. This allows the formatter to interpret the message body.

The instance serialized in the message body must comply with one of the schemas represented in the type array. When you read the message using the **Receive** method, the method creates object of the type that corresponds to the schema identied and reads the message body into it.

Only one of the two properties needs to be set when reading from the queue, but you can set both. The set of types is the combined set from the two properties. The decision of which property to use is specific to your application. If the message body contains a type whose schema does not match any of the types in the array for either property, an exception will be thrown when the message is read.

The **XmlMessageFormatter** is a crucial component of loosely coupled XML-based messaging. The XSD.exe utility uses the XML

format is used to generate XML schema, such as when you use the utility to serialize a class used by your application. The format is used again in the reverse process when the utility generates a class based on the schema you distribute to describe your class data. The use of the utility and the XML schema it generates enables you to avoid redistributing .dll files every time you recompile a class after the implementation of your class has changed. As long as the schema does not change on the client or the server, other changes on either side do not affect the other.

Example

[Visual Basic, C#] The following example includes three pieces of code: a server component, an order class, and client code. The order class can be used by the XSD.exe utility to generate schema that the server recognizes within incoming messages. The schema is an XML formatted file that describes the "shape" of the class. This schema can then be used on the client side to generate a client-specific order class that shares the same schema as the server class.

[Visual Basic, C#] The following code represents a server component that receives orders through a message queue. The body of the message should be an order object whose schema matches the Order.cs class below. The server process or application deserializes the order.

```
[Visual Basic]
Imports System
Imports System.Messaging

Public Class Server

    Public Shared Sub Main()

        Console.WriteLine("Processing Orders")

        Dim queuePath As String = ".\orders"
        EnsureQueueExists(queuePath)
        Dim queue As New MessageQueue(queuePath)
        CType(queue.Formatter, XmlMessageFormatter).        ⏎
TargetTypeNames = New String() {"Order"}

        While True
            Dim newOrder As Order = CType(queue.Receive().Body, Order)
            newOrder.ShipItems()
        End While
    End Sub 'Main

    ' Creates the queue if it does not already exist.
    Public Shared Sub EnsureQueueExists(path As String)
        If Not MessageQueue.Exists(path) Then
            MessageQueue.Create(path)
        End If
    End Sub 'EnsureQueueExists
End Class 'Server

[C#]
using System;
using System.Messaging;

public class Server{

    public static void Main(){

        Console.WriteLine("Processing Orders");

        string queuePath = ".\\orders";
        EnsureQueueExists(queuePath);
        MessageQueue queue = new MessageQueue(queuePath);
        ((XmlMessageFormatter)queue.Formatter).TargetTypeNames   ⏎
= new string[]("Order");

        while(true){
            Order newOrder = (Order)queue.Receive().Body;
```

```
            newOrder.ShipItems();
        }
    }

    // Creates the queue if it does not already exist.
    public static void EnsureQueueExists(string path){
        if(!MessageQueue.Exists(path)){
            MessageQueue.Create(path);
        }
    }
}
```

[Visual Basic, C#] This code sample represents the order class that provides a schema for the order objects that the application on the server receives and deserializes:

[Visual Basic]
```
Imports System
Imports Microsoft.VisualBasic

Public Class Order

    Public itemId As Integer
    Public quantity As Integer
    Public address As String


    Public Sub ShipItems()

        Console.WriteLine("Order Placed:")
        Console.WriteLine(ControlChars.Tab & "Item ID  : {0}", itemId)
        Console.WriteLine(ControlChars.Tab & "Quantity : {0}",           ⌐
quantity)
        Console.WriteLine(ControlChars.Tab & "Ship To  : {0}", address)

        ' Add order to the database.
        ' Insert code here.

    End Sub 'ShipItems
End Class 'Order
```

[C#]
```
using System;

public class Order{

    public int itemId;
    public int quantity;
    public string address;

    public void ShipItems(){

        Console.WriteLine("Order Placed:");
        Console.WriteLine("\tItem ID  : {0}",itemId);
        Console.WriteLine("\tQuantity : {0}",quantity);
        Console.WriteLine("\tShip To  : {0}",address);

        // Add order to the database.
        /* Insert code here. */


    }
}
```

[Visual Basic, C#] Any client application that interacts with the application on the server must send messages to the server by serializing information in a locally defined order class into the message body. The locally defined order class must have the same schema as the server-defined order class into which the application on the server will attempt to deserialize the message body. The XSD.exe utility lets the manager of the application on the server create and distribute the schema the client must use to serialize messages going to the server.

[Visual Basic, C#] When the manager of the client application receives the schema for the order class, the XSD.exe utility is used

again to generate a client-specific order class from the schema. It is this class that is used in the client code example below, not the server's order class (the XSD.exe utility causes the schema-generated class to have the same name as the original class). This new order class is used to serialize the order into the message body.

[Visual Basic, C#] The following code is the client-side processing, used to serialize an order and send the information associated with the order to a queue. The code associates Item, Quantity, and Address information with elements of the schema that were generated for the Order.cs class by the XSD.exe utility. An order is sent to the "orders" queue on the local computer.

[Visual Basic]
```
Imports System
Imports System.Messaging

Class Client

    Public Shared Sub Main()

        Dim queuePath As String = ".\orders"
        EnsureQueueExists(queuePath)
        Dim queue As New MessageQueue(queuePath)

        Dim orderRequest As New Order()
        orderRequest.itemId = 1025
        orderRequest.quantity = 5
        orderRequest.address = "One Microsoft Way"

        queue.Send(orderRequest)
        ' This line uses a new method you define on the Order class:
        ' orderRequest.PrintReceipt()

    End Sub 'Main

    ' Creates the queue if it does not already exist.
    Public Shared Sub EnsureQueueExists(path As String)
        If Not MessageQueue.Exists(path) Then
            MessageQueue.Create(path)
        End If
    End Sub 'EnsureQueueExists
End Class 'Client
```

[C#]
```
using System;
using System.Messaging;

class Client{

    public static void Main(){

        string queuePath = ".\\orders";
        EnsureQueueExists(queuePath);
        MessageQueue queue = new MessageQueue(queuePath);

        Order orderRequest = new Order();
        orderRequest.itemId = 1025;
        orderRequest.quantity = 5;
        orderRequest.address = "One Microsoft Way";

        queue.Send(orderRequest);
        // This line uses a new method you define on the Order class:
        // orderRequest.PrintReceipt();
    }

    // Creates the queue if it does not already exist.
    public static void EnsureQueueExists(string path){
        if(!MessageQueue.Exists(path)){
            MessageQueue.Create(path);
        }
    }
}
```

[Visual Basic, C#] After the schema is generated from the order class on the server, you can modify the class. Unless the schema changes, you do not need to redistribute the schema. After you have distributed the schema and generated a client-side order class, that client class can also be modified independently of the server's order class, as long as the schema itself is not modified. The two classes have become loosely coupled.

Requirements

Namespace: System.Messaging

Platforms: Windows 98, Windows NT 4.0, Windows Millennium Edition, Windows 2000, Windows XP Home Edition, Windows XP Professional, Windows .NET Server family

Assembly: System.Messaging (in System.Messaging.dll)

XmlMessageFormatter Constructor

Initializes a new instance of the **XmlMessageFormatter** class.

Overload List

Initializes a new instance of the **XmlMessageFormatter** class, without target types set.

> [Visual Basic] **Public Sub New()**
>
> [C#] **public XmlMessageFormatter();**
>
> [C++] **public: XmlMessageFormatter();**
>
> [JScript] **public function XmlMessageFormatter();**

Initializes a new instance of the **XmlMessageFormatter** class, setting target types passed in as an array of (fully qualified) string values.

> [Visual Basic] **Public Sub New(String())**
>
> [C#] **public XmlMessageFormatter(string[]);**
>
> [C++] **public: XmlMessageFormatter(String*[]);**
>
> [JScript] **public function XmlMessageFormatter(String[]);**

Initializes a new instance of the **XmlMessageFormatter** class, setting target types passed in as an array of object types.

> [Visual Basic] **Public Sub New(Type())**
>
> [C#] **public XmlMessageFormatter(Type[]);**
>
> [C++] **public: XmlMessageFormatter(Type*[]);**
>
> [JScript] **public function XmlMessageFormatter(Type[]);**

Example

See related example in the **System.Messaging.XMLMessageFormatter** class topic.

XmlMessageFormatter Constructor ()

Initializes a new instance of the **XmlMessageFormatter** class, without target types set.

```
[Visual Basic]
Public Sub New()
[C#]
public XmlMessageFormatter();
[C++]
public: XmlMessageFormatter();
[JScript]
public function XmlMessageFormatter();
```

Remarks

This overload of the constructor is used most frequently when writing to the queue, as target types are not required when writing.

To read a message from a queue using an instance of **XmlMessageFormatter** created using this constructor, you must set the **TargetTypeNames** or **TargetTypes** properties so the formatter knows what types to attempt to deserialize.

When you create a new **MessageQueue**, a default **XmlMessageFormatter** instance is created, without the target types set. As with a formatter created using this constructor, you must set target types for that formatter instance if you want to read from the queue.

Requirements

Platforms: Windows 98, Windows NT 4.0, Windows Millennium Edition, Windows 2000, Windows XP Home Edition, Windows XP Professional, Windows .NET Server family

.NET Framework Security:

- Full trust for the immediate caller. This member cannot be used by partially trusted code.

XmlMessageFormatter Constructor (String[])

Initializes a new instance of the **XmlMessageFormatter** class, setting target types passed in as an array of (fully qualified) string values.

```
[Visual Basic]
Public Sub New( _
    ByVal targetTypeNames() As String _
)
[C#]
public XmlMessageFormatter(
    string[] targetTypeNames
);
[C++]
public: XmlMessageFormatter(
    String* targetTypeNames __gc[]
);
[JScript]
public function XmlMessageFormatter(
    targetTypeNames : String[]
);
```

Parameters

targetTypeNames
> An array of type **String** that specifies the set of possible types that will be deserialized by the formatter from the message provided. These values must be fully qualified, for example, "MyNamespace.MyOrders, MyOrdersAssemblyName".

Exceptions

Exception Type	Condition
ArgumentNullException	The *targetTypeNames* parameter is a null reference (**Nothing** in Visual Basic).

Remarks

The constructors with target types parameters are most frequently used when reading from the queue. When writing, it is not necessary to specify target types.

This overload of the **ctor** constructor sets the **TargetTypeNames** property to the array values passed in through the *targetTypeNames* parameter. Setting this property enables a **MessageQueue** using this **XmlMessageFormatter** instance to read messages containing objects of given types.

Both the **TargetTypeNames** and **TargetTypes** properties tell the formatter what schemas to attempt to match when deserializing a message. This allows the formatter to interpret the message body.

The instance serialized in the message body must comply with one of the schemas represented in the type array. When you read the message using the **Receive** method, the method creates object of the type that corresponds to the schema identied and reads the message body into it.

Only one of the two properties needs to be set when reading from the queue, but you can set both. The set of types is the combined set from the two properties. The decision of which one to use is specific to your application. If the message body contains a type whose schema does not match any of the types in the array for either property, an exception will be thrown at read time.

Example

See related example in the **System.Messaging.XMLMessageFormatter** class topic.

Requirements

Platforms: Windows 98, Windows NT 4.0, Windows Millennium Edition, Windows 2000, Windows XP Home Edition, Windows XP Professional, Windows .NET Server family

.NET Framework Security:

- Full trust for the immediate caller. This member cannot be used by partially trusted code.

XmlMessageFormatter Constructor (Type[])

Initializes a new instance of the **XmlMessageFormatter** class, setting target types passed in as an array of object types.

```
[Visual Basic]
Public Sub New( _
   ByVal targetTypes() As Type _
)
[C#]
public XmlMessageFormatter(
   Type[] targetTypes
);
[C++]
public: XmlMessageFormatter(
   Type* targetTypes[]
);
[JScript]
public function XmlMessageFormatter(
   targetTypes : Type[]
);
```

Parameters

targetTypes
    An array of type **Type** that specifies the set of possible types that will be deserialized by the formatter from the message provided.

Exceptions

Exception Type	Condition
ArgumentNullException	The *targetTypes* parameter is a null reference (**Nothing** in Visual Basic).

Remarks

The constructors with target types parameters are most frequently used when reading from the queue. When writing, it is not necessary to specify target types.

This overload of the **ctor** constructor sets the **TargetTypes** property to the array values passed in through the *targetTypes* parameter. Setting this property enables a **MessageQueue** using this **XmlMessageFormatter** instance to read messages containing objects of the given types.

Both the **TargetTypeNames** and **TargetTypes** properties tell the formatter what schemas to attempt to match when deserializing a message. This allows the formatter to interpret the message body.

The instance serialized in the message body must comply with one of the schemas represented in the type array. When you read the message using the **Receive** method, the method creates object of the type that corresponds to the schema identied and reads the message body into it.

Only one of the two properties needs to be set when reading from the queue, but you can set both. The set of types is the combined set from the two properties. The decision of which one to use is specific to your application. If the message body contains a type whose schema does not match any of the types in the array for either property, an exception will be thrown at read time.

When specifying **TargetTypes** rather than **TargetTypeNames**, type existence is checked at compile time rather than read time, reducing possibility for error. **TargetTypeNames** requires every entry to be fully qualified, specifying its assembly name. Further, when working with multiple concurrent versions, the version number must also be appended to the target type name as well.

When using **TargetTypes**, you can add each object (say, MyClass) to the list in a way demonstrated by the following C# code.

```
TargetTypes = new Type[]{typeof(MyClass)}
```

Requirements

Platforms: Windows 98, Windows NT 4.0, Windows Millennium Edition, Windows 2000, Windows XP Home Edition, Windows XP Professional, Windows .NET Server family

.NET Framework Security:

- Full trust for the immediate caller. This member cannot be used by partially trusted code.

XmlMessageFormatter.TargetTypeNames Property

Specifies the set of possible types that will be deserialized by the formatter from the message provided.

```
[Visual Basic]
Public Property TargetTypeNames As String ()
[C#]
public string[] TargetTypeNames {get; set;}
```

```
[C++]
public: __property String* get_TargetTypeNames();
public: __property void set_TargetTypeNames(String* __gc[]);
[JScript]
public function get TargetTypeNames() : String[];
public function set TargetTypeNames(String[]);
```

Property Value

An array of type **String** that specifies the types of objects to deserialize from the message body when reading the message.

Exceptions

Exception Type	Condition
ArgumentNullException	The **TargetTypeNames** property is a null reference (**Nothing** in Visual Basic).

Remarks

Both the **TargetTypeNames** and **TargetTypes** properties tell the formatter what schemas to attempt to match when deserializing a message. This allows the formatter to interpret the message body.

The instance serialized in the message body must comply with one of the schemas represented in the type array. When you read the message using the **Receive** method, the method creates object of the type that corresponds to the schema identied and reads the message body into it.

Only one of the two properties needs to be set when reading from the queue, but you can set both. The set of types is the combined set from the two properties. The decision of which property to use is specific to your application. If the message body contains a type whose schema does not match any of the types in the array for either property, an exception will be thrown when the message is read.

TargetTypeNames requires every entry to be fully qualified, specifying its assembly name. Further, when working with multiple concurrent versions, the version number must also be appended to the target type name as well.

> **Note** The target types are only required when reading from the queue. The **TargetTypeNames** and **TargetTypes** properties do not need to be set to write to the queue.

Requirements

Platforms: Windows 98, Windows NT 4.0, Windows Millennium Edition, Windows 2000, Windows XP Home Edition, Windows XP Professional, Windows .NET Server family

.NET Framework Security:
- Full trust for the immediate caller. This member cannot be used by partially trusted code.

XmlMessageFormatter.TargetTypes Property

Specifies the set of possible types that will be deserialized by the formatter from the message provided.

```
[Visual Basic]
Public Property TargetTypes As Type ()
[C#]
public Type[] TargetTypes {get; set;}
```

```
[C++]
public: __property Type* get_TargetTypes();
public: __property void set_TargetTypes(Type*[]);
[JScript]
public function get TargetTypes() : Type[];
public function set TargetTypes(Type[]);
```

Property Value

An array of type **Type** that specifies the types of objects to deserialize from the message body when reading the message.

Exceptions

Exception Type	Condition
ArgumentNullException	The **TargetTypes** property is a null reference (**Nothing** in Visual Basic).

Remarks

Both the **TargetTypeNames** and **TargetTypes** properties tell the formatter what schemas to attempt to match when deserializing a message. This allows the formatter to interpret the message body.

The instance serialized in the message body must comply with one of the schemas represented in the type array. When you read the message using the **Receive** method, the method creates object of the type that corresponds to the schema identied and reads the message body into it.

Only one of the two properties needs to be set when reading from the queue, but you can set both. The set of types is the combined set from the two properties. The decision of which property to use is specific to your application. If the message body contains a type whose schema does not match any of the types in the array for either property, an exception will be thrown when the message is read.

> **Note** The target types are only required when reading from the queue. The **TargetTypeNames** and **TargetTypes** properties do not need to be set to write to the queue.

When specifying **TargetTypes** rather than **TargetTypeNames**, type existence is checked at compile time rather than read time, reducing possibility for error.

When using **TargetTypes**, you can add each object (say, MyClass) to the list in a way demonstrated by the C# code TargetTypes = new Type[]{typeof(MyClass), typeof

(MyOtherClass)};.

Example

See related example in the **System.Messaging.XMLMessageFormatter** class topic.

Requirements

Platforms: Windows 98, Windows NT 4.0, Windows Millennium Edition, Windows 2000, Windows XP Home Edition, Windows XP Professional, Windows .NET Server family

.NET Framework Security:
- Full trust for the immediate caller. This member cannot be used by partially trusted code.

XmlMessageFormatter.CanRead Method

Determines whether the formatter can deserialize the message.

```
[Visual Basic]
Public Overridable Function CanRead( _
    ByVal message As Message _
) As Boolean Implements IMessageFormatter.CanRead
[C#]
public virtual bool CanRead(
    Message message
);
[C++]
public: virtual bool CanRead(
    Message* message
);
[JScript]
public function CanRead(
    message : Message
) : Boolean;
```

Parameters

message
> The **Message** to inspect.

Return Value

true if the XML formatter can deserialize the message; otherwise, **false**.

Implements

IMessageFormatter.CanRead

Exceptions

Exception Type	Condition
InvalidOperationException	Neither the **TargetTypeNames** nor **TargetTypes** property has been set.
ArgumentNullException	The *message* parameter is a null reference (**Nothing** in Visual Basic).

Remarks

When **CanRead** is called, the formatter attempts to determine if the contents of the message are something it can deserialize. The formatter can only deserialize the message if the type in the message body has the same schema as one of the types in the array represented by the **TargetTypeNames** and **TargetTypes** properties. **CanRead** returns **false** under the following two circumstances:

1. The message was not formatted using the **XmlMessageFormatter**.
2. The schema of the message body is not among those listed in either the **TargetTypeNames** or **TargetTypes** property.

The **TargetTypeNames** and **TargetTypes** properties tell the formatter what types of objects it must be able to deserialize. If any type is missing from the list, yet is found within the message, **CanRead** returns **false**.

Requirements

Platforms: Windows 98, Windows NT 4.0, Windows Millennium Edition, Windows 2000, Windows XP Home Edition, Windows XP Professional, Windows .NET Server family

.NET Framework Security:
- Full trust for the immediate caller. This member cannot be used by partially trusted code.

XmlMessageFormatter.Clone Method

Creates an instance of the **XmlMessageFormatter** class whose read/write properties (the sets of target types) are the same as the current **XmlMessageFormatter** instance.

```
[Visual Basic]
Public Overridable Function Clone() As Object Implements _
    ICloneable.Clone
[C#]
public virtual object Clone();
[C++]
public: virtual Object* Clone();
[JScript]
public function Clone() : Object;
```

Return Value

An object whose properties are identical to those of this **XmlMessageFormatter** instance, but whose metadata does not specify it to be a formatter class instance.

Implements

ICloneable.Clone

Remarks

This method creates a copy of the formatter and initializes all its properties to the values of this **XmlMessageFormatter** object.

Requirements

Platforms: Windows 98, Windows NT 4.0, Windows Millennium Edition, Windows 2000, Windows XP Home Edition, Windows XP Professional, Windows .NET Server family

.NET Framework Security:
- Full trust for the immediate caller. This member cannot be used by partially trusted code.

XmlMessageFormatter.Read Method

Reads the contents from the given message and creates an object containing the deserialized message.

```
[Visual Basic]
Public Overridable Function Read( _
    ByVal message As Message _
) As Object Implements IMessageFormatter.Read
[C#]
public virtual object Read(
    Message message
);
[C++]
public: virtual Object* Read(
    Message* message
);
[JScript]
public function Read(
    message : Message
) : Object;
```

Parameters

message
> The **Message**, in XML format, to deserialize.

Return Value

The deserialized message.

Implements

IMessageFormatter.Read

Exceptions

Exception Type	Condition
InvalidOperationException	Neither the **TargetTypeNames** nor **TargetTypes** property has been set. -or- The instance serialized in the message body doesn't comply with any of the schemas represented by the types in the **TargetTypeNames** and **TargetTypes** properties.
ArgumentNullException	The *message* parameter is a null reference (**Nothing** in Visual Basic).

Remarks

Both the **TargetTypeNames** and **TargetTypes** properties tell the formatter what schemas to attempt to match when deserializing a message. One of these properties must be set before the message can be deserialized.

The instance serialized in the message body must comply with one of the schemas represented in the type array. When you read the message using the **Receive** method, the method creates object of the type that corresponds to the schema identied and reads the message body into it.

The target types do not have to be specified in order to write to the queue.

Requirements

Platforms: Windows 98, Windows NT 4.0, Windows Millennium Edition, Windows 2000, Windows XP Home Edition, Windows XP Professional, Windows .NET Server family

.NET Framework Security:
- Full trust for the immediate caller. This member cannot be used by partially trusted code.

XmlMessageFormatter.Write Method

Serializes an object into the body of the message.

```
[Visual Basic]
Public Overridable Sub Write( _
   ByVal message As Message, _
   ByVal obj As Object _
) Implements IMessageFormatter.Write
[C#]
public virtual void Write(
   Message message,
   object obj
);
[C++]
public: virtual void Write(
   Message* message,
   Object* obj
);
```

```
[JScript]
public function Write(
   message : Message,
   obj : Object
);
```

Parameters

message
   The **Message** whose **Body** property will contain the serialized object.

obj
   The **Object** to be serialized into the message body.

Implements

IMessageFormatter.Write

Exceptions

Exception Type	Condition
ArgumentNullException	The *message* parameter is a null reference (**Nothing** in Visual Basic). -or- The *obj* parameter is a null reference (**Nothing**).

Remarks

The target types need not be specified to write to the queue as they must be when reading. The **TargetTypeNames** or **TargetTypes** property is used by the formatter only when deserializing a message.

The **XmlMessageFormatter** makes use of the **XmlSerializer** class, which defines what can be serialized. Only public fields and public properties can be serialized. Structures, structures with arrays, and arrays of structures are all serializable, as long as they do not use the encoded style with the SOAP protocol.

Requirements

Platforms: Windows 98, Windows NT 4.0, Windows Millennium Edition, Windows 2000, Windows XP Home Edition, Windows XP Professional, Windows .NET Server family

.NET Framework Security:
- Full trust for the immediate caller. This member cannot be used by partially trusted code.

System.Net Namespace

The **System.Net** namespace provides a simple programming interface for many of the protocols used on networks today. The **WebRequest** and **WebResponse** classes form the basis of what are called pluggable protocols, an implementation of network services that enables you to develop applications that use Internet resources without worrying about the specific details of the individual protocols.

AuthenticationManager Class

Manages the authentication modules called during the client authentication process.

System.Object
  System.Net.AuthenticationManager

[Visual Basic]
Public Class AuthenticationManager
[C#]
public class AuthenticationManager
[C++]
public __gc class AuthenticationManager
[JScript]
public class AuthenticationManager

Thread Safety

Any public static (**Shared** in Visual Basic) members of this type are safe for multithreaded operations. Any instance members are not guaranteed to be thread safe.

Remarks

AuthenticationManager is a static class that manages the authentication modules that an application uses. When a request is made to protected resources, the **AuthenticationManager** calls the **Authenticate** method to get an **Authorization** instance to use in subsequent requests.

The **AuthenticationManager** queries each registered authentication module by calling the **IAuthenticationModule.Authenticate** method for each module. The first authentication module to return an **Authorization** instance is used to authenticate the request.

Modules that provide the basic, digest, negotiate, NTLM, and Kerberos authentication types are registered with the **AuthenticationManager** by default. Additional authentication modules that implement the **IAuthenticationModule** interface can be added using the **Register** method. Authentication modules are called in the order in which they were added to the list.

Note The Kerberos and negotiate authentication type is not supported on Windows 95/98 or Windows NT 4.0.

Example

[Visual Basic]
```
' The following example shows how to create a custom Basic
authentication module,
' how to register it using the AuthenticationManager class
and how to authorize
' users to access a Web site.
' Note: To run this program you must create a test Web site
that performs
' Basic authentication. Also you must add to your server
```

```
machine a user whose
' credentials are the same as the ones you use in this program.
' Attention: Basic authentication sends the user's credentials
over HTTP.
' Passwords and user names are encoded using Base64 encoding.
Although the
' user information is encoded, it is considered insecure because
it could be deciphered
' relatively easily.
' If you must use Basic authentication you are strongly advised
to use strong
' security mechanisms, such as SSL, when transferring
sensitive information.

Imports System
Imports System.Net
Imports System.IO
Imports System.Text
Imports System.Collections
Imports Microsoft.VisualBasic

Namespace Mssc.Services.Authentication

    Module TestingAuthentication

    ' The ClientAuthentication class performs the following main tasks:
    ' 1) Obtains the user's credentials.
    ' 2) Unregisters the standard Basic authentication.
    ' 3) Registers the custom Basic authentication.
    ' 4) Reads the selected page and displays it on the console.

    Class TestAuthentication

        Private Shared username, password, domain, uri As String

        'This method invoked when the user does not enter the
required input parameters.
        Private Shared Sub showusage()
            Console.WriteLine("Attempts to authenticate to a URL")
            Console.WriteLine(ControlChars.Cr + ControlChars.Lf +
"Use one of the following:")
            Console.WriteLine(ControlChars.Tab +
"customBasicAuthentication URL username password domain")
            Console.WriteLine(ControlChars.Tab +
"customBasicAuthentication URL username password")
        End Sub 'showusage

        ' Display registered authentication modules.
        Private Shared Sub displayRegisteredModules()
            ' The AuthenticationManager calls all authentication
modules sequentially
            ' until one of them responds with an authorization
instance. Show
            ' the current registered modules.
            Dim registeredModules As IEnumerator =
AuthenticationManager.RegisteredModules
            Console.WriteLine(ControlChars.Cr + ControlChars.Lf +
"The following authentication modules are now registered with the
system:")
            While registeredModules.MoveNext()
                Console.WriteLine(ControlChars.Cr + " " +
ControlChars.Lf + " Module : {0}", registeredModules.Current)
                Dim currentAuthenticationModule As
IAuthenticationModule = CType(registeredModules.Current,
IAuthenticationModule)
                Console.WriteLine(ControlChars.Tab + "
CanPreAuthenticate : {0}",
currentAuthenticationModule.CanPreAuthenticate)
            End While
        End Sub 'displayRegisteredModules

        ' The getPage method accesses the selected page and
displays its content
        ' on the console.
        Private Shared Sub getPage(ByVal url As [String])
```

```vb
    Try
        ' Create the Web request object.
        Dim req As HttpWebRequest =                                    ↵
CType(WebRequest.Create(url), HttpWebRequest)

        ' Define the request access method.
        req.Method = "GET"

        ' Define the request credentials according to the          ↵
user's input.
        If domain = [String].Empty Then
            req.Credentials = New NetworkCredential(username, password)
            ' If the user does not specify the Internet            ↵
resource domain, this usually
            ' is by default the name of the sever hosting          ↵
the resource.
        Else
            req.Credentials = New NetworkCredential             ↵
(username, password, domain)
        End If
        ' Issue the request.
        Dim result As HttpWebResponse = CType              ↵
(req.GetResponse(), HttpWebResponse)

        Console.WriteLine(ControlChars.Lf + "Authentication        ↵
Succeeded:")

        ' Store the response.
        Dim sData As Stream = result.GetResponseStream()

        ' Display the response.
        displayPageContent(sData)
    Catch e As WebException
        ' Display any errors. In particular, display any        ↵
protocol-related error.
        If e.Status = WebExceptionStatus.ProtocolError Then
            Dim hresp As HttpWebResponse = CType(e.Response,    ↵
HttpWebResponse)
            Console.WriteLine((ControlChars.Lf +               ↵
"Authentication Failed, " + hresp.StatusCode))
            Console.WriteLine(("Status Code: " +              ↵
Fix(hresp.StatusCode)))
            Console.WriteLine(("Status Description: " +        ↵
hresp.StatusDescription))
            Return
        End If
        Console.WriteLine(("Caught Exception: " + e.Message))
        Console.WriteLine(("Stack: " + e.StackTrace))
    End Try
End Sub 'getPage

' The displayPageContent method display the content of the
' selected page.
Private Shared Sub displayPageContent(ByVal ReceiveStream    ↵
As Stream)
    ' Create an ASCII encoding object.
    Dim ASCII As Encoding = Encoding.ASCII

    ' Define the byte array to temporarily hold the current    ↵
read bytes.
    Dim read(511) As [Byte]

    Console.WriteLine(ControlChars.Cr + ControlChars.Lf +      ↵
"Page Content..." + ControlChars.Cr + ControlChars.Lf)

    ' Read the page content and display it on the console.
    ' Read the first 512 bytes.
    Dim bytes As Integer = ReceiveStream.Read(read, 0, 512)
    While bytes > 0
        Console.Write(ASCII.GetString(read, 0, bytes))
        bytes = ReceiveStream.Read(read, 0, 512)
    End While
    Console.WriteLine("")
End Sub 'displayPageContent
```

```vb
'Entry point which delegates to C-style main Private Function
'Public Overloads Sub Main(ByVal args() As String)
' Main(System.Environment.GetCommandLineArgs())
'End Sub

' This is the program entry point. It allows the user to enter
' her credentials and the Internet resource (Web page) to access.
' It also unregisters the standard and registers the           ↵
customized Basic
' authentication.
Public Shared Sub Main(ByVal args() As String)

    If args.Length < 3 Then
        showusage()
    Else

        ' Read the user's credentials.
        uri = args(0)
        username = args(1)
        password = args(2)

        If args.Length = 3 Then
            domain = String.Empty
            ' If the domain exists, store it. Usually the domain name
            ' is by default the name of the server hosting the Internet
            ' resource.
        Else
            domain = args(3)
        End If

        ' Instantiate the custom Basic authentication module.
        Dim customBasicModule As New CustomBasic()

        ' Unregister the standard Basic authentication module.
        AuthenticationManager.Unregister("Basic")

        ' Register the custom Basic authentication module.
        AuthenticationManager.Register(customBasicModule)

        ' Display registered authorization modules.
        displayRegisteredModules()

        ' Read the specified page and display it on the console.
        getPage(uri)
    End If
    Return
End Sub 'Main

' The CustomBasic class creates a custom Basic               ↵
authentication by implementing the
' IAuthenticationModule interface. It performs the following
' tasks:
' 1) Defines and initializes the required properties.
' 2) Implements the Authenticate and PreAuthenticate methods.

Public Class CustomBasic
    Implements IAuthenticationModule

    Private m_authenticationType As String
    Private m_canPreAuthenticate As Boolean

    ' The CustomBasic constructor initializes the properties    ↵
of the customized
    ' authentication.
    Public Sub New()
        m_authenticationType = "Basic"
        m_canPreAuthenticate = False
    End Sub 'New

    ' Define the authentication type. This type is then        ↵
used to identify this
    ' custom authentication module. The default is set to Basic.

    Public ReadOnly Property AuthenticationType() As String _
        Implements IAuthenticationModule.AuthenticationType
```

```
      Get
         Return m_authenticationType
      End Get
   End Property

   ' Define the pre-authentication capabilities for the        ⏎
module. The default is set
   ' to false.

   Public ReadOnly Property CanPreAuthenticate() As Boolean _
      Implements IAuthenticationModule.CanPreAuthenticate

      Get
         Return m_canPreAuthenticate
      End Get
   End Property

   ' The checkChallenge method checks whether the challenge     ⏎
sent by the HttpWebRequest
   ' contains the correct type (Basic) and the correct domain name.
   ' Note: The challenge is in the form BASIC REALM="DOMAINNAME";
   ' the Internet Web site must reside on a server whose
   ' domain name is equal to DOMAINNAME.
   Public Function checkChallenge(ByVal Challenge As String,     ⏎
ByVal domain As String) As Boolean
      Dim challengePasses As Boolean = False

      Dim tempChallenge As [String] = Challenge.ToUpper()

      ' Verify that this is a Basic authorization request and     ⏎
that the requested domain
      ' is correct.
      ' Note: When the domain is an empty string, the following    ⏎
code only checks
      ' whether the authorization type is Basic.
      If tempChallenge.IndexOf("BASIC") <> -1 Then
         If domain <> [String].Empty Then
            If tempChallenge.IndexOf(domain.ToUpper()) <> -1 Then
               challengePasses = True
               ' The domain is not allowed and the authorization   ⏎
type is Basic.
            Else
               challengePasses = False
            End If
            ' The domain is a blank string and the authorization  ⏎
type is Basic.
         Else
            challengePasses = True
         End If
      End If
      Return challengePasses
   End Function 'checkChallenge

   ' The PreAuthenticate method specifies whether the           ⏎
authentication implemented
   ' by this class allows pre-authentication.
   ' Even if you do not use it, this method must be             ⏎
implemented to obey to the rules
   ' of interface implementation.
   ' In this case it always returns false.
   Public Function PreAuthenticate(ByVal request As            ⏎
WebRequest, ByVal credentials As ICredentials) As Authorization _
      Implements IAuthenticationModule.PreAuthenticate

      Return Nothing
   End Function 'PreAuthenticate

   ' Authenticate is the core method for this custom authentication.
   ' When an Internet resource requests authentication,         ⏎
the WebRequest.GetResponse
   ' method calls the AuthenticationManager.Authenticate        ⏎
method. This method, in
   ' turn, calls the Authenticate method on each of the         ⏎
registered authentication
   ' modules, in the order in which they were registered.       ⏎
```

```
   When the authentication is
   ' complete an Authorization object is returned to the WebRequest.
   Public Function Authenticate(ByVal challenge As String,      ⏎
ByVal request As WebRequest, ByVal credentials As ICredentials)  ⏎
As Authorization _
      Implements IAuthenticationModule.Authenticate

      Dim ASCII As Encoding = Encoding.ASCII

      ' Get the username and password from the credentials
      Dim MyCreds As NetworkCredential =
credentials.GetCredential(request.RequestUri, "Basic")

      If PreAuthenticate(request, credentials) Is Nothing Then
         Console.WriteLine(ControlChars.Lf + "               ⏎
Pre-authentication is not allowed.")
      Else
         Console.WriteLine(ControlChars.Lf + "               ⏎
Pre-authentication is allowed.")
      End If
      ' Verify that the challenge satisfies the                ⏎
authorization requirements.
      Dim challengeOk As Boolean = checkChallenge              ⏎
(challenge, MyCreds.Domain)

      If Not challengeOk Then
         Return Nothing
      End If

      ' Create the encrypted string according to the Basic      ⏎
authentication format as
      ' follows:
      ' a)Concatenate the username and password separated by colon;
      ' b)Apply ASCII encoding to obtain a stream of bytes;
      ' c)Apply Base64 encoding to this array of bytes to        ⏎
obtain the encoded
      ' authorization.
      Dim BasicEncrypt As String = MyCreds.UserName + ":" +     ⏎
MyCreds.Password

      Dim BasicToken As String = "Basic " +                   ⏎
Convert.ToBase64String(ASCII.GetBytes(BasicEncrypt))

      ' Create an Authorization object using the encoded        ⏎
authorization above.
      Dim resourceAuthorization As New Authorization(BasicToken)

      ' Get the Message property, which contains the           ⏎
authorization string that the
      ' client returns to the server when accessing            ⏎
protected resources.
      Console.WriteLine(ControlChars.Lf + " Authorization      ⏎
Message:{0}", resourceAuthorization.Message)

      ' Get the Complete property, which is set to true         ⏎
when the authentication process
      ' between the client and the server is finished.
      Console.WriteLine(ControlChars.Lf + " Authorization      ⏎
Complete:{0}", resourceAuthorization.Complete)

      Console.WriteLine(ControlChars.Lf + " Authorization      ⏎
ConnectionGroupId:{0}", resourceAuthorization.ConnectionGroupId)

      Return resourceAuthorization
   End Function 'Authenticate
   End Class 'CustomBasic
   End Module
End Namespace

[C#]
// The following example shows how to create a custom Basic      ⏎
authentication module,
// how to register it using the AuthenticationManager class and  ⏎
how to authorize
// users to access a Web site.
```

```
// Note: To run this program you must create a test Web site
that performs
// Basic authentication. Also you must add to your server
machine a user whose
// credentials are the same as the ones you use in this program.
// Attention: Basic authentication sends the user's credentials
over HTTP.
// Passwords and user names are encoded using Base64 encoding.
Although the
// user information is encoded, it is considered insecure
because it could be deciphered
// relatively easily.
// If you must use Basic authentication you are strongly advised
to use strong
// security mechanisms, such as SSL, when transferring
sensitive information.

using System;
using System.Net;
using System.IO;
using System.Text;
using System.Collections;

namespace Mssc.Services.Authentication
{
    // The ClientAuthentication class performs the following main tasks:
    // 1) Obtains the user's credentials.
    // 2) Unregisters the standard Basic authentication.
    // 3) Registers the custom Basic authentication.
    // 4) Reads the selected page and displays it on the console.
    class TestAuthentication
    {

        private static string username, password, domain, uri;

        // This method invoked when the user does not enter
the required input parameters.
        private static void showusage()
        {
            Console.WriteLine("Attempts to authenticate to a URL");
            Console.WriteLine("\r\nUse one of the following:");
            Console.WriteLine("\tcustomBasicAuthentication URL
username password domain");
            Console.WriteLine("\tcustomBasicAuthentication URL
username password");
        }

        // Display registered authentication modules.
        private static void displayRegisteredModules()
        {
            // The AuthenticationManager calls all authentication
modules sequentially
            // until one of them responds with an authorization
instance.  Show
            // the current registered modules.
            IEnumerator registeredModules =
AuthenticationManager.RegisteredModules;
            Console.WriteLine("\r\nThe following authentication
modules are now registered with the system:");
            while(registeredModules.MoveNext())
            {
                Console.WriteLine("\r \n Module :
{0}",registeredModules.Current);
                IAuthenticationModule currentAuthenticationModule =
(IAuthenticationModule)registeredModules.Current;
                Console.WriteLine("\t  CanPreAuthenticate :
{0}",currentAuthenticationModule.CanPreAuthenticate);
            }
        }

        // The getPage method accesses the selected page and
displays its content
        // on the console.
        private static void getPage(String url)
        {
```

```
            try
            {
                // Create the Web request object.
                HttpWebRequest req = (HttpWebRequest) WebRequest.Create(url);

                // Define the request access method.
                req.Method = "GET";

                // Define the request credentials according to the
user's input.
                if (domain == String.Empty)
                    req.Credentials = new NetworkCredential(username, password);
                else
                    // If the user does not specify the Internet resource
domain, this usually
                    // is by default the name of the sever hosting the resource.
                    req.Credentials = new NetworkCredential(username,
password, domain);

                // Issue the request.
                HttpWebResponse result = (HttpWebResponse) req.GetResponse();

                Console.WriteLine("\nAuthentication Succeeded:");

                // Store the response.
                Stream sData = result.GetResponseStream();

                // Display the response.
                displayPageContent(sData);
            }
            catch (WebException e)
            {
                // Display any errors. In particular, display any
protocol-related error.
                if (e.Status == WebExceptionStatus.ProtocolError)
                {
                    HttpWebResponse hresp = (HttpWebResponse) e.Response;
                    Console.WriteLine("\nAuthentication Failed, " +
hresp.StatusCode);
                    Console.WriteLine("Status Code: " + (int) hresp.StatusCode);
                    Console.WriteLine("Status Description: " +
hresp.StatusDescription);
                    return;
                }
                Console.WriteLine("Caught Exception: " + e.Message);
                Console.WriteLine("Stack: " + e.StackTrace);
            }
        }

        // The displayPageContent method display the content of the
        // selected page.
        private static void displayPageContent(Stream ReceiveStream)
        {
            // Create an ASCII encoding object.
            Encoding ASCII = Encoding.ASCII;

            // Define the byte array to temporarily hold the
current read bytes.
            Byte[] read = new Byte[512];

            Console.WriteLine("\r\nPage Content...\r\n");

            // Read the page content and display it on the console.
            // Read the first 512 bytes.
            int bytes = ReceiveStream.Read(read, 0, 512);
            while (bytes > 0)
            {
                Console.Write(ASCII.GetString(read, 0, bytes));
                bytes = ReceiveStream.Read(read, 0, 512);
            }
            Console.WriteLine("");
        }

        // This is the program entry point. It allows the user to enter
        // her credentials and the Internet resource (Web page) to access.
```

```csharp
    // It also unregisters the standard and registers the
customized Basic
    // authentication.
    public static void Main(string[] args)
    {

        if (args.Length < 3)
            showusage();
        else
        {

            // Read the user's credentials.
            uri = args[0];
            username = args[1];
            password = args[2];

            if (args.Length == 3)
                domain = string.Empty;
            else
                // If the domain exists, store it. Usually the domain name
                // is by default the name of the server hosting the Internet
                // resource.
                domain = args[3];

            // Instantiate the custom Basic authentication module.
            CustomBasic customBasicModule = new CustomBasic();

            // Unregister the standard Basic authentication module.
            AuthenticationManager.Unregister("Basic");

            // Register the custom Basic authentication module.
            AuthenticationManager.Register(customBasicModule);

            // Display registered authorization modules.
            displayRegisteredModules();

            // Read the specified page and display it on the console.
            getPage(uri);
        }
        return;
    }
}

// The CustomBasic class creates a custom Basic
authentication by implementing the
// IAuthenticationModule interface. It performs the
following
// tasks:
// 1) Defines and initializes the required properties.
// 2) Implements the Authenticate method.

public class CustomBasic : IAuthenticationModule
{

    private string m_authenticationType ;
    private bool m_canPreAuthenticate ;

    // The CustomBasic constructor initializes the
properties of the customized
    // authentication.
    public CustomBasic()
    {
        m_authenticationType = "Basic";
        m_canPreAuthenticate = false;
    }

    // Define the authentication type. This type is then
used to identify this
    // custom authentication module. The default is set to Basic.
    public string AuthenticationType
    {
        get
        {
            return m_authenticationType;
```

```csharp
        }
    }

    // Define the pre-authentication capabilities for the
module. The default is set
    // to false.
    public bool CanPreAuthenticate
    {
        get
        {
            return m_canPreAuthenticate;
        }
    }

    // The checkChallenge method checks whether the challenge
sent by the HttpWebRequest
    // contains the correct type (Basic) and the correct domain name.
    // Note: The challenge is in the form BASIC REALM="DOMAINNAME";
    // the Internet Web site must reside on a server whose
    // domain name is equal to DOMAINNAME.
    public bool checkChallenge(string Challenge, string domain)
    {
        bool challengePasses = false;

        String tempChallenge = Challenge.ToUpper();

        // Verify that this is a Basic authorization request
and that the requested domain
        // is correct.
        // Note: When the domain is an empty string, the
following code only checks
        // whether the authorization type is Basic.

        if (tempChallenge.IndexOf("BASIC") != -1)
            if (domain != String.Empty)
                if (tempChallenge.IndexOf(domain.ToUpper()) != -1)
                    challengePasses = true;
                else
                    // The domain is not allowed and the authorization
type is Basic.
                    challengePasses = false;
            else
                // The domain is a blank string and the authorization
type is Basic.
                challengePasses = true;

        return challengePasses;
    }

    // The PreAuthenticate method specifies whether the
authentication implemented
    // by this class allows pre-authentication.
    // Even if you do not use it, this method must be
implemented to obey to the rules
    // of interface implementation.
    // In this case it always returns false.
    public Authorization PreAuthenticate(WebRequest request,
ICredentials credentials)
    {
        return null;
    }

    // Authenticate is the core method for this custom authentication.
    // When an Internet resource requests authentication, the
WebRequest.GetResponse
    // method calls the AuthenticationManager.Authenticate
method. This method, in
    // turn, calls the Authenticate method on each of the
registered authentication
    // modules, in the order in which they were registered.
When the authentication is
    // complete an Authorization object is returned to the WebRequest.
    public Authorization Authenticate(String challenge,
WebRequest request, ICredentials credentials)
```

```
    {
        Encoding ASCII = Encoding.ASCII;

        // Get the username and password from the credentials
        NetworkCredential MyCreds =
credentials.GetCredential(request.RequestUri, "Basic");

        if (PreAuthenticate(request, credentials) == null)
            Console.WriteLine("\n Pre-authentication is not allowed.");
        else
            Console.WriteLine("\n Pre-authentication is allowed.");

        // Verify that the challenge satisfies the authorization
requirements.
        bool challengeOk = checkChallenge(challenge, MyCreds.Domain);

        if (!challengeOk)
            return null;

        // Create the encrypted string according to the Basic
authentication format as
        // follows:
        // a)Concatenate the username and password separated by colon;
        // b)Apply ASCII encoding to obtain a stream of bytes;
        // c)Apply Base64 encoding to this array of bytes to
obtain the encoded
        // authorization.
        string BasicEncrypt = MyCreds.UserName + ":" + MyCreds.Password;

        string BasicToken = "Basic " +
Convert.ToBase64String(ASCII.GetBytes(BasicEncrypt));

        // Create an Authorization object using the encoded
authorization above.
        Authorization resourceAuthorization = new
Authorization(BasicToken);

        // Get the Message property, which contains the
authorization string that the
        // client returns to the server when accessing
protected resources.
        Console.WriteLine("\n Authorization
Message:{0}",resourceAuthorization.Message);

        // Get the Complete property, which is set to true
when the authentication process
        // between the client and the server is finished.
        Console.WriteLine("\n Authorization
Complete:{0}",resourceAuthorization.Complete);

        Console.WriteLine("\n Authorization
ConnectionGroupId:{0}",resourceAuthorization.ConnectionGroupId);

        return resourceAuthorization;
    }
  }
}

[C++]
// This program shows how to create a custom Basic
authentication module,
// how to register it via the AuthenticationManager
class and how to authorize
// users to access a Web site.
// Note: In order to run this program you must create
a test Web site that performs
// Basic authentication. Also you must add to your
server machine a user whose
// credentials are the same you use in this program.
// Attention: Basic authentication sends the user's
credentials over HTTP.
// Passwords and user names are encoded using Base64
encoding. Although the
// user information is encoded, it is considered insecure
due to the fact that it
```

```
// could be deciphered relatively easily.
// If you must use basic authentication you are strongly
advised to use strong
// security mechanisms, such as SSL, when transferring
sensitive information on
// the wire.

#using <mscorlib.dll>
#using <System.dll>
using namespace System;
using namespace System::Net;
using namespace System::IO;
using namespace System::Text;
using namespace System::Collections;

// The ClientAuthentication class performs the following main tasks:
// 1) It obtains the user's credentials.
// 2) Unregisters the standard Basic authentication.
// 3) Registers the customized Basic authentication.
// 4) Reads the selected page and displays it on the console.
__gc class TestAuthentication {
public:
    static String *username, *password, *domain, *uri;

    // Show how to use this program.
    static void showusage() {
        Console::WriteLine(S"Attempts to authenticate to a URL");
        Console::WriteLine(S"\r\nUse one of the following:");
        Console::WriteLine(S"\tcustomBasicAuthentication URL
username password domain");
        Console::WriteLine(S"\tcustomBasicAuthentication URL
username password");
        Console::WriteLine(S"\r\nExample:");
        Console::WriteLine(S"\tcustomBasicAuthentication
http://ndpue/ncl/ basicuser basic.101 ndpue");
    }

    // Display registered authentication modules.
    static void displayRegisteredModules() {
        // The AuthenticationManager calls all authentication
modules sequentially
        // until one of them responds with an authorization
instance.  Show
        // the current registered modules, for testing purposes.
        IEnumerator* registeredModules =
AuthenticationManager::RegisteredModules;
        Console::WriteLine(S"\r\nThe following authentication
modules are now registered with the system");
        while(registeredModules->MoveNext()) {
            Console::WriteLine(S"\r \n Module : {0}",
            registeredModules->Current);
            IAuthenticationModule* currentAuthenticationModule =
                dynamic_cast<IAuthenticationModule*>
(registeredModules->Current);
            Console::WriteLine(S"\t  CanPreAuthenticate : {0}",
                __box(currentAuthenticationModule->CanPreAuthenticate));
        }
    }

    // The getPage method accesses the selected page an
displays its content
    // on the console.
    static void getPage(String* url) {
        try {
            // Create the Web request Object*.

            HttpWebRequest* req = dynamic_cast<HttpWebRequest*>
(WebRequest::Create(url));

            // Define the request access method.
            req->Method = S"GET";

            // Define the request credentials according to
the user's input.
            if (String::Compare(domain, String::Empty) == 0 )
```

```
        req->Credentials = new NetworkCredential
(username, password);
        else
            // If the user's specifies the Internet
resource domain, this usually
            // is by default the name of the sever
hosting the resource.
            req->Credentials = new NetworkCredential
(username, password, domain);

        // Issue the request.

        // req->GetResponse();

        HttpWebResponse* result = dynamic_cast<HttpWebResponse*>
(req->GetResponse());
        Console::WriteLine(S"\nAuthentication Succeeded:");

        // Store the response.
        Stream*  sData = result->GetResponseStream();

        // Display the response.
        displayPageContent(sData);
    } catch (WebException* e) {
        // Display the error, if any. In particular display protocol
        // related error.
        if (e->Status == WebExceptionStatus::ProtocolError) {
            HttpWebResponse* hresp = dynamic_cast
<HttpWebResponse*> (e->Response);
            Console::WriteLine(S"\nAuthentication Failed, {0}",
__box(hresp->StatusCode));
            Console::WriteLine(S"Status Code: {0}", __box((int)
hresp->StatusCode));
            Console::WriteLine(S"Status Description: {0}",
hresp->StatusDescription);
            return;
        }
        Console::WriteLine(S"Caught Exception: {0}", e->Message);
        Console::WriteLine(S"Stack: {0}", e->StackTrace);
    }
}

// The displayPageContent method display the content of the
// selected page.
static void displayPageContent(Stream* ReceiveStream) {
    // Create an ASCII encoding Object*.
    Encoding*  ASCII = Encoding::ASCII;

    // Define the Byte array to temporary hold the current
read bytes.
    Byte read[] = new Byte[512];

    Console::WriteLine(S"\r\nPage Content...\r\n");

    // Read the page content and display it on the console.
    // Read the first 512 bytes.
    int bytes = ReceiveStream->Read(read, 0, 512);
    while (bytes > 0) {
        Console::Write(ASCII->GetString(read, 0, bytes));
        bytes = ReceiveStream->Read(read, 0, 512);
    }
    Console::WriteLine(S"");
}
};

// The CustomBasic class creates a custom Basic
authentication by implementing the
// IAuthenticationModule* interface. In particular it
performs the following
// tasks:
// 1) Defines and initializes the required properties.
// 2) Impements the Authenticate method.

public __gc class CustomBasic : public IAuthenticationModule {
private:
```

```
    String* m_authenticationType;
    bool m_canPreAuthenticate;

    // The CustomBasic constructor initializes the properties
of the customized
    // authentication.
public:
    CustomBasic() {
        m_authenticationType = S"Basic";
        m_canPreAuthenticate = false;
    }

    // Define the authentication type. This type is then
used to identify this
    // custom authentication module. The default is set to Basic.
    __property String* get_AuthenticationType() {
        return m_authenticationType;
    }

    // Define the pre-authentication capabilities for the
module. The default is set
    // to false.
    __property bool get_CanPreAuthenticate() {
        return m_canPreAuthenticate;
    }

    // The checkChallenge method checks if the challenge
sent by the HttpWebRequest
    // contains the correct type (Basic) and the correct domain name.
    // Note: the challenge is in the form BASIC REALM=S"DOMAINNAME"
    // and you must assure that the Internet Web site resides
on a server whose
    // domain name is equal to DOMAINAME.
    bool checkChallenge(String* Challenge, String* domain) {
        bool challengePasses = false;

        String* tempChallenge = Challenge->ToUpper();
        // Verify that this is a Basic authorization request
and the requested domain
        // is correct.
        // Note: When the domain is an empty String* the
following code only checks
        // whether the authorization type is Basic.
        if (tempChallenge->IndexOf(S"BASIC") != -1)
            if (String::Compare(domain,String::Empty)!=0 )
                if (tempChallenge->IndexOf(domain->ToUpper()) != -1)
                    challengePasses = true;
                else
                    // The domain is not allowed and the
authorization type is Basic.
                    challengePasses = false;
            else
                // The domain is a blank String* and the
authorization type is Basic.
                challengePasses = true;

        return challengePasses;
    }

    // The PreAuthenticate method specifies if the
authentication implemented
    // by this class allows pre-authentication.
    // Even if you do not use it, this method must be
implemented to obey to the rules
    // of interface implementation.
    // In this case it always returns false.
    Authorization * PreAuthenticate(WebRequest* request, ICredentials*
credentials) {
        return 0;
    }

    // Authenticate is the core method for this custom authentication.
    // When an internet resource requests authentication, the
WebRequest::GetResponse
    // method calls the AuthenticationManager::Authenticate
```

```
method. This method, in
    // turn, calls the Authenticate method on each of the     ↵
registered authentication
    // modules, in the order they were registered. When the   ↵
authentication is
    // complete an Authorization Object* is returned to the   ↵
WebRequest, as
    // shown by this routine's retun type.
    Authorization * Authenticate(String* challenge, WebRequest*  ↵
request, ICredentials* credentials) {
        Encoding* ASCII = Encoding::ASCII;

        // Get the username and password from the credentials
        NetworkCredential * MyCreds = credentials->GetCredential  ↵
(request->RequestUri, S"Basic");

        if (PreAuthenticate(request, credentials) == 0)
            Console::WriteLine(S"\n Pre-authentication is not allowed.");
        else
            Console::WriteLine(S"\n Pre-authentication is allowed.");

        // Verify that the challenge satisfies the authorization   ↵
requirements.
        bool challengeOk = checkChallenge(challenge, MyCreds->Domain);

        if (!challengeOk)
            return 0;

        // Create the encrypted String* according to the Basic    ↵
authentication format as
        // follows:
        // a)Concatenate username and password separated by colon;
        // b)Apply ASCII encoding to obtain a stream of bytes;
        // c)Apply Base64 Encoding to this array of bytes to       ↵
obtain the encoded
        // authorization.
        String* BasicEncrypt = String::Concat(MyCreds->UserName,  ↵
S":", MyCreds->Password);

        String* BasicToken =
            String::Concat(S"Basic ", Convert::ToBase64String     ↵
(ASCII->GetBytes(BasicEncrypt)));

        // Create an Authorization Object* using the above         ↵
encoded authorization.
        Authorization* resourceAuthorization = new                ↵
Authorization(BasicToken);

        // Get the Message property which contains the            ↵
authorization String* that the
        // client returns to the server when accessing           ↵
protected resources
        Console::WriteLine(S"\n Authorization Message: {0}",       ↵
resourceAuthorization->Message);

        // Get the Complete property which is set to true        ↵
when the authentication process
        // between the client and the server is finished.
        Console::WriteLine(S"\n Authorization Complete: {0}",
            __box(resourceAuthorization->Complete));

        Console::WriteLine(S"\n Authorization ConnectionGroupId: {0}",
            resourceAuthorization->ConnectionGroupId);
        return resourceAuthorization;
    }
};

// This is the program entry point. It allows the user to enter
// her credentials and the Internet resource (Web page) to access.
// It also unregisters the standard and registers the customized basic
// authentication.
int main() {
    String* args[] = Environment::GetCommandLineArgs();
```

```
    if (args->Length < 4)
        TestAuthentication::showusage();
    else {
        // Read the user's credentials.
        TestAuthentication::uri = args[1];
        TestAuthentication::username = args[2];
        TestAuthentication::password = args[3];

        if (args->Length == 4)
            TestAuthentication::domain = String::Empty;
        else
            // If the domain exists, store it. Usually the domain name
            // is by default the name of the server hosting the Internet
            // resource.
            TestAuthentication::domain = args[4];

        // Instantiate the custom Basic authentication module.
        CustomBasic* customBasicModule = new CustomBasic();

        // Unregister the standard Basic authentication module.
        AuthenticationManager::Unregister(S"Basic");

        // Register the custom Basic authentication module.
        AuthenticationManager::Register(customBasicModule);

        // Display registered Authorization modules.
        TestAuthentication::displayRegisteredModules();

        // Read the specified page and display it on the console.
        TestAuthentication::getPage(TestAuthentication::uri);
    }
}
```

Requirements

Namespace: System.Net

Platforms: Windows 98, Windows NT 4.0, Windows Millennium Edition, Windows 2000, Windows XP Home Edition, Windows XP Professional, Windows .NET Server family, .NET Compact Framework - Windows CE .NET

Assembly: System (in System.dll)

AuthenticationManager.RegisteredModules Property

Gets a list of authentication modules that are registered with the authentication manager.

```
[Visual Basic]
Public Shared ReadOnly Property RegisteredModules As IEnumerator
[C#]
public static IEnumerator RegisteredModules {get;}
[C++]
public: __property static IEnumerator* get_RegisteredModules();
[JScript]
public static function get RegisteredModules() : IEnumerator;
```

Property Value

An **IEnumerator** that enables the registered authentication modules to be read.

Remarks

The **RegisteredModules** property provides an **IEnumerator** instance that enables the list of registered authentication modules to be read. The **Register** method adds modules to the list, and the **Unregister** method removes modules from it.

Example

See related example in the **System.Net.AuthenticationManager** class topic.

Requirements

Platforms: Windows 98, Windows NT 4.0,
Windows Millennium Edition, Windows 2000,
Windows XP Home Edition, Windows XP Professional,
Windows .NET Server family,
.NET Compact Framework - Windows CE .NET,
Common Language Infrastructure (CLI) Standard

AuthenticationManager.Authenticate Method

Calls each registered authentication module to find the first module that can respond to the authentication request.

```
[Visual Basic]
Public Shared Function Authenticate( _
   ByVal challenge As String, _
   ByVal request As WebRequest, _
   ByVal credentials As ICredentials _
) As Authorization
[C#]
public static Authorization Authenticate(
   string challenge,
   WebRequest request,
   ICredentials credentials
);
[C++]
public: static Authorization* Authenticate(
   String* challenge,
   WebRequest* request,
   ICredentials* credentials
);
[JScript]
public static function Authenticate(
   challenge : String,
   request : WebRequest,
   credentials : ICredentials
) : Authorization;
```

Parameters

challenge
   The challenge returned by the Internet resource.
request
   The **WebRequest** that initiated the authentication challenge.
credentials
   The **ICredentials** associated with this request.

Return Value

An instance of the **Authorization** class containing the result of the authorization attempt. If there is no authentication module to respond to the challenge, this method returns a null reference (**Nothing** in Visual Basic).

Exceptions

Exception Type	Condition
ArgumentNullException	*challenge* is a null reference (**Nothing** in Visual Basic). -or- *request* is a null reference (**Nothing**). -or- *credentials* is a null reference (**Nothing**).

Remarks

The **Authenticate** method calls the **IAuthenticationModule.Authenticate** method on each registered authentication module until one of the module responds with an **Authorization** instance.

The first **Authorization** instance returned is used to authenticate the request. If no authentication module can authenticate the request, the **Authenticate** method returns a null reference (**Nothing** in Visual Basic).

Authentication modules are called in the order in which they are registered with the **AuthenticationManager**.

Requirements

Platforms: Windows 98, Windows NT 4.0,
Windows Millennium Edition, Windows 2000,
Windows XP Home Edition, Windows XP Professional,
Windows .NET Server family,
.NET Compact Framework - Windows CE .NET,
Common Language Infrastructure (CLI) Standard

AuthenticationManager.PreAuthenticate Method

Preauthenticates a request.

```
[Visual Basic]
Public Shared Function PreAuthenticate( _
   ByVal request As WebRequest, _
   ByVal credentials As ICredentials _
) As Authorization
[C#]
public static Authorization PreAuthenticate(
   WebRequest request,
   ICredentials credentials
);
[C++]
public: static Authorization* PreAuthenticate(
   WebRequest* request,
   ICredentials* credentials
);
[JScript]
public static function PreAuthenticate(
   request : WebRequest,
   credentials : ICredentials
) : Authorization;
```

Parameters

request

A **WebRequest** to an Internet resource.

credentials

The **ICredentials** associated with the request.

Return Value

An instance of the **Authorization** class if the request can be preauthenticated; otherwise, a null reference (**Nothing** in Visual Basic). If *credentials* is a null reference (**Nothing**), this method returns a null reference (**Nothing**).

Exceptions

Exception Type	Condition
ArgumentNullException	*request* is **null.**

Remarks

If the authentication module can preauthenticate the request, the PreAuthenticate method returns an Authentication instance and sends the authorization information to the server preemptively instead of waiting for the resource to issue a challenge. This behavior is outlined in section 3.3 of RFC 2617 (HTTP Authentication: Basic and Digest Access Authentication). Authentication modules that support preauthentication allow clients to improve server efficiency by avoiding extra round trips caused by authentication challenges.

Authorization modules that can preauthenticate requests set the **IAuthenticationModule.CanPreAuthenticate** property to **true**.

Requirements

Platforms: Windows 98, Windows NT 4.0, Windows Millennium Edition, Windows 2000, Windows XP Home Edition, Windows XP Professional, Windows .NET Server family, .NET Compact Framework - Windows CE .NET, Common Language Infrastructure (CLI) Standard

AuthenticationManager.Register Method

Registers an authentication module with the authentication manager.

```
[Visual Basic]
Public Shared Sub Register( _
   ByVal authenticationModule As IAuthenticationModule _
)
[C#]
public static void Register(
   IAuthenticationModule authenticationModule
);
[C++]
public: static void Register(
   IAuthenticationModule* authenticationModule
);
[JScript]
public static function Register(
   authenticationModule : IAuthenticationModule
);
```

Parameters

authenticationModule

The **IAuthenticationModule** to register with the authentication manager.

Exceptions

Exception Type	Condition
ArgumentNullException	*authenticationModule* is a null reference (**Nothing** in Visual Basic).

Remarks

The **Register** method adds authentication modules to the end of the list of modules called by the **Authenticate** method. Authentication modules are called in the order in which they were added to the list. If a module with the same **AuthenticationType** is already registered, this method removes the registered module and adds *authenticationModule* to the end of the list.

Example

See related example in the **System.Net.AuthenticationManager** class topic.

Requirements

Platforms: Windows 98, Windows NT 4.0, Windows Millennium Edition, Windows 2000, Windows XP Home Edition, Windows XP Professional, Windows .NET Server family, .NET Compact Framework - Windows CE .NET, Common Language Infrastructure (CLI) Standard

AuthenticationManager.Unregister Method

Removes authentication modules from the list of registered modules.

Overload List

Removes the specified authentication module from the list of registered modules.

Supported by the .NET Compact Framework.

[Visual Basic] **Overloads Public Shared Sub Unregister (IAuthenticationModule)**

[C#] **public static void Unregister(IAuthenticationModule);**

[C++] **public: static void Unregister(IAuthenticationModule*);**

[JScript] **public static function Unregister (IAuthenticationModule);**

Removes authentication modules with the specified authentication scheme from the list of registered modules.

Supported by the .NET Compact Framework.

[Visual Basic] **Overloads Public Shared Sub Unregister (String)**

[C#] **public static void Unregister(string);**

[C++] **public: static void Unregister(String*);**

[JScript] **public static function Unregister(String);**

Example

See related example in the **System.Net.AuthenticationManager** class topic.

AuthenticationManager.Unregister Method (IAuthenticationModule)

Removes the specified authentication module from the list of registered modules.

```
[Visual Basic]
Overloads Public Shared Sub Unregister( _
   ByVal authenticationModule As IAuthenticationModule _
)
[C#]
public static void Unregister(
   IAuthenticationModule authenticationModule
);
[C++]
public: static void Unregister(
   IAuthenticationModule* authenticationModule
);
[JScript]
public static function Unregister(
   authenticationModule : IAuthenticationModule
);
```

Parameters

authenticationModule
   The **IAuthenticationModule** to remove from the list of registered modules.

Exceptions

Exception Type	Condition
ArgumentNullException	*authenticationModule* is a null reference (**Nothing** in Visual Basic).
InvalidOperation-Exception	The specified **IAuthenticationModule** is not registered.

Remarks

The **Unregister** method removes the specified authentication module from the list of authentication modules called by the **Authenticate** method. The module must have been added to the list using the **Register** method before it can be removed from the list.

Example

See related example in the **System.Net.AuthenticationManager** class topic.

Requirements

Platforms: Windows 98, Windows NT 4.0, Windows Millennium Edition, Windows 2000, Windows XP Home Edition, Windows XP Professional, Windows .NET Server family, .NET Compact Framework - Windows CE .NET, Common Language Infrastructure (CLI) Standard

AuthenticationManager.Unregister Method (String)

Removes authentication modules with the specified authentication scheme from the list of registered modules.

```
[Visual Basic]
Overloads Public Shared Sub Unregister( _
   ByVal authenticationScheme As String _
)
```

```
[C#]
public static void Unregister(
   string authenticationScheme
);
[C++]
public: static void Unregister(
   String* authenticationScheme
);
[JScript]
public static function Unregister(
   authenticationScheme : String
);
```

Parameters

authenticationScheme
   The authentication scheme of the module to remove.

Exceptions

Exception Type	Condition
ArgumentNullException	*authenticationScheme* is a null reference (**Nothing** in Visual Basic).
InvalidOperation-Exception	A module for this authentication scheme is not registered.

Remarks

The **Unregister** method removes the authentication module with the specified authentication scheme from the list of authentication modules called by the **Authenticate** method. The module must have been added to the list using the **Register** method before it can be removed from the list.

Example

See related example in the **System.Net.AuthenticationManager** class topic.

Requirements

Platforms: Windows 98, Windows NT 4.0, Windows Millennium Edition, Windows 2000, Windows XP Home Edition, Windows XP Professional, Windows .NET Server family, .NET Compact Framework - Windows CE .NET, Common Language Infrastructure (CLI) Standard

Authorization Class

Contains an authentication message for an Internet server.

System.Object
  System.Net.Authorization

```
[Visual Basic]
Public Class Authorization
[C#]
public class Authorization
[C++]
public __gc class Authorization
[JScript]
public class Authorization
```

Thread Safety

Any public static (**Shared** in Visual Basic) members of this type are safe for multithreaded operations. Any instance members are not guaranteed to be thread safe.

Remarks

The **AuthenticationManager** returns an instance of the **Authorization** class containing the authentication message that is sent to the Internet server to indicate that the client (such as **WebRequest** or one of its descendants) is authorized to access the server.

The **Authorization** instance is created by the authentication module that the **AuthenticationManager** designates to handle the request.

Requirements

Namespace: System.Net

Platforms: Windows 98, Windows NT 4.0, Windows Millennium Edition, Windows 2000, Windows XP Home Edition, Windows XP Professional, Windows .NET Server family, .NET Compact Framework - Windows CE .NET

Assembly: System (in System.dll)

Authorization Constructor

Creates a new instance of the **Authorization** class.

Overload List

Creates a new instance of the **Authorization** class with the specified authorization message.

Supported by the .NET Compact Framework.

  [Visual Basic] **Public Sub New(String)**

  [C#] **public Authorization(string);**

  [C++] **public: Authorization(String*);**

  [JScript] **public function Authorization(String);**

Creates a new instance of the **Authorization** class with the specified authorization message and completion status.

Supported by the .NET Compact Framework.

  [Visual Basic] **Public Sub New(String, Boolean)**

  [C#] **public Authorization(string, bool);**

  [C++] **public: Authorization(String*, bool);**

  [JScript] **public function Authorization(String, Boolean);**

Creates a new instance of the **Authorization** class with the specified authorization message, completion status, and connection group identifier.

  [Visual Basic] **Public Sub New(String, Boolean, String)**

  [C#] **public Authorization(string, bool, string);**

  [C++] **public: Authorization(String*, bool, String*);**

  [JScript] **public function Authorization(String, Boolean, String);**

Example

[Visual Basic, C#, C++] The following example creates a new instance of the **Authorization** class with the specified authorization message, completion status, and connection group identifier.

> [Visual Basic, C#, C++] **Note** This example shows how to use one of the overloaded versions of the **Authorization** constructor. For other examples that might be available, see the individual overload topics.

```
[Visual Basic]
Public Function Authenticate(challenge As String, request As      ⏎
WebRequest, credentials As ICredentials) As Authorization         ⏎
Implements IAuthenticationModule.Authenticate
    Try
        Dim message As String
        ' Check if Challenge string was raised by a site        ⏎
which requires CloneBasic authentication.
        If challenge Is Nothing Or                              ⏎
Not challenge.StartsWith("CloneBasic") Then
            Return Nothing
        End If
        Dim myCredentials As NetworkCredential
        If TypeOf credentials Is CredentialCache Then
            myCredentials = credentials.GetCredential          ⏎
(request.RequestUri, "CloneBasic")
            If myCredentials Is Nothing Then
                Return Nothing
            End If
        Else
            myCredentials = CType(credentials, NetworkCredential)
        End If 'Message encryption scheme :
'        a)Concatenate username and password seperated by space
'        b)Apply ASCII encoding to obtain a stream of bytes
'        c)Apply Base64 Encoding to this array of bytes to      ⏎
obtain our encoded authorization message

        message = myCredentials.UserName + " " + myCredentials.Password
        'Apply AsciiEncoding to our user name and password to    ⏎
obtain it as an array of bytes
        Dim asciiEncoding As Encoding = Encoding.ASCII
        Dim byteArray(asciiEncoding.GetByteCount(message)) As Byte
        byteArray = asciiEncoding.GetBytes(message)

        'Perform Base64 transform
        message = Convert.ToBase64String(byteArray)
        'The following overloaded contructor sets the           ⏎
'Message' property of authorization to the base64 string
'        *that  we just formed and it also sets the             ⏎
'Complete' property to true and the connection group id
'        *to the domain of the NetworkCredential object
        Dim myAuthorization As New Authorization              ⏎
"CloneBasic " + message, True, request.ConnectionGroupName)
        Return myAuthorization
    Catch e As Exception
        Console.WriteLine(("Exception Raised ...:" + e.Message))
        Return Nothing
    End Try
End Function 'Authenticate
```

```
[C#]
public Authorization Authenticate( string challenge,WebRequest
request,ICredentials credentials)
{
    try
    {
        string message;
        // Check if Challenge string was raised by a site
which requires CloneBasic authentication.
        if ((challenge == null) || (!challenge.StartsWith("CloneBasic")))
            return null;
        NetworkCredential myCredentials;
        if (credentials is CredentialCache)
        {
            myCredentials =
credentials.GetCredential(request.RequestUri,"CloneBasic");
            if (myCredentials == null)
                return null;
        }
        else
            myCredentials = (NetworkCredential)credentials;
        // Message encryption scheme :
        // a)Concatenate username and password seperated by space;
        // b)Apply ASCII encoding to obtain a stream of bytes;
        // c)Apply Base64 Encoding to this array of bytes to obtain
our encoded authorization message.

        message = myCredentials.UserName + " " +
myCredentials.Password;
        // Apply AsciiEncoding to our user name and password to
obtain it as an array of bytes.
        Encoding asciiEncoding = Encoding.ASCII;
        byte[] byteArray = new byte[asciiEncoding.GetByteCount(message)];
        byteArray = asciiEncoding.GetBytes(message);

        // Perform Base64 transform.
        message = Convert.ToBase64String(byteArray);
        // The following overloaded contructor sets the 'Message'
property of authorization to the base64 string;
        // that  we just formed and it also sets the 'Complete'
property to true and the connection group id;
        // to the domain of the NetworkCredential object.
        Authorization myAuthorization = new Authorization
("CloneBasic " + message,true,request.ConnectionGroupName);
        return myAuthorization;
    }
    catch(Exception e)
    {
        Console.WriteLine("Exception Raised ...:"+e.Message);
        return null;
    }
}

[C++]
Authorization * Authenticate(String* challenge, WebRequest*
request, ICredentials* credentials)
{
    try
    {
        String* message;
        // Check if Challenge String* was raised by a site which
requires CloneBasic authentication.
        if ((challenge == 0) || (!challenge->StartsWith(S"CloneBasic")))
            return 0;
        NetworkCredential* myCredentials;
        if (dynamic_cast<CredentialCache*>(credentials) == 0)
        {
            myCredentials = credentials->GetCredential(request-
>RequestUri, S"CloneBasic");
            if (myCredentials == 0)
                return 0;
        }
        else
            myCredentials = dynamic_cast<NetworkCredential*>(credentials);
        // Message encryption scheme :
        // a)Concatenate username and password seperated by space;
        // b)Apply ASCII encoding to obtain a stream of bytes;
```

```
        // c)Apply Base64 Encoding to this array of bytes to obtain
our encoded authorization message.

        message = String::Concat(myCredentials->UserName, S" ",
myCredentials->Password);
        // Apply AsciiEncoding to our user name and password to
obtain it as an array of bytes.
        Encoding*  asciiEncoding = Encoding::ASCII;
        Byte byteArray[] = new Byte[asciiEncoding->GetByteCount(message)];
        byteArray = asciiEncoding->GetBytes(message);

        // Perform Base64 transform.
        message = Convert::ToBase64String(byteArray);
        // The following overloaded contructor sets the 'Message'
property of authorization to the base64 String*;
        // that  we just formed and it also sets the 'Complete'
property to true and the connection group id;
        // to the domain of the NetworkCredential Object*.
        Authorization* myAuthorization =
            new Authorization(String::Concat(S"CloneBasic ",
message, __box(true), request->ConnectionGroupName));
        return myAuthorization;
    }
    catch (Exception* e)
    {
        Console::WriteLine(S"Exception Raised ...: {0}", e->Message);
        return 0;
    }
}
```

Authorization Constructor (String)

Creates a new instance of the **Authorization** class with the specified authorization message.

```
[Visual Basic]
Public Sub New( _
    ByVal token As String _
)
[C#]
public Authorization(
    string token
);
[C++]
public: Authorization(
    String* token
);
[JScript]
public function Authorization(
    token : String
);
```

Parameters

token

The encrypted authorization message expected by the server.

Remarks

The **Authorization** instance is created with the **Message** property set to *token* and the **Complete** property set to **true**.

Example

See related example in the **System.Net.AuthenticationManager** class topic.

Requirements

Platforms: Windows 98, Windows NT 4.0, Windows Millennium Edition, Windows 2000, Windows XP Home Edition, Windows XP Professional, Windows .NET Server family, .NET Compact Framework - Windows CE .NET, Common Language Infrastructure (CLI) Standard

Authorization Constructor (String, Boolean)

Creates a new instance of the **Authorization** class with the specified authorization message and completion status.

```
[Visual Basic]
Public Sub New( _
   ByVal token As String, _
   ByVal finished As Boolean _
)
[C#]
public Authorization(
   string token,
   bool finished
);
[C++]
public: Authorization(
   String* token,
   bool finished
);
[JScript]
public function Authorization(
   token : String,
   finished : Boolean
);
```

Parameters

token

The encrypted authorization message expected by the server .

finished

The completion status of the authorization attempt. **true** if the authorization attempt is complete; otherwise, **false**.

Remarks

The **Authorization** instance is created with the **Message** property set to *token* and the **Complete** property set to *finished*.

Example

See related example in the **System.Net.AuthenticationManager** class topic.

Requirements

Platforms: Windows 98, Windows NT 4.0, Windows Millennium Edition, Windows 2000, Windows XP Home Edition, Windows XP Professional, Windows .NET Server family, .NET Compact Framework - Windows CE .NET, Common Language Infrastructure (CLI) Standard

Authorization Constructor (String, Boolean, String)

Creates a new instance of the **Authorization** class with the specified authorization message, completion status, and connection group identifier.

```
[Visual Basic]
Public Sub New( _
   ByVal token As String, _
   ByVal finished As Boolean, _
   ByVal connectionGroupId As String _
)
[C#]
public Authorization(
   string token,
```

```
   bool finished,
   string connectionGroupId
);
[C++]
public: Authorization(
   String* token,
   bool finished,
   String* connectionGroupId
);
[JScript]
public function Authorization(
   token : String,
   finished : Boolean,
   connectionGroupId : String
);
```

Parameters

token

The encrypted authorization message expected by the server .

finished

The completion status of the authorization attempt. **true** if the authorization attempt is complete; otherwise, **false**.

connectionGroupId

A unique identifier that can be used to create private Client-Server connections, that would only be bound to this authentication scheme.

Example

See related example in the **System.Net.AuthenticationManager** class topic.

Requirements

Platforms: Windows 98, Windows NT 4.0, Windows Millennium Edition, Windows 2000, Windows XP Home Edition, Windows XP Professional, Windows .NET Server family, Common Language Infrastructure (CLI) Standard

Authorization.Complete Property

Gets the completion status of the authorization.

```
[Visual Basic]
Public ReadOnly Property Complete As Boolean
[C#]
public bool Complete {get;}
[C++]
public: __property bool get_Complete();
[JScript]
public function get Complete() : Boolean;
```

Property Value

true if the authentication process is complete; otherwise, **false**.

Remarks

The **Complete** property is set to **true** when the authentication process between the client and the server is finished. Some authentication modules, such as the Kerberos module, use multiple round trips between the client and server to complete the authentication process. To keep the **WebRequest** or descendant that initiated the authentication process from interrupting while authorization is taking place, the authentication module sets the **Complete** property to **false**.

Example

See related example in the **System.Net.AuthenticationManager** class topic.

Requirements

Platforms: Windows 98, Windows NT 4.0, Windows Millennium Edition, Windows 2000, Windows XP Home Edition, Windows XP Professional, Windows .NET Server family, .NET Compact Framework - Windows CE .NET, Common Language Infrastructure (CLI) Standard

Authorization.ConnectionGroupId Property

Gets a unique identifier for user-specific connections.

```
[Visual Basic]
Public ReadOnly Property ConnectionGroupId As String
[C#]
public string ConnectionGroupId {get;}
[C++]
public: __property String* get_ConnectionGroupId();
[JScript]
public function get ConnectionGroupId() : String;
```

Property Value

A unique string associating a connection with an authenticating entity.

Remarks

The **ConnectionGroupId** property is a unique string that associates a connection with a specific authenticating entity. For example, the NTLM authorization module ties the authentication credential information to a specific connection to prevent invalid reuse of the connection.

Example

See related example in the **System.Net.AuthenticationManager** class topic.

Requirements

Platforms: Windows 98, Windows NT 4.0, Windows Millennium Edition, Windows 2000, Windows XP Home Edition, Windows XP Professional, Windows .NET Server family, Common Language Infrastructure (CLI) Standard

Authorization.Message Property

Gets the message returned to the server in response to an authentication challenge.

```
[Visual Basic]
Public ReadOnly Property Message As String
[C#]
public string Message {get;}
[C++]
public: __property String* get_Message();
[JScript]
public function get Message() : String;
```

Property Value

The message that will be returned to the server in response to an authentication challenge.

Remarks

The **Message** property contains the authorization string that the client will return to the server when accessing protected resources. The actual contents of the message is defined by the authentication type the client and server are using. Basic HTTP authentication, for example, uses a different message than Kerberos authentication.

When an authentication module supports preauthentication, the **Message** property is sent with the initial request.

Example

See related example in the **System.Net.AuthenticationManager** class topic.

Requirements

Platforms: Windows 98, Windows NT 4.0, Windows Millennium Edition, Windows 2000, Windows XP Home Edition, Windows XP Professional, Windows .NET Server family, .NET Compact Framework - Windows CE .NET, Common Language Infrastructure (CLI) Standard

Authorization.ProtectionRealm Property

Gets or sets the prefix for uniform resource identifiers (URIs) that can be authenticated with the **Message** property.

```
[Visual Basic]
Public Property ProtectionRealm As String ()
[C#]
public string[] ProtectionRealm {get; set;}
[C++]
public: __property String* get_ProtectionRealm();
public: __property void set_ProtectionRealm(String* __gc[]);
[JScript]
public function get ProtectionRealm() : String[];
public function set ProtectionRealm(String[]);
```

Property Value

An array of strings that contains URI prefixes.

Remarks

The **ProtectionRealm** property contains a list of URI prefixes that the **Message** property can be used to authenticate. **WebRequest** and descendants compare a URI to this list to determine if the **Authorization** is valid for a particular URI.

Example

See related example in the **System.Net.AuthenticationManager** class topic.

Requirements

Platforms: Windows 98, Windows NT 4.0, Windows Millennium Edition, Windows 2000, Windows XP Home Edition, Windows XP Professional, Windows .NET Server family, .NET Compact Framework - Windows CE .NET, Common Language Infrastructure (CLI) Standard

Cookie Class

Provides a set of properties and methods used to manage cookies. This class cannot be inherited.

System.Object
  System.Net.Cookie

```
[Visual Basic]
<Serializable>
NotInheritable Public Class Cookie
[C#]
[Serializable]
public sealed class Cookie
[C++]
[Serializable]
public __gc __sealed class Cookie
[JScript]
public
    Serializable
class Cookie
```

Thread Safety

Any public static (**Shared** in Visual Basic) members of this type are safe for multithreaded operations. Any instance members are not guaranteed to be thread safe.

Remarks

The **Cookie** class is used by a client application to retrieve information about cookies received with HTTP responses. The following cookie formats are supported during parsing the HTTP resonse headers: Netscape, RFC 2109, and RFC 2965.

For a list of initial property values for an instance of **Cookie**, see the various **Cookie** constructors.

Requirements

Namespace: System.Net

Platforms: Windows 98, Windows NT 4.0, Windows Millennium Edition, Windows 2000, Windows XP Home Edition, Windows XP Professional, Windows .NET Server family

Assembly: System (in System.dll)

Cookie Constructor

Initializes a new instance of the **Cookie** class, conforming to the Netscape specification. In general, an application doesn't need to construct a **Cookie** class since it is created automatically based on the Set-Cookie header received with the HTTP response.

Overload List

Initializes a new instance of the **Cookie** class.

  [Visual Basic] **Public Sub New()**
  [C#] **public Cookie();**
  [C++] **public: Cookie();**
  [JScript] **public function Cookie();**

Initializes a new instance of the **Cookie** class with a specified **Name** and **Value**.

  [Visual Basic] **Public Sub New(String, String)**
  [C#] **public Cookie(string, string);**
  [C++] **public: Cookie(String*, String*);**
  [JScript] **public function Cookie(String, String);**

Initializes a new instance of the **Cookie** class with a specified **Name**, **Value**, and **Path**.

  [Visual Basic] **Public Sub New(String, String, String)**
  [C#] **public Cookie(string, string, string);**
  [C++] **public: Cookie(String*, String*, String*);**
  [JScript] **public function Cookie(String, String, String);**

Initializes a new instance of the **Cookie** class with a specified **Name**, **Value**, **Path**, and **Domain**.

  [Visual Basic] **Public Sub New(String, String, String, String)**
  [C#] **public Cookie(string, string, string, string);**
  [C++] **public: Cookie(String*, String*, String*, String*);**
  [JScript] **public function Cookie(String, String, String, String);**

Cookie Constructor ()

Initializes a new instance of the **Cookie** class.

```
[Visual Basic]
Public Sub New()
[C#]
public Cookie();
[C++]
public: Cookie();
[JScript]
public function Cookie();
```

Remarks

The default constructor initializes all fields to their default values, using empty strings ("") for *name, value, path,* and *domain.* Note that at least the **Name** property must be initialized before using an instance of the **Cookie** class.

Requirements

Platforms: Windows 98, Windows NT 4.0, Windows Millennium Edition, Windows 2000, Windows XP Home Edition, Windows XP Professional, Windows .NET Server family

Cookie Constructor (String, String)

Initializes a new instance of the **Cookie** class with a specified **Name** and **Value**.

```
[Visual Basic]
Public Sub New( _
    ByVal name As String, _
    ByVal value As String _
)
[C#]
public Cookie(
    string name,
    string value
);
[C++]
public: Cookie(
    String* name,
    String* value
);
```

```
[JScript]
public function Cookie(
    name : String,
    value : String
);
```

Parameters

name

> The name of a **Cookie**. The following characters must not be used inside *name*: equal sign, semicolon, comma, newline (\n), return (\r), tab (\t). The dollarsign character cannot be the first character.

value

> The value of a **Cookie**. The following characters must not be used inside *value*: semicolon, comma.

Remarks

The default for the *value* parameter uses the empty string ("") .

Requirements

Platforms: Windows 98, Windows NT 4.0, Windows Millennium Edition, Windows 2000, Windows XP Home Edition, Windows XP Professional, Windows .NET Server family

Cookie Constructor (String, String, String)

Initializes a new instance of the **Cookie** class with a specified **Name**, **Value**, and **Path**.

```
[Visual Basic]
Public Sub New( _
    ByVal name As String, _
    ByVal value As String, _
    ByVal path As String _
)
[C#]
public Cookie(
    string name,
    string value,
    string path
);
[C++]
public: Cookie(
    String* name,
    String* value,
    String* path
);
[JScript]
public function Cookie(
    name : String,
    value : String,
    path : String
);
```

Parameters

name

> The name of a **Cookie**. The following characters must not be used inside *name*: equal sign, semicolon, comma, newline (\n), return (\r), tab (\t). The dollarsign character cannot be the first character.

value

> The value of a **Cookie**. The following characters must not be used inside *value*: semicolon, comma.

path

> The subset of URIs on the origin server to which this **Cookie** applies. The default value is "/".

Remarks

The default for the *path* parameter uses the empty string ("") .

Requirements

Platforms: Windows 98, Windows NT 4.0, Windows Millennium Edition, Windows 2000, Windows XP Home Edition, Windows XP Professional, Windows .NET Server family

Cookie Constructor (String, String, String, String)

Initializes a new instance of the **Cookie** class with a specified **Name**, **Value**, **Path**, and **Domain**.

```
[Visual Basic]
Public Sub New( _
    ByVal name As String, _
    ByVal value As String, _
    ByVal path As String, _
    ByVal domain As String _
)
[C#]
public Cookie(
    string name,
    string value,
    string path,
    string domain
);
[C++]
public: Cookie(
    String* name,
    String* value,
    String* path,
    String* domain
);
[JScript]
public function Cookie(
    name : String,
    value : String,
    path : String,
    domain : String
);
```

Parameters

name

> The name of a **Cookie**. The following characters must not be used inside *name*: equal sign, semicolon, comma, newline (\n), return (\r), tab (\t). The dollarsign character cannot be the first character.

value

> The value of a **Cookie** object. The following characters must not be used inside *value*: semicolon, comma.

path

> The subset of URIs on the origin server to which this **Cookie** applies. The default value is "/".

domain

> The optional internet domain for which this **Cookie** is valid. The default value is the host this **Cookie** has been received from.

Remarks

The default for the *domain* and *path* parameters uses the empty string ("") .

Requirements

Platforms: Windows 98, Windows NT 4.0, Windows Millennium Edition, Windows 2000, Windows XP Home Edition, Windows XP Professional, Windows .NET Server family

Cookie.Comment Property

Gets or sets a comment that the server can add to a **Cookie**.

```
[Visual Basic]
Public Property Comment As String
[C#]
public string Comment {get; set;}
[C++]
public: __property String* get_Comment();
public: __property void set_Comment(String*);
[JScript]
public function get Comment() : String;
public function set Comment(String);
```

Property Value

An optional comment to document intended usage for this **Cookie**.

Remarks

The client can inspect this optional comment for information added by the server. For example, the server could include information about issues such as the privacy policy or intended usage.

Requirements

Platforms: Windows 98, Windows NT 4.0, Windows Millennium Edition, Windows 2000, Windows XP Home Edition, Windows XP Professional, Windows .NET Server family

Cookie.CommentUri Property

Gets or sets a URI comment that the server can provide with a **Cookie**.

```
[Visual Basic]
Public Property CommentUri As Uri
[C#]
public Uri CommentUri {get; set;}
[C++]
public: __property Uri* get_CommentUri();
public: __property void set_CommentUri(Uri*);
[JScript]
public function get CommentUri() : Uri;
public function set CommentUri(Uri);
```

Property Value

An optional comment representing the intended usage of the URI reference for this **Cookie**. The value must conform to URI format.

Remarks

The URI can provide optional information, such as how the server uses the **Cookie**.

Requirements

Platforms: Windows 98, Windows NT 4.0, Windows Millennium Edition, Windows 2000, Windows XP Home Edition, Windows XP Professional, Windows .NET Server family

Cookie.Discard Property

Gets or sets the discard flag set by the server.

```
[Visual Basic]
Public Property Discard As Boolean
[C#]
public bool Discard {get; set;}
[C++]
public: __property bool get_Discard();
public: __property void set_Discard(bool);
[JScript]
public function get Discard() : Boolean;
public function set Discard(Boolean);
```

Property Value

true if the client is to discard the **Cookie** at the end of the current session; otherwise, **false**. The default is **false**.

Remarks

When **true**, this property instructs the client application not to save the **Cookie** on the user's hard disk when a session ends.

Requirements

Platforms: Windows 98, Windows NT 4.0, Windows Millennium Edition, Windows 2000, Windows XP Home Edition, Windows XP Professional, Windows .NET Server family

Cookie.Domain Property

Gets or sets the URI for which the **Cookie** is valid.

```
[Visual Basic]
Public Property Domain As String
[C#]
public string Domain {get; set;}
[C++]
public: __property String* get_Domain();
public: __property void set_Domain(String*);
[JScript]
public function get Domain() : String;
public function set Domain(String);
```

Property Value

The URI for which the **Cookie** is valid.

Remarks

A server cannot indicate a domain other than its own URI. However, it can indicate more than one server in the domain. The default value is the host this cookie has been received from.

Requirements

Platforms: Windows 98, Windows NT 4.0,
Windows Millennium Edition, Windows 2000,
Windows XP Home Edition, Windows XP Professional,
Windows .NET Server family

Cookie.Expired Property

Gets or sets the current state of the **Cookie**.

```
[Visual Basic]
Public Property Expired As Boolean
[C#]
public bool Expired {get; set;}
[C++]
public: __property bool get_Expired();
public: __property void set_Expired(bool);
[JScript]
public function get Expired() : Boolean;
public function set Expired(Boolean);
```

Property Value

true if the **Cookie** has expired; otherwise, **false**. The default is **false**.

Remarks

Expired Cookies, if received, should be destroyed by the client application.

Requirements

Platforms: Windows 98, Windows NT 4.0,
Windows Millennium Edition, Windows 2000,
Windows XP Home Edition, Windows XP Professional,
Windows .NET Server family

Cookie.Expires Property

Gets or sets the expiration date and time for the **Cookie** as a **DateTime**.

```
[Visual Basic]
Public Property Expires As DateTime
[C#]
public DateTime Expires {get; set;}
[C++]
public: __property DateTime get_Expires();
public: __property void set_Expires(DateTime);
[JScript]
public function get Expires() : DateTime;
public function set Expires(DateTime);
```

Property Value

The expiration date and time for the **Cookie** as a **DateTime** instance.

Remarks

Setting the **Expires** property to **MinValue** makes this a session **Cookie**, which is its default value.

Requirements

Platforms: Windows 98, Windows NT 4.0,
Windows Millennium Edition, Windows 2000,
Windows XP Home Edition, Windows XP Professional,
Windows .NET Server family

Cookie.Name Property

Gets or sets the name for the **Cookie**.

```
[Visual Basic]
Public Property Name As String
[C#]
public string Name {get; set;}
[C++]
public: __property String* get_Name();
public: __property void set_Name(String*);
[JScript]
public function get Name() : String;
public function set Name(String);
```

Property Value

The name for the **Cookie**.

Remarks

The **Name** property must be initialized before using an instance of the **Cookie** class. The following characters are reserved and cannot be used for this attribute value: equal sign, semicolon, comma, newline (\n),return (\r), tab (\t). The dollarsign ($) character cannot be the first character.

Requirements

Platforms: Windows 98, Windows NT 4.0,
Windows Millennium Edition, Windows 2000,
Windows XP Home Edition, Windows XP Professional,
Windows .NET Server family

Cookie.Path Property

Gets or sets the URIs to which the **Cookie** applies .

```
[Visual Basic]
Public Property Path As String
[C#]
public string Path {get; set;}
[C++]
public: __property String* get_Path();
public: __property void set_Path(String*);
[JScript]
public function get Path() : String;
public function set Path(String);
```

Property Value

The URIs to which the **Cookie** applies .

Remarks

The **Path** property specifies the subset of URIs on the origin server to which this **Cookie** applies. If not specified then this **Cookie** will be sent to all pages on the origin server or servers.

Requirements

Platforms: Windows 98, Windows NT 4.0,
Windows Millennium Edition, Windows 2000,
Windows XP Home Edition, Windows XP Professional,
Windows .NET Server family

Cookie.Port Property

Gets or sets a list of TCP ports that the **Cookie** applies to.

```
[Visual Basic]
Public Property Port As String
[C#]
public string Port {get; set;}
```

```
[C++]
public: __property String* get_Port();
public: __property void set_Port(String*);
[JScript]
public function get Port() : String;
public function set Port(String);
```

Property Value

The list of TCP ports that the **Cookie** applies to.

Remarks

This attribute restricts the ports to which this **Cookie** may be sent. The default value means no restriction. Setting this to the empty string ("") will restrict the port to the one used in the HTTP response. Otherwise the value must be a double-quoted string that contains port values delimited with commas.

Requirements

Platforms: Windows 98, Windows NT 4.0, Windows Millennium Edition, Windows 2000, Windows XP Home Edition, Windows XP Professional, Windows .NET Server family

Cookie.Secure Property

Gets or sets the security level of a **Cookie**.

```
[Visual Basic]
Public Property Secure As Boolean
[C#]
public bool Secure {get; set;}
[C++]
public: __property bool get_Secure();
public: __property void set_Secure(bool);
[JScript]
public function get Secure() : Boolean;
public function set Secure(Boolean);
```

Property Value

true if the client is only to return the cookie in subsequent requests if those requests are secure; otherwise, **false**. The default is **false**.

Remarks

In effect, when this property is **true** this cookie may be sent only with https:// requests.

Requirements

Platforms: Windows 98, Windows NT 4.0, Windows Millennium Edition, Windows 2000, Windows XP Home Edition, Windows XP Professional, Windows .NET Server family

Cookie.TimeStamp Property

Gets the time when the cookie was issued as a **DateTime**.

```
[Visual Basic]
Public ReadOnly Property TimeStamp As DateTime
[C#]
public DateTime TimeStamp {get;}
[C++]
public: __property DateTime get_TimeStamp();
[JScript]
public function get TimeStamp() : DateTime;
```

Property Value

The time when the cookie was issued as a **DateTime**.

Remarks

This is a read-only property.

Requirements

Platforms: Windows 98, Windows NT 4.0, Windows Millennium Edition, Windows 2000, Windows XP Home Edition, Windows XP Professional, Windows .NET Server family

Cookie.Value Property

Gets or sets the **Value** for the **Cookie**.

```
[Visual Basic]
Public Property Value As String
[C#]
public string Value {get; set;}
[C++]
public: __property String* get_Value();
public: __property void set_Value(String*);
[JScript]
public function get Value() : String;
public function set Value(String);
```

Property Value

The **Value** for the **Cookie**.

Remarks

The **Value** of a **Cookie** must not be null. The following characters are reserved and cannot be used for this property: semicolon, comma.

Requirements

Platforms: Windows 98, Windows NT 4.0, Windows Millennium Edition, Windows 2000, Windows XP Home Edition, Windows XP Professional, Windows .NET Server family

Cookie.Version Property

Gets or sets the version of HTTP state maintenance to which the cookie conforms.

```
[Visual Basic]
Public Property Version As Integer
[C#]
public int Version {get; set;}
[C++]
public: __property int get_Version();
public: __property void set_Version(int);
[JScript]
public function get Version() : int;
public function set Version(int);
```

Property Value

The version of HTTP state maintenance to which the cookie conforms.

Remarks

The default cookie version is Netscape. If the value is explicitly set to 1, than this **Cookie** must conform to RFC 2109. Note that if a **Cookie** was created automatically by receiving a Set-Cookie2 HTTP response header, the conformance is set to RFC 2965.

Requirements

Platforms: Windows 98, Windows NT 4.0,
Windows Millennium Edition, Windows 2000,
Windows XP Home Edition, Windows XP Professional,
Windows .NET Server family

Cookie.Equals Method

Overrides the **Equals** method.

```
[Visual Basic]
Overrides Public Function Equals( _
   ByVal comparand As Object _
) As Boolean
[C#]
public override bool Equals(
   object comparand
);
[C++]
public: bool Equals(
   Object* comparand
);
[JScript]
public override function Equals(
   comparand : Object
) : Boolean;
```

Parameters

comparand
   A reference to a **Cookie**.

Return Value

Returns **true** if the **Cookie** is equal to *comparand*. Two **Cookie**
instances are equal if their **Name**, **Value**, **Path**, **Domain** and
Version properties are equal. **Name** and **Domain** string comparisons
are case-insensitive.

Requirements

Platforms: Windows 98, Windows NT 4.0,
Windows Millennium Edition, Windows 2000,
Windows XP Home Edition, Windows XP Professional,
Windows .NET Server family

Cookie.GetHashCode Method

Overrides the **GetHashCode** method.

```
[Visual Basic]
Overrides Public Function GetHashCode() As Integer
[C#]
public override int GetHashCode();
[C++]
public: int GetHashCode();
[JScript]
public override function GetHashCode() : int;
```

Return Value

The 32-bit signed integer hash code for this instance.

Remarks

Classes that might be used as a key in a hash table must provide this
override, because objects that are used as keys in a hash table are
required to generate their own hash code through this method.

Requirements

Platforms: Windows 98, Windows NT 4.0,
Windows Millennium Edition, Windows 2000,
Windows XP Home Edition, Windows XP Professional,
Windows .NET Server family

Cookie.ToString Method

Overrides the **ToString** method.

```
[Visual Basic]
Overrides Public Function ToString() As String
[C#]
public override string ToString();
[C++]
public: String* ToString();
[JScript]
public override function ToString() : String;
```

Return Value

Returns a string representation of this **Cookie** object suitable for
including in a HTTP Cookie: request header.

Remarks

The exact format of the string depends on the RFC this cookie
conforms to.

Requirements

Platforms: Windows 98, Windows NT 4.0,
Windows Millennium Edition, Windows 2000,
Windows XP Home Edition, Windows XP Professional,
Windows .NET Server family

CookieCollection Class

Provides a collection container for instances of the **Cookie** class.

System.Object
  System.Net.CookieCollection

```
[Visual Basic]
<Serializable>
Public Class CookieCollection
   Implements ICollection, IEnumerable
[C#]
[Serializable]
public class CookieCollection : ICollection, IEnumerable
[C++]
[Serializable]
public __gc class CookieCollection : public ICollection,
   IEnumerable
[JScript]
public
   Serializable
class CookieCollection implements ICollection, IEnumerable
```

Thread Safety

Any public static (**Shared** in Visual Basic) members of this type are safe for multithreaded operations. Any instance members are not guaranteed to be thread safe.

Remarks

The **CookieCollection** class implements an **ICollection** interface to provide a general mechanism for handling collections of cookies. For example, this is useful in the case where an application is designed to store cookies for multiple servers.

Requirements

Namespace: System.Net

Platforms: Windows 98, Windows NT 4.0, Windows Millennium Edition, Windows 2000, Windows XP Home Edition, Windows XP Professional, Windows .NET Server family

Assembly: System (in System.dll)

CookieCollection Constructor

Initializes a new instance of the **CookieCollection** class.

```
[Visual Basic]
Public Sub New()
[C#]
public CookieCollection();
[C++]
public: CookieCollection();
[JScript]
public function CookieCollection();
```

Remarks

The following table shows initial property values for an instance of **CookieCollection**.

Property	Default
IsReadOnly	**true**
Count	0
IsSynchronized	**false**

Requirements

Platforms: Windows 98, Windows NT 4.0, Windows Millennium Edition, Windows 2000, Windows XP Home Edition, Windows XP Professional, Windows .NET Server family

CookieCollection.Count Property

Gets the number of cookies contained in a **CookieCollection**.

```
[Visual Basic]
Public Overridable ReadOnly Property Count As Integer  Implements _
   ICollection.Count
[C#]
public virtual int Count {get;}
[C++]
public: __property virtual int get_Count();
[JScript]
public function get Count() : int;
```

Property Value

The number of cookies contained in a **CookieCollection**

Implements

ICollection.Count

Requirements

Platforms: Windows 98, Windows NT 4.0, Windows Millennium Edition, Windows 2000, Windows XP Home Edition, Windows XP Professional, Windows .NET Server family

CookieCollection.IsReadOnly Property

Gets a value indicating whether a **CookieCollection** is read-only.

```
[Visual Basic]
Public ReadOnly Property IsReadOnly As Boolean
[C#]
public bool IsReadOnly {get;}
[C++]
public: __property bool get_IsReadOnly();
[JScript]
public function get IsReadOnly() : Boolean;
```

Property Value

true if this is a read-only **CookieCollection**; otherwise, **false**. The default is **true**.

Requirements

Platforms: Windows 98, Windows NT 4.0, Windows Millennium Edition, Windows 2000, Windows XP Home Edition, Windows XP Professional, Windows .NET Server family

CookieCollection.IsSynchronized Property

Gets a value indicating whether access to a **CookieCollection** is thread safe.

```
[Visual Basic]
Public Overridable ReadOnly Property IsSynchronized As Boolean  _
   Implements ICollection.IsSynchronized
[C#]
public virtual bool IsSynchronized {get;}
```

```
[C++]
public: __property virtual bool get_IsSynchronized();
[JScript]
public function get IsSynchronized() : Boolean;
```

Property Value

true if access to the **CookieCollection** is thread safe; otherwise, **false**. The default is **false**.

Implements

ICollection.IsSynchronized

Requirements

Platforms: Windows 98, Windows NT 4.0, Windows Millennium Edition, Windows 2000, Windows XP Home Edition, Windows XP Professional, Windows .NET Server family

CookieCollection.Item Property

Gets a specific **Cookie** from a **CookieCollection**.

[C#] In C#, this property is the indexer for the **CookieCollection** class.

Overload List

Gets the **Cookie** with a specific index from a **CookieCollection**.

> [Visual Basic] **Overloads Public Default ReadOnly Property Item(Integer) As Cookie**
>
> [C#] **public Cookie this[int] {get;}**
>
> [C++] **public: __property Cookie* get_Item(int);**
>
> [JScript] **CookieCollection.Item (int)**

Gets the **Cookie** with a specific name from a **CookieCollection**.

> [Visual Basic] **Overloads Public Default ReadOnly Property Item(String) As Cookie**
>
> [C#] **public Cookie this[string] {get;}**
>
> [C++] **public: __property Cookie* get_Item(String*);**
>
> [JScript] **CookieCollection.Item (String)**

CookieCollection.Item Property (Int32)

Gets the **Cookie** with a specific index from a **CookieCollection**.

[C#] In C#, this property is the indexer for the **CookieCollection** class.

```
[Visual Basic]
Overloads Public Default ReadOnly Property Item( _
   ByVal index As Integer _
) As Cookie
[C#]
public Cookie this[
   int index
] {get;}
[C++]
public: __property Cookie* get_Item(
   int index
);
[JScript]
returnValue = CookieCollectionObject.Item(index);
-or-
returnValue = CookieCollectionObject(index);
```

[JScript] In JScript, you can use the default indexed properties defined by a type, but you cannot explicitly define your own. However, specifying the **expando** attribute on a class automatically provides a default indexed property whose type is **Object** and whose index type is **String**.

Arguments [JScript]

index
> The zero-based index of the **Cookie** to be found.

Parameters [Visual Basic, C#, C++]

index
> The zero-based index of the **Cookie** to be found.

Property Value

A **Cookie** with a specific index from a **CookieCollection**.

Exceptions

Exception Type	Condition
ArgumentOutOfRange-Exception	index < 0 or index >= Count

Remarks

You can use this to iterate over the contents of a **CookieCollection**.

Requirements

Platforms: Windows 98, Windows NT 4.0, Windows Millennium Edition, Windows 2000, Windows XP Home Edition, Windows XP Professional, Windows .NET Server family

CookieCollection.Item Property (String)

Gets the **Cookie** with a specific name from a **CookieCollection**.

[C#] In C#, this property is the indexer for the **CookieCollection** class.

```
[Visual Basic]
Overloads Public Default ReadOnly Property Item( _
   ByVal name As String _
) As Cookie
[C#]
public Cookie this[
   string name
] {get;}
[C++]
public: __property Cookie* get_Item(
   String* name
);
[JScript]
returnValue = CookieCollectionObject.Item(name);
-or-
returnValue = CookieCollectionObject(name);
```

[JScript] In JScript, you can use the default indexed properties defined by a type, but you cannot explicitly define your own. However, specifying the **expando** attribute on a class automatically provides a default indexed property whose index type is **String**.

Arguments [JScript]

name
> The name of the **Cookie** to be found.

Parameters [Visual Basic, C#, C++]

name
> The name of the **Cookie** to be found.

Property Value

The **Cookie** with a specific name from a **CookieCollection**.

Exceptions

Exception Type	Condition
ArgumentNullException	*name* is null.

Remarks

You can use this to iterate over the contents of a **CookieCollection**.

Requirements

Platforms: Windows 98, Windows NT 4.0,
Windows Millennium Edition, Windows 2000,
Windows XP Home Edition, Windows XP Professional,
Windows .NET Server family

CookieCollection.SyncRoot Property

Gets an object that you can use to synchronize access to the **CookieCollection**.

```
[Visual Basic]
Public Overridable ReadOnly Property SyncRoot As Object  Implements _
   ICollection.SyncRoot
[C#]
public virtual object SyncRoot {get;}
[C++]
public: _property virtual Object* get_SyncRoot();
[JScript]
public function get SyncRoot() : Object;
```

Property Value

An object that you can use to synchronize access to the **CookieCollection**.

Implements

ICollection.SyncRoot

Remarks

The **SyncRoot** property returns an object that can be used to synchronize access to the **CookieCollection**.

Requirements

Platforms: Windows 98, Windows NT 4.0,
Windows Millennium Edition, Windows 2000,
Windows XP Home Edition, Windows XP Professional,
Windows .NET Server family

CookieCollection.Add Method

Adds a **Cookie** to a **CookieCollection**.

Overload List

Adds a **Cookie** to a **CookieCollection**.

> [Visual Basic] **Overloads Public Sub Add(Cookie)**
> [C#] **public void Add(Cookie);**
> [C++] **public: void Add(Cookie*);**
> [JScript] **public function Add(Cookie);**

Adds the contents of a **CookieCollection** to the current instance.

> [Visual Basic] **Overloads Public Sub Add(CookieCollection)**
> [C#] **public void Add(CookieCollection);**
> [C++] **public: void Add(CookieCollection*);**
> [JScript] **public function Add(CookieCollection);**

CookieCollection.Add Method (Cookie)

Adds a **Cookie** to a **CookieCollection**.

```
[Visual Basic]
Overloads Public Sub Add( _
   ByVal cookie As Cookie _
)
[C#]
public void Add(
   Cookie cookie
);
[C++]
public: void Add(
   Cookie* cookie
);
[JScript]
public function Add(
   cookie : Cookie
);
```

Parameters

cookie
> The **Cookie** to be added to a **CookieCollection**

Exceptions

Exception Type	Condition
ArgumentNullException	*cookie* is null

Requirements

Platforms: Windows 98, Windows NT 4.0,
Windows Millennium Edition, Windows 2000,
Windows XP Home Edition, Windows XP Professional,
Windows .NET Server family

CookieCollection.Add Method (CookieCollection)

Adds the contents of a **CookieCollection** to the current instance.

```
[Visual Basic]
Overloads Public Sub Add( _
   ByVal cookies As CookieCollection _
)
[C#]
public void Add(
   CookieCollection cookies
);
[C++]
public: void Add(
   CookieCollection* cookies
);
[JScript]
public function Add(
   cookies : CookieCollection
);
```

Parameters

cookies
> The **CookieCollection** to be added .

Exceptions

Exception Type	Condition
ArgumentNullException	*cookies* is null

Remarks

Each **Cookie** is read from the **CookieCollection** *cookies* and added to the current instance.

Requirements

Platforms: Windows 98, Windows NT 4.0, Windows Millennium Edition, Windows 2000, Windows XP Home Edition, Windows XP Professional, Windows .NET Server family

CookieCollection.CopyTo Method

Copies the elements of a **CookieCollection** to an instance of the **Array** class, starting at a particular index.

```
[Visual Basic]
Public Overridable Sub CopyTo( _
   ByVal array As Array, _
   ByVal index As Integer _
) Implements ICollection.CopyTo
[C#]
public virtual void CopyTo(
   Array array,
   int index
);
[C++]
public: virtual void CopyTo(
   Array* array,
   int index
);
[JScript]
public function CopyTo(
   array : Array,
   index : int
);
```

Parameters

array
> The target **Array** to which the **CookieCollection** will be copied.

index
> The zero-based index in the target **Array** where copying begins.

Implements

ICollection.CopyTo

Remarks

The **Array** *array* must be one-dimensional with zero-based indexing.

Requirements

Platforms: Windows 98, Windows NT 4.0, Windows Millennium Edition, Windows 2000, Windows XP Home Edition, Windows XP Professional, Windows .NET Server family

CookieCollection.GetEnumerator Method

Gets an enumerator that can iterate through a **CookieCollection**.

```
[Visual Basic]
Public Overridable Function GetEnumerator() As IEnumerator _
   Implements IEnumerable.GetEnumerator
[C#]
public virtual IEnumerator GetEnumerator();
[C++]
public: virtual IEnumerator* GetEnumerator();
[JScript]
public function GetEnumerator() : IEnumerator;
```

Return Value

An instance of an implemention of an **IEnumerator** interface that can iterate through a **CookieCollection**.

Implements

IEnumerable.GetEnumerator

Remarks

You should use an **IEnumerator** only to read data in the collection. Enumerators cannot be used to modify the underlying collection. The enumerator does not have exclusive access to the collection.

When an enumerator is created, it takes a snapshot of the current state of the collection. If changes such as adding, modifying, or deleting elements are made to the collection, the snapshot gets out of sync and the enumerator throws an **InvalidOperationException**. Two enumerators created from the same collection at the same time can produce different snapshots of the collection.

Requirements

Platforms: Windows 98, Windows NT 4.0, Windows Millennium Edition, Windows 2000, Windows XP Home Edition, Windows XP Professional, Windows .NET Server family

CookieContainer Class

Provides a container for a collection of **CookieCollection** objects.

System.Object
    System.Net.CookieContainer

```
[Visual Basic]
<Serializable>
Public Class CookieContainer
[C#]
[Serializable]
public class CookieContainer
[C++]
[Serializable]
public __gc class CookieContainer
[JScript]
public
    Serializable
class CookieContainer
```

Thread Safety

Any public static (**Shared** in Visual Basic) members of this type are safe for multithreaded operations. Any instance members are not guaranteed to be thread safe.

Remarks

A **CookieContainer** is a data structure that provides storage for instances of the **Cookie** class, and which is accessed in a database-like manner. The **CookieContainer** has a capacity limit which is set when the container is created, or changed by a property.

An instance of the **Cookie** class is added to the container based on its originating URI. It is added to an internal **CookieCollection** associated with the URI. A **Cookie** is retrieved from the container based on the URI as a **CookieCollection**, or as a string which can be used to submit HTTP WebRequests.

The **CookieContainer** has three properties that govern the volume of the content of the container: **Capacity**, **MaxCookieSize**, and **PerDomainCapacity**. These values have the default settings of 300, 4096, and 20 respectively. When a **Cookie** is added to the container, these properties are used to determine whether a **Cookie** already contained in the **CookieContainer** should be discarded to make room for the new one. The **CookieContainer** keeps track of each addition to ensure that neither the **Capacity** nor the **PerDomainCapacity** limits are exceeded. If one or both are exceeded, then **Cookie** instances held by the **CookieContainer** are removed. First, any expired **Cookie** is removed. If further capacity must be recaptured, then the least-recently-used **CookieCollection** is purged.

Requirements

Namespace: System.Net

Platforms: Windows 98, Windows NT 4.0, Windows Millennium Edition, Windows 2000, Windows XP Home Edition, Windows XP Professional, Windows .NET Server family

Assembly: System (in System.dll)

CookieContainer Constructor

Initializes a new instance of the **CookieContainer** class.

Overload List

Initializes a new instance of the **CookieContainer** class.

> [Visual Basic] **Public Sub New()**
> [C#] **public CookieContainer();**
> [C++] **public: CookieContainer();**
> [JScript] **public function CookieContainer();**

Initializes a new instance of the **CookieContainer** class with a specified value for the number of **Cookie** instances the container can hold.

> [Visual Basic] **Public Sub New(Integer)**
> [C#] **public CookieContainer(int);**
> [C++] **public: CookieContainer(int);**
> [JScript] **public function CookieContainer(int);**

Initializes a new instance of the **CookieContainer** class with specific properties.

> [Visual Basic] **Public Sub New(Integer, Integer, Integer)**
> [C#] **public CookieContainer(int, int, int);**
> [C++] **public: CookieContainer(int, int, int);**
> [JScript] **public function CookieContainer(int, int, int);**

CookieContainer Constructor ()

Initializes a new instance of the **CookieContainer** class.

```
[Visual Basic]
Public Sub New()
[C#]
public CookieContainer();
[C++]
public: CookieContainer();
[JScript]
public function CookieContainer();
```

Remarks

The default constructor initializes all fields to their default values. **DefaultCookieLimit** is used to initialize **Capacity**, **DefaultCookieLengthLimit** is used for **MaxCookieSize**, and **DefaultPerDomainCookieLimit** is used for **PerDomainCapacity**.

Requirements

Platforms: Windows 98, Windows NT 4.0, Windows Millennium Edition, Windows 2000, Windows XP Home Edition, Windows XP Professional, Windows .NET Server family

CookieContainer Constructor (Int32)

Initializes a new instance of the **CookieContainer** class with a specified value for the number of **Cookie** instances the container can hold.

```
[Visual Basic]
Public Sub New( _
    ByVal capacity As Integer _
)
```

```
[C#]
public CookieContainer(
   int capacity
);
[C++]
public: CookieContainer(
   int capacity
);
[JScript]
public function CookieContainer(
   capacity : int
);
```

Parameters

capacity
    The number of **Cookie** instances the **CookieContainer** can hold.

Exceptions

Exception Type	Condition
ArgumentException	*capacity* is less than or equal to zero

Remarks

PerDomainCapacity is initialized to 20, and **MaxCookieSize** is initialized to 4096.

Requirements

Platforms: Windows 98, Windows NT 4.0, Windows Millennium Edition, Windows 2000, Windows XP Home Edition, Windows XP Professional, Windows .NET Server family

CookieContainer Constructor (Int32, Int32, Int32)

Initializes a new instance of the **CookieContainer** class with specific properties.

```
[Visual Basic]
Public Sub New( _
   ByVal capacity As Integer, _
   ByVal perDomainCapacity As Integer, _
   ByVal maxCookieSize As Integer _
)
[C#]
public CookieContainer(
   int capacity,
   int perDomainCapacity,
   int maxCookieSize
);
[C++]
public: CookieContainer(
   int capacity,
   int perDomainCapacity,
   int maxCookieSize
);
[JScript]
public function CookieContainer(
   capacity : int,
   perDomainCapacity : int,
   maxCookieSize : int
);
```

Parameters

capacity
    The number of **Cookie** instances the **CookieContainer** can hold.
perDomainCapacity
    The number of **Cookie** instances per domain.
maxCookieSize
    The maximum size in bytes for any single **Cookie** in a **CookieContainer**.

Exceptions

Exception Type	Condition
ArgumentException	*perDomainCapacity* is not equal to **MaxValue** and (*perDomainCapacity* is less than or equal to zero or *perDomainCapacity* is greater than *capacity*)
ArgumentException	*maxCookieSize* is less than or equal to zero

Remarks

The parameters specify values for **Capacity**, **MaxCookieSize**, and **PerDomainCapacity**.

Requirements

Platforms: Windows 98, Windows NT 4.0, Windows Millennium Edition, Windows 2000, Windows XP Home Edition, Windows XP Professional, Windows .NET Server family

CookieContainer.DefaultCookieLengthLimit Field

Represents the default maximum size, in bytes, of the **Cookie** instances the **CookieContainer** can hold. This field is constant.

```
[Visual Basic]
Public Const DefaultCookieLengthLimit As Integer
[C#]
public const int DefaultCookieLengthLimit;
[C++]
public: const int DefaultCookieLengthLimit;
[JScript]
public var DefaultCookieLengthLimit : int;
```

Remarks

The default maximum **Cookie** size is 4096.

Requirements

Platforms: Windows 98, Windows NT 4.0, Windows Millennium Edition, Windows 2000, Windows XP Home Edition, Windows XP Professional, Windows .NET Server family

CookieContainer.DefaultCookieLimit Field

Represents the default maximum number of **Cookie** instances the **CookieContainer** can hold. This field is constant.

```
[Visual Basic]
Public Const DefaultCookieLimit As Integer
[C#]
public const int DefaultCookieLimit;
```

```
[C++]
public: const int DefaultCookieLimit;
[JScript]
public var DefaultCookieLimit : int;
```

Remarks

The default maximum number of **Cookie** instances is 300.

Requirements

Platforms: Windows 98, Windows NT 4.0,
Windows Millennium Edition, Windows 2000,
Windows XP Home Edition, Windows XP Professional,
Windows .NET Server family

CookieContainer.DefaultPerDomainCookieLimit Field

Represents the default maximum number of **Cookie** instances the
CookieContainer can reference per domain. This field is constant.

```
[Visual Basic]
Public Const DefaultPerDomainCookieLimit As Integer
[C#]
public const int DefaultPerDomainCookieLimit;
[C++]
public: const int DefaultPerDomainCookieLimit;
[JScript]
public var DefaultPerDomainCookieLimit : int;
```

Remarks

The default maximum number of **Cookie** instances per domain is 20.

Requirements

Platforms: Windows 98, Windows NT 4.0,
Windows Millennium Edition, Windows 2000,
Windows XP Home Edition, Windows XP Professional,
Windows .NET Server family

CookieContainer.Capacity Property

Gets and sets the number of **Cookie** instances a **CookieContainer**
can hold.

```
[Visual Basic]
Public Property Capacity As Integer
[C#]
public int Capacity {get; set;}
[C++]
public: __property int get_Capacity();
public: __property void set_Capacity(int);
[JScript]
public function get Capacity() : int;
public function set Capacity(int);
```

Property Value

The number of **Cookie** instances a **CookieContainer** can hold. This
is a hard limit and cannot be exceeded by adding a **Cookie**.

Exceptions

Exception Type	Condition
ArgumentOutOfRange-Exception	*Capacity* is less than or equal to zero or (value is less than **PerDomainCapacity** and **PerDomainCapacity** is not equal to **MaxValue**).

Remarks

If **Count** equals or exceeds **Capacity**, one or more **Cookie** instances
are removed from the container. Enough instances are removed to
bring **Count** below **Capacity** as follows: if there are expired **Cookie**
instances in scope they are cleaned up. If not, then the least recently
used **CookieCollection** is found and removed from the container.

Capacity must be greater than or equal to **PerDomainCapacity**. If
you set **PerDomainCapacity** and the current **Count** of **Cookie**
instances is less than the new value, the excess is removed from the
container. Enough instances are removed to bring **Count** below
Capacity as follows: if there are expired **Cookie** instances in scope
they are cleaned up. If not, or if there are still more than the new
value of **PerDomainCapacity**, then the least recently used
CookieCollection is found and removed from the container.

Requirements

Platforms: Windows 98, Windows NT 4.0,
Windows Millennium Edition, Windows 2000,
Windows XP Home Edition, Windows XP Professional,
Windows .NET Server family

CookieContainer.Count Property

Gets the number of **Cookie** instances a **CookieContainer** currently
holds.

```
[Visual Basic]
Public ReadOnly Property Count As Integer
[C#]
public int Count {get;}
[C++]
public: __property int get_Count();
[JScript]
public function get Count() : int;
```

Property Value

The number of **Cookie** instances a **CookieContainer** currently
holds. This is the total of **Cookie** instances in all domains.

Remarks

The default value of this property is **DefaultCookieLimit**. If **Count**
equals or exceeds **Capacity**, one or more **Cookie** instances are
removed from the container. Enough instances are removed to bring
Count below **Capacity** as follows: if there are expired **Cookie**
instances in scope they are cleaned up. If not, then the least recently
used **CookieCollection** is found and removed from the container.

Requirements

Platforms: Windows 98, Windows NT 4.0,
Windows Millennium Edition, Windows 2000,
Windows XP Home Edition, Windows XP Professional,
Windows .NET Server family

CookieContainer.MaxCookieSize Property

Represents the maximum allowed length of a **Cookie**.

```
[Visual Basic]
Public Property MaxCookieSize As Integer
[C#]
public int MaxCookieSize {get; set;}
[C++]
public: __property int get_MaxCookieSize();
public: __property void set_MaxCookieSize(int);
[JScript]
public function get MaxCookieSize() : int;
public function set MaxCookieSize(int);
```

Property Value

The maximum allowed length, in bytes, of a **Cookie**.

Exceptions

Exception Type	Condition
ArgumentOutOfRange-Exception	*MaxCookieSize* is less than or equal to zero

Remarks

If the new value of **MaxCookieSize** is less than the current value, any **Cookie** with length exceeding the new value will be truncated.

Requirements

Platforms: Windows 98, Windows NT 4.0, Windows Millennium Edition, Windows 2000, Windows XP Home Edition, Windows XP Professional, Windows .NET Server family

CookieContainer.PerDomainCapacity Property

Gets and sets the number of **Cookie** instances a **CookieContainer** can hold per domain.

```
[Visual Basic]
Public Property PerDomainCapacity As Integer
[C#]
public int PerDomainCapacity {get; set;}
[C++]
public: __property int get_PerDomainCapacity();
public: __property void set_PerDomainCapacity(int);
[JScript]
public function get PerDomainCapacity() : int;
public function set PerDomainCapacity(int);
```

Property Value

The number of **Cookie** instances allowed per domain.

Exceptions

Exception Type	Condition
ArgumentOutOfRange-Exception	*PerDomainCapacity* is less than or equal to zero or (*PerDomainCapacity* is greater than the maximum allowable number of cookies instances, 300, and is not equal to **MaxValue**)

Remarks

If the new **PerDomainCapacity** value is less than the current value, and if any of the domain collections contain more **Cookie** instances than the new value, the collections are pruned to fit. This uses the same basic rules as described in the **Capacity** property. However, this does the clean-up only on the collection for this domain.

Requirements

Platforms: Windows 98, Windows NT 4.0, Windows Millennium Edition, Windows 2000, Windows XP Home Edition, Windows XP Professional, Windows .NET Server family

CookieContainer.Add Method

Adds a **Cookie** to a **CookieContainer**.

Overload List

Adds a **Cookie** to a **CookieContainer**. This method uses the domain from the **Cookie** to determine which domain collection to associate the **Cookie** with.

> [Visual Basic] **Overloads Public Sub Add(Cookie)**
> [C#] **public void Add(Cookie);**
> [C++] **public: void Add(Cookie*);**
> [JScript] **public function Add(Cookie);**

Adds the contents of a **CookieCollection** to the **CookieContainer**.

> [Visual Basic] **Overloads Public Sub Add(CookieCollection)**
> [C#] **public void Add(CookieCollection);**
> [C++] **public: void Add(CookieCollection*);**
> [JScript] **public function Add(CookieCollection);**

Adds a **Cookie** to the **CookieContainer** for a particular URI.

> [Visual Basic] **Overloads Public Sub Add(Uri, Cookie)**
> [C#] **public void Add(Uri, Cookie);**
> [C++] **public: void Add(Uri*, Cookie*);**
> [JScript] **public function Add(Uri, Cookie);**

Adds the contents of a **CookieCollection** to the **CookieContainer** for a particular URI.

> [Visual Basic] **Overloads Public Sub Add(Uri, CookieCollection)**
> [C#] **public void Add(Uri, CookieCollection);**
> [C++] **public: void Add(Uri*, CookieCollection*);**
> [JScript] **public function Add(Uri, CookieCollection);**

CookieContainer.Add Method (Cookie)

Adds a **Cookie** to a **CookieContainer**. This method uses the domain from the **Cookie** to determine which domain collection to associate the **Cookie** with.

```
[Visual Basic]
Overloads Public Sub Add( _
   ByVal cookie As Cookie _
)
[C#]
public void Add(
   Cookie cookie
);
```

```
[C++]
public: void Add(
    Cookie* cookie
);
[JScript]
public function Add(
    cookie : Cookie
);
```

Parameters

cookie
> The **Cookie** to be added to the **CookieContainer**.

Exceptions

Exception Type	Condition
ArgumentNullException	*cookie* is a null reference (**Nothing** in Visual Basic)
ArgumentException	domain for *cookie* is a null reference (**Nothing** in Visual Basic)
CookieException	*cookie* is larger than *maxCookieSize*

Remarks

If the **Count** property equals or exceeds the **Capacity** property, one or more **Cookie** instances are removed from the container before adding the *cookie* parameter. Enough **Cookie** instances are removed to bring **Count** below **Capacity** as follows: if there are expired instances in given scope they are cleaned up. If not, then the least recently used **CookieCollection** is found and removed from the container.

Requirements

Platforms: Windows 98, Windows NT 4.0, Windows Millennium Edition, Windows 2000, Windows XP Home Edition, Windows XP Professional, Windows .NET Server family

CookieContainer.Add Method (CookieCollection)

Adds the contents of a **CookieCollection** to the **CookieContainer**.

```
[Visual Basic]
Overloads Public Sub Add( _
    ByVal cookies As CookieCollection _
)
[C#]
public void Add(
    CookieCollection cookies
);
[C++]
public: void Add(
    CookieCollection* cookies
);
[JScript]
public function Add(
    cookies : CookieCollection
);
```

Parameters

cookies
> The **CookieCollection** to be added to the **CookieContainer**.

Exceptions

Exception Type	Condition
ArgumentNullException	*cookies* is a null reference (**Nothing** in Visual Basic)

Remarks

If the **Count** property equals the **Capacity** property, one or more **Cookie** instances are removed from the container before adding the contents of the *cookies* parameter. Enough **Cookie** instances are removed to make room for *cookies* as follows: if there are expired instances they are cleaned up. If not, or if more room is needed, then the least recently used **CookieCollection** is found and removed from the container.

Requirements

Platforms: Windows 98, Windows NT 4.0, Windows Millennium Edition, Windows 2000, Windows XP Home Edition, Windows XP Professional, Windows .NET Server family

CookieContainer.Add Method (Uri, Cookie)

Adds a **Cookie** to the **CookieContainer** for a particular URI.

```
[Visual Basic]
Overloads Public Sub Add( _
    ByVal uri As Uri, _
    ByVal cookie As Cookie _
)
[C#]
public void Add(
    Uri uri,
    Cookie cookie
);
[C++]
public: void Add(
    Uri* uri,
    Cookie* cookie
);
[JScript]
public function Add(
    uri : Uri,
    cookie : Cookie
);
```

Parameters

uri
> The URI of the **Cookie** to be added to the **CookieContainer**.

cookie
> The **Cookie** to be added to the **CookieContainer**.

Exceptions

Exception Type	Condition
ArgumentNullException	*uri* is a null reference (**Nothing** in Visual Basic)
ArgumentNullException	*cookie* is a null reference (**Nothing** in Visual Basic)

Remarks

If you add a **Cookie** instance for just one specific host, don't set the **Domain** property of the **Cookie** instance. This is set automatically, based on the URI.

If your URI corresponds to your local domain and sends to all the hosts on the local domain, set the **Cookie Domain** property equal to ".local". Otherwise, make sure it matches the host name used in the URI.

If the **Cookie Version** is Netscape, the **Path** property of the **Cookie**, if not set explicitly, is derived from the URI and is the complete path from the URI, including the page name.

If the **Count** property equals the **Capacity** property, one or more **Cookie** instances are removed from the container before adding the *cookie* parameter. Enough **Cookie** instances are removed to bring **Count** below **Capacity** as follows: if there are expired instances in scope they are cleaned up. If not, then the least recently used **CookieCollection** is found and removed from the container.

Requirements

Platforms: Windows 98, Windows NT 4.0, Windows Millennium Edition, Windows 2000, Windows XP Home Edition, Windows XP Professional, Windows .NET Server family

CookieContainer.Add Method (Uri, CookieCollection)

Adds the contents of a **CookieCollection** to the **CookieContainer** for a particular URI.

```
[Visual Basic]
Overloads Public Sub Add( _
   ByVal uri As Uri, _
   ByVal cookies As CookieCollection _
)
[C#]
public void Add(
   Uri uri,
   CookieCollection cookies
);
[C++]
public: void Add(
   Uri* uri,
   CookieCollection* cookies
);
[JScript]
public function Add(
   uri : Uri,
   cookies : CookieCollection
);
```

Parameters

uri
The URI of the **CookieCollection** to be added to the **CookieContainer**.

cookies
The **CookieCollection** to be added to the **CookieContainer**.

Exceptions

Exception Type	Condition
ArgumentNullException	*uri* is a null reference (**Nothing** in Visual Basic)
ArgumentNullException	*cookies* is a null reference (**Nothing** in Visual Basic)

Remarks

If you add a **Cookie** instance for just one specific host, don't set the **Domain** property of the **Cookie** instance. This is set automatically, based on the URI.

If your URI corresponds to your local domain and sends to all the hosts on the local domain, set the **Cookie Domain** property equal to ".local". Otherwise, make sure it matches the host name used in the URI.

If **Count** equals **Capacity**, one or more **Cookie** instances is removed from the container before adding the *cookie* parameter. Enough **Cookie** instances are removed to bring **Count** below **Capacity** as follows: if there are expired instances in scope they are cleaned up. If not, then the least recently used **CookieCollection** is found and removed from the container.

Requirements

Platforms: Windows 98, Windows NT 4.0, Windows Millennium Edition, Windows 2000, Windows XP Home Edition, Windows XP Professional, Windows .NET Server family

CookieContainer.GetCookieHeader Method

Gets the HTTP cookie header containing the HTTP cookies representing the **Cookie** instances associated with a specific URI.

```
[Visual Basic]
Public Function GetCookieHeader( _
   ByVal uri As Uri _
) As String
[C#]
public string GetCookieHeader(
   Uri uri
);
[C++]
public: String* GetCookieHeader(
   Uri* uri
);
[JScript]
public function GetCookieHeader(
   uri : Uri
) : String;
```

Parameters

uri
The URI of the **Cookie** instances desired.

Return Value

An HTTP cookie header, with strings representing **Cookie** instances delimited by semicolons.

Exceptions

Exception Type	Condition
ArgumentNullException	*uri* is a null reference (**Nothing** in Visual Basic)

Remarks

GetCookieHeader returns a string that holds the HTTP cookie header for the **Cookie** instances specified by *uri*. The HTTP header is built by adding a string representation of each **Cookie** associated with *uri*. Note the exact format of the string depends on the RFC the **Cookie** conforms to. The strings for all the **Cookie** instances associated with *uri* are combined and delimited by semicolons.

This string is not in the correct format for use as the second parameter of the **SetCookies** method.

Requirements

Platforms: Windows 98, Windows NT 4.0, Windows Millennium Edition, Windows 2000, Windows XP Home Edition, Windows XP Professional, Windows .NET Server family

CookieContainer.GetCookies Method

Gets A **CookieCollection** containing the **Cookie** instances associated with a specific URI.

```
[Visual Basic]
Public Function GetCookies( _
   ByVal uri As Uri _
) As CookieCollection
[C#]
public CookieCollection GetCookies(
   Uri uri
);
[C++]
public: CookieCollection* GetCookies(
   Uri* uri
);
[JScript]
public function GetCookies(
   uri : Uri
) : CookieCollection;
```

Parameters

uri
   The URI of the **Cookie** instances desired.

Return Value

A **CookieCollection** containing the **Cookie** instances associated with a specific URI.

Exceptions

Exception Type	Condition
ArgumentNullException	*uri* is a null reference (**Nothing** in Visual Basic)

Remarks

A new instance of a **CookieCollection** is created. Then the **Cookie** instances in the internal collection associated with the specified URI are read out and added to the new **CookieCollection**.

Requirements

Platforms: Windows 98, Windows NT 4.0, Windows Millennium Edition, Windows 2000, Windows XP Home Edition, Windows XP Professional, Windows .NET Server family

CookieContainer.SetCookies Method

Adds **Cookie** instances for one or more cookies from an HTTP cookie header to the **CookieContainer** for a specific URI.

```
[Visual Basic]
Public Sub SetCookies( _
   ByVal uri As Uri, _
   ByVal cookieHeader As String _
)
```

```
[C#]
public void SetCookies(
   Uri uri,
   string cookieHeader
);
[C++]
public: void SetCookies(
   Uri* uri,
   String* cookieHeader
);
[JScript]
public function SetCookies(
   uri : Uri,
   cookieHeader : String
);
```

Parameters

uri
   The URI of the **CookieCollection**.
cookieHeader
   The contents of an HTTP set-cookie header as returned by a HTTP server, with **Cookie** instances delimited by commas.

Exceptions

Exception Type	Condition
ArgumentNullException	*uri* is a null reference (**Nothing** in Visual Basic)
ArgumentNullException	*cookieHeader* is a null reference (**Nothing** in Visual Basic)

Remarks

SetCookies pulls all the HTTP cookies out of the HTTP cookie header, builds a **Cookie** for each one, and then adds each **Cookie** to the internal **CookieCollection** associated with the URI. The HTTP cookies in the *cookieHeader* string must be delimited by commas.

Requirements

Platforms: Windows 98, Windows NT 4.0, Windows Millennium Edition, Windows 2000, Windows XP Home Edition, Windows XP Professional, Windows .NET Server family

CookieException Class

The exception that is thrown when an error is made adding a **Cookie** to a **CookieContainer**.

System.Object
  System.Exception
    System.SystemException
      System.FormatException
        System.Net.CookieException

```
[Visual Basic]
<Serializable>
Public Class CookieException
   Inherits FormatException
[C#]
[Serializable]
public class CookieException : FormatException
[C++]
[Serializable]
public __gc class CookieException : public FormatException
[JScript]
public
   Serializable
class CookieException extends FormatException
```

Thread Safety

Any public static (**Shared** in Visual Basic) members of this type are safe for multithreaded operations. Any instance members are not guaranteed to be thread safe.

Remarks

This exception is thrown if an attempt is made to **Add** a **Cookie** with length greater than **MaxCookieSize** to a **CookieContainer**.

Requirements

Namespace: System.Net

Platforms: Windows 98, Windows NT 4.0, Windows Millennium Edition, Windows 2000, Windows XP Home Edition, Windows XP Professional, Windows .NET Server family

Assembly: System (in System.dll)

CookieException Constructor

Initializes a new instance of the **CookieException** class.

Overload List

Initializes a new instance of the **CookieException** class.

[Visual Basic] **Public Sub New()**
[C#] **public CookieException();**
[C++] **public: CookieException();**
[JScript] **public function CookieException();**

Initializes a new instance of the **CookieException** class with specific values of *serializationInfo* and *streamingContext*.

[Visual Basic] **Protected Sub New(SerializationInfo, StreamingContext)**
[C#] **protected CookieException(SerializationInfo, StreamingContext);**
[C++] **protected: CookieException(SerializationInfo*, StreamingContext);**
[JScript] **protected function CookieException (SerializationInfo, StreamingContext);**

CookieException Constructor ()

Initializes a new instance of the **CookieException** class.

```
[Visual Basic]
Public Sub New()
[C#]
public CookieException();
[C++]
public: CookieException();
[JScript]
public function CookieException();
```

Remarks

The default constructor for **CookieException**.

Requirements

Platforms: Windows 98, Windows NT 4.0, Windows Millennium Edition, Windows 2000, Windows XP Home Edition, Windows XP Professional, Windows .NET Server family

CookieException Constructor (SerializationInfo, StreamingContext)

Initializes a new instance of the **CookieException** class with specific values of *serializationInfo* and *streamingContext*.

```
[Visual Basic]
Protected Sub New( _
   ByVal serializationInfo As SerializationInfo, _
   ByVal streamingContext As StreamingContext _
)
[C#]
protected CookieException(
   SerializationInfo serializationInfo,
   StreamingContext streamingContext
);
[C++]
protected: CookieException(
   SerializationInfo* serializationInfo,
   StreamingContext streamingContext
);
[JScript]
protected function CookieException(
   serializationInfo : SerializationInfo,
   streamingContext : StreamingContext
);
```

Parameters

serializationInfo
  The **SerializationInfo** to be used.
streamingContext
  The **StreamingContext** to be used.

Remarks

Allows you to set up custom serialization.

Requirements

Platforms: Windows 98, Windows NT 4.0, Windows Millennium Edition, Windows 2000, Windows XP Home Edition, Windows XP Professional, Windows .NET Server family

CookieException.ISerializable.GetObjectData Method

This member supports the .NET Framework infrastructure and is not intended to be used directly from your code.

```
[Visual Basic]
Private Sub GetObjectData( _
    ByVal serializationInfo As SerializationInfo, _
    ByVal streamingContext As StreamingContext _
) Implements ISerializable.GetObjectData
[C#]
void ISerializable.GetObjectData(
    SerializationInfo serializationInfo,
    StreamingContext streamingContext
);
[C++]
private: void ISerializable::GetObjectData(
    SerializationInfo* serializationInfo,
    StreamingContext streamingContext
);
[JScript]
private function ISerializable.GetObjectData(
    serializationInfo : SerializationInfo,
    streamingContext : StreamingContext
);
```

CredentialCache Class

Provides storage for multiple credentials.

System.Object
   System.Net.CredentialCache

```
[Visual Basic]
Public Class CredentialCache
   Implements ICredentials, IEnumerable
[C#]
public class CredentialCache : ICredentials, IEnumerable
[C++]
public __gc class CredentialCache : public ICredentials,
   IEnumerable
[JScript]
public class CredentialCache implements ICredentials, IEnumerable
```

Thread Safety

Any public static (**Shared** in Visual Basic) members of this type are safe for multithreaded operations. Any instance members are not guaranteed to be thread safe.

Remarks

The **CredentialCache** class stores credentials for multiple Internet resources. Applications that need to access multiple resources can store the credentials for those resources in a **CredentialCache** instance that then provides the proper set of credentials to the Internet resource when required. When the **GetCredential** method is called, it compares the URI and authentication type provided with those stored in the cache and returns the first set of credentials that match.

The **DefaultCredentials** property contains the system credentials of the current security context. For client applications, these represent the user name, password, and domain of the user who is currently logged in. For ASP.NET applications, the default credentials are the user credentials of the logged-in user or the user being impersonated.

Example

[Visual Basic, C#] The following example initializes a **CredentialCache** with multiple security credentials and uses those credentials with a **WebRequest**:

```
[Visual Basic]
Dim myCache As New CredentialCache()

myCache.Add(New Uri("http://www.contoso.com/"), "Basic",    ⌐
New NetworkCredential(UserName, SecurelyStoredPassword))
myCache.Add(New Uri("http://www.contoso.com/"), "Digest",   ⌐
New NetworkCredential(UserName, SecurelyStoredPassword, Domain))

wReq.Credentials = myCache

[C#]
CredentialCache myCache = new CredentialCache();

myCache.Add(new Uri("http://www.contoso.com/"),"Basic",new    ⌐
NetworkCredential(UserName,SecurelyStoredPassword));
myCache.Add(new Uri("http://www.contoso.com/"),"Digest", new  ⌐
NetworkCredential(UserName,SecurelyStoredPassword,Domain));

wReq.Credentials = myCache;
```

Requirements

Namespace: System.Net

Platforms: Windows 98, Windows NT 4.0,
Windows Millennium Edition, Windows 2000,
Windows XP Home Edition, Windows XP Professional,
Windows .NET Server family

Assembly: System (in System.dll)

CredentialCache Constructor

Creates a new instance of the **CredentialCache** class.

```
[Visual Basic]
Public Sub New()
[C#]
public CredentialCache();
[C++]
public: CredentialCache();
[JScript]
public function CredentialCache();
```

Remarks

The constructor creates a **CredentialCache** instance.

Example

[Visual Basic, C#] The following example initializes a **CredentialCache** with multiple security credentials and uses those credentials with a **WebRequest**:

```
[Visual Basic]
Dim myCache As New CredentialCache()

myCache.Add(New Uri("http://www.contoso.com/"), "Basic",    ⌐
etworkCredential(UserName, SecurelyStoredPassword))
myCache.Add(New Uri("http://www.contoso.com/"), "Digest",   ⌐
New NetworkCredential(UserName, SecurelyStoredPassword, Domain))

wReq.Credentials = myCache

[C#]
CredentialCache myCache = new CredentialCache();

myCache.Add(new Uri("http://www.contoso.com/"),"Basic",new    ⌐
NetworkCredential(UserName,SecurelyStoredPassword));
myCache.Add(new Uri("http://www.contoso.com/"),"Digest", new  ⌐
NetworkCredential(UserName,SecurelyStoredPassword,Domain));

wReq.Credentials = myCache;
```

Requirements

Platforms: Windows 98, Windows NT 4.0,
Windows Millennium Edition, Windows 2000,
Windows XP Home Edition, Windows XP Professional,
Windows .NET Server family,
Common Language Infrastructure (CLI) Standard

CredentialCache.DefaultCredentials Property

Gets the system credentials of the application.

```
[Visual Basic]
Public Shared ReadOnly Property DefaultCredentials As ICredentials
[C#]
public static ICredentials DefaultCredentials {get;}
[C++]
public: __property static ICredentials* get_DefaultCredentials();
[JScript]
public static function get DefaultCredentials() : ICredentials;
```

Property Value

An **ICredentials** that represents the system credentials of the application.

Remarks

The **DefaultCredentials** property applies only to NTLM, negotiate, and Kerberos-based authentication.

DefaultCredentials represents the system credentials for the current security context in which the application is running. For a client-side application, these are usually the Windows credentials (user name, password, and domain) of the user running the application. For ASP.NET applications, the default credentials are the user credentials of the logged-in user, or the user being impersonated.

> **Note** The **ICredentials** instance returned by **DefaultCredentials** cannot be used to view the user name, password, or domain of the current security context.

Example

[Visual Basic, C#, C++] The following example uses the **DefaultCredentials** method to get the system credentials of the application.

```
[Visual Basic]
' Assuming "Windows Authentication" has been set as;
' Directory Security settings for default web site in IIS.
Dim url As String = "http://localhost"
' Create a 'HttpWebRequest' object with the specified url.
Dim myHttpWebRequest As HttpWebRequest = CType( _
WebRequest.Create(url), HttpWebRequest)
' Assign the credentials of the logged in user or the user
being impersonated.
myHttpWebRequest.Credentials = CredentialCache.DefaultCredentials
' Send the 'HttpWebRequest' and wait for response.
Dim myHttpWebResponse As HttpWebResponse = _
CType(myHttpWebRequest.GetResponse(), HttpWebResponse)
Console.WriteLine("Authentication successful")
Console.WriteLine("Response received successfully")
```

```
[C#]
// Ensure Directory Security settings for default web site in
IIS is "Windows Authentication".
string url = "http://localhost";
// Create a 'HttpWebRequest' object with the specified url.
HttpWebRequest myHttpWebRequest =
(HttpWebRequest)WebRequest.Create(url);
// Assign the credentials of the logged in user or the user
being impersonated.
myHttpWebRequest.Credentials = CredentialCache.DefaultCredentials;
// Send the 'HttpWebRequest' and wait for response.
HttpWebResponse myHttpWebResponse =
(HttpWebResponse)myHttpWebRequest.GetResponse();
Console.WriteLine("Authentication successful");
Console.WriteLine("Response received successfully");
```

```
[C++]
// Ensure Directory Security settings for default web site in
IIS is S"Windows Authentication".
String* url = S"http://localhost";
// Create a 'HttpWebRequest' Object* with the specified url.
HttpWebRequest* myHttpWebRequest =
dynamic_cast<HttpWebRequest*>(WebRequest::Create(url));
// Assign the credentials of the logged in user or the user
being impersonated.
myHttpWebRequest->Credentials = CredentialCache::DefaultCredentials;
// Send the 'HttpWebRequest' and wait for response.
HttpWebResponse* myHttpWebResponse =
dynamic_cast<HttpWebResponse*>(myHttpWebRequest->GetResponse());
Console::WriteLine(S"Authentication successful");
Console::WriteLine(S"Response received successfully");
```

Requirements

Platforms: Windows 98, Windows NT 4.0, Windows Millennium Edition, Windows 2000, Windows XP Home Edition, Windows XP Professional, Windows .NET Server family, Common Language Infrastructure (CLI) Standard

.NET Framework Security:

- **EnvironmentPermission** for reading the user's system credentials. Associated enumeration: **EnvironmentPermissionAccess**

CredentialCache.Add Method

Adds a **NetworkCredential** instance to the credential cache.

```
[Visual Basic]
Public Sub Add( _
    ByVal uriPrefix As Uri, _
    ByVal authType As String, _
    ByVal cred As NetworkCredential _
)
[C#]
public void Add(
    Uri uriPrefix,
    string authType,
    NetworkCredential cred
);
[C++]
public: void Add(
    Uri* uriPrefix,
    String* authType,
    NetworkCredential* cred
);
[JScript]
public function Add(
    uriPrefix : Uri,
    authType : String,
    cred : NetworkCredential
);
```

Parameters

uriPrefix
> A **Uri** that specifies the URI prefix of the resources that the credential grants access to.

authType
> The authentication scheme used by the resource named in *uriPrefix*.

cred
> The **NetworkCredential** to add to the credential cache.

Exceptions

Exception Type	Condition
ArgumentNullException	*uriPrefix* is a null reference (**Nothing** in Visual Basic) -or- *authType* is a null reference (**Nothing**).
ArgumentException	The same credentials are added more than once.

Remarks

The **Add** method places a **NetworkCredential** instance into the **CredentialCache**. The cache stores credentials in the order in which they are added to it. When the **GetCredential** method is called, it returns the proper matching **NetworkCredential** instance.

Example

[Visual Basic, C#] The following example initializes a **CredentialCache** with multiple security credentials and uses those credentials with a **WebRequest**:

[Visual Basic]
```
Dim myCache As New CredentialCache()

myCache.Add(New Uri("http://www.contoso.com/"), "Basic", New
NetworkCredential(UserName, SecurelyStoredPassword))
myCache.Add(New Uri("http://www.contoso.com/"), "Digest", New
NetworkCredential(UserName, SecurelyStoredPassword, Domain))

wReq.Credentials = myCache
```

[C#]
```
CredentialCache myCache = new CredentialCache();

myCache.Add(new Uri("http://www.contoso.com/"),"Basic",new
NetworkCredential(UserName,SecurelyStoredPassword));
myCache.Add(new Uri("http://www.contoso.com/"),"Digest", new
NetworkCredential(UserName,SecurelyStoredPassword,Domain));

wReq.Credentials = myCache;
```

Requirements

Platforms: Windows 98, Windows NT 4.0, Windows Millennium Edition, Windows 2000, Windows XP Home Edition, Windows XP Professional, Windows .NET Server family, Common Language Infrastructure (CLI) Standard

CredentialCache.GetCredential Method

Returns the **NetworkCredential** instance associated with the specified URI and authentication type.

[Visual Basic]
```
Public Overridable Function GetCredential( _
   ByVal uriPrefix As Uri, _
   ByVal authType As String _
) As NetworkCredential Implements ICredentials.GetCredential
```
[C#]
```
public virtual NetworkCredential GetCredential(
   Uri uriPrefix,
   string authType
);
```
[C++]
```
public: virtual NetworkCredential* GetCredential(
   Uri* uriPrefix,
   String* authType
);
```
[JScript]
```
public function GetCredential(
   uriPrefix : Uri,
   authType : String
) : NetworkCredential;
```

Parameters

uriPrefix
   A **Uri** that specifies the URI prefix of the resources that the credential grants access to.
authType
   The authentication scheme used by the resource named in *uriPrefix*.

Return Value

A **NetworkCredential** or, if there is no matching credential in the cache, a null reference (**Nothing** in Visual Basic).

Implements

ICredentials.GetCredential

Remarks

The **GetCredential** method searches the **CredentialCache** and returns the **NetworkCredential** instance for the specified URI and authorization type. If the **CredentialCache** contains no matching **NetworkCredential** instance, a null reference (**Nothing** in Visual Basic) is returned.

GetCredential uses the longest matching URI prefix in the cache to determine which set of credentials to return for an authorization type. The following table shows examples.

URI Prefix	Matches
http://www.contoso.com/portal/news.htm	Requests for the specific Web page news.htm.
http://www.contoso.com/portal/	Requests for all content in the portal path, except the page news.htm.
http://www.contoso.com/	Requests for all resources at www.contoso.com, except those in the portal path.

Example

[Visual Basic, C#, C++] The following example uses the **GetCredential** method to return the **NetworkCredential** instance associated with the specified URI and authentication type.

[Visual Basic]
```
Public Shared Sub GetPage(url As String, userName As String, password As String, domainName As String)
   Try
      Dim myCredentialCache As New CredentialCache()
      ' Dummy names used as credentials
      myCredentialCache.Add(New Uri("http://microsoft.com/"),
"Basic", New NetworkCredential("user1", "passwd1", "domain1"))
      myCredentialCache.Add(New Uri("http://msdn.com/"),
"Basic", New NetworkCredential("user2", "passwd2", "domain2"))
      myCredentialCache.Add(New Uri(url), "Basic", New
NetworkCredential(userName, password, domainName))
      ' Creates a webrequest with the specified url.
      Dim myWebRequest As WebRequest = WebRequest.Create(url)
      ' Call 'GetCredential' to obtain the credentials specific
to our Uri.
      Dim myCredential As NetworkCredential =
myCredentialCache.GetCredential(New Uri(url), "Basic")
      Display(myCredential)
      myWebRequest.Credentials = myCredential 'Associating only
our credentials
      ' Sends the request and waits for response.
      Dim myWebResponse As WebResponse = myWebRequest.GetResponse()
      ' Process response here.
      Console.WriteLine(ControlChars.Cr + "Response Received.")
      myWebResponse.Close()

   Catch e As WebException
      If Not (e.Response Is Nothing) Then
```

```vb
                Console.WriteLine(ControlChars.Lf +
ControlChars.Cr + "Failed to obtain a response. The
following error occured : {0}", CType(e.Response,
HttpWebResponse).StatusDescription)
            Else
                Console.WriteLine(ControlChars.Lf +
ControlChars.Cr + "Failed to obtain a response. The
following error occured : {0}", e.Status)
            End If
        Catch e As Exception
            Console.WriteLine(ControlChars.Cr + "The
following exception was raised : {0}", e.Message)
        End Try
End Sub 'GetPage

Public Shared Sub Display(credential As NetworkCredential)
    Console.WriteLine("The credentials are: ")
Console.WriteLine(ControlChars.Cr + "Username : {0} ,Password
: {1} ,Domain : {2}", credential.UserName, credential.
Password, credential.Domain)
End Sub 'Display
```

[C#]
```csharp
public static void GetPage(string url,string userName,string
password,string domainName)
{
    try
    {
        CredentialCache myCredentialCache = new CredentialCache();
        // Dummy names used as credentials.
        myCredentialCache.Add(new Uri("http://microsoft.com/")
,"Basic", new NetworkCredential("user1","passwd1","domain1"));
        myCredentialCache.Add(new Uri("http://msdn.com/"),
"Basic", new NetworkCredential("user2","passwd2","domain2"));
        myCredentialCache.Add(new Uri(url),"Basic", new
NetworkCredential(userName,password,domainName));
        // Create a webrequest with the specified url.
        WebRequest myWebRequest = WebRequest.Create(url);
        // Call 'GetCredential' to obtain the credentials
specific to our Uri.
        NetworkCredential myCredential =
myCredentialCache.GetCredential(new Uri(url),"Basic");
        Display(myCredential);
        // Associating only our credentials.
        myWebRequest.Credentials = myCredential;
        // Sends the request and waits for response.
        WebResponse myWebResponse = myWebRequest.GetResponse();

        // Process response here.

        Console.WriteLine("\nResponse Received.");
        myWebResponse.Close();

    }
    catch(WebException e)
    {
        if (e.Response != null)
            Console.WriteLine("\r\nFailed to obtain a response.
The following error occured :
{0}",((HttpWebResponse)(e.Response)).StatusDescription);
        else
            Console.WriteLine("\r\nFailed to obtain a response.
The following error occured : {0}",e.Status);
    }
    catch(Exception e)
    {
        Console.WriteLine("\nThe following exception was
raised : {0}",e.Message);
    }
}
    public static void Display(NetworkCredential credential)
    {
Console.WriteLine("\nThe credentials are:");
Console.WriteLine("\nUsername : {0} ,Password : {1} ,
Domain :
{2}",credential.UserName,credential.Password,credential.Domain);
    }
```

[C++]
```cpp
void Display(NetworkCredential* credential)
{
    Console::WriteLine(S"\nThe credentials are:");
    Console::WriteLine(S"\nUsername : {0} , Password : {1} ,
Domain : {2}",
        credential->UserName, credential->Password, credential->Domain);
}

void GetPage(String* url, String* userName, String* password,
String* domainName)
{
    try
    {
        CredentialCache* myCredentialCache = new CredentialCache();
        // Dummy names used as credentials.
        myCredentialCache->Add(new Uri(S"http://microsoft.com/"),
        S"Basic", new NetworkCredential(S"user1", S"passwd1",
S"domain1"));
        myCredentialCache->Add(new Uri(S"http://msdn.com/"), S"Basic",
            new NetworkCredential(S"user2", S"passwd2", S"domain2"));
        myCredentialCache->Add(new Uri(url), S"Basic", new
NetworkCredential(userName, password, domainName));
        // Create a webrequest with the specified url.
        WebRequest* myWebRequest = WebRequest::Create(url);
        // Call 'GetCredential' to obtain the credentials
specific to our Uri.
        NetworkCredential* myCredential = myCredentialCache-
>GetCredential(new Uri(url), S"Basic");
        Display(myCredential);
        // Associating only our credentials.
        myWebRequest->Credentials = myCredential;
        // Sends the request and waits for response.
        WebResponse* myWebResponse = myWebRequest->GetResponse();

        // Process response here.

        Console::WriteLine(S"\nResponse Received.");
        myWebResponse->Close();
    }
    catch (WebException* e)
    {
        if (e->Response != 0)
            Console::WriteLine(S"\r\nFailed to obtain a
response. The following error occured : {0}",
            (dynamic_cast<HttpWebResponse*>(e->Response))-
>StatusDescription);
        else
            Console::WriteLine(S"\r\nFailed to obtain a
response. The following error occured : {0}",
            __box( e->Status));
    }
    catch (Exception* e)
    {
        Console::WriteLine(S"\nThe following exception was
raised : {0}", e->Message);
    }
}
```

Requirements

Platforms: Windows 98, Windows NT 4.0,
Windows Millennium Edition, Windows 2000,
Windows XP Home Edition, Windows XP Professional,
Windows .NET Server family,
Common Language Infrastructure (CLI) Standard

CredentialCache.GetEnumerator Method

Returns an enumerator that can iterate through the **CredentialCache** instance.

```
[Visual Basic]
Public Overridable Function GetEnumerator() As IEnumerator _
    Implements IEnumerable.GetEnumerator
[C#]
public virtual IEnumerator GetEnumerator();
[C++]
public: virtual IEnumerator* GetEnumerator();
[JScript]
public function GetEnumerator() : IEnumerator;
```

Return Value

An **IEnumerator** for the **CredentialCache**.

Implements

IEnumerable.GetEnumerator

Example

See related example in the **System.Net.CredentialCache.GetCredential** method topic.

Requirements

Platforms: Windows 98, Windows NT 4.0, Windows Millennium Edition, Windows 2000, Windows XP Home Edition, Windows XP Professional, Windows .NET Server family, Common Language Infrastructure (CLI) Standard

CredentialCache.Remove Method

Deletes a **NetworkCredential** instance from the cache.

```
[Visual Basic]
Public Sub Remove( _
    ByVal uriPrefix As Uri, _
    ByVal authType As String _
)
[C#]
public void Remove(
    Uri uriPrefix,
    string authType
);
[C++]
public: void Remove(
    Uri* uriPrefix,
    String* authType
);
[JScript]
public function Remove(
    uriPrefix : Uri,
    authType : String
);
```

Parameters

uriPrefix
    A **Uri** that specifies the URI prefix of the resources that the credential is used for.
authType
    The authentication scheme used by the host named in *uriPrefix*.

Remarks

The **Remove** method removes the specified **NetworkCredential** instance from the **CredentialCache**. Multiple calls to the **Remove** method for the same **NetworkCredential** have no effect.

Example

See related example in the **System.Net.CredentialCache.GetCredential** method topic.

Requirements

Platforms: Windows 98, Windows NT 4.0, Windows Millennium Edition, Windows 2000, Windows XP Home Edition, Windows XP Professional, Windows .NET Server family, Common Language Infrastructure (CLI) Standard

Dns Class

Provides simple domain name resolution functionality.

System.Object
  System.Net.Dns

```
[Visual Basic]
NotInheritable Public Class Dns
[C#]
public sealed class Dns
[C++]
public __gc __sealed class Dns
[JScript]
public class Dns
```

Thread Safety

Any public static (**Shared** in Visual Basic) members of this type are safe for multithreaded operations. Any instance members are not guaranteed to be thread safe.

Remarks

The **Dns** class is a static class that retrieves information about a specific host from the Internet Domain Name System (DNS).

The host information from the DNS query is returned in an instance of the **IPHostEntry** class. If the specified host has more than one entry in the DNS database, **IPHostEntry** contains multiple IP addresses and aliases.

Example

[Visual Basic, C#] The following example queries the DNS database for information on the host www.contoso.com:

```
[Visual Basic]
Dim hostInfo As IPHostEntry = Dns.GetHostByName("www.contoso.com")
```

```
[C#]
IPHostEntry hostInfo = Dns.GetHostByName("www.contoso.com");
```

Requirements

Namespace: System.Net

Platforms: Windows 98, Windows NT 4.0, Windows Millennium Edition, Windows 2000, Windows XP Home Edition, Windows XP Professional, Windows .NET Server family, .NET Compact Framework - Windows CE .NET

Assembly: System (in System.dll)

.NET Framework Security:
- **DnsPermission** to allow the use of **Dns**.

Dns.BeginGetHostByName Method

Begins an asynchronous request for **IPHostEntry** information about the specified DNS host name.

```
[Visual Basic]
Public Shared Function BeginGetHostByName( _
   ByVal hostName As String, _
   ByVal requestCallback As AsyncCallback, _
   ByVal stateObject As Object _
) As IAsyncResult
[C#]
public static IAsyncResult BeginGetHostByName(
   string hostName,
```
```
   AsyncCallback requestCallback,
   object stateObject
);
[C++]
public: static IAsyncResult* BeginGetHostByName(
   String* hostName,
   AsyncCallback* requestCallback,
   Object* stateObject
);
[JScript]
public static function BeginGetHostByName(
   hostName : String,
   requestCallback : AsyncCallback,
   stateObject : Object
) : IAsyncResult;
```

Parameters

hostName
    A string containing the DNS name of the host.
requestCallback
    The **AsyncCallback**.
stateObject
    The State object.

Return Value

An **IAsyncResult** instance that references the asynchronous request.

Exceptions

Exception Type	Condition
ArgumentNullException	*hostName* is a null reference (**Nothing** in Visual Basic).
SecurityException	The caller does not have permission to access DNS information.
SocketException	An error was encountered executing the DNS query.

Remarks

The **BeginGetHostByName** method starts an asynchronous request for DNS host information. The asynchronous callback method uses the **EndGetHostByName** method to return the actual host information.

Requirements

Platforms: Windows 98, Windows NT 4.0, Windows Millennium Edition, Windows 2000, Windows XP Home Edition, Windows XP Professional, Windows .NET Server family, .NET Compact Framework - Windows CE .NET, Common Language Infrastructure (CLI) Standard

.NET Framework Security:
- **DnsPermission** for accessing DNS. Associated enumeration: **PermissionState.Unrestricted**

Dns.BeginResolve Method

Begins an asynchronous request to resolve a DNS host name or IP address to an **IPAddress** instance.

```
[Visual Basic]
Public Shared Function BeginResolve( _
   ByVal hostName As String, _
   ByVal requestCallback As AsyncCallback, _
   ByVal stateObject As Object _
) As IAsyncResult
```

```
[C#]
public static IAsyncResult BeginResolve(
   string hostName,
   AsyncCallback requestCallback,
   object stateObject
);
[C++]
public: static IAsyncResult* BeginResolve(
   String* hostName,
   AsyncCallback* requestCallback,
   Object* stateObject
);
[JScript]
public static function BeginResolve(
   hostName : String,
   requestCallback : AsyncCallback,
   stateObject : Object
) : IAsyncResult;
```

Parameters

hostName

   A string containing the DNS name of the host.

requestCallback

   The **AsyncCallback**.

stateObject

   The State object.

Return Value

An **IAsyncResult** instance that references the asynchronous request.

Exceptions

Exception Type	Condition
ArgumentNullException	*hostName* is a null reference (**Nothing** in Visual Basic).
SocketException	The caller does not have permission to access DNS information.
SecurityException	An error occurred when executing the DNS query.

Remarks

The **BeginResolve** method starts an asynchronous request for DNS host information. The asynchronous callback method uses the **EndResolve** method to return the actual host information.

Example

[Visual Basic, C#, C++] The following example uses **BeginResolve** to resolve a DNS host name to an **IPAddress**.

```
[Visual Basic]
Class DnsBeginGetHostByName

   Class RequestState
      Public host As IPHostEntry

      Public Sub New()
         host = Nothing
      End Sub 'New
   End Class 'RequestState

   Public Shared Sub Main()
    Try
       ' Create an instance of the RequestState class.
       Dim myRequestState As New RequestState()

       ' Begin an asynchronous request for information such
as the host name, IP addresses,
```

```
       ' or aliases for the specified URI.
       Dim asyncResult As IAsyncResult =              ⅃
CType(Dns.BeginResolve("www.contoso.com", AddressOf    ⅃
RespCallback, myRequestState),IAsyncResult)

       ' Wait until asynchronous call completes.
       While asyncResult.IsCompleted <> True
       End While

       Console.WriteLine(("Host name : " +            ⅃
myRequestState.host.HostName))
       Console.WriteLine(ControlChars.Cr + "IP address list : ")
       Dim index As Integer
       For index = 0 To myRequestState.host.AddressList.Length - 1
          Console.WriteLine(myRequestState.host.AddressList(index))
       Next index
       Console.WriteLine(ControlChars.Cr + "Aliases : ")

       For index = 0 To myRequestState.host.Aliases.Length - 1
          Console.WriteLine(myRequestState.host.Aliases(index))
       Next index
    catch e as Exception
       Console.WriteLine("Exception caught!!!")
       Console.WriteLine(("Source : " + e.Source))
       Console.WriteLine(("Message : " + e.Message))
    End Try
   End Sub 'Main

   Private Shared Sub RespCallback(ar As IAsyncResult)
      Try
         ' Convert the IAsyncResult object to a RequestState object.
         Dim tempRequestState As RequestState = CType(   ⅃
(ar.AsyncState, RequestState)

         ' End the asynchronous request.
         tempRequestState.host = Dns.EndResolve(ar)
      Catch e As ArgumentNullException
         Console.WriteLine("ArgumentNullException caught!!!")
         Console.WriteLine(("Source : " + e.Source))
         Console.WriteLine(("Message : " + e.Message))
      Catch e As Exception
         Console.WriteLine("Exception caught!!!")
         Console.WriteLine(("Source : " + e.Source))
         Console.WriteLine(("Message : " + e.Message))
      End Try
   End Sub 'RespCallback
```

```
[C#]
class DnsBeginGetHostByName
{
   public static System.Threading.ManualResetEvent allDone = null;

   class RequestState
   {
      public IPHostEntry host;
      public RequestState()
      {
         host = null;
      }
   }

   public static void Main()
   {
      allDone = new ManualResetEvent(false);
      // Create an instance of the RequestState class.
      RequestState myRequestState = new RequestState();

      // Begin an asynchronous request for information like host  ⅃
name, IP addresses, or
      // aliases for specified the specified URI.
      IAsyncResult asyncResult = Dns.BeginResolve            ⅃
("www.contoso.com", new AsyncCallback(RespCallback), myRequestState );

      // Wait until asynchronous call completes.
      allDone.WaitOne();
      Console.WriteLine("Host name : " + myRequestState.host.HostName);
      Console.WriteLine("\nIP address list : ");
      for(int index=0; index <                               ⅃
```

```
myRequestState.host.AddressList.Length; index++)
    {
        Console.WriteLine(myRequestState.host.AddressList[index]);
    }
    Console.WriteLine("\nAliases : ");
    for(int index=0; index
< myRequestState.host.Aliases.Length; index++)
    {
        Console.WriteLine(myRequestState.host.Aliases[index]);
    }
}

private static void RespCallback(IAsyncResult ar)
{
    try
    {
        // Convert the IAsyncResult object to a RequestState object.
        RequestState tempRequestState = (RequestState)ar.AsyncState;
        // End the asynchronous request.
        tempRequestState.host = Dns.EndResolve(ar);
        allDone.Set();
    }
    catch(ArgumentNullException e)
    {
        Console.WriteLine("ArgumentNullException caught!!!");
        Console.WriteLine("Source : " + e.Source);
        Console.WriteLine("Message : " + e.Message);
    }
    catch(Exception e)
    {
        Console.WriteLine("Exception caught!!!");
        Console.WriteLine("Source : " + e.Source);
        Console.WriteLine("Message : " + e.Message);
    }
}
}

[C++]
public __gc class DnsBeginGetHostByName
{
public:
    static System::Threading::ManualResetEvent* allDone = 0;
    __gc class RequestState
    {
    public:
        IPHostEntry* host;
        RequestState()
        {
            host = 0;
        }
    };

    static void RespCallback(IAsyncResult* ar)
    {
        try
        {
            // Convert the IAsyncResult* Object* to a
RequestState Object*.
            RequestState* tempRequestState =
                dynamic_cast<RequestState*>(ar->AsyncState);
            // End the asynchronous request.
            tempRequestState->host = Dns::EndResolve(ar);
            allDone->Set();
        }
        catch (ArgumentNullException* e)
        {
            Console::WriteLine(S"ArgumentNullException caught!!!");
            Console::WriteLine(S"Source : {0}", e->Source);
            Console::WriteLine(S"Message : {0}", e->Message);
        }
        catch (Exception* e)
        {
            Console::WriteLine(S"Exception caught!!!");
            Console::WriteLine(S"Source : {0}", e->Source);
            Console::WriteLine(S"Message : {0}", e->Message);
        }
    }
};
```

Requirements

Platforms: Windows 98, Windows NT 4.0,
Windows Millennium Edition, Windows 2000,
Windows XP Home Edition, Windows XP Professional,
Windows .NET Server family,
.NET Compact Framework - Windows CE .NET,
Common Language Infrastructure (CLI) Standard

.NET Framework Security:

- **DnsPermission** for accessing DNS. Associated enumeration:
  PermissionState.Unrestricted

Dns.EndGetHostByName Method

Ends an asynchronous request for DNS information.

```
[Visual Basic]
Public Shared Function EndGetHostByName( _
    ByVal asyncResult As IAsyncResult _
) As IPHostEntry
[C#]
public static IPHostEntry EndGetHostByName(
    IAsyncResult asyncResult
);
[C++]
public: static IPHostEntry* EndGetHostByName(
    IAsyncResult* asyncResult
);
[JScript]
public static function EndGetHostByName(
    asyncResult : IAsyncResult
) : IPHostEntry;
```

Parameters

asyncResult
    The pending request for DNS information.

Return Value

An **IPHostEntry** object containin DNS information about a host.

Exceptions

Exception Type	Condition
ArgumentNullException	*asyncResult* is a null reference (**Nothing** in Visual Basic).

Remarks

The **EndGetHostByName** method completes an asynchronous
request for DNS information that was started with a call to
BeginGetHostByName.

Requirements

Platforms: Windows 98, Windows NT 4.0,
Windows Millennium Edition, Windows 2000,
Windows XP Home Edition, Windows XP Professional,
Windows .NET Server family,
.NET Compact Framework - Windows CE .NET,
Common Language Infrastructure (CLI) Standard

Dns.EndResolve Method

Ends an asynchronous request for DNS information.

```
[Visual Basic]
Public Shared Function EndResolve( _
    ByVal asyncResult As IAsyncResult _
) As IPHostEntry
```

```
[C#]
public static IPHostEntry EndResolve(
    IAsyncResult asyncResult
);
[C++]
public: static IPHostEntry* EndResolve(
    IAsyncResult* asyncResult
);
[JScript]
public static function EndResolve(
    asyncResult : IAsyncResult
) : IPHostEntry;
```

Parameters

asyncResult
   The pending request for DNS information.

Return Value

An **IPHostEntry** object that contains DNS information about a host.

Exceptions

Exception Type	Condition
ArgumentNullException	*asyncResult* is a null reference (**Nothing** in Visual Basic).

Remarks

The **EndResolve** method completes an asynchronous request for DNS information that was started with a call to **BeginResolve**.

Example

See related example in the **System.Net.Dns.BeginResolve** method topic.

Requirements

Platforms: Windows 98, Windows NT 4.0, Windows Millennium Edition, Windows 2000, Windows XP Home Edition, Windows XP Professional, Windows .NET Server family, .NET Compact Framework - Windows CE .NET, Common Language Infrastructure (CLI) Standard

Dns.GetHostByAddress Method

Gets DNS host information for an IP address.

Overload List

Creates an **IPHostEntry** instance from the specified **IPAddress**.
Supported by the .NET Compact Framework.

   [Visual Basic] **Overloads Public Shared Function GetHostByAddress(IPAddress) As IPHostEntry**
   [C#] **public static IPHostEntry GetHostByAddress (IPAddress);**
   [C++] **public: static IPHostEntry* GetHostByAddress (IPAddress*);**
   [JScript] **public static function GetHostByAddress (IPAddress) : IPHostEntry;**

Creates an **IPHostEntry** instance from an IP address.
Supported by the .NET Compact Framework.

   [Visual Basic] **Overloads Public Shared Function GetHostByAddress(String) As IPHostEntry**
   [C#] **public static IPHostEntry GetHostByAddress(string);**

   [C++] **public: static IPHostEntry* GetHostByAddress(String*);**
   [JScript] **public static function GetHostByAddress(String) : IPHostEntry;**

Dns.GetHostByAddress Method (IPAddress)

Creates an **IPHostEntry** instance from the specified **IPAddress**.

```
[Visual Basic]
Overloads Public Shared Function GetHostByAddress( _
    ByVal address As IPAddress _
) As IPHostEntry
[C#]
public static IPHostEntry GetHostByAddress(
    IPAddress address
);
[C++]
public: static IPHostEntry* GetHostByAddress(
    IPAddress* address
);
[JScript]
public static function GetHostByAddress(
    address : IPAddress
) : IPHostEntry;
```

Parameters

address
   An **IPAddress**.

Return Value

An **IPHostEntry**.

Exceptions

Exception Type	Condition
ArgumentNullException	*address* is a null reference (**Nothing** in Visual Basic).
SocketException	An error is encountered when resolving *address*.
SecurityException	The caller does not have permission to access DNS information.

Requirements

Platforms: Windows 98, Windows NT 4.0, Windows Millennium Edition, Windows 2000, Windows XP Home Edition, Windows XP Professional, Windows .NET Server family, .NET Compact Framework - Windows CE .NET, Common Language Infrastructure (CLI) Standard

.NET Framework Security:

*   **DnsPermission** for accessing DNS. Associated enumeration: **PermissionState.Unrestricted**

Dns.GetHostByAddress Method (String)

Creates an **IPHostEntry** instance from an IP address.

```
[Visual Basic]
Overloads Public Shared Function GetHostByAddress( _
    ByVal address As String _
) As IPHostEntry
```

```
[C#]
public static IPHostEntry GetHostByAddress(
   string address
);
[C++]
public: static IPHostEntry* GetHostByAddress(
   String* address
);
[JScript]
public static function GetHostByAddress(
   address : String
) : IPHostEntry;
```

Parameters

address

A string that represents an IP address.

Return Value

An **IPHostEntry** instance.

Exceptions

Exception Type	Condition
ArgumentNullException	*address* is a null reference (**Nothing** in Visual Basic).
SocketException	An error is encountered when resolving *address*.
FormatException	*address* is not a valid IP address.
SecurityException	The caller does not have permission to access DNS information.

Requirements

Platforms: Windows 98, Windows NT 4.0,
Windows Millennium Edition, Windows 2000,
Windows XP Home Edition, Windows XP Professional,
Windows .NET Server family,
.NET Compact Framework - Windows CE .NET,
Common Language Infrastructure (CLI) Standard

.NET Framework Security:

- **DnsPermission** for accessing DNS. Associated enumeration: **PermissionState.Unrestricted**

Dns.GetHostByName Method

Gets the DNS information for the specified DNS host name.

```
[Visual Basic]
Public Shared Function GetHostByName( _
   ByVal hostName As String _
) As IPHostEntry
[C#]
public static IPHostEntry GetHostByName(
   string hostName
);
[C++]
public: static IPHostEntry* GetHostByName(
   String* hostName
);
[JScript]
public static function GetHostByName(
   hostName : String
) : IPHostEntry;
```

Parameters

hostName

A string containing the DNS name of the host.

Return Value

An **IPHostEntry** object containing host information for the address specified in *hostName*.

Exceptions

Exception Type	Condition
ArgumentNullException	*hostName* is a null reference (**Nothing** in Visual Basic).
SocketException	An error is encountered when resolving *hostName*.
SecurityException	The caller does not have permission to access DNS information.

Remarks

The **GetHostByName** method queries the Internet DNS server for host information.

For asychronous access to DNS information, use the **BeginGetHostByName** and **EndGetHostByName** methods.

Example

[Visual Basic, C#, C++] The following example uses the **GetHostByName** to gets the DNS information for the specified DNS host name.

```
[Visual Basic]
Public Sub DisplayHostName(hostName As [String])
   Try
      ' Call the GetHostByName method, passing a DNS style
host name(for example,
      ' "www.contoso.com") as an argument to obtain an
IPHostEntry instance, that
      ' contains information for the specified host.

      Dim hostInfo As IPHostEntry = Dns.GetHostByName(hostName)
      ' Get the IP address list that resolves to the host
names contained in
      ' the Alias property.
      Dim address As IPAddress() = hostInfo.AddressList
      ' Get the alias names of the the addresses in the IP
address list.
      Dim [alias] As [String]() = hostInfo.Aliases

      Console.WriteLine(("Host name : " + hostInfo.HostName))
      Console.WriteLine(ControlChars.Cr + "Aliases : ")
      Dim index As Integer
      For index = 0 To [alias].Length - 1
         Console.WriteLine([alias](index))
      Next index
      Console.WriteLine(ControlChars.Cr + "IP address list : ")

      For index = 0 To address.Length - 1
         Console.WriteLine(address(index))
      Next index
   Catch e As SocketException
      Console.WriteLine("SocketException caught!!!")
      Console.WriteLine(("Source : " + e.Source))
      Console.WriteLine(("Message : " + e.Message))
   Catch e As ArgumentNullException
      Console.WriteLine("ArgumentNullException caught!!!")
      Console.WriteLine(("Source : " + e.Source))
      Console.WriteLine(("Message : " + e.Message))
   Catch e As Exception
      Console.WriteLine("Exception caught!!!")
      Console.WriteLine(("Source : " + e.Source))
      Console.WriteLine(("Message : " + e.Message))
   End Try
```

[C#]
```csharp
try
{
    IPHostEntry hostInfo = Dns.GetHostByName(hostName);
    // Get the IP address list that resolves to the host
names contained in the
    // Alias property.
    IPAddress[] address = hostInfo.AddressList;
    // Get the alias names of the addresses in the IP address list.
    String[] alias = hostInfo.Aliases;

    Console.WriteLine("Host name : " + hostInfo.HostName);
    Console.WriteLine("\nAliases : ");
    for(int index=0; index < alias.Length; index++) {
        Console.WriteLine(alias[index]);
    }
    Console.WriteLine("\nIP address list : ");
    for(int index=0; index < address.Length; index++) {
        Console.WriteLine(address[index]);
    }
}
catch(SocketException e)
{
    Console.WriteLine("SocketException caught!!!");
    Console.WriteLine("Source : " + e.Source);
    Console.WriteLine("Message : " + e.Message);
}
catch(ArgumentNullException e)
{
    Console.WriteLine("ArgumentNullException caught!!!");
    Console.WriteLine("Source : " + e.Source);
    Console.WriteLine("Message : " + e.Message);
}
catch(Exception e)
{
    Console.WriteLine("Exception caught!!!");
    Console.WriteLine("Source : " + e.Source);
    Console.WriteLine("Message : " + e.Message);
}
```

[C++]
```cpp
try {
    IPHostEntry* hostInfo = Dns::GetHostByName(hostName);
    // Get the IP address list that resolves to the host
names contained in the
    // Alias property.
    IPAddress* address[] = hostInfo->AddressList;
    // Get the alias names of the addresses in the IP address list.
    String* alias[] = hostInfo->Aliases;

    Console::WriteLine(S"Host name : {0}", hostInfo->HostName);
    Console::WriteLine(S"\nAliases : ");
    for (int index=0; index < alias->Length; index++)
        Console::WriteLine(alias->Item[index]);

    Console::WriteLine(S"\nIP address list : ");
    for (int index=0; index < address->Length; index++)
        Console::WriteLine(address->Item[index]);

} catch (SocketException* e) {
    Console::WriteLine(S"SocketException caught!!!");
    Console::WriteLine(S"Source : {0}", e->Source);
    Console::WriteLine(S"Message : {0}", e->Message);
} catch (ArgumentNullException* e) {
    Console::WriteLine(S"ArgumentNullException caught!!!");
    Console::WriteLine(S"Source : {0}", e->Source);
    Console::WriteLine(S"Message : {0}", e->Message);
} catch (Exception* e) {
    Console::WriteLine(S"Exception caught!!!");
    Console::WriteLine(S"Source : {0}", e->Source);
    Console::WriteLine(S"Message : {0}", e->Message);
}
```

Requirements

Platforms: Windows 98, Windows NT 4.0, Windows Millennium Edition, Windows 2000, Windows XP Home Edition, Windows XP Professional, Windows .NET Server family, .NET Compact Framework - Windows CE .NET, Common Language Infrastructure (CLI) Standard

.NET Framework Security:

- **DnsPermission** for accessing DNS. Associated enumeration: **PermissionState.Unrestricted**

Dns.GetHostName Method

Gets the host name of the local computer.

```
[Visual Basic]
Public Shared Function GetHostName() As String
[C#]
public static string GetHostName();
[C++]
public: static String* GetHostName();
[JScript]
public static function GetHostName() : String;
```

Return Value

A string containing the DNS host name of the local computer.

Exceptions

Exception Type	Condition
SocketException	An error is encountered when resolving the local host name.
SecurityException	The caller does not have permission to access DNS information.

Example

[Visual Basic, C#, C++] The following example uses the **GetHostName** method to obtain the host name of the local computer.

```vbnet
[Visual Basic]
Public Sub DisplayLocalHostName()
    Try
        ' Get the local computer host name.
        Dim hostName As [String] = Dns.GetHostName()
        Console.WriteLine(("Computer name :" + hostName))
    Catch e As SocketException
        Console.WriteLine("SocketException caught!!!")
        Console.WriteLine(("Source : " + e.Source))
        Console.WriteLine(("Message : " + e.Message))
    Catch e As Exception
        Console.WriteLine("Exception caught!!!")
        Console.WriteLine(("Source : " + e.Source))
        Console.WriteLine(("Message : " + e.Message))
    End Try
```

```csharp
[C#]
public void DisplayLocalHostName()
{
    try {
        // Get the local computer host name.
        String hostName = Dns.GetHostName();
        Console.WriteLine("Computer name :" + hostName);
    }
    catch(SocketException e) {
        Console.WriteLine("SocketException caught!!!");
        Console.WriteLine("Source : " + e.Source);
```

```
        Console.WriteLine("Message : " + e.Message);
    }
    catch(Exception e)
    {
        Console.WriteLine("Exception caught!!!");
        Console.WriteLine("Source : " + e.Source);
        Console.WriteLine("Message : " + e.Message);
    }
}
```

```
[C++]
public:
    void DisplayLocalHostName()
    {
        try {
            // Get the local computer host name.
            String*  hostName = Dns::GetHostName();
            Console::WriteLine(S"Computer name : {0}", hostName);
        } catch (SocketException* e) {
            Console::WriteLine(S"SocketException caught!!!");
            Console::WriteLine(S"Source : {0}", e->Source);
            Console::WriteLine(S"Message : {0}", e->Message);
        } catch (Exception* e) {
            Console::WriteLine(S"Exception caught!!!");
            Console::WriteLine(S"Source : {0}", e->Source);
            Console::WriteLine(S"Message : {0}", e->Message);
        }
    }
```

Requirements

Platforms: Windows 98, Windows NT 4.0,
Windows Millennium Edition, Windows 2000,
Windows XP Home Edition, Windows XP Professional,
Windows .NET Server family,
.NET Compact Framework - Windows CE .NET,
Common Language Infrastructure (CLI) Standard

.NET Framework Security:

- **DnsPermission** for accessing DNS. Associated enumeration: **PermissionState.Unrestricted**

Dns.Resolve Method

Resolves a DNS host name or IP address to an **IPHostEntry** instance.

```
[Visual Basic]
Public Shared Function Resolve( _
    ByVal hostName As String _
) As IPHostEntry
[C#]
public static IPHostEntry Resolve(
    string hostName
);
[C++]
public: static IPHostEntry* Resolve(
    String* hostName
);
[JScript]
public static function Resolve(
    hostName : String
) : IPHostEntry;
```

Parameters

hostName
    A DNS-style host name or IP address.

Return Value

An **IPHostEntry** instance containing address information about the host specified in *hostName*.

Exceptions

Exception Type	Condition
ArgumentNullException	*hostName* is a null reference (**Nothing** in Visual Basic).
SocketException	An error is encountered when resolving *hostName*.
SecurityException	The caller does not have permission to access DNS information.

Remarks

The **Resolve** method queries a DNS server for the IP address associated with a host name or IP address.

When *hostName* is a DNS-style host name associated with multiple IP addresses, only the first IP address that resolves to that host name is returned.

Example

[Visual Basic, C#, C++] The following example uses the Resolve method to resolve an IP address to an **IPHostEntry** instance.

```
[Visual Basic]
Public Sub DisplayHostAddress(hostString As [String])
    Try
        ' Call the Resolve method passing a DNS style host    ⏎
name or an IP address in
        ' dotted-quad notation (for example, "www.contoso.com"  ⏎
or "207.46.131.199") to
        ' obtain an IPHostEntry instance that contains         ⏎
address information for the
        ' specified host.
        Dim hostInfo As IPHostEntry = Dns.Resolve(hostString)
        ' Get the IP address list that resolves to the         ⏎
host names contained in the Alias
        ' property.
        Dim address As IPAddress() = hostInfo.AddressList
        ' Get the alias names of the addresses in the IP address list.
        Dim [alias] As [String]() = hostInfo.Aliases

        Console.WriteLine(("Host name : " + hostInfo.HostName))
        Console.WriteLine(ControlChars.Cr + "Aliases : ")
        Dim index As Integer
        For index = 0 To [alias].Length - 1
            Console.WriteLine([alias](index))
        Next index
        Console.WriteLine(ControlChars.Cr + "IP Address list :")

        For index = 0 To address.Length - 1
            Console.WriteLine(address(index))
        Next index
    Catch e As SocketException
        Console.WriteLine("SocketException caught!!!")
        Console.WriteLine(("Source : " + e.Source))
        Console.WriteLine(("Message : " + e.Message))
    Catch e As ArgumentNullException
        Console.WriteLine("ArgumentNullException caught!!!")
        Console.WriteLine(("Source : " + e.Source))
        Console.WriteLine(("Message : " + e.Message))
    Catch e As NullReferenceException
        Console.WriteLine("NullReferenceException caught!!!")
        Console.WriteLine(("Source : " + e.Source))
        Console.WriteLine(("Message : " + e.Message))
    Catch e As Exception
        Console.WriteLine("Exception caught!!!")
        Console.WriteLine(("Source : " + e.Source))
        Console.WriteLine(("Message : " + e.Message))
    End Try
```

```csharp
[C#]
try {
    IPHostEntry hostInfo = Dns.Resolve(hostString);
    // Get the IP address list that resolves to the host
names contained in the
    // Alias property.
    IPAddress[] address = hostInfo.AddressList;
    // Get the alias names of the addresses in the IP address list.
    String[] alias = hostInfo.Aliases;

    Console.WriteLine("Host name : " + hostInfo.HostName);
    Console.WriteLine("\nAliases : ");
    for(int index=0; index < alias.Length; index++) {
        Console.WriteLine(alias[index]);
    }
    Console.WriteLine("\nIP Address list :");
    for(int index=0; index < address.Length; index++) {
        Console.WriteLine(address[index]);
    }
}
catch(SocketException e)
{
    Console.WriteLine("SocketException caught!!!");
    Console.WriteLine("Source : " + e.Source);
    Console.WriteLine("Message : " + e.Message);
}
catch(ArgumentNullException e)
{
Console.WriteLine("ArgumentNullException caught!!!");
    Console.WriteLine("Source : " + e.Source);
    Console.WriteLine("Message : " + e.Message);
}
catch(NullReferenceException e)
{
    Console.WriteLine("NullReferenceException caught!!!");
    Console.WriteLine("Source : " + e.Source);
    Console.WriteLine("Message : " + e.Message);
}
catch(Exception e)
{
    Console.WriteLine("Exception caught!!!");
    Console.WriteLine("Source : " + e.Source);
    Console.WriteLine("Message : " + e.Message);
}
```

```cpp
[C++]
try {
    IPHostEntry* hostInfo = Dns::Resolve(hostString);
    // Get the IP address list that resolves to the host
names contained in the
    // Alias property.
    IPAddress* address[] = hostInfo->AddressList;
    // Get the alias names of the addresses in the IP address list.
    String* alias[] = hostInfo->Aliases;

    Console::WriteLine(S"Host name : {0}", hostInfo->HostName);
    Console::WriteLine(S"\nAliases : ");
    for (int index=0; index < alias->Length; index++) {
        Console::WriteLine(alias->Item[index]);
    }
    Console::WriteLine(S"\nIP Address list :");
    for (int index=0; index < address->Length; index++) {
        Console::WriteLine(address->Item[index]);
    }
} catch (SocketException* e) {
Console::WriteLine(S"SocketException caught!!!");
Console::WriteLine(S"Source : {0}", e->Source);
Console::WriteLine(S"Message : {0}", e->Message);
} catch (ArgumentNullException* e) {
Console::WriteLine(S"ArgumentNullException caught!!!");
Console::WriteLine(S"Source : {0}", e->Source);
Console::WriteLine(S"Message : {0}", e->Message);
} catch (NullReferenceException* e) {
Console::WriteLine(S"NullReferenceException caught!!!");
Console::WriteLine(S"Source : {0}", e->Source);
```

```cpp
Console::WriteLine(S"Message : {0}", e->Message);
} catch (Exception* e) {
Console::WriteLine(S"Exception caught!!!");
Console::WriteLine(S"Source : {0}", e->Source);
Console::WriteLine(S"Message : {0}", e->Message);
}
```

Requirements

Platforms: Windows 98, Windows NT 4.0,
Windows Millennium Edition, Windows 2000,
Windows XP Home Edition, Windows XP Professional,
Windows .NET Server family,
.NET Compact Framework - Windows CE .NET,
Common Language Infrastructure (CLI) Standard

.NET Framework Security:

- **DnsPermission** for accessing DNS. Associated enumeration:
  PermissionState.Unrestricted

DnsPermission Class

Controls rights to access Domain Name System (DNS) servers on the network.

System.Object
  System.Security.CodeAccessPermission
    System.Net.DnsPermission

```
[Visual Basic]
<Serializable>
NotInheritable Public Class DnsPermission
   Inherits CodeAccessPermission
   Implements IUnrestrictedPermission
[C#]
[Serializable]
public sealed class DnsPermission : CodeAccessPermission,
   IUnrestrictedPermission
[C++]
[Serializable]
public __gc __sealed class DnsPermission : public
   CodeAccessPermission, IUnrestrictedPermission
[JScript]
public
   Serializable
class DnsPermission extends CodeAccessPermission implements
   IUnrestrictedPermission
```

Thread Safety

Any public static (**Shared** in Visual Basic) members of this type are safe for multithreaded operations. Any instance members are not guaranteed to be thread safe.

Remarks

The default permissions allow all local and Intranet zone applications to access DNS services, and no DNS permission for Internet zone applications.

Requirements

Namespace: System.Net

Platforms: Windows 98, Windows NT 4.0, Windows Millennium Edition, Windows 2000, Windows XP Home Edition, Windows XP Professional, Windows .NET Server family

Assembly: System (in System.dll)

DnsPermission Constructor

Creates a new instance of the **DnsPermission** class that either allows unrestricted DNS access or disallows DNS access.

```
[Visual Basic]
Public Sub New( _
   ByVal state As PermissionState _
)
[C#]
public DnsPermission(
   PermissionState state
);
[C++]
public: DnsPermission(
   PermissionState state
);
```

```
[JScript]
public function DnsPermission(
   state : PermissionState
);
```

Parameters

state
    One of the **PermissionState** values.

Exceptions

Exception Type	Condition
ArgumentException	*state* is not a valid **PermissionState** value.

Remarks

If *state* is **Unrestricted** the **DnsPermission** instance passes all demands. If *state* contains any other value, the **DnsPermission** instance fails all demands.

Example

[Visual Basic, C#, C++] The following example creates an instance of the **DnsPermission** class.

```
[Visual Basic]
Public Sub useDns()
   ' Create a DnsPermission instance.
   Dim permission As New DnsPermission(PermissionState.Unrestricted)

   ' Check for permission.
   permission.Demand()
   ' Create a SecurityElement object to hold XML encoding of
the DnsPermission instance.
   Dim securityElementObj As SecurityElement = permission.ToXml()
   Console.WriteLine("Tag, Attributes and Values of 'DnsPermission'
instance :")
   Console.WriteLine((ControlChars.Cr + ControlChars.Tab + "Tag
:" + securityElementObj.Tag))
   ' Print the attributes and values.
   PrintKeysAndValues(securityElementObj.Attributes)
End Sub 'useDns

Private Sub PrintKeysAndValues(myList As Hashtable)
   ' Get the enumerator that can iterate through the hash table.
   Dim myEnumerator As IDictionaryEnumerator = myList.GetEnumerator()
   Console.WriteLine(ControlChars.Cr + ControlChars.Tab +
"-KEY-" + ControlChars.Tab + "-VALUE-")
   While myEnumerator.MoveNext()
      Console.WriteLine(ControlChars.Tab + "{0}:" +
ControlChars.Tab + "{1}", myEnumerator.Key, myEnumerator.Value)
   End While
   Console.WriteLine()
End Sub 'PrintKeysAndValues

[C#]
public void useDns() {

   // Create a DnsPermission instance.
   DnsPermission permission = new
DnsPermission(PermissionState.Unrestricted);

   // Check for permission.
   permission.Demand();
   // Create a SecurityElement object to hold XML encoding of
the DnsPermission instance.
   SecurityElement securityElementObj = permission.ToXml();
   Console.WriteLine("Tag, Attributes and Values of
'DnsPermission' instance :");
   Console.WriteLine("\n\tTag :" + securityElementObj.Tag);
   // Print the attributes and values.
   PrintKeysAndValues(securityElementObj.Attributes);
}
```

```
private void PrintKeysAndValues(Hashtable myList) {
    // Get the enumerator that can iterate through the hash table.
    IDictionaryEnumerator myEnumerator = myList.GetEnumerator();
    Console.WriteLine("\n\t-KEY-\t-VALUE-");
    while (myEnumerator.MoveNext())
        Console.WriteLine("\t{0}:\t{1}", myEnumerator.Key,
myEnumerator.Value);
    Console.WriteLine();
}
```

```
[C++]
public:
    void useDns()
    {
        // Create a DnsPermission instance.
        DnsPermission* permission = new
DnsPermission(PermissionState::Unrestricted);

        // Check for permission.
        permission->Demand();
        // Create a SecurityElement Object* to hold XML encoding
of the DnsPermission instance.
        SecurityElement*  securityElementObj = permission->ToXml();
        Console::WriteLine(S"Tag, Attributes and Values of
'DnsPermission' instance :");
        Console::WriteLine(S"\n\tTag : {0}", securityElementObj->Tag);
        // Print the attributes and values.
        PrintKeysAndValues(securityElementObj->Attributes);
    }

private:
    void PrintKeysAndValues(Hashtable* myList)
    {
        // Get the enumerator that can iterate through the hash table.
        IDictionaryEnumerator* myEnumerator = myList->GetEnumerator();
        Console::WriteLine(S"\n\t-KEY-\t-VALUE-");
        while (myEnumerator->MoveNext())
            Console::WriteLine(S"\t {0}:\t {1}", myEnumerator->Key,
myEnumerator->Value);
        Console::WriteLine();
    }
```

Requirements

Platforms: Windows 98, Windows NT 4.0,
Windows Millennium Edition, Windows 2000,
Windows XP Home Edition, Windows XP Professional,
Windows .NET Server family,
Common Language Infrastructure (CLI) Standard

DnsPermission.Copy Method

Creates an identical copy of the current permission instance.

```
[Visual Basic]
Overrides Public Function Copy() As IPermission Implements _
    IPermission.Copy
[C#]
public override IPermission Copy();
[C++]
public: IPermission* Copy();
[JScript]
public override function Copy() : IPermission;
```

Return Value

A new instance of the **DnsPermission** class that is an identical copy of the current instance.

Implements

IPermission.Copy

Remarks

A copy of a **DnsPermission** instance provides the same access to DNS servers as the original permission instance.

Example

[Visual Basic, C#, C++] The following example creates an identical copy of an existing **DnsPermission** instance.

```
[Visual Basic]
Public Sub UseDns()
    ' Create a DnsPermission instance.
    Dim myPermission As New DnsPermission(PermissionState.Unrestricted)
    ' Check for permission.
    myPermission.Demand()
    ' Create an identical copy of the above DnsPermission object.
    Dim myPermissionCopy As DnsPermission =
CType(myPermission.Copy(), DnsPermission)
    Console.WriteLine("Attributes and Values of 'DnsPermission'
instance :")
    ' Print the attributes and values.
    PrintKeysAndValues(myPermission.ToXml().Attributes)
    Console.WriteLine("Attribute and values of copied instance :")
    PrintKeysAndValues(myPermissionCopy.ToXml().Attributes)
End Sub 'UseDns

Private Sub PrintKeysAndValues(myHashtable As Hashtable)
    ' Get the enumerator that can iterate through he hash table.
    Dim myEnumerator As IDictionaryEnumerator =
myHashtable.GetEnumerator()
    Console.WriteLine(ControlChars.Tab + "-KEY-" +
ControlChars.Tab + "-VALUE-")
    While myEnumerator.MoveNext()
        Console.WriteLine(ControlChars.Tab + "{0}:" +
ControlChars.Tab + "{1}", myEnumerator.Key, myEnumerator.Value)
    End While
    Console.WriteLine()
End Sub 'PrintKeysAndValues
```

```
[C#]
public void UseDns() {
    // Create a DnsPermission instance.
    DnsPermission myPermission = new
DnsPermission(PermissionState.Unrestricted);
    // Check for permission.
    myPermission.Demand();
    // Create an identical copy of the above 'DnsPermission' object.
    DnsPermission myPermissionCopy = (DnsPermission)myPermission.Copy();
    Console.WriteLine("Attributes and Values of 'DnsPermission'
instance :");
    // Print the attributes and values.
    PrintKeysAndValues(myPermission.ToXml().Attributes);
    Console.WriteLine("Attribute and values of copied instance :");
    PrintKeysAndValues(myPermissionCopy.ToXml().Attributes);
}

private void PrintKeysAndValues(Hashtable myHashtable) {
    // Get the enumerator that can iterate through the hash table.
    IDictionaryEnumerator myEnumerator = myHashtable.GetEnumerator();
    Console.WriteLine("\t-KEY-\t-VALUE-");
    while (myEnumerator.MoveNext())
        Console.WriteLine("\t{0}:\t{1}", myEnumerator.Key,
myEnumerator.Value);
    Console.WriteLine();
}
```

```
[C++]
public:
    void UseDns()
    {
        // Create a DnsPermission instance.
        DnsPermission* myPermission = new
DnsPermission(PermissionState::Unrestricted);
        // Check for permission.
        myPermission->Demand();
```

```
        // Create an identical copy of the above 'DnsPermission' Object*.
        DnsPermission* myPermissionCopy =                                    ⏎
dynamic_cast<DnsPermission*>(myPermission->Copy());
        Console::WriteLine(S"Attributes and Values of                       ⏎
'DnsPermission' instance :");
        // Print the attributes and values.
        PrintKeysAndValues(myPermission->ToXml()->Attributes);
        Console::WriteLine(S"Attribute and values of copied instance :");
        PrintKeysAndValues(myPermissionCopy->ToXml()->Attributes);
    }

private:
    void PrintKeysAndValues(Hashtable* myHashtable)
    {
        // Get the enumerator that can iterate through the hash table.
        IDictionaryEnumerator* myEnumerator = myHashtable-                   ⏎
>GetEnumerator();
        Console::WriteLine(S"\t-KEY-\t-VALUE-");
        while (myEnumerator->MoveNext())
            Console::WriteLine(S"\t {0}:\t {1}", myEnumerator->Key,          ⏎
myEnumerator->Value);
        Console::WriteLine();
    }
```

Requirements

Platforms: Windows 98, Windows NT 4.0,
Windows Millennium Edition, Windows 2000,
Windows XP Home Edition, Windows XP Professional,
Windows .NET Server family,
Common Language Infrastructure (CLI) Standard

DnsPermission.FromXml Method

Reconstructs a **DnsPermission** instance from an XML encoding.

```
[Visual Basic]
Overrides Public Sub FromXml( _
    ByVal securityElement As SecurityElement _
) Implements ISecurityEncodable.FromXml
[C#]
public override void FromXml(
    SecurityElement securityElement
);
[C++]
public: void FromXml(
    SecurityElement* securityElement
);
[JScript]
public override function FromXml(
    securityElement : SecurityElement
);
```

Parameters

securityElement
    The XML encoding to use to reconstruct the **DnsPermission**
    instance.

Implements

ISecurityEncodable.FromXml

Exceptions

Exception Type	Condition
ArgumentNullException	*securityElement* is a null reference (**Nothing** in Visual Basic).
ArgumentException	*securityElement* is not a **DnsPermission** element.

Remarks

The **FromXml** method reconstructs a **DnsPermission** instance from
an XML encoding defined by **SecurityElement** class.

Use the **ToXml** method to XML-encode the **DnsPermission**
instance, including state information.

Example

[Visual Basic, C#, C++] The following example reconstructs a
DnsPermission instance from an XML encoding.

```
[Visual Basic]
Public Sub ConstructDnsPermission()
    Try
        ' Create a DnsPermission instance.
        Dim permission As New DnsPermission(PermissionState.None)
        ' Create a SecurityElement instance by calling the ToXml          ⏎
method on the
        ' DnsPermission instance and print its attributes,
        ' which hold the  XML encoding of the DnsPermission instance.
        Console.WriteLine("Attributes and Values of
'DnsPermission' instance :")
        PrintKeysAndValues(permission.ToXml().Attributes)

        ' Create a SecurityElement instacnce .
        Dim securityElementObj As New SecurityElement("IPermission")
        ' Add attributes and values of the SecurityElement              ⏎
instance corresponding to
        ' teh permission instance.
        securityElementObj.AddAttribute("version", "1")
        securityElementObj.AddAttribute("Unrestricted", "true")
        securityElementObj.AddAttribute("class",                         ⏎
"System.Net.DnsPermission")

        ' Reconstruct a DnsPermission instance from an XML encoding.
        Dim permission1 As New DnsPermission(PermissionState.None)
        permission1.FromXml(securityElementObj)

        ' Print the attributes and values of the constructed             ⏎
DnsPermission object.
        Console.WriteLine("After reconstruction Attributes and          ⏎
Values of new DnsPermission instance :")
        PrintKeysAndValues(permission1.ToXml().Attributes)
    Catch e As NullReferenceException
        Console.WriteLine("NullReferenceException caught!!!")
        Console.WriteLine(("Source : " + e.Source))
        Console.WriteLine(("Message : " + e.Message))
    Catch e As SecurityException
        Console.WriteLine("SecurityException caught!!!")
        Console.WriteLine(("Source : " + e.Source))
        Console.WriteLine(("Message : " + e.Message))
    Catch e As ArgumentNullException
        Console.WriteLine("ArgumentNullException caught!!!")
        Console.WriteLine(("Source : " + e.Source))
        Console.WriteLine(("Message : " + e.Message))
    Catch e As Exception
        Console.WriteLine("Exception caught!!!")
        Console.WriteLine(("Source : " + e.Source))
        Console.WriteLine(("Message : " + e.Message))
    End Try
End Sub 'ConstructDnsPermission

Private Sub PrintKeysAndValues(myList As Hashtable)
    ' Get the enumerator that can iterate through the hash table.
    Dim myEnumerator As IDictionaryEnumerator = myList.GetEnumerator()
    Console.WriteLine(ControlChars.Tab + "-KEY-" +                       ⏎
ControlChars.Tab + "-VALUE-")
    While myEnumerator.MoveNext()
        Console.WriteLine(ControlChars.Tab + "{0}:" +                    ⏎
ControlChars.Tab + "{1}", myEnumerator.Key, myEnumerator.Value)
    End While
    Console.WriteLine()
End Sub 'PrintKeysAndValues
```

```csharp
[C#]
public void ConstructDnsPermission() {
  try
  {
    // Create a DnsPermission instance.
    DnsPermission permission = new DnsPermission(PermissionState.None);
    // Create a SecurityElement instance by calling the
ToXml method on the
    // DnsPermission instance.
    // Print its attributes, which hold the  XML encoding
of the DnsPermission
    // instance.
    Console.WriteLine("Attributes and Values of
'DnsPermission' instance :");
    PrintKeysAndValues(permission.ToXml().Attributes);

    // Create a SecurityElement instance.
    SecurityElement securityElementObj = new
SecurityElement("IPermission");
    // Add attributes and values of the SecurityElement
instance corresponding to
    // the permission instance.
    securityElementObj.AddAttribute("version", "1");
    securityElementObj.AddAttribute("Unrestricted", "true");
    securityElementObj.AddAttribute("class","System.Net.DnsPermission");

    // Reconstruct a DnsPermission instance from an XML encoding.
    DnsPermission permission1 = new
DnsPermission(PermissionState.None);
    permission1.FromXml(securityElementObj);

    // Print the attributes and values of the constructed
DnsPermission object.
    Console.WriteLine("After reconstruction Attributes and
Values of new DnsPermission instance :");
    PrintKeysAndValues(permission1.ToXml().Attributes);
  }
  catch(NullReferenceException e)
  {
    Console.WriteLine("NullReferenceException caught!!!");
    Console.WriteLine("Source : " + e.Source);
    Console.WriteLine("Message : " + e.Message);
  }
  catch(SecurityException e)
  {
    Console.WriteLine("SecurityException caught!!!");
    Console.WriteLine("Source : " + e.Source);
    Console.WriteLine("Message : " + e.Message);
  }
  catch(ArgumentNullException e)
  {
    Console.WriteLine("ArgumentNullException caught!!!");
    Console.WriteLine("Source : " + e.Source);
    Console.WriteLine("Message : " + e.Message);
  }
  catch(Exception e)
  {
    Console.WriteLine("Exception caught!!!");
    Console.WriteLine("Source : " + e.Source);
    Console.WriteLine("Message : " + e.Message);
  }
}

private void PrintKeysAndValues(Hashtable myList) {
  // Get the enumerator that can iterate through the hash table.
  IDictionaryEnumerator myEnumerator = myList.GetEnumerator();
  Console.WriteLine("\t-KEY-\t-VALUE-");
  while (myEnumerator.MoveNext())
    Console.WriteLine("\t{0}:\t{1}", myEnumerator.Key,
myEnumerator.Value);
  Console.WriteLine();
}

[C++]
public:
  void ConstructDnsPermission()
```

```cpp
{
  try
  {
    // Create a DnsPermission instance.
    DnsPermission* permission = new
DnsPermission(PermissionState::None);
    // Create a SecurityElement instance by calling
the ToXml method on the
    // DnsPermission instance.
    // Print its attributes, which hold the  XML encoding
of the DnsPermission
    // instance.
    Console::WriteLine(S"Attributes and Values of
'DnsPermission' instance :");
    PrintKeysAndValues(permission->ToXml()->Attributes);

    // Create a SecurityElement instance.
    SecurityElement* securityElementObj = new
SecurityElement(S"IPermission");
    // Add attributes and values of the SecurityElement
instance corresponding to
    // the permission instance.
    securityElementObj->AddAttribute(S"version", S"1");
    securityElementObj->AddAttribute(S"Unrestricted", S"true");
    securityElementObj->AddAttribute(S"class",
S"System.Net.DnsPermission");

    // Reconstruct a DnsPermission instance from an XML encoding.
    DnsPermission* permission1 = new
DnsPermission(PermissionState::None);
    permission1->FromXml(securityElementObj);

    // Print the attributes and values of the
constructed DnsPermission Object*.
    Console::WriteLine(S"After reconstruction
Attributes and Values of new DnsPermission instance :");
    PrintKeysAndValues(permission1->ToXml()->Attributes);
  }
  catch (NullReferenceException* e)
  {
    Console::WriteLine(S"NullReferenceException caught!!!");
    Console::WriteLine(S"Source : {0}", e->Source);
    Console::WriteLine(S"Message : {0}", e->Message);
  }
  catch (SecurityException* e)
  {
    Console::WriteLine(S"SecurityException caught!!!");
    Console::WriteLine(S"Source : {0}", e->Source);
    Console::WriteLine(S"Message : {0}", e->Message);
  }
  catch (ArgumentNullException* e)
  {
    Console::WriteLine(S"ArgumentNullException caught!!!");
    Console::WriteLine(S"Source : {0}", e->Source);
    Console::WriteLine(S"Message : {0}", e->Message);
  }
  catch (Exception* e)
  {
    Console::WriteLine(S"Exception caught!!!");
    Console::WriteLine(S"Source : {0}", e->Source);
    Console::WriteLine(S"Message : {0}", e->Message);
  }
}

private:
  void PrintKeysAndValues(Hashtable * myList)
  {
    // Get the enumerator that can iterate through the hash table.
    IDictionaryEnumerator* myEnumerator = myList->GetEnumerator();
    Console::WriteLine(S"\t-KEY-\t-VALUE-");
    while (myEnumerator->MoveNext())
      Console::WriteLine(S"\t {0}:\t {1}",
      myEnumerator->Key, myEnumerator->Value);
    Console::WriteLine();
  }
```

Requirements

Platforms: Windows 98, Windows NT 4.0,
Windows Millennium Edition, Windows 2000,
Windows XP Home Edition, Windows XP Professional,
Windows .NET Server family,
Common Language Infrastructure (CLI) Standard

DnsPermission.Intersect Method

Creates a permission instance that is the intersection of the current
permission instance and the specified permission instance.

```
[Visual Basic]
Overrides Public Function Intersect( _
   ByVal target As IPermission _
) As IPermission Implements IPermission.Intersect
[C#]
public override IPermission Intersect(
   IPermission target
);
[C++]
public: IPermission* Intersect(
   IPermission* target
);
[JScript]
public override function Intersect(
   target : IPermission
) : IPermission;
```

Parameters

target

The **DnsPermission** instance to combine with the current
instance.

Return Value

A **DnsPermission** instance that represents the intersection of the
current **DnsPermission** instance with the specified **DnsPermission**
instance, or a null reference (**Nothing** in Visual Basic) if the
intersection is empty. If both the current instance and *target* are
unrestricted, this method returns a new **DnsPermission** instance that
is unrestricted; otherwise, it returns a null reference (**Nothing**).

Implements

IPermission.Intersect

Exceptions

Exception Type	Condition
ArgumentException	*target* is neither a **DnsPermission** nor a null reference (**Nothing** in Visual Basic).

Remarks

The **Intersect** method returns a **DnsPermission** instance that allows
the access defined by both the current **DnsPermission** instance and
the specified **DnsPermission** instance. Any demand must pass both
permissions to pass their intersection.

Example

[Visual Basic, C#, C++] The following example creates a
permission instance that is the intersection of the current permission
instance and the specified permission instance.

```
[Visual Basic]
Public Sub useDns()
    ' Create a DnsPermission instance.
    dnsPermission1 = New DnsPermission(PermissionState.Unrestricted)
    dnsPermission2 = New DnsPermission(PermissionState.None)
    ' Check for permission.
    dnsPermission1.Demand()
    dnsPermission2.Demand()
    Console.WriteLine("Attributes and Values of first          ⏎
DnsPermission instance :")
    PrintKeysAndValues(dnsPermission1.ToXml().Attributes)
    Console.WriteLine("Attributes and Values of second         ⏎
DnsPermission instance :")
    PrintKeysAndValues(dnsPermission2.ToXml().Attributes)
    Console.WriteLine("Union of both instances : ")
    MyUnion()
    Console.WriteLine("Intersection of both instances : ")
    MyIntersection()
End Sub 'useDns

Private Sub PrintKeysAndValues(myList As Hashtable)
    ' Get the enumerator that can iterate through the hash table.
    Dim myEnumerator As IDictionaryEnumerator = myList.GetEnumerator()
    Console.WriteLine(ControlChars.Tab + "-KEY-" +              ⏎
ControlChars.Tab + "-VALUE-")
    While myEnumerator.MoveNext()
        Console.WriteLine(ControlChars.Tab + "{0}:" +           ⏎
ControlChars.Tab + "{1}", myEnumerator.Key, myEnumerator.Value)
    End While
    Console.WriteLine()
End Sub 'PrintKeysAndValues

Private Sub MyIntersection()
    ' Create a DnsPermission instance that is the              ⏎
intersection of the current
    ' DnsPermission instance and the specified DnsPermission instance.
    Dim permission As DnsPermission =                          ⏎
CType(dnsPermission1.Intersect(dnsPermission2), DnsPermission)
    ' Print the attributes and values of the intersection      ⏎
instance of DnsPermission.
    PrintKeysAndValues(permission.ToXml().Attributes)
End Sub 'MyIntersection

[C#]
public void useDns() {
    // Create a DnsPermission instance.
    dnsPermission1 = new DnsPermission(PermissionState.Unrestricted);
    dnsPermission2 = new DnsPermission(PermissionState.None);
    // Check for permission.
    dnsPermission1.Demand();
    dnsPermission2.Demand();
    Console.WriteLine("Attributes and Values of first          ⏎
nsPermission instance :");
    PrintKeysAndValues(dnsPermission1.ToXml().Attributes);
    Console.WriteLine("Attributes and Values of second         ⏎
DnsPermission instance :");
    PrintKeysAndValues(dnsPermission2.ToXml().Attributes);
    Console.WriteLine("Union of both instances : ");
    MyUnion();
    Console.WriteLine("Intersection of both instances : ");
    MyIntersection();
}

private void PrintKeysAndValues(Hashtable myList) {
    // Get the enumerator that can iterate through the hash tabble.
    IDictionaryEnumerator myEnumerator = myList.GetEnumerator();
    Console.WriteLine("\t-KEY-\t-VALUE-");
    while (myEnumerator.MoveNext())
        Console.WriteLine("\t{0}:\t{1}", myEnumerator.Key,      ⏎
myEnumerator.Value);
    Console.WriteLine();
}

    // Create a DnsPermission instance that is the             ⏎
intersection of current
    // DnsPermission instance and the specified DnsPermission instance.
```

```
private void MyIntersection()
{
    DnsPermission permission =
(DnsPermission)dnsPermission1.Intersect(dnsPermission2);
    // Print the attributes and the values of the intersection
instance of
    // DnsPermission.
    PrintKeysAndValues(permission.ToXml().Attributes);
}

[C++]
public:
    void useDns()
    {
        // Create a DnsPermission instance.
    dnsPermission1 = new DnsPermission(PermissionState::Unrestricted);
    dnsPermission2 = new DnsPermission(PermissionState::None);
        // Check for permission.
        dnsPermission1->Demand();
        dnsPermission2->Demand();
        Console::WriteLine(S"Attributes and Values of first
DnsPermission instance :");
        PrintKeysAndValues(dnsPermission1->ToXml()->Attributes);
        Console::WriteLine(S"Attributes and Values of second
DnsPermission instance :");
        PrintKeysAndValues(dnsPermission2->ToXml()->Attributes);
        Console::WriteLine(S"Union of both instances : ");
        MyUnion();
        Console::WriteLine(S"Intersection of both instances : ");
        MyIntersection();
    }

private:
    void PrintKeysAndValues(Hashtable* myList)
    {
        // Get the enumerator that can iterate through the hash tabble.
        IDictionaryEnumerator* myEnumerator = myList->GetEnumerator();
        Console::WriteLine(S"\t-KEY-\t-VALUE-");
        while (myEnumerator->MoveNext())
            Console::WriteLine(S"\t {0}:\t {1}",
            myEnumerator->Key, myEnumerator->Value);
        Console::WriteLine();
    }

    // Create a DnsPermission instance that is the
intersection of current
    // DnsPermission instance and the specified
DnsPermission instance.
private:
    void MyIntersection()
    {
        DnsPermission* permission =
            dynamic_cast<DnsPermission*>(dnsPermission1-
>Intersect(dnsPermission2));
        // Print the attributes and the values of the
intersection instance of
        // DnsPermission.
        PrintKeysAndValues(permission->ToXml()->Attributes);
    }
```

Requirements

Platforms: Windows 98, Windows NT 4.0,
Windows Millennium Edition, Windows 2000,
Windows XP Home Edition, Windows XP Professional,
Windows .NET Server family,
Common Language Infrastructure (CLI) Standard

DnsPermission.IsSubsetOf Method

Determines whether the current permission instance is a subset of the specified permission instance.

```
[Visual Basic]
Overrides Public Function IsSubsetOf( _
    ByVal target As IPermission _
) As Boolean Implements IPermission.IsSubsetOf
[C#]
public override bool IsSubsetOf(
    IPermission target
);
[C++]
public: bool IsSubsetOf(
    IPermission* target
);
[JScript]
public override function IsSubsetOf(
    target : IPermission
) : Boolean;
```

Parameters

target
    The second **DnsPermission** instance to be tested for the subset relationship.

Return Value

false if the current instance is unrestricted and *target* is either a null reference (**Nothing** in Visual Basic) or unrestricted, otherwise **true**.

Implements

IPermission.IsSubsetOf

Exceptions

Exception Type	Condition
ArgumentException	*target* is neither a **DnsPermission** nor a null reference (**Nothing** in Visual Basic).

Remarks

The current **DnsPermission** instance is a subset of the specified **DnsPermission** instance if the current **DnsPermission** instance specifies a set of operations that is wholly contained by the specified **DnsPermission** instance.

If the **IsSubsetOf** method returns **true**, the current **DnsPermission** instance allows no more access to DNS servers than does the specified **DnsPermission** instance.

Example

See related example in the **System.Net.DnsPermission.Intersect** method topic.

Requirements

Platforms: Windows 98, Windows NT 4.0,
Windows Millennium Edition, Windows 2000,
Windows XP Home Edition, Windows XP Professional,
Windows .NET Server family,
Common Language Infrastructure (CLI) Standard

DnsPermission.IsUnrestricted Method

Checks the overall permission state of the object.

```
[Visual Basic]
Public Overridable Function IsUnrestricted() As Boolean Implements _
   IUnrestrictedPermission.IsUnrestricted
[C#]
public virtual bool IsUnrestricted();
[C++]
public: virtual bool IsUnrestricted();
[JScript]
public function IsUnrestricted() : Boolean;
```

Return Value

true if the **DnsPermission** instance was created with
PermissionState.Unrestricted; otherwise, **false**.

Implements

IUnrestrictedPermission.IsUnrestricted

Example

See related example in the **System.Net.DnsPermission.Intersect**
method topic.

Requirements

Platforms: Windows 98, Windows NT 4.0,
Windows Millennium Edition, Windows 2000,
Windows XP Home Edition, Windows XP Professional,
Windows .NET Server family

DnsPermission.ToXml Method

Creates an XML encoding of a **DnsPermission** instance and its
current state.

```
[Visual Basic]
Overrides Public Function ToXml() As SecurityElement Implements _
   ISecurityEncodable.ToXml
[C#]
public override SecurityElement ToXml();
[C++]
public: SecurityElement* ToXml();
[JScript]
public override function ToXml() : SecurityElement;
```

Return Value

A **SecurityElement** instance containing an XML-encoded
representation of the security object, including state information.

Implements

ISecurityEncodable.ToXml

Remarks

The **ToXml** method creates a **SecurityElement** instance to XML-
encode a representation of the **DnsPermission** instance, including
state information.

Use **FromXml** method to restore the state information from a
SecurityElement instance.

Example

See related example in the **System.Net.DnsPermission.Intersect**
method topic.

Requirements

Platforms: Windows 98, Windows NT 4.0,
Windows Millennium Edition, Windows 2000,
Windows XP Home Edition, Windows XP Professional,
Windows .NET Server family,
Common Language Infrastructure (CLI) Standard

DnsPermission.Union Method

Creates a permission instance that is the union of the current
permission instance and the specified permission instance.

```
[Visual Basic]
Overrides Public Function Union( _
   ByVal target As IPermission _
) As IPermission Implements IPermission.Union
[C#]
public override IPermission Union(
   IPermission target
);
[C++]
public: IPermission* Union(
   IPermission* target
);
[JScript]
public override function Union(
   target : IPermission
) : IPermission;
```

Parameters

target
> The **DnsPermission** instance to combine with the current
> instance.

Return Value

A **DnsPermission** instance that represents the union of the current
DnsPermission instance with the specified **DnsPermission**
instance. If *target* is a null reference (**Nothing** in Visual Basic), this
method returns a copy of the current instance. If the current instance
or *target* is unrestricted, this method returns a **DnsPermission**
instance that is unrestricted; otherwise, it returns a **DnsPermission**
instance that is not unrestricted.

Implements

IPermission.Union

Exceptions

Exception Type	Condition
ArgumentException	*target* is neither a **DnsPermission** nor a null reference (**Nothing** in Visual Basic).

Remarks

The **Union** method returns a **DnsPermission** instance that allows the
access defined by either the current **DnsPermission** instance or the
specified **DnsPermission** instance. Any demand that passes either
permission passes their union.

Example

[Visual Basic, C#, C++] The following example creates a
permission instance that is the union of the current permission
instance and the specified permission instance.

```
[Visual Basic]
Private Sub MyUnion()
    ' Create a DnsPermission instance which is the union of
the current DnsPermission instance and the specified
DnsPermission instance.
    Dim permission As DnsPermission =
CType(dnsPermission1.Union(dnsPermission2), DnsPermission)
    ' Print the attributes and values of the union
instance of DnsPermission.
    PrintKeysAndValues(permission.ToXml().Attributes)
End Sub 'MyUnion
Public Sub useDns()
    ' Create a DnsPermission instance.
    dnsPermission1 = New DnsPermission(PermissionState.Unrestricted)
    dnsPermission2 = New DnsPermission(PermissionState.None)
    ' Check for permission.
    dnsPermission1.Demand()
    dnsPermission2.Demand()
    Console.WriteLine("Attributes and Values of first
DnsPermission instance :")
    PrintKeysAndValues(dnsPermission1.ToXml().Attributes)
    Console.WriteLine("Attributes and Values of second
DnsPermission instance :")
    PrintKeysAndValues(dnsPermission2.ToXml().Attributes)
    Console.WriteLine("Union of both instances : ")
    MyUnion()
    Console.WriteLine("Intersection of both instances : ")
    MyIntersection()
End Sub 'useDns

Private Sub PrintKeysAndValues(myList As Hashtable)
    ' Get the enumerator that can iterate through the hash table.
    Dim myEnumerator As IDictionaryEnumerator = myList.GetEnumerator()
    Console.WriteLine(ControlChars.Tab + "-KEY-" +
ControlChars.Tab + "-VALUE-")
    While myEnumerator.MoveNext()
        Console.WriteLine(ControlChars.Tab + "{0}:" +
ControlChars.Tab + "{1}", myEnumerator.Key, myEnumerator.Value)
    End While
    Console.WriteLine()
End Sub 'PrintKeysAndValues
```

```
[C#]
private void MyUnion()
{
    // Create a DnsPermission instance that is the union of
the current DnsPermission
    // instance and the specified DnsPermission instance.
    DnsPermission permission =
(DnsPermission)dnsPermission1.Union(dnsPermission2);
    // Print the attributes and the values of the union
instance of DnsPermission.
    PrintKeysAndValues(permission.ToXml().Attributes);
}
public void useDns() {
    // Create a DnsPermission instance.
    dnsPermission1 = new DnsPermission(PermissionState.Unrestricted);
    dnsPermission2 = new DnsPermission(PermissionState.None);
    // Check for permission.
    dnsPermission1.Demand();
    dnsPermission2.Demand();
    Console.WriteLine("Attributes and Values of first
DnsPermission instance :");
    PrintKeysAndValues(dnsPermission1.ToXml().Attributes);
    Console.WriteLine("Attributes and Values of second
DnsPermission instance :");
    PrintKeysAndValues(dnsPermission2.ToXml().Attributes);
    Console.WriteLine("Union of both instances : ");
    MyUnion();
    Console.WriteLine("Intersection of both instances : ");
    MyIntersection();
}

private void PrintKeysAndValues(Hashtable myList) {
    // Get the enumerator that can iterate through the hash table.
```

```
    IDictionaryEnumerator myEnumerator = myList.GetEnumerator();
    Console.WriteLine("\t-KEY-\t-VALUE-");
    while (myEnumerator.MoveNext())
        Console.WriteLine("\t{0}:\t{1}", myEnumerator.Key,
myEnumerator.Value);
    Console.WriteLine();
}
```

```
[C++]
void MyUnion()
    {
    // Create a DnsPermission instance that is the union of the
current DnsPermission
    // instance and the specified DnsPermission instance.
    DnsPermission* permission =
dynamic_cast<DnsPermission*>(dnsPermission1->Union(dnsPermission2));
    // Print the attributes and the values of the union instance
of DnsPermission.
    PrintKeysAndValues(permission->ToXml()->Attributes);
    }
public:
void useDns()
    {
    // Create a DnsPermission instance.
    dnsPermission1 = new DnsPermission(PermissionState::Unrestricted);
    dnsPermission2 = new DnsPermission(PermissionState::None);
    // Check for permission.
    dnsPermission1->Demand();
    dnsPermission2->Demand();
    Console::WriteLine(S"Attributes and Values of first
DnsPermission instance :");
    PrintKeysAndValues(dnsPermission1->ToXml()->Attributes);
    Console::WriteLine(S"Attributes and Values of second
DnsPermission instance :");
    PrintKeysAndValues(dnsPermission2->ToXml()->Attributes);
    Console::WriteLine(S"Union of both instances : ");
    MyUnion();
    Console::WriteLine(S"Intersection of both instances : ");
    MyIntersection();
    }

private:
void PrintKeysAndValues(Hashtable* myList)
    {
    // Get the enumerator that can iterate through the hash tabble.
    IDictionaryEnumerator* myEnumerator = myList->GetEnumerator();
    Console::WriteLine(S"\t-KEY-\t-VALUE-");
    while (myEnumerator->MoveNext())
        Console::WriteLine(S"\t {0}:\t {1}",
        myEnumerator->Key, myEnumerator->Value);
    Console::WriteLine();
    }
```

Requirements

Platforms: Windows 98, Windows NT 4.0,
Windows Millennium Edition, Windows 2000,
Windows XP Home Edition, Windows XP Professional,
Windows .NET Server family,
Common Language Infrastructure (CLI) Standard

DnsPermissionAttribute Class

Specifies permission to request information from Domain Name Servers.

System.Object
  System.Attribute
    System.Security.Permissions.SecurityAttribute
      System.Security.Permissions.CodeAccessSecurityAttribute
        System.Net.DnsPermissionAttribute

```
[Visual Basic]
<AttributeUsage(AttributeTargets.Assembly Or AttributeTargets.Class _
   Or AttributeTargets.Struct Or AttributeTargets.Constructor Or _
   AttributeTargets.Method)>
<Serializable>
NotInheritable Public Class DnsPermissionAttribute
   Inherits CodeAccessSecurityAttribute
[C#]
[AttributeUsage(AttributeTargets.Assembly | AttributeTargets.Class
   | AttributeTargets.Struct | AttributeTargets.Constructor |
   AttributeTargets.Method)]
[Serializable]
public sealed class DnsPermissionAttribute :
   CodeAccessSecurityAttribute
[C++]
[AttributeUsage(AttributeTargets::Assembly |
   AttributeTargets::Class | AttributeTargets::Struct |
   AttributeTargets::Constructor | AttributeTargets::Method)]
[Serializable]
public __gc __sealed class DnsPermissionAttribute : public
   CodeAccessSecurityAttribute
[JScript]
public
   AttributeUsage(AttributeTargets.Assembly | AttributeTargets.Class |
   AttributeTargets.Struct | AttributeTargets.Constructor |
   AttributeTargets.Method)
   Serializable
class DnsPermissionAttribute extends
   CodeAccessSecurityAttribute
```

Thread Safety

Any public static (**Shared** in Visual Basic) members of this type are safe for multithreaded operations. Any instance members are not guaranteed to be thread safe.

Remarks

The security information declared by **DnsPermissionAttribute** is stored in the metadata of the attribute target, which is the class to which the **DnsPermissionAttribute** is applied. The system then accesses this information at run-time. The **SecurityAction** passed to the constructor determines the allowable DNS targets.

These security attributes are used only for **Declarative Security**. For **Imperative Security**, use the corresponding **DnsPermission** class.

Security access is either fully restricted, or fully unrestricted. Set the **Unrestricted** property to **true** to grant access, or **false** for no access. Set this property as a named parameter.

Example

[Visual Basic, C#] The following example uses **DnsPermissionAttribute** to apply declarative security to a custom class.

```
[Visual Basic]
' Uses the DnsPermissionAttribute to restrict access only to
those who have permission.
<DnsPermission(SecurityAction.Demand, Unrestricted := true)> _
Public Class MyClass1

   Public Shared Function GetIPAddress() As IPAddress
      Dim ipAddress As IPAddress =
Dns.Resolve("localhost").AddressList(0)
      Return ipAddress
   End Function 'GetIPAddress

   Public Shared Sub Main()
      Try
         ' Grants Access.
         Console.WriteLine(("Access granted" +
ControlChars.NewLine + " The local host IP Address is :" +
MyClass1.GetIPAddress().ToString()))
         ' Denies Access.
      Catch securityException As SecurityException
         Console.WriteLine("Access denied")
         Console.WriteLine(securityException.ToString())
      End Try
```

```
[C#]
//Uses the DnsPermissionAttribute to restrict access only to
those who have permission.
[DnsPermission(SecurityAction.Demand, Unrestricted = true)]
public class MyClass{

public static IPAddress GetIPAddress(){
      IPAddress ipAddress = Dns.Resolve("localhost").AddressList[0];
      return ipAddress;
}
public static void Main(){
try{
   //Grants Access.
   Console.WriteLine(" Access granted\n The local host IP
Address is :" +
                           MyClass.GetIPAddress().ToString());
}
// Denies Access.
catch(SecurityException securityException){
      Console.WriteLine("Access denied");
      Console.WriteLine(securityException.ToString());
}
```

Requirements

Namespace: System.Net

Platforms: Windows 98, Windows NT 4.0, Windows Millennium Edition, Windows 2000, Windows XP Home Edition, Windows XP Professional, Windows .NET Server family

Assembly: System (in System.dll)

DnsPermissionAttribute Constructor

Initializes a new instance of the **DnsPermissionAttribute** class with the specified **SecurityAction** value.

```
[Visual Basic]
Public Sub New( _
   ByVal action As SecurityAction _
)
[C#]
public DnsPermissionAttribute(
   SecurityAction action
);
```

```
[C++]
public: DnsPermissionAttribute(
    SecurityAction action
);
[JScript]
public function DnsPermissionAttribute(
    action : SecurityAction
);
```

Parameters

action
> One of the **SecurityAction** values.

Exceptions

Exception Type	Condition
ArgumentException	The *action* parameter is not a valid **SecurityAction**.

Remarks

The **SecurityAction** value passed to this constructor specifies the allowable **DnsPermissionAttribute** targets.

Example

[Visual Basic, C#] The following example uses **DnsPermission-Attribute** to apply declarative security to a custom class.

```
[Visual Basic]
' Uses the DnsPermissionAttribute to restrict access only to
those who have permission.
<DnsPermission(SecurityAction.Demand, Unrestricted := true)> _
Public Class MyClass1

    Public Shared Function GetIPAddress() As IPAddress
        Dim ipAddress As IPAddress =
Dns.Resolve("localhost").AddressList(0)
        Return ipAddress
    End Function 'GetIPAddress

    Public Shared Sub Main()
        Try
            ' Grants Access.
            Console.WriteLine(("Access granted" +
ControlChars.NewLine + " The local host IP Address is :" +
MyClass1.GetIPAddress().ToString()))
            ' Denies Access.
        Catch securityException As SecurityException
            Console.WriteLine("Access denied")
            Console.WriteLine(securityException.ToString())
        End Try
```

```
[C#]
//Uses the DnsPermissionAttribute to restrict access only to
those who have permission.
[DnsPermission(SecurityAction.Demand, Unrestricted = true)]
public class MyClass{

public static IPAddress GetIPAddress(){
    IPAddress ipAddress = Dns.Resolve("localhost").AddressList[0];
    return ipAddress;
}
public static void Main(){
try{
    //Grants Access.
    Console.WriteLine(" Access granted\n The local host IP
Address is :" +
                    MyClass.GetIPAddress().ToString());
}
// Denies Access.
catch(SecurityException securityException){
    Console.WriteLine("Access denied");
    Console.WriteLine(securityException.ToString());
}
}
```

Requirements

Platforms: Windows 98, Windows NT 4.0,
Windows Millennium Edition, Windows 2000,
Windows XP Home Edition, Windows XP Professional,
Windows .NET Server family,
Common Language Infrastructure (CLI) Standard

DnsPermissionAttribute.CreatePermission Method

Creates and returns a new instance of the **DnsPermission** class.

```
[Visual Basic]
Overrides Public Function CreatePermission() As IPermission
[C#]
public override IPermission CreatePermission();
[C++]
public: IPermission* CreatePermission();
[JScript]
public override function CreatePermission() : IPermission;
```

Return Value

A **DnsPermission** corresponding to the security declaration.

Remarks

The **CreatePermission** method is called by the security system, not by application code. The security information described by **DnsPermissionAttribute** is stored in the metadata of the attribute target. which is the class to which **DnsPermissionAttribute** is applied. The system then accesses the information at run time and calls **CreatePermission**. The system uses the returned **IPermission** to enforce the specified security requirements.

Requirements

Platforms: Windows 98, Windows NT 4.0,
Windows Millennium Edition, Windows 2000,
Windows XP Home Edition, Windows XP Professional,
Windows .NET Server family,
Common Language Infrastructure (CLI) Standard

EndPoint Class

Identifies a network address. This is an abstract (**MustInherit** in Visual Basic) class.

System.Object
  System.Net.EndPoint
    System.Net.IPEndPoint
    System.Net.IrDAEndPoint

```
[Visual Basic]
<Serializable>
MustInherit Public Class EndPoint
[C#]
[Serializable]
public abstract class EndPoint
[C++]
[Serializable]
public __gc __abstract class EndPoint
[JScript]
public
    Serializable
abstract class EndPoint
```

Thread Safety

Any public static (**Shared** in Visual Basic) members of this type are safe for multithreaded operations. Any instance members are not guaranteed to be thread safe.

Remarks

The **EndPoint** class provides an abstract (**MustInherit** in Visual Basic) base class that represents a network resource or service. Descendant classes combine network connection information to form a connection point to a service.

Requirements

Namespace: System.Net

Platforms: Windows 98, Windows NT 4.0, Windows Millennium Edition, Windows 2000, Windows XP Home Edition, Windows XP Professional, Windows .NET Server family, .NET Compact Framework - Windows CE .NET

Assembly: System (in System.dll)

EndPoint Constructor

Initializes a new instance of the **EndPoint** class.

```
[Visual Basic]
Protected Sub New()
[C#]
protected EndPoint();
[C++]
protected: EndPoint();
[JScript]
protected function EndPoint();
```

Remarks

This constructor is called by derived class constructors to initialize state in this type.

Requirements

Platforms: Windows 98, Windows NT 4.0, Windows Millennium Edition, Windows 2000, Windows XP Home Edition, Windows XP Professional, Windows .NET Server family, .NET Compact Framework - Windows CE .NET, Common Language Infrastructure (CLI) Standard

EndPoint.AddressFamily Property

Gets the address family to which the endpoint belongs.

```
[Visual Basic]
Public Overridable ReadOnly Property AddressFamily As AddressFamily
[C#]
public virtual AddressFamily AddressFamily {get;}
[C++]
public: __property virtual AddressFamily get_AddressFamily();
[JScript]
public function get AddressFamily() : AddressFamily;
```

Property Value

One of the **AddressFamily** values.

Exceptions

Exception Type	Condition
NotImplemented-Exception	Any attempt is made to get or set the property when the property is not overridden in a descendant class.

Remarks

The **AddressFamily** property specifies the addressing scheme used by the endpoint's underlying network protocol.

Requirements

Platforms: Windows 98, Windows NT 4.0, Windows Millennium Edition, Windows 2000, Windows XP Home Edition, Windows XP Professional, Windows .NET Server family, .NET Compact Framework - Windows CE .NET, Common Language Infrastructure (CLI) Standard

EndPoint.Create Method

Creates an **EndPoint** instance from a **SocketAddress** instance.

```
[Visual Basic]
Public Overridable Function Create( _
    ByVal socketAddress As SocketAddress _
) As EndPoint
[C#]
public virtual EndPoint Create(
    SocketAddress socketAddress
);
[C++]
public: virtual EndPoint* Create(
    SocketAddress* socketAddress
);
[JScript]
public function Create(
    socketAddress : SocketAddress
) : EndPoint;
```

Parameters

socketAddress
 The socket address that serves as the endpoint for a connection.

Return Value

A new **EndPoint** instance initialized from the specified **SocketAddress** instance.

Exceptions

Exception Type	Condition
NotImplemented-Exception	Any attempt is made to access the method when the method is not overridden in a descendant class.

Requirements

Platforms: Windows 98, Windows NT 4.0, Windows Millennium Edition, Windows 2000, Windows XP Home Edition, Windows XP Professional, Windows .NET Server family, .NET Compact Framework - Windows CE .NET, Common Language Infrastructure (CLI) Standard

EndPoint.Serialize Method

Serializes endpoint information into a **SocketAddress** instance.

```
[Visual Basic]
Public Overridable Function Serialize() As SocketAddress
[C#]
public virtual SocketAddress Serialize();
[C++]
public: virtual SocketAddress* Serialize();
[JScript]
public function Serialize() : SocketAddress;
```

Return Value

A **SocketAddress** instance containing the endpoint information.

Exceptions

Exception Type	Condition
NotImplemented-Exception	Any attempt is made to access the method when the method is not overridden in a descendant class.

Requirements

Platforms: Windows 98, Windows NT 4.0, Windows Millennium Edition, Windows 2000, Windows XP Home Edition, Windows XP Professional, Windows .NET Server family, .NET Compact Framework - Windows CE .NET

EndpointPermission Class

Defines an endpoint that is authorized by a **SocketPermission** instance.

System.Object
  System.Net.EndpointPermission

```
[Visual Basic]
<Serializable>
Public Class EndpointPermission
[C#]
[Serializable]
public class EndpointPermission
[C++]
[Serializable]
public __gc class EndpointPermission
[JScript]
public
    Serializable
class EndpointPermission
```

Thread Safety

Any public static (**Shared** in Visual Basic) members of this type are safe for multithreaded operations. Any instance members are not guaranteed to be thread safe.

Remarks

The **EndpointPermission** class defines a network endpoint, including host name, network port number, and transport type used to make the connection.

Requirements

Namespace: System.Net

Platforms: Windows 98, Windows NT 4.0, Windows Millennium Edition, Windows 2000, Windows XP Home Edition, Windows XP Professional, Windows .NET Server family

Assembly: System (in System.dll)

EndpointPermission.Hostname Property

Gets the DNS host name or IP address of the server associated with this endpoint.

```
[Visual Basic]
Public ReadOnly Property Hostname As String
[C#]
public string Hostname {get;}
[C++]
public: __property String* get_Hostname();
[JScript]
public function get Hostname() : String;
```

Property Value

A string containing the DNS host name or IP address of the server.

Requirements

Platforms: Windows 98, Windows NT 4.0, Windows Millennium Edition, Windows 2000, Windows XP Home Edition, Windows XP Professional, Windows .NET Server family

EndpointPermission.Port Property

Gets the network port number associated with this endpoint.

```
[Visual Basic]
Public ReadOnly Property Port As Integer
[C#]
public int Port {get;}
[C++]
public: __property int get_Port();
[JScript]
public function get Port() : int;
```

Property Value

The network port number associated with this request, or **SocketPermission.AllPorts**.

Requirements

Platforms: Windows 98, Windows NT 4.0, Windows Millennium Edition, Windows 2000, Windows XP Home Edition, Windows XP Professional, Windows .NET Server family

EndpointPermission.Transport Property

Gets the transport type associated with this endpoint.

```
[Visual Basic]
Public ReadOnly Property Transport As TransportType
[C#]
public TransportType Transport {get;}
[C++]
public: __property TransportType get_Transport();
[JScript]
public function get Transport() : TransportType;
```

Property Value

One of the **TransportType** values.

Requirements

Platforms: Windows 98, Windows NT 4.0, Windows Millennium Edition, Windows 2000, Windows XP Home Edition, Windows XP Professional, Windows .NET Server family

EndpointPermission.Equals Method

This member overrides **Object.Equals**.

```
[Visual Basic]
Overrides Public Function Equals( _
    ByVal obj As Object _
) As Boolean
[C#]
public override bool Equals(
    object obj
);
[C++]
public: bool Equals(
    Object* obj
);
[JScript]
public override function Equals(
    obj : Object
) : Boolean;
```

Requirements

Platforms: Windows 98, Windows NT 4.0,
Windows Millennium Edition, Windows 2000,
Windows XP Home Edition, Windows XP Professional,
Windows .NET Server family

EndpointPermission.GetHashCode Method

This member overrides **Object.GetHashCode**.

```
[Visual Basic]
Overrides Public Function GetHashCode() As Integer
[C#]
public override int GetHashCode();
[C++]
public: int GetHashCode();
[JScript]
public override function GetHashCode() : int;
```

Requirements

Platforms: Windows 98, Windows NT 4.0,
Windows Millennium Edition, Windows 2000,
Windows XP Home Edition, Windows XP Professional,
Windows .NET Server family

EndpointPermission.ToString Method

Returns a string that represents the current **EndpointPermission**
instance.

```
[Visual Basic]
Overrides Public Function ToString() As String
[C#]
public override string ToString();
[C++]
public: String* ToString();
[JScript]
public override function ToString() : String;
```

Return Value

A string that represents the current **EndpointPermission** instance.

Remarks

The **ToString** method returns a string representing the contents for
the **EndpointPermission** instance. The string is in the form
Hostname # Port # Transport.

Requirements

Platforms: Windows 98, Windows NT 4.0,
Windows Millennium Edition, Windows 2000,
Windows XP Home Edition, Windows XP Professional,
Windows .NET Server family

FileWebRequest Class

Provides a file system implementation of the **WebRequest** class.

System.Object
  System.MarshalByRefObject
    System.Net.WebRequest
      System.Net.FileWebRequest

```
[Visual Basic]
<Serializable>
Public Class FileWebRequest
    Inherits WebRequest
[C#]
[Serializable]
public class FileWebRequest : WebRequest
[C++]
[Serializable]
public __gc class FileWebRequest : public WebRequest
[JScript]
public
    Serializable
class FileWebRequest extends WebRequest
```

Thread Safety

Any public static (**Shared** in Visual Basic) members of this type are safe for multithreaded operations. Any instance members are not guaranteed to be thread safe.

Remarks

The **FileWebRequest** class implements the **WebRequest** abstract (**MustInherit** in Visual Basic) base class for URIs that use the file:/ / scheme to request local files.

Do not use the **FileWebRequest** constructor. Use the **WebRequest.Create** method to initialize new instances of the **FileWebRequest** class. If the URI scheme is file://, the **Create** method returns a **FileWebRequest** instance.

The **GetResponse** method makes a synchronous request for the file specified in the **RequestUri** property and returns a **FileWebResponse** instance containing the response. You can make an asynchronous request for the file using the **BeginGetResponse** and **EndGetResponse** methods.

When you want to write data to a file, the **GetRequestStream** method returns a **Stream** instance to write to. The **BeginGetRequestStream** and **EndGetRequestStream** methods provide asynchronous access to the write data stream.

The **FileWebRequest** class relies on the **File** class for error handling and code access security.

Example

[Visual Basic]

```
' This example creates or opens a text file and stores a string in it.
' Both the file and the string are passed by the user.
' Note. For this program to work, the folder containing the test file
' must be shared, with its permissions set to allow write access.

Imports System.Net
Imports System
Imports System.IO
Imports System.Text

Namespace Mssc.PluggableProtocols.File

Module TestGetRequestStream
```

```
Class TestGetRequestStream

    Private Shared myFileWebRequest As FileWebRequest

    ' Show how to use this program.
    Private Shared Sub showUsage()
        Console.WriteLine(ControlChars.Lf + "Please enter        ↵
file name
and timeout :")
        Console.WriteLine("Usage: vb_getrequeststream         ↵
<systemname>/<sharedfoldername>/<filename> timeout")
        Console.WriteLine("Example: vb_getrequestream          ↵
ngetrequestrtream() ndpue/temp/hello.txt  1000")
        Console.WriteLine("Small time-out values
(for example, 3 or less) cause a time-out exception.")
    End Sub

    Private Shared Sub makeFileRequest(ByVal fileName As String,     ↵
ByVal timeout As Integer)
        Try
            ' Create a Uri object.to access the file requested by the user.
            Dim myUrl As New Uri("file://" + fileName)

            ' Create a FileWebRequest object.for the requeste file.
            myFileWebRequest = CType(WebRequest.CreateDefault       ↵
(myUrl), FileWebRequest)

            ' Set the time-out to the value selected by the user.
            myFileWebRequest.Timeout = timeout

            ' Set the Method property to POST
            myFileWebRequest.Method = "POST"

        Catch e As WebException
            Console.WriteLine(("WebException is: " + e.Message))
        Catch e As UriFormatException
            Console.WriteLine(("UriFormatWebException is: " + e.Message))
        End Try

    End Sub

    Private Shared Sub writeToFile()
        Try
            ' Enter the string to write to the file.
            Console.WriteLine("Enter the string you want to write:")
            Dim userInput As String = Console.ReadLine()

            ' Convert the string to a byte array.
            Dim encoder As New ASCIIEncoding()
            Dim byteArray As Byte() = encoder.GetBytes(userInput)

            ' Set the ContentLength property.
            myFileWebRequest.ContentLength = byteArray.Length

            Dim contentLength As String =                      ↵
myFileWebRequest.ContentLength.ToString()

            Console.WriteLine(ControlChars.Lf + "The content length    ↵
is {0}.", contentLength)

            ' Get the file stream handler to write to the file.
            Dim readStream As Stream = myFileWebRequest.GetRequestStream()

            ' Write to the stream.
            ' Note. For this to work the file must be accessible
            ' on the network. This can be accomplished by          ↵
setting the property
            ' sharing of the folder containg the file.
            ' FileWebRequest.Credentials property cannot be used
for this purpose.
            readStream.Write(byteArray, 0, userInput.Length)

            Console.WriteLine(ControlChars.Lf + "The String you
entered was successfully written to the file.")
```

```
        readStream.Close()

      Catch e As WebException
        Console.WriteLine(("WebException is: " + e.Message))
      Catch e As UriFormatException
        Console.WriteLine(("UriFormatWebException is: " + e.Message))
      End Try

    End Sub

    Public Shared Sub Main(ByVal args() As String)

      If args.Length < 2 Then
        showUsage()
      Else
        makeFileRequest(args(0), Integer.Parse(args(1)))
        writeToFile()
      End If

    End Sub 'Main

  End Class 'TestGetRequestStream

End Module

End Namespace
```

[C#]
```
// This example creates or opens a text file and stores a string in it.
// Both the file and the string are passed by the user.
// Note. For this program to work, the folder containing the test file
// must be shared, with its permissions set to allow write access.

using System.Net;
using System;
using System.IO;
using System.Text;

namespace Mssc.PluggableProtocols.File
{
  class TestGetRequestStream
  {
    private static FileWebRequest myFileWebRequest;

    private static void showUsage()
    {
      Console.WriteLine("\nPlease enter file name and timeout :");
      Console.WriteLine("Usage: cs_getrequeststream
<systemname>/<sharedfoldername>/<filename> timeout");
      Console.WriteLine("Example: cs_getrequeststream
ngetrequestrtream() ndpue/temp/hello.txt  1000");
      Console.WriteLine("Small time-out values
(for example, 3 or less) cause a time-out exception.");
    }

    private static void makeFileRequest(string fileName, int timeout)
    {
      try
      {
        // Create a Uri object.
        Uri myUrl=new Uri("file://" + fileName);
        // Create a FileWebRequest object.
        myFileWebRequest =
(FileWebRequest)WebRequest.CreateDefault(myUrl);
        // Set the time-out to the value selected by the user.
        myFileWebRequest.Timeout = timeout;
        // Set the Method property to POST
        myFileWebRequest.Method="POST";
      }
      catch(WebException e)
      {
        Console.WriteLine("WebException: "+e.Message);
      }
      catch(UriFormatException e)
      {
```

```
        Console.WriteLine("UriFormatWebException: "+e.Message);
      }
    }

    private static void writeToFile()
    {
      try
      {
        // Enter the string to write to the file.
        Console.WriteLine("Enter the string you want to write:");
        string userInput = Console.ReadLine();
        // Convert the string to a byte array.
        ASCIIEncoding encoder = new ASCIIEncoding();
        byte[] byteArray = encoder.GetBytes(userInput);
        // Set the ContentLength property.
        myFileWebRequest.ContentLength=byteArray.Length;
        string contentLength = myFileWebRequest.ContentLength.ToString();
        Console.WriteLine("\nThe content length is {0}.",
contentLength);
        // Get the file stream handler to write to the file.
        Stream readStream=myFileWebRequest.GetRequestStream();

        // Write to the file stream.
        // Note.  For this to work, the file must be accessible
        // on the network. This can be accomplished by setting
the property
        // sharing of the folder containg the file.
        // FileWebRequest.Credentials property cannot be used
for this purpose.
        readStream.Write(byteArray,0,userInput.Length);

        Console.WriteLine("\nThe String you entered was
successfully written to the file.");

        readStream.Close();

      }
      catch(WebException e)
      {
        Console.WriteLine("The WebException: "+e.Message);
      }
      catch(UriFormatException e)
      {
        Console.WriteLine("The UriFormatWebException: "+e.Message);
      }
    }

    public static void Main(String[] args)
    {
      if (args.Length < 2)
        showUsage();
      else
      {
        makeFileRequest(args[0], int.Parse(args[1]));
        writeToFile();
      }
    }
  }
}
```

[C++]
```
// This program creates or open a text file in which it stores a
String*.
// Both file and String* are passed by the user.
// Note. In order for this program to work, the folder containing
the test file
// must be shared with its permissions set to allow write access.

#using <mscorlib.dll>
#using <System.dll>

using namespace System;
using namespace System::IO;
using namespace System::Text;
using namespace System::Net;
```

```
__gc class TestGetRequestStream {
private:
    static FileWebRequest* myFileWebRequest;

    static void showUsage() {
        Console::WriteLine(S"\nPlease enter file name and timeout :");

        Console::WriteLine(S"Usage: cs_getrequeststream          ↵
<systemname>/<sharedfoldername>/<filename> timeout");
        Console::WriteLine(S"Example: cs_getrequeststream        ↵
ndpue/temp/hello.txt 1000");
        Console::WriteLine(S"Small timeout values                ↵
(for instance 3 or less) cause a timeout exception.");
    }

    static void makeFileRequest(String* fileName, int timeout) {
        try {
            // Create a Uri Object*.
            Uri* myUrl = new Uri(String::Format(S"file://{0}", fileName));
            // Create a FileWebRequest Object*.
            myFileWebRequest =
dynamic_cast<FileWebRequest*>(WebRequest::CreateDefault(myUrl));
            // Set the timeout to the value selected by the user.
            myFileWebRequest->Timeout = timeout;
            // Set the Method property to POST
            myFileWebRequest->Method=S"POST";
        } catch (WebException* e) {
            Console::WriteLine(S"WebException: {0}", e->Message);
        } catch (UriFormatException* e) {
            Console::WriteLine(S"UriFormatWebException: {0}", e->Message);
        }
    }

    static void writeToFile() {
        try {
            // Enter the String* to write into the file.
            Console::WriteLine(S"Enter the string you want to write:");
            String* userInput = Console::ReadLine();
            // Convert the String* to Byte array.
            ASCIIEncoding* encoder = new ASCIIEncoding();
            Byte byteArray[] = encoder->GetBytes(userInput);
            // Set the ContentLength property.
            myFileWebRequest->ContentLength=byteArray->Length;
            String* contentLength = myFileWebRequest-         ↵
>ContentLength.ToString();
            Console::WriteLine(S"\nThe content length is {0}.",  ↵
contentLength);
            // Get the file stream handler to write into the file.
            Stream* readStream=myFileWebRequest->GetRequestStream();

            // Write to the file stream.
            // Note. In order for this to work the file must be accessible
            // on the network. This can be accomplished by setting   ↵
the property
            // sharing of the folder containg the file. The permissions
            // can be set so everyone can modify the file.
            // FileWebRequest::Credentials property cannot be used   ↵
for this purpose.
            readStream->Write(byteArray, 0, userInput->Length);

            Console::WriteLine(S"\nThe String you entered was       ↵
successfully written into the file.");

            readStream->Close();

        } catch (WebException* e) {
            Console::WriteLine(S"The WebException: {0}", e->Message);
        } catch (UriFormatException* e) {
            Console::WriteLine(S"The UriFormatWebException:         ↵
{0}", e->Message);
        }
    }

public:
    static void main() {
```

```
        String* args[] = Environment::GetCommandLineArgs();
        if (args->Length < 3)
            showUsage();
        else {
            makeFileRequest(args[1], Int32::Parse(args[2]));
            writeToFile();
        }
    }
};

int main()
{
    TestGetRequestStream::main();
}
```

Requirements

Namespace: System.Net

Platforms: Windows 98, Windows NT 4.0,
Windows Millennium Edition, Windows 2000,
Windows XP Home Edition, Windows XP Professional,
Windows .NET Server family

Assembly: System (in System.dll)

FileWebRequest Constructor

Initializes a new instance of the **FileWebRequest** class from the
specified instances of the **SerializationInfo** and **StreamingContext**
classes.

```
[Visual Basic]
Protected Sub New( _
    ByVal serializationInfo As SerializationInfo, _
    ByVal streamingContext As StreamingContext _
)
[C#]
protected FileWebRequest(
    SerializationInfo serializationInfo,
    StreamingContext streamingContext
);
[C++]
protected: FileWebRequest(
    SerializationInfo* serializationInfo,
    StreamingContext streamingContext
);
[JScript]
protected function FileWebRequest(
    serializationInfo : SerializationInfo,
    streamingContext : StreamingContext
);
```

Parameters

serializationInfo
>   A **SerializationInfo** instance that contains the information
>   required to serialize the new **FileWebRequest** instance.

streamingContext
>   An instance of the **StreamingContext** class that contains the
>   source of the serialized stream associated with the new
>   **FileWebRequest** instance.

Remarks

This constructor implements the **ISerializable** interface for the
FileWebRequest class.

Requirements

Platforms: Windows 98, Windows NT 4.0,
Windows Millennium Edition, Windows 2000,
Windows XP Home Edition, Windows XP Professional,
Windows .NET Server family

FileWebRequest.ConnectionGroupName Property

Gets or sets the name of the connection group for the request. This
property is reserved for future use.

```
[Visual Basic]
Overrides Public Property ConnectionGroupName As String
[C#]
public override string ConnectionGroupName {get; set;}
[C++]
public: __property String* get_ConnectionGroupName();
public: __property void set_ConnectionGroupName(String*);
[JScript]
public override function get ConnectionGroupName() : String;
public override function set ConnectionGroupName(String);
```

Property Value

The name of the connection group for the request.

Remarks

The **ConnectionGroupName** property is currently not used by the
FileWebRequest class.

Requirements

Platforms: Windows 98, Windows NT 4.0,
Windows Millennium Edition, Windows 2000,
Windows XP Home Edition, Windows XP Professional,
Windows .NET Server family

FileWebRequest.ContentLength Property

Gets or sets the content length of the data being sent.

```
[Visual Basic]
Overrides Public Property ContentLength As Long
[C#]
public override long ContentLength {get; set;}
[C++]
public: __property __int64 get_ContentLength();
public: __property void set_ContentLength(__int64);
[JScript]
public override function get ContentLength() : long;
public override function set ContentLength(long);
```

Property Value

The number of bytes of request data being sent.

Exceptions

Exception Type	Condition
ArgumentException	ContentLength is less than 0.

Example

See related example in the **System.Net.FileWebRequest** class topic.

Requirements

Platforms: Windows 98, Windows NT 4.0,
Windows Millennium Edition, Windows 2000,
Windows XP Home Edition, Windows XP Professional,
Windows .NET Server family

FileWebRequest.ContentType Property

Gets or sets the content type of the data being sent. This property is
reserved for future use.

```
[Visual Basic]
Overrides Public Property ContentType As String
[C#]
public override string ContentType {get; set;}
[C++]
public: __property String* get_ContentType();
public: __property void set_ContentType(String*);
[JScript]
public override function get ContentType() : String;
public override function set ContentType(String);
```

Property Value

The content type of the data being sent.

Remarks

The **ContentType** property contains the media type of the data
being sent. This is typically the MIME encoding of the content. The
ContentType property is currently not used by the **FileWebRequest**
class.

Requirements

Platforms: Windows 98, Windows NT 4.0,
Windows Millennium Edition, Windows 2000,
Windows XP Home Edition, Windows XP Professional,
Windows .NET Server family

FileWebRequest.Credentials Property

Gets or sets the credentials associated with this request. This
property is reserved for future use.

```
[Visual Basic]
Overrides Public Property Credentials As ICredentials
[C#]
public override ICredentials Credentials {get; set;}
[C++]
public: __property ICredentials* get_Credentials();
public: __property void set_Credentials(ICredentials*);
[JScript]
public override function get Credentials() : ICredentials;
public override function set Credentials(ICredentials);
```

Property Value

An **ICredentials** that contains the authentication credentials
associated with this request. The default is a null reference (**Nothing**
in Visual Basic).

Remarks

Because the **FileWebRequest** class does not authenticate requests
for files from the local file system, it ignores the contents, if any, of
the **Credentials** property. Authentication for **FileWebRequest** is
handled by the access control lists for the file resource in the
underlying file system.

Requirements

Platforms: Windows 98, Windows NT 4.0,
Windows Millennium Edition, Windows 2000,
Windows XP Home Edition, Windows XP Professional,
Windows .NET Server family

FileWebRequest.Headers Property

Gets a collection of the name/value pairs associated with the request.
This property is reserved for future use.

```
[Visual Basic]
Overrides Public ReadOnly Property Headers As WebHeaderCollection
[C#]
public override WebHeaderCollection Headers {get;}
[C++]
public: __property WebHeaderCollection* get_Headers();
[JScript]
public override function get Headers() : WebHeaderCollection;
```

Property Value

A **WebHeaderCollection** that contains header name/value pairs
associated with this request.

Remarks

The **Headers** property is currently not used by the **FileWebRequest**
class.

Requirements

Platforms: Windows 98, Windows NT 4.0,
Windows Millennium Edition, Windows 2000,
Windows XP Home Edition, Windows XP Professional,
Windows .NET Server family

FileWebRequest.Method Property

Gets or sets the protocol method used for the request. This property
is reserved for future use.

```
[Visual Basic]
Overrides Public Property Method As String
[C#]
public override string Method {get; set;}
[C++]
public: __property String* get_Method();
public: __property void set_Method(String*);
[JScript]
public override function get Method() : String;
public override function set Method(String);
```

Property Value

The protocol method to use in this request.

Remarks

The **Method** property is currently not used by the **FileWebRequest**
class.

Example

See related example in the **System.Net.FileWebRequest** class topic.

Requirements

Platforms: Windows 98, Windows NT 4.0,
Windows Millennium Edition, Windows 2000,
Windows XP Home Edition, Windows XP Professional,
Windows .NET Server family

FileWebRequest.PreAuthenticate Property

Gets or sets a value indicating whether to preauthenticate a request.
This property is reserved for future use.

```
[Visual Basic]
Overrides Public Property PreAuthenticate As Boolean
[C#]
public override bool PreAuthenticate {get; set;}
[C++]
public: __property bool get_PreAuthenticate();
public: __property void set_PreAuthenticate(bool);
[JScript]
public override function get PreAuthenticate() : Boolean;
public override function set PreAuthenticate(Boolean);
```

Property Value

true to preauthenticate; otherwise, **false**.

Remarks

The **PreAuthenticate** property is currently not used by the
FileWebRequest class.

Requirements

Platforms: Windows 98, Windows NT 4.0,
Windows Millennium Edition, Windows 2000,
Windows XP Home Edition, Windows XP Professional,
Windows .NET Server family

FileWebRequest.Proxy Property

Gets or sets the network proxy to use for this request. This property
is reserved for future use.

```
[Visual Basic]
Overrides Public Property Proxy As IWebProxy
[C#]
public override IWebProxy Proxy {get; set;}
[C++]
public: __property IWebProxy* get_Proxy();
public: __property void set_Proxy(IWebProxy*);
[JScript]
public override function get Proxy() : IWebProxy;
public override function set Proxy(IWebProxy);
```

Property Value

An **IWebProxy** that indicates the network proxy to use for this
request.

Remarks

The **Proxy** property is currently not used by the **FileWebRequest**
class.

Requirements

Platforms: Windows 98, Windows NT 4.0,
Windows Millennium Edition, Windows 2000,
Windows XP Home Edition, Windows XP Professional,
Windows .NET Server family

FileWebRequest.RequestUri Property

Gets the URI of the request.

```
[Visual Basic]
Overrides Public ReadOnly Property RequestUri As Uri
[C#]
public override Uri RequestUri {get;}
```

```
[C++]
public: __property Uri* get_RequestUri();
[JScript]
public override function get RequestUri() : Uri;
```

Property Value

A **Uri** containing the URI of the request.

Example

See related example in the **System.Net.FileWebRequest** class topic.

Requirements

Platforms: Windows 98, Windows NT 4.0,
Windows Millennium Edition, Windows 2000,
Windows XP Home Edition, Windows XP Professional,
Windows .NET Server family

FileWebRequest.Timeout Property

Gets or sets the length of time until the request times out.

```
[Visual Basic]
Overrides Public Property Timeout As Integer
[C#]
public override int Timeout {get; set;}
[C++]
public: __property int get_Timeout();
public: __property void set_Timeout(int);
[JScript]
public override function get Timeout() : int;
public override function set Timeout(int);
```

Property Value

The time, in milliseconds, until the request times out, or the value **Timeout.Infinite** to indicate that the request does not time out.

Exceptions

Exception Type	Condition
ArgumentException	**Timeout** is set to less than 0.

Example

See related example in the **System.Net.FileWebRequest** class topic.

Requirements

Platforms: Windows 98, Windows NT 4.0,
Windows Millennium Edition, Windows 2000,
Windows XP Home Edition, Windows XP Professional,
Windows .NET Server family

FileWebRequest.BeginGetRequestStream Method

Begins an asynchronous request for a **Stream** instance to use to write data.

```
[Visual Basic]
Overrides Public Function BeginGetRequestStream( _
    ByVal callback As AsyncCallback, _
    ByVal state As Object _
) As IAsyncResult
[C#]
public override IAsyncResult BeginGetRequestStream(
    AsyncCallback callback,
    object state
);
```

```
[C++]
public: IAsyncResult* BeginGetRequestStream(
    AsyncCallback* callback,
    Object* state
);
[JScript]
public override function BeginGetRequestStream(
    callback : AsyncCallback,
    state : Object
) : IAsyncResult;
```

Parameters

callback
    The **AsyncCallback** delegate.
state
    An object containing state information for this request.

Return Value

An **IAsyncResult** that references the asynchronous request.

Exceptions

Exception Type	Condition
ProtocolViolation-Exception	The **Method** property is GET and the application writes to the stream.
InvalidOperation-Exception	The stream is being used by a previous call to **BeginGetRequestStream**
ApplicationException	No write stream is available.

Remarks

The **BeginGetRequestStream** method starts an asynchronous request for a stream used to send data to a file system resource. The callback method that implements the **AsyncCallback** delegate uses the **EndGetRequestStream** method to return the request stream.

Example

See related example in the **System.Net.FileWebRequest** class topic.

Requirements

Platforms: Windows 98, Windows NT 4.0,
Windows Millennium Edition, Windows 2000,
Windows XP Home Edition, Windows XP Professional,
Windows .NET Server family

FileWebRequest.BeginGetResponse Method

Begins an asynchronous request for a file system resource.

```
[Visual Basic]
Overrides Public Function BeginGetResponse( _
    ByVal callback As AsyncCallback, _
    ByVal state As Object _
) As IAsyncResult
[C#]
public override IAsyncResult BeginGetResponse(
    AsyncCallback callback,
    object state
);
[C++]
public: IAsyncResult* BeginGetResponse(
    AsyncCallback* callback,
    Object* state
);
```

```
[JScript]
public override function BeginGetResponse(
    callback : AsyncCallback,
    state : Object
) : IAsyncResult;
```

Parameters

callback

The **AsyncCallback** delegate.

state

An object containing state information for this request.

Return Value

An **IAsyncResult** that references the asynchronous request.

Exceptions

Exception Type	Condition
InvalidOperation-Exception	The stream is already in use by a previous call to **BeginGetResponse**.

Remarks

The **BeginGetResponse** method starts an asynchronous request for a file system resource. The asynchronous callback method that implements the **AsyncCallback** delegate uses the **EndGetResponse** method to return the actual **FileWebResponse**.

Example

See related example in the **System.Net.FileWebRequest** class topic.

Requirements

Platforms: Windows 98, Windows NT 4.0, Windows Millennium Edition, Windows 2000, Windows XP Home Edition, Windows XP Professional, Windows .NET Server family

FileWebRequest.EndGetRequestStream Method

Ends an asynchronous request for a **Stream** instance that the application uses to write data.

```
[Visual Basic]
Overrides Public Function EndGetRequestStream( _
    ByVal asyncResult As IAsyncResult _
) As Stream
[C#]
public override Stream EndGetRequestStream(
    IAsyncResult asyncResult
);
[C++]
public: Stream* EndGetRequestStream(
    IAsyncResult* asyncResult
);
[JScript]
public override function EndGetRequestStream(
    asyncResult : IAsyncResult
) : Stream;
```

Parameters

asyncResult

An **IAsyncResult** referencing the pending request for a stream.

Return Value

A **Stream** instance that the application uses to write data.

Exceptions

Exception Type	Condition
ArgumentNullException	*asyncResult* is a null reference (**Nothing** in Visual Basic).

Remarks

The **EndGetRequestStream** method completes an asynchronous stream request that was started by the **BeginGetRequestStream** method.

> **Note** To avoid timing issues with garbage collection, be sure to close the response stream by calling the **Close** method on the stream returned by **GetResponseStream** after calling **EndGetResponse**.

Example

See related example in the **System.Net.FileWebRequest** class topic.

Requirements

Platforms: Windows 98, Windows NT 4.0, Windows Millennium Edition, Windows 2000, Windows XP Home Edition, Windows XP Professional, Windows .NET Server family

FileWebRequest.EndGetResponse Method

Ends an asynchronous request for a file system resource.

```
[Visual Basic]
Overrides Public Function EndGetResponse( _
    ByVal asyncResult As IAsyncResult _
) As WebResponse
[C#]
public override WebResponse EndGetResponse(
    IAsyncResult asyncResult
);
[C++]
public: WebResponse* EndGetResponse(
    IAsyncResult* asyncResult
);
[JScript]
public override function EndGetResponse(
    asyncResult : IAsyncResult
) : WebResponse;
```

Parameters

asyncResult

An **IAsyncResult** referencing the pending request for a response.

Return Value

A **WebResponse** that contains the response from the file system resource.

Exceptions

Exception Type	Condition
ArgumentNullException	*asyncResult* is a null reference (**Nothing** in Visual Basic).

Remarks

The **EndGetResponse** method completes an asynchronous request for a file system resource that was started with the **BeginGetResponse** method.

Example

See related example in the **System.Net.FileWebRequest** class topic.

Requirements

Platforms: Windows 98, Windows NT 4.0,
Windows Millennium Edition, Windows 2000,
Windows XP Home Edition, Windows XP Professional,
Windows .NET Server family

FileWebRequest.GetRequestStream Method

Returns a **Stream** instance for writing data to the file system resource.

```
[Visual Basic]
Overrides Public Function GetRequestStream() As Stream
[C#]
public override Stream GetRequestStream();
[C++]
public: Stream* GetRequestStream();
[JScript]
public override function GetRequestStream() : Stream;
```

Return Value

A **Stream** for writing data to the file system resource.

Exceptions

Exception Type	Condition
WebException	The request times out.

Remarks

The **GetRequestStream** method returns a **Stream** instance for writing data to the file system resource.

The **GetRequestStream** method provides synchronous access to the **Stream**. For asynchronous access, use the **BeginGetRequestStream** and **EndGetRequestStream** methods.

Requirements

Platforms: Windows 98, Windows NT 4.0,
Windows Millennium Edition, Windows 2000,
Windows XP Home Edition, Windows XP Professional,
Windows .NET Server family

FileWebRequest.GetResponse Method

Returns a response to a file system request.

```
[Visual Basic]
Overrides Public Function GetResponse() As WebResponse
[C#]
public override WebResponse GetResponse();
[C++]
public: WebResponse* GetResponse();
[JScript]
public override function GetResponse() : WebResponse;
```

Return Value

A **WebResponse** that contains the response from the file system resource.

Exceptions

Exception Type	Condition
WebException	The request timed out.

Remarks

The **GetResponse** method returns a **WebResponse** instance containing the response from the file system resource.

The **GetResponse** method provides synchronous access to the **WebResponse**. For asynchronous access, use the **BeginGetResponse** and **EndGetResponse** methods.

Example

See related example in the **System.Net.FileWebRequest** class topic.

Requirements

Platforms: Windows 98, Windows NT 4.0,
Windows Millennium Edition, Windows 2000,
Windows XP Home Edition, Windows XP Professional,
Windows .NET Server family

FileWebRequest.ISerializable.GetObjectData Method

This member supports the .NET Framework infrastructure and is not intended to be used directly from your code.

```
[Visual Basic]
Private Sub GetObjectData( _
    ByVal serializationInfo As SerializationInfo, _
    ByVal streamingContext As StreamingContext _
) Implements ISerializable.GetObjectData
[C#]
void ISerializable.GetObjectData(
    SerializationInfo serializationInfo,
    StreamingContext streamingContext
);
[C++]
private: void ISerializable::GetObjectData(
    SerializationInfo* serializationInfo,
    StreamingContext streamingContext
);
[JScript]
private function ISerializable.GetObjectData(
    serializationInfo : SerializationInfo,
    streamingContext : StreamingContext
);
```

FileWebResponse Class

Provides a file system implementation of the **WebResponse** class.

System.Object
  System.MarshalByRefObject
    System.Net.WebResponse
      System.Net.FileWebResponse

```
[Visual Basic]
<Serializable>
Public Class FileWebResponse
    Inherits WebResponse
[C#]
[Serializable]
public class FileWebResponse : WebResponse
[C++]
[Serializable]
public __gc class FileWebResponse : public WebResponse
[JScript]
public
    Serializable
class FileWebResponse extends WebResponse
```

Thread Safety

Any public static (**Shared** in Visual Basic) members of this type are safe for multithreaded operations. Any instance members are not guaranteed to be thread safe.

Remarks

The **FileWebResponse** class implements the **WebResponse** abstract (**MustInherit** in Visual Basic) base class to return file system resources for the **FileWebRequest** class.

Client applications do not create **FileWebResponse** instances directly; instead, they are created by calling the **GetResponse** method on a **FileWebRequest** instance.

The **GetResponseStream** method returns a **Stream** instance that provides read-only access to a file system resource.

The **FileWebResponse** class relies on the **File** class for error handling and code access security.

Requirements

Namespace: System.Net

Platforms: Windows 98, Windows NT 4.0, Windows Millennium Edition, Windows 2000, Windows XP Home Edition, Windows XP Professional, Windows .NET Server family

Assembly: System (in System.dll)

FileWebResponse Constructor

Initializes a new instance of the **FileWebResponse** class from the specified instances of the **SerializationInfo** and **StreamingContext** classes.

```
[Visual Basic]
Protected Sub New( _
    ByVal serializationInfo As SerializationInfo, _
    ByVal streamingContext As StreamingContext _
)
```

```
[C#]
protected FileWebResponse(
    SerializationInfo serializationInfo,
    StreamingContext streamingContext
);
[C++]
protected: FileWebResponse(
    SerializationInfo* serializationInfo,
    StreamingContext streamingContext
);
[JScript]
protected function FileWebResponse(
    serializationInfo : SerializationInfo,
    streamingContext : StreamingContext
);
```

Parameters

serializationInfo
    A **SerializationInfo** instance that contains the information required to serialize the new **FileWebResponse** instance.

streamingContext
    An instance of the **StreamingContext** class that contains the source of the serialized stream associated with the new **FileWebResponse** instance.

Remarks

This constructor implements the **ISerializable** interface for the **FileWebResponse** class.

Requirements

Platforms: Windows 98, Windows NT 4.0, Windows Millennium Edition, Windows 2000, Windows XP Home Edition, Windows XP Professional, Windows .NET Server family

FileWebResponse.ContentLength Property

Gets the length of the content in the file system resource.

```
[Visual Basic]
Overrides Public ReadOnly Property ContentLength As Long
[C#]
public override long ContentLength {get;}
[C++]
public: __property __int64 get_ContentLength();
[JScript]
public override function get ContentLength() : long;
```

Property Value

The number of bytes returned from the file system resource.

Remarks

The **ContentLength** property contains the length, in bytes, of the file system resource.

Example

[Visual Basic, C#, C++] The following example uses the **ContentLength** property to obtain the content length of the file system resource.

```
[Visual Basic]
Public Shared Sub GetPage(url As [String])

    Try
        Dim fileUrl As New Uri("file://" + url)
```

```
  ' Create a 'FileWebrequest' object with the specified Uri
  Dim myFileWebRequest As FileWebRequest =
CType(WebRequest.Create(fileUrl), FileWebRequest)
      ' Send the 'fileWebRequest' and wait for response.
  Dim myFileWebResponse As FileWebResponse =
CType(myFileWebRequest.GetResponse(), FileWebResponse)

      ' The ContentLength and ContentType received as
headers in the response object are also exposed as properties.
      ' These provide information about the length and
type of the entity body in the response.
      Console.WriteLine(ControlChars.Cr + "Content length
:{0}, Content Type : {1}", myFileWebResponse.ContentLength,
myFileWebResponse.ContentType)
      myFileWebResponse.Close()
  Catch e As WebException
      Console.WriteLine(ControlChars.Lf + ControlChars.Cr +
"The Reason for failure is : {0}", e.Status)
  Catch e As Exception
      Console.WriteLine(ControlChars.Cr + "The following
exception was raised : {0}", e.Message)
  End Try
```

[C#]
```
public static void GetPage(String url)
{
  try
    {
      Uri fileUrl = new Uri("file://"+url);
      // Create a 'FileWebrequest' object with the specified Uri.
      FileWebRequest myFileWebRequest =
(FileWebRequest)WebRequest.Create(fileUrl);
      // Send the 'fileWebRequest' and wait for response.
      FileWebResponse myFileWebResponse =
(FileWebResponse)myFileWebRequest.GetResponse();
      // Print the ContentLength and ContentType properties received
as headers in the response object.
      Console.WriteLine("\nContent length :{0}, Content Type
: {1}",myFileWebResponse.ContentLength,myFileWebResponse.ContentType);
      // Release resources of response object.
      myFileWebResponse.Close();
    }
  catch(WebException e)
    {
      Console.WriteLine("\r\nWebException thrown.The
Reason for failure is : {0}",e.Status);
    }
  catch(Exception e)
    {
      Console.WriteLine("\nThe following Exception
was raised : {0}",e.Message);
    }
}
```

[C++]
```
void GetPage(String* url) {
  try {
      Uri* fileUrl = new Uri(String::Concat(S"file://", url));
      // Create a 'FileWebRequest' Object* with the specified Uri.
      FileWebRequest* myFileWebRequest =
dynamic_cast<FileWebRequest*>(WebRequest::Create(fileUrl));
      // Send the 'fileWebRequest' and wait for response.
      FileWebResponse* myFileWebResponse =
dynamic_cast<FileWebResponse*>(myFileWebRequest->GetResponse());
      // Print the ContentLength and ContentType properties received as
headers in the response Object*.
      Console::WriteLine(S"\nContent length : {0}, Content Type
: {1}", __box(myFileWebResponse->ContentLength),
myFileWebResponse->ContentType);
      // Release resources of response Object*.
      myFileWebResponse->Close();
  } catch (WebException* e) {
      Console::WriteLine(S"\r\nWebException thrown.The Reason
  for failure is : {0}", __box( e->Status));
  } catch (Exception* e) {
```

```
      Console::WriteLine(S"\nThe following Exception was raised
: {0}", e->Message);
  }
}
```

Requirements

Platforms: Windows 98, Windows NT 4.0,
Windows Millennium Edition, Windows 2000,
Windows XP Home Edition, Windows XP Professional,
Windows .NET Server family

FileWebResponse.ContentType Property

Gets the content type of the file system resource.

```
[Visual Basic]
Overrides Public ReadOnly Property ContentType As String
[C#]
public override string ContentType {get;}
[C++]
public: __property String* get_ContentType();
[JScript]
public override function get ContentType() : String;
```

Property Value

The value "binary/octet-stream".

Remarks

The **ContentType** property contains the content type of the file
system resource. The value of **ContentType** is always "binary/octet-
stream".

Example

See related example in the **System.Net.FileWebResponse** class
topic.

Requirements

Platforms: Windows 98, Windows NT 4.0,
Windows Millennium Edition, Windows 2000,
Windows XP Home Edition, Windows XP Professional,
Windows .NET Server family

FileWebResponse.Headers Property

Gets a collection of header name/value pairs associated with the
response.

```
[Visual Basic]
Overrides Public ReadOnly Property Headers As WebHeaderCollection
[C#]
public override WebHeaderCollection Headers {get;}
[C++]
public: __property WebHeaderCollection* get_Headers();
[JScript]
public override function get Headers() : WebHeaderCollection;
```

Property Value

A **WebHeaderCollection** that contains the header name/value pairs
associated with the response.

Remarks

The **Headers** property contains two name/value pairs, one for
content length and one for content type, both of which are also
exposed as properties, **ContentLength** and **ContentType**.

Example

See related example in the **System.Net.FileWebResponse** class topic.

Requirements

Platforms: Windows 98, Windows NT 4.0, Windows Millennium Edition, Windows 2000, Windows XP Home Edition, Windows XP Professional, Windows .NET Server family

FileWebResponse.ResponseUri Property

Gets the URI of the file system resource that provided the response.

```
[Visual Basic]
Overrides Public ReadOnly Property ResponseUri As Uri
[C#]
public override Uri ResponseUri {get;}
[C++]
public: __property Uri* get_ResponseUri();
[JScript]
public override function get ResponseUri() : Uri;
```

Property Value

A **Uri** that contains the URI of the file system resource that provided the response.

Remarks

The **ResponseUri** property contains the URI of the file system resource that provided the response. This is always the file system resource that was requested.

Example

See related example in the **System.Net.FileWebResponse** class topic.

Requirements

Platforms: Windows 98, Windows NT 4.0, Windows Millennium Edition, Windows 2000, Windows XP Home Edition, Windows XP Professional, Windows .NET Server family

FileWebResponse.Close Method

Closes the response stream.

```
[Visual Basic]
Overrides Public Sub Close()
[C#]
public override void Close();
[C++]
public: void Close();
[JScript]
public override function Close();
```

Remarks

The **Close** method cleans up the resources used by a **FileWebResponse** and closes the response stream by calling the **Stream.Close** method.

Note The response stream must be closed to avoid running out of system resources. You can closes the response stream by calling either **Stream.Close** or **Close**

Example

See related example in the **System.Net.FileWebResponse** class topic.

Requirements

Platforms: Windows 98, Windows NT 4.0, Windows Millennium Edition, Windows 2000, Windows XP Home Edition, Windows XP Professional, Windows .NET Server family

FileWebResponse.Dispose Method

Releases the unmanaged resources used by the **FileWebResponse** and optionally releases the managed resources.

```
[Visual Basic]
Protected Overridable Sub Dispose( _
    ByVal disposing As Boolean _
)
[C#]
protected virtual void Dispose(
    bool disposing
);
[C++]
protected: virtual void Dispose(
    bool disposing
);
[JScript]
protected function Dispose(
    disposing : Boolean
);
```

Parameters

disposing
> **true** to release both managed and unmanaged resources; **false** to release only unmanaged resources.

Remarks

This method is called by the public **Dispose()** method and the **Finalize** method. **Dispose()** invokes the protected **Dispose(Boolean)** method with the *disposing* parameter set to **true**. **Finalize** invokes **Dispose** with *disposing* set to **false**.

When the *disposing* parameter is **true**, this method releases all resources held by any managed objects that this **FileWebResponse** references. This method invokes the **Dispose()** method of each referenced object.

Notes to Inheritors: **Dispose** can be called multiple times by other objects. When overriding **Dispose(Boolean)**, be careful not to reference objects that have been previously disposed of in an earlier call to **Dispose**.

Requirements

Platforms: Windows 98, Windows NT 4.0, Windows Millennium Edition, Windows 2000, Windows XP Home Edition, Windows XP Professional, Windows .NET Server family

FileWebResponse.GetResponseStream Method

Returns the data stream from the file system resource.

```
[Visual Basic]
Overrides Public Function GetResponseStream() As Stream
[C#]
public override Stream GetResponseStream();
[C++]
public: Stream* GetResponseStream();
[JScript]
public override function GetResponseStream() : Stream;
```

Return Value

A **Stream** for reading data from the file system resource.

Remarks

The **GetResponseStream** method returns the data stream from the file system resource.

> **Note** The response stream must be closed to avoid running out of system resources. The response stream can be closed by calling **Stream.Close** or **Close**

Example

See related example in the **System.Net.FileWebResponse** class topic.

Requirements

Platforms: Windows 98, Windows NT 4.0, Windows Millennium Edition, Windows 2000, Windows XP Home Edition, Windows XP Professional, Windows .NET Server family

FileWebResponse.IDisposable.Dispose Method

This member supports the .NET Framework infrastructure and is not intended to be used directly from your code.

```
[Visual Basic]
Private Sub Dispose() Implements IDisposable.Dispose
[C#]
void IDisposable.Dispose();
[C++]
private: void IDisposable::Dispose();
[JScript]
private function IDisposable.Dispose();
```

FileWebResponse.ISerializable.GetObjectData Method

This member supports the .NET Framework infrastructure and is not intended to be used directly from your code.

```
[Visual Basic]
Private Sub GetObjectData( _
    ByVal serializationInfo As SerializationInfo, _
    ByVal streamingContext As StreamingContext _
) Implements ISerializable.GetObjectData
[C#]
void ISerializable.GetObjectData(
    SerializationInfo serializationInfo,
    StreamingContext streamingContext
);
```

```
[C++]
private: void ISerializable::GetObjectData(
    SerializationInfo* serializationInfo,
    StreamingContext streamingContext
);
[JScript]
private function ISerializable.GetObjectData(
    serializationInfo : SerializationInfo,
    streamingContext : StreamingContext
);
```

GlobalProxySelection Class

Contains a global default proxy instance for all HTTP requests.

System.Object
    System.Net.GlobalProxySelection

```
[Visual Basic]
Public Class GlobalProxySelection
[C#]
public class GlobalProxySelection
[C++]
public __gc class GlobalProxySelection
[JScript]
public class GlobalProxySelection
```

Thread Safety

Any public static (**Shared** in Visual Basic) members of this type are safe for multithreaded operations. Any instance members are not guaranteed to be thread safe.

Remarks

The **GlobalProxySelection** stores the proxy settings for the default proxy that **WebRequest** instances use to contact Internet sites beyond the local network. The default proxy setting is initialized from the global or application configuration file, and can be overridden for individual requests, or disabled by setting the **HttpWebRequest.Proxy** property to the result of the **GetEmptyWebProxy** method.

The proxy settings stored in **GlobalProxySelection** are used by any **HttpWebRequest** instances whose **Proxy** property is not set to another value.

> **Note** Changes to the **GlobalProxySelection** after a request is made are not reflected in a **WebRequest**.

Example

[Visual Basic, C#] The following example sets the **GlobalProxySelection** for an HTTP proxy named "webproxy" on port 80.

```
[Visual Basic]
Dim proxyURI As New Uri("http://webproxy:80")
GlobalProxySelection.Select = New WebProxy(proxyURI)
```

```
[C#]
Uri proxyURI = new Uri("http://webproxy:80");
 GlobalProxySelection.Select = new WebProxy(proxyURI);
```

Requirements

Namespace: System.Net

Platforms: Windows 98, Windows NT 4.0, Windows Millennium Edition, Windows 2000, Windows XP Home Edition, Windows XP Professional, Windows .NET Server family, .NET Compact Framework - Windows CE .NET

Assembly: System (in System.dll)

GlobalProxySelection Constructor

Initializes a new instance of the **GlobalProxySelection** class.

```
[Visual Basic]
Public Sub New()
```

```
[C#]
public GlobalProxySelection();
[C++]
public: GlobalProxySelection();
[JScript]
public function GlobalProxySelection();
```

Remarks

The default constructor initializes any fields to their default values.

Requirements

Platforms: Windows 98, Windows NT 4.0, Windows Millennium Edition, Windows 2000, Windows XP Home Edition, Windows XP Professional, Windows .NET Server family, .NET Compact Framework - Windows CE .NET, Common Language Infrastructure (CLI) Standard

GlobalProxySelection.Select Property

Gets or sets the global HTTP proxy.

```
[Visual Basic]
Public Shared Property Select As IWebProxy
[C#]
public static IWebProxy Select {get; set;}
[C++]
public: __property static IWebProxy* get_Select();
public: __property static void set_Select(IWebProxy*);
[JScript]
public static function get Select() : IWebProxy;
public static function set Select(IWebProxy);
```

Property Value

An **IWebProxy** that every call to **HttpWebRequest.GetResponse** uses.

Exceptions

Exception Type	Condition
SecurityException	The caller does not have permission for the requested operation.

Remarks

The **Select** method sets the proxy that all **HttpWebRequest** instances use.

Requirements

Platforms: Windows 98, Windows NT 4.0, Windows Millennium Edition, Windows 2000, Windows XP Home Edition, Windows XP Professional, Windows .NET Server family, .NET Compact Framework - Windows CE .NET, Common Language Infrastructure (CLI) Standard

.NET Framework Security:
• **WebPermission** To get or set the global HTTP proxy. Associated enumeration: **PermissionState**

GlobalProxySelection.GetEmptyWebProxy Method

Returns an empty proxy instance.

```
[Visual Basic]
Public Shared Function GetEmptyWebProxy() As IWebProxy
[C#]
public static IWebProxy GetEmptyWebProxy();
[C++]
public: static IWebProxy* GetEmptyWebProxy();
[JScript]
public static function GetEmptyWebProxy() : IWebProxy;
```

Return Value

An **IWebProxy** that contains no information.

Remarks

The **GetEmptyWebProxy** method returns a blank **IWebProxy** instance to indicate that no proxy is used to access an Internet resource.

Example

[Visual Basic, C#] The following example creates a **WebRequest** instance that does not use a proxy to contact an Internet resource.

```
[Visual Basic]
Dim myReq As WebRequest = WebRequest.Create("http://www.contoso.com/")
myReq.Proxy = GlobalProxySelection.GetEmptyWebProxy()

[C#]
WebRequest myReq = WebRequest.Create("http://www.contoso.com/");
myReq.Proxy = GlobalProxySelection.GetEmptyWebProxy();
```

Requirements

Platforms: Windows 98, Windows NT 4.0, Windows Millennium Edition, Windows 2000, Windows XP Home Edition, Windows XP Professional, Windows .NET Server family, .NET Compact Framework - Windows CE .NET, Common Language Infrastructure (CLI) Standard

HttpContinueDelegate Delegate

Represents the method that notifies callers when a continue response is received by the client.

```vb
[Visual Basic]
<Serializable>
Public Delegate Sub HttpContinueDelegate( _
   ByVal StatusCode As Integer, _
   ByVal httpHeaders As WebHeaderCollection _
)
```
```csharp
[C#]
[Serializable]
public delegate void HttpContinueDelegate(
   int StatusCode,
   WebHeaderCollection httpHeaders
);
```
```cpp
[C++]
[Serializable]
public __gc __delegate void HttpContinueDelegate(
   int StatusCode,
   WebHeaderCollection* httpHeaders
);
```

[JScript] In JScript, you can use the delegates in the .NET Framework, but you cannot define your own.

Parameters [Visual Basic, C#, C++]

The declaration of your callback method must have the same parameters as the **HttpContinueDelegate** delegate declaration.

StatusCode
   The numeric value of the HTTP status from the server.

httpHeaders
   The headers returned with the 100-continue response from the server.

Remarks

Use **HttpContinueDelegate** to specify the callback method to be called when an HTTP 100-continue response is received from the server. When set, the delegate is called whenever protocol responses of type **HttpStatusCode.Continue** are received. Your event handler must declare the same parameters as the **HttpContinueDelegate**.

Note   *StatusCode* is always **HttpStatusCode.Continue**.

This is useful when the client wants to display the status of data being received from the server.

Requirements

Namespace: System.Net

Platforms: Windows 98, Windows NT 4.0, Windows Millennium Edition, Windows 2000, Windows XP Home Edition, Windows XP Professional, Windows .NET Server family, .NET Compact Framework - Windows CE .NET

Assembly: System (in System.dll)

HttpStatusCode Enumeration

Contains the values of status codes defined for HTTP.

```
[Visual Basic]
<Serializable>
Public Enum HttpStatusCode
[C#]
[Serializable]
public enum HttpStatusCode
[C++]
[Serializable]
__value public enum HttpStatusCode
[JScript]
public
    Serializable
enum HttpStatusCode
```

Remarks

The **HttpStatusCode** enumeration contains the values of the status codes defined in RFC 2616 for HTTP 1.1.

The status of an HTTP request is contained in the **HttpWebResponse.StatusCode** property.

Members

Member name	Description
Accepted Supported by the .NET Compact Framework.	Equivalent to HTTP status 202. **Accepted** indicates that the request has been accepted for further processing.
Ambiguous Supported by the .NET Compact Framework.	Equivalent to HTTP status 300. **Ambiguous** indicates that the requested information has multiple representations. The default action is to treat this status as a redirect and follow the contents of the Location header associated with this response. If the **HttpWebRequest.AllowAutoRedirect** property is **false**, **Ambiguous** will cause an exception to be thrown. **Ambiguous** is a synonym for **MultipleChoices**.
BadGateway Supported by the .NET Compact Framework.	Equivalent to HTTP status 502. **BadGateway** indicates that an intermediate proxy server received a bad response from another proxy or the origin server.
BadRequest Supported by the .NET Compact Framework.	Equivalent to HTTP status 400. **BadRequest** indicates that the request could not be understood by the server. **BadRequest** is sent when no other error is applicable, or if the exact error is unknown or does not have its own error code.
Conflict Supported by the .NET Compact Framework.	Equivalent to HTTP status 409. **Conflict** indicates that the request could not be carried out due to a conflict on the server.

Member name	Description
Continue Supported by the .NET Compact Framework.	Equivalent to HTTP status 100. **Continue** indicates that the client may continue with its request.
Created Supported by the .NET Compact Framework.	Equivalent to HTTP status 201. **Created** indicates that the request resulted in a new resource created before the response was sent.
ExpectationFailed Supported by the .NET Compact Framework.	Equivalent to HTTP status 417. **ExpectationFailed** indicates that an expectation given in an Expect header could not be met by the server.
Forbidden Supported by the .NET Compact Framework.	Equivalent to HTTP status 403. **Forbidden** indicates that the server refuses to fulfill the request.
Found Supported by the .NET Compact Framework.	Equivalent to HTTP status 302. **Found** indicates that the requested information is located at the URI specified in the Location header. The default action when this status is received is to follow the Location header associated with the response. When the original request method was POST, the redirected request will use the GET method. If the **HttpWebRequest.AllowAutoRedirect** property is **false**, **Found** will cause an exception to be thrown. **Found** is a synonym for **Redirect**.
GatewayTimeout Supported by the .NET Compact Framework.	Equivalent to HTTP status 504. **GatewayTimeout** indicates that an intermediate proxy server timed out while waiting for a response from another proxy or the origin server.
Gone Supported by the .NET Compact Framework.	Equivalent to HTTP status 410. **Gone** indicates that the requested resource is not longer available.
HttpVersionNot-Supported Supported by the .NET Compact Framework.	Equivalent to HTTP status 505. **HttpVersionNotSupported** indicates that the requested HTTP version is not supported by the server.
InternalServerError Supported by the .NET Compact Framework.	Equivalent to HTTP status 500. **InternalServerError** indicates that a generic error has occurred on the server.
LengthRequired Supported by the .NET Compact Framework.	Equivalent to HTTP status 411. **LengthRequired** indicates that the required Content-length header is missing.
MethodNotAllowed Supported by the .NET Compact Framework.	Equivalent to HTTP status 405. **MethodNotAllowed** indicates that the request method (POST or GET) is not allowed on the requested resource.

Member name	Description
Moved Supported by the .NET Compact Framework.	Equivalent to HTTP status 301. **Moved** indicates that the requested information has been moved to the URI specified in the Location header. The default action when this status is received is to follow the Location header associated with the response. When the original request method was POST, the redirected request will use the GET method. **Moved** is a synonym for **MovedPermanently**.
MovedPermanently Supported by the .NET Compact Framework.	Equivalent to HTTP status 301. **MovedPermanently** indicates that the requested information has been moved to the URI specified in the Location header. The default action when this status is received is to follow the Location header associated with the response. **MovedPermanently** is a synonym for **Moved**.
MultipleChoices Supported by the .NET Compact Framework.	Equivalent to HTTP status 300. **MultipleChoices** indicates that the requested information has multiple representations. The default action is to treat this status as a redirect and follow the contents of the Location header associated with this response. If the **HttpWebRequest.AllowAutoRedirect** property is **false**, **MultipleChoices** will cause an exception to be thrown. **MultipleChoices** is a synonym for **Ambiguous**.
NoContent Supported by the .NET Compact Framework.	Equivalent to HTTP status 204. **NoContent** indicates that the request has been successfully processed and that the response is intentionally blank.
NonAuthoritative-Information Supported by the .NET Compact Framework.	Equivalent to HTTP status 203. **NonAuthoritativeInformation** indicates that the returned metainformation is from a cached copy instead of the origin server and therefore may be incorrect.
NotAcceptable Supported by the .NET Compact Framework.	Equivalent to HTTP status 406. **NotAcceptable** indicates that the client has indicated with Accept headers that it will not accept any of the available representations of the resource.
NotFound Supported by the .NET Compact Framework.	Equivalent to HTTP status 404. **NotFound** indicates that the requested resource does not exist on the server.

Member name	Description
NotImplemented Supported by the .NET Compact Framework.	Equivalent to HTTP status 501. **NotImplemented** indicates the server does not support the requested function.
NotModified Supported by the .NET Compact Framework.	Equivalent to HTTP status 304. **NotModified** indicates that the client's cached copy is up to date. The contents of the resource is not transferred.
OK Supported by the .NET Compact Framework.	Equivalent to HTTP status 200. **OK** indicates that the request succeeded and the requested information is in the response. This is the most common status code to receive.
PartialContent Supported by the .NET Compact Framework.	Equivalent to HTTP status 206. **PartialContent** indicates that the response is a partial response as requested by a GET request that includes a byte range.
PaymentRequired Supported by the .NET Compact Framework.	Equivalent to HTTP status 402. **PaymentRequired** is reserved for future use.
PreconditionFailed Supported by the .NET Compact Framework.	Equivalent to HTTP status 412. **PreconditionFailed** indicates that a condition set for this request failed, and the request cannot be carried out. Conditions are set with conditional request headers such as If-Match, If-None-Match, or If-Unmodified-Since.
ProxyAuthentication-Required Supported by the .NET Compact Framework.	Equivalent to HTTP status 407. **ProxyAuthenticationRequired** indicates that the requested proxy requires authentication. The Proxy-authenticate header contains the details of how to perform the authentication.
Redirect Supported by the .NET Compact Framework.	Equivalent to HTTP status 302. **Redirect** indicates that the requested information is located at the URI specified in the Location header. The default action when this status is received is to follow the Location header associated with the response. When the original request method was POST, the redirected request will use the GET method. If the **HttpWebRequest.AllowAutoRedirect** property is **false**, **Redirect** will cause an exception to be thrown. **Redirect** is a synonym for **Found**.

Member name	Description
RedirectKeepVerb Supported by the .NET Compact Framework.	Equivalent to HTTP status 307. **RedirectKeepVerb** indicates that the request information is located at the URI specified in the Location header. The default action when this status is received is to follow the Location header associated with the response. When the original request method was POST, the redirected request will also use the POST method. If the **HttpWebRequest.Allow-AutoRedirect** property is **false**, **RedirectKeepVerb** will cause an exception to be thrown. **RedirectKeepVerb** is a synonym for **TemporaryRedirect**.
RedirectMethod Supported by the .NET Compact Framework.	Equivalent to HTTP status 303. **RedirectMethod** automatically redirects the client to the URI specified in the Location header as the result of a POST. The request to the resource specified by the Location header will be made with a GET. If the **HttpWebRequest.AllowAutoRedirect** property is **false**, **RedirectMethod** will cause an exception to be thrown. **RedirectMethod** is a synonym for **SeeOther**.
RequestedRangeNot-Satisfiable Supported by the .NET Compact Framework.	Equivalent to HTTP status 416. **RequestedRangeNotSatisfiable** indicates that the range of data requested from the resource cannot be returned, either because the beginning of the range is before the beginning of the resource, or the end of the range is after the end of the resource.
RequestEntityTooLarge Supported by the .NET Compact Framework.	Equivalent to HTTP status 413. **RequestEntityTooLarge** indicates that the request is too large for the server to process.
RequestTimeout Supported by the .NET Compact Framework.	Equivalent to HTTP status 408. **RequestTimeout** indicates that the client did not send a request within the time the server was expecting the request.
RequestUriTooLong Supported by the .NET Compact Framework.	Equivalent to HTTP status 414. **RequestUriTooLong** indicates that the URI is too long.
ResetContent Supported by the .NET Compact Framework.	Equivalent to HTTP status 205. **ResetContent** indicates that the client should reset (not reload) the current resource.

Member name	Description
SeeOther Supported by the .NET Compact Framework.	Equivalent to HTTP status 303. **SeeOther** automatically redirects the client to the URI specified in the Location header as the result of a POST. The request to the resource specified by the Location header will be made with a GET. If the **HttpWebRequest.Allow-AutoRedirect** property is **false**, **SeeOther** will cause an exception to be thrown. **SeeOther** is a synonym for **RedirectMethod**.
ServiceUnavailable Supported by the .NET Compact Framework.	Equivalent to HTTP status 503. **ServiceUnavailable** indicates that the server is temporarily unavailable, usually due to high load or maintenance.
SwitchingProtocols Supported by the .NET Compact Framework.	Equivalent to HTTP status 101. **SwitchingProtocols** indicates that the protocol version or protocol is being changed.
TemporaryRedirect Supported by the .NET Compact Framework.	Equivalent to HTTP status 307. **TemporaryRedirect** indicates that the request information is located at the URI specified in the Location header. The default action when this status is received is to follow the Location header associated with the response. When the original request method was POST, the redirected request will also use the POST method. If the **HttpWebRequest.Allow-AutoRedirect** property is **false**, **TemporaryRedirect** will cause an exception to be thrown. **TemporaryRedirect** is a synonym for **RedirectKeepVerb**.
Unauthorized Supported by the .NET Compact Framework.	Equivalent to HTTP status 401. **Unauthorized** indicates that the requested resource requires authentication. The WWW-Authenticate header contains the details of how to perform the authentication.
UnsupportedMediaType Supported by the .NET Compact Framework.	Equivalent to HTTP status 415. **UnsupportedMediaType** indicates that the request is an unsupported type.
Unused Supported by the .NET Compact Framework.	Equivalent to HTTP status 306. **Unused** is a proposed extension to the HTTP/1.1 specification that is not fully specified.

Member name	Description
UseProxy Supported by the .NET Compact Framework.	Equivalent to HTTP status 305. **UseProxy** indicates that the request should use the proxy server at the URI specified in the Location header.

Example

[Visual Basic, C#, JScript] The following example compares the status returned by an **HttpWebResponse** with a member of the **HttpStatusCode** class to determine the status of a response.

[Visual Basic]
```
Dim httpReq As HttpWebRequest =                                          ┘
CType(WebRequest.Create("http://www.contoso.com"), HttpWebRequest)
httpReq.AllowAutoRedirect = False

Dim httpRes As HttpWebResponse = CType                                    ┘
(httpReq.GetResponse(), HttpWebResponse)

If httpRes.StatusCode = HttpStatusCode.Moved Then
    ' Code for moved resources goes here.
End If

httpRes.Close()
```

[C#]
```
HttpWebRequest httpReq =                                                 ┘
(HttpWebRequest)WebRequest.Create("http://www.contoso.com");
httpReq.AllowAutoRedirect = false;

HttpWebResponse httpRes = (HttpWebResponse)httpReq.GetResponse();

if (httpRes.StatusCode==HttpStatusCode.Moved)
{
    // Code for moved resources goes here.
}

// Close the response.
httpRes.Close();
```

[JScript]
```
var httpReq : HttpWebRequest =                                           ┘
HttpWebRequest(WebRequest.Create("http://www.contoso.com"))
httpReq.AllowAutoRedirect = false

var httpRes : HttpWebResponse = HttpWebResponse(httpReq.GetResponse())

if(httpRes.StatusCode == HttpStatusCode.Moved){
    // Code for moved resources goes here.
}

httpRes.Close()
```

Requirements

Namespace: System.Net

Platforms: Windows 98, Windows NT 4.0, Windows Millennium Edition, Windows 2000, Windows XP Home Edition, Windows XP Professional, Windows .NET Server family, .NET Compact Framework - Windows CE .NET

Assembly: System (in System.dll)

HttpVersion Class

Defines the HTTP version numbers supported by the
HttpWebRequest and **HttpWebResponse** classes.

System.Object
  System.Net.HttpVersion

```
[Visual Basic]
Public Class HttpVersion
[C#]
public class HttpVersion
[C++]
public __gc class HttpVersion
[JScript]
public class HttpVersion
```

Thread Safety

Any public static (**Shared** in Visual Basic) members of this type are
safe for multithreaded operations. Any instance members are not
guaranteed to be thread safe.

Remarks

The **HttpVersion** class defines the HTTP versions supported by the
HttpWebRequest and **HttpWebResponse** classes. The HTTP
version number is used to control version-specific features of HTTP,
such as pipelining and chunking.

Example

[Visual Basic, C#, C++] The following example demonstrates the
use of **HttpVersion**.

```
[Visual Basic]
' Create a 'HttpWebRequest' object.
Dim myHttpWebRequest As HttpWebRequest =
CType(WebRequest.Create("http://www.microsoft.com"), HttpWebRequest)
Console.WriteLine(ControlChars.Cr + "The 'ProtocolVersion'
of the protocol before assignment is :{0}",
myHttpWebRequest.ProtocolVersion)
' Assign Version10 to ProtocolVersion.
myHttpWebRequest.ProtocolVersion = HttpVersion.Version10
' The response object of 'HttpWebRequest' is assigned
to a 'HttpWebResponse' variable.
Dim myHttpWebResponse As HttpWebResponse =
CType(myHttpWebRequest.GetResponse(), HttpWebResponse)
Console.WriteLine(ControlChars.Cr + "The 'ProtocolVersion'
of the protocol after  assignment is :{0}",
myHttpWebRequest.ProtocolVersion)
Console.WriteLine(ControlChars.Cr + "The 'ProtocolVersion'
 of the response object is :{0}", myHttpWebResponse.ProtocolVersion)

[C#]
// Create a 'HttpWebRequest' object.
HttpWebRequest myHttpWebRequest=(HttpWebRequest)WebRequest.Create
("http://www.microsoft.com");
Console.WriteLine("\nThe 'ProtocolVersion' of the protocol
before assignment is :{0}",myHttpWebRequest.ProtocolVersion);
// Assign Version10 to ProtocolVersion.
myHttpWebRequest.ProtocolVersion=HttpVersion.Version10;
// Assign the response object of 'HttpWebRequest' to a
'HttpWebResponse' variable.
HttpWebResponse
myHttpWebResponse=(HttpWebResponse)myHttpWebRequest.GetResponse();
Console.WriteLine("\nThe 'ProtocolVersion' of the protocol
after  assignment is :{0}",myHttpWebRequest.ProtocolVersion);
Console.WriteLine("\nThe 'ProtocolVersion' of the response
object is :{0}",myHttpWebResponse.ProtocolVersion);

[C++]
// Create a 'HttpWebRequest' Object*.
HttpWebRequest* myHttpWebRequest =
   dynamic_cast<HttpWebRequest*>(WebRequest::Create
(S"http://www.microsoft.com"));
Console::WriteLine(S"\nThe 'ProtocolVersion' of the protocol
before assignment is : {0}",
   myHttpWebRequest->ProtocolVersion);
// Assign Version10 to ProtocolVersion.
myHttpWebRequest->ProtocolVersion=HttpVersion::Version10;
// Assign the response Object* of 'HttpWebRequest' to a
'HttpWebResponse' variable.
HttpWebResponse* myHttpWebResponse=dynamic_cast<HttpWebResponse*>
(myHttpWebRequest->GetResponse());
Console::WriteLine(S"\nThe 'ProtocolVersion' of the protocol
after  assignment is : {0}",
   myHttpWebRequest->ProtocolVersion);
Console::WriteLine(S"\nThe 'ProtocolVersion' of the response
Object* is : {0}",
   myHttpWebResponse->ProtocolVersion);
```

Requirements

Namespace: System.Net

Platforms: Windows 98, Windows NT 4.0,
Windows Millennium Edition, Windows 2000,
Windows XP Home Edition, Windows XP Professional,
Windows .NET Server family,
.NET Compact Framework - Windows CE .NET

Assembly: System (in System.dll)

HttpVersion Constructor

Initializes a new instance of the **HttpVersion** class.

```
[Visual Basic]
Public Sub New()
[C#]
public HttpVersion();
[C++]
public: HttpVersion();
[JScript]
public function HttpVersion();
```

Remarks

The default constructor initializes any fields to their default values.

Requirements

Platforms: Windows 98, Windows NT 4.0,
Windows Millennium Edition, Windows 2000,
Windows XP Home Edition, Windows XP Professional,
Windows .NET Server family,
.NET Compact Framework - Windows CE .NET,
Common Language Infrastructure (CLI) Standard

HttpVersion.Version10 Field

Defines a **Version** instance for HTTP 1.0.

```
[Visual Basic]
Public Shared ReadOnly Version10 As Version
[C#]
public static readonly Version Version10;
[C++]
public: static Version* Version10;
[JScript]
public static var Version10 : Version;
```

Requirements

Platforms: Windows 98, Windows NT 4.0,
Windows Millennium Edition, Windows 2000,
Windows XP Home Edition, Windows XP Professional,
Windows .NET Server family,
.NET Compact Framework - Windows CE .NET,
Common Language Infrastructure (CLI) Standard

HttpVersion.Version11 Field

Defines a **Version** instance for HTTP 1.1.

```
[Visual Basic]
Public Shared ReadOnly Version11 As Version
[C#]
public static readonly Version Version11;
[C++]
public: static Version* Version11;
[JScript]
public static var Version11 : Version;
```

Requirements

Platforms: Windows 98, Windows NT 4.0,
Windows Millennium Edition, Windows 2000,
Windows XP Home Edition, Windows XP Professional,
Windows .NET Server family,
.NET Compact Framework - Windows CE .NET,
Common Language Infrastructure (CLI) Standard

HttpWebRequest Class

Provides an HTTP-specific implementation of the **WebRequest** class.

System.Object
  System.MarshalByRefObject
    System.Net.WebRequest
      System.Net.HttpWebRequest

[Visual Basic]
```
<Serializable>
Public Class HttpWebRequest
    Inherits WebRequest
```
[C#]
```
[Serializable]
public class HttpWebRequest : WebRequest
```
[C++]
```
[Serializable]
public __gc class HttpWebRequest : public WebRequest
```
[JScript]
```
public
    Serializable
class HttpWebRequest extends WebRequest
```

Thread Safety

An application must run in full trust mode when using serialization.

Remarks

The **HttpWebRequest** class provides support for the properties and methods defined in **WebRequest** and for additional properties and methods that enable the user to interact directly with servers using HTTP.

Do not use the **HttpWebRequest** constructor. Use the **WebRequest.Create** method to initialize new **HttpWebRequest** instances. If the scheme for the URI is http:// or https://, **Create** returns an **HttpWebRequest** instance.

The **GetResponse** method makes a synchronous request to the Internet resource specified in the **RequestUri** property and returns an **HttpWebResponse** instance containing the response. You can make an asynchronous request to the Internet resource using the **BeginGetResponse** and **EndGetResponse** methods.

When you want to send data to the Internet resource, the **GetRequestStream** method returns a **Stream** instance to use to send data. The **BeginGetRequestStream** and **EndGetRequestStream** methods provide asynchronous access to the send data stream.

The **HttpWebRequest** class throws a **WebException** when errors occur while accessing an Internet resource. The **WebException.Status** property is one of the **WebExceptionStatus** values that indicates the source of the error. When **WebException.Status** is **WebExceptionStatus.ProtocolError**, the **Response** property contains the **HttpWebResponse** received from the Internet resource.

HttpWebRequest exposes common HTTP header values sent to the Internet resource as properties, set by methods, or set by the system; the following table contains a complete list. You can set other headers in the **Headers** property as name/value pairs.

The following table lists the HTTP headers that are set either by properties or methods or the system.

Header	Set by
Accept	Set by the **Accept** property.
Connection	Set by the **Connection** property, **KeepAlive** property.
Content-Length	Set by the **ContentLength** property.
Content-Type	Set by the **ContentType** property.
Expect	Set by the **Expect** property.
Date	Set by the system to current date.
Host	Set by the system to current host information.
If-Modified-Since	Set by the **IfModifiedSince** property.
Range	Set by the **AddRange** method.
Referer	Set by the **Referer** property.
Transfer-Encoding	Set by the **TransferEncoding** property (the **SendChunked** property must be true).
User-Agent	Set by the **UserAgent** property.

Note **HttpWebRequest** is registered automatically. You do not need to call **RegisterPrefix** to register **System.Net.HttpWebRequest** before using URIs beginning with http:// or https://.

Example

[Visual Basic, C#, JScript] The following example creates an **HttpWebRequest** for the URI http://www.contoso.com/ .

[Visual Basic]
```
Dim myReq As HttpWebRequest = _
    CType(WebRequest.Create("http://www.contoso.com/"),
HttpWebRequest)
```

[C#]
```
HttpWebRequest myReq =
  (HttpWebRequest)WebRequest.Create("http://www.contoso.com/");
```

[JScript]
```
var myReq : HttpWebRequest =
HttpWebRequest(WebRequest.Create("http://www.contoso.com/"))
```

Requirements

Namespace: System.Net

Platforms: Windows 98, Windows NT 4.0, Windows Millennium Edition, Windows 2000, Windows XP Home Edition, Windows XP Professional, Windows .NET Server family, .NET Compact Framework - Windows CE .NET

Assembly: System (in System.dll)

.NET Framework Security:
- **WebPermission** to access the requested URI or any URI that the request is redirected to. Associated enumeration: **Connect**.

HttpWebRequest Constructor

Initializes a new instance of the **HttpWebRequest** class from the specified instances of the **SerializationInfo** and **StreamingContext** classes.

```
[Visual Basic]
Protected Sub New( _
   ByVal serializationInfo As SerializationInfo, _
   ByVal streamingContext As StreamingContext _
)
[C#]
protected HttpWebRequest(
   SerializationInfo serializationInfo,
   StreamingContext streamingContext
);
[C++]
protected: HttpWebRequest(
   SerializationInfo* serializationInfo,
   StreamingContext streamingContext
);
[JScript]
protected function HttpWebRequest(
   serializationInfo : SerializationInfo,
   streamingContext : StreamingContext
);
```

Parameters

serializationInfo
> A **SerializationInfo** instance containing the information required to serialize the new **HttpWebRequest** instance.

streamingContext
> A **StreamingContext** instance containing the source and destination of the serialized stream associated with the new **HttpWebRequest** instance.

Remarks

This constructor implements the **ISerializable** interface for the **HttpWebRequest** class.

An application must run in full trust mode when using serialization.

Requirements

Platforms: Windows 98, Windows NT 4.0, Windows Millennium Edition, Windows 2000, Windows XP Home Edition, Windows XP Professional, Windows .NET Server family

HttpWebRequest.Accept Property

Gets or sets the value of the **Accept** HTTP header.

```
[Visual Basic]
Public Property Accept As String
[C#]
public string Accept {get; set;}
[C++]
public: __property String* get_Accept();
public: __property void set_Accept(String*);
[JScript]
public function get Accept() : String;
public function set Accept(String);
```

Property Value

The value of the **Accept** HTTP header. The default value is a null reference (**Nothing** in Visual Basic).

Remarks

To clear the **Accept** HTTP header, set the **Accept** property to a null reference (**Nothing** in Visual Basic).

Example

[Visual Basic, C#, C++] The following example sets the **Accept** property.

```
[Visual Basic]
' Create a 'HttpWebRequest' object.
Dim myHttpWebRequest As HttpWebRequest =
CType(WebRequest.Create(myUri), HttpWebRequest)
' Set the 'Accept' property to accept an image of any type.
myHttpWebRequest.Accept = "image/*"
' The response object of 'HttpWebRequest' is assigned
to a 'HttpWebResponse' variable.
Dim myHttpWebResponse As HttpWebResponse =
CType(myHttpWebRequest.GetResponse(), HttpWebResponse)

[C#]
// Create a 'HttpWebRequest' object.
HttpWebRequest
myHttpWebRequest=(HttpWebRequest)WebRequest.Create(myUri);
// Set the 'Accept' property to accept an image of any type.
myHttpWebRequest.Accept="image/*";
// The response object of 'HttpWebRequest' is assigned
to a 'HttpWebResponse' variable.
HttpWebResponse
myHttpWebResponse=(HttpWebResponse)myHttpWebRequest.GetResponse();

[C++]
// Create a 'HttpWebRequest' Object*.
HttpWebRequest* myHttpWebRequest =
   dynamic_cast<HttpWebRequest*>(WebRequest::Create(myUri));
// Set the 'Accept' property to accept an image of any type.
myHttpWebRequest->Accept=S"image/*";
// The response Object* of 'HttpWebRequest' is assigned
to a 'HttpWebResponse' variable.
HttpWebResponse* myHttpWebResponse =
   dynamic_cast<HttpWebResponse*>(myHttpWebRequest->GetResponse());
```

Requirements

Platforms: Windows 98, Windows NT 4.0, Windows Millennium Edition, Windows 2000, Windows XP Home Edition, Windows XP Professional, Windows .NET Server family, .NET Compact Framework - Windows CE .NET, Common Language Infrastructure (CLI) Standard

HttpWebRequest.Address Property

Gets the URI of the Internet resource that actually responds to the request.

```
[Visual Basic]
Public ReadOnly Property Address As Uri
[C#]
public Uri Address {get;}
[C++]
public: __property Uri* get_Address();
[JScript]
public function get Address() : Uri;
```

Property Value

A **Uri** identifying the Internet resource that actually responds to the request. The default is the URI used by the **WebRequest.Create** method to initialize the request.

Remarks

The **Address** property is set to the URI that actually responds to a request, after any redirections that might happen during the request are complete.

The URI of the original request is kept in the **RequestUri** property.

Example

[Visual Basic, C#, JScript] The following example checks to see if the **HttpWebRequest** instance req was redirected to another location to fulfill the request, and sets the value of the hasChanged variable to **true** if the request was redirected; otherwise hasChanged is set to **false**.

```
[Visual Basic]
Dim hasChanged As Boolean = _
  (req.RequestUri.ToString() <> req.Address.ToString())
```

```
[C#]
bool hasChanged = (req.RequestUri != req.Address);
```

```
[JScript]
var hasChanged : Boolean = (req.RequestUri.ToString()
= req.Address.ToString())
```

Requirements

Platforms: Windows 98, Windows NT 4.0, Windows Millennium Edition, Windows 2000, Windows XP Home Edition, Windows XP Professional, Windows .NET Server family, .NET Compact Framework - Windows CE .NET, Common Language Infrastructure (CLI) Standard

HttpWebRequest.AllowAutoRedirect Property

Gets or sets a value that indicates whether the request should follow redirection responses.

```
[Visual Basic]
Public Property AllowAutoRedirect As Boolean
[C#]
public bool AllowAutoRedirect {get; set;}
[C++]
public: __property bool get_AllowAutoRedirect();
public: __property void set_AllowAutoRedirect(bool);
[JScript]
public function get AllowAutoRedirect() : Boolean;
public function set AllowAutoRedirect(Boolean);
```

Property Value

true if the request should automatically follow redirection responses from the Internet resource; otherwise **false**. The default value is **true**.

Remarks

Set **AllowAutoRedirect** to **true** if you want the request to automatically follow HTTP redirection headers to the new location of the resource. The maximum number of redirections to follow is set by the **MaximumAutomaticRedirections** property.

If **AllowAutoRedirect** is set to false all responses with an HTTP status code from 300 to 399 will be returned to the application.

Example

[Visual Basic, C#, C++] The following example uses the **AllowAutoRedirect** property to allow the request to follow redirection responses.

```
[Visual Basic]
    'This method creates a new HttpWebRequest Object to
the mentioned URL.
        Dim myHttpWebRequest As HttpWebRequest =
CType(WebRequest.Create("http://www.contoso.com"), HttpWebRequest)
            myHttpWebRequest.MaximumAutomaticRedirections = 1
            myHttpWebRequest.AllowAutoRedirect = True
        Dim myHttpWebResponse As HttpWebResponse =
CType(myHttpWebRequest.GetResponse(), HttpWebResponse)
```

```
[C#]
// Create a new HttpWebRequest Object to the mentioned URL.
HttpWebRequest
myHttpWebRequest=(HttpWebRequest)WebRequest.Create("http://
www.contoso.com");
myHttpWebRequest.MaximumAutomaticRedirections=1;
myHttpWebRequest.AllowAutoRedirect=true;
HttpWebResponse
myHttpWebResponse=(HttpWebResponse)myHttpWebRequest.GetResponse();
```

```
[C++]
// Create a new HttpWebRequest Object to the mentioned URL.
HttpWebRequest* myHttpWebRequest =
    dynamic_cast<HttpWebRequest*>(WebRequest::Create
(S"http://www.contoso.com"));
myHttpWebRequest->MaximumAutomaticRedirections=1;
myHttpWebRequest->AllowAutoRedirect=true;
HttpWebResponse* myHttpWebResponse =
    dynamic_cast<HttpWebResponse*>(myHttpWebRequest->GetResponse());
```

Requirements

Platforms: Windows 98, Windows NT 4.0, Windows Millennium Edition, Windows 2000, Windows XP Home Edition, Windows XP Professional, Windows .NET Server family, .NET Compact Framework - Windows CE .NET, Common Language Infrastructure (CLI) Standard

HttpWebRequest.AllowWriteStreamBuffering Property

Gets or sets a value that indicates whether to buffer the data sent to the Internet resource.

```
[Visual Basic]
Public Property AllowWriteStreamBuffering As Boolean
[C#]
public bool AllowWriteStreamBuffering {get; set;}
[C++]
public: __property bool get_AllowWriteStreamBuffering();
public: __property void set_AllowWriteStreamBuffering(bool);
[JScript]
public function get AllowWriteStreamBuffering() : Boolean;
public function set AllowWriteStreamBuffering(Boolean);
```

Property Value

true to enable buffering of the data sent to the Internet resource; **false** to disable buffering. The default is **true**.

Remarks

When **AllowWriteStreamBuffering** is **true**, the data is buffered in memory so it is ready to be resent in the event of redirections or authentication requests.

Notes to Implementers: Setting **AllowWriteStreamBuffering true** might cause performance problems when uploading large datasets because the data buffer could use all available memory.

.NET Compact Framework - Windows CE .NET Platform Note: For performance considerations, the default value for **AllowWriteStreamBuffering** is false; however, it is important to note that if verbs require entity data (such as POST), redirection and authentication might not occur. To implement the full .NET Framework behavior for HTTP requests, set **AllowWriteStreamBuffering** to **true**.

Example

[Visual Basic, C#, C++] The following example uses the **AllowWriteStreamBuffering** property to disable data buffering.

[Visual Basic]
```
' A new 'HttpWebRequest' object is created
Dim myHttpWebRequest As HttpWebRequest =                        ⌐
CType(WebRequest.Create                                          ⌐
("http://www.contoso.com/codesnippets/next.asp"), HttpWebRequest)
          ' AllowWriteStreamBuffering is set to 'false'
myHttpWebRequest.AllowWriteStreamBuffering = False
Console.WriteLine(ControlChars.Cr + "Please Enter the data to be  ⌐
posted to the (http://www.contoso.com/codesnippets/next.asp) uri:")
Dim inputData As String = Console.ReadLine()
Dim postData As String = "firstone" + ChrW(61) + inputData
' 'Method' property of 'HttpWebRequest' class is set to POST.
myHttpWebRequest.Method = "POST"
Dim encodedData As New ASCIIEncoding()
Dim byteArray As Byte() = encodedData.GetBytes(postData)
' 'ContentType' property of the 'HttpWebRequest' class is
set to "application/x-www-form-urlencoded".
myHttpWebRequest.ContentType = "application/x-www-form-urlencoded"
' If the AllowWriteStreamBuffering property of HttpWebRequest
is set to false,then contentlength has to be set to length of  ⌐
data to be posted else Exception(411) Length required is raised. ⌐
 myHttpWebRequest.ContentLength=byteArray.Length
Dim newStream As Stream = myHttpWebRequest.GetRequestStream()
newStream.Write(byteArray, 0, byteArray.Length)
newStream.Close()
Console.WriteLine(ControlChars.Cr + "Data has been posted to the ⌐
Uri" + ControlChars.Cr + ControlChars.Cr + "Please wait for the  ⌐
response..........")
' The response object of 'HttpWebRequest' is assigned to a      ⌐
'HttpWebResponse' variable.
Dim myHttpWebResponse As HttpWebResponse =                       ⌐
CType(myHttpWebRequest.GetResponse(), HttpWebResponse)
```

[C#]
```
          // Create a new 'HttpWebRequest' object to the        ⌐
mentioned Uri.
          HttpWebRequest
myHttpWebRequest=(HttpWebRequest)WebRequest.Create             ⌐
("http://www.contoso.com/codesnippets/next.asp");
          // Set AllowWriteStreamBuffering to 'false'.
          myHttpWebRequest.AllowWriteStreamBuffering=false;
          Console.WriteLine("\nPlease Enter the data to         ⌐
be posted to the (http://www.contoso.com/codesnippets/next.asp) uri:");
          string inputData =Console.ReadLine();
          string postData="firstone="+inputData;
          // Set 'Method' property of 'HttpWebRequest' class to POST.
          myHttpWebRequest.Method="POST";
          ASCIIEncoding encodedData=new ASCIIEncoding();
          byte[] byteArray=encodedData.GetBytes(postData);
          // Set 'ContentType' property of the 'HttpWebRequest'
class to "application/x-www-form-urlencoded".
          myHttpWebRequest.ContentType="application/x-www-form- ⌐
```

```
urlencoded";
          // If the AllowWriteStreamBuffering property of       ⌐
HttpWebRequest is set to false,the contentlength has to be     ⌐
set to length of data to be posted else Exception(411) is raised.
          myHttpWebRequest.ContentLength=byteArray.Length;
          Stream newStream=myHttpWebRequest.GetRequestStream();
          newStream.Write(byteArray,0,byteArray.Length);
          newStream.Close();
          Console.WriteLine("\nData has been posted to the      ⌐
Uri\n\nPlease wait for the response..........");
          // Assign the response object of 'HttpWebRequest'     ⌐
to a 'HttpWebResponse' variable.
          HttpWebResponse
myHttpWebResponse=(HttpWebResponse)myHttpWebRequest.GetResponse();
```

[C++]
```
          // Create a new 'HttpWebRequest' Object* to the mentioned Uri.
          HttpWebRequest* myHttpWebRequest =
               dynamic_cast<HttpWebRequest*>(WebRequest::Create  ⌐
(S"http://www.contoso.com/codesnippets/next.asp"));
          // Set AllowWriteStreamBuffering to 'false'.
          myHttpWebRequest->AllowWriteStreamBuffering=false;
          Console::WriteLine(S"\nPlease Enter the data to be posted ⌐
to the (http://www.contoso.com/codesnippets/next.asp) uri:");
          String* inputData =Console::ReadLine();
          String* postData = String::Concat(S"firstone= ", inputData);
          // Set 'Method' property of 'HttpWebRequest' class to POST.
          myHttpWebRequest->Method=S"POST";
          ASCIIEncoding* encodedData = new ASCIIEncoding();
          Byte byteArray[]=encodedData->GetBytes(postData);
          // Set 'ContentType' property of the 'HttpWebRequest'  ⌐
class to S"application/x-www-form-urlencoded";
          myHttpWebRequest->ContentType = S"application/x-www-form- ⌐
urlencoded";
          // If the AllowWriteStreamBuffering property of       ⌐
HttpWebRequest is set to false, the contentlength has to        ⌐
be set to length of data to be posted else Exception(411) is raised.
          myHttpWebRequest->ContentLength=byteArray->Length;
          Stream* newStream=myHttpWebRequest->GetRequestStream();
          newStream->Write(byteArray, 0, byteArray->Length);
          newStream->Close();
          Console::WriteLine(S"\nData has been posted to the    ⌐
Uri\n\nPlease wait for the response..........");
          // Assign the response Object* of 'HttpWebRequest' to a ⌐
'HttpWebResponse' variable.
          HttpWebResponse* myHttpWebResponse =
               dynamic_cast<HttpWebResponse*>(myHttpWebRequest-  ⌐
>GetResponse());
```

Requirements

Platforms: Windows 98, Windows NT 4.0, Windows Millennium Edition, Windows 2000, Windows XP Home Edition, Windows XP Professional, Windows .NET Server family, .NET Compact Framework - Windows CE .NET, Common Language Infrastructure (CLI) Standard

HttpWebRequest.ClientCertificates Property

Gets the collection of security certificates associated with this request.

[Visual Basic]
```
Public ReadOnly Property ClientCertificates As _
    X509CertificateCollection
```
[C#]
```
public X509CertificateCollection ClientCertificates {get;}
```
[C++]
```
public: __property X509CertificateCollection*
    get_ClientCertificates();
```

```
[JScript]
public function get ClientCertificates() :
    X509CertificateCollection;
```

Property Value

The **X509CertificateCollection** containing the security certificates associated with this request.

Remarks

In order for an application to use a certificate contained in the collection it must have access rights to this certificate. The mere fact that an application adds a certificate to the collection does not assure that it can access it. The application must have the same access rigths of the entity that issued the certificate.

Requirements

Platforms: Windows 98, Windows NT 4.0, Windows Millennium Edition, Windows 2000, Windows XP Home Edition, Windows XP Professional, Windows .NET Server family

HttpWebRequest.Connection Property

Gets or sets the value of the **Connection** HTTP header.

```
[Visual Basic]
Public Property Connection As String
[C#]
public string Connection {get; set;}
[C++]
public: __property String* get_Connection();
public: __property void set_Connection(String*);
[JScript]
public function get Connection() : String;
public function set Connection(String);
```

Property Value

The value of the **Connection** HTTP header. The default value is a null reference (**Nothing** in Visual Basic).

Exceptions

Exception Type	Condition
ArgumentException	The value of **Connection** is set to Keep-alive or Close.

Remarks

The request sends the **Connection** property to the Internet resource as the **Connection** HTTP header. If **KeepAlive** is true, the value "Keep-alive" is appended to the end of the **Connection** header.

To clear the **Connection** HTTP header, set the **Connection** property to a null reference (**Nothing** in Visual Basic).

Changing the **Connection** property after the request has been started by calling **GetRequestStream**, **BeginGetRequestStream**, **GetResponse**, or **BeginGetResponse** method will throw an **InvalidOperationException**.

Example

[Visual Basic, C#, C++] The following example uses the **Connection** property to set the value of the Connection HTTP Header.

```
[Visual Basic]
Class HttpWebRequest_Connection

  Shared Sub Main()
    Try

      ' Create a new 'HttpWebRequest' object for the
  specified Uri. Make sure that
      ' a default proxy is set if you are behind a fire wall.
      Dim myHttpWebRequest1 As HttpWebRequest =
  CType(WebRequest.Create("http://www.contoso.com"), HttpWebRequest)
      myHttpWebRequest1.KeepAlive = False
      ' Assign the response object of 'HttpWebRequest' to a
  'HttpWebResponse' variable.
      Dim myHttpWebResponse1 As HttpWebResponse =
  CType(myHttpWebRequest1.GetResponse(), HttpWebResponse)

      Console.WriteLine(ControlChars.Cr + "The HTTP request
  Headers for the first request are {0}", myHttpWebRequest1.Headers)
      Console.WriteLine("Press Enter Key to Continue.........")
      Console.Read()
      Dim streamResponse As Stream =
  myHttpWebResponse1.GetResponseStream()
      Dim streamRead As New StreamReader(streamResponse)
      Dim readBuff(256) As [Char]
      Dim count As Integer = streamRead.Read(readBuff, 0, 256)
      Console.WriteLine("The contents of the Html page are
  ......." + ControlChars.Cr)
      While count > 0
        Dim outputData As New [String](readBuff, 0, count)
        Console.Write(outputData)
        count = streamRead.Read(readBuff, 0, 256)
      End While
      ' Close the Stream object.
      streamResponse.Close()
      streamRead.Close()
      ' Release the resources held by response object.
      myHttpWebResponse1.Close()
      Console.WriteLine()
      ' Create a new 'HttpWebRequest' object  to the specified Uri.
      Dim myHttpWebRequest2 As HttpWebRequest =
  CType(WebRequest.Create("http://www.contoso.com"), HttpWebRequest)
      myHttpWebRequest2.Connection = "Close"
      ' Assign the response object of 'HttpWebRequest' to a
  'HttpWebResponse' variable.
      Dim myHttpWebResponse2 As HttpWebResponse =
  CType(myHttpWebRequest2.GetResponse(), HttpWebResponse)
      ' Release the resources held by response object.
      myHttpWebResponse2.Close()
      Console.WriteLine(ControlChars.Cr + "The Http
  RequestHeaders are " + ControlChars.Cr + "{0}",
  myHttpWebRequest2.Headers)
      Console.WriteLine(ControlChars.Cr + "Press 'Enter'
  Key to Continue........")
      Console.Read()
    Catch e As ArgumentException
      Console.WriteLine(ControlChars.Cr + "The second
  HttpWebRequest object has raised an Argument Exception as
  'Connection' Property is set to 'Close'")
      Console.WriteLine(ControlChars.Cr + "{0}", e.Message)
    Catch e As WebException
      Console.WriteLine("WebException raised!")
      Console.WriteLine(ControlChars.Cr + "{0}", e.Message)
      Console.WriteLine(ControlChars.Cr + "{0}", e.Status)
    Catch e As Exception
      Console.WriteLine("Exception raised!")
      Console.WriteLine("Source :{0} ", e.Source)
      Console.WriteLine("Message : {0}", e.Message)
    End Try
  End Sub ' Main
End Class ' HttpWebRequest_Connection
```

```csharp
[C#]
using System;
using System.IO;
using System.Net;
using System.Text;

class HttpWebRequest_Connection
{
  static void Main()
  {
    try
    {

      // Create a new HttpWebRequest object.Make sure that
      // a default proxy is set if you are behind a fire wall.
      HttpWebRequest myHttpWebRequest1 =
        (HttpWebRequest)WebRequest.Create("http://www.contoso.com");

      myHttpWebRequest1.KeepAlive=false;
      // Assign the response object of HttpWebRequest to a
HttpWebResponse variable.
      HttpWebResponse myHttpWebResponse1 =
        (HttpWebResponse)myHttpWebRequest1.GetResponse();

      Console.WriteLine("\nThe HTTP request Headers for the
first request are: \n{0}",myHttpWebRequest1.Headers);
      Console.WriteLine("Press Enter Key to Continue.........");
      Console.Read();

      Stream streamResponse=myHttpWebResponse1.GetResponseStream();
      StreamReader streamRead = new StreamReader( streamResponse );
      Char[] readBuff = new Char[256];
      int count = streamRead.Read( readBuff, 0, 256 );
      Console.WriteLine("The contents of the Html page are.......\n");
      while (count > 0)
      {
        String outputData = new String(readBuff, 0, count);
        Console.Write(outputData);
        count = streamRead.Read(readBuff, 0, 256);
      }
      Console.WriteLine();
      // Close the Stream object.
      streamResponse.Close();
      streamRead.Close();
      // Release the resources held by response object.
      myHttpWebResponse1.Close();
      // Create a new HttpWebRequest object for the specified Uri.
      HttpWebRequest myHttpWebRequest2 =
        (HttpWebRequest)WebRequest.Create("http://www.contoso.com");
      myHttpWebRequest2.Connection="Close";
      // Assign the response object of 'HttpWebRequest' to a
'HttpWebResponse' variable.
      HttpWebResponse myHttpWebResponse2 =
        (HttpWebResponse)myHttpWebRequest2.GetResponse();
      // Release the resources held by response object.
      myHttpWebResponse2.Close();
      Console.WriteLine("\nThe Http RequestHeaders are
\n{0}",myHttpWebRequest2.Headers);
      Console.WriteLine("\nPress 'Enter' Key to Continue.........");
      Console.Read();
    }
    catch(ArgumentException e)
    {
      Console.WriteLine("\nThe second HttpWebRequest object
has raised an Argument Exception as 'Connection' Property is
set to 'Close'");
      Console.WriteLine("\n{0}",e.Message);
    }
    catch(WebException e)
    {
      Console.WriteLine("WebException raised!");
      Console.WriteLine("\n{0}",e.Message);
      Console.WriteLine("\n{0}",e.Status);
    }
    catch(Exception e)
```

```
    {
      Console.WriteLine("Exception raised!");
      Console.WriteLine("Source :{0} " , e.Source);
      Console.WriteLine("Message :{0} " , e.Message);
    }
  }
}
```

```cpp
[C++]
int main() {
  try {

    // Create a new HttpWebRequest Object*.Make sure that
    // a default proxy is set if you are behind a fure wall.
    HttpWebRequest* myHttpWebRequest1 =
      dynamic_cast<HttpWebRequest*>(WebRequest::Create
(S"http://www.contoso.com"));

    myHttpWebRequest1->KeepAlive=false;
    // Assign the response Object* of HttpWebRequest to a
HttpWebResponse variable.
    HttpWebResponse* myHttpWebResponse1 =
      dynamic_cast<HttpWebResponse*>(myHttpWebRequest1-
>GetResponse());

    Console::WriteLine(S"\nThe HTTP request Headers for the
first request are: \n {0}",
      myHttpWebRequest1->Headers);
    Console::WriteLine(S"Press Enter Key to Continue.........");
    Console::Read();

    Stream* streamResponse = myHttpWebResponse1->GetResponseStream();
    StreamReader* streamRead = new StreamReader(streamResponse);
    Char readBuff[] = new Char[256];
    int count = streamRead->Read(readBuff, 0, 256);
    Console::WriteLine(S"The contents of the Html page
are.......\n");
    while (count > 0) {
      String* outputData = new String(readBuff, 0, count);
      Console::Write(outputData);
      count = streamRead->Read(readBuff, 0, 256);
    }
    Console::WriteLine();
    // Close the Stream Object*.
    streamResponse->Close();
    streamRead->Close();
    // Release the resources held by response Object*.
    myHttpWebResponse1->Close();
    // Create a new HttpWebRequest Object* for the specified Uri.
    HttpWebRequest* myHttpWebRequest2 =
      dynamic_cast<HttpWebRequest*>(WebRequest::Create
(S"http://www.contoso.com"));
    myHttpWebRequest2->Connection=S"Close";
    // Assign the response Object* of 'HttpWebRequest'
to a 'HttpWebResponse' variable.
    HttpWebResponse* myHttpWebResponse2 =
      dynamic_cast<HttpWebResponse*>(myHttpWebRequest2-
>GetResponse());
    // Release the resources held by response Object*.
    myHttpWebResponse2->Close();
    Console::WriteLine(S"\nThe Http RequestHeaders are \n {0}",
      myHttpWebRequest2->Headers);
    Console::WriteLine(S"\nPress 'Enter' Key to Continue.........");
    Console::Read();
  } catch (ArgumentException* e) {
    Console::WriteLine(S"\nThe second HttpWebRequest
Object* has raised an Argument Exception as 'Connection'
Property is set to 'Close'");
    Console::WriteLine(S"\n {0}", e->Message);
  } catch (WebException* e) {
    Console::WriteLine(S"WebException raised!");
    Console::WriteLine(S"\n {0}", e->Message);
    Console::WriteLine(S"\n {0}", __box( e->Status));
  } catch (Exception* e) {
    Console::WriteLine(S"Exception raised!");
```

```
        Console::WriteLine(S"Source : {0} " , e->Source);
        Console::WriteLine(S"Message : {0} " , e->Message);
    }
}
```

Requirements

Platforms: Windows 98, Windows NT 4.0,
Windows Millennium Edition, Windows 2000,
Windows XP Home Edition, Windows XP Professional,
Windows .NET Server family,
.NET Compact Framework - Windows CE .NET,
Common Language Infrastructure (CLI) Standard

HttpWebRequest.ConnectionGroupName Property

Gets or sets the name of the connection group for the request.

```
[Visual Basic]
Overrides Public Property ConnectionGroupName As String
[C#]
public override string ConnectionGroupName {get; set;}
[C++]
public: __property String* get_ConnectionGroupName();
public: __property void set_ConnectionGroupName(String*);
[JScript]
public override function get ConnectionGroupName() : String;
public override function set ConnectionGroupName(String);
```

Property Value

The name of the connection group for this request. The default value
is a null reference (**Nothing** in Visual Basic).

Remarks

The **ConnectionGroupName** property enables you to associate a
request with a connection group. This is useful when your
application makes requests to one server for different users, such as
a Web site that retrieves customer information from a database
server.

Notes to Implementers: Each connection group creates additional
connections for a server. This may result in exceeding
ServicePoint.ConnectionLimit for that server.

Example

[Visual Basic, C#, JScript] The following example show how to use
user information to form a connection group, assuming that the
variables *username*, *password*, and *domain* are set by the application
before this code is called.

```
[Visual Basic]
' Create a secure group name.
Dim Sha1 As New SHA1Managed()
Dim updHash As [Byte]() =
Sha1.ComputeHash(Encoding.UTF8.GetBytes(("username" +
"password" + "domain")))
Dim secureGroupName As [String] = Encoding.Default.GetString(updHash)

' Create a request for a specific URL.
Dim myWebRequest As WebRequest = WebRequest.Create("http://
www.contoso.com")

' Set the authentication credentials for the request.
myWebRequest.Credentials = New NetworkCredential
("username", "password", "domain")
myWebRequest.ConnectionGroupName = secureGroupName
```

```
' Get the response.
Dim myWebResponse As WebResponse = myWebRequest.GetResponse()

' Insert the code that uses myWebResponse here.
' Close the response.
myWebResponse.Close()
```

```
[C#]
// Create a secure group name.
SHA1Managed Sha1 = new SHA1Managed();
Byte[] updHash = Sha1.ComputeHash(Encoding.UTF8.GetBytes
("username" + "password" + "domain"));
String secureGroupName = Encoding.Default.GetString(updHash);

// Create a request for a specific URL.
WebRequest myWebRequest=WebRequest.Create("http://www.contoso.com");

// Set the authentication credentials for the request.
myWebRequest.Credentials = new NetworkCredential
("username", "password", "domain");
myWebRequest.ConnectionGroupName = secureGroupName;

// Get the response.
WebResponse myWebResponse=myWebRequest.GetResponse();

// Insert the code that uses myWebResponse here.

// Close the response.
myWebResponse.Close();
```

```
[JScript]
//Create a WebRequest
var wReq : WebRequest = WebRequest.Create("http://www.contoso.com/")

// Set the Authentication credentials for the request.
wReq.Credentials = new NetworkCredential(username, password, domain)
// Assign the request to a connection group based on the user//s name
wReq.ConnectionGroupName = username

//Get the response
var wResp : WebResponse = wReq.GetResponse()

//Use the response and then close.
wResp.Close()
```

Requirements

Platforms: Windows 98, Windows NT 4.0,
Windows Millennium Edition, Windows 2000,
Windows XP Home Edition, Windows XP Professional,
Windows .NET Server family,
.NET Compact Framework - Windows CE .NET,
Common Language Infrastructure (CLI) Standard

HttpWebRequest.ContentLength Property

Gets or sets the **Content-length** HTTP header.

```
[Visual Basic]
Overrides Public Property ContentLength As Long
[C#]
public override long ContentLength {get; set;}
[C++]
public: __property __int64 get_ContentLength();
public: __property void set_ContentLength(__int64);
[JScript]
public override function get ContentLength() : long;
public override function set ContentLength(long);
```

Property Value

The number of bytes of data to send to the Internet resource. The default is -1, which indicates the property has not been set and that there is no request data to send.

Exceptions

Exception Type	Condition
InvalidOperation-Exception	The request has been started by calling the **GetRequestStream**, **BeginGetRequestStream**, **GetResponse**, or **BeginGetResponse** method.
ArgumentOutOfRange-Exception	The new **ContentLength** value is less than 0.

Remarks

The **ContentLength** property contains the value to send as the **Content-length** HTTP header with the request.

Any value other than -1 in the **ContentLength** property indicates that the request will upload data and that only methods that upload data are allowed to be set in the **Method** property.

Once the **ContentLength** property is set to a value, that number of bytes must be written to the request stream that is returned by calling **GetRequestStream** or both **BeginGetRequestStream** and **EndGetRequestStream**.

Example

[Visual Basic, C#, C++] The following example sets the **ContentLength** property to the length of the string being posted.

```
[Visual Basic]
Console.WriteLine(ControlChars.Cr + "Please enter the data
to be posted to the
(http://www.contoso.com/codesnippets/next.asp) Uri :")
' Create a new string object to POST data to the Url.
Dim inputData As String = Console.ReadLine()
Dim postData As String = "firstone" + ChrW(61) + inputData
Dim encoding As New ASCIIEncoding()
Dim byte1 As Byte() = encoding.GetBytes(postData)
' Set the content type of the data being posted.
myHttpWebRequest.ContentType = "application/x-www-form-urlencoded"
' Set the content length of the string being posted.
myHttpWebRequest.ContentLength = postData.Length
Dim newStream As Stream = myHttpWebRequest.GetRequestStream()
newStream.Write(byte1, 0, byte1.Length)
Console.WriteLine("The value of 'ContentLength' property after
sending the data is {0}", myHttpWebRequest.ContentLength)
newStream.Close()
```

```
[C#]
string postData="firstone="+inputData;
ASCIIEncoding encoding=new ASCIIEncoding();
byte[] byte1=encoding.GetBytes(postData);
// Set the content type of the data being posted.
myHttpWebRequest.ContentType="application/x-www-form-urlencoded";
// Set the content length of the string being posted.
myHttpWebRequest.ContentLength=postData.Length;
Stream newStream=myHttpWebRequest.GetRequestStream();
newStream.Write(byte1,0,byte1.Length);
Console.WriteLine("The value of 'ContentLength' property after
sending the data is {0}",myHttpWebRequest.ContentLength);
// Close the Stream object.
          newStream.Close();
```

```
[C++]
String* postData = String::Concat(S"firstone= ", inputData);
ASCIIEncoding* encoding = new ASCIIEncoding();
Byte byte1[] = encoding->GetBytes(postData);
// Set the content type of the data being posted.
```

```
myHttpWebRequest->ContentType = S"application/x-www-form-urlencoded";
// Set the content length of the String* being posted.
myHttpWebRequest->ContentLength=postData->Length;
Stream* newStream = myHttpWebRequest->GetRequestStream();
newStream->Write(byte1, 0, byte1->Length);
Console::WriteLine(S"The value of 'ContentLength' property
after sending the data is {0}",
    __box(myHttpWebRequest->ContentLength));
// Close the Stream Object*.
newStream->Close();
```

Requirements

Platforms: Windows 98, Windows NT 4.0, Windows Millennium Edition, Windows 2000, Windows XP Home Edition, Windows XP Professional, Windows .NET Server family, .NET Compact Framework - Windows CE .NET, Common Language Infrastructure (CLI) Standard

HttpWebRequest.ContentType Property

Gets or sets the value of the **Content-type** HTTP header.

```
[Visual Basic]
Overrides Public Property ContentType As String
[C#]
public override string ContentType {get; set;}
[C++]
public: __property String* get_ContentType();
public: __property void set_ContentType(String*);
[JScript]
public override function get ContentType() : String;
public override function set ContentType(String);
```

Property Value

The value of the **Content-type** HTTP header. The default value is a null reference (**Nothing** in Visual Basic).

Remarks

The **ContentType** property contains the media type of the request. Values assigned to the **ContentType** property replace any existing contents when the request sends the **Content-type** HTTP header.

To clear the **Content-type** HTTP header, set the **ContentType** property to a null reference (**Nothing** in Visual Basic).

Example

[Visual Basic, C#, C++] The following example sets the **ContentType** property.

```
[Visual Basic]
' Set the 'Method' property of the 'Webrequest' to 'POST'.
myHttpWebRequest.Method = "POST"
Console.WriteLine(ControlChars.Cr + "Please enter the data
to be posted to the
(http://www.contoso.com/codesnippets/next.asp) Uri :")
' Create a new string object to POST data to the Url.
Dim inputData As String = Console.ReadLine()
Dim postData As String = "firstone" + ChrW(61) + inputData
Dim encoding As New ASCIIEncoding()
Dim byte1 As Byte() = encoding.GetBytes(postData)
' Set the content type of the data being posted.
myHttpWebRequest.ContentType = "application/x-www-form-urlencoded"
' Set the content length of the string being posted.
myHttpWebRequest.ContentLength = postData.Length
Dim newStream As Stream = myHttpWebRequest.GetRequestStream()
newStream.Write(byte1, 0, byte1.Length)
Console.WriteLine("The value of 'ContentLength' property after sending
the data is {0}", myHttpWebRequest.ContentLength)
newStream.Close()
```

```
[C#]
// Set the 'Method' property of the 'Webrequest' to 'POST'.
myHttpWebRequest.Method="POST";
Console.WriteLine("\nPlease enter the data to be posted
to the (http://www.contoso.com/codesnippets/next.asp) Uri :");
// Create a new string object to POST data to the Url.
string inputData=Console.ReadLine();
string postData="firstone="+inputData;
ASCIIEncoding encoding=new ASCIIEncoding();
byte[] byte1=encoding.GetBytes(postData);
// Set the content type of the data being posted.
myHttpWebRequest.ContentType="application/x-www-form-urlencoded";
// Set the content length of the string being posted.
myHttpWebRequest.ContentLength=postData.Length;
Stream newStream=myHttpWebRequest.GetRequestStream();
newStream.Write(byte1,0,byte1.Length);
Console.WriteLine("The value of 'ContentLength' property
after sending the data is {0}",myHttpWebRequest.ContentLength);
// Close the Stream object.
            newStream.Close();

[C++]
// Set the 'Method' property of the 'Webrequest' to 'POST'.
myHttpWebRequest->Method=S"POST";
Console::WriteLine(S"\nPlease enter the data to be posted
to the (http://www.contoso.com/codesnippets/next.asp) Uri :");
// Create a new String* Object to POST data to the Url.
String* inputData = Console::ReadLine();
String* postData = String::Concat(S"firstone= ", inputData);
ASCIIEncoding* encoding = new ASCIIEncoding();
Byte byte1[] = encoding->GetBytes(postData);
// Set the content type of the data being posted.
myHttpWebRequest->ContentType = S"application/x-www-form-urlencoded";
// Set the content length of the String* being posted.
myHttpWebRequest->ContentLength=postData->Length;
Stream* newStream = myHttpWebRequest->GetRequestStream();
newStream->Write(byte1, 0, byte1->Length);
Console::WriteLine(S"The value of 'ContentLength'
property after sending the data is {0}",
    __box(myHttpWebRequest->ContentLength));
// Close the Stream Object*.
newStream->Close();
```

Requirements

Platforms: Windows 98, Windows NT 4.0,
Windows Millennium Edition, Windows 2000,
Windows XP Home Edition, Windows XP Professional,
Windows .NET Server family,
.NET Compact Framework - Windows CE .NET,
Common Language Infrastructure (CLI) Standard

HttpWebRequest.ContinueDelegate Property

Gets or sets the delegate method called when an HTTP 100-continue response is received from the Internet resource.

```
[Visual Basic]
Public Property ContinueDelegate As HttpContinueDelegate
[C#]
public HttpContinueDelegate ContinueDelegate {get; set;}
[C++]
public: __property HttpContinueDelegate* get_ContinueDelegate();
public: __property void set_ContinueDelegate(HttpContinueDelegate*);
[JScript]
public function get ContinueDelegate() : HttpContinueDelegate;
public function set ContinueDelegate(HttpContinueDelegate);
```

Property Value

A delegate that implements the callback method that executes when an HTTP Continue response is returned from the Internet resource. The default value is a null reference (**Nothing** in Visual Basic).

Remarks

The **ContinueDelegate** property specifies the callback method to call when the client receives a 100-Continue response.

When the **ContinueDelegate** property is set, the client calls the delegate whenever protocol responses of type **HttpStatusCode.Continue** (100) are received. This is useful if you want the client to display the status of the data being received from the Internet resource.

Requirements

Platforms: Windows 98, Windows NT 4.0,
Windows Millennium Edition, Windows 2000,
Windows XP Home Edition, Windows XP Professional,
Windows .NET Server family,
.NET Compact Framework - Windows CE .NET,
Common Language Infrastructure (CLI) Standard

HttpWebRequest.CookieContainer Property

Gets or sets the cookies associated with the request.

```
[Visual Basic]
Public Property CookieContainer As CookieContainer
[C#]
public CookieContainer CookieContainer {get; set;}
[C++]
public: __property CookieContainer* get_CookieContainer();
public: __property void set_CookieContainer(CookieContainer*);
[JScript]
public function get CookieContainer() : CookieContainer;
public function set CookieContainer(CookieContainer);
```

Property Value

A **CookieContainer** containing the cookies associated with this request.

Remarks

The **CookieContainer** property provides an instance of the **CookieContainer** class that contains the cookies associated with this request.

CookieContainer is a null reference (**Nothing** in Visual Basic) by default. You must assign a **CookieContainer** instance to the property to have cookies returned in the **Cookies** property of the **HttpWebResponse** returned by **GetResponse**.

Requirements

Platforms: Windows 98, Windows NT 4.0,
Windows Millennium Edition, Windows 2000,
Windows XP Home Edition, Windows XP Professional,
Windows .NET Server family

HttpWebRequest.Credentials Property

Provides authentication information for the request.

```
[Visual Basic]
Overrides Public Property Credentials As ICredentials
[C#]
public override ICredentials Credentials {get; set;}
```

```
[C++]
public: __property ICredentials* get_Credentials();
public: __property void set_Credentials(ICredentials*);
[JScript]
public override function get Credentials() : ICredentials;
public override function set Credentials(ICredentials);
```

Property Value

An **ICredentials** containing the authentication credentials associated with the request. The default is a null reference (**Nothing** in Visual Basic).

Remarks

The **Credentials** property contains authentication information to identify the maker of the request. The **Credentials** property can be either an instance of **NetworkCredential**, in which case the user, password, and domain information contained in the **NetworkCredential** instance is used to authenticate the request, or it can be an instance of **CredentialCache**, in which case the uniform resource identifier (URI) of the request is used to determine the user, password, and domain information to use to authenticate the request.

Requirements

Platforms: Windows 98, Windows NT 4.0, Windows Millennium Edition, Windows 2000, Windows XP Home Edition, Windows XP Professional, Windows .NET Server family, .NET Compact Framework - Windows CE .NET, Common Language Infrastructure (CLI) Standard

HttpWebRequest.DefaultMaximumResponse-HeadersLength Property

Note: This namespace, class, or member is supported only in version 1.1 of the .NET Framework.

Gets or sets the default for the **MaximumResponseHeadersLength** property.

```
[Visual Basic]
Public Shared Property DefaultMaximumResponseHeadersLength As _
    Integer
[C#]
public static int DefaultMaximumResponseHeadersLength {get; set;}
[C++]
public: __property static int
get_DefaultMaximumResponseHeadersLength();
public: __property static void
    set_DefaultMaximumResponseHeadersLength(int);
[JScript]
public static function get DefaultMaximumResponseHeadersLength() : int;
public static function set DefaultMaximumResponseHeadersLength(int);
```

Property Value

The configuration file sets this value to 64 kilobytes.

Exceptions

Exception Type	Condition
ArgumentOutOfRange-Exception	The value is less than 0 and is not equal to -1.

Remarks

This value can be changed in the configuration file or can be overridden using the **MaximumResponseHeadersLength** property.

Requirements

Platforms: Windows 98, Windows NT 4.0, Windows Millennium Edition, Windows 2000, Windows XP Home Edition, Windows XP Professional, Windows .NET Server family

HttpWebRequest.Expect Property

Gets or sets the value of the **Expect** HTTP header.

```
[Visual Basic]
Public Property Expect As String
[C#]
public string Expect {get; set;}
[C++]
public: __property String* get_Expect();
public: __property void set_Expect(String*);
[JScript]
public function get Expect() : String;
public function set Expect(String);
```

Property Value

The contents of the **Expect** HTTP header. The default value is a null reference (**Nothing** in Visual Basic).

Exceptions

Exception Type	Condition
ArgumentException	Expect is set to a string that contains "100-continue" as a substring.

Requirements

Platforms: Windows 98, Windows NT 4.0, Windows Millennium Edition, Windows 2000, Windows XP Home Edition, Windows XP Professional, Windows .NET Server family, .NET Compact Framework - Windows CE .NET, Common Language Infrastructure (CLI) Standard

HttpWebRequest.HaveResponse Property

Gets a value indicating whether a response has been received from an Internet resource.

```
[Visual Basic]
Public ReadOnly Property HaveResponse As Boolean
[C#]
public bool HaveResponse {get;}
[C++]
public: __property bool get_HaveResponse();
[JScript]
public function get HaveResponse() : Boolean;
```

Property Value

true if a response has been received; otherwise **false**.

Example

[Visual Basic, C#, C++] The following example checks the **HaveResponse** property to determine if a response has been received from an Internet resource.

```
[Visual Basic]
' Create a new 'HttpWebRequest' Object.
Dim myHttpWebRequest As HttpWebRequest =
CType(WebRequest.Create("http://www.contoso.com"), HttpWebRequest)
```

```
Dim myHttpWebResponse As HttpWebResponse
' Display the 'HaveResponse' property of the 'HttpWebRequest'
object to the console.
Console.WriteLine(ControlChars.Cr + "The value of
'HaveResponse' property before a response object is
obtained :{0}", myHttpWebRequest.HaveResponse)
' Assign the response object of 'HttpWebRequest' to a
'HttpWebResponse' variable.
myHttpWebResponse = CType
(myHttpWebRequest.GetResponse(), HttpWebResponse)
If myHttpWebRequest.HaveResponse Then
    Dim streamResponse As Stream =
myHttpWebResponse.GetResponseStream()
    Dim streamRead As New StreamReader(streamResponse)
    Dim readBuff(256) As [Char]
    Dim count As Integer = streamRead.Read(readBuff, 0, 256)
    Console.WriteLine(ControlChars.Cr +
"The contents of Html Page are :  " + ControlChars.Cr)
    While count > 0
        Dim outputData As New [String](readBuff, 0, count)
        Console.Write(outputData)
        count = streamRead.Read(readBuff, 0, 256)
    End While
    '  Close the Stream object.
    streamResponse.Close()
    streamRead.Close()
    ' Release the HttpWebResponse Resource.
    myHttpWebResponse.Close()
    Console.WriteLine(ControlChars.Cr + "Press 'Enter'
key to continue..........")
    Console.Read()

Else
    Console.WriteLine(ControlChars.Cr + "The response is
not received ")
End If
```

```
[C#]
// Create a new 'HttpWebRequest' Object.
HttpWebRequest myHttpWebRequest=(HttpWebRequest)WebRequest.Create
("http://www.contoso.com");
HttpWebResponse myHttpWebResponse;
// Display the 'HaveResponse' property of the 'HttpWebRequest'
object to the console.
Console.WriteLine("\nThe value of 'HaveResponse' property
before a response object is obtained
:{0}",myHttpWebRequest.HaveResponse);
// Assign the response object of 'HttpWebRequest' to a
'HttpWebResponse' variable.
myHttpWebResponse=(HttpWebResponse)myHttpWebRequest.GetResponse();
if (myHttpWebRequest.HaveResponse)
{
    Stream streamResponse=myHttpWebResponse.GetResponseStream();
    StreamReader streamRead = new StreamReader( streamResponse );
    Char[] readBuff = new Char[256];
    int count = streamRead.Read( readBuff, 0, 256 );
    Console.WriteLine("\nThe contents of Html Page are :  \n");
    while (count > 0)
    {
        String outputData = new String(readBuff, 0, count);
        Console.Write(outputData);
        count = streamRead.Read(readBuff, 0, 256);
    }
    // Close the Stream object.
    streamResponse.Close();
    streamRead.Close();
    // Release the HttpWebResponse Resource.
    myHttpWebResponse.Close();
    Console.WriteLine("\nPress 'Enter' key to continue..........");
    Console.Read();
}
else
{
    Console.WriteLine("\nThe response is not received ");
}
```

```
[C++]
// Create a new 'HttpWebRequest' Object.
HttpWebRequest* myHttpWebRequest =
    dynamic_cast<HttpWebRequest*>(WebRequest::Create
(S"http://www.contoso.com"));
HttpWebResponse* myHttpWebResponse;
// Display the 'HaveResponse' property of the
'HttpWebRequest' Object* to the console.
Console::WriteLine(S"\nThe value of 'HaveResponse'
property before a response Object* is obtained : {0}",
    __box(myHttpWebRequest->HaveResponse));
// Assign the response Object* of 'HttpWebRequest' to a
'HttpWebResponse' variable.
myHttpWebResponse =
    dynamic_cast<HttpWebResponse*>(myHttpWebRequest->GetResponse());
if (myHttpWebRequest->HaveResponse) {
    Stream* streamResponse = myHttpWebResponse->GetResponseStream();
    StreamReader* streamRead = new StreamReader(streamResponse);
    Char readBuff[] = new Char[256];
    int count = streamRead->Read(readBuff, 0, 256);
    Console::WriteLine(S"\nThe contents of Html Page are :  \n");
    while (count > 0) {
        String* outputData = new String(readBuff, 0, count);
        Console::Write(outputData);
        count = streamRead->Read(readBuff, 0, 256);
    }
    // Close the Stream Object*.
    streamResponse->Close();
    streamRead->Close();
    // Release the HttpWebResponse Resource.
    myHttpWebResponse->Close();
    Console::WriteLine(S"\nPress 'Enter' key to continue..........");
    Console::Read();
} else {
    Console::WriteLine(S"\nThe response is not received ");
}
```

Requirements

Platforms: Windows 98, Windows NT 4.0,
Windows Millennium Edition, Windows 2000,
Windows XP Home Edition, Windows XP Professional,
Windows .NET Server family,
.NET Compact Framework - Windows CE .NET,
Common Language Infrastructure (CLI) Standard

HttpWebRequest.Headers Property

Gets a collection of the name/value pairs that make up the HTTP
headers.

```
[Visual Basic]
Overrides Public Property Headers As WebHeaderCollection
[C#]
public override WebHeaderCollection Headers {get; set;}
[C++]
public: __property WebHeaderCollection* get_Headers();
public: __property void set_Headers(WebHeaderCollection*);
[JScript]
public override function get Headers() : WebHeaderCollection;
public override function set Headers(WebHeaderCollection);
```

Property Value

A **WebHeaderCollection** containing the name/value pairs that make
up the headers for the HTTP request.

Exceptions

Exception Type	Condition
InvalidOperation-Exception	The request has been started by calling the **GetRequestStream**, **BeginGetRequestStream**, **GetResponse**, or **BeginGetResponse** method.

Remarks

The **Headers** collection contains the protocol headers associated with the request. The following table lists the HTTP headers that are not stored in the **Headers** collection but are either set by the system or set by properties or methods.

Header	Set by
Accept	Set by the **Accept** property.
Connection	Set by the **Connection** property and **KeepAlive** property.
Content-Length	Set by the **ContentLength** property.
Content-Type	Set by the **ContentType** property.
Expect	Set by the **Expect** property.
Date	Set by the system to the current date.
Host	Set by the system to the current host information.
If-Modified-Since	Set by the **IfModifiedSince** property.
Range	Set by the **AddRange** method.
Referer	Set by the **Referer** property.
Transfer-Encoding	Set by the **TransferEncoding** property (the **SendChunked** property must be true).
User-Agent	Set by the **UserAgent** property.

The **Add** method throws an **ArgumentException** if you try to set one of these protected headers.

Changing the **Headers** property after the request has been started by calling **GetRequestStream**, **BeginGetRequestStream**, **GetResponse**, or **BeginGetResponse** method will throw an **InvalidOperationException**.

Example

[Visual Basic, C#, C++] The following example uses the **Headers** property to print the HTTP header name/value pairs to the console.

```
[Visual Basic]
' Create a new 'HttpWebRequest' Object to the mentioned URL.
Dim myHttpWebRequest As HttpWebRequest =
CType(WebRequest.Create("http://www.contoso.com"), HttpWebRequest)
' Assign the response object of 'HttpWebRequest' to a
'HttpWebResponse' variable.
Dim myHttpWebResponse As HttpWebResponse =
CType(myHttpWebRequest.GetResponse(), HttpWebResponse)
Console.WriteLine(ControlChars.Cr + "The HttpHeaders are " +
ControlChars.Cr + ControlChars.Cr + ControlChars.Tab + "Name" +
ControlChars.Tab + ControlChars.Tab +
"Value" + ControlChars.Cr + "{0}", myHttpWebRequest.Headers)

' Print the HTML contents of the page to the console.
Dim streamResponse As Stream = myHttpWebResponse.GetResponseStream()
Dim streamRead As New StreamReader(streamResponse)
Dim readBuff(256) As [Char]
Dim count As Integer = streamRead.Read(readBuff, 0, 256)
Console.WriteLine(ControlChars.Cr + "The HTML contents of page
the are  : " + ControlChars.Cr + ControlChars.Cr + " ")
While count > 0
    Dim outputData As New [String](readBuff, 0, count)
```

```
Console.Write(outputData)
    count = streamRead.Read(readBuff, 0, 256)
End While
    ' Close the Stream object.
    streamResponse.Close()
    streamRead.Close()
    ' Release the HttpWebResponse Resource.
    myHttpWebResponse.Close()
```

```
[C#]
// Create a new 'HttpWebRequest' Object to the mentioned URL.
HttpWebRequest myHttpWebRequest=(HttpWebRequest)WebRequest.Create
("http://www.contoso.com");
// Assign the response object of 'HttpWebRequest' to a
'HttpWebResponse' variable.
HttpWebResponse
myHttpWebResponse=(HttpWebResponse)myHttpWebRequest.GetResponse();
Console.WriteLine("\nThe HttpHeaders are
\n\n\tName\t\tValue\n{0}",myHttpWebRequest.Headers);
// Print the HTML contents of the page to the console.
Stream streamResponse=myHttpWebResponse.GetResponseStream();
StreamReader streamRead = new StreamReader( streamResponse );
Char[] readBuff = new Char[256];
int count = streamRead.Read( readBuff, 0, 256 );
Console.WriteLine("\nThe HTML contents of page the are  : \n\n ");
while (count > 0)
{
    String outputData = new String(readBuff, 0, count);
    Console.Write(outputData);
    count = streamRead.Read(readBuff, 0, 256);
}
// Close the Stream object.
streamResponse.Close();
streamRead.Close();
// Release the HttpWebResponse Resource.
myHttpWebResponse.Close();
```

```
[C++]
// Create a new 'HttpWebRequest' Object to the mentioned URL.
HttpWebRequest* myHttpWebRequest =
    dynamic_cast<HttpWebRequest*>(WebRequest::Create
(S"http://www.contoso.com"));
// Assign the response Object* of 'HttpWebRequest' to a
'HttpWebResponse' variable.
HttpWebResponse* myHttpWebResponse =
    dynamic_cast<HttpWebResponse*>(myHttpWebRequest->GetResponse());
Console::WriteLine(S"\nThe HttpHeaders are \n\n\tName\t\tValue\n {0}",
    myHttpWebRequest->Headers);
// Print the HTML contents of the page to the console.
Stream* streamResponse = myHttpWebResponse->GetResponseStream();
StreamReader* streamRead = new StreamReader(streamResponse);
Char readBuff[] = new Char[256];
int count = streamRead->Read(readBuff, 0, 256);
Console::WriteLine(S"\nThe HTML contents of page the are  : \n\n ");
while (count > 0) {
    String* outputData = new String(readBuff, 0, count);
    Console::Write(outputData);
    count = streamRead->Read(readBuff, 0, 256);
}
// Close the Stream Object*.
streamResponse->Close();
streamRead->Close();
// Release the HttpWebResponse Resource.
myHttpWebResponse->Close();
```

Requirements

Platforms: Windows 98, Windows NT 4.0, Windows Millennium Edition, Windows 2000, Windows XP Home Edition, Windows XP Professional, Windows .NET Server family, .NET Compact Framework - Windows CE .NET, Common Language Infrastructure (CLI) Standard

HttpWebRequest.IfModifiedSince Property

Gets or sets the value of the **If-Modified-Since** HTTP header.

```
[Visual Basic]
Public Property IfModifiedSince As DateTime
[C#]
public DateTime IfModifiedSince {get; set;}
[C++]
public: __property DateTime get_IfModifiedSince();
public: __property void set_IfModifiedSince(DateTime);
[JScript]
public function get IfModifiedSince() : DateTime;
public function set IfModifiedSince(DateTime);
```

Property Value

A **DateTime** that contains the contents of the **If-Modified-Since** HTTP header. The default value is the current date and time.

Remarks

The **IfModifiedSince** property is assumed to be local time.

Example

[Visual Basic, C#, C++] The following example checks the **IfModifiedSince** property.

```vb
[Visual Basic]
' Create a new 'Uri' object with the mentioned string.
Dim myUri As New Uri("http://www.contoso.com")
' Create a new 'HttpWebRequest' object with the above 'Uri' object.
Dim myHttpWebRequest As HttpWebRequest =
CType(WebRequest.Create(myUri), HttpWebRequest)
' Create a new 'DateTime' object.
Dim today As DateTime = DateTime.Now
If DateTime.Compare(today, myHttpWebRequest.IfModifiedSince) = 0 Then
    ' Assign the response object of 'HttpWebRequest' to a
'HttpWebResponse' variable.
    Dim myHttpWebResponse As HttpWebResponse =
CType(myHttpWebRequest.GetResponse(), HttpWebResponse)
    Console.WriteLine("Response headers " + ControlChars.Cr +
"{0}" + ControlChars.Cr, myHttpWebResponse.Headers)
    Dim streamResponse As Stream = myHttpWebResponse.GetResponseStream()
    Dim streamRead As New StreamReader(streamResponse)
    Dim readBuff(256) As [Char]
    Dim count As Integer = streamRead.Read(readBuff, 0, 256)
    Console.WriteLine(ControlChars.Cr + "The contents of Html
Page are :  " + ControlChars.Cr)
    While count > 0
        Dim outputData As New [String](readBuff, 0, count)
        Console.Write(outputData)
        count = streamRead.Read(readBuff, 0, 256)
    End While
        ' Close the Stream object.
    streamResponse.Close()
    streamRead.Close()
        ' Release the HttpWebResponse Resource.
    myHttpWebResponse.Close()
    Console.WriteLine(ControlChars.Cr + "Press 'Enter' key to
continue...............")
    Console.Read()
Else
    Console.WriteLine((ControlChars.Cr + "The page has
been modified since " + today))
End If
```

```csharp
[C#]
// Create a new 'Uri' object with the mentioned string.
Uri myUri =new Uri("http://www.contoso.com");
// Create a new 'HttpWebRequest' object with the above 'Uri' object.
HttpWebRequest myHttpWebRequest=
(HttpWebRequest)WebRequest.Create(myUri);
// Create a new 'DateTime' object.
```

```csharp
DateTime today= DateTime.Now;
if (DateTime.Compare(today,myHttpWebRequest.IfModifiedSince)==0)
{
    // Assign the response object of 'HttpWebRequest' to a
'HttpWebResponse' variable.
    HttpWebResponse
myHttpWebResponse=(HttpWebResponse)myHttpWebRequest.GetResponse();
    Console.WriteLine("Response headers
\n{0}\n",myHttpWebResponse.Headers);
    Stream streamResponse=myHttpWebResponse.GetResponseStream();
    StreamReader streamRead = new StreamReader( streamResponse );
    Char[] readBuff = new Char[256];
    int count = streamRead.Read( readBuff, 0, 256 );
    Console.WriteLine("\nThe contents of Html Page are :  \n");
    while (count > 0)
    {
        String outputData = new String(readBuff, 0, count);
        Console.Write(outputData);
        count = streamRead.Read(readBuff, 0, 256);
    }
    // Close the Stream object.
    streamResponse.Close();
    streamRead.Close();
    // Release the HttpWebResponse Resource.
    myHttpWebResponse.Close();
    Console.WriteLine("\nPress 'Enter' key to
continue................");
    Console.Read();
}
else
{
    Console.WriteLine("\nThe page has been modified since "+today);
}
```

```cpp
[C++]
// Create a new 'Uri' Object* with the mentioned String*.
Uri* myUri = new Uri(S"http://www.contoso.com");
// Create a new 'HttpWebRequest' Object* with the above 'Uri' Object*.
HttpWebRequest* myHttpWebRequest =
    dynamic_cast<HttpWebRequest*>(WebRequest::Create(myUri));
// Create a new 'DateTime' Object*.
DateTime today = DateTime::Now;
if (DateTime::Compare(today, myHttpWebRequest->IfModifiedSince)==0) {
    // Assign the response Object* of 'HttpWebRequest' to a
'HttpWebResponse' variable.
    HttpWebResponse* myHttpWebResponse =
        dynamic_cast<HttpWebResponse*>(myHttpWebRequest->GetResponse());
    Console::WriteLine(S"Response headers \n {0}\n",
        myHttpWebResponse->Headers);
    Stream* streamResponse = myHttpWebResponse->GetResponseStream();
    StreamReader* streamRead = new StreamReader(streamResponse);
    Char readBuff[] = new Char[256];
    int count = streamRead->Read(readBuff, 0, 256);
    Console::WriteLine(S"\nThe contents of Html Page are :  \n");
    while (count > 0) {
        String* outputData = new String(readBuff, 0, count);
        Console::Write(outputData);
        count = streamRead->Read(readBuff, 0, 256);
    }
    // Close the Stream Object*.
    streamResponse->Close();
    streamRead->Close();
    // Release the HttpWebResponse Resource.
    myHttpWebResponse->Close();
    Console::WriteLine(S"\nPress 'Enter' key to
continue................");
    Console::Read();
} else {
    Console::WriteLine(S"\nThe page has been modified since {0}", __box(
today));
}
```

Requirements

Platforms: Windows 98, Windows NT 4.0,
Windows Millennium Edition, Windows 2000,
Windows XP Home Edition, Windows XP Professional,
Windows .NET Server family,
.NET Compact Framework - Windows CE .NET,
Common Language Infrastructure (CLI) Standard

HttpWebRequest.KeepAlive Property

Gets or sets a value indicating whether to make a persistent
connection to the Internet resource.

```
[Visual Basic]
Public Property KeepAlive As Boolean
[C#]
public bool KeepAlive {get; set;}
[C++]
public: __property bool get_KeepAlive();
public: __property void set_KeepAlive(bool);
[JScript]
public function get KeepAlive() : Boolean;
public function set KeepAlive(Boolean);
```

Property Value

true if the request to the Internet resource should contain a
Connection HTTP header with the value Keep-alive; otherwise,
false. The default is **true**.

Remarks

Set this property to **true** to send an **Connection** HTTP header with
the value Keep-alive. An application uses **KeepAlive** to indicate a
preference for persistent connections. When the **KeepAlive** property
is **true**, the application makes persistent connections to the servers
that support them.

> **Note**   When using HTTP/1.1, Keep-Alive is on by default.
> Setting **KeepAlive** false may result in sending a **Connection:
> Close** header to the server.

Requirements

Platforms: Windows 98, Windows NT 4.0,
Windows Millennium Edition, Windows 2000,
Windows XP Home Edition, Windows XP Professional,
Windows .NET Server family,
.NET Compact Framework - Windows CE .NET,
Common Language Infrastructure (CLI) Standard

HttpWebRequest.MaximumAutomatic-Redirections Property

Gets or sets the maximum number of redirects that the request will
follow.

```
[Visual Basic]
Public Property MaximumAutomaticRedirections As Integer
[C#]
public int MaximumAutomaticRedirections {get; set;}
[C++]
public: __property int get_MaximumAutomaticRedirections();
public: __property void set_MaximumAutomaticRedirections(int);
[JScript]
public function get MaximumAutomaticRedirections() : int;
public function set MaximumAutomaticRedirections(int);
```

Property Value

The maximum number of redirection responses that the request will
follow. The default value is 50.

Exceptions

Exception Type	Condition
ArgumentException	The value is set to 0 or less.

Remarks

The **MaximumAutomaticRedirections** method property sets the
maximum number of redirections for the request to follow if the
AllowAutoRedirect property is **true**.

Requirements

Platforms: Windows 98, Windows NT 4.0,
Windows Millennium Edition, Windows 2000,
Windows XP Home Edition, Windows XP Professional,
Windows .NET Server family,
.NET Compact Framework - Windows CE .NET,
Common Language Infrastructure (CLI) Standard

HttpWebRequest.MaximumResponseHeaders-Length Property

Note: This namespace, class, or member is supported only in
version 1.1 of the .NET Framework.

Gets or sets the maximum allowed length of the response headers.

```
[Visual Basic]
Public Property MaximumResponseHeadersLength As Integer
[C#]
public int MaximumResponseHeadersLength {get; set;}
[C++]
public: __property int get_MaximumResponseHeadersLength();
public: __property void set_MaximumResponseHeadersLength(int);
[JScript]
public function get MaximumResponseHeadersLength() : int;
public function set MaximumResponseHeadersLength(int);
```

Property Value

The length in kilobytes (1024 bytes) of the response headers.

Exceptions

Exception Type	Condition
InvalidOperation-Exception	The property is set after the request has already been submitted.
ArgumentOutOfRange-Exception	The value is less than 0 and is not equal to -1.

Remarks

The length is measured in kilobytes (1024 bytes) and it includes the
response status line and the response headers as well as all extra
control characters received as part of the HTTP protocol. A value of
-1 means no such limit will be imposed on the response headers, a
value of 0 means that all requests will fail.

Requirements

Platforms: Windows 98, Windows NT 4.0,
Windows Millennium Edition, Windows 2000,
Windows XP Home Edition, Windows XP Professional,
Windows .NET Server family

HttpWebRequest.MediaType Property

Gets or sets the media type of the request.

```
[Visual Basic]
Public Property MediaType As String
[C#]
public string MediaType {get; set;}
[C++]
public: __property String* get_MediaType();
public: __property void set_MediaType(String*);
[JScript]
public function get MediaType() : String;
public function set MediaType(String);
```

Property Value

The media type of the request. The default value is a null reference (**Nothing** in Visual Basic).

Remarks

The value of the **MediaType** property affects the **CharacterSet** property. When you set the **MediaType** in the request, the corresponding media type is chosen from the list of character sets returned in the response **Content-type** HTTP header.

Requirements

Platforms: Windows 98, Windows NT 4.0, Windows Millennium Edition, Windows 2000, Windows XP Home Edition, Windows XP Professional, Windows .NET Server family, .NET Compact Framework - Windows CE .NET, Common Language Infrastructure (CLI) Standard

HttpWebRequest.Method Property

Gets or sets the method for the request.

```
[Visual Basic]
Overrides Public Property Method As String
[C#]
public override string Method {get; set;}
[C++]
public: __property String* get_Method();
public: __property void set_Method(String*);
[JScript]
public override function get Method() : String;
public override function set Method(String);
```

Property Value

The request method to use to contact the Internet resource. The default value is GET.

Exceptions

Exception Type	Condition
ArgumentException	No method is supplied. -or- The method string contains invalid characters.

Remarks

The **Method** property can be set to any of the HTTP 1.1 protocol verbs: GET, HEAD, POST, PUT, DELETE, TRACE, or OPTIONS.

If the **ContentLength** property is set to any value other than -1, the **Method** property must be set to a protocol property that uploads data.

Requirements

Platforms: Windows 98, Windows NT 4.0, Windows Millennium Edition, Windows 2000, Windows XP Home Edition, Windows XP Professional, Windows .NET Server family, .NET Compact Framework - Windows CE .NET, Common Language Infrastructure (CLI) Standard

HttpWebRequest.Pipelined Property

Gets or sets a value indicating whether to pipeline the request to the Internet resource.

```
[Visual Basic]
Public Property Pipelined As Boolean
[C#]
public bool Pipelined {get; set;}
[C++]
public: __property bool get_Pipelined();
public: __property void set_Pipelined(bool);
[JScript]
public function get Pipelined() : Boolean;
public function set Pipelined(Boolean);
```

Property Value

true if the request should be pipelined; otherwise, **false**. The default is **true**.

Remarks

An application uses the **Pipelined** property to indicate a preference for pipelined connections. When **Pipelined** is **true**, an application makes pipelined connections to the servers that support them.

Pipelined connections are made only when the **KeepAlive** property is also **true**.

Requirements

Platforms: Windows 98, Windows NT 4.0, Windows Millennium Edition, Windows 2000, Windows XP Home Edition, Windows XP Professional, Windows .NET Server family, .NET Compact Framework - Windows CE .NET, Common Language Infrastructure (CLI) Standard

HttpWebRequest.PreAuthenticate Property

Gets or sets a value indicating whether to send a preauthentication header with the request.

```
[Visual Basic]
Overrides Public Property PreAuthenticate As Boolean
[C#]
public override bool PreAuthenticate {get; set;}
[C++]
public: __property bool get_PreAuthenticate();
public: __property void set_PreAuthenticate(bool);
[JScript]
public override function get PreAuthenticate() : Boolean;
public override function set PreAuthenticate(Boolean);
```

Property Value

true to send a **WWW-authenticate** HTTP header with the initial request; otherwise, **false**. The default is **false**.

Remarks

When **PreAuthenticate** is **true** and credentials are supplied, the **WWW-authenticate** HTTP header is sent with the initial request if its value is known; otherwise the request uses standard authentication procedures. If the authentication scheme does not support preauthentication, this property is ignored.

Requirements

Platforms: Windows 98, Windows NT 4.0, Windows Millennium Edition, Windows 2000, Windows XP Home Edition, Windows XP Professional, Windows .NET Server family, .NET Compact Framework - Windows CE .NET, Common Language Infrastructure (CLI) Standard

HttpWebRequest.ProtocolVersion Property

Gets or sets the version of HTTP to use for the request.

```
[Visual Basic]
Public Property ProtocolVersion As Version
[C#]
public Version ProtocolVersion {get; set;}
[C++]
public: __property Version* get_ProtocolVersion();
public: __property void set_ProtocolVersion(Version*);
[JScript]
public function get ProtocolVersion() : Version;
public function set ProtocolVersion(Version);
```

Property Value

The HTTP version to use for the request. The default is **HttpVersion.Version11**.

Exceptions

Exception Type	Condition
ArgumentException	The HTTP version is set to a value other than 1.0 or 1.1.

Remarks

The **HttpWebRequest** class supports only versions 1.0 and 1.1 of HTTP. Setting **ProtocolVersion** to a different version throws an exception.

Note To set the HTTP version of the current request, use the **Version10** and **Version11** fields of the **HttpVersion** class.

Requirements

Platforms: Windows 98, Windows NT 4.0, Windows Millennium Edition, Windows 2000, Windows XP Home Edition, Windows XP Professional, Windows .NET Server family, .NET Compact Framework - Windows CE .NET, Common Language Infrastructure (CLI) Standard

HttpWebRequest.Proxy Property

Gets or sets proxy information for the request.

```
[Visual Basic]
Overrides Public Property Proxy As IWebProxy
[C#]
public override IWebProxy Proxy {get; set;}
[C++]
public: __property IWebProxy* get_Proxy();
public: __property void set_Proxy(IWebProxy*);
[JScript]
public override function get Proxy() : IWebProxy;
public override function set Proxy(IWebProxy);
```

Property Value

The **WebProxy** instance to use to proxy the request. The default value is set by calling **GlobalProxySelection.Select**.

Exceptions

Exception Type	Condition
ArgumentNullException	**Proxy** is set to a null reference (**Nothing** in Visual Basic).
InvalidOperationException	The request has been started by calling **GetRequestStream**, **BeginGetRequestStream**, **GetResponse**, **BeginGetResponse**.
SecurityException	The caller does not have permission for the requested operation.

Remarks

The **Proxy** property identifies the **WebProxy** instance to use to process requests to Internet resources. To specify that no proxy should be used, set the **Proxy** property to the proxy instance returned by the **GlobalProxySelection.GetEmptyWebProxy** method.

Changing the **Proxy** property after the request has been started by calling **GetRequestStream**, **BeginGetRequestStream**, **GetResponse**, or **BeginGetResponse** method will throw an **InvalidOperationException**.

Requirements

Platforms: Windows 98, Windows NT 4.0, Windows Millennium Edition, Windows 2000, Windows XP Home Edition, Windows XP Professional, Windows .NET Server family, .NET Compact Framework - Windows CE .NET, Common Language Infrastructure (CLI) Standard

.NET Framework Security:
- **WebPermission** to get or set the **Proxy** property. Associated enumeration: **Unrestricted**.

HttpWebRequest.ReadWriteTimeout Property

Note: This namespace, class, or member is supported only in version 1.1 of the .NET Framework.

```
[Visual Basic]
Public Property ReadWriteTimeout As Integer
[C#]
public int ReadWriteTimeout {get; set;}
[C++]
public: __property int get_ReadWriteTimeout();
public: __property void set_ReadWriteTimeout(int);
```

```
[JScript]
public function get ReadWriteTimeout() : int;
public function set ReadWriteTimeout(int);
```

Requirements

Platforms: Windows 98, Windows NT 4.0,
Windows Millennium Edition, Windows 2000,
Windows XP Home Edition, Windows XP Professional,
Windows .NET Server family

HttpWebRequest.Referer Property

Gets or sets the value of the **Referer** HTTP header.

```
[Visual Basic]
Public Property Referer As String
[C#]
public string Referer {get; set;}
[C++]
public: __property String* get_Referer();
public: __property void set_Referer(String*);
[JScript]
public function get Referer() : String;
public function set Referer(String);
```

Property Value

The value of the **Referer** HTTP header. The default value is a null
reference (**Nothing** in Visual Basic).

Remarks

If the **AllowAutoRedirect** property is **true**, the **Referer** property is
set automatically when the request is redirected to another site.

To clear the **Referer** HTTP header, set the **Referer** property to a null
reference (**Nothing** in Visual Basic).

Requirements

Platforms: Windows 98, Windows NT 4.0,
Windows Millennium Edition, Windows 2000,
Windows XP Home Edition, Windows XP Professional,
Windows .NET Server family,
.NET Compact Framework - Windows CE .NET,
Common Language Infrastructure (CLI) Standard

HttpWebRequest.RequestUri Property

Gets the original URI of the request.

```
[Visual Basic]
Overrides Public ReadOnly Property RequestUri As Uri
[C#]
public override Uri RequestUri {get;}
[C++]
public: __property Uri* get_RequestUri();
[JScript]
public override function get RequestUri() : Uri;
```

Property Value

A **Uri** containing the URI of the Internet resource passed to the
WebRequest.Create method.

Remarks

The **Uri** instance passed to **HttpWebRequest** by the call to
WebRequest.Create.

Following a redirection header does not change the **RequestUri**
property. To get the actual URI that responded to the request,
examine the **Address** property.

Example

[Visual Basic, C#, JScript] The following example checks to see if
the **HttpWebRequest** instance req was redirected to another location
to fulfill the request, and sets the value of the hasChanged variable to
true if the request was redirected; otherwise hasChanged is set to **false**.

```
[Visual Basic]
Dim hasChanged As Boolean = _
    (req.RequestUri.ToString() <> req.Address.ToString())

[C#]
bool hasChanged = (req.RequestUri != req.Address);

[JScript]
var hasChanged : Boolean = (req.RequestUri.ToString() !=
req.Address.ToString())
```

Requirements

Platforms: Windows 98, Windows NT 4.0,
Windows Millennium Edition, Windows 2000,
Windows XP Home Edition, Windows XP Professional,
Windows .NET Server family,
.NET Compact Framework - Windows CE .NET,
Common Language Infrastructure (CLI) Standard

HttpWebRequest.SendChunked Property

Gets or sets a value indicating whether to send data in segments to
the Internet resource.

```
[Visual Basic]
Public Property SendChunked As Boolean
[C#]
public bool SendChunked {get; set;}
[C++]
public: __property bool get_SendChunked();
public: __property void set_SendChunked(bool);
[JScript]
public function get SendChunked() : Boolean;
public function set SendChunked(Boolean);
```

Property Value

true to send data to the Internet resource in segments; otherwise,
false. The default value is **false**.

Exceptions

Exception Type	Condition
InvalidOperation-Exception	The request has been started by calling the **GetRequestStream**, **BeginGetRequestStream**, **GetResponse**, or **BeginGetResponse** method.

Remarks

When **SendChunked** is **true**, the request sends data to the Internet
resource in segments. The Internet resource must support receiving
chunked data.

Changing the **SendChunked** property after the request has been
started by calling **GetRequestStream**, **BeginGetRequestStream**,

GetResponse, or **BeginGetResponse** method will throw an **InvalidOperationException**.

Requirements

Platforms: Windows 98, Windows NT 4.0, Windows Millennium Edition, Windows 2000, Windows XP Home Edition, Windows XP Professional, Windows .NET Server family, .NET Compact Framework - Windows CE .NET, Common Language Infrastructure (CLI) Standard

HttpWebRequest.ServicePoint Property

Gets the service point to use for the request.

```
[Visual Basic]
Public ReadOnly Property ServicePoint As ServicePoint
[C#]
public ServicePoint ServicePoint {get;}
[C++]
public: __property ServicePoint* get_ServicePoint();
[JScript]
public function get ServicePoint() : ServicePoint;
```

Property Value

A **ServicePoint** that represents the network connection to the Internet resource.

Remarks

The **ServicePoint.Address** property may be different from **HttpWebRequest.Address** if the request is redirected.

Requirements

Platforms: Windows 98, Windows NT 4.0, Windows Millennium Edition, Windows 2000, Windows XP Home Edition, Windows XP Professional, Windows .NET Server family, .NET Compact Framework - Windows CE .NET, Common Language Infrastructure (CLI) Standard

HttpWebRequest.Timeout Property

Gets or sets the time-out value for a request.

```
[Visual Basic]
Overrides Public Property Timeout As Integer
[C#]
public override int Timeout {get; set;}
[C++]
public: __property int get_Timeout();
public: __property void set_Timeout(int);
[JScript]
public override function get Timeout() : int;
public override function set Timeout(int);
```

Property Value

The number of milliseconds to wait before the request times out.

Remarks

Timeout is the number of milliseconds that a synchronous request made with the **GetResponse** method waits for a response, and the **GetRequestStream** methods waits for a stream. If a resource does not respond within the time-out period, the request throws a **WebException** with the **Status** property set to **WebExceptionStatus.Timeout**.

The **Timeout** property has no effect on asynchronous requests made with the **BeginGetResponse** or **BeginGetRequestStream** methods.

> **CAUTION** In the case of asynchronous requests, it is the responsibility of the client application to implement its own timeout mechanism. Refer to the example in the **BeginGetResponse** method.

Example

[Visual Basic, C#, C++] The following example sets the **Timeout** property of the **HttpWebRequest** instance.

```
[Visual Basic]
' Create a new 'HttpWebRequest' Object to the mentioned URL.
    Dim myHttpWebRequest As HttpWebRequest =          ┘
CType(WebRequest.Create("http://www.contoso.com"), HttpWebRequest)
    Console.WriteLine(ControlChars.Cr + "The timeout       ┘
time of the request before setting the property is {0}    ┘
milliSeconds", myHttpWebRequest.Timeout)
    ' Set the 'Timeout' property of the HttpWebRequest
to 10 milli seconds.
    myHttpWebRequest.Timeout = 10
    ' Display the 'Timeout' property of the               ┘
'HttpWebRequest' on the console.
    Console.WriteLine(ControlChars.Cr + "The timeout       ┘
time of the request after setting the timeout is {0}     ┘
milliSeconds", myHttpWebRequest.Timeout)
    ' A HttpWebResponse object is created and is           ┘
GetResponse Property of the HttpWebRequest associated with it
    Dim myHttpWebResponse As HttpWebResponse =            ┘
CType(myHttpWebRequest.GetResponse(), HttpWebResponse)

[C#]
// Create a new 'HttpWebRequest' Object to the mentioned URL.
HttpWebRequest myHttpWebRequest=(HttpWebRequest)WebRequest.Create  ┘
("http://www.contoso.com");
Console.WriteLine("\nThe timeout time of the request before
setting the property is {0} milliSeconds.",myHttpWebRequest.Timeout);
// Set the 'Timeout' property of the HttpWebRequest to 10 milli   ┘
seconds.
myHttpWebRequest.Timeout=10;
// Display the 'Timeout' property of the 'HttpWebRequest' on the  ┘
console.
Console.WriteLine("\nThe timeout time of the request after
setting the timeout is {0}  milliSeconds.",myHttpWebRequest.Timeout);
// A HttpWebResponse object is created and is GetResponse          ┘
Property of the HttpWebRequest associated with it
HttpWebResponse
myHttpWebResponse=(HttpWebResponse)myHttpWebRequest.GetResponse();

[C++]
// Create a new 'HttpWebRequest' Object to the mentioned URL.
HttpWebRequest* myHttpWebRequest =
    dynamic_cast<HttpWebRequest*>(WebRequest::Create        ┘
(S"http://www.contoso.com"));
Console::WriteLine(S"\nThe time->Item[Out] time* of         ┘
the request before setting the property is {0}  milliSeconds.",
    __box(myHttpWebRequest->Timeout));
// Set the 'Timeout' property of the HttpWebRequest to       ┘
10 milli seconds.
myHttpWebRequest->Timeout = 10;
// Display the 'Timeout' property of the 'HttpWebRequest'    ┘
on the console.
Console::WriteLine(S"\nThe timeout time of the request       ┘
after setting the timeout is {0}  milliSeconds.",
    __box(myHttpWebRequest->Timeout));
// A HttpWebResponse Object* is created and is GetResponse   ┘
Property of the HttpWebRequest associated with it
HttpWebResponse* myHttpWebResponse =
    dynamic_cast<HttpWebResponse*>(myHttpWebRequest->GetResponse());
```

Requirements

Platforms: Windows 98, Windows NT 4.0,
Windows Millennium Edition, Windows 2000,
Windows XP Home Edition, Windows XP Professional,
Windows .NET Server family,
.NET Compact Framework - Windows CE .NET,
Common Language Infrastructure (CLI) Standard

HttpWebRequest.TransferEncoding Property

Gets or sets the value of the **Transfer-encoding** HTTP header.

```
[Visual Basic]
Public Property TransferEncoding As String
[C#]
public string TransferEncoding {get; set;}
[C++]
public: __property String* get_TransferEncoding();
public: __property void set_TransferEncoding(String*);
[JScript]
public function get TransferEncoding() : String;
public function set TransferEncoding(String);
```

Property Value

The value of the **Transfer-encoding** HTTP header. The default
value is a null reference (**Nothing** in Visual Basic).

Exceptions

Exception Type	Condition
InvalidOperation-Exception	**TransferEncoding** is set when **SendChunked** is **false**.
ArgumentException	**TransferEncoding** is set to the value "Chunked".

Remarks

Before you can set the **TransferEncoding** property, you must first
set the **SendChunked** property to **true**. Clearing **TransferEncoding**
by setting it to a null reference (**Nothing** in Visual Basic) has no
effect on the value of **SendChunked**.

Values assigned to the **TransferEncoding** property replace any
existing contents.

Requirements

Platforms: Windows 98, Windows NT 4.0,
Windows Millennium Edition, Windows 2000,
Windows XP Home Edition, Windows XP Professional,
Windows .NET Server family,
.NET Compact Framework - Windows CE .NET,
Common Language Infrastructure (CLI) Standard

HttpWebRequest.UnsafeAuthenticated-ConnectionSharing Property

Note: This namespace, class, or member is supported only in
version 1.1 of the .NET Framework.

Gets or sets a value indicating whether to allow high-speed NTLM-
authenticated connection sharing.

```
[Visual Basic]
Public Property UnsafeAuthenticatedConnectionSharing As Boolean
[C#]
public bool UnsafeAuthenticatedConnectionSharing {get; set;}
```

```
[C++]
public: __property bool get_UnsafeAuthenticatedConnectionSharing();
public: __property void
set_UnsafeAuthenticatedConnectionSharing(bool);
[JScript]
public function get UnsafeAuthenticatedConnectionSharing() : Boolean;
public function set UnsafeAuthenticatedConnectionSharing(Boolean);
```

Property Value

true, to keep the authenticated connection open; otherwise, **false**.

Remarks

The default value for this property is **false**, which causes the current
connection to be closed after a request is completed. Your
application must go through the authentication sequence every time
it issues a new request.

If this property is set to **true**, the connection used to retrieve the
response remains open after the authentication sequence has been
performed. In this case, other requests that have this property set to
true may use the connection without repeating the authentication
sequence. In other words, if a connection has been authenticated for
user A, user B can use the same connection using the credentials of
user A.

Caution[note] Because it is possible for an application to use the
connection without being authenticated, you need to be sure that
there is no security breach in your system when setting this property
to **true**.

You may want to consider enabling this mechanism if your are
having performance problems and your application is running on a
Web server with Windows Integrated Authentication.

Enabling this setting opens the system to security risks. If you set the
UnsafeAuthenticatedConnectionSharing to **true** be sure to take
the following precautions:

- Use the **ConnectionGroupName** to manage connections for
  different users. This avoids the potential use of the connection by
  non-authenticated applications.

- Run your application in a protected environment to avoid
  possible connection exploits.

If you control the back-end server, as an alternative you might
consider turning off the authentication persistence. This will
increase the perfomance to a lesser degree but it is safer. For more
details, search for AuthPersistence in the MSDN library.

Requirements

Platforms: Windows 98, Windows NT 4.0,
Windows Millennium Edition, Windows 2000,
Windows XP Home Edition, Windows XP Professional,
Windows .NET Server family

.NET Framework Security:

- **WebPermission** Unrestricted Web permission is required to set
  this property.

HttpWebRequest.UserAgent Property

Gets or sets the value of the **User-agent** HTTP header.

```
[Visual Basic]
Public Property UserAgent As String
[C#]
public string UserAgent {get; set;}
```

```
[C++]
public: __property String* get_UserAgent();
public: __property void set_UserAgent(String*);
[JScript]
public function get UserAgent() : String;
public function set UserAgent(String);
```

Property Value

The value of the **User-agent** HTTP header. The default value is a null reference (**Nothing** in Visual Basic).

Requirements

Platforms: Windows 98, Windows NT 4.0,
Windows Millennium Edition, Windows 2000,
Windows XP Home Edition, Windows XP Professional,
Windows .NET Server family,
.NET Compact Framework - Windows CE .NET,
Common Language Infrastructure (CLI) Standard

HttpWebRequest.Abort Method

Cancels a request to an Internet resource.

```
[Visual Basic]
Overrides Public Sub Abort()
[C#]
public override void Abort();
[C++]
public: void Abort();
[JScript]
public override function Abort();
```

Remarks

Abort cancels a request to a resource. After a request is canceled, calling **GetResponse**, **BeginGetResponse**, **EndGetResponse**, **GetRequestStream**, **BeginGetRequestStream**, or **EndGetRequestStream** will cause a **WebException** with **Status** set to **RequestCanceled**.

Requirements

Platforms: Windows 98, Windows NT 4.0,
Windows Millennium Edition, Windows 2000,
Windows XP Home Edition, Windows XP Professional,
Windows .NET Server family,
.NET Compact Framework - Windows CE .NET,
Common Language Infrastructure (CLI) Standard

HttpWebRequest.AddRange Method

Adds a range header to the request.

Overload List

Adds a byte range header to a request for a specific range from the beginning or end of the requested data.

Supported by the .NET Compact Framework.

[Visual Basic] **Overloads Public Sub AddRange(Integer)**

[C#] **public void AddRange(int);**

[C++] **public: void AddRange(int);**

[JScript] **public function AddRange(int);**

Adds a byte range header to the request for a specified range.

Supported by the .NET Compact Framework.

[Visual Basic] **Overloads Public Sub AddRange(Integer, Integer)**

[C#] **public void AddRange(int, int);**

[C++] **public: void AddRange(int, int);**

[JScript] **public function AddRange(int, int);**

Adds a range header to a request for a specific range from the beginning or end of the requested data.

Supported by the .NET Compact Framework.

[Visual Basic] **Overloads Public Sub AddRange(String, Integer)**

[C#] **public void AddRange(string, int);**

[C++] **public: void AddRange(String*, int);**

[JScript] **public function AddRange(String, int);**

Adds a range header to a request for a specified range.

Supported by the .NET Compact Framework.

[Visual Basic] **Overloads Public Sub AddRange(String, Integer, Integer)**

[C#] **public void AddRange(string, int, int);**

[C++] **public: void AddRange(String*, int, int);**

[JScript] **public function AddRange(String, int, int);**

HttpWebRequest.AddRange Method (Int32)

Adds a byte range header to a request for a specific range from the beginning or end of the requested data.

```
[Visual Basic]
Overloads Public Sub AddRange( _
    ByVal range As Integer _
)
[C#]
public void AddRange(
    int range
);
[C++]
public: void AddRange(
    int range
);
[JScript]
public function AddRange(
    range : int
);
```

Parameters

range
    The starting or ending point of the range.

Exceptions

Exception Type	Condition
InvalidOperation-Exception	The range header could not be added.

Remarks

AddRange adds a byte range header to the request.

If *range* is positive, the range is from the start of the data to *range*.

If *range* is negative, the range is from *range* to the end of the data.

Requirements

Platforms: Windows 98, Windows NT 4.0,
Windows Millennium Edition, Windows 2000,
Windows XP Home Edition, Windows XP Professional,
Windows .NET Server family,
.NET Compact Framework - Windows CE .NET,
Common Language Infrastructure (CLI) Standard

HttpWebRequest.AddRange Method (Int32, Int32)

Adds a byte range header to the request for a specified range.

```
[Visual Basic]
Overloads Public Sub AddRange( _
   ByVal from As Integer, _
   ByVal to As Integer _
)
[C#]
public void AddRange(
   int from,
   int to
);
[C++]
public: void AddRange(
   int from,
   int to
);
[JScript]
public function AddRange(
   from : int,
   to : int
);
```

Parameters
from
   The position at which to start sending data.
to
   The position at which to stop sending data.

Exceptions

Exception Type	Condition
ArgumentOutOfRange-Exception	*from* is greater than *to* -or- *from* or *to* is less than 0.
InvalidOperation-Exception	The range header could not be added.

Remarks

AddRange adds a byte range header to the request.

Requirements

Platforms: Windows 98, Windows NT 4.0,
Windows Millennium Edition, Windows 2000,
Windows XP Home Edition, Windows XP Professional,
Windows .NET Server family,
.NET Compact Framework - Windows CE .NET,
Common Language Infrastructure (CLI) Standard

HttpWebRequest.AddRange Method (String, Int32)

Adds a range header to a request for a specific range from the beginning or end of the requested data.

```
[Visual Basic]
Overloads Public Sub AddRange( _
   ByVal rangeSpecifier As String, _
   ByVal range As Integer _
)
[C#]
public void AddRange(
   string rangeSpecifier,
   int range
);
[C++]
public: void AddRange(
   String* rangeSpecifier,
   int range
);
[JScript]
public function AddRange(
   rangeSpecifier : String,
   range : int
);
```

Parameters
rangeSpecifier
   The description of the range.
range
   The starting or ending point of the range.

Exceptions

Exception Type	Condition
ArgumentNullException	*rangeSpecifier* is a null reference (**Nothing** in Visual Basic).
ArgumentException	*rangeSpecifier* is invalid.
InvalidOperation-Exception	The range header could not be added.

Remarks

If *range* is positive, the range is from the start of the data to *range*.

If *range* is negative, the range is from *range* to the end of the data.

Requirements

Platforms: Windows 98, Windows NT 4.0,
Windows Millennium Edition, Windows 2000,
Windows XP Home Edition, Windows XP Professional,
Windows .NET Server family,
.NET Compact Framework - Windows CE .NET,
Common Language Infrastructure (CLI) Standard

HttpWebRequest.AddRange Method (String, Int32, Int32)

Adds a range header to a request for a specified range.

```
[Visual Basic]
Overloads Public Sub AddRange( _
   ByVal rangeSpecifier As String, _
   ByVal from As Integer, _
   ByVal to As Integer _
)
```

```
[C#]
public void AddRange(
   string rangeSpecifier,
   int from,
   int to
);
[C++]
public: void AddRange(
   String* rangeSpecifier,
   int from,
   int to
);
[JScript]
public function AddRange(
   rangeSpecifier : String,
   from : int,
   to : int
);
```

Parameters
rangeSpecifier
   The description of the range.
from
   The position at which to start sending data.
to
   The position at which to stop sending data.

Exceptions

Exception Type	Condition
ArgumentNullException	*rangeSpecifier* is a null reference (**Nothing** in Visual Basic).
ArgumentOutOfRange-Exception	*from* is greater than *to* -or- *from* or *to* is less than 0.
ArgumentException	*rangeSpecifier* is invalid.
InvalidOperation-Exception	The range header could not be added.

Requirements
Platforms: Windows 98, Windows NT 4.0, Windows Millennium Edition, Windows 2000, Windows XP Home Edition, Windows XP Professional, Windows .NET Server family, .NET Compact Framework - Windows CE .NET, Common Language Infrastructure (CLI) Standard

HttpWebRequest.BeginGetRequestStream Method

Begins an asynchronous request for a **Stream** instance to use to write data.

```
[Visual Basic]
Overrides Public Function BeginGetRequestStream( _
   ByVal callback As AsyncCallback, _
   ByVal state As Object _
) As IAsyncResult
[C#]
public override IAsyncResult BeginGetRequestStream(
   AsyncCallback callback,
   object state
);
```

```
[C++]
public: IAsyncResult* BeginGetRequestStream(
   AsyncCallback* callback,
   Object* state
);
[JScript]
public override function BeginGetRequestStream(
   callback : AsyncCallback,
   state : Object
) : IAsyncResult;
```

Parameters
callback
   The **AsyncCallback** delegate.
state
   The state object for this request.

Return Value
An **IAsyncResult** that references the asynchronous request.

Exceptions

Exception Type	Condition
ProtocolViolation-Exception	The **Method** property is GET or HEAD. -or- **KeepAlive** is **true**, **AllowWriteStreamBuffering** is **false**, **ContentLength** is -1, **SendChunked** is **false**, and **Method** is POST or PUT.
InvalidOperation-Exception	The stream is being used by a previous call to **BeginGetRequestStream** -or- **TransferEncoding** is set to a value and **SendChunked** is **false**.
WebException	**Abort** was previously called.

Remarks
The **BeginGetRequestStream** method starts an asynchronous request for a stream used to send data for the **HttpWebRequest**. The asynchronous callback method uses the **EndGetRequestStream** method to return the actual stream.

Requirements
Platforms: Windows 98, Windows NT 4.0, Windows Millennium Edition, Windows 2000, Windows XP Home Edition, Windows XP Professional, Windows .NET Server family, .NET Compact Framework - Windows CE .NET, Common Language Infrastructure (CLI) Standard

HttpWebRequest.BeginGetResponse Method

Begins an asynchronous request to an Internet resource.

```
[Visual Basic]
Overrides Public Function BeginGetResponse( _
   ByVal callback As AsyncCallback, _
   ByVal state As Object _
) As IAsyncResult
```

```
[C#]
public override IAsyncResult BeginGetResponse(
   AsyncCallback callback,
   object state
);
[C++]
public: IAsyncResult* BeginGetResponse(
   AsyncCallback* callback,
   Object* state
);
[JScript]
public override function BeginGetResponse(
   callback : AsyncCallback,
   state : Object
) : IAsyncResult;
```

Parameters

callback
   The **AsyncCallback** delegate
state
   The state object for this request.

Return Value

An **IAsyncResult** that references the asynchronous request for a response.

Exceptions

Exception Type	Condition
InvalidOperation-Exception	The stream is already in use by a previous call to **BeginGetResponse**
	-or-
	TransferEncoding is set to a value and **SendChunked** is **false**.
ProtocolViolation-Exception	**Method** is GET or HEAD, and either **ContentLength** is greater than zero or **SendChunked** is **true**.
	-or-
	KeepAlive is **true**, **AllowWriteStreamBuffering** is **false**, and either **ContentLength** is -1, **SendChunked** is **false** and **Method** is POST or PUT.
WebException	**Abort** was previously called.

Remarks

The **BeginGetResponse** method starts an asynchronous request for a response from the Internet resource. The asynchronous callback method uses the **EndGetResponse** method to return the actual **WebResponse**.

Requirements

Platforms: Windows 98, Windows NT 4.0, Windows Millennium Edition, Windows 2000, Windows XP Home Edition, Windows XP Professional, Windows .NET Server family, .NET Compact Framework - Windows CE .NET, Common Language Infrastructure (CLI) Standard

HttpWebRequest.EndGetRequestStream Method

Ends an asynchronous request for a **Stream** instance to use to write data.

```
[Visual Basic]
Overrides Public Function EndGetRequestStream( _
   ByVal asyncResult As IAsyncResult _
) As Stream
[C#]
public override Stream EndGetRequestStream(
   IAsyncResult asyncResult
);
[C++]
public: Stream* EndGetRequestStream(
   IAsyncResult* asyncResult
);
[JScript]
public override function EndGetRequestStream(
   asyncResult : IAsyncResult
) : Stream;
```

Parameters

asyncResult
   The pending request for a stream.

Return Value

A **Stream** to use to write request data.

Exceptions

Exception Type	Condition
ArgumentNullException	*asyncResult* is a null reference (**Nothing** in Visual Basic).
IOException	The request did not complete, and no stream is available.
ArgumentException	*asyncResult* was not returned by the current instance from a call to **BeginGetRequestStream**.
InvalidOperation-Exception	This method was called previously using *asyncResult*.
WebException	**Abort** was previously called.
	-or-
	An error occurred while processing the request.

Remarks

The **EndGetRequestStream** method completes an asynchronous request for a stream that was started by the **BeginGetRequestStream** method. Once the **Stream** instance has been returned, you can send data with the **HttpWebRequest** by using the **Stream.Write** method.

Note You must set the value of the **ContentLength** property before writing data to the stream.

CAUTION You must call the **Stream.Close** method to close the stream and release the connection for reuse. Failure to close the stream will cause your application to run out of connections.

Requirements

Platforms: Windows 98, Windows NT 4.0,
Windows Millennium Edition, Windows 2000,
Windows XP Home Edition, Windows XP Professional,
Windows .NET Server family,
.NET Compact Framework - Windows CE .NET,
Common Language Infrastructure (CLI) Standard

HttpWebRequest.EndGetResponse Method

Ends an asynchronous request to an Internet resource.

```
[Visual Basic]
Overrides Public Function EndGetResponse( _
   ByVal asyncResult As IAsyncResult _
) As WebResponse
[C#]
public override WebResponse EndGetResponse(
   IAsyncResult asyncResult
);
[C++]
public: WebResponse* EndGetResponse(
   IAsyncResult* asyncResult
);
[JScript]
public override function EndGetResponse(
   asyncResult : IAsyncResult
) : WebResponse;
```

Parameters

asyncResult
    The pending request for a response.

Return Value

A **WebResponse** containing the response from the Internet resource.

Exceptions

Exception Type	Condition
ArgumentNullException	*asyncResult* is a null reference (**Nothing** in Visual Basic).
InvalidOperation-Exception	This method was called previously using *asyncResult*.
	-or-
	The **ContentLength** property is greater than 0 but the data has not been written to the request stream.
WebException	**Abort** was previously called.
	-or-
	An error occurred while processing the request.
ArgumentException	*asyncResult* was not returned by the current instance from a call to **BeginGetResponse**.

Remarks

The **EndGetResponse** method completes an asynchronous request for an Internet resource that was started by calling **BeginGetResponse**.

> **CAUTION** You must call the **Close** method to close the stream and release the connection. Failure to do so may cause your application to run out of connections.

Requirements

Platforms: Windows 98, Windows NT 4.0,
Windows Millennium Edition, Windows 2000,
Windows XP Home Edition, Windows XP Professional,
Windows .NET Server family,
.NET Compact Framework - Windows CE .NET,
Common Language Infrastructure (CLI) Standard

HttpWebRequest.GetHashCode Method

Gets the hash code for this **HttpWebRequest**.

```
[Visual Basic]
Overrides Public Function GetHashCode() As Integer
[C#]
public override int GetHashCode();
[C++]
public: int GetHashCode();
[JScript]
public override function GetHashCode() : int;
```

Return Value

The hash code for the **HttpWebRequest**.

Remarks

The hash codes for **HttpWebRequest** A and B are guaranteed to be the same when A.Equals(B) is **true**.

This method implements the **Object.GetHashCode**.

Requirements

Platforms: Windows 98, Windows NT 4.0,
Windows Millennium Edition, Windows 2000,
Windows XP Home Edition, Windows XP Professional,
Windows .NET Server family,
.NET Compact Framework - Windows CE .NET,
Common Language Infrastructure (CLI) Standard

HttpWebRequest.GetRequestStream Method

Gets a **Stream** instance to use to write request data.

```
[Visual Basic]
Overrides Public Function GetRequestStream() As Stream
[C#]
public override Stream GetRequestStream();
[C++]
public: Stream* GetRequestStream();
[JScript]
public override function GetRequestStream() : Stream;
```

Return Value

A **Stream** to use to write request data.

Exceptions

Exception Type	Condition
ProtocolViolation-Exception	The **Method** property is GET or HEAD.
	-or-
	KeepAlive is **true**, **AllowWriteStreamBuffering** is **false**, **ContentLength** is -1, **SendChunked** is **false**, and **Method** is POST or PUT.
InvalidOperation-Exception	The **GetRequestStream** method is called more than once.
	-or-
	TransferEncoding is set to a value and **SendChunked** is **false**.
WebException	**Abort** was previously called.
	-or-
	The time-out period for the request expired.
	-or-
	An error occurred while processing the request.

Remarks

The **GetRequestStream** method returns a stream to use to send data for the **HttpWebRequest**. Once the **Stream** instance has been returned, you can send data with the **HttpWebRequest** by using the **Stream.Write** method.

> **Note** You must set the value of the **ContentLength** property before writing data to the stream.

> **CAUTION** You must call the **Stream.Close** method to close the stream and release the connection for reuse. Failure to close the stream will cause your application to run out of connections.

Requirements

Platforms: Windows 98, Windows NT 4.0, Windows Millennium Edition, Windows 2000, Windows XP Home Edition, Windows XP Professional, Windows .NET Server family, .NET Compact Framework - Windows CE .NET, Common Language Infrastructure (CLI) Standard

HttpWebRequest.GetResponse Method

Returns a response from an Internet resource.

```
[Visual Basic]
Overrides Public Function GetResponse() As WebResponse
[C#]
public override WebResponse GetResponse();
[C++]
public: WebResponse* GetResponse();
[JScript]
public override function GetResponse() : WebResponse;
```

Return Value

A **WebResponse** containing the response from the Internet resource.

Exceptions

Exception Type	Condition
InvalidOperation-Exception	The stream is already in use by a previous call to **BeginGetResponse**.
	-or-
	TransferEncoding is set to a value and **SendChunked** is **false**.
ProtocolViolation-Exception	**Method** is GET or HEAD, and either **ContentLength** is greater or equal to zero or **SendChunked** is **true**.
	-or-
	KeepAlive is **true**, **AllowWriteStreamBuffering** is **false**, **ContentLength** is -1, **SendChunked** is **false**, and **Method** is POST or PUT.
WebException	**Abort** was previously called.
	-or-
	The time-out period for the request expired.
	-or-
	An error occurred while processing the request.

Remarks

The **GetResponse** method returns a **WebResponse** instance containing the response from the Internet resource. The actual instance returned is an instance of **HttpWebResponse**, and can be typecast to that class to access HTTP-specific properties.

> **CAUTION** You must call the **Close** method to close the stream and release the connection. Failure to do so may cause your application to run out of connections.

Requirements

Platforms: Windows 98, Windows NT 4.0, Windows Millennium Edition, Windows 2000, Windows XP Home Edition, Windows XP Professional, Windows .NET Server family, .NET Compact Framework - Windows CE .NET, Common Language Infrastructure (CLI) Standard

HttpWebRequest.ISerializable.GetObjectData Method

Populates a **SerializationInfo** with the data needed to serialize the target object.

```
[Visual Basic]
Private Sub GetObjectData( _
   ByVal serializationInfo As SerializationInfo, _
   ByVal streamingContext As StreamingContext _
) Implements ISerializable.GetObjectData
[C#]
void ISerializable.GetObjectData(
   SerializationInfo serializationInfo,
   StreamingContext streamingContext
);
```

```
[C++]
private: void ISerializable::GetObjectData(
   SerializationInfo* serializationInfo,
   StreamingContext streamingContext
);
[JScript]
private function ISerializable.GetObjectData(
   serializationInfo : SerializationInfo,
   streamingContext : StreamingContext
);
```

Parameters

serializationInfo

   The **SerializationInfo** to populate with data.

streamingContext

   The destination (see **StreamingContext**) for this serialization.

Implements

ISerializable.GetObjectData

Remarks

Any objects included in the **SerializationInfo** are automatically tracked and serialized by the formatter.

Requirements

Platforms: Windows 98, Windows NT 4.0, Windows Millennium Edition, Windows 2000, Windows XP Home Edition, Windows XP Professional, Windows .NET Server family

HttpWebResponse Class

Provides an HTTP-specific implementation of the **WebResponse** class.

System.Object
  System.MarshalByRefObject
    System.Net.WebResponse
      System.Net.HttpWebResponse

```
[Visual Basic]
<Serializable>
Public Class HttpWebResponse
    Inherits WebResponse
[C#]
[Serializable]
public class HttpWebResponse : WebResponse
[C++]
[Serializable]
public __gc class HttpWebResponse : public WebResponse
[JScript]
public
    Serializable
class HttpWebResponse extends WebResponse
```

Thread Safety

Any public static (**Shared** in Visual Basic) members of this type are safe for multithreaded operations. Any instance members are not guaranteed to be thread safe.

Remarks

This class contains support for HTTP-specific uses of the properties and methods of the **WebResponse** class. The **HttpWebResponse** class is used to build HTTP stand-alone client applications which send HTTP requests and receive HTTP responses.

> **Note** Do not confuse **HttpWebResponse** with the **HttpResponse** which is used in ASP.NET applications and whose methods and properties are exposed through the ASP.NET's intrinsic **HttpResponse** object.

You should never directly create an instance of the **HttpWebResponse** class. Instead, use the instance returned by a call to **HttpWebRequest.GetResponse**.

Common header information returned from the Internet resource is exposed as properties of the class. See the following table for a complete list. Other headers can be read from the **Headers** property as name/value pairs.

The following table shows the common HTTP headers that are available through properties of the **HttpWebResponse** class.

Header	Property
Content-Encoding	**ContentEncoding**
Content-Length	**ContentLength**
Content-Type	**ContentType**
Last-Modified	**LastModified**
Server	**Server**

The contents of the response from the Internet resource are returned as a **Stream** by calling the **GetResponseStream** method.

Example

[Visual Basic, C#, JScript] The following example returns an **HttpWebResponse** from an **HttpWebRequest**:

```
[Visual Basic]
Dim HttpWReq As HttpWebRequest = _
    CType(WebRequest.Create("http://www.contoso.com"), HttpWebRequest)

Dim HttpWResp As HttpWebResponse = _
    CType(HttpWReq.GetResponse(), HttpWebResponse)
' Insert code that uses the response object.
HttpWResp.Close()
```

```
[C#]
HttpWebRequest HttpWReq =
(HttpWebRequest)WebRequest.Create("http://www.contoso.com");

HttpWebResponse HttpWResp = (HttpWebResponse)HttpWReq.GetResponse();
// Insert code that uses the response object.
HttpWResp.Close();
```

```
[JScript]
var httpWReq : HttpWebRequest =
HttpWebRequest(WebRequest.Create("http://www.contoso.com"))

var httpWResp : HttpWebResponse =
HttpWebResponse(httpWReq.GetResponse())
// Insert code to use response object.
httpWResp.Close()
```

Requirements

Namespace: System.Net

Platforms: Windows 98, Windows NT 4.0, Windows Millennium Edition, Windows 2000, Windows XP Home Edition, Windows XP Professional, Windows .NET Server family, .NET Compact Framework - Windows CE .NET

Assembly: System (in System.dll)

HttpWebResponse Constructor

Initializes a new instance of the **HttpWebResponse** class from the specified **SerializationInfo** and **StreamingContext** instances.

```
[Visual Basic]
Protected Sub New( _
    ByVal serializationInfo As SerializationInfo, _
    ByVal streamingContext As StreamingContext _
)
[C#]
protected HttpWebResponse(
    SerializationInfo serializationInfo,
    StreamingContext streamingContext
);
[C++]
protected: HttpWebResponse(
    SerializationInfo* serializationInfo,
    StreamingContext streamingContext
);
[JScript]
protected function HttpWebResponse(
    serializationInfo : SerializationInfo,
    streamingContext : StreamingContext
);
```

Parameters

serializationInfo

A **SerializationInfo** containing the information required to serialize the new **HttpWebRequest**.

streamingContext

A **StreamingContext** containing the source of the serialized stream associated with the new **HttpWebRequest**.

Remarks

This constructor implements the **ISerializable** interface for the **HttpWebRequest** class.

Requirements

Platforms: Windows 98, Windows NT 4.0, Windows Millennium Edition, Windows 2000, Windows XP Home Edition, Windows XP Professional, Windows .NET Server family

HttpWebResponse.CharacterSet Property

Gets the character set of the response.

```
[Visual Basic]
Public ReadOnly Property CharacterSet As String
[C#]
public string CharacterSet {get;}
[C++]
public: __property String* get_CharacterSet();
[JScript]
public function get CharacterSet() : String;
```

Property Value

A string containing the character set of the response.

Exceptions

Exception Type	Condition
ObjectDisposedException	The current instance has been disposed.

Remarks

The **CharacterSet** property contains a value describing the character set of the response. This character set information is taken from the header returned with the response.

Example

[Visual Basic, C#, C++] The following example obtains the character set of the response.

```
[Visual Basic]
Try
    Dim myHttpWebRequest As HttpWebRequest =
CType(WebRequest.Create(url), HttpWebRequest)
    Dim myHttpWebResponse As HttpWebResponse =
CType(myHttpWebRequest.GetResponse(), HttpWebResponse)

    Console.WriteLine(("The encoding method used is: " +
myHttpWebResponse.ContentEncoding))
    Console.WriteLine(("The character set used is :" +
myHttpWebResponse.CharacterSet))

    Dim seperator As Char = "/"c
    Dim contenttype As [String] = myHttpWebResponse.ContentType
    ' Retrieve 'text' if the content type is of 'text/html.
    Dim maintype As [String] = contenttype.Substring(0,
contenttype.IndexOf(seperator))
    ' Display only 'text' type.
    If [String].Compare(maintype, "text") = 0 Then
        Console.WriteLine(ControlChars.NewLine + " Content
type is 'text'.")
```

```
[C#]
try
    {
        HttpWebRequest myHttpWebRequest =
    (HttpWebRequest)WebRequest.Create(url);
        HttpWebResponse myHttpWebResponse =
    (HttpWebResponse)myHttpWebRequest.GetResponse();

        Console.WriteLine("The encoding method used is: " +
    myHttpWebResponse.ContentEncoding);
        Console.WriteLine("The character set used is :" +
    myHttpWebResponse.CharacterSet);

        char seperator = '/';
        String contenttype = myHttpWebResponse.ContentType;
        // Retrieve 'text' if the content type is of 'text/html.
        String maintype =
    contenttype.Substring(0,contenttype.IndexOf(seperator));
        // Display only 'text' type.
        if (String.Compare(maintype,"text") == 0)
            {
                Console.WriteLine("\n Content type is 'text'.");
```

```
[C++]
try {
    HttpWebRequest* myHttpWebRequest =
        dynamic_cast<HttpWebRequest*>(WebRequest::Create(url));
    HttpWebResponse* myHttpWebResponse =
        dynamic_cast<HttpWebResponse*>(myHttpWebRequest->GetResponse());

    Console::WriteLine(S"The encoding method used is: {0}",
        myHttpWebResponse->ContentEncoding);
    Console::WriteLine(S"The character set used is : {0}",
        myHttpWebResponse->CharacterSet);

    char seperator = '/';
    String* contenttype = myHttpWebResponse->ContentType;
    // Retrieve 'text' if the content type is of 'text/html.
    String* maintype = contenttype->Substring(0, contenttype-
>IndexOf(seperator));
    // Display only 'text' type.
    if (String::Compare(maintype, S"text") == 0) {
        Console::WriteLine(S"\n Content type is 'text'.");
```

Requirements

Platforms: Windows 98, Windows NT 4.0, Windows Millennium Edition, Windows 2000, Windows XP Home Edition, Windows XP Professional, Windows .NET Server family, .NET Compact Framework - Windows CE .NET, Common Language Infrastructure (CLI) Standard

HttpWebResponse.ContentEncoding Property

Gets the method used to encode the body of the response.

```
[Visual Basic]
Public ReadOnly Property ContentEncoding As String
[C#]
public string ContentEncoding {get;}
[C++]
public: __property String* get_ContentEncoding();
[JScript]
public function get ContentEncoding() : String;
```

Property Value

A string describing the method used to encode the body of the response.

Exceptions

Exception Type	Condition
ObjectDisposedException	The current instance has been disposed.

Remarks

The **ContentEncoding** property contains the value of the Content-Encoding header returned with the response.

Example

[Visual Basic, C#, C++] The following example uses the **ContentEncoding** property to obtain the value of the Content-Encoding header returned with the response.

```
[Visual Basic]
Try
    Dim myHttpWebRequest As HttpWebRequest =
CType(WebRequest.Create(url), HttpWebRequest)
    Dim myHttpWebResponse As HttpWebResponse =
CType(myHttpWebRequest.GetResponse(), HttpWebResponse)

    Console.WriteLine(("The encoding method used is: " +
myHttpWebResponse.ContentEncoding))
    Console.WriteLine(("The character set used is :" +
myHttpWebResponse.CharacterSet))

    Dim seperator As Char = "/"c
    Dim contenttype As [String] = myHttpWebResponse.ContentType
    ' Retrieve 'text' if the content type is of 'text/html.
    Dim maintype As [String] = contenttype.Substring(0,
contenttype.IndexOf(seperator))
    ' Display only 'text' type.
    If [String].Compare(maintype, "text") = 0 Then
        Console.WriteLine(ControlChars.NewLine + " Content
type is 'text'.")
```

```
[C#]
try
    {
        HttpWebRequest myHttpWebRequest =
(HttpWebRequest)WebRequest.Create(url);
        HttpWebResponse myHttpWebResponse =
(HttpWebResponse)myHttpWebRequest.GetResponse();

        Console.WriteLine("The encoding method used is: " +
myHttpWebResponse.ContentEncoding);
        Console.WriteLine("The character set used is :" +
myHttpWebResponse.CharacterSet);

        char seperator = '/';
        String contenttype = myHttpWebResponse.ContentType;
        // Retrieve 'text' if the content type is of 'text/html.
        String maintype =
contenttype.Substring(0,contenttype.IndexOf(seperator));
        // Display only 'text' type.
        if (String.Compare(maintype,"text") == 0)
            {
                Console.WriteLine("\n Content type is 'text'.");
```

```
[C++]
try {
    HttpWebRequest* myHttpWebRequest =
        dynamic_cast<HttpWebRequest*>(WebRequest::Create(url));
    HttpWebResponse* myHttpWebResponse =
        dynamic_cast<HttpWebResponse*>(myHttpWebRequest->GetResponse());

    Console::WriteLine(S"The encoding method used is: {0}",
        myHttpWebResponse->ContentEncoding);
    Console::WriteLine(S"The character set used is : {0}",
        myHttpWebResponse->CharacterSet);
```

```
    char seperator = '/';
    String* contenttype = myHttpWebResponse->ContentType;
    // Retrieve 'text' if the content type is of 'text/html.
    String* maintype = contenttype->Substring(0, contenttype-
>IndexOf(seperator));
    // Display only 'text' type.
    if (String::Compare(maintype, S"text") == 0) {
        Console::WriteLine(S"\n Content type is 'text'.");
```

Requirements

Platforms: Windows 98, Windows NT 4.0, Windows Millennium Edition, Windows 2000, Windows XP Home Edition, Windows XP Professional, Windows .NET Server family, .NET Compact Framework - Windows CE .NET, Common Language Infrastructure (CLI) Standard

HttpWebResponse.ContentLength Property

Gets the length of the content returned by the request.

```
[Visual Basic]
Overrides Public ReadOnly Property ContentLength As Long
[C#]
public override long ContentLength {get;}
[C++]
public: __property __int64 get_ContentLength();
[JScript]
public override function get ContentLength() : long;
```

Property Value

The number of bytes returned by the request. Content length does not include header information.

Exceptions

Exception Type	Condition
ObjectDisposedException	The current instance has been disposed.

Remarks

The **ContentLength** property contains the value of the Content-Length header returned with the response. If the Content-Length header is not set in the response, **ContentLength** is set to the value -1.

Requirements

Platforms: Windows 98, Windows NT 4.0, Windows Millennium Edition, Windows 2000, Windows XP Home Edition, Windows XP Professional, Windows .NET Server family, .NET Compact Framework - Windows CE .NET, Common Language Infrastructure (CLI) Standard

HttpWebResponse.ContentType Property

Gets the content type of the response.

```
[Visual Basic]
Overrides Public ReadOnly Property ContentType As String
[C#]
public override string ContentType {get;}
[C++]
public: __property String* get_ContentType();
[JScript]
public override function get ContentType() : String;
```

Property Value

A string containing the content type of the response.

Exceptions

Exception Type	Condition
ObjectDisposedException	The current instance has been disposed.

Remarks

The **ContentType** property contains the value of the Content-Type header returned with the response.

Requirements

Platforms: Windows 98, Windows NT 4.0, Windows Millennium Edition, Windows 2000, Windows XP Home Edition, Windows XP Professional, Windows .NET Server family, .NET Compact Framework - Windows CE .NET, Common Language Infrastructure (CLI) Standard

HttpWebResponse.Cookies Property

Gets or sets the cookies associated with this request.

```
[Visual Basic]
Public Property Cookies As CookieCollection
[C#]
public CookieCollection Cookies {get; set;}
[C++]
public: __property CookieCollection* get_Cookies();
public: __property void set_Cookies(CookieCollection*);
[JScript]
public function get Cookies() : CookieCollection;
public function set Cookies(CookieCollection);
```

Property Value

A **CookieCollection** containing the cookies associated with this request.

Remarks

The **Cookies** property provides an instance of the **CookieCollection** class holding the cookies associated with this response.

If the **CookieContainer** property of the associated **HttpWebRequest** is a null reference (**Nothing** in Visual Basic), the **Cookies** property will also be a null reference (**Nothing**). Any cookie information sent by the server will be available in the **Headers** property, however.

Requirements

Platforms: Windows 98, Windows NT 4.0, Windows Millennium Edition, Windows 2000, Windows XP Home Edition, Windows XP Professional, Windows .NET Server family

HttpWebResponse.Headers Property

Gets the headers associated with this response from the server.

```
[Visual Basic]
Overrides Public ReadOnly Property Headers As WebHeaderCollection
[C#]
public override WebHeaderCollection Headers {get;}
```

```
[C++]
public: __property WebHeaderCollection* get_Headers();
[JScript]
public override function get Headers() : WebHeaderCollection;
```

Property Value

A **WebHeaderCollection** containing the header information returned with the response.

Exceptions

Exception Type	Condition
ObjectDisposedException	The current instance has been disposed.

Remarks

The **Headers** property is a collection of name/value pairs containing the HTTP header values returned with the response. Common header information returned from the Internet resource is exposed as properties of the **HttpWebResponse** class. The following table lists common headers that the API exposes as properties.

Header	Property
Content-Encoding	**ContentEncoding**
Content-Length	**ContentLength**
Content-Type	**ContentType**
Last-Modified	**LastModified**
Server	**Server**

Requirements

Platforms: Windows 98, Windows NT 4.0, Windows Millennium Edition, Windows 2000, Windows XP Home Edition, Windows XP Professional, Windows .NET Server family, .NET Compact Framework - Windows CE .NET, Common Language Infrastructure (CLI) Standard

HttpWebResponse.LastModified Property

Gets the last date and time that the contents of the response were modified.

```
[Visual Basic]
Public ReadOnly Property LastModified As DateTime
[C#]
public DateTime LastModified {get;}
[C++]
public: __property DateTime get_LastModified();
[JScript]
public function get LastModified() : DateTime;
```

Property Value

A **DateTime** containing the date and time the contents of the response were modified.

Exceptions

Exception Type	Condition
ObjectDisposedException	The current instance has been disposed.

Remarks

The **LastModified** property contains the value of the Last-Modified header received with the response. The date and time are assumed to be local time.

Requirements

Platforms: Windows 98, Windows NT 4.0,
Windows Millennium Edition, Windows 2000,
Windows XP Home Edition, Windows XP Professional,
Windows .NET Server family,
.NET Compact Framework - Windows CE .NET,
Common Language Infrastructure (CLI) Standard

HttpWebResponse.Method Property

Gets the method used to return the response.

```
[Visual Basic]
Public ReadOnly Property Method As String
[C#]
public string Method {get;}
[C++]
public: __property String* get_Method();
[JScript]
public function get Method() : String;
```

Property Value

A string containing the HTTP method used to return the response.

Exceptions

Exception Type	Condition
ObjectDisposedException	The current instance has been disposed.

Remarks

Method returns the method used to return the response. Common HTTP methods are GET, HEAD, POST, PUT, and DELETE.

ORDER=0> in the upper-left corner of the page.

Requirements

Platforms: Windows 98, Windows NT 4.0,
Windows Millennium Edition, Windows 2000,
Windows XP Home Edition, Windows XP Professional,
Windows .NET Server family,
.NET Compact Framework - Windows CE .NET,
Common Language Infrastructure (CLI) Standard

HttpWebResponse.ProtocolVersion Property

Gets the version of the HTTP protocol used in the response.

```
[Visual Basic]
Public ReadOnly Property ProtocolVersion As Version
[C#]
public Version ProtocolVersion {get;}
[C++]
public: __property Version* get_ProtocolVersion();
[JScript]
public function get ProtocolVersion() : Version;
```

Property Value

A **Version** containing the HTTP protocol version of the response.

Exceptions

Exception Type	Condition
ObjectDisposedException	The current instance has been disposed.

Remarks

The **ProtocolVersion** property contains the HTTP protocol version number of the response sent by the Internet resource.

Requirements

Platforms: Windows 98, Windows NT 4.0,
Windows Millennium Edition, Windows 2000,
Windows XP Home Edition, Windows XP Professional,
Windows .NET Server family,
.NET Compact Framework - Windows CE .NET,
Common Language Infrastructure (CLI) Standard

HttpWebResponse.ResponseUri Property

Gets the URI of the Internet resource that responded to the request.

```
[Visual Basic]
Overrides Public ReadOnly Property ResponseUri As Uri
[C#]
public override Uri ResponseUri {get;}
[C++]
public: __property Uri* get_ResponseUri();
[JScript]
public override function get ResponseUri() : Uri;
```

Property Value

A **Uri** containing the URI of the Internet resource that responded to the request.

Exceptions

Exception Type	Condition
ObjectDisposedException	The current instance has been disposed.

Remarks

The **ResponseUri** property contains the URI of the Internet resource that actually responded to the request. This URI might not be the same as the originally requested URI, if the original server redirected the request.

Requirements

Platforms: Windows 98, Windows NT 4.0,
Windows Millennium Edition, Windows 2000,
Windows XP Home Edition, Windows XP Professional,
Windows .NET Server family,
.NET Compact Framework - Windows CE .NET,
Common Language Infrastructure (CLI) Standard

HttpWebResponse.Server Property

Gets the name of the server that sent the response.

```
[Visual Basic]
Public ReadOnly Property Server As String
[C#]
public string Server {get;}
[C++]
public: __property String* get_Server();
[JScript]
public function get Server() : String;
```

Property Value

A string containing the name of the server that sent the response.

Exceptions

Exception Type	Condition
ObjectDisposedException	The current instance has been disposed.

Remarks

The **Server** property contains the value of the Server header returned with the response.

Requirements

Platforms: Windows 98, Windows NT 4.0,
Windows Millennium Edition, Windows 2000,
Windows XP Home Edition, Windows XP Professional,
Windows .NET Server family,
.NET Compact Framework - Windows CE .NET,
Common Language Infrastructure (CLI) Standard

HttpWebResponse.StatusCode Property

Gets the status of the response.

```
[Visual Basic]
Public ReadOnly Property StatusCode As HttpStatusCode
[C#]
public HttpStatusCode StatusCode {get;}
[C++]
public: __property HttpStatusCode get_StatusCode();
[JScript]
public function get StatusCode() : HttpStatusCode;
```

Property Value

One of the **HttpStatusCode** values.

Exceptions

Exception Type	Condition
ObjectDisposedException	The current instance has been disposed.

Remarks

The **StatusCode** parameter is a number indicating the status of the HTTP response. The expected values for status are defined in the **HttpStatusCode** class.

Requirements

Platforms: Windows 98, Windows NT 4.0,
Windows Millennium Edition, Windows 2000,
Windows XP Home Edition, Windows XP Professional,
Windows .NET Server family,
.NET Compact Framework - Windows CE .NET,
Common Language Infrastructure (CLI) Standard

HttpWebResponse.StatusDescription Property

Gets the status description returned with the response.

```
[Visual Basic]
Public ReadOnly Property StatusDescription As String
[C#]
public string StatusDescription {get;}
[C++]
public: __property String* get_StatusDescription();
[JScript]
public function get StatusDescription() : String;
```

Property Value

A string describing the status of the response.

Exceptions

Exception Type	Condition
ObjectDisposedException	The current instance has been disposed.

Remarks

A common status message is OK.

Requirements

Platforms: Windows 98, Windows NT 4.0,
Windows Millennium Edition, Windows 2000,
Windows XP Home Edition, Windows XP Professional,
Windows .NET Server family,
.NET Compact Framework - Windows CE .NET,
Common Language Infrastructure (CLI) Standard

HttpWebResponse.Close Method

Closes the response stream.

```
[Visual Basic]
Overrides Public Sub Close()
[C#]
public override void Close();
[C++]
public: void Close();
[JScript]
public override function Close();
```

Remarks

The **Close** method closes the response stream and releases the connection to the Internet resource for reuse by other requests.

> **Note** You must call either the **Stream.Close** or the **HttpWebResponse.Close** method to close the stream and release the connection for reuse. It is not necessary to call both **Stream.Close** and **HttpWebResponse.Close**, but doing so does not cause an error. Failure to close the stream will cause your application to run out of connections.

Requirements

Platforms: Windows 98, Windows NT 4.0,
Windows Millennium Edition, Windows 2000,
Windows XP Home Edition, Windows XP Professional,
Windows .NET Server family,
.NET Compact Framework - Windows CE .NET,
Common Language Infrastructure (CLI) Standard

HttpWebResponse.Dispose Method

This member supports the .NET Framework infrastructure and is not intended to be used directly from your code.

```
[Visual Basic]
Protected Overridable Sub Dispose( _
   ByVal disposing As Boolean _
)
[C#]
protected virtual void Dispose(
   bool disposing
);
```

```
[C++]
protected: virtual void Dispose(
    bool disposing
);
[JScript]
protected function Dispose(
    disposing : Boolean
);
```

HttpWebResponse.GetHashCode Method

This member overrides **Object.GetHashCode**.

```
[Visual Basic]
Overrides Public Function GetHashCode() As Integer
[C#]
public override int GetHashCode();
[C++]
public: int GetHashCode();
[JScript]
public override function GetHashCode() : int;
```

Requirements

Platforms: Windows 98, Windows NT 4.0,
Windows Millennium Edition, Windows 2000,
Windows XP Home Edition, Windows XP Professional,
Windows .NET Server family,
.NET Compact Framework - Windows CE .NET,
Common Language Infrastructure (CLI) Standard

HttpWebResponse.GetResponseHeader Method

Gets the contents of a header that was returned with the response.

```
[Visual Basic]
Public Function GetResponseHeader( _
    ByVal headerName As String _
) As String
[C#]
public string GetResponseHeader(
    string headerName
);
[C++]
public: String* GetResponseHeader(
    String* headerName
);
[JScript]
public function GetResponseHeader(
    headerName : String
) : String;
```

Parameters

headerName
  The header value to return.

Return Value

The contents of the specified header.

Exceptions

Exception Type	Condition
ObjectDisposedException	The current instance has been disposed.

Remarks

Use **GetResponseHeader** to retrieve the contents of particular headers. You must specify which header you wish to return.

Requirements

Platforms: Windows 98, Windows NT 4.0,
Windows Millennium Edition, Windows 2000,
Windows XP Home Edition, Windows XP Professional,
Windows .NET Server family,
.NET Compact Framework - Windows CE .NET,
Common Language Infrastructure (CLI) Standard

HttpWebResponse.GetResponseStream Method

Gets the stream used to read the body of the response from the server.

```
[Visual Basic]
Overrides Public Function GetResponseStream() As Stream
[C#]
public override Stream GetResponseStream();
[C++]
public: Stream* GetResponseStream();
[JScript]
public override function GetResponseStream() : Stream;
```

Return Value

A **Stream** containing the body of the response.

Exceptions

Exception Type	Condition
ProtocolViolation- Exception	There is no response stream.
ObjectDisposedException	The current instance has been disposed.

Remarks

The **GetResponseStream** method returns the data stream from the requested Internet resource.

> **Note** You must call either the **Stream.Close** or **HttpWebResponse.Close** method to close the stream and release the connection for reuse. It is not necessary to call both **Stream.Close** and **HttpWebResponse.Close**, but doing so does not cause an error. Failure to close the stream will cause your application to run out of connections.

Requirements

Platforms: Windows 98, Windows NT 4.0,
Windows Millennium Edition, Windows 2000,
Windows XP Home Edition, Windows XP Professional,
Windows .NET Server family,
.NET Compact Framework - Windows CE .NET,
Common Language Infrastructure (CLI) Standard

HttpWebResponse.IDisposable.Dispose Method

This member supports the .NET Framework infrastructure and is not intended to be used directly from your code.

```
[Visual Basic]
Private Sub Dispose() Implements IDisposable.Dispose
[C#]
void IDisposable.Dispose();
```

```
[C++]
private: void IDisposable::Dispose();
[JScript]
private function IDisposable.Dispose();
```

HttpWebResponse.ISerializable.GetObjectData Method

This member supports the .NET Framework infrastructure and is not
intended to be used directly from your code.

```
[Visual Basic]
Private Sub GetObjectData( _
   ByVal serializationInfo As SerializationInfo, _
   ByVal streamingContext As StreamingContext _
) Implements ISerializable.GetObjectData
[C#]
void ISerializable.GetObjectData(
   SerializationInfo serializationInfo,
   StreamingContext streamingContext
);
[C++]
private: void ISerializable::GetObjectData(
   SerializationInfo* serializationInfo,
   StreamingContext streamingContext
);
[JScript]
private function ISerializable.GetObjectData(
   serializationInfo : SerializationInfo,
   streamingContext : StreamingContext
);
```

IAuthenticationModule Interface

Provides the base authentication interface for Web client authentication modules.

```
[Visual Basic]
Public Interface IAuthenticationModule
[C#]
public interface IAuthenticationModule
[C++]
public __gc __interface IAuthenticationModule
[JScript]
public interface IAuthenticationModule
```

Remarks

The **IAuthenticationModule** interface defines the properties and methods that custom authentication modules must use.

Authentication modules conduct the entire authentication process with a server, responding to an authentication challenge as appropriate. This process may consist of requests to an authentication server separate from the resource server, as well as any other activities required to properly authenticate a request for a URI.

Custom authentication modules should implement the **IAuthenticationModule** interface and then register with the **AuthenticationManager.Register** method. Authentication modules are also registered at program initialization by reading the configuration file.

Example

[Visual Basic, C#, C++] The following example creates creates a customized authentication class by implementing the **IAuthenticationModule** interface. For a complete example refer to the **AuthenticationManager** class.

```
[Visual Basic]
' The CustomBasic class creates a custom Basic
authentication by implementing the
' IAuthenticationModule interface. It performs the following
tasks:
' 1) Defines and initializes the required properties.
' 2) Implements the Authenticate and PreAuthenticate methods.

Public Class CustomBasic
    Implements IAuthenticationModule

    Private m_authenticationType As String
    Private m_canPreAuthenticate As Boolean

    ' The CustomBasic constructor initializes the properties
of the customized
    ' authentication.
    Public Sub New()
        m_authenticationType = "Basic"
        m_canPreAuthenticate = False
    End Sub 'New

    ' Define the authentication type. This type is then used to
identify this
    ' custom authentication module. The default is set to Basic.

    Public ReadOnly Property AuthenticationType() As String _
        Implements IAuthenticationModule.AuthenticationType
```

```
        Get
            Return m_authenticationType
        End Get
    End Property

    ' Define the pre-authentication capabilities for the module.
The default is set
    ' to false.

    Public ReadOnly Property CanPreAuthenticate() As Boolean _
        Implements IAuthenticationModule.CanPreAuthenticate

        Get
            Return m_canPreAuthenticate
        End Get
    End Property

    ' The checkChallenge method checks whether the challenge
sent by the HttpWebRequest
    ' contains the correct type (Basic) and the correct domain name.
    ' Note: The challenge is in the form BASIC REALM="DOMAINNAME";
    ' the Internet Web site must reside on a server whose
    ' domain name is equal to DOMAINNAME.
    Public Function checkChallenge(ByVal Challenge As String, _
ByVal domain As String) As Boolean
        Dim challengePasses As Boolean = False

        Dim tempChallenge As [String] = Challenge.ToUpper()

        ' Verify that this is a Basic authorization request and
that the requested domain
        ' is correct.
        ' Note: When the domain is an empty string, the following
code only checks
        ' whether the authorization type is Basic.
        If tempChallenge.IndexOf("BASIC") <> -1 Then
            If domain <> [String].Empty Then
                If tempChallenge.IndexOf(domain.ToUpper()) <> -1 Then
                    challengePasses = True
                    ' The domain is not allowed and the authorization
type is Basic.
                Else
                    challengePasses = False
                End If
                ' The domain is a blank string and the authorization
type is Basic.
            Else
                challengePasses = True
            End If
        End If
        Return challengePasses
    End Function 'checkChallenge

    ' The PreAuthenticate method specifies whether the
authentication implemented
    ' by this class allows pre-authentication.
    ' Even if you do not use it, this method must be implemented
to obey to the rules
    ' of interface implementation.
    ' In this case it always returns false.
    Public Function PreAuthenticate(ByVal request As WebRequest, _
ByVal credentials As ICredentials) As Authorization _
        Implements IAuthenticationModule.PreAuthenticate

        Return Nothing
    End Function 'PreAuthenticate

    ' Authenticate is the core method for this custom authentication.
    ' When an Internet resource requests authentication, the
WebRequest.GetResponse
    ' method calls the AuthenticationManager.Authenticate method.
This method, in
    ' turn, calls the Authenticate method on each of the
registered authentication
```

```
' modules, in the order in which they were registered.
When the authentication is
' complete an Authorization object is returned to the WebRequest.
Public Function Authenticate(ByVal challenge As String, ByVal
request As WebRequest, ByVal credentials As ICredentials) As
Authorization _
    Implements IAuthenticationModule.Authenticate

    Dim ASCII As Encoding = Encoding.ASCII

    ' Get the username and password from the credentials
    Dim MyCreds As NetworkCredential =
credentials.GetCredential(request.RequestUri, "Basic")

    If PreAuthenticate(request, credentials) Is Nothing Then
        Console.WriteLine(ControlChars.Lf + " Pre-authentication
is not allowed.")
    Else
        Console.WriteLine(ControlChars.Lf + " Pre-authentication
is allowed.")
    End If
    ' Verify that the challenge satisfies the authorization
requirements.
    Dim challengeOk As Boolean = checkChallenge(challenge,
MyCreds.Domain)

    If Not challengeOk Then
        Return Nothing
    End If

    ' Create the encrypted string according to the Basic
authentication format as
    ' follows:
    ' a)Concatenate the username and password separated by colon;
    ' b)Apply ASCII encoding to obtain a stream of bytes;
    ' c)Apply Base64 encoding to this array of bytes to obtain
the encoded
    ' authorization.
    Dim BasicEncrypt As String = MyCreds.UserName + ":" +
MyCreds.Password

    Dim BasicToken As String = "Basic " +
Convert.ToBase64String(ASCII.GetBytes(BasicEncrypt))

    ' Create an Authorization object using the encoded
authorization above.
    Dim resourceAuthorization As New Authorization(BasicToken)

    ' Get the Message property, which contains the authorization
string that the
    ' client returns to the server when accessing protected resources.
    Console.WriteLine(ControlChars.Lf + " Authorization Message
:{0}", resourceAuthorization.Message)

    ' Get the Complete property, which is set to true when the
authentication process
    ' between the client and the server is finished.
    Console.WriteLine(ControlChars.Lf + " Authorization Complete
:{0}", resourceAuthorization.Complete)

    Console.WriteLine(ControlChars.Lf + " Authorization
ConnectionGroupId:{0}", resourceAuthorization.ConnectionGroupId)

    Return resourceAuthorization
End Function 'Authenticate
End Class 'CustomBasic
```

[C#]
```
// The CustomBasic class creates a custom Basic authentication
by implementing the
// IAuthenticationModule interface. It performs the following
// tasks:
// 1) Defines and initializes the required properties.
// 2) Implements the Authenticate method.
```

```
public class CustomBasic : IAuthenticationModule
{
    private string m_authenticationType ;
    private bool m_canPreAuthenticate ;

    // The CustomBasic constructor initializes the properties
of the customized
    // authentication.
    public CustomBasic()
    {
        m_authenticationType = "Basic";
        m_canPreAuthenticate = false;
    }

    // Define the authentication type. This type is then used to
identify this
    // custom authentication module. The default is set to Basic.
    public string AuthenticationType
    {
        get
        {
            return m_authenticationType;
        }
    }

    // Define the pre-authentication capabilities for the module.
The default is set
    // to false.
    public bool CanPreAuthenticate
    {
        get
        {
            return m_canPreAuthenticate;
        }
    }

    // The checkChallenge method checks whether the challenge sent
by the HttpWebRequest
    // contains the correct type (Basic) and the correct domain name.
    // Note: The challenge is in the form BASIC REALM="DOMAINNAME";
    // the Internet Web site must reside on a server whose
    // domain name is equal to DOMAINNAME.
    public bool checkChallenge(string Challenge, string domain)
    {
        bool challengePasses = false;

        String tempChallenge = Challenge.ToUpper();

        // Verify that this is a Basic authorization request and
that the requested domain
        // is correct.
        // Note: When the domain is an empty string, the following
code only checks
        // whether the authorization type is Basic.

        if (tempChallenge.IndexOf("BASIC") != -1)
            if (domain != String.Empty)
                if (tempChallenge.IndexOf(domain.ToUpper()) != -1)
                    challengePasses = true;
                else
                    // The domain is not allowed and the authorization
type is Basic.
                    challengePasses = false;
            else
                // The domain is a blank string and the authorization
type is Basic.
                challengePasses = true;

        return challengePasses;
    }

    // The PreAuthenticate method specifies whether the
authentication implemented
    // by this class allows pre-authentication.
```

```
    // Even if you do not use it, this method must be implemented
to obey to the rules
    // of interface implementation.
    // In this case it always returns false.
    public Authorization PreAuthenticate(WebRequest request,
ICredentials credentials)
    {
      return null;
    }

    // Authenticate is the core method for this custom authentication.
    // When an Internet resource requests authentication, the
WebRequest.GetResponse
    // method calls the AuthenticationManager.Authenticate method.
This method, in
    // turn, calls the Authenticate method on each of the
registered authentication
    // modules, in the order in which they were registered.
When the authentication is
    // complete an Authorization object is returned to the WebRequest.
    public Authorization Authenticate(String challenge, WebRequest
request, ICredentials credentials)
    {
      Encoding ASCII = Encoding.ASCII;

      // Get the username and password from the credentials
      NetworkCredential MyCreds =
credentials.GetCredential(request.RequestUri, "Basic");

      if (PreAuthenticate(request, credentials) == null)
        Console.WriteLine("\n Pre-authentication is not allowed.");
      else
        Console.WriteLine("\n Pre-authentication is allowed.");

      // Verify that the challenge satisfies the authorization
requirements.
      bool challengeOk = checkChallenge(challenge, MyCreds.Domain);

      if (!challengeOk)
        return null;

      // Create the encrypted string according to the Basic
authentication format as
      // follows:
      // a)Concatenate the username and password separated by colon;
      // b)Apply ASCII encoding to obtain a stream of bytes;
      // c)Apply Base64 encoding to this array of bytes to
obtain the encoded
      // authorization.
      string BasicEncrypt = MyCreds.UserName + ":" + MyCreds.Password;

      string BasicToken = "Basic " +
Convert.ToBase64String(ASCII.GetBytes(BasicEncrypt));

      // Create an Authorization object using the encoded
authorization above.
      Authorization resourceAuthorization = new
Authorization(BasicToken);

      // Get the Message property, which contains the
authorization string that the
      // client returns to the server when accessing protected resources.
      Console.WriteLine("\n Authorization
Message:{0}",resourceAuthorization.Message);

      // Get the Complete property, which is set to true
when the authentication process
      // between the client and the server is finished.
      Console.WriteLine("\n Authorization
Complete:{0}",resourceAuthorization.Complete);

      Console.WriteLine("\n Authorization
ConnectionGroupId:{0}",resourceAuthorization.ConnectionGroupId);
```

```
      return resourceAuthorization;
    }
}

[C++]
// The CustomBasic class creates a custom Basic
authentication by implementing the
// IAuthenticationModule* interface. In particular it
performs the following
// tasks:
// 1) Defines and initializes the required properties.
// 2) Impements the Authenticate method.

public __gc class CustomBasic : public IAuthenticationModule {
private:
    String* m_authenticationType;
    bool m_canPreAuthenticate;

    // The CustomBasic constructor initializes the properties
of the customized
    // authentication.
public:
    CustomBasic() {
      m_authenticationType = S"Basic";
      m_canPreAuthenticate = false;
    }

    // Define the authentication type. This type is then
used to identify this
    // custom authentication module. The default is set to Basic.
    __property String* get_AuthenticationType() {
      return m_authenticationType;
    }

    // Define the pre-authentication capabilities for the
module. The default is set
    // to false.
    __property bool get_CanPreAuthenticate() {
      return m_canPreAuthenticate;
    }

    // The checkChallenge method checks if the challenge sent
by the HttpWebRequest
    // contains the correct type (Basic) and the correct domain name.
    // Note: the challenge is in the form BASIC REALM=S"DOMAINNAME"
    // and you must assure that the Internet Web site resides
on a server whose
    // domain name is equal to DOMAINNAME.
    bool checkChallenge(String* Challenge, String* domain) {
      bool challengePasses = false;

      String* tempChallenge = Challenge->ToUpper();
      // Verify that this is a Basic authorization request
and the requested domain
      // is correct.
      // Note: When the domain is an empty String* the
following code only checks
      // whether the authorization type is Basic.
      if (tempChallenge->IndexOf(S"BASIC") != -1)
        if (String::Compare(domain,String::Empty)!=0 )
          if (tempChallenge->IndexOf(domain->ToUpper()) != -1)
            challengePasses = true;
          else
            // The domain is not allowed and the authorization
type is Basic.
            challengePasses = false;
        else
          // The domain is a blank String* and the
authorization type is Basic.
          challengePasses = true;

      return challengePasses;
    }

    // The PreAuthenticate method specifies if the
authentication implemented
```

```
// by this class allows pre-authentication.
// Even if you do not use it, this method must be
implemented to obey to the rules
// of interface implemebtation.
// In this case it always returns false.
Authorization * PreAuthenticate(WebRequest* request,
ICredentials* credentials) {
    return 0;
}

// Authenticate is the core method for this custom authentication.
// When an internet resource requests authentication,
the WebRequest::GetResponse
// method calls the AuthenticationManager::Authenticate
method. This method, in
// turn, calls the Authenticate method on each of the
registered authentication
// modules, in the order they were registered. When the
authentication is
// complete an Authorization Object* is returned to the
WebRequest, as
// shown by this routine's retun type.
Authorization * Authenticate(String* challenge, WebRequest*
request, ICredentials* credentials) {
    Encoding*  ASCII = Encoding::ASCII;

    // Get the username and password from the credentials
    NetworkCredential * MyCreds = credentials->GetCredential
(request->RequestUri, S"Basic");

    if (PreAuthenticate(request, credentials) == 0)
        Console::WriteLine(S"\n Pre-authentication is not allowed.");
    else
        Console::WriteLine(S"\n Pre-authentication is allowed.");

    // Verify that the challenge satisfies the authorization
requirements.
    bool challengeOk = checkChallenge(challenge, MyCreds->Domain);

    if (!challengeOk)
        return 0;

    // Create the encrypted String* according to the Basic
authentication format as
    // follows:
    // a)Concatenate username and password separated by colon;
    // b)Apply ASCII encoding to obtain a stream of bytes;
    // c)Apply Base64 Encoding to this array of bytes to obtain
the encoded
    // authorization.
    String* BasicEncrypt = String::Concat(MyCreds->UserName,
S":", MyCreds->Password);

    String* BasicToken =
        String::Concat(S"Basic ", Convert::ToBase64String(ASCII-
>GetBytes(BasicEncrypt)));

    // Create an Authorization Object* using the above encoded
authorization.
    Authorization* resourceAuthorization = new
Authorization(BasicToken);

    // Get the Message property which contains the
authorization String* that the
    // client returns to the server when accessing protected
resources
    Console::WriteLine(S"\n Authorization Message: {0}",
resourceAuthorization->Message);

    // Get the Complete property which is set to true when the
authentication process
    // between the client and the server is finished.
    Console::WriteLine(S"\n Authorization Complete: {0}",
        __box(resourceAuthorization->Complete));
```

```
        Console::WriteLine(S"\n Authorization ConnectionGroupId: {0}",
            resourceAuthorization->ConnectionGroupId);
        return resourceAuthorization;
    }
};

// This is the program entry point. It allows the user to enter
// her credentials and the Internet resource (Web page) to access.
// It also unregisters the standard and registers the customized basic
// authentication.
int main() {
    String* args[] = Environment::GetCommandLineArgs();

    if (args->Length < 4)
        TestAuthentication::showusage();
    else {
        // Read the user's credentials.
        TestAuthentication::uri = args[1];
        TestAuthentication::username = args[2];
        TestAuthentication::password = args[3];

        if (args->Length == 4)
            TestAuthentication::domain = String::Empty;
        else
            // If the domain exists, store it. Usually the domain name
            // is by default the name of the server hosting the Internet
            // resource.
            TestAuthentication::domain = args[4];

        // Instantiate the custom Basic authentication module.
        CustomBasic* customBasicModule = new CustomBasic();

        // Unregister the standard Basic authentication module.
        AuthenticationManager::Unregister(S"Basic");

        // Register the custom Basic authentication module.
        AuthenticationManager::Register(customBasicModule);

        // Display registered Authorization modules.
        TestAuthentication::displayRegisteredModules();

        // Read the specified page and display it on the console.
        TestAuthentication::getPage(TestAuthentication::uri);
    }
}
```

Requirements

Namespace: System.Net

Platforms: Windows 98, Windows NT 4.0,
Windows Millennium Edition, Windows 2000,
Windows XP Home Edition, Windows XP Professional,
Windows .NET Server family,
.NET Compact Framework - Windows CE .NET

Assembly: System (in System.dll)

IAuthenticationModule.AuthenticationType Property

Gets the authentication type provided by this authentication module.

```
[Visual Basic]
ReadOnly Property AuthenticationType As String
[C#]
string AuthenticationType {get;}
[C++]
__property String* get_AuthenticationType();
[JScript]
function get AuthenticationType() : String;
```

Property Value

A string indicating the authentication type provided by this authentication module.

Remarks

The **AuthenticationType** property identifies the authentication type implemented by this authentication module. The **AuthenticationType** property is used by the **AuthenticationManager.Register** method to determine if the authentication module has been registered, and by the **AuthenticationManager.Unregister** method to remove a registered authentication module.

Example

See related example in the **System.Net.AuthenticationManager** class topic.

Requirements

Platforms: Windows 98, Windows NT 4.0, Windows Millennium Edition, Windows 2000, Windows XP Home Edition, Windows XP Professional, Windows .NET Server family, .NET Compact Framework - Windows CE .NET, Common Language Infrastructure (CLI) Standard

IAuthenticationModule.CanPreAuthenticate Property

Gets a value indicating whether the authentication module supports preauthentication.

```
[Visual Basic]
ReadOnly Property CanPreAuthenticate As Boolean
[C#]
bool CanPreAuthenticate {get;}
[C++]
__property bool get_CanPreAuthenticate();
[JScript]
function get CanPreAuthenticate() : Boolean;
```

Property Value

true if the authorization module supports preauthentication; otherwise **false**.

Remarks

The **CanPreAuthenticate** property is set to **true** to indicate that the authentication module can respond with a valid **Authorization** instance when the **PreAuthenticate** method is called.

Notes to Implementers: This is typically a fixed value; either the authentication module can preauthenticate, or it cannot.

Example

See related example in the **System.Net.AuthenticationManager** class topic.

Requirements

Platforms: Windows 98, Windows NT 4.0, Windows Millennium Edition, Windows 2000, Windows XP Home Edition, Windows XP Professional, Windows .NET Server family, .NET Compact Framework - Windows CE .NET, Common Language Infrastructure (CLI) Standard

IAuthenticationModule.Authenticate Method

Returns an instance of the **Authorization** class in respose to an authentication challenge from a server.

```
[Visual Basic]
Function Authenticate( _
    ByVal challenge As String, _
    ByVal request As WebRequest, _
    ByVal credentials As ICredentials _
) As Authorization
[C#]
Authorization Authenticate(
    string challenge,
    WebRequest request,
    ICredentials credentials
);
[C++]
Authorization* Authenticate(
    String* challenge,
    WebRequest* request,
    ICredentials* credentials
);
[JScript]
function Authenticate(
    challenge : String,
    request : WebRequest,
    credentials : ICredentials
) : Authorization;
```

Parameters

challenge
   The authentication challenge sent by the server.
request
   The **WebRequest** instance associated with the challenge.
credentials
   The credentials associated with the challenge.

Return Value

An **Authorization** instance containing the authorization message for the request, or a null reference (**Nothing** in Visual Basic) if the challenge cannot be handled.

Remarks

The **Authenticate** method conducts the authentication process with the server and returns an **Authorization** instance to the **AuthenticationManager**.

Notes to Implementers: The **AuthenticationManager** calls the **Authenticate** method on registered authentication modules to determine which module handles the challenge. If the authentication module cannot handle the challenge, the **Authenticate** method must return a null reference (**Nothing** in Visual Basic). If the authentication module encounters an error while conducting the authentication process, **Authenticate** must throw an exception.

Example

See related example in the **System.Net.AuthenticationManager** class topic.

Requirements

Platforms: Windows 98, Windows NT 4.0, Windows Millennium Edition, Windows 2000, Windows XP Home Edition, Windows XP Professional, Windows .NET Server family, .NET Compact Framework - Windows CE .NET, Common Language Infrastructure (CLI) Standard

IAuthenticationModule.PreAuthenticate Method

Returns an instance of the **Authorization** class for an authentication request to a server.

```
[Visual Basic]
Function PreAuthenticate( _
   ByVal request As WebRequest, _
   ByVal credentials As ICredentials _
) As Authorization
[C#]
Authorization PreAuthenticate(
   WebRequest request,
   ICredentials credentials
);
[C++]
Authorization* PreAuthenticate(
   WebRequest* request,
   ICredentials* credentials
);
[JScript]
function PreAuthenticate(
   request : WebRequest,
   credentials : ICredentials
) : Authorization;
```

Parameters

request

The **WebRequest** instance associated with the authentication request.

credentials

The credentials associated with the authentication request.

Return Value

An **Authorization** instance containing the authorization message for the request.

Remarks

When the **CanPreAuthenticate** property is **true**, the **PreAuthenticate** method will return an instance of the **Authorization** class containing an authentication message.

Example

See related example in the **System.Net.AuthenticationManager** class topic.

Requirements

Platforms: Windows 98, Windows NT 4.0, Windows Millennium Edition, Windows 2000, Windows XP Home Edition, Windows XP Professional, Windows .NET Server family, .NET Compact Framework - Windows CE .NET, Common Language Infrastructure (CLI) Standard

ICertificatePolicy Interface

Validates a server certificate.

```
[Visual Basic]
Public Interface ICertificatePolicy
[C#]
public interface ICertificatePolicy
[C++]
public __gc __interface ICertificatePolicy
[JScript]
public interface ICertificatePolicy
```

Remarks

The **ICertificatePolicy** interface is used to provide custom security certificate validation for an application. The default policy is to allow valid certificates, as well as valid certificates that have expired. To change this policy, implement the **ICertificatePolicy** interface with a different policy, and then assign that policy to **ServicePointManager.CertificatePolicy**.

ICertificatePolicy uses the Security Support Provider Interface (SSPI). For more information, see the SSPI documentation in MSDN.

Example

[Visual Basic, C#] The following example creates a certificate policy returns that false for any certificate problem and prints a message indicating the problem on the console. The CertificateProblem enum defines SSPI constants for certificate problems, and the private GetProblemMessage method creates a printable message about the problem.

```
[Visual Basic]
Public Enum CertificateProblem As Long
    CertEXPIRED                = 2148204801   ' 0x800B0101
    CertVALIDITYPERIODNESTING  = 2148204802   ' 0x800B0102
    CertROLE                   = 2148204803   ' 0x800B0103
    CertPATHLENCONST           = 2148204804   ' 0x800B0104
    CertCRITICAL               = 2148204805   ' 0x800B0105
    CertPURPOSE                = 2148204806   ' 0x800B0106
    CertISSUERCHAINING         = 2148204807   ' 0x800B0107
    CertMALFORMED              = 2148204808   ' 0x800B0108
    CertUNTRUSTEDROOT          = 2148204809   ' 0x800B0109
    CertCHAINING               = 2148204810   ' 0x800B010A
    CertREVOKED                = 2148204812   ' 0x800B010C
    CertUNTRUSTEDTESTROOT      = 2148204813   ' 0x800B010D
    CertREVOCATION_FAILURE     = 2148204814   ' 0x800B010E
    CertCN_NO_MATCH            = 2148204815   ' 0x800B010F
    CertWRONG_USAGE            = 2148204816   ' 0x800B0110
    CertUNTRUSTEDCA            = 2148204818   ' 0x800B0112
End Enum

Public Class MyCertificateValidation
    Implements ICertificatePolicy

    ' Default policy for certificate validation.
    Public Shared DefaultValidate As Boolean = False

    Public Function CheckValidationResult(srvPoint As ServicePoint, _
        cert As X509Certificate, request As WebRequest, problem _
    As Integer) _
        As Boolean Implements ICertificatePolicy.CheckValidationResult

        Dim ValidationResult As Boolean = False
        Console.WriteLine(("Certificate Problem with accessing " & _
            request.RequestUri.ToString()))
        Console.Write("Problem code 0x{0:X8},", CInt(problem))
        Console.WriteLine(GetProblemMessage(CType(problem, _
            CertificateProblem)))
```

```
        ValidationResult = DefaultValidate
        Return ValidationResult
    End Function

    Private Function GetProblemMessage _
(Problem As CertificateProblem) As String
        Dim ProblemMessage As String = ""
        Dim problemList As New CertificateProblem()
        Dim ProblemCodeName As String = System.Enum.GetName( _
            problemList.GetType(), Problem)
        If Not (ProblemCodeName Is Nothing) Then
            ProblemMessage = ProblemMessage + _
"-Certificateproblem:" & _
                ProblemCodeName
        Else
            ProblemMessage = "Unknown Certificate Problem"
        End If
        Return ProblemMessage
    End Function
End Class

[C#]
public enum  CertificateProblem : long
{
    CertEXPIRED                = 0x800B0101,
    CertVALIDITYPERIODNESTING  = 0x800B0102,
    CertROLE                   = 0x800B0103,
    CertPATHLENCONST           = 0x800B0104,
    CertCRITICAL               = 0x800B0105,
    CertPURPOSE                = 0x800B0106,
    CertISSUERCHAINING         = 0x800B0107,
    CertMALFORMED              = 0x800B0108,
    CertUNTRUSTEDROOT          = 0x800B0109,
    CertCHAINING               = 0x800B010A,
    CertREVOKED                = 0x800B010C,
    CertUNTRUSTEDTESTROOT      = 0x800B010D,
    CertREVOCATION_FAILURE     = 0x800B010E,
    CertCN_NO_MATCH            = 0x800B010F,
    CertWRONG_USAGE            = 0x800B0110,
    CertUNTRUSTEDCA            = 0x800B0112
}

public class MyCertificateValidation : ICertificatePolicy
{
    // Default policy for certificate validation.
    public static bool DefaultValidate = false;

    public bool CheckValidationResult(ServicePoint sp,
X509Certificate cert,
        WebRequest request, int problem)
    {
        bool ValidationResult=false;
        Console.WriteLine("Certificate Problem with accessing " +
            request.RequestUri);
        Console.Write("Problem code 0x{0:X8},",(int)problem);

Console.WriteLine(GetProblemMessage((CertificateProblem)problem));

        ValidationResult = DefaultValidate;
        return ValidationResult;
    }

    private String GetProblemMessage(CertificateProblem Problem)
    {
        String ProblemMessage = "";
        CertificateProblem problemList = new CertificateProblem();
        String ProblemCodeName =
Enum.GetName(problemList.GetType(),Problem);
        if(ProblemCodeName != null)
            ProblemMessage = ProblemMessage + "-Certificateproblem:" +
                ProblemCodeName;
        else
            ProblemMessage = "Unknown Certificate Problem";
        return ProblemMessage;
    }
}
```

Requirements

Namespace: System.Net

Platforms: Windows 98, Windows NT 4.0,
Windows Millennium Edition, Windows 2000,
Windows XP Home Edition, Windows XP Professional,
Windows .NET Server family,
.NET Compact Framework - Windows CE .NET

Assembly: System (in System.dll)

ICertificatePolicy.CheckValidationResult Method

Validates a server certificate.

```
[Visual Basic]
Function CheckValidationResult( _
   ByVal srvPoint As ServicePoint, _
   ByVal certificate As X509Certificate, _
   ByVal request As WebRequest, _
   ByVal certificateProblem As Integer _
) As Boolean
[C#]
bool CheckValidationResult(
   ServicePoint srvPoint,
   X509Certificate certificate,
   WebRequest request,
   int certificateProblem
);
[C++]
bool CheckValidationResult(
   ServicePoint* srvPoint,
   X509Certificate* certificate,
   WebRequest* request,
   int certificateProblem
);
[JScript]
function CheckValidationResult(
   srvPoint : ServicePoint,
   certificate : X509Certificate,
   request : WebRequest,
   certificateProblem : int
) : Boolean;
```

Parameters

srvPoint
   The **ServicePoint** that will use the certificate.
certificate
   The certificate to validate.
request
   The request that received the certificate.
certificateProblem
   The problem encountered when using the certificate.

Return Value

true if the certificate should be honored; otherwise, **false**.

Remarks

The **CheckValidationResult** method implements the application
certificate validation policy. The method can examine the *srvPoint*,
certificate, *request*, and *certificateProblem* parameters to determine
whether the certificate should be honored.

The *certificateProblem* parameter is a Security Support Provider
Interface (SSPI) status code. For more information, see the SSPI
documentation on MSDN.

Requirements

Platforms: Windows 98, Windows NT 4.0,
Windows Millennium Edition, Windows 2000,
Windows XP Home Edition, Windows XP Professional,
Windows .NET Server family,
.NET Compact Framework - Windows CE .NET

ICredentials Interface

Provides the base authentication interface for retrieving credentials for Web client authentication.

```
[Visual Basic]
Public Interface ICredentials
[C#]
public interface ICredentials
[C++]
public __gc __interface ICredentials
[JScript]
public interface ICredentials
```

Classes that Implement ICredentials

Class	Description
CredentialCache	Provides storage for multiple credentials.
NetworkCredential	Provides credentials for password-based authentication schemes such as basic, digest, NTLM, and Kerberos authentication.

Remarks

The **ICredentials** interface provides the **GetCredential** method to objects that supply network credentials to applications.

Example

[Visual Basic, C#, C++] The following example illustrates how to use the **ICredentials** interface.

```
[Visual Basic]
Class CredentialInfo
    Public uriObj As Uri
    Public authenticationType As [String]
    Public networkCredentialObj As NetworkCredential

    Public Sub New(uriObj As Uri, authenticationType _
As [String], networkCredentialObj As NetworkCredential)
        Me.uriObj = uriObj
        Me.authenticationType = authenticationType
        Me.networkCredentialObj = networkCredentialObj
    End Sub 'New
End Class 'CredentialInfo

Private arrayListObj As ArrayList


Public Sub New()
    arrayListObj = New ArrayList()
End Sub 'New


Public Sub Add(uriObj As Uri, authenticationType As _
[String], credential As NetworkCredential)
    ' adds a 'CredentialInfo' object into a list
    arrayListObj.Add(New CredentialInfo(uriObj, _
authenticationType, credential))
End Sub 'Add

' Remove the 'CredentialInfo' object from the list _
which matches to the given 'Uri' and 'AuthenticationType'
Public Sub Remove(uriObj As Uri, authenticationType As [String])
    Dim index As Integer
    For index = 0 To arrayListObj.Count - 1
        Dim credentialInfo As CredentialInfo = _
CType(arrayListObj(index), CredentialInfo)
        If uriObj.Equals(credentialInfo.uriObj) And _
authenticationType.Equals(credentialInfo.authenticationType) Then
            arrayListObj.RemoveAt(index)
```

```
        End If
    Next index
End Sub 'Remove

Public Function GetCredential(uriObj As Uri, _
authenticationType As [String]) As NetworkCredential _
Implements ICredentials.GetCredential
    Dim index As Integer
    For index = 0 To arrayListObj.Count - 1
        Dim credentialInfoObj As CredentialInfo = _
CType(arrayListObj(index), CredentialInfo)
        If uriObj.Equals(credentialInfoObj.uriObj) And _
authenticationType.Equals(credentialInfoObj.authenticationType) Then
            Return credentialInfoObj.networkCredentialObj
        End If
    Next index
    Return Nothing
End Function 'GetCredential


[C#]
class CredentialList : ICredentials
{
    class CredentialInfo
    {
        public Uri uriObj;
        public String authenticationType;
        public NetworkCredential networkCredentialObj;

        public CredentialInfo(Uri uriObj, String _
authenticationType, NetworkCredential networkCredentialObj)
        {
            this.uriObj = uriObj;
            this.authenticationType = authenticationType;
            this.networkCredentialObj = networkCredentialObj;
        }
    }

    private ArrayList arrayListObj;

    public CredentialList()
    {
        arrayListObj = new ArrayList();
    }

    public void Add (Uri uriObj, String _
authenticationType, NetworkCredential credential)
    {
        // Add a 'CredentialInfo' object into a list.
        arrayListObj.Add (new CredentialInfo(uriObj, _
authenticationType, credential));
    }
    // Remove the 'CredentialInfo' object from the list _
    that matches to the given 'Uri' and 'AuthenticationType'
    public void Remove (Uri uriObj, String authenticationType)
    {
        for(int index=0;index < arrayListObj.Count; index++)
        {
            CredentialInfo credentialInfo = _
(CredentialInfo)arrayListObj[index];
            if(uriObj.Equals(credentialInfo.uriObj)&&
authenticationType.Equals(credentialInfo.authenticationType))
                arrayListObj.RemoveAt(index);
        }
    }
    public NetworkCredential GetCredential (Uri uriObj, _
String authenticationType)
    {
        for(int index=0;index < arrayListObj.Count; index++)
        {
            CredentialInfo credentialInfoObj = _
(CredentialInfo)arrayListObj[index];
            if(uriObj.Equals(credentialInfoObj.uriObj) && _
authenticationType.Equals(credentialInfoObj.authenticationType))
                return credentialInfoObj.networkCredentialObj;
        }
        return null;
```

```
    }
};

[C++]
__gc class CredentialList : public ICredentials {
    __gc class CredentialInfo {
    public:
        Uri* uriObj;
        String* authenticationType;
        NetworkCredential* networkCredentialObj;

        CredentialInfo(Uri* uriObj, String* authenticationType,
    NetworkCredential* networkCredentialObj) {
            this->uriObj = uriObj;
            this->authenticationType = authenticationType;
            this->networkCredentialObj = networkCredentialObj;
        }
    };

private:
    ArrayList*  arrayListObj;

public:
    CredentialList() {
        arrayListObj = new ArrayList();
    }

    void Add (Uri* uriObj, String* authenticationType,
NetworkCredential* credential) {
        // Add a 'CredentialInfo' Object* into a list.
        arrayListObj->Add (new CredentialInfo(uriObj,
authenticationType, credential));
    }

    // Remove the 'CredentialInfo' Object* from the list that
matches to the given 'Uri' and 'AuthenticationType'
    void Remove (Uri* uriObj, String* authenticationType) {
        for (int index=0;index < arrayListObj->Count; index++) {
            CredentialInfo* credentialInfo =
dynamic_cast<CredentialInfo*>(arrayListObj->Item[index]);
            if (uriObj->Equals(credentialInfo->uriObj)&&
authenticationType->Equals(credentialInfo->authenticationType))
                arrayListObj->RemoveAt(index);
        }
    }

    NetworkCredential * GetCredential (Uri* uriObj, String*
authenticationType) {
        for (int index=0;index < arrayListObj->Count; index++) {
            CredentialInfo* credentialInfoObj =
dynamic_cast<CredentialInfo*>(arrayListObj->Item[index]);
            if (uriObj->Equals(credentialInfoObj->uriObj) &&
authenticationType->Equals(credentialInfoObj->authenticationType))
                return credentialInfoObj->networkCredentialObj;
        }
        return 0;
    }
};
```

Requirements

Namespace: System.Net

Platforms: Windows 98, Windows NT 4.0,
Windows Millennium Edition, Windows 2000,
Windows XP Home Edition, Windows XP Professional,
Windows .NET Server family,
.NET Compact Framework - Windows CE .NET

Assembly: System (in System.dll)

ICredentials.GetCredential Method

Returns a **NetworkCredential** object that is associated with the specified URI, and authentication type.

[Visual Basic]
```
Function GetCredential( _
    ByVal uri As Uri, _
    ByVal authType As String _
) As NetworkCredential
```
[C#]
```
NetworkCredential GetCredential(
    Uri uri,
    string authType
);
```
[C++]
```
NetworkCredential* GetCredential(
    Uri* uri,
    String* authType
);
```
[JScript]
```
function GetCredential(
    uri : Uri,
    authType : String
) : NetworkCredential;
```

Parameters

uri

    The **Uri** that the client is providing authentication for.

authType

    The type of authentication, as defined in the **IAuthenticationModule.AuthenticationType** property.

Return Value

The **NetworkCredential** associated with the specified URI and authentication type, or if no credentials are available, a null reference (**Nothing** in Visual Basic).

Remarks

The **GetCredential** method returns a **NetworkCredential** instance that contains the credentials associated with the specified URI and authorization scheme. When no credentials are available, the **GetCredential** method returns a null reference (**Nothing** in Visual Basic).

Example

[Visual Basic, C#, C++] The following uses **GetCredential** to retrieve a **NetworkCredential** instance.

[Visual Basic]
```
Class CredentialInfo
    Public uriObj As Uri
    Public authenticationType As [String]
    Public networkCredentialObj As NetworkCredential

    Public Sub New(uriObj As Uri, authenticationType As
[String], networkCredentialObj As NetworkCredential)
        Me.uriObj = uriObj
        Me.authenticationType = authenticationType
        Me.networkCredentialObj = networkCredentialObj
    End Sub 'New
End Class 'CredentialInfo

Private arrayListObj As ArrayList

Public Sub New()
    arrayListObj = New ArrayList()
End Sub 'New

Public Sub Add(uriObj As Uri, authenticationType As [String],
credential As NetworkCredential)
    ' adds a 'CredentialInfo' object into a list
    arrayListObj.Add(New CredentialInfo(uriObj,
```

```
authenticationType, credential))
    End Sub 'Add

' Remove the 'CredentialInfo' object from the list which
matches to the given 'Uri' and 'AuthenticationType'
Public Sub Remove(uriObj As Uri, authenticationType As [String])
    Dim index As Integer
    For index = 0 To arrayListObj.Count - 1
        Dim credentialInfo As CredentialInfo =
CType(arrayListObj(index), CredentialInfo)
        If uriObj.Equals(credentialInfo.uriObj) And
authenticationType.Equals(credentialInfo.authenticationType) Then
            arrayListObj.RemoveAt(index)
        End If
    Next index
End Sub 'Remove

Public Function GetCredential(uriObj As Uri, authenticationType As
[String]) As NetworkCredential  Implements ICredentials.GetCredential
    Dim index As Integer
    For index = 0 To arrayListObj.Count - 1
        Dim credentialInfoObj As CredentialInfo =
CType(arrayListObj(index), CredentialInfo)
        If uriObj.Equals(credentialInfoObj.uriObj) And
authenticationType.Equals(credentialInfoObj.authenticationType) Then
            Return credentialInfoObj.networkCredentialObj
        End If
    Next index
    Return Nothing
End Function 'GetCredential
```

[C#]
```
class CredentialList : ICredentials
{
    class CredentialInfo
    {
        public Uri uriObj;
        public String authenticationType;
        public NetworkCredential networkCredentialObj;

        public CredentialInfo(Uri uriObj,
String authenticationType, NetworkCredential networkCredentialObj)
        {
            this.uriObj = uriObj;
            this.authenticationType = authenticationType;
            this.networkCredentialObj = networkCredentialObj;
        }
    }

    private ArrayList arrayListObj;

    public CredentialList()
    {
        arrayListObj = new ArrayList();
    }

    public void Add (Uri uriObj, String
authenticationType, NetworkCredential credential)
    {
        // Add a 'CredentialInfo' object into a list.
        arrayListObj.Add (new CredentialInfo(uriObj, authenticationType,
credential));
    }
    // Remove the 'CredentialInfo' object from the list that
matches to the given 'Uri' and 'AuthenticationType'
    public void Remove (Uri uriObj, String authenticationType)
    {
        for(int index=0;index < arrayListObj.Count; index++)
        {
            CredentialInfo credentialInfo =
(CredentialInfo)arrayListObj[index];
            if(uriObj.Equals(credentialInfo.uriObj)&&
authenticationType.Equals(credentialInfo.authenticationType))
                arrayListObj.RemoveAt(index);
        }
    }
    public NetworkCredential GetCredential (Uri uriObj,
String authenticationType)
```

```
    {
        for(int index=0;index < arrayListObj.Count; index++)
        {
            CredentialInfo credentialInfoObj =
(CredentialInfo)arrayListObj[index];
            if(uriObj.Equals(credentialInfoObj.uriObj) &&
authenticationType.Equals(credentialInfoObj.authenticationType))
                return credentialInfoObj.networkCredentialObj;
        }
        return null;
    }
};
```

[C++]
```
__gc class CredentialList : public ICredentials {
    __gc class CredentialInfo {
    public:
        Uri* uriObj;
        String* authenticationType;
        NetworkCredential* networkCredentialObj;

        CredentialInfo(Uri* uriObj, String*
authenticationType, NetworkCredential* networkCredentialObj) {
            this->uriObj = uriObj;
            this->authenticationType = authenticationType;
            this->networkCredentialObj = networkCredentialObj;
        }
    };

private:
    ArrayList* arrayListObj;

public:
    CredentialList() {
        arrayListObj = new ArrayList();
    }

    void Add (Uri* uriObj, String* authenticationType,
NetworkCredential* credential) {
        // Add a 'CredentialInfo' Object* into a list.
        arrayListObj->Add (new CredentialInfo(uriObj,
authenticationType, credential));
    }

    // Remove the 'CredentialInfo' Object* from the list
that matches to the given 'Uri' and 'AuthenticationType'
    void Remove (Uri* uriObj, String* authenticationType) {
        for (int index=0;index < arrayListObj->Count; index++) {
            CredentialInfo* credentialInfo =
dynamic_cast<CredentialInfo*>(arrayListObj->Item[index]);
            if (uriObj->Equals(credentialInfo->uriObj)&& authenticationType-
>Equals(credentialInfo->authenticationType))
                arrayListObj->RemoveAt(index);
        }
    }

    NetworkCredential * GetCredential (Uri* uriObj, String*
authenticationType) {
        for (int index=0;index < arrayListObj->Count; index++) {
            CredentialInfo* credentialInfoObj =
dynamic_cast<CredentialInfo*>(arrayListObj->Item[index]);
            if (uriObj->Equals(credentialInfoObj->uriObj) &&
authenticationType->Equals(credentialInfoObj->authenticationType))
                return credentialInfoObj->networkCredentialObj;
        }
        return 0;
    }
};
```

Requirements

Platforms: Windows 98, Windows NT 4.0,
Windows Millennium Edition, Windows 2000,
Windows XP Home Edition, Windows XP Professional,
Windows .NET Server family,
.NET Compact Framework - Windows CE .NET,
Common Language Infrastructure (CLI) Standard

IPAddress Class

Provides an Internet Protocol (IP) address.

System.Object
    System.Net.IPAddress

```
[Visual Basic]
<Serializable>
Public Class IPAddress
[C#]
[Serializable]
public class IPAddress
[C++]
[Serializable]
public __gc class IPAddress
[JScript]
public
    Serializable
class IPAddress
```

Thread Safety

Any public static (**Shared** in Visual Basic) members of this type are safe for multithreaded operations. Any instance members are not guaranteed to be thread safe.

Remarks

The **IPAddress** class contains the address of a computer on an IP network.

Example

[Visual Basic, C#, C++] The following code example shows how to query a server to obtain the family addresses and the IP addresses it supports.

```
[Visual Basic]
' This program shows how to use the IPAddress class to obtain a server
' IP addressess and related information.
Imports System
Imports System.Net
Imports System.Net.Sockets
Imports System.Text.RegularExpressions
Imports Microsoft.VisualBasic

Namespace Mssc.Services.ConnectionManagement
  Module M_TestIPAddress

    Class TestIPAddress

      'The IPAddresses method obtains the selected server        ⌐
IP address information.
      'It then displays the type of address family supported      ⌐
by the server and
      'its IP address in standard and byte format.
      Private Shared Sub IPAddresses(ByVal server As String)
        Try
          Dim ASCII As New System.Text.ASCIIEncoding()

          ' Get server related information.
          Dim heserver As IPHostEntry = Dns.Resolve(server)

          ' Loop on the AddressList
          Dim curAdd As IPAddress
          For Each curAdd In heserver.AddressList

            ' Display the type of address family supported       ⌐
by the server. If the
            ' server is IPv6-enabled this value is:              ⌐
InternNetworkV6. If the server
            ' is also IPv4-enabled there will be an additional   ⌐
value of InterNetwork.
```

```
            Console.WriteLine(("AddressFamily: " +
curAdd.AddressFamily.ToString()))                                ⌐

            ' Display the ScopeId property in case of IPV6 addresses.
            If curAdd.AddressFamily.ToString() =                ⌐
ProtocolFamily.InterNetworkV6.ToString() Then
              Console.WriteLine(("Scope Id: " +                 ⌐
curAdd.ScopeId.ToString()))
            End If

            ' Display the server IP address in the standard format. In
            ' IPv4 the format will be dotted-quad notation,     ⌐
in IPv6 it will be
            ' in colon-hexadecimal notation.
            Console.WriteLine(("Address: " + curAdd.ToString()))

            ' Display the server IP address in byte format.
            Console.Write("AddressBytes: ")

            Dim bytes As [Byte]() = curAdd.GetAddressBytes()
            Dim i As Integer
            For i = 0 To bytes.Length - 1
              Console.Write(bytes(i))
            Next i
            Console.WriteLine(ControlChars.Cr + ControlChars.Lf)
          Next curAdd

        Catch e As Exception
          Console.WriteLine(("[DoResolve] Exception: " + e.ToString()))
        End Try
      End Sub 'IPAddresses

      ' This IPAddressAdditionalInfo displays additional        ⌐
server address information.
      Private Shared Sub IPAddressAdditionalInfo()
        Try
          ' Display the flags that show if the server supports  ⌐
IPv4 or IPv6
          ' address schemas.
          Console.WriteLine((ControlChars.Cr + ControlChars.Lf + ⌐
"SupportsIPv4: " + Socket.SupportsIPv4.ToString()))
          Console.WriteLine(("SupportsIPv6: " +                 ⌐
Socket.SupportsIPv6.ToString()))

          If Socket.SupportsIPv6 Then
            ' Display the server Any address. This IP address   ⌐
indicates that the server
            ' should listen for client activity on all network  ⌐
interfaces.
            Console.WriteLine((ControlChars.Cr +                ⌐
ControlChars.Lf + "IPv6Any: " + IPAddress.IPv6Any.ToString()))

            ' Display the server loopback address.
            Console.WriteLine(("IPv6Loopback: " +               ⌐
IPAddress.IPv6Loopback.ToString()))

            ' Used during autoconfiguration first phase.
            Console.WriteLine(("IPv6None: " +                   ⌐
IPAddress.IPv6None.ToString()))

            Console.WriteLine(("IsLoopback(IPv6Loopback)
: " + IPAddress.IsLoopback(IPAddress.IPv6Loopback).ToString()))
          End If
          Console.WriteLine(("IsLoopback(Loopback): " +         ⌐
IPAddress.IsLoopback(IPAddress.Loopback).ToString()))
        Catch e As Exception
          Console.WriteLine(("[IPAddresses] Exception: " +      ⌐
e.ToString()))
        End Try
      End Sub 'IPAddressAdditionalInfo

      Public Shared Sub Main(ByVal args() As String)
        Dim server As String = Nothing

        ' Define a regular expression to parse user's input.
        ' This is a security check. It allows only
```

```vb
        ' alphanumeric input string between 2 to 40 character long.
        'Define a regular expression to parse user's input.
        'This is a security check. It allows only
        'alphanumeric input string between 2 to 40 character long.
        Dim rex As New Regex("^[a-zA-Z]\w{1,39}$")

        If args.Length < 1 Then
            ' If no server name is passed as an argument to
this program, use the current
            ' server name as default.
            server = Dns.GetHostName()
            Console.WriteLine(("Using current host: " + server))
        Else
            server = args(0)
            If Not rex.Match(server).Success Then
                Console.WriteLine("Input string format not allowed.")
                Return
            End If
        End If

        ' Get the list of the addresses associated with
the requested server.
        IPAddresses(server)

        ' Get additonal address information.
        IPAddressAdditionalInfo()
    End Sub 'Main
    End Class 'TestIPAddress
  End Module
End Namespace
```

```
[C#]
// This program shows how to use the IPAddress class to obtain a server
// IP addressess and related information.

using System;
using System.Net;
using System.Net.Sockets;
using System.Text.RegularExpressions;

namespace Mssc.Services.ConnectionManagement
{

  class TestIPAddress
  {

    /**
      * The IPAddresses method obtains the selected server
IP address information.
      * It then displays the type of address family supported
by the server and its
      * IP address in standard and byte format.
      **/
    private static void IPAddresses(string server)
    {
      try
      {
        System.Text.ASCIIEncoding ASCII = new
System.Text.ASCIIEncoding();

        // Get server related information.
        IPHostEntry heserver = Dns.Resolve(server);

        // Loop on the AddressList
        foreach (IPAddress curAdd in heserver.AddressList)
        {

          // Display the type of address family supported
by the server. If the
          // server is IPv6-enabled this value is:
InternNetworkV6. If the server
          // is also IPv4-enabled there will be an
additional value of InterNetwork.
          Console.WriteLine("AddressFamily: " +
curAdd.AddressFamily.ToString());

          // Display the ScopeId property in case of IPV6 addresses.
          if(curAdd.AddressFamily.ToString() ==
ProtocolFamily.InterNetworkV6.ToString())
            Console.WriteLine("Scope Id: " +
curAdd.ScopeId.ToString());

          // Display the server IP address in the standard format. In
          // IPv4 the format will be dotted-quad notation,
in IPv6 it will be
          // in in colon-hexadecimal notation.
          Console.WriteLine("Address: " + curAdd.ToString());

          // Display the server IP address in byte format.
          Console.Write("AddressBytes: ");

          Byte[] bytes = curAdd.GetAddressBytes();
          for (int i = 0; i < bytes.Length; i++)
          {
            Console.Write(bytes[i]);
          }

          Console.WriteLine("\r\n");

        }

      }
      catch (Exception e)
      {
        Console.WriteLine("[DoResolve] Exception: " + e.ToString());
      }
    }

    // This IPAddressAdditionalInfo displays additional
server address information.
    private static void IPAddressAdditionalInfo()
    {
      try
      {
        // Display the flags that show if the server
supports IPv4 or IPv6
        // address schemas.
        Console.WriteLine("\r\nSupportsIPv4: " + Socket.SupportsIPv4);
        Console.WriteLine("SupportsIPv6: " + Socket.SupportsIPv6);

        if (Socket.SupportsIPv6)
        {
          // Display the server Any address. This IP address
indicates that the server
          // should listen for client activity on all network
interfaces.
          Console.WriteLine("\r\nIPv6Any: " +
IPAddress.IPv6Any.ToString());

          // Display the server loopback address.
          Console.WriteLine("IPv6Loopback: " +
IPAddress.IPv6Loopback.ToString());

          // Used during autoconfiguration first phase.
          Console.WriteLine("IPv6None: " +
IPAddress.IPv6None.ToString());

          Console.WriteLine("IsLoopback(IPv6Loopback): "
+ IPAddress.IsLoopback(IPAddress.IPv6Loopback));
        }
        Console.WriteLine("IsLoopback(Loopback): " +
IPAddress.IsLoopback(IPAddress.Loopback));
      }
      catch (Exception e)
      {
        Console.WriteLine("[IPAddresses] Exception: " + e.ToString());
      }
    }

    public static void Main(string[] args)
    {
      string server = null;
```

```
      // Define a regular expression to parse user's input.
      // This is a security check. It allows only
      // alphanumeric input string between 2 to 40 character long.
      Regex rex = new Regex(@"^[a-zA-Z]\w{1,39}$");

      if (args.Length < 1)
      {
        // If no server name is passed as an argument to
this program, use the current
        // server name as default.
        server = Dns.GetHostName();
        Console.WriteLine("Using current host: " + server);
      }
      else
      {
        server = args[0];
        if (!(rex.Match(server)).Success)
        {
          Console.WriteLine("Input string format not allowed.");
          return;
        }
      }

      // Get the list of the addresses associated with the
requested server.
      IPAddresses(server);

      // Get additonal address information.
      IPAddressAdditionalInfo();
    }

  }
}

[C++]
#using <mscorlib.dll>
#using <System.dll>
using namespace System;
using namespace System::Net;
using namespace System::Net::Sockets;

/**
* The IPAddresses method obtains the selected server IP
address information.
* It then displays the type of address family supported by
the server and its
* IP address in standard and Byte format.
**/
void IPAddresses(String* server) {
  try {
      System::Text::ASCIIEncoding* ASCII = new
System::Text::ASCIIEncoding();

      // Get server related information.
      IPHostEntry* heserver = Dns::Resolve(server);

      // Loop on the AddressList
      System::Collections::IEnumerator* myEnum =
heserver->AddressList->GetEnumerator();
      while (myEnum->MoveNext()) {
          IPAddress* curAdd = __try_cast<IPAddress*>(myEnum->Current);

      // Display the type of address family supported by
the server. If the
      // server is IPv6-enabled this value is:
InternNetworkV6. If the server
      // is also IPv4-enabled there will be an additional
value of InterNetwork.
          Console::WriteLine(S"AddressFamily: {0}", __box( curAdd-
>AddressFamily));

      // Display the server IP address in the standard format. In
      // IPv4 the format will be dotted-quad notation, in
IPv6 it will be
      // in in colon-hexadecimal notation.
          Console::WriteLine(S"Address: {0}", curAdd);
```

```
      // Display the server IP address in Byte format.
      Console::Write(S"AddressBytes: ");

      Byte bytes[] = curAdd->GetAddressBytes();
      for (int i = 0; i < bytes->Length; i++) {
        Console::Write(bytes->Item[i]);
      }
      Console::WriteLine(S"\r\n");
    }

  } catch (Exception* e) {
    Console::WriteLine(S"->Item[DoResolve] Exception: {0}", e);
  }
}

// This IPAddressAdditionalInfo displays additional server
address information.
void IPAddressAdditionalInfo() {
  try {
    // Display the flags that show if the server supports
IPv4 or IPv6
    // address schemas.
    Console::WriteLine(S"\r\nSupportsIPv4: {0}", __box(
Socket::SupportsIPv4));
    Console::WriteLine(S"SupportsIPv6: {0}", __box(
Socket::SupportsIPv6));

    if (Socket::SupportsIPv6) {
      // Display the server Any address. This IP address
indicates that the server
      // should listen for client activity on all network
interfaces.
      Console::WriteLine(S"\r\nIPv6Any: {0}", IPAddress::IPv6Any);

      // Display the server loopback address.
      Console::WriteLine(S"IPv6Loopback: {0}",
IPAddress::IPv6Loopback);

      // Used during autoconfiguration first phase.
      Console::WriteLine(S"IPv6None: {0}", IPAddress::IPv6None);

      Console::WriteLine(S"IsLoopback(IPv6Loopback): {0}",
__box( IPAddress::IsLoopback(IPAddress::IPv6Loopback)));
    }
    Console::WriteLine(S"IsLoopback(Loopback): {0}", __box(
IPAddress::IsLoopback(IPAddress::Loopback)));
  } catch (Exception* e) {
    Console::WriteLine(S"->Item[IPAddresses] Exception: {0}", e);
  }
}

int main() {
  String* args[] = Environment::GetCommandLineArgs();
  String* server;

  if (args->Length == 1)
    // If no server name is passed as an argument to this
program, use the current
    // server name as default.
    server = Dns::GetHostName();
  else
    server = args[1];

  // Get the list of the addresses associated with the
requested server.
  IPAddresses(server);

  // Get additonal address information.
  IPAddressAdditionalInfo();
}
```

Requirements

Namespace: System.Net

Platforms: Windows 98, Windows NT 4.0,
Windows Millennium Edition, Windows 2000,
Windows XP Home Edition, Windows XP Professional,
Windows .NET Server family,
.NET Compact Framework - Windows CE .NET

Assembly: System (in System.dll)

IPAddress Constructor

Note: This namespace, class, or member is supported only in
version 1.1 of the .NET Framework.

Overload List

Initializes a new instance of the **IPAddress** class with the specified
address and scope equal to 0.

    [Visual Basic] **Public Sub New(Byte())**

    [C#] **public IPAddress(byte[]);**

    [C++] **public: IPAddress(unsigned char __gc[]);**

    [JScript] **public function IPAddress(Byte[]);**

Initializes a new instance of the **IPAddress** class with the specified
address.

Supported by the .NET Compact Framework.

    [Visual Basic] **Public Sub New(Long)**

    [C#] **public IPAddress(long);**

    [C++] **public: IPAddress(__int64);**

    [JScript] **public function IPAddress(long);**

Initializes a new instance of the **IPAddress** class with the specified
address and scope.

    [Visual Basic] **Public Sub New(Byte(), Long)**

    [C#] **public IPAddress(byte[], long);**

    [C++] **public: IPAddress(unsigned char __gc[], __int64);**

    [JScript] **public function IPAddress(Byte[], long);**

IPAddress Constructor (Byte[])

Note: This namespace, class, or member is supported only in
version 1.1 of the .NET Framework.

Initializes a new instance of the **IPAddress** class with the specified
address and scope equal to 0.

```
[Visual Basic]
Public Sub New( _
    ByVal address() As Byte _
)
[C#]
public IPAddress(
    byte[] address
);
[C++]
public: IPAddress(
    unsigned char address __gc[]
);
[JScript]
public function IPAddress(
    address : Byte[]
);
```

Parameters

address
    The byte array value of the IP address.

Remarks

The **IPAddress** is created with the **Address** property set to *address*.

Requirements

Platforms: Windows 98, Windows NT 4.0,
Windows Millennium Edition, Windows 2000,
Windows XP Home Edition, Windows XP Professional,
Windows .NET Server family

IPAddress Constructor (Int64)

Initializes a new instance of the **IPAddress** class with the specified
address.

```
[Visual Basic]
Public Sub New( _
    ByVal newAddress As Long _
)
[C#]
public IPAddress(
    long newAddress
);
[C++]
public: IPAddress(
    __int64 newAddress
);
[JScript]
public function IPAddress(
    newAddress : long
);
```

Parameters

newAddress
    The long value of the IP address.

Remarks

The **IPAddress** instance is created with the **Address** property set to
newAddress.

Requirements

Platforms: Windows 98, Windows NT 4.0,
Windows Millennium Edition, Windows 2000,
Windows XP Home Edition, Windows XP Professional,
Windows .NET Server family,
.NET Compact Framework - Windows CE .NET,
Common Language Infrastructure (CLI) Standard

IPAddress Constructor (Byte[], Int64)

Note: This namespace, class, or member is supported only in
version 1.1 of the .NET Framework.

Initializes a new instance of the **IPAddress** class with the specified
address and scope.

```
[Visual Basic]
Public Sub New( _
    ByVal address() As Byte, _
    ByVal scopeid As Long _
)
```

```
[C#]
public IPAddress(
   byte[] address,
   long scopeid
);
[C++]
public: IPAddress(
   unsigned char address __gc[],
   __int64 scopeid
);
[JScript]
public function IPAddress(
   address : Byte[],
   scopeid : long
);
```

Parameters

address
> The byte array value of the IP address

scopeid
> The long value of the scope identifier.

Exceptions

Exception Type	Condition
ArgumentNullException	*address* is a null reference (**Nothing** in Visual Basic).
	-or-
	address length != 16 .
ArgumentOutOfRange-Exception	*scopeid* < 0 or
	scopeid > 0x00000000FFFFFFFF

Remarks

The *scopeid* identifies a network interface in the case of a link-local address. The scope is only valid for link-local and site-local addresses.

Requirements

Platforms: Windows 98, Windows NT 4.0, Windows Millennium Edition, Windows 2000, Windows XP Home Edition, Windows XP Professional, Windows .NET Server family

IPAddress.Any Field

Provides an IP address indicating that the server should listen for client activity on all network interfaces. This field is read-only.

```
[Visual Basic]
Public Shared ReadOnly Any As IPAddress
[C#]
public static readonly IPAddress Any;
[C++]
public: static IPAddress* Any;
[JScript]
public static var Any : IPAddress;
```

Remarks

The **Socket.Bind** method uses the **Any** field to indicate that a **Socket** instance should listen for client activity on all network interfaces.

The **Any** field is equivalent to 0.0.0.0 in dotted-quad notation.

Requirements

Platforms: Windows 98, Windows NT 4.0, Windows Millennium Edition, Windows 2000, Windows XP Home Edition, Windows XP Professional, Windows .NET Server family, .NET Compact Framework - Windows CE .NET, Common Language Infrastructure (CLI) Standard

IPAddress.Broadcast Field

Provides the IP broadcast address. This field is read-only.

```
[Visual Basic]
Public Shared ReadOnly Broadcast As IPAddress
[C#]
public static readonly IPAddress Broadcast;
[C++]
public: static IPAddress* Broadcast;
[JScript]
public static var Broadcast : IPAddress;
```

Remarks

The **Broadcast** field is equivalent to 255.255.255.255 in dotted-quad notation.

Requirements

Platforms: Windows 98, Windows NT 4.0, Windows Millennium Edition, Windows 2000, Windows XP Home Edition, Windows XP Professional, Windows .NET Server family, .NET Compact Framework - Windows CE .NET, Common Language Infrastructure (CLI) Standard

IPAddress.IPv6Any Field

Note: This namespace, class, or member is supported only in version 1.1 of the .NET Framework.

The **Socket.Bind** method uses the **IPv6Any** field to indicate that a **Socket** should listen for client activity on all network interfaces.

```
[Visual Basic]
Public Shared ReadOnly IPv6Any As IPAddress
[C#]
public static readonly IPAddress IPv6Any;
[C++]
public: static IPAddress* IPv6Any;
[JScript]
public static var IPv6Any : IPAddress;
```

Remarks

The **IPv6Any** field is equivalent to 0:0:0:0:0:0:0:0 in colon-hexadecimal notation, or to:: in compact notation.

Requirements

Platforms: Windows 98, Windows NT 4.0, Windows Millennium Edition, Windows 2000, Windows XP Home Edition, Windows XP Professional, Windows .NET Server family

IPAddress.IPv6Loopback Field

Note: This namespace, class, or member is supported only in version 1.1 of the .NET Framework.

Provides the IP loopback address. This property is read-only.

```
[Visual Basic]
Public Shared ReadOnly IPv6Loopback As IPAddress
[C#]
public static readonly IPAddress IPv6Loopback;
[C++]
public: static IPAddress* IPv6Loopback;
[JScript]
public static var IPv6Loopback : IPAddress;
```

Remarks

The **IPv6Loopback** field is equivalent to 0:0:0:0:0:0:0:1 in colon-hexadecimal notation, or to::1 in compact notation.

Requirements

Platforms: Windows 98, Windows NT 4.0, Windows Millennium Edition, Windows 2000, Windows XP Home Edition, Windows XP Professional, Windows .NET Server family

IPAddress.IPv6None Field

Note: This namespace, class, or member is supported only in version 1.1 of the .NET Framework.

Provides an IP address indicating that no network interface should be used. This property is read-only.

```
[Visual Basic]
Public Shared ReadOnly IPv6None As IPAddress
[C#]
public static readonly IPAddress IPv6None;
[C++]
public: static IPAddress* IPv6None;
[JScript]
public static var IPv6None : IPAddress;
```

Remarks

The **Socket.Bind** method uses the **IPv6None** field to indicate that a **Socket** should not listen for client activity. The **IPv6None** field is equivalent to 0:0:0:0:0:0:0:0 in colon-hexadecimal notation, or to::0 in compact notation.

Requirements

Platforms: Windows 98, Windows NT 4.0, Windows Millennium Edition, Windows 2000, Windows XP Home Edition, Windows XP Professional, Windows .NET Server family

IPAddress.Loopback Field

Provides the IP loopback address. This field is read-only.

```
[Visual Basic]
Public Shared ReadOnly Loopback As IPAddress
[C#]
public static readonly IPAddress Loopback;
[C++]
public: static IPAddress* Loopback;
[JScript]
public static var Loopback : IPAddress;
```

Remarks

The **Loopback** field is equivalent to 127.0.0.1 in dotted-quad notation.

Requirements

Platforms: Windows 98, Windows NT 4.0, Windows Millennium Edition, Windows 2000, Windows XP Home Edition, Windows XP Professional, Windows .NET Server family, .NET Compact Framework - Windows CE .NET, Common Language Infrastructure (CLI) Standard

IPAddress.None Field

Provides an IP address indicating that no network interface should be used. This field is read-only.

```
[Visual Basic]
Public Shared ReadOnly None As IPAddress
[C#]
public static readonly IPAddress None;
[C++]
public: static IPAddress* None;
[JScript]
public static var None : IPAddress;
```

Remarks

The **Socket.Bind** method uses the **None** field to indicate that a **Socket** should not listen for client activity. The **None** field is equivalent to 255.255.255.255 in dotted-quad notation.

Requirements

Platforms: Windows 98, Windows NT 4.0, Windows Millennium Edition, Windows 2000, Windows XP Home Edition, Windows XP Professional, Windows .NET Server family, .NET Compact Framework - Windows CE .NET, Common Language Infrastructure (CLI) Standard

IPAddress.Address Property

Note: This member is now obsolete.

IPAddress.Address is address family dependant, use Equals method for comparison.

An Internet Protocol (IP) address.

```
[Visual Basic]
<Obsolete("IPAddress.Address is address family dependant, use _
    Equals method for comparison.", False)>
Public Property Address As Long
[C#]
[Obsolete("IPAddress.Address is address family dependant, use
    Equals method for comparison.", false)]
public long Address {get; set;}
[C++]
[Obsolete("IPAddress.Address is address family dependant, use
    Equals method for comparison.", false)]
public: __property __int64 get_Address();
public: __property void set_Address(__int64);
[JScript]
public
    Obsolete("IPAddress.Address is address family dependant, use Equals
    method for comparison.", false)
```

```
function get Address() : long;
public function set Address(long);
```

Property Value

The long value of the IP address.

Remarks

This property is obsolete. Use **GetAddressBytes**.

To convert **Address** to dotted-quad notation, use the **ToString** method.

Requirements

Platforms: Windows 98, Windows NT 4.0,
Windows Millennium Edition, Windows 2000,
Windows XP Home Edition, Windows XP Professional,
Windows .NET Server family,
.NET Compact Framework - Windows CE .NET,
Common Language Infrastructure (CLI) Standard

IPAddress.AddressFamily Property

Gets the address family of the IP address.

```
[Visual Basic]
Public ReadOnly Property AddressFamily As AddressFamily
[C#]
public AddressFamily AddressFamily {get;}
[C++]
public: _property AddressFamily get_AddressFamily();
[JScript]
public function get AddressFamily() : AddressFamily;
```

Property Value

Returns **AddressFamily.InterNetwork** in for IPv4 or
AddressFamily.InterNetworkV6 for IPv6.

Example

Refer to the example in the **IPAddress** class topic.

Requirements

Platforms: Windows 98, Windows NT 4.0,
Windows Millennium Edition, Windows 2000,
Windows XP Home Edition, Windows XP Professional,
Windows .NET Server family,
Common Language Infrastructure (CLI) Standard

IPAddress.ScopeId Property

Note: This namespace, class, or member is supported only in version 1.1 of the .NET Framework.

Gets or sets the IPv6 address scope identifier.

```
[Visual Basic]
Public Property ScopeId As Long
[C#]
public long ScopeId {get; set;}
[C++]
public: _property __int64 get_ScopeId();
public: _property void set_ScopeId(__int64);
[JScript]
public function get ScopeId() : long;
public function set ScopeId(long);
```

Property Value

A long integer specifying the scope of the address.

Exceptions

Exception Type	Condition
SocketException	AddressFamily = InterNetwork.
ArgumentOutOfRange-Exception	ScopeId is less than 0. -or- ScopeId is greater than 0x00000000FFFFFFFF.

Remarks

The meaning of **ScopeId** changes depending on the context in which it is used.

- Link-local address. On a host with multiple interfaces connected to separate links, the same link-local address can be assigned to multiple interfaces. To eliminate this ambiguity, a scope identifier is used to specify the interface over which messages are exchanged.

   Note Link-local addresses, identified by the Format Prefix (FP) FE80, are used by nodes when communicating with neighboring nodes on the same link.

- Site-local addresses. A host can be connected to multiple sites. In this case, a scope identifier is used to indicate a specific site to communicate with.

   Note Site-local addresses, identified by the Format Prefix (FP) FEC0, are used by nodes when communicating on private intranets.

The notation that is used to specify the *ScopeId* with an address is `Address%ScopeId`. For example, `FE80::5EFE:192.168.41.30%2` .

Requirements

Platforms: Windows 98, Windows NT 4.0,
Windows Millennium Edition, Windows 2000,
Windows XP Home Edition, Windows XP Professional,
Windows .NET Server family

IPAddress.Equals Method

Compares two IP addresses.

```
[Visual Basic]
Overrides Public Function Equals( _
   ByVal comparand As Object _
) As Boolean
[C#]
public override bool Equals(
   object comparand
);
[C++]
public: bool Equals(
   Object* comparand
);
[JScript]
public override function Equals(
   comparand : Object
) : Boolean;
```

Parameters

comparand

An **IPAddress** instance to compare to the current instance.

Return Value

true if the two addresses are equal; otherwise, **false**.

Remarks

The **Equals** method compares the current **IPAddress** instance with the *comparand* parameter and returns **true** if the two instances contain the same IP address.

Requirements

Platforms: Windows 98, Windows NT 4.0, Windows Millennium Edition, Windows 2000, Windows XP Home Edition, Windows XP Professional, Windows .NET Server family, .NET Compact Framework - Windows CE .NET, Common Language Infrastructure (CLI) Standard

IPAddress.GetAddressBytes Method

Note: This namespace, class, or member is supported only in version 1.1 of the .NET Framework.

Provides a copy of the **IPAddress** as an array of bytes.

```
[Visual Basic]
Public Function GetAddressBytes() As Byte()
[C#]
public byte[] GetAddressBytes();
[C++]
public: unsigned char GetAddressBytes() __gc[];
[JScript]
public function GetAddressBytes() : Byte[];
```

Return Value

Array of bytes.

Example

[Visual Basic, C#, C++] The following code example shows how to get a server IP address in byte format.

```
[Visual Basic]
Dim bytes As [Byte]() = curAdd.GetAddressBytes()
Dim i As Integer
For i = 0 To bytes.Length - 1
   Console.Write(bytes(i))
Next i

[C#]
Byte[] bytes = curAdd.GetAddressBytes();
for (int i = 0; i < bytes.Length; i++)
{
   Console.Write(bytes[i]);
}

[C++]
Byte bytes[] = curAdd->GetAddressBytes();
for (int i = 0; i < bytes->Length; i++) {
   Console::Write(bytes->Item[i]);
}
Console::WriteLine(S"\r\n");
```

Requirements

Platforms: Windows 98, Windows NT 4.0, Windows Millennium Edition, Windows 2000, Windows XP Home Edition, Windows XP Professional, Windows .NET Server family

IPAddress.GetHashCode Method

Returns a hash value for an IP address.

```
[Visual Basic]
Overrides Public Function GetHashCode() As Integer
[C#]
public override int GetHashCode();
[C++]
public: int GetHashCode();
[JScript]
public override function GetHashCode() : int;
```

Return Value

An integer hash value.

Remarks

The **GetHashCode** method returns a hash code of the IP address. This value can be used as a key in hash tables.

Requirements

Platforms: Windows 98, Windows NT 4.0, Windows Millennium Edition, Windows 2000, Windows XP Home Edition, Windows XP Professional, Windows .NET Server family, .NET Compact Framework - Windows CE .NET, Common Language Infrastructure (CLI) Standard

IPAddress.HostToNetworkOrder Method

Converts a value from host byte order to network byte order.

Overload List

Converts a short value from host byte order to network byte order.

Supported by the .NET Compact Framework.

[Visual Basic] **Overloads Public Shared Function HostToNetworkOrder(Short) As Short**

[C#] **public static short HostToNetworkOrder(short);**

[C++] **public: static short HostToNetworkOrder(short);**

[JScript] **public static function HostToNetworkOrder(Int16) : Int16;**

Converts an integer value from host byte order to network byte order.

Supported by the .NET Compact Framework.

[Visual Basic] **Overloads Public Shared Function HostToNetworkOrder(Integer) As Integer**

[C#] **public static int HostToNetworkOrder(int);**

[C++] **public: static int HostToNetworkOrder(int);**

[JScript] **public static function HostToNetworkOrder(int) : int;**

Converts a long value from host byte order to network byte order.

Supported by the .NET Compact Framework.

[Visual Basic] **Overloads Public Shared Function HostToNetworkOrder(Long) As Long**

[C#] **public static long HostToNetworkOrder(long);**

[C++] **public: static __int64 HostToNetworkOrder(__int64);**

[JScript] **public static function HostToNetworkOrder(long) : long;**

IPAddress.HostToNetworkOrder Method (Int16)

Converts a short value from host byte order to network byte order.

```
[Visual Basic]
Overloads Public Shared Function HostToNetworkOrder( _
  ByVal host As Short _
) As Short
[C#]
public static short HostToNetworkOrder(
   short host
);
[C++]
public: static short HostToNetworkOrder(
   short host
);
[JScript]
public static function HostToNetworkOrder(
   host : Int16
) : Int16;
```

Parameters

host
   The number to convert, expressed in host byte order.

Return Value

A short value, expressed in network byte order.

Remarks

Different computers use different conventions for ordering the bytes within multibyte integer values. Some computers put the most significant byte first (known as big-endian order) and others put the least-significant byte first (known as little-endian order). To work with computers that use different byte ordering, all integer values sent over the network are sent in network byte order.

The **HostToNetworkOrder** method converts multibyte integer values stored on the host system from the byte order used by the host to the byte order used by the network.

Requirements

Platforms: Windows 98, Windows NT 4.0, Windows Millennium Edition, Windows 2000, Windows XP Home Edition, Windows XP Professional, Windows .NET Server family, .NET Compact Framework - Windows CE .NET, Common Language Infrastructure (CLI) Standard

IPAddress.HostToNetworkOrder Method (Int32)

Converts an integer value from host byte order to network byte order.

```
[Visual Basic]
Overloads Public Shared Function HostToNetworkOrder( _
  ByVal host As Integer _
) As Integer
[C#]
public static int HostToNetworkOrder(
   int host
);
[C++]
public: static int HostToNetworkOrder(
   int host
);
```

```
[JScript]
public static function HostToNetworkOrder(
   host : int
) : int;
```

Parameters

host
   The number to convert, expressed in host byte order.

Return Value

An integer value, expressed in network byte order.

Remarks

Different computers use different conventions for ordering the bytes within multibyte integer values. Some computers put the most significant byte first (known as big-endian order) and others put the least-significant byte first (known as little-endian order). To work with computers that use different byte ordering, all integer values sent over the network are sent in network byte order.

The **HostToNetworkOrder** method converts multibyte integer values stored on the host system from the byte order used by the host to the byte order used by the network.

Requirements

Platforms: Windows 98, Windows NT 4.0, Windows Millennium Edition, Windows 2000, Windows XP Home Edition, Windows XP Professional, Windows .NET Server family, .NET Compact Framework - Windows CE .NET, Common Language Infrastructure (CLI) Standard

IPAddress.HostToNetworkOrder Method (Int64)

Converts a long value from host byte order to network byte order.

```
[Visual Basic]
Overloads Public Shared Function HostToNetworkOrder( _
  ByVal host As Long _
) As Long
[C#]
public static long HostToNetworkOrder(
   long host
);
[C++]
public: static __int64 HostToNetworkOrder(
   __int64 host
);
[JScript]
public static function HostToNetworkOrder(
   host : long
) : long;
```

Parameters

host
   The number to convert, expressed in host byte order.

Return Value

A long value, expressed in network byte order.

Remarks

Different computers use different conventions for ordering the bytes within multibyte integer values. Some computers put the most significant byte first (known as big-endian order) and others put the least-significant byte first (known as little-endian order). To work with computers that use different byte ordering, all integer values sent over the network are sent in network byte order.

The **HostToNetworkOrder** method converts multibyte integer values stored on the host system from the byte order used by the host to the byte order used by the network.

Requirements

Platforms: Windows 98, Windows NT 4.0, Windows Millennium Edition, Windows 2000, Windows XP Home Edition, Windows XP Professional, Windows .NET Server family, .NET Compact Framework - Windows CE .NET, Common Language Infrastructure (CLI) Standard

IPAddress.IsLoopback Method

Indicates whether the specified IP address is the loopback address.

```
[Visual Basic]
Public Shared Function IsLoopback( _
   ByVal address As IPAddress _
) As Boolean
[C#]
public static bool IsLoopback(
   IPAddress address
);
[C++]
public: static bool IsLoopback(
   IPAddress* address
);
[JScript]
public static function IsLoopback(
   address : IPAddress
) : Boolean;
```

Parameters

address
   An IP address.

Return Value

true if *address* is the loopback address; otherwise, **false**.

Remarks

The **IsLoopback** method compares *address* to **Loopback** and returns **true** if the two IP addresses are the same.

Notice, in the case of IPv4, the **IsLoopback** returns **true** for any IP address of the form 127.X.Y.Z (where X, Y, and Z are in the range 0-255), not just **Loopback** (127.0.0.1).

Requirements

Platforms: Windows 98, Windows NT 4.0, Windows Millennium Edition, Windows 2000, Windows XP Home Edition, Windows XP Professional, Windows .NET Server family, .NET Compact Framework - Windows CE .NET, Common Language Infrastructure (CLI) Standard

IPAddress.NetworkToHostOrder Method

Converts a number from network byte order to host byte order.

Overload List

Converts a short value from network byte order to host byte order.

Supported by the .NET Compact Framework.

   [Visual Basic] **Overloads Public Shared Function NetworkToHostOrder(Short) As Short**

   [C#] **public static short NetworkToHostOrder(short);**

   [C++] **public: static short NetworkToHostOrder(short);**

   [JScript] **public static function NetworkToHostOrder(Int16) : Int16;**

Converts an integer value from network byte order to host byte order.

Supported by the .NET Compact Framework.

   [Visual Basic] **Overloads Public Shared Function NetworkToHostOrder(Integer) As Integer**

   [C#] **public static int NetworkToHostOrder(int);**

   [C++] **public: static int NetworkToHostOrder(int);**

   [JScript] **public static function NetworkToHostOrder(int) : int;**

Converts a long value from network byte order to host byte order.

Supported by the .NET Compact Framework.

   [Visual Basic] **Overloads Public Shared Function NetworkToHostOrder(Long) As Long**

   [C#] **public static long NetworkToHostOrder(long);**

   [C++] **public: static __int64 NetworkToHostOrder(__int64);**

   [JScript] **public static function NetworkToHostOrder(long) : long;**

Example

[Visual Basic, C#, C++] The following example uses the **NetworkToHostOrder** method to convert a long value from network byte order to host byte order.

> [Visual Basic, C#, C++] **Note** This example shows how to use one of the overloaded versions of **NetworkToHostOrder**. For other examples that might be available, see the individual overload topics.

```
[Visual Basic]
Public Sub NetworkToHostOrder_Long(networkByte As Long)
    Dim hostByte As Long
    ' Converts a long value from network byte order to host byte order.
    hostByte = IPAddress.NetworkToHostOrder(networkByte)
    Console.WriteLine("Network byte order to Host byte order of      ↵
{0} is {1}", networkByte, hostByte)
End Sub 'NetworkToHostOrder_Long
```

```
[C#]
public void NetworkToHostOrder_Long(long networkByte)
{
    long hostByte;
    // Converts a long value from network byte order to host byte order.
    hostByte = IPAddress.NetworkToHostOrder(networkByte);
    Console.WriteLine("Network byte order to Host byte order of {0}      ↵
is {1}", networkByte, hostByte);
}
```

```
[C++]
void NetworkToHostOrder_Long(__int64 networkByte) {
    __int64 hostByte;
    // Converts a long value from network Byte order to host Byte order.
    hostByte = IPAddress::NetworkToHostOrder(networkByte);
    Console::WriteLine(S"Network Byte order to Host Byte order of      ↵
{0} is {1}",
        __box(networkByte), __box( hostByte));
}
```

IPAddress.NetworkToHostOrder Method (Int16)

Converts a short value from network byte order to host byte order.

```
[Visual Basic]
Overloads Public Shared Function NetworkToHostOrder( _
   ByVal network As Short _
) As Short
[C#]
public static short NetworkToHostOrder(
   short network
);
[C++]
public: static short NetworkToHostOrder(
   short network
);
[JScript]
public static function NetworkToHostOrder(
   network : Int16
) : Int16;
```

Parameters

network
   The number to convert, expressed in network byte order.

Return Value

A short value, expressed in host byte order.

Remarks

Different computers use different conventions for ordering the bytes within multibyte integer values. Some computers put the most significant byte first (known as big-endian order) and others put the least-significant byte first (known as little-endian order). To wprk with computers that use different byte ordering, all integer values sent over the network are sent in network byte order.

The **NetworkToHostOrder** method converts multibyte integer values stored on the host system from the byte order used by the network to the byte order used by the host.

Example

[Visual Basic, C#, C++] The following example uses the **NetworkToHostOrder** method to convert a short value from network byte order to host byte order.

```
[Visual Basic]
Public Sub NetworkToHostOrder_Short(networkByte As Short)
   Dim hostByte As Short
   ' Converts a short value from network byte order to host
byte order.
   hostByte = IPAddress.NetworkToHostOrder(networkByte)
   Console.WriteLine("Network byte order to Host byte order of
{0} is {1}", networkByte, hostByte)
End Sub 'NetworkToHostOrder_Short
```

```
[C#]
public void NetworkToHostOrder_Short(short networkByte)
{
   short hostByte;
   // Converts a short value from network byte order to host byte order.
   hostByte = IPAddress.NetworkToHostOrder(networkByte);
   Console.WriteLine("Network byte order to Host byte order of
{0} is {1}", networkByte, hostByte);
}
```

```
[C++]
void NetworkToHostOrder_Short(short networkByte) {
   short hostByte;
   // Converts a short value from network Byte order to host Byte order.
   hostByte = IPAddress::NetworkToHostOrder(networkByte);
```

```
   Console::WriteLine(S"Network Byte order to Host Byte order of
{0} is {1}",
      __box(networkByte), __box( hostByte));
}
```

Requirements

Platforms: Windows 98, Windows NT 4.0, Windows Millennium Edition, Windows 2000, Windows XP Home Edition, Windows XP Professional, Windows .NET Server family, .NET Compact Framework - Windows CE .NET, Common Language Infrastructure (CLI) Standard

IPAddress.NetworkToHostOrder Method (Int32)

Converts an integer value from network byte order to host byte order.

```
[Visual Basic]
Overloads Public Shared Function NetworkToHostOrder( _
   ByVal network As Integer _
) As Integer
[C#]
public static int NetworkToHostOrder(
   int network
);
[C++]
public: static int NetworkToHostOrder(
   int network
);
[JScript]
public static function NetworkToHostOrder(
   network : int
) : int;
```

Parameters

network
   The number to convert, expressed in network byte order.

Return Value

An integer value, expressed in host byte order.

Remarks

Different computers use different conventions for ordering the bytes within multibyte integer values. Some computers put the most significant byte first (known as big-endian order) and others put the least-significant byte first (known as little-endian order). To work with computers that use different byte ordering, all integer values sent over the network are sent in network byte order.

The **NetworkToHostOrder** method converts multibyte integer values stored on the host system from the byte order used by the network to the byte order used by the host.

Example

[Visual Basic, C#, C++] The following example uses the **NetworkToHostOrder** method to convert an integer value from network byte order to host byte order.

```
[Visual Basic]
Public Sub NetworkToHostOrder_Integer(networkByte As Integer)
   Dim hostByte As Integer
   ' Converts an integer value from network byte order to
host byte order.
   hostByte = IPAddress.NetworkToHostOrder(networkByte)
   Console.WriteLine("Network byte order to Host byte order
of {0} is {1}", networkByte, hostByte)
End Sub 'NetworkToHostOrder_Integer
```

```
[C#]
public void NetworkToHostOrder_Integer(int networkByte)
{
   int hostByte;
   // Converts an integer value from network byte order to
host byte order.
   hostByte = IPAddress.NetworkToHostOrder(networkByte);
   Console.WriteLine("Network byte order to Host byte order of
{0} is {1}", networkByte, hostByte);
}
```

```
[C++]
void NetworkToHostOrder_Integer(int networkByte) {
   int hostByte;
   // Converts an integer value from network Byte order to
host Byte order.
   hostByte = IPAddress::NetworkToHostOrder(networkByte);
   Console::WriteLine(S"Network Byte order to Host Byte order
of {0} is {1}",
       __box(networkByte), __box( hostByte));
}
```

Requirements

Platforms: Windows 98, Windows NT 4.0,
Windows Millennium Edition, Windows 2000,
Windows XP Home Edition, Windows XP Professional,
Windows .NET Server family,
.NET Compact Framework - Windows CE .NET,
Common Language Infrastructure (CLI) Standard

IPAddress.NetworkToHostOrder Method (Int64)

Converts a long value from network byte order to host byte order.

```
[Visual Basic]
Overloads Public Shared Function NetworkToHostOrder( _
   ByVal network As Long _
) As Long
[C#]
public static long NetworkToHostOrder(
   long network
);
[C++]
public: static __int64 NetworkToHostOrder(
   __int64 network
);
[JScript]
public static function NetworkToHostOrder(
   network : long
) : long;
```

Parameters

network
   The number to convert, expressed in network byte order.

Return Value

A long value, expressed in host byte order.

Remarks

Different computers use different conventions for ordering the bytes
within multibyte integer values. Some computers put the most
significant byte first (known as big-endian order) and others put the
least-significant byte first (known as little-endian order). To worj
with computers that use different byte ordering, all integer values
sent over the network are sent in network byte order.

The **NetworkToHostOrder** method converts multibyte integer
values stored on the host system from the byte order used by the
network to the byte order used by the host.

Example

[Visual Basic, C#, C++] The following example uses the
NetworkToHostOrder method to convert a long value from
network byte order to host byte order.

```
[Visual Basic]
Public Sub NetworkToHostOrder_Long(networkByte As Long)
    Dim hostByte As Long
    ' Converts a long value from network byte order to host byte order.
    hostByte = IPAddress.NetworkToHostOrder(networkByte)
    Console.WriteLine("Network byte order to Host byte order
of {0} is {1}", networkByte, hostByte)
End Sub 'NetworkToHostOrder_Long
```

```
[C#]
public void NetworkToHostOrder_Long(long networkByte)
{
   long hostByte;
   // Converts a long value from network byte order to host byte order.
   hostByte = IPAddress.NetworkToHostOrder(networkByte);
   Console.WriteLine("Network byte order to Host byte order of
{0} is {1}", networkByte, hostByte);
}
```

```
[C++]
void NetworkToHostOrder_Long(__int64 networkByte) {
   __int64 hostByte;
   // Converts a long value from network Byte order to host Byte order.
   hostByte = IPAddress::NetworkToHostOrder(networkByte);
   Console::WriteLine(S"Network Byte order to Host Byte order
of {0} is {1}",
       __box(networkByte), __box( hostByte));
}
```

Requirements

Platforms: Windows 98, Windows NT 4.0,
Windows Millennium Edition, Windows 2000,
Windows XP Home Edition, Windows XP Professional,
Windows .NET Server family,
.NET Compact Framework - Windows CE .NET,
Common Language Infrastructure (CLI) Standard

IPAddress.Parse Method

Converts an IP address string to an **IPAddress** instance.

```
[Visual Basic]
Public Shared Function Parse( _
   ByVal ipString As String _
) As IPAddress
[C#]
public static IPAddress Parse(
   string ipString
);
[C++]
public: static IPAddress* Parse(
   String* ipString
);
[JScript]
public static function Parse(
   ipString : String
) : IPAddress;
```

Parameters

ipString

A string containing an IP address in dotted-quad notation in case of IPv4 and in colon-hexadecimal notation, in case of IPv6.

Return Value

An **IPAddress** instance.

Exceptions

Exception Type	Condition
ArgumentNullException	*ipString* is a null reference (**Nothing** in Visual Basic).
FormatException	*ipString* is not a valid IP address.

Remarks

The static **Parse** method creates an **IPAddress** instance from an IP address expressed in dotted-quad notation in case of IPv4 and in colon-hexadecimal notation, in case of IPv6.

Requirements

Platforms: Windows 98, Windows NT 4.0,
Windows Millennium Edition, Windows 2000,
Windows XP Home Edition, Windows XP Professional,
Windows .NET Server family,
.NET Compact Framework - Windows CE .NET,
Common Language Infrastructure (CLI) Standard

IPAddress.ToString Method

Converts an Internet address to its standard notation.

```
[Visual Basic]
Overrides Public Function ToString() As String
[C#]
public override string ToString();
[C++]
public: String* ToString();
[JScript]
public override function ToString() : String;
```

Return Value

A string containing the IP address in either IPv4 dotted-quad or in IPv6 colon-hexadecimal notation.

Remarks

The **ToString** method converts the IP address stored in the **Address** property to either IPv4 dotted-quad or to IPv6 colon-hexadecimal notation.

Requirements

Platforms: Windows 98, Windows NT 4.0,
Windows Millennium Edition, Windows 2000,
Windows XP Home Edition, Windows XP Professional,
Windows .NET Server family,
.NET Compact Framework - Windows CE .NET,
Common Language Infrastructure (CLI) Standard

IPEndPoint Class

Represents a network endpoint as an IP address and a port number.

System.Object
  System.Net.EndPoint
    System.Net.IPEndPoint

[Visual Basic]
```
<Serializable>
Public Class IPEndPoint
    Inherits EndPoint
```
[C#]
```
[Serializable]
public class IPEndPoint : EndPoint
```
[C++]
```
[Serializable]
public __gc class IPEndPoint : public EndPoint
```
[JScript]
```
public
    Serializable
class IPEndPoint extends EndPoint
```

Thread Safety

Any public static (**Shared** in Visual Basic) members of this type are safe for multithreaded operations. Any instance members are not guaranteed to be thread safe.

Remarks

The **IPEndPoint** class contains the host and port information needed by an application to connect to a service on a host. By combining the host's IP address and port number of a service, the **IPEndPoint** class forms a connection point to a service.

Example

[Visual Basic]
```
' This example uses the IPEndPoint class and its members to
display the home page                                                     ⏎
' of the server selected by the user.

Imports System
Imports System.Text
Imports System.IO
Imports System.Net
Imports System.Net.Sockets
Imports System.Text.RegularExpressions

Namespace Mssc.Services.ConnectionManagement
    Module M_TestIPEndPoint

        Public Class TestIPEndPoint

        'The getPage method gets the server's home page content by
            'recreating the server's endpoint from the original        ⏎
serialized endpoint.
            'Then it creates a new socket and connects it to the endpoint.
            Private Shared Function getPage(ByVal server As String,    ⏎
ByVal socketAddress As SocketAddress) As String
                'Set up variables and String to write to the server.
                Dim ASCII As Encoding = Encoding.ASCII
                Dim [Get] As String = "GET / HTTP/1.1" + ControlChars
.Cr + ControlChars.Lf + "Host: " + server + ControlChars.Cr +          ⏎
ControlChars.Lf + "Connection: Close" + ControlChars.Cr +              ⏎
ControlChars.Lf + ControlChars.Cr + ControlChars.Lf
                Dim ByteGet As [Byte]() = ASCII.GetBytes([Get])
                Dim RecvBytes(255) As [Byte]
                Dim strRetPage As [String] = Nothing

                Dim socket As Socket = Nothing
```
```
                ' Recreate the connection endpoint from the serialized  ⏎
information.
                Dim endpoint As New IPEndPoint(0, 0)
                Dim clonedIPEndPoint As IPEndPoint =                   ⏎
CType(endpoint.Create(socketAddress), IPEndPoint)
                Console.WriteLine(("clonedIPEndPoint: " +              ⏎
clonedIPEndPoint.ToString()))
                Console.WriteLine("Press any key to continue.")
                Console.ReadLine()

                Try
                    ' Create a socket object to establish a connection with ⏎
the server.
                    socket = New Socket(endpoint.AddressFamily,        ⏎
SocketType.Stream, ProtocolType.Tcp)

                    ' Connect to the cloned end point.
                    socket.Connect(clonedIPEndPoint)
                Catch e As SocketException
                    Console.WriteLine(("Source : " + e.Source))
                    Console.WriteLine(("Message : " + e.Message))
                Catch e As Exception
                    Console.WriteLine(("Source : " + e.Source))
                    Console.WriteLine(("Message : " + e.Message))
                End Try

                If socket Is Nothing Then
                    Return "Connection to cloned endpoint failed"
                End If
                ' Send request to the server.
                socket.Send(ByteGet, ByteGet.Length, 0)

                ' Receive the server  home page content.
                Dim bytes As Int32 = socket.Receive(RecvBytes,         ⏎
RecvBytes.Length, 0)

                ' Read the first 256 bytes.
                strRetPage = "Default HTML page on " + server + ":" +  ⏎
ControlChars.Cr + ControlChars.Lf
                strRetPage = strRetPage + ASCII.GetString(RecvBytes, 0, bytes)

                While bytes > 0
                    bytes = socket.Receive(RecvBytes, RecvBytes.Length, 0)
                    strRetPage = strRetPage + ASCII.GetString(RecvBytes, ⏎
0, bytes)
                End While

                socket.Close()

                Return strRetPage
            End Function 'getPage

            ' The serializeEndpoint method serializes the endpoint     ⏎
and returns the
            ' SocketAddress containing the serialized endpoint data.
            Private Shared Function serializeEndpoint(ByVal endpoint   ⏎
As IPEndPoint) As SocketAddress

                ' Serialize IPEndPoint details to a SocketAddress instance.
                Dim socketAddress As SocketAddress = endpoint.Serialize()

                ' Display the serialized endpoint information.
                Console.WriteLine("Endpoint Serialize() : " +          ⏎
socketAddress.ToString())

                Console.WriteLine("Socket Family : " +                 ⏎
socketAddress.Family.ToString())
                Console.WriteLine("Socket Size : " + socketAddress.ToString())

                Console.WriteLine("Press any key to continue.")
                Console.ReadLine()

                Return socketAddress
            End Function 'serializeEndpoint
```

```
        Private Shared Sub displayEndpointInfo(ByVal
endpoint As IPEndPoint)
            Console.WriteLine("Endpoint Address : " +
endpoint.Address.ToString())
            Console.WriteLine("Endpoint AddressFamily : " +
endpoint.AddressFamily.ToString())
            Console.WriteLine("Endpoint Port : " +
endpoint.Port.ToString())
            Console.WriteLine("Endpoint ToString() : " +
endpoint.ToString())

            Console.WriteLine("Press any key to continue.")
            Console.ReadLine()
        End Sub 'displayEndpointInfo

        ' The following method determines the server endpoint and then
        ' serializes it to obtain the related SocketAddress object.
        ' Note that in the for loop a temporary socket is
created to ensure that
        ' the current IP address format matches the AddressFamily type.
        ' In fact, in the case of servers supporting both IPv4 and IPv6, an
exception
        ' may arise if an IP address format does not match the
address family type.
        Private Shared Function getSocketAddress(ByVal server As
String, ByVal port As Integer) As SocketAddress
            Dim tempSocket As Socket = Nothing
            Dim host As IPHostEntry = Nothing
            Dim serializedSocketAddress As SocketAddress = Nothing

            Try
                ' Get the object containing Internet host information.
                host = Dns.Resolve(server)

                ' Obtain the IP address from the list of IP
addresses associated with the server.
                Dim address As IPAddress
                For Each address In host.AddressList
                    Dim endpoint As New IPEndPoint(address, port)

                    tempSocket = New Socket(endpoint.AddressFamily,
SocketType.Stream, ProtocolType.Tcp)

                    tempSocket.Connect(endpoint)

                    If tempSocket.Connected Then
                        ' Display the endpoint information.
                        displayEndpointInfo(endpoint)
                        ' Serialize the endpoint to obtain a
SocketAddress object.
                        serializedSocketAddress = serializeEndpoint(endpoint)
                        Exit For

                    End If

                Next address

                'Close the temporary socket.
                tempSocket.Close()

            Catch e As SocketException
                Console.WriteLine(("Source : " + e.Source))
                Console.WriteLine(("Message : " + e.Message))
            Catch e As Exception
                Console.WriteLine(("Source : " + e.Source))
                Console.WriteLine(("Message : " + e.Message))
            End Try

            Return serializedSocketAddress

        End Function 'getSocketAddress

        ' The requestServerHomePage obtains the server's home
page and returns
        ' its content.
```

```
        Private Shared Function requestServerHomePage(ByVal
server As String, ByVal port As Integer) As String
            Dim strRetPage As [String] = Nothing

            ' Get a socket address using the specified server and port.
            Dim socketAddress As SocketAddress = getSocketAddress
(server, port)

            If socketAddress Is Nothing Then
                strRetPage = "Connection failed"
                ' Obtain the server's home page content.
            Else
                strRetPage = getPage(server, socketAddress)
            End If
            Return strRetPage
        End Function 'requestServerHomePage

        ' Show to the user how to use this program when wrong
input parameters are entered.
        Private Shared Sub showusage()
            Console.WriteLine("Enter the server name as follows:")
            Console.WriteLine(ControlChars.Tab + "vb_ipendpoint
servername")
        End Sub 'showusage

        ' This is the program entry point. It allows the user to enter
        ' a server name that is used to locate its current homepage.
        Public Shared Sub Main(ByVal args() As String)
            Dim host As String = Nothing
            Dim port As Integer = 80

            'Define a regular expression to parse user's input.
            'This is a security check. It allows only
            'alphanumeric input string between 2 to 40 character long.
            Dim rex As New Regex("^[a-zA-Z]\w{1,39}$")

            If args.Length = 0 Then
                ' Show how to use this program.
                showusage()
            Else
                host = args(0)
                If ((rex.Match(host)).Success) Then
                    ' Get the specified server home_page and
display its content.
                    Dim result As String = requestServerHomePage(host, port)
                    Console.WriteLine(result)
                Else
                    Console.WriteLine("Input string format not allowed.")
                End If
            End If
        End Sub 'Main

    End Class 'TestIPEndPoint
  End Module
End Namespace

[C#]
// This example uses the IPEndPoint class and its members
to display the home page
// of the server selected by the user.

using System;
using System.Text;
using System.IO;
using System.Net;
using System.Net.Sockets;
using System.Text.RegularExpressions;

namespace Mssc.Services.ConnectionManagement
{
  public class TestIPEndPoint
  {

    // The getPage method gets the server's home page content by
    // recreating the server's endpoint from the original
```

```
serialized endpoint.
    // Then it creates a new socket and connects it to the endpoint.
    private static string getPage(string server, SocketAddress
socketAddress)
    {
        //Set up variables and string to write to the server.
        Encoding ASCII = Encoding.ASCII;
        string Get = "GET / HTTP/1.1\r\nHost: " + server +
            "\r\nConnection: Close\r\n\r\n";
        Byte[] ByteGet = ASCII.GetBytes(Get);
        Byte[] RecvBytes = new Byte[256];
        String strRetPage = null;

        Socket socket = null;

        // Recreate the connection endpoint from the
serialized information.
        IPEndPoint endpoint = new IPEndPoint(0,0);
        IPEndPoint clonedIPEndPoint = (IPEndPoint)
endpoint.Create(socketAddress);
        Console.WriteLine("clonedIPEndPoint: " +
clonedIPEndPoint.ToString());

        Console.WriteLine("Press any key to continue.");
        Console.ReadLine();

        try
        {
            // Create a socket object to establish a
connection with the server.
            socket =
                new Socket(endpoint.AddressFamily,
SocketType.Stream, ProtocolType.Tcp);

            // Connect to the cloned end point.
            socket.Connect(clonedIPEndPoint);
        }
        catch(SocketException e)
        {
            Console.WriteLine("Source : " + e.Source);
            Console.WriteLine("Message : " + e.Message);
        }
        catch(Exception e)
        {
            Console.WriteLine("Source : " + e.Source);
            Console.WriteLine("Message : " + e.Message);
        }

        if (socket == null)
            return ("Connection to cloned endpoint failed");

        // Send request to the server.
        socket.Send(ByteGet, ByteGet.Length, 0);

        // Receive the server  home page content.
        Int32 bytes = socket.Receive(RecvBytes, RecvBytes.Length, 0);

        // Read the first 256 bytes.
        strRetPage = "Default HTML page on " + server + ":\r\n";
        strRetPage = strRetPage + ASCII.GetString(RecvBytes, 0, bytes);

        while (bytes > 0)
        {
            bytes = socket.Receive(RecvBytes, RecvBytes.Length, 0);
            strRetPage = strRetPage + ASCII.GetString(RecvBytes, 0, bytes);
        }

        socket.Close();

        return strRetPage;
    }

    // The serializeEndpoint method serializes the endpoint
and returns the
    // SocketAddress containing the serialized endpoint data.

    private static SocketAddress serializeEndpoint(IPEndPoint endpoint)
    {
        // Serialize IPEndPoint details to a SocketAddress instance.
        SocketAddress socketAddress = endpoint.Serialize();

        // Display the serialized endpoint information.
        Console.WriteLine("Endpoint.Serialize() : " +
socketAddress.ToString());

        Console.WriteLine("Socket.Family : " + socketAddress.Family);
        Console.WriteLine("Socket.Size : " + socketAddress.Size);

        Console.WriteLine("Press any key to continue.");
        Console.ReadLine();

        return socketAddress;
    }

    private static void displayEndpointInfo(IPEndPoint endpoint)
    {
        Console.WriteLine("Endpoint.Address : " + endpoint.Address);
        Console.WriteLine("Endpoint.AddressFamily : " +
endpoint.AddressFamily);
        Console.WriteLine("Endpoint.Port : " + endpoint.Port);
        Console.WriteLine("Endpoint.ToString() : " +
endpoint.ToString());

        Console.WriteLine("Press any key to continue.");
        Console.ReadLine();
    }

    // The serializeEndpoint method determines the server
endpoint and then
    // serializes it to obtain the related SocketAddress object.
    // Note that in the for loop a temporary socket is
created to ensure that
    // the current IP address format matches the AddressFamily type.
    // In fact, in the case of servers supporting both IPv4
and IPv6, an exception
    // may arise if an IP address format does not match the
address family type.
    private static SocketAddress getSocketAddress
(string server, int port)
    {
        Socket tempSocket = null;
        IPHostEntry host = null;
        SocketAddress serializedSocketAddress = null;

        try
        {
            // Get the object containing Internet host information.
            host = Dns.Resolve(server);

            // Obtain the IP address from the list of IP
addresses associated with the server.
            foreach(IPAddress address in host.AddressList)
            {
                IPEndPoint endpoint = new IPEndPoint(address, port);

                tempSocket =
                    new Socket(endpoint.AddressFamily,
SocketType.Stream, ProtocolType.Tcp);

                tempSocket.Connect(endpoint);

                if(tempSocket.Connected)
                {
                    // Display the endpoint information.
                    displayEndpointInfo(endpoint);
                    // Serialize the endpoint to obtain a SocketAddress object.
                    serializedSocketAddress = serializeEndpoint(endpoint);
                    break;
                }
                else
```

```
            continue;
        }

        // Close the temporary socket.
        tempSocket.Close();
    }

    catch(SocketException e)
    {
        Console.WriteLine("Source : " + e.Source);
        Console.WriteLine("Message : " + e.Message);
    }
    catch(Exception e)
    {
        Console.WriteLine("Source : " + e.Source);
        Console.WriteLine("Message : " + e.Message);
    }
    return serializedSocketAddress;

}

// The requestServerHomePage method obtains the server's
home page and returns
// its content.
private static string requestServerHomePage(string
server, int port)
{
    String strRetPage = null;

    // Get a socket address using the specified server and port.
    SocketAddress socketAddress = getSocketAddress(server, port);

    if (socketAddress == null)
        strRetPage = "Connection failed";
    else
        // Obtain the server's home page content.
        strRetPage = getPage(server, socketAddress);

    return strRetPage;
}

// Show to the user how to use this program when
wrong input parameters are entered.
private static void showUsage()
{
    Console.WriteLine("Enter the server name as follows:");
    Console.WriteLine("\tcs_ipendpoint servername");
}

// This is the program entry point. It allows the user to enter
// a server name that is used to locate its current homepage.
public static void Main(string[] args)
{
    string host= null;
    int port = 80;

    // Define a regular expression to parse user's input.
    // This is a security check. It allows only
    // alphanumeric input string between 2 to 40 character long.
    Regex rex = new Regex(@"^[a-zA-Z]\w{1,39}$");

    if (args.Length < 1)
        showUsage();
    else
    {
        string message = args[0];
        if ((rex.Match(message)).Success)
        {
            host = args[0];
            // Get the specified server home_page and
display its content.
            string result = requestServerHomePage(host, port);
            Console.WriteLine(result);
        }
        else
```

```
            Console.WriteLine("Input string format not allowed.");
        }

    }

}
}
```

[C++]
```
// This program displays the home page of the server selected
by the user.
// To do that it uses the IPEndPoint and shows how to use its
methods and
// properties.

#using <mscorlib.dll>
#using <System.dll>

using namespace System;
using namespace System::Text;
using namespace System::IO;
using namespace System::Net;
using namespace System::Net::Sockets;
using namespace System::Text::RegularExpressions;

public __gc class TestIPEndPoint {

private:
    // This method gets the server's home page content. It does so by
    // recreating the server's endpoint from the original
serialized endpoint.
    // Then creating a socket and connecting it to the above endpoint.
    static String* getPage(String* server, SocketAddress*
socketAddress) {
        //Set up variables and String to write to the server.
        Encoding* ASCII = Encoding::ASCII;
        String* Get = String::Format(S"GET / HTTP/1.1\r\nHost:
{0}\r\nConnection: Close\r\n\r\n", server);
        Byte ByteGet[] = ASCII->GetBytes(Get);
        Byte RecvBytes[] = new Byte[256];
        String* strRetPage = 0;

        Socket* socket = 0;

        // Recreate the connection endpoint from the
serialized information.
        IPEndPoint* endpoint = new IPEndPoint((__int64)0, 0);
        IPEndPoint* clonedIPEndPoint =
            dynamic_cast<IPEndPoint*> (endpoint->Create(socketAddress));
        Console::WriteLine(S"clonedIPEndPoint: {0}", clonedIPEndPoint);

        Console::WriteLine(S"Press any key to continue.");
        Console::ReadLine();

        try {
            // Create a socket Object* to establish a connection
with the server.
            socket =
                new Socket(endpoint->AddressFamily, SocketType::
Stream, ProtocolType::Tcp);

            // Connect to the cloned end point.
            socket->Connect(clonedIPEndPoint);
        } catch (SocketException* e) {
            Console::WriteLine(S"SocketException caught!!!");
            Console::WriteLine(S"Source : {0}", e->Source);
            Console::WriteLine(S"Message : {0}", e->Message);
        } catch (Exception* e) {
            Console::WriteLine(S"Exception caught!!!");
            Console::WriteLine(S"Source : {0}", e->Source);
            Console::WriteLine(S"Message : {0}", e->Message);
        }

        if (socket == 0)
            return (S"Connection to cloned endpoint failed");
```

```
        // Send request to the server.
        socket->Send(ByteGet, ByteGet-          ⏎
>Length,static_cast<SocketFlags>(0));

        // Receive the server  home page content.
        Int32 bytes = socket->Receive(RecvBytes, RecvBytes-  ⏎
>Length,static_cast<SocketFlags>(0));

        // Read the first 256 bytes.
        strRetPage = String::Format(S"Default HTML page on  ⏎
{0}:\r\n", server);
        strRetPage = String::Concat(strRetPage, ASCII-  ⏎
>GetString(RecvBytes, 0, bytes));

        while (bytes > 0) {
            bytes = socket->Receive(RecvBytes, RecvBytes-  ⏎
>Length,static_cast<SocketFlags>(0));
            strRetPage = String::Concat(strRetPage, ASCII-  ⏎
>GetString(RecvBytes, 0, bytes));
        }

        socket->Close();

        return strRetPage;
    }

    // This method serialize the endpoint and returns the
    // SocketAddress containing the serialized endpoint data.
    static SocketAddress* serializeEndpoint(IPEndPoint* endpoint) {

        // Serialize IPEndPoint details to a SocketAddress instance.
        SocketAddress* socketAddress = endpoint->Serialize();

        // Display the serialized endpoint information.
        Console::WriteLine(S"Endpoint::Serialize() : {0}",  ⏎
socketAddress);

        Console::WriteLine(S"Socket::Family : {0}", __box(socketAddress-
>Family));
        Console::WriteLine(S"Socket::Size : {0}", __box(socketAddress-
>Size));

        Console::WriteLine(S"Press any key to continue.");
        Console::ReadLine();

        return socketAddress;
    }

    static void displayEndpointInfo(IPEndPoint* endpoint) {
        Console::WriteLine(S"Endpoint->Address : {0}", endpoint->Address);
        Console::WriteLine(S"Endpoint->AddressFamily : {0}",  ⏎
__box(endpoint->AddressFamily));
        Console::WriteLine(S"Endpoint::Port : {0}", __box  ⏎
(endpoint->Port));
        Console::WriteLine(S"Endpoint : {0}", endpoint);

        Console::WriteLine(S"Press any key to continue.");
        Console::ReadLine();
    }

    // The following method determines the server endpoint and then
    // serializes it to obtain the related SockeAddress Object*.
    // Note that in the for loop a temporary socket is created to  ⏎
make sure that
    // the current IP address format matches the AddressFamily type.
    // In fact in the case of servers supporting both IPv4 and  ⏎
IPv6, an exception
    // may arise in the case an IP address format does not matches
    // the address family type.
    static SocketAddress* getSocketAddress(String* server, int port) {
        Socket* tempSocket = 0;
        IPHostEntry* host = 0;
        SocketAddress* serializedSocketAddress = 0;

        try {
            // Get the Object* containing Internet host information.
            host = Dns::Resolve(server);

            // Obtain the IP address from the list of IP associated  ⏎
with the server.
            System::Collections::IEnumerator* myEnum = host->  ⏎
AddressList->GetEnumerator();
            while (myEnum->MoveNext()) {
              IPAddress* address = __try_cast<IPAddress*>(myEnum->Current);

                IPEndPoint* endpoint = new IPEndPoint(address, port);
                tempSocket =
                    new Socket(endpoint->AddressFamily, SocketType::  ⏎
Stream, ProtocolType::Tcp);

                tempSocket->Connect(endpoint);

                if (tempSocket->Connected) {
                    // Display the endpoint information.
                    displayEndpointInfo(endpoint);
                    // Serialize the endpoint to obtain a SocketAddress
Object*.
                    serializedSocketAddress = serializeEndpoint(endpoint);
                    break;
                } else
                    continue;
            }

            // Close the temporary socket.
            tempSocket->Close();
        } catch (SocketException* e) {
            Console::WriteLine(S"SocketException caught!!!");
            Console::WriteLine(S"Source : {0}", e->Source);
            Console::WriteLine(S"Message : {0}", e->Message);
        } catch (Exception* e) {
            Console::WriteLine(S"Exception caught!!!");
            Console::WriteLine(S"Source : {0}", e->Source);
            Console::WriteLine(S"Message : {0}", e->Message);
        }
        return serializedSocketAddress;

    }

    // This method obtains the server's home page and returns
    // its content.
    static String* requestServerHomePage(String* server, int port) {
        String* strRetPage = 0;

        // Get a socket address using the specified server and port.
        SocketAddress* socketAddress = getSocketAddress(server, port);

        if (socketAddress == 0)
            strRetPage = S"Connection failed";
        else
            // Obtain the server's home page content.
            strRetPage = getPage(server, socketAddress);

        return strRetPage;
    }

    // Show how to use this program.
    static void showUsage() {
        Console::WriteLine(S"Enter the server name as follows:");
        Console::WriteLine(S"\tcs_ipendpoint server");
        Console::WriteLine(S"\r\nExample:");
        Console::WriteLine(S"\tcs_ipendpoint ndpue");
    }

public:
    // This is the program entry point. It allows the user to enter
    // a server name that is used to locate its current homepage.
    static void main() {
        String* args[] = Environment::GetCommandLineArgs();
```

```
String* host = 0;
int port = 80;

// Define a regular expression to parse user's input.
// This is a security check. It allows only
// alphanumeric input String* between 2 to 40 character long.
Regex* rex = new Regex(S"^[a-zA-Z]\\w{1,39}$");

if (args->Length < 2)
    showUsage();
else {
    String* message = args[1];
    if ((rex->Match(message))->Success) {
        host = args[1];
        // Get the selected server homepage and display its    ⌐
content.
        String* result = requestServerHomePage(host, port);
        Console::WriteLine(result);
    } else
        Console::WriteLine(S"Input string format not allowed.");
    }
    }
};

int main()
{
    TestIPEndPoint::main();
}
```

Requirements

Namespace: System.Net

Platforms: Windows 98, Windows NT 4.0,
Windows Millennium Edition, Windows 2000,
Windows XP Home Edition, Windows XP Professional,
Windows .NET Server family,
.NET Compact Framework - Windows CE .NET

Assembly: System (in System.dll)

IPEndPoint Constructor

Initializes a new instance of the **IPEndPoint** class.

Overload List

Initializes a new instance of the **IPEndPoint** class with the specified address and port number.

Supported by the .NET Compact Framework.

　[Visual Basic] **Public Sub New(Long, Integer)**

　[C#] **public IPEndPoint(long, int);**

　[C++] **public: IPEndPoint(__int64, int);**

　[JScript] **public function IPEndPoint(long, int);**

Initializes a new instance of the **IPEndPoint** class with the specified address and port number.

Supported by the .NET Compact Framework.

　[Visual Basic] **Public Sub New(IPAddress, Integer)**

　[C#] **public IPEndPoint(IPAddress, int);**

　[C++] **public: IPEndPoint(IPAddress*, int);**

　[JScript] **public function IPEndPoint(IPAddress, int);**

IPEndPoint Constructor (Int64, Int32)

Initializes a new instance of the **IPEndPoint** class with the specified address and port number.

```
[Visual Basic]
Public Sub New( _
    ByVal address As Long, _
    ByVal port As Integer _
)
[C#]
public IPEndPoint(
    long address,
    int port
);
[C++]
public: IPEndPoint(
    __int64 address,
    int port
);
[JScript]
public function IPEndPoint(
    address : long,
    port : int
);
```

Parameters

address
　The IP address of the Internet host.

port
　The port number associated with the address, or 0 to specify any available port.

Exceptions

Exception Type	Condition
ArgumentOutOfRange-Exception	*port* is less than **MinPort**. -or- *port* is greater than **MaxPort**. -or- *address* is less than 0 or greater than 0x00000000FFFFFFFF.

Requirements

Platforms: Windows 98, Windows NT 4.0,
Windows Millennium Edition, Windows 2000,
Windows XP Home Edition, Windows XP Professional,
Windows .NET Server family,
.NET Compact Framework - Windows CE .NET,
Common Language Infrastructure (CLI) Standard

IPEndPoint Constructor (IPAddress, Int32)

Initializes a new instance of the **IPEndPoint** class with the specified address and port number.

```
[Visual Basic]
Public Sub New( _
    ByVal address As IPAddress, _
    ByVal port As Integer _
)
[C#]
public IPEndPoint(
    IPAddress address,
    int port
);
```

```
[C++]
public: IPEndPoint(
    IPAddress* address,
    int port
);
[JScript]
public function IPEndPoint(
    address : IPAddress,
    port : int
);
```

Parameters

address
    An **IPAddress**.
port
    The port number associated with *address*.

Exceptions

Exception Type	Condition
ArgumentOutOfRange-Exception	*port* is less than **MinPort**. -or- *port* is greater than **MaxPort**. -or- *address* is less than 0 or greater than 0x00000000FFFFFFFF.

Requirements

Platforms: Windows 98, Windows NT 4.0, Windows Millennium Edition, Windows 2000, Windows XP Home Edition, Windows XP Professional, Windows .NET Server family, .NET Compact Framework - Windows CE .NET, Common Language Infrastructure (CLI) Standard

IPEndPoint.MaxPort Field

Specifies the maximum value that can be assigned to the **Port** property. This field is read-only.

```
[Visual Basic]
Public Const MaxPort As Integer
[C#]
public const int MaxPort;
[C++]
public: const int MaxPort;
[JScript]
public var MaxPort : int;
```

Requirements

Platforms: Windows 98, Windows NT 4.0, Windows Millennium Edition, Windows 2000, Windows XP Home Edition, Windows XP Professional, Windows .NET Server family, .NET Compact Framework - Windows CE .NET, Common Language Infrastructure (CLI) Standard

IPEndPoint.MinPort Field

Specifies the minimum value that can be assigned to the **Port** property. This field is read-only.

```
[Visual Basic]
Public Const MinPort As Integer
[C#]
public const int MinPort;
[C++]
public: const int MinPort;
[JScript]
public var MinPort : int;
```

Requirements

Platforms: Windows 98, Windows NT 4.0, Windows Millennium Edition, Windows 2000, Windows XP Home Edition, Windows XP Professional, Windows .NET Server family, .NET Compact Framework - Windows CE .NET, Common Language Infrastructure (CLI) Standard

IPEndPoint.Address Property

Gets or sets the IP address of the endpoint.

```
[Visual Basic]
Public Property Address As IPAddress
[C#]
public IPAddress Address {get; set;}
[C++]
public: __property IPAddress* get_Address();
public: __property void set_Address(IPAddress*);
[JScript]
public function get Address() : IPAddress;
public function set Address(IPAddress);
```

Property Value

An **IPAddress** instance containing the IP address of the endpoint.

Example

[Visual Basic, C#, C++] The following example sets the **Address** property using the **IPAddress** specified.

```
[Visual Basic]
Private Shared Sub displayEndpointInfo(ByVal endpoint As IPEndPoint)
    Console.WriteLine("Endpoint Address : " + _
endpoint.Address.ToString())
    Console.WriteLine("Endpoint AddressFamily : " + _
endpoint.AddressFamily.ToString())
    Console.WriteLine("Endpoint Port : " + endpoint.Port.ToString())
    Console.WriteLine("Endpoint ToString() : " + endpoint.ToString())

    Console.WriteLine("Press any key to continue.")
    Console.ReadLine()
End Sub 'displayEndpointInfo

[C#]
private static void displayEndpointInfo(IPEndPoint endpoint)
{
    Console.WriteLine("Endpoint.Address : " + endpoint.Address);
    Console.WriteLine("Endpoint.AddressFamily : " + _
endpoint.AddressFamily);
    Console.WriteLine("Endpoint.Port : " + endpoint.Port);
    Console.WriteLine("Endpoint.ToString() : " + endpoint.ToString());

    Console.WriteLine("Press any key to continue.");
    Console.ReadLine();
}

[C++]
static void displayEndpointInfo(IPEndPoint* endpoint) {
    Console::WriteLine(S"Endpoint->Address : {0}", endpoint->Address);
```

```
  Console::WriteLine(S"Endpoint->AddressFamily : {0}",                      ⏎
_box(endpoint->AddressFamily));
  Console::WriteLine(S"Endpoint::Port : {0}", _box(endpoint->Port));
  Console::WriteLine(S"Endpoint : {0}", endpoint);

  Console::WriteLine(S"Press any key to continue.");
  Console::ReadLine();
}
```

Requirements

Platforms: Windows 98, Windows NT 4.0,
Windows Millennium Edition, Windows 2000,
Windows XP Home Edition, Windows XP Professional,
Windows .NET Server family,
.NET Compact Framework - Windows CE .NET,
Common Language Infrastructure (CLI) Standard

IPEndPoint.AddressFamily Property

Gets the Internet Protocol (IP) address family.

```
[Visual Basic]
Overrides Public ReadOnly Property AddressFamily As AddressFamily
[C#]
public override AddressFamily AddressFamily {get;}
[C++]
public: _property AddressFamily get_AddressFamily();
[JScript]
public override function get AddressFamily() : AddressFamily;
```

Property Value

Returns **AddressFamily.InterNetwork**.

Example

[Visual Basic, C#, C++] The following example uses the
AddressFamily property to return the **AddressFamily** to which the
IPEndPoint belongs. In this case it is the **InterNetwork**
AddressFamily.

```
[Visual Basic]
Private Shared Sub displayEndpointInfo(ByVal endpoint As IPEndPoint)
  Console.WriteLine("Endpoint Address : " +                               ⏎
endpoint.Address.ToString())
  Console.WriteLine("Endpoint AddressFamily : " +                        ⏎
endpoint.AddressFamily.ToString())
  Console.WriteLine("Endpoint Port : " + endpoint.Port.ToString())
  Console.WriteLine("Endpoint ToString() : " + endpoint.ToString())

  Console.WriteLine("Press any key to continue.")
  Console.ReadLine()
End Sub 'displayEndpointInfo
```

```
[C#]
private static void displayEndpointInfo(IPEndPoint endpoint)
{
  Console.WriteLine("Endpoint.Address : " + endpoint.Address);
  Console.WriteLine("Endpoint.AddressFamily : " +                         ⏎
endpoint.AddressFamily);
  Console.WriteLine("Endpoint.Port : " + endpoint.Port);
  Console.WriteLine("Endpoint.ToString() : " + endpoint.ToString());

  Console.WriteLine("Press any key to continue.");
  Console.ReadLine();
}
```

```
[C++]
static void displayEndpointInfo(IPEndPoint* endpoint) {
  Console::WriteLine(S"Endpoint->Address : {0}", endpoint->Address);
  Console::WriteLine(S"Endpoint->AddressFamily : {0}", _box             ⏎
(endpoint->AddressFamily));
```

```
  Console::WriteLine(S"Endpoint::Port : {0}", _box(endpoint->Port));
  Console::WriteLine(S"Endpoint : {0}", endpoint);

  Console::WriteLine(S"Press any key to continue.");
  Console::ReadLine();
}
```

Requirements

Platforms: Windows 98, Windows NT 4.0,
Windows Millennium Edition, Windows 2000,
Windows XP Home Edition, Windows XP Professional,
Windows .NET Server family,
.NET Compact Framework - Windows CE .NET,
Common Language Infrastructure (CLI) Standard

IPEndPoint.Port Property

Gets or sets the TCP port number of the endpoint.

```
[Visual Basic]
Public Property Port As Integer
[C#]
public int Port {get; set;}
[C++]
public: _property int get_Port();
public: _property void set_Port(int);
[JScript]
public function get Port() : int;
public function set Port(int);
```

Property Value

An integer value in the range **MinPort** to **MaxPort** indicating the
TCP port number of the endpoint.

Exceptions

Exception Type	Condition
ArgumentOutOfRange-Exception	The value that was specified for a set operation is less than **MinPort** or greater than **MaxPort**.

Requirements

Platforms: Windows 98, Windows NT 4.0,
Windows Millennium Edition, Windows 2000,
Windows XP Home Edition, Windows XP Professional,
Windows .NET Server family,
.NET Compact Framework - Windows CE .NET,
Common Language Infrastructure (CLI) Standard

IPEndPoint.Create Method

Creates an endpoint from a socket address.

```
[Visual Basic]
Overrides Public Function Create( _
   ByVal socketAddress As SocketAddress _
) As EndPoint
[C#]
public override EndPoint Create(
   SocketAddress socketAddress
);
[C++]
public: EndPoint* Create(
   SocketAddress* socketAddress
);
```

```
[JScript]
public override function Create(
    socketAddress : SocketAddress
) : EndPoint;
```

Parameters

socketAddress
> The **SocketAddress** to use for the endpoint.

Return Value

An **EndPoint** instance using the specified socket address.

Exceptions

Exception Type	Condition
ArgumentException	The AddressFamily of *socketAddress* is not equal to the AddressFamily of the current instance.
	-or-
	socketAddress.Size < 8.

Example

[Visual Basic, C#, C++] The following example uses the specified **SocketAddress** to create an **IPEndPoint**.

```
[Visual Basic]
' Recreate the connection endpoint from the serialized information.
Dim endpoint As New IPEndPoint(0, 0)
Dim clonedIPEndPoint As IPEndPoint =
CType(endpoint.Create(socketAddress), IPEndPoint)
Console.WriteLine(("clonedIPEndPoint: " + clonedIPEndPoint.ToString()))
```

```
[C#]
// Recreate the connection endpoint from the serialized information.
IPEndPoint endpoint = new IPEndPoint(0,0);
IPEndPoint clonedIPEndPoint = (IPEndPoint)
endpoint.Create(socketAddress);
Console.WriteLine("clonedIPEndPoint: " + clonedIPEndPoint.ToString());
```

```
[C++]
// Recreate the connection endpoint from the serialized information.
IPEndPoint* endpoint = new IPEndPoint((__int64)0, 0);
IPEndPoint* clonedIPEndPoint =
    dynamic_cast<IPEndPoint*> (endpoint->Create(socketAddress));
Console::WriteLine(S"clonedIPEndPoint: {0}", clonedIPEndPoint);
```

Requirements

Platforms: Windows 98, Windows NT 4.0, Windows Millennium Edition, Windows 2000, Windows XP Home Edition, Windows XP Professional, Windows .NET Server family, .NET Compact Framework - Windows CE .NET, Common Language Infrastructure (CLI) Standard

IPEndPoint.Equals Method

This member overrides **Object.Equals**.

```
[Visual Basic]
Overrides Public Function Equals( _
    ByVal comparand As Object _
) As Boolean
[C#]
public override bool Equals(
    object comparand
);
```

```
[C++]
public: bool Equals(
    Object* comparand
);
[JScript]
public override function Equals(
    comparand : Object
) : Boolean;
```

Requirements

Platforms: Windows 98, Windows NT 4.0, Windows Millennium Edition, Windows 2000, Windows XP Home Edition, Windows XP Professional, Windows .NET Server family, .NET Compact Framework - Windows CE .NET, Common Language Infrastructure (CLI) Standard

IPEndPoint.GetHashCode Method

This member overrides **Object.GetHashCode**.

```
[Visual Basic]
Overrides Public Function GetHashCode() As Integer
[C#]
public override int GetHashCode();
[C++]
public: int GetHashCode();
[JScript]
public override function GetHashCode() : int;
```

Requirements

Platforms: Windows 98, Windows NT 4.0, Windows Millennium Edition, Windows 2000, Windows XP Home Edition, Windows XP Professional, Windows .NET Server family, .NET Compact Framework - Windows CE .NET, Common Language Infrastructure (CLI) Standard

IPEndPoint.Serialize Method

Serializes endpoint information into a **SocketAddress** instance.

```
[Visual Basic]
Overrides Public Function Serialize() As SocketAddress
[C#]
public override SocketAddress Serialize();
[C++]
public: SocketAddress* Serialize();
[JScript]
public override function Serialize() : SocketAddress;
```

Return Value

A **SocketAddress** instance containing the socket address for the endpoint.

Example

[Visual Basic, C#, C++] The following example uses the **Serialize** method to serialize endpoint information into a **SocketAddress** instance.

[Visual Basic]
```
' The serializeEndpoint method serializes the endpoint and returns the
' SocketAddress containing the serialized endpoint data.
Private Shared Function serializeEndpoint                              ⅃
(ByVal endpoint As IPEndPoint) As SocketAddress

    ' Serialize IPEndPoint details to a SocketAddress instance.
    Dim socketAddress As SocketAddress = endpoint.Serialize()

    ' Display the serialized endpoint information.
    Console.WriteLine("Endpoint Serialize() : " +                     ⅃
socketAddress.ToString())

    Console.WriteLine("Socket Family : " +                            ⅃
socketAddress.Family.ToString())
    Console.WriteLine("Socket Size : " + socketAddress.ToString())

    Console.WriteLine("Press any key to continue.")
    Console.ReadLine()

    Return socketAddress
End Function 'serializeEndpoint
```

[C#]
```
// The serializeEndpoint method serializes the endpoint and returns the
// SocketAddress containing the serialized endpoint data.
private static SocketAddress serializeEndpoint(IPEndPoint endpoint)
{

    // Serialize IPEndPoint details to a SocketAddress instance.
    SocketAddress socketAddress = endpoint.Serialize();

    // Display the serialized endpoint information.
    Console.WriteLine("Endpoint.Serialize() : " +                     ⅃
socketAddress.ToString());

    Console.WriteLine("Socket.Family : " + socketAddress.Family);
    Console.WriteLine("Socket.Size : " + socketAddress.Size);

    Console.WriteLine("Press any key to continue.");
    Console.ReadLine();

    return socketAddress;
}
```

[C++]
```
// This method serialize the endpoint and returns the
// SocketAddress containing the serialized endpoint data.
static SocketAddress* serializeEndpoint(IPEndPoint* endpoint) {

    // Serialize IPEndPoint details to a SocketAddress instance.
    SocketAddress* socketAddress = endpoint->Serialize();

    // Display the serialized endpoint information.
    Console::WriteLine(S"Endpoint::Serialize() : {0}", socketAddress);

    Console::WriteLine(S"Socket::Family : {0}", __box           ⅃
(socketAddress->Family));
    Console::WriteLine(S"Socket::Size : {0}", __box             ⅃
(socketAddress->Size));

    Console::WriteLine(S"Press any key to continue.");
    Console::ReadLine();

    return socketAddress;
}
```

Requirements

Platforms: Windows 98, Windows NT 4.0,
Windows Millennium Edition, Windows 2000,
Windows XP Home Edition, Windows XP Professional,
Windows .NET Server family,
.NET Compact Framework - Windows CE .NET

IPEndPoint.ToString Method

Returns the IP address and port number of the specified endpoint.

```
[Visual Basic]
Overrides Public Function ToString() As String
[C#]
public override string ToString();
[C++]
public: String* ToString();
[JScript]
public override function ToString() : String;
```

Return Value

A string containing the IP address and the port number of the
specified endpoint (for example, 192.168.1.2:23).

Example

[Visual Basic, C#, C++] The following example returns a string
representation of the IP address and port number of the specified
IPEndPoint.

[Visual Basic]
```
Private Shared Sub displayEndpointInfo(ByVal endpoint As IPEndPoint)
    Console.WriteLine("Endpoint Address : " +                         ⅃
endpoint.Address.ToString())
    Console.WriteLine("Endpoint AddressFamily : " +                   ⅃
endpoint.AddressFamily.ToString())
    Console.WriteLine("Endpoint Port : " + endpoint.Port.ToString())
    Console.WriteLine("Endpoint ToString() : " + endpoint.ToString())

    Console.WriteLine("Press any key to continue.")
    Console.ReadLine()
End Sub 'displayEndpointInfo
```

[C#]
```
private static void displayEndpointInfo(IPEndPoint endpoint)
{
    Console.WriteLine("Endpoint.Address : " + endpoint.Address);
    Console.WriteLine("Endpoint.AddressFamily : " +                   ⅃
endpoint.AddressFamily);
    Console.WriteLine("Endpoint.Port : " + endpoint.Port);
    Console.WriteLine("Endpoint.ToString() : " + endpoint.ToString());

    Console.WriteLine("Press any key to continue.");
    Console.ReadLine();
}
```

[C++]
```
static void displayEndpointInfo(IPEndPoint* endpoint) {
    Console::WriteLine(S"Endpoint->Address : {0}", endpoint->Address);
    Console::WriteLine(S"Endpoint->AddressFamily : {0}",              ⅃
__box(endpoint->AddressFamily));
    Console::WriteLine(S"Endpoint::Port : {0}", __box(endpoint->Port));
    Console::WriteLine(S"Endpoint : {0}", endpoint);

    Console::WriteLine(S"Press any key to continue.");
    Console::ReadLine();
}
```

Requirements

Platforms: Windows 98, Windows NT 4.0,
Windows Millennium Edition, Windows 2000,
Windows XP Home Edition, Windows XP Professional,
Windows .NET Server family,
.NET Compact Framework - Windows CE .NET,
Common Language Infrastructure (CLI) Standard

IPHostEntry Class

Provides a container class for Internet host address information.
For a list of all members of this type, see **IPHostEntry Members**.

System.Object
  System.Net.IPHostEntry

```
[Visual Basic]
Public Class IPHostEntry
[C#]
public class IPHostEntry
[C++]
public __gc class IPHostEntry
[JScript]
public class IPHostEntry
```

Thread Safety

Any public static (**Shared** in Visual Basic) members of this type are safe for multithreaded operations. Any instance members are not guaranteed to be thread safe.

Remarks

The **IPHostEntry** class associates a Domain Name System (DNS) host name with an array of aliases and an array of matching IP addresses.

The **IPHostEntry** class is used as a helper class with the **Dns** class.

Example

[Visual Basic, C#] The following example queries the DNS database for information on the host www.contoso.com and returns the information in an **IPHostEntry** instance.

```
[Visual Basic]
Dim hostInfo As IPHostEntry = Dns.GetHostByName("www.contoso.com")

[C#]
IPHostEntry hostInfo = Dns.GetHostByName("www.contoso.com");
```

Requirements

Namespace: System.Net

Platforms: Windows 98, Windows NT 4.0, Windows Millennium Edition, Windows 2000, Windows XP Home Edition, Windows XP Professional, Windows .NET Server family, .NET Compact Framework - Windows CE .NET

Assembly: System (in System.dll)

IPHostEntry Constructor

Initializes a new instance of the **IPHostEntry** class.

```
[Visual Basic]
Public Sub New()
[C#]
public IPHostEntry();
[C++]
public: IPHostEntry();
[JScript]
public function IPHostEntry();
```

Remarks

The default constructor initializes any fields to their default values.

Requirements

Platforms: Windows 98, Windows NT 4.0, Windows Millennium Edition, Windows 2000, Windows XP Home Edition, Windows XP Professional, Windows .NET Server family, .NET Compact Framework - Windows CE .NET, Common Language Infrastructure (CLI) Standard

IPHostEntry.AddressList Property

Gets or sets a list of IP addresses associated with a host.

```
[Visual Basic]
Public Property AddressList As IPAddress ()
[C#]
public IPAddress[] AddressList {get; set;}
[C++]
public: __property IPAddress* get_AddressList();
public: __property void set_AddressList(IPAddress*[]);
[JScript]
public function get AddressList() : IPAddress[];
public function set AddressList(IPAddress[]);
```

Property Value

An array of type **IPAddress** containing IP addresses that resolve to the host names contained in the **Aliases** property.

Example

[Visual Basic, C#, C++] The following example uses the **AddressList** property to access the IP addresses associated with the **IPHostEntry**.

```
[Visual Basic]
Public Sub GetIpAddressList(hostString As [String])
    Try
        ' Get 'IPHostEntry' object which contains information      ↵
like host name, IP addresses, aliases
        ' for specified url
        Dim hostInfo As IPHostEntry = Dns.GetHostByName(hostString)
        Console.WriteLine(("Host name : " + hostInfo.HostName))
        Console.WriteLine("IP address List : ")
        Dim index As Integer
        For index = 0 To hostInfo.AddressList.Length - 1
            Console.WriteLine(hostInfo.AddressList(index))
        Next index
    Catch e As SocketException
        Console.WriteLine("SocketException caught!!!")
        Console.WriteLine(("Source : " + e.Source))
        Console.WriteLine(("Message : " + e.Message))
    Catch e As ArgumentNullException
        Console.WriteLine("ArgumentNullException caught!!!")
        Console.WriteLine(("Source : " + e.Source))
        Console.WriteLine(("Message : " + e.Message))
    Catch e As Exception
        Console.WriteLine("Exception caught!!!")
        Console.WriteLine(("Source : " + e.Source))
        Console.WriteLine(("Message : " + e.Message))
    End Try
End Sub 'GetIpAddressList

[C#]
public void GetIpAddressList(String hostString)
{
    try
    {
        // Get 'IPHostEntry' object containing information       ↵
like host name, IP addresses, aliases for a host.
        IPHostEntry hostInfo = Dns.GetHostByName(hostString);
        Console.WriteLine("Host name : " + hostInfo.HostName);
```

```
        Console.WriteLine("IP address List : ");
        for(int index=0; index < hostInfo.AddressList.Length; index++)
        {
            Console.WriteLine(hostInfo.AddressList[index]);
        }
    }
    catch(SocketException e)
    {
        Console.WriteLine("SocketException caught!!!");
        Console.WriteLine("Source : " + e.Source);
        Console.WriteLine("Message : " + e.Message);
    }
    catch(ArgumentNullException e)
    {
        Console.WriteLine("ArgumentNullException caught!!!");
        Console.WriteLine("Source : " + e.Source);
        Console.WriteLine("Message : " + e.Message);
    }
    catch(Exception e)
    {
        Console.WriteLine("Exception caught!!!");
        Console.WriteLine("Source : " + e.Source);
        Console.WriteLine("Message : " + e.Message);
    }
}
```

```
[C++]
void GetIpAddressList(String* hostString) {
    try {
        // Get 'IPHostEntry' Object* containing information
        // like host name, IP addresses, aliases for a host.
        IPHostEntry* hostInfo = Dns::GetHostByName(hostString);
        Console::WriteLine(S"Host name : {0}", hostInfo->HostName);
        Console::WriteLine(S"IP address List : ");
        for (int index = 0 ; index < hostInfo->AddressList->
    ength ; index++)
            Console::WriteLine(hostInfo->AddressList->Item[index]);

    } catch (SocketException* e) {
        Console::WriteLine(S"SocketException caught!!!");
        Console::WriteLine(S"Source : {0}", e->Source);
        Console::WriteLine(S"Message : {0}", e->Message);
    } catch (ArgumentNullException* e) {
        Console::WriteLine(S"ArgumentNullException caught!!!");
        Console::WriteLine(S"Source : {0}", e->Source);
        Console::WriteLine(S"Message : {0}", e->Message);
    } catch (Exception* e) {
        Console::WriteLine(S"Exception caught!!!");
        Console::WriteLine(S"Source : {0}", e->Source);
        Console::WriteLine(S"Message : {0}", e->Message);
    }
}
```

Requirements

Platforms: Windows 98, Windows NT 4.0,
Windows Millennium Edition, Windows 2000,
Windows XP Home Edition, Windows XP Professional,
Windows .NET Server family,
.NET Compact Framework - Windows CE .NET,
Common Language Infrastructure (CLI) Standard

IPHostEntry.Aliases Property

Gets or sets a list of aliases associated with a host.

```
[Visual Basic]
Public Property Aliases As String ()
[C#]
public string[] Aliases {get; set;}
[C++]
public: __property String* get_Aliases();
public: __property void set_Aliases(String* __gc[]);
```

```
[JScript]
public function get Aliases() : String[];
public function set Aliases(String[]);
```

Property Value

An array of strings containing DNS names that resolve to the IP addresses in the **AddressList** property.

Requirements

Platforms: Windows 98, Windows NT 4.0,
Windows Millennium Edition, Windows 2000,
Windows XP Home Edition, Windows XP Professional,
Windows .NET Server family,
.NET Compact Framework - Windows CE .NET,
Common Language Infrastructure (CLI) Standard

IPHostEntry.HostName Property

Gets or sets the DNS name of the host.

```
[Visual Basic]
Public Property HostName As String
[C#]
public string HostName {get; set;}
[C++]
public: __property String* get_HostName();
public: __property void set_HostName(String*);
[JScript]
public function get HostName() : String;
public function set HostName(String);
```

Property Value

A string containing the primary host name for the server.

Remarks

The **HostName** property contains the primary host name for a server. If the DNS entry for the server defines additional aliases, they will be available in the **Aliases** property.

Example

[Visual Basic, C#, C++] The following example uses the **HostName** property to retrieve the primary host name.

```
[Visual Basic]
Public Sub GetIpAddressList(hostString As [String])
    Try
        ' Get 'IPHostEntry' object which contains information
like host name, IP addresses, aliases
        ' for specified url
        Dim hostInfo As IPHostEntry = Dns.GetHostByName(hostString)
        Console.WriteLine(("Host name : " + hostInfo.HostName))
        Console.WriteLine("IP address List : ")
        Dim index As Integer
        For index = 0 To hostInfo.AddressList.Length - 1
            Console.WriteLine(hostInfo.AddressList(index))
        Next index
    Catch e As SocketException
        Console.WriteLine("SocketException caught!!!")
        Console.WriteLine(("Source : " + e.Source))
        Console.WriteLine(("Message : " + e.Message))
    Catch e As ArgumentNullException
        Console.WriteLine("ArgumentNullException caught!!!")
        Console.WriteLine(("Source : " + e.Source))
        Console.WriteLine(("Message : " + e.Message))
    Catch e As Exception
        Console.WriteLine("Exception caught!!!")
        Console.WriteLine(("Source : " + e.Source))
        Console.WriteLine(("Message : " + e.Message))
    End Try
End Sub 'GetIpAddressList
```

```
[C#]
public void GetIpAddressList(String hostString)
{
    try
    {
        // Get 'IPHostEntry' object containing information          ⏎
        like host name, IP addresses, aliases for a host.
        IPHostEntry hostInfo = Dns.GetHostByName(hostString);
        Console.WriteLine("Host name : " + hostInfo.HostName);
        Console.WriteLine("IP address List : ");
        for(int index=0; index < hostInfo.AddressList.Length; index++)
        {
            Console.WriteLine(hostInfo.AddressList[index]);
        }
    }
    catch(SocketException e)
    {
        Console.WriteLine("SocketException caught!!!");
        Console.WriteLine("Source : " + e.Source);
        Console.WriteLine("Message : " + e.Message);
    }
    catch(ArgumentNullException e)
    {
        Console.WriteLine("ArgumentNullException caught!!!");
        Console.WriteLine("Source : " + e.Source);
        Console.WriteLine("Message : " + e.Message);
    }
    catch(Exception e)
    {
        Console.WriteLine("Exception caught!!!");
        Console.WriteLine("Source : " + e.Source);
        Console.WriteLine("Message : " + e.Message);
    }
}
```

```
[C++]
void GetIpAddressList(String* hostString) {
    try {
        // Get 'IPHostEntry' Object* containing information
        // like host name, IP addresses, aliases for a host.
        IPHostEntry* hostInfo = Dns::GetHostByName(hostString);
        Console::WriteLine(S"Host name : {0}", hostInfo->HostName);
        Console::WriteLine(S"IP address List : ");
        for (int index = 0 ; index < hostInfo->AddressList->          ⏎
Length ; index++)
            Console::WriteLine(hostInfo->AddressList->Item[index]);

    } catch (SocketException* e) {
        Console::WriteLine(S"SocketException caught!!!");
        Console::WriteLine(S"Source : {0}", e->Source);
        Console::WriteLine(S"Message : {0}", e->Message);
    } catch (ArgumentNullException* e) {
        Console::WriteLine(S"ArgumentNullException caught!!!");
        Console::WriteLine(S"Source : {0}", e->Source);
        Console::WriteLine(S"Message : {0}", e->Message);
    } catch (Exception* e) {
        Console::WriteLine(S"Exception caught!!!");
        Console::WriteLine(S"Source : {0}", e->Source);
        Console::WriteLine(S"Message : {0}", e->Message);
    }
}
```

Requirements

Platforms: Windows 98, Windows NT 4.0,
Windows Millennium Edition, Windows 2000,
Windows XP Home Edition, Windows XP Professional,
Windows .NET Server family,
.NET Compact Framework - Windows CE .NET,
Common Language Infrastructure (CLI) Standard

IrDAEndPoint Class

Note: This namespace, class, or member is supported only in version 1.1 of the .NET Framework.

This class establishes connections to a server and provides infrared port information.

System.Object
  System.Net.EndPoint
    System.Net.IrDAEndPoint

```
[Visual Basic]
Public Class IrDAEndPoint
   Inherits EndPoint
[C#]
public class IrDAEndPoint : EndPoint
[C++]
public __gc class IrDAEndPoint : public EndPoint
[JScript]
public class IrDAEndPoint extends EndPoint
```

Thread Safety

Any public static (**Shared** in Visual Basic) members of this type are safe for multithreaded operations. Any instance members are not guaranteed to be thread safe.

Remarks

Represents a network infrared service.

Requirements

Namespace: System.Net

Platforms: .NET Compact Framework - Windows CE .NET

Assembly: System.Net.Irda (in System.Net.Irda.dll)

IrDAEndPoint Constructor

Note: This namespace, class, or member is supported only in version 1.1 of the .NET Framework.

Initializes a new instance of the **IrDAEndPoint** class.

```
[Visual Basic]
Public Sub New( _
   ByVal irdaDeviceID() As Byte, _
   ByVal serviceName As String _
)
[C#]
public IrDAEndPoint(
   byte[] irdaDeviceID,
   string serviceName
);
[C++]
public: IrDAEndPoint(
   unsigned char irdaDeviceID __gc[],
   String* serviceName
);
[JScript]
public function IrDAEndPoint(
   irdaDeviceID : Byte[],
   serviceName : String
);
```

Parameters

irdaDeviceID
  The device identifier.
serviceName
  The name of the service to connect to.

Requirements

Platforms: .NET Compact Framework - Windows CE .NET

.NET Framework Security:
- Full trust for the immediate caller. This member cannot be used by partially trusted code.

IrDAEndPoint.AddressFamily Property

Note: This namespace, class, or member is supported only in version 1.1 of the .NET Framework.

Gets the address family to which the endpoint belongs.

```
[Visual Basic]
Overrides Public ReadOnly Property AddressFamily As AddressFamily
[C#]
public override AddressFamily AddressFamily {get;}
[C++]
public: __property AddressFamily get_AddressFamily();
[JScript]
public override function get AddressFamily() : AddressFamily;
```

Property Value

One of the **AddressFamily** values.

Remarks

An **AddressFamily** member specifies the addressing scheme that a **Socket** uses to resolve an address.

Requirements

Platforms: .NET Compact Framework - Windows CE .NET

.NET Framework Security:
- Full trust for the immediate caller. This member cannot be used by partially trusted code.

IrDAEndPoint.DeviceID Property

Note: This namespace, class, or member is supported only in version 1.1 of the .NET Framework.

Gets or sets an indentifier for the device.

```
[Visual Basic]
Public Property DeviceID As Byte ()
[C#]
public byte[] DeviceID {get; set;}
[C++]
public: __property unsigned char get_DeviceID();
public: __property void set_DeviceID(unsigned char __gc[]);
[JScript]
public function get DeviceID() : Byte[];
public function set DeviceID(Byte[]);
```

Property Value

A 4-byte value.

Requirements

Platforms: .NET Compact Framework - Windows CE .NET

.NET Framework Security:

* Full trust for the immediate caller. This member cannot be used by partially trusted code.

IrDAEndPoint.ServiceName Property

Note: This namespace, class, or member is supported only in version 1.1 of the .NET Framework.

Gets or sets the name of the service.

```
[Visual Basic]
Public Property ServiceName As String
[C#]
public string ServiceName {get; set;}
[C++]
public: __property String* get_ServiceName();
public: __property void set_ServiceName(String*);
[JScript]
public function get ServiceName() : String;
public function set ServiceName(String);
```

Property Value

The name of the service, such as ChatService.

Requirements

Platforms: .NET Compact Framework - Windows CE .NET

.NET Framework Security:

* Full trust for the immediate caller. This member cannot be used by partially trusted code.

IrDAEndPoint.Create Method

Note: This namespace, class, or member is supported only in version 1.1 of the .NET Framework.

Creates an **IrDAEndPoint** from a socket address.

```
[Visual Basic]
Overrides Public Function Create( _
    ByVal sockaddr As SocketAddress _
) As EndPoint
[C#]
public override EndPoint Create(
    SocketAddress sockaddr
);
[C++]
public: EndPoint* Create(
    SocketAddress* sockaddr
);
[JScript]
public override function Create(
    sockaddr : SocketAddress
) : EndPoint;
```

Parameters

sockaddr
    A **SocketAddress**.

Exceptions

Exception Type	Condition
NotSupportedException	Any attempt is made to access the method when the method is not overridden in a descendant class.

Requirements

Platforms: .NET Compact Framework - Windows CE .NET

.NET Framework Security:

* Full trust for the immediate caller. This member cannot be used by partially trusted code.

IrDAEndPoint.Serialize Method

Note: This namespace, class, or member is supported only in version 1.1 of the .NET Framework.

Serializes endpoint information into a **SocketAddress**.

```
[Visual Basic]
Overrides Public Function Serialize() As SocketAddress
[C#]
public override SocketAddress Serialize();
[C++]
public: SocketAddress* Serialize();
[JScript]
public override function Serialize() : SocketAddress;
```

Return Value

A **SocketAddress** containing the endpoint information.

Exceptions

Exception Type	Condition
NotSupportedException	An attempt is made to access the method when the method is not overridden in a descendant class.

Requirements

Platforms: .NET Compact Framework - Windows CE .NET

.NET Framework Security:

* Full trust for the immediate caller. This member cannot be used by partially trusted code.

IWebProxy Interface

Provides the base interface for implementation of proxy access for the **WebRequest** class.

```
[Visual Basic]
Public Interface IWebProxy
[C#]
public interface IWebProxy
[C++]
public __gc __interface IWebProxy
[JScript]
public interface IWebProxy
```

Classes that Implement IWebProxy

Class	Description
WebProxy	Contains HTTP proxy settings for the **WebRequest** class.

Remarks

The **IWebProxy** interface provides the methods and properties required by the **WebRequest** class to access proxy servers.

The **WebProxy** class is the base implementation of the **IWebProxy** interface.

Notes to Implementers: The **GetProxy** method can be used to control proxy use based on the destination URI. Use the **IsBypassed** method to indicate that the proxy should not be used to reach the destination server.

Requirements

Namespace: System.Net

Platforms: Windows 98, Windows NT 4.0, Windows Millennium Edition, Windows 2000, Windows XP Home Edition, Windows XP Professional, Windows .NET Server family, .NET Compact Framework - Windows CE .NET

Assembly: System (in System.dll)

IWebProxy.Credentials Property

The credentials to submit to the proxy server for authentication.

```
[Visual Basic]
Property Credentials As ICredentials
[C#]
ICredentials Credentials {get; set;}
[C++]
__property ICredentials* get_Credentials();
__property void set_Credentials(ICredentials*);
[JScript]
function get Credentials() : ICredentials;function set
Credentials(ICredentials);
```

Property Value

An **ICredentials** that contains the credentials needed to authenticate a request to the proxy server.

Remarks

The **Credentials** property is an **ICredentials** instance containing the authorization credentials to send to the proxy server in response to an HTTP 407 (proxy authorization) status code.

```
[Visual Basic]
Public Class WebProxy_Interface
    Implements IWebProxy

    'The credentials to be used with the web proxy.
    Private iCredentials As ICredentials

    'Uri of the associated proxy server.
    Private webProxyUri As Uri

    Sub New(proxyUri As Uri)

        webProxyUri = proxyUri
    End Sub 'New

    'Get and Set the Credentials property.

    Public Property Credentials() As ICredentials
Implements IWebProxy.Credentials
        Get
            Return iCredentials
        End Get
        Set
            If iCredentials Is value Then
                iCredentials = value
            End If
        End Set
    End Property

    'Returns the web proxy for the specified destination(destUri).
    Public Function GetProxy(destUri As Uri) As Uri
Implements IWebProxy.GetProxy

        'Always use the same proxy.
        Return webProxyUri
    End Function 'GetProxy

    'Returns whether the web proxy should be bypassed for the
specified destination(hostUri).
    Public Function IsBypassed(hostUri As Uri) As Boolean
Implements IWebProxy.IsBypassed
        'Never bypass the proxy.
        Return False
    End Function 'IsBypassed
End Class 'WebProxy_Interface

[C#]
public class WebProxy_Interface : IWebProxy

{

    // The credentials to be used with the web proxy.
    private ICredentials iCredentials;

    // Uri of the associated proxy server.
    private Uri webProxyUri;

    public WebProxy_Interface(Uri proxyUri) {

        webProxyUri = proxyUri;

    }

    // Get and Set the Credentials property.
    public ICredentials Credentials {
        get {
            return iCredentials;
        }
        set {
            if(iCredentials != value)
                iCredentials = value;
        }
    }
}
```

```
// Return the web proxy for the specified destination(destUri).
public Uri GetProxy(Uri destUri) {

    // Always use the same proxy.
    return webProxyUri;

}

// Return whether the web proxy should be bypassed
for the specified destination(hostUri).
    public bool IsBypassed(Uri hostUri) {

        // Never bypass the proxy.
        return false;

    }
};

[C++]
public __gc class WebProxy_Interface : public IWebProxy {
private:
    // The credentials to be used with the web proxy.
    ICredentials* iCredentials;

    // Uri of the associated proxy server.
    Uri* webProxyUri;

public:
    WebProxy_Interface(Uri* proxyUri) {
        webProxyUri = proxyUri;
    }

    // Get and Set the Credentials property.
    __property ICredentials* get_Credentials() {
        return iCredentials;
    }
    __property void set_Credentials(ICredentials* value) {
        if (iCredentials != value)
            iCredentials = value;
    }

    // Return the web proxy for the specified destination(destUri).
    Uri* GetProxy(Uri* destUri) {
        // Always use the same proxy.
        return webProxyUri;
    }

    // Return whether the web proxy should be bypassed for
the specified destination(hostUri).
    bool IsBypassed(Uri* hostUri) {
        // Never bypass the proxy.
        return false;
    }
};
```

Example

The following example uses the **Credentials** property to set the credentials that will be submitted to the proxy server for authentication.

Requirements

Platforms: Windows 98, Windows NT 4.0,
Windows Millennium Edition, Windows 2000,
Windows XP Home Edition, Windows XP Professional,
Windows .NET Server family,
.NET Compact Framework - Windows CE .NET,
Common Language Infrastructure (CLI) Standard

IWebProxy.GetProxy Method

Returns the URI of a proxy.

```
[Visual Basic]
Function GetProxy( _
    ByVal destination As Uri _
) As Uri
[C#]
Uri GetProxy(
    Uri destination
);
[C++]
Uri* GetProxy(
    Uri* destination
);
[JScript]
function GetProxy(
    destination : Uri
) : Uri;
```

Parameters

destination
    A **Uri** specifying the requested Internet resource.

Return Value

A **Uri** containing the URI of the proxy used to contact *destination*.

Remarks

The **GetProxy** method returns the URI of the proxy server that handles requests to the Internet resource specified in the *destination* parameter.

Example

The following example uses the **GetProxy** method to return the URI that the **WebRequest** uses to access the Internet resource.

Requirements

Platforms: Windows 98, Windows NT 4.0,
Windows Millennium Edition, Windows 2000,
Windows XP Home Edition, Windows XP Professional,
Windows .NET Server family,
.NET Compact Framework - Windows CE .NET,
Common Language Infrastructure (CLI) Standard

IWebProxy.IsBypassed Method

Indicates that the proxy should not be used for the specified host.

```
[Visual Basic]
Function IsBypassed( _
    ByVal host As Uri _
) As Boolean
[C#]
bool IsBypassed(
    Uri host
);
[C++]
bool IsBypassed(
    Uri* host
);
[JScript]
function IsBypassed(
    host : Uri
) : Boolean;
```

Parameters

host

> The **Uri** of the host to check for proxy use.

Return Value

true if the proxy server should not be used for *host*; otherwise, **false**.

Remarks

The **IsBypassed** method indicates whether to use the proxy server to access the host specified in the *host* parameter. If **IsBypassed** is **true**, the proxy is not used to contact the host and the request is passed directly to the server.

Example

The following example uses the **IsBypassed** property to determine if the proxy server should be used for the specified host.

Requirements

Platforms: Windows 98, Windows NT 4.0,
Windows Millennium Edition, Windows 2000,
Windows XP Home Edition, Windows XP Professional,
Windows .NET Server family,
.NET Compact Framework - Windows CE .NET,
Common Language Infrastructure (CLI) Standard

IWebRequestCreate Interface

Provides the base interface for creating **WebRequest** instances.

```
[Visual Basic]
Public Interface IWebRequestCreate
[C#]
public interface IWebRequestCreate
[C++]
public __gc __interface IWebRequestCreate
[JScript]
public interface IWebRequestCreate
```

Remarks

The **IWebRequestCreate** interface defines the method that **WebRequest** descendants must use to register with the **WebRequest.Create** method.

Classes that implement the **IWebRequestCreate** interface can be registered with the **WebRequest** class and associated with a specific URI scheme so that the **WebRequest** calls the class's **Create** method when a URI matching that scheme is requested.

Requirements

Namespace: System.Net

Platforms: Windows 98, Windows NT 4.0, Windows Millennium Edition, Windows 2000, Windows XP Home Edition, Windows XP Professional, Windows .NET Server family, .NET Compact Framework - Windows CE .NET

Assembly: System (in System.dll)

IWebRequestCreate.Create Method

Creates a **WebRequest** instance.

```
[Visual Basic]
Function Create( _
    ByVal uri As Uri _
) As WebRequest
[C#]
WebRequest Create(
    Uri uri
);
[C++]
WebRequest* Create(
    Uri* uri
);
[JScript]
function Create(
    uri : Uri
) : WebRequest;
```

Parameters

uri
> The uniform resource identifier (URI) of the Web resource.

Return Value

A **WebRequest** instance.

Remarks

The **Create** method must return an initialized instance of the **WebRequest** descendant capable of performing a standard request/response transaction for the protocol without needing any protocol-specific fields modified.

Requirements

Platforms: Windows 98, Windows NT 4.0, Windows Millennium Edition, Windows 2000, Windows XP Home Edition, Windows XP Professional, Windows .NET Server family, .NET Compact Framework - Windows CE .NET, Common Language Infrastructure (CLI) Standard

NetworkAccess Enumeration

Specifies network access permissions.

```
[Visual Basic]
<Serializable>
Public Enum NetworkAccess
[C#]
[Serializable]
public enum NetworkAccess
[C++]
[Serializable]
__value public enum NetworkAccess
[JScript]
public
    Serializable
enum NetworkAccess
```

Remarks

The **NetworkAccess** enumeration is used with the **WebPermission** and **SocketPermission** classes.

Members

Member name	Description
Accept	Indicates that the application is allowed to accept connections from the Internet on a local resource. Notice that this is a protection for the local host that uses Accept to grant access to a local resource (address/port). At the time a socket tries to bind to this local resource a permission check is performed to see if an Accept exists on that resource.
Connect	Indicates that the application is allowed to connect to specific Internet resources. Notice that, in the case of remote host resource, no check is performed to see that Connect permissions exist. This is because the port of a connecting remote host is unknown and not suitable permissions can be built in advance. It is the application responsibility to check the permissions of the remote host trying to connect to a listening socket.

Requirements

Namespace: System.Net

Platforms: Windows 98, Windows NT 4.0, Windows Millennium Edition, Windows 2000, Windows XP Home Edition, Windows XP Professional, Windows .NET Server family

Assembly: System (in System.dll)

NetworkCredential Class

Provides credentials for password-based authentication schemes such as basic, digest, NTLM, and Kerberos authentication.

System.Object
  System.Net.NetworkCredential

```
[Visual Basic]
Public Class NetworkCredential
   Implements ICredentials
[C#]
public class NetworkCredential : ICredentials
[C++]
public __gc class NetworkCredential : public ICredentials
[JScript]
public class NetworkCredential implements ICredentials
```

Thread Safety

Any public static (**Shared** in Visual Basic) members of this type are safe for multithreaded operations. Any instance members are not guaranteed to be thread safe.

Remarks

The **NetworkCredential** class is a base class that supplies credentials in password-based authentication schemes such as basic, digest, NTLM, and Kerberos. Classes that implement the **ICredentials** interface, such as the **CredentialCache** class, return **NetworkCredential** instances.

This class does not support public key-based authentication methods such as SSL client authentication.

Requirements

Namespace: System.Net

Platforms: Windows 98, Windows NT 4.0, Windows Millennium Edition, Windows 2000, Windows XP Home Edition, Windows XP Professional, Windows .NET Server family, .NET Compact Framework - Windows CE .NET

Assembly: System (in System.dll)

NetworkCredential Constructor

Initializes a new instance of the **NetworkCredential** class.

Overload List

Initializes a new instance of the **NetworkCredential** class.

Supported by the .NET Compact Framework.

> [Visual Basic] **Public Sub New()**
> [C#] **public NetworkCredential();**
> [C++] **public: NetworkCredential();**
> [JScript] **public function NetworkCredential();**

Initializes a new instance of the **NetworkCredential** class with the specified user name and password.

Supported by the .NET Compact Framework.

> [Visual Basic] **Public Sub New(String, String)**
> [C#] **public NetworkCredential(string, string);**
> [C++] **public: NetworkCredential(String*, String*);**
> [JScript] **public function NetworkCredential(String, String);**

Initializes a new instance of the **NetworkCredential** class with the specified user name, password, and domain.

Supported by the .NET Compact Framework.

> [Visual Basic] **Public Sub New(String, String, String)**
> [C#] **public NetworkCredential(string, string, string);**
> [C++] **public: NetworkCredential(String*, String*, String*);**
> [JScript] **public function NetworkCredential(String, String, String);**

Example

[Visual Basic, C#, C++] The following example creates a **NetworkCredential** instance using the specified user name and password.

> [Visual Basic, C#, C++] **Note** This example shows how to use one of the overloaded versions of the **NetworkCredential** constructor. For other examples that might be available, see the individual overload topics.

```
[Visual Basic]
' Call the constructor  to create an instance of                 ↵
NetworkCredential with the
' specified user name and password.
Dim myCredentials As New NetworkCredential(username, passwd)
' Create a WebRequest with the specified URL.
Dim myWebRequest As WebRequest = WebRequest.Create(url)
myCredentials.Domain = domain
myWebRequest.Credentials = myCredentials
Console.WriteLine(ControlChars.Cr + ControlChars.Cr +           ↵
"Credentials Domain : {0} , UserName : {1} , Password : {2}",    ↵
myCredentials.Domain, myCredentials.UserName, myCredentials.Password)
Console.WriteLine(ControlChars.Cr + ControlChars.Cr + "Request  ↵
to Url is sent.Waiting for response...")
' Send the request and wait for a response.
Dim myWebResponse As WebResponse = myWebRequest.GetResponse()
' Process the response.
Console.WriteLine(ControlChars.Cr + "Response received successfully.")
' Release the resources of the response object.
myWebResponse.Close()


[C#]
// Call the onstructor  to create an instance of                 ↵
NetworkCredential with the
// specified user name and password.
NetworkCredential myCredentials = new
NetworkCredential(username,passwd);

    // Create a WebRequest with the specified URL.
    WebRequest myWebRequest = WebRequest.Create(url);
    myCredentials.Domain = domain;
    myWebRequest.Credentials = myCredentials;
    Console.WriteLine("\n\nCredentials Domain : {0} ,            ↵
UserName : {1} , Password : {2}",
    myCredentials.Domain, myCredentials.UserName,
myCredentials.Password);
    Console.WriteLine("\n\nRequest to Url is sent.Waiting        ↵
for response...");

    // Send the request and wait for a response.
    WebResponse myWebResponse = myWebRequest.GetResponse();

    // Process the response.
    Console.WriteLine("\nResponse received successfully.");
    // Release the resources of the response object.
    myWebResponse.Close();


[C++]
// Call the onstructor  to create an instance of                 ↵
NetworkCredential with the
// specified user name and password.
```

```
NetworkCredential* myCredentials = new
    NetworkCredential(username, passwd);

// Create a WebRequest with the specified URL.
WebRequest* myWebRequest = WebRequest::Create(url);
myCredentials->Domain = domain;
myWebRequest->Credentials = myCredentials;
Console::WriteLine(S"\n\nCredentials Domain : {0} , UserName
: {1} , Password : {2}",
    myCredentials->Domain, myCredentials->UserName,
myCredentials->Password);
Console::WriteLine(S"\n\nRequest to Url is sent.Waiting
for response...");

// Send the request and wait for a response.
WebResponse* myWebResponse = myWebRequest->GetResponse();

// Process the response.
Console::WriteLine(S"\nResponse received successfully.");
// Release the resources of the response Object*.
myWebResponse->Close();
```

NetworkCredential Constructor ()

Initializes a new instance of the **NetworkCredential** class.

```
[Visual Basic]
Public Sub New()
[C#]
public NetworkCredential();
[C++]
public: NetworkCredential();
[JScript]
public function NetworkCredential();
```

Remarks

The default constructor for the **NetworkCredential** class initializes all properties to a null reference (**Nothing** in Visual Basic).

Requirements

Platforms: Windows 98, Windows NT 4.0,
Windows Millennium Edition, Windows 2000,
Windows XP Home Edition, Windows XP Professional,
Windows .NET Server family,
.NET Compact Framework - Windows CE .NET,
Common Language Infrastructure (CLI) Standard

NetworkCredential Constructor (String, String)

Initializes a new instance of the **NetworkCredential** class with the specified user name and password.

```
[Visual Basic]
Public Sub New( _
    ByVal userName As String, _
    ByVal password As String _
)
[C#]
public NetworkCredential(
    string userName,
    string password
);
[C++]
public: NetworkCredential(
    String* userName,
    String* password
);
```

```
[JScript]
public function NetworkCredential(
    userName : String,
    password : String
);
```

Parameters

userName
   The user name associated with the credentials.
password
   The password for the user name associated with the credentials.

Remarks

The constructor initializes a **NetworkCredential** instance with the **UserName** property set to *userName* and the **Password** property set to *password*.

Example

[Visual Basic, C#, C++] The following example creates a **NetworkCredential** instance using the specified user name and password.

```
[Visual Basic]
' Call the constructor  to create an instance of
NetworkCredential with the
' specified user name and password.
Dim myCredentials As New NetworkCredential(username, passwd)
' Create a WebRequest with the specified URL.
Dim myWebRequest As WebRequest = WebRequest.Create(url)
myCredentials.Domain = domain
myWebRequest.Credentials = myCredentials
Console.WriteLine(ControlChars.Cr + ControlChars.Cr +
"Credentials Domain : {0} , UserName : {1} , Password : {2}",
myCredentials.Domain, myCredentials.UserName, myCredentials.Password)
Console.WriteLine(ControlChars.Cr + ControlChars.Cr + "Request
to Url is sent.Waiting for response...")
' Send the request and wait for a response.
Dim myWebResponse As WebResponse = myWebRequest.GetResponse()
' Process the response.
Console.WriteLine(ControlChars.Cr + "Response received successfully.")
' Release the resources of the response object.
myWebResponse.Close()
```

```
[C#]
// Call the onstructor  to create an instance of
NetworkCredential with the
// specified user name and password.
NetworkCredential myCredentials = new
NetworkCredential(username,passwd);

    // Create a WebRequest with the specified URL.
    WebRequest myWebRequest = WebRequest.Create(url);
    myCredentials.Domain = domain;
    myWebRequest.Credentials = myCredentials;
    Console.WriteLine("\n\nCredentials Domain : {0} ,
UserName : {1} , Password : {2}",
    myCredentials.Domain, myCredentials.UserName,
myCredentials.Password);
    Console.WriteLine("\n\nRequest to Url is sent.Waiting
for response...");

    // Send the request and wait for a response.
    WebResponse myWebResponse = myWebRequest.GetResponse();

    // Process the response.
    Console.WriteLine("\nResponse received successfully.");
    // Release the resources of the response object.
    myWebResponse.Close();
```

```
[C++]
// Call the onstructor  to create an instance of
NetworkCredential with the
// specified user name and password.
NetworkCredential* myCredentials = new
   NetworkCredential(username, passwd);

// Create a WebRequest with the specified URL.
WebRequest* myWebRequest = WebRequest::Create(url);
myCredentials->Domain = domain;
myWebRequest->Credentials = myCredentials;
Console::WriteLine(S"\n\nCredentials Domain : {0} ,
UserName : {1} , Password : {2}",
   myCredentials->Domain, myCredentials->UserName,
myCredentials->Password);
Console::WriteLine(S"\n\nRequest to Url is sent.Waiting
for response...");

// Send the request and wait for a response.
WebResponse* myWebResponse = myWebRequest->GetResponse();

// Process the response.
Console::WriteLine(S"\nResponse received successfully.");
// Release the resources of the response Object*.
myWebResponse->Close();
```

Requirements

Platforms: Windows 98, Windows NT 4.0,
Windows Millennium Edition, Windows 2000,
Windows XP Home Edition, Windows XP Professional,
Windows .NET Server family,
.NET Compact Framework - Windows CE .NET,
Common Language Infrastructure (CLI) Standard

NetworkCredential Constructor (String, String, String)

Initializes a new instance of the **NetworkCredential** class with the specified user name, password, and domain.

```
[Visual Basic]
Public Sub New( _
   ByVal userName As String, _
   ByVal password As String, _
   ByVal domain As String _
)
[C#]
public NetworkCredential(
   string userName,
   string password,
   string domain
);
[C++]
public: NetworkCredential(
   String* userName,
   String* password,
   String* domain
);
[JScript]
public function NetworkCredential(
   userName : String,
   password : String,
   domain : String
);
```

Parameters

userName
    The user name associated with the credentials.
password
    The password for the user name associated with the credentials.
domain
    The domain associated with these credentials.

Remarks

The constructor initializes a **NetworkCredential** instance with the **UserName** property set to *userName*, the **Password** property set to *password*, and the **Domain** property set to *domain*.

Requirements

Platforms: Windows 98, Windows NT 4.0,
Windows Millennium Edition, Windows 2000,
Windows XP Home Edition, Windows XP Professional,
Windows .NET Server family,
.NET Compact Framework - Windows CE .NET,
Common Language Infrastructure (CLI) Standard

NetworkCredential.Domain Property

Gets or sets the domain or computer name that verifies the credentials.

```
[Visual Basic]
Public Property Domain As String
[C#]
public string Domain {get; set;}
[C++]
public: __property String* get_Domain();
public: __property void set_Domain(String*);
[JScript]
public function get Domain() : String;
public function set Domain(String);
```

Property Value

The name of the domain associated with the credentials.

Remarks

The **Domain** property specifies the domain or realm to which the user name belongs. Typically, this is the host computer name where the application runs or the user domain for the currently logged in user.

Requirements

Platforms: Windows 98, Windows NT 4.0,
Windows Millennium Edition, Windows 2000,
Windows XP Home Edition, Windows XP Professional,
Windows .NET Server family,
.NET Compact Framework - Windows CE .NET,
Common Language Infrastructure (CLI) Standard

.NET Framework Security:

- **EnvironmentPermission** to get the system domain. Associated enumeration: **EnvironmentPermissionAccess.Read**

NetworkCredential.Password Property

Gets or sets the password for the user name associated with the credentials.

```
[Visual Basic]
Public Property Password As String
[C#]
public string Password {get; set;}
[C++]
public: __property String* get_Password();
public: __property void set_Password(String*);
[JScript]
public function get Password() : String;
public function set Password(String);
```

Property Value

The he password associated with the credentials.

Requirements

Platforms: Windows 98, Windows NT 4.0,
Windows Millennium Edition, Windows 2000,
Windows XP Home Edition, Windows XP Professional,
Windows .NET Server family,
.NET Compact Framework - Windows CE .NET,
Common Language Infrastructure (CLI) Standard

.NET Framework Security:

- **SecurityPermission** to get the user password. Associated enumeration: **SecurityPermissionFlag.UnmanagedCode**

NetworkCredential.UserName Property

Gets or sets the user name associated with the credentials.

```
[Visual Basic]
Public Property UserName As String
[C#]
public string UserName {get; set;}
[C++]
public: __property String* get_UserName();
public: __property void set_UserName(String*);
[JScript]
public function get UserName() : String;
public function set UserName(String);
```

Property Value

The user name associated with the credentials.

Requirements

Platforms: Windows 98, Windows NT 4.0,
Windows Millennium Edition, Windows 2000,
Windows XP Home Edition, Windows XP Professional,
Windows .NET Server family,
.NET Compact Framework - Windows CE .NET,
Common Language Infrastructure (CLI) Standard

.NET Framework Security:

- **EnvironmentPermission** to read the user name from the system. Associated enumeration: **EnvironmentPermissionAccess.Read**

NetworkCredential.GetCredential Method

Returns an instance of the **NetworkCredential** class for the specified URI and authentication type.

```
[Visual Basic]
Public Overridable Function GetCredential( _
   ByVal uri As Uri, _
   ByVal authType As String _
) As NetworkCredential Implements ICredentials.GetCredential
[C#]
public virtual NetworkCredential GetCredential(
   Uri uri,
   string authType
);
[C++]
public: virtual NetworkCredential* GetCredential(
   Uri* uri,
   String* authType
);
[JScript]
public function GetCredential(
   uri : Uri,
   authType : String
) : NetworkCredential;
```

Parameters

uri
    The URI that the client is providing authentication for.
authType
    The type of authentication requested, as defined in the **IAuthenticationModule.AuthenticationType** property.

Return Value

A **NetworkCredential** instance.

Implements

ICredentials.GetCredential

Example

See related example in the **System.Net.NetworkCredential** class topic.

Requirements

Platforms: Windows 98, Windows NT 4.0,
Windows Millennium Edition, Windows 2000,
Windows XP Home Edition, Windows XP Professional,
Windows .NET Server family,
.NET Compact Framework - Windows CE .NET,
Common Language Infrastructure (CLI) Standard

ProtocolViolationException Class

The exception that is thrown when an error is made while using a network protocol.

System.Object
  System.Exception
    System.SystemException
      System.InvalidOperationException
        System.Net.ProtocolViolationException

[Visual Basic]
```
<Serializable>
Public Class ProtocolViolationException
  Inherits InvalidOperationException
```
[C#]
```
[Serializable]
public class ProtocolViolationException :
    InvalidOperationException
```
[C++]
```
[Serializable]
public __gc class ProtocolViolationException : public
    InvalidOperationException
```
[JScript]
```
public
    Serializable
class ProtocolViolationException extends
    InvalidOperationException
```

Thread Safety

Any public static (**Shared** in Visual Basic) members of this type are safe for multithreaded operations. Any instance members are not guaranteed to be thread safe.

Remarks

A **ProtocolViolationException** is thrown by descendants of **WebRequest** and **WebResponse** to indicate an error using the underlying protocol. For example, the **HttpWebRequest** and **HttpWebResponse** classes throw a **ProtocolViolationException** to indicate an error using HTTP.

Requirements

Namespace: System.Net

Platforms: Windows 98, Windows NT 4.0, Windows Millennium Edition, Windows 2000, Windows XP Home Edition, Windows XP Professional, Windows .NET Server family, .NET Compact Framework - Windows CE .NET

Assembly: System (in System.dll)

ProtocolViolationException Constructor

Initializes a new instance of the **ProtocolViolationException** class.

Overload List

Initializes a new instance of the **ProtocolViolationException** class.

Supported by the .NET Compact Framework.

  [Visual Basic] **Public Sub New()**
  [C#] **public ProtocolViolationException();**
  [C++] **public: ProtocolViolationException();**

  [JScript] **public function ProtocolViolationException();**

Initializes a new instance of the **ProtocolViolationException** class with the specified message.

Supported by the .NET Compact Framework.

  [Visual Basic] **Public Sub New(String)**
  [C#] **public ProtocolViolationException(string);**
  [C++] **public: ProtocolViolationException(String*);**
  [JScript] **public function ProtocolViolationException(String);**

Initializes a new instance of the **ProtocolViolationException** class from the specified specified **SerializationInfo** and **StreamingContext** instances.

  [Visual Basic] **Protected Sub New(SerializationInfo, StreamingContext)**
  [C#] **protected ProtocolViolationException(SerializationInfo, StreamingContext);**
  [C++] **protected: ProtocolViolationException (SerializationInfo*, StreamingContext);**
  [JScript] **protected function ProtocolViolationException (SerializationInfo, StreamingContext);**

ProtocolViolationException Constructor ( )

Initializes a new instance of the **ProtocolViolationException** class.

[Visual Basic]
```
Public Sub New()
```
[C#]
```
public ProtocolViolationException();
```
[C++]
```
public: ProtocolViolationException();
```
[JScript]
```
public function ProtocolViolationException();
```

Remarks

The **Message** property is initialized to a system-supplied message that describes the error. The InnerException property is initialized to a null reference (**Nothing** in Visual Basic).

Requirements

Platforms: Windows 98, Windows NT 4.0, Windows Millennium Edition, Windows 2000, Windows XP Home Edition, Windows XP Professional, Windows .NET Server family, .NET Compact Framework - Windows CE .NET, Common Language Infrastructure (CLI) Standard

ProtocolViolationException Constructor (String)

Initializes a new instance of the **ProtocolViolationException** class with the specified message.

[Visual Basic]
```
Public Sub New( _
    ByVal message As String _
)
```
[C#]
```
public ProtocolViolationException(
    string message
);
```

```
[C++]
public: ProtocolViolationException(
    String* message
);
[JScript]
public function ProtocolViolationException(
    message : String
);
```

Parameters

message
> The error message string.

Remarks

This constructor initializes a new instance of the
ProtocolViolationException class with the **Message** property set to
the value of the *message* parameter. If *message* is a null reference,
the **Message** property is initialized to a system-supplied message.
The **InnerException** property is initialized to a null reference
(**Nothing** in Visual Basic).

Requirements

Platforms: Windows 98, Windows NT 4.0,
Windows Millennium Edition, Windows 2000,
Windows XP Home Edition, Windows XP Professional,
Windows .NET Server family,
.NET Compact Framework - Windows CE .NET,
Common Language Infrastructure (CLI) Standard

ProtocolViolationException Constructor (SerializationInfo, StreamingContext)

Initializes a new instance of the **ProtocolViolationException** class
from the specified specified **SerializationInfo** and
StreamingContext instances.

```
[Visual Basic]
Protected Sub New( _
    ByVal serializationInfo As SerializationInfo, _
    ByVal streamingContext As StreamingContext _
)
[C#]
protected ProtocolViolationException(
    SerializationInfo serializationInfo,
    StreamingContext streamingContext
);
[C++]
protected: ProtocolViolationException(
    SerializationInfo* serializationInfo,
    StreamingContext streamingContext
);
[JScript]
protected function ProtocolViolationException(
    serializationInfo : SerializationInfo,
    streamingContext : StreamingContext
);
```

Parameters

serializationInfo
> A **SerializationInfo** containing the information required to
> serialize the new **ProtocolViolationException**.

streamingContext
> A **StreamingContext** containing the source of the serialized
> stream associated with the new **ProtocolViolationException**.

Remarks

This constructor implements the **ISerializable** interface for the
ProtocolViolationException class.

Requirements

Platforms: Windows 98, Windows NT 4.0,
Windows Millennium Edition, Windows 2000,
Windows XP Home Edition, Windows XP Professional,
Windows .NET Server family

ProtocolViolationException.ISerializable.GetObjectData Method

This member supports the .NET Framework infrastructure and is not
intended to be used directly from your code.

```
[Visual Basic]
Private Sub GetObjectData( _
    ByVal serializationInfo As SerializationInfo, _
    ByVal streamingContext As StreamingContext _
) Implements ISerializable.GetObjectData
[C#]
void ISerializable.GetObjectData(
    SerializationInfo serializationInfo,
    StreamingContext streamingContext
);
[C++]
private: void ISerializable::GetObjectData(
    SerializationInfo* serializationInfo,
    StreamingContext streamingContext
);
[JScript]
private function ISerializable.GetObjectData(
    serializationInfo : SerializationInfo,
    streamingContext : StreamingContext
);
```

SecurityProtocolType Enumeration

Note: This namespace, class, or member is supported only in version 1.1 of the .NET Framework.

This enumeration has a **FlagsAttribute** attribute that allows a bitwise combination of its member values.

```
[Visual Basic]
<Flags>
<Serializable>
Public Enum SecurityProtocolType
[C#]
[Flags]
[Serializable]
public enum SecurityProtocolType
[C++]
[Flags]
[Serializable]
__value public enum SecurityProtocolType
[JScript]
public
    Flags
    Serializable
enum SecurityProtocolType
```

Members

Member name	Description	Value
Ssl3		48
Tls		192

Requirements

Namespace: System.Net

Platforms: Windows 98, Windows NT 4.0, Windows Millennium Edition, Windows 2000, Windows XP Home Edition, Windows XP Professional, Windows .NET Server family

Assembly: System (in System.dll)

ServicePoint Class

Provides connection management for HTTP connections.

For a list of all members of this type, see **ServicePoint Members**.

System.Object
  System.Net.ServicePoint

```
[Visual Basic]
Public Class ServicePoint
[C#]
public class ServicePoint
[C++]
public __gc class ServicePoint
[JScript]
public class ServicePoint
```

Thread Safety

Any public static (**Shared** in Visual Basic) members of this type are safe for multithreaded operations. Any instance members are not guaranteed to be thread safe.

Remarks

The **ServicePoint** class handles connections to an Internet resource based on the host information passed in the resource's URI. The initial connection to the resource determines the information the **ServicePoint** maintains, which is then shared by all subsequent requests to that resource.

ServicePoint instances are managed by the **ServicePointManager** class and are created, if necessary, by the **ServicePointManager.FindServicePoint** method. The maximum number of **ServicePoint** instances that can be created is set by the **ServicePointManager.MaxServicePoints** property.

Each **ServicePoint** instance maintains its connection to an Internet resource until it has been idle longer than the time specified in the **MaxIdleTime** property. Once a ServicePoint exceeds the **MaxIdleTime**, it can be recycled to another connection. The default value of **MaxIdleTime** is set by the **ServicePointManager.MaxServicePointIdleTime** property.

Requirements

Namespace: System.Net

Platforms: Windows 98, Windows NT 4.0, Windows Millennium Edition, Windows 2000, Windows XP Home Edition, Windows XP Professional, Windows .NET Server family, .NET Compact Framework - Windows CE .NET

Assembly: System (in System.dll)

ServicePoint.Address Property

Gets the URI of the **ServicePoint**.

```
[Visual Basic]
Public ReadOnly Property Address As Uri
[C#]
public Uri Address {get;}
[C++]
public: __property Uri* get_Address();
[JScript]
public function get Address() : Uri;
```

Property Value

An instance of the **Uri** class containing the URI of the Internet server that this **ServicePoint** connects to.

Requirements

Platforms: Windows 98, Windows NT 4.0, Windows Millennium Edition, Windows 2000, Windows XP Home Edition, Windows XP Professional, Windows .NET Server family, .NET Compact Framework - Windows CE .NET, Common Language Infrastructure (CLI) Standard

ServicePoint.Certificate Property

Gets the certificate received for this **ServicePoint**.

```
[Visual Basic]
Public ReadOnly Property Certificate As X509Certificate
[C#]
public X509Certificate Certificate {get;}
[C++]
public: __property X509Certificate* get_Certificate();
[JScript]
public function get Certificate() : X509Certificate;
```

Property Value

An instance of the **X509Certificate** class containing the security certificate received for this **ServicePoint**.

Remarks

Although a **ServicePoint** can make multiple connections to an Internet resource, it can maintain only one certificate.

Requirements

Platforms: Windows 98, Windows NT 4.0, Windows Millennium Edition, Windows 2000, Windows XP Home Edition, Windows XP Professional, Windows .NET Server family, .NET Compact Framework - Windows CE .NET

ServicePoint.ClientCertificate Property

Gets the last client certificate sent to the server.

```
[Visual Basic]
Public ReadOnly Property ClientCertificate As X509Certificate
[C#]
public X509Certificate ClientCertificate {get;}
[C++]
public: __property X509Certificate* get_ClientCertificate();
[JScript]
public function get ClientCertificate() : X509Certificate;
```

Property Value

An **X509Certificate** containing the public values of the last client certificate sent to the server.

Requirements

Platforms: Windows 98, Windows NT 4.0, Windows Millennium Edition, Windows 2000, Windows XP Home Edition, Windows XP Professional, Windows .NET Server family

ServicePoint.ConnectionLimit Property

Gets or sets the maximum number of connections allowed on this **ServicePoint**.

```
[Visual Basic]
Public Property ConnectionLimit As Integer
[C#]
public int ConnectionLimit {get; set;}
[C++]
public: __property int get_ConnectionLimit();
public: __property void set_ConnectionLimit(int);
[JScript]
public function get ConnectionLimit() : int;
public function set ConnectionLimit(int);
```

Property Value

The maximum number of connections allowed on this **ServicePoint**.

Exceptions

Exception Type	Condition
ArgumentOutOfRange-Exception	The connection limit is 0 or less than 0.

Remarks

The **ConnectionLimit** property sets the maximum number of connections that the **ServicePoint** can make to an Internet resource. The value of the **ConnectionLimit** property is set to the value of the **ServicePointManager.DefaultConnectionLimit** property when the **ServicePoint** is created; subsequent changes to **DefaultConnectionLimit** have no effect on existing **ServicePoint** instances.

Requirements

Platforms: Windows 98, Windows NT 4.0, Windows Millennium Edition, Windows 2000, Windows XP Home Edition, Windows XP Professional, Windows .NET Server family, .NET Compact Framework - Windows CE .NET, Common Language Infrastructure (CLI) Standard

ServicePoint.ConnectionName Property

Gets the connection group name established by the **WebRequest** that created the connection.

```
[Visual Basic]
Public ReadOnly Property ConnectionName As String
[C#]
public string ConnectionName {get;}
[C++]
public: __property String* get_ConnectionName();
[JScript]
public function get ConnectionName() : String;
```

Property Value

A string containing the connection group name assigned by the **WebRequest** instance that created the connection.

Remarks

The **ConnectionName** property contains the connection group assigned to the **ConnectionGroupName** property of the **WebRequest** that initiated the connection provided by this **ServicePoint**. If the **ConnectionName** property is set, only **WebRequest** instances with the same **ConnectionGroupName** can use this **ServicePoint**.

Requirements

Platforms: Windows 98, Windows NT 4.0, Windows Millennium Edition, Windows 2000, Windows XP Home Edition, Windows XP Professional, Windows .NET Server family, .NET Compact Framework - Windows CE .NET, Common Language Infrastructure (CLI) Standard

ServicePoint.CurrentConnections Property

Gets the number of connections associated with this **ServicePoint**.

```
[Visual Basic]
Public ReadOnly Property CurrentConnections As Integer
[C#]
public int CurrentConnections {get;}
[C++]
public: __property int get_CurrentConnections();
[JScript]
public function get CurrentConnections() : int;
```

Property Value

The number of connections associated with this **ServicePoint**.

Remarks

The **CurrentConnections** property contains the number of active Internet connections associated with this **ServicePoint**. The value of **CurrentConnections** cannot exceed that of **ConnectionLimit**.

Requirements

Platforms: Windows 98, Windows NT 4.0, Windows Millennium Edition, Windows 2000, Windows XP Home Edition, Windows XP Professional, Windows .NET Server family, .NET Compact Framework - Windows CE .NET, Common Language Infrastructure (CLI) Standard

ServicePoint.IdleSince Property

Gets the date and time that the **ServicePoint** was last connected to a host.

```
[Visual Basic]
Public ReadOnly Property IdleSince As DateTime
[C#]
public DateTime IdleSince {get;}
[C++]
public: __property DateTime get_IdleSince();
[JScript]
public function get IdleSince() : DateTime;
```

Property Value

A **DateTime** instance containing the date and time at which the **ServicePoint** was last connected.

Remarks

The **IdleSince** property records the last date and time at which a service point was disconnected from a host. When the difference between the current time and **IdleSince** exceeds the value of **MaxIdleTime**, the **ServicePoint** is available for recycling to another connection.

Requirements

Platforms: Windows 98, Windows NT 4.0,
Windows Millennium Edition, Windows 2000,
Windows XP Home Edition, Windows XP Professional,
Windows .NET Server family,
.NET Compact Framework - Windows CE .NET,
Common Language Infrastructure (CLI) Standard

ServicePoint.MaxIdleTime Property

Gets or sets the amount of time the **ServicePoint** can remain idle
(unconnected to a host).

```
[Visual Basic]
Public Property MaxIdleTime As Integer
[C#]
public int MaxIdleTime {get; set;}
[C++]
public: __property int get_MaxIdleTime();
public: __property void set_MaxIdleTime(int);
[JScript]
public function get MaxIdleTime() : int;
public function set MaxIdleTime(int);
```

Property Value

The length of time, in milliseconds, that the **ServicePoint** can
remain idle before it is reused for another connection.

Exceptions

Exception Type	Condition
ArgumentOutOfRange-Exception	**MaxIdleTime** is set to less than **Timeout.Infinite** or greater than **Int32.MaxValue**.

Remarks

The **MaxIdleTime** property contains the length of time, in
milliseconds, that the **ServicePoint** is allowed to maintain an idle
connection to an Internet resource before it is recycled for use in
another connection.

You can set **MaxIdleTime** to **Timeout.Infinite** to indicate that the
ServicePoint should never timeout.

The default value of the **MaxIdleTime** property is the value of the
ServicePointManager.MaxServicePointIdleTime property when
the **ServicePoint** is created. Subsequent changes to the
MaxServicePointIdleTime property have no effect on existing
ServicePoint instances.

Requirements

Platforms: Windows 98, Windows NT 4.0,
Windows Millennium Edition, Windows 2000,
Windows XP Home Edition, Windows XP Professional,
Windows .NET Server family,
.NET Compact Framework - Windows CE .NET,
Common Language Infrastructure (CLI) Standard

ServicePoint.ProtocolVersion Property

Gets the version of the HTTP protocol that the **ServicePoint** uses.

```
[Visual Basic]
Public Overridable ReadOnly Property ProtocolVersion As Version
[C#]
public virtual Version ProtocolVersion {get;}
```

```
[C++]
public: __property virtual Version* get_ProtocolVersion();
[JScript]
public function get ProtocolVersion() : Version;
```

Property Value

A **Version** instance containing the HTTP protocol version that the
ServicePoint uses.

Requirements

Platforms: Windows 98, Windows NT 4.0,
Windows Millennium Edition, Windows 2000,
Windows XP Home Edition, Windows XP Professional,
Windows .NET Server family,
.NET Compact Framework - Windows CE .NET,
Common Language Infrastructure (CLI) Standard

ServicePoint.SupportsPipelining Property

Indicates whether the **ServicePoint** supports pipelined connections.

```
[Visual Basic]
Public ReadOnly Property SupportsPipelining As Boolean
[C#]
public bool SupportsPipelining {get;}
[C++]
public: __property bool get_SupportsPipelining();
[JScript]
public function get SupportsPipelining() : Boolean;
```

Property Value

true if the **ServicePoint** supports pipelined connections; otherwise,
false.

Requirements

Platforms: Windows 98, Windows NT 4.0,
Windows Millennium Edition, Windows 2000,
Windows XP Home Edition, Windows XP Professional,
Windows .NET Server family,
.NET Compact Framework - Windows CE .NET,
Common Language Infrastructure (CLI) Standard

ServicePoint.UseNagleAlgorithm Property

Note: This namespace, class, or member is supported only in
version 1.1 of the .NET Framework.

```
[Visual Basic]
Public Property UseNagleAlgorithm As Boolean
[C#]
public bool UseNagleAlgorithm {get; set;}
[C++]
public: __property bool get_UseNagleAlgorithm();
public: __property void set_UseNagleAlgorithm(bool);
[JScript]
public function get UseNagleAlgorithm() : Boolean;
public function set UseNagleAlgorithm(Boolean);
```

Requirements

Platforms: Windows 98, Windows NT 4.0,
Windows Millennium Edition, Windows 2000,
Windows XP Home Edition, Windows XP Professional,
Windows .NET Server family

ServicePoint.GetHashCode Method

Gets the hash code for the **ServicePoint**.

```
[Visual Basic]
Overrides Public Function GetHashCode() As Integer
[C#]
public override int GetHashCode();
[C++]
public: int GetHashCode();
[JScript]
public override function GetHashCode() : int;
```

Return Value

The hash code for the **ServicePoint**.

Remarks

The hash code for **ServicePoint** A and B is the same if A.Equals(B) is **true**.

This method implements the **Object.GetHashCode** method.

Example

[Visual Basic, C#, C++] The following example uses the **GetHashCode** method to determine if two **HttpWebRequest** instances are pointing to the same **ServicePoint**.

```
[Visual Basic]
' Create the first 'HttpWebRequest' object.
Dim myWebRequest1 As HttpWebRequest =
CType(WebRequest.Create("http://www.microsoft.com"), HttpWebRequest)
' The response object of 'HttpWebRequest' is assigned to a
'HttpWebResponse' variable.
Dim myWebResponse1 As HttpWebResponse =
CType(myWebRequest1.GetResponse(), HttpWebResponse)
Dim myServicePoint1 As ServicePoint = myWebRequest1.ServicePoint

' Create the second 'HttpWebRequest' object with the same
hostfragment as above.
Dim myWebRequest2 As HttpWebRequest =
CType(WebRequest.Create("http://www.microsoft.com/windows"),
HttpWebRequest)
Dim myWebResponse2 As HttpWebResponse =
CType(myWebRequest2.GetResponse(), HttpWebResponse)
Dim myServicePoint2 As ServicePoint = myWebRequest2.ServicePoint

Console.WriteLine("The 'HashCode' for the first connection is
:" + myServicePoint1.GetHashCode().ToString())

Console.WriteLine("The 'HashCode' for the second connection is:
" + myServicePoint2.GetHashCode().ToString())
' Check whether the first and second 'HttpWebRequest' objects
connecting to the same internet
' server are using the same 'ServicePoint'  or not
If myServicePoint1.GetHashCode().Equals(
myServicePoint2.GetHashCode()) Then
     Console.WriteLine(ControlChars.Cr + "Two connections are
created to the same Internet Server")
     Console.WriteLine("So same 'ServicePoint' is used for
both the Connections")
End If

[C#]
// Create the first 'HttpWebRequest' object.
HttpWebRequest myWebRequest1 = (HttpWebRequest)
WebRequest.Create("http://www.microsoft.com");
// The response object of 'HttpWebRequest' is assigned to a
'HttpWebResponse' variable.
HttpWebResponse myWebResponse1
=(HttpWebResponse)myWebRequest1.GetResponse();
ServicePoint myServicePoint1 = myWebRequest1.ServicePoint;
```

```
// Create the second 'HttpWebRequest' object with the
same hostfragment as above.
HttpWebRequest myWebRequest2 =(HttpWebRequest)
WebRequest.Create("http://www.microsoft.com/windows");
HttpWebResponse myWebResponse2
=(HttpWebResponse)myWebRequest2.GetResponse();
ServicePoint myServicePoint2 = myWebRequest2.ServicePoint;

Console.WriteLine("\nThe 'HashCode' for the first
connection is:"+myServicePoint1.GetHashCode());

Console.WriteLine("The 'HashCode' for the second
connection is:"+myServicePoint2.GetHashCode());

// Check whether the first and second 'HttpWebRequest'
objects  connecting to the same internet
// server are using the same 'ServicePoint' or not

if(myServicePoint1.GetHashCode().Equals(myServicePoint2.GetHashCode()))
          {
                Console.WriteLine("\nTwo connections are
created to the same Internet Server");
                Console.WriteLine("So same 'ServicePoint'
is used for both the Connections");
          }

// Release all the response object resources.
myWebResponse1.Close();
myWebResponse2.Close();

[C++]
// Create the first 'HttpWebRequest' Object*.
HttpWebRequest* myWebRequest1 =
     dynamic_cast<HttpWebRequest*> (WebRequest::Create(S"http://
www.microsoft.com"));
// The response Object* of 'HttpWebRequest' is assigned
to a 'HttpWebResponse' variable.
HttpWebResponse* myWebResponse1 =
     dynamic_cast<HttpWebResponse*>(myWebRequest1->GetResponse());
ServicePoint* myServicePoint1 = myWebRequest1->ServicePoint;

// Create the second 'HttpWebRequest' Object* with the same
hostfragment as above.
HttpWebRequest* myWebRequest2 =
     dynamic_cast<HttpWebRequest*> (WebRequest::Create(S"http://
www.microsoft.com/windows"));
HttpWebResponse* myWebResponse2 =
     dynamic_cast<HttpWebResponse*>(myWebRequest2->GetResponse());
ServicePoint* myServicePoint2 = myWebRequest2->ServicePoint;

Console::WriteLine(S"\nThe 'HashCode' for the first
connection is: {0}",
     __box(myServicePoint1->GetHashCode()));

Console::WriteLine(S"The 'HashCode' for the second connection
is: {0}",
     __box(myServicePoint2->GetHashCode()));

// Check whether the first and second 'HttpWebRequest'
objects  connecting to the same internet
// server are using the same 'ServicePoint' or not
if ( __box(myServicePoint1->GetHashCode()) ->
Equals(__box(myServicePoint2->GetHashCode()) ) ) {
     Console::WriteLine(S"\nTwo connections are created to
the same Internet Server");
     Console::WriteLine(S"So same 'ServicePoint' is used for
both the Connections");
}

// Release all the response Object* resources.
myWebResponse1->Close();
myWebResponse2->Close();
```

Requirements

Platforms: Windows 98, Windows NT 4.0,
Windows Millennium Edition, Windows 2000,
Windows XP Home Edition, Windows XP Professional,
Windows .NET Server family,
.NET Compact Framework - Windows CE .NET,
Common Language Infrastructure (CLI) Standard

ServicePointManager Class

Manages the collection of **ServicePoint** instances.

For a list of all members of this type, see **ServicePointManager Members**.

System.Object
  System.Net.ServicePointManager

```
[Visual Basic]
Public Class ServicePointManager
[C#]
public class ServicePointManager
[C++]
public __gc class ServicePointManager
[JScript]
public class ServicePointManager
```

Thread Safety

Any public static (**Shared** in Visual Basic) members of this type are safe for multithreaded operations. Any instance members are not guaranteed to be thread safe.

Remarks

ServicePointManager is a static class used to create, maintain, and delete instances of the **ServicePoint** class.

When an application requests a connection to an Internet resource URI through the **ServicePointManager**, the **ServicePointManager** returns a **ServicePoint** instance containing connection information for the host identified by the URI. If there is an existing **ServicePoint** for that host, the **ServicePointManager** returns the existing **ServicePoint**, otherwise the **ServicePointManager** creates a new **ServicePoint** instance.

Example

[Visual Basic, C#] The following example creates a **ServicePoint** instance for connections to the URI www.contoso.com .

```
[Visual Basic]
Dim myUri As New Uri("http://www.contoso.com/")

Dim mySP As ServicePoint = ServicePointManager.FindServicePoint(myUri)

[C#]
Uri myUri = new Uri("http://www.contoso.com/");

  ServicePoint mySP = ServicePointManager.FindServicePoint(myUri);
```

Requirements

Namespace: System.Net

Platforms: Windows 98, Windows NT 4.0, Windows Millennium Edition, Windows 2000, Windows XP Home Edition, Windows XP Professional, Windows .NET Server family, .NET Compact Framework - Windows CE .NET

Assembly: System (in System.dll)

ServicePointManager.DefaultNonPersistentConnectionLimit Field

The default number of nonpersistent connections (4) allowed on a **ServicePoint** connected to an HTTP/1.0 or later server. This field is constant.

```
[Visual Basic]
Public Const DefaultNonPersistentConnectionLimit As Integer
[C#]
public const int DefaultNonPersistentConnectionLimit;
[C++]
public: const int DefaultNonPersistentConnectionLimit;
[JScript]
public var DefaultNonPersistentConnectionLimit : int;
```

Requirements

Platforms: Windows 98, Windows NT 4.0, Windows Millennium Edition, Windows 2000, Windows XP Home Edition, Windows XP Professional, Windows .NET Server family, Common Language Infrastructure (CLI) Standard

ServicePointManager.DefaultPersistentConnectionLimit Field

The default number of persistent connections (2) allowed on a **ServicePoint** connected to an HTTP/1.1 or later server. This field is constant.

```
[Visual Basic]
Public Const DefaultPersistentConnectionLimit As Integer
[C#]
public const int DefaultPersistentConnectionLimit;
[C++]
public: const int DefaultPersistentConnectionLimit;
[JScript]
public var DefaultPersistentConnectionLimit : int;
```

Requirements

Platforms: Windows 98, Windows NT 4.0, Windows Millennium Edition, Windows 2000, Windows XP Home Edition, Windows XP Professional, Windows .NET Server family, .NET Compact Framework - Windows CE .NET, Common Language Infrastructure (CLI) Standard

ServicePointManager.CertificatePolicy Property

Gets or sets policy for server certificates.

```
[Visual Basic]
Public Shared Property CertificatePolicy As ICertificatePolicy
[C#]
public static ICertificatePolicy CertificatePolicy {get; set;}
[C++]
public: __property static ICertificatePolicy* get_CertificatePolicy();
public: __property static void
set_CertificatePolicy(ICertificatePolicy*);
[JScript]
public static function get CertificatePolicy() : ICertificatePolicy;
public static function set CertificatePolicy(ICertificatePolicy);
```

Property Value

An instance implementing the **ICertificatePolicy** interface.

Remarks

When the **CertificatePolicy** property is set to an **ICertificatePolicy** interface instance, the **ServicePointManager** uses the certificate policy defined in that instance instead of the default certificate policy.

The default certificate policy allows valid certificates, as well as valid certificates that have expired.

Example

[Visual Basic, C#] The following example shows how to catch a certificate policy exception for a custom certificate policy. It assumes that the certificate policy object has been defined, that the URI for the Web resource is contained in the variable *myUri*, and that there is a method named ProcessResponse that performs the work of the application.

```
[Visual Basic]
ServicePointManager.CertificatePolicy = New MyCertificatePolicy()

' Create the request and receive the response
Try
    Dim myRequest As WebRequest = WebRequest.Create(myUri)
    Dim myResponse As WebResponse = myRequest.GetResponse()

    ProcessResponse(myResponse)

    myResponse.Close()

' Catch any exceptions
Catch e As WebException
    If e.Status = WebExceptionStatus.TrustFailure Then
        ' Code for handling security certificate problems goes here.
    End If
    ' Other exception handling goes here
End Try
```

```
[C#]
ServicePointManager.CertificatePolicy = new MyCertificatePolicy();

    // Create the request and receive the response
    try
    {
    WebRequest myRequest = WebRequest.Create(myUri);
    WebResponse myResponse = myRequest.GetResponse();
    ProcessResponse(myResponse);
    myResponse.Close();
    }
    // Catch any exceptions
    catch(WebException e)
    {
    if (e.Status == WebExceptionStatus.TrustFailure)
    {
    // Code for handling security certificate problems goes here.
    }
    // Other exception handling goes here
    }
```

Requirements

Platforms: Windows 98, Windows NT 4.0, Windows Millennium Edition, Windows 2000, Windows XP Home Edition, Windows XP Professional, Windows .NET Server family, .NET Compact Framework - Windows CE .NET

.NET Framework Security:

- **SecurityPermission** to set the CertificatePolicy property. Associated enumeration: **SecurityPermissionFlag.UnmanagedCode**

ServicePointManager.CheckCertificate-RevocationList Property

Note: This namespace, class, or member is supported only in version 1.1 of the .NET Framework.

```
[Visual Basic]
Public Shared Property CheckCertificateRevocationList As Boolean
[C#]
public static bool CheckCertificateRevocationList {get; set;}
[C++]
public: __property static bool get_CheckCertificateRevocationList();
public: __property static void
set_CheckCertificateRevocationList(bool);
[JScript]
public static function get CheckCertificateRevocationList() : Boolean;
public static function set CheckCertificateRevocationList(Boolean);
```

Requirements

Platforms: Windows 98, Windows NT 4.0, Windows Millennium Edition, Windows 2000, Windows XP Home Edition, Windows XP Professional, Windows .NET Server family

ServicePointManager.DefaultConnectionLimit Property

The maximum number of concurrent connections allowed by a **ServicePoint** instance.

```
[Visual Basic]
Public Shared Property DefaultConnectionLimit As Integer
[C#]
public static int DefaultConnectionLimit {get; set;}
[C++]
public: __property static int get_DefaultConnectionLimit();
public: __property static void set_DefaultConnectionLimit(int);
[JScript]
public static function get DefaultConnectionLimit() : int;
public static function set DefaultConnectionLimit(int);
```

Property Value

The maximum number of concurrent connections allowed by a **ServicePoint** instance.

Exceptions

Exception Type	Condition
ArgumentOutOfRange-Exception	**DefaultConnectionLimit** is less than or equal to 0.

Remarks

The **DefaultConnectionLimit** property sets the default maximum number of concurrent connections that the **ServicePointManager** assigns to the **ConnectionLimit** property when creating **ServicePoint** instances.

Changing the **DefaultConnectionLimit** property has no effect on existing **ServicePoint** instances; it affects only **ServicePoint** instances that are initialized after the change.

Requirements

Platforms: Windows 98, Windows NT 4.0,
Windows Millennium Edition, Windows 2000,
Windows XP Home Edition, Windows XP Professional,
Windows .NET Server family,
.NET Compact Framework - Windows CE .NET,
Common Language Infrastructure (CLI) Standard

ServicePointManager.MaxServicePointIdleTime Property

Gets or sets the maximum idle time of a **ServicePoint** instance.

```
[Visual Basic]
Public Shared Property MaxServicePointIdleTime As Integer
[C#]
public static int MaxServicePointIdleTime {get; set;}
[C++]
public: __property static int get_MaxServicePointIdleTime();
public: __property static void set_MaxServicePointIdleTime(int);
[JScript]
public static function get MaxServicePointIdleTime() : int;
public static function set MaxServicePointIdleTime(int);
```

Property Value

The maximum idle time, in milliseconds, of a **ServicePoint** instance.

Exceptions

Exception Type	Condition
ArgumentOutOfRange-Exception	**MaxServicePointIdleTime** is less than **Timeout.Infinite** or greater than **Int32.MaxValue**

Remarks

The **MaxServicePointIdleTime** property sets the maximum idle time that the **ServicePointManager** assigns to the **MaxIdleTime** property when creating **ServicePoint** instances. Changes to this value will affect only **ServicePoint** instances that are initialized after the value is changed.

After a **ServicePoint** has been idle for the time specified in **MaxIdleTime**, it is eligible for garbage collection. A **ServicePoint** is idle when the list of connections associated with the **ServicePoint** is empty.

Default value is 900,000 milliseconds (15 minutes).

Requirements

Platforms: Windows 98, Windows NT 4.0,
Windows Millennium Edition, Windows 2000,
Windows XP Home Edition, Windows XP Professional,
Windows .NET Server family,
.NET Compact Framework - Windows CE .NET,
Common Language Infrastructure (CLI) Standard

ServicePointManager.MaxServicePoints Property

Gets or sets the maximum number of **ServicePoint** instances to maintain at any time.

```
[Visual Basic]
Public Shared Property MaxServicePoints As Integer
[C#]
public static int MaxServicePoints {get; set;}
[C++]
public: __property static int get_MaxServicePoints();
public: __property static void set_MaxServicePoints(int);
[JScript]
public static function get MaxServicePoints() : int;
public static function set MaxServicePoints(int);
```

Property Value

The maximum number of **ServicePoint** instances to maintain. The default value is 0, which means there is no limit to the number of **ServicePoint** instances.

Exceptions

Exception Type	Condition
ArgumentOutOfRange-Exception	**MaxServicePoints** is less than 0 or greater than **Int32.MaxValue**.

Remarks

When you reduce the **MaxServicePoints** property below the number of **ServicePoint** instances currently in existence, the **ServicePointManager** deletes the **ServicePoint** instances with the longest idle times. If the number of **ServicePoint** instances with active connections is greater than the value of **MaxServicePoints**, the **ServicePointManager** will delete the **ServicePoint** instances as they become idle.

Requirements

Platforms: Windows 98, Windows NT 4.0,
Windows Millennium Edition, Windows 2000,
Windows XP Home Edition, Windows XP Professional,
Windows .NET Server family,
Common Language Infrastructure (CLI) Standard

ServicePointManager.SecurityProtocol Property

Note: This namespace, class, or member is supported only in version 1.1 of the .NET Framework.

```
[Visual Basic]
Public Shared Property SecurityProtocol As SecurityProtocolType
[C#]
public static SecurityProtocolType SecurityProtocol {get; set;}
[C++]
public: __property static SecurityProtocolType get_SecurityProtocol();
public: __property static void
set_SecurityProtocol(SecurityProtocolType);
[JScript]
public static function get SecurityProtocol() : SecurityProtocolType;
public static function set SecurityProtocol(SecurityProtocolType);
```

Requirements

Platforms: Windows 98, Windows NT 4.0,
Windows Millennium Edition, Windows 2000,
Windows XP Home Edition, Windows XP Professional,
Windows .NET Server family

ServicePointManager.FindServicePoint Method

Finds an existing **ServicePoint** or creates a new **ServicePoint** to manage communication for this request.

Overload List

Finds an existing **ServicePoint** or creates a new **ServicePoint** to manage communications with the specified **Uri**.

Supported by the .NET Compact Framework.

> [Visual Basic] **Overloads Public Shared Function FindServicePoint(Uri) As ServicePoint**
>
> [C#] **public static ServicePoint FindServicePoint(Uri);**
>
> [C++] **public: static ServicePoint* FindServicePoint(Uri*);**
>
> [JScript] **public static function FindServicePoint(Uri) : ServicePoint;**

Finds an existing **ServicePoint** or creates a new **ServicePoint** to manage communications with the specified URI.

Supported by the .NET Compact Framework.

> [Visual Basic] **Overloads Public Shared Function FindServicePoint(String, IWebProxy) As ServicePoint**
>
> [C#] **public static ServicePoint FindServicePoint(string, IWebProxy);**
>
> [C++] **public: static ServicePoint* FindServicePoint(String*, IWebProxy*);**
>
> [JScript] **public static function FindServicePoint(String, IWebProxy) : ServicePoint;**

Finds an existing **ServicePoint** or creates a new **ServicePoint** to manage communications with the specified **Uri** instance.

Supported by the .NET Compact Framework.

> [Visual Basic] **Overloads Public Shared Function FindServicePoint(Uri, IWebProxy) As ServicePoint**
>
> [C#] **public static ServicePoint FindServicePoint(Uri, IWebProxy);**
>
> [C++] **public: static ServicePoint* FindServicePoint(Uri*, IWebProxy*);**
>
> [JScript] **public static function FindServicePoint(Uri, IWebProxy) : ServicePoint;**

ServicePointManager.FindServicePoint Method (Uri)

Finds an existing **ServicePoint** or creates a new **ServicePoint** to manage communications with the specified **Uri**.

```
[Visual Basic]
Overloads Public Shared Function FindServicePoint( _
   ByVal address As Uri _
) As ServicePoint
[C#]
public static ServicePoint FindServicePoint(
   Uri address
);
[C++]
public: static ServicePoint* FindServicePoint(
   Uri* address
);
[JScript]
public static function FindServicePoint(
   address : Uri
) : ServicePoint;
```

Parameters

address
> The **Uri** of the Internet resource to contact.

Return Value

The **ServicePoint** that manages communications for the request.

Exceptions

Exception Type	Condition
ArgumentNullException	*address* is a null reference (**Nothing** in Visual Basic).
InvalidOperation-Exception	The maximum number of service points defined in **MaxServicePoints** has been reached.

Remarks

The **FindServicePoint** method returns the **ServicePoint** instance associated with the specified Internet host name. If no **ServicePoint** exists for that host, the **ServicePointManager** creates one.

Requirements

Platforms: Windows 98, Windows NT 4.0, Windows Millennium Edition, Windows 2000, Windows XP Home Edition, Windows XP Professional, Windows .NET Server family, .NET Compact Framework - Windows CE .NET, Common Language Infrastructure (CLI) Standard

ServicePointManager.FindServicePoint Method (String, IWebProxy)

Finds an existing **ServicePoint** or creates a new **ServicePoint** to manage communications with the specified URI.

```
[Visual Basic]
Overloads Public Shared Function FindServicePoint( _
   ByVal uriString As String, _
   ByVal proxy As IWebProxy _
) As ServicePoint
[C#]
public static ServicePoint FindServicePoint(
   string uriString,
   IWebProxy proxy
);
[C++]
public: static ServicePoint* FindServicePoint(
   String* uriString,
   IWebProxy* proxy
);
[JScript]
public static function FindServicePoint(
   uriString : String,
   proxy : IWebProxy
) : ServicePoint;
```

Parameters

uriString
> The URI of the Internet resource to be contacted.

proxy
> Proxy data for this request.

Return Value

The **ServicePoint** that manages communications for the request.

Exceptions

Exception Type	Condition
UriFormatException	The URI specified in *uriString* is invalid.

Exception Type	Condition
InvalidOperation-Exception	The maximum number of service points defined in **MaxServicePoints** has been reached.

Remarks

The **FindServicePoint** method returns the **ServicePoint** instance associated with the specified Internet host name. If no **ServicePoint** exists for that host, the **ServicePointManager** creates one.

Requirements

Platforms: Windows 98, Windows NT 4.0, Windows Millennium Edition, Windows 2000, Windows XP Home Edition, Windows XP Professional, Windows .NET Server family, .NET Compact Framework - Windows CE .NET, Common Language Infrastructure (CLI) Standard

Remarks

The **FindServicePoint** method returns the **ServicePoint** instance associated with the specified Internet host name. If no **ServicePoint** exists for that host, the **ServicePointManager** creates one.

Requirements

Platforms: Windows 98, Windows NT 4.0, Windows Millennium Edition, Windows 2000, Windows XP Home Edition, Windows XP Professional, Windows .NET Server family, .NET Compact Framework - Windows CE .NET, Common Language Infrastructure (CLI) Standard

ServicePointManager.FindServicePoint Method (Uri, IWebProxy)

Finds an existing **ServicePoint** or creates a new **ServicePoint** to manage communications with the specified **Uri** instance.

```
[Visual Basic]
Overloads Public Shared Function FindServicePoint( _
   ByVal address As Uri, _
   ByVal proxy As IWebProxy _
) As ServicePoint
[C#]
public static ServicePoint FindServicePoint(
   Uri address,
   IWebProxy proxy
);
[C++]
public: static ServicePoint* FindServicePoint(
   Uri* address,
   IWebProxy* proxy
);
[JScript]
public static function FindServicePoint(
   address : Uri,
   proxy : IWebProxy
) : ServicePoint;
```

Parameters

address
    A **Uri** instance containing the address of the Internet resource to contact.

proxy
    Proxy data for this request.

Return Value

The **ServicePoint** that manages communications for the request.

Exceptions

Exception Type	Condition
ArgumentNullException	*address* is a null reference (**Nothing** in Visual Basic).
InvalidOperation-Exception	The maximum number of service points defined in **MaxServicePoints** has been reached.

SocketAddress Class

Stores serialized information from **EndPoint** derived classes.

System.Object
  System.Net.SocketAddress

```
[Visual Basic]
Public Class SocketAddress
[C#]
public class SocketAddress
[C++]
public __gc class SocketAddress
[JScript]
public class SocketAddress
```

Thread Safety

Any public static (**Shared** in Visual Basic) members of this type are safe for multithreaded operations. Any instance members are not guaranteed to be thread safe.

Remarks

The first two bytes of the underlying buffer are reserved for the **AddressFamily** enumerated value. When the **SocketAddress** is used to store a serialized **IPEndPoint**. The third and fourth bytes are used to store port number information. The next bytes are used to store the IP address. You can access any information within this underlying byte buffer by referring to its byte position; the byte buffer uses zero-based indexing. You can also use the **Family** and **Size** properties to get the **AddressFamily** value and the buffer size, respectively. To view any of this information as a string, use the **ToString** method.

Example

[Visual Basic, C#, C++] The following example demonstrates how to use **SocketAddress** to serialize an instance of the **EndPoint** class. After serialization, the underlying byte buffer of the **SocketAddress** contains all of the **IPEndPoint** state information.

```
[Visual Basic]
'Creates an IpEndPoint.
Dim ipAddress As IPAddress =
Dns.Resolve("www.contoso.com").AddressList(0)
Dim ipLocalEndPoint As New IPEndPoint(ipAddress, 11000)

'Serializes the IPEndPoint.
Dim socketAddress As SocketAddress = ipLocalEndPoint.Serialize()

'Verifies that ipLocalEndPoint is now serialized by printing
its contents.
Console.WriteLine(("Contents of socketAddress are: " +
socketAddress.ToString()))
'Checks the Family property.
Console.WriteLine(("The address family of socketAddress is: "
" + socketAddress.Family.ToString()))
'Checks the underlying buffer size.
Console.WriteLine(("The size of the underlying buffer is: "
" + socketAddress.Size.ToString()))
    End Sub 'MySerializeIPEndPointClassMethod
```

```
[C#]
//Creates an IpEndPoint.
IPAddress ipAddress = Dns.Resolve("www.contoso.com").AddressList[0];
IPEndPoint ipLocalEndPoint = new IPEndPoint(ipAddress, 11000);

//Serializes the IPEndPoint.
SocketAddress socketAddress = ipLocalEndPoint.Serialize();
```

```
//Verifies that ipLocalEndPoint is now serialized by printing
its contents.
Console.WriteLine("Contents of the socketAddress are: " +
socketAddress.ToString());
//Checks the Family property.
Console.WriteLine("The address family of the socketAddress is:
" + socketAddress.Family.ToString());
//Checks the underlying buffer size.
Console.WriteLine("The size of the underlying buffer is: " +
socketAddress.Size.ToString());
```

```
[C++]
//Creates an IpEndPoint.
IPAddress* ipAddress = Dns::Resolve(S"www.contoso.com")-
>AddressList[0];
IPEndPoint* ipLocalEndPoint = new IPEndPoint(ipAddress, 11000);

//Serializes the IPEndPoint.
SocketAddress* socketAddress = ipLocalEndPoint->Serialize();

//Verifies that ipLocalEndPoint is now serialized by printing
its contents.
Console::WriteLine(S"Contents of the socketAddress are: {0}",
socketAddress);
//Checks the Family property.
Console::WriteLine(S"The address family of the socketAddress is: {0}",
    __box( socketAddress->Family));
//Checks the underlying buffer size.
Console::WriteLine(S"The size of the underlying buffer is: {0}",
    __box( socketAddress->Size));
```

Requirements

Namespace: System.Net

Platforms: Windows 98, Windows NT 4.0, Windows Millennium Edition, Windows 2000, Windows XP Home Edition, Windows XP Professional, Windows .NET Server family, .NET Compact Framework - Windows CE .NET

Assembly: System (in System.dll)

SocketAddress Constructor

Creates a new instance of the **SocketAddress** class.

Overload List

Creates a new instance of the **SocketAddress** class for the given address family.

Supported by the .NET Compact Framework.

[Visual Basic] **Public Sub New(AddressFamily)**

[C#] **public SocketAddress(AddressFamily);**

[C++] **public: SocketAddress(AddressFamily);**

[JScript] **public function SocketAddress(AddressFamily);**

Creates a new instance of the **SocketAddress** class using the specified address family and buffer size.

Supported by the .NET Compact Framework.

[Visual Basic] **Public Sub New(AddressFamily, Integer)**

[C#] **public SocketAddress(AddressFamily, int);**

[C++] **public: SocketAddress(AddressFamily, int);**

[JScript] **public function SocketAddress(AddressFamily, int);**

SocketAddress Constructor (AddressFamily)

Creates a new instance of the **SocketAddress** class for the given address family.

```
[Visual Basic]
Public Sub New( _
    ByVal family As AddressFamily _
)
[C#]
public SocketAddress(
    AddressFamily family
);
[C++]
public: SocketAddress(
    AddressFamily family
);
[JScript]
public function SocketAddress(
    family : AddressFamily
);
```

Parameters

family
   An **AddressFamily** enumerated value.

Remarks

This overload sets the underlying buffer size to 32 bytes.

Requirements

Platforms: Windows 98, Windows NT 4.0,
Windows Millennium Edition, Windows 2000,
Windows XP Home Edition, Windows XP Professional,
Windows .NET Server family,
.NET Compact Framework - Windows CE .NET,
Common Language Infrastructure (CLI) Standard

SocketAddress Constructor (AddressFamily, Int32)

Creates a new instance of the **SocketAddress** class using the specified address family and buffer size.

```
[Visual Basic]
Public Sub New( _
    ByVal family As AddressFamily, _
    ByVal size As Integer _
)
[C#]
public SocketAddress(
    AddressFamily family,
    int size
);
[C++]
public: SocketAddress(
    AddressFamily family,
    int size
);
[JScript]
public function SocketAddress(
    family : AddressFamily,
    size : int
);
```

Parameters

family
   An **AddressFamily** enumerated value.
size
   The number of bytes to allocate for the underlying buffer.

Exceptions

Exception Type	Condition
ArgumentOutOfRange-Exception	*size* is less than 2. These two bytes are needed to store *family*.

Remarks

Use this overload to create a new instance of the **SocketAddress** class with a particular underlying buffer size.

Requirements

Platforms: Windows 98, Windows NT 4.0,
Windows Millennium Edition, Windows 2000,
Windows XP Home Edition, Windows XP Professional,
Windows .NET Server family,
.NET Compact Framework - Windows CE .NET,
Common Language Infrastructure (CLI) Standard

SocketAddress.Family Property

Gets the **AddressFamily** enumerated value of the current **SocketAddress**.

```
[Visual Basic]
Public ReadOnly Property Family As AddressFamily
[C#]
public AddressFamily Family {get;}
[C++]
public: __property AddressFamily get_Family();
[JScript]
public function get Family() : AddressFamily;
```

Property Value

One of the **AddressFamily** enumerated values.

Remarks

This method gets the **AddressFamily** enumerated value representing the addressing scheme of the current **SocketAddress**. If you want to view the corresponding string representation of **AddressFamily**, use the **ToString** method.

Requirements

Platforms: Windows 98, Windows NT 4.0,
Windows Millennium Edition, Windows 2000,
Windows XP Home Edition, Windows XP Professional,
Windows .NET Server family,
.NET Compact Framework - Windows CE .NET,
Common Language Infrastructure (CLI) Standard

SocketAddress.Item Property

Gets or sets the specified index element in the underlying buffer.

[C#] In C#, this property is the indexer for the **SocketAddress** class.

```
[Visual Basic]
Public Default Property Item( _
    ByVal offset As Integer _
) As Byte
```

```
[C#]
public byte this[
   int offset
] {get; set;}
[C++]
public: __property unsigned char get_Item(
   int offset
);
public: __property void set_Item(
   int offset,
   unsigned char
);
[JScript]
returnValue = SocketAddressObject.Item(offset);
SocketAddressObject.Item(offset) = returnValue;
-or-
returnValue = SocketAddressObject(offset);
SocketAddressObject(offset) = returnValue;
```

[JScript] In JScript, you can use the default indexed properties defined by a type, but you cannot explicitly define your own. However, specifying the **expando** attribute on a class automatically provides a default indexed property whose type is **Object** and whose index type is **String**.

Arguments [JScript]
offset
   The array index element of the desired information.

Parameters [Visual Basic, C#, C++]
offset
   The array index element of the desired information.

Property Value
The value of the specified index element in the underlying buffer.

Exceptions

Exception Type	Condition
IndexOutOfRange-Exception	The specified index does not exist in the buffer.

Remarks
This property gets or sets the specified byte position in the underlying buffer.

> **Note** Be sure to call **Size** before referring to elements in the underlying buffer. Referring to an index that does not exist will cause the **SocketAddress** to throw an **IndexOutOfRangeException**.

Requirements
Platforms: Windows 98, Windows NT 4.0, Windows Millennium Edition, Windows 2000, Windows XP Home Edition, Windows XP Professional, Windows .NET Server family, Common Language Infrastructure (CLI) Standard

SocketAddress.Size Property

Gets the underlying buffer size of the **SocketAddress**.

```
[Visual Basic]
Public ReadOnly Property Size As Integer
[C#]
public int Size {get;}
```

```
[C++]
public: __property int get_Size();
[JScript]
public function get Size() : int;
```

Property Value
The underlying buffer size of the **SocketAddress**.

Remarks
This property gets the underlying buffer size of the **SocketAddress** in bytes.

Requirements
Platforms: Windows 98, Windows NT 4.0, Windows Millennium Edition, Windows 2000, Windows XP Home Edition, Windows XP Professional, Windows .NET Server family, .NET Compact Framework - Windows CE .NET, Common Language Infrastructure (CLI) Standard

SocketAddress.Equals Method

This member overrides **Object.Equals**.

```
[Visual Basic]
Overrides Public Function Equals( _
   ByVal comparand As Object _
) As Boolean
[C#]
public override bool Equals(
   object comparand
);
[C++]
public: bool Equals(
   Object* comparand
);
[JScript]
public override function Equals(
   comparand : Object
) : Boolean;
```

Requirements
Platforms: Windows 98, Windows NT 4.0, Windows Millennium Edition, Windows 2000, Windows XP Home Edition, Windows XP Professional, Windows .NET Server family, .NET Compact Framework - Windows CE .NET, Common Language Infrastructure (CLI) Standard

SocketAddress.GetHashCode Method

This member overrides **Object.GetHashCode**.

```
[Visual Basic]
Overrides Public Function GetHashCode() As Integer
[C#]
public override int GetHashCode();
[C++]
public: int GetHashCode();
[JScript]
public override function GetHashCode() : int;
```

Requirements

Platforms: Windows 98, Windows NT 4.0,
Windows Millennium Edition, Windows 2000,
Windows XP Home Edition, Windows XP Professional,
Windows .NET Server family,
.NET Compact Framework - Windows CE .NET,
Common Language Infrastructure (CLI) Standard

SocketAddress.ToString Method

Returns information about the socket address.

```
[Visual Basic]
Overrides Public Function ToString() As String
[C#]
public override string ToString();
[C++]
public: String* ToString();
[JScript]
public override function ToString() : String;
```

Return Value

A string containing information about the **SocketAddress**.

Remarks

The **ToString** method returns a string containing the
AddressFamily enumerated value, the size of the underlying buffer
of the **SocketAddress** structure, and the remaining contents of the
buffer.

Requirements

Platforms: Windows 98, Windows NT 4.0,
Windows Millennium Edition, Windows 2000,
Windows XP Home Edition, Windows XP Professional,
Windows .NET Server family,
.NET Compact Framework - Windows CE .NET,
Common Language Infrastructure (CLI) Standard

SocketPermission Class

Controls rights to make or accept connections on a transport address.

System.Object
  System.Security.CodeAccessPermission
    System.Net.SocketPermission

[Visual Basic]
```
<Serializable>
NotInheritable Public Class SocketPermission
    Inherits CodeAccessPermission
    Implements IUnrestrictedPermission
```
[C#]
```
[Serializable]
public sealed class SocketPermission : CodeAccessPermission,
    IUnrestrictedPermission
```
[C++]
```
[Serializable]
public __gc __sealed class SocketPermission : public
    CodeAccessPermission, IUnrestrictedPermission
```
[JScript]
```
public
    Serializable
class SocketPermission extends CodeAccessPermission
    implements IUnrestrictedPermission
```

Thread Safety

Any public static (**Shared** in Visual Basic) members of this type are safe for multithreaded operations. Any instance members are not guaranteed to be thread safe.

Remarks

SocketPermission instances control permission to accept connections or initiate **Socket** connections. A **Socket** permission can secure access based on host name or IP address, a port number, and a transport protocol.

Example

[Visual Basic, C#, C++] The following example demonstrates how to use the **SocketPermission** class to set, change, and enforce various socket access restrictions.

[Visual Basic]
```
' Creates a SocketPermission restricting access to and from all URIs.
Dim mySocketPermission1 As New SocketPermission(PermissionState.None)

' The socket to which this permission will apply will allow
connections from www.contoso.com.
mySocketPermission1.AddPermission(NetworkAccess.Accept,
TransportType.Tcp, "www.contoso.com", 11000)

' Creates a SocketPermission which will allow the target
Socket to connect with www.southridgevideo.com.
Dim mySocketPermission2 As New SocketPermission
(NetworkAccess.Connect, TransportType.Tcp,
"www.southridgevideo.com", 11002)

' Creates a SocketPermission from the union of two SocketPermissions.
Dim mySocketPermissionUnion As SocketPermission =
CType(mySocketPermission1.Union(mySocketPermission2), SocketPermission)

' Checks to see if the union was successfully created by
using the IsSubsetOf method.
If mySocketPermission1.IsSubsetOf(mySocketPermissionUnion)
And mySocketPermission2.IsSubsetOf(mySocketPermissionUnion) Then
    Console.WriteLine("This union contains permissions
from both mySocketPermission1 and mySocketPermission2")
```

```
' Prints the allowable accept URIs to the console.
Console.WriteLine("This union accepts connections on :")

Dim myEnumerator As IEnumerator = mySocketPermissionUnion.AcceptList
While myEnumerator.MoveNext()
    Console.WriteLine(CType(myEnumerator.Current,
EndpointPermission).ToString())
End While

Console.WriteLine("This union establishes connections on : ")

    ' Prints the allowable connect URIs to the console.
Console.WriteLine("This union permits connections to :")

myEnumerator = mySocketPermissionUnion.ConnectList
While myEnumerator.MoveNext()
    Console.WriteLine(CType(myEnumerator.Current,
EndpointPermission).ToString())
    End While
End If
' Creates a SocketPermission from the intersect of two
SocketPermissions.
Dim mySocketPermissionIntersect As SocketPermission =
CType(mySocketPermission1.Intersect
(mySocketPermissionUnion), SocketPermission)

' mySocketPermissionIntersect should now contain the
permissions of mySocketPermission1.
If mySocketPermission1.IsSubsetOf(mySocketPermissionIntersect)
Then
    Console.WriteLine("This is expected")
End If
' mySocketPermissionIntersect should not contain the
permissios of mySocketPermission2.
If mySocketPermission2.IsSubsetOf(mySocketPermissionIntersect) Then
    Console.WriteLine("This should not print")
End If

' Creates a copy of the intersect SocketPermission.
Dim mySocketPermissionIntersectCopy As SocketPermission =
CType(mySocketPermissionIntersect.Copy(), SocketPermission)

If mySocketPermissionIntersectCopy.Equals
(mySocketPermissionIntersect) Then
    Console.WriteLine("Copy successfull")
End If
' Converts a SocketPermission to XML format and then
immediately converts it back to a SocketPermission.
mySocketPermission1.FromXml(mySocketPermission1.ToXml())

' Checks to see if permission for this socket resource is
unrestricted.  If it is, then there is no need to
' demand that permissions be enforced.
If mySocketPermissionUnion.IsUnrestricted() Then

'Do nothing.  There are no restrictions.
Else
    ' Enforces the permissions found in mySocketPermissionUnion
on any Socket Resources used below this statement.
    mySocketPermissionUnion.Demand()
End If

Dim myIpHostEntry As IPHostEntry = Dns.Resolve("www.contoso.com")
Dim myLocalEndPoint As New IPEndPoint
(myIpHostEntry.AddressList(0), 11000)

Dim s As New Socket(myLocalEndPoint.Address.AddressFamily,
SocketType.Stream, ProtocolType.Tcp)
Try
    s.Connect(myLocalEndPoint)
Catch e As Exception
    Console.WriteLine(("Exception Thrown: " + e.ToString()))
End Try

' Perform all socket operations in here.
s.Close()
    End Sub 'MySocketPermission
```

```csharp
[C#]
    // Creates a SocketPermission restricting access to and
from all URIs.
    SocketPermission mySocketPermission1 = new
SocketPermission(PermissionState.None);

    // The socket to which this permission will apply
will allow connections from www.contoso.com.
    mySocketPermission1.AddPermission(NetworkAccess.Accept,
TransportType.Tcp, "www.contoso.com", 11000);

    // Creates a SocketPermission which will allow the target
Socket to connect with www.southridgevideo.com.
    SocketPermission mySocketPermission2 =
                    new SocketPermission(NetworkAccess.Connect,
TransportType.Tcp,
"www.southridgevideo.com", 11002);

    // Creates a SocketPermission from the union of two
SocketPermissions.
    SocketPermission mySocketPermissionUnion =

(SocketPermission)mySocketPermission1.Union(mySocketPermission2);

    // Checks to see if the union was successfully created by
using the IsSubsetOf method.
    if (mySocketPermission1.IsSubsetOf(mySocketPermissionUnion) &&
        mySocketPermission2.IsSubsetOf(mySocketPermissionUnion)){
        Console.WriteLine("This union contains permissions
from both mySocketPermission1 and mySocketPermission2");

        // Prints the allowable accept URIs to the console.
        Console.WriteLine("This union accepts connections on :");

        IEnumerator myEnumerator =
mySocketPermissionUnion.AcceptList;
        while (myEnumerator.MoveNext()) {

Console.WriteLine(((EndpointPermission)myEnumerator.Current).ToString());
        }
                // Prints the allowable connect URIs to the console.
        Console.WriteLine("This union permits connections to :");

        myEnumerator = mySocketPermissionUnion.ConnectList;
        while (myEnumerator.MoveNext()) {

Console.WriteLine(((EndpointPermission)myEnumerator.Current).ToString());
        }

    }

    // Creates a SocketPermission from the intersect of two
SocketPermissions.
    SocketPermission mySocketPermissionIntersect =

(SocketPermission)mySocketPermission1.Intersect
(mySocketPermissionUnion);

    // mySocketPermissionIntersect should now contain the
permissions of mySocketPermission1.
    if (mySocketPermission1.IsSubsetOf(mySocketPermissionIntersect)){
        Console.WriteLine("This is expected");
    }
    // mySocketPermissionIntersect should not contain the
permissions of mySocketPermission2.
    if (mySocketPermission2.IsSubsetOf(mySocketPermissionIntersect)){
        Console.WriteLine("This should not print");
    }

// Creates a copy of the intersect SocketPermission.
    SocketPermission mySocketPermissionIntersectCopy =
(SocketPermission)mySocketPermissionIntersect.Copy();

    if
(mySocketPermissionIntersectCopy.Equals(mySocketPermissionIntersect)){
```

```csharp
        Console.WriteLine("Copy successfull");
    }

    // Converts a SocketPermission to XML format and then
immediately converts it back to a SocketPermission.
    mySocketPermission1.FromXml(mySocketPermission1.ToXml());

    // Checks to see if permission for this socket resource
is unrestricted.  If it is, then there is no need to
    // demand that permissions be enforced.
    if (mySocketPermissionUnion.IsUnrestricted()){

        //Do nothing.  There are no restrictions.

    }
    else{
        // Enforces the permissions found in
mySocketPermissionUnion on any Socket Resources used below
this statement.
        mySocketPermissionUnion.Demand();
    }

    IPHostEntry myIpHostEntry = Dns.Resolve("www.contoso.com");
    IPEndPoint myLocalEndPoint = new
IPEndPoint(myIpHostEntry.AddressList[0], 11000);

    Socket s = new Socket(myLocalEndPoint.Address.AddressFamily,
                            SocketType.Stream,
                            ProtocolType.Tcp);
    try{
        s.Connect(myLocalEndPoint);
    }
    catch (Exception e){
        Console.WriteLine("Exception Thrown: " + e.ToString());
    }

    // Perform all socket operations in here.

    s.Close();
```

```cpp
[C++]
    // Creates a SocketPermission restricting access
to and from all URIs.
    SocketPermission *mySocketPermission1 = new
SocketPermission(PermissionState::None);

    // The socket to which this permission will apply will
allow connections from www.contoso.com.
    mySocketPermission1->AddPermission
(NetworkAccess::Accept, TransportType::Tcp, "www.contoso.com", 11000);

    // Creates a SocketPermission which will allow
the target Socket to connect with www.southridgevideo.com.
    SocketPermission *mySocketPermission2 =
        new SocketPermission(NetworkAccess::Connect,
TransportType::Tcp, "www.southridgevideo.com", 11002);

    // Creates a SocketPermission from the union of two
SocketPermissions.
    SocketPermission *mySocketPermissionUnion =
        __try_cast<SocketPermission *>
(mySocketPermission1->Union(mySocketPermission2));

    // Checks to see if the union was successfully
created by using the IsSubsetOf method.
    if (mySocketPermission1->IsSubsetOf(mySocketPermissionUnion) &&
        mySocketPermission2->IsSubsetOf(mySocketPermissionUnion)){
        Console::WriteLine("This union contains
permissions from both mySocketPermission1 and mySocketPermission2");

        // Prints the allowable accept URIs to the console.
        Console::WriteLine("This union accepts
connections on :");

        IEnumerator *myEnumerator =
mySocketPermissionUnion->AcceptList;
        while (myEnumerator->MoveNext()) {
```

```
                    Console::WriteLine
(__try_cast<EndpointPermission *>(myEnumerator->Current)->ToString());
                }

                // Prints the allowable connect URIs to the console.
                Console::WriteLine("This union permits
connections to :");

                myEnumerator = mySocketPermissionUnion->ConnectList;
                while (myEnumerator->MoveNext()) {
                    Console::WriteLine(__try_cast
<EndpointPermission *>(myEnumerator->Current)->ToString());
                }

            }

                // Creates a SocketPermission from the
intersect of two SocketPermissions.
                SocketPermission *mySocketPermissionIntersect =
                    __try_cast<SocketPermission *>
(mySocketPermission1->Intersect(mySocketPermissionUnion));

                // mySocketPermissionIntersect should now
contain the permissions of mySocketPermission1.
                if (mySocketPermission1-
>IsSubsetOf(mySocketPermissionIntersect)){
                    Console::WriteLine("This is expected");
                }
                // mySocketPermissionIntersect should not
contain the permissios of mySocketPermission2.
                if (mySocketPermission2-
>IsSubsetOf(mySocketPermissionIntersect)){
                    Console::WriteLine("This should not print");
                }

                // Creates a copy of the intersect SocketPermission.
                SocketPermission *mySocketPermissionIntersectCopy =
                    __try_cast<SocketPermission
*>(mySocketPermissionIntersect->Copy());

                if (mySocketPermissionIntersectCopy-
>Equals(mySocketPermissionIntersect)){
                    Console::WriteLine("Copy successfull");
                }

                // Converts a SocketPermission to XML format
and then immediately converts it back to a SocketPermission.
                mySocketPermission1->FromXml(mySocketPermission1->ToXml());

                // Checks to see if permission for this socket
resource is unrestricted.  If it is, then there is no need to
                // demand that permissions be enforced.
                if (mySocketPermissionUnion->IsUnrestricted()){

                    //Do nothing.  There are no restrictions.

                }
                else{
                    // Enforces the permissions found in
mySocketPermissionUnion on any Socket Resources used
below this statement.
                    mySocketPermissionUnion->Demand();
                }

                IPHostEntry *myIpHostEntry =
Dns::Resolve("www.contoso.com");
                IPEndPoint *myLocalEndPoint = new IPEndPoint
(myIpHostEntry->AddressList[0], 11000);

                Socket *s = new Socket(myLocalEndPoint->Address-
>AddressFamily,
                    SocketType::Stream, ProtocolType::Tcp);
                try{
                    s->Connect(myLocalEndPoint);
                }
                catch (Exception *e){
                    Console::Write("Exception Thrown: ");
```

```
                Console::WriteLine(e->ToString());
            }

            // Perform all socket operations in here.

            s->Close();
```

Requirements

Namespace: System.Net

Platforms: Windows 98, Windows NT 4.0,
Windows Millennium Edition, Windows 2000,
Windows XP Home Edition, Windows XP Professional,
Windows .NET Server family

Assembly: System (in System.dll)

SocketPermission Constructor

Initializes a new instance of the **SocketPermission** class.

Overload List

Initializes a new instance of the **SocketPermission** class that allows
unrestricted access to the **Socket** or disallows access to the **Socket**.

> [Visual Basic] **Public Sub New(PermissionState)**
> [C#] **public SocketPermission(PermissionState);**
> [C++] **public: SocketPermission(PermissionState);**
> [JScript] **public function SocketPermission(PermissionState);**

Initializes a new instance of the **SocketPermission** class for the
given transport address with the specified permission.

> [Visual Basic] **Public Sub New(NetworkAccess,
> TransportType, String, Integer)**
> [C#] **public SocketPermission(NetworkAccess,
> TransportType, string, int);**
> [C++] **public: SocketPermission(NetworkAccess,
> TransportType, String*, int);**
> [JScript] **public function SocketPermission(NetworkAccess,
> TransportType, String, int);**

Example

See related example in the **System.Nete.SocketPermission** class
topic.

SocketPermission Constructor (PermissionState)

Initializes a new instance of the **SocketPermission** class that allows
unrestricted access to the **Socket** or disallows access to the **Socket**.

```
[Visual Basic]
Public Sub New( _
   ByVal state As PermissionState _
)
[C#]
public SocketPermission(
   PermissionState state
);
[C++]
public: SocketPermission(
   PermissionState state
);
[JScript]
public function SocketPermission(
   state : PermissionState
);
```

Parameters

state

    One of the **PermissionState** values.

Remarks

If the **SocketPermission** instance was created with the **Unrestricted** value from **PermissionState** then the **SocketPermission** instance will pass all demands. Any other value for *state* will result in a **SocketPermission** instance that will fail all demands unless a transport address permission is added with **AddPermission**.

Example

See related example in the **System.Nete.SocketPermission** class topic.

Requirements

Platforms: Windows 98, Windows NT 4.0, Windows Millennium Edition, Windows 2000, Windows XP Home Edition, Windows XP Professional, Windows .NET Server family, Common Language Infrastructure (CLI) Standard

SocketPermission Constructor (NetworkAccess, TransportType, String, Int32)

Initializes a new instance of the **SocketPermission** class for the given transport address with the specified permission.

```
[Visual Basic]
Public Sub New( _
    ByVal access As NetworkAccess, _
    ByVal transport As TransportType, _
    ByVal hostName As String, _
    ByVal portNumber As Integer _
)
[C#]
public SocketPermission(
    NetworkAccess access,
    TransportType transport,
    string hostName,
    int portNumber
);
[C++]
public: SocketPermission(
    NetworkAccess access,
    TransportType transport,
    String* hostName,
    int portNumber
);
[JScript]
public function SocketPermission(
    access : NetworkAccess,
    transport : TransportType,
    hostName : String,
    portNumber : int
);
```

Parameters

access

    One of the **NetworkAccess** values.

transport

    One of the **TransportType** values.

hostName

    The host name for the transport address.

portNumber

    The port number for the transport address.

Exceptions

Exception Type	Condition
ArgumentNullException	*hostName* is a null reference (**Nothing** in Visual Basic).

Remarks

This constructor creates a **SocketPermission** that controls access to the specified *hostName* and *portNumber* using the specified *transport*.

The *hostName* can be a DNS name, an IP address, or a specified IP subnet using, such as 192.168.1.*.

The *portNumber* can be any valid port number defined by the transport, or **SocketPermission.AllPorts**.

Example

See related example in the **System.Nete.SocketPermission** class topic.

Requirements

Platforms: Windows 98, Windows NT 4.0, Windows Millennium Edition, Windows 2000, Windows XP Home Edition, Windows XP Professional, Windows .NET Server family, Common Language Infrastructure (CLI) Standard

SocketPermission.AllPorts Field

Defines a constant representing all ports.

```
[Visual Basic]
Public Const AllPorts As Integer
[C#]
public const int AllPorts;
[C++]
public: const int AllPorts;
[JScript]
public var AllPorts : int;
```

Remarks

This field is read-only. The value of this field is -1.

Example

See related example in the **System.Nete.SocketPermission** class topic.

Requirements

Platforms: Windows 98, Windows NT 4.0, Windows Millennium Edition, Windows 2000, Windows XP Home Edition, Windows XP Professional, Windows .NET Server family, Common Language Infrastructure (CLI) Standard

SocketPermission.AcceptList Property

Gets a list of **EndpointPermission** instances identifying the endpoints that can be accepted under this permission instance.

```
[Visual Basic]
Public ReadOnly Property AcceptList As IEnumerator
[C#]
public IEnumerator AcceptList {get;}
```

```
[C++]
public: __property IEnumerator* get_AcceptList();
[JScript]
public function get AcceptList() : IEnumerator;
```

Property Value

An instance implementing the **IEnumerator** interface containing **EndpointPermission** instances.

Example

The following example uses the **AcceptList** property to return a list of endpoints to which accept priveledges are granted.

Requirements

Platforms: Windows 98, Windows NT 4.0, Windows Millennium Edition, Windows 2000, Windows XP Home Edition, Windows XP Professional, Windows .NET Server family

SocketPermission.ConnectList Property

Gets a list of **EndpointPermission** instances identifying the endpoints that can be connected to under this permission instance.

```
[Visual Basic]
Public ReadOnly Property ConnectList As IEnumerator
[C#]
public IEnumerator ConnectList {get;}
[C++]
public: __property IEnumerator* get_ConnectList();
[JScript]
public function get ConnectList() : IEnumerator;
```

Property Value

An instance implementing the **IEnumerator** interface containing **EndpointPermission** instances.

Example

See related example in the **System.Nete.SocketPermission** class topic.

Requirements

Platforms: Windows 98, Windows NT 4.0, Windows Millennium Edition, Windows 2000, Windows XP Home Edition, Windows XP Professional, Windows .NET Server family

SocketPermission.AddPermission Method

Adds a permission to the set of permissions for a transport address.

```
[Visual Basic]
Public Sub AddPermission( _
   ByVal access As NetworkAccess, _
   ByVal transport As TransportType, _
   ByVal hostName As String, _
   ByVal portNumber As Integer _
)
[C#]
public void AddPermission(
   NetworkAccess access,
   TransportType transport,
   string hostName,
   int portNumber
);
```

```
[C++]
public: void AddPermission(
   NetworkAccess access,
   TransportType transport,
   String* hostName,
   int portNumber
);
[JScript]
public function AddPermission(
   access : NetworkAccess,
   transport : TransportType,
   hostName : String,
   portNumber : int
);
```

Parameters

access
   One of the **NetworkAccess** values.
transport
   One of the **TransportType** values.
hostName
   The host name for the transport address.
portNumber
   The port number for the transport address.

Remarks

The *hostName* can be a DNS name, an IP address, or a specified IP subnet using, such as 192.168.1.*.

Example

See related example in the **System.Nete.SocketPermission** class topic.

Requirements

Platforms: Windows 98, Windows NT 4.0, Windows Millennium Edition, Windows 2000, Windows XP Home Edition, Windows XP Professional, Windows .NET Server family

SocketPermission.Copy Method

Creates a copy of a **SocketPermission** instance.

```
[Visual Basic]
Overrides Public Function Copy() As IPermission Implements _
   IPermission.Copy
[C#]
public override IPermission Copy();
[C++]
public: IPermission* Copy();
[JScript]
public override function Copy() : IPermission;
```

Return Value

A new instance of the **SocketPermission** class that is a copy of the current instance.

Implements

IPermission.Copy

Remarks

The object returned by this method represents the same level of access as the current instance. This method overrides **Copy** and is implemented to support the **IPermission** interface.

Example

The following example creates a **SocketPermission** by taking a copy of an existing **SocketPermission**.

Requirements

Platforms: Windows 98, Windows NT 4.0, Windows Millennium Edition, Windows 2000, Windows XP Home Edition, Windows XP Professional, Windows .NET Server family, Common Language Infrastructure (CLI) Standard

SocketPermission.FromXml Method

Reconstructs a **SocketPermission** instance for an XML encoding.

```
[Visual Basic]
Overrides Public Sub FromXml( _
    ByVal securityElement As SecurityElement _
) Implements ISecurityEncodable.FromXml
[C#]
public override void FromXml(
    SecurityElement securityElement
);
[C++]
public: void FromXml(
    SecurityElement* securityElement
);
[JScript]
public override function FromXml(
    securityElement : SecurityElement
);
```

Parameters

securityElement
    The XML encoding used to reconstruct the **SocketPermission** instance.

Implements

ISecurityEncodable.FromXml

Exceptions

Exception Type	Condition
ArgumentNullException	The *securityElement* is a null reference (**Nothing** in Visual Basic).
ArgumentException	The *securityElement* is not a permission element for this type.

Remarks

The **FromXml** method reconstructs a **SocketPermission** instance from an XML encoding defined by the **SecurityElement** class.

Use the **ToXml** method to encode the **SocketPermission** instance, including state information, in XML.

Example

See related example in the **System.Nete.SocketPermission** class topic.

Requirements

Platforms: Windows 98, Windows NT 4.0, Windows Millennium Edition, Windows 2000, Windows XP Home Edition, Windows XP Professional, Windows .NET Server family, Common Language Infrastructure (CLI) Standard

SocketPermission.Intersect Method

Returns the logical intersection between two **SocketPermission** instances.

```
[Visual Basic]
Overrides Public Function Intersect( _
    ByVal target As IPermission _
) As IPermission Implements IPermission.Intersect
[C#]
public override IPermission Intersect(
    IPermission target
);
[C++]
public: IPermission* Intersect(
    IPermission* target
);
[JScript]
public override function Intersect(
    target : IPermission
) : IPermission;
```

Parameters

target
    The **SocketPermission** instance to intersect with the current instance.

Return Value

The **SocketPermission** instance that represents the intersection of two **SocketPermission** instances. If the intersection is empty, the method returns a null reference (**Nothing** in Visual Basic). If the *target* parameter is a null reference, the method returns a null reference (**Nothing**).

Implements

IPermission.Intersect

Exceptions

Exception Type	Condition
ArgumentException	The *target* parameter is not a **SocketPermission**.
SecurityException	**DnsPermission** is not granted to the method caller.

Remarks

The intersection of two permissions is a permission that secures the resources and operations secured by both permissions. Specifically, it represents the minimum permission such that any demand that passes both permissions will also pass their intersection. This method overrides **Intersect** and is implemented to support the **IPermission** interface.

Example

See related example in the **System.Nete.SocketPermission** class topic.

Requirements

Platforms: Windows 98, Windows NT 4.0, Windows Millennium Edition, Windows 2000, Windows XP Home Edition, Windows XP Professional, Windows .NET Server family, Common Language Infrastructure (CLI) Standard

SocketPermission.IsSubsetOf Method

Determines if the current permission is a subset of the specified permission.

```
[Visual Basic]
Overrides Public Function IsSubsetOf( _
    ByVal target As IPermission _
) As Boolean Implements IPermission.IsSubsetOf
[C#]
public override bool IsSubsetOf(
    IPermission target
);
[C++]
public: bool IsSubsetOf(
    IPermission* target
);
[JScript]
public override function IsSubsetOf(
    target : IPermission
) : Boolean;
```

Parameters

target
> A **SocketPermission** that is to be tested for the subset relationship.

Return Value

If *target* is a null reference (**Nothing** in Visual Basic), this method returns **true** if the current instance defines no permissions; otherwise, **false**. If *target* is not a null reference (**Nothing**), this method returns **true** if the current instance defines a subset of *target* permissions; otherwise, **false**.

Implements

IPermission.IsSubsetOf

Exceptions

Exception Type	Condition
ArgumentException	*target* is not a **SocketException**.
SecurityException	**DnsPermission** is not granted to the method caller.

Remarks

The current permission is a subset of the specified permission if the current permission specifies a set of operations that is wholly contained by the specified permission.

For example, a permission that represents access to 192.168.1.1:80 is a subset of a permission that represents access to 192.168.1.1:Any. If this method returns **true**, the current permission represents no more access to the protected resource than does the specified permission.

Requirements

Platforms: Windows 98, Windows NT 4.0, Windows Millennium Edition, Windows 2000, Windows XP Home Edition, Windows XP Professional, Windows .NET Server family, Common Language Infrastructure (CLI) Standard

SocketPermission.IsUnrestricted Method

Checks the overall permission state of the object.

```
[Visual Basic]
Public Overridable Function IsUnrestricted() As Boolean Implements _
    IUnrestrictedPermission.IsUnrestricted
[C#]
public virtual bool IsUnrestricted();
[C++]
public: virtual bool IsUnrestricted();
[JScript]
public function IsUnrestricted() : Boolean;
```

Return Value

true if the **SocketPermission** instance was created with the **Unrestricted** value from **PermissionState**; otherwise, **false**.

Implements

IUnrestrictedPermission.IsUnrestricted

Example

See related example in the **System.Nete.SocketPermission** class topic.

Requirements

Platforms: Windows 98, Windows NT 4.0, Windows Millennium Edition, Windows 2000, Windows XP Home Edition, Windows XP Professional, Windows .NET Server family

SocketPermission.ToXml Method

Creates an XML encoding of a **SocketPermission** instance and its current state.

```
[Visual Basic]
Overrides Public Function ToXml() As SecurityElement Implements _
    ISecurityEncodable.ToXml
[C#]
public override SecurityElement ToXml();
[C++]
public: SecurityElement* ToXml();
[JScript]
public override function ToXml() : SecurityElement;
```

Return Value

A **SecurityElement** instance containing an XML-encoded representation of the **SocketPermission** instance, including state information.

Implements

ISecurityEncodable.ToXml

Remarks

The **ToXml** method creates a **SecurityElement** instance to encode a representation of the **SocketPermission** instance, including state information, in XML.

Use the **FromXml** method to restore the state information from a **SecurityElement** instance.

Example

See related example in the **System.Nete.SocketPermission** class topic.

Requirements

Platforms: Windows 98, Windows NT 4.0,
Windows Millennium Edition, Windows 2000,
Windows XP Home Edition, Windows XP Professional,
Windows .NET Server family,
Common Language Infrastructure (CLI) Standard

SocketPermission.Union Method

Returns the logical union between two **SocketPermission** instances.

```
[Visual Basic]
Overrides Public Function Union( _
   ByVal target As IPermission _
) As IPermission Implements IPermission.Union
[C#]
public override IPermission Union(
   IPermission target
);
[C++]
public: IPermission* Union(
   IPermission* target
);
[JScript]
public override function Union(
   target : IPermission
) : IPermission;
```

Parameters

target
> The **SocketPermission** instance to combine with the current
> instance.

Return Value

The **SocketPermission** instance that represents the union of two
SocketPermission instances. If *target* parameter is a null reference
(**Nothing** in Visual Basic), it returns a copy of the current instance.

Implements

IPermission.Union

Exceptions

Exception Type	Condition
ArgumentException	*target* is not a **SocketPermission**.

Remarks

The result of a call to **Union** is a permission that represents all of the
access to **Socket** connections represented by the current instance as
well as the access represented by *target*. Any demand that passes
either the current instance or *target* passes their union. This method
overrides **Union** and is implemented to support the **IPermission**
interface.

Requirements

Platforms: Windows 98, Windows NT 4.0,
Windows Millennium Edition, Windows 2000,
Windows XP Home Edition, Windows XP Professional,
Windows .NET Server family,
Common Language Infrastructure (CLI) Standard

SocketPermissionAttribute Class

Specifies security actions to control **Socket** connections. This class cannot be inherited.

System.Object
  System.Attribute
    System.Security.Permissions.SecurityAttribute
      System.Security.Permissions.CodeAccessSecurityAttribute
        System.Net.SocketPermissionAttribute

```
[Visual Basic]
<AttributeUsage(AttributeTargets.Assembly Or AttributeTargets.Class _
   Or AttributeTargets.Struct Or AttributeTargets.Constructor Or _
   AttributeTargets.Method)>
<Serializable>
NotInheritable Public Class SocketPermissionAttribute
   Inherits CodeAccessSecurityAttribute
[C#]
[AttributeUsage(AttributeTargets.Assembly | AttributeTargets.Class
   | AttributeTargets.Struct | AttributeTargets.Constructor |
   AttributeTargets.Method)]
[Serializable]
public sealed class SocketPermissionAttribute :
   CodeAccessSecurityAttribute
[C++]
[AttributeUsage(AttributeTargets::Assembly |
   AttributeTargets::Class | AttributeTargets::Struct |
   AttributeTargets::Constructor | AttributeTargets::Method)]
[Serializable]
public __gc __sealed class SocketPermissionAttribute : public
   CodeAccessSecurityAttribute
[JScript]
public
   AttributeUsage(AttributeTargets.Assembly | AttributeTargets.Class |
   AttributeTargets.Struct | AttributeTargets.Constructor |
   AttributeTargets.Method)
   Serializable
class SocketPermissionAttribute extends
   CodeAccessSecurityAttribute
```

Thread Safety

Any public static (**Shared** in Visual Basic) members of this type are safe for multithreaded operations. Any instance members are not guaranteed to be thread safe.

Remarks

To use this attribute, your **Socket** connection must conform to the properties specified in your **SocketPermissionAttribute**. For example, to secure a **Socket** connection on port 80, set the **Port** property of the **SocketPermissionAttribute** to "80". The security information specified in **SocketPermissionAttribute** is stored in the metadata of the attribute target, which is the class to which the **SocketPermissionAttribute** is applied. The system then accesses the information at run time. The **SecurityAction** passed to the constructor determines the allowable **SocketPermissionAttribute** targets.

> **Note** The properties of a **SocketPermissionAttribute** must have values that are not a null reference (**Nothing** in Visual Basic). Also, once set, the values of the properties cannot be changed.

> **Note** For more information about using attributes, see **Extending Metadata Using Attributes**.

Example

See related example in the **System.Net.SocketPermission** class topic.

Requirements

Namespace: System.Net

Platforms: Windows 98, Windows NT 4.0, Windows Millennium Edition, Windows 2000, Windows XP Home Edition, Windows XP Professional, Windows .NET Server family

Assembly: System (in System.dll)

SocketPermissionAttribute Constructor

Initializes a new instance of the **SocketPermissionAttribute** class with the specified **SecurityAction** value.

```
[Visual Basic]
Public Sub New( _
   ByVal action As SecurityAction _
)
[C#]
public SocketPermissionAttribute(
   SecurityAction action
);
[C++]
public: SocketPermissionAttribute(
   SecurityAction action
);
[JScript]
public function SocketPermissionAttribute(
   action : SecurityAction
);
```

Parameters

action
    One of the **SecurityAction** values.

Exceptions

Exception Type	Condition
ArgumentException	*action* is not a valid **SecurityAction** value.

Remarks

The **SecurityAction** value passed to this constructor specifies the allowable **SocketPermissionAttribute** targets.

Requirements

Platforms: Windows 98, Windows NT 4.0, Windows Millennium Edition, Windows 2000, Windows XP Home Edition, Windows XP Professional, Windows .NET Server family, Common Language Infrastructure (CLI) Standard

SocketPermissionAttribute.Access Property

Gets or sets the network access method allowed by this **SocketPermissionAttribute**.

```
[Visual Basic]
Public Property Access As String
[C#]
public string Access {get; set;}
[C++]
public: __property String* get_Access();
public: __property void set_Access(String*);
[JScript]
public function get Access() : String;
public function set Access(String);
```

Property Value

A string containing the network access method allowed by this instance of **SocketPermissionAttribute**. Valid values are "Accept" and "Connect."

Exceptions

Exception Type	Condition
ArgumentException	The **Access** property is not a null reference (**Nothing** in Visual Basic) when you attempt to set the value. To specify more than one Access method, use an additional attribute declaration statement.

Remarks

This property is write-once. Valid values for this property correspond to **NetworkAccess** enumeration values.

Requirements

Platforms: Windows 98, Windows NT 4.0, Windows Millennium Edition, Windows 2000, Windows XP Home Edition, Windows XP Professional, Windows .NET Server family, Common Language Infrastructure (CLI) Standard

SocketPermissionAttribute.Host Property

Gets or sets the DNS host name or IP address specified by this **SocketPermissionAttribute**.

```
[Visual Basic]
Public Property Host As String
[C#]
public string Host {get; set;}
[C++]
public: __property String* get_Host();
public: __property void set_Host(String*);
[JScript]
public function get Host() : String;
public function set Host(String);
```

Property Value

A string containing the DNS host name or IP address associated with this instance of **SocketPermissionAttribute**.

Exceptions

Exception Type	Condition
ArgumentException	**Host** is not a null reference (**Nothing** in Visual Basic) when you attempt to set the value. To specify more than one host, use an additional attribute declaration statement.

Remarks

This property is write-once and specifies the Domain Name Services (DNS) host name to which this permission applies.

Requirements

Platforms: Windows 98, Windows NT 4.0, Windows Millennium Edition, Windows 2000, Windows XP Home Edition, Windows XP Professional, Windows .NET Server family, Common Language Infrastructure (CLI) Standard

SocketPermissionAttribute.Port Property

Gets or sets the port number associated with this **SocketPermissionAttribute**.

```
[Visual Basic]
Public Property Port As String
[C#]
public string Port {get; set;}
[C++]
public: __property String* get_Port();
public: __property void set_Port(String*);
[JScript]
public function get Port() : String;
public function set Port(String);
```

Property Value

A string containing the port number associated with this instance of **SocketPermissionAttribute**.

Exceptions

Exception Type	Condition
ArgumentException	The **Port** property is a null reference (**Nothing** in Visual Basic) when attempt to set the value. To specify more than one port, use an additional attribute declaration statement.

Remarks

This property is write-once and specifies the port number to which this permission applies. The valid values are a string-encoded integer, or the string "All".

Requirements

Platforms: Windows 98, Windows NT 4.0, Windows Millennium Edition, Windows 2000, Windows XP Home Edition, Windows XP Professional, Windows .NET Server family, Common Language Infrastructure (CLI) Standard

SocketPermissionAttribute.Transport Property

Gets or sets the **TransportType** specified by this **SocketPermissionAttribute**.

```
[Visual Basic]
Public Property Transport As String
[C#]
public string Transport {get; set;}
[C++]
public: __property String* get_Transport();
public: __property void set_Transport(String*);
[JScript]
public function get Transport() : String;
public function set Transport(String);
```

Property Value

A string containing the **TransportType** associated with this **SocketPermissionAttribute**.

Exceptions

Exception Type	Condition
ArgumentException	**Transport** is not a null reference (**Nothing** in Visual Basic) when you attempt to set the value. To specify more than one transport type, use an additional attribute declaration statement.

Remarks

Possible string values of this property are **All**, **Connectionless**, **ConnectionOriented**, **Tcp**, **Udp**.

Requirements

Platforms: Windows 98, Windows NT 4.0, Windows Millennium Edition, Windows 2000, Windows XP Home Edition, Windows XP Professional, Windows .NET Server family, Common Language Infrastructure (CLI) Standard

SocketPermissionAttribute.CreatePermission Method

Creates and returns a new instance of the **SocketPermission** class.

```
[Visual Basic]
Overrides Public Function CreatePermission() As IPermission
[C#]
public override IPermission CreatePermission();
[C++]
public: IPermission* CreatePermission();
[JScript]
public override function CreatePermission() : IPermission;
```

Return Value

An instance of the **SocketPermission** class corresponding to the security declaration.

Exceptions

Exception Type	Condition
ArgumentException	One or more of the current instance's **Access**, **Host**, **Transport**, or **Port** properties is a null reference (**Nothing** in Visual Basic).

Remarks

The **CreatePermission** method is called by the security system, not by the application code. The security information described by **SocketPermissionAttribute** is stored in the metadata of the attribute target, which is the class to which the **SocketPermissionAttribute** is applied. The system then accesses the information at run_time and calls **CreatePermission**. The system uses the returned **IPermission** to enforce the specified security requirements.

Requirements

Platforms: Windows 98, Windows NT 4.0, Windows Millennium Edition, Windows 2000, Windows XP Home Edition, Windows XP Professional, Windows .NET Server family, Common Language Infrastructure (CLI) Standard

TransportType Enumeration

Defines transport types for the **SocketPermission** and **Socket** classes.

```
[Visual Basic]
<Serializable>
Public Enum TransportType
[C#]
[Serializable]
public enum TransportType
[C++]
[Serializable]
__value public enum TransportType
[JScript]
public
   Serializable
enum TransportType
```

Remarks

The **TransportType** enumeration defines transport types for the **SocketPermission** and **Socket** classes.

Members

Member name	Description
All	All transport types.
Connectionless	The transport type is connectionless, such as UDP.
ConnectionOriented	The transport is connection oriented, such as TCP.
Tcp	TCP transport.
Udp	UDP transport.

Requirements

Namespace: System.Net

Platforms: Windows 98, Windows NT 4.0, Windows Millennium Edition, Windows 2000, Windows XP Home Edition, Windows XP Professional, Windows .NET Server family

Assembly: System (in System.dll)

WebClient Class

Provides common methods for sending data to and receiving data from a resource identified by a URI. This class cannot be inherited.

System.Object
  System.MarshalByRefObject
    System.ComponentModel.Component
      System.Net.WebClient

```
[Visual Basic]
<ComVisible(True)>
NotInheritable Public Class WebClient
   Inherits Component
[C#]
[ComVisible(true)]
public sealed class WebClient : Component
[C++]
[ComVisible(true)]
public __gc __sealed class WebClient : public Component
[JScript]
public
   ComVisible(true)
class WebClient extends Component
```

Thread Safety

Any public static (**Shared** in Visual Basic) members of this type are safe for multithreaded operations. Any instance members are not guaranteed to be thread safe.

Remarks

The **WebClient** class provides common methods for sending data to or receiving data from any local, intranet, or Internet resource identified by a URI.

The **WebClient** class uses the **WebRequest** class to provide access to Internet resources. **WebClient** instances can access data with any **WebRequest** descendant registered with the **WebRequest.RegisterPrefix** method.

> **Note** By default, the .NET Framework supports URIs that begin with http:, https:, and file: scheme identifiers.

The **WebClient** class provides four methods for uploading data to a resource:

- **OpenWrite** returns a **Stream** used to send data to the resource.
- **UploadData** sends a byte array to the resource and returns a byte array containing any response.
- **UploadFile** sends a local file to the resource and returns a byte array containing any response.
- **UploadValues** sends a **NameValueCollection** to the resource and returns a byte array containing any response.

The **WebClient** class also provides three methods for downloading data from a resource:

- **DownloadData** downloads data from a resource and returns a byte array.
- **DownloadFile** downloads data from a resource to a local file.
- **OpenRead** returns the data from the resource as a **Stream**.

Requirements

Namespace: System.Net

Platforms: Windows 98, Windows NT 4.0, Windows Millennium Edition, Windows 2000, Windows XP Home Edition, Windows XP Professional, Windows .NET Server family

Assembly: System (in System.dll)

.NET Framework Security:

- **WebPermission** to access the requested URI or any URI that the request is redirected to. Associated enumeration: **Connect**.

WebClient Constructor

Initializes a new instance of the **WebClient** class.

```
[Visual Basic]
Public Sub New()
[C#]
public WebClient();
[C++]
public: WebClient();
[JScript]
public function WebClient();
```

Remarks

The default constructor creates a new instance of the **WebClient** class with each field set to a null reference (**Nothing** in Visual Basic).

Example

[Visual Basic, C#] The following example creates a **WebClient** instance and then uses it to download data from a server and display it on the system console, to download data from a server and write it to a file, and to upload form values to a server and receive the response.

```
[Visual Basic]
Public Shared Sub Main()

    Try
        Dim client As New WebClient()
        Dim pageData As [Byte]() =          ⏎
client.DownloadData("http://www.contoso.com")
        Dim pageHtml As String = Encoding.ASCII.GetString(pageData)

        ' Download the data to a buffer.
        Console.WriteLine(pageHtml)

        ' Download the data to a file.
        client.DownloadFile("http://www.contoso.com", "page.htm")

        ' Upload some form post values.
        dim form as New NameValueCollection()
        form.Add("MyName", "MyValue")

        ' Note that you need to replace          ⏎
"http://localhost/somefile.aspx" with the name of
        ' a file that is available to your computer.
        Dim responseData As [Byte]() =          ⏎
client.UploadValues("http://www.contoso.com/form.aspx", form)
        Console.WriteLine(Encoding.ASCII.GetString(responseData))

    Catch webEx As WebException
        if webEx.Status = WebExceptionStatus.ConnectFailure then
            Console.WriteLine("Are you behind a firewall?          ⏎
If so, go through the proxy server.")
        end if
        Console.Write(webEx.ToString())
    End Try

End Sub 'Main
```

```
[C#]
try {

// Download the data to a buffer.
      WebClient client = new WebClient();

  Byte[] pageData = client.DownloadData("http://www.contoso.com");
string pageHtml = Encoding.ASCII.GetString(pageData);
Console.WriteLine(pageHtml);

// Download the data to a file.
      client.DownloadFile("http://www.contoso.com", "page.htm");

// Upload some form post values.
NameValueCollection form = new NameValueCollection();
form.Add("MyName", "MyValue");
Byte[] responseData = client.UploadValues("http://www.contoso.com/
form.aspx", form);

}
catch (WebException webEx) {
      Console.WriteLine(webEx.ToString());
        if(webEx.Status == WebExceptionStatus.ConnectFailure) {
            Console.WriteLine("Are you behind a firewall?
If so, go through the proxy server.");
        }
}
```

Requirements

Platforms: Windows 98, Windows NT 4.0,
Windows Millennium Edition, Windows 2000,
Windows XP Home Edition, Windows XP Professional,
Windows .NET Server family,
Common Language Infrastructure (CLI) Standard

WebClient.BaseAddress Property

Gets or sets the base URI for requests made by a **WebClient**.

```
[Visual Basic]
Public Property BaseAddress As String
[C#]
public string BaseAddress {get; set;}
[C++]
public: __property String* get_BaseAddress();
public: __property void set_BaseAddress(String*);
[JScript]
public function get BaseAddress() : String;
public function set BaseAddress(String);
```

Property Value

The base URI for requests made by a **WebClient**.

Exceptions

Exception Type	Condition
ArgumentException	**BaseAddress** is set to an invalid URI.

Remarks

The **BaseAddress** property contains a base URI that is combined
with the relative address specified when calling an upload or
download method.

If the **BaseAddress** property is set, the URI specified when calling
the following methods must be a relative URI:

- **DownloadData**
- **DownloadFile**
- **OpenRead**

- **OpenWrite**
- **UploadData**
- **UploadFile**
- **UploadValues**

Example

[Visual Basic, C#, C++] The following example downloads data
from an Internet server and displays it on the console. It assumes that
the server's address (such as http://www.contoso.com) is in hostUri
and that the path to the resource (such as/default.htm) is in uriSuffix.

```
[Visual Basic]
' Create a new WebClient instance.
Dim myWebClient As New WebClient()

' Set the BaseAddress of the Web resource in the WebClient.
myWebClient.BaseAddress = hostUri
Console.WriteLine(("Downloading from " + hostUri + "/" + uriSuffix))
Console.WriteLine(ControlChars.Cr + "Press Enter key to continue")
Console.ReadLine()

' Download the target Web resource into a byte array.
Dim myDatabuffer As Byte() = myWebClient.DownloadData(uriSuffix)

' Display the downloaded data.
      Dim download As String = Encoding.ASCII.GetString(myDatabuffer)
      Console.WriteLine(download)

Console.WriteLine(("Download of " +
myWebClient.BaseAddress.ToString() + uriSuffix + " was successful."))
```

```
[C#]
// Create a new WebClient instance.
WebClient myWebClient = new WebClient();

// Set the BaseAddress of the Web Resource in the WebClient.
myWebClient.BaseAddress = hostUri;
Console.WriteLine("Downloading from " + hostUri + "/" + uriSuffix);
Console.WriteLine("\nPress Enter key to continue");
Console.ReadLine();

// Download the target Web Resource into a byte array.
byte[] myDatabuffer = myWebClient.DownloadData (uriSuffix);

// Display the downloaded data.
string download = Encoding.ASCII.GetString(myDatabuffer);
Console.WriteLine(download);

Console.WriteLine("Download of " +
myWebClient.BaseAddress.ToString() + uriSuffix + " was successful.");
```

```
[C++]
// Create a new WebClient instance.
WebClient* myWebClient = new WebClient();

// Set the BaseAddress of the Web Resource in the WebClient.
myWebClient->BaseAddress = hostUri;
Console::WriteLine(S"Downloading from {0}/ {1}", hostUri, uriSuffix);
Console::WriteLine(S"\nPress Enter key to continue");
Console::ReadLine();

// Download the target Web Resource into a Byte array.
Byte myDatabuffer[] = myWebClient->DownloadData (uriSuffix);

// Display the downloaded data.
String* download = Encoding::ASCII->GetString(myDatabuffer);
Console::WriteLine(download);

Console::WriteLine(S"Download of {0}{1} was successful.",
myWebClient->BaseAddress, uriSuffix);
```

Requirements

Platforms: Windows 98, Windows NT 4.0,
Windows Millennium Edition, Windows 2000,
Windows XP Home Edition, Windows XP Professional,
Windows .NET Server family,
Common Language Infrastructure (CLI) Standard

WebClient.Credentials Property

Gets or sets the network credentials used to authenticate the request
with the Internet resource.

```
[Visual Basic]
Public Property Credentials As ICredentials
[C#]
public ICredentials Credentials {get; set;}
[C++]
public: __property ICredentials* get_Credentials();
public: __property void set_Credentials(ICredentials*);
[JScript]
public function get Credentials() : ICredentials;
public function set Credentials(ICredentials);
```

Property Value

An **ICredentials** containing the authentication credentials for the
request. The default is a null reference (**Nothing** in Visual Basic).

Remarks

The **Credentials** property contains the authentication credentials
required to access the Internet resource.

Example

The following example uses the user's system credentials to
authenticate a request.

```
[Visual Basic]
Public Shared Sub Main()
    Try
        Dim client As New WebClient()

        client.Credentials = CredentialCache.DefaultCredentials

        Dim pageData As [Byte]() =
client.DownloadData("http://www.contoso.com")
        Dim pageHtml As String = Encoding.ASCII.GetString(pageData)

        Console.WriteLine(pageHtml)

    Catch webEx As WebException
        Console.Write(webEx.ToString())
    End Try
End Sub

[C#]
public static void Main()
{
    try {

        WebClient client = new WebClient();

        client.Credentials = CredentialCache.DefaultCredentials;

        Byte[] pageData =
client.DownloadData("http://www.contoso.com");
        string pageHtml = Encoding.ASCII.GetString(pageData);
        Console.WriteLine(pageHtml);

    } catch (WebException webEx) {
        Console.Write(webEx.ToString());
```

```
    }
}

[C++]
int main()
{
    try
    {
        WebClient* client = new WebClient();
        client -> Credentials = CredentialCache::DefaultCredentials;
        Byte pageData[] = client ->
DownloadData(S"http://www.contoso.com");
        String* pageHtml = Encoding::ASCII -> GetString(pageData);
        Console::WriteLine(pageHtml);

    }
    catch (WebException* webEx)
    {
        Console::Write(webEx);
    }
}

[JScript]
public static function Main()
{
    try {

        var client : WebClient = new WebClient();

        client.Credentials = CredentialCache.DefaultCredentials;

        var pageData : Byte[] =
client.DownloadData("http://www.contoso.com");
        var pageHtml : String = Encoding.ASCII.GetString(pageData);
        Console.WriteLine(pageHtml);

    } catch (webEx : WebException) {
        Console.Write(webEx.ToString());
    }
}
```

Requirements

Platforms: Windows 98, Windows NT 4.0,
Windows Millennium Edition, Windows 2000,
Windows XP Home Edition, Windows XP Professional,
Windows .NET Server family,
Common Language Infrastructure (CLI) Standard

WebClient.Headers Property

Gets or sets a collection of header name/value pairs associated with
the request.

```
[Visual Basic]
Public Property Headers As WebHeaderCollection
[C#]
public WebHeaderCollection Headers {get; set;}
[C++]
public: __property WebHeaderCollection* get_Headers();
public: __property void set_Headers(WebHeaderCollection*);
[JScript]
public function get Headers() : WebHeaderCollection;
public function set Headers(WebHeaderCollection);
```

Property Value

A **WebHeaderCollection** containing header name/value pairs
associated with this request.

Remarks

The **Headers** property contains a **WebHeaderCollection** instance containing header informationthat the **WebClient** sends to the Internet resource. This is an unrestricted collection of headers, so setting headers that are restricted by **WebRequest** descendants such as **HttpWebRequest** is allowed.

Example

[Visual Basic, C#, C++] The following example uses the **Headers** collection to set the HTTP Content-Type header to "application/x-www-form-urlencoded" to notify the server that form data is attached to the post.

[Visual Basic]
```
Dim uriString As String
Console.Write(ControlChars.Cr + "Please enter the URI
to post data to{for example, http://www.contoso.com} : ")
uriString = Console.ReadLine()
' Create a new WebClient instance.
Dim myWebClient As New WebClient()
Console.WriteLine(ControlChars.Cr + "Please enter the data
to be posted to the URI {0}:", uriString)
Dim postData As String = Console.ReadLine()
myWebClient.Headers.Add("Content-Type",
"application/x-www-form-urlencoded")
' Apply ASCII Encoding to obtain the string as a byte array.
Dim byteArray As Byte() = Encoding.ASCII.GetBytes(postData)
Console.WriteLine("Uploading to {0} ...", uriString)
' Upload the input string using the HTTP 1.0 POST method.
Dim responseArray As Byte() = myWebClient.UploadData(uriString,
"POST", byteArray)
' Decode and display the response.
Console.WriteLine(ControlChars.Cr + "Response received was
:{0}", Encoding.ASCII.GetString(responseArray))
```

[C#]
```
string uriString;
Console.Write("\nPlease enter the URI to post data to
{for example, http://www.contoso.com} : ");
uriString = Console.ReadLine();
// Create a new WebClient instance.
WebClient myWebClient = new WebClient();
Console.WriteLine("\nPlease enter the data to be posted to
the URI {0}:",uriString);
string postData = Console.ReadLine();
myWebClient.Headers.Add("Content-Type","application/x-www-form-
urlencoded");
// Apply ASCII Encoding to obtain the string as a byte array.
byte[] byteArray = Encoding.ASCII.GetBytes(postData);
Console.WriteLine("Uploading to {0} ...", uriString);
// Upload the input string using the HTTP 1.0 POST method.
byte[] responseArray =
myWebClient.UploadData(uriString,"POST",byteArray);
// Decode and display the response.
Console.WriteLine("\nResponse received was {0}",
    Encoding.ASCII.GetString(responseArray));
```

[C++]
```
String* uriString;
Console::Write(S"\nPlease enter the URI to post data to
{for example, http://www.contoso.com} : ");
uriString = Console::ReadLine();
// Create a new WebClient instance.
WebClient* myWebClient = new WebClient();
Console::WriteLine(S"\nPlease enter the data to be posted to
the URI {0}:", uriString);
String* postData = Console::ReadLine();
myWebClient->Headers->Add(S"Content-Type",
S"application/x-www-form-urlencoded");
// Apply ASCII Encoding to obtain the String* as a Byte array.
Byte byteArray[] = Encoding::ASCII->GetBytes(postData);
Console::WriteLine(S"Uploading to {0} ...", uriString);
// Upload the input String* using the HTTP 1.0 POST method.
```

```
Byte responseArray[] = myWebClient->UploadData(uriString,
S"POST", byteArray);
// Decode and display the response.
Console::WriteLine(S"\nResponse received was {0}",
    Encoding::ASCII->GetString(responseArray));
```

Requirements

Platforms: Windows 98, Windows NT 4.0, Windows Millennium Edition, Windows 2000, Windows XP Home Edition, Windows XP Professional, Windows .NET Server family, Common Language Infrastructure (CLI) Standard

WebClient.QueryString Property

Gets or sets a collection of query name/value pairs associated with the request.

```
[Visual Basic]
Public Property QueryString As NameValueCollection
[C#]
public NameValueCollection QueryString {get; set;}
[C++]
public: __property NameValueCollection* get_QueryString();
public: __property void set_QueryString(NameValueCollection*);
[JScript]
public function get QueryString() : NameValueCollection;
public function set QueryString(NameValueCollection);
```

Property Value

A **NameValueCollection** that contains query name/value pairs associated with the request.

Remarks

The **QueryString** property contains a **NameValueCollection** instance containing name/value pairs that are appended to the URI as a query string. The contents of the **QueryString** property are preceded by a question mark (?), and name/value pairs are separated from one another by an ampersand (&).

Example

[Visual Basic, C#, C++] The following example takes user input from the command line and builds a **NameValueCollection** that is assigned to the **QueryString** property. It then downloads the response from the server to a local file.

[Visual Basic]
```
Dim uriString As String = "http://www.contoso.com/search"
' Create a new WebClient instance.
Dim myWebClient As New WebClient()
' Create a new NameValueCollection instance to hold the
QueryString parameters and values.
Dim myQueryStringCollection As New NameValueCollection()
Console.Write(("Enter the word(s), separated by space
characters, to search for in " + uriString + ": "))
' Read user input phrase to search in uriString.
Dim searchPhrase As String = Console.ReadLine()
' Append necessary parameter/value pairs to the name/value container.
' as QueryString = "?q=Microsoft&btnG=Google+Search".
If searchPhrase.Length > 1 Then
    'Assign the user-defined search phrase.
    myQueryStringCollection.Add("q", searchPhrase)
' If error, default to search 'Microsoft'.
Else
    myQueryStringCollection.Add("q", "Microsoft")
End If
' Assign auxilliary parameters required for the search.
myQueryStringCollection.Add("btnG", "Google" + ChrW(43) + "Search")
```

```
Console.WriteLine(("Searching " + uriString + " ......."))
' Attach QueryString to the WebClient.
myWebClient.QueryString = myQueryStringCollection
' Download the search results Web page into
'searchresult.htm' for inspection.
myWebClient.DownloadFile(uriString, "searchresult.htm")
Console.WriteLine((ControlChars.Cr + "Download of " + uriString +
" was successful. Please see 'searchresult.htm' for results."))
```

[C#]
```
string uriString = "http://www.contoso.com/search";
// Create a new WebClient instance.
WebClient myWebClient = new WebClient();
// Create a new NameValueCollection instance to hold the
QueryString parameters and values.
NameValueCollection myQueryStringCollection = new
NameValueCollection();
Console.Write("Enter the word(s), separated by space
character to search for in " + uriString + ": ");
// Read user input phrase to search for at uriString.
string searchPhrase = Console.ReadLine();
if (searchPhrase.Length > 1)
    // Assign the user-defined search phrase.
    myQueryStringCollection.Add("q",searchPhrase);
else
    // If error, default to search for 'Microsoft'.
    myQueryStringCollection.Add("q","Microsoft");
// Assign auxilliary parameters required for the search.
Console.WriteLine("Searching " + uriString + " .......");
// Attach QueryString to the WebClient.
myWebClient.QueryString = myQueryStringCollection;
// Download the search results Web page into
'searchresult.htm' for inspection.
myWebClient.DownloadFile (uriString, "searchresult.htm");
Console.WriteLine("\nDownload of " + uriString + "
was successful. Please see 'searchresult.htm' for results.");
```

[C++]
```
String* uriString = S"http://www.contoso.com/search";
// Create a new WebClient instance.
WebClient* myWebClient = new WebClient();
// Create a new NameValueCollection instance to hold the
QueryString parameters and values.
NameValueCollection* myQueryStringCollection =
    new NameValueCollection();
Console::Write(S"Enter the word(s), separated by space
character to search for in {0}: ", uriString);
// Read user input phrase to search for at uriString.
String* searchPhrase = Console::ReadLine();
if (searchPhrase->Length > 1)
    // Assign the user-defined search phrase.
    myQueryStringCollection->Add(S"q", searchPhrase);
else
    // If error, default to search for 'Microsoft'.
    myQueryStringCollection->Add(S"q", S"Microsoft");
// Assign auxilliary parameters required for the search.
Console::WriteLine(S"Searching {0} .......", uriString);
// Attach QueryString to the WebClient.
myWebClient->QueryString = myQueryStringCollection;
// Download the search results Web page into
'searchresult.htm' for inspection.
myWebClient->DownloadFile (uriString, S"searchresult.htm");
Console::WriteLine(S"\nDownload of {0} was successful.
Please see 'searchresult.htm' for results.", uriString);
```

Requirements

Platforms: Windows 98, Windows NT 4.0,
Windows Millennium Edition, Windows 2000,
Windows XP Home Edition, Windows XP Professional,
Windows .NET Server family,
Common Language Infrastructure (CLI) Standard

WebClient.ResponseHeaders Property

Gets a collection of header name/value pairs associated with the
response.

```
[Visual Basic]
Public ReadOnly Property ResponseHeaders As WebHeaderCollection
[C#]
public WebHeaderCollection ResponseHeaders {get;}
[C++]
public: __property WebHeaderCollection* get_ResponseHeaders();
[JScript]
public function get ResponseHeaders() : WebHeaderCollection;
```

Property Value

A **WebHeaderCollection** containing header name/value pairs
associated with this response.

Remarks

The **ResponseHeaders** property contains a **WebHeaderCollection**
instance containing header information the **WebClient** receives
from the Internet resource.

Example

See related example in the **System.Net.WebClient** class topic.

Requirements

Platforms: Windows 98, Windows NT 4.0,
Windows Millennium Edition, Windows 2000,
Windows XP Home Edition, Windows XP Professional,
Windows .NET Server family,
Common Language Infrastructure (CLI) Standard

WebClient.DownloadData Method

Downloads data from a resource with the specified URI.

```
[Visual Basic]
Public Function DownloadData( _
   ByVal address As String _
) As Byte()
[C#]
public byte[] DownloadData(
   string address
);
[C++]
public: unsigned char DownloadData(
   String* address
) __gc[];
[JScript]
public function DownloadData(
   address : String
) : Byte[];
```

Parameters

address
    The URI to download data from.

Return Value

A byte array containing the data downloaded from the resource
specified in the *address* parameter.

Exceptions

Exception Type	Condition
WebException	The URI formed by combining **BaseAddress** and *address* is invalid. -or- An error occurred while downloading data.

Remarks

The **DownloadData** method downloads the data from the URI specified by the *address* parameter to a local byte array.

If the **BaseAddress** property is not empty, *address* must be a relative URI that is combined with **BaseAddress** to form the absolute URI of the requested data. If the **QueryString** property is not empty, it is appended to *address*.

Example

See related example in the **System.Net.WebClient** class topic.

Requirements

Platforms: Windows 98, Windows NT 4.0, Windows Millennium Edition, Windows 2000, Windows XP Home Edition, Windows XP Professional, Windows .NET Server family, Common Language Infrastructure (CLI) Standard

WebClient.DownloadFile Method

Downloads data from a resource with the specified URI to a local file.

```
[Visual Basic]
Public Sub DownloadFile( _
   ByVal address As String, _
   ByVal fileName As String _
)
[C#]
public void DownloadFile(
   string address,
   string fileName
);
[C++]
public: void DownloadFile(
   String* address,
   String* fileName
);
[JScript]
public function DownloadFile(
   address : String,
   fileName : String
);
```

Parameters

address
    The URI to download data from.
fileName
    The name of the local file to receive the data.

Exceptions

Exception Type	Condition
WebException	The URI formed by combining **BaseAddress** and *address* is invalid. -or- *filename* is a null reference (**Nothing** in Visual Basic), or **Empty**. -or- An error occurred while downloading data.
SecurityException	The caller does not have permission to write to local file.

Remarks

The **DownloadFile** method downloads data from the URI specified by in the *address* parameter to a local file.

If the **BaseAddress** property is not empty, *address* must be a relative URI that is combined with **BaseAddress** to form the absolute URI of the requested data. If the **QueryString** property is not empty, it is appended to *address*.

Requirements

Platforms: Windows 98, Windows NT 4.0, Windows Millennium Edition, Windows 2000, Windows XP Home Edition, Windows XP Professional, Windows .NET Server family, Common Language Infrastructure (CLI) Standard

WebClient.OpenRead Method

Opens a readable stream for the data downloaded from a resource with the specified URI.

```
[Visual Basic]
Public Function OpenRead( _
   ByVal address As String _
) As Stream
[C#]
public Stream OpenRead(
   string address
);
[C++]
public: Stream* OpenRead(
   String* address
);
[JScript]
public function OpenRead(
   address : String
) : Stream;
```

Parameters

address
    The URI to download data from.

Return Value

A **Stream** used to read data from a resource.

Exceptions

Exception Type	Condition
WebException	The URI formed by combining **BaseAddress**, *address* is invalid. -or- An error occurred while downloading data.

Remarks

The **OpenRead** method creates a **Stream** instance used to access the data specified by the *address* parameter.

If the **BaseAddress** property is not empty, *address* must be a relative URI that is combined with **BaseAddress** to form the absolute URI of the requested data. If the **QueryString** property is not a null reference (**Nothing** in Visual Basic), it is appended to *address*.

> **Note** You must call **Stream.Close** when finished with the **Stream** to avoid running out of system resources.

Example

See related example in the **System.Net.WebClient** class topic.

Requirements

Platforms: Windows 98, Windows NT 4.0, Windows Millennium Edition, Windows 2000, Windows XP Home Edition, Windows XP Professional, Windows .NET Server family, Common Language Infrastructure (CLI) Standard

WebClient.OpenWrite Method

Opens a stream for writing data to a resource with the specified URI.

Overload List

Opens a stream for writing data to the specified resource.

[Visual Basic] **Overloads Public Function OpenWrite(String) As Stream**

[C#] **public Stream OpenWrite(string);**

[C++] **public: Stream* OpenWrite(String*);**

[JScript] **public function OpenWrite(String) : Stream;**

Opens a stream for writing data to the specified resource with using the specified method.

[Visual Basic] **Overloads Public Function OpenWrite(String, String) As Stream**

[C#] **public Stream OpenWrite(string, string);**

[C++] **public: Stream* OpenWrite(String*, String*);**

[JScript] **public function OpenWrite(String, String) : Stream;**

Example

See related example in the **System.Net.WebClient** class topic.

WebClient.OpenWrite Method (String)

Opens a stream for writing data to the specified resource.

```
[Visual Basic]
Overloads Public Function OpenWrite( _
   ByVal address As String _
) As Stream
```

```
[C#]
public Stream OpenWrite(
   string address
);
```
```
[C++]
public: Stream* OpenWrite(
   String* address
);
```
```
[JScript]
public function OpenWrite(
   address : String
) : Stream;
```

Parameters

address
   The URI of the resource to receive the data.

Return Value

A **Stream** used to write data to the resource.

Exceptions

Exception Type	Condition
WebException	The URI formed by combining **BaseAddress**, and *address* is invalid. -or- An error occurred while opening the stream.

Remarks

The **OpenWrite** method returns a writable stream that is used to send data to a resource. The underlying request is made with the POST method.

If the **BaseAddress** property is not empty, *address* must be a relative URI that is combined with **BaseAddress** to form the absolute URI of the requested data. If the **QueryString** property is not empty, it is appended to *address*.

Example

See related example in the **System.Net.WebClient** class topic.

Requirements

Platforms: Windows 98, Windows NT 4.0, Windows Millennium Edition, Windows 2000, Windows XP Home Edition, Windows XP Professional, Windows .NET Server family, Common Language Infrastructure (CLI) Standard

WebClient.OpenWrite Method (String, String)

Opens a stream for writing data to the specified resource with using the specified method.

```
[Visual Basic]
Overloads Public Function OpenWrite( _
   ByVal address As String, _
   ByVal method As String _
) As Stream
```
```
[C#]
public Stream OpenWrite(
   string address,
   string method
);
```

```
[C++]
public: Stream* OpenWrite(
    String* address,
    String* method
);
[JScript]
public function OpenWrite(
    address : String,
    method : String
) : Stream;
```

Parameters

address
    The URI of the resource to receive the data.
method
    The method used to send the data to the resource.

Return Value

A **Stream** used to write data to the resource.

Exceptions

Exception Type	Condition
WebException	The URI formed by combining **BaseAddress**, and *address* is invalid. -or- An error occurred while opening the stream.

Remarks

The **OpenWrite** method returns a writable stream that is used to send data to a resource. The underlying request is made with the method specified in the *method* parameter.

If the *method* parameter specifies a method that is not understood by the server, the underlying protocol classes determine what occurs. Typically, a **WebException** is thrown with the **Status** property set to indicate the error.

If the **BaseAddress** property is not empty, *address* must be a relative URI that is combined with **BaseAddress** to form the absolute URI of the requested data. If the **QueryString** property is not empty, it is appended to *address*.

Requirements

Platforms: Windows 98, Windows NT 4.0, Windows Millennium Edition, Windows 2000, Windows XP Home Edition, Windows XP Professional, Windows .NET Server family, Common Language Infrastructure (CLI) Standard

WebClient.UploadData Method

Uploads a data buffer to a resource with the specified URI.

Overload List

Uploads a data buffer to a resource identified by a URI.

[Visual Basic] **Overloads Public Function UploadData(String, Byte()) As Byte()**

[C#] **public byte[] UploadData(string, byte[]);**

[C++] **public: unsigned char UploadData(String*, unsigned char __gc[]) __gc[];**

[JScript] **public function UploadData(String, Byte[]) : Byte[];**

This member supports the .NET Framework infrastructure and is not intended to be used directly from your code.

[Visual Basic] **Overloads Public Function UploadData(String, String, Byte()) As Byte()**

[C#] **public byte[] UploadData(string, string, byte[]);**

[C++] **public: unsigned char UploadData(String*, String*, unsigned char __gc[]) __gc[];**

[JScript] **public function UploadData(String, String, Byte[]) : Byte[];**

Example

See related example in the **System.Net.WebClient** class topic.

WebClient.UploadData Method (String, Byte[])

Uploads a data buffer to a resource identified by a URI.

```
[Visual Basic]
Overloads Public Function UploadData( _
    ByVal address As String, _
    ByVal data() As Byte _
) As Byte()
[C#]
public byte[] UploadData(
    string address,
    byte[] data
);
[C++]
public: unsigned char UploadData(
    String* address,
    unsigned char data __gc[]
) __gc[];
[JScript]
public function UploadData(
    address : String,
    data : Byte[]
) : Byte[];
```

Parameters

address
    The URI of the resource to receive the data.
data
    The data buffer to send to the resource.

Return Value

An array of bytes containing the body of any response from the resource.

Exceptions

Exception Type	Condition
WebException	The URI formed by combining **BaseAddress**, and *address* is invalid. -or- An error occurred while opening the stream. -or- There was no response from the server hosting the resource.

Remarks

The **UploadData** method sends a data buffer to a resource. The underlying request is made using the POST method verb.

The POST verb is defined by HTTP. If the underlying request does not use HTTP and POST is not understood by the server, the underlying protocol classes determine what occurs. Typically, a **WebException** is thrown with the **Status** property set to indicate the error.

The **UploadData** method sends the content of *data* to the server without encoding it.

If the **BaseAddress** property is not empty, *address* must be a relative URI that is combined with **BaseAddress** to form the absolute URI of the requested data. If the **QueryString** property is not empty, it is appended to *address*.

Example

See related example in the **System.Net.WebClient** class topic.

Requirements

Platforms: Windows 98, Windows NT 4.0, Windows Millennium Edition, Windows 2000, Windows XP Home Edition, Windows XP Professional, Windows .NET Server family, Common Language Infrastructure (CLI) Standard

WebClient.UploadData Method (String, String, Byte[])

This member supports the .NET Framework infrastructure and is not intended to be used directly from your code.

```
[Visual Basic]
Overloads Public Function UploadData( _
   ByVal address As String, _
   ByVal method As String, _
   ByVal data() As Byte _
) As Byte()
[C#]
public byte[] UploadData(
   string address,
   string method,
   byte[] data
);
[C++]
public: unsigned char UploadData(
   String* address,
   String* method,
   unsigned char data __gc[]
) __gc[];
[JScript]
public function UploadData(
   address : String,
   method : String,
   data : Byte[]
) : Byte[];
```

WebClient.UploadFile Method

Uploads a local file to a resource with the specified URI.

Overload List

Uploads the specified local file to a resource with the specified URI.

[Visual Basic] **Overloads Public Function UploadFile(String, String) As Byte()**

[C#] **public byte[] UploadFile(string, string);**

[C++] **public: unsigned char UploadFile(String*, String*) __gc[];**

[JScript] **public function UploadFile(String, String) : Byte[];**

Uploads the specified local file to the specified resource using the specified method.

[Visual Basic] **Overloads Public Function UploadFile(String, String, String) As Byte()**

[C#] **public byte[] UploadFile(string, string, string);**

[C++] **public: unsigned char UploadFile(String*, String*, String*) __gc[];**

[JScript] **public function UploadFile(String, String, String) : Byte[];**

Example

See related example in the **System.Net.WebClient** class topic.

WebClient.UploadFile Method (String, String)

Uploads the specified local file to a resource with the specified URI.

```
[Visual Basic]
Overloads Public Function UploadFile( _
   ByVal address As String, _
   ByVal fileName As String _
) As Byte()
[C#]
public byte[] UploadFile(
   string address,
   string fileName
);
[C++]
public: unsigned char UploadFile(
   String* address,
   String* fileName
) __gc[];
[JScript]
public function UploadFile(
   address : String,
   fileName : String
) : Byte[];
```

Parameters

address
    The URI of the resource to receive the file.
fileName
    The file to send to the resource.

Return Value

An array of bytes containing the body of any response from the resource.

Exceptions

Exception Type	Condition
WebException	The URI formed by combining **BaseAddress**, and *address* is invalid. -or- *fileName* is a null reference (**Nothing** in Visual Basic), **Empty**, or contains invalid character, or the specified path to the file does not exixts. -or- An error occurred while opening the stream. -or- There was no response from the server hosting the resource. -or- The **Content-type** header begins with "multipart".
SecurityException	Local file access has not been granted.

Remarks

The **UploadFile** method sends a local file to a resource. The underlying request is made using the POST method verb.

The POST verb is defined by HTTP. If the underlying request does not use HTTP and POST is not understood by the server, the underlying protocol classes determine what occurs. Typically, a **WebException** is thrown with the **Status** property set to indicate the error.

If the **BaseAddress** property is not empty, *address* must be a relative URI that is combined with **BaseAddress** to form the absolute URI of the requested data. If the **QueryString** property is not empty, it is appended to *address*.

Example

See related example in the **System.Net.WebClient** class topic.

Requirements

Platforms: Windows 98, Windows NT 4.0, Windows Millennium Edition, Windows 2000, Windows XP Home Edition, Windows XP Professional, Windows .NET Server family, Common Language Infrastructure (CLI) Standard

WebClient.UploadFile Method (String, String, String)

Uploads the specified local file to the specified resource using the specified method.

```
[Visual Basic]
Overloads Public Function UploadFile( _
   ByVal address As String, _
   ByVal method As String, _
   ByVal fileName As String _
) As Byte()
[C#]
public byte[] UploadFile(
   string address,
   string method,
   string fileName
);
[C++]
public: unsigned char UploadFile(
   String* address,
   String* method,
   String* fileName
) __gc[];
[JScript]
public function UploadFile(
   address : String,
   method : String,
   fileName : String
) : Byte[];
```

Parameters

address
 The URI of the resource to receive the file.
method
 The method verb used to send the file to the resource.
fileName
 The file to send to the resource.

Return Value

An array of bytes containing the body of any response from the resource.

Exceptions

Exception Type	Condition
WebException	The URI formed by combining **BaseAddress**, and *address* is invalid. -or- *fileName* is a null reference (**Nothing** in Visual Basic), **Empty**, or contains invalid character, or the specified path to the file does not exixts. -or- An error occurred while opening the stream. -or- There was no response from the server hosting the resource. -or- The **Content-type** header begins with "multipart".
SecurityException	Local file access has not been granted

Remarks

The **UploadFile** method sends a local file to a resource using the method verb specified in the *method* parameter and returns any response from the server.

If the *method* parameter specifies a verb that is not understood by the server, the underlying protocol classes determine what occurs. Typically, a **WebException** is thrown with the **Status** property set to indicate the error.

If the **BaseAddress** property is not empty, *address* must be a relative URI that is combined with **BaseAddress** to form the absolute URI of the requested data. If the **QueryString** property is not empty, it is appended to *address*.

Example

See related example in the **System.Net.WebClient** class topic.

Requirements

Platforms: Windows 98, Windows NT 4.0, Windows Millennium Edition, Windows 2000, Windows XP Home Edition, Windows XP Professional, Windows .NET Server family, Common Language Infrastructure (CLI) Standard

WebClient.UploadValues Method

Uploads a name/value collection to a resource with the specified URI.

Overload List

Uploads the specified name/value collection to the specified resource identified by a URI.

> [Visual Basic] **Overloads Public Function UploadValues (String, NameValueCollection) As Byte()**
>
> [C#] **public byte[] UploadValues(string, NameValueCollection);**
>
> [C++] **public: unsigned char UploadValues(String*, NameValueCollection*) __gc[];**
>
> [JScript] **public function UploadValues(String, NameValueCollection) : Byte[];**

Uploads the specified name/value collection to the specified resource with the specified URI using the specified method.

> [Visual Basic] **Overloads Public Function UploadValues (String, String, NameValueCollection) As Byte()**
>
> [C#] **public byte[] UploadValues(string, string, NameValueCollection);**
>
> [C++] **public: unsigned char UploadValues(String*, String*, NameValueCollection*) __gc[];**
>
> [JScript] **public function UploadValues(String, String, NameValueCollection) : Byte[];**

Example

See related example in the **System.Net.WebClient** class topic.

WebClient.UploadValues Method (String, NameValueCollection)

Uploads the specified name/value collection to the specified resource identified by a URI.

```
[Visual Basic]
Overloads Public Function UploadValues( _
   ByVal address As String, _
   ByVal data As NameValueCollection _
) As Byte()
[C#]
public byte[] UploadValues(
   string address,
   NameValueCollection data
);
```

```
[C++]
public: unsigned char UploadValues(
   String* address,
   NameValueCollection* data
) __gc[];
[JScript]
public function UploadValues(
   address : String,
   data : NameValueCollection
) : Byte[];
```

Parameters

address
> The URI of the resource to receive the collection.

data
> The **NameValueCollection** to send to the resource.

Return Value

An array of bytes containing the body of any response from the resource.

Exceptions

Exception Type	Condition
WebException	The URI formed by combining **BaseAddress**, and *address* is invalid. -or- *data* is a null reference (**Nothing** in Visual Basic). -or- There was no response from the server hosting the resource. -or- An error occured while opening the stream. -or- The **Content-type** header is not a null reference (**Nothing**) or "application/x-www-form-urlencoded".

Remarks

The **UploadValues** method sends a **NameValueCollection** to an Internet server. The underlying request is made using the POST method verb.

The POST verb is defined by HTTP. If the underlying request does not use HTTP and POST is not understood by the server, the underlying protocol classes determine what occurs. Typically, a **WebException** is thrown with the **Status** property set to indicate the error.

If the Content-type header is a null reference (**Nothing** in Visual Basic), the **UploadValues** method sets it to "application/x-www-form-urlencoded".

If the **BaseAddress** property is not empty, *address* must be a relative URI that is combined with **BaseAddress** to form the absolute URI of the requested data. If the **QueryString** property is not empty, it is appended to *address*.

Example

See related example in the **System.Net.WebClient** class topic.

Requirements

Platforms: Windows 98, Windows NT 4.0,
Windows Millennium Edition, Windows 2000,
Windows XP Home Edition, Windows XP Professional,
Windows .NET Server family,
Common Language Infrastructure (CLI) Standard

WebClient.UploadValues Method (String, String, NameValueCollection)

Uploads the specified name/value collection to the specified resource with the specified URI using the specified method.

```
[Visual Basic]
Overloads Public Function UploadValues( _
   ByVal address As String, _
   ByVal method As String, _
   ByVal data As NameValueCollection _
) As Byte()
[C#]
public byte[] UploadValues(
   string address,
   string method,
   NameValueCollection data
);
[C++]
public: unsigned char UploadValues(
   String* address,
   String* method,
   NameValueCollection* data
) __gc[];
[JScript]
public function UploadValues(
   address : String,
   method : String,
   data : NameValueCollection
) : Byte[];
```

Parameters

address
   The URI of the resource to receive the collection.
method
   The method verb used to send the file to the resource.
data
   The **NameValueCollection** to send to the resource.

Return Value

An array of bytes containing the body of any response from the resource.

Exceptions

Exception Type	Condition
WebException	The URI formed by combining **BaseAddress**, and *address* is invalid. -or- *data* is a null reference (**Nothing** in Visual Basic). -or- An error occurred while opening the stream. -or- There was no response from the server hosting the resource. -or- The **Content-type** header is not "application/x-www-form-urlencoded".

Remarks

The **UploadValues** method sends a **NameValueCollection** to a resource using the method verb specified in the *method* parameter and returns any response from the server.

If the Content-type header is a null reference (**Nothing** in Visual Basic), the **UploadValues** method sets it to "application/x-www-form-urlencoded".

If the *method* parameter specifies a verb that is not understood by the server, the underlying protocol classes determine what occurs. Typically, a **WebException** is thrown with the **Status** property set to indicate the error.

If the **BaseAddress** property is not empty, *address* must be a relative URI that is combined with **BaseAddress** to form the absolute URI of the requested data. If the **QueryString** property is not empty, it is appended to *address*.

Example

See related example in the **System.Net.WebClient** class topic.

Requirements

Platforms: Windows 98, Windows NT 4.0,
Windows Millennium Edition, Windows 2000,
Windows XP Home Edition, Windows XP Professional,
Windows .NET Server family,
Common Language Infrastructure (CLI) Standard

WebException Class

The exception that is thrown when an error occurs while accessing the network through a pluggable protocol.

System.Object
  System.Exception
    System.SystemException
      System.InvalidOperationException
        System.Net.WebException

```
[Visual Basic]
<Serializable>
Public Class WebException
   Inherits InvalidOperationException
[C#]
[Serializable]
public class WebException : InvalidOperationException
[C++]
[Serializable]
public __gc class WebException : public InvalidOperationException
[JScript]
public
   Serializable
class WebException extends InvalidOperationException
```

Thread Safety

Any public static (**Shared** in Visual Basic) members of this type are safe for multithreaded operations. Any instance members are not guaranteed to be thread safe.

Remarks

The **WebException** class is thrown by classes descended from **WebRequest** and **WebResponse** that implement pluggable protocols for accessing the Internet.

When **WebException** is thrown by a descendant of the **WebRequest** class, the **Response** property provides the Internet response to the application.

Requirements

Namespace: System.Net

Platforms: Windows 98, Windows NT 4.0, Windows Millennium Edition, Windows 2000, Windows XP Home Edition, Windows XP Professional, Windows .NET Server family, .NET Compact Framework - Windows CE .NET

Assembly: System (in System.dll)

WebException Constructor

Initializes a new instance of the **WebException** class.

Overload List

Initializes a new instance of the **WebException** class.

Supported by the .NET Compact Framework.

  [Visual Basic] **Public Sub New()**
  [C#] **public WebException();**
  [C++] **public: WebException();**
  [JScript] **public function WebException();**

Initializes a new instance of the **WebException** class with the specified error message.

Supported by the .NET Compact Framework.

  [Visual Basic] **Public Sub New(String)**
  [C#] **public WebException(string);**
  [C++] **public: WebException(String*);**
  [JScript] **public function WebException(String);**

Initializes a new instance of the **WebException** class from the specified **SerializationInfo** and **StreamingContext** instances.

  [Visual Basic] **Protected Sub New(SerializationInfo, StreamingContext)**
  [C#] **protected WebException(SerializationInfo, StreamingContext);**
  [C++] **protected: WebException(SerializationInfo*, StreamingContext);**
  [JScript] **protected function WebException(SerializationInfo, StreamingContext);**

Initializes a new instance of the **WebException** class with the specified error message and nested exception.

Supported by the .NET Compact Framework.

  [Visual Basic] **Public Sub New(String, Exception)**
  [C#] **public WebException(string, Exception);**
  [C++] **public: WebException(String*, Exception*);**
  [JScript] **public function WebException(String, Exception);**

Initializes a new instance of the **WebException** class with the specified error message and status.

Supported by the .NET Compact Framework.

  [Visual Basic] **Public Sub New(String, WebExceptionStatus)**
  [C#] **public WebException(string, WebExceptionStatus);**
  [C++] **public: WebException(String*, WebExceptionStatus);**
  [JScript] **public function WebException(String, WebExceptionStatus);**

Initializes a new instance of the **WebException** class with the specified error message, nested exception, status, and response.

Supported by the .NET Compact Framework.

  [Visual Basic] **Public Sub New(String, Exception, WebExceptionStatus, WebResponse)**
  [C#] **public WebException(string, Exception, WebExceptionStatus, WebResponse);**
  [C++] **public: WebException(String*, Exception*, WebExceptionStatus, WebResponse*);**
  [JScript] **public function WebException(String, Exception, WebExceptionStatus, WebResponse);**

Example

[Visual Basic, C#, C++] The following example throws a **WebException** by specifying an error message and a **WebExceptionStatus**.

> [Visual Basic, C#, C++] **Note** This example shows how to use one of the overloaded versions of the **WebException** constructor. For other examples that might be available, see the individual overload topics.

```
[Visual Basic]
    ' Send the data.
    Dim ASCII As Encoding = Encoding.ASCII
    Dim requestPage As String = "GET /nhjj.htm HTTP/1.1"
+ ControlChars.Lf + ControlChars.Cr + "Host: " + connectUri
```

```vb
   + ControlChars.Lf + ControlChars.Cr + "Connection: Close" + ↵
ControlChars.Lf + ControlChars.Cr + ControlChars.Lf + ControlChars.Cr
       Dim byteGet As [Byte]() = ASCII.GetBytes(requestPage)
       Dim recvBytes(256) As [Byte]

       ' Create an 'IPEndPoint' object.
       Dim hostEntry As IPHostEntry = Dns.Resolve(connectUri)
       Dim serverAddress As IPAddress = hostEntry.AddressList(0)
       Dim endPoint As New IPEndPoint(serverAddress, 80)

       ' Create a 'Socket' object  for sending data.
       Dim connectSocket As New Socket ↵
(AddressFamily.InterNetwork, SocketType.Stream, ProtocolType.Tcp)

       ' Connect to host using 'IPEndPoint' object.
       connectSocket.Connect(endPoint)

       ' Sent the 'requestPage' text to the host.
       connectSocket.Send(byteGet, byteGet.Length, 0)

       ' Receive the information sent by the server.
       Dim bytesReceived As Int32 = connectSocket.Receive ↵
(recvBytes, recvBytes.Length, 0)
       Dim headerString As [String] = ASCII.GetString ↵
(recvBytes, 0, bytesReceived)

       ' Check whether 'status 404' is there or not in the ↵
information sent by server.
       If headerString.IndexOf("404") <> False Then
           bytesReceived = connectSocket.Receive(recvBytes, ↵
recvBytes.Length, 0)
           Dim memoryStream As New MemoryStream(recvBytes)
           getStream = CType(memoryStream, Stream)

           ' Create a 'WebResponse' object.
           Dim myWebResponse As WebResponse = CType(New ↵
HttpConnect(getStream), WebResponse)
           Dim myException As New Exception("File Not found")

           ' Throw the 'WebException' object with a message ↵
string, message status,InnerException and WebResponse.
           Throw New WebException("The Requested page is not ↵
found.", myException, WebExceptionStatus.ProtocolError, myWebResponse)
       End If

   connectSocket.Close()
```

```csharp
[C#]
// Send the data.
Encoding ASCII = Encoding.ASCII;
string requestPage = "GET /nhjj.htm HTTP/1.1\r\nHost: " + ↵
connectUri + "\r\nConnection: Close\r\n\r\n";
Byte[] byteGet = ASCII.GetBytes(requestPage);
Byte[] recvBytes = new Byte[256];

// Create an 'IPEndPoint' object.

IPHostEntry hostEntry = Dns.Resolve(connectUri);
IPAddress serverAddress = hostEntry.AddressList[0];
IPEndPoint endPoint = new IPEndPoint(serverAddress, 80);

// Create a 'Socket' object  for sending data.
Socket connectSocket = new Socket ↵
(AddressFamily.InterNetwork, SocketType.Stream,ProtocolType.Tcp);

// Connect to host using 'IPEndPoint' object.

connectSocket.Connect(endPoint);

// Sent the 'requestPage' text to the host.
connectSocket.Send(byteGet, byteGet.Length, 0);

// Receive the information sent by the server.
Int32 bytesReceived = connectSocket.Receive(recvBytes, ↵
```

```
recvBytes.Length, 0);
String headerString = ASCII.GetString(recvBytes, 0, bytesReceived);

        // Check whether 'status 404' is there or not ↵
in the information sent by server.
        if(headerString.IndexOf("404")!=-1)
        {
   bytesReceived = connectSocket.Receive(recvBytes, ↵
recvBytes.Length, 0);
   MemoryStream memoryStream = new MemoryStream(recvBytes);
   getStream = (Stream) memoryStream;

   // Create a 'WebResponse' object
   WebResponse myWebResponse = (WebResponse) new ↵
HttpConnect(getStream);
   Exception myException = new Exception("File Not found");

   // Throw the 'WebException' object with a message string, ↵
message status,InnerException and WebResponse
   throw new WebException("The Requested page is not ↵
found.",myException,WebExceptionStatus.ProtocolError,myWebResponse);

        }

        connectSocket.Close();
```

```cpp
[C++]
// Send the data.
Encoding* ASCII = Encoding::ASCII;
String* requestPage = String::Concat ↵
(S"GET /nhjj.htm HTTP/1.1\r\nHost: ", connectUri, ↵
S"\r\nConnection: Close\r\n\r\n");
Byte byteGet[] = ASCII->GetBytes(requestPage);
Byte recvBytes[] = new Byte[256];

// Create an 'IPEndPoint' Object*.
IPHostEntry* hostEntry = Dns::Resolve(connectUri);
IPAddress* serverAddress = hostEntry->AddressList[0];
IPEndPoint* endPoint = new IPEndPoint(serverAddress, 80);

// Create a 'Socket' Object*  for sending data.
Socket* connectSocket = new Socket(AddressFamily:: ↵
InterNetwork, SocketType::Stream, ProtocolType::Tcp);

// Connect to host using 'IPEndPoint' Object*.
connectSocket->Connect(endPoint);

// Sent the 'requestPage' text to the host.
connectSocket->Send(byteGet, byteGet- ↵
>Length,static_cast<SocketFlags>(0));

// Receive the information sent by the server.
Int32 bytesReceived = connectSocket->Receive(recvBytes, ↵
recvBytes->Length,static_cast<SocketFlags>(0));
String* headerString = ASCII->GetString(recvBytes, 0, bytesReceived);

// Check whether 'status 404' is there or not in the ↵
information sent by server.
if (headerString->IndexOf(S"404")!=-1) {
   bytesReceived = connectSocket->Receive(recvBytes, recvBytes- ↵
>Length,static_cast<SocketFlags>(0));
   MemoryStream* memoryStream = new MemoryStream(recvBytes);
   getStream = dynamic_cast<System::IO::Stream*>(memoryStream);

   // Create a 'WebResponse' Object*
   WebResponse * myWebResponse = dynamic_cast<WebResponse*> ↵
(new HttpConnect(getStream));
   Exception* myException = new Exception(S"File Not found");

   // Throw the 'WebException' Object* with a message String*, ↵
message status, InnerException and WebResponse
   throw new WebException(S"The Requested page is not found.",
      myException, WebExceptionStatus::ProtocolError, myWebResponse);
}

connectSocket->Close();
```

WebException Constructor ()

Initializes a new instance of the **WebException** class.

```
[Visual Basic]
Public Sub New()
[C#]
public WebException();
[C++]
public: WebException();
[JScript]
public function WebException();
```

Remarks

The default constructor initializes a new instance of the **WebException** class. The **Message** property is initialized to a system-supplied message that describes the error. This message takes into account the current system culture. The **InnerException** and **Response** properties are initialized to a null reference (**Nothing** in Visual Basic). The **Status** property is initialized to **RequestCanceled**.

Example

See the related example in the **System.Net.WebException** constructor topic.

Requirements

Platforms: Windows 98, Windows NT 4.0, Windows Millennium Edition, Windows 2000, Windows XP Home Edition, Windows XP Professional, Windows .NET Server family, .NET Compact Framework - Windows CE .NET, Common Language Infrastructure (CLI) Standard

WebException Constructor (String)

Initializes a new instance of the **WebException** class with the specified error message.

```
[Visual Basic]
Public Sub New( _
   ByVal message As String _
)
[C#]
public WebException(
   string message
);
[C++]
public: WebException(
   String* message
);
[JScript]
public function WebException(
   message : String
);
```

Parameters

message
  The text of the error message.

Remarks

The **WebException** instance is initialized with the **Message** property set to the value of *message*. If *message* is a null reference (**Nothing** in Visual Basic), the **Message** property is initialized to a system-supplied message. The **InnerException** and **Response**

properties are initialized to a null reference (**Nothing**). The **Status** property is initialized to **RequestCanceled**.

Example

See the related example in the **System.Net.WebException** constructor topic.

Requirements

Platforms: Windows 98, Windows NT 4.0, Windows Millennium Edition, Windows 2000, Windows XP Home Edition, Windows XP Professional, Windows .NET Server family, .NET Compact Framework - Windows CE .NET, Common Language Infrastructure (CLI) Standard

WebException Constructor (SerializationInfo, StreamingContext)

Initializes a new instance of the **WebException** class from the specified **SerializationInfo** and **StreamingContext** instances.

```
[Visual Basic]
Protected Sub New( _
   ByVal serializationInfo As SerializationInfo, _
   ByVal streamingContext As StreamingContext _
)
[C#]
protected WebException(
   SerializationInfo serializationInfo,
   StreamingContext streamingContext
);
[C++]
protected: WebException(
   SerializationInfo* serializationInfo,
   StreamingContext streamingContext
);
[JScript]
protected function WebException(
   serializationInfo : SerializationInfo,
   streamingContext : StreamingContext
);
```

Parameters

serializationInfo
  A **SerializationInfo** containing the information required to serialize the new **WebException**.

streamingContext
  A **StreamingContext** containing the source of the serialized stream associated with the new **WebException**.

Remarks

This constructor implements the **ISerializable** interface for the **WebException** class.

Requirements

Platforms: Windows 98, Windows NT 4.0, Windows Millennium Edition, Windows 2000, Windows XP Home Edition, Windows XP Professional, Windows .NET Server family

WebException Constructor (String, Exception)

Initializes a new instance of the **WebException** class with the specified error message and nested exception.

```
[Visual Basic]
Public Sub New( _
   ByVal message As String, _
   ByVal innerException As Exception _
)
[C#]
public WebException(
   string message,
   Exception innerException
);
[C++]
public: WebException(
   String* message,
   Exception* innerException
);
[JScript]
public function WebException(
   message : String,
   innerException : Exception
);
```

Parameters

message
    The text of the error message.
innerException
    A nested exception.

Remarks

The **WebException** instance is initialized with the **Message** property set to the value of *message* and the **InnerException** property set to the value of *innerException*. If *message* is a null reference (**Nothing** in Visual Basic), the **Message** property is initialized to a system-supplied message.The **InnerException** and **Response** properties are initialized to a null reference (**Nothing**). The **Status** property is initialized to **RequestCanceled**.

Example

See the related example in the **System.Net.WebException** constructor topic.

Requirements

Platforms: Windows 98, Windows NT 4.0, Windows Millennium Edition, Windows 2000, Windows XP Home Edition, Windows XP Professional, Windows .NET Server family, .NET Compact Framework - Windows CE .NET, Common Language Infrastructure (CLI) Standard

WebException Constructor (String, WebExceptionStatus)

Initializes a new instance of the **WebException** class with the specified error message and status.

```
[Visual Basic]
Public Sub New( _
   ByVal message As String, _
   ByVal status As WebExceptionStatus _
)
```

```
[C#]
public WebException(
   string message,
   WebExceptionStatus status
);
[C++]
public: WebException(
   String* message,
   WebExceptionStatus status
);
[JScript]
public function WebException(
   message : String,
   status : WebExceptionStatus
);
```

Parameters

message
    The text of the error message.
status
    One of the **WebExceptionStatus** values.

Remarks

The **WebException** instance is initialized with the **Message** property set to the value of *message* and the **Status** property set to the value of *status*. If *message* is a null reference (**Nothing** in Visual Basic), the **Message** property is initialized to a system-supplied message.The **InnerException** and **Response** properties are initialized to a null reference (**Nothing**).

Example

See the related example in the **System.Net.WebException** constructor topic.

Requirements

Platforms: Windows 98, Windows NT 4.0, Windows Millennium Edition, Windows 2000, Windows XP Home Edition, Windows XP Professional, Windows .NET Server family, .NET Compact Framework - Windows CE .NET, Common Language Infrastructure (CLI) Standard

WebException Constructor (String, Exception, WebExceptionStatus, WebResponse)

Initializes a new instance of the **WebException** class with the specified error message, nested exception, status, and response.

```
[Visual Basic]
Public Sub New( _
   ByVal message As String, _
   ByVal innerException As Exception, _
   ByVal status As WebExceptionStatus, _
   ByVal response As WebResponse _
)
[C#]
public WebException(
   string message,
   Exception innerException,
   WebExceptionStatus status,
   WebResponse response
);
```

```
[C++]
public: WebException(
   String* message,
   Exception* innerException,
   WebExceptionStatus status,
   WebResponse* response
);
[JScript]
public function WebException(
   message : String,
   innerException : Exception,
   status : WebExceptionStatus,
   response : WebResponse
);
```

Parameters

message
   The text of the error message.
innerException
   A nested exception.
status
   One of the **WebExceptionStatus** values.
response
   A **WebResponse** instance containing the response from the remote host.

Remarks

The **WebException** instance is initialized with the **Message** property set to the value of *message*, the **InnerException** property set to the value of *innerException*, the **Status** property set to the value of *status*, and the **Response** property set to *response*. If *message* is a null reference (**Nothing** in Visual Basic), the **Message** property is initialized to a system-supplied message.

Example

See the related example in the **System.Net.WebException** constructor topic.

Requirements

Platforms: Windows 98, Windows NT 4.0, Windows Millennium Edition, Windows 2000, Windows XP Home Edition, Windows XP Professional, Windows .NET Server family, .NET Compact Framework - Windows CE .NET, Common Language Infrastructure (CLI) Standard

WebException.Response Property

Gets the response that the remote host returned.

```
[Visual Basic]
Public ReadOnly Property Response As WebResponse
[C#]
public WebResponse Response {get;}
[C++]
public: __property WebResponse* get_Response();
[JScript]
public function get Response() : WebResponse;
```

Property Value

If a response is available from the Internet resource, a **WebResponse** instance containing the error response from an Internet resource; otherwise, a null reference (**Nothing** in Visual Basic).

Remarks

Some Internet protocols, such as HTTP, return otherwise valid responses indicating that an error has occurred at the protocol level. When the response to an Internet request indicates an error, **WebRequest.GetResponse** sets the **Status** property to **WebExceptionStatus.ProtocolError** and provides the **WebResponse** containing the error message in the **Response** property of the **WebException** that was thrown. The application can examine the **WebResponse** to determine the actual error.

Example

See the related example in the **System.Net.WebException** constructor topic.

Requirements

Platforms: Windows 98, Windows NT 4.0, Windows Millennium Edition, Windows 2000, Windows XP Home Edition, Windows XP Professional, Windows .NET Server family, .NET Compact Framework - Windows CE .NET, Common Language Infrastructure (CLI) Standard

WebException.Status Property

Gets the status of the response.

```
[Visual Basic]
Public ReadOnly Property Status As WebExceptionStatus
[C#]
public WebExceptionStatus Status {get;}
[C++]
public: __property WebExceptionStatus get_Status();
[JScript]
public function get Status() : WebExceptionStatus;
```

Property Value

One of the **WebExceptionStatus** values.

Remarks

The **Status** property indicates the reason for the **WebException**.

The value of **Status** is one of the **WebExceptionStatus** values.

Example

See the related example in the **System.Net.WebException** constructor topic.

Requirements

Platforms: Windows 98, Windows NT 4.0, Windows Millennium Edition, Windows 2000, Windows XP Home Edition, Windows XP Professional, Windows .NET Server family, .NET Compact Framework - Windows CE .NET, Common Language Infrastructure (CLI) Standard

WebException.ISerializable.GetObjectData Method

This member supports the .NET Framework infrastructure and is not intended to be used directly from your code.

```
[Visual Basic]
Private Sub GetObjectData( _
   ByVal serializationInfo As SerializationInfo, _
   ByVal streamingContext As StreamingContext _
) Implements ISerializable.GetObjectData
```

```
[C#]
void ISerializable.GetObjectData(
   SerializationInfo serializationInfo,
   StreamingContext streamingContext
);
[C++]
private: void ISerializable::GetObjectData(
   SerializationInfo* serializationInfo,
   StreamingContext streamingContext
);
[JScript]
private function ISerializable.GetObjectData(
   serializationInfo : SerializationInfo,
   streamingContext : StreamingContext
);
```

WebExceptionStatus Enumeration

Defines status codes for the **WebException** class.

```
[Visual Basic]
<Serializable>
Public Enum WebExceptionStatus
[C#]
[Serializable]
public enum WebExceptionStatus
[C++]
[Serializable]
__value public enum WebExceptionStatus
[JScript]
public
    Serializable
enum WebExceptionStatus
```

Remarks

The **WebExceptionStatus** enumeration defines the status codes assigned to the **Status** property.

Members

Member name	Description
ConnectFailure Supported by the .NET Compact Framework.	The remote service point could not be contacted at the transport level.
ConnectionClosed Supported by the .NET Compact Framework.	The connection was prematurely closed.
KeepAliveFailure Supported by the .NET Compact Framework.	The connection for a request that specifies the Keep-alive header was closed unexpectedly.
MessageLengthLimit-Exceeded	A message was received that exceeded the specified limit when sending a request or receiving a response from the server.
NameResolutionFailure Supported by the .NET Compact Framework.	The name resolver service could not resolve the host name.
Pending Supported by the .NET Compact Framework.	An internal asynchronous request is pending.
PipelineFailure Supported by the .NET Compact Framework.	This member supports the .NET Framework infrastructure and is not intended to be used directly from your code.
ProtocolError Supported by the .NET Compact Framework.	The response received from the server was complete but indicated a protocol-level error. For example, an HTTP protocol error such as 401 Access Denied would use this status.
ProxyNameResolution-Failure Supported by the .NET Compact Framework.	The name resolver service could not resolve the proxy host name.

Member name	Description
ReceiveFailure Supported by the .NET Compact Framework.	A complete response was not received from the remote server.
RequestCanceled Supported by the .NET Compact Framework.	The request was canceled, the **WebRequest.Abort** method was called, or an unclassifiable error occurred. This is the default value for **Status**.
SecureChannelFailure Supported by the .NET Compact Framework.	An error occurred in a secure channel link.
SendFailure Supported by the .NET Compact Framework.	A complete request could not be sent to the remote server.
ServerProtocolViolation Supported by the .NET Compact Framework.	The server response was not a valid HTTP response.
Success Supported by the .NET Compact Framework.	No error was encountered.
Timeout Supported by the .NET Compact Framework.	No response was received during the time-out period for a request.
TrustFailure Supported by the .NET Compact Framework.	A server certificate could not be validated.
UnknownError	An exception of unknown type has occurred.

Requirements

Namespace: System.Net

Platforms: Windows 98, Windows NT 4.0, Windows Millennium Edition, Windows 2000, Windows XP Home Edition, Windows XP Professional, Windows .NET Server family, .NET Compact Framework - Windows CE .NET

Assembly: System (in System.dll)

WebHeaderCollection Class

Contains protocol headers associated with a request or response.

System.Object
   System.Collections.Specialized.NameObjectCollectionBase
     System.Collections.Specialized.NameValueCollection
       System.Net.WebHeaderCollection

```
[Visual Basic]
<Serializable>
<ComVisible(True)>
Public Class WebHeaderCollection
   Inherits NameValueCollection
[C#]
[Serializable]
[ComVisible(true)]
public class WebHeaderCollection : NameValueCollection
[C++]
[Serializable]
[ComVisible(true)]
public __gc class WebHeaderCollection : public
   NameValueCollection
[JScript]
public
   Serializable
   ComVisible(true)
class WebHeaderCollection extends NameValueCollection
```

Thread Safety

Any public static (**Shared** in Visual Basic) members of this type are safe for multithreaded operations. Any instance members are not guaranteed to be thread safe.

Remarks

The **WebHeaderCollection** class is generally accessed through **WebRequest.Headers** or **WebResponse.Headers**. Some common headers are considered restricted and are either exposed directly by the API (such as **Content-Type**) or protected by the system and cannot be changed.

The restricted headers are:

- Accept
- Connection
- Content-Length
- Content-Type
- Date
- Expect
- Host
- If-Modified-Since
- Range
- Referer
- Transfer-Encoding
- User-Agent

Requirements

Namespace: System.Net

Platforms: Windows 98, Windows NT 4.0,
Windows Millennium Edition, Windows 2000,
Windows XP Home Edition, Windows XP Professional,
Windows .NET Server family,
.NET Compact Framework - Windows CE .NET

Assembly: System (in System.dll)

WebHeaderCollection Constructor

Initializes a new instance of the **WebHeaderCollection** class.

Overload List

Initializes a new instance of the **WebHeaderCollection** class.

Supported by the .NET Compact Framework.

   [Visual Basic] **Public Sub New()**

   [C#] **public WebHeaderCollection();**

   [C++] **public: WebHeaderCollection();**

   [JScript] **public function WebHeaderCollection();**

Initializes a new instance of the **WebHeaderCollection** class from the specified instances of the **SerializationInfo** and **StreamingContext** classes.

   [Visual Basic] **Protected Sub New(SerializationInfo, StreamingContext)**

   [C#] **protected WebHeaderCollection(SerializationInfo, StreamingContext);**

   [C++] **protected: WebHeaderCollection(SerializationInfo*, StreamingContext);**

   [JScript] **protected function WebHeaderCollection(SerializationInfo, StreamingContext);**

WebHeaderCollection Constructor ( )

Initializes a new instance of the **WebHeaderCollection** class.

```
[Visual Basic]
Public Sub New()
[C#]
public WebHeaderCollection();
[C++]
public: WebHeaderCollection();
[JScript]
public function WebHeaderCollection();
```

Requirements

Platforms: Windows 98, Windows NT 4.0,
Windows Millennium Edition, Windows 2000,
Windows XP Home Edition, Windows XP Professional,
Windows .NET Server family,
.NET Compact Framework - Windows CE .NET,
Common Language Infrastructure (CLI) Standard

WebHeaderCollection Constructor (SerializationInfo, StreamingContext)

Initializes a new instance of the **WebHeaderCollection** class from the specified instances of the **SerializationInfo** and **StreamingContext** classes.

```
[Visual Basic]
Protected Sub New( _
   ByVal serializationInfo As SerializationInfo, _
   ByVal streamingContext As StreamingContext _
)
[C#]
protected WebHeaderCollection(
   SerializationInfo serializationInfo,
   StreamingContext streamingContext
);
```

```
[C++]
protected: WebHeaderCollection(
   SerializationInfo* serializationInfo,
   StreamingContext streamingContext
);
[JScript]
protected function WebHeaderCollection(
   serializationInfo : SerializationInfo,
   streamingContext : StreamingContext
);
```

Parameters
serializationInfo
> A **SerializationInfo** containing the information required to serialize the **WebHeaderCollection**.

streamingContext
> A **StreamingContext** containing the source of the serialized stream associated with the new **WebHeaderCollection**.

Exceptions

Exception Type	Condition
ArgumentException	*headerName* contains invalid characters.
ArgumentNullException	*headerName* is a null reference or **Empty**.

Remarks
This constructor implements the **ISerializable** interface for the **WebHeaderCollection** class.

Requirements
Platforms: Windows 98, Windows NT 4.0, Windows Millennium Edition, Windows 2000, Windows XP Home Edition, Windows XP Professional, Windows .NET Server family

WebHeaderCollection.Add Method
Inserts a new header into the collection.

Overload List
Inserts the specified header into the collection.
Supported by the .NET Compact Framework.

> [Visual Basic] **Overloads Public Sub Add(String)**
> [C#] **public void Add(string);**
> [C++] **public: void Add(String*);**
> [JScript] **public function Add(String);**

Inserts a header with the specified name and value into the collection.
Supported by the .NET Compact Framework.

> [Visual Basic] **Overloads Overrides Public Sub Add(String, String)**
> [C#] **public override void Add(string, string);**
> [C++] **public: void Add(String*, String*);**
> [JScript] **public override function Add(String, String);**

Inherited from **NameValueCollection**.
Supported by the .NET Compact Framework.

> [Visual Basic] **Overloads Public Sub Add(NameValueCollection)**
> [C#] **public void Add(NameValueCollection);**

> [C++] **public: void Add(NameValueCollection*);**
> [JScript] **public function Add(NameValueCollection);**

Example
[Visual Basic, C#, C++] The following example adds a name/value pair to a **WebHeaderCollection** using the **Add** Method.

> [Visual Basic, C#, C++] **Note** This example shows how to use one of the overloaded versions of **Add**. For other examples that might be available, see the individual overload topics.

```
[Visual Basic]
Public Shared Sub Main()

Try
      'Create a web request for "www.msn.com".
      Dim myHttpWebRequest As HttpWebRequest =
CType(WebRequest.Create("http://www.msn.com"), HttpWebRequest)

      'Get the headers associated with the request.
      Dim myWebHeaderCollection As WebHeaderCollection =
myHttpWebRequest.Headers

      Console.WriteLine("Configuring Webrequest to accept
Danish and English language using 'Add' method")

      'Add the Accept-Language header (for Danish) in the request.
      myWebHeaderCollection.Add("Accept-Language:da")

      'Include English in the Accept-Langauge header.
      myWebHeaderCollection.Add("Accept-Language:en;q" +
ChrW(61) + "0.8")

      'Get the associated response for the above request.
      Dim myHttpWebResponse As HttpWebResponse =
CType(myHttpWebRequest.GetResponse(), HttpWebResponse)

      'Print the headers for the request.
      printHeaders(myWebHeaderCollection)
      myHttpWebResponse.Close()
   'Catch exception if trying to add a restricted header.
   Catch e As ArgumentException
      Console.WriteLine(e.Message)
   Catch e As WebException
      Console.WriteLine(e.Message)
      If e.Status = WebExceptionStatus.ProtocolError Then
         Console.WriteLine("Status Code : {0}", CType
(e.Response, HttpWebResponse).StatusCode)
         Console.WriteLine("Status Description : {0}",
CType(e.Response, HttpWebResponse).StatusDescription)
         Console.WriteLine("Server : {0}", CType
(e.Response, HttpWebResponse).Server)
      End If
   Catch e As Exception
      Console.WriteLine(e.Message)
   End Try
End Sub 'Main

[C#]
try {
   //Create a web request for "www.msn.com".
   HttpWebRequest myHttpWebRequest = (HttpWebRequest)
WebRequest.Create("http://www.msn.com");

   //Get the headers associated with the request.
   WebHeaderCollection myWebHeaderCollection =
myHttpWebRequest.Headers;

   Console.WriteLine("Configuring Webrequest to accept
Danish and English language using 'Add' method");

   //Add the Accept-Language header (for Danish) in the request.
   myWebHeaderCollection.Add("Accept-Language:da");

   //Include English in the Accept-Langauge header.
   myWebHeaderCollection.Add("Accept-Language:en;q=0.8");
```

```
//Get the associated response for the above request.
  HttpWebResponse myHttpWebResponse = (HttpWebResponse)
myHttpWebRequest.GetResponse();

  //Print the headers for the request.
  printHeaders(myWebHeaderCollection);
  myHttpWebResponse.Close();
}
//Catch exception if trying to add a restricted header.
catch(ArgumentException e) {
  Console.WriteLine(e.Message);
}
catch(WebException e) {
  Console.WriteLine("\nWebException is thrown. \nMessage
is :" + e.Message);
  if(e.Status == WebExceptionStatus.ProtocolError) {
    Console.WriteLine("Status Code : {0}",
((HttpWebResponse)e.Response).StatusCode);
    Console.WriteLine("Status Description : {0}",
((HttpWebResponse)e.Response).StatusDescription);
    Console.WriteLine("Server : {0}",
((HttpWebResponse)e.Response).Server);
  }
}
catch(Exception e) {
  Console.WriteLine("Exception is thrown. Message is :" + e.Message);
}

[C++]
try {
  //Create a web request for S"www.msn.com".
  HttpWebRequest* myHttpWebRequest =
    dynamic_cast<HttpWebRequest*> (WebRequest::Create(S"http://
www.msn.com"));

  //Get the headers associated with the request.
  WebHeaderCollection* myWebHeaderCollection =
myHttpWebRequest->Headers;

  Console::WriteLine(S"Configuring Webrequest to
accept Danish and English language using 'Add' method");

  //Add the Accept-Language header (for Danish) in the request.
  myWebHeaderCollection->Add(S"Accept-Language:da");

  //Include English in the Accept-Langauge header.
  myWebHeaderCollection->Add(S"Accept-Language:en;q=0.8");

  //Get the associated response for the above request.
  HttpWebResponse* myHttpWebResponse =
dynamic_cast<HttpWebResponse*> (myHttpWebRequest->GetResponse());

  //Print the headers for the request.
  printHeaders(myWebHeaderCollection);
  myHttpWebResponse->Close();
}
//Catch exception if trying to add a restricted header.
catch(ArgumentException* e) {
  Console::WriteLine(e->Message);
} catch (WebException* e) {
  Console::WriteLine(S"\nWebException is thrown. \nMessage is
: {0}", e->Message);
  if (e->Status == WebExceptionStatus::ProtocolError) {
    Console::WriteLine(S"Status Code : {0}",
      __box((dynamic_cast<HttpWebResponse*>(e->Response))-
>StatusCode));
    Console::WriteLine(S"Status Description : {0}",
      (dynamic_cast<HttpWebResponse*>(e->Response))-
>StatusDescription);
    Console::WriteLine(S"Server : {0}",
      (dynamic_cast<HttpWebResponse*>(e->Response))->Server);
  }
} catch (Exception* e) {
  Console::WriteLine(S"Exception is thrown. Message is : {0}",
e->Message);
}
```

WebHeaderCollection.Add Method (String)

Inserts the specified header into the collection.

```
[Visual Basic]
Overloads Public Sub Add( _
  ByVal header As String _
)
[C#]
public void Add(
  string header
);
[C++]
public: void Add(
  String* header
);
[JScript]
public function Add(
  header : String
);
```

Parameters

header
  The header to add, with the name and value separated by a colon.

Exceptions

Exception Type	Condition
ArgumentNullException	*header* is a null reference (**Nothing in Visual Basic**) or **Empty**.
ArgumentException	*header* does not contain a colon (:) character. -or- The name part of *header* is **Empty** or contains invalid characters. -or- *header* is a restricted header that should be set with a property. -or- The value part of *header* contains invalid characters.

Remarks

The *header* parameter must be specified in the format "name:value". If the specified header does not exist in the collection, a new header is added to the collection.

If the header specified in *header* is already present in the collection, the value part of the *header* is concatenated with the existing value.

Example

[Visual Basic, C#, C++] The following example adds a name/value pair to a **WebHeaderCollection** using the **Add** Method.

```
[Visual Basic]
Public Shared Sub Main()

  Try
      'Create a web request for "www.msn.com".
      Dim myHttpWebRequest As HttpWebRequest =
CType(WebRequest.Create("http://www.msn.com"), HttpWebRequest)

      'Get the headers associated with the request.
      Dim myWebHeaderCollection As WebHeaderCollection =
myHttpWebRequest.Headers
```

```
        Console.WriteLine("Configuring Webrequest to accept
Danish and English language using 'Add' method")

        'Add the Accept-Language header (for Danish) in the request.
            myWebHeaderCollection.Add("Accept-Language:da")

        'Include English in the Accept-Langauge header.
            myWebHeaderCollection.Add("Accept-Language:en;q" +
ChrW(61) + "0.8")

        'Get the associated response for the above request.
            Dim myHttpWebResponse As HttpWebResponse =
CType(myHttpWebRequest.GetResponse(), HttpWebResponse)

        'Print the headers for the request.
            printHeaders(myWebHeaderCollection)
            myHttpWebResponse.Close()
    'Catch exception if trying to add a restricted header.
    Catch e As ArgumentException
        Console.WriteLine(e.Message)
    Catch e As WebException
        Console.WriteLine(e.Message)
        If e.Status = WebExceptionStatus.ProtocolError Then
            Console.WriteLine("Status Code : {0}", CType
(e.Response, HttpWebResponse).StatusCode)
            Console.WriteLine("Status Description : {0}",
CType(e.Response, HttpWebResponse).StatusDescription)
            Console.WriteLine("Server : {0}", CType(e.Response,
HttpWebResponse).Server)
        End If
    Catch e As Exception
        Console.WriteLine(e.Message)
    End Try
End Sub 'Main
```

[C#]
```
try {
    //Create a web request for "www.msn.com".
     HttpWebRequest myHttpWebRequest = (HttpWebRequest)
WebRequest.Create("http://www.msn.com");

    //Get the headers associated with the request.
    WebHeaderCollection myWebHeaderCollection =
myHttpWebRequest.Headers;

    Console.WriteLine("Configuring Webrequest to accept
Danish and English language using 'Add' method");

    //Add the Accept-Language header (for Danish) in the request.
    myWebHeaderCollection.Add("Accept-Language:da");

    //Include English in the Accept-Langauge header.
    myWebHeaderCollection.Add("Accept-Language:en;q=0.8");

    //Get the associated response for the above request.
     HttpWebResponse myHttpWebResponse = (HttpWebResponse)
myHttpWebRequest.GetResponse();

    //Print the headers for the request.
    printHeaders(myWebHeaderCollection);
    myHttpWebResponse.Close();
}
//Catch exception if trying to add a restricted header.
catch(ArgumentException e) {
    Console.WriteLine(e.Message);
}
catch(WebException e) {
    Console.WriteLine("\nWebException is thrown. \nMessage is
:" + e.Message);
    if(e.Status == WebExceptionStatus.ProtocolError) {
        Console.WriteLine("Status Code : {0}",
((HttpWebResponse)e.Response).StatusCode);
        Console.WriteLine("Status Description : {0}",
((HttpWebResponse)e.Response).StatusDescription);
        Console.WriteLine("Server : {0}",
```

```
((HttpWebResponse)e.Response).Server);
    }
}
catch(Exception e) {
    Console.WriteLine("Exception is thrown. Message is
:" + e.Message);
}
```

[C++]
```
try {
    //Create a web request for S"www.msn.com".
    HttpWebRequest* myHttpWebRequest =
        dynamic_cast<HttpWebRequest*> (WebRequest::Create(S"http://
www.msn.com"));

    //Get the headers associated with the request.
    WebHeaderCollection* myWebHeaderCollection =
myHttpWebRequest->Headers;

    Console::WriteLine(S"Configuring Webrequest to accept
Danish and English language using 'Add' method");

    //Add the Accept-Language header (for Danish) in the request.
    myWebHeaderCollection->Add(S"Accept-Language:da");

    //Include English in the Accept-Langauge header.
    myWebHeaderCollection->Add(S"Accept-Language:en;q=0.8");

    //Get the associated response for the above request.
    HttpWebResponse* myHttpWebResponse = dynamic_cast
<HttpWebResponse*> (myHttpWebRequest->GetResponse());

    //Print the headers for the request.
    printHeaders(myWebHeaderCollection);
    myHttpWebResponse->Close();
}
//Catch exception if trying to add a restricted header.
catch(ArgumentException* e) {
    Console::WriteLine(e->Message);
} catch (WebException* e) {
    Console::WriteLine(S"\nWebException is thrown. \nMessage
is : {0}", e->Message);
    if (e->Status == WebExceptionStatus::ProtocolError) {
        Console::WriteLine(S"Status Code : {0}",
            __box((dynamic_cast<HttpWebResponse*>(e->Response)-
>StatusCode));
        Console::WriteLine(S"Status Description : {0}",
            (dynamic_cast<HttpWebResponse*>(e->Response))-
>StatusDescription);
        Console::WriteLine(S"Server : {0}",
            (dynamic_cast<HttpWebResponse*>(e->Response))->Server);
} catch (Exception* e) {
    Console::WriteLine(S"Exception is thrown. Message is :
{0}", e->Message);
}
```

Requirements

Platforms: Windows 98, Windows NT 4.0,
Windows Millennium Edition, Windows 2000,
Windows XP Home Edition, Windows XP Professional,
Windows .NET Server family,
.NET Compact Framework - Windows CE .NET,
Common Language Infrastructure (CLI) Standard

WebHeaderCollection.Add Method (String, String)

Inserts a header with the specified name and value into the collection.

```
[Visual Basic]
Overrides Overloads Public Sub Add( _
   ByVal name As String, _
   ByVal value As String _
)
[C#]
public override void Add(
   string name,
   string value
);
[C++]
public: void Add(
   String* name,
   String* value
);
[JScript]
public override function Add(
   name : String,
   value : String
);
```

Parameters

name
   The header to add to the collection.
value
   The content of the header.

Exceptions

Exception Type	Condition
ArgumentException	*name* is a null reference (**Nothing** in Visual Basic), **Empty**, or contains invalid characters. -or- *name* is a restricted header that must be set with a property setting. -or- *value* contains invalid characters.

Remarks

If the header specified in *name* does not exist, the **Add** method inserts a new header into the list of header name/value pairs.

If the header specified in *name* is already present, *value* is added to the existing comma-separated list of values associated with *name*.

Example

See related example in the **System.Net.WebHeader.Add** method topic.

Requirements

Platforms: Windows 98, Windows NT 4.0, Windows Millennium Edition, Windows 2000, Windows XP Home Edition, Windows XP Professional, Windows .NET Server family, .NET Compact Framework - Windows CE .NET, Common Language Infrastructure (CLI) Standard

WebHeaderCollection.AddWithoutValidate Method

Inserts a header into the collection without checking whether the header is on the restricted header list.

```
[Visual Basic]
Protected Sub AddWithoutValidate( _
   ByVal headerName As String, _
   ByVal headerValue As String _
)
[C#]
protected void AddWithoutValidate(
   string headerName,
   string headerValue
);
[C++]
protected: void AddWithoutValidate(
   String* headerName,
   String* headerValue
);
[JScript]
protected function AddWithoutValidate(
   headerName : String,
   headerValue : String
);
```

Parameters

headerName
   The header to add to the collection.
headerValue
   The content of the header.

Exceptions

Exception Type	Condition
ArgumentException	*headerName* is a null reference (**Nothing** in Visual Basic), **Empty**, or contains invalid characters. -or- *headerValue* contains invalid characters.

Remarks

The **AddWithoutValidate** method adds a header to the collection without checking whether the header is on the restricted header list.

Notes to Inheritors: Use the **AddWithoutValidate** method to add headers that are normally exposed through properties.

Requirements

Platforms: Windows 98, Windows NT 4.0, Windows Millennium Edition, Windows 2000, Windows XP Home Edition, Windows XP Professional, Windows .NET Server family, .NET Compact Framework - Windows CE .NET, Common Language Infrastructure (CLI) Standard

WebHeaderCollection.GetValues Method

Gets an array of header values stored in a header.

Overload List

Gets an array of header values stored in a header.

Supported by the .NET Compact Framework.

> [Visual Basic] **Overloads Overrides Public Function GetValues(String) As String()**
>
> [C#] **public override string[] GetValues(string);**
>
> [C++] **public: String* GetValues(String*) __gc[];**
>
> [JScript] **public override function GetValues(String) : String[];**

Inherited from **NameValueCollection**.

Supported by the .NET Compact Framework.

> [Visual Basic] **Overloads Public Overridable Function GetValues(Integer) As String()**
>
> [C#] **public virtual string[] GetValues(int);**
>
> [C++] **public: virtual String* GetValues(int) __gc[];**
>
> [JScript] **public function GetValues(int) : String[];**

Example

See related example in the **System.Net.WebHeader.Add** method topic.

WebHeaderCollection.GetValues Method (String)

Gets an array of header values stored in a header.

```
[Visual Basic]
Overrides Overloads Public Function GetValues( _
   ByVal header As String _
) As String()
[C#]
public override string[] GetValues(
   string header
);
[C++]
public: String* GetValues(
   String* header
) __gc[];
[JScript]
public override function GetValues(
   header : String
) : String[];
```

Parameters

header
> The header to return.

Return Value

An array of header strings.

Remarks

GetValues returns the contents of the specified header as an array.

Example

See related example in the **System.Net.WebHeader.Add** method topic.

Requirements

Platforms: Windows 98, Windows NT 4.0, Windows Millennium Edition, Windows 2000, Windows XP Home Edition, Windows XP Professional, Windows .NET Server family,

.NET Compact Framework - Windows CE .NET, Common Language Infrastructure (CLI) Standard

WebHeaderCollection.ISerializable.GetObjectData Method

This member supports the .NET Framework infrastructure and is not intended to be used directly from your code.

```
[Visual Basic]
Private Sub GetObjectData( _
   ByVal serializationInfo As SerializationInfo, _
   ByVal streamingContext As StreamingContext _
) Implements ISerializable.GetObjectData
[C#]
void ISerializable.GetObjectData(
   SerializationInfo serializationInfo,
   StreamingContext streamingContext
);
[C++]
private: void ISerializable::GetObjectData(
   SerializationInfo* serializationInfo,
   StreamingContext streamingContext
);
[JScript]
private function ISerializable.GetObjectData(
   serializationInfo : SerializationInfo,
   streamingContext : StreamingContext
);
```

WebHeaderCollection.IsRestricted Method

Tests whether the specified HTTP header can be set.

```
[Visual Basic]
Public Shared Function IsRestricted( _
   ByVal headerName As String _
) As Boolean
[C#]
public static bool IsRestricted(
   string headerName
);
[C++]
public: static bool IsRestricted(
   String* headerName
);
[JScript]
public static function IsRestricted(
   headerName : String
) : Boolean;
```

Parameters

headerName
> The header to test.

Return Value

true if the header is restricted; otherwise **false**.

Exceptions

Exception Type	Condition
ArgumentNullException	*headerName* is a null reference (**Nothing** in Visual Basic) or **Empty**.
ArgumentException	*headerName* contains invalid characters.

Remarks

The **IsRestricted** method returns **true** to indicate that a header is restricted and must be set using properties instead of directly or is set by the system. The restricted headers are:

- Accept
- Connection
- Content-Length
- Content-Type
- Date
- Expect
- Host
- If-Modified-Since
- Range
- Referer
- Transfer-Encoding
- User-Agent

Example

See related example in the **System.Net.WebHeader.Add** method topic.

Requirements

Platforms: Windows 98, Windows NT 4.0, Windows Millennium Edition, Windows 2000, Windows XP Home Edition, Windows XP Professional, Windows .NET Server family, .NET Compact Framework - Windows CE .NET, Common Language Infrastructure (CLI) Standard

WebHeaderCollection.OnDeserialization Method

This member overrides **NameObjectCollectionBase.OnDeserialization**.

```
[Visual Basic]
Overrides Public Sub OnDeserialization( _
    ByVal sender As Object _
) Implements IDeserializationCallback.OnDeserialization
[C#]
public override void OnDeserialization(
    object sender
);
[C++]
public: void OnDeserialization(
    Object* sender
);
[JScript]
public override function OnDeserialization(
    sender : Object
);
```

Requirements

Platforms: Windows 98, Windows NT 4.0, Windows Millennium Edition, Windows 2000, Windows XP Home Edition, Windows XP Professional, Windows .NET Server family

WebHeaderCollection.Remove Method

Removes the specified header from the collection.

```
[Visual Basic]
Overrides Public Sub Remove( _
    ByVal name As String _
)
[C#]
public override void Remove(
    string name
);
[C++]
public: void Remove(
    String* name
);
[JScript]
public override function Remove(
    name : String
);
```

Parameters

name
    The name of the header to remove from the collection.

Exceptions

Exception Type	Condition
ArgumentNullException	*name* is a null reference (**Nothing** in Visual Basic) **Empty**.
ArgumentException	*name* is a restricted header.
	-or-
	name contains invalid characters.

Remarks

Remove deletes the specified header from the collection. If the specified header does not exist, the method returns.

Example

See related example in the **System.Net.WebHeader.Add** method topic.

Requirements

Platforms: Windows 98, Windows NT 4.0, Windows Millennium Edition, Windows 2000, Windows XP Home Edition, Windows XP Professional, Windows .NET Server family, .NET Compact Framework - Windows CE .NET, Common Language Infrastructure (CLI) Standard

WebHeaderCollection.Set Method

Sets the specified header to the specified value.

```
[Visual Basic]
Overrides Public Sub Set( _
    ByVal name As String, _
    ByVal value As String _
)
[C#]
public override void Set(
    string name,
    string value
);
```

```
[C++]
public: void Set(
   String* name,
   String* value
);
[JScript]
public override function Set(
   name : String,
   value : String
);
```

Parameters

name
> The header to set.

value
> The content of the header to set.

Exceptions

Exception Type	Condition
ArgumentNullException	*name* is a null reference (**Nothing** in Visual Basic) or **Empty**.
ArgumentException	*name* is a restricted header.
	-or-
	name or *value* contain invalid characters.

Remarks

If the header specified in the header does not exist, the **Set** method inserts a new header into the list of header name/value pairs.

If the header specified in *header* is already present, *value* replaces the existing value.

Example

See related example in the **System.Net.WebHeader.Add** method topic.

Requirements

Platforms: Windows 98, Windows NT 4.0, Windows Millennium Edition, Windows 2000, Windows XP Home Edition, Windows XP Professional, Windows .NET Server family, .NET Compact Framework - Windows CE .NET, Common Language Infrastructure (CLI) Standard

WebHeaderCollection.ToByteArray Method

This member supports the .NET Framework infrastructure and is not intended to be used directly from your code.

```
[Visual Basic]
Public Function ToByteArray() As Byte()
[C#]
public byte[] ToByteArray();
[C++]
public: unsigned char ToByteArray() __gc[];
[JScript]
public function ToByteArray() : Byte[];
```

WebHeaderCollection.ToString Method

This member overrides **Object.ToString**.

```
[Visual Basic]
Overrides Public Function ToString() As String
[C#]
public override string ToString();
[C++]
public: String* ToString();
[JScript]
public override function ToString() : String;
```

Requirements

Platforms: Windows 98, Windows NT 4.0, Windows Millennium Edition, Windows 2000, Windows XP Home Edition, Windows XP Professional, Windows .NET Server family, .NET Compact Framework - Windows CE .NET

WebPermission Class

Controls rights to access HTTP Internet resources.

System.Object
  System.Security.CodeAccessPermission
    System.Net.WebPermission

```
[Visual Basic]
<Serializable>
NotInheritable Public Class WebPermission
    Inherits CodeAccessPermission
    Implements IUnrestrictedPermission
[C#]
[Serializable]
public sealed class WebPermission : CodeAccessPermission,
    IUnrestrictedPermission
[C++]
[Serializable]
public __gc __sealed class WebPermission : public
    CodeAccessPermission, IUnrestrictedPermission
[JScript]
public
    Serializable
class WebPermission extends CodeAccessPermission implements
    IUnrestrictedPermission
```

Thread Safety

Any public static (**Shared** in Visual Basic) members of this type are safe for multithreaded operations. Any instance members are not guaranteed to be thread safe.

Remarks

WebPermission provides a set of methods and properties to control access to Internet resources. You can use a **WebPermission** to provide either restricted or unrestricted access to your resource, based on the **PermissionState** set when the **WebPermission** is created.

Create a **WebPermission** instance by calling its constructor using one of the following sets of parameters:

- No parameters. The default **PermissionState** is **None**.
- A **PermissionState**. Specify either **Unrestricted** to allow any URI to be used in the target class, or **None** to allow access only to URIs you specify through the use of the **AddPermission** method.
- A **NetworkAccess** value and a URI string. The specified URI has permissions granted by the **NetworkAccess** value.
- A **NetworkAccess** specifier and URI regular expression.

The **ConnectList** and **AcceptList** hold the URIs to which you have granted access permission. To add a URI to either of these lists, use **AddPermission**. If you pass **Accept** as the **NetworkAccess** parameter, the URI will be added to the **AcceptList**. **WebPermission** will allow connections to your target class with URIs matching the **AcceptList**.

> **CAUTION** To **Deny** access to an Internet resource you must **Deny** access to all the possible paths to that resource. A better approach is to allow access to the specific resource only. For more information on this subject refer to the TBD topic.

> **Note** You only need to **Deny** access using the resource canonical path. There is no need to use all the path's syntactical variations.

Example

[Visual Basic, C#] The following example demonstrates how to create a new instance of **WebPermission** using a **Regex**. Additional hosts are added to the connect and accept list of **WebPermission**. Finally the connect and accept list are displayed to the console.

```
[Visual Basic]
' Create a Regex that accepts all the URLs contianing the
host fragment www.contoso.com.
Dim myRegex As New Regex("http://www\.contoso\.com/.*")

' Create a WebPermission that gives permission to all the
hosts containing same host fragment.
Dim myWebPermission As New WebPermission
(NetworkAccess.Connect, myRegex)
' Add connect privileges for a www.adventure-works.com.
myWebPermission.AddPermission(NetworkAccess.Connect,
"http://www.adventure-works.com")
' Add accept privileges for www.alpineskihouse.com.
myWebPermission.AddPermission(NetworkAccess.Accept,
"http://www.alpineskihouse.com/")
' Check whether all callers higher in the call stack have been
 granted the permission.
myWebPermission.Demand()

' Get all the URIs with Connect permission.
Dim myConnectEnum As IEnumerator = myWebPermission.ConnectList
Console.WriteLine(ControlChars.NewLine + "The 'URIs' with
'Connect' permission are :" + ControlChars.NewLine)
While myConnectEnum.MoveNext()
    Console.WriteLine((ControlChars.Tab +
myConnectEnum.Current.ToString()))
End While

' Get all the URIs with Accept permission.
Dim myAcceptEnum As IEnumerator = myWebPermission.AcceptList
Console.WriteLine(ControlChars.NewLine + ControlChars.NewLine
+ "The 'URIs' with 'Accept' permission is :" + ControlChars.NewLine)

While myAcceptEnum.MoveNext()
    Console.WriteLine((ControlChars.Tab + myAcceptEnum.Current))
End While

[C#]
//  Create a Regex that accepts all URLs containing the
host fragment www.contoso.com.
    Regex myRegex = new Regex(@"http://www\.contoso\.com/.*");

    // Create a WebPermission that gives permissions to all
the hosts containing the same host fragment.
    WebPermission myWebPermission = new
WebPermission(NetworkAccess.Connect,myRegex);

    //Add connect privileges for a www.adventure-works.com.
    myWebPermission.AddPermission(NetworkAccess.Connect,
"http://www.adventure-works.com");

    //Add accept privileges for www.alpineskihouse.com.
    myWebPermission.AddPermission(NetworkAccess.Accept,
"http://www.alpineskihouse.com/");

    // Check whether all callers higher in the call stack
have been granted the permission.
    myWebPermission.Demand();

    // Get all the URIs with Connect permission.
    IEnumerator myConnectEnum = myWebPermission.ConnectList;
    Console.WriteLine("\nThe 'URIs' with 'Connect' permission
```

```
are :\n");
   while (myConnectEnum.MoveNext())
   {Console.WriteLine("\t" + myConnectEnum.Current);}

   // Get all the URIs with Accept permission.
   IEnumerator myAcceptEnum = myWebPermission.AcceptList;
   Console.WriteLine("\n\nThe 'URIs' with 'Accept'
permission is :\n");

   while (myAcceptEnum.MoveNext())
     {Console.WriteLine("\t" + myAcceptEnum.Current);}
```

Requirements

Namespace: System.Net

Platforms: Windows 98, Windows NT 4.0,
Windows Millennium Edition, Windows 2000,
Windows XP Home Edition, Windows XP Professional,
Windows .NET Server family

Assembly: System (in System.dll)

WebPermission Constructor

Creates a new instance of the **WebPermission** class.

Overload List

Creates a new instance of the **WebPermission** class.

[Visual Basic] **Public Sub New()**

[C#] **public WebPermission();**

[C++] **public: WebPermission();**

[JScript] **public function WebPermission();**

Creates a new instance of the **WebPermission** class that passes all
demands or fails all demands.

[Visual Basic] **Public Sub New(PermissionState)**

[C#] **public WebPermission(PermissionState);**

[C++] **public: WebPermission(PermissionState);**

[JScript] **public function WebPermission(PermissionState);**

Initializes a new instance of the **WebPermission** class with the
specified access rights for the specified URI regular expression.

[Visual Basic] **Public Sub New(NetworkAccess, Regex)**

[C#] **public WebPermission(NetworkAccess, Regex);**

[C++] **public: WebPermission(NetworkAccess, Regex*);**

[JScript] **public function WebPermission(NetworkAccess,
Regex);**

Initializes a new instance of the **WebPermission** class with the
specified access rights for the specified URI.

[Visual Basic] **Public Sub New(NetworkAccess, String)**

[C#] **public WebPermission(NetworkAccess, string);**

[C++] **public: WebPermission(NetworkAccess, String*);**

[JScript] **public function WebPermission(NetworkAccess,
String);**

Example

[Visual Basic, C#, C++] The following example creates a new
instance of **WebPermission** with connect rights for the specified
URI.

> [Visual Basic, C#, C++] **Note** This example shows how to use
> one of the overloaded versions of the **WebPermission**
> constructor. For other examples that might be available, see the
> individual overload topics.

```
[Visual Basic]
' Create a WebPermission.instance.
Dim myWebPermission1 As New WebPermission
 (NetworkAccess.Connect, "http://www.contoso.com/default.htm")
myWebPermission1.Demand()
```

```
[C#]
   // Create a WebPermission.instance.
   WebPermission myWebPermission1 = new
WebPermission(NetworkAccess.Connect,
"http://www.contoso.com/default.htm");
   myWebPermission1.Demand();
```

```
[C++]
// Create a WebPermission::instance.
WebPermission* myWebPermission1 = new
WebPermission(NetworkAccess::Connect,
S"http://www.contoso.com/default.htm");
myWebPermission1->Demand();
```

WebPermission Constructor ()

Creates a new instance of the **WebPermission** class.

```
[Visual Basic]
Public Sub New()
[C#]
public WebPermission();
[C++]
public: WebPermission();
[JScript]
public function WebPermission();
```

Remarks

Creates a new instance of the **WebPermission** class. This
constructor creates an empty permission that does not grant any
rights.

Requirements

Platforms: Windows 98, Windows NT 4.0,
Windows Millennium Edition, Windows 2000,
Windows XP Home Edition, Windows XP Professional,
Windows .NET Server family

WebPermission Constructor (PermissionState)

Creates a new instance of the **WebPermission** class that passes all
demands or fails all demands.

```
[Visual Basic]
Public Sub New( _
   ByVal state As PermissionState _
)
[C#]
public WebPermission(
   PermissionState state
);
[C++]
public: WebPermission(
   PermissionState state
);
[JScript]
public function WebPermission(
   state : PermissionState
);
```

Parameters

state

A **PermissionState** value.

Remarks

The value of the *state* parameter is either **PermissionState.None** or **PermissionState.Unrestricted**, respectively yielding fully restricted or fully unrestricted access to all security variables. If you specify **PermissionState.None**, then you may give access to individual URI's using **AddPermission**.

Example

[Visual Basic, C#, C++] The following example creates an instance of **WebPermission** and gives access rights to specific URLs.

```
[Visual Basic]
' Create a WebPermission instance.
Dim myWebPermission1 As New WebPermission(PermissionState.None)

' Allow access to the first set of URL's.
myWebPermission1.AddPermission(NetworkAccess.Connect,
"http://www.microsoft.com/default.htm")
myWebPermission1.AddPermission(NetworkAccess.Connect,
"http://www.msn.com")

' Check whether all callers higher in the call stack have
  been granted the permissionor not.
myWebPermission1.Demand()
```

```
[C#]
// Create a WebPermission instance.
WebPermission myWebPermission1 = new
WebPermission(PermissionState.None);

// Allow access to the first set of URL's.
myWebPermission1.AddPermission(NetworkAccess.Connect,
"http://www.microsoft.com/default.htm");
myWebPermission1.AddPermission(NetworkAccess.Connect,
"http://www.msn.com");

// Check whether all callers higher in the call stack have been
   granted the permissionor not.
myWebPermission1.Demand();
```

```
[C++]
// Create a WebPermission instance.
WebPermission* myWebPermission1 = new
WebPermission(PermissionState::None);

// Allow access to the first set of URL's.
myWebPermission1->AddPermission(NetworkAccess::Connect,
S"http://www.microsoft.com/default.htm");
myWebPermission1->AddPermission(NetworkAccess::Connect,
S"http://www.msn.com");

// Check whether all callers higher in the call stack have
   been granted the permissionor not.
myWebPermission1->Demand();
```

Requirements

Platforms: Windows 98, Windows NT 4.0, Windows Millennium Edition, Windows 2000, Windows XP Home Edition, Windows XP Professional, Windows .NET Server family, Common Language Infrastructure (CLI) Standard

WebPermission Constructor (NetworkAccess, Regex)

Initializes a new instance of the **WebPermission** class with the specified access rights for the specified URI regular expression.

```
[Visual Basic]
Public Sub New( _
    ByVal access As NetworkAccess, _
    ByVal uriRegex As Regex _
)
[C#]
public WebPermission(
    NetworkAccess access,
    Regex uriRegex
);
[C++]
public: WebPermission(
    NetworkAccess access,
    Regex* uriRegex
);
[JScript]
public function WebPermission(
    access : NetworkAccess,
    uriRegex : Regex
);
```

Parameters

access

A **NetworkAccess** value indicating what kind of access to grant to the specified URI. **Accept** indicates that the application is allowed to accept connections from the Internet on a local resource. **Connect** indicates that the application is allowed to connect to specific Internet resources.

uriRegex

A regular expression describing the URI to which acess is to be granted.

Remarks

This constructor initializes a **WebPermission** and grants its target permission to either make a remote host connection or to accept a remote host connection using the URI described by the *uriRegex* parameter.

> **Note** It is recommended to create *uriRegex* using the **RegexOptions.IgnoreCase**, **RegexOptions.Compiled**, and **RegexOptions.Singleline** flags.

Example

[Visual Basic, C#, C++] The following example creates a new instance of **WebPermission** with connect rights for the specified **System.Text.RegularExpressions.Regex**.

```
[Visual Basic]
' Creates an instance of 'Regex' that accepts all  URL's
containing the host fragment 'www.contoso.com'.
Dim myRegex As New Regex("http://www\.contoso\.com/.*")

  ' Creates a 'WebPermission' that gives the permissions to all
the hosts containing same host fragment.
  Dim myWebPermission As New WebPermission
(NetworkAccess.Connect, myRegex)

  ' Checks all callers higher in the call stack have been
granted the permission.
  myWebPermission.Demand()
```

```
[C#]
    // Create an instance of 'Regex' that accepts all
URL's containing the host
    // fragment 'www.contoso.com'.
    Regex myRegex = new Regex(@"http://www\.contoso\.com/.*");

    // Create a WebPermission that gives the permissions to
all the hosts containing
    // the same fragment.
    WebPermission myWebPermission = new
WebPermission(NetworkAccess.Connect,myRegex);

    // Checks all callers higher in the call stack have been
granted the permission.
    myWebPermission.Demand();

[C++]
// Create an instance of 'Regex' that accepts all   URL's
containing the host
// fragment 'www.contoso.com'.
Regex* myRegex = new Regex(S"http://www.contoso.com/.*");

// Create a WebPermission that gives the permissions to all
the hosts containing
// the same fragment.
WebPermission* myWebPermission = new
WebPermission(NetworkAccess::Connect, myRegex);

// Checks all callers higher in the call stack have been
granted the permission.
myWebPermission->Demand();
```

Requirements

Platforms: Windows 98, Windows NT 4.0,
Windows Millennium Edition, Windows 2000,
Windows XP Home Edition, Windows XP Professional,
Windows .NET Server family

WebPermission Constructor (NetworkAccess, String)

Initializes a new instance of the **WebPermission** class with the
specified access rights for the specified URI.

```
[Visual Basic]
Public Sub New( _
   ByVal access As NetworkAccess, _
   ByVal uriString As String _
)
[C#]
public WebPermission(
   NetworkAccess access,
   string uriString
);
[C++]
public: WebPermission(
   NetworkAccess access,
   String* uriString
);
[JScript]
public function WebPermission(
   access : NetworkAccess,
   uriString : String
);
```

Parameters

access

A NetworkAccess value indicating what kind of access to grant
to the specified URI. **Accept** indicates that the application is
allowed to accept connections from the Internet on a local
resource. **Connect** indicates that the application is allowed to
connect to specific Internet resources.

uriString

A URI string to which access rights are granted.

Exceptions

Exception Type	Condition
ArgumentNullException	*uriString* is a null reference (**Nothing** in Visual Basic).

Remarks

This constructor initializes a **WebPermission** and grants its target
permission to either make a remote host connection or to accept a
remote host connection using the URI described by the *uriString*
parameter.

Example

[Visual Basic, C#, C++] The following example creates a new
instance of **WebPermission** with connect rights for the specified
URI.

```
[Visual Basic]
' Create a WebPermission.instance.
Dim myWebPermission1 As New WebPermission
  (NetworkAccess.Connect, "http://www.contoso.com/default.htm")
myWebPermission1.Demand()

[C#]
    // Create a WebPermission.instance.
    WebPermission myWebPermission1 = new
WebPermission(NetworkAccess.Connect,
"http://www.contoso.com/default.htm");
    myWebPermission1.Demand();

[C++]
// Create a WebPermission::instance.
WebPermission* myWebPermission1 = new
WebPermission(NetworkAccess::Connect,
S"http://www.contoso.com/default.htm");
myWebPermission1->Demand();
```

Requirements

Platforms: Windows 98, Windows NT 4.0,
Windows Millennium Edition, Windows 2000,
Windows XP Home Edition, Windows XP Professional,
Windows .NET Server family,
Common Language Infrastructure (CLI) Standard

WebPermission.AcceptList Property

This property returns an enumeration of a single accept permissions
held by this **WebPermission**. The possible objects types contained
in the returned enumeration are **String** and
System.Text.RegularExpressions.Regex.

```
[Visual Basic]
Public ReadOnly Property AcceptList As IEnumerator
[C#]
public IEnumerator AcceptList {get;}
[C++]
public: __property IEnumerator* get_AcceptList();
```

```
[JScript]
public function get AcceptList() : IEnumerator;
```

Property Value

The **IEnumerator** interface containing accept permissions.

Remarks

This property gets a list of local resources permitted by this **WebPermission**. The class to which you have applied **WebPermission** only has permission to receive an incoming connection to local resources found in this list.

> **Note**   You can add URIs to this list using **AddPermission**.

Example

[Visual Basic, C#, C++] The following example prints the URL's in the **AcceptList** to the console.

```
[Visual Basic]
' Get all URI's with Accept permission.
Dim myEnum1 As IEnumerator = myWebPermission1.AcceptList
Console.WriteLine(ControlChars.Cr + ControlChars.Cr + "The  ⌐
  URIs with Accept permission are :" + ControlChars.Cr)
While myEnum1.MoveNext()
    Console.WriteLine((ControlChars.Tab + "The URI is : " +  ⌐
myEnum1.Current))
End While
```

```
[C#]
// Get all URI's with Accept permission.
IEnumerator myEnum1 = myWebPermission1.AcceptList;
Console.WriteLine("\n\nThe URIs with Accept permission are :\n");
while (myEnum1.MoveNext())
{ Console.WriteLine("\tThe URI is : "+myEnum1.Current); }
```

```
[C++]
// Get all URI's with Accept permission.
IEnumerator* myEnum1 = myWebPermission1->AcceptList;
Console::WriteLine(S"\n\nThe URIs with Accept permission are :\n");  ⌐
while (myEnum1->MoveNext()) { Console::WriteLine(S"\tThe URI is  ⌐
: {0}", myEnum1->Current); }
```

Requirements

Platforms: Windows 98, Windows NT 4.0, Windows Millennium Edition, Windows 2000, Windows XP Home Edition, Windows XP Professional, Windows .NET Server family

WebPermission.ConnectList Property

This property returns an enumeration of a single connect permissions held by this **WebPermission**. The possible objects types contained in the returned enumeration are **String** and **System.Text.RegularExpressions.Regex**.

```
[Visual Basic]
Public ReadOnly Property ConnectList As IEnumerator
[C#]
public IEnumerator ConnectList {get;}
[C++]
public: __property IEnumerator* get_ConnectList();
[JScript]
public function get ConnectList() : IEnumerator;
```

Property Value

The **IEnumerator** interface containing connect permissions.

Remarks

This property gets a list of remote resources permitted by this **WebPermission**. The class to which you have applied **WebPermission** only has permission to connect with resources found in this list.

> **Note**   You can add URIs to this list using **AddPermission**.

Example

[Visual Basic, C#, C++] The following example prints the URL's in the **ConnectList** to the console.

```
[Visual Basic]
' Gets all URIs with Connect permission.
Dim myEnum As IEnumerator = myWebPermission1.ConnectList
Console.WriteLine(ControlChars.Cr + "The URIs with Connect  ⌐
permission are :" + ControlChars.Cr)
While myEnum.MoveNext()
    Console.WriteLine((ControlChars.Tab + "The URI is : " +  ⌐
myEnum.Current))
End While
```

```
[C#]
// Gets all URIs with Connect permission.
IEnumerator myEnum = myWebPermission1.ConnectList;
Console.WriteLine("\nThe URIs with Connect permission are :\n");
while (myEnum.MoveNext())
{ Console.WriteLine("\tThe URI is : "+myEnum.Current); }
```

```
[C++]
// Gets all URIs with Connect permission.
IEnumerator* myEnum = myWebPermission1->ConnectList;
Console::WriteLine(S"\nThe URIs with Connect permission are :\n");
while (myEnum->MoveNext()) { Console::WriteLine(S"\tThe URI is  ⌐
: {0}", myEnum->Current); }
```

Requirements

Platforms: Windows 98, Windows NT 4.0, Windows Millennium Edition, Windows 2000, Windows XP Home Edition, Windows XP Professional, Windows .NET Server family

WebPermission.AddPermission Method

Adds the specified URI with the specified access rights to the current **WebPermission**.

Overload List

Adds the specified URI with the specified access rights to the current **WebPermission**.

[Visual Basic] **Overloads Public Sub AddPermission(NetworkAccess, Regex)**

[C#] **public void AddPermission(NetworkAccess, Regex);**

[C++] **public: void AddPermission(NetworkAccess, Regex*);**

[JScript] **public function AddPermission(NetworkAccess, Regex);**

Adds the specified URI string with the specified access rights to the current **WebPermission**.

[Visual Basic] **Overloads Public Sub AddPermission(NetworkAccess, String)**

[C#] **public void AddPermission(NetworkAccess, string);**

[C++] **public: void AddPermission(NetworkAccess, String*);**

[JScript] **public function AddPermission(NetworkAccess, String);**

Example

[Visual Basic, C#, C++] The following example demonstrates how to add access rights to particular URL strings.

> [Visual Basic, C#, C++] **Note** This example shows how to use one of the overloaded versions of **AddPermission**. For other examples that might be available, see the individual overload topics.

[Visual Basic]
```
' Allow access to the first set of resources.
myWebPermission1.AddPermission(NetworkAccess.Connect,
"http://www.contoso.com/default.htm")
myWebPermission1.AddPermission(NetworkAccess.Connect,
"http://www.adventure-works.com/default.htm")

' Check whether if the callers higher in the call stack
have been granted
' access permissions.
myWebPermission1.Demand()
```

[C#]
```
    // Allow access to the first set of resources.
    myWebPermission1.AddPermission(NetworkAccess.Connect,
"http://www.contoso.com/default.htm");
    myWebPermission1.AddPermission(NetworkAccess.Connect,
"http://www.adventure-works.com/default.htm");

    // Check whether if the callers higher in the call stack
have been granted
    // access permissions.
    myWebPermission1.Demand();
```

[C++]
```
// Allow access to the first set of resources.
myWebPermission1->AddPermission(NetworkAccess::Connect,
    S"http://www.contoso.com/default.htm");
myWebPermission1->AddPermission(NetworkAccess::Connect,
    S"http://www.adventure-works.com/default.htm");

// Check whether if the callers higher in the call stack have
been granted
// access permissions.
myWebPermission1->Demand();
```

WebPermission.AddPermission Method (NetworkAccess, Regex)

Adds the specified URI with the specified access rights to the current **WebPermission**.

[Visual Basic]
```
Overloads Public Sub AddPermission( _
   ByVal access As NetworkAccess, _
   ByVal uriRegex As Regex _
)
```
[C#]
```
public void AddPermission(
   NetworkAccess access,
   Regex uriRegex
);
```
[C++]
```
public: void AddPermission(
   NetworkAccess access,
   Regex* uriRegex
);
```

[JScript]
```
public function AddPermission(
   access : NetworkAccess,
   uriRegex : Regex
);
```

Parameters

access
> A NetworkAccess specifying the access rights granted to the URI.

uriRegex
> A regular expression describing the set of URI's to which access rights are granted.

Exceptions

Exception Type	Condition
ArgumentNullException	The *uriRegex* parameter is a null reference (**Nothing** in Visual Basic).

Remarks

If you have specified **None** as the **PermissionState**, use **AddPermission** to allow the use of *uriRegex* in the target class. Specify **Accept** as the *access* parameter to add the URI specified by the *uriRegex* parameter to the list of URI accept strings, or specify **Connect** as the access parameter to add the URI to the list of URI connect strings.

> **Note** Calling **AddPermission** on an **Unrestricted WebPermission** instance will have no effect as permission is granted to all URI's.

> **Note** It is recommended to create *uriRegex* using the **RegexOptions.IgnoreCase**, **RegexOptions.Compiled**, and **RegexOptions.Singleline** flags.

Example

[Visual Basic, C#, C++] The following example uses **AddPermission** to give access rights for the specified URI.

[Visual Basic]
```
' Create a WebPermission.
Dim myWebPermission1 As New WebPermission()

' Allow Connect access to the specified URLs.
myWebPermission1.AddPermission(NetworkAccess.Connect, New
Regex("http://www\.contoso\.com/.*", RegexOptions.Compiled Or
RegexOptions.IgnoreCase Or RegexOptions.Singleline))

myWebPermission1.Demand()
```

[C#]
```
// Create a WebPermission.
WebPermission myWebPermission1 = new WebPermission();

// Allow Connect access to the specified URLs.
myWebPermission1.AddPermission(NetworkAccess.Connect,new
Regex("http://www\\.contoso\\.com/.*",
   RegexOptions.Compiled | RegexOptions.IgnoreCase |
RegexOptions.Singleline));

myWebPermission1.Demand();
```

[C++]
```
// Create a WebPermission.
WebPermission* myWebPermission1 = new WebPermission();
```

```
// Allow Connect access to the specified URLs.
myWebPermission1->AddPermission(NetworkAccess::Connect,
    new Regex(S"http://www\\.contoso\\.com/.*",
    static_cast<RegexOptions>(RegexOptions::Compiled |
RegexOptions::IgnoreCase | RegexOptions::Singleline)));

myWebPermission1->Demand();
```

Requirements

Platforms: Windows 98, Windows NT 4.0,
Windows Millennium Edition, Windows 2000,
Windows XP Home Edition, Windows XP Professional,
Windows .NET Server family

WebPermission.AddPermission Method (NetworkAccess, String)

Adds the specified URI string with the specified access rights to the current **WebPermission**.

```
[Visual Basic]
Overloads Public Sub AddPermission( _
    ByVal access As NetworkAccess, _
    ByVal uriString As String _
)
[C#]
public void AddPermission(
    NetworkAccess access,
    string uriString
);
[C++]
public: void AddPermission(
    NetworkAccess access,
    String* uriString
);
[JScript]
public function AddPermission(
    access : NetworkAccess,
    uriString : String
);
```

Parameters

access
    A **NetworkAccess** specifying the access rights granted to the URI
uriString
    A string describing the URI to which access rights are granted.

Exceptions

Exception Type	Condition
ArgumentNullException	*uriString* is **null.**

Remarks

If you have specified **None** as the **PermissionState**, use **AddPermission** to permit the use of *uriString* in the target class. The way that *uriString* can be used by the target class is specified by *access*. Specify **Accept** as the access parameter to add the URI specified by the *uriString* parameter to the list of URI accept strings, or specify **Connect** as the access parameter to add the URI to the list of URI connect strings.

> **Note** Calling **AddPermission** on **Unrestricted WebPermission** will have no effect, as permission is granted to all URI's.

Example

[Visual Basic, C#, C++] The following example demonstrates how to add access rights to particular URL strings.

```
[Visual Basic]
' Allow access to the first set of resources.
myWebPermission1.AddPermission(NetworkAccess.Connect,
"http://www.contoso.com/default.htm")
myWebPermission1.AddPermission(NetworkAccess.Connect,
"http://www.adventure-works.com/default.htm")

' Check whether if the callers higher in the call stack have
been granted
' access permissions.
myWebPermission1.Demand()

[C#]
    // Allow access to the first set of resources.
    myWebPermission1.AddPermission(NetworkAccess.Connect,
"http://www.contoso.com/default.htm");
    myWebPermission1.AddPermission(NetworkAccess.Connect,
"http://www.adventure-works.com/default.htm");

    // Check whether if the callers higher in the call stack
have been granted
    // access permissions.
    myWebPermission1.Demand();

[C++]
// Allow access to the first set of resources.
myWebPermission1->AddPermission(NetworkAccess::Connect,
    S"http://www.contoso.com/default.htm");
myWebPermission1->AddPermission(NetworkAccess::Connect,
    S"http://www.adventure-works.com/default.htm");

// Check whether if the callers higher in the call stack have
been granted
// access permissions.
myWebPermission1->Demand();
```

Requirements

Platforms: Windows 98, Windows NT 4.0,
Windows Millennium Edition, Windows 2000,
Windows XP Home Edition, Windows XP Professional,
Windows .NET Server family

WebPermission.Copy Method

Creates a copy of a **WebPermission**.

```
[Visual Basic]
Overrides Public Function Copy() As IPermission Implements _
    IPermission.Copy
[C#]
public override IPermission Copy();
[C++]
public: IPermission* Copy();
[JScript]
public override function Copy() : IPermission;
```

Return Value

A new instance of the **WebPermission** class that has the same values as the original

Implements

IPermission.Copy

Remarks

The **IPermission** returned by this method represents the same access to resources as the original **WebPermission**. This method overrides **Copy** and is implemented to support the **IPermission** interface.

Example

[Visual Basic, C#, C++] The following example demonstrates how to create a second instance of **WebPermission** using **Copy**. This second instance is identical to the first.

```
[Visual Basic]
' Create another WebPermission instance that is the copy of
the above WebPermission instance.
Dim myWebPermission2 As WebPermission = CType
 (myWebPermission1.Copy(), WebPermission)

' Check whether all callers higher in the call stack have been
granted the permissionor not.
myWebPermission2.Demand()
```

```
[C#]
// Create another WebPermission instance that is the copy of
the above WebPermission instance.
 WebPermission myWebPermission2 = (WebPermission)
myWebPermission1.Copy();

// Check whether all callers higher in the call stack have been
granted the permissionor not.
myWebPermission2.Demand();
```

```
[C++]
// Create another WebPermission instance that is the copy of the
 above WebPermission instance.
WebPermission* myWebPermission2 = dynamic_cast<WebPermission*>
 (myWebPermission1->Copy());

// Check whether all callers higher in the call stack have been
 granted the permissionor not.
myWebPermission2->Demand();
```

Requirements

Platforms: Windows 98, Windows NT 4.0, Windows Millennium Edition, Windows 2000, Windows XP Home Edition, Windows XP Professional, Windows .NET Server family, Common Language Infrastructure (CLI) Standard

WebPermission.FromXml Method

Reconstructs a **WebPermission** from an XML encoding.

```
[Visual Basic]
Overrides Public Sub FromXml( _
   ByVal securityElement As SecurityElement _
) Implements ISecurityEncodable.FromXml
[C#]
public override void FromXml(
   SecurityElement securityElement
);
[C++]
public: void FromXml(
   SecurityElement* securityElement
);
[JScript]
public override function FromXml(
   securityElement : SecurityElement
);
```

Parameters

securityElement
   The XML encoding from which to reconstruct the **WebPermission**.

Implements

ISecurityEncodable.FromXml

Exceptions

Exception Type	Condition
ArgumentNullException	The *securityElement* parameter is a null reference (**Nothing** in Visual Basic)
ArgumentException	*securityElement* is not a permission element for this type.

Remarks

The **FromXml** method reconstructs a **WebPermission** from an XML encoding defined by the **SecurityElement** class.

Use the **ToXml** method to XML-encode the **WebPermission**, including state information.

Example

[Visual Basic, C#, C++] The following example creates a **System.Security.SecurityElement**, populates its attributes, and uses **FromXml** to transfer this information to an instance of **WebPermission**.

```
[Visual Basic]
' Create  a WebPermission without permission on the protected resource.
Dim myWebPermission1 As New WebPermission(PermissionState.None)

' Create a SecurityElement by calling the ToXml method on the
WebPermission
' instance and display its attributes (which hold the XML encoding of
' the WebPermission).
Console.WriteLine("Attributes and Values of the WebPermission are :")
myWebPermission1.ToXml().ToString()

' Create another WebPermission with no permission on the
protected resource.
Dim myWebPermission2 As New WebPermission(PermissionState.None)

'Converts the new WebPermission from XML using myWebPermission1.
myWebPermission2.FromXml(myWebPermission1.ToXml())
```

```
[C#]
   // Create  a WebPermission without permission on the
protected resource.
   WebPermission myWebPermission1 = new
WebPermission(PermissionState.None);

   // Create a SecurityElement by calling the ToXml method on
the WebPermission
   // instance and display its attributes (which hold the XML
encoding of
   // the WebPermission).
   Console.WriteLine("Attributes and Values of the WebPermission
are :");
   myWebPermission1.ToXml().ToString();

   // Create another WebPermission with no permission on the
protected resource.
   WebPermission myWebPermission2 = new
WebPermission(PermissionState.None);

   //Converts the new WebPermission from XML using myWebPermission1.
   myWebPermission2.FromXml(myWebPermission1.ToXml());
```

```
[C++]
// Create  a WebPermission with->Item[Out] permission* on the        ↵
protected resource
   WebPermission* myWebPermission1 =
   new WebPermission(PermissionState::None);

// Create a SecurityElement by calling the ToXml method on the        ↵
WebPermission
// instance and display its attributes (which hold the XML encoding of
// the WebPermission).
Console::WriteLine(S"Attributes and Values of the WebPermission       ↵
 are :");
myWebPermission1->ToXml();

// Create another WebPermission with no permission on the             ↵
protected resource
   WebPermission* myWebPermission2 =
   new WebPermission(PermissionState::None);

//Converts the new WebPermission from XML using myWebPermission1.
myWebPermission2->FromXml(myWebPermission1->ToXml());
```

Requirements

Platforms: Windows 98, Windows NT 4.0,
Windows Millennium Edition, Windows 2000,
Windows XP Home Edition, Windows XP Professional,
Windows .NET Server family,
Common Language Infrastructure (CLI) Standard

WebPermission.Intersect Method

Returns the logical intersection of two **WebPermission** instances.

```
[Visual Basic]
Overrides Public Function Intersect( _
   ByVal target As IPermission _
) As IPermission Implements IPermission.Intersect
[C#]
public override IPermission Intersect(
   IPermission target
);
[C++]
public: IPermission* Intersect(
   IPermission* target
);
[JScript]
public override function Intersect(
   target : IPermission
) : IPermission;
```

Parameters

target
    The **WebPermission** to compare with the current instance.

Return Value

A new **WebPermission** that represents the intersection of the current instance and the *target* parameter. If the intersection is empty, the method returns a null reference (**Nothing** in Visual Basic).

Implements

IPermission.Intersect

Exceptions

Exception Type	Condition
ArgumentException	*target* is not a null reference (**Nothing** in Visual Basic) or of type **WebPermission**

Remarks

Intersect returns a **WebPermission** that contains those permissions that are common in both *target* and the current instance.

This method overrides **Intersect** and is implemented to support the **IPermission** interface.

Example

[Visual Basic, C#, C++] The following example shows how to create an instance of **WebPermission** using the logical intersection of two exisiting **WebPermission** instances.

```
[Visual Basic]
' Create a third WebPermission instance via the logical       ↵
intersection of the previous
' two WebPermission instances.
Dim myWebPermission3 As WebPermission =                       ↵
CType(myWebPermission1.Intersect(myWebPermission2), WebPermission)
Console.WriteLine(ControlChars.Cr + "Attributes and Values of  ↵
 the WebPermission instance after the Intersect are:" +        ↵
ControlChars.Cr)
Console.WriteLine(myWebPermission3.ToXml().ToString())
    End Sub 'CreateIntersect

[C#]
    // Create a third WebPermission instance via the          ↵
logical intersection of the previous
    // two WebPermission instances.
    WebPermission myWebPermission3 =(WebPermission)            ↵
myWebPermission1.Intersect(myWebPermission2);
    Console.WriteLine("\nAttributes and Values of  the         ↵
WebPermission instance after the Intersect are:\n");
    Console.WriteLine(myWebPermission3.ToXml().ToString());

[C++]
// Create a third WebPermission instance via the logical       ↵
intersection of the previous
// two WebPermission instances.
WebPermission* myWebPermission3 =dynamic_cast                 ↵
<WebPermission*> (myWebPermission1->Intersect(myWebPermission2));
Console::WriteLine(S"\nAttributes and Values of  the           ↵
WebPermission instance after the Intersect are:\n");
Console::WriteLine(myWebPermission3->ToXml());
```

Requirements

Platforms: Windows 98, Windows NT 4.0,
Windows Millennium Edition, Windows 2000,
Windows XP Home Edition, Windows XP Professional,
Windows .NET Server family,
Common Language Infrastructure (CLI) Standard

WebPermission.IsSubsetOf Method

Determines whether the current **WebPermission** is a subset of the specified object.

```
[Visual Basic]
Overrides Public Function IsSubsetOf( _
   ByVal target As IPermission _
) As Boolean Implements IPermission.IsSubsetOf
[C#]
public override bool IsSubsetOf(
   IPermission target
);
[C++]
public: bool IsSubsetOf(
   IPermission* target
);
```

```
[JScript]
public override function IsSubsetOf(
    target : IPermission
) : Boolean;
```

Parameters

target

The **WebPermission** to compare to the current **WebPermission**.

Return Value

true if the current instance is a subset of the *target* parameter; otherwise, **false**. If the target is a null reference (**Nothing** in Visual Basic), the method returns **true** for an empty current permission that is not unrestricted and **false** otherwise.

Implements

IPermission.IsSubsetOf

Exceptions

Exception Type	Condition
ArgumentException	the target parameter is not an instance of **WebPermission**.
NotSupportedException	If the current instance contains a Regex-encoded right and there is not exactly same right found in the target instance.

Remarks

If the current **WebPermission** specifies a set of associated resources that is wholly contained by the *target* parameter, then the current **WebPermission** is a subset of *target*. This method overrides **IsSubsetOf** and is implemented to support the **IPermission** interface.

Example

[Visual Basic, C#, C++] The following example uses **IsSubsetOf** to determine if the access rights found in one instance of **WebPermission** are found in another instance of **WebPermission**.

```
[Visual Basic]
' Create the target permission.
Dim targetPermission As New WebPermission()
targetPermission.AddPermission(NetworkAccess.Connect,
New Regex("www\.contoso\.com/Public/.*"))
' Create the permission for a URI matching target.
Dim connectPermission As New WebPermission()
connectPermission.AddPermission(NetworkAccess.Connect,
"www.contoso.com/Public/default.htm")
'The following statement prints true.
Console.WriteLine(("Is the second URI a subset of the
first one?: " & connectPermission.IsSubsetOf(targetPermission)))
    End Sub 'myIsSubsetExample
```

```
[C#]
    // Create the target permission.
    WebPermission targetPermission = new WebPermission();
    targetPermission.AddPermission(NetworkAccess.Connect,
new Regex("www\\.contoso\\.com/Public/.*"));
    // Create the permission for a URI matching target.
    WebPermission connectPermission = new WebPermission();
    connectPermission.AddPermission
(NetworkAccess.Connect, "www.contoso.com/Public/default.htm");
    //The following statement prints true.
    Console.WriteLine("Is the second URI a subset of the
first one?: " + connectPermission.IsSubsetOf(targetPermission));
```

```
[C++]
// Create the target permission.
WebPermission* targetPermission = new WebPermission();
```

```
targetPermission->AddPermission(NetworkAccess::Connect,
new Regex(S"www\\.contoso\\.com/Public/.*"));
// Create the permission for a URI matching target.
WebPermission* connectPermission = new WebPermission();
connectPermission->AddPermission(NetworkAccess::Connect,
S"www.contoso.com/Public/default.htm");
//The following statement prints true.
Console::WriteLine(S"Is the second URI a subset of the first
one?: {0}", __box(connectPermission->IsSubsetOf(targetPermission)));
```

Requirements

Platforms: Windows 98, Windows NT 4.0, Windows Millennium Edition, Windows 2000, Windows XP Home Edition, Windows XP Professional, Windows .NET Server family, Common Language Infrastructure (CLI) Standard

WebPermission.IsUnrestricted Method

Checks the overall permission state of the **WebPermission**.

```
[Visual Basic]
Public Overridable Function IsUnrestricted() As Boolean Implements _
    IUnrestrictedPermission.IsUnrestricted
[C#]
public virtual bool IsUnrestricted();
[C++]
public: virtual bool IsUnrestricted();
[JScript]
public function IsUnrestricted() : Boolean;
```

Return Value

true if the **WebPermission** was created with the **Unrestricted PermissionState**; otherwise, **false**.

Implements

IUnrestrictedPermission.IsUnrestricted

Remarks

If **WebPermission** is **Unrestricted**, then the target class can use all URIs. Otherwise, specific permission must be given for any URI you want to use with the target class.

> **Note** Use **AddPermission** to add a URI and specify its permissions.

Requirements

Platforms: Windows 98, Windows NT 4.0, Windows Millennium Edition, Windows 2000, Windows XP Home Edition, Windows XP Professional, Windows .NET Server family

WebPermission.ToXml Method

Creates an XML encoding of a **WebPermission** and its current state.

```
[Visual Basic]
Overrides Public Function ToXml() As SecurityElement Implements _
    ISecurityEncodable.ToXml
[C#]
public override SecurityElement ToXml();
[C++]
public: SecurityElement* ToXml();
[JScript]
public override function ToXml() : SecurityElement;
```

Return Value

A **SecurityElement** containing an XML-encoded representation of the **WebPermission**, including state information.

Implements

ISecurityEncodable.ToXml

Remarks

Use the **FromXml** method to restore the state information from a **SecurityElement**.

Example

[Visual Basic, C#, C++] The following example demonstrates how to use **ToXml** to create a **System.Security.SecurityElement** and print its attributes to the console.

```
[Visual Basic]
' Create a WebPermission without permission on the protected resource.
Dim myWebPermission1 As New WebPermission(PermissionState.None)
' Create a SecurityElement by calling the ToXml method on the
'WebPermission
' instance and display its attributes (which hold the XML encoding of
' the WebPermission).
Console.WriteLine("Attributes and Values of the WebPermission are :")
myWebPermission1.ToXml().ToString()
' Create another WebPermission with no permission on the
'protected resource.
Dim myWebPermission2 As New WebPermission(PermissionState.None)
'Converts the new WebPermission from XML using myWebPermission1.
myWebPermission2.FromXml(myWebPermission1.ToXml())
```

```
[C#]
    // Create a WebPermission without permission on the
'protected resource.
    WebPermission myWebPermission1 = new
WebPermission(PermissionState.None);
    // Create a SecurityElement by calling the ToXml method
on the WebPermission
    // instance and display its attributes (which hold the
XML encoding of
    // the WebPermission).
    Console.WriteLine("Attributes and Values of the WebPermission
are :");
    myWebPermission1.ToXml().ToString();
    // Create another WebPermission with no permission on the
'protected resource.
    WebPermission myWebPermission2 = new
WebPermission(PermissionState.None);
    //Converts the new WebPermission from XML using myWebPermission1.
    myWebPermission2.FromXml(myWebPermission1.ToXml());
```

```
[C++]
// Create a WebPermission with->Item[Out] permission* on the
'protected resource
    WebPermission* myWebPermission1 =
    new WebPermission(PermissionState::None);
// Create a SecurityElement by calling the ToXml method on
the WebPermission
// instance and display its attributes (which hold the XML encoding of
// the WebPermission).
Console::WriteLine(S"Attributes and Values of the WebPermission
are :");
myWebPermission1->ToXml();
// Create another WebPermission with no permission on the
protected resource
    WebPermission* myWebPermission2 =
    new WebPermission(PermissionState::None);

//Converts the new WebPermission from XML using myWebPermission1.
myWebPermission2->FromXml(myWebPermission1->ToXml());
```

Requirements

Platforms: Windows 98, Windows NT 4.0, Windows Millennium Edition, Windows 2000, Windows XP Home Edition, Windows XP Professional, Windows .NET Server family, Common Language Infrastructure (CLI) Standard

WebPermission.Union Method

Returns the logical union between two instances of the **WebPermission** class.

```
[Visual Basic]
Overrides Public Function Union( _
   ByVal target As IPermission _
) As IPermission Implements IPermission.Union
[C#]
public override IPermission Union(
   IPermission target
);
[C++]
public: IPermission* Union(
   IPermission* target
);
[JScript]
public override function Union(
   target : IPermission
) : IPermission;
```

Parameters

target
> The **WebPermission** to combine with the current **WebPermission**.

Return Value

A **WebPermission** that represents the union of the current instance and the *target* parameter. If either WebPermission is **Unrestricted**, the method returns a **WebPermission** that is **Unrestricted**. If the target is a null reference (**Nothing** in Visual Basic), returns a copy of current **WebPermission**.

Implements

IPermission.Union

Exceptions

Exception Type	Condition
ArgumentException	target is not a null reference (**Nothing** in Visual Basic) or of type **WebPermission**.

Remarks

Union returns a **WebPermission** that contains all the permissions in both *target* and the current instance.

Example

[Visual Basic, C#, C++] The following example takes the logical union of two **WebPermission** instances to create a third instance of **WebPermission**.

```
[Visual Basic]
' Create another WebPermission that is the Union of previous
  two WebPermission
' instances.
Dim myWebPermission3 As WebPermission =
CType(myWebPermission1.Union(myWebPermission2), WebPermission)
```

```
Console.WriteLine(ControlChars.Cr + "Attributes and values        ⏎
of the WebPermission after the Union are : ")
' Display the attributes,values and children.
Console.WriteLine(myWebPermission3.ToXml().ToString())
   End Sub 'CreateUnion
```

[C#]
```
   // Create another WebPermission that is the Union of        ⏎
previous two WebPermission
   // instances.
   WebPermission myWebPermission3 =(WebPermission)              ⏎
myWebPermission1.Union(myWebPermission2);
   Console.WriteLine("\nAttributes and values of the            ⏎
WebPermission after the Union are : ");
   // Display the attributes,values and children.
   Console.WriteLine(myWebPermission3.ToXml().ToString());
```

[C++]
```
// Create another WebPermission that is the Union of previous   ⏎
  two WebPermission
// instances.
WebPermission* myWebPermission3 =dynamic_cast<WebPermission*>    ⏎
  (myWebPermission1->Union(myWebPermission2));
Console::WriteLine(S"\nAttributes and values of the             ⏎
WebPermission after the Union are : ");
// Display the attributes, values and children.
Console::WriteLine(myWebPermission3->ToXml());
```

Requirements

Platforms: Windows 98, Windows NT 4.0,
Windows Millennium Edition, Windows 2000,
Windows XP Home Edition, Windows XP Professional,
Windows .NET Server family,
Common Language Infrastructure (CLI) Standard

WebPermissionAttribute Class

Specifies permission to access Internet resources. This class cannot be inherited.

System.Object
  System.Attribute
    System.Security.Permissions.SecurityAttribute
      System.Security.Permissions.CodeAccessSecurityAttribute
        System.Net.WebPermissionAttribute

[Visual Basic]
```
<AttributeUsage(AttributeTargets.Assembly Or AttributeTargets.Class _
   Or AttributeTargets.Struct Or AttributeTargets.Constructor Or _
   AttributeTargets.Method)>
<Serializable>
NotInheritable Public Class WebPermissionAttribute
   Inherits CodeAccessSecurityAttribute
```
[C#]
```
[AttributeUsage(AttributeTargets.Assembly | AttributeTargets.Class
   | AttributeTargets.Struct | AttributeTargets.Constructor |
   AttributeTargets.Method)]
[Serializable]
public sealed class WebPermissionAttribute :
   CodeAccessSecurityAttribute
```
[C++]
```
[AttributeUsage(AttributeTargets::Assembly |
   AttributeTargets::Class | AttributeTargets::Struct |
   AttributeTargets::Constructor | AttributeTargets::Method)]
[Serializable]
public __gc __sealed class WebPermissionAttribute : public
   CodeAccessSecurityAttribute
```
[JScript]
```
public
   AttributeUsage(AttributeTargets.Assembly | AttributeTargets.Class |
   AttributeTargets.Struct | AttributeTargets.Constructor |
   AttributeTargets.Method)
   Serializable
class WebPermissionAttribute extends
   CodeAccessSecurityAttribute
```

Thread Safety

Any public static (**Shared** in Visual Basic) members of this type are safe for multithreaded operations. Any instance members are not guaranteed to be thread safe.

Remarks

WebPermissionAttribute allows you to declaratively specify which URI strings and regular expression strings your class can use.

The security information specified in the **WebPermissionAttribute** is stored in the metadata of the attribute target, which is the class to which **WebPermissionAttribute** is applied. The system accesses this information at run time. The **System.Security.Permissions.SecurityAction** passed to the constructor determines the allowable **WebPermissionAttribute** targets. The system uses the **WebPermission** returned by the **CreatePermission** method to convert the security information of the attribute target to a serializable form stored in metadata.

> **Note** **WebPermissionAttribute** is used only for **Declarative Security**. For **Imperative Security**, use the corresponding **WebPermission**.

Example

[Visual Basic, C#, C++] The following example demonstrates how to apply **WebPermissionAttribute** to a method.

[Visual Basic]
```
' Deny access to a specific resource by setting the          ⏎
ConnectPattern property.
   <WebPermission(SecurityAction.Deny, ConnectPattern :=      ⏎
"http://www\.contoso\.com/.*")> Public Sub Connect()

   ' Create a Connection.
   Dim myWebRequest As HttpWebRequest =                       ⏎
CType(WebRequest.Create("http://www.contoso.com"), HttpWebRequest)
   Console.WriteLine("This line should never be printed")
```

[C#]
```
   // Deny access to a specific resource by setting the       ⏎
ConnectPattern property.
   [WebPermission(SecurityAction.Deny,                        ⏎
ConnectPattern=@"http://www\.contoso\.com/")]

public void Connect()
   {
      // Create a Connection.
      HttpWebRequest myWebRequest =                           ⏎
(HttpWebRequest)WebRequest.Create("http://www.contoso.com");
         Console.WriteLine("This line should never be printed");
   }
```

[C++]
```
// Deny access to a specific resource by setting the          ⏎
ConnectPattern property.
[method:WebPermission(SecurityAction::Deny,                   ⏎
ConnectPattern="http://www.contoso.com/")]
void Connect() {
   // Create a Connection.
   HttpWebRequest* myWebRequest =
      dynamic_cast<HttpWebRequest*>(WebRequest::Create        ⏎
(S"http://www.contoso.com"));
   Console::WriteLine(S"This line should never be printed");
}
```

Requirements

Namespace: System.Net

Platforms: Windows 98, Windows NT 4.0, Windows Millennium Edition, Windows 2000, Windows XP Home Edition, Windows XP Professional, Windows .NET Server family

Assembly: System (in System.dll)

WebPermissionAttribute Constructor

Initializes a new instance of the **WebPermissionAttribute** class with a value that specifies the security actions that can be performed on this class.

[Visual Basic]
```
Public Sub New( _
   ByVal action As SecurityAction _
)
```
[C#]
```
public WebPermissionAttribute(
   SecurityAction action
);
```

```
[C++]
public: WebPermissionAttribute(
  SecurityAction action
);
[JScript]
public function WebPermissionAttribute(
  action : SecurityAction
);
```

Parameters

action

One of the **SecurityAction** values.

Exceptions

Exception Type	Condition
ArgumentException	*action* is not a valid **SecurityAction** value.

Remarks

The **SecurityAction** value passed to this constructor specifies the allowable security actions that can be performed on this class.

Example

[Visual Basic, C#, C++] The following example demonstrates how to apply **WebPermissionAttribute** to a method.

```
[Visual Basic]
' Set the declarative security for the URI.
<WebPermission(SecurityAction.Deny, Connect :=
"http://www.contoso.com/")> _
Public Sub Connect()
  ' Throw an exception.
  Try
    Dim myWebRequest As HttpWebRequest =
CType(WebRequest.Create("http://www.contoso.com"), HttpWebRequest)
  Catch e As Exception
    Console.WriteLine(("Exception : " + e.ToString()))
  End Try
End Sub 'Connect
```

```
[C#]
// Set the declarative security for the URI.
  [WebPermission(SecurityAction.Deny, Connect =
@"http://www.contoso.com/")]
  public void Connect()
  {
    // Throw an exception.
    try
    {
      HttpWebRequest myWebRequest =
(HttpWebRequest)WebRequest.Create("http://www.contoso.com/");
    }
    catch(Exception e)
    {
      Console.WriteLine("Exception : " + e.ToString());
    }
```

```
[C++]
// Set the declarative security for the URI.
[WebPermission(SecurityAction::Deny, Connect =
S"http://www.contoso.com/")]
void Connect() {
  // Throw an exception.
  try {
    HttpWebRequest* myWebRequest =
      dynamic_cast<HttpWebRequest*>(WebRequest::Create
(S"http://www.contoso.com/"));
  } catch (Exception* e) {
    Console::WriteLine(S"Exception : {0}", e);
  }
```

Requirements

Platforms: Windows 98, Windows NT 4.0, Windows Millennium Edition, Windows 2000, Windows XP Home Edition, Windows XP Professional, Windows .NET Server family, Common Language Infrastructure (CLI) Standard

WebPermissionAttribute.Accept Property

Gets or sets the URI string accepted by the current **WebPermissionAttribute**.

```
[Visual Basic]
Public Property Accept As String
[C#]
public string Accept {get; set;}
[C++]
public: __property String* get_Accept();
public: __property void set_Accept(String*);
[JScript]
public function get Accept() : String;
public function set Accept(String);
```

Property Value

A string containing the URI accepted by the current **WebPermissionAttribute**.

Exceptions

Exception Type	Condition
ArgumentException	**Accept** is not a null reference (**Nothing** in Visual Basic) when you attempt to set the value. If you wish to specify more than one Accept URI, use an additional attribute declaration statement.

Remarks

When applying **WebPermissionAttribute** to your class, this property specifies what URI string will be accepted for use within your class. This permission is applied when the security system calls **CreatePermission**. This property is write-once.

Example

See related example in the **System.Net.WebPermissionAttribute** constructor topic.

Requirements

Platforms: Windows 98, Windows NT 4.0, Windows Millennium Edition, Windows 2000, Windows XP Home Edition, Windows XP Professional, Windows .NET Server family, Common Language Infrastructure (CLI) Standard

WebPermissionAttribute.AcceptPattern Property

Gets or sets a regular expression pattern that describes the URI accepted by the current **WebPermissionAttribute**.

```
[Visual Basic]
Public Property AcceptPattern As String
[C#]
public string AcceptPattern {get; set;}
```

```
[C++]
public: __property String* get_AcceptPattern();
public: __property void set_AcceptPattern(String*);
[JScript]
public function get AcceptPattern() : String;
public function set AcceptPattern(String);
```

Property Value

A string containing a regular expression pattern that describes the URI accepted by the current **WebPermissionAttribute**. This string must be escaped according to the rules for encoding a **System.Text.RegularExpressions.Regex** constructor string.

Exceptions

Exception Type	Condition
ArgumentException	**AcceptPattern** is not a null reference (**Nothing** in Visual Basic) when you attempt to set the value. If you wish to specify more than one Accept URI, use an additional attribute declaration statement.

Remarks

When applying **WebPermissionAttribute** to your class, this property specifies what regular expression string will be accepted for use within your class. This property is write-once.

Example

[Visual Basic, C#, C++] The following example demonstrates how to use **WebPermissionAttribute** to specify an allowable **AcceptPattern**.

[Visual Basic]
```
<WebPermission(SecurityAction.Deny, AcceptPattern := _
"http://www\.contoso\.com/Private/.*")> _
   Public Shared Sub        CheckAcceptPermission(uriToCheck As String)
      Dim re As New Regex("http://www\.contoso\.com/Public/.*")
      Dim con As New WebPermission(NetworkAccess.Connect, re)
      con.Assert()
      Dim permissionToCheck As New WebPermission()
      permissionToCheck.AddPermission(NetworkAccess.Accept, uriToCheck)
      permissionToCheck.Demand()
   End Sub 'CheckAcceptPermission

   Public Shared Sub demoDenySite()
      'Passes a security check.
      CheckAcceptPermission("http://www.contoso.com/Public/page.htm")
      Console.WriteLine("Public page has passed Accept permission
check")

      Try
         'Throws a SecurityException.
         CheckAcceptPermission("http://www.contoso.com/Private/page.htm")
         Console.WriteLine("This line will not be printed")
      Catch e As SecurityException
         Console.WriteLine(("Expected exception" + e.Message))
      End Try
   End Sub 'demoDenySite
```

[C#]
```
[WebPermission(SecurityAction.Deny,
AcceptPattern=@"http://www\.contoso\.com/Private/.*")]

public static void CheckAcceptPermission(string uriToCheck) {

    WebPermission permissionToCheck = new WebPermission();
    permissionToCheck.AddPermission(NetworkAccess.Accept, uriToCheck);
    permissionToCheck.Demand();

}
```

```
public static void demoDenySite() {
    //Passes a security check.
    CheckAcceptPermission("http://www.contoso.com/Public/page.htm");
    Console.WriteLine("Public page has passed Accept permission
check");

    try {
        //Throws a SecurityException.
        CheckAcceptPermission("http://www.contoso.com/Private/
page.htm");
        Console.WriteLine("This line will not be printed");
    }

    catch (SecurityException e) {
        Console.WriteLine("Expected exception: " + e.Message);
    }

}
```

[C++]
```
[method:WebPermission(SecurityAction::Deny,
AcceptPattern=S"http://www\\.contoso\\.com/Private/.*")]
static void CheckAcceptPermission(String* uriToCheck) {
    WebPermission* permissionToCheck = new WebPermission();
    permissionToCheck->AddPermission(NetworkAccess::Accept, uriToCheck);
    permissionToCheck->Demand();
}
```

```
public:
static void demoDenySite() {
    // Passes a security check.
    CheckAcceptPermission(S"http://www.contoso.com/Public/page.htm");
    Console::WriteLine(S"Public page has passed Accept permission
check");

    try {
        // Throws a SecurityException.
        CheckAcceptPermission(S"http://www.contoso.com/Private/page.htm");
        Console::WriteLine(S"This line will not be printed");
    } catch (SecurityException* e) {
        Console::WriteLine(S"Expected exception: {0}", e->Message);
    }
}
```

Requirements

Platforms: Windows 98, Windows NT 4.0, Windows Millennium Edition, Windows 2000, Windows XP Home Edition, Windows XP Professional, Windows .NET Server family

WebPermissionAttribute.Connect Property

Gets or sets the URI connection string controlled by the current **WebPermissionAttribute**.

```
[Visual Basic]
Public Property Connect As String
[C#]
public string Connect {get; set;}
[C++]
public: __property String* get_Connect();
public: __property void set_Connect(String*);
[JScript]
public function get Connect() : String;
public function set Connect(String);
```

Property Value

A string containing the URI connection controlled by the current **WebPermissionAttribute**.

Exceptions

Exception Type	Condition
ArgumentException	**Connect** is not a null reference (**Nothing** in Visual Basic) when you attempt to set the value. If you wish to specify more than one Connect URI, use an additional attribute declaration statement.

Remarks

When applying **WebPermissionAttribute** to your class, this property specifies what URI connection is accepted for use within your class. This property is write-once.

Example

[Visual Basic, C#, C++] The following example demonstrates how to use WebPermissionAttribute to specify an allowable **Connect** string.

```
[Visual Basic]
    ' Set the WebPermissionAttribute  Connect property.
    <WebPermission(SecurityAction.Deny, Connect :=
"http://www.contoso.com/Private.htm")> _
        Public Shared Sub CheckConnectPermission(uriToCheck As String)
        Dim permissionToCheck As New WebPermission()
        permissionToCheck.AddPermission(NetworkAccess.Connect,
uriToCheck)
        permissionToCheck.Demand()
    End Sub 'CheckConnectPermission

    Public Shared Sub demoDenySite()
        'Pass the security check.
        CheckConnectPermission("http://www.contoso.com/Public.htm")
        Console.WriteLine("Public page has passed Connect
permission check")
        Try
            'Throw a SecurityException.
            CheckConnectPermission("http://www.contoso.com/Private.htm")
            Console.WriteLine("This line will not be printed")
        Catch e As SecurityException
            Console.WriteLine(("Expected exception" + e.Message))
        End Try
    End Sub 'demoDenySite
```

```
[C#]
// Set the WebPermissionAttribute  Connect property.
[WebPermission(SecurityAction.Deny, Connect=@"http://www.contoso.com/
Private.htm")]

public static void demoDenySite()
{
    //Pass the security check.
    CheckConnectPermission("http://www.contoso.com/Public.htm");
    Console.WriteLine("Public page has passed connect
permission check");

    try
    {
        //Throw a SecurityException.
        CheckConnectPermission("http://www.contoso.com/Private.htm");
        Console.WriteLine("This line will not be printed");
    }
    catch (SecurityException e) {
        Console.WriteLine("Expected exception" + e.Message);
    }

}

public static void CheckConnectPermission(string uriToCheck) {
    WebPermission permissionToCheck = new WebPermission();
    permissionToCheck.AddPermission(NetworkAccess.Connect, uriToCheck);
    permissionToCheck.Demand();
}
```

```
[C++]
// Set the WebPermissionAttribute  Connect property.
[method:WebPermission(SecurityAction::Deny, Connect=S"http://
www.contoso.com/Private.htm")]
static void demoDenySite() {
    //Pass the security check.
    CheckConnectPermission(S"http://www.contoso.com/Public.htm");
    Console::WriteLine(S"Public page has passed connect
permission check");

    try {
        //Throw a SecurityException.
        CheckConnectPermission(S"http://www.contoso.com/Private.htm");
        Console::WriteLine(S"This line will not be printed");
    } catch (SecurityException* e) {
        Console::WriteLine(S"Expected exception {0}", e->Message);
    }
}

static void CheckConnectPermission(String* uriToCheck) {
    WebPermission* permissionToCheck = new WebPermission();
    permissionToCheck->AddPermission(NetworkAccess::
Connect, uriToCheck);
    permissionToCheck->Demand();
}
```

Requirements

Platforms: Windows 98, Windows NT 4.0, Windows Millennium Edition, Windows 2000, Windows XP Home Edition, Windows XP Professional, Windows .NET Server family, Common Language Infrastructure (CLI) Standard

WebPermissionAttribute.ConnectPattern Property

Gets or sets a regular expression pattern that describes the URI connection controlled by the current **WebPermissionAttribute**.

```
[Visual Basic]
Public Property ConnectPattern As String
[C#]
public string ConnectPattern {get; set;}
[C++]
public: __property String* get_ConnectPattern();
public: __property void set_ConnectPattern(String*);
[JScript]
public function get ConnectPattern() : String;
public function set ConnectPattern(String);
```

Property Value

A string containing a regular expression pattern that describes the URI connection controlled by this **WebPermissionAttribute**.

Exceptions

Exception Type	Condition
ArgumentException	**ConnectPattern** is not a null reference (**Nothing** in Visual Basic) when you attempt to set the value. If you wish to specify more than one connect URI, use an additional attribute declaration statement.

Remarks

When applying **WebPermissionAttribute** to your class, this property specifies what regular expression connect string is accepted for use within your class. This property is write-once.

Example

[Visual Basic, C#, C++] The following example demonstrates how to use **WebPermissionAttribute** to specify an allowable **ConnectPattern**.

[Visual Basic]
```
' Set the WebPermissionAttribute  ConnectPattern property.
<WebPermission(SecurityAction.Deny, ConnectPattern :=
"http://www\.contoso\.com/Private/.*")> _
    Public Shared Sub CheckConnectPermission(uriToCheck As String)
    Dim re As New Regex("http://www\.contoso\.com/Public/.*")
    Dim con As New WebPermission(NetworkAccess.Connect, re)
    con.Assert()
    Dim permissionToCheck As New WebPermission()
    permissionToCheck.AddPermission
(NetworkAccess.Connect, uriToCheck)
    permissionToCheck.Demand()
    End Sub 'CheckConnectPermission

    Public Shared Sub demoDenySite()
        'Pass the security check.
        CheckConnectPermission("http://www.contoso.com/Public/page.htm")
        Console.WriteLine("Public page has passed Connect
permission check")

        Try
            'Throw a SecurityException.
            CheckConnectPermission("http://www.contoso.com/Private/
page.htm")
            Console.WriteLine("This line will not be printed")
        Catch e As SecurityException
            Console.WriteLine(("Expected exception" + e.Message))
        End Try
    End Sub 'demoDenySite
```

[C#]
```
// Set the WebPermissionAttribute  ConnectPattern property.
[WebPermission(SecurityAction.Deny,
ConnectPattern=@"http://www\.contoso\.com/Private/.*")]

public static void CheckConnectPermission(string uriToCheck)
{
    WebPermission permissionToCheck = new WebPermission();
    permissionToCheck.AddPermission(NetworkAccess.Connect, uriToCheck);
    permissionToCheck.Demand();
}

public static void demoDenySite() {
    //Pass the security check.
    CheckConnectPermission("http://www.contoso.com/Public/page.htm");
    Console.WriteLine("Public page has passed Connect permission check");

    try
    {
        //Throw a SecurityException.
        CheckConnectPermission("http://www.contoso.com/Private/page.htm");
        Console.WriteLine("This line will not be printed");
    }
    catch (SecurityException e)
    {
        Console.WriteLine("Expected exception" + e.Message);
    }

}
```

[C++]
```
// Set the WebPermissionAttribute  ConnectPattern property.
[WebPermission(SecurityAction::Deny,
ConnectPattern=S"http://www\\.contoso\\.com/Private/.*")]
void CheckConnectPermission(String* uriToCheck) {
    WebPermission* permissionToCheck = new WebPermission();
    permissionToCheck->AddPermission(NetworkAccess::
Connect, uriToCheck);
    permissionToCheck->Demand();
```

```
void demoDenySite() {
    //Pass the security check.
    CheckConnectPermission(S"http://www.contoso.com/Public/page.htm");
    Console::WriteLine(S"Public page has passed Connect
permission check");

    try {
        //Throw a SecurityException.
        CheckConnectPermission(S"http://www.contoso.com/Private/
page.htm");
        Console::WriteLine(S"This line will not be printed");
    } catch (SecurityException* e) {
        Console::WriteLine(S"Expected exception {0}", e->Message);
    }
}
```

Requirements

Platforms: Windows 98, Windows NT 4.0, Windows Millennium Edition, Windows 2000, Windows XP Home Edition, Windows XP Professional, Windows .NET Server family

WebPermissionAttribute.CreatePermission Method

Creates and returns a new instance of the **WebPermission** class.

```
[Visual Basic]
Overrides Public Function CreatePermission() As IPermission
[C#]
public override IPermission CreatePermission();
[C++]
public: IPermission* CreatePermission();
[JScript]
public override function CreatePermission() : IPermission;
```

Return Value

A **WebPermission** corresponding to the security declaration.

Remarks

The **CreatePermission** method is called by the security system, not by application code.

The security information described by **WebPermissionAttribute** is stored in the metadata of the attribute target, which is the class to which **WebPermissionAttribute** is applied. The system accesses the information at run time. The system uses the **WebPermission** returned by **CreatePermission** to convert the security information of the attribute target to a serializable form stored in metadata.

Requirements

Platforms: Windows 98, Windows NT 4.0, Windows Millennium Edition, Windows 2000, Windows XP Home Edition, Windows XP Professional, Windows .NET Server family, Common Language Infrastructure (CLI) Standard

WebProxy Class

Contains HTTP proxy settings for the **WebRequest** class.

System.Object
  System.Net.WebProxy

```
[Visual Basic]
<Serializable>
Public Class WebProxy
   Implements IWebProxy, ISerializable
[C#]
[Serializable]
public class WebProxy : IWebProxy, ISerializable
[C++]
[Serializable]
public __gc class WebProxy : public IWebProxy, ISerializable
[JScript]
public
   Serializable
class WebProxy implements IWebProxy, ISerializable
```

Thread Safety

Any public static (**Shared** in Visual Basic) members of this type are safe for multithreaded operations. Any instance members are not guaranteed to be thread safe.

Remarks

The **WebProxy** class contains the proxy settings that **WebRequest** instances use to override the proxy settings in **GlobalProxySelection**.

The **WebProxy** class is the base implementation of the **IWebProxy** interface.

Example

[Visual Basic, C#] The following example assigns a **WebProxy** to a **WebRequest**. The **WebRequest** instance uses the proxy to connect to external Internet resources.

```
[Visual Basic]
Dim proxyObject As New WebProxy("http://proxyserver:80/", True)
Dim req As WebRequest = WebRequest.Create("http://www.contoso.com")
req.Proxy = proxyObject
```

```
[C#]
WebProxy proxyObject = new WebProxy("http://proxyserver:80/",true);
WebRequest req = WebRequest.Create("http://www.contoso.com");
req.Proxy = proxyObject;
```

Requirements

Namespace: System.Net

Platforms: Windows 98, Windows NT 4.0, Windows Millennium Edition, Windows 2000, Windows XP Home Edition, Windows XP Professional, Windows .NET Server family, .NET Compact Framework - Windows CE .NET

Assembly: System (in System.dll)

WebProxy Constructor

Initializes a new instance of the **WebProxy** class.

Overload List

Initializes an empty instance of the **WebProxy** class.
Supported by the .NET Compact Framework.

> [Visual Basic] **Public Sub New()**
> [C#] **public WebProxy();**
> [C++] **public: WebProxy();**
> [JScript] **public function WebProxy();**

Initializes a new instance of the **WebProxy** class with the specified URI.
Supported by the .NET Compact Framework.

> [Visual Basic] **Public Sub New(String)**
> [C#] **public WebProxy(string);**
> [C++] **public: WebProxy(String*);**
> [JScript] **public function WebProxy(String);**

Initializes a new instance of the **WebProxy** class from the specified **Uri**.
Supported by the .NET Compact Framework.

> [Visual Basic] **Public Sub New(Uri)**
> [C#] **public WebProxy(Uri);**
> [C++] **public: WebProxy(Uri*);**
> [JScript] **public function WebProxy(Uri);**

This member supports the .NET Framework infrastructure and is not intended to be used directly from your code.

> [Visual Basic] **Protected Sub New(SerializationInfo, StreamingContext)**
> [C#] **protected WebProxy(SerializationInfo, StreamingContext);**
> [C++] **protected: WebProxy(SerializationInfo*, StreamingContext);**
> [JScript] **protected function WebProxy(SerializationInfo, StreamingContext);**

Initializes a new instance of the **WebProxy** class with the specified URI and bypass setting.
Supported by the .NET Compact Framework.

> [Visual Basic] **Public Sub New(String, Boolean)**
> [C#] **public WebProxy(string, bool);**
> [C++] **public: WebProxy(String*, bool);**
> [JScript] **public function WebProxy(String, Boolean);**

Initializes a new instance of the **WebProxy** class with the specified host and port number.
Supported by the .NET Compact Framework.

> [Visual Basic] **Public Sub New(String, Integer)**
> [C#] **public WebProxy(string, int);**
> [C++] **public: WebProxy(String*, int);**
> [JScript] **public function WebProxy(String, int);**

Initializes a new instance of the **WebProxy** class with the **Uri** and bypass setting.
Supported by the .NET Compact Framework.

> [Visual Basic] **Public Sub New(Uri, Boolean)**
> [C#] **public WebProxy(Uri, bool);**
> [C++] **public: WebProxy(Uri*, bool);**
> [JScript] **public function WebProxy(Uri, Boolean);**

Initializes a new instance of the **WebProxy** class with the specified URI, bypass setting, and list of URIs to bypass.

    [Visual Basic] **Public Sub New(String, Boolean, String())**

    [C#] **public WebProxy(string, bool, string[]);**

    [C++] **public: WebProxy(String*, bool, String*[]);**

    [JScript] **public function WebProxy(String, Boolean, String[]);**

Initializes a new instance of the **WebProxy** class with the specified **Uri**, bypass setting, and list of URIs to bypass.

    [Visual Basic] **Public Sub New(Uri, Boolean, String())**

    [C#] **public WebProxy(Uri, bool, string[]);**

    [C++] **public: WebProxy(Uri*, bool, String[]);**

    [JScript] **public function WebProxy(Uri, Boolean, String[]);**

Initializes a new instance of the **WebProxy** class with the specified URI, bypass setting, list of URIs to bypass, and credentials.

    [Visual Basic] **Public Sub New(String, Boolean, String(), ICredentials)**

    [C#] **public WebProxy(string, bool, string[], ICredentials);**

    [C++] **public: WebProxy(String*, bool, String*[], ICredentials*);**

    [JScript] **public function WebProxy(String, Boolean, String[], ICredentials);**

Initializes a new instance of the **WebProxy** class with the specified **Uri**, bypass setting, list of URIs to bypass, and credentials.

    [Visual Basic] **Public Sub New(Uri, Boolean, String(), ICredentials)**

    [C#] **public WebProxy(Uri, bool, string[], ICredentials);**

    [C++] **public: WebProxy(Uri*, bool, String[], ICredentials*);**

    [JScript] **public function WebProxy(Uri, Boolean, String[], ICredentials);**

WebProxy Constructor ()

Initializes an empty instance of the **WebProxy** class.

```
[Visual Basic]
Public Sub New()
[C#]
public WebProxy();
[C++]
public: WebProxy();
[JScript]
public function WebProxy();
```

Remarks

The default constructor initializes an empty instance of the **WebProxy** class with the **Address** property set to a null reference.

When the **Address** property is a null reference, the **IsBypassed** method returns **true**, and the **GetProxy** method returns the destination address.

Requirements

Platforms: Windows 98, Windows NT 4.0, Windows Millennium Edition, Windows 2000, Windows XP Home Edition, Windows XP Professional, Windows .NET Server family, .NET Compact Framework - Windows CE .NET, Common Language Infrastructure (CLI) Standard

WebProxy Constructor (String)

Initializes a new instance of the **WebProxy** class with the specified URI.

```
[Visual Basic]
Public Sub New( _
    ByVal Address As String _
)
[C#]
public WebProxy(
    string Address
);
[C++]
public: WebProxy(
    String* Address
);
[JScript]
public function WebProxy(
    Address : String
);
```

Parameters

Address
    The URI of the proxy server.

Exceptions

Exception Type	Condition
UriFormatException	*Address* is an invalid URI.

Remarks

The **WebProxy** instance is initialized with the **Address** property set to a **Uri** instance containing *Address*.

Requirements

Platforms: Windows 98, Windows NT 4.0, Windows Millennium Edition, Windows 2000, Windows XP Home Edition, Windows XP Professional, Windows .NET Server family, .NET Compact Framework - Windows CE .NET, Common Language Infrastructure (CLI) Standard

WebProxy Constructor (Uri)

Initializes a new instance of the **WebProxy** class from the specified **Uri**.

```
[Visual Basic]
Public Sub New( _
    ByVal Address As Uri _
)
[C#]
public WebProxy(
    Uri Address
);
[C++]
public: WebProxy(
    Uri* Address
);
[JScript]
public function WebProxy(
    Address : Uri
);
```

Parameters

Address

A **Uri** containing the address of the proxy server.

Remarks

The **WebProxy** instance is initialized with the **Address** property set to the *Address* parameter.

Requirements

Platforms: Windows 98, Windows NT 4.0, Windows Millennium Edition, Windows 2000, Windows XP Home Edition, Windows XP Professional, Windows .NET Server family, .NET Compact Framework - Windows CE .NET, Common Language Infrastructure (CLI) Standard

WebProxy Constructor (SerializationInfo, StreamingContext)

This member supports the .NET Framework infrastructure and is not intended to be used directly from your code.

```
[Visual Basic]
Protected Sub New( _
   ByVal serializationInfo As SerializationInfo, _
   ByVal streamingContext As StreamingContext _
)
[C#]
protected WebProxy(
   SerializationInfo serializationInfo,
   StreamingContext streamingContext
);
[C++]
protected: WebProxy(
   SerializationInfo* serializationInfo,
   StreamingContext streamingContext
);
[JScript]
protected function WebProxy(
   serializationInfo : SerializationInfo,
   streamingContext : StreamingContext
);
```

WebProxy Constructor (String, Boolean)

Initializes a new instance of the **WebProxy** class with the specified URI and bypass setting.

```
[Visual Basic]
Public Sub New( _
   ByVal Address As String, _
   ByVal BypassOnLocal As Boolean _
)
[C#]
public WebProxy(
   string Address,
   bool BypassOnLocal
);
[C++]
public: WebProxy(
   String* Address,
   bool BypassOnLocal
);
```

```
[JScript]
public function WebProxy(
   Address : String,
   BypassOnLocal : Boolean
);
```

Parameters

Address

The URI of the proxy server.

BypassOnLocal

true to bypass the proxy for local addresses; otherwise, **false**.

Exceptions

Exception Type	Condition
UriFormatException	*Address* is an invalid URI.

Remarks

The **WebProxy** instance is initialized with the **Address** property set to a **Uri** instance containing *Address* and the **BypassProxyOnLocal** property set to *BypassOnLocal*.

Requirements

Platforms: Windows 98, Windows NT 4.0, Windows Millennium Edition, Windows 2000, Windows XP Home Edition, Windows XP Professional, Windows .NET Server family, .NET Compact Framework - Windows CE .NET, Common Language Infrastructure (CLI) Standard

WebProxy Constructor (String, Int32)

Initializes a new instance of the **WebProxy** class with the specified host and port number.

```
[Visual Basic]
Public Sub New( _
   ByVal Host As String, _
   ByVal Port As Integer _
)
[C#]
public WebProxy(
   string Host,
   int Port
);
[C++]
public: WebProxy(
   String* Host,
   int Port
);
[JScript]
public function WebProxy(
   Host : String,
   Port : int
);
```

Parameters

Host

The name of the proxy host.

Port

The port number on *Host* to use.

Exceptions

Exception Type	Condition
UriFormatException	The URI formed by combining *Host* and *Port* is not a valid URI.

Remarks

The **WebProxy** instance is initialized with the **Address** property set to a **Uri** instance of the form http:// *Host*: *Port*.

Requirements

Platforms: Windows 98, Windows NT 4.0,
Windows Millennium Edition, Windows 2000,
Windows XP Home Edition, Windows XP Professional,
Windows .NET Server family,
.NET Compact Framework - Windows CE .NET,
Common Language Infrastructure (CLI) Standard

WebProxy Constructor (Uri, Boolean)

Initializes a new instance of the **WebProxy** class with the **Uri** and bypass setting.

```
[Visual Basic]
Public Sub New( _
   ByVal Address As Uri, _
   ByVal BypassOnLocal As Boolean _
)
[C#]
public WebProxy(
   Uri Address,
   bool BypassOnLocal
);
[C++]
public: WebProxy(
   Uri* Address,
   bool BypassOnLocal
);
[JScript]
public function WebProxy(
   Address : Uri,
   BypassOnLocal : Boolean
);
```

Parameters

Address
   A **Uri** containing the address of the proxy server.
BypassOnLocal
   true to bypass the proxy for local addresses; otherwise, **false**.

Remarks

The **WebProxy** instance is initialized with the **Address** property set to *Address* and with the **BypassProxyOnLocal** property set to *BypassOnLocal*.

Requirements

Platforms: Windows 98, Windows NT 4.0,
Windows Millennium Edition, Windows 2000,
Windows XP Home Edition, Windows XP Professional,
Windows .NET Server family,
.NET Compact Framework - Windows CE .NET,
Common Language Infrastructure (CLI) Standard

WebProxy Constructor (String, Boolean, String[])

Initializes a new instance of the **WebProxy** class with the specified URI, bypass setting, and list of URIs to bypass.

```
[Visual Basic]
Public Sub New( _
   ByVal Address As String, _
   ByVal BypassOnLocal As Boolean, _
   ByVal BypassList() As String _
)
[C#]
public WebProxy(
   string Address,
   bool BypassOnLocal,
   string[] BypassList
);
[C++]
public: WebProxy(
   String* Address,
   bool BypassOnLocal,
   String* BypassList __gc[]
);
[JScript]
public function WebProxy(
   Address : String,
   BypassOnLocal : Boolean,
   BypassList : String[]
);
```

Parameters

Address
   The URI of the proxy server.
BypassOnLocal
   true to bypass the proxy for local addresses; otherwise, **false**.
BypassList
   An array of regular expression strings containing the URIs of the servers to bypass.

Exceptions

Exception Type	Condition
UriFormatException	*Address* is an invalid URI.

Remarks

The **WebProxy** instance is initialized with the **Address** property set to a **Uri** instance containing *Address*, the **BypassProxyOnLocal** property set to *BypassOnLocal*, and the **BypassList** property set to *BypassList*.

Requirements

Platforms: Windows 98, Windows NT 4.0,
Windows Millennium Edition, Windows 2000,
Windows XP Home Edition, Windows XP Professional,
Windows .NET Server family,
Common Language Infrastructure (CLI) Standard

WebProxy Constructor (Uri, Boolean, String[])

Initializes a new instance of the **WebProxy** class with the specified **Uri**, bypass setting, and list of URIs to bypass.

```
[Visual Basic]
Public Sub New( _
   ByVal Address As Uri, _
```

```
  ByVal BypassOnLocal As Boolean, _
  ByVal BypassList() As String _
)
[C#]
public WebProxy(
  Uri Address,
  bool BypassOnLocal,
  string[] BypassList
);
[C++]
public: WebProxy(
  Uri* Address,
  bool BypassOnLocal,
  String* BypassList __gc[]
);
[JScript]
public function WebProxy(
  Address : Uri,
  BypassOnLocal : Boolean,
  BypassList : String[]
);
```

Parameters

Address
   A **Uri** containing the address of the proxy server.
BypassOnLocal
   true to bypass the proxy for local addresses; otherwise, **false**.
BypassList
   An array of regular expression strings containing the URIs of the
   servers to bypass.

Remarks

The **WebProxy** instance is initialized with the **Address** property set
to *Address*, the **BypassProxyOnLocal** property set to
BypassOnLocal, and the **BypassList** property set to *BypassList*.

Requirements

Platforms: Windows 98, Windows NT 4.0,
Windows Millennium Edition, Windows 2000,
Windows XP Home Edition, Windows XP Professional,
Windows .NET Server family,
Common Language Infrastructure (CLI) Standard

WebProxy Constructor (String, Boolean, String[], ICredentials)

Initializes a new instance of the **WebProxy** class with the specified
URI, bypass setting, list of URIs to bypass, and credentials.

```
[Visual Basic]
Public Sub New( _
  ByVal Address As String, _
  ByVal BypassOnLocal As Boolean, _
  ByVal BypassList() As String, _
  ByVal Credentials As ICredentials _
)
[C#]
public WebProxy(
  string Address,
  bool BypassOnLocal,
  string[] BypassList,
  ICredentials Credentials
);
```

```
[C++]
public: WebProxy(
  String* Address,
  bool BypassOnLocal,
  String* BypassList __gc[],
  ICredentials* Credentials
);
[JScript]
public function WebProxy(
  Address : String,
  BypassOnLocal : Boolean,
  BypassList : String[],
  Credentials : ICredentials
);
```

Parameters

Address
   The URI of the proxy server.
BypassOnLocal
   true to bypass the proxy for local addresses; otherwise, **false**.
BypassList
   An array of regular expression strings containing the URIs of the
   servers to bypass.
Credentials
   An **ICredentials** to submit to the proxy server for authentication.

Exceptions

Exception Type	Condition
UriFormatException	*Address* is an invalid URI.

Remarks

The **WebProxy** instance is initialized with the **Address** property set
to a **Uri** instance containing *Address*, the **BypassProxyOnLocal**
property set to *BypassOnLocal*, the **BypassList** property set to
BypassList, and the **Credentials** property set to *Credentials*.

Requirements

Platforms: Windows 98, Windows NT 4.0,
Windows Millennium Edition, Windows 2000,
Windows XP Home Edition, Windows XP Professional,
Windows .NET Server family,
Common Language Infrastructure (CLI) Standard

WebProxy Constructor (Uri, Boolean, String[], ICredentials)

Initializes a new instance of the **WebProxy** class with the specified
Uri, bypass setting, list of URIs to bypass, and credentials.

```
[Visual Basic]
Public Sub New( _
  ByVal Address As Uri, _
  ByVal BypassOnLocal As Boolean, _
  ByVal BypassList() As String, _
  ByVal Credentials As ICredentials _
)
[C#]
public WebProxy(
  Uri Address,
  bool BypassOnLocal,
  string[] BypassList,
  ICredentials Credentials
);
```

```
[C++]
public: WebProxy(
    Uri* Address,
    bool BypassOnLocal,
    String* BypassList __gc[],
    ICredentials* Credentials
);
[JScript]
public function WebProxy(
    Address : Uri,
    BypassOnLocal : Boolean,
    BypassList : String[],
    Credentials : ICredentials
);
```

Parameters

Address

    A **Uri** containing the address of the proxy server.

BypassOnLocal

    true to bypass the proxy for local addresses; otherwise, **false**.

BypassList

    An array of regular expression strings containing the URIs of the servers to bypass.

Credentials

    An **ICredentials** to submit to the proxy server for authentication.

Remarks

The **WebProxy** instance is initialized with the **Address** property set to *Address*, the **BypassProxyOnLocal** property set to *BypassOnLocal*, the **BypassList** property set to *BypassList*, and the **Credentials** property set to *Credentials*

Requirements

Platforms: Windows 98, Windows NT 4.0, Windows Millennium Edition, Windows 2000, Windows XP Home Edition, Windows XP Professional, Windows .NET Server family, Common Language Infrastructure (CLI) Standard

WebProxy.Address Property

Gets or sets the address of the proxy server.

```
[Visual Basic]
Public Property Address As Uri
[C#]
public Uri Address {get; set;}
[C++]
public: __property Uri* get_Address();
public: __property void set_Address(Uri*);
[JScript]
public function get Address() : Uri;
public function set Address(Uri);
```

Property Value

A **Uri** containing the address of the proxy server.

Remarks

The **Address** property contains the address of the proxy server. When **Address** is a null reference (**Nothing** in Visual Basic), all requests bypass the proxy and connect directly to the destination host.

Requirements

Platforms: Windows 98, Windows NT 4.0, Windows Millennium Edition, Windows 2000, Windows XP Home Edition, Windows XP Professional, Windows .NET Server family, .NET Compact Framework - Windows CE .NET, Common Language Infrastructure (CLI) Standard

WebProxy.BypassArrayList Property

Gets a list of addresses that do not use the proxy server.

```
[Visual Basic]
Public ReadOnly Property BypassArrayList As ArrayList
[C#]
public ArrayList BypassArrayList {get;}
[C++]
public: __property ArrayList* get_BypassArrayList();
[JScript]
public function get BypassArrayList() : ArrayList;
```

Property Value

An **ArrayList** containing a list of **BypassList** arrays representing URIs that will not use the proxy server when accessed.

Remarks

The **BypassList** is an array list of regular expression strings describing the URIs that a **WebRequest** instance accesses directly instead of through the proxy server.

Requirements

Platforms: Windows 98, Windows NT 4.0, Windows Millennium Edition, Windows 2000, Windows XP Home Edition, Windows XP Professional, Windows .NET Server family, Common Language Infrastructure (CLI) Standard

WebProxy.BypassList Property

Gets or sets an array of addresses that do not use the proxy server.

```
[Visual Basic]
Public Property BypassList As String ()
[C#]
public string[] BypassList {get; set;}
[C++]
public: __property String* get_BypassList();
public: __property void set_BypassList(String* __gc[]);
[JScript]
public function get BypassList() : String[];
public function set BypassList(String[]);
```

Property Value

An array containing a list of regular expressions that describe URIs that will not use the proxy server when accessed.

Remarks

The **BypassList** property contains an array of regular expressions that describe URIs that a **WebRequest** instance accesses directly instead of through the proxy server.

Requirements

Platforms: Windows 98, Windows NT 4.0,
Windows Millennium Edition, Windows 2000,
Windows XP Home Edition, Windows XP Professional,
Windows .NET Server family,
Common Language Infrastructure (CLI) Standard

WebProxy.BypassProxyOnLocal Property

Gets or sets a value indicating whether to bypass the proxy server for local addresses.

```
[Visual Basic]
Public Property BypassProxyOnLocal As Boolean
[C#]
public bool BypassProxyOnLocal {get; set;}
[C++]
public: __property bool get_BypassProxyOnLocal();
public: __property void set_BypassProxyOnLocal(bool);
[JScript]
public function get BypassProxyOnLocal() : Boolean;
public function set BypassProxyOnLocal(Boolean);
```

Property Value

true to bypass the proxy server for local addresses; otherwise, **false**. The default value is **false**.

Remarks

The setting of the **BypassProxyOnLocal** property determines whether **WebRequest** instances use the proxy server when accessing local Internet resources.

If **BypassProxyOnLocal** is **true**, requests to local Internet resources do not use the proxy server. Local requests are identified by the lack of a period (.) in the URI, as in http://webserver/ or access the local server, including http://localhost, http://loopback, or http://127.0.0.1 . When **BypassProxyOnLocal** is **false**, all Internet requests are made through the proxy server.

> **Note** Requests to a local host with a URI containing a period use the proxy. To avoid using a proxy in these cases, create an entry for the host in the **BypassList**.

Requirements

Platforms: Windows 98, Windows NT 4.0,
Windows Millennium Edition, Windows 2000,
Windows XP Home Edition, Windows XP Professional,
Windows .NET Server family,
.NET Compact Framework - Windows CE .NET,
Common Language Infrastructure (CLI) Standard

WebProxy.Credentials Property

Gets or sets the credentials to submit to the proxy server for authentication.

```
[Visual Basic]
Public Overridable Property Credentials As ICredentials  Implements _
   IWebProxy.Credentials
[C#]
public virtual ICredentials Credentials {get; set;}
[C++]
public: __property virtual ICredentials* get_Credentials();
public: __property virtual void set_Credentials(ICredentials*);
```

```
[JScript]
public function get Credentials() : ICredentials;
public function set Credentials(ICredentials);
```

Property Value

An **ICredentials** containing the credentials to submit to the proxy server for authentication.

Implements

IWebProxy.Credentials

Remarks

The **Credentials** property contains the authentication credentials to send to the proxy server in response to an HTTP 407 (proxy authorization) status code.

Requirements

Platforms: Windows 98, Windows NT 4.0,
Windows Millennium Edition, Windows 2000,
Windows XP Home Edition, Windows XP Professional,
Windows .NET Server family,
.NET Compact Framework - Windows CE .NET,
Common Language Infrastructure (CLI) Standard

WebProxy.GetDefaultProxy Method

Reads the Internet Explorer nondynamic proxy settings.

```
[Visual Basic]
Public Shared Function GetDefaultProxy() As WebProxy
[C#]
public static WebProxy GetDefaultProxy();
[C++]
public: static WebProxy* GetDefaultProxy();
[JScript]
public static function GetDefaultProxy() : WebProxy;
```

Return Value

A **WebProxy** instance containing the nondynamic proxy settings from Internet Explorer 5.5.

Remarks

The **GetDefaultProxy** method reads the nondynamic proxy settings stored by Internet Explorer 5.5 and creates a **WebProxy** instance with those settings.

The **GetDefaultProxy** does not pick up any dynamic settings that are generated from script run by Internet Explorer, from automatic configuration entries, or from DHCP or DNS lookups.

Requirements

Platforms: Windows 98, Windows NT 4.0,
Windows Millennium Edition, Windows 2000,
Windows XP Home Edition, Windows XP Professional,
Windows .NET Server family,
.NET Compact Framework - Windows CE .NET,
Common Language Infrastructure (CLI) Standard

WebProxy.GetProxy Method

Returns the proxied URI for a request.

```
[Visual Basic]
Public Overridable Function GetProxy( _
   ByVal destination As Uri _
) As Uri Implements IWebProxy.GetProxy
```

```
[C#]
public virtual Uri GetProxy(
   Uri destination
);
[C++]
public: virtual Uri* GetProxy(
   Uri* destination
);
[JScript]
public function GetProxy(
   destination : Uri
) : Uri;
```

Parameters
destination
   The **Uri** of the requested Internet resource.

Return Value

The **Uri** of the Internet resource, if the resource is on the bypass list; otherwise, the **Uri** of the proxy.

Implements

IWebProxy.GetProxy

Remarks

The **GetProxy** method returns the URI that the **WebRequest** uses to access the Internet resource.

GetProxy compares *destination* with the contents of **BypassList** using the **IsBypassed** method. If **IsBypassed** returns **true**, **GetProxy** returns *destination* and the **WebRequest** does not use the proxy server.

If *destination* is not in **BypassList**, the **WebRequest** uses the proxy server, and the **Address** property is returned.

Example

Requirements

Platforms: Windows 98, Windows NT 4.0, Windows Millennium Edition, Windows 2000, Windows XP Home Edition, Windows XP Professional, Windows .NET Server family, .NET Compact Framework - Windows CE .NET, Common Language Infrastructure (CLI) Standard

WebProxy.IsBypassed Method

Indicates whether to use the proxy server for the specified host.

```
[Visual Basic]
Public Overridable Function IsBypassed( _
   ByVal host As Uri _
) As Boolean Implements IWebProxy.IsBypassed
[C#]
public virtual bool IsBypassed(
   Uri host
);
[C++]
public: virtual bool IsBypassed(
   Uri* host
);
[JScript]
public function IsBypassed(
   host : Uri
) : Boolean;
```

Parameters
host
   The **Uri** of the host to check for proxy use.

Return Value

true if the proxy server should not be used for *host*; otherwise, **false**.

Implements

IWebProxy.IsBypassed

Remarks

The **IsBypassed** method is used to determine whether to bypass the proxy server when accessing an Internet resource.

The **BypassProxyOnLocal** and **BypassList** properties control the return value of the **IsBypassed** method.

IsBypassed returns **true** under any of the following conditions.

- If **BypassProxyOnLocal** is **true** and *host* is a local URI. Local requests are identified by the lack of a period (.) in the URI, as in "http://webserver/".
- If *host* matches a regular expression in **BypassList**.
- If **Address** is a null reference (**Nothing** in Visual Basic).

All other conditions return **false**.

Requirements

Platforms: Windows 98, Windows NT 4.0, Windows Millennium Edition, Windows 2000, Windows XP Home Edition, Windows XP Professional, Windows .NET Server family, .NET Compact Framework - Windows CE .NET, Common Language Infrastructure (CLI) Standard

.NET Framework Security:

- **ArgumentException BypassList** contains an invalid regular expression.

WebProxy.ISerializable.GetObjectData Method

This member supports the .NET Framework infrastructure and is not intended to be used directly from your code.

```
[Visual Basic]
Private Sub GetObjectData( _
   ByVal serializationInfo As SerializationInfo, _
   ByVal streamingContext As StreamingContext _
) Implements ISerializable.GetObjectData
[C#]
void ISerializable.GetObjectData(
   SerializationInfo serializationInfo,
   StreamingContext streamingContext
);
[C++]
private: void ISerializable::GetObjectData(
   SerializationInfo* serializationInfo,
   StreamingContext streamingContext
);
[JScript]
private function ISerializable.GetObjectData(
   serializationInfo : SerializationInfo,
   streamingContext : StreamingContext
);
```

WebRequest Class

Makes a request to a Uniform Resource Identifier (URI). This is an abstract (**MustInherit** in Visual Basic) class.

System.Object
  System.MarshalByRefObject
    System.Net.WebRequest
      System.Net.FileWebRequest
      System.Net.HttpWebRequest

```
[Visual Basic]
<Serializable>
MustInherit Public Class WebRequest
   Inherits MarshalByRefObject
   Implements ISerializable
[C#]
[Serializable]
public abstract class WebRequest : MarshalByRefObject,
   ISerializable
[C++]
[Serializable]
public __gc __abstract class WebRequest : public
   MarshalByRefObject, ISerializable
[JScript]
public
   Serializable
abstract class WebRequest extends MarshalByRefObject
   implements ISerializable
```

Thread Safety

An application must run in full trust mode when using serialization.

Remarks

WebRequest is the abstract (**MustInherit** in Visual Basic) base class for the .NET Framework's request/response model for accessing data from the Internet. An application that uses the request/response model can request data from the Internet in a protocol-agnostic manner, in which the application works with instances of the **WebRequest** class while protocol-specific descendant classes carry out the details of the request.

Requests are sent from an application to a particular URI, such as a Web page on a server. The URI determines the proper descendant class to create from a list of **WebRequest** descendants registered for the application. **WebRequest** descendants are typically registered to handle a specific protocol, such as HTTP or FTP, but can be registered to handle a request to a specific server or path on a server.

The **WebRequest** class throws a **WebException** when errors occur while accessing an Internet resource. The **WebException.Status** property is one of the **WebExceptionStatus** values that indicates the source of the error. When **WebException.Status** is **WebExceptionStatus.ProtocolError**, the **Response** property contains the **WebResponse** received from the Internet resource.

Because the **WebRequest** class is an abstract (**MustInherit** in Visual Basic) class, the actual behavior of **WebRequest** instances at run time is determined by the descendant class returned by **WebRequest.Create** method. For more information about default values and exceptions, see the documentation for the descendant classes, such as **HttpWebRequest** and **FileWebRequest**.

> **Note** Use the **Create** method to initialize new **WebRequest** instances. Do not use the **WebRequest** constructor.

Notes to Inheritors: When you inherit from **WebRequest**, you must override the following members: **Method, RequestUri, Headers, ContentLength, ContentType, Credentials, PreAuthenticate, GetRequestStream, BeginGetRequestStream, EndGetRequestStream, GetResponse, BeginGetResponse,** and **EndGetResponse**. In addition, you must provide an implementation of the **IWebRequestCreate** interface, which defines the **Create** method used when you call **Create**. You must register the class that implements the **IWebRequestCreate** interface, using the **RegisterPrefix** method or the configuration file.

Example

[Visual Basic, C#] The following example shows how to create a **WebRequest** instance and return the response.

```
[Visual Basic]
' Initialize the WebRequest.
Dim myRequest As WebRequest =
WebRequest.Create("http://www.contoso.com")

' Return the response.
Dim myResponse As WebResponse = myRequest.GetResponse()

' Code to use the WebResponse goes here.
' Close the response to free resources.
myResponse.Close()
```

```
[C#]
// Initialize the WebRequest.
WebRequest myRequest = WebRequest.Create("http://www.contoso.com");

// Return the response.
WebResponse myResponse = myRequest.GetResponse();

// Code to use the WebResponse goes here.

// Close the response to free resources.
myResponse.Close();
```

Requirements

Namespace: System.Net

Platforms: Windows 98, Windows NT 4.0, Windows Millennium Edition, Windows 2000, Windows XP Home Edition, Windows XP Professional, Windows .NET Server family, .NET Compact Framework - Windows CE .NET

Assembly: System (in System.dll)

.NET Framework Security:
- **WebPermission** to access the requested URI or any URI that the request is redirected to. Associated enumeration: **Connect**.

WebRequest Constructor

Initializes a new instance of the **WebRequest** class.

Overload List

Initializes a new instance of the **WebRequest** class.

Supported by the .NET Compact Framework.

  [Visual Basic] **Protected Sub New()**

  [C#] **protected WebRequest();**

  [C++] **protected: WebRequest();**

  [JScript] **protected function WebRequest();**

Initializes a new instance of the **WebRequest** class from the specified instances of the **SerializationInfo** and **StreamingContext** classes.

> [Visual Basic] **Protected Sub New(SerializationInfo, StreamingContext)**
>
> [C#] **protected WebRequest(SerializationInfo, StreamingContext);**
>
> [C++] **protected: WebRequest(SerializationInfo*, StreamingContext);**
>
> [JScript] **protected function WebRequest(SerializationInfo, StreamingContext);**

Example

[Visual Basic, C#] The following example shows how to create a **WebRequest** instance by calling the **Create** method on the **WebRequest** class.

> [Visual Basic, C#] **Note** This example shows how to use one of the overloaded versions of the **WebRequest** constructor. For other examples that might be available, see the individual overload topics.

```
[Visual Basic]
Dim myRequest As WebRequest =
WebRequest.Create("http://www.contoso.com")
```

```
[C#]
WebRequest myRequest = WebRequest.Create("http://www.contoso.com");
```

WebRequest Constructor ()

Initializes a new instance of the **WebRequest** class.

```
[Visual Basic]
Protected Sub New()
[C#]
protected WebRequest();
[C++]
protected: WebRequest();
[JScript]
protected function WebRequest();
```

Remarks

Use the **Create** method to initialize new **WebRequest** instances. Do not use the constructor.

Example

[Visual Basic, C#] The following example shows how to create a **WebRequest** instance by calling the **Create** method on the **WebRequest** class.

```
[Visual Basic]
Dim myRequest As WebRequest =
WebRequest.Create("http://www.contoso.com")
```

```
[C#]
WebRequest myRequest = WebRequest.Create("http://www.contoso.com");
```

Requirements

Platforms: Windows 98, Windows NT 4.0, Windows Millennium Edition, Windows 2000, Windows XP Home Edition, Windows XP Professional, Windows .NET Server family, .NET Compact Framework - Windows CE .NET, Common Language Infrastructure (CLI) Standard

WebRequest Constructor (SerializationInfo, StreamingContext)

Initializes a new instance of the **WebRequest** class from the specified instances of the **SerializationInfo** and **StreamingContext** classes.

```
[Visual Basic]
Protected Sub New( _
   ByVal serializationInfo As SerializationInfo, _
   ByVal streamingContext As StreamingContext _
)
[C#]
protected WebRequest(
   SerializationInfo serializationInfo,
   StreamingContext streamingContext
);
[C++]
protected: WebRequest(
   SerializationInfo* serializationInfo,
   StreamingContext streamingContext
);
[JScript]
protected function WebRequest(
   serializationInfo : SerializationInfo,
   streamingContext : StreamingContext
);
```

Parameters

serializationInfo
> A **SerializationInfo** that contains the information required to serialize the new **WebRequest** instance.

streamingContext
> A **StreamingContext** that indicates the source of the serialized stream associated with the new **WebRequest** instance.

Exceptions

Exception Type	Condition
NotSupportedException	Any attempt is made to access the constructor, when the constructor is not overridden in a descendant class.

Remarks

When implemented by a descendant class, this constructor implements the **ISerializable** interface for the **WebRequest** descendant.

Notice that an application must run in full trust mode when using serialization.

Requirements

Platforms: Windows 98, Windows NT 4.0, Windows Millennium Edition, Windows 2000, Windows XP Home Edition, Windows XP Professional, Windows .NET Server family

WebRequest.ConnectionGroupName Property

When overridden in a descendant class, gets or sets the name of the connection group for the request.

```
[Visual Basic]
Public Overridable Property ConnectionGroupName As String
[C#]
public virtual string ConnectionGroupName {get; set;}
```

```
[C++]
public: __property virtual String* get_ConnectionGroupName();
public: __property virtual void set_ConnectionGroupName(String*);
[JScript]
public function get ConnectionGroupName() : String;
public function set ConnectionGroupName(String);
```

Property Value

The name of the connection group for the request.

Exceptions

Exception Type	Condition
NotSupportedException	Any attempt is made to get or set the property, when the property is not overridden in a descendant class.

Remarks

The **ConnectionGroupName** property associates specific requests within an application to one or more connection pools.

> **Note** The **WebRequest** class is an abstract (**MustInherit** in Visual Basic) class. The actual behavior of **WebRequest** instances at run time is determined by the descendant class returned by the **WebRequest.Create** method. For more information about default values and exceptions, see the documentation for the descendant classes, such as **HttpWebRequest** and **FileWebRequest**.

Notes to Inheritors: The **ConnectionGroupName** property typically associates a group of requests that share a set of credentials with a connection to an Internet resource to avoid potential security failures.

Requirements

Platforms: Windows 98, Windows NT 4.0, Windows Millennium Edition, Windows 2000, Windows XP Home Edition, Windows XP Professional, Windows .NET Server family, .NET Compact Framework - Windows CE .NET, Common Language Infrastructure (CLI) Standard

WebRequest.ContentLength Property

When overridden in a descendant class, gets or sets the content length of the request data being sent.

```
[Visual Basic]
Public Overridable Property ContentLength As Long
[C#]
public virtual long ContentLength {get; set;}
[C++]
public: __property virtual __int64 get_ContentLength();
public: __property virtual void set_ContentLength(__int64);
[JScript]
public function get ContentLength() : long;
public function set ContentLength(long);
```

Property Value

The number of bytes of request data being sent.

Exceptions

Exception Type	Condition
NotSupportedException	Any attempt is made to get or set the property, when the property is not overridden in a descendant class.

Remarks

The **ContentLength** property contains the number of bytes of data sent to the Internet resource by the **WebRequest** instance.

> **Note** The **WebRequest** class is an abstract (**MustInherit** in Visual Basic) class. The actual behavior of **WebRequest** instances at run time is determined by the descendant class returned by the **WebRequest.Create** method. For more information about default values and exceptions, see the documentation for the descendant classes, such as **HttpWebRequest** and **FileWebRequest**.

Example

The following example sets the **ContentLength** property to the amount of bytes in the outgoing byte buffer.

Requirements

Platforms: Windows 98, Windows NT 4.0, Windows Millennium Edition, Windows 2000, Windows XP Home Edition, Windows XP Professional, Windows .NET Server family, .NET Compact Framework - Windows CE .NET, Common Language Infrastructure (CLI) Standard

WebRequest.ContentType Property

When overridden in a descendant class, gets or sets the content type of the request data being sent.

```
[Visual Basic]
Public Overridable Property ContentType As String
[C#]
public virtual string ContentType {get; set;}
[C++]
public: __property virtual String* get_ContentType();
public: __property virtual void set_ContentType(String*);
[JScript]
public function get ContentType() : String;
public function set ContentType(String);
```

Property Value

The content type of the request data.

Exceptions

Exception Type	Condition
NotSupportedException	Any attempt is made to get or set the property, when the property is not overridden in a descendant class.

Remarks

The **ContentType** property contains the media type of the request. This is typically the MIME encoding of the content.

> **Note** The **WebRequest** class is an abstract (**MustInherit** in Visual Basic) class. The actual behavior of **WebRequest** instances at run time is determined by the descendant class returned by the **WebRequest.Create** method. For more information about default values and exceptions, see the documentation for the descendant classes, such as **HttpWebRequest** and **FileWebRequest**.

Example

The following example sets the **ContentType** property to the appropriate media type.

Requirements

Platforms: Windows 98, Windows NT 4.0, Windows Millennium Edition, Windows 2000, Windows XP Home Edition, Windows XP Professional, Windows .NET Server family, .NET Compact Framework - Windows CE .NET, Common Language Infrastructure (CLI) Standard

WebRequest.Credentials Property

When overridden in a descendant class, gets or sets the network credentials used for authenticating the request with the Internet resource.

```
[Visual Basic]
Public Overridable Property Credentials As ICredentials
[C#]
public virtual ICredentials Credentials {get; set;}
[C++]
public: __property virtual ICredentials* get_Credentials();
public: __property virtual void set_Credentials(ICredentials*);
[JScript]
public function get Credentials() : ICredentials;
public function set Credentials(ICredentials);
```

Property Value

An **ICredentials** containing the authentication credentials associated with the request. The default is a null reference (**Nothing** in Visual Basic).

Exceptions

Exception Type	Condition
NotSupportedException	Any attempt is made to get or set the property, when the property is not overridden in a descendant class.

Remarks

The **Credentials** property contains the authentication credentials required to access the Internet resource.

> **Note** The **WebRequest** class is an abstract (**MustInherit** in Visual Basic) class. The actual behavior of **WebRequest** instances at run time is determined by the descendant class returned by the **WebRequest.Create** method. For more information about default values and exceptions, see the documentation for the descendant classes, such as **HttpWebRequest** and **FileWebRequest**.

Example

[Visual Basic, C#, C++] The following example collects username and password information from the user and creates a NetworkCredential with this information. The Credentials property is set with this NetworkCredential. When the request is made, credentials stored in this property are used to validate the requesters access.

```
[Visual Basic]
' Create a new webrequest to the mentioned URL.
Dim myWebRequest As WebRequest = WebRequest.Create(url)
```

```
' Set 'Preauthenticate' property to true.
myWebRequest.PreAuthenticate = True
Console.WriteLine(ControlChars.Cr + "Please Enter ur credentials
for the requested Url")
Console.WriteLine("UserName")
Dim UserName As String = Console.ReadLine()
Console.WriteLine("Password")
Dim Password As String = Console.ReadLine()

' Create a New 'NetworkCredential' object.
Dim networkCredential As New NetworkCredential(UserName, Password)

' Associate the 'NetworkCredential' object with the
'WebRequest' object.
myWebRequest.Credentials = networkCredential

' Assign the response object of 'WebRequest' to a
'WebResponse' variable.
Dim myWebResponse As WebResponse = myWebRequest.GetResponse()
```

```
[C#]
            // Create a new webrequest to the mentioned URL.
        WebRequest myWebRequest=WebRequest.Create(url);

            // Set 'Preauthenticate' property to true.
Credentials will be sent with the request.
        myWebRequest.PreAuthenticate=true;

        Console.WriteLine("\nPlease Enter ur credentials
for the requested Url");
        Console.WriteLine("UserName");
        string UserName=Console.ReadLine();
        Console.WriteLine("Password");
        string Password=Console.ReadLine();

            // Create a New 'NetworkCredential' object.
        NetworkCredential networkCredential=new
NetworkCredential(UserName,Password);

            // Associate the 'NetworkCredential'
object with the 'WebRequest' object.
        myWebRequest.Credentials=networkCredential;

            // Assign the response object of 'WebRequest'
to a 'WebResponse' variable.
        WebResponse myWebResponse=myWebRequest.GetResponse();
```

```
[C++]
// Create a new webrequest to the mentioned URL.
WebRequest* myWebRequest=WebRequest::Create(url);

// Set 'Preauthenticate' property to true. Credentials
will be sent with the request.
myWebRequest->PreAuthenticate=true;

Console::WriteLine(S"\nPlease Enter ur credentials for
the requested Url");
Console::WriteLine(S"UserName");
String* UserName=Console::ReadLine();
Console::WriteLine(S"Password");
String* Password=Console::ReadLine();

// Create a New 'NetworkCredential' object.
NetworkCredential* networkCredential =
    new NetworkCredential(UserName, Password);

// Associate the 'NetworkCredential' object with the
'WebRequest' object.
myWebRequest->Credentials=networkCredential;

// Assign the response object of 'WebRequest' to a
'WebResponse' variable.
WebResponse* myWebResponse=myWebRequest->GetResponse();
```

Requirements

Platforms: Windows 98, Windows NT 4.0,
Windows Millennium Edition, Windows 2000,
Windows XP Home Edition, Windows XP Professional,
Windows .NET Server family,
.NET Compact Framework - Windows CE .NET,
Common Language Infrastructure (CLI) Standard

WebRequest.Headers Property

When overridden in a descendant class, gets or sets the collection of
header name/value pairs associated with the request.

```
[Visual Basic]
Public Overridable Property Headers As WebHeaderCollection
[C#]
public virtual WebHeaderCollection Headers {get; set;}
[C++]
public: __property virtual WebHeaderCollection* get_Headers();
public: __property virtual void set_Headers(WebHeaderCollection*);
[JScript]
public function get Headers() : WebHeaderCollection;
public function set Headers(WebHeaderCollection);
```

Property Value

A **WebHeaderCollection** containing the header name/value pairs
associated with this request.

Exceptions

Exception Type	Condition
NotSupportedException	Any attempt is made to get or set the property, when the property is not overridden in a descendant class.

Remarks

The **Headers** property contains a **WebHeaderCollection** instance
containing the header information to send to the Internet resource.

> **Note** The **WebRequest** class is an abstract (**MustInherit** in
> Visual Basic) class. The actual behavior of **WebRequest**
> instances at run time is determined by the descendant class
> returned by the **WebRequest.Create** method. For more
> information about default values and exceptions, see the
> documentation for the descendant classes, such as
> **HttpWebRequest** and **FileWebRequest**.

Example

[Visual Basic, C#, C++] The following example displays the header
name/value pairs associated with this request.

```
[Visual Basic]
' Create a new request to the mentioned URL.
Dim myWebRequest As WebRequest =
WebRequest.Create("http://www.contoso.com")

        ' Assign the response object of 'WebRequest'
to a 'WebResponse' variable.

Dim myWebResponse As WebResponse = myWebRequest.GetResponse()
        ' Release the resources of response object.

    myWebResponse.Close()
        Console.WriteLine(ControlChars.Cr + "The HttpHeaders are
" + ControlChars.Cr + "{0}", myWebRequest.Headers)
```

```
[C#]
        // Create a new request to the mentioned URL.
        WebRequest myWebRequest=WebRequest.Create("http://
www.contoso.com");

        // Assign the response object of 'WebRequest'
to a 'WebResponse' variable.
        WebResponse myWebResponse=myWebRequest.GetResponse();

        // Release the resources of response object.
        myWebResponse.Close();
        Console.WriteLine("\nThe HttpHeaders are
\n{0}",myWebRequest.Headers);
```

```
[C++]
// Create a new request to the mentioned URL.
WebRequest* myWebRequest=WebRequest::Create(S"http://www.contoso.com");

// Assign the response Object* of 'WebRequest' to a
'WebResponse' variable.
WebResponse* myWebResponse=myWebRequest->GetResponse();

// Release the resources of response Object*.
myWebResponse->Close();
Console::WriteLine(S"\nThe HttpHeaders are \n {0}",
myWebRequest->Headers);
```

Requirements

Platforms: Windows 98, Windows NT 4.0,
Windows Millennium Edition, Windows 2000,
Windows XP Home Edition, Windows XP Professional,
Windows .NET Server family,
.NET Compact Framework - Windows CE .NET,
Common Language Infrastructure (CLI) Standard

WebRequest.Method Property

When overridden in a descendant class, gets or sets the protocol
method to use in this request.

```
[Visual Basic]
Public Overridable Property Method As String
[C#]
public virtual string Method {get; set;}
[C++]
public: __property virtual String* get_Method();
public: __property virtual void set_Method(String*);
[JScript]
public function get Method() : String;
public function set Method(String);
```

Property Value

The protocol method to use in this request.

Exceptions

Exception Type	Condition
NotSupportedException	If the property is not overridden in a descendant class, any attempt is made to get or set the property.

Remarks

When overridden in a descendant class, the **Method** property
contains the request method to use in this request.

Note The **WebRequest** class is an abstract (**MustInherit** in Visual Basic) class. The actual behavior of **WebRequest** instances at run time is determined by the descendant class returned by the **WebRequest.Create** method. For more information about default values and exceptions, see the documentation for the descendant classes, such as **HttpWebRequest** and **FileWebRequest**.

Notes to Inheritors: The **Method** property can contain any valid request method for the protocol implemented. The default value must provide a default request/response transaction that does not require protocol-specific properties to be set.

Example

[Visual Basic, C#, C++] The following example sets the **Method** property to POST to indicate that the request will post data to the target host.

[Visual Basic]
```
    ' Create a new request to the mentioned URL.
        Dim myWebRequest As WebRequest =
WebRequest.Create("http://www.contoso.com/codesnippets/next.asp")

        ' Create an instance of the RequestState and assign
'myWebRequest' to it's request field.
        Dim myRequestState As New RequestState()
        myRequestState.request = myWebRequest
        myWebRequest.ContentType =
"application/x-www-form-urlencoded"

        ' Set the 'Method' prperty  to 'POST' to post
data to a Uri.
        myRequestState.request.Method = "POST"
        myRequestState.request.ContentType =
"application/x-www-form-urlencoded"

        ' Start the Asynchronous 'BeginGetRequestStream'
method call.
        Dim r As IAsyncResult =
CType(myWebRequest.BeginGetRequestStream(AddressOf
ReadCallback, myRequestState), IAsyncResult)

        ' Assign the response object of 'WebRequest'
to a 'WebResponse' variable.
        Dim myWebResponse As WebResponse =
myWebRequest.GetResponse()
        Console.WriteLine(ControlChars.Cr + "The string
entered has been successfully posted to the Uri")
        Console.WriteLine("Please wait for the response.......")
        Dim streamResponse As Stream =
myWebResponse.GetResponseStream()
        Dim streamRead As New StreamReader(streamResponse)
        Dim readBuff(256) As [Char]
        Dim count As Integer = streamRead.Read(readBuff, 0, 256)
        Console.WriteLine(ControlChars.Cr + "The contents of the HTML
page are ")
        While count > 0
            Dim outputData As New [String](readBuff, 0, count)
            Console.WriteLine(outputData)
            count = streamRead.Read(readBuff, 0, 256)
        End While

        ' Close the Stream Object.
    streamResponse.Close()
    streamRead.Close()
    allDone.WaitOne()

    ' Release the HttpWebResponse Resource.
     myWebResponse.Close()
    Catch e As WebException
        Console.WriteLine(ControlChars.Cr + "WebException Caught!")
        Console.WriteLine("Message :{0}", e.Message)
```

```
    Catch e As Exception
        Console.WriteLine(ControlChars.Cr + "Exception Caught!")
        Console.WriteLine("Message :{0}", e.Message)
    End Try
End Sub ' Main

    Private Shared Sub ReadCallback(asynchronousResult As IAsyncResult)
      Try

        ' State of request is set to asynchronous.
        Dim myRequestState As RequestState =
CType(asynchronousResult.AsyncState, RequestState)
        Dim myWebRequest2 As WebRequest = myRequestState.request

        ' End of the Asynchronus request.
        Dim streamResponse As Stream =
myWebRequest2.EndGetRequestStream(asynchronousResult)

        ' Create a string that is to be posted to the uri.
        Console.WriteLine(ControlChars.Cr + "Please enter a
string to be posted to
(http://www.contoso.com/codesnippets/next.asp) Uri:")
        Dim inputData As String = Console.ReadLine()
        Dim postData As String = "firstone" + ChrW(61) + inputData
        Dim encoder As New ASCIIEncoding()

        ' Convert  the string into a byte array.
        Dim ByteArray As Byte() = encoder.GetBytes(postData)

        ' Write data to the stream.
        streamResponse.Write(ByteArray, 0, postData.Length)
        streamResponse.Close()
        allDone.Set()

    Catch e As WebException
        Console.WriteLine(ControlChars.Cr + "WebException Caught!")
        Console.WriteLine("Message :{0}", e.Message)
    Catch e As Exception
        Console.WriteLine(ControlChars.Cr + "Exception Caught!")
        Console.WriteLine("Message :{0}", e.Message)
    End Try

    End Sub ' ReadCallback
```

[C#]
```
// Create a new request to the mentioned URL.
WebRequest myWebRequest= WebRequest.Create("http://www.contoso.com");

// Create an instance of the RequestState and assign
'myWebRequest' to it's request field.
RequestState myRequestState = new RequestState();
myRequestState.request = myWebRequest;
myWebRequest.ContentType="application/x-www-form-urlencoded";

// Set the 'Method' prperty  to 'POST' to post data to a Uri.
myRequestState.request.Method="POST";
myRequestState.request.ContentType="application/x-www-form-urlencoded";

// Start the Asynchronous 'BeginGetRequestStream' method call.
IAsyncResult r=(IAsyncResult)
myWebRequest.BeginGetRequestStream(new
AsyncCallback(ReadCallback),myRequestState);

// Assign the response object of 'WebRequest' to a 'WebResponse'
variable.
WebResponse myWebResponse=myWebRequest.GetResponse();
Console.WriteLine("\nThe string entered has been successfully
posted to the Uri");
Console.WriteLine("Please wait for the response.......");

Stream streamResponse=myWebResponse.GetResponseStream();
StreamReader streamRead = new StreamReader( streamResponse );
Char[] readBuff = new Char[256];
int count = streamRead.Read( readBuff, 0, 256 );
Console.WriteLine("\nThe contents of the HTML page are ");
```

```
while (count > 0)
{
    String outputData = new String(readBuff, 0, count);
    Console.Write(outputData);
    count = streamRead.Read(readBuff, 0, 256);
}

// Close the Stream Object.
streamResponse.Close();
streamRead.Close();
allDone.WaitOne();

// Release the HttpWebResponse Resource.
myWebResponse.Close();

    }
    catch(Exception e)
    {
Console.WriteLine(e.ToString());
    }

}
private static void ReadCallback(IAsyncResult asynchronousResult)
{
    try
    {

// State of request is set to asynchronous.
RequestState myRequestState=(RequestState)
asynchronousResult.AsyncState;
WebRequest  myWebRequest2=myRequestState.request;

// End of the Asynchronus request.
Stream
streamResponse=myWebRequest2.EndGetRequestStream(asynchronousResult);

// Create a string that is to be posted to the uri.
Console.WriteLine("\nPlease enter a string to be posted to
(http://www.contoso.com) Uri:");
string inputData=Console.ReadLine();
string postData="firstone="+inputData;
ASCIIEncoding encoder = new ASCIIEncoding();

// Convert  the string into a byte array.
byte[] ByteArray = encoder.GetBytes(postData);

// Write data to the stream.
streamResponse.Write(ByteArray,0,postData.Length);
streamResponse.Close();
allDone.Set();
    }
    catch(Exception e)
    {
Console.WriteLine(e.ToString());
    }
}
```

```
[C++]
// Create a new request to the mentioned URL.
WebRequest* myWebRequest=
WebRequest::Create(S"http://www.contoso.com");

// Create an instance of the RequestState and assign
'myWebRequest' to it's request field.
RequestState* myRequestState = new RequestState();
myRequestState->request = myWebRequest;
myWebRequest->ContentType=S"application/x-www-form-urlencoded";

// Set the 'Method' prperty  to 'POST' to post data to a Uri.
myRequestState->request->Method=S"POST";
myRequestState->request->
ContentType=S"application/x-www-form-urlencoded";

// Start the Asynchronous 'BeginGetRequestStream' method call.
IAsyncResult* r =
```

```
        dynamic_cast<IAsyncResult*> (myWebRequest->
    BeginGetRequestStream(new AsyncCallback(r,
        WebRequest_BeginGetRequeststream::ReadCallback), myRequestState));

    // Assign the response Object* of 'WebRequest' to a
    'WebResponse' variable.
    WebResponse* myWebResponse = myWebRequest->GetResponse();
    Console::WriteLine(S"\nThe String* entered has been successfully
    posted to the Uri");
    Console::WriteLine(S"Please wait for the response.......");

    Stream* streamResponse = myWebResponse->GetResponseStream();
    StreamReader* streamRead = new StreamReader(streamResponse);
    Char readBuff[] = new Char[256];
    int count = streamRead->Read(readBuff, 0, 256);
    Console::WriteLine(S"\nThe contents of the HTML page are ");

    while (count > 0) {
        String* outputData = new String(readBuff, 0, count);
        Console::Write(outputData);
        count = streamRead->Read(readBuff, 0, 256);
    }

    // Close the Stream Object.
    streamResponse->Close();
    streamRead->Close();
    WebRequest_BeginGetRequeststream::allDone->WaitOne();

    // Release the HttpWebResponse Resource.
    myWebResponse->Close();

    } catch (Exception* e) {
    Console::WriteLine(e);
    }
}
```

Requirements

Platforms: Windows 98, Windows NT 4.0,
Windows Millennium Edition, Windows 2000,
Windows XP Home Edition, Windows XP Professional,
Windows .NET Server family,
.NET Compact Framework - Windows CE .NET,
Common Language Infrastructure (CLI) Standard

WebRequest.PreAuthenticate Property

When overridden in a descendant class, indicates whether to
preauthenticate the request.

```
[Visual Basic]
Public Overridable Property PreAuthenticate As Boolean
[C#]
public virtual bool PreAuthenticate {get; set;}
[C++]
public: __property virtual bool get_PreAuthenticate();
public: __property virtual void set_PreAuthenticate(bool);
[JScript]
public function get PreAuthenticate() : Boolean;
public function set PreAuthenticate(Boolean);
```

Property Value

true to preauthenticate; otherwise, **false**.

Exceptions

Exception Type	Condition
NotSupportedException	Any attempt is made to get or set the property, when the property is not overridden in a descendant class.

Remarks

The **PreAuthenticate** property indicates whether to send authentication information with the initial request. When **PreAuthenticate** is **false**, the **WebRequest** waits for an authentication challenge before sending authentication information.

> **Note** The **WebRequest** class is an abstract (**MustInherit** in Visual Basic) class. The actual behavior of **WebRequest** instances at run time is determined by the descendant class returned by the **WebRequest.Create** method. For more information about default values and exceptions, see the documentation for the descendant classes, such as **HttpWebRequest** and **FileWebRequest**.

Example

See related example in the **System.Net.WebRequest** method topic.

Requirements

Platforms: Windows 98, Windows NT 4.0, Windows Millennium Edition, Windows 2000, Windows XP Home Edition, Windows XP Professional, Windows .NET Server family, .NET Compact Framework - Windows CE .NET, Common Language Infrastructure (CLI) Standard

WebRequest.Proxy Property

When overridden in a descendant class, gets or sets the network proxy to use to access this Internet resource.

```
[Visual Basic]
Public Overridable Property Proxy As IWebProxy
[C#]
public virtual IWebProxy Proxy {get; set;}
[C++]
public: __property virtual IWebProxy* get_Proxy();
public: __property virtual void set_Proxy(IWebProxy*);
[JScript]
public function get Proxy() : IWebProxy;
public function set Proxy(IWebProxy);
```

Property Value

The **IWebProxy** to use to access the Internet resource.

Exceptions

Exception Type	Condition
NotSupportedException	Any attempt is made to get or set the property, when the property is not overridden in a descendant class.

Remarks

The **Proxy** property identifies the network proxy that the request uses to access the Internet resource. The request is made through the proxy server rather than directly to the Internet resource.

> **Note** The **WebRequest** class is an abstract (**MustInherit** in Visual Basic) class. The actual behavior of **WebRequest** instances at run time is determined by the descendant class returned by the **WebRequest.Create** method. For more information about default values and exceptions, see the documentation for the descendant classes, such as **HttpWebRequest** and **FileWebRequest**.

Requirements

Platforms: Windows 98, Windows NT 4.0, Windows Millennium Edition, Windows 2000, Windows XP Home Edition, Windows XP Professional, Windows .NET Server family, .NET Compact Framework - Windows CE .NET, Common Language Infrastructure (CLI) Standard

WebRequest.RequestUri Property

When overridden in a descendant class, gets the URI of the Internet resource associated with the request.

```
[Visual Basic]
Public Overridable ReadOnly Property RequestUri As Uri
[C#]
public virtual Uri RequestUri {get;}
[C++]
public: __property virtual Uri* get_RequestUri();
[JScript]
public function get RequestUri() : Uri;
```

Property Value

A **Uri** representing the resource associated with the request

Exceptions

Exception Type	Condition
NotSupportedException	Any attempt is made to get or set the property, when the property is not overridden in a descendant class.

Remarks

When overridden in a descendant class, the **RequestUri** property contains the **Uri** instance that **Create** method uses to create the request.

> **Note** The **WebRequest** class is an abstract (**MustInherit** in Visual Basic) class. The actual behavior of **WebRequest** instances at run time is determined by the descendant class returned by the **WebRequest.Create** method. For more information about default values and exceptions, see the documentation for the descendant classes, such as **HttpWebRequest** and **FileWebRequest**.

Notes to Inheritors: **RequestUri** must contain the original **Uri** instance passed to the **Create** method. If the protocol is able to redirect the request to a different URI to service the request, the descendant must provide a property to contain the URI that actually services the request

Example

[Visual Basic, C#, C++] The following example checks the **RequestUri** property to determine the site originally requested.

```
[Visual Basic]
' Create a new WebRequest Object to the mentioned URL.
Dim myWebRequest As WebRequest =                              ⌐
WebRequest.Create("http://www.example.com")
Console.WriteLine(ControlChars.Cr + "The Uri that responded  ⌐
for the Request is   {0}", myWebRequest.RequestUri)
' Assign the response object of 'WebRequest' to a            ⌐
'WebResponse' variable.
Dim myWebResponse As WebResponse = myWebRequest.GetResponse()
' Print the HTML contents of the page to the console.
Dim streamResponse As Stream = myWebResponse.GetResponseStream()
```

```
Dim streamRead As New StreamReader(streamResponse)
Dim readBuff(256) As [Char]
Dim count As Integer = streamRead.Read(readBuff, 0, 256)
Console.WriteLine(ControlChars.Cr + "The Uri that responded
for the Request is  {0}", myWebRequest.RequestUri)
```

```
[C#]
// Create a new WebRequest Object to the mentioned URL.
WebRequest myWebRequest=WebRequest.Create("http://www.example.com");
Console.WriteLine("\nThe Uri that responded for the Request
is  {0}",myWebRequest.RequestUri);
// Assign the response object of 'WebRequest' to a
'WebResponse' variable.
WebResponse myWebResponse=myWebRequest.GetResponse();
// Print the HTML contents of the page to the console.
Stream streamResponse=myWebResponse.GetResponseStream();
StreamReader streamRead = new StreamReader( streamResponse );
Char[] readBuff = new Char[256];
int count = streamRead.Read( readBuff, 0, 256 );
Console.WriteLine("\nThe Uri that responded for the Request
is '{0}'",myWebRequest.RequestUri);
```

```
[C++]
// Create a new WebRequest Object to the mentioned URL.
WebRequest* myWebRequest=WebRequest::Create(S"http://www.google.com");
Console::WriteLine(S"\nThe Uri that responded for the Request is {0}",
    myWebRequest->RequestUri);

// Assign the response Object* of 'WebRequest' to a
'WebResponse' variable.
WebResponse* myWebResponse = myWebRequest->GetResponse();

// Print the HTML contents of the page to the console.
Stream* streamResponse = myWebResponse->GetResponseStream();
StreamReader* streamRead = new StreamReader(streamResponse);
Char readBuff[] = new Char[256];
int count = streamRead->Read(readBuff, 0, 256);
Console::WriteLine(S"\nThe Uri that responded for the
Request is ' {0}'",
    myWebRequest->RequestUri);
```

Requirements

Platforms: Windows 98, Windows NT 4.0, Windows Millennium Edition, Windows 2000, Windows XP Home Edition, Windows XP Professional, Windows .NET Server family, .NET Compact Framework - Windows CE .NET, Common Language Infrastructure (CLI) Standard

WebRequest.Timeout Property

Gets or sets the length of time before the request times out.

```
[Visual Basic]
Public Overridable Property Timeout As Integer
[C#]
public virtual int Timeout {get; set;}
[C++]
public: __property virtual int get_Timeout();
public: __property virtual void set_Timeout(int);
[JScript]
public function get Timeout() : int;
public function set Timeout(int);
```

Property Value

The length of time, in milliseconds, until the request times out, or the value **Timeout.Infinite** to indicate that the request does not time out.

Exceptions

Exception Type	Condition
NotSupportedException	Any attempt is made to get or set the property, when the property is not overridden in a descendant class.

Remarks

The **Timeout** property indicates the length of time, in milliseconds, until the request times out and throws a **WebException**. The **Timeout** property affects only synchronous requests made with the **GetResponse** method. To time out asynchronous requests, use the **Abort** method.

> **Note** The **WebRequest** class is an abstract (**MustInherit** in Visual Basic) class. The actual behavior of **WebRequest** instances at run time is determined by the descendant class returned by the **WebRequest.Create** method. For more information about default values and exceptions, see the documentation for the descendant classes, such as **HttpWebRequest** and **FileWebRequest**.

Notes to Inheritors: Descendant classes signal a timeout by throwing a **WebException** with the **Status** field set to **WebExceptionStatus.Timeout**. When **Timeout** is set to **Timeout.Infinite** the descendant class does not time out.

Requirements

Platforms: Windows 98, Windows NT 4.0, Windows Millennium Edition, Windows 2000, Windows XP Home Edition, Windows XP Professional, Windows .NET Server family, .NET Compact Framework - Windows CE .NET, Common Language Infrastructure (CLI) Standard

WebRequest.Abort Method

Cancels an asynchronous request to an Internet resource.

```
[Visual Basic]
Public Overridable Sub Abort()
[C#]
public virtual void Abort();
[C++]
public: virtual void Abort();
[JScript]
public function Abort();
```

Exceptions

Exception Type	Condition
NotSupportedException	Any attempt is made to access the method, when the method is not overridden in a descendant class.

Remarks

The **Abort** method cancels asynchronous requests to Internet resources started with the **BeginGetResponse** method.

> **Note** The **WebRequest** class is an abstract (**MustInherit** in Visual Basic) class. The actual behavior of **WebRequest** instances at run time is determined by the descendant class returned by the **WebRequest.Create** method. For more information about default values and exceptions, see the documentation for the descendant classes, such as **HttpWebRequest** and **FileWebRequest**.

Requirements

Platforms: Windows 98, Windows NT 4.0,
Windows Millennium Edition, Windows 2000,
Windows XP Home Edition, Windows XP Professional,
Windows .NET Server family,
.NET Compact Framework - Windows CE .NET,
Common Language Infrastructure (CLI) Standard

WebRequest.BeginGetRequestStream Method

When overridden in a descendant class, provides an asynchronous
version of the **GetRequestStream** method.

```
[Visual Basic]
Public Overridable Function BeginGetRequestStream( _
   ByVal callback As AsyncCallback, _
   ByVal state As Object _
) As IAsyncResult
[C#]
public virtual IAsyncResult BeginGetRequestStream(
   AsyncCallback callback,
   object state
);
[C++]
public: virtual IAsyncResult* BeginGetRequestStream(
   AsyncCallback* callback,
   Object* state
);
[JScript]
public function BeginGetRequestStream(
   callback : AsyncCallback,
   state : Object
) : IAsyncResult;
```

Parameters

callback
   The **AsyncCallback** delegate.

state
   An object containing state information for this asynchronous
   request.

Return Value

An **IAsyncResult** that references the asynchronous request.

Exceptions

Exception Type	Condition
NotSupportedException	Any attempt is made to access the method, when the method is not overridden in a descendant class.

Remarks

The **BeginGetRequestStream** method starts an asynchronous
request for a stream used to send data to an Internet resource. The
callback method that implements the **AsyncCallback** delegate uses
the **EndGetRequestStream** method to return the request stream.

> **Note** The **WebRequest** class is an abstract (**MustInherit** in
> Visual Basic) class. The actual behavior of **WebRequest**
> instances at run time is determined by the descendant class
> returned by the **WebRequest.Create** method. For more
> information about default values and exceptions, see the
> documentation for the descendant classes, such as
> **HttpWebRequest** and **FileWebRequest**.

Requirements

Platforms: Windows 98, Windows NT 4.0,
Windows Millennium Edition, Windows 2000,
Windows XP Home Edition, Windows XP Professional,
Windows .NET Server family,
.NET Compact Framework - Windows CE .NET,
Common Language Infrastructure (CLI) Standard

WebRequest.BeginGetResponse Method

When overridden in a descendant class, begins an asynchronous
request for an Internet resource.

```
[Visual Basic]
Public Overridable Function BeginGetResponse( _
   ByVal callback As AsyncCallback, _
   ByVal state As Object _
) As IAsyncResult
[C#]
public virtual IAsyncResult BeginGetResponse(
   AsyncCallback callback,
   object state
);
[C++]
public: virtual IAsyncResult* BeginGetResponse(
   AsyncCallback* callback,
   Object* state
);
[JScript]
public function BeginGetResponse(
   callback : AsyncCallback,
   state : Object
) : IAsyncResult;
```

Parameters

callback
   The **AsyncCallback** delegate.

state
   An object containing state information for this asynchronous
   request.

Return Value

An **IAsyncResult** that references the asynchronous request.

Exceptions

Exception Type	Condition
NotSupportedException	Any attempt is made to access the method, when the method is not overridden in a descendant class.

Remarks

The **BeginGetResponse** method starts an asynchronous request for
a response. The callback method that implements the
AsyncCallback delegate uses the **EndGetResponse** method to
return the **WebResponse** from the Internet resource.

> **Note** The **WebRequest** class is an abstract (**MustInherit** in
> Visual Basic) class. The actual behavior of **WebRequest**
> instances at run time is determined by the descendant class
> returned by the **WebRequest.Create** method. For more
> information about default values and exceptions, see the
> documentation for the descendant classes, such as
> **HttpWebRequest** and **FileWebRequest**.

Requirements

Platforms: Windows 98, Windows NT 4.0,
Windows Millennium Edition, Windows 2000,
Windows XP Home Edition, Windows XP Professional,
Windows .NET Server family,
.NET Compact Framework - Windows CE .NET,
Common Language Infrastructure (CLI) Standard

WebRequest.Create Method

Initializes a new **WebRequest**.

Overload List

Initializes a new **WebRequest** instance for the specified URI scheme.

Supported by the .NET Compact Framework.

[Visual Basic] **Overloads Public Shared Function Create(String) As WebRequest**

[C#] **public static WebRequest Create(string);**

[C++] **public: static WebRequest* Create(String*);**

[JScript] **public static function Create(String) : WebRequest;**

Initializes a new **WebRequest** instance for the specified URI scheme.

Supported by the .NET Compact Framework.

[Visual Basic] **Overloads Public Shared Function Create(Uri) As WebRequest**

[C#] **public static WebRequest Create(Uri);**

[C++] **public: static WebRequest* Create(Uri*);**

[JScript] **public static function Create(Uri) : WebRequest;**

Example

[Visual Basic, C#, C++] The following example uses **Create** to instantiate an **HttpWebRequest** instance. A Uri representing the target url is used as the constructor parameter.

[Visual Basic, C#, C++] **Note** This example shows how to use one of the overloaded versions of **Create**. For other examples that might be available, see the individual overload topics.

```
[Visual Basic]
' Create a new 'Uri' object with the specified string.
Dim myUri As New Uri("http://www.contoso.com")
' Create a new request to the above mentioned URL.
Dim myWebRequest As WebRequest = WebRequest.Create(myUri)
'  Assign the response object of 'WebRequest' to a
'WebResponse' variable.
Dim myWebResponse As WebResponse = myWebRequest.GetResponse()
```

```
[C#]
// Create a new 'Uri' object with the specified string.
Uri myUri =new Uri("http://www.contoso.com");
// Create a new request to the above mentioned URL.
WebRequest myWebRequest= WebRequest.Create(myUri);
// Assign the response object of 'WebRequest' to a
'WebResponse' variable.
WebResponse myWebResponse= myWebRequest.GetResponse();
```

```
[C++]
// Create a new 'Uri' object with the specified String*.
Uri* myUri = new Uri(S"http://www.contoso.com");
// Create a new request to the above mentioned URL.
WebRequest* myWebRequest= WebRequest::Create(myUri);
// Assign the response object of 'WebRequest' to a
'WebResponse' variable.
WebResponse* myWebResponse = myWebRequest->GetResponse();
```

WebRequest.Create Method (String)

Initializes a new **WebRequest** instance for the specified URI scheme.

```
[Visual Basic]
Overloads Public Shared Function Create( _
   ByVal requestUriString As String _
) As WebRequest
[C#]
public static WebRequest Create(
   string requestUriString
);
[C++]
public: static WebRequest* Create(
   String* requestUriString
);
[JScript]
public static function Create(
   requestUriString : String
) : WebRequest;
```

Parameters

requestUriString
   The URI that identifies the Internet resource.

Return Value

A **WebRequest** descendant for the specific URI scheme.

Exceptions

Exception Type	Condition
NotSupportedException	The request scheme specified in *requestUriString* has not been registered.
ArgumentNullException	*requestUriString* is a null reference (**Nothing** in Visual Basic).
SecurityException	The caller does not have permission to connect to the requested URI or a URI that the request is redirected to.
UriFormatException	The URI specified in *requestUriString* is not a valid URI.

Remarks

The **Create** method returns a descendant of the **WebRequest** class determined at run time as the closest registered match for *requestUri*.

For example, when a URI beginning with http:// is passed in *requestUri*, an **HttpWebRequest** is returned by **Create**. If a URI beginning with file:// is passed instead, the **Create** method will return a **FileWebRequest** instance.

The .NET Framework includes support for the http://, https://, and file:// URI schemes. Custom **WebRequest** descendants to handle other requests are registered with the **RegisterPrefix** method.

The **Create** method uses the *requestUriString* parameter to create a **Uri** instance that it passes to the new **WebRequest**.

Example

[Visual Basic, C#, C++] The following example uses **Create** to instantiate an **HttpWebRequest** instance. A string representing the target url is used as the constructor parameter.

```
[Visual Basic]
Dim ourUri As New Uri(url)
' Create a 'WebRequest' object with the specified url.

Dim myWebRequest As WebRequest = WebRequest.Create(url)

' Send the 'WebRequest' and wait for response.
Dim myWebResponse As WebResponse = myWebRequest.GetResponse()

' "ResponseUri" property is used to get the actual Uri from
' where the response was attained.
If ourUri.Equals(myWebResponse.ResponseUri) Then
    Console.WriteLine(ControlChars.Cr + "Request Url : {0}
was not redirected", url)
Else
    Console.WriteLine(ControlChars.Cr + "Request Url : {0}
was redirected to {1}", url, myWebResponse.ResponseUri)
End If

' Release resources of response object.
myWebResponse.Close()

[C#]
Uri ourUri = new Uri(url);

// Create a 'WebRequest' object with the specified url.
WebRequest myWebRequest = WebRequest.Create(url);

// Send the 'WebRequest' and wait for response.
WebResponse myWebResponse = myWebRequest.GetResponse();

// Use "ResponseUri" property to get the actual Uri from
// where the response was attained.
if (ourUri.Equals(myWebResponse.ResponseUri))
    Console.WriteLine("\nRequest Url : {0} was not redirected",url);
else
    Console.WriteLine("\nRequest Url : {0} was redirected to
{1}",url,myWebResponse.ResponseUri);
// Release resources of response object.
myWebResponse.Close();

[C++]
Uri* ourUri = new Uri(url);

// Create a 'WebRequest' Object* with the specified url.
WebRequest* myWebRequest = WebRequest::Create(url);

// Send the 'WebRequest' and wait for response.
WebResponse* myWebResponse = myWebRequest->GetResponse();

// Use S"ResponseUri" property to get the actual Uri from
// where the response was attained.
if (ourUri->Equals(myWebResponse->ResponseUri))
    Console::WriteLine(S"\nRequest Url : {0} was not redirected", url);
else
    Console::WriteLine(S"\nRequest Url : {0} was redirected
to {1}", url, myWebResponse->ResponseUri);
// Release resources of response Object*.
myWebResponse->Close();
```

Requirements

Platforms: Windows 98, Windows NT 4.0,
Windows Millennium Edition, Windows 2000,
Windows XP Home Edition, Windows XP Professional,
Windows .NET Server family,
.NET Compact Framework - Windows CE .NET,
Common Language Infrastructure (CLI) Standard

WebRequest.Create Method (Uri)

Initializes a new **WebRequest** instance for the specified URI scheme.

```
[Visual Basic]
Overloads Public Shared Function Create( _
    ByVal requestUri As Uri _
) As WebRequest
[C#]
public static WebRequest Create(
    Uri requestUri
);
[C++]
public: static WebRequest* Create(
    Uri* requestUri
);
[JScript]
public static function Create(
    requestUri : Uri
) : WebRequest;
```

Parameters

requestUri
    A **Uri** containing the URI of the requested resource.

Return Value

A **WebRequest** descendant for the specified URI scheme.

Exceptions

Exception Type	Condition
NotSupportedException	The request scheme specified in *requestUri* is not registered.
ArgumentNullException	*requestUri* is a null reference (**Nothing** in Visual Basic).
SecurityException	The caller does not have permission to connect to the requested URI or a URI that the request is redirected to.

Remarks

The **Create** method returns a descendant of the **WebRequest** class determined at run time as the closest registered match for *requestUri*.

For example, if you create a **WebRequest** descendant, Handler1, to handle requests to http://www.contoso.com/text/ and another named Handler2 to handle requests to http://www.contoso.com/code/, you can use **Create** method to return the WebRequest descendant associated with either specified URI.

To return a descendant of the **WebRequest** class based on only the scheme portion of a URI, use the **CreateDefault** method.

The .NET Framework includes support for the http://, https://, and file:// URI schemes. Custom **WebRequest** descendants to handle other requests are registered with the **RegisterPrefix** method.

Example

[Visual Basic, C#, C++] The following example uses **Create** to instantiate an **HttpWebRequest** instance. A Uri representing the target url is used as the constructor parameter.

```
[Visual Basic]
' Create a new 'Uri' object with the specified string.
Dim myUri As New Uri("http://www.contoso.com")
' Create a new request to the above mentioned URL.
Dim myWebRequest As WebRequest = WebRequest.Create(myUri)
```

```
' Assign the response object of 'WebRequest' to a
'WebResponse' variable.
Dim myWebResponse As WebResponse = myWebRequest.GetResponse()

[C#]
// Create a new 'Uri' object with the specified string.
Uri myUri =new Uri("http://www.contoso.com");
// Create a new request to the above mentioned URL.
WebRequest myWebRequest= WebRequest.Create(myUri);
// Assign the response object of 'WebRequest' to a
'WebResponse' variable.
WebResponse myWebResponse= myWebRequest.GetResponse();

[C++]
// Create a new 'Uri' object with the specified String*.
Uri* myUri = new Uri(S"http://www.contoso.com");
// Create a new request to the above mentioned URL.
WebRequest* myWebRequest= WebRequest::Create(myUri);
// Assign the response object of 'WebRequest' to a
'WebResponse' variable.
WebResponse* myWebResponse = myWebRequest->GetResponse();
```

Requirements

Platforms: Windows 98, Windows NT 4.0,
Windows Millennium Edition, Windows 2000,
Windows XP Home Edition, Windows XP Professional,
Windows .NET Server family,
.NET Compact Framework - Windows CE .NET,
Common Language Infrastructure (CLI) Standard

WebRequest.CreateDefault Method

Initializes a new **WebRequest** instance for the specified URI
scheme.

```
[Visual Basic]
Public Shared Function CreateDefault( _
   ByVal requestUri As Uri _
) As WebRequest
[C#]
public static WebRequest CreateDefault(
   Uri requestUri
);
[C++]
public: static WebRequest* CreateDefault(
   Uri* requestUri
);
[JScript]
public static function CreateDefault(
   requestUri : Uri
) : WebRequest;
```

Parameters
requestUri
   A **Uri** containing the URI of the requested resource.

Return Value
A **WebRequest** descendant for the specified URI scheme.

Exceptions

Exception Type	Condition
NotSupportedException	The request scheme specified in *requestUri* is not registered.
ArgumentNullException	*requestUri* is a null reference (**Nothing** in Visual Basic).
SecurityException	The caller does not have permission to connect to the requested URI or a URI that the request is redirected to.

Remarks

The **CreateDefault** method returns a **WebRequest** descendant
instance based on only the scheme portion of a URI.

For example, when a URI beginning with http:// is passed in
requestUri, an **HttpWebRequest** is returned by **CreateDefault**. If a
URI beginning with file:// is passed instead, the **CreateDefault**
method will return a **FileWebRequest**.

Requirements

Platforms: Windows 98, Windows NT 4.0,
Windows Millennium Edition, Windows 2000,
Windows XP Home Edition, Windows XP Professional,
Windows .NET Server family,
.NET Compact Framework - Windows CE .NET,
Common Language Infrastructure (CLI) Standard

WebRequest.EndGetRequestStream Method

When overridden in a descendant class, returns a **Stream** for writing
data to the Internet resource.

```
[Visual Basic]
Public Overridable Function EndGetRequestStream( _
   ByVal asyncResult As IAsyncResult _
) As Stream
[C#]
public virtual Stream EndGetRequestStream(
   IAsyncResult asyncResult
);
[C++]
public: virtual Stream* EndGetRequestStream(
   IAsyncResult* asyncResult
);
[JScript]
public function EndGetRequestStream(
   asyncResult : IAsyncResult
) : Stream;
```

Parameters
asyncResult
   An **IAsyncResult** that references a pending request for a stream.

Return Value
A **Stream** to write data to.

Exceptions

Exception Type	Condition
NotSupportedException	Any attempt is made to access the method, when the method is not overridden in a descendant class.

Remarks

The **EndGetRequestStream** method completes an asynchronous
stream request that was started by the **BeginGetRequestStream**
method.

> **Note** To avoid timing issues with garbage collection, be sure to
> close the response stream by calling the **Close** method on the
> stream returned by **GetResponseStream** after calling
> **EndGetResponse**.

Note The **WebRequest** class is an abstract (**MustInherit** in Visual Basic) class. The actual behavior of **WebRequest** instances at run time is determined by the descendant class returned by the **WebRequest.Create** method. For more information about default values and exceptions, see the documentation for the descendant classes, such as **HttpWebRequest** and **FileWebRequest**.

Requirements

Platforms: Windows 98, Windows NT 4.0, Windows Millennium Edition, Windows 2000, Windows XP Home Edition, Windows XP Professional, Windows .NET Server family, .NET Compact Framework - Windows CE .NET, Common Language Infrastructure (CLI) Standard

WebRequest.EndGetResponse Method

When overridden in a descendant class, returns a **WebResponse**.

```
[Visual Basic]
Public Overridable Function EndGetResponse( _
    ByVal asyncResult As IAsyncResult _
) As WebResponse
[C#]
public virtual WebResponse EndGetResponse(
    IAsyncResult asyncResult
);
[C++]
public: virtual WebResponse* EndGetResponse(
    IAsyncResult* asyncResult
);
[JScript]
public function EndGetResponse(
    asyncResult : IAsyncResult
) : WebResponse;
```

Parameters

asyncResult

An **IAsyncResult** that references a pending request for a response.

Return Value

A **WebResponse** that contains a response to the Internet request.

Exceptions

Exception Type	Condition
NotSupportedException	Any attempt is made to access the method, when the method is not overridden in a descendant class.

Remarks

The **EndGetResponse** method completes an asynchronous request for an Internet resource that was started with the **BeginGetResponse** method.

Note The **WebRequest** class is an abstract (**MustInherit** in Visual Basic) class. The actual behavior of **WebRequest** instances at run time is determined by the descendant class returned by the **WebRequest.Create** method. For more information about default values and exceptions, see the documentation for the descendant classes, such as **HttpWebRequest** and **FileWebRequest**.

Requirements

Platforms: Windows 98, Windows NT 4.0, Windows Millennium Edition, Windows 2000, Windows XP Home Edition, Windows XP Professional, Windows .NET Server family, .NET Compact Framework - Windows CE .NET, Common Language Infrastructure (CLI) Standard

WebRequest.GetRequestStream Method

When overridden in a descendant class, returns a **Stream** for writing data to the Internet resource.

```
[Visual Basic]
Public Overridable Function GetRequestStream() As Stream
[C#]
public virtual Stream GetRequestStream();
[C++]
public: virtual Stream* GetRequestStream();
[JScript]
public function GetRequestStream() : Stream;
```

Return Value

A **Stream** for writing data to the Internet resource.

Exceptions

Exception Type	Condition
NotSupportedException	Any attempt is made to access the method, when the method is not overridden in a descendant class.

Remarks

The **GetRequestStream** method initiates a request to send data to the Internet resource and returns a **Stream** instance for sending data to the Internet resource.

The **GetRequestStream** method provides synchronous access to the **Stream**. For asynchronous access, use the **BeginGetRequestStream** and **EndGetRequestStream** methods.

Note The **WebRequest** class is an abstract (**MustInherit** in Visual Basic) class. The actual behavior of **WebRequest** instances at run time is determined by the descendant class returned by the **WebRequest.Create** method. For more information about default values and exceptions, see the documentation for the descendant classes, such as **HttpWebRequest** and **FileWebRequest**.

Example

The following example uses the **GetRequestStream** method to obtain a stream and then writes data that stream.

Requirements

Platforms: Windows 98, Windows NT 4.0, Windows Millennium Edition, Windows 2000, Windows XP Home Edition, Windows XP Professional, Windows .NET Server family, .NET Compact Framework - Windows CE .NET, Common Language Infrastructure (CLI) Standard

WebRequest.GetResponse Method

When overridden in a descendant class, returns a response to an Internet request.

```
[Visual Basic]
Public Overridable Function GetResponse() As WebResponse
[C#]
public virtual WebResponse GetResponse();
[C++]
public: virtual WebResponse* GetResponse();
[JScript]
public function GetResponse() : WebResponse;
```

Return Value

A **WebResponse** containing the response to the Internet request.

Exceptions

Exception Type	Condition
NotSupportedException	Any attempt is made to access the method, when the method is not overridden in a descendant class.

Remarks

The **GetResponse** method sends a request to an Internet resource and returns a **WebResponse** instance. If the request has already been initiated by a call to **GetRequestStream**, the **GetResponse** method completes the request and returns any response.

The **GetResponse** method provides synchronous access to the **WebResponse**. For asynchronous access, use the **BeginGetResponse** and **EndGetResponse** methods.

> **Note** The **WebRequest** class is an abstract (**MustInherit** in Visual Basic) class. The actual behavior of **WebRequest** instances at run time is determined by the descendant class returned by the **WebRequest.Create** method. For more information about default values and exceptions, see the documentation for the descendant classes, such as **HttpWebRequest** and **FileWebRequest**.

Example

[Visual Basic, C#, C++] The following example sets the **Timeout** property to 10000 milliseconds. If the timeout period expires before the resource can be returned, a **WebException** is thrown.

```
[Visual Basic]
' Create a new WebRequest Object to the mentioned URL.
Dim myWebRequest As WebRequest =
WebRequest.Create("http://www.contoso.com")
Console.WriteLine(ControlChars.Cr + "The Timeout time of
the request before setting is : {0} milliseconds",
myWebRequest.Timeout)

' Set the 'Timeout' property in Milliseconds.
        myWebRequest.Timeout = 10000

        ' Assign the response object of 'WebRequest'
to a 'WebResponse' variable.
Dim myWebResponse As WebResponse = myWebRequest.GetResponse()

[C#]
            // Create a new WebRequest Object to
the mentioned URL.
        WebRequest myWebRequest=WebRequest.Create("http://
www.contoso.com");
        Console.WriteLine("\nThe Timeout time of the request
before setting is : {0} milliseconds",myWebRequest.Timeout);
```

```
// Set the 'Timeout' property in Milliseconds.
myWebRequest.Timeout=10000;

        // This request will throw a WebException if it
reaches the timeout limit before it is able to fetch the resource.
            WebResponse myWebResponse=myWebRequest.GetResponse();

[C++]
// Create a new WebRequest Object to the mentioned URL.
WebRequest* myWebRequest = WebRequest::Create(S"http://
www.contoso.com");
Console::WriteLine(S"\nThe Timeout time of the request
before setting is : {0} milliseconds",
    __box(myWebRequest->Timeout));

// Set the 'Timeout' property in Milliseconds.
myWebRequest->Timeout=10000;

// This request will throw a WebException if it reaches the
timeout limit
// before it is able to fetch the resource.
WebResponse* myWebResponse = myWebRequest->GetResponse();
```

Requirements

Platforms: Windows 98, Windows NT 4.0, Windows Millennium Edition, Windows 2000, Windows XP Home Edition, Windows XP Professional, Windows .NET Server family, .NET Compact Framework - Windows CE .NET, Common Language Infrastructure (CLI) Standard

WebRequest.ISerializable.GetObjectData Method

This member supports the .NET Framework infrastructure and is not intended to be used directly from your code.

```
[Visual Basic]
Private Sub GetObjectData( _
   ByVal serializationInfo As SerializationInfo, _
   ByVal streamingContext As StreamingContext _
) Implements ISerializable.GetObjectData
[C#]
void ISerializable.GetObjectData(
   SerializationInfo serializationInfo,
   StreamingContext streamingContext
);
[C++]
private: void ISerializable::GetObjectData(
   SerializationInfo* serializationInfo,
   StreamingContext streamingContext
);
[JScript]
private function ISerializable.GetObjectData(
   serializationInfo : SerializationInfo,
   streamingContext : StreamingContext
);
```

WebRequest.RegisterPrefix Method

Registers a **WebRequest** descendant for the specified URI.

```
[Visual Basic]
Public Shared Function RegisterPrefix( _
   ByVal prefix As String, _
   ByVal creator As IWebRequestCreate _
) As Boolean
[C#]
public static bool RegisterPrefix(
   string prefix,
   IWebRequestCreate creator
);
[C++]
public: static bool RegisterPrefix(
   String* prefix,
   IWebRequestCreate* creator
);
[JScript]
public static function RegisterPrefix(
   prefix : String,
   creator : IWebRequestCreate
) : Boolean;
```

Parameters

prefix
   The complete URI or URI prefix that the **WebRequest** descendant services.

creator
   The create method that the **WebRequest** calls to create the **WebRequest** descendant.

Return Value

true if registration is successful; otherwise, **false**.

Exceptions

Exception Type	Condition
ArgumentNullException	*prefix* is a null reference (**Nothing** in Visual Basic) -or- *creator* is a null reference (**Nothing**).

Remarks

The **RegisterPrefix** method registers **WebRequest** descendants to service requests. **WebRequest** descendants are typically registered to handle a specific protocol, such HTTP or FTP, but can be registered to handle a request to a specific server or path on a server.

Duplicate prefixes are not allowed. **RegisterPrefix** returns **false** if an attempt is made to register a duplicate prefix.

> **Note** The **HttpWebRequest** class is registered to service requests for HTTP and HTTPS schemes by default. Attempts to register a different **WebRequest** descendant for these schemes will fail.

Requirements

Platforms: Windows 98, Windows NT 4.0, Windows Millennium Edition, Windows 2000, Windows XP Home Edition, Windows XP Professional, Windows .NET Server family, .NET Compact Framework - Windows CE .NET, Common Language Infrastructure (CLI) Standard

WebResponse Class

Provides a response from a Uniform Resource Identifier (URI). This is an abstract (**MustInherit** in Visual Basic) class.

System.Object
  System.MarshalByRefObject
    System.Net.WebResponse
      System.Net.FileWebResponse
      System.Net.HttpWebResponse

```
[Visual Basic]
<Serializable>
MustInherit Public Class WebResponse
   Inherits MarshalByRefObject
   Implements ISerializable, IDisposable
[C#]
[Serializable]
public abstract class WebResponse : MarshalByRefObject,
   ISerializable, IDisposable
[C++]
[Serializable]
public __gc __abstract class WebResponse : public
   MarshalByRefObject, ISerializable, IDisposable
[JScript]
public
   Serializable
abstract class WebResponse extends MarshalByRefObject
   implements ISerializable, IDisposable
```

Thread Safety

Any public static (**Shared** in Visual Basic) members of this type are safe for multithreaded operations. Any instance members are not guaranteed to be thread safe.

Remarks

The **WebResponse** class is the abstract (**MustInherit** in Visual Basic) base class from which protocol-specific response classes are derived. Applications can participate in request and response transactions in a protocol-agnostic manner using instances of the **WebResponse** class while protocol-specific classes derived from **WebResponse** carry out the details of the request.

Client applications do not create **WebResponse** objects directly, they are created by calling the **GetResponse** method on a **WebRequest** instance.

Notes to Inheritors: When you inherit from **WebResponse**, you must override the following members: **ContentLength**, **ContentType**, **GetResponseStream**, **ResponseUri**, and **Headers**.

Example

[Visual Basic, C#] The following example creates a **WebResponse** instance from a **WebRequest**.

```
[Visual Basic]
' Initialize the WebRequest.
Dim myRequest As WebRequest =
WebRequest.Create("http://www.contoso.com")

' Return the response.
Dim myResponse As WebResponse = myRequest.GetResponse()

' Code to use the WebResponse goes here.
' Close the response to free resources.
myResponse.Close()
```

```
[C#]
// Initialize the WebRequest.
WebRequest myRequest = WebRequest.Create("http://www.contoso.com");

// Return the response.
WebResponse myResponse = myRequest.GetResponse();

// Code to use the WebResponse goes here.

// Close the response to free resources.
myResponse.Close();
```

Requirements

Namespace: System.Net

Platforms: Windows 98, Windows NT 4.0, Windows Millennium Edition, Windows 2000, Windows XP Home Edition, Windows XP Professional, Windows .NET Server family, .NET Compact Framework - Windows CE .NET

Assembly: System (in System.dll)

WebResponse Constructor

Initializes a new instance of the **WebResponse** class.

Overload List

Initializes a new instance of the **WebResponse** class.

Supported by the .NET Compact Framework.

  [Visual Basic] **Protected Sub New()**
  [C#] **protected WebResponse();**
  [C++] **protected: WebResponse();**
  [JScript] **protected function WebResponse();**

Initializes a new instance of the **WebResponse** class from the specified instances of the **SerializationInfo** and **StreamingContext** classes.

  [Visual Basic] **Protected Sub New(SerializationInfo, StreamingContext)**
  [C#] **protected WebResponse(SerializationInfo, StreamingContext);**
  [C++] **protected: WebResponse(SerializationInfo*, StreamingContext);**
  [JScript] **protected function WebResponse(SerializationInfo, StreamingContext);**

WebResponse Constructor ()

Initializes a new instance of the **WebResponse** class.

```
[Visual Basic]
Protected Sub New()
[C#]
protected WebResponse();
[C++]
protected: WebResponse();
[JScript]
protected function WebResponse();
```

Remarks

Applications do not call the **WebResponse** constructor directly, use the **GetResponse** method on a **WebRequest** instance.

Notes to Implementers: This constructor creates and initializes the required fields for descendant classes.

Requirements

Platforms: Windows 98, Windows NT 4.0, Windows Millennium Edition, Windows 2000, Windows XP Home Edition, Windows XP Professional, Windows .NET Server family, .NET Compact Framework - Windows CE .NET, Common Language Infrastructure (CLI) Standard

WebResponse Constructor (SerializationInfo, StreamingContext)

Initializes a new instance of the **WebResponse** class from the specified instances of the **SerializationInfo** and **StreamingContext** classes.

```
[Visual Basic]
Protected Sub New( _
    ByVal serializationInfo As SerializationInfo, _
    ByVal streamingContext As StreamingContext _
)
[C#]
protected WebResponse(
    SerializationInfo serializationInfo,
    StreamingContext streamingContext
);
[C++]
protected: WebResponse(
    SerializationInfo* serializationInfo,
    StreamingContext streamingContext
);
[JScript]
protected function WebResponse(
    serializationInfo : SerializationInfo,
    streamingContext : StreamingContext
);
```

Parameters

serializationInfo
  An instance of the **SerializationInfo** class containing the information required to serialize the new **WebRequest** instance.
streamingContext
  An instance of the **StreamingContext** class indicating the source of the serialized stream associated with the new **WebRequest** instance.

Exceptions

Exception Type	Condition
NotSupportedException	Any attempt is made to access the constructor, when the constructor is not overridden in a descendant class.

Remarks

When implemented by a descendant class, this constructor implements the **ISerializable** interface for the **WebResponse** descendant.

Requirements

Platforms: Windows 98, Windows NT 4.0, Windows Millennium Edition, Windows 2000, Windows XP Home Edition, Windows XP Professional, Windows .NET Server family

WebResponse.ContentLength Property

When overridden in a descendant class, gets or sets the content length of data being received.

```
[Visual Basic]
Public Overridable Property ContentLength As Long
[C#]
public virtual long ContentLength {get; set;}
[C++]
public: __property virtual __int64 get_ContentLength();
public: __property virtual void set_ContentLength(__int64);
[JScript]
public function get ContentLength() : long;
public function set ContentLength(long);
```

Property Value

The number of bytes returned from the Internet resource.

Exceptions

Exception Type	Condition
NotSupportedException	Any attempt is made to get or set the property, when the property is not overridden in a descendant class.

Remarks

The **ContentLength** property contains the length, in bytes, of the response from the Internet resource. For request methods that contain header information, the **ContentLength** does not include the length of the header information.

> **Note** The **WebResponse** class is an abstract (**MustInherit** in Visual Basic) class. The actual behavior of **WebResponse** instances at run time is determined by the descendant class returned by **WebRequest.GetResponse**. For more information about default values and exceptions, please see the documentation for the descendant classes, such as **HttpWebResponse** and **FileWebResponse**.

Example

[Visual Basic, C#, C++] The following example uses the **ContentLength** property to obtain the Length of the resource returned.

```
[Visual Basic]
' Create a 'WebRequest' with the specified url.
Dim myWebRequest As WebRequest = WebRequest.Create("www.contoso.com")

' Send the 'WebRequest' and wait for response.
Dim myWebResponse As WebResponse = myWebRequest.GetResponse()

' The ContentLength and ContentType received as headers in the
response object are also exposed as properties.
' These provide information about the length and type of the
entity body in the response.
Console.WriteLine(ControlChars.Cr + "Content length :{0}, Content
Type : {1}", myWebResponse.ContentLength, myWebResponse.ContentType)
myWebResponse.Close()

[C#]
        // Create a 'WebRequest' with the specified url.
        WebRequest myWebRequest =
WebRequest.Create("http://www.contoso.com");

        // Send the 'WebRequest' and wait for response.
        WebResponse myWebResponse = myWebRequest.GetResponse();
```

```
                // Display the content length and content type
received as headers in the response object.
               Console.WriteLine("\nContent length :{0}, Content
Type : {1}",
                                   myWebResponse.ContentLength,
                                   myWebResponse.ContentType);

                // Release resources of response object.
                myWebResponse.Close();
```

```
[C++]
// Create a 'WebRequest' with the specified url.
WebRequest* myWebRequest = WebRequest::Create(S"http://
www.contoso.com");

// Send the 'WebRequest' and wait for response.
WebResponse* myWebResponse = myWebRequest->GetResponse();

// Display the content length and content type received as
headers in the response Object*.
Console::WriteLine(S"\nContent length : {0}, Content Type :
{1}", __box(myWebResponse->ContentLength),
    myWebResponse->ContentType);

// Release resources of response Object*.
myWebResponse->Close();
```

Requirements

Platforms: Windows 98, Windows NT 4.0,
Windows Millennium Edition, Windows 2000,
Windows XP Home Edition, Windows XP Professional,
Windows .NET Server family,
.NET Compact Framework - Windows CE .NET,
Common Language Infrastructure (CLI) Standard

WebResponse.ContentType Property

When overridden in a derived class, gets or sets the content type of
the data being received.

```
[Visual Basic]
Public Overridable Property ContentType As String
[C#]
public virtual string ContentType {get; set;}
[C++]
public: __property virtual String* get_ContentType();
public: __property virtual void set_ContentType(String*);
[JScript]
public function get ContentType() : String;
public function set ContentType(String);
```

Property Value

A string containing the content type of the response.

Exceptions

Exception Type	Condition
NotSupportedException	Any attempt is made to get or set the property, when the property is not overridden in a descendant class.

Remarks

The **ContentType** property contains the MIME content type of the
response from the Internet resource, if known.

Note The **WebResponse** class is an abstract (**MustInherit** in
Visual Basic) class. The actual behavior of **WebResponse**
instances at run time is determined by the descendant class
returned by **WebRequest.GetResponse**. For more information
about default values and exceptions, please see the
documentation for the descendant classes, such as
HttpWebResponse and **FileWebResponse**.

Example

[Visual Basic, C#, C++] The following example uses the
ContentType property to obtain the content type of the response.

```
[Visual Basic]
' Create a 'WebRequest' with the specified url.
Dim myWebRequest As WebRequest = WebRequest.Create("www.contoso.com")

' Send the 'WebRequest' and wait for response.
Dim myWebResponse As WebResponse = myWebRequest.GetResponse()

' The ContentLength and ContentType received as headers in the
response object are also exposed as properties.
' These provide information about the length and type of the
entity body in the response.
Console.WriteLine(ControlChars.Cr + "Content length :{0},
Content Type : {1}", myWebResponse.ContentLength,
myWebResponse.ContentType)
myWebResponse.Close()
```

```
[C#]
                // Create a 'WebRequest' with the specified url.
        WebRequest myWebRequest =
WebRequest.Create("http://www.contoso.com");

                // Send the 'WebRequest' and wait for response.
        WebResponse myWebResponse = myWebRequest.GetResponse();

                // Display the content length and content
type received as headers in the response object.
                Console.WriteLine("\nContent length :{0},
Content Type : {1}",
                                   myWebResponse.ContentLength,
                                   myWebResponse.ContentType);

                // Release resources of response object.
                myWebResponse.Close();
```

```
[C++]
// Create a 'WebRequest' with the specified url.
WebRequest* myWebRequest =
WebRequest::Create(S"http://www.contoso.com");

// Send the 'WebRequest' and wait for response.
WebResponse* myWebResponse = myWebRequest->GetResponse();

// Display the content length and content type received as
headers in the response Object*.
Console::WriteLine(S"\nContent length : {0}, Content Type :
{1}", __box(myWebResponse->ContentLength),
    myWebResponse->ContentType);

// Release resources of response Object*.
myWebResponse->Close();
```

Requirements

Platforms: Windows 98, Windows NT 4.0,
Windows Millennium Edition, Windows 2000,
Windows XP Home Edition, Windows XP Professional,
Windows .NET Server family,
.NET Compact Framework - Windows CE .NET,
Common Language Infrastructure (CLI) Standard

WebResponse.Headers Property

When overridden in a derived class, gets a collection of header name-value pairs associated with this request.

```
[Visual Basic]
Public Overridable ReadOnly Property Headers As WebHeaderCollection
[C#]
public virtual WebHeaderCollection Headers {get;}
[C++]
public: __property virtual WebHeaderCollection* get_Headers();
[JScript]
public function get Headers() : WebHeaderCollection;
```

Property Value

An instance of the **WebHeaderCollection** class containing header values associated with this response.

Exceptions

Exception Type	Condition
NotSupportedException	Any attempt is made to get or set the property, when the property is not overridden in a descendant class.

Remarks

The **Headers** property contains the name-value header pairs returned in the response.

> **Note** The **WebResponse** class is an abstract (**MustInherit** in Visual Basic) class. The actual behavior of **WebResponse** instances at run time is determined by the descendant class returned by **WebRequest.GetResponse**. For more information about default values and exceptions, please see the documentation for the descendant classes, such as **HttpWebResponse** and **FileWebResponse**.

Example

[Visual Basic, C#, C++] The following example displays all of the header name-value pairs returned in the **WebResponse**.

```
[Visual Basic]
' Create a 'WebRequest' object with the specified url
Dim myWebRequest As WebRequest = WebRequest.Create("www.contoso.com")

' Send the 'WebRequest' and wait for response.
Dim myWebResponse As WebResponse = myWebRequest.GetResponse()

' Display all the Headers present in the response received
from the URl.
Console.WriteLine(ControlChars.Cr + "The following headers
were received in the response")

' Headers property is a 'WebHeaderCollection'. Use it's
properties to traverse the collection and display each header
Dim i As Integer

While i < myWebResponse.Headers.Count
    Console.WriteLine(ControlChars.Cr + "Header Name:{0}, Header
value :{1}", myWebResponse.Headers.Keys(i), myWebResponse.Headers(i))
    i = i + 1
End While

' Release resources of response object.
myWebResponse.Close()

[C#]
        // Create a 'WebRequest' object with the specified url.
        WebRequest myWebRequest =
WebRequest.Create("http://www.contoso.com");
```

```
        // Send the 'WebRequest' and wait for response.
        WebResponse myWebResponse = myWebRequest.GetResponse();

        // Display all the Headers present in the response
received from the URl.
        Console.WriteLine("\nThe following headers were
received in the response");

        // Display each header and it's key , associated with
the response object.
        for(int i=0; i < myWebResponse.Headers.Count; ++i)
            Console.WriteLine("\nHeader Name:{0}, Header
value :{1}",myWebResponse.Headers.Keys[i],myWebResponse.Headers[i]);

        // Release resources of response object.
        myWebResponse.Close();

[C++]
// Create a 'WebRequest' Object* with the specified url.
WebRequest* myWebRequest =
WebRequest::Create(S"http://www.contoso.com");

// Send the 'WebRequest' and wait for response.
WebResponse* myWebResponse = myWebRequest->GetResponse();

// Display all the Headers present in the response received
from the URl.
Console::WriteLine(S"\nThe following headers were received
in the response");

// Display each header and it's key , associated with the
response Object*.
for (int i = 0 ; i < myWebResponse->Headers->Count ; ++i)
    Console::WriteLine(S"\nHeader Name: {0}, Header value : {1}",
    myWebResponse->Headers->Keys->Item[i], myWebResponse->
Headers->Item[i]);

// Release resources of response Object*.
myWebResponse->Close();
```

Requirements

Platforms: Windows 98, Windows NT 4.0, Windows Millennium Edition, Windows 2000, Windows XP Home Edition, Windows XP Professional, Windows .NET Server family, .NET Compact Framework - Windows CE .NET, Common Language Infrastructure (CLI) Standard

WebResponse.ResponseUri Property

When overridden in a derived class, gets the URI of the Internet resource that actually responded to the request.

```
[Visual Basic]
Public Overridable ReadOnly Property ResponseUri As Uri
[C#]
public virtual Uri ResponseUri {get;}
[C++]
public: __property virtual Uri* get_ResponseUri();
[JScript]
public function get ResponseUri() : Uri;
```

Property Value

An instance of the **Uri** class that contains the URI of the Internet resource that actually responded to the request.

Exceptions

Exception Type	Condition
NotSupportedException	Any attempt is made to get or set the property, when the property is not overridden in a descendant class.

Remarks

The **ResponseUri** property contains the URI of the Internet resource that actually provided the response data. This resource may not be the originally requested URI if the underlying protocol allows redirection of the request.

> **Note** The **WebResponse** class is an abstract (**MustInherit** in Visual Basic) class. The actual behavior of **WebResponse** instances at run time is determined by the descendant class returned by **WebRequest.GetResponse**. For more information about default values and exceptions, please see the documentation for the descendant classes, such as **HttpWebResponse** and **FileWebResponse**.

Example

[Visual Basic, C#, C++] The following example uses the **ResponseUri** property to determine if the location from which the **WebResponse** originated.

```
[Visual Basic]
Dim ourUri As New Uri(url)
' Create a 'WebRequest' object with the specified url.

Dim myWebRequest As WebRequest = WebRequest.Create(url)

' Send the 'WebRequest' and wait for response.
Dim myWebResponse As WebResponse = myWebRequest.GetResponse()

' "ResponseUri" property is used to get the actual Uri from
where the response was attained.
If ourUri.Equals(myWebResponse.ResponseUri) Then
    Console.WriteLine(ControlChars.Cr + "Request Url : {0}
was not redirected", url)
Else
    Console.WriteLine(ControlChars.Cr + "Request Url : {0}
was redirected to {1}", url, myWebResponse.ResponseUri)
End If

' Release resources of response object.
myWebResponse.Close()

[C#]
Uri ourUri = new Uri(url);

// Create a 'WebRequest' object with the specified url.
WebRequest myWebRequest = WebRequest.Create(url);

// Send the 'WebRequest' and wait for response.
WebResponse myWebResponse = myWebRequest.GetResponse();

// Use "ResponseUri" property to get the actual Uri from
where the response was attained.
if (ourUri.Equals(myWebResponse.ResponseUri))
    Console.WriteLine("\nRequest Url : {0} was not redirected",url);
else
    Console.WriteLine("\nRequest Url : {0} was redirected to
{1}",url,myWebResponse.ResponseUri);
// Release resources of response object.
myWebResponse.Close();

[C++]
Uri* ourUri = new Uri(url);

// Create a 'WebRequest' Object* with the specified url.
WebRequest* myWebRequest = WebRequest::Create(url);

// Send the 'WebRequest' and wait for response.
WebResponse* myWebResponse = myWebRequest->GetResponse();

// Use S"ResponseUri" property to get the actual Uri from where
the response was attained.
```

```
if (ourUri->Equals(myWebResponse->ResponseUri))
    Console::WriteLine(S"\nRequest Url : {0} was not redirected", url);
else
    Console::WriteLine(S"\nRequest Url : {0} was redirected to
{1}", url, myWebResponse->ResponseUri);
// Release resources of response Object*.
myWebResponse->Close();
```

Requirements

Platforms: Windows 98, Windows NT 4.0, Windows Millennium Edition, Windows 2000, Windows XP Home Edition, Windows XP Professional, Windows .NET Server family, .NET Compact Framework - Windows CE .NET, Common Language Infrastructure (CLI) Standard

WebResponse.Close Method

When overridden by a descendant class, closes the response stream.

```
[Visual Basic]
Public Overridable Sub Close()
[C#]
public virtual void Close();
[C++]
public: virtual void Close();
[JScript]
public function Close();
```

Exceptions

Exception Type	Condition
NotSupportedException	Any attempt is made to access the method, when the method is not overridden in a descendant class.

Remarks

The **Close** method cleans up the resources used by a **WebResponse** and closes the underlying stream by calling the **Stream.Close** method.

> **Note** The response must be closed to avoid running out of system resources. The response stream can be closed by calling **Stream.Close** or **Close**.

> **Note** The **WebResponse** class is an abstract (**MustInherit** in Visual Basic) class. The actual behavior of **WebResponse** instances at run time is determined by the descendant class returned by **WebRequest.GetResponse**. For more information about default values and exceptions, please see the documentation for the descendant classes, such as **HttpWebResponse** and **FileWebResponse**.

Example

[Visual Basic, C#, C++] The following example uses the **Close** method to close the WebResponse.

```
[Visual Basic]
' Create a 'WebRequest' object with the specified url
Dim myWebRequest As WebRequest = WebRequest.Create("www.contoso.com")
' Send the 'WebRequest' and wait for response.
Dim myWebResponse As WebResponse = myWebRequest.GetResponse()

' Process the response here
Console.WriteLine(ControlChars.Cr + "Response Received.Trying to
Close the response stream..")
```

```
  Release resources of response object
myWebResponse.Close()
Console.WriteLine(ControlChars.Cr + "Response Stream
successfully closed")
```

```
[C#]
// Create a 'WebRequest' object with the specified url.
WebRequest myWebRequest = WebRequest.Create("http://www.contoso.com");
// Send the 'WebRequest' and wait for response.
WebResponse myWebResponse = myWebRequest.GetResponse();

// Process the response here.
Console.WriteLine("\nResponse Received.Trying to Close
the response stream..");
// Release resources of response object.
myWebResponse.Close();
Console.WriteLine("\nResponse Stream successfully closed");
```

```
[C++]
// Create a 'WebRequest' Object* with the specified url.
WebRequest* myWebRequest = WebRequest::Create(S"http://
www.contoso.com");
// Send the 'WebRequest' and wait for response.
WebResponse* myWebResponse = myWebRequest->GetResponse();

// Process the response here.
Console::WriteLine(S"\nResponse Received::Trying to Close
the response stream..");
// Release resources of response Object*.
myWebResponse->Close();
Console::WriteLine(S"\nResponse Stream successfully closed");
```

Requirements

Platforms: Windows 98, Windows NT 4.0,
Windows Millennium Edition, Windows 2000,
Windows XP Home Edition, Windows XP Professional,
Windows .NET Server family,
.NET Compact Framework - Windows CE .NET,
Common Language Infrastructure (CLI) Standard

WebResponse.GetResponseStream Method

When overridden in a descendant class, returns the data stream from
the Internet resource.

```
[Visual Basic]
Public Overridable Function GetResponseStream() As Stream
[C#]
public virtual Stream GetResponseStream();
[C++]
public: virtual Stream* GetResponseStream();
[JScript]
public function GetResponseStream() : Stream;
```

Return Value

An instance of the **Stream** class for reading data from the Internet
resource.

Exceptions

Exception Type	Condition
NotSupportedException	Any attempt is made to access the method, when the method is not overridden in a descendant class.

Remarks

The **GetResponseStream** method returns the data stream from the
Internet resource.

Note The response stream must be closed to avoid running out
of system resources. The response stream can be closed by
calling **Stream.Close** or **Close**

Example

[Visual Basic, C#, C++] The following example uses
GetResponseStream to return a **StreamReader** instance. A small
local buffer is used to read data from the **StreamReader** and output
it to the console.

```
[Visual Basic]
' Create a 'WebRequest' object with the specified url
Dim myWebRequest As WebRequest = WebRequest.Create("www.contoso.com")

' Send the 'WebRequest' and wait for response.
Dim myWebResponse As WebResponse = myWebRequest.GetResponse()

' Call method 'GetResponseStream' to obtain stream associated
with the response object
Dim ReceiveStream As Stream = myWebResponse.GetResponseStream()

Dim encode As Encoding = System.Text.Encoding.GetEncoding("utf-8")

' Pipe the stream to a higher level stream reader with the
required encoding format.
Dim readStream As New StreamReader(ReceiveStream, encode)
Console.WriteLine(ControlChars.Cr + "Response stream received")
Dim read(256) As [Char]

' Read 256 charcters at a time    .
Dim count As Integer = readStream.Read(read, 0, 256)
Console.WriteLine("HTML..." + ControlChars.Lf + ControlChars.Cr)
While count > 0

    ' Dump the 256 characters on a string and display the
string onto the console.
    Dim str As New [String](read, 0, count)
    Console.Write(str)
    count = readStream.Read(read, 0, 256)

End While
Console.WriteLine("")

' Release the resources of stream object.
readStream.Close()

' Release the resources of response object.
myWebResponse.Close()
```

```
[C#]
    // Create a 'WebRequest' object with the specified url.
    WebRequest myWebRequest = WebRequest.Create("http://
www.constoso.com");

    // Send the 'WebRequest' and wait for response.
    WebResponse myWebResponse = myWebRequest.GetResponse();

    // Obtain a 'Stream' object associated with the response object.
    Stream ReceiveStream = myWebResponse.GetResponseStream();

    Encoding encode = System.Text.Encoding.GetEncoding("utf-8");

    // Pipe the stream to a higher level stream reader
with the required encoding format.
    StreamReader readStream = new StreamReader( ReceiveStream,
encode );
    Console.WriteLine("\nResponse stream received");
    Char[] read = new Char[256];

    // Read 256 charcters at a time.
    int count = readStream.Read( read, 0, 256 );
    Console.WriteLine("HTML...\r\n");
```

```
    while (count > 0)
    {
            // Dump the 256 characters on a string and
display the string onto the console.
        String str = new String(read, 0, count);
        Console.Write(str);
        count = readStream.Read(read, 0, 256);
    }

    Console.WriteLine("");
    // Release the resources of stream object.
    readStream.Close();

    // Release the resources of response object.
    myWebResponse.Close();
```

[C++]
```
// Create a 'WebRequest' Object* with the specified url.
WebRequest* myWebRequest =
WebRequest::Create(S"http://www.constoso.com");

// Send the 'WebRequest' and wait for response.
WebResponse* myWebResponse = myWebRequest->GetResponse();

// Obtain a 'Stream' Object* associated with the response Object*.
Stream* ReceiveStream = myWebResponse->GetResponseStream();

Encoding* encode = System::Text::Encoding::GetEncoding(S"utf-8");

// Pipe the stream to a higher level stream reader with the required
encoding format.
StreamReader* readStream = new StreamReader(ReceiveStream, encode);
Console::WriteLine(S"\nResponse stream received");
Char read[] = new Char[256];

// Read 256 charcters at a time.
int count = readStream->Read(read, 0, 256);
Console::WriteLine(S"HTML...\r\n");

while (count > 0) {
    // Dump the 256 characters on a String* and display the
String* onto the console.
    String* str = new String(read, 0, count);
    Console::Write(str);
    count = readStream->Read(read, 0, 256);
}

Console::WriteLine(S"");
// Release the resources of stream Object*.
readStream->Close();

// Release the resources of response Object*.
myWebResponse->Close();
```

Requirements

Platforms: Windows 98, Windows NT 4.0,
Windows Millennium Edition, Windows 2000,
Windows XP Home Edition, Windows XP Professional,
Windows .NET Server family,
.NET Compact Framework - Windows CE .NET,
Common Language Infrastructure (CLI) Standard

WebResponse.IDisposable.Dispose Method

This member supports the .NET Framework infrastructure and is not
intended to be used directly from your code.

[Visual Basic]
```
Private Sub Dispose() Implements IDisposable.Dispose
```
[C#]
```
void IDisposable.Dispose();
```

[C++]
```
private: void IDisposable::Dispose();
```
[JScript]
```
private function IDisposable.Dispose();
```

WebResponse.ISerializable.GetObjectData Method

This member supports the .NET Framework infrastructure and is not
intended to be used directly from your code.

[Visual Basic]
```
Private Sub GetObjectData( _
    ByVal serializationInfo As SerializationInfo, _
    ByVal streamingContext As StreamingContext _
) Implements ISerializable.GetObjectData
```
[C#]
```
void ISerializable.GetObjectData(
    SerializationInfo serializationInfo,
    StreamingContext streamingContext
);
```
[C++]
```
private: void ISerializable::GetObjectData(
    SerializationInfo* serializationInfo,
    StreamingContext streamingContext
);
```
[JScript]
```
private function ISerializable.GetObjectData(
    serializationInfo : SerializationInfo,
    streamingContext : StreamingContext
);
```

System.Net.Sockets Namespace

The **System.Net.Sockets** namespace provides a managed implementation of the Windows Sockets (Winsock) interface for developers who need to tightly control access to the network.

The **TCPClient**, **TCPListener**, and **UDPClient** classes encapsulate the details of creating TCP and UDP connections to the Internet.

AddressFamily Enumeration

Specifies the addressing scheme that an instance of the **Socket** class can use.

```
[Visual Basic]
<Serializable>
Public Enum AddressFamily
[C#]
[Serializable]
public enum AddressFamily
[C++]
[Serializable]
__value public enum AddressFamily
[JScript]
public
    Serializable
enum AddressFamily
```

Remarks

An **AddressFamily** member specifies the addressing scheme that a **Socket** will use to resolve an address. For example, **InterNetwork** indicates that an IP version 4 address is expected when a **Socket** connects to an endpoint.

Members

Member name	Description
AppleTalk Supported by the .NET Compact Framework.	AppleTalk address.
Atm Supported by the .NET Compact Framework.	Native ATM services address.
Banyan Supported by the .NET Compact Framework.	Banyan address.
Ccitt Supported by the .NET Compact Framework.	Addresses for CCITT protocols, such as X.25.
Chaos Supported by the .NET Compact Framework.	Address for MIT CHAOS protocols.
Cluster Supported by the .NET Compact Framework.	Address for Microsoft cluster products.

Member name	Description
DataKit Supported by the .NET Compact Framework.	Address for Datakit protocols.
DataLink Supported by the .NET Compact Framework.	Direct data-link interface address.
DecNet Supported by the .NET Compact Framework.	DECnet address.
Ecma Supported by the .NET Compact Framework.	European Computer Manufacturers Association (ECMA) address.
FireFox Supported by the .NET Compact Framework.	FireFox address.
HyperChannel Supported by the .NET Compact Framework.	NSC Hyperchannel address.
Ieee12844 Supported by the .NET Compact Framework.	IEEE 1284.4 workgroup address.
ImpLink Supported by the .NET Compact Framework.	ARPANET IMP address.
InterNetwork Supported by the .NET Compact Framework.	Address for IP version 4.
InterNetworkV6 Supported by the .NET Compact Framework.	Address for IP version 6.
Ipx Supported by the .NET Compact Framework.	IPX or SPX address.
Irda Supported by the .NET Compact Framework.	IrDA address.
Iso Supported by the .NET Compact Framework.	Address for ISO protocols.
Lat Supported by the .NET Compact Framework.	LAT address.
Max Supported by the .NET Compact Framework.	MAX address.
NetBios Supported by the .NET Compact Framework.	NetBios address.
NetworkDesigners Supported by the .NET Compact Framework.	Address for Network Designers OSI gateway-enabled protocols.

Member name	Description
NS Supported by the .NET Compact Framework.	Address for Xerox NS protocols.
Osi Supported by the .NET Compact Framework.	Address for ISO protocols.
Pup Supported by the .NET Compact Framework.	Address for PUP protocols.
Sna Supported by the .NET Compact Framework.	IBM SNA address.
Unix Supported by the .NET Compact Framework.	Unix local to host address.
Unknown Supported by the .NET Compact Framework.	Unknown address family.
Unspecified Supported by the .NET Compact Framework.	Unspecified address family.
VoiceView Supported by the .NET Compact Framework.	VoiceView address.

Example

The following example creates a **Socket** using the **InterNetwork AddressFamily**.

Requirements

Namespace: System.Net.Sockets

Platforms: Windows 98, Windows NT 4.0, Windows Millennium Edition, Windows 2000, Windows XP Home Edition, Windows XP Professional, Windows .NET Server family, .NET Compact Framework - Windows CE .NET

Assembly: System (in System.dll)

IPv6MulticastOption Class

Note: This namespace, class, or member is supported only in version 1.1 of the .NET Framework.

Contains option values for joining an IPv6 multicast group.

System.Object
   System.Net.Sockets.IPv6MulticastOption

```
[Visual Basic]
Public Class IPv6MulticastOption
[C#]
public class IPv6MulticastOption
[C++]
public __gc class IPv6MulticastOption
[JScript]
public class IPv6MulticastOption
```

Thread Safety

Any public static (**Shared** in Visual Basic) members of this type are safe for multithreaded operations. Any instance members are not guaranteed to be thread safe.

Requirements

Namespace: System.Net.Sockets

Platforms: Windows 98, Windows NT 4.0, Windows Millennium Edition, Windows 2000, Windows XP Home Edition, Windows XP Professional, Windows .NET Server family

Assembly: System (in System.dll)

IPv6MulticastOption Constructor

Note: This namespace, class, or member is supported only in version 1.1 of the .NET Framework.

Initializes a new instance of the **IPv6MulticastOption** class.

Overload List

Initializes a new version of the **IPv6MulticastOption** class for the specified IP multicast group.

   [Visual Basic] **Public Sub New(IPAddress)**
   [C#] **public IPv6MulticastOption(IPAddress);**
   [C++] **public: IPv6MulticastOption(IPAddress*);**
   [JScript] **public function IPv6MulticastOption(IPAddress);**

Initializes a new instance of the **IPv6MulticastOption** class with the specified IP multicast group and the local interface address.

   [Visual Basic] **Public Sub New(IPAddress, Long)**
   [C#] **public IPv6MulticastOption(IPAddress, long);**
   [C++] **public: IPv6MulticastOption(IPAddress*, __int64);**
   [JScript] **public function IPv6MulticastOption(IPAddress, long);**

IPv6MulticastOption Constructor (IPAddress)

Note: This namespace, class, or member is supported only in version 1.1 of the .NET Framework.

Initializes a new version of the **IPv6MulticastOption** class for the specified IP multicast group.

```
[Visual Basic]
Public Sub New( _
    ByVal group As IPAddress _
)
[C#]
public IPv6MulticastOption(
    IPAddress group
);
[C++]
public: IPv6MulticastOption(
    IPAddress* group
);
[JScript]
public function IPv6MulticastOption(
    group : IPAddress
);
```

Parameters

group
   The **IPAddress** of the multicast group.

Exceptions

Exception Type	Condition
System.ArgumentNull-Exception	*group* is a null reference (**Nothing** in Visual Basic).

Requirements

Platforms: Windows 98, Windows NT 4.0, Windows Millennium Edition, Windows 2000, Windows XP Home Edition, Windows XP Professional, Windows .NET Server family

IPv6MulticastOption Constructor (IPAddress, Int64)

Note: This namespace, class, or member is supported only in version 1.1 of the .NET Framework.

Initializes a new instance of the **IPv6MulticastOption** class with the specified IP multicast group and the local interface address.

```
[Visual Basic]
Public Sub New( _
    ByVal group As IPAddress, _
    ByVal ifindex As Long _
)
[C#]
public IPv6MulticastOption(
    IPAddress group,
    long ifindex
);
[C++]
public: IPv6MulticastOption(
    IPAddress* group,
    __int64 ifindex
);
```

```
[JScript]
public function IPv6MulticastOption(
    group : IPAddress,
    ifindex : long
);
```

Parameters

group
> The group **IPAddress**.

ifindex
> The local interface address.

Exceptions

Exception Type	Condition
System.ArgumentOutOf-RangeException	*ifindex* is less than 0. -or- *ifindex* is greater than 0x00000000FFFFFFFF.
System.ArgumentNull-Exception	*group* is a null reference (**Nothing** in Visual Basic).

Remarks

The *ifindex* parameter specifies the interface on which data is received or sent.

Requirements

Platforms: Windows 98, Windows NT 4.0, Windows Millennium Edition, Windows 2000, Windows XP Home Edition, Windows XP Professional, Windows .NET Server family

IPv6MulticastOption.Group Property

Note: This namespace, class, or member is supported only in version 1.1 of the .NET Framework.

Gets or sets the IP address of a multicast group.

```
[Visual Basic]
Public Property Group As IPAddress
[C#]
public IPAddress Group {get; set;}
[C++]
public: __property IPAddress* get_Group();
public: __property void set_Group(IPAddress*);
[JScript]
public function get Group() : IPAddress;
public function set Group(IPAddress);
```

Property Value

An **IPAddress** containing the Internet address of a multicast group.

Exceptions

Exception Type	Condition
System.ArgumentNull-Exception	*group* is a null reference (**Nothing** in Visual Basic).

Requirements

Platforms: Windows 98, Windows NT 4.0, Windows Millennium Edition, Windows 2000, Windows XP Home Edition, Windows XP Professional, Windows .NET Server family

IPv6MulticastOption.InterfaceIndex Property

Note: This namespace, class, or member is supported only in version 1.1 of the .NET Framework.

Gets or sets the interface index associated with a multicast group.

```
[Visual Basic]
Public Property InterfaceIndex As Long
[C#]
public long InterfaceIndex {get; set;}
[C++]
public: __property __int64 get_InterfaceIndex();
public: __property void set_InterfaceIndex(__int64);
[JScript]
public function get InterfaceIndex() : long;
public function set InterfaceIndex(long);
```

Exceptions

Exception Type	Condition
System.ArgumentOutOf-RangeException	*ifindex* is less than 0. -or- *ifindex* is greater than 0x00000000FFFFFFFF.

Remarks

The *ifindex* parameter specifies the interface on which data is received or sent.

Requirements

Platforms: Windows 98, Windows NT 4.0, Windows Millennium Edition, Windows 2000, Windows XP Home Edition, Windows XP Professional, Windows .NET Server family

IrDACharacterSet Enumeration

Note: This namespace, class, or member is supported only in version 1.1 of the .NET Framework.

Describes the character sets supported by the device.

```
[Visual Basic]
<Serializable>
Public Enum IrDACharacterSet
[C#]
[Serializable]
public enum IrDACharacterSet
[C++]
[Serializable]
__value public enum IrDACharacterSet
[JScript]
public
    Serializable
enum IrDACharacterSet
```

Remarks

The **IrDACharacterSet** enumeration describes the following character sets, which are used by the **IrDAClient** and **IrDADeviceInfo** classes.

Members

Member name	Description
ASCII Supported only by the .NET Compact Framework.	The ASCII character set.
ISO8859Arabic Supported only by the .NET Compact Framework.	The Arabic graphic character set.
ISO8859Cyrillic Supported only by the .NET Compact Framework.	The Cyrillic graphic character set.
ISO8859Greek Supported only by the .NET Compact Framework.	The Greek graphic character set.
ISO8859Hebrew Supported only by the .NET Compact Framework.	The Hebrew graphic character set.
ISO8859Latin1 Supported only by the .NET Compact Framework.	The western European graphic character set.
ISO8859Latin2 Supported only by the .NET Compact Framework.	The eastern European graphic character set.

Member name	Description
ISO8859Latin3 Supported only by the .NET Compact Framework.	The southern European graphic character set.
ISO8859Latin4 Supported only by the .NET Compact Framework.	The northern European graphic character set.
ISO8859Latin5 Supported only by the .NET Compact Framework.	The Turkish graphic character set.
Unicode Supported only by the .NET Compact Framework.	The Unicode character set.

Requirements

Namespace: System.Net.Sockets

Platforms: .NET Compact Framework - Windows CE .NET

Assembly: System.Net.Irda (in System.Net.Irda.dll)

IrDAClient Class

Note: This namespace, class, or member is supported only in version 1.1 of the .NET Framework.

Provides connection information, and creates client connection objects for opening and closing connections to a server.

System.Object
  System.Net.Sockets.IrDAClient

```
[Visual Basic]
Public Class IrDAClient
[C#]
public class IrDAClient
[C++]
public __gc class IrDAClient
[JScript]
public class IrDAClient
```

Thread Safety

Any public static (**Shared** in Visual Basic) members of this type are safe for multithreaded operations. Any instance members are not guaranteed to be thread safe.

Requirements

Namespace: System.Net.Sockets

Platforms: .NET Compact Framework - Windows CE .NET

Assembly: System.Net.Irda (in System.Net.Irda.dll)

IrDAClient Constructor

Note: This namespace, class, or member is supported only in version 1.1 of the .NET Framework.

Initializes a new instance of the **IrDAClient** class.

Overload List

Initializes a new instance of the **IrDAClient** class.

Supported only by the .NET Compact Framework.

  [Visual Basic] **Public Sub New()**
  [C#] **public IrDAClient();**
  [C++] **public: IrDAClient();**
  [JScript] **public function IrDAClient();**

Initializes a new instance of the **IrDAClient** class for connecting to a specified endpoint.

Supported only by the .NET Compact Framework.

  [Visual Basic] **Public Sub New(IrDAEndPoint)**
  [C#] **public IrDAClient(IrDAEndPoint);**
  [C++] **public: IrDAClient(IrDAEndPoint*);**
  [JScript] **public function IrDAClient(IrDAEndPoint);**

Initializes a new instance of the **IrDAClient** class for connecting to a specified service.

Supported only by the .NET Compact Framework.

  [Visual Basic] **Public Sub New(String)**
  [C#] **public IrDAClient(string);**
  [C++] **public: IrDAClient(String*);**
  [JScript] **public function IrDAClient(String);**

IrDAClient Constructor ( )

Note: This namespace, class, or member is supported only in version 1.1 of the .NET Framework.

Initializes a new instance of the **IrDAClient** class.

```
[Visual Basic]
Public Sub New()
[C#]
public IrDAClient();
[C++]
public: IrDAClient();
[JScript]
public function IrDAClient();
```

Requirements

Platforms: .NET Compact Framework - Windows CE .NET

.NET Framework Security:

- Full trust for the immediate caller. This member cannot be used by partially trusted code.

IrDAClient Constructor (IrDAEndPoint)

Note: This namespace, class, or member is supported only in version 1.1 of the .NET Framework.

Initializes a new instance of the **IrDAClient** class for connecting to a specified endpoint.

```
[Visual Basic]
Public Sub New( _
   ByVal remoteEP As IrDAEndPoint _
)
[C#]
public IrDAClient(
   IrDAEndPoint remoteEP
);
[C++]
public: IrDAClient(
   IrDAEndPoint* remoteEP
);
[JScript]
public function IrDAClient(
   remoteEP : IrDAEndPoint
);
```

Parameters

remoteEP
  An **IrDAEndPoint**.

Requirements

Platforms: .NET Compact Framework - Windows CE .NET

.NET Framework Security:

- Full trust for the immediate caller. This member cannot be used by partially trusted code.

IrDAClient Constructor (String)

Note: This namespace, class, or member is supported only in version 1.1 of the .NET Framework.

Initializes a new instance of the **IrDAClient** class for connecting to a specified service.

```
[Visual Basic]
Public Sub New( _
   ByVal service As String _
)
[C#]
public IrDAClient(
   string service
);
[C++]
public: IrDAClient(
   String* service
);
[JScript]
public function IrDAClient(
   service : String
);
```

Parameters

service
   The name of a service to connect to.

Requirements

Platforms: .NET Compact Framework - Windows CE .NET

.NET Framework Security:
- Full trust for the immediate caller. This member cannot be used by partially trusted code.

IrDAClient.RemoteMachineName Property

Note: This namespace, class, or member is supported only in version 1.1 of the .NET Framework.

Gets the name of the device the connected device.

```
[Visual Basic]
Public ReadOnly Property RemoteMachineName As String
[C#]
public string RemoteMachineName {get;}
[C++]
public: __property String* get_RemoteMachineName();
[JScript]
public function get RemoteMachineName() : String;
```

Property Value

A string value of the computer or device name.

Requirements

Platforms: .NET Compact Framework - Windows CE .NET

.NET Framework Security:
- Full trust for the immediate caller. This member cannot be used by partially trusted code.

IrDAClient.Close Method

Note: This namespace, class, or member is supported only in version 1.1 of the .NET Framework.

Closes the socket of the connection.

```
[Visual Basic]
Public Sub Close()
[C#]
public void Close();
[C++]
public: void Close();
[JScript]
public function Close();
```

Requirements

Platforms: .NET Compact Framework - Windows CE .NET

.NET Framework Security:
- Full trust for the immediate caller. This member cannot be used by partially trusted code.

IrDAClient.Connect Method

Note: This namespace, class, or member is supported only in version 1.1 of the .NET Framework.

Connects a client to a specified service.

Overload List

Connects a client to a specified endpoint.

Supported only by the .NET Compact Framework.
   [Visual Basic] **Overloads Public Sub Connect(IrDAEndPoint)**
   [C#] **public void Connect(IrDAEndPoint);**
   [C++] **public: void Connect(IrDAEndPoint*);**
   [JScript] **public function Connect(IrDAEndPoint);**

Connects a client to a specified service.

Supported only by the .NET Compact Framework.
   [Visual Basic] **Overloads Public Sub Connect(String)**
   [C#] **public void Connect(string);**
   [C++] **public: void Connect(String*);**
   [JScript] **public function Connect(String);**

IrDAClient.Connect Method (IrDAEndPoint)

Note: This namespace, class, or member is supported only in version 1.1 of the .NET Framework.

Connects a client to a specified endpoint.

```
[Visual Basic]
Overloads Public Sub Connect( _
   ByVal remoteEP As IrDAEndPoint _
)
[C#]
public void Connect(
   IrDAEndPoint remoteEP
);
[C++]
public: void Connect(
   IrDAEndPoint* remoteEP
);
```

```
[JScript]
public function Connect(
    remoteEP : IrDAEndPoint
);
```

Parameters

remoteEP

An **IrDAEndPoint** that represents the remote device.

Requirements

Platforms: .NET Compact Framework - Windows CE .NET

.NET Framework Security:

- Full trust for the immediate caller. This member cannot be used by partially trusted code.

IrDAClient.Connect Method (String)

Note: This namespace, class, or member is supported only in version 1.1 of the .NET Framework.

Connects a client to a specified service.

```
[Visual Basic]
Overloads Public Sub Connect( _
    ByVal service As String _
)
[C#]
public void Connect(
    string service
);
[C++]
public: void Connect(
    String* service
);
[JScript]
public function Connect(
    service : String
);
```

Parameters

service

The name of the service to connect to.

Requirements

Platforms: .NET Compact Framework - Windows CE .NET

.NET Framework Security:

- Full trust for the immediate caller. This member cannot be used by partially trusted code.

IrDAClient.DiscoverDevices Method

Note: This namespace, class, or member is supported only in version 1.1 of the .NET Framework.

Obtains information about devices using a particular socket.

Overload List

Obtains information about a specified number of devices.

Supported only by the .NET Compact Framework.

[Visual Basic] **Overloads Public Function DiscoverDevices(Integer) As IrDADeviceInfo()**

[C#] **public IrDADeviceInfo[] DiscoverDevices(int);**

[C++] **public: IrDADeviceInfo* DiscoverDevices(int) [];**

[JScript] **public function DiscoverDevices(int) : IrDADeviceInfo[];**

Obtains information about available devices using a socket.

Supported only by the .NET Compact Framework.

[Visual Basic] **Overloads Public Shared Function DiscoverDevices(Integer, Socket) As IrDADeviceInfo()**

[C#] **public static IrDADeviceInfo[] DiscoverDevices(int, Socket);**

[C++] **public: static IrDADeviceInfo* DiscoverDevices(int, Socket*) [];**

[JScript] **public static function DiscoverDevices(int, Socket) : IrDADeviceInfo[];**

IrDAClient.DiscoverDevices Method (Int32)

Note: This namespace, class, or member is supported only in version 1.1 of the .NET Framework.

Obtains information about a specified number of devices.

```
[Visual Basic]
Overloads Public Function DiscoverDevices( _
    ByVal maxDevices As Integer _
) As IrDADeviceInfo()
[C#]
public IrDADeviceInfo[] DiscoverDevices(
    int maxDevices
);
[C++]
public: IrDADeviceInfo* DiscoverDevices(
    int maxDevices
) [];
[JScript]
public function DiscoverDevices(
    maxDevices : int
) : IrDADeviceInfo[];
```

Parameters

maxDevices

The maximum number of devices to get information about.

Return Value

An **IrDADeviceInfo** interface.

Requirements

Platforms: .NET Compact Framework - Windows CE .NET

.NET Framework Security:

- Full trust for the immediate caller. This member cannot be used by partially trusted code.

IrDAClient.DiscoverDevices Method (Int32, Socket)

Note: This namespace, class, or member is supported only in version 1.1 of the .NET Framework.

Obtains information about available devices using a socket.

```
[Visual Basic]
Overloads Public Shared Function DiscoverDevices( _
    ByVal maxDevices As Integer, _
    ByVal irdaSocket As Socket _
) As IrDADeviceInfo()
[C#]
public static IrDADeviceInfo[] DiscoverDevices(
    int maxDevices,
    Socket irdaSocket
);
```

```
[C++]
public: static IrDADeviceInfo* DiscoverDevices(
    int maxDevices,
    Socket* irdaSocket
) [];
[JScript]
public static function DiscoverDevices(
    maxDevices : int,
    irdaSocket : Socket
) : IrDADeviceInfo[];
```

Parameters

maxDevices

The maximum number of devices to get information about.

irdaSocket

The IrDA socket.

Return Value

Returns an instance of the **IrDADeviceInfo** class.

Requirements

Platforms: .NET Compact Framework - Windows CE .NET

.NET Framework Security:

- Full trust for the immediate caller. This member cannot be used by partially trusted code.

IrDAClient.GetRemoteMachineName Method

Note: This namespace, class, or member is supported only in version 1.1 of the .NET Framework.

Gets the name of a device by a specified socket.

```
[Visual Basic]
Public Shared Function GetRemoteMachineName( _
    ByVal s As Socket _
) As String
[C#]
public static string GetRemoteMachineName(
    Socket s
);
[C++]
public: static String* GetRemoteMachineName(
    Socket* s
);
[JScript]
public static function GetRemoteMachineName(
    s : Socket
) : String;
```

Parameters

s

A **Socket**.

Return Value

Returns a string value of the computer or device name.

Requirements

Platforms: .NET Compact Framework - Windows CE .NET

.NET Framework Security:

- Full trust for the immediate caller. This member cannot be used by partially trusted code.

IrDAClient.GetStream Method

Note: This namespace, class, or member is supported only in version 1.1 of the .NET Framework.

Gets the underlying stream of data.

```
[Visual Basic]
Public Function GetStream() As Stream
[C#]
public Stream GetStream();
[C++]
public: Stream* GetStream();
[JScript]
public function GetStream() : Stream;
```

Requirements

Platforms: .NET Compact Framework - Windows CE .NET

.NET Framework Security:

- Full trust for the immediate caller. This member cannot be used by partially trusted code.

IrDADeviceInfo Class

Note: This namespace, class, or member is supported only in version 1.1 of the .NET Framework.

Provides information about available servers and ports obtained by the client during a discovery query.

System.Object
   System.Net.Sockets.IrDADeviceInfo

```
[Visual Basic]
Public Class IrDADeviceInfo
[C#]
public class IrDADeviceInfo
[C++]
public __gc class IrDADeviceInfo
[JScript]
public class IrDADeviceInfo
```

Thread Safety

Any public static (**Shared** in Visual Basic) members of this type are safe for multithreaded operations. Any instance members are not guaranteed to be thread safe.

Requirements

Namespace: System.Net.Sockets

Platforms: .NET Compact Framework - Windows CE .NET

Assembly: System.Net.Irda (in System.Net.Irda.dll)

IrDADeviceInfo.CharacterSet Property

Note: This namespace, class, or member is supported only in version 1.1 of the .NET Framework.

Gets the character set used by the server, such as ASCII.

```
[Visual Basic]
Public ReadOnly Property CharacterSet As IrDACharacterSet
[C#]
public IrDACharacterSet CharacterSet {get;}
[C++]
public: __property IrDACharacterSet get_CharacterSet();
[JScript]
public function get CharacterSet() : IrDACharacterSet;
```

Property Value

A value of the **IrDACharacterSet** enumeration.

Requirements

Platforms: .NET Compact Framework - Windows CE .NET

.NET Framework Security:

- Full trust for the immediate caller. This member cannot be used by partially trusted code.

IrDADeviceInfo.DeviceID Property

Note: This namespace, class, or member is supported only in version 1.1 of the .NET Framework.

Gets the device identifier.

```
[Visual Basic]
Public ReadOnly Property DeviceID As Byte ()
[C#]
public byte[] DeviceID {get;}
```

```
[C++]
public: __property unsigned char get_DeviceID();
[JScript]
public function get DeviceID() : Byte[];
```

Property Value

A 4-byte value.

Requirements

Platforms: .NET Compact Framework - Windows CE .NET

.NET Framework Security:

- Full trust for the immediate caller. This member cannot be used by partially trusted code.

IrDADeviceInfo.DeviceName Property

Note: This namespace, class, or member is supported only in version 1.1 of the .NET Framework.

Gets a name of a device.

```
[Visual Basic]
Public ReadOnly Property DeviceName As String
[C#]
public string DeviceName {get;}
[C++]
public: __property String* get_DeviceName();
[JScript]
public function get DeviceName() : String;
```

Property Value

A string value identifying the device type, such as "fax."

Requirements

Platforms: .NET Compact Framework - Windows CE .NET

.NET Framework Security:

- Full trust for the immediate caller. This member cannot be used by partially trusted code.

IrDADeviceInfo.Hints Property

Note: This namespace, class, or member is supported only in version 1.1 of the .NET Framework.

Gets the type of the device, such as **Computer**.

```
[Visual Basic]
Public ReadOnly Property Hints As IrDAHints
[C#]
public IrDAHints Hints {get;}
[C++]
public: __property IrDAHints get_Hints();
[JScript]
public function get Hints() : IrDAHints;
```

Property Value

A value of the **IrDAHints** enumeration.

Requirements

Platforms: .NET Compact Framework - Windows CE .NET

.NET Framework Security:

- Full trust for the immediate caller. This member cannot be used by partially trusted code.

IrDAHints Enumeration

Note: This namespace, class, or member is supported only in version 1.1 of the .NET Framework.

Describes an enumeration of possible device types, such as **Fax**.

This enumeration has a **FlagsAttribute** attribute that allows a bitwise combination of its member values.

```
[Visual Basic]
<Flags>
<Serializable>
Public Enum IrDAHints
[C#]
[Flags]
[Serializable]
public enum IrDAHints
[C++]
[Flags]
[Serializable]
__value public enum IrDAHints
[JScript]
public
    Flags
    Serializable
enum IrDAHints
```

Members

Member name	Description	Value
Computer Supported only by the .NET Compact Framework.	A personal computer	4
Fax Supported only by the .NET Compact Framework.	A fax	32
FileServer Supported only by the .NET Compact Framework.	A personal computer file server	512
LanAccess Supported only by the .NET Compact Framework.	A local area network access	64
Modem Supported only by the .NET Compact Framework.	A modem	16
None Supported only by the .NET Compact Framework.	A name indicating no device	0
PdaAndPalmtop Supported only by the .NET Compact Framework.	A Pocket PC	2
PnP Supported only by the .NET Compact Framework.	A Plug and Play interface	1
Printer Supported only by the .NET Compact Framework.	A printer	8
Telephony Supported only by the .NET Compact Framework.	A telephonic device	256

Requirements

Namespace: System.Net.Sockets

Platforms: .NET Compact Framework - Windows CE .NET

Assembly: System.Net.Irda (in System.Net.Irda.dll)

IrDAListener Class

Note: This namespace, class, or member is supported only in version 1.1 of the .NET Framework.

Places a socket in a listening state to monitor connections from a specified service or network address.

System.Object
   System.Net.Sockets.IrDAListener

```
[Visual Basic]
Public Class IrDAListener
[C#]
public class IrDAListener
[C++]
public __gc class IrDAListener
[JScript]
public class IrDAListener
```

Thread Safety

Any public static (**Shared** in Visual Basic) members of this type are safe for multithreaded operations. Any instance members are not guaranteed to be thread safe.

Remarks

You can monitor a service by specifying a service name or a network address. The listener will not listen until you call the **Start** method.

Requirements

Namespace: System.Net.Sockets

Platforms: .NET Compact Framework - Windows CE .NET

Assembly: System.Net.Irda (in System.Net.Irda.dll)

IrDAListener Constructor

Note: This namespace, class, or member is supported only in version 1.1 of the .NET Framework.

Initializes a new instance of the **IrDAListener** class.

Overload List

Initializes a new instance of the **IrDAListener** class.

Supported only by the .NET Compact Framework.

   [Visual Basic] **Public Sub New(IrDAEndPoint)**
   [C#] **public IrDAListener(IrDAEndPoint);**
   [C++] **public: IrDAListener(IrDAEndPoint*);**
   [JScript] **public function IrDAListener(IrDAEndPoint);**

Initializes a new instance of the **IrDAListener** class.

Supported only by the .NET Compact Framework.

   [Visual Basic] **Public Sub New(String)**
   [C#] **public IrDAListener(string);**
   [C++] **public: IrDAListener(String*);**
   [JScript] **public function IrDAListener(String);**

IrDAListener Constructor (IrDAEndPoint)

Note: This namespace, class, or member is supported only in version 1.1 of the .NET Framework.

Initializes a new instance of the **IrDAListener** class.

```
[Visual Basic]
Public Sub New( _
    ByVal ep As IrDAEndPoint _
)
[C#]
public IrDAListener(
    IrDAEndPoint ep
);
[C++]
public: IrDAListener(
    IrDAEndPoint* ep
);
[JScript]
public function IrDAListener(
    ep : IrDAEndPoint
);
```

Parameters

ep
   The network address to monitor for making a connection.

Requirements

Platforms: .NET Compact Framework - Windows CE .NET

.NET Framework Security:

• Full trust for the immediate caller. This member cannot be used by partially trusted code.

IrDAListener Constructor (String)

Note: This namespace, class, or member is supported only in version 1.1 of the .NET Framework.

Initializes a new instance of the **IrDAListener** class.

```
[Visual Basic]
Public Sub New( _
    ByVal service As String _
)
[C#]
public IrDAListener(
    string service
);
[C++]
public: IrDAListener(
    String* service
);
[JScript]
public function IrDAListener(
    service : String
);
```

Parameters

service
   The name of the service to listen for.

Requirements

Platforms: .NET Compact Framework - Windows CE .NET

.NET Framework Security:

• Full trust for the immediate caller. This member cannot be used by partially trusted code.

IrDAListener.LocalEndpoint Property

Note: This namespace, class, or member is supported only in version 1.1 of the .NET Framework.

Gets a new instance of the **IrDAListener** class.

```
[Visual Basic]
Public ReadOnly Property LocalEndpoint As IrDAEndPoint
[C#]
public IrDAEndPoint LocalEndpoint {get;}
[C++]
public: __property IrDAEndPoint* get_LocalEndpoint();
[JScript]
public function get LocalEndpoint() : IrDAEndPoint;
```

Property Value

A socket.

Requirements

Platforms: .NET Compact Framework - Windows CE .NET

.NET Framework Security:

- Full trust for the immediate caller. This member cannot be used by partially trusted code.

IrDAListener.AcceptIrDAClient Method

Note: This namespace, class, or member is supported only in version 1.1 of the .NET Framework.

Creates a client object for a connection when the specified service or endpoint is detected by the listener component.

```
[Visual Basic]
Public Function AcceptIrDAClient() As IrDAClient
[C#]
public IrDAClient AcceptIrDAClient();
[C++]
public: IrDAClient* AcceptIrDAClient();
[JScript]
public function AcceptIrDAClient() : IrDAClient;
```

Return Value

An **IrDAClient** component.

Requirements

Platforms: .NET Compact Framework - Windows CE .NET

.NET Framework Security:

- Full trust for the immediate caller. This member cannot be used by partially trusted code.

IrDAListener.AcceptSocket Method

Note: This namespace, class, or member is supported only in version 1.1 of the .NET Framework.

Creates a new socket for a connection.

```
[Visual Basic]
Public Function AcceptSocket() As Socket
[C#]
public Socket AcceptSocket();
[C++]
public: Socket* AcceptSocket();
[JScript]
public function AcceptSocket() : Socket;
```

Return Value

A socket.

Requirements

Platforms: .NET Compact Framework - Windows CE .NET

.NET Framework Security:

- Full trust for the immediate caller. This member cannot be used by partially trusted code.

IrDAListener.Pending Method

Note: This namespace, class, or member is supported only in version 1.1 of the .NET Framework.

Determines if there is a connection pending.

```
[Visual Basic]
Public Function Pending() As Boolean
[C#]
public bool Pending();
[C++]
public: bool Pending();
[JScript]
public function Pending() : Boolean;
```

Return Value

true if there is a connection pending; otherwise, **false**.

Requirements

Platforms: .NET Compact Framework - Windows CE .NET

.NET Framework Security:

- Full trust for the immediate caller. This member cannot be used by partially trusted code.

IrDAListener.Start Method

Note: This namespace, class, or member is supported only in version 1.1 of the .NET Framework.

Starts the socket to listen for incoming connections.

```
[Visual Basic]
Public Sub Start()
[C#]
public void Start();
[C++]
public: void Start();
[JScript]
public function Start();
```

Requirements

Platforms: .NET Compact Framework - Windows CE .NET

.NET Framework Security:

- Full trust for the immediate caller. This member cannot be used by partially trusted code.

IrDAListener.Stop Method

Note: This namespace, class, or member is supported only in version 1.1 of the .NET Framework.

Stops the socket from monitoring connections.

```
[Visual Basic]
Public Sub Stop()
[C#]
public void Stop();
[C++]
public: void Stop();
[JScript]
public function Stop();
```

Requirements

Platforms: .NET Compact Framework - Windows CE .NET

.NET Framework Security:

- Full trust for the immediate caller. This member cannot be used by partially trusted code.

LingerOption Class

Specifies whether a **Socket** will remain connected after a call to **Close** and the length of time it will remain connected, if data remains to be sent.

For a list of all members of this type, see **LingerOption Members**.

System.Object
   System.Net.Sockets.LingerOption

```
[Visual Basic]
Public Class LingerOption
[C#]
public class LingerOption
[C++]
public __gc class LingerOption
[JScript]
public class LingerOption
```

Thread Safety

Any public static (**Shared** in Visual Basic) members of this type are safe for multithreaded operations. Any instance members are not guaranteed to be thread safe.

Remarks

There may still be data available in the outgoing network buffer after you close the **Socket**. If you want to specify the amount of time that the **Socket** will attempt to transmit unsent data after closing, create a **LingerOption** with the *enabled* parameter set to **true**, and the *seconds* parameter set to the desired amount of time. The *seconds* parameter is used to indicate how long you would like the **Socket** to remain connected before timing out. If you do not want the **Socket** to stay connected for any length of time after closing, create a **LingerOption** with the *enabled* parameter set to **false**. In this case, the **Socket** will close immediately and any unsent data will be lost. Once created, pass the **LingerOption** to the **Socket.SetSocketOption** method. If you are sending and receiving data with a **TcpClient**, then pass the **LingerOption** to the **TcpClient.LingerState** method.

By default, lingering is enabled with a zero time-out. As a result, the **Socket** will attempt to send pending data until there is no data left in the outgoing network buffer.

Example

[Visual Basic, C#] The following example sets a previously created **Socket** to linger one second after calling the **Close** method.

```
[Visual Basic]
Dim myOpts As New LingerOption(True, 1)

mySocket.SetSocketOption(SocketOptionLevel.Socket,
SocketOptionName.Linger, _
    myOpts)

[C#]
LingerOption myOpts = new LingerOption(true,1);

mySocket.SetSocketOption(SocketOptionLevel.Socket,
SocketOptionName.Linger, myOpts);
```

Requirements

Namespace: System.Net.Sockets

Platforms: Windows 98, Windows NT 4.0, Windows Millennium Edition, Windows 2000, Windows XP Home Edition, Windows XP Professional, Windows .NET Server family, .NET Compact Framework - Windows CE .NET

Assembly: System (in System.dll)

LingerOption Constructor

Initializes a new instance of the **LingerOption** class.

```
[Visual Basic]
Public Sub New( _
    ByVal enable As Boolean, _
    ByVal seconds As Integer _
)
[C#]
public LingerOption(
    bool enable,
    int seconds
);
[C++]
public: LingerOption(
    bool enable,
    int seconds
);
[JScript]
public function LingerOption(
    enable : Boolean,
    seconds : int
);
```

Parameters

enable
    true to remain connected after the **Socket.Close** method is called; otherwise, **false**.

seconds
    The number of seconds to remain connected after the **Socket.Close** method is called.

Remarks

There may still be data available in the outgoing network buffer after you close the **Socket**. Use the *enable* parameter to specify whether you would like the **Socket** to continue transmitting unsent data after the close method is called. Use the *seconds* parameter to indicate how long you would like the **Socket** to attempt transferring unsent data before timing out. If you specify **true** for the *enable* parameter and 0 for the *seconds* peramter, the **Socket** will attempt to send data until there is no data left in the outgoing network buffer. If you specify **false** for the *enable* peramter, the **Socket** will close immediately and any unsent data will be lost.

Requirements

Platforms: Windows 98, Windows NT 4.0, Windows Millennium Edition, Windows 2000, Windows XP Home Edition, Windows XP Professional, Windows .NET Server family, .NET Compact Framework - Windows CE .NET, Common Language Infrastructure (CLI) Standard

LingerOption.Enabled Property

Gets or sets a value indicating whether to linger after the **Socket** is closed.

```
[Visual Basic]
Public Property Enabled As Boolean
[C#]
public bool Enabled {get; set;}
[C++]
public: __property bool get_Enabled();
public: __property void set_Enabled(bool);
[JScript]
public function get Enabled() : Boolean;
public function set Enabled(Boolean);
```

Property Value

true if the **Socket** should linger after **Socket.Close** is called; otherwise **false**.

Remarks

You can use the **Enabled** property to determine whether the **Socket** will linger after closing. Change this value to **true** or **false** and pass the altered **LingerOption** to the **SetSocketOption** or **LingerState** method to disable or enable lingering.

Requirements

Platforms: Windows 98, Windows NT 4.0, Windows Millennium Edition, Windows 2000, Windows XP Home Edition, Windows XP Professional, Windows .NET Server family, .NET Compact Framework - Windows CE .NET, Common Language Infrastructure (CLI) Standard

LingerOption.LingerTime Property

Gets or sets the amount of time to remain connected after calling the **Socket.Close** method if data remains to be sent.

```
[Visual Basic]
Public Property LingerTime As Integer
[C#]
public int LingerTime {get; set;}
[C++]
public: __property int get_LingerTime();
public: __property void set_LingerTime(int);
[JScript]
public function get LingerTime() : int;
public function set LingerTime(int);
```

Property Value

The amount of time, in seconds, to remain connected after calling **Socket.Close**.

Remarks

Use this value if you want to determine how long a closed **Socket** will attempt transferring unsent data before timing out. You can also set this value to the desired time-out period, in seconds. If the **Enabled** property is **true**, and you set **LingerTime** to 0, the **Socket** will attempt to send data until there is no data left in the outgoing network buffer. If you change this value, you must pass the altered **LingerOption** to the **SetSocketOption** or **LingerState** method.

Requirements

Platforms: Windows 98, Windows NT 4.0, Windows Millennium Edition, Windows 2000, Windows XP Home Edition, Windows XP Professional, Windows .NET Server family, .NET Compact Framework - Windows CE .NET, Common Language Infrastructure (CLI) Standard

MulticastOption Class

Contains **IPAddress** values used for joining and dropping multicast groups.

System.Object
  System.Net.Sockets.MulticastOption

[Visual Basic]
```
Public Class MulticastOption
```
[C#]
```
public class MulticastOption
```
[C++]
```
public __gc class MulticastOption
```
[JScript]
```
public class MulticastOption
```

Thread Safety

Any public static (**Shared** in Visual Basic) members of this type are safe for multithreaded operations. Any instance members are not guaranteed to be thread safe.

Remarks

Use a **MulticastOption** to store the **IPAddress** of a multicast group you want to join or drop. Use the **Socket.SetSocketOption** method with the following parameters to join a multicast group.

Parameter	Value
socketOptionLevel	**SocketOptionLevel.Udp**
socketOptionName	**AddMembership**
object	**MulticastOption**

Use **DropMembership** to drop a multicast group.

Example

[Visual Basic, C#, C++] The following examples join the default IP interface to an IP multicast group. They assume the IP multicast group address in the range 224.0.0.0 to 239.255.255.255.

[Visual Basic]
```
' This is the listener example that shows how to use the
MulticastOption class.
' In particular, it shows how to use the MulticastOption
(IPAddress, IPAddress)
' constructor, which you need to use if you have a host with
more than one
' network card.
' The first parameter specifies the multicast group address,
and the second
' specifies the local address of the network card you want to
use for the data
' exchange.
' You must run this program in conjunction with the sender
program as
' follows:
' Open a console window and run the listener from the command line.
' In another console window run the sender. In both cases you
must specify
' the local IPAddress to use. To obtain this address run the
ipconfig comand
' from the command line.

Imports System
Imports System.Net
Imports System.Net.Sockets
Imports System.Text
Imports Microsoft.VisualBasic

Namespace Mssc.TransportProtocols.Utilities
```

```
Module M_TestMulticastOption

  Public Class TestMulticastOption

    Private Shared mcastAddress As IPAddress
    Private Shared mcastPort As Integer
    Private Shared mcastSocket As Socket
    Private Shared mcastOption As MulticastOption

    Private Shared Sub MulticastOptionProperties()
      Console.WriteLine(("Current multicast group is:
" + mcastOption.Group.ToString()))
      Console.WriteLine(("Current multicast local address
is: " + mcastOption.LocalAddress.ToString()))
    End Sub 'MulticastOptionProperties

    Private Shared Sub StartMulticast()

      Try
        mcastSocket = New Socket
(AddressFamily.InterNetwork, SocketType.Dgram, ProtocolType.Udp)

        Console.Write("Enter the local IP address: ")

        Dim localIPAddr As IPAddress =
IPAddress.Parse(Console.ReadLine())

        'IPAddress localIP = IPAddress.Any;
        Dim localEP As EndPoint = CType
(New IPEndPoint(localIPAddr, mcastPort), EndPoint)

        mcastSocket.Bind(localEP)

        ' Define a MulticastOption object specifying
the multicast group
        ' address and the local IPAddress.
        ' The multicast group address is the same as the
address used by the server.
        mcastOption = New MulticastOption(mcastAddress, localIPAddr)

        mcastSocket.SetSocketOption(SocketOptionLevel.IP,
SocketOptionName.AddMembership, mcastOption)

      Catch e As Exception
        Console.WriteLine(e.ToString())
      End Try
    End Sub 'StartMulticast

    Private Shared Sub ReceiveBroadcastMessages()
      Dim done As Boolean = False
      Dim bytes() As Byte = New [Byte](99) {}
      Dim groupEP As New IPEndPoint(mcastAddress, mcastPort)
      Dim remoteEP As EndPoint = CType(New IPEndPoint
(IPAddress.Any, 0), EndPoint)

      Try
        While Not done
          Console.WriteLine("Waiting for multicast packets.....")
          Console.WriteLine("Enter ^C to terminate.")

          mcastSocket.ReceiveFrom(bytes, remoteEP)

          Console.WriteLine("Received broadcast from {0}
:" + ControlChars.Lf + " {1}" + ControlChars.Lf,
groupEP.ToString(), Encoding.ASCII.GetString(bytes, 0, bytes.Length))
        End While

        mcastSocket.Close()

      Catch e As Exception
        Console.WriteLine(e.ToString())
      End Try
    End Sub 'ReceiveBrodcastMessages
```

```vb
      Public Shared Sub Main(ByVal args() As String)
         ' Initialize the multicast address group and multicast port.
         ' Both address and port are selected from the allowed sets as
         ' defined in the related RFC documents. These are the same
         ' as the values used by the sender.
         mcastAddress = IPAddress.Parse("224.168.100.2")
         mcastPort = 11000

         ' Start a multicast group.
         StartMulticast()

         ' Display MulticastOption properties.
         MulticastOptionProperties()

         ' Receive broadcast messages.
         ReceiveBroadcastMessages()
      End Sub 'Main
   End Class 'TestMulticastOption

  End Module

End Namespace
```

```csharp
[C#]
using System;
using System.Net;
using System.Net.Sockets;
using System.Text;

// This is the listener example that shows how to use the
MulticastOption class.
// In particular, it shows how to use the MulticastOption
(IPAddress, IPAddress)
// constructor, which you need to use if you have a host with
more than one
// network card.
// The first parameter specifies the multicast group address,
and the second
// specifies the local address of the network card you want to
use for the data
// exchange.
// You must run this program in conjunction with the sender program as
// follows:
// Open a console window and run the listener from the command line.
// In another console window run the sender. In both cases you
must specify
// the local IPAddress to use. To obtain this address run the
ipconfig comand
// from the command line.
//
namespace Mssc.TransportProtocols.Utilities
{

  public class TestMulticastOption
  {

    private static IPAddress mcastAddress;
    private static int mcastPort;
    private static Socket mcastSocket;
    private static MulticastOption mcastOption;

    private static void MulticastOptionProperties()
    {
      Console.WriteLine("Current multicast group is: " +
mcastOption.Group);
      Console.WriteLine("Current multicast local address is:
" + mcastOption.LocalAddress);
    }

    private static void StartMulticast()
    {

      try
      {
        mcastSocket = new Socket(AddressFamily.InterNetwork,
                      SocketType.Dgram,
                      ProtocolType.Udp);

        Console.Write("Enter the local IP address: ");

        IPAddress localIPAddr = IPAddress.Parse(Console.ReadLine());

        //IPAddress localIP = IPAddress.Any;
        EndPoint localEP = (EndPoint)new IPEndPoint
(localIPAddr, mcastPort);

        mcastSocket.Bind(localEP);

        // Define a MulticastOption object specifying the
multicast group
        // address and the local IPAddress.
        // The multicast group address is the same as the
address used by the server.
        mcastOption = new MulticastOption(mcastAddress, localIPAddr);

        mcastSocket.SetSocketOption(SocketOptionLevel.IP,
                         SocketOptionName.AddMembership,
                         mcastOption);

      }

      catch (Exception e)
      {
        Console.WriteLine(e.ToString());
      }
    }

    private static void ReceiveBroadcastMessages()
    {
      bool done = false;
      byte[] bytes = new Byte[100];
      IPEndPoint groupEP = new IPEndPoint(mcastAddress, mcastPort);
      EndPoint remoteEP = (EndPoint) new IPEndPoint(IPAddress.Any,0);

      try
      {
        while (!done)
        {
          Console.WriteLine("Waiting for multicast packets...");
          Console.WriteLine("Enter ^C to terminate.");

          mcastSocket.ReceiveFrom(bytes, ref remoteEP);

          Console.WriteLine("Received broadcast from {0} :\n {1}\n",
            groupEP.ToString(),
            Encoding.ASCII.GetString(bytes,0,bytes.Length));

        }

        mcastSocket.Close();
      }

      catch (Exception e)
      {
        Console.WriteLine(e.ToString());
      }
    }

    public static void Main(String[] args)
    {
      // Initialize the multicast address group and multicast port.
      // Both address and port are selected from the allowed sets as
      // defined in the related RFC documents. These are the same
      // as the values used by the sender.
      mcastAddress = IPAddress.Parse("224.168.100.2");
      mcastPort = 11000;

      // Start a multicast group.
      StartMulticast();
```

```
        // Display MulticastOption properties.
        MulticastOptionProperties();

        // Receive broadcast messages.
        ReceiveBroadcastMessages();
    }
  }
}
```

[C++]
```cpp
#using <mscorlib.dll>
#using <System.dll>

using namespace System;
using namespace System::Net;
using namespace System::Net::Sockets;
using namespace System::Text;

// This program shows how to use the MultiCastOption type.
In particular,
// it shows how to use the MultiCastOption
(IPAddress, IPAddress) constructor.
// You need to use this constructor, in the case of
multihomed host (i.e.,
// a host with more than one network card). With the first
parameter you
// specify the multicast group address, with the second you specify the
// local address of one of the network cards you want to use
for the data
// exchange.
// You must run this program in conjunction with the sender program as
// follows:
// Open a console window and run the listener from the command line.
// In another console window run the sender. In both cases
you must specify
// the local IPAddress to use. To obtain this address run the
ipconfig from
// the command line.
//

public __gc class TestMulticastOption {
private:
    static IPAddress* mcastAddress;
    static int  mcastPort;
    static Socket* mcastSocket;
    static MulticastOption* mcastOption;

    static void MulticastOptionProperties() {
        Console::WriteLine(S"Current multicast group is:
{0}", mcastOption->Group);
        Console::WriteLine(S"Current multicast local address
is: {0}", mcastOption->LocalAddress);
    }

    static void StartMulticast() {

        try {
            mcastSocket = new Socket(AddressFamily::InterNetwork,
                SocketType::Dgram,
                ProtocolType::Udp);

            Console::Write(S"Enter the local IP Address: ");

            IPAddress* localIPAddr =
IPAddress::Parse(Console::ReadLine());

            //IPAddress localIP = IPAddress::Any;
            EndPoint* localEP = dynamic_cast<EndPoint*>(new
IPEndPoint(localIPAddr, mcastPort));

            mcastSocket->Bind(localEP);

            // Define a MuticastOption Object* specifying the
multicast group
            // address and the local IPAddress.
```
```cpp
            // The multicast group address is the same one used
by the server.
            mcastOption = new MulticastOption(mcastAddress, localIPAddr);

            mcastSocket->SetSocketOption(SocketOptionLevel::IP,
                SocketOptionName::AddMembership,
                mcastOption);

        } catch (Exception* e) {
            Console::WriteLine(e);
        }
    }

    static void ReceiveBrodcastMessages() {
        bool done = false;
        Byte bytes[] = new Byte[100];
        IPEndPoint* groupEP = new IPEndPoint(mcastAddress, mcastPort);
        EndPoint* remoteEP = dynamic_cast<EndPoint*> (new
IPEndPoint(IPAddress::Any, 0));

        try {
            while (!done) {
                Console::WriteLine(S"Waiting for Multicast
packets.......");
                Console::WriteLine(S"Enter ^C to terminate.");

                mcastSocket->ReceiveFrom(bytes, &remoteEP);

                Console::WriteLine(S"Received broadcast from {0} :\n {1}\n",
                    groupEP,
                    Encoding::ASCII->GetString(bytes, 0, bytes->Length));
            }
            mcastSocket->Close();
        } catch (Exception* e) {
            Console::WriteLine(e);
        }
    }

public:
    static void Main() {
        // Initialize multicast address group and multicast port.
        // Both address and port are selected from the allowed sets as
        // defined in the related RFC documents. These are the
same values
        // used by the sender.
        mcastAddress = IPAddress::Parse(S"224.168.100.2");
        mcastPort = 11000;

        // Start a multicast group.
        StartMulticast();

        // Display multicast option properties.
        MulticastOptionProperties();

        // Receive brodcast messages.
        ReceiveBrodcastMessages();
    }
};

int main()
{
    TestMulticastOption::Main();
}
```

[Visual Basic]
```vbnet
' This sender example must be used in conjunction with the
listener program.
' You must run this program as follows:
' Open a console window and run the listener from the command line.
' In another console window run the sender. In both cases
you must specify
' the local IPAddress to use. To obtain this address, run the
ipconfig command
' from the command line.
'
```

```vbnet
Imports System
Imports System.Net.Sockets
Imports System.Net
Imports System.Text
Imports Microsoft.VisualBasic

Namespace Mssc.TransportProtocols.Utilities

  Module M_TestMulticastOption

    Class TestMulticastOption

      Private Shared mcastAddress As IPAddress
      Private Shared mcastPort As Integer
      Private Shared mcastSocket As Socket

      Shared Sub JoinMulticastGroup()
        Try
          ' Create a multicast socket.
          mcastSocket = New Socket(AddressFamily.InterNetwork, _
SocketType.Dgram, ProtocolType.Udp)

          ' Get the local IP address used by the listener and _
the sender to
          ' exchange multicast messages.
          Console.Write(ControlChars.Lf + "Enter local IPAddress _
for sending multicast packets: ")
          Dim localIPAddr As IPAddress = _
IPAddress.Parse(Console.ReadLine())

          ' Create an IPEndPoint object.
          Dim IPlocal As New IPEndPoint(localIPAddr, 0)

          ' Bind this endpoint to the multicast socket.
          mcastSocket.Bind(IPlocal)

          ' Define a MulticastOption object specifying the _
multicast group
          ' address and the local IP address.
          ' The multicast group address is the same as the _
address used by the listener.
          Dim mcastOption As MulticastOption
          mcastOption = New MulticastOption(mcastAddress, localIPAddr)

          mcastSocket.SetSocketOption(SocketOptionLevel.IP, _
SocketOptionName.AddMembership, mcastOption)

        Catch e As Exception
          Console.WriteLine((ControlChars.Lf + e.ToString()))
        End Try
      End Sub 'JoinMulticast

      Shared Sub BroadcastMessage(ByVal message As String)
        Dim endPoint As IPEndPoint

        Try
          'Send multicast packets to the listener.
          endPoint = New IPEndPoint(mcastAddress, mcastPort)
          mcastSocket.SendTo _
(ASCIIEncoding.ASCII.GetBytes(message), endPoint)
          Console.WriteLine("Multicast data sent.....")
        Catch e As Exception
          Console.WriteLine((ControlChars.Lf + e.ToString()))
        End Try

        mcastSocket.Close()
      End Sub 'BrodcastMessage

      Public Shared Sub Main(ByVal args() As String)
        ' Initialize the multicast address group and multicast port.
        ' Both address and port are selected from the allowed sets as
        ' defined in the related RFC documents. These are the _
same as the
        ' values used by the sender.
```

```vbnet
        mcastAddress = IPAddress.Parse("224.168.100.2")
        mcastPort = 11000

        ' Join the listener multicast group.
        JoinMulticastGroup()

        ' Broadcast the message to the listener.
        BroadcastMessage("Hello multicast listener.")
      End Sub 'Main
    End Class 'TestMulticastOption

  End Module

End Namespace
```

```csharp
[C#]
using System;
using System.Net.Sockets;
using System.Net;
using System.Text;

// This sender example must be used in conjunction with the
// listener program.
// You must run this program as follows:
// Open a console window and run the listener from the command line.
// In another console window run the sender. In both cases
you must specify
// the local IPAddress to use. To obtain this address,
run the ipconfig command
// from the command line.
//
namespace Mssc.TransportProtocols.Utilities
{
  class TestMulticastOption
  {

    static IPAddress mcastAddress;
    static int mcastPort;
    static Socket mcastSocket;

    static void JoinMulticastGroup()
    {
      try
      {
        // Create a multicast socket.
        mcastSocket = new Socket(AddressFamily.InterNetwork,
                                 SocketType.Dgram,
                                 ProtocolType.Udp);

        // Get the local IP address used by the listener
and the sender to
        // exchange multicast messages.
        Console.Write("\nEnter local IPAddress for sending
multicast packets: ");
        IPAddress  localIPAddr = IPAddress.Parse(Console.ReadLine());

        // Create an IPEndPoint object.
        IPEndPoint IPlocal = new IPEndPoint(localIPAddr, 0);

        // Bind this endpoint to the multicast socket.
        mcastSocket.Bind(IPlocal);

        // Define a MulticastOption object specifying the
multicast group
        // address and the local IP address.
        // The multicast group address is the same as the
address used by the listener.
        MulticastOption mcastOption;
        mcastOption = new MulticastOption(mcastAddress, localIPAddr);

        mcastSocket.SetSocketOption(SocketOptionLevel.IP,
                                    SocketOptionName.AddMembership,
                                    mcastOption);
```

```
    }
    catch (Exception e)
    {
      Console.WriteLine("\n" + e.ToString());
    }
  }

  static void BroadcastMessage(string message)
  {
    IPEndPoint endPoint;

    try
    {
      //Send multicast packets to the listener.
      endPoint = new IPEndPoint(mcastAddress,mcastPort);
      mcastSocket.SendTo(ASCIIEncoding.ASCII.GetBytes
(message), endPoint);
      Console.WriteLine("Multicast data sent.....");
    }
    catch (Exception e)
    {
      Console.WriteLine("\n" + e.ToString());
    }

    mcastSocket.Close();
  }

  static void Main(string[] args)
  {
    // Initialize the multicast address group and multicast port.
    // Both address and port are selected from the allowed sets as
    // defined in the related RFC documents. These are the same
    // as the values used by the sender.
    mcastAddress = IPAddress.Parse("224.168.100.2");
    mcastPort = 11000;

    // Join the listener multicast group.
    JoinMulticastGroup();

    // Broadcast the message to the listener.
    BroadcastMessage("Hello multicast listener.");
  }
 }
}

[C++]
#using <mscorlib.dll>
#using <System.dll>

using namespace System;
using namespace System::Net::Sockets;
using namespace System::Net;
using namespace System::Text;

// This is an auxiliary program to be used in conjunction
with a listener
// program.
// You must run this program as follows:
// Open a console window and run the listener from the command line.
// In another console window run the sender. In both cases you
must specify
// the local IPAddress to use. To obtain this address run the ipconfig
// from the command line.
//

__gc class TestMulticastOption {

  static IPAddress* mcastAddress;
  static int mcastPort;
  static Socket* mcastSocket;

  static void JoinMulticast() {
    try {
      // Create multicast socket.
      mcastSocket = new Socket(AddressFamily::InterNetwork,
        SocketType::Dgram,
        ProtocolType::Udp);

      // Get the local IP address used by the listener
and the sender to
      // exchange data in a multicast fashion.
      Console::Write(S"\nEnter local IPAddress for sending
multicast packets: ");
      IPAddress* localIPAddr =
IPAddress::Parse(Console::ReadLine());

      // Create an IPEndPoint Object*.
      IPEndPoint* IPlocal = new IPEndPoint(localIPAddr, 0);

      // Bind this end point to the multicast socket.
      mcastSocket->Bind(IPlocal);

      // Define a MuticastOption Object* specifying the
multicast group
      // address and the local IPAddress.
      // The multicast group address is the same one used
by the listener.
      MulticastOption* mcastOption;
      mcastOption = new MulticastOption(mcastAddress, localIPAddr);

      mcastSocket->SetSocketOption(SocketOptionLevel::IP,
        SocketOptionName::AddMembership,
        mcastOption);

    } catch (Exception* e) {
      Console::WriteLine(S"\n {0}", e);
    }
  }

  static void BrodcastMessage(String* message) {
    IPEndPoint* endPoint;

    try {
      //Send multicast packets to the listener.
      endPoint = new IPEndPoint(mcastAddress, mcastPort);
      mcastSocket->SendTo(ASCIIEncoding::ASCII->GetBytes
(message), endPoint);
      Console::WriteLine(S"Multicast data sent.....");
    } catch (Exception* e) {
      Console::WriteLine(S"\n {0}", e);
    }

    mcastSocket->Close();
  }

public:
  static void main() {
    // Initialize multicast address group and multicast port.
    // Both address and port are selected from the allowed sets as
    // defined in the related RFC documents. These are the
same values
    // used by the sender.
    mcastAddress = IPAddress::Parse(S"224.168.100.2");
    mcastPort = 11000;

    // Join the listener multicast group.
    JoinMulticast();

    // Broadcast message to the listener.
    BrodcastMessage(S"Hello multicast listener.");
  }
};

int main()
{
  TestMulticastOption::main();
}
```

Requirements

Namespace: System.Net.Sockets

Platforms: Windows 98, Windows NT 4.0,
Windows Millennium Edition, Windows 2000,
Windows XP Home Edition, Windows XP Professional,
Windows .NET Server family,
.NET Compact Framework - Windows CE .NET

Assembly: System (in System.dll)

MulticastOption Constructor

Initializes a new instance of the **MulticastOption** class.

Overload List

Initializes a new version of the **MulticastOption** class for the
specified IP multicast group.

Supported by the .NET Compact Framework.

[Visual Basic] **Public Sub New(IPAddress)**
[C#] **public MulticastOption(IPAddress);**
[C++] **public: MulticastOption(IPAddress*);**
[JScript] **public function MulticastOption(IPAddress);**

Initializes a new instance of the **MulticastOption** class with the
specified IP multicast group address and local IP address associated
with a network interface.

Supported by the .NET Compact Framework.

[Visual Basic] **Public Sub New(IPAddress, IPAddress)**
[C#] **public MulticastOption(IPAddress, IPAddress);**
[C++] **public: MulticastOption(IPAddress*, IPAddress*);**
[JScript] **public function MulticastOption(IPAddress,
IPAddress);**

Example

[Visual Basic, C#, C++] **Note** This example shows how to use
one of the overloaded versions of the **MulticastOption**
constructor. For other examples that might be available, see the
individual overload topics.

[Visual Basic]
```
' Define a MulticastOption object specifying the multicast group
' address and the local IPAddress.
' The multicast group address is the same as the address used by
the server.
mcastOption = New MulticastOption(mcastAddress, localIPAddr)

mcastSocket.SetSocketOption(SocketOptionLevel.IP,
SocketOptionName.AddMembership, mcastOption)
```

[C#]
```
    // Define a MulticastOption object specifying the
multicast group
    // address and the local IPAddress.
    // The multicast group address is the same as the
address used by the server.
    mcastOption = new MulticastOption(mcastAddress, localIPAddr);

    mcastSocket.SetSocketOption(SocketOptionLevel.IP,
                                SocketOptionName.AddMembership,
                                mcastOption);
```

[C++]
```
    // Define a MulticastOption Object* specifying the
multicast group
```

// address and the local IPAddress.
// The multicast group address is the same one used
by the server.
```
    mcastOption = new MulticastOption(mcastAddress, localIPAddr);

    mcastSocket->SetSocketOption(SocketOptionLevel::IP,
        SocketOptionName::AddMembership,
        mcastOption);
```

MulticastOption Constructor (IPAddress)

Initializes a new version of the **MulticastOption** class for the
specified IP multicast group.

```
[Visual Basic]
Public Sub New( _
   ByVal group As IPAddress _
)
[C#]
public MulticastOption(
   IPAddress group
);
[C++]
public: MulticastOption(
   IPAddress* group
);
[JScript]
public function MulticastOption(
   group : IPAddress
);
```

Parameters

group
     The **IPAddress** of the multicast group.

Exceptions

Exception Type	Condition
ArgumentNullException	*group* is a null reference (**Nothing** in Visual Basic).

Requirements

Platforms: Windows 98, Windows NT 4.0,
Windows Millennium Edition, Windows 2000,
Windows XP Home Edition, Windows XP Professional,
Windows .NET Server family,
.NET Compact Framework - Windows CE .NET,
Common Language Infrastructure (CLI) Standard

MulticastOption Constructor (IPAddress, IPAddress)

Initializes a new instance of the **MulticastOption** class with the
specified IP multicast group address and local IP address associated
with a network interface.

```
[Visual Basic]
Public Sub New( _
   ByVal group As IPAddress, _
   ByVal mcint As IPAddress _
)
[C#]
public MulticastOption(
   IPAddress group,
   IPAddress mcint
);
```

```
[C++]
public: MulticastOption(
    IPAddress* group,
    IPAddress* mcint
);
[JScript]
public function MulticastOption(
    group : IPAddress,
    mcint : IPAddress
);
```

Parameters

group

    The group **IPAddress**.

mcint

    The local **IPAddress**.

Exceptions

Exception Type	Condition
ArgumentNullException	*group* is a null reference (**Nothing** in Visual Basic).
	-or-
	mcint is a null reference (**Nothing**).

Example

```
[Visual Basic]
' Define a MulticastOption object specifying the multicast group
' address and the local IPAddress.
' The multicast group address is the same as the address      ⌐
used by the server.
mcastOption = New MulticastOption(mcastAddress, localIPAddr)

mcastSocket.SetSocketOption(SocketOptionLevel.IP,             ⌐
SocketOptionName.AddMembership, mcastOption)

[C#]
    // Define a MulticastOption object specifying         ⌐
the multicast group
    // address and the local IPAddress.
    // The multicast group address is the same as the    ⌐
address used by the server.
    mcastOption = new MulticastOption(mcastAddress, localIPAddr);

    mcastSocket.SetSocketOption(SocketOptionLevel.IP,
                    SocketOptionName.AddMembership,
                    mcastOption);

[C++]
    // Define a MuticastOption Object* specifying the     ⌐
multicast group
    // address and the local IPAddress.
    // The multicast group address is the same one used  ⌐
by the server.
    mcastOption = new MulticastOption(mcastAddress, localIPAddr);

    mcastSocket->SetSocketOption(SocketOptionLevel::IP,
        SocketOptionName::AddMembership,
        mcastOption);
```

Requirements

Platforms: Windows 98, Windows NT 4.0, Windows Millennium Edition, Windows 2000, Windows XP Home Edition, Windows XP Professional, Windows .NET Server family, .NET Compact Framework - Windows CE .NET, Common Language Infrastructure (CLI) Standard

MulticastOption.Group Property

Gets or sets the IP address of a multicast group.

```
[Visual Basic]
Public Property Group As IPAddress
[C#]
public IPAddress Group {get; set;}
[C++]
public: __property IPAddress* get_Group();
public: __property void set_Group(IPAddress*);
[JScript]
public function get Group() : IPAddress;
public function set Group(IPAddress);
```

Property Value

An **IPAddress** containing the Internet address of a multicast group.

Remarks

Valid IP addresses for multicast packets are in the range 224.0.0.0 to 239.255.255.255.

Example

```
[Visual Basic]
Private Shared Sub MulticastOptionProperties()
    Console.WriteLine(("Current multicast group is: " +       ⌐
mcastOption.Group.ToString()))
    Console.WriteLine(("Current multicast local address is: " + ⌐
mcastOption.LocalAddress.ToString()))
End Sub 'MulticastOptionProperties

[C#]
    private static void MulticastOptionProperties()
    {
        Console.WriteLine("Current multicast group is: " +      ⌐
mcastOption.Group);
        Console.WriteLine("Current multicast local address is:  ⌐
" + mcastOption.LocalAddress);
    }

[C++]
static void MulticastOptionProperties() {
    Console::WriteLine(S"Current multicast group is: {0}",      ⌐
mcastOption->Group);
    Console::WriteLine(S"Current multicast local address is:    ⌐
{0}", mcastOption->LocalAddress);
}
```

Requirements

Platforms: Windows 98, Windows NT 4.0, Windows Millennium Edition, Windows 2000, Windows XP Home Edition, Windows XP Professional, Windows .NET Server family, .NET Compact Framework - Windows CE .NET, Common Language Infrastructure (CLI) Standard

MulticastOption.LocalAddress Property

Gets or sets the local address associated with a multicast group.

```
[Visual Basic]
Public Property LocalAddress As IPAddress
[C#]
public IPAddress LocalAddress {get; set;}
[C++]
public: __property IPAddress* get_LocalAddress();
public: __property void set_LocalAddress(IPAddress*);
```

```
[JScript]
public function get LocalAddress() : IPAddress;
public function set LocalAddress(IPAddress);
```

Property Value

An **IPAddress** containing the local address associated with a multicast group.

Remarks

The **LocalAddress** property contains the IP address of the interface associated with the multicast group membership. If **LocalAddress** is set to **Any**, the default interface is used.

Example

```
[Visual Basic]
Private Shared Sub MulticastOptionProperties()
  Console.WriteLine(("Current multicast group is: " +        ⌐
mcastOption.Group.ToString()))
  Console.WriteLine(("Current multicast local address is: " +      ⌐
mcastOption.LocalAddress.ToString()))
End Sub 'MulticastOptionProperties
```

```
[C#]
    private static void MulticastOptionProperties()
    {
      Console.WriteLine("Current multicast group is: " +         ⌐
mcastOption.Group);
      Console.WriteLine("Current multicast local address       ⌐
is: " + mcastOption.LocalAddress);
    }
```

```
[C++]
static void MulticastOptionProperties() {
  Console::WriteLine(S"Current multicast group is: {0}",       ⌐
mcastOption->Group);
  Console::WriteLine(S"Current multicast local address is:    ⌐
{0}", mcastOption->LocalAddress);
}
```

Requirements

Platforms: Windows 98, Windows NT 4.0, Windows Millennium Edition, Windows 2000, Windows XP Home Edition, Windows XP Professional, Windows .NET Server family, .NET Compact Framework - Windows CE .NET, Common Language Infrastructure (CLI) Standard

NetworkStream Class

Provides the underlying stream of data for network access.

System.Object
  System.MarshalByRefObject
    System.IO.Stream
      System.Net.Sockets.NetworkStream

```
[Visual Basic]
Public Class NetworkStream
   Inherits Stream
[C#]
public class NetworkStream : Stream
[C++]
public __gc class NetworkStream : public Stream
[JScript]
public class NetworkStream extends Stream
```

Thread Safety

Any public static (**Shared** in Visual Basic) members of this type are safe for multithreaded operations. Any instance members are not guaranteed to be thread safe.

Remarks

The **NetworkStream** class provides methods for sending and receiving data over **Stream** sockets in blocking mode. For more information of blocking versus non-blocking **Socket**, see **Using an Asynchronous Client Socket**.You can use the **NetworkStream** class for both synchronous and asynchronous data transfer. For more information on asynchronous versus synchronous communication, see **Sockets**. In order to create a **NetworkStream**, you must provide a connected **Socket**. You can also specify what **FileAccess** permission the **NetworkStream** has over the provided **Socket**. By default, closing the **NetworkStream** does not close the provided **Socket**. If you want the **NetworkStream** to have permission to close the provided **Socket**, you must specify **true** for the value of the *ownsSocket* constructor parameter.

Use the **Write** and **Read** methods for simple single thread synchronous blocking I/O. If you want to process your I/O using separate threads, consider using the **BeginWrite/ EndWrite** and **BeginRead/ EndRead** methods for communication.

The **NetworkStream** does not support random access to the network data stream. The value of the **CanSeek** property, which indicates whether the stream supports seeking, is always **false**; reading the **Position** property, reading the **Length** property, or calling the **Seek** method will throw a **NotSupportedException**.

Example

[Visual Basic, C#, C++] The following example demonstrates how to create a **NetworkStream** from a connected **Stream Socket** and perform basic synchronous blocking I/O.

```
[Visual Basic]
' Create the NetworkStream for communicating with the remote host.
Dim myNetworkStream As NetworkStream

If networkStreamOwnsSocket Then
   myNetworkStream = New NetworkStream(mySocket, True)
Else
   myNetworkStream = New NetworkStream(mySocket)
End If
```

```
[C#]
// Create the NetworkStream for communicating with the remote host.
NetworkStream myNetworkStream;

if (networkStreamOwnsSocket){
   myNetworkStream = new NetworkStream(mySocket, true);
}
else{
   myNetworkStream = new NetworkStream(mySocket);
}
```

```
[C++]
   // Create the NetworkStream for communicating with the
remote host.
   NetworkStream* myNetworkStream;

   if (networkStreamOwnsSocket) {
      myNetworkStream = new NetworkStream(mySocket, true);
   } else {
      myNetworkStream = new NetworkStream(mySocket);
   }
```

Requirements

Namespace: System.Net.Sockets

Platforms: Windows 98, Windows NT 4.0, Windows Millennium Edition, Windows 2000, Windows XP Home Edition, Windows XP Professional, Windows .NET Server family, .NET Compact Framework - Windows CE .NET

Assembly: System (in System.dll)

NetworkStream Constructor

Creates a new instance of the **NetworkStream** class.

Overload List

Creates a new instance of the **NetworkStream** class for the specified **Socket**.

Supported by the .NET Compact Framework.

  [Visual Basic] **Public Sub New(Socket)**
  [C#] **public NetworkStream(Socket);**
  [C++] **public: NetworkStream(Socket*);**
  [JScript] **public function NetworkStream(Socket);**

Initializes a new instance of the **NetworkStream** class for the specified **Socket** with the specified **Socket** ownership.

Supported by the .NET Compact Framework.

  [Visual Basic] **Public Sub New(Socket, Boolean)**
  [C#] **public NetworkStream(Socket, bool);**
  [C++] **public: NetworkStream(Socket*, bool);**
  [JScript] **public function NetworkStream(Socket, Boolean);**

Creates a new instance of the **NetworkStream** class for the specified **Socket** with the specified access rights.

Supported by the .NET Compact Framework.

  [Visual Basic] **Public Sub New(Socket, FileAccess)**
  [C#] **public NetworkStream(Socket, FileAccess);**
  [C++] **public: NetworkStream(Socket*, FileAccess);**
  [JScript] **public function NetworkStream(Socket, FileAccess);**

Creates a new instance of the **NetworkStream** class for the specified **Socket** with the specified access rights and the specified **Socket** ownership.

Supported by the .NET Compact Framework.

[Visual Basic] **Public Sub New(Socket, FileAccess, Boolean)**

[C#] **public NetworkStream(Socket, FileAccess, bool);**

[C++] **public: NetworkStream(Socket*, FileAccess, bool);**

[JScript] **public function NetworkStream(Socket, FileAccess, Boolean);**

Example

[Visual Basic, C#, C++] The following example creates a **NetworkStream** with the ability to read and write to the **Socket**. Ownership of the **Socket** is given to this **NetworkStream** by specifying **true** for *ownsSocket*.

[Visual Basic, C#, C++] **Note** This example shows how to use one of the overloaded versions of the **NetworkStream** constructor. For other examples that might be available, see the individual overload topics.

```
[Visual Basic]
mySocket.Connect(myIpEndPoint)

' Create the NetworkStream for communicating with the remote host.
Dim myNetworkStream As NetworkStream

If networkStreamOwnsSocket Then
    myNetworkStream = New NetworkStream(mySocket,
FileAccess.ReadWrite, True)
Else
    myNetworkStream = New NetworkStream(mySocket, FileAccess.ReadWrite)
End If
```

```
[C#]
mySocket.Connect(myIpEndPoint);

// Create the NetworkStream for communicating with the remote host.
NetworkStream myNetworkStream;

if (networkStreamOwnsSocket){
    myNetworkStream = new NetworkStream(mySocket,
FileAccess.ReadWrite, true);
}
else{
    myNetworkStream = new NetworkStream(mySocket,
FileAccess.ReadWrite);
}
```

```
[C++]
mySocket->Connect(myIpEndPoint);

// Create the NetworkStream for communicating with the remote host.
NetworkStream* myNetworkStream;

if (networkStreamOwnsSocket) {
    myNetworkStream = new NetworkStream(mySocket,
FileAccess::ReadWrite, true);
} else {
    myNetworkStream = new NetworkStream(mySocket,
FileAccess::ReadWrite);
}
```

NetworkStream Constructor (Socket)

Creates a new instance of the **NetworkStream** class for the specified **Socket**.

```
[Visual Basic]
Public Sub New( _
    ByVal socket As Socket _
)
```

```
[C#]
public NetworkStream(
    Socket socket
);
[C++]
public: NetworkStream(
    Socket* socket
);
[JScript]
public function NetworkStream(
    socket : Socket
);
```

Parameters

socket

The **Socket** that the **NetworkStream** will use to send and receive data.

Exceptions

Exception Type	Condition
ArgumentNullException	*socket* is a null reference (**Nothing** in Visual Basic).
IOException	*socket* is not connected.
	-or-
	The **SocketType** property of *socket* is not **SocketType.Stream**.
	-or-
	socket is in a nonblocking state.

Remarks

The **NetworkStream** is created with read/write access to the specified **Socket**. The **NetworkStream** does not own the underlying **Socket**, so calling the **Close** method will not close the **Socket**.

Example

[Visual Basic, C#, C++] The following example illustrates how to create a **NetworkStream** with a **Socket**.

```
[Visual Basic]
' Create the NetworkStream for communicating with the remote host.
Dim myNetworkStream As NetworkStream

If networkStreamOwnsSocket Then
    myNetworkStream = New NetworkStream(mySocket, True)
Else
    myNetworkStream = New NetworkStream(mySocket)
End If
```

```
[C#]
// Create the NetworkStream for communicating with the remote host.
NetworkStream myNetworkStream;

if (networkStreamOwnsSocket){
    myNetworkStream = new NetworkStream(mySocket, true);
}
else{
    myNetworkStream = new NetworkStream(mySocket);
}
```

```
[C++]
    // Create the NetworkStream for communicating with the
remote host.
    NetworkStream* myNetworkStream;

    if (networkStreamOwnsSocket) {
        myNetworkStream = new NetworkStream(mySocket, true);
    } else {
        myNetworkStream = new NetworkStream(mySocket);
    }
```

Requirements

Platforms: Windows 98, Windows NT 4.0,
Windows Millennium Edition, Windows 2000,
Windows XP Home Edition, Windows XP Professional,
Windows .NET Server family,
.NET Compact Framework - Windows CE .NET,
Common Language Infrastructure (CLI) Standard

NetworkStream Constructor (Socket, Boolean)

Initializes a new instance of the **NetworkStream** class for the
specified **Socket** with the specified **Socket** ownership.

```
[Visual Basic]
Public Sub New( _
   ByVal socket As Socket, _
   ByVal ownsSocket As Boolean _
)
[C#]
public NetworkStream(
   Socket socket,
   bool ownsSocket
);
[C++]
public: NetworkStream(
   Socket* socket,
   bool ownsSocket
);
[JScript]
public function NetworkStream(
   socket : Socket,
   ownsSocket : Boolean
);
```

Parameters

socket
> The **Socket** that **NetworkStream** will use to send and receive data.

ownsSocket
> **true** to indicate that the **NetworkStream** will take ownership of the **Socket**; otherwise, **false**.

Exceptions

Exception Type	Condition
ArgumentNullException	*socket* is a null reference (**Nothing** in Visual Basic).
IOException	*socket* is not connected.
	-or-
	The value of the **SocketType** property of *socket* is not **SocketType.Stream**.
	-or-
	socket is in a nonblocking state.

Remarks

The **NetworkStream** is created with read/write access to the
specified **Socket**. If *ownsSocket* is **true**, the **NetworkStream** takes
ownership of the underlying **Socket**, and calling the
NetworkStream's **Close** method will also close the underlying
Socket.

Example

[Visual Basic, C#, C++] The following example creates a
NetworkStream with ownership of the **Socket**.

```
[Visual Basic]
' Create the NetworkStream for communicating with the remote host.
Dim myNetworkStream As NetworkStream

If networkStreamOwnsSocket Then
    myNetworkStream = New NetworkStream(mySocket, True)
Else
    myNetworkStream = New NetworkStream(mySocket)
End If
```

```
[C#]
// Create the NetworkStream for communicating with the remote host.
NetworkStream myNetworkStream;

if (networkStreamOwnsSocket){
    myNetworkStream = new NetworkStream(mySocket, true);
}
else{
    myNetworkStream = new NetworkStream(mySocket);
}
```

```
[C++]
    // Create the NetworkStream for communicating with the
remote host.
    NetworkStream* myNetworkStream;

    if (networkStreamOwnsSocket) {
        myNetworkStream = new NetworkStream(mySocket, true);
    } else {
        myNetworkStream = new NetworkStream(mySocket);
    }
```

Requirements

Platforms: Windows 98, Windows NT 4.0,
Windows Millennium Edition, Windows 2000,
Windows XP Home Edition, Windows XP Professional,
Windows .NET Server family,
.NET Compact Framework - Windows CE .NET,
Common Language Infrastructure (CLI) Standard

NetworkStream Constructor (Socket, FileAccess)

Creates a new instance of the **NetworkStream** class for the
specified **Socket** with the specified access rights.

```
[Visual Basic]
Public Sub New( _
   ByVal socket As Socket, _
   ByVal access As FileAccess _
)
[C#]
public NetworkStream(
   Socket socket,
   FileAccess access
);
[C++]
public: NetworkStream(
   Socket* socket,
   FileAccess access
);
```

```
[JScript]
public function NetworkStream(
    socket : Socket,
    access : FileAccess
);
```

Parameters

socket

The **Socket** that **NetworkStream** will use to send and receive data.

access

A bitwise combination of the **FileAccess** values. specifying the type of access given to the **NetworkStream** over the provided **Socket**.

Exceptions

Exception Type	Condition
ArgumentNullException	*socket* is a null reference (**Nothing** in Visual Basic).
IOException	*socket* is not connected.
	-or-
	The **SocketType** property of *socket* is not **SocketType.Stream**.
	-or-
	socket is in a nonblocking state.

Remarks

The **NetworkStream** is created with the specified access to the specified **Socket**. With this constructor, the **NetworkStream** does not own the underlying **Socket**, so calling the NetworkStream's **Close** method will not close the underlying **Socket**.

The *access* parameter sets the **CanRead** and **CanWrite** properties of the **NetworkStream**. If you specify **Write**, then the **NetworkStream** will allow calls to the **Write** method. If you specify **Read**, then the **NetworkStream** will allow calls to the **Read** method. If you specify **ReadWrite**, both method calls will be allowed.

Example

[Visual Basic, C#, C++] The following example creates a **NetworkStream** with the ability to read and write to the **Socket**.

[Visual Basic]
```
mySocket.Connect(myIpEndPoint)

' Create the NetworkStream for communicating with the remote host.
Dim myNetworkStream As NetworkStream

If networkStreamOwnsSocket Then
    myNetworkStream = New NetworkStream(mySocket, FileAccess.ReadWrite, True)
Else
    myNetworkStream = New NetworkStream(mySocket, FileAccess.ReadWrite)
End If
```

[C#]
```
mySocket.Connect(myIpEndPoint);

// Create the NetworkStream for communicating with the remote host.
NetworkStream myNetworkStream;

if (networkStreamOwnsSocket){
    myNetworkStream = new NetworkStream(mySocket, FileAccess.ReadWrite, true);
}
```

```
else{
    myNetworkStream = new NetworkStream(mySocket, FileAccess.ReadWrite);
}
```

[C++]
```
mySocket->Connect(myIpEndPoint);

// Create the NetworkStream for communicating with the remote host.
NetworkStream* myNetworkStream;

if (networkStreamOwnsSocket) {
    myNetworkStream = new NetworkStream(mySocket, FileAccess::ReadWrite, true);
} else {
    myNetworkStream = new NetworkStream(mySocket, FileAccess::ReadWrite);
}
```

[JScript] No example is available for JScript. To view a Visual Basic, C#, or C++ example, click the Language Filter button <IMG SRC="filter1a.gif" ALT="Language Filter" BORDER=0> in the upper-left corner of the page.

Requirements

Platforms: Windows 98, Windows NT 4.0, Windows Millennium Edition, Windows 2000, Windows XP Home Edition, Windows XP Professional, Windows .NET Server family, .NET Compact Framework - Windows CE .NET, Common Language Infrastructure (CLI) Standard

NetworkStream Constructor (Socket, FileAccess, Boolean)

Creates a new instance of the **NetworkStream** class for the specified **Socket** with the specified access rights and the specified **Socket** ownership.

```
[Visual Basic]
Public Sub New( _
    ByVal socket As Socket, _
    ByVal access As FileAccess, _
    ByVal ownsSocket As Boolean _
)
[C#]
public NetworkStream(
    Socket socket,
    FileAccess access,
    bool ownsSocket
);
[C++]
public: NetworkStream(
    Socket* socket,
    FileAccess access,
    bool ownsSocket
);
[JScript]
public function NetworkStream(
    socket : Socket,
    access : FileAccess,
    ownsSocket : Boolean
);
```

Parameters

socket

> The **Socket** that **NetworkStream** will use to send and receive data.

access

> A bitwise combination of the **FileAccess** values that specifies the type of access given to the **NetworkStream** over the provided **Socket**.

ownsSocket

> **true** to indicate that the **NetworkStream** will take ownership of the **Socket**; otherwise, **false**.

Exceptions

Exception Type	Condition
ArgumentNullException	*socket* is a null reference (**Nothing** in Visual Basic).
IOException	*socket* is not connected.
	-or-
	The **SocketType** property of *socket* is not **SocketType.Stream**.
	-or-
	socket is in a nonblocking state.

Remarks

The **NetworkStream** is created with read/write access to the specified **Socket**. If the value of the *ownsSocket* parameter is **true**, the **NetworkStream** takes ownership of the underlying **Socket**, and calling the **NetworkStream.Close** method will also close the underlying **Socket**.

The *access* parameter sets the **CanRead** and **CanWrite** properties of the **NetworkStream**. If you specify **Write**, then **NetworkStream** will allow calls to the **Write** method. If you specify **Read**, then **NetworkStream** will allow calls to the **Read** method. If you specify **ReadWrite**, both method calls will be allowed.

Example

[Visual Basic, C#, C++] The following example creates a **NetworkStream** with the ability to read and write to the **Socket**. Ownership of the **Socket** is given to this **NetworkStream** by specifying **true** for *ownsSocket*.

```
[Visual Basic]
mySocket.Connect(myIpEndPoint)

' Create the NetworkStream for communicating with the remote host.
Dim myNetworkStream As NetworkStream

If networkStreamOwnsSocket Then
    myNetworkStream = New NetworkStream(mySocket, _
FileAccess.ReadWrite, True)
Else
    myNetworkStream = New NetworkStream(mySocket, FileAccess.ReadWrite)
End If

[C#]
mySocket.Connect(myIpEndPoint);

// Create the NetworkStream for communicating with the remote host.
NetworkStream myNetworkStream;

if (networkStreamOwnsSocket){
    myNetworkStream = new NetworkStream(mySocket, _
FileAccess.ReadWrite, true);
}
```

```
else{
    myNetworkStream = new NetworkStream(mySocket, _
FileAccess.ReadWrite);
}

[C++]
mySocket->Connect(myIpEndPoint);

// Create the NetworkStream for communicating with the remote host.
NetworkStream* myNetworkStream;

if (networkStreamOwnsSocket) {
    myNetworkStream = new NetworkStream(mySocket, _
FileAccess::ReadWrite, true);
} else {
    myNetworkStream = new NetworkStream(mySocket, _
FileAccess::ReadWrite);
}
```

Requirements

Platforms: Windows 98, Windows NT 4.0, Windows Millennium Edition, Windows 2000, Windows XP Home Edition, Windows XP Professional, Windows .NET Server family, .NET Compact Framework - Windows CE .NET, Common Language Infrastructure (CLI) Standard

NetworkStream.CanRead Property

Gets a value indicating whether the **NetworkStream** supports reading.

```
[Visual Basic]
Overrides Public ReadOnly Property CanRead As Boolean
[C#]
public override bool CanRead {get;}
[C++]
public: __property bool get_CanRead();
[JScript]
public override function get CanRead() : Boolean;
```

Property Value

true if data can be read from the stream; otherwise, **false**. The default value is **true**.

Remarks

If **CanRead** is **true**, **NetworkStream** will allow calls to the **Read** method. Provide the appropriate **FileAccess** enumerated value in the constructor to set the readablity and writability of the **NetworkStream**. The **CanRead** property is set when the **NetworkStream** is initialized.

Example

[Visual Basic, C#, C++] The following example checks **CanRead** to verify that the **NetworkStream** is readable. It then performs a read operation on the **NetworkStream**.

```
[Visual Basic]
' Check to see if this NetworkStream is readable.
If myNetworkStream.CanRead Then
    Dim myReadBuffer(1024) As Byte
    Dim myCompleteMessage As [String] = ""
    Dim numberOfBytesRead As Integer = 0

    ' Incoming message may be larger than the buffer size.
    Do
        numberOfBytesRead = myNetworkStream.Read _
(myReadBuffer, 0, myReadBuffer.Length)
```

```
      myCompleteMessage = [String].Concat
(myCompleteMessage, Encoding.ASCII.GetString
(myReadBuffer, 0, numberOfBytesRead))
   Loop While myNetworkStream.DataAvailable

   ' Print out the received message to the console.
   Console.WriteLine(("You received the following
message : " + myCompleteMessage))
Else
   Console.WriteLine("Sorry.  You cannot read from
this NetworkStream.")
End If


[C#]
 // Check to see if this NetworkStream is readable.
 if(myNetworkStream.CanRead){
     byte[] myReadBuffer = new byte[1024];
     String myCompleteMessage = "";
     int numberOfBytesRead = 0;

     // Incoming message may be larger than the buffer size.
     do{
         numberOfBytesRead = myNetworkStream.Read
(myReadBuffer, 0, myReadBuffer.Length);
         myCompleteMessage =
             String.Concat(myCompleteMessage,
Encoding.ASCII.GetString(myReadBuffer, 0, numberOfBytesRead));
     }
     while(myNetworkStream.DataAvailable);

     // Print out the received message to the console.
     Console.WriteLine("You received the following message : " +
                         myCompleteMessage);
 }
 else{
     Console.WriteLine("Sorry.  You cannot read from
this NetworkStream.");
 }


[C++]
     // Check to see if this NetworkStream is readable.
     if (myNetworkStream->CanRead) {
         Byte myReadBuffer[] = new Byte[1024];
         String* myCompleteMessage = S"";
         int numberOfBytesRead = 0;

         // Incoming message may be larger than the buffer size.
         do{
             numberOfBytesRead = myNetworkStream->Read
(myReadBuffer, 0, myReadBuffer->Length);
             myCompleteMessage =
                 String::Concat(myCompleteMessage,
Encoding::ASCII->GetString(myReadBuffer, 0, numberOfBytesRead));
         } while (myNetworkStream->DataAvailable);

         // Print out the received message to the console.
         Console::WriteLine(S"You received the following
message : {0}", myCompleteMessage);
     } else {
         Console::WriteLine(S"Sorry.  You cannot read
from this NetworkStream.");
     }
```

Requirements

Platforms: Windows 98, Windows NT 4.0,
Windows Millennium Edition, Windows 2000,
Windows XP Home Edition, Windows XP Professional,
Windows .NET Server family,
.NET Compact Framework - Windows CE .NET,
Common Language Infrastructure (CLI) Standard

NetworkStream.CanSeek Property

Gets a value indicating whether the stream supports seeking. This
property always returns **false**.

```
[Visual Basic]
Overrides Public ReadOnly Property CanSeek As Boolean
[C#]
public override bool CanSeek {get;}
[C++]
public: __property bool get_CanSeek();
[JScript]
public override function get CanSeek() : Boolean;
```

Property Value

false to indicate that **NetworkStream** cannot seek a specific
location in the stream.

Remarks

This property is not currently supported and will always return **false**

Requirements

Platforms: Windows 98, Windows NT 4.0,
Windows Millennium Edition, Windows 2000,
Windows XP Home Edition, Windows XP Professional,
Windows .NET Server family,
.NET Compact Framework - Windows CE .NET,
Common Language Infrastructure (CLI) Standard

NetworkStream.CanWrite Property

Gets a value that indicates whether the **NetworkStream** supports
writing.

```
[Visual Basic]
Overrides Public ReadOnly Property CanWrite As Boolean
[C#]
public override bool CanWrite {get;}
[C++]
public: __property bool get_CanWrite();
[JScript]
public override function get CanWrite() : Boolean;
```

Property Value

true if data can be written to the **NetworkStream**; otherwise, **false**.
The default value is **true**.

Remarks

If **CanWrite** is **true**, **NetworkStream** will allow calls to the **Write**
method. Provide the appropriate **FileAccess** enumerated value in the
constructor to set the readablity and writability of the
NetworkStream. The **CanWrite** property is set when the
NetworkStream is initialized.

Example

[Visual Basic, C#, C++] The following example checks **CanWrite**
to verify that the **NetworkStream** is writable. It then performs a
write operation on the **NetworkStream**.

```
[Visual Basic]
' Check to see if this NetworkStream is writable.
If myNetworkStream.CanWrite Then

   Dim myWriteBuffer As Byte() = Encoding.ASCII.GetBytes
("Are you receiving this message?")
   myNetworkStream.Write(myWriteBuffer, 0, myWriteBuffer.Length)
Else
```

```
      Console.WriteLine("Sorry.  You cannot write to this NetworkStream.")
End If
```

```
[C#]
// Check to see if this NetworkStream is writable.
if (myNetworkStream.CanWrite){

      byte[] myWriteBuffer = Encoding.ASCII.GetBytes("Are you       ⏎
receiving this message?");
      myNetworkStream.Write(myWriteBuffer, 0, myWriteBuffer.Length);
}
else{
      Console.WriteLine("Sorry.  You cannot write to this             ⏎
NetworkStream.");
}
```

```
[C++]
      // Check to see if this NetworkStream is writable.
      if (myNetworkStream->CanWrite) {
          Byte myWriteBuffer[] = Encoding::ASCII->GetBytes            ⏎
(S"Are you receiving this message?");
          myNetworkStream->Write(myWriteBuffer, 0,                    ⏎
myWriteBuffer->Length);
      } else {
          Console::WriteLine(S"Sorry.  You cannot write              ⏎
to this NetworkStream.");
      }
```

Requirements

Platforms: Windows 98, Windows NT 4.0,
Windows Millennium Edition, Windows 2000,
Windows XP Home Edition, Windows XP Professional,
Windows .NET Server family,
.NET Compact Framework - Windows CE .NET,
Common Language Infrastructure (CLI) Standard

NetworkStream.DataAvailable Property

Gets a value indicating whether data is available on the
NetworkStream to be read.

```
[Visual Basic]
Public Overridable ReadOnly Property DataAvailable As Boolean
[C#]
public virtual bool DataAvailable {get;}
[C++]
public: __property virtual bool get_DataAvailable();
[JScript]
public function get DataAvailable() : Boolean;
```

Property Value

true if data is available on the stream to be read; otherwise, **false**.

Exceptions

Exception Type	Condition
ObjectDisposed-Exception	The **NetworkStream** is closed.
IOException	The underlying **Socket** is closed.
SocketException	Use **SocketException.ErrorCode** to obtain the specific error code. Once you have obtained this code, you can refer to the Windows Socket Version 2 API error code documentation in MSDN for a detailed description of the error.

Remarks

The **Read** method blocks execution until data is received from the
remote host and queued in the network buffer for reading. If you
want to avoid blocking, use the **DataAvailable** method to determine
if this data is available. If **DataAvailable** is **true**, a call to **Read** will
return immediately. If the remote host shuts down or closes the
connection, **DataAvailable** throws a **SocketException**.

Example

[Visual Basic, C#, C++] The following example reads from the
NetworkStream as long as data is available.

```
[Visual Basic]
' Check to see if this NetworkStream is readable.
If myNetworkStream.CanRead Then
    Dim myReadBuffer(1024) As Byte
    Dim myCompleteMessage As [String] = ""
    Dim numberOfBytesRead As Integer = 0

    ' Incoming message may be larger than the buffer size.
    Do
        numberOfBytesRead = myNetworkStream.Read              ⏎
(myReadBuffer, 0, myReadBuffer.Length)
        myCompleteMessage = [String].Concat(myCompleteMessage, ⏎
Encoding.ASCII.GetString(myReadBuffer, 0, numberOfBytesRead))
    Loop While myNetworkStream.DataAvailable

    ' Print out the received message to the console.
    Console.WriteLine(("You received the following           ⏎
message : " + myCompleteMessage))
Else
    Console.WriteLine("Sorry.  You cannot read from this     ⏎
NetworkStream.")
End If
```

```
[C#]
// Check to see if this NetworkStream is readable.
 if(myNetworkStream.CanRead){
      byte[] myReadBuffer = new byte[1024];
      String myCompleteMessage = "";
      int numberOfBytesRead = 0;

      // Incoming message may be larger than the buffer size.
      do{
          numberOfBytesRead = myNetworkStream.Read           ⏎
(myReadBuffer, 0, myReadBuffer.Length);
          myCompleteMessage =
              String.Concat(myCompleteMessage,               ⏎
Encoding.ASCII.GetString(myReadBuffer, 0, numberOfBytesRead));
      }
      while(myNetworkStream.DataAvailable);

      // Print out the received message to the console.
      Console.WriteLine("You received the following message : " +
                            myCompleteMessage);
}
else{
      Console.WriteLine("Sorry.  You cannot read from         ⏎
this NetworkStream.");
}
```

```
[C++]
      // Check to see if this NetworkStream is readable.
      if (myNetworkStream->CanRead) {
          Byte myReadBuffer[] = new Byte[1024];
          String* myCompleteMessage = S"";
          int numberOfBytesRead = 0;

          // Incoming message may be larger than the buffer size.
          do{
              numberOfBytesRead = myNetworkStream->Read        ⏎
(myReadBuffer, 0, myReadBuffer->Length);
              myCompleteMessage =
```

```
                String::Concat(myCompleteMessage, Encoding
::ASCII->GetString(myReadBuffer, 0, numberOfBytesRead));
           } while (myNetworkStream->DataAvailable);

           // Print out the received message to the console.
           Console::WriteLine(S"You received the following
message : {0}", myCompleteMessage);
        } else {
           Console::WriteLine(S"Sorry.  You cannot read from
this NetworkStream.");
        }
```

Requirements

Platforms: Windows 98, Windows NT 4.0,
Windows Millennium Edition, Windows 2000,
Windows XP Home Edition, Windows XP Professional,
Windows .NET Server family,
.NET Compact Framework - Windows CE .NET,
Common Language Infrastructure (CLI) Standard

NetworkStream.Length Property

Gets the length of the data available on the stream. This property
always throws a **NotSupportedException**.

```
[Visual Basic]
Overrides Public ReadOnly Property Length As Long
[C#]
public override long Length {get;}
[C++]
public: __property __int64 get_Length();
[JScript]
public override function get Length() : long;
```

Property Value

The length of the data available on the stream. This property is not
currently supported, and will throw a **NotSupportedException**.

Exceptions

Exception Type	Condition
NotSupportedException	Any access.

Requirements

Platforms: Windows 98, Windows NT 4.0,
Windows Millennium Edition, Windows 2000,
Windows XP Home Edition, Windows XP Professional,
Windows .NET Server family,
.NET Compact Framework - Windows CE .NET,
Common Language Infrastructure (CLI) Standard

NetworkStream.Position Property

Gets or sets the current position in the stream. This property always
throws a **NotSupportedException**.

```
[Visual Basic]
Overrides Public Property Position As Long
[C#]
public override long Position {get; set;}
[C++]
public: __property __int64 get_Position();
public: __property void set_Position(__int64);
[JScript]
public override function get Position() : long;
public override function set Position(long);
```

Property Value

The current position in the stream. This property is not currently
supported, and will throw a **NotSupportedException**.

Exceptions

Exception Type	Condition
NotSupportedException	Any access.

Requirements

Platforms: Windows 98, Windows NT 4.0,
Windows Millennium Edition, Windows 2000,
Windows XP Home Edition, Windows XP Professional,
Windows .NET Server family,
.NET Compact Framework - Windows CE .NET,
Common Language Infrastructure (CLI) Standard

NetworkStream.Readable Property

Gets or sets a value indicating whether the **NetworkStream** can be
read.

```
[Visual Basic]
Protected Property Readable As Boolean
[C#]
protected bool Readable {get; set;}
[C++]
protected: __property bool get_Readable();
protected: __property void set_Readable(bool);
[JScript]
protected function get Readable() : Boolean;
protected function set Readable(Boolean);
```

Property Value

true to indicate that the **NetworkStream** can be read; otherwise,
false. The default value is **true**.

Remarks

You must derive from the **NetworkStream** class to use the
Readable property. If **Readable** is **true**, **NetworkStream** will allow
calls to the **Read** method. You can also determine whether a
NetworkStream is readable by checking the publically accessible
CanRead property.

The **Readable** property is set when the **NetworkStream** is
initialized.

Requirements

Platforms: Windows 98, Windows NT 4.0,
Windows Millennium Edition, Windows 2000,
Windows XP Home Edition, Windows XP Professional,
Windows .NET Server family

NetworkStream.Socket Property

Gets the underlying **Socket**.

```
[Visual Basic]
Protected ReadOnly Property Socket As Socket
[C#]
protected Socket Socket {get;}
[C++]
protected: __property Socket* get_Socket();
[JScript]
protected function get Socket() : Socket;
```

Property Value

A **Socket** that represents the underlying network connection.

Remarks

Classes deriving from **NetworkStream** can use this property to get the underlying **Socket**. Use the underlying **Socket** returned from the **Socket** property if you require access beyond that which **NetworkStream** provides.

> **Note** This property is accessible only through this class or a derived class.

Requirements

Platforms: Windows 98, Windows NT 4.0, Windows Millennium Edition, Windows 2000, Windows XP Home Edition, Windows XP Professional, Windows .NET Server family

NetworkStream.Writeable Property

Gets a value that indicates whether the **NetworkStream** is writable.

```
[Visual Basic]
Protected Property Writeable As Boolean
[C#]
protected bool Writeable {get; set;}
[C++]
protected: __property bool get_Writeable();
protected: __property void set_Writeable(bool);
[JScript]
protected function get Writeable() : Boolean;
protected function set Writeable(Boolean);
```

Property Value

true if data can be written to the stream; otherwise, **false**. The default value is **true**.

Remarks

You must derive from the **NetworkStream** class to use the **Writeable** property. If **Writeable** is **true**, **NetworkStream** will allow calls to the **Write** method. You can also determine whether a **NetworkStream** is writable by checking the publicly accessible **CanWrite** property.

The **Writeable** property is set when the **NetworkStream** is initialized.

Requirements

Platforms: Windows 98, Windows NT 4.0, Windows Millennium Edition, Windows 2000, Windows XP Home Edition, Windows XP Professional, Windows .NET Server family

NetworkStream.BeginRead Method

Begins an asynchronous read from the **NetworkStream**.

```
[Visual Basic]
Overrides Public Function BeginRead( _
    ByVal buffer() As Byte, _
    ByVal offset As Integer, _
    ByVal size As Integer, _
    ByVal callback As AsyncCallback, _
    ByVal state As Object _
) As IAsyncResult
```

```
[C#]
public override IAsyncResult BeginRead(
    byte[] buffer,
    int offset,
    int size,
    AsyncCallback callback,
    object state
);
[C++]
public: IAsyncResult* BeginRead(
    unsigned char buffer __gc[],
    int offset,
    int size,
    AsyncCallback* callback,
    Object* state
);
[JScript]
public override function BeginRead(
    buffer : Byte[],
    offset : int,
    size : int,
    callback : AsyncCallback,
    state : Object
) : IAsyncResult;
```

Parameters

buffer
  An array of type **Byte** that is the location in memory to store data read from the **NetworkStream**.
offset
  The location in *buffer* to begin storing the data.
size
  The number of bytes to read from the **NetworkStream**.
callback
  The **AsyncCallback** delegate that is executed when **BeginRead** completes.
state
  An object containing any additional user defined data.

Return Value

An **IAsyncResult** representing the asynchronous call.

Exceptions

Exception Type	Condition
ArgumentNullException	*buffer* is a null reference (**Nothing** in Visual Basic).
ArgumentOutOfRange-Exception	*offset* is less than 0.
	-or-
	offset is greater than the length of *buffer*.
	-or-
	size is less than 0.
	-or-
	size is greater than the length of *buffer* minus the value of the *offset* parameter.

Exception Type	Condition
IOException	The underlying **Socket** is closed.
	-or-
	There is a failure while reading from the network.
ObjectDisposed-Exception	The **NetworkStream** is closed.
IOException	An error occurred when accessing the socket. See the Remarks section for more information.

Remarks

The **BeginRead** method starts asynchronously reading data from the incoming network buffers. Calling the **BeginRead** method gives you the ability to receive data within a separate execution thread.

You must create a callback method that implements the **AsyncCallback** delegate and pass its name to the **BeginRead** method. At the very minimum, your *state* parameter must contain the **NetworkStream**. Since you will want to obtain the received data within your callback method, you should create a small class or structure to hold a read buffer and any other useful information. Pass the structure or class instance to the **BeginRead** method through the *state* parameter.

Your callback method should implement the **EndRead** method. When your application calls **BeginRead**, the system will use a separate thread to execute the specified callback method, and will block on **EndRead** until the provided **NetworkStream** reads data or throws an exception. If you want the original thread to block after you call the **BeginRead** method, use **WaitOne**. Call **Set** in the callback method when you want the original thread to continue executing.

The **BeginRead** method will read as much data as is available, up to the number of bytes specified by the *size* parameter.

> **Note** If you receive a **IOException** check the **InnerException** property to determine if it was caused by a **SocketException**. If so, use **ErrorCode** to obtain the specific error code. Once you have obtained this code, you can refer to the Windows Socket Version 2 API error code documentation in MSDN for a detailed description of the error.

Example

[Visual Basic, C#, C++] The following example uses **BeginRead** to read data asynchronously from the network stream. The method myReadCallBack implements the **AsyncCallback** delegate and will be called by the system when **BeginRead** returns.

```
[Visual Basic]
' Check to see if this NetworkStream is readable.
If myNetworkStream.CanRead Then

    Dim myReadBuffer(1024) As Byte
    myNetworkStream.BeginRead(myReadBuffer, 0,
myReadBuffer.Length, New AsyncCallback(AddressOf
NetworkStream_ASync_Send_Receive.myReadCallBack), myNetworkStream)

    allDone.WaitOne()
Else
    Console.WriteLine("Sorry.  You cannot read from this
NetworkStream.")
End If
```

```
[C#]
// Check to see if this NetworkStream is readable.
if(myNetworkStream.CanRead){

    byte[] myReadBuffer = new byte[1024];
    myNetworkStream.BeginRead(myReadBuffer, 0, myReadBuffer.Length,
                              new
AsyncCallback(NetworkStream_ASync_Send_Receive.myReadCallBack),
                              myNetworkStream);

    allDone.WaitOne();
}
else{
    Console.WriteLine("Sorry.  You cannot read from this
NetworkStream.");
}
```

```
[C++]
// Check to see if this NetworkStream is readable.
if (myNetworkStream->CanRead) {
    Byte myReadBuffer[] = new Byte[1024];
    myNetworkStream->BeginRead(myReadBuffer, 0, myReadBuffer->Length,
        new AsyncCallback(0, &MyNetworkStreamClass::myReadCallBack),
        myNetworkStream);
    allDone->WaitOne();
} else {
    Console::WriteLine(S"Sorry.  You cannot read from this
NetworkStream.");
}
```

Requirements

Platforms: Windows 98, Windows NT 4.0, Windows Millennium Edition, Windows 2000, Windows XP Home Edition, Windows XP Professional, Windows .NET Server family, .NET Compact Framework - Windows CE .NET, Common Language Infrastructure (CLI) Standard

NetworkStream.BeginWrite Method

Begins an asynchronous write to a stream.

```
[Visual Basic]
Overrides Public Function BeginWrite( _
    ByVal buffer() As Byte, _
    ByVal offset As Integer, _
    ByVal size As Integer, _
    ByVal callback As AsyncCallback, _
    ByVal state As Object _
) As IAsyncResult
```

```
[C#]
public override IAsyncResult BeginWrite(
    byte[] buffer,
    int offset,
    int size,
    AsyncCallback callback,
    object state
);
```

```
[C++]
public: IAsyncResult* BeginWrite(
    unsigned char buffer __gc[],
    int offset,
    int size,
    AsyncCallback* callback,
    Object* state
);
```

```
[JScript]
public override function BeginWrite(
    buffer : Byte[],
    offset : int,
    size : int,
    callback : AsyncCallback,
    state : Object
) : IAsyncResult;
```

Parameters

buffer
    An array of type **Byte** that contains the data to write to the
    NetworkStream.

offset
    The location in *buffer* to begin sending the data.

size
    The number of bytes to write to the **NetworkStream**.

callback
    The **AsyncCallback** delegate that is executed when **BeginWrite**
    completes.

state
    An object containing any additional user defined data.

Return Value

An **IAsyncResult** representing the asynchronous call.

Exceptions

Exception Type	Condition
ArgumentNullException	*buffer* is a null reference (**Nothing** in Visual Basic).
ArgumentOutOfRange-Exception	*offset* is less than 0.
	-or-
	offset is greater than the length of *buffer*.
	-or-
	size is less than 0.
	-or-
	size is greater than the length of *buffer* minus the value of the *offset* parameter.
IOException	The underlying **Socket** is closed.
	-or-
	There is a failure while writing to the network.
ObjectDisposed-Exception	The **NetworkStream** is closed.
IOException	An error occurred when accessing the socket. See the Remarks section for more information.

Remarks

The **BeginWrite** method starts an asynchronous send operation to the remote host. Calling the **BeginWrite** method gives you the ability to send data within a separate execution thread.

You must create acallback method that implements the **AsyncCallback** delegate and pass its name to the **BeginWrite** method. At the very minimum, your *state* parameter must contain the **NetworkStream**. If your callback needs more information, you can create a small class or structure to hold the **NetworkStream** and

the other required information. Pass the structure or class instance to the **BeginWrite** method through the *state* parameter.

Your callback method should implement the **EndWrite** method. When your application calls **BeginWrite**, the system will use a separate thread to execute the specified callback method, and will block on **EndWrite** until the **NetworkStream** sends the number of bytes requested or throws an exception. If you want the original thread to block after you call the **BeginWrite** method, use **WaitOne**. Call **Set** in the callback method when you want the original thread to continue executing. For additional information on writing callback methods, see **Callback Sample**.

> **Note** If you receive a **IOException** check the **InnerException** property to determine if it was caused by a **SocketException**. If so, use **ErrorCode** to obtain the specific error code. Once you have obtained this code, you can refer to the Windows Socket Version 2 API error code documentation in MSDN for a detailed description of the error.

Example

[Visual Basic, C#, C++] The following example uses **BeginWrite** to write data asynchronously to a network stream. The method m yWriteCallBack implements the **AsyncCallback** delegate and will be called by the system when **BeginWrite** returns.

```
[Visual Basic]
' Check to see if this NetworkStream is writable.
If myNetworkStream.CanWrite Then

    Dim myWriteBuffer As Byte() = Encoding.ASCII.GetBytes
("Are you receiving this message?")
    myNetworkStream.BeginWrite(myWriteBuffer, 0,
myWriteBuffer.Length, New AsyncCallback(AddressOf
NetworkStream_ASync_Send_Receive.myWriteCallBack), myNetworkStream)
    allDone.WaitOne()
Else
    Console.WriteLine("Sorry.  You cannot write to this NetworkStream.")
End If

[C#]
// Check to see if this NetworkStream is writable.
if (myNetworkStream.CanWrite){

    byte[] myWriteBuffer = Encoding.ASCII.GetBytes("Are you
receiving this message?");
    myNetworkStream.BeginWrite(myWriteBuffer, 0,
myWriteBuffer.Length,
                                              new
AsyncCallback(NetworkStream_ASync_Send_Receive.myWriteCallBack),
                                      myNetworkStream);
    allDone.WaitOne();
}
else{
    Console.WriteLine("Sorry.  You cannot write to this
NetworkStream.");
}

[C++]
// Check to see if this NetworkStream is writable.
if (myNetworkStream->CanWrite) {
    Byte myWriteBuffer[] = Encoding::ASCII->GetBytes(S"Are you
receiving this message?");
    myNetworkStream->BeginWrite(myWriteBuffer, 0, myWriteBuffer-
>Length,
        new AsyncCallback(0, &MyNetworkStreamClass::myWriteCallBack),
        myNetworkStream);
    allDone->WaitOne();
} else {
    Console::WriteLine(S"Sorry.  You cannot write to this
NetworkStream.");
}
```

Requirements

Platforms: Windows 98, Windows NT 4.0,
Windows Millennium Edition, Windows 2000,
Windows XP Home Edition, Windows XP Professional,
Windows .NET Server family,
.NET Compact Framework - Windows CE .NET,
Common Language Infrastructure (CLI) Standard

NetworkStream.Close Method

Closes the **NetworkStream**.

```
[Visual Basic]
Overrides Public Sub Close()
[C#]
public override void Close();
[C++]
public: void Close();
[JScript]
public override function Close();
```

Remarks

The **Close** method frees both unmanaged and managed resources
associated with the **NetworkStream**. If the **NetworkStream** owns
the underlying **Socket**, it is closed as well.

Example

[Visual Basic, C#, C++] The following example closes the
NetworkStream.

```
[Visual Basic]
' Close the NetworkStream
myNetworkStream.Close()

[C#]
// Close the NetworkStream
myNetworkStream.Close();

[C++]
        // Close the NetworkStream
        myNetworkStream->Close();
```

Requirements

Platforms: Windows 98, Windows NT 4.0,
Windows Millennium Edition, Windows 2000,
Windows XP Home Edition, Windows XP Professional,
Windows .NET Server family,
.NET Compact Framework - Windows CE .NET,
Common Language Infrastructure (CLI) Standard

NetworkStream.Dispose Method

Releases the unmanaged resources used by the **NetworkStream** and
optionally releases the managed resources.

```
[Visual Basic]
Protected Overridable Sub Dispose( _
    ByVal disposing As Boolean _
)
[C#]
protected virtual void Dispose(
    bool disposing
);
[C++]
protected: virtual void Dispose(
    bool disposing
);
```

```
[JScript]
protected function Dispose(
    disposing : Boolean
);
```

Parameters

disposing
> **true** to release both managed and unmanaged resources; **false** to
> release only unmanaged resources.

Remarks

This method is called by the public **Dispose()** method and the
Finalize method. **Dispose()** invokes the protected **Dispose(Boolean)**
method with the *disposing* parameter set to **true**. **Finalize** invokes
Dispose with *disposing* set to **false**.

When the *disposing* parameter is **true**, this method releases all
resources held by any managed objects that this **NetworkStream**
references. This method invokes the **Dispose()** method of each
referenced object.

Notes to Inheritors: **Dispose** can be called multiple times by other
objects. When overriding **Dispose(Boolean)**, be careful not to
reference objects that have been previously disposed of in an earlier
call to **Dispose**.

Requirements

Platforms: Windows 98, Windows NT 4.0,
Windows Millennium Edition, Windows 2000,
Windows XP Home Edition, Windows XP Professional,
Windows .NET Server family,
.NET Compact Framework - Windows CE .NET,
Common Language Infrastructure (CLI) Standard

NetworkStream.EndRead Method

Handles the end of an asynchronous read.

```
[Visual Basic]
Overrides Public Function EndRead( _
    ByVal asyncResult As IAsyncResult _
) As Integer
[C#]
public override int EndRead(
    IAsyncResult asyncResult
);
[C++]
public: int EndRead(
    IAsyncResult* asyncResult
);
[JScript]
public override function EndRead(
    asyncResult : IAsyncResult
) : int;
```

Parameters

asyncResult
> An **IAsyncResult** representing an asynchronous call.

Return Value

The number of bytes read from the **NetworkStream**.

Exceptions

Exception Type	Condition
ArgumentException	*asyncResult* is a null reference (**Nothing** in Visual Basic).
IOException	The underlying **Socket** is closed.
	-or-
	An error occurs while reading the network.
ObjectDisposed-Exception	The **NetworkStream** is closed.
IOException	An error occurred when accessing the socket. See the Remarks section for more information.

Remarks

The **EndRead** method completes the asynchronous read operation started in the **BeginRead** method.

Before calling **BeginRead**, you need to create a callback method that implements the **AsyncCallback** delegate. This callback method executes in a separate thread and is called by the system after **BeginRead** returns. The callback method must accept the **IAsyncResult** returned from the **BeginRead** method as a parameter.

Within the callback method, call the **AsyncState** method of the **IAsyncResult** to obtain the state object passed to the **BeginRead** method. Extract the receiving **NetworkStream** from this state object. After obtaining the **NetworkStream**, you can call the **EndRead** method to successfully complete the read operation and return the number of bytes read.

The **EndRead** method will block until data is available. The **EndRead** method will read as much data as is available up to the number of bytes specified in the *size* parameter of the **BeginRead** method. If the remote host shuts down the **Socket** connection and all available data has been received, the **EndRead** method will complete immediately and return zero bytes.

To obtain the received data, call the **AsyncState** method of the **IAsyncResult**, and extract the buffer contained in the resulting state object.

> **Note** If you receive a **IOException** check the **InnerException** property to determine if it was caused by a **SocketException**. If so, use **ErrorCode** to obtain the specific error code. Once you have obtained this code, you can refer to the Windows Socket Version 2 API error code documentation in MSDN for a detailed description of the error.

Example

[Visual Basic, C#, C++] In the following example, myReadCallback is provided to **BeginRead** as the callback method. **EndRead** is implemented in myReadCallback to complete the asynchronous read call started by **BeginRead**.

[Visual Basic]
```
Public Shared Sub myReadCallBack(ar As IAsyncResult)

   Dim myNetworkStream As NetworkStream = CType(ar.AsyncState, _
NetworkStream)
   Dim myReadBuffer(1024) As Byte
   Dim myCompleteMessage As [String] = ""
   Dim numberOfBytesRead As Integer

   numberOfBytesRead = myNetworkStream.EndRead(ar)
   myCompleteMessage = [String].Concat(myCompleteMessage, _
Encoding.ASCII.GetString(myReadBuffer, 0, numberOfBytesRead))
```

```
   ' message received may be larger than buffer size so loop _
through until you have it all.
   While myNetworkStream.DataAvailable

      myNetworkStream.BeginRead(myReadBuffer, 0, _
myReadBuffer.Length, New AsyncCallback(AddressOf _
NetworkStream_ASync_Send_Receive.myReadCallBack), myNetworkStream)
   End While

   ' Print out the received message to the console.
   Console.WriteLine(("You received the following message _
: " + myCompleteMessage))
End Sub 'myReadCallBack

'Entry point which delegates to C-style main Private Function
Public Overloads Shared Sub Main()
   Main(System.Environment.GetCommandLineArgs())
End Sub
```

[C#]
```
public static void myReadCallBack(IAsyncResult ar ){

    NetworkStream myNetworkStream = (NetworkStream)ar.AsyncState;
    byte[] myReadBuffer = new byte[1024];
    String myCompleteMessage = "";
    int numberOfBytesRead;

    numberOfBytesRead = myNetworkStream.EndRead(ar);
    myCompleteMessage =
       String.Concat(myCompleteMessage,
Encoding.ASCII.GetString(myReadBuffer, 0, numberOfBytesRead));

    // message received may be larger than buffer size _
so loop through until you have it all.
    while(myNetworkStream.DataAvailable){

       myNetworkStream.BeginRead(myReadBuffer, 0, myReadBuffer.Length,
                                 new
AsyncCallback(NetworkStream_ASync_Send_Receive.myReadCallBack),
                                 myNetworkStream);

    }

    // Print out the received message to the console.
    Console.WriteLine("You received the following message : " +
                      myCompleteMessage);
}
```

[C++]
```
static void myReadCallBack(IAsyncResult* ar) {
    NetworkStream* myNetworkStream = __try_cast
<NetworkStream*>(ar->AsyncState);
    Byte myReadBuffer[] = new Byte[1024];
    String* myCompleteMessage = S"";
    int numberOfBytesRead;

    numberOfBytesRead = myNetworkStream->EndRead(ar);
    myCompleteMessage =
        String::Concat(myCompleteMessage, Encoding::ASCII-
>GetString(myReadBuffer, 0, numberOfBytesRead));

    // message received may be larger than buffer size _
so loop through until you have it all.
    while (myNetworkStream->DataAvailable) {
        AsyncCallback* pasync = new AsyncCallback(0, &myReadCallBack);
        myNetworkStream->BeginRead(myReadBuffer, 0, _
myReadBuffer->Length,
            pasync,
            myNetworkStream);
    }

    // Print out the received message to the console.
    Console::WriteLine(S"You received the following message : {0}",
myCompleteMessage);
}
```

Requirements

Platforms: Windows 98, Windows NT 4.0,
Windows Millennium Edition, Windows 2000,
Windows XP Home Edition, Windows XP Professional,
Windows .NET Server family,
.NET Compact Framework - Windows CE .NET,
Common Language Infrastructure (CLI) Standard

NetworkStream.EndWrite Method

Handles the end of an asynchronous write.

```
[Visual Basic]
Overrides Public Sub EndWrite( _
   ByVal asyncResult As IAsyncResult _
)
[C#]
public override void EndWrite(
   IAsyncResult asyncResult
);
[C++]
public: void EndWrite(
   IAsyncResult* asyncResult
);
[JScript]
public override function EndWrite(
   asyncResult : IAsyncResult
);
```

Parameters

asyncResult
  The **IAsyncResult** representing the asynchronous call.

Exceptions

Exception Type	Condition
ArgumentNullException	*asyncResult* is a null reference (**Nothing** in Visual Basic).
IOException	The underlying **Socket** is closed. -or- An error occurs while writing to the network.
ObjectDisposed-Exception	The **NetworkStream** is closed.
IOException	An error occurred when accessing the socket. See the Remarks section for more information.

Remarks

EndWrite completes the asynchronous send operation started in **BeginWrite**.

Before calling **BeginWrite**, you need to create a callback method that implements the **AsyncCallback** delegate. This callback method executes in a separate thread and is called by the system after **BeginWrite** returns. The callback method must accept the **IAsyncResult** returned from the **BeginWrite** method as a parameter.

Within the callback method, call the **AsyncState** method of the *IAsyncResult* parameter to obtain the **NetworkStream**. After obtaining the **NetworkStream**, you can call the **EndWrite** method to successfully complete the send operation and return the number of bytes sent.

The **EndWrite** method will block until the requested number of bytes are sent.

> **Note** If you receive a **IOException** check the **InnerException** property to determine if it was caused by a **SocketException**. If so, use **ErrorCode** to obtain the specific error code. Once you have obtained this code, you can refer to the Windows Socket Version 2 API error code documentation in MSDN for a detailed description of the error.

Example

[Visual Basic, C#, C++] In the following example, myWriteCallback is provided to **BeginWrite** as the callback method. **EndWrite** is implemented in myWriteCallback to complete the asynchronous write call started by **BeginWrite**.

```
[Visual Basic]
Public Shared Sub myWriteCallBack(ar As IAsyncResult)

   Dim myNetworkStream As NetworkStream =
CType(ar.AsyncState, NetworkStream)
   myNetworkStream.EndWrite(ar)
End Sub 'myWriteCallBack

[C#]
public static void myWriteCallBack(IAsyncResult ar){

   NetworkStream myNetworkStream = (NetworkStream)ar.AsyncState;
   myNetworkStream.EndWrite(ar);
}

[C++]
static void myWriteCallBack(IAsyncResult* ar) {
   NetworkStream* myNetworkStream = __try_cast
<NetworkStream*>(ar->AsyncState);
   myNetworkStream->EndWrite(ar);
}
```

Requirements

Platforms: Windows 98, Windows NT 4.0,
Windows Millennium Edition, Windows 2000,
Windows XP Home Edition, Windows XP Professional,
Windows .NET Server family,
.NET Compact Framework - Windows CE .NET,
Common Language Infrastructure (CLI) Standard

NetworkStream.Finalize Method

Releases all resources used by the **NetworkStream**.

[C#] In C#, finalizers are expressed using destructor syntax.

[C++] In C++, finalizers are expressed using destructor syntax.

```
[Visual Basic]
Overrides Protected Sub Finalize()
[C#]
~NetworkStream();
[C++]
~NetworkStream();
[JScript]
protected override function Finalize();
```

Remarks

This method overrides **Object.Finalize**. Application code should not call this method; an object's **Finalize** method is automatically invoked during garbage collection, unless finalization by the garbage collector has been disabled by a call to the **GC.SuppressFinalize** method.

Requirements

Platforms: Windows 98, Windows NT 4.0,
Windows Millennium Edition, Windows 2000,
Windows XP Home Edition, Windows XP Professional,
Windows .NET Server family,
.NET Compact Framework - Windows CE .NET,
Common Language Infrastructure (CLI) Standard

NetworkStream.Flush Method

Flushes data from the stream. This method is reserved for future use.

```
[Visual Basic]
Overrides Public Sub Flush()
[C#]
public override void Flush();
[C++]
public: void Flush();
[JScript]
public override function Flush();
```

Remarks

The **Flush** method implements the **Stream.Flush** method; however, because **NetworkStream** is not buffered, it has no affect on network streams. Calling the **Flush** method will not throw an exception.

Requirements

Platforms: Windows 98, Windows NT 4.0,
Windows Millennium Edition, Windows 2000,
Windows XP Home Edition, Windows XP Professional,
Windows .NET Server family,
.NET Compact Framework - Windows CE .NET,
Common Language Infrastructure (CLI) Standard

NetworkStream.IDisposable.Dispose Method

This member supports the .NET Framework infrastructure and is not intended to be used directly from your code.

```
[Visual Basic]
Private Sub Dispose() Implements IDisposable.Dispose
[C#]
void IDisposable.Dispose();
[C++]
private: void IDisposable::Dispose();
[JScript]
private function IDisposable.Dispose();
```

NetworkStream.Read Method

Reads data from the **NetworkStream**.

```
[Visual Basic]
Overrides Public Function Read( _
   <InteropServices.In(), _
   Out()> ByVal buffer() As Byte, _
   ByVal offset As Integer, _
   ByVal size As Integer _
) As Integer
[C#]
public override int Read(
   [
   In,
```

```
   Out
] byte[] buffer,
   int offset,
   int size
);
[C++]
public: int Read(
   [
   In,
   Out
] unsigned char buffer __gc[],
   int offset,
   int size
);
[JScript]
public override function Read(
   buffer : Byte[],
   offset : int,
   size : int
) : int;
```

Parameters

buffer
   An array of type **Byte** that is the location in memory to store data read from the **NetworkStream**.
offset
   The location in *buffer* to begin storing the data to.
size
   The number of bytes to read from the **NetworkStream**.

Return Value

The number of bytes read from the **NetworkStream**.

Exceptions

Exception Type	Condition
ArgumentNullException	*buffer* is a null reference (**Nothing** in Visual Basic).
ArgumentOutOfRange-Exception	*offset* is less than 0.
	-or-
	offset is greater than the length of *buffer*.
	-or-
	size is less than 0.
	-or-
	size is less than the length of *buffer* minus the value of the *offset* parameter.
IOException	The underlying **Socket** is closed.
ObjectDisposed-Exception	The **NetworkStream** is closed.
	-or-
	There is a failure reading from the network.
IOException	An error occurred when accessing the socket. See the Remarks section for more information.

Remarks

This method reads data into the *buffer* parameter and returns the number of bytes successfully read. If no data is available for reading, the **NetworkStream.Read** method will block until data is available. To avoid blocking, you can use the **DataAvailable** property to determine if data is queued in the incoming network buffer for reading. If **DataAvailable** returns **true**, the **Read** operation will complete immediately. The **Read** operation will read as much data as is available, up to the number of bytes specified by the *size* parameter. If the remote host shuts down the connection, and all available data has been received, the **Read** method will complete immediately and return zero bytes.

> **Note** Check to see if the **NetworkStream** is readable by calling **CanRead**. If you attempt to read from a **NetworkStream** that is not readable, you will get an **IOException**.

> **Note** If you receive a **IOException** check the **InnerException** property to determine if it was caused by a **SocketException**. If so, use **ErrorCode** to obtain the specific error code. Once you have obtained this code, you can refer to the Windows Socket Version 2 API error code documentation in MSDN for a detailed description of the error.

Example

[Visual Basic, C#, C++] The following example uses **DataAvailable** to determine if data is available to be read. If data is available, it reads from the **NetworkStream**.

[Visual Basic]
```
' Check to see if this NetworkStream is readable.
If myNetworkStream.CanRead Then
Dim myReadBuffer(1024) As Byte
Dim myCompleteMessage As [String] = ""
Dim numberOfBytesRead As Integer = 0

' Incoming message may be larger than the buffer size.
Do
    numberOfBytesRead = myNetworkStream.Read(myReadBuffer, 0, myReadBuffer.Length)
    myCompleteMessage = [String].Concat(myCompleteMessage, Encoding.ASCII.GetString(myReadBuffer, 0, numberOfBytesRead))
    Loop While myNetworkStream.DataAvailable

' Print out the received message to the console.
Console.WriteLine(("You received the following message : " + myCompleteMessage))
Else
    Console.WriteLine("Sorry.  You cannot read from this NetworkStream.")
End If
```

[C#]
```
// Check to see if this NetworkStream is readable.
 if(myNetworkStream.CanRead){
    byte[] myReadBuffer = new byte[1024];
    String myCompleteMessage = "";
    int numberOfBytesRead = 0;

    // Incoming message may be larger than the buffer size.
    do{
        numberOfBytesRead = myNetworkStream.Read(myReadBuffer, 0, myReadBuffer.Length);
        myCompleteMessage =
            String.Concat(myCompleteMessage, Encoding.ASCII.GetString(myReadBuffer, 0, numberOfBytesRead));
    }
    while(myNetworkStream.DataAvailable);

    // Print out the received message to the console.
    Console.WriteLine("You received the following message : " +
                        myCompleteMessage);
}
```

```
else{
    Console.WriteLine("Sorry.  You cannot read from this NetworkStream.");
}
```

[C++]
```
    // Check to see if this NetworkStream is readable.
    if (myNetworkStream->CanRead) {
        Byte myReadBuffer[] = new Byte[1024];
        String* myCompleteMessage = S"";
        int numberOfBytesRead = 0;

        // Incoming message may be larger than the buffer size.
        do{
            numberOfBytesRead = myNetworkStream->Read(myReadBuffer, 0, myReadBuffer->Length);
            myCompleteMessage =
                String::Concat(myCompleteMessage, Encoding::ASCII->GetString(myReadBuffer, 0, numberOfBytesRead));
        } while (myNetworkStream->DataAvailable);

        // Print out the received message to the console.
        Console::WriteLine(S"You received the following message : {0}", myCompleteMessage);
    } else {
        Console::WriteLine(S"Sorry.  You cannot read from this NetworkStream.");
    }
```

Requirements

Platforms: Windows 98, Windows NT 4.0, Windows Millennium Edition, Windows 2000, Windows XP Home Edition, Windows XP Professional, Windows .NET Server family, .NET Compact Framework - Windows CE .NET, Common Language Infrastructure (CLI) Standard

NetworkStream.Seek Method

Sets the current position of the stream to the given value. This method always throws a **NotSupportedException**.

[Visual Basic]
```
Overrides Public Function Seek( _
   ByVal offset As Long, _
   ByVal origin As SeekOrigin _
) As Long
```
[C#]
```
public override long Seek(
   long offset,
   SeekOrigin origin
);
```
[C++]
```
public: __int64 Seek(
   __int64 offset,
   SeekOrigin origin
);
```
[JScript]
```
public override function Seek(
   offset : long,
   origin : SeekOrigin
) : long;
```

Parameters

offset
   This parameter is not used.
origin
   This parameter is not used.

Return Value

The position in the stream. This method is not currently supported, and will throw a **NotSupportedException**.

Exceptions

Exception Type	Condition
NotSupportedException	Any access.

Requirements

Platforms: Windows 98, Windows NT 4.0,
Windows Millennium Edition, Windows 2000,
Windows XP Home Edition, Windows XP Professional,
Windows .NET Server family,
.NET Compact Framework - Windows CE .NET,
Common Language Infrastructure (CLI) Standard

NetworkStream.SetLength Method

Sets the length of the stream. This method always throws a **NotSupportedException**.

```
[Visual Basic]
Overrides Public Sub SetLength( _
   ByVal value As Long _
)
[C#]
public override void SetLength(
   long value
);
[C++]
public: void SetLength(
   __int64 value
);
[JScript]
public override function SetLength(
   value : long
);
```

Parameters

value
   This parameter is not used.

Exceptions

Exception Type	Condition
NotSupportedException	Any access.

Requirements

Platforms: Windows 98, Windows NT 4.0,
Windows Millennium Edition, Windows 2000,
Windows XP Home Edition, Windows XP Professional,
Windows .NET Server family,
.NET Compact Framework - Windows CE .NET,
Common Language Infrastructure (CLI) Standard

NetworkStream.Write Method

Writes data to the **NetworkStream**.

```
[Visual Basic]
Overrides Public Sub Write( _
   ByVal buffer() As Byte, _
   ByVal offset As Integer, _
   ByVal size As Integer _
)
```

```
[C#]
public override void Write(
   byte[] buffer,
   int offset,
   int size
);
[C++]
public: void Write(
   unsigned char buffer __gc[],
   int offset,
   int size
);
[JScript]
public override function Write(
   buffer : Byte[],
   offset : int,
   size : int
);
```

Parameters

buffer
   An array of type **Byte** that contains the data to write to the **NetworkStream**.
offset
   The location in *buffer* from which to start writing data.
size
   The number of bytes to write to the **NetworkStream**.

Exceptions

Exception Type	Condition
ArgumentNullException	*buffer* is a null reference (**Nothing** in Visual Basic).
ArgumentOutOfRange-Exception	*offset* is less than 0.
	-or-
	offset is greater than the length of *buffer*.
	-or-
	size is less than 0.
	-or-
	size is greater than the length of *buffer* minus the value of the *offset* parameter.
IOException	There is a failure while writing to the network.
ObjectDisposed-Exception	The **NetworkStream** is closed.
	-or-
	There is a failure reading from the network.
IOException	An error occurred when accessing the socket. See the Remarks section for more information.

Remarks

The **Write** method starts at the specified *offset* and sends *size* bytes from the contents of *buffer* to the network. The **Write** method blocks until the requested number of bytes are sent or a **SocketException** is thrown. If you receive a **SocketException**, use **SocketException.ErrorCode** to obtain the specific error code.

Once you have obtained this code, you can refer to the Windows Socket Version 2 API error code documentation in MSDN for a detailed description of the error.

Note Check to see if the **NetworkStream** is writable by accessing the **CanWrite** property. If you attempt to write to a **NetworkStream** that is not writable, you will get an **IOException**. If you receive a **IOException** check the **InnerException** property to determine if it was caused by a **SocketException**. If so, use **ErrorCode** to obtain the specific error code. Once you have obtained this code, you can refer to the Windows Socket Version 2 API error code documentation in MSDN for a detailed description of the error.

Example

[Visual Basic, C#, C++] The following example checks to see whether the **NetworkStream** is writable. If it is, then **Write** is used to write a small message.

[Visual Basic]
```
' Check to see if this NetworkStream is writable.
If myNetworkStream.CanWrite Then

   Dim myWriteBuffer As Byte() = Encoding.ASCII.GetBytes          ⌐
("Are you receiving this message?")
   myNetworkStream.Write(myWriteBuffer, 0, myWriteBuffer.Length)
Else
   Console.WriteLine("Sorry.  You cannot write to this NetworkStream.")
End If
```

[C#]
```
// Check to see if this NetworkStream is writable.
 if (myNetworkStream.CanWrite){

      byte[] myWriteBuffer = Encoding.ASCII.GetBytes("Are you     ⌐
receiving this message?");
      myNetworkStream.Write(myWriteBuffer, 0, myWriteBuffer.Length);
 }
 else{
      Console.WriteLine("Sorry.  You cannot write to this          ⌐
NetworkStream.");
 }
```

[C++]
```
      // Check to see if this NetworkStream is writable.
      if (myNetworkStream->CanWrite) {
         Byte myWriteBuffer[] = Encoding::ASCII->GetBytes          ⌐
(S"Are you receiving this message?");
         myNetworkStream->Write(myWriteBuffer, 0,                  ⌐
myWriteBuffer->Length);
      } else {
         Console::WriteLine(S"Sorry.  You cannot write to          ⌐
this NetworkStream.");
      }
```

Requirements

Platforms: Windows 98, Windows NT 4.0,
Windows Millennium Edition, Windows 2000,
Windows XP Home Edition, Windows XP Professional,
Windows .NET Server family,
.NET Compact Framework - Windows CE .NET,
Common Language Infrastructure (CLI) Standard

ProtocolFamily Enumeration

Specifies the type of protocol that an instance of the **Socket** class can use.

```
[Visual Basic]
<Serializable>
Public Enum ProtocolFamily
[C#]
[Serializable]
public enum ProtocolFamily
[C++]
[Serializable]
__value public enum ProtocolFamily
[JScript]
public
    Serializable
enum ProtocolFamily
```

Remarks

The **ProtocolFamily** enumeration specifies the protocol scheme used by the **Socket** class to resolve an address. For example, **InterNetwork** indicates that the IP version 4 protocol is expected when a **Socket** connects to an endpoint.

Members

Member name	Description
AppleTalk Supported by the .NET Compact Framework.	AppleTalk protocol.
Atm Supported by the .NET Compact Framework.	Native ATM services protocol.
Banyan Supported by the .NET Compact Framework.	Banyan protocol.
Ccitt Supported by the .NET Compact Framework.	CCITT protocol, such as X.25.
Chaos Supported by the .NET Compact Framework.	MIT CHAOS protocol.
Cluster Supported by the .NET Compact Framework.	Microsoft Cluster products protocol.
DataKit Supported by the .NET Compact Framework.	DataKit protocol.
DataLink Supported by the .NET Compact Framework.	Direct data link protocol.
DecNet Supported by the .NET Compact Framework.	DECNet protocol.
Ecma Supported by the .NET Compact Framework.	European Computer Manufactures Association (ECMA) protocol.

Member name	Description
FireFox Supported by the .NET Compact Framework.	FireFox protocol.
HyperChannel Supported by the .NET Compact Framework.	NSC HyperChannel protocol.
Ieee12844 Supported by the .NET Compact Framework.	IEEE 1284.4 workgroup protocol.
ImpLink Supported by the .NET Compact Framework.	ARPANET IMP protocol.
InterNetwork Supported by the .NET Compact Framework.	IP version 4 protocol.
InterNetworkV6 Supported by the .NET Compact Framework.	IP version 6 protocol.
Ipx Supported by the .NET Compact Framework.	IPX or SPX protocol.
Irda Supported by the .NET Compact Framework.	IrDA protocol.
Iso Supported by the .NET Compact Framework.	ISO protocol.
Lat Supported by the .NET Compact Framework.	LAT protocol.
Max Supported by the .NET Compact Framework.	MAX protocol.
NetBios Supported by the .NET Compact Framework.	NetBios protocol.
NetworkDesigners Supported by the .NET Compact Framework.	Network Designers OSI gateway enabled protocol.
NS Supported by the .NET Compact Framework.	Xerox NS protocol.
Osi Supported by the .NET Compact Framework.	OSI protocol.
Pup Supported by the .NET Compact Framework.	PUP protocol.
Sna Supported by the .NET Compact Framework.	IBM SNA protocol.

Member name	Description
Unix Supported by the .NET Compact Framework.	Unix local to host protocol.
Unknown Supported by the .NET Compact Framework.	Unknown protocol.
Unspecified Supported by the .NET Compact Framework.	Unspecified protocol.
VoiceView Supported by the .NET Compact Framework.	VoiceView protocol.

Requirements

Namespace: System.Net.Sockets

Platforms: Windows 98, Windows NT 4.0,
Windows Millennium Edition, Windows 2000,
Windows XP Home Edition, Windows XP Professional,
Windows .NET Server family,
.NET Compact Framework - Windows CE .NET

Assembly: System (in System.dll)

ProtocolType Enumeration

Specifies the protocols that the **Socket** class supports.

```
[Visual Basic]
<Serializable>
Public Enum ProtocolType
[C#]
[Serializable]
public enum ProtocolType
[C++]
[Serializable]
_value public enum ProtocolType
[JScript]
public
    Serializable
enum ProtocolType
```

Remarks

The **Socket** class uses the **ProtocolType** enumeration to inform the Windows Socket API of the requested protocol. Low-level driver software for the requested protocol must be present on the computer for the **Socket** to be created successfully.

Members

Member name	Description
Ggp Supported by the .NET Compact Framework.	Gateway To Gateway Protocol.
Icmp Supported by the .NET Compact Framework.	Internet Control Message Protocol.
Idp Supported by the .NET Compact Framework.	IDP Protocol.
Igmp Supported by the .NET Compact Framework.	Internet Group Management Protocol.
IP Supported by the .NET Compact Framework.	Internet Protocol.
IPv6	Internet Protocol v6.
Ipx Supported by the .NET Compact Framework.	IPX Protocol.
ND Supported by the .NET Compact Framework.	Net Disk Protocol (unofficial).
Pup Supported by the .NET Compact Framework.	PUP Protocol.
Raw Supported by the .NET Compact Framework.	Raw UP packet protocol.
Spx Supported by the .NET Compact Framework.	SPX Protocol.

Member name	Description
SpxII Supported by the .NET Compact Framework.	SPX Version 2 Protocol.
Tcp Supported by the .NET Compact Framework.	Transmission Control Protocol.
Udp Supported by the .NET Compact Framework.	User Datagram Protocol.
Unknown Supported by the .NET Compact Framework.	Unknown protocol.
Unspecified Supported by the .NET Compact Framework.	Unspecified protocol.

Example

[Visual Basic, C#, C++] The following example demonstrates how to use **ProtocolType** to instantiate a **Socket**.

```
[Visual Basic]
Imports System
Imports System.Text
Imports System.IO
Imports System.Net
Imports System.Net.Sockets

-

Public Class Sample

    Public Shared Function DoSocketGet(server As String) As String
        'Set up variables and String to write to the server.
        Dim ASCII As Encoding = Encoding.ASCII
        Dim [Get] As String = "GET / HTTP/1.1" + ControlChars.Lf    ⅃
+ ControlChars.NewLine + "Host: " + server + ControlChars.Lf       ⅃
+ ControlChars.NewLine + "Connection: Close" + ControlChars.Lf     ⅃
+ ControlChars.NewLine + ControlChars.Lf + ControlChars.NewLine
        Dim ByteGet As [Byte]() = ASCII.GetBytes([Get])
        Dim RecvBytes(256) As [Byte]
        Dim strRetPage As [String] = Nothing

        ' IPAddress and IPEndPoint represent the endpoint that will
        '   receive the request.
        ' Get first IPAddress in list return by DNS.
        Try

            ' Define those variables to be evaluated in the next     ⅃
for loop and
            ' then used to connect to the server. These variables    ⅃
are defined
            ' outside the for loop to make them accessible there after.
            Dim s As Socket = Nothing
            Dim hostEndPoint As IPEndPoint
            Dim hostAddress As IPAddress = Nothing
            Dim conPort As Integer = 80

            ' Get DNS host information.
            Dim hostInfo As IPHostEntry = Dns.Resolve(server)
            ' Get the DNS IP addresses associated with the host.
            Dim IPaddresses As IPAddress() = hostInfo.AddressList

            ' Evaluate the socket and receiving host IPAddress       ⅃
and IPEndPoint.
            Dim index As Integer = 0
            For index = 0 To IPaddresses.Length - 1
```

```
        hostAddress = IPaddresses(index)
        hostEndPoint = New IPEndPoint(hostAddress, conPort)

        ' Creates the Socket to send data over a TCP connection.
        s = New Socket(AddressFamily.InterNetwork,
SocketType.Stream, ProtocolType.Tcp)

        ' Connect to the host using its IPEndPoint.
        s.Connect(hostEndPoint)

        If Not s.Connected Then
          ' Connection failed, try next IPaddress.
          strRetPage = "Unable to connect to host"
          s = Nothing
          GoTo ContinueFor1
        End If

        ' Sent the GET request to the host.
        s.Send(ByteGet, ByteGet.Length, 0)

ContinueFor1:
      Next index  ' End of the for loop.

      ' Receive the host home page content and loop until
all the data is received.

        'Dim bytes As Int32 = s.Receive(RecvBytes, RecvBytes.Length, 0)
        Dim bytes As Int32 = s.Receive(RecvBytes, RecvBytes.Length, 0)

        strRetPage = "Default HTML page on " + server + ":\r\n"
        strRetPage = "Default HTML page on " + server + ":" +
ControlChars.Lf + ControlChars.NewLine

        Dim i As Integer

        While bytes > 0

          bytes = s.Receive(RecvBytes, RecvBytes.Length, 0)

          strRetPage = strRetPage + ASCII.GetString(RecvBytes, 0, bytes)

        End While

      ' End of the try block.
      Catch e As SocketException
        Console.WriteLine("SocketException caught!!!")
        Console.WriteLine(("Source : " + e.Source))
        Console.WriteLine(("Message : " + e.Message))
      Catch e As ArgumentNullException
        Console.WriteLine("ArgumentNullException caught!!!")
        Console.WriteLine(("Source : " + e.Source))
        Console.WriteLine(("Message : " + e.Message))
      Catch e As NullReferenceException
        Console.WriteLine("NullReferenceException caught!!!")
        Console.WriteLine(("Source : " + e.Source))
        Console.WriteLine(("Message : " + e.Message))
      Catch e As Exception
        Console.WriteLine("Exception caught!!!")
        Console.WriteLine(("Source : " + e.Source))
        Console.WriteLine(("Message : " + e.Message))
      End Try

      Return strRetPage
    End Function 'DoSocketGet

    Public Shared Sub Main()
      Console.WriteLine(DoSocketGet("localhost"))
    End Sub 'Main
End Class 'Sample

[C#]
using System;
using System.Text;
using System.IO;
```

```
using System.Net;
using System.Net.Sockets;

public class Sample
{

  public static string DoSocketGet(string server)
  {
    //Set up variables and String to write to the server.
    Encoding ASCII = Encoding.ASCII;
    string Get = "GET / HTTP/1.1\r\nHost: " + server +
                  "\r\nConnection: Close\r\n\r\n";
    Byte[] ByteGet = ASCII.GetBytes(Get);
    Byte[] RecvBytes = new Byte[256];
    String strRetPage = null;

    // IPAddress and IPEndPoint represent the endpoint that will
    //   receive the request.
    // Get first IPAddress in list return by DNS.

    try
    {
      // Define those variables to be evaluated in the next
for loop and
      // then used to connect to the server. These variables
are defined
      // outside the for loop to make them accessible there after.
      Socket s = null;
      IPEndPoint hostEndPoint;
      IPAddress hostAddress = null;
      int conPort = 80;

      // Get DNS host information.
      IPHostEntry hostInfo = Dns.Resolve(server);
      // Get the DNS IP addresses associated with the host.
      IPAddress[] IPaddresses = hostInfo.AddressList;

      // Evaluate the socket and receiving host IPAddress and
IPEndPoint.
        for (int index=0; index<IPaddresses.Length; index++)
        {
          hostAddress = IPaddresses[index];
          hostEndPoint = new IPEndPoint(hostAddress, conPort);

          // Creates the Socket to send data over a TCP connection.
          s = new Socket(AddressFamily.InterNetwork,
SocketType.Stream, ProtocolType.Tcp );

          // Connect to the host using its IPEndPoint.
          s.Connect(hostEndPoint);

          if (!s.Connected)
          {
            // Connection failed, try next IPaddress.
            strRetPage = "Unable to connect to host";
            s = null;
            continue;
          }

          // Sent the GET request to the host.
          s.Send(ByteGet, ByteGet.Length, 0);

        } // End of the for loop.

      // Receive the host home page content and loop until
all the data is received.
        Int32 bytes = s.Receive(RecvBytes, RecvBytes.Length, 0);
        strRetPage = "Default HTML page on " + server + ":\r\n";
        strRetPage = strRetPage + ASCII.GetString(RecvBytes, 0, bytes);

        while (bytes > 0)
        {
          bytes = s.Receive(RecvBytes, RecvBytes.Length, 0);
```

```
      strRetPage = strRetPage + ASCII.GetString(RecvBytes, 0, bytes);
    }

  } // End of the try block.

  catch(SocketException e)
  {
    Console.WriteLine("SocketException caught!!!");
    Console.WriteLine("Source : " + e.Source);
    Console.WriteLine("Message : " + e.Message);
  }
  catch(ArgumentNullException e)
  {
    Console.WriteLine("ArgumentNullException caught!!!");
    Console.WriteLine("Source : " + e.Source);
    Console.WriteLine("Message : " + e.Message);
  }
  catch(NullReferenceException e)
  {
    Console.WriteLine("NullReferenceException caught!!!");
    Console.WriteLine("Source : " + e.Source);
    Console.WriteLine("Message : " + e.Message);
  }
  catch(Exception e)
  {
    Console.WriteLine("Exception caught!!!");
    Console.WriteLine("Source : " + e.Source);
    Console.WriteLine("Message : " + e.Message);
  }

  return strRetPage;

}
  public static void Main()
  {
    Console.WriteLine(DoSocketGet("localhost"));
  }
}

[C++]
#using <mscorlib.dll>
#using <System.dll>
#include <stdlib.h>

using namespace System;
using namespace System::Text;
using namespace System::IO;
using namespace System::Net;
using namespace System::Net::Sockets;

public __gc class Sample
{
public:

  String *DoSocketGet(String *server)
  {
    //Set up variables and String to write to the server.
    Encoding *ASCII = Encoding::ASCII;
    String *Get = "GET / HTTP/1.1\r\nHost: ";
    Get->Concat(server, "\r\nConnection: Close\r\n\r\n");
    Byte ByteGet[] = ASCII->GetBytes(Get);
    Byte RecvBytes[] = new Byte[256];
    String *strRetPage = NULL;

    // IPAddress and IPEndPoint represent the endpoint that will
    //   receive the request.
    // Get first IPAddress in list return by DNS.

    try
    {

      // Define those variables to be evaluated in the         ⏎
next for loop and
      // then used to connect to the server. These             ⏎
variables are defined
```

```
      // outside the for loop to make them accessible          ⏎
there after.
      Socket *s = NULL;
      IPEndPoint *hostEndPoint;
      IPAddress *hostAddress = NULL;
      int conPort = 80;

      // Get DNS host information.
      IPHostEntry *hostInfo = Dns::Resolve(server);
      // Get the DNS IP addresses associated with the host.
      IPAddress *IPaddresses[] = hostInfo->AddressList;

      // Evaluate the socket and receiving host IPAddress       ⏎
and IPEndPoint.
      for (int index=0; index<IPaddresses->Length; index++)
      {
        hostAddress = IPaddresses[index];
        hostEndPoint = new IPEndPoint(hostAddress, conPort);

        // Creates the Socket to send data over a TCP           ⏎
connection.
        s = new Socket(AddressFamily::InterNetwork,            ⏎
SocketType::Stream, ProtocolType::Tcp );

        // Connect to the host using its IPEndPoint.
        s->Connect(hostEndPoint);

        if (!s->Connected)
        {
          // Connection failed, try next IPaddress.
          strRetPage = "Unable to connect to host";
          s = NULL;
          continue;
        }

        // Sent the GET request to the host.
        s->Send(ByteGet, ByteGet->Length, SocketFlags::None);

      } // End of the for loop.

      // Receive the host home page content and loop            ⏎
until all the data is received.
      Int32 bytes = s->Receive(RecvBytes,                       ⏎
RecvBytes->Length, SocketFlags::None);
      strRetPage = "Default HTML page on ";
      strRetPage->Concat(server, ":\r\n", ASCII-              ⏎
>GetString(RecvBytes, 0, bytes));

      while (bytes > 0)
      {
        bytes = s->Receive(RecvBytes,                          ⏎
RecvBytes->Length, SocketFlags::None);
        strRetPage->Concat(ASCII->GetString                    ⏎
(RecvBytes, 0, bytes));
      }

    } // End of the try block.

    catch(SocketException *e)
    {
      Console::WriteLine("SocketException caught!!!");
      Console::Write("Source : ");
      Console::WriteLine(e->Source);
      Console::Write("Message : ");
      Console::WriteLine(e->Message);
    }
    catch(ArgumentNullException *e)
    {
      Console::WriteLine("ArgumentNULLException caught!!!");
      Console::Write("Source : ");
      Console::WriteLine(e->Source);
      Console::Write("Message : ");
      Console::WriteLine(e->Message);
    }
    catch(NullReferenceException *e)
```

```
        {
            Console::WriteLine("NULLReferenceException caught!!!");
            Console::Write("Source : ");
            Console::WriteLine(e->Source);
            Console::Write("Message : ");
            Console::WriteLine(e->Message);
        }
        catch(Exception *e)
        {
            Console::WriteLine("Exception caught!!!");
            Console::Write("Source : ");
            Console::WriteLine(e->Source);
            Console::Write("Message : ");
            Console::WriteLine(e->Message);
        }

        return strRetPage;
    }

    Sample()
    {
        Console::WriteLine(DoSocketGet("localhost"));
    }
};
```

Requirements

Namespace: System.Net.Sockets

Platforms: Windows 98, Windows NT 4.0,
Windows Millennium Edition, Windows 2000,
Windows XP Home Edition, Windows XP Professional,
Windows .NET Server family,
.NET Compact Framework - Windows CE .NET

Assembly: System (in System.dll)

SelectMode Enumeration

Defines the polling modes for the **Socket.Poll** method.

[Visual Basic]
```
<Serializable>
Public Enum SelectMode
```
[C#]
```
[Serializable]
public enum SelectMode
```
[C++]
```
[Serializable]
__value public enum SelectMode
```
[JScript]
```
public
    Serializable
enum SelectMode
```

Remarks

The **SelectMode** enumeration defines the polling modes that can be passed to the **Socket.Poll** method. Use the **SelectRead** value to determine if a listening **Socket** has incoming connection requests. Use the **SelectWrite** value to determine if a **Socket** is writeable. Use the **SelectError** value to determine if there is an error condition present on the **Socket**. For explanations of writeablity, readability, and the presence of error conditions, see the **Socket.Poll** method.

Members

Member name	Description
SelectError Supported by the .NET Compact Framework.	Error status mode.
SelectRead Supported by the .NET Compact Framework.	Read status mode.
SelectWrite Supported by the .NET Compact Framework.	Write status mode.

Example

[Visual Basic, C#, C++] The following example checks the status of a **Socket** using all three **SelectMode** enumeration values. A call to **Poll** using the **SelectWrite** enumerated value should return **true**.

[Visual Basic]
```
'Creates the Socket for sending data over TCP.
Dim s As New Socket(AddressFamily.InterNetwork,
SocketType.Stream, ProtocolType.Tcp)

' Connects to host using IPEndPoint.
s.Connect(EPhost)
If Not s.Connected Then
    strRetPage = "Unable to connect to host"
End If
' Use the SelectWrite enumeration to obtain Socket status.
If s.Poll(- 1, SelectMode.SelectWrite) Then
    Console.WriteLine("This Socket is writable.")
Else
    If s.Poll(- 1, SelectMode.SelectRead) Then
        Console.WriteLine(("This should not print.  Because
this is not a listening Socket," + " no incoming connecton
requests are expected. "))
    Else
        If s.Poll(- 1, SelectMode.SelectError) Then
            Console.WriteLine("This Socket has an error.")
```
```
        End If
    End If
```

[C#]
```
//Creates the Socket for sending data over TCP.
Socket s = new Socket(AddressFamily.InterNetwork, SocketType.Stream,
    ProtocolType.Tcp );

// Connects to host using IPEndPoint.
s.Connect(EPhost);
if (!s.Connected)
{
    strRetPage = "Unable to connect to host";
}
// Use the SelectWrite enumeration to obtain Socket status.
if(s.Poll(-1, SelectMode.SelectWrite)){
    Console.WriteLine("This Socket is writable.");
}
else if (s.Poll(-1, SelectMode.SelectRead)){
    Console.WriteLine("This should not print.
Because this is not a listening Socket," +
            " no incoming connecton requests are expected. " );
}
else if (s.Poll(-1, SelectMode.SelectError)){
    Console.WriteLine("This Socket has an error.");
}
```

[C++]
```
//Creates the Socket for sending data over TCP.
Socket* s = new Socket(AddressFamily::InterNetwork,
SocketType::Stream, ProtocolType::Tcp );

// Connects to host using IPEndPoint.
s->Connect(EPhost);
if (!s->Connected) {
    strRetPage = S"Unable to connect to host";
}
// Use the SelectWrite enumeration to obtain Socket status.
if (s->Poll(-1, SelectMode::SelectWrite)) {
    Console::WriteLine(S"This Socket is writable.");
} else if (s->Poll(-1, SelectMode::SelectRead)) {
    Console::WriteLine(S"This should not print.
Because this is not a listening Socket, {0}",
        S" no incoming connecton requests are expected.");
} else if (s->Poll(-1, SelectMode::SelectError)) {
    Console::WriteLine(S"This Socket has an error.");
}
```

Requirements

Namespace: System.Net.Sockets

Platforms: Windows 98, Windows NT 4.0, Windows Millennium Edition, Windows 2000, Windows XP Home Edition, Windows XP Professional, Windows .NET Server family, .NET Compact Framework - Windows CE .NET

Assembly: System (in System.dll)

Socket Class

Implements the Berkeley sockets interface.

System.Object
  System.Net.Sockets.Socket

```
[Visual Basic]
Public Class Socket
   Implements IDisposable
[C#]
public class Socket : IDisposable
[C++]
public __gc class Socket : public IDisposable
[JScript]
public class Socket implements IDisposable
```

Thread Safety

Any public static (**Shared** in Visual Basic) members of this type are safe for multithreaded operations. Any instance members are not guaranteed to be thread safe.

Remarks

The **Socket** class provides a rich set of methods and properties for network communications. The **Socket** class allows you to perform both synchronous and asynchronous data transfer using any of the communication protocols listed in the **ProtocolType** enumeration. The **Socket** class follows the .NET Framework naming pattern for asynchronous methods; for example, the synchronous **Receive** method corresponds to the asynchronous **BeginReceive** and **EndReceive** methods.

If your application only requires one thread during execution, use the following methods, which are designed for synchronous operation mode.

- If you are using a connection-oriented protocol such as TCP, your server can listen for connections using the **Listen** method. The **Accept** method processes any incoming connection requests and returns a **Socket** that you can use to communicate data with the remote host. Use this returned **Socket** to call the **Send** or **Receive** method. Call the **Bind** method prior to calling the **Listen** method if you would like to specify the local IP address and port number. If you do not call **Bind**, the underlying service provider will assign these values for you. You can later use the **LocalEndPoint** property to identify the IP address and port number assigned to your **Socket**. If you would like to connect to a listening host, call the **Connect** method. To communicate data, call the **Send** or **Receive** method.

- If you are using a connectionless protocol such as UDP, you do not need to listen for connections at all. Call the **ReceiveFrom** method to accept any incoming datagrams. Use the **SendTo** method to send datagrams to a remote host.

To process communications using separate threads during execution, use the following methods, which are designed for asynchronous operation mode.

- If you are using a connection-oriented protocol such as TCP, use the **Socket**, **BeginConnect**, and **EndConnect** methods to connect with a listening host. Use the **BeginSend** and **EndSend** or **BeginReceive** and **EndReceive** methods to communicate data asynchronously. Incoming connection requests can be processed using **BeginAccept** and **EndAccept**.

- If you are using a connectionless protocol such as UDP, you can use **BeginSendTo** and **EndSendTo** to send datagrams and **BeginReceiveFrom** and **EndReceiveFrom** to receive datagrams.

When you are finished sending and receiving data, use the **Shutdown** method to disable the **Socket**. After calling **Shutdown**, call the **Close** method to release all resources associated with the **Socket**.

The **Socket** class allows you to configure your **Socket** using the **SetSocketOption** methods. Retrieve these settings using the **GetSocketOption** methods.

> **Note** If you are writing a relatively simple application and only require synchronous data transfer, consider using **TcpClient**, **TcpListener**, and **UdpClient**. These classes provide a simpler and more user-friendly interface to **Socket** communications.

Example

[Visual Basic, C#, C++] The following example shows how the **Socket** class can be used to send data to an HTTP server and receive the response.

```
[Visual Basic]
Imports System
Imports System.Text
Imports System.IO
Imports System.Net
Imports System.Net.Sockets
Imports Microsoft.VisualBasic

Public Class mySocket

    Private Shared Function connectSocket(server As String,       ↵
port As Integer) As Socket
        Dim s As Socket = Nothing
        Dim iphe As IPHostEntry = Nothing

        Try
            ' Get host related information.
            iphe = Dns.Resolve(server)

            ' Loop through the AddressList to obtain the         ↵
supported AddressFamily. This is to avoid
            ' an exception to be thrown if the host IP Address   ↵
is not compatible with the address family
            ' (typical in the IPv6 case).
            Dim ipad As IPAddress

            For Each ipad In iphe.AddressList
                Dim ipe As New IPEndPoint(ipad, port)

                Dim tmpS As New Socket(ipe.AddressFamily,       ↵
SocketType.Stream, ProtocolType.Tcp)

                tmpS.Connect(ipe)

                If tmpS.Connected Then
                    s = tmpS
                    Exit For
                End If

            Next ipad

        Catch e As SocketException
            Console.WriteLine("SocketException caught!!!")
            Console.WriteLine(("Source : " + e.Source))
            Console.WriteLine(("Message : " + e.Message))
        Catch e As Exception
            Console.WriteLine("Exception caught!!!")
            Console.WriteLine(("Source : " + e.Source))
            Console.WriteLine(("Message : " + e.Message))
        End Try
        Return s
    End Function 'connectSocket
```

```vbnet
' This method requests the home page content for the passed server.
' It displays the number of bytes received and the page content.
   Private Shared Function socketSendReceive(server As String, port As
Integer) As String
      'Set up variables and String to write to the server.
      Dim ASCII As Encoding = Encoding.ASCII
      Dim [Get] As String = "GET / HTTP/1.1" + ControlChars.Cr +
ControlChars.Lf + "Host: " + server + ControlChars.Cr +
ControlChars.Lf + "Connection: Close" + ControlChars.Cr +
ControlChars.Lf + ControlChars.Cr + ControlChars.Lf
      Dim ByteGet As [Byte]() = ASCII.GetBytes([Get])
      Dim RecvBytes(255) As [Byte]
      Dim strRetPage As [String] = Nothing

      ' Create a socket connection with the specified server and port.
      Dim s As Socket = connectSocket(server, port)

      If s Is Nothing Then
         Return "Connection failed"
      End If
      ' Send request to the server.
      s.Send(ByteGet, ByteGet.Length, 0)

      ' Receive the server  home page content.
      Dim bytes As Int32 = s.Receive(RecvBytes, RecvBytes.Length, 0)

      ' Read the first 256 bytes.
      strRetPage = "Default HTML page on " + server + ":" +
ControlChars.Cr + ControlChars.Lf
      strRetPage = strRetPage + ASCII.GetString(RecvBytes, 0, bytes)

      While bytes > 0
         bytes = s.Receive(RecvBytes, RecvBytes.Length, 0)
         strRetPage = strRetPage + ASCII.GetString(RecvBytes, 0, bytes)
      End While

      Return strRetPage
   End Function 'socketSendReceive

   'Entry point which delegates to C-style main Private Function
   Public Overloads Shared Sub Main()
      Main(System.Environment.GetCommandLineArgs())
   End Sub

   Overloads Private Shared Sub Main(args() As String)
      Dim host As String
      Dim port As Integer = 80

      If args.Length = 1 Then
         ' If no server name is passed as argument to this
program, use the current
         ' host name as default.
         host = Dns.GetHostName()
      Else
         host = args(1)
      End If

      Dim result As String = socketSendReceive(host, port)

      Console.WriteLine(result)
   End Sub 'Main
End Class 'mySocket
```

```csharp
[C#]
using System;
using System.Text;
using System.IO;
using System.Net;
using System.Net.Sockets;

public class mySocket
{
   private static Socket connectSocket(string server, int port)
   {
      Socket s = null;
      IPHostEntry iphe = null;

      try
      {
         // Get host related information.
         iphe = Dns.Resolve(server);

         // Loop through the AddressList to obtain the
supported AddressFamily. This is to avoid
         // an exception to be thrown if the host IP Address
is not compatible with the address family
         // (typical in the IPv6 case).
         foreach(IPAddress ipad in iphe.AddressList)
         {
            IPEndPoint ipe = new IPEndPoint(ipad, port);

            Socket tmpS =
               new Socket(ipe.AddressFamily,
SocketType.Stream, ProtocolType.Tcp);

            tmpS.Connect(ipe);

            if(tmpS.Connected)
            {
               s = tmpS;
               break;
            }
            else
               continue;
         }
      }

      catch(SocketException e)
      {
         Console.WriteLine("SocketException caught!!!");
         Console.WriteLine("Source : " + e.Source);
         Console.WriteLine("Message : " + e.Message);
      }
      catch(Exception e)
      {
         Console.WriteLine("Exception caught!!!");
         Console.WriteLine("Source : " + e.Source);
         Console.WriteLine("Message : " + e.Message);
      }
      return s;

   }

   // This method requests the home page content for the passed server.
   // It displays the number of bytes received and the page content.
   private static string socketSendReceive(string server, int port)
   {
      //Set up variables and String to write to the server.
      Encoding ASCII = Encoding.ASCII;
      string Get = "GET / HTTP/1.1\r\nHost: " + server +
                   "\r\nConnection: Close\r\n\r\n";
      Byte[] ByteGet = ASCII.GetBytes(Get);
      Byte[] RecvBytes = new Byte[256];
      String strRetPage = null;

      // Create a socket connection with the specified server and port.
      Socket s = connectSocket(server, port);

      if (s == null)
         return ("Connection failed");

      // Send request to the server.
      s.Send(ByteGet, ByteGet.Length, 0);

      // Receive the server  home page content.
      Int32 bytes = s.Receive(RecvBytes, RecvBytes.Length, 0);

      // Read the first 256 bytes.
      strRetPage = "Default HTML page on " + server + ":\r\n";
      strRetPage = strRetPage + ASCII.GetString(RecvBytes, 0, bytes);

      while (bytes > 0)
      {
```

```
        bytes = s.Receive(RecvBytes, RecvBytes.Length, 0);
        strRetPage = strRetPage + ASCII.GetString(RecvBytes, 0, bytes);
    }

    return strRetPage;
}

public static void Main(string[] args)
{
    string host;
    int port = 80;

    if (args.Length == 0)
        // If no server name is passed as argument to
this program, use the current
        // host name as default.
        host = Dns.GetHostName();
    else
        host = args[0];

    string result = socketSendReceive(host, port);

    Console.WriteLine(result);
}

}

[C++]
#using <mscorlib.dll>
#using <System.dll>
using namespace System;
using namespace System::Text;
using namespace System::IO;
using namespace System::Net;
using namespace System::Net::Sockets;

Socket * connectSocket(String* server, int port) {
    Socket* s = 0;
    IPHostEntry* iphe = 0;

    try {
        // Get host related information.
        iphe = Dns::Resolve(server);

        // Loop through the AddressList to obtain the
supported AddressFamily. This is to avoid
        // an exception to be thrown if the host IP
Address is not compatible with the address family
        // (typical in the IPv6 case).
        System::Collections::IEnumerator* myEnum = iphe->
AddressList->GetEnumerator();
        while (myEnum->MoveNext()) {
            IPAddress* ipad = __try_cast<IPAddress*>(myEnum->Current);

            IPEndPoint* ipe = new IPEndPoint(ipad, port);
            Socket* tmpS = new Socket(ipe->AddressFamily,
SocketType::Stream, ProtocolType::Tcp);
            tmpS->Connect(ipe);
            if (tmpS->Connected) {
                s = tmpS;
                break;
            } else
                continue;
        }
    } catch (SocketException* e) {
        Console::WriteLine(S"SocketException caught!!!");
        Console::WriteLine(S"Source : {0}", e->Source);
        Console::WriteLine(S"Message : {0}", e->Message);
    } catch (Exception* e) {
        Console::WriteLine(S"Exception caught!!!");
        Console::WriteLine(S"Source : {0}", e->Source);
        Console::WriteLine(S"Message : {0}", e->Message);
    }
    return s;
}
```

```
// This method requests the home page content for the passed server.
// It displays the number of bytes received and the page content.
String* socketSendReceive(String* server, int port) {
    //Set up variables and String to write to the server.
    Encoding* ASCII = Encoding::ASCII;
    String* Get = String::Concat(S"GET / HTTP/1.1\r\nHost: ", server,
        S"\r\nConnection: Close\r\n\r\n");
    Byte ByteGet[] = ASCII->GetBytes(Get);
    Byte RecvBytes[] = new Byte[256];
    String* strRetPage = 0;

    // Create a socket connection with the specified server and port.
    Socket* s = connectSocket(server, port);
    if (s == 0)
        return (S"Connection failed");

    // Send request to the server.
    s->Send(ByteGet, ByteGet->Length, static_cast<SocketFlags>(0));

    // Receive the server  home page content.
    Int32 bytes = s->Receive(RecvBytes, RecvBytes->Length,
static_cast<SocketFlags>(0));

    // Read the first 256 bytes.
    strRetPage = String::Concat(S"Default HTML page on ", server,
S":\r\n");
    strRetPage = String::Concat(strRetPage, ASCII->GetString
(RecvBytes, 0, bytes));
    while (bytes > 0) {
        bytes = s->Receive(RecvBytes, RecvBytes->Length,
static_cast<SocketFlags>(0));
        strRetPage = String::Concat(strRetPage, ASCII-
>GetString(RecvBytes, 0, bytes));
    }
    return strRetPage;
}

int main() {
    String* args[] = Environment::GetCommandLineArgs();
    String* host;
    int port = 80;

    if (args->Length == 1)
        // If no server name is passed as argument to this
program, use the current
        // host name as default.
        host = Dns::GetHostName();
    else
        host = args[1];

    String* result = socketSendReceive(host, port);
    Console::WriteLine(result);
}
```

Requirements

Namespace: System.Net.Sockets

Platforms: Windows 98, Windows NT 4.0,
Windows Millennium Edition, Windows 2000,
Windows XP Home Edition, Windows XP Professional,
Windows .NET Server family,
.NET Compact Framework - Windows CE .NET

Assembly: System (in System.dll)

.NET Framework Security:

- **SocketPermission** to establish an outgoing connection or accept
  an incoming request.

Socket Constructor

Initializes a new instance of the **Socket** class.

```
[Visual Basic]
Public Sub New( _
   ByVal addressFamily As AddressFamily, _
   ByVal socketType As SocketType, _
   ByVal protocolType As ProtocolType _
)
[C#]
public Socket(
   AddressFamily addressFamily,
   SocketType socketType,
   ProtocolType protocolType
);
[C++]
public: Socket(
   AddressFamily addressFamily,
   SocketType socketType,
   ProtocolType protocolType
);
[JScript]
public function Socket(
   addressFamily : AddressFamily,
   socketType : SocketType,
   protocolType : ProtocolType
);
```

Parameters

addressFamily
   One of the **AddressFamily** values.
socketType
   One of the **SocketType** values.
protocolType
   One of the **ProtocolType** values.

Exceptions

Exception Type	Condition
SocketException	The combination of *addressFamily*, *socketType*, and *protocolType* results in an invalid socket.

Remarks

The *addressFamily* parameter specifies the addressing scheme that the **Socket** uses, the *socketType* parameter specifies the type of the **Socket**, and the *protocolType* parameter specifies the protocol used by the **Socket**. The three parameters are not independent. Some address families restrict which protocols can be used with them, and often the **Socket** type is implicit in the protocol. If the combination of address family, **Socket** type, and protocol type results in an invalid **Socket**, this constructor will throw a **SocketException**.

> **Note** If this constructor throws a **SocketException**, use **SocketException.ErrorCode** to obtain the specific error code. Once you have obtained this code, you can refer to the Windows Socket Version 2 API error code documentation in MSDN for a detailed description of the error.

Example

See related example in the **System.Net.Sockets.Socket** class topic.

Requirements

Platforms: Windows 98, Windows NT 4.0, Windows Millennium Edition, Windows 2000, Windows XP Home Edition, Windows XP Professional, Windows .NET Server family, .NET Compact Framework - Windows CE .NET, Common Language Infrastructure (CLI) Standard

Socket.AddressFamily Property

Gets the address family of the **Socket**.

```
[Visual Basic]
Public ReadOnly Property AddressFamily As AddressFamily
[C#]
public AddressFamily AddressFamily {get;}
[C++]
public: __property AddressFamily get_AddressFamily();
[JScript]
public function get AddressFamily() : AddressFamily;
```

Property Value

One of the **AddressFamily** values.

Remarks

AddressFamily specifies the addressing scheme that an instance of the **Socket** class can use. This property is read-only and is set when the **Socket** is created.

Example

See related example in the **System.Net.Sockets.Socket** class topic.

Requirements

Platforms: Windows 98, Windows NT 4.0, Windows Millennium Edition, Windows 2000, Windows XP Home Edition, Windows XP Professional, Windows .NET Server family, .NET Compact Framework - Windows CE .NET, Common Language Infrastructure (CLI) Standard

Socket.Available Property

Gets the amount of data that has been received from the network and is available to be read.

```
[Visual Basic]
Public ReadOnly Property Available As Integer
[C#]
public int Available {get;}
[C++]
public: __property int get_Available();
[JScript]
public function get Available() : int;
```

Property Value

The number of bytes of data received from the network and available to be read.

Exceptions

Exception Type	Condition
SocketException	An error occurred when attempting to access the socket. See the Remarks section for more information.
ObjectDisposed-Exception	The **Socket** has been closed.

Remarks

If you are using a non-blocking **Socket**, **Available** is a good way to determine whether data is queued for reading, before calling **Receive**. With **Stream Socket** types, the available data is the total amount of data queued in the network buffer for reading. If you are using a message-oriented **Socket** type such as **Dgram**, the available data is the first message in that buffer. If no data is queued in the network buffer, **Available** returns 0.

If the remote host shuts down or closes the connection, **Available** throws a **SocketException**. If you receive a **SocketException**, use **SocketException.ErrorCode** to obtain the specific error code. Once you have obtained this code, you can refer to the Windows Socket Version 2 API error code documentation in MSDN for a detailed description of the error.

Example

See related example in the **System.Net.Sockets.Socket** class topic.

Requirements

Platforms: Windows 98, Windows NT 4.0, Windows Millennium Edition, Windows 2000, Windows XP Home Edition, Windows XP Professional, Windows .NET Server family, .NET Compact Framework - Windows CE .NET, Common Language Infrastructure (CLI) Standard

Socket.Blocking Property

Gets or sets a value that indicates whether the **Socket** is in blocking mode.

```
[Visual Basic]
Public Property Blocking As Boolean
[C#]
public bool Blocking {get; set;}
[C++]
public: __property bool get_Blocking();
public: __property void set_Blocking(bool);
[JScript]
public function get Blocking() : Boolean;
public function set Blocking(Boolean);
```

Property Value

true if the **Socket** will block; otherwise, **false**. The default is **true**.

Exceptions

Exception Type	Condition
SocketException	An error occurred when attempting to access the socket. See the Remarks section for more information.
ObjectDisposed-Exception	The **Socket** has been closed.

Remarks

The **Blocking** property indicates whether a **Socket** is in blocking mode.

If you are in blocking mode, and you make a method call which does not complete immediately, your application will block execution until the requested operation completes. If you want execution to continue even though the requested operation is not complete, change the **Blocking** property to **false**. The **Blocking** property has no effect on asynchronous methods. If you are sending and receiving data asynchronously and want to block execution, use the **ManualResetEvent** class.

> **Note** If you receive a **SocketException**, use **SocketException.ErrorCode** to obtain the specific error code. Once you have obtained this code, you can refer to the Windows Socket Version 2 API error code documentation in MSDN for a detailed description of the error.

Requirements

Platforms: Windows 98, Windows NT 4.0, Windows Millennium Edition, Windows 2000, Windows XP Home Edition, Windows XP Professional, Windows .NET Server family, .NET Compact Framework - Windows CE .NET, Common Language Infrastructure (CLI) Standard

Socket.Connected Property

Gets a value indicating whether a **Socket** is connected to a remote host.

```
[Visual Basic]
Public ReadOnly Property Connected As Boolean
[C#]
public bool Connected {get;}
[C++]
public: __property bool get_Connected();
[JScript]
public function get Connected() : Boolean;
```

Property Value

true if the **Socket** is connected to a remote resource; otherwise, **false**.

Remarks

The **Connected** property gets the connection state of the **Socket**. This property will return the latest known state of the **Socket**. When it returns **false**, the **Socket** was either never connected, or is no longer connected.

There is no guarantee that the **Socket** is still **Connected** even if **Connected** returns **true**. A value of **true** simply means that the **Socket** was connected at the time of the last I/O operation.

Example

[Visual Basic, C#] The following example connects to a remote endpoint and then verifies the connection.

```
[Visual Basic]
aSocket.Connect(anEndPoint)
If Not aSocket.Connected Then
    Console.WriteLine("Winsock error: " _
        + Convert.ToString(System.Runtime.InteropServices.Marshal. ↵
GetLastWin32Error()))
End If

[C#]
aSocket.Connect(anEndPoint);
if (!aSocket.Connected) {
    Console.WriteLine("Winsock error: "
        + Convert.ToString(System.Runtime.InteropServices.Marshal. ↵
GetLastWin32Error()));
}
```

Requirements

Platforms: Windows 98, Windows NT 4.0,
Windows Millennium Edition, Windows 2000,
Windows XP Home Edition, Windows XP Professional,
Windows .NET Server family,
.NET Compact Framework - Windows CE .NET,
Common Language Infrastructure (CLI) Standard

Socket.Handle Property

Gets the operating system handle for the **Socket**.

```
[Visual Basic]
Public ReadOnly Property Handle As IntPtr
[C#]
public IntPtr Handle {get;}
[C++]
public: __property IntPtr get_Handle();
[JScript]
public function get Handle() : IntPtr;
```

Property Value

An **IntPtr** representing the operating system handle for the **Socket**.

Requirements

Platforms: Windows 98, Windows NT 4.0,
Windows Millennium Edition, Windows 2000,
Windows XP Home Edition, Windows XP Professional,
Windows .NET Server family,
.NET Compact Framework - Windows CE .NET,
Common Language Infrastructure (CLI) Standard

Socket.LocalEndPoint Property

Gets the local endpoint.

```
[Visual Basic]
Public ReadOnly Property LocalEndPoint As EndPoint
[C#]
public EndPoint LocalEndPoint {get;}
[C++]
public: __property EndPoint* get_LocalEndPoint();
[JScript]
public function get LocalEndPoint() : EndPoint;
```

Property Value

The **EndPoint** that the **Socket** is using for communications.

Exceptions

Exception Type	Condition
SocketException	An error occurred when attempting to access the socket. See the Remarks section for more information.
ObjectDisposed-Exception	The **Socket** has been closed.

Remarks

The **LocalEndPoint** property gets an **EndPoint** containing the local IP address and port number to which your **Socket** is bound. You must cast this **EndPoint** to an **IPEndPoint** before retrieving any information. You can then call the **IPEndPoint.Address** method to retrieve the local **IPAddress**, and the **IPEndPoint.Port** method to retrieve the local port number.

The **LocalEndPoint** property is usually set after you make a call to the **Bind** method. If you allow the system to assign your socket's local IP address and port number, the **LocalEndPoint** property will be set after the first I/O operation. For connection-oriented protocols, the first I/O operation would be a call to the **Connect** or **Accept** method. For connectionless protocols, the first I/O operation would be any of the send or receive calls.

> **Note** If you receive a **SocketException**, use **SocketException.ErrorCode** to obtain the specific error code. Once you have obtained this code, you can refer to the Windows Socket Version 2 API error code documentation in MSDN for a detailed description of the error.

Example

See related example in the **System.Net.Sockets.Socket** class topic.

Requirements

Platforms: Windows 98, Windows NT 4.0,
Windows Millennium Edition, Windows 2000,
Windows XP Home Edition, Windows XP Professional,
Windows .NET Server family,
.NET Compact Framework - Windows CE .NET,
Common Language Infrastructure (CLI) Standard

Socket.ProtocolType Property

Gets the protocol type of the **Socket**.

```
[Visual Basic]
Public ReadOnly Property ProtocolType As ProtocolType
[C#]
public ProtocolType ProtocolType {get;}
[C++]
public: __property ProtocolType get_ProtocolType();
[JScript]
public function get ProtocolType() : ProtocolType;
```

Property Value

One of the **ProtocolType** values.

Remarks

The **ProtocolType** property is set when the **Socket** is created, and specifies the protocol used by that **Socket**.

Requirements

Platforms: Windows 98, Windows NT 4.0,
Windows Millennium Edition, Windows 2000,
Windows XP Home Edition, Windows XP Professional,
Windows .NET Server family,
.NET Compact Framework - Windows CE .NET,
Common Language Infrastructure (CLI) Standard

Socket.RemoteEndPoint Property

Gets the remote endpoint.

```
[Visual Basic]
Public ReadOnly Property RemoteEndPoint As EndPoint
[C#]
public EndPoint RemoteEndPoint {get;}
[C++]
public: __property EndPoint* get_RemoteEndPoint();
```

```
[JScript]
public function get RemoteEndPoint() : EndPoint;
```

Property Value

The **EndPoint** with which the **Socket** is communicating.

Exceptions

Exception Type	Condition
SocketException	An error occurred when attempting to access the socket. See the Remarks section for more information.
ObjectDisposed-Exception	The **Socket** has been closed.

Remarks

If you are using a connection-oriented protocol, the **RemoteEndPoint** property gets the **EndPoint** containing the remote IP address and port number to which the **Socket** is connected. If you are using a connectionless protocol, **RemoteEndPoint** contains the default remote IP address and port number with which the **Socket** will communicate. You must cast this **EndPoint** to an **IPEndPoint** before retrieving any information. You can then call the **IPEndPoint.Address** method to retrieve the remote **IPAddress**, and the **IPEndPoint.Port** method to retrieve the remote port number.

The **RemoteEndPoint** is set after a call to either **Accept** or **Connect**. If you try to access this property earlier, **RemoteEndPoint** will throw a **SocketException**. If you receive a **SocketException**, use **SocketException.ErrorCode** to obtain the specific error code. Once you have obtained this code, you can refer to the Windows Socket Version 2 API error code documentation in MSDN for a detailed description of the error.

Example

See related example in the **System.Net.Sockets.Socket** class topic.

Requirements

Platforms: Windows 98, Windows NT 4.0, Windows Millennium Edition, Windows 2000, Windows XP Home Edition, Windows XP Professional, Windows .NET Server family, .NET Compact Framework - Windows CE .NET, Common Language Infrastructure (CLI) Standard

Socket.SocketType Property

Gets the type of the **Socket**.

```
[Visual Basic]
Public ReadOnly Property SocketType As SocketType
[C#]
public SocketType SocketType {get;}
[C++]
public: __property SocketType get_SocketType();
[JScript]
public function get SocketType() : SocketType;
```

Property Value

One of the **SocketType** values.

Remarks

SocketType is read-only and is set when the **Socket** is created.

Example

See related example in the **System.Net.Sockets.Socket** class topic.

Requirements

Platforms: Windows 98, Windows NT 4.0, Windows Millennium Edition, Windows 2000, Windows XP Home Edition, Windows XP Professional, Windows .NET Server family, .NET Compact Framework - Windows CE .NET, Common Language Infrastructure (CLI) Standard

Socket.SupportsIPv4 Property

Note: This namespace, class, or member is supported only in version 1.1 of the .NET Framework.

Gets a value indicating whether IPv4 support is available and enabled on the current host.

```
[Visual Basic]
Public Shared ReadOnly Property SupportsIPv4 As Boolean
[C#]
public static bool SupportsIPv4 {get;}
[C++]
public: __property static bool get_SupportsIPv4();
[JScript]
public static function get SupportsIPv4() : Boolean;
```

Property Value

true if the current host supports the IPv4 protocol; otherwise, **false**.

Remarks

The value of this property is a function of the Operating System's support for the IPv4 protocol.

Requirements

Platforms: Windows 98, Windows NT 4.0, Windows Millennium Edition, Windows 2000, Windows XP Home Edition, Windows XP Professional, Windows .NET Server family

Socket.SupportsIPv6 Property

Note: This namespace, class, or member is supported only in version 1.1 of the .NET Framework.

Gets a value indicating whether IPv6 support is available and enabled on the current host.

```
[Visual Basic]
Public Shared ReadOnly Property SupportsIPv6 As Boolean
[C#]
public static bool SupportsIPv6 {get;}
[C++]
public: __property static bool get_SupportsIPv6();
[JScript]
public static function get SupportsIPv6() : Boolean;
```

Property Value

true if the current host supports the IPv6 protocol; otherwise, **false**.

Remarks

The value of this property is a function of the Operating System's support for the IPv6 protocol and of the **config.ipv6Enabled** field defined by the configuration file.

Note A host can support both IPv4 and IPv6 protocols.

Requirements

Platforms: Windows 98, Windows NT 4.0,
Windows Millennium Edition, Windows 2000,
Windows XP Home Edition, Windows XP Professional,
Windows .NET Server family

Socket.Accept Method

Creates a new **Socket** for a newly created connection.

```
[Visual Basic]
Public Function Accept() As Socket
[C#]
public Socket Accept();
[C++]
public: Socket* Accept();
[JScript]
public function Accept() : Socket;
```

Return Value

A **Socket** for a newly created connection.

Exceptions

Exception Type	Condition
SocketException	An error occurred when attempting to access the socket. See the Remarks section for more information.
ObjectDisposed-Exception	The **Socket** has been closed.
InvalidOperation-Exception	The **Socket** is not bound. You must call **Bind** before calling **Accept**.

Remarks

Accept synchronously extracts the first pending connection request
from the connection request queue of the listening socket, and then
creates and returns a new **Socket**. You cannot use this returned
Socket to accept any additional connections from the connection
queue. However, you can call the **RemoteEndPoint** method of the
returned **Socket** to identify the remote host's network address and
port number.

In blocking mode, **Accept** will block until an incoming connection
attempt is queued. After accepting a connection, the original **Socket**
will continue queuing incoming connection requests until you close
it.

If you call this method using a non-blocking **Socket**, and no
connection requests are queued, **Accept** will throw a
SocketException. If you receive a **SocketException**, use
SocketException.ErrorCode to obtain the specific error code.
Once you have obtained this code, you can refer to the Windows
Socket Version 2 API error code documentation in MSDN for a
detailed description of the error.

Note Before calling the **Accept** method, you must first call the
Listen method to listen for and queue incoming connection
requests.

Example

See related example in the **System.Net.Sockets.Socket** class topic.

Requirements

Platforms: Windows 98, Windows NT 4.0,
Windows Millennium Edition, Windows 2000,
Windows XP Home Edition, Windows XP Professional,
Windows .NET Server family,
.NET Compact Framework - Windows CE .NET,
Common Language Infrastructure (CLI) Standard

Socket.BeginAccept Method

Begins an asynchronous operation to accept an incoming connection
attempt.

```
[Visual Basic]
Public Function BeginAccept( _
    ByVal callback As AsyncCallback, _
    ByVal state As Object _
) As IAsyncResult
[C#]
public IAsyncResult BeginAccept(
    AsyncCallback callback,
    object state
);
[C++]
public: IAsyncResult* BeginAccept(
    AsyncCallback* callback,
    Object* state
);
[JScript]
public function BeginAccept(
    callback : AsyncCallback,
    state : Object
) : IAsyncResult;
```

Parameters

callback
    The **AsyncCallback** delegate.
state
    An object containing state information for this request.

Return Value

An **IAsyncResult** that references the asynchronous **Socket** creation.

Exceptions

Exception Type	Condition
SocketException	An error occurred when attempting to access the socket. See the Remarks section for more information.
ObjectDisposed-Exception	The **Socket** has been closed.

Remarks

Connection-oriented protocols can use the **BeginAccept** method to
asynchronously process incoming connection attempts. Accepting
connections asynchronously gives you the ability to send and receive
data within a separate execution thread. Before calling the
BeginAccept method, you must call the **Listen** method to listen for
and queue incoming connection requests.

You must create a callback method that implements the
AsyncCallback delegate and pass its name to the **BeginAccept**
method. To do this, at the very minimum, you must pass the listening
Socket to **BeginAccept** through the *state* parameter. If your callback
needs more information, you can create a small class to hold the

Socket and the other required information. Pass an instance of this class to the **BeginAccept** method through the *state* parameter.

Your callback method should implement the **EndAccept** method. When your application calls **BeginAccept**, the system will use a separate thread to execute the specified callback method, and will block on **EndAccept** until a pending connection is retrieved. **EndAccept** will return a new **Socket** that you can use to send and receive data with the remote host. You cannot use this returned **Socket** to accept any additional connections from the connection queue. If you want the original thread to block after you call the **BeginAccept** method, use **WaitHandle.WaitOne**. Call **ManualResetEvent.Set** in the callback method when you want the original thread to continue executing.

> **Note** You can call the **RemoteEndPoint** method of the returned **Socket** to identify the remote host's network address and port number.

> **Note** If you receive a **SocketException**, use **SocketException.ErrorCode** to obtain the specific error code. Once you have obtained this code, you can refer to the Windows Socket Version 2 API error code documentation in MSDN for a detailed description of the error.

Example

See related example in the **System.Net.Sockets.Socket** class topic.

Requirements

Platforms: Windows 98, Windows NT 4.0, Windows Millennium Edition, Windows 2000, Windows XP Home Edition, Windows XP Professional, Windows .NET Server family, .NET Compact Framework - Windows CE .NET, Common Language Infrastructure (CLI) Standard

Socket.BeginConnect Method

Begins an asynchronous request for a remote host connection.

```
[Visual Basic]
Public Function BeginConnect( _
   ByVal remoteEP As EndPoint, _
   ByVal callback As AsyncCallback, _
   ByVal state As Object _
) As IAsyncResult
[C#]
public IAsyncResult BeginConnect(
   EndPoint remoteEP,
   AsyncCallback callback,
   object state
);
[C++]
public: IAsyncResult* BeginConnect(
   EndPoint* remoteEP,
   AsyncCallback* callback,
   Object* state
);
[JScript]
public function BeginConnect(
   remoteEP : EndPoint,
   callback : AsyncCallback,
   state : Object
) : IAsyncResult;
```

Parameters

remoteEP
   An **EndPoint** that represents the remote host.
callback
   The **AsyncCallback** delegate.
state
   An object that contains state information for this request.

Return Value

An **IAsyncResult** that references the asynchronous connection.

Exceptions

Exception Type	Condition
ArgumentNullException	*remoteEP* is a null reference (**Nothing** in Visual Basic).
SocketException	An error occurred when attempting to access the socket. See the Remarks section for more information.
ObjectDisposed-Exception	The **Socket** has been closed.
SecurityException	A caller higher in the call stack does not have permission for the requested operation.

Remarks

If you are using a connection-oriented protocol, the **BeginConnect** method starts an asynchronous request for a connection to the *remoteEP* parameter. If you are using a connectionless protocol, **BeginConnect** establishes a default remote host. Connecting or setting the default remote host asynchronously gives you the ability to send and receive data within a separate execution thread.

You can create acallback method that implements the **AsyncCallback** delegate and pass its name to the **BeginConnect** method. At the very minimum, you must pass the **Socket** to **BeginConnect** through the *state* parameter. If your callback needs more information, you can create a small class to hold the **Socket**, and the other required information. Pass an instance of this class to the **BeginConnect** method through the *state* parameter.

Your callback method should implement the **EndConnect** method. When your application calls **BeginConnect**, the system will use a separate thread to execute the specified callback method, and will block on **EndConnect** until the **Socket** connects successfully or throws an exception. If you want the original thread to block after you call the **BeginConnect** method, use **WaitOne**. Call **Set** in the callback method when you want the original thread to continue executing. For additional information on writing callback methods see **Callback Sample**.

If you are using a connectionless protocol such as UDP, you do not have to call **BeginConnect** before sending and receiving data. You can use **BeginSendTo** and **BeginReceiveFrom** to communicate with a remote host. If you do call **BeginConnect**, any datagrams that arrive from an address other than the specified default will be discarded. If you wish to set your default remote host to a broadcast address, you must first call **SetSocketOption** and set Broadcast to **true**. If you cannot, **BeginConnect** will throw a **SocketException**.

If you are using a connection-oriented protocol and do not call **Bind** before calling **BeginConnect**, the underlying service provider will assign the most appropriate local network address and port number. If you are using a connectionless protocol, the service provider will not assign a local network address and port number until you call the **BeginSend** or **ReceiveFrom** method. If you want to change the default remote host, call the **BeginConnect** method again with the desired endpoint.

Note If you receive a **SocketException**, use **SocketException.ErrorCode** to obtain the specific error code. Once you have obtained this code, you can refer to the Windows Socket Version 2 API error code documentation in MSDN for a detailed description of the error.

Example

See related example in the **System.Net.Sockets.Socket** class topic.

Requirements

Platforms: Windows 98, Windows NT 4.0, Windows Millennium Edition, Windows 2000, Windows XP Home Edition, Windows XP Professional, Windows .NET Server family, .NET Compact Framework - Windows CE .NET, Common Language Infrastructure (CLI) Standard

Socket.BeginReceive Method

Begins to asynchronously receive data from a connected **Socket**.

```
[Visual Basic]
Public Function BeginReceive( _
    ByVal buffer() As Byte, _
    ByVal offset As Integer, _
    ByVal size As Integer, _
    ByVal socketFlags As SocketFlags, _
    ByVal callback As AsyncCallback, _
    ByVal state As Object _
) As IAsyncResult
[C#]
public IAsyncResult BeginReceive(
    byte[] buffer,
    int offset,
    int size,
    SocketFlags socketFlags,
    AsyncCallback callback,
    object state
);
[C++]
public: IAsyncResult* BeginReceive(
    unsigned char buffer __gc[],
    int offset,
    int size,
    SocketFlags socketFlags,
    AsyncCallback* callback,
    Object* state
);
[JScript]
public function BeginReceive(
    buffer : Byte[],
    offset : int,
    size : int,
    socketFlags : SocketFlags,
    callback : AsyncCallback,
    state : Object
) : IAsyncResult;
```

Parameters

buffer
  An array of type **Byte** that is the storage location for the received data.
offset
  The zero-based position in the *buffer* parameter at which to store the received data.
size
  The number of bytes to receive.
socketFlags
  A bitwise combination of the **SocketFlags** values.
callback
  The **AsyncCallback** delegate.
state
  An object containing state information for this request.

Return Value

An **IAsyncResult** that references the asynchronous read.

Exceptions

Exception Type	Condition
ArgumentNullException	*buffer* is a null reference (**Nothing** in Visual Basic).
SocketException	An error occurred when attempting to access the socket. See the Remarks section for more information.
ObjectDisposed-Exception	**Socket** has been closed.
ArgumentOutOfRange-Exception	*offset* is less than 0.
	-or-
	offset is greater than the length of *buffer*.
	-or-
	size is less than 0.
	-or-
	size is greater than the length of *buffer* minus the value of the *offset* parameter.

Remarks

The **BeginReceive** method starts asynchronously reading data from the **Socket** returned by **EndAccept**. Calling the **BeginReceive** method gives you the ability to receive data within a separate execution thread.

You can create a callback method that implements the **AsyncCallback** delegate and pass its name to the **BeginReceive** method. To do this, at the very minimum, your *state* parameter must contain the connected or default **Socket** being used for communication. Since you will want to obtain the received data within your callback method, you should create a small class or structure to hold a read buffer, and any other useful information. Pass the structure or class instance to the **BeginReceive** method through the *state* parameter.

Your callback method should implement the **EndReceive** method. When your application calls **BeginReceive**, the system will use a separate thread to execute the specified callback method, and will block on **EndReceive** until the **Socket** reads data or throws an exception. If you want the original thread to block after you call the **BeginReceive** method, use **WaitHandle.WaitOne**. Call

ManualResetEvent.Set in the callback method when you want the original thread to continue executing. .

You can call **BeginReceive** from both connection-oriented and connectionless sockets. You must call the **Connect**, **BeginConnect**, **Accept**, or **BeginAccept** method before calling the **BeginReceive** method, because the **BeginReceive** method will only read data which arrives from the remote host you specify in one of these methods. If you are using a connectionless protocol, you can also use the **BeginReceiveFrom** method. **BeginReceiveFrom** will allow you to receive data arriving from any host.

If you are using a connection-oriented **Socket**, the **BeginReceive** method will read as much data as is available, up to the number of bytes specified by the *size* parameter.

If you are using a connectionless **Socket**, **BeginReceive** will read the first enqueued datagram from the destination address you specify in the **Connect** or **BeginConnect** method. If the datagram you receive is larger than the size of the *buffer* parameter, *buffer* gets filled with the first part of the message, and a **SocketException** is thrown. With unreliable protocols the excess data is lost; with reliable protocols, the data is retained by the service provider and you can retrieve the rest by calling the **BeginReceive** method with a large enough buffer.

If you specify the **OutOfBand** flag as the *socketFlags* parameter and the **Socket** is configured for in-line reception of out-of-band (OOB) data (using **OutOfBandInline**) and OOB data is available, **BeginReceive** will return only OOB data. The OOB data is a logically independent transmission channel associated with each pair of connected stream sockets. This data is delivered with higher priority and independently of the normal data. If you specify the **Peek** flag, the available data is copied into the receive buffer but not removed from the system buffer.

Note If you receive a **SocketException**, use **SocketException.ErrorCode** to obtain the specific error code. Once you have obtained this code, you can refer to the Windows Socket Version 2 API error code documentation in MSDN for a detailed description of the error.

Example

See related example in the **System.Net.Sockets.Socket** class topic.

Requirements

Platforms: Windows 98, Windows NT 4.0,
Windows Millennium Edition, Windows 2000,
Windows XP Home Edition, Windows XP Professional,
Windows .NET Server family,
.NET Compact Framework - Windows CE .NET,
Common Language Infrastructure (CLI) Standard

Socket.BeginReceiveFrom Method

Begins to asynchronously receive data from a specified network device.

```
[Visual Basic]
Public Function BeginReceiveFrom( _
   ByVal buffer() As Byte, _
   ByVal offset As Integer, _
   ByVal size As Integer, _
   ByVal socketFlags As SocketFlags, _
   ByRef remoteEP As EndPoint, _
   ByVal callback As AsyncCallback, _
   ByVal state As Object _
) As IAsyncResult
```

```
[C#]
public IAsyncResult BeginReceiveFrom(
   byte[] buffer,
   int offset,
   int size,
   SocketFlags socketFlags,
   ref EndPoint remoteEP,
   AsyncCallback callback,
   object state
);
```

```
[C++]
public: IAsyncResult* BeginReceiveFrom(
   unsigned char buffer __gc[],
   int offset,
   int size,
   SocketFlags socketFlags,
   EndPoint** remoteEP,
   AsyncCallback* callback,
   Object* state
);
```

```
[JScript]
public function BeginReceiveFrom(
   buffer : Byte[],
   offset : int,
   size : int,
   socketFlags : SocketFlags,
   remoteEP : EndPoint,
   callback : AsyncCallback,
   state : Object
) : IAsyncResult;
```

Parameters

buffer
   An array of type **Byte** that is the storage location for the received data.
offset
   The zero-based position in the *buffer* parameter at which to store the data.
size
   The number of bytes to receive.
socketFlags
   A bitwise combination of the **SocketFlags** values.
remoteEP
   An **EndPoint** that represents the source of the data.
callback
   The **AsyncCallback** delegate.
state
   An object containing state information for this request.

Return Value

An **IAsyncResult** that references the asynchronous read.

Exceptions

Exception Type	Condition
ArgumentNullException	*buffer* is a null reference (**Nothing** in Visual Basic).
	-or-
	remoteEP is a null reference (**Nothing**).

Exception Type	Condition
SocketException	An error occurred when attempting to access the socket. See the Remarks section for more information.
ArgumentOutOfRange-Exception	*offset* is less than 0. -or- *offset* is greater than the length of *buffer*. -or- *size* is less than 0. -or- *size* is greater than the length of *buffer* minus the value of the *offset* parameter.
ObjectDisposed-Exception	The **Socket** has been closed.
SecurityException	A caller higher in the call stack does not have permission for the requested operation.

Remarks

The **BeginReceiveFrom** method starts asynchronously reading connectionless datagrams from a remote host. Calling the **BeginReceiveFrom** method gives you the ability to receive data within a separate execution thread.

You can create a *callback* method that implements the **AsyncCallback** delegate and pass its name to the **BeginReceiveFrom** method. To do this, at the very minimum, your *state* parameter must contain the connected or default **Socket** being used for communication. If your callback needs more information, you can create a small class to hold the **Socket** and the other required information. Pass an instance of this class to the **BeginReceiveFrom** method through the *state* parameter.

Your callback method should implement the **EndReceiveFrom** method. When your application calls **BeginReceiveFrom**, the system will use a separate thread to execute the specified callback method, and it will block on **EndReceiveFrom** until the **Socket** reads data or throws an exception. If you want the original thread to block after you call the **BeginReceiveFrom** method, use **WaitHandle.WaitOne**. Call **ManualResetEvent.Set** in the callback method when you want the original thread to continue executing. .

> **Note** Before calling **BeginReceiveFrom**, you must explicitly bind the **Socket** to a local endpoint using the **Bind** method, or **BeginReceiveFrom** will throw a **SocketException**.

This method reads data into the *buffer* parameter, and captures the remote host endpoint from which the data is sent. For information on how to retrieve this endpoint, refer to **EndReceiveFrom**. This method is most useful if you intend to asynchronously receive connectionless datagrams from an unknown host or multiple hosts. In these cases, **BeginReceiveFrom** will read the first enqueued datagram received into the local network buffer. If the datagram you receive is larger than the size of *buffer*, the **BeginReceiveFrom** method will fill *buffer* with as much of the message as is possible, and throw a **SocketException**. If you are using an unreliable protocol, the excess data will be lost. If you are using a reliable protocol, the excess data will be retained by the service provider and you can retrieve it by calling the **BeginReceiveFrom** method with a large enough buffer.

Although **BeginReceiveFrom** is intended for connectionless protocols, you can use a connection-oriented protocol as well. If you choose to do so, you must first either establish a remote host connection by calling the **Connect/ BeginConnect** method or accept an incoming connection request by calling the **Accept** or **BeginAccept** method. If you call the **BeginReceiveFrom** method before establishing or accepting a connection, you will get a **SocketException**. You can also establish a default remote host for a connectionless protocol prior to calling the **BeginReceiveFrom** method. In either of these cases, the **BeginReceiveFrom** method will ignore the *remoteEP* parameter and only receive data from the connected or default remote host.

With connection-oriented sockets, **BeginReceiveFrom** will read as much data as is available up to the number of bytes specified by the *size* parameter.If you specify the **OutOfBand** flag as the *socketFlags* parameter and the **Socket** is configured for in-line reception of out-of-band (OOB) data (using **OutOfBandInline**) and OOB data is available, **BeginReceiveFrom** returns only OOB data. The OOB data is a logically independent transmission channel associated with each pair of connected stream sockets. This data is delivered with higher priority and independently of the normal data. If you specify the **Peek** flag as the *socketFlags* parameter, the available data is copied into the receive buffer but not removed from the system buffer.

> **Note** If you receive a **SocketException**, use **SocketException.ErrorCode** to obtain the specific error code. Once you have obtained this code, you can refer to the Windows Socket Version 2 API error code documentation in MSDN for a detailed description of the error.

Example

See related example in the **System.Net.Sockets.Socket** class topic.

Requirements

Platforms: Windows 98, Windows NT 4.0, Windows Millennium Edition, Windows 2000, Windows XP Home Edition, Windows XP Professional, Windows .NET Server family, .NET Compact Framework - Windows CE .NET, Common Language Infrastructure (CLI) Standard

Socket.BeginSend Method

Sends data asynchronously to a connected **Socket**.

```
[Visual Basic]
Public Function BeginSend( _
   ByVal buffer() As Byte, _
   ByVal offset As Integer, _
   ByVal size As Integer, _
   ByVal socketFlags As SocketFlags, _
   ByVal callback As AsyncCallback, _
   ByVal state As Object _
) As IAsyncResult
[C#]
public IAsyncResult BeginSend(
   byte[] buffer,
   int offset,
   int size,
   SocketFlags socketFlags,
   AsyncCallback callback,
   object state
);
```

```
[C++]
public: IAsyncResult* BeginSend(
    unsigned char buffer __gc[],
    int offset,
    int size,
    SocketFlags socketFlags,
    AsyncCallback* callback,
    Object* state
);
[JScript]
public function BeginSend(
    buffer : Byte[],
    offset : int,
    size : int,
    socketFlags : SocketFlags,
    callback : AsyncCallback,
    state : Object
) : IAsyncResult;
```

Parameters

buffer

An array of type **Byte** that contains the data to send.

offset

The zero-based position in the *buffer* parameter at which to begin sending data.

size

The number of bytes to send.

socketFlags

A bitwise combination of the **SocketFlags** values.

callback

The **AsyncCallback** delegate.

state

An object containing state information for this request.

Return Value

An **IAsyncResult** that references the asynchronous send.

Exceptions

Exception Type	Condition
ArgumentNullException	*buffer* is a null reference (**Nothing** in Visual Basic).
SocketException	An error occurred when attempting to access the socket. See remarks section below.
ArgumentOutOfRange- Exception	*offset* is less than 0. -or- *offset* is less than the length of *buffer*. -or- *size* is less than 0. -or- *size* is greater than the length of *buffer* minus the value of the *offset* parameter.
ObjectDisposed- Exception	The **Socket** has been closed.

Remarks

The **BeginSend** method starts an asynchronous send operation to the remote host established in the **Connect**, **BeginConnect**, **Accept**, **BeginAccept** method. **BeginSend** will throw an exception if you do not first call **Accept**, **BeginAccept**, **Connect**, or **BeginConnect**. Calling the **BeginSend** method gives you the ability to send data within a separate execution thread.

You can create a callback method that implements the **AsyncCallback** delegate and pass its name to the **BeginSend** method. To do this, at the very minimum, your *state* parameter must contain the connected or default **Socket** being used for communication. If your callback needs more information, you can create a small class or structure to hold the **Socket** and the other required information. Pass an instance of this class to the **BeginSend** method through the *state* parameter.

Your callback method should implement the **EndSend** method. When your application calls **BeginSend**, the system will use a separate thread to execute the specified callback method, and will block on **EndSend** until the **Socket** sends the number of bytes requested or throws an exception. If you want the original thread to block after you call the **BeginSend** method, use the **WaitHandle. WaitOne** method. Call **Set** in the callback method when you want the original thread to continue executing. For additional information on writing callback methods see **Callback Sample**.

Although intended for connection-oriented protocols, **BeginSend** also works for connectionless protocols, provided that you first call the **Connect** or **BeginConnect** method to establish a default remote host. If you are using a connectionless protocol and plan to send data to several different hosts, you should use **BeginSendTo**. It is okay to use **BeginSendTo** even after you have established a default remote host with **Connect**. You can also change the default remote host prior to calling **BeginSend** by making another call to **Connect** or **BeginConnect**. With connectionless protocols, you must also be sure that the size of your buffer does not exceed the maximum packet size of the underlying service provider. If it does, the datagram will not be sent and **BeginSend** will throw a **SocketException**.

If you specify the **DontRoute** flag as the *socketflags* parameter, the data you are sending will not be routed. If you specify the **OutOfBand** flag as the *socketflags* parameter, only out-of-band (OOB) data is sent.

> **Note** If you receive a **SocketException**, use **SocketException.ErrorCode** to obtain the specific error code. Once you have obtained this code, you can refer to the Windows Socket Version 2 API error code documentation in MSDN for a detailed description of the error.

Example

See related example in the **System.Net.Sockets.Socket** class topic.

Requirements

Platforms: Windows 98, Windows NT 4.0, Windows Millennium Edition, Windows 2000, Windows XP Home Edition, Windows XP Professional, Windows .NET Server family, .NET Compact Framework - Windows CE .NET, Common Language Infrastructure (CLI) Standard

Socket.BeginSendTo Method

Sends data asynchronously to a specific remote host.

```
[Visual Basic]
Public Function BeginSendTo( _
   ByVal buffer() As Byte, _
   ByVal offset As Integer, _
   ByVal size As Integer, _
   ByVal socketFlags As SocketFlags, _
   ByVal remoteEP As EndPoint, _
   ByVal callback As AsyncCallback, _
   ByVal state As Object _
) As IAsyncResult
[C#]
public IAsyncResult BeginSendTo(
   byte[] buffer,
   int offset,
   int size,
   SocketFlags socketFlags,
   EndPoint remoteEP,
   AsyncCallback callback,
   object state
);
[C++]
public: IAsyncResult* BeginSendTo(
   unsigned char buffer __gc[],
   int offset,
   int size,
   SocketFlags socketFlags,
   EndPoint* remoteEP,
   AsyncCallback* callback,
   Object* state
);
[JScript]
public function BeginSendTo(
   buffer : Byte[],
   offset : int,
   size : int,
   socketFlags : SocketFlags,
   remoteEP : EndPoint,
   callback : AsyncCallback,
   state : Object
) : IAsyncResult;
```

Parameters

buffer
   An array of type **Byte** that contains the data to send.
offset
   The zero-based position in *buffer* at which to begin sending data.
size
   The number of bytes to send.
socketFlags
   A bitwise combination of the **SocketFlags** values.
remoteEP
   An **EndPoint** that represents the remote device.
callback
   The **AsyncCallback** delegate.
state
   An object containing state information for this request.

Return Value

An **IAsyncResult** that references the asynchronous send.

Exceptions

Exception Type	Condition
ArgumentNullException	*buffer* is a null reference (**Nothing** in Visual Basic). -or- *remoteEP* is a null reference (**Nothing**).
SocketException	An error occurred when attempting to access the socket. See the Remarks section for more information.
ArgumentOutOfRange-Exception	*offset* is less than 0. -or- *offset* is greater than the length of *buffer*. -or- *size* is less than 0. -or- *size* is greater than the length of *buffer* minus the value of the *offset* parameter.
ObjectDisposed-Exception	The **Socket** has been closed.
SecurityException	A caller higher in the call stack does not have permission for the requested operation.

Remarks

The **BeginSendTo** method starts an asynchronous send operation to the remote host specified in the *remoteEP* parameter. Calling the **BeginSendTo** method gives you the ability to send data within a separate execution thread. Although intended for connectionless protocols, **BeginSendTo** works with both connectionless and connection-oriented protocols.

You can create a callback method that implements the **AsyncCallback** delegate and pass its name to the **BeginSendTo** method. To do this, at the very minimum, your *state* parameter must contain the connected or default **Socket** being used for communication. If your callback needs more information, you can create a small class to hold the **Socket**, and the other required information. Pass an instance of this class to the **BeginSendTo** method through the *state* parameter.

Your callback method should implement the **EndSendTo** method. When your application calls **BeginSendTo**, the system will use a separate thread to execute the specified callback method, and will block on **EndSendTo** until the **Socket** sends the number of bytes requested or throws an exception. If you want the original thread to block after you call the **BeginSendTo** method, use the **WaitHandle.WaitOne** method. Call **ManualResetEvent.Set** in the callback method when you want the original thread to continue executing. For additional information on writing callback methods see **Callback Sample**.

If you are using a connection-oriented protocol, you must first call the **Connect**, **BeginConnect**, **Accept**, or **BeginAccept** method, or **BeginSendTo** will throw a **SocketException**. **BeginSendTo** will ignore the *remoteEP* parameter and send data to the **EndPoint** established in the **Connect**, **BeginConnect**, **Accept**, or **BeginAccept** method.

If you are using a connectionless protocol, you do not need to establish a default remote host with the **Connect** or **BeginConnect** method prior to calling **SendTo**. You only need to do this if you intend to call the **BeginSend** method. If you do call the **Connect** or **BeginConnect** method prior to calling **SendTo**, the *remoteEP* parameter will override the specified default remote host for that send operation only. You are also not required to call the **Bind** method. In this case, the underlying service provider will assign the most appropriate local network address and port number. If you need to identify the assigned local network address and port number, you can use the **LocalEndPoint** property after the **EndSendTo** method successfully completes.

If you want to send data to a broadcast address, you must first call the **SetSocketOption** method and set the socket option to **SocketOptionName.Broadcast**. -You must also be sure that the size of your buffer does not exceed the maximum packet size of the underlying service provider. If it does, the datagram will not be sent and **EndSendTo** will throw a **SocketException**.

If you specify the **DontRoute** flag as the *socketflags* parameter, the data you are sending will not be routed. If you specify the **OutOfBand** flag as the *socketflags* parameter, only out-of-band (OOB) data is sent. The OOB data is a logically independent transmission channel associated with each pair of connected stream sockets. This data is delivered with higher priority and independently of the normal data.

> **Note** If you receive a **SocketException**, use **SocketException.ErrorCode** to obtain the specific error code. Once you have obtained this code, you can refer to the Windows Socket Version 2 API error code documentation in MSDN for a detailed description of the error.

Example

See related example in the **System.Net.Sockets.Socket** class topic.

Requirements

Platforms: Windows 98, Windows NT 4.0, Windows Millennium Edition, Windows 2000, Windows XP Home Edition, Windows XP Professional, Windows .NET Server family, .NET Compact Framework - Windows CE .NET, Common Language Infrastructure (CLI) Standard

Socket.Bind Method

Associates a **Socket** with a local endpoint.

```
[Visual Basic]
Public Sub Bind( _
   ByVal localEP As EndPoint _
)
[C#]
public void Bind(
   EndPoint localEP
);
[C++]
public: void Bind(
   EndPoint* localEP
);
[JScript]
public function Bind(
   localEP : EndPoint
);
```

Parameters

localEP
   The local **EndPoint** to associate with the **Socket**.

Exceptions

Exception Type	Condition
ArgumentNullException	*localEP* is a null reference (**Nothing** in Visual Basic).
SocketException	An error occurred when attempting to access the socket. See the Remarks section for more information.
ObjectDisposed-Exception	The **Socket** has been closed.
SecurityException	A caller higher in the call stack does not have permission for the requested operation.

Remarks

Use the **Bind** method if you need to use a specific local endpoint. You must call **Bind** before you can call the **Listen** method. You do not need to call **Bind** before using the **Connect** method unless you need to use a specific local endpoint. You can use the **Bind** method on both connectionless and connection-oriented protocols.

Before calling **Bind**, you must first create the local **IPEndPoint** from which you intend to communicate data. If you do not care which local address is assigned, you can create an **IPEndPoint** using **IPAddress.Any** as the address parameter, and the underlying service provider will assign the most appropriate network address. This might help simplify your application if you have multiple network interfaces. If you do not care which local port is used, you can create an **IPEndPoint** using 0 for the port number. In this case, the service provider will assign an available port number between 1024 and 5000.

If you use the above approach, you can discover what local network address and port number has been assigned by calling the **LocalEndPoint**. If you are using a connection-oriented protocol, **LocalEndPoint** will not return the locally assigned network address until after you have made a call to the **Connect** or **EndConnect** method. If you are using a connectionless protocol, you will not have access to this information until you have completed a send or receive.

> **Note** If you intend to receive multicasted datagrams, you must call the **Bind** method with a multicast port number.

> **Note** You must call the **Bind** method if you intend to receive connectionless datagrams using the **ReceiveFrom** method.

> **Note** If you receive a **SocketException** when calling the **Bind** method, use **SocketException.ErrorCode** to obtain the specific error code. Once you have obtained this code, you can refer to the Windows Socket Version 2 API error code documentation in MSDN for a detailed description of the error

Example

See related example in the **System.Net.Sockets.Socket** class topic.

[Visual Basic, C#] The following example binds a **Socket** using the specified local endpoint.

Visual Basic]
```
ry
    aSocket.Bind(anEndPoint)
atch e As Exception
    Console.WriteLine("Winsock error: " & e.ToString())
nd Try
```

C#]
```
ry {
    aSocket.Bind(anEndPoint);
}
atch (Exception e) {
    Console.WriteLine("Winsock error: " + e.ToString());
```

Requirements

Platforms: Windows 98, Windows NT 4.0,
Windows Millennium Edition, Windows 2000,
Windows XP Home Edition, Windows XP Professional,
Windows .NET Server family,
NET Compact Framework - Windows CE .NET,
Common Language Infrastructure (CLI) Standard

NET Framework Security:

• **SocketPermission** for accepting connections from the host
  defined by *localEP*. Associated enumeration:
  NetworkAccess.Accept

Socket.Close Method

Closes the **Socket** connection and releases all associated resources.

```
[Visual Basic]
Public Sub Close()
[C#]
public void Close();
[C++]
public: void Close();
[JScript]
public function Close();
```

Remarks

The **Close** method closes the the remote host connection and releases all managed and unmanaged resources associated with the **Socket**. Upon closing, the **Connected** property is set to **false**.

For connection-oriented protocols, it is recommended that you call **Shutdown** before calling the **Close** method. This ensures that all data is sent and received on the connected socket before it is closed.

If you need to call **Close** without first calling **Shutdown**, you can ensure that data queued for outgoing transmission will be sent by setting the **DontLinger Socket** option to **false** and specifying a non-zero time-out interval. **Close** will then block until this data is sent or until the specified time-out expires. If you set **DontLinger** to **false** and specify a zero time-out interval, **Close** releases the connection and automatically discards outgoing queued data.

> **Note** To set the **DontLinger** socket option to **false**, create a **LingerOption**, set the enabled property to **false**, and set the **LingerTime** property to the desired time out period. Use this **LingerOption** along with the **DontLinger** socket option to call the **SetSocketOption** method.

Example

[Visual Basic, C#] The following example closes a **Socket**.

```
[Visual Basic]
aSocket.Shutdown(SocketShutdown.Both)
aSocket.Close()
If aSocket.Connected Then
    Console.WriteLine("Winsock error: " _
        + Convert.ToString(System.Runtime.InteropServices.Marshal. ⤶
GetLastWin32Error()))
End If
```

```
[C#]
aSocket.Shutdown(SocketShutdown.Both);
aSocket.Close();
if (aSocket.Connected) {
    Console.WriteLine("Winsock error: " +                           ⤶
Convert.ToString
(System.Runtime.InteropServices.Marshal.GetLastWin32Error()) );    ⤶
}
```

Requirements

Platforms: Windows 98, Windows NT 4.0,
Windows Millennium Edition, Windows 2000,
Windows XP Home Edition, Windows XP Professional,
Windows .NET Server family,
.NET Compact Framework - Windows CE .NET,
Common Language Infrastructure (CLI) Standard

Socket.Connect Method

Establishes a connection to a remote host.

```
[Visual Basic]
Public Sub Connect( _
    ByVal remoteEP As EndPoint _
)
[C#]
public void Connect(
    EndPoint remoteEP
);
[C++]
public: void Connect(
    EndPoint* remoteEP
);
[JScript]
public function Connect(
    remoteEP : EndPoint
);
```

Parameters

remoteEP
    An **EndPoint** that represents the remote device.

Exceptions

Exception Type	Condition
ArgumentNullException	*remoteEP* is a null reference (**Nothing** in Visual Basic).
SocketException	An error occurred when attempting to access the socket. See the Remarks section for more information.
ObjectDisposed-Exception	The **Socket** has been closed.
SecurityException	A caller higher in the call stack does not have permission for the requested operation.

Remarks

If you are using a connection-oriented protocol such as TCP, the **Connect** method synchronously establishes a network connection between **LocalEndPoint** and the specified remote endpoint. If you are using a connectionless protocol, **Connect** establishes a default remote host. After you call **Connect**, you can send data to the remote device with the **Send** method, or receive data from the remote device with the **Receive** method.

If you are using a connectionless protocol such as UDP, you do not have to call **Connect** before sending and receiving data. You can use **SendTo** and **ReceiveFrom** to synchronously communicate with a remote host. If you do call **Connect**, any datagrams that arrive from an address other than the specified default will be discarded. If you want to set your default remote host to a broadcast address, you must first call the **SetSocketOption** method and set the socket option to **SocketOptionName.Broadcast**, or **Connect** will throw a **SocketException**. If you receive a **SocketException**, use **SocketException.ErrorCode** to obtain the specific error code. Once you have obtained this code, you can refer to the Windows Socket Version 2 API error code documentation in MSDN for a detailed description of the error.

The **Connect** method will block, unless you specifically set the **Blocking** property to **false** prior to calling **Connect**. If you are using a connection-oriented protocol like TCP and you do disable blocking, **Connect** will throw a **SocketException** because it needs time to make the connection. Connectionless protocols will not throw an exception because they simply establish a default remote host. You can use **SocketException.ErrorCode** to obtain the specific error code. Once you have obtained this code, you can refer to the Windows Socket Version 2 API error code documentation in MSDN for a detailed description of the error. If the error returned WSAEWOULDBLOCK, the remote host connection has been initiated by a connection-oriented **Socket**, but has not yet completed successfully. Use the **Poll** method to determine when the **Socket** is finished connecting.

> **Note** If you are using a connection-oriented protocol and did not call **Bind** before calling **Connect**, the underlying service provider will assign the local network address and port number. If you are using a connectionless protocol, the service provider will not assign a local network address and port number until you complete a send or receive operation. If you want to change the default remote host, call **Connect** again with the desired endpoint.

Example

[Visual Basic, C#] The following example connects to a remote endpoint and then verifies the connection.

[Visual Basic]
```
aSocket.Connect(anEndPoint)
If Not aSocket.Connected Then
    Console.WriteLine("Winsock error: " _
    + Convert.ToString(
System.Runtime.InteropServices.Marshal.GetLastWin32Error()))
End If
```

[C#]
```
aSocket.Connect(anEndPoint);
if (!aSocket.Connected) {
    Console.WriteLine("Winsock error: "
    + Convert.ToString
(System.Runtime.InteropServices.Marshal.GetLastWin32Error()));
}
```

Requirements

Platforms: Windows 98, Windows NT 4.0, Windows Millennium Edition, Windows 2000, Windows XP Home Edition, Windows XP Professional, Windows .NET Server family, .NET Compact Framework - Windows CE .NET, Common Language Infrastructure (CLI) Standard

.NET Framework Security:
- **SocketPermission** for connecting to the remote host. Associated enumeration: **NetworkAccess.Connect**

Socket.Dispose Method

Releases the unmanaged resources used by the **Socket**, and optionally disposes of the managed resources.

```
[Visual Basic]
Protected Overridable Sub Dispose( _
    ByVal disposing As Boolean _
)
[C#]
protected virtual void Dispose(
    bool disposing
);
[C++]
protected: virtual void Dispose(
    bool disposing
);
[JScript]
protected function Dispose(
    disposing : Boolean
);
```

Parameters

disposing
> **true** to release both managed and unmanaged resources; **false** to releases only unmanaged resources.

Remarks

This method is called by the public **Dispose()** method and the **Finalize** method. **Dispose()** invokes the protected **Dispose(Boolean)** method with the *disposing* parameter set to **true**. **Finalize** invokes **Dispose** with *disposing* set to **false**.

When the *disposing* parameter is **true**, this method releases all resources held by any managed objects that this **Socket** references. This method invokes the **Dispose()** method of each referenced object.

Notes to Inheritors: **Dispose** can be called multiple times by other objects. When overriding **Dispose(Boolean)**, be careful not to reference objects that have been previously disposed of in an earlier call to **Dispose**.

Requirements

Platforms: Windows 98, Windows NT 4.0, Windows Millennium Edition, Windows 2000, Windows XP Home Edition, Windows XP Professional, Windows .NET Server family, .NET Compact Framework - Windows CE .NET, Common Language Infrastructure (CLI) Standard

Socket.EndAccept Method

Asynchronously accepts an incoming connection attempt and creates a new **Socket** to handle remote host communication.

```
[Visual Basic]
Public Function EndAccept( _
   ByVal asyncResult As IAsyncResult _
) As Socket
[C#]
public Socket EndAccept(
   IAsyncResult asyncResult
);
[C++]
public: Socket* EndAccept(
   IAsyncResult* asyncResult
);
[JScript]
public function EndAccept(
   asyncResult : IAsyncResult
) : Socket;
```

Parameters

asyncResult

> An **IAsyncResult** that stores state information for this asynchronous operation as well as any user defined data.

Return Value

A **Socket** to handle communication with the remote host.

Exceptions

Exception Type	Condition
ArgumentNullException	*asyncResult* is a null reference (**Nothing** in Visual Basic).
ArgumentException	*asyncResult* was not created by a call to **BeginAccept**.
SocketException	An error occurred when attempting to access the socket. See the Remarks section for more information.
ObjectDisposed-Exception	The **Socket** has been closed.

Remarks

EndAccept completes a call to **BeginAccept**. Before calling **BeginAccept**, you need to create a callback method that implements the **AsyncCallback** delegate. This callback method executes in a separate thread, and is called by the system after the **BeginAccept** method returns. It must accept the *asyncResult* parameter returned from the **BeginAccept** method.

Within the callback method, call the **AsyncState** method of the *asyncResult* parameter to obtain the **Socket** on which the connection attempt is being made. After obtaining the **Socket**, you can call the **EndAccept** method to successfully complete the connection attempt. The **EndAccept** method blocks until a connection is pending in the incoming connection queue. The **EndAccept** method accepts the incoming connection and returns a new **Socket** that can be used to send data to and receive data from the remote host.

> **Note** If you receive a **SocketException**, use **SocketException.ErrorCode** to obtain the specific error code. Once you have obtained this code, you can refer to the Windows Socket Version 2 API error code documentation in MSDN for a detailed description of the error.

Example

[Visual Basic, C#, C++] The following example ends an asynchronous request and creates a new **Socket** to accept an incoming connection request.

```
[Visual Basic]
allDone.Set()
Dim s As Socket = CType(ar.AsyncState, Socket)
Dim s2 As Socket = s.EndAccept(ar)
Dim so2 As New StateObject()
so2.workSocket = s2
s2.BeginReceive(so2.buffer, 0, StateObject.BUFFER_SIZE, 0, _
New AsyncCallback(AddressOf Async_Send_Receive.Read_Callback), so2)
      End Sub 'Listen_Callback
```

```
[C#]
allDone.Set();
Socket s = (Socket) ar.AsyncState;
Socket s2 = s.EndAccept(ar);
StateObject so2 = new StateObject();
so2.workSocket = s2;
s2.BeginReceive(so2.buffer, 0, StateObject.BUFFER_SIZE,0,
               new AsyncCallback(Async_Send_Receive.Read_Callback),
so2);
```

```
[C++]
allDone->Set();
Socket* s = __try_cast<Socket*>(ar->AsyncState);
Socket* s2 = s->EndAccept(ar);
StateObject* so2 = new StateObject();
so2->workSocket = s2;
s2->BeginReceive(so2->buffer, 0, StateObject::BUFFER_SIZE,
SocketFlags::None,
      new AsyncCallback(0, &Async_Send_Receive::Read_Callback), so2);
```

Requirements

Platforms: Windows 98, Windows NT 4.0, Windows Millennium Edition, Windows 2000, Windows XP Home Edition, Windows XP Professional, Windows .NET Server family, .NET Compact Framework - Windows CE .NET, Common Language Infrastructure (CLI) Standard

Socket.EndConnect Method

Ends a pending asynchronous connection request.

```
[Visual Basic]
Public Sub EndConnect( _
   ByVal asyncResult As IAsyncResult _
)
[C#]
public void EndConnect(
   IAsyncResult asyncResult
);
[C++]
public: void EndConnect(
   IAsyncResult* asyncResult
);
[JScript]
public function EndConnect(
   asyncResult : IAsyncResult
);
```

Parameters

asyncResult

An **IAsyncResult** that stores state information and any user defined data for this asynchronous operation.

Exceptions

Exception Type	Condition
ArgumentNullException	*asyncResult* is a null reference (**Nothing** in Visual Basic).
ArgumentException	*asyncResult* was not returned by a call to the **BeginConnect** method.
InvalidOperation-Exception	**EndConnect** was previously called for the asynchronous connection.
SocketException	An error occurred when attempting to access the socket. See the Remarks section for more information.
ObjectDisposed-Exception	The **Socket** has been closed.

Remarks

EndConnect is a blocking method that completes the asynchronous remote host connection request started in the **BeginConnect** method.

Before calling **BeginConnect**, you need to create a callback method that implements the **AsyncCallback** delegate. This callback method executes in a separate thread and is called by the system after **BeginConnect** returns. The callback method must accept the **IAsyncResult** returned by the **BeginConnect** method as a parameter.

Within the callback method, call the **AsyncState** method of the **IAsyncResult** parameter to obtain the **Socket** on which the connection attempt is being made. After obtaining the **Socket**, you can call the **EndConnect** method to successfully complete the connection attempt.

> **Note** If you receive a **SocketException**, use **SocketException.ErrorCode** to obtain the specific error code. Once you have obtained this code, you can refer to the Windows Socket Version 2 API error code documentation in MSDN for a detailed description of the error.

Example

[Visual Basic, C#, C++] The following example ends the asynchronous connection attempt.

```
[Visual Basic]
allDone.Set()
Dim s As Socket = CType(ar.AsyncState, Socket)
s.EndConnect(ar)
Dim so2 As New StateObject()
so2.workSocket = s
Dim buff As Byte() = Encoding.ASCII.GetBytes("This is a test")
s.BeginSend(buff, 0, buff.Length, 0, New AsyncCallback _
(AddressOf Async_Send_Receive.Send_Callback), so2)
    End Sub 'Connect_Callback
```

```
[C#]
allDone.Set();
Socket s = (Socket) ar.AsyncState;
s.EndConnect(ar);
StateObject so2 = new StateObject();
so2.workSocket = s;
byte[] buff = Encoding.ASCII.GetBytes("This is a test");
s.BeginSend(buff, 0, buff.Length,0,
            new AsyncCallback(Async_Send_Receive.Send_Callback),
so2);
```

```
[C++]
allDone->Set();
Socket* s = __try_cast<Socket*>(ar->AsyncState);
s->EndConnect(ar);
StateObject* so2 = new StateObject();
so2->workSocket = s;
Byte buff[] = Encoding::ASCII->GetBytes(S"This is a test");
s->BeginSend(buff, 0, buff->Length, SocketFlags::None,
    new AsyncCallback(0, &Async_Send_Receive::Send_Callback), so2);
```

Requirements

Platforms: Windows 98, Windows NT 4.0, Windows Millennium Edition, Windows 2000, Windows XP Home Edition, Windows XP Professional, Windows .NET Server family, .NET Compact Framework - Windows CE .NET, Common Language Infrastructure (CLI) Standard

Socket.EndReceive Method

Ends a pending asynchronous read.

```
[Visual Basic]
Public Function EndReceive( _
    ByVal asyncResult As IAsyncResult _
) As Integer
[C#]
public int EndReceive(
    IAsyncResult asyncResult
);
[C++]
public: int EndReceive(
    IAsyncResult* asyncResult
);
[JScript]
public function EndReceive(
    asyncResult : IAsyncResult
) : int;
```

Parameters

asyncResult

An **IAsyncResult** that stores state information and any user defined data for this asynchronous operation.

Return Value

The number of bytes received.

Exceptions

Exception Type	Condition
ArgumentNullException	*asyncResult* is a null reference (**Nothing** in Visual Basic).
ArgumentException	*asyncResult* was not returned by a call to the **BeginReceive** method.
InvalidOperation-Exception	**EndReceive** was previously called for the asynchronous read.
SocketException	An error occurred when attempting to access the socket. See the Remarks section for more information.
ObjectDisposed-Exception	The **Socket** has been closed.

Remarks

The **EndReceive** method completes the asynchronous read operation started in the **BeginReceive** method.

Before calling **BeginReceive**, you need to create a callback method that implements the **AsyncCallback** delegate. This callback method executes in a separate thread and is called by the system after **BeginReceive** returns. The callback method must accept the **IAsyncResult** returned by the **BeginReceive** method as a parameter.

Within the callback method, call the **AsyncState** method of the **IAsyncResult** to obtain the state object passed to the **BeginReceive** method. Extract the receiving **Socket** from this state object. After obtaining the **Socket**, you can call the **EndReceive** method to successfully complete the read operation and return the number of bytes read.

The **EndReceive** method will block until data is available. If you are using a connectionless protocol, **EndReceive** will read the first enqueued datagram available in the incoming network buffer. If you are using a connection-oriented protocol, the **EndReceive** method will read as much data as is available up to the number of bytes you specified in the *size* parameter of the **BeginReceive** method. If the remote host shuts down the **Socket** connection with the **Shutdown** method, and all available data has been received, the **EndReceive** method will complete immediately and return zero bytes.To obtain the received data, call the **AsyncState** method of the **IAsyncResult**, and extract the buffer contained in the resulting state object.

Note If you receive a **SocketException**, use **SocketException.ErrorCode** to obtain the specific error code. Once you have obtained this code, you can refer to the Windows Socket Version 2 API error code documentation in MSDN for a detailed description of the error.

Example

[Visual Basic, C#, C++] The following example ends a pending asynchronous read.

[Visual Basic]
```
Dim so As StateObject = CType(ar.AsyncState, StateObject)
Dim s As Socket = so.workSocket

Dim read As Integer = s.EndReceive(ar)

If read > 0 Then
    so.sb.Append(Encoding.ASCII.GetString(so.buffer, 0, read))
    s.BeginReceive(so.buffer, 0, StateObject.BUFFER_SIZE, 0,
New AsyncCallback(AddressOf Async_Send_Receive.Read_Callback), so)
Else
    If so.sb.Length > 1 Then
        'All the data has been read, so displays it to the console
        Dim strContent As String
        strContent = so.sb.ToString()
        Console.WriteLine([String].Format("Read {0} byte
from socket" + "data = {1} ", strContent.Length, strContent))
    End If
    s.Close()
End If
    End Sub 'Read_Callback
```

[C#]
```
StateObject so = (StateObject) ar.AsyncState;
Socket s = so.workSocket;

int read = s.EndReceive(ar);

if (read > 0) {
        so.sb.Append(Encoding.ASCII.GetString(so.buffer, 0, read));
        s.BeginReceive(so.buffer, 0, StateObject.BUFFER_SIZE, 0,
                            new
AsyncCallback(Async_Send_Receive.Read_Callback), so);
}
else{
```

```
if (so.sb.Length > 1) {
        //All of the data has been read, so displays
it to the console
        string strContent;
        strContent = so.sb.ToString();
        Console.WriteLine(String.Format("Read {0} byte from socket" +
                            "data = {1} ", strContent.Length,
strContent));
    }
    s.Close();
}
```

[C++]
```
StateObject* so = __try_cast<StateObject*>(ar->AsyncState);
Socket* s = so->workSocket;

int read = s->EndReceive(ar);

if (read > 0) {
    so->sb->Append(Encoding::ASCII->GetString(so->buffer, 0, read));
    s->BeginReceive(so->buffer, 0, StateObject::BUFFER_SIZE,
SocketFlags::None,
        new AsyncCallback(0, &Async_Send_Receive::Read_Callback), so);
} else {
    if (so->sb->Length > 1) {
        //All of the data has been read, so displays it to the console
        String* strContent = so->sb->ToString();
        Console::WriteLine(String::Format(S"Read {0} byte
from socket data = {1} ",
            __box(strContent->Length), strContent));
    }
    s->Close();
}
```

Requirements

Platforms: Windows 98, Windows NT 4.0, Windows Millennium Edition, Windows 2000, Windows XP Home Edition, Windows XP Professional, Windows .NET Server family, .NET Compact Framework - Windows CE .NET, Common Language Infrastructure (CLI) Standard

Socket.EndReceiveFrom Method

Ends a pending asynchronous read from a specific endpoint.

```
[Visual Basic]
Public Function EndReceiveFrom( _
    ByVal asyncResult As IAsyncResult, _
    ByRef endPoint As EndPoint _
) As Integer
[C#]
public int EndReceiveFrom(
    IAsyncResult asyncResult,
    ref EndPoint endPoint
);
[C++]
public: int EndReceiveFrom(
    IAsyncResult* asyncResult,
    EndPoint** endPoint
);
[JScript]
public function EndReceiveFrom(
    asyncResult : IAsyncResult,
    endPoint : EndPoint
) : int;
```

Parameters

asyncResult

An **IAsyncResult** that stores state information and any user defined data for this asynchronous operation.

endPoint

The source **EndPoint**.

Return Value

If successful, the number of bytes received. If unsuccessful, returns 0.

Exceptions

Exception Type	Condition
ArgumentNullException	*asyncResult* is a null reference (**Nothing** in Visual Basic).
ArgumentException	*asyncResult* was not returned by a call to the **BeginReceiveFrom** method.
InvalidOperation-Exception	**EndReceiveFrom** was previously called for the asynchronous read.
SocketException	An error occurred when attempting to access the socket. See the Remarks section for more information.
ObjectDisposed-Exception	The **Socket** has been closed.

Remarks

The **EndReceiveFrom** method completes the asynchronous read operation started in the **BeginReceiveFrom** method.

Before calling **BeginReceiveFrom**, you need to create a callback method that implements the **AsyncCallback** delegate. This callback method executes in a separate thread and is called by the system after **BeginReceiveFrom** returns. The callback method must accept the **IAsyncResult** returned by the **BeginReceiveFrom** method as a parameter.

Within the callback method, call the **AsyncState** method of the **IAsyncResult** to obtain the state object passed to the **BeginReceiveFrom** method. Extract the receiving **Socket** from this state object. After obtaining the **Socket**, you can call the **EndReceiveFrom** method to successfully complete the read operation and return the number of bytes read.

The **EndReceiveFrom** method will block until data is available. If you are using a connectionless protocol, **EndReceiveFrom** will read the first enqueued datagram available in the incoming network buffer. If you are using a connection-oriented protocol, the **EndReceiveFrom** method will read as much data as is available up to the number of bytes you specified in the *size* parameter of the **BeginReceiveFrom** method. If the remote host shuts down the **Socket** connection with the **Shutdown** method, and all available data has been received, the **EndReceiveFrom** method will complete immediately and return zero bytes. To obtain the received data, call the **AsyncState** method of the **IAsyncResult** object, and extract the buffer contained in the resulting state object. To identify the originating host, extract the **EndPoint** and cast it to an **IPEndPoint**. Use the **IPEndPoint.Address** method to obtain the IP address and the **IPEndPoint.Port** method to obtain the port number.

Note If you receive a **SocketException**, use **SocketException.ErrorCode** to obtain the specific error code. Once you have obtained this code, you can refer to the Windows Socket Version 2 API error code documentation in MSDN for a detailed description of the error.

Requirements

Platforms: Windows 98, Windows NT 4.0, Windows Millennium Edition, Windows 2000, Windows XP Home Edition, Windows XP Professional, Windows .NET Server family, .NET Compact Framework - Windows CE .NET, Common Language Infrastructure (CLI) Standard

Socket.EndSend Method

Ends a pending asynchronous send.

```
[Visual Basic]
Public Function EndSend( _
   ByVal asyncResult As IAsyncResult _
) As Integer
[C#]
public int EndSend(
   IAsyncResult asyncResult
);
[C++]
public: int EndSend(
   IAsyncResult* asyncResult
);
[JScript]
public function EndSend(
    asyncResult : IAsyncResult
) : int;
```

Parameters

asyncResult

An **IAsyncResult** that stores state information for this asynchronous operation.

Return Value

If successful, the number of bytes sent to the **Socket**; otherwise, an invalid **Socket** error.

Exceptions

Exception Type	Condition
ArgumentNullException	*asyncResult* is a null reference (**Nothing** in Visual Basic).
ArgumentException	*asyncResult* was not returned by a call to the **BeginSend** method.
InvalidOperation-Exception	**EndSend** was previously called for the asynchronous read.
SocketException	An error occurred when attempting to access the socket. See the Remarks section for more information.
ObjectDisposed-Exception	The **Socket** has been closed.

Remarks

EndSend completes the asynchronous send operation started in **BeginSend**.

Before calling **BeginSend**, you need to create a callback method that implements the **AsyncCallback** delegate. This callback method executes in a separate thread and is called by the system after **BeginSend** returns. The callback method must accept the **IAsyncResult** returned by the **BeginSend** method as a parameter.

Within the callback method, call the **AsyncState** method of the **IAsyncResult** parameter to obtain the sending **Socket**. After obtaining the **Socket**, you can call the **EndSend** method to successfully complete the send operation and return the number of bytes sent.If you are using a connectionless protocol, **EndSend** will block until the datagram is sent. If you are using a connection-oriented protocol, **EndSend** will block until the requested number of bytes are sent. There is no guarantee that the data you send will appear on the network immediately. To increase network efficiency, the underlying system may delay transmission until a significant amount of outgoing data is collected. A successful completion of the **BeginSend** method means that the underlying system has had room to buffer your data for a network send. If it is important to your application to send every byte to the remote host immediately, you can use **SetSocketOption** to enable **SocketOptionName.NoDelay**. For more information about buffering for network efficiency, refer to the Nagle algorithm in MSDN.

> **Note** If you receive a **SocketException**, use **SocketException.ErrorCode** to obtain the specific error code. Once you have obtained this code, you can refer to the Windows Socket Version 2 API error code documentation in MSDN for a detailed description of the error.

Example

[Visual Basic, C#, C++] The following example ends a pending asynchronous send.

```
[Visual Basic]
Dim so As StateObject = CType(ar.AsyncState, StateObject)
Dim s As Socket = so.workSocket

Dim send As Integer = s.EndSend(ar)

Console.WriteLine(("The size of the message sent was :" +
send.ToString()))

s.Close()
    End Sub 'Send_Callback
```

```
[C#]
StateObject so = (StateObject) ar.AsyncState;
Socket s = so.workSocket;

int send = s.EndSend(ar);

    Console.WriteLine("The size of the message sent
was :" + send.ToString());

s.Close();
```

```
[C++]
StateObject* so = __try_cast<StateObject*>(ar->AsyncState);
Socket* s = so->workSocket;

int send = s->EndSend(ar);

Console::WriteLine(S"The size of the message sent was
: {0}", __box(send));

s->Close();
```

Requirements

Platforms: Windows 98, Windows NT 4.0, Windows Millennium Edition, Windows 2000, Windows XP Home Edition, Windows XP Professional, Windows .NET Server family, .NET Compact Framework - Windows CE .NET, Common Language Infrastructure (CLI) Standard

Socket.EndSendTo Method

Ends a pending asynchronous send to a specific location.

```
[Visual Basic]
Public Function EndSendTo( _
    ByVal asyncResult As IAsyncResult _
) As Integer
[C#]
public int EndSendTo(
    IAsyncResult asyncResult
);
[C++]
public: int EndSendTo(
    IAsyncResult* asyncResult
);
[JScript]
public function EndSendTo(
    asyncResult : IAsyncResult
) : int;
```

Parameters

asyncResult

> An **IAsyncResult** that stores state information and any user defined data for this asynchronous operation.

Return Value

If successful, the number of bytes sent; otherwise, an invalid **Socket** error.

Exceptions

Exception Type	Condition
ArgumentNullException	*asyncResult* is a null reference (**Nothing** in Visual Basic).
ArgumentException	*asyncResult* was not returned by a call to the **BeginSendTo** method.
InvalidOperation-Exception	**EndSendTo** was previously called for the asynchronous read.
SocketException	An error occurred when attempting to access the socket. See the Remarks section for more information.
ObjectDisposed-Exception	The **Socket** has been closed.

Remarks

EndSendTo completes the asynchronous send operation started in **BeginSendTo**.

Before calling **BeginSendTo**, you need to create a callback method that implements the **AsyncCallback** delegate. This callback method executes in a separate thread and is called by the system after **BeginReceive** returns. The callback method must accept the **IAsyncResult** returned by the **BeginSendTo** method as a parameter.

Within the callback method, call the **AsyncState** method of the **IAsyncResult** parameter to obtain the sending **Socket**. After obtaining the **Socket**, you can call the **EndSendTo** method to successfully complete the send operation and return the number of bytes sent.

If you are using a connectionless protocol, **EndSendTo** will block until the datagram is sent. If you are using a connection-oriented protocol, **EndSendTo** will block until the requested number of bytes are sent. There is no guarantee that the data you send will appear on the network immediately. To increase network efficiency, the underlying system may delay transmission until a significant amount of outgoing data is collected. A successful completion of the **BeginSendTo** method means that the underlying system has had room to buffer your data for a network send. If it is important to your application to send every byte to the remote host immediately, you can use **SetSocketOption** to enable **SocketOptionName.NoDelay**. For more information about buffering for network efficiency, refer to the Nagle algorithm in MSDN.

> **Note** If you receive a **SocketException**, use **SocketException.ErrorCode** to obtain the specific error code. Once you have obtained this code, you can refer to the Windows Socket Version 2 API error code documentation in MSDN for a detailed description of the error.

Example

[Visual Basic, C#, C++] The following example ends an asynchronous send to a specific location.

```
[Visual Basic]
Dim so As StateObject = CType(ar.AsyncState, StateObject)
Dim s As Socket = so.workSocket

Dim send As Integer = s.EndSendTo(ar)

Console.WriteLine(("The size of the message sent was :" +
send.ToString()))

s.Close()
    End Sub 'SendTo_Callback
```

```
[C#]
StateObject so = (StateObject) ar.AsyncState;
Socket s = so.workSocket;

int send = s.EndSendTo(ar);

    Console.WriteLine("The size of the message sent was :" +
send.ToString());

s.Close();
```

```
[C++]
StateObject* so = __try_cast<StateObject*>(ar->AsyncState);
Socket* s = so->workSocket;

int send = s->EndSendTo(ar);

Console::WriteLine(S"The size of the message sent was
: {0}", __box(send));

s->Close();
```

Requirements

Platforms: Windows 98, Windows NT 4.0, Windows Millennium Edition, Windows 2000, Windows XP Home Edition, Windows XP Professional, Windows .NET Server family, .NET Compact Framework - Windows CE .NET, Common Language Infrastructure (CLI) Standard

Socket.Finalize Method

Frees resources used by the **Socket** class.

[C#] In C#, finalizers are expressed using destructor syntax.

[C++] In C++, finalizers are expressed using destructor syntax.

```
[Visual Basic]
Overrides Protected Sub Finalize()
```

```
[C#]
~Socket();
[C++]
~Socket();
[JScript]
protected override function Finalize();
```

Remarks

The **Socket** class finalizer calls the **Close** method to close the **Socket** and free resources associated with the **Socket**.

Requirements

Platforms: Windows 98, Windows NT 4.0, Windows Millennium Edition, Windows 2000, Windows XP Home Edition, Windows XP Professional, Windows .NET Server family, .NET Compact Framework - Windows CE .NET, Common Language Infrastructure (CLI) Standard

Socket.GetHashCode Method

This member overrides **Object.GetHashCode**.

```
[Visual Basic]
Overrides Public Function GetHashCode() As Integer
[C#]
public override int GetHashCode();
[C++]
public: int GetHashCode();
[JScript]
public override function GetHashCode() : int;
```

Requirements

Platforms: Windows 98, Windows NT 4.0, Windows Millennium Edition, Windows 2000, Windows XP Home Edition, Windows XP Professional, Windows .NET Server family, .NET Compact Framework - Windows CE .NET, Common Language Infrastructure (CLI) Standard

Socket.GetSocketOption Method

Returns the value of a **Socket** option.

Overload List

Returns the value of a specified **Socket** option, represented as an object.

Supported by the .NET Compact Framework.

> [Visual Basic] **Overloads Public Function GetSocketOption (SocketOptionLevel, SocketOptionName) As Object**
>
> [C#] **public object GetSocketOption(SocketOptionLevel, SocketOptionName);**
>
> [C++] **public: Object* GetSocketOption(SocketOptionLevel, SocketOptionName);**
>
> [JScript] **public function GetSocketOption(SocketOptionLevel, SocketOptionName) : Object;**

Returns the specified **Socket** option setting, represented as a byte array.

Supported by the .NET Compact Framework.

> [Visual Basic] **Overloads Public Sub GetSocketOption (SocketOptionLevel, SocketOptionName, Byte())**

[C#] **public void GetSocketOption(SocketOptionLevel, SocketOptionName, byte[]);**

[C++] **public: void GetSocketOption(SocketOptionLevel, SocketOptionName, unsigned char __gc[]);**

[JScript] **public function GetSocketOption(SocketOptionLevel, SocketOptionName, Byte[]);**

Returns the value of the specified **Socket** option in an array.

Supported by the .NET Compact Framework.

[Visual Basic] **Overloads Public Function GetSocketOption (SocketOptionLevel, SocketOptionName, Integer) As Byte()**

[C#] **public byte[] GetSocketOption(SocketOptionLevel, SocketOptionName, int);**

[C++] **public: unsigned char GetSocketOption(SocketOptionLevel, SocketOptionName, int) __gc[];**

[JScript] **public function GetSocketOption(SocketOptionLevel, SocketOptionName, int) : Byte[];**

Socket.GetSocketOption Method (SocketOptionLevel, SocketOptionName)

Returns the value of a specified **Socket** option, represented as an object.

```
[Visual Basic]
Overloads Public Function GetSocketOption( _
   ByVal optionLevel As SocketOptionLevel, _
   ByVal optionName As SocketOptionName _
) As Object
[C#]
public object GetSocketOption(
   SocketOptionLevel optionLevel,
   SocketOptionName optionName
);
[C++]
public: Object* GetSocketOption(
   SocketOptionLevel optionLevel,
   SocketOptionName optionName
);
[JScript]
public function GetSocketOption(
   optionLevel : SocketOptionLevel,
   optionName : SocketOptionName
) : Object;
```

Parameters

optionLevel
   One of the **SocketOptionLevel** values.

optionName
   One of the **SocketOptionName** values.

Return Value

An object representing the value of the option. When the *optionName* parameter is set to **Linger** the return value is an instance of the **LingerOption** class. When *optionName* is set to **AddMembership** or **DropMembership**, the return value is an instance of the **MulticastOption** class. When *optionName* is any other value, the return value is an integer.

Exceptions

Exception Type	Condition
SocketException	An error occurred when attempting to access the socket. See the Remarks section for more information.
ObjectDisposed-Exception	The **Socket** has been closed.

Remarks

Socket options determine the behavior of the current **Socket**. Use this overload to get the **Linger**, **AddMembership**, and **DropMembership Socket** options. For the **Linger** option, use **Socket** for the *optionLevel* parameter. For **AddMembership** and **DropMembership**, use **IP**. If you want to set the value of any of the options listed above, use the **SetSocketOption** method.

> **Note** If you receive a **SocketException**, use **SocketException.ErrorCode** to obtain the specific error code. Once you have obtained this code, you can refer to the Windows Socket Version 2 API error code documentation in MSDN for a detailed description of the error.

Requirements

Platforms: Windows 98, Windows NT 4.0, Windows Millennium Edition, Windows 2000, Windows XP Home Edition, Windows XP Professional, Windows .NET Server family, .NET Compact Framework - Windows CE .NET, Common Language Infrastructure (CLI) Standard

Socket.GetSocketOption Method (SocketOptionLevel, SocketOptionName, Byte[])

Returns the specified **Socket** option setting, represented as a byte array.

```
[Visual Basic]
Overloads Public Sub GetSocketOption( _
   ByVal optionLevel As SocketOptionLevel, _
   ByVal optionName As SocketOptionName, _
   ByVal optionValue() As Byte _
)
[C#]
public void GetSocketOption(
   SocketOptionLevel optionLevel,
   SocketOptionName optionName,
   byte[] optionValue
);
[C++]
public: void GetSocketOption(
   SocketOptionLevel optionLevel,
   SocketOptionName optionName,
   unsigned char optionValue __gc[]
);
[JScript]
public function GetSocketOption(
   optionLevel : SocketOptionLevel,
   optionName : SocketOptionName,
   optionValue : Byte[]
);
```

Parameters

optionLevel

    One of the **SocketOptionLevel** values.

optionName

    One of the **SocketOptionName** values.

optionValue

    An array of type **Byte** that is to receive the option setting.

Exceptions

Exception Type	Condition
SocketException	An error occurred when attempting to access the socket. See the Remarks section for more information.
ObjectDisposed-Exception	The **Socket** has been closed.

Remarks

Socket options determine the behavior of the current **Socket**. Upon successful completion of this method, the array specified by the *optionValue* parameter contains the value of the specified **Socket** option. When the length of the *optionValue* array is smaller than the number of bytes required to store the value of the specified **Socket** option, **GetSocketOption** will throw a **SocketException**. If you receive a **SocketException**, use **SocketException.ErrorCode** to obtain the specific error code. Once you have obtained this code, you can refer to the Windows Socket Version 2 API error code documentation in MSDN for a detailed description of the error. Use this overload for any sockets that are represented by Boolean values or integers.

Requirements

Platforms: Windows 98, Windows NT 4.0, Windows Millennium Edition, Windows 2000, Windows XP Home Edition, Windows XP Professional, Windows .NET Server family, .NET Compact Framework - Windows CE .NET, Common Language Infrastructure (CLI) Standard

Socket.GetSocketOption Method (SocketOptionLevel, SocketOptionName, Int32)

Returns the value of the specified **Socket** option in an array.

```
[Visual Basic]
Overloads Public Function GetSocketOption( _
   ByVal optionLevel As SocketOptionLevel, _
   ByVal optionName As SocketOptionName, _
   ByVal optionLength As Integer _
) As Byte()
[C#]
public byte[] GetSocketOption(
   SocketOptionLevel optionLevel,
   SocketOptionName optionName,
   int optionLength
);
[C++]
public: unsigned char GetSocketOption(
   SocketOptionLevel optionLevel,
   SocketOptionName optionName,
   int optionLength
) __gc[];
```

```
[JScript]
public function GetSocketOption(
   optionLevel : SocketOptionLevel,
   optionName : SocketOptionName,
   optionLength : int
) : Byte[];
```

Parameters

optionLevel

    One of the **SocketOptionLevel** values.

optionName

    One of the **SocketOptionName** values.

optionLength

    The length, in bytes, of the expected return value.

Return Value

An array of type **Byte** that contains the value of the socket option.

Exceptions

Exception Type	Condition
SocketException	An error occurred when attempting to access the socket. See the Remarks section for more information.
ObjectDisposed-Exception	The **Socket** has been closed.

Remarks

The *optionLength* parameter sets the maximum size of the returned byte array. If the option value requires fewer bytes, the array will contain only that many bytes. If the option value requires more bytes, **GetSocketOption** will throw a **SocketException**. Use this overload for any sockets that are represented by Boolean values or integers.

> **Note** If you receive a **SocketException**, use **SocketException.ErrorCode** to obtain the specific error code. Once you have obtained this code, you can refer to the Windows Socket Version 2 API error code documentation in MSDN for a detailed description of the error.

Requirements

Platforms: Windows 98, Windows NT 4.0, Windows Millennium Edition, Windows 2000, Windows XP Home Edition, Windows XP Professional, Windows .NET Server family, .NET Compact Framework - Windows CE .NET, Common Language Infrastructure (CLI) Standard

Socket.IDisposable.Dispose Method

This member supports the .NET Framework infrastructure and is not intended to be used directly from your code.

```
[Visual Basic]
Private Sub Dispose() Implements IDisposable.Dispose
[C#]
void IDisposable.Dispose();
[C++]
private: void IDisposable::Dispose();
[JScript]
private function IDisposable.Dispose();
```

Socket.IOControl Method

Sets low-level operating modes for the **Socket**.

```
[Visual Basic]
Public Function IOControl( _
   ByVal ioControlCode As Integer, _
   ByVal optionInValue() As Byte, _
   ByVal optionOutValue() As Byte _
) As Integer
[C#]
public int IOControl(
   int ioControlCode,
   byte[] optionInValue,
   byte[] optionOutValue
);
[C++]
public: int IOControl(
   int ioControlCode,
   unsigned char optionInValue __gc[],
   unsigned char optionOutValue __gc[]
);
[JScript]
public function IOControl(
   ioControlCode : int,
   optionInValue : Byte[],
   optionOutValue : Byte[]
) : int;
```

Parameters

ioControlCode
   The control code of the operation to perform.

optionInValue
   An array of type **Byte** that contains the input data required by the operation.

optionOutValue
   An array of type **Byte** that contains the output data returned by the operation.

Return Value

The number of bytes in the *optionOutValue* parameter.

Exceptions

Exception Type	Condition
SocketException	An error occurred when attempting to access the socket. See the Remarks section for more information.
ObjectDisposed-Exception	The **Socket** has been closed.
InvalidOperation-Exception	An attempt was made to change the blocking mode without using the **Blocking** property.
SecurityException	A caller in the call stack does not have the required permissions.

Remarks

The **IOControl** method provides low-level access to the operating system **Socket** underlying the current instance of the **Socket** class. For more information about **IOControl**, see the WSAIoct documentation in MSDN.

Note If you receive a **SocketException**, use **SocketException.ErrorCode** to obtain the specific error code. Once you have obtained this code, you can refer to the Windows Socket Version 2 API error code documentation in MSDN for a detailed description of the error.

Example

See related example in the **System.Sockets.Socket** class topic.

Requirements

Platforms: Windows 98, Windows NT 4.0, Windows Millennium Edition, Windows 2000, Windows XP Home Edition, Windows XP Professional, Windows .NET Server family, .NET Compact Framework - Windows CE .NET, Common Language Infrastructure (CLI) Standard

Socket.Listen Method

Places a **Socket** in a listening state.

```
[Visual Basic]
Public Sub Listen( _
   ByVal backlog As Integer _
)
[C#]
public void Listen(
   int backlog
);
[C++]
public: void Listen(
   int backlog
);
[JScript]
public function Listen(
   backlog : int
);
```

Parameters

backlog
   The maximum length of the pending connections queue.

Exceptions

Exception Type	Condition
SocketException	An error occurred when attempting to access the socket. See the Remarks section for more information.
ObjectDisposed-Exception	The **Socket** has been closed.

Remarks

Listen causes a connection-oriented **Socket** to listen for incoming connection attempts. The *backlog* parameter specifies the number of incoming connections that can be queued for acceptance. To determine the maximum number of connections you can specify, retrieve the **MaxConnections** value. **Listen** does not block.

If you receive a **SocketException**, use **ErrorCode** to obtain the specific error code. Once you have obtained this code, you can refer to the Windows Socket Version 2 API error code documentation in MSDN for a detailed description of the error. Use **Accept** or **BeginAccept** to accept a connection from the queue.

Note You must call the **Bind** method before calling **Listen**, or **Listen** will throw a **SocketException**.

Example

See related example in the **System.Sockets.Socket** class topic.

Requirements

Platforms: Windows 98, Windows NT 4.0, Windows Millennium Edition, Windows 2000, Windows XP Home Edition, Windows XP Professional, Windows .NET Server family, .NET Compact Framework - Windows CE .NET, Common Language Infrastructure (CLI) Standard

Socket.Poll Method

Determines the status of the **Socket**.

```
[Visual Basic]
Public Function Poll( _
   ByVal microSeconds As Integer, _
   ByVal mode As SelectMode _
) As Boolean
[C#]
public bool Poll(
   int microSeconds,
   SelectMode mode
);
[C++]
public: bool Poll(
   int microSeconds,
   SelectMode mode
);
[JScript]
public function Poll(
   microSeconds : int,
   mode : SelectMode
) : Boolean;
```

Parameters

microSeconds
   The time to wait for a response, in microseconds.
mode
   One of the **SelectMode** values.

Return Value

Mode	Return Value
SelectRead	**true** if **Listen** has been called and a connection is pending; -or- **true** if data is available for reading; -or- **true** if the connection has been closed, reset, or terminated; otherwise, returns **false**.

Mode	Return Value
SelectWrite	**true**, if processing a **Connect**, and the connection has succeeded; -or- **true** if data can be sent; otherwise, returns **false**.
SelectError	**true** if processing a **Connect** that does not block, and the connection has failed; -or- **true** if **OutOfBandInline** is not set and out-of-band data is available; otherwise, returns **false**.

Exceptions

Exception Type	Condition
NotSupportedException	The *mode* parameter is not one of the **SelectMode** values.
SocketException	An error occurred when attempting to access the socket. See remarks below.
ObjectDisposed-Exception	The **Socket** has been closed.

Remarks

The **Poll** method will check the state of the **Socket**. Specify **SelectMode.SelectRead** for the *selectMode* parameter to determine if the **Socket** is readable. Specify **SelectMode.SelectWrite** to determine if the **Socket** is writable. Use **SelectMode.SelectError** to detect an error condition. **Poll** will block execution until the specified time period, measured in *microseconds,* elapses. Set the *microSeconds* parameter to a negative integer if you would like to wait indefinitely for a response. If you want to check the status of multiple sockets, you might prefer to use the **Select** method.

Note If you receive a **SocketException**, use **SocketException.ErrorCode** to obtain the specific error code. Once you have obtained this code, you can refer to the Windows Socket Version 2 API error code documentation in MSDN for a detailed description of the error.

Example

See related example in the **System.Sockets.Socket** class topic.

Requirements

Platforms: Windows 98, Windows NT 4.0, Windows Millennium Edition, Windows 2000, Windows XP Home Edition, Windows XP Professional, Windows .NET Server family, .NET Compact Framework - Windows CE .NET, Common Language Infrastructure (CLI) Standard

Socket.Receive Method

Receives data from a bound **Socket**.

Overload List

Receives data from a bound **Socket** into a receive buffer.

Supported by the .NET Compact Framework.

[Visual Basic] **Overloads Public Function Receive(Byte()) As Integer**

[C#] **public int Receive(byte[]);**

[C++] **public: int Receive(unsigned char __gc[]);**

[JScript] **public function Receive(Byte[]) : int;**

Receives data from a bound **Socket** into a receive buffer, using the specified **SocketFlags**.

Supported by the .NET Compact Framework.

[Visual Basic] **Overloads Public Function Receive(Byte(), SocketFlags) As Integer**

[C#] **public int Receive(byte[], SocketFlags);**

[C++] **public: int Receive(unsigned char __gc[], SocketFlags);**

[JScript] **public function Receive(Byte[], SocketFlags) : int;**

Receives the specified number of bytes of data from a bound **Socket** into a receive buffer, using the specified **SocketFlags**.

Supported by the .NET Compact Framework.

[Visual Basic] **Overloads Public Function Receive(Byte(), Integer, SocketFlags) As Integer**

[C#] **public int Receive(byte[], int, SocketFlags);**

[C++] **public: int Receive(unsigned char __gc[], int, SocketFlags);**

[JScript] **public function Receive(Byte[], int, SocketFlags) : int;**

Receives the specified number of bytes from a bound **Socket** into the specified offset position of the receive buffer, using the specified **SocketFlags**.

Supported by the .NET Compact Framework.

[Visual Basic] **Overloads Public Function Receive(Byte(), Integer, Integer, SocketFlags) As Integer**

[C#] **public int Receive(byte[], int, int, SocketFlags);**

[C++] **public: int Receive(unsigned char __gc[], int, int, SocketFlags);**

[JScript] **public function Receive(Byte[], int, int, SocketFlags) : int;**

Example

See related example in the **System.Sockets.Socket** class topic.

Socket.Receive Method (Byte[])

Receives data from a bound **Socket** into a receive buffer.

```
[Visual Basic]
Overloads Public Function Receive( _
   ByVal buffer() As Byte _
) As Integer
[C#]
public int Receive(
   byte[] buffer
);
[C++]
public: int Receive(
   unsigned char buffer __gc[]
);
[JScript]
public function Receive(
   buffer : Byte[]
) : int;
```

Parameters

buffer

An array of type **Byte** that is the storage location for the received data.

Return Value

The number of bytes received.

Exceptions

Exception Type	Condition
ArgumentNullException	*buffer* is a null reference (**Nothing** in Visual Basic).
SocketException	An error occurred when attempting to access the socket. See the Remarks section for more information.
ObjectDisposed-Exception	The **Socket** has been closed.
SecurityException	A caller in the call stack does not have the required permissions.

Remarks

The **Receive** method reads data into the buffer parameter and returns the number of bytes successfully read. You can call **Receive** from both connection-oriented and connectionless sockets.

This overload only requires you to provide a receive buffer. The buffer offset defaults to 0, the size defaults to the length of the buffer parameter, and the **SocketFlags** value defaults to **None**.

If you are using a connection-oriented protocol, You must either call **Connect** to establish a remote host connection, or **Accept** to accept an incoming connection prior to calling **Receive**. The **Receive** method will only read data that arrives from the remote host established in the **Connect** or **Accept** method. If you are using a connectionless protocol, you can also use the **ReceiveFrom** method. **ReceiveFrom** will allow you to receive data arriving from any host.

If no data is available for reading, the **Receive** method will block until data is available. If you are in non-blocking mode, and there is no data available in the in the protocol stack buffer, the **Receive** method will complete immediately and throw a **SocketException**. You can use the **Available** property to determine if data is available for reading. When **Available** is non-zero, retry the receive operation.

If you are using a connection-oriented **Socket**, the **Receive** method will read as much data as is available, up to the size of the buffer. If the remote host shuts down the **Socket** connection with the **Shutdown** method, and all available data has been received, the **Receive** method will complete immediately and return zero bytes.

If you are using a connectionless **Socket**, **Receive** will read the first enqueued datagram from the destination address you specify in the **Connect** method. If the datagram you receive is larger than the size of the *buffer* parameter, *buffer* gets filled with the first part of the message, the excess data is lost and a **SocketException** is thrown.

> **Note** If you receive a **SocketException**, use **SocketException.ErrorCode** to obtain the specific error code. Once you have obtained this code, you can refer to the Windows Socket Version 2 API error code documentation in MSDN for a detailed description of the error.

Example

See related example in the **System.Sockets.Socket** class topic.

Requirements

Platforms: Windows 98, Windows NT 4.0,
Windows Millennium Edition, Windows 2000,
Windows XP Home Edition, Windows XP Professional,
Windows .NET Server family,
.NET Compact Framework - Windows CE .NET,
Common Language Infrastructure (CLI) Standard

.NET Framework Security:

*   **SocketPermission** for accepting connections from the network.
    Associated enumeration: **Accept**.

Socket.Receive Method (Byte[], SocketFlags)

Receives data from a bound **Socket** into a receive buffer, using the
specified **SocketFlags**.

```
[Visual Basic]
Overloads Public Function Receive( _
   ByVal buffer() As Byte, _
   ByVal socketFlags As SocketFlags _
) As Integer
[C#]
public int Receive(
   byte[] buffer,
   SocketFlags socketFlags
);
[C++]
public: int Receive(
   unsigned char buffer __gc[],
   SocketFlags socketFlags
);
[JScript]
public function Receive(
   buffer : Byte[],
   socketFlags : SocketFlags
) : int;
```

Parameters

buffer
   An array of type **Byte** that is the storage location for the received
   data.
socketFlags
   A bitwise combination of the **SocketFlags** values.

Return Value

The number of bytes received.

Exceptions

Exception Type	Condition
ArgumentNullException	*buffer* is a null reference (**Nothing** in Visual Basic).
SocketException	An error occurred when attempting to access the socket. See the Remarks section for more information.
ObjectDisposed-Exception	The **Socket** has been closed.
SecurityException	A caller in the call stack does not have the required permissions.

Remarks

The **Receive** method reads data into the buffer parameter and returns
the number of bytes successfully read. You can call **Receive** from
both connection-oriented and connectionless sockets.

This overload only requires you to provide a receive buffer and the
necessary **SocketFlags**. The buffer offset defaults to 0, and the size
defaults to the length of the byte parameter. If you specify the **Peek**
flag as the *socketFlags* parameter, the available data is copied into
the receive buffer but not removed from the system buffer. If you
specify the **OutOfBand** flag as the *socketFlags* parameter and the
Socket is configured for in-line reception of out-of-band (OOB) data
(using **OutOfBandInline**) and OOB data is available, **Receive** will
return only OOB data. The OOB data is a logically independent
transmission channel associated with each pair of connected stream
sockets. This data is delivered with higher priority and
independently of the normal data.

If you are using a connection-oriented protocol, You must either call
Connect to establish a remote host connection, or **Accept** to accept
an incoming connection prior to calling **Receive**. The **Receive**
method will only read data that arrives from the remote host
established in the **Connect** or **Accept** method. If you are using a
connectionless protocol, you can also use the **ReceiveFrom** method.
ReceiveFrom will allow you to receive data arriving from any host.

If no data is available for reading, the **Receive** method will block
until data is available. If you are in non-blocking mode, and there is
no data available in the protocol stack buffer, the **Receive** method
will complete immediately and throw a **SocketException**. You can
use the **Available** property to determine if data is available for
reading. When **Available** is non-zero, retry your receive operation.

If you are using a connection-oriented **Socket**, the **Receive** method
will read as much data as is available up to the size of the buffer. If
the remote host shuts down the **Socket** connection with the
Shutdown method, and all available data has been received, the
Receive method will complete immediately and return zero bytes.

If you are using a connectionless **Socket**, **Receive** will read the first
enqueued datagram from the destination address you specify in the
Connect method. If the datagram you receive is larger than the size
of the *buffer* parameter, *buffer* gets filled with the first part of the
message, the excess data is lost and a **SocketException** is thrown.

> **Note** If you receive a **SocketException**, use
> **SocketException.ErrorCode** to obtain the specific error code.
> Once you have obtained this code, you can refer to the
> Windows Socket Version 2 API error code documentation in
> MSDN for a detailed description of the error.

Example

See related example in the **System.Sockets.Socket** class topic.

Requirements

Platforms: Windows 98, Windows NT 4.0,
Windows Millennium Edition, Windows 2000,
Windows XP Home Edition, Windows XP Professional,
Windows .NET Server family,
.NET Compact Framework - Windows CE .NET,
Common Language Infrastructure (CLI) Standard

.NET Framework Security:

*   **SocketPermission** for accepting connections from the network.
    Associated enumeration: **Accept**.

Socket.Receive Method (Byte[], Int32, SocketFlags)

Receives the specified number of bytes of data from a bound **Socket** into a receive buffer, using the specified **SocketFlags**.

[Visual Basic]
```
Overloads Public Function Receive( _
    ByVal buffer() As Byte, _
    ByVal size As Integer, _
    ByVal socketFlags As SocketFlags _
) As Integer
```
[C#]
```
public int Receive(
    byte[] buffer,
    int size,
    SocketFlags socketFlags
);
```
[C++]
```
public: int Receive(
    unsigned char buffer __gc[],
    int size,
    SocketFlags socketFlags
);
```
[JScript]
```
public function Receive(
    buffer : Byte[],
    size : int,
    socketFlags : SocketFlags
) : int;
```

Parameters

buffer
    An array of type **Byte** that is the storage location for the received data.
size
    The number of bytes to receive.
socketFlags
    A bitwise combination of the **SocketFlags** values.

Return Value

The number of bytes received.

Exceptions

Exception Type	Condition
ArgumentNullException	*buffer* is a null reference (**Nothing** in Visual Basic).
ArgumentOutOfRange-Exception	*size* exceeds the size of *buffer*.
SocketException	An error occurred when attempting to access the socket. See the Remarks section for more information.
ObjectDisposed-Exception	The **Socket** has been closed.
SecurityException	A caller in the call stack does not have the required permissions.

Remarks

The **Receive** This method reads data into the *buffer* parameter and returns the number of bytes successfully read. You can call **Receive** from both connection-oriented and connectionless sockets.

This overload only requires you to provide a receive buffer, the number of bytes you want to receive, and the necessary **SocketFlags**. The buffer offset defaults to 0. If you specify the **Peek** flag as the *socketFlags* parameter, the available data is copied into the receive buffer but not removed from the system buffer. If you specify the **OutOfBand** flag as the *socketFlags* parameter and the **Socket** is configured for in-line reception of out-of-band (OOB) data (using **OutOfBandInline**) and OOB data is available, **Receive** will return only OOB data. The OOB data is a logically independent transmission channel associated with each pair of connected stream sockets. This data is delivered with higher priority and independently of the normal data.

If you are using a connection-oriented protocol, You must either call **Connect** to establish a remote host connection, or **Accept** to accept an incoming connection prior to calling **Receive**. The **Receive** method will only read data that arrives from the remote host established in the **Connect** or **Accept** method. If you are using a connectionless protocol, you can also use the **ReceiveFrom** method. **ReceiveFrom** will allow you to receive data arriving from any host.

If no data is available for reading, the **Receive** method will block until data is available. If you are in non-blocking mode, and there is no data available in the in the protocol stack buffer, The **Receive** method will complete immediately and throw a **SocketException**. You can use the **Available** property to determine if data is available for reading. When **Available** is non-zero, retry your receive operation.

If you are using a connection-oriented **Socket**, the **Receive** method will read as much data as is available, up to the number of bytes specified by the *size* parameter. If the remote host shuts down the **Socket** connection with the **Shutdown** method, and all available data has been received, the **Receive** method will complete immediately and return zero bytes.

If you are using a connectionless **Socket**, **Receive** will read the first enqueued datagram from the destination address you specify in the **Connect** method. If the datagram you receive is larger than the size of the *buffer* parameter, *buffer* gets filled with the first part of the message, the excess data is lost and a **SocketException** is thrown.

> **Note** If you receive a **SocketException**, use **SocketException.ErrorCode** to obtain the specific error code. Once you have obtained this code, you can refer to the Windows Socket Version 2 API error code documentation in MSDN for a detailed description of the error.

Example

See related example in the **System.Sockets.Socket** class topic.

Requirements

Platforms: Windows 98, Windows NT 4.0, Windows Millennium Edition, Windows 2000, Windows XP Home Edition, Windows XP Professional, Windows .NET Server family, .NET Compact Framework - Windows CE .NET, Common Language Infrastructure (CLI) Standard

.NET Framework Security:
- **SocketPermission** for accepting connections from the network. Associated enumeration: **Accept**.

Socket.Receive Method (Byte[], Int32, Int32, SocketFlags)

Receives the specified number of bytes from a bound **Socket** into the specified offset position of the receive buffer, using the specified **SocketFlags**.

```
[Visual Basic]
Overloads Public Function Receive( _
   ByVal buffer() As Byte, _
   ByVal offset As Integer, _
   ByVal size As Integer, _
   ByVal socketFlags As SocketFlags _
) As Integer
[C#]
public int Receive(
   byte[] buffer,
   int offset,
   int size,
   SocketFlags socketFlags
);
[C++]
public: int Receive(
   unsigned char buffer __gc[],
   int offset,
   int size,
   SocketFlags socketFlags
);
[JScript]
public function Receive(
   buffer : Byte[],
   offset : int,
   size : int,
   socketFlags : SocketFlags
) : int;
```

Parameters

buffer

An array of type **Byte** that is the storage location for received data.

offset

The location in *buffer* to store the received data.

size

The number of bytes to receive.

socketFlags

A bitwise combination of the **SocketFlags** values.

Return Value

The number of bytes received.

Exceptions

Exception Type	Condition
ArgumentNullException	*buffer* is a null reference (**Nothing** in Visual Basic).
ArgumentOutOfRange-Exception	*offset* is less than 0.
	-or-
	offset is greater than the length of *buffer*.
	-or-
	size is less than 0.
	-or-
	size is greater than the length of *buffer* minus the value of the *offset* parameter.

Exception Type	Condition
SocketException	*socketFlags* is not a valid combination of values.
	-or-
	The **LocalEndPoint** property was not set.
	-or-
	An operating system error occurs while accessing the **Socket**.
ObjectDisposed-Exception	The **Socket** has been closed.
SecurityException	A caller in the call stack does not have the required permissions.

Remarks

The **Receive** method reads data into the buffer parameter and returns the number of bytes successfully read. You can call **Receive** from both connection-oriented and connectionless sockets.

If you specify the **Peek** flag as the *socketFlags* parameter, the available data is copied into the receive buffer but not removed from the system buffer. If you specify the **OutOfBand** flag as the *socketFlags* parameter and the **Socket** is configured for in-line reception of out-of-band (OOB) data (using **OutOfBandInline**) and OOB data is available, **Receive** will return only OOB data. The OOB data is a logically independent transmission channel associated with each pair of connected stream sockets. This data is delivered with higher priority and independently of the normal data.

If you are using a connection-oriented protocol, You must either call **Connect** to establish a remote host connection, or **Accept** to accept an incoming connection prior to calling **Receive**. The **Receive** method will only read data that arrives from the remote host established in the **Connect** or **Accept** method. If you are using a connectionless protocol, you can also use the **ReceiveFrom** method. **ReceiveFrom** will allow you to receive data arriving from any host.

If no data is available for reading, the **Receive** method will block until data is available. If you are in non-blocking mode, and there is no data available in the in the protocol stack buffer, the **Receive** method will complete immediately and throw a **SocketException**. An error occurred when attempting to access the socket. See Remarks below. You can use the **Available** property to determine if data is available for reading. When **Available** is non-zero, retry the receive operation.

If you are using a connection-oriented **Socket**, the **Receive** method will read as much data as is available, up to the number of bytes specified by the size parameter. If the remote host shuts down the **Socket** connection with the **Shutdown** method, and all available data has been received, the **Receive** method will complete immediately and return zero bytes.

If you are using a connectionless **Socket**, **Receive** will read the first enqueued datagram from the destination address you specify in the **Connect** method. If the datagram you receive is larger than the size of the *buffer* parameter, *buffer* gets filled with the first part of the message, the excess data is lost and a **SocketException** is thrown.

> **Note** If you receive a **SocketException**, use **SocketException.ErrorCode** to obtain the specific error code. Once you have obtained this code, you can refer to the Windows Socket Version 2 API error code documentation in MSDN for a detailed description of the error.

Example

See related example in the **System.Sockets.Socket** class topic.

Requirements

Platforms: Windows 98, Windows NT 4.0,
Windows Millennium Edition, Windows 2000,
Windows XP Home Edition, Windows XP Professional,
Windows .NET Server family,
.NET Compact Framework - Windows CE .NET,
Common Language Infrastructure (CLI) Standard

.NET Framework Security:

- **SocketPermission** for accepting connections from the network. Associated enumeration: **Accept**.

Socket.ReceiveFrom Method

Receives a datagram and stores the source endpoint.

Overload List

Receives a datagram into the data buffer and stores the endpoint.

Supported by the .NET Compact Framework.

[Visual Basic] **Overloads Public Function ReceiveFrom(Byte(), ByRef EndPoint) As Integer**

[C#] **public int ReceiveFrom(byte[], ref EndPoint);**

[C++] **public: int ReceiveFrom(unsigned char __gc[], EndPoint**);**

[JScript] **public function ReceiveFrom(Byte[], EndPoint) : int;**

Receives a datagram into the data buffer, using the specified **SocketFlags**, and stores the endpoint.

Supported by the .NET Compact Framework.

[Visual Basic] **Overloads Public Function ReceiveFrom (Byte(), SocketFlags, ByRef EndPoint) As Integer**

[C#] **public int ReceiveFrom(byte[], SocketFlags, ref EndPoint);**

[C++] **public: int ReceiveFrom(unsigned char __gc[], SocketFlags, EndPoint**);**

[JScript] **public function ReceiveFrom(Byte[], SocketFlags, EndPoint) : int;**

Receives the specified number of bytes into the data buffer, using the specified **SocketFlags**, and stores the endpoint.

Supported by the .NET Compact Framework.

[Visual Basic] **Overloads Public Function ReceiveFrom (Byte(), Integer, SocketFlags, ByRef EndPoint) As Integer**

[C#] **public int ReceiveFrom(byte[], int, SocketFlags, ref EndPoint);**

[C++] **public: int ReceiveFrom(unsigned char __gc[], int, SocketFlags, EndPoint**);**

[JScript] **public function ReceiveFrom(Byte[], int, SocketFlags, EndPoint) : int;**

Receives the specified number of bytes of data into the specified location of the data buffer, using the specified **SocketFlags**, and stores the endpoint.

Supported by the .NET Compact Framework.

[Visual Basic] **Overloads Public Function ReceiveFrom (Byte(), Integer, Integer, SocketFlags, ByRef EndPoint) As Integer**

[C#] **public int ReceiveFrom(byte[], int, int, SocketFlags, ref EndPoint);**

[C++] **public: int ReceiveFrom(unsigned char __gc[], int, int, SocketFlags, EndPoint**);**

[JScript] **public function ReceiveFrom(Byte[], int, int, SocketFlags, EndPoint) : int;**

Example

See related example in the **System.Sockets.Socket** class topic.

Socket.ReceiveFrom Method (Byte[], EndPoint)

Receives a datagram into the data buffer and stores the endpoint.

```
[Visual Basic]
Overloads Public Function ReceiveFrom( _
   ByVal buffer() As Byte, _
   ByRef remoteEP As EndPoint _
) As Integer
[C#]
public int ReceiveFrom(
   byte[] buffer,
   ref EndPoint remoteEP
);
[C++]
public: int ReceiveFrom(
   unsigned char buffer __gc[],
   EndPoint** remoteEP
);
[JScript]
public function ReceiveFrom(
   buffer : Byte[],
   remoteEP : EndPoint
) : int;
```

Parameters

buffer
  An array of type **Byte** that is the storage location for received data.
remoteEP
  An **EndPoint**, passed by reference, that represents the remote server.

Return Value

The number of bytes received.

Exceptions

Exception Type	Condition
ArgumentNullException	*buffer* is a null reference (**Nothing** in Visual Basic). -or- *remoteEP* is a null reference (**Nothing**).
SocketException	An error occurred when attempting to access the socket. See the Remarks section for more information.
ObjectDisposed-Exception	The **Socket** has been closed.
SecurityException	A caller in the call stack does not have the required permissions.

Remarks

The **ReceiveFrom** method reads data into the *buffer* parameter, returns the number of bytes successfully read, and captures the remote host endpoint from which the data was sent. This method is useful if you intend to receive connectionless datagrams from an unknown host or multiple hosts.

This overload only requires you to provide a receive *buffer*, and an **EndPoint** representing the remote host. The buffer offset defaults to 0. The size defaults to the length of the *buffer* parameterand the *socketFlags* value defaults to **None**.

> **Note** Before calling **ReceiveFrom**, you must explicitly bind the **Socket** to a local endpoint using the **Bind** method. If you do not, **ReceiveFrom** will throw a **SocketException**.

With connectionless protocols, **ReceiveFrom** will read the first enqueued datagram received into the local network buffer. If the datagram you receive is larger than the size of *buffer*, the **ReceiveFrom** method will fill *buffer* with as much of the message as is possible, and throw a **SocketException**. If you are using an unreliable protocol, the excess data will be lost. If you are using a reliable protocol, the excess data will be retained by the service provider and you can retreive it by calling the **ReceiveFrom** method with a large enough buffer.

If no data is available for reading, the **ReceiveFrom** method will block until data is available. If you are in non-blocking mode, and there is no data available in the in the protocol stack buffer, the **ReceiveFrom** method will complete immediately and throw a **SocketException**. You can use the **Available** property to determine if data is available for reading. When **Available** is non-zero, retry the receive operation.

Although **ReceiveFrom** is intended for connectionless protocols, you can use a connection-oriented protocol as well. If you choose to do so, you must first either establish a remote host connection by calling the **Connect** method or accept an incoming remote host connection by calling the **Accept** method. If you do not establish or accept a connection before calling the **ReceiveFrom** method, you will get a **SocketException**. You can also establish a default remote host for a connectionless protocol prior to calling the **ReceiveFrom** method. In either of these cases, the **ReceiveFrom** method will ignore the *remoteEP* parameter and only receive data from the connected or default remote host.

With connection-oriented sockets, **ReceiveFrom** will read as much data as is available up to the size of *buffer*. If the remote host shuts down the **Socket** connection with the **Shutdown** method, and all available data has been received, the **ReceiveFrom** method will complete immediately and return zero bytes.

> **Note** If you receive a **SocketException**, use **SocketException.ErrorCode** to obtain the specific error code. Once you have obtained this code, you can refer to the Windows Socket Version 2 API error code documentation in MSDN for a detailed description of the error.

> **Note** The AddressFamily of the EndPoint used in ReceiveFrom needs to match the AddressFamily of the EndPoint used in SendTo.

Example

See related example in the **System.Sockets.Socket** class topic.

Requirements

Platforms: Windows 98, Windows NT 4.0, Windows Millennium Edition, Windows 2000, Windows XP Home Edition, Windows XP Professional, Windows .NET Server family, .NET Compact Framework - Windows CE .NET, Common Language Infrastructure (CLI) Standard

.NET Framework Security:

- **SocketPermission** for accepting connections from the network. Associated enumeration: **Accept**.

Socket.ReceiveFrom Method (Byte[], SocketFlags, EndPoint)

Receives a datagram into the data buffer, using the specified **SocketFlags**, and stores the endpoint.

```
[Visual Basic]
Overloads Public Function ReceiveFrom( _
   ByVal buffer() As Byte, _
   ByVal socketFlags As SocketFlags, _
   ByRef remoteEP As EndPoint _
) As Integer
[C#]
public int ReceiveFrom(
   byte[] buffer,
   SocketFlags socketFlags,
   ref EndPoint remoteEP
);
[C++]
public: int ReceiveFrom(
   unsigned char buffer __gc[],
   SocketFlags socketFlags,
   EndPoint** remoteEP
);
[JScript]
public function ReceiveFrom(
   buffer : Byte[],
   socketFlags : SocketFlags,
   remoteEP : EndPoint
) : int;
```

Parameters

buffer
> An array of type **Byte** that is the storage location for the received data.

socketFlags
> A bitwise combination of the **SocketFlags** values.

remoteEP
> An **EndPoint**, passed by reference, that represents the remote server.

Return Value

The number of bytes received.

Exceptions

Exception Type	Condition
ArgumentNullException	*buffer* is a null reference (**Nothing** in Visual Basic). -or- *remoteEP* is a null reference (**Nothing**).

Exception Type	Condition
SocketException	An error occurred when attempting to access the socket. See the Remarks section for more information.
ObjectDisposed-Exception	The Socket has been closed.
SecurityException	A caller in the call stack does not have the required permissions.

Remarks

The **ReceiveFrom** method reads data into the *buffer* parameter, returns the number of bytes successfully read, and captures the remote host endpoint from which the data was sent. This method is useful if you intend to receive connectionless datagrams from an unknown host or multiple hosts.

This overload only requires you to provide a receive buffer, the necessary **SocketFlags**, and an **EndPoint** representing the remote host. The offset defaults to 0 and the size defaults to the length of the buffer parameter. If you specify the **OutOfBand** flag as the *socketFlags* parameter and the **Socket** is configured for in-line reception of out-of-band (OOB) data (using **OutOfBandInline**) and OOB data is available, **ReceiveFrom** will return only OOB data. If you specify the **Peek** flag, the available data is copied into the receive buffer but not removed from the system buffer.

> **Note** Before calling **ReceiveFrom**, you must explicitly bind the **Socket** to a local endpoint using the **Bind** method. If you do not, **ReceiveFrom** will throw a **SocketException**.

With connectionless protocols, **ReceiveFrom** will read the first enqueued datagram received into the local network buffer. If the datagram you receive is larger than the size of *buffer*, the **ReceiveFrom** method will fill *buffer* with as much of the message as is possible, and throw a **SocketException**. If you are using an unreliable protocol, the excess data will be lost. If you are using a reliable protocol, the excess data will be retained by the service provider and you can retreive it by calling the **ReceiveFrom** method with a large enough buffer.

If no data is available for reading, the **ReceiveFrom** method will block until data is available. If you are in non-blocking mode, and there is no data available in the in the protocol stack buffer, the **ReceiveFrom** method will complete immediately and throw a **SocketException**. You can use the **Available** property to determine if data is available for reading. When **Available** is non-zero, retry the receive operation.

Although **ReceiveFrom** is intended for connectionless protocols, you can use a connection-oriented protocol as well. If you choose to do so, you must first either establish a remote host connection by calling the **Connect** method or accept an incoming remote host connection by calling the **Accept** method. If you do not establish or accept a connection before calling the **ReceiveFrom** method, you will get a **SocketException**. You can also establish a default remote host for a connectionless protocol prior to calling the **ReceiveFrom** method. In either of these cases, the **ReceiveFrom** method will ignore the *remoteEP* parameter and only receive data from the connected or default remote host.

With connection-oriented sockets, **ReceiveFrom** will read as much data as is available up to the size of *buffer*. If the remote host shuts down the **Socket** connection with the **Shutdown** method, and all available data has been Received, the **ReceiveFrom** method will complete immediately and return zero bytes.

> **Note** If you receive a **SocketException**, use **SocketException.ErrorCode** to obtain the specific error code. Once you have obtained this code, you can refer to the Windows Socket Version 2 API error code documentation in MSDN for a detailed description of the error.

> **Note** The AddressFamily of the EndPoint used in ReceiveFrom needs to match the AddressFamily of the EndPoint used in SendTo.

Example

See related example in the **System.Sockets.Socket** class topic.

Requirements

Platforms: Windows 98, Windows NT 4.0, Windows Millennium Edition, Windows 2000, Windows XP Home Edition, Windows XP Professional, Windows .NET Server family, .NET Compact Framework - Windows CE .NET, Common Language Infrastructure (CLI) Standard

.NET Framework Security:
- **SocketPermission** for accepting connections from the network. Associated enumeration: **Accept**.

Socket.ReceiveFrom Method (Byte[], Int32, SocketFlags, EndPoint)

Receives the specified number of bytes into the data buffer, using the specified **SocketFlags**, and stores the endpoint.

```
[Visual Basic]
Overloads Public Function ReceiveFrom( _
   ByVal buffer() As Byte, _
   ByVal size As Integer, _
   ByVal socketFlags As SocketFlags, _
   ByRef remoteEP As EndPoint _
) As Integer
[C#]
public int ReceiveFrom(
   byte[] buffer,
   int size,
   SocketFlags socketFlags,
   ref EndPoint remoteEP
);
[C++]
public: int ReceiveFrom(
   unsigned char buffer __gc[],
   int size,
   SocketFlags socketFlags,
   EndPoint** remoteEP
);
[JScript]
public function ReceiveFrom(
   buffer : Byte[],
   size : int,
   socketFlags : SocketFlags,
   remoteEP : EndPoint
) : int;
```

Parameters

buffer
> An array of type **Byte** that is the storage location for received data.

size
> The number of bytes to receive.

socketFlags
> A bitwise combination of the **SocketFlags** values.

remoteEP
> An **EndPoint**, passed by reference, that represents the remote server.

Return Value

The number of bytes received.

Exceptions

Exception Type	Condition
ArgumentNullException	*buffer* is a null reference (**Nothing** in Visual Basic). - or- *remoteEP* is a null reference (**Nothing**).
ArgumentOutOfRange-Exception	*size* is less than 0. -or- *size* is greater than the length of *buffer*.
SocketException	*socketFlags* is not a valid combination of values. -or- The **LocalEndPoint** property was not set. -or- An operating system error occurs while accessing the **Socket**.
ObjectDisposed-Exception	The **Socket** has been closed.
SecurityException	A caller in the call stack does not have the required permissions.

Remarks

The **ReceiveFrom** method reads data into the *buffer* parameter, returns the number of bytes successfully read, and captures the remote host endpoint from which the data was sent. This method is useful if you intend to receive connectionless datagrams from an unknown host or multiple hosts.

This overload only requires you to provide a receive buffer, the number of bytes you want to receive, the necessary **SocketFlags**, and an **EndPoint** representing the remote host. The buffer offset defaults to 0. If you specify the **OutOfBand** flag as the *socketFlags* parameter and the **Socket** is configured for in-line reception of out-of-band (OOB) data (using **OutOfBandInline**) and OOB data is available, **ReceiveFrom** will return only OOB data. The OOB data is a logically independent transmission channel associated with each pair of connected stream sockets. This data is delivered with higher priority and independently of the normal data. If you specify the **Peek** flag as the *socketFlags* parameter, the available data is copied into the receive buffer but not removed from the system buffer.

With connectionless protocols, **ReceiveFrom** will read the first enqueued datagram received into the local network buffer. If the datagram you receive is larger than the size of *buffer*, the **ReceiveFrom** method will fill *buffer* with as much of the message as is possible, and throw a **SocketException**. If you are using an unreliable protocol, the excess data will be lost. If you are using a

reliable protocol, the excess data will be retained by the service provider and you can retreive it by calling the **ReceiveFrom** method with a large enough buffer.

If no data is available for reading, the **ReceiveFrom** method will block until data is available. If you are in non-blocking mode, and there is no data available in the in the protocol stack buffer, the **ReceiveFrom** method will complete immediately and throw a **SocketException**. You can use the **Available** property to determine if data is available for reading. When **Available** is non-zero, retry the receive operation.

Although **ReceiveFrom** is intended for connectionless protocols, you can use a connection-oriented protocol as well. If you choose to do so, you must first either establish a remote host connection by calling the **Connect** method or accept an incoming remote host connection by calling the **Accept** method. If you do not establish or accept a connection before calling the **ReceiveFrom** method, you will get a **SocketException**. You can also establish a default remote host for a connectionless protocol prior to calling the **ReceiveFrom** method. In either of these cases, the **ReceiveFrom** method will ignore the *remoteEP* parameter and only receive data from the connected or default remote host.

With connection-oriented sockets, **ReceiveFrom** will read as much data as is available up to the number of bytes specified by the *size* parameter. If the remote host shuts down the **Socket** connection with the **Shutdown** method, and all available data has been received, the **ReceiveFrom** method will complete immediately and return zero bytes.

> **Note** Before calling **ReceiveFrom**, you must explicitly bind the **Socket** to a local endpoint using the **Bind** method. If you do not, **ReceiveFrom** will throw a **SocketException**. If you receive a **SocketException**, use **SocketException.ErrorCode** to obtain the specific error code. Once you have obtained this code, you can refer to the Windows Socket Version 2 API error code documentation in MSDN for a detailed description of the error.

> **Note** The AddressFamily of the EndPoint used in ReceiveFrom needs to match the AddressFamily of the EndPoint used in SendTo.

Example

See related example in the **System.Sockets.Socket** class topic.

Requirements

Platforms: Windows 98, Windows NT 4.0, Windows Millennium Edition, Windows 2000, Windows XP Home Edition, Windows XP Professional, Windows .NET Server family, .NET Compact Framework - Windows CE .NET, Common Language Infrastructure (CLI) Standard

.NET Framework Security:
- **SocketPermission** for accepting connections from the network. Associated enumeration: **Accept**.

Socket.ReceiveFrom Method (Byte[], Int32, Int32, SocketFlags, EndPoint)

Receives the specified number of bytes of data into the specified location of the data buffer, using the specified **SocketFlags**, and stores the endpoint.

Visual Basic]
```
verloads Public Function ReceiveFrom( _
    ByVal buffer() As Byte, _
    ByVal offset As Integer, _
    ByVal size As Integer, _
    ByVal socketFlags As SocketFlags, _
    ByRef remoteEP As EndPoint _
) As Integer
```
[C#]
```
public int ReceiveFrom(
    byte[] buffer,
    int offset,
    int size,
    SocketFlags socketFlags,
    ref EndPoint remoteEP
);
```
[C++]
```
public: int ReceiveFrom(
    unsigned char buffer __gc[],
    int offset,
    int size,
    SocketFlags socketFlags,
    EndPoint** remoteEP
);
```
[JScript]
```
public function ReceiveFrom(
    buffer : Byte[],
    offset : int,
    size : int,
    socketFlags : SocketFlags,
    remoteEP : EndPoint
) : int;
```

Parameters

buffer
An array of type **Byte** that is the storage location for received data.

offset
The position in the *buffer* parameter to store the received data.

size
The number of bytes to receive.

socketFlags
A bitwise combination of the **SocketFlags** values.

remoteEP
An **EndPoint**, passed by reference, that represents the remote server.

Return Value

The number of bytes received.

Exceptions

Exception Type	Condition
ArgumentNullException	*buffer* is a null reference (**Nothing** in Visual Basic). -or- *remoteEP* is a null reference (**Nothing**).

Exception Type	Condition
ArgumentOutOfRange-Exception	*offset* is less than 0. -or- *offset* is greater than the length of *buffer*. -or- *size* is less than 0. -or- *size* is greater than the length of the *buffer* minus the value of the offset parameter.
SocketException	*socketFlags* is not a valid combination of values. -or- The **LocalEndPoint** property was not set. -or- An error occurred when attempting to access the socket. See the Remarks section for more information.
ObjectDisposed-Exception	The **Socket** has been closed.
SecurityException	A caller in the call stack does not have the required permissions.

Remarks

The **ReceiveFrom** method reads data into the *buffer* parameter, returns the number of bytes successfully read, and captures the remote host endpoint from which the data was sent. This method is useful if you intend to receive connectionless datagrams from an unknown host or multiple hosts.

If you specify the **OutOfBand** flag as the *socketFlags* parameter and the **Socket** is configured for in-line reception of out-of-band (OOB) data (using **OutOfBandInline**) and OOB data is available, **ReceiveFrom** will return only OOB data. The OOB data is a logically independent transmission channel associated with each pair of connected stream sockets. This data is delivered with higher priority and independently of the normal data. If you specify the **Peek** flag as the *socketFlags* parameter, the available data is copied into the receive buffer but not removed from the system buffer.

With connectionless protocols, **ReceiveFrom** will read the first enqueued datagram received into the local network buffer. If the datagram you receive is larger than the size of *buffer*, the **ReceiveFrom** method will fill *buffer* with as much of the message as is possible, and throw a **SocketException**. If you are using an unreliable protocol, the excess data will be lost. If you are using a reliable protocol, the excess data will be retained by the service provider and you can retreive it by calling the **ReceiveFrom** method with a large enough buffer.

If no data is available for reading, the **ReceiveFrom** method will block until data is available. If you are in non-blocking mode, and there is no data available in the in the protocol stack buffer, the **ReceiveFrom** method will complete immediately and throw a **SocketException**. You can use the **Available** property to determine if data is available for reading. When **Available** is non-zero, retry the receive operation.

Although **ReceiveFrom** is intended for connectionless protocols, you can use a connection-oriented protocol as well. If you choose to do so, you must first either establish a remote host connection by calling the **Connect** method or accept an incoming remote host connection by calling the **Accept** method. If you do not establish or accept a connection before calling the **ReceiveFrom** method, you will get a **SocketException**. You can also establish a default remote host for a connectionless protocol prior to calling the **ReceiveFrom** method. In either of these cases, the **ReceiveFrom** method will ignore the *remoteEP* parameter and only receive data from the connected or default remote host.

With connection-oriented sockets, **ReceiveFrom** will read as much data as is available up to the amount of bytes specified by the size parameter. If the remote host shuts down the **Socket** connection with the **Shutdown** method, and all available data has been Received, the **ReceiveFrom** method will complete immediately and return zero bytes.

Note Before calling **ReceiveFrom**, you must explicitly bind the **Socket** to a local endpoint using the **Bind** method. If you do not, **ReceiveFrom** will throw a **SocketException**. If you receive a **SocketException**, use **SocketException.ErrorCode** to obtain the specific error code. Once you have obtained this code, you can refer to the Windows Socket Version 2 API error code documentation in MSDN for a detailed description of the error.

Note The AddressFamily of the EndPoint used in ReceiveFrom needs to match the AddressFamily of the EndPoint used in SendTo.

Example

See related example in the **System.Sockets.Socket** class topic.

Requirements

Platforms: Windows 98, Windows NT 4.0, Windows Millennium Edition, Windows 2000, Windows XP Home Edition, Windows XP Professional, Windows .NET Server family, .NET Compact Framework - Windows CE .NET, Common Language Infrastructure (CLI) Standard

.NET Framework Security:

- **SocketPermission** for accepting connections from the network. Associated enumeration: **Accept**.

Socket.Select Method

Determines the status of one or more sockets.

```
[Visual Basic]
Public Shared Sub Select( _
   ByVal checkRead As IList, _
   ByVal checkWrite As IList, _
   ByVal checkError As IList, _
   ByVal microSeconds As Integer _
)
[C#]
public static void Select(
   IList checkRead,
   IList checkWrite,
   IList checkError,
   int microSeconds
);
```

```
[C++]
public: static void Select(
   IList* checkRead,
   IList* checkWrite,
   IList* checkError,
   int microSeconds
);
[JScript]
public static function Select(
   checkRead : IList,
   checkWrite : IList,
   checkError : IList,
   microSeconds : int
);
```

Parameters

checkRead
   An **IList** of **Socket** instances to check for readability.
checkWrite
   An **IList** of **Socket** instances to check for writeability.
checkError
   An **IList** of **Socket** instances to check for errors.
microSeconds
   The time to wait for a response, in microseconds.

Exceptions

Exception Type	Condition
ArgumentNullException	The *checkRead* parameter is a null reference (**Nothing** in Visual Basic) or empty.
	-and-
	The *checkWrite* parameter is a null reference (**Nothing**) or empty
	-and-
	The *checkError* parameter is a null reference (**Nothing**) or empty.
SocketException	An error occurred when attempting to access the socket. See the Remakrs section for more information.

Remarks

Select is a static method that determines the status of one or more **Socket** instances. You must place one or more sockets into an **IList** before you can use the **Select** method. Check for readability by calling **Select** with the **IList** as the *checkread* parameter. To check your sockets for writeability, use the *checkwrite* parameter. For detecting error conditions, use *Checkerror*. After calling **Select**, the **IList** will be filled with only those sockets that satisfy the conditions.

If you are in a listening state, readability means that a call to **Accept** will succeed without blocking. If you have already accepted the connection, readability means that data is available for reading. In these cases, all receive operations will succeed without blocking. Readability can also indicate whether the remote **Socket** has shut down the connection; in that case a call to **Receive** will return immediately, with zero bytes returned.

If you make a nonblocking call to **Connect**, writability means that you have connected successfully. If you already have a connection established, writeability means that all send operations will succeed without blocking.

f you have made a non-blocking call to **Connect**, the checkerror parameter identifies sockets that have not connected successfully.

> **Note** Use the **Poll** method if you only want to determine the status of a single **Socket**.

> **Note** If you receive a **SocketException**, use **SocketException.ErrorCode** to obtain the specific error code. Once you have obtained this code, you can refer to the Windows Socket Version 2 API error code documentation in MSDN for a detailed description of the error.

Example

See related example in the **System.Sockets.Socket** class topic.

Requirements

Platforms: Windows 98, Windows NT 4.0, Windows Millennium Edition, Windows 2000, Windows XP Home Edition, Windows XP Professional, Windows .NET Server family, .NET Compact Framework - Windows CE .NET, Common Language Infrastructure (CLI) Standard

Socket.Send Method

Sends data to a connected **Socket**.

Overload List

Sends data to a connected **Socket**.

Supported by the .NET Compact Framework.

> [Visual Basic] **Overloads Public Function Send(Byte()) As Integer**
> [C#] **public int Send(byte[]);**
> [C++] **public: int Send(unsigned char __gc[]);**
> [JScript] **public function Send(Byte[]) : int;**

Sends data to a connected **Socket** using the specified **SocketFlags**.

Supported by the .NET Compact Framework.

> [Visual Basic] **Overloads Public Function Send(Byte(), SocketFlags) As Integer**
> [C#] **public int Send(byte[], SocketFlags);**
> [C++] **public: int Send(unsigned char __gc[], SocketFlags);**
> [JScript] **public function Send(Byte[], SocketFlags) : int;**

Sends the specified number of bytes of data to a connected **Socket**, using the specified **SocketFlags**.

Supported by the .NET Compact Framework.

> [Visual Basic] **Overloads Public Function Send(Byte(), Integer, SocketFlags) As Integer**
> [C#] **public int Send(byte[], int, SocketFlags);**
> [C++] **public: int Send(unsigned char __gc[], int, SocketFlags);**
> [JScript] **public function Send(Byte[], int, SocketFlags) : int;**

Sends the specified number of bytes of data to a connected **Socket**, starting at the specified offset, and using the specified **SocketFlags**.

Supported by the .NET Compact Framework.

> [Visual Basic] **Overloads Public Function Send(Byte(), Integer, Integer, SocketFlags) As Integer**
> [C#] **public int Send(byte[], int, int, SocketFlags);**

> [C++] **public: int Send(unsigned char __gc[], int, int, SocketFlags);**
> [JScript] **public function Send(Byte[], int, int, SocketFlags) : int;**

Example

See related example in the **System.Sockets.Socket** class topic.

Socket.Send Method (Byte[])

Sends data to a connected **Socket**.

```
[Visual Basic]
Overloads Public Function Send( _
   ByVal buffer() As Byte _
) As Integer
[C#]
public int Send(
   byte[] buffer
);
[C++]
public: int Send(
   unsigned char buffer __gc[]
);
[JScript]
public function Send(
   buffer : Byte[]
) : int;
```

Parameters

buffer
> An array of of type **Byte** that contains the data to be sent.

Return Value

The number of bytes sent to the **Socket**.

Exceptions

Exception Type	Condition
ArgumentNullException	*buffer* is a null reference (**Nothing** in Visual Basic).
SocketException	An error occurred when attempting to access the socket. See the Remarks section for more information.
ObjectDisposed- Exception	The **Socket** has been closed.

Remarks

Send synchronously sends data to the remote host specified in the **Connect** or **Accept** method and returns the number of bytes successfully sent. **Send** can be used for both connection-oriented and connectionless protocols.

This overload requires a buffer containing the data you want to send. The **SocketFlags** value defaults to 0, the buffer offset defaults to 0, and the number of bytes to send defaults to the size of the buffer.

If you are using a connectionless protocol, you must call **Connect** before calling this method, or **Send** will throw a **SocketException**. If you are using a connection-oriented protocol, you must either use **Connect** to establish a remote host connection, or use **Accept** to accept an incoming connection.

If you are using a connectionless protocol and plan to send data to several different hosts, you should use the **SendTo** method. If you do not use the **SendTo** method, you will have to call **Connect** before each call to **Send**. You can use **SendTo** even after you have established a default remote host with **Connect**. You can also change the default remote host prior to calling **Send** by making another call to **Connect**.

If you are using a connection-oriented protocol, **Send** will block until all of the bytes in the buffer are sent. In nonblocking mode, **Send** may complete successfully even if it sends less than the number of bytes in the buffer. It is your application's responsibility to keep track of the number of bytes sent and to retry the operation until the application sends the bytes in the buffer. There is also no guarantee that the data you send will appear on the network immediately. To increase network efficiency, the underlying system may delay transmission until a significant amount of outgoing data is collected. A successful completion of the **Send** method means that the underlying system has had room to buffer your data for a network send. If it is important to your application to send every byte to the remote host immediately, you can use **SetSocketOption** to enable **SocketOptionName.NoDelay**. For more information about buffering for network efficiency, refer to the Nagle algorithm in MSDN.

> **Note** If you receive a **SocketException**, use **SocketException.ErrorCode** to obtain the specific error code. Once you have obtained this code, you can refer to the Windows Socket Version 2 API error code documentation in MSDN for a detailed description of the error.

.NET Compact Framework - Windows CE .NET Platform
Note: The consequence of sending zero-length data with this method is determined by the native operating system and not by the .NET Compact Framework.

Example
See related example in the **System.Sockets.Socket** class topic.

Requirements
Platforms: Windows 98, Windows NT 4.0, Windows Millennium Edition, Windows 2000, Windows XP Home Edition, Windows XP Professional, Windows .NET Server family, .NET Compact Framework - Windows CE .NET, Common Language Infrastructure (CLI) Standard

Socket.Send Method (Byte[], SocketFlags)

Sends data to a connected **Socket** using the specified **SocketFlags**.

```
[Visual Basic]
Overloads Public Function Send( _
    ByVal buffer() As Byte, _
    ByVal socketFlags As SocketFlags _
) As Integer
[C#]
public int Send(
    byte[] buffer,
    SocketFlags socketFlags
);
[C++]
public: int Send(
    unsigned char buffer __gc[],
    SocketFlags socketFlags
);
[JScript]
public function Send(
    buffer : Byte[],
    socketFlags : SocketFlags
) : int;
```

Parameters
buffer
> An array of type **Byte** that contains the data to be sent.

socketFlags
> A bitwise combination of the **SocketFlags** values.

Return Value
The number of bytes sent to the **Socket**.

Exceptions

Exception Type	Condition
ArgumentNullException	*buffer* is a null reference (**Nothing** in Visual Basic).
SocketException	An error occurred when attempting to access the socket. See the Remarks section for more information.
ObjectDisposed-Exception	The **Socket** has been closed.

Remarks

Send synchronously sends data to the remote host established in the **Connect** or **Accept** method and returns the number of bytes successfully sent. The **Send** method can be used for both connection-oriented and connectionless protocols.

This overload requires a buffer containing the data you want to send and a bitwise combination of **SocketFlags**. The buffer offset defaults to 0, and the number of bytes to send defaults to the size of the buffer. If you specify the **DontRoute** flag as the *socketflags* parameter value, the data you are sending will not be routed. If you specify the **OutOfBand** flag as the *socketflags* parameter, **Send** will only send out-of-band (OOB) data. The OOB data is a logically independent transmission channel associated with each pair of connected stream sockets. This data is delivered with higher priority and independently of the normal data.

If you are using a connectionless protocol, you must call **Connect** before calling this method, or **Send** will throw a **SocketException**. If you are using a connection-oriented protocol, you must either use **Connect** to establish a remote host connection, or use **Accept** to accept an incoming connection.

If you are using a connectionless protocol and plan to send data to several different hosts, you should use the **SendTo** method. If you do not use the **SendTo** method, you will have to call the **Connect** method before each call to **Send**. You can use **SendTo** even after you have established a default remote host with **Connect**. You can also change the default remote host prior to calling **Send** by making another call to **Connect**.

If you are using a connection-oriented protocol, **Send** will block until all of the bytes in the buffer are sent. In nonblocking mode, **Send** may complete successfully even if it sends less than the number of bytes in the buffer. It is your application's responsibility to keep track of the number of bytes sent and to retry the operation until the application sends the requested number of bytes. There is also no guarantee that the data you send will appear on the network immediately. To increase network efficiency, the underlying system may delay transmission until a significant amount of outgoing data is collected. A successful completion of the **Send** method means that the underlying system has had room to buffer your data for a network send. If it is important to your application to send every byte to the remote host immediately, you can use **SetSocketOption** to enable **SocketOptionName.NoDelay**. For more information about buffering for network efficiency, refer to the Nagle algorithm in MSDN.

Note You must ensure that the size of your buffer does not exceed the maximum packet size of the underlying service provider. If it does, the datagram will not be sent and **Send** will throw a **SocketException**. If you receive a **SocketException**, use **SocketException.ErrorCode** to obtain the specific error code. Once you have obtained this code, you can refer to the Windows Socket Version 2 API error code documentation in MSDN for a detailed description of the error.

.NET Compact Framework - Windows CE .NET Platform

Note: The consequence of sending zero-length data with this method is determined by the native operating system and not by the .NET Compact Framework.

Example

See related example in the **System.Sockets.Socket** class topic.

Requirements

Platforms: Windows 98, Windows NT 4.0, Windows Millennium Edition, Windows 2000, Windows XP Home Edition, Windows XP Professional, Windows .NET Server family, .NET Compact Framework - Windows CE .NET, Common Language Infrastructure (CLI) Standard

Socket.Send Method (Byte[], Int32, SocketFlags)

Sends the specified number of bytes of data to a connected **Socket**, using the specified **SocketFlags**.

```
[Visual Basic]
Overloads Public Function Send( _
   ByVal buffer() As Byte, _
   ByVal size As Integer, _
   ByVal socketFlags As SocketFlags _
) As Integer
[C#]
public int Send(
   byte[] buffer,
   int size,
   SocketFlags socketFlags
);
[C++]
public: int Send(
   unsigned char buffer __gc[],
   int size,
   SocketFlags socketFlags
);
[JScript]
public function Send(
   buffer : Byte[],
   size : int,
   socketFlags : SocketFlags
) : int;
```

Parameters

buffer
    An array of type **Byte** that contains the data to be sent.

size
    The number of bytes to send.

socketFlags
    A bitwise combination of the **SocketFlags** values.

Return Value

The number of bytes sent to the **Socket**.

Exceptions

Exception Type	Condition
ArgumentNullException	*buffer* is a null reference (**Nothing** in Visual Basic).
ArgumentOutOfRange-Exception	*size* is less than 0 or exceeds the size of the buffer.
SocketException	*socketFlags* is not a valid combination of values. -or- An operating system error occurs while accessing the socket. See the Remarks section for more information.
ObjectDisposed-Exception	The **Socket** has been closed.

Remarks

Send synchronously sends data to the remote host established in the **Connect** or **Accept** method and returns the number of bytes successfully sent. **Send** can be used for both connection-oriented and connectionless protocols.

This overload requires a buffer containing the data you want to send, the number of bytes you want to send, and a bitwise combination of any **SocketFlags**. If you specify the **DontRoute** flag as the *socketflags* parameter, the data you are sending will not be routed. If you specify the **OutOfBand** flag as the *socketflags* parameter, **Send** will only send out-of-band (OOB) data. The OOB data is a logically independent transmission channel associated with each pair of connected stream sockets. This data is delivered with higher priority and independently of the normal data.

If you are using a connectionless protocol, you must call **Connect** before calling this method, or **Send** will throw a **SocketException**. If you are using a connection-oriented protocol, you must either use **Connect** to establish a remote host connection, or use **Accept** to accept an incoming connection.

If you are using a connectionless protocol and plan to send data to several different hosts, you should use the **SendTo** method. If you do not use the **SendTo** method, you will have to call the **Connect** method before each call to the **Send** method. You can use **SendTo** even after you have established a default remote host with **Connect**. You can also change the default remote host prior to calling **Send** by making another call to **Connect**.

With a connection-oriented protocol, **Send** will block until the requested number of bytes are sent. In nonblocking mode, **Send** may complete successfully even if it sends less than the number of bytes you request. It is your application's responsibility to keep track of the number of bytes sent and to retry the operation until the application sends the requested number of bytes. There is also no guarantee that the data you send will appear on the network immediately. To increase network efficiency, the underlying system may delay transmission until a significant amount of outgoing data is collected. A successful completion of the **Send** method means that the underlying system has had room to buffer your data for a network send. If it is important to your application to send every byte to the remote host immediately, you can use **SetSocketOption** to enable **SocketOptionName.NoDelay**. For more information about

buffering for network efficiency, refer to the Nagle algorithm in
MSDN.

> **Note** You must ensure that the size does not exceed the
> maximum packet size of the underlying service provider. If it
> does, the datagram will not be sent and **Send** will throw a
> **SocketException**. If you receive a **SocketException**, use
> **SocketException.ErrorCode** to obtain the specific error code.
> Once you have obtained this code, you can refer to the
> Windows Socket Version 2 API error code documentation in
> MSDN for a detailed description of the error.

.NET Compact Framework - Windows CE .NET Platform
Note: The consequence of sending zero-length data with this
method is determined by the native operating system and not by the
.NET Compact Framework.

Example

See related example in the **System.Sockets.Socket** class topic.

Requirements

Platforms: Windows 98, Windows NT 4.0,
Windows Millennium Edition, Windows 2000,
Windows XP Home Edition, Windows XP Professional,
Windows .NET Server family,
.NET Compact Framework - Windows CE .NET,
Common Language Infrastructure (CLI) Standard

Socket.Send Method (Byte[], Int32, Int32, SocketFlags)

Sends the specified number of bytes of data to a connected **Socket**,
starting at the specified offset, and using the specified **SocketFlags**.

```
[Visual Basic]
Overloads Public Function Send( _
   ByVal buffer() As Byte, _
   ByVal offset As Integer, _
   ByVal size As Integer, _
   ByVal socketFlags As SocketFlags _
) As Integer
[C#]
public int Send(
   byte[] buffer,
   int offset,
   int size,
   SocketFlags socketFlags
);
[C++]
public: int Send(
   unsigned char buffer __gc[],
   int offset,
   int size,
   SocketFlags socketFlags
);
[JScript]
public function Send(
   buffer : Byte[],
   offset : int,
   size : int,
   socketFlags : SocketFlags
) : int;
```

Parameters
buffer
> An array of type **Byte** that contains the data to be sent.

offset
> The position in the data buffer at which to begin sending data.

size
> The number of bytes to send.

socketFlags
> A bitwise combination of the **SocketFlags** values.

Return Value

The number of bytes sent to the **Socket**.

Exceptions

Exception Type	Condition
ArgumentNullException	*buffer* is a null reference (**Nothing** in Visual Basic).
ArgumentOutOfRange-Exception	*offset* is less than 0.
	-or-
	offset is greaterthan the length of *buffer*.
	-or-
	size is less than 0.
	-or-
	size is greaterthan the length of *buffer* minus the value of the *offset* parameter.
SocketException	*socketFlags* is not a valid combination of values.
	-or-
	An operating system error occurs while accessing the **Socket**. See the Remarks section for more information.
ObjectDisposed-Exception	The **Socket** has been closed.

Remarks

Send synchronously sends data to the remote host specified in the
Connect or **Accept** method and returns the number of bytes
successfully sent. **Send** can be used for both connection-oriented
and connectionless protocols.

In this overload, if you specify the **DontRoute** flag as the *socketflags*
parameter, the data you are sending will not be routed. If you specify
the **OutOfBand** flag as the *socketflags* parameter, **Send** will only
send out-of-band (OOB) data. The OOB data is a logically
independent transmission channel associated with each pair of
connected stream sockets. This data is delivered with higher priority
and independently of the normal data.

If you are using a connectionless protocol, you must call **Connect**
before calling this method or **Send** will throw a **SocketException**. If
you are using a connection-oriented protocol, you must either use
Connect to establish a remote host connection, or use **Accept** to
accept an incoming connection.

If you are using a connectionless protocol and plan to send data to
several different hosts, you should use **SendTo**. If you do not use
SendTo, you will have to call **Connect** before each call to **Send**. It is
okay to use **SendTo** even after you have established a default remote

ost with **Connect**. You can also change the default remote host rior to calling **Send** by making another call to **Connect**.

'ou must also be sure that the size does not exceed the maximum acket size of the underlying service provider. If it does, the atagram will not be sent and **Send** will throw a **SocketException**.

f you are using a connection-oriented protocol, **Send** will block ntil the requested number of bytes are sent. In nonblocking mode, **Send** may complete successfully even if it sends less than the umber of bytes you request. It is your application's responsibility to eep track of the number of bytes sent and to retry the operation ntil the application sends the requested number of bytes. There is lso no guarantee that the data you send will appear on the network mmediately. To increase network efficiency, the underlying system nay delay transmission until a significant amount of outgoing data s collected. A successful completion of the **Send** method means that he underlying system has had room to buffer your data for a etwork send. If it is important to your application to send every byte o the remote host immediately, you can use **SetSocketOption** to nable **SocketOptionName.NoDelay**. For more information about uffering for network efficiency, refer to the Nagle algorithm in /1SDN.

> **Note** If you receive a **SocketException**, use
> **SocketException.ErrorCode** to obtain the specific error code.
> Once you have obtained this code, you can refer to the
> Windows Socket Version 2 API error code documentation in
> MSDN for a detailed description of the error.

NET Compact Framework - Windows CE .NET Platform
Note: The consequence of sending zero-length data with this method is determined by the native operating system and not by the NET Compact Framework.

Example

See related example in the **System.Sockets.Socket** class topic.

Requirements

Platforms: Windows 98, Windows NT 4.0,
Windows Millennium Edition, Windows 2000,
Windows XP Home Edition, Windows XP Professional,
Windows .NET Server family,
NET Compact Framework - Windows CE .NET,
Common Language Infrastructure (CLI) Standard

Socket.SendTo Method

Sends data to a specific endpoint.

Overload List

Sends data to the specified endpoint.

Supported by the .NET Compact Framework.

> [Visual Basic] **Overloads Public Function SendTo(Byte(), EndPoint) As Integer**
> [C#] **public int SendTo(byte[], EndPoint);**
> [C++] **public: int SendTo(unsigned char __gc[], EndPoint*);**
> [JScript] **public function SendTo(Byte[], EndPoint) : int;**

Sends data to a specific endpoint using the specified **SocketFlags**.

Supported by the .NET Compact Framework.

> [Visual Basic] **Overloads Public Function SendTo(Byte(), SocketFlags, EndPoint) As Integer**
> [C#] **public int SendTo(byte[], SocketFlags, EndPoint);**

> [C++] **public: int SendTo(unsigned char __gc[], SocketFlags, EndPoint*);**
> [JScript] **public function SendTo(Byte[], SocketFlags, EndPoint) : int;**

Sends the specified number of bytes of data to the specified endpoint using the specified **SocketFlags**.

Supported by the .NET Compact Framework.

> [Visual Basic] **Overloads Public Function SendTo(Byte(), Integer, SocketFlags, EndPoint) As Integer**
> [C#] **public int SendTo(byte[], int, SocketFlags, EndPoint);**
> [C++] **public: int SendTo(unsigned char __gc[], int, SocketFlags, EndPoint*);**
> [JScript] **public function SendTo(Byte[], int, SocketFlags, EndPoint) : int;**

Sends the specified number of bytes of data to the specified endpoint, starting at the specified location in the buffer, and using the specified **SocketFlags**.

Supported by the .NET Compact Framework.

> [Visual Basic] **Overloads Public Function SendTo(Byte(), Integer, Integer, SocketFlags, EndPoint) As Integer**
> [C#] **public int SendTo(byte[], int, int, SocketFlags, EndPoint);**
> [C++] **public: int SendTo(unsigned char __gc[], int, int, SocketFlags, EndPoint*);**
> [JScript] **public function SendTo(Byte[], int, int, SocketFlags, EndPoint) : int;**

Example

See related example in the **System.Sockets.Socket** class topic.

Socket.SendTo Method (Byte[], EndPoint)

Sends data to the specified endpoint.

```
[Visual Basic]
Overloads Public Function SendTo( _
    ByVal buffer() As Byte, _
    ByVal remoteEP As EndPoint _
) As Integer
[C#]
public int SendTo(
    byte[] buffer,
    EndPoint remoteEP
);
[C++]
public: int SendTo(
    unsigned char buffer __gc[],
    EndPoint* remoteEP
);
[JScript]
public function SendTo(
    buffer : Byte[],
    remoteEP : EndPoint
) : int;
```

Parameters
buffer
    An array of type **Byte** that contains the data to be sent.
remoteEP
    The **EndPoint** representing the destination for the data.

Return Value

The number of bytes sent.

Exceptions

Exception Type	Condition
ArgumentNullException	*buffer* is a null reference (**Nothing** in Visual Basic). -or- *remoteEP* is a null reference (**Nothing**).
SocketException	An error occurred when attempting to access the socket. See the Remarks section for more information.
ObjectDisposed-Exception	The **Socket** has been closed.

Remarks

In this overload, the buffer offset defaults to 0, the number of bytes to send defaults to the size of the *buffer* parameter, and the **SocketFlags** value defaults to 0.

If you are using a connectionless protocol, you do not need to establish a default remote host with the **Connect** method prior to calling **SendTo**. You only need to do this if you intend to call the **Send** method. If you do call the **Connect** method prior to calling **SendTo**, the *remoteEP* parameter will override the specified default remote host for that send operation only. You are also not required to call the **Bind** method, because the underlying service provider will assign the most appropriate local network address and port number. If you need to identify the assigned local network address and port number, you can use the **LocalEndPoint** property after the **SendTo** method successfully completes.

Although intended for connectionless protocols, **SendTo** also works with connection-oriented protocols. If you are using a connection-oriented protocol, you must first establish a remote host connection by calling the **Connect** method or accept an incoming connection request using the **Accept** method. If you do not establish or accept a remote host connection, **SendTo** will throw a **SocketException**. You can also establish a default remote host for a connectionless protocol prior to calling the **SendTo** method. In either of these cases, **SendTo** will ignore the *remoteEP* parameter and only send data to the connected or default remote host.

Blocking sockets will block until the all of the bytes in the buffer are sent. Since a nonblocking **Socket** completes immediately, it might not send all of the bytes in the *buffer*. It is your application's responsibility to keep track of the number of bytes sent and to retry the operation until the application sends all of the bytes in the *buffer*. There is also no guarantee that the data you send will appear on the network immediately. To increase network efficiency, the underlying system may delay transmission until a significant amount of outgoing data is collected. A successful completion of the **SendTo** method means that the underlying system has had room to buffer your data for a network send. If it is important to your application to send every byte to the remote host immediately, you can use **SetSocketOption** to enable **SocketOptionName.NoDelay**. For more information about buffering for network efficiency, refer to the Nagle algorithm on MSDN. If you are using a connectionless protocol in blocking mode, **SendTo** will block until the datagram is sent. If you want to send data to a broadcast address, you must first call the **SetSocketOption** method and set the socket option to **SocketOptionName.Broadcast**. You must also be sure that the

number of bytes sent does not exceed the maximum packet size of the underlying service provider. If it does, the datagram will not be sent and **SendTo** will throw a **SocketException**.

> **Note** If you receive a **SocketException**, use **SocketException.ErrorCode** to obtain the specific error code. Once you have obtained this code, you can refer to the Windows Socket Version 2 API error code documentation in MSDN for a detailed description of the error.

.NET Compact Framework - Windows CE .NET Platform Note: The consequence of sending zero-length data with this method is determined by the native operating system and not by the .NET Compact Framework.

Example

See related example in the **System.Sockets.Socket** class topic.

Requirements

Platforms: Windows 98, Windows NT 4.0, Windows Millennium Edition, Windows 2000, Windows XP Home Edition, Windows XP Professional, Windows .NET Server family, .NET Compact Framework - Windows CE .NET, Common Language Infrastructure (CLI) Standard

Socket.SendTo Method (Byte[], SocketFlags, EndPoint)

Sends data to a specific endpoint using the specified **SocketFlags**.

```
[Visual Basic]
Overloads Public Function SendTo( _
   ByVal buffer() As Byte, _
   ByVal socketFlags As SocketFlags, _
   ByVal remoteEP As EndPoint _
) As Integer
[C#]
public int SendTo(
   byte[] buffer,
   SocketFlags socketFlags,
   EndPoint remoteEP
);
[C++]
public: int SendTo(
   unsigned char buffer __gc[],
   SocketFlags socketFlags,
   EndPoint* remoteEP
);
[JScript]
public function SendTo(
   buffer : Byte[],
   socketFlags : SocketFlags,
   remoteEP : EndPoint
) : int;
```

Parameters

buffer
   An array of type **Byte** that contains the data to be sent.
socketFlags
   A bitwise combination of the **SocketFlags** values.
remoteEP
   The **EndPoint** that represents the destination location for the data.

Return Value

The number of bytes sent.

Exceptions

Exception Type	Condition
ArgumentNullException	*buffer* is a null reference (**Nothing** in Visual Basic). -or- *remoteEP* is a null reference (**Nothing**).
SocketException	An error occurred when attempting to access the socket. See the Remarks section for more information.
ObjectDisposed-Exception	The **Socket** has been closed.

Remarks

In this overload, the buffer offset defaults to 0, and the number of bytes to send defaults to the size of the *buffer*. If you specify the **DontRoute** flag as the *socketflags* parameter, the data you are sending will not be routed. If you specify the **OutOfBand** flag as the *socketflags* parameter, **Send** will only send out-of-band (OOB) data. The OOB data is a logically independent transmission channel associated with each pair of connected stream sockets. This data is delivered with higher priority and independently of the normal data.

If you are using a connectionless protocol, you do not need to establish a default remote host with the **Connect** method prior to calling **SendTo**. You only need to do this if you intend to call the **Send** method. If you do call the **Connect** method prior to calling **SendTo**, the *remoteEP* parameter will override the specified default remote host for that send operation only. You are also not required to call the **Bind** method, because the underlying service provider will assign the most appropriate local network address and port number. If you need to identify the assigned local network address and port number, you can use the **LocalEndPoint** property after the **SendTo** method successfully completes.

Although intended for connectionless protocols, **SendTo** also works with connection-oriented protocols. If you are using a connection-oriented protocol, you must first establish a remote host connection by calling the **Connect** method or accept an incoming connection request using the **Accept** method. If you do not establish or accept a remote host connection, **SendTo** will throw a **SocketException**. You can also establish a default remote host for a connectionless protocol prior to calling the **SendTo** method. In either of these cases, **SendTo** will ignore the *remoteEP* parameter and only send data to the connected or default remote host.

Blocking sockets will block until the requested all of the bytes in the *buffer* are sent. Since a nonblocking **Socket** completes immediately, it might not send all of the bytes in the *buffer*. It is your application's responsibility to keep track of the number of bytes sent and to retry the operation until the application sends all of the bytes in the *buffer*. There is also no guarantee that the data you send will appear on the network immediately. To increase network efficiency, the underlying system may delay transmission until a significant amount of outgoing data is collected. A successful completion of the **SendTo** method means that the underlying system has had room to buffer your data for a network send. If it is important to your application to send every byte to the remote host immediately, you can use **SetSocketOption** to enable **SocketOptionName.NoDelay**. For more information about buffering for network efficiency, refer to the Nagle algorithm on MSDN.

If you are using a connectionless protocol in blocking mode, **SendTo** will block until the datagram is sent. If you want to send data to a broadcast address, you must first call the **SetSocketOption** method and set the socket option to **SocketOptionName.Broadcast**. You must also be sure that the number of bytes sent does not exceed the maximum packet size of the underlying service provider. If it does, the datagram will not be sent and **SendTo** will throw a **SocketException**.

> **Note** If you receive a **SocketException**, use **SocketException.ErrorCode** to obtain the specific error code. Once you have obtained this code, you can refer to the Windows Socket Version 2 API error code documentation in MSDN for a detailed description of the error.

.NET Compact Framework - Windows CE .NET Platform Note: The consequence of sending zero-length data with this method is determined by the native operating system and not by the .NET Compact Framework.

Example

See related example in the **System.Sockets.Socket** class topic.

Requirements

Platforms: Windows 98, Windows NT 4.0, Windows Millennium Edition, Windows 2000, Windows XP Home Edition, Windows XP Professional, Windows .NET Server family, .NET Compact Framework - Windows CE .NET, Common Language Infrastructure (CLI) Standard

Socket.SendTo Method (Byte[], Int32, SocketFlags, EndPoint)

Sends the specified number of bytes of data to the specified endpoint using the specified **SocketFlags**.

```
[Visual Basic]
Overloads Public Function SendTo( _
   ByVal buffer() As Byte, _
   ByVal size As Integer, _
   ByVal socketFlags As SocketFlags, _
   ByVal remoteEP As EndPoint _
) As Integer
[C#]
public int SendTo(
   byte[] buffer,
   int size,
   SocketFlags socketFlags,
   EndPoint remoteEP
);
[C++]
public: int SendTo(
   unsigned char buffer __gc[],
   int size,
   SocketFlags socketFlags,
   EndPoint* remoteEP
);
[JScript]
public function SendTo(
   buffer : Byte[],
   size : int,
   socketFlags : SocketFlags,
   remoteEP : EndPoint
) : int;
```

Parameters

buffer

An array of type **Byte** that contains the data to be sent.

size

The number of bytes to send.

socketFlags

A bitwise combination of the **SocketFlags** values.

remoteEP

The **EndPoint** representing the destination location for the data.

Return Value

The number of bytes sent.

Exceptions

Exception Type	Condition
ArgumentNullException	*buffer* is a null reference (**Nothing** in Visual Basic). -or- *remoteEP* is a null reference (**Nothing**).
ArgumentOutOfRange-Exception	The specified *size* exceeds the size of *buffer*.
SocketException	An error occurred when attempting to access the socket. See the Remarks section for more information.
ObjectDisposed-Exception	The **Socket** has been closed.

Remarks

In this overload, the buffer offset defaults to 0. If you specify the **DontRoute** flag as the *socketflags* parameter, the data you are sending will not be routed. If you specify the **OutOfBand** flag as the *socketflags* parameter, **Send** will only send out-of-band (OOB) data. The OOB data is a logically independent transmission channel associated with each pair of connected stream sockets. This data is delivered with higher priority and independently of the normal data.

If you are using a connectionless protocol, you do not need to establish a default remote host with the **Connect** method prior to calling **SendTo**. You only need to do this if you intend to call the **Send** method. If you do call the **Connect** method prior to calling **SendTo**, the *remoteEP* parameter will override the specified default remote host for that send operation only. You are also not required to call the **Bind** method, because the underlying service provider will assign the most appropriate local network address and port number. If you need to identify the assigned local network address and port number, you can use the **LocalEndPoint** property after the **SendTo** method successfully completes.

Although intended for connectionless protocols, **SendTo** also works with connection-oriented protocols. If you are using a connection-oriented protocol, you must first establish a remote host connection by calling the **Connect** method or accept an incoming connection request using the **Accept** method. If you do not establish or accept a remote host connection, **SendTo** will throw a **SocketException**. You can also establish a default remote host for a connectionless protocol prior to calling the **SendTo** method. In either of these cases, **SendTo** will ignore the *remoteEP* parameter and only send data to the connected or default remote host.

Blocking sockets will block until the requested number of bytes are sent. Since a nonblocking **Socket** completes immediately, it might not send all of the bytes requested in a single operation. It is your application's responsibility to keep track of the number of bytes sent and to retry the operation until the application sends the requested number of bytes. There is also no guarantee that the data you send will appear on the network immediately. To increase network efficiency, the underlying system may delay transmission until a significant amount of out-going data is collected. A successful completion of the **SendTo** method means that the underlying system has had room to buffer your data for a network send. If it is important to your application to send every byte to the remote host immediately, you can use **SetSocketOption** to enable **SocketOptionName.NoDelay**. For more information about buffering for network efficiency, refer to the Nagle algorithm on MSDN.

If you are using a connectionless protocol in blocking mode, **SendTo** will block until the datagram is sent. If you want to send data to a broadcast address, you must first call the **SetSocketOption** method and set the socket option to **SocketOptionName.Broadcast**. You must also be sure that the number of bytes sent does not exceed the maximum packet size of the underlying service provider. If it does, the datagram will not be sent and **SendTo** will throw a **SocketException**.

> **Note** If you receive a **SocketException**, use **SocketException.ErrorCode** to obtain the specific error code. Once you have obtained this code, you can refer to the Windows Socket Version 2 API error code documentation in MSDN for a detailed description of the error.

.NET Compact Framework - Windows CE .NET Platform Note: The consequence of sending zero-length data with this method is determined by the native operating system and not by the .NET Compact Framework.

Example

See related example in the **System.Sockets.Socket** class topic.

Requirements

Platforms: Windows 98, Windows NT 4.0, Windows Millennium Edition, Windows 2000, Windows XP Home Edition, Windows XP Professional, Windows .NET Server family, .NET Compact Framework - Windows CE .NET, Common Language Infrastructure (CLI) Standard

Socket.SendTo Method (Byte[], Int32, Int32, SocketFlags, EndPoint)

Sends the specified number of bytes of data to the specified endpoint, starting at the specified location in the buffer, and using the specified **SocketFlags**.

```
[Visual Basic]
Overloads Public Function SendTo( _
    ByVal buffer() As Byte, _
    ByVal offset As Integer, _
    ByVal size As Integer, _
    ByVal socketFlags As SocketFlags, _
    ByVal remoteEP As EndPoint _
) As Integer
[C#]
public int SendTo(
    byte[] buffer,
    int offset,
    int size,
    SocketFlags socketFlags,
    EndPoint remoteEP
);
```

```
[C++]
public: int SendTo(
    unsigned char buffer __gc[],
    int offset,
    int size,
    SocketFlags socketFlags,
    EndPoint* remoteEP
);
[JScript]
public function SendTo(
    buffer : Byte[],
    offset : int,
    size : int,
    socketFlags : SocketFlags,
    remoteEP : EndPoint
) : int;
```

Parameters

buffer
> An array of type **Byte** that contains the data to be sent.

offset
> The position in the data buffer at which to begin sending data.

size
> The number of bytes to send.

socketFlags
> A bitwise combination of the **SocketFlags** values.

remoteEP
> The **EndPoint** representing the destination location for the data.

Return Value

The number of bytes sent.

Exceptions

Exception Type	Condition
ArgumentNullException	*buffer* is a null reference (**Nothing** in Visual Basic).
	-or-
	remoteEP is a null reference (**Nothing**).
ArgumentOutOf-RangeException	*offset* is less than 0.
	-or-
	offset is greater than the length of *buffer*.
	-or-
	size is less than 0.
	-or-
	size is greater than the length of *buffer* minus the value of the *offset* parameter.
SocketException	*socketFlags* is not a valid combination of values.
	-or-
	An operating system error occurs while accessing the **Socket**. See the Remarks section for more information.
ObjectDisposed-Exception	The **Socket** has been closed.
SecurityException	A caller in the call stack does not have the required permissions.

Remarks

In this overload, if you specify the **DontRoute** flag as the *socketflags* parameter, the data you are sending will not be routed. If you specify the **OutOfBand** flag as the *socketflags* parameter, **Send** will only send out-of-band (OOB) data. The OOB data is a logically independent transmission channel associated with each pair of connected stream sockets. This data is delivered with higher priority and independently of the normal data.

If you are using a connectionless protocol, you do not need to establish a default remote host with the **Connect** method prior to calling **SendTo**. You only need to do this if you intend to call the **Send** method. If you do call the **Connect** method prior to calling **SendTo**, the *remoteEP* parameter will override the specified default remote host for that send operation only. You are also not required to call the **Bind** method, because the underlying service provider will assign the most appropriate local network address and port number. If you need to identify the assigned local network address and port number, you can use the **LocalEndPoint** property after the **SendTo** method successfully completes.

Although intended for connectionless protocols, **SendTo** also works with connection-oriented protocols. If you are using a connection-oriented protocol, you must first establish a remote host connection by calling the **Connect** method or accept an incoming connection request using the **Accept** method. If you do not establish or accept a remote host connection, **SendTo** will throw a **SocketException**. You can also establish a default remote host for a connectionless protocol prior to calling the **SendTo** method. In either of these cases, **SendTo** will ignore the *remoteEP* parameter and only send data to the connected or default remote host.

Blocking sockets will block until the requested number of bytes are sent. Since a nonbocking **Socket** completes immediately, it might not send all of the bytes requested in a single operation. It is your applications responsibility to keep track of the number of bytes sent and to retry the operation until the application sends the requested number of bytes. There is also no guarantee that the data you send will appear on the network immediately. To increase network efficiency, the underlying system may delay transmission until a significant amount of out-going data is collected. A successful completion of the **SendTo** method means that the underlying system has had room to buffer your data for a network send. If it is important to your application to send every byte to the remote host immediately, you can use **SetSocketOption** to enable **SocketOptionName.NoDelay**. For more information about buffering for network efficiency, refer to the Nagle algorithm in MSDN.

If you are using a connectionless protocol in blocking mode, **SendTo** will block until the datagram is sent. If you want to send data to a broadcast address, you must first call the **SetSocketOption** method and set the socket option to **SocketOptionName.Broadcast**. You must also be sure that the size does not exceed the maximum packet size of the underlying service provider. If it does, the datagram will not be sent and **SendTo** will throw a **SocketException**.

> **Note** If you receive a **SocketException**, use **SocketException.ErrorCode** to obtain the specific error code. Once you have obtained this code, you can refer to the Windows Socket Version 2 API error code documentation in MSDN for a detailed description of the error.

.NET Compact Framework - Windows CE .NET Platform Note: The consequence of sending zero-length data with this method is determined by the native operating system and not by the .NET Compact Framework.

Example

See related example in the **System.Sockets.Socket** class topic.

Requirements

Platforms: Windows 98, Windows NT 4.0, Windows Millennium Edition, Windows 2000, Windows XP Home Edition, Windows XP Professional, Windows .NET Server family, .NET Compact Framework - Windows CE .NET, Common Language Infrastructure (CLI) Standard

Socket.SetSocketOption Method

Sets a **Socket** option.

Overload List

Sets the specified **Socket** option to the specified value, represented as a byte array.

Supported by the .NET Compact Framework.

[Visual Basic] **Overloads Public Sub SetSocketOption (SocketOptionLevel, SocketOptionName, Byte())**

[C#] **public void SetSocketOption(SocketOptionLevel, SocketOptionName, byte[]);**

[C++] **public: void SetSocketOption(SocketOptionLevel, SocketOptionName, unsigned char __gc[]);**

[JScript] **public function SetSocketOption(SocketOptionLevel, SocketOptionName, Byte[]);**

Sets the specified **Socket** option to the specified integer value.

Supported by the .NET Compact Framework.

[Visual Basic] **Overloads Public Sub SetSocketOption (SocketOptionLevel, SocketOptionName, Integer)**

[C#] **public void SetSocketOption(SocketOptionLevel, SocketOptionName, int);**

[C++] **public: void SetSocketOption(SocketOptionLevel, SocketOptionName, int);**

[JScript] **public function SetSocketOption(SocketOptionLevel, SocketOptionName, int);**

Sets the specified **Socket** option to the specified value, represented as an object.

Supported by the .NET Compact Framework.

[Visual Basic] **Overloads Public Sub SetSocketOption (SocketOptionLevel, SocketOptionName, Object)**

[C#] **public void SetSocketOption(SocketOptionLevel, SocketOptionName, object);**

[C++] **public: void SetSocketOption(SocketOptionLevel, SocketOptionName, Object*);**

[JScript] **public function SetSocketOption(SocketOptionLevel, SocketOptionName, Object);**

Example

See related example in the **System.Sockets.Socket** class topic.

Socket.SetSocketOption Method (SocketOptionLevel, SocketOptionName, Byte[])

Sets the specified **Socket** option to the specified value, represented as a byte array.

```
[Visual Basic]
Overloads Public Sub SetSocketOption( _
    ByVal optionLevel As SocketOptionLevel, _
    ByVal optionName As SocketOptionName, _
    ByVal optionValue() As Byte _
)
[C#]
public void SetSocketOption(
    SocketOptionLevel optionLevel,
    SocketOptionName optionName,
    byte[] optionValue
);
[C++]
public: void SetSocketOption(
    SocketOptionLevel optionLevel,
    SocketOptionName optionName,
    unsigned char optionValue __gc[]
);
[JScript]
public function SetSocketOption(
    optionLevel : SocketOptionLevel,
    optionName : SocketOptionName,
    optionValue : Byte[]
);
```

Parameters

optionLevel
   One of the **SocketOptionLevel** values.
optionName
   One of the **SocketOptionName** values.
optionValue
   An array of type **Byte** that represents the value of the option.

Exceptions

Exception Type	Condition
SocketException	An error occurred when attempting to access the socket. See the Remarks section for more information.
ObjectDisposed-Exception	The **Socket** has been closed.

Remarks

Socket options determine the behavior of the current **Socket**. Use this overload to set those **Socket** options that require a byte array as an option value.

> **Note** If you receive a **SocketException**, use **SocketException.ErrorCode** to obtain the specific error code. Once you have obtained this code, you can refer to the Windows Socket Version 2 API error code documentation in MSDN for a detailed description of the error.

Windows 98, Windows NT 4.0 Platform Note: You must call the **Bind** method before using **AddMembership** as the *optionName* parameter.

Example

See related example in the **System.Sockets.Socket** class topic.

Requirements

Platforms: Windows 98, Windows NT 4.0,
Windows Millennium Edition, Windows 2000,
Windows XP Home Edition, Windows XP Professional,
Windows .NET Server family,
.NET Compact Framework - Windows CE .NET,
Common Language Infrastructure (CLI) Standard

Socket.SetSocketOption Method (SocketOptionLevel, SocketOptionName, Int32)

Sets the specified **Socket** option to the specified integer value.

```
[Visual Basic]
Overloads Public Sub SetSocketOption( _
   ByVal optionLevel As SocketOptionLevel, _
   ByVal optionName As SocketOptionName, _
   ByVal optionValue As Integer _
)
[C#]
public void SetSocketOption(
   SocketOptionLevel optionLevel,
   SocketOptionName optionName,
   int optionValue
);
[C++]
public: void SetSocketOption(
   SocketOptionLevel optionLevel,
   SocketOptionName optionName,
   int optionValue
);
[JScript]
public function SetSocketOption(
   optionLevel : SocketOptionLevel,
   optionName : SocketOptionName,
   optionValue : int
);
```

Parameters

optionLevel
   One of the **SocketOptionLevel** values.
optionName
   One of the **SocketOptionName** values.
optionValue
   A value of the option.

Exceptions

Exception Type	Condition
SocketException	An error occurred when attempting to access the socket. See the Remarks section for more information.
ObjectDisposed-Exception	The **Socket** has been closed.

Remarks

Socket options determine the behavior of the current **Socket**. For an option with a **Boolean** data type, specify a nonzero value to enable the option, and a zero value to disable the option. For an option with an integer data type, specify the appropriate value. **Socket** options are grouped by level of protocol support.

Listed below are the various **Socket** options that can be set using this overload. These options are grouped by the appropriate

SocketOptionLevel. If you intend to set any of these options, be sure to use the appropriate **SocketOptionLevel** for the *optionLevel* parameter. The option you choose to set must be specified in the *optionName* parameter. If you want to get the current value of any of the options listed, use the **GetSocketOption** method.

SocketOptionLevel.Socket options that can be set using this overload.
- **Broadcast**
- **DontLinger**
- **Debug**
- **Error**
- **KeepAlive**
- **OutOfBandInline**
- **ReceiveBuffer**
- **ReceiveTimeout**
- **ReuseAddress**
- **SendBuffer**
- **SendTimeout**
- **Type**

SocketOptionLevel.IP options that can be set using this overload.
- **HeaderIncluded**
- **IPOptions**
- **IpTimeToLive**
- **MulticastInterface**
- **MulticastLoopback**
- **MulticastTimeToLive**
- **TypeOfService**
- **UseLoopback**

SocketOptionLevel.Tcp options that can be set using this overload.
- **BsdUrgent**
- **Expedited**
- **NoDelay**

SocketOptionLevel.Udp options that can be set using this overload.
- **ChecksumCoverage**
- **NoChecksum**

For more information on these options, refer to the **SocketOptionName** enumeration.

> **Note** If you receive a **SocketException**, use **SocketException.ErrorCode** to obtain the specific error code. Once you have obtained this code, you can refer to the Windows Socket Version 2 API error code documentation in MSDN for a detailed description of the error.

Windows 98, Windows NT 4.0 Platform Note: You must call the **Bind** method before using **AddMembership** as the *optionName* parameter.

Example

See related example in the **System.Sockets.Socket** class topic.

Requirements

Platforms: Windows 98, Windows NT 4.0,
Windows Millennium Edition, Windows 2000,
Windows XP Home Edition, Windows XP Professional,
Windows .NET Server family,
.NET Compact Framework - Windows CE .NET,
Common Language Infrastructure (CLI) Standard

Socket.SetSocketOption Method (SocketOptionLevel, SocketOptionName, Object)

Sets the specified **Socket** option to the specified value, represented as an object.

```
[Visual Basic]
Overloads Public Sub SetSocketOption( _
   ByVal optionLevel As SocketOptionLevel, _
   ByVal optionName As SocketOptionName, _
   ByVal optionValue As Object _
)
[C#]
public void SetSocketOption(
   SocketOptionLevel optionLevel,
   SocketOptionName optionName,
   object optionValue
);
[C++]
public: void SetSocketOption(
   SocketOptionLevel optionLevel,
   SocketOptionName optionName,
   Object* optionValue
);
[JScript]
public function SetSocketOption(
   optionLevel : SocketOptionLevel,
   optionName : SocketOptionName,
   optionValue : Object
);
```

Parameters

optionLevel
   One of the **SocketOptionLevel** values.
optionName
   One of the **SocketOptionName** values.
optionValue
   A **LingerOption** or **MulticastOption** containing the value of the option.

Exceptions

Exception Type	Condition
ArgumentNullException	*optionValue* is a null reference (**Nothing** in Visual Basic).
SocketException	An error occurred when attempting to access the socket. See the Remarks section for more information.
ObjectDisposed-Exception	The **Socket** has been closed.

Remarks

Socket options determine the behavior of the current **Socket**. Use this overload to set the **Linger**, **AddMembership**, and **DropMembership Socket** options. For the **Linger** option, use **Socket** for the *optionLevel* parameter. For **AddMembership** and **DropMembership**, use **IP**. If you want to get the current value of any of the options listed above, use the **GetSocketOption** method.

> **Note** If you receive a **SocketException**, use **SocketException.ErrorCode** to obtain the specific error code. Once you have obtained this code, you can refer to the Windows Socket Version 2 API error code documentation in MSDN for a detailed description of the error.

Windows 98, Windows NT 4.0 Platform Note: You must call the **Bind** method before using **AddMembership** as the *optionName* parameter.

Example

See related example in the **System.Sockets.Socket** class topic.

Requirements

Platforms: Windows 98, Windows NT 4.0, Windows Millennium Edition, Windows 2000, Windows XP Home Edition, Windows XP Professional, Windows .NET Server family, .NET Compact Framework - Windows CE .NET, Common Language Infrastructure (CLI) Standard

Socket.Shutdown Method

Disables sends and receives on a **Socket**.

```
[Visual Basic]
Public Sub Shutdown( _
   ByVal how As SocketShutdown _
)
[C#]
public void Shutdown(
   SocketShutdown how
);
[C++]
public: void Shutdown(
   SocketShutdown how
);
[JScript]
public function Shutdown(
   how : SocketShutdown
);
```

Parameters

how
   One of the **SocketShutdown** values that specifies the operation that will no longer be allowed.

Exceptions

Exception Type	Condition
SocketException	An error occurred when attempting to access the socket. See the Remarks section for more information.
ObjectDisposed-Exception	The **Socket** has been closed.

Remarks

When using a connection-oriented **Socket**, always call the **Shutdown** method before closing the **Socket**. This ensures that all data is sent and received on the connected socket before it is closed.

Call the **Close** method to free all managed and unmanaged resources associated with the **Socket**. Do not attempt to reuse the **Socket** after closing.

The following table shows the **SocketShutdown** enumeration values that are valid for the *how* parameter.

Value	Description
Send	Disable sending on this **Socket**.
Receive	Disable receiving on this **Socket**.

Value	Description
Both	Disable both sending and receiving on this **Socket**.

Setting *how* to **Send** specifies that subsequent calls to **Send** are not allowed. If you are using a connectionless **Socket**, specifying **Send** will have no effect.

Setting *how* to **Receive** specifies that subsequent calls to **Receive** are not allowed. This has no effect on lower protocol layers. If you are using a connection-oriented protocol, the connection is terminated if either of the following conditions exist after a call to **Shutdown**:

- Data is in the incoming network buffer waiting to be received.

- More data has arrived.

If you are using a connectionless protocol, datagrams are accepted and queued. However, if no buffer space is available for additional incoming datagrams, they will be discarded and no error will be returned to the sender. Using **Shutdown** on a connectionless **Socket** is not recommended.

Setting *how* to **Both** disables both sends and receives as described above.

> **Note** If you receive a **SocketException** when calling the **Shutdown** method, use **SocketException.ErrorCode** to obtain the specific error code. Once you have obtained this code, you can refer to the Windows Socket Version 2 API error code documentation in MSDN for a detailed description of the error.

Example

See related example in the **System.Sockets.Socket** class topic.

Requirements

Platforms: Windows 98, Windows NT 4.0,
Windows Millennium Edition, Windows 2000,
Windows XP Home Edition, Windows XP Professional,
Windows .NET Server family,
.NET Compact Framework - Windows CE .NET,
Common Language Infrastructure (CLI) Standard

SocketException Class

The exception that is thrown when a socket error occurs.

System.Object
  System.Exception
    System.SystemException
      System.Runtime.InteropServices.ExternalException
        System.ComponentModel.Win32Exception
          System.Net.Sockets.SocketException

```
[Visual Basic]
<Serializable>
Public Class SocketException
    Inherits Win32Exception
[C#]
[Serializable]
public class SocketException : Win32Exception
[C++]
[Serializable]
public __gc class SocketException : public Win32Exception
[JScript]
public
    Serializable
class SocketException extends Win32Exception
```

Thread Safety

Any public static (**Shared** in Visual Basic) members of this type are safe for multithreaded operations. Any instance members are not guaranteed to be thread safe.

Remarks

A **SocketException** is thrown by the **Socket** and **Dns** classes when an error occurs with the network.

The default constructor for the **SocketException** class sets the **ErrorCode** property to the last operating system socket error that occurred. For more information about socket error codes, see the Windows Socket Version 2 API error code documentation in MSDN.

Requirements

Namespace: System.Net.Sockets

Platforms: Windows 98, Windows NT 4.0, Windows Millennium Edition, Windows 2000, Windows XP Home Edition, Windows XP Professional, Windows .NET Server family, .NET Compact Framework - Windows CE .NET

Assembly: System (in System.dll)

SocketException Constructor

Initializes a new instance of the **SocketException** class.

Overload List

Initializes a new instance of the **SocketException** class with the last operating system error code.

Supported by the .NET Compact Framework.

[Visual Basic] **Public Sub New()**
[C#] **public SocketException();**
[C++] **public: SocketException();**
[JScript] **public function SocketException();**

Initializes a new instance of the **SocketException** class with the specified error code.

Supported by the .NET Compact Framework.

[Visual Basic] **Public Sub New(Integer)**
[C#] **public SocketException(int);**
[C++] **public: SocketException(int);**
[JScript] **public function SocketException(int);**

Initializes a new instance of the **SocketException** class from the specified instances of the **SerializationInfo** and **StreamingContext** classes.

[Visual Basic] **Protected Sub New(SerializationInfo, StreamingContext)**
[C#] **protected SocketException(SerializationInfo, StreamingContext);**
[C++] **protected: SocketException(SerializationInfo*, StreamingContext);**
[JScript] **protected function SocketException(SerializationInfo, StreamingContext);**

SocketException Constructor ( )

Initializes a new instance of the **SocketException** class with the last operating system error code.

```
[Visual Basic]
Public Sub New()
[C#]
public SocketException();
[C++]
public: SocketException();
[JScript]
public function SocketException();
```

Remarks

The **ctor** constructor sets the **ErrorCode** property to the last operating system socket error that occurred. For more information about socket error codes, see the Windows Socket Version 2 API error code documentation in MSDN.

Requirements

Platforms: Windows 98, Windows NT 4.0, Windows Millennium Edition, Windows 2000, Windows XP Home Edition, Windows XP Professional, Windows .NET Server family, .NET Compact Framework - Windows CE .NET, Common Language Infrastructure (CLI) Standard

SocketException Constructor (Int32)

Initializes a new instance of the **SocketException** class with the specified error code.

```
[Visual Basic]
Public Sub New( _
    ByVal errorCode As Integer _
)
[C#]
public SocketException(
    int errorCode
);
```

```
[C++]
public: SocketException(
    int errorCode
);
[JScript]
public function SocketException(
    errorCode : int
);
```

Parameters

errorCode
    The error code indicating the error that occurred.

Remarks

The **ctor** constructor sets the **ErrorCode** property to *errorCode*.

Requirements

Platforms: Windows 98, Windows NT 4.0,
Windows Millennium Edition, Windows 2000,
Windows XP Home Edition, Windows XP Professional,
Windows .NET Server family,
.NET Compact Framework - Windows CE .NET

SocketException Constructor (SerializationInfo, StreamingContext)

Initializes a new instance of the **SocketException** class from the specified instances of the **SerializationInfo** and **StreamingContext** classes.

```
[Visual Basic]
Protected Sub New( _
    ByVal serializationInfo As SerializationInfo, _
    ByVal streamingContext As StreamingContext _
)
[C#]
protected SocketException(
    SerializationInfo serializationInfo,
    StreamingContext streamingContext
);
[C++]
protected: SocketException(
    SerializationInfo* serializationInfo,
    StreamingContext streamingContext
);
[JScript]
protected function SocketException(
    serializationInfo : SerializationInfo,
    streamingContext : StreamingContext
);
```

Parameters

serializationInfo
    A **SerializationInfo** instance containing the information required to serialize the new **SocketException** instance.

streamingContext
    A **StreamingContext** containing the source of the serialized stream associated with the new **SocketException** instance.

Remarks

This constructor implements the **ISerializable** interface for the **SocketException** class.

Requirements

Platforms: Windows 98, Windows NT 4.0,
Windows Millennium Edition, Windows 2000,
Windows XP Home Edition, Windows XP Professional,
Windows .NET Server family

SocketException.ErrorCode Property

Gets the error code associated with this exception.

```
[Visual Basic]
Overrides Public ReadOnly Property ErrorCode As Integer
[C#]
public override int ErrorCode {get;}
[C++]
public: __property int get_ErrorCode();
[JScript]
public override function get ErrorCode() : int;
```

Property Value

An integer error code associated with this exception.

Remarks

The **ErrorCode** property contains the error code associated with the error that caused the exception.

The default constructor for **SocketException** sets the **ErrorCode** property to the last operating system error that occurred. For more information about socket error codes, see the Windows Socket Version 2 API error code documentation in MSDN.

Requirements

Platforms: Windows 98, Windows NT 4.0,
Windows Millennium Edition, Windows 2000,
Windows XP Home Edition, Windows XP Professional,
Windows .NET Server family,
.NET Compact Framework - Windows CE .NET

SocketFlags Enumeration

Provides constant values for **Socket** messages.

This enumeration has a **FlagsAttribute** attribute that allows a bitwise combination of its member values.

```
[Visual Basic]
<Flags>
<Serializable>
Public Enum SocketFlags
[C#]
[Flags]
[Serializable]
public enum SocketFlags
[C++]
[Flags]
[Serializable]
__value public enum SocketFlags
[JScript]
public
   Flags
   Serializable
enum SocketFlags
```

Members

Member name	Description	Value
DontRoute Supported by the .NET Compact Framework.	Send without using routing tables.	4
MaxIOVectorLength Supported by the .NET Compact Framework.	Provides a standard value for the number of WSABUF structures used to send and receive data.	16
None Supported by the .NET Compact Framework.	Use no flags for this call.	0
OutOfBand Supported by the .NET Compact Framework.	Process out-of-band data.	1
Partial Supported by the .NET Compact Framework.	Partial send or receive for message.	32768
Peek Supported by the .NET Compact Framework.	Peek at incoming message.	2

Requirements

Namespace: System.Net.Sockets

Platforms: Windows 98, Windows NT 4.0, Windows Millennium Edition, Windows 2000, Windows XP Home Edition, Windows XP Professional, Windows .NET Server family, .NET Compact Framework - Windows CE .NET

Assembly: System (in System.dll)

SocketOptionLevel Enumeration

Defines socket option levels for the **Socket.SetSocketOption** and **Socket.GetSocketOption** methods.

```
[Visual Basic]
<Serializable>
Public Enum SocketOptionLevel
[C#]
[Serializable]
public enum SocketOptionLevel
[C++]
[Serializable]
__value public enum SocketOptionLevel
[JScript]
public
   Serializable
enum SocketOptionLevel
```

Remarks

The **SocketOptionLevel** enumeration defines the socket option levels that can be passed to the **Socket.SetSocketOption** and **Socket.GetSocketOption** methods. **SocketOptionName** enumerated values are grouped by **SocketOptionLevel**.

Members

Member name	Description
IP Supported by the .NET Compact Framework.	**Socket** options apply only to IP sockets.
IPv6	**Socket** options apply only to IPv6 sockets.
Socket Supported by the .NET Compact Framework.	**Socket** options apply to all sockets.
Tcp Supported by the .NET Compact Framework.	**Socket** options apply only to TCP sockets.
Udp Supported by the .NET Compact Framework.	**Socket** options apply only to UDP sockets.

Example

[Visual Basic, C#, C++] The following example uses the **Tcp** enumerated value to specify that **SetSocketOption** must select a **SocketOptionName** which pertains to **Tcp** sockets only.

```
[Visual Basic]
'Send operations will timeout of confirmation is not received
  within 1000 milliseconds.
s.SetSocketOption(SocketOptionLevel.Socket,
SocketOptionName.SendTimeout, 1000)

'Socket will linger for 10 seconds after close is called.
Dim lingerOption As New LingerOption(True, 10)
s.SetSocketOption(SocketOptionLevel.Socket,
SocketOptionName.Linger, lingerOption)
```

```
[C#]
//Send operations will timeout of confirmation is not
received within 1000 milliseconds.
s.SetSocketOption(SocketOptionLevel.Socket,
SocketOptionName.SendTimeout, 1000);

//Socket will linger for 10 seconds after close is called.
LingerOption lingerOption = new LingerOption(true, 10);
s.SetSocketOption(SocketOptionLevel.Socket,
SocketOptionName.Linger, lingerOption);
```

```
[C++]
//Specifies that send operations will time out if confirmation
is not received within 1000 milliseconds.
s->SetSocketOption(SocketOptionLevel::Socket,
SocketOptionName::SendTimeout, 1000);

//Specifies that the Socket will linger for 10 seconds after
Close is called.
LingerOption *lingerOption = new LingerOption(true, 10);
s->SetSocketOption(SocketOptionLevel::Socket, SocketOptionName::
Linger, lingerOption);
```

Requirements

Namespace: System.Net.Sockets

Platforms: Windows 98, Windows NT 4.0, Windows Millennium Edition, Windows 2000, Windows XP Home Edition, Windows XP Professional, Windows .NET Server family, .NET Compact Framework - Windows CE .NET

Assembly: System (in System.dll)

SocketOptionName Enumeration

Defines **Socket** configuration option names for the **Socket** class.

```
[Visual Basic]
<Serializable>
Public Enum SocketOptionName
[C#]
[Serializable]
public enum SocketOptionName
[C++]
[Serializable]
__value public enum SocketOptionName
[JScript]
public
    Serializable
enum SocketOptionName
```

Remarks

SocketOptionName defines the names of each **Socket** configuration option. Sockets can be configured with the **Socket.SetSocketOption** method.

Members

Member name	Description
AcceptConnection Supported by the .NET Compact Framework.	Socket is listening.
AddMembership Supported by the .NET Compact Framework.	Add an IP group membership.
AddSourceMembership Supported by the .NET Compact Framework.	Join a source group.
BlockSource Supported by the .NET Compact Framework.	Block data from a source.
Broadcast Supported by the .NET Compact Framework.	Permit sending broadcast messages on the socket.
BsdUrgent Supported by the .NET Compact Framework.	Use urgent data as defined in RFC-1222. This option can be set only once, and once set, cannot be turned off.
ChecksumCoverage Supported by the .NET Compact Framework.	Set or get UDP checksum coverage.
Debug Supported by the .NET Compact Framework.	Record debugging information.
DontFragment Supported by the .NET Compact Framework.	Do not fragment IP datagrams.

Member name	Description
DontLinger Supported by the .NET Compact Framework.	Close socket gracefully without lingering.
DontRoute Supported by the .NET Compact Framework.	Do not route; send directly to interface addresses.
DropMembership Supported by the .NET Compact Framework.	Drop an IP group membership.
DropSourceMembership Supported by the .NET Compact Framework.	Drop a source group.
Error Supported by the .NET Compact Framework.	Get error status and clear.
ExclusiveAddressUse Supported by the .NET Compact Framework.	Enables a socket to be bound for exclusive access.
Expedited Supported by the .NET Compact Framework.	Use expedited data as defined in RFC-1222. This option can be set only once, and once set, cannot be turned off.
HeaderIncluded Supported by the .NET Compact Framework.	Indicates application is providing the IP header for outgoing datagrams.
IPOptions Supported by the .NET Compact Framework.	Specifies IP options to be inserted into outgoing datagrams.
IpTimeToLive Supported by the .NET Compact Framework.	Set the IP header time-to-live field.
KeepAlive Supported by the .NET Compact Framework.	Send keep-alives.
Linger Supported by the .NET Compact Framework.	Linger on close if unsent data is present.
MaxConnections Supported by the .NET Compact Framework.	Maximum queue length that can be specified by **Listen**.
MulticastInterface Supported by the .NET Compact Framework.	Set the interface for outgoing multicast packets.
MulticastLoopback Supported by the .NET Compact Framework.	IP multicast loopback.
MulticastTimeToLive Supported by the .NET Compact Framework.	IP multicast time to live.
NoChecksum Supported by the .NET Compact Framework.	Send UDP datagrams with checksum set to zero.

Member name	Description
NoDelay Supported by the .NET Compact Framework.	Disables the Nagle algorithm for send coalescing.
OutOfBandInline Supported by the .NET Compact Framework.	Receives out-of-band data in the normal data stream.
PacketInformation Supported by the .NET Compact Framework.	Return information about received packets.
ReceiveBuffer Supported by the .NET Compact Framework.	Send low water mark.
ReceiveLowWater Supported by the .NET Compact Framework.	Receive low water mark.
ReceiveTimeout Supported by the .NET Compact Framework.	Receive time out.
ReuseAddress Supported by the .NET Compact Framework.	Allows the socket to be bound to an address that is already in use.
SendBuffer Supported by the .NET Compact Framework.	Specifies the total per-socket buffer space reserved for sends. This is unrelated to the maximum message size or the size of a TCP window.
SendLowWater Supported by the .NET Compact Framework.	Specifies the total per-socket buffer space reserved for receives. This is unrelated to the maximum message size or the size of a TCP window.
SendTimeout Supported by the .NET Compact Framework.	Send timeout.
Type Supported by the .NET Compact Framework.	Get socket type.
TypeOfService Supported by the .NET Compact Framework.	Change the IP header type of service field.
UnblockSource Supported by the .NET Compact Framework.	Unblock a previously blocked source.
UseLoopback Supported by the .NET Compact Framework.	Bypass hardware when possible.

Example

[Visual Basic, C#, C++] The following example uses the **Linger** enumerated value to set the linger time of the **Socket**.

[Visual Basic]
```
'Creates the Socket for sending data over TCP.
Dim s As New Socket(AddressFamily.InterNetwork,
SocketType.Stream, ProtocolType.Tcp)

' Connects to host using IPEndPoint.
s.Connect(EPhost)
```

```
If Not s.Connected Then
    strRetPage = "Unable to connect to host"
End If
' Use the SelectWrite enumeration to obtain Socket status.
If s.Poll(- 1, SelectMode.SelectWrite) Then
    Console.WriteLine("This Socket is writable.")
Else
    If s.Poll(- 1, SelectMode.SelectRead) Then
        Console.WriteLine(("This should not print. Because
this is not a listening Socket," + " no incoming connecton
requests are expected. "))
    Else
        If s.Poll(- 1, SelectMode.SelectError) Then
            Console.WriteLine("This Socket has an error.")
        End If
    End If
End If
```

[C#]
```
//Creates the Socket for sending data over TCP.
Socket s = new Socket(AddressFamily.InterNetwork, SocketType.Stream,
    ProtocolType.Tcp );

// Connects to host using IPEndPoint.
s.Connect(EPhost);
if (!s.Connected)
{
    strRetPage = "Unable to connect to host";
}
// Use the SelectWrite enumeration to obtain Socket status.
if(s.Poll(-1, SelectMode.SelectWrite)){
    Console.WriteLine("This Socket is writable.");
}
else if (s.Poll(-1, SelectMode.SelectRead)){
    Console.WriteLine("This should not print. Because
this is not a listening Socket," +
                    " no incoming connecton
requests are expected. " );
}
else if (s.Poll(-1, SelectMode.SelectError)){
    Console.WriteLine("This Socket has an error.");
}
```

[C++]
```
//Creates the Socket for sending data over TCP.
Socket* s = new Socket(AddressFamily::InterNetwork,
SocketType::Stream, ProtocolType::Tcp );

// Connects to host using IPEndPoint.
s->Connect(EPhost);
if (!s->Connected) {
    strRetPage = S"Unable to connect to host";
}
// Use the SelectWrite enumeration to obtain Socket status.
if (s->Poll(-1, SelectMode::SelectWrite)) {
    Console::WriteLine(S"This Socket is writable.");
} else if (s->Poll(-1, SelectMode::SelectRead)) {
    Console::WriteLine(S"This should not print. Because
this is not a listening Socket, {0}",
        S" no incoming connecton requests are expected.");
} else if (s->Poll(-1, SelectMode::SelectError)) {
    Console::WriteLine(S"This Socket has an error.");
}
```

Requirements

Namespace: System.Net.Sockets

Platforms: Windows 98, Windows NT 4.0, Windows Millennium Edition, Windows 2000, Windows XP Home Edition, Windows XP Professional, Windows .NET Server family, .NET Compact Framework - Windows CE .NET

Assembly: System (in System.dll)

SocketShutdown Enumeration

Defines constants used by the **Socket.Shutdown** method.

```
[Visual Basic]
<Serializable>
Public Enum SocketShutdown
[C#]
[Serializable]
public enum SocketShutdown
[C++]
[Serializable]
__value public enum SocketShutdown
[JScript]
public
   Serializable
enum SocketShutdown
```

Remarks

The **SocketShutdown** enumeration defines the values that can be passed to the **Socket.Shutdown** method.

Members

Member name	Description
Both Supported by the .NET Compact Framework.	Disables a **Socket** for both sending and receiving. This field is constant.
Receive Supported by the .NET Compact Framework.	Disables a **Socket** for receiving. This field is constant.
Send Supported by the .NET Compact Framework.	Disables a **Socket** for sending. This field is constant.

Requirements

Namespace: System.Net.Sockets

Platforms: Windows 98, Windows NT 4.0, Windows Millennium Edition, Windows 2000, Windows XP Home Edition, Windows XP Professional, Windows .NET Server family, .NET Compact Framework - Windows CE .NET

Assembly: System (in System.dll)

SocketType Enumeration

Specifies the type of socket an instance of the **Socket** class represents.

```
[Visual Basic]
<Serializable>
Public Enum SocketType
[C#]
[Serializable]
public enum SocketType
[C++]
[Serializable]
__value public enum SocketType
[JScript]
public
    Serializable
enum SocketType
```

Remarks

Before a **Socket** can send and receive data, it must first be created using an **AddressFamily**, a **SocketType**, and a **ProtocolType**. The **SocketType** enumeration provides several options for defining the type of **Socket** that you intend to open.

> **Note** **SocketType** will sometimes implicitly indicate which **ProtocolType** will be used within an **AddressFamily**. For example when the **SocketType** is **Dgram**, the **ProtocolType** is always **Udp**. When the **SocketType** is **Stream**, the **ProtocolType** is always **Tcp**. If you try to create a **Socket** with an incompatible combination, **Socket** will throw a **SocketException**.

Members

Member name	Description
Dgram Supported by the .NET Compact Framework.	Supports datagrams, which are connectionless, unreliable messages of a fixed (typically small) maximum length. Messages might be lost or duplicated and might arrive out of order. A **Socket** of type **Dgram** requires no connection prior to sending and receiving data, and can communicate with multiple peers. **Dgram** uses the Datagram Protocol (**Udp**) and the **InterNetwork AddressFamily**.
Raw Supported by the .NET Compact Framework.	Supports access to the underlying transport protocol. Using the **SocketType Raw**, you can communicate using protocols such as, Internet Control Message Protocol (**Icmp**) and Internet Group Management Protocol (**Igmp**). Your application must provide a complete IP header when sending. Received datagrams return with the IP header and options intact.

Member name	Description
Rdm Supported by the .NET Compact Framework.	Supports connectionless, message-oriented, reliably delivered messages, and preserves message boundaries in data. Rdm (Reliably-Delivered Messages) messages arrive unduplicated and in order. Furthermore, the sender is notified if messages are lost. If you initialize a **Socket** using **Rdm**, you do not require a remote host connection before sending and receiving data. With **Rdm**, you can communicate with multiple peers.
Seqpacket Supported by the .NET Compact Framework.	Provides connection-oriented and reliable two-way transfer of ordered byte streams across a network. **Seqpacket** does not duplicate data, and it preserves boundaries within the data stream. A **Socket** of type **Seqpacket** communicates with a single peer and requires a remote host connection before communication can begin.
Stream Supported by the .NET Compact Framework.	Supports reliable, two-way, connection-based byte streams without the duplication of data and without preservation of boundaries. A **Socket** of this type communicates with a single peer and requires a remote host connection before communication can begin. **Stream** uses the Transmission Control Protocol (**Tcp**) **ProtocolType** and the **InterNetwork AddressFamily**.
Unknown Supported by the .NET Compact Framework.	Specifies an unknown **Socket** type.

Example

[Visual Basic, C#, C++] The following example uses the **Stream** enumerated member as a parameter to the **Socket** constructor.

```
[Visual Basic]
'Creates the Socket for sending data over TCP.
Dim s As New Socket(AddressFamily.InterNetwork,
SocketType.Stream, ProtocolType.Tcp)

' Connects to host using IPEndPoint.
s.Connect(EPhost)
If Not s.Connected Then
    strRetPage = "Unable to connect to host"
End If
' Use the SelectWrite enumeration to obtain Socket status.
If s.Poll(- 1, SelectMode.SelectWrite) Then
    Console.WriteLine("This Socket is writable.")
Else
    If s.Poll(- 1, SelectMode.SelectRead) Then
        Console.WriteLine("This should not print.
Because this is not a listening Socket," + " no incoming
connecton requests are expected. "))
    Else
        If s.Poll(- 1, SelectMode.SelectError) Then
            Console.WriteLine("This Socket has an error.")
        End If
    End If
End If
```

```csharp
[C#]
//Creates the Socket for sending data over TCP.
Socket s = new Socket(AddressFamily.InterNetwork, SocketType.Stream,
    ProtocolType.Tcp );

// Connects to host using IPEndPoint.
s.Connect(EPhost);
if (!s.Connected)
{
   strRetPage = "Unable to connect to host";
}
// Use the SelectWrite enumeration to obtain Socket status.
 if(s.Poll(-1, SelectMode.SelectWrite)){
      Console.WriteLine("This Socket is writable.");
 }
 else if (s.Poll(-1, SelectMode.SelectRead)){
        Console.WriteLine("This should not print.  Because
" no incoming connecton requests are expected. " );
 }
 else if (s.Poll(-1, SelectMode.SelectError)){
      Console.WriteLine("This Socket has an error.");
 }
```

```cpp
[C++]
//Creates the Socket for sending data over TCP.
Socket* s = new Socket(AddressFamily::InterNetwork,
SocketType::Stream, ProtocolType::Tcp );

// Connects to host using IPEndPoint.
s->Connect(EPhost);
if (!s->Connected) {
   strRetPage = S"Unable to connect to host";
}
// Use the SelectWrite enumeration to obtain Socket status.
if (s->Poll(-1, SelectMode::SelectWrite)) {
   Console::WriteLine(S"This Socket is writable.");
} else if (s->Poll(-1, SelectMode::SelectRead)) {
   Console::WriteLine(S"This should not print.  Because
this is not a listening Socket, {0}",
      S" no incoming connecton requests are expected.");
} else if (s->Poll(-1, SelectMode::SelectError)) {
   Console::WriteLine(S"This Socket has an error.");
}
```

Requirements

Namespace: System.Net.Sockets

Platforms: Windows 98, Windows NT 4.0,
Windows Millennium Edition, Windows 2000,
Windows XP Home Edition, Windows XP Professional,
Windows .NET Server family,
.NET Compact Framework - Windows CE .NET

Assembly: System (in System.dll)

TcpClient Class

Provides client connections for TCP network services.

System.Object
   System.Net.Sockets.TcpClient

```
[Visual Basic]
Public Class TcpClient
   Implements IDisposable
[C#]
public class TcpClient : IDisposable
[C++]
public __gc class TcpClient : public IDisposable
[JScript]
public class TcpClient implements IDisposable
```

Thread Safety

Any public static (**Shared** in Visual Basic) members of this type are safe for multithreaded operations. Any instance members are not guaranteed to be thread safe.

Remarks

The **TcpClient** class provides simple methods for connecting, sending, and receiving stream data over a network in synchronous blocking mode.

In order for **TcpClient** to connect and exchange data, a **TcpListener** or **Socket** created with the TCP **ProtocolType** must be listening for incoming connection requests. You can connect to this listener in one of the following two ways:

- Create a **TcpClient** and call one of the three available **Connect** methods.

- Create a **TcpClient** using the host name and port number of the remote host. This constructor will automatically attempt a connection.

> **Note** If you want to send connectionless datagrams in synchronous blocking mode, use the **UdpClient** class.

Notes to Inheritors: To send and receive data, use the **GetStream** method to obtain a **NetworkStream**. Call the **Write** and **Read** methods of the **NetworkStream** to send and receive data with the remote host. Use the **Close** method to release all resources associated with the **TcpClient**.

Example

[Visual Basic, C#, C++] The following example establishes a **TcpClient** connection.

```vbnet
[Visual Basic]
Shared Sub Connect(server As [String], message As [String])
   Try
      ' Create a TcpClient.
      ' Note, for this client to work you need to have a TcpServer
      ' connected to the same address as specified by the server, port
      ' combination.
      Dim port As Int32 = 13000
      Dim client As New TcpClient(server, port)

      ' Translate the passed message into ASCII and store it as
      a Byte array.
      Dim data As [Byte]() =
System.Text.Encoding.ASCII.GetBytes(message)

      ' Get a client stream for reading and writing.
      '  Stream stream = client.GetStream();
      Dim stream As NetworkStream = client.GetStream()

      ' Send the message to the connected TcpServer.
      stream.Write(data, 0, data.Length)

      Console.WriteLine("Sent: {0}", message)

      ' Receive the TcpServer.response.
      ' Buffer to store the response bytes.
      data = New [Byte](256) {}

      ' String to store the response ASCII representation.
      Dim responseData As [String] = [String].Empty

      ' Read the first batch of the TcpServer response bytes.
      Dim bytes As Int32 = stream.Read(data, 0, data.Length)
      responseData = System.Text.Encoding.ASCII.GetString
(data, 0, bytes)
      Console.WriteLine("Received: {0}", responseData)

      ' Close everything.
      client.Close()
   Catch e As ArgumentNullException
      Console.WriteLine("ArgumentNullException: {0}", e)
   Catch e As SocketException
      Console.WriteLine("SocketException: {0}", e)
   End Try

   Console.WriteLine(ControlChars.Cr + " Press Enter to continue...")
   Console.Read()
End Sub 'Connect
```

```csharp
[C#]
static void Connect(String server, String message)
{
   try
   {
      // Create a TcpClient.
      // Note, for this client to work you need to have a TcpServer
      // connected to the same address as specified by the server, port
      // combination.
      Int32 port = 13000;
      TcpClient client = new TcpClient(server, port);

      // Translate the passed message into ASCII and store it as
      a Byte array.
      Byte[] data = System.Text.Encoding.ASCII.GetBytes(message);

      // Get a client stream for reading and writing.
      //  Stream stream = client.GetStream();

      NetworkStream stream = client.GetStream();

      // Send the message to the connected TcpServer.
      stream.Write(data, 0, data.Length);

      Console.WriteLine("Sent: {0}", message);

      // Receive the TcpServer.response.

      // Buffer to store the response bytes.
      data = new Byte[256];

      // String to store the response ASCII representation.
      String responseData = String.Empty;

      // Read the first batch of the TcpServer response bytes.
      Int32 bytes = stream.Read(data, 0, data.Length);
      responseData = System.Text.Encoding.ASCII.GetString
(data, 0, bytes);
      Console.WriteLine("Received: {0}", responseData);

      // Close everything.
      client.Close();
   }
   catch (ArgumentNullException e)
   {
```

```
    Console.WriteLine("ArgumentNullException: {0}", e);
}
catch (SocketException e)
{
    Console.WriteLine("SocketException: {0}", e);
}

Console.WriteLine("\n Press Enter to continue...");
Console.Read();
}
```

```
[C++]
void Connect(String* server, String* message) {
    try {
        // Create a TcpClient.
        // Note, for this client to work you need to have a TcpServer
        // connected to the same address as specified by the        ⌐
server, port
        // combination.
        Int32 port = 13000;
        TcpClient* client = new TcpClient(server, port);

        // Translate the passed message into ASCII and store
it as a Byte array.
        Byte data[] = Text::Encoding::ASCII->GetBytes(message);

        // Get a client stream for reading and writing.
        //  Stream stream = client->GetStream();

        NetworkStream* stream = client->GetStream();

        // Send the message to the connected TcpServer.
        stream->Write(data, 0, data->Length);

        Console::WriteLine(S"Sent: {0}", message);

        // Receive the TcpServer::response.

        // Buffer to store the response bytes. data = new Byte[256];

        // String to store the response ASCII representation.
        String* responseData = String::Empty;

        // Read the first batch of the TcpServer response bytes.
        Int32 bytes = stream->Read(data, 0, data->Length);
        responseData = Text::Encoding::ASCII->GetString        ⌐
(data, 0, bytes);
        Console::WriteLine(S"Received: {0}", responseData);

        // Close everything.
        client->Close();
    } catch (ArgumentNullException* e) {
        Console::WriteLine(S"ArgumentNullException: {0}", e);
    } catch (SocketException* e) {
        Console::WriteLine(S"SocketException: {0}", e);
    }

    Console::WriteLine(S"\n Press Enter to continue...");
    Console::Read();
}
```

Requirements

Namespace: System.Net.Sockets

Platforms: Windows 98, Windows NT 4.0,
Windows Millennium Edition, Windows 2000,
Windows XP Home Edition, Windows XP Professional,
Windows .NET Server family,
.NET Compact Framework - Windows CE .NET

Assembly: System (in System.dll)

.NET Framework Security:

- **SocketPermission** to establish an outgoing connection or accept an incoming request.

TcpClient Constructor

Initializes a new instance of the **TcpClient** class.

Overload List

Initializes a new instance of the **TcpClient** class.

Supported by the .NET Compact Framework.

> [Visual Basic] **Public Sub New()**
> [C#] **public TcpClient();**
> [C++] **public: TcpClient();**
> [JScript] **public function TcpClient();**

Initializes a new instance of the **TcpClient** class with the specified family.

> [Visual Basic] **Public Sub New(AddressFamily)**
> [C#] **public TcpClient(AddressFamily);**
> [C++] **public: TcpClient(AddressFamily);**
> [JScript] **public function TcpClient(AddressFamily);**

Initializes a new instance of the **TcpClient** class and binds it to the specified local endpoint.

Supported by the .NET Compact Framework.

> [Visual Basic] **Public Sub New(IPEndPoint)**
> [C#] **public TcpClient(IPEndPoint);**
> [C++] **public: TcpClient(IPEndPoint*);**
> [JScript] **public function TcpClient(IPEndPoint);**

Initializes a new instance of the **TcpClient** class and connects to the specified port on the specified host.

Supported by the .NET Compact Framework.

> [Visual Basic] **Public Sub New(String, Integer)**
> [C#] **public TcpClient(string, int);**
> [C++] **public: TcpClient(String*, int);**
> [JScript] **public function TcpClient(String, int);**

Example

See related example in the **System.Net.Sockets.TCPClient** class topic.

TcpClient Constructor ( )

Initializes a new instance of the **TcpClient** class.

```
[Visual Basic]
Public Sub New()
[C#]
public TcpClient();
[C++]
public: TcpClient();
[JScript]
public function TcpClient();
```

Remarks

This constructor creates a new **TcpClient** and allows the underlying service provider to assign the most appropriate local IP address and port number. You must first call the **Connect** method before sending and receiving data.

> **Note** This constructor works only with IPv4 address types.

Example

[Visual Basic, C#] The following example demonstrates how to use the default constructor to create a new **TcpClient**.

[Visual Basic]
```
'Creates a TCPClient using the default constructor.
Dim tcpClientC As New TcpClient()
```
[C#]
```
//Creates a TCPClient using the default constructor.
TcpClient tcpClientC = new TcpClient();
```

Requirements

Platforms: Windows 98, Windows NT 4.0,
Windows Millennium Edition, Windows 2000,
Windows XP Home Edition, Windows XP Professional,
Windows .NET Server family,
.NET Compact Framework - Windows CE .NET

TcpClient Constructor (AddressFamily)

Note: This namespace, class, or member is supported only in version 1.1 of the .NET Framework.

Initializes a new instance of the **TcpClient** class with the specified family.

[Visual Basic]
```
Public Sub New( _
   ByVal family As AddressFamily _
)
```
[C#]
```
public TcpClient(
   AddressFamily family
);
```
[C++]
```
public: TcpClient(
   AddressFamily family
);
```
[JScript]
```
public function TcpClient(
   family : AddressFamily
);
```

Parameters

family
    The **AddressFamily** of the IP protocol.

Exceptions

Exception Type	Condition
System.Argument-Exception	*family* != **AddressFamily.InterNetwork** -or- *family* != **AddressFamily.InterNetworkV6**

Requirements

Platforms: Windows 98, Windows NT 4.0,
Windows Millennium Edition, Windows 2000,
Windows XP Home Edition, Windows XP Professional,
Windows .NET Server family

TcpClient Constructor (IPEndPoint)

Initializes a new instance of the **TcpClient** class and binds it to the specified local endpoint.

[Visual Basic]
```
Public Sub New( _
   ByVal localEP As IPEndPoint _
)
```
[C#]
```
public TcpClient(
   IPEndPoint localEP
);
```
[C++]
```
public: TcpClient(
   IPEndPoint* localEP
);
```
[JScript]
```
public function TcpClient(
   localEP : IPEndPoint
);
```

Parameters

localEP
    The **IPEndPoint** to which you bind the TCP **Socket**.

Exceptions

Exception Type	Condition
ArgumentNullException	*localEP* is a null reference (**Nothing** in Visual Basic).

Remarks

This constructor creates a new **TcpClient** and binds it to the **IPEndPoint** specified by the *localEP* parameter. Before you call this constructor, you must create an **IPEndPoint** using the IP address and port number from which you intend to send and receive data. You do not need to specify a local IP address and port number before connecting and communcating. If you create a **TcpClient** using any other constructor, the underlying service provider will assign the most appropriate local IP address and port number.

You must call the **Connect** method before sending and receiving data.

Example

See related example in the **System.Net.Sockets.TCPClient** class topic.

Requirements

Platforms: Windows 98, Windows NT 4.0,
Windows Millennium Edition, Windows 2000,
Windows XP Home Edition, Windows XP Professional,
Windows .NET Server family,
.NET Compact Framework - Windows CE .NET

TcpClient Constructor (String, Int32)

Initializes a new instance of the **TcpClient** class and connects to the specified port on the specified host.

[Visual Basic]
```
Public Sub New( _
   ByVal hostname As String, _
   ByVal port As Integer _
)
```

```
[C#]
public TcpClient(
    string hostname,
    int port
);
[C++]
public: TcpClient(
    String* hostname,
    int port
);
[JScript]
public function TcpClient(
    hostname : String,
    port : int
);
```

Parameters

hostname

The DNS name of the remote host to which you intend to connect.

port

The port number of the remote host to which you intend to connect.

Exceptions

Exception Type	Condition
ArgumentNullException	*hostname* is a null reference (**Nothing** in Visual Basic).
ArgumentOutOfRange-Exception	*port* is not between **MinPort** and **MaxPort**.
SocketException	An error occurred when accessing the socket. See the Remarks section for more information.

Remarks

This constructor creates a new **TcpClient** and makes a synchronous connection attempt to the provided host name and port number. The underlying service provider will assign the most appropriate local IP address and port number. **TcpClient** will block until it either connects or fails. This constructor allows you to initialize, resolve the DNS host name, and connect in one convenient step.

> **Note** If you receive a **SocketException**, use **SocketException.ErrorCode** to obtain the specific error code. Once you have obtained this code, you can refer to the Windows Socket Version 2 API error code documentation in MSDN for a detailed description of the error.

Example

[Visual Basic, C#] The following example demonstrates how to create an instance of the **TcpClient** class using a host name and port number.

```
[Visual Basic]
'Creates a TCPClient using hostname and port.
Try
    Dim tcpClientB As New TcpClient("www.contoso.com", 11000)
Catch e As Exception
    Console.WriteLine(e.ToString())
End Try
```

```
[C#]
//Creates a TCPClient using hostname and port.
try{
```

```
    TcpClient tcpClientB = new TcpClient("www.contoso.com", 11000);
}
catch (Exception e ) {
        Console.WriteLine(e.ToString());
}
```

Requirements

Platforms: Windows 98, Windows NT 4.0, Windows Millennium Edition, Windows 2000, Windows XP Home Edition, Windows XP Professional, Windows .NET Server family, .NET Compact Framework - Windows CE .NET

TcpClient.Active Property

Gets or set a value that indicates whether a connection has been made.

```
[Visual Basic]
Protected Property Active As Boolean
[C#]
protected bool Active {get; set;}
[C++]
protected: __property bool get_Active();
protected: __property void set_Active(bool);
[JScript]
protected function get Active() : Boolean;
protected function set Active(Boolean);
```

Property Value

true if the connection has been made; otherwise, **false**.

Remarks

Classes deriving from **TcpClient** can use this property to determine if a connection attempt has succeeded. It does not monitor the ongoing connection state of **TcpClient**. If the remote host closes the connection, **Active** will not be updated. If you are deriving from **TcpClient** and require closer attention to the connection state, use the **Connected** property of the **Socket** returned by the **Client** method.

Example

See related example in the **System.Net.Sockets.TCPClient** class topic.

Requirements

Platforms: Windows 98, Windows NT 4.0, Windows Millennium Edition, Windows 2000, Windows XP Home Edition, Windows XP Professional, Windows .NET Server family

TcpClient.Client Property

Gets or sets the underlying **Socket**.

```
[Visual Basic]
Protected Property Client As Socket
[C#]
protected Socket Client {get; set;}
[C++]
protected: __property Socket* get_Client();
protected: __property void set_Client(Socket*);
[JScript]
protected function get Client() : Socket;
protected function set Client(Socket);
```

Property Value

The underlying network **Socket**.

Remarks

TcpClient creates a **Socket** to send and receive data over a network. Classes deriving from **TcpClient** can use this property to get or set this **Socket**. Use the underlying **Socket** returned from **Client** if you require access beyond that which **TcpClient** provides. You can also use **Client** to set the underlying **Socket** to an existing **Socket**. This might be useful if you want to take advantage of the simplicity of **TcpClient** using a pre-existing **Socket**.

Example

See related example in the **System.Net.Sockets.TCPClient** class topic.

Requirements

Platforms: Windows 98, Windows NT 4.0, Windows Millennium Edition, Windows 2000, Windows XP Home Edition, Windows XP Professional, Windows .NET Server family

TcpClient.LingerState Property

Gets or sets information about the sockets linger time.

```
[Visual Basic]
Public Property LingerState As LingerOption
[C#]
public LingerOption LingerState {get; set;}
[C++]
public: __property LingerOption* get_LingerState();
public: __property void set_LingerState(LingerOption*);
[JScript]
public function get LingerState() : LingerOption;
public function set LingerState(LingerOption);
```

Property Value

A **LingerOption**. By default, lingering is enabled with a linger time of 0 seconds.

Remarks

This property controls the length of time that the TCP connection will remain open after a call to **Close** when data remains to be sent. When you call the **Write** method, data is placed in the outgoing network buffer. This property can be used to ensure that this data is sent to the remote host before the **Close** method drops the connection.

To enable lingering, create a **LingerOption** containing the disired values, and set this property to that **LingerOption**. If the **Enabled** property of the **LingerOption** is **true**, then data is sent to the network with a time-out of **LingerOption.LingerTime** seconds. Once the data is sent, or if the time-out expires, the connection is closed and any unsent data is lost. If the **Enabled** property of the **LingerOption** is **false**, then the connection closes immediately after a call to the **Close** method, even if data remains to be sent.

Example

See related example in the **System.Net.Sockets.TCPClient** class topic.

Requirements

Platforms: Windows 98, Windows NT 4.0, Windows Millennium Edition, Windows 2000, Windows XP Home Edition, Windows XP Professional, Windows .NET Server family, .NET Compact Framework - Windows CE .NET

TcpClient.NoDelay Property

Gets or sets a value that disables a delay when send or receive buffers are not full.

```
[Visual Basic]
Public Property NoDelay As Boolean
[C#]
public bool NoDelay {get; set;}
[C++]
public: __property bool get_NoDelay();
public: __property void set_NoDelay(bool);
[JScript]
public function get NoDelay() : Boolean;
public function set NoDelay(Boolean);
```

Property Value

true if the delay is disabled, otherwise **false**. The default value is **false**.

Remarks

When **NoDelay** is **false**, a **TcpClient** does not send a packet over the network until it has collected a significant amount of outgoing data. Because of the amount of overhead in a TCP segment, sending small amounts of data is inefficient. However, situations do exist where you need to send very small amounts of data or expect immediate responses from each packet you send. Your decision should weigh the relative importance of network efficiency versus application requirements.

Example

[Visual Basic, C#] The following example enables the delay. It then checks the value of **NoDelay** to verify that the property was successfully set.

```
[Visual Basic]
' Sends data immediately upon calling NetworkStream.Write.
tcpClient.NoDelay = True

' Determines if the delay is enabled by using the NoDelay property.
If tcpClient.NoDelay = True Then
   Console.WriteLine(("The delay was set successfully to " +
tcpClient.NoDelay.ToString()))
End If
```

```
[C#]
// Sends data immediately upon calling NetworkStream.Write.
tcpClient.NoDelay = true;

// Determines if the delay is enabled by using the NoDelay property.
if (tcpClient.NoDelay == true)
   Console.WriteLine("The delay was set successfully to " +
      tcpClient.NoDelay.ToString());
```

Requirements

Platforms: Windows 98, Windows NT 4.0, Windows Millennium Edition, Windows 2000, Windows XP Home Edition, Windows XP Professional, Windows .NET Server family, .NET Compact Framework - Windows CE .NET

TcpClient.ReceiveBufferSize Property

Gets or sets the size of the receive buffer.

```
[Visual Basic]
Public Property ReceiveBufferSize As Integer
[C#]
public int ReceiveBufferSize {get; set;}
[C++]
public: __property int get_ReceiveBufferSize();
public: __property void set_ReceiveBufferSize(int);
[JScript]
public function get ReceiveBufferSize() : int;
public function set ReceiveBufferSize(int);
```

Property Value

The size of the receive buffer, in bytes. The default value is 8192 bytes.

Remarks

The **ReceiveBufferSize** property gets or sets the number of bytes that you are expecting to store in the receive buffer for each read operation. This property actually manipulates the network buffer space allocated for receiving incoming data.

Your network buffer should be at least as large as your application buffer to ensure that the desired data will be available when you call the **NetworkStream.Read** method. Use the **ReceiveBufferSize** property to set this size. If your application will be receiving bulk data, you should pass the **Read** method a very large application buffer.

If the network buffer is smaller than the amount of data you request in the **Read** method, you will not be able to retrieve the desired amount of data in one read operation. This incurs the overhead of additional calls to the **Read** method.

Example

[Visual Basic, C#] The following example sets and gets the receive buffer size.

```
[Visual Basic]
' Sets the receive buffer size using the ReceiveBufferSize
public property.
tcpClient.ReceiveBufferSize = 1024

' Gets the receive buffer size using the ReceiveBufferSize
public property.
If tcpClient.ReceiveBufferSize = 1024 Then
   Console.WriteLine(("The receive buffer was successfully
set to " + tcpClient.ReceiveBufferSize.ToString()))
End If
```

```
[C#]
// sets the receive buffer size using the ReceiveBufferSize
public property.
tcpClient.ReceiveBufferSize = 1024;

// gets the receive buffer size using the ReceiveBufferSize
public property.
if (tcpClient.ReceiveBufferSize == 1024)
   Console.WriteLine("The receive buffer was successfully
set to " +
      tcpClient.ReceiveBufferSize.ToString());
```

Requirements

Platforms: Windows 98, Windows NT 4.0, Windows Millennium Edition, Windows 2000, Windows XP Home Edition, Windows XP Professional, Windows .NET Server family, .NET Compact Framework - Windows CE .NET

TcpClient.ReceiveTimeout Property

Gets or sets the amount of time a **TcpClient** will wait to receive data once a read operation is initiated.

```
[Visual Basic]
Public Property ReceiveTimeout As Integer
[C#]
public int ReceiveTimeout {get; set;}
[C++]
public: __property int get_ReceiveTimeout();
public: __property void set_ReceiveTimeout(int);
[JScript]
public function get ReceiveTimeout() : int;
public function set ReceiveTimeout(int);
```

Property Value

The time-out value of the connection in milliseconds. The default value is 0.

Remarks

The **ReceiveTimeout** property determines the amount of time that the **Read** method will block until it is able to receive data. This time is measured in milliseconds. If the time-out expires before **Read** successfully completes, **TcpClient** will throw a **SocketException**. There is no time-out by default.

Example

[Visual Basic, C#] The following example sets and gets the receive time out.

```
[Visual Basic]
' Sets the receive time out using the ReceiveTimeout public property.
tcpClient.ReceiveTimeout = 5

' Gets the receive time out using the ReceiveTimeout public property.
If tcpClient.ReceiveTimeout = 5 Then
   Console.WriteLine(("The receive time out limit was
successfully set " + tcpClient.ReceiveTimeout.ToString()))
End If
```

```
[C#]
// Sets the receive time out using the ReceiveTimeout public property.
tcpClient.ReceiveTimeout = 5;

// Gets the receive time out using the ReceiveTimeout public property.
if (tcpClient.ReceiveTimeout == 5)
   Console.WriteLine("The receive time out limit was
successfully set " +
      tcpClient.ReceiveTimeout.ToString());
```

Requirements

Platforms: Windows 98, Windows NT 4.0, Windows Millennium Edition, Windows 2000, Windows XP Home Edition, Windows XP Professional, Windows .NET Server family

TcpClient.SendBufferSize Property

Gets or sets the size of the send buffer.

```
[Visual Basic]
Public Property SendBufferSize As Integer
[C#]
public int SendBufferSize {get; set;}
[C++]
public: __property int get_SendBufferSize();
public: __property void set_SendBufferSize(int);
```

```
[JScript]
public function get SendBufferSize() : int;
public function set SendBufferSize(int);
```

Property Value

The size of the send buffer, in bytes. The default value is 8192 bytes.

Remarks

The **SendBufferSize** property gets or sets the number of bytes that you are expecting to send in each call to the **NetworkStream.Write** method. This property actually manipulates the network buffer space allocated for send operation.

Your network buffer should be at least as large as your application buffer to ensure that the desired data will be stored and sent in one operation. Use the **SendBufferSize** property to set this size. If your application will be sending bulk data, you should pass the **Write** method a very large application buffer.

If the network buffer is smaller than the amount of data you provide the **Write** method, several network send operations will be performed for every call you make to the **Write** method. You can achieve greater data throughput by ensuring that your network buffer is at least as large as your application buffer.

Example

[Visual Basic, C#] The following example sets and gets the send buffer size.

```
[Visual Basic]
'Sets the send buffer size using the SendBufferSize public property.
tcpClient.SendBufferSize = 1024

' Gets the send buffer size using the SendBufferSize public property.
If tcpClient.SendBufferSize = 1024 Then
    Console.WriteLine(("The send buffer was successfully set
to " + tcpClient.SendBufferSize.ToString()))
End If
```

```
[C#]
//sets the send buffer size using the SendBufferSize public property.
tcpClient.SendBufferSize = 1024;

// gets the send buffer size using the SendBufferSize public property.
if (tcpClient.SendBufferSize == 1024)
    Console.WriteLine("The send buffer was successfully set to " +
        tcpClient.SendBufferSize.ToString());
```

Requirements

Platforms: Windows 98, Windows NT 4.0, Windows Millennium Edition, Windows 2000, Windows XP Home Edition, Windows XP Professional, Windows .NET Server family, .NET Compact Framework - Windows CE .NET

TcpClient.SendTimeout Property

Gets or sets the amount of time a **TcpClient** will wait for a send operation to complete successfully.

```
[Visual Basic]
Public Property SendTimeout As Integer
[C#]
public int SendTimeout {get; set;}
[C++]
public: __property int get_SendTimeout();
public: __property void set_SendTimeout(int);
```

```
[JScript]
public function get SendTimeout() : int;
public function set SendTimeout(int);
```

Property Value

The send time-out value, in milliseconds. The default is 0.

Remarks

The **SendTimeout** property determines the amount of time that the **Send** method will block until it is able to return successfully. This time is measured in milliseconds.

After you call the **Write** method, the underlying **Socket** returns the number of bytes actually sent to the host. The **SendTimeout** property determines the amount of time a **TcpClient** will wait before receiving the number of bytes returned. If the time-out expires before the **Send** method successfully completes, **TcpClient** will throw a **SocketException**. There is no time-out by default.

Example

[Visual Basic, C#] The following example sets and gets the **SendTimeout** value.

```
[Visual Basic]
' Sets the send time out using the SendTimeout public property.
tcpClient.SendTimeout = 5

' Gets the send time out using the SendTimeout public property.
If tcpClient.SendTimeout = 5 Then
    Console.WriteLine(("The send time out limit was
successfully set " + tcpClient.SendTimeout.ToString()))
End If
```

```
[C#]
// sets the send time out using the SendTimeout public property.
tcpClient.SendTimeout = 5;

// gets the send time out using the SendTimeout public property.
if (tcpClient.SendTimeout == 5)
    Console.WriteLine("The send time out limit was
successfully set " +
        tcpClient.SendTimeout.ToString());
```

Requirements

Platforms: Windows 98, Windows NT 4.0, Windows Millennium Edition, Windows 2000, Windows XP Home Edition, Windows XP Professional, Windows .NET Server family

TcpClient.Close Method

Closes the TCP connection and releases all resources associated with the **TcpClient**.

```
[Visual Basic]
Public Sub Close()
[C#]
public void Close();
[C++]
public: void Close();
[JScript]
public function Close();
```

Exceptions

Exception Type	Condition
SocketException	An error occurred when accessing the socket. See the Remarks section for more information.

Remarks

The **Close** method closes the TCP connection. It calls the **Dispose** method passing a **true** value to release all managed and unmanaged resources associated with the **TcpClient**. These resources include the underlying **Socket** used for connecting with the remote host, and the **NetworkStream** used to send and receive data.

> **Note** If you receive a **SocketException**, use **SocketException.ErrorCode** to obtain the specific error code. Once you have obtained this code, you can refer to the Windows Socket Version 2 API error code documentation in MSDN for a detailed description of the error.

Example

[Visual Basic, C#] The following example demonstrates closing a **TcpClient** by calling the **Close** method.

```
[Visual Basic]
' Uses the Close public method to close the network stream and socket.
tcpClient.Close()
    End Sub 'MyTcpClientCommunicator
```

```
[C#]
// Uses the Close public method to close the network stream and socket.
tcpClient.Close();
```

Requirements

Platforms: Windows 98, Windows NT 4.0, Windows Millennium Edition, Windows 2000, Windows XP Home Edition, Windows XP Professional, Windows .NET Server family, .NET Compact Framework - Windows CE .NET

TcpClient.Connect Method

Connects the client to a remote TCP host using the specified host name and port number.

Overload List

Connects the client to a remote TCP host using the specified remote network endpoint.

Supported by the .NET Compact Framework.

> [Visual Basic] **Overloads Public Sub Connect(IPEndPoint)**
> [C#] **public void Connect(IPEndPoint);**
> [C++] **public: void Connect(IPEndPoint*);**
> [JScript] **public function Connect(IPEndPoint);**

Connects the client to a remote TCP host using the specified IP address and port number.

Supported by the .NET Compact Framework.

> [Visual Basic] **Overloads Public Sub Connect(IPAddress, Integer)**
> [C#] **public void Connect(IPAddress, int);**
> [C++] **public: void Connect(IPAddress*, int);**
> [JScript] **public function Connect(IPAddress, int);**

Connects the client to the specified port on the specified host.

Supported by the .NET Compact Framework.

> [Visual Basic] **Overloads Public Sub Connect(String, Integer)**
> [C#] **public void Connect(string, int);**
> [C++] **public: void Connect(String*, int);**
> [JScript] **public function Connect(String, int);**

Example

[Visual Basic, C#] The following example uses the host name and port number to connect with a remote host.

> [Visual Basic, C#] **Note** This example shows how to use one of the overloaded versions of **Connect**. For other examples that might be available, see the individual overload topics.

```
[Visual Basic]
'Uses a host name and port number to establish a socket connection.
Dim tcpClient As New TcpClient()
Try
    tcpClient.Connect("www.contoso.com", 11002)
Catch e As Exception
    Console.WriteLine(e.ToString())
End Try
```

```
[C#]
//Uses a host name and port number to establish a socket connection.
    TcpClient tcpClient = new TcpClient();
    try{
    tcpClient.Connect("www.contoso.com", 11002);
    }
    catch (Exception e ) {
        Console.WriteLine(e.ToString());
    }
```

TcpClient.Connect Method (IPEndPoint)

Connects the client to a remote TCP host using the specified remote network endpoint.

```
[Visual Basic]
Overloads Public Sub Connect( _
    ByVal remoteEP As IPEndPoint _
)
[C#]
public void Connect(
    IPEndPoint remoteEP
);
[C++]
public: void Connect(
    IPEndPoint* remoteEP
);
[JScript]
public function Connect(
    remoteEP : IPEndPoint
);
```

Parameters

remoteEP
    The **IPEndPoint** to which you intend to connect.

Exceptions

Exception Type	Condition
ArgumentNullException	*remoteEp* is a null reference (**Nothing** in Visual Basic).
SocketException	An error occurred when accessing the socket. See the Remarks section for more information.
ObjectDisposedException	The **TcpClient** is closed.

Remarks

Call this method to establish a synchronous remote host connection to the specified **IPEndPoint**. Before you call **Connect** you must create an instance of the **IPEndPoint** class using an IP address and a port number. Use this **IPEndPoint** as the *remoteEP* parameter. The **Connect** method will block until it either connects or fails. After connecting with the remote host, use the **GetStream** method to obtain the underlying **NetworkStream**. Use this **NetworkStream** to send and receive data.

> **Note** If you receive a **SocketException**, use **SocketException.ErrorCode** to obtain the specific error code. Once you have obtained this code, you can refer to the Windows Socket Version 2 API error code documentation in MSDN for a detailed description of the error.

Example

[Visual Basic, C#] The following example uses an **IPEndPoint** to connect with a remote host.

[Visual Basic]
```
Uses a remote end point to establish a socket connection.
Dim tcpClient As New TcpClient()
Dim ipAddress As IPAddress = _
Dns.Resolve("www.contoso.com").AddressList(0)
Dim ipEndPoint As New IPEndPoint(ipAddress, 11004)
Try
    tcpClient.Connect(ipEndPoint)
Catch e As Exception
    Console.WriteLine(e.ToString())
End Try
```

[C#]
```
//Uses a remote end point to establish a socket connection.
TcpClient tcpClient = new TcpClient();
IPAddress ipAddress = Dns.Resolve("www.contoso.com").AddressList[0];
IPEndPoint ipEndPoint = new IPEndPoint(ipAddress, 11004);
try{
    tcpClient.Connect(ipEndPoint);
}
catch (Exception e ) {
        Console.WriteLine(e.ToString());
        }
```

Requirements

Platforms: Windows 98, Windows NT 4.0, Windows Millennium Edition, Windows 2000, Windows XP Home Edition, Windows XP Professional, Windows .NET Server family, .NET Compact Framework - Windows CE .NET

TcpClient.Connect Method (IPAddress, Int32)

Connects the client to a remote TCP host using the specified IP address and port number.

[Visual Basic]
```
Overloads Public Sub Connect( _
   ByVal address As IPAddress, _
   ByVal port As Integer _
)
```
[C#]
```
public void Connect(
   IPAddress address,
   int port
);
```

[C++]
```
public: void Connect(
   IPAddress* address,
   int port
);
```
[JScript]
```
public function Connect(
   address : IPAddress,
   port : int
);
```

Parameters

address
   The **IPAddress** of the host to which you intend to connect.
port
   The port number to which you intend to connect.

Exceptions

Exception Type	Condition
ArgumentNullException	*address* parameter is a null reference (**Nothing** in Visual Basic).
ArgumentOutOfRange-Exception	The *port* is not between **MinPort** and **MaxPort**.
SocketException	An error occurred when accessing the socket. See the Remarks section for more information.
ObjectDisposedException	**TcpClient** is closed.

Remarks

Call this method to establish a synchronous remote host connection to the specified **IPAddress** and port number. The **Connect** method will block until it either connects or fails. After connecting with the remote host, use the **GetStream** method to obtain the underlying **NetworkStream**. Use this **NetworkStream** to send and receive data.

> **Note** If you receive a **SocketException**, use **SocketException.ErrorCode** to obtain the specific error code. Once you have obtained this code, you can refer to the Windows Socket Version 2 API error code documentation in MSDN for a detailed description of the error.

Example

[Visual Basic, C#] The following example uses an IP Address and port number to connect with a remote host.

[Visual Basic]
```
'Uses the IP address and port number to establish a socket connection.
Dim tcpClient As New TcpClient()
Dim ipAddress As IPAddress = _
Dns.Resolve("www.contoso.com").AddressList(0)
Try
    tcpClient.Connect(ipAddress, 11003)
Catch e As Exception
    Console.WriteLine(e.ToString())
End Try
```

[C#]
```
//Uses the IP address and port number to establish a socket connection.
TcpClient tcpClient = new TcpClient();
IPAddress ipAddress = Dns.Resolve("www.contoso.com").AddressList[0];
try{
    tcpClient.Connect(ipAddress, 11003);
}
catch (Exception e ) {
        Console.WriteLine(e.ToString());
}
```

Requirements

Platforms: Windows 98, Windows NT 4.0,
Windows Millennium Edition, Windows 2000,
Windows XP Home Edition, Windows XP Professional,
Windows .NET Server family,
.NET Compact Framework - Windows CE .NET

TcpClient.Connect Method (String, Int32)

Connects the client to the specified port on the specified host.

```
[Visual Basic]
Overloads Public Sub Connect( _
   ByVal hostname As String, _
   ByVal port As Integer _
)
[C#]
public void Connect(
   string hostname,
   int port
);
[C++]
public: void Connect(
   String* hostname,
   int port
);
[JScript]
public function Connect(
   hostname : String,
   port : int
);
```

Parameters

hostname
> The DNS name of the remote host to which you intend to
> connect.

port
> The port number of the remote host to which you intend to
> connect.

Exceptions

Exception Type	Condition
ArgumentNullException	*hostname* is a null reference (**Nothing** in Visual Basic).
ArgumentOutOfRange-Exception	*port* is not between **MinPort** and **MaxPort**.
SocketException	An error occurred when accessing the socket. See the Remarks section for more information.
ObjectDisposedException	**TcpClient** is closed.

Remarks

Call this method to establish a synchronous remote host connection to
the specified host name and port number. The **Connect** method will
block until it either connects or fails. After connecting with the remote
host, use the **GetStream** method to obtain the underlying
NetworkStream. Use this **NetworkStream** to send and receive data.

> **Note** If you receive a **SocketException**, use
> **SocketException.ErrorCode** to obtain the specific error code.
> Once you have obtained this code, you can refer to the
> Windows Socket Version 2 API error code documentation in
> MSDN for a detailed description of the error.

Example

[Visual Basic, C#] The following example uses the host name and
port number to connect with a remote host.

```
[Visual Basic]
'Uses a host name and port number to establish a socket connection.
Dim tcpClient As New TcpClient()
Try
   tcpClient.Connect("www.contoso.com", 11002)
Catch e As Exception
   Console.WriteLine(e.ToString())
End Try

[C#]
//Uses a host name and port number to establish a socket connection.
   TcpClient tcpClient = new TcpClient();
   try{
   tcpClient.Connect("www.contoso.com", 11002);
   }
   catch (Exception e ) {
       Console.WriteLine(e.ToString());
   }
```

Requirements

Platforms: Windows 98, Windows NT 4.0,
Windows Millennium Edition, Windows 2000,
Windows XP Home Edition, Windows XP Professional,
Windows .NET Server family,
.NET Compact Framework - Windows CE .NET

TcpClient.Dispose Method

Releases the unmanaged resources used by the **TcpClient** and
optionally releases the managed resources.

```
[Visual Basic]
Protected Overridable Sub Dispose( _
   ByVal disposing As Boolean _
)
[C#]
protected virtual void Dispose(
   bool disposing
);
[C++]
protected: virtual void Dispose(
   bool disposing
);
[JScript]
protected function Dispose(
   disposing : Boolean
);
```

Parameters

disposing
> **true** to release both managed and unmanaged resources; **false** to
> release only unmanaged resources.

Remarks

This method is called by the public **Dispose()** method and the **Finalize** method. **Dispose()** invokes this method with the *disposing* parameter set to **true**. **Finalize** invokes this method with *disposing* set to **false**.

When the *disposing* parameter is **true**, this method releases all resources held by any managed objects that this **TcpClient** references. It does this by invoking the **Dispose()** method of each referenced object.

Notes to Inheritors: **Dispose** can be called multiple times by other objects. When overriding **Dispose(Boolean)**, be careful not to reference objects that have been previously disposed of in an earlier call to **Dispose**. For more information about how to implement **Dispose(Boolean)**, see **Implementing a Dispose Method**.

For more information about **Dispose** and **Finalize**, see **Cleaning Up Unmanaged Resources** and **Overriding the Finalize Method**.

Example

The following example uses a derived class to demonstrate the **Dispose** method. Specifying **true** causes both managed and unmanaged resources to be released.

[Visual Basic]
```
' This derived class demonstrates the use of three protected
properties belonging to the TcpClient Class.
Public Class MyTcpClientDerivedClass
    Inherits TcpClient

    Public Sub New()
    End Sub 'New

    Public Sub UsingProtectedMethods()

        'Uses the protected 'Active' property  belonging to
the TcpClient base class
        'to determine if a connection is established.
        If Me.Active Then
            ' Calls the protected 'Client' property belonging
to the TcpClient base class.
            Dim s As Socket = Me.Client
            'Uses the Socket returned by Client to set an option
that is not available using TcpClient.
            s.SetSocketOption(SocketOptionLevel.Socket,
SocketOptionName.Broadcast, 1)
        End If
        'To free all resources, calls protected virtual
method Dispose belonging to the TcpClient base class.
        Me.Dispose(True)
        GC.SuppressFinalize(Me)
    End Sub 'UsingProtectedMethods
End Class 'MyTcpClientDerivedClass
```

[C#]
```
// This derived class demonstrates the use of three protected
methods belonging to the TcpClient class
public class MyTcpClientDerivedClass : TcpClient{

// Constructor for the derived class.
public MyTcpClientDerivedClass() : base(){
}
public void UsingProtectedMethods(){

// Uses the protected 'Active' property belonging to the
TcpClient base class
// to determine if a connection is established.
if (this.Active){
    // Calls the protected 'Client' property belonging to
the TcpClient base class.
    Socket s = this.Client;
    // Uses the Socket returned by Client to set an option
```

that is not available using TcpClient.
```
    s.SetSocketOption(SocketOptionLevel.Socket,
SocketOptionName.Broadcast, 1);
    }
    // To free all resources, calls the protected virtual
method Dispose belonging to the TcpClient base class.
    this.Dispose(true);
    GC.SuppressFinalize(this);

}

}
```

[C++]
```
// This derived class demonstrates the use of three protected
methods belonging to the TcpClient class
__gc public class MyTcpClientDerivedClass : public TcpClient{

    // Constructor for the derived class.
public:
    void UsingProtectedMethods() {

        // Uses the protected 'Active' property belonging to
the TcpClient base class
        // to determine if a connection is established.
        if (this->Active) {
            // Calls the protected 'Client' property belonging
to the TcpClient base class.
            Socket* s = this->Client;
            // Uses the Socket returned by Client to set an
option that is not available using TcpClient.
            s->SetSocketOption(SocketOptionLevel::Socket,
SocketOptionName::Broadcast, 1);
        }
        // To free all resources, calls the protected virtual
method Dispose belonging to the TcpClient base class.
        this->Dispose(true);
        GC::SuppressFinalize(this);
    }
};
```

[JScript]
```
// The purpose of this class is to demonstrate the use of
three protected methods belonging to the TcpClient Class
public class MyTcpClientDerivedClass extends TcpClient{

// constructor
public function MyTcpClientDerivedClass(){
    super();
}

public function importProtectedMethods(){

    //Use the protected property 'Active' belonging to the
TcpClient base class.
    //This determines if connection is established.
    if (this.Active){
        //Calling the protected property 'client' belonging to
the TcpClient base class.
        var s : Socket = this.Client;
        //Suppose you want to set an option that is not available
by just import TcpClient object.
        s.SetSocketOption(SocketOptionLevel.Socket,
SocketOptionName.Broadcast, 1);
    }
    //Call protected virtual method Dispose belonging to the
TcpClient base class to free all resources.
    this.Dispose(true);
    GC.SuppressFinalize(this);

}

}
```

Requirements

Platforms: Windows 98, Windows NT 4.0,
Windows Millennium Edition, Windows 2000,
Windows XP Home Edition, Windows XP Professional,
Windows .NET Server family,
.NET Compact Framework - Windows CE .NET

TcpClient.Finalize Method

Frees resources used by the **TcpClient** class.

[C#] In C#, finalizers are expressed using destructor syntax.

[C++] In C++, finalizers are expressed using destructor syntax.

```
[Visual Basic]
Overrides Protected Sub Finalize()
[C#]
~TcpClient();
[C++]
~TcpClient();
[JScript]
protected override function Finalize();
```

Remarks

This method overrides **Object.Finalize**. Application code should not
call this method; an object's **Finalize** method is automatically
invoked during garbage collection, unless finalization by the garbage
collector has been disabled by a call to the **GC.SuppressFinalize**
method.

The **TcpClient** class finalizer closes the TCP connection and
releases all managed resources associated with the **TcpClient**. These
resources include the underlying **Socket** used for connecting with
the remote host, and the **NetworkStream** used to send and receive
data. The finalizer does not release any unmanaged resources.

Requirements

Platforms: Windows 98, Windows NT 4.0,
Windows Millennium Edition, Windows 2000,
Windows XP Home Edition, Windows XP Professional,
Windows .NET Server family,
.NET Compact Framework - Windows CE .NET

TcpClient.GetStream Method

Returns the **NetworkStream** used to send and receive data.

```
[Visual Basic]
Public Function GetStream() As NetworkStream
[C#]
public NetworkStream GetStream();
[C++]
public: NetworkStream* GetStream();
[JScript]
public function GetStream() : NetworkStream;
```

Return Value

The underlying **NetworkStream**.

Exceptions

Exception Type	Condition
InvalidOperationException	The **TcpClient** is not connected to a remote host.

Exception Type	Condition
ObjectDisposedException	The **TcpClient** has been closed.

Remarks

GetStream returns a **NetworkStream** that you can use to send and
receive data. The **NetworkStream** class inherits from the **Stream**
class, which provides a rich collection of methods and properties
used to facilitate network communications.

You must call the **Connect** method first, or the **GetStream** method
will throw an **InvalidOperationException**. Once you have obtained
the **NetworkStream**, call the **Write** method to send data to the
remote host. Call the **Read** method to receive data arriving from the
remote host. Both of these methods block until the specified
operation is performed. You can avoid blocking on a read operation
by checking the **DataAvailable** property. A **true** value means that
data has arrived from the remote host and is available for reading. In
this case, **Read** is guaranteed to complete immediately. If the remote
host has shutdown its connection, **Read** will immediately return
with zero bytes.

> **Note** You do not need to close the **NetworkStream** when you
> are through sending and receiving data. Closing **TcpClient** will
> release the **NetworkStream** to the garbage collector.

> **Note** If you receive a **SocketException**, use
> **SocketException.ErrorCode** to obtain the specific error code.
> Once you have obtained this code, you can refer to the
> Windows Socket Version 2 API error code documentation in
> MSDN for a detailed description of the error.

Example

[Visual Basic, C#] The following example uses **GetStream** to obtain
the underlying **NetworkStream**. After obtaining the
NetworkStream, it sends and receives using its **Write** and **Read**
methods.

```
[Visual Basic]
Dim tcpClient As New TcpClient()
' Uses the GetStream public method to return the NetworkStream.
Try
    Dim networkStream As NetworkStream = tcpClient.GetStream()
    If networkStream.CanWrite Then
        Dim sendBytes As [Byte]() = Encoding.ASCII.GetBytes         ⌐
("Is anybody there?")
        networkStream.Write(sendBytes, 0, sendBytes.Length)
    Else
        Console.WriteLine("You cannot write data to this stream.")
        tcpClient.Close()
        Return
    End If
    If networkStream.CanRead Then

        ' Reads the NetworkStream into a byte buffer.
        Dim bytes(tcpClient.ReceiveBufferSize) As Byte
        ' Read can return anything from 0 to numBytesToRead.
        ' This method blocks until at least one byte is read.
        networkStream.Read(bytes, 0, CInt(tcpClient.ReceiveBufferSize))

        ' Returns the data received from the host to the console.
        Dim returndata As String = Encoding.ASCII.GetString(bytes)
        Console.WriteLine(("This is what the host returned to        ⌐
you: " + returndata))
    Else
        Console.WriteLine("You cannot read data from this stream.")
        tcpClient.Close()
        Return
```

```
  End If
atch e As Exception
   Console.WriteLine(e.ToString())
nd Try

C#]
cpClient tcpClient = new TcpClient();
/ Uses the GetStream public method to return the NetworkStream.
ry{
    NetworkStream networkStream = tcpClient.GetStream();
    if(networkStream.CanWrite){
        Byte[] sendBytes = Encoding.ASCII.GetBytes("Is
nybody there?");
        networkStream.Write(sendBytes, 0, sendBytes.Length);
    }
    else{
        Console.WriteLine("You cannot write data to this stream.");
        tcpClient.Close();
        return;
    }
    if(networkStream.CanRead){

        // Reads NetworkStream into a byte buffer.
        byte[] bytes = new byte[tcpClient.ReceiveBufferSize];
        // Read can return anything from 0 to numBytesToRead.
        // This method blocks until at least one byte is read.
        networkStream.Read(bytes, 0, (int) tcpClient.ReceiveBufferSize);

        // Returns the data received from the host to the console.
        string returndata = Encoding.ASCII.GetString(bytes);
        Console.WriteLine("This is what the host returned to
ou: " + returndata);
    }
    else{
        Console.WriteLine("You cannot read data from this stream.");
        tcpClient.Close();
        return;
    }
}
catch (Exception e ) {
            Console.WriteLine(e.ToString());
    }
```

Requirements

Platforms: Windows 98, Windows NT 4.0,
Windows Millennium Edition, Windows 2000,
Windows XP Home Edition, Windows XP Professional,
Windows .NET Server family,
.NET Compact Framework - Windows CE .NET

TcpClient.IDisposable.Dispose Method

This member supports the .NET Framework infrastructure and is not
intended to be used directly from your code.

```
[Visual Basic]
Private Sub Dispose() Implements IDisposable.Dispose
[C#]
void IDisposable.Dispose();
[C++]
private: void IDisposable::Dispose();
[JScript]
private function IDisposable.Dispose();
```

TcpListener Class

Listens for connections from TCP network clients.

System.Object
  System.Net.Sockets.TcpListener

```
[Visual Basic]
Public Class TcpListener
[C#]
public class TcpListener
[C++]
public __gc class TcpListener
[JScript]
public class TcpListener
```

Thread Safety

Any public static (**Shared** in Visual Basic) members of this type are safe for multithreaded operations. Any instance members are not guaranteed to be thread safe.

Remarks

The **TcpListener** class provides simple methods that listen for and accept incoming connection requests in blocking synchronous mode. You can use either a **TcpClient** or a **Socket** to connect with a **TcpListener**. Create a **TcpListener** using an **IPEndPoint**, a Local IP address and port number, or just a port number. Specify **Any** for the local IP address and 0 for the local port number if you want the underlying service provider to assign those values for you. If you choose to do this, you can use the **LocalEndpoint** to identify the assigned information.

Use the **Start** method to begin listening for incoming connection requests. **Start** will queue incoming connections until you either call the **Stop** method or it has queued **MaxConnections**. Use either **AcceptSocket** or **AcceptTcpClient** to pull a connection from the incoming connection request queue. These two methods will block. If you want to avoid blocking, you can use the **Pending** method first to determine if connection requests are available in the queue.

Call the **Stop** method to close the **TcpListener**.

> **Note** The **Stop** method does not close any accepted connections. You are responsible for closing these separately.

Example

[Visual Basic, C#, C++] The following example creates a **TcpListener**.

```
[Visual Basic]
Public Shared Sub Main()

  Try
      ' Set the TcpListener on port 13000.
      Dim port As Int32 = 13000
      Dim localAddr As IPAddress = IPAddress.Parse("127.0.0.1")

      Dim server As New TcpListener(localAddr, port)

      ' Start listening for client requests.
      server.Start()

      ' Buffer for reading data
      Dim bytes(1024) As [Byte]
      Dim data As [String] = Nothing

      ' Enter the listening loop.
      While True
         Console.Write("Waiting for a connection... ")

         ' Perform a blocking call to accept requests.
         ' You could also user server.AcceptSocket() here.
         Dim client As TcpClient = server.AcceptTcpClient()
         Console.WriteLine("Connected!")

         data = Nothing

         ' Get a stream object for reading and writing
         Dim stream As NetworkStream = client.GetStream()

         Dim i As Int32

         ' Loop to receive all the data sent by the client.
         i = stream.Read(bytes, 0, bytes.Length)
         While (i <> 0)
            ' Translate data bytes to a ASCII string.
            data = System.Text.Encoding.ASCII.GetString(bytes, 0, i)
            Console.WriteLine([String].Format("Received: {0}", data))

            ' Process the data sent by the client.
            data = data.ToUpper()

            Dim msg As [Byte]() =
System.Text.Encoding.ASCII.GetBytes(data)

            ' Send back a response.
            stream.Write(msg, 0, msg.Length)
            Console.WriteLine([String].Format("Sent: {0}", data))

            i = stream.Read(bytes, 0, bytes.Length)

         End While

         ' Shutdown and end connection
         client.Close()
      End While
   Catch e As SocketException
      Console.WriteLine("SocketException: {0}", e)
   End Try

   Console.WriteLine(ControlChars.Cr + "Hit enter to continue...")
   Console.Read()
End Sub 'Main
```

```
[C#]
public static void Main()
{

  try
  {
    // Set the TcpListener on port 13000.
    Int32 port = 13000;
    IPAddress localAddr = IPAddress.Parse("127.0.0.1");

    // TcpListener server = new TcpListener(port);
    TcpListener server = new TcpListener(localAddr, port);

    // Start listening for client requests.
    server.Start();

    // Buffer for reading data
    Byte[] bytes = new Byte[256];
    String data = null;

    // Enter the listening loop.
    while(true)
    {
      Console.Write("Waiting for a connection... ");

      // Perform a blocking call to accept requests.
      // You could also user server.AcceptSocket() here.
      TcpClient client = server.AcceptTcpClient();
      Console.WriteLine("Connected!");

      data = null;
```

```
// Get a stream object for reading and writing
NetworkStream stream = client.GetStream();

Int32 i;

// Loop to receive all the data sent by the client.
while((i = stream.Read(bytes, 0, bytes.Length))!=0)
{
  // Translate data bytes to a ASCII string.
  data = System.Text.Encoding.ASCII.GetString(bytes, 0, i);
  Console.WriteLine(String.Format("Received: {0}", data));

  // Process the data sent by the client.
  data = data.ToUpper();

  Byte[] msg = System.Text.Encoding.ASCII.GetBytes(data);

  // Send back a response.
  stream.Write(msg, 0, msg.Length);
  Console.WriteLine(String.Format("Sent: {0}", data));
}

// Shutdown and end connection
client.Close();
}
}
catch(SocketException e)
{
  Console.WriteLine("SocketException: {0}", e);
}

Console.WriteLine("\nHit enter to continue...");
Console.Read();
```

```
[C++]
void main() {
  try {
    // Set the TcpListener on port 13000.
    Int32 port = 13000;
    IPAddress* localAddr = IPAddress::Parse(S"127.0.0.1");

    // TcpListener* server = new TcpListener(port);
    TcpListener* server = new TcpListener(localAddr, port);

    // Start listening for client requests.
    server->Start();

    // Buffer for reading data
    Byte bytes[] = new Byte[256];
    String* data = 0;

    // Enter the listening loop.
    while (true) {
      Console::Write(S"Waiting for a connection... ");

      // Perform a blocking call to accept requests.
      // You could also user server.AcceptSocket() here.
      TcpClient* client = server->AcceptTcpClient();
      Console::WriteLine(S"Connected!");

      data = 0;

      // Get a stream Object* for reading and writing
      NetworkStream* stream = client->GetStream();

      Int32 i;

      // Loop to receive all the data sent by the client.
      while (i = stream->Read(bytes, 0, bytes->Length)) {
        // Translate data bytes to a ASCII String*.
        data = Text::Encoding::ASCII->GetString(bytes, 0, i);
        Console::WriteLine(String::Format(S"Received: {0}",
data));
```

```
        // Process the data sent by the client.
        data = data->ToUpper();

        Byte msg[] = Text::Encoding::ASCII->GetBytes(data);

        // Send back a response.
        stream->Write(msg, 0, msg->Length);
        Console::WriteLine(String::Format(S"Sent: {0}", data));
      }

      // Shutdown and end connection
      client->Close();
    }
  } catch (SocketException* e) {
    Console::WriteLine(S"SocketException: {0}", e);
  }

  Console::WriteLine(S"\nHit enter to continue...");
  Console::Read();
}
```

Requirements

Namespace: System.Net.Sockets

Platforms: Windows 98, Windows NT 4.0,
Windows Millennium Edition, Windows 2000,
Windows XP Home Edition, Windows XP Professional,
Windows .NET Server family,
.NET Compact Framework - Windows CE .NET

Assembly: System (in System.dll)

.NET Framework Security:

- **SocketPermission** to establish an outgoing connection or accept an incoming request.

TcpListener Constructor

Initializes a new instance of the **TcpListener** class.

Overload List

Obsolete: Initializes a new instance of the **TcpListener** class that listens on the specified port.

Supported by the .NET Compact Framework.

> [Visual Basic] **Public Sub New(Integer)**
>
> [C#] **public TcpListener(int);**
>
> [C++] **public: TcpListener(int);**
>
> [JScript] **public function TcpListener(int);**

Initializes a new instance of the **TcpListener** class with the specified local endpoint.

Supported by the .NET Compact Framework.

> [Visual Basic] **Public Sub New(IPEndPoint)**
>
> [C#] **public TcpListener(IPEndPoint);**
>
> [C++] **public: TcpListener(IPEndPoint*);**
>
> [JScript] **public function TcpListener(IPEndPoint);**

Initializes a new instance of the **TcpListener** class that listens for incoming connection attempts on the specified local IP address and port number.

Supported by the .NET Compact Framework.

> [Visual Basic] **Public Sub New(IPAddress, Integer)**
>
> [C#] **public TcpListener(IPAddress, int);**
>
> [C++] **public: TcpListener(IPAddress*, int);**
>
> [JScript] **public function TcpListener(IPAddress, int);**

TcpListener Constructor (Int32)

NOTE: This member is now obsolete.

Use TcpListener(IPAddress localaddr, int port).

Initializes a new instance of the **TcpListener** class that listens on the specified port.

```
[Visual Basic]
<Obsolete("Use TcpListener(IPAddress localaddr, int port).", _
    False)>
Public Sub New( _
    ByVal port As Integer _
)
[C#]
[Obsolete("Use TcpListener(IPAddress localaddr, int port).",
    false)]
public TcpListener(
    int port
);
[C++]
[Obsolete("Use TcpListener(IPAddress localaddr, int port).",
    false)]
public: TcpListener(
    int port
);
[JScript]
public
    Obsolete("Use TcpListener(IPAddress localaddr, int port).", false)
function TcpListener(
    port : int
);
```

Parameters

port

The port on which to listen for incoming connection attempts.

Exceptions

Exception Type	Condition
ArgumentOutOfRange-Exception	*port* is not between **MinPort** and **MaxPort**.

Remarks

This constructor is obsolete. Use **TcpListener** and **TcpListener**.

This constructor allows you to specify the port number on which to listen for incoming connection attempts. With this constructor, the underlying service provider assigns the most appropriate network address. If you do not care which local port is used, you can specify 0 for the port number. In this case, the service provider will assign an available port number between 1024 and 5000. If you use this approach, you can discover what local network address and port number has been assigned by using the **LocalEndpoint** property.

Call the **Start** method to begin listening for incoming connection attempts.

Requirements

Platforms: Windows 98, Windows NT 4.0, Windows Millennium Edition, Windows 2000, Windows XP Home Edition, Windows XP Professional, Windows .NET Server family, .NET Compact Framework - Windows CE .NET

TcpListener Constructor (IPEndPoint)

Initializes a new instance of the **TcpListener** class with the specified local endpoint.

```
[Visual Basic]
Public Sub New( _
    ByVal localEP As IPEndPoint _
)
[C#]
public TcpListener(
    IPEndPoint localEP
);
[C++]
public: TcpListener(
    IPEndPoint* localEP
);
[JScript]
public function TcpListener(
    localEP : IPEndPoint
);
```

Parameters

localEP

An **IPEndPoint** that represents the local endpoint to which to bind the listener **Socket**.

Exceptions

Exception Type	Condition
ArgumentNullException	*localEP* is a null reference (**Nothing** in Visual Basic).

Remarks

This constructor allows you to specify the local IP address and port number on which to listen for incoming connection attempts. Before using this construcor, you must create an **IPEndPoint** using the desired local IP address and port number. Pass this **IPEndPoint** to the constructor as the *localEP* parameter.

If you do not care which local address is assigned, you can create an **IPEndPoint** using **IPAddress.Any** as the address parameter, and the underlying service provider will assign the most appropriate network address. This might help simplify your application if you have multiple network interfaces. If you do not care which local port is used, you can create an **IPEndPoint** using 0 for the port number. In this case, the service provider will assign an available port number between 1024 and 5000. If you use this approach, you can discover what local network address and port number has been assigned by using the **LocalEndpoint** property.

Call the **Start** method to begin listening for incoming connection attempts.

Requirements

Platforms: Windows 98, Windows NT 4.0, Windows Millennium Edition, Windows 2000, Windows XP Home Edition, Windows XP Professional, Windows .NET Server family, .NET Compact Framework - Windows CE .NET

TcpListener Constructor (IPAddress, Int32)

Initializes a new instance of the **TcpListener** class that listens for incoming connection attempts on the specified local IP address and port number.

```
[Visual Basic]
Public Sub New( _
    ByVal localaddr As IPAddress, _
    ByVal port As Integer _
)
[C#]
public TcpListener(
    IPAddress localaddr,
    int port
);
[C++]
public: TcpListener(
    IPAddress* localaddr,
    int port
);
[JScript]
public function TcpListener(
    localaddr : IPAddress,
    port : int
);
```

Parameters

localaddr
    An **IPAddress** that represents the local IP address.

port
    The port on which to listen for incoming connection attempts.

Exceptions

Exception Type	Condition
ArgumentNullException	*localaddr* is a null reference (**Nothing** in Visual Basic).
ArgumentOutOfRange-Exception	*port* is not between **MinPort** and **MaxPort**.

Remarks

This constructor allows you to specify the local IP address and port number on which to listen for incoming connection attempts. Before calling this constructor you must first create an **IPAddress** using the desired local address. Pass this **IPAddress** to the constructor as the *localaddr* parameter. If you do not care which local address is assigned, specify **IPAddress.Any** for the *localaddr* parameter, and the underlying service provider will assign the most appropriate network address. This might help simplify your application if you have multiple network interfaces. If you do not care which local port is used, you can specify 0 for the port number. In this case, the service provider will assign an available port number between 1024 and 5000. If you use this approach, you can discover what local network address and port number has been assigned by using the **LocalEndpoint** property.

Call the **Start** method to begin listening for incoming connection attempts.

Requirements

Platforms: Windows 98, Windows NT 4.0, Windows Millennium Edition, Windows 2000, Windows XP Home Edition, Windows XP Professional, Windows .NET Server family, .NET Compact Framework - Windows CE .NET

TcpListener.Active Property

Gets a value that indicates whether **TcpListener** is actively listening for client connections.

```
[Visual Basic]
Protected ReadOnly Property Active As Boolean
[C#]
protected bool Active {get;}
[C++]
protected: __property bool get_Active();
[JScript]
protected function get Active() : Boolean;
```

Property Value

true if **TcpListener** is actively listening; otherwise **false**.

Remarks

Classes deriving from **TcpListener** can use this property to determine if the **Socket** is currently listening for incoming connection attempts. The **Active** property can be used to avoid redundant **Start** attempts.

Requirements

Platforms: Windows 98, Windows NT 4.0, Windows Millennium Edition, Windows 2000, Windows XP Home Edition, Windows XP Professional, Windows .NET Server family

TcpListener.LocalEndpoint Property

Gets the underlying **EndPoint** of the current **TcpListener**.

```
[Visual Basic]
Public ReadOnly Property LocalEndpoint As EndPoint
[C#]
public EndPoint LocalEndpoint {get;}
[C++]
public: __property EndPoint* get_LocalEndpoint();
[JScript]
public function get LocalEndpoint() : EndPoint;
```

Property Value

The **EndPoint** to which the **Socket** is bound.

Remarks

You can use **LocalEndpoint** to identify the local network interface and port number being used to listen for incoming client connection requests. You must first cast this **EndPoint** to an **IPEndPoint**. You can then call the **IPEndPoint.Address** method to retrieve the local IP address, and the **IPEndPoint.Port** method to retreive the local port number.

Requirements

Platforms: Windows 98, Windows NT 4.0, Windows Millennium Edition, Windows 2000, Windows XP Home Edition, Windows XP Professional, Windows .NET Server family, .NET Compact Framework - Windows CE .NET

TcpListener.Server Property

Gets the underlying network **Socket**.

```
[Visual Basic]
Protected ReadOnly Property Server As Socket
```

```
[C#]
protected Socket Server {get;}
[C++]
protected: __property Socket* get_Server();
[JScript]
protected function get Server() : Socket;
```

Property Value

The underlying **Socket**.

Remarks

TcpListener creates a **Socket** to listen for incoming client connection requests. Classes deriving from **TcpListener** can use this property to get this **Socket**. Use the underlying **Socket** returned by the **Server** property if you require access beyond that which **TcpListener** provides.

> **Note** **Server** only returns the **Socket** used to listen for incoming client connection requests. Use the **AcceptSocket** method to accept a pending connection request and obtain a **Socket** for sending and receiving data. You can also use the **AcceptTcpClient** method to accept a pending connection request and obtain a **TcpClient** for sending and receiving data.

Requirements

Platforms: Windows 98, Windows NT 4.0, Windows Millennium Edition, Windows 2000, Windows XP Home Edition, Windows XP Professional, Windows .NET Server family

TcpListener.AcceptSocket Method

Accepts a pending connection request.

```
[Visual Basic]
Public Function AcceptSocket() As Socket
[C#]
public Socket AcceptSocket();
[C++]
public: Socket* AcceptSocket();
[JScript]
public function AcceptSocket() : Socket;
```

Return Value

A **Socket** used to send and receive data.

Exceptions

Exception Type	Condition
InvalidOperationException	The listener has not been started with a call to **Start**.

Remarks

AcceptSocket is a blocking method that returns a **Socket** you can use to send and receive data. If you want to avoid blocking, use the **Pending** method to determine if connections requests are available in the incoming connection queue.

The **Socket** returned is initialized with the IP address and port number of the remote host. You can use any of the **Send** and **Receive** methods available in the **Socket** class to communicate with the remote host. When you are finished using the **Socket**, be sure to call its **Close** method. If your application is relatively simple, consider using the **AcceptTcpClient** method rather than the **AcceptSocket** method. **TcpClient** provides you with simple methods for sending and receiving data over a network in blocking synchronous mode.

Requirements

Platforms: Windows 98, Windows NT 4.0, Windows Millennium Edition, Windows 2000, Windows XP Home Edition, Windows XP Professional, Windows .NET Server family, .NET Compact Framework - Windows CE .NET

TcpListener.AcceptTcpClient Method

Accepts a pending connection request

```
[Visual Basic]
Public Function AcceptTcpClient() As TcpClient
[C#]
public TcpClient AcceptTcpClient();
[C++]
public: TcpClient* AcceptTcpClient();
[JScript]
public function AcceptTcpClient() : TcpClient;
```

Return Value

A **TcpClient** used to send and receive data.

Exceptions

Exception Type	Condition
InvalidOperationException	The listener has not been started with a call to **Start**.

Remarks

AcceptTcpClient is a blocking method that returns a **TcpClient** you can use to send and receive data. Use the **Pending** method to determine if connections requests are available in the incoming connection queue if you want to avoid blocking.

Use **TcpClient.GetStream** to obtain the underlying **NetworkStream** of the returned **TcpClient**. The **NetworkStream** will provide you with methods for sending and receiving with the remote host. When you are through with the **TcpClient**, be sure to call its **Close** method. If you want greater flexibility than a **TcpClient** offers, consider using **AcceptSocket**.

Requirements

Platforms: Windows 98, Windows NT 4.0, Windows Millennium Edition, Windows 2000, Windows XP Home Edition, Windows XP Professional, Windows .NET Server family, .NET Compact Framework - Windows CE .NET

TcpListener.Finalize Method

Frees resources used by the **TcpClient** class.

[C#] In C#, finalizers are expressed using destructor syntax.

[C++] In C++, finalizers are expressed using destructor syntax.

```
[Visual Basic]
Overrides Protected Sub Finalize()
[C#]
~TcpListener();
[C++]
~TcpListener();
[JScript]
protected override function Finalize();
```

Remarks

The finalizer for the **TcpListener** class calls the **Stop** method to close the **TcpListener**.

Requirements

Platforms: Windows 98, Windows NT 4.0,
Windows Millennium Edition, Windows 2000,
Windows XP Home Edition, Windows XP Professional,
Windows .NET Server family,
.NET Compact Framework - Windows CE .NET

TcpListener.Pending Method

Determines if there are pending connection requests.

```
[Visual Basic]
Public Function Pending() As Boolean
[C#]
public bool Pending();
[C++]
public: bool Pending();
[JScript]
public function Pending() : Boolean;
```

Return Value

true if connections are pending; otherwise, **false**.

Exceptions

Exception Type	Condition
InvalidOperationException	The listener has not been started with a call to **Start**.

Remarks

This non-blocking method determines if there are any pending connection requests. Because the **AcceptSocket** and **AcceptTcpClient** methods block execution until **Start** has queued an incoming connection request, the **Pending** method can be used to determine if connections are available before attempting to accept them.

Requirements

Platforms: Windows 98, Windows NT 4.0,
Windows Millennium Edition, Windows 2000,
Windows XP Home Edition, Windows XP Professional,
Windows .NET Server family,
.NET Compact Framework - Windows CE .NET

TcpListener.Start Method

Starts listening for incoming connection requests.

```
[Visual Basic]
Public Sub Start()
[C#]
public void Start();
[C++]
public: void Start();
[JScript]
public function Start();
```

Exceptions

Exception Type	Condition
SocketException	Use **SocketException.ErrorCode** to obtain the specific error code. Once you have obtained this code, you can refer to the Windows Socket Version 2 API error code documentation in MSDN for a detailed description of the error.

Remarks

The **Start** method initializes the underlying **Socket**, binds it to a local endpoint, and listens for incoming connection attempts. If a connection request is received, **Start** will queue the request and continue listening for additional requests until you call the **Stop** method. If **TcpListener** receives a connection request after it has already queued the maximum number of connections it will throw a **SocketException**.

To remove a connection from the incoming connection queue, use either the **AcceptTcpClient** method or the **AcceptSocket** method. The **AcceptTcpClient** method will remove a connection from the queue and return a **TcpClient** that you can use to send and receive data. The **AcceptSocket** method will return a **Socket** that you can use to do the same. If your application only requires basic blocking synchronous I/O, use **AcceptTcpClient**. For more detailed behavioral control, use **AcceptSocket**. Both of these methods block execution until a connection request is available in the queue. Use the **Pending** method if you want to be sure a connection is available before attempting to accept.

Use the **Stop** method to close the **TcpListener** and stop listening. You are responsible for closing your accepted connections separately.

Requirements

Platforms: Windows 98, Windows NT 4.0,
Windows Millennium Edition, Windows 2000,
Windows XP Home Edition, Windows XP Professional,
Windows .NET Server family,
.NET Compact Framework - Windows CE .NET

TcpListener.Stop Method

Closes the listener.

```
[Visual Basic]
Public Sub Stop()
[C#]
public void Stop();
[C++]
public: void Stop();
[JScript]
public function Stop();
```

Exceptions

Exception Type	Condition
SocketException	Use **SocketException.ErrorCode** to obtain the specific error code. Once you have obtained this code, you can refer to the Windows Socket Version 2 API error code documentation in MSDN for a detailed description of the error.

Remarks

Stop closes the listener. Any unaccepted connection requests in the queue will be lost. Remote hosts waiting for a connection to be accepted will throw a **SocketException**. You are responsible for closing your accepted connections separately.

Requirements

Platforms: Windows 98, Windows NT 4.0,
Windows Millennium Edition, Windows 2000,
Windows XP Home Edition, Windows XP Professional,
Windows .NET Server family,
.NET Compact Framework - Windows CE .NET

UdpClient Class

Provides User Datagram Protocol (UDP) network services.

System.Object
   System.Net.Sockets.UdpClient

[Visual Basic]
```
Public Class UdpClient
   Implements IDisposable
```
[C#]
```
public class UdpClient : IDisposable
```
[C++]
```
public __gc class UdpClient : public IDisposable
```
[JScript]
```
public class UdpClient implements IDisposable
```

Thread Safety

Any public static (**Shared** in Visual Basic) members of this type are safe for multithreaded operations. Any instance members are not guaranteed to be thread safe.

Remarks

The **UdpClient** class provides simple methods for sending and receiving connectionless UDP datagrams in blocking synchronous mode. For more information of blocking versus nonblocking sockets, see TBD. For information on asynchronous versus synchronous communication, see TBD. Because UDP is a connectionless transport protocol, you do not need to establish a remote host connection prior to sending and receiving data. You do, however, have the option of establishing a default remote host in one of the following two ways:

- Create an instance of the **UdpClient** class using the remote host name and port number as parameters.
- Create an instance of the **UdpClient** class and then call the **Connect** method.

You can use any of the send methods provided in the **UdpClient** to send data to a remote device. Use the **Receive** method to receive data from remote hosts.

> **Note** Do not call **Send** using a host name or **IPEndPoint** if you have already specified a default remote host. If you do, **UdpClient** will throw an exception.

UdpClient methods also allow you to send and receive multicasted datagrams. Use The **JoinMulticastGroup** method to subscribe a **UdpClient** to a multicast group. Use the **DropMulticastGroup** method to unsubscribe a **UdpClient** from a multicast group.

Example

[Visual Basic, C#] The following example establishes a **UdpClient** connection using the host name www.contoso.com on port 11000. A small string message is sent to two separate remote host machines. The **Receive** method blocks execution until a message is received. Using the **IPEndPoint** passed to **Receive**, the identity of the responding host is revealed.

[Visual Basic]
```
' This constructor arbitrarily assigns the local port number.
Dim udpClient As New UdpClient()
Try
    udpClient.Connect("www.contoso.com", 11000)

    ' Sends a message to the host to which you have connected.
    Dim sendBytes As [Byte]() = Encoding.ASCII.GetBytes
("Is anybody there?")

    udpClient.Send(sendBytes, sendBytes.Length)

    ' Sends message to a different host using optional hostname
and port parameters.
    Dim udpClientB As New UdpClient()
    udpClientB.Send(sendBytes, sendBytes.Length,
"AlternateHostMachineName", 11000)

    'Blocks until a message returns on this socket from a remote host.
    Dim RemoteIpEndPoint As New IPEndPoint(IPAddress.Any, 0)

    ' Blocks until a message returns on this socket from a remote host.
    Dim receiveBytes As [Byte]() = udpClient.Receive(RemoteIpEndPoint)
    Dim returnData As String = Encoding.ASCII.GetString(receiveBytes)

    ' Which one of these two hosts responded?
    Console.WriteLine(("This is the message you received " + _
                       returnData.ToString()))
    Console.WriteLine(("This message was sent from " + _
          RemoteIpEndPoint.Address.ToString() + _
                    " on their port number " + _
                    RemoteIpEndPoint.Port.ToString()))
    udpClient.Close()
    udpClientB.Close()

Catch e As Exception
    Console.WriteLine(e.ToString())
End Try
    End Sub
```

[C#]
```
// This constructor arbitrarily assigns the local port number.
UdpClient udpClient = new UdpClient();
    try{
        udpClient.Connect("www.contoso.com", 11000);

        // Sends a message to the host to which you have connected.
        Byte[] sendBytes = Encoding.ASCII.GetBytes
("Is anybody there?");

        udpClient.Send(sendBytes, sendBytes.Length);

        // Sends a message to a different host using optional
hostname and port parameters.
        UdpClient udpClientB = new UdpClient();
        udpClientB.Send(sendBytes, sendBytes.Length,
"AlternateHostMachineName", 11000);

        //IPEndPoint object will allow us to read datagrams
sent from any source.
        IPEndPoint RemoteIpEndPoint = new IPEndPoint
(IPAddress.Any, 0);

        // Blocks until a message returns on this socket from
a remote host.
        Byte[] receiveBytes = udpClient.Receive(ref RemoteIpEndPoint);
        string returnData = Encoding.ASCII.GetString(receiveBytes);

        // Uses the IPEndPoint object to determine which of
these two hosts responded.
        Console.WriteLine("This is the message you received " +
                          returnData.ToString());
        Console.WriteLine("This message was sent from " +
                    RemoteIpEndPoint.Address.ToString() +
                    " on their port number " +
                    RemoteIpEndPoint.Port.ToString());

        udpClient.Close();
        udpClientB.Close();

    }
    catch (Exception e ) {
            Console.WriteLine(e.ToString());
    }
```

Requirements

Namespace: System.Net.Sockets

Platforms: Windows 98, Windows NT 4.0,
Windows Millennium Edition, Windows 2000,
Windows XP Home Edition, Windows XP Professional,
Windows .NET Server family,
.NET Compact Framework - Windows CE .NET

Assembly: System (in System.dll)

.NET Framework Security:

- **SocketPermission** To establish an outgoing connection or accept an incoming request.

UdpClient Constructor

Initializes a new instance of the **UdpClient** class.

Overload List

Initializes a new instance of the **UdpClient** class.

Supported by the .NET Compact Framework.

[Visual Basic] **Public Sub New()**

[C#] **public UdpClient();**

[C++] **public: UdpClient();**

[JScript] **public function UdpClient();**

Initializes a new instance of the **UdpClient** class.

[Visual Basic] **Public Sub New(AddressFamily)**

[C#] **public UdpClient(AddressFamily);**

[C++] **public: UdpClient(AddressFamily);**

[JScript] **public function UdpClient(AddressFamily);**

Initializes a new instance of the **UdpClient** class and binds it to the local port number provided.

Supported by the .NET Compact Framework.

[Visual Basic] **Public Sub New(Integer)**

[C#] **public UdpClient(int);**

[C++] **public: UdpClient(int);**

[JScript] **public function UdpClient(int);**

Initializes a new instance of the **UdpClient** class and binds it to the specified local endpoint.

Supported by the .NET Compact Framework.

[Visual Basic] **Public Sub New(IPEndPoint)**

[C#] **public UdpClient(IPEndPoint);**

[C++] **public: UdpClient(IPEndPoint*);**

[JScript] **public function UdpClient(IPEndPoint);**

Initializes a new instance of the **UdpClient** class and binds it to the local port number provided.

[Visual Basic] **Public Sub New(Integer, AddressFamily)**

[C#] **public UdpClient(int, AddressFamily);**

[C++] **public: UdpClient(int, AddressFamily);**

[JScript] **public function UdpClient(int, AddressFamily);**

Initializes a new instance of the **UdpClient** class and establishes a default remote host.

Supported by the .NET Compact Framework.

[Visual Basic] **Public Sub New(String, Integer)**

[C#] **public UdpClient(string, int);**

[C++] **public: UdpClient(String*, int);**

[JScript] **public function UdpClient(String, int);**

Example

[Visual Basic, C#] The following example demonstrates how to create an instance of the **UdpClient** class using a host name and port number.

> [Visual Basic, C#] **Note** This example shows how to use one of the overloaded versions of the **UdpClient** constructor. For other examples that might be available, see the individual overload topics.

```
[Visual Basic]
'Creates an instance of the UdpClient class with a remote host
 name and a port number.
Try
    Dim udpClient As New UdpClient("www.contoso.com", 11000)
Catch e As Exception
    Console.WriteLine(e.ToString())
End Try
```

```
[C#]
        //Creates an instance of the UdpClient class
with a remote host name and a port number.
        try{
                UdpClient udpClient = new
UdpClient("www.contoso.com",11000);
        }
        catch (Exception e ) {
                Console.WriteLine(e.ToString());
        }
```

UdpClient Constructor ()

Initializes a new instance of the **UdpClient** class.

```
[Visual Basic]
Public Sub New()
[C#]
public UdpClient();
[C++]
public: UdpClient();
[JScript]
public function UdpClient();
```

Exceptions

Exception Type	Condition
SocketException	An error occurred when accessing the socket. See the Remarks section for more information.

Remarks

This constructor creates a new **UdpClient** and allows the underlying service provider to assign the most appropriate local IP address and port number.

> **Note** If you receive a **SocketException**, use **SocketException.ErrorCode** to obtain the specific error code. Once you have obtained this code, you can refer to the Windows Socket Version 2 API error code documentation in MSDN for a detailed description of the error.

This constructor is not suitable for joining a multicast group because it does not perform socket binding. Also, it works only with IPv4 address types.

Example

[Visual Basic, C#] The following example demonstrates how to use the default constructor to create an instance of the **UdpClient** class.

```
[Visual Basic]
'Creates an instance of the UdpClient class using the    ⅃
  default constructor.
Dim udpClient As New UdpClient()
```

```
[C#]
//Creates an instance of the UdpClient class using the    ⅃
  default constructor.
UdpClient udpClient = new UdpClient();
```

Requirements

Platforms: Windows 98, Windows NT 4.0, Windows Millennium Edition, Windows 2000, Windows XP Home Edition, Windows XP Professional, Windows .NET Server family, .NET Compact Framework - Windows CE .NET

UdpClient Constructor (AddressFamily)

Note: This namespace, class, or member is supported only in version 1.1 of the .NET Framework.

Initializes a new instance of the **UdpClient** class.

```
[Visual Basic]
Public Sub New( _
   ByVal family As AddressFamily _
)
[C#]
public UdpClient(
   AddressFamily family
);
[C++]
public: UdpClient(
   AddressFamily family
);
[JScript]
public function UdpClient(
   family : AddressFamily
);
```

Parameters

family
> One of the **AddressFamily** values that specifies the addressing scheme of the socket.

Exceptions

Exception Type	Condition
System.Argument-Exception	*family* is not **InterNetwork** or **InterNetwork6**.
Sockets.SocketException	An error occurred when accessing the socket. See the Remarks section for more information.

Remarks

The *family* parameter determines whether the listener uses an IP version 4 address (IPv4) or an IP version 6 (IPv6) address. To use an IPv4 address, pass the **InterNetwork** value. To use an IPv6 address, pass the **InterNetworkV6** value. Passing any other value will cause the method to throw an **ArgumentException**.

> **Note** If you receive a **SocketException**, use **SocketException.ErrorCode** to obtain the specific error code. Once you have obtained this code, you can refer to the Windows Socket Version 2 API error code documentation in MSDN for a detailed description of the error.

The **ctor** is not suitable for joining a multicast group because it does not perform socket binding.

Requirements

Platforms: Windows 98, Windows NT 4.0, Windows Millennium Edition, Windows 2000, Windows XP Home Edition, Windows XP Professional, Windows .NET Server family

UdpClient Constructor (Int32)

Initializes a new instance of the **UdpClient** class and binds it to the local port number provided.

```
[Visual Basic]
Public Sub New( _
   ByVal port As Integer _
)
[C#]
public UdpClient(
   int port
);
[C++]
public: UdpClient(
   int port
);
[JScript]
public function UdpClient(
   port : int
);
```

Parameters

port
> The local port number from which you intend to communicate.

Exceptions

Exception Type	Condition
ArgumentOutOfRange-Exception	The *port* parameter is greater than **MaxPort** or less than **MinPort**.
SocketException	An error occurred when accessing the socket. See the Remarks section for more information.

Remarks

This constructor creates an underlying **Socket** and binds it to the port number from which you intend to communicate. Use this constructor if you are only interested in setting the local port number. The underlying service provider will assign the local IP address.

> **Note** If you receive a **SocketException**, use **SocketException.ErrorCode** to obtain the specific error code. Once you have obtained this code, you can refer to the Windows Socket Version 2 API error code documentation in MSDN for a detailed description of the error.

This constructor works only with IPv4 address types.

Example

[Visual Basic, C#] The following example demonstrates using a local port number to create an instance of the **UdpClient** class.

```
[Visual Basic]
'Creates an instance of the UdpClient class to listen on
'the default interface using a particular port.
Try
    Dim udpClient As New UdpClient(11000)
Catch e As Exception
    Console.WriteLine(e.ToString())
End Try
```

```
[C#]
//Creates an instance of the UdpClient class to listen on
// the default interface using a particular port.
try{
        UdpClient udpClient = new UdpClient(11000);
}
catch (Exception e ) {
        Console.WriteLine(e.ToString());
    }
```

Requirements

Platforms: Windows 98, Windows NT 4.0, Windows Millennium Edition, Windows 2000, Windows XP Home Edition, Windows XP Professional, Windows .NET Server family, .NET Compact Framework - Windows CE .NET

UdpClient Constructor (IPEndPoint)

Initializes a new instance of the **UdpClient** class and binds it to the specified local endpoint.

```
[Visual Basic]
Public Sub New( _
    ByVal localEP As IPEndPoint _
)
[C#]
public UdpClient(
    IPEndPoint localEP
);
[C++]
public: UdpClient(
    IPEndPoint* localEP
);
[JScript]
public function UdpClient(
    localEP : IPEndPoint
);
```

Parameters

localEP

An **IPEndPoint** that respresents the local endpoint to which you bind the UDP connection.

Exceptions

Exception Type	Condition
ArgumentNullException	*localEP* is a null reference (**Nothing** in Visual Basic).
SocketException	An error occurred when accessing the socket. See the Remarks section for more information.

Remarks

This constructor creates a new **UdpClient** and binds it to the **IPEndPoint** specified by the *localEP* parameter. Before you call this constructor, you must create an **IPEndPoint** using the IP address and port number from which you intend to send and receive data. You do not need to specify a local IP address and port number for sending and receiving data. If you do not, the underlying service provider will assign the most appropriate local IP address and port number.

> **Note** If you receive a **SocketException**, use **SocketException.ErrorCode** to obtain the specific error code. Once you have obtained this code, you can refer to the Windows Socket Version 2 API error code documentation in MSDN for a detailed description of the error.

Example

[Visual Basic, C#] The following example demonstrates how to create an instance of the **UdpClient** class using a local endpoint.

```
[Visual Basic]
'Creates an instance of the UdpClient class using a local endpoint.
Dim ipAddress As IPAddress =                                          ⏎
Dns.Resolve(Dns.GetHostName()).AddressList(0)
Dim ipLocalEndPoint As New IPEndPoint(ipAddress, 11000)

Try
    Dim udpClient As New UdpClient(ipLocalEndPoint)
Catch e As Exception
    Console.WriteLine(e.ToString())
End Try
```

```
[C#]
        //Creates an instance of the UdpClient class              ⏎
using a local endpoint.
        IPAddress ipAddress =                                     ⏎
Dns.Resolve(Dns.GetHostName()).AddressList[0];
        IPEndPoint ipLocalEndPoint = new IPEndPoint               ⏎
(ipAddress, 11000);

        try{
            UdpClient udpClient = new UdpClient(ipLocalEndPoint);
        }
        catch (Exception e ) {
                Console.WriteLine(e.ToString());
        }
```

Requirements

Platforms: Windows 98, Windows NT 4.0, Windows Millennium Edition, Windows 2000, Windows XP Home Edition, Windows XP Professional, Windows .NET Server family, .NET Compact Framework - Windows CE .NET

UdpClient Constructor (Int32, AddressFamily)

Note: This namespace, class, or member is supported only in version 1.1 of the .NET Framework.

Initializes a new instance of the **UdpClient** class and binds it to the local port number provided.

```
[Visual Basic]
Public Sub New( _
    ByVal port As Integer, _
    ByVal family As AddressFamily _
)
```

```
[C#]
public UdpClient(
   int port,
   AddressFamily family
);
[C++]
public: UdpClient(
   int port,
   AddressFamily family
);
[JScript]
public function UdpClient(
   port : int,
   family : AddressFamily
);
```

Parameters

port
   The port on which to listen for incoming connection attempts.
family
   One of the **AddressFamily** values that specifies the addressing
   scheme of the socket.

Exceptions

Exception Type	Condition
System.Argument-Exception	*family* is not **InterNetwork** or **InterNetwork6**.
System.ArgumentOutOfRangeException	*port* is greater than **MaxPort** or less than **MinPort**.
Sockets.SocketException	An error occurred when accessing the socket. See the Remarks section for more information.

Remarks

The **ctor** creates an underlying **Socket** and binds it to the port
number from which you intend to communicate.

The *family* parameter determines whether the listener uses an IP
version 4 address (IPv4) or an IP version 6 (IPv6) address. To use an
IPv4 address, pass the **InterNetwork** value. To use an IPv6 address,
pass the **InterNetworkV6** value. Passing any other value will cause
the method to throw an **ArgumentException**.

> **Note** If you receive a **SocketException**, use
> **SocketException.ErrorCode** to obtain the specific error code.
> Once you have obtained this code, refer to the Windows Socket
> Version 2 API error code documentation in MSDN for a
> detailed description of the error.

Example

[Visual Basic, C#, C++] The following code example shows how to
create a UDP client to use in a multicast group. For a complete
example, see the **JoinMulticastGroup** method topic.

```
[Visual Basic]
' Bind and listen on port 2000. This constructor creates a socket
' and binds it to the port on which to receive data. The family
' parameter specifies that this connection uses an IPv6 address.
clientOriginator = New UdpClient(2000, AddressFamily.InterNetworkV6)

' Join or create a multicast group. The multicast address ranges
' to use are specified in RFC#2375. You are free to use
' different addresses.
' Transform the string address into the internal format.
m_GrpAddr = IPAddress.Parse("FF01::1")
```

```
' Display the multicast address used.
Console.WriteLine(("Multicast Address:
[" + m_GrpAddr.ToString() + "]"))

' Exercise the use of the IPv6MulticastOption.
Console.WriteLine("Instantiate IPv6MulticastOption(IPAddress)")

' Instantiate IPv6MulticastOption using one of the
' overloaded constructors.
Dim ipv6MulticastOption As New IPv6MulticastOption(m_GrpAddr)

' Store the IPAdress multicast options.
Dim group As IPAddress = ipv6MulticastOption.Group
Dim interfaceIndex As Long = ipv6MulticastOption.InterfaceIndex

' Display IPv6MulticastOption properties.
Console.WriteLine(("IPv6MulticastOption.Group:
[" + group.ToString() + "]"))
Console.WriteLine(("IPv6MulticastOption.InterfaceIndex:
[" + interfaceIndex.ToString() + "]"))

' Instantiate IPv6MulticastOption using another
' overloaded constructor.
Dim ipv6MulticastOption2 As New
IPv6MulticastOption(group, interfaceIndex)

' Store the IPAdress multicast options.
group = ipv6MulticastOption2.Group
interfaceIndex = ipv6MulticastOption2.InterfaceIndex

' Display the IPv6MulticastOption2 properties.
Console.WriteLine(("IPv6MulticastOption.Group:
[" + group.ToString() + "]"))
Console.WriteLine(("IPv6MulticastOption.InterfaceIndex:
[" + interfaceIndex.ToString() + "]"))

' Join the specified multicast group using one of the
' JoinMulticastGroup overloaded methods.
clientOriginator.JoinMulticastGroup(Fix(interfaceIndex), group)

' Define the endpoint data port. Note that this port number
' must match the ClientTarget UDP port number which is the
' port on which the ClientTarget is receiving data.
m_ClientTargetdest = New IPEndPoint(m_GrpAddr, 1000)
```

```
[C#]
      // Bind and listen on port 2000. This constructor
creates a socket
      // and binds it to the port on which to receive
data. The family
      // parameter specifies that this connection uses
an IPv6 address.
      clientOriginator = new UdpClient(2000,
AddressFamily.InterNetworkV6);

      // Join or create a multicast group. The multicast
address ranges
      // to use are specified in RFC#2375. You are free to use
      // different addresses.

      // Transform the string address into the internal format.
      m_GrpAddr = IPAddress.Parse("FF01::1");

      // Display the multicast address used.
      Console.WriteLine("Multicast Address:
[" + m_GrpAddr.ToString() + "]");

      // Exercise the use of the IPv6MulticastOption.
      Console.WriteLine("Instantiate
IPv6MulticastOption(IPAddress)");

      // Instantiate IPv6MulticastOption using one of the
      // overloaded constructors.
      IPv6MulticastOption ipv6MulticastOption = new
IPv6MulticastOption(m_GrpAddr);
```

```
        // Store the IPAddress multicast options.
        IPAddress group = ipv6MulticastOption.Group;
        long interfaceIndex = ipv6MulticastOption.InterfaceIndex;

        // Display IPv6MulticastOption properties.
        Console.WriteLine("IPv6MulticastOption.Group:
[" + group  + "]");
        Console.WriteLine("IPv6MulticastOption.InterfaceIndex:
[" + interfaceIndex + "]");

        // Instantiate IPv6MulticastOption using another
        // overloaded constructor.
        IPv6MulticastOption ipv6MulticastOption2 = new
IPv6MulticastOption(group, interfaceIndex);

        // Store the IPAddress multicast options.
        group = ipv6MulticastOption2.Group;
        interfaceIndex = ipv6MulticastOption2.InterfaceIndex;

        // Display the IPv6MulticastOption2 properties.
        Console.WriteLine("IPv6MulticastOption.Group:
[" + group  + "]");
        Console.WriteLine("IPv6MulticastOption.InterfaceIndex:
[" + interfaceIndex + "]");

        // Join the specified multicast group using one of the
        // JoinMulticastGroup overloaded methods.
        clientOriginator.JoinMulticastGroup
((int)interfaceIndex, group);

        // Define the endpoint data port. Note that this port number
        // must match the ClientTarget UDP port number which is the
        // port on which the ClientTarget is receiving data.
        m_ClientTargetdest = new IPEndPoint(m_GrpAddr, 1000);

[C++]
// Bind and listen on port 2000. This constructor creates a socket
// and binds it to the port on which to receive data. The family
// parameter specifies that this connection uses an IPv6 address.
clientOriginator = new UdpClient(2000, AddressFamily::InterNetworkV6);

// Join or create a multicast group. The multicast address ranges
// to use are specified in RFC#2375. You are free to use
// different addresses.

// Transform the String* address into the internal format.
m_GrpAddr = IPAddress::Parse(S"FF01::1");

// Display the multicast address used.
Console::WriteLine(S"Multicast Address: [ {0}]", m_GrpAddr);

// Exercise the use of the IPv6MulticastOption.
Console::WriteLine(S"Instantiate IPv6MulticastOption(IPAddress)");

// Instantiate IPv6MulticastOption using one of the
// overloaded constructors.
IPv6MulticastOption* ipv6MulticastOption = new
IPv6MulticastOption(m_GrpAddr);

// Store the IPAddress multicast options.
IPAddress * group = ipv6MulticastOption->Group;
__int64 interfaceIndex = ipv6MulticastOption->InterfaceIndex;

// Display IPv6MulticastOption properties.
Console::WriteLine(S"IPv6MulticastOption::Group: [ {0}]", group);
Console::WriteLine(S"IPv6MulticastOption::InterfaceIndex:
[ {0}]", __box(interfaceIndex));

// Instantiate IPv6MulticastOption using another
// overloaded constructor.
IPv6MulticastOption* ipv6MulticastOption2 =
   new IPv6MulticastOption(group, interfaceIndex);
```

```
        // Store the IPAddress multicast options.
        group = ipv6MulticastOption2->Group;
        interfaceIndex = ipv6MulticastOption2->InterfaceIndex;

        // Display the IPv6MulticastOption2 properties.
        Console::WriteLine(S"IPv6MulticastOption::Group: [ {0} ]", group);
        Console::WriteLine(S"IPv6MulticastOption::InterfaceIndex:
[ {0} ]", __box(interfaceIndex));

        // Join the specified multicast group using one of the
        // JoinMulticastGroup overloaded methods.
        clientOriginator->JoinMulticastGroup((int)interfaceIndex, group);

        // Define the endpoint data port. Note that this port number
        // must match the ClientTarget UDP port number which is the
        // port on which the ClientTarget is receiving data.
        m_ClientTargetdest = new IPEndPoint(m_GrpAddr, 1000);
```

Requirements

Platforms: Windows 98, Windows NT 4.0,
Windows Millennium Edition, Windows 2000,
Windows XP Home Edition, Windows XP Professional,
Windows .NET Server family

UdpClient Constructor (String, Int32)

Initializes a new instance of the **UdpClient** class and establishes a
default remote host.

```
[Visual Basic]
Public Sub New( _
   ByVal hostname As String, _
   ByVal port As Integer _
)
[C#]
public UdpClient(
   string hostname,
   int port
);
[C++]
public: UdpClient(
   String* hostname,
   int port
);
[JScript]
public function UdpClient(
   hostname : String,
   port : int
);
```

Parameters

hostname
   The name of the remote DNS host to which you intend to
   connect.
port
   The remote port number to which you intend to connect.

Exceptions

Exception Type	Condition
ArgumentNullException	*hostname* is a null reference (**Nothing** in Visual Basic).
ArgumentOutOfRange-Exception	*port* is not between **MinPort** and **MaxPort**.

Exception Type	Condition
SocketException	An error occured when accessing the socket. See the Remarks section for more information.

Remarks

This constructor initializes a new **UdpClient** and establishes a remote host using the *hostname* and *port* parameters. Establishing a default remote host is optional. If you use this constructor, you do not have to specify a remote host in each call to the **Send** method. Specifying a default remote host limits you to that host only. You can change the default remote host at any time by calling the **Connect** method. If you want to specify a remote host in your call to the **Send** method, do not use this constructor.

> **Note** If you receive a **SocketException**, use **SocketException.ErrorCode** to obtain the specific error code. Once you have obtained this code, you can refer to the Windows Socket Version 2 API error code documentation in MSDN for a detailed description of the error.

Example

[Visual Basic, C#] The following example demonstrates how to create an instance of the **UdpClient** class using a host name and port number.

```
[Visual Basic]
'Creates an instance of the UdpClient class with a remote host    ↵
name and a port number.
Try
   Dim udpClient As New UdpClient("www.contoso.com", 11000)
Catch e As Exception
   Console.WriteLine(e.ToString())
End Try

[C#]
        //Creates an instance of the UdpClient class with        ↵
a remote host name and a port number.
        try{
            UdpClient udpClient = new                            ↵
UdpClient("www.contoso.com",11000);
        }
        catch (Exception e ) {
                Console.WriteLine(e.ToString());
        }
```

Requirements

Platforms: Windows 98, Windows NT 4.0, Windows Millennium Edition, Windows 2000, Windows XP Home Edition, Windows XP Professional, Windows .NET Server family, .NET Compact Framework - Windows CE .NET

UdpClient.Active Property

Gets or sets a value indicating whether a default remote host has been established.

```
[Visual Basic]
Protected Property Active As Boolean
[C#]
protected bool Active {get; set;}
[C++]
protected: __property bool get_Active();
protected: __property void set_Active(bool);
```

```
[JScript]
protected function get Active() : Boolean;
protected function set Active(Boolean);
```

Property Value

true if a connection is active; otherwise, **false**.

Remarks

Classes deriving from **UdpClient** can use this property to determine if a default remote host has been established. You can establish a default remote host by using the appropriate constructor or by calling the **Connect** method. If you do establish a default remote host, you cannot specify a remote host in your call to **Send**.

Example

[Visual Basic, C#] The following example demonstrates a derived class using the protected property **Active**. In this example, MyUdpClientDerivedClass verifies that the connection is active before obtaining the underlying **Socket**.

```
[Visual Basic]
' This derived class demonstrates the use of three protected     ↵
methods belonging to the UdpClient class.
Public Class MyUdpClientDerivedClass
    Inherits UdpClient

    Public Sub New()
    End Sub 'New

    Public Sub UsingProtectedMethods()

        'Uses the protected Active property belonging to the
UdpClient base class to determine if a connection is established.
        If Me.Active Then
            ' Calls the protected Client property belonging to    ↵
the UdpClient base class.
            Dim s As Socket = Me.Client
                'Uses the Socket returned by Client to set an     ↵
option that is not available using UdpClient.
            s.SetSocketOption(SocketOptionLevel.Socket,           ↵
SocketOptionName.Broadcast, 1)
        End If
    End Sub 'UsingProtectedMethods
End Class 'MyUdpClientDerivedClass

[C#]
// This derived class demonstrate the use of three protected      ↵
methods belonging to the UdpClient class.
public class MyUdpClientDerivedClass : UdpClient{

public MyUdpClientDerivedClass() : base(){
}
public void UsingProtectedMethods(){

    //Uses the protected Active property belonging to the         ↵
UdpClient base class to determine if a connection is established.
    if (this.Active){
        //Calls the protected Client property belonging to the    ↵
UdpClient base class.
        Socket s = this.Client;
        //Uses the Socket returned by Client to set an option     ↵
that is not available using UdpClient.
        s.SetSocketOption(SocketOptionLevel.Socket,               ↵
SocketOptionName.Broadcast, 1);
    }

  }

}
```

Requirements

Platforms: Windows 98, Windows NT 4.0,
Windows Millennium Edition, Windows 2000,
Windows XP Home Edition, Windows XP Professional,
Windows .NET Server family,
.NET Compact Framework - Windows CE .NET

UdpClient.Client Property

Gets or sets the underlying network **Socket**.

```
[Visual Basic]
Protected Property Client As Socket
[C#]
protected Socket Client {get; set;}
[C++]
protected: __property Socket* get_Client();
protected: __property void set_Client(Socket*);
[JScript]
protected function get Client() : Socket;
protected function set Client(Socket);
```

Property Value

The underlying Network **Socket**.

Remarks

UdpClient creates a **Socket** used to send and receive data over a
network. Classes deriving from **UdpClient** can use this property to
get or set this **Socket**. Use the underlying **Socket** returned from
Client if you require access beyond that which **UdpClient** provides.
You can also use **Client** to set the underlying **Socket** to an existing
Socket. This is useful if you want to take advantage of the simplicity
of **UdpClient** using a pre-existing **Socket**.

Example

[Visual Basic, C#] The following example demonstrates a derived
class using the protected property **Client**. In this example,
MyUdpClientDerivedClass obtains the underlying **Socket** to enable
broadcasting.

```
[Visual Basic]
' This derived class demonstrates the use of three protected
 methods belonging to the UdpClient class.
Public Class MyUdpClientDerivedClass
    Inherits UdpClient

    Public Sub New()
    End Sub 'New

    Public Sub UsingProtectedMethods()

        'Uses the protected Active property belonging to the
 UdpClient base class to determine if a connection is established.
        If Me.Active Then
            ' Calls the protected Client property belonging to the
 UdpClient base class.
            Dim s As Socket = Me.Client
            'Uses the Socket returned by Client to set an
 option that is not available using UdpClient.
            s.SetSocketOption(SocketOptionLevel.Socket,
SocketOptionName.Broadcast, 1)
        End If
    End Sub 'UsingProtectedMethods
End Class 'MyUdpClientDerivedClass

[C#]
// This derived class demonstrate the use of three protected
 methods belonging to the UdpClient class.
public class MyUdpClientDerivedClass : UdpClient{
```

```
public MyUdpClientDerivedClass() : base(){
}
public void UsingProtectedMethods(){

    //Uses the protected Active property belonging to the
UdpClient base class to determine if a connection is established.
    if (this.Active){
        //Calls the protected Client property belonging to the
UdpClient base class.
        Socket s = this.Client;
        //Uses the Socket returned by Client to set an option that
is not available using UdpClient.
        s.SetSocketOption(SocketOptionLevel.Socket,
SocketOptionName.Broadcast, 1);
    }

}

}
```

Requirements

Platforms: Windows 98, Windows NT 4.0,
Windows Millennium Edition, Windows 2000,
Windows XP Home Edition, Windows XP Professional,
Windows .NET Server family,
.NET Compact Framework - Windows CE .NET

UdpClient.Close Method

Closes the UDP connection.

```
[Visual Basic]
Public Sub Close()
[C#]
public void Close();
[C++]
public: void Close();
[JScript]
public function Close();
```

Exceptions

Exception Type	Condition
SocketException	An error occurred when accessing the socket. See the Remarks section for more information.

Remarks

The **Close** disables the underlying **Socket** and releases all managed
and unmanaged resources associated with the **UdpClient**.

> **Note** If you receive a **SocketException**, use
> **SocketException.ErrorCode** to obtain the specific error code.
> Once you have obtained this code, you can refer to the
> Windows Socket Version 2 API error code documentation in
> MSDN for a detailed description of the error.

Example

[Visual Basic, C#] The following example demonstrates closing a
UdpClient by calling the **Close** method.

```
[Visual Basic]
' Closes the UDP client by calling the public method Close().
udpClient.Close()

[C#]
// Closes the UDP client by calling the public method Close().
udpClient.Close();
```

Requirements

Platforms: Windows 98, Windows NT 4.0, Windows Millennium Edition, Windows 2000, Windows XP Home Edition, Windows XP Professional, Windows .NET Server family, .NET Compact Framework - Windows CE .NET

UdpClient.Connect Method

Establishes a default remote host.

Overload List

Establishes a default remote host using the specified network endpoint.

Supported by the .NET Compact Framework.

    [Visual Basic] **Overloads Public Sub Connect(IPEndPoint)**

    [C#] **public void Connect(IPEndPoint);**

    [C++] **public: void Connect(IPEndPoint*);**

    [JScript] **public function Connect(IPEndPoint);**

Establishes a default remote host using the specified IP address and port number.

Supported by the .NET Compact Framework.

    [Visual Basic] **Overloads Public Sub Connect(IPAddress, Integer)**

    [C#] **public void Connect(IPAddress, int);**

    [C++] **public: void Connect(IPAddress*, int);**

    [JScript] **public function Connect(IPAddress, int);**

Establishes a default remote host using the specified host name and port number.

Supported by the .NET Compact Framework.

    [Visual Basic] **Overloads Public Sub Connect(String, Integer)**

    [C#] **public void Connect(string, int);**

    [C++] **public: void Connect(String*, int);**

    [JScript] **public function Connect(String, int);**

Example

[Visual Basic, C#] The following example uses the host name and port number to connect to a remote host.

[Visual Basic, C#] **Note** This example shows how to use one of the overloaded versions of **Connect**. For other examples that might be available, see the individual overload topics.

```
[Visual Basic]
'Uses a host name and port number to establish a socket connection.
Dim udpClient As New UdpClient()
Try
    udpClient.Connect("www.contoso.com", 11002)
Catch e As Exception
    Console.WriteLine(e.ToString())
End Try

[C#]
//Uses a host name and port number to establish a socket connection.
    UdpClient udpClient = new UdpClient();
    try{
    udpClient.Connect("www.contoso.com", 11002);
    }
    catch (Exception e ) {
        Console.WriteLine(e.ToString());
    }
```

UdpClient.Connect Method (IPEndPoint)

Establishes a default remote host using the specified network endpoint.

```
[Visual Basic]
Overloads Public Sub Connect( _
    ByVal endPoint As IPEndPoint _
)
[C#]
public void Connect(
    IPEndPoint endPoint
);
[C++]
public: void Connect(
    IPEndPoint* endPoint
);
[JScript]
public function Connect(
    endPoint : IPEndPoint
);
```

Parameters

endPoint
    An **IPEndPoint** that specifies the network endpoint to which you intend to send data.

Exceptions

Exception Type	Condition
SocketException	An error occurred when accessing the socket. See the Remarks section for more information.
ArgumentNullException	*endPoint* is a null reference (**Nothing** in Visual Basic).
ObjectDisposedException	The **UdpClient** is closed.

Remarks

The **Connect** method establishes a default remote host using the value specified in the *endPoint* parameter. Once established, you do not have to specify a remote host in each call to the **Send** method.

Establishing a default remote host is optional. Specifying a default remote host limits you to that host only. If you want to send datagrams to a different remote host, you must make another call to the **Connect** method or create another **UdpClient** without a default remote host. If you have established a default remote host and you also provide a remote host in your call to the **Send** method, **Send** will throw a **SocketException**. If you receive a **SocketException**, use **SocketException.ErrorCode** to obtain the specific error code. Once you have obtained this code, you can refer to the Windows Socket Version 2 API error code documentation in MSDN for a detailed description of the error.

If you call the **Connect** method, any datagrams that arrive from an address other than the specified default will be discarded. You cannot set the default remote host to a broadcast address using this method unless you inherit from **UdpClient**, use the Client method to obtain the underlying **Socket**, and set the socket option to **SocketOptionName.Broadcast**.

You can however, broadcast data to the default broadcast address, 255.255.255.255, if you specify **IPAddress.Broadcast** in your call to the **Send** method. If your application requires greater control over broadcast addresses, you can also revert to using the **Socket** class.

Note Since the UDP protocol is connectionless, the **Connect** method does not block. Do not call the **Connect** method if you intend to receive multicasted datagrams.

Example

[Visual Basic, C#] The following example uses an **IPEndPoint** to establish a default remote host.

[Visual Basic]
```
'Uses a remote endpoint to establish a socket connection.
Dim udpClient As New UdpClient()
Dim ipAddress As IPAddress =
Dns.Resolve("www.contoso.com").AddressList(0)
Dim ipEndPoint As New IPEndPoint(ipAddress, 11004)
Try
    udpClient.Connect(ipEndPoint)
Catch e As Exception
    Console.WriteLine(e.ToString())
End Try
```

[C#]
```
//Uses a remote endpoint to establish a socket connection.
UdpClient udpClient = new UdpClient();
IPAddress ipAddress = Dns.Resolve("www.contoso.com").AddressList[0];
IPEndPoint ipEndPoint = new IPEndPoint(ipAddress, 11004);
try{
    udpClient.Connect(ipEndPoint);
}
catch (Exception e ) {
        Console.WriteLine(e.ToString());
    }
```

Requirements

Platforms: Windows 98, Windows NT 4.0, Windows Millennium Edition, Windows 2000, Windows XP Home Edition, Windows XP Professional, Windows .NET Server family, .NET Compact Framework - Windows CE .NET

UdpClient.Connect Method (IPAddress, Int32)

Establishes a default remote host using the specified IP address and port number.

[Visual Basic]
```
Overloads Public Sub Connect( _
    ByVal addr As IPAddress, _
    ByVal port As Integer _
)
```
[C#]
```
public void Connect(
    IPAddress addr,
    int port
);
```
[C++]
```
public: void Connect(
    IPAddress* addr,
    int port
);
```
[JScript]
```
public function Connect(
    addr : IPAddress,
    port : int
);
```

Parameters

addr
> The **IPAddress** of the remote host to which you intend to send data.

port
> The port number to which you intend send data.

Exceptions

Exception Type	Condition
ObjectDisposedException	**UdpClient** is closed.
ArgumentNullException	*addr* is **null.**
ArgumentOutOfRangeException	*port* is not between **MinPort** and **MaxPort**.
SocketException	An error occurred when accessing the socket. See the Remarks section for more information.

Remarks

The **Connect** method establishes a default remote host using the values specified in the *addr* and *port* parameters. Once established, you do not have to specify a remote host in each call to the **Send** method.

Establishing a default remote host is optional. Specifying a default remote host limits you to that host only. If you want to send datagrams to a different remote host, you must make another call to the **Connect** method or create another **UdpClient** without a default remote host. If you have established a default remote host and you also provide a remote host in your call to the **Send** method, **Send** will throw a **SocketException**. If you receive a **SocketException**, use **SocketException.ErrorCode** to obtain the specific error code. Once you have obtained this code, you can refer to the Windows Socket Version 2 API error code documentation in MSDN for a detailed description of the error.

If you call the **Connect** method, any datagrams that arrive from an address other than the specified default will be discarded. You cannot set the default remote host to a broadcast address using this method unless you inherit from **UdpClient**, use the client method to obtain the underlying **Socket**, and set the socket option to **SocketOptionName.Broadcast**.

You can however, broadcast data to the default broadcast address, **255.255.255.255**, if you specify **IPAddress.Broadcast** in your call to the **Send** method. If your application requires greater control over broadcast addresses, you can also revert to using the **Socket** class.

Note Since the UDP protocol is connectionless, the **Connect** method does not block. Do not call the **Connect** method if you intend to receive multicasted datagrams.

Example

[Visual Basic, C#] The following example uses an IP address and port number to connect with a remote host.

[Visual Basic]
```
'Uses the IP address and port number to establish a socket connection.
Dim udpClient As New UdpClient()
Dim ipAddress As IPAddress =
Dns.Resolve("www.contoso.com").AddressList(0)
Try
    udpClient.Connect(ipAddress, 11003)
Catch e As Exception
```

```
    Console.WriteLine(e.ToString())
End Try
```

[C#]
```
//Uses the IP address and port number to establish a socket connection.
UdpClient udpClient = new UdpClient();
IPAddress ipAddress = Dns.Resolve("www.contoso.com").AddressList[0];
try{
     udpClient.Connect(ipAddress, 11003);
}
catch (Exception e ) {
          Console.WriteLine(e.ToString());
}
```

Requirements

Platforms: Windows 98, Windows NT 4.0,
Windows Millennium Edition, Windows 2000,
Windows XP Home Edition, Windows XP Professional,
Windows .NET Server family,
.NET Compact Framework - Windows CE .NET

UdpClient.Connect Method (String, Int32)

Establishes a default remote host using the specified host name and
port number.

[Visual Basic]
```
Overloads Public Sub Connect( _
   ByVal hostname As String, _
   ByVal port As Integer _
)
```
[C#]
```
public void Connect(
   string hostname,
   int port
);
```
[C++]
```
public: void Connect(
   String* hostname,
   int port
);
```
[JScript]
```
public function Connect(
   hostname : String,
   port : int
);
```

Parameters

hostname
    The DNS name of the remote host to which you intend send data.
port
    The port number on the remote host to which you intend to send
    data.

Exceptions

Exception Type	Condition
ObjectDisposedException	The **UdpClient** is closed.
ArgumentOutOfRange-Exception	*port* is not between **MinPort** and **MaxPort**.
SocketException	An error occurred when accessing the socket. See the Remarks section for more information.

Remarks

The **Connect** method establishes a default remote host using the
values specified in the *port* and *hostname* parameters. Once
established, you do not have to specify a remote host in each call to
the **Send** method.

Establishing a default remote host is optional. Specifying a default
remote host limits you to that host only. If you want to send
datagrams to a different remote host, you must make another call to
the **Connect** method or create another **UdpClient** without a default
remote host.

If you have established a default remote host and you also provide a
remote host in your call to the **Send** method, **Send** will throw a
SocketException. If you receive a **SocketException**, use
SocketException.ErrorCode to obtain the specific error code.
Once you have obtained this code, you can refer to the Windows
Socket Version 2 API error code documentation in MSDN for a
detailed description of the error.

If you call the **Connect** method, any datagrams that arrive from an
address other than the specified default will be discarded. You
cannot set the default remote host to a broadcast address using this
method unless you inherit from **UdpClient**, use the client method to
obtain the underlying **Socket**, and set the socket option to
SocketOptionName.Broadcast.

You can however, broadcast data to the default broadcast address,
255.255.255.255, if you specify **IPAddress.Broadcast** in your call
to the **Send** method. If your application requires greater control over
broadcast addresses, you can also revert to using the **Socket** class.

> **Note** Since the UDP protocol is connectionless, the **Connect**
> method does not block. Do not call the **Connect** method if you
> intend to receive multicasted datagrams.

Example

[Visual Basic, C#] The following example uses the host name and
port number to connect to a remote host.

[Visual Basic]
```
'Uses a host name and port number to establish a socket connection.
Dim udpClient As New UdpClient()
Try
    udpClient.Connect("www.contoso.com", 11002)
Catch e As Exception
    Console.WriteLine(e.ToString())
End Try
```

[C#]
```
//Uses a host name and port number to establish a socket connection.
   UdpClient udpClient = new UdpClient();
   try{
   udpClient.Connect("www.contoso.com", 11002);
   }
   catch (Exception e ) {
        Console.WriteLine(e.ToString());
   }
```

Requirements

Platforms: Windows 98, Windows NT 4.0,
Windows Millennium Edition, Windows 2000,
Windows XP Home Edition, Windows XP Professional,
Windows .NET Server family,
.NET Compact Framework - Windows CE .NET

UdpClient.DropMulticastGroup Method

Leaves a multicast group.

Overload List

Leaves a multicast group.

Supported by the .NET Compact Framework.

> [Visual Basic] **Overloads Public Sub DropMulticast Group(IPAddress)**
> [C#] **public void DropMulticastGroup(IPAddress);**
> [C++] **public: void DropMulticastGroup(IPAddress*);**
> [JScript] **public function DropMulticastGroup(IPAddress);**

Leaves a multicast group.

> [Visual Basic] **Overloads Public Sub DropMulticast Group(IPAddress, Integer)**
> [C#] **public void DropMulticastGroup(IPAddress, int);**
> [C++] **public: void DropMulticastGroup(IPAddress*, int);**
> [JScript] **public function DropMulticastGroup(IPAddress, int);**

Example

[Visual Basic, C#, C++] The following example demonstrates how to drop a multicast group by providing a multicast address.

[Visual Basic, C#, C++] **Note** This example shows how to use one of the overloaded versions of **DropMulticastGroup**. For other examples that might be available, see the individual overload topics.

```
[Visual Basic]
' Send data to ClientTarget.
Console.WriteLine(ControlChars.Lf + "The
ClientOriginator sent:" + ControlChars.Lf)
Send.OriginatorSendData(clientOriginator, m_ClientTargetdest)

' Receive data from ClientTarget
Ret = Receive.ReceiveUntilStop(clientOriginator)

' Stop the ClientTarget thread
m_t.Abort()

' Abandon the multicast group.
clientOriginator.DropMulticastGroup(m_GrpAddr)
```

```
[C#]
    // Send data to ClientTarget.
    Console.WriteLine("\nThe ClientOriginator sent:\n");
    Send.OriginatorSendData(clientOriginator, m_ClientTargetdest);

    // Receive data from ClientTarget
    Ret = Receive.ReceiveUntilStop(clientOriginator);

    // Stop the ClientTarget thread
    m_t.Abort();

    // Abandon the multicast group.
    clientOriginator.DropMulticastGroup(m_GrpAddr);
```

```
[C++]
// Send data to ClientTarget.
Console::WriteLine(S"\nThe ClientOriginator sent:\n");
Send::OriginatorSendData(clientOriginator, m_ClientTargetdest);

// Receive data from ClientTarget
Ret = Receive::ReceiveUntilStop(clientOriginator);

// Stop the ClientTarget thread
m_t->Abort();

// Abandon the multicast group.
clientOriginator->DropMulticastGroup(m_GrpAddr);
```

UdpClient.DropMulticastGroup Method (IPAddress)

Leaves a multicast group.

```
[Visual Basic]
Overloads Public Sub DropMulticastGroup( _
   ByVal multicastAddr As IPAddress _
)
[C#]
public void DropMulticastGroup(
   IPAddress multicastAddr
);
[C++]
public: void DropMulticastGroup(
   IPAddress* multicastAddr
);
[JScript]
public function DropMulticastGroup(
   multicastAddr : IPAddress
);
```

Parameters

multicastAddr
> The **IPAddress** of the multicast group to leave.

Exceptions

Exception Type	Condition
ObjectDisposedException	The underlying **Socket** has been closed.
SocketException	An error occurred when accessing the socket. See the Remarks section for more information.
ArgumentException	The IP address is not compatible with the **AddressFamily** value that defines the addressing scheme of the socket.
ArgumentNullException	*multicastAddr* is a null reference (**Nothing** in Visual Basic).

Remarks

The **DropMulticastGroup** method withdraws the **UdpClient** from the multicast group identified by the specified **IPAddress**. After calling the **DropMulticastGroup** method, the underlying **Socket** sends an Internet Group Management Protocol (IGMP) packet to the router, removing the router from the multicast group. After a **UdpClient** withdraws from the group, it will no longer be able to receive datagrams sent to that group.

> **Note** If you receive a **SocketException**, use **SocketException.ErrorCode** to obtain the specific error code. Once you have obtained this code, you can refer to the Windows Socket Version 2 API error code documentation in MSDN for a detailed description of the error.

Example

[Visual Basic, C#, C++] The following example demonstrates how to drop a multicast group by providing a multicast address.

```
[Visual Basic]
' Send data to ClientTarget.
Console.WriteLine(ControlChars.Lf + "The
ClientOriginator sent:" + ControlChars.Lf)
Send.OriginatorSendData(clientOriginator, m_ClientTargetdest)
```

```
' Receive data from ClientTarget
Ret = Receive.ReceiveUntilStop(clientOriginator)

' Stop the ClientTarget thread
m_t.Abort()

' Abandon the multicast group.
clientOriginator.DropMulticastGroup(m_GrpAddr)
```

[C#]
```
    // Send data to ClientTarget.
    Console.WriteLine("\nThe ClientOriginator sent:\n");
    Send.OriginatorSendData(clientOriginator, m_ClientTargetdest);

    // Receive data from ClientTarget
    Ret = Receive.ReceiveUntilStop(clientOriginator);

    // Stop the ClientTarget thread
    m_t.Abort();

    // Abandon the multicast group.
    clientOriginator.DropMulticastGroup(m_GrpAddr);
```

[C++]
```
// Send data to ClientTarget.
Console::WriteLine(S"\nThe ClientOriginator sent:\n");
Send::OriginatorSendData(clientOriginator, m_ClientTargetdest);

// Receive data from ClientTarget
Ret = Receive::ReceiveUntilStop(clientOriginator);

// Stop the ClientTarget thread
m_t->Abort();

// Abandon the multicast group.
clientOriginator->DropMulticastGroup(m_GrpAddr);
```

Requirements

Platforms: Windows 98, Windows NT 4.0,
Windows Millennium Edition, Windows 2000,
Windows XP Home Edition, Windows XP Professional,
Windows .NET Server family,
.NET Compact Framework - Windows CE .NET

UdpClient.DropMulticastGroup Method (IPAddress, Int32)

Note: This namespace, class, or member is supported only in
version 1.1 of the .NET Framework.

Leaves a multicast group.

```
[Visual Basic]
Overloads Public Sub DropMulticastGroup( _
    ByVal multicastAddr As IPAddress, _
    ByVal ifindex As Integer _
)
[C#]
public void DropMulticastGroup(
    IPAddress multicastAddr,
    int ifindex
);
[C++]
public: void DropMulticastGroup(
    IPAddress* multicastAddr,
    int ifindex
);
[JScript]
public function DropMulticastGroup(
    multicastAddr : IPAddress,
    ifindex : int
);
```

Parameters

multicastAddr
>   The **IPAddress** of the multicast group to leave.

ifindex
>   The local address of the multicast group to leave.

Requirements

Platforms: Windows 98, Windows NT 4.0,
Windows Millennium Edition, Windows 2000,
Windows XP Home Edition, Windows XP Professional,
Windows .NET Server family

UdpClient.IDisposable.Dispose Method

This member supports the .NET Framework infrastructure and is not
intended to be used directly from your code.

```
[Visual Basic]
Private Sub Dispose() Implements IDisposable.Dispose
[C#]
void IDisposable.Dispose();
[C++]
private: void IDisposable::Dispose();
[JScript]
private function IDisposable.Dispose();
```

UdpClient.JoinMulticastGroup Method

Adds a **UdpClient** to a multicast group.

Overload List

Adds a **UdpClient** to a multicast group.

>   [Visual Basic] **Overloads Public Sub JoinMulticastGroup
>   (IPAddress)**
>   [C#] **public void JoinMulticastGroup(IPAddress);**
>   [C++] **public: void JoinMulticastGroup(IPAddress*);**
>   [JScript] **public function JoinMulticastGroup(IPAddress);**

Adds a **UdpClient** to a multicast group.

>   [Visual Basic] **Overloads Public Sub JoinMulticastGroup
>   (Integer, IPAddress)**
>   [C#] **public void JoinMulticastGroup(int, IPAddress);**
>   [C++] **public: void JoinMulticastGroup(int, IPAddress*);**
>   [JScript] **public function JoinMulticastGroup(int,
>   IPAddress);**

Adds a **UdpClient** to a multicast group with the specified Time to
Live (TTL).

Supported by the .NET Compact Framework.

>   [Visual Basic] **Overloads Public Sub JoinMulticastGroup
>   (IPAddress, Integer)**
>   [C#] **public void JoinMulticastGroup(IPAddress, int);**
>   [C++] **public: void JoinMulticastGroup(IPAddress*, int);**
>   [JScript] **public function JoinMulticastGroup(IPAddress,
>   int);**

Example

[Visual Basic, C#] The following example demonstrates how to join
a multicast group by providing two parameters, a multicast address,
and a number representing the TTL.

[Visual Basic, C#] **Note** This example shows how to use one of the overloaded versions of **JoinMulticastGroup**. For other examples that might be available, see the individual overload topics.

```
[Visual Basic]
Dim udpClient As New UdpClient()
' Creates an IP address to use to join and drop the multicast group.
Dim multicastIpAddress As IPAddress =
IPAddress.Parse("239.255.255.255")

Try
    ' The packet dies after 50 router hops.
    udpClient.JoinMulticastGroup(multicastIpAddress, 50)
Catch e As Exception
    Console.WriteLine(e.ToString())
End Try
```

```
[C#]
UdpClient udpClient = new UdpClient();
// Creates an IPAddress to use to join and drop the multicast group.
IPAddress multicastIpAddress = IPAddress.Parse("239.255.255.255");

try{
    // The packet dies after 50 router hops.
    udpClient.JoinMulticastGroup(multicastIpAddress, 50);
}
catch ( Exception e ){
    Console.WriteLine( e.ToString());
}
```

UdpClient.JoinMulticastGroup Method (IPAddress)

Adds a **UdpClient** to a multicast group.

```
[Visual Basic]
Overloads Public Sub JoinMulticastGroup( _
    ByVal multicastAddr As IPAddress _
)
[C#]
public void JoinMulticastGroup(
    IPAddress multicastAddr
);
[C++]
public: void JoinMulticastGroup(
    IPAddress* multicastAddr
);
[JScript]
public function JoinMulticastGroup(
    multicastAddr : IPAddress
);
```

Parameters

multicastAddr
    The multicast **IPAddress** of the group you want to join.

Exceptions

Exception Type	Condition
ObjectDisposedException	The underlying **Socket** has been closed.
SocketException	An error occurred when accessing the socket. See the Remarks section for more information.
ArgumentException	The IP address is not compatible with the **AddressFamily** value that defines the addressing scheme of the socket.

Remarks

The **JoinMulticastGroup** method subscribes the **UdpClient** to a multicast group using the specified **IPAddress**. After calling the **JoinMulticastGroup** method, the underlying **Socket** sends an Internet Group Management Protocol (IGMP) packet to the router requesting membership to the multicast group. The multicast address range is 224.0.0.0 to 239.255.255.255. If you specify an address outside this range or if the router to which the request is made is not multicast enabled, **UdpClient** will throw a **SocketException**. If you receive a **SocketException**, use **SocketException.ErrorCode** to obtain the specific error code. Once you have obtained this code, you can refer to the Windows Socket Version 2 API error code documentation in MSDN for a detailed description of the error. Once the **UdpClient** is listed with the router as a member of the multicast group, it will be able to receive multicasted datagrams sent to the specified **IPAddress**.

Note You must create the **UdpClient** using the multicast port number; otherwise, you will not be able to receive multicasted datagrams. Do not call the **Connect** method prior to calling the **JoinMulticastGroup** method, or the **Receive** method will not work. You do not need to belong to a multicast group to send datagrams to a multicast IP address.

Before joining a multicast group make sure the socket is bound to the port or end point. You do that by calling one of the constructors that accept as parameter a port or an end point.

To stop receiving multicasted datagrams, call the **DropMulticastGroup** method and provide the **IPAddress** of the group from which you would like to withdraw.

Note In the IPv6 case, there are several multicast address ranges you can choose from. Please, refer to the IETF RFC 2375.

Example

[Visual Basic, C#, C++] The following example demonstrates how to join a multicast group by providing a multicast address.

```
[Visual Basic]
Imports System
Imports System.Net
Imports System.Net.Sockets
Imports System.Text
Imports System.IO
Imports System.Threading
Imports Microsoft.VisualBasic

' The following Receive class is used by both the ClientOriginator and
' the ClientTarget class to receive data from one another..

Public Class Receive

    ' The following static method performs the actual data
    ' exchange. In particular, it performs the following tasks:
    ' 1)Establishes a communication endpoint.
    ' 2)Receive data through this end point on behalf of the
    ' caller.
    ' 3) Returns the received data in ASCII format.
    Public Shared Function ReceiveUntilStop(c As UdpClient) As String
        Dim strData As [String] = ""
        Dim Ret As [String] = ""
        Dim ASCII As New ASCIIEncoding()

        ' Establish the communication endpoint.
        Dim endpoint As New IPEndPoint(IPAddress.IPv6Any, 50)
```

```vbnet
            While Not strData.Equals("Over")
                Dim data As [Byte]() = c.Receive(endpoint)
                strData = ASCII.GetString(data)
                Ret += strData + ControlChars.Lf
            End While
            Return Ret
        End Function 'ReceiveUntilStop
End Class 'Receive

' The following Send class is used by both the ClientOriginator and
' ClientTarget classes to send data to one another.

Public Class Send
    Private Shared greetings As Char() = {"H"c, "e"c, "l"c,
"l"c, "o"c, " "c, "T"c, "a"c, "r"c, "g"c, "e"c, "t"c, "."c}
    Private Shared nice As Char() = {"H"c, "a"c, "v"c, "e"c,
" "c, "a"c, " "c, "n"c, "i"c, "c"c, "e"c, " "c, "d"c, "a"c,
"y"c, "."c}
    Private Shared eom As Char() = {"O"c, "v"c, "e"c, "r"c}

    Private Shared tGreetings As Char() = {"H"c, "e"c, "l"c,
"l"c, "o"c, " "c, "O"c, "r"c, "i"c, "g"c, "i"c, "n"c, "a"c,
"t"c, "o"c, "r"c, "!"c}
    Private Shared tNice As Char() = {"Y"c, "o"c, "u"c, " "
"c, "t"c, "o"c, "o"c, "."c}

    ' The following static method sends data to the ClientTarget on
    ' behalf of the ClientOriginator.
    Public Shared Sub OriginatorSendData(c As UdpClient,
ep As IPEndPoint)
        Console.WriteLine(New String(greetings))
        c.Send(GetByteArray(greetings), greetings.Length, ep)
        Thread.Sleep(1000)

        Console.WriteLine(New [String](nice))
        c.Send(GetByteArray(nice), nice.Length, ep)

        Thread.Sleep(1000)
        Console.WriteLine(New [String](eom))
        c.Send(GetByteArray(eom), eom.Length, ep)
    End Sub 'OriginatorSendData

    ' The following static method sends data to the ClientOriginator on
    ' behalf of the ClientTarget.
    Public Shared Sub TargetSendData(c As UdpClient, ep As IPEndPoint)
        Console.WriteLine(New String(tGreetings))
        c.Send(GetByteArray(tGreetings), tGreetings.Length, ep)
        Thread.Sleep(1000)

        Console.WriteLine(New [String](tNice))
        c.Send(GetByteArray(tNice), tNice.Length, ep)

        Thread.Sleep(1000)
        Console.WriteLine(New [String](eom))
        c.Send(GetByteArray(eom), eom.Length, ep)
    End Sub 'TargetSendData

    ' Internal utility
    Public Shared Function GetByteArray(ChArray() As [Char]) As [Byte]()
        Dim Ret(ChArray.Length) As [Byte]

        Dim i As Integer
        For i = 0 To ChArray.Length - 1
            Ret(i) = AscW(ChArray(i))
        Next i
        Return Ret
    End Function 'GetByteArray

End Class 'Send

' The ClientTarget class is the receiver of the ClientOriginator
' messages. The StartMulticastConversation method contains the
' logic for exchanging data between the ClientTarget and its
' counterpart ClientOriginator in a multicast operation.

Public Class ClientTarget
    Private Shared m_ClientTarget As UdpClient
    Private Shared m_GrpAddr As IPAddress

    ' The following StartMulticastConversation method connects the UDP
    ' ClientTarget with the ClientOriginator.
    ' It performs the following main tasks:
    ' 1)Creates a UDP client to receive data on a specific port
and using
    ' IPv6 addresses. The port is the same one used by the
ClientOriginator
    ' to define its communication endpoint.
    ' 2)Joins or creates a multicast group at the specified address.
    ' 3)Defines the endpoint port to send data to the ClientOriginator.
    ' 4)Receives data from the ClientOriginator until the end of the
    ' communication.
    ' 5)Sends data to the ClientOriginator.
    ' Note this method is the counterpart of the
    ' ClientOriginator.ConnectOriginatorAndTarget().
    Public Shared Sub StartMulticastConversation()
        Dim Ret As String

        ' Bind and listen on port 1000. Specify the IPv6 address
family type.
        m_ClientTarget = New UdpClient(1000,
AddressFamily.InterNetworkV6)

        ' Join or create a multicast group
        m_GrpAddr = IPAddress.Parse("FF01::1")

        ' Use the overloaded JoinMulticastGroup method.
        ' Refer to the ClientOriginator method to see how to use
the other
        ' methods.
        m_ClientTarget.JoinMulticastGroup(m_GrpAddr)

        ' Define the endpoint data port. Note that this port number
        ' must match the ClientOriginator UDP port number which is the
        ' port on which the ClientOriginator is receiving data.
        Dim ClientOriginatordest As New IPEndPoint(m_GrpAddr, 2000)

        ' Receive data from the ClientOriginator.
        Ret = Receive.ReceiveUntilStop(m_ClientTarget)
        Console.WriteLine((ControlChars.Lf + "The ClientTarget
received: " + ControlChars.Lf + ControlChars.Lf + Ret +
ControlChars.Lf))

        ' Done receiving, now respond to the ClientOriginator.
        ' Wait to make sure the ClientOriginator is ready to receive.
        Thread.Sleep(2000)

        Console.WriteLine(ControlChars.Lf + "The ClientTarget
sent:" + ControlChars.Lf)

        Send.TargetSendData(m_ClientTarget, ClientOriginatordest)

        ' Exit the multicast conversation.
        m_ClientTarget.DropMulticastGroup(m_GrpAddr)
    End Sub 'StartMulticastConversation
End Class 'ClientTarget

' The following ClientOriginator class starts the multicast
conversation
' with the ClientTarget class..
' It performs the following main tasks:
' 1)Creates a socket and binds it to the port on which to communicate.
' 2)Specifies that the connection must use an IPv6 address.
' 3)Joins or create a multicast group.
'   Note that the multicast address ranges to use are specified
'   in the RFC#2375.
' 4)Defines the endpoint to send the data to and starts the
' client target (ClientTarget) thread.

Public Class ClientOriginator
    Private Shared clientOriginator As UdpClient
```

```
        Private Shared m_GrpAddr As IPAddress
        Private Shared m_ClientTargetdest As IPEndPoint
        Private Shared m_t As Thread


        ' The ConnectOriginatorAndTarget method connects the
        ' ClientOriginator with the ClientTarget.
        ' It performs the following main tasks:
        ' 1)Creates a UDP client to receive data on a specific port
        '   using IPv6 addresses.
        ' 2)Joins or create a multicast group at the specified address.
        ' 3)Defines the endpoint port to send data to on the ClientTarget.
        ' 4)Starts the ClientTarget thread that also creates the
ClientTarget object.
        ' Note this method is the counterpart of the
        ' ClientTarget.StartMulticastConversation().
        Public Shared Function ConnectOriginatorAndTarget() As Boolean
            Try
                ' Bind and listen on port 2000. This constructor
creates a socket
                ' and binds it to the port on which to receive data.
The family
                ' parameter specifies that this connection uses an IPv6
address.
                clientOriginator = New UdpClient(2000,
AddressFamily.InterNetworkV6)

                ' Join or create a multicast group. The multicast
address ranges
                ' to use are specified in RFC#2375. You are free to use
                ' different addresses.
                ' Transform the string address into the internal format.
                m_GrpAddr = IPAddress.Parse("FF01::1")

                ' Display the multicast address used.
                Console.WriteLine(("Multicast Address: [" +
m_GrpAddr.ToString() + "]"))

                ' Exercise the use of the IPv6MulticastOption.
                Console.WriteLine("Instantiate IPv6MulticastOption(IPAddress)")

                ' Instantiate IPv6MulticastOption using one of the
                ' overloaded constructors.
                Dim ipv6MulticastOption As New IPv6MulticastOption(m_GrpAddr)

                ' Store the IPAddress multicast options.
                Dim group As IPAddress = ipv6MulticastOption.Group
                Dim interfaceIndex As Long =
ipv6MulticastOption.InterfaceIndex

                ' Display IPv6MulticastOption properties.
                Console.WriteLine(("IPv6MulticastOption.Group: [" +
group.ToString() + "]"))
                Console.WriteLine(("IPv6MulticastOption.InterfaceIndex:
[" + interfaceIndex.ToString() + "]"))

                ' Instantiate IPv6MulticastOption using another
                ' overloaded constructor.
                Dim ipv6MulticastOption2 As New
IPv6MulticastOption(group, interfaceIndex)

                ' Store the IPAdress multicast options.
                group = ipv6MulticastOption2.Group
                interfaceIndex = ipv6MulticastOption2.InterfaceIndex

                ' Display the IPv6MulticastOption2 properties.
                Console.WriteLine(("IPv6MulticastOption.Group: [" +
group.ToString() + "]"))
                Console.WriteLine(("IPv6MulticastOption.InterfaceIndex:
[" + interfaceIndex.ToString() + "]"))

                ' Join the specified multicast group using one of the
                ' JoinMulticastGroup overloaded methods.
                clientOriginator.JoinMulticastGroup
(Fix(interfaceIndex), group)
```

```
                ' Define the endpoint data port. Note that this port number
                ' must match the ClientTarget UDP port number which is the
                ' port on which the ClientTarget is receiving data.
                m_ClientTargetdest = New IPEndPoint(m_GrpAddr, 1000)

                ' Start the ClientTarget thread so it is ready to receive.
                m_t = New Thread(New ThreadStart(AddressOf
ClientTarget.StartMulticastConversation))
                m_t.Start()

                ' Make sure that the thread has started.
                Thread.Sleep(2000)

                Return True
            Catch e As Exception
                Console.WriteLine(("[ClientOriginator.ConnectClients]
Exception: " + e.ToString()))
                Return False
            End Try
        End Function 'ConnectOriginatorAndTarget

        ' The SendAndReceive performs the data exchange
        ' between the ClientOriginator and the ClientTarget classes.
        Public Shared Function SendAndReceive() As String
            Dim Ret As String = ""

            ' Send data to ClientTarget.
            Console.WriteLine(ControlChars.Lf + "The ClientOriginator
sent:" + ControlChars.Lf)
            Send.OriginatorSendData(clientOriginator, m_ClientTargetdest)

            ' Receive data from ClientTarget
            Ret = Receive.ReceiveUntilStop(clientOriginator)

            ' Stop the ClientTarget thread
            m_t.Abort()

            ' Abandon the multicast group.
            clientOriginator.DropMulticastGroup(m_GrpAddr)

            Return Ret
        End Function 'SendAndReceive

        'This is the console application entry point.
        Public Shared Sub Main()
            ' Join the multicast group.
            If ConnectOriginatorAndTarget() Then
                ' Perform a multicast conversation with the ClientTarget.
                Dim Ret As String = SendAndReceive()
                Console.WriteLine((ControlChars.Lf + "The
ClientOriginator received: " + ControlChars.Lf + ControlChars.Lf
+ Ret))
            Else
                Console.WriteLine("Unable to Join the multicast group")
            End If
        End Sub 'Main
End Class 'ClientOriginator

[C#]
using System;
using System.Net;
using System.Net.Sockets;
using System.Text;
using System.IO;
using System.Threading;

namespace Mssc.TransportProtocols.Utilities
{

    // The following Receive class is used by both the
ClientOriginator and
    // the ClientTarget class to receive data from one another..
    public class Receive
    {
        // The following static method performs the actual data
```

```
// exchange. In particular, it performs the following tasks:
// 1)Establishes a communication endpoint.
// 2)Receive data through this end point on behalf of the
// caller.
// 3) Returns the received data in ASCII format.
public static string ReceiveUntilStop(UdpClient c)
{
  String strData = "";
  String Ret = "";
  ASCIIEncoding ASCII = new ASCIIEncoding();

  // Establish the communication endpoint.
  IPEndPoint endpoint = new IPEndPoint(IPAddress.IPv6Any, 50);

  while (!strData.Equals("Over"))
  {
    Byte[] data = c.Receive(ref endpoint);
    strData = ASCII.GetString(data);
    Ret += strData + "\n";
  }
  return Ret;
}
}

// The following Send class is used by both the ClientOriginator and
// ClientTarget classes to send data to one another.
public class Send
{
  private static char[] greetings = { 'H', 'e', 'l', 'l', 'o', ' ',
                                       'T', 'a', 'r', 'g', 'e',
't', '.' };
  private static char[] nice     = { 'H', 'a', 'v', 'e', ' ',
'a', ' ', 'n', 'i',
                                     'c', 'e', ' ', 'd', 'a',
'y', '.' };
  private static char [] eom      = { 'O', 'v', 'e', 'r' };

  private static char[] tGreetings = { 'H', 'e', 'l', 'l', 'o', ' ',
                                       'O', 'r', 'i', 'g', 'i',
'n', 'a', 't', 'o', 'r', '!' };
  private static char[] tNice  = { 'Y', 'o', 'u', ' ', 't',
'o', 'o', '.'};

  // The following static method sends data to the ClientTarget on
  // behalf of the ClientOriginator.
  public static void OriginatorSendData(UdpClient c, IPEndPoint ep)
  {
    Console.WriteLine(new string(greetings));
    c.Send(GetByteArray(greetings), greetings.Length, ep);
    Thread.Sleep(1000);

    Console.WriteLine(new String(nice));
    c.Send(GetByteArray(nice), nice.Length, ep);

    Thread.Sleep(1000);
    Console.WriteLine(new String(eom));
    c.Send(GetByteArray(eom), eom.Length, ep);
  }

  // The following static method sends data to the
  // ClientOriginator on
  // behalf of the ClientTarget.
  public static void TargetSendData(UdpClient c, IPEndPoint ep)
  {
    Console.WriteLine(new string(tGreetings));
    c.Send(GetByteArray(tGreetings), tGreetings.Length, ep);
    Thread.Sleep(1000);

    Console.WriteLine(new String(tNice));
    c.Send(GetByteArray(tNice), tNice.Length, ep);

    Thread.Sleep(1000);
    Console.WriteLine(new String(eom));
    c.Send(GetByteArray(eom), eom.Length, ep);
  }
```

```
  // Internal utility
  private static Byte[] GetByteArray(Char[] ChArray)
  {
    Byte[] Ret = new Byte[ChArray.Length];
    for (int i = 0; i < ChArray.Length; i++)
      Ret[i] = (Byte) ChArray[i];
    return Ret;
  }
}

// The ClientTarget class is the receiver of the ClientOriginator
// messages. The StartMulticastConversation method contains the
// logic for exchanging data between the ClientTarget and its
// counterpart ClientOriginator in a multicast operation.
public class ClientTarget
{
  private static UdpClient m_ClientTarget;
  private static IPAddress m_GrpAddr;

  // The following StartMulticastConversation method connects the UDP
  // ClientTarget with the ClientOriginator.
  // It performs the following main tasks:
  // 1)Creates a UDP client to receive data on a specific port
and using
  // IPv6 addresses. The port is the same one used by the
ClientOriginator
  // to define its communication endpoint.
  // 2)Joins or creates a multicast group at the specified address.
  // 3)Defines the endpoint port to send data to the
ClientOriginator.
  // 4)Receives data from the ClientOriginator until the end of the
  // communication.
  // 5)Sends data to the ClientOriginator.
  // Note this method is the counterpart of the
  // ClientOriginator.ConnectOriginatorAndTarget().
  public static void StartMulticastConversation()
  {
    string Ret;

    // Bind and listen on port 1000. Specify the IPv6 address
family type.
    m_ClientTarget = new UdpClient(1000, AddressFamily.InterNetworkV6);

    // Join or create a multicast group
    m_GrpAddr = IPAddress.Parse("FF01::1");

    // Use the overloaded JoinMulticastGroup method.
    // Refer to the ClientOriginator method to see how to use
the other
    // methods.
    m_ClientTarget.JoinMulticastGroup(m_GrpAddr);

    // Define the endpoint data port. Note that this port number
    // must match the ClientOriginator UDP port number which is the
    // port on which the ClientOriginator is receiving data.
    IPEndPoint ClientOriginatordest = new IPEndPoint
(m_GrpAddr, 2000);

    // Receive data from the ClientOriginator.
    Ret = Receive.ReceiveUntilStop(m_ClientTarget);
    Console.WriteLine("\nThe ClientTarget received: " + "\n\n"
+ Ret + "\n");

    // Done receiving, now respond to the ClientOriginator.

    // Wait to make sure the ClientOriginator is ready to receive.
    Thread.Sleep(2000);

    Console.WriteLine("\nThe ClientTarget sent:\n");

    Send.TargetSendData(m_ClientTarget, ClientOriginatordest);

    // Exit the multicast conversation.
    m_ClientTarget.DropMulticastGroup(m_GrpAddr);
```

```
    }
  }

  // The following ClientOriginator class starts the
multicast conversation
  // with the ClientTarget class..
  // It performs the following main tasks:
  // 1)Creates a socket and binds it to the port on which to
communicate.
  // 2)Specifies that the connection must use an IPv6 address.
  // 3)Joins or create a multicast group.
  //    Note that the multicast address ranges to use are specified
  //    in the RFC#2375.
  // 4)Defines the endpoint to send the data to and starts the
  // client target (ClientTarget) thread.
  public class ClientOriginator
  {
    private static UdpClient clientOriginator;
    private static IPAddress m_GrpAddr;
    private static IPEndPoint m_ClientTargetdest;
    private static Thread m_t;

    // The ConnectOriginatorAndTarget method connects the
    // ClientOriginator with the ClientTarget.
    // It performs the following main tasks:
    // 1)Creates a UDP client to receive data on a specific port
    //   using IPv6 addresses.
    // 2)Joins or create a multicast group at the specified address.
    // 3)Defines the endpoint port to send data to on the ClientTarget.
    // 4)Starts the ClientTarget thread that also creates the
ClientTarget object.
    // Note this method is the counterpart of the
    // ClientTarget.StartMulticastConversation().
    public static bool ConnectOriginatorAndTarget()
    {
      try
      {

        // Bind and listen on port 2000. This constructor
creates a socket
        // and binds it to the port on which to receive
data. The family
        // parameter specifies that this connection uses an
IPv6 address.
        clientOriginator = new UdpClient(2000,
AddressFamily.InterNetworkV6);

        // Join or create a multicast group. The multicast
address ranges
        // to use are specified in RFC#2375. You are free to use
        // different addresses.

        // Transform the string address into the internal format.
        m_GrpAddr = IPAddress.Parse("FF01::1");

        // Display the multicast address used.
        Console.WriteLine("Multicast Address:
[" + m_GrpAddr.ToString() + "]");

        // Exercise the use of the IPv6MulticastOption.
        Console.WriteLine("Instantiate IPv6MulticastOption(IPAddress)");

        // Instantiate IPv6MulticastOption using one of the
        // overloaded constructors.
        IPv6MulticastOption ipv6MulticastOption = new
IPv6MulticastOption(m_GrpAddr);

        // Store the IPAdress multicast options.
        IPAddress group = ipv6MulticastOption.Group;
        long interfaceIndex = ipv6MulticastOption.InterfaceIndex;

        // Display IPv6MulticastOption properties.
        Console.WriteLine("IPv6MulticastOption.Group:
[" + group  + "]");
```

```
        Console.WriteLine("IPv6MulticastOption.InterfaceIndex:
[" + interfaceIndex + "]");

        // Instantiate IPv6MulticastOption using another
        // overloaded constructor.
        IPv6MulticastOption ipv6MulticastOption2 = new
IPv6MulticastOption(group, interfaceIndex);

        // Store the IPAdress multicast options.
        group = ipv6MulticastOption2.Group;
        interfaceIndex = ipv6MulticastOption2.InterfaceIndex;

        // Display the IPv6MulticastOption2 properties.
        Console.WriteLine("IPv6MulticastOption.Group:
[" + group  + "]");
        Console.WriteLine("IPv6MulticastOption.InterfaceIndex:
[" + interfaceIndex + "]");

        // Join the specified multicast group using one of the
        // JoinMulticastGroup overloaded methods.
        clientOriginator.JoinMulticastGroup((int)
interfaceIndex, group);

        // Define the endpoint data port. Note that this port number
        // must match the ClientTarget UDP port number which is the
        // port on which the ClientTarget is receiving data.
        m_ClientTargetdest = new IPEndPoint(m_GrpAddr, 1000);

        // Start the ClientTarget thread so it is ready to receive.
        m_t = new Thread(new
ThreadStart(ClientTarget.StartMulticastConversation));
        m_t.Start();

        // Make sure that the thread has started.
        Thread.Sleep(2000);

        return true;
      }
      catch (Exception e)
      {
        Console.WriteLine("[ClientOriginator.ConnectClients]
Exception: " + e.ToString());
        return false;
      }
    }

    // The SendAndReceive performs the data exchange
    // between the ClientOriginator and the ClientTarget classes.
    public static string SendAndReceive()
    {
      string Ret = "";

      // Send data to ClientTarget.
      Console.WriteLine("\nThe ClientOriginator sent:\n");
      Send.OriginatorSendData(clientOriginator, m_ClientTargetdest);

      // Receive data from ClientTarget
      Ret = Receive.ReceiveUntilStop(clientOriginator);

      // Stop the ClientTarget thread
      m_t.Abort();

      // Abandon the multicast group.
      clientOriginator.DropMulticastGroup(m_GrpAddr);

      return Ret;
    }

    //This is the console application entry point.
    public static void Main()
    {
      // Join the multicast group.
      if (ConnectOriginatorAndTarget())
      {
        // Perform a multicast conversation with the ClientTarget.
```

```
        string Ret = SendAndReceive();
        Console.WriteLine("\nThe ClientOriginator received:
+ "\n\n" + Ret);
    }
    else
    {
        Console.WriteLine("Unable to Join the multicast group");
    }
}
```

```
[C++]
#using <mscorlib.dll>
#using <System.dll>
using namespace System;
using namespace System::Net;
using namespace System::Net::Sockets;
using namespace System::Text;
using namespace System::IO;
using namespace System::Threading;

//namespace Mssc::TransportProtocols::Utilities {
    // The following Receive class is used by both the
ClientOriginator and
    // the ClientTarget class to receive data from one another..
    public __gc class Receive {
        // The following static method performs the actual data
        // exchange. In particular, it performs the following tasks:
        // 1)Establishes a communication endpoint.
        // 2)Receive data through this end point on behalf of the
        // caller.
        // 3) Returns the received data in ASCII format.
    public:
        static String* ReceiveUntilStop(UdpClient* c) {
            String* strData = S"";
            String* Ret = S"";
            ASCIIEncoding* ASCII = new ASCIIEncoding();

            // Establish the communication endpoint.
            IPEndPoint* endpoint = new IPEndPoint(IPAddress::IPv6Any, 50);

            while (!strData->Equals(S"Over")) {
                Byte data[] = c->Receive(&endpoint);

                strData = ASCII->GetString(data);
                Ret = String::Concat(Ret, strData, S"\n");
            }
            return Ret;
        }
    };

    // The following Send class is used by both the ClientOriginator and
    // ClientTarget classes to send data to one another.
    public __gc class Send {
    private:
        static Char greetings [] = { 'H', 'e', 'l', 'l', 'o', ' ',
            'T', 'a', 'r', 'g', 'e', 't', '->' };
    private:
        static Char nice[]    = { 'H', 'a', 'v', 'e', ' ', 'a',
' ', 'n', 'i',
            'c', 'e', ' ', 'd', 'a', 'y', '->' };
    private:
        static Char eom[]    = { 'O', 'v', 'e', 'r'};

    private:
        static Char tGreetings[] = { 'H', 'e', 'l', 'l', 'o', ' ',
            'O', 'r', 'i', 'g', 'i', 'n', 'a', 't', 'o', 'r', '!' };
    private:
        static Char tNice[]   = { 'Y', 'o', 'u', ' ', 't',
'o', 'o', '->'};
    private:
        // The following static method sends data to the ClientTarget on
        // behalf of the ClientOriginator.
    public:
```

```
        static void OriginatorSendData(UdpClient * c, IPEndPoint * ep) {
            Console::WriteLine(new String (greetings));
            c->Send(GetByteArray(greetings), greetings->Length, ep);
            Thread::Sleep(1000);

            Console::WriteLine(new String(nice));
            c->Send(GetByteArray(nice), nice->Length, ep);

            Thread::Sleep(1000);
            Console::WriteLine(new String(eom));
            c->Send(GetByteArray(eom), eom->Length, ep);
        }

        // The following static method sends data to the
ClientOriginator on
        // behalf of the ClientTarget.
    public:
        static void TargetSendData(UdpClient * c, IPEndPoint * ep) {
            Console::WriteLine(new String (tGreetings));
            c->Send(GetByteArray(tGreetings), tGreetings->Length, ep);
            Thread::Sleep(1000);

            Console::WriteLine(new String(tNice));
            c->Send(GetByteArray(tNice), tNice->Length, ep);

            Thread::Sleep(1000);
            Console::WriteLine(new String(eom));
            c->Send(GetByteArray(eom), eom->Length, ep);
        }
        // Internal utility
    private:
        static Byte GetByteArray(Char ChArray[])[] {
            Byte Ret[] = new Byte[ChArray->Length];
            for (int i = 0; i < ChArray->Length; i++)
                Ret[i] = (Byte) ChArray[i];
            return Ret;
        }
    };

    // The ClientTarget class is the receiver of the ClientOriginator
    // messages. The StartMulticastConversation method contains the
    // logic for exchanging data between the ClientTarget and its
    // counterpart ClientOriginator in a multicast operation.
    public __gc class ClientTarget {
    private:
        static UdpClient* m_ClientTarget;
    private:
        static IPAddress* m_GrpAddr;

        // The following StartMulticastConversation method
connects the UDP
        // ClientTarget with the ClientOriginator.
        // It performs the following main tasks:
        // 1)Creates a UDP client to receive data on a
specific port and using
        // IPv6 addresses. The port is the same one used
by the ClientOriginator
        // to define its communication endpoint.
        // 2)Joins or creates a multicast group at the specified address.
        // 3)Defines the endpoint port to send data to the
ClientOriginator.
        // 4)Receives data from the ClientOriginator until
the end of the
        // communication.
        // 5)Sends data to the ClientOriginator.
        // Note this method is the counterpart of the
        // ClientOriginator::ConnectOriginatorAndTarget().
    public:
        static void StartMulticastConversation() {
            String* Ret;

            // Bind and listen on port 1000. Specify the IPv6
address family type.
            m_ClientTarget = new UdpClient(1000,
AddressFamily::InterNetworkV6);
```

```
          // Join or create a multicast group
          m_GrpAddr = IPAddress::Parse(S"FF01::1");

          // Use the overloaded JoinMulticastGroup method.
          // Refer to the ClientOriginator method to see how
to use the other
          // methods.
          m_ClientTarget->JoinMulticastGroup(m_GrpAddr);

          // Define the endpoint data port. Note that this port number
          // must match the ClientOriginator UDP port number
which is the
          // port on which the ClientOriginator is receiving data.
          IPEndPoint* ClientOriginatordest = new IPEndPoint
(m_GrpAddr, 2000);

          // Receive data from the ClientOriginator.
          Ret = Receive::ReceiveUntilStop(m_ClientTarget);
          Console::WriteLine(S"\nThe ClientTarget received:
\n\n {0}\n", Ret);

          // Done receiving, now respond to the ClientOriginator.
          // Wait to make sure the ClientOriginator is ready to receive.
          Thread::Sleep(2000);
          Console::WriteLine(S"\nThe ClientTarget sent:\n");
          Send::TargetSendData(m_ClientTarget, ClientOriginatordest);

          // Exit the multicast conversation.
          m_ClientTarget->DropMulticastGroup(m_GrpAddr);
       }
    };

    // The following ClientOriginator class starts the multicast
conversation
    // with the ClientTarget class..
    // It performs the following main tasks:
    // 1)Creates a socket and binds it to the port on which to
communicate.
    // 2)Specifies that the connection must use an IPv6 address.
    // 3)Joins or create a multicast group.
    //   Note that the multicast address ranges to use are specified
    //   in the RFC#2375.
    // 4)Defines the endpoint to send the data to and starts the
    // client target (ClientTarget) thread.
    public __gc class ClientOriginator {
    private:
       static UdpClient* clientOriginator;
    private:
       static IPAddress* m_GrpAddr;
    private:
       static IPEndPoint* m_ClientTargetdest;
    private:
       static Thread* m_t;

       // The ConnectOriginatorAndTarget method connects the
       // ClientOriginator with the ClientTarget.
       // It performs the following main tasks:
       // 1)Creates a UDP client to receive data on a specific port
       //   using IPv6 addresses.
       // 2)Joins or create a multicast group at the specified address.
       // 3)Defines the endpoint port to send data to on the
ClientTarget.
       // 4)Starts the ClientTarget thread that also creates
the ClientTarget Object*.
       // Note this method is the counterpart of the
       // ClientTarget::StartMulticastConversation().
    public:
       static bool ConnectOriginatorAndTarget() {
          try {

             // Bind and listen on port 2000. This constructor
creates a socket
             // and binds it to the port on which to receive
data. The family
             // parameter specifies that this connection uses
```

```
an IPv6 address.
             clientOriginator = new UdpClient(2000,
AddressFamily::InterNetworkV6);

             // Join or create a multicast group. The multicast
address ranges
             // to use are specified in RFC#2375. You are free to use
             // different addresses.

             // Transform the String* address into the internal format.
             m_GrpAddr = IPAddress::Parse(S"FF01::1");

             // Display the multicast address used.
             Console::WriteLine(S"Multicast Address: [ {0}]",
m_GrpAddr);

             // Exercise the use of the IPv6MulticastOption.
             Console::WriteLine(S"Instantiate
IPv6MulticastOption(IPAddress)");

             // Instantiate IPv6MulticastOption using one of the
             // overloaded constructors.
             IPv6MulticastOption* ipv6MulticastOption =
new IPv6MulticastOption(m_GrpAddr);

             // Store the IPAddress multicast options.
             IPAddress * group = ipv6MulticastOption->Group;
             __int64 interfaceIndex = ipv6MulticastOption-
>InterfaceIndex;

             // Display IPv6MulticastOption properties.
             Console::WriteLine(S"IPv6MulticastOption::Group:
[ {0}]", group);
             Console::WriteLine(S"IPv6MulticastOption::
InterfaceIndex: [ {0}]", __box(interfaceIndex));

             // Instantiate IPv6MulticastOption using another
             // overloaded constructor.
             IPv6MulticastOption* ipv6MulticastOption2 =
                new IPv6MulticastOption(group, interfaceIndex);

             // Store the IPAdress multicast options.
             group = ipv6MulticastOption2->Group;
             interfaceIndex = ipv6MulticastOption2->InterfaceIndex;

             // Display the IPv6MulticastOption2 properties.
             Console::WriteLine(S"IPv6MulticastOption::Group:
[ {0} ]", group);
             Console::WriteLine(S"IPv6MulticastOption::
InterfaceIndex: [ {0} ]", __box(interfaceIndex));

             // Join the specified multicast group using one of the
             // JoinMulticastGroup overloaded methods.
             clientOriginator->JoinMulticastGroup((int)
interfaceIndex, group);

             // Define the endpoint data port. Note that this
port number
             // must match the ClientTarget UDP port number which is the
             // port on which the ClientTarget is receiving data.
             m_ClientTargetdest = new IPEndPoint(m_GrpAddr, 1000);

             // Start the ClientTarget thread so it is ready to receive.
             m_t = new Thread(new ThreadStart(0,
ClientTarget::StartMulticastConversation));
             m_t->Start();

             // Make sure that the thread has started.
             Thread::Sleep(2000);

             return true;
          } catch (Exception* e) {
             Console::WriteLine(S"[ClientOriginator::
ConnectClients] Exception: {0}", e);
             return false;
```

```
        }
    }

    // The SendAndReceive performs the data exchange
    // between the ClientOriginator and the ClientTarget classes.
public:
    static String* SendAndReceive() {
        String* Ret = S"";

        // Send data to ClientTarget.
        Console::WriteLine(S"\nThe ClientOriginator sent:\n");
        Send::OriginatorSendData(clientOriginator,
m_ClientTargetdest);

        // Receive data from ClientTarget
        Ret = Receive::ReceiveUntilStop(clientOriginator);

        // Stop the ClientTarget thread
        m_t->Abort();

        // Abandon the multicast group.
        clientOriginator->DropMulticastGroup(m_GrpAddr);

        return Ret;
    }
};
//}

//This is the console application entry point.
int main() {
    // Join the multicast group.
    if (ClientOriginator::ConnectOriginatorAndTarget()) {
        // Perform a multicast conversation with the ClientTarget.
        String* Ret = ClientOriginator::SendAndReceive();
        Console::WriteLine(S"\nThe ClientOriginator received:
\n\n {0}", Ret);
    } else {
        Console::WriteLine(S"Unable to Join the multicast group");
    }
}
```

Requirements

Platforms: Windows 98, Windows NT 4.0,
Windows Millennium Edition, Windows 2000,
Windows XP Home Edition, Windows XP Professional,
Windows .NET Server family

UdpClient.JoinMulticastGroup Method (Int32, IPAddress)

Note: This namespace, class, or member is supported only in version 1.1 of the .NET Framework.

Adds a **UdpClient** to a multicast group.

```
[Visual Basic]
Overloads Public Sub JoinMulticastGroup( _
    ByVal ifindex As Integer, _
    ByVal multicastAddr As IPAddress _
)
[C#]
public void JoinMulticastGroup(
    int ifindex,
    IPAddress multicastAddr
);
[C++]
public: void JoinMulticastGroup(
    int ifindex,
    IPAddress* multicastAddr
);
```

```
[JScript]
public function JoinMulticastGroup(
    ifindex : int,
    multicastAddr : IPAddress
);
```

Parameters

ifindex
    The local address.
multicastAddr
    The multicast **IPAddress** of the group you want to join.

Exceptions

Exception Type	Condition
System.ObjectDisposed-Exception	The underlying **Socket** has been closed.
Sockets.SocketException	An error occurred when accessing the socket. See the Remarks section for more information.

Remarks

Before joining a multicast group, be sure the socket is bound to the port or endpoint. You can do this by calling one of the constructors that accepts a port or an end point as parameter.

The *infindex* parameter is used to identify a hardware interface on the same link.

Note There are several multicast address ranges to choose from. Refer to the IETF RFC 2375.

Requirements

Platforms: Windows 98, Windows NT 4.0,
Windows Millennium Edition, Windows 2000,
Windows XP Home Edition, Windows XP Professional,
Windows .NET Server family

UdpClient.JoinMulticastGroup Method (IPAddress, Int32)

Adds a **UdpClient** to a multicast group with the specified Time to Live (TTL).

```
[Visual Basic]
Overloads Public Sub JoinMulticastGroup( _
    ByVal multicastAddr As IPAddress, _
    ByVal timeToLive As Integer _
)
[C#]
public void JoinMulticastGroup(
    IPAddress multicastAddr,
    int timeToLive
);
[C++]
public: void JoinMulticastGroup(
    IPAddress* multicastAddr,
    int timeToLive
);
[JScript]
public function JoinMulticastGroup(
    multicastAddr : IPAddress,
    timeToLive : int
);
```

Parameters

multicastAddr

The **IPAddress** of the multicast group to join.

timeToLive

The Time to Live (TTL), measured in router hops.

Exceptions

Exception Type	Condition
ArgumentOutOfRange-Exception	The TTL provided is not between 0 and 255
ObjectDisposedException	The underlying **Socket** has been closed.
SocketException	An error occurred when accessing the socket. See the Remarks section for more information.
ArgumentNullException	*multicastAddr* is a null reference (**Nothing** in Visual Basic).
ArgumentException	The IP address is not compatible with the **AddressFamily** value that defines the addressing scheme of the socket.

Remarks

The **JoinMulticastGroup** method subscribes the **UdpClient** to a multicast group using the specified **IPAddress**. After calling the **JoinMulticastGroup** method, the underlying **Socket** sends an Internet Group Management Protocol (IGMP) packet to the router requesting membership to the multicast group. The multicast address range is 224.0.0.0 to 239.255.255.255. If you specify an address outside this range or if the router to which the request is made is not multicast enabled, **UdpClient** will throw a **SocketException**. If you receive a **SocketException**, use **SocketException.ErrorCode** to obtain the specific error code. Once you have obtained this code, you can refer to the Windows Socket Version 2 API error code documentation in MSDN for a detailed description of the error. The *timeToLive* parameter specifies how many router hops will be allowed for a multicasted datagram before being discarded. Once the **UdpClient** is listed with the router as a member of the multicast group, it will be able to receive multicasted datagrams sent to the specified **IPAddress**.

> **Note** You must create the **UdpClient** using the multicast port number otherwise you will not be able to receive multicasted datagrams. Do not call the **Connect** method prior to calling the **JoinMulticastGroup** method or the receive method will not work. You do not need to belong to a multicast group to send datagrams to a multicast IP address.

Before joining a multicast group make sure the socket is bound to the port or end point. You do that by calling one of the constructors that accept as parameter a port or an end point.

To stop receiving multicasted datagrams, call the **DropMulticastGroup** method and provide the **IPAddress** of the group from which you would like to withdraw.

Example

[Visual Basic, C#] The following example demonstrates how to join a multicast group by providing two parameters, a multicast address, and a number representing the TTL.

```
[Visual Basic]
Dim udpClient As New UdpClient()
' Creates an IP address to use to join and drop the multicast group.
Dim multicastIpAddress As IPAddress =
IPAddress.Parse("239.255.255.255")

Try
    ' The packet dies after 50 router hops.
    udpClient.JoinMulticastGroup(multicastIpAddress, 50)
Catch e As Exception
    Console.WriteLine(e.ToString())
End Try
```

```
[C#]
UdpClient udpClient = new UdpClient();
// Creates an IPAddress to use to join and drop the multicast group.
IPAddress multicastIpAddress = IPAddress.Parse("239.255.255.255");

try{
    // The packet dies after 50 router hops.
    udpClient.JoinMulticastGroup(multicastIpAddress, 50);
}
catch ( Exception e ){
    Console.WriteLine( e.ToString());
}
```

Requirements

Platforms: Windows 98, Windows NT 4.0, Windows Millennium Edition, Windows 2000, Windows XP Home Edition, Windows XP Professional, Windows .NET Server family, .NET Compact Framework - Windows CE .NET

UdpClient.Receive Method

Returns a UDP datagram that was sent by a remote host.

```
[Visual Basic]
Public Function Receive( _
    ByRef remoteEP As IPEndPoint _
) As Byte()
[C#]
public byte[] Receive(
    ref IPEndPoint remoteEP
);
[C++]
public: unsigned char Receive(
    IPEndPoint** remoteEP
) __gc[];
[JScript]
public function Receive(
    remoteEP : IPEndPoint
) : Byte[];
```

Parameters

remoteEP

An **IPEndPoint** representing the remote host from which the data was sent.

Return Value

An array of type **Byte** that contains datagram data.

Exceptions

Exception Type	Condition
ObjectDisposedException	The underlying **Socket** has been closed.

Exception Type	Condition
SocketException	An error occurred when accessing the socket. See the Remarks section for more information.

Remarks

The **Receive** method will block until a datagram arrives from a remote host. When data is available, the **Receive** method will read the first enqueued datagram and return the data portion as a byte array. This method populates the *remoteEP* parameter with the **IPAddress** and port number of the sender.

If you specify a default remote host in the **Connect** method, the **Receive** method will accept datagrams from that host only. All other datagrams will be discarded.

If the datagram you receive is larger than the size of the *buffer* parameter, *buffer* gets filled with the first part of the message, and the **Receive** method throws a **SocketException**. The remaining data is discarded. If you receive a **SocketException**, use **SocketException.ErrorCode** to obtain the specific error code. Once you have obtained this code, you can refer to the Windows Socket Version 2 API error code documentation in MSDN for a detailed description of the error.

> **Note** If you intend to receive multicasted datagrams, do not call the **Connect** method prior to calling the **Receive** method. The **UdpClient** you use to receive datagrams must be created using the multicast port number.

Example

[Visual Basic, C#] The following example demonstrates the **Receive** method. The **Receive** method blocks execution until it receives a message. Using the **IPEndPoint** passed to **Receive**, the identity of the responding host is revealed.

```
[Visual Basic]
'Creates a UdpClient for reading incoming data.
Dim receivingUdpClient As New UdpClient()

'Creates an IPEndPoint to record the IP address and port number
of the sender.
' The IPEndPoint will allow you to read datagrams sent from any source.
Dim RemoteIpEndPoint As New IPEndPoint(IPAddress.Any, 0)
Try

    ' Blocks until a message returns on this socket from a remote host.
    Dim receiveBytes As [Byte]() =
receivingUdpClient.Receive(RemoteIpEndPoint)

    Dim returnData As String = Encoding.ASCII.GetString(receiveBytes)

    Console.WriteLine(("This is the message you
received " + returnData.ToString()))
    Console.WriteLine(("This message was sent from " +
RemoteIpEndPoint.Address.ToString() + " on their port
 number " + RemoteIpEndPoint.Port.ToString()))
Catch e As Exception
    Console.WriteLine(e.ToString())
End Try
    End Sub 'MyUdpClientCommunicator

[C#]
//Creates a UdpClient for reading incoming data.
UdpClient receivingUdpClient = new UdpClient();

//Creates an IPEndPoint to record the IP Address and port
number of the sender.
    // The IPEndPoint will allow you to read datagrams sent
```

```
from any source.
IPEndPoint RemoteIpEndPoint = new IPEndPoint(IPAddress.Any, 0);
try{

    // Blocks until a message returns on this socket
from a remote host.
    Byte[] receiveBytes = receivingUdpClient.Receive(ref
RemoteIpEndPoint);

    string returnData = Encoding.ASCII.GetString(receiveBytes);

    Console.WriteLine("This is the message you received " +
                                returnData.ToString());
    Console.WriteLine("This message was sent from " +
                        RemoteIpEndPoint.Address.ToString() +
                        " on their port number " +
                        RemoteIpEndPoint.Port.ToString());
}
catch ( Exception e ){
    Console.WriteLine(e.ToString());
}
```

Requirements

Platforms: Windows 98, Windows NT 4.0, Windows Millennium Edition, Windows 2000, Windows XP Home Edition, Windows XP Professional, Windows .NET Server family, .NET Compact Framework - Windows CE .NET

UdpClient.Send Method

Sends a UDP datagram to a remote host.

Overload List

Sends a UDP datagram to a remote host.

Supported by the .NET Compact Framework.

> [Visual Basic] **Overloads Public Function Send(Byte(), Integer) As Integer**
> [C#] **public int Send(byte[], int);**
> [C++] **public: int Send(unsigned char __gc[], int);**
> [JScript] **public function Send(Byte[], int) : int;**

Sends a UDP datagram to the host at the specified remote endpoint.

Supported by the .NET Compact Framework.

> [Visual Basic] **Overloads Public Function Send(Byte(), Integer, IPEndPoint) As Integer**
> [C#] **public int Send(byte[], int, IPEndPoint);**
> [C++] **public: int Send(unsigned char __gc[], int, IPEndPoint*);**
> [JScript] **public function Send(Byte[], int, IPEndPoint) : int;**

Sends a UDP datagram to a specified port on a specified remote host.

Supported by the .NET Compact Framework.

> [Visual Basic] **Overloads Public Function Send(Byte(), Integer, String, Integer) As Integer**
> [C#] **public int Send(byte[], int, string, int);**
> [C++] **public: int Send(unsigned char __gc[], int, String*, int);**
> [JScript] **public function Send(Byte[], int, String, int) : int;**

Example

[Visual Basic, C#] The following example demonstrates the **Send** method. This example uses a host name and a port number to identify the target host.

[Visual Basic, C#] **Note** This example shows how to use one of the overloaded versions of **Send**. For other examples that might be available, see the individual overload topics.

[Visual Basic]
```
Dim udpClient As New UdpClient()

Dim sendBytes As [Byte]() = Encoding.ASCII.GetBytes("Is anybody there")
Try
    udpClient.Send(sendBytes, sendBytes.Length, _
"www.contoso.com", 11000)
Catch e As Exception
    Console.WriteLine(e.ToString())
End Try
```

[C#]
```
UdpClient udpClient = new UdpClient();

Byte[] sendBytes = Encoding.ASCII.GetBytes("Is anybody there");
try{
    udpClient.Send(sendBytes, sendBytes.Length, _
"www.contoso.com", 11000);
}
catch ( Exception e ){
    Console.WriteLine(e.ToString());
}
```

UdpClient.Send Method (Byte[], Int32)

Sends a UDP datagram to a remote host.

[Visual Basic]
```
Overloads Public Function Send( _
    ByVal dgram() As Byte, _
    ByVal bytes As Integer _
) As Integer
```
[C#]
```
public int Send(
    byte[] dgram,
    int bytes
);
```
[C++]
```
public: int Send(
    unsigned char dgram __gc[],
    int bytes
);
```
[JScript]
```
public function Send(
    dgram : Byte[],
    bytes : int
) : int;
```

Parameters

dgram

An array of type **Byte** that specifies the UDP datagram that you intend to send represented as an array of bytes.

bytes

The number of bytes in the datagram.

Return Value

The number of bytes sent.

Exceptions

Exception Type	Condition
ArgumentNullException	*dgram* is a null reference (**Nothing** in Visual Basic).
InvalidOperationException	The **UdpClient** has already established a default remote host.
ObjectDisposedException	The **UdpClient** is closed.
SocketException	An error occurred when accessing the socket. See the Remarks section for more information.

Remarks

This overload sends datagrams to the remote host established in the **Connect** method and returns the number of bytes sent. If you do not call **Connect** before calling this overload, the **Send** method will throw a **SocketException**. If you receive a **SocketException**, use **SocketException.ErrorCode** to obtain the specific error code. Once you have obtained this code, you can refer to the Windows Socket Version 2 API error code documentation in MSDN for a detailed description of the error.

If you want to send datagrams to a different remote host, you must call the **Connect** method and specify the desired remote host. Use either of the other **Send** method overloads to send datagrams to a broadcast address.

Example

[Visual Basic, C#] The following example demonstrates the **Send** method. You must establish a default remote host prior to using this overload.

[Visual Basic]
```
Dim udpClient As New UdpClient("www.contoso.com", 11000)
Dim sendBytes As [Byte]() = Encoding.ASCII.GetBytes("Is anybody there")
Try
    udpClient.Send(sendBytes, sendBytes.Length)
Catch e As Exception
    Console.WriteLine(e.ToString())
End Try
```

[C#]
```
UdpClient udpClient = new UdpClient("www.contoso.com", 11000);
Byte[] sendBytes = Encoding.ASCII.GetBytes("Is anybody there");
try{
    udpClient.Send(sendBytes, sendBytes.Length);
}
catch ( Exception e ){
    Console.WriteLine( e.ToString());
}
```

Requirements

Platforms: Windows 98, Windows NT 4.0, Windows Millennium Edition, Windows 2000, Windows XP Home Edition, Windows XP Professional, Windows .NET Server family, .NET Compact Framework - Windows CE .NET

UdpClient.Send Method (Byte[], Int32, IPEndPoint)

Sends a UDP datagram to the host at the specified remote endpoint.

[Visual Basic]
```
Overloads Public Function Send( _
    ByVal dgram() As Byte, _
    ByVal bytes As Integer, _
```

```
    ByVal endPoint As IPEndPoint _
) As Integer
[C#]
public int Send(
    byte[] dgram,
    int bytes,
    IPEndPoint endPoint
);
[C++]
public: int Send(
    unsigned char dgram __gc[],
    int bytes,
    IPEndPoint* endPoint
);
[JScript]
public function Send(
    dgram : Byte[],
    bytes : int,
    endPoint : IPEndPoint
) : int;
```

Parameters

dgram
    An array of type **Byte** that specifies the UDP datagram that you intend to send, represented as an array of bytes.

bytes
    The number of bytes in the datagram.

endPoint
    An **IPEndPoint** that represents the host and port to which to send the datagram.

Return Value

The number of bytes sent.

Exceptions

Exception Type	Condition
ArgumentNullException	*dgram* is a null reference (**Nothing** in Visual Basic).
InvalidOperationException	**UdpClient** has already established a default remote host.
ObjectDisposedException	**UdpClient** is closed.
SocketException	An error occurred when accessing the socket. See the Remarks section for more information.

Remarks

The **Send** method sends datagrams to the specified endpoint and returns the number of bytes successfully sent. Before calling this overload, you must first create an **IPEndPoint** using the IP address and port number of the remote host to which your datagrams will be delivered. You can send datagrams to the default broadcast address, 255.255.255.255, by specifying **SocketOptionName.Broadcast** for the **Address** property of the **IPEndPoint**. After you have created this **IPEndPoint**, pass it to the **Send** method as the *endPoint* parameter.

If you want to send datagrams to any other broadcast address, use the **Client** method to obtain the underlying **Socket**, and set the socket option to **SocketOptionName.Broadcast**. You can also revert to using the **Socket** class.

Note Do not provide an *endPoint* parameter to this method if you have already established a remote host with the **Connect** method. If you do, the **Send** method will throw a **SocketException**. If you receive a **SocketException**, use **SocketException.ErrorCode** to obtain the specific error code. Once you have obtained this code, you can refer to the Windows Socket Version 2 API error code documentation in MSDN for a detailed description of the error.

Example

[Visual Basic, C#] The following example demonstrates the **Send** method. This example uses an **IPEndPoint** to specify the target host.

```
[Visual Basic]
Dim udpClient As New UdpClient()
Dim ipAddress As IPAddress =
Dns.Resolve("www.contoso.com").AddressList(0)
Dim ipEndPoint As New IPEndPoint(ipAddress, 11004)

Dim sendBytes As [Byte]() = Encoding.ASCII.GetBytes
("Is anybody there?")
Try
    udpClient.Send(sendBytes, sendBytes.Length, ipEndPoint)
Catch e As Exception
    Console.WriteLine(e.ToString())
End Try

[C#]
UdpClient udpClient = new UdpClient();
IPAddress ipAddress = Dns.Resolve("www.contoso.com").AddressList[0];
IPEndPoint ipEndPoint = new IPEndPoint(ipAddress, 11004);

Byte[] sendBytes = Encoding.ASCII.GetBytes("Is anybody there?");
try{
    udpClient.Send(sendBytes, sendBytes.Length, ipEndPoint);
}
catch ( Exception e ){
    Console.WriteLine(e.ToString());
}
```

Requirements

Platforms: Windows 98, Windows NT 4.0, Windows Millennium Edition, Windows 2000, Windows XP Home Edition, Windows XP Professional, Windows .NET Server family, .NET Compact Framework - Windows CE .NET

UdpClient.Send Method (Byte[], Int32, String, Int32)

Sends a UDP datagram to a specified port on a specified remote host.

```
[Visual Basic]
Overloads Public Function Send( _
    ByVal dgram() As Byte, _
    ByVal bytes As Integer, _
    ByVal hostname As String, _
    ByVal port As Integer _
) As Integer
[C#]
public int Send(
    byte[] dgram,
    int bytes,
    string hostname,
    int port
);
```

```
[C++]
public: int Send(
    unsigned char dgram __gc[],
    int bytes,
    String* hostname,
    int port
);
[JScript]
public function Send(
    dgram : Byte[],
    bytes : int,
    hostname : String,
    port : int
) : int;
```

Parameters

dgram

An array of type **Byte** that specifies the UDP datagram that you intend to send represented as an array of bytes.

bytes

The number of bytes in the datagram.

hostname

The name of the remote host to which you intend to send the datagram.

port

The remote port number with which you intend to communicate.

Return Value

The number of bytes sent.

Exceptions

Exception Type	Condition
ArgumentNullException	*dgram* is a null reference (**Nothing** in Visual Basic).
InvalidOperationException	The **UdpClient** has already established a default remote host.
ObjectDisposedException	The **UdpClient** is closed.
SocketException	An error occurred when accessing the socket. See the Remarks section for more information.

Remarks

The **Send** method sends datagrams to the values specified by the *hostname* and *port* parameters and returns the number of bytes successfully sent. You can send datagrams to the default broadcast address by specifying "255.255.255.255" for the *hostname* parameter value.

If you want to send datagrams to any other broadcast address, use the **Client** method to obtain the underlying **Socket**, and set the socket option to **SocketOptionName.Broadcast**. You can also revert to using the **Socket** class.

> **Note** Do not provide a host name or port number to this method if you have already established a remote host with the **Connect** method. If you do, the **Send** method will throw a **SocketException**. If you receive a **SocketException**, use **SocketException.ErrorCode** to obtain the specific error code. Once you have obtained this code, you can refer to the Windows Socket Version 2 API error code documentation in MSDN for a detailed description of the error.

Example

[Visual Basic, C#] The following example demonstrates the **Send** method. This example uses a host name and a port number to identify the target host.

```
[Visual Basic]
Dim udpClient As New UdpClient()

Dim sendBytes As [Byte]() = Encoding.ASCII.GetBytes("Is anybody there")
Try
    udpClient.Send(sendBytes, sendBytes.Length,
"www.contoso.com", 11000)
Catch e As Exception
    Console.WriteLine(e.ToString())
End Try

[C#]
UdpClient udpClient = new UdpClient();

Byte[] sendBytes = Encoding.ASCII.GetBytes("Is anybody there");
try{
    udpClient.Send(sendBytes, sendBytes.Length,
"www.contoso.com", 11000);
}
catch ( Exception e ){
    Console.WriteLine(e.ToString());
}
```

Requirements

Platforms: Windows 98, Windows NT 4.0, Windows Millennium Edition, Windows 2000, Windows XP Home Edition, Windows XP Professional, Windows .NET Server family, .NET Compact Framework - Windows CE .NET

System.Reflection Namespace

The System.Reflection namespace contains classes and interfaces that provide a managed view of loaded types, methods, and fields, with the ability to dynamically create and invoke types.

AmbiguousMatchException Class

The exception that is thrown when binding to a method results in more than one method matching the binding criteria. This class cannot be inherited.

System.Object
  System.Exception
    System.SystemException
      System.Reflection.AmbiguousMatchException

```
[Visual Basic]
<Serializable>
NotInheritable Public Class AmbiguousMatchException
    Inherits SystemException
[C#]
[Serializable]
public sealed class AmbiguousMatchException : SystemException
[C++]
[Serializable]
public __gc __sealed class AmbiguousMatchException : public
    SystemException
[JScript]
public
    Serializable
class AmbiguousMatchException extends SystemException
```

Thread Safety

Any public static (**Shared** in Visual Basic) members of this type are safe for multithreaded operations. Any instance members are not guaranteed to be thread safe.

Remarks

AmbiguousMatchException uses the HRESULT COR_E_AMBIGUOUSMATCH which has the value 0x8000211D.

An **AmbiguousMatchException** is thrown if the application calls upon a class and it cannot determine which class or overloaded class to utilize. The binding attempts to locate the proper class to use, determined by the number of parameters and the type of parameters. If multiple acceptable classes are located, **AmbiguousMatchException** is thrown.

Overload resolution is a mechanism for selecting the best function member to invoke given an argument list and a set of candidate function members. Overload resolution selects the function member to invoke. If a selection cannot be determined, an **AmbiguousMatchException** is thrown.

Requirements

Namespace: System.Reflection

Platforms: Windows 98, Windows NT 4.0, Windows Millennium Edition, Windows 2000, Windows XP Home Edition, Windows XP Professional, Windows .NET Server family, .NET Compact Framework - Windows CE .NET

Assembly: Mscorlib (in Mscorlib.dll)

AmbiguousMatchException Constructor

Initializes a new instance of the **AmbiguousMatchException** class.

Overload List

Initializes a new instance of the **AmbiguousMatchException** class with an empty message string and the root cause exception set to a null reference (**Nothing** in Visual Basic).

Supported by the .NET Compact Framework.

  [Visual Basic] **Public Sub New()**
  [C#] **public AmbiguousMatchException();**
  [C++] **public: AmbiguousMatchException();**
  [JScript] **public function AmbiguousMatchException();**

Initializes a new instance of the **AmbiguousMatchException** class with its message string set to the given message and the root cause exception set to a null reference (**Nothing** in Visual Basic).

Supported by the .NET Compact Framework.

  [Visual Basic] **Public Sub New(String)**
  [C#] **public AmbiguousMatchException(string);**
  [C++] **public: AmbiguousMatchException(String*);**
  [JScript] **public function AmbiguousMatchException(String);**

Initializes a new instance of the **AmbiguousMatchException** class with a specified error message and a reference to the inner exception that is the cause of this exception.

Supported by the .NET Compact Framework.

  [Visual Basic] **Public Sub New(String, Exception)**
  [C#] **public AmbiguousMatchException(string, Exception);**
  [C++] **public: AmbiguousMatchException(String*, Exception*);**
  [JScript] **public function AmbiguousMatchException(String, Exception);**

Example

[Visual Basic, C#, C++] The following example shows two classes, each named Mymethod. One class takes an integer and the other takes a string. If an integer is passed to Mymethod, the first class is used. If a string is passed, the second class is used. If it cannot be determined which Mymethod to use, **AmbiguousMatchException** is thrown.

> [Visual Basic, C#, C++] **Note** This example shows how to use one of the overloaded versions of the **AmbiguousMatchException** constructor. For other examples that might be available, see the individual overload topics.

```vb
[Visual Basic]
Class Myambiguous

    'The first overload is typed to an Int32
    Overloads Public Shared Sub Mymethod(number As Int32)
        Console.Write(ControlChars.Cr + "{0}", "I am from ↵
Int32 method")
    End Sub 'Mymethod

    'The second overload is typed to a string
    Overloads Public Shared Sub Mymethod(alpha As String)
        Console.Write(ControlChars.Cr + "{0}", "I am from a string.")
    End Sub 'Mymethod

    Public Shared Sub Main()
        Try
            'The following does not cause as exception
            Mymethod(2) ' goes to Mymethod (Int32)
            Mymethod("3") ' goes to Mymethod (string)
            Dim Mytype As Type = Type.GetType("Myambiguous")

            Dim Mymethodinfo32 As MethodInfo = ↵
Mytype.GetMethod("Mymethod", New Type() {GetType(Int32)})
            Dim Mymethodinfostr As MethodInfo = ↵
Mytype.GetMethod("Mymethod", New Type() {GetType(System.String)})

            'Invoke a method, utilizing a Int32 integer
            Mymethodinfo32.Invoke(Nothing, New Object() {2})

            'Invoke the method utilizing a string
            Mymethodinfostr.Invoke(Nothing, New Object() {"1"})

            'The following line causes an ambiguious exception
            Dim Mymethodinfo As MethodInfo = ↵
Mytype.GetMethod("Mymethod")
        ' end of try block
        Catch theException As System.Reflection.AmbiguousMatchException
            Console.Write(ControlChars.Cr & ↵
"AmbiguousMatchException message - {0}", theException.Message)
        Catch
        End Try
        Return
    End Sub 'Main
End Class 'Myambiguous

'This code produces the following output:
'I am from Int32 method
'I am from a string.
'I am from Int32 method
'I am from a string.
'AmbiguousMatchException message - Ambiguous match found.
```

```csharp
[C#]
class Myambiguous {
    //The first overload is typed to an Int32
    public static void Mymethod (Int32 number){
        Console.Write("\n{0}", "I am from Int32 method");
    }

    //The second overload is typed to a string
    public static void Mymethod (string alpha) {
        Console.Write("\n{0}", "I am from a string.");
    }

    public static void Main() {
        try {
            //The following does not cause as exception
            Mymethod (2); // goes to Mymethod (Int32)
            Mymethod ("3"); // goes to Mymethod (string)

            Type Mytype = Type.GetType("Myambiguous");

            MethodInfo Mymethodinfo32 = Mytype.GetMethod ↵
("Mymethod", new Type[]{typeof(Int32)});
```

```csharp
            MethodInfo Mymethodinfostr = Mytype.GetMethod
("Mymethod", new Type[]{typeof(System.String)});

            //Invoke a method, utilizing a Int32 integer
            Mymethodinfo32.Invoke(null, new Object[]{2});

            //Invoke the method utilizing a string
            Mymethodinfostr.Invoke(null, new Object[]{"1"});

            //The following line causes an ambiguious exception
            MethodInfo Mymethodinfo = Mytype.GetMethod("Mymethod");
        } // end of try block

        catch(System.Reflection.AmbiguousMatchException theException) {
            Console.Write("\nAmbiguousMatchException
message - {0}", theException.Message);
        }
        catch {
            Console.Write("\nError thrown");
        }
        return;
    }
}

//This code produces the following output:
//I am from Int32 method
//I am from a string.
//I am from Int32 method
//I am from a string.
//AmbiguousMatchException message - Ambiguous match found.
```

```cpp
[C++]
__gc class Myambiguous {
    //The first overload is typed to an Int32
public:
    static void Mymethod (Int32 number) {
        Console::Write(S"\nI am from Int32 method");
    }

    //The second overload is typed to a String*
    static void Mymethod (String* alpha) {
        Console::Write(S"\nI am from a String*.");
    }

    static void main() {
        try {
            //The following does not cause as exception
            Mymethod (2); // goes to Mymethod (Int32)
            Mymethod (S"3"); // goes to Mymethod (String*)

            Type* Mytype = Type::GetType(S"Myambiguous");

            Type* temp0 [] = {__typeof(Int32)};
            MethodInfo* Mymethodinfo32 = Mytype->GetMethod
(S"Mymethod", temp0);

            Type* temp1 [] = {__typeof(System::String)};
            MethodInfo* Mymethodinfostr = Mytype->GetMethod
(S"Mymethod", temp1);

            //Invoke a method, utilizing a Int32 integer

            Object* temp2 [] = {__box(2)};
            Mymethodinfo32->Invoke(0, temp2);

            //Invoke the method utilizing a String*

            Object* temp3 [] = {S"1"};
            Mymethodinfostr->Invoke(0, temp3);

            //The following line causes an ambiguous exception
            MethodInfo* Mymethodinfo = Mytype->GetMethod(S"Mymethod");
        } // end of try block
```

```
    catch(System::Reflection::AmbiguousMatchException* theException) {
        Console::Write(S"\nAmbiguousMatchException message      ↵
  {0}", theException->Message);
    } catch (Exception*) {
        Console::Write(S"\nError thrown");
    }
    return;
}
}

nt main() {
    Myambiguous::main();
}

//This code produces the following output:
//I am from Int32 method
//I am from a String*.
//I am from Int32 method
//I am from a String*.
//AmbiguousMatchException message - Ambiguous match found.
```

AmbiguousMatchException Constructor ( )

Initializes a new instance of the **AmbiguousMatchException** class with an empty message string and the root cause exception set to a null reference (**Nothing** in Visual Basic).

```
[Visual Basic]
Public Sub New()
[C#]
public AmbiguousMatchException();
[C++]
public: AmbiguousMatchException();
[JScript]
public function AmbiguousMatchException();
```

Remarks

AmbiguousMatchException inherits from **Exception**. This constructor sets the properties of the **Exception** object as shown in the following table.

Property	Value
InnerException	A null reference (**Nothing** in Visual Basic)
Message	The empty string ("").

Requirements

Platforms: Windows 98, Windows NT 4.0,
Windows Millennium Edition, Windows 2000,
Windows XP Home Edition, Windows XP Professional,
Windows .NET Server family,
.NET Compact Framework - Windows CE .NET,
Common Language Infrastructure (CLI) Standard

AmbiguousMatchException Constructor (String)

Initializes a new instance of the **AmbiguousMatchException** class with its message string set to the given message and the root cause exception set to a null reference (**Nothing** in Visual Basic).

```
[Visual Basic]
Public Sub New( _
    ByVal message As String _
)
[C#]
public AmbiguousMatchException(
    string message
);
```

```
[C++]
public: AmbiguousMatchException(
    String* message
);
[JScript]
public function AmbiguousMatchException(
    message : String
);
```

Parameters

message
　　A string indicating the reason this exception was thrown.

Remarks

AmbiguousMatchException inherits from **Exception**. This constructor sets the properties of the **Exception** object as shown in the following table.

Property	Value
InnerException	A null reference (**Nothing** in Visual Basic)
Message	The *message* string.

Requirements

Platforms: Windows 98, Windows NT 4.0,
Windows Millennium Edition, Windows 2000,
Windows XP Home Edition, Windows XP Professional,
Windows .NET Server family,
.NET Compact Framework - Windows CE .NET,
Common Language Infrastructure (CLI) Standard

AmbiguousMatchException Constructor (String, Exception)

Initializes a new instance of the **AmbiguousMatchException** class with a specified error message and a reference to the inner exception that is the cause of this exception.

```
[Visual Basic]
Public Sub New( _
    ByVal message As String, _
    ByVal inner As Exception _
)
[C#]
public AmbiguousMatchException(
    string message,
    Exception inner
);
[C++]
public: AmbiguousMatchException(
    String* message,
    Exception* inner
);
[JScript]
public function AmbiguousMatchException(
    message : String,
    inner : Exception
);
```

Parameters

message
　　The error message that explains the reason for the exception.

inner

> The exception that is the cause of the current exception. If the *inner* parameter is not a null reference (**Nothing** in Visual Basic), the current exception is raised in a **catch** block that handles the inner exception.

Remarks

An exception that is thrown as a direct result of a previous exception should include a reference to the previous exception in the **InnerException** property. The **InnerException** property returns the same value that is passed into the constructor, or a null reference (**Nothing** in Visual Basic) if the **InnerException** property does not supply the inner exception value to the constructor.

The following table shows the initial property values for an instance of **AmbiguousMatchException**.

Property	Value
InnerException	The inner exception reference.
Message	The error message string.

Example

See related example in the **System.Reflection.AmbiguousMatchException** constructor topic.

Requirements

Platforms: Windows 98, Windows NT 4.0, Windows Millennium Edition, Windows 2000, Windows XP Home Edition, Windows XP Professional, Windows .NET Server family, .NET Compact Framework - Windows CE .NET, Common Language Infrastructure (CLI) Standard

Assembly Class

Defines an **Assembly**, which is a reusable, versionable, and self-describing building block of a common language runtime application.

System.Object
  System.Reflection.Assembly
    System.Reflection.Emit.AssemblyBuilder

[Visual Basic]
```
<Serializable>
<ClassInterface(ClassInterfaceType.AutoDual)>
Public Class Assembly
    Implements IEvidenceFactory, ICustomAttributeProvider, _
    ISerializable
```
[C#]
```
[Serializable]
[ClassInterface(ClassInterfaceType.AutoDual)]
public class Assembly : IEvidenceFactory,
    ICustomAttributeProvider, ISerializable
```
[C++]
```
[Serializable]
[ClassInterface(ClassInterfaceType::AutoDual)]
public __gc class Assembly : public IEvidenceFactory,
    ICustomAttributeProvider, ISerializable
```
[JScript]
```
public
    Serializable
    ClassInterface(ClassInterfaceType.AutoDual)
class Assembly implements IEvidenceFactory,
    ICustomAttributeProvider, ISerializable
```

Thread Safety

This type is safe for multithreaded operations.

Remarks

Assemblies provide the infrastructure that allows the runtime to fully understand the contents of an application and to enforce the versioning and dependency rules defined by the application. These concepts are crucial for solving the versioning problem and for simplifying the deployment of runtime applications.

Example

[Visual Basic]
```
' LoadInvoke loads MyAssembly.dll and invokes the MyMethod1 method.
' After compiling this class, run LoadInvoke.exe with MyAssembly.dll
' as the command line argument, as shown below:
' LoadInvoke Myassembly.dll
Imports System
Imports System.Reflection

Public Class LoadInvoke
    Public Shared Sub Main(ByVal args() As String)
        Dim a As [Assembly] = [Assembly].LoadFrom(args(0))
        Dim mytypes As Type() = a.GetTypes()
        Dim flags As BindingFlags = BindingFlags.NonPublic _
Or BindingFlags.Public Or BindingFlags.Static Or _
            BindingFlags.Instance Or BindingFlags.DeclaredOnly

        Dim t As Type
        For Each t In mytypes
            Dim mi As MethodInfo() = t.GetMethods(flags)
            Dim obj As [Object] = Activator.CreateInstance(t)

            Dim m As MethodInfo
            For Each m In mi
                m.Invoke(obj, Nothing)
            Next m
        Next t
    End Sub 'Main
End Class 'LoadInvoke
```

[C#]
```
// LoadInvoke loads MyAssembly.dll and invokes the MyMethod1 method.
// After compiling this class, run LoadInvoke.exe with MyAssembly.dll
// as the command line argument, as shown below:
// LoadInvoke Myassembly.dll

using System;
using System.Reflection;
public class LoadInvoke
{
    public static void Main(string[] args)
    {
        Assembly a = Assembly.LoadFrom(args[0]);
        Type[] mytypes = a.GetTypes();
        BindingFlags flags = (BindingFlags.NonPublic |
BindingFlags.Public |
            BindingFlags.Static | BindingFlags.Instance |
BindingFlags.DeclaredOnly);

        foreach(Type t in mytypes)
        {
            MethodInfo[] mi = t.GetMethods(flags);
            Object obj = Activator.CreateInstance(t);

            foreach(MethodInfo m in mi)
            {
                m.Invoke(obj, null);
            }
        }
    }
}
```

[C++]
```
// LoadInvoke loads MyAssembly.dll and invokes the MyMethod1 method.
// After compiling this class, run LoadInvoke.exe with MyAssembly.dll
// as the command line argument, as shown below:
// LoadInvoke Myassembly.dll

#using <mscorlib.dll>

using namespace System;
using namespace System::Reflection;

int main() {
    String* args[] = Environment::GetCommandLineArgs();
    Assembly* a = Assembly::LoadFrom(args[0]);
    Type* mytypes[] = a->GetTypes();
    BindingFlags flags =
static_cast<BindingFlags>(BindingFlags::NonPublic |
BindingFlags::Public |
        BindingFlags::Static | BindingFlags::Instance |
BindingFlags::DeclaredOnly);

    System::Collections::IEnumerator* myEnum = mytypes->GetEnumerator();
    while (myEnum->MoveNext()) {
        Type* t = __try_cast<Type*>(myEnum->Current);

        MethodInfo* mi[] = t->GetMethods(flags);
        Object* obj = Activator::CreateInstance(t);

        System::Collections::IEnumerator* myEnum = mi->GetEnumerator();
        while (myEnum->MoveNext()) {
            MethodInfo* m = __try_cast<MethodInfo*>(myEnum->Current);
            m->Invoke(obj, 0);
        }
    }
}
```

[Visual Basic]
```
' Use this class with the LoadInvoke program.
```

```
' Compile this class using vbc /t:library MyAssembly.vb
' to obtain MyAssembly.dll.
Imports System
Imports Microsoft.VisualBasic

Public Class MyAssembly
    Public Sub MyMethod1()
        Console.WriteLine("Invoking MyAssembly.MyMethod1")
    End Sub 'MyMethod1
End Class 'MyAssembly

[C#]
// Use this class with the LoadInvoke program.
// Compile this class using csc /t:library MyAssembly.cs
// to obtain MyAssembly.dll.
using System;

public class MyAssembly
{
    public void MyMethod1()
    {
        Console.WriteLine("Invoking MyAssembly.MyMethod1");
    }
}
```

Requirements

Namespace: System.Reflection

Platforms: Windows 98, Windows NT 4.0,
Windows Millennium Edition, Windows 2000,
Windows XP Home Edition, Windows XP Professional,
Windows .NET Server family,
.NET Compact Framework - Windows CE .NET

Assembly: Mscorlib (in Mscorlib.dll)

Assembly.CodeBase Property

Gets the location of the assembly as specified originally, for
example, in an **AssemblyName** object.

```
[Visual Basic]
Public Overridable ReadOnly Property CodeBase As String
[C#]
public virtual string CodeBase {get;}
[C++]
public: __property virtual String* get_CodeBase();
[JScript]
public function get CodeBase() : String;
```

Property Value

The location of the assembly as specified originally.

Exceptions

Exception Type	Condition
SecurityException	The caller does not have the required permission.

Remarks

To get the absolute path to the loaded manifest-containing file, use
the **Assembly.Location** property instead.

If the assembly was loaded as a byte array, this property returns the
location of the caller of the **Load** method, not the assembly.

Example

The following example shows an expression that uses the **CodeBase**
property.

```
[Visual Basic]
Dim SampleAssembly As [Assembly]
' Instantiate a target object.
Dim Integer1 As New Int32()
Dim Type1 As Type
' Set the Type instance to the target class type.
Type1 = Integer1.GetType()
' Instantiate an Assembly class to the assembly housing the
  Integer type.
SampleAssembly = [Assembly].GetAssembly(Integer1.GetType())
' Gets the location of the assembly using file: protocol.
Console.WriteLine(("CodeBase=" + SampleAssembly.CodeBase))
        End Sub 'Snippet1

[C#]
Assembly SampleAssembly;
// Instantiate a target object.
Int32 Integer1 = new Int32();
Type Type1;
// Set the Type instance to the target class type.
Type1 = Integer1.GetType();
// Instantiate an Assembly class to the assembly housing the
   Integer type.
SampleAssembly = Assembly.GetAssembly(Integer1.GetType());
// Gets the location of the assembly using file: protocol.
Console.WriteLine("CodeBase=" + SampleAssembly.CodeBase);

[C++]
Assembly* SampleAssembly;
// Instantiate a target Object*.
Int32 Integer1(0);
Type* Type1;
// Set the Type instance to the target class type.
Type1 = __box(Integer1)->GetType();
// Instantiate an Assembly class to the assembly housing
the Integer type.
SampleAssembly = Assembly::GetAssembly(__box(Integer1)->GetType());
// Gets the location of the assembly using file: protocol.
Console::WriteLine(S"CodeBase= {0}", SampleAssembly->CodeBase);

[JScript]
var SampleAssembly : Assembly;
// Instantiate a target object.
var Integer1 : Int32 = 0;
var Type1 : Type;
// Set the Type instance to the target class type.
Type1 = Integer1.GetType();
// Instantiate an Assembly class to the assembly housing
the Integer type.
SampleAssembly = Assembly.GetAssembly(Integer1.GetType());
// Gets the location of the assembly using file: protocol.
Console.WriteLine("CodeBase=" + SampleAssembly.CodeBase);
```

Requirements

Platforms: Windows 98, Windows NT 4.0,
Windows Millennium Edition, Windows 2000,
Windows XP Home Edition, Windows XP Professional,
Windows .NET Server family

.NET Framework Security:

- **FileIOPermission** for access to the path. Associated
  enumeration: **FileIOPermissionAccess.PathDiscovery**.

Assembly.EntryPoint Property

Gets the entry point of this assembly.

```
[Visual Basic]
Public Overridable ReadOnly Property EntryPoint As MethodInfo
[C#]
public virtual MethodInfo EntryPoint {get;}
```

```
[C++]
public: __property virtual MethodInfo* get_EntryPoint();
[JScript]
public function get EntryPoint() : MethodInfo;
```

Property Value

A **MethodInfo** object that represents the entry point of this assembly. If no entry point is found (for example, the assembly is a DLL), a null reference (**Nothing** in Visual Basic) is returned.

Requirements

Platforms: Windows 98, Windows NT 4.0, Windows Millennium Edition, Windows 2000, Windows XP Home Edition, Windows XP Professional, Windows .NET Server family

Assembly.EscapedCodeBase Property

Gets the URI, including escape characters, that represents the codebase.

```
[Visual Basic]
Public Overridable ReadOnly Property EscapedCodeBase As String
[C#]
public virtual string EscapedCodeBase {get;}
[C++]
public: __property virtual String* get_EscapedCodeBase();
[JScript]
public function get EscapedCodeBase() : String;
```

Property Value

A URI with escape characters.

Exceptions

Exception Type	Condition
SecurityException	The caller does not have the required permission.

Requirements

Platforms: Windows 98, Windows NT 4.0, Windows Millennium Edition, Windows 2000, Windows XP Home Edition, Windows XP Professional, Windows .NET Server family

.NET Framework Security:
- **FileIOPermission** for access to the path. Associated enumeration: **FileIOPermissionAccess.PathDiscovery**.

Assembly.Evidence Property

Gets the evidence for this assembly.

```
[Visual Basic]
Public Overridable ReadOnly Property Evidence As Evidence _
    Implements IEvidenceFactory.Evidence
[C#]
public virtual Evidence Evidence {get;}
[C++]
public: __property virtual Evidence* get_Evidence();
[JScript]
public function get Evidence() : Evidence;
```

Property Value

An **Evidence** object for this assembly.

Implements

IEvidenceFactory.Evidence

Exceptions

Exception Type	Condition
SecurityException	The caller does not have the required permission.

Remarks

Evidence is the set of information that constitutes input to security policy decisions, such as what permissions can be granted to code.

Requirements

Platforms: Windows 98, Windows NT 4.0, Windows Millennium Edition, Windows 2000, Windows XP Home Edition, Windows XP Professional, Windows .NET Server family

.NET Framework Security:
- **SecurityPermission** to load an assembly with evidence. Associated enumeration: **SecurityPermissionFlag.ControlEvidence**.

Assembly.FullName Property

Gets the display name of the assembly.

```
[Visual Basic]
Public Overridable ReadOnly Property FullName As String
[C#]
public virtual string FullName {get;}
[C++]
public: __property virtual String* get_FullName();
[JScript]
public function get FullName() : String;
```

Property Value

The display name of the assembly.

Remarks

See **AssemblyName** for a description of the format of the display name of an assembly.

Example

The following example retrieves the full name of an assembly.

```
[Visual Basic]
Dim SampleAssembly As [Assembly]
' Instantiate a target object.
Dim Integer1 As New Int32()
Dim Type1 As Type
' Set the Type instance to the target class type.
Type1 = Integer1.GetType()
' Instantiate an Assembly class to the assembly housing
the Integer type.
SampleAssembly = [Assembly].GetAssembly(Integer1.GetType())
' Write the display name of assembly including base name and version.
Console.WriteLine(("FullName=" + SampleAssembly.FullName))
        End Sub 'Snippet2
```

```
[C#]
Assembly SampleAssembly;
// Instantiate a target object.
Int32 Integer1 = new Int32();
Type Type1;
// Set the Type instance to the target class type.
Type1 = Integer1.GetType();
// Instantiate an Assembly class to the assembly housing
```

```
the Integer type.
SampleAssembly = Assembly.GetAssembly(Integer1.GetType());
// Write the display name of assembly including base name and version.
Console.WriteLine("FullName=" + SampleAssembly.FullName);
```

```
[C++]
Assembly* SampleAssembly;
// Instantiate a target Object*.
Int32 Integer1(0);
Type* Type1;
// Set the Type instance to the target class type.
Type1 = __box(Integer1)->GetType();
// Instantiate an Assembly class to the assembly housing       ⏎
 the Integer type.
SampleAssembly = Assembly::GetAssembly(__box(Integer1)->GetType());
// Write the display name of assembly including base name and version.
Console::WriteLine(S"FullName= {0}", SampleAssembly->FullName);
```

```
[JScript]
var SampleAssembly : Assembly;
// Instantiate a target object.
var Integer1 : Int32 = 0;
var Type1 : Type;
// Set the Type instance to the target class type.
Type1 = Integer1.GetType();
// Instantiate an Assembly class to the assembly housing       ⏎
the Integer type.
SampleAssembly = Assembly.GetAssembly(Integer1.GetType());
// Write the display name of assembly including base name and version.
Console.WriteLine("FullName=" + SampleAssembly.FullName);
```

Requirements

Platforms: Windows 98, Windows NT 4.0,
Windows Millennium Edition, Windows 2000,
Windows XP Home Edition, Windows XP Professional,
Windows .NET Server family,
.NET Compact Framework - Windows CE .NET,
Common Language Infrastructure (CLI) Standard

Assembly.GlobalAssemblyCache Property

Gets a value indicating whether the assembly was loaded from the
global assembly cache.

```
[Visual Basic]
Public ReadOnly Property GlobalAssemblyCache As Boolean
[C#]
public bool GlobalAssemblyCache {get;}
[C++]
public: __property bool get_GlobalAssemblyCache();
[JScript]
public function get GlobalAssemblyCache() : Boolean;
```

Property Value

true if the assembly was loaded from the global assembly cache;
otherwise, **false**.

Requirements

Platforms: Windows 98, Windows NT 4.0,
Windows Millennium Edition, Windows 2000,
Windows XP Home Edition, Windows XP Professional,
Windows .NET Server family

Assembly.ImageRuntimeVersion Property

Note: This namespace, class, or member is supported only in
version 1.1 of the .NET Framework.</I></Font>

Gets the version of the common language runtime (CLR) saved in
the file containing the manifest.

```
[Visual Basic]
<ComVisible(False)>
Public Overridable ReadOnly Property ImageRuntimeVersion As String
[C#]
[ComVisible(false)]
public virtual string ImageRuntimeVersion {get;}
[C++]
[ComVisible(false)]
public: __property virtual String* get_ImageRuntimeVersion();
[JScript]
public
   ComVisible(false)
function get ImageRuntimeVersion() : String;
```

Property Value

A string representing the CLR version.

Remarks

Some .NET Framework version 1.0 common language runtime
DLLs have incorrect versions such as v1.x86ret and "retail."

Requirements

Platforms: Windows 98, Windows NT 4.0,
Windows Millennium Edition, Windows 2000,
Windows XP Home Edition, Windows XP Professional,
Windows .NET Server family

Assembly.Location Property

Gets the location, in codebase format, of the loaded file that contains
the manifest if not shadow-copied.

```
[Visual Basic]
Public Overridable ReadOnly Property Location As String
[C#]
public virtual string Location {get;}
[C++]
public: __property virtual String* get_Location();
[JScript]
public function get Location() : String;
```

Property Value

The location of the loaded file that contains the manifest. If the
loaded file was shadow-copied, the **Location** is that of the file before
being shadow-copied. If the assembly is loaded from a byte array,
such as when using the **Load(Byte[])** method, **Location** is an empty
string ("").

Exceptions

Exception Type	Condition
SecurityException	The caller does not have the required permission.

Example

See related example in the **System.Reflection.Assembly.FullName**
property topic.

Requirements

Platforms: Windows 98, Windows NT 4.0,
Windows Millennium Edition, Windows 2000,
Windows XP Home Edition, Windows XP Professional,
Windows .NET Server family

NET Framework Security:

- **FileIOPermission** for access to the path. Associated enumeration: **FileIOPermissionAccess.PathDiscovery**.

Assembly.CreateInstance Method

Locates a type from this assembly and creates an instance of it using the system activator.

Overload List

Locates the specified type from this assembly and creates an instance of it using the system activator, using case-sensitive search.

Supported by the .NET Compact Framework.

   [Visual Basic] **Overloads Public Function CreateInstance(String) As Object**

   [C#] **public object CreateInstance(string);**

   [C++] **public: Object* CreateInstance(String*);**

   [JScript] **public function CreateInstance(String) : Object;**

Locates the specified type from this assembly and creates an instance of it using the system activator, with optional case-sensitive search.

   [Visual Basic] **Overloads Public Function CreateInstance(String, Boolean) As Object**

   [C#] **public object CreateInstance(string, bool);**

   [C++] **public: Object* CreateInstance(String*, bool);**

   [JScript] **public function CreateInstance(String, Boolean) : Object;**

Locates the specified type from this assembly and creates an instance of it using the system activator, with optional case-sensitive search and having the specified culture, arguments, and binding and activation attributes.

   [Visual Basic] **Overloads Public Function CreateInstance(String, Boolean, BindingFlags, Binder, Object(), CultureInfo, Object()) As Object**

   [C#] **public object CreateInstance(string, bool, BindingFlags, Binder, object[], CultureInfo, object[]);**

   [C++] **public: Object* CreateInstance(String*, bool, BindingFlags, Binder*, Object[], CultureInfo*, Object[]);**

   [JScript] **public function CreateInstance(String, Boolean, BindingFlags, Binder, Object[], CultureInfo, Object[]) : Object;**

Assembly.CreateInstance Method (String)

Locates the specified type from this assembly and creates an instance of it using the system activator, using case-sensitive search.

```
[Visual Basic]
Overloads Public Function CreateInstance( _
   ByVal typeName As String _
) As Object
[C#]
public object CreateInstance(
   string typeName
);
[C++]
public: Object* CreateInstance(
   String* typeName
);
```

```
[JScript]
public function CreateInstance(
   typeName : String
) : Object;
```

Parameters

typeName
   The **Type.FullName** of the type to locate.

Return Value

An instance of **Object** representing the type, with culture, arguments, binder, and activation attributes set to a null reference (**Nothing** in Visual Basic), and **BindingFlags** set to Public or Instance, or a null reference (**Nothing**) if *typeName* is not found.

Exceptions

Exception Type	Condition
ArgumentException	*typeName* is the empty string ("") or "\0anything" -or- The length of *typeName* exceeds 1024 characters.
ArgumentNullException	*typeName* is a null reference (**Nothing** in Visual Basic).
MissingMethodException	No matching constructor was found.

Requirements

Platforms: Windows 98, Windows NT 4.0, Windows Millennium Edition, Windows 2000, Windows XP Home Edition, Windows XP Professional, Windows .NET Server family, .NET Compact Framework - Windows CE .NET, Common Language Infrastructure (CLI) Standard

.NET Framework Security:

- **ReflectionPermission** to enhance security and performance when invoked late-bound through mechanisms such as **Type.InvokeMember**. Associated enumeration: **ReflectionPermissionFlag.MemberAccess**.

Assembly.CreateInstance Method (String, Boolean)

Locates the specified type from this assembly and creates an instance of it using the system activator, with optional case-sensitive search.

```
[Visual Basic]
Overloads Public Function CreateInstance( _
   ByVal typeName As String, _
   ByVal ignoreCase As Boolean _
) As Object
[C#]
public object CreateInstance(
   string typeName,
   bool ignoreCase
);
[C++]
public: Object* CreateInstance(
   String* typeName,
   bool ignoreCase
);
```

```
[JScript]
public function CreateInstance(
    typeName : String,
    ignoreCase : Boolean
) : Object;
```

Parameters

typeName

The **Type.FullName** of the type to locate.

ignoreCase

true to ignore the case of the type name; otherwise, **false**.

Return Value

An instance of **Object** representing the type, with culture, arguments, binder, and activation attributes set to a null reference (**Nothing** in Visual Basic), and **BindingFlags** set to Public or Instance, or a null reference (**Nothing**) if *typeName* is not found.

Exceptions

Exception Type	Condition
ArgumentException	*typeName* is the empty string ("") or "\0anything"
	-or-
	The length of *typeName* exceeds 1024 characters.
MissingMethodException	No matching constructor was found.
ArgumentNullException	*typeName* is a null reference (**Nothing** in Visual Basic).

Requirements

Platforms: Windows 98, Windows NT 4.0, Windows Millennium Edition, Windows 2000, Windows XP Home Edition, Windows XP Professional, Windows .NET Server family

.NET Framework Security:

- **ReflectionPermission** to enhance security and performance when invoked late-bound through mechanisms such as **Type.InvokeMember**. Associated enumeration: **ReflectionPermissionFlag.MemberAccess**.

Assembly.CreateInstance Method (String, Boolean, BindingFlags, Binder, Object[], CultureInfo, Object[])

Locates the specified type from this assembly and creates an instance of it using the system activator, with optional case-sensitive search and having the specified culture, arguments, and binding and activation attributes.

```
[Visual Basic]
Overloads Public Function CreateInstance( _
    ByVal typeName As String, _
    ByVal ignoreCase As Boolean, _
    ByVal bindingAttr As BindingFlags, _
    ByVal binder As Binder, _
    ByVal args() As Object, _
    ByVal culture As CultureInfo, _
    ByVal activationAttributes() As Object _
) As Object
[C#]
public object CreateInstance(
    string typeName,
    bool ignoreCase,
```

```
    BindingFlags bindingAttr,
    Binder binder,
    object[] args,
    CultureInfo culture,
    object[] activationAttributes
);
[C++]
public: Object* CreateInstance(
    String* typeName,
    bool ignoreCase,
    BindingFlags bindingAttr,
    Binder* binder,
    Object* args __gc[],
    CultureInfo* culture,
    Object* activationAttributes __gc[]
);
[JScript]
public function CreateInstance(
    typeName : String,
    ignoreCase : Boolean,
    bindingAttr : BindingFlags,
    binder : Binder,
    args : Object[],
    culture : CultureInfo,
    activationAttributes : Object[]
) : Object;
```

Parameters

typeName

The **Type.FullName** of the type to locate.

ignoreCase

true to ignore the case of the type name; otherwise, **false**.

bindingAttr

A bitmask that affects the way in which the search is conducted. The value is a combination of bit flags from **BindingFlags**.

binder

An object that enables the binding, coercion of argument types, invocation of members, and retrieval of **MemberInfo** objects via reflection. If *binder* is a null reference (**Nothing** in Visual Basic), the default binder is used.

args

An array of type **Object** containing the arguments to be passed to the constructor. This array of arguments must match in number, order, and type the parameters of the constructor to be invoked. If the default constructor is desired, *args* must be an empty array or a null reference (**Nothing** in Visual Basic).

culture

An instance of **CultureInfo** used to govern the coercion of types. If this is a null reference (**Nothing** in Visual Basic), the **CultureInfo** for the current thread is used. (This is necessary to convert a **String** that represents 1000 to a **Double** value, for example, since 1000 is represented differently by different cultures.)

activationAttributes

An array of type **Object** containing one or more activation attributes that can participate in the activation. An example of an activation attribute is:

URLAttribute(http://hostname/appname/objectURI)

Return Value

An instance of **Object** representing the type and matching the specified criteria, or a null reference (**Nothing** in Visual Basic) if *typeName* is not found.

Exceptions

Exception Type	Condition
ArgumentException	*typeName* is the empty string ("") or "\0anything"
	-or-
	The length of *typeName* exceeds 1024 characters.
ArgumentNullException	*typeName* is a null reference (**Nothing** in Visual Basic).
MissingMethodException	No matching constructor was found.
NotSupportedException	A non-empty activation attributes array is passed to a type that does not inherit from **MarshalByRefObject**.
SecurityException	The caller does not have the required permission.

Requirements

Platforms: Windows 98, Windows NT 4.0, Windows Millennium Edition, Windows 2000, Windows XP Home Edition, Windows XP Professional, Windows .NET Server family

.NET Framework Security:

- **ReflectionPermission** to enhance security and performance when invoked late-bound through mechanisms such as **Type.InvokeMember**. Associated enumeration: **ReflectionPermissionFlag.MemberAccess**.
- **SecurityPermission** to create an instance of a delegate. Associated enumeration: **SecurityPermissionFlag.UnmanagedCode**.

Assembly.CreateQualifiedName Method

Creates the name of a type qualified by the display name of its assembly.

```
[Visual Basic]
Public Shared Function CreateQualifiedName( _
   ByVal assemblyName As String, _
   ByVal typeName As String _
) As String
[C#]
public static string CreateQualifiedName(
   string assemblyName,
   string typeName
);
[C++]
public: static String* CreateQualifiedName(
   String* assemblyName,
   String* typeName
);
[JScript]
public static function CreateQualifiedName(
   assemblyName : String,
   typeName : String
) : String;
```

Parameters

assemblyName
   The display name of an assembly.
typeName
   The full name of a type.

Return Value

A **String** that is the full name of the type qualified by the display name of the assembly.

Remarks

The format of the returned string is:

<FullTypeName>, <AssemblyDisplayName>

See **AssemblyName** for a description of the format of the display name of an assembly.

Requirements

Platforms: Windows 98, Windows NT 4.0, Windows Millennium Edition, Windows 2000, Windows XP Home Edition, Windows XP Professional, Windows .NET Server family

.NET Framework Security:

- **ReflectionPermission** to enhance security and performance when invoked late-bound through mechanisms such as **Type.InvokeMember**. Associated enumeration: **ReflectionPermissionFlag.MemberAccess**.

Assembly.GetAssembly Method

Gets the assembly in which the specified class is defined.

```
[Visual Basic]
Public Shared Function GetAssembly( _
   ByVal type As Type _
) As Assembly
[C#]
public static Assembly GetAssembly(
   Type type
);
[C++]
public: static Assembly* GetAssembly(
   Type* type
);
[JScript]
public static function GetAssembly(
   type : Type
) : Assembly;
```

Parameters

type
   A **Type** object representing a class in the assembly that will be returned.

Return Value

The assembly in which the specified class is defined.

Exceptions

Exception Type	Condition
ArgumentNullException	*type* is a null reference (**Nothing** in Visual Basic).

Example

See related example in the **System.Reflection.Assembly.FullName** property topic.

Requirements

Platforms: Windows 98, Windows NT 4.0, Windows Millennium Edition, Windows 2000, Windows XP Home Edition, Windows XP Professional, Windows .NET Server family

.NET Framework Security:

- **ReflectionPermission** to enhance security and performance when invoked late-bound through mechanisms such as **Type.InvokeMember**. Associated enumeration: **ReflectionPermissionFlag.MemberAccess**.

Assembly.GetCallingAssembly Method

Returns the **Assembly** of the method that invoked the currently executing method.

```
[Visual Basic]
Public Shared Function GetCallingAssembly() As Assembly
[C#]
public static Assembly GetCallingAssembly();
[C++]
public: static Assembly* GetCallingAssembly();
[JScript]
public static function GetCallingAssembly() : Assembly;
```

Return Value

The **Assembly** object of the method that invoked the currently executing method.

Example

See related example in the **System.Reflection.Assembly.FullName** property topic.

Requirements

Platforms: Windows 98, Windows NT 4.0, Windows Millennium Edition, Windows 2000, Windows XP Home Edition, Windows XP Professional, Windows .NET Server family, .NET Compact Framework - Windows CE .NET

.NET Framework Security:

- **ReflectionPermission** to enhance security and performance when invoked late-bound through mechanisms such as **Type.InvokeMember**. Associated enumeration: **ReflectionPermissionFlag.MemberAccess**.

Assembly.GetCustomAttributes Method

Gets the custom attributes for this assembly.

Overload List

Gets all the custom attributes for this assembly.

[Visual Basic] **Overloads Public Overridable Function GetCustomAttributes(Boolean) As Object() Implements ICustomAttributeProvider.GetCustomAttributes**

[C#] **public virtual object[] GetCustomAttributes(bool);**

[C++] **public: virtual Object* GetCustomAttributes(bool) __gc[];**

[JScript] **public function GetCustomAttributes(Boolean) : Object[];**

Gets the custom attributes for this assembly as specified by type.

[Visual Basic] **Overloads Public Overridable Function GetCustomAttributes(Type, Boolean) As Object() Implements ICustomAttributeProvider.GetCustomAttributes**

[C#] **public virtual object[] GetCustomAttributes(Type, bool);**

[C++] **public: virtual Object* GetCustomAttributes(Type*, bool) __gc[];**

[JScript] **public function GetCustomAttributes(Type, Boolean) : Object[];**

Assembly.GetCustomAttributes Method (Boolean)

Gets all the custom attributes for this assembly.

```
[Visual Basic]
Overloads Public Overridable Function GetCustomAttributes( _
   ByVal inherit As Boolean _
) As Object() Implements ICustomAttributeProvider.GetCustomAttributes
[C#]
public virtual object[] GetCustomAttributes(
   bool inherit
);
[C++]
public: virtual Object* GetCustomAttributes(
   bool inherit
) __gc[];
[JScript]
public function GetCustomAttributes(
   inherit : Boolean
) : Object[];
```

Parameters

inherit
   This argument is ignored for objects of type **Assembly**.

Return Value

An array of type **Object** containing the custom attributes for this assembly.

Implements

ICustomAttributeProvider.GetCustomAttributes

Remarks

This method implements the corresponding **ICustomAttributeProvider** interface method. Therefore, the *inherit* parameter must be specified even though it is ignored.

A pseudo-attribute indicates bits of the core metadata that must be set when the attribute is present. Unlike a custom attribute that extends the metadata for a type and is saved along with the type, a pseudo-attribute modifies the metadata for the type and then is discarded. Some of the resulting bits cannot be accessed using existing reflection APIs.

The following table summarizes the different pseudo-attributes and the accessors for the bits that are available in reflection.

Pseudo-Attribute	Metadata Bits	Reflection Accessor
DllImportAttribute	CorPInvokeMap DLL name	No accessor for PInvokeMap for ordinary method/ global method attributes. No accessor for DLL name.
GuidAttribute	Stored as a real custom attribute.	Accessed as a real custom attribute.
ComImportAttribute	CorType-Attr.tdImport	Type.Attri-butes.Import
SerializableAttribute	CorType-Attr.tdSerializable	Type.Attri-butes.Serializable
NonSerializedAttribute	CorField-Attr.fdNotSeria-lized	FieldInfo. Attributes.Not-Serialized
MethodImplAttribute	CorMethodImpl	MethodInfo.Get-MethodImplemen-tationFlags() Constructor-Info.GetMethod-Implementation-Flags()
MarshalAsAttribute	Various bits.	No accessor.
PreserveSigAttribute	CorMethod-Impl.miOLE	MethodInfo.Get-MethodImplemen-tationFlags().OLE ConstructorInfo. GetMethodImple-mentationFlags(). OLE
InAttribute	CorParamAttr.pdIn	ParameterInfo. Attributes.In
OutAttribute	CorParam-Attr.pdOut	ParameterInfo. Attributes.Out
StructLayoutAttribute	CorType-Attr.tdLayout-Sequential	Type.Attri-butes.Layout-Sequential
	CorType-Attr.tdExplicit-Layout	Type.Attri-butes.Explicit-Layout
	CorType-Attr.tdAnsiClass	Type.Attri-butes.AnsiClass
	CorType-Attr.tdUnicode-Class	Type.Attri-butes.UnicodeClass
	CorType-Attr.tdAutoClass	Type.Attri-butes.AutoClass
	Class packing.	No accessor.
FieldOffsetAttribute	Field offset.	No accessor.
AssemblyLoadAttri-bute	CorAssemblyFlags	No accessor or enumerator.

Requirements

Platforms: Windows 98, Windows NT 4.0, Windows Millennium Edition, Windows 2000, Windows XP Home Edition, Windows XP Professional, Windows .NET Server family

.NET Framework Security:

- **ReflectionPermission** to enhance security and performance when invoked late-bound through mechanisms such as **Type.InvokeMember**. Associated enumeration: **ReflectionPermissionFlag.MemberAccess**.

Assembly.GetCustomAttributes Method (Type, Boolean)

Gets the custom attributes for this assembly as specified by type.

```
[Visual Basic]
Overloads Public Overridable Function GetCustomAttributes( _
    ByVal attributeType As Type, _
    ByVal inherit As Boolean _
) As Object() Implements ICustomAttributeProvider.GetCustomAttributes
[C#]
public virtual object[] GetCustomAttributes(
    Type attributeType,
    bool inherit
);
[C++]
public: virtual Object* GetCustomAttributes(
    Type* attributeType,
    bool inherit
) __gc[];
[JScript]
public function GetCustomAttributes(
    attributeType : Type,
    inherit : Boolean
) : Object[];
```

Parameters

attributeType
    The **Type** for which the custom attributes are to be returned.
inherit
    This argument is ignored for objects of type **Assembly**.

Return Value

An array of type **Object** containing the custom attributes for this assembly as specified by *attributeType*.

Implements

ICustomAttributeProvider.GetCustomAttributes

Exceptions

Exception Type	Condition
ArgumentNullException	*attributeType* is a null reference (**Nothing** in Visual Basic).
ArgumentException	*attributeType* is not a runtime type.

Remarks

This method implements the corresponding **ICustomAttributeProvider** interface method. Therefore, the *inherit* parameter must be specified even though it is ignored.

A pseudo-attribute indicates bits of the core metadata that must be set when the attribute is present. Unlike a custom attribute that extends the metadata for a type and is saved along with the type, a pseudo-attribute modifies the metadata for the type and then is discarded. Some of the resulting bits cannot be accessed using existing reflection APIs.

The following table summarizes the different pseudo-attributes and the accessors for the bits that are available in reflection.

Pseudo-Attribute	Metadata Bits	Reflection Accessor
DllImportAttribute	CorPInvokeMap DLL name	No accessor for PInvokeMap for ordinary method/global method attributes. No accessor for DLL name.
GuidAttribute	Stored as a real custom attribute.	Accessed as a real custom attribute.
ComImportAttribute	CorType-Attr.tdImport	Type.Attributes.Import
SerializableAttribute	CorType-Attr.tdSerializable	Type.Attributes.Serializable
NonSerializedAttribute	CorField-Attr.fdNotSerialized	FieldInfo.Attributes.NotSerialized
MethodImplAttribute	CorMethodImpl	MethodInfo.GetMethodImplementationFlags() ConstructorInfo.GetMethodImplementationFlags()
MarshalAsAttribute	Various bits.	No accessor.
PreserveSigAttribute	CorMethod-Impl.miOLE	MethodInfo.GetMethodImplementationFlags().OLE ConstructorInfo.GetMethodImplementationFlags().OLE
InAttribute	CorParamAttr.pdIn	ParameterInfo.Attributes.In
OutAttribute	CorParam-Attr.pdOut	ParameterInfo.Attributes.Out
StructLayoutAttribute	CorType-Attr.tdLayout-Sequential	Type.Attributes.LayoutSequential
	CorType-Attr.tdExplicit-Layout	Type.Attributes.ExplicitLayout
	CorType-Attr.tdAnsiClass	Type.Attributes.AnsiClass
	CorType-Attr.tdUnicode-Class	Type.Attributes.UnicodeClass
	CorType-Attr.tdAutoClass	Type.Attributes.AutoClass
	Class packing.	No accessor.
FieldOffsetAttribute	Field offset.	No accessor.
AssemblyLoadAttribute	CorAssemblyFlags	No accessor or enumerator.

Requirements

Platforms: Windows 98, Windows NT 4.0, Windows Millennium Edition, Windows 2000, Windows XP Home Edition, Windows XP Professional, Windows .NET Server family

.NET Framework Security:

- **ReflectionPermission** to enhance security and performance when invoked late-bound through mechanisms such as **Type.InvokeMember**. Associated enumeration: **ReflectionPermissionFlag.MemberAccess**.

Assembly.GetEntryAssembly Method

Gets the process executable in the default application domain. In other application domains, this is the first executable that was executed by **AppDomain.ExecuteAssembly**.

```
[Visual Basic]
Public Shared Function GetEntryAssembly() As Assembly
[C#]
public static Assembly GetEntryAssembly();
[C++]
public: static Assembly* GetEntryAssembly();
[JScript]
public static function GetEntryAssembly() : Assembly;
```

Return Value

The **Assembly** that is the process executable in the default application domain, or the first executable that was executed by **AppDomain.ExecuteAssembly**.

Requirements

Platforms: Windows 98, Windows NT 4.0, Windows Millennium Edition, Windows 2000, Windows XP Home Edition, Windows XP Professional, Windows .NET Server family

.NET Framework Security:

- **ReflectionPermission** to enhance security and performance when invoked late-bound through mechanisms such as **Type.InvokeMember**. Associated enumeration: **ReflectionPermissionFlag.MemberAccess**.

Assembly.GetExecutingAssembly Method

Gets the **Assembly** that the current code is running from.

```
[Visual Basic]
Public Shared Function GetExecutingAssembly() As Assembly
[C#]
public static Assembly GetExecutingAssembly();
[C++]
public: static Assembly* GetExecutingAssembly();
[JScript]
public static function GetExecutingAssembly() : Assembly;
```

Return Value

The assembly that the current code is running from.

Example

See related example in the **System.Reflection.Assembly.FullName** property topic.

Requirements

Platforms: Windows 98, Windows NT 4.0,
Windows Millennium Edition, Windows 2000,
Windows XP Home Edition, Windows XP Professional,
Windows .NET Server family,
NET Compact Framework - Windows CE .NET

NET Framework Security:

- **ReflectionPermission** to enhance security and performance
  when invoked late-bound through mechanisms such as
  Type.InvokeMember. Associated enumeration:
  ReflectionPermissionFlag.MemberAccess.

Assembly.GetExportedTypes Method

Gets the exported types defined in this assembly.

```
[Visual Basic]
Public Overridable Function GetExportedTypes() As Type()
[C#]
public virtual Type[] GetExportedTypes();
[C++]
public: virtual Type* GetExportedTypes() [];
[JScript]
public function GetExportedTypes() : Type[];
```

Return Value

An array of type **Type** containing the exported types defined in this
assembly.

Requirements

Platforms: Windows 98, Windows NT 4.0,
Windows Millennium Edition, Windows 2000,
Windows XP Home Edition, Windows XP Professional,
Windows .NET Server family

.NET Framework Security:

- **ReflectionPermission** to enhance security and performance
  when invoked late-bound through mechanisms such as
  Type.InvokeMember. Associated enumeration:
  ReflectionPermissionFlag.MemberAccess.

Assembly.GetFile Method

Gets a **FileStream** for the specified file in the file table of the
manifest of this assembly.

```
[Visual Basic]
Public Overridable Function GetFile( _
   ByVal name As String _
) As FileStream
[C#]
public virtual FileStream GetFile(
   string name
);
[C++]
public: virtual FileStream* GetFile(
   String* name
);
[JScript]
public function GetFile(
   name : String
) : FileStream;
```

Parameters

name
    The name of the specified file.

Return Value

A **FileStream** for the specified file, or a null reference (**Nothing** in
Visual Basic) if the file is not found.

Exceptions

Exception Type	Condition
FileLoadException	A file that was found could not be loaded.
ArgumentNullException	The *name* parameter is a null reference (**Nothing** in Visual Basic).
SecurityException	The caller does not have the required permission.
ArgumentException	The *name* parameter is the empty string ("").

Remarks

This method works on both public and private resources. *name*
should not include the path to the file.

Requirements

Platforms: Windows 98, Windows NT 4.0,
Windows Millennium Edition, Windows 2000,
Windows XP Home Edition, Windows XP Professional,
Windows .NET Server family

.NET Framework Security:

- **ReflectionPermission** to enhance security and performance
  when invoked late-bound through mechanisms such as
  Type.InvokeMember. Associated enumeration:
  ReflectionPermissionFlag.MemberAccess.

- **FileIOPermission** for access to the path and for reading the
  specified file. Associated enumerations:
  FileIOPermissionAccess.PathDiscovery and
  FileIOPermissionAccess.Read

Assembly.GetFiles Method

Gets the files in the file table of an assembly manifest.

Overload List

Gets the files in the file table of an assembly manifest.

   [Visual Basic] **Overloads Public Overridable Function
   GetFiles() As FileStream()**

   [C#] **public virtual FileStream[] GetFiles();**

   [C++] **public: virtual FileStream* GetFiles() [];**

   [JScript] **public function GetFiles() : FileStream[];**

Gets the files in the file table of an assembly manifest, specifying
whether to include resource modules.

   [Visual Basic] **Overloads Public Overridable Function
   GetFiles(Boolean) As FileStream()**

   [C#] **public virtual FileStream[] GetFiles(bool);**

   [C++] **public: virtual FileStream* GetFiles(bool) [];**

   [JScript] **public function GetFiles(Boolean) : FileStream[];**

Assembly.GetFiles Method ()

Gets the files in the file table of an assembly manifest.

```
[Visual Basic]
Overloads Public Overridable Function GetFiles() As FileStream()
[C#]
public virtual FileStream[] GetFiles();
[C++]
public: virtual FileStream* GetFiles() [];
[JScript]
public function GetFiles() : FileStream[];
```

Return Value

An array of **FileStream** objects.

Remarks

This method only works on public resources.

Requirements

Platforms: Windows 98, Windows NT 4.0,
Windows Millennium Edition, Windows 2000,
Windows XP Home Edition, Windows XP Professional,
Windows .NET Server family

.NET Framework Security:

- **ReflectionPermission** to enhance security and performance when invoked late-bound through mechanisms such as **Type.InvokeMember**. Associated enumeration: **ReflectionPermissionFlag.MemberAccess**.

Assembly.GetFiles Method (Boolean)

Gets the files in the file table of an assembly manifest, specifying whether to include resource modules.

```
[Visual Basic]
Overloads Public Overridable Function GetFiles( _
    ByVal getResourceModules As Boolean _
) As FileStream()
[C#]
public virtual FileStream[] GetFiles(
    bool getResourceModules
);
[C++]
public: virtual FileStream* GetFiles(
    bool getResourceModules
) [];
[JScript]
public function GetFiles(
    getResourceModules : Boolean
) : FileStream[];
```

Parameters

getResourceModules
    true to include resource modules; otherwise, **false**.

Return Value

An array of **FileStream** objects.

Remarks

This method only works on public resources.

Requirements

Platforms: Windows 98, Windows NT 4.0,
Windows Millennium Edition, Windows 2000,
Windows XP Home Edition, Windows XP Professional,
Windows .NET Server family

.NET Framework Security:

- **ReflectionPermission** to enhance security and performance when invoked late-bound through mechanisms such as **Type.InvokeMember**. Associated enumeration: **ReflectionPermissionFlag.MemberAccess**.

Assembly.GetLoadedModules Method

Gets all the loaded modules that are part of this assembly.

Overload List

Gets all the loaded modules that are part of this assembly.

[Visual Basic] **Overloads Public Function GetLoadedModules() As Module()**
[C#] **public Module[] GetLoadedModules();**
[C++] **public: Module* GetLoadedModules() [];**
[JScript] **public function GetLoadedModules() : Module[];**

Gets all the loaded modules that are part of this assembly, specifying whether to include resource modules.

[Visual Basic] **Overloads Public Function GetLoadedModules(Boolean) As Module()**
[C#] **public Module[] GetLoadedModules(bool);**
[C++] **public: Module* GetLoadedModules(bool) [];**
[JScript] **public function GetLoadedModules(Boolean) : Module[];**

Assembly.GetLoadedModules Method ()

Gets all the loaded modules that are part of this assembly.

```
[Visual Basic]
Overloads Public Function GetLoadedModules() As Module()
[C#]
public Module[] GetLoadedModules();
[C++]
public: Module* GetLoadedModules() [];
[JScript]
public function GetLoadedModules() : Module[];
```

Return Value

An array of modules.

Remarks

A type can be retrieved from a specific module using **Module.GetType**. Calling **Module.GetType** on the module containing the manifest will not initiate a search of the entire assembly. To retrieve a type from an assembly, regardless of which module it is in, you must call **Assembly.GetType**.

Requirements

Platforms: Windows 98, Windows NT 4.0,
Windows Millennium Edition, Windows 2000,
Windows XP Home Edition, Windows XP Professional,
Windows .NET Server family

.NET Framework Security:

- **ReflectionPermission** to enhance security and performance when invoked late-bound through mechanisms such as **Type.InvokeMember**. Associated enumeration: **ReflectionPermissionFlag.MemberAccess**.

Assembly.GetLoadedModules Method (Boolean)

Gets all the loaded modules that are part of this assembly, specifying whether to include resource modules.

```
[Visual Basic]
Overloads Public Function GetLoadedModules( _
    ByVal getResourceModules As Boolean _
) As Module()
[C#]
public Module[] GetLoadedModules(
    bool getResourceModules
);
[C++]
public: Module* GetLoadedModules(
    bool getResourceModules
) [];
[JScript]
public function GetLoadedModules(
    getResourceModules : Boolean
) : Module[];
```

Parameters

getResourceModules
  true to include resource modules; otherwise, **false**.

Return Value

An array of modules.

Requirements

Platforms: Windows 98, Windows NT 4.0, Windows Millennium Edition, Windows 2000, Windows XP Home Edition, Windows XP Professional, Windows .NET Server family

.NET Framework Security:

- **ReflectionPermission** to enhance security and performance when invoked late-bound through mechanisms such as **Type.InvokeMember**. Associated enumeration: **ReflectionPermissionFlag.MemberAccess**.

Assembly.GetManifestResourceInfo Method

Returns information about how the given resource has been persisted.

```
[Visual Basic]
Public Overridable Function GetManifestResourceInfo( _
    ByVal resourceName As String _
) As ManifestResourceInfo
[C#]
public virtual ManifestResourceInfo GetManifestResourceInfo(
    string resourceName
);
[C++]
public: virtual ManifestResourceInfo* GetManifestResourceInfo(
    String* resourceName
);
[JScript]
public function GetManifestResourceInfo(
    resourceName : String
) : ManifestResourceInfo;
```

Parameters

resourceName
  The name of the resource.

Return Value

ManifestResourceInfo populated with information about the resource's topology, or a null reference (**Nothing** in Visual Basic) if the resource is not found.

Exceptions

Exception Type	Condition
ArgumentNullException	*resourceName* is a null reference (**Nothing** in Visual Basic).
ArgumentException	The *resourceName* parameter is the empty string ("").

Remarks

This method works on both public and private resources.

Requirements

Platforms: Windows 98, Windows NT 4.0, Windows Millennium Edition, Windows 2000, Windows XP Home Edition, Windows XP Professional, Windows .NET Server family

.NET Framework Security:

- **ReflectionPermission** to enhance security and performance when invoked late-bound through mechanisms such as **Type.InvokeMember**. Associated enumeration: **ReflectionPermissionFlag.MemberAccess**.

Assembly.GetManifestResourceNames Method

Returns the names of all the resources in this assembly.

```
[Visual Basic]
Public Overridable Function GetManifestResourceNames() As String()
[C#]
public virtual string[] GetManifestResourceNames();
[C++]
public: virtual String* GetManifestResourceNames() __gc[];
[JScript]
public function GetManifestResourceNames() : String[];
```

Return Value

An array of type **String** containing the names of all the resources.

Remarks

This method works on both public and private resources.

Requirements

Platforms: Windows 98, Windows NT 4.0, Windows Millennium Edition, Windows 2000, Windows XP Home Edition, Windows XP Professional, Windows .NET Server family, .NET Compact Framework - Windows CE .NET

.NET Framework Security:

- **ReflectionPermission** to enhance security and performance when invoked late-bound through mechanisms such as **Type.InvokeMember**. Associated enumeration: **ReflectionPermissionFlag.MemberAccess**.

Assembly.GetManifestResourceStream Method

Loads the specified manifest resource from this assembly.

Overload List

Loads the specified manifest resource from this assembly.

Supported by the .NET Compact Framework.

[Visual Basic] **Overloads Public Overridable Function GetManifestResourceStream(String) As Stream**

[C#] **public virtual Stream GetManifestResource-Stream(string);**

[C++] **public: virtual Stream* GetManifestResource-Stream(String*);**

[JScript] **public function GetManifestResource-Stream(String) : Stream;**

Loads the specified manifest resource, scoped by the namespace of the specified type, from this assembly.

Supported by the .NET Compact Framework.

[Visual Basic] **Overloads Public Overridable Function GetManifestResourceStream(Type, String) As Stream**

[C#] **public virtual Stream GetManifestResource-Stream(Type, string);**

[C++] **public: virtual Stream* GetManifestResource-Stream(Type*, String*);**

[JScript] **public function GetManifestResourceStream(Type, String) : Stream;**

Example

If the full name of *type* is "MyNameSpace.MyClasses" and *name* is "Net", **GetManifestResourceStream** will search for a resource named MyNameSpace.Net.

Assembly.GetManifestResourceStream Method (String)

Loads the specified manifest resource from this assembly.

```
[Visual Basic]
Overloads Public Overridable Function GetManifestResourceStream( _
   ByVal name As String _
) As Stream
[C#]
public virtual Stream GetManifestResourceStream(
   string name
);
[C++]
public: virtual Stream* GetManifestResourceStream(
   String* name
);
[JScript]
public function GetManifestResourceStream(
   name : String
) : Stream;
```

Parameters

name
    The name of the manifest resource being requested.

Return Value

A **Stream** representing this manifest resource.

Exceptions

Exception Type	Condition
ArgumentNullException	The *name* parameter is a null reference (**Nothing** in Visual Basic).
ArgumentException	The *name* parameter is the empty string ("").
SecurityException	The caller does not have the required permission.

Remarks

This method works on both public and private resources.

Requirements

Platforms: Windows 98, Windows NT 4.0, Windows Millennium Edition, Windows 2000, Windows XP Home Edition, Windows XP Professional, Windows .NET Server family, .NET Compact Framework - Windows CE .NET

.NET Framework Security:

- **ReflectionPermission** to enhance security and performance when invoked late-bound through mechanisms such as **Type.InvokeMember**. Associated enumeration: **ReflectionPermissionFlag.MemberAccess**.

Assembly.GetManifestResourceStream Method (Type, String)

Loads the specified manifest resource, scoped by the namespace of the specified type, from this assembly.

```
[Visual Basic]
Overloads Public Overridable Function GetManifestResourceStream( _
   ByVal type As Type, _
   ByVal name As String _
) As Stream
[C#]
public virtual Stream GetManifestResourceStream(
   Type type,
   string name
);
[C++]
public: virtual Stream* GetManifestResourceStream(
   Type* type,
   String* name
);
[JScript]
public function GetManifestResourceStream(
   type : Type,
   name : String
) : Stream;
```

Parameters

type
    The type whose namespace is used to scope the manifest resource name.
name
    The name of the manifest resource being requested.

Return Value

A **Stream** representing this manifest resource.

Exceptions

Exception Type	Condition
ArgumentNullException	The *name* parameter is a null reference (**Nothing** in Visual Basic).
ArgumentException	The *name* parameter is the empty string ("").
SecurityException	The caller does not have the required permission.

Remarks

This method works on both public and private resources.

Example

If the full name of *type* is "MyNameSpace.MyClasses" and *name* is "Net", **GetManifestResourceStream** will search for a resource named MyNameSpace.Net.

Requirements

Platforms: Windows 98, Windows NT 4.0, Windows Millennium Edition, Windows 2000, Windows XP Home Edition, Windows XP Professional, Windows .NET Server family, .NET Compact Framework - Windows CE .NET

.NET Framework Security:

- **ReflectionPermission** to enhance security and performance when invoked late-bound through mechanisms such as **Type.InvokeMember**. Associated enumeration: **ReflectionPermissionFlag.MemberAccess**.

Assembly.GetModule Method

Gets the specified module in this assembly.

```
[Visual Basic]
Public Function GetModule( _
   ByVal name As String _
) As Module
[C#]
public Module GetModule(
   string name
);
[C++]
public: Module* GetModule(
   String* name
);
[JScript]
public function GetModule(
   name : String
) : Module;
```

Parameters

name
   The name of the module being requested.

Return Value

The module being requested, or a null reference (**Nothing** in Visual Basic) if the module is not found.

Exceptions

Exception Type	Condition
ArgumentNullException	The *name* parameter is a null reference (**Nothing** in Visual Basic).

Exception Type	Condition
ArgumentException	The *name* parameter is the empty string ("").
SecurityException	The caller does not have the required permission.

Remarks

This method works on file names.

Classes in the **Reflection.Emit** namespace emit the scope name for a dynamic module. The scope name can be determined by the **Module.ScopeName** property. Pass the kind of module you want to **Assembly.GetModule**. For example, if you want the module that contains the assembly manifest, pass the scope name of the module to **GetModule**. Otherwise, pass the file name of the module. Assemblies loaded by one of the **Load** methods that have a byte[] parameter have only one module, and that is the manifest module. Always seek these modules using the scope name.

A type can be retrieved from a specific module using **Module.GetType**. Calling **Module.GetType** on the module containing the manifest will not initiate a search of the entire assembly. To retrieve a type from an assembly, regardless of which module it is in, you must call **Assembly.GetType**.

Requirements

Platforms: Windows 98, Windows NT 4.0, Windows Millennium Edition, Windows 2000, Windows XP Home Edition, Windows XP Professional, Windows .NET Server family

.NET Framework Security:

- **ReflectionPermission** to enhance security and performance when invoked late-bound through mechanisms such as **Type.InvokeMember**. Associated enumeration: **ReflectionPermissionFlag.MemberAccess**.

Assembly.GetModules Method

Gets all the modules that are part of this assembly.

Overload List

Gets all the modules that are part of this assembly.

Supported by the .NET Compact Framework.

   [Visual Basic] **Overloads Public Function GetModules() As Module()**
   [C#] **public Module[] GetModules();**
   [C++] **public: Module* GetModules() [];**
   [JScript] **public function GetModules() : Module[];**

Gets all the modules that are part of this assembly, specifying whether to include resource modules.

   [Visual Basic] **Overloads Public Function GetModules(Boolean) As Module()**
   [C#] **public Module[] GetModules(bool);**
   [C++] **public: Module* GetModules(bool) [];**
   [JScript] **public function GetModules(Boolean) : Module[];**

Example

The following example displays the name of the module in the returned array that contains the assembly manifest.

```
[Visual Basic]
Imports System
Imports System.Reflection

Public Class Form1

    Public Shared Sub Main()
        Dim mainAssembly As [Assembly] =
[Assembly].GetExecutingAssembly()
        Dim mainMod As [Module] = mainAssembly.GetModules()(0)
        Console.WriteLine("The executing assembly is {0}.",
mainAssembly)
    End Sub 'Main
End Class 'Form1

[C#]
using System;
using System.Reflection;

public class Form1
{
    public static void Main()
    {
        Assembly mainAssembly = Assembly.GetExecutingAssembly();
        Module mainMod = mainAssembly.GetModules()[0];
        Console.WriteLine("The executing assembly is {0}.",
mainAssembly);
    }
}

[C++]
#using <mscorlib.dll>

using namespace System;
using namespace System::Reflection;

int main() {
    Assembly* mainAssembly = Assembly::GetExecutingAssembly();
    Module* mainMod = mainAssembly->GetModules()[0];
    Console::WriteLine(S"The executing assembly is {0}.", mainAssembly);
}

[JScript]
var mainAssembly : Assembly = Assembly.GetExecutingAssembly();
var mainMod : Module = mainAssembly.GetModules()[0];
Console.WriteLine("Module name: {0}", mainMod.Name);
```

Assembly.GetModules Method ()

Gets all the modules that are part of this assembly.

```
[Visual Basic]
Overloads Public Function GetModules() As Module()
[C#]
public Module[] GetModules();
[C++]
public: Module* GetModules() [];
[JScript]
public function GetModules() : Module[];
```

Return Value

An array of modules.

Exceptions

Exception Type	Condition
FileNotFoundException	The module to be loaded does not specify a file name extension.

Remarks

A type can be retrieved from a specific module using
Module.GetType. Calling **Module.GetType** on the module

containing the manifest will not initiate a search of the entire
assembly. To retrieve a type from an assembly, regardless of which
module it is in, you must call **Assembly.GetType**.

Note Modules must be emitted with file name extensions.

Example

The following example displays the name of the module in the
returned array that contains the assembly manifest.

```
[Visual Basic]
Imports System
Imports System.Reflection

Public Class Form1

    Public Shared Sub Main()
        Dim mainAssembly As [Assembly] =
[Assembly].GetExecutingAssembly()
        Dim mainMod As [Module] = mainAssembly.GetModules()(0)
        Console.WriteLine("The executing assembly is {0}.
", mainAssembly)
    End Sub 'Main
End Class 'Form1

[C#]
using System;
using System.Reflection;

public class Form1
{
    public static void Main()
    {
        Assembly mainAssembly = Assembly.GetExecutingAssembly();
        Module mainMod = mainAssembly.GetModules()[0];
        Console.WriteLine("The executing assembly is {0}.
", mainAssembly);
    }
}

[C++]
#using <mscorlib.dll>

using namespace System;
using namespace System::Reflection;

int main() {
    Assembly* mainAssembly = Assembly::GetExecutingAssembly();
    Module* mainMod = mainAssembly->GetModules()[0];
    Console::WriteLine(S"The executing assembly is {0}.", mainAssembly);
}

[JScript]
var mainAssembly : Assembly = Assembly.GetExecutingAssembly();
var mainMod : Module = mainAssembly.GetModules()[0];
Console.WriteLine("Module name: {0}", mainMod.Name);
```

Requirements

Platforms: Windows 98, Windows NT 4.0,
Windows Millennium Edition, Windows 2000,
Windows XP Home Edition, Windows XP Professional,
Windows .NET Server family,
.NET Compact Framework - Windows CE .NET

.NET Framework Security:

• **ReflectionPermission** to enhance security and performance
when invoked late-bound through mechanisms such as
Type.InvokeMember. Associated enumeration:
ReflectionPermissionFlag.MemberAccess.

ssembly.GetModules Method (Boolean)

Gets all the modules that are part of this assembly, specifying whether to include resource modules.

```
[Visual Basic]
Overloads Public Function GetModules( _
    ByVal getResourceModules As Boolean _
) As Module()
[C#]
public Module[] GetModules(
    bool getResourceModules
);
[C++]
public: Module* GetModules(
    bool getResourceModules
) [];
[JScript]
public function GetModules(
    getResourceModules : Boolean
) : Module[];
```

Parameters

getResourceModules
    true to include resource modules; otherwise, false.

Return Value

An array of modules.

Remarks

Note Modules must be emitted with file name extensions.

Requirements

Platforms: Windows 98, Windows NT 4.0, Windows Millennium Edition, Windows 2000, Windows XP Home Edition, Windows XP Professional, Windows .NET Server family

.NET Framework Security:
*   **ReflectionPermission** to enhance security and performance when invoked late-bound through mechanisms such as **Type.InvokeMember**. Associated enumeration: **ReflectionPermissionFlag.MemberAccess**.

Assembly.GetName Method

Gets an **AssemblyName** for this assembly.

Overload List

Gets an **AssemblyName** for this assembly.

Supported by the .NET Compact Framework.

> [Visual Basic] **Overloads Public Overridable Function GetName() As AssemblyName**
> [C#] **public virtual AssemblyName GetName();**
> [C++] **public: virtual AssemblyName* GetName();**
> [JScript] **public function GetName() : AssemblyName;**

Gets an **AssemblyName** for this assembly, setting the codebase as specified by *copiedName*.

Supported by the .NET Compact Framework.

> [Visual Basic] **Overloads Public Overridable Function GetName(Boolean) As AssemblyName**
> [C#] **public virtual AssemblyName GetName(bool);**

> [C++] **public: virtual AssemblyName* GetName(bool);**
> [JScript] **public function GetName(Boolean) : AssemblyName;**

Assembly.GetName Method ()

Gets an **AssemblyName** for this assembly.

```
[Visual Basic]
Overloads Public Overridable Function GetName() As AssemblyName
[C#]
public virtual AssemblyName GetName();
[C++]
public: virtual AssemblyName* GetName();
[JScript]
public function GetName() : AssemblyName;
```

Return Value

An **AssemblyName** for this assembly.

Exceptions

Exception Type	Condition
SecurityException	The caller does not have the required permission.

Requirements

Platforms: Windows 98, Windows NT 4.0, Windows Millennium Edition, Windows 2000, Windows XP Home Edition, Windows XP Professional, Windows .NET Server family, .NET Compact Framework - Windows CE .NET

.NET Framework Security:
*   **FileIOPermission** for access to the path of the assembly. Associated enumeration: **FileIOPermissionAccess.PathDiscovery**
*   **ReflectionPermission** to enhance security and performance when invoked late-bound through mechanisms such as **Type.InvokeMember**. Associated enumeration: **ReflectionPermissionFlag.MemberAccess**.

Assembly.GetName Method (Boolean)

Gets an **AssemblyName** for this assembly, setting the codebase as specified by *copiedName*.

```
[Visual Basic]
Overloads Public Overridable Function GetName( _
    ByVal copiedName As Boolean _
) As AssemblyName
[C#]
public virtual AssemblyName GetName(
    bool copiedName
);
[C++]
public: virtual AssemblyName* GetName(
    bool copiedName
);
[JScript]
public function GetName(
    copiedName : Boolean
) : AssemblyName;
```

Parameters

copiedName
> **true** to set the **CodeBase** to the location of the assembly after it was shadow copied; **false** to set **CodeBase** to the original location.

Return Value

An **AssemblyName** for this assembly.

Exceptions

Exception Type	Condition
SecurityException	The caller does not have the required permission.

Requirements

Platforms: Windows 98, Windows NT 4.0, Windows Millennium Edition, Windows 2000, Windows XP Home Edition, Windows XP Professional, Windows .NET Server family, .NET Compact Framework - Windows CE .NET

.NET Framework Security:

- **FileIOPermission** for access to the path of the assembly. Associated enumeration: **FileIOPermissionAccess.PathDiscovery**
- **ReflectionPermission** to enhance security and performance when invoked late-bound through mechanisms such as **Type.InvokeMember**. Associated enumeration: **ReflectionPermissionFlag.MemberAccess**.

Assembly.GetObjectData Method

Gets serialization information with all of the data needed to reinstantiate this assembly.

```
[Visual Basic]
Public Overridable Sub GetObjectData( _
    ByVal info As SerializationInfo, _
    ByVal context As StreamingContext _
) Implements ISerializable.GetObjectData
[C#]
public virtual void GetObjectData(
    SerializationInfo info,
    StreamingContext context
);
[C++]
public: virtual void GetObjectData(
    SerializationInfo* info,
    StreamingContext context
);
[JScript]
public function GetObjectData(
    info : SerializationInfo,
    context : StreamingContext
);
```

Parameters

info
> The object to be populated with serialization information.

context
> The destination context of the serialization.

Implements

ISerializable.GetObjectData

Exceptions

Exception Type	Condition
ArgumentNullException	*info* is a null reference (**Nothing** in Visual Basic).

Requirements

Platforms: Windows 98, Windows NT 4.0, Windows Millennium Edition, Windows 2000, Windows XP Home Edition, Windows XP Professional, Windows .NET Server family

.NET Framework Security:

- **ReflectionPermission** to enhance security and performance when invoked late-bound through mechanisms such as **Type.InvokeMember**. Associated enumeration: **ReflectionPermissionFlag.MemberAccess**.

Assembly.GetReferencedAssemblies Method

Gets the **AssemblyName** objects for all the assemblies referenced by this assembly.

```
[Visual Basic]
Public Function GetReferencedAssemblies() As AssemblyName()
[C#]
public AssemblyName[] GetReferencedAssemblies();
[C++]
public: AssemblyName* GetReferencedAssemblies() [];
[JScript]
public function GetReferencedAssemblies() : AssemblyName[];
```

Return Value

An array of type **AssemblyName** containing all the assemblies referenced by this assembly.

Requirements

Platforms: Windows 98, Windows NT 4.0, Windows Millennium Edition, Windows 2000, Windows XP Home Edition, Windows XP Professional, Windows .NET Server family

.NET Framework Security:

- **ReflectionPermission** to enhance security and performance when invoked late-bound through mechanisms such as **Type.InvokeMember**. Associated enumeration: **ReflectionPermissionFlag.MemberAccess**.

Assembly.GetSatelliteAssembly Method

Gets the satellite assembly.

Overload List

Gets the satellite assembly for the specified culture.

Supported by the .NET Compact Framework.

> [Visual Basic] **Overloads Public Function GetSatelliteAssembly(CultureInfo) As Assembly**
>
> [C#] **public Assembly GetSatelliteAssembly(CultureInfo);**
>
> [C++] **public: Assembly* GetSatelliteAssembly(CultureInfo*);**
>
> [JScript] **public function GetSatelliteAssembly(CultureInfo) : Assembly;**

Gets the specified version of the satellite assembly for the specified culture.

Supported by the .NET Compact Framework.

[Visual Basic] **Overloads Public Function GetSatelliteAssembly(CultureInfo, Version) As Assembly**

[C#] **public Assembly GetSatelliteAssembly(CultureInfo, Version);**

[C++] **public: Assembly* GetSatelliteAssembly(CultureInfo*, Version*);**

[JScript] **public function GetSatelliteAssembly(CultureInfo, Version) : Assembly;**

Assembly.GetSatelliteAssembly Method (CultureInfo)

Gets the satellite assembly for the specified culture.

```
[Visual Basic]
Overloads Public Function GetSatelliteAssembly( _
   ByVal culture As CultureInfo _
) As Assembly
[C#]
public Assembly GetSatelliteAssembly(
   CultureInfo culture
);
[C++]
public: Assembly* GetSatelliteAssembly(
   CultureInfo* culture
);
[JScript]
public function GetSatelliteAssembly(
   culture : CultureInfo
) : Assembly;
```

Parameters

culture
   The specified culture.

Return Value

The specified satellite assembly.

Exceptions

Exception Type	Condition
ArgumentNullException	*culture* is a null reference (**Nothing** in Visual Basic).
FileNotFoundException	The assembly cannot be found.
FileLoadException	The satellite assembly with a matching file name was found, but the **CultureInfo** did not match the one specified.

Remarks

Satellite assemblies contain localized resources, as distinct from main application assemblies, which contain non-localizable executable code and resources for a single culture that serve as the default or neutral culture.

Call this method to use your current assembly version.

Requirements

Platforms: Windows 98, Windows NT 4.0, Windows Millennium Edition, Windows 2000, Windows XP Home Edition, Windows XP Professional, Windows .NET Server family, .NET Compact Framework - Windows CE .NET

.NET Framework Security:

• **ReflectionPermission** to enhance security and performance when invoked late-bound through mechanisms such as **Type.InvokeMember**. Associated enumeration: **ReflectionPermissionFlag.MemberAccess**.

Assembly.GetSatelliteAssembly Method (CultureInfo, Version)

Gets the specified version of the satellite assembly for the specified culture.

```
[Visual Basic]
Overloads Public Function GetSatelliteAssembly( _
   ByVal culture As CultureInfo, _
   ByVal version As Version _
) As Assembly
[C#]
public Assembly GetSatelliteAssembly(
   CultureInfo culture,
   Version version
);
[C++]
public: Assembly* GetSatelliteAssembly(
   CultureInfo* culture,
   Version* version
);
[JScript]
public function GetSatelliteAssembly(
   culture : CultureInfo,
   version : Version
) : Assembly;
```

Parameters

culture
   The specified culture.
version
   The version of the satellite assembly.

Return Value

The specified satellite assembly.

Exceptions

Exception Type	Condition
ArgumentNullException	*culture* is a null reference (**Nothing** in Visual Basic).
FileLoadException	The satellite assembly with a matching file name was found, but the **CultureInfo** or the version did not match the one specified.
FileNotFoundException	The assembly cannot be found.

Remarks

Satellite assemblies contain localized resources, as distinct from main application assemblies, which contain non-localizable executable code and resources for a single culture that serve as the default or neutral culture.

Call **GetSatelliteAssembly(CultureInfo)** to use your current assembly version.

If *version* is a null reference (**Nothing** in Visual Basic), the current assembly version is used if both the resource and main assemblies are signed.

Requirements

Platforms: Windows 98, Windows NT 4.0,
Windows Millennium Edition, Windows 2000,
Windows XP Home Edition, Windows XP Professional,
Windows .NET Server family,
.NET Compact Framework - Windows CE .NET

.NET Framework Security:

- **ReflectionPermission** to enhance security and performance
  when invoked late-bound through mechanisms such as
  Type.InvokeMember. Associated enumeration:
  ReflectionPermissionFlag.MemberAccess.

Assembly.GetType Method

Gets the **Type** object that represents the specified type.

Overload List

Gets the **Type** object with the specified name in the assembly
instance.

Supported by the .NET Compact Framework.

[Visual Basic] **Overloads Public Overridable Function
GetType(String) As Type**
[C#] **public virtual Type GetType(string);**
[C++] **public: virtual Type* GetType(String*);**
[JScript] **public function GetType(String) : Type;**

Gets the **Type** object with the specified name in the assembly
instance and optionally throws an exception.

Supported by the .NET Compact Framework.

[Visual Basic] **Overloads Public Overridable Function
GetType(String, Boolean) As Type**
[C#] **public virtual Type GetType(string, bool);**
[C++] **public: virtual Type* GetType(String*, bool);**
[JScript] **public function GetType(String, Boolean) : Type;**

Gets the **Type** object with the specified name in the assembly
instance, with the options of ignoring the case, and throwing an
exception.

[Visual Basic] **Overloads Public Function GetType(String,
Boolean, Boolean) As Type**
[C#] **public Type GetType(string, bool, bool);**
[C++] **public: Type* GetType(String*, bool, bool);**
[JScript] **public function GetType(String, Boolean, Boolean) :
Type;**

Inherited from **Object**.

Supported by the .NET Compact Framework.

[Visual Basic] **Overloads Public Function GetType() As Type**
[C#] **public Type GetType();**
[C++] **public: Type* GetType();**
[JScript] **public function GetType() : Type;**

Assembly.GetType Method (String)

Gets the **Type** object with the specified name in the assembly
instance.

```
[Visual Basic]
Overloads Public Overridable Function GetType( _
   ByVal name As String _
) As Type
```

```
[C#]
public virtual Type GetType(
   string name
);
```
```
[C++]
public: virtual Type* GetType(
   String* name
);
```
```
[JScript]
public function GetType(
   name : String
) : Type;
```

Parameters

name
> The full name of the type.

Return Value

A **Type** object that represents the specified class, or a null reference
(**Nothing** in Visual Basic) if the class is not found.

Exceptions

Exception Type	Condition
ArgumentException	*name* is invalid.
	-or-
	The length of *name* exceeds 1024 characters.
ArgumentNullException	*name* is a null reference (**Nothing** in Visual Basic).
SecurityException	The caller does not have the required permission.

Remarks

Unlike **Type.GetType**, which requires a string that includes both the
type name and the assembly name, this method requires only the
type name because only the assembly on which you are calling
GetType is used.

Requirements

Platforms: Windows 98, Windows NT 4.0,
Windows Millennium Edition, Windows 2000,
Windows XP Home Edition, Windows XP Professional,
Windows .NET Server family,
.NET Compact Framework - Windows CE .NET,
Common Language Infrastructure (CLI) Standard

.NET Framework Security:

- **ReflectionPermission** to enhance security and performance
  when invoked late-bound through mechanisms such as
  Type.InvokeMember. Associated enumeration:
  ReflectionPermissionFlag.MemberAccess.

- **ReflectionPermission** for reflecting methods that are not public.
  Associated enumerations: **ReflectionPermissionFlag.Mem-
  berAccess, ReflectionPermissionFlag.TypeInformation**

Assembly.GetType Method (String, Boolean)

Gets the **Type** object with the specified name in the assembly
instance and optionally throws an exception.

[Visual Basic]
```
Overloads Public Overridable Function GetType( _
    ByVal name As String, _
    ByVal throwOnError As Boolean _
) As Type
```
[C#]
```
public virtual Type GetType(
    string name,
    bool throwOnError
);
```
[C++]
```
public: virtual Type* GetType(
    String* name,
    bool throwOnError
);
```
[JScript]
```
public function GetType(
    name : String,
    throwOnError : Boolean
) : Type;
```

Parameters

name

 The full name of the type.

throwOnError

 true to throw an exception if the type is not found; otherwise, a null reference (**Nothing** in Visual Basic).

Return Value

A **Type** object that represents the specified class.

Exceptions

Exception Type	Condition
ReflectionTypeLoad-Exception	The type is not in the assembly instance you are calling the method on.
ArgumentException	*name* is invalid. -or- The length of *name* exceeds 1024 characters.
ArgumentNullException	*name* is a null reference (**Nothing** in Visual Basic).
SecurityException	The caller does not have the required permission.

Remarks

Unlike **Type.GetType**, which requires a string that includes both the type name and the assembly name, this method requires only the type name because only the assembly on which you are calling **GetType** is used.

Requirements

Platforms: Windows 98, Windows NT 4.0, Windows Millennium Edition, Windows 2000, Windows XP Home Edition, Windows XP Professional, Windows .NET Server family, .NET Compact Framework - Windows CE .NET

.NET Framework Security:

• **ReflectionPermission** to enhance security and performance when invoked late-bound through mechanisms such as

Type.InvokeMember. Associated enumeration: **ReflectionPermissionFlag.MemberAccess**.

• **ReflectionPermission** for reflecting methods that are not public. Associated enumerations: **ReflectionPermissionFlag.MemberAccess**, **ReflectionPermissionFlag.TypeInformation**

Assembly.GetType Method (String, Boolean, Boolean)

Gets the **Type** object with the specified name in the assembly instance, with the options of ignoring the case, and throwing an exception.

[Visual Basic]
```
Overloads Public Function GetType( _
    ByVal name As String, _
    ByVal throwOnError As Boolean, _
    ByVal ignoreCase As Boolean _
) As Type
```
[C#]
```
public Type GetType(
    string name,
    bool throwOnError,
    bool ignoreCase
);
```
[C++]
```
public: Type* GetType(
    String* name,
    bool throwOnError,
    bool ignoreCase
);
```
[JScript]
```
public function GetType(
    name : String,
    throwOnError : Boolean,
    ignoreCase : Boolean
) : Type;
```

Parameters

name

 The full name of the type.

throwOnError

 true to throw an exception if the type is not found; otherwise, a null reference (**Nothing** in Visual Basic).

ignoreCase

 true to ignore the case of the type name; otherwise, **false**.

Return Value

A **Type** object that represents the specified class.

Exceptions

Exception Type	Condition
ReflectionTypeLoad-Exception	The type is not in the assembly instance you are calling the method on.
ArgumentException	*name* is invalid. -or- The length of *name* exceeds 1024 characters.
ArgumentNullException	*name* is a null reference (**Nothing** in Visual Basic).

Exception Type	Condition
SecurityException	The caller does not have the required permission.

Remarks

Unlike **Type.GetType**, which requires a string that includes both the type name and the assembly name, this method requires only the type name because only the assembly on which you are calling **GetType** is used.

Requirements

Platforms: Windows 98, Windows NT 4.0, Windows Millennium Edition, Windows 2000, Windows XP Home Edition, Windows XP Professional, Windows .NET Server family

.NET Framework Security:

- **ReflectionPermission** to enhance security and performance when invoked late-bound through mechanisms such as **Type.InvokeMember**. Associated enumeration: **ReflectionPermissionFlag.MemberAccess**.
- **ReflectionPermission** for reflecting methods that are not public. Associated enumerations: **ReflectionPermissionFlag.MemberAccess**, **ReflectionPermissionFlag.TypeInformation**

Assembly.GetTypes Method

Gets the types defined in this assembly.

```
[Visual Basic]
Public Overridable Function GetTypes() As Type()
[C#]
public virtual Type[] GetTypes();
[C++]
public: virtual Type* GetTypes() [];
[JScript]
public function GetTypes() : Type[];
```

Return Value

An array of type **Type** containing objects for all the types defined in this assembly.

Example

The following example displays the types in the specified assembly.

```
[Visual Basic]
Dim SampleAssembly As [Assembly]
SampleAssembly = [Assembly].LoadFrom("c:\Sample.Assembly.dll")
' Obtain a reference to a method known to exist in assembly.
Dim Method As MethodInfo =
SampleAssembly.GetTypes()(0).GetMethod("Method1")
' Obtain a reference to the parameters collection of the MethodInfo
instance.
Dim Params As ParameterInfo() = Method.GetParameters()
' Display information about method parameters.
' Param = sParam1
'    Type = System.String
'    Position = 0
'    Optional=False
Dim Param As ParameterInfo
For Each Param In Params
    Console.WriteLine(("Param=" + Param.Name.ToString()))
    Console.WriteLine(("  Type=" + Param.ParameterType.ToString()))
    Console.WriteLine(("  Position=" + Param.Position.ToString()))
    Console.WriteLine(("  Optional=" + Param.IsOptional.ToString()))
Next Param
```

```
[C#]
Assembly SampleAssembly;
SampleAssembly = Assembly.LoadFrom("c:\\Sample.Assembly.dll");
// Obtain a reference to a method known to exist in assembly.
MethodInfo Method = SampleAssembly.GetTypes()[0].GetMethod("Method1");
// Obtain a reference to the parameters collection of the
MethodInfo instance.
ParameterInfo[] Params = Method.GetParameters();
// Display information about method parameters.
// Param = sParam1
//    Type = System.String
//    Position = 0
//    Optional=False
foreach (ParameterInfo Param in Params)
{
    Console.WriteLine("Param=" + Param.Name.ToString());
    Console.WriteLine("  Type=" + Param.ParameterType.ToString());
    Console.WriteLine("  Position=" + Param.Position.ToString());
    Console.WriteLine("  Optional=" + Param.IsOptional.ToString());
}
```

```
[C++]
Assembly* SampleAssembly;
SampleAssembly = Assembly::LoadFrom(S"c:\\Sample::Assembly.dll");
// Obtain a reference to a method known to exist in assembly.
MethodInfo* Method = SampleAssembly->GetTypes()[0]-
>GetMethod(S"Method1");
// Obtain a reference to the parameters collection of the
 MethodInfo instance.
ParameterInfo* Params[] = Method->GetParameters();
// Display information ab->Item[Out] method* parameters.
// Param = sParam1
//    Type = System::String
//    Position = 0
//    Optional=False
IEnumerator* myEnum = Params->GetEnumerator();
while (myEnum->MoveNext()) {
    ParameterInfo* Param = __try_cast<ParameterInfo*>(myEnum->Current);

    Console::WriteLine(S"Param= {0}", Param->Name);
    Console::WriteLine(S"  Type= {0}", Param->ParameterType);
    Console::WriteLine(S"  Position= {0}", __box(Param->Position));
    Console::WriteLine(S"  Optional= {0}", __box(Param->IsOptional));
}
```

```
[JScript]
var SampleAssembly : Assembly;
SampleAssembly = Assembly.LoadFrom("c:\\Sample.Assembly.dll");
// Obtain a reference to a method known to exist in assembly.
var Method : MethodInfo =
SampleAssembly.GetTypes()[0].GetMethod("Method1");
// Obtain a reference to the parameters collection of the
MethodInfo instance.
var Params : ParameterInfo[] = Method.GetParameters();
// Display information about method parameters.
// Param = sParam1
//    Type = System.String
//    Position = 0
//    Optional=False
for (var i : int in Params){
    var Param : ParameterInfo = Params[i];
    Console.WriteLine("Param=" + Param.Name.ToString());
    Console.WriteLine("  Type=" + Param.ParameterType.ToString());
    Console.WriteLine("  Position=" + Param.Position.ToString());
    Console.WriteLine("  Optional=" + Param.IsOptional.ToString());
}
```

Requirements

Platforms: Windows 98, Windows NT 4.0, Windows Millennium Edition, Windows 2000, Windows XP Home Edition, Windows XP Professional, Windows .NET Server family, .NET Compact Framework - Windows CE .NET, Common Language Infrastructure (CLI) Standard

.NET Framework Security:

> **ReflectionPermission** to enhance security and performance when invoked late-bound through mechanisms such as **Type.InvokeMember**. Associated enumeration: **ReflectionPermissionFlag.MemberAccess**.
>
> **ReflectionPermission** for reflecting methods that are not public. Associated enumerations: **ReflectionPermissionFlag.MemberAccess**, **ReflectionPermissionFlag.TypeInformation**

Assembly.IsDefined Method

Indicates whether a custom attribute identified by the specified **Type** is defined.

```
[Visual Basic]
Public Overridable Function IsDefined( _
   ByVal attributeType As Type, _
   ByVal inherit As Boolean _
) As Boolean Implements ICustomAttributeProvider.IsDefined
[C#]
public virtual bool IsDefined(
   Type attributeType,
   bool inherit
);
[C++]
public: virtual bool IsDefined(
   Type* attributeType,
   bool inherit
);
[JScript]
public function IsDefined(
   attributeType : Type,
   inherit : Boolean
) : Boolean;
```

Parameters

attributeType
> The **Type** of the custom attribute to be checked for this assembly.

inherit
> This argument is ignored for objects of this type.

Return Value

true if a custom attribute identified by the specified **Type** is defined; otherwise, **false**.

Implements

ICustomAttributeProvider.IsDefined

Exceptions

Exception Type	Condition
ArgumentNullException	*attributeType* is a null reference (**Nothing** in Visual Basic).

Requirements

Platforms: Windows 98, Windows NT 4.0, Windows Millennium Edition, Windows 2000, Windows XP Home Edition, Windows XP Professional, Windows .NET Server family

.NET Framework Security:

- **ReflectionPermission** to enhance security and performance when invoked late-bound through mechanisms such as **Type.InvokeMember**. Associated enumeration: **ReflectionPermissionFlag.MemberAccess**.

Assembly.Load Method

Loads an assembly.

Overload List

Loads an assembly given its **AssemblyName**.

Supported by the .NET Compact Framework.

> [Visual Basic] **Overloads Public Shared Function Load(AssemblyName) As Assembly**
>
> [C#] **public static Assembly Load(AssemblyName);**
>
> [C++] **public: static Assembly* Load(AssemblyName*);**
>
> [JScript] **public static function Load(AssemblyName) : Assembly;**

Loads the assembly with a Common Object File Format (COFF)-based image containing an emitted assembly. The assembly is loaded into the domain of the caller.

> [Visual Basic] **Overloads Public Shared Function Load(Byte()) As Assembly**
>
> [C#] **public static Assembly Load(byte[]);**
>
> [C++] **public: static Assembly* Load(unsigned char __gc[]);**
>
> [JScript] **public static function Load(Byte[]) : Assembly;**

Loads an assembly given the long form of its name.

Supported by the .NET Compact Framework.

> [Visual Basic] **Overloads Public Shared Function Load(String) As Assembly**
>
> [C#] **public static Assembly Load(string);**
>
> [C++] **public: static Assembly* Load(String*);**
>
> [JScript] **public static function Load(String) : Assembly;**

Loads an assembly given its **AssemblyName**. The assembly is loaded into the domain of the caller using the supplied evidence.

> [Visual Basic] **Overloads Public Shared Function Load(AssemblyName, Evidence) As Assembly**
>
> [C#] **public static Assembly Load(AssemblyName, Evidence);**
>
> [C++] **public: static Assembly* Load(AssemblyName*, Evidence*);**
>
> [JScript] **public static function Load(AssemblyName, Evidence) : Assembly;**

Loads the assembly with a Common Object File Format (COFF)-based image containing an emitted assembly.

> [Visual Basic] **Overloads Public Shared Function Load(Byte(), Byte()) As Assembly**
>
> [C#] **public static Assembly Load(byte[], byte[]);**
>
> [C++] **public: static Assembly* Load(unsigned char __gc[], unsigned char __gc[]);**
>
> [JScript] **public static function Load(Byte[], Byte[]) : Assembly;**

Loads an assembly given its display name, loading the assembly into the domain of the caller using the supplied evidence.

> [Visual Basic] **Overloads Public Shared Function Load(String, Evidence) As Assembly**
>
> [C#] **public static Assembly Load(string, Evidence);**
>
> [C++] **public: static Assembly* Load(String*, Evidence*);**
>
> [JScript] **public static function Load(String, Evidence) : Assembly;**

Loads the assembly with a Common Object File Format (COFF)-based image containing an emitted assembly.

[Visual Basic] **Overloads Public Shared Function Load(Byte(), Byte(), Evidence) As Assembly**

[C#] **public static Assembly Load(byte[], byte[], Evidence);**

[C++] **public: static Assembly* Load(unsigned char __gc[], unsigned char __gc[], Evidence*);**

[JScript] **public static function Load(Byte[], Byte[], Evidence) : Assembly;**

Example

[Visual Basic, C#, C++] The following example loads an assembly given its fully qualified name, and lists all the types contained in the specified assembly. For this code example to run, you must provide the fully qualified assembly name. For information about how to obtain the fully qualified assembly name, see **Assembly Names**.

[Visual Basic, C#, C++] **Note** This example shows how to use one of the overloaded versions of **Load**. For other examples that might be available, see the individual overload topics.

```
[Visual Basic]
Imports System
Imports System.Reflection

Class Class1
    Public Shared Sub Main()
        Dim SampleAssembly As [Assembly]
        ' You must supply a valid fully qualified assembly name here.
        SampleAssembly = [Assembly].Load("Assembly text name, Version, Culture, PublicKeyToken")
        Dim Types As Type() = SampleAssembly.GetTypes()
        Dim oType As Type
        ' Display all the types contained in the specified assembly.
        For Each oType In Types
            Console.WriteLine(oType.Name.ToString())
        Next oType
    End Sub 'LoadSample
End Class 'Class1
```

```
[C#]
using System;
using System.Reflection;

class Class1
{
    public static void Main()
    {
        Assembly SampleAssembly;
        // You must supply a valid fully qualified assembly name here.
        SampleAssembly = Assembly.Load("Assembly text name, Version, Culture, PublicKeyToken");
        Type[] Types = SampleAssembly.GetTypes();
        // Display all the types contained in the specified assembly.
        foreach (Type oType in Types)
        {
            Console.WriteLine(oType.Name.ToString());
        }
    }
}
```

```
[C++]
#using <mscorlib.dll>

using namespace System;
using namespace System::Collections;
using namespace System::Reflection;

void main()
{
```

```
    Assembly* SampleAssembly;
    // You must supply a valid fully qualified assembly name here.
    SampleAssembly = Assembly::Load(S"Assembly text name, Version, Culture, PublicKeyToken");
    Type* Types[] = SampleAssembly->GetTypes();
    // Display all the types contained in the specified assembly.
    IEnumerator* myEnum = Types->GetEnumerator();
    while (myEnum->MoveNext())
    {
        Type* oType = __try_cast<Type*>(myEnum->Current);
        Console::WriteLine(oType->Name);
    }
}
```

Assembly.Load Method (AssemblyName)

Loads an assembly given its **AssemblyName**.

```
[Visual Basic]
Overloads Public Shared Function Load( _
    ByVal assemblyRef As AssemblyName _
) As Assembly
[C#]
public static Assembly Load(
    AssemblyName assemblyRef
);
[C++]
public: static Assembly* Load(
    AssemblyName* assemblyRef
);
[JScript]
public static function Load(
    assemblyRef : AssemblyName
) : Assembly;
```

Parameters

assemblyRef
> The **AssemblyName** object that describes the assembly to be loaded.

Return Value

The loaded assembly.

Exceptions

Exception Type	Condition
ArgumentNullException	*assemblyRef* is a null reference (**Nothing** in Visual Basic).
FileNotFoundException	*assemblyRef* is not found.
BadImageFormatException	*assemblyFile* is not a valid assembly.
SecurityException	The caller does not have the required permission.

Remarks

The **Load** methods use the default load context, which records the assembly name and assembly instance information for the set of assemblies that is the transitive closure of the assemblies referenced by a managed application. The default load context applies to assemblies that are loaded with a **Load** method and that use a fully qualified assembly reference.

Whether certain permissions are granted or not granted to an assembly is based on evidence. The rules for assembly and security evidence merging are as follows:

- When you use a **Load** method with no **Evidence** parameter, the assembly is loaded with the evidence that the loader supplies.

When you use a **Load** method with an **Evidence** parameter, pieces of evidence are merged. Pieces of evidence supplied as an argument to the **Load** method supersede pieces of evidence supplied by the loader.

When you use a **Load** method with a **Byte[]** parameter to load a common object file format (COFF) image, evidence is combined. **Zone**, **Url** and **Site** are inherited from the calling assembly, and **Hash** and **StrongName** are taken from the COFF assembly.

When you use a **Load** method with a **Byte[]** parameter and **Evidence** to load a common object file format (COFF) image, only the supplied evidence is used. Evidence of the calling assembly and evidence of the COFF image is ignored.

Reflecting on Managed Extensions for C++ executable files might throw a **BadImageFormatException**. This is most likely caused by C++ compiler stripping the relocation addresses or the .Reloc section from your executable file. To preserve the .reloc address for your C++ executable file, specify **/fixed:no** when you are linking.

Requirements

Platforms: Windows 98, Windows NT 4.0, Windows Millennium Edition, Windows 2000, Windows XP Home Edition, Windows XP Professional, Windows .NET Server family, NET Compact Framework - Windows CE .NET

NET Framework Security:

- **ReflectionPermission** to enhance security and performance when invoked late-bound through mechanisms such as **Type.InvokeMember**. Associated enumeration: **ReflectionPermissionFlag.MemberAccess**.

- **FileIOPermission** for access to read from a file or directory, and for access to the information in the path itself. Associated enumerations: **FileIOPermissionAccess.Read**, **FileIOPermissionAccess.PathDiscovery**.

- **WebPermission** for reading a URI that does not begin with "file://".

- **SecurityPermission** to load an assembly with evidence. Associated enumeration: **SecurityPermissionFlag.ControlEvidence**.

Assembly.Load Method (Byte[])

Loads the assembly with a Common Object File Format (COFF)-based image containing an emitted assembly. The assembly is loaded into the domain of the caller.

```
[Visual Basic]
Overloads Public Shared Function Load( _
   ByVal rawAssembly() As Byte _
) As Assembly
[C#]
public static Assembly Load(
   byte[] rawAssembly
);
[C++]
public: static Assembly* Load(
   unsigned char rawAssembly __gc[]
);
[JScript]
public static function Load(
   rawAssembly : Byte[]
) : Assembly;
```

Parameters

rawAssembly
> An array of type **byte** that is a COFF-based image containing an emitted assembly.

Return Value

The loaded assembly.

Exceptions

Exception Type	Condition
ArgumentNullException	*rawAssembly* is a null reference (**Nothing** in Visual Basic).
BadImageFormatException	*rawAssembly* is not a valid assembly.
SecurityException	The caller does not have the required permission.

Remarks

The **Load** methods use the default load context, which records the assembly name and assembly instance information for the set of assemblies that is the transitive closure of the assemblies referenced by a managed application. The default load context applies to assemblies that are loaded with a **Load** method and that use a fully qualified assembly reference.

Whether certain permissions are granted or not granted to an assembly is based on evidence. The rules for assembly and security evidence merging are as follows:

- When you use a **Load** method with no **Evidence** parameter, the assembly is loaded with the evidence that the loader supplies.

- When you use a **Load** method with an **Evidence** parameter, pieces of evidence are merged. Pieces of evidence supplied as an argument to the **Load** method supersede pieces of evidence supplied by the loader.

- When you use a **Load** method with a **Byte[]** parameter to load a common object file format (COFF) image, evidence is combined. **Zone**, **Url** and **Site** are inherited from the calling assembly, and **Hash** and **StrongName** are taken from the COFF assembly.

- When you use a **Load** method with a **Byte[]** parameter and **Evidence** to load a common object file format (COFF) image, only the supplied evidence is used. Evidence of the calling assembly and evidence of the COFF image is ignored.

Reflecting on Managed Extensions for C++ executable files might throw a **BadImageFormatException**. This is most likely caused by C++ compiler stripping the relocation addresses or the .Reloc section from your executable file. To preserve the .reloc address for your C++ executable file, specify **/fixed:no** when you are linking.

Requirements

Platforms: Windows 98, Windows NT 4.0, Windows Millennium Edition, Windows 2000, Windows XP Home Edition, Windows XP Professional, Windows .NET Server family

.NET Framework Security:

- **ReflectionPermission** to enhance security and performance when invoked late-bound through mechanisms such as **Type.InvokeMember**. Associated enumeration: **ReflectionPermissionFlag.MemberAccess**.

- **FileIOPermission** for access to read from a file or directory, and for access to the information in the path itself. Associated enumerations: **FileIOPermissionAccess.Read**, **FileIOPermissionAccess.PathDiscovery**.

- **WebPermission** for reading a URI that does not begin with "file://".
- **SecurityPermission** to load an assembly with evidence. Associated enumeration: **SecurityPermissionFlag.ControlEvidence**.

Assembly.Load Method (String)

Loads an assembly given the long form of its name.

```
[Visual Basic]
Overloads Public Shared Function Load( _
   ByVal assemblyString As String _
) As Assembly
[C#]
public static Assembly Load(
   string assemblyString
);
[C++]
public: static Assembly* Load(
   String* assemblyString
);
[JScript]
public static function Load(
   assemblyString : String
) : Assembly;
```

Parameters

assemblyString
    The long form of the assembly name.

Return Value

The loaded assembly.

Exceptions

Exception Type	Condition
ArgumentNullException	*assemblyString* is a null reference (**Nothing** in Visual Basic).
FileNotFoundException	*assemblyString* is not found.
BadImageFormatException	*assemblyFile* is not a valid assembly.
SecurityException	The caller does not have the required permission.

Remarks

The **Load** methods use the default load context, which records the assembly name and assembly instance information for the set of assemblies that is the transitive closure of the assemblies referenced by a managed application. The default load context applies to assemblies that are loaded with a **Load** method and that use a fully qualified assembly reference.

Whether certain permissions are granted or not granted to an assembly is based on evidence. The rules for assembly and security evidence merging are as follows:

- When you use a **Load** method with no **Evidence** parameter, the assembly is loaded with the evidence that the loader supplies.
- When you use a **Load** method with an **Evidence** parameter, pieces of evidence are merged. Pieces of evidence supplied as an argument to the **Load** method supersede pieces of evidence supplied by the loader.
- When you use a **Load** method with a **Byte[]** parameter to load a common object file format (COFF) image, evidence is combined.

Zone, **Url** and **Site** are inherited from the calling assembly, and **Hash** and **StrongName** are taken from the COFF assembly.

- When you use a **Load** method with a **Byte[]** parameter and **Evidence** to load a common object file format (COFF) image, only the supplied evidence is used. Evidence of the calling assembly and evidence of the COFF image is ignored.

Reflecting on Managed Extensions for C++ executable files might throw a **BadImageFormatException**. This is most likely caused by C++ compiler stripping the relocation addresses or the .Reloc section from your executable file. To preserve the .reloc address for your C++ executable file, specify **/fixed:no** when you are linking.

Example

See related example in the **System.Reflection.Assembly.Load** method topic.

Requirements

Platforms: Windows 98, Windows NT 4.0, Windows Millennium Edition, Windows 2000, Windows XP Home Edition, Windows XP Professional, Windows .NET Server family, .NET Compact Framework - Windows CE .NET, Common Language Infrastructure (CLI) Standard

.NET Framework Security:

- **ReflectionPermission** to enhance security and performance when invoked late-bound through mechanisms such as **Type.InvokeMember**. Associated enumeration: **ReflectionPermissionFlag.MemberAccess**.
- **FileIOPermission** for access to read from a file or directory, and for access to the information in the path itself. Associated enumerations: **FileIOPermissionAccess.Read**, **FileIOPermissionAccess.PathDiscovery**.
- **WebPermission** for reading a URI that does not begin with "file://".
- **SecurityPermission** to load an assembly with evidence. Associated enumeration: **SecurityPermissionFlag.ControlEvidence**.

Assembly.Load Method (AssemblyName, Evidence)

Loads an assembly given its **AssemblyName**. The assembly is loaded into the domain of the caller using the supplied evidence.

```
[Visual Basic]
Overloads Public Shared Function Load( _
   ByVal assemblyRef As AssemblyName, _
   ByVal assemblySecurity As Evidence _
) As Assembly
[C#]
public static Assembly Load(
   AssemblyName assemblyRef,
   Evidence assemblySecurity
);
[C++]
public: static Assembly* Load(
   AssemblyName* assemblyRef,
   Evidence* assemblySecurity
);
[JScript]
public static function Load(
   assemblyRef : AssemblyName,
   assemblySecurity : Evidence
) : Assembly;
```

Parameters

assemblyRef

The **AssemblyName** object that describes the assembly to be loaded.

assemblySecurity

Evidence for loading the assembly.

Return Value

The loaded assembly.

Exceptions

Exception Type	Condition
ArgumentNullException	*assemblyRef* is a null reference (**Nothing** in Visual Basic).
FileNotFoundException	*assemblyRef* is not found.
BadImageFormatException	*assemblyFile* is not a valid assembly.
FileLoadException	An assembly or module was loaded twice with two different evidences.
SecurityException	The caller does not have the required permission.

Remarks

The **Load** methods use the default load context, which records the assembly name and assembly instance information for the set of assemblies that is the transitive closure of the assemblies referenced by a managed application. The default load context applies to assemblies that are loaded with a **Load** method and that use a fully qualified assembly reference.

Whether certain permissions are granted or not granted to an assembly is based on evidence. The rules for assembly and security evidence merging are as follows:

- When you use a **Load** method with no **Evidence** parameter, the assembly is loaded with the evidence that the loader supplies.
- When you use a **Load** method with an **Evidence** parameter, pieces of evidence are merged. Pieces of evidence supplied as an argument to the **Load** method supersede pieces of evidence supplied by the loader.
- When you use a **Load** method with a **Byte[]** parameter to load a common object file format (COFF) image, evidence is combined. **Zone**, **Url** and **Site** are inherited from the calling assembly, and **Hash** and **StrongName** are taken from the COFF assembly.
- When you use a **Load** method with a **Byte[]** parameter and **Evidence** to load a common object file format (COFF) image, only the supplied evidence is used. Evidence of the calling assembly and evidence of the COFF image is ignored.

Reflecting on Managed Extensions for C++ executable files might throw a **BadImageFormatException**. This is most likely caused by C++ compiler stripping the relocation addresses or the .Reloc section from your executable file. To preserve the .reloc address for your C++ executable file, specify **/fixed:no** when you are linking.

Requirements

Platforms: Windows 98, Windows NT 4.0, Windows Millennium Edition, Windows 2000, Windows XP Home Edition, Windows XP Professional, Windows .NET Server family

.NET Framework Security:

- **ReflectionPermission** to enhance security and performance when invoked late-bound through mechanisms such as **Type.InvokeMember**. Associated enumeration: **ReflectionPermissionFlag.MemberAccess**.
- **FileIOPermission** for access to read from a file or directory, and for access to the information in the path itself. Associated enumerations: **FileIOPermissionAccess.Read**, **FileIOPermissionAccess.PathDiscovery**.
- **WebPermission** for reading a URI that does not begin with "file://".
- **SecurityPermission** to load an assembly with evidence. Associated enumeration: **SecurityPermissionFlag.ControlEvidence**.

Assembly.Load Method (Byte[], Byte[])

Loads the assembly with a Common Object File Format (COFF)-based image containing an emitted assembly.

```
[Visual Basic]
Overloads Public Shared Function Load( _
    ByVal rawAssembly() As Byte, _
    ByVal rawSymbolStore() As Byte _
) As Assembly
[C#]
public static Assembly Load(
    byte[] rawAssembly,
    byte[] rawSymbolStore
);
[C++]
public: static Assembly* Load(
    unsigned char rawAssembly __gc[],
    unsigned char rawSymbolStore __gc[]
);
[JScript]
public static function Load(
    rawAssembly : Byte[],
    rawSymbolStore : Byte[]
) : Assembly;
```

Parameters

rawAssembly

An array of type **byte** that is a COFF-based image containing an emitted assembly.

rawSymbolStore

An array of type **byte** containing the raw bytes representing the symbols for the assembly.

Return Value

The loaded assembly.

Exceptions

Exception Type	Condition
ArgumentNullException	*rawAssembly* is a null reference (**Nothing** in Visual Basic).
SecurityException	The caller does not have the required permission.
BadImageFormatException	*assemblyFile* is not a valid assembly.

Remarks

The assembly is loaded into the domain of the caller, and the raw bytes representing the symbols for the assembly are also loaded.

The **Load** methods use the default load context, which records the assembly name and assembly instance information for the set of assemblies that is the transitive closure of the assemblies referenced by a managed application. The default load context applies to assemblies that are loaded with a **Load** method and that use a fully qualified assembly reference.

Whether certain permissions are granted or not granted to an assembly is based on evidence. The rules for assembly and security evidence merging are as follows:

- When you use a **Load** method with no **Evidence** parameter, the assembly is loaded with the evidence that the loader supplies.

- When you use a **Load** method with an **Evidence** parameter, pieces of evidence are merged. Pieces of evidence supplied as an argument to the **Load** method supersede pieces of evidence supplied by the loader.

- When you use a **Load** method with a **Byte[]** parameter to load a common object file format (COFF) image, evidence is combined. **Zone**, **Url** and **Site** are inherited from the calling assembly, and **Hash** and **StrongName** are taken from the COFF assembly.

- When you use a **Load** method with a **Byte[]** parameter and **Evidence** to load a common object file format (COFF) image, only the supplied evidence is used. Evidence of the calling assembly and evidence of the COFF image is ignored.

Reflecting on Managed Extensions for C++ executable files might throw a **BadImageFormatException**. This is most likely caused by C++ compiler stripping the relocation addresses or the .Reloc section from your executable file. To preserve the .reloc address for your C++ executable file, specify **/fixed:no** when you are linking.

Requirements

Platforms: Windows 98, Windows NT 4.0, Windows Millennium Edition, Windows 2000, Windows XP Home Edition, Windows XP Professional, Windows .NET Server family

.NET Framework Security:

- **ReflectionPermission** to enhance security and performance when invoked late-bound through mechanisms such as **Type.InvokeMember**. Associated enumeration: **ReflectionPermissionFlag.MemberAccess**.

- **FileIOPermission** for access to read from a file or directory, and for access to the information in the path itself. Associated enumerations: **FileIOPermissionAccess.Read**, **FileIOPermissionAccess.PathDiscovery**.

- **WebPermission** for reading a URI that does not begin with "file://".

- **SecurityPermission** to load an assembly with evidence. Associated enumeration: **SecurityPermissionFlag.ControlEvidence**.

Assembly.Load Method (String, Evidence)

Loads an assembly given its display name, loading the assembly into the domain of the caller using the supplied evidence.

```
[Visual Basic]
Overloads Public Shared Function Load( _
   ByVal assemblyString As String, _
   ByVal assemblySecurity As Evidence _
) As Assembly
```

```
[C#]
public static Assembly Load(
   string assemblyString,
   Evidence assemblySecurity
);
```

```
[C++]
public: static Assembly* Load(
   String* assemblyString,
   Evidence* assemblySecurity
);
```

```
[JScript]
public static function Load(
   assemblyString : String,
   assemblySecurity : Evidence
) : Assembly;
```

Parameters

assemblyString
  The display name of the assembly.

assemblySecurity
  Evidence for loading the assembly.

Return Value

The loaded assembly.

Exceptions

Exception Type	Condition
ArgumentNullException	*assemblyString* is a null reference (**Nothing** in Visual Basic).
FileNotFoundException	*assemblyString* is not found.
BadImageFormatException	*assemblyFile* is not a valid assembly.
FileLoadException	An assembly or module was loaded twice with two different evidences.
SecurityException	The caller does not have the required permission.

Remarks

The **Load** methods use the default load context, which records the assembly name and assembly instance information for the set of assemblies that is the transitive closure of the assemblies referenced by a managed application. The default load context applies to assemblies that are loaded with a **Load** method and that use a fully qualified assembly reference.

Whether certain permissions are granted or not granted to an assembly is based on evidence. The rules for assembly and security evidence merging are as follows:

- When you use a **Load** method with no **Evidence** parameter, the assembly is loaded with the evidence that the loader supplies.

- When you use a **Load** method with an **Evidence** parameter, pieces of evidence are merged. Pieces of evidence supplied as an argument to the **Load** method supersede pieces of evidence supplied by the loader.

- When you use a **Load** method with a **Byte[]** parameter to load a common object file format (COFF) image, evidence is combined. **Zone**, **Url** and **Site** are inherited from the calling assembly, and **Hash** and **StrongName** are taken from the COFF assembly.

- When you use a **Load** method with a **Byte[]** parameter and **Evidence** to load a common object file format (COFF) image, only the supplied evidence is used. Evidence of the calling assembly and evidence of the COFF image is ignored.

eflecting on Managed Extensions for C++ executable files might row a **BadImageFormatException**. This is most likely caused by ++ compiler stripping the relocation addresses or the .Reloc ection from your executable file. To preserve the .reloc address for ur C++ executable file, specify **/fixed:no** when you are linking.

equirements

latforms: Windows 98, Windows NT 4.0, indows Millennium Edition, Windows 2000, indows XP Home Edition, Windows XP Professional, indows .NET Server family

NET Framework Security:

ReflectionPermission to enhance security and performance when invoked late-bound through mechanisms such as **Type.InvokeMember**. Associated enumeration: **ReflectionPermissionFlag.MemberAccess**.

FileIOPermission for access to read from a file or directory, and for access to the information in the path itself. Associated enumerations: **FileIOPermissionAccess.Read**, **FileIOPermissionAccess.PathDiscovery**.

WebPermission for reading a URI that does not begin with "file://".

SecurityPermission to load an assembly with evidence. Associated enumeration: **SecurityPermissionFlag.ControlEvidence**.

ssembly.Load Method (Byte[], Byte[], Evidence)

oads the assembly with a Common Object File Format (COFF)-ased image containing an emitted assembly.

[Visual Basic]
```
Overloads Public Shared Function Load( _
    ByVal rawAssembly() As Byte, _
    ByVal rawSymbolStore() As Byte, _
    ByVal securityEvidence As Evidence _
) As Assembly
```
[C#]
```
public static Assembly Load(
    byte[] rawAssembly,
    byte[] rawSymbolStore,
    Evidence securityEvidence
);
```
[C++]
```
public: static Assembly* Load(
    unsigned char rawAssembly __gc[],
    unsigned char rawSymbolStore __gc[],
    Evidence* securityEvidence
);
```
[JScript]
```
public static function Load(
    rawAssembly : Byte[],
    rawSymbolStore : Byte[],
    securityEvidence : Evidence
) : Assembly;
```

arameters

awAssembly
An array of type **byte** that is a COFF-based image containing an emitted assembly.

awSymbolStore
An array of type **byte** containing the raw bytes representing the symbols for the assembly.

securityEvidence
Evidence for loading the assembly.

Return Value

The loaded assembly.

Exceptions

Exception Type	Condition
ArgumentNullException	*rawAssembly* is a null reference (**Nothing** in Visual Basic).
BadImageFormat-Exception	*assemblyFile* is not a valid assembly.
FileLoadException	An assembly or module was loaded twice with two different evidences.
SecurityException	The caller does not have the required permission.

Remarks

The assembly is loaded into the domain of the caller using the supplied evidence. The raw bytes representing the symbols for the assembly are also loaded.

The **Load** methods use the default load context, which records the assembly name and assembly instance information for the set of assemblies that is the transitive closure of the assemblies referenced by a managed application. The default load context applies to assemblies that are loaded with a **Load** method and that use a fully qualified assembly reference.

Whether certain permissions are granted or not granted to an assembly is based on evidence. The rules for assembly and security evidence merging are as follows:

- When you use a **Load** method with no **Evidence** parameter, the assembly is loaded with the evidence that the loader supplies.
- When you use a **Load** method with an **Evidence** parameter, pieces of evidence are merged. Pieces of evidence supplied as an argument to the **Load** method supersede pieces of evidence supplied by the loader.
- When you use a **Load** method with a **Byte[]** parameter to load a common object file format (COFF) image, evidence is combined. **Zone**, **Url** and **Site** are inherited from the calling assembly, and **Hash** and **StrongName** are taken from the COFF assembly.
- When you use a **Load** method with a **Byte[]** parameter and **Evidence** to load a common object file format (COFF) image, only the supplied evidence is used. Evidence of the calling assembly and evidence of the COFF image is ignored.

Reflecting on Managed Extensions for C++ executable files might throw a **BadImageFormatException**. This is most likely caused by C++ compiler stripping the relocation addresses or the .Reloc section from your executable file. To preserve the .reloc address for your C++ executable file, specify **/fixed:no** when you are linking.

Requirements

Platforms: Windows 98, Windows NT 4.0, Windows Millennium Edition, Windows 2000, Windows XP Home Edition, Windows XP Professional, Windows .NET Server family

.NET Framework Security:

- **ReflectionPermission** to enhance security and performance when invoked late-bound through mechanisms such as **Type.InvokeMember**. Associated enumeration: **ReflectionPermissionFlag.MemberAccess**.

- **FileIOPermission** for access to read from a file or directory, and for access to the information in the path itself. Associated enumerations: **FileIOPermissionAccess.Read**, **FileIOPermissionAccess.PathDiscovery**.
- **WebPermission** for reading a URI that does not begin with "file://".
- **SecurityPermission** to load an assembly with evidence. Associated enumeration: **SecurityPermissionFlag.ControlEvidence**.

Assembly.LoadFile Method

Note: This namespace, class, or member is supported only in version 1.1 of the .NET Framework.

Loads the contents of an assembly file.

Overload List

Loads the contents of an assembly file on the specified path.

[Visual Basic] **Overloads Public Shared Function LoadFile(String) As Assembly**

[C#] **public static Assembly LoadFile(string);**

[C++] **public: static Assembly* LoadFile(String*);**

[JScript] **public static function LoadFile(String) : Assembly;**

Loads an assembly given its path, loading the assembly into the domain of the caller using the supplied evidence.

[Visual Basic] **Overloads Public Shared Function LoadFile(String, Evidence) As Assembly**

[C#] **public static Assembly LoadFile(string, Evidence);**

[C++] **public: static Assembly* LoadFile(String*, Evidence*);**

[JScript] **public static function LoadFile(String, Evidence) : Assembly;**

Assembly.LoadFile Method (String)

Note: This namespace, class, or member is supported only in version 1.1 of the .NET Framework.

Loads the contents of an assembly file on the specified path.

```
[Visual Basic]
Overloads Public Shared Function LoadFile( _
   ByVal path As String _
) As Assembly
[C#]
public static Assembly LoadFile(
   string path
);
[C++]
public: static Assembly* LoadFile(
   String* path
);
[JScript]
public static function LoadFile(
   path : String
) : Assembly;
```

Parameters

path
    The path of the file to load.

Return Value

The loaded assembly.

Exceptions

Exception Type	Condition
ArgumentNullException	The *path* parameter is a null reference (**Nothing** in Visual Basic).
FileNotFoundException	The *path* parameter is the empty string ("") or does not exist.
SecurityException	The caller does not have the required permission.

Requirements

Platforms: Windows 98, Windows NT 4.0, Windows Millennium Edition, Windows 2000, Windows XP Home Edition, Windows XP Professional, Windows .NET Server family

.NET Framework Security:

- **ReflectionPermission** to enhance security and performance when invoked late-bound through mechanisms such as **Type.InvokeMember**. Associated enumeration: **ReflectionPermissionFlag.MemberAccess**.
- **FileIOPermission** for access to read from a file or directory, and for access to the information in the path itself. Associated enumerations: **FileIOPermissionAccess.Read**, **FileIOPermissionAccess.PathDiscovery**.
- **SecurityPermission** to load an assembly with evidence. Associated enumeration: **SecurityPermissionFlag.ControlEvidence**.

Assembly.LoadFile Method (String, Evidence)

Note: This namespace, class, or member is supported only in version 1.1 of the .NET Framework.

Loads an assembly given its path, loading the assembly into the domain of the caller using the supplied evidence.

```
[Visual Basic]
Overloads Public Shared Function LoadFile( _
   ByVal path As String, _
   ByVal securityEvidence As Evidence _
) As Assembly
[C#]
public static Assembly LoadFile(
   string path,
   Evidence securityEvidence
);
[C++]
public: static Assembly* LoadFile(
   String* path,
   Evidence* securityEvidence
);
[JScript]
public static function LoadFile(
   path : String,
   securityEvidence : Evidence
) : Assembly;
```

Parameters

path
    The path of the assembly file.
securityEvidence
    Evidence for loading the assembly.

eturn Value

...e loaded assembly.

.ceptions

.xception Type	Condition
.rgumentNullException	The *path* parameter is a null reference (**Nothing** in Visual Basic).
.ecurityException	The caller does not have the required permission.
.ileNotFoundException	The *path* parameter is the empty string ("") or does not exist.

.quirements

.atforms: Windows 98, Windows NT 4.0,
...indows Millennium Edition, Windows 2000,
...indows XP Home Edition, Windows XP Professional,
...indows .NET Server family

.ET Framework Security:

ReflectionPermission to enhance security and performance
when invoked late-bound through mechanisms such as
Type.InvokeMember. Associated enumeration:
ReflectionPermissionFlag.MemberAccess.

FileIOPermission for access to read from a file or directory, and
for access to the information in the path itself. Associated
enumerations: **FileIOPermissionAccess.Read**,
FileIOPermissionAccess.PathDiscovery.

SecurityPermission to load an assembly with evidence. Associated enumeration: **SecurityPermissionFlag.ControlEvidence**.

..ssembly.LoadFrom Method

...oads an assembly.

.verload List

...oads an assembly given its file name or path.

...upported by the .NET Compact Framework.

[Visual Basic] **Overloads Public Shared Function
LoadFrom(String) As Assembly**

[C#] **public static Assembly LoadFrom(string);**

[C++] **public: static Assembly* LoadFrom(String*);**

[JScript] **public static function LoadFrom(String) : Assembly;**

...oads an assembly given its file name or path and supplying security
...vidence.

[Visual Basic] **Overloads Public Shared Function
LoadFrom(String, Evidence) As Assembly**

[C#] **public static Assembly LoadFrom(string, Evidence);**

[C++] **public: static Assembly* LoadFrom(String*,
Evidence*);**

[JScript] **public static function LoadFrom(String, Evidence) :
Assembly;**

...oads an assembly given its file name or path, security evidence
...ash value, and hash algorithm.

[Visual Basic] **Overloads Public Shared Function
LoadFrom(String, Evidence, Byte(),
AssemblyHashAlgorithm) As Assembly**

[C#] **public static Assembly LoadFrom(string, Evidence,
byte[], AssemblyHashAlgorithm);**

[C++] **public: static Assembly* LoadFrom(String*,
Evidence*, unsigned char __gc[], AssemblyHashAlgorithm);**

[JScript] **public static function LoadFrom(String, Evidence,
Byte[], AssemblyHashAlgorithm) : Assembly;**

Example

The following example loads an assembly given its file name or
path.

```
[Visual Basic]
Dim SampleAssembly As [Assembly]
SampleAssembly = [Assembly].LoadFrom("c:\Sample.Assembly.dll")
' Obtain a reference to a method known to exist in assembly.
Dim Method As MethodInfo =                                         ↵
SampleAssembly.GetTypes()(0).GetMethod("Method1")
' Obtain a reference to the parameters collection of the           ↵
MethodInfo instance.
Dim Params As ParameterInfo() = Method.GetParameters()
' Display information about method parameters.
' Param = sParam1
'    Type = System.String
'    Position = 0
'    Optional=False
Dim Param As ParameterInfo
For Each Param In Params
    Console.WriteLine(("Param=" + Param.Name.ToString()))
    Console.WriteLine(("   Type=" + Param.ParameterType.ToString()))
    Console.WriteLine(("   Position=" + Param.Position.ToString()))
    Console.WriteLine(("   Optional=" + Param.IsOptional.ToString()))
Next Param
```

```
[C#]
Assembly SampleAssembly;
SampleAssembly = Assembly.LoadFrom("c:\\Sample.Assembly.dll");
// Obtain a reference to a method known to exist in assembly.
MethodInfo Method = SampleAssembly.GetTypes()[0].GetMethod("Method1");
// Obtain a reference to the parameters collection of the MethodInfo
instance.
ParameterInfo[] Params = Method.GetParameters();
// Display information about method parameters.
// Param = sParam1
//    Type = System.String
//    Position = 0
//    Optional=False
foreach (ParameterInfo Param in Params)
{
    Console.WriteLine("Param=" + Param.Name.ToString());
    Console.WriteLine("   Type=" + Param.ParameterType.ToString());
    Console.WriteLine("   Position=" + Param.Position.ToString());
    Console.WriteLine("   Optional=" + Param.IsOptional.ToString());
}
```

```
[C++]
Assembly* SampleAssembly;
SampleAssembly = Assembly::LoadFrom(S"c:\\Sample::Assembly.dll");
// Obtain a reference to a method known to exist in assembly.
MethodInfo* Method = SampleAssembly->GetTypes()[0]-             ↵
>GetMethod(S"Method1");
// Obtain a reference to the parameters collection of the       ↵
 MethodInfo instance.
ParameterInfo* Params[] = Method->GetParameters();
// Display information ab->Item[Out] method* parameters.
// Param = sParam1
//    Type = System::String
//    Position = 0
//    Optional=False
IEnumerator* myEnum = Params->GetEnumerator();
while (myEnum->MoveNext()) {
    ParameterInfo* Param = __try_cast<ParameterInfo*>(myEnum->Current);

    Console::WriteLine(S"Param= {0}", Param->Name);
    Console::WriteLine(S"   Type= {0}", Param->ParameterType);
    Console::WriteLine(S"   Position= {0}", __box(Param->Position));
    Console::WriteLine(S"   Optional= {0}", __box(Param->IsOptional));
}
```

```
[JScript]
var SampleAssembly : Assembly;
SampleAssembly = Assembly.LoadFrom("c:\\Sample.Assembly.dll");
// Obtain a reference to a method known to exist in assembly.
var Method : MethodInfo =
SampleAssembly.GetTypes()[0].GetMethod("Method1");
// Obtain a reference to the parameters collection of
the MethodInfo instance.
var Params : ParameterInfo[] = Method.GetParameters();
// Display information about method parameters.
// Param = sParam1
//    Type = System.String
//    Position = 0
//    Optional=False
for (var i : int in Params){
    var Param : ParameterInfo = Params[i];
    Console.WriteLine("Param=" + Param.Name.ToString());
    Console.WriteLine("  Type=" + Param.ParameterType.ToString());
    Console.WriteLine("  Position=" + Param.Position.ToString());
    Console.WriteLine("  Optional=" + Param.IsOptional.ToString());
}
```

Assembly.LoadFrom Method (String)

Loads an assembly given its file name or path.

```
[Visual Basic]
Overloads Public Shared Function LoadFrom( _
    ByVal assemblyFile As String _
) As Assembly
[C#]
public static Assembly LoadFrom(
    string assemblyFile
);
[C++]
public: static Assembly* LoadFrom(
    String* assemblyFile
);
[JScript]
public static function LoadFrom(
    assemblyFile : String
) : Assembly;
```

Parameters

assemblyFile
    The name or path of the file that contains the manifest of the
    assembly.

Return Value

The loaded assembly.

Exceptions

Exception Type	Condition
ArgumentNullException	*assemblyFile* is a null reference (Nothing in Visual Basic).
FileNotFoundException	*assemblyFile* is not found, or the module you are trying to load does not specify a filename extension.
BadImageFormatException	*assemblyFile* is not a valid assembly.
SecurityException	A codebase that does not start with "file://" was specified without the required WebPermission.

Exception Type	Condition
PathTooLongException	An assembly or module was loaded twice with two different evidences, or the assembly name is longer than MAX_PATH characters.
ArgumentException	The *assemblyFile* parameter is the empty string ("").

Remarks

The *assemblyFile* parameter must refer to a URI without escape
characters. This method supplies escape characters for all invalid
characters in the URI.

assemblyFile is relative to the current directory, and the assembly is
loaded into the domain of the caller.

The **LoadFrom** methods use a load context that records the
assembly name and the assembly instance information for the set of
assemblies that is the transitive closure of the assemblies loaded by
the application using **LoadFrom**. The **LoadFrom** load context
applies to assemblies that are loaded using their locations.

Whether certain permissions are granted or not granted to an
assembly is based on evidence. The rules for assembly and security
evidence merging are as follows:

- When you use a **LoadFrom** method with no **Evidence**
  parameter, the assembly is loaded with the evidence that the
  loader supplies.

- When you use a **LoadFrom** method with an **Evidence**
  parameter, pieces of evidence are merged. Pieces of evidence
  supplied as an argument to the **LoadFrom** method supersede
  pieces of evidence supplied by the loader.

- When you use a **LoadFrom** method with a **Byte[]** parameter to
  load a common object file format (COFF) image, evidence is
  combined. **Zone**, **Url** and **Site** are inherited from the calling
  assembly, and **Hash** and **StrongName** are taken from the COFF
  assembly.

- When you use a **LoadFrom** method with a **Byte[]** parameter and
  Evidence to load a common object file format (COFF) image,
  only the supplied evidence is used. Evidence of the calling
  assembly and evidence of the COFF image is ignored.

Example

The following example loads an assembly given its file name or
path.

```
[Visual Basic]
Dim SampleAssembly As [Assembly]
SampleAssembly = [Assembly].LoadFrom("c:\Sample.Assembly.dll")
' Obtain a reference to a method known to exist in assembly.
Dim Method As MethodInfo =
SampleAssembly.GetTypes()(0).GetMethod("Method1")
' Obtain a reference to the parameters collection of the
MethodInfo instance.
Dim Params As ParameterInfo() = Method.GetParameters()
' Display information about method parameters.
' Param = sParam1
'    Type = System.String
'    Position = 0
'    Optional=False
Dim Param As ParameterInfo
For Each Param In Params
    Console.WriteLine(("Param=" + Param.Name.ToString()))
    Console.WriteLine(("  Type=" + Param.ParameterType.ToString()))
    Console.WriteLine(("  Position=" + Param.Position.ToString()))
    Console.WriteLine(("  Optional=" + Param.IsOptional.ToString()))
Next Param
```

```
[C#]
Assembly SampleAssembly;
SampleAssembly = Assembly.LoadFrom("c:\\Sample.Assembly.dll");
// Obtain a reference to a method known to exist in assembly.
MethodInfo Method = SampleAssembly.GetTypes()[0].GetMethod("Method1");
// Obtain a reference to the parameters collection of the
// MethodInfo instance.
ParameterInfo[] Params = Method.GetParameters();
// Display information about method parameters.
// Param = sParam1
//   Type = System.String
//   Position = 0
//   Optional=False
foreach (ParameterInfo Param in Params)
{
    Console.WriteLine("Param=" + Param.Name.ToString());
    Console.WriteLine("   Type=" + Param.ParameterType.ToString());
    Console.WriteLine("   Position=" + Param.Position.ToString());
    Console.WriteLine("   Optional=" + Param.IsOptional.ToString());
}
```

```
[C++]
Assembly* SampleAssembly;
SampleAssembly = Assembly::LoadFrom(S"c:\\Sample::Assembly.dll");
// Obtain a reference to a method known to exist in assembly.
MethodInfo* Method = SampleAssembly->GetTypes()[0]-
GetMethod(S"Method1");
// Obtain a reference to the parameters collection of the
// MethodInfo instance.
ParameterInfo* Params[] = Method->GetParameters();
// Display information ab->Item[Out] method* parameters.
// Param = sParam1
//   Type = System::String
//   Position = 0
//   Optional=False
IEnumerator* myEnum = Params->GetEnumerator();
while (myEnum->MoveNext()) {
    ParameterInfo* Param = __try_cast<ParameterInfo*>(myEnum->Current);

    Console::WriteLine(S"Param= {0}", Param->Name);
    Console::WriteLine(S"   Type= {0}", Param->ParameterType);
    Console::WriteLine(S"   Position= {0}", __box(Param->Position));
    Console::WriteLine(S"   Optional= {0}", __box(Param->IsOptional));
}
```

```
[JScript]
var SampleAssembly : Assembly;
SampleAssembly = Assembly.LoadFrom("c:\\Sample.Assembly.dll");
// Obtain a reference to a method known to exist in assembly.
var Method : MethodInfo =
SampleAssembly.GetTypes()[0].GetMethod("Method1");
// Obtain a reference to the parameters collection of the
// MethodInfo instance.
var Params : ParameterInfo[] = Method.GetParameters();
// Display information about method parameters.
// Param = sParam1
//   Type = System.String
//   Position = 0
//   Optional=False
for (var i : int in Params){
    var Param : ParameterInfo = Params[i];
    Console.WriteLine("Param=" + Param.Name.ToString());
    Console.WriteLine("   Type=" + Param.ParameterType.ToString());
    Console.WriteLine("   Position=" + Param.Position.ToString());
    Console.WriteLine("   Optional=" + Param.IsOptional.ToString());
}
```

Requirements

Platforms: Windows 98, Windows NT 4.0,
Windows Millennium Edition, Windows 2000,
Windows XP Home Edition, Windows XP Professional,
Windows .NET Server family,
.NET Compact Framework - Windows CE .NET

.NET Framework Security:

- **ReflectionPermission** to enhance security and performance when invoked late-bound through mechanisms such as **Type.InvokeMember**. Associated enumeration: **ReflectionPermissionFlag.MemberAccess**.
- **FileIOPermission** for reading a URI that begins with "file://". Associated enumeration: **FileIOPermissionAccess.Read**
- **WebPermission** for reading a URI that does not begin with "file://".

Assembly.LoadFrom Method (String, Evidence)

Loads an assembly given its file name or path and supplying security evidence.

```
[Visual Basic]
Overloads Public Shared Function LoadFrom( _
    ByVal assemblyFile As String, _
    ByVal securityEvidence As Evidence _
) As Assembly
[C#]
public static Assembly LoadFrom(
    string assemblyFile,
    Evidence securityEvidence
);
[C++]
public: static Assembly* LoadFrom(
    String* assemblyFile,
    Evidence* securityEvidence
);
[JScript]
public static function LoadFrom(
    assemblyFile : String,
    securityEvidence : Evidence
) : Assembly;
```

Parameters

assemblyFile
The name or path of the file that contains the manifest of the assembly.

securityEvidence
Evidence for loading the assembly.

Return Value

The loaded assembly.

Exceptions

Exception Type	Condition
ArgumentNullException	*assemblyFile* is a null reference (**Nothing** in Visual Basic).
FileNotFoundException	*assemblyFile* is not found, or the module you are trying to load does not specify a filename extension.
BadImageFormatException	*assemblyFile* is not a valid assembly.
SecurityException	A codebase that does not start with "file://" was specified without the required **WebPermission**.
PathTooLongException	An assembly or module was loaded twice with two different evidences, or the assembly name is longer than MAX_PATH characters.

Exception Type	Condition
ArgumentException	The *assemblyFile* parameter is the empty string ("").

Remarks

The *assemblyFile* parameter must refer to a URI without escape characters. This method supplies escape characters for all invalid characters in the URI.

assemblyFile is relative to the current directory, and the assembly is loaded into the domain of the caller.

The **LoadFrom** methods use a load context that records the assembly name and the assembly instance information for the set of assemblies that is the transitive closure of the assemblies loaded by the application using **LoadFrom**. The **LoadFrom** load context applies to assemblies that are loaded using their locations.

Whether certain permissions are granted or not granted to an assembly is based on evidence. The rules for assembly and security evidence merging are as follows:

- When you use a **LoadFrom** method with no **Evidence** parameter, the assembly is loaded with the evidence that the loader supplies.
- When you use a **LoadFrom** method with an **Evidence** parameter, pieces of evidence are merged. Pieces of evidence supplied as an argument to the **LoadFrom** method supersede pieces of evidence supplied by the loader.
- When you use a **LoadFrom** method with a **Byte[]** parameter to load a common object file format (COFF) image, evidence is combined. **Zone**, **Url** and **Site** are inherited from the calling assembly, and **Hash** and **StrongName** are taken from the COFF assembly.
- When you use a **LoadFrom** method with a **Byte[]** parameter and **Evidence** to load a common object file format (COFF) image, only the supplied evidence is used. Evidence of the calling assembly and evidence of the COFF image is ignored.

Requirements

Platforms: Windows 98, Windows NT 4.0, Windows Millennium Edition, Windows 2000, Windows XP Home Edition, Windows XP Professional, Windows .NET Server family

.NET Framework Security:

- **ReflectionPermission** to enhance security and performance when invoked late-bound through mechanisms such as **Type.InvokeMember**. Associated enumeration: **ReflectionPermissionFlag.MemberAccess**.
- **SecurityPermission** to load an assembly with evidence. Associated enumeration: **SecurityPermissionFlag.ControlEvidence**.
- **FileIOPermission** for reading a URI that begins with "file://". Associated enumeration: **FileIOPermissionAccess.Read**
- **WebPermission** for reading a URI that does not begin with "file://".

Assembly.LoadFrom Method (String, Evidence, Byte[], AssemblyHashAlgorithm)

Note: This namespace, class, or member is supported only in version 1.1 of the .NET Framework.

Loads an assembly given its file name or path, security evidence hash value, and hash algorithm.

[Visual Basic]
```
Overloads Public Shared Function LoadFrom( _
    ByVal assemblyFile As String, _
    ByVal securityEvidence As Evidence, _
    ByVal hashValue() As Byte, _
    ByVal hashAlgorithm As AssemblyHashAlgorithm _
) As Assembly
```
[C#]
```
public static Assembly LoadFrom(
    string assemblyFile,
    Evidence securityEvidence,
    byte[] hashValue,
    AssemblyHashAlgorithm hashAlgorithm
);
```
[C++]
```
public: static Assembly* LoadFrom(
    String* assemblyFile,
    Evidence* securityEvidence,
    unsigned char hashValue __gc[],
    AssemblyHashAlgorithm hashAlgorithm
);
```
[JScript]
```
public static function LoadFrom(
    assemblyFile : String,
    securityEvidence : Evidence,
    hashValue : Byte[],
    hashAlgorithm : AssemblyHashAlgorithm
) : Assembly;
```

Parameters

assemblyFile
    The name or path of the file that contains the manifest of the assembly.

securityEvidence
    Evidence for loading the assembly.

hashValue
    The value of the computed hash code.

hashAlgorithm
    The hash algorithm used for hashing files and for generating the strong name.

Return Value

The loaded assembly.

Exceptions

Exception Type	Condition
ArgumentNullException	*assemblyFile* is a null reference (**Nothing** in Visual Basic).
FileNotFoundException	*assemblyFile* is not found, or the module you are trying to load does not specify a filename extension.
BadImageFormatException	*assemblyFile* is not a valid assembly.
SecurityException	A codebase that does not start with "file://" was specified without the required **WebPermission**.
PathTooLongException	An assembly or module was loaded twice with two different evidences, or the assembly name is longer than MAX_PATH characters.

Exception Type	Condition
ArgumentException	The *assemblyFile* parameter is the empty string ("").

Remarks

The *assemblyFile* parameter must refer to a URI without escape characters. This method supplies escape characters for all invalid characters in the URI.

assemblyFile is relative to the current directory, and the assembly is loaded into the domain of the caller.

The **LoadFrom** methods use a load context that records the assembly name and the assembly instance information for the set of assemblies that is the transitive closure of the assemblies loaded by the application using **LoadFrom**. The **LoadFrom** load context applies to assemblies that are loaded using their locations.

Whether certain permissions are granted or not granted to an assembly is based on evidence. The rules for assembly and security evidence merging are as follows:

- When you use a **LoadFrom** method with no **Evidence** parameter, the assembly is loaded with the evidence that the loader supplies.

- When you use a **LoadFrom** method with an **Evidence** parameter, pieces of evidence are merged. Pieces of evidence supplied as an argument to the **LoadFrom** method supersede pieces of evidence supplied by the loader.

- When you use a **LoadFrom** method with a **Byte[]** parameter to load a common object file format (COFF) image, evidence is combined. **Zone**, **Url** and **Site** are inherited from the calling assembly, and **Hash** and **StrongName** are taken from the COFF assembly.

- When you use a **LoadFrom** method with a **Byte[]** parameter and **Evidence** to load a common object file format (COFF) image, only the supplied evidence is used. Evidence of the calling assembly and evidence of the COFF image is ignored.

Requirements

Platforms: Windows 98, Windows NT 4.0, Windows Millennium Edition, Windows 2000, Windows XP Home Edition, Windows XP Professional, Windows .NET Server family

NET Framework Security:

- **SecurityPermission** to load an assembly with evidence. Associated enumeration: **SecurityPermissionFlag.ControlEvidence**.
- **ReflectionPermission** to enhance security and performance when invoked late-bound through mechanisms such as **Type.InvokeMember**. Associated enumeration: **ReflectionPermissionFlag.MemberAccess**.
- **FileIOPermission** for reading a URI that begins with "file://". Associated enumeration: **FileIOPermissionAccess.Read**
- **WebPermission** for reading a URI that does not begin with "file://".

Assembly.LoadModule Method

Loads the module internal to this assembly.

Overload List

Loads the module, internal to this assembly, with a Common Object File Format (COFF)-based image containing an emitted module, or a resource file.

[Visual Basic] **Overloads Public Function LoadModule(String, Byte()) As Module**

[C#] **public Module LoadModule(string, byte[]);**

[C++] **public: Module* LoadModule(String*, unsigned char __gc[]);**

[JScript] **public function LoadModule(String, Byte[]) : Module;**

Loads the module, internal to this assembly, with a Common Object File Format (COFF)-based image containing an emitted module, or a resource file. The raw bytes representing the symbols for the module are also loaded.

[Visual Basic] **Overloads Public Function LoadModule(String, Byte(), Byte()) As Module**

[C#] **public Module LoadModule(string, byte[], byte[]);**

[C++] **public: Module* LoadModule(String*, unsigned char __gc[], unsigned char __gc[]);**

[JScript] **public function LoadModule(String, Byte[], Byte[]) : Module;**

Assembly.LoadModule Method (String, Byte[])

Loads the module, internal to this assembly, with a Common Object File Format (COFF)-based image containing an emitted module, or a resource file.

```
[Visual Basic]
Overloads Public Function LoadModule( _
   ByVal moduleName As String, _
   ByVal rawModule() As Byte _
) As Module
[C#]
public Module LoadModule(
   string moduleName,
   byte[] rawModule
);
[C++]
public: Module* LoadModule(
   String* moduleName,
   unsigned char rawModule __gc[]
);
[JScript]
public function LoadModule(
   moduleName : String,
   rawModule : Byte[]
) : Module;
```

Parameters

moduleName
   Name of the module. Must correspond to a file name in this assembly's manifest.
rawModule
   A byte array that is a COFF-based image containing an emitted module, or a resource.

Return Value

The loaded Module.

Exceptions

Exception Type	Condition
ArgumentNullException	*moduleName* or *rawModule* is a null reference (**Nothing** in Visual Basic).
ArgumentException	*moduleName* does not match a file entry in this assembly's manifest.
BadImageFormatException	*rawModule* is not a valid module.
SecurityException	The caller does not have the required permission.

Requirements

Platforms: Windows 98, Windows NT 4.0, Windows Millennium Edition, Windows 2000, Windows XP Home Edition, Windows XP Professional, Windows .NET Server family

.NET Framework Security:

- **ReflectionPermission** to enhance security and performance when invoked late-bound through mechanisms such as **Type.InvokeMember**. Associated enumeration: **ReflectionPermissionFlag.MemberAccess**.
- **SecurityPermission** to provide evidence. Associated enumeration: **SecurityPermissionFlag.ControlEvidence**.

Assembly.LoadModule Method (String, Byte[], Byte[])

Loads the module, internal to this assembly, with a Common Object File Format (COFF)-based image containing an emitted module, or a resource file. The raw bytes representing the symbols for the module are also loaded.

```
[Visual Basic]
Overloads Public Function LoadModule( _
   ByVal moduleName As String, _
   ByVal rawModule() As Byte, _
   ByVal rawSymbolStore() As Byte _
) As Module
[C#]
public Module LoadModule(
   string moduleName,
   byte[] rawModule,
   byte[] rawSymbolStore
);
[C++]
public: Module* LoadModule(
   String* moduleName,
   unsigned char rawModule __gc[],
   unsigned char rawSymbolStore __gc[]
);
[JScript]
public function LoadModule(
   moduleName : String,
   rawModule : Byte[],
   rawSymbolStore : Byte[]
) : Module;
```

Parameters

moduleName
Name of the module. Must correspond to a file name in this assembly's manifest.

rawModule
A byte array that is a COFF-based image containing an emitted module, or a resource.

rawSymbolStore
A byte array containing the raw bytes representing the symbols for the module. Must be a null reference (**Nothing** in Visual Basic) if this is a resource file.

Return Value

The loaded module.

Exceptions

Exception Type	Condition
ArgumentNullException	*moduleName* or *rawModule* is a null reference (**Nothing** in Visual Basic).
ArgumentException	*moduleName* does not match a file entry in this assembly's manifest.
BadImageFormatException	*rawModule* is not a valid module.
SecurityException	The caller does not have the required permission.

Requirements

Platforms: Windows 98, Windows NT 4.0, Windows Millennium Edition, Windows 2000, Windows XP Home Edition, Windows XP Professional, Windows .NET Server family

.NET Framework Security:

- **ReflectionPermission** to enhance security and performance when invoked late-bound through mechanisms such as **Type.InvokeMember**. Associated enumeration: **ReflectionPermissionFlag.MemberAccess**.
- **SecurityPermission** to provide evidence. Associated enumeration: **SecurityPermissionFlag.ControlEvidence**.

Assembly.LoadWithPartialName Method

Loads an assembly from the application directory or from the global assembly cache using a partial name.

Overload List

Loads an assembly from the application directory or from the global assembly cache using a partial name.

[Visual Basic] **Overloads Public Shared Function LoadWithPartialName(String) As Assembly**
[C#] **public static Assembly LoadWithPartialName(string);**
[C++] **public: static Assembly* LoadWithPartialName(String*);**
[JScript] **public static function LoadWithPartialName(String) : Assembly;**

Loads an assembly from the application directory or from the global assembly cache using a partial name. The assembly is loaded into the domain of the caller using the supplied evidence.

[Visual Basic] **Overloads Public Shared Function LoadWithPartialName(String, Evidence) As Assembly**
[C#] **public static Assembly LoadWithPartialName(string, Evidence);**
[C++] **public: static Assembly* LoadWithPartialName(String*, Evidence*);**
[JScript] **public static function LoadWithPartialName(String, Evidence) : Assembly;**

Assembly.LoadWithPartialName Method (String)

Loads an assembly from the application directory or from the global assembly cache using a partial name.

```
[Visual Basic]
Overloads Public Shared Function LoadWithPartialName( _
    ByVal partialName As String _
) As Assembly
[C#]
public static Assembly LoadWithPartialName(
    string partialName
);
[C++]
public: static Assembly* LoadWithPartialName(
    String* partialName
);
[JScript]
public static function LoadWithPartialName(
    partialName : String
) : Assembly;
```

Parameters

partialName
    The partial name of the assembly.

Return Value

The loaded assembly. If *partialName* is not found, this method returns a null reference (**Nothing** in Visual Basic).

Exceptions

Exception Type	Condition
SecurityException	The caller does not have the required permission.
NullReferenceException	The *partialName* parameter is a null reference (**Nothing** in Visual Basic).

Remarks

Applications that load assemblies with this method will be impacted by upgrades of those assemblies. Therefore, do not use this method unless necessary, and even then, consider redesigning the application to use **Load** or **LoadFrom**.

Requirements

Platforms: Windows 98, Windows NT 4.0, Windows Millennium Edition, Windows 2000, Windows XP Home Edition, Windows XP Professional, Windows .NET Server family

.NET Framework Security:

- **ReflectionPermission** to enhance security and performance when invoked late-bound through mechanisms such as **Type.InvokeMember**. Associated enumeration: **ReflectionPermissionFlag.MemberAccess**.

- **FileIOPermission** for access to read from a file or directory, and for access to the information in the path itself. Associated enumerations: **FileIOPermissionAccess.Read**, **FileIOPermissionAccess.PathDiscovery**.

- **WebPermission** for reading a URI that does not begin with "file://".

- **SecurityPermission** for calling unmanaged code and to load an assembly with evidence. Associated enumerations: **SecurityPermissionFlag.UnmanagedCode**, **SecurityPermissionFlag.ControlEvidence**.

Assembly.LoadWithPartialName Method (String, Evidence)

Loads an assembly from the application directory or from the global assembly cache using a partial name. The assembly is loaded into the domain of the caller using the supplied evidence.

```
[Visual Basic]
Overloads Public Shared Function LoadWithPartialName( _
    ByVal partialName As String, _
    ByVal securityEvidence As Evidence _
) As Assembly
[C#]
public static Assembly LoadWithPartialName(
    string partialName,
    Evidence securityEvidence
);
[C++]
public: static Assembly* LoadWithPartialName(
    String* partialName,
    Evidence* securityEvidence
);
[JScript]
public static function LoadWithPartialName(
    partialName : String,
    securityEvidence : Evidence
) : Assembly;
```

Parameters

partialName
    The partial name of the assembly.
securityEvidence
    Evidence for loading the assembly.

Return Value

The loaded assembly. If *partialName* is not found, this method returns a null reference (**Nothing** in Visual Basic).

Exceptions

Exception Type	Condition
FileLoadException	An assembly or module was loaded twice with two different evidences.
SecurityException	The caller does not have the required permission.
NullReferenceException	The *partialName* parameter is a null reference (**Nothing** in Visual Basic).

Remarks

Evidence is the set of information that constitutes input to security policy decisions, such as what permissions can be granted to code.

Applications that load assemblies with this method will be impacted by upgrades of those assemblies. Therefore, do not use this method unless necessary, and even then, consider redesigning the application to use **Load** or **LoadFrom**.

Requirements

Platforms: Windows 98, Windows NT 4.0, Windows Millennium Edition, Windows 2000, Windows XP Home Edition, Windows XP Professional, Windows .NET Server family

.NET Framework Security:

- **ReflectionPermission** to enhance security and performance when invoked late-bound through mechanisms such as **Type.InvokeMember**. Associated enumeration: **ReflectionPermissionFlag.MemberAccess**.
- **FileIOPermission** for access to read from a file or directory, and for access to the information in the path itself. Associated enumerations: **FileIOPermissionAccess.Read**, **FileIOPermissionAccess.PathDiscovery**.
- **WebPermission** for reading a URI that does not begin with "file://".
- **SecurityPermission** for calling unmanaged code and to load an assembly with evidence. Associated enumerations: **SecurityPermissionFlag.UnmanagedCode**, **SecurityPermissionFlag.ControlEvidence**.

Assembly.ToString Method

Returns the full name of the assembly, also known as the display name.

```
[Visual Basic]
Overrides Public Function ToString() As String
[C#]
public override string ToString();
[C++]
public: String* ToString();
[JScript]
public override function ToString() : String;
```

Return Value

The full name of the assembly, or the class name if the full name of the assembly cannot be determined.

Requirements

Platforms: Windows 98, Windows NT 4.0, Windows Millennium Edition, Windows 2000, Windows XP Home Edition, Windows XP Professional, Windows .NET Server family, .NET Compact Framework - Windows CE .NET, Common Language Infrastructure (CLI) Standard

.NET Framework Security:

- **ReflectionPermission** to enhance security and performance when invoked late-bound through mechanisms such as **Type.InvokeMember**. Associated enumeration: **ReflectionPermissionFlag.MemberAccess**.

Assembly.ModuleResolve Event

Occurs when the common language runtime class loader cannot resolve a reference to an internal module of an assembly through normal means.

```
[Visual Basic]
Public Event ModuleResolve As ModuleResolveEventHandler
[C#]
public event ModuleResolveEventHandler ModuleResolve;
[C++]
public: __event ModuleResolveEventHandler* ModuleResolve;
```

[JScript] In JScript, you can handle the events defined by a class, but you cannot define your own.

Event Data

The event handler receives an argument of type **ResolveEventArgs** containing data related to this event.

Remarks

This event gives the callback a chance to find and load the module itself and return it.

Requirements

Platforms: Windows 98, Windows NT 4.0, Windows Millennium Edition, Windows 2000, Windows XP Home Edition, Windows XP Professional, Windows .NET Server family

.NET Framework Security:

- **SecurityPermission** to create and manipulate an application domain. Associated enumeration: **SecurityPermissionFlag.ControlAppDomain**.

AssemblyAlgorithmIdAttribute Class

Specifies an algorithm to hash all files in an assembly. This class cannot be inherited.

System.Object
  System.Attribute
    System.Reflection.AssemblyAlgorithmIdAttribute

```
[Visual Basic]
<AttributeUsage(AttributeTargets.Assembly)>
NotInheritable Public Class AssemblyAlgorithmIdAttribute
    Inherits Attribute
[C#]
[AttributeUsage(AttributeTargets.Assembly)]
public sealed class AssemblyAlgorithmIdAttribute : Attribute
[C++]
[AttributeUsage(AttributeTargets::Assembly)]
public __gc __sealed class AssemblyAlgorithmIdAttribute : public
    Attribute
[JScript]
public
    AttributeUsage(AttributeTargets.Assembly)
class AssemblyAlgorithmIdAttribute extends Attribute
```

Thread Safety

Any public static (**Shared** in Visual Basic) members of this type are safe for multithreaded operations. Any instance members are not guaranteed to be thread safe.

Remarks

The file hash values and names in the assembly are stored in the assembly manifest. When a file is loaded, the hash value is used to verify that a file has not been changed since the manifest was built.

Requirements

Namespace: System.Reflection

Platforms: Windows 98, Windows NT 4.0,
Windows Millennium Edition, Windows 2000,
Windows XP Home Edition, Windows XP Professional,
Windows .NET Server family,
.NET Compact Framework - Windows CE .NET

Assembly: Mscorlib (in Mscorlib.dll)

AssemblyAlgorithmIdAttribute Constructor

Initializes a new instance of the **AssemblyAlgorithmIdAttribute** class.

Overload List

Initializes a new instance of the **AssemblyAlgorithmIdAttribute** class with the specified hash algorithm, using one of the members of **AssemblyHashAlgorithm** to represent the hash algorithm.

Supported by the .NET Compact Framework.

[Visual Basic] **Public Sub New(AssemblyHashAlgorithm)**

[C#] **public AssemblyAlgorithmIdAttribute(AssemblyHashAlgorithm);**

[C++] **public: AssemblyAlgorithmIdAttribute(AssemblyHashAlgorithm);**

[JScript] **public function AssemblyAlgorithmIdAttribute(AssemblyHashAlgorithm);**

Initializes a new instance of the **AssemblyAlgorithmIdAttribute** class with the specified hash algorithm, using an unsigned integer to represent the hash algorithm.

This constructor is not CLS-compliant. For more information about CLS compliance, see **What is the Common Language Specification?**. This constructor is not CLS-compliant.

Supported by the .NET Compact Framework.

[Visual Basic] **Public Sub New(UInt32)**

[C#] **public AssemblyAlgorithmIdAttribute(uint);**

[C++] **public: AssemblyAlgorithmIdAttribute(unsigned int);**

[JScript] **public function AssemblyAlgorithmIdAttribute(UInt32);**

AssemblyAlgorithmIdAttribute Constructor (AssemblyHashAlgorithm)

Initializes a new instance of the **AssemblyAlgorithmIdAttribute** class with the specified hash algorithm, using one of the members of **AssemblyHashAlgorithm** to represent the hash algorithm.

```
[Visual Basic]
Public Sub New( _
    ByVal algorithmId As AssemblyHashAlgorithm _
)
[C#]
public AssemblyAlgorithmIdAttribute(
    AssemblyHashAlgorithm algorithmId
);
[C++]
public: AssemblyAlgorithmIdAttribute(
    AssemblyHashAlgorithm algorithmId
);
[JScript]
public function AssemblyAlgorithmIdAttribute(
    algorithmId : AssemblyHashAlgorithm
);
```

Parameters

algorithmId
    A member of **AssemblyHashAlgorithm** that represents the hash algorithm.

Requirements

Platforms: Windows 98, Windows NT 4.0,
Windows Millennium Edition, Windows 2000,
Windows XP Home Edition, Windows XP Professional,
Windows .NET Server family,
.NET Compact Framework - Windows CE .NET

AssemblyAlgorithmIdAttribute Constructor (UInt32)

Initializes a new instance of the **AssemblyAlgorithmIdAttribute** class with the specified hash algorithm, using an unsigned integer to represent the hash algorithm.

This constructor is not CLS-compliant.

```
[Visual Basic]
<CLSCompliant(False)>
Public Sub New( _
   ByVal algorithmId As UInt32 _
)
[C#]
[CLSCompliant(false)]
public AssemblyAlgorithmIdAttribute(
   uint algorithmId
);
[C++]
[CLSCompliant(false)]
public: AssemblyAlgorithmIdAttribute(
   unsigned int algorithmId
);
[JScript]
public
   CLSCompliant(false)
function AssemblyAlgorithmIdAttribute(
   algorithmId : UInt32
);
```

Parameters

algorithmId

An unsigned integer representing the hash algorithm.

Requirements

Platforms: Windows 98, Windows NT 4.0,
Windows Millennium Edition, Windows 2000,
Windows XP Home Edition, Windows XP Professional,
Windows .NET Server family,
.NET Compact Framework - Windows CE .NET

AssemblyAlgorithmIdAttribute.AlgorithmId Property

Gets the hash algorithm of an assembly manifest's contents.

This property is not CLS-compliant.

```
[Visual Basic]
<CLSCompliant(False)>
Public ReadOnly Property AlgorithmId As UInt32
[C#]
[CLSCompliant(false)]
public uint AlgorithmId {get;}
[C++]
[CLSCompliant(false)]
public: __property unsigned int get_AlgorithmId();
[JScript]
public
   CLSCompliant(false)
function get AlgorithmId() : UInt32;
```

Property Value

An unsigned integer representing the assembly hash algorithm.

Requirements

Platforms: Windows 98, Windows NT 4.0,
Windows Millennium Edition, Windows 2000,
Windows XP Home Edition, Windows XP Professional,
Windows .NET Server family,
.NET Compact Framework - Windows CE .NET

AssemblyCompanyAttribute Class

Defines a company name custom attribute for an assembly manifest.

System.Object
  System.Attribute
    System.Reflection.AssemblyCompanyAttribute

[Visual Basic]
```
<AttributeUsage(AttributeTargets.Assembly)>
NotInheritable Public Class AssemblyCompanyAttribute
   Inherits Attribute
```
[C#]
```
[AttributeUsage(AttributeTargets.Assembly)]
public sealed class AssemblyCompanyAttribute : Attribute
```
[C++]
```
[AttributeUsage(AttributeTargets::Assembly)]
public __gc __sealed class AssemblyCompanyAttribute : public
   Attribute
```
[JScript]
```
public
       AttributeUsage(AttributeTargets.Assembly)
class AssemblyCompanyAttribute extends Attribute
```

Thread Safety

Any public static (**Shared** in Visual Basic) members of this type are safe for multithreaded operations. Any instance members are not guaranteed to be thread safe.

Example

[Visual Basic]
```
Imports System
Imports System.Threading
Imports System.Reflection
Imports System.Reflection.Emit
Imports System.Resources

Public Class MyEmitTest
   Public Shared Sub Main()
      Dim myAssembly As AssemblyBuilder = _
         CType(CreateAssembly(Thread.GetDomain()). _
Assembly, AssemblyBuilder)

      Dim myResourceWriter As IResourceWriter = _
         myAssembly.DefineResource("myResourceFile", _
         "A sample Resource File", "MyResourceFile.resources")
      myResourceWriter.AddResource("AddResource test", _
"Test resource added")

      ' Define unmanaged version information resources.
      myAssembly.DefineVersionInfoResource()
      myAssembly.Save("MyEmittedAssembly.dll")
   End Sub 'Main

   ' Create the callee transient dynamic assembly.
   Private Shared Function CreateAssembly(myDomain As AppDomain) _
As Type
      Dim myAssemblyName As New AssemblyName()
      myAssemblyName.Name = "MyEmittedAssembly"

      Dim myAssembly As AssemblyBuilder = _
         myDomain.DefineDynamicAssembly(myAssemblyName, _
AssemblyBuilderAccess.Save)

      ' Set Company Attribute to the assembly.
      Dim companyAttribute As Type = GetType(AssemblyCompanyAttribute)
      Dim myConstructorInfo1 As ConstructorInfo = _
```

```
companyAttribute.GetConstructor(New Type() {GetType(String)})
      Dim attributeBuilder1 As _
             New CustomAttributeBuilder(myConstructorInfo1, _
New Object(0) {"Microsoft Corporation"})
      myAssembly.SetCustomAttribute(attributeBuilder1)

      ' Set Copyright Attribute to the assembly.
      Dim copyrightAttribute As Type = _
GetType(AssemblyCopyrightAttribute)
      Dim myConstructorInfo2 As ConstructorInfo = _
copyrightAttribute.GetConstructor(New Type() {GetType(String)})
      Dim attributeBuilder2 As _
             New CustomAttributeBuilder(myConstructorInfo2, _
             New Object(0) {"@Copyright Microsoft Corp. 1990-2001"})
      myAssembly.SetCustomAttribute(attributeBuilder2)

      Dim myModule As ModuleBuilder = _
             myAssembly.DefineDynamicModule("EmittedModule", _
"EmittedModule.mod")

      ' Define a public class named "HelloWorld" in the assembly.
      Dim helloWorldClass As TypeBuilder = _
myModule.DefineType("HelloWorld", TypeAttributes.Public)
      ' Define the Display method.
      Dim myMethod As MethodBuilder = _
         helloWorldClass.DefineMethod("Display", _
MethodAttributes.Public, GetType(String), Nothing)

      ' Generate IL for GetGreeting.
      Dim methodIL As ILGenerator = myMethod.GetILGenerator()
      methodIL.Emit(OpCodes.Ldstr, "Display method get called.")
      methodIL.Emit(OpCodes.Ret)

      ' Returns the type HelloWorld.
      Return helloWorldClass.CreateType()
   End Function 'CreateAssembly
End Class 'MyEmitTest
```

[C#]
```
using System;
using System.Threading;
using System.Reflection;
using System.Reflection.Emit;
using System.Resources;

public class MyEmitTest
{
   public static void Main()
   {
      AssemblyBuilder myAssembly =
         (AssemblyBuilder)CreateAssembly(Thread.GetDomain()).Assembly;

      IResourceWriter myResourceWriter =
myAssembly.DefineResource("myResourceFile",
         "A sample Resource File", "MyResourceFile.resources");
      myResourceWriter.AddResource("AddResource test",
"Test resource added");

      // Define unmanaged version information resources .
      myAssembly.DefineVersionInfoResource();
      myAssembly.Save("MyEmittedAssembly.dll");
   }

   // Create the callee transient dynamic assembly.
   private static Type CreateAssembly(AppDomain myDomain)
   {
      AssemblyName myAssemblyName = new AssemblyName();
      myAssemblyName.Name = "MyEmittedAssembly";

      AssemblyBuilder myAssembly =
myDomain.DefineDynamicAssembly(myAssemblyName,
         AssemblyBuilderAccess.Save);

      // Set Company Attribute to the assembly.
      Type companyAttribute = typeof(AssemblyCompanyAttribute);
```

```
        ConstructorInfo myConstructorInfo1 =
companyAttribute.GetConstructor(new Type[]{typeof(String)});
        CustomAttributeBuilder attributeBuilder1 =
            new CustomAttributeBuilder(myConstructorInfo1,
    new object[1]{"Microsoft Corporation"});
        myAssembly.SetCustomAttribute(attributeBuilder1);

        // Set Copyright Attribute to the assembly.
        Type copyrightAttribute = typeof(AssemblyCopyrightAttribute);
        ConstructorInfo myConstructorInfo2 =
copyrightAttribute.GetConstructor(new Type[]{typeof(String)});
        CustomAttributeBuilder attributeBuilder2 =
            new CustomAttributeBuilder(myConstructorInfo2,
            new object[1]{"@Copyright Microsoft Corp. 1990-2001"});
        myAssembly.SetCustomAttribute(attributeBuilder2);

        ModuleBuilder myModule =
myAssembly.DefineDynamicModule("EmittedModule",
        "EmittedModule.mod");

        // Define a public class named "HelloWorld" in the assembly.
        TypeBuilder helloWorldClass =
            myModule.DefineType("HelloWorld", TypeAttributes.Public);
        // Define the Display method.
        MethodBuilder myMethod = helloWorldClass.DefineMethod("Display",
            MethodAttributes.Public, typeof(String), null);

        // Generate IL for GetGreeting.
        ILGenerator methodIL = myMethod.GetILGenerator();
        methodIL.Emit(OpCodes.Ldstr, "Display method get called.");
        methodIL.Emit(OpCodes.Ret);

        // Returns the type HelloWorld.

        return(helloWorldClass.CreateType());
    }
}

[C++]
#using <mscorlib.dll>

using namespace System;
using namespace System::Threading;
using namespace System::Reflection;
using namespace System::Reflection::Emit;
using namespace System::Resources;

// Create the callee transient dynamic assembly.
static Type* CreateAssembly(AppDomain* myDomain) {
    AssemblyName* myAssemblyName = new AssemblyName();
    myAssemblyName->Name = S"MyEmittedAssembly";

    AssemblyBuilder* myAssembly = myDomain-
>DefineDynamicAssembly(myAssemblyName,
        AssemblyBuilderAccess::Save);

    // Set Company Attribute to the assembly.
    Type* companyAttribute = __typeof(AssemblyCompanyAttribute);
    Type* types1[] = {__typeof(String)};
    ConstructorInfo* myConstructorInfo1 = companyAttribute-
>GetConstructor(types1);
    Object* obj1[] = {S"Microsoft Corporation"};
    CustomAttributeBuilder* attributeBuilder1 = new
CustomAttributeBuilder(myConstructorInfo1, obj1);
    myAssembly->SetCustomAttribute(attributeBuilder1);

    // Set Copyright Attribute to the assembly.
    Type* copyrightAttribute = __typeof(AssemblyCopyrightAttribute);
    Type* types2[] = {__typeof(String)};
    ConstructorInfo* myConstructorInfo2 = copyrightAttribute-
>GetConstructor(types2);
    Object* obj2[] = {S"@Copyright Microsoft Corp. 1990-2001"};
    CustomAttributeBuilder* attributeBuilder2 = new
CustomAttributeBuilder(myConstructorInfo2, obj2);
    myAssembly->SetCustomAttribute(attributeBuilder2);
```

```
    ModuleBuilder* myModule = myAssembly-
>DefineDynamicModule(S"EmittedModule",
        S"EmittedModule::mod");

    // Define a public class named S"HelloWorld" in the assembly.
    TypeBuilder* helloWorldClass =
        myModule->DefineType(S"HelloWorld", TypeAttributes::Public);
    // Define the Display method.
    MethodBuilder* myMethod = helloWorldClass->DefineMethod(S"Display",
        MethodAttributes::Public, __typeof(String), 0);

    // Generate IL for GetGreeting.
    ILGenerator* methodIL = myMethod->GetILGenerator();
    methodIL->Emit(OpCodes::Ldstr, S"Display method get called.");
    methodIL->Emit(OpCodes::Ret);

    // Returns the type HelloWorld.

    return(helloWorldClass->CreateType());
}

void main()
{
    AssemblyBuilder* myAssembly =
        __try_cast<AssemblyBuilder*>(CreateAssembly
(Thread::GetDomain())->Assembly);

    IResourceWriter* myResourceWriter = myAssembly-
>DefineResource(S"myResourceFile",
        S"A sample Resource File", S"MyResourceFile::resources");
    myResourceWriter->AddResource(S"AddResource test",
S"Test resource added");

    // Define unmanaged version information resources .
    myAssembly->DefineVersionInfoResource();
    myAssembly->Save(S"MyEmittedAssembly.dll");
}
```

Requirements

Namespace: System.Reflection

Platforms: Windows 98, Windows NT 4.0,
Windows Millennium Edition, Windows 2000,
Windows XP Home Edition, Windows XP Professional,
Windows .NET Server family,
.NET Compact Framework - Windows CE .NET

Assembly: Mscorlib (in Mscorlib.dll)

AssemblyCompanyAttribute Constructor

Initializes a new instance of the **AssemblyCompanyAttribute** class.

```
[Visual Basic]
Public Sub New( _
    ByVal company As String _
)
[C#]
public AssemblyCompanyAttribute(
    string company
);
[C++]
public: AssemblyCompanyAttribute(
    String* company
);
[JScript]
public function AssemblyCompanyAttribute(
    company : String
);
```

Parameters

company

    The company name information.

Requirements

Platforms: Windows 98, Windows NT 4.0,
Windows Millennium Edition, Windows 2000,
Windows XP Home Edition, Windows XP Professional,
Windows .NET Server family,
.NET Compact Framework - Windows CE .NET

AssemblyCompanyAttribute.Company Property

Gets company name information.

```
[Visual Basic]
Public ReadOnly Property Company As String
[C#]
public string Company {get;}
[C++]
public: __property String* get_Company();
[JScript]
public function get Company() : String;
```

Property Value

A string containing the company name.

Requirements

Platforms: Windows 98, Windows NT 4.0,
Windows Millennium Edition, Windows 2000,
Windows XP Home Edition, Windows XP Professional,
Windows .NET Server family,
.NET Compact Framework - Windows CE .NET

AssemblyConfiguration-Attribute Class

Defines an assembly configuration custom attribute (such as retail or debug) for an assembly manifest.

System.Object
  System.Attribute
    System.Reflection.AssemblyConfigurationAttribute

```
[Visual Basic]
<AttributeUsage(AttributeTargets.Assembly)>
NotInheritable Public Class AssemblyConfigurationAttribute
    Inherits Attribute
[C#]
[AttributeUsage(AttributeTargets.Assembly)]
public sealed class AssemblyConfigurationAttribute : Attribute
[C++]
[AttributeUsage(AttributeTargets::Assembly)]
public __gc __sealed class AssemblyConfigurationAttribute : public
    Attribute
[JScript]
public
    AttributeUsage(AttributeTargets.Assembly)
class AssemblyConfigurationAttribute extends Attribute
```

Thread Safety

Any public static (**Shared** in Visual Basic) members of this type are safe for multithreaded operations. Any instance members are not guaranteed to be thread safe.

Requirements

Namespace: System.Reflection

Platforms: Windows 98, Windows NT 4.0, Windows Millennium Edition, Windows 2000, Windows XP Home Edition, Windows XP Professional, Windows .NET Server family, .NET Compact Framework - Windows CE .NET

Assembly: Mscorlib (in Mscorlib.dll)

AssemblyConfigurationAttribute Constructor

Initializes a new instance of the **AssemblyConfigurationAttribute** class.

```
[Visual Basic]
Public Sub New( _
    ByVal configuration As String _
)
[C#]
public AssemblyConfigurationAttribute(
    string configuration
);
[C++]
public: AssemblyConfigurationAttribute(
    String* configuration
);
[JScript]
public function AssemblyConfigurationAttribute(
    configuration : String
);
```

Parameters

configuration
    The assembly configuration.

Requirements

Platforms: Windows 98, Windows NT 4.0, Windows Millennium Edition, Windows 2000, Windows XP Home Edition, Windows XP Professional, Windows .NET Server family, .NET Compact Framework - Windows CE .NET

AssemblyConfigurationAttribute.Configuration Property

Gets assembly configuration information.

```
[Visual Basic]
Public ReadOnly Property Configuration As String
[C#]
public string Configuration {get;}
[C++]
public: __property String* get_Configuration();
[JScript]
public function get Configuration() : String;
```

Property Value

A string containing the assembly configuration information.

Requirements

Platforms: Windows 98, Windows NT 4.0, Windows Millennium Edition, Windows 2000, Windows XP Home Edition, Windows XP Professional, Windows .NET Server family, .NET Compact Framework - Windows CE .NET

AssemblyCopyrightAttribute Class

Defines a copyright custom attribute for an assembly manifest.

System.Object
  System.Attribute
    System.Reflection.AssemblyCopyrightAttribute

```
[Visual Basic]
<AttributeUsage(AttributeTargets.Assembly)>
NotInheritable Public Class AssemblyCopyrightAttribute
    Inherits Attribute
[C#]
[AttributeUsage(AttributeTargets.Assembly)]
public sealed class AssemblyCopyrightAttribute : Attribute
[C++]
[AttributeUsage(AttributeTargets::Assembly)]
public __gc __sealed class AssemblyCopyrightAttribute : public
    Attribute
[JScript]
public
    AttributeUsage(AttributeTargets.Assembly)
class AssemblyCopyrightAttribute extends Attribute
```

Thread Safety

Any public static (**Shared** in Visual Basic) members of this type are safe for multithreaded operations. Any instance members are not guaranteed to be thread safe.

Example

```
[Visual Basic]
Imports System
Imports System.Threading
Imports System.Reflection
Imports System.Reflection.Emit
Imports System.Resources

Public Class MyEmitTest
    Public Shared Sub Main()
        Dim myAssembly As AssemblyBuilder = _
                CType(CreateAssembly(Thread.GetDomain()).
Assembly, AssemblyBuilder)

        Dim myResourceWriter As IResourceWriter = _
            myAssembly.DefineResource("myResourceFile", _
            "A sample Resource File", "MyResourceFile.resources")
        myResourceWriter.AddResource("AddResource test", _
"Test resource added")

        ' Define unmanaged version information resources.
        myAssembly.DefineVersionInfoResource()
        myAssembly.Save("MyEmittedAssembly.dll")
    End Sub 'Main

    ' Create the callee transient dynamic assembly.
    Private Shared Function CreateAssembly(myDomain As AppDomain) _
As Type
        Dim myAssemblyName As New AssemblyName()
        myAssemblyName.Name = "MyEmittedAssembly"

        Dim myAssembly As AssemblyBuilder = _
            myDomain.DefineDynamicAssembly(myAssemblyName,
AssemblyBuilderAccess.Save)

        ' Set Company Attribute to the assembly.
        Dim companyAttribute As Type = GetType(AssemblyCompanyAttribute)
        Dim myConstructorInfo1 As ConstructorInfo =
```

```
companyAttribute.GetConstructor(New Type() {GetType(String)})
        Dim attributeBuilder1 As _
                New CustomAttributeBuilder(myConstructorInfo1,
New Object(0) {"Microsoft Corporation"})
        myAssembly.SetCustomAttribute(attributeBuilder1)

        ' Set Copyright Attribute to the assembly.
        Dim copyrightAttribute As Type =
GetType(AssemblyCopyrightAttribute)
        Dim myConstructorInfo2 As ConstructorInfo =
copyrightAttribute.GetConstructor(New Type() {GetType(String)})
        Dim attributeBuilder2 As _
                New CustomAttributeBuilder(myConstructorInfo2, _
                New Object(0) {"@Copyright Microsoft Corp. 1990-2001"})
        myAssembly.SetCustomAttribute(attributeBuilder2)

        Dim myModule As ModuleBuilder = _
                myAssembly.DefineDynamicModule("EmittedModule",
"EmittedModule.mod")

        ' Define a public class named "HelloWorld" in the assembly.
        Dim helloWorldClass As TypeBuilder =
myModule.DefineType("HelloWorld", TypeAttributes.Public)
        ' Define the Display method.
        Dim myMethod As MethodBuilder = _
            helloWorldClass.DefineMethod("Display",
MethodAttributes.Public, GetType(String), Nothing)

        ' Generate IL for GetGreeting.
        Dim methodIL As ILGenerator = myMethod.GetILGenerator()
        methodIL.Emit(OpCodes.Ldstr, "Display method get called.")
        methodIL.Emit(OpCodes.Ret)

        ' Returns the type HelloWorld.
        Return helloWorldClass.CreateType()
    End Function 'CreateAssembly
End Class 'MyEmitTest

[C#]
using System;
using System.Threading;
using System.Reflection;
using System.Reflection.Emit;
using System.Resources;

public class MyEmitTest
{
    public static void Main()
    {
        AssemblyBuilder myAssembly =
            (AssemblyBuilder)CreateAssembly(Thread.GetDomain()).Assembly;

        IResourceWriter myResourceWriter =
myAssembly.DefineResource("myResourceFile",
            "A sample Resource File", "MyResourceFile.resources");
        myResourceWriter.AddResource("AddResource test",
"Test resource added");

        // Define unmanaged version information resources .
        myAssembly.DefineVersionInfoResource();
        myAssembly.Save("MyEmittedAssembly.dll");
    }

    // Create the callee transient dynamic assembly.
    private static Type CreateAssembly(AppDomain myDomain)
    {
        AssemblyName myAssemblyName = new AssemblyName();
        myAssemblyName.Name = "MyEmittedAssembly";

        AssemblyBuilder myAssembly =
myDomain.DefineDynamicAssembly(myAssemblyName,
            AssemblyBuilderAccess.Save);

        // Set Company Attribute to the assembly.
        Type companyAttribute = typeof(AssemblyCompanyAttribute);
```

```
      ConstructorInfo myConstructorInfo1 =
companyAttribute.GetConstructor(new Type[]{typeof(String)}));
      CustomAttributeBuilder attributeBuilder1 =
         new CustomAttributeBuilder(myConstructorInfo1, new
object[1]{"Microsoft Corporation"});
      myAssembly.SetCustomAttribute(attributeBuilder1);

      // Set Copyright Attribute to the assembly.
      Type copyrightAttribute = typeof(AssemblyCopyrightAttribute);
      ConstructorInfo myConstructorInfo2 =
copyrightAttribute.GetConstructor(new Type[]{typeof(String)}));
      CustomAttributeBuilder attributeBuilder2 =
         new CustomAttributeBuilder(myConstructorInfo2,
         new object[1]{"@Copyright Microsoft Corp. 1990-2001"});
      myAssembly.SetCustomAttribute(attributeBuilder2);

      ModuleBuilder myModule =
myAssembly.DefineDynamicModule("EmittedModule",
         "EmittedModule.mod");

      // Define a public class named "HelloWorld" in the assembly.
      TypeBuilder helloWorldClass =
         myModule.DefineType("HelloWorld", TypeAttributes.Public);
      // Define the Display method.
      MethodBuilder myMethod = helloWorldClass.DefineMethod("Display",
         MethodAttributes.Public, typeof(String), null);

      // Generate IL for GetGreeting.
      ILGenerator methodIL = myMethod.GetILGenerator();
      methodIL.Emit(OpCodes.Ldstr, "Display method get called.");
      methodIL.Emit(OpCodes.Ret);

      // Returns the type HelloWorld.

      return(helloWorldClass.CreateType());
   }
}

[C++]
#using <mscorlib.dll>

using namespace System;
using namespace System::Threading;
using namespace System::Reflection;
using namespace System::Reflection::Emit;
using namespace System::Resources;

// Create the callee transient dynamic assembly.
static Type* CreateAssembly(AppDomain* myDomain) {
   AssemblyName* myAssemblyName = new AssemblyName();
   myAssemblyName->Name = S"MyEmittedAssembly";

   AssemblyBuilder* myAssembly = myDomain-
>DefineDynamicAssembly(myAssemblyName,
      AssemblyBuilderAccess::Save);

   // Set Company Attribute to the assembly.
   Type* companyAttribute = __typeof(AssemblyCompanyAttribute);
   Type* types1[] = {__typeof(String)};
   ConstructorInfo* myConstructorInfo1 = companyAttribute-
>GetConstructor(types1);
   Object* obj1[] = {S"Microsoft Corporation"};
   CustomAttributeBuilder* attributeBuilder1 = new
CustomAttributeBuilder(myConstructorInfo1, obj1);
   myAssembly->SetCustomAttribute(attributeBuilder1);

   // Set Copyright Attribute to the assembly.
   Type* copyrightAttribute = __typeof(AssemblyCopyrightAttribute);
   Type* types2[] = {__typeof(String)};
   ConstructorInfo* myConstructorInfo2 = copyrightAttribute-
>GetConstructor(types2);
   Object* obj2[] = {S"@Copyright Microsoft Corp. 1990-2001"};
   CustomAttributeBuilder* attributeBuilder2 = new
CustomAttributeBuilder(myConstructorInfo2, obj2);
   myAssembly->SetCustomAttribute(attributeBuilder2);
```

```
   ModuleBuilder* myModule = myAssembly-
>DefineDynamicModule(S"EmittedModule",
      S"EmittedModule::mod");

   // Define a public class named S"HelloWorld" in the assembly.
   TypeBuilder* helloWorldClass =
      myModule->DefineType(S"HelloWorld", TypeAttributes::Public);
   // Define the Display method.
   MethodBuilder* myMethod = helloWorldClass->DefineMethod(S"Display",
      MethodAttributes::Public, __typeof(String), 0);

   // Generate IL for GetGreeting.
   ILGenerator* methodIL = myMethod->GetILGenerator();
   methodIL->Emit(OpCodes::Ldstr, S"Display method get called.");
   methodIL->Emit(OpCodes::Ret);

   // Returns the type HelloWorld.

   return(helloWorldClass->CreateType());
}

void main()
{
   AssemblyBuilder* myAssembly =
      __try_cast<AssemblyBuilder*>(CreateAssembly
(Thread::GetDomain())->Assembly);

   IResourceWriter* myResourceWriter = myAssembly-
>DefineResource(S"myResourceFile",
      S"A sample Resource File", S"MyResourceFile::resources");
   myResourceWriter->AddResource(S"AddResource test", S"Test
resource added");

   // Define unmanaged version information resources .
   myAssembly->DefineVersionInfoResource();
   myAssembly->Save(S"MyEmittedAssembly.dll");
}
```

Requirements

Namespace: System.Reflection

Platforms: Windows 98, Windows NT 4.0,
Windows Millennium Edition, Windows 2000,
Windows XP Home Edition, Windows XP Professional,
Windows .NET Server family,
.NET Compact Framework - Windows CE .NET

Assembly: Mscorlib (in Mscorlib.dll)

AssemblyCopyrightAttribute Constructor

Initializes a new instance of the **AssemblyCopyrightAttribute**
class.

```
[Visual Basic]
Public Sub New( _
   ByVal copyright As String _
)
[C#]
public AssemblyCopyrightAttribute(
   string copyright
);
[C++]
public: AssemblyCopyrightAttribute(
   String* copyright
);
```

```
[JScript]
public function AssemblyCopyrightAttribute(
    copyright : String
);
```

Parameters

copyright
    The copyright information.

Requirements

Platforms: Windows 98, Windows NT 4.0,
Windows Millennium Edition, Windows 2000,
Windows XP Home Edition, Windows XP Professional,
Windows .NET Server family,
.NET Compact Framework - Windows CE .NET

AssemblyCopyrightAttribute.Copyright Property

Gets copyright information.

```
[Visual Basic]
Public ReadOnly Property Copyright As String
[C#]
public string Copyright {get;}
[C++]
public: __property String* get_Copyright();
[JScript]
public function get Copyright() : String;
```

Property Value

A string containing the copyright information.

Requirements

Platforms: Windows 98, Windows NT 4.0,
Windows Millennium Edition, Windows 2000,
Windows XP Home Edition, Windows XP Professional,
Windows .NET Server family,
.NET Compact Framework - Windows CE .NET

AssemblyCultureAttribute Class

Specifies which culture the assembly supports.

System.Object
  System.Attribute
    System.Reflection.AssemblyCultureAttribute

```
[Visual Basic]
<AttributeUsage(AttributeTargets.Assembly)>
NotInheritable Public Class AssemblyCultureAttribute
   Inherits Attribute
[C#]
[AttributeUsage(AttributeTargets.Assembly)]
public sealed class AssemblyCultureAttribute : Attribute
[C++]
[AttributeUsage(AttributeTargets::Assembly)]
public __gc __sealed class AssemblyCultureAttribute : public
   Attribute
[JScript]
public
      AttributeUsage(AttributeTargets.Assembly)
class AssemblyCultureAttribute extends Attribute
```

Thread Safety

Any public static (**Shared** in Visual Basic) members of this type are safe for multithreaded operations. Any instance members are not guaranteed to be thread safe.

Remarks

The attribute is used by compilers to distinguish between a main assembly and a satellite assembly. A main assembly contains code and the neutral culture's resources. A satellite assembly contains only resources for a particular culture, as in [assembly:AssemblyCultureAttribute("de")]. Putting this attribute on an assembly and using something other than the empty string ("") for the culture name will make this assembly look like a satellite assembly, rather than a main assembly that contains executable code. Labeling a traditional code library with this attribute will break it, because no other code will be able to find the library's entry points at runtime.

For more detail, see the specifications for the common language runtime architecture, metadata, Microsoft intermediate language instruction set, file format, and Microsoft intermediate language assembly reference in the "Tool Developers Guide" folder of the SDK.

Requirements

Namespace: System.Reflection

Platforms: Windows 98, Windows NT 4.0, Windows Millennium Edition, Windows 2000, Windows XP Home Edition, Windows XP Professional, Windows .NET Server family, .NET Compact Framework - Windows CE .NET

Assembly: Mscorlib (in Mscorlib.dll)

AssemblyCultureAttribute Constructor

Initializes a new instance of the **AssemblyCultureAttribute** class with the culture supported by the assembly being attributed.

```
[Visual Basic]
Public Sub New( _
   ByVal culture As String _
)
[C#]
public AssemblyCultureAttribute(
   string culture
);
[C++]
public: AssemblyCultureAttribute(
   String* culture
);
[JScript]
public function AssemblyCultureAttribute(
   culture : String
);
```

Parameters

culture
    The culture supported by the attributed assembly.

Remarks

The culture names follow the RFC1766 names. The format is as follows: "language"-"country/region". For example, the format for US English is "en-US".

Requirements

Platforms: Windows 98, Windows NT 4.0, Windows Millennium Edition, Windows 2000, Windows XP Home Edition, Windows XP Professional, Windows .NET Server family, .NET Compact Framework - Windows CE .NET

AssemblyCultureAttribute.Culture Property

Gets the supported culture of the attributed assembly.

```
[Visual Basic]
Public ReadOnly Property Culture As String
[C#]
public string Culture {get;}
[C++]
public: __property String* get_Culture();
[JScript]
public function get Culture() : String;
```

Property Value

A string containing the name of the supported culture.

Requirements

Platforms: Windows 98, Windows NT 4.0, Windows Millennium Edition, Windows 2000, Windows XP Home Edition, Windows XP Professional, Windows .NET Server family, .NET Compact Framework - Windows CE .NET

AssemblyDefaultAliasAttribute Class

Defines a friendly default alias for an assembly manifest.

System.Object
  System.Attribute
    System.Reflection.AssemblyDefaultAliasAttribute

[Visual Basic]
```
<AttributeUsage(AttributeTargets.Assembly)>
NotInheritable Public Class AssemblyDefaultAliasAttribute
    Inherits Attribute
```
[C#]
```
[AttributeUsage(AttributeTargets.Assembly)]
public sealed class AssemblyDefaultAliasAttribute : Attribute
```
[C++]
```
[AttributeUsage(AttributeTargets::Assembly)]
public __gc __sealed class AssemblyDefaultAliasAttribute : public
    Attribute
```
[JScript]
```
public
    AttributeUsage(AttributeTargets.Assembly)
class AssemblyDefaultAliasAttribute extends Attribute
```

Thread Safety

Any public static (**Shared** in Visual Basic) members of this type are
safe for multithreaded operations. Any instance members are not
guaranteed to be thread safe.

Remarks

This is a friendly default alias in cases where the assembly name is
not friendly or is a GUID.

Requirements

Namespace: System.Reflection

Platforms: Windows 98, Windows NT 4.0,
Windows Millennium Edition, Windows 2000,
Windows XP Home Edition, Windows XP Professional,
Windows .NET Server family,
.NET Compact Framework - Windows CE .NET

Assembly: Mscorlib (in Mscorlib.dll)

AssemblyDefaultAliasAttribute Constructor

Initializes a new instance of the **AssemblyDefaultAliasAttribute**
class.

[Visual Basic]
```
Public Sub New( _
    ByVal defaultAlias As String _
)
```
[C#]
```
public AssemblyDefaultAliasAttribute(
    string defaultAlias
);
```
[C++]
```
public: AssemblyDefaultAliasAttribute(
    String* defaultAlias
);
```
[JScript]
```
public function AssemblyDefaultAliasAttribute(
    defaultAlias : String
);
```

Parameters

defaultAlias
    The assembly default alias information.

Requirements

Platforms: Windows 98, Windows NT 4.0,
Windows Millennium Edition, Windows 2000,
Windows XP Home Edition, Windows XP Professional,
Windows .NET Server family,
.NET Compact Framework - Windows CE .NET

AssemblyDefaultAliasAttribute.DefaultAlias Property

Gets default alias information.

[Visual Basic]
```
Public ReadOnly Property DefaultAlias As String
```
[C#]
```
public string DefaultAlias {get;}
```
[C++]
```
public: __property String* get_DefaultAlias();
```
[JScript]
```
public function get DefaultAlias() : String;
```

Property Value

A string containing the default alias information.

Requirements

Platforms: Windows 98, Windows NT 4.0,
Windows Millennium Edition, Windows 2000,
Windows XP Home Edition, Windows XP Professional,
Windows .NET Server family,
.NET Compact Framework - Windows CE .NET

AssemblyDelaySignAttribute Class

Specifies that the assembly is not fully signed when created.

System.Object
  System.Attribute
    System.Reflection.AssemblyDelaySignAttribute

```
[Visual Basic]
<AttributeUsage(AttributeTargets.Assembly)>
NotInheritable Public Class AssemblyDelaySignAttribute
   Inherits Attribute
[C#]
[AttributeUsage(AttributeTargets.Assembly)]
public sealed class AssemblyDelaySignAttribute : Attribute
[C++]
[AttributeUsage(AttributeTargets::Assembly)]
public __gc __sealed class AssemblyDelaySignAttribute : public
   Attribute
[JScript]
public
   AttributeUsage(AttributeTargets.Assembly)
class AssemblyDelaySignAttribute extends Attribute
```

Thread Safety

Any public static (**Shared** in Visual Basic) members of this type are safe for multithreaded operations. Any instance members are not guaranteed to be thread safe.

Remarks

When this attribute is used on an assembly, space is reserved for the signature which is later filled by a signing tool such as the Sn.exe utility. Delayed signing is used when the author of the assembly does not have access to the private key that will be used to generate the signature, as in `[assembly:AssemblyDelaySignAttribute(true)]`.

The classes in **System.Runtime.CompilerServices** are intended for use by compilers only. Do not use them unless you are building a compiler. For more detail, see the specifications for the common language runtime architecture, metadata, Microsoft intermediate language instruction set, file format, and Microsoft intermediate language assembly reference in the "Tool Developers Guide" folder of the SDK.

Requirements

Namespace: System.Reflection

Platforms: Windows 98, Windows NT 4.0, Windows Millennium Edition, Windows 2000, Windows XP Home Edition, Windows XP Professional, Windows .NET Server family, .NET Compact Framework - Windows CE .NET

Assembly: Mscorlib (in Mscorlib.dll)

AssemblyDelaySignAttribute Constructor

Initializes a new instance of the **AssemblyDelaySignAttribute** class.

```
[Visual Basic]
Public Sub New( _
   ByVal delaySign As Boolean _
)
[C#]
public AssemblyDelaySignAttribute(
   bool delaySign
);
[C++]
public: AssemblyDelaySignAttribute(
   bool delaySign
);
[JScript]
public function AssemblyDelaySignAttribute(
   delaySign : Boolean
);
```

Parameters

delaySign
    true if the feature this attribute represents is activated; otherwise, **false**.

Requirements

Platforms: Windows 98, Windows NT 4.0, Windows Millennium Edition, Windows 2000, Windows XP Home Edition, Windows XP Professional, Windows .NET Server family, .NET Compact Framework - Windows CE .NET

AssemblyDelaySignAttribute.DelaySign Property

Gets a value indicating the state of the attribute.

```
[Visual Basic]
Public ReadOnly Property DelaySign As Boolean
[C#]
public bool DelaySign {get;}
[C++]
public: __property bool get_DelaySign();
[JScript]
public function get DelaySign() : Boolean;
```

Property Value

true if this assembly has been built as delay-signed; otherwise, **false**.

Requirements

Platforms: Windows 98, Windows NT 4.0, Windows Millennium Edition, Windows 2000, Windows XP Home Edition, Windows XP Professional, Windows .NET Server family, .NET Compact Framework - Windows CE .NET

AssemblyDescriptionAttribute Class

Defines an assembly description custom attribute for an assembly manifest.

System.Object
  System.Attribute
    System.Reflection.AssemblyDescriptionAttribute

```
[Visual Basic]
<AttributeUsage(AttributeTargets.Assembly)>
NotInheritable Public Class AssemblyDescriptionAttribute
    Inherits Attribute
[C#]
[AttributeUsage(AttributeTargets.Assembly)]
public sealed class AssemblyDescriptionAttribute : Attribute
[C++]
[AttributeUsage(AttributeTargets::Assembly)]
public __gc __sealed class AssemblyDescriptionAttribute : public
    Attribute
[JScript]
public
    AttributeUsage(AttributeTargets.Assembly)
class AssemblyDescriptionAttribute extends Attribute
```

Thread Safety

Any public static (**Shared** in Visual Basic) members of this type are safe for multithreaded operations. Any instance members are not guaranteed to be thread safe.

Example

```
[Visual Basic]
Imports System
Imports System.Threading
Imports System.Reflection
Imports System.Reflection.Emit
Imports System.Resources

Public Class MyEmitTest
    Public Shared Sub Main()
        Dim myAssembly As AssemblyBuilder = _
            CType(CreateAssembly(Thread.GetDomain()).Assembly, _
AssemblyBuilder)

        Dim myResourceWriter As IResourceWriter = _
            myAssembly.DefineResource("myResourceFile", _
            "A sample Resource File", "MyResourceFile.resources")
        myResourceWriter.AddResource("AddResource test", _
"Test resource added")

        ' Define unmanaged version information resources.
        myAssembly.DefineVersionInfoResource()
        myAssembly.Save("MyEmittedAssembly.dll")
    End Sub 'Main

    ' Create the callee transient dynamic assembly.
    Private Shared Function CreateAssembly(myDomain As AppDomain) _
As Type
        Dim myAssemblyName As New AssemblyName()
        myAssemblyName.Name = "MyEmittedAssembly"

        Dim myAssembly As AssemblyBuilder = _
            myDomain.DefineDynamicAssembly(myAssemblyName, _
AssemblyBuilderAccess.Save)

        ' Set Company Attribute to the assembly.
        Dim companyAttribute As Type = GetType(AssemblyCompanyAttribute)
```

```
        Dim myConstructorInfo1 As ConstructorInfo =
companyAttribute.GetConstructor(New Type() {GetType(String)})
        Dim attributeBuilder1 As _
                New CustomAttributeBuilder(myConstructorInfo1, _
New Object(0) {"Microsoft Corporation"})
        myAssembly.SetCustomAttribute(attributeBuilder1)

        ' Set Copyright Attribute to the assembly.
        Dim copyrightAttribute As Type =
GetType(AssemblyCopyrightAttribute)
        Dim myConstructorInfo2 As ConstructorInfo =
copyrightAttribute.GetConstructor(New Type() {GetType(String)})
        Dim attributeBuilder2 As _
                New CustomAttributeBuilder(myConstructorInfo2, _
                New Object(0) {"@Copyright Microsoft Corp. 1990-2001"})
        myAssembly.SetCustomAttribute(attributeBuilder2)

        Dim myModule As ModuleBuilder = _
                myAssembly.DefineDynamicModule( _
"EmittedModule", "EmittedModule.mod")

        ' Define a public class named "HelloWorld" in the assembly.
        Dim helloWorldClass As TypeBuilder =
myModule.DefineType("HelloWorld", TypeAttributes.Public)
        ' Define the Display method.
        Dim myMethod As MethodBuilder = _
            helloWorldClass.DefineMethod("Display", _
MethodAttributes.Public, GetType(String), Nothing)

        ' Generate IL for GetGreeting.
        Dim methodIL As ILGenerator = myMethod.GetILGenerator()
        methodIL.Emit(OpCodes.Ldstr, "Display method get called.")
        methodIL.Emit(OpCodes.Ret)

        ' Returns the type HelloWorld.
        Return helloWorldClass.CreateType()
    End Function 'CreateAssembly
End Class 'MyEmitTest

[C#]
using System;
using System.Threading;
using System.Reflection;
using System.Reflection.Emit;
using System.Resources;

public class MyEmitTest
{
    public static void Main()
    {
        AssemblyBuilder myAssembly =
            (AssemblyBuilder)CreateAssembly(Thread.GetDomain()).Assembly;

        IResourceWriter myResourceWriter =
myAssembly.DefineResource("myResourceFile",
            "A sample Resource File", "MyResourceFile.resources");
        myResourceWriter.AddResource("AddResource test", "Test resource
added");

        // Define unmanaged version information resources  .
        myAssembly.DefineVersionInfoResource();
        myAssembly.Save("MyEmittedAssembly.dll");
    }

    // Create the callee transient dynamic assembly.
    private static Type CreateAssembly(AppDomain myDomain)
    {
        AssemblyName myAssemblyName = new AssemblyName();
        myAssemblyName.Name = "MyEmittedAssembly";

        AssemblyBuilder myAssembly =
myDomain.DefineDynamicAssembly(myAssemblyName,
            AssemblyBuilderAccess.Save);
```

```
        // Set Company Attribute to the assembly.
        Type companyAttribute = typeof(AssemblyCompanyAttribute);
        ConstructorInfo myConstructorInfo1 =                                    ⌐
companyAttribute.GetConstructor(new Type[]{typeof(String)});
        CustomAttributeBuilder attributeBuilder1 =
            new CustomAttributeBuilder(myConstructorInfo1, new               ⌐
object[1]{"Microsoft Corporation"});
        myAssembly.SetCustomAttribute(attributeBuilder1);

        // Set Copyright Attribute to the assembly.
        Type copyrightAttribute = typeof(AssemblyCopyrightAttribute);
        ConstructorInfo myConstructorInfo2 =                                    ⌐
copyrightAttribute.GetConstructor(new Type[]{typeof(String)});
        CustomAttributeBuilder attributeBuilder2 =
            new CustomAttributeBuilder(myConstructorInfo2,
            new object[1]{"@Copyright Microsoft Corp. 1990-2001"});
        myAssembly.SetCustomAttribute(attributeBuilder2);

        ModuleBuilder myModule =                                                ⌐
myAssembly.DefineDynamicModule("EmittedModule",
            "EmittedModule.mod");

        // Define a public class named "HelloWorld" in the assembly.
        TypeBuilder helloWorldClass =
            myModule.DefineType("HelloWorld", TypeAttributes.Public);
        // Define the Display method.
        MethodBuilder myMethod = helloWorldClass.DefineMethod("Display",
            MethodAttributes.Public, typeof(String), null);

        // Generate IL for GetGreeting.
        ILGenerator methodIL = myMethod.GetILGenerator();
        methodIL.Emit(OpCodes.Ldstr, "Display method get called.");
        methodIL.Emit(OpCodes.Ret);

        // Returns the type HelloWorld.

        return(helloWorldClass.CreateType());
    }
}

[C++]
#using <mscorlib.dll>

using namespace System;
using namespace System::Threading;
using namespace System::Reflection;
using namespace System::Reflection::Emit;
using namespace System::Resources;

// Create the callee transient dynamic assembly.
static Type* CreateAssembly(AppDomain* myDomain) {
    AssemblyName* myAssemblyName = new AssemblyName();
    myAssemblyName->Name = S"MyEmittedAssembly";

    AssemblyBuilder* myAssembly = myDomain-                                     ⌐
>DefineDynamicAssembly(myAssemblyName,
        AssemblyBuilderAccess::Save);

    // Set Company Attribute to the assembly.
    Type* companyAttribute = __typeof(AssemblyCompanyAttribute);
    Type* types1[] = {__typeof(String)};
    ConstructorInfo* myConstructorInfo1 =                                       ⌐
companyAttribute->GetConstructor(types1);
    Object* obj1[] = {S"Microsoft Corporation"};
    CustomAttributeBuilder* attributeBuilder1 = new
CustomAttributeBuilder(myConstructorInfo1, obj1);
    myAssembly->SetCustomAttribute(attributeBuilder1);

    // Set Copyright Attribute to the assembly.
    Type* copyrightAttribute = __typeof(AssemblyCopyrightAttribute);
    Type* types2[] = {__typeof(String)};
    ConstructorInfo* myConstructorInfo2 = copyrightAttribute-                   ⌐
>GetConstructor(types2);
    Object* obj2[] = {S"@Copyright Microsoft Corp. 1990-2001"};
    CustomAttributeBuilder* attributeBuilder2 = new                            ⌐
```

```
CustomAttributeBuilder(myConstructorInfo2, obj2);
    myAssembly->SetCustomAttribute(attributeBuilder2);

    ModuleBuilder* myModule = myAssembly-                                       ⌐
>DefineDynamicModule(S"EmittedModule",
        S"EmittedModule::mod");

    // Define a public class named S"HelloWorld" in the assembly.
    TypeBuilder* helloWorldClass =
        myModule->DefineType(S"HelloWorld", TypeAttributes::Public);
    // Define the Display method.
    MethodBuilder* myMethod = helloWorldClass->DefineMethod(S"Display",
        MethodAttributes::Public, __typeof(String), 0);

    // Generate IL for GetGreeting.
    ILGenerator* methodIL = myMethod->GetILGenerator();
    methodIL->Emit(OpCodes::Ldstr, S"Display method get called.");
    methodIL->Emit(OpCodes::Ret);

    // Returns the type HelloWorld.

    return(helloWorldClass->CreateType());
}

void main()
{
    AssemblyBuilder* myAssembly =
        __try_cast<AssemblyBuilder*>(CreateAssembly                            ⌐
(Thread::GetDomain())->Assembly);

    IResourceWriter* myResourceWriter = myAssembly-                             ⌐
>DefineResource(S"myResourceFile",
        S"A sample Resource File", S"MyResourceFile::resources");
    myResourceWriter->AddResource(S"AddResource test",                         ⌐
S"Test resource added");

    // Define unmanaged version information resources  .
    myAssembly->DefineVersionInfoResource();
    myAssembly->Save(S"MyEmittedAssembly.dll");
}
```

Requirements

Namespace: System.Reflection

Platforms: Windows 98, Windows NT 4.0,
Windows Millennium Edition, Windows 2000,
Windows XP Home Edition, Windows XP Professional,
Windows .NET Server family,
.NET Compact Framework - Windows CE .NET

Assembly: Mscorlib (in Mscorlib.dll)

AssemblyDescriptionAttribute Constructor

Initializes a new instance of the **AssemblyDescriptionAttribute**
class.

```
[Visual Basic]
Public Sub New( _
    ByVal description As String _
)
[C#]
public AssemblyDescriptionAttribute(
    string description
);
[C++]
public: AssemblyDescriptionAttribute(
    String* description
);
```

```
JScript]
ublic function AssemblyDescriptionAttribute(
    description : String
);
```

arameters

escription
  The assembly description.

equirements

latforms: Windows 98, Windows NT 4.0,
Windows Millennium Edition, Windows 2000,
Windows XP Home Edition, Windows XP Professional,
Windows .NET Server family,
NET Compact Framework - Windows CE .NET

AssemblyDescriptionAttribute.Description Property

Gets assembly description information.

```
[Visual Basic]
Public ReadOnly Property Description As String
[C#]
public string Description {get;}
[C++]
public: __property String* get_Description();
[JScript]
public function get Description() : String;
```

Property Value

A string containing the assembly description.

Requirements

Platforms: Windows 98, Windows NT 4.0,
Windows Millennium Edition, Windows 2000,
Windows XP Home Edition, Windows XP Professional,
Windows .NET Server family,
 NET Compact Framework - Windows CE .NET

AssemblyFileVersionAttribute Class

Instructs a compiler to use a specific version number for the Win32 file version resource. The Win32 file version is not required to be the same as the assembly's version number.

System.Object
  System.Attribute
    System.Reflection.AssemblyFileVersionAttribute

```
[Visual Basic]
<AttributeUsage(AttributeTargets.Assembly)>
NotInheritable Public Class AssemblyFileVersionAttribute
   Inherits Attribute
[C#]
[AttributeUsage(AttributeTargets.Assembly)]
public sealed class AssemblyFileVersionAttribute : Attribute
[C++]
[AttributeUsage(AttributeTargets::Assembly)]
public __gc __sealed class AssemblyFileVersionAttribute : public
   Attribute
[JScript]
public
   AttributeUsage(AttributeTargets.Assembly)
class AssemblyFileVersionAttribute extends Attribute
```

Thread Safety

Any public static (**Shared** in Visual Basic) members of this type are safe for multithreaded operations. Any instance members are not guaranteed to be thread safe.

Requirements

Namespace: System.Reflection

Platforms: Windows 98, Windows NT 4.0, Windows Millennium Edition, Windows 2000, Windows XP Home Edition, Windows XP Professional, Windows .NET Server family

Assembly: Mscorlib (in Mscorlib.dll)

AssemblyFileVersionAttribute Constructor

Initializes a new instance of the **AssemblyFileVersionAttribute** class, specifiying the file version.

```
[Visual Basic]
Public Sub New( _
   ByVal version As String _
)
[C#]
public AssemblyFileVersionAttribute(
   string version
);
[C++]
public: AssemblyFileVersionAttribute(
   String* version
);
[JScript]
public function AssemblyFileVersionAttribute(
   version : String
);
```

Parameters

version
  The file version.

Exceptions

Exception Type	Condition
ArgumentNullException	*version* is a null reference (**Nothing** in Visual Basic).

Requirements

Platforms: Windows 98, Windows NT 4.0, Windows Millennium Edition, Windows 2000, Windows XP Home Edition, Windows XP Professional, Windows .NET Server family

AssemblyFileVersionAttribute.Version Property

Gets the Win32 file version resource name.

```
[Visual Basic]
Public ReadOnly Property Version As String
[C#]
public string Version {get;}
[C++]
public: __property String* get_Version();
[JScript]
public function get Version() : String;
```

Property Value

A string containing the file version resource name.

Requirements

Platforms: Windows 98, Windows NT 4.0, Windows Millennium Edition, Windows 2000, Windows XP Home Edition, Windows XP Professional, Windows .NET Server family

AssemblyFlagsAttribute Class

Specifies whether an assembly supports side-by-side execution on the same computer, in the same process, or in the same application domain. This class cannot be inherited.

System.Object
 System.Attribute
  System.Reflection.AssemblyFlagsAttribute

[Visual Basic]
```
<AttributeUsage(AttributeTargets.Assembly)>
NotInheritable Public Class AssemblyFlagsAttribute
    Inherits Attribute
```
[C#]
```
[AttributeUsage(AttributeTargets.Assembly)]
public sealed class AssemblyFlagsAttribute : Attribute
```
[C++]
```
[AttributeUsage(AttributeTargets::Assembly)]
public __gc __sealed class AssemblyFlagsAttribute : public
    Attribute
```
[JScript]
```
public
    AttributeUsage(AttributeTargets.Assembly)
class AssemblyFlagsAttribute extends Attribute
```

Thread Safety

Any public static (**Shared** in Visual Basic) members of this type are safe for multithreaded operations. Any instance members are not guaranteed to be thread safe.

Remarks

The **AssemblyVersionCompatibility** enumeration defines the compatibility of an assembly with other versions of the same assembly, indicating if it cannot execute side-by-side with other versions.

Requirements

Namespace: System.Reflection

Platforms: Windows 98, Windows NT 4.0, Windows Millennium Edition, Windows 2000, Windows XP Home Edition, Windows XP Professional, Windows .NET Server family, .NET Compact Framework - Windows CE .NET

Assembly: Mscorlib (in Mscorlib.dll)

AssemblyFlagsAttribute Constructor

Note: This namespace, class, or member is supported only in version 1.1 of the .NET Framework.

Initializes a new instance of the **AssemblyFlagsAttribute** class.

Overload List

Initializes a new instance of the **AssemblyFlagsAttribute** class with the specified assembly flag.

Supported by the .NET Compact Framework.

[Visual Basic] **Public Sub New(Integer)**
[C#] **public AssemblyFlagsAttribute(int);**
[C++] **public: AssemblyFlagsAttribute(int);**
[JScript] **public function AssemblyFlagsAttribute(int);**

Initializes a new instance of the **AssemblyFlagsAttribute** class with the specified side-by-side execution flag.

This constructor is not CLS-compliant. For more information about CLS compliance, see **What is the Common Language Specification?**. This constructor is not CLS-compliant.

Supported by the .NET Compact Framework.

[Visual Basic] **Public Sub New(UInt32)**
[C#] **public AssemblyFlagsAttribute(uint);**
[C++] **public: AssemblyFlagsAttribute(unsigned int);**
[JScript] **public function AssemblyFlagsAttribute(UInt32);**

AssemblyFlagsAttribute Constructor (Int32)

Note: This namespace, class, or member is supported only in version 1.1 of the .NET Framework.

Initializes a new instance of the **AssemblyFlagsAttribute** class with the specified assembly flag.

[Visual Basic]
```
Public Sub New( _
    ByVal assemblyFlags As Integer _
)
```
[C#]
```
public AssemblyFlagsAttribute(
    int assemblyFlags
);
```
[C++]
```
public: AssemblyFlagsAttribute(
    int assemblyFlags
);
```
[JScript]
```
public function AssemblyFlagsAttribute(
    assemblyFlags : int
);
```

Parameters

assemblyFlags
  A value representing the kind of side-by-side execution allowed (same machine, same process, or same application domain).

Requirements

Platforms: Windows 98, Windows NT 4.0, Windows Millennium Edition, Windows 2000, Windows XP Home Edition, Windows XP Professional, Windows .NET Server family, .NET Compact Framework - Windows CE .NET

AssemblyFlagsAttribute Constructor (UInt32)

Initializes a new instance of the **AssemblyFlagsAttribute** class with the specified side-by-side execution flag.

This constructor is not CLS-compliant.

[Visual Basic]
```
<CLSCompliant(False)>
Public Sub New( _
    ByVal flags As UInt32 _
)
```
[C#]
```
[CLSCompliant(false)]
public AssemblyFlagsAttribute(
    uint flags
);
```

```
[C++]
[CLSCompliant(false)]
public: AssemblyFlagsAttribute(
    unsigned int flags
);
[JScript]
public
    CLSCompliant(false)
function AssemblyFlagsAttribute(
    flags : UInt32
);
```

Parameters

flags

    A value representing the kind of side-by-side execution allowed (same machine, same process, or same application domain).

Remarks

The **AssemblyVersionCompatibility** enumeration defines the compatibility of an assembly with other versions of the same assembly, indicating if it cannot execute side-by-side with other versions.

Requirements

Platforms: Windows 98, Windows NT 4.0, Windows Millennium Edition, Windows 2000, Windows XP Home Edition, Windows XP Professional, Windows .NET Server family, .NET Compact Framework - Windows CE .NET

AssemblyFlagsAttribute.AssemblyFlags Property

Note: This namespace, class, or member is supported only in version 1.1 of the .NET Framework.

Gets the value representing the kind of side-by-side execution allowed (same machine, same process, or same application domain).

```
[Visual Basic]
Public ReadOnly Property AssemblyFlags As Integer
[C#]
public int AssemblyFlags {get;}
[C++]
public: __property int get_AssemblyFlags();
[JScript]
public function get AssemblyFlags() : int;
```

Property Value

A value representing the allowed side-by-side execution.

Requirements

Platforms: Windows 98, Windows NT 4.0, Windows Millennium Edition, Windows 2000, Windows XP Home Edition, Windows XP Professional, Windows .NET Server family, .NET Compact Framework - Windows CE .NET

AssemblyFlagsAttribute.Flags Property

Gets the value representing the kind of side-by-side execution allowed (same machine, same process, or same application domain).

```
[Visual Basic]
<CLSCompliant(False)>
Public ReadOnly Property Flags As UInt32
[C#]
[CLSCompliant(false)]
public uint Flags {get;}
[C++]
[CLSCompliant(false)]
public: __property unsigned int get_Flags();
[JScript]
public
    CLSCompliant(false)
function get Flags() : UInt32;
```

Property Value

A value representing the allowed side-by-side execution.

Requirements

Platforms: Windows 98, Windows NT 4.0, Windows Millennium Edition, Windows 2000, Windows XP Home Edition, Windows XP Professional, Windows .NET Server family, .NET Compact Framework - Windows CE .NET

AssemblyInformationalVersion Attribute Class

Defines additional version information for an assembly manifest.

System.Object
  System.Attribute
    System.Reflection.AssemblyInformationalVersionAttribute

[Visual Basic]
```
<AttributeUsage(AttributeTargets.Assembly)>
NotInheritable Public Class AssemblyInformationalVersionAttribute
    Inherits Attribute
```
[C#]
```
[AttributeUsage(AttributeTargets.Assembly)]
public sealed class AssemblyInformationalVersionAttribute :
    Attribute
```
[C++]
```
[AttributeUsage(AttributeTargets::Assembly)]
public __gc __sealed class AssemblyInformationalVersionAttribute :
    public Attribute
```
[JScript]
```
public
    AttributeUsage(AttributeTargets.Assembly)
class AssemblyInformationalVersionAttribute extends
    Attribute
```

Thread Safety

Any public static (**Shared** in Visual Basic) members of this type are safe for multithreaded operations. Any instance members are not guaranteed to be thread safe.

Remarks

The attribute defined by this class attaches additional version information to an assembly for documentation purposes only. This data is never used at runtime.

Requirements

Namespace: System.Reflection

Platforms: Windows 98, Windows NT 4.0,
Windows Millennium Edition, Windows 2000,
Windows XP Home Edition, Windows XP Professional,
Windows .NET Server family,
.NET Compact Framework - Windows CE .NET

Assembly: Mscorlib (in Mscorlib.dll)

AssemblyInformationalVersionAttribute Constructor

Initializes a new instance of the
AssemblyInformationalVersionAttribute class.

[Visual Basic]
```
Public Sub New( _
    ByVal informationalVersion As String _
)
```
[C#]
```
public AssemblyInformationalVersionAttribute(
    string informationalVersion
);
```
[C++]
```
public: AssemblyInformationalVersionAttribute(
    String* informationalVersion
);
```
[JScript]
```
public function AssemblyInformationalVersionAttribute(
    informationalVersion : String
);
```

Parameters

informationalVersion
    The assembly version information.

Requirements

Platforms: Windows 98, Windows NT 4.0,
Windows Millennium Edition, Windows 2000,
Windows XP Home Edition, Windows XP Professional,
Windows .NET Server family,
.NET Compact Framework - Windows CE .NET

AssemblyInformationalVersionAttribute.InformationalVersion Property

Gets version information.

[Visual Basic]
```
Public ReadOnly Property InformationalVersion As String
```
[C#]
```
public string InformationalVersion {get;}
```
[C++]
```
public: __property String* get_InformationalVersion();
```
[JScript]
```
public function get InformationalVersion() : String;
```

Property Value

A string containing the version information.

Requirements

Platforms: Windows 98, Windows NT 4.0,
Windows Millennium Edition, Windows 2000,
Windows XP Home Edition, Windows XP Professional,
Windows .NET Server family,
.NET Compact Framework - Windows CE .NET

AssemblyKeyFileAttribute Class

Specifies the name of a file containing the key pair used to generate a strong name.

System.Object
    System.Attribute
        System.Reflection.AssemblyKeyFileAttribute

[Visual Basic]
```
<AttributeUsage(AttributeTargets.Assembly)>
NotInheritable Public Class AssemblyKeyFileAttribute
    Inherits Attribute
```
[C#]
```
[AttributeUsage(AttributeTargets.Assembly)]
public sealed class AssemblyKeyFileAttribute : Attribute
```
[C++]
```
[AttributeUsage(AttributeTargets::Assembly)]
public __gc __sealed class AssemblyKeyFileAttribute : public
    Attribute
```
[JScript]
```
public
    AttributeUsage(AttributeTargets.Assembly)
class AssemblyKeyFileAttribute extends Attribute
```

Thread Safety

Any public static (**Shared** in Visual Basic) members of this type are safe for multithreaded operations. Any instance members are not guaranteed to be thread safe.

Remarks

When building a strong-named assembly, the author must supply either this attribute or **AssemblyKeyNameAttribute**. If **AssemblyDelaySignAttribute** has also been specified, it is likely that this file will only contain the public key. An example of the syntax is [assembly:AssemblyKeyFileAttribute("myKey.snk")].

> **CAUTION** Since the path and file name persist, ensure that the string you use with **AssemblyKeyFileAttribute** does not contain sensitive information.

The classes in **System.Runtime.CompilerServices** are intended for use by compilers only. Do not use them unless you are building a compiler.For more detail, see the specifications for the common language runtime architecture, metadata, Microsoft intermediate language instruction set, file format, and Microsoft intermediate language assembly reference in the "Tool Developers Guide" folder of the SDK.

Requirements

Namespace: System.Reflection

Platforms: Windows 98, Windows NT 4.0, Windows Millennium Edition, Windows 2000, Windows XP Home Edition, Windows XP Professional, Windows .NET Server family, .NET Compact Framework - Windows CE .NET

Assembly: Mscorlib (in Mscorlib.dll)

AssemblyKeyFileAttribute Constructor

Initializes a new instance of the **AssemblyKeyFileAttribute** class with the name of the file containing the key pair to generate a strong name for the assembly being attributed.

[Visual Basic]
```
Public Sub New( _
    ByVal keyFile As String _
)
```
[C#]
```
public AssemblyKeyFileAttribute(
    string keyFile
);
```
[C++]
```
public: AssemblyKeyFileAttribute(
    String* keyFile
);
```
[JScript]
```
public function AssemblyKeyFileAttribute(
    keyFile : String
);
```

Parameters

keyFile
    The name of the file containing the key pair.

Remarks

> **CAUTION** Since the path and file name persist, ensure that the string you use with **AssemblyKeyFileAttribute** does not contain sensitive information.

Requirements

Platforms: Windows 98, Windows NT 4.0, Windows Millennium Edition, Windows 2000, Windows XP Home Edition, Windows XP Professional, Windows .NET Server family, .NET Compact Framework - Windows CE .NET

AssemblyKeyFileAttribute.KeyFile Property

Gets the name of the file containing the key pair used to generate a strong name for the attributed assembly.

[Visual Basic]
```
Public ReadOnly Property KeyFile As String
```
[C#]
```
public string KeyFile {get;}
```
[C++]
```
public: __property String* get_KeyFile();
```
[JScript]
```
public function get KeyFile() : String;
```

Property Value

A string containing the name of the file that contains the key pair.

Remarks

> **CAUTION** Since the path and file name persist, ensure that the string you use with **AssemblyKeyFileAttribute** does not contain sensitive information.

Requirements

Platforms: Windows 98, Windows NT 4.0, Windows Millennium Edition, Windows 2000, Windows XP Home Edition, Windows XP Professional, Windows .NET Server family, .NET Compact Framework - Windows CE .NET

AssemblyKeyNameAttribute Class

Specifies the name of a key container within the CSP containing the key pair used to generate a strong name.

System.Object
  System.Attribute
    System.Reflection.AssemblyKeyNameAttribute

[Visual Basic]
```
<AttributeUsage(AttributeTargets.Assembly)>
NotInheritable Public Class AssemblyKeyNameAttribute
    Inherits Attribute
```
[C#]
```
[AttributeUsage(AttributeTargets.Assembly)]
public sealed class AssemblyKeyNameAttribute : Attribute
```
[C++]
```
[AttributeUsage(AttributeTargets::Assembly)]
public __gc __sealed class AssemblyKeyNameAttribute : public
    Attribute
```
[JScript]
```
public
    AttributeUsage(AttributeTargets.Assembly)
class AssemblyKeyNameAttribute extends Attribute
```

Thread Safety

Any public static (**Shared** in Visual Basic) members of this type are safe for multithreaded operations. Any instance members are not guaranteed to be thread safe.

Remarks

When building a strong-named assembly, the author must supply either this attribute or **AssemblyKeyFileAttribute**.

An example of the syntax is `[assembly:AssemblyKeyNameAttribute("myContainer")]`.

The classes in **System.Runtime.CompilerServices** are intended for use by compilers only. Do not use them unless you are building a compiler. For more detail, see the specifications for the common language runtime architecture, metadata, Microsoft intermediate language instruction set, file format, and Microsoft intermediate language assembly reference in the "Tool Developers Guide" folder of the SDK.

Requirements

Namespace: System.Reflection

Platforms: Windows 98, Windows NT 4.0,
Windows Millennium Edition, Windows 2000,
Windows XP Home Edition, Windows XP Professional,
Windows .NET Server family,
.NET Compact Framework - Windows CE .NET

Assembly: Mscorlib (in Mscorlib.dll)

AssemblyKeyNameAttribute Constructor

Initializes a new instance of the **AssemblyKeyNameAttribute** class with the name of the container holding the key pair used to generate a strong name for the assembly being attributed.

[Visual Basic]
```
Public Sub New( _
    ByVal keyName As String _
)
```
[C#]
```
public AssemblyKeyNameAttribute(
    string keyName
);
```
[C++]
```
public: AssemblyKeyNameAttribute(
    String* keyName
);
```
[JScript]
```
public function AssemblyKeyNameAttribute(
    keyName : String
);
```

Parameters

keyName
    The name of the container containing the key pair.

Requirements

Platforms: Windows 98, Windows NT 4.0,
Windows Millennium Edition, Windows 2000,
Windows XP Home Edition, Windows XP Professional,
Windows .NET Server family,
.NET Compact Framework - Windows CE .NET

AssemblyKeyNameAttribute.KeyName Property

Gets the name of the container having the key pair that is used to generate a strong name for the attributed assembly.

[Visual Basic]
```
Public ReadOnly Property KeyName As String
```
[C#]
```
public string KeyName {get;}
```
[C++]
```
public: __property String* get_KeyName();
```
[JScript]
```
public function get KeyName() : String;
```

Property Value

A string containing the name of the container that has the relevant key pair.

Requirements

Platforms: Windows 98, Windows NT 4.0,
Windows Millennium Edition, Windows 2000,
Windows XP Home Edition, Windows XP Professional,
Windows .NET Server family,
.NET Compact Framework - Windows CE .NET

AssemblyName Class

Describes an assembly's unique identity in full.

System.Object
    System.Reflection.AssemblyName

[Visual Basic]
\<Serializable\>
NotInheritable Public Class AssemblyName
    Implements ICloneable, ISerializable, IDeserializationCallback
[C#]
[Serializable]
public sealed class AssemblyName : ICloneable, ISerializable,
    IDeserializationCallback
[C++]
[Serializable]
public __gc __sealed class AssemblyName : public ICloneable,
    ISerializable, IDeserializationCallback
[JScript]
public
    Serializable
class AssemblyName implements ICloneable, ISerializable,
    IDeserializationCallback

Thread Safety

Any public static (**Shared** in Visual Basic) members of this type are
safe for multithreaded operations. Any instance members are not
guaranteed to be thread safe.

Remarks

The assembly cache manager uses **AssemblyName** objects for binding and retrieving information about an assembly. An assembly's
identity consists of a simple name, a version number, a cryptographic key pair, and a supported culture. The simple name is the
unencrypted name, as distinguished from the strong name. The
strong name is an assembly name secured with a public and private
cryptographic key pair.

All compilers that support the common language runtime will emit
the simple name of a nested class, and reflection constructs a
mangled name when queried, in accordance with the following
conventions.

Delimiter	Meaning
Backslash (\\)	Escape character.
Comma (,)	Precedes the Assembly name.
Plus sign (+)	Precedes a nested class.
Period (.)	Denotes namespace identifiers.

For example, the fully qualified name for a class might look like
this:

TopNamespace.SubNameSpace.ContainingClass+NestedClass,MyA
ssembly

If the namespace were TopNamespace.Sub+Namespace, then the
string would have to precede the plus sign (+) with an escape
character (\\) to prevent it from being interpreted as a nesting
separator. Reflection emits this string as follows:

TopNamespace.Sub\\+Namespace.ContainingClass+NestedClass,M
yAssembly

A "++" becomes "\\+\\+", and a "\\" becomes "\\\\".

This qualified name can be persisted and later used to load the **Type**.
To search for and load a **Type**, use **GetType** either with the type
name only or with the assembly qualified type name. **GetType** wit
the type name only will look for the **Type** in the caller's assembly
and then in the System assembly. **GetType** with the assembly
qualified type name will look for the **Type** in any assembly.

Type names may include trailing characters that denote additional
information about the type, such as whether the type is a reference
type, a pointer type or an array type. To retrieve the type name
without these trailing characters, use t.GetElementType().ToString(),
where *t* is the type.

Spaces are relevant in all type name components except the
assembly name. In the assembly name, spaces before the ',' separato
are relevant, but spaces after the ',' separator are ignored.

A fully specified **AssemblyName** must have, in this order, the name
culture, public key or public key token, major version, minor
version, build number, and revision number parameters. The last
four are packaged in the **Version** type. However, an **AssemblyNam**
may specify a partial query when an insufficient number of
parameters is supplied to explicitly determine a unique assembly.
The assembly cache manager returns the first assembly that matche
the specified **AssemblyName**. The parameter order for partial
assembly name references must be the order specified above. For
example, you may specify and match on the name, culture, and
public key or public key token with the version parameters omitted
but you may not match on the name and public key or public key
token, omitting both the culture and the version. When used for
binding, the name is the minimum requirement.

To create a simple name, create an **AssemblyName** object using th
default constructor and set the **Name**. The other properties are
optional.

To create a full strong name, create an **AssemblyName** object usin
the default constructor and set the **Name** and **KeyPair**. The other
properties are optional. Use **SetPublicKey** and **SetPublicKeyToke**
to set the public key and the strong name. The strong name signing
always uses the **SHA1** hash algorithm.

For a partially specified strong name, create an **AssemblyName**
object using the default constructor and set the name and public key
The other properties are optional. An assembly created using such a
AssemblyName can be signed later using the Assembly Linker
(Al.exe).

It is possible to specify a public key and a **KeyPair** with inconsisten
values. This can be useful in developer scenarios. In this case, the
public key retrieved with **GetPublicKey** specifies the correct public
key, while the **KeyPair** specifies the public and private keys used
during development. When the runtime detects a mismatch betweer
the **KeyPair** and the public key, it looks up in the registry the correc
key that matches the public key.

The format of the display name of an **AssemblyName** is a comma-
delimited Unicode string that begins with the name, as follows:
Name \<,Culture =
            CultureInfo\> \<,Version =
            Major.Minor.Build.Revision\> \<, StrongName\>
            \<,PublicKeyToken\> '\0'

Name is the textual name of the assembly. CultureInfo is the RFC1766
format-defined culture. Major, Minor, Build, and Revision are the major
version, minor version, build number, and revision number of the
assembly. StrongName is the hexadecimal-encoded low-order 64 bits of
the hash value of the public key generated using the SHA-1 hashing
algorithm and the public key specified by **SetPublicKey**.

blicKeyToken is the hexadecimal-encoded public key specified by
tPublicKey.

uoted values are optional. Hexadecimal encoding is defined as the
nversion of each byte of a binary object to two hexadecimal
aracters, progressing from least to most significant byte.
dditional display values will be added as deemed necessary.

the full public key is known, then PublicKey may be substituted
r StrongName.

lso note that except for Name, which must come first, the lexical
der of parameters is unimportant. However, any parameter
ersion, Culture, StrongName or PublicKey) not specifically set is
nsidered to be omitted, and the **AssemblyName** is then considered
rtial. When specifying partial information, Name parameters must
e specified in the order described above.

hen supplying a display name, the convention StrongName =null or
blicKey= null indicates that binding and matching against a simply
amed assembly is required. Additionally, the convention Culture= ""
ouble quote representing an empty string) indicates matching
;ainst the default culture.

he following code example shows an **AssemblyName** for a simply
amed assembly with default culture.

m.microsoft.crypto,
        Culture=""

ne following code example shows a fully specified reference for a
rongly named assembly with culture "en".

m.microsoft.crypto, Culture=en, PublicKeyToken=a5d015c7d5a0b012,
rsion=1.0.0.0

he following code examples each show a partially specified
ssemblyName, which can be satisfied by either a strong or a
mply named assembly.

m.microsoft.crypto
m.microsoft.crypto, Culture=""
m.microsoft.crypto, Culture=en

he following code examples each show a partially specified
ssemblyName, which must be satisfied by a simply named
ssembly.

m.microsoft.crypto, Culture="", PublicKeyToken=null
m.microsoft.crypto, Culture=en, PublicKeyToken=null

he following code examples each show a partially specified
ssemblyName, which must be satisfied by a strongly named
ssembly.

m.microsoft.crypto, Culture="", PublicKeyToken=a5d015c7d5a0b012
m.microsoft.crypto, Culture=en, PublicKeyToken=a5d015c7d5a0b012,
rsion=1.0.0.0

equirements

amespace: System.Reflection

latforms: Windows 98, Windows NT 4.0,
Vindows Millennium Edition, Windows 2000,
Vindows XP Home Edition, Windows XP Professional,
Vindows .NET Server family,
NET Compact Framework - Windows CE .NET

ssembly: Mscorlib (in Mscorlib.dll)

AssemblyName Constructor

Initializes a new instance of the **AssemblyName** class.

```
[Visual Basic]
Public Sub New()
[C#]
public AssemblyName();
[C++]
public: AssemblyName();
[JScript]
public function AssemblyName();
```

Remarks [Visual Basic, C#, C++]

```
[Visual Basic]
Imports System
Imports System.Reflection
Imports System.Threading
Imports System.Reflection.Emit
Imports Microsoft.VisualBasic

Public Class AssemblyName_Constructor

    Public Shared Sub MakeAssembly(myAssemblyName As           ⏎
AssemblyName, fileName As String)
        ' Get the assembly builder from the application domain
associated with the current thread.
        Dim myAssemblyBuilder As AssemblyBuilder =             ⏎
Thread.GetDomain().DefineDynamicAssembly(myAssemblyName,       ⏎
AssemblyBuilderAccess.RunAndSave)
        ' Create a dynamic module in the assembly.
        Dim myModuleBuilder As ModuleBuilder =                 ⏎
myAssemblyBuilder.DefineDynamicModule("MyModule", fileName)
        ' Create a type in the module.
        Dim myTypeBuilder As TypeBuilder =                     ⏎
myModuleBuilder.DefineType("MyType")
        ' Create a method called 'Main'.
        Dim myMethodBuilder As MethodBuilder =                 ⏎
myTypeBuilder.DefineMethod("Main", MethodAttributes.Public     ⏎
Or MethodAttributes.HideBySig Or MethodAttributes.Static,      ⏎
GetType(object), Nothing)
        Dim myILGenerator As ILGenerator =                     ⏎
myMethodBuilder.GetILGenerator()
        ' Use the utility method to generate the IL instructions ⏎
that print a string to the console.
        myILGenerator.EmitWriteLine("Hello World!")
        ' Generate the 'ret' IL instruction.
        myILGenerator.Emit(OpCodes.Ret)
        ' End the creation of the type.
        myTypeBuilder.CreateType()
        ' Set the method with name 'Main' as the entry point   ⏎
in the assembly.
        myAssemblyBuilder.SetEntryPoint(myMethodBuilder)
        myAssemblyBuilder.Save(fileName)
    End Sub 'MakeAssembly


    Public Shared Sub Main()

        ' Create a dynamic assembly with name 'MyAssembly'     ⏎
and build version '1.0.0.2001'.
        Dim myAssemblyName As New AssemblyName()
        myAssemblyName.Name = "MyAssembly"
        myAssemblyName.Version = New Version("1.0.0.2001")
        MakeAssembly(myAssemblyName, "MyAssembly.exe")

        ' Get all the assemblies currently loaded in the       ⏎
application domain.
        Dim myAssemblies As [Assembly]() =                     ⏎
Thread.GetDomain().GetAssemblies()
```

```vb
' Get the dynamic assembly named 'MyAssembly'.
Dim myAssembly As [Assembly] = Nothing
Dim i As Integer
For i = 0 To myAssemblies.Length - 1
    If [String].Compare(myAssemblies(i).GetName().Name, _
"MyAssembly") = 0 Then
        myAssembly = myAssemblies(i)
    End If
Next i
If Not (myAssembly Is Nothing) Then
    Console.WriteLine(ControlChars.Cr + "Displaying the _
assembly name" + ControlChars.Cr)
    Console.WriteLine(myAssembly)
End If
End Sub 'Main
End Class 'AssemblyName_Constructor
```

[C#]

```csharp
using System;
using System.Reflection;
using System.Threading;
using System.Reflection.Emit;

public class AssemblyName_Constructor
{
    public static void MakeAssembly(AssemblyName _
myAssemblyName, string fileName)
    {
        // Get the assembly builder from the application
domain associated with the current thread.
        AssemblyBuilder myAssemblyBuilder =
Thread.GetDomain().DefineDynamicAssembly(myAssemblyName, _
AssemblyBuilderAccess.RunAndSave);
        // Create a dynamic module in the assembly.
        ModuleBuilder myModuleBuilder =
myAssemblyBuilder.DefineDynamicModule("MyModule", fileName); _
        // Create a type in the module.
        TypeBuilder myTypeBuilder = myModuleBuilder.DefineType("MyType");
        // Create a method called 'Main'.
        MethodBuilder myMethodBuilder =
myTypeBuilder.DefineMethod("Main", MethodAttributes.Public | _
MethodAttributes.HideBySig |
            MethodAttributes.Static, typeof(void), null);
        // Get the Intermediate Language generator for the method.
        ILGenerator myILGenerator = myMethodBuilder.GetILGenerator();
        // Use the utility method to generate the IL
instructions that print a string to the console. _
        myILGenerator.EmitWriteLine("Hello World!");
        // Generate the 'ret' IL instruction.
        myILGenerator.Emit(OpCodes.Ret);
        // End the creation of the type.
        myTypeBuilder.CreateType();
        // Set the method with name 'Main' as the entry _
point in the assembly.
        myAssemblyBuilder.SetEntryPoint(myMethodBuilder);
        myAssemblyBuilder.Save(fileName);
    }

    public static void Main()
    {
        // Create a dynamic assembly with name 'MyAssembly'
and build version '1.0.0.2001'. _
        AssemblyName myAssemblyName = new AssemblyName();
        myAssemblyName.Name = "MyAssembly";
        myAssemblyName.Version = new Version("1.0.0.2001");
        MakeAssembly(myAssemblyName, "MyAssembly.exe");

        // Get all the assemblies currently loaded in the _
application domain.
        Assembly[] myAssemblies = Thread.GetDomain().GetAssemblies();

        // Get the dynamic assembly named 'MyAssembly'.
        Assembly myAssembly = null;
```

```csharp
        for(int i = 0; i < myAssemblies.Length; i++)
        {
            if(String.Compare(myAssemblies[i].GetName().Name,
"MyAssembly") == 0)
                myAssembly = myAssemblies[i];
        }
        if(myAssembly != null)
        {
            Console.WriteLine("\nDisplaying the assembly name\n");
            Console.WriteLine(myAssembly);
        }
    }
}
```

[C++]

```cpp
#using <mscorlib.dll>

using namespace System;
using namespace System::Reflection;
using namespace System::Threading;
using namespace System::Reflection::Emit;

static void MakeAssembly(AssemblyName* myAssemblyName,
 String* fileName)
{
    // Get the assembly builder from the application domain
associated with the current thread.
    AssemblyBuilder* myAssemblyBuilder = Thread::GetDomain()-
>DefineDynamicAssembly(myAssemblyName,
AssemblyBuilderAccess::RunAndSave);
    // Create a dynamic module in the assembly.
    ModuleBuilder* myModuleBuilder = myAssemblyBuilder-
>DefineDynamicModule(S"MyModule", fileName);
    // Create a type in the module.
    TypeBuilder* myTypeBuilder = myModuleBuilder->DefineType(S"MyType");
    // Create a method called 'Main'.
    MethodBuilder* myMethodBuilder = myTypeBuilder-
>DefineMethod(S"Main",
        static_cast<MethodAttributes>( MethodAttributes::Public |
MethodAttributes::HideBySig | MethodAttributes::Static ),
        __typeof(void), 0);
    // Get the Intermediate Language generator for the method.
    ILGenerator* myILGenerator = myMethodBuilder->GetILGenerator();
    // Use the utility method to generate the IL instructions
that print a String* to the console.
    myILGenerator->EmitWriteLine(S"Hello World!");
    // Generate the 'ret' IL instruction.
    myILGenerator->Emit(OpCodes::Ret);
    // End the creation of the type.
    myTypeBuilder->CreateType();
    // Set the method with name 'Main' as the entry point
in the assembly.
    myAssemblyBuilder->SetEntryPoint(myMethodBuilder);
    myAssemblyBuilder->Save(fileName);
}

void main()
{
    // Create a dynamic assembly with name 'MyAssembly'
and build version '1.0.0.2001'.
    AssemblyName* myAssemblyName = new AssemblyName();
    myAssemblyName->Name = S"MyAssembly";
    myAssemblyName->Version = new Version(S"1.0.0.2001");
    MakeAssembly(myAssemblyName, S"MyAssembly.exe");

    // Get all the assemblies currently loaded in the
application domain.
    Assembly* myAssemblies[] = Thread::GetDomain()->GetAssemblies();

    // Get the dynamic assembly named 'MyAssembly'.
    Assembly* myAssembly = 0;
    for (int i = 0; i < myAssemblies->Length; i++) {
        if (String::Compare(myAssemblies[i]->GetName()->Name,
S"MyAssembly") == 0)
            myAssembly = myAssemblies[i];
```

```
}
if (myAssembly != 0) {
   Console::WriteLine("\nDisplaying the assembly name\n");
   Console::WriteLine(myAssembly);
}
```

Requirements

Platforms: Windows 98, Windows NT 4.0,
Windows Millennium Edition, Windows 2000,
Windows XP Home Edition, Windows XP Professional,
Windows .NET Server family,
.NET Compact Framework - Windows CE .NET

AssemblyName.CodeBase Property

Gets or sets the location of the assembly as a URL.

[Visual Basic]
```
Public Property CodeBase As String
```
[C#]
```
public string CodeBase {get; set;}
```
[C++]
```
public: __property String* get_CodeBase();
public: __property void set_CodeBase(String*);
```
[JScript]
```
public function get CodeBase() : String;
public function set CodeBase(String);
```

Property Value

A string that is the URL location of the assembly. If the assembly is
loaded from a byte array, such as when using the **Load(Byte[])**
method, **CodeBase** is an empty string ("").

Example

[Visual Basic]
```
Imports System
Imports Microsoft.VisualBasic
Imports System.Reflection
Imports System.Threading
Imports System.IO
Imports System.Globalization
Imports System.Reflection.Emit
Imports System.Configuration.Assemblies

Public Class AssemblyName_CodeBase

   Public Shared Sub MakeAssembly(myAssemblyName As
AssemblyName, fileName As String)
      ' Get the assembly builder from the application domain
associated with the current thread.
      Dim myAssemblyBuilder As AssemblyBuilder =
Thread.GetDomain().DefineDynamicAssembly(myAssemblyName,
AssemblyBuilderAccess.RunAndSave)
      ' Create a dynamic module in the assembly.
      Dim myModuleBuilder As ModuleBuilder =
myAssemblyBuilder.DefineDynamicModule("MyModule", fileName)
      ' Create a type in the module.
      Dim myTypeBuilder As TypeBuilder =
myModuleBuilder.DefineType("MyType")
      ' Create a method called 'Main'.
      Dim myMethodBuilder As MethodBuilder =
myTypeBuilder.DefineMethod("Main", MethodAttributes.
Public Or MethodAttributes.HideBySig Or MethodAttributes.
Static, GetType(object), Nothing)
      ' Get the Intermediate Language generator for the method.
      Dim myILGenerator As ILGenerator =
myMethodBuilder.GetILGenerator()
      ' Use the utility method to generate the IL
```

```
instructions that print a string to the console.
      myILGenerator.EmitWriteLine("Hello World!")
      ' Generate the 'ret' IL instruction.
      myILGenerator.Emit(OpCodes.Ret)
      ' End the creation of the type.
      myTypeBuilder.CreateType()
      ' Set the method with name 'Main' as the entry
point in the assembly.
      myAssemblyBuilder.SetEntryPoint(myMethodBuilder)
      myAssemblyBuilder.Save(fileName)
   End Sub 'MakeAssembly


   Public Shared Sub Main()

      ' Create a dynamic assembly with name 'MyAssembly'
and build version '1.0.0.2001'.
      Dim myAssemblyName As New AssemblyName()
      ' Set the codebase to the physical directory were the
assembly resides.
      myAssemblyName.CodeBase = [String].Concat("file:///",
Directory.GetCurrentDirectory())
      ' Set the culture information of the assembly to
'English-American'.
      myAssemblyName.CultureInfo = New CultureInfo("en-US")
      ' Set the hash algoritm to 'SHA1'.
      myAssemblyName.HashAlgorithm = AssemblyHashAlgorithm.SHA1
      myAssemblyName.Name = "MyAssembly"
      myAssemblyName.Version = New Version("1.0.0.2001")
      MakeAssembly(myAssemblyName, "MyAssembly.exe")

      ' Get all the assemblies currently loaded in the
application domain.
      Dim myAssemblies As [Assembly]() =
Thread.GetDomain().GetAssemblies()

      ' Get the dynamic assembly named 'MyAssembly'.
      Dim myAssembly As [Assembly] = Nothing
      Dim i As Integer
      For i = 0 To myAssemblies.Length - 1
         If [String].Compare(myAssemblies(i).GetName()
.Name, "MyAssembly") = 0 Then
            myAssembly = myAssemblies(i)
         End If
      Next i ' Display the full assembly information to the console.
      If Not (myAssembly Is Nothing) Then
         Console.WriteLine(ControlChars.Cr + "Displaying
the full assembly name" + ControlChars.Cr)
            Console.WriteLine(myAssembly.GetName().FullName)
      End If
   End Sub 'Main
End Class 'AssemblyName_CodeBase
```

[C#]
```
using System;
using System.Reflection;
using System.Threading;
using System.IO;
using System.Globalization;
using System.Reflection.Emit;
using System.Configuration.Assemblies;

public class AssemblyName_CodeBase
{
   public static void MakeAssembly(AssemblyName myAssemblyName,
   string fileName)
   {
      // Get the assembly builder from the application domain
associated with the current thread.
      AssemblyBuilder myAssemblyBuilder =
Thread.GetDomain().DefineDynamicAssembly(myAssemblyName,
AssemblyBuilderAccess.RunAndSave);
      // Create a dynamic module in the assembly.
      ModuleBuilder myModuleBuilder =
myAssemblyBuilder.DefineDynamicModule("MyModule", fileName);
```

```
        // Create a type in the module.
        TypeBuilder myTypeBuilder = myModuleBuilder.DefineType("MyType");
        // Create a method called 'Main'.
        MethodBuilder myMethodBuilder =
myTypeBuilder.DefineMethod("Main", MethodAttributes.Public |
MethodAttributes.HideBySig |
            MethodAttributes.Static, typeof(void), null);
        // Get the Intermediate Language generator for the method.
        ILGenerator myILGenerator = myMethodBuilder.GetILGenerator();
        // Use the utility method to generate the IL
instructions that print a string to the console.
        myILGenerator.EmitWriteLine("Hello World!");
        // Generate the 'ret' IL instruction.
        myILGenerator.Emit(OpCodes.Ret);
        // End the creation of the type.
        myTypeBuilder.CreateType();
        // Set the method with name 'Main' as the entry point
in the assembly.
        myAssemblyBuilder.SetEntryPoint(myMethodBuilder);
        myAssemblyBuilder.Save(fileName);
    }

    public static void Main()
    {

        // Create a dynamic assembly with name 'MyAssembly'
and build version '1.0.0.2001'.
        AssemblyName myAssemblyName = new AssemblyName();
        // Set the codebase to the physical directory were
the assembly resides.
        myAssemblyName.CodeBase = String.Concat("file:///",
Directory.GetCurrentDirectory());
        // Set the culture information of the assembly to
'English-American'.
        myAssemblyName.CultureInfo = new CultureInfo("en-US");
        // Set the hash algoritm to 'SHA1'.
        myAssemblyName.HashAlgorithm = AssemblyHashAlgorithm.SHA1;
        myAssemblyName.Name = "MyAssembly";
        myAssemblyName.Version = new Version("1.0.0.2001");
        MakeAssembly(myAssemblyName, "MyAssembly.exe");

        // Get all the assemblies currently loaded in the
application domain.
        Assembly[] myAssemblies = Thread.GetDomain().GetAssemblies();

        // Get the dynamic assembly named 'MyAssembly'.
        Assembly myAssembly = null;
        for(int i = 0; i < myAssemblies.Length; i++)
        {
            if(String.Compare(myAssemblies[i].GetName().Name,
"MyAssembly") == 0)
                myAssembly = myAssemblies[i];
        }
        // Display the full assembly information to the console.
        if(myAssembly != null)
        {
            Console.WriteLine("\nDisplaying the full assembly name\n");
            Console.WriteLine(myAssembly.GetName().FullName);
        }
    }
}

[C++]
#using <mscorlib.dll>

using namespace System;
using namespace System::Reflection;
using namespace System::Threading;
using namespace System::IO;
using namespace System::Globalization;
using namespace System::Reflection::Emit;
using namespace System::Configuration::Assemblies;

static void MakeAssembly(AssemblyName* myAssemblyName, String*
fileName)
{
    // Get the assembly builder from the application domain
```

```
associated with the current thread.
    AssemblyBuilder* myAssemblyBuilder = Thread::GetDomain()-
>DefineDynamicAssembly(myAssemblyName,
AssemblyBuilderAccess::RunAndSave);
    // Create a dynamic module in the assembly.
    ModuleBuilder* myModuleBuilder = myAssemblyBuilder-
>DefineDynamicModule(S"MyModule", fileName);
    // Create a type in the module.
    TypeBuilder* myTypeBuilder = myModuleBuilder->DefineType(S"MyType");
    // Create a method called 'Main'.
    MethodBuilder* myMethodBuilder = myTypeBuilder-
>DefineMethod(S"Main",
        static_cast<MethodAttributes>( MethodAttributes::Public |
MethodAttributes::HideBySig | MethodAttributes::Static ),
        __typeof(void), 0);
    // Get the Intermediate Language generator for the method.
    ILGenerator* myILGenerator = myMethodBuilder->GetILGenerator();
    // Use the utility method to generate the IL instructions that
print a String* to the console.
    myILGenerator->EmitWriteLine(S"Hello World!");
    // Generate the 'ret' IL instruction.
    myILGenerator->Emit(OpCodes::Ret);
    // End the creation of the type.
    myTypeBuilder->CreateType();
    // Set the method with name 'Main' as the entry point in
the assembly.
    myAssemblyBuilder->SetEntryPoint(myMethodBuilder);
    myAssemblyBuilder->Save(fileName);
}

void main()
{
    // Create a dynamic assembly with name 'MyAssembly' and
build version '1.0.0.2001'.
    AssemblyName* myAssemblyName = new AssemblyName();
    // Set the codebase to the physical directory were the
assembly resides.
    myAssemblyName->CodeBase = String::Concat(S"file:///",
Directory::GetCurrentDirectory());
    // Set the culture information of the assembly to
'English-American'.
    myAssemblyName->CultureInfo = new CultureInfo(S"en-US");
    // Set the hash algoritm to 'SHA1'.
    myAssemblyName->HashAlgorithm = AssemblyHashAlgorithm::SHA1;
    myAssemblyName->Name = S"MyAssembly";
    myAssemblyName->Version = new Version(S"1.0.0.2001");
    MakeAssembly(myAssemblyName, S"MyAssembly.exe");

    // Get all the assemblies currently loaded in the
application domain.
    Assembly* myAssemblies[] = Thread::GetDomain()->GetAssemblies();

    // Get the dynamic assembly named 'MyAssembly'.
    Assembly* myAssembly = 0;
    for (int i = 0; i < myAssemblies->Length; i++)
    {
        if (String::Compare(myAssemblies[i]->GetName()->Name,
S"MyAssembly") == 0)
            myAssembly = myAssemblies[i];
    }
    // Display the full assembly information to the console.
    if (myAssembly != 0)
    {
        Console::WriteLine(S"\nDisplaying the full assembly name\n");
        Console::WriteLine(myAssembly->GetName()->FullName);
    }
}
```

Requirements

Platforms: Windows 98, Windows NT 4.0,
Windows Millennium Edition, Windows 2000,
Windows XP Home Edition, Windows XP Professional,
Windows .NET Server family,
.NET Compact Framework - Windows CE .NET

AssemblyName.CultureInfo Property

Gets or sets the culture supported by the assembly.

```
[Visual Basic]
Public Property CultureInfo As CultureInfo
[C#]
public CultureInfo CultureInfo {get; set;}
[C++]
public: __property CultureInfo* get_CultureInfo();
public: __property void set_CultureInfo(CultureInfo*);
[JScript]
public function get CultureInfo() : CultureInfo;
public function set CultureInfo(CultureInfo);
```

Property Value

A **CultureInfo** object representing the culture supported by the assembly.

Example

See related example in the **AssemblyName.CodeBase** property topic.

Requirements

Platforms: Windows 98, Windows NT 4.0,
Windows Millennium Edition, Windows 2000,
Windows XP Home Edition, Windows XP Professional,
Windows .NET Server family,
.NET Compact Framework - Windows CE .NET

AssemblyName.EscapedCodeBase Property

Gets the URI, including escape characters, that represents the codebase.

```
[Visual Basic]
Public ReadOnly Property EscapedCodeBase As String
[C#]
public string EscapedCodeBase {get;}
[C++]
public: __property String* get_EscapedCodeBase();
[JScript]
public function get EscapedCodeBase() : String;
```

Property Value

A URI with escape characters.

Requirements

Platforms: Windows 98, Windows NT 4.0,
Windows Millennium Edition, Windows 2000,
Windows XP Home Edition, Windows XP Professional,
Windows .NET Server family

AssemblyName.Flags Property

Gets or sets the attributes of the assembly.

```
[Visual Basic]
Public Property Flags As AssemblyNameFlags
[C#]
public AssemblyNameFlags Flags {get; set;}
[C++]
public: __property AssemblyNameFlags get_Flags();
public: __property void set_Flags(AssemblyNameFlags);
[JScript]
public function get Flags() : AssemblyNameFlags;
public function set Flags(AssemblyNameFlags);
```

Property Value

An **AssemblyNameFlags** object representing the attributes of the assembly.

Example

See related example in the **AssemblyName.CodeBase** property topic.

Requirements

Platforms: Windows 98, Windows NT 4.0,
Windows Millennium Edition, Windows 2000,
Windows XP Home Edition, Windows XP Professional,
Windows .NET Server family,
.NET Compact Framework - Windows CE .NET

AssemblyName.FullName Property

Gets the full name of the assembly, also known as the display name.

```
[Visual Basic]
Public ReadOnly Property FullName As String
[C#]
public string FullName {get;}
[C++]
public: __property String* get_FullName();
[JScript]
public function get FullName() : String;
```

Property Value

A string that is the full name of the assembly, also known as the display name.

Example

See related example in the **AssemblyName.CodeBase** property topic.

Requirements

Platforms: Windows 98, Windows NT 4.0,
Windows Millennium Edition, Windows 2000,
Windows XP Home Edition, Windows XP Professional,
Windows .NET Server family,
.NET Compact Framework - Windows CE .NET

AssemblyName.HashAlgorithm Property

Gets or sets the hash algorithm used by the assembly manifest.

```
[Visual Basic]
Public Property HashAlgorithm As AssemblyHashAlgorithm
[C#]
public AssemblyHashAlgorithm HashAlgorithm {get; set;}
[C++]
public: __property AssemblyHashAlgorithm get_HashAlgorithm();
public: __property void set_HashAlgorithm(AssemblyHashAlgorithm);
[JScript]
public function get HashAlgorithm() : AssemblyHashAlgorithm;
public function set HashAlgorithm(AssemblyHashAlgorithm);
```

Property Value

An **AssemblyHashAlgorithm** object representing the hash algorithm used by the assembly manifest.

Example

See related example in the **AssemblyName.CodeBase** property topic.

Requirements

Platforms: Windows 98, Windows NT 4.0, Windows Millennium Edition, Windows 2000, Windows XP Home Edition, Windows XP Professional, Windows .NET Server family, .NET Compact Framework - Windows CE .NET

AssemblyName.KeyPair Property

Gets or sets the public and private cryptographic key pair generated by the public key or public key token of the assembly.

```
[Visual Basic]
Public Property KeyPair As StrongNameKeyPair
[C#]
public StrongNameKeyPair KeyPair {get; set;}
[C++]
public: __property StrongNameKeyPair* get_KeyPair();
public: __property void set_KeyPair(StrongNameKeyPair*);
[JScript]
public function get KeyPair() : StrongNameKeyPair;
public function set KeyPair(StrongNameKeyPair);
```

Property Value

A **StrongNameKeyPair** object containing the public and private cryptographic key pair generated by the public key or public key token of the assembly.

Remarks

When the runtime loads an assembly, it does not set the **AssemblyName.KeyPair** property. The getter for the property is only useful if the user set the property after the assembly was loaded and wants to subsequently retrieve the property.

Example

See related example in the **AssemblyName.CodeBase** property topic.

Requirements

Platforms: Windows 98, Windows NT 4.0, Windows Millennium Edition, Windows 2000, Windows XP Home Edition, Windows XP Professional, Windows .NET Server family

AssemblyName.Name Property

Gets or sets the simple, unencrypted name of the assembly.

```
[Visual Basic]
Public Property Name As String
[C#]
public string Name {get; set;}
[C++]
public: __property String* get_Name();
public: __property void set_Name(String*);
```

```
[JScript]
public function get Name() : String;
public function set Name(String);
```

Property Value

A **String** that is the simple, unencrypted name of the assembly.

Remarks

Assembly names are limited to the number of characters as defined by MAX_PATH.

Example

See related example in the **AssemblyName.CodeBase** property topic.

Requirements

Platforms: Windows 98, Windows NT 4.0, Windows Millennium Edition, Windows 2000, Windows XP Home Edition, Windows XP Professional, Windows .NET Server family, .NET Compact Framework - Windows CE .NET

AssemblyName.Version Property

Gets or sets the major, minor, revision, and build numbers of the assembly.

```
[Visual Basic]
Public Property Version As Version
[C#]
public Version Version {get; set;}
[C++]
public: __property Version* get_Version();
public: __property void set_Version(Version*);
[JScript]
public function get Version() : Version;
public function set Version(Version);
```

Property Value

A **Version** object representing the major, minor, revision, and build numbers of the assembly.

Example

See related example in the **AssemblyName.CodeBase** property topic.

Requirements

Platforms: Windows 98, Windows NT 4.0, Windows Millennium Edition, Windows 2000, Windows XP Home Edition, Windows XP Professional, Windows .NET Server family, .NET Compact Framework - Windows CE .NET

AssemblyName.VersionCompatibility Property

Gets or sets the information related to the assembly's compatibility with other assemblies.

```
[Visual Basic]
Public Property VersionCompatibility As _
    AssemblyVersionCompatibility
[C#]
public AssemblyVersionCompatibility VersionCompatibility {get;
    set;}
```

```
[C++]
public: __property AssemblyVersionCompatibility get_
VersionCompatibility();
public: __property void set_
VersionCompatibility(AssemblyVersionCompatibility);
[JScript]
public function get VersionCompatibility() :
AssemblyVersionCompatibility;
public function set VersionCompatibility(AssemblyVersionCompatibility);
```

Property Value

An **AssemblyVersionCompatibility** object representing information about the assembly's compatibility with other assemblies.

Remarks

VersionCompatibility information indicates, for example, that the assembly cannot execute side-by-side with other versions due to conflicts over a device driver.

Currently, **VersionCompatibility** always returns **SameMachine**, and is not used by the loader. This property is reserved for a future feature.

Example

See related example in the **AssemblyName.CodeBase** property topic.

Requirements

Platforms: Windows 98, Windows NT 4.0, Windows Millennium Edition, Windows 2000, Windows XP Home Edition, Windows XP Professional, Windows .NET Server family, .NET Compact Framework - Windows CE .NET

AssemblyName.Clone Method

Makes a copy of this **AssemblyName** object.

```
[Visual Basic]
Public Overridable Function Clone() As Object Implements _
    ICloneable.Clone
[C#]
public virtual object Clone();
[C++]
public: virtual Object* Clone();
[JScript]
public function Clone() : Object;
```

Return Value

An object that is a copy of this **AssemblyName** object.

Implements

ICloneable.Clone

Remarks

A new object is created, identical to the original.

Requirements

Platforms: Windows 98, Windows NT 4.0, Windows Millennium Edition, Windows 2000, Windows XP Home Edition, Windows XP Professional, Windows .NET Server family, .NET Compact Framework - Windows CE .NET

AssemblyName.GetAssemblyName Method

Gets the **AssemblyName** for a given file.

```
[Visual Basic]
Public Shared Function GetAssemblyName( _
    ByVal assemblyFile As String _
) As AssemblyName
[C#]
public static AssemblyName GetAssemblyName(
    string assemblyFile
);
[C++]
public: static AssemblyName* GetAssemblyName(
    String* assemblyFile
);
[JScript]
public static function GetAssemblyName(
    assemblyFile : String
) : AssemblyName;
```

Parameters

assemblyFile
    The assembly file for which to get the **AssemblyName**.

Return Value

An **AssemblyName** object representing the given file.

Exceptions

Exception Type	Condition
ArgumentNullException	*assemblyFile* is a null reference (**Nothing** in Visual Basic).
ArgumentException	*assemblyFile* is empty.
FileNotFoundException	*assemblyFile* is not found.
SecurityException	The caller does not have path discovery permission.
BadImageFormatException	*assemblyFile* is not a valid assembly.

Remarks

This will only work if the file contains an assembly manifest. This method causes the file to be opened and closed, but the assembly is not added to this domain.

Requirements

Platforms: Windows 98, Windows NT 4.0, Windows Millennium Edition, Windows 2000, Windows XP Home Edition, Windows XP Professional, Windows .NET Server family

.NET Framework Security:
- **FileIOPermission** for access to information in the path. Associated enumeration: **FileIOPermissionAccess.PathDiscovery**.

AssemblyName.GetObjectData Method

Gets serialization information with all of the data needed to recreate an instance of this **AssemblyName**.

```
[Visual Basic]
Public Overridable Sub GetObjectData( _
    ByVal info As SerializationInfo, _
    ByVal context As StreamingContext _
) Implements ISerializable.GetObjectData
```

```
[C#]
public virtual void GetObjectData(
    SerializationInfo info,
    StreamingContext context
);
[C++]
public: virtual void GetObjectData(
    SerializationInfo* info,
    StreamingContext context
);
[JScript]
public function GetObjectData(
    info : SerializationInfo,
    context : StreamingContext
);
```

Parameters

info
   The object to be populated with serialization information.
context
   The destination context of the serialization.

Implements

ISerializable.GetObjectData

Exceptions

Exception Type	Condition
ArgumentNullException	*info* is a null reference (**Nothing** in Visual Basic).

Requirements

Platforms: Windows 98, Windows NT 4.0, Windows Millennium Edition, Windows 2000, Windows XP Home Edition, Windows XP Professional, Windows .NET Server family

AssemblyName.GetPublicKey Method

Gets the public key of the assembly.

```
[Visual Basic]
Public Function GetPublicKey() As Byte()
[C#]
public byte[] GetPublicKey();
[C++]
public: unsigned char GetPublicKey() __gc[];
[JScript]
public function GetPublicKey() : Byte[];
```

Return Value

An array of type **byte** containing the public key of the assembly.

Example

See related example in the **AssemblyName.CodeBase** property topic.

Requirements

Platforms: Windows 98, Windows NT 4.0, Windows Millennium Edition, Windows 2000, Windows XP Home Edition, Windows XP Professional, Windows .NET Server family, .NET Compact Framework - Windows CE .NET

AssemblyName.GetPublicKeyToken Method

Gets the public key token, which is the last 8 bytes of the SHA-1 hash of the public key under which the application or assembly is signed.

```
[Visual Basic]
Public Function GetPublicKeyToken() As Byte()
[C#]
public byte[] GetPublicKeyToken();
[C++]
public: unsigned char GetPublicKeyToken() __gc[];
[JScript]
public function GetPublicKeyToken() : Byte[];
```

Return Value

An array of type **byte** containing the public key token.

Example

See related example in the **AssemblyName.CodeBase** property topic.

Requirements

Platforms: Windows 98, Windows NT 4.0, Windows Millennium Edition, Windows 2000, Windows XP Home Edition, Windows XP Professional, Windows .NET Server family, .NET Compact Framework - Windows CE .NET

AssemblyName.OnDeserialization Method

Implements the **ISerializable** interface and is called back by the deserialization event when deserialization is complete.

```
[Visual Basic]
Public Overridable Sub OnDeserialization( _
    ByVal sender As Object _
) Implements IDeserializationCallback.OnDeserialization
[C#]
public virtual void OnDeserialization(
    object sender
);
[C++]
public: virtual void OnDeserialization(
    Object* sender
);
[JScript]
public function OnDeserialization(
    sender : Object
);
```

Parameters

sender
   The source of the deserialization event.

Implements

IDeserializationCallback.OnDeserialization

Requirements

Platforms: Windows 98, Windows NT 4.0, Windows Millennium Edition, Windows 2000, Windows XP Home Edition, Windows XP Professional, Windows .NET Server family

AssemblyName.SetPublicKey Method

Sets the public key identifying the assembly.

```
[Visual Basic]
Public Sub SetPublicKey( _
    ByVal publicKey() As Byte _
)
[C#]
public void SetPublicKey(
    byte[] publicKey
);
[C++]
public: void SetPublicKey(
    unsigned char publicKey __gc[]
);
[JScript]
public function SetPublicKey(
    publicKey : Byte[]
);
```

Parameters

publicKey

A byte array containing the public key of the assembly.

Example

See related example in the **AssemblyName.CodeBase** property topic.

Requirements

Platforms: Windows 98, Windows NT 4.0, Windows Millennium Edition, Windows 2000, Windows XP Home Edition, Windows XP Professional, Windows .NET Server family, .NET Compact Framework - Windows CE .NET

AssemblyName.SetPublicKeyToken Method

Sets the public key, which is the last 8 bytes of the SHA-1 hash of the public key under which the application or assembly is signed.

```
[Visual Basic]
Public Sub SetPublicKeyToken( _
    ByVal publicKeyToken() As Byte _
)
[C#]
public void SetPublicKeyToken(
    byte[] publicKeyToken
);
[C++]
public: void SetPublicKeyToken(
    unsigned char publicKeyToken __gc[]
);
[JScript]
public function SetPublicKeyToken(
    publicKeyToken : Byte[]
);
```

Parameters

publicKeyToken

A byte array containing the public key token of the assembly.

Example

See related example in the **AssemblyName.CodeBase** property topic.

Requirements

Platforms: Windows 98, Windows NT 4.0, Windows Millennium Edition, Windows 2000, Windows XP Home Edition, Windows XP Professional, Windows .NET Server family, .NET Compact Framework - Windows CE .NET

AssemblyName.ToString Method

Returns the full name of the assembly, also known as the display name.

```
[Visual Basic]
Overrides Public Function ToString() As String
[C#]
public override string ToString();
[C++]
public: String* ToString();
[JScript]
public override function ToString() : String;
```

Return Value

A **String** that is the full name of the assembly, or the class name if the full name of the assembly cannot be determined.

Remarks

See the description of **AssemblyName** for the format of the returned string.

Requirements

Platforms: Windows 98, Windows NT 4.0, Windows Millennium Edition, Windows 2000, Windows XP Home Edition, Windows XP Professional, Windows .NET Server family, .NET Compact Framework - Windows CE .NET

AssemblyNameFlags Enumeration

Provides information about an **Assembly** reference.

This enumeration has a **FlagsAttribute** attribute that allows a bitwise combination of its member values.

```
[Visual Basic]
<Flags>
<Serializable>
Public Enum AssemblyNameFlags
[C#]
[Flags]
[Serializable]
public enum AssemblyNameFlags
[C++]
[Flags]
[Serializable]
__value public enum AssemblyNameFlags
[JScript]
public
    Flags
    Serializable
enum AssemblyNameFlags
```

Remarks

These flags are not used in the **AssemblyName** for a loaded assembly. They describe whether the user has provided a full or compressed public key in an **AssemblyName** that will be used to load an assembly.

Members

Member name	Description	Value
None Supported by the .NET Compact Framework.	Specifies that no flags are in effect.	0
PublicKey Supported by the .NET Compact Framework.	Specifies that a public key is formed from the full public key rather than the public key token.	1
Retargetable Supported by the .NET Compact Framework.	Specifies that the assembly can be retargeted at runtime to an assembly from a different publisher.	256

Requirements

Namespace: System.Reflection

Platforms: Windows 98, Windows NT 4.0, Windows Millennium Edition, Windows 2000, Windows XP Home Edition, Windows XP Professional, Windows .NET Server family, .NET Compact Framework - Windows CE .NET

Assembly: Mscorlib (in Mscorlib.dll)

AssemblyNameProxy Class

Provides a remotable version of the **AssemblyName**.

System.Object
  System.MarshalByRefObject
    System.Reflection.AssemblyNameProxy

[Visual Basic]
```
Public Class AssemblyNameProxy
    Inherits MarshalByRefObject
```
[C#]
```
public class AssemblyNameProxy : MarshalByRefObject
```
[C++]
```
public __gc class AssemblyNameProxy : public MarshalByRefObject
```
[JScript]
```
public class AssemblyNameProxy extends MarshalByRefObject
```

Thread Safety

Any public static (**Shared** in Visual Basic) members of this type are safe for multithreaded operations. Any instance members are not guaranteed to be thread safe.

Requirements

Namespace: System.Reflection

Platforms: Windows 98, Windows NT 4.0,
Windows Millennium Edition, Windows 2000,
Windows XP Home Edition, Windows XP Professional,
Windows .NET Server family

Assembly: Mscorlib (in Mscorlib.dll)

AssemblyNameProxy Constructor

Initializes a new instance of the **AssemblyNameProxy** class.

[Visual Basic]
```
Public Sub New()
```
[C#]
```
public AssemblyNameProxy();
```
[C++]
```
public: AssemblyNameProxy();
```
[JScript]
```
public function AssemblyNameProxy();
```

Remarks

The default constructor initializes any fields to their default values.

Requirements

Platforms: Windows 98, Windows NT 4.0,
Windows Millennium Edition, Windows 2000,
Windows XP Home Edition, Windows XP Professional,
Windows .NET Server family

AssemblyNameProxy.GetAssemblyName Method

Gets the **AssemblyName** for a given file.

[Visual Basic]
```
Public Function GetAssemblyName( _
    ByVal assemblyFile As String _
) As AssemblyName
```
[C#]
```
public AssemblyName GetAssemblyName(
    string assemblyFile
);
```
[C++]
```
public: AssemblyName* GetAssemblyName(
    String* assemblyFile
);
```
[JScript]
```
public function GetAssemblyName(
    assemblyFile : String
) : AssemblyName;
```

Parameters

assemblyFile
    The assembly file for which to get the **AssemblyName**.

Return Value

An **AssemblyName** object representing the given file.

Exceptions

Exception Type	Condition
ArgumentNullException	*assemblyFile* is a null reference (**Nothing** in Visual Basic).
ArgumentException	*assemblyFile* is empty.
FileNotFoundException	*assemblyFile* is not found.
SecurityException	The caller does not have the required permission.
BadImageFormatException	*assemblyFile* is not a valid assembly.

Remarks

This will only work if the file contains an assembly manifest. This method causes the file to be opened and closed.

Example

[Visual Basic]

```
Imports System
Imports System.Reflection
Imports System.Text.RegularExpressions
Imports Microsoft.VisualBasic

Public Class AssemblyName_GetAssemblyName

    Public Shared Sub Main()

        ' Get the type of 'System.Object'.
        Dim myType As Type = GetType(System.Object)

        ' Get the path of 'System.dll'.
        Dim system As String = Regex.Replace         ┘
(myType.Assembly.CodeBase, "mscorlib.dll", "System.dll")
        system = Regex.Replace(system, "file:///", "")

        ' Get the assembly information and display to the console.
        Dim myAssemblyName As AssemblyName =          ┘
AssemblyName.GetAssemblyName(system)
        Console.WriteLine(ControlChars.Cr + "Displaying the   ┘
assembly information of 'System.dll'" + ControlChars.Cr)
        Console.WriteLine(myAssemblyName.ToString())
    End Sub 'Main
End Class 'AssemblyName_GetAssemblyName
```

```csharp
[C#]
using System;
using System.Reflection;
using System.Text.RegularExpressions;

public class AssemblyName_GetAssemblyName
{
   public static void Main()
   {

      // Get the type of 'System.Object'.
      Type myType = typeof(System.Object);

      // Get the path of 'System.dll'.
      string system = Regex.Replace
(myType.Assembly.CodeBase, "mscorlib.dll", "System.dll");
      system = Regex.Replace(system, "file:///", "");

      // Get the assembly information and display to the console.
      AssemblyName myAssemblyName =
AssemblyName.GetAssemblyName(system);
      Console.WriteLine("\nDisplaying the assembly information
 of 'System.dll'\n");
      Console.WriteLine(myAssemblyName.ToString());
   }
}
```

```cpp
[C++]
#using <mscorlib.dll>
#using <system.dll>

using namespace System;
using namespace System::Reflection;
using namespace System::Text::RegularExpressions;

void main()
{
   // Get the type of 'System::Object'.
   Type* myType = __typeof(System::Object);

   // Get the path of 'System.dll'.
   String* system = Regex::Replace(myType->Assembly->
CodeBase, S"mscorlib.dll", S"System.dll");
   system = Regex::Replace(system, S"file:///", S"");

   // Get the assembly information and display to the console.
   AssemblyName* myAssemblyName =
AssemblyName::GetAssemblyName(system);
   Console::WriteLine(S"\nDisplaying the assembly
information of 'System.dll'\n");
   Console::WriteLine(myAssemblyName);
}
```

Requirements

Platforms: Windows 98, Windows NT 4.0,
Windows Millennium Edition, Windows 2000,
Windows XP Home Edition, Windows XP Professional,
Windows .NET Server family

.NET Framework Security:

- **FileIOPermission** for access to information in the path. Associated enumeration: **FileIOPermissionAccess.PathDiscovery**.

AssemblyProductAttribute Class

Defines a product name custom attribute for an assembly manifest.

System.Object
   System.Attribute
      System.Reflection.AssemblyProductAttribute

```
[Visual Basic]
<AttributeUsage(AttributeTargets.Assembly)>
NotInheritable Public Class AssemblyProductAttribute
   Inherits Attribute
[C#]
[AttributeUsage(AttributeTargets.Assembly)]
public sealed class AssemblyProductAttribute : Attribute
[C++]
[AttributeUsage(AttributeTargets::Assembly)]
public __gc __sealed class AssemblyProductAttribute : public
   Attribute
[JScript]
public
   AttributeUsage(AttributeTargets.Assembly)
class AssemblyProductAttribute extends Attribute
```

Thread Safety

Any public static (**Shared** in Visual Basic) members of this type are safe for multithreaded operations. Any instance members are not guaranteed to be thread safe.

Requirements

Namespace: System.Reflection

Platforms: Windows 98, Windows NT 4.0, Windows Millennium Edition, Windows 2000, Windows XP Home Edition, Windows XP Professional, Windows .NET Server family, .NET Compact Framework - Windows CE .NET

Assembly: Mscorlib (in Mscorlib.dll)

AssemblyProductAttribute Constructor

Initializes a new instance of the **AssemblyProductAttribute** class.

```
[Visual Basic]
Public Sub New( _
   ByVal product As String _
)
[C#]
public AssemblyProductAttribute(
   string product
);
[C++]
public: AssemblyProductAttribute(
   String* product
);
[JScript]
public function AssemblyProductAttribute(
   product : String
);
```

Parameters

product
   The product name information.

Requirements

Platforms: Windows 98, Windows NT 4.0, Windows Millennium Edition, Windows 2000, Windows XP Home Edition, Windows XP Professional, Windows .NET Server family, .NET Compact Framework - Windows CE .NET

AssemblyProductAttribute.Product Property

Gets product name information.

```
[Visual Basic]
Public ReadOnly Property Product As String
[C#]
public string Product {get;}
[C++]
public: __property String* get_Product();
[JScript]
public function get Product() : String;
```

Property Value

A string containing the product name.

Requirements

Platforms: Windows 98, Windows NT 4.0, Windows Millennium Edition, Windows 2000, Windows XP Home Edition, Windows XP Professional, Windows .NET Server family, .NET Compact Framework - Windows CE .NET

AssemblyTitleAttribute Class

Defines an assembly title custom attribute for an assembly manifest.

System.Object
  System.Attribute
    System.Reflection.AssemblyTitleAttribute

[Visual Basic]
```
<AttributeUsage(AttributeTargets.Assembly)>
NotInheritable Public Class AssemblyTitleAttribute
   Inherits Attribute
```
[C#]
```
[AttributeUsage(AttributeTargets.Assembly)]
public sealed class AssemblyTitleAttribute : Attribute
```
[C++]
```
[AttributeUsage(AttributeTargets::Assembly)]
public __gc __sealed class AssemblyTitleAttribute : public
   Attribute
```
[JScript]
```
public
   AttributeUsage(AttributeTargets.Assembly)
class AssemblyTitleAttribute extends Attribute
```

Thread Safety

Any public static (**Shared** in Visual Basic) members of this type are safe for multithreaded operations. Any instance members are not guaranteed to be thread safe.

Remarks

The assembly title is a friendly name, which can include spaces.

Example

```
[Visual Basic]
Imports System
Imports System.Threading
Imports System.Reflection
Imports System.Reflection.Emit
Imports System.Resources

Public Class MyEmitTest
   Public Shared Sub Main()
      Dim myAssembly As AssemblyBuilder = _
            CType(CreateAssembly(Thread.GetDomain()).
Assembly, AssemblyBuilder)

      Dim myResourceWriter As IResourceWriter = _
         myAssembly.DefineResource("myResourceFile", _
         "A sample Resource File", "MyResourceFile.resources")
      myResourceWriter.AddResource("AddResource test", "Test
resource added")

      ' Define unmanaged version information resources.
      myAssembly.DefineVersionInfoResource()
      myAssembly.Save("MyEmittedAssembly.dll")
   End Sub 'Main

   ' Create the callee transient dynamic assembly.
   Private Shared Function CreateAssembly(myDomain As AppDomain)
As Type
      Dim myAssemblyName As New AssemblyName()
      myAssemblyName.Name = "MyEmittedAssembly"

      Dim myAssembly As AssemblyBuilder = _
            myDomain.DefineDynamicAssembly(myAssemblyName,
AssemblyBuilderAccess.Save)

      ' Set Company Attribute to the assembly.
      Dim companyAttribute As Type = GetType(AssemblyCompanyAttribute)
      Dim myConstructorInfo1 As ConstructorInfo = _
```

```
companyAttribute.GetConstructor(New Type() {GetType(String)})
      Dim attributeBuilder1 As _
            New CustomAttributeBuilder(myConstructorInfo1,
New Object(0) {"Microsoft Corporation"})
      myAssembly.SetCustomAttribute(attributeBuilder1)

      ' Set Copyright Attribute to the assembly.
      Dim copyrightAttribute As Type =
GetType(AssemblyCopyrightAttribute)
      Dim myConstructorInfo2 As ConstructorInfo =
copyrightAttribute.GetConstructor(New Type() {GetType(String)})
      Dim attributeBuilder2 As _
            New CustomAttributeBuilder(myConstructorInfo2, _
            New Object(0) {"@Copyright Microsoft Corp. 1990-2001"})
      myAssembly.SetCustomAttribute(attributeBuilder2)

      Dim myModule As ModuleBuilder = _
            myAssembly.DefineDynamicModule("EmittedModule",
"EmittedModule.mod")

      ' Define a public class named "HelloWorld" in the assembly.
      Dim helloWorldClass As TypeBuilder =
myModule.DefineType("HelloWorld", TypeAttributes.Public)
      ' Define the Display method.
      Dim myMethod As MethodBuilder = _
         helloWorldClass.DefineMethod("Display",
MethodAttributes.Public, GetType(String), Nothing)

      ' Generate IL for GetGreeting.
      Dim methodIL As ILGenerator = myMethod.GetILGenerator()
      methodIL.Emit(OpCodes.Ldstr, "Display method get called.")
      methodIL.Emit(OpCodes.Ret)

      ' Returns the type HelloWorld.
      Return helloWorldClass.CreateType()
   End Function 'CreateAssembly
End Class 'MyEmitTest
```

```
[C#]
using System;
using System.Threading;
using System.Reflection;
using System.Reflection.Emit;
using System.Resources;

public class MyEmitTest
{
   public static void Main()
   {
      AssemblyBuilder myAssembly =
         (AssemblyBuilder)CreateAssembly(Thread.GetDomain()).Assembly;

      IResourceWriter myResourceWriter =
myAssembly.DefineResource("myResourceFile",
         "A sample Resource File", "MyResourceFile.resources");
      myResourceWriter.AddResource("AddResource test", "Test resource
added");

      // Define unmanaged version information resources  .
      myAssembly.DefineVersionInfoResource();
      myAssembly.Save("MyEmittedAssembly.dll");
   }

   // Create the callee transient dynamic assembly.
   private static Type CreateAssembly(AppDomain myDomain)
   {
      AssemblyName myAssemblyName = new AssemblyName();
      myAssemblyName.Name = "MyEmittedAssembly";

      AssemblyBuilder myAssembly =
myDomain.DefineDynamicAssembly(myAssemblyName,
            AssemblyBuilderAccess.Save);

      // Set Company Attribute to the assembly.
      Type companyAttribute = typeof(AssemblyCompanyAttribute);
```

```
    ConstructorInfo myConstructorInfo1 =
ompanyAttribute.GetConstructor(new Type[]{typeof(String)});
    CustomAttributeBuilder attributeBuilder1 =
        new CustomAttributeBuilder(myConstructorInfo1,
new object[1]{"Microsoft Corporation"});
    myAssembly.SetCustomAttribute(attributeBuilder1);

    // Set Copyright Attribute to the assembly.
    Type copyrightAttribute = typeof(AssemblyCopyrightAttribute);
    ConstructorInfo myConstructorInfo2 =
opyrightAttribute.GetConstructor(new Type[]{typeof(String)});
    CustomAttributeBuilder attributeBuilder2 =
        new CustomAttributeBuilder(myConstructorInfo2,
        new object[1]{"@Copyright Microsoft Corp. 1990-2001"});
    myAssembly.SetCustomAttribute(attributeBuilder2);

    ModuleBuilder myModule =
myAssembly.DefineDynamicModule("EmittedModule",
        "EmittedModule.mod");

    // Define a public class named "HelloWorld" in the assembly.
    TypeBuilder helloWorldClass =
        myModule.DefineType("HelloWorld", TypeAttributes.Public);
    // Define the Display method.
    MethodBuilder myMethod = helloWorldClass.DefineMethod("Display",
        MethodAttributes.Public, typeof(String), null);

    // Generate IL for GetGreeting.
    ILGenerator methodIL = myMethod.GetILGenerator();
    methodIL.Emit(OpCodes.Ldstr, "Display method get called.");
    methodIL.Emit(OpCodes.Ret);

    // Returns the type HelloWorld.

    return(helloWorldClass.CreateType());
    }
}

[C++]
#using <mscorlib.dll>

using namespace System;
using namespace System::Threading;
using namespace System::Reflection;
using namespace System::Reflection::Emit;
using namespace System::Resources;

// Create the callee transient dynamic assembly.
static Type* CreateAssembly(AppDomain* myDomain) {
    AssemblyName* myAssemblyName = new AssemblyName();
    myAssemblyName->Name = S"MyEmittedAssembly";

    AssemblyBuilder* myAssembly = myDomain-
>DefineDynamicAssembly(myAssemblyName,
        AssemblyBuilderAccess::Save);

    // Set Company Attribute to the assembly.
    Type* companyAttribute = __typeof(AssemblyCompanyAttribute);
    Type* types1[] = {__typeof(String)};
    ConstructorInfo* myConstructorInfo1 = companyAttribute-
>GetConstructor(types1);
    Object* obj1[] = {S"Microsoft Corporation"};
    CustomAttributeBuilder* attributeBuilder1 = new
CustomAttributeBuilder(myConstructorInfo1, obj1);
    myAssembly->SetCustomAttribute(attributeBuilder1);

    // Set Copyright Attribute to the assembly.
    Type* copyrightAttribute = __typeof(AssemblyCopyrightAttribute);
    Type* types2[] = {__typeof(String)};
    ConstructorInfo* myConstructorInfo2 = copyrightAttribute-
>GetConstructor(types2);
    Object* obj2[] = {S"@Copyright Microsoft Corp. 1990-2001"};
    CustomAttributeBuilder* attributeBuilder2 = new
CustomAttributeBuilder(myConstructorInfo2, obj2);
    myAssembly->SetCustomAttribute(attributeBuilder2);
```

```
    ModuleBuilder* myModule = myAssembly-
>DefineDynamicModule(S"EmittedModule",
        S"EmittedModule::mod");

    // Define a public class named S"HelloWorld" in the assembly.
    TypeBuilder* helloWorldClass =
        myModule->DefineType(S"HelloWorld", TypeAttributes::Public);
    // Define the Display method.
    MethodBuilder* myMethod = helloWorldClass->DefineMethod(S"Display",
        MethodAttributes::Public, __typeof(String), 0);

    // Generate IL for GetGreeting.
    ILGenerator* methodIL = myMethod->GetILGenerator();
    methodIL->Emit(OpCodes::Ldstr, S"Display method get called.");
    methodIL->Emit(OpCodes::Ret);

    // Returns the type HelloWorld.

    return(helloWorldClass->CreateType());
}

void main()
{
    AssemblyBuilder* myAssembly =
        __try_cast<AssemblyBuilder*>(CreateAssembly
(Thread::GetDomain())->Assembly);

    IResourceWriter* myResourceWriter = myAssembly-
>DefineResource(S"myResourceFile",
        S"A sample Resource File", S"MyResourceFile::resources");
    myResourceWriter->AddResource(S"AddResource test", S"Test
resource added");

    // Define unmanaged version information resources  .
    myAssembly->DefineVersionInfoResource();
    myAssembly->Save(S"MyEmittedAssembly.dll");
}
```

Requirements

Namespace: System.Reflection

Platforms: Windows 98, Windows NT 4.0, Windows Millennium Edition, Windows 2000, Windows XP Home Edition, Windows XP Professional, Windows .NET Server family, .NET Compact Framework - Windows CE .NET

Assembly: Mscorlib (in Mscorlib.dll)

AssemblyTitleAttribute Constructor

Initializes a new instance of the **AssemblyTitleAttribute** class.

```
[Visual Basic]
Public Sub New( _
   ByVal title As String _
)
[C#]
public AssemblyTitleAttribute(
   string title
);
[C++]
public: AssemblyTitleAttribute(
   String* title
);
[JScript]
public function AssemblyTitleAttribute(
   title : String
);
```

Parameters

title

The assembly title.

Requirements

Platforms: Windows 98, Windows NT 4.0,
Windows Millennium Edition, Windows 2000,
Windows XP Home Edition, Windows XP Professional,
Windows .NET Server family,
.NET Compact Framework - Windows CE .NET

AssemblyTitleAttribute.Title Property

Gets assembly title information.

```
[Visual Basic]
Public ReadOnly Property Title As String
[C#]
public string Title {get;}
[C++]
public: __property String* get_Title();
[JScript]
public function get Title() : String;
```

Property Value

A string containing the assembly title.

Requirements

Platforms: Windows 98, Windows NT 4.0,
Windows Millennium Edition, Windows 2000,
Windows XP Home Edition, Windows XP Professional,
Windows .NET Server family,
.NET Compact Framework - Windows CE .NET

AssemblyTrademarkAttribute Class

Defines a trademark custom attribute for an assembly manifest.

System.Object
  System.Attribute
    System.Reflection.AssemblyTrademarkAttribute

```
[Visual Basic]
<AttributeUsage(AttributeTargets.Assembly)>
NotInheritable Public Class AssemblyTrademarkAttribute
   Inherits Attribute
[C#]
[AttributeUsage(AttributeTargets.Assembly)]
public sealed class AssemblyTrademarkAttribute : Attribute
[C++]
[AttributeUsage(AttributeTargets::Assembly)]
public __gc __sealed class AssemblyTrademarkAttribute : public
   Attribute
[JScript]
public
   AttributeUsage(AttributeTargets.Assembly)
class AssemblyTrademarkAttribute extends Attribute
```

Thread Safety

Any public static (**Shared** in Visual Basic) members of this type are safe for multithreaded operations. Any instance members are not guaranteed to be thread safe.

Requirements

Namespace: System.Reflection

Platforms: Windows 98, Windows NT 4.0, Windows Millennium Edition, Windows 2000, Windows XP Home Edition, Windows XP Professional, Windows .NET Server family, .NET Compact Framework - Windows CE .NET

Assembly: Mscorlib (in Mscorlib.dll)

AssemblyTrademarkAttribute Constructor

Initializes a new instance of the **AssemblyTrademarkAttribute** class.

```
[Visual Basic]
Public Sub New( _
   ByVal trademark As String _
)
[C#]
public AssemblyTrademarkAttribute(
   string trademark
);
[C++]
public: AssemblyTrademarkAttribute(
   String* trademark
);
[JScript]
public function AssemblyTrademarkAttribute(
   trademark : String
);
```

Parameters

trademark
  The trademark information.

Requirements

Platforms: Windows 98, Windows NT 4.0, Windows Millennium Edition, Windows 2000, Windows XP Home Edition, Windows XP Professional, Windows .NET Server family, .NET Compact Framework - Windows CE .NET

AssemblyTrademarkAttribute.Trademark Property

Gets trademark information.

```
[Visual Basic]
Public ReadOnly Property Trademark As String
[C#]
public string Trademark {get;}
[C++]
public: __property String* get_Trademark();
[JScript]
public function get Trademark() : String;
```

Property Value

A **String** containing trademark information.

Requirements

Platforms: Windows 98, Windows NT 4.0, Windows Millennium Edition, Windows 2000, Windows XP Home Edition, Windows XP Professional, Windows .NET Server family, .NET Compact Framework - Windows CE .NET

AssemblyVersionAttribute Class

Specifies the version of the assembly being attributed.

System.Object
  System.Attribute
    System.Reflection.AssemblyVersionAttribute

```
[Visual Basic]
<AttributeUsage(AttributeTargets.Assembly)>
NotInheritable Public Class AssemblyVersionAttribute
  Inherits Attribute
[C#]
[AttributeUsage(AttributeTargets.Assembly)]
public sealed class AssemblyVersionAttribute : Attribute
[C++]
[AttributeUsage(AttributeTargets::Assembly)]
public __gc __sealed class AssemblyVersionAttribute : public
  Attribute
[JScript]
public
  AttributeUsage(AttributeTargets.Assembly)
class AssemblyVersionAttribute extends Attribute
```

Thread Safety

Any public static (**Shared** in Visual Basic) members of this type are safe for multithreaded operations. Any instance members are not guaranteed to be thread safe.

Remarks

The assembly version number is part of an assembly's identity and plays a key part in binding to the assembly and in version policy. The default version policy for the runtime is that applications run only with the versions they were built and tested with, unless overridden by explicit version policy in configuration files (the application configuration file, the publisher policy file, and the computer's administrator configuration file). See **Assemblies Overview** for more information.

Note   Version checking only occurs with strong-named assemblies.

The version number has four parts, as follows:

<major version>.<minor version>.<build number>.<revision>

You can specify all the values or you can accept the default build number, revision number, or both by using an asterisk (*). For example, [assembly:AssemblyVersion("2.3.25.1")] indicates 2 as the major version, 3 as the minor version, 25 as the build number, and 1 as the revision number. A version number such as [assembly:AssemblyVersion("1.2.*")] specifies 1 as the major version, 2 as the minor version, and accepts the default build and revision numbers. A version number such as [assembly:AssemblyVersion("1.2.15.*")] specifies 1 as the major version, 2 as the minor version, 15 as the build number, and accepts the default revision number. A version number such as [assembly:AssemblyVersion("1.2.*.6")] specifies 1 as the major version, 2 as the minor version, accepts the default build number, and specifies 6 as the revision number.

The assembly major and minor versions are used as the type library version number when the assembly is exported. Some COM hosts do not accept type libraries with the version number 0.0. Therefore, if you want to expose an assembly to COM clients, set the assembly version explicitly to 1.0 in the **AssemblyVersionAttribute** page for projects created outside Visual Studio .NET and with no **AssemblyVersionAttribute** specified. Do this even when the assembly version is 0.0. All projects created in Visual Studio .NET have a default assembly version of 1.0*.

To get the name of an assembly you have loaded, call **GetName** on the assembly to get an **AssemblyName**, and then get the **Version** property. To get the name of an assembly you have not loaded, call **GetAssemblyName** from your client application to check the assembly version that your application uses.

Requirements

Namespace: System.Reflection

Platforms: Windows 98, Windows NT 4.0, Windows Millennium Edition, Windows 2000, Windows XP Home Edition, Windows XP Professional, Windows .NET Server family, .NET Compact Framework - Windows CE .NET

Assembly: Mscorlib (in Mscorlib.dll)

AssemblyVersionAttribute Constructor

Initializes a new instance of the **AssemblyVersionAttribute** class with the version number of the assembly being attributed.

```
[Visual Basic]
Public Sub New( _
  ByVal version As String _
)
[C#]
public AssemblyVersionAttribute(
  string version
);
[C++]
public: AssemblyVersionAttribute(
  String* version
);
[JScript]
public function AssemblyVersionAttribute(
  version : String
);
```

Parameters

version
    The version number of the attributed assembly.

Remarks

The format of the *version* string is: **major. minor. build. revision**.

When specifying a version, you have to at least specify **major**. If you specify **major** and **minor**, you can specify an asterisk (*) for **build**. This will cause **build** to be equal to the number of days since January 1, 2000 local time, and for **revision** to be equal to the number of seconds since midnight local time, divided by 2.

If you specify **major**, **minor**, and **build**, you can specify an asterisk for **revision**. This will cause **revision** to be equal to the number of seconds since midnight local time, divided by 2.

Examples of valid version strings include:

1

1.1

1.1.*

1.1.1

1.1.1.*

1.1.1.1

Requirements

Platforms: Windows 98, Windows NT 4.0,
Windows Millennium Edition, Windows 2000,
Windows XP Home Edition, Windows XP Professional,
Windows .NET Server family,
.NET Compact Framework - Windows CE .NET

AssemblyVersionAttribute.Version Property

Gets the version number of the attributed assembly.

```
[Visual Basic]
Public ReadOnly Property Version As String
[C#]
public string Version {get;}
[C++]
public: __property String* get_Version();
[JScript]
public function get Version() : String;
```

Property Value

A string containing the assembly version number.

Requirements

Platforms: Windows 98, Windows NT 4.0,
Windows Millennium Edition, Windows 2000,
Windows XP Home Edition, Windows XP Professional,
Windows .NET Server family,
.NET Compact Framework - Windows CE .NET

Binder Class

Selects a member from a list of candidates, and performs type conversion from actual argument type to formal argument type.

System.Object
  System.Reflection.Binder

```
[Visual Basic]
<Serializable>
<ClassInterface(ClassInterfaceType.AutoDual)>
MustInherit Public Class Binder
[C#]
[Serializable]
[ClassInterface(ClassInterfaceType.AutoDual)]
public abstract class Binder
[C++]
[Serializable]
[ClassInterface(ClassInterfaceType::AutoDual)]
public __gc __abstract class Binder
[JScript]
public
   Serializable
   ClassInterface(ClassInterfaceType.AutoDual)
abstract class Binder
```

Thread Safety

Any public static (**Shared** in Visual Basic) members of this type are safe for multithreaded operations. Any instance members are not guaranteed to be thread safe.

Remarks

Notes to Inheritors: When you inherit from **Binder**, you must override the following members: **BindToMethod**, **BindToField**, **SelectMethod**, **SelectProperty**, and **ChangeType**.

Example

[Visual Basic, C#, C++] The following example implements and demonstrates all members of the **Binder** class. The private method **CanConvertFrom** finds compatible types for a given type.

```
[Visual Basic]
Imports System
Imports System.Reflection
Imports System.Globalization
Imports Microsoft.VisualBasic

Public Class MyBinder
    Inherits Binder
    Public Sub New()
        MyBase.new()
    End Sub 'New
    Private Class BinderState
        Public args() As Object
    End Class 'BinderState

    Public Overrides Function BindToField(ByVal bindingAttr As
BindingFlags, ByVal match() As FieldInfo, ByVal value As Object,
ByVal culture As CultureInfo) As FieldInfo
        If match Is Nothing Then
            Throw New ArgumentNullException("match")
        End If
        ' Get a field for which the value parameter can be
converted to the specified field type.
        Dim i As Integer
        For i = 0 To match.Length - 1
            If Not (ChangeType(value, match(i).FieldType,
culture) Is Nothing) Then
                Return match(i)
```

```
            End If
        Next i
        Return Nothing
    End Function 'BindToField

    Public Overrides Function BindToMethod(ByVal bindingAttr As
BindingFlags, ByVal match() As MethodBase, ByRef args() As
Object, ByVal modifiers() As ParameterModifier, ByVal
culture As CultureInfo, ByVal names() As String, ByRef state
As Object) As MethodBase
        ' Store the arguments to the method in a state object.
        Dim myBinderState As New BinderState()
        Dim arguments() As Object = New [Object](args.Length) {}
        args.CopyTo(arguments, 0)
        myBinderState.args = arguments
        state = myBinderState

        If match Is Nothing Then
            Throw New ArgumentNullException()
        End If
        ' Find a method that has the same parameters as those of args.
        Dim i As Integer
        For i = 0 To match.Length - 1
            ' Count the number of parameters that match.
            Dim count As Integer = 0
            Dim parameters As ParameterInfo() =
match(i).GetParameters()
            ' Go on to the next method if the number of
parameters do not match.
            If args.Length <> parameters.Length Then
                GoTo ContinueFori
            End If
            ' Match each of the parameters that the user
expects the method to have.
            Dim j As Integer
            For j = 0 To args.Length - 1
                ' If names is not null, then reorder args.
                If Not (names Is Nothing) Then
                    If names.Length <> args.Length Then
                        Throw New ArgumentException("names
and args must have the same number of elements.")
                    End If
                    Dim k As Integer
                    For k = 0 To names.Length - 1
                        If String.Compare(parameters(j).Name,
names(k).ToString()) = 0 Then
                            args(j) = myBinderState.args(k)
                        End If
                    Next k
                End If ' Determine whether the types specified
by the user can be converted to parameter type.
                If Not (ChangeType(args(j),
parameters(j).ParameterType, culture) Is Nothing) Then
                    count += 1
                Else
                    Exit For
                End If
            Next j
            ' Determine whether the method has been found.
            If count = args.Length Then
                Return match(i)
            End If
ContinueFori:
        Next i
        Return Nothing
    End Function 'BindToMethod

    Public Overrides Function ChangeType(ByVal value As
Object, ByVal myChangeType As Type, ByVal culture As
CultureInfo) As Object
        ' Determine whether the value parameter can be
converted to a value of type myType.
        If CanConvertFrom(value.GetType(), myChangeType) Then
            ' Return the converted object.
            Return Convert.ChangeType(value, myChangeType)
```

```
                ' Return null.
        Else
                Return Nothing
        End If
End Function 'ChangeType

    Public Overrides Sub ReorderArgumentArray(ByRef args() _
As Object, ByVal state As Object)
            'Redimension the array to hold the state values.
            ReDim args(CType(state, BinderState).args.Length)
            ' Return the args that had been reordered by BindToMethod.
            CType(state, BinderState).args.CopyTo(args, 0)
    End Sub 'ReorderArgumentArray

    Public Overrides Function SelectMethod(ByVal bindingAttr _
As BindingFlags, ByVal match() As MethodBase, ByVal types() _
As Type, ByVal modifiers() As ParameterModifier) As MethodBase
            If match Is Nothing Then
                Throw New ArgumentNullException("match")
            End If
            Dim i As Integer
            For i = 0 To match.Length - 1
                ' Count the number of parameters that match.
                Dim count As Integer = 0
                Dim parameters As ParameterInfo() = _
match(i).GetParameters()
                ' Go on to the next method if the number of
parameters do not match.
                If types.Length <> parameters.Length Then
                    GoTo ContinueFori
                End If
                ' Match each of the parameters that the user expects
the method to have.
                Dim j As Integer
                For j = 0 To types.Length - 1
                    ' Determine whether the types specified by the
user can be converted to parameter type.
                    If CanConvertFrom(types(j), _
parameters(j).ParameterType) Then
                        count += 1
                    Else
                        Exit For
                    End If
                Next j ' Determine whether the method has been found.
                If count = types.Length Then
                    Return match(i)
                End If
ContinueFori:
            Next i
            Return Nothing
    End Function 'SelectMethod
    Public Overrides Function SelectProperty(ByVal _
bindingAttr As BindingFlags, ByVal match() As PropertyInfo, _
ByVal returnType As Type, ByVal indexes() As Type, ByVal _
modifiers() As ParameterModifier) As PropertyInfo
            If match Is Nothing Then
                Throw New ArgumentNullException("match")
            End If
            Dim i As Integer
            For i = 0 To match.Length - 1
                ' Count the number of indexes that match.
                Dim count As Integer = 0
                Dim parameters As ParameterInfo() = _
match(i).GetIndexParameters()
                ' Go on to the next property if the number of
indexes do not match.
                If indexes.Length <> parameters.Length Then
                    GoTo ContinueFori
                End If
                ' Match each of the indexes that the user expects
the property to have.
                Dim j As Integer
                For j = 0 To indexes.Length - 1
                    ' Determine whether the types specified by the
user can be converted to index type.
                    If CanConvertFrom(indexes(j), _
parameters(j).ParameterType) Then
                        count += 1
                    Else
                        Exit For
                    End If
                Next j ' Determine whether the property has been found.
                If count = indexes.Length Then
                    ' Determine whether the return type can be
converted to the properties type.
                    If CanConvertFrom(returnType, match(i).GetType()) Then
                        Return match(i)
                    Else
                        GoTo ContinueFori
                    End If
                End If
ContinueFori:
            Next i
            Return Nothing
    End Function 'SelectProperty

    ' Determine whether type1 can be converted to type2. Check
only for primitive types.
    Private Function CanConvertFrom(ByVal type1 As Type, ByVal _
type2 As Type) As Boolean
            If type1.IsPrimitive And type2.IsPrimitive Then
                Dim typeCode1 As TypeCode = Type.GetTypeCode(type1)
                Dim typeCode2 As TypeCode = Type.GetTypeCode(type2)
                ' If both type1 and type2 have same type, return true.
                If typeCode1 = typeCode2 Then
                    Return True
                End If ' Possible conversions from Char follow.
                If typeCode1 = TypeCode.Char Then
                    Select Case typeCode2
                        Case TypeCode.UInt16
                            Return True
                        Case TypeCode.UInt32
                            Return True
                        Case TypeCode.Int32
                            Return True
                        Case TypeCode.UInt64
                            Return True
                        Case TypeCode.Int64
                            Return True
                        Case TypeCode.Single
                            Return True
                        Case TypeCode.Double
                            Return True
                        Case Else
                            Return False
                    End Select
                End If ' Possible conversions from Byte follow.
                If typeCode1 = TypeCode.Byte Then
                    Select Case typeCode2
                        Case TypeCode.Char
                            Return True
                        Case TypeCode.UInt16
                            Return True
                        Case TypeCode.Int16
                            Return True
                        Case TypeCode.UInt32
                            Return True
                        Case TypeCode.Int32
                            Return True
                        Case TypeCode.UInt64
                            Return True
                        Case TypeCode.Int64
                            Return True
                        Case TypeCode.Single
                            Return True
                        Case TypeCode.Double
                            Return True
                        Case Else
                            Return False
```

```
        End Select
    End If ' Possible conversions from SByte follow.
    If typeCode1 = TypeCode.SByte Then
        Select Case typeCode2
            Case TypeCode.Int16
                Return True
            Case TypeCode.Int32
                Return True
            Case TypeCode.Int64
                Return True
            Case TypeCode.Single
                Return True
            Case TypeCode.Double
                Return True
            Case Else
                Return False
        End Select
    End If ' Possible conversions from UInt16 follow.
    If typeCode1 = TypeCode.UInt16 Then
        Select Case typeCode2
            Case TypeCode.UInt32
                Return True
            Case TypeCode.Int32
                Return True
            Case TypeCode.UInt64
                Return True
            Case TypeCode.Int64
                Return True
            Case TypeCode.Single
                Return True
            Case TypeCode.Double
                Return True
            Case Else
                Return False
        End Select
    End If ' Possible conversions from Int16 follow.
    If typeCode1 = TypeCode.Int16 Then
        Select Case typeCode2
            Case TypeCode.Int32
                Return True
            Case TypeCode.Int64
                Return True
            Case TypeCode.Single
                Return True
            Case TypeCode.Double
                Return True
            Case Else
                Return False
        End Select
    End If ' Possible conversions from UInt32 follow.
    If typeCode1 = TypeCode.UInt32 Then
        Select Case typeCode2
            Case TypeCode.UInt64
                Return True
            Case TypeCode.Int64
                Return True
            Case TypeCode.Single
                Return True
            Case TypeCode.Double
                Return True
            Case Else
                Return False
        End Select
    End If ' Possible conversions from Int32 follow.
    If typeCode1 = TypeCode.Int32 Then
        Select Case typeCode2
            Case TypeCode.Int64
                Return True
            Case TypeCode.Single
                Return True
            Case TypeCode.Double
                Return True
            Case Else
                Return False
        End Select
    End If ' Possible conversions from UInt64 follow.
    If typeCode1 = TypeCode.UInt64 Then
        Select Case typeCode2
            Case TypeCode.Single
                Return True
            Case TypeCode.Double
                Return True
            Case Else
                Return False
        End Select
    End If ' Possible conversions from Int64 follow.
    If typeCode1 = TypeCode.Int64 Then
        Select Case typeCode2
            Case TypeCode.Single
                Return True
            Case TypeCode.Double
                Return True
            Case Else
                Return False
        End Select
    End If ' Possible conversions from Single follow.
    If typeCode1 = TypeCode.Single Then
        Select Case typeCode2
            Case TypeCode.Double
                Return True
            Case Else
                Return False
        End Select
        End If
    End If
    Return False
    End Function 'CanConvertFrom
End Class 'MyBinder

Public Class MyClass1
    Public myFieldB As Short
    Public myFieldA As Integer

    Public Overloads Sub MyMethod(ByVal i As Long, ByVal k As Char)
        Console.WriteLine(ControlChars.NewLine & "This is
MyMethod(long i, char k).")
    End Sub 'MyMethod

    Public Overloads Sub MyMethod(ByVal i As Long, ByVal j As Long)
        Console.WriteLine(ControlChars.NewLine & "This is
MyMethod(long i, long j).")
    End Sub 'MyMethod
End Class 'MyClass1

Public Class Binder_Example
    Public Shared Sub Main()
        ' Get the type of MyClass1.
        Dim myType As Type = GetType(MyClass1)
        ' Get the instance of MyClass1.
        Dim myInstance As New MyClass1()
        Console.WriteLine(ControlChars.Cr & "Displaying the
results of using the MyBinder binder.")
        Console.WriteLine()
        ' Get the method information for MyMethod.
        Dim myMethod As MethodInfo = myType.GetMethod
("MyMethod", BindingFlags.Public Or BindingFlags.Instance,
New MyBinder(), New Type() {GetType(Short), GetType(Short)},
Nothing)
        Console.WriteLine(MyMethod)
        ' Invoke MyMethod.
        myMethod.Invoke(myInstance, BindingFlags.InvokeMethod,
New MyBinder(), New [Object]() {CInt(32), CInt(32)},
CultureInfo.CurrentCulture)
    End Sub 'Main
End Class 'Binder_Example
```

[C#]
```
using System;
using System.Reflection;
using System.Globalization;
```

```csharp
public class MyBinder : Binder
{
    public MyBinder() : base()
    {
    }
    private class BinderState
    {
        public object[] args;
    }
    public override FieldInfo BindToField(
        BindingFlags bindingAttr,
        FieldInfo[] match,
        object value,
        CultureInfo culture
        )
    {
        if(match == null)
            throw new ArgumentNullException("match");
        // Get a field for which the value parameter can be
        // converted to the specified field type.
        for(int i = 0; i < match.Length; i++)
            if(ChangeType(value, match[i].FieldType, culture) != null)
                return match[i];
        return null;
    }
    public override MethodBase BindToMethod(
        BindingFlags bindingAttr,
        MethodBase[] match,
        ref object[] args,
        ParameterModifier[] modifiers,
        CultureInfo culture,
        string[] names,
        out object state
        )
    {
        // Store the arguments to the method in a state object.
        BinderState myBinderState = new BinderState();
        object[] arguments = new Object[args.Length];
        args.CopyTo(arguments, 0);
        myBinderState.args = arguments;
        state = myBinderState;
        if(match == null)
            throw new ArgumentNullException();
        // Find a method that has the same parameters as those
        // of the args parameter.
        for(int i = 0; i < match.Length; i++)
        {
            // Count the number of parameters that match.
            int count = 0;
            ParameterInfo[] parameters = match[i].GetParameters();
            // Go on to the next method if the number of
            // parameters do not match.
            if(args.Length != parameters.Length)
                continue;
            // Match each of the parameters that the user
            // expects the method to have.
            for(int j = 0; j < args.Length; j++)
            {
                // If the names parameter is not null, then
                // reorder args.
                if(names != null)
                {
                    if(names.Length != args.Length)
                        throw new ArgumentException("names and args must have the same number of elements.");
                    for(int k = 0; k < names.Length; k++)
                        if(String.Compare(parameters[j].Name, names[k].ToString()) == 0)
                            args[j] = myBinderState.args[k];
                }
                // Determine whether the types specified by
                // the user can be converted to the parameter type.
                if(ChangeType(args[j], parameters[j].ParameterType, culture) != null)
                    count += 1;
                else
                    break;
            }
            // Determine whether the method has been found.
            if(count == args.Length)
                return match[i];
        }
        return null;
    }
    public override object ChangeType(
        object value,
        Type myChangeType,
        CultureInfo culture
        )
    {
        // Determine whether the value parameter can be converted
        // to a value of type myType.
        if(CanConvertFrom(value.GetType(), myChangeType))
            // Return the converted object.
            return Convert.ChangeType(value, myChangeType);
        else
            // Return null.
            return null;
    }
    public override void ReorderArgumentArray(
        ref object[] args,
        object state
        )
    {
        // Return the args that had been reordered by BindToMethod.
        ((BinderState)state).args.CopyTo(args, 0);
    }
    public override MethodBase SelectMethod(
        BindingFlags bindingAttr,
        MethodBase[] match,
        Type[] types,
        ParameterModifier[] modifiers
        )
    {
        if(match == null)
            throw new ArgumentNullException("match");
        for(int i = 0; i < match.Length; i++)
        {
            // Count the number of parameters that match.
            int count = 0;
            ParameterInfo[] parameters = match[i].GetParameters();
            // Go on to the next method if the number of
            // parameters do not match.
            if(types.Length != parameters.Length)
                continue;
            // Match each of the parameters that the user
            // expects the method to have.
            for(int j = 0; j < types.Length; j++)
                // Determine whether the types specified by
                // the user can be converted to parameter type.
                if(CanConvertFrom(types[j], parameters[j].ParameterType))
                    count += 1;
                else
                    break;
            // Determine whether the method has been found.
            if(count == types.Length)
                return match[i];
        }
        return null;
    }
    public override PropertyInfo SelectProperty(
        BindingFlags bindingAttr,
        PropertyInfo[] match,
        Type returnType,
        Type[] indexes,
        ParameterModifier[] modifiers
        )
    {
        if(match == null)
```

```
            throw new ArgumentNullException("match");
        for(int i = 0; i < match.Length; i++)
        {
            // Count the number of indexes that match.
            int count = 0;
            ParameterInfo[] parameters = match[i].GetIndexParameters();
            // Go on to the next property if the number of indexes do not
match.
            if(indexes.Length != parameters.Length)
                continue;
            // Match each of the indexes that the user expects         ⏎
the property to have.
            for(int j = 0; j < indexes.Length; j++)
                // Determine whether the types specified by the        ⏎
user can be converted to index type.
                if(CanConvertFrom(indexes[j],                          ⏎
parameters[j].ParameterType))
                    count += 1;
                else
                    break;
            // Determine whether the property has been found.
            if(count == indexes.Length)
                // Determine whether the return type can be            ⏎
converted to the properties type.
                if(CanConvertFrom(returnType, match[i].GetType()))
                    return match[i];
                else
                    continue;
        }
        return null;
    }
    // Determines whether type1 can be converted to type2.            ⏎
Check only for primitive types.
    private bool CanConvertFrom(Type type1, Type type2)
    {
        if(type1.IsPrimitive && type2.IsPrimitive)
        {
            TypeCode typeCode1 = Type.GetTypeCode(type1);
            TypeCode typeCode2 = Type.GetTypeCode(type2);
            // If both type1 and type2 have the same type, return true.
            if(typeCode1 == typeCode2)
                return true;
            // Possible conversions from Char follow.
            if(typeCode1 == TypeCode.Char)
                switch(typeCode2)
                {
                    case TypeCode.UInt16 : return true;
                    case TypeCode.UInt32 : return true;
                    case TypeCode.Int32  : return true;
                    case TypeCode.UInt64 : return true;
                    case TypeCode.Int64  : return true;
                    case TypeCode.Single : return true;
                    case TypeCode.Double : return true;
                    default              : return false;
                }
            // Possible conversions from Byte follow.
            if(typeCode1 == TypeCode.Byte)
                switch(typeCode2)
                {
                    case TypeCode.Char   : return true;
                    case TypeCode.UInt16 : return true;
                    case TypeCode.Int16  : return true;
                    case TypeCode.UInt32 : return true;
                    case TypeCode.Int32  : return true;
                    case TypeCode.UInt64 : return true;
                    case TypeCode.Int64  : return true;
                    case TypeCode.Single : return true;
                    case TypeCode.Double : return true;
                    default              : return false;
                }
            // Possible conversions from SByte follow.
            if(typeCode1 == TypeCode.SByte)
                switch(typeCode2)
                {
                    case TypeCode.Int16  : return true;

                    case TypeCode.Int32  : return true;
                    case TypeCode.Int64  : return true;
                    case TypeCode.Single : return true;
                    case TypeCode.Double : return true;
                    default              : return false;
                }
            // Possible conversions from UInt16 follow.
            if(typeCode1 == TypeCode.UInt16)
                switch(typeCode2)
                {
                    case TypeCode.UInt32 : return true;
                    case TypeCode.Int32  : return true;
                    case TypeCode.UInt64 : return true;
                    case TypeCode.Int64  : return true;
                    case TypeCode.Single : return true;
                    case TypeCode.Double : return true;
                    default              : return false;
                }
            // Possible conversions from Int16 follow.
            if(typeCode1 == TypeCode.Int16)
                switch(typeCode2)
                {
                    case TypeCode.Int32  : return true;
                    case TypeCode.Int64  : return true;
                    case TypeCode.Single : return true;
                    case TypeCode.Double : return true;
                    default              : return false;
                }
            // Possible conversions from UInt32 follow.
            if(typeCode1 == TypeCode.UInt32)
                switch(typeCode2)
                {
                    case TypeCode.UInt64 : return true;
                    case TypeCode.Int64  : return true;
                    case TypeCode.Single : return true;
                    case TypeCode.Double : return true;
                    default              : return false;
                }
            // Possible conversions from Int32 follow.
            if(typeCode1 == TypeCode.Int32)
                switch(typeCode2)
                {
                    case TypeCode.Int64  : return true;
                    case TypeCode.Single : return true;
                    case TypeCode.Double : return true;
                    default              : return false;
                }
            // Possible conversions from UInt64 follow.
            if(typeCode1 == TypeCode.UInt64)
                switch(typeCode2)
                {
                    case TypeCode.Single : return true;
                    case TypeCode.Double : return true;
                    default              : return false;
                }
            // Possible conversions from Int64 follow.
            if(typeCode1 == TypeCode.Int64)
                switch(typeCode2)
                {
                    case TypeCode.Single : return true;
                    case TypeCode.Double : return true;
                    default              : return false;
                }
            // Possible conversions from Single follow.
            if(typeCode1 == TypeCode.Single)
                switch(typeCode2)
                {
                    case TypeCode.Double : return true;
                    default              : return false;
                }
        }
        return false;
    }
}
public class MyClass1
```

```cpp
{
    public short myFieldB;
    public int myFieldA;
    public void MyMethod(long i, char k)
    {
        Console.WriteLine("\nThis is MyMethod(long i, char k)");
    }
    public void MyMethod(long i, long j)
    {
        Console.WriteLine("\nThis is MyMethod(long i, long j)");
    }
}
public class Binder_Example
{
    public static void Main()
    {
        // Get the type of MyClass1.
        Type myType = typeof(MyClass1);
        // Get the instance of MyClass1.
        MyClass1 myInstance = new MyClass1();
        Console.WriteLine("\nDisplaying the results of using
the MyBinder binder.\n");
        // Get the method information for MyMethod.
        MethodInfo myMethod = myType.GetMethod("MyMethod",
BindingFlags.Public | BindingFlags.Instance,
            new MyBinder(), new Type[] {typeof(short),
typeof(short)}, null);
        Console.WriteLine(myMethod);
        // Invoke MyMethod.
        myMethod.Invoke(myInstance, BindingFlags.InvokeMethod,
new MyBinder(), new Object[] {(int)32, (int)32},
CultureInfo.CurrentCulture);
    }
}

[C++]
#using <mscorlib.dll>

using namespace System;
using namespace System::Reflection;
using namespace System::Globalization;
using namespace System::Runtime::InteropServices;

public __gc class MyBinder : public Binder
{
public:
    MyBinder() : Binder()
    {
    }
private:
    __gc class BinderState
    {
    public:
        Object* args[];
    };
public:
    FieldInfo* BindToField(
        BindingFlags bindingAttr,
        FieldInfo* match[],
        Object* value,
        CultureInfo* culture)
    {
        if (match == 0)
            throw new ArgumentNullException(S"match");
        // Get a field for which the value parameter can be
converted to the specified field type.
        for (int i = 0; i < match->Length; i++)
            if (ChangeType(value, match[i]->FieldType, culture) != 0)
                return match[i];
        return 0;
    }
    virtual MethodBase* BindToMethod(
        BindingFlags bindingAttr,
        MethodBase* match[],
        Object* (*args)[],
        ParameterModifier modifiers[],
        CultureInfo* culture,
        String* names[],
        [Out] Object** state)
    {
        // Store the arguments to the method in a state Object*.
        BinderState* myBinderState = new BinderState();
        Object* arguments[] = new Object*[(*args)->Length];
        (*args)->CopyTo(arguments, 0);
        myBinderState->args = arguments;
        *state = myBinderState;
        if (match == 0)
            throw new ArgumentNullException();
        // Find a method that has the same parameters as those
of the args parameter.
        for (int i = 0; i < match->Length; i++) {
            // Count the number of parameters that match.
            int count = 0;
            ParameterInfo* parameters[] = match[i]->GetParameters();
            // Go on to the next method if the number of parameters
do not match.
            if ((*args)->Length != parameters->Length)
                continue;
            // Match each of the parameters that the user expects
the method to have.
            for (int j = 0; j < (*args)->Length; j++) {
                // If the names parameter is not 0, then reorder args.
                if (names != 0) {
                    if (names->Length != (*args)->Length)
                        throw new ArgumentException(S"names and
args must have the same number of elements.");
                    for (int k = 0; k < names->Length; k++)
                        if (String::Compare(parameters[j]->Name,
names[k]) == 0)
                            (*args)[j] = myBinderState->args->Item[k];
                }
                // Determine whether the types specified by the user
can be converted to the parameter type.
                if (ChangeType(args[j], parameters[j]->
ParameterType, culture) != 0)
                    count += 1;
                else
                    break;
            }
            // Determine whether the method has been found.
            if (count == (*args)->Length)
                return match[i];
        }
        return 0;
    }
    Object* ChangeType(Object* value, Type* myChangeType,
CultureInfo* culture)
    {
        // Determine whether the value parameter can be converted
to a value of type myType.
        if (CanConvertFrom(value->GetType(), myChangeType))
            // Return the converted Object*.
            return Convert::ChangeType(value, myChangeType);
        else
            // Return 0.
            return 0;
    }
    void ReorderArgumentArray(Object* (*args) __gc[], Object* state)
    {
        // Return the args that had been reordered by BindToMethod.
        (__try_cast<BinderState*>(state))->args->CopyTo((*args), 0);
    }
    MethodBase* SelectMethod(
        BindingFlags bindingAttr,
        MethodBase* match[],
        Type* types[],
        ParameterModifier modifiers[])
    {
        if (match == 0)
            throw new ArgumentNullException(S"match");
        for (int i = 0; i < match->Length; i++) {
            // Count the number of parameters that match.
```

```cpp
            int count = 0;
            ParameterInfo* parameters[] = match[i]->GetParameters();
            // Go on to the next method if the number of parameters        ⌐
do not match.
            if (types->Length != parameters->Length)
                continue;
            // Match each of the parameters that the user expects           ⌐
the method to have.
            for (int j = 0; j < types->Length; j++)
                // Determine whether the types specified by the user        ⌐
can be converted to parameter type.
                if (CanConvertFrom(types[j], parameters[j]->ParameterType))
                    count += 1;
                else
                    break;
            // Determine whether the method has been found.
            if (count == types->Length)
                return match[i];
        }
        return 0;
    }
    PropertyInfo* SelectProperty(
        BindingFlags bindingAttr,
        PropertyInfo* match[],
        Type* returnType,
        Type* indexes[],
        ParameterModifier modifiers[]) {
        if (match == 0)
            throw new ArgumentNullException(S"match");
        for (int i = 0; i < match->Length; i++) {
            // Count the number of indexes that match.
            int count = 0;
            ParameterInfo* parameters[] = match[i]-                         ⌐
>GetIndexParameters();
            // Go on to the next property if the number of                  ⌐
indexes do not match.
            if (indexes->Length != parameters->Length)
                continue;
            // Match each of the indexes that the user expects              ⌐
the property to have.
            for (int j = 0; j < indexes->Length; j++)
                // Determine whether the types specified by the             ⌐
user can be converted to index type.
                if (CanConvertFrom(indexes[j], parameters[j]-              ⌐
>ParameterType))
                    count += 1;
                else
                    break;
            // Determine whether the property has been found.
            if (count == indexes->Length)
                // Determine whether the return type can be                 ⌐
converted to the properties type.
                if (CanConvertFrom(returnType, match[i]->GetType()))
                    return match[i];
                else
                    continue;
        }
        return 0;
    }
    // Determines whether type1 can be converted to type2.                  ⌐
Check only for primitive types.
private:
    bool CanConvertFrom(Type* type1, Type* type2)
    {
        if (type1->IsPrimitive && type2->IsPrimitive)
        {
            TypeCode typeCode1 = Type::GetTypeCode(type1);
            TypeCode typeCode2 = Type::GetTypeCode(type2);
            // If both type1 and type2 have the same type, return true.
            if (typeCode1 == typeCode2)
                return true;
            // Possible conversions from Char follow.
            if (typeCode1 == TypeCode::Char){
                switch(typeCode2) {
                    case TypeCode::UInt16 : return true;
                    case TypeCode::UInt32 : return true;
                    case TypeCode::Int32  : return true;
                    case TypeCode::UInt64 : return true;
                    case TypeCode::Int64  : return true;
                    case TypeCode::Single : return true;
                    case TypeCode::Double : return true;
                    default               : return false;
                }
            }
            // Possible conversions from Byte follow.
            if (typeCode1 == TypeCode::Byte){
                switch(typeCode2) {
                    case TypeCode::Char   : return true;
                    case TypeCode::UInt16 : return true;
                    case TypeCode::Int16  : return true;
                    case TypeCode::UInt32 : return true;
                    case TypeCode::Int32  : return true;
                    case TypeCode::UInt64 : return true;
                    case TypeCode::Int64  : return true;
                    case TypeCode::Single : return true;
                    case TypeCode::Double : return true;
                    default               : return false;
                }
            }
            // Possible conversions from SByte follow.
            if (typeCode1 == TypeCode::SByte){
                switch(typeCode2) {
                    case TypeCode::Int16  : return true;
                    case TypeCode::Int32  : return true;
                    case TypeCode::Int64  : return true;
                    case TypeCode::Single : return true;
                    case TypeCode::Double : return true;
                    default               : return false;
                }
            }
            // Possible conversions from UInt16 follow.
            if (typeCode1 == TypeCode::UInt16){
                switch(typeCode2) {
                    case TypeCode::UInt32 : return true;
                    case TypeCode::Int32  : return true;
                    case TypeCode::UInt64 : return true;
                    case TypeCode::Int64  : return true;
                    case TypeCode::Single : return true;
                    case TypeCode::Double : return true;
                    default               : return false;
                }
            }
            // Possible conversions from Int16 follow.
            if (typeCode1 == TypeCode::Int16){
                switch(typeCode2) {
                    case TypeCode::Int32  : return true;
                    case TypeCode::Int64  : return true;
                    case TypeCode::Single : return true;
                    case TypeCode::Double : return true;
                    default               : return false;
                }
            }
            // Possible conversions from UInt32 follow.
            if (typeCode1 == TypeCode::UInt32){
                switch(typeCode2) {
                    case TypeCode::UInt64 : return true;
                    case TypeCode::Int64  : return true;
                    case TypeCode::Single : return true;
                    case TypeCode::Double : return true;
                    default               : return false;
                }
            }
            // Possible conversions from Int32 follow.
            if (typeCode1 == TypeCode::Int32){
                switch(typeCode2) {
                    case TypeCode::Int64  : return true;
                    case TypeCode::Single : return true;
                    case TypeCode::Double : return true;
                    default               : return false;
                }
            }
            // Possible conversions from UInt64 follow.
```

```
        if (typeCode1 == TypeCode::UInt64){
            switch(typeCode2) {
                case TypeCode::Single : return true;
                case TypeCode::Double : return true;
                default               : return false;
            }
        }
        // Possible conversions from Int64 follow.
        if (typeCode1 == TypeCode::Int64){
            switch(typeCode2) {
                case TypeCode::Single : return true;
                case TypeCode::Double : return true;
                default               : return false;
            }
        }
        // Possible conversions from Single follow.
        if (typeCode1 == TypeCode::Single){
            switch(typeCode2) {
                case TypeCode::Double : return true;
                default               : return false;
            }
        }
    }
    return false;
    }
};

public __gc class MyClass1
{
public:
    short myFieldB;
    int myFieldA;
    void MyMethod(long i, char k)
    {
        Console::WriteLine(S"\nThis is MyMethod(long i, char k)");
    }
    void MyMethod(long i, long j)
    {
        Console::WriteLine(S"\nThis is MyMethod(long i, long j)");
    }
};

void main()
{
    // Get the type of MyClass1.
    Type* myType = __typeof(MyClass1);
    // Get the instance of MyClass1.
    MyClass1* myInstance = new MyClass1();
    Console::WriteLine(S"\nDisplaying the results of using the
MyBinder binder.\n");
    // Get the method information for MyMethod.
    Type* types[] = {__typeof(short), __typeof(short)};
    MethodInfo* myMethod = myType->GetMethod(S"MyMethod",
        static_cast<BindingFlags>( BindingFlags::Public |
BindingFlags::Instance ),
        new MyBinder(), types, 0);
    Console::WriteLine(myMethod);
    // Invoke MyMethod.
    Object* obj[] = {__box(32), __box(32)};
    myMethod->Invoke(myInstance, BindingFlags::InvokeMethod,
 new MyBinder(), obj, CultureInfo::CurrentCulture);
}
```

Requirements

Namespace: System.Reflection

Platforms: Windows 98, Windows NT 4.0,
Windows Millennium Edition, Windows 2000,
Windows XP Home Edition, Windows XP Professional,
Windows .NET Server family,
.NET Compact Framework - Windows CE .NET

Assembly: Mscorlib (in Mscorlib.dll)

Binder Constructor

Initializes a new instance of the **Binder** class.

```
[Visual Basic]
Protected Sub New()
[C#]
protected Binder();
[C++]
protected: Binder();
[JScript]
protected function Binder();
```

Remarks

This constructor is called by derived class constructors to initialize state in this type.

Requirements

Platforms: Windows 98, Windows NT 4.0,
Windows Millennium Edition, Windows 2000,
Windows XP Home Edition, Windows XP Professional,
Windows .NET Server family,
.NET Compact Framework - Windows CE .NET,
Common Language Infrastructure (CLI) Standard

Binder.BindToField Method

Selects a field from the given set of fields, based on the specified criteria.

```
[Visual Basic]
Public MustOverride Function BindToField( _
    ByVal bindingAttr As BindingFlags, _
    ByVal match() As FieldInfo, _
    ByVal value As Object, _
    ByVal culture As CultureInfo _
) As FieldInfo
[C#]
public abstract FieldInfo BindToField(
    BindingFlags bindingAttr,
    FieldInfo[] match,
    object value,
    CultureInfo culture
);
[C++]
public: virtual FieldInfo* BindToField(
    BindingFlags bindingAttr,
    FieldInfo* match[],
    Object* value,
    CultureInfo* culture
) = 0;
[JScript]
public abstract function BindToField(
    bindingAttr : BindingFlags,
    match : FieldInfo[],
    value : Object,
    culture : CultureInfo
) : FieldInfo;
```

Parameters

bindingAttr
    One of the **BindingFlags** enumerators.

match

The set of fields Reflection has determined to be a possible match, typically because they have the correct member name.

value

The field value used to locate a matching field.

culture

An instance of **CultureInfo** used to control the coercion of data types. If *culture* is a null reference (**Nothing** in Visual Basic), the **CultureInfo** for the current thread is used.

Note For example, this parameter is necessary to convert a **String** that represents 1000 to a **Double** value, since 1000 is represented differently by different cultures.

Return Value

A **FieldInfo** object containing the matching field.

Remarks

This method controls the binding provided by Type.InvokeMember().

Requirements

Platforms: Windows 98, Windows NT 4.0, Windows Millennium Edition, Windows 2000, Windows XP Home Edition, Windows XP Professional, Windows .NET Server family, .NET Compact Framework - Windows CE .NET, Common Language Infrastructure (CLI) Standard

Binder.BindToMethod Method

Selects a method to invoke from the given set of methods, based on the actual arguments.

```
[Visual Basic]
Public MustOverride Function BindToMethod( _
   ByVal bindingAttr As BindingFlags, _
   ByVal match() As MethodBase, _
   ByRef args() As Object, _
   ByVal modifiers() As ParameterModifier, _
   ByVal culture As CultureInfo, _
   ByVal names() As String, _
   <Out()> ByRef state As Object _
) As MethodBase
[C#]
public abstract MethodBase BindToMethod(
   BindingFlags bindingAttr,
   MethodBase[] match,
   ref object[] args,
   ParameterModifier[] modifiers,
   CultureInfo culture,
   string[] names,
   out object state
);
[C++]
public: virtual MethodBase* BindToMethod(
   BindingFlags bindingAttr,
   MethodBase* match[],
   Object* args __gc[],
   ParameterModifier modifiers[],
   CultureInfo* culture,
   String* names __gc[],
   [
```

```
   Out
] Object** state
) = 0;
[JScript]
public abstract function BindToMethod(
   bindingAttr : BindingFlags,
   match : MethodBase[],
   args : Object[],
   modifiers : ParameterModifier[],
   culture : CultureInfo,
   names : String[],
   state : Object
) : MethodBase;
```

Parameters

bindingAttr

One of the **BindingFlags** enumerators.

match

The set of methods Reflection has determined to be a possible match, typically because they have the correct member name.

args

The actual arguments passed in. Both the types and values of the arguments can be changed.

modifiers

An array of parameter modifiers that enable binding to work with parameter signatures in which the types have been modified.

culture

An instance of **CultureInfo** used to control the coercion of data types. If *culture* is a null reference (**Nothing** in Visual Basic), the **CultureInfo** for the current thread is used.

Note For example, this parameter is necessary to convert a **String** that represents 1000 to a **Double** value, since 1000 is represented differently by different cultures.

---

names

The method name or names.

state

A binder-provided object that keeps track of argument reordering. The *state* parameter is a cookie that was passed to **BindToMethod** and represents an opaque object. The binder creates this object, and the binder is the sole consumer of this object. If *state* is not a null reference (**Nothing** in Visual Basic) when **BindToMethod** returns, the runtime calls **ReorderArgumentArray**.

Return Value

A **MethodBase** object containing the matching method.

Remarks

The binder allows a client to map the array of arguments back to its original form if the argument array has been manipulated by **BindToMethod**. Use this remap capability to get back by-reference arguments when such arguments are present. However, to get back by-reference arguments, you must be able to ensure that the argument order you used has not changed. When you pass arguments by name, the binder reorders the argument array, and that is what the calling methods see. The state parameter keeps track of argument reordering, thus enabling the binder to reorder the argument array to its original form.

Requirements

Platforms: Windows 98, Windows NT 4.0,
Windows Millennium Edition, Windows 2000,
Windows XP Home Edition, Windows XP Professional,
Windows .NET Server family,
.NET Compact Framework - Windows CE .NET,
Common Language Infrastructure (CLI) Standard

Binder.ChangeType Method

Changes the type of the given **Object** to the given **Type**.

```
[Visual Basic]
Public MustOverride Function ChangeType( _
   ByVal value As Object, _
   ByVal type As Type, _
   ByVal culture As CultureInfo _
) As Object
[C#]
public abstract object ChangeType(
   object value,
   Type type,
   CultureInfo culture
);
[C++]
public: virtual Object* ChangeType(
   Object* value,
   Type* type,
   CultureInfo* culture
) = 0;
[JScript]
public abstract function ChangeType(
   value : Object,
   type : Type,
   culture : CultureInfo
) : Object;
```

Parameters

value
   The value to change into a new **Type**.

type
   The new **Type** that *value* will become.

culture
   An instance of **CultureInfo** used to control the coercion of data
   types. If *culture* is a null reference (**Nothing** in Visual Basic), the
   CultureInfo for the current thread is used.

   Note   For example, this parameter is necessary to convert a
   String that represents 1000 to a **Double** value, since 1000 is
   represented differently by different cultures.

Return Value

An **Object** containing the given value as the new type.

Remarks

Reflection models the accessibility rules of the common type
system. For example, if the caller is in the same assembly, the caller
does not need special permissions for internal members. Otherwise,
the caller needs **ReflectionPermission**. This is consistent with
lookup of members that are protected, private, and so on.

The general principle is that **ChangeType** should perform only
widening coercions, which never lose data. An example of a

widening coercion is coercing a value that is a 32-bit signed integer
to a value that is a 64-bit signed integer. This is distinguished from a
narrowing coercion, which may lose data. An example of a
narrowing coercion is coercing a 64-bit signed integer to a 32-bit
signed integer.

The following table lists the coercions performed by the default
ChangeType.

Source Type	Target Type
Any type	Its base type.
Any type	The interface it implements.
Char	UInt16, UInt32, Int32, UInt64, Int64, Single, Double
Byte	Char, UInt16, Int16, UInt32, Int32, UInt64, Int64, Single, Double
SByte	Int16, Int32, Int64, Single, Double
UInt16	UInt32, Int32, UInt64, Int64, Single, Double
Int16	Int32, Int64, Single, Double
UInt32	UInt64, Int64, Single, Double
Int32	Int64, Single, Double
UInt64	Single, Double
Int64	Single, Double
Single	Double
Non-reference	By-reference.

Requirements

Platforms: Windows 98, Windows NT 4.0,
Windows Millennium Edition, Windows 2000,
Windows XP Home Edition, Windows XP Professional,
Windows .NET Server family,
.NET Compact Framework - Windows CE .NET,
Common Language Infrastructure (CLI) Standard

Binder.ReorderArgumentArray Method

Upon returning from **BindToMethod**, restores the *args* argument to
what it was when it came from **BindToMethod**.

```
[Visual Basic]
Public MustOverride Sub ReorderArgumentArray( _
   ByRef args() As Object, _
   ByVal state As Object _
)
[C#]
public abstract void ReorderArgumentArray(
   ref object[] args,
   object state
);
[C++]
public: virtual void ReorderArgumentArray(
   Object* args __gc[],
   Object* state
) = 0;
[JScript]
public abstract function ReorderArgumentArray(
   args : Object[],
   state : Object
);
```

Parameters

args

> The actual arguments passed in. Both the types and values of the arguments can be changed.

state

> A binder-provided object that keeps track of argument reordering.

Remarks

The common language runtime calls this method if *state* is not a null reference (**Nothing** in Visual Basic) after a return from **BindToMethod**.

Requirements

Platforms: Windows 98, Windows NT 4.0, Windows Millennium Edition, Windows 2000, Windows XP Home Edition, Windows XP Professional, Windows .NET Server family, .NET Compact Framework - Windows CE .NET, Common Language Infrastructure (CLI) Standard

Binder.SelectMethod Method

Selects a method from the given set of methods, based on the argument type.

```
[Visual Basic]
Public MustOverride Function SelectMethod( _
   ByVal bindingAttr As BindingFlags, _
   ByVal match() As MethodBase, _
   ByVal types() As Type, _
   ByVal modifiers() As ParameterModifier _
) As MethodBase
[C#]
public abstract MethodBase SelectMethod(
   BindingFlags bindingAttr,
   MethodBase[] match,
   Type[] types,
   ParameterModifier[] modifiers
);
[C++]
public: virtual MethodBase* SelectMethod(
   BindingFlags bindingAttr,
   MethodBase* match[],
   Type* types[],
   ParameterModifier modifiers[]
) = 0;
[JScript]
public abstract function SelectMethod(
   bindingAttr : BindingFlags,
   match : MethodBase[],
   types : Type[],
   modifiers : ParameterModifier[]
) : MethodBase;
```

Parameters

bindingAttr

> One of the **BindingFlags** enumerators.

match

> The set of methods Reflection has determined to be a possible match, typically because they have the correct member name.

types

> The values used to locate a matching method.

modifiers

> An array of parameter modifiers that enable binding to work with parameter signatures in which the types have been modified.

Return Value

A **MethodBase** object containing the matching method, if found; otherwise, a null reference (**Nothing** in Visual Basic).

Remarks

This method should return a null reference (**Nothing** in Visual Basic) if no method matches the criteria. This method controls the selection provided by the **GetConstructor** and **GetMethod** methods on **Type**.

Requirements

Platforms: Windows 98, Windows NT 4.0, Windows Millennium Edition, Windows 2000, Windows XP Home Edition, Windows XP Professional, Windows .NET Server family, .NET Compact Framework - Windows CE .NET, Common Language Infrastructure (CLI) Standard

Binder.SelectProperty Method

Selects a property from the given set of properties, based on the specified criteria.

```
[Visual Basic]
Public MustOverride Function SelectProperty( _
   ByVal bindingAttr As BindingFlags, _
   ByVal match() As PropertyInfo, _
   ByVal returnType As Type, _
   ByVal indexes() As Type, _
   ByVal modifiers() As ParameterModifier _
) As PropertyInfo
[C#]
public abstract PropertyInfo SelectProperty(
   BindingFlags bindingAttr,
   PropertyInfo[] match,
   Type returnType,
   Type[] indexes,
   ParameterModifier[] modifiers
);
[C++]
public: virtual PropertyInfo* SelectProperty(
   BindingFlags bindingAttr,
   PropertyInfo* match[],
   Type* returnType,
   Type* indexes[],
   ParameterModifier modifiers[]
) = 0;
[JScript]
public abstract function SelectProperty(
   bindingAttr : BindingFlags,
   match : PropertyInfo[],
   returnType : Type,
   indexes : Type[],
   modifiers : ParameterModifier[]
) : PropertyInfo;
```

Parameters

bindingAttr

> One of the **BindingFlags** enumerators.

match

> The set of properties Reflection has determined to be a possible match, typically because they have the correct member name.

returnType

> The return value the matching property must have.

indexes

> The index types of the property being searched for. Used for index properties such as the indexer for a class.

modifiers

> An array of parameter modifiers that enable binding to work with parameter signatures in which the types have been modified.

Return Value

A **PropertyInfo** object containing the matching property.

Remarks

This method controls the selection provided by the **GetProperty** method on **Type**.

Requirements

Platforms: Windows 98, Windows NT 4.0,
Windows Millennium Edition, Windows 2000,
Windows XP Home Edition, Windows XP Professional,
Windows .NET Server family,
.NET Compact Framework - Windows CE .NET,
Common Language Infrastructure (CLI) Standard

BindingFlags Enumeration

Specifies flags that control binding and the way in which the search for members and types is conducted by reflection.

This enumeration has a **FlagsAttribute** attribute that allows a bitwise combination of its member values.

```
[Visual Basic]
<Flags>
<Serializable>
Public Enum BindingFlags
[C#]
[Flags]
[Serializable]
public enum BindingFlags
[C++]
[Flags]
[Serializable]
__value public enum BindingFlags
[JScript]
public
    Flags
    Serializable
enum BindingFlags
```

Remarks

These **BindingFlags** control binding for a great many classes in the **System**, **System.Reflection**, and **System.Runtime** namespaces that invoke, create, get, set, and find members and types.

BindingFlags are used in the following **Type** methods and other places such as **MethodBase.Invoke**:

- **MethodBase.Invoke**
- **GetMembers**
- **GetEvents**
- **InvokeMember**
- **Activator.CreateInstance**
- **GetConstructor**
- **GetConstructors**
- **GetMethod**
- **GetMethods**
- **GetField**
- **GetFields**
- **GetEvent**
- **GetProperty**
- **GetProperties**
- **GetMember**
- **FindMembers**

InvokeMember and **GetMethod** are especially important.

The binding flags are categorized as follows.

Binding Flag	Purpose
DeclaredOnly	Access Control
FlattenHierarchy	Access Control
IgnoreCase	Access Control
IgnoreReturn	Access Control
Instance	Access Control
NonPublic	Access Control

Binding Flag	Purpose
Public	Access Control
Static	Access Control
ExactBinding	Change Type
OptionalParamBinding	Change Type
CreateInstance	Operation Type
GetField	Operation Type
SetField	Operation Type
GetProperty	Operation Type
SetProperty	Operation Type
InvokeMethod	Operation Type
PutDispProperty	Operation Type
PutRefDispProperty	Operation Type

Note You must specify **Instance** or **Static** along with **Public** or **NonPublic** or no members will be returned.

The following table lists the coercions performed by the default **Binder.ChangeType**. This table applies especially to the **ExactBinding** binding flag.

Source Type	Target Type
Any type	Its base type.
Any type	The interface it implements.
Char	**UInt16, UInt32, Int32, UInt64, Int64, Single, Double**
Byte	**Char, UInt16, Int16, UInt32, Int32, UInt64, Int64, Single, Double**
SByte	**Int16, Int32, Int64, Single, Double**
UInt16	**UInt32, Int32, UInt64, Int64, Single, Double**
Int16	**Int32, Int64, Single, Double**
UInt32	**UInt64, Int64, Single, Double**
Int32	**Int64, Single, Double**
UInt64	**Single, Double**
Int64	**Single, Double**
Single	**Double**
Non-reference	By-reference.

Members

Member name	Description	Value
CreateInstance Supported by the .NET Compact Framework.	Specifies that Reflection should create an instance of the specified type. Calls the constructor that matches the given arguments. The supplied member name is ignored. If the type of lookup is not specified, (Instance | Public) will apply. It is not possible to call a type initializer.	512

Member name	Description	Value
DeclaredOnly Supported by the .NET Compact Framework.	Specifies that only members declared at the level of the supplied type's hierarchy should be considered. Inherited members are not considered.	2
Default Supported by the .NET Compact Framework.	Specifies no binding flag.	0
ExactBinding Supported by the .NET Compact Framework.	Specifies that types of the supplied arguments must exactly match the types of the corresponding formal parameters. Reflection throws an exception if the caller supplies a non-null **Binder** object, since that implies that the caller is supplying **BindToXXX** implementations that will pick the appropriate method. Reflection models the accessibility rules of the common type system. For example, if the caller is in the same assembly, the caller does not need special permissions for internal members. Otherwise, the caller needs **ReflectionPermission**. This is consistent with lookup of members that are protected, private, and so on. The general principle is that **ChangeType** should perform only widening coercions, which never lose data. An example of a widening coercion is coercing a value that is a 32-bit signed integer to a value that is a 64-bit signed integer. This is distinguished from a narrowing coercion, which may lose data. An example of a narrowing coercion is coercing a 64-bit signed integer to a 32-bit signed integer. The default binder ignores this flag, while custom binders can implement the semantics of this flag.	65536

Member name	Description	Value
FlattenHierarchy Supported by the .NET Compact Framework.	Specifies that static members up the hierarchy should be returned. Static members include fields, methods, events, and properties. Nested types are not returned.	64
GetField Supported by the .NET Compact Framework.	Specifies that the value of the specified field should be returned.	1024
GetProperty Supported by the .NET Compact Framework.	Specifies that the value of the specified property should be returned.	4096
IgnoreCase Supported by the .NET Compact Framework.	Specifies that the case of the member name should not be considered when binding.	1
IgnoreReturn Supported by the .NET Compact Framework.	Used in COM interop to specify that the return value of the member can be ignored.	16777216
Instance Supported by the .NET Compact Framework.	Specifies that instance members are to be included in the search.	4
InvokeMethod Supported by the .NET Compact Framework.	Specifies that a method is to be invoked. This may not be a constructor or a type initializer.	256
NonPublic Supported by the .NET Compact Framework.	Specifies that non-public members are to be included in the search.	32
OptionalParamBinding Supported by the .NET Compact Framework.	Returns the set of members whose parameter count matches the number of supplied arguments. This binding flag is used for methods with parameters that have default values and methods with variable arguments (varargs). This flag should only be used with **Type.InvokeMember**. Parameters with default values are used only in calls where trailing arguments are omitted. They must be the last arguments.	262144
Public Supported by the .NET Compact Framework.	Specifies that public members are to be included in the search.	16

Member name	Description	Value
PutDispProperty Supported by the .NET Compact Framework.	Specifies that the **PROPPUT** member on a COM object should be invoked. **PROPPUT** specifies a property-setting function that uses a value. Use **PutDispProperty** if a property has both **PROPPUT** and **PROPPUTREF** and you need to distinguish which one is called.	16384
PutRefDispProperty Supported by the .NET Compact Framework.	Specifies that the **PROPPUTREF** member on a COM object should be invoked. **PROPPUTREF** specifies a property-setting function that uses a reference instead of a value. Use **PutRefDispProperty** if a property has both **PROPPUT** and **PROPPUTREF** and you need to distinguish which one is called.	32768
SetField Supported by the .NET Compact Framework.	Specifies that the value of the specified field should be set.	2048
SetProperty Supported by the .NET Compact Framework.	Specifies that the value of the specified property should be set. For COM properties, specifying this binding flag is equivalent to specifying **PutDispProperty** and **PutRefDispProperty**.	8192
Static Supported by the .NET Compact Framework.	Specifies that static members are to be included in the search.	8
SuppressChangeType Supported by the .NET Compact Framework.	Not implemented.	131072

Example

[Visual Basic, C#, C++] The following example demonstrates each binding flag.

```
[Visual Basic]
Imports System
Imports System.Reflection
Imports System.IO

Class EntryPoint
    Overloads Shared Sub Main(ByVal args() As String)
        Invoke.Go()
    End Sub 'Main
End Class 'EntryPoint

Class Invoke
```

```
Public Shared Sub Go()
    ' BindingFlags.InvokeMethod
    ' Call a static method.
    Dim t As Type = GetType(TestClass)

    Console.WriteLine()
    Console.WriteLine("Invoking a static method.")
    Console.WriteLine("------------------------")
    t.InvokeMember("SayHello", BindingFlags.InvokeMethod, _
Nothing, Nothing, New Object() {})

    ' BindingFlags.InvokeMethod
    ' Call an instance method.
    Dim c As New TestClass()
    Console.WriteLine()
    Console.WriteLine("Invoking an instance method.")
    Console.WriteLine("----------------------------")
    c.GetType().InvokeMember("AddUp", _
BindingFlags.InvokeMethod, Nothing, c, New Object() {})
    c.GetType().InvokeMember("AddUp", _
BindingFlags.InvokeMethod, Nothing, c, New Object() {})

    ' BindingFlags.InvokeMethod
    ' Call a method with parameters.
    Dim args() As Object = {100.09, 184.45}
    Dim result As Object
    Console.WriteLine()
    Console.WriteLine("Invoking a method with parameters.")
    Console.WriteLine("----------------------------------")
    result = t.InvokeMember("ComputeSum", BindingFlags.InvokeMethod, _
Nothing, Nothing, args)
    Console.WriteLine("{0} + {1} = {2}", args(0), args(1), result)

    ' BindingFlags.GetField, SetField
    Console.WriteLine()
    Console.WriteLine("Invoking a field (getting and setting.)")
    Console.WriteLine("---------------------------------------")
    ' Get a field value.
    result = t.InvokeMember("Name", BindingFlags.GetField, _
Nothing, c, New Object() {})
    Console.WriteLine("Name == {0}", result)
    ' Set a field.
    t.InvokeMember("Name", BindingFlags.SetField, _
Nothing, c, New Object() {"NewName"})
    result = t.InvokeMember("Name", BindingFlags.GetField, _
Nothing, c, New Object() {})
    Console.WriteLine("Name == {0}", result)

    Console.WriteLine()
    Console.WriteLine("Invoking an indexed property (getting _
and setting.)")
    Console.WriteLine("-------------------------------------------")
    ' BindingFlags.GetProperty
    ' Get an indexed property value.
    Dim index As Integer = 3
    result = t.InvokeMember("Item", _
BindingFlags.GetProperty, Nothing, c, New Object() {index})
    Console.WriteLine("Item[{0}] == {1}", index, result)
    ' BindingFlags.SetProperty
    ' Set an indexed property value.
    index = 3
    t.InvokeMember("Item", BindingFlags.SetProperty, _
Nothing, c, New Object() {index, "NewValue"})
    result = t.InvokeMember("Item", _
BindingFlags.GetProperty, Nothing, c, New Object() {index})
    Console.WriteLine("Item[{0}] == {1}", index, result)

    Console.WriteLine()
    Console.WriteLine("Getting a field or property.")
    Console.WriteLine("----------------------------")
    ' BindingFlags.GetField
    ' Get a field or property.
    result = t.InvokeMember("Name", _
BindingFlags.GetField Or BindingFlags.GetProperty, Nothing, c, _
New Object() {})
```

```vb
        Console.WriteLine("Name == {0}", result)
        ' BindingFlags.GetProperty
        result = t.InvokeMember("Value",                                      ┘
BindingFlags.GetField Or BindingFlags.GetProperty, Nothing,                   ┘
c, New Object() {})
        Console.WriteLine("Value == {0}", result)

        Console.WriteLine()
        Console.WriteLine("Invoking a method with named parameters.")
        Console.WriteLine("------------------------------------")
        ' BindingFlags.InvokeMethod
        ' Call a method using named parameters.
        Dim argValues() As Object = {"Mouse", "Micky"}
        Dim argNames() As [String] = {"lastName", "firstName"}
        t.InvokeMember("PrintName", BindingFlags.InvokeMethod,                 ┘
 Nothing, Nothing, argValues, Nothing, Nothing, argNames)

        Console.WriteLine()
        Console.WriteLine("Invoking a default member of a type.")
        Console.WriteLine("------------------------------------")
        ' BindingFlags.Default
        ' Call the default member of a type.
        Dim t3 As Type = GetType(TestClass2)
        t3.InvokeMember("", BindingFlags.InvokeMethod Or                       ┘
BindingFlags.Default, Nothing, New TestClass2(), New Object() {})

        Console.WriteLine()
        Console.WriteLine("Invoking a method by reference.")
        Console.WriteLine("-------------------------------")
        ' BindingFlags.Static, NonPublic, and Public
        ' Invoking a member by reference.
        Dim m As MethodInfo = t.GetMethod("Swap")
        args = New Object(1) {}
        args(0) = 1
        args(1) = 2
        m.Invoke(New TestClass(), args)
        Console.WriteLine("{0}, {1}", args(0), args(1))
        ' The string is case-sensitive.
        Dim type As Type = type.GetType("System.String")

        ' Check to see if the value is valid. If the object              ┘
is null, the type does not exist.
        If type Is Nothing Then
            Console.WriteLine("Please ensure that you specify             ┘
only valid types in the type field.")
            Console.WriteLine("The type name is case-sensitive.")
            Return
        End If
        ' Declare and populate the arrays to hold the information.
        ' You must declare either NonPublic or Public with              ┘
Static or the search will not work.
        Dim fi As FieldInfo() = type.GetFields                          ┘
 ((BindingFlags.Static Or BindingFlags.NonPublic Or                     ┘
BindingFlags.Public))
        ' BindingFlags.NonPublic
        Dim miNonPublic As MethodInfo() =                               ┘
type.GetMethods((BindingFlags.Static Or BindingFlags.NonPublic))
        ' BindingFlags.Public
        Dim miPublic As MethodInfo() =                                  ┘
type.GetMethods((BindingFlags.Static Or BindingFlags.Public))

        ' Iterate through all the nonpublic methods.
        Dim method As MethodInfo
        For Each method In miNonPublic
            Console.WriteLine(method)
        Next method
        ' Iterate through all the public methods.
        For Each method In miPublic
            Console.WriteLine(method)
        Next method
        ' Iterate through all the fields.
        Dim f As FieldInfo
        For Each f In fi
            Console.WriteLine(f)
        Next f
```

```vb
        ' Call an instance method.
        Dim tc As New TestClass()
        Console.WriteLine()
        Console.WriteLine("Invoking an Instance method.")
        Console.WriteLine("----------------------------")
        tc.GetType().InvokeMember("AddUp", BindingFlags.Public           ┘
Or BindingFlags.Instance Or BindingFlags.CreateInstance,                 ┘
Nothing, tc, New Object() {})

        ' BindingFlags.CreateInstance
        ' Calling and creating an instance method.
        Console.WriteLine()
        Console.WriteLine("Invoking and creating an instance method.")
        Console.WriteLine("-----------------------------------------")
        tc.GetType().InvokeMember("AddUp", BindingFlags.Public           ┘
Or BindingFlags.Instance Or BindingFlags.CreateInstance,                 ┘
Nothing, tc, New Object() {})

        ' BindingFlags.DeclaredOnly
        Dim tc2 As New TestClass()
        Console.WriteLine()
        Console.WriteLine("DeclaredOnly members")
        Console.WriteLine("-----------------------------")
        Dim memInfo As System.Reflection.MemberInfo() =                  ┘
tc2.GetType().GetMembers(BindingFlags.DeclaredOnly)
        Dim i As Integer
        For i = 0 To memInfo.Length - 1
            Console.WriteLine(memInfo(i).Name)
        Next i

        ' BindingFlags.SuppressChangeType
        Dim obj As New TestClass()
        Console.WriteLine()
        Console.WriteLine("Invoking static method - PrintName")
        Console.WriteLine("----------------------------------")
        Dim methInfo As System.Reflection.MethodInfo =                   ┘
obj.GetType().GetMethod("PrintName")
        methInfo.Invoke(obj, BindingFlags.SuppressChangeType            ┘
Or BindingFlags.InvokeMethod, Nothing, New Object() {"Brad",            ┘
"Smith"}, Nothing)

        ' BindingFlags.IgnoreCase
        Console.WriteLine()
        Console.WriteLine("Using IgnoreCase and invoking the            ┘
PrintName method.")
        Console.WriteLine("-------------------------------")
        methInfo = obj.GetType().GetMethod("PrintName")
        methInfo.Invoke(obj, BindingFlags.IgnoreCase Or                 ┘
BindingFlags.InvokeMethod, Nothing, New Object() {"brad",               ┘
"smith"}, Nothing)

        ' BindingFlags.IgnoreReturn
        Console.WriteLine()
        Console.WriteLine("Using IgnoreReturn and invoking              ┘
the PrintName method.")
        Console.WriteLine("--------------------------------------")
        methInfo = obj.GetType().GetMethod("PrintName")
        methInfo.Invoke(obj, BindingFlags.IgnoreReturn Or              ┘
BindingFlags.InvokeMethod, Nothing, New Object() {"Brad",              ┘
"Smith"}, Nothing)

        ' BindingFlags.OptionalParamBinding
        Console.WriteLine()
        Console.WriteLine("Using OptionalParamBinding and               ┘
invoking the PrintName method.")
        Console.WriteLine("-----------------------------------")
        methInfo = obj.GetType().GetMethod("PrintName")
        methInfo.Invoke(obj, BindingFlags.OptionalParamBinding Or
BindingFlags.InvokeMethod, Nothing, New Object() {"Brad",              ┘
 "Smith"}, Nothing)

        ' BindingFlags.ExactBinding
        Console.WriteLine()
        Console.WriteLine("Using ExactBinding and invoking              ┘
the PrintName method.")
```

```vb
        Console.WriteLine("-------------------------------------")
        methInfo = obj.GetType().GetMethod("PrintName")
        methInfo.Invoke(obj, BindingFlags.ExactBinding Or ↵
BindingFlags.InvokeMethod, Nothing, New Object() {"Brad", ↵
"Smith"}, Nothing)

        ' BindingFlags.FlattenHierarchy
        Console.WriteLine()
        Console.WriteLine("Using FlattenHierarchy and invoking ↵
the PrintName method.")
        Console.WriteLine("-------------------------------------")
        methInfo = obj.GetType().GetMethod("PrintName")
        methInfo.Invoke(obj, BindingFlags.FlattenHierarchy Or ↵
BindingFlags.InvokeMethod, Nothing, New Object() {"Brad", ↵
"Smith"}, Nothing)
    End Sub 'Go
End Class 'Invoke

Public Class TestClass
    Public Name As [String]
    Private values() As [Object] = {0, 1, 2, 3, 4, 5, 6, 7, 8, 9}

    Default Public Property Item(ByVal index As Integer) As [Object]
        Get
            Return values(index)
        End Get
        Set(ByVal Value As [Object])
            values(index) = Value
        End Set
    End Property

    Public ReadOnly Property Value() As [Object]
        Get
            Return "the value"
        End Get
    End Property

    Public Sub New()
        Name = "initialName"
    End Sub 'New

    Private methodCalled As Integer = 0

    Public Shared Sub SayHello()
        Console.WriteLine("Hello")
    End Sub 'SayHello

    Public Sub AddUp()
        methodCalled += 1
        Console.WriteLine("AddUp Called {0} times", methodCalled)
    End Sub 'AddUp

    Public Shared Function ComputeSum(ByVal d1 As Double, ByVal ↵
d2 As Double) As Double
        Return d1 + d2
    End Function 'ComputeSum

    Public Shared Sub PrintName(ByVal firstName As [String], ↵
ByVal lastName As [String])
        Console.WriteLine("{0},{1}", lastName, firstName)
    End Sub 'PrintName

    Public Sub PrintTime()
        Console.WriteLine(DateTime.Now)
    End Sub 'PrintTime

    Public Sub Swap(ByRef a As Integer, ByRef b As Integer)
        Dim x As Integer = a
        a = b
        b = x
    End Sub 'Swap
End Class 'TestClass

<DefaultMemberAttribute("PrintTime")> _
Public Class TestClass2
```

```vb
    Public Sub PrintTime()
        Console.WriteLine(DateTime.Now)
    End Sub 'PrintTime
End Class 'TestClass2
```

```csharp
[C#]
using System;
using System.Reflection;
using System.IO;

namespace BindingFlagsSnippet
{
    class EntryPoint
    {
        static void Main(string[] args)
        {
            Invoke.Go();
        }
    }

    class Invoke
    {
        public static void Go()
        {
            // BindingFlags.InvokeMethod
            // Call a static method.
            Type t = typeof (TestClass);

            Console.WriteLine();
            Console.WriteLine("Invoking a static method.");
            Console.WriteLine("-----------------------");
            t.InvokeMember ("SayHello", ↵
BindingFlags.InvokeMethod, null, null, new object [] {});

            // BindingFlags.InvokeMethod
            // Call an instance method.
            TestClass c = new TestClass ();
            Console.WriteLine();
            Console.WriteLine("Invoking an instance method.");
            Console.WriteLine("--------------------------");
            c.GetType().InvokeMember ("AddUp", BindingFlags.InvokeMethod,
null, c, new object [] {});
            c.GetType().InvokeMember ("AddUp", BindingFlags.InvokeMethod,
null, c, new object [] {});

            // BindingFlags.InvokeMethod
            // Call a method with parameters.
            object [] args = new object [] {100.09, 184.45};
            object result;
            Console.WriteLine();
            Console.WriteLine("Invoking a method with parameters.");
            Console.WriteLine("--------------------------------");
            result = t.InvokeMember ("ComputeSum", ↵
BindingFlags.InvokeMethod, null, null, args);
            Console.WriteLine ("{0} + {1} = {2}", args[0], ↵
args[1], result);

            // BindingFlags.GetField, SetField
            Console.WriteLine();
            Console.WriteLine("Invoking a field (getting and ↵
setting.)");
            Console.WriteLine("--------------------------");
            // Get a field value.
            result = t.InvokeMember ("Name", ↵
BindingFlags.GetField, null, c, new object [] {});
            Console.WriteLine ("Name == {0}", result);
            // Set a field.
            t.InvokeMember ("Name", BindingFlags.SetField, ↵
null, c, new object [] {"NewName"});
            result = t.InvokeMember ("Name", ↵
BindingFlags.GetField, null, c, new object [] {});
            Console.WriteLine ("Name == {0}", result);
```

```csharp
        Console.WriteLine();
        Console.WriteLine("Invoking an indexed property    ⌐
(getting and setting.)");
        Console.WriteLine("--------------------------------");
        // BindingFlags.GetProperty
        // Get an indexed property value.
        int  index = 3;
        result = t.InvokeMember ("Item",
BindingFlags.GetProperty, null, c, new object [] {index});
        Console.WriteLine ("Item[{0}] == {1}", index, result);
        // BindingFlags.SetProperty
        // Set an indexed property value.
        index = 3;
        t.InvokeMember ("Item", BindingFlags.SetProperty,    ⌐
null, c, new object [] {index, "NewValue"});
        result = t.InvokeMember ("Item",                     ⌐
BindingFlags.GetProperty , null, c, new object [] {index});
        Console.WriteLine ("Item[{0}] == {1}", index, result);

        Console.WriteLine();
        Console.WriteLine("Getting a field or property.");
        Console.WriteLine("---------------------------");
        // BindingFlags.GetField
        // Get a field or property.
        result = t.InvokeMember ("Name",                     ⌐
BindingFlags.GetField | BindingFlags.GetProperty, null,      ⌐
c, new object [] {});
        Console.WriteLine ("Name == {0}", result);
        // BindingFlags.GetProperty
        result = t.InvokeMember ("Value",                    ⌐
BindingFlags.GetField | BindingFlags.GetProperty, null, c,   ⌐
new object [] {});
        Console.WriteLine ("Value == {0}", result);

        Console.WriteLine();
        Console.WriteLine("Invoking a method with named      ⌐
parameters.");
        Console.WriteLine("---------------------------");
        // BindingFlags.InvokeMethod
        // Call a method using named parameters.
        object[] argValues = new object [] {"Mouse", "Micky"};
        String [] argNames = new String [] {"lastName",      ⌐
"firstName"};
        t.InvokeMember ("PrintName",                         ⌐
BindingFlags.InvokeMethod, null, null, argValues, null, null, ⌐
argNames);

        Console.WriteLine();
        Console.WriteLine("Invoking a default member of a type.");
        Console.WriteLine("---------------------------");
        // BindingFlags.Default
        // Call the default member of a type.
        Type t3 = typeof (TestClass2);
        t3.InvokeMember ("", BindingFlags.InvokeMethod |     ⌐
BindingFlags.Default, null, new TestClass2(), new object [] {});

        // BindingFlags.Static, NonPublic, and Public
        // Invoking a member by reference.
        Console.WriteLine();
        Console.WriteLine("Invoking a method by reference.");
        Console.WriteLine("-----------------------------");
        MethodInfo m = t.GetMethod("Swap");
        args = new object[2];
        args[0] = 1;
        args[1] = 2;
        m.Invoke(new TestClass(),args);
        Console.WriteLine ("{0}, {1}", args[0], args[1]);
        // The string is case-sensitive.
        Type type = Type.GetType("System.String");

        // Check to see if the value is valid. If the object  ⌐
is null, the type does not exist.
        if (type == null)
        {
            Console.WriteLine("Please ensure that you specify  ⌐
```

```csharp
only valid types in the type field.");
            Console.WriteLine("The type name is case-sensitive.");
            return;
        }
        // Declare and populate the arrays to hold the information.
        // You must declare either NonPublic or Public with    ⌐
Static or the search will not work.
        FieldInfo [] fi = type.GetFields (BindingFlags.Static |
            BindingFlags.NonPublic | BindingFlags.Public);
        // BindingFlags.NonPublic
        MethodInfo [] miNonPublic = type.GetMethods           ⌐
(BindingFlags.Static |
            BindingFlags.NonPublic);
        // BindingFlags.Public
        MethodInfo [] miPublic = type.GetMethods              ⌐
(BindingFlags.Static |
            BindingFlags.Public);

        // Iterate through all the nonpublic methods.
        foreach (MethodInfo method in miNonPublic)
        {
            Console.WriteLine(method);
        }
        // Iterate through all the public methods.
        foreach (MethodInfo method in miPublic)
        {
            Console.WriteLine(method);
        }
        // Iterate through all the fields.
        foreach (FieldInfo f in fi)
        {
            Console.WriteLine(f);
        }

        // BindingFlags.Instance
        // Call an instance method.
        TestClass tc = new TestClass ();
        Console.WriteLine();
        Console.WriteLine("Invoking an Instance method.");
        Console.WriteLine("---------------------------");
        tc.GetType().InvokeMember ("AddUp", BindingFlags.Public |
            BindingFlags.Instance | BindingFlags.CreateInstance,
            null, tc, new object [] {});

        // BindingFlags.CreateInstance
        // Calling and creating an instance method.
        Console.WriteLine();
        Console.WriteLine("Invoking and creating an instance    ⌐
method.");
        Console.WriteLine("----------------------");
        tc.GetType().InvokeMember ("AddUp", BindingFlags.Public |
            BindingFlags.Instance | BindingFlags.CreateInstance,
            null, tc, new object [] {});

        // BindingFlags.DeclaredOnly
        TestClass tc2 = new TestClass();
        Console.WriteLine();
        Console.WriteLine("DeclaredOnly members");
        Console.WriteLine("--------------------------------");
        System.Reflection.MemberInfo[] memInfo =
            tc2.GetType().GetMembers(BindingFlags.DeclaredOnly);
        for(int i=0;i<memInfo.Length;i++)
        {
            Console.WriteLine(memInfo[i].Name);
        }

        // BindingFlags.SuppressChangeType
        TestClass obj = new TestClass();
        Console.WriteLine();
        Console.WriteLine("Invoking static method - PrintName");
        Console.WriteLine("---------------------------------");
        System.Reflection.MethodInfo methInfo =
            obj.GetType().GetMethod("PrintName");
        methInfo.Invoke(obj,BindingFlags.SuppressChangeType |
```

```
            BindingFlags.InvokeMethod, null,new object[]
            {"Brad","Smith"},null);

        // BindingFlags.IgnoreCase
        Console.WriteLine();
        Console.WriteLine("Using IgnoreCase and invoking the     ↵
PrintName method.");
        Console.WriteLine("------------------------------------");
        methInfo = obj.GetType().GetMethod("PrintName");
        methInfo.Invoke(obj,BindingFlags.IgnoreCase |
            BindingFlags.InvokeMethod, null,new object[]
            {"brad","smith"},null);

        // BindingFlags.IgnoreReturn
        Console.WriteLine();
        Console.WriteLine("Using IgnoreReturn and              ↵
invoking the PrintName method.");
        Console.WriteLine("-----------------------------");
        methInfo = obj.GetType().GetMethod("PrintName");
        methInfo.Invoke(obj,BindingFlags.IgnoreReturn |
            BindingFlags.InvokeMethod, null,new object[]
            {"Brad","Smith"},null);

        // BindingFlags.OptionalParamBinding
        Console.WriteLine();
        Console.WriteLine("Using OptionalParamBinding          ↵
and invoking the PrintName method.");
        Console.WriteLine("---------------------------");
        methInfo = obj.GetType().GetMethod("PrintName");
        methInfo.Invoke(obj,BindingFlags.OptionalParamBinding |
            BindingFlags.InvokeMethod, null,new object[]
            {"Brad","Smith"},null);

        // BindingFlags.ExactBinding
        Console.WriteLine();
        Console.WriteLine("Using ExactBinding and invoking     ↵
the PrintName method.");
        Console.WriteLine("------------------------------");
        methInfo = obj.GetType().GetMethod("PrintName");
        methInfo.Invoke(obj,BindingFlags.ExactBinding |
            BindingFlags.InvokeMethod, null,new object[]
            {"Brad","Smith"},null);

        // BindingFlags.FlattenHierarchy
        Console.WriteLine();
        Console.WriteLine("Using FlattenHierarchy and          ↵
invoking the PrintName method.");
        Console.WriteLine("------------------------------");
        methInfo = obj.GetType().GetMethod("PrintName");
        methInfo.Invoke(obj,BindingFlags.FlattenHierarchy |
            BindingFlags.InvokeMethod, null,new object[]
            {"Brad","Smith"},null);
    }
}

public class TestClass
{
    public String Name;
    private Object [] values = new Object [] {0, 1,2,3,4,5,6,7,8,9};

    public Object this [int index]
    {
        get
        {
            return values[index];
        }
        set
        {
            values[index] = value;
        }
    }

    public Object Value
    {
        get
```

```
        {
            return "the value";
        }
    }

    public TestClass ()
    {
        Name = "initialName";
    }

    int methodCalled = 0;

    public static void SayHello ()
    {
        Console.WriteLine ("Hello");
    }

    public void AddUp ()
    {
        methodCalled++;
        Console.WriteLine ("AddUp Called {0} times", methodCalled);
    }

    public static double ComputeSum (double d1, double d2)
    {
        return d1 + d2;
    }

    public static void PrintName (String firstName, String lastName)
    {
        Console.WriteLine ("{0},{1}", lastName,firstName);
    }

    public void PrintTime ()
    {
        Console.WriteLine (DateTime.Now);
    }

    public void Swap(ref int a, ref int b)
    {
        int x = a;
        a = b;
        b = x;
    }
}

[DefaultMemberAttribute ("PrintTime")]
public class TestClass2
{
    public void PrintTime ()
    {
        Console.WriteLine (DateTime.Now);
    }
}
}

[C++]
#using <mscorlib.dll>

using namespace System;
using namespace System::Collections;
using namespace System::Reflection;
using namespace System::IO;

//namespace BindingFlagsSnippet {

    public __gc class TestClass
    {
    public:
        String* Name;
    private:
        Object* values[];

    public:
        __property Object* get_Item(int index)
```

```
   {
      return values->Item[index];
   }
   __property void set_Item(int index, Object* value)
   {
      values->Item[index] = value;
   }

   __property Object* get_Value() {
      return S"the value";
   }

   int methodCalled;

   TestClass ()
   {
      Name = S"initialName";
      Object* o[] = {__box(0), __box(1), __box(2),
__box(3), __box(4),
         __box(5), __box(6), __box(7), __box(8), __box(9)};
      values = o;
      methodCalled = 0;
   }

   static void SayHello () {
      Console::WriteLine (S"Hello");
   }

   void AddUp () {
      methodCalled++;
      Console::WriteLine (S"AddUp Called {0} times",
__box(methodCalled));
   }

   static double ComputeSum (double d1, double d2) {
      return d1 + d2;
   }

   static void PrintName (String* firstName, String* lastName) {
      Console::WriteLine (S"{0},{1}", lastName, firstName);
   }

   void PrintTime () {
      Console::WriteLine (__box(DateTime::Now));
   }

   void Swap(int __gc* a, int __gc* b) {
      int x = *a;
      *a = *b;
      *b = x;
   }
};

[DefaultMemberAttribute (S"PrintTime")]
public __gc class TestClass2
{
public:
   void PrintTime () {
      Console::WriteLine (__box(DateTime::Now));
   }
};

class Invoke
{
public:
   static void Go()
   {
      // BindingFlags::InvokeMethod
      // Call a static method.
      Type* t = __typeof (TestClass);

      Console::WriteLine();
      Console::WriteLine(S"Invoking a static method.");
      Console::WriteLine(S"------------------------");
      Object* obj1[];
```

```
      t->InvokeMember (S"SayHello",
BindingFlags::InvokeMethod, 0, 0, obj1);

      // BindingFlags::InvokeMethod
      // Call an instance method.
      TestClass* c = new TestClass ();
      Console::WriteLine();
      Console::WriteLine(S"Invoking an instance method.");
      Console::WriteLine(S"----------------------------");
      c->GetType()->InvokeMember (S"AddUp",
BindingFlags::InvokeMethod, 0, c, obj1);
      c->GetType()->InvokeMember (S"AddUp",
BindingFlags::InvokeMethod, 0, c, obj1);

      // BindingFlags::InvokeMethod
      // Call a method with parameters.
      Object* args[] = {__box(100.09), __box(184.45)};
      Object* result;
      Console::WriteLine();
      Console::WriteLine(S"Invoking a method with parameters.");
      Console::WriteLine(S"----------------------------------");
      result = t->InvokeMember (S"ComputeSum",
BindingFlags::InvokeMethod, 0, 0, args);
      Console::WriteLine (S" {0} + {1} = {2}", args->Item[0],
args->Item[1], result);

      // BindingFlags::GetField, SetField
      Console::WriteLine();
      Console::WriteLine(S"Invoking a field (getting and setting.)");
      Console::WriteLine(S"---------------------------------------");
      // Get a field value.
      result = t->InvokeMember (S"Name",
BindingFlags::GetField, 0, c, obj1);
      Console::WriteLine (S"Name == {0}", result);
      // Set a field.
      Object* obj2[] = {S"NewName"};
      t->InvokeMember (S"Name", BindingFlags::SetField, 0, c, obj2);
      result = t->InvokeMember (S"Name",
BindingFlags::GetField, 0, c, obj1);
      Console::WriteLine (S"Name == {0}", result);

      Console::WriteLine();
      Console::WriteLine(S"Invoking an indexed property
(getting and setting.)");
      Console::WriteLine(S"-----------------------------------");
      // BindingFlags::GetProperty
      // Get an indexed property value.
      int index = 3;
      Object* obj3[] = {__box(index)};
      result = t->InvokeMember (S"Item",
BindingFlags::GetProperty, 0, c, obj3);
      Console::WriteLine (S"Item->Item[ {0}] == {1}",
__box(index), result);
      // BindingFlags::SetProperty
      // Set an indexed property value.
      index = 3;
      Object* obj4[] = {__box(index), S"NewValue"};
      t->InvokeMember (S"Item", BindingFlags::SetProperty,
0, c, obj4);
      result = t->InvokeMember (S"Item",
BindingFlags::GetProperty , 0, c, obj3);
      Console::WriteLine (S"Item->Item[ {0}] == {1}",
__box(index), result);

      Console::WriteLine();
      Console::WriteLine(S"Getting a field or property.");
      Console::WriteLine(S"----------------------------");
      // BindingFlags::GetField
      // Get a field or property.
      result = t->InvokeMember (S"Name",
         static_cast<BindingFlags>(BindingFlags::GetField |
BindingFlags::GetProperty),
         0, c, obj1);
      Console::WriteLine (S"Name == {0}", result);
      // BindingFlags::GetProperty
```

```
        result = t->InvokeMember (S"Value",
            static_cast<BindingFlags>(BindingFlags::GetField |
BindingFlags::GetProperty),
            0, c, obj1);
        Console::WriteLine (S"Value == {0}", result);

        Console::WriteLine();
        Console::WriteLine(S"Invoking a method with named
parameters.");
        Console::WriteLine(S"------------------------");
        // BindingFlags::InvokeMethod
        // Call a method using named parameters.
        Object* argValues[] = {S"Mouse", S"Micky"};
        String* argNames[] = {S"lastName", S"firstName"};
        t->InvokeMember (S"PrintName",
BindingFlags::InvokeMethod, 0, 0, argValues, 0, 0, argNames);

        Console::WriteLine();
        Console::WriteLine(S"Invoking a default member of a type.");
        Console::WriteLine(S"----------------------------------");
        // BindingFlags::Default
        // Call the default member of a type.
        Type* t3 = __typeof (TestClass2);
        t3->InvokeMember (S"",
static_cast<BindingFlags>(BindingFlags::InvokeMethod |
BindingFlags::Default), 0, new TestClass2(), obj1);

        // BindingFlags::Static, NonPublic, and Public
        // Invoking a member by reference.
        Console::WriteLine();
        Console::WriteLine(S"Invoking a method by reference.");
        Console::WriteLine(S"-----------------------------");
        MethodInfo* m = t->GetMethod(S"Swap");
        args = new Object*[2];
        args[0] = __box(1);
        args[1] = __box(2);
        m->Invoke(new TestClass(), args);
        Console::WriteLine (S"{0}, {1}", args->Item[0],
args->Item[1]);
        // The String* is case-sensitive.
        Type* type = Type::GetType(S"System.String");

        // Check to see if the value is valid. If the
Object* is 0, the type does not exist.
        if (type == 0) {
            Console::WriteLine(S"Please ensure that you
specify only valid types in the type field.");
            Console::WriteLine(S"The type name is case-sensitive.");
            return;
        }
        // Declare and populate the arrays to hold the information.
        // You must declare either NonPublic or Public with
Static or the search will not work.
        FieldInfo* fi[] = type->GetFields
(static_cast<BindingFlags>(BindingFlags::Static |
            BindingFlags::NonPublic | BindingFlags::Public));
        // BindingFlags::NonPublic
        MethodInfo* miNonPublic[] = type->GetMethods
 (static_cast<BindingFlags>(BindingFlags::Static |
            BindingFlags::NonPublic));
        // BindingFlags::Public
        MethodInfo* miPublic[] = type->GetMethods
(static_cast<BindingFlags>(BindingFlags::Static |
            BindingFlags::Public));

        // Iterate through all the nonpublic methods.
        IEnumerator* myEnum1 = miNonPublic->GetEnumerator();
        while (myEnum1->MoveNext()) {
            MethodInfo* method = __try_cast<MethodInfo*>
(myEnum1->Current);

            Console::WriteLine(method);
        }
        // Iterate through all the public methods.
        IEnumerator* myEnum2 = miPublic->GetEnumerator();
```

```
        while (myEnum2->MoveNext()) {
            MethodInfo* method = __try_cast<MethodInfo*>
(myEnum2->Current);

            Console::WriteLine(method);
        }
        // Iterate through all the fields.
        IEnumerator* myEnum3 = fi->GetEnumerator();
        while (myEnum3->MoveNext()) {
            FieldInfo* f = __try_cast<FieldInfo*>(myEnum3->Current);

            Console::WriteLine(f);
        }

        // BindingFlags::Instance
        // Call an instance method.
        TestClass* tc = new TestClass ();
        Console::WriteLine();
        Console::WriteLine(S"Invoking an Instance method.");
        Console::WriteLine(S"-------------------------");
        tc->GetType()->InvokeMember (S"AddUp",
static_cast<BindingFlags>(BindingFlags::Public |
            BindingFlags::Instance | BindingFlags::CreateInstance),
            0, tc, obj1);

        // BindingFlags::CreateInstance
        // Calling and creating an instance method.
        Console::WriteLine();
        Console::WriteLine(S"Invoking and creating an
instance method.");
        Console::WriteLine(S"--------------------------");
        tc->GetType()->InvokeMember (S"AddUp",
static_cast<BindingFlags>(BindingFlags::Public |
            BindingFlags::Instance | BindingFlags::CreateInstance),
            0, tc, obj1);

        // BindingFlags::DeclaredOnly
        TestClass* tc2 = new TestClass();
        Console::WriteLine();
        Console::WriteLine(S"DeclaredOnly members");
        Console::WriteLine(S"-----------------------------------");
        System::Reflection::MemberInfo* memInfo[] =
            tc2->GetType()->GetMembers(BindingFlags::DeclaredOnly);
        for (int i=0;i<memInfo->Length;i++) {
            Console::WriteLine(memInfo[i]->Name);
        }

        // BindihgFlags::SuppressChangeType
        TestClass* obj = new TestClass();
        Console::WriteLine();
        Console::WriteLine(S"Invoking static method - PrintName");
        Console::WriteLine(S"-------------------------------");
        System::Reflection::MethodInfo* methInfo =
            obj->GetType()->GetMethod(S"PrintName");
        Object* args1[] = {S"Brad", S"Smith"};
        methInfo->Invoke(obj,
static_cast<BindingFlags>(BindingFlags::SuppressChangeType |
            BindingFlags::InvokeMethod), 0, args1, 0);

        // BindingFlags::IgnoreCase
        Console::WriteLine();
        Console::WriteLine(S"Using IgnoreCase and
invoking the PrintName method.");
        Console::WriteLine(S"---------------------------");
        methInfo = obj->GetType()->GetMethod(S"PrintName");
        Object* args2[] = {S"brad", S"smith"};
        methInfo->Invoke(obj,
static_cast<BindingFlags>(BindingFlags::IgnoreCase |
            BindingFlags::InvokeMethod), 0, args2, 0);

        // BindingFlags::IgnoreReturn
        Console::WriteLine();
        Console::WriteLine(S"Using IgnoreReturn and
invoking the PrintName method.");
        Console::WriteLine(S"--------------------------------");
```

```
      methInfo = obj->GetType()->GetMethod(S"PrintName");
      Object* args3[] = {S"Brad", S"Smith"};
      methInfo->Invoke(obj,
static_cast<BindingFlags>(BindingFlags::IgnoreReturn |
         BindingFlags::InvokeMethod), 0, args3, 0);

      // BindingFlags::OptionalParamBinding
      Console::WriteLine();
      Console::WriteLine(S"Using OptionalParamBinding and         ⌐
 invoking the PrintName method.");
      Console::WriteLine(S"------------------------------");
      methInfo = obj->GetType()->GetMethod(S"PrintName");
      Object* args4[] = {S"Brad", S"Smith"};
      methInfo->Invoke(obj,
static_cast<BindingFlags>(BindingFlags::OptionalParamBinding |
         BindingFlags::InvokeMethod), 0, args4, 0);

      // BindingFlags::ExactBinding
      Console::WriteLine();
      Console::WriteLine(S"Using ExactBinding and               ⌐
 invoking the PrintName method.");
      Console::WriteLine(S"-----------------------------");
      methInfo = obj->GetType()->GetMethod(S"PrintName");
      Object* args5[] = {S"Brad", S"Smith"};
      methInfo->Invoke(obj,
static_cast<BindingFlags>(BindingFlags::ExactBinding |
         BindingFlags::InvokeMethod), 0, args5, 0);

      // BindingFlags::FlattenHierarchy
      Console::WriteLine();
      Console::WriteLine(S"Using FlattenHierarchy and            ⌐
 invoking the PrintName method.");
      Console::WriteLine(S"-------------------------------------");
      methInfo = obj->GetType()->GetMethod(S"PrintName");
      Object* args6[] = {S"Brad", S"Smith"};
      methInfo->Invoke(obj,
static_cast<BindingFlags>(BindingFlags::FlattenHierarchy |
         BindingFlags::InvokeMethod), 0, args6, 0);
   }
 };

 void main()
 {
    String* args[] = Environment::GetCommandLineArgs();
    Invoke::Go();
 }
//}
```

Requirements

Namespace: System.Reflection

Platforms: Windows 98, Windows NT 4.0,
Windows Millennium Edition, Windows 2000,
Windows XP Home Edition, Windows XP Professional,
Windows .NET Server family,
.NET Compact Framework - Windows CE .NET

Assembly: Mscorlib (in Mscorlib.dll)

CallingConventions Enumeration

Defines the valid calling conventions for an enumeration.

This enumeration has a **FlagsAttribute** attribute that allows a bitwise combination of its member values.

```
[Visual Basic]
<Flags>
<Serializable>
Public Enum CallingConventions
[C#]
[Flags]
[Serializable]
public enum CallingConventions
[C++]
[Flags]
[Serializable]
__value public enum CallingConventions
[JScript]
public
   Flags
   Serializable
enum CallingConventions
```

Remarks

The native calling convention is the set of rules governing the order and layout of arguments passed to compiled methods. It also governs how to pass the return value, what registers to use for arguments, and whether the called or the calling method removes arguments from the stack.

Members

Member name	Description	Value
Any Supported by the .NET Compact Framework.	Specifies that either the **Standard** or the **VarArgs** calling convention may be used.	3
ExplicitThis Supported by the .NET Compact Framework.	Specifies that the signature is a function-pointer signature, representing a call to an instance or virtual method (not a static method). If **ExplicitThis** is set, **HasThis** must also be set. The first argument passed to the called method is still a **this** pointer, but the type of the first argument is now unknown. Therefore, a token that describes the type (or class) of the **this** pointer is explicitly stored into its metadata signature.	64
HasThis Supported by the .NET Compact Framework.	Specifies an instance or virtual method (not a static method). At run-time, the called method is passed a pointer to the target object as its first argument (the **this** pointer). The signature stored in metadata does not include the type of this first argument, because the method is known and its owner class can be discovered from metadata.	32

Member name	Description	Value
Standard Supported by the .NET Compact Framework.	Specifies the default calling convention as determined by the common language runtime.	1
VarArgs Supported by the .NET Compact Framework.	Specifies the calling convention for methods with variable arguments.	2

Example

```
[Visual Basic]
Public Class MyClass1
    Public Sub New(ByVal i As Integer)
    End Sub
    Public Shared Sub Main()
        Try
            Dim myType As Type = GetType(MyClass1)
            Dim types(0) As Type
            types(0) = GetType(Integer)
            ' Get the public instance constructor that takes an
integer parameter.
            Dim constructorInfoObj As ConstructorInfo = _
                        myType.GetConstructor
(BindingFlags.Instance Or _
                        BindingFlags.Public, Nothing, _
                        CallingConventions.HasThis, types, Nothing)
            If Not (constructorInfoObj Is Nothing) Then
                Console.WriteLine("The constructor of MyClass1
that " + _
                                "is a public instance method
and takes an " + _
                                "integer as a parameter is: ")
                Console.WriteLine(constructorInfoObj.ToString())
            Else
                Console.WriteLine("The constructor MyClass1 that " + _
                                "is a public instance method
and takes an " + _
                                "integer as a parameter is
not available.")
            End If
        Catch e As ArgumentNullException
            Console.WriteLine("ArgumentNullException: " + e.Message)
        Catch e As ArgumentException
            Console.WriteLine("ArgumentException: " + e.Message)
        Catch e As SecurityException
            Console.WriteLine("SecurityException: " + e.Message)
        Catch e As Exception
            Console.WriteLine("Exception: " + e.Message)
        End Try
    End Sub
End Class

[C#]
using System;
using System.Reflection;
using System.Security;

public class MyClass1
{
    public MyClass1(int i){}
    public static void Main()
    {
        try
        {
            Type  myType = typeof(MyClass1);
            Type[] types = new Type[1];
            types[0] = typeof(int);
            // Get the public instance constructor that
takes an integer parameter.
            ConstructorInfo constructorInfoObj = myType.GetConstructor(
                BindingFlags.Instance | BindingFlags.Public, null,
                CallingConventions.HasThis, types, null);
            if(constructorInfoObj != null)
```

```
                {
                        Console.WriteLine("The constructor of MyClass1
        that is a public " +
                                "instance method and takes an integer as
        a parameter is: ");
                        Console.WriteLine(constructorInfoObj.ToString());
                }
                else
                {
                        Console.WriteLine("The constructor of MyClass1
        that is a public instance " +
                                "method and takes an integer as a parameter
        is not available.");
                }
        }
        catch(ArgumentNullException e)
        {
                Console.WriteLine("ArgumentNullException: " + e.Message);
        }
        catch(ArgumentException e)
        {
                Console.WriteLine("ArgumentException: " + e.Message);
        }
        catch(SecurityException e)
        {
                Console.WriteLine("SecurityException: " + e.Message);
        }
        catch(Exception e)
        {
                Console.WriteLine("Exception: " + e.Message);
        }
    }
}

[C++]
#using <mscorlib.dll>

using namespace System;
using namespace System::Reflection;
using namespace System::Security;

public __gc class MyClass1 {
public:
    MyClass1(int i) {}
}
;
int main() {
    try {
        Type*  myType = __typeof(MyClass1);
        Type* types[] = new Type*[1];
        types->Item[0] = __typeof(int);
        // Get the public instance constructor that takes
    an integer parameter.
        ConstructorInfo*  constructorInfoObj = myType-
>GetConstructor(static_cast<BindingFlags>
(BindingFlags::Instance | BindingFlags::Public), 0,
        CallingConventions::HasThis, types, 0);
        if (constructorInfoObj != 0) {
            Console::WriteLine(S"The constructor of MyClass1
    that is a public instance method and takes an integer as a
    parameter is: ");
            Console::WriteLine(constructorInfoObj);
        } else {
            Console::WriteLine(S"The constructor of MyClass1
    that is a public instance method and takes an integer as a
     parameter is not available.");
        }
    } catch (ArgumentNullException* e) {
        Console::WriteLine(S"ArgumentNullException: {0}", e->Message);
    } catch (ArgumentException* e) {
        Console::WriteLine(S"ArgumentException: {0}", e->Message);
    } catch (SecurityException* e) {
        Console::WriteLine(S"SecurityException: {0}", e->Message);
    } catch (Exception* e) {
        Console::WriteLine(S"Exception: {0}", e->Message);
    }
}
```

Requirements

Namespace: System.Reflection

Platforms: Windows 98, Windows NT 4.0,
Windows Millennium Edition, Windows 2000,
Windows XP Home Edition, Windows XP Professional,
Windows .NET Server family,
.NET Compact Framework - Windows CE .NET

Assembly: Mscorlib (in Mscorlib.dll)

ConstructorInfo Class

Discovers the attributes of a class constructor and provides access to constructor metadata.

System.Object
  System.Reflection.MemberInfo
    System.Reflection.MethodBase
      System.Reflection.ConstructorInfo
        System.Reflection.Emit.ConstructorBuilder

```
[Visual Basic]
<Serializable>
<ClassInterface(ClassInterfaceType.AutoDual)>
MustInherit Public Class ConstructorInfo
   Inherits MethodBase
[C#]
[Serializable]
[ClassInterface(ClassInterfaceType.AutoDual)]
public abstract class ConstructorInfo : MethodBase
[C++]
[Serializable]
[ClassInterface(ClassInterfaceType::AutoDual)]
public __gc __abstract class ConstructorInfo : public MethodBase
[JScript]
public
   Serializable
   ClassInterface(ClassInterfaceType.AutoDual)
abstract class ConstructorInfo extends MethodBase
```

Thread Safety

This type is safe for multithreaded operations.

Remarks

ConstructorInfo is used to discover the attributes of a constructor as well as to invoke a constructor. Objects are created by calling **Invoke** on a **ConstructorInfo** returned by either the **GetConstructors** or **GetConstructor** method of a **Type** object.

Notes to Inheritors: When you inherit from **ConstructorInfo**, you must override the following member: **Invoke(BindingFlags, Binder, Object, CultureInfo)**.

Example

[Visual Basic, C#, C++] The following example uses **ConstructorInfo** with **GetConstructor** and **BindingFlags** to find the constructors that match the specified search criteria.

```
[Visual Basic]
Public Class MyClass1
    Public Sub New(ByVal i As Integer)
    End Sub
    Public Shared Sub Main()
        Try
            Dim myType As Type = GetType(MyClass1)
            Dim types(0) As Type
            types(0) = GetType(Integer)
            ' Get the public instance constructor that takes    ↵
an integer parameter.
            Dim constructorInfoObj As ConstructorInfo = _
                    myType.GetConstructor    ↵
(BindingFlags.Instance Or _
                    BindingFlags.Public, Nothing, _
                    CallingConventions.HasThis, types, Nothing)
            If Not (constructorInfoObj Is Nothing) Then
                Console.WriteLine("The constructor of MyClass1    ↵
that " + _
                                  "is a public instance method    ↵
and takes an " + _
                                  "integer as a parameter is: ")
                Console.WriteLine(constructorInfoObj.ToString())
            Else
                Console.WriteLine("The constructor MyClass1 that " + _
                                  "is a public instance method    ↵
and takes an " + _
                                  "integer as a parameter is not    ↵
available.")
            End If
        Catch e As ArgumentNullException
            Console.WriteLine("ArgumentNullException: " + e.Message)
        Catch e As ArgumentException
            Console.WriteLine("ArgumentException: " + e.Message)
        Catch e As SecurityException
            Console.WriteLine("SecurityException: " + e.Message)
        Catch e As Exception
            Console.WriteLine("Exception: " + e.Message)
        End Try
    End Sub
End Class

[C#]
using System;
using System.Reflection;
using System.Security;

public class MyClass1
{
    public MyClass1(int i){}
    public static void Main()
    {
        try
        {
            Type  myType = typeof(MyClass1);
            Type[] types = new Type[1];
            types[0] = typeof(int);
            // Get the public instance constructor that takes    ↵
an integer parameter.
            ConstructorInfo constructorInfoObj = myType.GetConstructor(
                BindingFlags.Instance | BindingFlags.Public, null,
                CallingConventions.HasThis, types, null);
            if(constructorInfoObj != null)
            {
                Console.WriteLine("The constructor of MyClass1    ↵
that is a public " +
                    "instance method and takes an integer as a    ↵
parameter is: ");
                Console.WriteLine(constructorInfoObj.ToString());
            }
            else
            {
                Console.WriteLine("The constructor of MyClass1    ↵
that is a public instance " +
                    "method and takes an integer as a parameter    ↵
is not available.");
            }
        }
        catch(ArgumentNullException e)
        {
            Console.WriteLine("ArgumentNullException: " + e.Message);
        }
        catch(ArgumentException e)
        {
            Console.WriteLine("ArgumentException: " + e.Message);
        }
        catch(SecurityException e)
        {
            Console.WriteLine("SecurityException: " + e.Message);
        }
        catch(Exception e)
        {
            Console.WriteLine("Exception: " + e.Message);
        }
    }
}
```

```
[C++]
#using <mscorlib.dll>

using namespace System;
using namespace System::Reflection;
using namespace System::Security;

public __gc class MyClass1 {
public:
    MyClass1(int i) {}
}
;
int main() {
    try {
        Type* myType = __typeof(MyClass1);
        Type* types[] = new Type*[1];
        types->Item[0] = __typeof(int);
        // Get the public instance constructor that takes an
integer parameter.
        ConstructorInfo* constructorInfoObj = myType-
>GetConstructor(static_cast<BindingFlags>
(BindingFlags::Instance | BindingFlags::Public), 0,
        CallingConventions::HasThis, types, 0);
        if (constructorInfoObj != 0) {
            Console::WriteLine(S"The constructor of MyClass1 that
is a public instance method and takes an integer as a parameter
is: ");
            Console::WriteLine(constructorInfoObj);
        } else {
            Console::WriteLine(S"The constructor of MyClass1 that
is a public instance method and takes an integer as a parameter
is not available.");
        }
    } catch (ArgumentNullException* e) {
        Console::WriteLine(S"ArgumentNullException: {0}", e->Message);
    } catch (ArgumentException* e) {
        Console::WriteLine(S"ArgumentException: {0}", e->Message);
    } catch (SecurityException* e) {
        Console::WriteLine(S"SecurityException: {0}", e->Message);
    } catch (Exception* e) {
        Console::WriteLine(S"Exception: {0}", e->Message);
    }
}
```

Requirements

Namespace: System.Reflection

Platforms: Windows 98, Windows NT 4.0, Windows Millennium Edition, Windows 2000, Windows XP Home Edition, Windows XP Professional, Windows .NET Server family, .NET Compact Framework - Windows CE .NET

Assembly: Mscorlib (in Mscorlib.dll)

ConstructorInfo Constructor

Initializes a new instance of the **ConstructorInfo** class.

```
[Visual Basic]
Protected Sub New()
[C#]
protected ConstructorInfo();
[C++]
protected: ConstructorInfo();
[JScript]
protected function ConstructorInfo();
```

Requirements

Platforms: Windows 98, Windows NT 4.0, Windows Millennium Edition, Windows 2000, Windows XP Home Edition, Windows XP Professional, Windows .NET Server family, .NET Compact Framework - Windows CE .NET, Common Language Infrastructure (CLI) Standard

.NET Framework Security:

- **ReflectionPermission** to enhance security and performance when invoked late-bound through mechanisms such as **Type.InvokeMember**. Associated enumeration: **ReflectionPermissionFlag.MemberAccess**.

ConstructorInfo.ConstructorName Field

Represents the name of the class constructor method as it is stored in metadata. This name is always ".ctor". This field is read-only.

```
[Visual Basic]
Public Shared ReadOnly ConstructorName As String
[C#]
public static readonly string ConstructorName;
[C++]
public: static String* ConstructorName;
[JScript]
public static var ConstructorName : String;
```

Requirements

Platforms: Windows 98, Windows NT 4.0, Windows Millennium Edition, Windows 2000, Windows XP Home Edition, Windows XP Professional, Windows .NET Server family, .NET Compact Framework - Windows CE .NET, Common Language Infrastructure (CLI) Standard

ConstructorInfo.TypeConstructorName Field

Represents the name of the type constructor method as it is stored in metadata. This name is always ".cctor". This property is read-only.

```
[Visual Basic]
Public Shared ReadOnly TypeConstructorName As String
[C#]
public static readonly string TypeConstructorName;
[C++]
public: static String* TypeConstructorName;
[JScript]
public static var TypeConstructorName : String;
```

Requirements

Platforms: Windows 98, Windows NT 4.0, Windows Millennium Edition, Windows 2000, Windows XP Home Edition, Windows XP Professional, Windows .NET Server family, .NET Compact Framework - Windows CE .NET, Common Language Infrastructure (CLI) Standard

ConstructorInfo.MemberType Property

Specifies the type of member that this instance reflects. This property is read-only.

```
[Visual Basic]
Overrides Public ReadOnly Property MemberType As MemberTypes
[C#]
public override MemberTypes MemberType {get;}
[C++]
public: __property MemberTypes get_MemberType();
[JScript]
public override function get MemberType() : MemberTypes;
```

Property Value

A **MemberTypes** object reflected by this instance.

Example

See related example in the **System.Reflection.ConstructorInfo** class topic.

Requirements

Platforms: Windows 98, Windows NT 4.0, Windows Millennium Edition, Windows 2000, Windows XP Home Edition, Windows XP Professional, Windows .NET Server family, .NET Compact Framework - Windows CE .NET

ConstructorInfo.Invoke Method

Invokes the constructor reflected by this instance.

Overload List

Invokes the constructor reflected by the instance that has the specified parameters, providing default values for the parameters not commonly used.

Supported by the .NET Compact Framework.

> [Visual Basic] **Overloads Public Function Invoke(Object()) As Object**
>
> [C#] **public object Invoke(object[]);**
>
> [C++] **public: Object* Invoke(Object*[]);**
>
> [JScript] **public function Invoke(Object[]) : Object;**

When implemented in a derived class, invokes the constructor reflected by this **ConstructorInfo** with the specified arguments, under the constraints of the specified **Binder**.

Supported by the .NET Compact Framework.

> [Visual Basic] **Overloads Public MustOverride Function Invoke(BindingFlags, Binder, Object(), CultureInfo) As Object**
>
> [C#] **public abstract object Invoke(BindingFlags, Binder, object[], CultureInfo);**
>
> [C++] **public: virtual Object* Invoke(BindingFlags, Binder*, Object[], CultureInfo*) = 0;**
>
> [JScript] **public abstract function Invoke(BindingFlags, Binder, Object[], CultureInfo) : Object;**

Inherited from **MethodBase**.

Supported by the .NET Compact Framework.

> [Visual Basic] **Overloads Public Function Invoke(Object, Object()) As Object**
>
> [C#] **public object Invoke(object, object[]);**
>
> [C++] **public: Object* Invoke(Object*, Object*[]);**
>
> [JScript] **public function Invoke(Object, Object[]) : Object;**

Inherited from **MethodBase**.

Supported by the .NET Compact Framework.

> [Visual Basic] **Overloads Public MustOverride Function Invoke(Object, BindingFlags, Binder, Object(), CultureInfo) As Object**
>
> [C#] **public abstract object Invoke(object, BindingFlags, Binder, object[], CultureInfo);**
>
> [C++] **public: virtual Object* Invoke(Object*, BindingFlags, Binder*, Object*[], CultureInfo*) = 0;**
>
> [JScript] **public abstract function Invoke(Object, BindingFlags, Binder, Object[], CultureInfo) : Object;**

ConstructorInfo.Invoke Method (Object[])

Invokes the constructor reflected by the instance that has the specified parameters, providing default values for the parameters not commonly used.

```
[Visual Basic]
Overloads Public Function Invoke( _
    ByVal parameters() As Object _
) As Object
[C#]
public object Invoke(
    object[] parameters
);
[C++]
public: Object* Invoke(
    Object* parameters __gc[]
);
[JScript]
public function Invoke(
    parameters : Object[]
) : Object;
```

Parameters

parameters

> An array of values that matches the number, order and type (under the constraints of the default binder) of the parameters for this constructor. If this constructor takes no parameters, then use either an array with zero elements or a null reference (**Nothing** in Visual Basic), as in Object[] parameters = new Object[0]. Any object in this array that is not explicitly initialized with a value will contain the default value for that object type. For reference-type elements, this value is a null reference (**Nothing**). For value-type elements, this value is 0, 0.0, or **false**, depending on the specific element type.

Return Value

An instance of the class associated with the constructor.

Exceptions

Exception Type	Condition
MethodAccessException	The attempt to access the constructor fails (that is, the class might be abstract), or the method is a class initializer. -or- The caller does not have permission to execute the constructor.
ArgumentException	The *parameters* array does not contain values that match the types accepted by this constructor.

Exception Type	Condition
TargetInvocationExcep-tion	The invoked constructor throws an exception.
TargetParameterCount-Exception	An incorrect number of parameters was passed.

Remarks

The number, type, and order of elements in the *parameters* array should be identical to the number, type, and order of parameters for the constructor reflected by this instance. Before calling the constructor, **Invoke** ensures that the caller has access permission and verify that the parameters are valid.

Access restrictions are ignored for fully trusted code. That is, private constructors, methods, fields, and properties can be accessed and invoked using reflection whenever the code is fully trusted.

This method is a convenience method for the following overloaded version, using default values. This method cannot be overridden.

Requirements

Platforms: Windows 98, Windows NT 4.0, Windows Millennium Edition, Windows 2000, Windows XP Home Edition, Windows XP Professional, Windows .NET Server family, .NET Compact Framework - Windows CE .NET, Common Language Infrastructure (CLI) Standard

.NET Framework Security:
- **ReflectionPermission** to enhance security and performance when invoked late-bound through mechanisms such as **Type.InvokeMember**. Associated enumeration: **ReflectionPermissionFlag.MemberAccess**.
- **ReflectionPermission** for reflecting non-public objects. Associated enumeration: **ReflectionPermissionFlag.MemberAccess**

ConstructorInfo.Invoke Method (BindingFlags, Binder, Object[], CultureInfo)

When implemented in a derived class, invokes the constructor reflected by this **ConstructorInfo** with the specified arguments, under the constraints of the specified **Binder**.

```
[Visual Basic]
Overloads Public MustOverride Function Invoke( _
    ByVal invokeAttr As BindingFlags, _
    ByVal binder As Binder, _
    ByVal parameters() As Object, _
    ByVal culture As CultureInfo _
) As Object
[C#]
public abstract object Invoke(
    BindingFlags invokeAttr,
    Binder binder,
    object[] parameters,
    CultureInfo culture
);
[C++]
public: virtual Object* Invoke(
    BindingFlags invokeAttr,
    Binder* binder,
    Object* parameters __gc[],
    CultureInfo* culture
) = 0;
```

```
[JScript]
public abstract function Invoke(
    invokeAttr : BindingFlags,
    binder : Binder,
    parameters : Object[],
    culture : CultureInfo
) : Object;
```

Parameters

invokeAttr
> One of the **BindingFlags** values that specifies the type of binding.

binder
> A **Binder** that defines a set of properties and enables the binding, coercion of argument types, and invocation of members using reflection. If *binder* is a null reference (**Nothing** in Visual Basic), then **Binder.DefaultBinding** is used.

parameters
> An array of type **Object** used to match the number, order and type of the parameters for this constructor, under the constraints of *binder*. If this constructor does not require parameters, pass an array with zero elements, as in Object[] parameters = new Object[0]. Any object in this array that is not explicitly initialized with a value will contain the default value for that object type. For reference-type elements, this value is a null reference (**Nothing** in Visual Basic). For value-type elements, this value is 0, 0.0, or **false**, depending on the specific element type.

culture
> A **CultureInfo** used to govern the coercion of types. If this is a null reference (**Nothing** in Visual Basic), the **CultureInfo** for the current thread is used.

Return Value

An instance of the class associated with the constructor.

Exceptions

Exception Type	Condition
MethodAccessException	The attempt to access the constructor fails (that is, the class might be abstract), or the method is a class initializer. -or- The caller does not have permission to execute the constructor.
ArgumentException	The *parameters* array does not contain values that match the types accepted by this constructor, under the constraints of the *binder*.
TargetInvocationExcep-tion	The invoked constructor throws an exception.
TargetParameter-CountException	An incorrect number of parameters was passed.

Remarks

The number, type, and order of elements in the *parameters* array should be identical to the number, type, and order of parameters for the constructor reflected by this instance.

Before calling the constructor, **Invoke** ensures that the caller has access permission and that the parameters are of the correct number, order and type.

Access restrictions are ignored for fully trusted code. That is, private constructors, methods, fields, and properties can be accessed and invoked using reflection whenever the code is fully trusted.

Requirements

Platforms: Windows 98, Windows NT 4.0,
Windows Millennium Edition, Windows 2000,
Windows XP Home Edition, Windows XP Professional,
Windows .NET Server family,
.NET Compact Framework - Windows CE .NET,
Common Language Infrastructure (CLI) Standard

.NET Framework Security:

- **ReflectionPermission** to enhance security and performance when invoked late-bound through mechanisms such as **Type.InvokeMember**. Associated enumeration: **ReflectionPermissionFlag.MemberAccess**.

- **ReflectionPermission** for reflecting non-public objects. Associated enumeration: **ReflectionPermissionFlag.MemberAccess**

CustomAttributeFormat-Exception Class

The exception that is thrown when the binary format of a custom attribute is invalid.

System.Object
  System.Exception
    System.SystemException
      System.FormatException
        System.Reflection.CustomAttributeFormatException

```
[Visual Basic]
<Serializable>
Public Class CustomAttributeFormatException
   Inherits FormatException
[C#]
[Serializable]
public class CustomAttributeFormatException : FormatException
[C++]
[Serializable]
public __gc class CustomAttributeFormatException : public
   FormatException
[JScript]
public
   Serializable
class CustomAttributeFormatException extends FormatException
```

Thread Safety

Any public static (**Shared** in Visual Basic) members of this type are safe for multithreaded operations. Any instance members are not guaranteed to be thread safe.

Remarks

CustomAttributeFormatException uses the HRESULT COR_E_FORMAT which has the value 0x80131537.

CustomAttributeFormatException is thrown if a custom attribute on a data type is formatted incorrectly, possibly because of a bug in the tool used to create the data type.

Requirements

Namespace: System.Reflection

Platforms: Windows 98, Windows NT 4.0, Windows Millennium Edition, Windows 2000, Windows XP Home Edition, Windows XP Professional, Windows .NET Server family, .NET Compact Framework - Windows CE .NET

Assembly: Mscorlib (in Mscorlib.dll)

CustomAttributeFormatException Constructor

Initializes a new instance of the **CustomAttributeFormatException** class.

Overload List

Initializes a new instance of the **CustomAttributeFormatException** class with the default properties.

Supported by the .NET Compact Framework.

  [Visual Basic] **Public Sub New()**

  [C#] **public CustomAttributeFormatException();**
  [C++] **public: CustomAttributeFormatException();**
  [JScript] **public function CustomAttributeFormatException();**

Initializes a new instance of the **CustomAttributeFormatException** class with the specified message.

Supported by the .NET Compact Framework.

  [Visual Basic] **Public Sub New(String)**
  [C#] **public CustomAttributeFormatException(string);**
  [C++] **public: CustomAttributeFormatException(String*);**
  [JScript] **public function CustomAttributeFormatException(String);**

Initializes a new instance of the **CustomAttributeFormatException** class with the specified serialization and context information.

  [Visual Basic] **Protected Sub New(SerializationInfo, StreamingContext)**
  [C#] **protected CustomAttributeFormatException(SerializationInfo, StreamingContext);**
  [C++] **protected: CustomAttributeFormatException(SerializationInfo*, StreamingContext);**
  [JScript] **protected function CustomAttributeFormatException(SerializationInfo, StreamingContext);**

Initializes a new instance of the **CustomAttributeFormatException** class with a specified error message and a reference to the inner exception that is the cause of this exception.

Supported by the .NET Compact Framework.

  [Visual Basic] **Public Sub New(String, Exception)**
  [C#] **public CustomAttributeFormatException(string, Exception);**
  [C++] **public: CustomAttributeFormatException(String*, Exception*);**
  [JScript] **public function CustomAttributeFormatException(String, Exception);**

CustomAttributeFormatException Constructor ()

Initializes a new instance of the **CustomAttributeFormatException** class with the default properties.

```
[Visual Basic]
Public Sub New()
[C#]
public CustomAttributeFormatException();
[C++]
public: CustomAttributeFormatException();
[JScript]
public function CustomAttributeFormatException();
```

Remarks

This constructor initializes an instance of **CustomAttributeFormatException** with an empty message string and the root cause exception set to a null reference (**Nothing** in Visual Basic).

This constructor sets the properties of the **Exception** object as follows:

Property	Value
InnerException	null
Message	The empty string ("").

Requirements

Platforms: Windows 98, Windows NT 4.0,
Windows Millennium Edition, Windows 2000,
Windows XP Home Edition, Windows XP Professional,
Windows .NET Server family,
.NET Compact Framework - Windows CE .NET

CustomAttributeFormatException Constructor (String)

Initializes a new instance of the
CustomAttributeFormatException class with the specified
message.

```
[Visual Basic]
Public Sub New( _
   ByVal message As String _
)
[C#]
public CustomAttributeFormatException(
   string message
);
[C++]
public: CustomAttributeFormatException(
   String* message
);
[JScript]
public function CustomAttributeFormatException(
   message : String
);
```

Parameters

message
    The message that indicates the reason this exception was thrown.

Remarks

This constructor sets the properties of the Exception object as
follows:

Property	Value
InnerException	A null reference (**Nothing** in Visual Basic)

Requirements

Platforms: Windows 98, Windows NT 4.0,
Windows Millennium Edition, Windows 2000,
Windows XP Home Edition, Windows XP Professional,
Windows .NET Server family,
.NET Compact Framework - Windows CE .NET

CustomAttributeFormatException Constructor (SerializationInfo, StreamingContext)

Initializes a new instance of the
CustomAttributeFormatException class with the specified
serialization and context information.

```
[Visual Basic]
Protected Sub New( _
   ByVal info As SerializationInfo, _
   ByVal context As StreamingContext _
)
[C#]
protected CustomAttributeFormatException(
   SerializationInfo info,
   StreamingContext context
);
[C++]
protected: CustomAttributeFormatException(
   SerializationInfo* info,
   StreamingContext context
);
[JScript]
protected function CustomAttributeFormatException(
   info : SerializationInfo,
   context : StreamingContext
);
```

Parameters

info
    The data for serializing or deserializing the custom attribute.
context
    The source and destination for the custom attribute.

Requirements

Platforms: Windows 98, Windows NT 4.0,
Windows Millennium Edition, Windows 2000,
Windows XP Home Edition, Windows XP Professional,
Windows .NET Server family

CustomAttributeFormatException Constructor (String, Exception)

Initializes a new instance of the
CustomAttributeFormatException class with a specified error
message and a reference to the inner exception that is the cause of
this exception.

```
[Visual Basic]
Public Sub New( _
   ByVal message As String, _
   ByVal inner As Exception _
)
[C#]
public CustomAttributeFormatException(
   string message,
   Exception inner
);
[C++]
public: CustomAttributeFormatException(
   String* message,
   Exception* inner
);
[JScript]
public function CustomAttributeFormatException(
   message : String,
   inner : Exception
);
```

Parameters

message
> The error message that explains the reason for the exception.

inner
> The exception that is the cause of the current exception. If the *inner* parameter is not a null reference (**Nothing** in Visual Basic), the current exception is raised in a **catch** block that handles the inner exception.

Remarks

An exception that is thrown as a direct result of a previous exception should include a reference to the previous exception in the **InnerException** property. The **InnerException** property returns the same value that is passed into the constructor, or a null reference (**Nothing** in Visual Basic) if the **InnerException** property does not supply the inner exception value to the constructor.

The following table shows the initial property values for an instance of **CustomAttributeFormatException**.

Property	Value
InnerException	The *inner* exception.
Message	The error message string.

Requirements

Platforms: Windows 98, Windows NT 4.0, Windows Millennium Edition, Windows 2000, Windows XP Home Edition, Windows XP Professional, Windows .NET Server family, .NET Compact Framework - Windows CE .NET

DefaultMemberAttribute Class

Defines the member of a type that is the default member used by **InvokeMember**. The default member is a name given to a type.

System.Object
  System.Attribute
    System.Reflection.DefaultMemberAttribute

```
[Visual Basic]
<AttributeUsage(AttributeTargets.Class Or AttributeTargets.Struct _
   Or AttributeTargets.Interface)>
<Serializable>
NotInheritable Public Class DefaultMemberAttribute
   Inherits Attribute
[C#]
[AttributeUsage(AttributeTargets.Class | AttributeTargets.Struct |
   AttributeTargets.Interface)]
[Serializable]
public sealed class DefaultMemberAttribute : Attribute
[C++]
[AttributeUsage(AttributeTargets::Class | AttributeTargets::Struct
   | AttributeTargets::Interface)]
[Serializable]
public __gc __sealed class DefaultMemberAttribute : public
   Attribute
[JScript]
public
   AttributeUsage(AttributeTargets.Class | AttributeTargets.Struct |
   AttributeTargets.Interface)
   Serializable
class DefaultMemberAttribute extends Attribute
```

Thread Safety

Any public static (**Shared** in Visual Basic) members of this type are safe for multithreaded operations. Any instance members are not guaranteed to be thread safe.

Example

```
[Visual Basic]
Imports System
Imports System.Reflection
Imports System.IO
Imports Microsoft.VisualBasic

<DefaultMemberAttribute("Age")> Public Class [MyClass]

   Public Sub Name(ByVal s As String)
   End Sub 'Name

   Public ReadOnly Property Age() As Integer
      Get
         Return 20
      End Get
   End Property

   Public Shared Sub Main()
      Try
         Dim myType As Type = GetType([MyClass])
         Dim memberInfoArray As MemberInfo() =          ↵
myType.GetDefaultMembers()
         If memberInfoArray.Length > 0 Then
            Dim memberInfoObj As MemberInfo
            For Each memberInfoObj In memberInfoArray
               Console.WriteLine("The default member name  ↵
is: " + memberInfoObj.ToString())
            Next memberInfoObj
         Else
            Console.WriteLine("No default members are available.")
         End If
      Catch e As InvalidOperationException
         Console.WriteLine("InvalidOperationException:       ↵
" + e.Message)
      Catch e As IOException
         Console.WriteLine("IOException: " + e.Message)
      Catch e As Exception
         Console.WriteLine("Exception: " + e.Message)
      End Try
   End Sub 'Main
End Class '[MyClass]

[C#]
using System;
using System.Reflection;
using System.IO;

[DefaultMemberAttribute("Age")]
public class MyClass
{
   public void Name(String s) {}
   public int Age
   {
      get
      {
         return 20;
      }
   }
   public static void Main()
   {
      try
      {
         Type  myType = typeof(MyClass);
         MemberInfo[] memberInfoArray = myType.GetDefaultMembers();
         if (memberInfoArray.Length > 0)
         {
            foreach(MemberInfo memberInfoObj in memberInfoArray)
            {
               Console.WriteLine("The default member name    ↵
is: " + memberInfoObj.ToString());
            }
         }
         else
         {
            Console.WriteLine("No default members are available.");
         }
      }
      catch(InvalidOperationException e)
      {
         Console.WriteLine("InvalidOperationException: " +       ↵
e.Message);
      }
      catch(IOException e)
      {
         Console.WriteLine("IOException: " + e.Message);
      }
      catch(Exception e)
      {
         Console.WriteLine("Exception: " + e.Message);
      }
   }
}

[C++]
#using <mscorlib.dll>

using namespace System;
using namespace System::Reflection;
using namespace System::IO;
```

```
[DefaultMemberAttribute(S"Age")]
public __gc class MyClass {
public:
   void Name(String* s) {}

   __property int get_Age() {
      return 20;
   }
};

int main() {
   try {
      Type*  myType = __typeof(MyClass);
      MemberInfo*  memberInfoArray[] = myType->GetDefaultMembers();
      if (memberInfoArray->Length > 0) {
         System::Collections::IEnumerator* myEnum =
memberInfoArray->GetEnumerator();
         while (myEnum->MoveNext()) {
            MemberInfo* memberInfoObj = __try_cast<MemberInfo*>
(myEnum->Current);

            Console::WriteLine(S"The default member name is:
{0}", memberInfoObj);
         }
      } else {
         Console::WriteLine(S"No default members are available.");
      }
   } catch (InvalidOperationException* e) {
      Console::WriteLine(S"InvalidOperationException: {0}", e-
>Message);
   } catch (IOException* e) {
      Console::WriteLine(S"IOException: {0}", e->Message);
   } catch (Exception* e) {
      Console::WriteLine(S"Exception: {0}", e->Message);
   }
}
```

Requirements

Namespace: System.Reflection

Platforms: Windows 98, Windows NT 4.0,
Windows Millennium Edition, Windows 2000,
Windows XP Home Edition, Windows XP Professional,
Windows .NET Server family,
.NET Compact Framework - Windows CE .NET

Assembly: Mscorlib (in Mscorlib.dll)

DefaultMemberAttribute Constructor

Initializes a new instance of the **DefaultMemberAttribute** class.

```
[Visual Basic]
Public Sub New( _
   ByVal memberName As String _
)
[C#]
public DefaultMemberAttribute(
   string memberName
);
[C++]
public: DefaultMemberAttribute(
   String* memberName
);
[JScript]
public function DefaultMemberAttribute(
   memberName : String
);
```

Parameters

memberName

> A **String** containing the name of the member to invoke. This
> may be a constructor, method, property, or field. A suitable
> invocation attribute must be specified. The default member of a
> class can be invoked by passing an empty **String** as the name of
> the member.
>
> The default member of a type is marked with the **Default-
> MemberAttribute** custom attribute or marked in COM in the
> usual way.

Requirements

Platforms: Windows 98, Windows NT 4.0,
Windows Millennium Edition, Windows 2000,
Windows XP Home Edition, Windows XP Professional,
Windows .NET Server family, .NET Compact Framework -
Windows CE .NET,
Common Language Infrastructure (CLI) Standard

DefaultMemberAttribute.MemberName Property

Gets the name from the attribute.

```
[Visual Basic]
Public ReadOnly Property MemberName As String
[C#]
public string MemberName {get;}
[C++]
public: __property String* get_MemberName();
[JScript]
public function get MemberName() : String;
```

Property Value

A string representing the member name.

Remarks

There is no set accessor because the name must be provided to the
constructor. The name is not optional.

Requirements

Platforms: Windows 98, Windows NT 4.0,
Windows Millennium Edition, Windows 2000,
Windows XP Home Edition, Windows XP Professional,
Windows .NET Server family,
.NET Compact Framework - Windows CE .NET,
Common Language Infrastructure (CLI) Standard

EventAttributes Enumeration

Specifies the attributes of an event.

This enumeration has a **FlagsAttribute** attribute that allows a bitwise combination of its member values.

```
[Visual Basic]
<Flags>
<Serializable>
Public Enum EventAttributes
[C#]
[Flags]
[Serializable]
public enum EventAttributes
[C++]
[Flags]
[Serializable]
__value public enum EventAttributes
[JScript]
public
    Flags
    Serializable
enum EventAttributes
```

Remarks

EventAttributes values may be combined using the bitwise OR operation to get the appropriate combination.

These enums are defined in the corhdr.h file and are a combination of bits and enumerators.

Members

Member name	Description	Value
None Supported by the .NET Compact Framework.	Specifies that the event has no attributes.	0
ReservedMask Supported by the .NET Compact Framework.	Specifies a reserved flag for common language runtime use only.	1024
RTSpecialName Supported by the .NET Compact Framework.	Specifies that the common language runtime should check name encoding.	1024
SpecialName Supported by the .NET Compact Framework.	Specifies that the event is special in a way described by the name.	512

Example

```
[Visual Basic]
Imports System
Imports System.Threading
Imports System.Reflection
Imports System.Reflection.Emit

Public Class MyApplication

    Delegate Sub MyEvent(temp As Object)

    Public Shared Sub Main()
        Dim helloWorldClass As TypeBuilder =
CreateCallee(Thread.GetDomain())

        Dim info As EventInfo() =
helloWorldClass.GetEvents(BindingFlags.Public Or _
```

```
BindingFlags.Instance)
        Console.WriteLine("'HelloWorld' type has following events :")
        Dim i As Integer
        For i = 0 To info.Length - 1
            Console.WriteLine(info(i).Name)
        Next i
    End Sub 'Main

    ' Create the callee transient dynamic assembly.
    Private Shared Function CreateCallee(myDomain As AppDomain) _
As TypeBuilder
        Dim myAssemblyName As New AssemblyName()
        myAssemblyName.Name = "EmittedAssembly"

        ' Create the callee dynamic assembly.
        Dim myAssembly As AssemblyBuilder = myDomain.DefineDynamicAssembly _
                                (myAssemblyName, _
AssemblyBuilderAccess.Run)
        ' Create a dynamic module named "CalleeModule" in the callee
        Dim myModule As ModuleBuilder = _
myAssembly.DefineDynamicModule("EmittedModule")

        ' Define a public class named "HelloWorld" in the assembly.
        Dim helloWorldClass As TypeBuilder = myModule.DefineType _
                                ("HelloWorld", _
TypeAttributes.Public)

        Dim myMethod1 As MethodBuilder = helloWorldClass.DefineMethod _
                ("OnClick", MethodAttributes.Public, _
Nothing, New Type() {GetType(Object)})
        Dim methodIL1 As ILGenerator = myMethod1.GetILGenerator()
        methodIL1.Emit(OpCodes.Ret)
        Dim myMethod2 As MethodBuilder = helloWorldClass.DefineMethod _
                ("OnMouseUp", MethodAttributes.Public, _
Nothing, New Type() {GetType(Object)})
        Dim methodIL2 As ILGenerator = myMethod2.GetILGenerator()
        methodIL2.Emit(OpCodes.Ret)

        ' Create the events.
        Dim myEvent1 As EventBuilder = helloWorldClass.DefineEvent _
                                ("Click", _
EventAttributes.None, GetType(MyEvent))
        myEvent1.SetRaiseMethod(myMethod1)
        Dim myEvent2 As EventBuilder = helloWorldClass.DefineEvent _
                                ("MouseUp", _
EventAttributes.None, GetType(MyEvent))
        myEvent2.SetRaiseMethod(myMethod2)

        helloWorldClass.CreateType()
        Return helloWorldClass
    End Function 'CreateCallee
End Class 'MyApplication

[C#]
using System;
using System.Threading;
using System.Reflection;
using System.Reflection.Emit;

public class MyApplication
{
    public delegate void MyEvent(Object temp);
    public static void Main()
    {
        TypeBuilder helloWorldClass = CreateCallee(Thread.GetDomain());

        EventInfo[] info =
            helloWorldClass.GetEvents(BindingFlags.Public |
BindingFlags.Instance);
        Console.WriteLine("'HelloWorld' type has following events :");
        for(int i=0; i < info.Length; i++)
            Console.WriteLine(info[i].Name);
    }
```

```
    // Create the callee transient dynamic assembly.
    private static TypeBuilder CreateCallee(AppDomain myDomain)
    {
        AssemblyName assemblyName = new AssemblyName();
        assemblyName.Name = "EmittedAssembly";

        // Create the callee dynamic assembly.
        AssemblyBuilder myAssembly =
            myDomain.DefineDynamicAssembly(assemblyName,
AssemblyBuilderAccess.Run);
        // Create a dynamic module named "CalleeModule" in the callee.
        ModuleBuilder myModule =
myAssembly.DefineDynamicModule("EmittedModule");

        // Define a public class named "HelloWorld" in the assembly.
        TypeBuilder helloWorldClass =
            myModule.DefineType("HelloWorld", TypeAttributes.Public);

        MethodBuilder myMethod1 = helloWorldClass.DefineMethod("OnClick",
            MethodAttributes.Public, typeof(void), new
Type[]{typeof(Object)});
        ILGenerator methodIL1 = myMethod1.GetILGenerator();
        methodIL1.Emit(OpCodes.Ret);
        MethodBuilder myMethod2 =
helloWorldClass.DefineMethod("OnMouseUp",
            MethodAttributes.Public, typeof(void), new
Type[]{typeof(Object)});
        ILGenerator methodIL2 = myMethod2.GetILGenerator();
        methodIL2.Emit(OpCodes.Ret);

        // Create the events.
        EventBuilder myEvent1 = helloWorldClass.DefineEvent("Click",
EventAttributes.None,
            typeof(MyEvent));
        myEvent1.SetRaiseMethod(myMethod1);
        EventBuilder myEvent2 = helloWorldClass.DefineEvent
("MouseUp", EventAttributes.None,
            typeof(MyEvent));
        myEvent2.SetRaiseMethod(myMethod2);

        helloWorldClass.CreateType();
        return(helloWorldClass);
    }
}
```

```
[C++]
#using <mscorlib.dll>

using namespace System;
using namespace System::Threading;
using namespace System::Reflection;
using namespace System::Reflection::Emit;

__gc class MyApplication
{
private:
        __delegate void MyEvent(Object* temp);
public:
    // Create the callee transient dynamic assembly.
    static TypeBuilder* CreateCallee(AppDomain* myDomain)
    {
        AssemblyName* assemblyName = new AssemblyName();
        assemblyName->Name = S"EmittedAssembly";

        // Create the callee dynamic assembly.
        AssemblyBuilder* myAssembly = myDomain-
>DefineDynamicAssembly(assemblyName, AssemblyBuilderAccess::Run);

        // Create a dynamic module
        ModuleBuilder* myModule = myAssembly-
>DefineDynamicModule(S"EmittedModule");

        // Define a public class named S"HelloWorld" in the assembly.
        TypeBuilder* helloWorldClass = myModule-
>DefineType(S"HelloWorld", TypeAttributes::Public);
```

```
        Type* typeArray __gc[] = new Type* __gc[1];
        typeArray[0] = __typeof(Object);
        MethodBuilder* myMethod1 = helloWorldClass-
>DefineMethod(S"OnClick", MethodAttributes::Public,
    __typeof(void), typeArray);

        ILGenerator* methodIL1 = myMethod1->GetILGenerator();
        methodIL1->Emit(OpCodes::Ret);
        MethodBuilder* myMethod2 = helloWorldClass-
>DefineMethod(S"OnMouseUp", MethodAttributes::Public,
    __typeof(void), typeArray);
        ILGenerator* methodIL2 = myMethod2->GetILGenerator();
        methodIL2->Emit(OpCodes::Ret);

        // Create the events.
        EventBuilder* myEvent1 = helloWorldClass->
DefineEvent(S"Click", EventAttributes::None,
    __typeof(MyEvent));
        myEvent1->SetRaiseMethod(myMethod1);
        EventBuilder* myEvent2 = helloWorldClass-
>DefineEvent(S"MouseUp", EventAttributes::None,
    __typeof(MyEvent));
        myEvent2->SetRaiseMethod(myMethod2);

        helloWorldClass->CreateType();
        return(helloWorldClass);
    }
};

int main()
{
    TypeBuilder* helloWorldClass =
MyApplication::CreateCallee(Thread::GetDomain());

    EventInfo* info[] = helloWorldClass-
>GetEvents(static_cast<BindingFlags>(BindingFlags::Public |
BindingFlags::Instance));
    Console::WriteLine(S"'HelloWorld' type has following events :");

    for (int i=0; i < info->Length; i++)
        Console::WriteLine(info[i]->Name);

    return 0;
}
```

Requirements

Namespace: System.Reflection

Platforms: Windows 98, Windows NT 4.0,
Windows Millennium Edition, Windows 2000,
Windows XP Home Edition, Windows XP Professional,
Windows .NET Server family,
.NET Compact Framework - Windows CE .NET

Assembly: Mscorlib (in Mscorlib.dll)

EventInfo Class

Discovers the attributes of an event and provides access to event metadata.

System.Object
  System.Reflection.MemberInfo
    System.Reflection.EventInfo

[Visual Basic]
```
<ClassInterface(ClassInterfaceType.AutoDual)>
MustInherit Public Class EventInfo
   Inherits MemberInfo
```
[C#]
```
[ClassInterface(ClassInterfaceType.AutoDual)]
public abstract class EventInfo : MemberInfo
```
[C++]
```
[ClassInterface(ClassInterfaceType::AutoDual)]
public __gc __abstract class EventInfo : public MemberInfo
```
[JScript]
```
public
   ClassInterface(ClassInterfaceType.AutoDual)
abstract class EventInfo extends MemberInfo
```

Thread Safety

This type is safe for multithreaded operations.

Remarks

Events are used with delegates. An event listener instantiates an event-handler delegate that is invoked whenever the event is raised by an event source. In order to connect to the event source, the event listener adds this delegate to the invocation list on the source. When the event is raised, the invoke method of the event-handler delegate is called. Both multicast and single-cast event notifications are supported. The **Add** and **Remove** methods, as well as the event-handler delegate class associated with an event, must be marked in the metadata.

Delegates are object-oriented function pointers. In C or C++, a function pointer is a reference to a method. In contrast to the C or C++ function pointer, a delegate contains two references: a reference to a method and a reference to an object that supports the method. Delegates can invoke a method without knowing the class type that declares or inherits the method. Delegates need only know the return type and parameter list of the method.

The event model works equally well for single-cast and multicast delegates. When the delegate's invoke method is called, only a single object will have a method called on it. A multicast modifier can be applied to a delegate declaration, which allows multiple methods to be called when the invoke method of the delegate is called.

Calling **ICustomAttributeProvider.GetCustomAttributes** on **EventInfo** when the *inherit* parameter of **GetCustomAttributes** is **true** does not walk the type hierarchy. Use **System.Attribute** to inherit custom attributes.

Notes to Inheritors: When you inherit from **EventInfo**, you must override the following members: **GetAddMethod**, **GetRemoveMethod**, and **GetRaiseMethod**.

Example

[Visual Basic]
```
Imports System
Imports System.Reflection
Imports System.Security
Imports Microsoft.VisualBasic
```

```
' Compile this sample using the following command line:
' vbc type_getevent.vb /r:"System.Windows.Forms.dll" /r:"System.dll"

Class MyEventExample
    Public Shared Sub Main()
        Try
            ' Creates a bitmask comprising  BindingFlags.
            Dim myBindingFlags As BindingFlags =
        BindingFlags.Instance Or BindingFlags.Public _
                                                 Or
        BindingFlags.NonPublic
            Dim myTypeBindingFlags As Type =
        GetType(System.Windows.Forms.Button)
            Dim myEventBindingFlags As EventInfo =
        myTypeBindingFlags.GetEvent("Click", myBindingFlags)
            If Not (myEventBindingFlags Is Nothing) Then
                Console.WriteLine("Looking for the Click event
        in the Button class with the specified BindingFlags.")
                Console.WriteLine(myEventBindingFlags.ToString())
            Else
                Console.WriteLine("The Click event is not
        available with the Button class.")
            End If
        Catch e As SecurityException
            Console.WriteLine("An exception occurred.")
            Console.WriteLine("Message :" + e.Message)
        Catch e As ArgumentNullException
            Console.WriteLine("An exception occurred.")
            Console.WriteLine("Message :" + e.Message)
        Catch e As Exception
            Console.WriteLine("The following exception
        was raised : {0}", e.Message)
        End Try
    End Sub 'Main
End Class 'MyEventExample
```

[C#]
```
using System;
using System.Reflection;
using System.Security;

class MyEventExample
{
    public static void Main()
    {
        try
        {

            // Creates a bitmask based on BindingFlags.
            BindingFlags myBindingFlags =
        BindingFlags.Instance | BindingFlags.Public | BindingFlags.NonPublic;
            Type myTypeBindingFlags =
        typeof(System.Windows.Forms.Button);
            EventInfo myEventBindingFlags =
        myTypeBindingFlags.GetEvent("Click", myBindingFlags);
            if(myEventBindingFlags != null)
            {
                Console.WriteLine("Looking for the Click
        event in the Button class with the specified BindingFlags.");
                Console.WriteLine(myEventBindingFlags.ToString());
            }
            else
                Console.WriteLine("The Click event is not
        available with the Button class.");
        }
        catch(SecurityException e)
        {
            Console.WriteLine("An exception occurred.");
            Console.WriteLine("Message :"+e.Message);
        }
        catch(ArgumentNullException e)
        {
            Console.WriteLine("An exception occurred.");
            Console.WriteLine("Message :"+e.Message);
        }
```

```
        catch(Exception e)
        {
             Console.WriteLine("The following exception
was raised : {0}",e.Message);
        }
    }
}

[C++]
#using <mscorlib.dll>
#using <System.dll>
#using <System.Windows.Forms.dll>

using namespace System;
using namespace System::Reflection;
using namespace System::Security;
using namespace System::Windows::Forms;

int main() {
    try {

        // Creates a bitmask based on BindingFlags.
        BindingFlags myBindingFlags =
static_cast<BindingFlags>(BindingFlags::Instance | BindingFlags:
:Public | BindingFlags::NonPublic);
        Type* myTypeBindingFlags =
_typeof(System::Windows::Forms::Button);
        EventInfo* myEventBindingFlags = myTypeBindingFlags-
>GetEvent(S"Click", myBindingFlags);
        if (myEventBindingFlags != 0) {
            Console::WriteLine(S"Looking for the Click event in
the Button class with the specified BindingFlags.");
            Console::WriteLine(myEventBindingFlags);
        } else
            Console::WriteLine(S"The Click event is not available
with the Button class.");
    } catch (SecurityException* e) {
        Console::WriteLine(S"An exception occurred.");
        Console::WriteLine(S"Message : {0}", e->Message);
    } catch (ArgumentNullException* e) {
        Console::WriteLine(S"An exception occurred.");
        Console::WriteLine(S"Message : {0}", e->Message);
    } catch (Exception* e) {
        Console::WriteLine(S"The following exception was raised :
{0}", e->Message);
    }
}
```

Requirements

Namespace: System.Reflection

Platforms: Windows 98, Windows NT 4.0,
Windows Millennium Edition, Windows 2000,
Windows XP Home Edition, Windows XP Professional,
Windows .NET Server family,
.NET Compact Framework - Windows CE .NET

Assembly: Mscorlib (in Mscorlib.dll)

EventInfo Constructor

Initializes a new instance of the **EventInfo** class.

```
[Visual Basic]
Protected Sub New()
[C#]
protected EventInfo();
[C++]
protected: EventInfo();
[JScript]
protected function EventInfo();
```

Requirements

Platforms: Windows 98, Windows NT 4.0,
Windows Millennium Edition, Windows 2000,
Windows XP Home Edition, Windows XP Professional,
Windows .NET Server family,
.NET Compact Framework - Windows CE .NET,
Common Language Infrastructure (CLI) Standard

.NET Framework Security:

- **ReflectionPermission** to enhance security and performance
  when invoked late-bound through mechanisms such as
  Type.InvokeMember. Associated enumeration:
  ReflectionPermissionFlag.MemberAccess.

EventInfo.Attributes Property

Gets the attributes for this event.

```
[Visual Basic]
Public MustOverride ReadOnly Property Attributes As EventAttributes
[C#]
public abstract EventAttributes Attributes {get;}
[C++]
public: __property virtual EventAttributes get_Attributes() = 0;
[JScript]
public abstract function get Attributes() : EventAttributes;
```

Property Value

The read-only attributes for this event.

Remarks

The attributes are returned in a 4-byte integer representing a bitmap
of the attributes set for the event reflected by this instance.

Requirements

Platforms: Windows 98, Windows NT 4.0,
Windows Millennium Edition, Windows 2000,
Windows XP Home Edition, Windows XP Professional,
Windows .NET Server family,
.NET Compact Framework - Windows CE .NET,
Common Language Infrastructure (CLI) Standard

EventInfo.EventHandlerType Property

Gets the **Type** object of the underlying event-handler delegate
associated with this event.

```
[Visual Basic]
Public ReadOnly Property EventHandlerType As Type
[C#]
public Type EventHandlerType {get;}
[C++]
public: __property Type* get_EventHandlerType();
[JScript]
public function get EventHandlerType() : Type;
```

Property Value

A read-only **Type** object representing the delegate event handler.

Exceptions

Exception Type	Condition
SecurityException	The caller does not have the required permission.

Example

```
[Visual Basic]
' The following example uses instances of classes in
' the System.Reflection namespace to discover an event argument type.
Imports System
Imports System.Reflection
Imports Microsoft.VisualBasic

Public Class MainClass
    Delegate Sub MyDelegate(ByVal i As Integer)
    Public Event ev As MyDelegate
    Public Sub Fire(ByVal i As Integer)
        AddHandler ev, AddressOf Me.Fire
    End Sub 'Fire

    Public Shared Sub Main()
        Dim deleg As Type = _
GetType(MainClass).GetEvent("ev").EventHandlerType
        Dim invoke As MethodInfo = deleg.GetMethod("Invoke")
        Dim pars As ParameterInfo() = invoke.GetParameters()
        Dim p As ParameterInfo
        For Each p In pars
            Console.WriteLine(p.ParameterType)
        Next p
    End Sub 'Main
End Class 'MainClass
```

```
[C#]
// The following example uses instances of classes in
// the System.Reflection namespace to discover an event argument type.
using System;
using System.Reflection;

public delegate void MyDelegate(int i);
public class MainClass
{
    public event MyDelegate ev;
    public void Fire(int i)
    {
        ev += new MyDelegate(this.Fire);
    }

    public static void Main()
    {
        Type deleg = typeof(MainClass).GetEvent("ev").EventHandlerType;
        MethodInfo invoke = deleg.GetMethod("Invoke");
        ParameterInfo[] pars = invoke.GetParameters();
        foreach (ParameterInfo p in pars)
        {
            Console.WriteLine(p.ParameterType);
        }
    }
}
```

```
[C++]
// The following example uses instances of classes in
// the System::Reflection namespace to discover an event argument type.
#using <mscorlib.dll>

using namespace System;
using namespace System::Reflection;

public __delegate void MyDelegate(int i);

public __gc class MainClass {
public:
    __event MyDelegate* ev;
public:
    void Fire(int i) {
        ev += new MyDelegate(this, Fire);
    }
};
```

```
int main() {
    Type* deleg = __typeof(MainClass)->GetEvent(S"ev")-
>EventHandlerType;
    MethodInfo* invoke = deleg->GetMethod(S"Invoke");
    ParameterInfo* pars[] = invoke->GetParameters();
    System::Collections::IEnumerator* myEnum = pars->GetEnumerator();
    while (myEnum->MoveNext()) {
        ParameterInfo* p = __try_cast<ParameterInfo*>(myEnum->Current);
        Console::WriteLine(p->ParameterType);
    }
}
```

Requirements

Platforms: Windows 98, Windows NT 4.0, Windows Millennium Edition, Windows 2000, Windows XP Home Edition, Windows XP Professional, Windows .NET Server family, .NET Compact Framework - Windows CE .NET, Common Language Infrastructure (CLI) Standard

.NET Framework Security:

- **ReflectionPermission** for returning properties that are not public. Associated enumeration: **ReflectionPermissionFlag.TypeInformation**

EventInfo.IsMulticast Property

Gets a value indicating whether the event is multicast.

```
[Visual Basic]
Public ReadOnly Property IsMulticast As Boolean
[C#]
public bool IsMulticast {get;}
[C++]
public: __property bool get_IsMulticast();
[JScript]
public function get IsMulticast() : Boolean;
```

Property Value

true if the delegate is an instance of a multicast delegate; otherwise, **false**.

Exceptions

Exception Type	Condition
SecurityException	The caller does not have the required permission.

Requirements

Platforms: Windows 98, Windows NT 4.0, Windows Millennium Edition, Windows 2000, Windows XP Home Edition, Windows XP Professional, Windows .NET Server family, .NET Compact Framework - Windows CE .NET

.NET Framework Security:

- **ReflectionPermission** for returning properties that are not public. Associated enumeration: **ReflectionPermissionFlag.TypeInformation**

EventInfo.IsSpecialName Property

Gets a value indicating whether the **EventInfo** has a name with a special meaning.

```
[Visual Basic]
Public ReadOnly Property IsSpecialName As Boolean
```

```
[C#]
public bool IsSpecialName {get;}
[C++]
public: __property bool get_IsSpecialName();
[JScript]
public function get IsSpecialName() : Boolean;
```

Property Value

true if this event has a special name; otherwise, **false**.

Remarks

This property determines whether the event's name has a special meaning. Names that begin with or contain an underscore character (_), property accessors, and operator overloading methods are examples of names that might require special treatment by some compilers.

Requirements

Platforms: Windows 98, Windows NT 4.0, Windows Millennium Edition, Windows 2000, Windows XP Home Edition, Windows XP Professional, Windows .NET Server family, .NET Compact Framework - Windows CE .NET

EventInfo.MemberType Property

Gets the member type of this event.

```
[Visual Basic]
Overrides Public ReadOnly Property MemberType As MemberTypes
[C#]
public override MemberTypes MemberType {get;}
[C++]
public: __property MemberTypes get_MemberType();
[JScript]
public override function get MemberType() : MemberTypes;
```

Property Value

The **MemberTypes.Event** value. The default is 0x02.

Remarks

Overrides **MemberType**.

Requirements

Platforms: Windows 98, Windows NT 4.0, Windows Millennium Edition, Windows 2000, Windows XP Home Edition, Windows XP Professional, Windows .NET Server family, .NET Compact Framework - Windows CE .NET

EventInfo.AddEventHandler Method

Adds an event handler to an event source.

```
[Visual Basic]
Public Sub AddEventHandler( _
   ByVal target As Object, _
   ByVal handler As Delegate _
)
[C#]
public void AddEventHandler(
   object target,
   Delegate handler
);
```

```
[C++]
public: void AddEventHandler(
   Object* target,
   Delegate* handler
);
[JScript]
public function AddEventHandler(
   target : Object,
   handler : Delegate
);
```

Parameters

target
    The event source.
handler
    Encapsulates a method or methods to be invoked when the event is raised by the target.

Exceptions

Exception Type	Condition
InvalidOperationException	The **MethodInfo** returned by **GetAddMethod** is a null reference (**Nothing** in Visual Basic).
ArgumentException	The handler that was passed in cannot be used.
MethodAccessException	The caller does not have access permission to the member.
TargetException	The *target* parameter is a null reference (**Nothing** in Visual Basic) and the event is not static. -or- The **EventInfo** is not declared on the target.

Remarks

This method attempts to add a delegate to synchronize the event on the target object.Each time the event is raised by the target parameter, the method or methods encapsulated by the handler will be invoked.

Requirements

Platforms: Windows 98, Windows NT 4.0, Windows Millennium Edition, Windows 2000, Windows XP Home Edition, Windows XP Professional, Windows .NET Server family, .NET Compact Framework - Windows CE .NET, Common Language Infrastructure (CLI) Standard

.NET Framework Security:

• **ReflectionPermission** to enhance security and performance when invoked late-bound through mechanisms such as **Type.InvokeMember**. Associated enumeration: **ReflectionPermissionFlag.MemberAccess**.

• **ReflectionPermission** for reflecting non-public objects. Associated enumeration: **ReflectionPermissionFlag.MemberAccess**

EventInfo.GetAddMethod Method

Returns the method used to add an event handler delegate to the event source.

Overload List

Returns the method used to add an event handler delegate to the event source.

Supported by the .NET Compact Framework.

[Visual Basic] **Overloads Public Function GetAddMethod() As MethodInfo**

[C#] **public MethodInfo GetAddMethod();**

[C++] **public: MethodInfo* GetAddMethod();**

[JScript] **public function GetAddMethod() : MethodInfo;**

When overridden in a derived class, retrieves the **MethodInfo** object for the **AddEventHandler** method of the event, specifying whether to return non-public methods.

Supported by the .NET Compact Framework.

[Visual Basic] **Overloads Public MustOverride Function GetAddMethod(Boolean) As MethodInfo**

[C#] **public abstract MethodInfo GetAddMethod(bool);**

[C++] **public: virtual MethodInfo* GetAddMethod(bool) = 0;**

[JScript] **public abstract function GetAddMethod(Boolean) : MethodInfo;**

Example

Typically, the method has the following signature:

```
add_<EventName>(<EventHandlerType> handler)
```

EventInfo.GetAddMethod Method ()

Returns the method used to add an event handler delegate to the event source.

```
[Visual Basic]
Overloads Public Function GetAddMethod() As MethodInfo
[C#]
public MethodInfo GetAddMethod();
[C++]
public: MethodInfo* GetAddMethod();
[JScript]
public function GetAddMethod() : MethodInfo;
```

Return Value

A **MethodInfo** object representing the method used to add an event handler delegate to the event source.

Remarks

GetAddMethod initializes and adds the event subscribe method. The **AddEventHandler** method is used to add an event-handler delegate to the invocation list of an event source.

Example

Typically, the method has the following signature:

```
add_<EventName>(<EventHandlerType> handler)
```

Requirements

Platforms: Windows 98, Windows NT 4.0, Windows Millennium Edition, Windows 2000, Windows XP Home Edition, Windows XP Professional, Windows .NET Server family, .NET Compact Framework - Windows CE .NET, Common Language Infrastructure (CLI) Standard

.NET Framework Security:

- **ReflectionPermission** to enhance security and performance when invoked late-bound through mechanisms such as **Type.InvokeMember**. Associated enumeration: **ReflectionPermissionFlag.MemberAccess**.

EventInfo.GetAddMethod Method (Boolean)

When overridden in a derived class, retrieves the **MethodInfo** object for the **AddEventHandler** method of the event, specifying whether to return non-public methods.

```
[Visual Basic]
Overloads Public MustOverride Function GetAddMethod( _
   ByVal nonOverloads Public As Boolean _
) As MethodInfo
[C#]
public abstract MethodInfo GetAddMethod(
   bool nonPublic
);
[C++]
public: virtual MethodInfo* GetAddMethod(
   bool nonPublic
) = 0;
[JScript]
public abstract function GetAddMethod(
   nonPublic : Boolean
) : MethodInfo;
```

Parameters

nonPublic
   true if non-public methods can be returned; otherwise, **false**.

Return Value

A **MethodInfo** object representing the method used to add an event handler delegate to the event source.

Exceptions

Exception Type	Condition
MethodAccessException	*nonPublic* is **true**, the method used to add an event handler delegate is non-public, and the caller does not have permission to reflect on non-public methods.

Remarks

The **GetAddMethod** initializes and adds the event subscribe method as a Boolean value. The **AddEventHandler** method is used to add an event-handler delegate to the invocation list of an event source.

Example

Typically, the method has the following signature:

```
add_<EventName>(<EventHandlerType> handler)
```

Requirements

Platforms: Windows 98, Windows NT 4.0, Windows Millennium Edition, Windows 2000, Windows XP Home Edition, Windows XP Professional, Windows .NET Server family, .NET Compact Framework - Windows CE .NET, Common Language Infrastructure (CLI) Standard

.NET Framework Security:

- **ReflectionPermission** to enhance security and performance when invoked late-bound through mechanisms such as **Type.InvokeMember**. Associated enumeration: **ReflectionPermissionFlag.MemberAccess**.
- **ReflectionPermission** for returning methods that are not public. Associated enumeration: **ReflectionPermissionFlag.TypeInformation**

EventInfo.GetRaiseMethod Method

Returns the method that is called when the event is raised.

Overload List

Returns the method that is called when the event is raised.

Supported by the .NET Compact Framework.

> [Visual Basic] **Overloads Public Function GetRaiseMethod() As MethodInfo**
>
> [C#] **public MethodInfo GetRaiseMethod();**
>
> [C++] **public: MethodInfo* GetRaiseMethod();**
>
> [JScript] **public function GetRaiseMethod() : MethodInfo;**

When overridden in a derived class, returns the method that is called when the event is raised, specifying whether to return non-public methods.

Supported by the .NET Compact Framework.

> [Visual Basic] **Overloads Public MustOverride Function GetRaiseMethod(Boolean) As MethodInfo**
>
> [C#] **public abstract MethodInfo GetRaiseMethod(bool);**
>
> [C++] **public: virtual MethodInfo* GetRaiseMethod(bool) = 0;**
>
> [JScript] **public abstract function GetRaiseMethod(Boolean) : MethodInfo;**

EventInfo.GetRaiseMethod Method ()

Returns the method that is called when the event is raised.

```
[Visual Basic]
Overloads Public Function GetRaiseMethod() As MethodInfo
[C#]
public MethodInfo GetRaiseMethod();
[C++]
public: MethodInfo* GetRaiseMethod();
[JScript]
public function GetRaiseMethod() : MethodInfo;
```

Return Value

The method that is called when the event is raised.

Requirements

Platforms: Windows 98, Windows NT 4.0, Windows Millennium Edition, Windows 2000, Windows XP Home Edition, Windows XP Professional, Windows .NET Server family, .NET Compact Framework - Windows CE .NET, Common Language Infrastructure (CLI) Standard

.NET Framework Security:

- **ReflectionPermission** to enhance security and performance when invoked late-bound through mechanisms such as **Type.InvokeMember**. Associated enumeration: **ReflectionPermissionFlag.MemberAccess**.

EventInfo.GetRaiseMethod Method (Boolean)

When overridden in a derived class, returns the method that is called when the event is raised, specifying whether to return non-public methods.

```
[Visual Basic]
Overloads Public MustOverride Function GetRaiseMethod( _
   ByVal nonOverloads Public As Boolean _
) As MethodInfo
[C#]
public abstract MethodInfo GetRaiseMethod(
   bool nonPublic
);
[C++]
public: virtual MethodInfo* GetRaiseMethod(
   bool nonPublic
) = 0;
[JScript]
public abstract function GetRaiseMethod(
   nonPublic : Boolean
) : MethodInfo;
```

Parameters

nonPublic
> **true** if non-public methods can be returned; otherwise, **false**.

Return Value

A **MethodInfo** object that was called when the event was raised.

Exceptions

Exception Type	Condition
MethodAccessException	*nonPublic* is **true**, the method used to add an event handler delegate is non-public, and the caller does not have permission to reflect on non-public methods.

Requirements

Platforms: Windows 98, Windows NT 4.0, Windows Millennium Edition, Windows 2000, Windows XP Home Edition, Windows XP Professional, Windows .NET Server family, .NET Compact Framework - Windows CE .NET, Common Language Infrastructure (CLI) Standard

.NET Framework Security:

- **ReflectionPermission** to enhance security and performance when invoked late-bound through mechanisms such as **Type.InvokeMember**. Associated enumeration: **ReflectionPermissionFlag.MemberAccess**.
- **ReflectionPermission** for returning methods that are not public. Associated enumeration: **ReflectionPermissionFlag.TypeInformation**

EventInfo.GetRemoveMethod Method

Returns the method used to remove an event handler delegate from the event source.

Overload List

Returns the method used to remove an event handler delegate from the event source.

Supported by the .NET Compact Framework.

> [Visual Basic] **Overloads Public Function GetRemoveMethod() As MethodInfo**
>
> [C#] **public MethodInfo GetRemoveMethod();**
>
> [C++] **public: MethodInfo* GetRemoveMethod();**
>
> [JScript] **public function GetRemoveMethod() : MethodInfo;**

When overridden in a derived class, retrieves the **MethodInfo** object for removing a method of the event, specifying whether to return non-public methods.

Supported by the .NET Compact Framework.

> [Visual Basic] **Overloads Public MustOverride Function GetRemoveMethod(Boolean) As MethodInfo**
>
> [C#] **public abstract MethodInfo GetRemoveMethod(bool);**
>
> [C++] **public: virtual MethodInfo* GetRemoveMethod(bool) = 0;**
>
> [JScript] **public abstract function GetRemoveMethod(Boolean) : MethodInfo;**

Example

Typically, the method has the following signature:

```
remove_<EventName>(<EventHandlerType> handler)
```

EventInfo.GetRemoveMethod Method ()

Returns the method used to remove an event handler delegate from the event source.

```
[Visual Basic]
Overloads Public Function GetRemoveMethod() As MethodInfo
[C#]
public MethodInfo GetRemoveMethod();
[C++]
public: MethodInfo* GetRemoveMethod();
[JScript]
public function GetRemoveMethod() : MethodInfo;
```

Return Value

A **MethodInfo** object representing the method used to remove an event handler delegate from the event source.

Example

Typically, the method has the following signature:

```
remove_<EventName>(<EventHandlerType> handler)
```

Requirements

Platforms: Windows 98, Windows NT 4.0, Windows Millennium Edition, Windows 2000, Windows XP Home Edition, Windows XP Professional, Windows .NET Server family, .NET Compact Framework - Windows CE .NET, Common Language Infrastructure (CLI) Standard

.NET Framework Security:

- **ReflectionPermission** to enhance security and performance when invoked late-bound through mechanisms such as **Type.InvokeMember**. Associated enumeration: **ReflectionPermissionFlag.MemberAccess.**

EventInfo.GetRemoveMethod Method (Boolean)

When overridden in a derived class, retrieves the **MethodInfo** object for removing a method of the event, specifying whether to return non-public methods.

```
[Visual Basic]
Overloads Public MustOverride Function GetRemoveMethod( _
    ByVal nonOverloads Public As Boolean _
) As MethodInfo
[C#]
public abstract MethodInfo GetRemoveMethod(
    bool nonPublic
);
[C++]
public: virtual MethodInfo* GetRemoveMethod(
    bool nonPublic
) = 0;
[JScript]
public abstract function GetRemoveMethod(
    nonPublic : Boolean
) : MethodInfo;
```

Parameters

nonPublic
> **true** if non-public methods can be returned; otherwise, **false.**

Return Value

A **MethodInfo** object representing the method used to remove an event handler delegate from the event source.

Exceptions

Exception Type	Condition
MethodAccessException	*nonPublic* is **true**, the method used to add an event handler delegate is non-public, and the caller does not have permission to reflect on non-public methods.

Example

Typically, the method has the following signature:

```
remove_<EventName>(<EventHandlerType> handler)
```

Requirements

Platforms: Windows 98, Windows NT 4.0, Windows Millennium Edition, Windows 2000, Windows XP Home Edition, Windows XP Professional, Windows .NET Server family, .NET Compact Framework - Windows CE .NET, Common Language Infrastructure (CLI) Standard

.NET Framework Security:

- **ReflectionPermission** to enhance security and performance when invoked late-bound through mechanisms such as **Type.InvokeMember**. Associated enumeration: **ReflectionPermissionFlag.MemberAccess.**

- **ReflectionPermission** for returning methods that are not public. Associated enumeration: **ReflectionPermissionFlag.TypeInformation**

EventInfo.RemoveEventHandler Method

Removes an event handler from an event source.

```
[Visual Basic]
Public Sub RemoveEventHandler( _
   ByVal target As Object, _
   ByVal handler As Delegate _
)
[C#]
public void RemoveEventHandler(
   object target,
   Delegate handler
);
[C++]
public: void RemoveEventHandler(
   Object* target,
   Delegate* handler
);
[JScript]
public function RemoveEventHandler(
   target : Object,
   handler : Delegate
);
```

Parameters

target
   The event source.
handler
   The delegate to be disassociated from the events raised by target.

Exceptions

Exception Type	Condition
InvalidOperationException	The **MethodInfo** returned by **GetAddMethod** is a null reference (**Nothing** in Visual Basic).
ArgumentException	The handler that was passed in cannot be used.
TargetException	The *target* parameter is a null reference (**Nothing** in Visual Basic) and the event is not static. -or- The **EventInfo** is not declared on the target.
MethodAccessException	The caller does not have access permission to the member.

Remarks

This method attempts to remove the delegate that may synchronize this event on the target object.

When an event is raised by target, the method or methods encapsulated by *handler* will no longer be invoked.

Requirements

Platforms: Windows 98, Windows NT 4.0, Windows Millennium Edition, Windows 2000, Windows XP Home Edition, Windows XP Professional, Windows .NET Server family, .NET Compact Framework - Windows CE .NET, Common Language Infrastructure (CLI) Standard

.NET Framework Security:

- **ReflectionPermission** to enhance security and performance when invoked late-bound through mechanisms such as **Type.InvokeMember**. Associated enumeration: **ReflectionPermissionFlag.MemberAccess**.
- **ReflectionPermission** for reflecting non-public objects. Associated enumeration: **ReflectionPermissionFlag.MemberAccess**

FieldAttributes Enumeration

Specifies flags that describe the attributes of a field.

This enumeration has a **FlagsAttribute** attribute that allows a bitwise combination of its member values.

```
[Visual Basic]
<Flags>
<Serializable>
Public Enum FieldAttributes
[C#]
[Flags]
[Serializable]
public enum FieldAttributes
[C++]
[Flags]
[Serializable]
__value public enum FieldAttributes
[JScript]
public
    Flags
    Serializable
enum FieldAttributes
```

Remarks

FieldAttributes uses the value from **FieldAccessMask** to mask off only the parts of the attribute value that is the accessibility. For example, the following code determines if **Attributes** has the public bit set:

(Attributes & FieldAttributes.FieldAccessMask) == FieldAttributes.Public

To get the **FieldAttributes**, first get the class **Type**. From the **Type**, get the **FieldInfo**. From the **FieldInfo**, get the **Attributes**.

The enumerated value is a number representing the bitwise OR of the attributes implemented on the field.

Members

Member name	Description	Value
Assembly Supported by the .NET Compact Framework.	Specifies that the field is accessible throughout the assembly.	3
FamANDAssem Supported by the .NET Compact Framework.	Specifies that the field is accessible only by subtypes in this assembly.	2
Family Supported by the .NET Compact Framework.	Specifies that the field is accessible only by type and subtypes.	4
FamORAssem Supported by the .NET Compact Framework.	Specifies that the field is accessible by subtypes anywhere, as well as throughout this assembly.	5
FieldAccessMask Supported by the .NET Compact Framework.	Specifies the access level of a given field.	7
HasDefault Supported by the .NET Compact Framework.	Specifies that the field has a default value.	32768

Member name	Description	Value
HasFieldMarshal Supported by the .NET Compact Framework.	Specifies that the field has marshalling information.	4096
HasFieldRVA Supported by the .NET Compact Framework.	Specifies that the field has a Relative Virtual Address (RVA). The RVA is the location of the method body in the current image, as an address relative to the start of the image file in which it is located.	256
InitOnly Supported by the .NET Compact Framework.	Specifies that the field is initialized only, and cannot be written after initialization.	32
Literal Supported by the .NET Compact Framework.	Specifies that the field's value is a compile-time (static or early bound) constant. No set accessor.	64
NotSerialized Supported by the .NET Compact Framework.	Specifies that the field does not have to be serialized when the type is remoted.	128
PinvokeImpl Supported by the .NET Compact Framework.	Reserved for future use.	8192
Private Supported by the .NET Compact Framework.	Specifies that the field is accessible only by the parent type.	1
PrivateScope Supported by the .NET Compact Framework.	Specifies that the field cannot be referenced.	0
Public Supported by the .NET Compact Framework.	Specifies that the field is accessible by any member for whom this scope is visible.	6
ReservedMask Supported by the .NET Compact Framework.	Reserved.	38144
RTSpecialName Supported by the .NET Compact Framework.	Specifies that the common language runtime (metadata internal APIs) should check the name encoding.	1024
SpecialName Supported by the .NET Compact Framework.	Specifies a special method, with the name describing how the method is special.	512
Static Supported by the .NET Compact Framework.	Specifies that the field represents the defined type, or else it is per-instance.	16

Example

[Visual Basic, C#] In this example, three fields are built and the **FieldAttributes** value is displayed when it is exactly defined. A **FieldAttributes** may contain more than one attribute, such as both **Public** and **Literal**, as shown in the third field below.

```
[Visual Basic]
Imports System
Imports System.Reflection
Imports Microsoft.VisualBasic

Module Module1
    Public Class Myfieldattributes
        Public Shared Sub Main()
            Console.WriteLine(ControlChars.Cr +                      ↵
"Reflection.FieldAttributes")
            Dim Myfieldx As New Myfielda()
            Dim Myfieldy As New Myfieldb()
            Dim Myfieldz As New Myfieldc()

            'Get the Type and FieldInfo for each of the three fields.
            Dim MyTypea As Type
'Use GetType on an instance of a type instead of calling Type.GetType.
            MyTypea = Myfieldx.GetType()
            Dim Myfieldinfoa As FieldInfo = MyTypea.GetField       ↵
("m_field", _
                BindingFlags.NonPublic Or BindingFlags.Instance)
            Dim MyTypeb As Type = Myfieldy.GetType()
            Dim Myfieldinfob As FieldInfo = MyTypeb.GetField       ↵
("m_field", _
                BindingFlags.Public Or BindingFlags.Instance)
            Dim MyTypec As Type = Myfieldz.GetType()
            Dim Myfieldinfoc As FieldInfo = MyTypec.GetField       ↵
("m_field", _
                BindingFlags.Public Or BindingFlags.Static)

            'For the first field,
            'get and display the Name, m_field, and attributes.
            Console.Write(ControlChars.CrLf + "{0} - ", MyTypea.Name)
            Console.Write("{0}; ", Myfieldinfoa.GetValue(Myfieldx))
            Dim Myattributesa As FieldAttributes =                 ↵
Myfieldinfoa.Attributes

            'If the FieldAttributes are exactly defined,
            'display them. Otherwise, describe as not defined.
            If [Enum].IsDefined(GetType(FieldAttributes),          ↵
Myattributesa) Then
                Console.Write("it has a {0} field attribute.", _
                    Myattributesa.ToString())
            Else
                Console.Write("it is not exactly defined.")
            End If

            'For the second field,
            'get and display the Name, field, and attributes.
            Console.Write(ControlChars.CrLf + "{0} - ", MyTypeb.Name)
            Console.Write("{0}; ", Myfieldinfob.GetValue(Myfieldy))
            Dim Myattributesb As FieldAttributes =                 ↵
Myfieldinfob.Attributes

            'If the FieldAttributes are exactly defined,
            'display them; otherwise, describe as not defined.
            If [Enum].IsDefined(GetType(FieldAttributes),          ↵
Myattributesb) Then
                Console.Write("it has a {0} field attribute.", _
                    Myattributesb.ToString())
            Else
                Console.Write("it is not exactly defined.")
            End If

            'For the third field,
            'get and display the Name, field, and attributes.
            Console.Write(ControlChars.CrLf + "{0} - ", MyTypec.Name)
            Console.Write("{0}; ", Myfieldinfoc.GetValue(Myfieldz))
            Dim Myattributesc As FieldAttributes =                 ↵
Myfieldinfoc.Attributes

            'If the FieldAttributes are exactly defined,
            'display them; otherwise, describe as not defined.
            If [Enum].IsDefined(GetType(FieldAttributes),          ↵
Myattributesc) Then
                Console.Write("it has a {0} field attribute.", _
                    Myattributesc.ToString())
            Else
                Console.Write("it is not exactly defined.")
            End If
        End Sub
    End Class
    'Make three fields
    'The first field is private
    Public Class Myfielda
        Private m_field As String = "A private field"

        Public Property Field() As String
            Get
                Return m_field
            End Get
            Set(ByVal Value As String)
                If m_field <> Value Then
                    m_field = Value + "---"
                End If
            End Set
        End Property
    End Class

    'The second field is public.
    Public Class Myfieldb
        Public m_field As String = "B public field"

        Public Property Field() As String
            Get
                Return m_field
            End Get
            Set(ByVal Value As String)
                If m_field <> Value Then
                    m_field = Value
                End If
            End Set
        End Property
    End Class

    'The third field is public and literal, which is not     ↵
exactly defined.
    Public Class Myfieldc
        Public Const m_field As String = "C constant field"

        Public ReadOnly Property Field() As String
            Get
                Return m_field
            End Get
        End Property
    End Class
End Module

[C#]
using System;
using System.Reflection;

//Make three fields
//The first field is private
public class Myfielda
{
    private string field = "A private field";
    public string Field{
        get{return field;}
        set{if(field!=value) {field=value + "---";}}
    }
}
//The second field is public
public class Myfieldb
{
    public string field = "B public field";
    public string Field{
        get{return field;}
        set{if(field!=value) {field=value;}}
    }
}
```

```
//The third field is public and literal, which is not exactly defined.
public class Myfieldc
{
    public const string field = "C constant field";
    public string Field{
        get{return field;}
    }
}
public class Myfieldattributes
{
    public static int Main()
    {
        Console.WriteLine ("\nReflection.FieldAttributes");
        Myfielda Myfielda = new Myfielda();
        Myfieldb Myfieldb = new Myfieldb();
        Myfieldc Myfieldc = new Myfieldc();

        //Get the Type and FieldInfo for each of the three fields
        Type MyTypea = Type.GetType("Myfielda");
        FieldInfo Myfieldinfoa = MyTypea.GetField("field",
            BindingFlags.NonPublic | BindingFlags.Instance);
        Type MyTypeb = Type.GetType("Myfieldb");
        FieldInfo Myfieldinfob = MyTypeb.GetField("field",
            BindingFlags.Public | BindingFlags.Instance);
        Type MyTypec = Type.GetType("Myfieldc");
        FieldInfo Myfieldinfoc = MyTypec.GetField("field",
            BindingFlags.Public | BindingFlags.Static);

        //For the first field;
        //Get and Display the Name, field, and attributes
        Console.Write ("\n{0} - ", MyTypea.FullName);
        Console.Write ("{0}; ", Myfieldinfoa.GetValue(Myfielda));
        FieldAttributes Myattributesa = Myfieldinfoa.Attributes;

        //If the FieldAttributes is exactly defined,
        // print it out, otherwise say it is not defined
        if (Enum.IsDefined(typeof(FieldAttributes),
            Myattributesa))
            Console.Write ("it has a {0} field attribute.",
                Myattributesa.ToString());
        else
            Console.Write ("it is not exactly defined.");

        //For the second field;
        //Get and Display the Name, field, and attributes
        Console.Write ("\n{0} - ", MyTypeb.FullName);
        Console.Write ("{0}; ", Myfieldinfob.GetValue(Myfieldb));
        FieldAttributes Myattributesb = Myfieldinfob.Attributes;

        //If the FieldAttributes is exactly defined,
        // print it out, otherwise say it is not defined
        if (Enum.IsDefined(typeof(FieldAttributes),
            Myattributesb))
            Console.Write ("it has a {0} field attribute.",
                Myattributesb.ToString());
        else
            Console.Write ("it is not exactly defined.");

        //For the third field;
        //Get and Display the Name, field, and attributes
        Console.Write ("\n{0} - ", MyTypec.FullName);
        Console.Write ("{0}; ", Myfieldinfoc.GetValue(Myfieldc));
        FieldAttributes Myattributesc = Myfieldinfoc.Attributes;

        //If the FieldAttributes is exactly defined,
        // print it out, otherwise say it is not defined
        if (Enum.IsDefined(typeof(FieldAttributes),
            Myattributesc))
            Console.Write ("it has a {0} field attribute.",
                Myattributesc.ToString());
        else
            Console.Write ("it is not exactly defined.");

        return 0;
    }
}
```

[Visual Basic, C#] This code produces the following output:

[Visual Basic, C#] Reflection.FieldAttributes

[Visual Basic, C#] Myfielda - A private field; it has a Private field attribute.

[Visual Basic, C#] Myfieldb - B public field; it has a Public field attribute.

[Visual Basic, C#] Myfieldc - C constant field; it is not exactly defined.

Requirements

Namespace: System.Reflection

Platforms: Windows 98, Windows NT 4.0, Windows Millennium Edition, Windows 2000, Windows XP Home Edition, Windows XP Professional, Windows .NET Server family, .NET Compact Framework - Windows CE .NET

Assembly: Mscorlib (in Mscorlib.dll)

FieldInfo Class

Discovers the attributes of a field and provides access to field metadata.

System.Object
   System.Reflection.MemberInfo
      System.Reflection.FieldInfo
         System.Reflection.Emit.FieldBuilder

```
[Visual Basic]
<Serializable>
<ClassInterface(ClassInterfaceType.AutoDual)>
MustInherit Public Class FieldInfo
    Inherits MemberInfo
[C#]
[Serializable]
[ClassInterface(ClassInterfaceType.AutoDual)]
public abstract class FieldInfo : MemberInfo
[C++]
[Serializable]
[ClassInterface(ClassInterfaceType::AutoDual)]
public __gc __abstract class FieldInfo : public MemberInfo
[JScript]
public
    Serializable
    ClassInterface(ClassInterfaceType.AutoDual)
abstract class FieldInfo extends MemberInfo
```

Thread Safety

Any public static (**Shared** in Visual Basic) members of this type are safe for multithreaded operations. Any instance members are not guaranteed to be thread safe.

Remarks

The field information is obtained from metadata. **FieldInfo** does not have a public constructor. **FieldInfo** objects are obtained by calling either the **GetFields** or **GetField** method of a **Type** object.

Fields are variables defined in the class. **FieldInfo** provides access to the metadata for a field within a class and provides dynamic set and get functionality for the field. The class is not loaded into memory until invoke or get is called on the object.

Notes to Inheritors: When you inherit from **FieldInfo**, you must override the following members: **GetValue** and **SetValue**.

Example

[Visual Basic, C#, C++] The following example uses **Type.GetFields** to get the field-related information from FieldInfoClass, and then displays field attributes.

```
[Visual Basic]
Imports System
Imports System.Reflection
Imports Microsoft.VisualBasic

Public Class FieldInfoClass
    Public myField1 As Integer = 0
    Protected myField2 As String = Nothing

    Public Shared Sub Main()
        Dim myFieldInfo() As FieldInfo
        Dim myType As Type = GetType(FieldInfoClass)
        ' Get the type and fields of FieldInfoClass.
        myFieldInfo = myType.GetFields(BindingFlags.NonPublic Or _
                      BindingFlags.Instance Or BindingFlags.Public)
        Console.WriteLine(ControlChars.NewLine & "The fields of " & _
                      "FieldInfoClass class are " &
ControlChars.NewLine)
        ' Display the field information of FieldInfoClass.
        Dim i As Integer
        For i = 0 To myFieldInfo.Length - 1
            Console.WriteLine(ControlChars.NewLine + "Name
: {0}", myFieldInfo(i).Name)
            Console.WriteLine("Declaring Type  : {0}",
myFieldInfo(i).DeclaringType)
            Console.WriteLine("IsPublic        : {0}",
myFieldInfo(i).IsPublic)
            Console.WriteLine("MemberType      : {0}",
myFieldInfo(i).MemberType)
            Console.WriteLine("FieldType       : {0}",
myFieldInfo(i).FieldType)
            Console.WriteLine("IsFamily        : {0}",
myFieldInfo(i).IsFamily)
        Next i
    End Sub
End Class
```

```
[C#]
using System;
using System.Reflection;

public class FieldInfoClass
{
    public int myField1 = 0;
    protected string myField2 = null;
    public static void Main()
    {
        FieldInfo[] myFieldInfo;
        Type myType = typeof(FieldInfoClass);
        // Get the type and fields of FieldInfoClass.
        myFieldInfo = myType.GetFields(BindingFlags.NonPublic
| BindingFlags.Instance
            | BindingFlags.Public);
        Console.WriteLine("\nThe fields of " +
            "FieldInfoClass are \n");
        // Display the field information of FieldInfoClass.
        for(int i = 0; i < myFieldInfo.Length; i++)
        {
            Console.WriteLine("\nName          : {0}",
myFieldInfo[i].Name);
            Console.WriteLine("Declaring Type : {0}",
myFieldInfo[i].DeclaringType);
            Console.WriteLine("IsPublic        : {0}",
myFieldInfo[i].IsPublic);
            Console.WriteLine("MemberType      : {0}",
myFieldInfo[i].MemberType);
            Console.WriteLine("FieldType       : {0}",
myFieldInfo[i].FieldType);
            Console.WriteLine("IsFamily        : {0}",
myFieldInfo[i].IsFamily);
        }
    }
}
```

```
[C++]
#using <mscorlib.dll>

using namespace System;
using namespace System::Reflection;

public __gc class FieldInfoClass
{
public:
    int myField1;
protected:
    String* myField2;
};
```

```
void main()
{
    FieldInfo* myFieldInfo[];
    Type* myType = __typeof(FieldInfoClass);
    // Get the type and fields of FieldInfoClass.
    myFieldInfo = myType-
>GetFields(static_cast<BindingFlags>(BindingFlags::NonPublic |    ⏎
BindingFlags::Instance
        | BindingFlags::Public));
    Console::WriteLine(S"\nThe fields of FieldInfoClass are \n");
    // Display the field information of FieldInfoClass.
    for (int i = 0; i < myFieldInfo->Length; i++) {
        Console::WriteLine(S"\nName         : {0}",         ⏎
myFieldInfo[i]->Name);
        Console::WriteLine(S"Declaring Type : {0}",         ⏎
myFieldInfo[i]->DeclaringType);
        Console::WriteLine(S"IsPublic       {0}",           ⏎
__box(myFieldInfo[i]->IsPublic));
        Console::WriteLine(S"MemberType    : {0}",          ⏎
__box(myFieldInfo[i]->MemberType));
        Console::WriteLine(S"FieldType     : {0}",          ⏎
myFieldInfo[i]->FieldType);
        Console::WriteLine(S"IsFamily      : {0}",          ⏎
__box(myFieldInfo[i]->IsFamily));
    }
}
```

Requirements

Namespace: System.Reflection

Platforms: Windows 98, Windows NT 4.0,
Windows Millennium Edition, Windows 2000,
Windows XP Home Edition, Windows XP Professional,
Windows .NET Server family,
.NET Compact Framework - Windows CE .NET

Assembly: Mscorlib (in Mscorlib.dll)

FieldInfo Constructor

Initializes a new instance of the **FieldInfo** class.

```
[Visual Basic]
Protected Sub New()
[C#]
protected FieldInfo();
[C++]
protected: FieldInfo();
[JScript]
protected function FieldInfo();
```

Requirements

Platforms: Windows 98, Windows NT 4.0,
Windows Millennium Edition, Windows 2000,
Windows XP Home Edition, Windows XP Professional,
Windows .NET Server family,
.NET Compact Framework - Windows CE .NET,
Common Language Infrastructure (CLI) Standard

.NET Framework Security:

- **ReflectionPermission** to enhance security and performance
  when invoked late-bound through mechanisms such as
  Type.InvokeMember. Associated enumeration:
  ReflectionPermissionFlag.MemberAccess.

FieldInfo.Attributes Property

Gets the attributes associated with this field.

```
[Visual Basic]
Public MustOverride ReadOnly Property Attributes As FieldAttributes
[C#]
public abstract FieldAttributes Attributes {get;}
[C++]
public: __property virtual FieldAttributes get_Attributes() = 0;
[JScript]
public abstract function get Attributes() : FieldAttributes;
```

Property Value

The **FieldAttributes** for this field.

Remarks

All members have a set of attributes, which are defined in relation to
the specific type of member. **FieldAttributes** informs the user
whether this field is the private field, a static field, and so on.

To get the **Attributes** property, first get the class **Type**. From the
Type, get the **FieldInfo**. From the **FieldInfo**, get the **Attributes**.

Requirements

Platforms: Windows 98, Windows NT 4.0,
Windows Millennium Edition, Windows 2000,
Windows XP Home Edition, Windows XP Professional,
Windows .NET Server family,
.NET Compact Framework - Windows CE .NET,
Common Language Infrastructure (CLI) Standard

FieldInfo.FieldHandle Property

Gets a **RuntimeFieldHandle**, which is a handle to the internal
metadata representation of a field.

```
[Visual Basic]
Public MustOverride ReadOnly Property FieldHandle As _
    RuntimeFieldHandle
[C#]
public abstract RuntimeFieldHandle FieldHandle {get;}
[C++]
public: __property virtual RuntimeFieldHandle get_FieldHandle() = 0;
[JScript]
public abstract function get FieldHandle() : RuntimeFieldHandle;
```

Property Value

A handle to the internal metadata representation of a field.

Remarks

The handles are valid only in the appdomain in which they were
obtained.

Example

See related example in the **System.Reflection.FieldInfo** class topic.

Requirements

Platforms: Windows 98, Windows NT 4.0,
Windows Millennium Edition, Windows 2000,
Windows XP Home Edition, Windows XP Professional,
Windows .NET Server family,
.NET Compact Framework - Windows CE .NET

FieldInfo.FieldType Property

Gets the type of this field object.

```
[Visual Basic]
Public MustOverride ReadOnly Property FieldType As Type
[C#]
public abstract Type FieldType {get;}
[C++]
public: _property virtual Type* get_FieldType() = 0;
[JScript]
public abstract function get FieldType() : Type;
```

Property Value

The type of this field object.

Remarks

The type is some primitive data type, such as **String**, **Boolean**, or **GUID**.

To get the **FieldType** property, first get the class **Type**. From the **Type**, get the **FieldInfo**. From the **FieldInfo**, get the **FieldType** value.

Example

See related example in the **System.Reflection.FieldInfo** class topic.

Requirements

Platforms: Windows 98, Windows NT 4.0,
Windows Millennium Edition, Windows 2000,
Windows XP Home Edition, Windows XP Professional,
Windows .NET Server family,
.NET Compact Framework - Windows CE .NET,
Common Language Infrastructure (CLI) Standard

FieldInfo.IsAssembly Property

Gets a value indicating whether this field has Assembly level visibility.

```
[Visual Basic]
Public ReadOnly Property IsAssembly As Boolean
[C#]
public bool IsAssembly {get;}
[C++]
public: _property bool get_IsAssembly();
[JScript]
public function get IsAssembly() : Boolean;
```

Property Value

true if the field has the **Assembly** attribute set; otherwise, **false**.

Remarks

If a field has **Assembly** level visibility, it can be called from any member within that assembly, but none outside of it.

The **IsAssembly** property is set when the **FieldAttributes.Assembly** attribute is set. In C#, you can declare the field as **internal** to set this property to limit the access of this field to this project.

Example

See related example in the **System.Reflection.FieldInfo** class topic.

Requirements

Platforms: Windows 98, Windows NT 4.0,
Windows Millennium Edition, Windows 2000,
Windows XP Home Edition, Windows XP Professional,
Windows .NET Server family,
.NET Compact Framework - Windows CE .NET

FieldInfo.IsFamily Property

Gets a value indicating whether this field has Family level visibility.

```
[Visual Basic]
Public ReadOnly Property IsFamily As Boolean
[C#]
public bool IsFamily {get;}
[C++]
public: _property bool get_IsFamily();
[JScript]
public function get IsFamily() : Boolean;
```

Property Value

true if the field has the **Family** attribute set; otherwise, **false**.

Remarks

This property can be called from any member in a derived class, but not from any other type.

To get the **IsFamily** property, first get the class **Type**. From the **Type**, get the **FieldInfo**. From the **FieldInfo**, get the **IsFamily** value.

The **IsFamily** property is set when the **FieldAttributes.Family** attribute is set.

Example

See related example in the **System.Reflection.FieldInfo** class topic.

Requirements

Platforms: Windows 98, Windows NT 4.0,
Windows Millennium Edition, Windows 2000,
Windows XP Home Edition, Windows XP Professional,
Windows .NET Server family,
.NET Compact Framework - Windows CE .NET

FieldInfo.IsFamilyAndAssembly Property

Gets a value indicating whether this field has **FamilyAndAssembly** level visibility.

```
[Visual Basic]
Public ReadOnly Property IsFamilyAndAssembly As Boolean
[C#]
public bool IsFamilyAndAssembly {get;}
[C++]
public: _property bool get_IsFamilyAndAssembly();
[JScript]
public function get IsFamilyAndAssembly() : Boolean;
```

Property Value

true if the field has the **FamANDAssem** attribute set; otherwise, **false**.

Remarks

If a field has **FamilyAndAssembly** level visibility, it can be called from any member in a derived class that is also in the same assembly, but not from any other type.

The **IsFamilyAndAssembly** property is set when the
FieldAttributes.FamANDAssem attribute is set.

Example

See related example in the **System.Reflection.FieldInfo** class topic.

Requirements

Platforms: Windows 98, Windows NT 4.0,
Windows Millennium Edition, Windows 2000,
Windows XP Home Edition, Windows XP Professional,
Windows .NET Server family,
.NET Compact Framework - Windows CE .NET

FieldInfo.IsFamilyOrAssembly Property

Gets a value indicating whether this field has **FamilyOrAssembly**
level visibility.

```
[Visual Basic]
Public ReadOnly Property IsFamilyOrAssembly As Boolean
[C#]
public bool IsFamilyOrAssembly {get;}
[C++]
public: __property bool get_IsFamilyOrAssembly();
[JScript]
public function get IsFamilyOrAssembly() : Boolean;
```

Property Value

true if the field has the **FamORAssem** attribute set; otherwise,
false.

Remarks

If a field has **FamilyOrAssembly** level visibility, it can be called
from any member in a derived class or any member in the same
assembly, but not from any other type.

The **IsFamilyOrAssembly** property is set when the
FieldAttributes.FamORAssem attribute is set.

Example

See related example in the **System.Reflection.FieldInfo** class topic.

Requirements

Platforms: Windows 98, Windows NT 4.0,
Windows Millennium Edition, Windows 2000,
Windows XP Home Edition, Windows XP Professional,
Windows .NET Server family,
.NET Compact Framework - Windows CE .NET

FieldInfo.IsInitOnly Property

Gets a value indicating whether the field can only be set in the body
of the constructor.

```
[Visual Basic]
Public ReadOnly Property Is As Boolean
[C#]
public bool IsInitOnly {get;}
[C++]
public: __property bool get_IsInitOnly();
[JScript]
public function get IsInitOnly() : Boolean;
```

Property Value

true if the field has the **InitOnly** attribute set; otherwise, **false**.

Remarks

If the returned value is **true**, the field can only be initialized, and is
read-only thereafter.

To get the **IsInitOnly** property, first get the class **Type**. From the
Type, get the **FieldInfo**. From the **FieldInfo**, get the **IsInitOnly**
property. To access a non-public field, set the **BindingFlags** to
NonPublic and choose either **Static** or **Instance BindingFlags** in
the **GetField** method.

The **IsInitOnly** property is set when the **FieldAttributes.InitOnly**
attribute is set.

Example

See related example in the **System.Reflection.FieldInfo** class topic.

Requirements

Platforms: Windows 98, Windows NT 4.0,
Windows Millennium Edition, Windows 2000,
Windows XP Home Edition, Windows XP Professional,
Windows .NET Server family,
.NET Compact Framework - Windows CE .NET

FieldInfo.IsLiteral Property

Gets a value indicating whether the value is written at compile time
and cannot be changed.

```
[Visual Basic]
Public ReadOnly Property IsLiteral As Boolean
[C#]
public bool IsLiteral {get;}
[C++]
public: __property bool get_IsLiteral();
[JScript]
public function get IsLiteral() : Boolean;
```

Property Value

true if the field has the **Literal** attribute set; otherwise, **false**.

Remarks

The **IsLiteral** property is set when the **FieldAttributes.Literal**
attribute is set. If this attribute is set, the field cannot be changed and
is constant.

Requirements

Platforms: Windows 98, Windows NT 4.0,
Windows Millennium Edition, Windows 2000,
Windows XP Home Edition, Windows XP Professional,
Windows .NET Server family,
.NET Compact Framework - Windows CE .NET

FieldInfo.IsNotSerialized Property

Gets a value indicating whether this field has the **NotSerialized**
attribute.

```
[Visual Basic]
Public ReadOnly Property IsNotSerialized As Boolean
[C#]
public bool IsNotSerialized {get;}
[C++]
public: __property bool get_IsNotSerialized();
[JScript]
public function get IsNotSerialized() : Boolean;
```

Property Value

true if the field has the **NotSerialized** attribute set; otherwise, **false**.

Remarks

The **IsNotSerialized** property returns **true** when the field is marked with the **FieldAttributes.NotSerialized** flag. When this flag is set on a field, it indicates that the field does not have to be serialized when the type is remoted.

Example

See related example in the **System.Reflection.FieldInfo** class topic.

Requirements

Platforms: Windows 98, Windows NT 4.0, Windows Millennium Edition, Windows 2000, Windows XP Home Edition, Windows XP Professional, Windows .NET Server family, .NET Compact Framework - Windows CE .NET

FieldInfo.IsPinvokeImpl Property

Gets a value indicating whether the corresponding **PinvokeImpl** attribute is set in **FieldAttributes**.

```
[Visual Basic]
Public ReadOnly Property IsPinvokeImpl As Boolean
[C#]
public bool IsPinvokeImpl {get;}
[C++]
public: __property bool get_IsPinvokeImpl();
[JScript]
public function get IsPinvokeImpl() : Boolean;
```

Property Value

true if the **PinvokeImpl** attribute is set in **FieldAttributes**; otherwise, **false**.

Example

See related example in the **System.Reflection.FieldInfo** class topic.

Requirements

Platforms: Windows 98, Windows NT 4.0, Windows Millennium Edition, Windows 2000, Windows XP Home Edition, Windows XP Professional, Windows .NET Server family, .NET Compact Framework - Windows CE .NET

FieldInfo.IsPrivate Property

Gets a value indicating whether the field is private.

```
[Visual Basic]
Public ReadOnly Property IsPrivate As Boolean
[C#]
public bool IsPrivate {get;}
[C++]
public: __property bool get_IsPrivate();
[JScript]
public function get IsPrivate() : Boolean;
```

Property Value

true if the field is private; otherwise; **false**.

Remarks

Private fields are accessible only from member functions.

The **IsPrivate** property is set when the **FieldAttributes.Private** attribute is set.

To get the **IsPrivate** property, first get the class **Type**. From the **Type**, get the **FieldInfo**. From the **FieldInfo**, get the **IsPrivate** property. To access a non-public field, set the **BindingFlags** to **NonPublic**, and either **Static** or **Instance** in the **GetField** method.

Example

See related example in the **System.Reflection.FieldInfo** class topic.

Requirements

Platforms: Windows 98, Windows NT 4.0, Windows Millennium Edition, Windows 2000, Windows XP Home Edition, Windows XP Professional, Windows .NET Server family, .NET Compact Framework - Windows CE .NET

FieldInfo.IsPublic Property

Gets a value indicating whether the field is public.

```
[Visual Basic]
Public ReadOnly Property IsPublic As Boolean
[C#]
public bool IsPublic {get;}
[C++]
public: __property bool get_IsPublic();
[JScript]
public function get IsPublic() : Boolean;
```

Property Value

true if this field is public; otherwise, **false**.

Remarks

Public fields are accessible everywhere their corresponding classes are visible.

The **IsPublic** property is set when the **FieldAttributes.Public** attribute is set.

To get the **IsPublic** property, first get the class **Type**. From the **Type**, get the **FieldInfo**. From the **FieldInfo**, get the **IsPublic** property. If the field is other than public, it is protected and cannot be readily accessed. To access a nonpublic field, set the **BindingFlags** to **NonPublic**, specify either **BindingFlags.Instance** or **BindingFlags.Static**, and use this for the **GetField** method.

Example

See related example in the **System.Reflection.FieldInfo** class topic.

Requirements

Platforms: Windows 98, Windows NT 4.0, Windows Millennium Edition, Windows 2000, Windows XP Home Edition, Windows XP Professional, Windows .NET Server family, .NET Compact Framework - Windows CE .NET

FieldInfo.IsSpecialName Property

Gets a value indicating whether the corresponding **SpecialName** attribute is set in the **FieldAttributes** enumerator.

```
[Visual Basic]
Public ReadOnly Property IsSpecialName As Boolean
[C#]
public bool IsSpecialName {get;}
```

```
[C++]
public: __property bool get_IsSpecialName();
[JScript]
public function get IsSpecialName() : Boolean;
```

Property Value

true if the **SpecialName** attribute is set in **FieldAttributes**; otherwise, **false**.

Remarks

Names that begin with or contain an underscore character (_), property accessors, and operator overloading methods are examples of names that might require special treatment by some compilers.

Example

See related example in the **System.Reflection.FieldInfo** class topic.

Requirements

Platforms: Windows 98, Windows NT 4.0, Windows Millennium Edition, Windows 2000, Windows XP Home Edition, Windows XP Professional, Windows .NET Server family, .NET Compact Framework - Windows CE .NET

FieldInfo.IsStatic Property

Gets a value indicating whether the field is static.

```
[Visual Basic]
Public ReadOnly Property IsStatic As Boolean
[C#]
public bool IsStatic {get;}
[C++]
public: __property bool get_IsStatic();
[JScript]
public function get IsStatic() : Boolean;
```

Property Value

true if this field is static; otherwise, **false**.

Remarks

When a field is static, one copy of the field is shared by all instances of the type.

The **IsStatic** property is set when the **FieldAttributes.Static** attribute is set.

To get the **IsStatic** property, first get the class **Type**. From the **Type**, get the **FieldInfo**. From the **FieldInfo**, get the **IsStatic** property. To access a non-public field, set the **BindingFlags** to **NonPublic** in the **GetField** method and set the accessibility to **Instance** or **Static**.

Example

See related example in the **System.Reflection.FieldInfo** class topic.

Requirements

Platforms: Windows 98, Windows NT 4.0, Windows Millennium Edition, Windows 2000, Windows XP Home Edition, Windows XP Professional, Windows .NET Server family, .NET Compact Framework - Windows CE .NET

FieldInfo.MemberType Property

Gets the **Type** of property reflected by this **FieldInfo** object. The retrieved value indicates that this member is a field.

```
[Visual Basic]
Overrides Public ReadOnly Property MemberType As MemberTypes
[C#]
public override MemberTypes MemberType {get;}
[C++]
public: __property MemberTypes get_MemberType();
[JScript]
public override function get MemberType() : MemberTypes;
```

Property Value

A **MemberTypes.Field** object.

Remarks

This property is used when this field is being tested as a generic member.

Example

See related example in the **System.Reflection.FieldInfo** class topic.

Requirements

Platforms: Windows 98, Windows NT 4.0, Windows Millennium Edition, Windows 2000, Windows XP Home Edition, Windows XP Professional, Windows .NET Server family, .NET Compact Framework - Windows CE .NET

FieldInfo.GetFieldFromHandle Method

Gets a **FieldInfo** containing the value of the field reflected by this instance.

```
[Visual Basic]
Public Shared Function GetFieldFromHandle( _
    ByVal handle As RuntimeFieldHandle _
) As FieldInfo
[C#]
public static FieldInfo GetFieldFromHandle(
    RuntimeFieldHandle handle
);
[C++]
public: static FieldInfo* GetFieldFromHandle(
    RuntimeFieldHandle handle
);
[JScript]
public static function GetFieldFromHandle(
    handle : RuntimeFieldHandle
) : FieldInfo;
```

Parameters

handle
    A handle to the internal metadata representation of a field.

Return Value

A **FieldInfo** containing the value of the field reflected by this instance.

Remarks

The handles are valid only in the application domain in which they were obtained.

Example

See related example in the **System.Reflection.FieldInfo** class topic.

Requirements

Platforms: Windows 98, Windows NT 4.0, Windows Millennium Edition, Windows 2000, Windows XP Home Edition, Windows XP Professional, Windows .NET Server family, .NET Compact Framework - Windows CE .NET

.NET Framework Security:

- **ReflectionPermission** to enhance security and performance when invoked late-bound through mechanisms such as **Type.InvokeMember**. Associated enumeration: **ReflectionPermissionFlag.MemberAccess**.

FieldInfo.GetValue Method

When overridden in a derived class, returns the value of a field supported by a given object.

```
[Visual Basic]
Public MustOverride Function GetValue( _
   ByVal obj As Object _
) As Object
[C#]
public abstract object GetValue(
   object obj
);
[C++]
public: virtual Object* GetValue(
   Object* obj
) = 0;
[JScript]
public abstract function GetValue(
   obj : Object
) : Object;
```

Parameters

obj
   The object whose field value will be returned.

Return Value

An object containing the value of the field reflected by this instance.

Exceptions

Exception Type	Condition
TargetException	The field is non-static and *obj* is a null reference (**Nothing** in Visual Basic).
NotSupportedException	A field is marked literal, but the field does not have one of the accepted literal types.
FieldAccessException	The caller does not have permission to access this field.
ArgumentException	The method is neither declared nor inherited by the class of *obj*.

Remarks

If the field is static, *obj* is ignored. For non-static fields, *obj* should be an instance of a class that inherits or declares the field. Note that the return type of **GetValue** is **Object**. For example, if the field holds a Boolean primitive value, an instance of **Object** with the appropriate Boolean value is returned. Before returning the value, **GetValue** checks to see if the user has access permission.

Note Access restrictions are ignored for fully trusted code. That is, private constructors, methods, fields, and properties can be accessed and invoked through reflection whenever the code is fully trusted.

Example

See related example in the **System.Reflection.FieldInfo** class topic.

Requirements

Platforms: Windows 98, Windows NT 4.0, Windows Millennium Edition, Windows 2000, Windows XP Home Edition, Windows XP Professional, Windows .NET Server family, .NET Compact Framework - Windows CE .NET, Common Language Infrastructure (CLI) Standard

.NET Framework Security:

- **ReflectionPermission** to enhance security and performance when invoked late-bound through mechanisms such as **Type.InvokeMember**. Associated enumeration: **ReflectionPermissionFlag.MemberAccess**.

FieldInfo.GetValueDirect Method

Returns the value of a field supported by a given object.

This method is not CLS-compliant. The CLS-compliant alternative is the **GetValue** member.

```
[Visual Basic]
<CLSCompliant(False)>
Public Overridable Function GetValueDirect( _
   ByVal obj As TypedReference _
) As Object
[C#]
[CLSCompliant(false)]
public virtual object GetValueDirect(
   TypedReference obj
);
[C++]
[CLSCompliant(false)]
public: virtual Object* GetValueDirect(
   TypedReference obj
);
[JScript]
public
   CLSCompliant(false)
function GetValueDirect(
   obj : TypedReference
) : Object;
```

Parameters

obj
   A managed pointer to a location and a runtime representation of the type that might be stored at that location.

Return Value

An **Object** containing a field value.

Exceptions

Exception Type	Condition
NotSupportedException	The caller requires the CLS alternative, but called this method instead.

Requirements

Platforms: Windows 98, Windows NT 4.0,
Windows Millennium Edition, Windows 2000,
Windows XP Home Edition, Windows XP Professional,
Windows .NET Server family

.NET Framework Security:

• **ReflectionPermission** to enhance security and performance
  when invoked late-bound through mechanisms such as
  Type.InvokeMember. Associated enumeration:
  ReflectionPermissionFlag.MemberAccess.

FieldInfo.SetValue Method

Sets the value of the field for the given object to the given value.

Overload List

Sets the value of the field supported by the given object.

Supported by the .NET Compact Framework.

[Visual Basic] **Overloads Public Sub SetValue(Object, Object)**

[C#] **public void SetValue(object, object);**

[C++] **public: void SetValue(Object*, Object*);**

[JScript] **public function SetValue(Object, Object);**

When overridden in a derived class, sets the value of the field
supported by the given object.

Supported by the .NET Compact Framework.

[Visual Basic] **Overloads Public MustOverride Sub
SetValue(Object, Object, BindingFlags, Binder, CultureInfo)**

[C#] **public abstract void SetValue(object, object,
BindingFlags, Binder, CultureInfo);**

[C++] **public: virtual void SetValue(Object*, Object*,
BindingFlags, Binder*, CultureInfo*) = 0;**

[JScript] **public abstract function SetValue(Object, Object,
BindingFlags, Binder, CultureInfo);**

Example

See related example in the **System.Reflection.FieldInfo** class topic.

FieldInfo.SetValue Method (Object, Object)

Sets the value of the field supported by the given object.

```
[Visual Basic]
Overloads Public Sub SetValue( _
   ByVal obj As Object, _
   ByVal value As Object _
)
[C#]
public void SetValue(
   object obj,
   object value
);
[C++]
public: void SetValue(
   Object* obj,
   Object* value
);
```

```
[JScript]
public function SetValue(
   obj : Object,
   value : Object
);
```

Parameters

obj
  The object whose field value will be set.
value
  The value to assign to the field.

Exceptions

Exception Type	Condition
FieldAccessException	The caller does not have permission to access this field.
TargetException	The *obj* parameter is a null reference (**Nothing** in Visual Basic) and the field is an instance field.
ArgumentException	The field does not exist on the object. -or- The *value* parameter cannot be converted and stored in the field.

Remarks

This method will assign *value* to the field reflected by this instance
on object *obj*. If the field is static, *obj* will be ignored. For non-static
fields, *obj* should be an instance of a class that inherits or declares
the field. The new value is passed as an **Object**. For example, if the
field's type is Boolean, an instance of **Object** with the appropriate
Boolean value is passed. Before setting the value, **SetValue** checks
to see if the user has access permission. This final method is a
convenience method for calling the following **SetValue** method.

> **Note** Access restrictions are ignored for fully trusted code.
> That is, private constructors, methods, fields, and properties
> can be accessed and invoked using reflection whenever the
> code is fully trusted.

Example

See related example in the **System.Reflection.FieldInfo** class topic.

Requirements

Platforms: Windows 98, Windows NT 4.0,
Windows Millennium Edition, Windows 2000,
Windows XP Home Edition, Windows XP Professional,
Windows .NET Server family,
.NET Compact Framework - Windows CE .NET,
Common Language Infrastructure (CLI) Standard

.NET Framework Security:

• **ReflectionPermission** to enhance security and performance
  when invoked late-bound through mechanisms such as
  Type.InvokeMember. Associated enumeration:
  ReflectionPermissionFlag.MemberAccess.

• **ReflectionPermission** for returning fields that are not public.
  Associated enumeration:
  ReflectionPermissionFlag.MemberAccess.

• **SecurityPermission** for updating init-only fields. Associated
  enumeration: **SecurityPermissionFlag.SerializationFormatter**.

FieldInfo.SetValue Method (Object, Object, BindingFlags, Binder, CultureInfo)

When overridden in a derived class, sets the value of the field supported by the given object.

```
[Visual Basic]
Overloads Public MustOverride Sub SetValue( _
    ByVal obj As Object, _
    ByVal value As Object, _
    ByVal invokeAttr As BindingFlags, _
    ByVal binder As Binder, _
    ByVal culture As CultureInfo _
)
[C#]
public abstract void SetValue(
    object obj,
    object value,
    BindingFlags invokeAttr,
    Binder binder,
    CultureInfo culture
);
[C++]
public: virtual void SetValue(
    Object* obj,
    Object* value,
    BindingFlags invokeAttr,
    Binder* binder,
    CultureInfo* culture
) = 0;
[JScript]
public abstract function SetValue(
    obj : Object,
    value : Object,
    invokeAttr : BindingFlags,
    binder : Binder,
    culture : CultureInfo
);
```

Parameters

obj

   The object whose field value will be set.

value

   The value to assign to the field.

invokeAttr

   A field of **Binder** that specifies the type of binding that is desired (for example, **Binder.CreateInstance** or **Binder.ExactBinding**).

binder

   A set of properties that enables the binding, coercion of argument types, and invocation of members through reflection. If *binder* is a null reference (**Nothing** in Visual Basic), then **Binder.DefaultBinding** is used.

culture

   The software preferences of a particular culture.

Exceptions

Exception Type	Condition
FieldAccessException	The caller does not have permission to access this field.
TargetException	The *obj* parameter is a null reference (**Nothing** in Visual Basic) and the field is an instance field.

Exception Type	Condition
ArgumentException	The field does not exist on the object. -or- The *value* parameter cannot be converted and stored in the field.

Remarks

This method will assign *value* to the field reflected by this instance on *obj*. If the field is static, *obj* will be ignored. For non-static fields, *obj* should be an instance of a class that inherits or declares the field. The new value is passed as an **Object**. For example, if the field's type is **Boolean**, an instance of **Object** with the appropriate Boolean value is passed. Before setting the value, **SetValue** checks to see if the user has access permission.

> **Note** Access restrictions are ignored for fully trusted code. That is, private constructors, methods, fields, and properties can be accessed and invoked using reflection whenever the code is fully trusted.

Requirements

Platforms: Windows 98, Windows NT 4.0, Windows Millennium Edition, Windows 2000, Windows XP Home Edition, Windows XP Professional, Windows .NET Server family, .NET Compact Framework - Windows CE .NET, Common Language Infrastructure (CLI) Standard

.NET Framework Security:

- **ReflectionPermission** to enhance security and performance when invoked late-bound through mechanisms such as **Type.InvokeMember**. Associated enumeration: **ReflectionPermissionFlag.MemberAccess**.
- **ReflectionPermission** for returning fields that are not public. Associated enumeration: **ReflectionPermissionFlag.MemberAccess**
- **SecurityPermission** for updating init-only fields. Associated enumeration: **SecurityPermissionFlag.SerializationFormatter**.

FieldInfo.SetValueDirect Method

Sets the value of the field supported by the given object.

This method is not CLS-compliant. The CLS-compliant alternative is the **SetValue** member.

```
[Visual Basic]
<CLSCompliant(False)>
Public Overridable Sub SetValueDirect( _
    ByVal obj As TypedReference, _
    ByVal value As Object _
)
[C#]
[CLSCompliant(false)]
public virtual void SetValueDirect(
    TypedReference obj,
    object value
);
[C++]
[CLSCompliant(false)]
public: virtual void SetValueDirect(
    TypedReference obj,
    Object* value
);
```

```
[JScript]
public
    CLSCompliant(false)
function SetValueDirect(
    obj : TypedReference,
    value : Object
);
```

Parameters

obj

> A managed pointer to a location and a runtime representation of the type that can be stored at that location.

value

> The value to assign to the field.

Exceptions

Exception Type	Condition
NotSupportedException	The caller requires the CLS alternative, but called this method instead.

Requirements

Platforms: Windows 98, Windows NT 4.0, Windows Millennium Edition, Windows 2000, Windows XP Home Edition, Windows XP Professional, Windows .NET Server family

.NET Framework Security:

• **ReflectionPermission** to enhance security and performance when invoked late-bound through mechanisms such as **Type.InvokeMember**. Associated enumeration: **ReflectionPermissionFlag.MemberAccess**.

ICustomAttributeProvider Interface

Provides custom attributes for reflection objects that support them.

```
[Visual Basic]
Public Interface ICustomAttributeProvider
[C#]
public interface ICustomAttributeProvider
[C++]
public __gc __interface ICustomAttributeProvider
[JScript]
public interface ICustomAttributeProvider
```

Classes that Implement ICustomAttributeProvider

Class	Description
Assembly	Defines an **Assembly**, which is a reusable, versionable, and self-describing building block of a common language runtime application.
MemberInfo	Discovers the attributes of a member and provides access to member metadata.
Module	Performs reflection on a module.
ParameterInfo	Discovers the attributes of a parameter and provides access to parameter metadata.

Remarks

Nearly all the Reflection classes can have attributes associated with them. Attributes can be standard (public, private, HelpString) or custom.

Requirements

Namespace: System.Reflection

Platforms: Windows 98, Windows NT 4.0, Windows Millennium Edition, Windows 2000, Windows XP Home Edition, Windows XP Professional, Windows .NET Server family, .NET Compact Framework - Windows CE .NET

Assembly: Mscorlib (in Mscorlib.dll)

ICustomAttributeProvider.GetCustomAttributes Method

Returns custom attributes defined on this member.

Overload List

Returns an array of all of the custom attributes defined on this member, excluding named attributes, or an empty array if there are no custom attributes.

Supported by the .NET Compact Framework.

[Visual Basic] **Overloads Function GetCustomAttributes(Boolean) As Object()**

[C#] **object[] GetCustomAttributes(bool);**

[C++] **Object* GetCustomAttributes(bool) __gc[];**

[JScript] **function GetCustomAttributes(Boolean) : Object[];**

Returns an array of custom attributes defined on this member, identified by type, or an empty array if there are no custom attributes of that type.

Supported by the .NET Compact Framework.

[Visual Basic] **Overloads Function GetCustomAttributes(Type, Boolean) As Object()**

[C#] **object[] GetCustomAttributes(Type, bool);**

[C++] **Object* GetCustomAttributes(Type*, bool) __gc[];**

[JScript] **function GetCustomAttributes(Type, Boolean) : Object[];**

ICustomAttributeProvider.GetCustomAttributes Method (Boolean)

Returns an array of all of the custom attributes defined on this member, excluding named attributes, or an empty array if there are no custom attributes.

```
[Visual Basic]
Function GetCustomAttributes( _
   ByVal inherit As Boolean _
) As Object()
[C#]
object[] GetCustomAttributes(
   bool inherit
);
[C++]
Object* GetCustomAttributes(
   bool inherit
) __gc[];
[JScript]
function GetCustomAttributes(
   inherit : Boolean
) : Object[];
```

Parameters

inherit
When **true**, look up the hierarchy chain for the inherited custom attribute.

Return Value

An array of Objects representing custom attributes, or an empty array.

Exceptions

Exception Type	Condition
TypeLoadException	The custom attribute type cannot be loaded.
AmbiguousMatchException	There is more than one attribute of type *attributeType* defined on this member.

Remarks

Calling **ICustomAttributeProvider.GetCustomAttributes** on **PropertyInfo** or **EventInfo** when the *inherit* parameter of **GetCustomAttributes** is **true** does not walk the type hierarchy. Use **System.Attribute** to inherit custom attributes.

This method returns custom attributes defined directly on a non-inherited member only.

Requirements

Platforms: Windows 98, Windows NT 4.0,
Windows Millennium Edition, Windows 2000,
Windows XP Home Edition, Windows XP Professional,
Windows .NET Server family,
.NET Compact Framework - Windows CE .NET

ICustomAttributeProvider.GetCustomAttributes Method (Type, Boolean)

Returns an array of custom attributes defined on this member,
identified by type, or an empty array if there are no custom attributes
of that type.

```
[Visual Basic]
Function GetCustomAttributes( _
   ByVal attributeType As Type, _
   ByVal inherit As Boolean _
) As Object()
[C#]
object[] GetCustomAttributes(
   Type attributeType,
   bool inherit
);
[C++]
Object* GetCustomAttributes(
   Type* attributeType,
   bool inherit
) __gc[];
[JScript]
function GetCustomAttributes(
   attributeType : Type,
   inherit : Boolean
) : Object[];
```

Parameters

attributeType
   The type of the custom attributes.
inherit
   When **true**, look up the hierarchy chain for the inherited custom
   attribute.

Return Value

An array of Objects representing custom attributes, or an empty
array.

Exceptions

Exception Type	Condition
TypeLoadException	The custom attribute type cannot be loaded.
AmbiguousMatchException	There is more than one attribute of type *attributeType* defined on this member.

Remarks

If *attributeType* is a base class or interface, this method returns any
implementation of that type.

This method returns custom attributes defined directly on a non-
inherited member only.

Calling **ICustomAttributeProvider.GetCustomAttributes** on
PropertyInfo or **EventInfo** when the *inherit* parameter of
GetCustomAttributes is **true** does not walk the type hierarchy. Use
System.Attribute to inherit custom attributes.

Requirements

Platforms: Windows 98, Windows NT 4.0,
Windows Millennium Edition, Windows 2000,
Windows XP Home Edition, Windows XP Professional,
Windows .NET Server family,
.NET Compact Framework - Windows CE .NET

ICustomAttributeProvider.IsDefined Method

Indicates whether one or more instance of *attributeType* is defined
on this member.

```
[Visual Basic]
Function IsDefined( _
   ByVal attributeType As Type, _
   ByVal inherit As Boolean _
) As Boolean
[C#]
bool IsDefined(
   Type attributeType,
   bool inherit
);
[C++]
bool IsDefined(
   Type* attributeType,
   bool inherit
);
[JScript]
function IsDefined(
   attributeType : Type,
   inherit : Boolean
) : Boolean;
```

Parameters

attributeType
   The type of the custom attributes.
inherit
   When **true**, look up the hierarchy chain for the inherited custom
   attribute.

Return Value

true if the *attributeType* is defined on this member; **false** otherwise.

Requirements

Platforms: Windows 98, Windows NT 4.0,
Windows Millennium Edition, Windows 2000,
Windows XP Home Edition, Windows XP Professional,
Windows .NET Server family,
.NET Compact Framework - Windows CE .NET

InterfaceMapping Structure

Retrieves the mapping of an interface into the actual methods on a class that implements that interface.

System.Object
  System.ValueType
    System.Reflection.InterfaceMapping

```
[Visual Basic]
Public Structure InterfaceMapping
[C#]
public struct InterfaceMapping
[C++]
public __value struct InterfaceMapping
```

[JScript] In JScript, you can use the structures in the .NET Framework, but you cannot define your own.

Thread Safety

Any public static (**Shared** in Visual Basic) members of this type are safe for multithreaded operations. Any instance members are not guaranteed to be thread safe.

Requirements

Namespace: System.Reflection

Platforms: Windows 98, Windows NT 4.0, Windows Millennium Edition, Windows 2000, Windows XP Home Edition, Windows XP Professional, Windows .NET Server family

Assembly: Mscorlib (in Mscorlib.dll)

InterfaceMapping.InterfaceMethods Field

Shows the methods that are defined on the interface.

```
[Visual Basic]
Public InterfaceMethods() As MethodInfo
[C#]
public MethodInfo[] InterfaceMethods;
[C++]
public: MethodInfo* InterfaceMethods[];
[JScript]
public var InterfaceMethods : MethodInfo[];
```

Remarks

The elements returned in the **InterfaceMethods** array match their counterpart elements returned from the **TargetMethods** array. That is, the elements are in the same array indexing order.

Requirements

Platforms: Windows 98, Windows NT 4.0, Windows Millennium Edition, Windows 2000, Windows XP Home Edition, Windows XP Professional, Windows .NET Server family

InterfaceMapping.InterfaceType Field

Shows the type that represents the interface.

```
[Visual Basic]
Public InterfaceType As Type
[C#]
public Type InterfaceType;
```

```
[C++]
public: Type* InterfaceType;
[JScript]
public var InterfaceType : Type;
```

Requirements

Platforms: Windows 98, Windows NT 4.0, Windows Millennium Edition, Windows 2000, Windows XP Home Edition, Windows XP Professional, Windows .NET Server family

InterfaceMapping.TargetMethods Field

Shows the methods that implement the interface.

```
[Visual Basic]
Public TargetMethods() As MethodInfo
[C#]
public MethodInfo[] TargetMethods;
[C++]
public: MethodInfo* TargetMethods[];
[JScript]
public var TargetMethods : MethodInfo[];
```

Remarks

The elements returned in the **InterfaceMethods** array match their counterpart elements returned from the **TargetMethods** array. That is, the elements are in the same array indexing order.

Requirements

Platforms: Windows 98, Windows NT 4.0, Windows Millennium Edition, Windows 2000, Windows XP Home Edition, Windows XP Professional, Windows .NET Server family

InterfaceMapping.TargetType Field

Represents the type that implements the interface.

```
[Visual Basic]
Public TargetType As Type
[C#]
public Type TargetType;
[C++]
public: Type* TargetType;
[JScript]
public var TargetType : Type;
```

Requirements

Platforms: Windows 98, Windows NT 4.0, Windows Millennium Edition, Windows 2000, Windows XP Home Edition, Windows XP Professional, Windows .NET Server family

InvalidFilterCriteriaException Class

The exception that is thrown in **FindMembers** when the filter criteria is not valid for the type of filter you are using.

System.Object
  System.Exception
    System.ApplicationException
      System.Reflection.InvalidFilterCriteriaException

```
[Visual Basic]
<Serializable>
Public Class InvalidFilterCriteriaException
  Inherits ApplicationException
[C#]
[Serializable]
public class InvalidFilterCriteriaException : ApplicationException
[C++]
[Serializable]
public __gc class InvalidFilterCriteriaException : public
  ApplicationException
[JScript]
public
  Serializable
class InvalidFilterCriteriaException extends
  ApplicationException
```

Thread Safety

Any public static (**Shared** in Visual Basic) members of this type are safe for multithreaded operations. Any instance members are not guaranteed to be thread safe.

Remarks

InvalidFilterCriteriaException uses the HRESULT COR_E_INVALIDFILTERCRITERIA which has the value 0x80131601.

Requirements

Namespace: System.Reflection

Platforms: Windows 98, Windows NT 4.0, Windows Millennium Edition, Windows 2000, Windows XP Home Edition, Windows XP Professional, Windows .NET Server family

Assembly: Mscorlib (in Mscorlib.dll)

InvalidFilterCriteriaException Constructor

Initializes an instance of the **InvalidFilterCriteriaException** class.

Overload List

Initializes a new instance of the **InvalidFilterCriteriaException** class with the default properties.

  [Visual Basic] **Public Sub New()**

  [C#] **public InvalidFilterCriteriaException();**

  [C++] **public: InvalidFilterCriteriaException();**

  [JScript] **public function InvalidFilterCriteriaException();**

Initializes a new instance of the **InvalidFilterCriteriaException** class with the given HRESULT and message string.

  [Visual Basic] **Public Sub New(String)**

  [C#] **public InvalidFilterCriteriaException(string);**

  [C++] **public: InvalidFilterCriteriaException(String*);**

  [JScript] **public function InvalidFilterCriteriaException(String);**

Initializes a new instance of the **InvalidFilterCriteriaException** class with the specified serialization and context information.

  [Visual Basic] **Protected Sub New(SerializationInfo, StreamingContext)**

  [C#] **protected InvalidFilterCriteriaException(SerializationInfo, StreamingContext);**

  [C++] **protected: InvalidFilterCriteriaException(SerializationInfo*, StreamingContext);**

  [JScript] **protected function InvalidFilterCriteriaException(SerializationInfo, StreamingContext);**

Initializes a new instance of the **InvalidFilterCriteriaException** class with a specified error message and a reference to the inner exception that is the cause of this exception.

  [Visual Basic] **Public Sub New(String, Exception)**

  [C#] **public InvalidFilterCriteriaException(string, Exception);**

  [C++] **public: InvalidFilterCriteriaException(String*, Exception*);**

  [JScript] **public function InvalidFilterCriteriaException(String, Exception);**

InvalidFilterCriteriaException Constructor ( )

Initializes a new instance of the **InvalidFilterCriteriaException** class with the default properties.

```
[Visual Basic]
Public Sub New()
[C#]
public InvalidFilterCriteriaException();
[C++]
public: InvalidFilterCriteriaException();
[JScript]
public function InvalidFilterCriteriaException();
```

Remarks

This constructor initializes an instance of **InvalidFilterCriteriaException** with an empty message string and the root cause exception set to a null reference (**Nothing** in Visual Basic).

This constructor sets the properties of the **Exception** object as follows:

Property	Value
InnerException	null
Message	The empty string ("").

Requirements

Platforms: Windows 98, Windows NT 4.0, Windows Millennium Edition, Windows 2000, Windows XP Home Edition, Windows XP Professional, Windows .NET Server family

InvalidFilterCriteriaException Constructor (String)

Initializes a new instance of the **InvalidFilterCriteriaException** class with the given HRESULT and message string.

```
[Visual Basic]
Public Sub New( _
    ByVal message As String _
)
[C#]
public InvalidFilterCriteriaException(
    string message
);
[C++]
public: InvalidFilterCriteriaException(
    String* message
);
[JScript]
public function InvalidFilterCriteriaException(
    message : String
);
```

Parameters

message
> The message text for the exception.

Remarks

An exception that is thrown as a direct result of a previous exception should include a reference to the previous exception in the **InnerException** property. The **InnerException** property returns the same value that is passed into the constructor, or a null reference (**Nothing** in Visual Basic) if the **InnerException** property does not supply the inner exception value to the constructor.

The following table shows the initial property values for an instance of **InvalidFilterCriteriaException**.

Property	Value
InnerException	A null reference (**Nothing**)
Message	The error message string.

Requirements

Platforms: Windows 98, Windows NT 4.0, Windows Millennium Edition, Windows 2000, Windows XP Home Edition, Windows XP Professional, Windows .NET Server family

InvalidFilterCriteriaException Constructor (SerializationInfo, StreamingContext)

Initializes a new instance of the **InvalidFilterCriteriaException** class with the specified serialization and context information.

```
[Visual Basic]
Protected Sub New( _
    ByVal info As SerializationInfo, _
    ByVal context As StreamingContext _
)
[C#]
protected InvalidFilterCriteriaException(
    SerializationInfo info,
    StreamingContext context
);
```

```
[C++]
protected: InvalidFilterCriteriaException(
    SerializationInfo* info,
    StreamingContext context
);
[JScript]
protected function InvalidFilterCriteriaException(
    info : SerializationInfo,
    context : StreamingContext
);
```

Parameters

info
> A **SerializationInfo** object that contains the information required to serialize this instance.

context
> A **StreamingContext** object that contains the source and destination of the serialized stream associated with this instance.

Requirements

Platforms: Windows 98, Windows NT 4.0, Windows Millennium Edition, Windows 2000, Windows XP Home Edition, Windows XP Professional, Windows .NET Server family

InvalidFilterCriteriaException Constructor (String, Exception)

Initializes a new instance of the **InvalidFilterCriteriaException** class with a specified error message and a reference to the inner exception that is the cause of this exception.

```
[Visual Basic]
Public Sub New( _
    ByVal message As String, _
    ByVal inner As Exception _
)
[C#]
public InvalidFilterCriteriaException(
    string message,
    Exception inner
);
[C++]
public: InvalidFilterCriteriaException(
    String* message,
    Exception* inner
);
[JScript]
public function InvalidFilterCriteriaException(
    message : String,
    inner : Exception
);
```

Parameters

message
> The error message that explains the reason for the exception.

inner
> The exception that is the cause of the current exception. If the *inner* parameter is not a null reference (**Nothing** in Visual Basic), the current exception is raised in a **catch** block that handles the inner exception.

Remarks

An exception that is thrown as a direct result of a previous exception should include a reference to the previous exception in the **InnerException** property. The **InnerException** property returns the same value that is passed into the constructor, or a null reference (**Nothing** in Visual Basic) if the **InnerException** property does not supply the inner exception value to the constructor.

The following table shows the initial property values for an instance of **InvalidFilterCriteriaException**.

Property	Value
InnerException	The inner exception reference.
Message	The error message string.

Requirements

Platforms: Windows 98, Windows NT 4.0, Windows Millennium Edition, Windows 2000, Windows XP Home Edition, Windows XP Professional, Windows .NET Server family

IReflect Interface

Allows objects to return **MemberInfo** objects that represent an object.

```
[Visual Basic]
<Guid("AFBF15E5-C37C-11d2-B88E-00A0C9B471B8")>
Public Interface IReflect
[C#]
[Guid("AFBF15E5-C37C-11d2-B88E-00A0C9B471B8")]
public interface IReflect
[C++]
[Guid("AFBF15E5-C37C-11d2-B88E-00A0C9B471B8")]
public __gc __interface IReflect
[JScript]
public
   Guid("AFBF15E5-C37C-11d2-B88E-00A0C9B471B8")
interface IReflect
```

Classes that Implement IReflect

Class	Description
AccessibleObject	Provides information that accessibility applications use to adjust an application's UI for users with impairments.
Type	Represents type declarations: class types, interface types, array types, value types, and enumeration types.

Remarks

IReflect defines a subset of the **Type** reflection methods. Use **IReflect** to access and invoke members of a type.

Requirements

Namespace: System.Reflection

Platforms: Windows 98, Windows NT 4.0, Windows Millennium Edition, Windows 2000, Windows XP Home Edition, Windows XP Professional, Windows .NET Server family

Assembly: Mscorlib (in Mscorlib.dll)

IReflect.UnderlyingSystemType Property

Gets the underlying type that represents the **IReflect** object.

```
[Visual Basic]
ReadOnly Property UnderlyingSystemType As Type
[C#]
Type UnderlyingSystemType {get;}
[C++]
__property Type* get_UnderlyingSystemType();
[JScript]
function get UnderlyingSystemType() : Type;
```

Property Value

The underlying type that represents the **IReflect** object.

Requirements

Platforms: Windows 98, Windows NT 4.0, Windows Millennium Edition, Windows 2000, Windows XP Home Edition, Windows XP Professional, Windows .NET Server family

IReflect.GetField Method

Returns the **FieldInfo** object corresponding to the specified field and **BindingFlag**.

```
[Visual Basic]
Function GetField( _
   ByVal name As String, _
   ByVal bindingAttr As BindingFlags _
) As FieldInfo
[C#]
FieldInfo GetField(
   string name,
   BindingFlags bindingAttr
);
[C++]
FieldInfo* GetField(
   String* name,
   BindingFlags bindingAttr
);
[JScript]
function GetField(
   name : String,
   bindingAttr : BindingFlags
) : FieldInfo;
```

Parameters

name
  The name of the field to find.
bindingAttr
  The binding attributes used to control the search.

Return Value

A **FieldInfo** object containing the field information for the named object that meets the search constraints specified in *bindingAttr*.

Exceptions

Exception Type	Condition
AmbiguousMatchException	The object implements multiple fields with the same name.

Requirements

Platforms: Windows 98, Windows NT 4.0, Windows Millennium Edition, Windows 2000, Windows XP Home Edition, Windows XP Professional, Windows .NET Server family

IReflect.GetFields Method

Returns an array of **FieldInfo** objects corresponding to all fields of the current class.

```
[Visual Basic]
Function GetFields( _
   ByVal bindingAttr As BindingFlags _
) As FieldInfo()
[C#]
FieldInfo[] GetFields(
   BindingFlags bindingAttr
);
[C++]
FieldInfo* GetFields(
   BindingFlags bindingAttr
) [];
```

```
[JScript]
function GetFields(
    bindingAttr : BindingFlags
) : FieldInfo[];
```

Parameters

bindingAttr
> The binding attributes used to control the search.

Return Value

An array of **FieldInfo** objects containing all the field information for this reflection object that meets the search constraints specified in *bindingAttr*.

Remarks

The match is based upon a name. Each field must have a unique name. The **BindingFlags.NonPublic** flag specifies that non-public methods are included in the search. The **BindingFlags.Public** flag specifies that public methods are included in the search.

Requirements

Platforms: Windows 98, Windows NT 4.0, Windows Millennium Edition, Windows 2000, Windows XP Home Edition, Windows XP Professional, Windows .NET Server family

IReflect.GetMember Method

Retrieves an array of **MemberInfo** objects corresponding to all public members or to all members that match a specified name.

```
[Visual Basic]
Function GetMember( _
    ByVal name As String, _
    ByVal bindingAttr As BindingFlags _
) As MemberInfo()
[C#]
MemberInfo[] GetMember(
    string name,
    BindingFlags bindingAttr
);
[C++]
MemberInfo* GetMember(
    String* name,
    BindingFlags bindingAttr
) [];
[JScript]
function GetMember(
    name : String,
    bindingAttr : BindingFlags
) : MemberInfo[];
```

Parameters

name
> The name of the member to find.

bindingAttr
> The binding attributes used to control the search.

Return Value

An array of **MemberInfo** objects matching the *name* parameter.

Remarks

The **GetMember** method retrieves an array of **MemberInfo** objects by using the name and binding attribute that correspond to all public members or to all members that match a specified name. The case of

the specified name is observed or ignored, as specified by **BindingFlags.IgnoreCase**.

Requirements

Platforms: Windows 98, Windows NT 4.0, Windows Millennium Edition, Windows 2000, Windows XP Home Edition, Windows XP Professional, Windows .NET Server family

IReflect.GetMembers Method

Retrieves an array of **MemberInfo** objects corresponding either to all public members or to all members of the current class.

```
[Visual Basic]
Function GetMembers( _
    ByVal bindingAttr As BindingFlags _
) As MemberInfo()
[C#]
MemberInfo[] GetMembers(
    BindingFlags bindingAttr
);
[C++]
MemberInfo* GetMembers(
    BindingFlags bindingAttr
) [];
[JScript]
function GetMembers(
    bindingAttr : BindingFlags
) : MemberInfo[];
```

Parameters

bindingAttr
> The binding attributes used to control the search.

Return Value

An array of **MemberInfo** objects containing all the member information for this reflection object.

Remarks

This method retrieves an array of **MemberInfo** objects by using the binding attribute that corresponds either to all public members or to all members of the current class. It returns an array of all of the members defined for this object.

Requirements

Platforms: Windows 98, Windows NT 4.0, Windows Millennium Edition, Windows 2000, Windows XP Home Edition, Windows XP Professional, Windows .NET Server family

IReflect.GetMethod Method

Retrieves a **MethodInfo** object corresponding to a specified method.

Overload List

Retrieves a **MethodInfo** object corresponding to a specified method under specified search constraints.

> [Visual Basic] **Overloads Function GetMethod(String, BindingFlags) As MethodInfo**
>
> [C#] **MethodInfo GetMethod(string, BindingFlags);**
>
> [C++] **MethodInfo* GetMethod(String*, BindingFlags);**
>
> [JScript] **function GetMethod(String, BindingFlags) : MethodInfo;**

Retrieves a **MethodInfo** object corresponding to a specified method, using a **Type** array to choose from among overloaded methods.

> [Visual Basic] **Overloads Function GetMethod(String, BindingFlags, Binder, Type(), ParameterModifier()) As MethodInfo**
>
> [C#] **MethodInfo GetMethod(string, BindingFlags, Binder, Type[], ParameterModifier[]);**
>
> [C++] **MethodInfo* GetMethod(String*, BindingFlags, Binder*, Type[], ParameterModifier[]);**
>
> [JScript] **function GetMethod(String, BindingFlags, Binder, Type[], ParameterModifier[]) : MethodInfo;**

IReflect.GetMethod Method (String, BindingFlags)

Retrieves a **MethodInfo** object corresponding to a specified method under specified search constraints.

```
[Visual Basic]
Function GetMethod( _
   ByVal name As String, _
   ByVal bindingAttr As BindingFlags _
) As MethodInfo
[C#]
MethodInfo GetMethod(
   string name,
   BindingFlags bindingAttr
);
[C++]
MethodInfo* GetMethod(
   String* name,
   BindingFlags bindingAttr
);
[JScript]
function GetMethod(
   name : String,
   bindingAttr : BindingFlags
) : MethodInfo;
```

Parameters

name
> The name of the member to find.

bindingAttr
> The binding attributes used to control the search.

Return Value

A **MethodInfo** object containing the method information, with the match being based on the method name and search constraints specified in *bindingAttr*.

Exceptions

Exception Type	Condition
AmbiguousMatchException	The object implements multiple methods with the same name.

Requirements

Platforms: Windows 98, Windows NT 4.0, Windows Millennium Edition, Windows 2000, Windows XP Home Edition, Windows XP Professional, Windows .NET Server family

IReflect.GetMethod Method (String, BindingFlags, Binder, Type[], ParameterModifier[])

Retrieves a **MethodInfo** object corresponding to a specified method, using a **Type** array to choose from among overloaded methods.

```
[Visual Basic]
Function GetMethod( _
   ByVal name As String, _
   ByVal bindingAttr As BindingFlags, _
   ByVal binder As Binder, _
   ByVal types() As Type, _
   ByVal modifiers() As ParameterModifier _
) As MethodInfo
[C#]
MethodInfo GetMethod(
   string name,
   BindingFlags bindingAttr,
   Binder binder,
   Type[] types,
   ParameterModifier[] modifiers
);
[C++]
MethodInfo* GetMethod(
   String* name,
   BindingFlags bindingAttr,
   Binder* binder,
   Type* types[],
   ParameterModifier modifiers[]
);
[JScript]
function GetMethod(
   name : String,
   bindingAttr : BindingFlags,
   binder : Binder,
   types : Type[],
   modifiers : ParameterModifier[]
) : MethodInfo;
```

Parameters

name
> The name of the member to find.

bindingAttr
> The binding attributes used to control the search.

binder
> An object that implements **Binder**, containing properties related to this method.

types
> An array used to choose among overloaded methods.

modifiers
> An array of parameter modifiers used to make binding work with parameter signatures in which the types have been modified.

Return Value

The requested method that matches all the specified parameters.

Exceptions

Exception Type	Condition
AmbiguousMatchException	The object implements multiple methods with the same name.

Remarks

The return value is a match based on the method name, **BindingFlags** enum member, the kind of type conversion specified by the *binder* parameter, the overload, and the **ParameterInfo** that describes the signature of the method.

Requirements

Platforms: Windows 98, Windows NT 4.0, Windows Millennium Edition, Windows 2000, Windows XP Home Edition, Windows XP Professional, Windows .NET Server family

IReflect.GetMethods Method

Retrieves an array of **MethodInfo** objects with all public methods or all methods of the current class.

```
[Visual Basic]
Function GetMethods( _
   ByVal bindingAttr As BindingFlags _
) As MethodInfo()
[C#]
MethodInfo[] GetMethods(
   BindingFlags bindingAttr
);
[C++]
MethodInfo* GetMethods(
   BindingFlags bindingAttr
) [];
[JScript]
function GetMethods(
   bindingAttr : BindingFlags
) : MethodInfo[];
```

Parameters

bindingAttr
   The binding attributes used to control the search.

Return Value

An array of **MethodInfo** objects containing all the methods defined for this reflection object that meet the search constraints specified in *bindingAttr*.

Remarks

The non-public attribute of *bindingAttr* is indicated only if public methods are returned.

Requirements

Platforms: Windows 98, Windows NT 4.0, Windows Millennium Edition, Windows 2000, Windows XP Home Edition, Windows XP Professional, Windows .NET Server family

IReflect.GetProperties Method

Retrieves an array of **PropertyInfo** objects corresponding to all public properties or to all properties of the current class.

```
[Visual Basic]
Function GetProperties( _
   ByVal bindingAttr As BindingFlags _
) As PropertyInfo()
[C#]
PropertyInfo[] GetProperties(
   BindingFlags bindingAttr
);
```

```
[C++]
PropertyInfo* GetProperties(
   BindingFlags bindingAttr
) [];
[JScript]
function GetProperties(
   bindingAttr : BindingFlags
) : PropertyInfo[];
```

Parameters

bindingAttr
   The binding attribute used to control the search.

Return Value

An array of **PropertyInfo** objects for all the properties defined on the reflection object.

Requirements

Platforms: Windows 98, Windows NT 4.0, Windows Millennium Edition, Windows 2000, Windows XP Home Edition, Windows XP Professional, Windows .NET Server family

IReflect.GetProperty Method

Retrieves a **PropertyInfo** object corresponding to a specified property.

Overload List

Retrieves a **PropertyInfo** object corresponding to a specified property under specified search constraints.

   [Visual Basic] **Overloads Function GetProperty(String, BindingFlags) As PropertyInfo**

   [C#] **PropertyInfo GetProperty(string, BindingFlags);**

   [C++] **PropertyInfo* GetProperty(String*, BindingFlags);**

   [JScript] **function GetProperty(String, BindingFlags) : PropertyInfo;**

Retrieves a **PropertyInfo** object corresponding to a specified property with specified search constraints.

   [Visual Basic] **Overloads Function GetProperty(String, BindingFlags, Binder, Type, Type(), ParameterModifier()) As PropertyInfo**

   [C#] **PropertyInfo GetProperty(string, BindingFlags, Binder, Type, Type[], ParameterModifier[]);**

   [C++] **PropertyInfo* GetProperty(String*, BindingFlags, Binder*, Type*, Type[], ParameterModifier[]);**

   [JScript] **function GetProperty(String, BindingFlags, Binder, Type, Type[], ParameterModifier[]) : PropertyInfo;**

IReflect.GetProperty Method (String, BindingFlags)

Retrieves a **PropertyInfo** object corresponding to a specified property under specified search constraints.

```
[Visual Basic]
Function GetProperty( _
   ByVal name As String, _
   ByVal bindingAttr As BindingFlags _
) As PropertyInfo
```

```
[C#]
PropertyInfo GetProperty(
    string name,
    BindingFlags bindingAttr
);
[C++]
PropertyInfo* GetProperty(
    String* name,
    BindingFlags bindingAttr
);
[JScript]
function GetProperty(
    name : String,
    bindingAttr : BindingFlags
) : PropertyInfo;
```

Parameters

name
    The name of the property to find.
bindingAttr
    The binding attributes used to control the search.

Return Value

A **PropertyInfo** object for the located property that meets the search
constraints specified in *bindingAttr*, or a null reference (**Nothing** in
Visual Basic) if the property was not located.

Exceptions

Exception Type	Condition
AmbiguousMatchException	The object implements multiple fields with the same name.

Requirements

Platforms: Windows 98, Windows NT 4.0,
Windows Millennium Edition, Windows 2000,
Windows XP Home Edition, Windows XP Professional,
Windows .NET Server family

IReflect.GetProperty Method (String, BindingFlags, Binder, Type, Type[], ParameterModifier[])

Retrieves a **PropertyInfo** object corresponding to a specified
property with specified search constraints.

```
[Visual Basic]
Function GetProperty( _
    ByVal name As String, _
    ByVal bindingAttr As BindingFlags, _
    ByVal binder As Binder, _
    ByVal returnType As Type, _
    ByVal types() As Type, _
    ByVal modifiers() As ParameterModifier _
) As PropertyInfo
[C#]
PropertyInfo GetProperty(
    string name,
    BindingFlags bindingAttr,
    Binder binder,
    Type returnType,
    Type[] types,
    ParameterModifier[] modifiers
);
```

```
[C++]
PropertyInfo* GetProperty(
    String* name,
    BindingFlags bindingAttr,
    Binder* binder,
    Type* returnType,
    Type* types[],
    ParameterModifier modifiers[]
);
[JScript]
function GetProperty(
    name : String,
    bindingAttr : BindingFlags,
    binder : Binder,
    returnType : Type,
    types : Type[],
    modifiers : ParameterModifier[]
) : PropertyInfo;
```

Parameters

name
    The name of the member to find.
bindingAttr
    The binding attribute used to control the search.
binder
    An object that implements **Binder**, containing properties related
    to this method.
returnType
    The type of the property.
types
    An array used to choose among overloaded methods with the
    same name.
modifiers
    An array used to choose the parameter modifiers.

Return Value

A **PropertyInfo** object for the located property, if a property with
the specified name was located in this reflection object, or a null
reference (**Nothing** in Visual Basic) if the property was not located.

Remarks

This method retrieves a **PropertyInfo** object corresponding to a
specified property under specified search constraints. A type array is
used to choose from among overloaded methods.

Requirements

Platforms: Windows 98, Windows NT 4.0,
Windows Millennium Edition, Windows 2000,
Windows XP Home Edition, Windows XP Professional,
Windows .NET Server family

IReflect.InvokeMember Method

Invokes a specified member.

```
[Visual Basic]
Function InvokeMember( _
    ByVal name As String, _
    ByVal invokeAttr As BindingFlags, _
    ByVal binder As Binder, _
    ByVal target As Object, _
    ByVal args() As Object, _
    ByVal modifiers() As ParameterModifier, _
```

```
      ByVal culture As CultureInfo, _
      ByVal namedParameters() As String _
) As Object
[C#]
object InvokeMember(
   string name,
   BindingFlags invokeAttr,
   Binder binder,
   object target,
   object[] args,
   ParameterModifier[] modifiers,
   CultureInfo culture,
   string[] namedParameters
);
[C++]
Object* InvokeMember(
   String* name,
   BindingFlags invokeAttr,
   Binder* binder,
   Object* target,
   Object* args __gc[],
   ParameterModifier modifiers[],
   CultureInfo* culture,
   String* namedParameters __gc[]
);
[JScript]
function InvokeMember(
   name : String,
   invokeAttr : BindingFlags,
   binder : Binder,
   target : Object,
   args : Object[],
   modifiers : ParameterModifier[],
   culture : CultureInfo,
   namedParameters : String[]
) : Object;
```

Parameters

name

The name of the member to find.

invokeAttr

One of the **BindingFlags** invocation attributes. The *invokeAttr* parameter may be a constructor, method, property, or field. A suitable invocation attribute must be specified. Invoke the default member of a class by passing the empty string ("") as the name of the member.

binder

One of the **BindingFlags** bit flags. Implements **Binder**, containing properties related to this method.

target

The object on which to invoke the specified member. This parameter is ignored for static members.

args

An array of objects that contains the number, order, and type of the parameters of the member to be invoked. This is an empty array if there are no parameters.

modifiers

An array of **ParameterModifier** objects. This array has the same length as the *args* parameter, representing the invoked member's argument attributes in the metadata. A parameter can have the following attributes: **pdIn**, **pdOut**, **pdRetval**, **pdOptional**, and

pdHasDefault. These represent [In], [Out], [retval], [optional], and a default parameter, respectively. These attributes are used by various interoperability services.

culture

An instance of **CultureInfo** used to govern the coercion of types. For example, *culture* converts a **String** that represents 1000 to a **Double** value, since 1000 is represented differently by different cultures. If this parameter is a null reference (**Nothing** in Visual Basic), the **CultureInfo** for the current thread is used.

namedParameters

A **String** array of parameters.

Return Value

The specified member.

Exceptions

Exception Type	Condition
ArgumentException	*invokeAttr* is **BindingFlags.CreateInstance** and another bit flag is also set.
ArgumentException	*invokeAttr* is not **BindingFlags.CreateInstance** and *name* is a null reference (**Nothing** in Visual Basic).
ArgumentException	*invokeAttr* is not an invocation attribute from **BindingFlags**.
ArgumentException	*invokeAttr* specifies both **get** and **set** for a property or field.
ArgumentException	*invokeAttr* specifies both a field **set** and an **Invoke** method. *args* are provided for a field **get**.
ArgumentException	More than one argument is specified for a field **set**.
MissingFieldException	The field or property cannot be found.
MissingMethodException	The method cannot be found.
SecurityException	A private member is invoked without the necessary **ReflectionPermission**.

Remarks

The method that is to be invoked must be accessible and provide the most specific match with the specified argument list, under the constraints of the specified binder and invocation attributes.

A method is invoked if the number of parameters in the method declaration equals the number of arguments in the specified argument list, and the type of each argument can be converted by the binder to the type of the parameter.

> **Note** The array of parameter modifiers passed in to **InvokeMember** must contain a single parameter modifier. Only the first parameter modifier is considered when determining which argument needs to be passed by reference when exposed to COM.

The binder finds all matching methods, in accordance with the type of binding requested (**BindingFlags.InvokeMethod**, **GetProperties**, and so on). The set of methods is filtered by the name, number of arguments, and a set of search modifiers defined in the binder. After the method is selected, it is invoked, and accessibility is checked at that point. The search may control which set of methods is searched based upon the accessibility attribute associated with the method. **BindToMethod** selects the method to be invoked. The default binder selects the most specific match.

Access restrictions are ignored for fully trusted code. That is, private constructors, methods, fields, and properties can be accessed and invoked through reflection whenever the code is fully trusted.

Example

[Visual Basic, C#, C++] The following example obtains the value of the **Now** property.

```
[Visual Basic]
Imports System
Imports System.Reflection
Imports Microsoft.VisualBasic

Public Class MainClass
    Public Overloads Shared Sub Main(ByVal args() As String)
        Dim tDate As Type = Type.GetType("System.DateTime")
        Dim result As [Object] = tDate.InvokeMember("Now",
BindingFlags.GetProperty, Nothing, Nothing, New [Object](-1) {})
        Console.WriteLine(result.ToString())
    End Sub 'Main
End Class 'MainClass
```

```
[C#]
using System;
using System.Reflection;

public class MainClass
{
    public static void Main(string[] args)
    {
        Type tDate = Type.GetType("System.DateTime");
        Object result = tDate.InvokeMember("Now",
BindingFlags.GetProperty, null, null, new Object[0]);
        Console.WriteLine(result.ToString());
    }
}
```

```
[C++]
#using <mscorlib.dll>
#using <System.DLL>
using namespace System;
using namespace System::Reflection;

#define NULL 0

void main()
{
    Type *tDate = Type::GetType(L"System.DateTime");
    Object* result = tDate->InvokeMember(L"Now",
BindingFlags::GetProperty, NULL, NULL, new Object*[0]);
    Console::WriteLine(result->ToString());
}
```

Requirements

Platforms: Windows 98, Windows NT 4.0, Windows Millennium Edition, Windows 2000, Windows XP Home Edition, Windows XP Professional, Windows .NET Server family

ManifestResourceInfo Class

Contains manifest resource topology information.

System.Object
   System.Reflection.ManifestResourceInfo

```
[Visual Basic]
Public Class ManifestResourceInfo
[C#]
public class ManifestResourceInfo
[C++]
public __gc class ManifestResourceInfo
[JScript]
public class ManifestResourceInfo
```

Thread Safety

This type is safe for multithreaded operations.

Requirements

Namespace: System.Reflection

Platforms: Windows 98, Windows NT 4.0,
Windows Millennium Edition, Windows 2000,
Windows XP Home Edition, Windows XP Professional,
Windows .NET Server family

Assembly: Mscorlib (in Mscorlib.dll)

ManifestResourceInfo.FileName Property

Indicates the name of the file containing the manifest resource, if not the same as the manifest file. This property is read-only.

```
[Visual Basic]
Public Overridable ReadOnly Property FileName As String
[C#]
public virtual string FileName {get;}
[C++]
public: __property virtual String* get_FileName();
[JScript]
public function get FileName() : String;
```

Property Value

A **String** that is the manifest resource's file name.

Requirements

Platforms: Windows 98, Windows NT 4.0,
Windows Millennium Edition, Windows 2000,
Windows XP Home Edition, Windows XP Professional,
Windows .NET Server family

ManifestResourceInfo.ReferencedAssembly Property

Indicates the containing assembly. This property is read-only.

```
[Visual Basic]
Public Overridable ReadOnly Property ReferencedAssembly As Assembly
[C#]
public virtual Assembly ReferencedAssembly {get;}
[C++]
public: __property virtual Assembly* get_ReferencedAssembly();
[JScript]
public function get ReferencedAssembly() : Assembly;
```

Property Value

An **Assembly** object representing the manifest resource's containing assembly.

Requirements

Platforms: Windows 98, Windows NT 4.0,
Windows Millennium Edition, Windows 2000,
Windows XP Home Edition, Windows XP Professional,
Windows .NET Server family

ManifestResourceInfo.ResourceLocation Property

Indicates the manifest resource's location. This property is read-only.

```
[Visual Basic]
Public Overridable ReadOnly Property ResourceLocation As _
   ResourceLocation
[C#]
public virtual ResourceLocation ResourceLocation {get;}
[C++]
public: __property virtual ResourceLocation get_ResourceLocation();
[JScript]
public function get ResourceLocation() : ResourceLocation;
```

Property Value

A combination of the **ResourceLocation** flags.

Requirements

Platforms: Windows 98, Windows NT 4.0,
Windows Millennium Edition, Windows 2000,
Windows XP Home Edition, Windows XP Professional,
Windows .NET Server family

MemberFilter Delegate

Represents a delegate that is used to filter a list of members represented in an array of **MemberInfo** objects.

```
[Visual Basic]
<Serializable>
Public Delegate Function Sub MemberFilter( _
   ByVal m As MemberInfo, _
   ByVal filterCriteria As Object _
) As Boolean
[C#]
[Serializable]
public delegate bool MemberFilter(
   MemberInfo m,
   object filterCriteria
);
[C++]
[Serializable]
public __gc __delegate bool MemberFilter(
   MemberInfo* m,
   Object* filterCriteria
);
```

[JScript] In JScript, you can use the delegates in the .NET Framework, but you cannot define your own.

Parameters [Visual Basic, C#, C++]

The declaration of your callback method must have the same parameters as the **MemberFilter** delegate declaration.

m

   The **MemberInfo** object to which the filter is applied.

filterCriteria

   An arbitrary object used to filter the list.

Remarks

Every derived class of a **Delegate** and **MulticastDelegate** has a constructor and an **Invoke** method.

The **FindMembers** method uses this delegate to filter the list of members that it returns.

Requirements

Namespace: System.Reflection

Platforms: Windows 98, Windows NT 4.0, Windows Millennium Edition, Windows 2000, Windows XP Home Edition, Windows XP Professional, Windows .NET Server family

Assembly: Mscorlib (in Mscorlib.dll)

MemberInfo Class

Discovers the attributes of a member and provides access to member metadata.

System.Object
  System.Reflection.MemberInfo
    System.Reflection.EventInfo
    System.Reflection.FieldInfo
    System.Reflection.MethodBase
    System.Reflection.PropertyInfo
    System.Type

```
[Visual Basic]
<Serializable>
<ClassInterface(ClassInterfaceType.AutoDual)>
MustInherit Public Class MemberInfo
   Implements ICustomAttributeProvider
[C#]
[Serializable]
[ClassInterface(ClassInterfaceType.AutoDual)]
public abstract class MemberInfo : ICustomAttributeProvider
[C++]
[Serializable]
[ClassInterface(ClassInterfaceType::AutoDual)]
public __gc __abstract class MemberInfo : public
   ICustomAttributeProvider
[JScript]
public
   Serializable
   ClassInterface(ClassInterfaceType.AutoDual)
abstract class MemberInfo implements
   ICustomAttributeProvider
```

Thread Safety

This type is safe for multithreaded operations.

Remarks

The **MemberInfo** class is the abstract base class of the classes used to obtain information for all members of a class (constructors, events, fields, methods, and properties).

This class introduces the basic functionality that all members provide.

Notes to Inheritors: When you inherit from **MemberInfo**, you must override the following members: **GetCustomAttributes** and **IsDefined**.

Requirements

Namespace: System.Reflection

Platforms: Windows 98, Windows NT 4.0, Windows Millennium Edition, Windows 2000, Windows XP Home Edition, Windows XP Professional, Windows .NET Server family, .NET Compact Framework - Windows CE .NET

Assembly: Mscorlib (in Mscorlib.dll)

MemberInfo Constructor

Initializes a new instance of the **MemberInfo** class.

```
[Visual Basic]
Protected Sub New()
```

```
[C#]
protected MemberInfo();
[C++]
protected: MemberInfo();
[JScript]
protected function MemberInfo();
```

Remarks

Only a derived class can create this **MemberInfo** class.

Requirements

Platforms: Windows 98, Windows NT 4.0, Windows Millennium Edition, Windows 2000, Windows XP Home Edition, Windows XP Professional, Windows .NET Server family, .NET Compact Framework - Windows CE .NET, Common Language Infrastructure (CLI) Standard

MemberInfo.DeclaringType Property

Gets the class that declares this member.

```
[Visual Basic]
Public MustOverride ReadOnly Property DeclaringType As Type
[C#]
public abstract Type DeclaringType {get;}
[C++]
public: __property virtual Type* get_DeclaringType() = 0;
[JScript]
public abstract function get DeclaringType() : Type;
```

Property Value

The **Type** object for the class that declares this member.

Remarks

The **DeclaringType** property retrieves a reference to the **Type** object for the type that declares this member. A member of a class (or interface) is either declared or inherited from a base class (or interface). The returned class might not be the same as the **Type** object used to obtain this **MemberInfo** object.

- If the **Type** object from which this **MemberInfo** object was obtained did not declare this member, the **DeclaringType** will represent one of its base types.

- If the **MemberInfo** object is a global member, (that is, it was obtained from **Module.GetMethods**, which returns global methods on a module), then the returned **DeclaringType** will be a null reference (**Nothing** in Visual Basic).

Example

[Visual Basic, C#, JScript] The following example shows how **DeclaringType** works with classes and interfaces and retrieves the member names of the **System.IO.BufferedStream** class, along with the class in which those members are declared. Also note that when B overrides virtual method M from A, it essentially redefines (or redeclares) this method. Therefore, B.M's **MethodInfo** reports the declaring type as B rather than A, even though A is where this method was originally declared.

```
[Visual Basic]
Imports System
Imports System.IO
Imports System.Reflection
Imports Microsoft.VisualBasic
```

```
Namespace MyNamespace1

    Interface i
        Function MyVar() As Integer
    End Interface
    ' DeclaringType for MyVar is i.

    Class A
        Implements i
        Function MyVar() As Integer Implements i.MyVar
            Return 0
        End Function
    End Class
    ' DeclaringType for MyVar is A.

    Class B
        Inherits A
        Function MyVars() As Integer
            Return 0
        End Function
    End Class
    ' DeclaringType for MyVar is B.

    Class C
        Inherits A
    End Class
    ' DeclaringType for MyVar is A.
End Namespace

Namespace MyNamespace2

    Class A
        Public Overridable Sub M()
        End Sub
    End Class

    Class B
        Inherits A
        Public Overrides Sub M()
        End Sub
    End Class
End Namespace
Class Mymemberinfo

    Public Shared Sub Main()

        Console.WriteLine(ControlChars.Cr & "Reflection.MemberInfo")

        'Get the Type and MemberInfo.
        Dim MyType As Type = Type.GetType("System.IO.BufferedStream")

        Dim Mymemberinfoarray As MemberInfo() = MyType.GetMembers()

        'Get and display the DeclaringType method.
        Console.WriteLine(ControlChars.Cr & "There are {0}          ↵
members in {1}.", Mymemberinfoarray.Length, MyType.FullName)

        Dim Mymemberinfo As MemberInfo
        For Each Mymemberinfo In Mymemberinfoarray
            Console.WriteLine("The declaring type of {0} is        ↵
{1}.", Mymemberinfo.Name, Mymemberinfo.DeclaringType.ToString())
        Next Mymemberinfo
    End Sub
End Class
```

```
[C#]
using System;
using System.IO;
using System.Reflection;

namespace MyNamespace1
{
    interface i
    {
        int MyVar() ;
    };
    // DeclaringType for MyVar is i.

    class A : i
    {
        public int MyVar() { return 0; }
    };
    // DeclaringType for MyVar is A.

    class B : A
    {
        new int MyVar() { return 0; }
    };
    // DeclaringType for MyVar is B.

    class C : A
    {
    };
    // DeclaringType for MyVar is A.

}

namespace MyNamespace2
{
    class Mymemberinfo
    {

        public static void Main(string[] args)
        {

            Console.WriteLine ("\nReflection.MemberInfo");

            //Get the Type and MemberInfo.
            Type MyType =Type.GetType("System.IO.BufferedStream");
            MemberInfo[] Mymemberinfoarray = MyType.GetMembers();

            //Get and display the DeclaringType method.
            Console.WriteLine("\nThere are {0} members in {1}.      ↵
", Mymemberinfoarray.Length, MyType.FullName);

            foreach (MemberInfo Mymemberinfo in Mymemberinfoarray)
            {
                Console.WriteLine("Declaring type of {0} is {1}     ↵
.", Mymemberinfo.Name, Mymemberinfo.DeclaringType);
            }
        }
    }
}

namespace MyNamespace3
{
    class A
    {
        virtual public void M () {}
    }
    class B: A
    {
        override public void M () {}
    }
}
```

```
[JScript]

package MyPackage1 {

interface i {
function MyVar() : int ;
};
// DeclaringType for MyVar is i.

class A implements i {
public function MyVar() : int { return 0; }
};
// DeclaringType for MyVar is A.
```

```
class B extends A {
hide function MyVar() :  int{ return 0; }
};
// DeclaringType for MyVar is B.

class C extends A {
};
// DeclaringType for MyVar is A.
}

import System;
import System.IO;
import System.Reflection;

class Mymemberinfo {

   public static function Main() : void  {

      Console.WriteLine ("\nReflection.MemberInfo");

      //Get the Type and MemberInfo.
      var MyType : Type =Type.GetType("System.IO.BufferedStream");
      var Mymemberinfoarray : MemberInfo[] = MyType.GetMembers();

      //Get and display the DeclaringType method.
      Console.Write("\nThere are {0} members in ",
Mymemberinfoarray.Length);
      Console.Write("{0}.", MyType.FullName);

      for (var i : int in Mymemberinfoarray) {
         var Mymemberinfo : MemberInfo = Mymemberinfoarray[i];
         Console.Write("\n" + Mymemberinfo.Name + " declaring type - "
         + Mymemberinfo.DeclaringType);
      }
   }
}
Mymemberinfo.Main();

package MyPackage3 {
class A {
   public function M () : void  {}
}
class B extends A {
   override public function M () : void  {}
}
}
```

[Visual Basic, C#, JScript] **Note   DeclaringType** returns only the member names and the names of their declaring types. To return the member names with their prototypes, call **MemberInfo.ToString**.

Requirements

Platforms: Windows 98, Windows NT 4.0, Windows Millennium Edition, Windows 2000, Windows XP Home Edition, Windows XP Professional, Windows .NET Server family, .NET Compact Framework - Windows CE .NET, Common Language Infrastructure (CLI) Standard

MemberInfo.MemberType Property

Gets the type of this member, such as field, method, and so on.

```
[Visual Basic]
Public MustOverride ReadOnly Property MemberType As MemberTypes
[C#]
public abstract MemberTypes MemberType {get;}
[C++]
public: __property virtual MemberTypes get_MemberType() = 0;
```

```
[JScript]
public abstract function get MemberType() : MemberTypes;
```

Property Value

An enumerated value from the **MemberTypes** class, specifying a constructor, event, field, method, property, type information, all, or custom.

Remarks

To get the **MemberType** property, get the class **Type**. From the **Type**, get the **MethodInfo** array. From the **MethodInfo** array, get the **MemberTypes**.

Example

[Visual Basic, C#, JScript] The following example displays the member name and type of a specified class.

```
[Visual Basic]
Imports System
Imports System.Reflection
Imports Microsoft.VisualBasic

Class Mymemberinfo

    Public Shared Function Main() As Integer
        Console.WriteLine(ControlChars.Cr + "Reflection.MemberInfo")

        ' Get the Type and MemberInfo.
        Dim MyType As Type =
Type.GetType("System.Reflection.PropertyInfo")
        Dim Mymemberinfoarray As MemberInfo() = MyType.GetMembers()

        ' Get the MemberType method and display the elements.
        Console.Write(ControlChars.Cr + "There are {0} members in ", _
            Mymemberinfoarray.GetLength(0))
        Console.Write("{0}.", MyType.FullName)

        Dim counter As Integer
        For counter = 0 To Mymemberinfoarray.Length - 1
            Console.Write(ControlChars.CrLf + counter.ToString() + ". "
                + Mymemberinfoarray(counter).Name _
                + " Member type - " _
                + Mymemberinfoarray(counter).MemberType.ToString())
        Next counter
        Return 0
    End Function
End Class
```

```
[C#]
using System;
using System.Reflection;

class Mymemberinfo
{
    public static int Main()
    {
        Console.WriteLine ("\nReflection.MemberInfo");

        // Get the Type and MemberInfo.
        Type MyType = Type.GetType("System.Reflection.PropertyInfo");
        MemberInfo[] Mymemberinfoarray = MyType.GetMembers();

        // Get the MemberType method and display the elements.
        Console.Write("\nThere are {0} members in ",
Mymemberinfoarray.GetLength(0));
        Console.Write("{0}.", MyType.FullName);

        for (int counter = 0; counter <
Mymemberinfoarray.Length; counter++)
        {
            Console.Write("\n" + counter + ". "
                + Mymemberinfoarray[counter].Name
                + " Member type - " +
```

```
            Mymemberinfoarray[counter].MemberType.ToString());
        }
        return 0;
    }
}

[JScript]
import System;
import System.Reflection;

class Mymemberinfo
{
    public static function Main() : void
    {
        Console.WriteLine ("\nReflection.MemberInfo");

        //Get the Type and MemberInfo.
        var MyType : Type =
Type.GetType("System.Reflection.PropertyInfo");
        var Mymemberinfoarray : MemberInfo[] = MyType.GetMembers();

        //Get the MemberType method and display the elements.
        Console.Write("\nThere are {0} members in ",
            Mymemberinfoarray.GetLength(0));
        Console.Write("{0}.", MyType.FullName);

        for (var counter : int in Mymemberinfoarray)
        {
            Console.Write("\n" + counter + ". "
                + Mymemberinfoarray[counter].Name
                + " Member type - " +
                Mymemberinfoarray[counter].MemberType.ToString());
        }
    }
}
Mymemberinfo.Main();
```

Requirements

Platforms: Windows 98, Windows NT 4.0,
Windows Millennium Edition, Windows 2000,
Windows XP Home Edition, Windows XP Professional,
Windows .NET Server family,
.NET Compact Framework - Windows CE .NET

MemberInfo.Name Property

Gets the name of this member.

```
[Visual Basic]
Public MustOverride ReadOnly Property Name As String
[C#]
public abstract string Name {get;}
[C++]
public: __property virtual String* get_Name() = 0;
[JScript]
public abstract function get Name() : String;
```

Property Value

A **String** containing the name of this member.

Remarks

Only the simple name is returned, not the fully qualified name. For
example, for a member System.Reflection.MemberTypes.Field, the
Name property would be Field.

To get the Name property, get the class **Type**. From the **Type**, get the
MemberInfo array. From a **MemberInfo** element of the array,
obtain the **Name** property.

Example

[Visual Basic, C#, JScript] This example lists the **Name** and
DeclaringType property of each member of the specified class.

```
[Visual Basic]
Imports System
Imports System.Reflection
Imports Microsoft.VisualBasic

Class Mymemberinfo
    Public Shared Function Main() As Integer
        Console.WriteLine("Reflection.MemberInfo")

        ' Get the Type and MemberInfo.
        Dim MyType As Type = Type.GetType("System.Empty")
        Dim Mymemberinfoarray As MemberInfo() = MyType.GetMembers()

        ' Get and display the DeclaringType method.
        Console.WriteLine("There are {0} members in {1}",
Mymemberinfoarray.GetLength(0), MyType.FullName)

        Dim Mymemberinfo As MemberInfo
        For Each Mymemberinfo In Mymemberinfoarray
            Console.WriteLine(Mymemberinfo.Name & "
declaring type - " & Mymemberinfo.DeclaringType.ToString())
        Next Mymemberinfo

        Return 0
    End Function
End Class
```

```
[C#]
using System;
using System.Reflection;

class Mymemberinfo
{
    public static int Main()
    {
        Console.WriteLine ("\nReflection.MemberInfo");

        // Get the Type and MemberInfo.
        Type MyType = Type.GetType("System.Empty");
        MemberInfo[] Mymemberinfoarray = MyType.GetMembers();

        // Get and display the DeclaringType method.
        Console.Write("\nThere are {0} members in ",
            Mymemberinfoarray.GetLength(0));
        Console.Write("{0}.", MyType.FullName);

        foreach (MemberInfo Mymemberinfo in Mymemberinfoarray)
        {
            Console.Write("\n" + Mymemberinfo.Name
                + " declaring type - " +
                Mymemberinfo.DeclaringType);
        }

        return 0;
    }
}
```

```
[JScript]
import System;
import System.Reflection;

class Mymemberinfo
{
    public static function Main() : void
    {
        Console.WriteLine ("\nReflection.MemberInfo");

        //Get the Type and MemberInfo.
        var MyType : Type = Type.GetType("System.Empty");
        var Mymemberinfoarray : MemberInfo[] = MyType.GetMembers();
```

```
//Get and display the DeclaringType method.
Console.Write("\nThere are {0} members in ",
    Mymemberinfoarray.GetLength(0));
Console.Write("{0}.", MyType.FullName);

    for (var i : int in Mymemberinfoarray)
    {
        var Mymemberinfo : MemberInfo = Mymemberinfoarray[i];
        Console.Write("\n" + Mymemberinfo.Name
          + " declaring type - " +
            Mymemberinfo.DeclaringType);
    }
  }
}
Mymemberinfo.Main();
```

Requirements

Platforms: Windows 98, Windows NT 4.0,
Windows Millennium Edition, Windows 2000,
Windows XP Home Edition, Windows XP Professional,
Windows .NET Server family,
.NET Compact Framework - Windows CE .NET,
Common Language Infrastructure (CLI) Standard

MemberInfo.ReflectedType Property

Gets the class object that was used to obtain this instance of
MemberInfo.

```
[Visual Basic]
Public MustOverride ReadOnly Property ReflectedType As Type
[C#]
public abstract Type ReflectedType {get;}
[C++]
public: __property virtual Type* get_ReflectedType() = 0;
[JScript]
public abstract function get ReflectedType() : Type;
```

Property Value

The **Type** object through which this **MemberInfo** object was
obtained.

Remarks

The **ReflectedType** property retrieves the **Type** object that was used
to obtain this instance of **MemberInfo**. A **MemberInfo** object
represents a member of a particular class or interface.

In order to obtain a **MethodInfo** object:

- The **Type** object that represents the class or interface that
  supports the method is queried. This property holds a reference
  to that **Type** object.
- If the reflected type is the same class as the declaring class, the
  member is defined on the declaring class, not on a base class.
- If the **MemberInfo** object is a global member, (that is, it was
  obtained from **Module.GetMethods**, which returns global
  methods on a module), then the returned **DeclaringType** will be
  a null reference (**Nothing** in Visual Basic).

Example

[Visual Basic, C#] The following example gets **ReflectedType**
property for the specified type.

```
[Visual Basic]
Imports System
Imports System.IO
Imports System.Reflection
Imports Microsoft.VisualBasic
```

```
Class Mymemberinfo

    Public Shared Sub Main()

        Console.WriteLine(ControlChars.Cr & "Reflection.MemberInfo")

        ' Get the Type and MemberInfo.
        Dim MyType As Type = Type.GetType("System.IO.BufferedStream")
        Dim Mymemberinfoarray As MemberInfo() = MyType.GetMembers()

        ' Get and display the DeclaringType method.
        Console.WriteLine(ControlChars.Cr & "There are {0}
members in {1}:", _
            Mymemberinfoarray.Length, MyType.FullName)

        Dim Mymemberinfo As MemberInfo
        For Each Mymemberinfo In Mymemberinfoarray
            Console.WriteLine(ControlChars.Cr & Mymemberinfo.Name _
            & " reflected type - " &
Mymemberinfo.ReflectedType.ToString())
        Next Mymemberinfo
    End Sub
End Class

[C#]
using System;
using System.IO;
using System.Reflection;

class Mymemberinfo
{

    public static void Main(string[] args)
    {
        Console.WriteLine ("\nReflection.MemberInfo");

        // Get the Type and MemberInfo.
        Type MyType =Type.GetType("System.IO.BufferedStream");
        MemberInfo[] Mymemberinfoarray = MyType.GetMembers();

        // Get and display the DeclaringType method.
        Console.Write("\nThere are {0} members in ",
Mymemberinfoarray.Length);
        Console.Write("{0}.", MyType.FullName);

        foreach (MemberInfo Mymemberinfo in Mymemberinfoarray)
        {
            Console.Write("\n" + Mymemberinfo.Name + "
reflected type - " +
                Mymemberinfo.ReflectedType);
        }
    }
}
```

[Visual Basic, C#] This code produces the following output:

[Visual Basic, C#] Reflection.MemberInfo

[Visual Basic, C#] There are 31 members in
System.IO.BufferedStream.

[Visual Basic, C#] WriteByte reflected type -
System.IO.BufferedStream

Requirements

Platforms: Windows 98, Windows NT 4.0,
Windows Millennium Edition, Windows 2000,
Windows XP Home Edition, Windows XP Professional,
Windows .NET Server family,
.NET Compact Framework - Windows CE .NET,
Common Language Infrastructure (CLI) Standard

MemberInfo.GetCustomAttributes Method

When overridden in a derived class, returns all attributes defined on this member.

Overload List

When overridden in a derived class, returns an array of all of the custom attributes.

Supported by the .NET Compact Framework.

[Visual Basic] **Overloads Public MustOverride Function GetCustomAttributes(Boolean) As Object() Implements ICustomAttributeProvider.GetCustomAttributes**

[C#] **public abstract object[] GetCustomAttributes(bool);**

[C++] **public: virtual Object* GetCustomAttributes(bool) __gc[] = 0;**

[JScript] **public abstract function GetCustomAttributes(Boolean) : Object[];**

When overridden in a derived class, returns an array of custom attributes identified by **Type**.

Supported by the .NET Compact Framework.

[Visual Basic] **Overloads Public MustOverride Function GetCustomAttributes(Type, Boolean) As Object() Implements ICustomAttributeProvider.GetCustomAttributes**

[C#] **public abstract object[] GetCustomAttributes(Type, bool);**

[C++] **public: virtual Object* GetCustomAttributes(Type*, bool) __gc[] = 0;**

[JScript] **public abstract function GetCustomAttributes(Type, Boolean) : Object[];**

Example

[Visual Basic, C#, C++] The following example defines a custom attribute and associates the attribute with MyClass.MyMethod, retrieves the attribute at run time, and displays the result.

[Visual Basic, C#, C++] **Note** This example shows how to use one of the overloaded versions of **GetCustomAttributes**. For other examples that might be available, see the individual overload topics.

[Visual Basic]
```
Imports System
Imports System.Reflection
Imports Microsoft.VisualBasic

' Define a custom attribute with one named parameter.
<AttributeUsage(AttributeTargets.All)> Public Class MyAttribute
    Inherits Attribute
    Private myName As String

    Public Sub New(ByVal name As String)
        myName = name
    End Sub 'New

    Public ReadOnly Property Name() As String
        Get
            Return myName
        End Get
    End Property
End Class 'MyAttribute

' Define a class that has the custom attribute associated
' with one of its members.
Public Class MyClass1
```

```
    <MyAttribute("This is an example attribute.")> Public Sub
MyMethod(ByVal i As Integer)
        Return
    End Sub 'MyMethod
End Class 'MyClass1

Public Class MemberInfo_GetCustomAttributes

    Public Shared Sub Main()
        Try
            ' Get the type of MyClass1.
            Dim myType As Type = GetType(MyClass1)
            ' Get the members associated with MyClass1.
            Dim myMembers As MemberInfo() = myType.GetMembers()

            ' Display the attributes for each of the members
of MyClass1.
            Dim i As Integer
            For i = 0 To myMembers.Length - 1
                Dim myAttributes As [Object]() =
myMembers(i).GetCustomAttributes(False)
                If myAttributes.Length > 0 Then
                    Console.WriteLine("The attributes for the
member {0} are: ", myMembers(i))
                    Dim j As Integer
                    For j = 0 To myAttributes.Length - 1
                        Console.WriteLine("The type of the
attribute is: {0}", myAttributes(j))
                    Next j
                End If
            Next i
        Catch e As Exception
            Console.WriteLine("An exception occurred: {0}.", e.Message)
        End Try
    End Sub 'Main
End Class 'MemberInfo_GetCustomAttributes
```

[C#]
```
using System;
using System.Reflection;

// Define a custom attribute with one named parameter.
[AttributeUsage(AttributeTargets.All)]
public class MyAttribute : Attribute
{
    private string myName;
    public MyAttribute(string name)
    {
        myName = name;
    }
    public string Name
    {
        get
        {
            return myName;
        }
    }
}

// Define a class that has the custom attribute associated
// with one of its members.
public class MyClass1
{
    [MyAttribute("This is an example attribute.")]
    public void MyMethod(int i)
    {
        return;
    }
}

public class MemberInfo_GetCustomAttributes
{
    public static void Main()
    {
        try
```

```
        {
            // Get the type of MyClass1.
            Type myType = typeof(MyClass1);
            // Get the members associated with MyClass1.
            MemberInfo[] myMembers = myType.GetMembers();

            // Display the attributes for each of the
    members of MyClass1.
            for(int i = 0; i < myMembers.Length; i++)
            {
                Object[] myAttributes =
    myMembers[i].GetCustomAttributes(true);
                if(myAttributes.Length > 0)
                {
                    Console.WriteLine("\nThe attributes for
    the member {0} are: \n", myMembers[i]);
                    for(int j = 0; j < myAttributes.Length; j++)
                        Console.WriteLine("The type of the
    attribute is {0}.", myAttributes[j]);
                }
            }
        }
        catch(Exception e)
        {
            Console.WriteLine("An exception occurred: {0}", e.Message);
        }
    }
}
```

[C++]
```
#using <mscorlib.dll>

using namespace System;
using namespace System::Reflection;

// Define a custom attribute with one named parameter.
[AttributeUsage(AttributeTargets::All)]
public __gc class MyAttribute : public Attribute
{
private:
    String* myName;
public:
    MyAttribute(String* name) {
        myName = name;
    }
    __property String* get_Name()
    {
        return myName;
    }
};

// Define a class that has the custom attribute associated
with one of its members.
public __gc class MyClass1
{
public:
    [MyAttribute(S"This is an example attribute.")]
    void MyMethod(int i) {
        return;
    }
};

void main()
{
    try {
        // Get the type of MyClass1.
        Type* myType = __typeof(MyClass1);
        // Get the members associated with MyClass1.
        MemberInfo* myMembers[] = myType->GetMembers();

        // Display the attributes for each of the members of MyClass1.
        for (int i = 0; i < myMembers->Length; i++) {
            Object* myAttributes[] = myMembers[i]-
>GetCustomAttributes(true);
            if (myAttributes->Length > 0) {
```

```
                Console::WriteLine(S"\nThe attributes for the
    member {0} are: \n", myMembers->Item[i]);
                for (int j = 0; j < myAttributes->Length; j++)
                    Console::WriteLine(S"The type of the attribute
    is {0}.", myAttributes->Item[j]);
            }
        }
    } catch (Exception* e) {
        Console::WriteLine(S"An exception occurred: {0}", e->Message);
    }
}
```

MemberInfo.GetCustomAttributes Method (Boolean)

When overridden in a derived class, returns an array of all of the custom attributes.

```
[Visual Basic]
Overloads Public MustOverride Function GetCustomAttributes( _
    ByVal inherit As Boolean _
) As Object() Implements ICustomAttributeProvider.GetCustomAttributes
[C#]
public abstract object[] GetCustomAttributes(
    bool inherit
);
[C++]
public: virtual Object* GetCustomAttributes(
    bool inherit
) __gc[] = 0;
[JScript]
public abstract function GetCustomAttributes(
    inherit : Boolean
) : Object[];
```

Parameters

inherit

Specifies whether to search this member's inheritance chain to find the attributes.

Return Value

An array of all the custom attributes, or an array with zero elements if no attributes are defined.

Implements

ICustomAttributeProvider.GetCustomAttributes

Example

[Visual Basic, C#, C++] The following example defines a custom attribute and associates the attribute with MyClass.MyMethod, retrieves the attribute at run time, and displays the result.

```
[Visual Basic]
Imports System
Imports System.Reflection
Imports Microsoft.VisualBasic

' Define a custom attribute with one named parameter.
<AttributeUsage(AttributeTargets.All)> Public Class MyAttribute
    Inherits Attribute
    Private myName As String

    Public Sub New(ByVal name As String)
        myName = name
    End Sub 'New

    Public ReadOnly Property Name() As String
        Get
            Return myName
        End Get
```

```vb
        End Property
End Class 'MyAttribute

' Define a class that has the custom attribute associated         ↵
with one of its members.
Public Class MyClass1

    <MyAttribute("This is an example attribute.")> Public Sub      ↵
MyMethod(ByVal i As Integer)
        Return
    End Sub 'MyMethod
End Class 'MyClass1

Public Class MemberInfo_GetCustomAttributes

    Public Shared Sub Main()
        Try
            ' Get the type of MyClass1.
            Dim myType As Type = GetType(MyClass1)
            ' Get the members associated with MyClass1.
            Dim myMembers As MemberInfo() = myType.GetMembers()

            ' Display the attributes for each of the members of MyClass1.
            Dim i As Integer
            For i = 0 To myMembers.Length - 1
                Dim myAttributes As [Object]() =                   ↵
myMembers(i).GetCustomAttributes(False)
                If myAttributes.Length > 0 Then
                    Console.WriteLine("The attributes for          ↵
the member {0} are: ", myMembers(i))
                    Dim j As Integer
                    For j = 0 To myAttributes.Length - 1
                        Console.WriteLine("The type of the         ↵
attribute is: {0}", myAttributes(j))
                    Next j
                End If
            Next i
        Catch e As Exception
            Console.WriteLine("An exception occurred: {0}.", e.Message)
        End Try
    End Sub 'Main
End Class 'MemberInfo_GetCustomAttributes
```

[C#]
```csharp
using System;
using System.Reflection;

// Define a custom attribute with one named parameter.
[AttributeUsage(AttributeTargets.All)]
public class MyAttribute : Attribute
{
    private string myName;
    public MyAttribute(string name)
    {
        myName = name;
    }
    public string Name
    {
        get
        {
            return myName;
        }
    }
}

// Define a class that has the custom attribute associated          ↵
 with one of its members.
public class MyClass1
{
    [MyAttribute("This is an example attribute.")]
    public void MyMethod(int i)
    {
        return;
    }
}
```

```csharp
public class MemberInfo_GetCustomAttributes
{
    public static void Main()
    {
        try
        {
            // Get the type of MyClass1.
            Type myType = typeof(MyClass1);
            // Get the members associated with MyClass1.
            MemberInfo[] myMembers = myType.GetMembers();

            // Display the attributes for each of the              ↵
members of MyClass1.
            for(int i = 0; i < myMembers.Length; i++)
            {
                Object[] myAttributes =                           ↵
myMembers[i].GetCustomAttributes(true);
                if(myAttributes.Length > 0)
                {
                    Console.WriteLine("\nThe attributes for the member {0}
are: \n", myMembers[i]);
                    for(int j = 0; j < myAttributes.Length; j++)
                        Console.WriteLine("The type of the         ↵
attribute is {0}.", myAttributes[j]);
                }
            }
        }
        catch(Exception e)
        {
            Console.WriteLine("An exception occurred: {0}", e.Message);
        }
    }
}
```

[C++]
```cpp
#using <mscorlib.dll>

using namespace System;
using namespace System::Reflection;

// Define a custom attribute with one named parameter.
[AttributeUsage(AttributeTargets::All)]
public __gc class MyAttribute : public Attribute
{
private:
    String* myName;
public:
    MyAttribute(String* name) {
        myName = name;
    }
    __property String* get_Name()
    {
        return myName;
    }
};

// Define a class that has the custom attribute associated          ↵
 with one of its members.
public __gc class MyClass1
{
public:
    [MyAttribute(S"This is an example attribute.")]
    void MyMethod(int i) {
        return;
    }
};

void main()
{
    try {
        // Get the type of MyClass1.
        Type* myType = __typeof(MyClass1);
        // Get the members associated with MyClass1.
        MemberInfo* myMembers[] = myType->GetMembers();
```

```
   // Display the attributes for each of the members of MyClass1.
   for (int i = 0; i < myMembers->Length; i++) {
       Object* myAttributes[] = myMembers[i]-     ⏎
>GetCustomAttributes(true);
       if (myAttributes->Length > 0) {
           Console::WriteLine(S"\nThe attributes for the   ⏎
member {0} are: \n", myMembers->Item[i]);
           for (int j = 0; j < myAttributes->Length; j++)
               Console::WriteLine(S"The type of the attribute   ⏎
is {0}.", myAttributes->Item[j]);
       }
   }
   } catch (Exception* e) {
       Console::WriteLine(S"An exception occurred: {0}", e->Message);
   }
}
```

Requirements

Platforms: Windows 98, Windows NT 4.0,
Windows Millennium Edition, Windows 2000,
Windows XP Home Edition, Windows XP Professional,
Windows .NET Server family,
.NET Compact Framework - Windows CE .NET

MemberInfo.GetCustomAttributes Method (Type, Boolean)

When overridden in a derived class, returns an array of custom attributes identified by **Type**.

```
[Visual Basic]
Overloads Public MustOverride Function GetCustomAttributes( _
   ByVal attributeType As Type, _
   ByVal inherit As Boolean _
) As Object() Implements ICustomAttributeProvider.GetCustomAttributes
[C#]
public abstract object[] GetCustomAttributes(
   Type attributeType,
   bool inherit
);
[C++]
public: virtual Object* GetCustomAttributes(
   Type* attributeType,
   bool inherit
) __gc[] = 0;
[JScript]
public abstract function GetCustomAttributes(
   attributeType : Type,
   inherit : Boolean
) : Object[];
```

Parameters

attributeType
   The type of attribute to search for. Only attributes that are assignable to this type are returned.

inherit
   Specifies whether to search this member's inheritance chain to find the attributes.

Return Value

An array of custom attributes defined on this reflected member, or an array with zero (0) elements if no attributes are defined.

Implements

ICustomAttributeProvider.GetCustomAttributes

Exceptions

Exception Type	Condition
TypeLoadException	If the custom attribute type can not be loaded.

Requirements

Platforms: Windows 98, Windows NT 4.0,
Windows Millennium Edition, Windows 2000,
Windows XP Home Edition, Windows XP Professional,
Windows .NET Server family,
.NET Compact Framework - Windows CE .NET

MemberInfo.IsDefined Method

When overridden in a derived class, indicates whether one or more instance of *attributeType* is defined on this member.

```
[Visual Basic]
Public MustOverride Function IsDefined( _
   ByVal attributeType As Type, _
   ByVal inherit As Boolean _
) As Boolean Implements ICustomAttributeProvider.IsDefined
[C#]
public abstract bool IsDefined(
   Type attributeType,
   bool inherit
);
[C++]
public: virtual bool IsDefined(
   Type* attributeType,
   bool inherit
) = 0;
[JScript]
public abstract function IsDefined(
   attributeType : Type,
   inherit : Boolean
) : Boolean;
```

Parameters

attributeType
   The **Type** object to which the custom attributes are applied.

inherit
   Specifies whether to search this member's inheritance chain to find the attributes.

Return Value

true if one or more instance of *attributeType* is defined on this member; otherwise **false**.

Implements

ICustomAttributeProvider.IsDefined

Example

[Visual Basic, C#, C++] The following example determines whether the specified attribute is defined on the specified member.

```
[Visual Basic]
Imports System
Imports System.Reflection
Imports Microsoft.VisualBasic

' Define a custom attribute with one named parameter.
<AttributeUsage(AttributeTargets.All)> Public Class MyAttribute
   Inherits Attribute
   Private myName As String
```

```vb
    Public Sub New(ByVal name As String)
        myName = name
    End Sub 'New

    Public ReadOnly Property Name() As String
        Get
            Return myName
        End Get
    End Property
End Class 'MyAttribute

' Define a class that has the custom attribute associated with
one of its members.
Public Class MyClass1

    <MyAttribute("This is an example attribute.")> Public Sub
MyMethod(ByVal i As Integer)
        Return
    End Sub 'MyMethod
End Class 'MyClass1

Public Class MemberInfo_GetCustomAttributes_IsDefined

    Public Shared Sub Main()
        Try
            ' Get the type of MyClass1.
            Dim myType As Type = GetType(MyClass1)
            ' Get the members associated with MyClass1.
            Dim myMembers As MemberInfo() = myType.GetMembers()

            ' Display the attributes for each of the members of
MyClass1.
            Dim i As Integer
            For i = 0 To myMembers.Length - 1
                ' Display the attribute if it is of type MyAttribute.
                If myMembers(i).IsDefined(GetType(MyAttribute),
 False) Then
                    Dim myAttributes As [Object]() =
myMembers(i).GetCustomAttributes(GetType(MyAttribute), False)
                    Console.WriteLine(ControlChars.Cr +
"The attributes of type MyAttribute for the member {0} are: " +
ControlChars.Cr, myMembers(i))
                    Dim j As Integer
                    For j = 0 To myAttributes.Length - 1
                        ' Display the value associated with the
attribute.
                        Console.WriteLine("The value of the
attribute is : ""{0}""", CType(myAttributes(j), MyAttribute).Name)
                    Next j
                End If
            Next i
        Catch e As Exception
            Console.WriteLine("An exception occurred: {0}", e.Message)
        End Try
    End Sub 'Main
End Class 'MemberInfo_GetCustomAttributes_IsDefined
```

[C#]

```csharp
using System;
using System.Reflection;

// Define a custom attribute with one named parameter.
[AttributeUsage(AttributeTargets.All)]
public class MyAttribute : Attribute
{
    private string myName;
    public MyAttribute(string name)
    {
        myName = name;
    }
    public string Name
    {
        get
        {
            return myName;
        }
    }
}

// Define a class that has the custom attribute associated with
 one of its members.
public class MyClass1
{
    [MyAttribute("This is an example attribute.")]
    public void MyMethod(int i)
    {
        return;
    }
}

public class MemberInfo_GetCustomAttributes_IsDefined
{
    public static void Main()
    {
        try
        {
            // Get the type of MyClass1.
            Type myType = typeof(MyClass1);
            // Get the members associated with MyClass1.
            MemberInfo[] myMembers = myType.GetMembers();

            // Display the attributes for each of the members
 of MyClass1.
            for(int i = 0; i < myMembers.Length; i++)
            {
                // Display the attribute if it is of type MyAttribute.
                if(myMembers[i].IsDefined(typeof(MyAttribute), false))
                {
                    Object[] myAttributes =
myMembers[i].GetCustomAttributes(typeof(MyAttribute), false);
                    Console.WriteLine("\nThe attributes of type
MyAttribute for the member {0} are: \n",
                        myMembers[i]);
                    for(int j = 0; j < myAttributes.Length; j++)
                        // Display the value associated with the
attribute.
                        Console.WriteLine("The value of the
 attribute is : \"{0}\"",
                            ((MyAttribute)myAttributes[j]).Name);
                }
            }
        }
        catch(Exception e)
        {
            Console.WriteLine("An exception occurred: {0}", e.Message);
        }
    }
}
```

[C++]

```cpp
#using <mscorlib.dll>

using namespace System;
using namespace System::Reflection;

// Define a custom attribute with one named parameter.
[AttributeUsage(AttributeTargets::All)]
public __gc class MyAttribute : public Attribute
{
private:
    String* myName;
public:
    MyAttribute(String* name)
    {
        myName = name;
    }
    __property String* get_Name()
    {
```

```
      return myName;
   }
};

// Define a class that has the custom attribute associated with        ↵
 one of its members.
public __gc class MyClass1
{
public:
   [MyAttribute(S"This is an example attribute.")]
   void MyMethod(int i)
   {
   }
};

void main()
{
   try {
      // Get the type of MyClass1.
      Type* myType = __typeof(MyClass1);
      // Get the members associated with MyClass1.
      MemberInfo* myMembers[] = myType->GetMembers();

      // Display the attributes for each of the members of MyClass1.
      for (int i = 0; i < myMembers->Length; i++) {
         // Display the attribute if it is of type MyAttribute.
         if (myMembers[i]->IsDefined(__typeof(MyAttribute), false)) {
            Object* myAttributes[] = myMembers[i]-                     ↵
>GetCustomAttributes(__typeof(MyAttribute), false);
            Console::WriteLine(S"\nThe attributes of type             ↵
MyAttribute for the member {0} are: \n",
               myMembers->Item[i]);
            for (int j = 0; j < myAttributes->Length; j++)
               // Display the value associated with the attribute.
               Console::WriteLine(S"The value of the attribute        ↵
 is : \"{0}\"",
                  (__try_cast<MyAttribute*>(myAttributes[j]))->Name);
         }
      }
   } catch (Exception* e) {
      Console::WriteLine(S"An exception occurred: {0}", e->Message);
   }
}
```

Requirements

Platforms: Windows 98, Windows NT 4.0,
Windows Millennium Edition, Windows 2000,
Windows XP Home Edition, Windows XP Professional,
Windows .NET Server family,
.NET Compact Framework - Windows CE .NET

MemberTypes Enumeration

Marks each type of member that is defined as a derived class of **MemberInfo**.

This enumeration has a **FlagsAttribute** attribute that allows a bitwise combination of its member values.

```
[Visual Basic]
<Flags>
<Serializable>
Public Enum MemberTypes
[C#]
[Flags]
[Serializable]
public enum MemberTypes
[C++]
[Flags]
[Serializable]
__value public enum MemberTypes
[JScript]
public
    Flags
    Serializable
enum MemberTypes
```

Remarks

These enum values are returned by **MemberType** and are useful in **switch** statements. **MemberTypes** matches CorTypeAttr as defined in the corhdr.h file.

To obtain the **MemberTypes** value for a method:

- First get a **Type**.
- From the **Type**, get the **MemberInfo** array.
- From the **MemberInfo** array, get the **MemberType**.

Members

Member name	Description	Value
All Supported by the .NET Compact Framework.	Specifies all member types.	191
Constructor Supported by the .NET Compact Framework.	Specifies that the member is a constructor, representing a **ConstructorInfo** member. Hexadecimal value of 0x01.	1
Custom Supported by the .NET Compact Framework.	Specifies that the member is a custom member type. Hexadecimal value of 0x40.	64
Event Supported by the .NET Compact Framework.	Specifies that the member is an event, representing an **EventInfo** member. Hexadecimal value of 0x02.	2
Field Supported by the .NET Compact Framework.	Specifies that the member is a field, representing a **FieldInfo** member. Hexadecimal value of 0x04.	4
Method Supported by the .NET Compact Framework.	Specifies that the member is a method, representing a **MethodInfo** member. Hexadecimal value of 0x08.	8

Member name	Description	Value
NestedType Supported by the .NET Compact Framework.	Specifies that the member is a nested type, extending **MemberInfo**.	128
Property Supported by the .NET Compact Framework.	Specifies that the member is a property, representing a **PropertyInfo** member. Hexadecimal value of 0x10.	16
TypeInfo Supported by the .NET Compact Framework.	Specifies that the member is a type, representing a **TypeInfo** member. Hexadecimal value of 0x20.	32

Example

[Visual Basic, C#] The following example displays the member types for the specified class.

```
[Visual Basic]
Imports System
Imports System.Reflection
Imports Microsoft.VisualBasic

Class membertypesenum

    Public Overloads Shared Function Main(ByVal args() As String) ⏎
As Integer
        Console.WriteLine(ControlChars.Lf & "Reflection.MemberTypes")
        Dim Mymembertypes As MemberTypes

        ' Get the type of a chosen class.
        Dim Mytype As Type = _                                      ⏎
Type.GetType("System.Reflection.ReflectionTypeLoadException")

        ' Get the MemberInfo array.
        Dim Mymembersinfoarray As MemberInfo() = Mytype.GetMembers()

        ' Get and display the name and the MemberType for each member.
        Dim Mymemberinfo As MemberInfo
        For Each Mymemberinfo In Mymembersinfoarray
            Mymembertypes = Mymemberinfo.MemberType
            Console.WriteLine("The member {0} of {1} is a {2}.        ⏎
", Mymemberinfo.Name, Mytype, Mymembertypes.ToString())
        Next Mymemberinfo
        Return 0
    End Function 'Main
End Class 'membertypesenum

[C#]
using System;
using System.Reflection;

class membertypesenum
{
    public static int Main(string[] args)
    {
        Console.WriteLine ("\nReflection.MemberTypes");
        MemberTypes Mymembertypes;

        // Get the type of a chosen class.
        Type Mytype = Type.GetType
            ("System.Reflection.ReflectionTypeLoadException");

        // Get the MemberInfo array.
        MemberInfo[] Mymembersinfoarray = Mytype.GetMembers();

        // Get and display the name and the MemberType for each member.
        foreach (MemberInfo Mymemberinfo in Mymembersinfoarray)
        {
            Mymembertypes = Mymemberinfo.MemberType;
            Console.WriteLine("The member {0} of {1} is a {2}        ⏎
.", Mymemberinfo.Name, Mytype, Mymembertypes.ToString());
        }
        return 0;
    }
}
```

Requirements

Namespace: System.Reflection

Platforms: Windows 98, Windows NT 4.0,
Windows Millennium Edition, Windows 2000,
Windows XP Home Edition, Windows XP Professional,
Windows .NET Server family,
.NET Compact Framework - Windows CE .NET

Assembly: Mscorlib (in Mscorlib.dll)

MethodAttributes Enumeration

Specifies flags for method attributes. These flags are defined in the corhdr.h file.

This enumeration has a **FlagsAttribute** attribute that allows a bitwise combination of its member values.

```
[Visual Basic]
<Flags>
<Serializable>
Public Enum MethodAttributes
[C#]
[Flags]
[Serializable]
public enum MethodAttributes
[C++]
[Flags]
[Serializable]
__value public enum MethodAttributes
[JScript]
public
    Flags
    Serializable
enum MethodAttributes
```

Members

Member name	Description	Value
Abstract Supported by the .NET Compact Framework.	Indicates that the class does not provide an implementation of this method.	1024
Assembly Supported by the .NET Compact Framework.	Indicates that the method is accessible to any class of this assembly.	3
CheckAccessOnOverride Supported by the .NET Compact Framework.	Indicates that the method can only be overridden when it is also accessible.	512
FamANDAssem Supported by the .NET Compact Framework.	Indicates that the method is accessible to members of this type and its derived types that are in this assembly only.	2
Family Supported by the .NET Compact Framework.	Indicates that the method is accessible only to members of this class and its derived classes.	4
FamORAssem Supported by the .NET Compact Framework.	Indicates that the method is accessible to derived classes anywhere, as well as to any class in the assembly.	5
Final Supported by the .NET Compact Framework.	Indicates that the method cannot be overridden.	32
HasSecurity Supported by the .NET Compact Framework.	Indicates that the method has security associated with it. Reserved flag for runtime use only.	16384

Member name	Description	Value
HideBySig Supported by the .NET Compact Framework.	Indicates that the method hides by name and signature; otherwise, by name only.	128
MemberAccessMask Supported by the .NET Compact Framework.	Retrieves accessibility information.	7
NewSlot Supported by the .NET Compact Framework.	Indicates that the method always gets a new slot in the vtable.	256
PinvokeImpl Supported by the .NET Compact Framework.	Indicates that the method implementation is forwarded through PInvoke (Platform Invocation Services).	8192
Private Supported by the .NET Compact Framework.	Indicates that the method is accessible only to the current class.	1
PrivateScope Supported by the .NET Compact Framework.	Indicates that the member cannot be referenced.	0
Public Supported by the .NET Compact Framework.	Indicates that the method is accessible to any object for which this object is in scope.	6
RequireSecObject Supported by the .NET Compact Framework.	Indicates that the method calls another method containing security code. Reserved flag for runtime use only.	32768
ReservedMask Supported by the .NET Compact Framework.	Indicates a reserved flag for runtime use only.	53248
ReuseSlot Supported by the .NET Compact Framework.	Indicates that the method will reuse an existing slot in the vtable. This is the default behavior.	0
RTSpecialName Supported by the .NET Compact Framework.	Indicates that the common language runtime checks the name encoding.	4096
SpecialName Supported by the .NET Compact Framework.	Indicates that the method is special. The name describes how this method is special.	2048
Static Supported by the .NET Compact Framework.	Indicates that the method is defined on the type; otherwise, it is defined per instance.	16
UnmanagedExport Supported by the .NET Compact Framework.	Indicates that the managed method is exported by thunk to unmanaged code.	8
Virtual Supported by the .NET Compact Framework.	Indicates that the method is virtual.	64
VtableLayoutMask Supported by the .NET Compact Framework.	Retrieves vtable attributes.	256

Example

[Visual Basic, C#] The following example displays the attributes of the specified method.

```
[Visual Basic]
Imports System
Imports System.Reflection
Imports Microsoft.VisualBasic

Class AttributesSample

    Public Sub Mymethod(ByVal intlm As Integer, ByRef str2m _
As String, ByRef str3m As String)
        str2m = "in Mymethod"
    End Sub 'Mymethod

    Public Shared Function Main(ByVal args() As String) As Integer
        Console.WriteLine("Reflection.MethodBase.Attributes Sample")

        ' Get the type of a chosen class.
        Dim MyType As Type = Type.GetType("AttributesSample")

        ' Get the method Mymethod on the type.
        Dim Mymethodbase As MethodBase = MyType.GetMethod("Mymethod")

        ' Display the method name and signature.
        Console.WriteLine("Mymethodbase = {0}", Mymethodbase)

        ' Get the MethodAttribute enumerated value.
        Dim Myattributes As MethodAttributes = Mymethodbase.Attributes

        ' Display the flags that are set.
        PrintAttributes(GetType _
(System.Reflection.MethodAttributes), CInt(Myattributes))
        Return 0
    End Function 'Main

    Public Shared Sub PrintAttributes(ByVal attribType As Type, _
ByVal iAttribValue As Integer)
        If Not attribType.IsEnum Then
            Console.WriteLine("This type is not an enum.")
            Return
        End If
        Dim fields As FieldInfo() = _
attribType.GetFields((BindingFlags.Public Or BindingFlags.Static))
        Dim i As Integer
        For i = 0 To fields.Length - 1
            Dim fieldvalue As Integer = _
CType(fields(i).GetValue(Nothing), Int32)
            If (fieldvalue And iAttribValue) = fieldvalue Then
                Console.WriteLine(fields(i).Name)
            End If
        Next i
    End Sub 'PrintAttributes
End Class 'AttributesSample

[C#]
using System;
using System.Reflection;

class AttributesSample
{
    public void Mymethod (int intlm, out string str2m, ref _
string str3m)
    {
        str2m = "in Mymethod";
    }

    public static int Main(string[] args)
    {
        Console.WriteLine ("Reflection.MethodBase.Attributes Sample");

        // Get the type of the chosen class.
        Type MyType = Type.GetType("AttributesSample");
```

```
        // Get the method Mymethod on the type.
        MethodBase Mymethodbase = MyType.GetMethod("Mymethod");

        // Display the method name and signature.
        Console.WriteLine("Mymethodbase = " + Mymethodbase);

        // Get the MethodAttribute enumerated value.
        MethodAttributes Myattributes = Mymethodbase.Attributes;

        // Display the flags that are set.
        PrintAttributes(typeof
(System.Reflection.MethodAttributes), (int) Myattributes);
        return 0;
    }

    public static void PrintAttributes(Type attribType, int _
iAttribValue)
    {
        if (!attribType.IsEnum) {Console.WriteLine("This type _
is not an enum."); return;}

        FieldInfo[] fields = attribType.GetFields _
(BindingFlags.Public | BindingFlags.Static);
        for (int i = 0; i < fields.Length; i++)
        {
            int fieldvalue = (Int32)fields[i].GetValue(null);
            if ((fieldvalue & iAttribValue) == fieldvalue)
            {
                Console.WriteLine(fields[i].Name);
            }
        }
    }
}
```

Requirements

Namespace: System.Reflection

Platforms: Windows 98, Windows NT 4.0, Windows Millennium Edition, Windows 2000, Windows XP Home Edition, Windows XP Professional, Windows .NET Server family, .NET Compact Framework - Windows CE .NET

Assembly: Mscorlib (in Mscorlib.dll)

MethodBase Class

Provides information about methods and constructors.

System.Object
  System.Reflection.MemberInfo
    System.Reflection.MethodBase
      System.Reflection.ConstructorInfo
      System.Reflection.MethodInfo

```
[Visual Basic]
<Serializable>
<ClassInterface(ClassInterfaceType.AutoDual)>
MustInherit Public Class MethodBase
    Inherits MemberInfo
[C#]
[Serializable]
[ClassInterface(ClassInterfaceType.AutoDual)]
public abstract class MethodBase : MemberInfo
[C++]
[Serializable]
[ClassInterface(ClassInterfaceType::AutoDual)]
public __gc __abstract class MethodBase : public MemberInfo
[JScript]
public
    Serializable
    ClassInterface(ClassInterfaceType.AutoDual)
abstract class MethodBase extends MemberInfo
```

Thread Safety

Any public static (**Shared** in Visual Basic) members of this type are safe for multithreaded operations. Any instance members are not guaranteed to be thread safe.

Remarks

MethodBase is the base class of **MethodInfo** and **ConstructorInfo**.

Notes to Inheritors: When you inherit from **MethodBase**, you must override the following members: **GetParameters**, the abstract overload of **Invoke**, and **GetMethodImplementationFlags**.

Requirements

Namespace: System.Reflection

Platforms: Windows 98, Windows NT 4.0, Windows Millennium Edition, Windows 2000, Windows XP Home Edition, Windows XP Professional, Windows .NET Server family, .NET Compact Framework - Windows CE .NET

Assembly: Mscorlib (in Mscorlib.dll)

MethodBase Constructor

Initializes a new instance of the **MethodBase** class.

```
[Visual Basic]
Protected Sub New()
[C#]
protected MethodBase();
[C++]
protected: MethodBase();
[JScript]
protected function MethodBase();
```

Requirements

Platforms: Windows 98, Windows NT 4.0, Windows Millennium Edition, Windows 2000, Windows XP Home Edition, Windows XP Professional, Windows .NET Server family, .NET Compact Framework - Windows CE .NET, Common Language Infrastructure (CLI) Standard

.NET Framework Security:

- **ReflectionPermission** to enhance security and performance when invoked late-bound through mechanisms such as **Type.InvokeMember**. Associated enumeration: **ReflectionPermissionFlag.MemberAccess**.

MethodBase.Attributes Property

Gets the attributes associated with this method.

```
[Visual Basic]
Public MustOverride ReadOnly Property Attributes As _
    MethodAttributes
[C#]
public abstract MethodAttributes Attributes {get;}
[C++]
public: __property virtual MethodAttributes get_Attributes() = 0;
[JScript]
public abstract function get Attributes() : MethodAttributes;
```

Property Value

One of the **MethodAttributes** values.

Remarks

All members have a set of attributes, which are defined in relation to the specific type of member.

To get the **MethodAttributes**, first get the type. From the type, get the method. From the method, get the **MethodAttributes**.

Notes to Implementers: Use the **Attributes** property to determine whether a method is **public**, **private**, **final**, virtual (**Overridable** in Visual Basic), and so on.

Example

[Visual Basic, C#, JScript] The following code example displays the attributes of the user-defined method Mymethod.

```
[Visual Basic]
Imports System
Imports System.Reflection
Imports Microsoft.VisualBasic

Class AttributesSample

    Public Sub Mymethod(ByVal int1m As Integer, ByRef str2m As
String, ByRef str3m As String)
        str2m = "in Mymethod"
    End Sub 'Mymethod

    Public Shared Function Main(ByVal args() As String) As Integer
        Console.WriteLine("Reflection.MethodBase.Attributes Sample")

        ' Get the type.
        Dim MyType As Type = Type.GetType("AttributesSample")

        ' Get the method Mymethod on the type.
        Dim Mymethodbase As MethodBase = MyType.GetMethod("Mymethod")

        ' Display the method name.
        Console.WriteLine("Mymethodbase = {0}.", Mymethodbase)
```

```
        ' Get the MethodAttribute enumerated value.
        Dim Myattributes As MethodAttributes = Mymethodbase.Attributes

        ' Display the flags that are set.
        PrintAttributes(GetType                                           ⏎
(System.Reflection.MethodAttributes), CInt(Myattributes))
        Return 0
    End Function 'Main

    Public Shared Sub PrintAttributes(ByVal attribType As                 ⏎
Type, ByVal iAttribValue As Integer)
        If Not attribType.IsEnum Then
            Console.WriteLine("This type is not an enum.")
            Return
        End If
        Dim fields As FieldInfo() =                                       ⏎
attribType.GetFields((BindingFlags.Public Or BindingFlags.Static))
        Dim i As Integer
        For i = 0 To fields.Length - 1
            Dim fieldvalue As Integer =                                   ⏎
CType(fields(i).GetValue(Nothing), Int32)
            If (fieldvalue And iAttribValue) = fieldvalue Then
                Console.WriteLine(fields(i).Name)
            End If
        Next i
    End Sub 'PrintAttributes
End Class 'AttributesSample
```

[C#]

```
using System;
using System.Reflection;

class AttributesSample
{
    public void Mymethod (int int1m, out string str2m,                    ⏎
ref string str3m)
    {
        str2m = "in Mymethod";
    }

    public static int Main(string[] args)
    {
        Console.WriteLine ("Reflection.MethodBase.Attributes Sample");

        // Get the type.
        Type MyType = Type.GetType("AttributesSample");

        // Get the method Mymethod on the type.
        MethodBase Mymethodbase = MyType.GetMethod("Mymethod");

        // Display the method name.
        Console.WriteLine("Mymethodbase = " + Mymethodbase);

        // Get the MethodAttribute enumerated value.
        MethodAttributes Myattributes = Mymethodbase.Attributes;

        // Display the flags that are set.
        PrintAttributes(typeof                                            ⏎
(System.Reflection.MethodAttributes), (int) Myattributes);
        return 0;
    }

    public static void PrintAttributes(Type attribType,                   ⏎
int iAttribValue)
    {
        if (!attribType.IsEnum)
        {
            Console.WriteLine("This type is not an enum.");
            return;
        }

        FieldInfo[] fields = attribType.GetFields                         ⏎
(BindingFlags.Public | BindingFlags.Static);
        for (int i = 0; i < fields.Length; i++)
        {
```

```
            int fieldvalue = (Int32)fields[i].GetValue(null);
            if ((fieldvalue & iAttribValue) == fieldvalue)
            {
                Console.WriteLine(fields[i].Name);
            }
        }
    }
}
```

[JScript]

```
import System;
import System.Reflection;

class AttributesSample
{
    public function Mymethod (int1m : int) : void
    {
    }

    public static function Main() : void
    {
        Console.WriteLine ("Reflection.MethodBase.Attributes Sample");

        // Get our type
        var MyType : Type = Type.GetType("AttributesSample");

        // Get the method Mymethod on our type
        var Mymethodbase : MethodBase = MyType.GetMethod("Mymethod");

        // Print out the method
        Console.WriteLine("Mymethodbase = " + Mymethodbase);

        // Get the MethodAttribute enumerated value
        var Myattributes : MethodAttributes = Mymethodbase.Attributes;

        // print out the flags set
        PrintAttributes( System.Reflection.MethodAttributes,              ⏎
int(Myattributes) );
    }

    public static function PrintAttributes( attribType :                  ⏎
Type, iAttribValue : int ) : void
    {
        if ( ! attribType.IsEnum ) { Console.WriteLine                    ⏎
( "This type is not an enum" ); return; }

        var fields : FieldInfo[] =                                        ⏎
attribType.GetFields(BindingFlags.Public | BindingFlags.Static);
        for ( var i:int = 0; i < fields.Length; i++ )
        {
            var fieldvalue : int = int(fields[i].GetValue(null));
            if ( (fieldvalue & iAttribValue) == fieldvalue )
            {
                Console.WriteLine( "\t" + fields[i].Name );
            }
        }
    }
}
AttributesSample.Main();
/*
This code produces the following output:

Reflection.MethodBase.Attributes Sample
Mymethodbase = Void Mymethod(Int32)
        PrivateScope
        FamANDAssem
        Family
        Public
        Virtual
        HideBySig
        VtableLayoutMask
        ReuseSlot
        NewSlot
*/
```

[Visual Basic, C#, JScript] This code produces the following output:

[Visual Basic, C#, JScript] Reflection.MethodBase.Attributes Sample

[Visual Basic, C#, JScript] Mymethodbase = Void Mymethod(Int32, System.String ByRef, System.String ByRef)

[Visual Basic, C#, JScript] PrivateScope

[Visual Basic, C#, JScript] FamANDAssem

[Visual Basic, C#, JScript] Family

[Visual Basic, C#, JScript] Public

[Visual Basic, C#, JScript] HideBySig

[Visual Basic, C#, JScript] ReuseSlot

Requirements

Platforms: Windows 98, Windows NT 4.0,
Windows Millennium Edition, Windows 2000,
Windows XP Home Edition, Windows XP Professional,
Windows .NET Server family,
.NET Compact Framework - Windows CE .NET,
Common Language Infrastructure (CLI) Standard

MethodBase.CallingConvention Property

Gets a value indicating the calling conventions for this method.

```
[Visual Basic]
Public Overridable ReadOnly Property CallingConvention As _
    CallingConventions
[C#]
public virtual CallingConventions CallingConvention {get;}
[C++]
public: __property virtual CallingConventions
    get_CallingConvention();
[JScript]
public function get CallingConvention() : CallingConventions;
```

Property Value

The **CallingConventions** for this method.

Example

```
[Visual Basic]
Public Class MyClass1
    Public Sub New(ByVal i As Integer)
    End Sub
    Public Shared Sub Main()
        Try
            Dim myType As Type = GetType(MyClass1)
            Dim types(0) As Type
            types(0) = GetType(Integer)
            ' Get the public instance constructor that takes an ⌐
integer parameter.
            Dim constructorInfoObj As ConstructorInfo = _
                myType.GetConstructor _
 (BindingFlags.Instance Or _
                BindingFlags.Public, Nothing, _
                CallingConventions.HasThis, types, Nothing)
            If Not (constructorInfoObj Is Nothing) Then
                Console.WriteLine("The constructor of MyClass1 ⌐
that " + _
                            "is a public instance method ⌐
and takes an " + _
                        "integer as a parameter is: ")
                Console.WriteLine(constructorInfoObj.ToString())
            Else
                Console.WriteLine("The constructor MyClass1 that " + _
                            "is a public instance method ⌐
and takes an " + _
```

```
                    "integer as a parameter is    ⌐
not available.")
            End If
        Catch e As ArgumentNullException
            Console.WriteLine("ArgumentNullException: " + e.Message)
        Catch e As ArgumentException
            Console.WriteLine("ArgumentException: " + e.Message)
        Catch e As SecurityException
            Console.WriteLine("SecurityException: " + e.Message)
        Catch e As Exception
            Console.WriteLine("Exception: " + e.Message)
        End Try
    End Sub
End Class

[C#]
using System;
using System.Reflection;
using System.Security;

public class MyClass1
{
    public MyClass1(int i){}
    public static void Main()
    {
        try
        {
            Type  myType = typeof(MyClass1);
            Type[] types = new Type[1];
            types[0] = typeof(int);
            // Get the public instance constructor that takes  ⌐
an integer parameter.
            ConstructorInfo constructorInfoObj = myType.GetConstructor(
                BindingFlags.Instance | BindingFlags.Public, null,
                CallingConventions.HasThis, types, null);
            if(constructorInfoObj != null)
            {
                Console.WriteLine("The constructor of MyClass1  ⌐
that is a public " +
                            "instance method and takes an integer as a  ⌐
parameter is: ");
                Console.WriteLine(constructorInfoObj.ToString());
            }
            else
            {
                Console.WriteLine("The constructor of MyClass1  ⌐
that is a public instance " +
                            "method and takes an integer as a parameter  ⌐
is not available.");
            }
        }
        catch(ArgumentNullException e)
        {
            Console.WriteLine("ArgumentNullException: " + e.Message);
        }
        catch(ArgumentException e)
        {
            Console.WriteLine("ArgumentException: " + e.Message);
        }
        catch(SecurityException e)
        {
            Console.WriteLine("SecurityException: " + e.Message);
        }
        catch(Exception e)
        {
            Console.WriteLine("Exception: " + e.Message);
        }
    }
}

[C++]
#using <mscorlib.dll>

using namespace System;
using namespace System::Reflection;
using namespace System::Security;
```

```
public __gc class MyClass1 {
public:
   MyClass1(int i) {}
}
;
int main() {
   try {
      Type* myType = __typeof(MyClass1);
      Type* types[] = new Type*[1];
      types->Item[0] = __typeof(int);
      // Get the public instance constructor that takes an      ⏎
integer parameter.
      ConstructorInfo*  constructorInfoObj = myType-          ⏎
>GetConstructor(static_cast<BindingFlags>                     ⏎
(BindingFlags::Instance | BindingFlags::Public), 0,
         CallingConventions::HasThis, types, 0);
      if (constructorInfoObj != 0) {
         Console::WriteLine(S"The constructor of MyClass1      ⏎
that is a public instance method and takes an integer as a    ⏎
parameter is: ");
         Console::WriteLine(constructorInfoObj);
      } else {
         Console::WriteLine(S"The constructor of MyClass1      ⏎
that is a public instance method and takes an integer as a    ⏎
parameter is not available.");
      }
   } catch (ArgumentNullException* e) {
      Console::WriteLine(S"ArgumentNullException: {0}", e->Message);
   } catch (ArgumentException* e) {
      Console::WriteLine(S"ArgumentException: {0}", e->Message);
   } catch (SecurityException* e) {
      Console::WriteLine(S"SecurityException: {0}", e->Message);
   } catch (Exception* e) {
      Console::WriteLine(S"Exception: {0}", e->Message);
   }
}
```

Requirements

Platforms: Windows 98, Windows NT 4.0,
Windows Millennium Edition, Windows 2000,
Windows XP Home Edition, Windows XP Professional,
Windows .NET Server family,
.NET Compact Framework - Windows CE .NET

MethodBase.IsAbstract Property

Gets a value indicating whether the method is abstract.

```
[Visual Basic]
Public ReadOnly Property IsAbstract As Boolean
[C#]
public bool IsAbstract {get;}
[C++]
public: __property bool get_IsAbstract();
[JScript]
public function get IsAbstract() : Boolean;
```

Property Value

true if the method is abstract; otherwise, **false**.

Remarks

An abstract member is declared on a base class and has no
implementation supplied.

To get the **MethodBase**, first get the type. From the type, get the
method. From the method, get the **MethodBase**. If the **MethodBase**
or constructor is other than public, it is protected and cannot be
readily accessed. To access a non-public method, set the
BindingFlags mask to **NonPublic** in **GetMethod**.

Example

[Visual Basic, C#, JScript] The following example determines
whether specified the method is abstract and displays the result.

```
[Visual Basic]
Imports System
Imports System.Reflection
Imports Microsoft.VisualBasic

Class methodbase1

   Public Shared Function Main() As Integer
      Console.WriteLine("Reflection.MethodBase")
      Console.WriteLine()
      ' Get the types.
      Dim MyType1 As Type = _
         Type.GetType("System.Runtime.Serialization.Formatter")
      Dim MyType2 As Type = _
         Type.GetType("System.Reflection.MethodBase")

      ' Get and display the methods.
      Dim Mymethodbase1 As MethodBase = _
         MyType1.GetMethod("WriteInt32", BindingFlags.NonPublic  ⏎
Or BindingFlags.Instance)
      Dim Mymethodbase2 As MethodBase = _
         MyType2.GetMethod("GetCurrentMethod",                   ⏎
BindingFlags.Public Or BindingFlags.Static)

      Console.WriteLine("Mymethodbase = {0}",                    ⏎
Mymethodbase1.ToString())
      If Mymethodbase1.IsAbstract Then
         Console.WriteLine(ControlChars.CrLf & "Mymethodbase    ⏎
is an abstract method.")
      Else
         Console.WriteLine(ControlChars.CrLf & "Mymethodbase    ⏎
is not an abstract method.")
      End If
      Console.Write("Mymethodbase = {0}", Mymethodbase2.ToString())
      If Mymethodbase2.IsAbstract Then
         Console.WriteLine(ControlChars.CrLf & "Mymethodbase    ⏎
is an abstract method.")
      Else
         Console.WriteLine(ControlChars.CrLf & "Mymethodbase    ⏎
is not an abstract method.")
      End If
      Return 0
   End Function
End Class

[C#]
using System;
using System.Reflection;
// using System.Windows.Forms;

class methodbase
{
   public static int Main(string[] args)
   {
      Console.WriteLine ("\nReflection.MethodBase");

      // Get the types.
      Type MyType1 =
Type.GetType("System.Runtime.Serialization.Formatter");
      Type MyType2 = Type.GetType("System.Reflection.MethodBase");

      // Get and display the methods.
      MethodBase Mymethodbase1 =
         MyType1.GetMethod("WriteInt32",                         ⏎
BindingFlags.NonPublic|BindingFlags.Instance);

      MethodBase Mymethodbase2 =
         MyType2.GetMethod("GetCurrentMethod",                   ⏎
BindingFlags.Public|BindingFlags.Static);
```

```
        Console.Write("\nMymethodbase = " + Mymethodbase1.ToString());
        if (Mymethodbase1.IsAbstract)
            Console.Write ("\nMymethodbase is an abstract method.");
        else
            Console.Write ("\nMymethodbase is not an abstract     ⏎
method.");

        Console.Write("\n\nMymethodbase = " +              ⏎
Mymethodbase2.ToString());
        if (Mymethodbase2.IsAbstract)
            Console.Write ("\nMymethodbase is an abstract method.");
        else
            Console.Write ("\nMymethodbase is not an abstract     ⏎
method.");

        return 0;
    }
}

[JScript]
class methodbase
{
    public static function Main() : int
    {
        Console.WriteLine ("\nReflection.MethodBase");

        //Get the MethodBase of two methods.

        //Get the types
        var MyType1 : Type =                               ⏎
Type.GetType("System.Runtime.Serialization.Formatter");
        var MyType2 : Type = Type.GetType("System.Reflection.MethodBase");

        //Get and display the methods
        var Mymethodbase1 : MethodBase =
            MyType1.GetMethod("WriteInt32",                ⏎
BindingFlags.Instance|BindingFlags.NonPublic);

        var Mymethodbase2 : MethodBase =
            MyType2.GetMethod("GetCurrentMethod",          ⏎
BindingFlags.Static|BindingFlags.Public);

        Console.Write("\nMymethodbase = " + Mymethodbase1.ToString());
        if (Mymethodbase1.IsAbstract)
            Console.Write ("\nMymethodbase is an abstract method");
        else
            Console.Write ("\nMymethodbase is not an abstract method");

        Console.Write("\n\nMymethodbase = " + Mymethodbase2.ToString());
        if (Mymethodbase2.IsAbstract)
            Console.Write ("\nMymethodbase is an abstract method");
        else
            Console.Write ("\nMymethodbase is not an abstract method");

    }
}
methodbase.Main();
/*
Produces the following output
Reflection.MethodBase

Mymethodbase = Void WriteInt32 (Int32, System.String)
Mymethodbase is an abstract method

Mymethodbase = System.Reflection.MethodBase GetCurrentMethod ()
Mymethodbase is not an abstract method
*/
```

Requirements

Platforms: Windows 98, Windows NT 4.0, Windows Millennium Edition, Windows 2000, Windows XP Home Edition, Windows XP Professional, Windows .NET Server family, .NET Compact Framework - Windows CE .NET

MethodBase.IsAssembly Property

Gets a value indicating whether this method can be called by other classes in the same assembly.

```
[Visual Basic]
Public ReadOnly Property IsAssembly As Boolean
[C#]
public bool IsAssembly {get;}
[C++]
public: __property bool get_IsAssembly();
[JScript]
public function get IsAssembly() : Boolean;
```

Property Value

true if this method can be called by other classes in the same assembly; otherwise, **false**.

Remarks

If set, this method can be called by other classes in the same assembly.

To get the **MethodBase**, first get the type. From the type, get the method. From the method, get the **MethodBase**. If the **MethodBase** or constructor is other than public, it is protected and cannot be readily accessed. To access a non-public method, set the **BindingFlags** mask to **NonPublic** in **GetMethod**.

Example

The following example determines whether a specified method can be called by other classes in the same assembly, and displays the result.

Requirements

Platforms: Windows 98, Windows NT 4.0, Windows Millennium Edition, Windows 2000, Windows XP Home Edition, Windows XP Professional, Windows .NET Server family, .NET Compact Framework - Windows CE .NET

MethodBase.IsConstructor Property

Gets a value indicating whether the method is a constructor.

```
[Visual Basic]
Public ReadOnly Property IsConstructor As Boolean
[C#]
public bool IsConstructor {get;}
[C++]
public: __property bool get_IsConstructor();
[JScript]
public function get IsConstructor() : Boolean;
```

Property Value

true if this method is a constructor; otherwise, **false**.

Requirements

Platforms: Windows 98, Windows NT 4.0, Windows Millennium Edition, Windows 2000, Windows XP Home Edition, Windows XP Professional, Windows .NET Server family, .NET Compact Framework - Windows CE .NET

MethodBase.IsFamily Property

Gets a value indicating whether access to this method is restricted to members of the class and members of its derived classes.

```
[Visual Basic]
Public ReadOnly Property IsFamily As Boolean
[C#]
public bool IsFamily {get;}
[C++]
public: __property bool get_IsFamily();
[JScript]
public function get IsFamily() : Boolean;
```

Property Value

true if access to the class is restricted to members of the class itself and to members of its derived classes; otherwise, **false**.

Remarks

If a type member has **Family** level visibility it can be called from any member in a derived class, but not from any other type.

Requirements

Platforms: Windows 98, Windows NT 4.0, Windows Millennium Edition, Windows 2000, Windows XP Home Edition, Windows XP Professional, Windows .NET Server family, .NET Compact Framework - Windows CE .NET

MethodBase.IsFamilyAndAssembly Property

Gets a value indicating whether this method can be called by derived classes if they are in the same assembly.

```
[Visual Basic]
Public ReadOnly Property IsFamilyAndAssembly As Boolean
[C#]
public bool IsFamilyAndAssembly {get;}
[C++]
public: __property bool get_IsFamilyAndAssembly();
[JScript]
public function get IsFamilyAndAssembly() : Boolean;
```

Property Value

true if access to this method is restricted to members of the class itself and to members of derived classes that are in the same assembly; otherwise, **false**.

Requirements

Platforms: Windows 98, Windows NT 4.0, Windows Millennium Edition, Windows 2000, Windows XP Home Edition, Windows XP Professional, Windows .NET Server family, .NET Compact Framework - Windows CE .NET

MethodBase.IsFamilyOrAssembly Property

Gets a value indicating whether this method can be called by derived classes, wherever they are, and by all classes in the same assembly.

```
[Visual Basic]
Public ReadOnly Property IsFamilyOrAssembly As Boolean
[C#]
public bool IsFamilyOrAssembly {get;}
```

```
[C++]
public: __property bool get_IsFamilyOrAssembly();
[JScript]
public function get IsFamilyOrAssembly() : Boolean;
```

Property Value

true if access to this method is restricted to members of the class itself, members of derived classes wherever they are, and members of other classes in the same assembly; otherwise, **false**.

Remarks

If a type member has **FamilyOrAssembly** level visibility it can be called from any member in a derived class or any member in the same assembly, but not from any other type.

Requirements

Platforms: Windows 98, Windows NT 4.0, Windows Millennium Edition, Windows 2000, Windows XP Home Edition, Windows XP Professional, Windows .NET Server family, .NET Compact Framework - Windows CE .NET

MethodBase.IsFinal Property

Gets a value indicating whether this method is **final**.

```
[Visual Basic]
Public ReadOnly Property IsFinal As Boolean
[C#]
public bool IsFinal {get;}
[C++]
public: __property bool get_IsFinal();
[JScript]
public function get IsFinal() : Boolean;
```

Property Value

true if this method is **final**; otherwise, **false**.

Remarks

To determine if a method is overridable, it is not sufficient to check that **IsVirtual** is **true**. For a method to be overridable, **IsVirtual** must be **true** and **IsFinal** must be **false**. For example, a method might be non-virtual, but it implements an interface method. The common language runtime requires that all methods that implement interface members must be marked as virtual (**Overridable** in Visual Basic); therefore, the compiler marks the method virtual (**Overridable** in Visual Basic) **final**. So there are cases where a method is marked as virtual (**Overridable** in Visual Basic) but is still not overridable.

To establish with certainty whether a method is overridable, use code such as this: `if (MethodInfo.IsVirtual && !MethodInfo.IsFinal)`

If **IsVirtual** is **false** or **IsFinal** is **true**, then the method cannot be overridden.

Example

[Visual Basic, C#, JScript] The following example displays **false** for **IsFinal**, which might lead you to think that MyMethod is overridable. The code prints **false** even though MyMethod is not marked virtual (**Overridable** in Visual Basic) and thus cannot be overridden.

```
[Visual Basic]
Imports System
Imports System.Reflection
Imports Microsoft.VisualBasic

Public Class MyClass1

    Public Sub MyMethod()
    End Sub

    Public Shared Sub Main()
        Dim m As MethodBase = GetType(MyClass1).GetMethod("MyMethod")
        Console.WriteLine("The IsFinal property value of
MyMethod is {0}.", m.IsFinal)
        Console.WriteLine("The IsVirtual property value of
MyMethod is {0}.", m.IsVirtual)
    End Sub
End Class

[C#]
using System;
using System.Reflection;

public class MyClass
{
    public void MyMethod()
    {
    }
    public static void Main()
    {
        MethodBase m = typeof(MyClass).GetMethod("MyMethod");
        Console.WriteLine("The IsFinal property value of
MyMethod is {0}.", m.IsFinal);
        Console.WriteLine("The IsVirtual property value of
MyMethod is {0}.", m.IsVirtual);
    }
}

[JScript]
import System;
import System.Reflection;

 public class MyClass
 {
 public function MyMethod() : void
   {
   }
 public static function Main() : void
   {
    var m : MethodBase  = MyClass.GetMethod("MyMethod");
    Console.WriteLine(m.IsFinal);
   }
 }
 MyClass.Main();
```

Requirements

Platforms: Windows 98, Windows NT 4.0,
Windows Millennium Edition, Windows 2000,
Windows XP Home Edition, Windows XP Professional,
Windows .NET Server family,
.NET Compact Framework - Windows CE .NET

MethodBase.IsHideBySig Property

Gets a value indicating whether only a member of the same kind
with exactly the same signature is hidden in the derived class.

```
[Visual Basic]
Public ReadOnly Property IsHideBySig As Boolean
[C#]
public bool IsHideBySig {get;}
```

```
[C++]
public: __property bool get_IsHideBySig();
[JScript]
public function get IsHideBySig() : Boolean;
```

Property Value

true if the member is hidden by signature; otherwise, **false**.

Requirements

Platforms: Windows 98, Windows NT 4.0,
Windows Millennium Edition, Windows 2000,
Windows XP Home Edition, Windows XP Professional,
Windows .NET Server family,
.NET Compact Framework - Windows CE .NET

MethodBase.IsPrivate Property

Gets a value indicating whether this member is private.

```
[Visual Basic]
Public ReadOnly Property IsPrivate As Boolean
[C#]
public bool IsPrivate {get;}
[C++]
public: __property bool get_IsPrivate();
[JScript]
public function get IsPrivate() : Boolean;
```

Property Value

true if access to this method is restricted to other members of the
class itself; otherwise, **false**.

Remarks

If a type member has **Private** level visibility, it can be called from
any member in the same class and no others.

Requirements

Platforms: Windows 98, Windows NT 4.0,
Windows Millennium Edition, Windows 2000,
Windows XP Home Edition, Windows XP Professional,
Windows .NET Server family,
.NET Compact Framework - Windows CE .NET

MethodBase.IsPublic Property

Gets a value indicating whether this is a public method.

```
[Visual Basic]
Public ReadOnly Property IsPublic As Boolean
[C#]
public bool IsPublic {get;}
[C++]
public: __property bool get_IsPublic();
[JScript]
public function get IsPublic() : Boolean;
```

Property Value

true if this method is public; otherwise, **false**.

Remarks

To get the **MethodBase**, first get the type. From the type, get the
method. From the method, get the **MethodBase**. If the **MethodBase**
or constructor is other than public, it is protected and cannot be
readily accessed. To access a non-public method, set the
BindingFlags mask to **NonPublic** in **GetMethod**.

Example

[Visual Basic]
```
Class methodbase1

    Public Shared Function Main() As Integer

        Console.WriteLine(ControlChars.Cr + "Reflection.MethodBase")

        'Get the MethodBase of a method.

        'Get the type
        Dim MyType As Type = Type.GetType("System.MulticastDelegate")

        'Get and display the method
        Dim Mymethodbase As MethodBase = _
            MyType.GetMethod("RemoveImpl", BindingFlags.NonPublic)

        Console.Write(ControlChars.Cr _
            + "Mymethodbase = " + Mymethodbase.ToString())

        Dim Myispublic As Boolean = Mymethodbase.IsPublic
        If Myispublic Then
            Console.Write(ControlChars.Cr _
                + "Mymethodbase is a public method")
        Else
            Console.Write(ControlChars.Cr _
                + "Mymethodbase is not a public method")
        End If
        Return 0
    End Function
End Class
```

```
' Produces the following output
'
' Reflection.MethodBase
' Mymethodbase = System.Delegate RemoveImpl (System.Delegate)
' Mymethodbase is not a public method
```

[C#]
```
class methodbase
{
    public static int Main(string[] args)
    {

        Console.WriteLine("\nReflection.MethodBase");

        //Get the MethodBase of a method.

        //Get the type
        Type MyType = Type.GetType("System.MulticastDelegate");

        //Get and display the method
        MethodBase Mymethodbase =
            MyType.GetMethod("RemoveImpl",BindingFlags.NonPublic);

        Console.Write("\nMymethodbase = " + Mymethodbase);

        bool Myispublic = Mymethodbase.IsPublic;
        if (Myispublic)
            Console.Write ("\nMymethodbase is a public method");
        else
            Console.Write ("\nMymethodbase is not a public method");

        return 0;
    }
}
/*
Produces the following output

Reflection.MethodBase
Mymethodbase = System.Delegate RemoveImpl (System.Delegate)
Mymethodbase is not a public method
*/
```

[JScript]
```
class methodbase
{
    public static function Main() : void
    {

        Console.WriteLine("\nReflection.MethodBase");

        //Get the MethodBase of a method.

        //Get the type
        var MyType : Type = Type.GetType("System.MulticastDelegate");

        //Get and display the method
        var Mymethodbase : MethodBase =
            MyType.GetMethod("RemoveImpl",
BindingFlags.NonPublic|BindingFlags.Instance);

        Console.Write("\nMymethodbase = " + Mymethodbase);

        var Myispublic : boolean = Mymethodbase.IsPublic;
        if (Myispublic)
            Console.Write ("\nMymethodbase is a public method");
        else
            Console.Write ("\nMymethodbase is not a public method");
    }
}
methodbase.Main();
/*
Produces the following output

Reflection.MethodBase
Mymethodbase = System.Delegate RemoveImpl (System.Delegate)
Mymethodbase is not a public method
*/
```

Requirements

Platforms: Windows 98, Windows NT 4.0,
Windows Millennium Edition, Windows 2000,
Windows XP Home Edition, Windows XP Professional,
Windows .NET Server family,
.NET Compact Framework - Windows CE .NET

MethodBase.IsSpecialName Property

Gets a value indicating whether this method has a special name.

```
[Visual Basic]
Public ReadOnly Property IsSpecialName As Boolean
[C#]
public bool IsSpecialName {get;}
[C++]
public: __property bool get_IsSpecialName();
[JScript]
public function get IsSpecialName() : Boolean;
```

Property Value

true if this method has a special name; otherwise, **false**.

Remarks

The **SpecialName** bit is set to flag members that are treated in a
special way by some compilers (such as property accessors and
operator overloading methods).

Requirements

Platforms: Windows 98, Windows NT 4.0,
Windows Millennium Edition, Windows 2000,
Windows XP Home Edition, Windows XP Professional,
Windows .NET Server family,
.NET Compact Framework - Windows CE .NET

MethodBase.IsStatic Property

Gets a value indicating whether the method is static (**Shared** in Visual Basic) .

```
[Visual Basic]
Public ReadOnly Property IsStatic As Boolean
[C#]
public bool IsStatic {get;}
[C++]
public: __property bool get_IsStatic();
[JScript]
public function get IsStatic() : Boolean;
```

Property Value

true if this method is static (**Shared** in Visual Basic); otherwise, **false**.

Remarks

A static member cannot implicitly reference instance data in a class.

Requirements

Platforms: Windows 98, Windows NT 4.0, Windows Millennium Edition, Windows 2000, Windows XP Home Edition, Windows XP Professional, Windows .NET Server family, .NET Compact Framework - Windows CE .NET

MethodBase.IsVirtual Property

Gets a value indicating whether the method is virtual (**Overridable** in Visual Basic) .

```
[Visual Basic]
Public ReadOnly Property IsVirtual As Boolean
[C#]
public bool IsVirtual {get;}
[C++]
public: __property bool get_IsVirtual();
[JScript]
public function get IsVirtual() : Boolean;
```

Property Value

true if this method is virtual (**Overridable** in Visual Basic); otherwise, **false**.

Remarks

A virtual member may reference instance data in a class and must be referenced through an instance of the class.

To determine if a method is overridable, it is not sufficient to check that **IsVirtual** is **true**. For a method to be overridable, **IsVirtual** must be **true** and **IsFinal** must be **false**. For example, a method might be non-virtual, but it implements an interface method. The common language runtime requires that all methods that implement interface members must be marked as virtual (**Overridable** in Visual Basic); therefore, the compiler marks the method virtual (**Overridable** in Visual Basic) **final**. So there are cases where a method is marked as virtual (**Overridable** in Visual Basic) but is still not overridable.

To establish with certainty whether a method is overridable, use code such as this: if (MethodInfo.IsVirtual && !MethodInfo.IsFinal)

If **IsVirtual** is **false** or **IsFinal** is **true**, then the method cannot be overridden.

Example

[Visual Basic, C#, JScript] The following example displays **false** for **IsFinal**, which might lead you to think that MyMethod is overridable. The code prints **false** even though MyMethod is not marked virtual (**Overridable** in Visual Basic) and thus cannot be overridden.

```
[Visual Basic]
Imports System
Imports System.Reflection
Imports Microsoft.VisualBasic

Public Class MyClass1

    Public Sub MyMethod()
    End Sub

    Public Shared Sub Main()
        Dim m As MethodBase = GetType(MyClass1).GetMethod("MyMethod")
        Console.WriteLine("The IsFinal property value of MyMethod ↵
is {0}.", m.IsFinal)
        Console.WriteLine("The IsVirtual property value of ↵
MyMethod is {0}.", m.IsVirtual)
    End Sub
End Class
```

```
[C#]
using System;
using System.Reflection;

public class MyClass
{
    public void MyMethod()
    {
    }
    public static void Main()
    {
        MethodBase m = typeof(MyClass).GetMethod("MyMethod");
        Console.WriteLine("The IsFinal property value of ↵
MyMethod is {0}.", m.IsFinal);
        Console.WriteLine("The IsVirtual property value of ↵
MyMethod is {0}.", m.IsVirtual);
    }
}
```

```
[JScript]
import System;
import System.Reflection;

public class MyClass
{
public function MyMethod() : void
    {
    }
public static function Main() : void
    {
    var m : MethodBase  = MyClass.GetMethod("MyMethod");
    Console.WriteLine(m.IsFinal);
    }
}
MyClass.Main();
```

Requirements

Platforms: Windows 98, Windows NT 4.0, Windows Millennium Edition, Windows 2000, Windows XP Home Edition, Windows XP Professional, Windows .NET Server family, .NET Compact Framework - Windows CE .NET

MethodBase.MethodHandle Property

Gets a handle to the internal metadata representation of a method.

```
[Visual Basic]
Public MustOverride ReadOnly Property MethodHandle As _
   RuntimeMethodHandle
[C#]
public abstract RuntimeMethodHandle MethodHandle {get;}
[C++]
public: __property virtual RuntimeMethodHandle get_MethodHandle() =
   0;
[JScript]
public abstract function get MethodHandle() : RuntimeMethodHandle;
```

Property Value

A **RuntimeMethodHandle** object.

Remarks

The handles are valid only in the application domain in which they were obtained.

Requirements

Platforms: Windows 98, Windows NT 4.0, Windows Millennium Edition, Windows 2000, Windows XP Home Edition, Windows XP Professional, Windows .NET Server family, .NET Compact Framework - Windows CE .NET

MethodBase.GetCurrentMethod Method

Returns a **MethodBase** object representing the currently executing method.

```
[Visual Basic]
Public Shared Function GetCurrentMethod() As MethodBase
[C#]
public static MethodBase GetCurrentMethod();
[C++]
public: static MethodBase* GetCurrentMethod();
[JScript]
public static function GetCurrentMethod() : MethodBase;
```

Return Value

A **MethodBase** object representing the currently executing method.

Requirements

Platforms: Windows 98, Windows NT 4.0, Windows Millennium Edition, Windows 2000, Windows XP Home Edition, Windows XP Professional, Windows .NET Server family

.NET Framework Security:

- **ReflectionPermission** to enhance security and performance when invoked late-bound through mechanisms such as **Type.InvokeMember**. Associated enumeration: **ReflectionPermissionFlag.MemberAccess**.

MethodBase.GetMethodFromHandle Method

Gets method information by using the method's internal metadata representation (handle).

```
[Visual Basic]
Public Shared Function GetMethodFromHandle( _
   ByVal handle As RuntimeMethodHandle _
) As MethodBase
[C#]
public static MethodBase GetMethodFromHandle(
   RuntimeMethodHandle handle
);
[C++]
public: static MethodBase* GetMethodFromHandle(
   RuntimeMethodHandle handle
);
[JScript]
public static function GetMethodFromHandle(
   handle : RuntimeMethodHandle
) : MethodBase;
```

Parameters

handle
   The method's handle.

Return Value

MethodBase information about the method.

Remarks

The handles are valid only in the application domain in which they were obtained.

Requirements

Platforms: Windows 98, Windows NT 4.0, Windows Millennium Edition, Windows 2000, Windows XP Home Edition, Windows XP Professional, Windows .NET Server family, .NET Compact Framework - Windows CE .NET, Common Language Infrastructure (CLI) Standard

.NET Framework Security:

- **ReflectionPermission** to enhance security and performance when invoked late-bound through mechanisms such as **Type.InvokeMember**. Associated enumeration: **ReflectionPermissionFlag.MemberAccess**.

MethodBase.GetMethodImplementationFlags Method

When overridden in a derived class, returns the **MethodImplAttributes** flags.

```
[Visual Basic]
Public MustOverride Function GetMethodImplementationFlags() As _
   MethodImplAttributes
[C#]
public abstract MethodImplAttributes GetMethodImplementationFlags();
[C++]
public: virtual MethodImplAttributes GetMethodImplementationFlags()
   = 0;
[JScript]
public abstract function GetMethodImplementationFlags() :
   MethodImplAttributes;
```

Return Value

The **MethodImplAttributes** flags.

Example

[Visual Basic]
```
' Define a constructor of the dynamic class.
Dim myConstructorBuilder As ConstructorBuilder = _
    myTypeBuilder.DefineConstructor(MethodAttributes.Public,
CallingConventions.Standard, _
                        myConstructorArgs)
' Get a reference to the module that contains this constructor.
Dim myModule As [Module] = myConstructorBuilder.GetModule()
Console.WriteLine("Module Name : " + myModule.Name)
' Get the 'MethodToken' that represents the token for this constructor.
Dim myMethodToken As MethodToken = myConstructorBuilder.GetToken()
Console.WriteLine("Constructor Token is : " +
myMethodToken.Token.ToString())
' Get the method implementation flags for this constructor.
Dim myMethodImplAttributes As MethodImplAttributes = _
    myConstructorBuilder.GetMethodImplementationFlags()
Console.WriteLine("MethodImplAttributes : " +
myMethodImplAttributes.ToString())
```

[C#]
```
// Define a constructor of the dynamic class.
ConstructorBuilder myConstructorBuilder =
myTypeBuilder.DefineConstructor(
    MethodAttributes.Public, CallingConventions.Standard,
myConstructorArgs);
// Get a reference to the module that contains this constructor.
Module myModule = myConstructorBuilder.GetModule();
Console.WriteLine("Module Name : " + myModule.Name);
// Get the 'MethodToken' that represents the token for this
constructor.
MethodToken myMethodToken = myConstructorBuilder.GetToken();
Console.WriteLine("Constructor Token is : " + myMethodToken.Token);
// Get the method implementation flags for this constructor.
MethodImplAttributes myMethodImplAttributes =
myConstructorBuilder.GetMethodImplementationFlags();
Console.WriteLine("MethodImplAttributes : "  + myMethodImplAttributes);
```

Requirements

Platforms: Windows 98, Windows NT 4.0, Windows Millennium Edition, Windows 2000, Windows XP Home Edition, Windows XP Professional, Windows .NET Server family

.NET Framework Security:
- **ReflectionPermission** to enhance security and performance when invoked late-bound through mechanisms such as **Type.InvokeMember**. Associated enumeration: **ReflectionPermissionFlag.MemberAccess**.

MethodBase.GetParameters Method

When overridden in a derived class, gets the parameters of the specified method or constructor.

[Visual Basic]
```
Public MustOverride Function GetParameters() As ParameterInfo()
```
[C#]
```
public abstract ParameterInfo[] GetParameters();
```
[C++]
```
public: virtual ParameterInfo* GetParameters() [] = 0;
```
[JScript]
```
public abstract function GetParameters() : ParameterInfo[];
```

Return Value

An array of type **ParameterInfo** containing information that matches the signature of the method (or constructor) reflected by this **MethodBase** instance.

Example

[Visual Basic]
```
' The following example uses instances of classes in
' the System.Reflection namespace to discover an event argument type.
Imports System
Imports System.Reflection
Imports Microsoft.VisualBasic

Public Class MainClass
    Delegate Sub MyDelegate(ByVal i As Integer)
    Public Event ev As MyDelegate
    Public Sub Fire(ByVal i As Integer)
        AddHandler ev, AddressOf Me.Fire
    End Sub 'Fire

    Public Shared Sub Main()
        Dim deleg As Type =
GetType(MainClass).GetEvent("ev").EventHandlerType
        Dim invoke As MethodInfo = deleg.GetMethod("Invoke")
        Dim pars As ParameterInfo() = invoke.GetParameters()
        Dim p As ParameterInfo
        For Each p In pars
            Console.WriteLine(p.ParameterType)
        Next p
    End Sub 'Main
End Class 'MainClass
```

[C#]
```
// The following example uses instances of classes in
// the System.Reflection namespace to discover an event argument type.
using System;
using System.Reflection;

public delegate void MyDelegate(int i);
public class MainClass
{
    public event MyDelegate ev;
    public void Fire(int i)
    {
        ev += new MyDelegate(this.Fire);
    }

    public static void Main()
    {
        Type deleg = typeof(MainClass).GetEvent("ev").EventHandlerType;
        MethodInfo invoke = deleg.GetMethod("Invoke");
        ParameterInfo[] pars = invoke.GetParameters();
        foreach (ParameterInfo p in pars)
        {
            Console.WriteLine(p.ParameterType);
        }
    }
}
```

[C++]
```
// The following example uses instances of classes in
// the System::Reflection namespace to discover an event argument type.
#using <mscorlib.dll>

using namespace System;
using namespace System::Reflection;

public __delegate void MyDelegate(int  i);

public __gc class MainClass {
public:
    __event MyDelegate* ev;
public:
    void Fire(int i) {
        ev += new MyDelegate(this, Fire);
    }
};
```

```
int main() {
    Type* deleg = __typeof(MainClass)->GetEvent(S"ev")-
>EventHandlerType;
    MethodInfo* invoke = deleg->GetMethod(S"Invoke");
    ParameterInfo* pars[] = invoke->GetParameters();
    System::Collections::IEnumerator* myEnum = pars->GetEnumerator();
    while (myEnum->MoveNext()) {
        ParameterInfo* p = __try_cast<ParameterInfo*>(myEnum->Current);
        Console::WriteLine(p->ParameterType);
    }
}
```

Requirements

Platforms: Windows 98, Windows NT 4.0,
Windows Millennium Edition, Windows 2000,
Windows XP Home Edition, Windows XP Professional,
Windows .NET Server family,
.NET Compact Framework - Windows CE .NET,
Common Language Infrastructure (CLI) Standard

.NET Framework Security:

- **ReflectionPermission** to enhance security and performance
  when invoked late-bound through mechanisms such as
  Type.InvokeMember. Associated enumeration:
  ReflectionPermissionFlag.MemberAccess.

MethodBase.Invoke Method

Invokes the method or constructor reflected by this **MethodInfo**
instance.

Overload List

Invokes the underlying method or constructor represented by this
MethodInfo object with the specified parameters.

Supported by the .NET Compact Framework.

[Visual Basic] **Overloads Public Function Invoke(Object, Object()) As Object**

[C#] **public object Invoke(object, object[]);**

[C++] **public: Object* Invoke(Object*, Object*[]);**

[JScript] **public function Invoke(Object, Object[]) : Object;**

When overridden in a derived class, invokes the reflected method or
constructor with the given parameters.

Supported by the .NET Compact Framework.

[Visual Basic] **Overloads Public MustOverride Function Invoke(Object, BindingFlags, Binder, Object(), CultureInfo) As Object**

[C#] **public abstract object Invoke(object, BindingFlags, Binder, object[], CultureInfo);**

[C++] **public: virtual Object* Invoke(Object*, BindingFlags, Binder*, Object*[], CultureInfo*) = 0;**

[JScript] **public abstract function Invoke(Object, BindingFlags, Binder, Object[], CultureInfo) : Object;**

Example

[Visual Basic, C#, C++] The following example demonstrates all
members of the **System.Reflection.Binder** class using an overload
of **Type.InvokeMember**. The private method **CanConvertFrom**
finds compatible types for a given type. For another example of
invoking members in a custom binding scenario, see **Dynamically Loading and Using Types**.

[Visual Basic, C#, C++] **Note** This example shows how to use
one of the overloaded versions of **Invoke**. For other examples
that might be available, see the individual overload topics.

```
[Visual Basic]
Imports System
Imports System.Reflection
Imports System.Globalization
Imports Microsoft.VisualBasic

Public Class MyBinder
    Inherits Binder
    Public Sub New()
        MyBase.new()
    End Sub 'New
    Private Class BinderState
        Public args() As Object
    End Class 'BinderState

    Public Overrides Function BindToField(ByVal bindingAttr
As BindingFlags, ByVal match() As FieldInfo, ByVal value
As Object, ByVal culture As CultureInfo) As FieldInfo
        If match Is Nothing Then
            Throw New ArgumentNullException("match")
        End If
        ' Get a field for which the value parameter can be
converted to the specified field type.
        Dim i As Integer
        For i = 0 To match.Length - 1
            If Not (ChangeType(value, match(i).FieldType,
culture) Is Nothing) Then
                Return match(i)
            End If
        Next i
        Return Nothing
    End Function 'BindToField

    Public Overrides Function BindToMethod(ByVal bindingAttr As
BindingFlags, ByVal match() As MethodBase, ByRef args()
As Object, ByVal modifiers() As ParameterModifier, ByVal
culture As CultureInfo, ByVal names() As String, ByRef state
As Object) As MethodBase
        ' Store the arguments to the method in a state object.
        Dim myBinderState As New BinderState()
        Dim arguments() As Object = New [Object](args.Length) {}
        args.CopyTo(arguments, 0)
        myBinderState.args = arguments
        state = myBinderState

        If match Is Nothing Then
            Throw New ArgumentNullException()
        End If
        ' Find a method that has the same parameters as those of args.
        Dim i As Integer
        For i = 0 To match.Length - 1
            ' Count the number of parameters that match.
            Dim count As Integer = 0
            Dim parameters As ParameterInfo() =
match(i).GetParameters()
            ' Go on to the next method if the number of
parameters do not match.
            If args.Length <> parameters.Length Then
                GoTo ContinueFori
            End If
            ' Match each of the parameters that the user
expects the method to have.
            Dim j As Integer
            For j = 0 To args.Length - 1
                ' If names is not null, then reorder args.
                If Not (names Is Nothing) Then
                    If names.Length <> args.Length Then
                        Throw New ArgumentException("names
and args must have the same number of elements.")
                    End If
```

```
                Dim k As Integer
                For k = 0 To names.Length - 1
                    If String.Compare(parameters(j).
Name, names(k).ToString()) = 0 Then
                        args(j) = myBinderState.args(k)
                    End If
                Next k
            End If ' Determine whether the types specified
by the user can be converted to parameter type.
            If Not (ChangeType(args(j), parameters(j).ParameterType,
culture) Is Nothing) Then
                count += 1
            Else
                Exit For
            End If
        Next j
        ' Determine whether the method has been found.
        If count = args.Length Then
            Return match(i)
        End If
ContinueFori:
    Next i
    Return Nothing
End Function 'BindToMethod

    Public Overrides Function ChangeType(ByVal value As
Object, ByVal myChangeType As Type, ByVal culture As
CultureInfo) As Object
        ' Determine whether the value parameter can be
converted to a value of type myType.
        If CanConvertFrom(value.GetType(), myChangeType) Then
            ' Return the converted object.
            Return Convert.ChangeType(value, myChangeType)
            ' Return null.
        Else
            Return Nothing
        End If
    End Function 'ChangeType

    Public Overrides Sub ReorderArgumentArray(ByRef args() As
Object, ByVal state As Object)
        'Redimension the array to hold the state values.
        ReDim args(CType(state, BinderState).args.Length)
        ' Return the args that had been reordered by BindToMethod.
        CType(state, BinderState).args.CopyTo(args, 0)
    End Sub 'ReorderArgumentArray

    Public Overrides Function SelectMethod(ByVal bindingAttr
 As BindingFlags, ByVal match() As MethodBase, ByVal types()
As Type, ByVal modifiers() As ParameterModifier) As MethodBase
        If match Is Nothing Then
            Throw New ArgumentNullException("match")
        End If
        Dim i As Integer
        For i = 0 To match.Length - 1
            ' Count the number of parameters that match.
            Dim count As Integer = 0
            Dim parameters As ParameterInfo() =
match(i).GetParameters()
            ' Go on to the next method if the number of
parameters do not match.
            If types.Length <> parameters.Length Then
                GoTo ContinueFori
            End If
            ' Match each of the parameters that the user
expects the method to have.
            Dim j As Integer
            For j = 0 To types.Length - 1
                ' Determine whether the types specified by
the user can be converted to parameter type.
                If CanConvertFrom(types(j),
parameters(j).ParameterType) Then
                    count += 1
                Else
                    Exit For
                End If

            Next j ' Determine whether the method has been found.
            If count = types.Length Then
                Return match(i)
            End If
ContinueFori:
    Next i
    Return Nothing
End Function 'SelectMethod
    Public Overrides Function SelectProperty(ByVal
bindingAttr As BindingFlags, ByVal match() As PropertyInfo,
ByVal returnType As Type, ByVal indexes() As Type, ByVal
modifiers() As ParameterModifier) As PropertyInfo
        If match Is Nothing Then
            Throw New ArgumentNullException("match")
        End If
        Dim i As Integer
        For i = 0 To match.Length - 1
            ' Count the number of indexes that match.
            Dim count As Integer = 0
            Dim parameters As ParameterInfo() =
match(i).GetIndexParameters()

            ' Go on to the next property if the number of
indexes do not match.
            If indexes.Length <> parameters.Length Then
                GoTo ContinueFori
            End If
            ' Match each of the indexes that the user expects
the property to have.
            Dim j As Integer
            For j = 0 To indexes.Length - 1
                ' Determine whether the types specified by the
user can be converted to index type.
                If CanConvertFrom(indexes(j),
parameters(j).ParameterType) Then
                    count += 1
                Else
                    Exit For
                End If
            Next j ' Determine whether the property has been found.
            If count = indexes.Length Then
                ' Determine whether the return type can be
converted to the properties type.
                If CanConvertFrom(returnType, match(i).GetType()) Then
                    Return match(i)
                Else
                    GoTo ContinueFori
                End If
            End If
ContinueFori:
    Next i
    Return Nothing
End Function 'SelectProperty

    ' Determine whether type1 can be converted to type2. Check
only for primitive types.
    Private Function CanConvertFrom(ByVal type1 As Type, ByVal
type2 As Type) As Boolean
        If type1.IsPrimitive And type2.IsPrimitive Then
            Dim typeCode1 As TypeCode = Type.GetTypeCode(type1)
            Dim typeCode2 As TypeCode = Type.GetTypeCode(type2)
            ' If both type1 and type2 have same type, return true.
            If typeCode1 = typeCode2 Then
                Return True
            End If ' Possible conversions from Char follow.
            If typeCode1 = TypeCode.Char Then
                Select Case typeCode2
                    Case TypeCode.UInt16
                        Return True
                    Case TypeCode.UInt32
                        Return True
                    Case TypeCode.Int32
                        Return True
                    Case TypeCode.UInt64
                        Return True
                    Case TypeCode.Int64
```

```
                    Return True                                               Return True
            Case TypeCode.Single                                      Case Else
                    Return True                                               Return False
            Case TypeCode.Double                                   End Select
                    Return True                               End If ' Possible conversions from UInt32 follow.
            Case Else                                         If typeCode1 = TypeCode.UInt32 Then
                    Return False                                  Select Case typeCode2
        End Select                                                    Case TypeCode.UInt64
    End If ' Possible conversions from Byte follow.                           Return True
    If typeCode1 = TypeCode.Byte Then                                 Case TypeCode.Int64
        Select Case typeCode2                                                 Return True
            Case TypeCode.Char                                        Case TypeCode.Single
                    Return True                                               Return True
            Case TypeCode.UInt16                                      Case TypeCode.Double
                    Return True                                               Return True
            Case TypeCode.Int16                                       Case Else
                    Return True                                               Return False
            Case TypeCode.UInt32                                  End Select
                    Return True                               End If ' Possible conversions from Int32 follow.
            Case TypeCode.Int32                               If typeCode1 = TypeCode.Int32 Then
                    Return True                                  Select Case typeCode2
            Case TypeCode.UInt64                                     Case TypeCode.Int64
                    Return True                                              Return True
            Case TypeCode.Int64                                      Case TypeCode.Single
                    Return True                                              Return True
            Case TypeCode.Single                                     Case TypeCode.Double
                    Return True                                              Return True
            Case TypeCode.Double                                     Case Else
                    Return True                                              Return False
            Case Else                                            End Select
                    Return False                              End If ' Possible conversions from UInt64 follow.
        End Select                                            If typeCode1 = TypeCode.UInt64 Then
    End If ' Possible conversions from SByte follow.             Select Case typeCode2
    If typeCode1 = TypeCode.SByte Then                               Case TypeCode.Single
        Select Case typeCode2                                                Return True
            Case TypeCode.Int16                                      Case TypeCode.Double
                    Return True                                              Return True
            Case TypeCode.Int32                                      Case Else
                    Return True                                              Return False
            Case TypeCode.Int64                                  End Select
                    Return True                               End If ' Possible conversions from Int64 follow.
            Case TypeCode.Single                             If typeCode1 = TypeCode.Int64 Then
                    Return True                                  Select Case typeCode2
            Case TypeCode.Double                                     Case TypeCode.Single
                    Return True                                              Return True
            Case Else                                               Case TypeCode.Double
                    Return False                                             Return True
        End Select                                                   Case Else
    End If ' Possible conversions from UInt16 follow.                        Return False
    If typeCode1 = TypeCode.UInt16 Then                          End Select
        Select Case typeCode2                                 End If ' Possible conversions from Single follow.
            Case TypeCode.UInt32                             If typeCode1 = TypeCode.Single Then
                    Return True                                  Select Case typeCode2
            Case TypeCode.Int32                                      Case TypeCode.Double
                    Return True                                              Return True
            Case TypeCode.UInt64                                     Case Else
                    Return True                                              Return False
            Case TypeCode.Int64                                  End Select
                    Return True                               End If
            Case TypeCode.Single                             End If
                    Return True                               Return False
            Case TypeCode.Double                          End Function 'CanConvertFrom
                    Return True                       End Class 'MyBinder
            Case Else
                    Return False                      Public Class MyClass1
        End Select                                        Public myFieldB As Short
    End If ' Possible conversions from Int16 follow.      Public myFieldA As Integer
    If typeCode1 = TypeCode.Int16 Then
        Select Case typeCode2                             Public Overloads Sub MyMethod(ByVal i As Long, ByVal k As Char)
            Case TypeCode.Int32                                   Console.WriteLine(ControlChars.NewLine & "This is
                    Return True                           MyMethod(long i, char k).")
            Case TypeCode.Int64                               End Sub 'MyMethod
                    Return True
            Case TypeCode.Single                              Public Overloads Sub MyMethod(ByVal i As Long, ByVal j As Long)
                    Return True                                   Console.WriteLine(ControlChars.NewLine & "This is
            Case TypeCode.Double                          MyMethod(long i, long j).")
```

```
            End Sub 'MyMethod
End Class 'MyClass1

Public Class Binder_Example
    Public Shared Sub Main()
        ' Get the type of MyClass1.
        Dim myType As Type = GetType(MyClass1)
        ' Get the instance of MyClass1.
        Dim myInstance As New MyClass1()
        Console.WriteLine(ControlChars.Cr & "Displaying the      ⤶
results of using the MyBinder binder.")
        Console.WriteLine()
        ' Get the method information for MyMethod.
        Dim myMethod As MethodInfo = myType.GetMethod           ⤶
("MyMethod", BindingFlags.Public Or BindingFlags.Instance,      ⤶
New MyBinder(), New Type() {GetType(Short), GetType(Short)}, Nothing)
        Console.WriteLine(MyMethod)
        ' Invoke MyMethod.
        myMethod.Invoke(myInstance, BindingFlags.InvokeMethod,  ⤶
New [Object]() {CInt(32), CInt(32)},                            ⤶
CultureInfo.CurrentCulture)
    End Sub 'Main
End Class 'Binder_Example

[C#]
using System;
using System.Reflection;
using System.Globalization;

public class MyBinder : Binder
{
    public MyBinder() : base()
    {
    }
    private class BinderState
    {
        public object[] args;
    }
    public override FieldInfo BindToField(
        BindingFlags bindingAttr,
        FieldInfo[] match,
        object value,
        CultureInfo culture
        )
    {
        if(match == null)
            throw new ArgumentNullException("match");
        // Get a field for which the value parameter can be      ⤶
converted to the specified field type.
        for(int i = 0; i < match.Length; i++)
            if(ChangeType(value, match[i].FieldType, culture) != null)
                return match[i];
        return null;
    }
    public override MethodBase BindToMethod(
        BindingFlags bindingAttr,
        MethodBase[] match,
        ref object[] args,
        ParameterModifier[] modifiers,
        CultureInfo culture,
        string[] names,
        out object state
        )
    {
        // Store the arguments to the method in a state object.
        BinderState myBinderState = new BinderState();
        object[] arguments = new Object[args.Length];
        args.CopyTo(arguments, 0);
        myBinderState.args = arguments;
        state = myBinderState;
        if(match == null)
            throw new ArgumentNullException();
        // Find a method that has the same parameters as those   ⤶
of the args parameter.
        for(int i = 0; i < match.Length; i++)
        {
            // Count the number of parameters that match.
            int count = 0;
            ParameterInfo[] parameters = match[i].GetParameters();
            // Go on to the next method if the number of         ⤶
parameters do not match.
            if(args.Length != parameters.Length)
                continue;
            // Match each of the parameters that the user        ⤶
expects the method to have.
            for(int j = 0; j < args.Length; j++)
            {
                // If the names parameter is not null, then      ⤶
reorder args.
                if(names != null)
                {
                    if(names.Length != args.Length)
                        throw new ArgumentException("names       ⤶
and args must have the same number of elements.");
                    for(int k = 0; k < names.Length; k++)
                        if(String.Compare(parameters[j].Name,    ⤶
names[k].ToString()) == 0)
                            args[j] = myBinderState.args[k];
                }
                // Determine whether the types specified by      ⤶
the user can be converted to the parameter type.
                if(ChangeType(args[j], parameters[j]             ⤶
.ParameterType, culture) != null)
                    count += 1;
                else
                    break;
            }
            // Determine whether the method has been found.
            if(count == args.Length)
                return match[i];
        }
        return null;
    }
    public override object ChangeType(
        object value,
        Type myChangeType,
        CultureInfo culture
        )
    {
        // Determine whether the value parameter can be          ⤶
converted to a value of type myType.
        if(CanConvertFrom(value.GetType(), myChangeType))
            // Return the converted object.
            return Convert.ChangeType(value, myChangeType);
        else
            // Return null.
            return null;
    }
    public override void ReorderArgumentArray(
        ref object[] args,
        object state
        )
    {
        // Return the args that had been reordered by BindToMethod.
        ((BinderState)state).args.CopyTo(args, 0);
    }
    public override MethodBase SelectMethod(
        BindingFlags bindingAttr,
        MethodBase[] match,
        Type[] types,
        ParameterModifier[] modifiers
        )
    {
        if(match == null)
            throw new ArgumentNullException("match");
        for(int i = 0; i < match.Length; i++)
        {
            // Count the number of parameters that match.
            int count = 0;
            ParameterInfo[] parameters = match[i].GetParameters();
            // Go on to the next method if the number of         ⤶
parameters do not match.
```

```
                if(types.Length != parameters.Length)
                    continue;
                // Match each of the parameters that the user       ⏎
expects the method to have.
                for(int j = 0; j < types.Length; j++)
                    // Determine whether the types specified by      ⏎
the user can be converted to parameter type.
                    if(CanConvertFrom(types[j],                      ⏎
parameters[j].ParameterType))
                        count += 1;
                    else
                        break;
                // Determine whether the method has been found.
                if(count == types.Length)
                    return match[i];
            }
            return null;
        }
        public override PropertyInfo SelectProperty(
            BindingFlags bindingAttr,
            PropertyInfo[] match,
            Type returnType,
            Type[] indexes,
            ParameterModifier[] modifiers
            )
        {
            if(match == null)
                throw new ArgumentNullException("match");
            for(int i = 0; i < match.Length; i++)
            {
                // Count the number of indexes that match.
                int count = 0;
                ParameterInfo[] parameters = match[i].GetIndexParameters();
                // Go on to the next property if the number of       ⏎
indexes do not match.
                if(indexes.Length != parameters.Length)
                    continue;
                // Match each of the indexes that the user expects   ⏎
the property to have.
                for(int j = 0; j < indexes.Length; j++)
                    // Determine whether the types specified by      ⏎
the user can be converted to index type.
                    if(CanConvertFrom(indexes[j],
parameters[j].ParameterType))
                        count += 1;
                    else
                        break;
                // Determine whether the property has been found.
                if(count == indexes.Length)
                    // Determine whether the return type can         ⏎
be converted to the properties type.
                    if(CanConvertFrom(returnType, match[i].GetType()))
                        return match[i];
                    else
                        continue;
            }
            return null;
        }
        // Determines whether type1 can be converted to type2.       ⏎
Check only for primitive types.
        private bool CanConvertFrom(Type type1, Type type2)
        {
            if(type1.IsPrimitive && type2.IsPrimitive)
            {
                TypeCode typeCode1 = Type.GetTypeCode(type1);
                TypeCode typeCode2 = Type.GetTypeCode(type2);
                // If both type1 and type2 have the same type, return true.
                if(typeCode1 == typeCode2)
                    return true;
                // Possible conversions from Char follow.
                if(typeCode1 == TypeCode.Char)
                    switch(typeCode2)
                    {
                        case TypeCode.UInt16 : return true;
                        case TypeCode.UInt32 : return true;
                        case TypeCode.Int32  : return true;
                        case TypeCode.UInt64 : return true;
                        case TypeCode.Int64  : return true;
                        case TypeCode.Single : return true;
                        case TypeCode.Double : return true;
                        default              : return false;
                    }
                // Possible conversions from Byte follow.
                if(typeCode1 == TypeCode.Byte)
                    switch(typeCode2)
                    {
                        case TypeCode.Char   : return true;
                        case TypeCode.UInt16 : return true;
                        case TypeCode.Int16  : return true;
                        case TypeCode.UInt32 : return true;
                        case TypeCode.Int32  : return true;
                        case TypeCode.UInt64 : return true;
                        case TypeCode.Int64  : return true;
                        case TypeCode.Single : return true;
                        case TypeCode.Double : return true;
                        default              : return false;
                    }
                // Possible conversions from SByte follow.
                if(typeCode1 == TypeCode.SByte)
                    switch(typeCode2)
                    {
                        case TypeCode.Int16  : return true;
                        case TypeCode.Int32  : return true;
                        case TypeCode.Int64  : return true;
                        case TypeCode.Single : return true;
                        case TypeCode.Double : return true;
                        default              : return false;
                    }
                // Possible conversions from UInt16 follow.
                if(typeCode1 == TypeCode.UInt16)
                    switch(typeCode2)
                    {
                        case TypeCode.UInt32 : return true;
                        case TypeCode.Int32  : return true;
                        case TypeCode.UInt64 : return true;
                        case TypeCode.Int64  : return true;
                        case TypeCode.Single : return true;
                        case TypeCode.Double : return true;
                        default              : return false;
                    }
                // Possible conversions from Int16 follow.
                if(typeCode1 == TypeCode.Int16)
                    switch(typeCode2)
                    {
                        case TypeCode.Int32  : return true;
                        case TypeCode.Int64  : return true;
                        case TypeCode.Single : return true;
                        case TypeCode.Double : return true;
                        default              : return false;
                    }
                // Possible conversions from UInt32 follow.
                if(typeCode1 == TypeCode.UInt32)
                    switch(typeCode2)
                    {
                        case TypeCode.UInt64 : return true;
                        case TypeCode.Int64  : return true;
                        case TypeCode.Single : return true;
                        case TypeCode.Double : return true;
                        default              : return false;
                    }
                // Possible conversions from Int32 follow.
                if(typeCode1 == TypeCode.Int32)
                    switch(typeCode2)
                    {
                        case TypeCode.Int64  : return true;
                        case TypeCode.Single : return true;
                        case TypeCode.Double : return true;
                        default              : return false;
                    }
                // Possible conversions from UInt64 follow.
                if(typeCode1 == TypeCode.UInt64)
                    switch(typeCode2)
```

```
                {
                case TypeCode.Single : return true;
                case TypeCode.Double : return true;
                default              : return false;
                }
            }
            // Possible conversions from Int64 follow.
            if(typeCode1 == TypeCode.Int64)
                switch(typeCode2)
                {
                case TypeCode.Single : return true;
                case TypeCode.Double : return true;
                default              : return false;
                }
            // Possible conversions from Single follow.
            if(typeCode1 == TypeCode.Single)
                switch(typeCode2)
                {
                case TypeCode.Double : return true;
                default              : return false;
                }
            }
        }
        return false;
    }
}
public class MyClass1
{
    public short myFieldB;
    public int myFieldA;
    public void MyMethod(long i, char k)
    {
        Console.WriteLine("\nThis is MyMethod(long i, char k)");
    }
    public void MyMethod(long i, long j)
    {
        Console.WriteLine("\nThis is MyMethod(long i, long j)");
    }
}
public class Binder_Example
{
    public static void Main()
    {
        // Get the type of MyClass1.
        Type myType = typeof(MyClass1);
        // Get the instance of MyClass1.
        MyClass1 myInstance = new MyClass1();
        Console.WriteLine("\nDisplaying the results of using
the MyBinder binder.\n");
        // Get the method information for MyMethod.
        MethodInfo myMethod = myType.GetMethod("MyMethod",
BindingFlags.Public | BindingFlags.Instance,
            new MyBinder(), new Type[] {typeof(short),
typeof(short)}, null);
        Console.WriteLine(myMethod);
        // Invoke MyMethod.
        myMethod.Invoke(myInstance, BindingFlags.InvokeMethod,
 new MyBinder(), new Object[] {(int)32, (int)32},
CultureInfo.CurrentCulture);
    }
}

[C++]
#using <mscorlib.dll>

using namespace System;
using namespace System::Reflection;
using namespace System::Globalization;
using namespace System::Runtime::InteropServices;

public __gc class MyBinder : public Binder
{
public:
    MyBinder() : Binder()
    {
    }
private:
    __gc class BinderState
```

```
    {
    public:
        Object* args[];
    };
public:
    FieldInfo* BindToField(
        BindingFlags bindingAttr,
        FieldInfo* match[],
        Object* value,
        CultureInfo* culture)
    {
        if (match == 0)
            throw new ArgumentNullException(S"match");
        // Get a field for which the value parameter can be
converted to the specified field type.
        for (int i = 0; i < match->Length; i++)
            if (ChangeType(value, match[i]->FieldType, culture) != 0)
                return match[i];
        return 0;
    }
    virtual MethodBase* BindToMethod(
        BindingFlags bindingAttr,
        MethodBase* match[],
        Object* (*args)[],
        ParameterModifier modifiers[],
        CultureInfo* culture,
        String* names[],
        [Out] Object** state)
    {
        // Store the arguments to the method in a state Object*.
        BinderState* myBinderState = new BinderState();
        Object* arguments[] = new Object*[(*args)->Length];
        (*args)->CopyTo(arguments, 0);
        myBinderState->args = arguments;
        *state = myBinderState;
        if (match == 0)
            throw new ArgumentNullException();
        // Find a method that has the same parameters as
those of the args parameter.
        for (int i = 0; i < match->Length; i++) {
            // Count the number of parameters that match.
            int count = 0;
            ParameterInfo* parameters[] = match[i]->GetParameters();
            // Go on to the next method if the number of parameters
do not match.
            if ((*args)->Length != parameters->Length)
                continue;
            // Match each of the parameters that the user expects
the method to have.
            for (int j = 0; j < (*args)->Length; j++) {
                // If the names parameter is not 0, then reorder args.
                if (names != 0) {
                    if (names->Length != (*args)->Length)
                        throw new ArgumentException(S"names and
args must have the same number of elements.");
                    for (int k = 0; k < names->Length; k++)
                        if (String::Compare(parameters[j]->Name,
names[k]) == 0)
                            (*args)[j] = myBinderState->args->Item[k];
                }
                // Determine whether the types specified by the
user can be converted to the parameter type.
                if (ChangeType(args[j], parameters[j]->
ParameterType, culture) != 0)
                    count += 1;
                else
                    break;
            }
            // Determine whether the method has been found.
            if (count == (*args)->Length)
                return match[i];
        }
        return 0;
    }
    Object* ChangeType(Object* value, Type* myChangeType,
CultureInfo* culture)
```

```
   {
      // Determine whether the value parameter can be
converted to a value of type myType.
      if (CanConvertFrom(value->GetType(), myChangeType))
         // Return the converted Object*.
         return Convert::ChangeType(value, myChangeType);
      else
         // Return 0.
         return 0;
   }
   void ReorderArgumentArray(Object* (*args) __gc[], Object* state)
   {
      // Return the args that had been reordered by BindToMethod.
      (__try_cast<BinderState*>(state))->args->CopyTo((*args), 0);
   }
   MethodBase* SelectMethod(
      BindingFlags bindingAttr,
      MethodBase* match[],
      Type* types[],
      ParameterModifier modifiers[])
   {
      if (match == 0)
         throw new ArgumentNullException(S"match");
      for (int i = 0; i < match->Length; i++) {
         // Count the number of parameters that match.
         int count = 0;
         ParameterInfo* parameters[] = match[i]->GetParameters();
         // Go on to the next method if the number of
parameters do not match.
         if (types->Length != parameters->Length)
            continue;
         // Match each of the parameters that the user
expects the method to have.
         for (int j = 0; j < types->Length; j++)
            // Determine whether the types specified by the
user can be converted to parameter type.
            if (CanConvertFrom(types[j], parameters[j]->ParameterType))
               count += 1;
            else
               break;
         // Determine whether the method has been found.
         if (count == types->Length)
            return match[i];
      }
      return 0;
   }
   PropertyInfo* SelectProperty(
      BindingFlags bindingAttr,
      PropertyInfo* match[],
      Type* returnType,
      Type* indexes[],
      ParameterModifier modifiers[]) {
         if (match == 0)
            throw new ArgumentNullException(S"match");
         for (int i = 0; i < match->Length; i++) {
            // Count the number of indexes that match.
            int count = 0;
            ParameterInfo* parameters[] = match[i]-
>GetIndexParameters();
            // Go on to the next property if the number of
indexes do not match.
            if (indexes->Length != parameters->Length)
               continue;
            // Match each of the indexes that the user expects
the property to have.
            for (int j = 0; j < indexes->Length; j++)
               // Determine whether the types specified by the
user can be converted to index type.
               if (CanConvertFrom(indexes[j], parameters[j]-
>ParameterType))
                  count += 1;
               else
                  break;
            // Determine whether the property has been found.
            if (count == indexes->Length)
               // Determine whether the return type can be
converted to the properties type.
               if (CanConvertFrom(returnType, match[i]->GetType()))
                  return match[i];
               else
                  continue;
         }
         return 0;
   }
   // Determines whether type1 can be converted to type2.
Check only for primitive types.
private:
   bool CanConvertFrom(Type* type1, Type* type2)
   {
      if (type1->IsPrimitive && type2->IsPrimitive)
      {
         TypeCode typeCode1 = Type::GetTypeCode(type1);
         TypeCode typeCode2 = Type::GetTypeCode(type2);
         // If both type1 and type2 have the same type, return true.
         if (typeCode1 == typeCode2)
            return true;
         // Possible conversions from Char follow.
         if (typeCode1 == TypeCode::Char){
            switch(typeCode2) {
               case TypeCode::UInt16 : return true;
               case TypeCode::UInt32 : return true;
               case TypeCode::Int32  : return true;
               case TypeCode::UInt64 : return true;
               case TypeCode::Int64  : return true;
               case TypeCode::Single : return true;
               case TypeCode::Double : return true;
               default               : return false;
            }
         }
         // Possible conversions from Byte follow.
         if (typeCode1 == TypeCode::Byte){
            switch(typeCode2) {
               case TypeCode::Char   : return true;
               case TypeCode::UInt16 : return true;
               case TypeCode::Int16  : return true;
               case TypeCode::UInt32 : return true;
               case TypeCode::Int32  : return true;
               case TypeCode::UInt64 : return true;
               case TypeCode::Int64  : return true;
               case TypeCode::Single : return true;
               case TypeCode::Double : return true;
               default               : return false;
            }
         }
         // Possible conversions from SByte follow.
         if (typeCode1 == TypeCode::SByte){
            switch(typeCode2) {
               case TypeCode::Int16  : return true;
               case TypeCode::Int32  : return true;
               case TypeCode::Int64  : return true;
               case TypeCode::Single : return true;
               case TypeCode::Double : return true;
               default               : return false;
            }
         }
         // Possible conversions from UInt16 follow.
         if (typeCode1 == TypeCode::UInt16){
            switch(typeCode2) {
               case TypeCode::UInt32 : return true;
               case TypeCode::Int32  : return true;
               case TypeCode::UInt64 : return true;
               case TypeCode::Int64  : return true;
               case TypeCode::Single : return true;
               case TypeCode::Double : return true;
               default               : return false;
            }
         }
         // Possible conversions from Int16 follow.
         if (typeCode1 == TypeCode::Int16){
            switch(typeCode2) {
               case TypeCode::Int32  : return true;
               case TypeCode::Int64  : return true;
```

```
            case TypeCode::Single : return true;
            case TypeCode::Double : return true;
            default               : return false;
        }
    }
    // Possible conversions from UInt32 follow.
    if (typeCode1 == TypeCode::UInt32){
        switch(typeCode2) {
            case TypeCode::UInt64 : return true;
            case TypeCode::Int64  : return true;
            case TypeCode::Single : return true;
            case TypeCode::Double : return true;
            default               : return false;
        }
    }
    // Possible conversions from Int32 follow.
    if (typeCode1 == TypeCode::Int32){
        switch(typeCode2) {
            case TypeCode::Int64  : return true;
            case TypeCode::Single : return true;
            case TypeCode::Double : return true;
            default               : return false;
        }
    }
    // Possible conversions from UInt64 follow.
    if (typeCode1 == TypeCode::UInt64){
        switch(typeCode2) {
            case TypeCode::Single : return true;
            case TypeCode::Double : return true;
            default               : return false;
        }
    }
    // Possible conversions from Int64 follow.
    if (typeCode1 == TypeCode::Int64){
        switch(typeCode2) {
            case TypeCode::Single : return true;
            case TypeCode::Double : return true;
            default               : return false;
        }
    }
    // Possible conversions from Single follow.
    if (typeCode1 == TypeCode::Single){
        switch(typeCode2) {
            case TypeCode::Double : return true;
            default               : return false;
        }
    }
    }
    return false;
    }
};

public __gc class MyClass1
{
public:
    short myFieldB;
    int myFieldA;
    void MyMethod(long i, char k)
    {
        Console::WriteLine(S"\nThis is MyMethod(long i, char k)");
    }
    void MyMethod(long i, long j)
    {
        Console::WriteLine(S"\nThis is MyMethod(long i, long j)");
    }
};

void main()
{
    // Get the type of MyClass1.
    Type* myType = __typeof(MyClass1);
    // Get the instance of MyClass1.
    MyClass1* myInstance = new MyClass1();
    Console::WriteLine(S"\nDisplaying the results of using
the MyBinder binder.\n");
    // Get the method information for MyMethod.
```

```
    Type* types[] = {__typeof(short), __typeof(short)};
    MethodInfo* myMethod = myType->GetMethod(S"MyMethod",
        static_cast<BindingFlags>( BindingFlags::Public |
BindingFlags::Instance ),
        new MyBinder(), types, 0);
    Console::WriteLine(myMethod);
    // Invoke MyMethod.
    Object* obj[] = {__box(32), __box(32)};
    myMethod->Invoke(myInstance, BindingFlags::InvokeMethod,
    new MyBinder(), obj, CultureInfo::CurrentCulture);
}
```

MethodBase.Invoke Method (Object, Object[])

Invokes the underlying method or constructor represented by this
MethodInfo object with the specified parameters.

```
[Visual Basic]
Overloads Public Function Invoke( _
    ByVal obj As Object, _
    ByVal parameters() As Object _
) As Object
[C#]
public object Invoke(
    object obj,
    object[] parameters
);
[C++]
public: Object* Invoke(
    Object* obj,
    Object* parameters __gc[]
);
[JScript]
public function Invoke(
    obj : Object,
    parameters : Object[]
) : Object;
```

Parameters

obj

    The instance that created this method.

parameters

    An argument list for the invoked method or constructor. This is
an array of objects with the same number, order, and type as the
parameters of the method or constructor to be invoked. If there
are no parameters, this should be a null reference (**Nothing** in
Visual Basic).

    If the method or constructor represented by this instance takes a
ByRef parameter, there is no special attribute required for that
parameter in order to invoke the method or constructor using this
function. Any object in this array that is not explicitly initialized
with a value will contain the default value for that object type.
For reference-type elements, this value is a null reference
(**Nothing**). For value-type elements, this value is 0, 0.0, or **false**,
depending on the specific element type.

Return Value

An **Object** containing the return value of the invoked method, or a
re-initialized object in the case of a constructor.

Exceptions

Exception Type	Condition
TargetException	The *obj* parameter is a null reference (**Nothing** in Visual Basic) and the method is not static.
	-or-
	The method is not declared or inherited by the class of *obj*.
ArgumentException	The type of the *parameters* parameter does not match the signature of the method or constructor reflected by this instance.
TargetInvocationException	The invoked method or constructor throws an exception.
TargetParameter-CountException	The *parameters* array does not have the correct number of arguments.
MethodAccessException	The caller does not have permission to execute the constructor.

Remarks

Use this method to invoke methods with parameters that have default values. To bind to these methods, Reflection requires one of the binding flags **DefaultValueBinding**, **DefaultValueChangeType**, or **DefaultValueFull** to be specified explicitly. This is a requirement even in those cases where a value is passed for a parameter that has a default value.

For example, consider a method such as MyMethod(int x, float y = 2.0). To invoke this method with only the first argument as MyMethod(4), pass one of the above binding flags and pass two arguments, namely, 4 for the first argument and **Missing.Value** for the second argument. Unless you use **Missing.Value**, you may not omit optional parameters with the **Invoke** method. If you must do so, use **InvokeMember** instead.

This is a convenience method that calls the following **Invoke** method, passing a null reference (**Nothing** in Visual Basic) in the other parameters. If the invoked method throws an exception, **GetBaseException** returns the exception.

To invoke a static method using its **MethodInfo** object, the first parameter should be a null reference (**Nothing**), as shown in the following call:

```
Object myReturnValue =
          myMethodInfo.Invoke(null, myParametersArray);
```

Example

The following samples demonstrate dynamic method lookup using reflection. Note that all of the invocations return 1, because the method in classes A and B is virtual (**Overridable** in Visual Basic) .

```
[Visual Basic]
Public Class A
    Public Overridable Function method() As Integer
        Return 0
    End Function
End Class

Public Class B
    Public Overridable Function method() As Integer
        Return 1
    End Function
End Class
```

```
Class Mymethodinfo

    Public Shared Function Main() As Integer
        Console.WriteLine("Reflection.MethodInfo")
        Console.WriteLine()
        Dim MyA As New A()
        Dim MyB As New B()

        'Get the Type and MethodInfo
        Dim MyTypea As Type = Type.GetType("A")
        Dim Mymethodinfoa As MethodInfo = MyTypea.GetMethod("method")

        Dim MyTypeb As Type = Type.GetType("B")
        Dim Mymethodinfob As MethodInfo = MyTypeb.GetMethod("method")

        'Get and display the Invoke method
        Console.WriteLine("First method - {0} returns {1}", _
MyTypea.FullName, _
            Mymethodinfoa.Invoke(MyA, Nothing).ToString())
        Console.WriteLine("Second method - {0} returns {1}", _
MyTypeb.FullName, _
            Mymethodinfob.Invoke(MyB, Nothing).ToString())
        Return 0
    End Function
End Class
```

```
[C#]
using System;
using System.Reflection;
using System.Windows.Forms;

public class A
{
    public virtual int method () {return 0;}
}

public class B
{
    public virtual int method () {return 1;}
}

class Mymethodinfo
{
    public static int Main()
    {
        Console.WriteLine ("\nReflection.MethodInfo");
        A MyA = new A();
        B MyB = new B();

        // Get the Type and MethodInfo.
        Type MyTypea = Type.GetType("A");
        MethodInfo Mymethodinfoa = MyTypea.GetMethod("method");

        Type MyTypeb = Type.GetType("B");
        MethodInfo Mymethodinfob = MyTypeb.GetMethod("method");

        // Get and display the Invoke method.
        Console.Write("\nFirst method - " + MyTypea.FullName +
            " returns " + Mymethodinfoa.Invoke(MyA, null));
        Console.Write("\nSecond method - " + MyTypeb.FullName +
            " returns " + Mymethodinfob.Invoke(MyB, null));
        return 0;
    }
}
```

```
[C++]
#using <mscorlib.dll>
#using <System.DLL>

using namespace System;
using namespace System::Reflection;

#define NULL 0
```

```
_gc class A : public Object
{
    public:
    virtual int method() { return 0;}
};

_gc class B : public A
{
    public:
    virtual int method() { return 1;}
};

void main ()
{
    A *objA = new A();
    B *objB = new B();

    Type *typeA = objA->GetType();
    Type *typeB = objB->GetType();

    MethodInfo *methodA = typeA->GetMethod(L"method");
    MethodInfo *methodB = typeB->GetMethod(L"method");

    Console::WriteLine(S"\tUsing reflection to invoke A::method
on objB returns {0}.",
            dynamic_cast<Object *>(methodA->Invoke(objB, NULL)));
    Console::WriteLine(S"\tUsing Invoke on objB after
converting to type A returns {0}.",
            dynamic_cast<Object *>(methodA->Invoke
(dynamic_cast<A *>(objB), NULL)));

    Console::WriteLine(S"\r\nThe same behavior is seen when
the method ");
    Console::WriteLine(S"is invoked without reflection:\r\n");

    Console::WriteLine(S"\tDirectly invoking B::method on
objB returns {0}.",
            _box(objB->method()) );
    Console::WriteLine(S"\tDirectly invoking B::method on
objB after converting to type A returns {0}.",
            _box(dynamic_cast<A *>(objB)->method()));
};
```

[JScript]
```
public class A
{
    public function method () : int {return 0;}
}

public class B
{
    public function method () : int {return 1;}
}

class Mymethodinfo
{
    public static function Main() : void
    {
        Console.WriteLine ("\nReflection.MethodInfo");
        var MyA : A = new A();
        var MyB : B = new B();

        //Get the Type and MethodInfo
        var MyTypea : Type = Type.GetType("A");
        var Mymethodinfoa : MethodInfo = MyTypea.GetMethod("method");

        var MyTypeb : Type = Type.GetType("B");
        var Mymethodinfob : MethodInfo = MyTypeb.GetMethod("method");

        //Get and display the Invoke method
        Console.Write("\nFirst method - " + MyTypea.FullName +
            " returns " + Mymethodinfoa.Invoke(MyA, null));
        Console.Write("\nSecond method - " + MyTypeb.FullName +
            " returns " + Mymethodinfob.Invoke(MyB, null));
    }
}
Mymethodinfo.Main();
```

Requirements

Platforms: Windows 98, Windows NT 4.0,
Windows Millennium Edition, Windows 2000,
Windows XP Home Edition, Windows XP Professional,
Windows .NET Server family,
.NET Compact Framework - Windows CE .NET,
Common Language Infrastructure (CLI) Standard

.NET Framework Security:

- **ReflectionPermission** to enhance security and performance when invoked late-bound through mechanisms such as **Type.InvokeMember**. Associated enumeration: **ReflectionPermissionFlag.MemberAccess**.

- **ReflectionPermission** for reflecting non-public objects. Associated enumeration: **ReflectionPermissionFlag.MemberAccess**

MethodBase.Invoke Method (Object, BindingFlags, Binder, Object[], CultureInfo)

When overridden in a derived class, invokes the reflected method or constructor with the given parameters.

```
[Visual Basic]
Overloads Public MustOverride Function Invoke( _
    ByVal obj As Object, _
    ByVal invokeAttr As BindingFlags, _
    ByVal binder As Binder, _
    ByVal parameters() As Object, _
    ByVal culture As CultureInfo _
) As Object
[C#]
public abstract object Invoke(
    object obj,
    BindingFlags invokeAttr,
    Binder binder,
    object[] parameters,
    CultureInfo culture
);
[C++]
public: virtual Object* Invoke(
    Object* obj,
    BindingFlags invokeAttr,
    Binder* binder,
    Object* parameters _gc[],
    CultureInfo* culture
) = 0;
[JScript]
public abstract function Invoke(
    obj : Object,
    invokeAttr : BindingFlags,
    binder : Binder,
    parameters : Object[],
    culture : CultureInfo
) : Object;
```

Parameters

obj

The object on which to invoke the method or constructor. If the method or constructor is static, this argument is ignored.

invokeAttr

A bitmask that is a combination of 0 or more bit flags from **BindingFlags**, such as **DefaultBinding**, **NonPublic**, and so on.

If *binder* is a null reference (**Nothing** in Visual Basic), this parameter will be assigned the value **BindingFlags.Default-Binding**; thus, whatever you pass in is ignored.

binder

An object that enables the binding, coercion of argument types, invocation of members, and retrieval of **MemberInfo** objects via reflection. If *binder* is a null reference (**Nothing** in Visual Basic), the default binder is used.

parameters

An argument list for the invoked method or constructor. This is an array of objects with the same number, order, and type as the parameters of the method or constructor to be invoked. If there are no parameters, this should be a null reference (**Nothing** in Visual Basic).

If the method or constructor represented by this instance takes a ByRef parameter, there is no special attribute required for that parameter in order to invoke the method or constructor using this function. Any object in this array that is not explicitly initialized with a value will contain the default value for that object type. For reference-type elements, this value is a null reference (**Nothing**). For value-type elements, this value is 0, 0.0, or **false**, depending on the specific element type.

culture

An instance of **CultureInfo** used to govern the coercion of types. If this is a null reference (**Nothing** in Visual Basic), the **CultureInfo** for the current thread is used. (This is necessary to convert a **String** that represents 1000 to a **Double** value, for example, since 1000 is represented differently by different cultures.)

Return Value

An **Object** containing the return value of the invoked method, or a reinitialized object in the case of a constructor, or a null reference (**Nothing** in Visual Basic) if the method's return type is **void**. Before calling the method or constructor, **Invoke** checks to see if the user has access permission and verify that the parameters are valid.

Exceptions

Exception Type	Condition
TargetException	The *obj* parameter is a null reference (**Nothing** in Visual Basic) and the method is not static.
	-or-
	The method is not declared or inherited by the class of *obj*.
ArgumentException	The type of the *parameters* parameter does not match the signature of the method or constructor reflected by this instance.
TargetParameter-CountException	The *parameters* array does not have the correct number of arguments.
TargetInvocationException	The invoked method or constructor throws an exception.
MethodAccessException	The caller does not have permission to execute the constructor.

Remarks

Dynamically invokes the method reflected by this instance on *obj*, and passes along the specified parameters. If the method is static, the *obj* parameter is ignored. For non-static methods, *obj* should be an

instance of a class that inherits or declares the method and must be the same type as this class. If the method has no parameters, the value of *parameters* should be a null reference (**Nothing** in Visual Basic). Otherwise, the number, type, and order of elements in *parameters* should be identical to the number, type, and order of parameters for the method reflected by this instance.

You may not omit optional parameters in calls to **Invoke**. To invoke a method omitting optional parameters, you should call **Type.InvokeMember** instead.

For pass-by-value primitive parameters, normal widening is performed (Int16 -> Int32, for example). For pass-by-value reference parameters, normal reference widening is allowed (derived class to base class, and base class to interface type). However, for pass-by-reference primitive parameters, the types must match exactly. For pass-by-reference reference parameters, the normal widening still applies.

For example, if the method reflected by this instance is declared as
`public boolean`

Compare(String a, String b), then *parameters* should be an array of **Objects** with length 2 such that parameters[0] = new

Object("SomeString1") and parameters[1] = new
Object("SomeString2").

Reflection uses dynamic method lookup when invoking virtual methods. For example, suppose that class B inherits from class A and both implement a virtual method named M. Now suppose that you have a **MethodInfo** object that represents M on class A. If you use the **Invoke** method to invoke M on an object of type B, then reflection will use the implementation given by class B. Even if the object of type B is cast to A, the implementation given by class B is used (see code sample below).

On the other hand, if the method is non-virtual, then reflection will use the implementation given by the type from which the **MethodInfo** was obtained, regardless of the type of the object passed as the target.

Access restrictions are ignored for fully trusted code. That is, private constructors, methods, fields, and properties can be accessed and invoked via reflection whenever the code is fully trusted.

If the invoked method throws an exception, **TargetInvocationException.GetException** returns the exception. This implementation throws a **NotSupportedException**.

Example

See related example in the **System.Reflection.MethodBase.Invoke** method topic.

Requirements

Platforms: Windows 98, Windows NT 4.0, Windows Millennium Edition, Windows 2000, Windows XP Home Edition, Windows XP Professional, Windows .NET Server family, .NET Compact Framework - Windows CE .NET, Common Language Infrastructure (CLI) Standard

.NET Framework Security:

- **ReflectionPermission** to enhance security and performance when invoked late-bound through mechanisms such as **Type.InvokeMember**. Associated enumeration: **ReflectionPermissionFlag.MemberAccess**.

- **ReflectionPermission** for reflecting non-public objects. Associated enumeration: **ReflectionPermissionFlag.MemberAccess**

MethodImplAttributes Enumeration

Specifies flags for the attributes of a method implementation.

This enumeration has a **FlagsAttribute** attribute that allows a bitwise combination of its member values.

```
[Visual Basic]
<Flags>
<Serializable>
Public Enum MethodImplAttributes
[C#]
[Flags]
[Serializable]
public enum MethodImplAttributes
[C++]
[Flags]
[Serializable]
__value public enum MethodImplAttributes
[JScript]
public
    Flags
    Serializable
enum MethodImplAttributes
```

Remarks

The attributes are combined using the bitwise OR operation as follows:

Code Implementation Masks

- **CodeTypeMask**
- **IL**
- **Native**
- **OPTIL**
- **Runtime**

Managed Masks

- **ManagedMask**
- **Unmanaged**
- **Managed**

Implementation Information and Interop Masks

- **ForwardRef**
- **PreserveSig**
- **InternalCall**
- **Synchronized**
- **NoInlining**
- **MaxMethodImplVal**

Members

Member name	Description	Value
CodeTypeMask Supported by the .NET Compact Framework.	Specifies flags about code type.	3
ForwardRef Supported by the .NET Compact Framework.	Specifies that the method is not defined.	16
IL Supported by the .NET Compact Framework.	Specifies that the method implementation is in Microsoft intermediate language (MSIL).	0
InternalCall Supported by the .NET Compact Framework.	Specifies an internal call.	4096
Managed Supported by the .NET Compact Framework.	Specifies that the method implementation is managed, otherwise unmanaged.	0
ManagedMask Supported by the .NET Compact Framework.	Specifies whether the code is managed or unmanaged.	4
MaxMethodImplVal Supported by the .NET Compact Framework.	Specifies a range check value.	65535
Native Supported by the .NET Compact Framework.	Specifies that the method implementation is native.	1
NoInlining Supported by the .NET Compact Framework.	Specifies that the method cannot be inlined.	8
OPTIL Supported by the .NET Compact Framework.	This member supports the .NET Framework infrastructure and is not intended to be used directly from your code.	2
PreserveSig Supported by the .NET Compact Framework.	Specifies that the method signature is exported exactly as declared.	128
Runtime Supported by the .NET Compact Framework.	Specifies that the method implementation is provided by the runtime.	3
Synchronized Supported by the .NET Compact Framework.	Specifies that the method is single-threaded through the body. You can also use the C# **lock statement** or the Visual Basic **Lock function** for this purpose.	32
Unmanaged Supported by the .NET Compact Framework.	Specifies that the method implementation is unmanaged, otherwise managed.	4

Requirements

Namespace: System.Reflection

Platforms: Windows 98, Windows NT 4.0, Windows Millennium Edition, Windows 2000, Windows XP Home Edition, Windows XP Professional, Windows .NET Server family, .NET Compact Framework - Windows CE .NET

Assembly: Mscorlib (in Mscorlib.dll)

MethodInfo Class

Discovers the attributes of a method and provides access to method metadata.

System.Object
  System.Reflection.MemberInfo
    System.Reflection.MethodBase
      System.Reflection.MethodInfo
        System.Reflection.Emit.MethodBuilder

```
[Visual Basic]
<Serializable>
<ClassInterface(ClassInterfaceType.AutoDual)>
MustInherit Public Class MethodInfo
    Inherits MethodBase
[C#]
[Serializable]
[ClassInterface(ClassInterfaceType.AutoDual)]
public abstract class MethodInfo : MethodBase
[C++]
[Serializable]
[ClassInterface(ClassInterfaceType::AutoDual)]
public __gc __abstract class MethodInfo : public MethodBase
[JScript]
public
    Serializable
    ClassInterface(ClassInterfaceType.AutoDual)
abstract class MethodInfo extends MethodBase
```

Thread Safety

This type is safe for multithreaded operations.

Remarks

Instances of **MethodInfo** are obtained by calling either the **GetMethods** or **GetMethod** method of a **Type** object.

Notes to Inheritors: When you inherit from **MethodInfo**, you must override **GetBaseDefinition**.

Example

Requirements

Namespace: System.Reflection

Platforms: Windows 98, Windows NT 4.0, Windows Millennium Edition, Windows 2000, Windows XP Home Edition, Windows XP Professional, Windows .NET Server family, .NET Compact Framework - Windows CE .NET

Assembly: Mscorlib (in Mscorlib.dll)

MethodInfo Constructor

Initializes a new instance of the **MethodInfo** class.

```
[Visual Basic]
Protected Sub New()
[C#]
protected MethodInfo();
[C++]
protected: MethodInfo();
[JScript]
protected function MethodInfo();
```

Requirements

Platforms: Windows 98, Windows NT 4.0, Windows Millennium Edition, Windows 2000, Windows XP Home Edition, Windows XP Professional, Windows .NET Server family, .NET Compact Framework - Windows CE .NET, Common Language Infrastructure (CLI) Standard

MethodInfo.MemberType Property

Gets a value indicating that this member is a method.

```
[Visual Basic]
Overrides Public ReadOnly Property MemberType As MemberTypes
[C#]
public override MemberTypes MemberType {get;}
[C++]
public: __property MemberTypes get_MemberType();
[JScript]
public override function get MemberType() : MemberTypes;
```

Property Value

A **MemberTypes** object indicating that this member is a method.

Remarks

This is used when this method is being tested as generic member.

To get the **MemberType** property, first get the class **Type**. From the **Type**, get the **MethodInfo**. From the **MethodInfo**, get the **MemberType**.

Example

[Visual Basic, C#, JScript] The following example displays the type of the specified member.

```
[Visual Basic]
Imports System
Imports System.Reflection

Class MyMethodInfo

    Public Shared Function Main() As Integer
        Console.WriteLine("Reflection.MethodInfo")

        ' Get the Type and MethodInfo.
        Dim MyType As Type = _
Type.GetType("System.Reflection.FieldInfo")
        Dim Mymethodinfo As MethodInfo = MyType.GetMethod("GetValue")
        Console.WriteLine(MyType.FullName + "." + Mymethodinfo.Name)

        ' Get and display the MemberType property.
        Dim Mymembertypes As MemberTypes = Mymethodinfo.MemberType

        If MemberTypes.Constructor = Mymembertypes Then
            Console.WriteLine("MemberType is of type All.")

        ElseIf MemberTypes.Custom = Mymembertypes Then
            Console.WriteLine("MemberType is of type Custom.")

        ElseIf MemberTypes.Event = Mymembertypes Then
            Console.WriteLine("MemberType is of type Event.")

        ElseIf MemberTypes.Field = Mymembertypes Then
            Console.WriteLine("MemberType is of type Field.")

        ElseIf MemberTypes.Method = Mymembertypes Then
            Console.WriteLine("MemberType is of type Method.")

        ElseIf MemberTypes.Property = Mymembertypes Then
            Console.WriteLine("MemberType is of type Property.")
```

```
      ElseIf MemberTypes.TypeInfo = Mymembertypes Then
         Console.WriteLine("MemberType is of type TypeInfo.")

      End If
      Return 0
   End Function
End Class
[C#]
using System;
using System.Reflection;

class MyMethodInfo
{
    public static int Main()
    {
        Console.WriteLine("Reflection.MethodInfo");

        // Get the Type and MethodInfo.
        Type MyType = Type.GetType("System.Reflection.FieldInfo");
        MethodInfo Mymethodinfo = MyType.GetMethod("GetValue");
        Console.WriteLine(MyType.FullName + "." + Mymethodinfo.Name);

        // Get and display the MemberType property.
        MemberTypes Mymembertypes = Mymethodinfo.MemberType;

        if (MemberTypes.Constructor == Mymembertypes)
        {
            Console.WriteLine("MemberType is of type All.");
        }
        else if (MemberTypes.Custom == Mymembertypes)
        {
            Console.WriteLine("MemberType is of type Custom.");
        }
        else if (MemberTypes.Event == Mymembertypes)
        {
            Console.WriteLine("MemberType is of type Event.");
        }
        else if (MemberTypes.Field == Mymembertypes)
        {
            Console.WriteLine("MemberType is of type Field.");
        }
        else if (MemberTypes.Method == Mymembertypes)
        {
            Console.WriteLine("MemberType is of type Method.");
        }
        else if (MemberTypes.Property == Mymembertypes)
        {
            Console.WriteLine("MemberType is of type Property.");
        }
        else if (MemberTypes.TypeInfo == Mymembertypes)
        {
            Console.WriteLine("MemberType is of type TypeInfo.");
        }

        return 0;
    }
}

[JScript]
import System;
import System.Reflection;

 class MyMethodInfo
 {
   public static function Main() : void
   {
       Console.WriteLine("Reflection.MethodInfo");

       //Get the Type and MethodInfo.
       var MyType : Type = Type.GetType("System.Reflection.FieldInfo");
       var Mymethodinfo : MethodInfo = MyType.GetMethod("GetValue");
       Console.WriteLine(MyType.FullName + "." + Mymethodinfo.Name);
```

```
       //Get and display the MemberType property.
       var Mymembertypes : MemberTypes = Mymethodinfo.MemberType;

       if ( MemberTypes.Constructor == Mymembertypes )
       {
           Console.WriteLine( "MemberType is of type All" );
       }
       else if ( MemberTypes.Custom == Mymembertypes )
       {
           Console.WriteLine( "MemberType is of type Custom" );
       }
       else if ( MemberTypes.Event == Mymembertypes )
       {
           Console.WriteLine( "MemberType is of type Event" );
       }
       else if ( MemberTypes.Field == Mymembertypes )
       {
           Console.WriteLine( "MemberType is of type Field" );
       }
       else if ( MemberTypes.Method == Mymembertypes )
       {
           Console.WriteLine( "MemberType is of type Method" );
       }
       else if ( MemberTypes.Property == Mymembertypes )
       {
           Console.WriteLine( "MemberType is of type Property" );
       }
       else if ( MemberTypes.TypeInfo == Mymembertypes )
       {
           Console.WriteLine( "MemberType is of type TypeInfo" );
       }

   }
}
MyMethodInfo.Main();
/*
This code produces the following output:

Reflection.MethodInfo
System.Reflection.FieldInfo.GetValue
MemberType is of type Method
*/
```

Requirements

Platforms: Windows 98, Windows NT 4.0,
Windows Millennium Edition, Windows 2000,
Windows XP Home Edition, Windows XP Professional,
Windows .NET Server family,
.NET Compact Framework - Windows CE .NET

MethodInfo.ReturnType Property

Gets the return type of this method.

```
[Visual Basic]
Public MustOverride ReadOnly Property ReturnType As Type
[C#]
public abstract Type ReturnType {get;}
[C++]
public: __property virtual Type* get_ReturnType() = 0;
[JScript]
public abstract function get ReturnType() : Type;
```

Property Value

The return type of this method.

Remarks

To get the return type property, first get the class **Type**. From the
Type, get the **MethodInfo**. From the **MethodInfo**, get the
ReturnType.

Example

[Visual Basic, C#, JScript] The following example displays the return type of the specified method.

```
[Visual Basic]
Imports System
Imports System.Reflection
Imports Microsoft.VisualBasic

Class Mymethodinfo1

    Public Shared Function Main() As Integer
        Console.WriteLine(ControlChars.Cr + "Reflection.MethodInfo")

        'Get the Type and MethodInfo.
        Dim MyType As Type = _
Type.GetType("System.Reflection.FieldInfo")
        Dim Mymethodinfo As MethodInfo = MyType.GetMethod("GetValue")
        Console.Write(ControlChars.Cr _
            + MyType.FullName + "." + Mymethodinfo.Name)

        'Get and display the ReturnType.
        Console.Write(ControlChars.Cr _
            + "ReturnType = {0}", Mymethodinfo.ReturnType)
        Return 0
    End Function
End Class
```

```
[C#]
using System;
using System.Reflection;

class Mymethodinfo
{
    public static int Main()
    {
        Console.WriteLine ("\nReflection.MethodInfo");

        // Get the Type and MethodInfo.
        Type MyType = Type.GetType("System.Reflection.FieldInfo");
        MethodInfo Mymethodinfo = MyType.GetMethod("GetValue");
        Console.Write ("\n" + MyType.FullName + "." +
Mymethodinfo.Name);

        // Get and display the ReturnType.
        Console.Write ("\nReturnType = {0}", Mymethodinfo.ReturnType);
        return 0;
    }
}
```

```
[JScript]
class Mymethodinfo
{
    public static function Main() : void
    {
        Console.WriteLine ("\nReflection.MethodInfo");

        //Get the Type and MethodInfo.
        var MyType : Type = Type.GetType("System.Reflection.FieldInfo");
        var Mymethodinfo : MethodInfo = MyType.GetMethod("GetValue");
        Console.Write ("\n" + MyType.FullName + "." + Mymethodinfo.Name);

        //Get and display the ReturnType.
        Console.Write ("\nReturnType = {0}", Mymethodinfo.ReturnType);
    }
}
Mymethodinfo.Main();
/*
This code produces the following output:

Reflection.MethodInfo
System.Reflection.FieldInfo.GetValue
ReturnType - System.Object
*/
```

Requirements

Platforms: Windows 98, Windows NT 4.0, Windows Millennium Edition, Windows 2000, Windows XP Home Edition, Windows XP Professional, Windows .NET Server family, .NET Compact Framework - Windows CE .NET, Common Language Infrastructure (CLI) Standard

MethodInfo.ReturnTypeCustomAttributes Property

Gets the custom attributes for the return type.

```
[Visual Basic]
Public MustOverride ReadOnly Property ReturnTypeCustomAttributes As _
    _
    ICustomAttributeProvider
[C#]
public abstract ICustomAttributeProvider ReturnTypeCustomAttributes
    {get;}
[C++]
public: __property virtual ICustomAttributeProvider*
    get_ReturnTypeCustomAttributes() = 0;
[JScript]
public abstract function get ReturnTypeCustomAttributes() :
    ICustomAttributeProvider;
```

Property Value

An **ICustomAttributeProvider** object representing the custom attributes for the return type.

Requirements

Platforms: Windows 98, Windows NT 4.0, Windows Millennium Edition, Windows 2000, Windows XP Home Edition, Windows XP Professional, Windows .NET Server family, .NET Compact Framework - Windows CE .NET

MethodInfo.GetBaseDefinition Method

When overridden in a derived class, returns the **MethodInfo** object for the method on the direct or indirect base class in which the method represented by this instance was first declared.

```
[Visual Basic]
Public MustOverride Function GetBaseDefinition() As MethodInfo
[C#]
public abstract MethodInfo GetBaseDefinition();
[C++]
public: virtual MethodInfo* GetBaseDefinition() = 0;
[JScript]
public abstract function GetBaseDefinition() : MethodInfo;
```

Return Value

A **MethodInfo** object for the first implementation of this method.

Remarks

GetBaseDefinition returns the first definition of the specified method in the class hierarchy.

If the method is declared on an interface, **GetBaseDefinition** returns the method.

If the method is defined in a base class, then **GetBaseDefinition** works as follows:

- If a given method overrides a virtual definition in the base class, the virtual definition is returned.
- If a given method is specified with the **new** keyword (as in **newslot** as described in **Type Members**), the given method is returned.
- If the method is not defined in the type of the object on which **GetBaseDefinition** is called, the method definition highest in the class hierarchy is returned.

To get the **GetBaseDefinition** method, first get the class **Type**. From the **Type**, get the **MethodInfo**. From the **MethodInfo**, get the **GetBaseDefinition**.

Example

[Visual Basic, C#, JScript] This code example demonstrates the behavior of **GetBaseDefinition**.

```
[Visual Basic]
Imports System
Imports System.Reflection

Public Class GetBaseDef

    Public Shared Sub Main()
        Dim t As Type = GetType(B)
        Dim m As MethodInfo

        ' Print A Void B().
        m = t.GetMethod("B")
        Console.WriteLine(m.GetBaseDefinition().DeclaringType.ToString() _
+ " " _
            + m.GetBaseDefinition().ToString())

        ' Print A Void C().
        m = t.GetMethod("C")
        Console.WriteLine(m.GetBaseDefinition().DeclaringType.ToString() _
+ " " _
            + m.GetBaseDefinition().ToString())

        ' Print B Void D().
        m = t.GetMethod("D", BindingFlags.Public Or _
BindingFlags.Instance _
            Or BindingFlags.DeclaredOnly)
        Console.WriteLine(m.GetBaseDefinition().DeclaringType.ToString() _
 + " " _
            + m.GetBaseDefinition().ToString())
    End Sub

End Class

Public Class A

    Public Overridable Sub B()
        Console.WriteLine("C")
    End Sub

    Public Overridable Sub C()
        Console.WriteLine("C")
    End Sub

    Public Overridable Sub D()
        Console.WriteLine("E")
    End Sub
End Class

Public Class B
    Inherits A
```

```
    Public Overrides Sub C()
        Console.WriteLine("C")
    End Sub

    Public Shadows Sub D()
        Console.WriteLine("D")
    End Sub
End Class

[C#]
using System;
using System.Reflection;

public class GetBaseDef {
    public static void Main(String[] args)
    {
        Type t = typeof(B);
        MethodInfo m;

        // Print A Void B().
        m = t.GetMethod("B");
        Console.WriteLine(m.GetBaseDefinition().DeclaringType +
" " + m.GetBaseDefinition());

        // Print A Void C().
        m = t.GetMethod("C");
        Console.WriteLine(m.GetBaseDefinition().DeclaringType +
" " + m.GetBaseDefinition());

        // Print B Void D().
        m = t.GetMethod("D", (BindingFlags.Public |
                    BindingFlags.Instance |
                    BindingFlags.DeclaredOnly));
        Console.WriteLine(m.GetBaseDefinition().DeclaringType +
" " + m.GetBaseDefinition());
    }

}

public class A
{
    public virtual void B() { Console.WriteLine("C"); }
    public virtual void C() { Console.WriteLine("C"); }
    public virtual void D() { Console.WriteLine("E"); }
}

public class B : A
{
    public override void C() { Console.WriteLine("C"); }
    public new void D()  { Console.WriteLine("D"); }
}

[JScript]
import System;
import System.Reflection;

public class GetBaseDef {
    public static function Main() : void
    {
        var t : Type = B;
        var m : MethodInfo;

        // Print A Void B().
        m = t.GetMethod("B");
        Console.WriteLine(m.GetBaseDefinition().DeclaringType
+ " " + m.GetBaseDefinition());

        // Print A Void C().
        m = t.GetMethod("C");
        Console.WriteLine(m.GetBaseDefinition().DeclaringType
+ " " + m.GetBaseDefinition());

        // Print B Void D().
        m = t.GetMethod("D", (BindingFlags.Public |
                    BindingFlags.Instance |
```

```
                        BindingFlags.DeclaredOnly));
        Console.WriteLine(m.GetBaseDefinition().DeclaringType          ⌐
+ " " + m.GetBaseDefinition());
        }
    }
}

GetBaseDef.Main();

public class A
{
    public function B() : void  { Console.WriteLine("C"); }
    public function C() : void { Console.WriteLine("C"); }
    public function D() : void { Console.WriteLine("E"); }
}

public class B extends A
{
    public override function C() : void { Console.WriteLine("C"); }
    public hide function D() : void { Console.WriteLine("D"); }
}
```

Requirements

Platforms: Windows 98, Windows NT 4.0,
Windows Millennium Edition, Windows 2000,
Windows XP Home Edition, Windows XP Professional,
Windows .NET Server family,
.NET Compact Framework - Windows CE .NET,
Common Language Infrastructure (CLI) Standard

Missing Class

Represents a missing **Object**. This class cannot be inherited.

System.Object
   System.Reflection.Missing

```
[Visual Basic]
NotInheritable Public Class Missing
[C#]
public sealed class Missing
[C++]
public __gc __sealed class Missing
[JScript]
public class Missing
```

Thread Safety

Any public static (**Shared** in Visual Basic) members of this type are safe for multithreaded operations. Any instance members are not guaranteed to be thread safe.

Remarks

Missing is used to invoke a method with a default argument.

Only one instance of **Missing** ever exists.

Example

[Visual Basic] The following example shows a use of **Missing** to invoke a method with a default argument.

```
[Visual Basic]
Imports System
Imports System.Reflection
Imports Microsoft.VisualBasic

Public Class MissingSample

    Shared Sub Main()
        'To invoke MyMethod with a default argument, use the      ↵
following syntax:
        GetType(MissingSample).GetMethod("MyMethod").Invoke      ↵
(Nothing, New Object() {Missing.Value})
    End Sub

    Shared Function MyMethod(Optional k As Integer = 33) As Integer
        Console.WriteLine("k = " & k.ToString())
        Return 0
    End Function
End Class
```

Requirements

Namespace: System.Reflection

Platforms: Windows 98, Windows NT 4.0, Windows Millennium Edition, Windows 2000, Windows XP Home Edition, Windows XP Professional, Windows .NET Server family, .NET Compact Framework - Windows CE .NET

Assembly: Mscorlib (in Mscorlib.dll)

Missing.Value Field

Represents the sole instance of the **Missing** class.

```
[Visual Basic]
Public Shared ReadOnly Value As Missing
[C#]
public static readonly Missing Value;
[C++]
public: static Missing* Value;
[JScript]
public static var Value : Missing;
```

Requirements

Platforms: Windows 98, Windows NT 4.0, Windows Millennium Edition, Windows 2000, Windows XP Home Edition, Windows XP Professional, Windows .NET Server family, .NET Compact Framework - Windows CE .NET

Module Class

Performs reflection on a module.

System.Object
  System.Reflection.Module
    System.Reflection.Emit.ModuleBuilder

```
[Visual Basic]
<Serializable>
Public Class Module
    Implements ISerializable, ICustomAttributeProvider
[C#]
[Serializable]
public class Module : ISerializable, ICustomAttributeProvider
[C++]
[Serializable]
public __gc class Module : public ISerializable,
    ICustomAttributeProvider
[JScript]
public
    Serializable
class Module implements ISerializable,
    ICustomAttributeProvider
```

Thread Safety

Any public static (**Shared** in Visual Basic) members of this type are
safe for multithreaded operations. Any instance members are not
guaranteed to be thread safe.

Remarks

A module is a portable executable file of type .dll or .exe consisting
of one or more classes and interfaces. There may be multiple
namespaces contained in a single module, and a namespace may
span multiple modules.

One or more modules deployed as a unit compose an assembly.

Requirements

Namespace: System.Reflection

Platforms: Windows 98, Windows NT 4.0,
Windows Millennium Edition, Windows 2000,
Windows XP Home Edition, Windows XP Professional,
Windows .NET Server family,
.NET Compact Framework - Windows CE .NET

Assembly: Mscorlib (in Mscorlib.dll)

Module.FilterTypeName Field

A **TypeFilter** object that filters the list of types defined in this
module based upon the name. This field is case-sensitive and read-
only.

```
[Visual Basic]
Public Shared ReadOnly FilterTypeName As TypeFilter
[C#]
public static readonly TypeFilter FilterTypeName;
[C++]
public: static TypeFilter* FilterTypeName;
[JScript]
public static var FilterTypeName : TypeFilter;
```

Remarks

The filter supports a trailing "*" wildcard.

Example

[Visual Basic, C#, C++] The following example displays the module
names that match the specified search criteria.

```
[Visual Basic]
Imports System
Imports System.Reflection

Namespace ReflectionModule_Examples
    Class MyMainClass
        Shared Sub Main()
            Dim moduleArray() As [Module]

            moduleArray =                              ↵
[Assembly].GetExecutingAssembly().GetModules(False)

            ' In a simple project with only one module, the  ↵
module at index
            ' 0 will be the module containing these classes.
            Dim myModule As [Module] = moduleArray(0)

            Dim tArray() As Type

            tArray = myModule.FindTypes([Module].FilterTypeName, "My*")

            Dim t As Type
            For Each t In tArray
                Console.WriteLine("Found a module beginning with  ↵
My*: {0}", t.Name)
            Next t
        End Sub 'Main
    End Class 'MyMainClass

    Class MySecondClass
    End Class 'MySecondClass

    ' This class does not fit the filter criteria My*.
    Class YourClass
    End Class 'YourClass
End Namespace 'ReflectionModule_Examples

[C#]
using System;
using System.Reflection;

namespace ReflectionModule_Examples
{
    class MyMainClass
    {
        static void Main()
        {
            Module[] moduleArray;

            moduleArray =                              ↵
Assembly.GetExecutingAssembly().GetModules(false);

            // In a simple project with only one module, the  ↵
module at index
            // 0 will be the module containing these classes.
            Module myModule = moduleArray[0];

            Type[] tArray;

            tArray = myModule.FindTypes(Module.FilterTypeName, "My*");

            foreach(Type t in tArray)
            {
                Console.WriteLine("Found a module beginning with  ↵
My*: {0}.", t.Name);
            }
        }
    }
```

```
class MySecondClass
{
}

// This class does not fit the filter criteria My*.
class YourClass
{
}
}

[C++]
#using <mscorlib.dll>

using namespace System;
using namespace System::Reflection;
using namespace System::Collections;

public __gc class MySecondClass
{
};

// This class does not fit the filter criterion My*.
public __gc class YourClass
{
};

void main()
{
    Module* moduleArray[];

    moduleArray = Assembly::GetExecutingAssembly()->GetModules(false);

    // In a simple project with only one module, the module at index
    // 0 will be the module containing these classes.
    Module* myModule = moduleArray[0];

    Type* tArray[];

    tArray = myModule->FindTypes(Module::FilterTypeName, S"My*");
    IEnumerator* myEnum = tArray->GetEnumerator();
    while (myEnum->MoveNext()) {
        Type* t = __try_cast<Type*>(myEnum->Current);
        Console::WriteLine(S"Found a module beginning with My*: {0}
.", t->Name);
    }
}
```

Requirements

Platforms: Windows 98, Windows NT 4.0,
Windows Millennium Edition, Windows 2000,
Windows XP Home Edition, Windows XP Professional,
Windows .NET Server family

Module.FilterTypeNameIgnoreCase Field

A **TypeFilter** object that filters the list of types defined in this
module based upon the name. This field is case-insensitive and read-
only.

```
[Visual Basic]
Public Shared ReadOnly FilterTypeNameIgnoreCase As TypeFilter
[C#]
public static readonly TypeFilter FilterTypeNameIgnoreCase;
[C++]
public: static TypeFilter* FilterTypeNameIgnoreCase;
[JScript]
public static var FilterTypeNameIgnoreCase : TypeFilter;
```

Remarks

The filter supports a trailing "*" wildcard.

Example

[Visual Basic, C#, C++] The following example displays the module
names that match the specified search criteria, ignoring the case.

```
[Visual Basic]
Imports System
Imports System.Reflection

Namespace ReflectionModule_Examples
    Class MyMainClass
        Shared Sub Main()
            Dim moduleArray() As [Module]

            moduleArray = _
[Assembly].GetExecutingAssembly().GetModules(False)

            'In a simple project with only one module, the _
module at index
            ' 0 will be the module containing these classes.
            Dim myModule As [Module] = moduleArray(0)

            Dim tArray() As Type

            tArray = _
myModule.FindTypes([Module].FilterTypeNameIgnoreCase, "my*")

            Dim t As Type
            For Each t In tArray
                Console.WriteLine("Found a module beginning _
with my*: {0}", t.Name)
            Next t
        End Sub 'Main
    End Class 'MyMainClass

    Class MySecondClass
    End Class 'MySecondClass

    'This class does not fit the filter criteria my*
    Class YourClass
    End Class 'YourClass
End Namespace 'ReflectionModule_Examples

[C#]
using System;
using System.Reflection;

namespace ReflectionModule_Examples
{
    class MyMainClass
    {
        static void Main()
        {
            Module[] moduleArray;

            moduleArray = _
Assembly.GetExecutingAssembly().GetModules(false);

            // In a simple project with only one module, the _
module at index
            // 0 will be the module containing these classes.
            Module myModule = moduleArray[0];

            Type[] tArray;

            tArray = _
myModule.FindTypes(Module.FilterTypeNameIgnoreCase, "my*");

            foreach(Type t in tArray)
            {
                Console.WriteLine("Found a module beginning with _
my*: {0}", t.Name);
            }
        }
    }
```

```
class MySecondClass
{
}

// This class does not fit the filter criteria my*.
class YourClass
{
}
}

[C++]
#using <mscorlib.dll>

using namespace System;
using namespace System::Reflection;
using namespace System::Collections;

public __gc class MyMainClass
{
};

public __gc class MySecondClass
{
};

// This class does not fit the filter criteria my*.
public __gc class YourClass
{
};

void main()
{
    Module* moduleArray[];

    moduleArray = Assembly::GetExecutingAssembly()->GetModules(false);

    // In a simple project with only one module, the module at index
    // 0 will be the module containing these classes.
    Module* myModule = moduleArray[0];

    Type* tArray[];

    tArray = myModule->FindTypes
(Module::FilterTypeNameIgnoreCase, S"my*");

    IEnumerator* myEnum = tArray->GetEnumerator();
    while (myEnum->MoveNext()) {
        Type* t = __try_cast<Type*>(myEnum->Current);
        Console::WriteLine(S"Found a module beginning with my*:
{0}", t->Name);
    }
}
```

Requirements

Platforms: Windows 98, Windows NT 4.0,
Windows Millennium Edition, Windows 2000,
Windows XP Home Edition, Windows XP Professional,
Windows .NET Server family

Module.Assembly Property

Gets the appropriate **Assembly** for this instance of **Module**.

```
[Visual Basic]
Public ReadOnly Property Assembly As Assembly
[C#]
public Assembly Assembly {get;}
[C++]
public: __property Assembly* get_Assembly();
[JScript]
public function get Assembly() : Assembly;
```

Property Value

An **Assembly** object.

Requirements

Platforms: Windows 98, Windows NT 4.0,
Windows Millennium Edition, Windows 2000,
Windows XP Home Edition, Windows XP Professional,
Windows .NET Server family,
.NET Compact Framework - Windows CE .NET,
Common Language Infrastructure (CLI) Standard

Module.FullyQualifiedName Property

Gets a string representing the fully qualified name and path to this
module.

```
[Visual Basic]
Public Overridable ReadOnly Property FullyQualifiedName As String
[C#]
public virtual string FullyQualifiedName {get;}
[C++]
public: __property virtual String* get_FullyQualifiedName();
[JScript]
public function get FullyQualifiedName() : String;
```

Property Value

The fully qualified module name.

Exceptions

Exception Type	Condition
SecurityException	The caller does not have the required permissions.

Remarks

To get the name without the path, use **Name**.

If the assembly for this module was loaded from a byte array then
the **FullyQualifiedName** for the module will be: <Unknown>.

> **Note** The case of module name is platform-dependent.

Requirements

Platforms: Windows 98, Windows NT 4.0,
Windows Millennium Edition, Windows 2000,
Windows XP Home Edition, Windows XP Professional,
Windows .NET Server family,
.NET Compact Framework - Windows CE .NET,
Common Language Infrastructure (CLI) Standard

.NET Framework Security:
- **FileIOPermission** for access to information in the path.
  Associated enumeration:
  FileIOPermissionAccess.PathDiscovery.

Module.Name Property

Gets a **String** representing the name of the module with the path
removed.

```
[Visual Basic]
Public ReadOnly Property Name As String
[C#]
public string Name {get;}
```

```
[C++]
public: __property String* get_Name();
[JScript]
public function get Name() : String;
```

Property Value

The module name with no path.

Remarks

Name is a platform-dependent string.

To get the name and the path, use **FullyQualifiedName**.

Example

[Visual Basic, C#] This example shows the effect of the **ScopeName**, **FullyQualifiedName**, and **Name** properties.

```
[Visual Basic]
Imports System.Reflection
Imports System

Public Class Simple

    Public Shared Sub Main()
        Dim myMod As System.Reflection.Module = _
            [Assembly].GetExecutingAssembly().GetModules()(0)
        Console.WriteLine("Module Name is " + myMod.Name)
        Console.WriteLine("Module FullyQualifiedName is " _
            + myMod.FullyQualifiedName)
        Console.WriteLine("Module ScopeName is " + myMod.ScopeName)
    End Sub

End Class

' This code produces the following output:
'
' Module Name is modname.exe
' Module FullyQualifiedName is C:\Bin\modname.exe
' Module ScopeName is modname.exe

[C#]
using System.Reflection;
using System;

 public class Simple
 {
    public static void Main ()
    {
        Module mod = Assembly.GetExecutingAssembly().GetModules
() [0];
        Console.WriteLine ("Module Name is " + mod.Name);
        Console.WriteLine ("Module FullyQualifiedName is " +
mod.FullyQualifiedName);
        Console.WriteLine ("Module ScopeName is " + mod.ScopeName);
    }
 }
 /*
 This code produces the following output:

 Module Name is modname.exe
 Module FullyQualifiedName is C:\Bin\modname.exe
 Module ScopeName is modname.exe
 */
```

Requirements

Platforms: Windows 98, Windows NT 4.0,
Windows Millennium Edition, Windows 2000,
Windows XP Home Edition, Windows XP Professional,
Windows .NET Server family,
.NET Compact Framework - Windows CE .NET,
Common Language Infrastructure (CLI) Standard

Module.ScopeName Property

Gets a string representing the name of the module.

```
[Visual Basic]
Public ReadOnly Property ScopeName As String
[C#]
public string ScopeName {get;}
[C++]
public: __property String* get_ScopeName();
[JScript]
public function get ScopeName() : String;
```

Property Value

The module name.

Remarks

The **ScopeName** property is not used by the common language runtime, but you can use it to store any string you want in the property when you emit a module using the metadata APIs. Reflection itself does not allow you to set the **ScopeName** property.

Example

[Visual Basic, C#] This example shows the effect of the **ScopeName**, **FullyQualifiedName**, and **Name** properties.

```
[Visual Basic]
Imports System.Reflection
Imports System

Public Class Simple

    Public Shared Sub Main()
        Dim myMod As System.Reflection.Module = _
            [Assembly].GetExecutingAssembly().GetModules()(0)
        Console.WriteLine("Module Name is "
            + myMod.Name)
        Console.WriteLine("Module FullyQualifiedName is " _
            + myMod.FullyQualifiedName)
        Console.WriteLine("Module ScopeName is " _
            + myMod.ScopeName)
    End Sub
End Class

' Produces this output:
' Module Name is modname.exe
' Module FullyQualifiedName is C:\Bin\modname.exe
' Module ScopeName is modname.exe

[C#]
using System.Reflection;
using System;

public class Simple
{
    public static void Main ()
    {
        Module mod = Assembly.GetExecutingAssembly().GetModules () [0];
        Console.WriteLine ("Module Name is "
            + mod.Name);
        Console.WriteLine ("Module FullyQualifiedName is "
            + mod.FullyQualifiedName);
        Console.WriteLine ("Module ScopeName is "
            + mod.ScopeName);
    }
}
/*
Produces this output:
Module Name is modname.exe
Module FullyQualifiedName is C:\Bin\modname.exe
Module ScopeName is modname.exe
*/
```

Requirements

Platforms: Windows 98, Windows NT 4.0,
Windows Millennium Edition, Windows 2000,
Windows XP Home Edition, Windows XP Professional,
Windows .NET Server family

Module.FindTypes Method

Returns an array of classes accepted by the given filter and filter
criteria.

```
[Visual Basic]
Public Overridable Function FindTypes( _
   ByVal filter As TypeFilter, _
   ByVal filterCriteria As Object _
) As Type()
[C#]
public virtual Type[] FindTypes(
   TypeFilter filter,
   object filterCriteria
);
[C++]
public: virtual Type* FindTypes(
   TypeFilter* filter,
   Object* filterCriteria
) [];
[JScript]
public function FindTypes(
   filter : TypeFilter,
   filterCriteria : Object
) : Type[];
```

Parameters

filter
    The delegate used to filter the classes.
filterCriteria
    An Object used to filter the classes.

Return Value

An array of type **Type** containing classes that were accepted by the
filter.

Exceptions

Exception Type	Condition
ReflectionTypeLoadException	One or more classes in a module could not be loaded.

Remarks

ReflectionTypeLoadException is a special class load exception.
The **ReflectionTypeLoadException.Types** property contains the
array of classes that were defined in the module and were loaded.
This array may contain some null values. The **ReflectionTypeLoad-
Exception.LoaderExceptions** property is an array of exceptions
that represent the exceptions that were thrown by the class loader.
The holes in the class array line up with the exceptions.

The delegate given by *filter* is called for each class in the module,
passing along the **Type** object representing the class as well as the
given *filterCriteria*. If *filter* returns a particular class, that class will
be included in the returned array. If *filter* returns a null reference
(**Nothing** in Visual Basic), all classes are returned and *filterCriteria*
is ignored.

FindTypes cannot be used to look up parameterized types such as
arrays.

Example

See related example in the
System.Reflection.Module.Module.FilterTypeName field topic.

Requirements

Platforms: Windows 98, Windows NT 4.0,
Windows Millennium Edition, Windows 2000,
Windows XP Home Edition, Windows XP Professional,
Windows .NET Server family

Module.GetCustomAttributes Method

Returns custom attributes.

Overload List

Returns all custom attributes.

> [Visual Basic] **Overloads Public Overridable Function
> GetCustomAttributes(Boolean) As Object() Implements
> ICustomAttributeProvider.GetCustomAttributes**
>
> [C#] **public virtual object[] GetCustomAttributes(bool);**
>
> [C++] **public: virtual Object* GetCustomAttributes(bool)
> __gc[];**
>
> [JScript] **public function GetCustomAttributes(Boolean) :
> Object[];**

Gets custom attributes of the specified type.

> [Visual Basic] **Overloads Public Overridable Function
> GetCustomAttributes(Type, Boolean) As Object() Imple-
> ments ICustomAttributeProvider.GetCustomAttributes**
>
> [C#] **public virtual object[] GetCustomAttributes(Type,
> bool);**
>
> [C++] **public: virtual Object* GetCustomAttributes(Type*,
> bool) __gc[];**
>
> [JScript] **public function GetCustomAttributes(Type,
> Boolean) : Object[];**

Example

[Visual Basic, C#, C++] The following example displays the module
names of the specified type that match the specified search criteria.

> [Visual Basic, C#, C++] **Note** This example shows how to use
> one of the overloaded versions of **GetCustomAttributes**. For
> other examples that might be available, see the individual
> overload topics.

```
[Visual Basic]
Imports System
Imports System.Reflection
' Define a module-level attribute.
<Module: ReflectionModule_Examples.MySimpleAttribute("module-level")>
' This code assumes that the root namespace is set to empty("").
Namespace ReflectionModule_Examples
   Class MyMainClass
      Shared Sub Main()
         Dim moduleArray() As [Module]
         moduleArray =                                          ⏎
[Assembly].GetExecutingAssembly().GetModules(False)
         ' In a simple project with only one module, the       ⏎
module at index
         ' 0 will be the module containing these classes.
         Dim myModule As [Module] = moduleArray(0)
         Dim attributes() As Object
```

```
        ' Get only MySimpleAttribute attributes for this module.
        attributes = myModule.GetCustomAttributes( _

myModule.GetType("ReflectionModule_Examples.MySimpleAttribute", _
                False, False), True)
            Dim o As [Object]
            For Each o In attributes
                Console.WriteLine("Found this attribute on
myModule: {0}", o.ToString())
            Next o
        End Sub 'Main
    End Class 'MyMainClass
    ' Define a very simple custom attribute.
    <AttributeUsage(AttributeTargets.Class Or                   ⏎
AttributeTargets.Module)> _
    Public Class MySimpleAttribute
        Inherits Attribute
        Private name As String
        Public Sub New(ByVal newName As String)
            name = newName
        End Sub 'New
    End Class 'MySimpleAttribute
End Namespace 'ReflectionModule_Examples

[C#]
using System;
using System.Reflection;
//Define a module-level attribute.
[module: ReflectionModule_Examples.MySimpleAttribute("module-level")]
namespace ReflectionModule_Examples
{
    class MyMainClass
    {
        static void Main()
        {
            Module[] moduleArray;
            moduleArray =                                      ⏎
Assembly.GetExecutingAssembly().GetModules(false);
            // In a simple project with only one module,       ⏎
the module at index
            // 0 will be the module containing these classes.
            Module myModule = moduleArray[0];
            object[] attributes;
            //Get only MySimpleAttribute attributes for this module.
            attributes = myModule.GetCustomAttributes(

myModule.GetType("ReflectionModule_Examples.MySimpleAttribute", ⏎
false, false),
                    true);
            foreach(Object o in attributes)
            {
                Console.WriteLine("Found this attribute on      ⏎
myModule: {0}", o.ToString());
            }
        }
    }

    // Define a very simple custom attribute
    [AttributeUsage(AttributeTargets.Class | AttributeTargets.Module)]
    public class MySimpleAttribute : Attribute
    {
        private string name;

        public MySimpleAttribute(string newName)
        {
            name = newName;
        }
    }
}
```

```
[C++]
#using <mscorlib.dll>

using namespace System;
using namespace System::Reflection;
using namespace System::Collections;

namespace ReflectionModule_Examples
{
    // Define a very simple custom attribute
    [AttributeUsage(AttributeTargets::Class | AttributeTargets::Module)]
    public __gc class MySimpleAttribute : public Attribute
    {
    private:
        String* name;

    public:
        MySimpleAttribute(String* newName)
        {
            name = newName;
        }
    };
}

//Define a module-level attribute.
[module: ReflectionModule_Examples::MySimpleAttribute           ⏎
 (S"module-level")];

void main()
{
    System::Reflection::Module* moduleArray[];
    moduleArray = Assembly::GetExecutingAssembly()->GetModules(false);
    // In a simple project with only one module, the module at index
    // 0 will be the module containing these classes.
    System::Reflection::Module* myModule = moduleArray[0];
    Object* attributes[];
    //Get only MySimpleAttribute attributes for this module.
    attributes = myModule->GetCustomAttributes(myModule-        ⏎
>GetType(S"ReflectionModule_Examples.MySimpleAttribute", false, false),
        true);
    IEnumerator* myEnum = attributes->GetEnumerator();
    while (myEnum->MoveNext()) {
        Object* o = __try_cast<Object*>(myEnum->Current);
        Console::WriteLine(S"Found this attribute on myModule: {0}", o);
    }
}
```

Module.GetCustomAttributes Method (Boolean)

Returns all custom attributes.

```
[Visual Basic]
Overloads Public Overridable Function GetCustomAttributes( _
   ByVal inherit As Boolean _
) As Object() Implements ICustomAttributeProvider.GetCustomAttributes
[C#]
public virtual object[] GetCustomAttributes(
   bool inherit
);
[C++]
public: virtual Object* GetCustomAttributes(
   bool inherit
) __gc[];
[JScript]
public function GetCustomAttributes(
   inherit : Boolean
) : Object[];
```

Parameters

inherit
    This argument is ignored for objects of this type.

Return Value

An array of type **Object** containing all custom attributes.

Implements

ICustomAttributeProvider.GetCustomAttributes

Example

[Visual Basic, C#, C++] The following example displays the module names that match the specified search criteria.

```
[Visual Basic]
Imports System
Imports System.Reflection
' Define a module-level attribute.
<Module: ReflectionModule_Examples.MySimpleAttribute("module-level")>
Namespace ReflectionModule_Examples
    Class MyMainClass
        Shared Sub Main()
            Dim moduleArray() As [Module]
            moduleArray =
[Assembly].GetExecutingAssembly().GetModules(False)
            ' In a simple project with only one module, the
module at index
            ' 0 will be the module containing these classes.
            Dim myModule As [Module] = moduleArray(0)
            Dim attributes() As Object
            attributes = myModule.GetCustomAttributes(True)
            Dim o As [Object]
            For Each o In attributes
                Console.WriteLine("Found this attribute on
myModule: {0}", o.ToString())
            Next o
        End Sub 'Main
    End Class 'MyMainClass
    'A very simple custom attribute.
    <AttributeUsage(AttributeTargets.Class Or
AttributeTargets.Module)> _
    Public Class MySimpleAttribute
        Inherits Attribute
        Private name As String
        Public Sub New(ByVal newName As String)
            name = newName
        End Sub 'New
    End Class 'MySimpleAttribute
End Namespace 'ReflectionModule_Examples

[C#]
using System;
using System.Reflection;
//Define a module-level attribute.
[module: ReflectionModule_Examples.MySimpleAttribute("module-level")]
namespace ReflectionModule_Examples
{
    class MyMainClass
    {
        static void Main()
        {
            Module[] moduleArray;
            moduleArray =
Assembly.GetExecutingAssembly().GetModules(false);
            // In a simple project with only one module, the
module at index
            // 0 will be the module containing these classes.
            Module myModule = moduleArray[0];
            object[] attributes;
            attributes = myModule.GetCustomAttributes(true);
            foreach(Object o in attributes)
            {
                Console.WriteLine("Found this attribute on
myModule: {0}.", o.ToString());
            }
        }
    }
    //A very simple custom attribute.
    [AttributeUsage(AttributeTargets.Class | AttributeTargets.Module)]
```

```
public class MySimpleAttribute : Attribute
{
    private string name;

    public MySimpleAttribute(string newName)
    {
        name = newName;
    }
}
}
```

```
[C++]
#using <mscorlib.dll>

using namespace System;
using namespace System::Reflection;
using namespace System::Collections;

namespace ReflectionModule_Examples
{
    //Define a module-level attribute.
    //A very simple custom attribute.
    [AttributeUsage(AttributeTargets::Class | AttributeTargets::Module)]
    public __gc class MySimpleAttribute : public Attribute
    {
    private:
        String* name;

    public:
        MySimpleAttribute(String* newName)
        {
            name = newName;
        }
    };

    [module: MySimpleAttribute(S"module-level")];

    __gc class MyMainClass
    {
    };
}

void main()
{
    System::Reflection::Module* moduleArray[];
    moduleArray = Assembly::GetExecutingAssembly()->GetModules(false);
    // In a simple project with only one module, the module at index
    // 0 will be the module containing these classes.
    System::Reflection::Module* myModule = moduleArray[0];
    Object* attributes[];
    attributes = myModule->GetCustomAttributes(true);
    IEnumerator* myEnum = attributes->GetEnumerator();
    while (myEnum->MoveNext()) {
        Object* o = __try_cast<Object*>(myEnum->Current);
        Console::WriteLine(S"Found this attribute on myModule: {0}.", o);
    }
}
```

Requirements

Platforms: Windows 98, Windows NT 4.0, Windows Millennium Edition, Windows 2000, Windows XP Home Edition, Windows XP Professional, Windows .NET Server family

Module.GetCustomAttributes Method (Type, Boolean)

Gets custom attributes of the specified type.

```
[Visual Basic]
Overloads Public Overridable Function GetCustomAttributes( _
   ByVal attributeType As Type, _
   ByVal inherit As Boolean _
) As Object() Implements ICustomAttributeProvider.GetCustomAttributes
```

```
[C#]
public virtual object[] GetCustomAttributes(
    Type attributeType,
    bool inherit
);
[C++]
public: virtual Object* GetCustomAttributes(
    Type* attributeType,
    bool inherit
) __gc[];
[JScript]
public function GetCustomAttributes(
    attributeType : Type,
    inherit : Boolean
) : Object[];
```

Parameters

attributeType

The type of attribute to get.

inherit

This argument is ignored for objects of this type.

Return Value

An array of type **Object** containing all custom attributes of the
specified type.

Implements

ICustomAttributeProvider.GetCustomAttributes

Exceptions

Exception Type	Condition
ArgumentNullException	*attributeType* is a null reference (**Nothing** in Visual Basic).

Example

[Visual Basic, C#, C++] The following example displays the module
names of the specified type that match the specified search criteria.

```
[Visual Basic]
Imports System
Imports System.Reflection
' Define a module-level attribute.
<Module: ReflectionModule_Examples.MySimpleAttribute("module-level")>
' This code assumes that the root namespace is set to empty("").
Namespace ReflectionModule_Examples
    Class MyMainClass
        Shared Sub Main()
            Dim moduleArray() As [Module]
            moduleArray =
[Assembly].GetExecutingAssembly().GetModules(False)
            ' In a simple project with only one module, the
module at index
            ' 0 will be the module containing these classes.
            Dim myModule As [Module] = moduleArray(0)
            Dim attributes() As Object
            ' Get only MySimpleAttribute attributes for this module.
            attributes = myModule.GetCustomAttributes( _
myModule.GetType("ReflectionModule_Examples.MySimpleAttribute", _
            False, False), True)
            Dim o As [Object]
            For Each o In attributes
                Console.WriteLine("Found this attribute on
myModule: {0}", o.ToString())
            Next o
        End Sub 'Main
    End Class 'MyMainClass
    ' Define a very simple custom attribute.
```

```
    <AttributeUsage(AttributeTargets.Class Or
AttributeTargets.Module)> _
        Public Class MySimpleAttribute
            Inherits Attribute
            Private name As String
            Public Sub New(ByVal newName As String)
                name = newName
            End Sub 'New
        End Class 'MySimpleAttribute
End Namespace 'ReflectionModule_Examples

[C#]
using System;
using System.Reflection;
//Define a module-level attribute.
[module: ReflectionModule_Examples.MySimpleAttribute("module-level")]
namespace ReflectionModule_Examples
{
    class MyMainClass
    {
        static void Main()
        {
            Module[] moduleArray;
            moduleArray =
Assembly.GetExecutingAssembly().GetModules(false);
            // In a simple project with only one module,
the module at index
            // 0 will be the module containing these classes.
            Module myModule = moduleArray[0];
            object[] attributes;
            //Get only MySimpleAttribute attributes for this module.
            attributes = myModule.GetCustomAttributes(
myModule.GetType("ReflectionModule_Examples.MySimpleAttribute",
 false, false),
                true);
            foreach(Object o in attributes)
            {
                Console.WriteLine("Found this attribute on
myModule: {0}", o.ToString());
            }
        }
    }

    // Define a very simple custom attribute
    [AttributeUsage(AttributeTargets.Class | AttributeTargets.Module)]
    public class MySimpleAttribute : Attribute
    {
        private string name;

        public MySimpleAttribute(string newName)
        {
            name = newName;
        }
    }
}

[C++]
#using <mscorlib.dll>

using namespace System;
using namespace System::Reflection;
using namespace System::Collections;

namespace ReflectionModule_Examples
{
    // Define a very simple custom attribute
    [AttributeUsage(AttributeTargets::Class | AttributeTargets::Module)]
    public __gc class MySimpleAttribute : public Attribute
    {
    private:
        String* name;

    public:
        MySimpleAttribute(String* newName)
```

```
    {
        name = newName;
    }
};
}

//Define a module-level attribute.
[module: ReflectionModule_Examples::MySimpleAttribute
 (S"module-level")];

void main()
{
    System::Reflection::Module* moduleArray[];
    moduleArray = Assembly::GetExecutingAssembly()->GetModules(false);
    // In a simple project with only one module, the module at index
    // 0 will be the module containing these classes.
    System::Reflection::Module* myModule = moduleArray[0];
    Object* attributes[];
    //Get only MySimpleAttribute attributes for this module.
    attributes = myModule->GetCustomAttributes(myModule-
>GetType(S"ReflectionModule_Examples.MySimpleAttribute", false, false),
        true);
    IEnumerator* myEnum = attributes->GetEnumerator();
    while (myEnum->MoveNext()) {
        Object* o = __try_cast<Object*>(myEnum->Current);
        Console::WriteLine(S"Found this attribute on myModule: {0}", o);
    }
}
```

Requirements

Platforms: Windows 98, Windows NT 4.0,
Windows Millennium Edition, Windows 2000,
Windows XP Home Edition, Windows XP Professional,
Windows .NET Server family

Module.GetField Method

Returns a specified field.

Overload List

Returns a field having the specified name.

[Visual Basic] **Overloads Public Function GetField(String) As FieldInfo**

[C#] **public FieldInfo GetField(string);**

[C++] **public: FieldInfo* GetField(String*);**

[JScript] **public function GetField(String) : FieldInfo;**

Returns a field having the specified name and binding attributes.

[Visual Basic] **Overloads Public Function GetField(String, BindingFlags) As FieldInfo**

[C#] **public FieldInfo GetField(string, BindingFlags);**

[C++] **public: FieldInfo* GetField(String*, BindingFlags);**

[JScript] **public function GetField(String, BindingFlags) : FieldInfo;**

Module.GetField Method (String)

Returns a field having the specified name.

```
[Visual Basic]
Overloads Public Function GetField( _
    ByVal name As String _
) As FieldInfo
```

```
[C#]
public FieldInfo GetField(
    string name
);
[C++]
public: FieldInfo* GetField(
    String* name
);
[JScript]
public function GetField(
    name : String
) : FieldInfo;
```

Parameters

name
    The field name.

Return Value

A **FieldInfo** object having the specified name, or a null reference (**Nothing** in Visual Basic) if the field does not exist.

Exceptions

Exception Type	Condition
ArgumentNullException	The *name* parameter is a null reference (**Nothing** in Visual Basic).

Requirements

Platforms: Windows 98, Windows NT 4.0,
Windows Millennium Edition, Windows 2000,
Windows XP Home Edition, Windows XP Professional,
Windows .NET Server family,
Common Language Infrastructure (CLI) Standard

Module.GetField Method (String, BindingFlags)

Returns a field having the specified name and binding attributes.

```
[Visual Basic]
Overloads Public Function GetField( _
    ByVal name As String, _
    ByVal bindingAttr As BindingFlags _
) As FieldInfo
[C#]
public FieldInfo GetField(
    string name,
    BindingFlags bindingAttr
);
[C++]
public: FieldInfo* GetField(
    String* name,
    BindingFlags bindingAttr
);
[JScript]
public function GetField(
    name : String,
    bindingAttr : BindingFlags
) : FieldInfo;
```

Parameters

name
    The field name.
bindingAttr
    One of the **BindingFlags** bit flags used to control the search.

Return Value

A **FieldInfo** object having the specified name and binding attributes, or a null reference (**Nothing** in Visual Basic) if the field does not exist.

Exceptions

Exception Type	Condition
ArgumentNullException	The *name* parameter is a null reference (**Nothing** in Visual Basic).

Requirements

Platforms: Windows 98, Windows NT 4.0, Windows Millennium Edition, Windows 2000, Windows XP Home Edition, Windows XP Professional, Windows .NET Server family, Common Language Infrastructure (CLI) Standard

.NET Framework Security:

- **ReflectionPermission** for returning fields that are not public. Associated enumeration: **ReflectionPermissionFlag.TypeInformation**

Module.GetFields Method

Returns an array of fields implemented by a class.

```
[Visual Basic]
Public Function GetFields() As FieldInfo()
[C#]
public FieldInfo[] GetFields();
[C++]
public: FieldInfo* GetFields() [];
[JScript]
public function GetFields() : FieldInfo[];
```

Return Value

An array of type **FieldInfo** containing the fields implemented by a class, or a null reference (**Nothing** in Visual Basic) if the fields do not exist.

Requirements

Platforms: Windows 98, Windows NT 4.0, Windows Millennium Edition, Windows 2000, Windows XP Home Edition, Windows XP Professional, Windows .NET Server family, Common Language Infrastructure (CLI) Standard

Module.GetMethod Method

Returns a method having the specified criteria.

Overload List

Returns a method having the specified name.

[Visual Basic] **Overloads Public Function GetMethod(String) As MethodInfo**

[C#] **public MethodInfo GetMethod(string);**

[C++] **public: MethodInfo* GetMethod(String*);**

[JScript] **public function GetMethod(String) : MethodInfo;**

Returns a method having the specified name and parameter types.

[Visual Basic] **Overloads Public Function GetMethod(String, Type()) As MethodInfo**

[C#] **public MethodInfo GetMethod(string, Type[]);**

[C++] **public: MethodInfo* GetMethod(String*, Type[]);**

[JScript] **public function GetMethod(String, Type[]) : MethodInfo;**

Returns a method having the specified name, binding information, calling convention, and parameter types and modifiers.

[Visual Basic] **Overloads Public Function GetMethod(String, BindingFlags, Binder, CallingConventions, Type(), ParameterModifier()) As MethodInfo**

[C#] **public MethodInfo GetMethod(string, BindingFlags, Binder, CallingConventions, Type[], ParameterModifier[]);**

[C++] **public: MethodInfo* GetMethod(String*, BindingFlags, Binder*, CallingConventions, Type[], ParameterModifier[]);**

[JScript] **public function GetMethod(String, BindingFlags, Binder, CallingConventions, Type[], ParameterModifier[]) : MethodInfo;**

Module.GetMethod Method (String)

Returns a method having the specified name.

```
[Visual Basic]
Overloads Public Function GetMethod( _
   ByVal name As String _
) As MethodInfo
[C#]
public MethodInfo GetMethod(
   string name
);
[C++]
public: MethodInfo* GetMethod(
   String* name
);
[JScript]
public function GetMethod(
   name : String
) : MethodInfo;
```

Parameters

name
   The method name.

Return Value

A **MethodInfo** object having the specified name, or a null reference (**Nothing** in Visual Basic) if the method does not exist.

Exceptions

Exception Type	Condition
ArgumentNullException	*name* is a null reference (**Nothing** in Visual Basic).

Requirements

Platforms: Windows 98, Windows NT 4.0, Windows Millennium Edition, Windows 2000, Windows XP Home Edition, Windows XP Professional, Windows .NET Server family, Common Language Infrastructure (CLI) Standard

Module.GetMethod Method (String, Type[])

Returns a method having the specified name and parameter types.

```
[Visual Basic]
Overloads Public Function GetMethod( _
   ByVal name As String, _
   ByVal types() As Type _
) As MethodInfo
[C#]
public MethodInfo GetMethod(
   string name,
   Type[] types
);
[C++]
public: MethodInfo* GetMethod(
   String* name,
   Type* types[]
);
[JScript]
public function GetMethod(
   name : String,
   types : Type[]
) : MethodInfo;
```

Parameters

name
   The method name.
types
   The parameter types to search for.

Return Value

A **MethodInfo** object in accordance with the specified criteria, or a null reference (**Nothing** in Visual Basic) if the method does not exist.

Exceptions

Exception Type	Condition
ArgumentNullException	*name* is a null reference (**Nothing** in Visual Basic), *types* is a null reference (**Nothing**), or *types* (i) is a null reference (**Nothing**).

Requirements

Platforms: Windows 98, Windows NT 4.0, Windows Millennium Edition, Windows 2000, Windows XP Home Edition, Windows XP Professional, Windows .NET Server family, Common Language Infrastructure (CLI) Standard

Module.GetMethod Method (String, BindingFlags, Binder, CallingConventions, Type[], ParameterModifier[])

Returns a method having the specified name, binding information, calling convention, and parameter types and modifiers.

```
[Visual Basic]
Overloads Public Function GetMethod( _
   ByVal name As String, _
   ByVal bindingAttr As BindingFlags, _
   ByVal binder As Binder, _
   ByVal callConvention As CallingConventions, _
   ByVal types() As Type, _
   ByVal modifiers() As ParameterModifier _
) As MethodInfo
```

```
[C#]
public MethodInfo GetMethod(
   string name,
   BindingFlags bindingAttr,
   Binder binder,
   CallingConventions callConvention,
   Type[] types,
   ParameterModifier[] modifiers
);
[C++]
public: MethodInfo* GetMethod(
   String* name,
   BindingFlags bindingAttr,
   Binder* binder,
   CallingConventions callConvention,
   Type* types[],
   ParameterModifier modifiers[]
);
[JScript]
public function GetMethod(
   name : String,
   bindingAttr : BindingFlags,
   binder : Binder,
   callConvention : CallingConventions,
   types : Type[],
   modifiers : ParameterModifier[]
) : MethodInfo;
```

Parameters

name
   The method name.
bindingAttr
   One of the **BindingFlags** bit flags used to control the search.
binder
   An object that implements **Binder**, containing properties related to this method.
callConvention
   The calling convention for the method.
types
   The parameter types to search for.
modifiers
   An array of parameter modifiers used to make binding work with parameter signatures in which the types have been modified.

Return Value

A **MethodInfo** object in accordance with the specified criteria, or a null reference (**Nothing** in Visual Basic) if the method does not exist.

Exceptions

Exception Type	Condition
ArgumentNullException	*name* is a null reference (**Nothing** in Visual Basic), *types* is a null reference (**Nothing**), or *types* (i) is a null reference (**Nothing**).

Requirements

Platforms: Windows 98, Windows NT 4.0, Windows Millennium Edition, Windows 2000, Windows XP Home Edition, Windows XP Professional, Windows .NET Server family

Module.GetMethodImpl Method

Returns the method implementation in accordance with the specified criteria.

```
[Visual Basic]
Protected Overridable Function GetMethodImpl( _
   ByVal name As String, _
   ByVal bindingAttr As BindingFlags, _
   ByVal binder As Binder, _
   ByVal callConvention As CallingConventions, _
   ByVal types() As Type, _
   ByVal modifiers() As ParameterModifier _
) As MethodInfo
[C#]
protected virtual MethodInfo GetMethodImpl(
   string name,
   BindingFlags bindingAttr,
   Binder binder,
   CallingConventions callConvention,
   Type[] types,
   ParameterModifier[] modifiers
);
[C++]
protected: virtual MethodInfo* GetMethodImpl(
   String* name,
   BindingFlags bindingAttr,
   Binder* binder,
   CallingConventions callConvention,
   Type* types[],
   ParameterModifier modifiers[]
);
[JScript]
protected function GetMethodImpl(
   name : String,
   bindingAttr : BindingFlags,
   binder : Binder,
   callConvention : CallingConventions,
   types : Type[],
   modifiers : ParameterModifier[]
) : MethodInfo;
```

Parameters

name
    The method name.

bindingAttr
    One of the **BindingFlags** bit flags used to control the search.

binder
    An object that implements **Binder**, containing properties related to this method.

callConvention
    The calling convention for the method.

types
    The parameter types to search for.

modifiers
    An array of parameter modifiers used to make binding work with parameter signatures in which the types have been modified.

Return Value

A **MethodInfo** object containing implementation information as specified, or a null reference (**Nothing** in Visual Basic) if the method does not exist.

Exceptions

Exception Type	Condition
AmbiguousMatchException	*types* is a null reference (**Nothing** in Visual Basic).

Requirements

Platforms: Windows 98, Windows NT 4.0, Windows Millennium Edition, Windows 2000, Windows XP Home Edition, Windows XP Professional, Windows .NET Server family

Module.GetMethods Method

Returns an array of all the global methods defined on the module.

```
[Visual Basic]
Public Function GetMethods() As MethodInfo()
[C#]
public MethodInfo[] GetMethods();
[C++]
public: MethodInfo* GetMethods() [];
[JScript]
public function GetMethods() : MethodInfo[];
```

Return Value

An array of type **MethodInfo** containing all the global methods defined on the module, or a null reference (**Nothing** in Visual Basic) if the methods do not exist.

Requirements

Platforms: Windows 98, Windows NT 4.0, Windows Millennium Edition, Windows 2000, Windows XP Home Edition, Windows XP Professional, Windows .NET Server family, Common Language Infrastructure (CLI) Standard

Module.GetObjectData Method

Provides an **ISerializable** implementation for serialized objects.

```
[Visual Basic]
Public Overridable Sub GetObjectData( _
   ByVal info As SerializationInfo, _
   ByVal context As StreamingContext _
) Implements ISerializable.GetObjectData
[C#]
public virtual void GetObjectData(
   SerializationInfo info,
   StreamingContext context
);
[C++]
public: virtual void GetObjectData(
   SerializationInfo* info,
   StreamingContext context
);
[JScript]
public function GetObjectData(
   info : SerializationInfo,
   context : StreamingContext
);
```

Parameters

info

The information and data needed to serialize or deserialize an object.

context

The context for the serialization.

Implements

ISerializable.GetObjectData

Exceptions

Exception Type	Condition
ArgumentNullException	*info* is a null reference (**Nothing** in Visual Basic).

Requirements

Platforms: Windows 98, Windows NT 4.0, Windows Millennium Edition, Windows 2000, Windows XP Home Edition, Windows XP Professional, Windows .NET Server family

Module.GetSignerCertificate Method

Returns an **X509Certificate** object corresponding to the certificate included in the Authenticode signature of the assembly which this module belongs to. If the assembly has not been Authenticode signed, a null reference (**Nothing** in Visual Basic) is returned.

```
[Visual Basic]
Public Function GetSignerCertificate() As X509Certificate
[C#]
public X509Certificate GetSignerCertificate();
[C++]
public: X509Certificate* GetSignerCertificate();
[JScript]
public function GetSignerCertificate() : X509Certificate;
```

Return Value

An **X509Certificate** object, or a null reference (**Nothing** in Visual Basic) if the assembly to which this module belongs has not been Authenticode signed.

Requirements

Platforms: Windows 98, Windows NT 4.0, Windows Millennium Edition, Windows 2000, Windows XP Home Edition, Windows XP Professional, Windows .NET Server family

Module.GetType Method

Returns the specified class.

Overload List

Returns the specified class, performing a case-sensitive search.

Supported by the .NET Compact Framework.

[Visual Basic] **Overloads Public Overridable Function GetType(String) As Type**

[C#] **public virtual Type GetType(string);**

[C++] **public: virtual Type* GetType(String*);**

[JScript] **public function GetType(String) : Type;**

Returns the specified class, searching the module with the specified case sensitivity.

[Visual Basic] **Overloads Public Overridable Function GetType(String, Boolean) As Type**

[C#] **public virtual Type GetType(string, bool);**

[C++] **public: virtual Type* GetType(String*, bool);**

[JScript] **public function GetType(String, Boolean) : Type;**

Returns the specified class, searching the module with the specified case sensitivity and specifying whether to throw an exception if an error occurs while loading the **Type**.

[Visual Basic] **Overloads Public Overridable Function GetType(String, Boolean, Boolean) As Type**

[C#] **public virtual Type GetType(string, bool, bool);**

[C++] **public: virtual Type* GetType(String*, bool, bool);**

[JScript] **public function GetType(String, Boolean, Boolean) : Type;**

Inherited from **Object**.

Supported by the .NET Compact Framework.

[Visual Basic] **Overloads Public Function GetType() As Type**

[C#] **public Type GetType();**

[C++] **public: Type* GetType();**

[JScript] **public function GetType() : Type;**

Example

[Visual Basic, C#, C++] The following example displays the name of a class in the specified module. The *throwOnError* and *ignoreCase* parameters are specified as **false**.

> [Visual Basic, C#, C++] **Note** This example shows how to use one of the overloaded versions of **GetType**. For other examples that might be available, see the individual overload topics.

```
[Visual Basic]
Imports System
Imports System.Reflection

'This code assumes that the root namespace is set to empty("").
Namespace ReflectionModule_Examples
    Class MyMainClass
        Shared Sub Main()
            Dim moduleArray() As [Module]

            moduleArray =                                        ⏎
[Assembly].GetExecutingAssembly().GetModules(False)

            'In a simple project with only one module, the       ⏎
module at index
            ' 0 will be the module containing this class.
            Dim myModule As [Module] = moduleArray(0)

            Dim myType As Type
            myType =
myModule.GetType("ReflectionModule_Examples.MyMainClass", False, False)
            Console.WriteLine("Got type: {0}", myType.ToString())
        End Sub 'Main
    End Class 'MyMainClass
End Namespace 'ReflectionModule_Examples

[C#]
using System;
using System.Reflection;

namespace ReflectionModule_Examples
{
    class MyMainClass
```

```
    {
        static void Main()
        {
            Module[] moduleArray;

            moduleArray =
Assembly.GetExecutingAssembly().GetModules(false);

            //In a simple project with only one module, the
module at index
            // 0 will be the module containing this class.
            Module myModule = moduleArray[0];

            Type myType;
            myType =
myModule.GetType("ReflectionModule_Examples.MyMainClass",
false, false);
            Console.WriteLine("Got type: {0}", myType.ToString());
        }
    }
}

[C++]
#using <mscorlib.dll>

using namespace System;
using namespace System::Reflection;

namespace ReflectionModule_Examples
{
    public __gc class MyMainClass
    {
    };
}
void main()
{
    Module* moduleArray[];

    moduleArray = Assembly::GetExecutingAssembly()->GetModules(false);

    //In a simple project with only one module, the module at index
    // 0 will be the module containing this class.
    Module* myModule = moduleArray[0];

    Type* myType;
    myType = myModule->GetType
(S"ReflectionModule_Examples.MyMainClass", false, false);
    Console::WriteLine(S"Got type: {0}", myType);
}
```

Module.GetType Method (String)

Returns the specified class, performing a case-sensitive search.

```
[Visual Basic]
Overloads Public Overridable Function GetType( _
    ByVal className As String _
) As Type
[C#]
public virtual Type GetType(
    string className
);
[C++]
public: virtual Type* GetType(
    String* className
);
[JScript]
public function GetType(
    className : String
) : Type;
```

Parameters

className
> The name of the class to locate. The name must be fully qualified with the namespace.

Return Value

A **Type** object representing the given class name, if the class is in this module; otherwise, a null reference (**Nothing** in Visual Basic).

Exceptions

Exception Type	Condition
ArgumentNullException	*className* is a null reference (**Nothing** in Visual Basic).
TargetInvocationException	The class initializers are invoked and an exception is thrown.
ArgumentException	*className* is invalid, such as if it is greater than 1023 characters or if it is a zero-length string.
SecurityException	The caller does not have the required reflection permissions and attempts to reflect on a type that is not public.

Example

[Visual Basic, C#, C++] The following example displays the name of a class in the specified module.

```
[Visual Basic]
Imports System
Imports System.Reflection

'This code assumes that the root namespace is set to empty("").
Namespace ReflectionModule_Examples
    Class MyMainClass
        Shared Sub Main()
            Dim moduleArray() As [Module]

            moduleArray =
[Assembly].GetExecutingAssembly().GetModules(False)

            'In a simple project with only one module,
the module at index
            ' 0 will be the module containing these classes.
            Dim myModule As [Module] = moduleArray(0)

            Dim myType As Type

            myType =
myModule.GetType("ReflectionModule_Examples.MyMainClass")
            Console.WriteLine("Got type: {0}", myType.ToString())
        End Sub 'Main
    End Class 'MyMainClass
End Namespace 'ReflectionModule_Examples

[C#]
using System;
using System.Reflection;

namespace ReflectionModule_Examples
{
    class MyMainClass
    {
        static void Main()
        {
            Module[] moduleArray;

            moduleArray =
Assembly.GetExecutingAssembly().GetModules(false);
```

```
                    //In a simple project with only one module,
the module at index
                    // 0 will be the module containing these classes.
                    Module myModule = moduleArray[0];

            Type myType;

            myType =
myModule.GetType("ReflectionModule_Examples.MyMainClass");
                Console.WriteLine("Got type: {0}", myType.ToString());
            }
        }
}
```

```
[C++]
#using <mscorlib.dll>

using namespace System;
using namespace System::Reflection;

namespace ReflectionModule_Examples {
    public __gc class MyMainClass {
    };
}

void main()
{
    Module* moduleArray[];

    moduleArray = Assembly::GetExecutingAssembly()->GetModules(false);

    //In a simple project with only one module, the module at index
    // 0 will be the module containing these classes.
    Module* myModule = moduleArray[0];

    Type* myType;

    myType = myModule->GetType(S"ReflectionModule_Examples.MyMainClass");
    Console::WriteLine(S"Got type: {0}", myType);
}
```

Requirements

Platforms: Windows 98, Windows NT 4.0,
Windows Millennium Edition, Windows 2000,
Windows XP Home Edition, Windows XP Professional,
Windows .NET Server family,
.NET Compact Framework - Windows CE .NET

.NET Framework Security:
- **ReflectionPermission** for reflecting on types that are not public.
  Associated enumeration:
  ReflectionPermissionFlag.TypeInformation

Module.GetType Method (String, Boolean)

Returns the specified class, searching the module with the specified
case sensitivity.

```
[Visual Basic]
Overloads Public Overridable Function GetType( _
    ByVal className As String, _
    ByVal ignoreCase As Boolean _
) As Type
[C#]
public virtual Type GetType(
    string className,
    bool ignoreCase
);
```

```
[C++]
public: virtual Type* GetType(
    String* className,
    bool ignoreCase
);
[JScript]
public function GetType(
    className : String,
    ignoreCase : Boolean
) : Type;
```

Parameters

className
> The name of the class to locate. The name must be fully qualified
> with the namespace.

ignoreCase
> **true** for case-insensitive search; otherwise, **false**.

Return Value

A **Type** object representing the given class name, if the class is in
this module; otherwise, a null reference (**Nothing** in Visual Basic).

Exceptions

Exception Type	Condition
ArgumentNullException	*className* is a null reference (**Nothing** in Visual Basic).
TargetInvocationException	The class initializers are invoked and an exception is thrown.
ArgumentException	*className* is invalid, such as if it is greater than 1023 characters or if it is a zero-length string.
SecurityException	The caller does not have the required reflection permissions and attempts to reflect on a type that is not public.

Example

[Visual Basic, C#, C++] The following example displays the name
of a class in the specified module, specifying **false** for the
ignoreCase parameter so that case will not be ignored.

```
[Visual Basic]
Imports System
Imports System.Reflection

'This code assumes that the root namespace is set to empty("").
Namespace ReflectionModule_Examples
    Class MyMainClass
        Shared Sub Main()
            Dim moduleArray() As [Module]

            moduleArray =
[Assembly].GetExecutingAssembly().GetModules(False)

            'In a simple project with only one module,
the module at index
            ' 0 will be the module containing these classes.
            Dim myModule As [Module] = moduleArray(0)

            Dim myType As Type
            myType =
myModule.GetType("ReflectionModule_Examples.MyMainClass", False)
                Console.WriteLine("Got type: {0}", myType.ToString())
            End Sub 'Main
    End Class 'MyMainClass
End Namespace 'ReflectionModule_Examples
```

```
[C#]
using System;
using System.Reflection;

namespace ReflectionModule_Examples
{
    class MyMainClass
    {
        static void Main()
        {
            Module[] moduleArray;

            moduleArray =
Assembly.GetExecutingAssembly().GetModules(false);

            //In a simple project with only one module,
the module at index
            // 0 will be the module containing these classes.
            Module myModule = moduleArray[0];

            Type myType;
            myType =
myModule.GetType("ReflectionModule_Examples.MyMainClass", false);
            Console.WriteLine("Got type: {0}", myType.ToString());
        }
    }
}

[C++]
#using <mscorlib.dll>

using namespace System;
using namespace System::Reflection;

namespace ReflectionModule_Examples
{
    public __gc class MyMainClass
    {
    };
}
void main()
{
    Module* moduleArray[];

    moduleArray = Assembly::GetExecutingAssembly()->GetModules(false);

    //In a simple project with only one module, the module at index
    // 0 will be the module containing these classes.
    Module* myModule = moduleArray[0];

    Type* myType;
    myType = myModule->GetType
(S"ReflectionModule_Examples.MyMainClass", false);
    Console::WriteLine(S"Got type: {0}", myType);
}
```

Requirements

Platforms: Windows 98, Windows NT 4.0,
Windows Millennium Edition, Windows 2000,
Windows XP Home Edition, Windows XP Professional,
Windows .NET Server family

.NET Framework Security:

- **ReflectionPermission** for reflecting on types that are not public. Associated enumeration: **ReflectionPermissionFlag.TypeInformation**

Module.GetType Method (String, Boolean, Boolean)

Returns the specified class, searching the module with the specified case sensitivity and specifying whether to throw an exception if an error occurs while loading the **Type**.

```
[Visual Basic]
Overloads Public Overridable Function GetType( _
    ByVal className As String, _
    ByVal throwOnError As Boolean, _
    ByVal ignoreCase As Boolean _
) As Type
[C#]
public virtual Type GetType(
    string className,
    bool throwOnError,
    bool ignoreCase
);
[C++]
public: virtual Type* GetType(
    String* className,
    bool throwOnError,
    bool ignoreCase
);
[JScript]
public function GetType(
    className : String,
    throwOnError : Boolean,
    ignoreCase : Boolean
) : Type;
```

Parameters

className
> The name of the class to locate. The name must be fully qualified with the namespace.

throwOnError
> **true** to throw a **TypeLoadException** if an error occurs while loading the **Type**.
>
> -or-
>
> **false** to ignore errors while loading the **Type**.

ignoreCase
> **true** for case-insensitive search; otherwise, **false**.

Return Value

A **Type** object representing the given class name, if the class is in this module; otherwise, a null reference (**Nothing** in Visual Basic).

Exceptions

Exception Type	Condition
ArgumentNullException	*className* is a null reference (**Nothing** in Visual Basic).
TargetInvocationException	The class initializers are invoked and an exception is thrown.
ArgumentException	*className* is invalid, such as if it is greater than 1023 characters or if it is a zero-length string.
TypeLoadException	An error occurred while loading the type.
SecurityException	The caller does not have the required reflection permissions and attempts to reflect on a type that is not public.

Example

[Visual Basic, C#, C++] The following example displays the name of a class in the specified module. The *throwOnError* and *ignoreCase* parameters are specified as **false**.

```
[Visual Basic]
Imports System
Imports System.Reflection

'This code assumes that the root namespace is set to empty("").
Namespace ReflectionModule_Examples
    Class MyMainClass
        Shared Sub Main()
            Dim moduleArray() As [Module]

            moduleArray =
[Assembly].GetExecutingAssembly().GetModules(False)

            'In a simple project with only one module, the
module at index
            ' 0 will be the module containing this class.
            Dim myModule As [Module] = moduleArray(0)

            Dim myType As Type
            myType =
myModule.GetType("ReflectionModule_Examples.MyMainClass", False, False)
            Console.WriteLine("Got type: {0}", myType.ToString())
        End Sub 'Main
    End Class 'MyMainClass
End Namespace 'ReflectionModule_Examples

[C#]
using System;
using System.Reflection;

namespace ReflectionModule_Examples
{
    class MyMainClass
    {
        static void Main()
        {
            Module[] moduleArray;

            moduleArray =
Assembly.GetExecutingAssembly().GetModules(false);

            //In a simple project with only one module, the
module at index
            // 0 will be the module containing this class.
            Module myModule = moduleArray[0];

            Type myType;
            myType =
myModule.GetType("ReflectionModule_Examples.MyMainClass",
false, false);
            Console.WriteLine("Got type: {0}", myType.ToString());
        }
    }
}

[C++]
#using <mscorlib.dll>

using namespace System;
using namespace System::Reflection;

namespace ReflectionModule_Examples
{
    public __gc class MyMainClass
    {
    };
}
void main()
{
    Module* moduleArray[];

    moduleArray = Assembly::GetExecutingAssembly()->GetModules(false);

    //In a simple project with only one module, the module at index
    // 0 will be the module containing this class.
    Module* myModule = moduleArray[0];
```

```
    Type* myType;
    myType = myModule->GetType
(S"ReflectionModule_Examples.MyMainClass", false, false);
    Console::WriteLine(S"Got type: {0}", myType);
}
```

Requirements

Platforms: Windows 98, Windows NT 4.0,
Windows Millennium Edition, Windows 2000,
Windows XP Home Edition, Windows XP Professional,
Windows .NET Server family

.NET Framework Security:

- **ReflectionPermission** for reflecting on types that are not public.
  Associated enumeration:
  ReflectionPermissionFlag.TypeInformation

Module.GetTypes Method

Returns all the classes defined within this module.

```
[Visual Basic]
Public Overridable Function GetTypes() As Type()
[C#]
public virtual Type[] GetTypes();
[C++]
public: virtual Type* GetTypes() [];
[JScript]
public function GetTypes() : Type[];
```

Return Value

An array of type **Type** containing classes defined within the module
that is reflected by this instance.

Exceptions

Exception Type	Condition
ReflectionTypeLoadException	One or more classes in a module could not be loaded.
SecurityException	The caller does not have the required permission.

Remarks

ReflectionTypeLoadException is a special class load exception.
The **ReflectionTypeLoadException.Types** property contains the
array of classes that were defined in the module and were loaded.
This array may contain some null values. The
ReflectionTypeLoadException.LoaderExceptions property is an
array of exceptions that represent the exceptions that were thrown by
the class loader. The holes in the class array line up with the
exceptions.

For example, if the class initializers of one of the classes throws an
exception while it is being loaded, a **TargetInvocationException** is
stored in the corresponding element of the **LoaderExceptions** array.

Requirements

Platforms: Windows 98, Windows NT 4.0,
Windows Millennium Edition, Windows 2000,
Windows XP Home Edition, Windows XP Professional,
Windows .NET Server family,
.NET Compact Framework - Windows CE .NET

.NET Framework Security:

- **ReflectionPermission** Reflection permission for the current
  module.

Module.IsDefined Method

Determines if the specified *attributeType* is defined on this module.

```
[Visual Basic]
Public Overridable Function IsDefined( _
   ByVal attributeType As Type, _
   ByVal inherit As Boolean _
) As Boolean Implements ICustomAttributeProvider.IsDefined
[C#]
public virtual bool IsDefined(
   Type attributeType,
   bool inherit
);
[C++]
public: virtual bool IsDefined(
   Type* attributeType,
   bool inherit
);
[JScript]
public function IsDefined(
   attributeType : Type,
   inherit : Boolean
) : Boolean;
```

Parameters

attributeType
    The Type object to which the custom attribute is applied.

inherit
    This argument is ignored for objects of this type.

Return Value

true if one or more instance of *attributeType* is defined on this module; otherwise, **false**.

Implements

ICustomAttributeProvider.IsDefined

Exceptions

Exception Type	Condition
ArgumentNullException	*attributeType* is a null reference (**Nothing** in Visual Basic).

Example

[Visual Basic, C#, C++] The following example demonstrates a use of the **IsDefined** method.

```
[Visual Basic]
Imports System
Imports System.Reflection

'Define a module-level attribute.
<Module: ReflectionModule_Examples.MySimpleAttribute("module-level")>

'Define a module-level attribute.
Namespace ReflectionModule_Examples
    Class MyMainClass
        Shared Sub Main()
            Dim moduleArray() As [Module]

            moduleArray =
[Assembly].GetExecutingAssembly().GetModules(False)

            'In a simple project with only one module, the
module at index
            ' 0 will be the module containing these classes.
            Dim myModule As [Module] = moduleArray(0)
```

```
            Dim myType As Type
            myType =
myModule.GetType("ReflectionModule_Examples.MySimpleAttribute")
            Console.WriteLine("IsDefined(MySimpleAttribute)
= {0}", myModule.IsDefined(myType, False))
        End Sub 'Main
    End Class 'MyMainClass

    'A very simple custom attribute.
    <AttributeUsage
(AttributeTargets.Class Or AttributeTargets.Module)> _
    Public Class MySimpleAttribute
        Inherits Attribute
        Private name As String

        Public Sub New(ByVal newName As String)
            name = newName
        End Sub 'New
    End Class 'MySimpleAttribute
End Namespace 'ReflectionModule_Examples
```

```
[C#]
using System;
using System.Reflection;

//Define a module-level attribute.
[module: ReflectionModule_Examples.MySimpleAttribute("module-level")]

namespace ReflectionModule_Examples
{
    class MyMainClass
    {
        static void Main()
        {
            Module[] moduleArray;

            moduleArray =
Assembly.GetExecutingAssembly().GetModules(false);

            //In a simple project with only one module, the
module at index
            // 0 will be the module containing these classes.
            Module myModule = moduleArray[0];

            Type myType;
            myType =
myModule.GetType("ReflectionModule_Examples.MySimpleAttribute");
            Console.WriteLine("IsDefined(MySimpleAttribute)
= {0}", myModule.IsDefined(myType, false));
        }
    }

    //A very simple custom attribute.
    [AttributeUsage(AttributeTargets.Class | AttributeTargets.Module)]
    public class MySimpleAttribute : Attribute
    {
        private string name;

        public MySimpleAttribute(string newName)
        {
            name = newName;
        }
    }
}
```

```
[C++]
#using <mscorlib.dll>

using namespace System;
using namespace System::Reflection;

namespace ReflectionModule_Examples
{
    //A very simple custom attribute.
    [AttributeUsage(AttributeTargets::Class | AttributeTargets::Module)]
```

```
public __gc class MySimpleAttribute : public Attribute
{
private:
   String* name;

public:
   MySimpleAttribute(String* newName)
   {
      name = newName;
   }
};
}

//Define a module-level attribute.
[module: ReflectionModule_Examples::MySimpleAttribute
 (S"module-level")];

void main()
{
   System::Reflection::Module* moduleArray[];

   moduleArray = Assembly::GetExecutingAssembly()->GetModules(false);

   //In a simple project with only one module, the module at index
   // 0 will be the module containing these classes.
   System::Reflection::Module* myModule = moduleArray[0];

   Type* myType;
   myType = myModule-
>GetType(S"ReflectionModule_Examples.MySimpleAttribute");
   Console::WriteLine(S"IsDefined(MySimpleAttribute) = {0}",
__box(myModule->IsDefined(myType, false)));
}
```

Requirements

Platforms: Windows 98, Windows NT 4.0,
Windows Millennium Edition, Windows 2000,
Windows XP Home Edition, Windows XP Professional,
Windows .NET Server family

Module.IsResource Method

Gets a value indicating whether the object is a resource.

```
[Visual Basic]
Public Function IsResource() As Boolean
[C#]
public bool IsResource();
[C++]
public: bool IsResource();
[JScript]
public function IsResource() : Boolean;
```

Return Value

true if the object is a resource; otherwise, **false**.

Example

[Visual Basic, C#, C++] The following example demonstrates a use
of the **IsResource** method.

```
[Visual Basic]
Imports System
Imports System.Reflection

Namespace ReflectionModule_Examples
   Class MyMainClass
      Shared Sub Main()
         Dim moduleArray() As [Module]
```

```
         moduleArray = _
      [Assembly].GetExecutingAssembly().GetModules(False)

            'In a simple project with only one module, the
      module at index
            ' 0 will be the module containing this class.
         Dim myModule As [Module] = moduleArray(0)

         Console.WriteLine("myModule.IsResource() = {0}",
myModule.IsResource())
      End Sub 'Main
   End Class 'MyMainClass
End Namespace 'ReflectionModule_Examples
```

```
[C#]
using System;
using System.Reflection;

namespace ReflectionModule_Examples
{
   class MyMainClass
   {
      static void Main()
      {
         Module[] moduleArray;

         moduleArray =
Assembly.GetExecutingAssembly().GetModules(false);

            //In a simple project with only one module, the
      module at index
            // 0 will be the module containing this class.
         Module myModule = moduleArray[0];

         Console.WriteLine("myModule.IsResource() = {0}",
myModule.IsResource());
      }
   }
}
```

```
[C++]
#using <mscorlib.dll>

using namespace System;
using namespace System::Reflection;

void main()
{
   Module* moduleArray[];

   moduleArray = Assembly::GetExecutingAssembly()->GetModules(false);

   //In a simple project with only one module, the module at index
   // 0 will be the module containing this class.
   Module* myModule = moduleArray[0];

   Console::WriteLine(S"myModule->IsResource() = {0}",
__box(myModule->IsResource()));
}
```

Requirements

Platforms: Windows 98, Windows NT 4.0,
Windows Millennium Edition, Windows 2000,
Windows XP Home Edition, Windows XP Professional,
Windows .NET Server family

Module.ToString Method

Returns the name of the module.

```
[Visual Basic]
Overrides Public Function ToString() As String
```

```
[C#]
public override string ToString();
[C++]
public: String* ToString();
[JScript]
public override function ToString() : String;
```

Return Value

A **String** representing the name of this module.

Example

[Visual Basic, C#, C++] The following example demonstrates a use of the **ToString** method.

```
[Visual Basic]
Imports System
Imports System.Reflection

Namespace ReflectionModule_Examples
    Class MyMainClass
        Shared Sub Main()
            Dim moduleArray() As [Module]

            moduleArray = _
[Assembly].GetExecutingAssembly().GetModules(False)

            'In a simple project with only one module, the
module at index
            ' 0 will be the module containing this class.
            Dim myModule As [Module] = moduleArray(0)

            Console.WriteLine("myModule.ToString returns: {0}", _
myModule.ToString())
        End Sub 'Main
    End Class 'MyMainClass
End Namespace 'ReflectionModule_Examples

[C#]
using System;
using System.Reflection;

namespace ReflectionModule_Examples
{
    class MyMainClass
    {
        static void Main()
        {
            Module[] moduleArray;

            moduleArray = _
Assembly.GetExecutingAssembly().GetModules(false);

            //In a simple project with only one module, the
module at index
            // 0 will be the module containing this class.
            Module myModule = moduleArray[0];

            Console.WriteLine("myModule.ToString returns: {0}", _
myModule.ToString());
        }
    }
}
```

```
[C++]
#using <mscorlib.dll>

using namespace System;
using namespace System::Reflection;

void main()
{
    Module* moduleArray[];

    moduleArray = Assembly::GetExecutingAssembly()->GetModules(false);

    //In a simple project with only one module, the module at index
    // 0 will be the module containing this class.
    Module* myModule = moduleArray[0];

    Console::WriteLine(S"myModule->ToString returns: {0}", myModule);
}
```

Requirements

Platforms: Windows 98, Windows NT 4.0, Windows Millennium Edition, Windows 2000, Windows XP Home Edition, Windows XP Professional, Windows .NET Server family, .NET Compact Framework - Windows CE .NET, Common Language Infrastructure (CLI) Standard

ModuleResolveEventHandler Delegate

Represents the method that will handle the **ModuleResolve** event of an **Assembly**.

```
[Visual Basic]
<Serializable>
Public Delegate Function Sub ModuleResolveEventHandler( _
   ByVal sender As Object, _
   ByVal e As ResolveEventArgs _
) As Module
[C#]
[Serializable]
public delegate Module ModuleResolveEventHandler(
   object sender,
   ResolveEventArgs e
);
[C++]
[Serializable]
public __gc __delegate Module* ModuleResolveEventHandler(
   Object* sender,
   ResolveEventArgs* e
);
```

[JScript] In JScript, you can use the delegates in the .NET Framework, but you cannot define your own.

Parameters [Visual Basic, C#, C++]

The declaration of your event handler must have the same parameters as the **ModuleResolveEventHandler** delegate declaration.

sender
   The assembly that was the source of the event.

e
   The arguments supplied by the object describing the event.

Remarks

When you create an **Assembly** delegate, you identify the method that will handle the event. To associate the event with your event handler, add an instance of the delegate to the event. The event handler is called whenever the event occurs, unless you remove the delegate. For more information about event handler delegates, see **Events and Delegates**.

If the common language runtime class loader cannot resolve a reference to an internal module of an assembly through normal means, the event is raised to give the callback a chance to find or load the module itself and return it.

Each derived class of **Delegate** and **MulticastDelegate** has a constructor and an **Invoke** method. See the Managed Extensions for C++ code example given in the description for the **Delegate**.

Example

[C#] The following example demonstrates the sequence of execution in which an event handler is called. In this example, Server1 is an external module of the MySample class.

[C#] Compile and run this example as follows.

1. Compile Server1.
2. Compile MySample.
3. Run MySample. Note that the module file Server1.netmodule must be in a subfolder named "subfolder" for this to work.

[C#] Compile Server1 as follows:

[C#] csc

```
            /out:subfolder\Server1.netmodule /t:module Server1.cs
```

```
[C#]
using System;
using System.Reflection;
public class Server1 : MarshalByRefObject
{
    public int trivial()
    {
        Console.WriteLine ("server1.trivial");
        return 1;
    }
}
```

[C#] Compile MySample as follows:

[C#] csc /out:MySample.exe /t:exe

```
            /addmodule:subfolder\Server1.netmodule MySample.cs
```

```
[C#]
using System;
using System.IO;
using System.Reflection;
class MySample
{
    public static int Main(String[] args)
    {
        Assembly asm1 = Assembly.GetExecutingAssembly();
        asm1.ModuleResolve += new ModuleResolveEventHandler
(evModuleResolve);
        Console.WriteLine("Calling MySample.Test");
        Test();
        return 0;
    }
    private static Module evModuleResolve(object sender,
ResolveEventArgs e)
    {
        Console.WriteLine("MySample.evModuleResolve");
        FileStream fs = File.Open
(".\\subfolder\\server1.netmodule", FileMode.Open);
        byte [] rgFileBytes = new byte [1];
        long len = fs.Length;
        rgFileBytes = new byte[len];
        fs.Read(rgFileBytes, 0, (int)len);
        Assembly a = Assembly.GetExecutingAssembly();
        Module m = a.LoadModule("server1.netmodule", rgFileBytes);

        return m;
    }
    private static void Test()
    {
        Console.WriteLine("Instantiating Server1");
        Server1 s = new Server1();
        Console.WriteLine("Calling Server1.trivial");
        s.trivial();
    }
}
```

Requirements

Namespace: System.Reflection

Platforms: Windows 98, Windows NT 4.0, Windows Millennium Edition, Windows 2000, Windows XP Home Edition, Windows XP Professional, Windows .NET Server family

Assembly: Mscorlib (in Mscorlib.dll)

ParameterAttributes Enumeration

Defines the attributes that can be associated with a parameter. These are defined in CorHdr.h.

This enumeration has a **FlagsAttribute** attribute that allows a bitwise combination of its member values.

```
[Visual Basic]
<Flags>
<Serializable>
Public Enum ParameterAttributes
[C#]
[Flags]
[Serializable]
public enum ParameterAttributes
[C++]
[Flags]
[Serializable]
__value public enum ParameterAttributes
[JScript]
public
    Flags
    Serializable
enum ParameterAttributes
```

Remarks

To get the **ParameterAttributes** value, first get the **Type**. From the **Type**, get the **ParameterInfo** array. The **ParameterAttributes** value is within the array.

These enumerator values are dependent on optional metadata. Not all attributes are available from all compilers. See the appropriate compiler instructions to determine which enumerated values are available.

Members

Member name	Description	Value
HasDefault Supported by the .NET Compact Framework.	Specifies that the parameter has a default value.	4096
HasFieldMarshal Supported by the .NET Compact Framework.	Specifies that the parameter has field marshaling information.	8192
In Supported by the .NET Compact Framework.	Specifies that the parameter is an input parameter.	1
Lcid Supported by the .NET Compact Framework.	Specifies that the parameter is a locale identifier (lcid).	4
None Supported by the .NET Compact Framework.	Specifies that there is no parameter attribute.	0
Optional Supported by the .NET Compact Framework.	Specifies that the parameter is optional.	16
Out Supported by the .NET Compact Framework.	Specifies that the parameter is an output parameter.	2
Reserved3 Supported by the .NET Compact Framework.	Reserved.	16384
Reserved4 Supported by the .NET Compact Framework.	Reserved.	32768
ReservedMask Supported by the .NET Compact Framework.	Specifies that the parameter is reserved.	61440
Retval Supported by the .NET Compact Framework.	Specifies that the parameter is a return value.	8

Example

[Visual Basic, C#] The following example displays the attributes of the specified parameter.

```
[Visual Basic]
Imports System
Imports System.Reflection
Imports Microsoft.VisualBasic

Class paramatt

    Public Shared Sub mymethod(ByVal str1 As String, _
ByRef str2 As String, _
    ByRef str3 As String)
        str2 = "string"
    End Sub

    Public Shared Function Main() As Integer
        Console.WriteLine(ControlChars.CrLf + _
"Reflection.ParameterAttributes")

        ' Get the Type and the method.
        Dim Mytype As Type = Type.GetType("paramatt")
        Dim Mymethodbase As MethodBase = Mytype.GetMethod("mymethod")

        ' Display the method.
        Console.WriteLine("Mymethodbase = " + Mymethodbase.ToString())

        ' Get the ParameterInfo array.
        Dim Myarray As ParameterInfo() = Mymethodbase.GetParameters()

        ' Get and display the attributes for the second parameter.
        Dim Myparamattributes As ParameterAttributes = _
Myarray(1).Attributes

        Console.WriteLine("For the second parameter:" + _
ControlChars.CrLf _
            + "Myparamattributes = " + _
CInt(Myparamattributes).ToString() _
            + ", which is a " + Myparamattributes.ToString())

        Return 0
    End Function
End Class
```

```csharp
[C#]
using System;
using System.Reflection;

class paramatt
{
    public static void mymethod (string str1, out string str2,      ↵
ref string str3)
    {
        str2 = "string";
    }

    public static int Main(string[] args)
    {
        Console.WriteLine("\nReflection.ParameterAttributes");

        // Get the Type and the method.

        Type Mytype = Type.GetType("paramatt");
        MethodBase Mymethodbase = Mytype.GetMethod("mymethod");

        // Display the method.
        Console.Write("\nMymethodbase = " + Mymethodbase);

        // Get the ParameterInfo array.
        ParameterInfo[] Myarray = Mymethodbase.GetParameters();

        // Get and display the attributes for the second parameter.
        ParameterAttributes Myparamattributes = Myarray[1].Attributes;

        Console.Write("\nFor the second                               ↵
parameter:\nMyparamattributes = "
                + (int) Myparamattributes
                + ", which is an "
                + Myparamattributes.ToString());

        return 0;
    }
}
```

Requirements

Namespace: System.Reflection

Platforms: Windows 98, Windows NT 4.0,
Windows Millennium Edition, Windows 2000,
Windows XP Home Edition, Windows XP Professional,
Windows .NET Server family,
.NET Compact Framework - Windows CE .NET

Assembly: Mscorlib (in Mscorlib.dll)

ParameterInfo Class

Discovers the attributes of a parameter and provides access to parameter metadata.

System.Object
   System.Reflection.ParameterInfo

```
[Visual Basic]
<Serializable>
Public Class ParameterInfo
   Implements ICustomAttributeProvider
[C#]
[Serializable]
public class ParameterInfo : ICustomAttributeProvider
[C++]
[Serializable]
public __gc class ParameterInfo : public ICustomAttributeProvider
[JScript]
public
   Serializable
class ParameterInfo implements ICustomAttributeProvider
```

Thread Safety

This type is safe for multithreaded operations.

Remarks

Use an instance of **ParameterInfo** to obtain information about the parameter's data type, default value, and so on.

GetParameters returns an array of **ParameterInfo** objects representing the parameters of a method, in order.

Requirements

Namespace: System.Reflection

Platforms: Windows 98, Windows NT 4.0, Windows Millennium Edition, Windows 2000, Windows XP Home Edition, Windows XP Professional, Windows .NET Server family, .NET Compact Framework - Windows CE .NET

Assembly: Mscorlib (in Mscorlib.dll)

ParameterInfo Constructor

Initializes a new instance of the **ParameterInfo** class.

```
[Visual Basic]
Protected Sub New()
[C#]
protected ParameterInfo();
[C++]
protected: ParameterInfo();
[JScript]
protected function ParameterInfo();
```

Requirements

Platforms: Windows 98, Windows NT 4.0, Windows Millennium Edition, Windows 2000, Windows XP Home Edition, Windows XP Professional, Windows .NET Server family, .NET Compact Framework - Windows CE .NET, Common Language Infrastructure (CLI) Standard

ParameterInfo.AttrsImpl Field

The attributes of the parameter.

```
[Visual Basic]
Protected AttrsImpl As ParameterAttributes
[C#]
protected ParameterAttributes AttrsImpl;
[C++]
protected: ParameterAttributes AttrsImpl;
[JScript]
protected var AttrsImpl : ParameterAttributes;
```

Remarks

This field is intended only for users who are deriving classes from **ParameterInfo**.

Typical access to parameter attributes is through **Attributes**.

Requirements

Platforms: Windows 98, Windows NT 4.0, Windows Millennium Edition, Windows 2000, Windows XP Home Edition, Windows XP Professional, Windows .NET Server family, .NET Compact Framework - Windows CE .NET

ParameterInfo.ClassImpl Field

The **Type** of the parameter.

```
[Visual Basic]
Protected ClassImpl As Type
[C#]
protected Type ClassImpl;
[C++]
protected: Type* ClassImpl;
[JScript]
protected var ClassImpl : Type;
```

Remarks

This field is intended only for users who are deriving classes from **ParameterInfo**.

Typical access to parameter types is through **ParameterType**.

Requirements

Platforms: Windows 98, Windows NT 4.0, Windows Millennium Edition, Windows 2000, Windows XP Home Edition, Windows XP Professional, Windows .NET Server family, .NET Compact Framework - Windows CE .NET

ParameterInfo.DefaultValueImpl Field

The default value of the parameter.

```
[Visual Basic]
Protected DefaultValueImpl As Object
[C#]
protected object DefaultValueImpl;
[C++]
protected: Object* DefaultValueImpl;
[JScript]
protected var DefaultValueImpl : Object;
```

Remarks

This field is intended only for users who are deriving classes from **ParameterInfo**.

Typical access to the default value of the parameter is through **DefaultValue**.

Requirements

Platforms: Windows 98, Windows NT 4.0, Windows Millennium Edition, Windows 2000, Windows XP Home Edition, Windows XP Professional, Windows .NET Server family, .NET Compact Framework - Windows CE .NET

ParameterInfo.MemberImpl Field

The member in which the field is implemented.

```
[Visual Basic]
Protected MemberImpl As MemberInfo
[C#]
protected MemberInfo MemberImpl;
[C++]
protected: MemberInfo* MemberImpl;
[JScript]
protected var MemberImpl : MemberInfo;
```

Remarks

This field is intended only for users who are deriving classes from **ParameterInfo**.

Typical access to the parameter name is through the **Member**.

Requirements

Platforms: Windows 98, Windows NT 4.0, Windows Millennium Edition, Windows 2000, Windows XP Home Edition, Windows XP Professional, Windows .NET Server family, .NET Compact Framework - Windows CE .NET

ParameterInfo.NameImpl Field

The name of the parameter.

```
[Visual Basic]
Protected NameImpl As String
[C#]
protected string NameImpl;
[C++]
protected: String* NameImpl;
[JScript]
protected var NameImpl : String;
```

Remarks

This field is intended only for users who are deriving classes from **ParameterInfo**.

Typical access to the parameter name is through the **Name**.

Requirements

Platforms: Windows 98, Windows NT 4.0, Windows Millennium Edition, Windows 2000, Windows XP Home Edition, Windows XP Professional, Windows .NET Server family, .NET Compact Framework - Windows CE .NET

ParameterInfo.PositionImpl Field

The zero-based position of the parameter in the parameter list.

```
[Visual Basic]
Protected PositionImpl As Integer
[C#]
protected int PositionImpl;
[C++]
protected: int PositionImpl;
[JScript]
protected var PositionImpl : int;
```

Remarks

This field is intended only for users who are deriving classes from **ParameterInfo**.

Typical access to the name of the parameter is through **Position**.

Requirements

Platforms: Windows 98, Windows NT 4.0, Windows Millennium Edition, Windows 2000, Windows XP Home Edition, Windows XP Professional, Windows .NET Server family, .NET Compact Framework - Windows CE .NET

ParameterInfo.Attributes Property

Gets the attributes for this parameter.

```
[Visual Basic]
Public Overridable ReadOnly Property Attributes As _
    ParameterAttributes
[C#]
public virtual ParameterAttributes Attributes {get;}
[C++]
public: __property virtual ParameterAttributes get_Attributes();
[JScript]
public function get Attributes() : ParameterAttributes;
```

Property Value

A **ParameterAttributes** object representing the attributes for this parameter.

Remarks

This method utilizes the **AttrsImpl** method.

To get the **ParameterInfo** array, first get the method or the constructor and then call **MethodBase.GetParameters**.

Example

```
[Visual Basic]
Imports System
Imports System.Reflection
Imports Microsoft.VisualBasic

Public Class MyClass1

    Public Function MyMethod(i As Integer, ByRef j As Short, _
ByRef k As Long) As Integer
        j = 2
        Return 0
    End Function 'MyMethod
End Class 'MyClass1

Public Class ParameterInfo_Attributes

    Public Shared Sub Main()
        ' Get the type.
```

```
    Dim myType As Type = GetType(MyClass1)
    ' Get the method named 'MyMethod' from the type.
    Dim myMethodBase As MethodBase = myType.GetMethod("MyMethod")
    ' Get the parameters associated with the method.
    Dim myParameters As ParameterInfo() =
myMethodBase.GetParameters()
        Console.WriteLine(ControlChars.Cr + "The method {0}
has the {1} parameters :", "ParameterInfo_Example.MyMethod",
myParameters.Length)
        ' Print the attributes associated with each of the parameters.
        Dim i As Integer
        For i = 0 To myParameters.Length - 1
            Console.WriteLine(ControlChars.Tab + "The {0} parameter
 has the attribute : {1}", i + 1, myParameters(i).Attributes)
        Next i
    End Sub 'Main
End Class 'ParameterInfo_Attributes
```

```
[C#]
using System;
using System.Reflection;
public class MyClass1
{
    public int MyMethod( int i, out short j, ref long k)
    {
        j = 2;
        return 0;
    }
}

public class ParameterInfo_Attributes
{
    public static void Main()
    {
        // Get the type.
        Type myType = typeof(MyClass1);
        // Get the method named 'MyMethod' from the type.
        MethodBase myMethodBase = myType.GetMethod("MyMethod");
        // Get the parameters associated with the method.
        ParameterInfo[] myParameters = myMethodBase.GetParameters();
        Console.WriteLine("\nThe method {0} has the {1} parameters :",
                          "ParameterInfo_Example.MyMethod",
myParameters.Length);
        // Print the attributes associated with each of the parameters.
        for(int i = 0; i < myParameters.Length; i++)
            Console.WriteLine("\tThe {0} parameter has the
attribute : {1}",
                              i + 1, myParameters[i].Attributes);
    }
}
```

```
[C++]
#using <mscorlib.dll>

using namespace System;
using namespace System::Reflection;
using namespace System::Runtime::InteropServices;

public __gc class MyClass1
{
public:
    int MyMethod(int i, [Out] short* j, long* k)
    {
        *j = 2;
        return 0;
    }
};

void main()
{
    // Get the type.
    Type* myType = __typeof(MyClass1);
    // Get the method named 'MyMethod' from the type.
    MethodBase* myMethodBase = myType->GetMethod(S"MyMethod");
    // Get the parameters associated with the method.
```

```
    ParameterInfo* myParameters[] = myMethodBase->GetParameters();
    Console::WriteLine(S"\nThe method {0} has the {1} parameters :",
      S"ParameterInfo_Example::MyMethod", __box(myParameters->Length));
    // Print the attributes associated with each of the parameters.
    for (int i = 0; i < myParameters->Length; i++)
        Console::WriteLine(S"\tThe {0} parameter has the
attribute : {1}",
        __box(i + 1), __box(myParameters[i]->Attributes));
}
```

Requirements

Platforms: Windows 98, Windows NT 4.0,
Windows Millennium Edition, Windows 2000,
Windows XP Home Edition, Windows XP Professional,
Windows .NET Server family,
.NET Compact Framework - Windows CE .NET,
Common Language Infrastructure (CLI) Standard

ParameterInfo.DefaultValue Property

Gets a value indicating the default value if the parameter has a
default value.

```
[Visual Basic]
Public Overridable ReadOnly Property DefaultValue As Object
[C#]
public virtual object DefaultValue {get;}
[C++]
public: __property virtual Object* get_DefaultValue();
[JScript]
public function get DefaultValue() : Object;
```

Property Value

The default value of the parameter, or **Value** if the parameter has no
default value.

Remarks

The default value is used when an actual value is not specified in the
method call. A parameter can have a default value that is a null
reference (**Nothing** in Visual Basic). This is distinct from the case
where a default value is not defined.

This method utilizes the **DefaultValueImpl** method.

To get the **ParameterInfo** array, first get the method or the
constructor and then call **MethodBase.GetParameters**.

Requirements

Platforms: Windows 98, Windows NT 4.0,
Windows Millennium Edition, Windows 2000,
Windows XP Home Edition, Windows XP Professional,
Windows .NET Server family,
.NET Compact Framework - Windows CE .NET

ParameterInfo.IsIn Property

Gets a value indicating whether this is an input parameter.

```
[Visual Basic]
Public ReadOnly Property IsIn As Boolean
[C#]
public bool IsIn {get;}
[C++]
public: __property bool get_IsIn();
[JScript]
public function get IsIn() : Boolean;
```

Property Value

true if the parameter is an input parameter; otherwise, **false**.

Remarks

This method depends on an optional metadata flag. This flag can be inserted by compilers, but the compilers are not obligated to do so.

This method utilizes the **In** flag of the **ParameterAttributes** enumerator.

To get the **ParameterInfo** array, first get the method or the constructor and then call **MethodBase.GetParameters**.

Example

```
[Visual Basic]
Imports System
Imports System.Reflection
Imports System.Threading
Imports System.Reflection.Emit
Imports Microsoft.VisualBasic

Public Class ParameterInfo_IsIn_IsOut_IsOptional

    Public Shared Sub DefineMethod()
        Dim myAssemblyName As New AssemblyName()
        myAssemblyName.Name = "MyAssembly"
        ' Get the assembly builder from the application
domain associated with the current thread.
        Dim myAssemblyBuilder As AssemblyBuilder =
Thread.GetDomain().DefineDynamicAssembly(myAssemblyName,
AssemblyBuilderAccess.RunAndSave)
        ' Create a dynamic module in the assembly.
        Dim myModuleBuilder As ModuleBuilder =
myAssemblyBuilder.DefineDynamicModule("MyModule", "MyAssembly.dll")
        ' Create a type in the module.
        Dim myTypeBuilder As TypeBuilder =
myModuleBuilder.DefineType("MyType")
        ' Create a method called MyMethod.
        Dim myMethodBuilder As MethodBuilder =
myTypeBuilder.DefineMethod("MyMethod", MethodAttributes.Public
Or MethodAttributes.HideBySig Or MethodAttributes.Static,
GetType(String), New Type() {GetType(Integer),
GetType(Short), GetType(Long)})
        ' Set the attributes for the parameters of the method.
        ' Set the attribute for the first parameter to IN.
        Dim myParameterBuilder As ParameterBuilder =
myMethodBuilder.DefineParameter(1, ParameterAttributes.In,
"MyIntParameter")
        ' Set the attribute for the second parameter to OUT.
        myParameterBuilder =
myMethodBuilder.DefineParameter(2,
ParameterAttributes.Out, "MyShortParameter")
        ' Set the attribute for the third parameter to OPTIONAL.
        myParameterBuilder = myMethodBuilder.DefineParameter(3,
ParameterAttributes.Optional Or ParameterAttributes.HasDefault,
"MyLongParameter")
        ' Get the Microsoft Intermediate Language generator
for the method.
        Dim myILGenerator As ILGenerator =
myMethodBuilder.GetILGenerator()
        ' Use the utility method to generate the MSIL instructions
that print a string to the console.
        myILGenerator.EmitWriteLine("Hello World!")
        ' Generate the "ret" MSIL instruction.
        myILGenerator.Emit(OpCodes.Ret)
        ' End the creation of the type.
        myTypeBuilder.CreateType()
    End Sub 'DefineMethod

    Public Shared Sub Main()
        ' Create a dynamic assembly with a type named 'MyType'.
        DefineMethod()
```

```
        ' Get the assemblies currently loaded in the application domain.
        Dim myAssemblies As [Assembly]() =
Thread.GetDomain().GetAssemblies()
        Dim myAssembly As [Assembly] = Nothing
        ' Get the assembly named MyAssembly.
        Dim i As Integer
        For i = 0 To myAssemblies.Length - 1
            If [String].Compare
(myAssemblies(i).GetName(False).Name, "MyAssembly") = 0 Then
                myAssembly = myAssemblies(i)
            End If
        Next i
        If Not (myAssembly Is Nothing) Then
            ' Get a type named MyType.
            Dim myType As Type = myAssembly.GetType("MyType")
            ' Get a method named MyMethod from the type.
            Dim myMethodBase As MethodBase = myType.GetMethod("MyMethod")
            ' Get the parameters associated with the method.
            Dim myParameters As ParameterInfo() =
myMethodBase.GetParameters()
            Console.WriteLine(ControlChars.Cr + "The method {0}
has the {1} parameters :", myMethodBase, myParameters.Length)
            ' Print the IN, OUT and OPTIONAL attributes
associated with each of the parameters.
            For i = 0 To myParameters.Length - 1
                If myParameters(i).IsIn Then
                    Console.WriteLine(ControlChars.Tab +
"The {0} parameter has the In attribute", i + 1)
                End If
                If myParameters(i).IsOptional Then
                    Console.WriteLine(ControlChars.Tab + "The
{0} parameter has the Optional attribute", i + 1)
                End If
                If myParameters(i).IsOut Then
                    Console.WriteLine(ControlChars.Tab + "The
{0} parameter has the Out attribute", i + 1)
                End If
            Next i
        Else
            Console.WriteLine("Could not find a assembly named
'MyAssembly' for the current application domain")
        End If
    End Sub 'Main
End Class 'ParameterInfo_IsIn_IsOut_IsOptional

[C#]

using System;
using System.Reflection;
using System.Threading;
using System.Reflection.Emit;

public class ParameterInfo_IsIn_IsOut_IsOptional
{
    public static void DefineMethod()
    {
        AssemblyName myAssemblyName = new AssemblyName();
        myAssemblyName.Name = "MyAssembly";
        // Get the assembly builder from the application
domain associated with the current thread.
        AssemblyBuilder myAssemblyBuilder =
Thread.GetDomain().DefineDynamicAssembly(myAssemblyName,
AssemblyBuilderAccess.RunAndSave);
        // Create a dynamic module in the assembly.
        ModuleBuilder myModuleBuilder =
myAssemblyBuilder.DefineDynamicModule("MyModule", "MyAssembly.dll");
        // Create a type in the module.
        TypeBuilder myTypeBuilder = myModuleBuilder.DefineType("MyType");
        // Create a method called MyMethod.
        MethodBuilder myMethodBuilder =
myTypeBuilder.DefineMethod("MyMethod",MethodAttributes.Public |
MethodAttributes.HideBySig |

MethodAttributes.Static, typeof(string), new Type[]
{typeof(int), typeof(short), typeof(long)});
```

```csharp
        // Set the attributes for the parameters of the method.
        // Set the attribute for the first parameter to IN.
        ParameterBuilder myParameterBuilder =
myMethodBuilder.DefineParameter(1, ParameterAttributes.In,
"MyIntParameter");
        // Set the attribute for the second parameter to OUT.
        myParameterBuilder = myMethodBuilder.DefineParameter(2,
ParameterAttributes.Out, "MyShortParameter");
        // Set the attribute for the third parameter to OPTIONAL.
        myParameterBuilder = myMethodBuilder.DefineParameter(3,
ParameterAttributes.Optional | ParameterAttributes.HasDefault,
"MyLongParameter");
        // Get the Microsoft Intermediate Language generator
for the method.
        ILGenerator myILGenerator = myMethodBuilder.GetILGenerator();
        // Use the utility method to generate the MSIL instructions
    that print a string to the console.
        myILGenerator.EmitWriteLine("Hello World!");
        // Generate the "ret" MSIL instruction.
        myILGenerator.Emit(OpCodes.Ret);
        // End the creation of the type.
        myTypeBuilder.CreateType();
    }

    public static void Main()
    {
        // Create a dynamic assembly with a type named MyType.
        DefineMethod();

        // Get the assemblies currently loaded in the application domain.
        Assembly[] myAssemblies = Thread.GetDomain().GetAssemblies();
        Assembly myAssembly = null;
        // Get the assembly named MyAssembly.
        for(int i = 0; i < myAssemblies.Length; i++)
            if(String.Compare(myAssemblies[i].GetName(false).Name,
"MyAssembly") == 0)
                myAssembly = myAssemblies[i];

        if(myAssembly != null)
        {
            // Get a type named MyType.
            Type myType = myAssembly.GetType("MyType");
            // Get a method named MyMethod from the type.
            MethodBase myMethodBase = myType.GetMethod("MyMethod");
            // Get the parameters associated with the method.
            ParameterInfo[] myParameters = myMethodBase.GetParameters();
            Console.WriteLine("\nThe method {0} has the {1} parameters :",
                myMethodBase, myParameters.Length);
            // Print the IN, OUT and OPTIONAL attributes associated
with each of the parameters.
            for(int i = 0; i < myParameters.Length; i++)
            {
                if(myParameters[i].IsIn)
                    Console.WriteLine("\tThe {0} parameter has
the In attribute",
                                    i + 1);
                if(myParameters[i].IsOptional)
                    Console.WriteLine("\tThe {0} parameter has the
Optional attribute",
                                    i + 1);
                if(myParameters[i].IsOut)
                    Console.WriteLine("\tThe {0} parameter has
the Out attribute",
                                    i + 1);
            }
        }
        else
            Console.WriteLine("Could not find a assembly named
'MyAssembly' for the current application domain");
    }
}

[C++]

#using <mscorlib.dll>
```

```cpp
using namespace System;
using namespace System::Reflection;
using namespace System::Threading;
using namespace System::Reflection::Emit;

public __gc class ParameterInfo_IsIn_IsOut_IsOptional
{
public:
    static void DefineMethod()
    {
        AssemblyName* myAssemblyName = new AssemblyName();
        myAssemblyName->Name = S"MyAssembly";
        // Get the assembly builder from the application domain
associated with the current thread.
        AssemblyBuilder* myAssemblyBuilder = Thread::GetDomain()-
>DefineDynamicAssembly(myAssemblyName,
AssemblyBuilderAccess::RunAndSave);
        // Create a dynamic module in the assembly.
        ModuleBuilder* myModuleBuilder = myAssemblyBuilder-
>DefineDynamicModule(S"MyModule", S"MyAssembly.dll");
        // Create a type in the module.
        TypeBuilder* myTypeBuilder = myModuleBuilder-
>DefineType(S"MyType");
        // Create a method called MyMethod.
        Type* type1[] = {__typeof(int), __typeof(short), __typeof(long)};
        MethodBuilder* myMethodBuilder = myTypeBuilder-
>DefineMethod(S"MyMethod",
            static_cast<MethodAttributes>
(MethodAttributes::Public | MethodAttributes::HideBySig |
MethodAttributes::Static),
            __typeof(String), type1);
        // Set the attributes for the parameters of the method.
        // Set the attribute for the first parameter to IN.
        ParameterBuilder* myParameterBuilder = myMethodBuilder-
>DefineParameter(1, ParameterAttributes::In, S"MyIntParameter");
        // Set the attribute for the second parameter to OUT.
        myParameterBuilder = myMethodBuilder->DefineParameter
(2, ParameterAttributes::Out, S"MyShortParameter");
        // Set the attribute for the third parameter to OPTIONAL.
        myParameterBuilder = myMethodBuilder->DefineParameter(3,
            static_cast<ParameterAttributes>(ParameterAttributes:
:Optional | ParameterAttributes::HasDefault), S"MyLongParameter");
        // Get the Microsoft Intermediate Language generator for
the method.
        ILGenerator* myILGenerator = myMethodBuilder->GetILGenerator();
        // Use the utility method to generate the MSIL instructions
    that print a String* to the console.
        myILGenerator->EmitWriteLine(S"Hello World!");
        // Generate the S"ret" MSIL instruction.
        myILGenerator->Emit(OpCodes::Ret);
        // End the creation of the type.
        myTypeBuilder->CreateType();
    }
};
void main()
{
    // Create a dynamic assembly with a type named MyType.
    ParameterInfo_IsIn_IsOut_IsOptional::DefineMethod();

    // Get the assemblies currently loaded in the application domain.
    Assembly* myAssemblies[] = Thread::GetDomain()->GetAssemblies();
    Assembly* myAssembly = 0;
    // Get the assembly named MyAssembly.
    for (int i = 0; i < myAssemblies->Length; i++)
        if (String::Compare(myAssemblies[i]->GetName(false)->Name,
S"MyAssembly") == 0)
            myAssembly = myAssemblies[i];

    if (myAssembly != 0) {
        // Get a type named MyType.
        Type* myType = myAssembly->GetType(S"MyType");
        // Get a method named MyMethod from the type.
        MethodBase* myMethodBase = myType->GetMethod(S"MyMethod");
        // Get the parameters associated with the method.
        ParameterInfo* myParameters[] = myMethodBase->GetParameters();
```

```
      Console::WriteLine(S"\nThe method {0} has the {1} parameters :",
        myMethodBase, __box(myParameters->Length));
      // Print the IN, OUT and OPTIONAL attributes associated    ⌐
with each of the parameters.
      for (int i = 0; i < myParameters->Length; i++) {
        if (myParameters[i]->IsIn)
            Console::WriteLine(S"\tThe {0} parameter has the In    ⌐
attribute",
            __box(i + 1));
        if (myParameters[i]->IsOptional)
            Console::WriteLine(S"\tThe {0} parameter has the    ⌐
Optional attribute",
            __box(i + 1));
        if (myParameters[i]->IsOut)
            Console::WriteLine(S"\tThe {0} parameter has the    ⌐
 Out attribute",
            __box(i + 1));
      }
   } else
      Console::WriteLine(S"Could not find a assembly named    ⌐
'MyAssembly' for the current application domain");
}
```

Requirements

Platforms: Windows 98, Windows NT 4.0,
Windows Millennium Edition, Windows 2000,
Windows XP Home Edition, Windows XP Professional,
Windows .NET Server family

ParameterInfo.IsLcid Property

Gets a value indicating whether this parameter is a locale identifier
(lcid).

```
[Visual Basic]
Public ReadOnly Property IsLcid As Boolean
[C#]
public bool IsLcid {get;}
[C++]
public: __property bool get_IsLcid();
[JScript]
public function get IsLcid() : Boolean;
```

Property Value

true if the parameter is a locale identifier; otherwise, **false**.

Remarks

This method depends on an optional metadata flag. This flag can be
inserted by compilers, but the compilers are not obligated to do so.

This method utilizes the **Lcid** flag of the **ParameterAttributes**
enumerator.

To get the **ParameterInfo** array, first get the method or the
constructor and then call **MethodBase.GetParameters**.

Example

See related example in the **System.Reflection.ParameterInfo.IsIn**
property topic.

Requirements

Platforms: Windows 98, Windows NT 4.0,
Windows Millennium Edition, Windows 2000,
Windows XP Home Edition, Windows XP Professional,
Windows .NET Server family

ParameterInfo.IsOptional Property

Gets a value indicating whether this parameter is optional.

```
[Visual Basic]
Public ReadOnly Property IsOptional As Boolean
[C#]
public bool IsOptional {get;}
[C++]
public: __property bool get_IsOptional();
[JScript]
public function get IsOptional() : Boolean;
```

Property Value

true if the parameter is optional; otherwise, **false**.

Remarks

This method depends on an optional metadata flag. This flag can be
inserted by compilers, but the compilers are not obligated to do so.

This method utilizes the **Optional** flag of the **ParameterAttributes**
enumerator.

To get the **ParameterInfo** array, first get the method and then call
MethodBase.GetParameters.

Example

See related example in the **System.Reflection.ParameterInfo.IsIn**
property topic.

Requirements

Platforms: Windows 98, Windows NT 4.0,
Windows Millennium Edition, Windows 2000,
Windows XP Home Edition, Windows XP Professional,
Windows .NET Server family

ParameterInfo.IsOut Property

Gets a value indicating whether this is an output parameter.

```
[Visual Basic]
Public ReadOnly Property IsOut As Boolean
[C#]
public bool IsOut {get;}
[C++]
public: __property bool get_IsOut();
[JScript]
public function get IsOut() : Boolean;
```

Property Value

true if the parameter is an output parameter; otherwise, **false**.

Remarks

This method depends on an optional metadata flag. This flag can be
inserted by compilers, but the compilers are not obligated to do so.

This method utilizes the **Out** flag of the **ParameterAttributes**
enumerator.

To get the **ParameterInfo** array, first get the method or the
constructor and then call **MethodBase.GetParameters**.

Example

```
[Visual Basic]
Imports System
Imports System.Reflection
Imports Microsoft.VisualBasic

Class parminfo
```

```
    Public Shared Sub mymethod(int1m As Integer, ByRef str2m As String, _
    ByRef str3m As String)
        str2m = "in mymethod"
    End Sub

    Public Shared Function Main() As Integer
        Console.WriteLine(ControlChars.CrLf +
"Reflection.Parameterinfo")

        'Get the ParameterInfo parameter of a function.
        'Get the type.
        Dim Mytype As Type = Type.GetType("parminfo")

        'Get and display the method.
        Dim Mymethodbase As MethodBase = Mytype.GetMethod("mymethod")
        Console.Write(ControlChars.CrLf + "Mymethodbase = " _
            + Mymethodbase.ToString())

        'Get the ParameterInfo array.
        Dim Myarray As ParameterInfo() = Mymethodbase.GetParameters()

        'Get and display the IsOut of each parameter.
        Dim Myparam As ParameterInfo
        For Each Myparam In  Myarray
            Console.Write(ControlChars.CrLf _
                + "For parameter # " + Myparam.Position.ToString() _
                + ", the IsOut is - " + Myparam.IsOut.ToString())
        Next Myparam
        Return 0
    End Function
End Class

' This code produces the following output:
'
' Reflection.ParameterInfo
'
' Mymethodbase = Void mymethod (Int32, System.String ByRef,
System.String ByRef)
' For parameter # 0, the IsOut is - False
' For parameter # 1, the IsOut is - True
' For parameter # 2, the IsOut is - False

[C#]
using System;
using System.Reflection;

 class parminfo
 {
    public static void mymethod (
        int int1m, out string str2m, ref string str3m)
    {
        str2m = "in mymethod";
    }

    public static int Main(string[] args)
    {
        Console.WriteLine("\nReflection.Parameterinfo");

        //Get the ParameterInfo parameter of a function.

        //Get the type.
        Type Mytype = Type.GetType("parminfo");

        //Get and display the method.
        MethodBase Mymethodbase = Mytype.GetMethod("mymethod");
        Console.Write("\nMymethodbase = " + Mymethodbase);

        //Get the ParameterInfo array.
        ParameterInfo[] Myarray = Mymethodbase.GetParameters();

        //Get and display the IsOut of each parameter.
        foreach (ParameterInfo Myparam in Myarray)
        {
            Console.Write ("\nFor parameter # "  + Myparam.Position
                + ", the IsOut is - " + Myparam.IsOut );
```

```
        }
        return 0;
    }
}
/*
This code produces the following output:

Reflection.ParameterInfo

Mymethodbase = Void mymethod (Int32, System.String ByRef,
System.String ByRef)
For parameter # 0, the IsOut is - False
For parameter # 1, the IsOut is - True
For parameter # 2, the IsOut is - False
*/
```

Requirements

Platforms: Windows 98, Windows NT 4.0,
Windows Millennium Edition, Windows 2000,
Windows XP Home Edition, Windows XP Professional,
Windows .NET Server family

ParameterInfo.IsRetval Property

Gets a value indicating whether this is a **Retval** parameter.

```
[Visual Basic]
Public ReadOnly Property IsRetval As Boolean
[C#]
public bool IsRetval {get;}
[C++]
public: __property bool get_IsRetval();
[JScript]
public function get IsRetval() : Boolean;
```

Property Value

true if the parameter is a **Retval**; otherwise, **false**.

Remarks

This method depends on an optional metadata flag. This flag can be inserted by compilers, but the compilers are not obligated to do so.

This method utilizes the **Retval** flag of the **ParameterAttributes** enumerator.

To get the **ParameterInfo** array, first get the method or the constructor and then call **MethodBase.GetParameters**.

Requirements

Platforms: Windows 98, Windows NT 4.0,
Windows Millennium Edition, Windows 2000,
Windows XP Home Edition, Windows XP Professional,
Windows .NET Server family

ParameterInfo.Member Property

Gets a value indicating the member in which the parameter is implemented.

```
[Visual Basic]
Public Overridable ReadOnly Property Member As MemberInfo
[C#]
public virtual MemberInfo Member {get;}
[C++]
public: __property virtual MemberInfo* get_Member();
[JScript]
public function get Member() : MemberInfo;
```

Property Value

A **MemberInfo** object.

Requirements

Platforms: Windows 98, Windows NT 4.0,
Windows Millennium Edition, Windows 2000,
Windows XP Home Edition, Windows XP Professional,
Windows .NET Server family,
.NET Compact Framework - Windows CE .NET

ParameterInfo.Name Property

Gets the name of the parameter.

```
[Visual Basic]
Public Overridable ReadOnly Property Name As String
[C#]
public virtual string Name {get;}
[C++]
public: __property virtual String* get_Name();
[JScript]
public function get Name() : String;
```

Property Value

A **String** containing the simple name of this parameter.

Remarks

This method utilizes the protected **NameImpl** method, and depends on an optional metadata flag that might not be available in all compilers.

To get the **ParameterInfo** array, first get the method or the constructor and then call **MethodBase.GetParameters**.

Example

```
[Visual Basic]
Imports System
Imports System.Reflection
Imports Microsoft.VisualBasic

Class parminfo

    Public Shared Sub mymethod(intlm As Integer, _
ByRef str2m As String, _
    ByRef str3m As String)
        str2m = "in mymethod"
    End Sub

    Public Shared Function Main() As Integer
        Console.WriteLine(ControlChars.CrLf + _
"Reflection.Parameterinfo")

        'Get the ParameterInfo parameter of a function.
        'Get the type.
        Dim Mytype As Type = Type.GetType("parminfo")

        'Get and display the method.
        Dim Mymethodbase As MethodBase = Mytype.GetMethod("mymethod")
        Console.Write(ControlChars.CrLf _
            + "Mymethodbase = " + Mymethodbase.ToString())

        'Get the ParameterInfo array.
        Dim Myarray As ParameterInfo() = Mymethodbase.GetParameters()

        'Get and display the name of each parameter.
        Dim Myparam As ParameterInfo
        For Each Myparam In  Myarray
            Console.Write(ControlChars.CrLf _
                + "For parameter # " + Myparam.Position.ToString() _
```

```
            + ", the Name is - " + Myparam.Name)
        Next Myparam
        Return 0
    End Function
End Class
```

```
' This code produces the following output:
'
' Reflection.ParameterInfo
'
' Mymethodbase
' = Void mymethod (Int32, System.String ByRef, System.String ByRef)
' For parameter # 0, the Name is - intlm
' For parameter # 1, the Name is - str2m
' For parameter # 2, the Name is - str3m
```

```
[C#]
using System;
using System.Reflection;

class parminfo
{
    public static void mymethod (
        int intlm, out string str2m, ref string str3m)
    {
        str2m = "in mymethod";
    }

    public static int Main(string[] args)
    {
        Console.WriteLine("\nReflection.Parameterinfo");

        //Get the ParameterInfo parameter of a function.

        //Get the type.
        Type Mytype = Type.GetType("parminfo");

        //Get and display the method.
        MethodBase Mymethodbase = Mytype.GetMethod("mymethod");
        Console.Write("\nMymethodbase = " + Mymethodbase);

        //Get the ParameterInfo array.
        ParameterInfo[] Myarray = Mymethodbase.GetParameters();

        //Get and display the name of each parameter.
        foreach (ParameterInfo Myparam in Myarray)
        {
            Console.Write ("\nFor parameter # "  + Myparam.Position
                + ", the Name is - " + Myparam.Name);
        }
        return 0;
    }
}
/*
This code produces the following output:

Reflection.ParameterInfo

Mymethodbase
= Void mymethod (Int32, System.String ByRef, System.String ByRef)
For parameter # 0, the Name is - intlm
For parameter # 1, the Name is - str2m
For parameter # 2, the Name is - str3m
*/
```

Requirements

Platforms: Windows 98, Windows NT 4.0,
Windows Millennium Edition, Windows 2000,
Windows XP Home Edition, Windows XP Professional,
Windows .NET Server family,
.NET Compact Framework - Windows CE .NET,
Common Language Infrastructure (CLI) Standard

ParameterInfo.ParameterType Property

Gets the **Type** of this parameter.

```
[Visual Basic]
Public Overridable ReadOnly Property ParameterType As Type
[C#]
public virtual Type ParameterType {get;}
[C++]
public: __property virtual Type* get_ParameterType();
[JScript]
public function get ParameterType() : Type;
```

Property Value

The **Type** object that represents the **Type** of this parameter.

Remarks

This method depends on an optional metadata and might not be available in all compilers.

To get the **ParameterInfo** array, first get the method or the constructor and then call **MethodBase.GetParameters**.

Example

```
[Visual Basic]
Imports System
Imports System.Reflection
Imports Microsoft.VisualBasic

Class parminfo

    Public Shared Sub mymethod(int1m As Integer, _
  ByRef str2m As String, _
    ByRef str3m As String)
            str2m = "in mymethod"
    End Sub

    Public Shared Function Main() As Integer
        Console.WriteLine(ControlChars.CrLf + _
"Reflection.Parameterinfo")

        'Get the ParameterInfo parameter of a function.
        'Get the type.
        Dim Mytype As Type = Type.GetType("parminfo")

        'Get and display the method.
        Dim Mymethodbase As MethodBase = Mytype.GetMethod("mymethod")
        Console.Write(ControlChars.CrLf _
            + "Mymethodbase = " + Mymethodbase.ToString())

        'Get the ParameterInfo array.
        Dim Myarray As ParameterInfo() = Mymethodbase.GetParameters()

        'Get and display the ParameterInfo of each parameter.
        Dim Myparam As ParameterInfo
        For Each Myparam In  Myarray
            Console.Write(ControlChars.CrLf _
                + "For parameter # " + Myparam.Position.ToString() _
                + ", the ParameterType is - " + _
Myparam.ParameterType.ToString())
            Next Myparam
            Return 0
    End Function
End Class

' This code produces the following output:
'
' Reflection.Parameterinfo
'
' Mymethodbase = Void mymethod(Int32, System.String ByRef,
System.String ByRef)
' For parameter # 0, the ParameterType is - System.Int32
' For parameter # 1, the ParameterType is - System.String&
' For parameter # 2, the ParameterType is - System.String&
```

```
[C#]
using System;
using System.Reflection;

class parminfo
{
    public static void mymethod (
        int int1m, out string str2m, ref string str3m)
    {
        str2m = "in mymethod";
    }

    public static int Main(string[] args)
    {
        Console.WriteLine("\nReflection.Parameterinfo");

        //Get the ParameterInfo parameter of a function.

        //Get the type.
        Type Mytype = Type.GetType("parminfo");

        //Get and display the method.
        MethodBase Mymethodbase = Mytype.GetMethod("mymethod");
        Console.Write("\nMymethodbase = " + Mymethodbase);

        //Get the ParameterInfo array.
        ParameterInfo[]Myarray = Mymethodbase.GetParameters();

        //Get and display the ParameterInfo of each parameter.
        foreach (ParameterInfo Myparam in Myarray)
        {
            Console.Write ("\nFor parameter # " + Myparam.Position
                + ", the ParameterType is - " + Myparam.ParameterType);
        }
        return 0;
    }
}

/*
This code produces the following output:

Reflection.Parameterinfo

Mymethodbase = Void mymethod(Int32, System.String ByRef,
System.String ByRef)
For parameter # 0, the ParameterType is - System.Int32
For parameter # 1, the ParameterType is - System.String&
For parameter # 2, the ParameterType is - System.String&
*/
```

Requirements

Platforms: Windows 98, Windows NT 4.0, Windows Millennium Edition, Windows 2000, Windows XP Home Edition, Windows XP Professional, Windows .NET Server family, .NET Compact Framework - Windows CE .NET, Common Language Infrastructure (CLI) Standard

ParameterInfo.Position Property

Gets the signature position for the parameter.

```
[Visual Basic]
Public Overridable ReadOnly Property Position As Integer
[C#]
public virtual int Position {get;}
[C++]
public: __property virtual int get_Position();
[JScript]
public function get Position() : int;
```

Property Value

An integer representing the position this parameter occupies in the parameter list.

Remarks

This method utilizes the **PositionImpl** method.

To get the **ParameterInfo** array, first get the method or the constructor and then call **MethodBase.GetParameters**.

Requirements

Platforms: Windows 98, Windows NT 4.0, Windows Millennium Edition, Windows 2000, Windows XP Home Edition, Windows XP Professional, Windows .NET Server family, .NET Compact Framework - Windows CE .NET

ParameterInfo.GetCustomAttributes Method

Gets custom attributes defined on this parameter.

Overload List

Gets all the custom attributes defined on this parameter.

Supported by the .NET Compact Framework.

[Visual Basic] **Overloads Public Overridable Function GetCustomAttributes(Boolean) As Object() Implements ICustomAttributeProvider.GetCustomAttributes**

[C#] **public virtual object[] GetCustomAttributes(bool);**

[C++] **public: virtual Object* GetCustomAttributes(bool) __gc[];**

[JScript] **public function GetCustomAttributes(Boolean) : Object[];**

Gets the custom attributes of the specified type defined on this parameter.

Supported by the .NET Compact Framework.

[Visual Basic] **Overloads Public Overridable Function GetCustomAttributes(Type, Boolean) As Object() Implements ICustomAttributeProvider.GetCustomAttributes**

[C#] **public virtual object[] GetCustomAttributes(Type, bool);**

[C++] **public: virtual Object* GetCustomAttributes(Type*, bool) __gc[];**

[JScript] **public function GetCustomAttributes(Type, Boolean) : Object[];**

ParameterInfo.GetCustomAttributes Method (Boolean)

Gets all the custom attributes defined on this parameter.

```
[Visual Basic]
Overloads Public Overridable Function GetCustomAttributes( _
  ByVal inherit As Boolean _
) As Object() Implements ICustomAttributeProvider.GetCustomAttributes
[C#]
public virtual object[] GetCustomAttributes(
  bool inherit
);
[C++]
public: virtual Object* GetCustomAttributes(
  bool inherit
) __gc[];
```

```
[JScript]
public function GetCustomAttributes(
  inherit : Boolean
) : Object[];
```

Parameters

inherit
    This argument is ignored for object of this type.

Return Value

An array of type **Object** containing all the custom attributes defined on this parameter.

Implements

ICustomAttributeProvider.GetCustomAttributes

Requirements

Platforms: Windows 98, Windows NT 4.0, Windows Millennium Edition, Windows 2000, Windows XP Home Edition, Windows XP Professional, Windows .NET Server family, .NET Compact Framework - Windows CE .NET

ParameterInfo.GetCustomAttributes Method (Type, Boolean)

Gets the custom attributes of the specified type defined on this parameter.

```
[Visual Basic]
Overloads Public Overridable Function GetCustomAttributes( _
  ByVal attributeType As Type, _
  ByVal inherit As Boolean _
) As Object() Implements ICustomAttributeProvider.GetCustomAttributes
[C#]
public virtual object[] GetCustomAttributes(
  Type attributeType,
  bool inherit
);
[C++]
public: virtual Object* GetCustomAttributes(
  Type* attributeType,
  bool inherit
) __gc[];
[JScript]
public function GetCustomAttributes(
  attributeType : Type,
  inherit : Boolean
) : Object[];
```

Parameters

attributeType
    The custom attributes identified by type.
inherit
    This argument is ignored for objects of this type.

Return Value

An array of type **Object** containing the custom attributes of the specified type.

Implements

ICustomAttributeProvider.GetCustomAttributes

Requirements

Platforms: Windows 98, Windows NT 4.0,
Windows Millennium Edition, Windows 2000,
Windows XP Home Edition, Windows XP Professional,
Windows .NET Server family,
.NET Compact Framework - Windows CE .NET

ParameterInfo.IsDefined Method

Determines if the custom attribute of the specified type is defined on
this member.

```
[Visual Basic]
Public Overridable Function IsDefined( _
    ByVal attributeType As Type, _
    ByVal inherit As Boolean _
) As Boolean Implements ICustomAttributeProvider.IsDefined
[C#]
public virtual bool IsDefined(
    Type attributeType,
    bool inherit
);
[C++]
public: virtual bool IsDefined(
    Type* attributeType,
    bool inherit
);
[JScript]
public function IsDefined(
    attributeType : Type,
    inherit : Boolean
) : Boolean;
```

Parameters

attributeType
> The **Type** object to search for.

inherit
> This argument is ignored for objects of this type.

Return Value

true if one or more instance of *attributeType* is defined on this
member; otherwise, **false**.

Implements

ICustomAttributeProvider.IsDefined

Exceptions

Exception Type	Condition
ArgumentNullException	*attributeType* is a null reference (**Nothing** in Visual Basic).

Requirements

Platforms: Windows 98, Windows NT 4.0,
Windows Millennium Edition, Windows 2000,
Windows XP Home Edition, Windows XP Professional,
Windows .NET Server family,
.NET Compact Framework - Windows CE .NET

ParameterModifier Structure

Attaches a modifier to parameters so that binding can work with parameter signatures in which the types have been modified.

System.Object
  System.ValueType
    System.Reflection.ParameterModifier

```
[Visual Basic]
<Serializable>
Public Structure ParameterModifier
[C#]
[Serializable]
public struct ParameterModifier
[C++]
[Serializable]
public __value struct ParameterModifier
```

[JScript] In JScript, you can use the structures in the .NET Framework, but you cannot define your own.

Thread Safety

Any public static (**Shared** in Visual Basic) members of this type are safe for multithreaded operations. Any instance members are not guaranteed to be thread safe.

Requirements

Namespace: System.Reflection

Platforms: Windows 98, Windows NT 4.0, Windows Millennium Edition, Windows 2000, Windows XP Home Edition, Windows XP Professional, Windows .NET Server family, .NET Compact Framework - Windows CE .NET

Assembly: Mscorlib (in Mscorlib.dll)

ParameterModifier Constructor

Initializes a new instance of the **ParameterModifier** class with the number of parameters to modify.

```
[Visual Basic]
Public Sub New( _
   ByVal parameterCount As Integer _
)
[C#]
public ParameterModifier(
   int parameterCount
);
[C++]
public: ParameterModifier(
   int parameterCount
);
[JScript]
public function ParameterModifier(
   parameterCount : int
);
```

Parameters

parameterCount
   The number of parameters to modify.

Exceptions

Exception Type	Condition
ArgumentException	*parameterCount* is negative.

Requirements

Platforms: Windows 98, Windows NT 4.0, Windows Millennium Edition, Windows 2000, Windows XP Home Edition, Windows XP Professional, Windows .NET Server family, .NET Compact Framework - Windows CE .NET

ParameterModifier.Item Property

Gets or sets the index of the parameter array.

[C#] In C#, this property is the indexer for the **ParameterModifier** class.

```
[Visual Basic]
Public Default Property Item( _
   ByVal index As Integer _
) As Boolean
[C#]
public bool this[
   int index
] {get; set;}
[C++]
public: __property bool get_Item(
   int index
);
public: __property void set_Item(
   int index,
   bool
);
[JScript]
returnValue = ParameterModifierObject.Item(index);
ParameterModifierObject.Item(index) = returnValue;
-or-
returnValue = ParameterModifierObject(index);
ParameterModifierObject(index) = returnValue;
```

[JScript] In JScript, you can use the default indexed properties defined by a type, but you cannot explicitly define your own. However, specifying the **expando** attribute on a class automatically provides a default indexed property whose type is **Object** and whose index type is **String**.

Arguments [JScript]

index
   The integer representing the index position of the parameter array.

Parameters [Visual Basic, C#, C++]

index
   The integer representing the index position of the parameter array.

Property Value

An integer representing the index position of the parameter array.

Remarks

Indexers permit instances of a class to be indexed in the same way as arrays.

Requirements

Platforms: Windows 98, Windows NT 4.0, Windows Millennium Edition, Windows 2000, Windows XP Home Edition, Windows XP Professional, Windows .NET Server family

Pointer Class

Provides a wrapper class for pointers.

System.Object
   System.Reflection.Pointer

```
[Visual Basic]
<CLSCompliant(False)>
NotInheritable Public Class Pointer
   Implements ISerializable
[C#]
[CLSCompliant(false)]
public sealed class Pointer : ISerializable
[C++]
[CLSCompliant(false)]
public __gc __sealed class Pointer : public ISerializable
[JScript]
public
   CLSCompliant(false)
class Pointer implements ISerializable
```

Thread Safety

Any public static (**Shared** in Visual Basic) members of this type are safe for multithreaded operations. Any instance members are not guaranteed to be thread safe.

Requirements

Namespace: System.Reflection

Platforms: Windows 98, Windows NT 4.0, Windows Millennium Edition, Windows 2000, Windows XP Home Edition, Windows XP Professional, Windows .NET Server family

Assembly: Mscorlib (in Mscorlib.dll)

Pointer.Box Method

Boxes the supplied unmanaged memory pointer and the type associated with that pointer into a managed **Pointer** wrapper object. The value and the type are saved so they can be accessed from the native code during an invocation.

This method is not CLS-compliant. For more information about CLS compliance, see **What is the Common Language Specification**.

```
[C#]
public static object Box(
   void* ptr,
   Type type
);
[C++]
public: static Object* Box(
   void* ptr,
   Type* type
);
```

[Visual Basic] This method cannot be used in Visual Basic.

[JScript] This method cannot be used in JScript.

Parameters [C#, C++]

ptr
   The supplied unmanaged memory pointer.

type
   The type associated with the *ptr* parameter.

Return Value [C#, C++]

A pointer object.

Exceptions [C#, C++]

Exception Type	Condition
ArgumentException	*type* is not a pointer.
ArgumentNullException	*type* is a null reference (**Nothing** in Visual Basic).

Requirements [C#, C++]

Platforms: Windows 98, Windows NT 4.0, Windows Millennium Edition, Windows 2000, Windows XP Home Edition, Windows XP Professional, Windows .NET Server family

Pointer.ISerializable.GetObjectData Method

This member supports the .NET Framework infrastructure and is not intended to be used directly from your code.

```
[Visual Basic]
Private Sub GetObjectData( _
   ByVal info As SerializationInfo, _
   ByVal context As StreamingContext _
) Implements ISerializable.GetObjectData
[C#]
void ISerializable.GetObjectData(
   SerializationInfo info,
   StreamingContext context
);
[C++]
private: void ISerializable::GetObjectData(
   SerializationInfo* info,
   StreamingContext context
);
[JScript]
private function ISerializable.GetObjectData(
   info : SerializationInfo,
   context : StreamingContext
);
```

Pointer.Unbox Method

Returns the stored pointer.

This method is not CLS-compliant. For more information about CLS compliance, see **What is the Common Language Specification**.

```
[C#]
public static void* Unbox(
   object ptr
);
[C++]
public: static void* Unbox(
   Object* ptr
);
```

[Visual Basic] This method cannot be used in Visual Basic.

[JScript] This method cannot be used in JScript.

Parameters [C#, C++]

ptr
   The stored pointer.

Return Value [C#, C++]

This method returns void.

Exceptions [C#, C++]

Exception Type	Condition
ArgumentException	*ptr* is not a pointer.

Requirements [C#, C++]

Platforms: Windows 98, Windows NT 4.0,
Windows Millennium Edition, Windows 2000,
Windows XP Home Edition, Windows XP Professional,
Windows .NET Server family

PropertyAttributes Enumeration

Defines the attributes that can be associated with a property. These attribute values are defined in corhdr.h.

This enumeration has a **FlagsAttribute** attribute that allows a bitwise combination of its member values.

```
[Visual Basic]
<Flags>
<Serializable>
Public Enum PropertyAttributes
[C#]
[Flags]
[Serializable]
public enum PropertyAttributes
[C++]
[Flags]
[Serializable]
__value public enum PropertyAttributes
[JScript]
public
    Flags
    Serializable
enum PropertyAttributes
```

Remarks

To get the **PropertyAttributes**, first get the class **Type**. From the **Type**, get the **PropertyInfo**. From the **PropertyInfo**, get the **Attributes**.

The enumerated value is a number representing the bitwise OR of the attributes implemented on the method.

Members

Member name	Description	Value
HasDefault Supported by the .NET Compact Framework.	Specifies that the property has a default value.	4096
None Supported by the .NET Compact Framework.	Specifies that no attributes are associated with a property.	0
Reserved2 Supported by the .NET Compact Framework.	Reserved.	8192
Reserved3 Supported by the .NET Compact Framework.	Reserved.	16384
Reserved4 Supported by the .NET Compact Framework.	Reserved.	32768
ReservedMask Supported by the .NET Compact Framework.	Specifies a flag reserved for runtime use only.	62464
RTSpecialName Supported by the .NET Compact Framework.	Specifies that the metadata internal APIs check the name encoding.	1024
SpecialName Supported by the .NET Compact Framework.	Specifies that the property is special, with the name describing how the property is special.	512

Example

[Visual Basic, C#] The following example builds three properties and displays the **PropertyAttributes** enumerated value. Note that the read-only property has no setter and thus cannot be changed by `.Caption =`
statement.

```
[Visual Basic]
Imports System
Imports System.Reflection
Imports Microsoft.VisualBasic

' Make three properties, one read-write, one default,
' and one read-only.
Public Class Aproperty
    ' Define a read-write property.
    Private myCaption As String = "A Default caption"

    Public Property Caption() As String
        Get
            Return myCaption
        End Get
        Set(ByVal Value As String)
            If myCaption <> value Then
                myCaption = value
            End If
        End Set
    End Property
End Class

Public Class Bproperty
    ' Define a default property.
    Private myCaption As String = "B Default caption"

    Default Public ReadOnly Property Item(ByVal index As
Integer) As String
        Get
            Return "1"
        End Get
    End Property

    Public Property Caption() As String

        Get
            Return myCaption
        End Get
        Set(ByVal Value As String)
            If myCaption <> value Then
                myCaption = value
            End If
        End Set
    End Property
End Class

Public Class Cproperty
    ' Define a read-only property.
    Private myCaption As String = "C Default caption"

    Public ReadOnly Property Caption() As String
        Get
            Return myCaption
        End Get
        'No setting is allowed because this property is read-only.
    End Property
End Class
```

```
Class propertyattributesenum

    Public Shared Function Main() As Integer
        Console.WriteLine(ControlChars.CrLf &
"Reflection.PropertyAttributes")

        ' Determine whether a property exists, and change its value.
        Dim Mypropertya As New Aproperty()
        Dim Mypropertyb As New Bproperty()
        Dim Mypropertyc As New Cproperty()

        Console.Write(ControlChars.CrLf & "1. Mypropertya.Caption
= " & _
            Mypropertya.Caption)

        Console.Write(ControlChars.CrLf & "1. Mypropertyb.Caption
= " & _
            Mypropertyb.Caption)

        Console.Write(ControlChars.CrLf & "1. Mypropertyc.Caption
= " & _
            Mypropertyc.Caption)

        ' Only Mypropertya can be changed because Mypropertyb is
read-only.
        Mypropertya.Caption = "A- This is changed."
        Mypropertyb.Caption = "B- This is changed."
        ' Note that Mypropertyc is not changed, because it is
read-only.
        Console.Write(ControlChars.CrLf & ControlChars.CrLf & _
            "2. Mypropertya.Caption = " & Mypropertya.Caption)

        Console.Write(ControlChars.CrLf & "2.Mypropertyb.Caption
= " & _
            Mypropertyb.Caption)

        Console.Write(ControlChars.CrLf + "2. Mypropertyc.Caption
= " & _
            Mypropertyc.Caption)

        ' Get the PropertyAttributes Enumeration of the property.
        ' Get the type.
        Dim MyTypea As Type = Type.GetType("Aproperty")
        Dim MyTypeb As Type = Type.GetType("Bproperty")
        Dim MyTypec As Type = Type.GetType("Cproperty")

        ' Get the property attributes.
        Dim Mypropertyinfoa As PropertyInfo =
MyTypea.GetProperty("Caption")
        Dim Myattributesa As PropertyAttributes =
Mypropertyinfoa.Attributes
        Dim Mypropertyinfob As PropertyInfo =
MyTypeb.GetProperty("Item")
        Dim Myattributesb As PropertyAttributes =
Mypropertyinfob.Attributes
        Dim Mypropertyinfoc As PropertyInfo =
MyTypec.GetProperty("Caption")
        Dim Myattributesc As PropertyAttributes =
Mypropertyinfoc.Attributes

        ' Display the property attributes value.
        Console.Write(ControlChars.CrLf & ControlChars.CrLf & "a- " & _
            Myattributesa.ToString())

        Console.Write(ControlChars.CrLf & "b-" &
Myattributesb.ToString())

        Console.Write(ControlChars.CrLf & "c- " &
Myattributesc.ToString())
        Return 0
    End Function
End Class
```

```
[C#]
using System;
using System.Reflection;

// Define three properties: one read-write, one default,
// and one read only.
public class Aproperty
    // Define a read-write property.
{
    private string caption = "A Default caption";
    public string Caption
    {
        get{return caption;}
        set
        {
            if (caption != value){caption = value;}
        }
    }
}
public class Bproperty
    // Define a default property.
{
    private string caption  = "B Default caption";
    public string this [int index]
    {
        get {return "1";}
    }
    public string Caption
    {

        get{return caption;}
        set
        {
            if (caption != value){caption = value;}
        }
    }
}
public class Cproperty
    // Define a read-only property.
{
    private string caption = "C Default caption";
    public string Caption
    {
        get{return caption;}
        // No setting is allowed, because this is a read-only property.
    }
}

class propertyattributesenum
{
    public static int Main(string[] args)
    {
        Console.WriteLine("\nReflection.PropertyAttributes");

        // Determine whether a property exists, and change its value.
        Aproperty Mypropertya = new Aproperty();
        Bproperty Mypropertyb = new Bproperty();
        Cproperty Mypropertyc = new Cproperty();

        Console.Write("\n1. Mypropertya.Caption = " +
Mypropertya.Caption );

        Console.Write("\n1. Mypropertyb.Caption = " +
Mypropertyb.Caption );

        Console.Write("\n1. Mypropertyc.Caption = " +
Mypropertyc.Caption );

        // Only Mypropertya can be changed, as Mypropertyb is read-only.
        Mypropertya.Caption = "A- This is changed.";
        Mypropertyb.Caption = "B- This is changed.";
        // Note that Mypropertyc is not changed because it is read only
```

```
        Console.Write("\n\n2. Mypropertya.Caption = " +            ↵
Mypropertya.Caption );

        Console.Write("\n2.Mypropertyb.Caption = " +               ↵
Mypropertyb.Caption );

        Console.Write("\n2. Mypropertyc.Caption = " +              ↵
Mypropertyc.Caption );

        // Get the PropertyAttributes enumeration of the property.
        // Get the type.
        Type MyTypea = Type.GetType("Aproperty");
        Type MyTypeb = Type.GetType("Bproperty");
        Type MyTypec = Type.GetType("Cproperty");

        // Get the property attributes.
        PropertyInfo Mypropertyinfoa = MyTypea.GetProperty("Caption");
        PropertyAttributes Myattributesa = Mypropertyinfoa.Attributes;
        PropertyInfo Mypropertyinfob = MyTypeb.GetProperty("Item");
        PropertyAttributes Myattributesb = Mypropertyinfob.Attributes;
        PropertyInfo Mypropertyinfoc = MyTypec.GetProperty("Caption");
        PropertyAttributes Myattributesc = Mypropertyinfoc.Attributes;

        // Display the property attributes value.

        Console.Write("\n\na- " + Myattributesa.ToString());

        Console.Write("\nb-" + Myattributesb.ToString());

        Console.Write("\nc- " + Myattributesc.ToString());
        return 0;
    }
}
```

Requirements

Namespace: System.Reflection

Platforms: Windows 98, Windows NT 4.0,
Windows Millennium Edition, Windows 2000,
Windows XP Home Edition, Windows XP Professional,
Windows .NET Server family,
.NET Compact Framework - Windows CE .NET

Assembly: Mscorlib (in Mscorlib.dll)

PropertyInfo Class

Discovers the attributes of a property and provides access to property metadata.

System.Object
   System.Reflection.MemberInfo
      System.Reflection.PropertyInfo
         System.Reflection.Emit.PropertyBuilder

```
[Visual Basic]
<Serializable>
<ClassInterface(ClassInterfaceType.AutoDual)>
MustInherit Public Class PropertyInfo
   Inherits MemberInfo
[C#]
[Serializable]
[ClassInterface(ClassInterfaceType.AutoDual)]
public abstract class PropertyInfo : MemberInfo
[C++]
[Serializable]
[ClassInterface(ClassInterfaceType::AutoDual)]
public __gc __abstract class PropertyInfo : public MemberInfo
[JScript]
public
   Serializable
   ClassInterface(ClassInterfaceType.AutoDual)
abstract class PropertyInfo extends MemberInfo
```

Thread Safety

This type is safe for multithreaded operations.

Remarks

Properties are logically the same as fields. A property is a named aspect of an object's state whose value is typically accessible through **get** and **set** accessors. Properties may be read-only, in which case a set routine is not supported.

Several methods in this class assume that the getter and setter methods of a property have certain formats. The signatures of the **get** and **set** methods must match the following convention:

- The return type of the getter and the last argument of the setter must be identical. This is the type of the property.
- The getter and setter must have the same number, type, and order of indices.

If this format is not followed, the behavior of the **GetValue** and **SetValue** methods is undefined.

Calling **ICustomAttributeProvider.GetCustomAttributes** on **PropertyInfo** when the *inherit* parameter of **GetCustomAttributes** is **true** does not walk the type hierarchy. Use **System.Attribute** to inherit custom attributes.

Notes to Inheritors: When you inherit from **PropertyInfo**, you must override the following members: **GetValue**, **SetValue**, **GetAccessors**, **GetGetMethod**, **GetSetMethod**, and **GetIndexParameters**.

Requirements

Namespace: System.Reflection

Platforms: Windows 98, Windows NT 4.0, Windows Millennium Edition, Windows 2000, Windows XP Home Edition, Windows XP Professional, Windows .NET Server family, .NET Compact Framework - Windows CE .NET

Assembly: Mscorlib (in Mscorlib.dll)

PropertyInfo Constructor

Initializes a new instance of the **PropertyInfo** class.

```
[Visual Basic]
Protected Sub New()
[C#]
protected PropertyInfo();
[C++]
protected: PropertyInfo();
[JScript]
protected function PropertyInfo();
```

Requirements

Platforms: Windows 98, Windows NT 4.0, Windows Millennium Edition, Windows 2000, Windows XP Home Edition, Windows XP Professional, Windows .NET Server family, .NET Compact Framework - Windows CE .NET, Common Language Infrastructure (CLI) Standard

.NET Framework Security:

- **ReflectionPermission** to enhance security and performance when invoked late-bound through mechanisms such as **Type.InvokeMember**. Associated enumeration: **ReflectionPermissionFlag.MemberAccess**.

PropertyInfo.Attributes Property

Gets the attributes for this property.

```
[Visual Basic]
Public MustOverride ReadOnly Property Attributes As _
   PropertyAttributes
[C#]
public abstract PropertyAttributes Attributes {get;}
[C++]
public: __property virtual PropertyAttributes get_Attributes() = 0;
[JScript]
public abstract function get Attributes() : PropertyAttributes;
```

Property Value

Attributes of this property.

Remarks

This property represents the attributes associated with a member. All members have a set of attributes that are defined in relation to the specific type of member. The property attributes let the user know if this property is the default property, a **SpecialName** property, and so on.

To get the **Attributes** property, first get the class type. From the type, get the **PropertyInfo**. From the **PropertyInfo**, get the attributes.

Example

[Visual Basic, C#, JScript] The following example displays the attributes of the specified property.

```
[Visual Basic]
Imports System
Imports System.Reflection
Imports Microsoft.VisualBasic

Public Class Myproperty
    Private myCaption As String = "Default caption"

    Public Property Caption() As String
        Get
            Return myCaption
        End Get
        Set(ByVal Value As String)
            If myCaption <> value Then
                myCaption = value
            End If
        End Set
    End Property
End Class 'Myproperty

Class Mypropertyinfo

    Public Shared Function Main() As Integer
        Console.WriteLine(ControlChars.CrLf & _
"Reflection.PropertyInfo")

        ' Define a property.
        Dim Myproperty As New Myproperty()
        Console.Write(ControlChars.CrLf & "Myproperty.Caption = " & _
            Myproperty.Caption)

        ' Get the type and PropertyInfo.
        Dim MyType As Type = Type.GetType("Myproperty")
        Dim Mypropertyinfo As PropertyInfo = _
MyType.GetProperty("Caption")

        ' Get and display the attributes property.
        Dim Myattributes As PropertyAttributes = _
Mypropertyinfo.Attributes

        Console.Write(ControlChars.CrLf & "PropertyAttributes - " & _
            Myattributes.ToString())

        Return 0
    End Function
End Class
[C#]
using System;
using System.Reflection;

public class Myproperty
{
    private string caption = "Default caption";
    public string Caption
    {
        get{return caption;}
        set {if(caption!=value) {caption = value;}
        }
    }
}

class Mypropertyinfo
{
    public static int Main(string[] args)
    {
        Console.WriteLine("\nReflection.PropertyInfo");

        // Define a property.
        Myproperty Myproperty = new Myproperty();
        Console.Write("\nMyproperty.Caption = " + Myproperty.Caption);
```

```
        // Get the type and PropertyInfo.
        Type MyType = Type.GetType("Myproperty");
        PropertyInfo Mypropertyinfo = MyType.GetProperty("Caption");

        // Get and display the attributes property.
        PropertyAttributes Myattributes = Mypropertyinfo.Attributes;

        Console.Write("\nPropertyAttributes - " +
Myattributes.ToString());

        return 0;
    }
}

[JScript]
//Make a property, then display the PropertyInfo
import System;
import System.Reflection;

public class Myproperty
{
    private var caption : String = "Default caption";
    public function get Caption() : String {
        return caption;
    }
    public function set Caption(value:String) {
        if(caption!=value) caption = value;
    }
}

class Mypropertyinfo
{
    public static function Main() : void
    {
        Console.WriteLine("\nReflection.PropertyInfo");

        //Build a property
        var myproperty : Myproperty = new Myproperty();
        Console.Write("\nMyproperty.Caption = " + myproperty.Caption);

        //Get the type and PropertyInfo
        var MyType : Type = Type.GetType("Myproperty");
        var Mypropertyinfo : PropertyInfo =
MyType.GetProperty("Caption");

        //Get and display the attributes property
        var Myattributes : PropertyAttributes =
Mypropertyinfo.Attributes;

        Console.Write("\nPropertyAttributes - " +
Myattributes.ToString());

    }
}
Mypropertyinfo.Main();
/*
Produces the following output

Reflection.PropertyInfo
Myproperty.Caption = Default caption
PropertyAttributes - None
*/
```

Requirements

Platforms: Windows 98, Windows NT 4.0,
Windows Millennium Edition, Windows 2000,
Windows XP Home Edition, Windows XP Professional,
Windows .NET Server family,
.NET Compact Framework - Windows CE .NET,
Common Language Infrastructure (CLI) Standard

PropertyInfo.CanRead Property

Gets a value indicating whether the property can be read.

```
[Visual Basic]
Public MustOverride ReadOnly Property CanRead As Boolean
[C#]
public abstract bool CanRead {get;}
[C++]
public: __property virtual bool get_CanRead() = 0;
[JScript]
public abstract function get CanRead() : Boolean;
```

Property Value

true if this property can be read; otherwise, **false**.

Remarks

If the property does not have a **get** accessor, it cannot be read.

To get the **CanRead** property, first get the class **Type**. From the **Type**, get the **PropertyInfo**. From the **PropertyInfo**, get the **CanRead** value.

Example

[Visual Basic, C#, JScript] The following example defines two properties. The first property is readable and the **CanRead** property is **true**. The second property is not readable (there is no get accessor), and the **CanRead** property is **false**.

```
[Visual Basic]
Imports System
Imports System.Reflection
Imports Microsoft.VisualBasic

' Define one readable property and one not readable.
Public Class Mypropertya
    Private myCaption As String = "A Default caption"

    Public Property Caption() As String
        Get
            Return myCaption
        End Get
        Set(ByVal Value As String)
            If myCaption <> value Then
                myCaption = value
            End If
        End Set
    End Property
End Class

Public Class Mypropertyb
    Private myCaption As String = "B Default caption"

    Public WriteOnly Property Caption() As String
        Set(ByVal Value As String)
            If myCaption <> value Then
                myCaption = value
            End If
        End Set
    End Property
End Class

Class Mypropertyinfo

    Public Shared Function Main() As Integer
        Console.WriteLine(ControlChars.CrLf & _
"Reflection.PropertyInfo")

        ' Define two properties.
        Dim Mypropertya As New Mypropertya()
        Dim Mypropertyb As New Mypropertyb()
```

```
        Console.Write(ControlChars.Cr & "Mypropertya.Caption = " & _
            Mypropertya.Caption)
        ' Mypropertyb.Caption cannot be read because
        ' there is no get accessor.
        ' Get the type and PropertyInfo.
        Dim MyTypea As Type = Type.GetType("Mypropertya")
        Dim Mypropertyinfoa As PropertyInfo = _
MyTypea.GetProperty("Caption")
        Dim MyTypeb As Type = Type.GetType("Mypropertyb")
        Dim Mypropertyinfob As PropertyInfo = _
MyTypeb.GetProperty("Caption")

        ' Get and display the CanRead property.
        Console.Write(ControlChars.CrLf & "CanRead a - " & _
            Mypropertyinfoa.CanRead)

        Console.Write(ControlChars.CrLf & "CanRead b - " & _
            Mypropertyinfob.CanRead)

        Return 0
    End Function
End Class

[C#]
using System;
using System.Reflection;

// Define one readable property and one not readable.
public class Mypropertya
{
    private string caption = "A Default caption";
    public string Caption
    {
        get{return caption;}
        set {if(caption!=value) {caption = value;}
        }
    }
}
public class Mypropertyb
{
    private string caption = "B Default caption";
    public string Caption
    {
        set{if(caption!=value) {caption = value;}
        }
    }
}

class Mypropertyinfo
{
    public static int Main()
    {
        Console.WriteLine("\nReflection.PropertyInfo");

        // Define two properties.
        Mypropertya Mypropertya = new Mypropertya();
        Mypropertyb Mypropertyb = new Mypropertyb();

        Console.Write("\nMypropertya.Caption = " +
Mypropertya.Caption);
        // Mypropertyb.Caption cannot be read, because
        // there is no get accessor.

        // Get the type and PropertyInfo.
        Type MyTypea = Type.GetType("Mypropertya");
        PropertyInfo Mypropertyinfoa = MyTypea.GetProperty("Caption");
        Type MyTypeb = Type.GetType("Mypropertyb");
        PropertyInfo Mypropertyinfob = MyTypeb.GetProperty("Caption");

        // Get and display the CanRead property.
        Console.Write("\nCanRead a - " + Mypropertyinfoa.CanRead);
        Console.Write("\nCanRead b - " + Mypropertyinfob.CanRead);

        return 0;
    }
}
```

[JScript]
```
import System;
import System.Reflection;

//Make two properties, one readable and on not readable
public class Mypropertya
{
    private var caption : String = "A Default caption";
    public function get Caption() : String {
        return caption;
    }
    public function set Caption(value:String)
    {
        if(caption!=value) {caption = value;}
    }
}
public class Mypropertyb
{
    private var caption : String = "B Default caption";
    public function set Caption(value:String) {
        if(caption!=value) {caption = value;}
    }
}

class Mypropertyinfo
{
    public static function Main() : void
    {
        Console.WriteLine("\nReflection.PropertyInfo");

        //Build two properties
        var mypropertya : Mypropertya = new Mypropertya();
        var mypropertyb : Mypropertyb = new Mypropertyb();

        Console.Write("\nmypropertya.Caption = " + mypropertya.Caption);
        //Note: Mypropertyb.Caption cannot be read as
        // there is no get accessor

        //Get the type and PropertyInfo
        var MyTypea : Type = Type.GetType("Mypropertya");
        var Mypropertyinfoa : PropertyInfo =
MyTypea.GetProperty("Caption");
        var MyTypeb : Type = Type.GetType("Mypropertyb");
        var Mypropertyinfob : PropertyInfo =
MyTypeb.GetProperty("Caption");

        //Get and display the CanRead property

        Console.Write("\nCanRead a - " + Mypropertyinfoa.CanRead);

        Console.Write("\nCanRead b - " + Mypropertyinfob.CanRead);

    }
}
Mypropertyinfo.Main();
/*
Produces the following output

Reflection.PropertyInfo
Mypropertya.Caption = A Default caption
CanRead a - True
CanRead b - False
*/
```

Requirements

Platforms: Windows 98, Windows NT 4.0,
Windows Millennium Edition, Windows 2000,
Windows XP Home Edition, Windows XP Professional,
Windows .NET Server family,
.NET Compact Framework - Windows CE .NET,
Common Language Infrastructure (CLI) Standard

PropertyInfo.CanWrite Property

Gets a value indicating whether the property can be written to.

```
[Visual Basic]
Public MustOverride ReadOnly Property CanWrite As Boolean
[C#]
public abstract bool CanWrite {get;}
[C++]
public: _property virtual bool get_CanWrite() = 0;
[JScript]
public abstract function get CanWrite() : Boolean;
```

Property Value

true if this property can be written to; otherwise, **false**.

Remarks

If the property does not have a **set** accessor, it cannot be written to.

To get the **CanWrite** property, first get the class **Type**. From the **Type**, get the **PropertyInfo**. From the **PropertyInfo**, get the **CanWrite** value.

Example

[Visual Basic, C#, JScript] The following example defines two properties. The first property is writable and the **CanWrite** property is **true**. The second property is not writable (there is no **set** accessor), and the **CanWrite** property is **false**.

[Visual Basic]
```
Imports System
Imports System.Reflection
Imports Microsoft.VisualBasic

' Define one writable property and one not writable.
Public Class Mypropertya
    Private myCaption As String = "A Default caption"

    Public Property Caption() As String
        Get
            Return myCaption
        End Get
        Set(ByVal Value As String)
            If myCaption <> value Then
                myCaption = value
            End If
        End Set
    End Property
End Class

Public Class Mypropertyb
    Private myCaption As String = "B Default caption"

    Public ReadOnly Property Caption() As String
        Get
            Return myCaption
        End Get
    End Property
End Class

Class Mypropertyinfo

    Public Shared Function Main() As Integer
        Console.WriteLine(ControlChars.CrLf & _
"Reflection.PropertyInfo")

        ' Define two properties.
        Dim Mypropertya As New Mypropertya()
        Dim Mypropertyb As New Mypropertyb()

        ' Read and display the property.
        Console.Write(ControlChars.CrLf & "Mypropertya.Caption = " & _
```

```
        Mypropertya.Caption)
        Console.Write(ControlChars.CrLf & "Mypropertyb.Caption = " & _
           Mypropertyb.Caption)

        ' Write to the property.
        Mypropertya.Caption = "A- No Change"
        ' Mypropertyb.Caption cannot be written to because
        ' there is no set accessor.
        ' Read and display the property.
        Console.Write(ControlChars.CrLf & "Mypropertya.Caption = " & _
           Mypropertya.Caption)
        Console.Write(ControlChars.CrLf & "Mypropertyb.Caption = " & _
           Mypropertyb.Caption)

        ' Get the type and PropertyInfo.
        Dim MyTypea As Type = Type.GetType("Mypropertya")
        Dim Mypropertyinfoa As PropertyInfo = _
MyTypea.GetProperty("Caption")
        Dim MyTypeb As Type = Type.GetType("Mypropertyb")
        Dim Mypropertyinfob As PropertyInfo = _
MyTypeb.GetProperty("Caption")

        ' Get and display the CanWrite property.
        Console.Write(ControlChars.CrLf & "CanWrite a - " & _
           Mypropertyinfoa.CanWrite)

        Console.Write(ControlChars.CrLf & "CanWrite b - " & _
           Mypropertyinfob.CanWrite)

        Return 0
    End Function
End Class
```

```
[C#]
using System;
using System.Reflection;

// Define one writable property and one not writable.
public class Mypropertya
{
    private string caption = "A Default caption";
    public string Caption
    {
        get{return caption;}
        set {if(caption!=value) {caption = value;}
        }
    }
}
public class Mypropertyb
{
    private string caption = "B Default caption";
    public string Caption
    {
        get{return caption;}
    }
}

class Mypropertyinfo
{
    public static int Main()
    {
        Console.WriteLine("\nReflection.PropertyInfo");

        // Define two properties.
        Mypropertya Mypropertya = new Mypropertya();
        Mypropertyb Mypropertyb = new Mypropertyb();

        // Read and display the property.
        Console.Write("\nMypropertya.Caption = " +
Mypropertya.Caption);
        Console.Write("\nMypropertyb.Caption = " +
Mypropertyb.Caption);

        // Write to the property.
        Mypropertya.Caption = "A- No Change";
```

```
        // Mypropertyb.Caption cannot be written to because
        // there is no set accessor.

        // Read and display the property.
        Console.Write("\nMypropertya.Caption = " +
Mypropertya.Caption);
        Console.Write ("\nMypropertyb.Caption = " +
Mypropertyb.Caption);

        // Get the type and PropertyInfo.
        Type MyTypea = Type.GetType("Mypropertya");
        PropertyInfo Mypropertyinfoa = MyTypea.GetProperty("Caption");
        Type MyTypeb = Type.GetType("Mypropertyb");
        PropertyInfo Mypropertyinfob = MyTypeb.GetProperty("Caption");

        // Get and display the CanWrite property.

        Console.Write("\nCanWrite a - " + Mypropertyinfoa.CanWrite);

        Console.Write("\nCanWrite b - " + Mypropertyinfob.CanWrite);

        return 0;
    }
}
```

```
[JScript]
import System;
import System.Reflection;

//Make two properties, one writable and one not writable
public class Mypropertya
{
    private var caption : String = "A Default caption";
    public function get Caption() : String {
        return caption;
    }
    public function set Caption(value:String) {
        if(caption!=value) {caption = value;}
    }
}
public class Mypropertyb
{
    private var caption : String = "B Default caption";
    public function get Caption() : String {
        return caption;
    }
}

class Mypropertyinfo
{
    public static function Main() : void
    {
        Console.WriteLine("\nReflection.PropertyInfo");

        //Build two properties
        var mypropertya : Mypropertya = new Mypropertya();
        var mypropertyb : Mypropertyb = new Mypropertyb();

        //Read and display the property
        Console.Write("\nmypropertya.Caption = " + mypropertya.Caption);
        Console.Write("\nmypropertyb.Caption = " + mypropertyb.Caption);

        //Write to the property
        mypropertya.Caption = "A- I have been changed";
        //Note: Mypropertyb.Caption cannot be written as
        // there is no set accessor

        //Read and display the property
        Console.Write("\nmypropertya.Caption = " + mypropertya.Caption);
        Console.Write ("\nmypropertyb.Caption = " + mypropertyb.Caption);

        //Get the type and PropertyInfo
        var MyTypea : Type = Type.GetType("Mypropertya");
        var Mypropertyinfoa : PropertyInfo =
MyTypea.GetProperty("Caption");
```

```
    var MyTypeb : Type = Type.GetType("Mypropertyb");
    var Mypropertyinfob : PropertyInfo =                                ⌐
MyTypeb.GetProperty("Caption");

    //Get and display the CanWrite property

    Console.Write("\nCanWrite a - " + Mypropertyinfoa.CanWrite);

    Console.Write("\nCanWrite b - " + Mypropertyinfob.CanWrite);
    }
}
Mypropertyinfo.Main();
/*
This code produces the following output:

Reflection.PropertyInfo

mypropertya.Caption = A Default caption
mypropertyb.Caption = B Default caption
mypropertya.Caption = A- I have been changed
mypropertyb.Caption = B Default caption
CanWrite a - true
CanWrite b - false
*/
```

Requirements

Platforms: Windows 98, Windows NT 4.0,
Windows Millennium Edition, Windows 2000,
Windows XP Home Edition, Windows XP Professional,
Windows .NET Server family,
.NET Compact Framework - Windows CE .NET,
Common Language Infrastructure (CLI) Standard

PropertyInfo.IsSpecialName Property

Gets a value indicating whether the property is the special name.

```
[Visual Basic]
Public ReadOnly Property IsSpecialName As Boolean
[C#]
public bool IsSpecialName {get;}
[C++]
public: __property bool get_IsSpecialName();
[JScript]
public function get IsSpecialName() : Boolean;
```

Property Value

true if this property is the special name; otherwise, **false**.

Remarks

The **SpecialName** bit is set to flag members that are treated in a special way by some compilers (such as property accessors and operator overloading methods).

To get the **IsSpecialName** property, first get the class **Type**. From the **Type**, get the **PropertyInfo**. From the **PropertyInfo**, get the **IsSpecialName** value.

Requirements

Platforms: Windows 98, Windows NT 4.0,
Windows Millennium Edition, Windows 2000,
Windows XP Home Edition, Windows XP Professional,
Windows .NET Server family,
.NET Compact Framework - Windows CE .NET

PropertyInfo.MemberType Property

Gets the **Type** of property reflected by this **PropertyInfo** object.

```
[Visual Basic]
Overrides Public ReadOnly Property MemberType As MemberTypes
[C#]
public override MemberTypes MemberType {get;}
[C++]
public: __property MemberTypes get_MemberType();
[JScript]
public override function get MemberType() : MemberTypes;
```

Property Value

A **MemberTypes** object representing the type of the property.

Remarks

MemberType is a derived class of **MemberInfo** and specifies the type of member this is. Member types are constructors, properties, fields, and methods. Since this is a **PropertyInfo** property, the returned type is a property.

To get the **MemberType** property, first get the class **Type**. From the **Type**, get the **PropertyInfo**. From the **PropertyInfo**, get the **MemberType** value.

Example

[Visual Basic, C#, JScript] The following example displays the type of the specified member.

```
[Visual Basic]
Imports System
Imports System.Reflection
Imports Microsoft.VisualBasic

Class Mypropertyinfo

    Public Shared Function Main() As Integer
        Console.WriteLine(ControlChars.CrLf &                        ⌐
"Reflection.PropertyInfo")

        ' Get the type and PropertyInfo.
        Dim MyType As Type =                                         ⌐
Type.GetType("System.Reflection.MemberInfo")
        Dim Mypropertyinfo As PropertyInfo = MyType.GetProperty("Name")

        ' Read and display the MemberType property.
        Console.WriteLine("MemberType = " & _
            Mypropertyinfo.MemberType.ToString())

        Return 0
    End Function
End Class

[C#]
using System;
using System.Reflection;

class Mypropertyinfo
{
    public static int Main()
    {
        Console.WriteLine("\nReflection.PropertyInfo");

        // Get the type and PropertyInfo.
        Type MyType = Type.GetType("System.Reflection.MemberInfo");
        PropertyInfo Mypropertyinfo = MyType.GetProperty("Name");

        // Read and display the MemberType property.
        Console.Write("\nMemberType = " +                           ⌐
Mypropertyinfo.MemberType.ToString());
```

```
            return 0;
        }
    }
```

[JScript]
```
import System;
import System.Reflection;

class Mypropertyinfo
{
    public static function Main() : void
    {
        Console.WriteLine("\nReflection.PropertyInfo");

        //Get the type and PropertyInfo
        var MyType : Type = Type.GetType("System.Reflection.MemberInfo");
        var Mypropertyinfo : PropertyInfo = MyType.GetProperty("Name");

        //Read and display the MemberType property
        Console.Write("\nMemberType = " +
Mypropertyinfo.MemberType.ToString());
    }
}
Mypropertyinfo.Main();
/*
Produces the following output

Reflection.PropertyInfo
MemberType = Property
*/
```

Requirements

Platforms: Windows 98, Windows NT 4.0,
Windows Millennium Edition, Windows 2000,
Windows XP Home Edition, Windows XP Professional,
Windows .NET Server family,
.NET Compact Framework - Windows CE .NET

PropertyInfo.PropertyType Property

Gets the type of this property.

[Visual Basic]
```
Public MustOverride ReadOnly Property PropertyType As Type
```
[C#]
```
public abstract Type PropertyType {get;}
```
[C++]
```
public: __property virtual Type* get_PropertyType() = 0;
```
[JScript]
```
public abstract function get PropertyType() : Type;
```

Property Value

The type of this property.

Remarks

The **Type** is **String**, **Boolean**, **Int32**, and so on.

To get the **PropertyType** property, first get the class **Type**. From the
Type, get the **PropertyInfo**. From the **PropertyInfo**, get the
PropertyType value.

Example

[Visual Basic, C#, JScript] The following example displays the data
type of the specified property.

[Visual Basic]
```
Imports System
Imports System.Reflection
Imports Microsoft.VisualBasic
```

```
Class Mypropertyinfo

    Public Shared Function Main() As Integer
        Console.WriteLine(ControlChars.CrLf &
"Reflection.PropertyInfo")

        ' Get the type and PropertyInfo.
        Dim MyTypea As Type =
Type.GetType("System.Reflection.MemberInfo")
        Dim Mypropertyinfoa As PropertyInfo =
MyTypea.GetProperty("Name")
        Dim MyTypeb As Type =
Type.GetType("System.Reflection.MethodBase")
        Dim Mypropertyinfob As PropertyInfo =
MyTypeb.GetProperty("IsFinal")

        ' Read and display the PropertyType property.
        Console.WriteLine(MyTypea.FullName & "." & Mypropertyinfoa.Name &
_
            " has a PropertyType of " &
Mypropertyinfoa.PropertyType.ToString())
        Console.WriteLine(MyTypeb.FullName & "." &
Mypropertyinfob.Name & _
            " has a PropertyType of " &
Mypropertyinfob.PropertyType.ToString())

        Return 0
    End Function
End Class
```

[C#]
```
using System;
using System.Reflection;

class Mypropertyinfo
{
    public static int Main()
    {
        Console.WriteLine("\nReflection.PropertyInfo");

        // Get the type and PropertyInfo.
        Type MyTypea = Type.GetType("System.Reflection.MemberInfo");
        PropertyInfo Mypropertyinfoa = MyTypea.GetProperty("Name");
        Type MyTypeb = Type.GetType("System.Reflection.MethodBase");
        PropertyInfo Mypropertyinfob = MyTypeb.GetProperty("IsFinal");

        // Read and display the PropertyType property.
        Console.Write ("\n" + MyTypea.FullName + "." +
Mypropertyinfoa.Name +
            " has a PropertyType of " + Mypropertyinfoa.PropertyType);
        Console.Write("\n" + MyTypeb.FullName + "." +
Mypropertyinfob.Name +
            " has a PropertyType of " + Mypropertyinfob.PropertyType);

        return 0;
    }
}
```

[JScript]
```
import System;
import System.Reflection;

class Mypropertyinfo
{
    public static function Main() : void
    {
        Console.WriteLine("\nReflection.PropertyInfo");

        //Get the type and PropertyInfo
        var MyTypea : Type =
Type.GetType("System.Reflection.MemberInfo");
        var Mypropertyinfoa : PropertyInfo =
MyTypea.GetProperty("Name");
        var MyTypeb : Type =
Type.GetType("System.Reflection.MethodBase");
```

```
        var Mypropertyinfob : PropertyInfo =
MyTypeb.GetProperty("IsFinal");

        //Read and display the PropertyType property
        Console.Write ("\n" + MyTypea.FullName + "." +
Mypropertyinfoa.Name +
            " has a PropertyType of " + Mypropertyinfoa.PropertyType);
        Console.Write("\n" + MyTypeb.FullName + "." +
Mypropertyinfob.Name +
            " has a PropertyType of " + Mypropertyinfob.PropertyType);

    }
}
Mypropertyinfo.Main();
/*
Produces the following output

Reflection.PropertyInfo
System.Reflection.MemberInfo.Name has a PropertyType of System.String
System.Reflection.MethodBase.IsFinal has a PropertyType of Boolean
*/
```

Requirements

Platforms: Windows 98, Windows NT 4.0,
Windows Millennium Edition, Windows 2000,
Windows XP Home Edition, Windows XP Professional,
Windows .NET Server family,
.NET Compact Framework - Windows CE .NET,
Common Language Infrastructure (CLI) Standard

PropertyInfo.GetAccessors Method

Returns an array of the **get** and **set** accessors on this property.

Overload List

Returns an array whose elements reflect the public **get**, **set**, and other accessors of the property reflected by the current instance.

Supported by the .NET Compact Framework.

[Visual Basic] **Overloads Public Function GetAccessors() As MethodInfo()**

[C#] **public MethodInfo[] GetAccessors();**

[C++] **public: MethodInfo* GetAccessors() [];**

[JScript] **public function GetAccessors() : MethodInfo[];**

Returns an array whose elements reflect the public and, if specified, non-public **get**, **set**, and other accessors of the property reflected by the current instance.

Supported by the .NET Compact Framework.

[Visual Basic] **Overloads Public MustOverride Function GetAccessors(Boolean) As MethodInfo()**

[C#] **public abstract MethodInfo[] GetAccessors(bool);**

[C++] **public: virtual MethodInfo* GetAccessors(bool) [] = 0;**

[JScript] **public abstract function GetAccessors(Boolean) : MethodInfo[];**

Example

[Visual Basic, C#, JScript] The following example displays the accessors of the specified property.

> [Visual Basic, C#, JScript] **Note** This example shows how to use one of the overloaded versions of **GetAccessors**. For other examples that might be available, see the individual overload topics.

```
[Visual Basic]
Imports System
Imports System.Reflection
Imports Microsoft.VisualBasic

' Define a property.
Public Class Myproperty
    Private myCaption As String = "A Default caption"

    Public Property Caption() As String
        Get
            Return myCaption
        End Get
        Set(ByVal Value As String)
            If myCaption <> value Then
                myCaption = value
            End If
        End Set
    End Property
End Class

Class Mypropertyinfo

    Public Shared Function Main() As Integer
        Console.WriteLine(ControlChars.CrLf & _
"Reflection.PropertyInfo")

        ' Get the type and PropertyInfo.
        Dim MyType As Type = Type.GetType("Myproperty")
        Dim Mypropertyinfo As PropertyInfo = _
MyType.GetProperty("Caption")

        ' Get the public GetAccessors method.
        Dim Mymethodinfoarray As MethodInfo() = _
            Mypropertyinfo.GetAccessors(True)
        Console.Write(ControlChars.CrLf & "There are " & _
            Mymethodinfoarray.Length & " accessors (public).")

        Return 0
    End Function
End Class

[C#]
using System;
using System.Reflection;

// Define a property.
public class Myproperty
{
    private string caption = "A Default caption";
    public string Caption
    {
        get{return caption;}
        set {if(caption!=value) {caption = value;}
        }
    }
}

class Mypropertyinfo
{
    public static int Main()
    {
        Console.WriteLine ("\nReflection.PropertyInfo");

        // Get the type and PropertyInfo.
        Type MyType = Type.GetType("Myproperty");
        PropertyInfo Mypropertyinfo = MyType.GetProperty("Caption");

        // Get the public GetAccessors method.
        MethodInfo[] Mymethodinfoarray =
Mypropertyinfo.GetAccessors(true);
        Console.Write ("\nThere are "
            + Mymethodinfoarray.Length + " accessors (public).");

        return 0;
    }
}
```

```
[JScript]
import System;
import System.Reflection;

//Make a property
public class Myproperty
{
    private var caption : String = "A Default caption";
    public function get Caption() : String {
        return caption;
    }
    public function set Caption(value:String) {
        if(caption!=value) caption = value;
    }
}

class Mypropertyinfo
{
    public static function Main() : void
    {
        Console.WriteLine ("\nReflection.PropertyInfo");

        //Get the type and PropertyInfo
        var MyType : Type = Type.GetType("Myproperty");
        var Mypropertyinfo : PropertyInfo =
MyType.GetProperty("Caption");

        //Get the public GetAccessors Method
        var Mymethodinfoarray : MethodInfo[] =
Mypropertyinfo.GetAccessors(true);
        Console.Write ("\nThere are "
            + Mymethodinfoarray.Length + "accessors (public)");
    }
}
Mypropertyinfo.Main();
/*
Produces the following output

Reflection.PropertyInfo
There are 2 accessors (public)
*/
```

PropertyInfo.GetAccessors Method ()

Returns an array whose elements reflect the public **get**, **set**, and other accessors of the property reflected by the current instance.

```
[Visual Basic]
Overloads Public Function GetAccessors() As MethodInfo()
[C#]
public MethodInfo[] GetAccessors();
[C++]
public: MethodInfo* GetAccessors() [];
[JScript]
public function GetAccessors() : MethodInfo[];
```

Return Value

An array of **MethodInfo** objects that reflect the public **get**, **set**, and other accessors of the property reflected by the current instance, if found; otherwise, this method returns an array with zero (0) elements.

Requirements

Platforms: Windows 98, Windows NT 4.0, Windows Millennium Edition, Windows 2000, Windows XP Home Edition, Windows XP Professional, Windows .NET Server family, .NET Compact Framework - Windows CE .NET, Common Language Infrastructure (CLI) Standard

.NET Framework Security:

- **ReflectionPermission** to enhance security and performance when invoked late-bound through mechanisms such as **Type.InvokeMember**. Associated enumeration: **ReflectionPermissionFlag.MemberAccess**.

PropertyInfo.GetAccessors Method (Boolean)

Returns an array whose elements reflect the public and, if specified, non-public **get**, **set**, and other accessors of the property reflected by the current instance.

```
[Visual Basic]
Overloads Public MustOverride Function GetAccessors( _
    ByVal nonOverloads Public As Boolean _
) As MethodInfo()
[C#]
public abstract MethodInfo[] GetAccessors(
    bool nonPublic
);
[C++]
public: virtual MethodInfo* GetAccessors(
    bool nonPublic
) [] = 0;
[JScript]
public abstract function GetAccessors(
    nonPublic : Boolean
) : MethodInfo[];
```

Parameters

nonPublic

Indicates whether non-public methods should be returned in the **MethodInfo** array. **true** if non-public methods are to be included; otherwise, **false**.

Return Value

An array of **MethodInfo** objects whose elements reflect the **get**, **set**, and other accessors of the property reflected by the current instance. If *nonPublic* is **true**, this array contains public and non-public **get**, **set**, and other accessors. If *nonPublic* is **false**, this array contains only public **get**, **set**, and other accessors. If no accessors with the specified visibility are found, this method returns an array with zero (0) elements.

Remarks

To use the **GetAccessors** method, first get the class **Type**. From the **Type**, get the **PropertyInfo**. From the **PropertyInfo**, use the **GetAccessors** method.

Example

[Visual Basic, C#, JScript] The following example displays the accessors of the specified property.

```
[Visual Basic]
Imports System
Imports System.Reflection
Imports Microsoft.VisualBasic

' Define a property.
Public Class Myproperty
    Private myCaption As String = "A Default caption"

    Public Property Caption() As String
        Get
            Return myCaption
        End Get
        Set(ByVal Value As String)
```

```
            If myCaption <> value Then
                myCaption = value
            End If
        End Set
    End Property
End Class

Class Mypropertyinfo

    Public Shared Function Main() As Integer
        Console.WriteLine(ControlChars.CrLf & _
"Reflection.PropertyInfo")

        ' Get the type and PropertyInfo.
        Dim MyType As Type = Type.GetType("Myproperty")
        Dim Mypropertyinfo As PropertyInfo = _
MyType.GetProperty("Caption")

        ' Get the public GetAccessors method.
        Dim Mymethodinfoarray As MethodInfo() = _
            Mypropertyinfo.GetAccessors(True)
        Console.Write(ControlChars.CrLf & "There are " & _
            Mymethodinfoarray.Length & " accessors (public).")

        Return 0
    End Function
End Class

[C#]
using System;
using System.Reflection;

// Define a property.
public class Myproperty
{
    private string caption = "A Default caption";
    public string Caption
    {
        get{return caption;}
        set {if(caption!=value) {caption = value;}
        }
    }
}

class Mypropertyinfo
{
    public static int Main()
    {
        Console.WriteLine ("\nReflection.PropertyInfo");

        // Get the type and PropertyInfo.
        Type MyType = Type.GetType("Myproperty");
        PropertyInfo Mypropertyinfo = MyType.GetProperty("Caption");

        // Get the public GetAccessors method.
        MethodInfo[] Mymethodinfoarray =
Mypropertyinfo.GetAccessors(true);
        Console.Write ("\nThere are "
            + Mymethodinfoarray.Length + " accessors (public).");

        return 0;
    }
}

[JScript]
import System;
import System.Reflection;

//Make a property
public class Myproperty
{
    private var caption : String = "A Default caption";
    public function get Caption() : String {
        return caption;
    }
    public function set Caption(value:String) {
```

```
        if(caption!=value) caption = value;
    }
}

class Mypropertyinfo
{
    public static function Main() : void
    {
        Console.WriteLine ("\nReflection.PropertyInfo");

        //Get the type and PropertyInfo
        var MyType : Type = Type.GetType("Myproperty");
        var Mypropertyinfo : PropertyInfo =
MyType.GetProperty("Caption");

        //Get the public GetAccessors Method
        var Mymethodinfoarray : MethodInfo[] =
Mypropertyinfo.GetAccessors(true);
        Console.Write ("\nThere are "
            + Mymethodinfoarray.Length + "accessors (public)");
    }
}
Mypropertyinfo.Main();
/*
Produces the following output

Reflection.PropertyInfo
There are 2 accessors (public)
*/
```

Requirements

Platforms: Windows 98, Windows NT 4.0,
Windows Millennium Edition, Windows 2000,
Windows XP Home Edition, Windows XP Professional,
Windows .NET Server family,
.NET Compact Framework - Windows CE .NET,
Common Language Infrastructure (CLI) Standard

.NET Framework Security:

- **ReflectionPermission** to enhance security and performance when invoked late-bound through mechanisms such as **Type.InvokeMember**. Associated enumeration: **ReflectionPermissionFlag.MemberAccess**.

PropertyInfo.GetGetMethod Method

Returns a **MethodInfo** representing the **get** accessor for this property.

Overload List

Returns the public **get** accessor for this property.

Supported by the .NET Compact Framework.

[Visual Basic] **Overloads Public Function GetGetMethod() As MethodInfo**

[C#] **public MethodInfo GetGetMethod();**

[C++] **public: MethodInfo* GetGetMethod();**

[JScript] **public function GetGetMethod() : MethodInfo;**

When overridden in a derived class, returns the public or non-public **get** accessor for this property.

Supported by the .NET Compact Framework.

[Visual Basic] **Overloads Public MustOverride Function GetGetMethod(Boolean) As MethodInfo**

[C#] **public abstract MethodInfo GetGetMethod(bool);**

[C++] **public: virtual MethodInfo* GetGetMethod(bool) = 0;**

[JScript] **public abstract function GetGetMethod(Boolean) : MethodInfo;**

Example

[Visual Basic, C#, JScript] The following example displays the public or non-public **get** accessor for the specified property.

[Visual Basic, C#, JScript] **Note** This example shows how to use one of the overloaded versions of **GetGetMethod**. For other examples that might be available, see the individual overload topics.

[Visual Basic]
```
Imports System
Imports System.Reflection
Imports Microsoft.VisualBasic

' Define a property.
Public Class Myproperty
    Private myCaption As String = "A Default caption"

    Public Property Caption() As String
        Get
            Return myCaption
        End Get
        Set(ByVal Value As String)
            If myCaption <> value Then
                myCaption = value
            End If
        End Set
    End Property
End Class

Class Mypropertyinfo

    Public Shared Function Main() As Integer
        Console.WriteLine(ControlChars.CrLf & _
"Reflection.PropertyInfo")

        ' Get the type and PropertyInfo for two separate properties.
        Dim MyTypea As Type = Type.GetType("Myproperty")
        Dim Mypropertyinfoa As PropertyInfo = _
MyTypea.GetProperty("Caption")
        Dim MyTypeb As Type = _
Type.GetType("System.Reflection.MethodInfo")
        Dim Mypropertyinfob As PropertyInfo = _
MyTypeb.GetProperty("MemberType")

        ' Get and display the GetGetMethod Method for each property.
        Dim Mygetmethodinfoa As MethodInfo = _
Mypropertyinfoa.GetGetMethod()
        Console.WriteLine("GetAccessor for " & _
            Mypropertyinfoa.Name & " returns a " & _
            Mygetmethodinfoa.ReturnType.ToString())
        Dim Mygetmethodinfob As MethodInfo = _
Mypropertyinfob.GetGetMethod()
        Console.WriteLine("GetAccessor for " & _
            Mypropertyinfob.Name & " returns a " & _
            Mygetmethodinfob.ReturnType.ToString())

        ' Display the GetGetMethod without using the MethodInfo.
        Console.WriteLine(MyTypea.FullName & "." & _
            Mypropertyinfoa.Name & " GetGetMethod - " & _
            Mypropertyinfoa.GetGetMethod().ToString())
        Console.WriteLine(MyTypeb.FullName & "." & _
            Mypropertyinfob.Name & " GetGetMethod - " & _
            Mypropertyinfob.GetGetMethod().ToString())
        Return 0
    End Function
End Class
```

[C#]
```
using System;
using System.Reflection;

// Define a property.
public class Myproperty
{
    private string caption = "A Default caption";
    public string Caption
    {
        get{return caption;}
        set {if(caption!=value) {caption = value;}
        }
    }
}

class Mypropertyinfo
{
    public static int Main()
    {
        Console.WriteLine ("\nReflection.PropertyInfo");

        // Get the type and PropertyInfo for two separate properties.
        Type MyTypea = Type.GetType("Myproperty");
        PropertyInfo Mypropertyinfoa = MyTypea.GetProperty("Caption");
        Type MyTypeb = Type.GetType("System.Reflection.MethodInfo");
        PropertyInfo Mypropertyinfob =
MyTypeb.GetProperty("MemberType");

        // Get and display the GetGetMethod method for each property.
        MethodInfo Mygetmethodinfoa = Mypropertyinfoa.GetGetMethod();
        Console.Write ("\nGetAccessor for " + Mypropertyinfoa.Name
            + " returns a " + Mygetmethodinfoa.ReturnType);
        MethodInfo Mygetmethodinfob = Mypropertyinfob.GetGetMethod();
        Console.Write ("\nGetAccessor for " + Mypropertyinfob.Name
            + " returns a " + Mygetmethodinfob.ReturnType);

        // Display the GetGetMethod without using the MethodInfo.
        Console.Write ("\n" + MyTypea.FullName + "." +
Mypropertyinfoa.Name
            + " GetGetMethod - " + Mypropertyinfoa.GetGetMethod());
        Console.Write ("\n" + MyTypeb.FullName + "." +
Mypropertyinfob.Name
            + " GetGetMethod - " + Mypropertyinfob.GetGetMethod());
        return 0;
    }
}
```

[JScript]
```
import System;
import System.Reflection;

//Make a property
public class Myproperty
{
    private var caption : String = "A Default caption";
    public function get Caption() : String {
        return caption;
    }
    public function set Caption(value:String) {
        if(caption!=value) caption = value;
    }
}

class Mypropertyinfo
{
    public static function Main() : void
    {
        Console.WriteLine ("\nReflection.PropertyInfo");

        //Get the type and PropertyInfo for two separate properties
        var MyTypea : Type = Type.GetType("Myproperty");
        var Mypropertyinfoa : PropertyInfo =
MyTypea.GetProperty("Caption");
        var MyTypeb : Type =
Type.GetType("System.Reflection.MethodInfo");
        var Mypropertyinfob : PropertyInfo =
MyTypeb.GetProperty("MemberType");
```

```
//Get and display the GetGetMethod Method for each property
    var Mygetmethodinfoa : MethodInfo =
Mypropertyinfoa.GetGetMethod();
        Console.Write ("\nGetAccessor for " + Mypropertyinfoa.Name
            + " returns a " + Mygetmethodinfoa.ReturnType);
    var Mygetmethodinfob : MethodInfo =
Mypropertyinfob.GetGetMethod();
        Console.Write ("\nGetAccessor for " + Mypropertyinfob.Name
            + " returns a " + Mygetmethodinfob.ReturnType);

        //Display the GetGetMethod without using the MethodInfo
        Console.Write ("\n" + MyTypea.FullName + "." +
Mypropertyinfoa.Name
            + " GetGetMethod - " + Mypropertyinfoa.GetGetMethod());
        Console.Write ("\n" + MyTypeb.FullName + "." +
Mypropertyinfob.Name
            + " GetGetMethod - " + Mypropertyinfob.GetGetMethod());
    }
}
Mypropertyinfo.Main();
/*
Produces the following output

Reflection.PropertyInfo
GetAccessor for Caption returns a System.String
GetAccessor for MemberType returns a System.Reflection.MemberTypes
Myproperty.Caption GetGetMethod - System.String get_Caption()
System.Reflection.MethodInfo.MemberType GetGetMethod -
System.Reflection.MemberTypes get_MemberType()
*/
```

PropertyInfo.GetGetMethod Method ()

Returns the public **get** accessor for this property.

```
[Visual Basic]
Overloads Public Function GetGetMethod() As MethodInfo
[C#]
public MethodInfo GetGetMethod();
[C++]
public: MethodInfo* GetGetMethod();
[JScript]
public function GetGetMethod() : MethodInfo;
```

Return Value

A **MethodInfo** object representing the public **get** accessor for this property, or a null reference (**Nothing** in Visual Basic) if the **get** accessor is non-public or does not exist.

Remarks

This is a convenience method that provides an implementation for the abstract **GetGetMethod** method with the *nonPublic* parameter set to **false**.

To use the **GetGetMethod** method, first get the class **Type**. From the **Type**, get the **PropertyInfo**. From the **PropertyInfo**, use the **GetGetMethod** method.

Requirements

Platforms: Windows 98, Windows NT 4.0, Windows Millennium Edition, Windows 2000, Windows XP Home Edition, Windows XP Professional, Windows .NET Server family, .NET Compact Framework - Windows CE .NET, Common Language Infrastructure (CLI) Standard

.NET Framework Security:

- **ReflectionPermission** to enhance security and performance when invoked late-bound through mechanisms such as **Type.InvokeMember**. Associated enumeration: **ReflectionPermissionFlag.MemberAccess**.

PropertyInfo.GetGetMethod Method (Boolean)

When overridden in a derived class, returns the public or non-public **get** accessor for this property.

```
[Visual Basic]
Overloads Public MustOverride Function GetGetMethod( _
    ByVal nonOverloads Public As Boolean _
) As MethodInfo
[C#]
public abstract MethodInfo GetGetMethod(
    bool nonPublic
);
[C++]
public: virtual MethodInfo* GetGetMethod(
    bool nonPublic
) = 0;
[JScript]
public abstract function GetGetMethod(
    nonPublic : Boolean
) : MethodInfo;
```

Parameters

nonPublic
    Indicates whether a non-public **get** accessor should be returned. **true** if a non-public accessor is to be returned; otherwise, **false**.

Return Value

A **MethodInfo** object representing the **get** accessor for this property, if *nonPublic* is **true**. Returns a null reference (**Nothing** in Visual Basic) if *nonPublic* is **false** and the **get** accessor is non-public, or if *nonPublic* is **true** but no **get** accessors exist.

Exceptions

Exception Type	Condition
SecurityException	The requested method is non-public and the caller does not have **ReflectionPermission** to reflect on this non-public method.

Remarks

This property is the **MethodInfo** representing the get accessor.

To use the **GetGetMethod** method, first get the class **Type**. From the **Type**, get the **PropertyInfo**. From the **PropertyInfo**, use the **GetGetMethod** method.

Example

See related example in the **System.Reflection.PropertyInfo.GetGetMethod** method topic.

Requirements

Platforms: Windows 98, Windows NT 4.0, Windows Millennium Edition, Windows 2000, Windows XP Home Edition, Windows XP Professional, Windows .NET Server family, .NET Compact Framework - Windows CE .NET, Common Language Infrastructure (CLI) Standard

.NET Framework Security:

- **ReflectionPermission** to enhance security and performance when invoked late-bound through mechanisms such as **Type.InvokeMember**. Associated enumeration: **ReflectionPermissionFlag.MemberAccess**.

- **ReflectionPermission** for reflecting methods that are not public. Associated enumeration: **ReflectionPermissionFlag.TypeInformation**

PropertyInfo.GetIndexParameters Method

When overridden in a derived class, returns an array of all the index parameters for the property.

```
[Visual Basic]
Public MustOverride Function GetIndexParameters() As ParameterInfo()
[C#]
public abstract ParameterInfo[] GetIndexParameters();
[C++]
public: virtual ParameterInfo* GetIndexParameters() [] = 0;
[JScript]
public abstract function GetIndexParameters() : ParameterInfo[];
```

Return Value

An array of type **ParameterInfo** containing the parameters for the indexes.

Remarks

Extract any required parameter information from the returned array.

To use the **GetIndexParameters** method, first get the class **Type**. From the **Type**, get the **PropertyInfo**. From the **PropertyInfo**, use the **GetIndexParameters** method.

Example

See related example in the **System.Reflection.PropertyInfo.GetGetMethod** method topic.

Requirements

Platforms: Windows 98, Windows NT 4.0, Windows Millennium Edition, Windows 2000, Windows XP Home Edition, Windows XP Professional, Windows .NET Server family, .NET Compact Framework - Windows CE .NET, Common Language Infrastructure (CLI) Standard

.NET Framework Security:

- **ReflectionPermission** to enhance security and performance when invoked late-bound through mechanisms such as **Type.InvokeMember**. Associated enumeration: **ReflectionPermissionFlag.MemberAccess**.

- **ReflectionPermission** for reflecting objects that are not visible. Associated enumeration: **ReflectionPermissionFlag.TypeInformation**

PropertyInfo.GetSetMethod Method

Returns a **MethodInfo** representing the **set** accessor for this property.

Overload List

Returns the public **set** accessor for this property.

Supported by the .NET Compact Framework.

[Visual Basic] **Overloads Public Function GetSetMethod() As MethodInfo**

[C#] **public MethodInfo GetSetMethod();**

[C++] **public: MethodInfo* GetSetMethod();**

[JScript] **public function GetSetMethod() : MethodInfo;**

When overridden in a derived class, returns the **set** accessor for this property.

Supported by the .NET Compact Framework.

[Visual Basic] **Overloads Public MustOverride Function GetSetMethod(Boolean) As MethodInfo**

[C#] **public abstract MethodInfo GetSetMethod(bool);**

[C++] **public: virtual MethodInfo* GetSetMethod(bool) = 0;**

[JScript] **public abstract function GetSetMethod(Boolean) : MethodInfo;**

Example

See related example in the **System.Reflection.PropertyInfo.GetGetMethod** method topic.

PropertyInfo.GetSetMethod Method ()

Returns the public **set** accessor for this property.

```
[Visual Basic]
Overloads Public Function GetSetMethod() As MethodInfo
[C#]
public MethodInfo GetSetMethod();
[C++]
public: MethodInfo* GetSetMethod();
[JScript]
public function GetSetMethod() : MethodInfo;
```

Return Value

The **MethodInfo** object representing the **Set** method for this property if the **set** accessor is public, or a null reference (**Nothing** in Visual Basic) if the **set** accessor is not public.

Remarks

This is a convenience method that provides an implementation for the abstract **GetSetMethod** method with the *nonPublic* parameter set to **false**.

To use the **GetSetMethod** method, first get the class **Type**. From the **Type**, get the **PropertyInfo**. From the **PropertyInfo**, use the **GetSetMethod** method.

Requirements

Platforms: Windows 98, Windows NT 4.0, Windows Millennium Edition, Windows 2000, Windows XP Home Edition, Windows XP Professional, Windows .NET Server family, .NET Compact Framework - Windows CE .NET, Common Language Infrastructure (CLI) Standard

.NET Framework Security:

- **ReflectionPermission** to enhance security and performance when invoked late-bound through mechanisms such as **Type.InvokeMember**. Associated enumeration: **ReflectionPermissionFlag.MemberAccess**.

PropertyInfo.GetSetMethod Method (Boolean)

When overridden in a derived class, returns the **set** accessor for this property.

```
[Visual Basic]
Overloads Public MustOverride Function GetSetMethod( _
    ByVal nonOverloads Public As Boolean _
) As MethodInfo
[C#]
public abstract MethodInfo GetSetMethod(
    bool nonPublic
);
```

```
[C++]
public: virtual MethodInfo* GetSetMethod(
    bool nonPublic
) = 0;
[JScript]
public abstract function GetSetMethod(
    nonPublic : Boolean
) : MethodInfo;
```

Parameters

nonPublic

Indicates whether the accessor should be returned if it is non-public. **true** if a non-public accessor is to be returned; otherwise, **false**.

Return Value

Value	Condition
A **MethodInfo** object representing the **Set** method for this property.	The **set** accessor is public. -or- *nonPublic* is **true** and the **set** accessor is non-public.
A null reference (**Nothing** in Visual Basic)	*nonPublic* is **true**, but the property is read-only. -or- *nonPublic* is **false** and the **set** accessor is non-public. -or- There is no **set** accessor.

Exceptions

Exception Type	Condition
SecurityException	The requested method is non-public and the caller does not have **ReflectionPermission** to reflect on this non-public method.

Remarks

To use the **GetSetMethod** method, first get the class **Type**. From the **Type**, get the **PropertyInfo**. From the **PropertyInfo**, use the **GetSetMethod** method.

Example

See related example in the **System.Reflection.PropertyInfo.GetGetMethod** method topic.

Requirements

Platforms: Windows 98, Windows NT 4.0, Windows Millennium Edition, Windows 2000, Windows XP Home Edition, Windows XP Professional, Windows .NET Server family, .NET Compact Framework - Windows CE .NET, Common Language Infrastructure (CLI) Standard

.NET Framework Security:

• **ReflectionPermission** to enhance security and performance when invoked late-bound through mechanisms such as **Type.InvokeMember**. Associated enumeration: **ReflectionPermissionFlag.MemberAccess**.

• **ReflectionPermission** for reflecting methods that are not public. Associated enumeration: **ReflectionPermissionFlag.TypeInformation**

PropertyInfo.GetValue Method

Returns the value of the property.

Overload List

Returns the value of the property with optional index values for indexed properties.

Supported by the .NET Compact Framework.

[Visual Basic] **Overloads Public Overridable Function GetValue(Object, Object()) As Object**

[C#] **public virtual object GetValue(object, object[]);**

[C++] **public: virtual Object* GetValue(Object*, Object*[]);**

[JScript] **public function GetValue(Object, Object[]) : Object;**

When overridden in a derived class, returns the value of a property having the specified binding, index, and **CultureInfo**.

Supported by the .NET Compact Framework.

[Visual Basic] **Overloads Public MustOverride Function GetValue(Object, BindingFlags, Binder, Object(), CultureInfo) As Object**

[C#] **public abstract object GetValue(object, BindingFlags, Binder, object[], CultureInfo);**

[C++] **public: virtual Object* GetValue(Object*, BindingFlags, Binder*, Object*[], CultureInfo*) = 0;**

[JScript] **public abstract function GetValue(Object, BindingFlags, Binder, Object[], CultureInfo) : Object;**

PropertyInfo.GetValue Method (Object, Object[])

Returns the value of the property with optional index values for indexed properties.

```
[Visual Basic]
Overloads Public Overridable Function GetValue( _
    ByVal obj As Object, _
    ByVal index() As Object _
) As Object
[C#]
public virtual object GetValue(
    object obj,
    object[] index
);
[C++]
public: virtual Object* GetValue(
    Object* obj,
    Object* index __gc[]
);
[JScript]
public function GetValue(
    obj : Object,
    index : Object[]
) : Object;
```

Parameters

obj

The object whose property value will be returned.

index

Optional index values for indexed properties. This value should be a null reference (**Nothing** in Visual Basic) for non-indexed properties.

Return Value

The property value for the *obj* parameter.

Exceptions

Exception Type	Condition
ArgumentException	The *index* array does not contain the type of arguments needed.
	-or-
	The property's **Get** method is not found.
TargetException	The object does not match the target type, or a property is an instance property but *obj* is a null reference (**Nothing** in Visual Basic).
TargetParameterCount-Exception	The number of parameters in *index* does not match the number of parameters the indexed property takes.
MethodAccessException	There was an illegal attempt to access a private or protected method inside a class.

Remarks

This is a convenience method that provides an implementation for the abstract **GetValue** method with a **BindingFlags** parameter of **DefaultChangeType**, the **Binder** set to a null reference (**Nothing** in Visual Basic), and the **CultureInfo** set to a null reference (**Nothing**).

Because static properties belong to the type, not individual objects, get static properties by passing a null reference (**Nothing**) as the object argument. For example, use the following code to get the static **CurrentCulture** property of **CultureInfo**:

```
PropertyInfo CurCultProp =
            (typeof(CultureInfo)).GetProperty("CurrentCulture");
Console.WriteLine("CurrCult: " +
            CurCultProp.GetValue(null,null));
```

To use the **GetValue** method, first get the class **Type**. From the **Type**, get the **PropertyInfo**. From the **PropertyInfo**, use the **GetValue** method.

Requirements

Platforms: Windows 98, Windows NT 4.0, Windows Millennium Edition, Windows 2000, Windows XP Home Edition, Windows XP Professional, Windows .NET Server family, .NET Compact Framework - Windows CE .NET, Common Language Infrastructure (CLI) Standard

.NET Framework Security:

- **ReflectionPermission** to enhance security and performance when invoked late-bound through mechanisms such as **Type.InvokeMember**. Associated enumeration: **ReflectionPermissionFlag.MemberAccess**.
- **ReflectionPermission** for reflecting non-public objects. Associated enumeration: **ReflectionPermissionFlag.TypeInformation**

PropertyInfo.GetValue Method (Object, BindingFlags, Binder, Object[], CultureInfo)

When overridden in a derived class, returns the value of a property having the specified binding, index, and **CultureInfo**.

```
[Visual Basic]
Overloads Public MustOverride Function GetValue( _
    ByVal obj As Object, _
    ByVal invokeAttr As BindingFlags, _
    ByVal binder As Binder, _
    ByVal index() As Object, _
    ByVal culture As CultureInfo _
) As Object
[C#]
public abstract object GetValue(
    object obj,
    BindingFlags invokeAttr,
    Binder binder,
    object[] index,
    CultureInfo culture
);
[C++]
public: virtual Object* GetValue(
    Object* obj,
    BindingFlags invokeAttr,
    Binder* binder,
    Object* index __gc[],
    CultureInfo* culture
) = 0;
[JScript]
public abstract function GetValue(
    obj : Object,
    invokeAttr : BindingFlags,
    binder : Binder,
    index : Object[],
    culture : CultureInfo
) : Object;
```

Parameters

obj
    The object whose property value will be returned.

invokeAttr
    The invocation attribute. This must be a bit flag from **BindingFlags**: **InvokeMethod**, **CreateInstance**, **Static**, **GetField**, **SetField**, **GetProperty**, or **SetProperty**. A suitable invocation attribute must be specified. If a static member is to be invoked, the **Static** flag of **BindingFlags** must be set.

binder
    An object that enables the binding, coercion of argument types, invocation of members, and retrieval of **MemberInfo** objects via reflection. If *binder* is a null reference (**Nothing** in Visual Basic), the default binder is used.

index
    Optional index values for indexed properties. This value should be a null reference (**Nothing** in Visual Basic) for non-indexed properties.

culture
    The **CultureInfo** object that represents the culture for which the resource is to be localized. Note that if the resource is not localized for this culture, the **CultureInfo.Parent** method will be called successively in search of a match. If this value is a null reference (**Nothing** in Visual Basic), the **CultureInfo** is obtained from the **CultureInfo.CurrentUICulture** property.

Return Value

The property value for *obj*.

Exceptions

Exception Type	Condition
ArgumentException	The *index* array does not contain the type of arguments needed. -or- The property's **Get** method is not found.
TargetException	The object does not match the target type, or a property is an instance property but *obj* is a null reference (**Nothing** in Visual Basic).
TargetParameterCount-Exception	The number of parameters in *index* does not match the number of parameters the indexed property takes.
MethodAccessException	There was an illegal attempt to access a private or protected method inside a class.

Remarks

Because static properties belong to the type, not individual objects, get static properties by passing a null reference (**Nothing** in Visual Basic) as the object argument. For example, use the following code to get the static **CurrentCulture** property of **CultureInfo**:

```
PropertyInfo CurCultProp =
            (typeof(CultureInfo)).GetProperty("CurrentCulture");
Console.WriteLine("CurrCult: " +
            CurCultProp.GetValue(null,null));
```

To use the **GetValue** method, first get the class **Type**. From the **Type**, get the **PropertyInfo**. From the **PropertyInfo**, use the **GetValue** method.

Requirements

Platforms: Windows 98, Windows NT 4.0, Windows Millennium Edition, Windows 2000, Windows XP Home Edition, Windows XP Professional, Windows .NET Server family, .NET Compact Framework - Windows CE .NET, Common Language Infrastructure (CLI) Standard

.NET Framework Security:

- **ReflectionPermission** to enhance security and performance when invoked late-bound through mechanisms such as **Type.InvokeMember**. Associated enumeration: **ReflectionPermissionFlag.MemberAccess**.
- **ReflectionPermission** for reflecting non-public objects. Associated enumeration: **ReflectionPermissionFlag.TypeInformation**

PropertyInfo.SetValue Method

Sets the property value for the given object to the given value.

Overload List

Sets the value of the property with optional index values for index properties.

Supported by the .NET Compact Framework.

[Visual Basic] **Overloads Public Overridable Sub SetValue(Object, Object, Object())**

[C#] **public virtual void SetValue(object, object, object[]);**

[C++] **public: virtual void SetValue(Object*, Object*, Object*[]);**

[JScript] **public function SetValue(Object, Object, Object[]);**

When overridden in a derived class, sets the property value for the given object to the given value.

Supported by the .NET Compact Framework.

[Visual Basic] **Overloads Public MustOverride Sub SetValue(Object, Object, BindingFlags, Binder, Object(), CultureInfo)**

[C#] **public abstract void SetValue(object, object, BindingFlags, Binder, object[], CultureInfo);**

[C++] **public: virtual void SetValue(Object*, Object*, BindingFlags, Binder*, Object*[], CultureInfo*) = 0;**

[JScript] **public abstract function SetValue(Object, Object, BindingFlags, Binder, Object[], CultureInfo);**

Example

See related example in the **System.Reflection.PropertyInfo.GetGetMethod** method topic.

PropertyInfo.SetValue Method (Object, Object, Object[])

Sets the value of the property with optional index values for index properties.

```
[Visual Basic]
Overloads Public Overridable Sub SetValue( _
    ByVal obj As Object, _
    ByVal value As Object, _
    ByVal index() As Object _
)
[C#]
public virtual void SetValue(
    object obj,
    object value,
    object[] index
);
[C++]
public: virtual void SetValue(
    Object* obj,
    Object* value,
    Object* index __gc[]
);
[JScript]
public function SetValue(
    obj : Object,
    value : Object,
    index : Object[]
);
```

Parameters

obj
    The object whose property value will be set.

value
    The new value for this property.

index
    Optional index values for indexed properties. This value should be a null reference (**Nothing** in Visual Basic) for non-indexed properties.

Exceptions

Exception Type	Condition
ArgumentException	The *index* array does not contain the type of arguments needed. -or- The property's **Get** method is not found.
TargetException	The object does not match the target type, or a property is an instance property but *obj* is a null reference (**Nothing** in Visual Basic).
TargetParameterCount-Exception	The number of parameters in *index* does not match the number of parameters the indexed property takes.
MethodAccessException	There was an illegal attempt to access a private or protected method inside a class.

Remarks

This is a convenience method that provides an implementation for the abstract **SetValue** method with a **BindingFlags** parameter of **DefaultChangeType**, the **Binder** set to a null reference (**Nothing** in Visual Basic), and the **CultureInfo** set to a null reference (**Nothing**).

To use the **SetValue** method, first get the class **Type**. From the **Type**, get the **PropertyInfo**. From the **PropertyInfo**, use the **SetValue** method.

Requirements

Platforms: Windows 98, Windows NT 4.0, Windows Millennium Edition, Windows 2000, Windows XP Home Edition, Windows XP Professional, Windows .NET Server family, .NET Compact Framework - Windows CE .NET, Common Language Infrastructure (CLI) Standard

.NET Framework Security:

*   **ReflectionPermission** to enhance security and performance when invoked late-bound through mechanisms such as **Type.InvokeMember**. Associated enumeration: **ReflectionPermissionFlag.MemberAccess**.
*   **ReflectionPermission** for reflecting non-public objects. Associated enumerations: **ReflectionPermissionFlag.MemberAccess**, **ReflectionPermissionFlag.TypeInformation**

PropertyInfo.SetValue Method (Object, Object, BindingFlags, Binder, Object[], CultureInfo)

When overridden in a derived class, sets the property value for the given object to the given value.

```
[Visual Basic]
Overloads Public MustOverride Sub SetValue( _
   ByVal obj As Object, _
   ByVal value As Object, _
   ByVal invokeAttr As BindingFlags, _
   ByVal binder As Binder, _
   ByVal index() As Object, _
   ByVal culture As CultureInfo _
)
```

```
[C#]
public abstract void SetValue(
   object obj,
   object value,
   BindingFlags invokeAttr,
   Binder binder,
   object[] index,
   CultureInfo culture
);
```

```
[C++]
public: virtual void SetValue(
   Object* obj,
   Object* value,
   BindingFlags invokeAttr,
   Binder* binder,
   Object* index __gc[],
   CultureInfo* culture
) = 0;
```

```
[JScript]
public abstract function SetValue(
   obj : Object,
   value : Object,
   invokeAttr : BindingFlags,
   binder : Binder,
   index : Object[],
   culture : CultureInfo
);
```

Parameters

obj
    The object whose property value will be returned.
value
    The new value for this property.
invokeAttr
    The invocation attribute. This must be a bit flag from **BindingFlags**: **InvokeMethod**, **CreateInstance**, **Static**, **GetField**, **SetField**, **GetProperty**, or **SetProperty**. A suitable invocation attribute must be specified. If a static member is to be invoked, the **Static** flag of **BindingFlags** must be set.
binder
    An object that enables the binding, coercion of argument types, invocation of members, and retrieval of **MemberInfo** objects through reflection. If *binder* is a null reference (**Nothing** in Visual Basic), the default binder is used.
index
    Optional index values for indexed properties. This value should be a null reference (**Nothing** in Visual Basic) for non-indexed properties.
culture
    The **CultureInfo** object that represents the culture for which the resource is to be localized. Note that if the resource is not localized for this culture, the **CultureInfo.Parent** method will be called successively in search of a match. If this value is a null reference (**Nothing** in Visual Basic), the **CultureInfo** is obtained from the **CultureInfo.CurrentUICulture** property.

Return Value

An array of type **MethodInfo** containing the public accessors, or an empty array if there are no public accessors.

Exceptions

Exception Type	Condition
ArgumentException	The *index* array does not contain the type of arguments needed. -or- The property's **Get** method is not found.
TargetException	The object does not match the target type, or a property is an instance property but *obj* is a null reference (**Nothing** in Visual Basic).
TargetParameterCountEx ception	The number of parameters in *index* does not match the number of parameters the indexed property takes.
MethodAccessException	There was an illegal attempt to access a private or protected method inside a class.

Remarks

Access restrictions are ignored for fully trusted code. That is, private constructors, methods, fields, and properties can be accessed and invoked via Reflection whenever the code is fully trusted.

To use the **SetValue** method, first get the class **Type**. From the **Type**, get the **PropertyInfo**. From the **PropertyInfo**, use the **SetValue** method.

Example

See related example in the **System.Reflection.PropertyInfo.GetGetMethod** method topic.

Requirements

Platforms: Windows 98, Windows NT 4.0, Windows Millennium Edition, Windows 2000, Windows XP Home Edition, Windows XP Professional, Windows .NET Server family, .NET Compact Framework - Windows CE .NET, Common Language Infrastructure (CLI) Standard

.NET Framework Security:

- **ReflectionPermission** to enhance security and performance when invoked late-bound through mechanisms such as **Type.InvokeMember**. Associated enumeration: **ReflectionPermissionFlag.MemberAccess**.

- **ReflectionPermission** for reflecting non-public objects. Associated enumerations: **ReflectionPermissionFlag.MemberAccess**, **ReflectionPermissionFlag.TypeInformation**

ReflectionTypeLoadException Class

The exception that is thrown by the **Module.GetTypes** method if any of the classes in a module cannot be loaded. This class cannot be inherited.

System.Object
  System.Exception
    System.SystemException
      System.Reflection.ReflectionTypeLoadException

```
[Visual Basic]
<Serializable>
NotInheritable Public Class ReflectionTypeLoadException
    Inherits SystemException
[C#]
[Serializable]
public sealed class ReflectionTypeLoadException : SystemException
[C++]
[Serializable]
public __gc __sealed class ReflectionTypeLoadException : public
    SystemException
[JScript]
public
    Serializable
class ReflectionTypeLoadException extends SystemException
```

Thread Safety

Any public static (**Shared** in Visual Basic) members of this type are safe for multithreaded operations. Any instance members are not guaranteed to be thread safe.

Remarks

ReflectionTypeLoadException uses the HRESULT COR_E_REFLECTIONTYPELOAD that has the value 0x80131602.

An instance contains the array of classes (Types property) that were defined in the module and were loaded. The array can contain some null values. There is also another array of exceptions (**LoaderExceptions** property). This exception array represents the exceptions that were thrown by the class loader. The holes in the class array line up with the exceptions.

This exception exposes both the array of classes and the array of **TypeLoadExceptions**.

Requirements

Namespace: System.Reflection

Platforms: Windows 98, Windows NT 4.0, Windows Millennium Edition, Windows 2000, Windows XP Home Edition, Windows XP Professional, Windows .NET Server family

Assembly: Mscorlib (in Mscorlib.dll)

ReflectionTypeLoadException Constructor

Initializes a new instance of the **ReflectionTypeLoadException** class.

Overload List

Initializes a new instance of the **ReflectionTypeLoadException** class with the given classes and their associated exceptions.

> [Visual Basic] **Public Sub New(Type(), Exception())**
>
> [C#] **public ReflectionTypeLoadException(Type[], Exception[]);**
>
> [C++] **public: ReflectionTypeLoadException(Type*[], Exception[]);**
>
> [JScript] **public function ReflectionTypeLoadException(Type[], Exception[]);**

Initializes a new instance of the **ReflectionTypeLoadException** class with the given classes, their associated exceptions, and exception descriptions.

> [Visual Basic] **Public Sub New(Type(), Exception(), String)**
>
> [C#] **public ReflectionTypeLoadException(Type[], Exception[], string);**
>
> [C++] **public: ReflectionTypeLoadException(Type*[], Exception[], String*);**
>
> [JScript] **public function ReflectionTypeLoadException(Type[], Exception[], String);**

ReflectionTypeLoadException Constructor (Type[], Exception[])

Initializes a new instance of the **ReflectionTypeLoadException** class with the given classes and their associated exceptions.

```
[Visual Basic]
Public Sub New( _
    ByVal classes() As Type, _
    ByVal exceptions() As Exception _
)
[C#]
public ReflectionTypeLoadException(
    Type[] classes,
    Exception[] exceptions
);
[C++]
public: ReflectionTypeLoadException(
    Type* classes[],
    Exception* exceptions[]
);
[JScript]
public function ReflectionTypeLoadException(
    classes : Type[],
    exceptions : Exception[]
);
```

Parameters

classes

> An array of type **Type** containing the classes that were defined in the module and loaded. This array can contain null reference (**Nothing** in Visual Basic) values.

exceptions

An array of type **Exception** containing the exceptions that were thrown by the class loader. The null reference (**Nothing** in Visual Basic) values in the *classes* array line up with the exceptions in this *exceptions* array.

Requirements

Platforms: Windows 98, Windows NT 4.0, Windows Millennium Edition, Windows 2000, Windows XP Home Edition, Windows XP Professional, Windows .NET Server family

ReflectionTypeLoadException Constructor (Type[], Exception[], String)

Initializes a new instance of the **ReflectionTypeLoadException** class with the given classes, their associated exceptions, and exception descriptions.

```
[Visual Basic]
Public Sub New( _
   ByVal classes() As Type, _
   ByVal exceptions() As Exception, _
   ByVal message As String _
)
[C#]
public ReflectionTypeLoadException(
   Type[] classes,
   Exception[] exceptions,
   string message
);
[C++]
public: ReflectionTypeLoadException(
   Type* classes[],
   Exception* exceptions[],
   String* message
);
[JScript]
public function ReflectionTypeLoadException(
   classes : Type[],
   exceptions : Exception[],
   message : String
);
```

Parameters

classes

An array of type **Type** containing the classes that were defined in the module and loaded. This array can contain null reference (**Nothing** in Visual Basic) values.

exceptions

An array of type **Exception** containing the exceptions that were thrown by the class loader. The null reference (**Nothing** in Visual Basic) values in the *classes* array line up with the exceptions in this *exceptions* array.

message

A **String** describing the reason the exception was thrown.

Requirements

Platforms: Windows 98, Windows NT 4.0, Windows Millennium Edition, Windows 2000, Windows XP Home Edition, Windows XP Professional, Windows .NET Server family

ReflectionTypeLoadException.LoaderExceptions Property

Gets the array of exceptions thrown by the class loader.

```
[Visual Basic]
Public ReadOnly Property LoaderExceptions As Exception ()
[C#]
public Exception[] LoaderExceptions {get;}
[C++]
public: __property Exception* get_LoaderExceptions();
[JScript]
public function get LoaderExceptions() : Exception[];
```

Property Value

An array of type **Exception** containing the exceptions thrown by the class loader. The null values in the *classes* array of this instance line up with the exceptions in this array.

Remarks

The **LoaderExceptions** property retrieves an array of type **Exception** that is parallel to the **Types** array. This array will contain null values whenever reflection cannot load a class.

Requirements

Platforms: Windows 98, Windows NT 4.0, Windows Millennium Edition, Windows 2000, Windows XP Home Edition, Windows XP Professional, Windows .NET Server family

ReflectionTypeLoadException.Types Property

Gets the array of classes that were defined in the module and loaded.

```
[Visual Basic]
Public ReadOnly Property Types As Type ()
[C#]
public Type[] Types {get;}
[C++]
public: __property Type* get_Types();
[JScript]
public function get Types() : Type[];
```

Property Value

An array of type **Type** containing the classes that were defined in the module and loaded. This array can contain some a null reference (**Nothing** in Visual Basic) values.

Remarks

The **LoaderExceptions** property retrieves an array of type **Exception** that is parallel to this **Types** array. This array will contain null values whenever reflection cannot load a class.

Requirements

Platforms: Windows 98, Windows NT 4.0, Windows Millennium Edition, Windows 2000, Windows XP Home Edition, Windows XP Professional, Windows .NET Server family

ReflectionTypeLoadException.GetObjectData Method

Provides an **ISerializable** implementation for serialized objects.

```
[Visual Basic]
Overrides Public Sub GetObjectData( _
   ByVal info As SerializationInfo, _
   ByVal context As StreamingContext _
) Implements ISerializable.GetObjectData
[C#]
public override void GetObjectData(
   SerializationInfo info,
   StreamingContext context
);
[C++]
public: void GetObjectData(
   SerializationInfo* info,
   StreamingContext context
);
[JScript]
public override function GetObjectData(
   info : SerializationInfo,
   context : StreamingContext
);
```

Parameters

info
> The information and data needed to serialize or deserialize an object.

context
> The context for the serialization.

Implements

ISerializable.GetObjectData

Exceptions

Exception Type	Condition
ArgumentNullException	**info** is a null reference (**Nothing** in Visual Basic).

Requirements

Platforms: Windows 98, Windows NT 4.0, Windows Millennium Edition, Windows 2000, Windows XP Home Edition, Windows XP Professional, Windows .NET Server family

ResourceAttributes Enumeration

Specifies the attributes for a manifest resource.

This enumeration has a **FlagsAttribute** attribute that allows a bitwise combination of its member values.

```
[Visual Basic]
<Flags>
<Serializable>
Public Enum ResourceAttributes
[C#]
[Flags]
[Serializable]
public enum ResourceAttributes
[C++]
[Flags]
[Serializable]
__value public enum ResourceAttributes
[JScript]
public
   Flags
   Serializable
enum ResourceAttributes
```

Members

Member name	Description	Value
Private	A mask used to retrieve private manifest resources.	2
Public	A mask used to retrieve public manifest resources.	1

Requirements

Namespace: System.Reflection

Platforms: Windows 98, Windows NT 4.0, Windows Millennium Edition, Windows 2000, Windows XP Home Edition, Windows XP Professional, Windows .NET Server family

Assembly: Mscorlib (in Mscorlib.dll)

ResourceLocation Enumeration

Specifies the resource location.

This enumeration has a **FlagsAttribute** attribute that allows a bitwise combination of its member values.

```
[Visual Basic]
<Flags>
<Serializable>
Public Enum ResourceLocation
[C#]
[Flags]
[Serializable]
public enum ResourceLocation
[C++]
[Flags]
[Serializable]
__value public enum ResourceLocation
[JScript]
public
    Flags
    Serializable
enum ResourceLocation
```

Members

Member name	Description	Value
ContainedIn-AnotherAssembly	Specifies that the resource is contained in another assembly.	2
ContainedIn-ManifestFile	Specifies that the resource is contained in the manifest file.	4
Embedded	Specifies an embedded (that is, non-linked) resource.	1

Requirements

Namespace: System.Reflection

Platforms: Windows 98, Windows NT 4.0, Windows Millennium Edition, Windows 2000, Windows XP Home Edition, Windows XP Professional, Windows .NET Server family

Assembly: Mscorlib (in Mscorlib.dll)

StrongNameKeyPair Class

Encapsulates access to a public or private key pair used to sign strong name assemblies.

System.Object
  System.Reflection.StrongNameKeyPair

```
[Visual Basic]
<Serializable>
Public Class StrongNameKeyPair
[C#]
[Serializable]
public class StrongNameKeyPair
[C++]
[Serializable]
public __gc class StrongNameKeyPair
[JScript]
public
    Serializable
class StrongNameKeyPair
```

Thread Safety

Any public static (**Shared** in Visual Basic) members of this type are safe for multithreaded operations. Any instance members are not guaranteed to be thread safe.

Requirements

Namespace: System.Reflection

Platforms: Windows 98, Windows NT 4.0, Windows Millennium Edition, Windows 2000, Windows XP Home Edition, Windows XP Professional, Windows .NET Server family

Assembly: Mscorlib (in Mscorlib.dll)

StrongNameKeyPair Constructor

Initializes a new instance of the **StrongNameKeyPair** class.

Overload List

Initializes a new instance of the **StrongNameKeyPair** class, building the key pair from a **byte** array.

[Visual Basic] **Public Sub New(Byte())**

[C#] **public StrongNameKeyPair(byte[]);**

[C++] **public: StrongNameKeyPair(unsigned char __gc[]);**

[JScript] **public function StrongNameKeyPair(Byte[]);**

Initializes a new instance of the **StrongNameKeyPair** class, building the key pair from a **FileStream**.

[Visual Basic] **Public Sub New(FileStream)**

[C#] **public StrongNameKeyPair(FileStream);**

[C++] **public: StrongNameKeyPair(FileStream*);**

[JScript] **public function StrongNameKeyPair(FileStream);**

Initializes a new instance of the **StrongNameKeyPair** class, building the key pair from a **String**.

[Visual Basic] **Public Sub New(String)**

[C#] **public StrongNameKeyPair(string);**

[C++] **public: StrongNameKeyPair(String*);**

[JScript] **public function StrongNameKeyPair(String);**

StrongNameKeyPair Constructor (Byte[])

Initializes a new instance of the **StrongNameKeyPair** class, building the key pair from a **byte** array.

```
[Visual Basic]
Public Sub New( _
    ByVal keyPairArray() As Byte _
)
[C#]
public StrongNameKeyPair(
    byte[] keyPairArray
);
[C++]
public: StrongNameKeyPair(
    unsigned char keyPairArray __gc[]
);
[JScript]
public function StrongNameKeyPair(
    keyPairArray : Byte[]
);
```

Parameters

keyPairArray
    An array of type **byte** containing the key pair.

Exceptions

Exception Type	Condition
ArgumentNullException	*keyPairArray* is a null reference (**Nothing** in Visual Basic).
SecurityException	The caller does not have the required permission.

Requirements

Platforms: Windows 98, Windows NT 4.0, Windows Millennium Edition, Windows 2000, Windows XP Home Edition, Windows XP Professional, Windows .NET Server family

.NET Framework Security:

• **SecurityPermission** for access to unmanaged code. Associated enumeration: **SecurityPermissionFlag.UnmanagedCode**.

StrongNameKeyPair Constructor (FileStream)

Initializes a new instance of the **StrongNameKeyPair** class, building the key pair from a **FileStream**.

```
[Visual Basic]
Public Sub New( _
    ByVal keyPairFile As FileStream _
)
[C#]
public StrongNameKeyPair(
    FileStream keyPairFile
);
[C++]
public: StrongNameKeyPair(
    FileStream* keyPairFile
);
[JScript]
public function StrongNameKeyPair(
    keyPairFile : FileStream
);
```

Parameters

keyPairFile
    A **FileStream** containing the key pair.

Exceptions

Exception Type	Condition
ArgumentNullException	*keyPairFile* is a null reference (**Nothing** in Visual Basic).
SecurityException	The caller does not have the required permission.

Requirements

Platforms: Windows 98, Windows NT 4.0, Windows Millennium Edition, Windows 2000, Windows XP Home Edition, Windows XP Professional, Windows .NET Server family

.NET Framework Security:
- **SecurityPermission** for access to unmanaged code. Associated enumeration: **SecurityPermissionFlag.UnmanagedCode**.

StrongNameKeyPair Constructor (String)

Initializes a new instance of the **StrongNameKeyPair** class, building the key pair from a **String**.

```
[Visual Basic]
Public Sub New( _
   ByVal keyPairContainer As String _
)
[C#]
public StrongNameKeyPair(
   string keyPairContainer
);
[C++]
public: StrongNameKeyPair(
   String* keyPairContainer
);
[JScript]
public function StrongNameKeyPair(
   keyPairContainer : String
);
```

Parameters

keyPairContainer
    A string containing the key pair.

Exceptions

Exception Type	Condition
ArgumentNullException	*keyPairContainer* is a null reference (**Nothing** in Visual Basic).
SecurityException	The caller does not have the required permission.

Remarks

The key pair is in a named key container.

Requirements

Platforms: Windows 98, Windows NT 4.0, Windows Millennium Edition, Windows 2000, Windows XP Home Edition, Windows XP Professional, Windows .NET Server family

.NET Framework Security:
- **SecurityPermission** for access to unmanaged code. Associated enumeration: **SecurityPermissionFlag.UnmanagedCode**.

StrongNameKeyPair.PublicKey Property

Gets the public part of the public key or public key token of the key pair.

```
[Visual Basic]
Public ReadOnly Property PublicKey As Byte ()
[C#]
public byte[] PublicKey {get;}
[C++]
public: __property unsigned char get_PublicKey();
[JScript]
public function get PublicKey() : Byte[];
```

Property Value

An array of type **byte** containing the public key or public key token of the key pair.

Requirements

Platforms: Windows 98, Windows NT 4.0, Windows Millennium Edition, Windows 2000, Windows XP Home Edition, Windows XP Professional, Windows .NET Server family

TargetException Class

Represents the exception that is thrown when an attempt is made to invoke an invalid target.

System.Object
  System.Exception
    System.ApplicationException
      System.Reflection.TargetException

```
[Visual Basic]
<Serializable>
Public Class TargetException
  Inherits ApplicationException
[C#]
[Serializable]
public class TargetException : ApplicationException
[C++]
[Serializable]
public __gc class TargetException : public ApplicationException
[JScript]
public
  Serializable
class TargetException extends ApplicationException
```

Thread Safety

Any public static (**Shared** in Visual Basic) members of this type are safe for multithreaded operations. Any instance members are not guaranteed to be thread safe.

Remarks

A **TargetException** is thrown when an attempt is made to invoke a non-static method on a null object. This may occur because the caller does not have access to the member, or because the target does not define the member, and so on.

Requirements

Namespace: System.Reflection

Platforms: Windows 98, Windows NT 4.0, Windows Millennium Edition, Windows 2000, Windows XP Home Edition, Windows XP Professional, Windows .NET Server family

Assembly: Mscorlib (in Mscorlib.dll)

TargetException Constructor

Initializes a new instance of the **TargetException** class.

Overload List

Initializes a new instance of the **TargetException** class with an empty message and the root cause of the exception.

    [Visual Basic] **Public Sub New()**
    [C#] **public TargetException();**
    [C++] **public: TargetException();**
    [JScript] **public function TargetException();**

Initializes a new instance of the **TargetException** class with the given message and the root cause exception.

    [Visual Basic] **Public Sub New(String)**
    [C#] **public TargetException(string);**
    [C++] **public: TargetException(String*);**
    [JScript] **public function TargetException(String);**

Initializes a new instance of the **TargetException** class with the specified serialization and context information.

    [Visual Basic] **Protected Sub New(SerializationInfo, StreamingContext)**
    [C#] **protected TargetException(SerializationInfo, StreamingContext);**
    [C++] **protected: TargetException(SerializationInfo*, StreamingContext);**
    [JScript] **protected function TargetException(SerializationInfo, StreamingContext);**

Initializes a new instance of the **TargetException** class with a specified error message and a reference to the inner exception that is the cause of this exception.

    [Visual Basic] **Public Sub New(String, Exception)**
    [C#] **public TargetException(string, Exception);**
    [C++] **public: TargetException(String*, Exception*);**
    [JScript] **public function TargetException(String, Exception);**

TargetException Constructor ()

Initializes a new instance of the **TargetException** class with an empty message and the root cause of the exception.

```
[Visual Basic]
Public Sub New()
[C#]
public TargetException();
[C++]
public: TargetException();
[JScript]
public function TargetException();
```

Remarks

The **InnerException** property is set to a null reference (**Nothing** in Visual Basic) and the HRESULT error code is set to COR_E_TARGET.

TargetException inherits from the **Exception**. This constructor sets the properties of the **Exception** object as shown in the following table.

Property	Value
InnerException	A null reference (**Nothing**)
Message	The empty string ("").

Requirements

Platforms: Windows 98, Windows NT 4.0, Windows Millennium Edition, Windows 2000, Windows XP Home Edition, Windows XP Professional, Windows .NET Server family, Common Language Infrastructure (CLI) Standard

TargetException Constructor (String)

Initializes a new instance of the **TargetException** class with the given message and the root cause exception.

```
[Visual Basic]
Public Sub New( _
  ByVal message As String _
)
[C#]
public TargetException(
  string message
);
```

```
[C++]
public: TargetException(
   String* message
);
[JScript]
public function TargetException(
   message : String
);
```

Parameters

message
> A **String** describing the reason why the exception occurred.

Remarks

TargetException inherits from the **Exception**. This constructor sets the properties of the **Exception** object as shown in the following table.

Property	Value
InnerException	A null reference (**Nothing** in Visual Basic)
Message	The message string.

Requirements

Platforms: Windows 98, Windows NT 4.0, Windows Millennium Edition, Windows 2000, Windows XP Home Edition, Windows XP Professional, Windows .NET Server family, Common Language Infrastructure (CLI) Standard

TargetException Constructor (SerializationInfo, StreamingContext)

Initializes a new instance of the **TargetException** class with the specified serialization and context information.

```
[Visual Basic]
Protected Sub New( _
   ByVal info As SerializationInfo, _
   ByVal context As StreamingContext _
)
[C#]
protected TargetException(
   SerializationInfo info,
   StreamingContext context
);
[C++]
protected: TargetException(
   SerializationInfo* info,
   StreamingContext context
);
[JScript]
protected function TargetException(
   info : SerializationInfo,
   context : StreamingContext
);
```

Parameters

info
> The data for serializing or deserializing the object.

context
> The source of and destination for the object.

Requirements

Platforms: Windows 98, Windows NT 4.0, Windows Millennium Edition, Windows 2000, Windows XP Home Edition, Windows XP Professional, Windows .NET Server family

TargetException Constructor (String, Exception)

Initializes a new instance of the **TargetException** class with a specified error message and a reference to the inner exception that is the cause of this exception.

```
[Visual Basic]
Public Sub New( _
   ByVal message As String, _
   ByVal inner As Exception _
)
[C#]
public TargetException(
   string message,
   Exception inner
);
[C++]
public: TargetException(
   String* message,
   Exception* inner
);
[JScript]
public function TargetException(
   message : String,
   inner : Exception
);
```

Parameters

message
> The error message that explains the reason for the exception.

inner
> The exception that is the cause of the current exception. If the *inner* parameter is not a null reference (**Nothing** in Visual Basic), the current exception is raised in a **catch** block that handles the inner exception.

Remarks

An exception that is thrown as a direct result of a previous exception should include a reference to the previous exception in the **InnerException** property. The **InnerException** property returns the same value that is passed into the constructor, or a null reference (**Nothing** in Visual Basic) if the **InnerException** property does not supply the inner exception value to the constructor.

The following table shows the initial property values for an instance of **TargetException**.

Property	Value
InnerException	The inner exception reference.
Message	The error message string.

Requirements

Platforms: Windows 98, Windows NT 4.0, Windows Millennium Edition, Windows 2000, Windows XP Home Edition, Windows XP Professional, Windows .NET Server family, Common Language Infrastructure (CLI) Standard

TargetInvocationException Class

The exception that is thrown by methods invoked through reflection. This class cannot be inherited.

System.Object
  System.Exception
    System.ApplicationException
      System.Reflection.TargetInvocationException

```
[Visual Basic]
<Serializable>
NotInheritable Public Class TargetInvocationException
    Inherits ApplicationException
[C#]
[Serializable]
public sealed class TargetInvocationException :
    ApplicationException
[C++]
[Serializable]
public __gc __sealed class TargetInvocationException : public
    ApplicationException
[JScript]
public
    Serializable
class TargetInvocationException extends ApplicationException
```

Thread Safety

Any public static (**Shared** in Visual Basic) members of this type are safe for multithreaded operations. Any instance members are not guaranteed to be thread safe.

Remarks

TargetInvocationException uses the HRESULT COR_E_TARGETINVOCATION which has the value 0x80131604.

When created, the **TargetInvocationException** is passed a reference to the exception thrown by the method invoked through reflection. The **InnerException** property holds the underlying exception.

Requirements

Namespace: System.Reflection

Platforms: Windows 98, Windows NT 4.0, Windows Millennium Edition, Windows 2000, Windows XP Home Edition, Windows XP Professional, Windows .NET Server family, .NET Compact Framework - Windows CE .NET

Assembly: Mscorlib (in Mscorlib.dll)

TargetInvocationException Constructor

Initializes a new instance of the **TargetInvocationException** class.

Overload List

Initializes a new instance of the **TargetInvocationException** class with a reference to the inner exception that is the cause of this exception.

Supported by the .NET Compact Framework.

[Visual Basic] **Public Sub New(Exception)**

[C#] **public TargetInvocationException(Exception);**

[C++] **public: TargetInvocationException(Exception*);**

[JScript] **public function TargetInvocationException(Exception);**

Initializes a new instance of the **TargetInvocationException** class with a specified error message and a reference to the inner exception that is the cause of this exception.

Supported by the .NET Compact Framework.

[Visual Basic] **Public Sub New(String, Exception)**

[C#] **public TargetInvocationException(string, Exception);**

[C++] **public: TargetInvocationException(String*, Exception*);**

[JScript] **public function TargetInvocationException(String, Exception);**

TargetInvocationException Constructor (Exception)

Initializes a new instance of the **TargetInvocationException** class with a reference to the inner exception that is the cause of this exception.

```
[Visual Basic]
Public Sub New( _
    ByVal inner As Exception _
)
[C#]
public TargetInvocationException(
    Exception inner
);
[C++]
public: TargetInvocationException(
    Exception* inner
);
[JScript]
public function TargetInvocationException(
    inner : Exception
);
```

Parameters

inner

> The exception that is the cause of the current exception. If the *inner* parameter is not a null reference (**Nothing** in Visual Basic), the current exception is raised in a **catch** block that handles the inner exception.

Remarks

An exception that is thrown as a direct result of a previous exception should include a reference to the previous exception in the **InnerException** property. The **InnerException** property returns the same value that is passed into the constructor, or a null reference (**Nothing** in Visual Basic) if the **InnerException** property does not supply the inner exception value to the constructor.

The following table shows the initial property values for an instance of **TargetInvocationException**.

Property	Value
InnerException	The inner exception reference.
Message	The error message string.

Requirements

Platforms: Windows 98, Windows NT 4.0,
Windows Millennium Edition, Windows 2000,
Windows XP Home Edition, Windows XP Professional,
Windows .NET Server family,
.NET Compact Framework - Windows CE .NET,
Common Language Infrastructure (CLI) Standard

Requirements

Platforms: Windows 98, Windows NT 4.0,
Windows Millennium Edition, Windows 2000,
Windows XP Home Edition, Windows XP Professional,
Windows .NET Server family,
.NET Compact Framework - Windows CE .NET,
Common Language Infrastructure (CLI) Standard

TargetInvocationException Constructor (String, Exception)

Initializes a new instance of the **TargetInvocationException** class
with a specified error message and a reference to the inner exception
that is the cause of this exception.

```
[Visual Basic]
Public Sub New( _
   ByVal message As String, _
   ByVal inner As Exception _
)
[C#]
public TargetInvocationException(
   string message,
   Exception inner
);
[C++]
public: TargetInvocationException(
   String* message,
   Exception* inner
);
[JScript]
public function TargetInvocationException(
   message : String,
   inner : Exception
);
```

Parameters

message
   The error message that explains the reason for the exception.
inner
   The exception that is the cause of the current exception. If the
   inner parameter is not a null reference (**Nothing** in Visual Basic),
   the current exception is raised in a **catch** block that handles the
   inner exception.

Remarks

An exception that is thrown as a direct result of a previous exception
should include a reference to the previous exception in the
InnerException property. The **InnerException** property returns the
same value that is passed into the constructor, or a null reference
(**Nothing** in Visual Basic) if the **InnerException** property does not
supply the inner exception value to the constructor.

The following table shows the initial property values for an instance
of **TargetInvocationException**.

Property	Value
InnerException	The inner exception reference.
Message	The error message string.

TargetParameterCount-Exception Class

The exception that is thrown when the number of parameters for an invocation does not match the number expected. This class cannot be inherited.

System.Object
  System.Exception
    System.ApplicationException
      System.Reflection.TargetParameterCountException

```
[Visual Basic]
<Serializable>
NotInheritable Public Class TargetParameterCountException
   Inherits ApplicationException
[C#]
[Serializable]
public sealed class TargetParameterCountException :
   ApplicationException
[C++]
[Serializable]
public __gc __sealed class TargetParameterCountException : public
   ApplicationException
[JScript]
public
   Serializable
class TargetParameterCountException extends
   ApplicationException
```

Thread Safety

Any public static (**Shared** in Visual Basic) members of this type are safe for multithreaded operations. Any instance members are not guaranteed to be thread safe.

Remarks

TargetParameterCountException uses the HRESULT COR_E_TARGETPARAMCOUNT which has the value 0x8002000E.

Requirements

Namespace: System.Reflection

Platforms: Windows 98, Windows NT 4.0, Windows Millennium Edition, Windows 2000, Windows XP Home Edition, Windows XP Professional, Windows .NET Server family, .NET Compact Framework - Windows CE .NET

Assembly: Mscorlib (in Mscorlib.dll)

TargetParameterCountException Constructor

Initializes a new instance of the **TargetParameterCountException** class.

Overload List

Initializes a new instance of the **TargetParameterCountException** class with an empty message string and the root cause of the exception.

Supported by the .NET Compact Framework.

[Visual Basic] **Public Sub New()**
[C#] **public TargetParameterCountException();**
[C++] **public: TargetParameterCountException();**
[JScript] **public function TargetParameterCountException();**

Initializes a new instance of the **TargetParameterCountException** class with its message string set to the given message and the root cause exception.

Supported by the .NET Compact Framework.

[Visual Basic] **Public Sub New(String)**
[C#] **public TargetParameterCountException(string);**
[C++] **public: TargetParameterCountException(String*);**
[JScript] **public function TargetParameterCountException(String);**

Initializes a new instance of the **TargetParameterCountException** class with a specified error message and a reference to the inner exception that is the cause of this exception.

Supported by the .NET Compact Framework.

[Visual Basic] **Public Sub New(String, Exception)**
[C#] **public TargetParameterCountException(string, Exception);**
[C++] **public: TargetParameterCountException(String*, Exception*);**
[JScript] **public function TargetParameterCountException(String, Exception);**

TargetParameterCountException Constructor ( )

Initializes a new instance of the **TargetParameterCountException** class with an empty message string and the root cause of the exception.

```
[Visual Basic]
Public Sub New()
[C#]
public TargetParameterCountException();
[C++]
public: TargetParameterCountException();
[JScript]
public function TargetParameterCountException();
```

Remarks

TargetParameterCountException inherits from **Exception**. This constructor sets the properties of the Exception object as shown in the following table.

Property	Value
InnerException	A null reference (**Nothing** in Visual Basic)
Message	The empty string ("").

Requirements

Platforms: Windows 98, Windows NT 4.0, Windows Millennium Edition, Windows 2000, Windows XP Home Edition, Windows XP Professional, Windows .NET Server family, .NET Compact Framework - Windows CE .NET, Common Language Infrastructure (CLI) Standard

TargetParameterCountException Constructor (String)

Initializes a new instance of the **TargetParameterCountException** class with its message string set to the given message and the root cause exception.

```
[Visual Basic]
Public Sub New( _
   ByVal message As String _
)
[C#]
public TargetParameterCountException(
   string message
);
[C++]
public: TargetParameterCountException(
   String* message
);
[JScript]
public function TargetParameterCountException(
   message : String
);
```

Parameters
message
    A **String** describing the reason this exception was thrown.

Remarks

TargetParmeterCountException inherits from **Exception**. This constructor sets the properties of the **Exception** object as shown in the following table.

Property	Value
InnerException	A null reference (**Nothing** in Visual Basic)
Message	The message string.

Requirements

Platforms: Windows 98, Windows NT 4.0, Windows Millennium Edition, Windows 2000, Windows XP Home Edition, Windows XP Professional, Windows .NET Server family, .NET Compact Framework - Windows CE .NET, Common Language Infrastructure (CLI) Standard

TargetParameterCountException Constructor (String, Exception)

Initializes a new instance of the **TargetParameterCountException** class with a specified error message and a reference to the inner exception that is the cause of this exception.

```
[Visual Basic]
Public Sub New( _
   ByVal message As String, _
   ByVal inner As Exception _
)
[C#]
public TargetParameterCountException(
   string message,
   Exception inner
);
[C++]
public: TargetParameterCountException(
   String* message,
   Exception* inner
);
[JScript]
public function TargetParameterCountException(
   message : String,
   inner : Exception
);
```

Parameters
message
    The error message that explains the reason for the exception.
inner
    The exception that is the cause of the current exception. If the *inner* parameter is not a null reference (**Nothing** in Visual Basic), the current exception is raised in a **catch** block that handles the inner exception.

Remarks

An exception that is thrown as a direct result of a previous exception should include a reference to the previous exception in the **InnerException** property. The **InnerException** property returns the same value that is passed into the constructor, or a null reference (**Nothing** in Visual Basic) if the **InnerException** property does not supply the inner exception value to the constructor.

The following table shows the initial property values for an instance of **TargetParameterCountException**.

Property	Value
InnerException	The inner exception reference.
Message	The error message string.

Requirements

Platforms: Windows 98, Windows NT 4.0, Windows Millennium Edition, Windows 2000, Windows XP Home Edition, Windows XP Professional, Windows .NET Server family, .NET Compact Framework - Windows CE .NET, Common Language Infrastructure (CLI) Standard

TypeAttributes Enumeration

Specifies type attributes.

This enumeration has a **FlagsAttribute** attribute that allows a bitwise combination of its member values.

```
[Visual Basic]
<Flags>
<Serializable>
Public Enum TypeAttributes
[C#]
[Flags]
[Serializable]
public enum TypeAttributes
[C++]
[Flags]
[Serializable]
__value public enum TypeAttributes
[JScript]
public
    Flags
    Serializable
enum TypeAttributes
```

Remarks

The members of this enumerator class match the CorTypeAttr enumerator as defined in the corhdr.h file.

Members

Member name	Description	Value
Abstract Supported by the .NET Compact Framework.	Specifies that the type is abstract.	128
AnsiClass Supported by the .NET Compact Framework.	LPTSTR is interpreted as ANSI.	0
AutoClass Supported by the .NET Compact Framework.	LPTSTR is interpreted automatically.	131072
AutoLayout Supported by the .NET Compact Framework.	Specifies that class fields are automatically laid out by the common language runtime.	0
BeforeFieldInit Supported by the .NET Compact Framework.	Specifies that calling static methods of the type does not force the system to initialize the type.	1048576
Class Supported by the .NET Compact Framework.	Specifies that the type is a class.	0
ClassSemanticsMask Supported by the .NET Compact Framework.	Specifies class semantics information; the current class is contextful (else agile).	32
ExplicitLayout Supported by the .NET Compact Framework.	Specifies that class fields are laid out at the specified offsets.	16
HasSecurity Supported by the .NET Compact Framework.	Type has security associate with it.	262144

Member name	Description	Value
Import Supported by the .NET Compact Framework.	Specifies that the class or interface is imported from another module.	4096
Interface Supported by the .NET Compact Framework.	Specifies that the type is an interface.	32
LayoutMask Supported by the .NET Compact Framework.	Specifies class layout information.	24
NestedAssembly Supported by the .NET Compact Framework.	Specifies that the class is nested with assembly visibility, and is thus accessible only by methods within its assembly.	5
NestedFamANDAssem Supported by the .NET Compact Framework.	Specifies that the class is nested with assembly and family visibility, and is thus accessible only by methods lying in the intersection of its family and assembly.	6
NestedFamily Supported by the .NET Compact Framework.	Specifies that the class is nested with family visibility, and is thus accessible only by methods within its own type and any subtypes.	4
NestedFamORAssem Supported by the .NET Compact Framework.	Specifies that the class is nested with family or assembly visibility, and is thus accessible only by methods lying in the union of its family and assembly.	7
NestedPrivate Supported by the .NET Compact Framework.	Specifies that the class is nested with private visibility.	3
NestedPublic Supported by the .NET Compact Framework.	Specifies that the class is nested with public visibility.	2
NotPublic Supported by the .NET Compact Framework.	Specifies that the class is not public.	0
Public Supported by the .NET Compact Framework.	Specifies that the class is public.	1
ReservedMask Supported by the .NET Compact Framework.	Attributes reserved for runtime use.	264192
RTSpecialName Supported by the .NET Compact Framework.	Runtime should check name encoding.	2048
Sealed Supported by the .NET Compact Framework.	Specifies that the class is concrete and cannot be extended.	256

Member name	Description	Value
SequentialLayout Supported by the .NET Compact Framework.	Specifies that class fields are laid out sequentially, in the order that the fields were emitted to the metadata.	8
Serializable Supported by the .NET Compact Framework.	Specifies that the class can be serialized.	8192
SpecialName Supported by the .NET Compact Framework.	Specifies that the class is special in a way denoted by the name.	1024
StringFormatMask Supported by the .NET Compact Framework.	Used to retrieve string information for native interoperability.	196608
UnicodeClass Supported by the .NET Compact Framework.	LPTSTR is interpreted as UNICODE.	65536
VisibilityMask Supported by the .NET Compact Framework.	Specifies type visibility information.	7

Requirements

Namespace: System.Reflection

Platforms: Windows 98, Windows NT 4.0, Windows Millennium Edition, Windows 2000, Windows XP Home Edition, Windows XP Professional, Windows .NET Server family, .NET Compact Framework - Windows CE .NET

Assembly: Mscorlib (in Mscorlib.dll)

TypeDelegator Class

Wraps a **Type** object and delegates all methods to that **Type**.

System.Object
  System.Reflection.MemberInfo
    System.Type
      System.Reflection.TypeDelegator

```
[Visual Basic]
<Serializable>
Public Class TypeDelegator
   Inherits Type
[C#]
[Serializable]
public class TypeDelegator : Type
[C++]
[Serializable]
public __gc class TypeDelegator : public Type
[JScript]
public
   Serializable
class TypeDelegator extends Type
```

Thread Safety

Any public static (**Shared** in Visual Basic) members of this type are safe for multithreaded operations. Any instance members are not guaranteed to be thread safe.

Remarks

Delegates are used for the managed code objects to encapsulate method calls. They are used primarily in **Event** notifications and callbacks.

Derive from this type and only overload those methods you need to provide customization in.

Requirements

Namespace: System.Reflection

Platforms: Windows 98, Windows NT 4.0, Windows Millennium Edition, Windows 2000, Windows XP Home Edition, Windows XP Professional, Windows .NET Server family

Assembly: Mscorlib (in Mscorlib.dll)

TypeDelegator Constructor

Initializes a new instance of the **TypeDelegator** class.

Overload List

Initializes a new instance of the **TypeDelegator** class with default properties.

[Visual Basic] **Protected Sub New()**
[C#] **protected TypeDelegator();**
[C++] **protected: TypeDelegator();**
[JScript] **protected function TypeDelegator();**

Initializes a new instance of the **TypeDelegator** class specifying the encapsulating instance.

[Visual Basic] **Public Sub New(Type)**
[C#] **public TypeDelegator(Type);**
[C++] **public: TypeDelegator(Type*);**
[JScript] **public function TypeDelegator(Type);**

TypeDelegator Constructor ()

Initializes a new instance of the **TypeDelegator** class with default properties.

```
[Visual Basic]
Protected Sub New()
[C#]
protected TypeDelegator();
[C++]
protected: TypeDelegator();
[JScript]
protected function TypeDelegator();
```

Requirements

Platforms: Windows 98, Windows NT 4.0, Windows Millennium Edition, Windows 2000, Windows XP Home Edition, Windows XP Professional, Windows .NET Server family

TypeDelegator Constructor (Type)

Initializes a new instance of the **TypeDelegator** class specifying the encapsulating instance.

```
[Visual Basic]
Public Sub New( _
   ByVal delegatingType As Type _
)
[C#]
public TypeDelegator(
   Type delegatingType
);
[C++]
public: TypeDelegator(
   Type* delegatingType
);
[JScript]
public function TypeDelegator(
   delegatingType : Type
);
```

Parameters

delegatingType
  The instance of the class **Type** that encapsulates the call to the method of an object.

Exceptions

Exception Type	Condition
ArgumentNullException	*delegatingType* is a null reference (**Nothing** in Visual Basic).

Remarks

This constructor is called from a class to generate a delegate based upon the **Type** object for the class defining the method.

Requirements

Platforms: Windows 98, Windows NT 4.0, Windows Millennium Edition, Windows 2000, Windows XP Home Edition, Windows XP Professional, Windows .NET Server family

TypeDelegator.typeImpl Field

A value indicating type information.

```
[Visual Basic]
Protected typeImpl As Type
[C#]
protected Type typeImpl;
[C++]
protected: Type* typeImpl;
[JScript]
protected var typeImpl : Type;
```

Requirements

Platforms: Windows 98, Windows NT 4.0,
Windows Millennium Edition, Windows 2000,
Windows XP Home Edition, Windows XP Professional,
Windows .NET Server family

TypeDelegator.Assembly Property

Gets the assembly of the implemented type.

```
[Visual Basic]
Overrides Public ReadOnly Property Assembly As Assembly
[C#]
public override Assembly Assembly {get;}
[C++]
public: __property Assembly* get_Assembly();
[JScript]
public override function get Assembly() : Assembly;
```

Property Value

An **System.Reflection.Assembly** object representing the assembly
of the implemented type.

Remarks

Assemblies are the deployment units in the common language
runtime. Assemblies establish the namespace for resolving requests
and determine which resources are exposed externally and which are
accessible from within the assembly. The common language runtime
can determine and locate the assembly for any running object.

Requirements

Platforms: Windows 98, Windows NT 4.0,
Windows Millennium Edition, Windows 2000,
Windows XP Home Edition, Windows XP Professional,
Windows .NET Server family

TypeDelegator.AssemblyQualifiedName Property

Gets the assembly's fully qualified name.

```
[Visual Basic]
Overrides Public ReadOnly Property AssemblyQualifiedName As String
[C#]
public override string AssemblyQualifiedName {get;}
[C++]
public: __property String* get_AssemblyQualifiedName();
[JScript]
public override function get AssemblyQualifiedName() : String;
```

Property Value

A **String** containing the assembly's fully qualified name.

Requirements

Platforms: Windows 98, Windows NT 4.0,
Windows Millennium Edition, Windows 2000,
Windows XP Home Edition, Windows XP Professional,
Windows .NET Server family

TypeDelegator.BaseType Property

Gets the base type for the current type.

```
[Visual Basic]
Overrides Public ReadOnly Property BaseType As Type
[C#]
public override Type BaseType {get;}
[C++]
public: __property Type* get_BaseType();
[JScript]
public override function get BaseType() : Type;
```

Property Value

The base type for a type.

Remarks

The base type is the type from which this type directly inherits.
Since the **Object** class type is the ultimate base class of all the other
types, it is the only type that does not have a base type. In this case, a
null reference (**Nothing** in Visual Basic) is returned as the base type
of the **Object** type.

Requirements

Platforms: Windows 98, Windows NT 4.0,
Windows Millennium Edition, Windows 2000,
Windows XP Home Edition, Windows XP Professional,
Windows .NET Server family

TypeDelegator.FullName Property

Gets the fully qualified name of the implemented type.

```
[Visual Basic]
Overrides Public ReadOnly Property FullName As String
[C#]
public override string FullName {get;}
[C++]
public: __property String* get_FullName();
[JScript]
public override function get FullName() : String;
```

Property Value

A **String** containing the type's fully qualified name.

Remarks

A string containing the fully qualified name of the current
TypeDelegator.

Requirements

Platforms: Windows 98, Windows NT 4.0,
Windows Millennium Edition, Windows 2000,
Windows XP Home Edition, Windows XP Professional,
Windows .NET Server family

TypeDelegator.GUID Property

Gets the GUID (globally unique identifier) of the implemented type.

```
[Visual Basic]
Overrides Public ReadOnly Property GUID As Guid
[C#]
public override Guid GUID {get;}
[C++]
public: __property Guid get_GUID();
[JScript]
public override function get GUID() : Guid;
```

Property Value

A GUID.

Remarks

The GUID (globally unique identifier) is a 128-bit unique identification string used to identify a class or an interface. It is primarily useful for interoperability between the Microsoft .NET Framework and COM.

Requirements

Platforms: Windows 98, Windows NT 4.0, Windows Millennium Edition, Windows 2000, Windows XP Home Edition, Windows XP Professional, Windows .NET Server family

TypeDelegator.Module Property

Gets the module of the implemented type.

```
[Visual Basic]
Overrides Public ReadOnly Property Module As Module
[C#]
public override Module Module {get;}
[C++]
public: __property Module* get_Module();
[JScript]
public override function get Module() : Module;
```

Property Value

A **Module** object representing the module of the implemented type.

Remarks

A module is a loadable unit that can contain type declarations and implementations. Modules contain enough information to enable the common language runtime to locate all implementation bits when the module is loaded.

Requirements

Platforms: Windows 98, Windows NT 4.0, Windows Millennium Edition, Windows 2000, Windows XP Home Edition, Windows XP Professional, Windows .NET Server family

TypeDelegator.Name Property

Gets the name of the implemented type, with the path removed.

```
[Visual Basic]
Overrides Public ReadOnly Property Name As String
[C#]
public override string Name {get;}
```

```
[C++]
public: __property String* get_Name();
[JScript]
public override function get Name() : String;
```

Property Value

A **String** containing the type's non-qualified name.

Remarks

A string containing the name of the current **TypeDelegator**. Only the simple name, not the fully qualified name, is returned. To get the name and the path, use **FullName**.

Requirements

Platforms: Windows 98, Windows NT 4.0, Windows Millennium Edition, Windows 2000, Windows XP Home Edition, Windows XP Professional, Windows .NET Server family

TypeDelegator.Namespace Property

Gets the namespace of the implemented type.

```
[Visual Basic]
Overrides Public ReadOnly Property Namespace As String
[C#]
public override string Namespace {get;}
[C++]
public: __property String* get_Namespace();
[JScript]
public override function get Namespace() : String;
```

Property Value

A **String** containing the type's namespace.

Remarks

This property gets a string containing the namespace of the current **TypeDelegator**. For example, if the **TypeDelegator** is **TypeFilter**, the returned namespace is **System.Reflection**.

Requirements

Platforms: Windows 98, Windows NT 4.0, Windows Millennium Edition, Windows 2000, Windows XP Home Edition, Windows XP Professional, Windows .NET Server family

TypeDelegator.TypeHandle Property

Gets a handle to the internal metadata representation of an implemented type.

```
[Visual Basic]
Overrides Public ReadOnly Property TypeHandle As RuntimeTypeHandle
[C#]
public override RuntimeTypeHandle TypeHandle {get;}
[C++]
public: __property RuntimeTypeHandle get_TypeHandle();
[JScript]
public override function get TypeHandle() : RuntimeTypeHandle;
```

Property Value

A **RuntimeTypeHandle** object.

Remarks

A type handle is a unique integer value associated with each type. The handle is unique during the runtime.

Requirements

Platforms: Windows 98, Windows NT 4.0, Windows Millennium Edition, Windows 2000, Windows XP Home Edition, Windows XP Professional, Windows .NET Server family

TypeDelegator.UnderlyingSystemType Property

Gets the underlying **Type** that represents the implemented type.

```
[Visual Basic]
Overrides Public ReadOnly Property UnderlyingSystemType As Type  _
   Implements IReflect.UnderlyingSystemType
[C#]
public override Type UnderlyingSystemType {get;}
[C++]
public: __property Type* get_UnderlyingSystemType();
[JScript]
public override function get UnderlyingSystemType() : Type;
```

Property Value

The underlying type.

Implements

IReflect.UnderlyingSystemType

Requirements

Platforms: Windows 98, Windows NT 4.0, Windows Millennium Edition, Windows 2000, Windows XP Home Edition, Windows XP Professional, Windows .NET Server family

TypeDelegator.GetAttributeFlagsImpl Method

Gets the attributes assigned to the **TypeDelegator**.

```
[Visual Basic]
Overrides Protected Function GetAttributeFlagsImpl() As _
   TypeAttributes
[C#]
protected override TypeAttributes GetAttributeFlagsImpl();
[C++]
protected: TypeAttributes GetAttributeFlagsImpl();
[JScript]
protected override function GetAttributeFlagsImpl() :
   TypeAttributes;
```

Return Value

A **TypeAttributes** object representing the implementation attribute flags.

Remarks

This method can be used to determine if the **TypeDelegator** is abstract, public, and so on.

Requirements

Platforms: Windows 98, Windows NT 4.0, Windows Millennium Edition, Windows 2000, Windows XP Home Edition, Windows XP Professional, Windows .NET Server family

TypeDelegator.GetConstructorImpl Method

Gets the constructor that implemented the **TypeDelegator**.

```
[Visual Basic]
Overrides Protected Function GetConstructorImpl( _
   ByVal bindingAttr As BindingFlags, _
   ByVal binder As Binder, _
   ByVal callConvention As CallingConventions, _
   ByVal types() As Type, _
   ByVal modifiers() As ParameterModifier _
) As ConstructorInfo
[C#]
protected override ConstructorInfo GetConstructorImpl(
   BindingFlags bindingAttr,
   Binder binder,
   CallingConventions callConvention,
   Type[] types,
   ParameterModifier[] modifiers
);
[C++]
protected: ConstructorInfo* GetConstructorImpl(
   BindingFlags bindingAttr,
   Binder* binder,
   CallingConventions callConvention,
   Type* types[],
   ParameterModifier modifiers[]
);
[JScript]
protected override function GetConstructorImpl(
   bindingAttr : BindingFlags,
   binder : Binder,
   callConvention : CallingConventions,
   types : Type[],
   modifiers : ParameterModifier[]
) : ConstructorInfo;
```

Parameters

bindingAttr

A bitmask that affects the way in which the search is conducted. The value is a combination of zero or more bit flags from **BindingFlags**.

binder

An object that enables the binding, coercion of argument types, invocation of members, and retrieval of **MemberInfo** objects using reflection. If *binder* is a null reference (**Nothing** in Visual Basic), the default binder is used.

callConvention

The calling conventions.

types

An array of type **Type** containing a list of the parameter number, order, and types. Types cannot be a null reference (**Nothing** in Visual Basic); use an appropriate **GetMethod** method or an empty array to search for a method without parameters.

modifiers

An array of type **ParameterModifier** having the same length as the *types* array, whose elements represent the attributes associated with the parameters of the method to get.

Return Value

A **ConstructorInfo** object for the method that matches the specified criteria, or a null reference (**Nothing** in Visual Basic) if a match cannot be found.

Remarks

The *callConvention* parameter indicates the calling convention for the entry point. If no calling convention is specified, a default **CallingConventions** value of **Standard** is used.

Requirements

Platforms: Windows 98, Windows NT 4.0, Windows Millennium Edition, Windows 2000, Windows XP Home Edition, Windows XP Professional, Windows .NET Server family

TypeDelegator.GetConstructors Method

Overload List

Returns an array of **ConstructorInfo** objects representing constructors defined for the current class.

> [Visual Basic] **Overloads Overrides Public Function GetConstructors(BindingFlags) As ConstructorInfo()**
>
> [C#] **public override ConstructorInfo[] GetConstructors(BindingFlags);**
>
> [C++] **public: ConstructorInfo* GetConstructors(BindingFlags) [];**
>
> [JScript] **public override function GetConstructors(BindingFlags) : ConstructorInfo[];**

Inherited from **Type**.

> [Visual Basic] **Overloads Public Function GetConstructors() As ConstructorInfo()**
>
> [C#] **public ConstructorInfo[] GetConstructors();**
>
> [C++] **public: ConstructorInfo* GetConstructors() [];**
>
> [JScript] **public function GetConstructors() : ConstructorInfo[];**

TypeDelegator.GetConstructors Method (BindingFlags)

Returns an array of **ConstructorInfo** objects representing constructors defined for the current class.

```
[Visual Basic]
Overrides Overloads Public Function GetConstructors( _
   ByVal bindingAttr As BindingFlags _
) As ConstructorInfo()
[C#]
public override ConstructorInfo[] GetConstructors(
   BindingFlags bindingAttr
);
[C++]
public: ConstructorInfo* GetConstructors(
   BindingFlags bindingAttr
) [];
[JScript]
public override function GetConstructors(
   bindingAttr : BindingFlags
) : ConstructorInfo[];
```

Parameters

bindingAttr
> A bitmask that affects the way in which the search is conducted. The value is a combination of zero or more bit flags from **BindingFlags**.

Return Value

An array of type **ConstructorInfo** containing the specified constructors defined for this class. If no constructors are defined, an empty array is returned. Depending on the value of a specified parameter, only public constructors or both public and non-public constructors will be returned.

Remarks

Class initializers are available only through **GetMember**, **GetMembers**, **FindMembers**, and **GetConstructors**.

Requirements

Platforms: Windows 98, Windows NT 4.0, Windows Millennium Edition, Windows 2000, Windows XP Home Edition, Windows XP Professional, Windows .NET Server family

TypeDelegator.GetCustomAttributes Method

Returns all the custom attributes defined for this type.

Overload List

Returns all the custom attributes defined for this type, specifying whether to search the type's inheritance chain.

> [Visual Basic] **Overloads Overrides Public Function GetCustomAttributes(Boolean) As Object() Implements ICustomAttributeProvider.GetCustomAttributes**
>
> [C#] **public override object[] GetCustomAttributes(bool);**
>
> [C++] **public: Object* GetCustomAttributes(bool) __gc[];**
>
> [JScript] **public override function GetCustomAttributes(Boolean) : Object[];**

Returns an array of custom attributes identified by type.

> [Visual Basic] **Overloads Overrides Public Function GetCustomAttributes(Type, Boolean) As Object() Implements ICustomAttributeProvider.GetCustomAttributes**
>
> [C#] **public override object[] GetCustomAttributes(Type, bool);**
>
> [C++] **public: Object* GetCustomAttributes(Type*, bool) __gc[];**
>
> [JScript] **public override function GetCustomAttributes(Type, Boolean) : Object[];**

TypeDelegator.GetCustomAttributes Method (Boolean)

Returns all the custom attributes defined for this type, specifying whether to search the type's inheritance chain.

```
[Visual Basic]
Overrides Overloads Public Function GetCustomAttributes( _
   ByVal inherit As Boolean _
) As Object() Implements ICustomAttributeProvider.GetCustomAttributes
[C#]
public override object[] GetCustomAttributes(
   bool inherit
);
[C++]
public: Object* GetCustomAttributes(
   bool inherit
) __gc[];
```

```
[JScript]
public override function GetCustomAttributes(
    inherit : Boolean
) : Object[];
```

Parameters

inherit

Specifies whether to search this type's inheritance chain to find the attributes.

Return Value

An array of objects containing all the custom attributes defined for this type.

Implements

ICustomAttributeProvider.GetCustomAttributes

Exceptions

Exception Type	Condition
ReflectionTypeLoad-Exception	The custom attribute type cannot be loaded.

Requirements

Platforms: Windows 98, Windows NT 4.0, Windows Millennium Edition, Windows 2000, Windows XP Home Edition, Windows XP Professional, Windows .NET Server family

TypeDelegator.GetCustomAttributes Method (Type, Boolean)

Returns an array of custom attributes identified by type.

```
[Visual Basic]
Overrides Overloads Public Function GetCustomAttributes( _
    ByVal attributeType As Type, _
    ByVal inherit As Boolean _
) As Object() Implements ICustomAttributeProvider.GetCustomAttributes
[C#]
public override object[] GetCustomAttributes(
    Type attributeType,
    bool inherit
);
[C++]
public: Object* GetCustomAttributes(
    Type* attributeType,
    bool inherit
) __gc[];
[JScript]
public override function GetCustomAttributes(
    attributeType : Type,
    inherit : Boolean
) : Object[];
```

Parameters

attributeType

An array of custom attributes identified by type.

inherit

Specifies whether to search this type's inheritance chain to find the attributes.

Return Value

An array of objects containing the custom attributes defined in this type that match the *attributeType* parameter, specifying whether to

search the type's inheritance chain, or a null reference (**Nothing** in Visual Basic) if no custom attributes are defined on this type.

Implements

ICustomAttributeProvider.GetCustomAttributes

Exceptions

Exception Type	Condition
ArgumentException	*attributeType* is a null reference (**Nothing** in Visual Basic).
ReflectionTypeLoad-Exception	The custom attribute type cannot be loaded.

Requirements

Platforms: Windows 98, Windows NT 4.0, Windows Millennium Edition, Windows 2000, Windows XP Home Edition, Windows XP Professional, Windows .NET Server family

TypeDelegator.GetElementType Method

Returns the **Type** of the object encompassed or referred to by the current array, pointer or ByRef.

```
[Visual Basic]
Overrides Public Function GetElementType() As Type
[C#]
public override Type GetElementType();
[C++]
public: Type* GetElementType();
[JScript]
public override function GetElementType() : Type;
```

Return Value

The **Type** of the object encompassed or referred to by the current array, pointer or **ByRef**, or a null reference (**Nothing** in Visual Basic) if the current **Type** is not an array, a pointer or a **ByRef**.

Requirements

Platforms: Windows 98, Windows NT 4.0, Windows Millennium Edition, Windows 2000, Windows XP Home Edition, Windows XP Professional, Windows .NET Server family

TypeDelegator.GetEvent Method

Overload List

Returns the specified event.

[Visual Basic] **Overloads Overrides Public Function GetEvent(String, BindingFlags) As EventInfo**

[C#] **public override EventInfo GetEvent(string, BindingFlags);**

[C++] **public: EventInfo* GetEvent(String*, BindingFlags);**

[JScript] **public override function GetEvent(String, BindingFlags) : EventInfo;**

Inherited from **Type**.

[Visual Basic] **Overloads Public Function GetEvent(String) As EventInfo**

[C#] **public EventInfo GetEvent(string);**

[C++] **public: EventInfo* GetEvent(String*);**

[JScript] **public function GetEvent(String) : EventInfo;**

TypeDelegator.GetEvent Method (String, BindingFlags)

Returns the specified event.

```
[Visual Basic]
Overrides Overloads Public Function GetEvent( _
    ByVal name As String, _
    ByVal bindingAttr As BindingFlags _
) As EventInfo
[C#]
public override EventInfo GetEvent(
    string name,
    BindingFlags bindingAttr
);
[C++]
public: EventInfo* GetEvent(
    String* name,
    BindingFlags bindingAttr
);
[JScript]
public override function GetEvent(
    name : String,
    bindingAttr : BindingFlags
) : EventInfo;
```

Parameters

name

The name of the event to get.

bindingAttr

A bitmask that affects the way in which the search is conducted. The value is a combination of zero or more bit flags from **BindingFlags**.

Return Value

An **EventInfo** object representing the event declared or inherited by this type with the specified name. This method returns a null reference (**Nothing** in Visual Basic) if no such event is found.

Exceptions

Exception Type	Condition
ArgumentNullException	The *name* parameter is a null reference (**Nothing** in Visual Basic).

Remarks

If *bindingAttr* is **BindingFlags .IgnoreCase**, the case of the *name* parameter is ignored.

Requirements

Platforms: Windows 98, Windows NT 4.0, Windows Millennium Edition, Windows 2000, Windows XP Home Edition, Windows XP Professional, Windows .NET Server family

TypeDelegator.GetEvents Method

Returns an array of **EventInfo** objects representing all the public events declared or inherited by the current **TypeDelegator**.

Overload List

Returns an array of **EventInfo** objects representing all the public events declared or inherited by the current **TypeDelegator**.

[Visual Basic] **Overloads Overrides Public Function GetEvents() As EventInfo()**

[C#] **public override EventInfo[] GetEvents();**

[C++] **public: EventInfo* GetEvents() [];**

[JScript] **public override function GetEvents() : EventInfo[];**

Returns the events specified in *bindingAttr* that are declared or inherited by the current **TypeDelegator**.

[Visual Basic] **Overloads Overrides Public Function GetEvents(BindingFlags) As EventInfo()**

[C#] **public override EventInfo[] GetEvents(BindingFlags);**

[C++] **public: EventInfo* GetEvents(BindingFlags) [];**

[JScript] **public override function GetEvents(BindingFlags) : EventInfo[];**

TypeDelegator.GetEvents Method ()

Returns an array of **EventInfo** objects representing all the public events declared or inherited by the current **TypeDelegator**.

```
[Visual Basic]
Overrides Overloads Public Function GetEvents() As EventInfo()
[C#]
public override EventInfo[] GetEvents();
[C++]
public: EventInfo* GetEvents() [];
[JScript]
public override function GetEvents() : EventInfo[];
```

Return Value

Returns an array of type **EventInfo** containing all the events declared or inherited by the current type. If there are no events, an empty array is returned.

Requirements

Platforms: Windows 98, Windows NT 4.0, Windows Millennium Edition, Windows 2000, Windows XP Home Edition, Windows XP Professional, Windows .NET Server family

TypeDelegator.GetEvents Method (BindingFlags)

Returns the events specified in *bindingAttr* that are declared or inherited by the current **TypeDelegator**.

```
[Visual Basic]
Overrides Overloads Public Function GetEvents( _
    ByVal bindingAttr As BindingFlags _
) As EventInfo()
[C#]
public override EventInfo[] GetEvents(
    BindingFlags bindingAttr
);
[C++]
public: EventInfo* GetEvents(
    BindingFlags bindingAttr
) [];
[JScript]
public override function GetEvents(
    bindingAttr : BindingFlags
) : EventInfo[];
```

Parameters

bindingAttr

A bitmask that affects the way in which the search is conducted. The value is a combination of zero or more bit flags from **BindingFlags**.

Return Value

An array of type **EventInfo** containing the events specified in *bindingAttr*. If there are no events, an empty array is returned.

Requirements

Platforms: Windows 98, Windows NT 4.0, Windows Millennium Edition, Windows 2000, Windows XP Home Edition, Windows XP Professional, Windows .NET Server family

TypeDelegator.GetField Method

Overload List

Returns the **FieldInfo** object representing the field with the specified name.

[Visual Basic] **Overloads Overrides Public Function GetField(String, BindingFlags) As FieldInfo Implements IReflect.GetField**

[C#] **public override FieldInfo GetField(string, BindingFlags);**

[C++] **public: FieldInfo* GetField(String*, BindingFlags);**

[JScript] **public override function GetField(String, BindingFlags) : FieldInfo;**

Inherited from **Type**.

[Visual Basic] **Overloads Public Function GetField(String) As FieldInfo**

[C#] **public FieldInfo GetField(string);**

[C++] **public: FieldInfo* GetField(String*);**

[JScript] **public function GetField(String) : FieldInfo;**

TypeDelegator.GetField Method (String, BindingFlags)

Returns the **FieldInfo** object representing the field with the specified name.

```
[Visual Basic]
Overrides Overloads Public Function GetField( _
   ByVal name As String, _
   ByVal bindingAttr As BindingFlags _
) As FieldInfo Implements IReflect.GetField
[C#]
public override FieldInfo GetField(
   string name,
   BindingFlags bindingAttr
);
[C++]
public: FieldInfo* GetField(
   String* name,
   BindingFlags bindingAttr
);
[JScript]
public override function GetField(
   name : String,
   bindingAttr : BindingFlags
) : FieldInfo;
```

Parameters

name
   The name of the field to find.

bindingAttr
   A bitmask that affects the way in which the search is conducted. The value is a combination of zero or more bit flags from **BindingFlags**.

Return Value

A **FieldInfo** object representing the field declared or inherited by this **TypeDelegator** with the specified name. Returns a null reference (**Nothing** in Visual Basic) if no such field is found.

Implements

IReflect.GetField

Exceptions

Exception Type	Condition
ArgumentNullException	The *name* parameter is a null reference (**Nothing** in Visual Basic).

Remarks

Use a *bindingAttr* of **BindingFlags**.NonPublic to return all public and nonpublic fields. Use **BindingFlags.IgnoreCase** to ignore the case of the fields, as the search is case-sensitive by default.

Requirements

Platforms: Windows 98, Windows NT 4.0, Windows Millennium Edition, Windows 2000, Windows XP Home Edition, Windows XP Professional, Windows .NET Server family

TypeDelegator.GetFields Method

Overload List

Returns an array of **FieldInfo** objects representing the data fields defined for the current class.

[Visual Basic] **Overloads Overrides Public Function GetFields(BindingFlags) As FieldInfo() Implements IReflect.GetFields**

[C#] **public override FieldInfo[] GetFields(BindingFlags);**

[C++] **public: FieldInfo* GetFields(BindingFlags) [];**

[JScript] **public override function GetFields(BindingFlags) : FieldInfo[];**

Inherited from **Type**.

[Visual Basic] **Overloads Public Function GetFields() As FieldInfo()**

[C#] **public FieldInfo[] GetFields();**

[C++] **public: FieldInfo* GetFields() [];**

[JScript] **public function GetFields() : FieldInfo[];**

TypeDelegator.GetFields Method (BindingFlags)

Returns an array of **FieldInfo** objects representing the data fields defined for the current class.

```
[Visual Basic]
Overrides Overloads Public Function GetFields( _
   ByVal bindingAttr As BindingFlags _
) As FieldInfo() Implements IReflect.GetFields
[C#]
public override FieldInfo[] GetFields(
   BindingFlags bindingAttr
);
```

```
[C++]
public: FieldInfo* GetFields(
    BindingFlags bindingAttr
) [];
[JScript]
public override function GetFields(
    bindingAttr : BindingFlags
) : FieldInfo[];
```

Parameters

bindingAttr

A bitmask that affects the way in which the search is conducted. The value is a combination of zero or more bit flags from **BindingFlags**.

Return Value

An array of type **FieldInfo** containing the fields declared or inherited by the current **TypeDelegator**. An empty array is returned if there are no matched fields.

Implements

IReflect.GetFields

Remarks

Use a *bindingAttr* of **BindingFlags**.NonPublic to return all public and nonpublic fields.

Requirements

Platforms: Windows 98, Windows NT 4.0, Windows Millennium Edition, Windows 2000, Windows XP Home Edition, Windows XP Professional, Windows .NET Server family

TypeDelegator.GetInterface Method

Overload List

Returns the specified interface implemented by the current class.

[Visual Basic] **Overloads Overrides Public Function GetInterface(String, Boolean) As Type**

[C#] **public override Type GetInterface(string, bool);**

[C++] **public: Type* GetInterface(String*, bool);**

[JScript] **public override function GetInterface(String, Boolean) : Type;**

Inherited from **Type**.

[Visual Basic] **Overloads Public Function GetInterface(String) As Type**

[C#] **public Type GetInterface(string);**

[C++] **public: Type* GetInterface(String*);**

[JScript] **public function GetInterface(String) : Type;**

TypeDelegator.GetInterface Method (String, Boolean)

Returns the specified interface implemented by the current class.

```
[Visual Basic]
Overrides Overloads Public Function GetInterface( _
    ByVal name As String, _
    ByVal ignoreCase As Boolean _
) As Type
```

```
[C#]
public override Type GetInterface(
    string name,
    bool ignoreCase
);
[C++]
public: Type* GetInterface(
    String* name,
    bool ignoreCase
);
[JScript]
public override function GetInterface(
    name : String,
    ignoreCase : Boolean
) : Type;
```

Parameters

name

The fully qualified name of the interface implemented by the current class.

ignoreCase

true if the case is to be ignored; otherwise, **false**.

Return Value

A **Type** object representing the interface implemented (directly or indirectly) by the current class with the fully qualified name matching the specified name. If no interface that matches name is found, null is returned.

Exceptions

Exception Type	Condition
ArgumentNullException	The *name* parameter is a null reference (**Nothing** in Visual Basic).

Requirements

Platforms: Windows 98, Windows NT 4.0, Windows Millennium Edition, Windows 2000, Windows XP Home Edition, Windows XP Professional, Windows .NET Server family

TypeDelegator.GetInterfaceMap Method

Returns an interface mapping for the specified interface type.

```
[Visual Basic]
Overrides Public Function GetInterfaceMap( _
    ByVal interfaceType As Type _
) As InterfaceMapping
[C#]
public override InterfaceMapping GetInterfaceMap(
    Type interfaceType
);
[C++]
public: InterfaceMapping GetInterfaceMap(
    Type* interfaceType
);
[JScript]
public override function GetInterfaceMap(
    interfaceType : Type
) : InterfaceMapping;
```

Parameters

interfaceType

The **Type** of the interface to retrieve a mapping of.

Return Value

An **InterfaceMapping** object representing the interface mapping for *interfaceType*.

Remarks

The interface map denotes how an interface is mapped into the actual methods on a class that implements that interface.

Requirements

Platforms: Windows 98, Windows NT 4.0, Windows Millennium Edition, Windows 2000, Windows XP Home Edition, Windows XP Professional, Windows .NET Server family

TypeDelegator.GetInterfaces Method

Returns all the interfaces implemented on the current class and its base classes.

```
[Visual Basic]
Overrides Public Function GetInterfaces() As Type()
[C#]
public override Type[] GetInterfaces();
[C++]
public: Type* GetInterfaces() [];
[JScript]
public override function GetInterfaces() : Type[];
```

Return Value

An array of type **Type** containing all the interfaces implemented on the current class and its base classes. If none are defined, an empty array is returned.

Requirements

Platforms: Windows 98, Windows NT 4.0, Windows Millennium Edition, Windows 2000, Windows XP Home Edition, Windows XP Professional, Windows .NET Server family

TypeDelegator.GetMember Method

Overload List

Returns members (properties, methods, constructors, fields, events, and nested types) specified by the given *name*, *type*, and *bindingAttr*.

[Visual Basic] **Overloads Overrides Public Function GetMember(String, MemberTypes, BindingFlags) As MemberInfo()**

[C#] **public override MemberInfo[] GetMember(string, MemberTypes, BindingFlags);**

[C++] **public: MemberInfo* GetMember(String*, MemberTypes, BindingFlags) [];**

[JScript] **public override function GetMember(String, MemberTypes, BindingFlags) : MemberInfo[];**

Inherited from **Type**.

[Visual Basic] **Overloads Public Function GetMember(String) As MemberInfo()**

[C#] **public MemberInfo[] GetMember(string);**

[C++] **public: MemberInfo* GetMember(String*) [];**

[JScript] **public function GetMember(String) : MemberInfo[];**

Inherited from **Type**.

[Visual Basic] **Overloads Public Overridable Function GetMember(String, BindingFlags) As MemberInfo() Implements IReflect.GetMember**

[C#] **public virtual MemberInfo[] GetMember(string, BindingFlags);**

[C++] **public: virtual MemberInfo* GetMember(String*, BindingFlags) [];**

[JScript] **public function GetMember(String, BindingFlags) : MemberInfo[];**

TypeDelegator.GetMember Method (String, MemberTypes, BindingFlags)

Returns members (properties, methods, constructors, fields, events, and nested types) specified by the given *name*, *type*, and *bindingAttr*.

```
[Visual Basic]
Overrides Overloads Public Function GetMember( _
    ByVal name As String, _
    ByVal type As MemberTypes, _
    ByVal bindingAttr As BindingFlags _
) As MemberInfo()
[C#]
public override MemberInfo[] GetMember(
    string name,
    MemberTypes type,
    BindingFlags bindingAttr
);
[C++]
public: MemberInfo* GetMember(
    String* name,
    MemberTypes type,
    BindingFlags bindingAttr
) [];
[JScript]
public override function GetMember(
    name : String,
    type : MemberTypes,
    bindingAttr : BindingFlags
) : MemberInfo[];
```

Parameters

name

The name of the member to get.

type

The type of members to get.

bindingAttr

A bitmask that affects the way in which the search is conducted. The value is a combination of zero or more bit flags from **BindingFlags**.

Return Value

An array of type **MemberInfo** containing all the members of the current class and its base class meeting the specified criteria.

Exceptions

Exception Type	Condition
ArgumentNullException	The *name* parameter is a null reference (**Nothing** in Visual Basic).

Remarks

If *bindingAttr* is **BindingFlags**.NonPublic, all the members will be considered. If there are no matches, an empty array is returned.

Requirements

Platforms: Windows 98, Windows NT 4.0, Windows Millennium Edition, Windows 2000, Windows XP Home Edition, Windows XP Professional, Windows .NET Server family

TypeDelegator.GetMembers Method

Overload List

Returns members specified by *bindingAttr*.

[Visual Basic] **Overloads Overrides Public Function GetMembers(BindingFlags) As MemberInfo() Implements IReflect.GetMembers**

[C#] **public override MemberInfo[] GetMembers(BindingFlags);**

[C++] **public: MemberInfo* GetMembers(BindingFlags) [];**

[JScript] **public override function GetMembers(BindingFlags) : MemberInfo[];**

Inherited from **Type**.

[Visual Basic] **Overloads Public Function GetMembers() As MemberInfo()**

[C#] **public MemberInfo[] GetMembers();**

[C++] **public: MemberInfo* GetMembers() [];**

[JScript] **public function GetMembers() : MemberInfo[];**

TypeDelegator.GetMembers Method (BindingFlags)

Returns members specified by *bindingAttr*.

```
[Visual Basic]
Overrides Overloads Public Function GetMembers( _
   ByVal bindingAttr As BindingFlags _
) As MemberInfo() Implements IReflect.GetMembers
[C#]
public override MemberInfo[] GetMembers(
   BindingFlags bindingAttr
);
[C++]
public: MemberInfo* GetMembers(
   BindingFlags bindingAttr
) [];
[JScript]
public override function GetMembers(
   bindingAttr : BindingFlags
) : MemberInfo[];
```

Parameters

bindingAttr

A bitmask that affects the way in which the search is conducted. The value is a combination of zero or more bit flags from **BindingFlags**.

Return Value

An array of type **MemberInfo** containing all the members of the current class and its base classes that meet the *bindingAttr* filter.

Implements

IReflect.GetMembers

Remarks

If *bindingAttr* is **BindingFlags**.NonPublic, all the members will be considered. If there are no matches, an empty array is returned.

Requirements

Platforms: Windows 98, Windows NT 4.0, Windows Millennium Edition, Windows 2000, Windows XP Home Edition, Windows XP Professional, Windows .NET Server family

TypeDelegator.GetMethodImpl Method

Searches for the specified method whose parameters match the specified argument types and modifiers, using the specified binding constraints and the specified calling convention.

```
[Visual Basic]
Overrides Protected Function GetMethodImpl( _
   ByVal name As String, _
   ByVal bindingAttr As BindingFlags, _
   ByVal binder As Binder, _
   ByVal callConvention As CallingConventions, _
   ByVal types() As Type, _
   ByVal modifiers() As ParameterModifier _
) As MethodInfo
[C#]
protected override MethodInfo GetMethodImpl(
   string name,
   BindingFlags bindingAttr,
   Binder binder,
   CallingConventions callConvention,
   Type[] types,
   ParameterModifier[] modifiers
);
[C++]
protected: MethodInfo* GetMethodImpl(
   String* name,
   BindingFlags bindingAttr,
   Binder* binder,
   CallingConventions callConvention,
   Type* types[],
   ParameterModifier modifiers[]
);
[JScript]
protected override function GetMethodImpl(
   name : String,
   bindingAttr : BindingFlags,
   binder : Binder,
   callConvention : CallingConventions,
   types : Type[],
   modifiers : ParameterModifier[]
) : MethodInfo;
```

Parameters

name

The method name.

bindingAttr

A bitmask that affects the way in which the search is conducted. The value is a combination of zero or more bit flags from **BindingFlags**.

binder

An object that enables the binding, coercion of argument types, invocation of members, and retrieval of **MemberInfo** objects using reflection. If *binder* is a null reference (**Nothing** in Visual Basic), the default binder is used.

callConvention

The calling conventions.

types

An array of type **Type** containing a list of the parameter number, order, and types. Types cannot be a null reference (**Nothing** in Visual Basic); use an appropriate **GetMethod** method or an empty array to search for a method without parameters.

modifiers

An array of type **ParameterModifier** having the same length as the *types* array, whose elements represent the attributes associated with the parameters of the method to get.

Return Value

A **MethodInfoInfo** object for the implementation method that matches the specified criteria, or a null reference (**Nothing** in Visual Basic) if a match cannot be found.

Remarks

The *callConvention* parameter indicates the calling convention for the entry point. If no **CallingConventions** is specified, a default **CallingConventions** value of **Standard** is used.

Requirements

Platforms: Windows 98, Windows NT 4.0, Windows Millennium Edition, Windows 2000, Windows XP Home Edition, Windows XP Professional, Windows .NET Server family

TypeDelegator.GetMethods Method

Overload List

Returns an array of **MethodInfo** objects representing specified methods of the current **TypeDelegator**.

[Visual Basic] **Overloads Overrides Public Function GetMethods(BindingFlags) As MethodInfo() Implements IReflect.GetMethods**

[C#] **public override MethodInfo[] GetMethods(BindingFlags);**

[C++] **public: MethodInfo* GetMethods(BindingFlags) [];**

[JScript] **public override function GetMethods(BindingFlags) : MethodInfo[];**

Inherited from **Type**.

[Visual Basic] **Overloads Public Function GetMethods() As MethodInfo()**

[C#] **public MethodInfo[] GetMethods();**

[C++] **public: MethodInfo* GetMethods() [];**

[JScript] **public function GetMethods() : MethodInfo[];**

TypeDelegator.GetMethods Method (BindingFlags)

Returns an array of **MethodInfo** objects representing specified methods of the current **TypeDelegator**.

```
[Visual Basic]
Overrides Overloads Public Function GetMethods( _
    ByVal bindingAttr As BindingFlags _
) As MethodInfo() Implements IReflect.GetMethods
[C#]
public override MethodInfo[] GetMethods(
    BindingFlags bindingAttr
);
[C++]
public: MethodInfo* GetMethods(
    BindingFlags bindingAttr
) [];
[JScript]
public override function GetMethods(
    bindingAttr : BindingFlags
) : MethodInfo[];
```

Parameters

bindingAttr

A bitmask that affects the way in which the search is conducted. The value is a combination of zero or more bit flags from **BindingFlags**.

Return Value

An array of **MethodInfo** objects representing the methods defined on this **TypeDelegator**.

Implements

IReflect.GetMethods

Requirements

Platforms: Windows 98, Windows NT 4.0, Windows Millennium Edition, Windows 2000, Windows XP Home Edition, Windows XP Professional, Windows .NET Server family

TypeDelegator.GetNestedType Method

Overload List

Returns a nested type specified by *name* and in *bindingAttr* that are declared or inherited by the current **TypeDelegator**.

[Visual Basic] **Overloads Overrides Public Function GetNestedType(String, BindingFlags) As Type**

[C#] **public override Type GetNestedType(string, BindingFlags);**

[C++] **public: Type* GetNestedType(String*, BindingFlags);**

[JScript] **public override function GetNestedType(String, BindingFlags) : Type;**

Inherited from **Type**.

[Visual Basic] **Overloads Public Function GetNestedType(String) As Type**

[C#] **public Type GetNestedType(string);**

[C++] **public: Type* GetNestedType(String*);**

[JScript] **public function GetNestedType(String) : Type;**

TypeDelegator.GetNestedType Method (String, BindingFlags)

Returns a nested type specified by *name* and in *bindingAttr* that are declared or inherited by the current **TypeDelegator**.

```
[Visual Basic]
Overrides Overloads Public Function GetNestedType( _
   ByVal name As String, _
   ByVal bindingAttr As BindingFlags _
) As Type
[C#]
public override Type GetNestedType(
   string name,
   BindingFlags bindingAttr
);
[C++]
public: Type* GetNestedType(
   String* name,
   BindingFlags bindingAttr
);
[JScript]
public override function GetNestedType(
   name : String,
   bindingAttr : BindingFlags
) : Type;
```

Parameters

name
The nested type's name.

bindingAttr
A bitmask that affects the way in which the search is conducted. The value is a combination of zero or more bit flags from **BindingFlags**.

Return Value

A **Type** object representing the nested type.

Exceptions

Exception Type	Condition
ArgumentNullException	The *name* parameter is a null reference (**Nothing** in Visual Basic).

Requirements

Platforms: Windows 98, Windows NT 4.0, Windows Millennium Edition, Windows 2000, Windows XP Home Edition, Windows XP Professional, Windows .NET Server family

TypeDelegator.GetNestedTypes Method

Overload List

Returns the nested types specified in *bindingAttr* that are declared or inherited by the current **TypeDelegator**.

[Visual Basic] **Overloads Overrides Public Function GetNestedTypes(BindingFlags) As Type()**
[C#] **public override Type[] GetNestedTypes(BindingFlags);**
[C++] **public: Type* GetNestedTypes(BindingFlags) [];**
[JScript] **public override function GetNestedTypes(BindingFlags) : Type[];**

Inherited from **Type**.
[Visual Basic] **Overloads Public Function GetNestedTypes() As Type()**
[C#] **public Type[] GetNestedTypes();**
[C++] **public: Type* GetNestedTypes() [];**
[JScript] **public function GetNestedTypes() : Type[];**

TypeDelegator.GetNestedTypes Method (BindingFlags)

Returns the nested types specified in *bindingAttr* that are declared or inherited by the current **TypeDelegator**.

```
[Visual Basic]
Overrides Overloads Public Function GetNestedTypes( _
   ByVal bindingAttr As BindingFlags _
) As Type()
[C#]
public override Type[] GetNestedTypes(
   BindingFlags bindingAttr
);
[C++]
public: Type* GetNestedTypes(
   BindingFlags bindingAttr
) [];
[JScript]
public override function GetNestedTypes(
   bindingAttr : BindingFlags
) : Type[];
```

Parameters

bindingAttr
A bitmask that affects the way in which the search is conducted. The value is a combination of zero or more bit flags from **BindingFlags**.

Return Value

An array of type **Type** containing the nested types.

Requirements

Platforms: Windows 98, Windows NT 4.0, Windows Millennium Edition, Windows 2000, Windows XP Home Edition, Windows XP Professional, Windows .NET Server family

TypeDelegator.GetProperties Method

Overload List

Returns an array of **PropertyInfo** objects representing properties defined on this **TypeDelegator**.

[Visual Basic] **Overloads Overrides Public Function GetProperties(BindingFlags) As PropertyInfo() Implements IReflect.GetProperties**
[C#] **public override PropertyInfo[] GetProperties(BindingFlags);**
[C++] **public: PropertyInfo* GetProperties(BindingFlags) [];**
[JScript] **public override function GetProperties(BindingFlags) : PropertyInfo[];**

Inherited from **Type**.
[Visual Basic] **Overloads Public Function GetProperties() As PropertyInfo()**
[C#] **public PropertyInfo[] GetProperties();**
[C++] **public: PropertyInfo* GetProperties() [];**
[JScript] **public function GetProperties() : PropertyInfo[];**

TypeDelegator.GetProperties Method (BindingFlags)

Returns an array of **PropertyInfo** objects representing properties defined on this **TypeDelegator**.

```
[Visual Basic]
Overrides Overloads Public Function GetProperties( _
   ByVal bindingAttr As BindingFlags _
) As PropertyInfo() Implements IReflect.GetProperties
[C#]
public override PropertyInfo[] GetProperties(
   BindingFlags bindingAttr
);
[C++]
public: PropertyInfo* GetProperties(
   BindingFlags bindingAttr
) [];
[JScript]
public override function GetProperties(
   bindingAttr : BindingFlags
) : PropertyInfo[];
```

Parameters

bindingAttr
A bitmask that affects the way in which the search is conducted. The value is a combination of zero or more bit flags from **BindingFlags**.

Return Value

An array of **PropertyInfo** objects representing properties defined on this **TypeDelegator**.

Implements

IReflect.GetProperties

Requirements

Platforms: Windows 98, Windows NT 4.0, Windows Millennium Edition, Windows 2000, Windows XP Home Edition, Windows XP Professional, Windows .NET Server family

TypeDelegator.GetPropertyImpl Method

When overridden in a derived class, searches for the specified property whose parameters match the specified argument types and modifiers, using the specified binding constraints.

```
[Visual Basic]
Overrides Protected Function GetPropertyImpl( _
   ByVal name As String, _
   ByVal bindingAttr As BindingFlags, _
   ByVal binder As Binder, _
   ByVal returnType As Type, _
   ByVal types() As Type, _
   ByVal modifiers() As ParameterModifier _
) As PropertyInfo
[C#]
protected override PropertyInfo GetPropertyImpl(
   string name,
   BindingFlags bindingAttr,
   Binder binder,
   Type returnType,
   Type[] types,
   ParameterModifier[] modifiers
);
```

```
[C++]
protected: PropertyInfo* GetPropertyImpl(
   String* name,
   BindingFlags bindingAttr,
   Binder* binder,
   Type* returnType,
   Type* types[],
   ParameterModifier modifiers[]
);
[JScript]
protected override function GetPropertyImpl(
   name : String,
   bindingAttr : BindingFlags,
   binder : Binder,
   returnType : Type,
   types : Type[],
   modifiers : ParameterModifier[]
) : PropertyInfo;
```

Parameters

name
The property to get.
bindingAttr
A bitmask that affects the way in which the search is conducted. The value is a combination of zero or more bit flags from **BindingFlags**.
binder
An object that enables the binding, coercion of argument types, invocation of members, and retrieval of **MemberInfo** objects via reflection. If *binder* is a null reference (**Nothing** in Visual Basic), the default binder is used. See **Binder**.
returnType
The return type of the property.
types
A list of parameter types. The list represents the number, order, and types of the parameters. Types cannot be null; use an appropriate **GetMethod** method or an empty array to search for a method without parameters.
modifiers
An array of the same length as types with elements that represent the attributes associated with the parameters of the method to get.

Return Value

A **PropertyInfo** object for the property that matches the specified criteria, or null if a match cannot be found.

Requirements

Platforms: Windows 98, Windows NT 4.0, Windows Millennium Edition, Windows 2000, Windows XP Home Edition, Windows XP Professional, Windows .NET Server family

TypeDelegator.HasElementTypeImpl Method

Gets a value indicating whether the current **Type** encompasses or refers to another type; that is, whether the current **Type** is an array, a pointer or a ByRef.

```
[Visual Basic]
Overrides Protected Function HasElementTypeImpl() As Boolean
[C#]
protected override bool HasElementTypeImpl();
```

```
[C++]
protected: bool HasElementTypeImpl();
[JScript]
protected override function HasElementTypeImpl() : Boolean;
```

Return Value

true if the **Type** is an array, a pointer or a ByRef; otherwise, **false**.

Requirements

Platforms: Windows 98, Windows NT 4.0,
Windows Millennium Edition, Windows 2000,
Windows XP Home Edition, Windows XP Professional,
Windows .NET Server family

TypeDelegator.InvokeMember Method

Overload List

Invokes the specified member. The method that is to be invoked
must be accessible and provide the most specific match with the
specified argument list, under the constraints of the specified binder
and invocation attributes.

[Visual Basic] **Overloads Overrides Public Function
InvokeMember(String, BindingFlags, Binder, Object,
Object(), ParameterModifier(), CultureInfo, String()) As
Object Implements IReflect.InvokeMember**

[C#] **public override object InvokeMember(string,
BindingFlags, Binder, object, object[], ParameterModifier[],
CultureInfo, string[]);**

[C++] **public: Object* InvokeMember(String*,
BindingFlags, Binder*, Object*, Object[],
ParameterModifier[], CultureInfo*, String*[]);**

[JScript] **public override function InvokeMember(String,
BindingFlags, Binder, Object, Object[],
ParameterModifier[], CultureInfo, String[]) : Object;**

Inherited from **Type**.

[Visual Basic] **Overloads Public Function
InvokeMember(String, BindingFlags, Binder, Object,
Object()) As Object**

[C#] **public object InvokeMember(string, BindingFlags,
Binder, object, object[]);**

[C++] **public: Object* InvokeMember(String*,
BindingFlags, Binder*, Object*, Object[]);**

[JScript] **public function InvokeMember(String,
BindingFlags, Binder, Object, Object[]) : Object;**

Inherited from **Type**.

[Visual Basic] **Overloads Public Function
InvokeMember(String, BindingFlags, Binder, Object,
Object(), CultureInfo) As Object**

[C#] **public object InvokeMember(string, BindingFlags,
Binder, object, object[], CultureInfo);**

[C++] **public: Object* InvokeMember(String*,
BindingFlags, Binder*, Object*, Object[], CultureInfo*);**

[JScript] **public function InvokeMember(String,
BindingFlags, Binder, Object, Object[], CultureInfo) :
Object;**

TypeDelegator.InvokeMember Method (String, BindingFlags, Binder, Object, Object[], ParameterModifier[], CultureInfo, String[])

Invokes the specified member. The method that is to be invoked
must be accessible and provide the most specific match with the
specified argument list, under the constraints of the specified binder
and invocation attributes.

```
[Visual Basic]
Overrides Overloads Public Function InvokeMember( _
   ByVal name As String, _
   ByVal invokeAttr As BindingFlags, _
   ByVal binder As Binder, _
   ByVal target As Object, _
   ByVal args() As Object, _
   ByVal modifiers() As ParameterModifier, _
   ByVal culture As CultureInfo, _
   ByVal namedParameters() As String _
) As Object Implements IReflect.InvokeMember
[C#]
public override object InvokeMember(
   string name,
   BindingFlags invokeAttr,
   Binder binder,
   object target,
   object[] args,
   ParameterModifier[] modifiers,
   CultureInfo culture,
   string[] namedParameters
);
[C++]
public: Object* InvokeMember(
   String* name,
   BindingFlags invokeAttr,
   Binder* binder,
   Object* target,
   Object* args __gc[],
   ParameterModifier modifiers[],
   CultureInfo* culture,
   String* namedParameters __gc[]
);
[JScript]
public override function InvokeMember(
   name : String,
   invokeAttr : BindingFlags,
   binder : Binder,
   target : Object,
   args : Object[],
   modifiers : ParameterModifier[],
   culture : CultureInfo,
   namedParameters : String[]
) : Object;
```

Parameters

name

The name of the member to invoke. This may be a constructor,
method, property, or field. If an empty string ("") is passed, the
default member is invoked.

invokeAttr

The invocation attribute. This must be one of the following
BindingFlags: **InvokeMethod**, **CreateInstance**, **Static**,
GetField, **SetField**, **GetProperty**, or **SetProperty**. A suitable

invocation attribute must be specified. If a static member is to be invoked, the **Static** flag must be set.

binder

An object that enables the binding, coercion of argument types, invocation of members, and retrieval of **MemberInfo** objects via reflection. If *binder* is a null reference (**Nothing** in Visual Basic), the default binder is used. See **Binder**.

target

The object on which to invoke the specified member.

args

An array of type **Object** that contains the number, order, and type of the parameters of the member to be invoked. If *args* contains an uninitialized **Object**, it is treated as empty, which, with the default binder, can be widened to 0, 0.0 or a string.

modifiers

An array of type **ParameterModifer** that is the same length as *args*, with elements that represent the attributes associated with the arguments of the member to be invoked. A parameter has attributes associated with it in the member's signature. For ByRef, use **ParameterModifer.ByRef**, and for none, use **ParameterModifer.None**. The default binder does exact matching on these. Attributes such as **In** and **InOut** are not used in binding, and can be viewed using **ParameterInfo**.

culture

An instance of **CultureInfo** used to govern the coercion of types. This is necessary, for example, to convert a string that represents 1000 to a **Double** value, since 1000 is represented differently by different cultures. If *culture* is a null reference (**Nothing** in Visual Basic), the **CultureInfo** for the current thread's **CultureInfo** is used.

namedParameters

An array of type **String** containing parameter names that match up, starting at element zero, with the *args* array. There must be no holes in the array. If *args*. **Length** is greater than *namedParameters*. **Length**, the remaining parameters are filled in order.

Return Value

An **Object** representing the return value of the invoked member.

Implements

IReflect.InvokeMember

Remarks

A method will be invoked if both the following conditions are true:

- The number of parameters in the method declaration equals the number of arguments in the specified argument list (unless default arguments are defined on the member).
- The type of each arguments can be converted by the binder to the type of the parameter.

The binder will find all the matching methods. These methods are found based upon the type of binding requested (**BindingFlags.MethodInvoke**, **BindingFlags.GetProperties**, and so on). The set of methods is filtered by the name, number of arguments, and a set of search modifiers defined in the binder.

After the method is selected, it will be invoked. Accessibility is checked at that point. The search may control which set of methods are searched based upon the accessibility attribute associated with the method. The **Binder.BindToMethod** method is responsible for selecting the method to be invoked. The default binder selects the most specific match.

> **Note** Access restrictions are ignored for fully trusted code. That is, private constructors, methods, fields, and properties can be accessed and invoked using reflection whenever the code is fully trusted.

Currently, **InvokeMember** performs the Microsoft .NET Framework reflection semantics for every type of object.

If the member specified by name is an array and the **BindingFlags.GetField** flag is set on *invokeAttr*, the *args* array specifies the elements whose values are to be returned. For example, the following call through **Type** object **t** returns the value of the first element of the string array MyArray, which is a member of the calling object: String ret = (String) t.InvokeMember ("MyArray", BindingFlags.GetField, null,

this, new Variant[](0));

You can use **InvokeMember** to set one or more elements of a member array. All elements are set to the same value. The *args* array must be formatted as follows:

{index1,

index2, , value}

For example, to set the first member of MyArray from the previous example, the syntax is as follows:

```
t.InvokeMember ("MyArray", BindingFlags.SetField, null, this, new
                Variant[]{0,"Updated"});
```

Requirements

Platforms: Windows 98, Windows NT 4.0, Windows Millennium Edition, Windows 2000, Windows XP Home Edition, Windows XP Professional, Windows .NET Server family

TypeDelegator.IsArrayImpl Method

Gets a value indicating whether the **Type** is an array.

```
[Visual Basic]
Overrides Protected Function IsArrayImpl() As Boolean
[C#]
protected override bool IsArrayImpl();
[C++]
protected: bool IsArrayImpl();
[JScript]
protected override function IsArrayImpl() : Boolean;
```

Return Value

true if the **Type** is an array; otherwise, **false**.

Requirements

Platforms: Windows 98, Windows NT 4.0, Windows Millennium Edition, Windows 2000, Windows XP Home Edition, Windows XP Professional, Windows .NET Server family

TypeDelegator.IsByRefImpl Method

Gets a value indicating whether the **Type** is passed by reference.

```
[Visual Basic]
Overrides Protected Function IsByRefImpl() As Boolean
[C#]
protected override bool IsByRefImpl();
```

```
[C++]
protected: bool IsByRefImpl();
[JScript]
protected override function IsByRefImpl() : Boolean;
```

Return Value

true if the **Type** is passed by reference; otherwise, **false**.

Requirements

Platforms: Windows 98, Windows NT 4.0,
Windows Millennium Edition, Windows 2000,
Windows XP Home Edition, Windows XP Professional,
Windows .NET Server family

TypeDelegator.IsCOMObjectImpl Method

Gets a value indicating whether the **Type** is a COM object.

```
[Visual Basic]
Overrides Protected Function IsCOMObjectImpl() As Boolean
[C#]
protected override bool IsCOMObjectImpl();
[C++]
protected: bool IsCOMObjectImpl();
[JScript]
protected override function IsCOMObjectImpl() : Boolean;
```

Return Value

true if the **Type** is a COM object; otherwise, **false**.

Requirements

Platforms: Windows 98, Windows NT 4.0,
Windows Millennium Edition, Windows 2000,
Windows XP Home Edition, Windows XP Professional,
Windows .NET Server family

TypeDelegator.IsDefined Method

Indicates whether a custom attribute identified by *attributeType* is defined.

```
[Visual Basic]
Overrides Public Function IsDefined( _
   ByVal attributeType As Type, _
   ByVal inherit As Boolean _
) As Boolean Implements ICustomAttributeProvider.IsDefined
[C#]
public override bool IsDefined(
   Type attributeType,
   bool inherit
);
[C++]
public: bool IsDefined(
   Type* attributeType,
   bool inherit
);
[JScript]
public override function IsDefined(
   attributeType : Type,
   inherit : Boolean
) : Boolean;
```

Parameters

attributeType
   An array of custom attributes identified by type.
inherit
   Specifies whether to search this type's inheritance chain to find the attributes.

Return Value

true if a custom attribute identified by *attributeType* is defined; otherwise, **false**.

Implements

ICustomAttributeProvider.IsDefined

Exceptions

Exception Type	Condition
ArgumentException	*attributeType* is a null reference (**Nothing** in Visual Basic).
ReflectionTypeLoad-Exception	The custom attribute type cannot be loaded.

Requirements

Platforms: Windows 98, Windows NT 4.0,
Windows Millennium Edition, Windows 2000,
Windows XP Home Edition, Windows XP Professional,
Windows .NET Server family

TypeDelegator.IsPointerImpl Method

Gets a value indicating whether the **Type** is a pointer.

```
[Visual Basic]
Overrides Protected Function IsPointerImpl() As Boolean
[C#]
protected override bool IsPointerImpl();
[C++]
protected: bool IsPointerImpl();
[JScript]
protected override function IsPointerImpl() : Boolean;
```

Return Value

true if the **Type** is a pointer; otherwise, **false**.

Requirements

Platforms: Windows 98, Windows NT 4.0,
Windows Millennium Edition, Windows 2000,
Windows XP Home Edition, Windows XP Professional,
Windows .NET Server family

TypeDelegator.IsPrimitiveImpl Method

Gets a value indicating whether the **Type** is one of the primitive types.

```
[Visual Basic]
Overrides Protected Function IsPrimitiveImpl() As Boolean
[C#]
protected override bool IsPrimitiveImpl();
[C++]
protected: bool IsPrimitiveImpl();
[JScript]
protected override function IsPrimitiveImpl() : Boolean;
```

Return Value

true if the **Type** is one of the primitive types; otherwise, **false**.

Requirements

Platforms: Windows 98, Windows NT 4.0,
Windows Millennium Edition, Windows 2000,
Windows XP Home Edition, Windows XP Professional,
Windows .NET Server family

TypeDelegator.IsValueTypeImpl Method

Gets a value indicating whether the type is a value type; that is, not a
class or an interface.

```
[Visual Basic]
Overrides Protected Function IsValueTypeImpl() As Boolean
[C#]
protected override bool IsValueTypeImpl();
[C++]
protected: bool IsValueTypeImpl();
[JScript]
protected override function IsValueTypeImpl() : Boolean;
```

Return Value

true if the type is a value type; otherwise, **false**.

Requirements

Platforms: Windows 98, Windows NT 4.0,
Windows Millennium Edition, Windows 2000,
Windows XP Home Edition, Windows XP Professional,
Windows .NET Server family

TypeFilter Delegate

Filters the classes represented in an array of **Type** objects.

```
[Visual Basic]
<Serializable>
Public Delegate Function Sub TypeFilter( _
   ByVal m As Type, _
   ByVal filterCriteria As Object _
) As Boolean
[C#]
[Serializable]
public delegate bool TypeFilter(
   Type m,
   object filterCriteria
);
[C++]
[Serializable]
public __gc __delegate bool TypeFilter(
   Type* m,
   Object* filterCriteria
);
```

[JScript] In JScript, you can use the delegates in the .NET Framework, but you cannot define your own.

Parameters [Visual Basic, C#, C++]

The declaration of your callback method must have the same parameters as the **TypeFilter** delegate declaration.

m

　　The **Type** object to which the filter is applied.

filterCriteria

　　An arbitrary object used to filter the list.

Remarks

The **TypeFilter** delegate is used to filter a list of classes. Specifically, you use it to filter the classes represented in an array of **Type** objects. The **Type.FindInterfaces** method uses this delegate to filter the list of interfaces that it returns. Every derived class of **Delegate** and **MulticastDelegate** has a constructor and a **DynamicInvoke** method.

Requirements

Namespace: System.Reflection

Platforms: Windows 98, Windows NT 4.0, Windows Millennium Edition, Windows 2000, Windows XP Home Edition, Windows XP Professional, Windows .NET Server family

Assembly: Mscorlib (in Mscorlib.dll)

System.Reflection.Emit Namespace

The **System.Reflection.Emit** namespace contains classes that allow a compiler or tool to emit metadata and Microsoft intermediate language (MSIL) and optionally generate a PE file on disk. The primary clients of these classes are script engines and compilers.

AssemblyBuilder Class

Defines and represents a dynamic assembly.

System.Object
  System.Reflection.Assembly
    System.Reflection.Emit.AssemblyBuilder

```
[Visual Basic]
NotInheritable Public Class AssemblyBuilder
   Inherits Assembly
[C#]
public sealed class AssemblyBuilder : Assembly
[C++]
public __gc __sealed class AssemblyBuilder : public Assembly
[JScript]
public class AssemblyBuilder extends Assembly
```

Thread Safety

Reflection Emit is thread-safe when using assemblies that were created with the **AppDomain.DefineDynamicAssembly** method with the Boolean parameter *isSynchronized* set to **true**.

Remarks

A dynamic assembly is an assembly that is created using the Reflection Emit APIs. The dynamic modules in the assembly are saved when the dynamic assembly is saved using the **Save** method. To generate an executable, the **SetEntryPoint** method must be called to identify the method that is the entry point to the assembly. Assemblies are saved as DLL by default, unless **SetEntryPoint** requests the generation of a console application or a Windows-based application.

If a dynamic assembly contains more than one dynamic module, the assembly's manifest file name should match the module's name that is specified as the first argument to **DefineDynamicModule**.

Some methods on the base class **Assembly** such as **GetModules** and **GetLoadedModules** will not work correctly when called **AssemblyBuilder** objects. You can load the defined dynamic assembly and call the methods on the loaded assembly. For example, to ensure that resource modules are included in the returned module list, call **GetModules** on the loaded **Assembly** object.The signing of a dynamic assembly using **KeyPair** is not effective until the assembly is saved to disk. So, strong names will not work with transient dynamic assemblies.

Requirements

Namespace: System.Reflection.Emit

Platforms: Windows 98, Windows NT 4.0, Windows Millennium Edition, Windows 2000, Windows XP Home Edition, Windows XP Professional, Windows .NET Server family

Assembly: Mscorlib (in Mscorlib.dll)

.NET Framework Security:
- **ReflectionPermission** to enhance security and performance when invoked late-bound through mechanisms such as **Type.InvokeMember**. Associated enumeration: **ReflectionPermissionFlag.MemberAccess**.

AssemblyBuilder.CodeBase Property

Gets the location of the assembly, as specified originally (such as in an **AssemblyName** object).

```
[Visual Basic]
Overrides Public ReadOnly Property CodeBase As String
[C#]
public override string CodeBase {get;}
[C++]
public: __property String* get_CodeBase();
[JScript]
public override function get CodeBase() : String;
```

Property Value

The location of the assembly, as specified originally.

Exceptions

Exception Type	Condition
NotSupportedException	This method is not currently supported.
SecurityException	The caller does not have the required permission.

Remarks

To get the absolute path to the loaded manifest-containing file, use the **Assembly.Location** property.

Requirements

Platforms: Windows 98, Windows NT 4.0, Windows Millennium Edition, Windows 2000, Windows XP Home Edition, Windows XP Professional, Windows .NET Server family

.NET Framework Security:
- **ReflectionPermission** to enhance security and performance when invoked late-bound through mechanisms such as **Type.InvokeMember**. Associated enumeration: **ReflectionPermissionFlag.MemberAccess**.

AssemblyBuilder.EntryPoint Property

Returns the entry point of this assembly.

```
[Visual Basic]
Overrides Public ReadOnly Property EntryPoint As MethodInfo
[C#]
public override MethodInfo EntryPoint {get;}
[C++]
public: __property MethodInfo* get_EntryPoint();
[JScript]
public override function get EntryPoint() : MethodInfo;
```

Property Value

The entry point of this assembly.

Exceptions

Exception Type	Condition
SecurityException	The caller does not have the required permission.

Requirements

Platforms: Windows 98, Windows NT 4.0, Windows Millennium Edition, Windows 2000, Windows XP Home Edition, Windows XP Professional, Windows .NET Server family

.NET Framework Security:
* **ReflectionPermission** to enhance security and performance when invoked late-bound through mechanisms such as **Type.InvokeMember**. Associated enumeration: **ReflectionPermissionFlag.MemberAccess**.

AssemblyBuilder.ImageRuntimeVersion Property

Note: This namespace, class, or member is supported only in version 1.1 of the .NET Framework.

Gets the version of the common language runtime that will be saved in the file containing the manifest.

```
[Visual Basic]
Overrides Public ReadOnly Property ImageRuntimeVersion As String
[C#]
public override string ImageRuntimeVersion {get;}
[C++]
public: __property String* get_ImageRuntimeVersion();
[JScript]
public override function get ImageRuntimeVersion() : String;
```

Property Value

A string representing the common language runtime version.

Exceptions

Exception Type	Condition
SecurityException	The caller does not have the required permission.

Requirements

Platforms: Windows 98, Windows NT 4.0, Windows Millennium Edition, Windows 2000, Windows XP Home Edition, Windows XP Professional, Windows .NET Server family

.NET Framework Security:
* **ReflectionPermission** to enhance security and performance when invoked late-bound through mechanisms such as **Type.InvokeMember**. Associated enumeration: **ReflectionPermissionFlag.MemberAccess**.

AssemblyBuilder.Location Property

Gets the location, in codebase format, of the loaded file that contains the manifest if it is not shadow-copied.

```
[Visual Basic]
Overrides Public ReadOnly Property Location As String
[C#]
public override string Location {get;}
```

```
[C++]
public: __property String* get_Location();
[JScript]
public override function get Location() : String;
```

Property Value

The location of the loaded file that contains the manifest. If the loaded file has been shadow-copied, the **Location** is that of the file before being shadow-copied.

Exceptions

Exception Type	Condition
NotSupportedException	This method is not currently supported.
SecurityException	The caller does not have the required permission.

Requirements

Platforms: Windows 98, Windows NT 4.0, Windows Millennium Edition, Windows 2000, Windows XP Home Edition, Windows XP Professional, Windows .NET Server family

.NET Framework Security:
* **ReflectionPermission** to enhance security and performance when invoked late-bound through mechanisms such as **Type.InvokeMember**. Associated enumeration: **ReflectionPermissionFlag.MemberAccess**.

AssemblyBuilder.AddResourceFile Method

Adds an existing resource file to this assembly.

Overload List

Adds an existing resource file to this assembly.

> [Visual Basic] **Overloads Public Sub AddResourceFile (String, String)**
> [C#] **public void AddResourceFile(string, string);**
> [C++] **public: void AddResourceFile(String*, String*);**
> [JScript] **public function AddResourceFile(String, String);**

Adds an existing resource file to this assembly.

> [Visual Basic] **Overloads Public Sub AddResourceFile (String, String, ResourceAttributes)**
> [C#] **public void AddResourceFile(string, string, ResourceAttributes);**
> [C++] **public: void AddResourceFile(String*, String*, ResourceAttributes);**
> [JScript] **public function AddResourceFile(String, String, ResourceAttributes);**

Example

[Visual Basic, C#, C++] The following code sample demonstrates how to attach a resource file to a dynamically created assembly, using **AddResourceFile**.

> [Visual Basic, C#, C++] **Note** This example shows how to use one of the overloaded versions of **AddResourceFile**. For other examples that might be available, see the individual overload topics.

```
[Visual Basic]
Imports System
Imports System.IO
Imports System.Threading
Imports System.Reflection
Imports System.Reflection.Emit

_

Class AsmBuilderGetFileDemo

    Private Shared myResourceFileName As String = "MyResource.txt"

    Private Shared Function CreateResourceFile() As FileInfo

        Dim f As New FileInfo(myResourceFileName)
        Dim sw As StreamWriter = f.CreateText()

        sw.WriteLine("Hello, world!")

        sw.Close()

        Return f

    End Function 'CreateResourceFile

    Private Shared Function BuildDynAssembly() As AssemblyBuilder

        Dim myAsmFileName As String = "MyAsm.dll"

        Dim myDomain As AppDomain = Thread.GetDomain()
        Dim myAsmName As New AssemblyName()
        myAsmName.Name = "MyDynamicAssembly"

        Dim myAsmBuilder As AssemblyBuilder = _
myDomain.DefineDynamicAssembly(myAsmName, _
                    AssemblyBuilderAccess.RunAndSave)

        myAsmBuilder.AddResourceFile("MyResource", myResourceFileName)

        ' To confirm that the resource file has been added to the
manifest,
        ' we will save the assembly as MyAsm.dll. You can view the
manifest
        ' and confirm the presence of the resource file by running
        ' "ildasm MyAsm.dll" from the prompt in the directory
where you executed
        ' the compiled code.
        myAsmBuilder.Save(myAsmFileName)

        Return myAsmBuilder

    End Function 'BuildDynAssembly

    Public Shared Sub Main()

        Dim myResourceFS As FileStream = Nothing

        CreateResourceFile()

        Console.WriteLine("The contents of MyResource.txt, via GetFile:")

        Dim myAsm As AssemblyBuilder = BuildDynAssembly()

        Try

            myResourceFS = myAsm.GetFile(myResourceFileName)

        Catch nsException As NotSupportedException

        Console.WriteLine("---")
        Console.WriteLine _
("System.Reflection.Emit.AssemblyBuilder.GetFile is not
supported " + _
                "in this SDK build.")
```

```
        Console.WriteLine("The file data will now be retrieved
directly, via a new FileStream.")
        Console.WriteLine("---")
        myResourceFS = New FileStream(myResourceFileName, FileMode.Open)

        End Try

        Dim sr As New StreamReader(myResourceFS,
System.Text.Encoding.ASCII)
        Console.WriteLine(sr.ReadToEnd())
        sr.Close()

    End Sub 'Main

End Class 'AsmBuilderGetFileDemo

[C#]
using System;
using System.IO;
using System.Threading;
using System.Reflection;
using System.Reflection.Emit;

class AsmBuilderGetFileDemo

{
    private static string myResourceFileName = "MyResource.txt";

    private static FileInfo CreateResourceFile()
    {

        FileInfo f = new FileInfo(myResourceFileName);
        StreamWriter sw = f.CreateText();

        sw.WriteLine("Hello, world!");

        sw.Close();

        return f;

    }

    private static AssemblyBuilder BuildDynAssembly()
    {

        string myAsmFileName = "MyAsm.dll";

        AppDomain myDomain = Thread.GetDomain();
        AssemblyName myAsmName = new AssemblyName();
        myAsmName.Name = "MyDynamicAssembly";

        AssemblyBuilder myAsmBuilder = myDomain.DefineDynamicAssembly(
                    myAsmName,
                    AssemblyBuilderAccess.RunAndSave);

        myAsmBuilder.AddResourceFile("MyResource", myResourceFileName);

        // To confirm that the resource file has been added to the
manifest,
        // we will save the assembly as MyAsm.dll. You can view the
manifest
        // and confirm the presence of the resource file by running
        // "ildasm MyAsm.dll" from the prompt in the directory
where you executed
        // the compiled code.

        myAsmBuilder.Save(myAsmFileName);

        return myAsmBuilder;

    }

    public static void Main()
    {
```

```
FileStream myResourceFS = null;

CreateResourceFile();

Console.WriteLine("The contents of MyResource.txt, via GetFile:");

AssemblyBuilder myAsm = BuildDynAssembly();

try
    {
    myResourceFS = myAsm.GetFile(myResourceFileName);
    }
catch (NotSupportedException)
{
    Console.WriteLine("---");
    Console.WriteLine(
"System.Reflection.Emit.AssemblyBuilder.GetFile\nis not supported " +
            "in this SDK build.");
    Console.WriteLine("The file data will now be retrieved
directly, via a new FileStream.");
    Console.WriteLine("---");
    myResourceFS = new FileStream(myResourceFileName,
                FileMode.Open);
}

StreamReader sr = new StreamReader(myResourceFS,
System.Text.Encoding.ASCII);
    Console.WriteLine(sr.ReadToEnd());
    sr.Close();

}

}
```

[C++]
```
#using <mscorlib.dll>

using namespace System;
using namespace System::IO;
using namespace System::Threading;
using namespace System::Reflection;
using namespace System::Reflection::Emit;

__gc class AsmBuilderGetFileDemo {
public:
    static String* myResourceFileName = S"MyResource.txt";

    static FileInfo* CreateResourceFile() {
        FileInfo* f = new FileInfo(myResourceFileName);
        StreamWriter* sw = f->CreateText();

        sw->WriteLine(S"Hello, world!");
        sw->Close();
        return f;
    }

    static AssemblyBuilder* BuildDynAssembly() {

        String* myAsmFileName = S"MyAsm.dll";

        AppDomain* myDomain = Thread::GetDomain();
        AssemblyName* myAsmName = new AssemblyName();
        myAsmName->Name = S"MyDynamicAssembly";

        AssemblyBuilder* myAsmBuilder = myDomain-
>DefineDynamicAssembly(myAsmName,
            AssemblyBuilderAccess::RunAndSave);

        myAsmBuilder->AddResourceFile(S"MyResource", myResourceFileName);

        // To confirm that the resource file has been added to the
manifest,
        // we will save the assembly as MyAsm.dll. You can view
the manifest
        // and confirm the presence of the resource file by running
```

```
        // "ildasm MyAsm.dll" from the prompt in the directory
where you executed
        // the compiled code.

        myAsmBuilder->Save(myAsmFileName);

        return myAsmBuilder;
    }
};

int main() {

    FileStream* myResourceFS = 0;

    AsmBuilderGetFileDemo::CreateResourceFile();

    Console::WriteLine(S"The contents of MyResource.txt, via GetFile:");

    AssemblyBuilder* myAsm = AsmBuilderGetFileDemo::BuildDynAssembly();

    try {
        myResourceFS = myAsm-
>GetFile(AsmBuilderGetFileDemo::myResourceFileName);
    } catch (NotSupportedException*) {
        Console::WriteLine(S"---");
        Console::WriteLine
(S"System::Reflection::Emit::AssemblyBuilder::GetFile\nis
not supported in this SDK build.");
        Console::WriteLine(S"The file data will now be
retrieved directly, via a new FileStream.");
        Console::WriteLine(S"---");
        myResourceFS = new
FileStream(AsmBuilderGetFileDemo::myResourceFileName,
            FileMode::Open);
    }

    StreamReader* sr = new StreamReader(myResourceFS,
System::Text::Encoding::ASCII);
    Console::WriteLine(sr->ReadToEnd());
    sr->Close();
}
```

AssemblyBuilder.AddResourceFile Method (String, String)

Adds an existing resource file to this assembly.

[Visual Basic]
```
Overloads Public Sub AddResourceFile( _
    ByVal name As String, _
    ByVal fileName As String _
)
```
[C#]
```
public void AddResourceFile(
    string name,
    string fileName
);
```
[C++]
```
public: void AddResourceFile(
    String* name,
    String* fileName
);
```
[JScript]
```
public function AddResourceFile(
    name : String,
    fileName : String
);
```

Parameters

name

The logical name of the resource.

fileName

The physical file name (.resources file) to which the logical name is mapped. This should not include a path.

Exceptions

Exception Type	Condition
ArgumentException	*name* has been previously defined.
	-or-
	There is another file in the assembly named *fileName*.
	-or-
	The length of *name* is zero.
	-or-
	The length of *fileName* is zero, or if *fileName* includes a path.
ArgumentNullException	*name* or *fileName* is a null reference (**Nothing** in Visual Basic).
FileNotFoundException	If the file *fileName* is not found.
SecurityException	The caller does not have the required permission.

Remarks

fileName should not be the same as that of any other persistable module, standalone managed resource, or the standalone manifest file.

The managed resources in the file are assumed to be public.

Example

See related example in the **System.Reflection.Emit.AssemblyBuilder.AddResourceFile** method topic.

Requirements

Platforms: Windows 98, Windows NT 4.0, Windows Millennium Edition, Windows 2000, Windows XP Home Edition, Windows XP Professional, Windows .NET Server family

.NET Framework Security:

- **ReflectionPermission** SecurityAction.Demand, ReflectionEmit=true
- **ReflectionPermission** to enhance security and performance when invoked late-bound through mechanisms such as **Type.InvokeMember**. Associated enumeration: **ReflectionPermissionFlag.MemberAccess**.
- **FileIOPermission** The FileIOPermissionAccess.Read permission is needed to access the resource file *resourceFileName*.

AssemblyBuilder.AddResourceFile Method (String, String, ResourceAttributes)

Adds an existing resource file to this assembly.

```
[Visual Basic]
Overloads Public Sub AddResourceFile( _
   ByVal name As String, _
   ByVal fileName As String, _
   ByVal attribute As ResourceAttributes _
)
[C#]
public void AddResourceFile(
   string name,
   string fileName,
   ResourceAttributes attribute
);
[C++]
public: void AddResourceFile(
   String* name,
   String* fileName,
   ResourceAttributes attribute
);
[JScript]
public function AddResourceFile(
   name : String,
   fileName : String,
   attribute : ResourceAttributes
);
```

Parameters

name

The logical name of the resource.

fileName

The physical file name (.resources file) to which the logical name is mapped. This should not include a path.

attribute

The resource attributes.

Exceptions

Exception Type	Condition
ArgumentException	*name* has been previously defined.
	-or-
	There is another file in the assembly named *fileName*.
	-or-
	The length of *name* is zero or if the length of *fileName* is zero.
	-or-
	fileName includes a path.
ArgumentNullException	*name* or *fileName* is a null reference (**Nothing** in Visual Basic).
FileNotFoundException	If the file *fileName* is not found.
SecurityException	The caller does not have the required permission.

Remarks

fileName should not be the same as that of any other persistable module, standalone managed resource, or the standalone manifest file.

Attributes can be specified for the managed resource.

Example

See related example in the **System.Reflection.Emit.AssemblyBuilder.AddResourceFile** method topic.

Requirements

Platforms: Windows 98, Windows NT 4.0, Windows Millennium Edition, Windows 2000, Windows XP Home Edition, Windows XP Professional, Windows .NET Server family

.NET Framework Security:

- **ReflectionPermission** SecurityAction.Demand, ReflectionEmit=true
- **ReflectionPermission** to enhance security and performance when invoked late-bound through mechanisms such as **Type.InvokeMember**. Associated enumeration: **ReflectionPermissionFlag.MemberAccess**.
- **FileIOPermission** The FileIOPermissionAccess.Read permission is needed to access the resource file *resourceFileName*.

AssemblyBuilder.DefineDynamicModule Method

Defines a dynamic module in this assembly.

Overload List

Defines a named transient dynamic module in this assembly.

[Visual Basic] **Overloads Public Function DefineDynamic Module(String) As ModuleBuilder**

[C#] **public ModuleBuilder DefineDynamicModule(string);**

[C++] **public: ModuleBuilder* DefineDynamic Module(String*);**

[JScript] **public function DefineDynamicModule(String) : ModuleBuilder;**

Defines a named transient dynamic module in this assembly and specifies whether symbol information should be emitted.

[Visual Basic] **Overloads Public Function DefineDynamic Module(String, Boolean) As ModuleBuilder**

[C#] **public ModuleBuilder DefineDynamicModule(string, bool);**

[C++] **public: ModuleBuilder* DefineDynamicModule (String*, bool);**

[JScript] **public function DefineDynamicModule(String, Boolean) : ModuleBuilder;**

Defines a persistable dynamic module with the given name that will be saved to the specified file. No symbol information is emitted.

[Visual Basic] **Overloads Public Function DefineDynamic Module(String, String) As ModuleBuilder**

[C#] **public ModuleBuilder DefineDynamicModule(string, string);**

[C++] **public: ModuleBuilder* DefineDynamicModule (String*, String*);**

[JScript] **public function DefineDynamicModule(String, String) : ModuleBuilder;**

Defines a persistable dynamic module, specifying the module name, the name of the file to which the module will be saved, and whether symbol information should be emitted using the default symbol writer.

[Visual Basic] **Overloads Public Function DefineDynamic Module(String, String, Boolean) As ModuleBuilder**

[C#] **public ModuleBuilder DefineDynamicModule(string, string, bool);**

[C++] **public: ModuleBuilder* DefineDynamicModule (String*, String*, bool);**

[JScript] **public function DefineDynamicModule(String, String, Boolean) : ModuleBuilder;**

Example

The code example below demonstrates how to create a persistent dynamic module with symbol emission using **DefineDynamicModule**.

[Visual Basic, C#, C++] **Note** This example shows how to use one of the overloaded versions of **DefineDynamicModule**. For other examples that might be available, see the individual overload topics.

[Visual Basic]
```
Dim myAppDomain As AppDomain = Thread.GetDomain()
Dim myAsmName As New AssemblyName()
myAsmName.Name = "MyAssembly"
Dim myAsmBuilder As AssemblyBuilder =
myAppDomain.DefineDynamicAssembly(myAsmName, _
                    AssemblyBuilderAccess.Run)
' Create a dynamic module that can be saved as the specified
  DLL name. By
' specifying the third parameter as true, we can allow the
emission of symbol info.
Dim myModuleBuilder As ModuleBuilder =
myAsmBuilder.DefineDynamicModule("MyModule4", _
                    "MyModule4.dll", _
                    True)
```

[C#]
```
AppDomain myAppDomain = Thread.GetDomain();
AssemblyName myAsmName = new AssemblyName();
myAsmName.Name = "MyAssembly";
AssemblyBuilder myAsmBuilder = myAppDomain.DefineDynamicAssembly(
                    myAsmName,
                    AssemblyBuilderAccess.Run);
// Create a dynamic module that can be saved as the specified
   DLL name. By
// specifying the third parameter as true, we can allow the
emission of symbol info.
ModuleBuilder myModuleBuilder =
myAsmBuilder.DefineDynamicModule("MyModule4",
                    "MyModule4.dll",
                    true);
```

[C++]
```
AppDomain*  myAppDomain = Thread::GetDomain();
AssemblyName*  myAsmName = new AssemblyName();
myAsmName->Name = S"MyAssembly";
AssemblyBuilder*  myAsmBuilder = myAppDomain-
>DefineDynamicAssembly(myAsmName,
    AssemblyBuilderAccess::Run);
// Create a dynamic module that can be saved as the specified
   DLL name. By
// specifying the third parameter as true, we can allow the
emission of symbol info.
ModuleBuilder*  myModuleBuilder = myAsmBuilder-
>DefineDynamicModule(S"MyModule4",
    S"MyModule4.dll",
    true);
```

AssemblyBuilder.DefineDynamicModule Method (String)

Defines a named transient dynamic module in this assembly.

```
[Visual Basic]
Overloads Public Function DefineDynamicModule( _
   ByVal name As String _
) As ModuleBuilder
[C#]
public ModuleBuilder DefineDynamicModule(
   string name
);
[C++]
public: ModuleBuilder* DefineDynamicModule(
   String* name
);
[JScript]
public function DefineDynamicModule(
   name : String
) : ModuleBuilder;
```

Parameters

name

   The name of the dynamic module. Must be less than 260 characters in length.

Return Value

A **ModuleBuilder** representing the defined dynamic module.

Exceptions

Exception Type	Condition
ArgumentException	*name* begins with white space.
	-or-
	The length of *name* is zero.
	-or-
	The length of *name* is greater than or equal to 260.
ArgumentNullException	*name* is a null reference (**Nothing** in Visual Basic).
SecurityException	The caller does not have the required permission.

Remarks

It is an error to define multiple dynamic modules with the same name in an assembly.

The defined dynamic module is transient. The dynamic module is not saved, even if the parent dynamic assembly was created with **RunAndSave**.

Example

The code example below demonstrates how to create a transient dynamic module using **DefineDynamicModule**.

```
[Visual Basic]
Dim myAppDomain As AppDomain = Thread.GetDomain()
Dim myAsmName As New AssemblyName()
myAsmName.Name = "MyAssembly"
Dim myAsmBuilder As AssemblyBuilder =
myAppDomain.DefineDynamicAssembly(myAsmName, _
                  AssemblyBuilderAccess.Run)

' Create a transient dynamic module. Since no DLL name is
  specified with
' this constructor, it can not be saved.
```

```
Dim myModuleBuilder As ModuleBuilder =
myAsmBuilder.DefineDynamicModule("MyModule1")
```

```
[C#]
AppDomain myAppDomain = Thread.GetDomain();
AssemblyName myAsmName = new AssemblyName();
myAsmName.Name = "MyAssembly";
AssemblyBuilder myAsmBuilder = myAppDomain.DefineDynamicAssembly(
                myAsmName,
                AssemblyBuilderAccess.Run);

// Create a transient dynamic module. Since no DLL name is specified with
// this constructor, it can not be saved.
ModuleBuilder myModuleBuilder =
myAsmBuilder.DefineDynamicModule("MyModule1");
```

```
[C++]
AppDomain* myAppDomain = Thread::GetDomain();
AssemblyName* myAsmName = new AssemblyName();
myAsmName->Name = S"MyAssembly";
AssemblyBuilder* myAsmBuilder = myAppDomain-
>DefineDynamicAssembly(myAsmName,
   AssemblyBuilderAccess::Run);

// Create a transient dynamic module. Since no DLL name
is specified with
// this constructor, it cannot be saved.
ModuleBuilder* myModuleBuilder = myAsmBuilder-
>DefineDynamicModule(S"MyModule1");
```

Requirements

Platforms: Windows 98, Windows NT 4.0, Windows Millennium Edition, Windows 2000, Windows XP Home Edition, Windows XP Professional, Windows .NET Server family

.NET Framework Security:

*   **ReflectionPermission** SecurityAction.Demand, ReflectionEmit=true
*   **ReflectionPermission** to enhance security and performance when invoked late-bound through mechanisms such as **Type.InvokeMember**. Associated enumeration: **ReflectionPermissionFlag.MemberAccess**.

AssemblyBuilder.DefineDynamicModule Method (String, Boolean)

Defines a named transient dynamic module in this assembly and specifies whether symbol information should be emitted.

```
[Visual Basic]
Overloads Public Function DefineDynamicModule( _
   ByVal name As String, _
   ByVal emitSymbolInfo As Boolean _
) As ModuleBuilder
[C#]
public ModuleBuilder DefineDynamicModule(
   string name,
   bool emitSymbolInfo
);
[C++]
public: ModuleBuilder* DefineDynamicModule(
   String* name,
   bool emitSymbolInfo
);
```

```
[JScript]
public function DefineDynamicModule(
   name : String,
   emitSymbolInfo : Boolean
) : ModuleBuilder;
```

Parameters

name

The name of the dynamic module. Must be less than 260 characters in length.

emitSymbolInfo

true if symbol information is to be emitted; otherwise, **false**.

Return Value

A **ModuleBuilder** representing the defined dynamic module.

Exceptions

Exception Type	Condition
ArgumentException	*name* begins with white space.
	-or-
	The length of *name* is zero.
	-or-
	The length of *name* is greater than or equal to 260.
ArgumentNullException	*name* is a null reference (**Nothing** in Visual Basic).
ExecutionEngineException	The assembly for default symbol writer cannot be loaded.
	-or-
	The type that implements the default symbol writer interface cannot be found.
SecurityException	The caller does not have the required permission.

Remarks

It is an error to define multiple dynamic modules with the same name in an assembly.

The dynamic module is not saved, even if the parent dynamic assembly was created with **RunAndSave**.

Example

The code example below demonstrates how to create a transient dynamic module using **DefineDynamicModule**, suppressing symbol information.

```
[Visual Basic]
Dim myAppDomain As AppDomain = Thread.GetDomain()
Dim myAsmName As New AssemblyName()
myAsmName.Name = "MyAssembly"
Dim myAsmBuilder As AssemblyBuilder =          ⌐
myAppDomain.DefineDynamicAssembly(myAsmName, _
                   AssemblyBuilderAccess.Run)

' Create a transient dynamic module. Since no DLL name     ⌐
is specified with
' this constructor, it can not be saved. By specifying the  ⌐
second parameter
' of the constructor as false, we can suppress the emission  ⌐
of symbol info.
Dim myModuleBuilder As ModuleBuilder =          ⌐
myAsmBuilder.DefineDynamicModule("MyModule2", _
                   False)
```

```
[C#]
AppDomain myAppDomain = Thread.GetDomain();
AssemblyName myAsmName = new AssemblyName();
myAsmName.Name = "MyAssembly";
AssemblyBuilder myAsmBuilder = myAppDomain.DefineDynamicAssembly(
                   myAsmName,
                   AssemblyBuilderAccess.Run);

// Create a transient dynamic module. Since no DLL name     ⌐
is specified with
// this constructor, it can not be saved. By specifying     ⌐
the second parameter
// of the constructor as false, we can suppress the emission ⌐
of symbol info.
ModuleBuilder myModuleBuilder =          ⌐
myAsmBuilder.DefineDynamicModule("MyModule2",
                   false);
```

```
[C++]
AppDomain* myAppDomain = Thread::GetDomain();
AssemblyName* myAsmName = new AssemblyName();
myAsmName->Name = S"MyAssembly";
AssemblyBuilder* myAsmBuilder = myAppDomain-
>DefineDynamicAssembly(myAsmName,
   AssemblyBuilderAccess::Run);

// Create a transient dynamic module. Since no DLL name     ⌐
is specified with
// this constructor, it can not be saved. By specifying     ⌐
the second parameter
// of the constructor as false, we can suppress the emission ⌐
of symbol info.
ModuleBuilder* myModuleBuilder = myAsmBuilder-      ⌐
>DefineDynamicModule(S"MyModule2",
   false);
```

Requirements

Platforms: Windows 98, Windows NT 4.0, Windows Millennium Edition, Windows 2000, Windows XP Home Edition, Windows XP Professional, Windows .NET Server family

.NET Framework Security:

- **ReflectionPermission** SecurityAction.Demand, ReflectionEmit=true
- **ReflectionPermission** to enhance security and performance when invoked late-bound through mechanisms such as **Type.InvokeMember**. Associated enumeration: **ReflectionPermissionFlag.MemberAccess**.

AssemblyBuilder.DefineDynamicModule Method (String, String)

Defines a persistable dynamic module with the given name that will be saved to the specified file. No symbol information is emitted.

```
[Visual Basic]
Overloads Public Function DefineDynamicModule( _
   ByVal name As String, _
   ByVal fileName As String _
) As ModuleBuilder
[C#]
public ModuleBuilder DefineDynamicModule(
   string name,
   string fileName
);
```

```
[C++]
public: ModuleBuilder* DefineDynamicModule(
   String* name,
   String* fileName
);
[JScript]
public function DefineDynamicModule(
   name : String,
   fileName : String
) : ModuleBuilder;
```

Parameters

name

The name of the dynamic module. Must be less than 260 characters in length.

fileName

The name of the file to which the dynamic module should be saved.

Return Value

A **ModuleBuilder** object representing the defined dynamic module.

Exceptions

Exception Type	Condition
ArgumentNullException	*name* or *fileName* is a null reference (**Nothing** in Visual Basic).
ArgumentException	The length of *name* or *fileName* is zero.
	-or-
	The length of *name* is greater than or equal to 260.
	-or-
	fileName contains a path specification (a directory component, for example).
	-or-
	There is a conflict with the name of another file that belongs to this assembly.
InvalidOperationException	This assembly has been previously saved.
NotSupportedException	This assembly was called on a dynamic assembly with **Run** attribute.
SecurityException	The caller does not have the required permission.

Remarks

To define a persistable dynamic module, this assembly needs to be created with the **Save** or the **RunAndSave** attribute.

If a dynamic assembly contains more than one dynamic module, the assembly's manifest file name should match the module's name that is specified as the first argument to **DefineDynamicModule**.

Example

The code example below demonstrates how to create a persistent dynamic module using **DefineDynamicModule**.

```
[Visual Basic]
Dim myAppDomain As AppDomain = Thread.GetDomain()
Dim myAsmName As New AssemblyName()
myAsmName.Name = "MyAssembly"
Dim myAsmBuilder As AssemblyBuilder =                      ⏎
myAppDomain.DefineDynamicAssembly(myAsmName, _
                       AssemblyBuilderAccess.Run)
' Create a dynamic module that can be saved as the specified DLL name.
Dim myModuleBuilder As ModuleBuilder =                     ⏎
myAsmBuilder.DefineDynamicModule("MyModule3", _
                       "MyModule3.dll")
```

```
[C#]
AppDomain myAppDomain = Thread.GetDomain();
AssemblyName myAsmName = new AssemblyName();
myAsmName.Name = "MyAssembly";
AssemblyBuilder myAsmBuilder = myAppDomain.DefineDynamicAssembly(
                  myAsmName,
                  AssemblyBuilderAccess.Run);
// Create a dynamic module that can be saved as the specified DLL name.
ModuleBuilder myModuleBuilder =                            ⏎
myAsmBuilder.DefineDynamicModule("MyModule3",
                       "MyModule3.dll");
```

```
[C++]
AppDomain* myAppDomain = Thread::GetDomain();
AssemblyName* myAsmName = new AssemblyName();
myAsmName->Name = S"MyAssembly";
AssemblyBuilder* myAsmBuilder = myAppDomain-       ⏎
>DefineDynamicAssembly(myAsmName,
   AssemblyBuilderAccess::Run);
// Create a dynamic module that can be saved as the specified DLL name.
ModuleBuilder* myModuleBuilder = myAsmBuilder-     ⏎
>DefineDynamicModule(S"MyModule3",
   S"MyModule3.dll");
```

Requirements

Platforms: Windows 98, Windows NT 4.0, Windows Millennium Edition, Windows 2000, Windows XP Home Edition, Windows XP Professional, Windows .NET Server family

.NET Framework Security:

- **ReflectionPermission** SecurityAction.Demand, ReflectionEmit=true
- **ReflectionPermission** to enhance security and performance when invoked late-bound through mechanisms such as **Type.InvokeMember**. Associated enumeration: **ReflectionPermissionFlag.MemberAccess**.
- **FileIOPermission** Write=true or Append=true is needed to save the module

AssemblyBuilder.DefineDynamicModule Method (String, String, Boolean)

Defines a persistable dynamic module, specifying the module name, the name of the file to which the module will be saved, and whether symbol information should be emitted using the default symbol writer.

```
[Visual Basic]
Overloads Public Function DefineDynamicModule( _
   ByVal name As String, _
   ByVal fileName As String, _
   ByVal emitSymbolInfo As Boolean _
) As ModuleBuilder
```

```
[C#]
public ModuleBuilder DefineDynamicModule(
   string name,
   string fileName,
   bool emitSymbolInfo
);
[C++]
public: ModuleBuilder* DefineDynamicModule(
   String* name,
   String* fileName,
   bool emitSymbolInfo
);
[JScript]
public function DefineDynamicModule(
   name : String,
   fileName : String,
   emitSymbolInfo : Boolean
) : ModuleBuilder;
```

Parameters

name
> The name of the dynamic module. Must be less than 260 characters in length.

fileName
> The name of the file to which the dynamic module should be saved.

emitSymbolInfo
> If **true**, symbolic information is written using the default symbol writer.

Return Value

A **ModuleBuilder** object representing the defined dynamic module.

Exceptions

Exception Type	Condition
ArgumentNullException	*name* or *fileName* is a null reference (**Nothing** in Visual Basic).
ArgumentException	The length of *name* or *fileName* is zero. -or- The length of *name* is greater than or equal to 260. -or- *fileName* contains a path specification (a directory component, for example). -or- There is a conflict with the name of another file that belongs to this assembly.
InvalidOperationException	This assembly has been previously saved.
NotSupportedException	This assembly was called on a dynamic assembly with the **Run** attribute.

Exception Type	Condition
ExecutionEngineException	The assembly for default symbol writer cannot be loaded. -or- The type that implements the default symbol writer interface cannot be found.
SecurityException	The caller does not have the required permission.

Remarks

To define a persistable dynamic module, this assembly needs to be created with the **Save** or the **RunAndSave** attribute.

If a dynamic assembly contains more than one dynamic module, the assembly's manifest file name should match the module's name that is specified as the first argument to **DefineDynamicModule**.

Example

The code example below demonstrates how to create a persistent dynamic module with symbol emission using **DefineDynamicModule**.

```
[Visual Basic]
Dim myAppDomain As AppDomain = Thread.GetDomain()
Dim myAsmName As New AssemblyName()
myAsmName.Name = "MyAssembly"
Dim myAsmBuilder As AssemblyBuilder =                          ⅃
myAppDomain.DefineDynamicAssembly(myAsmName, _
                          AssemblyBuilderAccess.Run)
' Create a dynamic module that can be saved as the            ⅃
specified DLL name. By
' specifying the third parameter as true, we can allow the emission of
symbol info.
Dim myModuleBuilder As ModuleBuilder =                        ⅃
myAsmBuilder.DefineDynamicModule("MyModule4", _
                          "MyModule4.dll", _
                          True)
```

```
[C#]
AppDomain myAppDomain = Thread.GetDomain();
AssemblyName myAsmName = new AssemblyName();
myAsmName.Name = "MyAssembly";
AssemblyBuilder myAsmBuilder = myAppDomain.DefineDynamicAssembly(
                          myAsmName,
                          AssemblyBuilderAccess.Run);
// Create a dynamic module that can be saved as the specified ⅃
DLL name. By
// specifying the third parameter as true, we can allow the   ⅃
emission of symbol info.
ModuleBuilder myModuleBuilder =                               ⅃
myAsmBuilder.DefineDynamicModule("MyModule4",
                          "MyModule4.dll",
                          true);
```

```
[C++]
AppDomain* myAppDomain = Thread::GetDomain();
AssemblyName* myAsmName = new AssemblyName();
myAsmName->Name = S"MyAssembly";
AssemblyBuilder* myAsmBuilder = myAppDomain-           ⅃
>DefineDynamicAssembly(myAsmName,
   AssemblyBuilderAccess::Run);
// Create a dynamic module that can be saved as the specified ⅃
DLL name. By
// specifying the third parameter as true, we can allow       ⅃
the emission of symbol info.
ModuleBuilder* myModuleBuilder = myAsmBuilder-        ⅃
>DefineDynamicModule(S"MyModule4",
   S"MyModule4.dll",
   true);
```

Requirements

Platforms: Windows 98, Windows NT 4.0,
Windows Millennium Edition, Windows 2000,
Windows XP Home Edition, Windows XP Professional,
Windows .NET Server family

.NET Framework Security:

- **ReflectionPermission** SecurityAction.Demand,
  ReflectionEmit=true
- **ReflectionPermission** to enhance security and performance
  when invoked late-bound through mechanisms such as
  Type.InvokeMember. Associated enumeration:
  ReflectionPermissionFlag.MemberAccess.
- **FileIOPermission** Write=true or Append=true is needed to save
  this module

AssemblyBuilder.DefineResource Method

Defines a standalone managed resource for this assembly.

Overload List

Defines a standalone managed resource for this assembly with the
default public resource attribute.

> [Visual Basic] **Overloads Public Function DefineResource
> (String, String, String) As IResourceWriter**
>
> [C#] **public IResourceWriter DefineResource(string, string,
> string);**
>
> [C++] **public: IResourceWriter* DefineResource(String*,
> String*, String*);**
>
> [JScript] **public function DefineResource(String, String,
> String) : IResourceWriter;**

Defines a standalone managed resource for this assembly. Attributes
can be specified for the managed resource.

> [Visual Basic] **Overloads Public Function DefineResource
> (String, String, String, ResourceAttributes) As
> IResourceWriter**
>
> [C#] **public IResourceWriter DefineResource(string, string,
> string, ResourceAttributes);**
>
> [C++] **public: IResourceWriter* DefineResource(String*,
> String*, String*, ResourceAttributes);**
>
> [JScript] **public function DefineResource(String, String,
> String, ResourceAttributes) : IResourceWriter;**

Example

[Visual Basic, C#, C++]

> [Visual Basic, C#, C++] **Note** This example shows how to use
> one of the overloaded versions of **DefineResource**. For other
> examples that might be available, see the individual overload
> topics.

```
[Visual Basic]
Public Shared Sub Main()
   Dim myAssembly As AssemblyBuilder
   Dim myResourceWriter As IResourceWriter
   myAssembly = CType(CreateAssembly(Thread.GetDomain())
.Assembly, AssemblyBuilder)

   myResourceWriter = myAssembly.DefineResource("myResourceFile",
"A sample Resource File", _

"MyEmitAssembly.MyResource.resources")
```

```
   myResourceWriter.AddResource("AddResource 1", "First
added resource")
   myResourceWriter.AddResource("AddResource 2", "Second
added resource")
   myResourceWriter.AddResource("AddResource 3", "Third
added resource")

   myAssembly.DefineVersionInfoResource("AssemblySample",
"2:0:0:1", "Microsoft Corporation", _
        "@Copyright Microsoft Corp. 1990-2001", ".NET is a
trademark of Microsoft Corporation")
   myAssembly.Save("MyEmitAssembly.dll")
End Sub 'Main

' Create the callee transient dynamic assembly.
Private Shared Function CreateAssembly(myAppDomain As
AppDomain) As Type
   Dim myAssemblyName As New AssemblyName()
   myAssemblyName.Name = "MyEmitAssembly"
   Dim myAssembly As AssemblyBuilder =
myAppDomain.DefineDynamicAssembly(myAssemblyName, _

AssemblyBuilderAccess.Save)
   Dim myModule As ModuleBuilder =
myAssembly.DefineDynamicModule("EmittedModule", _

"EmittedModule.mod")

   ' Define a public class named "HelloWorld" in the assembly.
   Dim helloWorldClass As TypeBuilder =
myModule.DefineType("HelloWorld", TypeAttributes.Public)
   ' Define the Display method.
   Dim myMethod As MethodBuilder =
helloWorldClass.DefineMethod("Display", _
                            MethodAttributes.Public,
GetType(String), Nothing)

   ' Generate IL for GetGreeting.
   Dim methodIL As ILGenerator = myMethod.GetILGenerator()
   methodIL.Emit(OpCodes.Ldstr, "Display method get called.")
   methodIL.Emit(OpCodes.Ret)
   ' Returns the type HelloWorld.
   Return helloWorldClass.CreateType()
End Function 'CreateAssembly

[C#]
public static void Main()
{
   AssemblyBuilder myAssembly;
   IResourceWriter myResourceWriter;
   myAssembly =
(AssemblyBuilder)CreateAssembly(Thread.GetDomain()).Assembly;

   myResourceWriter = myAssembly.DefineResource("myResourceFile",
      "A sample Resource File", "MyEmitAssembly.MyResource.resources");
   myResourceWriter.AddResource("AddResource 1", "First added
resource");
   myResourceWriter.AddResource("AddResource 2", "Second added
resource");
   myResourceWriter.AddResource("AddResource 3", "Third added
resource");

   myAssembly.DefineVersionInfoResource("AssemblySample", "2:0:0:1",
      "Microsoft Corporation", "@Copyright Microsoft Corp. 1990-2001",
      ".NET is a trademark of Microsoft Corporation");
   myAssembly.Save("MyEmitAssembly.dll");
}

// Create the callee transient dynamic assembly.
private static Type CreateAssembly(AppDomain appDomain)
{
   AssemblyName myAssemblyName = new AssemblyName();
   myAssemblyName.Name = "MyEmitAssembly";
   AssemblyBuilder myAssembly =
appDomain.DefineDynamicAssembly(myAssemblyName,
```

```
    AssemblyBuilderAccess.Save);
    ModuleBuilder myModule =
myAssembly.DefineDynamicModule("EmittedModule",
    "EmittedModule.mod");

    // Define a public class named "HelloWorld" in the assembly.
    TypeBuilder helloWorldClass =
        myModule.DefineType("HelloWorld", TypeAttributes.Public);
    // Define the Display method.
    MethodBuilder myMethod = helloWorldClass.DefineMethod("Display",
        MethodAttributes.Public, typeof(String), null);

    // Generate IL for GetGreeting.
    ILGenerator methodIL = myMethod.GetILGenerator();
    methodIL.Emit(OpCodes.Ldstr, "Display method get called.");
    methodIL.Emit(OpCodes.Ret);

    // Returns the type HelloWorld.
    return(helloWorldClass.CreateType());
}

[C++]
#using <mscorlib.dll>
using namespace System;
using namespace System::Threading;
using namespace System::Reflection;
using namespace System::Reflection::Emit;
using namespace System::Resources;

/*
    The following program demonstrates the 'DefineResource'
and 'DefineVersionInfoResource'
    methods of 'AssemblyBuilder' class. It builds an assembly
and a resource file at runtime.
    The unmanaged version information like product, product
version, Company, Copyright,
    trademark are defined with 'DefineVersionInfoResource'
method.
*/

static Type* CreateAssembly(AppDomain *appDomain);

void main()
{
    AssemblyBuilder *myAssembly;
    IResourceWriter *myResourceWriter;
    myAssembly =
__try_cast<AssemblyBuilder*>(CreateAssembly(Thread::GetDomain())-
>Assembly);

    myResourceWriter = myAssembly->DefineResource(S"myResourceFile",
        S"A sample Resource File",
S"MyEmitAssembly.MyResource.resources");
    myResourceWriter->AddResource(S"AddResource 1", S"First
added resource");
    myResourceWriter->AddResource(S"AddResource 2", S"Second
added resource");
    myResourceWriter->AddResource(S"AddResource 3", S"Third
added resource");

    myAssembly->DefineVersionInfoResource(S"AssemblySample",
"2:0:0:1",
        S"Microsoft Corporation", S"@Copyright Microsoft Corp.
1990-2001",
        S".NET is a trademark of Microsoft Corporation");
    myAssembly->Save(S"MyEmitAssembly.dll");
}

    // Create the callee transient dynamic assembly.
    static Type* CreateAssembly(AppDomain *appDomain)
    {
        AssemblyName *myAssemblyName = new AssemblyName();
        myAssemblyName->Name = S"MyEmitAssembly";
        AssemblyBuilder *myAssembly = appDomain-
>DefineDynamicAssembly(myAssemblyName,
```

```
    AssemblyBuilderAccess::Save);
    ModuleBuilder *myModule = myAssembly-
>DefineDynamicModule(S"EmittedModule",
        S"EmittedModule.mod");

    // Define a public class named "HelloWorld" in the assembly.
    TypeBuilder *helloWorldClass =
        myModule->DefineType(S"HelloWorld", TypeAttributes::Public);
    // Define the Display method.
    MethodBuilder *myMethod = helloWorldClass-
>DefineMethod(S"Display",
        MethodAttributes::Public, __typeof(String), 0);

    // Generate IL for GetGreeting.
    ILGenerator *methodIL = myMethod->GetILGenerator();
    methodIL->Emit(OpCodes::Ldstr, S"Display method get called.");
    methodIL->Emit(OpCodes::Ret);

    // Returns the type HelloWorld.
    return(helloWorldClass->CreateType());
}
```

AssemblyBuilder.DefineResource Method (String, String, String)

Defines a standalone managed resource for this assembly with the default public resource attribute.

```
[Visual Basic]
Overloads Public Function DefineResource( _
    ByVal name As String, _
    ByVal description As String, _
    ByVal fileName As String _
) As IResourceWriter
[C#]
public IResourceWriter DefineResource(
    string name,
    string description,
    string fileName
);
[C++]
public: IResourceWriter* DefineResource(
    String* name,
    String* description,
    String* fileName
);
[JScript]
public function DefineResource(
    name : String,
    description : String,
    fileName : String
) : IResourceWriter;
```

Parameters

name
    The logical name of the resource.
description
    A textual description of the resource.
fileName
    The physical file name (.resources file) to which the logical name
    is mapped. This should not include a path.

Return Value

A **ResourceWriter** object for the specified resource.

Exceptions

Exception Type	Condition
ArgumentException	*name* has been previously defined.
	-or-
	There is another file in the assembly named *fileName*.
	-or-
	The length of *name* is zero.
	-or-
	The length of *fileName* is zero.
	-or-
	fileName includes a path.
ArgumentNullException	*name* or *fileName* is a null reference (**Nothing** in Visual Basic).
SecurityException	The caller does not have the required permission.

Remarks

Fine grain resources can be added with the returned **ResourceWriter** by calling **AddResource**.

fileName should not be the same as that of any other persistable module, stand-alone managed resource, or the stand-alone manifest file.

The runtime calls the **Close** method when the dynamic assembly is saved.

Example

[Visual Basic, C#, C++]

```
[Visual Basic]
Public Shared Sub Main()
    Dim myAssembly As AssemblyBuilder
    Dim myResourceWriter As IResourceWriter
    myAssembly = CType(CreateAssembly(Thread.GetDomain()). _
Assembly, AssemblyBuilder)

    myResourceWriter = myAssembly.DefineResource("myResourceFile", _
"A sample Resource File", _

"MyEmitAssembly.MyResource.resources")
    myResourceWriter.AddResource("AddResource 1", "First added
resource")
    myResourceWriter.AddResource("AddResource 2", "Second added
resource")
    myResourceWriter.AddResource("AddResource 3", "Third added
resource")

    myAssembly.DefineVersionInfoResource("AssemblySample", _
"2:0:0:1", "Microsoft Corporation", _
            "@Copyright Microsoft Corp. 1990-2001", ".NET is a
trademark of Microsoft Corporation")
    myAssembly.Save("MyEmitAssembly.dll")
End Sub 'Main

' Create the callee transient dynamic assembly.
Private Shared Function CreateAssembly(myAppDomain As AppDomain) _
As Type
    Dim myAssemblyName As New AssemblyName()
    myAssemblyName.Name = "MyEmitAssembly"
    Dim myAssembly As AssemblyBuilder =
myAppDomain.DefineDynamicAssembly(myAssemblyName, _

AssemblyBuilderAccess.Save)
    Dim myModule As ModuleBuilder =
myAssembly.DefineDynamicModule("EmittedModule", _
```

```
"EmittedModule.mod")

    ' Define a public class named "HelloWorld" in the assembly.
    Dim helloWorldClass As TypeBuilder =
myModule.DefineType("HelloWorld", TypeAttributes.Public)
    ' Define the Display method.
    Dim myMethod As MethodBuilder =
helloWorldClass.DefineMethod("Display", _
                            MethodAttributes.Public,
GetType(String), Nothing)

    ' Generate IL for GetGreeting.
    Dim methodIL As ILGenerator = myMethod.GetILGenerator()
    methodIL.Emit(OpCodes.Ldstr, "Display method get called.")
    methodIL.Emit(OpCodes.Ret)
    ' Returns the type HelloWorld.
    Return helloWorldClass.CreateType()
End Function 'CreateAssembly
```

```
[C#]
public static void Main()
{
    AssemblyBuilder myAssembly;
    IResourceWriter myResourceWriter;
    myAssembly =
(AssemblyBuilder)CreateAssembly(Thread.GetDomain()).Assembly;

    myResourceWriter = myAssembly.DefineResource("myResourceFile",
        "A sample Resource File", "MyEmitAssembly.MyResource.resources");
    myResourceWriter.AddResource("AddResource 1", "First added
resource");
    myResourceWriter.AddResource("AddResource 2", "Second added
resource");
    myResourceWriter.AddResource("AddResource 3", "Third added
resource");

    myAssembly.DefineVersionInfoResource("AssemblySample", "2:0:0:1",
        "Microsoft Corporation", "@Copyright Microsoft Corp. 1990-2001",
        ".NET is a trademark of Microsoft Corporation");
    myAssembly.Save("MyEmitAssembly.dll");
}

// Create the callee transient dynamic assembly.
private static Type CreateAssembly(AppDomain appDomain)
{
    AssemblyName myAssemblyName = new AssemblyName();
    myAssemblyName.Name = "MyEmitAssembly";
    AssemblyBuilder myAssembly =
appDomain.DefineDynamicAssembly(myAssemblyName,
        AssemblyBuilderAccess.Save);
    ModuleBuilder myModule =
myAssembly.DefineDynamicModule("EmittedModule",
        "EmittedModule.mod");

    // Define a public class named "HelloWorld" in the assembly.
    TypeBuilder helloWorldClass =
        myModule.DefineType("HelloWorld", TypeAttributes.Public);
    // Define the Display method.
    MethodBuilder myMethod = helloWorldClass.DefineMethod("Display",
        MethodAttributes.Public, typeof(String), null);

    // Generate IL for GetGreeting.
    ILGenerator methodIL = myMethod.GetILGenerator();
    methodIL.Emit(OpCodes.Ldstr, "Display method get called.");
    methodIL.Emit(OpCodes.Ret);

    // Returns the type HelloWorld.
    return(helloWorldClass.CreateType());
}

[C++]
#using <mscorlib.dll>
using namespace System;
using namespace System::Threading;
using namespace System::Reflection;
using namespace System::Reflection::Emit;
using namespace System::Resources;
```

```
/*
   The following program demonstrates the 'DefineResource' and
'DefineVersionInfoResource'
   methods of 'AssemblyBuilder' class. It builds an assembly
and a resource file at runtime.
   The unmanaged version information like product, product
version, Company, Copyright,
   trademark are defined with 'DefineVersionInfoResource' method.
*/

static Type* CreateAssembly(AppDomain *appDomain);

void main()
{
    AssemblyBuilder *myAssembly;
    IResourceWriter *myResourceWriter;
    myAssembly =
_try_cast<AssemblyBuilder*>(CreateAssembly(Thread::GetDomain
())->Assembly);

    myResourceWriter = myAssembly->DefineResource(S"myResourceFile",
        S"A sample Resource File",
S"MyEmitAssembly.MyResource.resources");
    myResourceWriter->AddResource(S"AddResource 1", S"First
added resource");
    myResourceWriter->AddResource(S"AddResource 2", S"Second
added resource");
    myResourceWriter->AddResource(S"AddResource 3", S"Third
added resource");

    myAssembly->DefineVersionInfoResource(S"AssemblySample",
"2:0:0:1",
        S"Microsoft Corporation", S"@Copyright Microsoft Corp.
1990-2001",
        S".NET is a trademark of Microsoft Corporation");
    myAssembly->Save(S"MyEmitAssembly.dll");
}

    // Create the callee transient dynamic assembly.
    static Type* CreateAssembly(AppDomain *appDomain)
    {
        AssemblyName *myAssemblyName = new AssemblyName();
        myAssemblyName->Name = S"MyEmitAssembly";
        AssemblyBuilder *myAssembly = appDomain-
>DefineDynamicAssembly(myAssemblyName,
            AssemblyBuilderAccess::Save);
        ModuleBuilder *myModule = myAssembly-
>DefineDynamicModule(S"EmittedModule",
            S"EmittedModule.mod");

        // Define a public class named "HelloWorld" in the assembly.
        TypeBuilder *helloWorldClass =
            myModule->DefineType(S"HelloWorld", TypeAttributes::Public);
        // Define the Display method.
        MethodBuilder *myMethod = helloWorldClass-
>DefineMethod(S"Display",
            MethodAttributes::Public, __typeof(String), 0);

        // Generate IL for GetGreeting.
        ILGenerator *methodIL = myMethod->GetILGenerator();
        methodIL->Emit(OpCodes::Ldstr, S"Display method get called.");
        methodIL->Emit(OpCodes::Ret);

        // Returns the type HelloWorld.
        return(helloWorldClass->CreateType());
    }
}
```

Requirements

Platforms: Windows 98, Windows NT 4.0,
Windows Millennium Edition, Windows 2000,
Windows XP Home Edition, Windows XP Professional,
Windows .NET Server family

.NET Framework Security:

- **ReflectionPermission** SecurityAction.Demand,
  ReflectionEmit=true

- **ReflectionPermission** to enhance security and performance
  when invoked late-bound through mechanisms such as
  Type.InvokeMember. Associated enumeration:
  ReflectionPermissionFlag.MemberAccess.

- **FileIOPermission** Write=true or Append=true

AssemblyBuilder.DefineResource Method (String, String, String, ResourceAttributes)

Defines a standalone managed resource for this assembly. Attributes
can be specified for the managed resource.

```
[Visual Basic]
Overloads Public Function DefineResource( _
   ByVal name As String, _
   ByVal description As String, _
   ByVal fileName As String, _
   ByVal attribute As ResourceAttributes _
) As IResourceWriter
[C#]
public IResourceWriter DefineResource(
   string name,
   string description,
   string fileName,
   ResourceAttributes attribute
);
[C++]
public: IResourceWriter* DefineResource(
   String* name,
   String* description,
   String* fileName,
   ResourceAttributes attribute
);
[JScript]
public function DefineResource(
   name : String,
   description : String,
   fileName : String,
   attribute : ResourceAttributes
) : IResourceWriter;
```

Parameters

name
   The logical name of the resource.
description
   A textual description of the resource.
fileName
   The physical file name (.resources file) to which the logical name
   is mapped. This should not include a path.
attribute
   The resource attributes.

Return Value

A **ResourceWriter** object for the specified resource.

Exceptions

Exception Type	Condition
ArgumentException	*name* has been previously defined or if there is another file in the assembly named *fileName*.
	-or-
	The length of *name* is zero.
	-or-
	The length of *fileName* is zero.
	-or-
	fileName includes a path.
ArgumentNullException	*name* or *fileName* is a null reference (**Nothing** in Visual Basic).
SecurityException	The caller does not have the required permission.

Remarks

Fine-grain resources can be added with the returned **ResourceWriter** by calling **AddResource**.

fileName should not be the same as that of any other persistable module, standalone managed resource, or the standalone manifest file.

The runtime calls the **Close** method when the dynamic assembly is saved.

Requirements

Platforms: Windows 98, Windows NT 4.0, Windows Millennium Edition, Windows 2000, Windows XP Home Edition, Windows XP Professional, Windows .NET Server family

.NET Framework Security:

- **ReflectionPermission** SecurityAction.Demand, ReflectionEmit=true
- **ReflectionPermission** to enhance security and performance when invoked late-bound through mechanisms such as **Type.InvokeMember**. Associated enumeration: **ReflectionPermissionFlag.MemberAccess**.
- **FileIOPermission** Write=true or Append=true

AssemblyBuilder.DefineUnmanagedResource Method

Defines an unmanaged resource for this assembly.

Overload List

Defines an unmanaged resource for this assembly as an opaque blob of bytes.

[Visual Basic] **Overloads Public Sub DefineUnmanaged Resource(Byte())**

[C#] **public void DefineUnmanagedResource(byte[]);**

[C++] **public: void DefineUnmanagedResource(unsigned char __gc[]);**

[JScript] **public function DefineUnmanagedResource(Byte[]);**

Defines an unmanaged resource file for this assembly given the name of the resource file.

[Visual Basic] **Overloads Public Sub DefineUnmanaged Resource(String)**

[C#] **public void DefineUnmanagedResource(string);**

[C++] **public: void DefineUnmanagedResource(String*);**

[JScript] **public function DefineUnmanagedResource(String);**

Example

[Visual Basic, C#, C++] The example below demonstrates a call to **DefineUnmanagedResource**, passing an external resource file.

[Visual Basic, C#, C++] **Note** This example shows how to use one of the overloaded versions of **DefineUnmanagedResource**. For other examples that might be available, see the individual overload topics.

[Visual Basic]
```
Public Shared Sub Main()
    Dim myAssembly As AssemblyBuilder =                         ⏎
CType(CreateAssembly(Thread.GetDomain()).Assembly, _
                                AssemblyBuilder)

    ' Defines a standalone managed resource for this assembly.
    Dim myResourceWriter As IResourceWriter =                   ⏎
myAssembly.DefineResource("myResourceFile", _
            "A sample Resource File", "MyAssemblyResource.       ⏎
resources", ResourceAttributes.Private)
    myResourceWriter.AddResource("AddResource Test", "Testing   ⏎
for the added resource")
    myAssembly.Save("MyEmitTestAssembly.dll")

    ' Defines an unmanaged resource file for this assembly.
    myAssembly.DefineUnmanagedResource("MyAssemblyResource.resources")
End Sub 'Main

Private Shared Function CreateAssembly(myDomain As AppDomain) As Type
    Dim myAssemblyName As New AssemblyName()
    myAssemblyName.Name = "MyEmitTestAssembly"
    Dim myAssembly As AssemblyBuilder =                         ⏎
myDomain.DefineDynamicAssembly(myAssemblyName, _
                            AssemblyBuilderAccess.Save)

    ' Define a dynamic module.
    Dim myModule As ModuleBuilder =                             ⏎
myAssembly.DefineDynamicModule("MyEmittedModule", _

"MyEmittedModule.mod")
    ' Define a public class named "EmitClass" in the assembly.
    Dim myEmitClass As TypeBuilder = myModule.DefineType        ⏎
("EmitClass", TypeAttributes.Public)

    ' Define the Display method.
    Dim myMethod As MethodBuilder = myEmitClass.DefineMethod    ⏎
("Display", MethodAttributes.Public, _
                        GetType(String), Nothing)

    ' Generate IL for Display method.
    Dim methodIL As ILGenerator = myMethod.GetILGenerator()
    methodIL.Emit(OpCodes.Ldstr, "Display method get called.")
    methodIL.Emit(OpCodes.Ret)

    ' Returns the type of EmitClass.
    Return myEmitClass.CreateType()
End Function 'CreateAssembly
```

[C#]
```
public static void Main()
{
    AssemblyBuilder myAssembly =
        (AssemblyBuilder)CreateAssembly(Thread.GetDomain()).Assembly;

    // Defines a standalone managed resource for this assembly.
    IResourceWriter myResourceWriter =                          ⏎
```

```
myAssembly.DefineResource("myResourceFile",
    "A sample Resource File", "MyAssemblyResource.resources",
    ResourceAttributes.Private);
myResourceWriter.AddResource("AddResource Test", "Testing
for the added resource");
myAssembly.Save("MyEmitTestAssembly.dll");

// Defines an unmanaged resource file for this assembly.
myAssembly.DefineUnmanagedResource("MyAssemblyResource.resources");
}

private static Type CreateAssembly(AppDomain myDomain)
{
    AssemblyName myAssemblyName = new AssemblyName();
    myAssemblyName.Name = "MyEmitTestAssembly";
    AssemblyBuilder myAssembly =
myDomain.DefineDynamicAssembly(myAssemblyName,
        AssemblyBuilderAccess.Save);

    // Define a dynamic module.
    ModuleBuilder myModule =
myAssembly.DefineDynamicModule("MyEmittedModule",
        "MyEmittedModule.mod");
    // Define a public class named "EmitClass" in the assembly.
    TypeBuilder myEmitClass = myModule.DefineType
("EmitClass", TypeAttributes.Public);

    // Define the Display method.
    MethodBuilder myMethod = myEmitClass.DefineMethod("Display",
        MethodAttributes.Public, typeof(String), null);

    // Generate IL for Display method.
    ILGenerator methodIL = myMethod.GetILGenerator();
    methodIL.Emit(OpCodes.Ldstr, "Display method get called.");
    methodIL.Emit(OpCodes.Ret);

    // Returns the type of EmitClass.
    return(myEmitClass.CreateType());
}
}
```

```
[C++]
public:
    static void Main()
    {
        AssemblyBuilder *myAssembly =
            __try_cast<AssemblyBuilder*>(CreateAssembly
(Thread::GetDomain())->Assembly);

        // Defines a standalone managed resource for this assembly.
        IResourceWriter *myResourceWriter = myAssembly-
>DefineResource(S"myResourceFile",
            S"A sample Resource File", S"MyAssemblyResource.resources",
            ResourceAttributes::Private);
        myResourceWriter->AddResource(S"AddResource Test",
S"Testing for the added resource");
        myAssembly->Save("MyEmitTestAssembly.dll");

        // Defines an unmanaged resource file for this assembly.
        myAssembly-
>DefineUnmanagedResource("MyAssemblyResource.resources");
    }

private:
    static Type* CreateAssembly(AppDomain *myDomain)
    {
        AssemblyName *myAssemblyName = new AssemblyName();
        myAssemblyName->Name = S"MyEmitTestAssembly";
        AssemblyBuilder *myAssembly = myDomain-
>DefineDynamicAssembly(myAssemblyName,
            AssemblyBuilderAccess::Save);

        // Define a dynamic module.
        ModuleBuilder *myModule = myAssembly-
>DefineDynamicModule(S"MyEmittedModule",
```

```
S"MyEmittedModule.mod");
        // Define a public class named "EmitClass" in the assembly.
        TypeBuilder *myEmitClass = myModule->DefineType
(S"EmitClass", TypeAttributes::Public);

        // Define the Display method.
        MethodBuilder *myMethod = myEmitClass->DefineMethod(S"Display",
            MethodAttributes::Public, __typeof(String), 0);

        // Generate IL for Display method.
        ILGenerator *methodIL = myMethod->GetILGenerator();
        methodIL->Emit(OpCodes::Ldstr, S"Display method get called.");
        methodIL->Emit(OpCodes::Ret);

        // Returns the type of EmitClass.
        return(myEmitClass->CreateType());
    }
};
```

AssemblyBuilder.DefineUnmanagedResource Method (Byte[])

Defines an unmanaged resource for this assembly as an opaque blob of bytes.

```
[Visual Basic]
Overloads Public Sub DefineUnmanagedResource( _
    ByVal resource() As Byte _
)
[C#]
public void DefineUnmanagedResource(
    byte[] resource
);
[C++]
public: void DefineUnmanagedResource(
    unsigned char resource __gc[]
);
[JScript]
public function DefineUnmanagedResource(
    resource : Byte[]
);
```

Parameters

resource

The opaque blob of bytes representing the unmanaged resource.

Exceptions

Exception Type	Condition
ArgumentException	An unmanaged resource was previously defined.
ArgumentNullException	*resource* is a null reference (**Nothing** in Visual Basic).
SecurityException	The caller does not have the required permission.

Remarks

An assembly can be associated with only one unmanaged resource. This means that calling **DefineVersionInfoResource** or **DefineUnmanagedResource** after either one of the methods was called previously will throw the System.ArgumentException being throw. Multiple unmanaged resources need to be merged with a tool such as the Microsoft ResMerge utility (not supplied with the common language runtime).

Example

See related example in the **System.Reflection.Emit.AssemblyBuilder.DefineUnmanagedRes ource** method topic.

Requirements

Platforms: Windows 98, Windows NT 4.0, Windows Millennium Edition, Windows 2000, Windows XP Home Edition, Windows XP Professional, Windows .NET Server family

.NET Framework Security:

- **ReflectionPermission** SecurityAction.Demand, ReflectionEmit=true
- **ReflectionPermission** to enhance security and performance when invoked late-bound through mechanisms such as **Type.InvokeMember**. Associated enumeration: **ReflectionPermissionFlag.MemberAccess.**

AssemblyBuilder.DefineUnmanagedResource Method (String)

Defines an unmanaged resource file for this assembly given the name of the resource file.

```
[Visual Basic]
Overloads Public Sub DefineUnmanagedResource( _
   ByVal resourceFileName As String _
)
[C#]
public void DefineUnmanagedResource(
   string resourceFileName
);
[C++]
public: void DefineUnmanagedResource(
   String* resourceFileName
);
[JScript]
public function DefineUnmanagedResource(
   resourceFileName : String
);
```

Parameters

resourceFileName
   The name of the resource file.

Exceptions

Exception Type	Condition
ArgumentException	An unmanaged resource was previously defined.
	-or-
	The file *resourceFileName* is not readable.
	-or-
	resourceFileName is the empty string ("").
ArgumentNullException	*resourceFileName* is a null reference (**Nothing** in Visual Basic).
FileNotFoundException	*resourceFileName* is not found.
	-or-
	resourceFileName is a directory.

Exception Type	Condition
SecurityException	The caller does not have the required permission.

Remarks

An assembly can be associated with only one unmanaged resource. This means that calling **DefineVersionInfoResource** or **DefineUnmanagedResource** after either one of the methods was called previously will throw the System.ArgumentException. Multiple unmanaged resources need to be merged with a tool such as the Microsoft ResMerge utility (not supplied with the common language runtime).

Example

See related example in the **System.Reflection.Emit.AssemblyBuilder.DefineUnmanagedRes ource** method topic.

Requirements

Platforms: Windows 98, Windows NT 4.0, Windows Millennium Edition, Windows 2000, Windows XP Home Edition, Windows XP Professional, Windows .NET Server family

.NET Framework Security:

- **ReflectionPermission** SecurityAction.Demand, ReflectionEmit=true
- **ReflectionPermission** to enhance security and performance when invoked late-bound through mechanisms such as **Type.InvokeMember**. Associated enumeration: **ReflectionPermissionFlag.MemberAccess.**
- **FileIOPermission** The FileIOPermissionAccess.Read permission is needed to access the resource file *resourceFileName*.

AssemblyBuilder.DefineVersionInfoResource Method

Defines an unmanaged version information resource for this assembly.

Overload List

Defines an unmanaged version information resource using the information specified in the assembly's AssemblyName object and the assembly's custom attributes.

   [Visual Basic] **Overloads Public Sub DefineVersionInfo Resource()**
   [C#] **public void DefineVersionInfoResource();**
   [C++] **public: void DefineVersionInfoResource();**
   [JScript] **public function DefineVersionInfoResource();**

Defines an unmanaged version information resource for this assembly with the given specifications.

   [Visual Basic] **Overloads Public Sub DefineVersionInfo Resource(String, String, String, String, String)**
   [C#] **public void DefineVersionInfoResource(string, string, string, string, string);**
   [C++] **public: void DefineVersionInfoResource(String*, String*, String*, String*, String*);**
   [JScript] **public function DefineVersionInfoResource(String, String, String, String, String);**

Example

[Visual Basic, C#, C++] The example below illustrates the usage of **DefineVersionInfoResource**.

[Visual Basic, C#, C++] **Note** This example shows how to use one of the overloaded versions of **DefineVersionInfoResource**. For other examples that might be available, see the individual overload topics.

[Visual Basic]
```
Imports System
Imports System.Threading
Imports System.Reflection
Imports System.Reflection.Emit
Imports System.Resources

Public Class MyEmitTest
    Public Shared Sub Main()
        Dim myAssembly As AssemblyBuilder = _
            CType(CreateAssembly(Thread.GetDomain()).Assembly, _
AssemblyBuilder)

        Dim myResourceWriter As IResourceWriter = _
            myAssembly.DefineResource("myResourceFile", _
            "A sample Resource File", "MyResourceFile.resources")
        myResourceWriter.AddResource("AddResource test", "Test
resource added")

        ' Define unmanaged version information resources.
        myAssembly.DefineVersionInfoResource()
        myAssembly.Save("MyEmittedAssembly.dll")
    End Sub 'Main

    ' Create the callee transient dynamic assembly.
    Private Shared Function CreateAssembly(myDomain As AppDomain) _
As Type
        Dim myAssemblyName As New AssemblyName()
        myAssemblyName.Name = "MyEmittedAssembly"

        Dim myAssembly As AssemblyBuilder = _
            myDomain.DefineDynamicAssembly(myAssemblyName, _
AssemblyBuilderAccess.Save)

        ' Set Company Attribute to the assembly.
        Dim companyAttribute As Type = GetType(AssemblyCompanyAttribute)
        Dim myConstructorInfo1 As ConstructorInfo = _
companyAttribute.GetConstructor(New Type() {GetType(String)})
        Dim attributeBuilder1 As _
            New CustomAttributeBuilder(myConstructorInfo1, _
New Object(0) {"Microsoft Corporation"})
        myAssembly.SetCustomAttribute(attributeBuilder1)

        ' Set Copyright Attribute to the assembly.
        Dim copyrightAttribute As Type = _
GetType(AssemblyCopyrightAttribute)
        Dim myConstructorInfo2 As ConstructorInfo = _
copyrightAttribute.GetConstructor(New Type() {GetType(String)})
        Dim attributeBuilder2 As _
            New CustomAttributeBuilder(myConstructorInfo2, _
            New Object(0) {"@Copyright Microsoft Corp. 1990-2001"})
        myAssembly.SetCustomAttribute(attributeBuilder2)

        Dim myModule As ModuleBuilder = _
            myAssembly.DefineDynamicModule("EmittedModule", _
"EmittedModule.mod")

        ' Define a public class named "HelloWorld" in the assembly.
        Dim helloWorldClass As TypeBuilder = _
myModule.DefineType("HelloWorld", TypeAttributes.Public)
        ' Define the Display method.
        Dim myMethod As MethodBuilder = _
            helloWorldClass.DefineMethod("Display", _
MethodAttributes.Public, GetType(String), Nothing)
```

```
        ' Generate IL for GetGreeting.
        Dim methodIL As ILGenerator = myMethod.GetILGenerator()
        methodIL.Emit(OpCodes.Ldstr, "Display method get called.")
        methodIL.Emit(OpCodes.Ret)

        ' Returns the type HelloWorld.
        Return helloWorldClass.CreateType()
    End Function 'CreateAssembly
End Class 'MyEmitTest
```

[C#]
```
using System;
using System.Threading;
using System.Reflection;
using System.Reflection.Emit;
using System.Resources;

public class MyEmitTest
{
    public static void Main()
    {
        AssemblyBuilder myAssembly =
            (AssemblyBuilder)CreateAssembly(Thread.GetDomain()).Assembly;

        IResourceWriter myResourceWriter =
myAssembly.DefineResource("myResourceFile",
            "A sample Resource File", "MyResourceFile.resources");
        myResourceWriter.AddResource("AddResource test",
"Test resource added");

        // Define unmanaged version information resources  .
        myAssembly.DefineVersionInfoResource();
        myAssembly.Save("MyEmittedAssembly.dll");
    }

    // Create the callee transient dynamic assembly.
    private static Type CreateAssembly(AppDomain myDomain)
    {
        AssemblyName myAssemblyName = new AssemblyName();
        myAssemblyName.Name = "MyEmittedAssembly";

        AssemblyBuilder myAssembly =
myDomain.DefineDynamicAssembly(myAssemblyName,
            AssemblyBuilderAccess.Save);

        // Set Company Attribute to the assembly.
        Type companyAttribute = typeof(AssemblyCompanyAttribute);
        ConstructorInfo myConstructorInfo1 =
companyAttribute.GetConstructor(new Type[]{typeof(String)});
        CustomAttributeBuilder attributeBuilder1 =
            new CustomAttributeBuilder(myConstructorInfo1,
new object[1]{"Microsoft Corporation"});
        myAssembly.SetCustomAttribute(attributeBuilder1);

        // Set Copyright Attribute to the assembly.
        Type copyrightAttribute = typeof(AssemblyCopyrightAttribute);
        ConstructorInfo myConstructorInfo2 =
copyrightAttribute.GetConstructor(new Type[]{typeof(String)});
        CustomAttributeBuilder attributeBuilder2 =
            new CustomAttributeBuilder(myConstructorInfo2,
            new object[1]{"@Copyright Microsoft Corp. 1990-2001"});
        myAssembly.SetCustomAttribute(attributeBuilder2);

        ModuleBuilder myModule =
myAssembly.DefineDynamicModule("EmittedModule",
            "EmittedModule.mod");

        // Define a public class named "HelloWorld" in the assembly.
        TypeBuilder helloWorldClass =
            myModule.DefineType("HelloWorld", TypeAttributes.Public);
        // Define the Display method.
        MethodBuilder myMethod = helloWorldClass.DefineMethod("Display",
            MethodAttributes.Public, typeof(String), null);
```

```
    // Generate IL for GetGreeting.
    ILGenerator methodIL = myMethod.GetILGenerator();
    methodIL.Emit(OpCodes.Ldstr, "Display method get called.");
    methodIL.Emit(OpCodes.Ret);

    // Returns the type HelloWorld.

    return(helloWorldClass.CreateType());
    }
}

[C++]
#using <mscorlib.dll>

using namespace System;
using namespace System::Threading;
using namespace System::Reflection;
using namespace System::Reflection::Emit;
using namespace System::Resources;

// Create the callee transient dynamic assembly.
static Type* CreateAssembly(AppDomain* myDomain) {
    AssemblyName* myAssemblyName = new AssemblyName();
    myAssemblyName->Name = S"MyEmittedAssembly";

    AssemblyBuilder* myAssembly = myDomain-
>DefineDynamicAssembly(myAssemblyName,
        AssemblyBuilderAccess::Save);

    // Set Company Attribute to the assembly.
    Type* companyAttribute = __typeof(AssemblyCompanyAttribute);
    Type* types1[] = {__typeof(String)};
    ConstructorInfo* myConstructorInfo1 = companyAttribute-
>GetConstructor(types1);
    Object* obj1[] = {S"Microsoft Corporation"};
    CustomAttributeBuilder* attributeBuilder1 = new
CustomAttributeBuilder(myConstructorInfo1, obj1);
    myAssembly->SetCustomAttribute(attributeBuilder1);

    // Set Copyright Attribute to the assembly.
    Type* copyrightAttribute = __typeof(AssemblyCopyrightAttribute);
    Type* types2[] = {__typeof(String)};
    ConstructorInfo* myConstructorInfo2 = copyrightAttribute-
>GetConstructor(types2);
    Object* obj2[] = {S"@Copyright Microsoft Corp. 1990-2001"};
    CustomAttributeBuilder* attributeBuilder2 = new
CustomAttributeBuilder(myConstructorInfo2, obj2);
    myAssembly->SetCustomAttribute(attributeBuilder2);

    ModuleBuilder* myModule = myAssembly-
>DefineDynamicModule(S"EmittedModule",
        S"EmittedModule::mod");

    // Define a public class named S"HelloWorld" in the assembly.
    TypeBuilder* helloWorldClass =
        myModule->DefineType(S"HelloWorld", TypeAttributes::Public);
    // Define the Display method.
    MethodBuilder* myMethod = helloWorldClass->DefineMethod(S"Display",
        MethodAttributes::Public, __typeof(String), 0);

    // Generate IL for GetGreeting.
    ILGenerator methodIL = myMethod->GetILGenerator();
    methodIL->Emit(OpCodes::Ldstr, S"Display method get called.");
    methodIL->Emit(OpCodes::Ret);

    // Returns the type HelloWorld.

    return(helloWorldClass->CreateType());
}

void main()
{
    AssemblyBuilder* myAssembly =
        __try_cast<AssemblyBuilder*>(CreateAssembly(Thread:
:GetDomain())->Assembly);
```

```
    IResourceWriter* myResourceWriter = myAssembly-
>DefineResource(S"myResourceFile",
        S"A sample Resource File", S"MyResourceFile::resources");
    myResourceWriter->AddResource(S"AddResource test",
S"Test resource added");

    // Define unmanaged version information resources  .
    myAssembly->DefineVersionInfoResource();
    myAssembly->Save(S"MyEmittedAssembly.dll");
}
```

AssemblyBuilder.DefineVersionInfoResource Method ()

Defines an unmanaged version information resource using the
information specified in the assembly's AssemblyName object and
the assembly's custom attributes.

```
[Visual Basic]
Overloads Public Sub DefineVersionInfoResource()
[C#]
public void DefineVersionInfoResource();
[C++]
public: void DefineVersionInfoResource();
[JScript]
public function DefineVersionInfoResource();
```

Exceptions

Exception Type	Condition
ArgumentException	An unmanaged version information resource was previously defined. -or- The unmanaged version information is too large to persist.
SecurityException	The caller does not have the required permission.

Remarks

An assembly can be associated with only one unmanaged resource.
This means that calling **DefineVersionInfoResource** or
DefineUnmanagedResource after either one of the methods was
called previously will throw the System.ArgumentException.
Multiple unmanaged resources need to be merged with a tool such as
the Microsoft ResMerge utility (not supplied with the common
language runtime SDK).

Empty argument strings get written as a single space. Spaces are
substituted for null characters in the argument strings.

The information is inferred from the **AssemblyName** object used to
define this dynamic assembly. This assembly's custom attributes
override information specified in the **AssemblyName** object.

Example

See related example in the
System.Reflection.Emit.AssemblyBuilder.DefineVersionInfoResource method topic.

Requirements

Platforms: Windows 98, Windows NT 4.0,
Windows Millennium Edition, Windows 2000,
Windows XP Home Edition, Windows XP Professional,
Windows .NET Server family

.NET Framework Security:

- **ReflectionPermission** SecurityAction.Demand, ReflectionEmit=true
- **ReflectionPermission** to enhance security and performance when invoked late-bound through mechanisms such as **Type.InvokeMember**. Associated enumeration: **ReflectionPermissionFlag.MemberAccess**.

AssemblyBuilder.DefineVersionInfoResource Method (String, String, String, String, String)

Defines an unmanaged version information resource for this assembly with the given specifications.

```
[Visual Basic]
Overloads Public Sub DefineVersionInfoResource( _
    ByVal product As String, _
    ByVal productVersion As String, _
    ByVal company As String, _
    ByVal copyright As String, _
    ByVal trademark As String _
)
[C#]
public void DefineVersionInfoResource(
    string product,
    string productVersion,
    string company,
    string copyright,
    string trademark
);
[C++]
public: void DefineVersionInfoResource(
    String* product,
    String* productVersion,
    String* company,
    String* copyright,
    String* trademark
);
[JScript]
public function DefineVersionInfoResource(
    product : String,
    productVersion : String,
    company : String,
    copyright : String,
    trademark : String
);
```

Parameters

product
    The name of the product with which this assembly is distributed.
productVersion
    The version of the product with which this assembly is distributed.
company
    The name of the company that produced this assembly.
copyright
    Describes all copyright notices, trademarks, and registered trademarks that apply to this assembly. This should include the full text of all notices, legal symbols, copyright dates, trademark numbers, and so on. In English, this string should be in the format "Copyright Microsoft Corp. 1990-2001".

trademark
    Describes all trademarks and registered trademarks that apply to this assembly. This should include the full text of all notices, legal symbols, trademark numbers, and so on. In English, this string should be in the format "Windows is a trademark of Microsoft Corporation".

Exceptions

Exception Type	Condition
ArgumentException	An unmanaged version information resource was previously defined.
	-or-
	The unmanaged version information is too large to persist.
SecurityException	The caller does not have the required permission.

Remarks

An assembly can be associated with only one unmanaged resource. This means that calling **DefineVersionInfoResource** or **DefineUnmanagedResource** after either one of the methods was called previously will throw the System.ArgumentException. Multiple unmanaged resources need to be merged with a tool such as the Microsoft **ResMerge** utility (not supplied with the common language runtime SDK).

Empty argument strings get written as a single space. Spaces are substituted for null characters in the argument strings.

The structure of the version resource includes data that identifies the version, language, and distribution of the file. Installation programs use the functions in the file installation library (VER.DLL) to retrieve the version information resource from a file and to extract the version information blocks from the resource.

Example

See related example in the **System.Reflection.Emit.AssemblyBuilder.DefineVersionInfoResource** method topic.

Requirements

Platforms: Windows 98, Windows NT 4.0, Windows Millennium Edition, Windows 2000, Windows XP Home Edition, Windows XP Professional, Windows .NET Server family

.NET Framework Security:

- **ReflectionPermission** SecurityAction.Demand, ReflectionEmit=true
- **ReflectionPermission** to enhance security and performance when invoked late-bound through mechanisms such as **Type.InvokeMember**. Associated enumeration: **ReflectionPermissionFlag.MemberAccess**.

AssemblyBuilder.GetDynamicModule Method

Returns the dynamic module with the specified name.

```
[Visual Basic]
Public Function GetDynamicModule( _
    ByVal name As String _
) As ModuleBuilder
```

```
[C#]
public ModuleBuilder GetDynamicModule(
    string name
);
[C++]
public: ModuleBuilder* GetDynamicModule(
    String* name
);
[JScript]
public function GetDynamicModule(
    name : String
) : ModuleBuilder;
```

Parameters

name
>   The name of the requested dynamic module.

Return Value

A ModuleBuilder object representing the requested dynamic module.

Exceptions

Exception Type	Condition
ArgumentNullException	*name* is a null reference (**Nothing** in Visual Basic).
ArgumentException	The length of *name* is zero.
SecurityException	The caller does not have the required permission.

Requirements

Platforms: Windows 98, Windows NT 4.0, Windows Millennium Edition, Windows 2000, Windows XP Home Edition, Windows XP Professional, Windows .NET Server family

.NET Framework Security:

*   **ReflectionPermission** to enhance security and performance when invoked late-bound through mechanisms such as **Type.InvokeMember**. Associated enumeration: **ReflectionPermissionFlag.MemberAccess**.

AssemblyBuilder.GetExportedTypes Method

Gets the exported types defined in this assembly.

```
[Visual Basic]
Overrides Public Function GetExportedTypes() As Type()
[C#]
public override Type[] GetExportedTypes();
[C++]
public: Type* GetExportedTypes() [];
[JScript]
public override function GetExportedTypes() : Type[];
```

Return Value

An array of **Type** containing the exported types defined in this assembly.

Exceptions

Exception Type	Condition
NotSupportedException	This method is not implemented.
SecurityException	The caller does not have the required permission.

Requirements

Platforms: Windows 98, Windows NT 4.0, Windows Millennium Edition, Windows 2000, Windows XP Home Edition, Windows XP Professional, Windows .NET Server family

.NET Framework Security:

*   **ReflectionPermission** to enhance security and performance when invoked late-bound through mechanisms such as **Type.InvokeMember**. Associated enumeration: **ReflectionPermissionFlag.MemberAccess**.

AssemblyBuilder.GetFile Method

Gets a **FileStream** for the specified file in the file table of the manifest of this assembly.

```
[Visual Basic]
Overrides Public Function GetFile( _
    ByVal name As String _
) As FileStream
[C#]
public override FileStream GetFile(
    string name
);
[C++]
public: FileStream* GetFile(
    String* name
);
[JScript]
public override function GetFile(
    name : String
) : FileStream;
```

Parameters

name
>   The name of the specified file.

Return Value

A **FileStream** for the specified file, or a null reference (**Nothing** in Visual Basic), if the file is not found.

Exceptions

Exception Type	Condition
NotSupportedException	This method is not currently supported.
SecurityException	The caller does not have the required permission.

Remarks

name should not include the path to the file.

Requirements

Platforms: Windows 98, Windows NT 4.0, Windows Millennium Edition, Windows 2000, Windows XP Home Edition, Windows XP Professional, Windows .NET Server family

.NET Framework Security:

*   **ReflectionPermission** to enhance security and performance when invoked late-bound through mechanisms such as **Type.InvokeMember**. Associated enumeration: **ReflectionPermissionFlag.MemberAccess**.

AssemblyBuilder.GetFiles Method

Overload List

Gets the files in the file table of an assembly manifest, specifying whether to include resource modules.

[Visual Basic] **Overloads Overrides Public Function GetFiles(Boolean) As FileStream()**

[C#] **public override FileStream[] GetFiles(bool);**

[C++] **public: FileStream* GetFiles(bool) [];**

[JScript] **public override function GetFiles(Boolean) : FileStream[];**

Inherited from **Assembly**.

[Visual Basic] **Overloads Public Overridable Function GetFiles() As FileStream()**

[C#] **public virtual FileStream[] GetFiles();**

[C++] **public: virtual FileStream* GetFiles() [];**

[JScript] **public function GetFiles() : FileStream[];**

AssemblyBuilder.GetFiles Method (Boolean)

Gets the files in the file table of an assembly manifest, specifying whether to include resource modules.

```
[Visual Basic]
Overrides Overloads Public Function GetFiles( _
    ByVal getResourceModules As Boolean _
) As FileStream()
[C#]
public override FileStream[] GetFiles(
    bool getResourceModules
);
[C++]
public: FileStream* GetFiles(
    bool getResourceModules
) [];
[JScript]
public override function GetFiles(
    getResourceModules : Boolean
) : FileStream[];
```

Parameters

getResourceModules
    true to include resource modules; otherwise, **false**.

Return Value

An array of **FileStream** objects.

Exceptions

Exception Type	Condition
NotSupportedException	This method is not currently supported.
SecurityException	The caller does not have the required permission.

Requirements

Platforms: Windows 98, Windows NT 4.0, Windows Millennium Edition, Windows 2000, Windows XP Home Edition, Windows XP Professional, Windows .NET Server family

.NET Framework Security:

- **ReflectionPermission** to enhance security and performance when invoked late-bound through mechanisms such as **Type.InvokeMember**. Associated enumeration: **ReflectionPermissionFlag.MemberAccess**.

AssemblyBuilder.GetManifestResourceInfo Method

Returns information about how the given resource has been persisted.

```
[Visual Basic]
Overrides Public Function GetManifestResourceInfo( _
    ByVal resourceName As String _
) As ManifestResourceInfo
[C#]
public override ManifestResourceInfo GetManifestResourceInfo(
    string resourceName
);
[C++]
public: ManifestResourceInfo* GetManifestResourceInfo(
    String* resourceName
);
[JScript]
public override function GetManifestResourceInfo(
    resourceName : String
) : ManifestResourceInfo;
```

Parameters

resourceName
    The name of the resource.

Return Value

ManifestResourceInfo populated with information about the resource's topology, or a null reference (**Nothing** in Visual Basic) if the resource is not found.

Exceptions

Exception Type	Condition
NotSupportedException	This method is not currently supported.
SecurityException	The caller does not have the required permission.

Requirements

Platforms: Windows 98, Windows NT 4.0, Windows Millennium Edition, Windows 2000, Windows XP Home Edition, Windows XP Professional, Windows .NET Server family

.NET Framework Security:

- **ReflectionPermission** to enhance security and performance when invoked late-bound through mechanisms such as **Type.InvokeMember**. Associated enumeration: **ReflectionPermissionFlag.MemberAccess**.

AssemblyBuilder.GetManifestResourceNames Method

Loads the specified manifest resource from this assembly.

```
[Visual Basic]
Overrides Public Function GetManifestResourceNames() As String()
[C#]
public override string[] GetManifestResourceNames();
[C++]
public: String* GetManifestResourceNames() __gc[];
[JScript]
public override function GetManifestResourceNames() : String[];
```

Return Value

An array of type **String** containing the names of all the resources.

Exceptions

Exception Type	Condition
NotSupportedException	This method is not supported on a dynamic assembly. To get the manifest resource names, use **GetManifestResourceNames**.
SecurityException	The caller does not have the required permission.

Requirements

Platforms: Windows 98, Windows NT 4.0, Windows Millennium Edition, Windows 2000, Windows XP Home Edition, Windows XP Professional, Windows .NET Server family

.NET Framework Security:
- **ReflectionPermission** to enhance security and performance when invoked late-bound through mechanisms such as **Type.InvokeMember**. Associated enumeration: **ReflectionPermissionFlag.MemberAccess**.

AssemblyBuilder.GetManifestResourceStream Method

Loads the specified manifest resource from this assembly.

Overload List

Loads the specified manifest resource from this assembly.

[Visual Basic] **Overloads Overrides Public Function GetManifestResourceStream(String) As Stream**

[C#] **public override Stream GetManifestResource Stream(string);**

[C++] **public: Stream* GetManifestResourceStream(String*);**

[JScript] **public override function GetManifestResource Stream(String) : Stream;**

Loads the specified manifest resource, scoped by the namespace of the specified type, from this assembly.

[Visual Basic] **Overloads Overrides Public Function GetManifestResourceStream(Type, String) As Stream**

[C#] **public override Stream GetManifestResource Stream(Type, string);**

[C++] **public: Stream* GetManifestResourceStream(Type*, String*);**

[JScript] **public override function GetManifestResource Stream(Type, String) : Stream;**

Example

If the full name of *type* is "MyNameSpace.MyClasses" and *name* is "Dot", **GetManifestResourceStream** will search for a resource named MyNameSpace.Dot.

AssemblyBuilder.GetManifestResourceStream Method (String)

Loads the specified manifest resource from this assembly.

```
[Visual Basic]
Overrides Overloads Public Function GetManifestResourceStream( _
    ByVal name As String _
) As Stream
[C#]
public override Stream GetManifestResourceStream(
    string name
);
[C++]
public: Stream* GetManifestResourceStream(
    String* name
);
[JScript]
public override function GetManifestResourceStream(
    name : String
) : Stream;
```

Parameters

name
    The name of the manifest resource being requested.

Return Value

A **Stream** representing this manifest resource.

Exceptions

Exception Type	Condition
NotSupportedException	This method is not currently supported.
SecurityException	The caller does not have the required permission.

Requirements

Platforms: Windows 98, Windows NT 4.0, Windows Millennium Edition, Windows 2000, Windows XP Home Edition, Windows XP Professional, Windows .NET Server family

.NET Framework Security:
- **ReflectionPermission** to enhance security and performance when invoked late-bound through mechanisms such as **Type.InvokeMember**. Associated enumeration: **ReflectionPermissionFlag.MemberAccess**.

AssemblyBuilder.GetManifestResourceStream Method (Type, String)

Loads the specified manifest resource, scoped by the namespace of the specified type, from this assembly.

```
[Visual Basic]
Overrides Overloads Public Function GetManifestResourceStream( _
    ByVal type As Type, _
    ByVal name As String _
) As Stream
```

```
[C#]
public override Stream GetManifestResourceStream(
    Type type,
    string name
);
[C++]
public: Stream* GetManifestResourceStream(
    Type* type,
    String* name
);
[JScript]
public override function GetManifestResourceStream(
    type : Type,
    name : String
) : Stream;
```

Parameters

type

The type whose namespace is used to scope the manifest resource name.

name

The name of the manifest resource being requested.

Return Value

A **Stream** representing this manifest resource.

Exceptions

Exception Type	Condition
NotSupportedException	This method is not currently supported.
SecurityException	The caller does not have the required permission.

Remarks

The returned **Stream** has its file pointer set to the beginning of the resource.

Example

If the full name of *type* is "MyNameSpace.MyClasses" and *name* is "Dot", **GetManifestResourceStream** will search for a resource named MyNameSpace.Dot.

Requirements

Platforms: Windows 98, Windows NT 4.0, Windows Millennium Edition, Windows 2000, Windows XP Home Edition, Windows XP Professional, Windows .NET Server family

.NET Framework Security:

- **ReflectionPermission** to enhance security and performance when invoked late-bound through mechanisms such as **Type.InvokeMember**. Associated enumeration: **ReflectionPermissionFlag.MemberAccess**.

AssemblyBuilder.Save Method

Saves this dynamic assembly to disk.

```
[Visual Basic]
Public Sub Save( _
    ByVal assemblyFileName As String _
)
```

```
[C#]
public void Save(
    string assemblyFileName
);
[C++]
public: void Save(
    String* assemblyFileName
);
[JScript]
public function Save(
    assemblyFileName : String
);
```

Parameters

assemblyFileName

The file name of the assembly.

Exceptions

Exception Type	Condition
ArgumentException	The length of *assemblyFileName* is 0. -or- There are two or more modules resource files in the assembly with the same name. -or- The target directory of the assembly is invalid. -or- *assemblyFileName* is not a simple file name (for example, has a directory or drive component) or more than unmanaged resource, including version information resource, was defined in this assembly. -or- The **CultureInfo** string in **AssemblyCultureAttribute** is not a valid string and **DefineVersionInfoResource** was called prior to calling this method.
ArgumentNullException	*assemblyFileName* is a null reference (**Nothing** in Visual Basic).
InvalidOperationException	This assembly has been saved before. -or- This assembly has access **Run AssemblyBuilderAccess**
IOException	If any output error occurs during the save.
NotSupportedException	If **CreateType** has not been called for any of the types in the modules of the assembly to be written to disk.
SecurityException	The caller does not have the required permission.

Remarks

This method saves all non-transient dynamic modules defined in this dynamic assembly. Transient dynamic modules are not saved. The assembly file name can be the same as one of the module's name. If so, the assemby information is stored within that module. *assemblyFileName* can be different from the names of all of the modules contained within the assembly. If so, the assembly is stored as a standalone.

For each **ResourceWriter** obtained using **DefineResource**, this method writes the .resources file and calls **Close** to close the stream.

The *assemblyFileName* needs to be a simple file name without a drive or directory component. To create an assembly in a specific directory, use one of the **DefineDynamicAssembly** methods that takes a target directory argument.

Example

[Visual Basic, C#, C++] The following code sample creates a dynamic assembly and then persists it to a local disk using **Save**.

```vbnet
[Visual Basic]
Imports System
Imports System.Text
Imports System.Threading
Imports System.Reflection
Imports System.Reflection.Emit

    _

' The Point class is the class we will reflect on and copy into our
' dynamic assembly. The public static function PointMain() will be used
' as our entry point.

' We are constructing the type seen here dynamically, and will write it
' out into a .exe file for later execution from the command-line.
' ---
' Class Point
'
'     Private x As Integer
'     Private y As Integer
'
'
'     Public Sub New(ix As Integer, iy As Integer)
'
'         Me.x = ix
'         Me.y = iy
'     End Sub 'New
'
'
'     Public Function DotProduct(p As Point) As Integer
'
'         Return Me.x * p.x + Me.y * p.y
'     End Function 'DotProduct
'
'
'     Public Shared Sub Main()
'
'         Console.Write("Enter the 'x' value for point 1: ")
'         Dim x1 As Integer = Convert.ToInt32(Console.ReadLine())
'
'         Console.Write("Enter the 'y' value for point 1: ")
'         Dim y1 As Integer = Convert.ToInt32(Console.ReadLine())
'
'         Console.Write("Enter the 'x' value for point 2: ")
'         Dim x2 As Integer = Convert.ToInt32(Console.ReadLine())
'
'         Console.Write("Enter the 'y' value for point 2: ")
'         Dim y2 As Integer = Convert.ToInt32(Console.ReadLine())
'
'         Dim p1 As New Point(x1, y1)
'         Dim p2 As New Point(x2, y2)
'
'         Console.WriteLine("({0}, {1}) . ({2}, {3}) = {4}.", x1, _
' y1, x2, y2, p1.DotProduct(p2))
'     End Sub 'Main
' End Class 'Point
' ---
Class AssemblyBuilderDemo

    Public Shared Function BuildDynAssembly() As Type

        Dim pointType As Type = Nothing

        Dim currentDom As AppDomain = Thread.GetDomain()

        Console.Write("Please enter a name for your new assembly: ")
        Dim asmFileNameBldr As New StringBuilder()
        asmFileNameBldr.Append(Console.ReadLine())
        asmFileNameBldr.Append(".exe")
        Dim asmFileName As String = asmFileNameBldr.ToString()

        Dim myAsmName As New AssemblyName()
        myAsmName.Name = "MyDynamicAssembly"

        Dim myAsmBldr As AssemblyBuilder = _
currentDom.DefineDynamicAssembly(myAsmName, _
                    AssemblyBuilderAccess.RunAndSave)

        ' We've created a dynamic assembly space - now, we need _
to create a module
        ' within it to reflect the type Point into.
        Dim myModuleBldr As ModuleBuilder = _
myAsmBldr.DefineDynamicModule(asmFileName, _
                    asmFileName)

        Dim myTypeBldr As TypeBuilder = myModuleBldr.DefineType("Point")

        Dim xField As FieldBuilder = myTypeBldr.DefineField _
("x", GetType(Integer), _
                    FieldAttributes.Private)
        Dim yField As FieldBuilder = myTypeBldr.DefineField _
("y", GetType(Integer), _
                    FieldAttributes.Private)

        ' Build the constructor.
        Dim objType As Type = Type.GetType("System.Object")
        Dim objCtor As ConstructorInfo = objType.GetConstructor _
(New Type() {})

        Dim ctorParams() As Type = {GetType(Integer), GetType(Integer)}
        Dim pointCtor As ConstructorBuilder = _
myTypeBldr.DefineConstructor( _
                    MethodAttributes.Public, _
                    CallingConventions.Standard, _
                    ctorParams)
        Dim ctorIL As ILGenerator = pointCtor.GetILGenerator()
        ctorIL.Emit(OpCodes.Ldarg_0)
        ctorIL.Emit(OpCodes.Call, objCtor)
        ctorIL.Emit(OpCodes.Ldarg_0)
        ctorIL.Emit(OpCodes.Ldarg_1)
        ctorIL.Emit(OpCodes.Stfld, xField)
        ctorIL.Emit(OpCodes.Ldarg_0)
        ctorIL.Emit(OpCodes.Ldarg_2)
        ctorIL.Emit(OpCodes.Stfld, yField)
        ctorIL.Emit(OpCodes.Ret)

        ' Build the DotProduct method.
        Console.WriteLine("Constructor built.")

        Dim pointDPBldr As MethodBuilder = _
myTypeBldr.DefineMethod("DotProduct", _
                    MethodAttributes.Public, _
                    GetType(Integer), _
                    New Type(0) {myTypeBldr})

        Dim dpIL As ILGenerator = pointDPBldr.GetILGenerator()
        dpIL.Emit(OpCodes.Ldarg_0)
```

```vbnet
        dpIL.Emit(OpCodes.Ldfld, xField)
        dpIL.Emit(OpCodes.Ldarg_1)
        dpIL.Emit(OpCodes.Ldfld, xField)
        dpIL.Emit(OpCodes.Mul_Ovf_Un)
        dpIL.Emit(OpCodes.Ldarg_0)
        dpIL.Emit(OpCodes.Ldfld, yField)
        dpIL.Emit(OpCodes.Ldarg_1)
        dpIL.Emit(OpCodes.Ldfld, yField)
        dpIL.Emit(OpCodes.Mul_Ovf_Un)
        dpIL.Emit(OpCodes.Add_Ovf_Un)
        dpIL.Emit(OpCodes.Ret)

        ' Build the PointMain method.
        Console.WriteLine("DotProduct built.")

        Dim pointMainBldr As MethodBuilder = _
myTypeBldr.DefineMethod("PointMain", _
                          MethodAttributes.Public Or _
                          MethodAttributes.Static, _
                          Nothing, Nothing)
        pointMainBldr.InitLocals = True
        Dim pmIL As ILGenerator = pointMainBldr.GetILGenerator()

        ' We have four methods that we wish to call, and must _
represent as
        ' MethodInfo tokens:
        ' - Sub Console.WriteLine(string)
        ' - Function Console.ReadLine() As String
        ' - Function Convert.Int32(string) As Int
        ' - Sub Console.WriteLine(string, object[])

        Dim writeMI As MethodInfo = GetType(Console).GetMethod("Write", _
                          New Type(0) {GetType(String)})

        Dim readLineMI As MethodInfo = _
GetType(Console).GetMethod("ReadLine", _
                          New Type() {})
        Dim convertInt32MI As MethodInfo = _
GetType(Convert).GetMethod("ToInt32", _
                          New Type(0) {GetType(String)})
        Dim wlParams() As Type = {GetType(String), GetType(Object())}
        Dim writeLineMI As MethodInfo = _
GetType(Console).GetMethod("WriteLine", wlParams)

        ' Although we could just refer to the local variables by
        ' index (short ints for Ldloc/Stloc, bytes for LdLoc_S/Stloc_S),
        ' this time, we'll use LocalBuilders for clarity and to
        ' demonstrate their usage and syntax.

        Dim x1LB As LocalBuilder = pmIL.DeclareLocal(GetType(Integer))
        Dim y1LB As LocalBuilder = pmIL.DeclareLocal(GetType(Integer))
        Dim x2LB As LocalBuilder = pmIL.DeclareLocal(GetType(Integer))
        Dim y2LB As LocalBuilder = pmIL.DeclareLocal(GetType(Integer))
        Dim point1LB As LocalBuilder = pmIL.DeclareLocal(myTypeBldr)
        Dim point2LB As LocalBuilder = pmIL.DeclareLocal(myTypeBldr)
        Dim tempObjArrLB As LocalBuilder = _
pmIL.DeclareLocal(GetType(Object()))

        pmIL.Emit(OpCodes.Ldstr, "Enter the 'x' value for point 1: ")
        pmIL.EmitCall(OpCodes.Call, writeMI, Nothing)
        pmIL.EmitCall(OpCodes.Call, readLineMI, Nothing)
        pmIL.EmitCall(OpCodes.Call, convertInt32MI, Nothing)
        pmIL.Emit(OpCodes.Stloc, x1LB)

        pmIL.Emit(OpCodes.Ldstr, "Enter the 'y' value for point 1: ")
        pmIL.EmitCall(OpCodes.Call, writeMI, Nothing)
        pmIL.EmitCall(OpCodes.Call, readLineMI, Nothing)
        pmIL.EmitCall(OpCodes.Call, convertInt32MI, Nothing)
        pmIL.Emit(OpCodes.Stloc, y1LB)

        pmIL.Emit(OpCodes.Ldstr, "Enter the 'x' value for point 2: ")
        pmIL.EmitCall(OpCodes.Call, writeMI, Nothing)
        pmIL.EmitCall(OpCodes.Call, readLineMI, Nothing)
        pmIL.EmitCall(OpCodes.Call, convertInt32MI, Nothing)
        pmIL.Emit(OpCodes.Stloc, x2LB)

        pmIL.Emit(OpCodes.Ldstr, "Enter the 'y' value for point 2: ")
        pmIL.EmitCall(OpCodes.Call, writeMI, Nothing)
        pmIL.EmitCall(OpCodes.Call, readLineMI, Nothing)
        pmIL.EmitCall(OpCodes.Call, convertInt32MI, Nothing)
        pmIL.Emit(OpCodes.Stloc, y2LB)

        pmIL.Emit(OpCodes.Ldloc, x1LB)
        pmIL.Emit(OpCodes.Ldloc, y1LB)
        pmIL.Emit(OpCodes.Newobj, pointCtor)
        pmIL.Emit(OpCodes.Stloc, point1LB)

        pmIL.Emit(OpCodes.Ldloc, x2LB)
        pmIL.Emit(OpCodes.Ldloc, y2LB)
        pmIL.Emit(OpCodes.Newobj, pointCtor)
        pmIL.Emit(OpCodes.Stloc, point2LB)

        pmIL.Emit(OpCodes.Ldstr, "({0}, {1}) . ({2}, {3}) = {4}.")
        pmIL.Emit(OpCodes.Ldc_I4_5)
        pmIL.Emit(OpCodes.Newarr, GetType([Object]))
        pmIL.Emit(OpCodes.Stloc, tempObjArrLB)

        pmIL.Emit(OpCodes.Ldloc, tempObjArrLB)
        pmIL.Emit(OpCodes.Ldc_I4_0)
        pmIL.Emit(OpCodes.Ldloc, x1LB)
        pmIL.Emit(OpCodes.Box, GetType(Integer))
        pmIL.Emit(OpCodes.Stelem_Ref)

        pmIL.Emit(OpCodes.Ldloc, tempObjArrLB)
        pmIL.Emit(OpCodes.Ldc_I4_1)
        pmIL.Emit(OpCodes.Ldloc, y1LB)
        pmIL.Emit(OpCodes.Box, GetType(Integer))
        pmIL.Emit(OpCodes.Stelem_Ref)

        pmIL.Emit(OpCodes.Ldloc, tempObjArrLB)
        pmIL.Emit(OpCodes.Ldc_I4_2)
        pmIL.Emit(OpCodes.Ldloc, x2LB)
        pmIL.Emit(OpCodes.Box, GetType(Integer))
        pmIL.Emit(OpCodes.Stelem_Ref)

        pmIL.Emit(OpCodes.Ldloc, tempObjArrLB)
        pmIL.Emit(OpCodes.Ldc_I4_3)
        pmIL.Emit(OpCodes.Ldloc, y2LB)
        pmIL.Emit(OpCodes.Box, GetType(Integer))
        pmIL.Emit(OpCodes.Stelem_Ref)

        pmIL.Emit(OpCodes.Ldloc, tempObjArrLB)
        pmIL.Emit(OpCodes.Ldc_I4_4)
        pmIL.Emit(OpCodes.Ldloc, point1LB)
        pmIL.Emit(OpCodes.Ldloc, point2LB)
        pmIL.EmitCall(OpCodes.Callvirt, pointDPBldr, Nothing)

        pmIL.Emit(OpCodes.Box, GetType(Integer))
        pmIL.Emit(OpCodes.Stelem_Ref)
        pmIL.Emit(OpCodes.Ldloc, tempObjArrLB)
        pmIL.EmitCall(OpCodes.Call, writeLineMI, Nothing)

        pmIL.Emit(OpCodes.Ret)

        Console.WriteLine("PointMain (entry point) built.")

        pointType = myTypeBldr.CreateType()

        Console.WriteLine("Type baked.")

        myAsmBldr.SetEntryPoint(pointMainBldr)

        myAsmBldr.Save(asmFileName)

        Console.WriteLine("Assembly saved as '{0}'.", asmFileName)
        Console.WriteLine("Type '{0}' at the prompt to run your _
new " + "dynamically generated dot product calculator.", asmFileName)

        ' After execution, this program will have generated and _
written to disk,
        ' in the directory you executed it from, a program named
```

```vb
        ' <name_you_entered_here>.exe. You can run it by typing
        ' the name you gave it during execution, in the same
directory where
        ' you executed this program.

        Return pointType

    End Function 'BuildDynAssembly

    Public Shared Sub Main()

        Dim myType As Type = BuildDynAssembly()
        Console.WriteLine("---")

        ' Let's invoke the type 'Point' created in our dynamic assembly.
        Dim ptInstance As Object = Activator.CreateInstance _
(myType, New Object(1) {0, 0})

        myType.InvokeMember("PointMain", BindingFlags.InvokeMethod, _
                Nothing, ptInstance, New Object() {})

    End Sub 'Main

End Class 'AssemblyBuilderDemo

[C#]
using System;
using System.Text;
using System.Threading;
using System.Reflection;
using System.Reflection.Emit;

// The Point class is the class we will reflect on and copy into our
// dynamic assembly. The public static function PointMain()
will be used
// as our entry point.
//
// We are constructing the type seen here dynamically, and will
 write it
// out into a .exe file for later execution from the command-line.
// ---
// class Point {
//
//    private int x;
//    private int y;
//
//    public Point(int ix, int iy) {
//
//        this.x = ix;
//        this.y = iy;
//
//    }
//
//    public int DotProduct (Point p) {
//
//        return ((this.x * p.x) + (this.y * p.y));
//
//    }
//
//    public static void PointMain() {
//
//        Console.Write("Enter the 'x' value for point 1: ");
//        int x1 = Convert.ToInt32(Console.ReadLine());
//
//        Console.Write("Enter the 'y' value for point 1: ");
//        int y1 = Convert.ToInt32(Console.ReadLine());
//
//        Console.Write("Enter the 'x' value for point 2: ");
//        int x2 = Convert.ToInt32(Console.ReadLine());
//
//        Console.Write("Enter the 'y' value for point 2: ");
//        int y2 = Convert.ToInt32(Console.ReadLine());
//
//        Point p1 = new Point(x1, y1);
//        Point p2 = new Point(x2, y2);
//
//        Console.WriteLine("({0}, {1}) . ({2}, {3}) = {4}.",
//            x1, y1, x2, y2, p1.DotProduct(p2));
//
//    }
//
// }
// ---

class AssemblyBuilderDemo {

    public static Type BuildDynAssembly() {

        Type pointType = null;

        AppDomain currentDom = Thread.GetDomain();

        Console.Write("Please enter a name for your new assembly: ");
        StringBuilder asmFileNameBldr = new StringBuilder();
            asmFileNameBldr.Append(Console.ReadLine());
        asmFileNameBldr.Append(".exe");
        string asmFileName = asmFileNameBldr.ToString();

        AssemblyName myAsmName = new AssemblyName();
        myAsmName.Name = "MyDynamicAssembly";

        AssemblyBuilder myAsmBldr = currentDom.DefineDynamicAssembly(
                        myAsmName,
                        AssemblyBuilderAccess.RunAndSave);

        // We've created a dynamic assembly space - now, we need
to create a module
        // within it to reflect the type Point into.

        ModuleBuilder myModuleBldr =
myAsmBldr.DefineDynamicModule(asmFileName,
                                asmFileName);

        TypeBuilder myTypeBldr = myModuleBldr.DefineType("Point");

        FieldBuilder xField = myTypeBldr.DefineField("x", typeof(int),
                    FieldAttributes.Private);
        FieldBuilder yField = myTypeBldr.DefineField("y", typeof(int),
                    FieldAttributes.Private);

        // Build the constructor.

        Type objType = Type.GetType("System.Object");
        ConstructorInfo objCtor = objType.GetConstructor(new Type[0]);

        Type[] ctorParams = new Type[] {typeof(int), typeof(int)};
        ConstructorBuilder pointCtor = myTypeBldr.DefineConstructor(
                            MethodAttributes.Public,
                            CallingConventions.Standard,
                            ctorParams);
        ILGenerator ctorIL = pointCtor.GetILGenerator();
        ctorIL.Emit(OpCodes.Ldarg_0);
        ctorIL.Emit(OpCodes.Call, objCtor);
        ctorIL.Emit(OpCodes.Ldarg_0);
        ctorIL.Emit(OpCodes.Ldarg_1);
        ctorIL.Emit(OpCodes.Stfld, xField);
        ctorIL.Emit(OpCodes.Ldarg_0);
        ctorIL.Emit(OpCodes.Ldarg_2);
        ctorIL.Emit(OpCodes.Stfld, yField);
        ctorIL.Emit(OpCodes.Ret);

        // Build the DotProduct method.

        Console.WriteLine("Constructor built.");

        MethodBuilder pointDPBldr = myTypeBldr.DefineMethod("DotProduct",
                        MethodAttributes.Public,
                        typeof(int),
                        new Type[] {myTypeBldr});
```

```
ILGenerator dpIL = pointDPBldr.GetILGenerator();
dpIL.Emit(OpCodes.Ldarg_0);
dpIL.Emit(OpCodes.Ldfld, xField);
dpIL.Emit(OpCodes.Ldarg_1);
dpIL.Emit(OpCodes.Ldfld, xField);
dpIL.Emit(OpCodes.Mul_Ovf_Un);
dpIL.Emit(OpCodes.Ldarg_0);
dpIL.Emit(OpCodes.Ldfld, yField);
dpIL.Emit(OpCodes.Ldarg_1);
dpIL.Emit(OpCodes.Ldfld, yField);
dpIL.Emit(OpCodes.Mul_Ovf_Un);
dpIL.Emit(OpCodes.Add_Ovf_Un);
dpIL.Emit(OpCodes.Ret);

    // Build the PointMain method.

    Console.WriteLine("DotProduct built.");

MethodBuilder pointMainBldr = myTypeBldr.DefineMethod("PointMain",
                        MethodAttributes.Public |
                        MethodAttributes.Static,
                        typeof(void),
                        null);
    pointMainBldr.InitLocals = true;
ILGenerator pmIL = pointMainBldr.GetILGenerator();

// We have four methods that we wish to call, and must represent as
// MethodInfo tokens:
// - void Console.WriteLine(string)
// - string Console.ReadLine()
// - int Convert.Int32(string)
// - void Console.WriteLine(string, object[])

MethodInfo writeMI = typeof(Console).GetMethod(
                    "Write",
                    new Type[] {typeof(string)});
MethodInfo readLineMI = typeof(Console).GetMethod(
                    "ReadLine",
                    new Type[0]);
MethodInfo convertInt32MI = typeof(Convert).GetMethod(
                    "ToInt32",
                        new Type[] {typeof(string)});
Type[] wlParams = new Type[] {typeof(string), typeof(object[])};
MethodInfo writeLineMI = typeof(Console).GetMethod(
                    "WriteLine",
                    wlParams);

// Although we could just refer to the local variables by
// index (short ints for Ldloc/Stloc, bytes for LdLoc_S/Stloc_S),
// this time, we'll use LocalBuilders for clarity and to
// demonstrate their usage and syntax.

LocalBuilder x1LB = pmIL.DeclareLocal(typeof(int));
LocalBuilder y1LB = pmIL.DeclareLocal(typeof(int));
LocalBuilder x2LB = pmIL.DeclareLocal(typeof(int));
LocalBuilder y2LB = pmIL.DeclareLocal(typeof(int));
LocalBuilder point1LB = pmIL.DeclareLocal(myTypeBldr);
LocalBuilder point2LB = pmIL.DeclareLocal(myTypeBldr);
LocalBuilder tempObjArrLB = pmIL.DeclareLocal(typeof(object[]));

pmIL.Emit(OpCodes.Ldstr, "Enter the 'x' value for point 1: ");
pmIL.EmitCall(OpCodes.Call, writeMI, null);
pmIL.EmitCall(OpCodes.Call, readLineMI, null);
pmIL.EmitCall(OpCodes.Call, convertInt32MI, null);
pmIL.Emit(OpCodes.Stloc, x1LB);

pmIL.Emit(OpCodes.Ldstr, "Enter the 'y' value for point 1: ");
pmIL.EmitCall(OpCodes.Call, writeMI, null);
pmIL.EmitCall(OpCodes.Call, readLineMI, null);
pmIL.EmitCall(OpCodes.Call, convertInt32MI, null);
pmIL.Emit(OpCodes.Stloc, y1LB);

pmIL.Emit(OpCodes.Ldstr, "Enter the 'x' value for point 2: ");
pmIL.EmitCall(OpCodes.Call, writeMI, null);
pmIL.EmitCall(OpCodes.Call, readLineMI, null);
```

```
pmIL.EmitCall(OpCodes.Call, convertInt32MI, null);
pmIL.Emit(OpCodes.Stloc, x2LB);

pmIL.Emit(OpCodes.Ldstr, "Enter the 'y' value for point 2: ");
pmIL.EmitCall(OpCodes.Call, writeMI, null);
pmIL.EmitCall(OpCodes.Call, readLineMI, null);
pmIL.EmitCall(OpCodes.Call, convertInt32MI, null);
pmIL.Emit(OpCodes.Stloc, y2LB);

pmIL.Emit(OpCodes.Ldloc, x1LB);
pmIL.Emit(OpCodes.Ldloc, y1LB);
pmIL.Emit(OpCodes.Newobj, pointCtor);
pmIL.Emit(OpCodes.Stloc, point1LB);

pmIL.Emit(OpCodes.Ldloc, x2LB);
pmIL.Emit(OpCodes.Ldloc, y2LB);
pmIL.Emit(OpCodes.Newobj, pointCtor);
pmIL.Emit(OpCodes.Stloc, point2LB);

pmIL.Emit(OpCodes.Ldstr, "({0}, {1}) . ({2}, {3}) = {4}.");
pmIL.Emit(OpCodes.Ldc_I4_5);
pmIL.Emit(OpCodes.Newarr, typeof(Object));
pmIL.Emit(OpCodes.Stloc, tempObjArrLB);

pmIL.Emit(OpCodes.Ldloc, tempObjArrLB);
pmIL.Emit(OpCodes.Ldc_I4_0);
pmIL.Emit(OpCodes.Ldloc, x1LB);
pmIL.Emit(OpCodes.Box, typeof(int));
pmIL.Emit(OpCodes.Stelem_Ref);

pmIL.Emit(OpCodes.Ldloc, tempObjArrLB);
pmIL.Emit(OpCodes.Ldc_I4_1);
pmIL.Emit(OpCodes.Ldloc, y1LB);
pmIL.Emit(OpCodes.Box, typeof(int));
pmIL.Emit(OpCodes.Stelem_Ref);

pmIL.Emit(OpCodes.Ldloc, tempObjArrLB);
pmIL.Emit(OpCodes.Ldc_I4_2);
pmIL.Emit(OpCodes.Ldloc, x2LB);
pmIL.Emit(OpCodes.Box, typeof(int));
pmIL.Emit(OpCodes.Stelem_Ref);

pmIL.Emit(OpCodes.Ldloc, tempObjArrLB);
pmIL.Emit(OpCodes.Ldc_I4_3);
pmIL.Emit(OpCodes.Ldloc, y2LB);
pmIL.Emit(OpCodes.Box, typeof(int));
pmIL.Emit(OpCodes.Stelem_Ref);

pmIL.Emit(OpCodes.Ldloc, tempObjArrLB);
pmIL.Emit(OpCodes.Ldc_I4_4);
pmIL.Emit(OpCodes.Ldloc, point1LB);
pmIL.Emit(OpCodes.Ldloc, point2LB);
pmIL.EmitCall(OpCodes.Callvirt, pointDPBldr, null);

pmIL.Emit(OpCodes.Box, typeof(int));
pmIL.Emit(OpCodes.Stelem_Ref);
pmIL.Emit(OpCodes.Ldloc, tempObjArrLB);
pmIL.EmitCall(OpCodes.Call, writeLineMI, null);

pmIL.Emit(OpCodes.Ret);

    Console.WriteLine("PointMain (entry point) built.");

    pointType = myTypeBldr.CreateType();

    Console.WriteLine("Type baked.");

myAsmBldr.SetEntryPoint(pointMainBldr);

    myAsmBldr.Save(asmFileName);

    Console.WriteLine("Assembly saved as '{0}'.", asmFileName);
    Console.WriteLine("Type '{0}' at the prompt to run your new " +
        "dynamically generated dot product calculator.",
        asmFileName);
```

```
    // After execution, this program will have generated and
written to disk,
            // in the directory you executed it from, a program named
    // <name_you_entered_here>.exe. You can run it by typing
    // the name you gave it during execution, in the same
directory where
    // you executed this program.

    return pointType;

  }


  public static void Main() {

    Type myType = BuildDynAssembly();
    Console.WriteLine("---");

    // Let's invoke the type 'Point' created in our dynamic assembly.

    object ptInstance = Activator.CreateInstance(myType,
new object[] {0,0});

    myType.InvokeMember("PointMain",
            BindingFlags.InvokeMethod,
            null,
            ptInstance,
            new object[0]);

  }
}

[C++]
#using <mscorlib.dll>

using namespace System;
using namespace System::Text;
using namespace System::Threading;
using namespace System::Reflection;
using namespace System::Reflection::Emit;

// The Point class is the class we will reflect on and copy into our
// dynamic assembly. The public static function PointMain()
will be used
// as our entry point.
//
// We are constructing the type seen here dynamically, and
will write it
// out into a .exe file for later execution from the command-line.
// ---
// class Point {
//
//    private:
//      int x;
//      int y;
//
//    public:
//      Point(int ix, int iy) {
//
//        this->x = ix;
//        this->y = iy;
//
//      }
//
//      int DotProduct (Point p) {
//
//        return ((this->x * p.x) + (this->y * p.y));
//
//      }
//
//      static void PointMain() {
//
//      Console::Write(S"Enter the 'x' value for point 1: ");
//      int x1 = Convert::ToInt32(Console::ReadLine());
//
//      Console::Write(S"Enter the 'y' value for point 1: ");
```

```
//      int y1 = Convert::ToInt32(Console::ReadLine());
//
//      Console::Write(S"Enter the 'x' value for point 2: ");
//      int x2 = Convert::ToInt32(Console::ReadLine());
//
//      Console::Write(S"Enter the 'y' value for point 2: ");
//      int y2 = Convert::ToInt32(Console::ReadLine());
//
//      Point p1 = new Point(x1, y1);
//      Point p2 = new Point(x2, y2);
//
//      Console::WriteLine(S"( {0}, {1}) . ( {2}, {3}) = {4}.",
//              x1, y1, x2, y2, p1.DotProduct(p2));
//
//    }
//
// }
// ---

Type* BuildDynAssembly() {

    Type* pointType = 0;

    AppDomain* currentDom = Thread::GetDomain();

    Console::Write(S"Please enter a name for your new assembly: ");
    StringBuilder* asmFileNameBldr = new StringBuilder();
    asmFileNameBldr->Append(Console::ReadLine());
    asmFileNameBldr->Append(S".exe");
    String* asmFileName = asmFileNameBldr->ToString();

    AssemblyName* myAsmName = new AssemblyName();
    myAsmName->Name = S"MyDynamicAssembly";

    AssemblyBuilder* myAsmBldr = currentDom-
>DefineDynamicAssembly(myAsmName,
        AssemblyBuilderAccess::RunAndSave);

    // We've created a dynamic assembly space - now, we need to
create a module
    // within it to reflect the type Point into.

    ModuleBuilder* myModuleBldr = myAsmBldr-
>DefineDynamicModule(asmFileName,
        asmFileName);

    TypeBuilder* myTypeBldr = myModuleBldr->DefineType(S"Point");

    FieldBuilder* xField = myTypeBldr->DefineField(S"x", __typeof(int),
        FieldAttributes::Private);
    FieldBuilder* yField = myTypeBldr->DefineField(S"y", __typeof(int),
        FieldAttributes::Private);

    // Build the constructor.

    Type* objType = Type::GetType(S"System.Object");
    ConstructorInfo* objCtor = objType->GetConstructor(new Type*[0]);

    Type* temp4 [] = {__typeof(int), __typeof(int)};
    Type* ctorParams[] = temp4;
    ConstructorBuilder* pointCtor = myTypeBldr-
>DefineConstructor(MethodAttributes::Public,
        CallingConventions::Standard,
        ctorParams);
    ILGenerator* ctorIL = pointCtor->GetILGenerator();
    ctorIL->Emit(OpCodes::Ldarg_0);
    ctorIL->Emit(OpCodes::Call, objCtor);
    ctorIL->Emit(OpCodes::Ldarg_0);
    ctorIL->Emit(OpCodes::Ldarg_1);
    ctorIL->Emit(OpCodes::Stfld, xField);
    ctorIL->Emit(OpCodes::Ldarg_0);
    ctorIL->Emit(OpCodes::Ldarg_2);
    ctorIL->Emit(OpCodes::Stfld, yField);
    ctorIL->Emit(OpCodes::Ret);
```

```
// Build the DotProduct method.

Console::WriteLine(S"Constructor built.");

Type* temp0 [] = {myTypeBldr};
MethodBuilder*  pointDPBldr = myTypeBldr-
>DefineMethod(S"DotProduct",
    MethodAttributes::Public,
    __typeof(int),
    temp0);

ILGenerator* dpIL = pointDPBldr->GetILGenerator();
dpIL->Emit(OpCodes::Ldarg_0);
dpIL->Emit(OpCodes::Ldfld, xField);
dpIL->Emit(OpCodes::Ldarg_1);
dpIL->Emit(OpCodes::Ldfld, xField);
dpIL->Emit(OpCodes::Mul_Ovf_Un);
dpIL->Emit(OpCodes::Ldarg_0);
dpIL->Emit(OpCodes::Ldfld, yField);
dpIL->Emit(OpCodes::Ldarg_1);
dpIL->Emit(OpCodes::Ldfld, yField);
dpIL->Emit(OpCodes::Mul_Ovf_Un);
dpIL->Emit(OpCodes->Add_Ovf_Un);
dpIL->Emit(OpCodes::Ret);

// Build the PointMain method.

Console::WriteLine(S"DotProduct built.");

MethodBuilder*  pointMainBldr = myTypeBldr->DefineMethod(
    S"PointMain",
    static_cast<MethodAttributes>(MethodAttributes:
:Public | MethodAttributes::Static),
    __typeof(void),
    0);
pointMainBldr->InitLocals = true;
ILGenerator* pmIL = pointMainBldr->GetILGenerator();

// We have four methods that we wish to call, and must represent as
// MethodInfo tokens:
// - void Console::WriteLine(String*)
// - String* Console::ReadLine()
// - int Convert::Int32(String*)
// - void Console::WriteLine(String*, Object*->Item[])

Type* temp1 [] = {__typeof(String)};
MethodInfo*  writeMI = __typeof(Console)->GetMethod
(S"Write", temp1);
MethodInfo*  readLineMI = __typeof(Console)->GetMethod
(S"ReadLine", new Type*[0]);
Type* temp2 [] = {__typeof(String)};
MethodInfo*  convertInt32MI = __typeof(Convert)-
>GetMethod(S"ToInt32", temp2);
Type* temp5 [] = {__typeof(String), __typeof(Object*[])};
Type* wlParams[] = temp5;
MethodInfo*  writeLineMI = __typeof(Console)-
>GetMethod(S"WriteLine", wlParams);

// Although we could just refer to the local variables by
// index (short ints for Ldloc/Stloc, bytes for LdLoc_S/Stloc_S),
// this time, we'll use LocalBuilders for clarity and to
// demonstrate their usage and syntax.

LocalBuilder*  x1LB = pmIL->DeclareLocal(__typeof(int));
LocalBuilder*  y1LB = pmIL->DeclareLocal(__typeof(int));
LocalBuilder*  x2LB = pmIL->DeclareLocal(__typeof(int));
LocalBuilder*  y2LB = pmIL->DeclareLocal(__typeof(int));
LocalBuilder*  point1LB = pmIL->DeclareLocal(myTypeBldr);
LocalBuilder*  point2LB = pmIL->DeclareLocal(myTypeBldr);
LocalBuilder*  tempObjArrLB = pmIL-
>DeclareLocal(__typeof(Object*[]));

pmIL->Emit(OpCodes::Ldstr, S"Enter the 'x' value for point 1: ");
pmIL->EmitCall(OpCodes::Call, writeMI, 0);
pmIL->EmitCall(OpCodes::Call, readLineMI, 0);
```

```
pmIL->EmitCall(OpCodes::Call, convertInt32MI, 0);
pmIL->Emit(OpCodes::Stloc, x1LB);

pmIL->Emit(OpCodes::Ldstr, S"Enter the 'y' value for point 1: ");
pmIL->EmitCall(OpCodes::Call, writeMI, 0);
pmIL->EmitCall(OpCodes::Call, readLineMI, 0);
pmIL->EmitCall(OpCodes::Call, convertInt32MI, 0);
pmIL->Emit(OpCodes::Stloc, y1LB);

pmIL->Emit(OpCodes::Ldstr, S"Enter the 'x' value for point 2: ");
pmIL->EmitCall(OpCodes::Call, writeMI, 0);
pmIL->EmitCall(OpCodes::Call, readLineMI, 0);
pmIL->EmitCall(OpCodes::Call, convertInt32MI, 0);
pmIL->Emit(OpCodes::Stloc, x2LB);

pmIL->Emit(OpCodes::Ldstr, S"Enter the 'y' value for point 2: ");
pmIL->EmitCall(OpCodes::Call, writeMI, 0);
pmIL->EmitCall(OpCodes::Call, readLineMI, 0);
pmIL->EmitCall(OpCodes::Call, convertInt32MI, 0);
pmIL->Emit(OpCodes::Stloc, y2LB);

pmIL->Emit(OpCodes::Ldloc, x1LB);
pmIL->Emit(OpCodes::Ldloc, y1LB);
pmIL->Emit(OpCodes::Newobj, pointCtor);
pmIL->Emit(OpCodes::Stloc, point1LB);

pmIL->Emit(OpCodes::Ldloc, x2LB);
pmIL->Emit(OpCodes::Ldloc, y2LB);
pmIL->Emit(OpCodes::Newobj, pointCtor);
pmIL->Emit(OpCodes::Stloc, point2LB);

pmIL->Emit(OpCodes::Ldstr, S"( {0}, {1}) . ( {2}, {3}) = {4}.");
pmIL->Emit(OpCodes::Ldc_I4_5);
pmIL->Emit(OpCodes::Newarr, __typeof(Object));
pmIL->Emit(OpCodes::Stloc, tempObjArrLB);

pmIL->Emit(OpCodes::Ldloc, tempObjArrLB);
pmIL->Emit(OpCodes::Ldc_I4_0);
pmIL->Emit(OpCodes::Ldloc, x1LB);
pmIL->Emit(OpCodes::Box, __typeof(int));
pmIL->Emit(OpCodes::Stelem_Ref);

pmIL->Emit(OpCodes::Ldloc, tempObjArrLB);
pmIL->Emit(OpCodes::Ldc_I4_1);
pmIL->Emit(OpCodes::Ldloc, y1LB);
pmIL->Emit(OpCodes::Box, __typeof(int));
pmIL->Emit(OpCodes::Stelem_Ref);

pmIL->Emit(OpCodes::Ldloc, tempObjArrLB);
pmIL->Emit(OpCodes::Ldc_I4_2);
pmIL->Emit(OpCodes::Ldloc, x2LB);
pmIL->Emit(OpCodes::Box, __typeof(int));
pmIL->Emit(OpCodes::Stelem_Ref);

pmIL->Emit(OpCodes::Ldloc, tempObjArrLB);
pmIL->Emit(OpCodes::Ldc_I4_3);
pmIL->Emit(OpCodes::Ldloc, y2LB);
pmIL->Emit(OpCodes::Box, __typeof(int));
pmIL->Emit(OpCodes::Stelem_Ref);

pmIL->Emit(OpCodes::Ldloc, tempObjArrLB);
pmIL->Emit(OpCodes::Ldc_I4_4);
pmIL->Emit(OpCodes::Ldloc, point1LB);
pmIL->Emit(OpCodes::Ldloc, point2LB);
pmIL->EmitCall(OpCodes::Callvirt, pointDPBldr, 0);

pmIL->Emit(OpCodes::Box, __typeof(int));
pmIL->Emit(OpCodes::Stelem_Ref);
pmIL->Emit(OpCodes::Ldloc, tempObjArrLB);
pmIL->EmitCall(OpCodes::Call, writeLineMI, 0);

pmIL->Emit(OpCodes::Ret);

Console::WriteLine(S"PointMain (entry point) built.");

pointType = myTypeBldr->CreateType();
```

Requirements

Platforms: Windows 98, Windows NT 4.0,
Windows Millennium Edition, Windows 2000,
Windows XP Home Edition, Windows XP Professional,
Windows .NET Server family

.NET Framework Security:
- **ReflectionPermission** SecurityAction.Demand,
  ReflectionEmit=true
- **ReflectionPermission** to enhance security and performance
  when invoked late-bound through mechanisms such as
  Type.InvokeMember. Associated enumeration:
  ReflectionPermissionFlag.MemberAccess.

.NET Framework Security:
- **ReflectionPermission** SecurityAction.Demand,
  ReflectionEmit=true
- **ReflectionPermission** to enhance security and performance
  when invoked late-bound through mechanisms such as
  Type.InvokeMember. Associated enumeration:
  ReflectionPermissionFlag.MemberAccess.

AssemblyBuilder.SetEntryPoint Method (MethodInfo, PEFileKinds)

Sets the entry point for this assembly and defines the type of the PE
being built.

```
[Visual Basic]
Overloads Public Sub SetEntryPoint( _
    ByVal entryMethod As MethodInfo, _
    ByVal fileKind As PEFileKinds _
)
[C#]
public void SetEntryPoint(
    MethodInfo entryMethod,
    PEFileKinds fileKind
);
[C++]
public: void SetEntryPoint(
    MethodInfo* entryMethod,
    PEFileKinds fileKind
);
[JScript]
public function SetEntryPoint(
    entryMethod : MethodInfo,
    fileKind : PEFileKinds
);
```

Parameters

entryMethod
  A reference to the method that represents the entry point for this
  dynamic assembly.
fileKind
  The type of the assembly executable being built.

Exceptions

Exception Type	Condition
ArgumentNullException	*entryMethod* is a null reference (**Nothing** in Visual Basic).
InvalidOperationException	*entryMethod* is not contained within this assembly.
SecurityException	The caller does not have the required permission.

Requirements

Platforms: Windows 98, Windows NT 4.0,
Windows Millennium Edition, Windows 2000,
Windows XP Home Edition, Windows XP Professional,
Windows .NET Server family

AssemblyBuilderAccess Enumeration

Defines the access modes for a dynamic assembly.

This enumeration has a **FlagsAttribute** attribute that allows a bitwise combination of its member values.

```
[Visual Basic]
<Flags>
<Serializable>
Public Enum AssemblyBuilderAccess
[C#]
[Flags]
[Serializable]
public enum AssemblyBuilderAccess
[C++]
[Flags]
[Serializable]
__value public enum AssemblyBuilderAccess
[JScript]
public
   Flags
   Serializable
enum AssemblyBuilderAccess
```

Members

Member name	Description	Value
Run	Represents that the dynamic assembly can be executed, but not saved.	1
RunAndSave	Represents that the dynamic assembly can be executed and saved.	3
Save	Represents that the dynamic assembly can be saved, but not executed.	2

Requirements

Namespace: System.Reflection.Emit

Platforms: Windows 98, Windows NT 4.0, Windows Millennium Edition, Windows 2000, Windows XP Home Edition, Windows XP Professional, Windows .NET Server family

Assembly: Mscorlib (in Mscorlib.dll)

ConstructorBuilder Class

Defines and represents a constructor of a dynamic class.

System.Object
  System.Reflection.MemberInfo
    System.Reflection.MethodBase
      System.Reflection.ConstructorInfo
        System.Reflection.Emit.ConstructorBuilder

```
[Visual Basic]
NotInheritable Public Class ConstructorBuilder
   Inherits ConstructorInfo
[C#]
public sealed class ConstructorBuilder : ConstructorInfo
[C++]
public __gc __sealed class ConstructorBuilder : public
   ConstructorInfo
[JScript]
public class ConstructorBuilder extends ConstructorInfo
```

Thread Safety

Reflection Emit is thread-safe when using assemblies that were created with the **AppDomain.DefineDynamicAssembly** method with the Boolean parameter *isSynchronized* set to **true**.

Remarks

ConstructorBuilder is used to fully describe a constructor in Microsoft intermediate language (MSIL), including the name, attributes, signature, and constructor body. It is used in conjunction with the **TypeBuilder** class to create classes at run time. Call **DefineConstructor** to get an instance of **ConstructorBuilder**.

The following code sample illustates the contextual usage of a **ConstructorBuilder**.

```
[Visual Basic]
Imports System
Imports System.Threading
Imports System.Reflection
Imports System.Reflection.Emit


Class TestCtorBuilder

    Public Shared Function DynamicPointTypeGen() As Type

        Dim pointType As Type = Nothing
        Dim ctorParams() As Type = {GetType(Integer),
GetType(Integer), GetType(Integer)}

        Dim myDomain As AppDomain = Thread.GetDomain()
        Dim myAsmName As New AssemblyName()
        myAsmName.Name = "MyDynamicAssembly"

        Dim myAsmBuilder As AssemblyBuilder =
myDomain.DefineDynamicAssembly(myAsmName,
AssemblyBuilderAccess.RunAndSave)

        Dim pointModule As ModuleBuilder =
myAsmBuilder.DefineDynamicModule("PointModule", "Point.dll")

        Dim pointTypeBld As TypeBuilder = pointModule.DefineType
("Point", TypeAttributes.Public)

        Dim xField As FieldBuilder = pointTypeBld.DefineField
("x", GetType(Integer), FieldAttributes.Public)
        Dim yField As FieldBuilder = pointTypeBld.DefineField
```

```
("y", GetType(Integer), FieldAttributes.Public)
        Dim zField As FieldBuilder = pointTypeBld.DefineField
("z", GetType(Integer), FieldAttributes.Public)

        Dim objType As Type = Type.GetType("System.Object")
        Dim objCtor As ConstructorInfo = objType.GetConstructor
(New Type() {})

        Dim pointCtor As ConstructorBuilder =
pointTypeBld.DefineConstructor(MethodAttributes.Public,
CallingConventions.Standard, ctorParams)
        Dim ctorIL As ILGenerator = pointCtor.GetILGenerator()

        ' NOTE: ldarg.0 holds the "this" reference - ldarg.1,
ldarg.2, and ldarg.3
        ' hold the actual passed parameters. ldarg.0 is used by
instance methods
        ' to hold a reference to the current calling object
instance. Static methods
        ' do not use arg.0, since they are not instantiated and
hence no reference
        ' is needed to distinguish them.
        ctorIL.Emit(OpCodes.Ldarg_0)

        ' Here, we wish to create an instance of System.Object by
invoking its
        ' constructor, as specified above.
        ctorIL.Emit(OpCodes.Call, objCtor)

        ' Now, we'll load the current instance ref in arg 0, along
        ' with the value of parameter "x" stored in arg 1, into stfld.
        ctorIL.Emit(OpCodes.Ldarg_0)
        ctorIL.Emit(OpCodes.Ldarg_1)
        ctorIL.Emit(OpCodes.Stfld, xField)

        ' Now, we store arg 2 "y" in the current instance with stfld.
        ctorIL.Emit(OpCodes.Ldarg_0)
        ctorIL.Emit(OpCodes.Ldarg_2)
        ctorIL.Emit(OpCodes.Stfld, yField)

        ' Last of all, arg 3 "z" gets stored in the current instance.
        ctorIL.Emit(OpCodes.Ldarg_0)
        ctorIL.Emit(OpCodes.Ldarg_3)
        ctorIL.Emit(OpCodes.Stfld, zField)

        ' Our work complete, we return.
        ctorIL.Emit(OpCodes.Ret)

        ' Now, let's create three very simple methods so we
can see our fields.
        Dim mthdNames() As String = {"GetX", "GetY", "GetZ"}

        Dim mthdName As String
        For Each mthdName In mthdNames
            Dim getFieldMthd As MethodBuilder =
pointTypeBld.DefineMethod(mthdName, MethodAttributes.Public,
GetType(Integer), Nothing)
            Dim mthdIL As ILGenerator = getFieldMthd.GetILGenerator()

            mthdIL.Emit(OpCodes.Ldarg_0)
            Select Case mthdName
                Case "GetX"
                    mthdIL.Emit(OpCodes.Ldfld, xField)
                Case "GetY"
                    mthdIL.Emit(OpCodes.Ldfld, yField)
                Case "GetZ"
                    mthdIL.Emit(OpCodes.Ldfld, zField)
            End Select

            mthdIL.Emit(OpCodes.Ret)
        Next mthdName
        ' Finally, we create the type.
        pointType = pointTypeBld.CreateType()
```

```vbnet
        ' Let's save it, just for posterity.
        myAsmBuilder.Save("Point.dll")

        Return pointType
    End Function 'DynamicPointTypeGen

    Public Shared Sub Main()

        Dim myDynamicType As Type = Nothing
        Dim aPoint As Object = Nothing
        Dim aPtypes() As Type = {GetType(Integer),
GetType(Integer), GetType(Integer)}
        Dim aPargs() As Object = {4, 5, 6}

        ' Call the  method to build our dynamic class.
        myDynamicType = DynamicPointTypeGen()

        Console.WriteLine("Some information about my new Type
'{0}':", myDynamicType.FullName)
        Console.WriteLine("Assembly: '{0}'", myDynamicType.Assembly)
        Console.WriteLine("Attributes: '{0}'", myDynamicType.Attributes)
        Console.WriteLine("Module: '{0}'", myDynamicType.Module)
        Console.WriteLine("Members: ")
        Dim member As MemberInfo
        For Each member In  myDynamicType.GetMembers()
            Console.WriteLine("-- {0} {1};", member.MemberType,
member.Name)
        Next member

        Console.WriteLine("---")

        ' Let's take a look at the constructor we created.
        Dim myDTctor As ConstructorInfo =
myDynamicType.GetConstructor(aPtypes)
        Console.WriteLine("Constructor: {0};", myDTctor.ToString())

        Console.WriteLine("---")

        ' Now, we get to use our dynamically-created class by
invoking the constructor.
        aPoint = myDTctor.Invoke(aPargs)
        Console.WriteLine("aPoint is type {0}.", aPoint.GetType())

        ' Finally, let's reflect on the instance of our new type
 - aPoint - and
        ' make sure everything proceeded according to plan.
        Console.WriteLine("aPoint.x = {0}",
myDynamicType.InvokeMember("GetX", BindingFlags.InvokeMethod,
Nothing, aPoint, New Object() {}))
        Console.WriteLine("aPoint.y = {0}",
myDynamicType.InvokeMember("GetY", BindingFlags.InvokeMethod,
Nothing, aPoint, New Object() {}))
        Console.WriteLine("aPoint.z = {0}",
myDynamicType.InvokeMember("GetZ", BindingFlags.InvokeMethod,
Nothing, aPoint, New Object() {}))
    End Sub 'Main
End Class 'TestCtorBuilder

' +++ OUTPUT +++
' Some information about my new Type 'Point':
' Assembly: 'MyDynamicAssembly, Version=0.0.0.0'
' Attributes: 'AutoLayout, AnsiClass, NotPublic, Public'
' Module: 'PointModule'
' Members:
' -- Field x;
' -- Field y;
' -- Field z;
' -- Method GetHashCode;
' -- Method Equals;
' -- Method ToString;
' -- Method GetType;
' -- Constructor .ctor;
' ---
' Constructor: Void .ctor(Int32, Int32, Int32);
' ---
```

```csharp
' aPoint is type Point.
' aPoint.x = 4
' aPoint.y = 5
' aPoint.z = 6

[C#]
using System;
using System.Threading;
using System.Reflection;
using System.Reflection.Emit;

class TestCtorBuilder {

    public static Type DynamicPointTypeGen() {

        Type pointType = null;
        Type[] ctorParams = new Type[] {typeof(int),
                    typeof(int),
                    typeof(int)};

        AppDomain myDomain = Thread.GetDomain();
        AssemblyName myAsmName = new AssemblyName();
        myAsmName.Name = "MyDynamicAssembly";

        AssemblyBuilder myAsmBuilder = myDomain.DefineDynamicAssembly(
                    myAsmName,
                    AssemblyBuilderAccess.RunAndSave);

        ModuleBuilder pointModule =
myAsmBuilder.DefineDynamicModule("PointModule",
                        "Point.dll");

        TypeBuilder pointTypeBld = pointModule.DefineType("Point",
                        TypeAttributes.Public);

        FieldBuilder xField = pointTypeBld.DefineField("x", typeof(int),
                        FieldAttributes.Public);
        FieldBuilder yField = pointTypeBld.DefineField("y", typeof(int),
                        FieldAttributes.Public);
        FieldBuilder zField = pointTypeBld.DefineField("z", typeof(int),
                        FieldAttributes.Public);

        Type objType = Type.GetType("System.Object");
        ConstructorInfo objCtor = objType.GetConstructor
(new Type[0]);

        ConstructorBuilder pointCtor = pointTypeBld.DefineConstructor(
                MethodAttributes.Public,
                CallingConventions.Standard,
                ctorParams);
        ILGenerator ctorIL = pointCtor.GetILGenerator();

        // NOTE: ldarg.0 holds the "this" reference - ldarg.1,
ldarg.2, and ldarg.3
        // hold the actual passed parameters. ldarg.0 is used by
instance methods
        // to hold a reference to the current calling object
instance. Static methods
        // do not use arg.0, since they are not instantiated
and hence no reference
        // is needed to distinguish them.

        ctorIL.Emit(OpCodes.Ldarg_0);

        // Here, we wish to create an instance of System.Object
by invoking its
        // constructor, as specified above.

        ctorIL.Emit(OpCodes.Call, objCtor);

        // Now, we'll load the current instance ref in arg 0, along
        // with the value of parameter "x" stored in arg 1, into stfld.
```

```
        ctorIL.Emit(OpCodes.Ldarg_0);
        ctorIL.Emit(OpCodes.Ldarg_1);
        ctorIL.Emit(OpCodes.Stfld, xField);

    // Now, we store arg 2 "y" in the current instance with stfld.

        ctorIL.Emit(OpCodes.Ldarg_0);
        ctorIL.Emit(OpCodes.Ldarg_2);
        ctorIL.Emit(OpCodes.Stfld, yField);

    // Last of all, arg 3 "z" gets stored in the current instance.

        ctorIL.Emit(OpCodes.Ldarg_0);
        ctorIL.Emit(OpCodes.Ldarg_3);
        ctorIL.Emit(OpCodes.Stfld, zField);

    // Our work complete, we return.

    ctorIL.Emit(OpCodes.Ret);

    // Now, let's create three very simple methods so we
can see our fields.

    string[] mthdNames = new string[] {"GetX", "GetY", "GetZ"};

        foreach (string mthdName in mthdNames) {
            MethodBuilder getFieldMthd = pointTypeBld.DefineMethod(
                    mthdName,
                    MethodAttributes.Public,
                            typeof(int),
                            null);
        ILGenerator mthdIL = getFieldMthd.GetILGenerator();

        mthdIL.Emit(OpCodes.Ldarg_0);
          switch (mthdName) {
            case "GetX": mthdIL.Emit(OpCodes.Ldfld, xField);
                break;
            case "GetY": mthdIL.Emit(OpCodes.Ldfld, yField);
                break;
            case "GetZ": mthdIL.Emit(OpCodes.Ldfld, zField);
                break;

          }
        mthdIL.Emit(OpCodes.Ret);

        }
    // Finally, we create the type.

     pointType = pointTypeBld.CreateType();

    // Let's save it, just for posterity.

    myAsmBuilder.Save("Point.dll");

    return pointType;

   }

   public static void Main() {

    Type myDynamicType = null;
        object aPoint = null;
    Type[] aPtypes = new Type[] {typeof(int), typeof(int),
typeof(int)};
        object[] aPargs = new object[] {4, 5, 6};

    // Call the  method to build our dynamic class.

    myDynamicType = DynamicPointTypeGen();

    Console.WriteLine("Some information about my new Type '{0}':",
            myDynamicType.FullName);
    Console.WriteLine("Assembly: '{0}'", myDynamicType.Assembly);
    Console.WriteLine("Attributes: '{0}'",
myDynamicType.Attributes);
```

```
    Console.WriteLine("Module: '{0}'", myDynamicType.Module);
    Console.WriteLine("Members: ");
    foreach (MemberInfo member in myDynamicType.GetMembers()) {
     Console.WriteLine("-- {0} {1};", member.MemberType,
member.Name);
    }

        Console.WriteLine("---");

    // Let's take a look at the constructor we created.

    ConstructorInfo myDTctor =
myDynamicType.GetConstructor(aPtypes);
        Console.WriteLine("Constructor: {0};", myDTctor.ToString());

        Console.WriteLine("---");

        // Now, we get to use our dynamically-created class
by invoking the constructor.

    aPoint = myDTctor.Invoke(aPargs);
        Console.WriteLine("aPoint is type {0}.", aPoint.GetType());

    // Finally, let's reflect on the instance of our new
type - aPoint - and
    // make sure everything proceeded according to plan.

    Console.WriteLine("aPoint.x = {0}",
            myDynamicType.InvokeMember("GetX",
                        BindingFlags.InvokeMethod,
                        null,
                        aPoint,
                        new object[0]));
    Console.WriteLine("aPoint.y = {0}",
            myDynamicType.InvokeMember("GetY",
                        BindingFlags.InvokeMethod,
                        null,
                        aPoint,
                        new object[0]));
    Console.WriteLine("aPoint.z = {0}",
            myDynamicType.InvokeMember("GetZ",
                        BindingFlags.InvokeMethod,
                        null,
                        aPoint,
                        new object[0]));

// +++ OUTPUT +++
// Some information about my new Type 'Point':
// Assembly: 'MyDynamicAssembly, Version=0.0.0.0'
// Attributes: 'AutoLayout, AnsiClass, NotPublic, Public'
// Module: 'PointModule'
// Members:
// -- Field x;
// -- Field y;
// -- Field z;
    // -- Method GetHashCode;
    // -- Method Equals;
    // -- Method ToString;
    // -- Method GetType;
    // -- Constructor .ctor;
// ---
// Constructor: Void .ctor(Int32, Int32, Int32);
// ---
// aPoint is type Point.
// aPoint.x = 4
// aPoint.y = 5
// aPoint.z = 6

   }

}
```

```cpp
[C++]
#using <mscorlib.dll>

using namespace System;
using namespace System::Threading;
using namespace System::Reflection;
using namespace System::Reflection::Emit;

Type* DynamicPointTypeGen() {

    Type* pointType = 0;
    Type* temp0 [] = {__typeof(int),
        __typeof(int),
        __typeof(int)};

    Type* ctorParams[] = temp0;

    AppDomain* myDomain = Thread::GetDomain();
    AssemblyName* myAsmName = new AssemblyName();
    myAsmName->Name = S"MyDynamicAssembly";

    AssemblyBuilder*  myAsmBuilder = myDomain-
>DefineDynamicAssembly(myAsmName,
        AssemblyBuilderAccess::RunAndSave);

    ModuleBuilder*  pointModule = myAsmBuilder-
>DefineDynamicModule(S"PointModule",
        S"Point.dll");

    TypeBuilder*  pointTypeBld = pointModule->DefineType(S"Point",
        TypeAttributes::Public);

    FieldBuilder*  xField = pointTypeBld->DefineField(S"x",
__typeof(int),
        FieldAttributes::Public);
    FieldBuilder*  yField = pointTypeBld->DefineField(S"y",
__typeof(int),
        FieldAttributes::Public);
    FieldBuilder*  zField = pointTypeBld->DefineField(S"z",
__typeof(int),
        FieldAttributes::Public);

    Type* objType = Type::GetType(S"System.Object");
    ConstructorInfo*  objCtor = objType->GetConstructor(new Type*[0]);

    ConstructorBuilder*  pointCtor = pointTypeBld-
>DefineConstructor(MethodAttributes::Public,
        CallingConventions::Standard,
        ctorParams);
    ILGenerator*  ctorIL = pointCtor->GetILGenerator();

    // NOTE: ldarg.0 holds the "this" reference - ldarg.1,
ldarg.2, and ldarg.3
    // hold the actual passed parameters. ldarg.0 is used by
instance methods
    // to hold a reference to the current calling Object*
instance. Static methods
    // do not use arg.0, since they are not instantiated and
hence no reference
    // is needed to distinguish them.

    ctorIL->Emit(OpCodes::Ldarg_0);

    // Here, we wish to create an instance of System::Object
by invoking its
    // constructor, as specified above.

    ctorIL->Emit(OpCodes::Call, objCtor);

    // Now, we'll load the current instance in arg 0, along
    // with the value of parameter "x" stored in arg 1, into stfld.

    ctorIL->Emit(OpCodes::Ldarg_0);
    ctorIL->Emit(OpCodes::Ldarg_1);
    ctorIL->Emit(OpCodes::Stfld, xField);
```

```cpp
    // Now, we store arg 2 "y" in the current instance with stfld.

    ctorIL->Emit(OpCodes::Ldarg_0);
    ctorIL->Emit(OpCodes::Ldarg_2);
    ctorIL->Emit(OpCodes::Stfld, yField);

    // Last of all, arg 3 "z" gets stored in the current instance.

    ctorIL->Emit(OpCodes::Ldarg_0);
    ctorIL->Emit(OpCodes::Ldarg_3);
    ctorIL->Emit(OpCodes::Stfld, zField);

    // Our work complete, we return.

    ctorIL->Emit(OpCodes::Ret);

    // Now, let's create three very simple methods so we can
see our fields.

    String* temp1 [] = {S"GetX", S"GetY", S"GetZ"};
    String* mthdNames[] = temp1;

    System::Collections::IEnumerator* myEnum = mthdNames-
>GetEnumerator();
    while (myEnum->MoveNext()) {
        String* mthdName = __try_cast<String*>(myEnum->Current);

        MethodBuilder* getFieldMthd = pointTypeBld-
>DefineMethod(mthdName,
            MethodAttributes::Public,
            __typeof(int),
            0);
        ILGenerator*  mthdIL = getFieldMthd->GetILGenerator();

        mthdIL->Emit(OpCodes::Ldarg_0);

        if( mthdName->Equals(S"GetX") ) mthdIL->Emit(OpCodes:
:Ldfld, xField);
        else if( mthdName->Equals(S"GetY") ) mthdIL->Emit(OpCodes:
:Ldfld, yField);
        else if( mthdName->Equals(S"GetZ") ) mthdIL->Emit(OpCodes:
:Ldfld, zField);
        mthdIL->Emit(OpCodes::Ret);

    }
    // Finally, we create the type.

    pointType = pointTypeBld->CreateType();

    // Let's save it, just for posterity.

    myAsmBuilder->Save(S"Point.dll");

    return pointType;
}

int main() {

    Type* myDynamicType = 0;
    Object* aPoint = 0;

    Type* temp2 [] = {__typeof(int), __typeof(int), __typeof(int)};
    Type* aPtypes[] = temp2;

    Object* temp3 [] = {__box(4), __box(5), __box(6)};
    Object* aPargs[] = temp3;

    // Call the  method to build our dynamic class.

    myDynamicType = DynamicPointTypeGen();

    Console::WriteLine(S"Some information about my new Type '{0}':",
        myDynamicType->FullName);
    Console::WriteLine(S"Assembly: '{0}'", myDynamicType->Assembly);
    Console::WriteLine(S"Attributes: '{0}'", __box(myDynamicType-
```

```
>Attributes));
    Console::WriteLine(S"Module: '{0}'", myDynamicType->Module);
    Console::WriteLine(S"Members: ");
    System::Collections::IEnumerator* myEnum = myDynamicType-
>GetMembers()->GetEnumerator();
    while (myEnum->MoveNext()) {
        MemberInfo* member = __try_cast<MemberInfo*>(myEnum->Current);
        Console::WriteLine(S"-- {0} {1};", __box
(member->MemberType), member->Name);
    }

    Console::WriteLine(S"---");

    // Let's take a look at the constructor we created.

    ConstructorInfo* myDTctor = myDynamicType->GetConstructor(aPtypes);
    Console::WriteLine(S"Constructor: {0};", myDTctor);

    Console::WriteLine(S"---");

    // Now, we get to use our dynamically-created class by
invoking the constructor.

    aPoint = myDTctor->Invoke(aPargs);
    Console::WriteLine(S"aPoint is type {0}.", aPoint->GetType());

    // Finally, let's reflect on the instance of our new type
 - aPoint - and
    // make sure everything proceeded according to plan.

    Console::WriteLine(S"aPoint.x = {0}",
        myDynamicType->InvokeMember(S"GetX",
        BindingFlags::InvokeMethod,
        0,
        aPoint,
        new Object*[0]));
    Console::WriteLine(S"aPoint.y = {0}",
        myDynamicType->InvokeMember(S"GetY",
        BindingFlags::InvokeMethod,
        0,
        aPoint,
        new Object*[0]));
    Console::WriteLine(S"aPoint.z = {0}",
        myDynamicType->InvokeMember(S"GetZ",
        BindingFlags::InvokeMethod,
        0,
        aPoint,
        new Object*[0]));

    // +++ OUTPUT +++
    // Some information ab->Item[Out] my* new Type 'Point':
    // Assembly: 'MyDynamicAssembly, Version=0.0.0.0'
    // Attributes: 'AutoLayout, AnsiClass, NotPublic, Public'
    // Module: 'PointModule'
    // Members:
    // -- Field x;
    // -- Field y;
    // -- Field z;
    // -- Method GetHashCode;
    // -- Method Equals;
    // -- Method ToString;
    // -- Method GetType;
    // -- Constructor .ctor;
    // ---
    // Constructor: Void .ctor(Int32, Int32, Int32);
    // ---
    // aPoint is type Point.
    // aPoint.x = 4
    // aPoint.y = 5
    // aPoint.z = 6
}
```

Requirements

Namespace: System.Reflection.Emit

Platforms: Windows 98, Windows NT 4.0,
Windows Millennium Edition, Windows 2000,
Windows XP Home Edition, Windows XP Professional,
Windows .NET Server family

Assembly: Mscorlib (in Mscorlib.dll)

ConstructorBuilder.Attributes Property

Retrieves the attributes for this constructor.

```
[Visual Basic]
Overrides Public ReadOnly Property Attributes As MethodAttributes
[C#]
public override MethodAttributes Attributes {get;}
[C++]
public: __property MethodAttributes get_Attributes();
[JScript]
public override function get Attributes() : MethodAttributes;
```

Property Value

Returns the attributes for this constructor.

Example

See related example in the
System.Reflection.Emit.ConstuctorBuilder class topic.

Requirements

Platforms: Windows 98, Windows NT 4.0,
Windows Millennium Edition, Windows 2000,
Windows XP Home Edition, Windows XP Professional,
Windows .NET Server family

ConstructorBuilder.DeclaringType Property

Retrieves a reference to the **Type** object for the type that declares
this member.

```
[Visual Basic]
Overrides Public ReadOnly Property DeclaringType As Type
[C#]
public override Type DeclaringType {get;}
[C++]
public: __property Type* get_DeclaringType();
[JScript]
public override function get DeclaringType() : Type;
```

Property Value

Returns the **Type** object for the type that declares this member.

Remarks

A member of a class (or interface) is either declared or inherited
from a base class (or interface).

Example

See related example in the
System.Reflection.Emit.ConstuctorBuilder class topic.

Requirements

Platforms: Windows 98, Windows NT 4.0,
Windows Millennium Edition, Windows 2000,
Windows XP Home Edition, Windows XP Professional,
Windows .NET Server family

ConstructorBuilder.InitLocals Property

Gets or sets whether the local variables in this constructor should be zero-initialized.

```
[Visual Basic]
Public Property InitLocals As Boolean
[C#]
public bool InitLocals {get; set;}
[C++]
public: __property bool get_InitLocals();
public: __property void set_InitLocals(bool);
[JScript]
public function get InitLocals() : Boolean;
public function set InitLocals(Boolean);
```

Property Value

Read/write. Gets or sets whether the local variables in this constructor should be zero-initialized.

Requirements

Platforms: Windows 98, Windows NT 4.0, Windows Millennium Edition, Windows 2000, Windows XP Home Edition, Windows XP Professional, Windows .NET Server family

ConstructorBuilder.MethodHandle Property

Retrieves the internal handle for the method. Use this handle to access the underlying metadata handle.

```
[Visual Basic]
Overrides Public ReadOnly Property MethodHandle As _
    RuntimeMethodHandle
[C#]
public override RuntimeMethodHandle MethodHandle {get;}
[C++]
public: __property RuntimeMethodHandle get_MethodHandle();
[JScript]
public override function get MethodHandle() : RuntimeMethodHandle;
```

Property Value

Returns the internal handle for the method. Use this handle to access the underlying metadata handle.

Exceptions

Exception Type	Condition
NotSupportedException	This property is not supported on this class.

Requirements

Platforms: Windows 98, Windows NT 4.0, Windows Millennium Edition, Windows 2000, Windows XP Home Edition, Windows XP Professional, Windows .NET Server family

ConstructorBuilder.Name Property

Retrieves the name of this constructor.

```
[Visual Basic]
Overrides Public ReadOnly Property Name As String
[C#]
public override string Name {get;}
```

```
[C++]
public: __property String* get_Name();
[JScript]
public override function get Name() : String;
```

Property Value

Returns the name of this constructor.

Example

See related example in the **System.Reflection.Emit.ConstuctorBuilder** class topic.

Requirements

Platforms: Windows 98, Windows NT 4.0, Windows Millennium Edition, Windows 2000, Windows XP Home Edition, Windows XP Professional, Windows .NET Server family

ConstructorBuilder.ReflectedType Property

Holds a reference to the **Type** object from which this object was obtained.

```
[Visual Basic]
Overrides Public ReadOnly Property ReflectedType As Type
[C#]
public override Type ReflectedType {get;}
[C++]
public: __property Type* get_ReflectedType();
[JScript]
public override function get ReflectedType() : Type;
```

Property Value

Returns the **Type** object from which this object was obtained.

Remarks

A **ConstructorBuilder** object represents a constructor on a particular class. In order to obtain a **ConstructorInfo** object, the **Type** object that represents the class that supports the constructor is queried. This property holds a reference to that **Type** object.

Requirements

Platforms: Windows 98, Windows NT 4.0, Windows Millennium Edition, Windows 2000, Windows XP Home Edition, Windows XP Professional, Windows .NET Server family

ConstructorBuilder.ReturnType Property

Retrieves the **Type** of this constructor's return value.

```
[Visual Basic]
Public ReadOnly Property ReturnType As Type
[C#]
public Type ReturnType {get;}
[C++]
public: __property Type* get_ReturnType();
[JScript]
public function get ReturnType() : Type;
```

Property Value

Returns the **Type** of this constructor's return value. This is always a null reference (**Nothing** in Visual Basic).

Remarks

This property might be removed in a future version.

Requirements

Platforms: Windows 98, Windows NT 4.0, Windows Millennium Edition, Windows 2000, Windows XP Home Edition, Windows XP Professional, Windows .NET Server family

ConstructorBuilder.Signature Property

Retrieves the signature of the field in the form of a string.

```
[Visual Basic]
Public ReadOnly Property Signature As String
[C#]
public string Signature {get;}
[C++]
public: __property String* get_Signature();
[JScript]
public function get Signature() : String;
```

Property Value

Returns the signature of the field.

Requirements

Platforms: Windows 98, Windows NT 4.0, Windows Millennium Edition, Windows 2000, Windows XP Home Edition, Windows XP Professional, Windows .NET Server family

ConstructorBuilder.AddDeclarativeSecurity Method

Adds declarative security to this constructor.

```
[Visual Basic]
Public Sub AddDeclarativeSecurity( _
    ByVal action As SecurityAction, _
    ByVal pset As PermissionSet _
)
[C#]
public void AddDeclarativeSecurity(
    SecurityAction action,
    PermissionSet pset
);
[C++]
public: void AddDeclarativeSecurity(
    SecurityAction action,
    PermissionSet* pset
);
[JScript]
public function AddDeclarativeSecurity(
    action : SecurityAction,
    pset : PermissionSet
);
```

Parameters

action
    The security action to be taken, such as Demand, Assert, and so on.

pset
    The set of permissions the action applies to.

Exceptions

Exception Type	Condition
ArgumentOutOfRange-Exception	*action* is invalid (RequestMinimum, RequestOptional, and RequestRefuse are invalid).
InvalidOperationExcep-tion	The containing type has been previously created using **CreateType**. -or- The permission set *pset* contains an action that was added earlier by **AddDeclarativeSecurity**.
ArgumentNullException	*pset* is a null reference (**Nothing** in Visual Basic).

Remarks

AddDeclarativeSecurity can be called several times, with each call specifying a security action (such as **Demand**, **Assert**, and **Deny**) and a set of permissions that the action applies to.

The following code sample illustrates the use of **AddDeclarativeSecurity**.

Example

See related example in the **System.Reflection.Emit.ConstuctorBuilder** class topic.

Requirements

Platforms: Windows 98, Windows NT 4.0, Windows Millennium Edition, Windows 2000, Windows XP Home Edition, Windows XP Professional, Windows .NET Server family

ConstructorBuilder.DefineParameter Method

Defines a parameter of this constructor.

```
[Visual Basic]
Public Function DefineParameter( _
    ByVal iSequence As Integer, _
    ByVal attributes As ParameterAttributes, _
    ByVal strParamName As String _
) As ParameterBuilder
[C#]
public ParameterBuilder DefineParameter(
    int iSequence,
    ParameterAttributes attributes,
    string strParamName
);
[C++]
public: ParameterBuilder* DefineParameter(
    int iSequence,
    ParameterAttributes attributes,
    String* strParamName
);
[JScript]
public function DefineParameter(
    iSequence : int,
    attributes : ParameterAttributes,
    strParamName : String
) : ParameterBuilder;
```

Parameters

iSequence

The position of the parameter in the parameter list. Parameters are indexed beginning with the number 1 for the first parameter.

attributes

The attributes of the parameter.

strParamName

The name of the parameter. The name can be the null string.

Return Value

Returns a **ParameterBuilder** object that represents the new parameter of this constructor.

Exceptions

Exception Type	Condition
ArgumentOutOfRange-Exception	*position* is less than or equal to zero, or it is greater than the number of parameters of the constructor.
InvalidOperationException	The containing type has been created using **CreateType**.

Remarks

See related example in the **System.Reflection.Emit.ConstuctorBuilder** class topic.

Requirements

Platforms: Windows 98, Windows NT 4.0, Windows Millennium Edition, Windows 2000, Windows XP Home Edition, Windows XP Professional, Windows .NET Server family

ConstructorBuilder.GetCustomAttributes Method

Returns the custom attributes defined for this constructor.

Overload List

Returns all the custom attributes defined for this constructor.

[Visual Basic] **Overloads Overrides Public Function GetCustomAttributes(Boolean) As Object() Implements ICustomAttributeProvider.GetCustomAttributes**

[C#] **public override object[] GetCustomAttributes(bool);**

[C++] **public: Object* GetCustomAttributes(bool) __gc[];**

[JScript] **public override function GetCustomAttributes (Boolean) : Object[];**

Returns the custom attributes identified by the given type.

[Visual Basic] **Overloads Overrides Public Function GetCustomAttributes(Type, Boolean) As Object() Implements ICustomAttributeProvider.GetCustomAttributes**

[C#] **public override object[] GetCustomAttributes(Type, bool);**

[C++] **public: Object* GetCustomAttributes(Type*, bool) __gc[];**

[JScript] **public override function GetCustomAttributes (Type, Boolean) : Object[];**

ConstructorBuilder.GetCustomAttributes Method (Boolean)

Returns all the custom attributes defined for this constructor.

```
[Visual Basic]
Overrides Overloads Public Function GetCustomAttributes( _
    ByVal inherit As Boolean _
) As Object() Implements ICustomAttributeProvider.GetCustomAttributes
[C#]
public override object[] GetCustomAttributes(
    bool inherit
);
[C++]
public: Object* GetCustomAttributes(
    bool inherit
) __gc[];
[JScript]
public override function GetCustomAttributes(
    inherit : Boolean
) : Object[];
```

Parameters

inherit

Controls inheritance of custom attributes from base classes. This parameter is ignored.

Return Value

Returns an array of objects representing all the custom attributes of the constructor represented by this **ConstructorBuilder** instance.

Implements

ICustomAttributeProvider.GetCustomAttributes

Remarks

The *inherit* parameter is ignored because a class never inherits constructors from base classes.

Requirements

Platforms: Windows 98, Windows NT 4.0, Windows Millennium Edition, Windows 2000, Windows XP Home Edition, Windows XP Professional, Windows .NET Server family

ConstructorBuilder.GetCustomAttributes Method (Type, Boolean)

Returns the custom attributes identified by the given type.

```
[Visual Basic]
Overrides Overloads Public Function GetCustomAttributes( _
    ByVal attributeType As Type, _
    ByVal inherit As Boolean _
) As Object() Implements ICustomAttributeProvider.GetCustomAttributes
[C#]
public override object[] GetCustomAttributes(
    Type attributeType,
    bool inherit
);
[C++]
public: Object* GetCustomAttributes(
    Type* attributeType,
    bool inherit
) __gc[];
```

```
[JScript]
public override function GetCustomAttributes(
    attributeType : Type,
    inherit : Boolean
) : Object[];
```

Parameters

attributeType

The custom attribute type.

inherit

Controls inheritance of custom attributes from base classes. This parameter is ignored.

Return Value

Returns an array of type **Object** representing the attributes of this constructor.

Implements

ICustomAttributeProvider.GetCustomAttributes

Remarks

The *inherit* parameter is ignored because a class never inherits constructors from base classes.

Requirements

Platforms: Windows 98, Windows NT 4.0, Windows Millennium Edition, Windows 2000, Windows XP Home Edition, Windows XP Professional, Windows .NET Server family

ConstructorBuilder.GetILGenerator Method

Gets an **ILGenerator** for this constructor.

```
[Visual Basic]
Public Function GetILGenerator() As ILGenerator
[C#]
public ILGenerator GetILGenerator();
[C++]
public: ILGenerator* GetILGenerator();
[JScript]
public function GetILGenerator() : ILGenerator;
```

Return Value

Returns an **ILGenerator** object for this constructor.

Exceptions

Exception Type	Condition
InvalidOperationException	If the constructor is a default constructor.

Remarks

The runtime generates the code for default constructors. Therefore, if an attempt is made to obtain an **ILGenerator**, an exception will be thrown.

Example

See related example in the **System.Reflection.Emit.ConstuctorBuilder** class topic.

Requirements

Platforms: Windows 98, Windows NT 4.0, Windows Millennium Edition, Windows 2000, Windows XP Home Edition, Windows XP Professional, Windows .NET Server family

ConstructorBuilder.GetMethodImplementation Flags Method

Returns the method implementation flags for this constructor.

```
[Visual Basic]
Overrides Public Function GetMethodImplementationFlags() As _
    MethodImplAttributes
[C#]
public override MethodImplAttributes GetMethodImplementationFlags();
[C++]
public: MethodImplAttributes GetMethodImplementationFlags();
[JScript]
public override function GetMethodImplementationFlags() :
    MethodImplAttributes;
```

Return Value

The method implementation flags for this constructor.

Example

See related example in the **System.Reflection.Emit.ConstuctorBuilder** class topic.

Requirements

Platforms: Windows 98, Windows NT 4.0, Windows Millennium Edition, Windows 2000, Windows XP Home Edition, Windows XP Professional, Windows .NET Server family

ConstructorBuilder.GetModule Method

Returns a reference to the module that contains this constructor.

```
[Visual Basic]
Public Function GetModule() As Module
[C#]
public Module GetModule();
[C++]
public: Module* GetModule();
[JScript]
public function GetModule() : Module;
```

Return Value

The module that contains this constructor.

Example

See related example in the **System.Reflection.Emit.ConstuctorBuilder** class topic.

Requirements

Platforms: Windows 98, Windows NT 4.0, Windows Millennium Edition, Windows 2000, Windows XP Home Edition, Windows XP Professional, Windows .NET Server family

ConstructorBuilder.GetParameters Method

Returns the parameters of this constructor.

```
[Visual Basic]
Overrides Public Function GetParameters() As ParameterInfo()
[C#]
public override ParameterInfo[] GetParameters();
[C++]
public: ParameterInfo* GetParameters() [];
```

[JScript]
```
public override function GetParameters() : ParameterInfo[];
```

Return Value

Returns an array of **ParameterInfo** objects that represent the parameters of this constructor.

Exceptions

Exception Type	Condition
InvalidOperationException	**CreateType** has not been called on this constructor's type.

Example

See related example in the **System.Reflection.Emit.ConstuctorBuilder** class topic.

Requirements

Platforms: Windows 98, Windows NT 4.0, Windows Millennium Edition, Windows 2000, Windows XP Home Edition, Windows XP Professional, Windows .NET Server family

ConstructorBuilder.GetToken Method

Returns the **MethodToken** that represents the token for this constructor.

[Visual Basic]
```
Public Function GetToken() As MethodToken
```
[C#]
```
public MethodToken GetToken();
```
[C++]
```
public: MethodToken GetToken();
```
[JScript]
```
public function GetToken() : MethodToken;
```

Return Value

Returns the **MethodToken** of this constructor.

Example

See related example in the **System.Reflection.Emit.ConstuctorBuilder** class topic.

Requirements

Platforms: Windows 98, Windows NT 4.0, Windows Millennium Edition, Windows 2000, Windows XP Home Edition, Windows XP Professional, Windows .NET Server family

ConstructorBuilder.Invoke Method

Invokes the constructor dynamically reflected by this instance.

Overload List

Invokes the constructor dynamically reflected by this instance on the given object, passing along the specified parameters, and under the constraints of the given binder.

[Visual Basic] **Overloads Overrides Public Function Invoke (BindingFlags, Binder, Object(), CultureInfo) As Object**

[C#] **public override object Invoke(BindingFlags, Binder, object[], CultureInfo);**

[C++] **public: Object* Invoke(BindingFlags, Binder*, Object[], CultureInfo*);**

[JScript] **public override function Invoke(BindingFlags, Binder, Object[], CultureInfo) : Object;**

Dynamically invokes the constructor reflected by this instance with the specified arguments, under the constraints of the specified **Binder**.

[Visual Basic] **Overloads Overrides Public Function Invoke (Object, BindingFlags, Binder, Object(), CultureInfo) As Object**

[C#] **public override object Invoke(object, BindingFlags, Binder, object[], CultureInfo);**

[C++] **public: Object* Invoke(Object*, BindingFlags, Binder*, Object*[], CultureInfo*);**

[JScript] **public override function Invoke(Object, BindingFlags, Binder, Object[], CultureInfo) : Object;**

Inherited from **ConstructorInfo**.

[Visual Basic] **Overloads Public Function Invoke(Object()) As Object**

[C#] **public object Invoke(object[]);**

[C++] **public: Object* Invoke(Object*[]);**

[JScript] **public function Invoke(Object[]) : Object;**

Inherited from **MethodBase**.

[Visual Basic] **Overloads Public Function Invoke(Object, Object()) As Object**

[C#] **public object Invoke(object, object[]);**

[C++] **public: Object* Invoke(Object*, Object*[]);**

[JScript] **public function Invoke(Object, Object[]) : Object;**

ConstructorBuilder.Invoke Method (BindingFlags, Binder, Object[], CultureInfo)

Invokes the constructor dynamically reflected by this instance on the given object, passing along the specified parameters, and under the constraints of the given binder.

[Visual Basic]
```
Overrides Overloads Public Function Invoke( _
    ByVal invokeAttr As BindingFlags, _
    ByVal binder As Binder, _
    ByVal parameters() As Object, _
    ByVal culture As CultureInfo _
) As Object
```
[C#]
```
public override object Invoke(
    BindingFlags invokeAttr,
    Binder binder,
    object[] parameters,
    CultureInfo culture
);
```
[C++]
```
public: Object* Invoke(
    BindingFlags invokeAttr,
    Binder* binder,
    Object* parameters __gc[],
    CultureInfo* culture
);
```

```
[JScript]
public override function Invoke(
    invokeAttr : BindingFlags,
    binder : Binder,
    parameters : Object[],
    culture : CultureInfo
) : Object;
```

Parameters

invokeAttr
This must be a bit flag from **BindingFlags**, such as InvokeMethod, NonPublic, and so on.

binder
An object that enables the binding, coercion of argument types, invocation of members, and retrieval of **MemberInfo** objects using reflection. If binder is a null reference (**Nothing** in Visual Basic), the default binder is used. See **Binder**.

parameters
An argument list. This is an array of arguments with the same number, order, and type as the parameters of the constructor to be invoked. If there are no parameters this should be a null reference (**Nothing** in Visual Basic).

culture
An instance of **CultureInfo** used to govern the coercion of types. If this is null, the **CultureInfo** for the current thread is used. (For example, this is necessary to convert a **String** that represents 1000 to a **Double** value, since 1000 is represented differently by different cultures.)

Return Value

Returns an **Object** that is the return value of the invoked constructor.

Exceptions

Exception Type	Condition
NotSupportedException	This method is not currently supported. You can retrieve the constructor using **GetConstructor** and call **Invoke** on the returned **ConstructorInfo**.

Remarks

If the constructor has no parameters, the value of the *parameters* parameter should be a null reference (**Nothing** in Visual Basic). Otherwise, the number, type, and order of elements in the *parameters* array should be identical to the number, type, and order of parameters for the constructor reflected by this instance.

For example, if the constructor reflected by this instance is declared as public class taking two strings, then the *parameters* parameter should be an array of **Object** with length 2.

> **Note** Access restrictions are ignored for fully-trusted code. That is, private constructors, methods, fields, and properties can be accessed and invoked using Reflection whenever the code is fully trusted.

Requirements

Platforms: Windows 98, Windows NT 4.0, Windows Millennium Edition, Windows 2000, Windows XP Home Edition, Windows XP Professional, Windows .NET Server family

ConstructorBuilder.Invoke Method (Object, BindingFlags, Binder, Object[], CultureInfo)

Dynamically invokes the constructor reflected by this instance with the specified arguments, under the constraints of the specified **Binder**.

```
[Visual Basic]
Overrides Overloads Public Function Invoke( _
    ByVal obj As Object, _
    ByVal invokeAttr As BindingFlags, _
    ByVal binder As Binder, _
    ByVal parameters() As Object, _
    ByVal culture As CultureInfo _
) As Object
[C#]
public override object Invoke(
    object obj,
    BindingFlags invokeAttr,
    Binder binder,
    object[] parameters,
    CultureInfo culture
);
[C++]
public: Object* Invoke(
    Object* obj,
    BindingFlags invokeAttr,
    Binder* binder,
    Object* parameters __gc[],
    CultureInfo* culture
);
[JScript]
public override function Invoke(
    obj : Object,
    invokeAttr : BindingFlags,
    binder : Binder,
    parameters : Object[],
    culture : CultureInfo
) : Object;
```

Parameters

obj
The object that needs to be reinitialized.

invokeAttr
One of the **BindingFlags** values that specifies the type of binding that is desired.

binder
A **Binder** that defines a set of properties and enables the binding, coercion of argument types, and invocation of members using reflection. If *binder* is a null reference (**Nothing** in Visual Basic), then Binder.DefaultBinding is used.

parameters
An argument list. This is an array of arguments with the same number, order, and type as the parameters of the constructor to be invoked. If there are no parameters, this should be a null reference (**Nothing** in Visual Basic).

culture
A **CultureInfo** used to govern the coercion of types. If this is null, the **CultureInfo** for the current thread is used.

Return Value

An instance of the class associated with the constructor.

Exceptions

Exception Type	Condition
NotSupportedException	This method is not currently supported. You can retrieve the constructor using **GetConstructor** and call **Invoke** on the returned **ConstructorInfo**.

Remarks

The number, type, and order of elements in the parameters array should be identical to the number, type, and order of parameters for the constructor reflected by this instance.

Before calling the constructor, **Invoke** ensures that the caller has access permission, and that the parameters are of the correct number, order and type.

Access restrictions are ignored for fully-trusted code. That is, private constructors, methods, fields, and properties can be accessed and invoked using Reflection whenever the code is fully trusted.

Requirements

Platforms: Windows 98, Windows NT 4.0, Windows Millennium Edition, Windows 2000, Windows XP Home Edition, Windows XP Professional, Windows .NET Server family

ConstructorBuilder.IsDefined Method

Checks if the specified custom attribute type is defined.

```
[Visual Basic]
Overrides Public Function IsDefined( _
   ByVal attributeType As Type, _
   ByVal inherit As Boolean _
) As Boolean Implements ICustomAttributeProvider.IsDefined
[C#]
public override bool IsDefined(
   Type attributeType,
   bool inherit
);
[C++]
public: bool IsDefined(
   Type* attributeType,
   bool inherit
);
[JScript]
public override function IsDefined(
   attributeType : Type,
   inherit : Boolean
) : Boolean;
```

Parameters

attributeType
   A custom attribute type.
inherit
   Controls inheritance of custom attributes from base classes. This parameter is ignored.

Return Value

true if the specified custom attribute type is defined; otherwise, **false**.

Implements

ICustomAttributeProvider.IsDefined

Exceptions

Exception Type	Condition
NotSupportedException	This method is not currently supported. You can retrieve the constructor using **GetConstructor** and call **IsDefined** on the returned **ConstructorInfo**.

Remarks

See the metadata specification for details on how to format *binaryAttribute*.

Requirements

Platforms: Windows 98, Windows NT 4.0, Windows Millennium Edition, Windows 2000, Windows XP Home Edition, Windows XP Professional, Windows .NET Server family

ConstructorBuilder.SetCustomAttribute Method

Sets a custom attribute.

Overload List

Set a custom attribute using a custom attribute builder.

> [Visual Basic] **Overloads Public Sub SetCustomAttribute (CustomAttributeBuilder)**
>
> [C#] **public void SetCustomAttribute(CustomAttribute Builder);**
>
> [C++] **public: void SetCustomAttribute(CustomAttribute Builder*);**
>
> [JScript] **public function SetCustomAttribute(Custom AttributeBuilder);**

Set a custom attribute using a specified custom attribute blob.

> [Visual Basic] **Overloads Public Sub SetCustomAttribute (ConstructorInfo, Byte())**
>
> [C#] **public void SetCustomAttribute(ConstructorInfo, byte[]);**
>
> [C++] **public: void SetCustomAttribute(ConstructorInfo*, unsigned char __gc[]);**
>
> [JScript] **public function SetCustomAttribute(Constructor-Info, Byte[]);**

Example

See related example in the **System.Reflection.Emit.ConstuctorBuilder** class topic.

ConstructorBuilder.SetCustomAttribute Method (CustomAttributeBuilder)

Set a custom attribute using a custom attribute builder.

```
[Visual Basic]
Overloads Public Sub SetCustomAttribute( _
   ByVal customBuilder As CustomAttributeBuilder _
)
[C#]
public void SetCustomAttribute(
   CustomAttributeBuilder customBuilder
);
```

```
[C++]
public: void SetCustomAttribute(
    CustomAttributeBuilder* customBuilder
);
[JScript]
public function SetCustomAttribute(
    customBuilder : CustomAttributeBuilder
);
```

Parameters

customBuilder
   An instance of a helper class to define the custom attribute.

Exceptions

Exception Type	Condition
ArgumentNullException	*customBuilder* is a null reference (**Nothing** in Visual Basic).

Example

See related example in the
System.Reflection.Emit.ConstuctorBuilder class topic.

Requirements

Platforms: Windows 98, Windows NT 4.0,
Windows Millennium Edition, Windows 2000,
Windows XP Home Edition, Windows XP Professional,
Windows .NET Server family

ConstructorBuilder.SetCustomAttribute Method (ConstructorInfo, Byte[])

Set a custom attribute using a specified custom attribute blob.

```
[Visual Basic]
Overloads Public Sub SetCustomAttribute( _
    ByVal con As ConstructorInfo, _
    ByVal binaryAttribute() As Byte _
)
[C#]
public void SetCustomAttribute(
    ConstructorInfo con,
    byte[] binaryAttribute
);
[C++]
public: void SetCustomAttribute(
    ConstructorInfo* con,
    unsigned char binaryAttribute __gc[]
);
[JScript]
public function SetCustomAttribute(
    con : ConstructorInfo,
    binaryAttribute : Byte[]
);
```

Parameters

con
   The constructor for the custom attribute.
binaryAttribute
   A byte blob representing the attributes.

Exceptions

Exception Type	Condition
ArgumentNullException	*con* or *binaryAttribute* is a null reference (**Nothing** in Visual Basic).

Remarks

See the metadata specification in the ECMA Partition II
documentation for details on how to format *binaryAttribute*. The
Partition II documentation is included with the .NET Framework
SDK installation, and can be found in the
%\Microsoft.NET\FrameworkSDK\Tool Developers Guide\docs
directory.

Example

See related example in the
System.Reflection.Emit.ConstuctorBuilder class topic.

Requirements

Platforms: Windows 98, Windows NT 4.0,
Windows Millennium Edition, Windows 2000,
Windows XP Home Edition, Windows XP Professional,
Windows .NET Server family

ConstructorBuilder.SetImplementationFlags Method

Sets the method implementation flags for this constructor.

```
[Visual Basic]
Public Sub SetImplementationFlags( _
    ByVal attributes As MethodImplAttributes _
)
[C#]
public void SetImplementationFlags(
    MethodImplAttributes attributes
);
[C++]
public: void SetImplementationFlags(
    MethodImplAttributes attributes
);
[JScript]
public function SetImplementationFlags(
    attributes : MethodImplAttributes
);
```

Parameters

attributes
   The method implementation flags.

Exceptions

Exception Type	Condition
InvalidOperationException	The containing type has been created using **CreateType**.

Example

See related example in the
System.Reflection.Emit.ConstuctorBuilder class topic.

Requirements

Platforms: Windows 98, Windows NT 4.0,
Windows Millennium Edition, Windows 2000,
Windows XP Home Edition, Windows XP Professional,
Windows .NET Server family

ConstructorBuilder.SetSymCustomAttribute Method

Sets this constructor's custom attribute associated with symbolic information.

```
[Visual Basic]
Public Sub SetSymCustomAttribute( _
   ByVal name As String, _
   ByVal data() As Byte _
)
[C#]
public void SetSymCustomAttribute(
   string name,
   byte[] data
);
[C++]
public: void SetSymCustomAttribute(
   String* name,
   unsigned char data __gc[]
);
[JScript]
public function SetSymCustomAttribute(
   name : String,
   data : Byte[]
);
```

Parameters

name
    The name of the custom attribute.
data
    The value of the custom attribute.

Exceptions

Exception Type	Condition
InvalidOperationException	The containing type has been created using **CreateType**. -or- The module does not have a symbol writer defined. For example, the module is not a debug module.

Example

See related example in the **System.Reflection.Emit.ConstuctorBuilder** class topic.

Requirements

Platforms: Windows 98, Windows NT 4.0, Windows Millennium Edition, Windows 2000, Windows XP Home Edition, Windows XP Professional, Windows .NET Server family

Return Value

Returns a **String** containing the name, attributes, and exceptions of this constructor, followed by the current Microsoft intermediate language (MSIL) stream.

Requirements

Platforms: Windows 98, Windows NT 4.0, Windows Millennium Edition, Windows 2000, Windows XP Home Edition, Windows XP Professional, Windows .NET Server family

ConstructorBuilder.ToString Method

Returns this **ConstructorBuilder** instance as a **String**.

```
[Visual Basic]
Overrides Public Function ToString() As String
[C#]
public override string ToString();
[C++]
public: String* ToString();
[JScript]
public override function ToString() : String;
```

CustomAttributeBuilder Class

Helps build custom attributes.

System.Object
  System.Reflection.Emit.CustomAttributeBuilder

```
[Visual Basic]
Public Class CustomAttributeBuilder
[C#]
public class CustomAttributeBuilder
[C++]
public __gc class CustomAttributeBuilder
[JScript]
public class CustomAttributeBuilder
```

Thread Safety

Reflection Emit is thread-safe when using assemblies that were created with the **AppDomain.DefineDynamicAssembly** method with the Boolean parameter *isSynchronized* set to **true**.

Remarks

Use the **CustomAttributeBuilder** object returned by the constructor to describe the custom attribute. Associate the **CustomAttribute** to a builder instance by calling the **SetCustomAttribute** method on that builder instance. For example, create a **CustomAttributeBuilder** to describe an instance of **AssemblyCultureAttribute** by supplying the constructor of **AssemblyCultureAttribute** and its argument. Then call **SetCustomAttribute** on an **AssemblyBuilder** to establish the association.

Example

[Visual Basic, C#, C++] The following code sample illustrates the use of **CustomAttributeBuilder**.

```
[Visual Basic]
Imports System
Imports System.Threading
Imports System.Reflection
Imports System.Reflection.Emit

–

' We will apply this custom attribute to our dynamic type.
Public Class ClassCreator

    Inherits Attribute

    Private creator As String

    Public ReadOnly Property GetCreator() As String
        Get
            Return creator
        End Get
    End Property

    Public Sub New(name As String)
        Me.creator = name
    End Sub 'New

End Class 'ClassCreator

–

' We will apply this dynamic attribute to our dynamic method.
Public Class DateLastUpdated

    Inherits Attribute

    Private dateUpdated As String
```

```
    Public ReadOnly Property GetDateUpdated() As String
        Get
            Return dateUpdated
        End Get
    End Property

    Public Sub New(theDate As String)
        Me.dateUpdated = theDate
    End Sub 'New

End Class 'DateLastUpdated

–

Class MethodBuilderCustomAttributesDemo

    Public Shared Function BuildTypeWithCustomAttributesOnMethod() _
    As Type

        Dim currentDomain As AppDomain = Thread.GetDomain()

        Dim myAsmName As New AssemblyName()
        myAsmName.Name = "MyAssembly"

        Dim myAsmBuilder As AssemblyBuilder = _
        currentDomain.DefineDynamicAssembly(myAsmName, _
                        AssemblyBuilderAccess.Run)

        Dim myModBuilder As ModuleBuilder = _
        myAsmBuilder.DefineDynamicModule("MyModule")

        ' First, we'll build a type with a custom attribute attached.
        Dim myTypeBuilder As TypeBuilder = _
        myModBuilder.DefineType("MyType", _
                        TypeAttributes.Public)

        Dim ctorParams() As Type = {GetType(String)}
        Dim classCtorInfo As ConstructorInfo = _
        GetType(ClassCreator).GetConstructor(ctorParams)

        Dim myCABuilder As New CustomAttributeBuilder(classCtorInfo, _
                        New Object() {"Joe Programmer"})

        myTypeBuilder.SetCustomAttribute(myCABuilder)

        ' Now, let's build a method and add a custom attribute to it.
        Dim myMethodBuilder As MethodBuilder = _
        myTypeBuilder.DefineMethod("HelloWorld", _
                        MethodAttributes.Public, Nothing, New Type() {})

        ctorParams = New Type() {GetType(String)}
        classCtorInfo = _
        GetType(DateLastUpdated).GetConstructor(ctorParams)

        Dim myCABuilder2 As New CustomAttributeBuilder(classCtorInfo, _
                        New Object() {DateTime.Now.ToString()})

        myMethodBuilder.SetCustomAttribute(myCABuilder2)

        Dim myIL As ILGenerator = myMethodBuilder.GetILGenerator()

        myIL.EmitWriteLine("Hello, world!")
        myIL.Emit(OpCodes.Ret)

        Return myTypeBuilder.CreateType()

    End Function 'BuildTypeWithCustomAttributesOnMethod

    Public Shared Sub Main()

        Dim myType As Type = BuildTypeWithCustomAttributesOnMethod()

        Dim myInstance As Object = Activator.CreateInstance(myType)

        Dim customAttrs As Object() = myType.GetCustomAttributes(True)
```

```
      Console.WriteLine("Custom Attributes for Type 'MyType':")

      Dim attrVal As Object = Nothing

      Dim customAttr As Object
      For Each customAttr In  customAttrs
         attrVal = GetType(ClassCreator).InvokeMember("GetCreator", _
                        BindingFlags.GetProperty, _
                        Nothing, customAttr, New Object() {})
         Console.WriteLine("-- Attribute: [{0} = ""{1}""]", _
customAttr, attrVal)
      Next customAttr

      Console.WriteLine("Custom Attributes for Method            _
'HelloWorld()' in 'MyType':")

      customAttrs =                                           _
myType.GetMember("HelloWorld")(0).GetCustomAttributes(True)

      For Each customAttr In  customAttrs
         attrVal =                                            _
GetType(DateLastUpdated).InvokeMember("GetDateUpdated", _
                        BindingFlags.GetProperty, _
                        Nothing, customAttr, New Object() {})
         Console.WriteLine("-- Attribute: [{0} = ""{1}""]", _
customAttr, attrVal)
      Next customAttr

      Console.WriteLine("---")

      Console.WriteLine(myType.InvokeMember("HelloWorld",     _
BindingFlags.InvokeMethod, _
                        Nothing, myInstance, New Object() {}))
   End Sub 'Main

End Class 'MethodBuilderCustomAttributesDemo
```

[C#]
```csharp
using System;
using System.Threading;
using System.Reflection;
using System.Reflection.Emit;

// We will apply this custom attribute to our dynamic type.
public class ClassCreator: Attribute

{
   private string creator;
   public string Creator
   {
    get
    {
      return creator;
    }
   }

   public ClassCreator(string name)
   {
      this.creator = name;
   }
}

// We will apply this dynamic attribute to our dynamic method.
public class DateLastUpdated: Attribute

{
   private string dateUpdated;
   public string DateUpdated
   {
      get
    {
      return dateUpdated;
    }
   }
```

```csharp
   public DateLastUpdated(string theDate)
   {
     this.dateUpdated = theDate;
   }
}

class MethodBuilderCustomAttributesDemo

{

   public static Type BuildTypeWithCustomAttributesOnMethod()
   {

    AppDomain currentDomain = Thread.GetDomain();

    AssemblyName myAsmName = new AssemblyName();
    myAsmName.Name = "MyAssembly";

    AssemblyBuilder myAsmBuilder = currentDomain.DefineDynamicAssembly(
                  myAsmName, AssemblyBuilderAccess.Run);

    ModuleBuilder myModBuilder =
myAsmBuilder.DefineDynamicModule("MyModule");

      // First, we'll build a type with a custom attribute attached.

    TypeBuilder myTypeBuilder = myModBuilder.DefineType("MyType",
                  TypeAttributes.Public);

    Type[] ctorParams = new Type[] { typeof(string) };
    ConstructorInfo classCtorInfo =
typeof(ClassCreator).GetConstructor(ctorParams);

    CustomAttributeBuilder myCABuilder = new CustomAttributeBuilder(
                  classCtorInfo,
                  new object[] { "Joe Programmer" });

    myTypeBuilder.SetCustomAttribute(myCABuilder);

      // Now, let's build a method and add a custom attribute to it.

    MethodBuilder myMethodBuilder =
myTypeBuilder.DefineMethod("HelloWorld",
                  MethodAttributes.Public,
                  null,
                  new Type[] { });

    ctorParams = new Type[] { typeof(string) };
    classCtorInfo = typeof(DateLastUpdated).GetConstructor(ctorParams);

    CustomAttributeBuilder myCABuilder2 = new CustomAttributeBuilder(
                  classCtorInfo,
                  new object[] { DateTime.Now.ToString() });

    myMethodBuilder.SetCustomAttribute(myCABuilder2);

    ILGenerator myIL = myMethodBuilder.GetILGenerator();

    myIL.EmitWriteLine("Hello, world!");
    myIL.Emit(OpCodes.Ret);

    return myTypeBuilder.CreateType();

   }

   public static void Main()
   {

    Type myType = BuildTypeWithCustomAttributesOnMethod();

    object myInstance = Activator.CreateInstance(myType);

    object[] customAttrs = myType.GetCustomAttributes(true);
```

```
    Console.WriteLine("Custom Attributes for Type 'MyType':");

    object attrVal = null;

    foreach (object customAttr in customAttrs)
        {
        attrVal = typeof(ClassCreator).InvokeMember("Creator",
                    BindingFlags.GetProperty,
                    null, customAttr, new object[] { });
        Console.WriteLine("-- Attribute: [{0} = \"{1}\"]",
customAttr, attrVal);
        }

    Console.WriteLine("Custom Attributes for Method 'HelloWorld()
' in 'MyType':");

    customAttrs =
myType.GetMember("HelloWorld")[0].GetCustomAttributes(true);

    foreach (object customAttr in customAttrs)
        {
        attrVal = typeof(DateLastUpdated).InvokeMember("DateUpdated",
                    BindingFlags.GetProperty,
                    null, customAttr, new object[] { });
        Console.WriteLine("-- Attribute: [{0} = \"{1}\"]",
customAttr, attrVal);
        }

    Console.WriteLine("---");

    Console.WriteLine(myType.InvokeMember("HelloWorld",
            BindingFlags.InvokeMethod,
            null, myInstance, new object[] { }));

    }

}

[C++]
#using <mscorlib.dll>

using namespace System;
using namespace System::Threading;
using namespace System::Reflection;
using namespace System::Reflection::Emit;

// We will apply this custom attribute to our dynamic type.
public __gc class ClassCreator : public Attribute {
private:
    String*  creator;
public:
    __property String* get_Creator() {
        return creator;
    }

public:
    ClassCreator(String* name) {
        this->creator = name;
    }
};

// We will apply this dynamic attribute to our dynamic method.
public __gc class DateLastUpdated : public Attribute {
private:
    String*  dateUpdated;
public:
    __property String* get_DateUpdated() {
        return dateUpdated;
    }
public:
    DateLastUpdated(String* theDate) {
        this->dateUpdated = theDate;
    }
};
```

```
Type* BuildTypeWithCustomAttributesOnMethod() {

    AppDomain*  currentDomain = Thread::GetDomain();

    AssemblyName* myAsmName = new AssemblyName();
    myAsmName->Name = S"MyAssembly";

    AssemblyBuilder*  myAsmBuilder = currentDomain
->DefineDynamicAssembly(myAsmName, AssemblyBuilderAccess::Run);

    ModuleBuilder*  myModBuilder = myAsmBuilder
->DefineDynamicModule(S"MyModule");

    // First, we'll build a type with a custom attribute attached.

    TypeBuilder*  myTypeBuilder = myModBuilder->DefineType(S"MyType",
        TypeAttributes::Public);

    Type* temp6 [] = {__typeof(String)};
    Type* ctorParams[] = temp6;
    ConstructorInfo  classCtorInfo = __typeof(ClassCreator)
->GetConstructor(ctorParams);

    Object* temp0 [] = {S"Joe Programmer"};
    CustomAttributeBuilder* myCABuilder = new
CustomAttributeBuilder(classCtorInfo, temp0);

    myTypeBuilder->SetCustomAttribute(myCABuilder);

    // Now, let's build a method and add a custom attribute to it.

    Type* temp1 [] = new Type*[0];
    MethodBuilder*  myMethodBuilder = myTypeBuilder
->DefineMethod(S"HelloWorld",
        MethodAttributes::Public,
        0,
        temp1);

    Type* temp7 [] = {__typeof(String)};
    ctorParams = temp7;
    classCtorInfo = __typeof(DateLastUpdated)-
>GetConstructor(ctorParams);

    Object* temp2 [] = {DateTime::Now.ToString()};
    CustomAttributeBuilder* myCABuilder2 = new
CustomAttributeBuilder(classCtorInfo, temp2);

    myMethodBuilder->SetCustomAttribute(myCABuilder2);

    ILGenerator*  myIL = myMethodBuilder->GetILGenerator();

    myIL->EmitWriteLine(S"Hello, world!");
    myIL->Emit(OpCodes::Ret);

    return myTypeBuilder->CreateType();
}

int main() {

    Type*  myType = BuildTypeWithCustomAttributesOnMethod();

    Object* myInstance = Activator::CreateInstance(myType);

    Object* customAttrs[] = myType->GetCustomAttributes(true);

    Console::WriteLine(S"Custom Attributes for Type 'MyType':");

    Object* attrVal = 0;

    System::Collections::IEnumerator* myEnum = customAttrs-
>GetEnumerator();
    while (myEnum->MoveNext()) {
        Object* customAttr = __try_cast<Object*>(myEnum->Current);
```

```
    Object* temp3 [] = new Object*[0];
    attrVal = __typeof(ClassCreator)->InvokeMember(S"Creator",
        BindingFlags::GetProperty,
        0, customAttr, temp3);
    Console::WriteLine(S"-- Attribute: [{0} = \"{1}\"]",        ⤶
customAttr, attrVal);
    }

    Console::WriteLine(S"Custom Attributes for Method        ⤶
'HelloWorld()' in 'MyType':");

    customAttrs = myType->GetMember(S"HelloWorld")[0]-        ⤶
>GetCustomAttributes(true);

    System::Collections::IEnumerator* myEnum2 = customAttrs-        ⤶
>GetEnumerator();
    while (myEnum2->MoveNext()) {
        Object* customAttr = __try_cast<Object*>(myEnum2->Current);
        Object* temp4 [] = new Object*[0];
        attrVal = __typeof(DateLastUpdated)->InvokeMember(S"DateUpdated",
            BindingFlags::GetProperty,
            0, customAttr, temp4);
        Console::WriteLine(S"-- Attribute: [{0} = \"{1}\"]",        ⤶
customAttr, attrVal);
    }

    Console::WriteLine(S"---");

    Object* temp5 [] = new Object*[0];
    Console::WriteLine(myType->InvokeMember(S"HelloWorld",
        BindingFlags::InvokeMethod,
        0, myInstance, temp5));
}
```

Requirements

Namespace: System.Reflection.Emit

Platforms: Windows 98, Windows NT 4.0,
Windows Millennium Edition, Windows 2000,
Windows XP Home Edition, Windows XP Professional,
Windows .NET Server family

Assembly: Mscorlib (in Mscorlib.dll)

CustomAttributeBuilder Constructor

Initializes an instances of the **CustomAttributeBuilder** class.

Overload List

Initializes an instance of the **CustomAttributeBuilder** class given
the constructor for the custom attribute and the arguments to the
constructor.

[Visual Basic] **Public Sub New(ConstructorInfo, Object())**

[C#] **public CustomAttributeBuilder(ConstructorInfo,
object[]);**

[C++] **public: CustomAttributeBuilder(ConstructorInfo*,
Object[]);**

[JScript] **public function
CustomAttributeBuilder(ConstructorInfo, Object[]);**

Initializes an instance of the **CustomAttributeBuilder** class given
the constructor for the custom attribute, the arguments to the
constructor, and a set of named field/value pairs.

[Visual Basic] **Public Sub New(ConstructorInfo, Object(),
FieldInfo(), Object())**

[C#] **public CustomAttributeBuilder(ConstructorInfo,
object[], FieldInfo[], object[]);**

[C++] **public: CustomAttributeBuilder(ConstructorInfo*,
Object[], FieldInfo[], Object[]);**

[JScript] **public function CustomAttributeBuilder
(ConstructorInfo, Object[], FieldInfo[], Object[]);**

Initializes an instance of the **CustomAttributeBuilder** class given
the constructor for the custom attribute, the arguments to the
constructor, and a set of named property or value pairs.

[Visual Basic] **Public Sub New(ConstructorInfo, Object(),
PropertyInfo(), Object())**

[C#] **public CustomAttributeBuilder(ConstructorInfo,
object[], PropertyInfo[], object[]);**

[C++] **public: CustomAttributeBuilder(ConstructorInfo*,
Object[], PropertyInfo[], Object[]);**

[JScript] **public function CustomAttributeBuilder
(ConstructorInfo, Object[], PropertyInfo[], Object[]);**

Initializes an instance of the **CustomAttributeBuilder** class given
the constructor for the custom attribute, the arguments to the
constructor, a set of named property or value pairs, and a set of
named field or value pairs.

[Visual Basic] **Public Sub New(ConstructorInfo, Object(),
PropertyInfo(), Object(), FieldInfo(), Object())**

[C#] **public CustomAttributeBuilder(ConstructorInfo,
object[], PropertyInfo[], object[], FieldInfo[], object[]);**

[C++] **public: CustomAttributeBuilder(ConstructorInfo*,
Object[], PropertyInfo[], Object[], FieldInfo[], Object[]);**

[JScript] **public function CustomAttributeBuilder
(ConstructorInfo, Object[], PropertyInfo[], Object[],
FieldInfo[], Object[]);**

CustomAttributeBuilder Constructor (ConstructorInfo, Object[])

Initializes an instance of the **CustomAttributeBuilder** class given
the constructor for the custom attribute and the arguments to the
constructor.

```
[Visual Basic]
Public Sub New( _
    ByVal con As ConstructorInfo, _
    ByVal constructorArgs() As Object _
)
[C#]
public CustomAttributeBuilder(
    ConstructorInfo con,
    object[] constructorArgs
);
[C++]
public: CustomAttributeBuilder(
    ConstructorInfo* con,
    Object* constructorArgs __gc[]
);
[JScript]
public function CustomAttributeBuilder(
    con : ConstructorInfo,
    constructorArgs : Object[]
);
```

Parameters

con

The constructor for the custom attribute.

constructorArgs

The arguments to the constructor of the custom attribute.

Exceptions

Exception Type	Condition
ArgumentException	*con* is static or private.
	-or-
	The number of supplied arguments does not match the number of parameters of the constructor as required by the calling convention of the constructor.
	-or-
	The type of supplied argument does not match the type of the parameter declared in the constructor
ArgumentNullException	*con*, *constructorArgs*, or any element of the *constructorArgs* array is a null reference (**Nothing** in Visual Basic).

Remarks

The elements of the *constructorArgs* array are restricted to element types. They can be **byte**, **sbyte**, **int**, **uint**, **long**, **ulong**, **float**, **double**, **String**, **char**, **bool**, an enum, a type, any of the previous types that was cast to an object, or a single dimension zero-based array of any of the previous types.

Requirements

Platforms: Windows 98, Windows NT 4.0, Windows Millennium Edition, Windows 2000, Windows XP Home Edition, Windows XP Professional, Windows .NET Server family

CustomAttributeBuilder Constructor (ConstructorInfo, Object[], FieldInfo[], Object[])

Initializes an instance of the **CustomAttributeBuilder** class given the constructor for the custom attribute, the arguments to the constructor, and a set of named field/value pairs.

```
[Visual Basic]
Public Sub New( _
   ByVal con As ConstructorInfo, _
   ByVal constructorArgs() As Object, _
   ByVal namedFields() As FieldInfo, _
   ByVal fieldValues() As Object _
)
[C#]
public CustomAttributeBuilder(
   ConstructorInfo con,
   object[] constructorArgs,
   FieldInfo[] namedFields,
   object[] fieldValues
);
```

```
[C++]
public: CustomAttributeBuilder(
   ConstructorInfo* con,
   Object* constructorArgs __gc[],
   FieldInfo* namedFields[],
   Object* fieldValues __gc[]
);
[JScript]
public function CustomAttributeBuilder(
   con : ConstructorInfo,
   constructorArgs : Object[],
   namedFields : FieldInfo[],
   fieldValues : Object[]
);
```

Parameters

con

The constructor for the custom attribute.

constructorArgs

The arguments to the constructor of the custom attribute.

namedFields

Named fields of the custom attribute.

fieldValues

Values for the named fields of the custom attribute.

Exceptions

Exception Type	Condition
ArgumentException	The lengths of the *namedFields* and *fieldValues* arrays are different.
	-or-
	con is static or private.
	-or-
	The number of supplied arguments does not match the number of parameters of the constructor as required by the calling convention of the constructor.
	-or-
	The type of supplied argument does not match the type of the parameter declared in the constructor.
	-or-
	The types of the field values do not match the types of the named fields.
	-or-
	The field does not belong to the same class or base class as the constructor.
ArgumentNullException	One of the parameters or any of the elements of the array parameters is a null reference (**Nothing** in Visual Basic).

Remarks

The elements of the *constructorArgs* and *fieldValues* arrays are restricted to element types. They can be **byte**, **sbyte**, **int**, **uint**, **long**, **ulong**, **float**, **double**, **String**, **char**, **bool**, an enum, a type, any of the previous types that was cast to an object, or a single dimension zero-based array of any of the previous types.

Requirements

Platforms: Windows 98, Windows NT 4.0,
Windows Millennium Edition, Windows 2000,
Windows XP Home Edition, Windows XP Professional,
Windows .NET Server family

CustomAttributeBuilder Constructor (ConstructorInfo, Object[], PropertyInfo[], Object[])

Initializes an instance of the **CustomAttributeBuilder** class given the constructor for the custom attribute, the arguments to the constructor, and a set of named property or value pairs.

```
[Visual Basic]
Public Sub New( _
   ByVal con As ConstructorInfo, _
   ByVal constructorArgs() As Object, _
   ByVal namedProperties() As PropertyInfo, _
   ByVal propertyValues() As Object _
)
[C#]
public CustomAttributeBuilder(
   ConstructorInfo con,
   object[] constructorArgs,
   PropertyInfo[] namedProperties,
   object[] propertyValues
);
[C++]
public: CustomAttributeBuilder(
   ConstructorInfo* con,
   Object* constructorArgs __gc[],
   PropertyInfo* namedProperties[],
   Object* propertyValues __gc[]
);
[JScript]
public function CustomAttributeBuilder(
   con : ConstructorInfo,
   constructorArgs : Object[],
   namedProperties : PropertyInfo[],
   propertyValues : Object[]
);
```

Parameters

con
> The constructor for the custom attribute.

constructorArgs
> The arguments to the constructor of the custom attribute.

namedProperties
> Named properties of the custom attribute.

propertyValues
> Values for the named properties of the custom attribute.

Exceptions

Exception Type	Condition
ArgumentException	The lengths of the *namedProperties* and *propertyValues* arrays are different.
	-or-
	con is static or private.
	-or-
	The number of supplied arguments does not match the number of parameters of the constructor as required by the calling convention of the constructor.
	-or-
	The type of supplied argument does not match the type of the parameter declared in the constructor.
	-or-
	The types of the property values do not match the types of the named properties.
	-or-
	A property has no setter method.
	-or-
	The property does not belong to the same class or base class as the constructor.
ArgumentNullException	One of the parameters is null or one of the elements of the array parameters is a null reference (**Nothing** in Visual Basic).

Remarks

The elements of the *constructorArgs* and *propertyValues* arrays are restricted to element types. They can be **byte**, **sbyte**, **int**, **uint**, **long**, **ulong**, **float**, **double**, **String**, **char**, **bool**, an enum, a type, any of the previous types that was cast to an object, or a single dimension zero-based array of any of the previous types.

Requirements

Platforms: Windows 98, Windows NT 4.0,
Windows Millennium Edition, Windows 2000,
Windows XP Home Edition, Windows XP Professional,
Windows .NET Server family

CustomAttributeBuilder Constructor (ConstructorInfo, Object[], PropertyInfo[], Object[], FieldInfo[], Object[])

Initializes an instance of the **CustomAttributeBuilder** class given the constructor for the custom attribute, the arguments to the constructor, a set of named property or value pairs, and a set of named field or value pairs.

```
[Visual Basic]
Public Sub New( _
    ByVal con As ConstructorInfo, _
    ByVal constructorArgs() As Object, _
    ByVal namedProperties() As PropertyInfo, _
    ByVal propertyValues() As Object, _
    ByVal namedFields() As FieldInfo, _
    ByVal fieldValues() As Object _
)
[C#]
public CustomAttributeBuilder(
    ConstructorInfo con,
    object[] constructorArgs,
    PropertyInfo[] namedProperties,
    object[] propertyValues,
    FieldInfo[] namedFields,
    object[] fieldValues
);
[C++]
public: CustomAttributeBuilder(
    ConstructorInfo* con,
    Object* constructorArgs __gc[],
    PropertyInfo* namedProperties[],
    Object* propertyValues __gc[],
    FieldInfo* namedFields[],
    Object* fieldValues __gc[]
);
[JScript]
public function CustomAttributeBuilder(
    con : ConstructorInfo,
    constructorArgs : Object[],
    namedProperties : PropertyInfo[],
    propertyValues : Object[],
    namedFields : FieldInfo[],
    fieldValues : Object[]
);
```

Parameters

con
    The constructor for the custom attribute.
constructorArgs
    The arguments to the constructor of the custom attribute.
namedProperties
    Named properties of the custom attribute.
propertyValues
    Values for the named properties of the custom attribute.
namedFields
    Named fields of the custom attribute.
fieldValues
    Values for the named fields of the custom attribute.

Exceptions

Exception Type	Condition
ArgumentException	The lengths of the *namedProperties* and *propertyValues* arrays are different.
	-or-
	The length of the *namedFields* and *namedValues* are different.
	-or-
	con is static or private.
	-or-
	The number of supplied arguments does not match the number of parameters of the constructor as required by the calling convention of the constructor.
	-or-
	The type of supplied argument does not match the type of the parameter declared in the constructor.
	-or-
	The types of the property values do not match the types of the named properties.
	-or-
	The types of the field values do not match the types of the corresponding field types.
	-or-
	A property has no setter.
	-or-
	The property or field does not belong to the same class or base class as the constructor.
ArgumentNullException	One of the parameters or any of the elements of the array parameters is a null reference (**Nothing** in Visual Basic).

Remarks

The elements of the *constructorArgs,*
    propertyValues, or *fieldValues* arrays are restricted to element types. They can be **byte, sbyte, int, uint, long, ulong, float, double, String, char, bool**, an enum, a type, any of the previous types that was cast to an object, or a single dimension zero-based array of any of the previous types.

Requirements

Platforms: Windows 98, Windows NT 4.0, Windows Millennium Edition, Windows 2000, Windows XP Home Edition, Windows XP Professional, Windows .NET Server family

EnumBuilder Class

Describes and represents an enumeration type.

System.Object
  System.Reflection.MemberInfo
    System.Type
      System.Reflection.Emit.EnumBuilder

```
[Visual Basic]
NotInheritable Public Class EnumBuilder
   Inherits Type
[C#]
public sealed class EnumBuilder : Type
[C++]
public __gc __sealed class EnumBuilder : public Type
[JScript]
public class EnumBuilder extends Type
```

Thread Safety

Reflection Emit is thread-safe when using assemblies that were created with the **AppDomain.DefineDynamicAssembly** method with the Boolean parameter *isSynchronized* set to **true**.

Example

[Visual Basic, C#] The following code sample demonstrates the construction of an enumeration within a dynamic assembly, using **EnumBuilder**.

```
[Visual Basic]
Imports System
Imports System.Collections
Imports System.Threading
Imports System.Reflection
Imports System.Reflection.Emit

Public Class MyEnumBuilderSample
   Private Shared myAssemblyBuilder As AssemblyBuilder
   Private Shared myModuleBuilder As ModuleBuilder
   Private Shared myEnumBuilder As EnumBuilder

   Public Shared Sub Main()
      Try
         CreateCallee(Thread.GetDomain(), AssemblyBuilderAccess.Save)
         Dim myTypeArray As Type() = myModuleBuilder.GetTypes()
         Dim myType As Type
         For Each myType In  myTypeArray
            Console.WriteLine("Enum Builder defined in the
module builder is: " + myType.Name)
         Next myType

         Console.WriteLine("Enum TypeToken is :" +
myEnumBuilder.TypeToken.ToString())
         Console.WriteLine("Enum UnderLyingField is :" +
myEnumBuilder.UnderlyingField.ToString())
         Console.WriteLine("Enum UnderLyingSystemType is :" +
myEnumBuilder.UnderlyingSystemType.ToString())
         Console.WriteLine("Enum GUID is :" +
myEnumBuilder.GUID.ToString())
         myAssemblyBuilder.Save("EmittedAssembly.dll")
      Catch ex As NotSupportedException
         Console.WriteLine("The following is the exception is
raised: " + ex.Message)
      Catch e As Exception
         Console.WriteLine("The following is the exception
raised: " + e.Message)
      End Try
   End Sub 'Main

   Private Shared Sub CreateCallee(myAppDomain As AppDomain,
access As AssemblyBuilderAccess)
```

```
      ' Create a name for the assembly.
      Dim myAssemblyName As New AssemblyName()
      myAssemblyName.Name = "EmittedAssembly"

      ' Create the dynamic assembly.
      myAssemblyBuilder =
myAppDomain.DefineDynamicAssembly(myAssemblyName, _
               AssemblyBuilderAccess.Save)
      ' Create a dynamic module.
      myModuleBuilder =
myAssemblyBuilder.DefineDynamicModule("EmittedModule",
"EmittedModule.mod")
      ' Create a dynamic Enum.
      myEnumBuilder = myModuleBuilder.DefineEnum
("MyNamespace.MyEnum", _
               TypeAttributes.Public, GetType(Int32))

      Dim myFieldBuilder1 As FieldBuilder =
myEnumBuilder.DefineLiteral("FieldOne", 1)
      Dim myFieldBuilder2 As FieldBuilder =
myEnumBuilder.DefineLiteral("FieldTwo", 2)

      myEnumBuilder.CreateType()
   End Sub 'CreateCallee
End Class 'MyEnumBuilderSample

[C#]
using System;
using System.Collections;
using System.Threading;
using System.Reflection;
using System.Reflection.Emit;

public class MyEnumBuilderSample
{
   static AssemblyBuilder myAssemblyBuilder;
   static ModuleBuilder myModuleBuilder;
   static EnumBuilder myEnumBuilder;

   public static void Main()
   {
      try
      {
         CreateCallee(Thread.GetDomain(), AssemblyBuilderAccess.Save);
         Type[] myTypeArray = myModuleBuilder.GetTypes();
         foreach(Type myType in myTypeArray)
         {
            Console.WriteLine("Enum Builder defined in the
module builder is: "
               + myType.Name);
         }

         Console.WriteLine("Enum TypeToken is :" +
               myEnumBuilder.TypeToken.ToString());
         Console.WriteLine("Enum UnderLyingField is :" +
               myEnumBuilder.UnderlyingField.ToString());
         Console.WriteLine("Enum UnderLyingSystemType is :" +
myEnumBuilder.UnderlyingSystemType.ToString());
         Console.WriteLine("Enum GUID is :" +
myEnumBuilder.GUID.ToString());
         myAssemblyBuilder.Save("EmittedAssembly.dll");
      }
      catch(NotSupportedException ex)
      {
         Console.WriteLine
("The following is the exception is raised: " + ex.Message);
      }
      catch(Exception e)
      {
         Console.WriteLine
("The following is the exception raised: " + e.Message);
      }
   }
```

```
    private static void CreateCallee(AppDomain myAppDomain,
AssemblyBuilderAccess access)
    {
        // Create a name for the assembly.
        AssemblyName myAssemblyName = new AssemblyName();
        myAssemblyName.Name = "EmittedAssembly";

        // Create the dynamic assembly.
        myAssemblyBuilder =
myAppDomain.DefineDynamicAssembly(myAssemblyName,
                            AssemblyBuilderAccess.Save);
        // Create a dynamic module.
        myModuleBuilder =
myAssemblyBuilder.DefineDynamicModule("EmittedModule",
                            "EmittedModule.mod");
        // Create a dynamic Enum.
        myEnumBuilder = myModuleBuilder.DefineEnum("MyNamespace.MyEnum",
                            TypeAttributes.Public, typeof(Int32));

        FieldBuilder myFieldBuilder1 =
myEnumBuilder.DefineLiteral("FieldOne", 1);
        FieldBuilder myFieldBuilder2 =
myEnumBuilder.DefineLiteral("FieldTwo", 2);

        myEnumBuilder.CreateType();
    }
}
```

Requirements

Namespace: System.Reflection.Emit

Platforms: Windows 98, Windows NT 4.0,
Windows Millennium Edition, Windows 2000,
Windows XP Home Edition, Windows XP Professional,
Windows .NET Server family

Assembly: Mscorlib (in Mscorlib.dll)

EnumBuilder.Assembly Property

Retrieves the dynamic assembly that contains this enum definition.

```
[Visual Basic]
Overrides Public ReadOnly Property Assembly As Assembly
[C#]
public override Assembly Assembly {get;}
[C++]
public: __property Assembly* get_Assembly();
[JScript]
public override function get Assembly() : Assembly;
```

Property Value

Read-only. The dynamic assembly that contains this enum definition.

Example

See related example in the System.Reflection.Emit.EnumBuilder class topic.

Requirements

Platforms: Windows 98, Windows NT 4.0,
Windows Millennium Edition, Windows 2000,
Windows XP Home Edition, Windows XP Professional,
Windows .NET Server family

EnumBuilder.AssemblyQualifiedName Property

Returns the full path of this enum qualified by the display name of the parent assembly.

```
[Visual Basic]
Overrides Public ReadOnly Property AssemblyQualifiedName As String
[C#]
public override string AssemblyQualifiedName {get;}
[C++]
public: __property String* get_AssemblyQualifiedName();
[JScript]
public override function get AssemblyQualifiedName() : String;
```

Property Value

Read-only. The full path of this enum qualified by the display name of the parent assembly.

Exceptions

Exception Type	Condition
NotSupportedException	If **CreateType** has not been called previously.

Remarks

The format of the returned string is:

<FullTypeName>, <AssemblyDisplayName>

See **AssemblyName** for a description of the format of the display name of an assembly.

Example

See related example in the **System.Reflection.Emit.EnumBuilder** class topic.

Requirements

Platforms: Windows 98, Windows NT 4.0,
Windows Millennium Edition, Windows 2000,
Windows XP Home Edition, Windows XP Professional,
Windows .NET Server family

EnumBuilder.BaseType Property

Returns the parent **Type** of this type which is always **Enum**.

```
[Visual Basic]
Overrides Public ReadOnly Property BaseType As Type
[C#]
public override Type BaseType {get;}
[C++]
public: __property Type* get_BaseType();
[JScript]
public override function get BaseType() : Type;
```

Property Value

Read-only. The parent **Type** of this type.

Requirements

Platforms: Windows 98, Windows NT 4.0,
Windows Millennium Edition, Windows 2000,
Windows XP Home Edition, Windows XP Professional,
Windows .NET Server family

EnumBuilder.DeclaringType Property

Returns the type that declared this **EnumBuilder**.

```
[Visual Basic]
Overrides Public ReadOnly Property DeclaringType As Type
[C#]
public override Type DeclaringType {get;}
[C++]
public: __property Type* get_DeclaringType();
[JScript]
public override function get DeclaringType() : Type;
```

Property Value

Read-only. The type that declared this **EnumBuilder**.

Requirements

Platforms: Windows 98, Windows NT 4.0,
Windows Millennium Edition, Windows 2000,
Windows XP Home Edition, Windows XP Professional,
Windows .NET Server family

EnumBuilder.FullName Property

Returns the full path of this enum.

```
[Visual Basic]
Overrides Public ReadOnly Property FullName As String
[C#]
public override string FullName {get;}
[C++]
public: __property String* get_FullName();
[JScript]
public override function get FullName() : String;
```

Property Value

Read-only. The full path of this enum.

Remarks

The returned format is "enclosingTypeFullName+nestedTypeName"
for nested types and "typeName" for non-nested types.

Requirements

Platforms: Windows 98, Windows NT 4.0,
Windows Millennium Edition, Windows 2000,
Windows XP Home Edition, Windows XP Professional,
Windows .NET Server family

EnumBuilder.GUID Property

Returns the GUID of this enum.

```
[Visual Basic]
Overrides Public ReadOnly Property GUID As Guid
[C#]
public override Guid GUID {get;}
[C++]
public: __property Guid get_GUID();
[JScript]
public override function get GUID() : Guid;
```

Property Value

Read-only. The GUID of this enum.

Exceptions

Exception Type	Condition
NotSupportedException	This method is not currently supported in types that are not complete.

Example

See related example in the **System.Reflection.Emit.EnumBuilder**
class topic.

Requirements

Platforms: Windows 98, Windows NT 4.0,
Windows Millennium Edition, Windows 2000,
Windows XP Home Edition, Windows XP Professional,
Windows .NET Server family

EnumBuilder.Module Property

Retrieves the dynamic module that contains this **EnumBuilder**
definition.

```
[Visual Basic]
Overrides Public ReadOnly Property Module As Module
[C#]
public override Module Module {get;}
[C++]
public: __property Module* get_Module();
[JScript]
public override function get Module() : Module;
```

Property Value

Read-only. The dynamic module that contains this **EnumBuilder**
definition.

Example

See related example in the **System.Reflection.Emit.EnumBuilder**
class topic.

Requirements

Platforms: Windows 98, Windows NT 4.0,
Windows Millennium Edition, Windows 2000,
Windows XP Home Edition, Windows XP Professional,
Windows .NET Server family

EnumBuilder.Name Property

Returns the name of this enum.

```
[Visual Basic]
Overrides Public ReadOnly Property Name As String
[C#]
public override string Name {get;}
[C++]
public: __property String* get_Name();
[JScript]
public override function get Name() : String;
```

Property Value

Read-only. The name of this enum.

Example

See related example in the **System.Reflection.Emit.EnumBuilder**
class topic.

Requirements

Platforms: Windows 98, Windows NT 4.0,
Windows Millennium Edition, Windows 2000,
Windows XP Home Edition, Windows XP Professional,
Windows .NET Server family

EnumBuilder.Namespace Property

Returns the namespace of this enum.

```
[Visual Basic]
Overrides Public ReadOnly Property Namespace As String
[C#]
public override string Namespace {get;}
[C++]
public: __property String* get_Namespace();
[JScript]
public override function get Namespace() : String;
```

Property Value

Read-only. The namespace of this enum.

Example

See related example in the **System.Reflection.Emit.EnumBuilder**
class topic.

Requirements

Platforms: Windows 98, Windows NT 4.0,
Windows Millennium Edition, Windows 2000,
Windows XP Home Edition, Windows XP Professional,
Windows .NET Server family

EnumBuilder.ReflectedType Property

Returns the type that was used to obtain this **EnumBuilder**.

```
[Visual Basic]
Overrides Public ReadOnly Property ReflectedType As Type
[C#]
public override Type ReflectedType {get;}
[C++]
public: __property Type* get_ReflectedType();
[JScript]
public override function get ReflectedType() : Type;
```

Property Value

Read-only. The type that was used to obtain this **EnumBuilder**.

Requirements

Platforms: Windows 98, Windows NT 4.0,
Windows Millennium Edition, Windows 2000,
Windows XP Home Edition, Windows XP Professional,
Windows .NET Server family

EnumBuilder.TypeHandle Property

Retrieves the internal handle for this enum.

```
[Visual Basic]
Overrides Public ReadOnly Property TypeHandle As RuntimeTypeHandle
[C#]
public override RuntimeTypeHandle TypeHandle {get;}
[C++]
public: __property RuntimeTypeHandle get_TypeHandle();
[JScript]
public override function get TypeHandle() : RuntimeTypeHandle;
```

Property Value

Read-only. The internal handle for this enum.

Exceptions

Exception Type	Condition
NotSupportedException	This property is not currently supported.

Remarks

You can retrieve the type using **Type.GetType** or
Assembly.GetType and use reflection on the retrieved type.

Use this handle to access the underlying metadata handle.

Requirements

Platforms: Windows 98, Windows NT 4.0,
Windows Millennium Edition, Windows 2000,
Windows XP Home Edition, Windows XP Professional,
Windows .NET Server family

EnumBuilder.TypeToken Property

Returns the internal metadata type token of this enum.

```
[Visual Basic]
Public ReadOnly Property TypeToken As TypeToken
[C#]
public TypeToken TypeToken {get;}
[C++]
public: __property TypeToken get_TypeToken();
[JScript]
public function get TypeToken() : TypeToken;
```

Property Value

Read-only. The type token of this enum.

Requirements

Platforms: Windows 98, Windows NT 4.0,
Windows Millennium Edition, Windows 2000,
Windows XP Home Edition, Windows XP Professional,
Windows .NET Server family

EnumBuilder.UnderlyingField Property

Returns the underlying field for this enum.

```
[Visual Basic]
Public ReadOnly Property UnderlyingField As FieldBuilder
[C#]
public FieldBuilder UnderlyingField {get;}
[C++]
public: __property FieldBuilder* get_UnderlyingField();
[JScript]
public function get UnderlyingField() : FieldBuilder;
```

Property Value

Read-only. The underlying field for this enum.

Requirements

Platforms: Windows 98, Windows NT 4.0,
Windows Millennium Edition, Windows 2000,
Windows XP Home Edition, Windows XP Professional,
Windows .NET Server family

EnumBuilder.UnderlyingSystemType Property

Returns the underlying system type for this enum.

```
[Visual Basic]
Overrides Public ReadOnly Property UnderlyingSystemType As Type _
    Implements IReflect.UnderlyingSystemType
[C#]
public override Type UnderlyingSystemType {get;}
[C++]
public: __property Type* get_UnderlyingSystemType();
[JScript]
public override function get UnderlyingSystemType() : Type;
```

Property Value

Read-only. Returns the underlying system type.

Implements

IReflect.UnderlyingSystemType

Requirements

Platforms: Windows 98, Windows NT 4.0,
Windows Millennium Edition, Windows 2000,
Windows XP Home Edition, Windows XP Professional,
Windows .NET Server family

EnumBuilder.CreateType Method

Creates a **Type** object for this enum.

```
[Visual Basic]
Public Function CreateType() As Type
[C#]
public Type CreateType();
[C++]
public: Type* CreateType();
[JScript]
public function CreateType() : Type;
```

Return Value

A **Type** object for this enum.

Exceptions

Exception Type	Condition
InvalidOperation-Exception	This type has been previously created. -or- The enclosing type has not been created.

Example

Requirements

Platforms: Windows 98, Windows NT 4.0,
Windows Millennium Edition, Windows 2000,
Windows XP Home Edition, Windows XP Professional,
Windows .NET Server family

EnumBuilder.DefineLiteral Method

Defines the named static field in an enumeration type with the
specified constant value.

```
[Visual Basic]
Public Function DefineLiteral( _
    ByVal literalName As String, _
    ByVal literalValue As Object _
) As FieldBuilder
```

```
[C#]
public FieldBuilder DefineLiteral(
    string literalName,
    object literalValue
);
[C++]
public: FieldBuilder* DefineLiteral(
    String* literalName,
    Object* literalValue
);
[JScript]
public function DefineLiteral(
    literalName : String,
    literalValue : Object
) : FieldBuilder;
```

Parameters

literalName
    The name of the static field.
literalValue
    The constant value of the literal.

Return Value

The defined field.

Remarks

The defined field will have the field attributes **Public**, **Static**, and
Literal set.

Requirements

Platforms: Windows 98, Windows NT 4.0,
Windows Millennium Edition, Windows 2000,
Windows XP Home Edition, Windows XP Professional,
Windows .NET Server family

EnumBuilder.GetAttributeFlagsImpl Method

Gets the implementation attribute flags.

```
[Visual Basic]
Overrides Protected Function GetAttributeFlagsImpl() As _
    TypeAttributes
[C#]
protected override TypeAttributes GetAttributeFlagsImpl();
[C++]
protected: TypeAttributes GetAttributeFlagsImpl();
[JScript]
protected override function GetAttributeFlagsImpl() :
    TypeAttributes;
```

Return Value

The implementation attribute flags.

Requirements

Platforms: Windows 98, Windows NT 4.0,
Windows Millennium Edition, Windows 2000,
Windows XP Home Edition, Windows XP Professional,
Windows .NET Server family

EnumBuilder.GetConstructorImpl Method

Searches for a constructor whose parameters match the specified argument types and modifiers, using the specified binding constraints and the specified calling convention.

```
[Visual Basic]
Overrides Protected Function GetConstructorImpl( _
   ByVal bindingAttr As BindingFlags, _
   ByVal binder As Binder, _
   ByVal callConvention As CallingConventions, _
   ByVal types() As Type, _
   ByVal modifiers() As ParameterModifier _
) As ConstructorInfo
[C#]
protected override ConstructorInfo GetConstructorImpl(
   BindingFlags bindingAttr,
   Binder binder,
   CallingConventions callConvention,
   Type[] types,
   ParameterModifier[] modifiers
);
[C++]
protected: ConstructorInfo* GetConstructorImpl(
   BindingFlags bindingAttr,
   Binder* binder,
   CallingConventions callConvention,
   Type* types[],
   ParameterModifier modifiers[]
);
[JScript]
protected override function GetConstructorImpl(
   bindingAttr : BindingFlags,
   binder : Binder,
   callConvention : CallingConventions,
   types : Type[],
   modifiers : ParameterModifier[]
) : ConstructorInfo;
```

Parameters

bindingAttr
   A bitmask comprised of one or more **BindingFlags** that specify how the search is conducted.
   -or-
   Zero, to conduct a case-sensitive search for public methods.

binder
   A **Binder** object that defines a set of properties and enables binding, which can involve selection of an overloaded method, coercion of argument types, and invocation of a member through reflection.
   -or-
   A null reference (**Nothing** in Visual Basic), to use the **DefaultBinder**.

callConvention
   The **CallingConventions** object that specifies the set of rules to use regarding the order and layout of arguments, how the return value is passed, what registers are used for arguments, and how the stack is cleaned up.

types
   An array of **Type** objects representing the number, order, and type of the parameters for the constructor to get.
   -or-
   An empty array of the type **Type** (that is, Type[] types = new Type[0]) to get a constructor that takes no parameters.

modifiers
   An array of **ParameterModifier** objects representing the attributes associated with the corresponding element in the *types* array.

Return Value

A **ConstructorInfo** object representing the constructor that matches the specified requirements, if found; otherwise, a null reference (**Nothing** in Visual Basic).

Exceptions

Exception Type	Condition
NotSupportedException	This method is not currently supported in types that are not complete.

Remarks

As a workaround to retrieve the constructor of a finished type, you can retrieve the type using **Type.GetType** or **Assembly.GetType** and use reflection on the retrieved type.

Requirements

Platforms: Windows 98, Windows NT 4.0, Windows Millennium Edition, Windows 2000, Windows XP Home Edition, Windows XP Professional, Windows .NET Server family

EnumBuilder.GetConstructors Method

Overload List

Returns an array of **ConstructorInfo** objects representing the public and non-public constructors defined for this class, as specified.

   [Visual Basic] **Overloads Overrides Public Function GetConstructors(BindingFlags) As ConstructorInfo()**
   [C#] **public override ConstructorInfo[] GetConstructors (BindingFlags);**
   [C++] **public: ConstructorInfo* GetConstructors (BindingFlags) [];**
   [JScript] **public override function GetConstructors (BindingFlags) : ConstructorInfo[];**

Inherited from **Type**.

   [Visual Basic] **Overloads Public Function GetConstructors() As ConstructorInfo()**
   [C#] **public ConstructorInfo[] GetConstructors();**
   [C++] **public: ConstructorInfo* GetConstructors() [];**
   [JScript] **public function GetConstructors() : ConstructorInfo[];**

EnumBuilder.GetConstructors Method (BindingFlags)

Returns an array of **ConstructorInfo** objects representing the public and non-public constructors defined for this class, as specified.

```
[Visual Basic]
Overrides Overloads Public Function GetConstructors( _
   ByVal bindingAttr As BindingFlags _
) As ConstructorInfo()
[C#]
public override ConstructorInfo[] GetConstructors(
   BindingFlags bindingAttr
);
```

```
[C++]
public: ConstructorInfo* GetConstructors(
   BindingFlags bindingAttr
) [];
[JScript]
public override function GetConstructors(
   bindingAttr : BindingFlags
) : ConstructorInfo[];
```

Parameters

bindingAttr

This must be a bit flag from **BindingFlags**: **InvokeMethod**,
NonPublic, and so on.

Return Value

Returns an array of **ConstructorInfo** objects representing the
specified constructors defined for this class. If no constructors are
defined, an empty array is returned.

Exceptions

Exception Type	Condition
NotSupportedException	This method is not currently supported in types that are not complete.

Remarks

As a workaround, to retrieve the constructor of a finished type, you
can retrieve the type using **Type.GetType** or **Assembly.GetType**
and use reflection on the retrieved type.

Requirements

Platforms: Windows 98, Windows NT 4.0,
Windows Millennium Edition, Windows 2000,
Windows XP Home Edition, Windows XP Professional,
Windows .NET Server family

EnumBuilder.GetCustomAttributes Method

Returns the custom attributes defined for this constructor.

Overload List

Returns all the custom attributes defined for this constructor.

[Visual Basic] **Overloads Overrides Public Function
GetCustomAttributes(Boolean) As Object() Implements
ICustomAttributeProvider.GetCustomAttributes**

[C#] **public override object[] GetCustomAttributes(bool);**

[C++] **public: Object* GetCustomAttributes(bool) __gc[];**

[JScript] **public override function GetCustomAttributes
(Boolean) : Object[];**

Returns the custom attributes identified by the given type.

[Visual Basic] **Overloads Overrides Public Function
GetCustomAttributes(Type, Boolean) As Object()
Implements ICustomAttributeProvider.GetCustom
Attributes**

[C#] **public override object[] GetCustomAttributes(Type,
bool);**

[C++] **public: Object* GetCustomAttributes(Type*, bool)
__gc[];**

[JScript] **public override function GetCustomAttributes
(Type, Boolean) : Object[];**

EnumBuilder.GetCustomAttributes Method (Boolean)

Returns all the custom attributes defined for this constructor.

```
[Visual Basic]
Overrides Overloads Public Function GetCustomAttributes( _
   ByVal inherit As Boolean _
) As Object() Implements ICustomAttributeProvider.GetCustomAttributes
[C#]
public override object[] GetCustomAttributes(
   bool inherit
);
[C++]
public: Object* GetCustomAttributes(
   bool inherit
) __gc[];
[JScript]
public override function GetCustomAttributes(
   inherit : Boolean
) : Object[];
```

Parameters

inherit

Specifies whether to search this member's inheritance chain to
find the attributes.

Return Value

Returns an array of objects representing all the custom attributes of
the constructor represented by this **ConstructorBuilder** instance.

Implements

ICustomAttributeProvider.GetCustomAttributes

Exceptions

Exception Type	Condition
NotSupportedException	This method is not currently supported in types that are not complete.

Remarks

See related example in the **System.Reflection.Emit.EnumBuilder**
class topic.

Requirements

Platforms: Windows 98, Windows NT 4.0,
Windows Millennium Edition, Windows 2000,
Windows XP Home Edition, Windows XP Professional,
Windows .NET Server family

EnumBuilder.GetCustomAttributes Method (Type, Boolean)

Returns the custom attributes identified by the given type.

```
[Visual Basic]
Overrides Overloads Public Function GetCustomAttributes( _
   ByVal attributeType As Type, _
   ByVal inherit As Boolean _
) As Object() Implements ICustomAttributeProvider.GetCustomAttributes
[C#]
public override object[] GetCustomAttributes(
   Type attributeType,
   bool inherit
);
```

```
[C++]
public: Object* GetCustomAttributes(
    Type* attributeType,
    bool inherit
) __gc[];
[JScript]
public override function GetCustomAttributes(
    attributeType : Type,
    inherit : Boolean
) : Object[];
```

Parameters

attributeType
 The **Type** object to which the custom attributes are applied.

inherit
 Specifies whether to search this member's inheritance chain to find the attributes.

Return Value

Returns an array of objects representing the attributes of this constructor that are of **Type** *attributeType*.

Implements

ICustomAttributeProvider.GetCustomAttributes

Exceptions

Exception Type	Condition
NotSupportedException	This method is not currently supported in types that are not complete.

Remarks

See related example in the **System.Reflection.Emit.EnumBuilder** class topic.

Requirements

Platforms: Windows 98, Windows NT 4.0, Windows Millennium Edition, Windows 2000, Windows XP Home Edition, Windows XP Professional, Windows .NET Server family

EnumBuilder.GetElementType Method

Calling this method always throws **NotSupportedException**.

```
[Visual Basic]
Overrides Public Function GetElementType() As Type
[C#]
public override Type GetElementType();
[C++]
public: Type* GetElementType();
[JScript]
public override function GetElementType() : Type;
```

Return Value

This method is not supported. No value is returned.

Exceptions

Exception Type	Condition
NotSupportedException	This method is not currently supported.

Requirements

Platforms: Windows 98, Windows NT 4.0, Windows Millennium Edition, Windows 2000, Windows XP Home Edition, Windows XP Professional, Windows .NET Server family

EnumBuilder.GetEvent Method

Overload List

Returns the event with the specified name.

 [Visual Basic] **Overloads Overrides Public Function GetEvent(String, BindingFlags) As EventInfo**

 [C#] **public override EventInfo GetEvent(string, BindingFlags);**

 [C++] **public: EventInfo* GetEvent(String*, BindingFlags);**

 [JScript] **public override function GetEvent(String, BindingFlags) : EventInfo;**

Inherited from **Type**.

 [Visual Basic] **Overloads Public Function GetEvent(String) As EventInfo**

 [C#] **public EventInfo GetEvent(string);**

 [C++] **public: EventInfo* GetEvent(String*);**

 [JScript] **public function GetEvent(String) : EventInfo;**

EnumBuilder.GetEvent Method (String, BindingFlags)

Returns the event with the specified name.

```
[Visual Basic]
Overrides Overloads Public Function GetEvent( _
    ByVal name As String, _
    ByVal bindingAttr As BindingFlags _
) As EventInfo
[C#]
public override EventInfo GetEvent(
    string name,
    BindingFlags bindingAttr
);
[C++]
public: EventInfo* GetEvent(
    String* name,
    BindingFlags bindingAttr
);
[JScript]
public override function GetEvent(
    name : String,
    bindingAttr : BindingFlags
) : EventInfo;
```

Parameters

name
 The name of the event to get.
bindingAttr
 This invocation attribute. This must be a bit flag from **BindingFlags**: **InvokeMethod**, **NonPublic**, and so on.

Return Value

Returns an **EventInfo** object representing the event declared or inherited by this type with the specified name. If there are no matches, then an empty array is returned.

Exceptions

Exception Type	Condition
NotSupportedException	This method is not currently supported in types that are not complete.

Remarks

As a workaround, to retrieve the event of a finished type, retrieve the type using **Type.GetType** or **Assembly.GetType** and use reflection on the retrieved type.

Requirements

Platforms: Windows 98, Windows NT 4.0, Windows Millennium Edition, Windows 2000, Windows XP Home Edition, Windows XP Professional, Windows .NET Server family

EnumBuilder.GetEvents Method

Overload List

Returns the events for the public events declared or inherited by this type.

[Visual Basic] **Overloads Overrides Public Function GetEvents() As EventInfo()**

[C#] **public override EventInfo[] GetEvents();**

[C++] **public: EventInfo* GetEvents() [];**

[JScript] **public override function GetEvents() : EventInfo[];**

Returns the public and non-public events that are declared by this type.

[Visual Basic] **Overloads Overrides Public Function GetEvents(BindingFlags) As EventInfo()**

[C#] **public override EventInfo[] GetEvents(BindingFlags);**

[C++] **public: EventInfo* GetEvents(BindingFlags) [];**

[JScript] **public override function GetEvents(BindingFlags) : EventInfo[];**

EnumBuilder.GetEvents Method ()

Returns the events for the public events declared or inherited by this type.

```
[Visual Basic]
Overrides Overloads Public Function GetEvents() As EventInfo()
[C#]
public override EventInfo[] GetEvents();
[C++]
public: EventInfo* GetEvents() [];
[JScript]
public override function GetEvents() : EventInfo[];
```

Return Value

Returns an array of **EventInfo** objects representing the public events declared or inherited by this type. An empty array is returned if there are no public events.

Exceptions

Exception Type	Condition
NotSupportedException	This method is not currently supported in types that are not complete.

Remarks

As a workaround, to retrieve the events of a finished type, retrieve the type using **Type.GetType** or **Assembly.GetType** and use reflection on the retrieved type.

Requirements

Platforms: Windows 98, Windows NT 4.0, Windows Millennium Edition, Windows 2000, Windows XP Home Edition, Windows XP Professional, Windows .NET Server family

EnumBuilder.GetEvents Method (BindingFlags)

Returns the public and non-public events that are declared by this type.

```
[Visual Basic]
Overrides Overloads Public Function GetEvents( _
    ByVal bindingAttr As BindingFlags _
) As EventInfo()
[C#]
public override EventInfo[] GetEvents(
    BindingFlags bindingAttr
);
[C++]
public: EventInfo* GetEvents(
    BindingFlags bindingAttr
) [];
[JScript]
public override function GetEvents(
    bindingAttr : BindingFlags
) : EventInfo[];
```

Parameters

bindingAttr

This must be a bit flag from **BindingFlags**, such as **InvokeMethod**, **NonPublic**, and so on.

Return Value

Returns an array of **EventInfo** objects representing the public and non-public events declared or inherited by this type. An empty array is returned if there are no events, as specified.

Exceptions

Exception Type	Condition
NotSupportedException	This method is not currently supported in types that are not complete.

Remarks

As a workaround, to retrieve the events of a finished type, retrieve the type using **Type.GetType** or **Assembly.GetType** and use reflection on the retrieved type to retrieve the events.

Requirements

Platforms: Windows 98, Windows NT 4.0, Windows Millennium Edition, Windows 2000, Windows XP Home Edition, Windows XP Professional, Windows .NET Server family

EnumBuilder.GetField Method

Overload List

Returns the field specified by the given name.

> [Visual Basic] **Overloads Overrides Public Function GetField (String, BindingFlags) As FieldInfo Implements IReflect.GetField**
>
> [C#] **public override FieldInfo GetField(string, BindingFlags);**
>
> [C++] **public: FieldInfo* GetField(String*, BindingFlags);**
>
> [JScript] **public override function GetField(String, BindingFlags) : FieldInfo;**

Inherited from **Type**.

> [Visual Basic] **Overloads Public Function GetField(String) As FieldInfo**
>
> [C#] **public FieldInfo GetField(string);**
>
> [C++] **public: FieldInfo* GetField(String*);**
>
> [JScript] **public function GetField(String) : FieldInfo;**

EnumBuilder.GetField Method (String, BindingFlags)

Returns the field specified by the given name.

```
[Visual Basic]
Overrides Overloads Public Function GetField( _
   ByVal name As String, _
   ByVal bindingAttr As BindingFlags _
) As FieldInfo Implements IReflect.GetField
[C#]
public override FieldInfo GetField(
   string name,
   BindingFlags bindingAttr
);
[C++]
public: FieldInfo* GetField(
   String* name,
   BindingFlags bindingAttr
);
[JScript]
public override function GetField(
   name : String,
   bindingAttr : BindingFlags
) : FieldInfo;
```

Parameters

name
> The name of the field to get.

bindingAttr
> This must be a bit flag from **BindingFlags**: **InvokeMethod**, **NonPublic**, and so on.

Return Value

Returns the **FieldInfo** object representing the field declared or inherited by this type with the specified name and public or non-public modifier. If there are no matches, then null is returned.

Implements

IReflect.GetField

Exceptions

Exception Type	Condition
NotSupportedException	This method is not currently supported in types that are not complete.

Remarks

As a workaround, to retrieve the field of a finished type, retrieve the type using **Type.GetType** or **GetType** and use reflection on the retrieved type.

Requirements

Platforms: Windows 98, Windows NT 4.0, Windows Millennium Edition, Windows 2000, Windows XP Home Edition, Windows XP Professional, Windows .NET Server family

EnumBuilder.GetFields Method

Overload List

Returns the public and non-public fields that are declared by this type.

> [Visual Basic] **Overloads Overrides Public Function GetFields(BindingFlags) As FieldInfo() Implements IReflect.GetFields**
>
> [C#] **public override FieldInfo[] GetFields(BindingFlags);**
>
> [C++] **public: FieldInfo* GetFields(BindingFlags) [];**
>
> [JScript] **public override function GetFields(BindingFlags) : FieldInfo[];**

Inherited from **Type**.

> [Visual Basic] **Overloads Public Function GetFields() As FieldInfo()**
>
> [C#] **public FieldInfo[] GetFields();**
>
> [C++] **public: FieldInfo* GetFields() [];**
>
> [JScript] **public function GetFields() : FieldInfo[];**

EnumBuilder.GetFields Method (BindingFlags)

Returns the public and non-public fields that are declared by this type.

```
[Visual Basic]
Overrides Overloads Public Function GetFields( _
   ByVal bindingAttr As BindingFlags _
) As FieldInfo() Implements IReflect.GetFields
[C#]
public override FieldInfo[] GetFields(
   BindingFlags bindingAttr
);
[C++]
public: FieldInfo* GetFields(
   BindingFlags bindingAttr
) [];
[JScript]
public override function GetFields(
   bindingAttr : BindingFlags
) : FieldInfo[];
```

Parameters

bindingAttr

This must be a bit flag from **BindingFlags**, such as InvokeMethod, NonPublic, and so on.

Return Value

Returns an array of **FieldInfo** objects representing the public and non-public fields declared or inherited by this type. An empty array is returned if there are no fields, as specified.

Implements

IReflect.GetFields

Exceptions

Exception Type	Condition
NotSupportedException	This method is not currently supported in types that are not complete.

Remarks

As a workaround, to retrieve the field of a finished type, retrieve the type using **Type.GetType** or **Assembly.GetType** and use reflection on the retrieved type.

Requirements

Platforms: Windows 98, Windows NT 4.0, Windows Millennium Edition, Windows 2000, Windows XP Home Edition, Windows XP Professional, Windows .NET Server family

EnumBuilder.GetInterface Method

Overload List

Returns the interface implemented (directly or indirectly) by this class with the fully-qualified name matching the given interface name.

[Visual Basic] **Overloads Overrides Public Function GetInterface(String, Boolean) As Type**

[C#] **public override Type GetInterface(string, bool);**

[C++] **public: Type* GetInterface(String*, bool);**

[JScript] **public override function GetInterface(String, Boolean) : Type;**

Inherited from **Type**.

[Visual Basic] **Overloads Public Function GetInterface (String) As Type**

[C#] **public Type GetInterface(string);**

[C++] **public: Type* GetInterface(String*);**

[JScript] **public function GetInterface(String) : Type;**

EnumBuilder.GetInterface Method (String, Boolean)

Returns the interface implemented (directly or indirectly) by this class with the fully-qualified name matching the given interface name.

```
[Visual Basic]
Overrides Overloads Public Function GetInterface( _
   ByVal name As String, _
   ByVal ignoreCase As Boolean _
) As Type
```

```
[C#]
public override Type GetInterface(
   string name,
   bool ignoreCase
);
```

```
[C++]
public: Type* GetInterface(
   String* name,
   bool ignoreCase
);
```

```
[JScript]
public override function GetInterface(
   name : String,
   ignoreCase : Boolean
) : Type;
```

Parameters

name

The name of the interface.

ignoreCase

If **true**, the search is case-insensitive. If **false**, the search is case-sensitive.

Return Value

Returns a **Type** object representing the implemented interface. Returns null if no interface matching name is found.

Exceptions

Exception Type	Condition
NotSupportedException	This method is not currently supported in types that are not complete.

Remarks

As a workaround, to retrieve the interface of a finished type, retrieve the type using **Type.GetType** or **Assembly.GetType** and use reflection on the retrieved type.

Requirements

Platforms: Windows 98, Windows NT 4.0, Windows Millennium Edition, Windows 2000, Windows XP Home Edition, Windows XP Professional, Windows .NET Server family

EnumBuilder.GetInterfaceMap Method

Returns an interface mapping for the interface requested.

```
[Visual Basic]
Overrides Public Function GetInterfaceMap( _
   ByVal interfaceType As Type _
) As InterfaceMapping
```

```
[C#]
public override InterfaceMapping GetInterfaceMap(
   Type interfaceType
);
```

```
[C++]
public: InterfaceMapping GetInterfaceMap(
   Type* interfaceType
);
```

```
[JScript]
public override function GetInterfaceMap(
   interfaceType : Type
) : InterfaceMapping;
```

Parameters

interfaceType

The type of the interface for which the interface mapping is to be retrieved.

Return Value

The requested interface mapping.

Exceptions

Exception Type	Condition
ArgumentException	The type does not implement the interface.

Remarks

As a workaround, to retrieve the interface mapping types of a finished type, retrieve the type using **Type.GetType** or **Assembly.GetType** and use reflection on the retrieved type.

Requirements

Platforms: Windows 98, Windows NT 4.0, Windows Millennium Edition, Windows 2000, Windows XP Home Edition, Windows XP Professional, Windows .NET Server family

EnumBuilder.GetInterfaces Method

Returns an array of all the interfaces implemented on this a class and its base classes.

```
[Visual Basic]
Overrides Public Function GetInterfaces() As Type()
[C#]
public override Type[] GetInterfaces();
[C++]
public: Type* GetInterfaces() [];
[JScript]
public override function GetInterfaces() : Type[];
```

Return Value

Returns an array of **Type** objects representing the implemented interfaces. If none are defined, an empty array is returned.

Remarks

As a workaround, to retrieve the interface of a finished type, retrieve the type using **Type.GetType** or **Assembly.GetType** and use reflection on the retrieved type.

Requirements

Platforms: Windows 98, Windows NT 4.0, Windows Millennium Edition, Windows 2000, Windows XP Home Edition, Windows XP Professional, Windows .NET Server family

EnumBuilder.GetMember Method

Overload List

Returns all the public and non-public members declared or inherited by this type, as specified.

[Visual Basic] **Overloads Overrides Public Function GetMember(String, MemberTypes, BindingFlags) As MemberInfo()**

[C#] **public override MemberInfo[] GetMember(string, MemberTypes, BindingFlags);**

[C++] **public: MemberInfo* GetMember(String*, MemberTypes, BindingFlags) [];**

[JScript] **public override function GetMember(String, MemberTypes, BindingFlags) : MemberInfo[];**

Inherited from **Type**.

[Visual Basic] **Overloads Public Function GetMember(String) As MemberInfo()**

[C#] **public MemberInfo[] GetMember(string);**

[C++] **public: MemberInfo* GetMember(String*) [];**

[JScript] **public function GetMember(String) : MemberInfo[];**

Inherited from **Type**.

[Visual Basic] **Overloads Public Overridable Function GetMember(String, BindingFlags) As MemberInfo() Implements IReflect.GetMember**

[C#] **public virtual MemberInfo[] GetMember(string, BindingFlags);**

[C++] **public: virtual MemberInfo* GetMember(String*, BindingFlags) [];**

[JScript] **public function GetMember(String, BindingFlags) : MemberInfo[];**

EnumBuilder.GetMember Method (String, MemberTypes, BindingFlags)

Returns all the public and non-public members declared or inherited by this type, as specified.

```
[Visual Basic]
Overrides Overloads Public Function GetMember( _
   ByVal name As String, _
   ByVal type As MemberTypes, _
   ByVal bindingAttr As BindingFlags _
) As MemberInfo()
[C#]
public override MemberInfo[] GetMember(
   string name,
   MemberTypes type,
   BindingFlags bindingAttr
);
[C++]
public: MemberInfo* GetMember(
   String* name,
   MemberTypes type,
   BindingFlags bindingAttr
) [];
[JScript]
public override function GetMember(
   name : String,
   type : MemberTypes,
   bindingAttr : BindingFlags
) : MemberInfo[];
```

Parameters

name

The name of the member.

type

The type of member that is to be returned.

bindingAttr

This must be a bit flag from **BindingFlags: InvokeMethod, NonPublic**, and so on.

Return Value

Returns an array of **MemberInfo** objects representing the public and non-public members defined on this type if *nonPublic* is used; otherwise, only the public members are returned.

Exceptions

Exception Type	Condition
NotSupportedException	This method is not currently supported in types that are not complete.

Remarks

As a workaround, to retrieve the member of a finished type, retrieve the type using **Type.GetType** or **Assembly.GetType** and use reflection on the retrieved type.

Requirements

Platforms: Windows 98, Windows NT 4.0, Windows Millennium Edition, Windows 2000, Windows XP Home Edition, Windows XP Professional, Windows .NET Server family

EnumBuilder.GetMembers Method

Overload List

Returns all the public and non-public members declared or inherited by this type, as specified.

[Visual Basic] **Overloads Overrides Public Function GetMembers(BindingFlags) As MemberInfo() Implements IReflect.GetMembers**

[C#] **public override MemberInfo[] GetMembers (BindingFlags);**

[C++] **public: MemberInfo* GetMembers(BindingFlags) [];**

[JScript] **public override function GetMembers(Binding Flags) : MemberInfo[];**

Inherited from **Type**.

[Visual Basic] **Overloads Public Function GetMembers() As MemberInfo()**

[C#] **public MemberInfo[] GetMembers();**

[C++] **public: MemberInfo* GetMembers() [];**

[JScript] **public function GetMembers() : MemberInfo[];**

EnumBuilder.GetMembers Method (BindingFlags)

Returns all the public and non-public members declared or inherited by this type, as specified.

```
[Visual Basic]
Overrides Overloads Public Function GetMembers( _
   ByVal bindingAttr As BindingFlags _
) As MemberInfo() Implements IReflect.GetMembers
[C#]
public override MemberInfo[] GetMembers(
   BindingFlags bindingAttr
);
[C++]
public: MemberInfo* GetMembers(
   BindingFlags bindingAttr
) [];
```

```
[JScript]
public override function GetMembers(
   bindingAttr : BindingFlags
) : MemberInfo[];
```

Parameters

bindingAttr

This must be a bit flag from **BindingFlags**: **InvokeMethod**, **NonPublic**, and so on.

Return Value

Returns an array of **MemberInfo** objects representing the public and non-public members declared or inherited by this type. An empty array is returned if there are no matching members.

Implements

IReflect.GetMembers

Exceptions

Exception Type	Condition
NotSupportedException	This method is not currently supported in types that are not complete.

Remarks

As a workaround, to retrieve the members of a finished type, retrieve the type using **Type.GetType** or **Assembly.GetType** and use reflection on the retrieved type.

Requirements

Platforms: Windows 98, Windows NT 4.0, Windows Millennium Edition, Windows 2000, Windows XP Home Edition, Windows XP Professional, Windows .NET Server family

EnumBuilder.GetMethodImpl Method

Searches for the specified method whose parameters match the specified argument types and modifiers, using the specified binding constraints and the specified calling convention.

```
[Visual Basic]
Overrides Protected Function GetMethodImpl( _
   ByVal name As String, _
   ByVal bindingAttr As BindingFlags, _
   ByVal binder As Binder, _
   ByVal callConvention As CallingConventions, _
   ByVal types() As Type, _
   ByVal modifiers() As ParameterModifier _
) As MethodInfo
[C#]
protected override MethodInfo GetMethodImpl(
   string name,
   BindingFlags bindingAttr,
   Binder binder,
   CallingConventions callConvention,
   Type[] types,
   ParameterModifier[] modifiers
);
[C++]
protected: MethodInfo* GetMethodImpl(
   String* name,
   BindingFlags bindingAttr,
   Binder* binder,
```

```
CallingConventions callConvention,
    Type* types[],
    ParameterModifier modifiers[]
);
[JScript]
protected override function GetMethodImpl(
    name : String,
    bindingAttr : BindingFlags,
    binder : Binder,
    callConvention : CallingConventions,
    types : Type[],
    modifiers : ParameterModifier[]
) : MethodInfo;
```

Parameters

name
> The **String** containing the name of the method to get.

bindingAttr
> A bitmask comprised of one or more **BindingFlags** that specify how the search is conducted.
>
> -or-
>
> Zero, to conduct a case-sensitive search for public methods.

binder
> A **Binder** object that defines a set of properties and enables binding, which can involve selection of an overloaded method, coercion of argument types, and invocation of a member through reflection.
>
> -or-
>
> A null reference (**Nothing** in Visual Basic), to use the **DefaultBinder**.

callConvention
> The **CallingConventions** object that specifies the set of rules to use regarding the order and layout of arguments, how the return value is passed, what registers are used for arguments, and what process cleans up the stack.

types
> An array of **Type** objects representing the number, order, and type of the parameters for the method to get.
>
> -or-
>
> An empty array of the type **Type** (that is, Type[] types = new Type[0]) to get a method that takes no parameters.

modifiers
> An array of **ParameterModifier** objects representing the attributes associated with the corresponding element in the *types* array.

Return Value

A **MethodInfo** object representing the method that matches the specified requirements, if found; otherwise, a null reference (**Nothing** in Visual Basic).

Exceptions

Exception Type	Condition
NotSupportedException	This method is not currently supported in types that are not complete.

Remarks

As a workaround, to retrieve the method, retrieve the type using **Type.GetType** or **Assembly.GetType** and use reflection on the retrieved type.

Requirements

Platforms: Windows 98, Windows NT 4.0, Windows Millennium Edition, Windows 2000, Windows XP Home Edition, Windows XP Professional, Windows .NET Server family

EnumBuilder.GetMethods Method

Overload List

Returns all the public and non-public methods declared or inherited by this type, as specified.

> [Visual Basic] **Overloads Overrides Public Function GetMethods(BindingFlags) As MethodInfo() Implements IReflect.GetMethods**
>
> [C#] **public override MethodInfo[] GetMethods (BindingFlags);**
>
> [C++] **public: MethodInfo* GetMethods(BindingFlags) [];**
>
> [JScript] **public override function GetMethods(BindingFlags) : MethodInfo[];**

Inherited from **Type**.

> [Visual Basic] **Overloads Public Function GetMethods() As MethodInfo()**
>
> [C#] **public MethodInfo[] GetMethods();**
>
> [C++] **public: MethodInfo* GetMethods() [];**
>
> [JScript] **public function GetMethods() : MethodInfo[];**

EnumBuilder.GetMethods Method (BindingFlags)

Returns all the public and non-public methods declared or inherited by this type, as specified.

```
[Visual Basic]
Overrides Overloads Public Function GetMethods( _
    ByVal bindingAttr As BindingFlags _
) As MethodInfo() Implements IReflect.GetMethods
[C#]
public override MethodInfo[] GetMethods(
    BindingFlags bindingAttr
);
[C++]
public: MethodInfo* GetMethods(
    BindingFlags bindingAttr
) [];
[JScript]
public override function GetMethods(
    bindingAttr : BindingFlags
) : MethodInfo[];
```

Parameters

bindingAttr
> This must be a bit flag from **BindingFlags**, such as **InvokeMethod**, **NonPublic**, and so on.

Return Value

Returns an array of **MethodInfo** objects representing the public and non-public methods defined on this type if *nonPublic* is used; otherwise, only the public methods are returned.

Implements

IReflect.GetMethods

Exceptions

Exception Type	Condition
NotSupportedException	This method is not currently supported in types that are not complete.

Remarks

As a workaround, to retrieve the methods of a finished type, retrieve the type using **Type.GetType** or **Assembly.GetType** and use reflection on the retrieved type.

Requirements

Platforms: Windows 98, Windows NT 4.0, Windows Millennium Edition, Windows 2000, Windows XP Home Edition, Windows XP Professional, Windows .NET Server family

EnumBuilder.GetNestedType Method

Overload List

Returns the public and non-public nested types that are declared by this type.

[Visual Basic] **Overloads Overrides Public Function GetNestedType(String, BindingFlags) As Type**

[C#] **public override Type GetNestedType(string, BindingFlags);**

[C++] **public: Type* GetNestedType(String*, BindingFlags);**

[JScript] **public override function GetNestedType(String, BindingFlags) : Type;**

Inherited from **Type**.

[Visual Basic] **Overloads Public Function GetNestedType (String) As Type**

[C#] **public Type GetNestedType(string);**

[C++] **public: Type* GetNestedType(String*);**

[JScript] **public function GetNestedType(String) : Type;**

EnumBuilder.GetNestedType Method (String, BindingFlags)

Returns the public and non-public nested types that are declared by this type.

```
[Visual Basic]
Overrides Overloads Public Function GetNestedType( _
   ByVal name As String, _
   ByVal bindingAttr As BindingFlags _
) As Type
[C#]
public override Type GetNestedType(
   string name,
   BindingFlags bindingAttr
);
[C++]
public: Type* GetNestedType(
   String* name,
   BindingFlags bindingAttr
);
```

```
[JScript]
public override function GetNestedType(
   name : String,
   bindingAttr : BindingFlags
) : Type;
```

Parameters

name
   The **String** containing the name of the nested type to get.
bindingAttr
   A bitmask comprised of one or more **BindingFlags** that specify how the search is conducted.
   -or-
   Zero, to conduct a case-sensitive search for public methods.

Return Value

A **Type** object representing the nested type that matches the specified requirements, if found; otherwise, a null reference (**Nothing** in Visual Basic).

Exceptions

Exception Type	Condition
NotSupportedException	This method is not currently supported in types that are not complete.

Remarks

As a workaround, to retrieve the nested type of a finished type, retrieve the type using **Type.GetType** or **Assembly.GetType** and use reflection on the retrieved type.

Requirements

Platforms: Windows 98, Windows NT 4.0, Windows Millennium Edition, Windows 2000, Windows XP Home Edition, Windows XP Professional, Windows .NET Server family

EnumBuilder.GetNestedTypes Method

Overload List

Returns the public and non-public nested types that are declared or inherited by this type.

[Visual Basic] **Overloads Overrides Public Function GetNestedTypes(BindingFlags) As Type()**

[C#] **public override Type[] GetNestedTypes(BindingFlags);**

[C++] **public: Type* GetNestedTypes(BindingFlags) [];**

[JScript] **public override function GetNestedTypes (BindingFlags) : Type[];**

Inherited from **Type**.

[Visual Basic] **Overloads Public Function GetNestedTypes() As Type()**

[C#] **public Type[] GetNestedTypes();**

[C++] **public: Type* GetNestedTypes() [];**

[JScript] **public function GetNestedTypes() : Type[];**

EnumBuilder.GetNestedTypes Method (BindingFlags)

Returns the public and non-public nested types that are declared or inherited by this type.

```
[Visual Basic]
Overrides Overloads Public Function GetNestedTypes( _
    ByVal bindingAttr As BindingFlags _
) As Type()
[C#]
public override Type[] GetNestedTypes(
    BindingFlags bindingAttr
);
[C++]
public: Type* GetNestedTypes(
    BindingFlags bindingAttr
) [];
[JScript]
public override function GetNestedTypes(
    bindingAttr : BindingFlags
) : Type[];
```

Parameters

bindingAttr

This must be a bit flag from **BindingFlags**, such as **InvokeMethod**, **NonPublic**, and so on.

Return Value

An array of **Type** objects representing all the types nested within the current **Type** that match the specified binding constraints.

An empty array of type **Type**, if no types are nested within the current **Type**, or if none of the nested types match the binding constraints.

Exceptions

Exception Type	Condition
NotSupportedException	This method is not currently supported in types that are not complete.

Remarks

As a workaround, to retrieve the nested types of a finished type, retrieve the type using **Type.GetType** or **Assembly.GetType** and use reflection on the retrieved type.

Requirements

Platforms: Windows 98, Windows NT 4.0, Windows Millennium Edition, Windows 2000, Windows XP Home Edition, Windows XP Professional, Windows .NET Server family

EnumBuilder.GetProperties Method

Overload List

Returns all the public and non-public properties declared or inherited by this type, as specified.

[Visual Basic] **Overloads Overrides Public Function GetProperties(BindingFlags) As PropertyInfo() Implements IReflect.GetProperties**

[C#] **public override PropertyInfo[] GetProperties (BindingFlags);**

[C++] **public: PropertyInfo* GetProperties(BindingFlags) [];**

[JScript] **public override function GetProperties (BindingFlags) : PropertyInfo[];**

Inherited from **Type**.

[Visual Basic] **Overloads Public Function GetProperties() As PropertyInfo()**

[C#] **public PropertyInfo[] GetProperties();**

[C++] **public: PropertyInfo* GetProperties() [];**

[JScript] **public function GetProperties() : PropertyInfo[];**

EnumBuilder.GetProperties Method (BindingFlags)

Returns all the public and non-public properties declared or inherited by this type, as specified.

```
[Visual Basic]
Overrides Overloads Public Function GetProperties( _
    ByVal bindingAttr As BindingFlags _
) As PropertyInfo() Implements IReflect.GetProperties
[C#]
public override PropertyInfo[] GetProperties(
    BindingFlags bindingAttr
);
[C++]
public: PropertyInfo* GetProperties(
    BindingFlags bindingAttr
) [];
[JScript]
public override function GetProperties(
    bindingAttr : BindingFlags
) : PropertyInfo[];
```

Parameters

bindingAttr

This invocation attribute. This must be a bit flag from **BindingFlags**: **InvokeMethod**, **NonPublic**, and so on.

Return Value

Returns an array of **PropertyInfo** objects representing the public and non-public properties defined on this type if *nonPublic* is used; otherwise, only the public properties are returned.

Implements

IReflect.GetProperties

Exceptions

Exception Type	Condition
NotSupportedException	This method is not currently supported in types that are not complete.

Remarks

As a workaround, to retrieve the properties of a finished type, retrieve the type using **Type.GetType** or **Assembly.GetType** and use reflection on the retrieved type.

Requirements

Platforms: Windows 98, Windows NT 4.0, Windows Millennium Edition, Windows 2000, Windows XP Home Edition, Windows XP Professional, Windows .NET Server family

EnumBuilder.GetPropertyImpl Method

Searches for the specified property whose parameters match the specified argument types and modifiers, using the specified binding constraints.

```
[Visual Basic]
Overrides Protected Function GetPropertyImpl( _
   ByVal name As String, _
   ByVal bindingAttr As BindingFlags, _
   ByVal binder As Binder, _
   ByVal returnType As Type, _
   ByVal types() As Type, _
   ByVal modifiers() As ParameterModifier _
) As PropertyInfo
[C#]
protected override PropertyInfo GetPropertyImpl(
   string name,
   BindingFlags bindingAttr,
   Binder binder,
   Type returnType,
   Type[] types,
   ParameterModifier[] modifiers
);
[C++]
protected: PropertyInfo* GetPropertyImpl(
   String* name,
   BindingFlags bindingAttr,
   Binder* binder,
   Type* returnType,
   Type* types[],
   ParameterModifier modifiers[]
);
[JScript]
protected override function GetPropertyImpl(
   name : String,
   bindingAttr : BindingFlags,
   binder : Binder,
   returnType : Type,
   types : Type[],
   modifiers : ParameterModifier[]
) : PropertyInfo;
```

Parameters

name
> The **String** containing the name of the property to get.

bindingAttr
> A bitmask comprised of one or more **BindingFlags** that specify how the search is conducted.
> -or-
> Zero, to conduct a case-sensitive search for public properties.

binder
> A **Binder** object that defines a set of properties and enables binding, which can involve selection of an overloaded member, coercion of argument types, and invocation of a member through reflection.
> -or-
> A null reference (**Nothing** in Visual Basic), to use the **DefaultBinder**.

returnType
> The return type of the property.

types
> An array of **Type** objects representing the number, order, and type of the parameters for the indexed property to get.
> -or-
> An empty array of the type **Type** (that is, Type[] types = new Type[0]) to get a property that is not indexed.

modifiers
> An array of **ParameterModifier** objects representing the attributes associated with the corresponding element in the *types* array.

Return Value

A **PropertyInfo** object representing the property that matches the specified requirements, if found; otherwise, a null reference (**Nothing** in Visual Basic).

Exceptions

Exception Type	Condition
NotSupportedException	This method is not currently supported in types that are not complete.

Remarks

As a workaround, to retrieve the property of a finished type, retrieve the type using **Type.GetType** or **Assembly.GetType** and use reflection on the retrieved type.

Requirements

Platforms: Windows 98, Windows NT 4.0, Windows Millennium Edition, Windows 2000, Windows XP Home Edition, Windows XP Professional, Windows .NET Server family

EnumBuilder.HasElementTypeImpl Method

Calling this method always throws **NotSupportedException**.

```
[Visual Basic]
Overrides Protected Function HasElementTypeImpl() As Boolean
[C#]
protected override bool HasElementTypeImpl();
[C++]
protected: bool HasElementTypeImpl();
[JScript]
protected override function HasElementTypeImpl() : Boolean;
```

Return Value

This method is not supported. No value is returned.

Exceptions

Exception Type	Condition
NotSupportedException	This method is not supported.

Remarks

Retrieve the type using **Type.GetType** or **Assembly.GetType** and use reflection on the retrieved type.

Requirements

Platforms: Windows 98, Windows NT 4.0, Windows Millennium Edition, Windows 2000, Windows XP Home Edition, Windows XP Professional, Windows .NET Server family

EnumBuilder.InvokeMember Method

Overload List

Invokes the specified member. The method that is to be invoked must be accessible and provide the most specific match with the specified argument list, under the contraints of the specified binder and invocation attributes.

[Visual Basic] **Overloads Overrides Public Function InvokeMember(String, BindingFlags, Binder, Object, Object(), ParameterModifier(), CultureInfo, String()) As Object Implements IReflect.InvokeMember**

[C#] **public override object InvokeMember(string, BindingFlags, Binder, object, object[], ParameterModifier[], CultureInfo, string[]);**

[C++] **public: Object* InvokeMember(String*, BindingFlags, Binder*, Object*, Object[], ParameterModifier[], CultureInfo*, String*[]);**

[JScript] **public override function InvokeMember(String, BindingFlags, Binder, Object, Object[], ParameterModifier[], CultureInfo, String[]) : Object;**

Inherited from **Type**.

[Visual Basic] **Overloads Public Function InvokeMember (String, BindingFlags, Binder, Object, Object()) As Object**

[C#] **public object InvokeMember(string, BindingFlags, Binder, object, object[]);**

[C++] **public: Object* InvokeMember(String*, BindingFlags, Binder*, Object*, Object[]);**

[JScript] **public function InvokeMember(String, BindingFlags, Binder, Object, Object[]) : Object;**

Inherited from **Type**.

[Visual Basic] **Overloads Public Function InvokeMember (String, BindingFlags, Binder, Object, Object(), CultureInfo) As Object**

[C#] **public object InvokeMember(string, BindingFlags, Binder, object, object[], CultureInfo);**

[C++] **public: Object* InvokeMember(String*, BindingFlags, Binder*, Object*, Object[], CultureInfo*);**

[JScript] **public function InvokeMember(String, Binding-Flags, Binder, Object, Object[], CultureInfo) : Object;**

EnumBuilder.InvokeMember Method (String, BindingFlags, Binder, Object, Object[], ParameterModifier[], CultureInfo, String[])

Invokes the specified member. The method that is to be invoked must be accessible and provide the most specific match with the specified argument list, under the contraints of the specified binder and invocation attributes.

```
[Visual Basic]
Overrides Overloads Public Function InvokeMember( _
    ByVal name As String, _
    ByVal invokeAttr As BindingFlags, _
    ByVal binder As Binder, _
    ByVal target As Object, _
    ByVal args() As Object, _
    ByVal modifiers() As ParameterModifier, _
    ByVal culture As CultureInfo, _
    ByVal namedParameters() As String _
) As Object Implements IReflect.InvokeMember
```

```
[C#]
public override object InvokeMember(
    string name,
    BindingFlags invokeAttr,
    Binder binder,
    object target,
    object[] args,
    ParameterModifier[] modifiers,
    CultureInfo culture,
    string[] namedParameters
);
```

```
[C++]
public: Object* InvokeMember(
    String* name,
    BindingFlags invokeAttr,
    Binder* binder,
    Object* target,
    Object* args __gc[],
    ParameterModifier modifiers[],
    CultureInfo* culture,
    String* namedParameters __gc[]
);
```

```
[JScript]
public override function InvokeMember(
    name : String,
    invokeAttr : BindingFlags,
    binder : Binder,
    target : Object,
    args : Object[],
    modifiers : ParameterModifier[],
    culture : CultureInfo,
    namedParameters : String[]
) : Object;
```

Parameters

name
The name of the member to invoke. This can be a constructor, method, property, or field. A suitable invocation attribute must be specified. Note that it is possible to invoke the default member of a class by passing an empty string as the name of the member.

invokeAttr
The invocation attribute. This must be a bit flag from **BindingFlags**.

binder
An object that enables the binding, coercion of argument types, invocation of members, and retrieval of **MemberInfo** objects using reflection. If binder is a null reference (**Nothing** in Visual Basic), the default binder is used. See **Binder**.

target
The object on which to invoke the specified member. If the member is static, this parameter is ignored.

args
An argument list. This is an array of objects that contains the number, order, and type of the parameters of the member to be invoked. If there are no parameters this should be null.

modifiers
An array of the same length as *args* with elements that represent the attributes associated with the arguments of the member to be invoked. A parameter has attributes associated with it in the metadata. They are used by various interoperability services. See the metadata specs for details such as this.

culture

> An instance of **CultureInfo** used to govern the coercion of types. If this is null, the **CultureInfo** for the current thread is used. (Note that this is necessary to, for example, convert a string that represents 1000 to a double value, since 1000 is represented differently by different cultures.)

namedParameters

> Each parameter in the *namedParameters* array gets the value in the corresponding element in the *args* array. If the length of *args* is greater than the length of *namedParameters*, the remaining argument values are passed in order.

Return Value

Returns the return value of the invoked member.

Implements

IReflect.InvokeMember

Exceptions

Exception Type	Condition
NotSupportedException	This method is not currently supported in types that are not complete.

Remarks

You can retrieve the type using **Type.GetType** or **Assembly.GetType** and use reflection on the retrieved type.

Requirements

Platforms: Windows 98, Windows NT 4.0, Windows Millennium Edition, Windows 2000, Windows XP Home Edition, Windows XP Professional, Windows .NET Server family

EnumBuilder.IsArrayImpl Method

Returns **false**.

```
[Visual Basic]
Overrides Protected Function IsArrayImpl() As Boolean
[C#]
protected override bool IsArrayImpl();
[C++]
protected: bool IsArrayImpl();
[JScript]
protected override function IsArrayImpl() : Boolean;
```

Return Value

The return value is **false**.

Requirements

Platforms: Windows 98, Windows NT 4.0, Windows Millennium Edition, Windows 2000, Windows XP Home Edition, Windows XP Professional, Windows .NET Server family

EnumBuilder.IsByRefImpl Method

Returns **false**.

```
[Visual Basic]
Overrides Protected Function IsByRefImpl() As Boolean
[C#]
protected override bool IsByRefImpl();
```

```
[C++]
protected: bool IsByRefImpl();
[JScript]
protected override function IsByRefImpl() : Boolean;
```

Return Value

The return value is **false**.

Requirements

Platforms: Windows 98, Windows NT 4.0, Windows Millennium Edition, Windows 2000, Windows XP Home Edition, Windows XP Professional, Windows .NET Server family

EnumBuilder.IsCOMObjectImpl Method

Returns **false**.

```
[Visual Basic]
Overrides Protected Function IsCOMObjectImpl() As Boolean
[C#]
protected override bool IsCOMObjectImpl();
[C++]
protected: bool IsCOMObjectImpl();
[JScript]
protected override function IsCOMObjectImpl() : Boolean;
```

Return Value

The return value is **false**.

Requirements

Platforms: Windows 98, Windows NT 4.0, Windows Millennium Edition, Windows 2000, Windows XP Home Edition, Windows XP Professional, Windows .NET Server family

EnumBuilder.IsDefined Method

Checks if the specified custom attribute type is defined.

```
[Visual Basic]
Overrides Public Function IsDefined( _
   ByVal attributeType As Type, _
   ByVal inherit As Boolean _
) As Boolean Implements ICustomAttributeProvider.IsDefined
[C#]
public override bool IsDefined(
   Type attributeType,
   bool inherit
);
[C++]
public: bool IsDefined(
   Type* attributeType,
   bool inherit
);
[JScript]
public override function IsDefined(
   attributeType : Type,
   inherit : Boolean
) : Boolean;
```

Parameters

attributeType

The **Type** object to which the custom attributes are applied.

inherit

Specifies whether to search this member's inheritance chain to find the attributes.

Return Value

true if one or more instance of *attributeType* is defined on this member; otherwise, **false**.

Implements

ICustomAttributeProvider.IsDefined

Exceptions

Exception Type	Condition
NotSupportedException	This method is not currently supported in types that are not complete.

Remarks

As a workaround, to check if a custom attribute is defined for a finished type, retrieve the type using **GetType** and call **GetCustomAttributes** on the returned **Type**.

Requirements

Platforms: Windows 98, Windows NT 4.0, Windows Millennium Edition, Windows 2000, Windows XP Home Edition, Windows XP Professional, Windows .NET Server family

EnumBuilder.IsPointerImpl Method

Returns **false**.

```
[Visual Basic]
Overrides Protected Function IsPointerImpl() As Boolean
[C#]
protected override bool IsPointerImpl();
[C++]
protected: bool IsPointerImpl();
[JScript]
protected override function IsPointerImpl() : Boolean;
```

Return Value

The return value is **false**.

Requirements

Platforms: Windows 98, Windows NT 4.0, Windows Millennium Edition, Windows 2000, Windows XP Home Edition, Windows XP Professional, Windows .NET Server family

EnumBuilder.IsPrimitiveImpl Method

Returns **false**.

```
[Visual Basic]
Overrides Protected Function IsPrimitiveImpl() As Boolean
[C#]
protected override bool IsPrimitiveImpl();
[C++]
protected: bool IsPrimitiveImpl();
[JScript]
protected override function IsPrimitiveImpl() : Boolean;
```

Return Value

The return value is **false**.

Requirements

Platforms: Windows 98, Windows NT 4.0, Windows Millennium Edition, Windows 2000, Windows XP Home Edition, Windows XP Professional, Windows .NET Server family

EnumBuilder.IsValueTypeImpl Method

Returns **true**.

```
[Visual Basic]
Overrides Protected Function IsValueTypeImpl() As Boolean
[C#]
protected override bool IsValueTypeImpl();
[C++]
protected: bool IsValueTypeImpl();
[JScript]
protected override function IsValueTypeImpl() : Boolean;
```

Return Value

The return value is **true**.

Requirements

Platforms: Windows 98, Windows NT 4.0, Windows Millennium Edition, Windows 2000, Windows XP Home Edition, Windows XP Professional, Windows .NET Server family

EnumBuilder.SetCustomAttribute Method

Sets custom attributes for this constructor.

Overload List

Sets a custom attribute using a custom attribute builder.

[Visual Basic] **Overloads Public Sub SetCustomAttribute(CustomAttributeBuilder)**

[C#] **public void SetCustomAttribute (CustomAttributeBuilder);**

[C++] **public: void SetCustomAttribute (CustomAttributeBuilder*);**

[JScript] **public function SetCustomAttribute (CustomAttributeBuilder);**

Sets a custom attribute using a specified custom attribute blob.

[Visual Basic] **Overloads Public Sub SetCustomAttribute (ConstructorInfo, Byte())**

[C#] **public void SetCustomAttribute(ConstructorInfo, byte[]);**

[C++] **public: void SetCustomAttribute(ConstructorInfo*, unsigned char __gc[]);**

[JScript] **public function SetCustomAttribute (ConstructorInfo, Byte[]);**

Example

See related example in the **System.Reflection.Emit.EnumBuilder** class topic.

EnumBuilder.SetCustomAttribute Method (CustomAttributeBuilder)

Sets a custom attribute using a custom attribute builder.

```
[Visual Basic]
Overloads Public Sub SetCustomAttribute( _
   ByVal customBuilder As CustomAttributeBuilder _
)
[C#]
public void SetCustomAttribute(
   CustomAttributeBuilder customBuilder
);
[C++]
public: void SetCustomAttribute(
   CustomAttributeBuilder* customBuilder
);
[JScript]
public function SetCustomAttribute(
   customBuilder : CustomAttributeBuilder
);
```

Parameters

customBuilder
    An instance of a helper class to define the custom attribute.

Exceptions

Exception Type	Condition
ArgumentNullException	*con* is a null reference (**Nothing** in Visual Basic).

Example

See related example in the **System.Reflection.Emit.EnumBuilder** class topic.

Requirements

Platforms: Windows 98, Windows NT 4.0, Windows Millennium Edition, Windows 2000, Windows XP Home Edition, Windows XP Professional, Windows .NET Server family

EnumBuilder.SetCustomAttribute Method (ConstructorInfo, Byte[])

Sets a custom attribute using a specified custom attribute blob.

```
[Visual Basic]
Overloads Public Sub SetCustomAttribute( _
   ByVal con As ConstructorInfo, _
   ByVal binaryAttribute() As Byte _
)
[C#]
public void SetCustomAttribute(
   ConstructorInfo con,
   byte[] binaryAttribute
);
[C++]
public: void SetCustomAttribute(
   ConstructorInfo* con,
   unsigned char binaryAttribute __gc[]
);
```

```
[JScript]
public function SetCustomAttribute(
   con : ConstructorInfo,
   binaryAttribute : Byte[]
);
```

Parameters

con
    The constructor for the custom attribute.
binaryAttribute
    A byte blob representing the attributes.

Exceptions

Exception Type	Condition
ArgumentNullException	*con* or *binaryAttribute* is a null reference (**Nothing** in Visual Basic).

Remarks

See the metadata specification in the ECMA Partition II documentation for details on how to format *binaryAttribute*. The Partition II documentation is included with the .NET Framework SDK installation, and can be found in the %\Microsoft.NET\FrameworkSDK\Tool Developers Guide\docs directory.

Example

See related example in the **System.Reflection.Emit.EnumBuilder** class topic.

Requirements

Platforms: Windows 98, Windows NT 4.0, Windows Millennium Edition, Windows 2000, Windows XP Home Edition, Windows XP Professional, Windows .NET Server family

EventBuilder Class

Defines events for a class.

System.Object
  System.Reflection.Emit.EventBuilder

```
[Visual Basic]
NotInheritable Public Class EventBuilder
[C#]
public sealed class EventBuilder
[C++]
public __gc __sealed class EventBuilder
[JScript]
public class EventBuilder
```

Thread Safety

Reflection Emit is thread-safe when using assemblies that were created with the **AppDomain.DefineDynamicAssembly** method with the Boolean parameter *isSynchronized* set to **true**.

Remarks

An **EventBuilder** is always associated with a **TypeBuilder**. The TypeBuilder.DefineEvent method will return a new **EventBuilder** to a client.

Requirements

Namespace: System.Reflection.Emit

Platforms: Windows 98, Windows NT 4.0, Windows Millennium Edition, Windows 2000, Windows XP Home Edition, Windows XP Professional, Windows .NET Server family

Assembly: Mscorlib (in Mscorlib.dll)

EventBuilder.AddOtherMethod Method

Adds one of the "other" methods associated with this event. "Other" methods are methods other than the "on" and "raise" methods associated with an event. This function can be called many times to add as many "other" methods.

```
[Visual Basic]
Public Sub AddOtherMethod( _
   ByVal mdBuilder As MethodBuilder _
)
[C#]
public void AddOtherMethod(
   MethodBuilder mdBuilder
);
[C++]
public: void AddOtherMethod(
   MethodBuilder* mdBuilder
);
[JScript]
public function AddOtherMethod(
   mdBuilder : MethodBuilder
);
```

Parameters

mdBuilder
  A **MethodBuilder** object that represents the other method.

Exceptions

Exception Type	Condition
ArgumentNullException	*mdBuilder* is a null reference (**Nothing** in Visual Basic).
InvalidOperationException	**CreateType** has been called on the enclosing type.

Requirements

Platforms: Windows 98, Windows NT 4.0, Windows Millennium Edition, Windows 2000, Windows XP Home Edition, Windows XP Professional, Windows .NET Server family

EventBuilder.GetEventToken Method

Returns the token for this event.

```
[Visual Basic]
Public Function GetEventToken() As EventToken
[C#]
public EventToken GetEventToken();
[C++]
public: EventToken GetEventToken();
[JScript]
public function GetEventToken() : EventToken;
```

Return Value

Returns the **EventToken** for this event.

Requirements

Platforms: Windows 98, Windows NT 4.0, Windows Millennium Edition, Windows 2000, Windows XP Home Edition, Windows XP Professional, Windows .NET Server family

EventBuilder.SetAddOnMethod Method

Sets the method used to subscribe to this event.

```
[Visual Basic]
Public Sub SetAddOnMethod( _
   ByVal mdBuilder As MethodBuilder _
)
[C#]
public void SetAddOnMethod(
   MethodBuilder mdBuilder
);
[C++]
public: void SetAddOnMethod(
   MethodBuilder* mdBuilder
);
[JScript]
public function SetAddOnMethod(
   mdBuilder : MethodBuilder
);
```

Parameters

mdBuilder
  A **MethodBuilder** object that represents the method used to subscribe to this event.

Exceptions

Exception Type	Condition
ArgumentNullException	*mdBuilder* is a null reference (**Nothing** in Visual Basic).
InvalidOperationException	**CreateType** has been called on the enclosing type.

Requirements

Platforms: Windows 98, Windows NT 4.0, Windows Millennium Edition, Windows 2000, Windows XP Home Edition, Windows XP Professional, Windows .NET Server family

EventBuilder.SetCustomAttribute Method

Sets custom attributes for this EventBuilder.

Overload List

Sets a custom attribute using a custom attribute builder.

[Visual Basic] **Overloads Public Sub SetCustomAttribute (CustomAttributeBuilder)**

[C#] **public void SetCustomAttribute (CustomAttributeBuilder);**

[C++] **public: void SetCustomAttribute (CustomAttributeBuilder*);**

[JScript] **public function SetCustomAttribute (CustomAttributeBuilder);**

Set a custom attribute using a specified custom attribute blob.

[Visual Basic] **Overloads Public Sub SetCustomAttribute (ConstructorInfo, Byte())**

[C#] **public void SetCustomAttribute(ConstructorInfo, byte[]);**

[C++] **public: void SetCustomAttribute(ConstructorInfo*, unsigned char __gc[]);**

[JScript] **public function SetCustomAttribute (ConstructorInfo, Byte[]);**

EventBuilder.SetCustomAttribute Method (CustomAttributeBuilder)

Sets a custom attribute using a custom attribute builder.

```
[Visual Basic]
Overloads Public Sub SetCustomAttribute( _
   ByVal customBuilder As CustomAttributeBuilder _
)
[C#]
public void SetCustomAttribute(
   CustomAttributeBuilder customBuilder
);
[C++]
public: void SetCustomAttribute(
   CustomAttributeBuilder* customBuilder
);
[JScript]
public function SetCustomAttribute(
   customBuilder : CustomAttributeBuilder
);
```

Parameters

customBuilder
    An instance of a helper class to describe the custom attribute.

Exceptions

Exception Type	Condition
ArgumentNullException	*con* is a null reference (**Nothing** in Visual Basic).
InvalidOperationException	**CreateType** has been called on the enclosing type.

Requirements

Platforms: Windows 98, Windows NT 4.0, Windows Millennium Edition, Windows 2000, Windows XP Home Edition, Windows XP Professional, Windows .NET Server family

EventBuilder.SetCustomAttribute Method (ConstructorInfo, Byte[])

Set a custom attribute using a specified custom attribute blob.

```
[Visual Basic]
Overloads Public Sub SetCustomAttribute( _
   ByVal con As ConstructorInfo, _
   ByVal binaryAttribute() As Byte _
)
[C#]
public void SetCustomAttribute(
   ConstructorInfo con,
   byte[] binaryAttribute
);
[C++]
public: void SetCustomAttribute(
   ConstructorInfo* con,
   unsigned char binaryAttribute __gc[]
);
[JScript]
public function SetCustomAttribute(
   con : ConstructorInfo,
   binaryAttribute : Byte[]
);
```

Parameters

con
    The constructor for the custom attribute.
binaryAttribute
    A byte blob representing the attributes.

Exceptions

Exception Type	Condition
ArgumentNullException	*con* or *binaryAttribute* is a null reference (**Nothing** in Visual Basic).
InvalidOperationException	**CreateType** has been called on the enclosing type.

Remarks

See the metadata specification in the ECMA Partition II documentation for details on how to format *binaryAttribute*. The Partition II documentation is included with the .NET Framework SDK installation, and can be found in the %\Microsoft.NET\FrameworkSDK\Tool Developers Guide\docs directory.

Requirements

Platforms: Windows 98, Windows NT 4.0, Windows Millennium Edition, Windows 2000, Windows XP Home Edition, Windows XP Professional, Windows .NET Server family

EventBuilder.SetRaiseMethod Method

Sets the method used to raise this event.

```
[Visual Basic]
Public Sub SetRaiseMethod( _
    ByVal mdBuilder As MethodBuilder _
)
[C#]
public void SetRaiseMethod(
    MethodBuilder mdBuilder
);
[C++]
public: void SetRaiseMethod(
    MethodBuilder* mdBuilder
);
[JScript]
public function SetRaiseMethod(
    mdBuilder : MethodBuilder
);
```

Parameters

mdBuilder
    A **MethodBuilder** object that represents the method used to raise this event.

Exceptions

Exception Type	Condition
ArgumentNullException	*mdBuilder* is a null reference (**Nothing** in Visual Basic).
InvalidOperationException	**CreateType** has been called on the enclosing type.

Requirements

Platforms: Windows 98, Windows NT 4.0, Windows Millennium Edition, Windows 2000, Windows XP Home Edition, Windows XP Professional, Windows .NET Server family

EventBuilder.SetRemoveOnMethod Method

Sets the method used to unsubscribe to this event.

```
[Visual Basic]
Public Sub SetRemoveOnMethod( _
    ByVal mdBuilder As MethodBuilder _
)
[C#]
public void SetRemoveOnMethod(
    MethodBuilder mdBuilder
);
[C++]
public: void SetRemoveOnMethod(
    MethodBuilder* mdBuilder
);
```

```
[JScript]
public function SetRemoveOnMethod(
    mdBuilder : MethodBuilder
);
```

Parameters

mdBuilder
    A **MethodBuilder** object that represents the method used to unsubscribe to this event.

Exceptions

Exception Type	Condition
ArgumentNullException	*mdBuilder* is a null reference (**Nothing** in Visual Basic).
InvalidOperationException	**CreateType** has been called on the enclosing type.

Requirements

Platforms: Windows 98, Windows NT 4.0, Windows Millennium Edition, Windows 2000, Windows XP Home Edition, Windows XP Professional, Windows .NET Server family

EventToken Structure

Represents the **Token** returned by the metadata to represent an event.

System.Object
　System.ValueType
　　System.Reflection.Emit.EventToken

```
[Visual Basic]
<Serializable>
Public Structure EventToken
[C#]
[Serializable]
public struct EventToken
[C++]
[Serializable]
public __value struct EventToken
```

[JScript] In JScript, you can use the structures in the .NET Framework, but you cannot define your own.

Thread Safety

Reflection Emit is thread-safe when using assemblies that were created with the **AppDomain.DefineDynamicAssembly** method with the Boolean parameter *isSynchronized* set to **true**.

Requirements

Namespace: System.Reflection.Emit

Platforms: Windows 98, Windows NT 4.0, Windows Millennium Edition, Windows 2000, Windows XP Home Edition, Windows XP Professional, Windows .NET Server family

Assembly: Mscorlib (in Mscorlib.dll)

EventToken.Empty Field

The default **EventToken** with **Token** value 0.

```
[Visual Basic]
Public Shared ReadOnly Empty As EventToken
[C#]
public static readonly EventToken Empty;
[C++]
public: static EventToken Empty;
[JScript]
public static var Empty : EventToken;
```

Requirements

Platforms: Windows 98, Windows NT 4.0, Windows Millennium Edition, Windows 2000, Windows XP Home Edition, Windows XP Professional, Windows .NET Server family

EventToken.Token Property

Retrieves the metadata token for this event.

```
[Visual Basic]
Public ReadOnly Property Token As Integer
[C#]
public int Token {get;}
[C++]
public: __property int get_Token();
```

```
[JScript]
public function get Token() : int;
```

Property Value

Read-only. Retrieves the metadata token for this event.

Requirements

Platforms: Windows 98, Windows NT 4.0, Windows Millennium Edition, Windows 2000, Windows XP Home Edition, Windows XP Professional, Windows .NET Server family

EventToken.Equals Method

Checks if the given object is an instance of **EventToken** and is equal to this instance.

```
[Visual Basic]
Overrides Public Function Equals( _
   ByVal obj As Object _
) As Boolean
[C#]
public override bool Equals(
   object obj
);
[C++]
public: bool Equals(
   Object* obj
);
[JScript]
public override function Equals(
   obj : Object
) : Boolean;
```

Parameters

obj
　　The object to be compared with this instance.

Return Value

Returns **true** if *obj* is an instance of **EventToken** and equals the current instance; otherwise, **false**.

Requirements

Platforms: Windows 98, Windows NT 4.0, Windows Millennium Edition, Windows 2000, Windows XP Home Edition, Windows XP Professional, Windows .NET Server family

EventToken.GetHashCode Method

Generates the hash code for this event.

```
[Visual Basic]
Overrides Public Function GetHashCode() As Integer
[C#]
public override int GetHashCode();
[C++]
public: int GetHashCode();
[JScript]
public override function GetHashCode() : int;
```

Return Value

Returns the hash code for this instance.

Requirements

Platforms: Windows 98, Windows NT 4.0,
Windows Millennium Edition, Windows 2000,
Windows XP Home Edition, Windows XP Professional,
Windows .NET Server family

FieldBuilder Class

Defines and represents a field. This class cannot be inherited.

System.Object
  System.Reflection.MemberInfo
    System.Reflection.FieldInfo
      System.Reflection.Emit.FieldBuilder

```
[Visual Basic]
NotInheritable Public Class FieldBuilder
   Inherits FieldInfo
[C#]
public sealed class FieldBuilder : FieldInfo
[C++]
public __gc __sealed class FieldBuilder : public FieldInfo
[JScript]
public class FieldBuilder extends FieldInfo
```

Thread Safety

Reflection Emit is thread-safe when using assemblies that were
created with the **AppDomain.DefineDynamicAssembly** method
with the Boolean parameter *isSynchronized* set to **true**.

Remarks

Get an instance of **FieldBuilder** by calling **DefineField**,
DefineInitializedData, or **DefineUninitializedData**.

> **Note** The **SetValue** method is currently not supported. As a
> workaround, retrieve the **FieldInfo** by reflecting on the
> finished type and call **SetValue** to set the value of the field.

Example

[Visual Basic, C#, C++] The following code sample illustrates the
use of **FieldBuilder**.

```
[Visual Basic]
Imports System
Imports System.Threading
Imports System.Reflection
Imports System.Reflection.Emit

Public Class FieldBuilder_Sample
   Private Shared Function CreateType(currentDomain As
AppDomain) As Type

      ' Create an assembly.
      Dim myAssemblyName As New AssemblyName()
      myAssemblyName.Name = "DynamicAssembly"
      Dim myAssembly As AssemblyBuilder =
currentDomain.DefineDynamicAssembly(myAssemblyName, _
                           AssemblyBuilderAccess.Run)
      ' Create a dynamic module in Dynamic Assembly.
      Dim myModuleBuilder As ModuleBuilder =
myAssembly.DefineDynamicModule("MyModule")
      ' Define a public class named "MyClass" in the assembly.
      Dim myTypeBuilder As TypeBuilder =
myModuleBuilder.DefineType("MyClass", _
                        TypeAttributes.Public)
      ' Define a private String field named "MyField" in the type.
      Dim myFieldBuilder As FieldBuilder =
myTypeBuilder.DefineField("MyField", _
                GetType(String), FieldAttributes.Private Or
FieldAttributes.Static)
      ' Create the constructor.
      Dim constructorArgs As Type() = {GetType(String)}
      Dim constructor As ConstructorBuilder = _

myTypeBuilder.DefineConstructor(MethodAttributes.Public, _
                     CallingConventions.Standard,
```

```
constructorArgs)
      Dim constructorIL As ILGenerator = constructor.GetILGenerator()
      constructorIL.Emit(OpCodes.Ldarg_0)
      Dim superConstructor As ConstructorInfo =
GetType(Object).GetConstructor(New Type() {})
      constructorIL.Emit(OpCodes.Call, superConstructor)
      constructorIL.Emit(OpCodes.Ldarg_0)
      constructorIL.Emit(OpCodes.Ldarg_1)
      constructorIL.Emit(OpCodes.Stfld, myFieldBuilder)
      constructorIL.Emit(OpCodes.Ret)

      ' Create the MyMethod method.
      Dim myMethodBuilder As MethodBuilder =
myTypeBuilder.DefineMethod("MyMethod", _
                     MethodAttributes.Public,
GetType(String), Nothing)
      Dim methodIL As ILGenerator = myMethodBuilder.GetILGenerator()
      methodIL.Emit(OpCodes.Ldarg_0)
      methodIL.Emit(OpCodes.Ldfld, myFieldBuilder)
      methodIL.Emit(OpCodes.Ret)
      Console.WriteLine("Name          :" + myFieldBuilder.Name)
      Console.WriteLine("DeclaringType : " +
myFieldBuilder.DeclaringType.ToString())
      Console.WriteLine("Type          :" +
myFieldBuilder.FieldType.ToString())
      Console.WriteLine("Token         :" +
myFieldBuilder.GetToken().Token.ToString())
      Return myTypeBuilder.CreateType()
   End Function 'CreateType
   Public Shared Sub Main()
      Try
         Dim myType As Type = CreateType(Thread.GetDomain())
         ' Create an instance of the "HelloWorld" class.
         Dim helloWorld As Object = Activator.CreateInstance _
(myType, New Object() {"HelloWorld"})
         ' Invoke the "MyMethod" method of the "MyClass" class.
         Dim myObject As Object = myType.InvokeMember("MyMethod", _
                     BindingFlags.InvokeMethod, Nothing, _
helloWorld, Nothing)
         Console.WriteLine("MyClass.MyMethod returned: " &
Microsoft.VisualBasic.Chr(34) & myObject &
Microsoft.VisualBasic.Chr(34) )
      Catch e as Exception
            Console.WriteLine("Exception Caught "+e.Message)
      End Try
   End Sub 'Main
End Class 'FieldBuilder_Sample

[C#]
using System;
using System.Threading;
using System.Reflection;
using System.Reflection.Emit;

public class FieldBuilder_Sample
{
   private static Type CreateType(AppDomain currentDomain)
   {

      // Create an assembly.
      AssemblyName myAssemblyName = new AssemblyName();
      myAssemblyName.Name = "DynamicAssembly";
      AssemblyBuilder myAssembly =
                  currentDomain.DefineDynamicAssembly(myAssemblyName,
AssemblyBuilderAccess.Run);
      // Create a dynamic module in Dynamic Assembly.
      ModuleBuilder
myModuleBuilder=myAssembly.DefineDynamicModule("MyModule");
      // Define a public class named "MyClass" in the assembly.
      TypeBuilder myTypeBuilder=
myModuleBuilder.DefineType("MyClass",TypeAttributes.Public);

      // Define a private String field named "MyField" in the type.
      FieldBuilder myFieldBuilder= myTypeBuilder.DefineField("MyField",
```

```
    typeof(string),FieldAttributes.Private|FieldAttributes.Static);
    // Create the constructor.
    Type[] constructorArgs = { typeof(String) };
    ConstructorBuilder constructor = myTypeBuilder.DefineConstructor(
        MethodAttributes.Public, CallingConventions.Standard,
constructorArgs);
    ILGenerator constructorIL = constructor.GetILGenerator();
    constructorIL.Emit(OpCodes.Ldarg_0);
    ConstructorInfo superConstructor =
typeof(Object).GetConstructor(new Type[0]);
    constructorIL.Emit(OpCodes.Call, superConstructor);
    constructorIL.Emit(OpCodes.Ldarg_0);
    constructorIL.Emit(OpCodes.Ldarg_1);
    constructorIL.Emit(OpCodes.Stfld, myFieldBuilder);
    constructorIL.Emit(OpCodes.Ret);

    // Create the MyMethod method.
    MethodBuilder myMethodBuilder=
myTypeBuilder.DefineMethod("MyMethod",
                    MethodAttributes.Public,typeof(String),null);
    ILGenerator methodIL = myMethodBuilder.GetILGenerator();
    methodIL.Emit(OpCodes.Ldarg_0);
    methodIL.Emit(OpCodes.Ldfld, myFieldBuilder);
    methodIL.Emit(OpCodes.Ret);
    Console.WriteLine("Name                    :"+myFieldBuilder.Name);
    Console.WriteLine("DeclaringType           :
"+myFieldBuilder.DeclaringType);
    Console.WriteLine("Type                    :"+myFieldBuilder.FieldType);
    Console.WriteLine("Token
:"+myFieldBuilder.GetToken().Token);
    return myTypeBuilder.CreateType();
}

public static void Main()
{
    try
    {
        Type myType = CreateType(Thread.GetDomain());
        // Create an instance of the "HelloWorld" class.
        Object helloWorld = Activator.CreateInstance(myType,
new Object[] { "HelloWorld" });
        // Invoke the "MyMethod" method of the "MyClass" class.
        Object myObject  = myType.InvokeMember("MyMethod",
                    BindingFlags.InvokeMethod, null,
helloWorld, null);
        Console.WriteLine("MyClass.MyMethod returned:
\"" + myObject + "\"");
    }
    catch( Exception e )
    {
        Console.WriteLine("Exception Caught "+e.Message);
    }
}
}

[C++]
#using <mscorlib.dll>

using namespace System;
using namespace System::Threading;
using namespace System::Reflection;
using namespace System::Reflection::Emit;

Type* CreateType(AppDomain* currentDomain)
{

    // Create an assembly.
    AssemblyName* myAssemblyName = new AssemblyName();
    myAssemblyName->Name = S"DynamicAssembly";
    AssemblyBuilder* myAssembly =
        currentDomain->DefineDynamicAssembly(myAssemblyName,
AssemblyBuilderAccess::Run);
    // Create a dynamic module in Dynamic Assembly.
    ModuleBuilder* myModuleBuilder=myAssembly-
>DefineDynamicModule(S"MyModule");
```

```
    // Define a public class named S"MyClass" in the assembly.
    TypeBuilder* myTypeBuilder= myModuleBuilder->DefineType
(S"MyClass", TypeAttributes::Public);

    // Define a private String field named S"MyField" in the type.
    FieldBuilder* myFieldBuilder= myTypeBuilder->DefineField(S"MyField",
        __typeof(String),
static_cast<FieldAttributes>(FieldAttributes::Private
|FieldAttributes::Static));
    // Create the constructor.
    Type* constructorArgs[] = { __typeof(String) };
    ConstructorBuilder* constructor = myTypeBuilder-
>DefineConstructor(MethodAttributes::Public,
CallingConventions::Standard, constructorArgs);
    ILGenerator* constructorIL = constructor->GetILGenerator();
    constructorIL->Emit(OpCodes::Ldarg_0);
    ConstructorInfo* superConstructor = __typeof(Object)-
>GetConstructor(new Type*[0]);
    constructorIL->Emit(OpCodes::Call, superConstructor);
    constructorIL->Emit(OpCodes::Ldarg_0);
    constructorIL->Emit(OpCodes::Ldarg_1);
    constructorIL->Emit(OpCodes::Stfld, myFieldBuilder);
    constructorIL->Emit(OpCodes::Ret);

    // Create the MyMethod method.
    MethodBuilder* myMethodBuilder= myTypeBuilder-
>DefineMethod(S"MyMethod",
        MethodAttributes::Public, __typeof(String), 0);
    ILGenerator* methodIL = myMethodBuilder->GetILGenerator();
    methodIL->Emit(OpCodes::Ldarg_0);
    methodIL->Emit(OpCodes::Ldfld, myFieldBuilder);
    methodIL->Emit(OpCodes::Ret);
    Console::WriteLine(S"Name                   : {0}",
myFieldBuilder->Name);
    Console::WriteLine(S"DeclaringType          : {0}",
myFieldBuilder->DeclaringType);
    Console::WriteLine(S"Type                   : {0}",
myFieldBuilder->FieldType);
    Console::WriteLine(S"Token                  : {0}",
__box(myFieldBuilder->GetToken().Token));
    return myTypeBuilder->CreateType();
}

void main() {
    try {
        Type* myType = CreateType(Thread::GetDomain());
        // Create an instance of the S"HelloWorld" class.
        Object* type[] = { S"HelloWorld" };
        Object* helloWorld = Activator::CreateInstance(myType, type);
        // Invoke the S"MyMethod" method of the S"MyClass" class.
        Object* myObject  = myType->InvokeMember(S"MyMethod",
            BindingFlags::InvokeMethod, 0, helloWorld, 0);
        Console::WriteLine(S"MyClass::MyMethod returned:
\"{0}\"", myObject);
    } catch (Exception* e) {
        Console::WriteLine(S"Exception Caught {0}", e->Message);
    }
}
```

Requirements

Namespace: System.Reflection.Emit

Platforms: Windows 98, Windows NT 4.0,
Windows Millennium Edition, Windows 2000,
Windows XP Home Edition, Windows XP Professional,
Windows .NET Server family

Assembly: Mscorlib (in Mscorlib.dll)

FieldBuilder.Attributes Property

Indicates the attributes of this field. This property is read-only.

```
[Visual Basic]
Overrides Public ReadOnly Property Attributes As FieldAttributes
[C#]
public override FieldAttributes Attributes {get;}
[C++]
public: __property FieldAttributes get_Attributes();
[JScript]
public override function get Attributes() : FieldAttributes;
```

Property Value

The attributes of this field.

Example

See related example in the **System.Reflection.Emit.FieldBuilder** class topic.

Requirements

Platforms: Windows 98, Windows NT 4.0, Windows Millennium Edition, Windows 2000, Windows XP Home Edition, Windows XP Professional, Windows .NET Server family

FieldBuilder.DeclaringType Property

Indicates a reference to the **Type** object for the type that declares this field. This property is read-only.

```
[Visual Basic]
Overrides Public ReadOnly Property DeclaringType As Type
[C#]
public override Type DeclaringType {get;}
[C++]
public: __property Type* get_DeclaringType();
[JScript]
public override function get DeclaringType() : Type;
```

Property Value

A reference to the **Type** object for the type that declares this field.

Requirements

Platforms: Windows 98, Windows NT 4.0, Windows Millennium Edition, Windows 2000, Windows XP Home Edition, Windows XP Professional, Windows .NET Server family

FieldBuilder.FieldHandle Property

Indicates the internal metadata handle for this field. This property is read-only.

```
[Visual Basic]
Overrides Public ReadOnly Property FieldHandle As _
    RuntimeFieldHandle
[C#]
public override RuntimeFieldHandle FieldHandle {get;}
[C++]
public: __property RuntimeFieldHandle get_FieldHandle();
[JScript]
public override function get FieldHandle() : RuntimeFieldHandle;
```

Property Value

The internal metadata handle for this field.

Exceptions

Exception Type	Condition
NotSupportedException	This method is not supported.

Requirements

Platforms: Windows 98, Windows NT 4.0, Windows Millennium Edition, Windows 2000, Windows XP Home Edition, Windows XP Professional, Windows .NET Server family

FieldBuilder.FieldType Property

Indicates the **Type** object that represents the type of this field. This property is read-only.

```
[Visual Basic]
Overrides Public ReadOnly Property FieldType As Type
[C#]
public override Type FieldType {get;}
[C++]
public: __property Type* get_FieldType();
[JScript]
public override function get FieldType() : Type;
```

Property Value

The **Type** object that represents the type of this field.

Requirements

Platforms: Windows 98, Windows NT 4.0, Windows Millennium Edition, Windows 2000, Windows XP Home Edition, Windows XP Professional, Windows .NET Server family

FieldBuilder.Name Property

Indicates the name of this field. This property is read-only.

```
[Visual Basic]
Overrides Public ReadOnly Property Name As String
[C#]
public override string Name {get;}
[C++]
public: __property String* get_Name();
[JScript]
public override function get Name() : String;
```

Property Value

A **String** containing the name of this field.

Example

See related example in the **System.Reflection.Emit.FieldBuilder** class topic.

Requirements

Platforms: Windows 98, Windows NT 4.0, Windows Millennium Edition, Windows 2000, Windows XP Home Edition, Windows XP Professional, Windows .NET Server family

FieldBuilder.ReflectedType Property

Indicates the reference to the **Type** object from which this object was obtained. This property is read-only.

```
[Visual Basic]
Overrides Public ReadOnly Property ReflectedType As Type
[C#]
public override Type ReflectedType {get;}
[C++]
public: __property Type* get_ReflectedType();
[JScript]
public override function get ReflectedType() : Type;
```

Property Value

A reference to the **Type** object from which this instance was obtained.

Remarks

A **FieldBuilder** object represents a field of a particular class. In order to obtain a **FieldBuilder** object, the **Type** object that represents the class that supports the field is queried. This property holds a reference to that **Type** object.

Example

See related example in the **System.Reflection.Emit.FieldBuilder** class topic.

Requirements

Platforms: Windows 98, Windows NT 4.0, Windows Millennium Edition, Windows 2000, Windows XP Home Edition, Windows XP Professional, Windows .NET Server family

FieldBuilder.GetCustomAttributes Method

Returns the custom attributes defined for this field.

Overload List

Returns all the custom attributes defined for this field.

[Visual Basic] **Overloads Overrides Public Function GetCustomAttributes(Boolean) As Object() Implements ICustomAttributeProvider.GetCustomAttributes**

[C#] **public override object[] GetCustomAttributes(bool);**

[C++] **public: Object* GetCustomAttributes(bool) __gc[];**

[JScript] **public override function GetCustomAttributes (Boolean) : Object[];**

Returns all the custom attributes defined for this field identified by the given type.

[Visual Basic] **Overloads Overrides Public Function GetCustomAttributes(Type, Boolean) As Object() Implements ICustomAttributeProvider.GetCustomAttributes**

[C#] **public override object[] GetCustomAttributes(Type, bool);**

[C++] **public: Object* GetCustomAttributes(Type*, bool) __gc[];**

[JScript] **public override function GetCustomAttributes (Type, Boolean) : Object[];**

FieldBuilder.GetCustomAttributes Method (Boolean)

Returns all the custom attributes defined for this field.

```
[Visual Basic]
Overrides Overloads Public Function GetCustomAttributes( _
    ByVal inherit As Boolean _
) As Object() Implements ICustomAttributeProvider.GetCustomAttributes
[C#]
public override object[] GetCustomAttributes(
    bool inherit
);
[C++]
public: Object* GetCustomAttributes(
    bool inherit
) __gc[];
[JScript]
public override function GetCustomAttributes(
    inherit : Boolean
) : Object[];
```

Parameters

inherit
Controls inheritance of custom attributes from base classes.

Return Value

An array of type **Object** representing all the custom attributes of the constructor represented by this **FieldBuilder** instance.

Implements

ICustomAttributeProvider.GetCustomAttributes

Exceptions

Exception Type	Condition
NotSupportedException	This method is not supported.

Requirements

Platforms: Windows 98, Windows NT 4.0, Windows Millennium Edition, Windows 2000, Windows XP Home Edition, Windows XP Professional, Windows .NET Server family

FieldBuilder.GetCustomAttributes Method (Type, Boolean)

Returns all the custom attributes defined for this field identified by the given type.

```
[Visual Basic]
Overrides Overloads Public Function GetCustomAttributes( _
    ByVal attributeType As Type, _
    ByVal inherit As Boolean _
) As Object() Implements ICustomAttributeProvider.GetCustomAttributes
[C#]
public override object[] GetCustomAttributes(
    Type attributeType,
    bool inherit
);
[C++]
public: Object* GetCustomAttributes(
    Type* attributeType,
    bool inherit
) __gc[];
[JScript]
public override function GetCustomAttributes(
    attributeType : Type,
    inherit : Boolean
) : Object[];
```

Parameters

attributeType
>   The custom attribute type.

inherit
>   Controls inheritance of custom attributes from base classes.

Return Value

An array of type **Object** representing all the custom attributes of the constructor represented by this **FieldBuilder** instance.

Implements

ICustomAttributeProvider.GetCustomAttributes

Exceptions

Exception Type	Condition
NotSupportedException	This method is not supported.

Requirements

Platforms: Windows 98, Windows NT 4.0, Windows Millennium Edition, Windows 2000, Windows XP Home Edition, Windows XP Professional, Windows .NET Server family

FieldBuilder.GetToken Method

Returns the token representing this field.

```
[Visual Basic]
Public Function GetToken() As FieldToken
[C#]
public FieldToken GetToken();
[C++]
public: FieldToken GetToken();
[JScript]
public function GetToken() : FieldToken;
```

Return Value

Returns the **FieldToken** object that represents the token for this field.

Requirements

Platforms: Windows 98, Windows NT 4.0, Windows Millennium Edition, Windows 2000, Windows XP Home Edition, Windows XP Professional, Windows .NET Server family

FieldBuilder.GetValue Method

Retrieves the value of the field supported by the given object.

```
[Visual Basic]
Overrides Public Function GetValue( _
   ByVal obj As Object _
) As Object
[C#]
public override object GetValue(
   object obj
);
[C++]
public: Object* GetValue(
   Object* obj
);
```

```
[JScript]
public override function GetValue(
   obj : Object
) : Object;
```

Parameters

obj
>   The object on which to access the field.

Return Value

An **Object** containing the value of the field reflected by this instance.

Exceptions

Exception Type	Condition
NotSupportedException	This method is not supported.

Remarks

If the field is static (**Shared** in Visual Basic), the *obj* parameter is ignored. For non-static fields, *obj* should be an instance of a class that inherits or declares the field.

The return type of **GetValue** is **Object**. For example, if the field holds a Boolean primitive value, an instance of **Object** with the appropriate Boolean value is returned. Before returning the value, **GetValue** checks to see if the user has access permission.

Access restrictions are ignored for fully-trusted code. **Private** constructors, methods, fields, and properties can be accessed and invoked using Reflection whenever the code is fully-trusted.

Requirements

Platforms: Windows 98, Windows NT 4.0, Windows Millennium Edition, Windows 2000, Windows XP Home Edition, Windows XP Professional, Windows .NET Server family

FieldBuilder.IsDefined Method

Indicates whether an attribute having the specified type is defined on a field.

```
[Visual Basic]
Overrides Public Function IsDefined( _
   ByVal attributeType As Type, _
   ByVal inherit As Boolean _
) As Boolean Implements ICustomAttributeProvider.IsDefined
[C#]
public override bool IsDefined(
   Type attributeType,
   bool inherit
);
[C++]
public: bool IsDefined(
   Type* attributeType,
   bool inherit
);
[JScript]
public override function IsDefined(
   attributeType : Type,
   inherit : Boolean
) : Boolean;
```

Parameters

attributeType
The type of the attribute.

inherit
Controls inheritance of custom attributes from base classes.

Return Value

true if one or more instance of *attributeType* is defined on this field; otherwise, **false**.

Implements

ICustomAttributeProvider.IsDefined

Exceptions

Exception Type	Condition
NotSupportedException	This method is not currently supported. Retrieve the field using **GetField** and call **IsDefined** on the returned **FieldInfo**.

Requirements

Platforms: Windows 98, Windows NT 4.0, Windows Millennium Edition, Windows 2000, Windows XP Home Edition, Windows XP Professional, Windows .NET Server family

FieldBuilder.SetConstant Method

Sets the default value of this field.

```
[Visual Basic]
Public Sub SetConstant( _
   ByVal defaultValue As Object _
)
[C#]
public void SetConstant(
   object defaultValue
);
[C++]
public: void SetConstant(
   Object* defaultValue
);
[JScript]
public function SetConstant(
   defaultValue : Object
);
```

Parameters

defaultValue
The new default value for this field.

Exceptions

Exception Type	Condition
InvalidOperationException	The containing type has been created using **CreateType**.

Remarks

defaultValue is restricted to the following types: **Boolean, SByte, Int16, Int32, Int64, Byte, UInt16, UInt32, UInt64, Single, Double, DateTime, Char, String,** and **Enum**. If the type of the field is **Decimal** or **Object**, *defaultValue* can only be null.

Requirements

Platforms: Windows 98, Windows NT 4.0, Windows Millennium Edition, Windows 2000, Windows XP Home Edition, Windows XP Professional, Windows .NET Server family

FieldBuilder.SetCustomAttribute Method

Sets a custom attribute.

Overload List

Sets a custom attribute using a custom attribute builder.

[Visual Basic] **Overloads Public Sub SetCustomAttribute (CustomAttributeBuilder)**

[C#] **public void SetCustomAttribute(Custom AttributeBuilder);**

[C++] **public: void SetCustomAttribute (CustomAttributeBuilder*);**

[JScript] **public function SetCustomAttribute (CustomAttributeBuilder);**

Sets a custom attribute using a specified custom attribute blob.

[Visual Basic] **Overloads Public Sub SetCustomAttribute (ConstructorInfo, Byte())**

[C#] **public void SetCustomAttribute(ConstructorInfo, byte[]);**

[C++] **public: void SetCustomAttribute(ConstructorInfo*, unsigned char __gc[]);**

[JScript] **public function SetCustomAttribute (ConstructorInfo, Byte[]);**

Example

See related example in the **System.Reflection.Emit.FieldBuilder** class topic.

FieldBuilder.SetCustomAttribute Method (CustomAttributeBuilder)

Sets a custom attribute using a custom attribute builder.

```
[Visual Basic]
Overloads Public Sub SetCustomAttribute( _
   ByVal customBuilder As CustomAttributeBuilder _
)
[C#]
public void SetCustomAttribute(
   CustomAttributeBuilder customBuilder
);
[C++]
public: void SetCustomAttribute(
   CustomAttributeBuilder* customBuilder
);
[JScript]
public function SetCustomAttribute(
   customBuilder : CustomAttributeBuilder
);
```

Parameters

customBuilder
An instance of a helper class to define the custom attribute.

Exceptions

Exception Type	Condition
ArgumentNullException	*con* is a null reference (**Nothing** in Visual Basic).
InvalidOperationException	The parent type of this field is complete.

Example

See related example in the **System.Reflection.Emit.FieldBuilder** class topic.

Requirements

Platforms: Windows 98, Windows NT 4.0, Windows Millennium Edition, Windows 2000, Windows XP Home Edition, Windows XP Professional, Windows .NET Server family

FieldBuilder.SetCustomAttribute Method (ConstructorInfo, Byte[])

Sets a custom attribute using a specified custom attribute blob.

```
[Visual Basic]
Overloads Public Sub SetCustomAttribute( _
   ByVal con As ConstructorInfo, _
   ByVal binaryAttribute() As Byte _
)
[C#]
public void SetCustomAttribute(
   ConstructorInfo con,
   byte[] binaryAttribute
);
[C++]
public: void SetCustomAttribute(
   ConstructorInfo* con,
   unsigned char binaryAttribute __gc[]
);
[JScript]
public function SetCustomAttribute(
   con : ConstructorInfo,
   binaryAttribute : Byte[]
);
```

Parameters

con
   The constructor for the custom attribute.
binaryAttribute
   A byte blob representing the attributes.

Exceptions

Exception Type	Condition
ArgumentNullException	*con* or *binaryAttribute* is a null reference (**Nothing** in Visual Basic).
InvalidOperationException	The parent type of this field is complete.

Remarks

See the metadata specification in the ECMA Partition II documentation for details on how to format *binaryAttribute*. The Partition II documentation is included with the .NET Framework SDK installation, and can be found in the %\Microsoft.NET\FrameworkSDK\Tool Developers Guide\docs directory.

Example

See related example in the **System.Reflection.Emit.FieldBuilder** class topic.

Requirements

Platforms: Windows 98, Windows NT 4.0, Windows Millennium Edition, Windows 2000, Windows XP Home Edition, Windows XP Professional, Windows .NET Server family

FieldBuilder.SetMarshal Method

Describes the native marshaling of the field.

```
[Visual Basic]
Public Sub SetMarshal( _
   ByVal unmanagedMarshal As UnmanagedMarshal _
)
[C#]
public void SetMarshal(
   UnmanagedMarshal unmanagedMarshal
);
[C++]
public: void SetMarshal(
   UnmanagedMarshal* unmanagedMarshal
);
[JScript]
public function SetMarshal(
   unmanagedMarshal : UnmanagedMarshal
);
```

Parameters

unmanagedMarshal
   A descriptor specifying the native marshalling of this field.

Exceptions

Exception Type	Condition
ArgumentNullException	*unmanagedMarshal* is a null reference (**Nothing** in Visual Basic).
InvalidOperationException	The containing type has been created using **CreateType**.

Remarks

See related example in the **System.Reflection.Emit.FieldBuilder** class topic.

Requirements

Platforms: Windows 98, Windows NT 4.0, Windows Millennium Edition, Windows 2000, Windows XP Home Edition, Windows XP Professional, Windows .NET Server family

FieldBuilder.SetOffset Method

Specifies the field layout.

```
[Visual Basic]
Public Sub SetOffset( _
   ByVal iOffset As Integer _
)
[C#]
public void SetOffset(
   int iOffset
);
```

```
[C++]
public: void SetOffset(
    int iOffset
);
[JScript]
public function SetOffset(
    iOffset : int
);
```

Parameters

iOffset

    The offset of the field within the type containing this field.

Exceptions

Exception Type	Condition
InvalidOperationException	The containing type has been created using **CreateType**.

Example

See related example in the **System.Reflection.Emit.FieldBuilder** class topic.

Requirements

Platforms: Windows 98, Windows NT 4.0, Windows Millennium Edition, Windows 2000, Windows XP Home Edition, Windows XP Professional, Windows .NET Server family

FieldBuilder.SetValue Method

Overload List

Sets the value of the field supported by the given object.

[Visual Basic] **Overloads Overrides Public Sub SetValue(Object, Object, BindingFlags, Binder, CultureInfo)**

[C#] **public override void SetValue(object, object, BindingFlags, Binder, CultureInfo);**

[C++] **public: void SetValue(Object*, Object*, BindingFlags, Binder*, CultureInfo*);**

[JScript] **public override function SetValue(Object, Object, BindingFlags, Binder, CultureInfo);**

Inherited from **FieldInfo**.

[Visual Basic] **Overloads Public Sub SetValue(Object, Object)**

[C#] **public void SetValue(object, object);**

[C++] **public: void SetValue(Object*, Object*);**

[JScript] **public function SetValue(Object, Object);**

FieldBuilder.SetValue Method (Object, Object, BindingFlags, Binder, CultureInfo)

Sets the value of the field supported by the given object.

```
[Visual Basic]
Overrides Overloads Public Sub SetValue( _
    ByVal obj As Object, _
    ByVal val As Object, _
    ByVal invokeAttr As BindingFlags, _
    ByVal binder As Binder, _
    ByVal culture As CultureInfo _
)
```

```
[C#]
public override void SetValue(
    object obj,
    object val,
    BindingFlags invokeAttr,
    Binder binder,
    CultureInfo culture
);
[C++]
public: void SetValue(
    Object* obj,
    Object* val,
    BindingFlags invokeAttr,
    Binder* binder,
    CultureInfo* culture
);
[JScript]
public override function SetValue(
    obj : Object,
    val : Object,
    invokeAttr : BindingFlags,
    binder : Binder,
    culture : CultureInfo
);
```

Parameters

obj

    The object on which to access the field.

val

    The value to assign to the field.

invokeAttr

    A member of **IBinder** that specifies the type of binding that is desired (for example, IBinder.CreateInstance, IBinder.ExactBinding).

binder

    A set of properties and enabling for binding, coercion of argument types, and invocation of members using reflection. If binder is null, then IBinder.DefaultBinding is used.

culture

    The software preferences of a particular culture.

Exceptions

Exception Type	Condition
NotSupportedException	This method is not supported.

Remarks

This method will assign the *val* parameter to the field reflected by this instance on **Object** *obj*. If the field is static, *obj* will be ignored. For non-static fields, *obj* should be an instance of a class that inherits or declares the field.

The new value is passed as an **Object**. For example, if the field's type is Boolean, an instance of **Object** with the appropriate Boolean value is passed. Before setting the value, **SetValue** checks to see if the user has access permission.

Access restrictions are ignored for fully-trusted code. **Private** constructors, methods, fields, and properties can be accessed and invoked using Reflection whenever the code is fully-trusted.

> **Note** This method is currently not supported. As a workaround, retrieve the **FieldInfo** by reflecting on the finished type and call **SetValue** to set the value of the field.

Requirements

Platforms: Windows 98, Windows NT 4.0,
Windows Millennium Edition, Windows 2000,
Windows XP Home Edition, Windows XP Professional,
Windows .NET Server family

FieldToken Structure

The **FieldToken** struct is an object representation of a token that represents a field.

System.Object
  System.ValueType
    System.Reflection.Emit.FieldToken

```
[Visual Basic]
<Serializable>
Public Structure FieldToken
[C#]
[Serializable]
public struct FieldToken
[C++]
[Serializable]
public __value struct FieldToken
```

[JScript] In JScript, you can use the structures in the .NET Framework, but you cannot define your own.

Thread Safety

Reflection Emit is thread-safe when using assemblies that were created with the **AppDomain.DefineDynamicAssembly** method with the Boolean parameter *isSynchronized* set to **true**.

Requirements

Namespace: System.Reflection.Emit

Platforms: Windows 98, Windows NT 4.0, Windows Millennium Edition, Windows 2000, Windows XP Home Edition, Windows XP Professional, Windows .NET Server family

Assembly: Mscorlib (in Mscorlib.dll)

FieldToken.Empty Field

The default FieldToken with **Token** value 0.

```
[Visual Basic]
Public Shared ReadOnly Empty As FieldToken
[C#]
public static readonly FieldToken Empty;
[C++]
public: static FieldToken Empty;
[JScript]
public static var Empty : FieldToken;
```

Requirements

Platforms: Windows 98, Windows NT 4.0, Windows Millennium Edition, Windows 2000, Windows XP Home Edition, Windows XP Professional, Windows .NET Server family

FieldToken.Token Property

Retrieves the metadata token for this field.

```
[Visual Basic]
Public ReadOnly Property Token As Integer
[C#]
public int Token {get;}
[C++]
public: __property int get_Token();
```
```
[JScript]
public function get Token() : int;
```

Property Value

Read-only. Retrieves the metadata token of this field.

Requirements

Platforms: Windows 98, Windows NT 4.0, Windows Millennium Edition, Windows 2000, Windows XP Home Edition, Windows XP Professional, Windows .NET Server family

FieldToken.Equals Method

Determines if an object is an instance of **FieldToken** and is equal to this instance.

```
[Visual Basic]
Overrides Public Function Equals( _
   ByVal obj As Object _
) As Boolean
[C#]
public override bool Equals(
   object obj
);
[C++]
public: bool Equals(
   Object* obj
);
[JScript]
public override function Equals(
   obj : Object
) : Boolean;
```

Parameters

obj
    The object to compare to this **FieldToken**.

Return Value

Returns **true** if *obj* is an instance of **FieldToken** and is equal to this object; otherwise, **false**.

Requirements

Platforms: Windows 98, Windows NT 4.0, Windows Millennium Edition, Windows 2000, Windows XP Home Edition, Windows XP Professional, Windows .NET Server family

FieldToken.GetHashCode Method

Generates the hash code for this field.

```
[Visual Basic]
Overrides Public Function GetHashCode() As Integer
[C#]
public override int GetHashCode();
[C++]
public: int GetHashCode();
[JScript]
public override function GetHashCode() : int;
```

Return Value

Returns the hash code for this instance.

Requirements

Platforms: Windows 98, Windows NT 4.0,
Windows Millennium Edition, Windows 2000,
Windows XP Home Edition, Windows XP Professional,
Windows .NET Server family

FlowControl Enumeration

Describes how an instruction alters the flow of control.

```
[Visual Basic]
<Serializable>
Public Enum FlowControl
[C#]
[Serializable]
public enum FlowControl
[C++]
[Serializable]
__value public enum FlowControl
[JScript]
public
    Serializable
enum FlowControl
```

Members

Member name	Description
Branch	Branch instruction.
Break	Break instruction.
Call	Call instruction.
Cond_Branch	Conditional branch instruction.
Meta	Provides information about a subsequent instruction. For example, the **Unaligned** instruction of **Reflection.Emit.Opcodes** has **FlowControl.Meta** and specifies that the subsequent pointer instruction might be unaligned.
Next	Normal flow of control.
Phi	This member supports the .NET Framework infrastructure and is not intended to be used directly from your code.
Return	Return instruction.
Throw	Exception throw instruction.

Requirements

Namespace: System.Reflection.Emit

Platforms: Windows 98, Windows NT 4.0, Windows Millennium Edition, Windows 2000, Windows XP Home Edition, Windows XP Professional, Windows .NET Server family

Assembly: Mscorlib (in Mscorlib.dll)

ILGenerator Class

Generates Microsoft intermediate language (MSIL) instructions.

System.Object
    System.Reflection.Emit.ILGenerator

```
[Visual Basic]
Public Class ILGenerator
[C#]
public class ILGenerator
[C++]
public __gc class ILGenerator
[JScript]
public class ILGenerator
```

Thread Safety

Reflection Emit is thread-safe when using assemblies that were created with the **AppDomain.DefineDynamicAssembly** method with the Boolean parameter *isSynchronized* set to **true**.

Remarks

MSIL is used as input to a just-in-time (JIT) compiler.

Requirements

Namespace: System.Reflection.Emit

Platforms: Windows 98, Windows NT 4.0, Windows Millennium Edition, Windows 2000, Windows XP Home Edition, Windows XP Professional, Windows .NET Server family

Assembly: Mscorlib (in Mscorlib.dll)

ILGenerator.BeginCatchBlock Method

Begins a catch block.

```
[Visual Basic]
Public Overridable Sub BeginCatchBlock( _
    ByVal exceptionType As Type _
)
[C#]
public virtual void BeginCatchBlock(
    Type exceptionType
);
[C++]
public: virtual void BeginCatchBlock(
    Type* exceptionType
);
[JScript]
public function BeginCatchBlock(
    exceptionType : Type
);
```

Parameters

exceptionType
    The Type object that represents the exception.

Exceptions

Exception Type	Condition
ArgumentException	The catch block is within a filtered exception.

Exception Type	Condition
ArgumentNullException	*exceptionType* is a null reference (**Nothing** in Visual Basic) and the exception filter block has not returned a value that indicates that finally blocks should be run until this catch block is located.
NotSupportedException	The Microsoft intermediate language (MSIL) being generated is not currently in an exception block.

Remarks

Emits a branch instruction to the end of the current exception block.

> **Note** If the filter exception block returns the **constant exception_execute_handler** (see the documentation for the Common Language Infrastructure Instruction Set), the argument to the **BeginCatchBlock** is not checked.

Example

[Visual Basic, C#, C++] The code sample below demonstrates the contextual usage of the **BeginCatchBlock** method.

```
[Visual Basic]
Imports System
Imports System.Threading
Imports System.Reflection
Imports System.Reflection.Emit

_

Class ILThrowExceptionDemo

    Public Shared Function BuildAdderType() As Type

        Dim myDomain As AppDomain = Thread.GetDomain()
        Dim myAsmName As New AssemblyName()
        myAsmName.Name = "AdderExceptionAsm"
        Dim myAsmBldr As AssemblyBuilder = _
myDomain.DefineDynamicAssembly(myAsmName, _
                        AssemblyBuilderAccess.Run)

        Dim myModBldr As ModuleBuilder = _
myAsmBldr.DefineDynamicModule("AdderExceptionMod")

        Dim myTypeBldr As TypeBuilder = myModBldr.DefineType("Adder")

        Dim adderParams() As Type = {GetType(Integer), GetType(Integer)}

        ' This method will add two numbers which are 100 or
    less. If either of the
        ' passed integer vales are greater than 100, it will
    throw an exception.
        Dim adderBldr As MethodBuilder = _
myTypeBldr.DefineMethod("DoAdd", _
                        MethodAttributes.Public Or
    MethodAttributes.Static, _
                        GetType(Integer), adderParams)
        Dim adderIL As ILGenerator = adderBldr.GetILGenerator()

        ' In order to successfully branch, we need to create labels
        ' representing the offset IL instruction block to branch to.
        ' These labels, when the MarkLabel(Label) method is invoked,
        ' will specify the IL instruction to branch to.
        Dim exCtorInfo As ConstructorInfo = _
GetType(OverflowException).GetConstructor( _
                        New Type() {GetType(String)})
        Dim exToStrMI As MethodInfo = _
GetType(OverflowException).GetMethod("ToString")
```

```
    Dim writeLineMI As MethodInfo = _                        ↵
GetType(Console).GetMethod("WriteLine", _
                        New Type() {GetType(String), _
                                GetType(Object)})

    Dim tmp1 As LocalBuilder = adderIL.DeclareLocal(GetType(Integer))
    Dim tmp2 As LocalBuilder = _
adderIL.DeclareLocal(GetType(OverflowException))

    Dim failed As Label = adderIL.DefineLabel()
    Dim endOfMthd As Label = adderIL.DefineLabel()

    ' First, load argument 0 and the integer value of "100" onto the
    ' stack. If arg0 > 100, branch to the label "failed",      ↵
which is marked
    ' as the address of the block that throws an exception.

    Dim exBlock As Label = adderIL.BeginExceptionBlock()
    adderIL.Emit(OpCodes.Ldarg_0)
    adderIL.Emit(OpCodes.Ldc_I4_S, 100)
    adderIL.Emit(OpCodes.Bgt_S, failed)

    ' Now, check to see if argument 1 was greater than 100.    ↵
If it was,
    ' branch to "failed." Otherwise, fall through and          ↵
perform the addition,
    ' branching unconditionally to the instruction at          ↵
the label "endOfMthd".

    adderIL.Emit(OpCodes.Ldarg_1)
    adderIL.Emit(OpCodes.Ldc_I4_S, 100)
    adderIL.Emit(OpCodes.Bgt_S, failed)

    adderIL.Emit(OpCodes.Ldarg_0)
    adderIL.Emit(OpCodes.Ldarg_1)
    adderIL.Emit(OpCodes.Add_Ovf_Un)
    adderIL.Emit(OpCodes.Stloc_S, tmp1)
    adderIL.Emit(OpCodes.Br_S, endOfMthd)

    ' If one of the arguments was greater than 100, we need    ↵
to throw an
    ' exception. We'll use "OverflowException" with a          ↵
customized message.
    ' First, we load our message onto the stack, and then      ↵
create a new
    ' exception object using the constructor overload that accepts a

    ' string message.
    adderIL.MarkLabel(failed)
    adderIL.Emit(OpCodes.Ldstr, "Cannot accept values over 100  ↵
for add.")
    adderIL.Emit(OpCodes.Newobj, exCtorInfo)

    ' We're going to need to refer to that exception object    ↵
later, so let's
    ' store it in a temporary variable. Since the store        ↵
function pops the
    ' the value/reference off the stack, and we'll need it     ↵
to throw the
    ' exception, we will subsequently load it back onto the    ↵
stack as well.

    adderIL.Emit(OpCodes.Stloc_S, tmp2)
    adderIL.Emit(OpCodes.Ldloc_S, tmp2)

    ' Throw the exception currently atop the stack.

    adderIL.ThrowException(GetType(OverflowException))

    ' Start the catch block.

    adderIL.BeginCatchBlock(GetType(OverflowException))

    ' First, we'll load a "wrapper" string, and then perform a
    ' late-bound call to the ToString() method of OverflowException,
```

```
    ' passing it the exception object we stored in local      ↵
variable tmp2.

    adderIL.Emit(OpCodes.Ldstr, "{0}")
    adderIL.Emit(OpCodes.Ldloc_S, tmp2)
    adderIL.EmitCall(OpCodes.Callvirt, exToStrMI, Nothing)

    ' Now, we should have the "wrapper" string atop the stack,
    ' along with the string result of the ToString() call. All
    ' conditions are met to call WriteLine(string, object).

    adderIL.EmitCall(OpCodes.Call, writeLineMI, Nothing)

    ' Since our function has to return an integer value,      ↵
we'll load -1 onto
    ' the stack to indicate an error, and store it in local   ↵
variable tmp1.

    adderIL.Emit(OpCodes.Ldc_I4_M1)
    adderIL.Emit(OpCodes.Stloc_S, tmp1)

    ' End the exception handling block.

    adderIL.EndExceptionBlock()

    ' The end of the method. If no exception was thrown,      ↵
the correct value
    ' will be saved in tmp1. If an exception was thrown,      ↵
tmp1 will be equal
    ' to -1. Either way, we'll load the value of tmp1 onto    ↵
the stack and return.

    adderIL.MarkLabel(endOfMthd)
    adderIL.Emit(OpCodes.Ldloc_S, tmp1)
    adderIL.Emit(OpCodes.Ret)

    Return myTypeBldr.CreateType()

End Function 'BuildAdderType

Public Shared Sub Main()

    Dim adderType As Type = BuildAdderType()

    Dim addIns As Object = Activator.CreateInstance(adderType)

    Dim addParams(1) As Object

    Console.Write("Enter an integer value: ")
    addParams(0) = CType(Convert.ToInt32(Console.ReadLine()), Object)

    Console.Write("Enter another integer value: ")
    addParams(1) = CType(Convert.ToInt32(Console.ReadLine()), Object)

    Console.WriteLine("If either integer was > 100, an         ↵
exception will be thrown.")
    Console.WriteLine("---")

    Console.WriteLine("{0} + {1} = {2}", addParams(0),         ↵
addParams(1), _
                adderType.InvokeMember("DoAdd", _
                        BindingFlags.InvokeMethod, _
                        Nothing, addIns, addParams))

    End Sub 'Main

End Class 'ILThrowExceptionDemo

[C#]
using System;
using System.Threading;
using System.Reflection;
using System.Reflection.Emit;

class ILThrowExceptionDemo {
```

```
public static Type BuildAdderType() {

    AppDomain myDomain = Thread.GetDomain();
    AssemblyName myAsmName = new AssemblyName();
    myAsmName.Name = "AdderExceptionAsm";
    AssemblyBuilder myAsmBldr =
myDomain.DefineDynamicAssembly(myAsmName,
                        AssemblyBuilderAccess.Run);

    ModuleBuilder myModBldr =
myAsmBldr.DefineDynamicModule("AdderExceptionMod");

    TypeBuilder myTypeBldr = myModBldr.DefineType("Adder");

    Type[] adderParams = new Type[] {typeof(int), typeof(int)};

    // This method will add two numbers which are 100 or
less. If either of the
    // passed integer vales are greater than 100, it will
throw an exception.

    MethodBuilder adderBldr = myTypeBldr.DefineMethod("DoAdd",
                    MethodAttributes.Public |
                    MethodAttributes.Static,
                    typeof(int),
                    adderParams);
    ILGenerator adderIL = adderBldr.GetILGenerator();

    // representing the offset IL instruction block to branch to.
    // These labels, when the MarkLabel(Label) method is invoked,
    // will specify the IL instruction to branch to.

    ConstructorInfo exCtorInfo =
typeof(OverflowException).GetConstructor(
                    new Type[]
                        {typeof(string)});
    MethodInfo exToStrMI =
typeof(OverflowException).GetMethod("ToString");
    MethodInfo writeLineMI = typeof(Console).GetMethod("WriteLine",
                    new Type[]
                        {typeof(string),
                         typeof(object)});

    LocalBuilder tmp1 = adderIL.DeclareLocal(typeof(int));
    LocalBuilder tmp2 =
adderIL.DeclareLocal(typeof(OverflowException));

    Label failed = adderIL.DefineLabel();
    Label endOfMthd = adderIL.DefineLabel();

    // First, load argument 0 and the integer value of "100" onto the
    // stack. If arg0 > 100, branch to the label "failed",
which is marked
    // as the address of the block that throws an exception.

    Label exBlock = adderIL.BeginExceptionBlock();
    adderIL.Emit(OpCodes.Ldarg_0);
    adderIL.Emit(OpCodes.Ldc_I4_S, 100);
    adderIL.Emit(OpCodes.Bgt_S, failed);

    // Now, check to see if argument 1 was greater than 100. If it was,
    // branch to "failed." Otherwise, fall through and
perform the addition,
    // branching unconditionally to the instruction at the
label "endOfMthd".

    adderIL.Emit(OpCodes.Ldarg_1);
    adderIL.Emit(OpCodes.Ldc_I4_S, 100);
    adderIL.Emit(OpCodes.Bgt_S, failed);

    adderIL.Emit(OpCodes.Ldarg_0);
    adderIL.Emit(OpCodes.Ldarg_1);
    adderIL.Emit(OpCodes.Add_Ovf_Un);
    adderIL.Emit(OpCodes.Stloc_S, tmp1);
    adderIL.Emit(OpCodes.Br_S, endOfMthd);

    // If one of the arguments was greater than 100, we need
to throw an
    // exception. We'll use "OverflowException" with a
customized message.
    // First, we load our message onto the stack, and then create a new
    // exception object using the constructor overload that accepts a
    // string message.

    adderIL.MarkLabel(failed);
    adderIL.Emit(OpCodes.Ldstr, "Cannot accept values over
100 for add.");
    adderIL.Emit(OpCodes.Newobj, exCtorInfo);

    // We're going to need to refer to that exception object
later, so let's
    // store it in a temporary variable. Since the store
function pops the
    // the value/reference off the stack, and we'll need it
to throw the
    // exception, we will subsequently load it back onto the
stack as well.

    adderIL.Emit(OpCodes.Stloc_S, tmp2);
    adderIL.Emit(OpCodes.Ldloc_S, tmp2);

    // Throw the exception currently atop the stack.

    adderIL.ThrowException(typeof(OverflowException));

    // Start the catch block.

    adderIL.BeginCatchBlock(typeof(OverflowException));

    // First, we'll load a "wrapper" string, and then perform a
    // late-bound call to the ToString() method of OverflowException,
    // passing it the exception object we stored in local
variable tmp2.

    adderIL.Emit(OpCodes.Ldstr, "{0}");
    adderIL.Emit(OpCodes.Ldloc_S, tmp2);
    adderIL.EmitCall(OpCodes.Callvirt, exToStrMI, null);

    // Now, we should have the "wrapper" string atop the stack,
    // along with the string result of the ToString() call. All
    // conditions are met to call WriteLine(string, object).

    adderIL.EmitCall(OpCodes.Call, writeLineMI, null);

    // Since our function has to return an integer value, we'll
load -1 onto
    // the stack to indicate an error, and store it in local
variable tmp1.

    adderIL.Emit(OpCodes.Ldc_I4_M1);
    adderIL.Emit(OpCodes.Stloc_S, tmp1);

    // End the exception handling block.

    adderIL.EndExceptionBlock();

    // The end of the method. If no exception was thrown, the
correct value
    // will be saved in tmp1. If an exception was thrown, tmp1
will be equal
    // to -1. Either way, we'll load the value of tmp1 onto
the stack and return.

    adderIL.MarkLabel(endOfMthd);
    adderIL.Emit(OpCodes.Ldloc_S, tmp1);
    adderIL.Emit(OpCodes.Ret);

    return myTypeBldr.CreateType();

}
```

```cpp
public static void Main() {

  Type adderType = BuildAdderType();

  object addIns = Activator.CreateInstance(adderType);

  object[] addParams = new object[2];

  Console.Write("Enter an integer value: ");
  addParams[0] = (object)Convert.ToInt32(Console.ReadLine());

  Console.Write("Enter another integer value: ");
  addParams[1] = (object)Convert.ToInt32(Console.ReadLine());

  Console.WriteLine("If either integer was > 100, an
exception will be thrown.");
  Console.WriteLine("---");

  Console.WriteLine("{0} + {1} = {2}",
          addParams[0], addParams[1],
          adderType.InvokeMember("DoAdd",
              BindingFlags.InvokeMethod,
              null,
              addIns,
              addParams));

  }

}
```

[C++]
```cpp
#using <mscorlib.dll>

using namespace System;
using namespace System::Threading;
using namespace System::Reflection;
using namespace System::Reflection::Emit;

Type* BuildAdderType() {

  AppDomain* myDomain = Thread::GetDomain();
  AssemblyName* myAsmName = new AssemblyName();
  myAsmName->Name = S"AdderExceptionAsm";
  AssemblyBuilder*  myAsmBldr = myDomain-
>DefineDynamicAssembly(myAsmName,
      AssemblyBuilderAccess::Run);

  ModuleBuilder* myModBldr = myAsmBldr-
>DefineDynamicModule(S"AdderExceptionMod");

  TypeBuilder*  myTypeBldr = myModBldr->DefineType(S"Adder");

  Type* adderParams[] = {__typeof(int), __typeof(int)};

  // This method will add two numbers which are 100 or less.
If either of the
  // passed integer vales are greater than 100, it will throw
an exception.

  MethodBuilder*  adderBldr = myTypeBldr->DefineMethod(
      S"DoAdd",
      static_cast<MethodAttributes>(MethodAttributes:
:Public | MethodAttributes::Static),
      __typeof(int),
      adderParams);
  ILGenerator*  adderIL = adderBldr->GetILGenerator();

  // representing the offset IL instruction block to branch to.
  // These labels, when the MarkLabel(Label) method is invoked,
  // will specify the IL instruction to branch to.

  Type* temp0 [] = {__typeof(String)};
  ConstructorInfo*  exCtorInfo = __typeof
(OverflowException)->GetConstructor(temp0);
```

```cpp
  MethodInfo*  exToStrMI = __typeof(OverflowException)-
>GetMethod(S"ToString");

  Type* temp1 [] = {__typeof(String), __typeof(Object)};
  MethodInfo*  writeLineMI = __typeof(Console)-
>GetMethod(S"WriteLine",
      temp1);

  LocalBuilder*  tmp1 = adderIL->DeclareLocal(__typeof(int));
  LocalBuilder*  tmp2 = adderIL-
>DeclareLocal(__typeof(OverflowException));

  Label failed = adderIL->DefineLabel();
  Label endOfMthd = adderIL->DefineLabel();

  // First, load argument 0 and the integer value of S"100" onto the
  // stack. If arg0 > 100, branch to the label S"failed",
which is marked
  // as the address of the block that throws an exception.

  Label exBlock = adderIL->BeginExceptionBlock();
  adderIL->Emit(OpCodes::Ldarg_0);
  adderIL->Emit(OpCodes::Ldc_I4_S, 100);
  adderIL->Emit(OpCodes::Bgt_S, failed);

  // Now, check to see if argument 1 was greater than 100. If it was,
  // branch to S"failed." Otherwise, fall through and
perform the addition,
  // branching unconditionally to the instruction at
the label S"endOfMthd".

  adderIL->Emit(OpCodes::Ldarg_1);
  adderIL->Emit(OpCodes::Ldc_I4_S, 100);
  adderIL->Emit(OpCodes::Bgt_S, failed);

  adderIL->Emit(OpCodes::Ldarg_0);
  adderIL->Emit(OpCodes::Ldarg_1);
  adderIL->Emit(OpCodes->Add_Ovf_Un);
  adderIL->Emit(OpCodes::Stloc_S, tmp1);
  adderIL->Emit(OpCodes::Br_S, endOfMthd);

  // If one of the arguments was greater than 100, we need to throw an
  // exception. We'll use "OverflowException" with a
customized message.
  // First, we load our message onto the stack, and then create a new
  // exception Object using the constructor overload that accepts a
  // String* message.

  adderIL->MarkLabel(failed);
  adderIL->Emit(OpCodes::Ldstr, S"Cannot accept values
over 100 for add.");
  adderIL->Emit(OpCodes::Newobj, exCtorInfo);

  // We're going to need to refer to that exception
Object later, so let's
  // store it in a temporary variable. Since the store
function pops the
  // the value/reference off the stack, and we'll need it
to throw the
  // exception, we will subsequently load it back onto the
stack as well.

  adderIL->Emit(OpCodes::Stloc_S, tmp2);
  adderIL->Emit(OpCodes::Ldloc_S, tmp2);

  // Throw the exception currently atop the stack.

  adderIL->ThrowException(__typeof(OverflowException));

  // Start the catch block.

  adderIL->BeginCatchBlock(__typeof(OverflowException));
```

```
// First, we'll load a "wrapper" String, and then perform a
// late-bound call to the ToString() method of OverflowException,
// passing it the exception Object we stored in local variable tmp2.

adderIL->Emit(OpCodes::Ldstr, S" {0}");
adderIL->Emit(OpCodes::Ldloc_S, tmp2);
adderIL->EmitCall(OpCodes::Callvirt, exToStrMI, 0);

// Now, we should have the "wrapper" String atop the stack,
// along with the String result of the ToString() call. All
// conditions are met to call WriteLine(String*, Object*).

adderIL->EmitCall(OpCodes::Call, writeLineMI, 0);

// Since our function has to return an integer value,
// we'll load -1 onto
// the stack to indicate an error, and store it in local
// variable tmp1.

adderIL->Emit(OpCodes::Ldc_I4_M1);
adderIL->Emit(OpCodes::Stloc_S, tmp1);

// End the exception handling block.

adderIL->EndExceptionBlock();

// The end of the method. If no exception was thrown,
// the correct value
// will be saved in tmp1. If an exception was thrown,
// tmp1 will be equal
// to -1. Either way, we'll load the value of tmp1 onto
// the stack and return.

adderIL->MarkLabel(endOfMthd);
adderIL->Emit(OpCodes::Ldloc_S, tmp1);
adderIL->Emit(OpCodes::Ret);

return myTypeBldr->CreateType();

}

int main() {

    Type*  adderType = BuildAdderType();

    Object* addIns = Activator::CreateInstance(adderType);

    Object* addParams[] = new Object*[2];

    Console::Write(S"Enter an integer value: ");
    addParams[0] = __box(Convert::ToInt32(Console::ReadLine()));

    Console::Write(S"Enter another integer value: ");
    addParams[1] = __box(Convert::ToInt32(Console::ReadLine()));

    Console::WriteLine(S"If either integer was > 100, an
exception will be thrown.");
    Console::WriteLine(S"---");

    Console::WriteLine(S" {0} + {1} = {2}",
        addParams[0], addParams[1],
        adderType->InvokeMember(S"DoAdd",
        BindingFlags::InvokeMethod,
        0,
        addIns,
        addParams));
}
```

Requirements

Platforms: Windows 98, Windows NT 4.0, Windows Millennium Edition, Windows 2000, Windows XP Home Edition, Windows XP Professional, Windows .NET Server family

ILGenerator.BeginExceptFilterBlock Method

Begins an exception block for a filtered exception.

```
[Visual Basic]
Public Overridable Sub BeginExceptFilterBlock()
[C#]
public virtual void BeginExceptFilterBlock();
[C++]
public: virtual void BeginExceptFilterBlock();
[JScript]
public function BeginExceptFilterBlock();
```

Exceptions

Exception Type	Condition
NotSupportedException	The Microsoft intermediate language (MSIL) being generated is not currently in an exception block.

Remarks

Emits a branch instruction to the end of the current exception block.

Requirements

Platforms: Windows 98, Windows NT 4.0, Windows Millennium Edition, Windows 2000, Windows XP Home Edition, Windows XP Professional, Windows .NET Server family

ILGenerator.BeginExceptionBlock Method

Begins an exception block for a non-filtered exception.

```
[Visual Basic]
Public Overridable Function BeginExceptionBlock() As Label
[C#]
public virtual Label BeginExceptionBlock();
[C++]
public: virtual Label BeginExceptionBlock();
[JScript]
public function BeginExceptionBlock() : Label;
```

Return Value

The label for the end of the block. This will leave you in the correct place to execute finally blocks or to finish the try.

Remarks

Creating an exception block records some information, but does not actually emit any Microsoft intermediate language (MSIL) onto the stream.

Example

See related example in the **System.Reflection.Emit.ILGenerator.BeginCatchBlock** method topic.

Requirements

Platforms: Windows 98, Windows NT 4.0, Windows Millennium Edition, Windows 2000, Windows XP Home Edition, Windows XP Professional, Windows .NET Server family

ILGenerator.BeginFaultBlock Method

Begins an exception fault block in the Microsoft intermediate language (MSIL) stream.

```
[Visual Basic]
Public Overridable Sub BeginFaultBlock()
[C#]
public virtual void BeginFaultBlock();
[C++]
public: virtual void BeginFaultBlock();
[JScript]
public function BeginFaultBlock();
```

Exceptions

Exception Type	Condition
NotSupportedException	The Microsoft intermediate language (MSIL) being generated is not currently in an exception block.

Example

See related example in the **System.Reflection.Emit.ILGenerator.BeginCatchBlock** method topic.

Requirements

Platforms: Windows 98, Windows NT 4.0, Windows Millennium Edition, Windows 2000, Windows XP Home Edition, Windows XP Professional, Windows .NET Server family

ILGenerator.BeginFinallyBlock Method

Begins a finally block in the Microsoft intermediate language (MSIL) instruction stream.

```
[Visual Basic]
Public Overridable Sub BeginFinallyBlock()
[C#]
public virtual void BeginFinallyBlock();
[C++]
public: virtual void BeginFinallyBlock();
[JScript]
public function BeginFinallyBlock();
```

Exceptions

Exception Type	Condition
NotSupportedException	The Microsoft intermediate language (MSIL) being generated is not currently in an exception block.

Example

See related example in the **System.Reflection.Emit.ILGenerator.BeginCatchBlock** method topic.

Requirements

Platforms: Windows 98, Windows NT 4.0, Windows Millennium Edition, Windows 2000, Windows XP Home Edition, Windows XP Professional, Windows .NET Server family

ILGenerator.BeginScope Method

Begins a lexical scope.

```
[Visual Basic]
Public Overridable Sub BeginScope()
[C#]
public virtual void BeginScope();
[C++]
public: virtual void BeginScope();
[JScript]
public function BeginScope();
```

Example

See related example in the **System.Reflection.Emit.ILGenerator.BeginCatchBlock** method topic.

Requirements

Platforms: Windows 98, Windows NT 4.0, Windows Millennium Edition, Windows 2000, Windows XP Home Edition, Windows XP Professional, Windows .NET Server family

ILGenerator.DeclareLocal Method

Declares a local variable.

```
[Visual Basic]
Public Function DeclareLocal( _
    ByVal localType As Type _
) As LocalBuilder
[C#]
public LocalBuilder DeclareLocal(
    Type localType
);
[C++]
public: LocalBuilder* DeclareLocal(
    Type* localType
);
[JScript]
public function DeclareLocal(
    localType : Type
) : LocalBuilder;
```

Parameters

localType
    The **Type** of the local variable.

Return Value

The declared local variable.

Exceptions

Exception Type	Condition
ArgumentNullException	*localType* is a null reference (**Nothing** in Visual Basic).
InvalidOperationException	The containing type has been created with **CreateType**.

Example

See related example in the **System.Reflection.Emit.ILGenerator.BeginCatchBlock** method topic.

Requirements

Platforms: Windows 98, Windows NT 4.0,
Windows Millennium Edition, Windows 2000,
Windows XP Home Edition, Windows XP Professional,
Windows .NET Server family

ILGenerator.DefineLabel Method

Declares a new label.

```
[Visual Basic]
Public Overridable Function DefineLabel() As Label
[C#]
public virtual Label DefineLabel();
[C++]
public: virtual Label DefineLabel();
[JScript]
public function DefineLabel() : Label;
```

Return Value

Returns a new label that can be used as a token for branching.

Remarks

In order to set the position of the label within the stream, you must call **MarkLabel**.

This is just a token and does not yet represent any particular location within the stream.

Example

See related example in the
System.Reflection.Emit.ILGenerator.BeginCatchBlock method topic.

Requirements

Platforms: Windows 98, Windows NT 4.0,
Windows Millennium Edition, Windows 2000,
Windows XP Home Edition, Windows XP Professional,
Windows .NET Server family

ILGenerator.Emit Method

Puts an instruction onto the Microsoft Intermediate Language (MSIL) stream for the just-in-time (JIT) compiler.

Overload List

Puts the specified instruction onto the stream of instructions.

[Visual Basic] **Overloads Public Overridable Sub Emit (OpCode)**

[C#] **public virtual void Emit(OpCode);**

[C++] **public: virtual void Emit(OpCode);**

[JScript] **public function Emit(OpCode);**

Puts the specified instruction and character argument onto the Microsoft intermediate language (MSIL) stream of instructions.

[Visual Basic] **Overloads Public Overridable Sub Emit (OpCode, Byte)**

[C#] **public virtual void Emit(OpCode, byte);**

[C++] **public: virtual void Emit(OpCode, unsigned char);**

[JScript] **public function Emit(OpCode, Byte);**

Puts the specified instruction and metadata token for the specified constructor onto the Microsoft intermediate language (MSIL) stream of instructions.

[Visual Basic] **Overloads Public Overridable Sub Emit (OpCode, ConstructorInfo)**

[C#] **public virtual void Emit(OpCode, ConstructorInfo);**

[C++] **public: virtual void Emit(OpCode, ConstructorInfo*);**

[JScript] **public function Emit(OpCode, ConstructorInfo);**

Puts the specified instruction and numerical argument onto the Microsoft intermediate language (MSIL) stream of instructions.

[Visual Basic] **Overloads Public Overridable Sub Emit (OpCode, Double)**

[C#] **public virtual void Emit(OpCode, double);**

[C++] **public: virtual void Emit(OpCode, double);**

[JScript] **public function Emit(OpCode, double);**

Puts the specified instruction and metadata token for the specified field onto the Microsoft intermediate language (MSIL) stream of instructions.

[Visual Basic] **Overloads Public Overridable Sub Emit (OpCode, FieldInfo)**

[C#] **public virtual void Emit(OpCode, FieldInfo);**

[C++] **public: virtual void Emit(OpCode, FieldInfo*);**

[JScript] **public function Emit(OpCode, FieldInfo);**

Puts the specified instruction and numerical argument onto the Microsoft intermediate language (MSIL) stream of instructions.

[Visual Basic] **Overloads Public Overridable Sub Emit (OpCode, Short)**

[C#] **public virtual void Emit(OpCode, short);**

[C++] **public: virtual void Emit(OpCode, short);**

[JScript] **public function Emit(OpCode, Int16);**

Puts the specified instruction and numerical argument onto the Microsoft intermediate language (MSIL) stream of instructions.

[Visual Basic] **Overloads Public Overridable Sub Emit (OpCode, Integer)**

[C#] **public virtual void Emit(OpCode, int);**

[C++] **public: virtual void Emit(OpCode, int);**

[JScript] **public function Emit(OpCode, int);**

Puts the specified instruction and numerical argument onto the Microsoft intermediate language (MSIL) stream of instructions.

[Visual Basic] **Overloads Public Overridable Sub Emit (OpCode, Long)**

[C#] **public virtual void Emit(OpCode, long);**

[C++] **public: virtual void Emit(OpCode, __int64);**

[JScript] **public function Emit(OpCode, long);**

Puts the specified instruction onto the Microsoft intermediate language (MSIL) stream and leaves space to include a label when fixes are done.

[Visual Basic] **Overloads Public Overridable Sub Emit (OpCode, Label)**

[C#] **public virtual void Emit(OpCode, Label);**

[C++] **public: virtual void Emit(OpCode, Label);**

[JScript] **public function Emit(OpCode, Label);**

Puts the specified instruction onto the Microsoft intermediate language (MSIL) stream and leaves space to include a label when fixes are done.

> [Visual Basic] **Overloads Public Overridable Sub Emit (OpCode, Label())**
>
> [C#] **public virtual void Emit(OpCode, Label[]);**
>
> [C++] **public: virtual void Emit(OpCode, Label[]);**
>
> [JScript] **public function Emit(OpCode, Label[]);**

Puts the specified instruction onto the Microsoft intermediate language (MSIL) stream followed by the index of the given local variable.

> [Visual Basic] **Overloads Public Overridable Sub Emit (OpCode, LocalBuilder)**
>
> [C#] **public virtual void Emit(OpCode, LocalBuilder);**
>
> [C++] **public: virtual void Emit(OpCode, LocalBuilder*);**
>
> [JScript] **public function Emit(OpCode, LocalBuilder);**

Puts the specified instruction onto the Microsoft intermediate language (MSIL) stream followed by the metadata token for the given method.

> [Visual Basic] **Overloads Public Overridable Sub Emit (OpCode, MethodInfo)**
>
> [C#] **public virtual void Emit(OpCode, MethodInfo);**
>
> [C++] **public: virtual void Emit(OpCode, MethodInfo*);**
>
> [JScript] **public function Emit(OpCode, MethodInfo);**

Puts the specified instruction and character argument onto the Microsoft intermediate language (MSIL) stream of instructions. This method is not CLS-compliant.

> [Visual Basic] **Overloads Public Sub Emit(OpCode, SByte)**
>
> [C#] **public void Emit(OpCode, sbyte);**
>
> [C++] **public: void Emit(OpCode, char);**
>
> [JScript] **public function Emit(OpCode, SByte);**

Puts the specified instruction and a signature token onto the Microsoft intermediate language (MSIL) stream of instructions.

> [Visual Basic] **Overloads Public Overridable Sub Emit (OpCode, SignatureHelper)**
>
> [C#] **public virtual void Emit(OpCode, SignatureHelper);**
>
> [C++] **public: virtual void Emit(OpCode, SignatureHelper*);**
>
> [JScript] **public function Emit(OpCode, SignatureHelper);**

Puts the specified instruction and numerical argument onto the Microsoft intermediate language (MSIL) stream of instructions.

> [Visual Basic] **Overloads Public Overridable Sub Emit (OpCode, Single)**
>
> [C#] **public virtual void Emit(OpCode, float);**
>
> [C++] **public: virtual void Emit(OpCode, float);**
>
> [JScript] **public function Emit(OpCode, float);**

Puts the specified instruction onto the Microsoft intermediate language (MSIL) stream followed by the metadata token for the given string.

> [Visual Basic] **Overloads Public Overridable Sub Emit (OpCode, String)**
>
> [C#] **public virtual void Emit(OpCode, string);**
>
> [C++] **public: virtual void Emit(OpCode, String*);**
>
> [JScript] **public function Emit(OpCode, String);**

Puts the specified instruction onto the Microsoft intermediate language (MSIL) stream followed by the metadata token for the given type.

> [Visual Basic] **Overloads Public Overridable Sub Emit (OpCode, Type)**
>
> [C#] **public virtual void Emit(OpCode, Type);**
>
> [C++] **public: virtual void Emit(OpCode, Type*);**
>
> [JScript] **public function Emit(OpCode, Type);**

Example

See related example in the **System.Reflection.Emit.ILGenerator. BeginCatchBlock** method topic.

ILGenerator.Emit Method (OpCode)

Puts the specified instruction onto the stream of instructions.

```
[Visual Basic]
Overloads Public Overridable Sub Emit( _
   ByVal opcode As OpCode _
)
[C#]
public virtual void Emit(
   OpCode opcode
);
[C++]
public: virtual void Emit(
   OpCode opcode
);
[JScript]
public function Emit(
   opcode : OpCode
);
```

Parameters

opcode
> The Microsoft Intermediate Language (MSIL) instruction to be put onto the stream.

Remarks

If the opcode requires an argument, the caller must ensure that the argument length matches the length of the declared parameter. Otherwise, results will be unpredictable. For example, if the Emit instruction requires a 2-byte operand and the caller supplies a 4-byte operand, the runtime will emit two additional bytes to the instruction stream. These extra bytes will be **Nop** instructions. The instruction values are defined in **OpCodes**.

Example

See related example in the **System.Reflection.Emit.ILGenerator.BeginCatchBlock** method topic.

Requirements

Platforms: Windows 98, Windows NT 4.0, Windows Millennium Edition, Windows 2000, Windows XP Home Edition, Windows XP Professional, Windows .NET Server family

ILGenerator.Emit Method (OpCode, Byte)

Puts the specified instruction and character argument onto the Microsoft intermediate language (MSIL) stream of instructions.

```
[Visual Basic]
Overloads Public Overridable Sub Emit( _
   ByVal opcode As OpCode, _
   ByVal arg As Byte _
)
[C#]
public virtual void Emit(
   OpCode opcode,
   byte arg
);
[C++]
public: virtual void Emit(
   OpCode opcode,
   unsigned char arg
);
[JScript]
public function Emit(
   opcode : OpCode,
   arg : Byte
);
```

Parameters

opcode

The Microsoft intermediate language (MSIL) instruction to be put onto the stream.

arg

The character argument pushed onto the stream immediately after the instruction.

Remarks

The instruction values are defined in the **OpCodes** enumeration.

Requirements

Platforms: Windows 98, Windows NT 4.0, Windows Millennium Edition, Windows 2000, Windows XP Home Edition, Windows XP Professional, Windows .NET Server family

ILGenerator.Emit Method (OpCode, ConstructorInfo)

Puts the specified instruction and metadata token for the specified constructor onto the Microsoft intermediate language (MSIL) stream of instructions.

```
[Visual Basic]
Overloads Public Overridable Sub Emit( _
   ByVal opcode As OpCode, _
   ByVal con As ConstructorInfo _
)
[C#]
public virtual void Emit(
   OpCode opcode,
   ConstructorInfo con
);
[C++]
public: virtual void Emit(
   OpCode opcode,
   ConstructorInfo* con
);
[JScript]
public function Emit(
   opcode : OpCode,
   con : ConstructorInfo
);
```

Parameters

opcode

The Microsoft intermediate language (MSIL) instruction to be emitted onto the stream.

con

A **ConstructorInfo** representing a constructor.

Remarks

The instruction values are defined in the **OpCodes** enumeration. The location of *con* is recorded so that the instruction stream can be patched if necessary when persisting the module to a PE.

Requirements

Platforms: Windows 98, Windows NT 4.0, Windows Millennium Edition, Windows 2000, Windows XP Home Edition, Windows XP Professional, Windows .NET Server family

ILGenerator.Emit Method (OpCode, Double)

Puts the specified instruction and numerical argument onto the Microsoft intermediate language (MSIL) stream of instructions.

```
[Visual Basic]
Overloads Public Overridable Sub Emit( _
   ByVal opcode As OpCode, _
   ByVal arg As Double _
)
[C#]
public virtual void Emit(
   OpCode opcode,
   double arg
);
[C++]
public: virtual void Emit(
   OpCode opcode,
   double arg
);
[JScript]
public function Emit(
   opcode : OpCode,
   arg : double
);
```

Parameters

opcode

The Microsoft intermediate language (MSIL) instruction to be put onto the stream. Defined in the **OpCodes** enumeration.

arg

The numerical argument pushed onto the stream immediately after the instruction.

Remarks

The instruction values are defined in the **OpCodes** enumeration.

Requirements

Platforms: Windows 98, Windows NT 4.0, Windows Millennium Edition, Windows 2000, Windows XP Home Edition, Windows XP Professional, Windows .NET Server family

ILGenerator.Emit Method (OpCode, FieldInfo)

Puts the specified instruction and metadata token for the specified field onto the Microsoft intermediate language (MSIL) stream of instructions.

```
[Visual Basic]
Overloads Public Overridable Sub Emit( _
   ByVal opcode As OpCode, _
   ByVal field As FieldInfo _
)
[C#]
public virtual void Emit(
   OpCode opcode,
   FieldInfo field
);
[C++]
public: virtual void Emit(
   OpCode opcode,
   FieldInfo* field
);
[JScript]
public function Emit(
   opcode : OpCode,
   field : FieldInfo
);
```

Parameters

opcode
> The Microsoft intermediate language (MSIL) instruction to be emitted onto the stream.

field
> A **FieldInfo** representing a field.

Remarks

The instruction values are defined in the **OpCodes** enumeration. The location of *field* is recorded so that the instruction stream can be patched if necessary when persisting the module to a portable executable (PE).

Requirements

Platforms: Windows 98, Windows NT 4.0, Windows Millennium Edition, Windows 2000, Windows XP Home Edition, Windows XP Professional, Windows .NET Server family

ILGenerator.Emit Method (OpCode, Int16)

Puts the specified instruction and numerical argument onto the Microsoft intermediate language (MSIL) stream of instructions.

```
[Visual Basic]
Overloads Public Overridable Sub Emit( _
   ByVal opcode As OpCode, _
   ByVal arg As Short _
)
[C#]
public virtual void Emit(
   OpCode opcode,
   short arg
);
[C++]
public: virtual void Emit(
   OpCode opcode,
   short arg
);
```

```
[JScript]
public function Emit(
   opcode : OpCode,
   arg : Int16
);
```

Parameters

opcode
> The Microsoft intermediate language (MSIL) instruction to be emitted onto the stream.

arg
> The **Int** argument pushed onto the stream immediately after the instruction.

Remarks

The instruction values are defined in the **OpCodes** enumeration.

Requirements

Platforms: Windows 98, Windows NT 4.0, Windows Millennium Edition, Windows 2000, Windows XP Home Edition, Windows XP Professional, Windows .NET Server family

ILGenerator.Emit Method (OpCode, Int32)

Puts the specified instruction and numerical argument onto the Microsoft intermediate language (MSIL) stream of instructions.

```
[Visual Basic]
Overloads Public Overridable Sub Emit( _
   ByVal opcode As OpCode, _
   ByVal arg As Integer _
)
[C#]
public virtual void Emit(
   OpCode opcode,
   int arg
);
[C++]
public: virtual void Emit(
   OpCode opcode,
   int arg
);
[JScript]
public function Emit(
   opcode : OpCode,
   arg : int
);
```

Parameters

opcode
> The Microsoft intermediate language (MSIL) instruction to be put onto the stream.

arg
> The numerical argument pushed onto the stream immediately after the instruction.

Remarks

The instruction values are defined in the **OpCodes** enumeration.

Requirements

Platforms: Windows 98, Windows NT 4.0, Windows Millennium Edition, Windows 2000, Windows XP Home Edition, Windows XP Professional, Windows .NET Server family

ILGenerator.Emit Method (OpCode, Int64)

Puts the specified instruction and numerical argument onto the Microsoft intermediate language (MSIL) stream of instructions.

```
[Visual Basic]
Overloads Public Overridable Sub Emit( _
   ByVal opcode As OpCode, _
   ByVal arg As Long _
)
[C#]
public virtual void Emit(
   OpCode opcode,
   long arg
);
[C++]
public: virtual void Emit(
   OpCode opcode,
   __int64 arg
);
[JScript]
public function Emit(
   opcode : OpCode,
   arg : long
);
```

Parameters

opcode
   The Microsoft intermediate language (MSIL) instruction to be put onto the stream.

arg
   The numerical argument pushed onto the stream immediately after the instruction.

Remarks

The instruction values are defined in the **OpCodes** enumeration.

Requirements

Platforms: Windows 98, Windows NT 4.0, Windows Millennium Edition, Windows 2000, Windows XP Home Edition, Windows XP Professional, Windows .NET Server family

ILGenerator.Emit Method (OpCode, Label)

Puts the specified instruction onto the Microsoft intermediate language (MSIL) stream and leaves space to include a label when fixes are done.

```
[Visual Basic]
Overloads Public Overridable Sub Emit( _
   ByVal opcode As OpCode, _
   ByVal label As Label _
)
[C#]
public virtual void Emit(
   OpCode opcode,
   Label label
);
[C++]
public: virtual void Emit(
   OpCode opcode,
   Label label
);
```

```
[JScript]
public function Emit(
   opcode : OpCode,
   label : Label
);
```

Parameters

opcode
   The Microsoft intermediate language (MSIL) instruction to be emitted onto the stream.

label
   The label to which to branch from this location.

Remarks

The instruction values are defined in the **OpCodes** enumeration. Labels are created using **DefineLabel** and their location within the stream is fixed by using **MarkLabel**. If a single-byte instruction is used, the label can represent a jump of at most 127 bytes along the stream. *instruction* must represent a branch instruction. Since branches are relative instructions, *label* will be replaced with the correct offset to branch during the fixup process.

Example

See related example in the **System.Reflection.Emit.ILGenerator.BeginCatchBlock** method topic.

Requirements

Platforms: Windows 98, Windows NT 4.0, Windows Millennium Edition, Windows 2000, Windows XP Home Edition, Windows XP Professional, Windows .NET Server family

ILGenerator.Emit Method (OpCode, Label[])

Puts the specified instruction onto the Microsoft intermediate language (MSIL) stream and leaves space to include a label when fixes are done.

```
[Visual Basic]
Overloads Public Overridable Sub Emit( _
   ByVal opcode As OpCode, _
   ByVal labels() As Label _
)
[C#]
public virtual void Emit(
   OpCode opcode,
   Label[] labels
);
[C++]
public: virtual void Emit(
   OpCode opcode,
   Label labels[]
);
[JScript]
public function Emit(
   opcode : OpCode,
   labels : Label[]
);
```

Parameters

opcode
   The Microsoft intermediate language (MSIL) instruction to be emitted onto the stream.

labels
>   The array of label objects to which to branch from this location. All of the labels will be used.

Remarks

Emits a switch table.

The instruction values are defined in the **OpCodes** enumeration.Labels are created using **DefineLabel** and their location within the stream is fixed by using **MarkLabel**. If a single-byte instruction is used, the label can represent a jump of at most 127 bytes along the stream. *instruction* must represent a branch instruction. Since branches are relative instructions, *label* will be replaced with the correct offset to branch during the fixup process.

Example

See related example in the **System.Reflection.Emit.ILGenerator.BeginCatchBlock** method topic.

Requirements

Platforms: Windows 98, Windows NT 4.0, Windows Millennium Edition, Windows 2000, Windows XP Home Edition, Windows XP Professional, Windows .NET Server family

ILGenerator.Emit Method (OpCode, LocalBuilder)

Puts the specified instruction onto the Microsoft intermediate language (MSIL) stream followed by the index of the given local variable.

```
[Visual Basic]
Overloads Public Overridable Sub Emit( _
    ByVal opcode As OpCode, _
    ByVal local As LocalBuilder _
)
[C#]
public virtual void Emit(
    OpCode opcode,
    LocalBuilder local
);
[C++]
public: virtual void Emit(
    OpCode opcode,
    LocalBuilder* local
);
[JScript]
public function Emit(
    opcode : OpCode,
    local : LocalBuilder
);
```

Parameters

opcode
>   The MSIL instruction to be emitted onto the stream.

local
>   A local variable.

Exceptions

Exception Type	Condition
ArgumentException	*local* 's parent method does not match the method associated with this ILGenerator.

Exception Type	Condition
ArgumentNullException	*local* is a null reference (**Nothing** in Visual Basic).
InvalidOperationException	*instruction* is a single-byte instruction and *local* represents a local with an index of greater than Byte.MaxValue.

Remarks

The instruction values are defined in the **OpCodes** enumeration.

Requirements

Platforms: Windows 98, Windows NT 4.0, Windows Millennium Edition, Windows 2000, Windows XP Home Edition, Windows XP Professional, Windows .NET Server family

ILGenerator.Emit Method (OpCode, MethodInfo)

Puts the specified instruction onto the Microsoft intermediate language (MSIL) stream followed by the metadata token for the given method.

```
[Visual Basic]
Overloads Public Overridable Sub Emit( _
    ByVal opcode As OpCode, _
    ByVal meth As MethodInfo _
)
[C#]
public virtual void Emit(
    OpCode opcode,
    MethodInfo meth
);
[C++]
public: virtual void Emit(
    OpCode opcode,
    MethodInfo* meth
);
[JScript]
public function Emit(
    opcode : OpCode,
    meth : MethodInfo
);
```

Parameters

opcode
>   The MSIL instruction to be emitted onto the stream.

meth
>   A **MethodInfo** representing a method.

Exceptions

Exception Type	Condition
ArgumentNullException	*meth* is a null reference (**Nothing** in Visual Basic).

Remarks

The instruction values are defined in the **OpCodes** enumeration.The location of *meth* is recorded so that the instruction stream can be patched if necessary when persisting the module to a portable executable file.

Requirements

Platforms: Windows 98, Windows NT 4.0, Windows Millennium Edition, Windows 2000, Windows XP Home Edition, Windows XP Professional, Windows .NET Server family

ILGenerator.Emit Method (OpCode, SByte)

Puts the specified instruction and character argument onto the Microsoft intermediate language (MSIL) stream of instructions.

This method is not CLS-compliant.

```
[Visual Basic]
<CLSCompliant(False)>
Overloads Public Sub Emit( _
   ByVal opcode As OpCode, _
   ByVal arg As SByte _
)
[C#]
[CLSCompliant(false)]
public void Emit(
   OpCode opcode,
   sbyte arg
);
[C++]
[CLSCompliant(false)]
public: void Emit(
   OpCode opcode,
   char arg
);
[JScript]
public
   CLSCompliant(false)
function Emit(
   opcode : OpCode,
   arg : SByte
);
```

Parameters

opcode
   The Microsoft intermediate language (MSIL) instruction to be put onto the stream.

arg
   The character argument pushed onto the stream immediately after the instruction.

Remarks

The instruction values are defined in the **OpCodes** enumeration.

Requirements

Platforms: Windows 98, Windows NT 4.0, Windows Millennium Edition, Windows 2000, Windows XP Home Edition, Windows XP Professional, Windows .NET Server family

ILGenerator.Emit Method (OpCode, SignatureHelper)

Puts the specified instruction and a signature token onto the Microsoft intermediate language (MSIL) stream of instructions.

```
[Visual Basic]
Overloads Public Overridable Sub Emit( _
   ByVal opcode As OpCode, _
   ByVal signature As SignatureHelper _
)
```

```
[C#]
public virtual void Emit(
   OpCode opcode,
   SignatureHelper signature
);
[C++]
public: virtual void Emit(
   OpCode opcode,
   SignatureHelper* signature
);
[JScript]
public function Emit(
   opcode : OpCode,
   signature : SignatureHelper
);
```

Parameters

opcode
   The Microsoft intermediate language (MSIL) instruction to be emitted onto the stream.

signature
   A helper for constructing a signature token.

Exceptions

Exception Type	Condition
ArgumentNullException	*signature* is a null reference (**Nothing** in Visual Basic).

Remarks

The instruction values are defined in the **OpCodes** enumeration.

Requirements

Platforms: Windows 98, Windows NT 4.0, Windows Millennium Edition, Windows 2000, Windows XP Home Edition, Windows XP Professional, Windows .NET Server family

ILGenerator.Emit Method (OpCode, Single)

Puts the specified instruction and numerical argument onto the Microsoft intermediate language (MSIL) stream of instructions.

```
[Visual Basic]
Overloads Public Overridable Sub Emit( _
   ByVal opcode As OpCode, _
   ByVal arg As Single _
)
[C#]
public virtual void Emit(
   OpCode opcode,
   float arg
);
[C++]
public: virtual void Emit(
   OpCode opcode,
   float arg
);
[JScript]
public function Emit(
   opcode : OpCode,
   arg : float
);
```

Parameters

opcode

The Microsoft intermediate language (MSIL) instruction to be put onto the stream.

arg

The **Single** argument pushed onto the stream immediately after the instruction.

Remarks

The instruction values are defined in the **OpCodes** enumeration.

Requirements

Platforms: Windows 98, Windows NT 4.0, Windows Millennium Edition, Windows 2000, Windows XP Home Edition, Windows XP Professional, Windows .NET Server family

ILGenerator.Emit Method (OpCode, String)

Puts the specified instruction onto the Microsoft intermediate language (MSIL) stream followed by the metadata token for the given string.

```
[Visual Basic]
Overloads Public Overridable Sub Emit( _
   ByVal opcode As OpCode, _
   ByVal str As String _
)
[C#]
public virtual void Emit(
   OpCode opcode,
   string str
);
[C++]
public: virtual void Emit(
   OpCode opcode,
   String* str
);
[JScript]
public function Emit(
   opcode : OpCode,
   str : String
);
```

Parameters

opcode

The MSIL instruction to be emitted onto the stream.

str

The **String** to be emitted.

Remarks

The instruction values are defined in the **OpCodes** enumeration. The location of *str* is recorded for future fixups if the module is persisted to a portable executable (PE).

Requirements

Platforms: Windows 98, Windows NT 4.0, Windows Millennium Edition, Windows 2000, Windows XP Home Edition, Windows XP Professional, Windows .NET Server family

ILGenerator.Emit Method (OpCode, Type)

Puts the specified instruction onto the Microsoft intermediate language (MSIL) stream followed by the metadata token for the given type.

```
[Visual Basic]
Overloads Public Overridable Sub Emit( _
   ByVal opcode As OpCode, _
   ByVal cls As Type _
)
[C#]
public virtual void Emit(
   OpCode opcode,
   Type cls
);
[C++]
public: virtual void Emit(
   OpCode opcode,
   Type* cls
);
[JScript]
public function Emit(
   opcode : OpCode,
   cls : Type
);
```

Parameters

opcode

The MSIL instruction to be put onto the stream.

cls

A **Type**.

Exceptions

Exception Type	Condition
ArgumentNullException	*cls* is a null reference (**Nothing** in Visual Basic).

Remarks

The instruction values are defined in the **OpCodes** enumeration. The location of *cls* is recorded so that the token can be patched if necessary when persisting the module to a portable executable (PE).

Requirements

Platforms: Windows 98, Windows NT 4.0, Windows Millennium Edition, Windows 2000, Windows XP Home Edition, Windows XP Professional, Windows .NET Server family

ILGenerator.EmitCall Method

Puts a call or callvirt instruction onto the Microsoft intermediate language (MSIL) stream.

```
[Visual Basic]
Public Sub EmitCall( _
   ByVal opcode As OpCode, _
   ByVal methodInfo As MethodInfo, _
   ByVal optionalParameterTypes() As Type _
)
[C#]
public void EmitCall(
   OpCode opcode,
   MethodInfo methodInfo,
   Type[] optionalParameterTypes
);
```

```
[C++]
public: void EmitCall(
   OpCode opcode,
   MethodInfo* methodInfo,
   Type* optionalParameterTypes[]
);
[JScript]
public function EmitCall(
   opcode : OpCode,
   methodInfo : MethodInfo,
   optionalParameterTypes : Type[]
);
```

Parameters

opcode
    The MSIL instruction to be emitted onto the stream.
methodInfo
    The method to be called.
optionalParameterTypes
    The types of the optional arguments if the method is a **varargs**
    method.

Exceptions

Exception Type	Condition
ArgumentNullException	*methodInfo* is a null reference (**Nothing** in Visual Basic).
InvalidOperationException	The calling convention for the method is not **varargs** but optional parameter types are supplied.

Remarks

This method cannot be used to call a constructor. Instead, use the
overloaded **Emit** method that takes a **ConstructorInfo** argument.

Example

See related example in the
System.Reflection.Emit.ILGenerator.BeginCatchBlock method
topic.

Requirements

Platforms: Windows 98, Windows NT 4.0,
Windows Millennium Edition, Windows 2000,
Windows XP Home Edition, Windows XP Professional,
Windows .NET Server family

ILGenerator.EmitCalli Method

Overload List

Puts a **Calli** instruction onto the Microsoft intermediate language
(MSIL) stream, specifying an unmanaged calling convention for the
indirect call.

   [Visual Basic] **Overloads Public Sub EmitCalli(OpCode,
CallingConvention, Type, Type())**

   [C#] **public void EmitCalli(OpCode, CallingConvention,
Type, Type[]);**

   [C++] **public: void EmitCalli(OpCode, CallingConvention,
Type*, Type[]);**

   [JScript] **public function EmitCalli(OpCode,
CallingConvention, Type, Type[]);**

Puts a **Calli** instruction onto the Microsoft intermediate language
(MSIL) stream, specifying a managed calling convention for the
indirect call.

   [Visual Basic] **Overloads Public Sub EmitCalli(OpCode,
CallingConventions, Type, Type(), Type())**

   [C#] **public void EmitCalli(OpCode, CallingConventions,
Type, Type[], Type[]);**

   [C++] **public: void EmitCalli(OpCode, CallingConventions,
Type*, Type[], Type[]);**

   [JScript] **public function EmitCalli(OpCode,
CallingConventions, Type, Type[], Type[]);**

Example

See related example in the
System.Reflection.Emit.ILGenerator.BeginCatchBlock method
topic.

ILGenerator.EmitCalli Method (OpCode, CallingConvention, Type, Type[])

Puts a **Calli** instruction onto the Microsoft intermediate language
(MSIL) stream, specifying an unmanaged calling convention for the
indirect call.

```
[Visual Basic]
Overloads Public Sub EmitCalli( _
   ByVal opcode As OpCode, _
   ByVal unmanagedCallConv As CallingConvention, _
   ByVal returnType As Type, _
   ByVal parameterTypes() As Type _
)
[C#]
public void EmitCalli(
   OpCode opcode,
   CallingConvention unmanagedCallConv,
   Type returnType,
   Type[] parameterTypes
);
[C++]
public: void EmitCalli(
   OpCode opcode,
   CallingConvention unmanagedCallConv,
   Type* returnType,
   Type* parameterTypes[]
);
[JScript]
public function EmitCalli(
   opcode : OpCode,
   unmanagedCallConv : CallingConvention,
   returnType : Type,
   parameterTypes : Type[]
);
```

Parameters

opcode
    The MSIL instruction to be emitted onto the stream.
unmanagedCallConv
    The unmanaged calling convention to be used.
returnType
    The **Type** of the result.
parameterTypes
    The types of the required arguments to the instruction.

Remarks

Use **EmitCalli** to put a **Calli** instruction onto the stream. Do not use **Emit**.

Example

See related example in the **System.Reflection.Emit.ILGenerator.BeginCatchBlock** method topic.

Requirements

Platforms: Windows 98, Windows NT 4.0, Windows Millennium Edition, Windows 2000, Windows XP Home Edition, Windows XP Professional, Windows .NET Server family

ILGenerator.EmitCalli Method (OpCode, CallingConventions, Type, Type[], Type[])

Puts a **Calli** instruction onto the Microsoft intermediate language (MSIL) stream, specifying a managed calling convention for the indirect call.

```
[Visual Basic]
Overloads Public Sub EmitCalli( _
   ByVal opcode As OpCode, _
   ByVal callingConvention As CallingConventions, _
   ByVal returnType As Type, _
   ByVal parameterTypes() As Type, _
   ByVal optionalParameterTypes() As Type _
)
[C#]
public void EmitCalli(
   OpCode opcode,
   CallingConventions callingConvention,
   Type returnType,
   Type[] parameterTypes,
   Type[] optionalParameterTypes
);
[C++]
public: void EmitCalli(
   OpCode opcode,
   CallingConventions callingConvention,
   Type* returnType,
   Type* parameterTypes[],
   Type* optionalParameterTypes[]
);
[JScript]
public function EmitCalli(
   opcode : OpCode,
   callingConvention : CallingConventions,
   returnType : Type,
   parameterTypes : Type[],
   optionalParameterTypes : Type[]
);
```

Parameters

opcode
>The MSIL instruction to be emitted onto the stream.

callingConvention
>The managed calling convention to be used.

returnType
>The **Type** of the result.

parameterTypes
>The types of the required arguments to the instruction.

optionalParameterTypes
>The types of the optional arguments for vararg calls.

Remarks

Use **EmitCalli** to put a **Calli** instruction onto the stream. Do not use **Emit**.

Requirements

Platforms: Windows 98, Windows NT 4.0, Windows Millennium Edition, Windows 2000, Windows XP Home Edition, Windows XP Professional, Windows .NET Server family

ILGenerator.EmitWriteLine Method

Helper functions to emit a call to **WriteLine** with different types of values.

Overload List

Emits the Microsoft intermediate language (MSIL) necessary to call **WriteLine** with the given field.

>[Visual Basic] **Overloads Public Overridable Sub EmitWriteLine(FieldInfo)**
>
>[C#] **public virtual void EmitWriteLine(FieldInfo);**
>
>[C++] **public: virtual void EmitWriteLine(FieldInfo*);**
>
>[JScript] **public function EmitWriteLine(FieldInfo);**

Emits the Microsoft intermediate language (MSIL) necessary to call **WriteLine** with the given local variable.

>[Visual Basic] **Overloads Public Overridable Sub EmitWriteLine(LocalBuilder)**
>
>[C#] **public virtual void EmitWriteLine(LocalBuilder);**
>
>[C++] **public: virtual void EmitWriteLine(LocalBuilder*);**
>
>[JScript] **public function EmitWriteLine(LocalBuilder);**

Emits the Microsoft intermediate language (MSIL) to call **WriteLine** with a string.

>[Visual Basic] **Overloads Public Overridable Sub EmitWriteLine(String)**
>
>[C#] **public virtual void EmitWriteLine(string);**
>
>[C++] **public: virtual void EmitWriteLine(String*);**
>
>[JScript] **public function EmitWriteLine(String);**

Example

See related example in the **System.Reflection.Emit.ILGenerator.BeginCatchBlock** method topic.

ILGenerator.EmitWriteLine Method (FieldInfo)

Emits the Microsoft intermediate language (MSIL) necessary to call **WriteLine** with the given field.

```
[Visual Basic]
Overloads Public Overridable Sub EmitWriteLine( _
   ByVal fld As FieldInfo _
)
[C#]
public virtual void EmitWriteLine(
   FieldInfo fld
);
```

```
[C++]
public: virtual void EmitWriteLine(
   FieldInfo* fld
);
[JScript]
public function EmitWriteLine(
   fld : FieldInfo
);
```

Parameters

fld
> The field whose value is to be written to the console.

Exceptions

Exception Type	Condition
ArgumentException	There is no TextWriter.WriteLine method for the type of the specified field.
ArgumentNullException	*fld* is a null reference (**Nothing** in Visual Basic).
NotSupportedException	The type of the field is **TypeBuilder** or **EnumBuilder**.

Example

See related example in the **System.Reflection.Emit.ILGenerator.BeginCatchBlock** method topic.

Requirements

Platforms: Windows 98, Windows NT 4.0, Windows Millennium Edition, Windows 2000, Windows XP Home Edition, Windows XP Professional, Windows .NET Server family

ILGenerator.EmitWriteLine Method (LocalBuilder)

Emits the Microsoft intermediate language (MSIL) necessary to call **WriteLine** with the given local variable.

```
[Visual Basic]
Overloads Public Overridable Sub EmitWriteLine( _
   ByVal localBuilder As LocalBuilder _
)
[C#]
public virtual void EmitWriteLine(
   LocalBuilder localBuilder
);
[C++]
public: virtual void EmitWriteLine(
   LocalBuilder* localBuilder
);
[JScript]
public function EmitWriteLine(
   localBuilder : LocalBuilder
);
```

Parameters

localBuilder
> The local variable whose value is to be written to the console.

Exceptions

Exception Type	Condition
ArgumentException	The type of *localBuilder* is not supported (**TypeBuilder**, for example).

Remarks

It is an error to call **EmitWriteLine** with a **LocalBuilder** which is not of one of the types for which **WriteLine** implements overloads.

Example

See related example in the **System.Reflection.Emit.ILGenerator.BeginCatchBlock** method topic.

Requirements

Platforms: Windows 98, Windows NT 4.0, Windows Millennium Edition, Windows 2000, Windows XP Home Edition, Windows XP Professional, Windows .NET Server family

ILGenerator.EmitWriteLine Method (String)

Emits the Microsoft intermediate language (MSIL) to call **WriteLine** with a string.

```
[Visual Basic]
Overloads Public Overridable Sub EmitWriteLine( _
   ByVal value As String _
)
[C#]
public virtual void EmitWriteLine(
   string value
);
[C++]
public: virtual void EmitWriteLine(
   String* value
);
[JScript]
public function EmitWriteLine(
   value : String
);
```

Parameters

value
> The string to be printed.

Remarks

The string must have already been defined.

Example

See related example in the **System.Reflection.Emit.ILGenerator.BeginCatchBlock** method topic.

Requirements

Platforms: Windows 98, Windows NT 4.0, Windows Millennium Edition, Windows 2000, Windows XP Home Edition, Windows XP Professional, Windows .NET Server family

ILGenerator.EndExceptionBlock Method

Ends an exception block.

```
[Visual Basic]
Public Overridable Sub EndExceptionBlock()
[C#]
public virtual void EndExceptionBlock();
[C++]
public: virtual void EndExceptionBlock();
[JScript]
public function EndExceptionBlock();
```

Exceptions

Exception Type	Condition
InvalidOperationException	The end exception block occurs in an unexpected place in the code stream.
NotSupportedException	The Microsoft intermediate language (MSIL) being generated is not currently in an exception block.

Example

See related example in the **System.Reflection.Emit.ILGenerator.BeginCatchBlock** method topic.

Requirements

Platforms: Windows 98, Windows NT 4.0, Windows Millennium Edition, Windows 2000, Windows XP Home Edition, Windows XP Professional, Windows .NET Server family

ILGenerator.EndScope Method

Ends a lexical scope.

```
[Visual Basic]
Public Overridable Sub EndScope()
[C#]
public virtual void EndScope();
[C++]
public: virtual void EndScope();
[JScript]
public function EndScope();
```

Remarks

This method is used to emit symbolic information. It is used with **BeginScope**.

Example

See related example in the **System.Reflection.Emit.ILGenerator.BeginCatchBlock** method topic.

Requirements

Platforms: Windows 98, Windows NT 4.0, Windows Millennium Edition, Windows 2000, Windows XP Home Edition, Windows XP Professional, Windows .NET Server family

ILGenerator.MarkLabel Method

Marks the Microsoft intermediate language (MSIL) stream's current position with the given label.

```
[Visual Basic]
Public Overridable Sub MarkLabel( _
    ByVal loc As Label _
)
[C#]
public virtual void MarkLabel(
    Label loc
);
[C++]
public: virtual void MarkLabel(
    Label loc
);
[JScript]
public function MarkLabel(
    loc : Label
);
```

Parameters

loc
> The label for which to set an index.

Exceptions

Exception Type	Condition
ArgumentException	*loc* represents an invalid index into the label array. -or- An index for *loc* has already been defined.

Remarks

A label cannot be defined more than once.

Example

See related example in the **System.Reflection.Emit.ILGenerator.BeginCatchBlock** method topic.

Requirements

Platforms: Windows 98, Windows NT 4.0, Windows Millennium Edition, Windows 2000, Windows XP Home Edition, Windows XP Professional, Windows .NET Server family

ILGenerator.MarkSequencePoint Method

Marks a sequence point in the Microsoft intermediate language (MSIL) stream.

```
[Visual Basic]
Public Overridable Sub MarkSequencePoint( _
    ByVal document As ISymbolDocumentWriter, _
    ByVal startLine As Integer, _
    ByVal startColumn As Integer, _
    ByVal endLine As Integer, _
    ByVal endColumn As Integer _
)
```

```
[C#]
public virtual void MarkSequencePoint(
   ISymbolDocumentWriter document,
   int startLine,
   int startColumn,
   int endLine,
   int endColumn
);
[C++]
public: virtual void MarkSequencePoint(
   ISymbolDocumentWriter* document,
   int startLine,
   int startColumn,
   int endLine,
   int endColumn
);
[JScript]
public function MarkSequencePoint(
   document : ISymbolDocumentWriter,
   startLine : int,
   startColumn : int,
   endLine : int,
   endColumn : int
);
```

Parameters

document
> The document for which the sequence point is being defined.
startLine
> The line where the sequence point begins.
startColumn
> The column in the line where the sequence point begins.
endLine
> The line where the sequence point ends.
endColumn
> The column in the line where the sequence point ends.

Exceptions

Exception Type	Condition
ArgumentOutOfRange-Exception	*startLine* or *endLine* is <= 0.

Remarks

Line numbers are indexed from 1. Columns are indexed from 0.

The symbolic information normally includes at least one Microsoft intermediate language (MSIL) offset for each source line. When the just-in-time (JIT) compiler is about to compile a method, it asks the profiling services for a list of MSIL offsets that should be preserved. These MSIL offsets are called *sequence points*.

Requirements

Platforms: Windows 98, Windows NT 4.0, Windows Millennium Edition, Windows 2000, Windows XP Home Edition, Windows XP Professional, Windows .NET Server family

ILGenerator.ThrowException Method

Emits an instruction to throw an exception.

```
[Visual Basic]
Public Overridable Sub ThrowException( _
   ByVal excType As Type _
)
```

```
[C#]
public virtual void ThrowException(
   Type excType
);
[C++]
public: virtual void ThrowException(
   Type* excType
);
[JScript]
public function ThrowException(
   excType : Type
);
```

Parameters

excType
> The class of the type of exception to throw.

Exceptions

Exception Type	Condition
ArgumentException	*excType* is not the **Exception** class or a derived class of **Exception**. -or- The type does not have a default constructor.
ArgumentNullException	*excType* is a null reference (**Nothing** in Visual Basic).

Example

See related example in the **System.Reflection.Emit.ILGenerator.BeginCatchBlock** method topic.

Requirements

Platforms: Windows 98, Windows NT 4.0, Windows Millennium Edition, Windows 2000, Windows XP Home Edition, Windows XP Professional, Windows .NET Server family

ILGenerator.UsingNamespace Method

Specifies the namespace to be used in evaluating locals and watches for the current active lexical scope.

```
[Visual Basic]
Public Sub UsingNamespace( _
   ByVal usingNamespace As String _
)
[C#]
public void UsingNamespace(
   string usingNamespace
);
[C++]
public: void UsingNamespace(
   String* usingNamespace
);
[JScript]
public function UsingNamespace(
   usingNamespace : String
);
```

Parameters

usingNamespace
> The namespace to be used in evaluating locals and watches for the current active lexical scope

Exceptions

Exception Type	Condition
ArgumentException	Length of *usingNamespace* is zero.
ArgumentNullException	*usingNamespace* is a null reference (**Nothing** in Visual Basic).

Requirements

Platforms: Windows 98, Windows NT 4.0, Windows Millennium Edition, Windows 2000, Windows XP Home Edition, Windows XP Professional, Windows .NET Server family

Label Structure

Represents a label in the instruction stream. **Label** is used in conjunction with the **ILGenerator** class.

System.Object
  System.ValueType
    System.Reflection.Emit.Label

```
[Visual Basic]
<Serializable>
Public Structure Label
[C#]
[Serializable]
public struct Label
[C++]
[Serializable]
public __value struct Label
```

[JScript] In JScript, you can use the structures in the .NET Framework, but you cannot define your own.

Thread Safety

Reflection Emit is thread-safe when using assemblies that were created with the **AppDomain.DefineDynamicAssembly** method with the Boolean parameter *isSynchronized* set to **true**.

Requirements

Namespace: System.Reflection.Emit

Platforms: Windows 98, Windows NT 4.0, Windows Millennium Edition, Windows 2000, Windows XP Home Edition, Windows XP Professional, Windows .NET Server family

Assembly: Mscorlib (in Mscorlib.dll)

Label.Equals Method

Checks if the given object is an instance of **Label** and is equal to this instance.

```
[Visual Basic]
Overrides Public Function Equals( _
   ByVal obj As Object _
) As Boolean
[C#]
public override bool Equals(
   object obj
);
[C++]
public: bool Equals(
   Object* obj
);
[JScript]
public override function Equals(
   obj : Object
) : Boolean;
```

Parameters

obj
    The object to compare with this **Label** instance.

Return Value

Returns **true** if *obj* is an instance of **Label** and is equal to this object; otherwise, **false**.

Requirements

Platforms: Windows 98, Windows NT 4.0, Windows Millennium Edition, Windows 2000, Windows XP Home Edition, Windows XP Professional, Windows .NET Server family

Label.GetHashCode Method

Generates a hash code for this instance.

```
[Visual Basic]
Overrides Public Function GetHashCode() As Integer
[C#]
public override int GetHashCode();
[C++]
public: int GetHashCode();
[JScript]
public override function GetHashCode() : int;
```

Return Value

Returns a hash code for this instance.

Requirements

Platforms: Windows 98, Windows NT 4.0, Windows Millennium Edition, Windows 2000, Windows XP Home Edition, Windows XP Professional, Windows .NET Server family

LocalBuilder Class

Represents a local variable within a method or constructor.

System.Object
   System.Reflection.Emit.LocalBuilder

```
[Visual Basic]
NotInheritable Public Class LocalBuilder
[C#]
public sealed class LocalBuilder
[C++]
public __gc __sealed class LocalBuilder
[JScript]
public class LocalBuilder
```

Thread Safety

Reflection Emit is thread-safe when using assemblies that were created with the **AppDomain.DefineDynamicAssembly** method with the Boolean parameter *isSynchronized* set to **true**.

Remarks

A **LocalBuilder** object can be defined using the **DeclareLocal** method.

Example

[Visual Basic, C#] The following example demonstrates the use of **LocalBuilder**.

```
[Visual Basic]
Imports System
Imports System.Reflection
Imports System.Reflection.Emit
Imports System.Threading

Class LocalBuilder_Sample

   Public Shared Sub Main()
      Try

         ' Create an assembly.
         Dim myAssemblyName As New AssemblyName()
         myAssemblyName.Name = "SampleAssembly"

         Dim myAssembly As AssemblyBuilder =
Thread.GetDomain().DefineDynamicAssembly _
                              (myAssemblyName,
AssemblyBuilderAccess.Run)

         ' Create a module 'myModule'.
         Dim myModule As ModuleBuilder =
myAssembly.DefineDynamicModule("SampleModule", True)

         ' Define a public class 'myClass'.
         Dim myTypeBuilder As TypeBuilder =
myModule.DefineType("myClass", TypeAttributes.Public)

         ' Define a private String field.
         Dim myField As FieldBuilder =
myTypeBuilder.DefineField("myMessage", GetType(String), _
                              FieldAttributes.Private)

         ' Create the constructor.
         Dim myConstructorArgs As Type() = {GetType(String)}
         Dim myConstructor As ConstructorBuilder =
myTypeBuilder.DefineConstructor _
                              (MethodAttributes.Public,
CallingConventions.Standard, myConstructorArgs)

         ' Generate IL for the method.
         Dim myConstructorIL As ILGenerator =
```

```
myConstructor.GetILGenerator()
         myConstructorIL.Emit(OpCodes.Ldarg_0)
         Dim mySuperConstructor As ConstructorInfo =
GetType(Object).GetConstructor(New Type() {})
         myConstructorIL.Emit(OpCodes.Call, mySuperConstructor)
         myConstructorIL.Emit(OpCodes.Ldarg_0)
         myConstructorIL.Emit(OpCodes.Ldarg_1)
         myConstructorIL.Emit(OpCodes.Stfld, myField)
         myConstructorIL.Emit(OpCodes.Ret)

         ' Create the 'Function1' public method.
         Dim myMethod As MethodBuilder =
myTypeBuilder.DefineMethod("Function1", MethodAttributes. _
                     Public, GetType(String), Nothing)

         ' Generate IL for 'Function1'.
         Dim myMethodIL As ILGenerator = myMethod.GetILGenerator()

         ' Create local variables.
         Dim myLB1 As LocalBuilder =
myMethodIL.DeclareLocal(GetType(String))
         myLB1.SetLocalSymInfo("myString")
         Console.WriteLine("'myLB1' type is :{0}", myLB1.LocalType)
         Dim myLB2 As LocalBuilder =
myMethodIL.DeclareLocal(GetType(Integer))
         myLB2.SetLocalSymInfo("myInt", 1, 2)
         Console.WriteLine("'myLB2' type is :{0}", myLB2.LocalType)

         myMethodIL.Emit(OpCodes.Ldstr, "Local value" )
         myMethodIL.Emit(OpCodes.Stloc_0 )
         myMethodIL.Emit(OpCodes.Ldloc_0 )
         myMethodIL.Emit(OpCodes.Stloc_1 )
         myMethodIL.Emit(OpCodes.Ldloc_1 )
         myMethodIL.Emit(OpCodes.Ret )

         ' Create "myClass" class.
         Dim myType1 As Type = myTypeBuilder.CreateType()

         Console.WriteLine("'myClass' is created.")
         ' Create an instance of the 'myClass'.
         Dim myObject1 As Object =
Activator.CreateInstance(myType1, New Object() {"HelloWorld"})

         ' Invoke 'Function1' method of 'myClass'.
         Dim myObject2 As Object =
myType1.InvokeMember("Function1", BindingFlags.InvokeMethod, _
                     Nothing, myObject1, Nothing)
         Console.WriteLine("myClass.Function1 is called.")
         Console.WriteLine("myClass.Function1 returned:
{0}", myObject2)
      Catch e As Exception
         Console.WriteLine("Exception :{0}", e.Message)
      End Try
   End Sub 'Main
End Class 'LocalBuilder_Sample

[C#]
using System;
using System.Reflection;
using System.Reflection.Emit;
using System.Threading;

class LocalBuilder_Sample
{
   public static void Main()
   {
      try
      {

         // Create an assembly.
         AssemblyName myAssemblyName = new AssemblyName();
         myAssemblyName.Name = "SampleAssembly";
```

```
        AssemblyBuilder myAssembly =
Thread.GetDomain().DefineDynamicAssembly(
        myAssemblyName, AssemblyBuilderAccess.Run);

        // Create a module 'myModule'.
        ModuleBuilder
myModule=myAssembly.DefineDynamicModule("SampleModule",true);

        // Define a public class 'myClass'.
        TypeBuilder myTypeBuilder =
myModule.DefineType("myClass", TypeAttributes.Public);

        // Define a private String field.
        FieldBuilder myField =
myTypeBuilder.DefineField("myMessage", typeof(String),
FieldAttributes.Private);

        // Create the constructor.
        Type[] myConstructorArgs = { typeof(String) };
        ConstructorBuilder myConstructor =
myTypeBuilder.DefineConstructor(
            MethodAttributes.Public,
CallingConventions.Standard, myConstructorArgs);

        // Generate IL for the method.
        ILGenerator myConstructorIL = myConstructor.GetILGenerator();
        myConstructorIL.Emit(OpCodes.Ldarg_0);
        ConstructorInfo mySuperConstructor =
typeof(Object).GetConstructor(new Type[0]);
        myConstructorIL.Emit(OpCodes.Call, mySuperConstructor);
        myConstructorIL.Emit(OpCodes.Ldarg_0);
        myConstructorIL.Emit(OpCodes.Ldarg_1);
        myConstructorIL.Emit(OpCodes.Stfld, myField);
        myConstructorIL.Emit(OpCodes.Ret);

        // Create the 'Function1' public method.
        MethodBuilder myMethod =
myTypeBuilder.DefineMethod("Function1",
        MethodAttributes.Public, typeof(String), null);

        // Generate IL for 'Function1'.
        ILGenerator myMethodIL = myMethod.GetILGenerator();

        // Create local variables.
        LocalBuilder myLB1 = myMethodIL.DeclareLocal(typeof(string));
        myLB1.SetLocalSymInfo("myString");
        Console.WriteLine("'myLB1' type is :{0}", myLB1.LocalType);
        LocalBuilder myLB2 = myMethodIL.DeclareLocal(typeof(int));
        myLB2.SetLocalSymInfo("myInt",1,2);
        Console.WriteLine("'myLB2' type is :{0}", myLB2.LocalType);
        myMethodIL.Emit(OpCodes.Ldstr, "Local value" );
        myMethodIL.Emit(OpCodes.Stloc_0 );
        myMethodIL.Emit(OpCodes.Ldloc_0 );
        myMethodIL.Emit(OpCodes.Stloc_1);
        myMethodIL.Emit(OpCodes.Ldloc_1 );
        myMethodIL.Emit(OpCodes.Ret );

        // Create "myClass" class.
        Type myType1 = myTypeBuilder.CreateType();

        Console.WriteLine("'myClass' is created.");
        // Create an instance of the 'myClass'.
        Object myObject1 = Activator.CreateInstance(myType1, new
Object[] { "HelloWorld" });

        // Invoke 'Function1' method of 'myClass'.
        Object myObject2 = myType1.InvokeMember
("Function1", BindingFlags.InvokeMethod, null, myObject1, null);
        Console.WriteLine("myClass.Function1 is called.");
        Console.WriteLine("myClass.Function1 returned:
{0}", myObject2);
    }
    catch(Exception e)
    {
        Console.WriteLine("Exception :{0}", e.Message );
    }
  }
}
```

LocalBuilder.LocalType Property

Returns the type of the local variable.

```
[Visual Basic]
Public ReadOnly Property LocalType As Type
[C#]
public Type LocalType {get;}
[C++]
public: __property Type* get_LocalType();
[JScript]
public function get LocalType() : Type;
```

Property Value

The type of the local variable.

Example

See related example in the **System.Reflection.Emit.LocalBuilder** class topic.

LocalBuilder.SetLocalSymInfo Method

Sets the local variable's symbolic information.

Overload List

Sets the name of this local variable.

[Visual Basic] **Overloads Public Sub SetLocalSymInfo (String)**

[C#] **public void SetLocalSymInfo(string);**

[C++] **public: void SetLocalSymInfo(String*);**

[JScript] **public function SetLocalSymInfo(String);**

Sets the name and lexical scope of this local variable.

[Visual Basic] **Overloads Public Sub SetLocalSymInfo (String, Integer, Integer)**

[C#] **public void SetLocalSymInfo(string, int, int);**

[C++] **public: void SetLocalSymInfo(String*, int, int);**

[JScript] **public function SetLocalSymInfo(String, int, int);**

Example

See related example in the **System.Reflection.Emit.LocalBuilder** class topic.

LocalBuilder.SetLocalSymInfo Method (String)

Sets the name of this local variable.

```
[Visual Basic]
Overloads Public Sub SetLocalSymInfo( _
   ByVal name As String _
)
[C#]
public void SetLocalSymInfo(
   string name
);
[C++]
public: void SetLocalSymInfo(
   String* name
);
[JScript]
public function SetLocalSymInfo(
   name : String
);
```

Parameters

name
    The name of the local variable.

Exceptions

Exception Type	Condition
InvalidOperation-Exception	The containing type has been created with **CreateType**. -or- There is no symbolic writer defined for the containing module.

Example

See related example in the **System.Reflection.Emit.LocalBuilder** class topic.

Requirements

Platforms: Windows 98, Windows NT 4.0, Windows Millennium Edition, Windows 2000, Windows XP Home Edition, Windows XP Professional, Windows .NET Server family

LocalBuilder.SetLocalSymInfo Method (String, Int32, Int32)

Sets the name and lexical scope of this local variable.

```
[Visual Basic]
Overloads Public Sub SetLocalSymInfo( _
   ByVal name As String, _
   ByVal startOffset As Integer, _
   ByVal endOffset As Integer _
)
[C#]
public void SetLocalSymInfo(
   string name,
   int startOffset,
   int endOffset
);
```

```
[C++]
public: void SetLocalSymInfo(
   String* name,
   int startOffset,
   int endOffset
);
[JScript]
public function SetLocalSymInfo(
   name : String,
   startOffset : int,
   endOffset : int
);
```

Parameters

name
    The name of the local variable.
startOffset
    The beginning offset of the lexical scope of the local variable.
endOffset
    The ending offset of the lexical scope of the local variable.

Exceptions

Exception Type	Condition
InvalidOperation-Exception	The containing type has been created with **CreateType**. -or- There is no symbolic writer defined for the containing module.

Example

See related example in the **System.Reflection.Emit.LocalBuilder** class topic.

Requirements

Platforms: Windows 98, Windows NT 4.0, Windows Millennium Edition, Windows 2000, Windows XP Home Edition, Windows XP Professional, Windows .NET Server family

MethodBuilder Class

Defines and represents a method (or constructor) on a dynamic class.

System.Object
   System.Reflection.MemberInfo
     System.Reflection.MethodBase
       System.Reflection.MethodInfo
         System.Reflection.Emit.MethodBuilder

```
[Visual Basic]
NotInheritable Public Class MethodBuilder
   Inherits MethodInfo
[C#]
public sealed class MethodBuilder : MethodInfo
[C++]
public __gc __sealed class MethodBuilder : public MethodInfo
[JScript]
public class MethodBuilder extends MethodInfo
```

Thread Safety

Reflection Emit is thread-safe when using assemblies that were created with the **AppDomain.DefineDynamicAssembly** method with the Boolean parameter *isSynchronized* set to **true**.

Remarks

MethodBuilder is used to fully describe a method in Microsoft intermediate language (MSIL), including the name, attributes, signature, and method body. It is used in conjunction with the **TypeBuilder** class to create classes at runtime.

Example

[Visual Basic, C#, C++] An example using the **MethodBuilder** class to create a method within a dynamic type is provided below.

```
[Visual Basic]
Imports System
Imports System.Threading
Imports System.Reflection
Imports System.Reflection.Emit

_

Class DemoMethodBuilder

   Public Shared Sub AddMethodDynamically(ByRef myTypeBld    ↵
As TypeBuilder, _
                      mthdName As String, _
                      mthdParams() As Type, _
                      returnType As Type, _
                      mthdAction As String)

   Dim myMthdBld As MethodBuilder = myTypeBld.DefineMethod(mthdName, _
                      MethodAttributes.Public Or    ↵
MethodAttributes.Static, _
                      returnType, _
                      mthdParams)

      Dim ILout As ILGenerator = myMthdBld.GetILGenerator()

      Dim numParams As Integer = mthdParams.Length

      Dim x As Byte
      For x = 0 To numParams - 1
        ILout.Emit(OpCodes.Ldarg_S, x)
      Next x

      If numParams > 1 Then
        Dim y As Integer
        For y = 0 To (numParams - 1) - 1
```

```
         Select Case mthdAction
           Case "A"
              ILout.Emit(OpCodes.Add)
           Case "M"
              ILout.Emit(OpCodes.Mul)
           Case Else
              ILout.Emit(OpCodes.Add)
         End Select
       Next y
     End If
     ILout.Emit(OpCodes.Ret)
   End Sub 'AddMethodDynamically

   Public Shared Sub Main()

      Dim myDomain As AppDomain = Thread.GetDomain()
      Dim asmName As New AssemblyName()
      asmName.Name = "DynamicAssembly1"

      Dim myAsmBuilder As AssemblyBuilder =              ↵
myDomain.DefineDynamicAssembly(asmName, _
                       AssemblyBuilderAccess.RunAndSave)

      Dim myModule As ModuleBuilder =
myAsmBuilder.DefineDynamicModule("DynamicModule1", _
                       "MyDynamicAsm.dll")

      Dim myTypeBld As TypeBuilder =                     ↵
myModule.DefineType("MyDynamicType", TypeAttributes.Public)

      ' Get info from the user to build the method dynamically.
      Console.WriteLine("Let's build a simple method dynamically!")
      Console.WriteLine("Please enter a few numbers,            ↵
separated by spaces.")
      Dim inputNums As String = Console.ReadLine()
      Console.Write("Do you want to [A]dd or [M]ultiply        ↵
these numbers? ")
      Dim myMthdAction As String = Console.ReadLine()
      Console.Write("Lastly, what do you want to name your     ↵
new dynamic method? ")
      Dim myMthdName As String = Console.ReadLine()

      ' Process inputNums into an array and create a           ↵
corresponding Type array
      Dim index As Integer = 0
      Dim inputNumsList As String() = inputNums.Split()

      Dim myMthdParams(inputNumsList.Length - 1) As Type
      Dim inputValsList(inputNumsList.Length - 1) As Object

      Dim inputNum As String
      For Each inputNum In  inputNumsList
         inputValsList(index) = CType(Convert.ToInt32(inputNum),  ↵
Object)
         myMthdParams(index) = GetType(Integer)
         index += 1
      Next inputNum

      ' Now, call the method building method with the          ↵
parameters, passing the
      ' TypeBuilder by reference.
      AddMethodDynamically(myTypeBld, myMthdName,              ↵
myMthdParams, GetType(Integer), myMthdAction)

      Dim myType As Type = myTypeBld.CreateType()

      Dim description as String
      If myMthdAction = "A" Then
      description = "adding"
      Else
      description = "multiplying"
      End If

      Console.WriteLine("---")
      Console.WriteLine("The result of {0} the inputted        ↵
```

```
values is: {1}", _
          description, _
        myType.InvokeMember(myMthdName, _
                    BindingFlags.InvokeMethod Or _
                        BindingFlags.Public Or _
                    BindingFlags.Static, _
                    Nothing, _
                    Nothing, _
                    inputValsList))
      Console.WriteLine("---")

    ' If you are interested in seeing the MSIL generated
dynamically for the method
    ' your program generated, change to the directory where
you ran the compiled
    ' code sample and type "ildasm MyDynamicAsm.dll" at the
prompt. When the list
    ' of manifest contents appears, click on "MyDynamicType"
and then on the name of
    ' of the method you provided during execution.

    myAsmBuilder.Save("MyDynamicAsm.dll")

    Dim myMthdInfo As MethodInfo = myType.GetMethod(myMthdName)
    Console.WriteLine("Your Dynamic Method: {0};",
myMthdInfo.ToString())
  End Sub 'Main
End Class 'DemoMethodBuilder

[C#]
using System;
using System.Threading;
using System.Reflection;
using System.Reflection.Emit;

class DemoMethodBuilder {

  public static void AddMethodDynamically (ref TypeBuilder myTypeBld,
                  string mthdName,
                  Type[] mthdParams,
                  Type returnType,
                  string mthdAction)
  {

    MethodBuilder myMthdBld = myTypeBld.DefineMethod(
                  mthdName,
                  MethodAttributes.Public |
                  MethodAttributes.Static,
                  returnType,
                  mthdParams);

    ILGenerator ILout = myMthdBld.GetILGenerator();

    int numParams = mthdParams.Length;

    for (byte x=0; x<numParams; x++) {
      ILout.Emit(OpCodes.Ldarg_S, x);
    }

      if (numParams > 1) {
          for (int y=0; y<(numParams-1); y++) {
      switch (mthdAction) {
        case "A": ILout.Emit(OpCodes.Add);
            break;
        case "M": ILout.Emit(OpCodes.Mul);
            break;
        default: ILout.Emit(OpCodes.Add);
            break;
      }
    }
  }
    ILout.Emit(OpCodes.Ret);

}
```

```
  public static void Main()
  {

    AppDomain myDomain = Thread.GetDomain();
    AssemblyName asmName = new AssemblyName();
    asmName.Name = "DynamicAssembly1";

    AssemblyBuilder myAsmBuilder = myDomain.DefineDynamicAssembly(
                  asmName,
                  AssemblyBuilderAccess.RunAndSave);

    ModuleBuilder myModule =
myAsmBuilder.DefineDynamicModule("DynamicModule1",
                  "MyDynamicAsm.dll");

    TypeBuilder myTypeBld = myModule.DefineType("MyDynamicType",
                  TypeAttributes.Public);

    // Get info from the user to build the method dynamically.

    Console.WriteLine("Let's build a simple method dynamically!");
    Console.WriteLine("Please enter a few numbers,
separated by spaces.");
    string inputNums = Console.ReadLine();
    Console.Write("Do you want to [A]dd or [M]ultiply these
numbers? ");
    string myMthdAction = Console.ReadLine();
    Console.Write("Lastly, what do you want to name your new
dynamic method? ");
    string myMthdName = Console.ReadLine();

    // Process inputNums into an array and create a
corresponding Type array

    int index = 0;
    string[] inputNumsList = inputNums.Split();

    Type[] myMthdParams = new Type[inputNumsList.Length];
    object[] inputValsList = new object[inputNumsList.Length];

    foreach (string inputNum in inputNumsList) {
      inputValsList[index] = (object)Convert.ToInt32(inputNum);
      myMthdParams[index] = typeof(int);
      index++;
    }

    // Now, call the method building method with the
parameters, passing the
    // TypeBuilder by reference.

    AddMethodDynamically(ref myTypeBld,
          myMthdName,
          myMthdParams,
          typeof(int),
          myMthdAction);

    Type myType = myTypeBld.CreateType();

    Console.WriteLine("---");
    Console.WriteLine("The result of {0} the inputted
values is: {1}",
              ((myMthdAction == "A") ? "adding" : "multiplying"),
              myType.InvokeMember(myMthdName,
              BindingFlags.InvokeMethod | BindingFlags.Public |
              BindingFlags.Static,
              null,
              null,
              inputValsList));
    Console.WriteLine("---");

    // Let's take a look at the method we created.

    // If you are interested in seeing the MSIL generated
dynamically for the method
        // your program generated, change to the directory
```

```
where you ran the compiled
        // code sample and type "ildasm MyDynamicAsm.dll" at
the prompt. When the list
    // of manifest contents appears, click on
"MyDynamicType" and then on the name of
        // of the method you provided during execution.

    myAsmBuilder.Save("MyDynamicAsm.dll");

    MethodInfo myMthdInfo = myType.GetMethod(myMthdName);
        Console.WriteLine("Your Dynamic Method: {0};",
myMthdInfo.ToString());

    }

}

[C++]
#using <mscorlib.dll>

using namespace System;
using namespace System::Threading;
using namespace System::Reflection;
using namespace System::Reflection::Emit;

void AddMethodDynamically (TypeBuilder* myTypeBld,
                           String* mthdName,
                           Type* mthdParams[],
                           Type* returnType,
                           String* mthdAction)
{
    MethodBuilder*  myMthdBld = myTypeBld->DefineMethod(
        mthdName,
        static_cast<MethodAttributes>(MethodAttributes::Public |
MethodAttributes::Static),
        returnType,
        mthdParams);

    ILGenerator* ILOut = myMthdBld->GetILGenerator();

    int numParams = mthdParams->Length;

    for (Byte x=0; x<numParams; x++) {
        ILOut->Emit(OpCodes::Ldarg_S, x);
    }

    if (numParams > 1) {
        for (int y=0; y<(numParams-1); y++) {
            if(mthdAction->Equals(S"A")) ILOut->Emit(OpCodes::Add);
            else if(mthdAction->Equals(S"M")) ILOut->Emit(OpCodes::Mul);
            else ILOut->Emit(OpCodes::Mul);
        }
    }
    ILOut->Emit(OpCodes::Ret);
}

int main() {

    AppDomain*  myDomain = Thread::GetDomain();
    AssemblyName* asmName = new AssemblyName();
    asmName->Name = S"DynamicAssembly1";

    AssemblyBuilder*  myAsmBuilder = myDomain-
>DefineDynamicAssembly(asmName,
        AssemblyBuilderAccess::RunAndSave);

    ModuleBuilder*  myModule = myAsmBuilder-
>DefineDynamicModule(S"DynamicModule1",
        S"MyDynamicAsm.dll");

    TypeBuilder*  myTypeBld = myModule->DefineType(S"MyDynamicType",
        TypeAttributes::Public);

    // Get info from the user to build the method dynamically.
```

```
    Console::WriteLine(S"Let's build a simple method dynamically!");
    Console::WriteLine(S"Please enter a few numbers,
separated by spaces.");
    String* inputNums = Console::ReadLine();
    Console::Write(S"Do you want to [A]dd or [M]ultiply
these numbers? ");
    String* myMthdAction = Console::ReadLine();
    Console::Write(S"Lastly, what do you want to name your
new dynamic method? ");
    String* myMthdName = Console::ReadLine();

    // Process inputNums into an array and create a
corresponding Type array

    int index = 0;
    String* inputNumsList[] = inputNums->Split(0);

    Type* myMthdParams[] = new Type*[inputNumsList->Length];
    Object* inputValsList[] = new Object*[inputNumsList->Length];

    System::Collections::IEnumerator* myEnum = inputNumsList-
>GetEnumerator();
    while (myEnum->MoveNext()) {
        String* inputNum = __try_cast<String*>(myEnum->Current);

        inputValsList[index] = __box(Convert::ToInt32(inputNum));
        myMthdParams[index] = __typeof(int);
        index++;
    }

    // Now, call the method building method with the parameters,
passing the
    // TypeBuilder by reference.

    AddMethodDynamically(myTypeBld,
        myMthdName,
        myMthdParams,
        __typeof(int),
        myMthdAction);

    Type*  myType = myTypeBld->CreateType();

    Console::WriteLine(S"---");
    Console::WriteLine(S"The result of {0} the inputted values is: {1}",
        ((myMthdAction->Equals(S"A")) ? S"adding" : S"multiplying"),
        myType-
>InvokeMember(myMthdName,static_cast<BindingFlags>(BindingFlags:
:InvokeMethod | BindingFlags::Public |
        BindingFlags::Static),
        0,
        0,
        inputValsList));
    Console::WriteLine(S"---");

    // Let's take a look at the method we created.

    // If you are interested in seeing the MSIL generated
dynamically for the method
    // your program generated, change to the directory where
you ran the compiled
    // code sample and type "ildasm MyDynamicAsm.dll" at the
prompt. When the list
    // of manifest contents appears, click on "MyDynamicType"
and then on the name of
    // of the method you provided during execution.

    myAsmBuilder->Save(S"MyDynamicAsm.dll");

    MethodInfo*  myMthdInfo = myType->GetMethod(myMthdName);
    Console::WriteLine(S"Your Dynamic Method: {0};", myMthdInfo);
}
```

Requirements

Namespace: System.Reflection.Emit

Platforms: Windows 98, Windows NT 4.0, Windows Millennium Edition, Windows 2000, Windows XP Home Edition, Windows XP Professional, Windows .NET Server family

Assembly: Mscorlib (in Mscorlib.dll)

MethodBuilder.Attributes Property

Retrieves the attributes for this method.

```
[Visual Basic]
Overrides Public ReadOnly Property Attributes As MethodAttributes
[C#]
public override MethodAttributes Attributes {get;}
[C++]
public: __property MethodAttributes get_Attributes();
[JScript]
public override function get Attributes() : MethodAttributes;
```

Property Value

Read-only. Retrieves the **MethodAttributes** for this method.

Requirements

Platforms: Windows 98, Windows NT 4.0, Windows Millennium Edition, Windows 2000, Windows XP Home Edition, Windows XP Professional, Windows .NET Server family

MethodBuilder.CallingConvention Property

Returns the calling convention of the method.

```
[Visual Basic]
Overrides Public ReadOnly Property CallingConvention As _
    CallingConventions
[C#]
public override CallingConventions CallingConvention {get;}
[C++]
public: __property CallingConventions get_CallingConvention();
[JScript]
public override function get CallingConvention() :
    CallingConventions;
```

Property Value

Read-only. The calling convention of the method.

Requirements

Platforms: Windows 98, Windows NT 4.0, Windows Millennium Edition, Windows 2000, Windows XP Home Edition, Windows XP Professional, Windows .NET Server family

MethodBuilder.DeclaringType Property

Returns the type that declares this method.

```
[Visual Basic]
Overrides Public ReadOnly Property DeclaringType As Type
[C#]
public override Type DeclaringType {get;}
```

```
[C++]
public: __property Type* get_DeclaringType();
[JScript]
public override function get DeclaringType() : Type;
```

Property Value

Read-only. The type that declares this method.

Example

See related example in the **System.Reflection.Emit.MethodBuilder** class topic.

Requirements

Platforms: Windows 98, Windows NT 4.0, Windows Millennium Edition, Windows 2000, Windows XP Home Edition, Windows XP Professional, Windows .NET Server family

MethodBuilder.InitLocals Property

Gets or sets whether the local variables in this method should be zero initialized. The default value of this property is **true**.

```
[Visual Basic]
Public Property InitLocals As Boolean
[C#]
public bool InitLocals {get; set;}
[C++]
public: __property bool get_InitLocals();
public: __property void set_InitLocals(bool);
[JScript]
public function get InitLocals() : Boolean;
public function set InitLocals(Boolean);
```

Property Value

Read/write. Gets or sets whether the local variables in this method should be zero initialized.

Remarks

If this property is set to **false**, the runtime will generate unverifiable code.

Requirements

Platforms: Windows 98, Windows NT 4.0, Windows Millennium Edition, Windows 2000, Windows XP Home Edition, Windows XP Professional, Windows .NET Server family

MethodBuilder.MethodHandle Property

Retrieves the internal handle for the method. Use this handle to access the underlying metadata handle.

```
[Visual Basic]
Overrides Public ReadOnly Property MethodHandle As _
    RuntimeMethodHandle
[C#]
public override RuntimeMethodHandle MethodHandle {get;}
[C++]
public: __property RuntimeMethodHandle get_MethodHandle();
[JScript]
public override function get MethodHandle() : RuntimeMethodHandle;
```

Property Value

Read-only. The internal handle for the method. Use this handle to access the underlying metadata handle.

Exceptions

Exception Type	Condition
NotSupportedException	This method is not currently supported. Retrieve the method using **GetMethod** and call **MethodHandle** on the returned **MethodInfo**.

Requirements

Platforms: Windows 98, Windows NT 4.0, Windows Millennium Edition, Windows 2000, Windows XP Home Edition, Windows XP Professional, Windows .NET Server family

MethodBuilder.Name Property

Retrieves the name of this method.

```
[Visual Basic]
Overrides Public ReadOnly Property Name As String
[C#]
public override string Name {get;}
[C++]
public: __property String* get_Name();
[JScript]
public override function get Name() : String;
```

Property Value

Read-only. Retrieves a string containing the simple name of this method.

Requirements

Platforms: Windows 98, Windows NT 4.0, Windows Millennium Edition, Windows 2000, Windows XP Home Edition, Windows XP Professional, Windows .NET Server family

MethodBuilder.ReflectedType Property

Retrieves the class that was used in reflection to obtain this object.

```
[Visual Basic]
Overrides Public ReadOnly Property ReflectedType As Type
[C#]
public override Type ReflectedType {get;}
[C++]
public: __property Type* get_ReflectedType();
[JScript]
public override function get ReflectedType() : Type;
```

Property Value

Read-only. The type used to obtain this method.

Requirements

Platforms: Windows 98, Windows NT 4.0, Windows Millennium Edition, Windows 2000, Windows XP Home Edition, Windows XP Professional, Windows .NET Server family

MethodBuilder.ReturnType Property

Retrieves the type of this method's return value.

```
[Visual Basic]
Overrides Public ReadOnly Property ReturnType As Type
[C#]
public override Type ReturnType {get;}
[C++]
public: __property Type* get_ReturnType();
[JScript]
public override function get ReturnType() : Type;
```

Property Value

Read-only. The type of object this method returns. If the **MethodBuilder** was defined as having the return type a null reference (**Nothing** in Visual Basic), the method will be defined to return void. However, **ReturnType** will return a null reference (**Nothing**).

Requirements

Platforms: Windows 98, Windows NT 4.0, Windows Millennium Edition, Windows 2000, Windows XP Home Edition, Windows XP Professional, Windows .NET Server family

MethodBuilder.ReturnTypeCustomAttributes Property

Returns the custom attributes of the method's return type.

```
[Visual Basic]
Overrides Public ReadOnly Property ReturnTypeCustomAttributes As _
    ICustomAttributeProvider
[C#]
public override ICustomAttributeProvider ReturnTypeCustomAttributes
    {get;}
[C++]
public: __property ICustomAttributeProvider*
    get_ReturnTypeCustomAttributes();
[JScript]
public override function get ReturnTypeCustomAttributes() :
    ICustomAttributeProvider;
```

Property Value

Read-only. The custom attributes of the method's return type.

Remarks

This method always returns a null reference (**Nothing** in Visual Basic). Get the **MethodInfo** after the containing **Type** has been created and invoked **ReturnTypeCustomAttributes** on the **MethodInfo**.

Requirements

Platforms: Windows 98, Windows NT 4.0, Windows Millennium Edition, Windows 2000, Windows XP Home Edition, Windows XP Professional, Windows .NET Server family

MethodBuilder.Signature Property

Retrieves the signature of the field.

```
[Visual Basic]
Public ReadOnly Property Signature As String
```

```
[C#]
public string Signature {get;}
[C++]
public: __property String* get_Signature();
[JScript]
public function get Signature() : String;
```

Property Value

Read-only. A String containing the signature of the method reflected by this **MethodBase** instance.

Requirements

Platforms: Windows 98, Windows NT 4.0, Windows Millennium Edition, Windows 2000, Windows XP Home Edition, Windows XP Professional, Windows .NET Server family

MethodBuilder.AddDeclarativeSecurity Method

Adds declarative security to this method.

```
[Visual Basic]
Public Sub AddDeclarativeSecurity( _
    ByVal action As SecurityAction, _
    ByVal pset As PermissionSet _
)
[C#]
public void AddDeclarativeSecurity(
    SecurityAction action,
    PermissionSet pset
);
[C++]
public: void AddDeclarativeSecurity(
    SecurityAction action,
    PermissionSet* pset
);
[JScript]
public function AddDeclarativeSecurity(
    action : SecurityAction,
    pset : PermissionSet
);
```

Parameters

action
    The security action to be taken (Demand, Assert, and so on).

pset
    The set of permissions the action applies to.

Exceptions

Exception Type	Condition
ArgumentOutOfRange-Exception	The *action* is invalid (**RequestMinimum**, **RequestOptional**, and **RequestRefuse** are invalid).
InvalidOperation-Exception	The containing type has been created using **CreateType** or if the permission set *pset* contains an action that was added earlier by AddDeclarativeSecurity.
ArgumentNullException	*pset* is a null reference (**Nothing** in Visual Basic).

Example

See related example in the **System.Reflection.Emit.MethodBuilder** class topic.

Requirements

Platforms: Windows 98, Windows NT 4.0, Windows Millennium Edition, Windows 2000, Windows XP Home Edition, Windows XP Professional, Windows .NET Server family

MethodBuilder.CreateMethodBody Method

Creates the body of the method using a supplied byte array of Microsoft Intermediate Language (MSIL) instructions.

```
[Visual Basic]
Public Sub CreateMethodBody( _
    ByVal il() As Byte, _
    ByVal count As Integer _
)
[C#]
public void CreateMethodBody(
    byte[] il,
    int count
);
[C++]
public: void CreateMethodBody(
    unsigned char il __gc[],
    int count
);
[JScript]
public function CreateMethodBody(
    il : Byte[],
    count : int
);
```

Parameters

il
    An array containing valid MSIL instructions. If this parameter is a null reference (**Nothing** in Visual Basic), the method's body is cleared.

count
    The number of valid bytes in the MSIL array. This value is ignored if MSIL is a null reference (**Nothing** in Visual Basic).

Exceptions

Exception Type	Condition
ArgumentOutOfRange-Exception	The *count* is not within the range of indexes of the supplied MSIL instruction array and *il* is not a null reference (**Nothing** in Visual Basic).
InvalidOperationException	The containing type was previously created using **CreateType**.
	-or-
	This method was called previously on this **MethodBuilder** with a non-a null reference (**Nothing** in Visual Basic) *il* argument.

Remarks

This method creates the method's body from *il*, an array containing MSIL instructions as opcodes. The number of bytes of valid MSIL is given by count.

> **Note** This is currently not fully supported. The user cannot supply the location of token fix ups and exception handlers.

Example

See related example in the **System.Reflection.Emit.MethodBuilder** class topic.

Requirements

Platforms: Windows 98, Windows NT 4.0, Windows Millennium Edition, Windows 2000, Windows XP Home Edition, Windows XP Professional, Windows .NET Server family

MethodBuilder.DefineParameter Method

Defines a parameter of this method.

```
[Visual Basic]
Public Function DefineParameter( _
   ByVal position As Integer, _
   ByVal attributes As ParameterAttributes, _
   ByVal strParamName As String _
) As ParameterBuilder
[C#]
public ParameterBuilder DefineParameter(
   int position,
   ParameterAttributes attributes,
   string strParamName
);
[C++]
public: ParameterBuilder* DefineParameter(
   int position,
   ParameterAttributes attributes,
   String* strParamName
);
[JScript]
public function DefineParameter(
   position : int,
   attributes : ParameterAttributes,
   strParamName : String
) : ParameterBuilder;
```

Parameters

position
   The position of the parameter in the parameter list. Parameters are indexed beginning with the number 1 for the first parameter.
attributes
   The attributes of the parameter.
strParamName
   The name of the parameter. The name can be the null string.

Return Value

Returns a **ParameterBuilder** object that represents the new parrameter of this method.

Exceptions

Exception Type	Condition
ArgumentOutOfRange-Exception	The method has no parameters. -or- *position* is less than or equal to zero. -or- *position* is greater than the number of the method's parameters.
InvalidOperationException	The containing type was previously created using **CreateType**

Requirements

Platforms: Windows 98, Windows NT 4.0, Windows Millennium Edition, Windows 2000, Windows XP Home Edition, Windows XP Professional, Windows .NET Server family

MethodBuilder.Equals Method

Determines whether the given object is equal to this instance.

```
[Visual Basic]
Overrides Public Function Equals( _
   ByVal obj As Object _
) As Boolean
[C#]
public override bool Equals(
   object obj
);
[C++]
public: bool Equals(
   Object* obj
);
[JScript]
public override function Equals(
   obj : Object
) : Boolean;
```

Parameters

obj
   The object to compare with this **MethodBuilder** instance.

Return Value

true if *obj* is an instance of **MethodBuilder** and is equal to this object; otherwise, **false**.

Remarks

Equality is determined by having the same name, attributes, and signature.

Requirements

Platforms: Windows 98, Windows NT 4.0, Windows Millennium Edition, Windows 2000, Windows XP Home Edition, Windows XP Professional, Windows .NET Server family

MethodBuilder.GetBaseDefinition Method

Return the base implementation for a method.

```
[Visual Basic]
Overrides Public Function GetBaseDefinition() As MethodInfo
```

```
[C#]
public override MethodInfo GetBaseDefinition();
[C++]
public: MethodInfo* GetBaseDefinition();
[JScript]
public override function GetBaseDefinition() : MethodInfo;
```

Return Value

The base implementation of this method.

Remarks

This always returns the current **MethodBuilder** object.

Requirements

Platforms: Windows 98, Windows NT 4.0, Windows Millennium Edition, Windows 2000, Windows XP Home Edition, Windows XP Professional, Windows .NET Server family

MethodBuilder.GetCustomAttributes Method

Returns the custom attributes defined for this method.

Overload List

Returns all the custom attributes defined for this method.

[Visual Basic] **Overloads Overrides Public Function GetCustomAttributes(Boolean) As Object() Implements ICustomAttributeProvider.GetCustomAttributes**

[C#] **public override object[] GetCustomAttributes(bool);**

[C++] **public: Object* GetCustomAttributes(bool) __gc[];**

[JScript] **public override function GetCustomAttributes (Boolean) : Object[];**

Returns the custom attributes identified by the given type.

[Visual Basic] **Overloads Overrides Public Function GetCustomAttributes(Type, Boolean) As Object() Implements ICustomAttributeProvider.GetCustomAttributes**

[C#] **public override object[] GetCustomAttributes(Type, bool);**

[C++] **public: Object* GetCustomAttributes(Type*, bool) __gc[];**

[JScript] **public override function GetCustomAttributes (Type, Boolean) : Object[];**

MethodBuilder.GetCustomAttributes Method (Boolean)

Returns all the custom attributes defined for this method.

```
[Visual Basic]
Overrides Overloads Public Function GetCustomAttributes( _
  ByVal inherit As Boolean _
) As Object() Implements ICustomAttributeProvider.GetCustomAttributes
[C#]
public override object[] GetCustomAttributes(
  bool inherit
);
[C++]
public: Object* GetCustomAttributes(
  bool inherit
) __gc[];
```

```
[JScript]
public override function GetCustomAttributes(
  inherit : Boolean
) : Object[];
```

Parameters

inherit
  Specifies whether to search this member's inheritance chain to find the custom attributes.

Return Value

Returns an array of objects representing all the custom attributes of this method.

Implements

ICustomAttributeProvider.GetCustomAttributes

Exceptions

Exception Type	Condition
NotSupportedException	This method is not currently supported. Retrieve the method using **GetMethod** and call **GetCustomAttributes** on the returned **MethodInfo**.

Requirements

Platforms: Windows 98, Windows NT 4.0, Windows Millennium Edition, Windows 2000, Windows XP Home Edition, Windows XP Professional, Windows .NET Server family

MethodBuilder.GetCustomAttributes Method (Type, Boolean)

Returns the custom attributes identified by the given type.

```
[Visual Basic]
Overrides Overloads Public Function GetCustomAttributes( _
  ByVal attributeType As Type, _
  ByVal inherit As Boolean _
) As Object() Implements ICustomAttributeProvider.GetCustomAttributes
[C#]
public override object[] GetCustomAttributes(
  Type attributeType,
  bool inherit
);
[C++]
public: Object* GetCustomAttributes(
  Type* attributeType,
  bool inherit
) __gc[];
[JScript]
public override function GetCustomAttributes(
  attributeType : Type,
  inherit : Boolean
) : Object[];
```

Parameters

attributeType
  The custom attribute type.
inherit
  Specifies whether to search this member's inheritance chain to find the custom attributes.

Return Value

Returns an array of objects representing the attributes of this method that are of **Type** attribute type.

Implements

ICustomAttributeProvider.GetCustomAttributes

Exceptions

Exception Type	Condition
NotSupportedException	This method is not currently supported. Retrieve the method using **GetMethod** and call **GetCustomAttributes** on the returned **MethodInfo**.

Requirements

Platforms: Windows 98, Windows NT 4.0, Windows Millennium Edition, Windows 2000, Windows XP Home Edition, Windows XP Professional, Windows .NET Server family

MethodBuilder.GetHashCode Method

Gets the hash code for this method.

```
[Visual Basic]
Overrides Public Function GetHashCode() As Integer
[C#]
public override int GetHashCode();
[C++]
public: int GetHashCode();
[JScript]
public override function GetHashCode() : int;
```

Return Value

The hash code for this method.

Requirements

Platforms: Windows 98, Windows NT 4.0, Windows Millennium Edition, Windows 2000, Windows XP Home Edition, Windows XP Professional, Windows .NET Server family

MethodBuilder.GetILGenerator Method

Returns an **ILGenerator** for this method.

Overload List

Returns an **ILGenerator** for this method with a default Microsoft intermediate language (MSIL) stream size of 64 bytes.

> [Visual Basic] **Overloads Public Function GetILGenerator() As ILGenerator**
>
> [C#] **public ILGenerator GetILGenerator();**
>
> [C++] **public: ILGenerator* GetILGenerator();**
>
> [JScript] **public function GetILGenerator() : ILGenerator;**

Returns an **ILGenerator** for this method with the specified Microsoft intermediate language (MSIL) stream size.

> [Visual Basic] **Overloads Public Function GetILGenerator(Integer) As ILGenerator**
>
> [C#] **public ILGenerator GetILGenerator(int);**
>
> [C++] **public: ILGenerator* GetILGenerator(int);**
>
> [JScript] **public function GetILGenerator(int) : ILGenerator;**

Example

See related example in the **System.Reflection.Emit.MethodBuilder** class topic.

MethodBuilder.GetILGenerator Method ()

Returns an **ILGenerator** for this method with a default Microsoft intermediate language (MSIL) stream size of 64 bytes.

```
[Visual Basic]
Overloads Public Function GetILGenerator() As ILGenerator
[C#]
public ILGenerator GetILGenerator();
[C++]
public: ILGenerator* GetILGenerator();
[JScript]
public function GetILGenerator() : ILGenerator;
```

Return Value

Returns an **ILGenerator** object for this method.

Exceptions

Exception Type	Condition
InvalidOperation-Exception	**MethodImplAttributes** indicates that the method body is not managed MSIL.

Example

See related example in the **System.Reflection.Emit.MethodBuilder** class topic.

Requirements

Platforms: Windows 98, Windows NT 4.0, Windows Millennium Edition, Windows 2000, Windows XP Home Edition, Windows XP Professional, Windows .NET Server family

MethodBuilder.GetILGenerator Method (Int32)

Returns an **ILGenerator** for this method with the specified Microsoft intermediate language (MSIL) stream size.

```
[Visual Basic]
Overloads Public Function GetILGenerator( _
   ByVal size As Integer _
) As ILGenerator
[C#]
public ILGenerator GetILGenerator(
   int size
);
[C++]
public: ILGenerator* GetILGenerator(
   int size
);
[JScript]
public function GetILGenerator(
   size : int
) : ILGenerator;
```

Parameters

size
> The size of the MSIL stream, in bytes.

Return Value

Returns an **ILGenerator** object for this method.

Exceptions

Exception Type	Condition
InvalidOperation-Exception	**MethodImplAttributes** indicates that the method body is not managed MSIL.

Example

See related example in the **System.Reflection.Emit.MethodBuilder** class topic.

Requirements

Platforms: Windows 98, Windows NT 4.0, Windows Millennium Edition, Windows 2000, Windows XP Home Edition, Windows XP Professional, Windows .NET Server family

MethodBuilder.GetMethodImplementation-Flags Method

Returns the implementation flags for the method.

```
[Visual Basic]
Overrides Public Function GetMethodImplementationFlags() As _
    MethodImplAttributes
[C#]
public override MethodImplAttributes GetMethodImplementationFlags();
[C++]
public: MethodImplAttributes GetMethodImplementationFlags();
[JScript]
public override function GetMethodImplementationFlags() :
    MethodImplAttributes;
```

Return Value

Returns the implementation flags for the method.

Requirements

Platforms: Windows 98, Windows NT 4.0, Windows Millennium Edition, Windows 2000, Windows XP Home Edition, Windows XP Professional, Windows .NET Server family

MethodBuilder.GetModule Method

Returns a reference to the module that contains this method.

```
[Visual Basic]
Public Function GetModule() As Module
[C#]
public Module GetModule();
[C++]
public: Module* GetModule();
[JScript]
public function GetModule() : Module;
```

Return Value

Returns a reference to the module that contains this method.

Example

See related example in the **System.Reflection.Emit.MethodBuilder** class topic.

Requirements

Platforms: Windows 98, Windows NT 4.0, Windows Millennium Edition, Windows 2000, Windows XP Home Edition, Windows XP Professional, Windows .NET Server family

MethodBuilder.GetParameters Method

Returns the parameters of this method.

```
[Visual Basic]
Overrides Public Function GetParameters() As ParameterInfo()
[C#]
public override ParameterInfo[] GetParameters();
[C++]
public: ParameterInfo* GetParameters() [];
[JScript]
public override function GetParameters() : ParameterInfo[];
```

Return Value

An array of **ParameterInfo** objects that represent the parameters of the method.

Exceptions

Exception Type	Condition
NotSupportedException	This method is not currently supported. Retrieve the method using **GetMethod** and call **GetParameters** on the returned **MethodInfo**.

Example

See related example in the **System.Reflection.Emit.MethodBuilder** class topic.

Requirements

Platforms: Windows 98, Windows NT 4.0, Windows Millennium Edition, Windows 2000, Windows XP Home Edition, Windows XP Professional, Windows .NET Server family

MethodBuilder.GetToken Method

Returns the **MethodToken** that represents the token for this method.

```
[Visual Basic]
Public Function GetToken() As MethodToken
[C#]
public MethodToken GetToken();
[C++]
public: MethodToken GetToken();
[JScript]
public function GetToken() : MethodToken;
```

Return Value

Returns the **MethodToken** of this method.

Requirements

Platforms: Windows 98, Windows NT 4.0, Windows Millennium Edition, Windows 2000, Windows XP Home Edition, Windows XP Professional, Windows .NET Server family

MethodBuilder.Invoke Method

Overload List

Dynamically invokes the method reflected by this instance on the given object, passing along the specified parameters, and under the constraints of the given binder.

[Visual Basic] **Overloads Overrides Public Function Invoke (Object, BindingFlags, Binder, Object(), CultureInfo) As Object**

[C#] **public override object Invoke(object, BindingFlags, Binder, object[], CultureInfo);**

[C++] **public: Object* Invoke(Object*, BindingFlags, Binder*, Object*[], CultureInfo*);**

[JScript] **public override function Invoke(Object, BindingFlags, Binder, Object[], CultureInfo) : Object;**

Inherited from **MethodBase**.

[Visual Basic] **Overloads Public Function Invoke(Object, Object()) As Object**

[C#] **public object Invoke(object, object[]);**

[C++] **public: Object* Invoke(Object*, Object*[]);**

[JScript] **public function Invoke(Object, Object[]) : Object;**

MethodBuilder.Invoke Method (Object, BindingFlags, Binder, Object[], CultureInfo)

Dynamically invokes the method reflected by this instance on the given object, passing along the specified parameters, and under the constraints of the given binder.

```
[Visual Basic]
Overrides Overloads Public Function Invoke( _
   ByVal obj As Object, _
   ByVal invokeAttr As BindingFlags, _
   ByVal binder As Binder, _
   ByVal parameters() As Object, _
   ByVal culture As CultureInfo _
) As Object
[C#]
public override object Invoke(
   object obj,
   BindingFlags invokeAttr,
   Binder binder,
   object[] parameters,
   CultureInfo culture
);
[C++]
public: Object* Invoke(
   Object* obj,
   BindingFlags invokeAttr,
   Binder* binder,
   Object* parameters __gc[],
   CultureInfo* culture
);
[JScript]
public override function Invoke(
   obj : Object,
   invokeAttr : BindingFlags,
   binder : Binder,
   parameters : Object[],
   culture : CultureInfo
) : Object;
```

Parameters

obj

The object on which to invoke the specified method. If the method is static, this parameter is ignored.

invokeAttr

This must be a bit flag from **BindingFlags**: **InvokeMethod**, **NonPublic**, and so on.

binder

An object that enables the binding, coercion of argument types, invocation of members, and retrieval of MemberInfo objects via reflection. If binder is a null reference (**Nothing** in Visual Basic), the default binder is used. For more details, see **Binder**.

parameters

An argument list. This is an array of arguments with the same number, order, and type as the parameters of the method to be invoked. If there are no parameters this should be a null reference (**Nothing** in Visual Basic).

culture

An instance of **CultureInfo** used to govern the coercion of types. If this is null, the **CultureInfo** for the current thread is used. (Note that this is necessary to, for example, convert a **String** that represents 1000 to a **Double** value, since 1000 is represented differently by different cultures.)

Return Value

Returns an object containing the return value of the invoked method.

Exceptions

Exception Type	Condition
NotSupportedException	This method is not currently supported. Retrieve the method using **GetMethod** and call **InvokeMember** on the returned **MethodInfo**.

Remarks

If the method is static, the *obj* parameter is ignored. For non-static methods, *obj* should be an instance of a class that inherits or declares the method and must be the same type as this class. If the method has no parameters, the value of *parameters* should be a null reference (**Nothing** in Visual Basic). Otherwise the number, type, and order of elements in the parameters array should be identical to the number, type, and order of parameters for the method reflected by this instance.

> **Note** Access restrictions are ignored for fully-trusted code. That is, private constructors, methods, fields, and properties can be accessed and invoked using Reflection whenever the code is fully-trusted.

Requirements

Platforms: Windows 98, Windows NT 4.0, Windows Millennium Edition, Windows 2000, Windows XP Home Edition, Windows XP Professional, Windows .NET Server family

MethodBuilder.IsDefined Method

Checks if the specified custom attribute type is defined.

```
[Visual Basic]
Overrides Public Function IsDefined( _
    ByVal attributeType As Type, _
    ByVal inherit As Boolean _
) As Boolean Implements ICustomAttributeProvider.IsDefined
[C#]
public override bool IsDefined(
    Type attributeType,
    bool inherit
);
[C++]
public: bool IsDefined(
    Type* attributeType,
    bool inherit
);
[JScript]
public override function IsDefined(
    attributeType : Type,
    inherit : Boolean
) : Boolean;
```

Parameters

attributeType
> The custom attribute type.

inherit
> Specifies whether to search this member's inheritance chain to find the custom attributes.

Return Value

true if the specified custom attribute type is defined; otherwise, **false**.

Implements

ICustomAttributeProvider.IsDefined

Exceptions

Exception Type	Condition
NotSupportedException	This method is not currently supported. Retrieve the method using **GetMethod** and call **IsDefined** on the returned **MethodInfo**.

Requirements

Platforms: Windows 98, Windows NT 4.0, Windows Millennium Edition, Windows 2000, Windows XP Home Edition, Windows XP Professional, Windows .NET Server family

MethodBuilder.SetCustomAttribute Method

Sets a custom attribute.

Overload List

Sets a custom attribute using a custom attribute builder.

> [Visual Basic] **Overloads Public Sub SetCustomAttribute (CustomAttributeBuilder)**

> [C#] **public void SetCustomAttribute (CustomAttributeBuilder);**

> [C++] **public: void SetCustomAttribute (CustomAttributeBuilder*);**

> [JScript] **public function SetCustomAttribute (CustomAttributeBuilder);**

Sets a custom attribute using a specified custom attribute blob.

> [Visual Basic] **Overloads Public Sub SetCustomAttribute (ConstructorInfo, Byte())**

> [C#] **public void SetCustomAttribute(ConstructorInfo, byte[]);**

> [C++] **public: void SetCustomAttribute(ConstructorInfo*, unsigned char __gc[]);**

> [JScript] **public function SetCustomAttribute (ConstructorInfo, Byte[]);**

MethodBuilder.SetCustomAttribute Method (CustomAttributeBuilder)

Sets a custom attribute using a custom attribute builder.

```
[Visual Basic]
Overloads Public Sub SetCustomAttribute( _
    ByVal customBuilder As CustomAttributeBuilder _
)
[C#]
public void SetCustomAttribute(
    CustomAttributeBuilder customBuilder
);
[C++]
public: void SetCustomAttribute(
    CustomAttributeBuilder* customBuilder
);
[JScript]
public function SetCustomAttribute(
    customBuilder : CustomAttributeBuilder
);
```

Parameters

customBuilder
> An instance of a helper class to describe the custom attribute.

Exceptions

Exception Type	Condition
ArgumentNullException	*customBuilder* is a null reference (**Nothing** in Visual Basic).

Requirements

Platforms: Windows 98, Windows NT 4.0, Windows Millennium Edition, Windows 2000, Windows XP Home Edition, Windows XP Professional, Windows .NET Server family

MethodBuilder.SetCustomAttribute Method (ConstructorInfo, Byte[])

Sets a custom attribute using a specified custom attribute blob.

```
[Visual Basic]
Overloads Public Sub SetCustomAttribute( _
    ByVal con As ConstructorInfo, _
    ByVal binaryAttribute() As Byte _
)
```

```
[C#]
public void SetCustomAttribute(
   ConstructorInfo con,
   byte[] binaryAttribute
);
[C++]
public: void SetCustomAttribute(
   ConstructorInfo* con,
   unsigned char binaryAttribute __gc[]
);
[JScript]
public function SetCustomAttribute(
   con : ConstructorInfo,
   binaryAttribute : Byte[]
);
```

Parameters

con
   The constructor for the custom attribute.
binaryAttribute
   A byte blob representing the attributes.

Exceptions

Exception Type	Condition
ArgumentNullException	*con* or *binaryAttribute* is a null reference (**Nothing** in Visual Basic).

Remarks

See the metadata specification in the ECMA Partition II documentation for details on how to format *binaryAttribute*. The Partition II documentation is included with the .NET Framework SDK installation, and can be found in the %\Microsoft.NET\FrameworkSDK\Tool Developers Guide\docs directory.

Requirements

Platforms: Windows 98, Windows NT 4.0, Windows Millennium Edition, Windows 2000, Windows XP Home Edition, Windows XP Professional, Windows .NET Server family

MethodBuilder.SetImplementationFlags Method

Sets the implementation flags for this method.

```
[Visual Basic]
Public Sub SetImplementationFlags( _
   ByVal attributes As MethodImplAttributes _
)
[C#]
public void SetImplementationFlags(
   MethodImplAttributes attributes
);
[C++]
public: void SetImplementationFlags(
   MethodImplAttributes attributes
);
[JScript]
public function SetImplementationFlags(
   attributes : MethodImplAttributes
);
```

Parameters

attributes
   The implementation flags to set.

Exceptions

Exception Type	Condition
InvalidOperation-Exception	The containing type was previously created using **CreateType**.

Example

See related example in the **System.Reflection.Emit.MethodBuilder** class topic.

Requirements

Platforms: Windows 98, Windows NT 4.0, Windows Millennium Edition, Windows 2000, Windows XP Home Edition, Windows XP Professional, Windows .NET Server family

MethodBuilder.SetMarshal Method

Sets marshaling information for the return type of this method.

```
[Visual Basic]
Public Sub SetMarshal( _
   ByVal unmanagedMarshal As UnmanagedMarshal _
)
[C#]
public void SetMarshal(
   UnmanagedMarshal unmanagedMarshal
);
[C++]
public: void SetMarshal(
   UnmanagedMarshal* unmanagedMarshal
);
[JScript]
public function SetMarshal(
   unmanagedMarshal : UnmanagedMarshal
);
```

Parameters

unmanagedMarshal
   Marshaling information for the return type of this method.

Exceptions

Exception Type	Condition
InvalidOperation-Exception	The containing type was previously created using **CreateType**

Example

See related example in the **System.Reflection.Emit.MethodBuilder** class topic.

Requirements

Platforms: Windows 98, Windows NT 4.0, Windows Millennium Edition, Windows 2000, Windows XP Home Edition, Windows XP Professional, Windows .NET Server family

MethodBuilder.SetSymCustomAttribute Method

Set a symbolic custom attribute using a blob.

```
[Visual Basic]
Public Sub SetSymCustomAttribute( _
    ByVal name As String, _
    ByVal data() As Byte _
)
[C#]
public void SetSymCustomAttribute(
    string name,
    byte[] data
);
[C++]
public: void SetSymCustomAttribute(
    String* name,
    unsigned char data __gc[]
);
[JScript]
public function SetSymCustomAttribute(
    name : String,
    data : Byte[]
);
```

Parameters

name
> The name of the symbolic custom attribute.

data
> The byte blob that represents the value of the symbolic custom attribute.

Exceptions

Exception Type	Condition
InvalidOperation-Exception	The containing type was previously created using **CreateType**. -or- The module that contains this method is not a debug module.

Remarks

Unlike the metadata custom attribute, this custom attribute is associated with a symbol writer.

Example

See related example in the **System.Reflection.Emit.MethodBuilder** class topic.

Requirements

Platforms: Windows 98, Windows NT 4.0, Windows Millennium Edition, Windows 2000, Windows XP Home Edition, Windows XP Professional, Windows .NET Server family

MethodBuilder.ToString Method

Returns this **MethodBuilder** instance as a string.

```
[Visual Basic]
Overrides Public Function ToString() As String
[C#]
public override string ToString();
[C++]
public: String* ToString();
[JScript]
public override function ToString() : String;
```

Return Value

Returns a string containing the name, attributes, method signature, exceptions, and local signature of this method followed by the current Microsoft intermediate language (MSIL) stream.

Requirements

Platforms: Windows 98, Windows NT 4.0, Windows Millennium Edition, Windows 2000, Windows XP Home Edition, Windows XP Professional, Windows .NET Server family

MethodRental Class

Provides a fast way to swap method body implementation given a method of a class.

System.Object
   System.Reflection.Emit.MethodRental

```
[Visual Basic]
NotInheritable Public Class MethodRental
[C#]
public sealed class MethodRental
[C++]
public __gc __sealed class MethodRental
[JScript]
public class MethodRental
```

Thread Safety

Reflection Emit is thread-safe when using assemblies that were created with the **AppDomain.DefineDynamicAssembly** method with the Boolean parameter *isSynchronized* set to **true**.

Requirements

Namespace: System.Reflection.Emit

Platforms: Windows 98, Windows NT 4.0, Windows Millennium Edition, Windows 2000, Windows XP Home Edition, Windows XP Professional, Windows .NET Server family

Assembly: Mscorlib (in Mscorlib.dll)

.NET Framework Security:
* **ReflectionPermission** to enhance security and performance when invoked late-bound through mechanisms such as **Type.InvokeMember**. Associated enumeration: **ReflectionPermissionFlag.MemberAccess**.

MethodRental.JitImmediate Field

Specifies that the method should be just-in-time (JIT) compiled immediately.

```
[Visual Basic]
Public Const JitImmediate As Integer
[C#]
public const int JitImmediate;
[C++]
public: const int JitImmediate;
[JScript]
public var JitImmediate : int;
```

Requirements

Platforms: Windows 98, Windows NT 4.0, Windows Millennium Edition, Windows 2000, Windows XP Home Edition, Windows XP Professional, Windows .NET Server family

.NET Framework Security:
* **ReflectionPermission** to enhance security and performance when invoked late-bound through mechanisms such as **Type.InvokeMember**. Associated enumeration: **ReflectionPermissionFlag.MemberAccess**.

MethodRental.JitOnDemand Field

Specifies that the method should be just-in-time (JIT) compiled when needed.

```
[Visual Basic]
Public Const JitOnDemand As Integer
[C#]
public const int JitOnDemand;
[C++]
public: const int JitOnDemand;
[JScript]
public var JitOnDemand : int;
```

Requirements

Platforms: Windows 98, Windows NT 4.0, Windows Millennium Edition, Windows 2000, Windows XP Home Edition, Windows XP Professional, Windows .NET Server family

.NET Framework Security:
* **ReflectionPermission** to enhance security and performance when invoked late-bound through mechanisms such as **Type.InvokeMember**. Associated enumeration: **ReflectionPermissionFlag.MemberAccess**.

MethodRental.SwapMethodBody Method

Swaps the body of a method.

```
[Visual Basic]
Public Shared Sub SwapMethodBody( _
    ByVal cls As Type, _
    ByVal methodtoken As Integer, _
    ByVal rgIL As IntPtr, _
    ByVal methodSize As Integer, _
    ByVal flags As Integer _
)
[C#]
public static void SwapMethodBody(
    Type cls,
    int methodtoken,
    IntPtr rgIL,
    int methodSize,
    int flags
);
[C++]
public: static void SwapMethodBody(
    Type* cls,
    int methodtoken,
    IntPtr rgIL,
    int methodSize,
    int flags
);
[JScript]
public static function SwapMethodBody(
    cls : Type,
    methodtoken : int,
    rgIL : IntPtr,
    methodSize : int,
    flags : int
);
```

Parameters

cls

The class containing the method.

methodtoken

The token for the method.

rgIL

A pointer to the method. This should include the method header.

methodSize

The size of the new method body in bytes.

flags

Flags that control the swapping. See the definitions of the constants.

Exceptions

Exception Type	Condition
ArgumentNullException	*cls* is a null reference (**Nothing** in Visual Basic).
NotSupportedException	The type *cls* is not complete.

Remarks

You cannot use this method to swap the body of a global method.

The method can only be called by the client that created the dynamic module that contains the type whose method's body is being swapped.

Example

[Visual Basic, C#] The following example illustrates how to swap a method body for a new body. It also illustrates how to obtain a method token for an existing method and how to construct a blob of bytes representing the Microsoft Intermediate Language (MSIL) code to be passed to **SwapMethodBody**.

[Visual Basic]
```vb
Imports System
Imports System.Reflection
Imports System.Reflection.Emit
Imports System.Runtime.InteropServices

Class SwapMethodBodySample

    ' First make a method that returns 0.
    ' Then swap the method body with a body that returns 1.
    Public Shared Sub Main()
        ' Construct a dynamic assembly
        Dim g As Guid = Guid.NewGuid()
        Dim asmname As New AssemblyName()
        asmname.Name = "tempfile" + g.ToString()
        Dim asmbuild As AssemblyBuilder = _
            System.Threading.Thread.GetDomain().DefineDynamicAssembly _
            (asmname, AssemblyBuilderAccess.Run)

        ' Add a dynamic module that contains one type that
has one method that
        ' has no arguments.
        Dim modbuild As ModuleBuilder = _
asmbuild.DefineDynamicModule("test")
        Dim tb As TypeBuilder = modbuild.DefineType("name of the Type")
        Dim somemethod As MethodBuilder = _
            tb.DefineMethod("My method Name", _
            MethodAttributes.Public Or(MethodAttributes.Static), _
            GetType(Integer), New Type() {})
        ' Define the body of the method to return 0.
        Dim ilg As ILGenerator = somemethod.GetILGenerator()
        ilg.Emit(OpCodes.Ldc_I4_0)
        ilg.Emit(OpCodes.Ret)
```

```vb
        ' Complete the type and verify that it returns 0.
        Dim tbBaked As Type = tb.CreateType()
        Dim res1 As Integer = _
            CInt(tbBaked.GetMethod("My method Name").Invoke _
            (Nothing, New Object() {}))
        If res1 <> 0 Then
            Console.WriteLine("Err_001a, should have returned 0")
        Else
            Console.WriteLine("Original method returned 0")
        End If

        ' Define a new method body that will return a 1 instead.
        Dim methodBytes As Byte() = _
            {&H3, &H30, &HA, &H0, &H2, &H0, &H0, &H0, &H0, &H0, &H0,
&H0, &H17, &H2A}
        '&H2      code size
        '&H17     ldc_i4_1
        '&H2A     ret

        ' Get the token for the method whose body you are replacing.
        Dim somemethodToken As MethodToken = somemethod.GetToken()

        ' Get the pointer to the method body.
        Dim hmem As GCHandle = _
            GCHandle.Alloc(CType(methodBytes, Object),
GCHandleType.Pinned)
        Dim addr As IntPtr = hmem.AddrOfPinnedObject()
        Dim cbSize As Integer = methodBytes.Length

        ' Swap the old method body with the new body.
        MethodRental.SwapMethodBody(tbBaked,
somemethodToken.Token, addr, _
            cbSize, MethodRental.JitImmediate)

        ' Verify that the modified method returns 1.
        Dim res2 As Integer = _
            CInt(tbBaked.GetMethod("My method Name").Invoke _
            (Nothing, New Object() {}))
        If res2 <> 1 Then
            Console.WriteLine("Err_001b, should have returned 1")
        Else
            Console.WriteLine("Swapped method body returned 1")
        End If
    End Sub
End Class
```

[C#]
```csharp
using System;
using System.Reflection;
using System.Reflection.Emit;
using System.Runtime.InteropServices;

class SwapMethodBodySample
{
    // First make a method that returns 0.
    // Then swap the method body with a body that returns 1.
    public static void Main(String [] args)
    {
        // Construct a dynamic assembly
        Guid g = Guid.NewGuid();
        AssemblyName asmname = new AssemblyName();
        asmname.Name = "tempfile" + g;
        AssemblyBuilder asmbuild = System.Threading.Thread.GetDomain().
            DefineDynamicAssembly(asmname, AssemblyBuilderAccess.Run);

        // Add a dynamic module that contains one type that has one
method that
        // has no arguments.
        ModuleBuilder modbuild = asmbuild.DefineDynamicModule( "test" );
        TypeBuilder tb = modbuild.DefineType( "name of the Type" );
        MethodBuilder somemethod = tb.DefineMethod
            ("My method Name",
            MethodAttributes.Public | MethodAttributes.Static,
            typeof(int),
            new Type[]{} );
```

```
    // Define the body of the method to return 0.
        ILGenerator ilg = somemethod.GetILGenerator();
    ilg.Emit(OpCodes.Ldc_I4_0);
    ilg.Emit(OpCodes.Ret);

    // Complete the type and verify that it returns 0.
    Type tbBaked = tb.CreateType();
    int res1 = (int)tbBaked.GetMethod
("My method Name").Invoke( null, new Object[]{} );
    if ( res1 != 0 ) {
        Console.WriteLine( "Err_001a, should have returned 0" );
    } else {
        Console.WriteLine("Original method returned 0");
    }

    // Define a new method body that will return a 1 instead.
    Byte[] methodBytes = {
        0x03,
        0x30,
        0x0A,
        0x00,
        0x02,                   // code size
        0x00,
        0x00,
        0x00,
        0x00,
        0x00,
        0x00,
        0x00,
        0x17,                   // ldc_i4_1
        0x2a                    // ret
    };

    // Get the token for the method whose body you are replacing.
    MethodToken somemethodToken = somemethod.GetToken();

    // Get the pointer to the method body.
        GCHandle hmem = GCHandle.Alloc((Object) methodBytes,
GCHandleType.Pinned);
        IntPtr addr = hmem.AddrOfPinnedObject();
    int cbSize = methodBytes.Length;

    // Swap the old method body with the new body.
    MethodRental.SwapMethodBody(
                    tbBaked,
                    somemethodToken.Token,
                    addr,
                    cbSize,
                    MethodRental.JitImmediate);

    // Verify that the modified method returns 1.
    int res2 = (int)tbBaked.GetMethod("My method Name").Invoke
( null, new Object[]{} );
    if ( res2 != 1 ) {
        Console.WriteLine( "Err_001b, should have returned 1" );
    } else {
        Console.WriteLine("Swapped method body returned 1");
    }
    }
}
```

Requirements

Platforms: Windows 98, Windows NT 4.0,
Windows Millennium Edition, Windows 2000,
Windows XP Home Edition, Windows XP Professional,
Windows .NET Server family

.NET Framework Security:

- **ReflectionPermission** to enhance security and performance
  when invoked late-bound through mechanisms such as
  Type.InvokeMember. Associated enumeration:
  ReflectionPermissionFlag.MemberAccess.

MethodToken Structure

The **MethodToken** struct is an object representation of a token that represents a method.

System.Object
  System.ValueType
    System.Reflection.Emit.MethodToken

```
[Visual Basic]
<Serializable>
Public Structure MethodToken
[C#]
[Serializable]
public struct MethodToken
[C++]
[Serializable]
public __value struct MethodToken
```

[JScript] In JScript, you can use the structures in the .NET Framework, but you cannot define your own.

Thread Safety

Reflection Emit is thread-safe when using assemblies that were created with the **AppDomain.DefineDynamicAssembly** method with the Boolean parameter *isSynchronized* set to **true**.

Requirements

Namespace: System.Reflection.Emit

Platforms: Windows 98, Windows NT 4.0, Windows Millennium Edition, Windows 2000, Windows XP Home Edition, Windows XP Professional, Windows .NET Server family

Assembly: Mscorlib (in Mscorlib.dll)

MethodToken.Empty Field

The default **MethodToken** with **Token** value 0.

```
[Visual Basic]
Public Shared ReadOnly Empty As MethodToken
[C#]
public static readonly MethodToken Empty;
[C++]
public: static MethodToken Empty;
[JScript]
public static var Empty : MethodToken;
```

Requirements

Platforms: Windows 98, Windows NT 4.0, Windows Millennium Edition, Windows 2000, Windows XP Home Edition, Windows XP Professional, Windows .NET Server family

MethodToken.Token Property

Returns the metadata token for this method.

```
[Visual Basic]
Public ReadOnly Property Token As Integer
[C#]
public int Token {get;}
[C++]
public: __property int get_Token();
[JScript]
public function get Token() : int;
```

Property Value

Read-only. Returns the metadata token for this method.

Requirements

Platforms: Windows 98, Windows NT 4.0, Windows Millennium Edition, Windows 2000, Windows XP Home Edition, Windows XP Professional, Windows .NET Server family

MethodToken.Equals Method

Tests whether the given object is equal to this **MethodToken** object.

```
[Visual Basic]
Overrides Public Function Equals( _
    ByVal obj As Object _
) As Boolean
[C#]
public override bool Equals(
    object obj
);
[C++]
public: bool Equals(
    Object* obj
);
[JScript]
public override function Equals(
    obj : Object
) : Boolean;
```

Parameters

obj
    The object to compare to this object.

Return Value

true if *obj* is an instance of **MethodToken** and is equal to this object; otherwise, **false**.

Requirements

Platforms: Windows 98, Windows NT 4.0, Windows Millennium Edition, Windows 2000, Windows XP Home Edition, Windows XP Professional, Windows .NET Server family

MethodToken.GetHashCode Method

Returns the generated hash code for this method.

```
[Visual Basic]
Overrides Public Function GetHashCode() As Integer
[C#]
public override int GetHashCode();
[C++]
public: int GetHashCode();
[JScript]
public override function GetHashCode() : int;
```

Return Value

Returns the hash code for this instance.

Requirements

Platforms: Windows 98, Windows NT 4.0, Windows Millennium Edition, Windows 2000, Windows XP Home Edition, Windows XP Professional, Windows .NET Server family

ModuleBuilder Class

Defines and represents a module. Get an instance of ModuleBuilder by calling **DefineDynamicModule**.

System.Object
  System.Reflection.Module
    System.Reflection.Emit.ModuleBuilder

```
[Visual Basic]
Public Class ModuleBuilder
   Inherits Module
[C#]
public class ModuleBuilder : Module
[C++]
public __gc class ModuleBuilder : public Module
[JScript]
public class ModuleBuilder extends Module
```

Thread Safety

Reflection Emit is thread-safe when using assemblies that were created with the **AppDomain.DefineDynamicAssembly** method with the Boolean parameter *isSynchronized* set to **true**.

Example

[Visual Basic, C#] The following code sample demonstrates the use of **ModuleBuilder** to create a dynamic module. Note that the ModuleBuilder is created by calling **DefineDynamicModule** in **AssemblyBuilder**, rather than through a constructor.

```
[Visual Basic]
Imports System
Imports System.Reflection
Imports System.Reflection.Emit

Public Class CodeGenerator
   Private myAssemblyBuilder As AssemblyBuilder

   Public Sub New()
      ' Get the current application domain for the current thread.
      Dim myCurrentDomain As AppDomain = AppDomain.CurrentDomain
      Dim myAssemblyName As New AssemblyName()
      myAssemblyName.Name = "TempAssembly"

      ' Define a dynamic assembly in the current application domain.
      myAssemblyBuilder = _
               myCurrentDomain.DefineDynamicAssembly
(myAssemblyName, AssemblyBuilderAccess.Run)

      ' Define a dynamic module in this assembly.
      Dim myModuleBuilder As ModuleBuilder = _
myAssemblyBuilder.DefineDynamicModule("TempModule")

      ' Define a runtime class with specified name and attributes.
      Dim myTypeBuilder As TypeBuilder = _
               myModuleBuilder.DefineType("TempClass",
TypeAttributes.Public)

      ' Add 'Greeting' field to the class, with the specified
attribute and type.
      Dim greetingField As FieldBuilder = _
               myTypeBuilder.DefineField("Greeting",
GetType(String), FieldAttributes.Public)
      Dim myMethodArgs As Type() = {GetType(String)}

      ' Add 'MyMethod' method to the class, with the specified
attribute and signature.
      Dim myMethod As MethodBuilder = _
               myTypeBuilder.DefineMethod("MyMethod",
MethodAttributes.Public, _
               CallingConventions.Standard, Nothing, myMethodArgs)
```

```
      Dim methodIL As ILGenerator = myMethod.GetILGenerator()
      methodIL.EmitWriteLine("In the method...")
      methodIL.Emit(OpCodes.Ldarg_0)
      methodIL.Emit(OpCodes.Ldarg_1)
      methodIL.Emit(OpCodes.Stfld, greetingField)
      methodIL.Emit(OpCodes.Ret)
      myTypeBuilder.CreateType()
   End Sub 'New

   Public ReadOnly Property MyAssembly() As AssemblyBuilder
      Get
         Return Me.myAssemblyBuilder
      End Get
   End Property
End Class 'CodeGenerator

Public Class TestClass
   Public Shared Sub Main()
      Dim myCodeGenerator As New CodeGenerator()
      ' Get the assembly builder for 'myCodeGenerator' object.
      Dim myAssemblyBuilder As AssemblyBuilder =
myCodeGenerator.MyAssembly
      ' Get the module builder for the above assembly builder object .
      Dim myModuleBuilder As ModuleBuilder =
myAssemblyBuilder.GetDynamicModule("TempModule")
      Console.WriteLine("The fully qualified name and path to
this " + _
                     "module is :" +
myModuleBuilder.FullyQualifiedName)
      Dim myType As Type = myModuleBuilder.GetType("TempClass")
      Dim myMethodInfo As MethodInfo = myType.GetMethod("MyMethod")
      ' Get the token used to identify the method within this module.
      Dim myMethodToken As MethodToken =
myModuleBuilder.GetMethodToken(myMethodInfo)
      Console.WriteLine("Token used to identify the method of
'myType'" + _
                     " within the module is {0:x}",
myMethodToken.Token)
      Dim args As Object() = {"Hello."}
      Dim myObject As Object = Activator.CreateInstance(myType,
Nothing, Nothing)
      myMethodInfo.Invoke(myObject, args)
   End Sub 'Main
End Class 'TestClass
```

```
[C#]
using System;
using System.Reflection;
using System.Reflection.Emit;

public class CodeGenerator
{
   AssemblyBuilder myAssemblyBuilder;
   public CodeGenerator()
   {
      // Get the current application domain for the current thread.
      AppDomain myCurrentDomain = AppDomain.CurrentDomain;
      AssemblyName myAssemblyName = new AssemblyName();
      myAssemblyName.Name = "TempAssembly";

      // Define a dynamic assembly in the current application domain.
      myAssemblyBuilder = myCurrentDomain.DefineDynamicAssembly
               (myAssemblyName, AssemblyBuilderAccess.Run);

      // Define a dynamic module in this assembly.
      ModuleBuilder myModuleBuilder = myAssemblyBuilder.
                           DefineDynamicModule("TempModule");

      // Define a runtime class with specified name and attributes.
      TypeBuilder myTypeBuilder = myModuleBuilder.DefineType
                           ("TempClass",TypeAttributes.Public);

      // Add 'Greeting' field to the class, with the
specified attribute and type.
      FieldBuilder greetingField =
```

```
myTypeBuilder.DefineField("Greeting",
                                        typeof(String),
FieldAttributes.Public);
        Type[] myMethodArgs = { typeof(String) };

        // Add 'MyMethod' method to the class, with the          ⌋
specified attribute and signature.
        MethodBuilder myMethod = myTypeBuilder.DefineMethod("MyMethod",
            MethodAttributes.Public, CallingConventions.Standard,     ⌋
null,myMethodArgs);

        ILGenerator methodIL = myMethod.GetILGenerator();
        methodIL.EmitWriteLine("In the method...");
        methodIL.Emit(OpCodes.Ldarg_0);
        methodIL.Emit(OpCodes.Ldarg_1);
        methodIL.Emit(OpCodes.Stfld, greetingField);
        methodIL.Emit(OpCodes.Ret);
        myTypeBuilder.CreateType();
    }
    public AssemblyBuilder MyAssembly
    {
        get
        {
            return this.myAssemblyBuilder;
        }
    }
}
public class TestClass
{
    public static void Main()
    {
        CodeGenerator myCodeGenerator = new CodeGenerator();
        // Get the assembly builder for 'myCodeGenerator' object.
        AssemblyBuilder myAssemblyBuilder = myCodeGenerator.MyAssembly;
        // Get the module builder for the above assembly builder object .
        ModuleBuilder myModuleBuilder = myAssemblyBuilder.

GetDynamicModule("TempModule");
        Console.WriteLine("The fully qualified name and path to this "
                            + "module is :"
+myModuleBuilder.FullyQualifiedName);
        Type myType = myModuleBuilder.GetType("TempClass");
        MethodInfo myMethodInfo =

myType.GetMethod("MyMethod");
        // Get the token used to identify the method within this module.
        MethodToken myMethodToken =
                        myModuleBuilder.GetMethodToken(myMethodInfo);
        Console.WriteLine("Token used to identify the method of 'myType'"
                        + " within the module is          ⌋
{0:x}",myMethodToken.Token);
        object[] args={"Hello."};
        object myObject = Activator.CreateInstance(myType,null,null);
        myMethodInfo.Invoke(myObject,args);
    }
}
```

Requirements

Namespace: System.Reflection.Emit

Platforms: Windows 98, Windows NT 4.0,
Windows Millennium Edition, Windows 2000,
Windows XP Home Edition, Windows XP Professional,
Windows .NET Server family

Assembly: Mscorlib (in Mscorlib.dll)

ModuleBuilder.FullyQualifiedName Property

Gets a **String** representing the fully-qualified name and path to this module.

```
[Visual Basic]
Overrides Public ReadOnly Property FullyQualifiedName As String
[C#]
public override string FullyQualifiedName {get;}
[C++]
public: __property String* get_FullyQualifiedName();
[JScript]
public override function get FullyQualifiedName() : String;
```

Property Value

The fully-qualified module name.

Remarks

To get the name without the path, use **Name**.

> **Note** The case of a module name is platform dependent.

Requirements

Platforms: Windows 98, Windows NT 4.0,
Windows Millennium Edition, Windows 2000,
Windows XP Home Edition, Windows XP Professional,
Windows .NET Server family

.NET Framework Security:

- **FileIOPermission** Accesses information in the path. Associated enumeration: **FileIOPermissionAccess.PathDiscovery**.

ModuleBuilder.CreateGlobalFunctions Method

Complete the global function definitions for this dynamic module.

```
[Visual Basic]
Public Sub CreateGlobalFunctions()
[C#]
public void CreateGlobalFunctions();
[C++]
public: void CreateGlobalFunctions();
[JScript]
public function CreateGlobalFunctions();
```

Exceptions

Exception Type	Condition
InvalidOperation- Exception	This method was called previously.

Remarks

This method should be called when the user is done with defining all of the global functions within this dynamic module. After calling this function, no more new global functions or new global data are allowed.

Example

See related example in the **System.Reflection.Emit.ModuleBuilder** class topic.

Requirements

Platforms: Windows 98, Windows NT 4.0,
Windows Millennium Edition, Windows 2000,
Windows XP Home Edition, Windows XP Professional,
Windows .NET Server family

.NET Framework Security:

- **ReflectionPermission** SecurityAction.Demand, ReflectionEmit

ModuleBuilder.DefineDocument Method

Define a document for source.

```
[Visual Basic]
Public Function DefineDocument( _
   ByVal url As String, _
   ByVal language As Guid, _
   ByVal languageVendor As Guid, _
   ByVal documentType As Guid _
) As ISymbolDocumentWriter
[C#]
public ISymbolDocumentWriter DefineDocument(
   string url,
   Guid language,
   Guid languageVendor,
   Guid documentType
);
[C++]
public: ISymbolDocumentWriter* DefineDocument(
   String* url,
   Guid language,
   Guid languageVendor,
   Guid documentType
);
[JScript]
public function DefineDocument(
   url : String,
   language : Guid,
   languageVendor : Guid,
   documentType : Guid
) : ISymbolDocumentWriter;
```

Parameters

url
   The URL for the document.

language
   The GUID identifying the document language. This can be null.

languageVendor
   The GUID identifying the document language vendor. This can be null.

documentType
   The GUID identifying the document type. This can be null.

Return Value

An **ISymbolDocumentWriter** object representing the defined document.

Exceptions

Exception Type	Condition
ArgumentNullException	*url* is a null reference (**Nothing** in Visual Basic).
InvalidOperationException	This method is called on a dynamic module that is not a debug module.

Example

See related example in the **System.Reflection.Emit.ModuleBuilder** class topic.

Requirements

Platforms: Windows 98, Windows NT 4.0, Windows Millennium Edition, Windows 2000, Windows XP Home Edition, Windows XP Professional, Windows .NET Server family

ModuleBuilder.DefineEnum Method

Defines an enumeration type with that is a value type with a single non-static field called *value__* of the specified type.

```
[Visual Basic]
Public Function DefineEnum( _
   ByVal name As String, _
   ByVal visibility As TypeAttributes, _
   ByVal underlyingType As Type _
) As EnumBuilder
[C#]
public EnumBuilder DefineEnum(
   string name,
   TypeAttributes visibility,
   Type underlyingType
);
[C++]
public: EnumBuilder* DefineEnum(
   String* name,
   TypeAttributes visibility,
   Type* underlyingType
);
[JScript]
public function DefineEnum(
   name : String,
   visibility : TypeAttributes,
   underlyingType : Type
) : EnumBuilder;
```

Parameters

name
   The full path of the enumeration type. *name* cannot contain embedded nulls.

visibility
   The type attributes for the enumeration. The attributes are any bits defined by **VisibilityMask**.

underlyingType
   The underlying type for the enumeration.

Return Value

Returns the defined enumeration.

Exceptions

Exception Type	Condition
ArgumentException	Attributes other than visibility attributes are provided.
	-or-
	An enum with the given name exists in the parent assembly of this module.
	-or-
	When the visibility attributes are incorrect for the scope of the enum. For example, if **NestedPublic** is specified as the *visibility* but the enum is not a nested type.
ArgumentNullException	*name* is a null reference (**Nothing** in Visual Basic).

Remarks

The defined enum is a derived class of **Enum**. The defined field has **Private** and **SpecialName** set.

Example

See related example in the **System.Reflection.Emit.ModuleBuilder** class topic.

Requirements

Platforms: Windows 98, Windows NT 4.0, Windows Millennium Edition, Windows 2000, Windows XP Home Edition, Windows XP Professional, Windows .NET Server family

.NET Framework Security:

- **ReflectionPermission** SecurityAction.Demand, ReflectionEmit

ModuleBuilder.DefineGlobalMethod Method

Defines a global method.

Overload List

Defines a global method given its name, attributes, return type, and parameter types.

[Visual Basic] **Overloads Public Function DefineGlobalMethod(String, MethodAttributes, Type, Type()) As MethodBuilder**

[C#] **public MethodBuilder DefineGlobalMethod(string, MethodAttributes, Type, Type[]);**

[C++] **public: MethodBuilder* DefineGlobalMethod(String*, MethodAttributes, Type*, Type[]);**

[JScript] **public function DefineGlobalMethod(String, MethodAttributes, Type, Type[]) : MethodBuilder;**

Defines a global method given its name, attributes, calling convention, return type, and parameter types.

[Visual Basic] **Overloads Public Function DefineGlobalMethod(String, MethodAttributes, CallingConventions, Type, Type()) As MethodBuilder**

[C#] **public MethodBuilder DefineGlobalMethod(string, MethodAttributes, CallingConventions, Type, Type[]);**

[C++] **public: MethodBuilder* DefineGlobalMethod(String*, MethodAttributes, CallingConventions, Type*, Type[]);**

[JScript] **public function DefineGlobalMethod(String, MethodAttributes, CallingConventions, Type, Type[]) : MethodBuilder;**

Example

See related example in the **System.Reflection.Emit.ModuleBuilder** class topic.

ModuleBuilder.DefineGlobalMethod Method (String, MethodAttributes, Type, Type[])

Defines a global method given its name, attributes, return type, and parameter types.

```
[Visual Basic]
Overloads Public Function DefineGlobalMethod( _
    ByVal name As String, _
    ByVal attributes As MethodAttributes, _
    ByVal returnType As Type, _
    ByVal parameterTypes() As Type _
) As MethodBuilder
```

```
[C#]
public MethodBuilder DefineGlobalMethod(
    string name,
    MethodAttributes attributes,
    Type returnType,
    Type[] parameterTypes
);
[C++]
public: MethodBuilder* DefineGlobalMethod(
    String* name,
    MethodAttributes attributes,
    Type* returnType,
    Type* parameterTypes[]
);
[JScript]
public function DefineGlobalMethod(
    name : String,
    attributes : MethodAttributes,
    returnType : Type,
    parameterTypes : Type[]
) : MethodBuilder;
```

Parameters

name
    The name of the method. *name* cannot contain embedded nulls.
attributes
    The attributes of the method.
returnType
    The return type of the method.
parameterTypes
    The types of the method's parameters.

Return Value

Returns the defined global method.

Exceptions

Exception Type	Condition
ArgumentException	The method is not static.
	-or-
	The length of *name* is zero
ArgumentNullException	*name* is a null reference (**Nothing** in Visual Basic).
InvalidOperation-Exception	**CreateGlobalFunctions** has been previously called.

Remarks

Notes to Implementers: The global method that this method defines is not usable until you call **CreateGlobalFunctions**.

Example

See related example in the **System.Reflection.Emit.ModuleBuilder** class topic.

Requirements

Platforms: Windows 98, Windows NT 4.0, Windows Millennium Edition, Windows 2000, Windows XP Home Edition, Windows XP Professional, Windows .NET Server family

.NET Framework Security:

- **ReflectionPermission** SecurityAction.Demand, ReflectionEmit

ModuleBuilder.DefineGlobalMethod Method (String, MethodAttributes, CallingConventions, Type, Type[])

Defines a global method given its name, attributes, calling convention, return type, and parameter types.

```
[Visual Basic]
Overloads Public Function DefineGlobalMethod( _
   ByVal name As String, _
   ByVal attributes As MethodAttributes, _
   ByVal callingConvention As CallingConventions, _
   ByVal returnType As Type, _
   ByVal parameterTypes() As Type _
) As MethodBuilder
[C#]
public MethodBuilder DefineGlobalMethod(
   string name,
   MethodAttributes attributes,
   CallingConventions callingConvention,
   Type returnType,
   Type[] parameterTypes
);
[C++]
public: MethodBuilder* DefineGlobalMethod(
   String* name,
   MethodAttributes attributes,
   CallingConventions callingConvention,
   Type* returnType,
   Type* parameterTypes[]
);
[JScript]
public function DefineGlobalMethod(
   name : String,
   attributes : MethodAttributes,
   callingConvention : CallingConventions,
   returnType : Type,
   parameterTypes : Type[]
) : MethodBuilder;
```

Parameters

name
    The name of the method. *name* cannot contain embedded nulls.
attributes
    The attributes of the method.
callingConvention
    The calling convention for the method.
returnType
    The return type of the method.
parameterTypes
    The types of the method's parameters.

Return Value

Returns the defined global method.

Exceptions

Exception Type	Condition
ArgumentException	The method is not static.
ArgumentNullException	*name* is a null reference (**Nothing** in Visual Basic).
InvalidOperation-Exception	**CreateGlobalFunctions** has been previously called.

Remarks

Notes to Implementers: You cannot use the global method that this method defines until you call **CreateGlobalFunctions**.

Example

See related example in the **System.Reflection.Emit.ModuleBuilder** class topic.

Requirements

Platforms: Windows 98, Windows NT 4.0, Windows Millennium Edition, Windows 2000, Windows XP Home Edition, Windows XP Professional, Windows .NET Server family

.NET Framework Security:

- **ReflectionPermission** SecurityAction.Demand, ReflectionEmit

ModuleBuilder.DefineInitializedData Method

Defines initialized data field in the .sdata section of the portable executable (PE) file.

```
[Visual Basic]
Public Function DefineInitializedData( _
   ByVal name As String, _
   ByVal data() As Byte, _
   ByVal attributes As FieldAttributes _
) As FieldBuilder
[C#]
public FieldBuilder DefineInitializedData(
   string name,
   byte[] data,
   FieldAttributes attributes
);
[C++]
public: FieldBuilder* DefineInitializedData(
   String* name,
   unsigned char data __gc[],
   FieldAttributes attributes
);
[JScript]
public function DefineInitializedData(
   name : String,
   data : Byte[],
   attributes : FieldAttributes
) : FieldBuilder;
```

Parameters

name
    The name used to refer to the data. *name* cannot contain embedded nulls.
data
    The blob of data.
attributes
    The attributes for the field. The default is **Static**.

Return Value

A field to reference the data.

Exceptions

Exception Type	Condition
ArgumentException	The length of *name* is zero. -or- The size of *data* is less than or equal to zero or greater than or equal to 0x3f0000.
ArgumentNullException	*name* or *data* is a null reference (**Nothing** in Visual Basic).
InvalidOperation-Exception	**CreateGlobalFunctions** has been previously called.

Example

See related example in the
System.Reflection.Emit.ModuleBuilder class topic.

Requirements

Platforms: Windows 98, Windows NT 4.0,
Windows Millennium Edition, Windows 2000,
Windows XP Home Edition, Windows XP Professional,
Windows .NET Server family

.NET Framework Security:

- **ReflectionPermission** SecurityAction.Demand, ReflectionEmit

ModuleBuilder.DefinePInvokeMethod Method

Defines a **PInvoke** method.

Overload List

Defines a **PInvoke** method given its name, the name of the DLL in which the method is defined, the attributes of the method, the calling convention of the method, the return type of the method, the types of the parameters of the method, and the **PInvoke** flags.

[Visual Basic] **Overloads Public Function DefinePInvoke Method(String, String, MethodAttributes, Calling Conventions, Type, Type(), CallingConvention, CharSet) As MethodBuilder**

[C#] **public MethodBuilder DefinePInvokeMethod(string, string, MethodAttributes, CallingConventions, Type, Type[], CallingConvention, CharSet);**

[C++] **public: MethodBuilder* DefinePInvokeMethod (String*, String*, MethodAttributes, CallingConventions, Type*, Type[], CallingConvention, CharSet);**

[JScript] **public function DefinePInvokeMethod(String, String, MethodAttributes, CallingConventions, Type, Type[], CallingConvention, CharSet) : MethodBuilder;**

Defines a **PInvoke** method given its name, the name of the DLL in which the method is defined, the attributes of the method, the calling convention of the method, the return type of the method, the types of the parameters of the method, and the **PInvoke** flags.

[Visual Basic] **Overloads Public Function DefinePInvoke Method(String, String, String, MethodAttributes, CallingConventions, Type, Type(), CallingConvention, CharSet) As MethodBuilder**

[C#] **public MethodBuilder DefinePInvokeMethod(string, string, string, MethodAttributes, CallingConventions, Type, Type[], CallingConvention, CharSet);**

[C++] **public: MethodBuilder* DefinePInvokeMethod (String*, String*, String*, MethodAttributes,**

CallingConventions, Type*, Type[], CallingConvention, CharSet);

[JScript] **public function DefinePInvokeMethod(String, String, String, MethodAttributes, CallingConventions, Type, Type[], CallingConvention, CharSet) : MethodBuilder;**

Example

See related example in the
System.Reflection.Emit.ModuleBuilder class topic.

ModuleBuilder.DefinePInvokeMethod Method (String, String, MethodAttributes, CallingConventions, Type, Type[], CallingConvention, CharSet)

Defines a **PInvoke** method given its name, the name of the DLL in which the method is defined, the attributes of the method, the calling convention of the method, the return type of the method, the types of the parameters of the method, and the **PInvoke** flags.

```
[Visual Basic]
Overloads Public Function DefinePInvokeMethod( _
   ByVal name As String, _
   ByVal dllName As String, _
   ByVal attributes As MethodAttributes, _
   ByVal callingConvention As CallingConventions, _
   ByVal returnType As Type, _
   ByVal parameterTypes() As Type, _
   ByVal nativeCallConv As CallingConvention, _
   ByVal nativeCharSet As CharSet _
) As MethodBuilder
[C#]
public MethodBuilder DefinePInvokeMethod(
   string name,
   string dllName,
   MethodAttributes attributes,
   CallingConventions callingConvention,
   Type returnType,
   Type[] parameterTypes,
   CallingConvention nativeCallConv,
   CharSet nativeCharSet
);
[C++]
public: MethodBuilder* DefinePInvokeMethod(
   String* name,
   String* dllName,
   MethodAttributes attributes,
   CallingConventions callingConvention,
   Type* returnType,
   Type* parameterTypes[],
   CallingConvention nativeCallConv,
   CharSet nativeCharSet
);
[JScript]
public function DefinePInvokeMethod(
   name : String,
   dllName : String,
   attributes : MethodAttributes,
   callingConvention : CallingConventions,
   returnType : Type,
   parameterTypes : Type[],
   nativeCallConv : CallingConvention,
   nativeCharSet : CharSet
) : MethodBuilder;
```

Parameters

name
> The name of the **PInvoke** method. *name* cannot contain embedded nulls.

dllName
> The name of the DLL in which the **PInvoke** method is defined.

attributes
> The attributes of the method.

callingConvention
> The method's calling convention.

returnType
> The method's return type.

parameterTypes
> The types of the method's parameters.

nativeCallConv
> The native calling convention.

nativeCharSet
> The method's native character set.

Return Value

The defined **PInvoke** method.

Exceptions

Exception Type	Condition
ArgumentException	The method is not static or if the containing type is an interface. -or- The method is abstract. -or- The method was previously defined.
ArgumentNullException	*name* or *dllName* is a null reference (**Nothing** in Visual Basic).
InvalidOperation-Exception	The containing type has been previously created using **CreateType**

Remarks

Some DLL import attributes (see the description of System.Runtime.InteropServices.DllImportAttribute) cannot be specified as arguments to this method. Such attributes should be set by emitting a custom attribute for the method. For example, the DLL import attribute **PreserveSig** is set by emitting a custom attribute.

Example

See related example in the **System.Reflection.Emit.ModuleBuilder** class topic.

Requirements

Platforms: Windows 98, Windows NT 4.0, Windows Millennium Edition, Windows 2000, Windows XP Home Edition, Windows XP Professional, Windows .NET Server family

.NET Framework Security:
• **ReflectionPermission** SecurityAction.Demand, ReflectionEmit

ModuleBuilder.DefinePInvokeMethod Method (String, String, String, MethodAttributes, CallingConventions, Type, Type[], CallingConvention, CharSet)

Defines a **PInvoke** method given its name, the name of the DLL in which the method is defined, the attributes of the method, the calling convention of the method, the return type of the method, the types of the parameters of the method, and the **PInvoke** flags.

```
[Visual Basic]
Overloads Public Function DefinePInvokeMethod( _
   ByVal name As String, _
   ByVal dllName As String, _
   ByVal entryName As String, _
   ByVal attributes As MethodAttributes, _
   ByVal callingConvention As CallingConventions, _
   ByVal returnType As Type, _
   ByVal parameterTypes() As Type, _
   ByVal nativeCallConv As CallingConvention, _
   ByVal nativeCharSet As CharSet _
) As MethodBuilder
[C#]
public MethodBuilder DefinePInvokeMethod(
   string name,
   string dllName,
   string entryName,
   MethodAttributes attributes,
   CallingConventions callingConvention,
   Type returnType,
   Type[] parameterTypes,
   CallingConvention nativeCallConv,
   CharSet nativeCharSet
);
[C++]
public: MethodBuilder* DefinePInvokeMethod(
   String* name,
   String* dllName,
   String* entryName,
   MethodAttributes attributes,
   CallingConventions callingConvention,
   Type* returnType,
   Type* parameterTypes[],
   CallingConvention nativeCallConv,
   CharSet nativeCharSet
);
[JScript]
public function DefinePInvokeMethod(
   name : String,
   dllName : String,
   entryName : String,
   attributes : MethodAttributes,
   callingConvention : CallingConventions,
   returnType : Type,
   parameterTypes : Type[],
   nativeCallConv : CallingConvention,
   nativeCharSet : CharSet
) : MethodBuilder;
```

Parameters

name
> The name of the **PInvoke** method. *name* cannot contain embedded nulls.

dllName
> The name of the DLL in which the **PInvoke** method is defined.

entryName
> The name of the entry point in the DLL.

attributes
> The attributes of the method.

callingConvention
> The method's calling convention.

returnType
> The method's return type.

parameterTypes
> The types of the method's parameters.

nativeCallConv
> The native calling convention.

nativeCharSet
> The method's native character set.

Return Value

The defined PInvoke method.

Exceptions

Exception Type	Condition
ArgumentException	The method is not static or if the containing type is an interface or if the method is abstract of if the method was previously defined.
ArgumentNullException	*name* or *dllName* is a null reference (**Nothing** in Visual Basic).
InvalidOperationException	The containing type has been previously created using **CreateType**

Remarks

Some DLL import attributes (see the description of System.Runtime.InteropServices.DllImportAttribute) cannot be specified as arguments to this method. Such attributes should be set by emitting a custom attribute for the method. For example, the DLL import attribute **PreserveSig** is set by emitting a custom attribute.

Example

See related example in the **System.Reflection.Emit.ModuleBuilder** class topic.

Requirements

Platforms: Windows 98, Windows NT 4.0, Windows Millennium Edition, Windows 2000, Windows XP Home Edition, Windows XP Professional, Windows .NET Server family

.NET Framework Security:
- **ReflectionPermission** SecurityAction.Demand, ReflectionEmit

ModuleBuilder.DefineResource Method

Defines a managed embedded resource to be stored in this module.

Overload List

Defines the named managed embedded resource to be stored in this module.

> [Visual Basic] **Overloads Public Function DefineResource (String, String) As IResourceWriter**
>
> [C#] **public IResourceWriter DefineResource(string, string);**
>
> [C++] **public: IResourceWriter* DefineResource(String*, String*);**

[JScript] **public function DefineResource(String, String) : IResourceWriter;**

Defines the named managed embedded resource with the given attributes that is to be stored in this module.

> [Visual Basic] **Overloads Public Function DefineResource (String, String, ResourceAttributes) As IResourceWriter**
>
> [C#] **public IResourceWriter DefineResource(string, string, ResourceAttributes);**
>
> [C++] **public: IResourceWriter* DefineResource(String*, String*, ResourceAttributes);**
>
> [JScript] **public function DefineResource(String, String, ResourceAttributes) : IResourceWriter;**

Example

See related example in the **System.Reflection.Emit.ModuleBuilder** class topic.

ModuleBuilder.DefineResource Method (String, String)

Defines the named managed embedded resource to be stored in this module.

```
[Visual Basic]
Overloads Public Function DefineResource( _
   ByVal name As String, _
   ByVal description As String _
) As IResourceWriter
[C#]
public IResourceWriter DefineResource(
   string name,
   string description
);
[C++]
public: IResourceWriter* DefineResource(
   String* name,
   String* description
);
[JScript]
public function DefineResource(
   name : String,
   description : String
) : IResourceWriter;
```

Parameters

name
> The name of the resource. *name* cannot contain embedded nulls.

description
> The description of the resource.

Return Value

Returns a resource writer for the defined resource.

Exceptions

Exception Type	Condition
ArgumentException	Length of *name* is zero.
ArgumentNullException	*name* is null.
InvalidOperationException	This module is transient. -or- The containing assembly is not persistable.

Remarks

The caller must not call the **ResourceWriter.Generate()** and **ResourceWriter.Close()** methods since these methods are called by **ModuleBuilder.Save** when the dynamic assembly is written to disk.

Example

See related example in the **System.Reflection.Emit.ModuleBuilder** class topic.

Requirements

Platforms: Windows 98, Windows NT 4.0, Windows Millennium Edition, Windows 2000, Windows XP Home Edition, Windows XP Professional, Windows .NET Server family

.NET Framework Security:
- **ReflectionPermission** SecurityAction.Demand, ReflectionEmit

ModuleBuilder.DefineResource Method (String, String, ResourceAttributes)

Defines the named managed embedded resource with the given attributes that is to be stored in this module.

```
[Visual Basic]
Overloads Public Function DefineResource( _
   ByVal name As String, _
   ByVal description As String, _
   ByVal attribute As ResourceAttributes _
) As IResourceWriter
[C#]
public IResourceWriter DefineResource(
   string name,
   string description,
   ResourceAttributes attribute
);
[C++]
public: IResourceWriter* DefineResource(
   String* name,
   String* description,
   ResourceAttributes attribute
);
[JScript]
public function DefineResource(
   name : String,
   description : String,
   attribute : ResourceAttributes
) : IResourceWriter;
```

Parameters

name
　　The name of the resource. *name* cannot contain embedded nulls.
description
　　The description of the resource.
attribute
　　The resource attributes.

Return Value

Returns a resource writer for the defined resource.

Exceptions

Exception Type	Condition
ArgumentException	Length of *name* is zero.

Exception Type	Condition
ArgumentNullException	*name* is null.
InvalidOperationException	This module is transient.
	-or-
	The containing assembly is not persistable.

Remarks

The caller must not call the **ResourceWriter.Generate()** and **ResourceWriter.Close()** methods since these methods are called by **ModuleBuilder.Save** when the dynamic assembly is written to disk.

Example

See related example in the **System.Reflection.Emit.ModuleBuilder** class topic.

Requirements

Platforms: Windows 98, Windows NT 4.0, Windows Millennium Edition, Windows 2000, Windows XP Home Edition, Windows XP Professional, Windows .NET Server family

.NET Framework Security:
- **ReflectionPermission** SecurityAction.Demand, ReflectionEmit

ModuleBuilder.DefineType Method

Constructs a **TypeBuilder**. To define a value type, define a type that is derives **ValueType**.

Overload List

Constructs a **TypeBuilder** for a type with the specified name.

　　[Visual Basic] **Overloads Public Function DefineType(String) As TypeBuilder**

　　[C#] **public TypeBuilder DefineType(string);**

　　[C++] **public: TypeBuilder* DefineType(String*);**

　　[JScript] **public function DefineType(String) : TypeBuilder;**

Constructs a **TypeBuilder** given the type name and the type attributes.

　　[Visual Basic] **Overloads Public Function DefineType(String, TypeAttributes) As TypeBuilder**

　　[C#] **public TypeBuilder DefineType(string, TypeAttributes);**

　　[C++] **public: TypeBuilder* DefineType(String*, TypeAttributes);**

　　[JScript] **public function DefineType(String, TypeAttributes) : TypeBuilder;**

Constructs a **TypeBuilder** given type name, its attributes, and the type that the defined type extends.

　　[Visual Basic] **Overloads Public Function DefineType(String, TypeAttributes, Type) As TypeBuilder**

　　[C#] **public TypeBuilder DefineType(string, TypeAttributes, Type);**

　　[C++] **public: TypeBuilder* DefineType(String*, TypeAttributes, Type*);**

　　[JScript] **public function DefineType(String, TypeAttributes, Type) : TypeBuilder;**

Constructs a **TypeBuilder** given the type name, the attributes, the type that the defined type extends, and the total size of the type.

[Visual Basic] **Overloads Public Function DefineType(String, TypeAttributes, Type, Integer) As TypeBuilder**

[C#] **public TypeBuilder DefineType(string, TypeAttributes, Type, int);**

[C++] **public: TypeBuilder* DefineType(String*, TypeAttributes, Type*, int);**

[JScript] **public function DefineType(String, TypeAttributes, Type, int) : TypeBuilder;**

Constructs a **TypeBuilder** given the type name, the attributes, the type that the defined type extends, and the packing size of the type.

[Visual Basic] **Overloads Public Function DefineType(String, TypeAttributes, Type, PackingSize) As TypeBuilder**

[C#] **public TypeBuilder DefineType(string, TypeAttributes, Type, PackingSize);**

[C++] **public: TypeBuilder* DefineType(String*, TypeAttributes, Type*, PackingSize);**

[JScript] **public function DefineType(String, TypeAttributes, Type, PackingSize) : TypeBuilder;**

Constructs a **TypeBuilder** given the type name, attributes, the type that the defined type extends, and the interfaces that the defined type implements.

[Visual Basic] **Overloads Public Function DefineType(String, TypeAttributes, Type, Type()) As TypeBuilder**

[C#] **public TypeBuilder DefineType(string, TypeAttributes, Type, Type[]);**

[C++] **public: TypeBuilder* DefineType(String*, TypeAttributes, Type*, Type[]);**

[JScript] **public function DefineType(String, TypeAttributes, Type, Type[]) : TypeBuilder;**

Constructs a **TypeBuilder** given the type name, attributes, the type that the defined type extends, the packing size of the defined type, and the total size of the defined type.

[Visual Basic] **Overloads Public Function DefineType(String, TypeAttributes, Type, PackingSize, Integer) As TypeBuilder**

[C#] **public TypeBuilder DefineType(string, TypeAttributes, Type, PackingSize, int);**

[C++] **public: TypeBuilder* DefineType(String*, TypeAttributes, Type*, PackingSize, int);**

[JScript] **public function DefineType(String, TypeAttributes, Type, PackingSize, int) : TypeBuilder;**

Example

See related example in the **System.Reflection.Emit.ModuleBuilder** class topic.

ModuleBuilder.DefineType Method (String)

Constructs a **TypeBuilder** for a type with the specified name.

```
[Visual Basic]
Overloads Public Function DefineType( _
   ByVal name As String _
) As TypeBuilder
[C#]
public TypeBuilder DefineType(
   string name
);
```

```
[C++]
public: TypeBuilder* DefineType(
   String* name
);
[JScript]
public function DefineType(
   name : String
) : TypeBuilder;
```

Parameters

name
  The full path of the type. *name* cannot contain embedded nulls.

Return Value

Returns the created **TypeBuilder**.

Exceptions

Exception Type	Condition
ArgumentException	A type with the given name exists in the parent assembly of this module. -or- Nested type attributes are set on a type that is not nested.
ArgumentNullException	*name* is null.

Remarks

Type names must be unique within an assembly. You cannot have two types with the same name in two different modules of an assembly.

Example

See related example in the **System.Reflection.Emit.ModuleBuilder** class topic.

Requirements

Platforms: Windows 98, Windows NT 4.0, Windows Millennium Edition, Windows 2000, Windows XP Home Edition, Windows XP Professional, Windows .NET Server family

.NET Framework Security:
- **ReflectionPermission** SecurityAction.Demand, ReflectionEmit

ModuleBuilder.DefineType Method (String, TypeAttributes)

Constructs a **TypeBuilder** given the type name and the type attributes.

```
[Visual Basic]
Overloads Public Function DefineType( _
   ByVal name As String, _
   ByVal attr As TypeAttributes _
) As TypeBuilder
[C#]
public TypeBuilder DefineType(
   string name,
   TypeAttributes attr
);
[C++]
public: TypeBuilder* DefineType(
   String* name,
   TypeAttributes attr
);
```

```
[JScript]
public function DefineType(
    name : String,
    attr : TypeAttributes
) : TypeBuilder;
```

Parameters

name
    The full path of the type. *name* cannot contain embedded nulls.
attr
    The attributes of the defined type.

Return Value

Returns a **TypeBuilder** created with all of the requested attributes.

Exceptions

Exception Type	Condition
ArgumentException	A type with the given name exists in the parent assembly of this module. -or- Nested type attributes are set on a type that is not nested.
ArgumentNullException	*name* is null.

Remarks

Type names must be unique within an assembly. You cannot have two types with the same name in two different modules of an assembly.

Example

See related example in the **System.Reflection.Emit.ModuleBuilder** class topic.

Requirements

Platforms: Windows 98, Windows NT 4.0, Windows Millennium Edition, Windows 2000, Windows XP Home Edition, Windows XP Professional, Windows .NET Server family

.NET Framework Security:
- **ReflectionPermission** SecurityAction.Demand, ReflectionEmit

ModuleBuilder.DefineType Method (String, TypeAttributes, Type)

Constructs a **TypeBuilder** given type name, its attributes, and the type that the defined type extends.

```
[Visual Basic]
Overloads Public Function DefineType( _
    ByVal name As String, _
    ByVal attr As TypeAttributes, _
    ByVal parent As Type _
) As TypeBuilder
[C#]
public TypeBuilder DefineType(
    string name,
    TypeAttributes attr,
    Type parent
);
[C++]
public: TypeBuilder* DefineType(
    String* name,
```

```
    TypeAttributes attr,
    Type* parent
);
[JScript]
public function DefineType(
    name : String,
    attr : TypeAttributes,
    parent : Type
) : TypeBuilder;
```

Parameters

name
    The full path of the type. *name* cannot contain embedded nulls.
attr
    The attribute to be associated with the type.
parent
    The Type that the defined type extends.

Return Value

Returns a **TypeBuilder** created with all of the requested attributes.

Exceptions

Exception Type	Condition
ArgumentException	A type with the given name exists in the parent assembly of this module. -or- Nested type attributes are set on a type that is not nested.
ArgumentNullException	*name* is null.

Remarks

Type names must be unique within an assembly. You cannot have two types with the same name in two different modules of an assembly.

Example

See related example in the **System.Reflection.Emit.ModuleBuilder** class topic.

Requirements

Platforms: Windows 98, Windows NT 4.0, Windows Millennium Edition, Windows 2000, Windows XP Home Edition, Windows XP Professional, Windows .NET Server family

.NET Framework Security:
- **ReflectionPermission** SecurityAction.Demand, ReflectionEmit

ModuleBuilder.DefineType Method (String, TypeAttributes, Type, Int32)

Constructs a **TypeBuilder** given the type name, the attributes, the type that the defined type extends, and the total size of the type.

```
[Visual Basic]
Overloads Public Function DefineType( _
    ByVal name As String, _
    ByVal attr As TypeAttributes, _
    ByVal parent As Type, _
    ByVal typesize As Integer _
) As TypeBuilder
```

```
[C#]
public TypeBuilder DefineType(
    string name,
    TypeAttributes attr,
    Type parent,
    int typesize
);
[C++]
public: TypeBuilder* DefineType(
    String* name,
    TypeAttributes attr,
    Type* parent,
    int typesize
);
[JScript]
public function DefineType(
    name : String,
    attr : TypeAttributes,
    parent : Type,
    typesize : int
) : TypeBuilder;
```

Parameters

name

 The full path of the type. *name* cannot contain embedded nulls.

attr

 The attributes of the defined type.

parent

 The Type that the defined type extends.

typesize

 The total size of the type.

Return Value

Returns a **TypeBuilder** object.

Exceptions

Exception Type	Condition
ArgumentException	A type with the given name exists in the parent assembly of this module.
	-or-
	Nested type attributes are set on a type that is not nested.
ArgumentNullException	*name* is null.

Remarks

Type names must be unique within an assembly. It is forbidden to have two types with the same name in two different modules of an assembly.

Example

See related example in the **System.Reflection.Emit.ModuleBuilder** class topic.

Requirements

Platforms: Windows 98, Windows NT 4.0, Windows Millennium Edition, Windows 2000, Windows XP Home Edition, Windows XP Professional, Windows .NET Server family

.NET Framework Security:

• **ReflectionPermission** SecurityAction.Demand, ReflectionEmit

ModuleBuilder.DefineType Method (String, TypeAttributes, Type, PackingSize)

Constructs a **TypeBuilder** given the type name, the attributes, the type that the defined type extends, and the packing size of the type.

```
[Visual Basic]
Overloads Public Function DefineType( _
    ByVal name As String, _
    ByVal attr As TypeAttributes, _
    ByVal parent As Type, _
    ByVal packsize As PackingSize _
) As TypeBuilder
[C#]
public TypeBuilder DefineType(
    string name,
    TypeAttributes attr,
    Type parent,
    PackingSize packsize
);
[C++]
public: TypeBuilder* DefineType(
    String* name,
    TypeAttributes attr,
    Type* parent,
    PackingSize packsize
);
[JScript]
public function DefineType(
    name : String,
    attr : TypeAttributes,
    parent : Type,
    packsize : PackingSize
) : TypeBuilder;
```

Parameters

name

 The full path of the type. *name* cannot contain embedded nulls.

attr

 The attributes of the defined type.

parent

 The Type that the defined type extends.

packsize

 The packing size of the type.

Return Value

Returns a **TypeBuilder** object.

Exceptions

Exception Type	Condition
ArgumentException	A type with the given name exists in the parent assembly of this module.
	-or-
	Nested type attributes are set on a type that is not nested.
ArgumentNullException	*name* is null.

Remarks

Type names must be unique within an assembly. You cannot have two types with the same name in two different modules of an assembly.

Example

See related example in the
System.Reflection.Emit.ModuleBuilder class topic.

Requirements

Platforms: Windows 98, Windows NT 4.0,
Windows Millennium Edition, Windows 2000,
Windows XP Home Edition, Windows XP Professional,
Windows .NET Server family

.NET Framework Security:

- **ReflectionPermission** SecurityAction.Demand, ReflectionEmit

ModuleBuilder.DefineType Method (String, TypeAttributes, Type, Type[])

Constructs a **TypeBuilder** given the type name, attributes, the type
that the defined type extends, and the interfaces that the defined type
implements.

```
[Visual Basic]
Overloads Public Function DefineType( _
   ByVal name As String, _
   ByVal attr As TypeAttributes, _
   ByVal parent As Type, _
   ByVal interfaces() As Type _
) As TypeBuilder
[C#]
public TypeBuilder DefineType(
   string name,
   TypeAttributes attr,
   Type parent,
   Type[] interfaces
);
[C++]
public: TypeBuilder* DefineType(
   String* name,
   TypeAttributes attr,
   Type* parent,
   Type* interfaces[]
);
[JScript]
public function DefineType(
   name : String,
   attr : TypeAttributes,
   parent : Type,
   interfaces : Type[]
) : TypeBuilder;
```

Parameters

name
   The full path of the type. *name* cannot contain embedded nulls.
attr
   The attributes to be associated with the type.
parent
   The type that the defined type extends.
interfaces
   The list of interfaces that the type implements.

Return Value

Returns a **TypeBuilder** created with all of the requested attributes.

Exceptions

Exception Type	Condition
ArgumentException	A type with the given name exists in the parent assembly of this module. -or- Nested type attributes are set on a type that is not nested.
ArgumentNullException	*name* is null.

Remarks

Type names must be unique within an assembly. You cannot have
two types with the same name in two different modules of an
assembly.

Example

See related example in the
System.Reflection.Emit.ModuleBuilder class topic.

Requirements

Platforms: Windows 98, Windows NT 4.0,
Windows Millennium Edition, Windows 2000,
Windows XP Home Edition, Windows XP Professional,
Windows .NET Server family

.NET Framework Security:

- **ReflectionPermission** SecurityAction.Demand, ReflectionEmit

ModuleBuilder.DefineType Method (String, TypeAttributes, Type, PackingSize, Int32)

Constructs a **TypeBuilder** given the type name, attributes, the type
that the defined type extends, the packing size of the defined type,
and the total size of the defined type.

```
[Visual Basic]
Overloads Public Function DefineType( _
   ByVal name As String, _
   ByVal attr As TypeAttributes, _
   ByVal parent As Type, _
   ByVal packingSize As PackingSize, _
   ByVal typesize As Integer _
) As TypeBuilder
[C#]
public TypeBuilder DefineType(
   string name,
   TypeAttributes attr,
   Type parent,
   PackingSize packingSize,
   int typesize
);
[C++]
public: TypeBuilder* DefineType(
   String* name,
   TypeAttributes attr,
   Type* parent,
   PackingSize packingSize,
   int typesize
);
[JScript]
public function DefineType(
   name : String,
   attr : TypeAttributes,
```

```
    parent : Type,
    packingSize : PackingSize,
    typesize : int
) : TypeBuilder;
```

Parameters

name
> The full path of the type. *name* cannot contain embedded nulls.

attr
> The attributes of the defined type.

parent
> The type that the defined type extends.

packingSize
> The packing size of the type.

typesize
> The total size of the type.

Return Value

Returns a **TypeBuilder** created with all of the requested attributes.

Exceptions

Exception Type	Condition
ArgumentException	A type with the given name exists in the parent assembly of this module.
	-or-
	Nested type attributes are set on a type that is not nested.
ArgumentNullException	*name* is null.

Remarks

Type names must be unique within an assembly. You cannot have two types with the same name in two different modules of an assembly.

Example

See related example in the **System.Reflection.Emit.ModuleBuilder** class topic.

Requirements

Platforms: Windows 98, Windows NT 4.0, Windows Millennium Edition, Windows 2000, Windows XP Home Edition, Windows XP Professional, Windows .NET Server family

.NET Framework Security:
- **ReflectionPermission** SecurityAction.Demand, ReflectionEmit

ModuleBuilder.DefineUninitializedData Method

Defines uninitialized data field in the .sdata section of the portable executable (PE) file.

```
[Visual Basic]
Public Function DefineUninitializedData( _
    ByVal name As String, _
    ByVal size As Integer, _
    ByVal attributes As FieldAttributes _
) As FieldBuilder
[C#]
public FieldBuilder DefineUninitializedData(
    string name,
    int size,
    FieldAttributes attributes
);
```

```
[C++]
public: FieldBuilder* DefineUninitializedData(
    String* name,
    int size,
    FieldAttributes attributes
);
[JScript]
public function DefineUninitializedData(
    name : String,
    size : int,
    attributes : FieldAttributes
) : FieldBuilder;
```

Parameters

name
> The name used to refer to the data. *name* cannot contain embedded nulls.

size
> The size of the data field.

attributes
> The attributes for the field.

Return Value

A field to reference the data.

Exceptions

Exception Type	Condition
ArgumentException	The length of *name* is zero.
	-or-
	size is less than or equal to zero or greater than or equal to 0x003f0000.
ArgumentNullException	*name* is a null reference (**Nothing** in Visual Basic).
InvalidOperation-Exception	**CreateGlobalFunctions** has been previously called.

Requirements

Platforms: Windows 98, Windows NT 4.0, Windows Millennium Edition, Windows 2000, Windows XP Home Edition, Windows XP Professional, Windows .NET Server family

.NET Framework Security:
- **ReflectionPermission** SecurityAction.Demand, ReflectionEmit

ModuleBuilder.DefineUnmanagedResource Method

Defines an unmanaged resource in this module. The blob must have the right format for a Win32 resource.

Overload List

Defines an unmanaged embedded resource given an opaque blob of bytes.

> [Visual Basic] **Overloads Public Sub DefineUnmanagedResource(Byte())**
>
> [C#] **public void DefineUnmanagedResource(byte[]);**
>
> [C++] **public: void DefineUnmanagedResource(unsigned char __gc[]);**
>
> [JScript] **public function DefineUnmanagedResource(Byte[]);**

Defines an unmanaged resource given the name of Win32 resource file.

[Visual Basic] **Overloads Public Sub DefineUnmanagedResource(String)**

[C#] **public void DefineUnmanagedResource(string);**

[C++] **public: void DefineUnmanagedResource(String*);**

[JScript] **public function DefineUnmanagedResource(String);**

ModuleBuilder.DefineUnmanagedResource Method (Byte[])

Defines an unmanaged embedded resource given an opaque blob of bytes.

```
[Visual Basic]
Overloads Public Sub DefineUnmanagedResource( _
   ByVal resource() As Byte _
)
[C#]
public void DefineUnmanagedResource(
   byte[] resource
);
[C++]
public: void DefineUnmanagedResource(
   unsigned char resource __gc[]
);
[JScript]
public function DefineUnmanagedResource(
   resource : Byte[]
);
```

Parameters
resource
  An opaque blob that represents an unmanaged resource

Exceptions

Exception Type	Condition
ArgumentException	An unmanaged resource has already been defined in the module's assembly.
ArgumentNullException	*resource* is a null reference (**Nothing** in Visual Basic).

Remarks

An assembly can be associated with only one unmanaged resource. This means that calling **DefineVersionInfoResource** or **DefineUnmanagedResource** after either one of the methods was called previously will result in the System.ArgumentException being throw. Multiple unmanaged resources need to be merged with a tool such as the Microsoft ResMerge utility (not supplied with the common language runtime).

Requirements

Platforms: Windows 98, Windows NT 4.0, Windows Millennium Edition, Windows 2000, Windows XP Home Edition, Windows XP Professional, Windows .NET Server family

.NET Framework Security:
- **ReflectionPermission** SecurityAction.Demand, ReflectionEmit

ModuleBuilder.DefineUnmanagedResource Method (String)

Defines an unmanaged resource given the name of Win32 resource file.

```
[Visual Basic]
Overloads Public Sub DefineUnmanagedResource( _
   ByVal resourceFileName As String _
)
[C#]
public void DefineUnmanagedResource(
   string resourceFileName
);
[C++]
public: void DefineUnmanagedResource(
   String* resourceFileName
);
[JScript]
public function DefineUnmanagedResource(
   resourceFileName : String
);
```

Parameters
resourceFileName
  The name of the unmanaged resource file

Exceptions

Exception Type	Condition
ArgumentException	An unmanaged resource has already been defined in the module's assembly. -or- *resourceFileName* is the empty string ("").
ArgumentNullException	*resource* is a null reference (**Nothing** in Visual Basic).
FileNotFoundException	*resourceFileName* is not found -or- *resourceFileName* is a directory

Remarks

An assembly can be associated with only one unmanaged resource. This means that calling **DefineVersionInfoResource** or **DefineUnmanagedResource** after either one of the methods was called previously will throw the System.ArgumentException. Multiple unmanaged resources need to be merged with a tool such as the Microsoft ResMerge utility (not supplied with the common language runtime).

Requirements

Platforms: Windows 98, Windows NT 4.0, Windows Millennium Edition, Windows 2000, Windows XP Home Edition, Windows XP Professional, Windows .NET Server family

.NET Framework Security:
- **ReflectionPermission** SecurityAction.Demand, ReflectionEmit

ModuleBuilder.GetArrayMethod Method

Returns the named method on an array class.

```
[Visual Basic]
Public Function GetArrayMethod( _
   ByVal arrayClass As Type, _
   ByVal methodName As String, _
   ByVal callingConvention As CallingConventions, _
   ByVal returnType As Type, _
   ByVal parameterTypes() As Type _
) As MethodInfo
[C#]
public MethodInfo GetArrayMethod(
   Type arrayClass,
   string methodName,
   CallingConventions callingConvention,
   Type returnType,
   Type[] parameterTypes
);
[C++]
public: MethodInfo* GetArrayMethod(
   Type* arrayClass,
   String* methodName,
   CallingConventions callingConvention,
   Type* returnType,
   Type* parameterTypes[]
);
[JScript]
public function GetArrayMethod(
   arrayClass : Type,
   methodName : String,
   callingConvention : CallingConventions,
   returnType : Type,
   parameterTypes : Type[]
) : MethodInfo;
```

Parameters

arrayClass
   An array class.
methodName
   The name of a method on the array class.
callingConvention
   The method's calling convention.
returnType
   The return type of the method.
parameterTypes
   The types of the method's parameters.

Return Value

The named method on an array class.

Exceptions

Exception Type	Condition
ArgumentException	*arrayClass* is not an array.
ArgumentNullException	*arrayClass* or *methodName* is a null reference (**Nothing** in Visual Basic).

Remarks

GetArrayMethod is useful when you have an array of a type whose definition has not been completed and you want to access methods defined on **Array**. For example, you might define a type and want to define a method that takes an array of the type as a parameter. In

order to access the elements of the array, you will need to call methods of the **Array** class.

Example

See related example in the **System.Reflection.Emit.ModuleBuilder** class topic.

Requirements

Platforms: Windows 98, Windows NT 4.0, Windows Millennium Edition, Windows 2000, Windows XP Home Edition, Windows XP Professional, Windows .NET Server family

ModuleBuilder.GetArrayMethodToken Method

Returns the token for the named method on an array class.

```
[Visual Basic]
Public Function GetArrayMethodToken( _
   ByVal arrayClass As Type, _
   ByVal methodName As String, _
   ByVal callingConvention As CallingConventions, _
   ByVal returnType As Type, _
   ByVal parameterTypes() As Type _
) As MethodToken
[C#]
public MethodToken GetArrayMethodToken(
   Type arrayClass,
   string methodName,
   CallingConventions callingConvention,
   Type returnType,
   Type[] parameterTypes
);
[C++]
public: MethodToken GetArrayMethodToken(
   Type* arrayClass,
   String* methodName,
   CallingConventions callingConvention,
   Type* returnType,
   Type* parameterTypes[]
);
[JScript]
public function GetArrayMethodToken(
   arrayClass : Type,
   methodName : String,
   callingConvention : CallingConventions,
   returnType : Type,
   parameterTypes : Type[]
) : MethodToken;
```

Parameters

arrayClass
   The **Type** object for the array.
methodName
   A string containing the name of the method.
callingConvention
   The calling convention for the method.
returnType
   The return type of the method.
parameterTypes
   The types of the parameters of the method.

Return Value

The token for the named method on an array class.

Exceptions

Exception Type	Condition
ArgumentException	*arrayClass* is not an array. -or- Length of *methodName* is zero.
ArgumentNullException	*arrayClass* or *methodName* is a null reference (**Nothing** in Visual Basic).

Remarks

This method is similar to **GetArrayMethod**, except that it returns the token of the array method instead of the method itself.

Example

See related example in the **System.Reflection.Emit.ModuleBuilder** class topic.

Requirements

Platforms: Windows 98, Windows NT 4.0, Windows Millennium Edition, Windows 2000, Windows XP Home Edition, Windows XP Professional, Windows .NET Server family

ModuleBuilder.GetConstructorToken Method

Returns the token used to identify the specified constructor within this module.

```
[Visual Basic]
Public Function GetConstructorToken( _
   ByVal con As ConstructorInfo _
) As MethodToken
[C#]
public MethodToken GetConstructorToken(
   ConstructorInfo con
);
[C++]
public: MethodToken GetConstructorToken(
   ConstructorInfo* con
);
[JScript]
public function GetConstructorToken(
   con : ConstructorInfo
) : MethodToken;
```

Parameters

con
   A **ConstructorInfo** object representing the constructor to get a token for.

Return Value

Returns the token used to identify the constructor represented by *con* within this module.

Exceptions

Exception Type	Condition
ArgumentNullException	*con* is a null reference (**Nothing** in Visual Basic).

Platforms: Windows 98, Windows NT 4.0, Windows Millennium Edition, Windows 2000, Windows XP Home Edition, Windows XP Professional, Windows .NET Server family

ModuleBuilder.GetFieldToken Method

Returns the token used to identify the specified field within this module.

```
[Visual Basic]
Public Function GetFieldToken( _
   ByVal field As FieldInfo _
) As FieldToken
[C#]
public FieldToken GetFieldToken(
   FieldInfo field
);
[C++]
public: FieldToken GetFieldToken(
   FieldInfo* field
);
[JScript]
public function GetFieldToken(
   field : FieldInfo
) : FieldToken;
```

Parameters

field
   A **FieldInfo** object representing the field to get a token for.

Return Value

Returns the token used to identify the field represented by *con* within this module.

Exceptions

Exception Type	Condition
ArgumentNullException	*con* is a null reference (**Nothing** in Visual Basic).
InvalidOperation-Exception	The field is defined in a different module.

Requirements

Platforms: Windows 98, Windows NT 4.0, Windows Millennium Edition, Windows 2000, Windows XP Home Edition, Windows XP Professional, Windows .NET Server family

ModuleBuilder.GetMethodToken Method

Returns the token used to identify the specified method within this module.

```
[Visual Basic]
Public Function GetMethodToken( _
   ByVal method As MethodInfo _
) As MethodToken
[C#]
public MethodToken GetMethodToken(
   MethodInfo method
);
```

```
[C++]
public: MethodToken GetMethodToken(
    MethodInfo* method
);
[JScript]
public function GetMethodToken(
    method : MethodInfo
) : MethodToken;
```

Parameters

method
> A **MethodToken** object representing the method to get a token for.

Return Value

Returns the token used to identify the method represented by method within this module.

Exceptions

Exception Type	Condition
ArgumentNullException	*method* is a null reference (**Nothing** in Visual Basic).
InvalidOperation-Exception	The declaring type for the method is not in this module.

Requirements

Platforms: Windows 98, Windows NT 4.0, Windows Millennium Edition, Windows 2000, Windows XP Home Edition, Windows XP Professional, Windows .NET Server family

ModuleBuilder.GetSignatureToken Method

Defines a signature token given a signature helper.

Overload List

Defines a signature token using the given **SignatureHelper** object.

> [Visual Basic] **Overloads Public Function GetSignatureToken (SignatureHelper) As SignatureToken**

> [C#] **public SignatureToken GetSignatureToken (SignatureHelper);**

> [C++] **public: SignatureToken GetSignatureToken (SignatureHelper*);**

> [JScript] **public function GetSignatureToken(SignatureHelper) : SignatureToken;**

Defines a signature token specified by the character array and signature length.

> [Visual Basic] **Overloads Public Function GetSignatureToken (Byte(), Integer) As SignatureToken**

> [C#] **public SignatureToken GetSignatureToken(byte[], int);**

> [C++] **public: SignatureToken GetSignatureToken(unsigned char __gc[], int);**

> [JScript] **public function GetSignatureToken(Byte[], int) : SignatureToken;**

ModuleBuilder.GetSignatureToken Method (SignatureHelper)

Defines a signature token using the given **SignatureHelper** object.

```
[Visual Basic]
Overloads Public Function GetSignatureToken( _
    ByVal sigHelper As SignatureHelper _
) As SignatureToken
[C#]
public SignatureToken GetSignatureToken(
    SignatureHelper sigHelper
);
[C++]
public: SignatureToken GetSignatureToken(
    SignatureHelper* sigHelper
);
[JScript]
public function GetSignatureToken(
    sigHelper : SignatureHelper
) : SignatureToken;
```

Parameters

sigHelper
> A reference to a **SignatureHelper**.

Return Value

A **SignatureToken** for the defined signature.

Exceptions

Exception Type	Condition
ArgumentNullException	*sigHelper* is a null reference (**Nothing** in Visual Basic).

Remarks

This will define a metadata token for the signature described by **SignatureHelper**.

Requirements

Platforms: Windows 98, Windows NT 4.0, Windows Millennium Edition, Windows 2000, Windows XP Home Edition, Windows XP Professional, Windows .NET Server family

ModuleBuilder.GetSignatureToken Method (Byte[], Int32)

Defines a signature token specified by the character array and signature length.

```
[Visual Basic]
Overloads Public Function GetSignatureToken( _
    ByVal sigBytes() As Byte, _
    ByVal sigLength As Integer _
) As SignatureToken
[C#]
public SignatureToken GetSignatureToken(
    byte[] sigBytes,
    int sigLength
);
[C++]
public: SignatureToken GetSignatureToken(
    unsigned char sigBytes __gc[],
    int sigLength
);
```

```
[JScript]
public function GetSignatureToken(
   sigBytes : Byte[],
   sigLength : int
) : SignatureToken;
```

Parameters

sigBytes
> The signature blob.

sigLength
> The length of the signature blob.

Return Value

A **SignatureToken** for the defined signature.

Requirements

Platforms: Windows 98, Windows NT 4.0,
Windows Millennium Edition, Windows 2000,
Windows XP Home Edition, Windows XP Professional,
Windows .NET Server family

ModuleBuilder.GetStringConstant Method

Returns the token of the given string in the module's constant pool.

```
[Visual Basic]
Public Function GetStringConstant( _
   ByVal str As String _
) As StringToken
[C#]
public StringToken GetStringConstant(
   string str
);
[C++]
public: StringToken GetStringConstant(
   String* str
);
[JScript]
public function GetStringConstant(
   str : String
) : StringToken;
```

Parameters

str
> The string to add to the module's constant pool.

Return Value

Returns the **StringToken** of the string added to the constant pool.

Exceptions

Exception Type	Condition
ArgumentNullException	*str* is a null reference (**Nothing** in Visual Basic).

Remarks

If *str* has already been defined, the existing token will be returned.

Requirements

Platforms: Windows 98, Windows NT 4.0,
Windows Millennium Edition, Windows 2000,
Windows XP Home Edition, Windows XP Professional,
Windows .NET Server family

ModuleBuilder.GetSymWriter Method

Returns the symbol writer associated with this dynamic module.

```
[Visual Basic]
Public Function GetSymWriter() As ISymbolWriter
[C#]
public ISymbolWriter GetSymWriter();
[C++]
public: ISymbolWriter* GetSymWriter();
[JScript]
public function GetSymWriter() : ISymbolWriter;
```

Return Value

Returns the symbol writer associated with this dynamic module.

Requirements

Platforms: Windows 98, Windows NT 4.0,
Windows Millennium Edition, Windows 2000,
Windows XP Home Edition, Windows XP Professional,
Windows .NET Server family

.NET Framework Security:

- **ReflectionPermission** SecurityAction.Demand, ReflectionEmit

ModuleBuilder.GetType Method

Gets a named type defined in the module.

Overload List

Gets the named type defined in the module.

> [Visual Basic] **Overloads Overrides Public Function GetType(String) As Type**
> [C#] **public override Type GetType(string);**
> [C++] **public: Type* GetType(String*);**
> [JScript] **public override function GetType(String) : Type;**

Gets the named type defined in the module optionally ignoring the case of the type name.

> [Visual Basic] **Overloads Overrides Public Function GetType (String, Boolean) As Type**
> [C#] **public override Type GetType(string, bool);**
> [C++] **public: Type* GetType(String*, bool);**
> [JScript] **public override function GetType(String, Boolean) : Type;**

Gets the named type defined in the module optionally ignoring the case of the type name. Optionally throws an exception if the type is not found.

> [Visual Basic] **Overloads Overrides Public Function GetType (String, Boolean, Boolean) As Type**
> [C#] **public override Type GetType(string, bool, bool);**
> [C++] **public: Type* GetType(String*, bool, bool);**
> [JScript] **public override function GetType(String, Boolean, Boolean) : Type;**

Inherited from **Object**.

> [Visual Basic] **Overloads Public Function GetType() As Type**
> [C#] **public Type GetType();**
> [C++] **public: Type* GetType();**
> [JScript] **public function GetType() : Type;**

ModuleBuilder.GetType Method (String)

Gets the named type defined in the module.

```
[Visual Basic]
Overrides Overloads Public Function GetType( _
    ByVal className As String _
) As Type
[C#]
public override Type GetType(
    string className
);
[C++]
public: Type* GetType(
    String* className
);
[JScript]
public override function GetType(
    className : String
) : Type;
```

Parameters

className
    The name of the **Type** to get.

Return Value

The requested type. Returns a null reference (**Nothing** in Visual Basic) if the type is not found.

Exceptions

Exception Type	Condition
ArgumentException	Length of *className* is zero or if length of *className* is greater than 1023.
ArgumentNullException	*className* is a null reference (**Nothing** in Visual Basic).
SecurityException	The requested **Type** is non-public and the caller does not have **ReflectionPermission** to reflect non-public objects outside the current assembly.
TargetInvocation-Exception	A class initializer is invoked and throws an exception.
TypeLoadException	An error is encountered while loading the **Type**.

Requirements

Platforms: Windows 98, Windows NT 4.0, Windows Millennium Edition, Windows 2000, Windows XP Home Edition, Windows XP Professional, Windows .NET Server family

.NET Framework Security:
* **ReflectionPermission** SecurityAction.Demand, ReflectionEmit

ModuleBuilder.GetType Method (String, Boolean)

Gets the named type defined in the module optionally ignoring the case of the type name.

```
[Visual Basic]
Overrides Overloads Public Function GetType( _
    ByVal className As String, _
    ByVal ignoreCase As Boolean _
) As Type
```

```
[C#]
public override Type GetType(
    string className,
    bool ignoreCase
);
[C++]
public: Type* GetType(
    String* className,
    bool ignoreCase
);
[JScript]
public override function GetType(
    className : String,
    ignoreCase : Boolean
) : Type;
```

Parameters

className
    The name of the **Type** to get.

ignoreCase
    If **true**, the search is case-insensitive. If **false**, the search is case-sensitive.

Return Value

The requested type. Returns a null reference (**Nothing** in Visual Basic) if the type is not found.

Exceptions

Exception Type	Condition
ArgumentException	Length of *className* is zero. -or- The length of *className* is greater than 1023.
ArgumentNullException	*className* is a null reference (**Nothing** in Visual Basic).
SecurityException	The requested **Type** is non-public and the caller does not have **ReflectionPermission** to reflect non-public objects outside the current assembly.
TargetInvocation-Exception	A class initializer is invoked and throws an exception.

Requirements

Platforms: Windows 98, Windows NT 4.0, Windows Millennium Edition, Windows 2000, Windows XP Home Edition, Windows XP Professional, Windows .NET Server family

.NET Framework Security:
* **ReflectionPermission** SecurityAction.Demand, ReflectionEmit

ModuleBuilder.GetType Method (String, Boolean, Boolean)

Gets the named type defined in the module optionally ignoring the case of the type name. Optionally throws an exception if the type is not found.

```
[Visual Basic]
Overrides Overloads Public Function GetType( _
    ByVal className As String, _
    ByVal throwOnError As Boolean, _
    ByVal ignoreCase As Boolean _
) As Type
```

```
[C#]
public override Type GetType(
    string className,
    bool throwOnError,
    bool ignoreCase
);
[C++]
public: Type* GetType(
    String* className,
    bool throwOnError,
    bool ignoreCase
);
[JScript]
public override function GetType(
    className : String,
    throwOnError : Boolean,
    ignoreCase : Boolean
) : Type;
```

Parameters

className
> The name of the **Type** to get.

throwOnError
> If **true**, throw a **TypeLoadException** when an error occurs while loading the **Type**. If **false**, ignore errors while loading the **Type**.

ignoreCase
> If **true**, the search is case-insensitive. If **false**, the search is case-sensitive.

Return Value

The requested type. Returns a null reference (**Nothing** in Visual Basic) if the type is not found.

Exceptions

Exception Type	Condition
ArgumentException	Length of *className* is zero.
	-or-
	The length of *className* is greater than 1023.
ArgumentNullException	*className* is a null reference (**Nothing** in Visual Basic).
SecurityException	The requested **Type** is non-public and the caller does not have **ReflectionPermission** to reflect non-public objects outside the current assembly.
TargetInvocation-Exception	A class initializer is invoked and throws an exception.
TypeLoadException	*throwOnError* is **true** and an error is encountered while loading the **Type**.

Requirements

Platforms: Windows 98, Windows NT 4.0, Windows Millennium Edition, Windows 2000, Windows XP Home Edition, Windows XP Professional, Windows .NET Server family

.NET Framework Security:
- **ReflectionPermission** SecurityAction.Demand, ReflectionEmit

ModuleBuilder.GetTypes Method

Returns all the classes defined within this module.

```
[Visual Basic]
Overrides Public Function GetTypes() As Type()
[C#]
public override Type[] GetTypes();
[C++]
public: Type* GetTypes() [];
[JScript]
public override function GetTypes() : Type[];
```

Return Value

An array of type **Type** containing classes defined within the module that is reflected by this instance.

Exceptions

Exception Type	Condition
ReflectionTypeLoad-Exception	One or more classes in a module could not be loaded.
SecurityException	The caller does not have the required permission.

Remarks

ReflectionTypeLoadException is a special class load exception. The **ReflectionTypeLoadException.Types** property contains the array of classes that were defined in the module and loaded. This array can contain some null values. The **ReflectionTypeLoadException.LoaderExceptions** property is an array of exceptions that represent the exceptions that were thrown by the class loader. The holes in the class array line up with the exceptions.

For example, if the class initializers of one of the classes throws an exception while it is being loaded, a **TargetInvocationException** is stored in the corresponding element of the **LoaderExceptions** array.

Requirements

Platforms: Windows 98, Windows NT 4.0, Windows Millennium Edition, Windows 2000, Windows XP Home Edition, Windows XP Professional, Windows .NET Server family

.NET Framework Security:
- **ReflectionPermission** Reflection permission for the current module.

ModuleBuilder.GetTypeToken Method

Returns a type token.

Overload List

Returns the token used to identify the type given its name.

> [Visual Basic] **Overloads Public Function GetTypeToken (String) As TypeToken**

> [C#] **public TypeToken GetTypeToken(string);**

> [C++] **public: TypeToken GetTypeToken(String*);**

> [JScript] **public function GetTypeToken(String) : TypeToken;**

Returns the token used to identify the specified type within this module.

> [Visual Basic] **Overloads Public Function GetTypeToken (Type) As TypeToken**

[C#] **public TypeToken GetTypeToken(Type);**
[C++] **public: TypeToken GetTypeToken(Type*);**
[JScript] **public function GetTypeToken(Type) : TypeToken;**

ModuleBuilder.GetTypeToken Method (String)

Returns the token used to identify the type given its name.

```
[Visual Basic]
Overloads Public Function GetTypeToken( _
   ByVal name As String _
) As TypeToken
[C#]
public TypeToken GetTypeToken(
   string name
);
[C++]
public: TypeToken GetTypeToken(
   String* name
);
[JScript]
public function GetTypeToken(
   name : String
) : TypeToken;
```

Parameters

name
   A string representing the name of the class.

Return Value

Returns the **TypeToken** used to identify the type given by name within this module.

Exceptions

Exception Type	Condition
ArgumentException	*type* is a **ByRef** or *type* is a **SymbolType** that is not a pointer or an array.
ArgumentNullException	*type* is null.
InvalidOperationException	This is a non-transient module that references a transient module.
TypeLoadException	The type named *name* cannot be found.

Remarks

This method is useful for clients of the **MethodRental** class who want to directly modify the body of a method.

Requirements

Platforms: Windows 98, Windows NT 4.0, Windows Millennium Edition, Windows 2000, Windows XP Home Edition, Windows XP Professional, Windows .NET Server family

ModuleBuilder.GetTypeToken Method (Type)

Returns the token used to identify the specified type within this module.

```
[Visual Basic]
Overloads Public Function GetTypeToken( _
   ByVal type As Type _
) As TypeToken
```

```
[C#]
public TypeToken GetTypeToken(
   Type type
);
[C++]
public: TypeToken GetTypeToken(
   Type* type
);
[JScript]
public function GetTypeToken(
   type : Type
) : TypeToken;
```

Parameters

type
   The type object that represents the class type.

Return Value

Returns the **TypeToken** used to identify the given type within this module.

Exceptions

Exception Type	Condition
ArgumentException	*type* is a **ByRef** or *type* is a **SymbolType** that is not a pointer or an array.
ArgumentNullException	*type* is null.
InvalidOperationException	A non-transient module that references a transient module.

Remarks

Tokens are used in Microsoft intermediate language (MSIL) instructions to identify objects. Tokens are relative to the module in which they are contained. For example, the token value for **String** is likely to be different from module to module. When **GetTypeToken** is invoked, a reference is added to the module. The reference becomes a permanent part of the module; multiple calls with the same argument have no additional affect.

Requirements

Platforms: Windows 98, Windows NT 4.0, Windows Millennium Edition, Windows 2000, Windows XP Home Edition, Windows XP Professional, Windows .NET Server family

ModuleBuilder.IsTransient Method

Checks if this dynamic module is transient.

```
[Visual Basic]
Public Function IsTransient() As Boolean
[C#]
public bool IsTransient();
[C++]
public: bool IsTransient();
[JScript]
public function IsTransient() : Boolean;
```

Return Value

Returns **true** if this dynamic module is transient; otherwise, **false**.

Requirements

Platforms: Windows 98, Windows NT 4.0,
Windows Millennium Edition, Windows 2000,
Windows XP Home Edition, Windows XP Professional,
Windows .NET Server family

ModuleBuilder.SetCustomAttribute Method

Sets a custom attribute.

Overload List

Set a custom attribute using a custom attribute builder.

[Visual Basic] **Overloads Public Sub SetCustomAttribute
(CustomAttributeBuilder)**

[C#] **public void SetCustomAttribute
(CustomAttributeBuilder);**

[C++] **public: void SetCustomAttribute
(CustomAttributeBuilder*);**

[JScript] **public function SetCustomAttribute
(CustomAttributeBuilder);**

Set a custom attribute using a specified custom attribute blob.

[Visual Basic] **Overloads Public Sub SetCustomAttribute
(ConstructorInfo, Byte())**

[C#] **public void SetCustomAttribute(ConstructorInfo,
byte[]);**

[C++] **public: void SetCustomAttribute(ConstructorInfo*,
unsigned char __gc[]);**

[JScript] **public function SetCustomAttribute
(ConstructorInfo, Byte[]);**

ModuleBuilder.SetCustomAttribute Method (CustomAttributeBuilder)

Set a custom attribute using a custom attribute builder.

```
[Visual Basic]
Overloads Public Sub SetCustomAttribute( _
   ByVal customBuilder As CustomAttributeBuilder _
)
[C#]
public void SetCustomAttribute(
   CustomAttributeBuilder customBuilder
);
[C++]
public: void SetCustomAttribute(
   CustomAttributeBuilder* customBuilder
);
[JScript]
public function SetCustomAttribute(
   customBuilder : CustomAttributeBuilder
);
```

Parameters

customBuilder

An instance of a helper class to define the custom attribute.

Exceptions

Exception Type	Condition
ArgumentNullException	*con* is a null reference (**Nothing** in Visual Basic).

Requirements

Platforms: Windows 98, Windows NT 4.0,
Windows Millennium Edition, Windows 2000,
Windows XP Home Edition, Windows XP Professional,
Windows .NET Server family

.NET Framework Security:

• **ReflectionPermission** SecurityAction.Demand, ReflectionEmit

ModuleBuilder.SetCustomAttribute Method (ConstructorInfo, Byte[])

Set a custom attribute using a specified custom attribute blob.

```
[Visual Basic]
Overloads Public Sub SetCustomAttribute( _
   ByVal con As ConstructorInfo, _
   ByVal binaryAttribute() As Byte _
)
[C#]
public void SetCustomAttribute(
   ConstructorInfo con,
   byte[] binaryAttribute
);
[C++]
public: void SetCustomAttribute(
   ConstructorInfo* con,
   unsigned char binaryAttribute __gc[]
);
[JScript]
public function SetCustomAttribute(
   con : ConstructorInfo,
   binaryAttribute : Byte[]
);
```

Parameters

con

The constructor for the custom attribute.

binaryAttribute

A byte blob representing the attributes.

Exceptions

Exception Type	Condition
ArgumentNullException	*con* or *binaryAttribute* is a null reference (**Nothing** in Visual Basic).

Remarks

See the metadata specification in the ECMA Partition II
documentation for details on how to format *binaryAttribute*. The
Partition II documentation is included with the .NET Framework
SDK installation, and can be found in the
%\Microsoft.NET\FrameworkSDK\Tool Developers Guide\docs
directory.

Requirements

Platforms: Windows 98, Windows NT 4.0,
Windows Millennium Edition, Windows 2000,
Windows XP Home Edition, Windows XP Professional,
Windows .NET Server family

.NET Framework Security:

• **ReflectionPermission** SecurityAction.Demand, ReflectionEmit

ModuleBuilder.SetSymCustomAttribute Method

Sets the custom attribute that is stored with the symbolic information.

```
[Visual Basic]
Public Sub SetSymCustomAttribute( _
    ByVal name As String, _
    ByVal data() As Byte _
)
[C#]
public void SetSymCustomAttribute(
    string name,
    byte[] data
);
[C++]
public: void SetSymCustomAttribute(
    String* name,
    unsigned char data __gc[]
);
[JScript]
public function SetSymCustomAttribute(
    name : String,
    data : Byte[]
);
```

Parameters

name
> The name of the custom attribute

data
> An opaque blob of bytes that represents the value of the custom attribute.

Exceptions

Exception Type	Condition
ArgumentNullException	*url* is a null reference (**Nothing** in Visual Basic).
InvalidOperationException	This method is called on a dynamic module that is not a debug module.

Remarks

The custom attribute that is set by this method is associated only with the symbolic information written by the symbol writer and is different from the custom attribute set using the **SetCustomAttribute** method.

Requirements

Platforms: Windows 98, Windows NT 4.0, Windows Millennium Edition, Windows 2000, Windows XP Home Edition, Windows XP Professional, Windows .NET Server family

.NET Framework Security:
- **ReflectionPermission** SecurityAction.Demand, ReflectionEmit

ModuleBuilder.SetUserEntryPoint Method

Sets the user entry point.

```
[Visual Basic]
Public Sub SetUserEntryPoint( _
    ByVal entryPoint As MethodInfo _
)
```
```
[C#]
public void SetUserEntryPoint(
    MethodInfo entryPoint
);
[C++]
public: void SetUserEntryPoint(
    MethodInfo* entryPoint
);
[JScript]
public function SetUserEntryPoint(
    entryPoint : MethodInfo
);
```

Parameters

entryPoint
> The user entry point.

Exceptions

Exception Type	Condition
ArgumentNullException	*entryPoint* is a null reference (**Nothing** in Visual Basic).
InvalidOperationException	This method is called on a dynamic module that is not a debug module.
	-or-
	entryPoint is not contained in this dynamic module.

Remarks

The compiler might generate a startup stub before calling user main. The startup stub will be the entry point. While the user main will be the user entry point so that debugger will not step into the compiler entry point.

Requirements

Platforms: Windows 98, Windows NT 4.0, Windows Millennium Edition, Windows 2000, Windows XP Home Edition, Windows XP Professional, Windows .NET Server family

.NET Framework Security:
- **ReflectionPermission** SecurityAction.Demand, ReflectionEmit

OpCode Structure

Describes a Microsoft intermediate language (MSIL) instruction.

System.Object
  System.ValueType
    System.Reflection.Emit.OpCode

```
[Visual Basic]
Public Structure OpCode
[C#]
public struct OpCode
[C++]
public __value struct OpCode
```

[JScript] In JScript, you can use the structures in the .NET Framework, but you cannot define your own.

Thread Safety

Reflection Emit is thread-safe when using assemblies that were created with the **AppDomain.DefineDynamicAssembly** method with the Boolean parameter *isSynchronized* set to **true**.

Requirements

Namespace: System.Reflection.Emit

Platforms: Windows 98, Windows NT 4.0, Windows Millennium Edition, Windows 2000, Windows XP Home Edition, Windows XP Professional, Windows .NET Server family

Assembly: Mscorlib (in Mscorlib.dll)

OpCode.FlowControl Property

The flow control characteristics of the Microsoft intermediate language (MSIL) instruction.

```
[Visual Basic]
Public ReadOnly Property FlowControl As FlowControl
[C#]
public FlowControl FlowControl {get;}
[C++]
public: __property FlowControl get_FlowControl();
[JScript]
public function get FlowControl() : FlowControl;
```

Property Value

Read-only. The type of flow control.

Requirements

Platforms: Windows 98, Windows NT 4.0, Windows Millennium Edition, Windows 2000, Windows XP Home Edition, Windows XP Professional, Windows .NET Server family

OpCode.Name Property

The name of the Microsoft intermediate language (MSIL) instruction.

```
[Visual Basic]
Public ReadOnly Property Name As String
[C#]
public string Name {get;}
[C++]
public: __property String* get_Name();
```

```
[JScript]
public function get Name() : String;
```

Property Value

Read-only. The name of the MSIL instruction.

Requirements

Platforms: Windows 98, Windows NT 4.0, Windows Millennium Edition, Windows 2000, Windows XP Home Edition, Windows XP Professional, Windows .NET Server family

OpCode.OpCodeType Property

The type of Microsoft intermediate language (MSIL) instruction.

```
[Visual Basic]
Public ReadOnly Property OpCodeType As OpCodeType
[C#]
public OpCodeType OpCodeType {get;}
[C++]
public: __property OpCodeType get_OpCodeType();
[JScript]
public function get OpCodeType() : OpCodeType;
```

Property Value

Read-only. The type of Microsoft intermediate language (MSIL) instruction.

Requirements

Platforms: Windows 98, Windows NT 4.0, Windows Millennium Edition, Windows 2000, Windows XP Home Edition, Windows XP Professional, Windows .NET Server family

OpCode.OperandType Property

The operand type of an Microsoft intermediate language (MSIL) instruction.

```
[Visual Basic]
Public ReadOnly Property OperandType As OperandType
[C#]
public OperandType OperandType {get;}
[C++]
public: __property OperandType get_OperandType();
[JScript]
public function get OperandType() : OperandType;
```

Property Value

Read-only. The operand type of an MSIL instruction.

Requirements

Platforms: Windows 98, Windows NT 4.0, Windows Millennium Edition, Windows 2000, Windows XP Home Edition, Windows XP Professional, Windows .NET Server family

OpCode.Size Property

The size of the Microsoft intermediate language (MSIL) instruction.

```
[Visual Basic]
Public ReadOnly Property Size As Integer
```

```
[C#]
public int Size {get;}
[C++]
public: __property int get_Size();
[JScript]
public function get Size() : int;
```

Property Value

Read-only. The size of the MSIL instruction.

Requirements

Platforms: Windows 98, Windows NT 4.0,
Windows Millennium Edition, Windows 2000,
Windows XP Home Edition, Windows XP Professional,
Windows .NET Server family

OpCode.StackBehaviourPop Property

How the Microsoft intermediate language (MSIL) instruction pops
the stack.

```
[Visual Basic]
Public ReadOnly Property StackBehaviourPop As StackBehaviour
[C#]
public StackBehaviour StackBehaviourPop {get;}
[C++]
public: __property StackBehaviour get_StackBehaviourPop();
[JScript]
public function get StackBehaviourPop() : StackBehaviour;
```

Property Value

Read-only. The way the MSIL instruction pops the stack.

Requirements

Platforms: Windows 98, Windows NT 4.0,
Windows Millennium Edition, Windows 2000,
Windows XP Home Edition, Windows XP Professional,
Windows .NET Server family

OpCode.StackBehaviourPush Property

How the Microsoft intermediate language (MSIL) instruction pushes
operand onto the stack.

```
[Visual Basic]
Public ReadOnly Property StackBehaviourPush As StackBehaviour
[C#]
public StackBehaviour StackBehaviourPush {get;}
[C++]
public: __property StackBehaviour get_StackBehaviourPush();
[JScript]
public function get StackBehaviourPush() : StackBehaviour;
```

Property Value

Read-only. The way the MSIL instruction pushes operand onto the
stack.

Requirements

Platforms: Windows 98, Windows NT 4.0,
Windows Millennium Edition, Windows 2000,
Windows XP Home Edition, Windows XP Professional,
Windows .NET Server family

OpCode.Value Property

The value of the immediate operand of the Microsoft intermediate
language (MSIL) instruction.

```
[Visual Basic]
Public ReadOnly Property Value As Short
[C#]
public short Value {get;}
[C++]
public: __property short get_Value();
[JScript]
public function get Value() : Int16;
```

Property Value

Read-only. The value of the immediate operand of the MSIL
instruction.

Requirements

Platforms: Windows 98, Windows NT 4.0,
Windows Millennium Edition, Windows 2000,
Windows XP Home Edition, Windows XP Professional,
Windows .NET Server family

OpCode.Equals Method

Tests whether the given object is equal to this **Opcode**.

```
[Visual Basic]
Overrides Public Function Equals( _
   ByVal obj As Object _
) As Boolean
[C#]
public override bool Equals(
   object obj
);
[C++]
public: bool Equals(
   Object* obj
);
[JScript]
public override function Equals(
   obj : Object
) : Boolean;
```

Parameters

obj
    The object to compare to this object.

Return Value

true if *obj* is an instance of **Opcode** and is equal to this object;
otherwise, **false**.

Requirements

Platforms: Windows 98, Windows NT 4.0,
Windows Millennium Edition, Windows 2000,
Windows XP Home Edition, Windows XP Professional,
Windows .NET Server family

OpCode.GetHashCode Method

Returns the generated hash code for this **Opcode**.

```
[Visual Basic]
Overrides Public Function GetHashCode() As Integer
[C#]
public override int GetHashCode();
[C++]
public: int GetHashCode();
[JScript]
public override function GetHashCode() : int;
```

Return Value

Returns the hash code for this instance.

Requirements

Platforms: Windows 98, Windows NT 4.0,
Windows Millennium Edition, Windows 2000,
Windows XP Home Edition, Windows XP Professional,
Windows .NET Server family

OpCode.ToString Method

Returns this **Opcode** as a **String**.

```
[Visual Basic]
Overrides Public Function ToString() As String
[C#]
public override string ToString();
[C++]
public: String* ToString();
[JScript]
public override function ToString() : String;
```

Return Value

Returns a **String** containing the name of this **Opcode**.

Requirements

Platforms: Windows 98, Windows NT 4.0,
Windows Millennium Edition, Windows 2000,
Windows XP Home Edition, Windows XP Professional,
Windows .NET Server family

OpCodes Class

Provides field representations of the Microsoft Intermediate Language (MSIL) instructions for emission by the **ILGenerator** class members (such as **Emit**).

System.Object
  System.Reflection.Emit.OpCodes

[Visual Basic]
```
Public Class OpCodes
```
[C#]
```
public class OpCodes
```
[C++]
```
public __gc class OpCodes
```
[JScript]
```
public class OpCodes
```

Thread Safety

Reflection Emit is thread-safe when using assemblies that were created with the **AppDomain.DefineDynamicAssembly** method with the Boolean parameter *isSynchronized* set to **true**.

Remarks

See the Common Language Infrastructure Instruction Set documentation in the Tool Developers Guide for a detailed description of the member opcodes.

Example

[Visual Basic, C#, C++] The following example demonstrates the construction of a dynamic method using **ILGenerator** to emit **OpCodes** into a **MethodBuilder**.

[Visual Basic]
```
Imports System
Imports System.Threading
Imports System.Reflection
Imports System.Reflection.Emit

_

Class EmitWriteLineDemo

    Public Shared Function CreateDynamicType() As Type

        Dim ctorParams() As Type = {GetType(Integer), GetType(Integer)}

        Dim myDomain As AppDomain = Thread.GetDomain()
        Dim myAsmName As New AssemblyName()
        myAsmName.Name = "MyDynamicAssembly"

        Dim myAsmBuilder As AssemblyBuilder = _
myDomain.DefineDynamicAssembly(myAsmName, _
AssemblyBuilderAccess.RunAndSave)

        Dim pointModule As ModuleBuilder = _
myAsmBuilder.DefineDynamicModule("PointModule", "Point.dll")

        Dim pointTypeBld As TypeBuilder = pointModule.DefineType _
("Point", _
                        TypeAttributes.Public)

        Dim xField As FieldBuilder = pointTypeBld.DefineField("x", _
                        GetType(Integer), _
                        FieldAttributes.Public)
        Dim yField As FieldBuilder = pointTypeBld.DefineField("y", _
                        GetType(Integer), _
                        FieldAttributes.Public)
```

```
        Dim objType As Type = Type.GetType("System.Object")
        Dim objCtor As ConstructorInfo = _
objType.GetConstructor(New Type(){})

        Dim pointCtor As ConstructorBuilder = _
pointTypeBld.DefineConstructor( _
                        MethodAttributes.Public, _
                        CallingConventions.Standard, _
                        ctorParams)
        Dim ctorIL As ILGenerator = pointCtor.GetILGenerator()

        ' First, you build the constructor.

        ctorIL.Emit(OpCodes.Ldarg_0)
        ctorIL.Emit(OpCodes.Call, objCtor)
        ctorIL.Emit(OpCodes.Ldarg_0)
        ctorIL.Emit(OpCodes.Ldarg_1)
        ctorIL.Emit(OpCodes.Stfld, xField)
        ctorIL.Emit(OpCodes.Ldarg_0)
        ctorIL.Emit(OpCodes.Ldarg_2)
        ctorIL.Emit(OpCodes.Stfld, yField)
        ctorIL.Emit(OpCodes.Ret)

        ' Now, you'll build a method to output some information on the
        ' inside your dynamic class. This method will have the following
        ' definition in C#:
        '   Public Sub WritePoint()

        Dim writeStrMthd As MethodBuilder = _
pointTypeBld.DefineMethod("WritePoint", _
                        MethodAttributes.Public, _
                        Nothing, Nothing)

        Dim writeStrIL As ILGenerator = writeStrMthd.GetILGenerator()

        ' The below ILGenerator created demonstrates a few ways to create
        ' string output through STDIN.
        ' ILGenerator.EmitWriteLine(string) will generate a ldstr and a
        ' call to WriteLine for you.

        writeStrIL.EmitWriteLine("The value of this current
instance is:")

        ' Here, you will do the hard work yourself. First, you
need to create
        ' the string we will be passing and obtain the correct
WriteLine overload
        ' for said string. In the below case, you are substituting
in two values,
        ' so the chosen overload is Console.WriteLine(string,
object, object).

        Dim inStr As [String] = "({0}, {1})"
        Dim wlParams() As Type = {GetType(String), GetType
(Object), GetType(Object)}

        ' We need the MethodInfo to pass into EmitCall later.

        Dim writeLineMI As MethodInfo = _
GetType(Console).GetMethod("WriteLine", wlParams)

        ' Push the string with the substitutions onto the stack.
        ' This is the first argument for WriteLine - the string one.

        writeStrIL.Emit(OpCodes.Ldstr, inStr)

        ' Since the second argument is an object, and it corresponds to
        ' to the substitution for the value of our integer field, you
        ' need to box that field to an object. First, push a reference
        ' to the current instance, and then push the value stored in
        ' field 'x'. We need the reference to the current instance
(stored
        ' in local argument index 0) so Ldfld can load from the correct
        ' instance (this one).
```

```
        writeStrIL.Emit(OpCodes.Ldarg_0)
        writeStrIL.Emit(OpCodes.Ldfld, xField)

        ' Now, we execute the box opcode, which pops the value of field 'x',
        ' returning a reference to the integer value boxed as an object.

        writeStrIL.Emit(OpCodes.Box, GetType(Integer))

        ' Atop the stack, you'll find our string inStr, followed
by a reference
        ' to the boxed value of 'x'. Now, you need to likewise box
field 'y'.

        writeStrIL.Emit(OpCodes.Ldarg_0)
        writeStrIL.Emit(OpCodes.Ldfld, yField)
        writeStrIL.Emit(OpCodes.Box, GetType(Integer))

        ' Now, you have all of the arguments for your call to
        ' Console.WriteLine(string, object, object) atop the stack:
        ' the string InStr, a reference to the boxed value of 'x', and
        ' a reference to the boxed value of 'y'.
        ' Call Console.WriteLine(string, object, object) with EmitCall.

        writeStrIL.EmitCall(OpCodes.Call, writeLineMI, Nothing)

        ' Lastly, EmitWriteLine can also output the value of a field
        ' using the overload EmitWriteLine(FieldInfo).

        writeStrIL.EmitWriteLine("The value of 'x' is:")
        writeStrIL.EmitWriteLine(xField)
        writeStrIL.EmitWriteLine("The value of 'y' is:")
        writeStrIL.EmitWriteLine(yField)

        ' Since we return no value (void), the the ret opcode will not
        ' return the top stack value.

        writeStrIL.Emit(OpCodes.Ret)

        Return pointTypeBld.CreateType()

    End Function 'CreateDynamicType

    Public Shared Sub Main()

        Dim ctorParams(1) As Object

        Console.Write("Enter a integer value for X: ")
        Dim myX As String = Console.ReadLine()
        Console.Write("Enter a integer value for Y: ")
        Dim myY As String = Console.ReadLine()

        Console.WriteLine("---")

        ctorParams(0) = Convert.ToInt32(myX)
        ctorParams(1) = Convert.ToInt32(myY)

        Dim ptType As Type = CreateDynamicType()

        Dim ptInstance As Object = Activator.CreateInstance
(ptType, ctorParams)

        ptType.InvokeMember("WritePoint", _
                BindingFlags.InvokeMethod, _
                Nothing, ptInstance, Nothing)

    End Sub 'Main

End Class 'EmitWriteLineDemo

[C#]
using System;
using System.Threading;
using System.Reflection;
using System.Reflection.Emit;
```

```
class EmitWriteLineDemo {

    public static Type CreateDynamicType() {
        Type[] ctorParams = new Type[] {typeof(int),
                typeof(int)};

        AppDomain myDomain = Thread.GetDomain();
        AssemblyName myAsmName = new AssemblyName();
        myAsmName.Name = "MyDynamicAssembly";

        AssemblyBuilder myAsmBuilder = myDomain.DefineDynamicAssembly(
                        myAsmName,
                        AssemblyBuilderAccess.RunAndSave);

        ModuleBuilder pointModule =
myAsmBuilder.DefineDynamicModule("PointModule",
                        "Point.dll");

        TypeBuilder pointTypeBld = pointModule.DefineType("Point",
                        TypeAttributes.Public);

    FieldBuilder xField = pointTypeBld.DefineField("x", typeof(int),
FieldAttributes.Public);
        FieldBuilder yField = pointTypeBld.DefineField("y", typeof(int),
FieldAttributes.Public);

        Type objType = Type.GetType("System.Object");
        ConstructorInfo objCtor = objType.GetConstructor(new Type[0]);

        ConstructorBuilder pointCtor = pointTypeBld.DefineConstructor(
                        MethodAttributes.Public,
                        CallingConventions.Standard,
                        ctorParams);
        ILGenerator ctorIL = pointCtor.GetILGenerator();

        // First, you build the constructor.
        ctorIL.Emit(OpCodes.Ldarg_0);
        ctorIL.Emit(OpCodes.Call, objCtor);
        ctorIL.Emit(OpCodes.Ldarg_0);
        ctorIL.Emit(OpCodes.Ldarg_1);
        ctorIL.Emit(OpCodes.Stfld, xField);
        ctorIL.Emit(OpCodes.Ldarg_0);
        ctorIL.Emit(OpCodes.Ldarg_2);
        ctorIL.Emit(OpCodes.Stfld, yField);
        ctorIL.Emit(OpCodes.Ret);

        // Now, you'll build a method to output some information on the
        // inside your dynamic class. This method will
have the following
        // definition in C#:
    //  public void WritePoint()

        MethodBuilder writeStrMthd = pointTypeBld.DefineMethod(
                        "WritePoint",
                        MethodAttributes.Public,
                        typeof(void),
                        null);

        ILGenerator writeStrIL = writeStrMthd.GetILGenerator();

        // The below ILGenerator created demonstrates a
few ways to create
        // string output through STDIN.

        // ILGenerator.EmitWriteLine(string) will generate a ldstr and a
        // call to WriteLine for you.

        writeStrIL.EmitWriteLine("The value of this current
instance is:");

        // Here, you will do the hard work yourself. First, you
need to create
        // the string we will be passing and obtain the correct
```

```
WriteLine overload
        // for said string. In the below case, you are
substituting in two values,
        // so the chosen overload is Console.WriteLine(string,
object, object).

        String inStr = "({0}, {1})";
        Type[] wlParams = new Type[] {typeof(string),
                        typeof(object),
                        typeof(object)};

        // We need the MethodInfo to pass into EmitCall later.

        MethodInfo writeLineMI = typeof(Console).GetMethod(
                        "WriteLine",
                    wlParams);

        // Push the string with the substitutions onto the stack.
        // This is the first argument for WriteLine - the string one.

        writeStrIL.Emit(OpCodes.Ldstr, inStr);

        // Since the second argument is an object, and it corresponds to
        // to the substitution for the value of our integer field, you
        // need to box that field to an object. First, push a reference
        // to the current instance, and then push the value stored in
        // field 'x'. We need the reference to the current instance
(stored
        // in local argument index 0) so Ldfld can load from the correct
        // instance (this one).

        writeStrIL.Emit(OpCodes.Ldarg_0);
        writeStrIL.Emit(OpCodes.Ldfld, xField);

        // Now, we execute the box opcode, which pops the value
of field 'x',
        // returning a reference to the integer value boxed as
an object.

        writeStrIL.Emit(OpCodes.Box, typeof(int));

        // Atop the stack, you'll find our string inStr, followed
by a reference
        // to the boxed value of 'x'. Now, you need to likewise
box field 'y'.

        writeStrIL.Emit(OpCodes.Ldarg_0);
        writeStrIL.Emit(OpCodes.Ldfld, yField);
        writeStrIL.Emit(OpCodes.Box, typeof(int));

        // Now, you have all of the arguments for your call to
        // Console.WriteLine(string, object, object) atop the stack:
        // the string InStr, a reference to the boxed value of 'x', and
        // a reference to the boxed value of 'y'.

        // Call Console.WriteLine(string, object, object) with EmitCall.

        writeStrIL.EmitCall(OpCodes.Call, writeLineMI, null);

        // Lastly, EmitWriteLine can also output the value of a field
        // using the overload EmitWriteLine(FieldInfo).

        writeStrIL.EmitWriteLine("The value of 'x' is:");
        writeStrIL.EmitWriteLine(xField);
        writeStrIL.EmitWriteLine("The value of 'y' is:");
        writeStrIL.EmitWriteLine(yField);

        // Since we return no value (void), the the ret opcode will not
        // return the top stack value.

        writeStrIL.Emit(OpCodes.Ret);

        return pointTypBld.CreateType();
    }
```

```
public static void Main() {

        object[] ctorParams = new object[2];

        Console.Write("Enter a integer value for X: ");
        string myX = Console.ReadLine();
        Console.Write("Enter a integer value for Y: ");
        string myY = Console.ReadLine();

        Console.WriteLine("---");

        ctorParams[0] = Convert.ToInt32(myX);
        ctorParams[1] = Convert.ToInt32(myY);

        Type ptType = CreateDynamicType();

        object ptInstance = Activator.CreateInstance(ptType, ctorParams);
        ptType.InvokeMember("WritePoint",
                BindingFlags.InvokeMethod,
                null,
                ptInstance,
                new object[0]);
    }
}

[C++]
#using <mscorlib.dll>

using namespace System;
using namespace System::Threading;
using namespace System::Reflection;
using namespace System::Reflection::Emit;

Type* CreateDynamicType() {
    Type* ctorParams[] = {__typeof(int),
        __typeof(int)};

    AppDomain*  myDomain = Thread::GetDomain();
    AssemblyName* myAsmName = new AssemblyName();
    myAsmName->Name = S"MyDynamicAssembly";

    AssemblyBuilder*  myAsmBuilder = myDomain-
>DefineDynamicAssembly(myAsmName,
        AssemblyBuilderAccess::RunAndSave);

    ModuleBuilder*  pointModule = myAsmBuilder-
>DefineDynamicModule(S"PointModule",
        S"Point.dll");

    TypeBuilder*  pointTypeBld = pointModule->DefineType(S"Point",
        TypeAttributes::Public);

    FieldBuilder*  xField = pointTypeBld->DefineField(S"x",
__typeof(int),
        FieldAttributes::Public);
    FieldBuilder*  yField = pointTypeBld->DefineField(S"y",
__typeof(int),
        FieldAttributes::Public);

    Type*  objType = Type::GetType(S"System.Object");
    ConstructorInfo*  objCtor = objType->GetConstructor(new Type*[0]);

    ConstructorBuilder*  pointCtor = pointTypeBld-
>DefineConstructor(MethodAttributes::Public,
        CallingConventions::Standard,
        ctorParams);
    ILGenerator*  ctorIL = pointCtor->GetILGenerator();

    // First, you build the constructor.
    ctorIL->Emit(OpCodes::Ldarg_0);
    ctorIL->Emit(OpCodes::Call, objCtor);
    ctorIL->Emit(OpCodes::Ldarg_0);
    ctorIL->Emit(OpCodes::Ldarg_1);
    ctorIL->Emit(OpCodes::Stfld, xField);
    ctorIL->Emit(OpCodes::Ldarg_0);
```

```
ctorIL->Emit(OpCodes::Ldarg_2);
ctorIL->Emit(OpCodes::Stfld, yField);
ctorIL->Emit(OpCodes::Ret);

// Now, you'll build a method to output some information on the
// inside your dynamic class. This method will have the following
// definition in C#:
// public void WritePoint()

MethodBuilder* writeStrMthd = pointTypeBld-          ⏎
>DefineMethod(S"WritePoint",
    MethodAttributes::Public,
    __typeof(void),
    0);

ILGenerator* writeStrIL = writeStrMthd->GetILGenerator();

// The below ILGenerator created demonstrates a few ways to create
// String* output through STDIN.

// ILGenerator::EmitWriteLine(String*) will generate a ldstr and a
// call to WriteLine for you.

writeStrIL->EmitWriteLine(S"The value of this current          ⏎
instance is:");

// Here, you will do the hard work yourself. First, you need      ⏎
to create
// the String* we will be passing and obtain the correct         ⏎
WriteLine overload
// for said String*. In the below case, you are substituting     ⏎
in two values,
// so the chosen overload is Console::WriteLine(String*,         ⏎
Object*, Object*).

String*  inStr = S"( {0}, {1})";
Type* wlParams[] = {__typeof(String),
    __typeof(Object),
    __typeof(Object)};

// We need the MethodInfo to pass into EmitCall later.

MethodInfo* writeLineMI = __typeof(Console)-                    ⏎
>GetMethod(S"WriteLine",
    wlParams);

// Push the String* with the substitutions onto the stack.
// This is the first argument for WriteLine - the String* one.

writeStrIL->Emit(OpCodes::Ldstr, inStr);

// Since the second argument is an Object*, and it corresponds to
// to the substitution for the value of our integer field, you
// need to box that field to an Object*. First, push a reference
// to the current instance, and then push the value stored in
// field 'x'. We need the reference to the current instance (stored
// in local argument index 0) so Ldfld can load from the correct
// instance (this one).

writeStrIL->Emit(OpCodes::Ldarg_0);
writeStrIL->Emit(OpCodes::Ldfld, xField);

// Now, we execute the box opcode, which pops the value of        ⏎
field 'x',
// returning a reference to the integer value boxed as an Object*.

writeStrIL->Emit(OpCodes::Box, __typeof(int));

// Atop the stack, you'll find our String* inStr, followed by     ⏎
a reference
// to the boxed value of 'x'. Now, you need to likewise box       ⏎
field 'y'.
```

```
writeStrIL->Emit(OpCodes::Ldarg_0);
writeStrIL->Emit(OpCodes::Ldfld, yField);
writeStrIL->Emit(OpCodes::Box, __typeof(int));

// Now, you have all of the arguments for your call to
// Console::WriteLine(String*, Object*, Object*) atop the stack:
// the String* InStr, a reference to the boxed value of 'x', and
// a reference to the boxed value of 'y'.

// Call Console::WriteLine(String*, Object*, Object*) with EmitCall.

writeStrIL->EmitCall(OpCodes::Call, writeLineMI, 0);

// Lastly, EmitWriteLine can also output the value of a field
// using the overload EmitWriteLine(FieldInfo).

writeStrIL->EmitWriteLine(S"The value of 'x' is:");
writeStrIL->EmitWriteLine(xField);
writeStrIL->EmitWriteLine(S"The value of 'y' is:");
writeStrIL->EmitWriteLine(yField);

// Since we return no value (void), the the ret opcode will not
// return the top stack value.

writeStrIL->Emit(OpCodes::Ret);

return pointTypeBld->CreateType();
}

int main() {

    Object* ctorParams[] = new Object*[2];

    Console::Write(S"Enter a integer value for X: ");
    String* myX = Console::ReadLine();
    Console::Write(S"Enter a integer value for Y: ");
    String* myY = Console::ReadLine();

    Console::WriteLine(S"---");

    ctorParams[0] = __box(Convert::ToInt32(myX));
    ctorParams[1] = __box(Convert::ToInt32(myY));

    Type*  ptType = CreateDynamicType();

    Object* ptInstance = Activator::CreateInstance(ptType, ctorParams);
    ptType->InvokeMember(S"WritePoint",
        BindingFlags::InvokeMethod,
        0,
        ptInstance,
        new Object*[0]);
}
```

Requirements

Namespace: System.Reflection.Emit

Platforms: Windows 98, Windows NT 4.0,
Windows Millennium Edition, Windows 2000,
Windows XP Home Edition, Windows XP Professional,
Windows .NET Server family

Assembly: Mscorlib (in Mscorlib.dll)

OpCodes.Add Field

Adds two values and pushes the result onto the evaluation stack.

```
[Visual Basic]
Public Shared ReadOnly Add As OpCode
[C#]
public static readonly OpCode Add;
[C++]
public: static OpCode Add;
```

[JScript]
```
public static var Add : OpCode;
```

Remarks

The following table lists the instruction's hexadecimal and Microsoft Intermediate Language (MSIL) assembly format, along with a brief reference summary:

Format	Assembly Format	Description
58	add	Adds two numeric values, returning a new numeric value.

The stack transitional behavior, in sequential order, is:

1. *value1* is pushed onto the stack.
2. *value2* is pushed onto the stack.
3. *value2* and *value1* are popped from the stack; *value1* is added to *value2*.
4. The result is pushed onto the stack.

Overflow is not detected for integer operations (for proper overflow handling, see **Add_Ovf**).

Integer addition wraps, rather than saturates. For example, assuming 8-bit integers where *value1* is set to 255 and *value2* is set to 1, the wrapped result is 0 rather than 256.

Floating-point overflow returns **+inf** (**PositiveInfinity**) or **-inf** (**NegativeInfinity**).

The acceptable operand types and their corresponding result data type are listed in the table below. If there is no entry for a particular type combination (for example, **int32** and **float**; **int32** and **int64**), it is an invalid Microsoft Intermediate Language (MSIL) and generates an error.

operand	value1 type	value2 type	result type
add	**int32**	**int32**	**int32**
add	**int32**	**natural int**	**natural int**
add	**int32**	**&**	**&**
add	**int32**	*****	*****
add	**int64**	**int64**	**int64**
add	**natural int**	**int32**	**natural int**
add	**natural int**	**natural int**	**natural int**
add	**natural int**	**&**	**&**
add	**natural int**	*****	*****
add	**F**	**F**	**F**
add	**&**	**int32**	**&**
add	**&**	**natural int**	**&**
add	*****	**int32**	*****
add	*****	**natural int**	*****

The following **Emit** constructor overload can use the **add** opcode:

- ILGenerator.Emit(OpCode)

Requirements

Platforms: Windows 98, Windows NT 4.0, Windows Millennium Edition, Windows 2000, Windows XP Home Edition, Windows XP Professional, Windows .NET Server family

OpCodes.Add_Ovf Field

Adds two integers, performs an overflow check, and pushes the result onto the evaluation stack.

```
[Visual Basic]
Public Shared ReadOnly Add_Ovf As OpCode
[C#]
public static readonly OpCode Add_Ovf;
[C++]
public: static OpCode Add_Ovf;
[JScript]
public static var Add_Ovf : OpCode;
```

Remarks

The following table lists the instruction's hexadecimal and Microsoft Intermediate Language (MSIL) assembly format, along with a brief reference summary:

Format	Assembly Format	Description
D6	add.ovf	Adds two signed integer values with an overflow check.

The stack transitional behavior, in sequential order, is:

1. *value1* is pushed onto the stack.
2. *value2* is pushed onto the stack.
3. *value2* and *value1* are popped from the stack; *value1* is added to *value2* with a check for overflow.
4. The result is pushed onto the stack.

OverflowException is thrown if the result is not represented in the result type.

You can perform this operation on signed integers. For floating-point values, use **Add**.

The acceptable operand types and their corresponding result data type are listed in the table below. If there is no entry for a particular type combination (for example, **int32** and **float**; **int32** and **int64**), it is an invalid Microsoft Intermediate Language (MSIL) instruction and generates an error.

operand	value1 type	value2 type	result type
add	**int32**	**int32**	**int32**
add	**int32**	**natural int**	**natural int**
add	**int32**	**&**	**&**
add	**int32**	*****	*****
add	**int64**	**int64**	**int64**
add	**natural int**	**int32**	**natural int**
add	**natural int**	**natural int**	**natural int**
add	**natural int**	**&**	**&**
add	**natural int**	*****	*****
add	**F**	**F**	**F**
add	**&**	**int32**	**&**
add	**&**	**natural int**	**&**
add	*****	**int32**	*****
add	*****	**natural int**	*****

The following **Emit** constructor overload can use the **add.ovf** opcode:

- ILGenerator.Emit(OpCode)

Requirements

Platforms: Windows 98, Windows NT 4.0, Windows Millennium Edition, Windows 2000, Windows XP Home Edition, Windows XP Professional, Windows .NET Server family

OpCodes.Add_Ovf_Un Field

Adds two unsigned integer values, performs an overflow check, and pushes the result onto the evaluation stack.

```
[Visual Basic]
Public Shared ReadOnly Add_Ovf_Un As OpCode
[C#]
public static readonly OpCode Add_Ovf_Un;
[C++]
public: static OpCode Add_Ovf_Un;
[JScript]
public static var Add_Ovf_Un : OpCode;
```

Remarks

The following table lists the instruction's hexadecimal and Microsoft Intermediate Language (MSIL) assembly format, along with a brief reference summary:

Format	Assembly Format	Description
D7	add.ovf.un	Adds two unsigned integer values with an overflow check.

The stack transitional behavior, in sequential order, is:

1. *value1* is pushed onto the stack.
2. *value2* is pushed onto the stack.
3. *value2* and *value1* are popped from the stack; *value1* is added to *value2* with a check for overflow.
4. The result is pushed onto the stack.

OverflowException is thrown if the result is not represented in the result type.

You can perform this operation on signed integers. For floating-point values, use **Add**.

The acceptable operand types and their corresponding result data type are listed in the table below. If there is no entry for a particular type combination (for example, **int32** and **float**; **int32** and **int64**), it is an invalid Microsoft Intermediate Language (MSIL) instruction and generates an error.

operand	value1 type	value2 type	result type
add	int32	int32	int32
add	int32	natural int	natural int
add	int32	&	&
add	int32	*	*
add	int64	int64	int64
add	natural int	int32	natural int
add	natural int	natural int	natural int
add	natural int	&	&
add	natural int	*	*
add	F	F	F
add	&	int32	&
add	&	natural int	&
add	*	int32	*
add	*	natural int	*

The following **Emit** constructor overload can use the **add.ovf.un** opcode:

- ILGenerator.Emit(OpCode)

Requirements

Platforms: Windows 98, Windows NT 4.0, Windows Millennium Edition, Windows 2000, Windows XP Home Edition, Windows XP Professional, Windows .NET Server family

OpCodes.And Field

Computes the bitwise AND of two values and pushes the result onto the evaluation stack.

```
[Visual Basic]
Public Shared ReadOnly And As OpCode
[C#]
public static readonly OpCode And;
[C++]
public: static OpCode And;
[JScript]
public static var And : OpCode;
```

Remarks

The following table lists the instruction's hexadecimal and Microsoft Intermediate Language (MSIL) assembly format, along with a brief reference summary:

Format	Instruction	Description
5F	and	Determines the bitwise AND of two integer values.

The stack transitional behavior, in sequential order, is:

1. *value1* is pushed onto the stack.
2. *value2* is pushed onto the stack.
3. *value1* and *value2* are popped from the stack; the bitwise AND of the two values is computed.
4. The result is pushed onto the stack.

The **and** instruction computes the bitwise AND of the top two values on the stack and leaves the result on the stack.

And is an integer-specific operation.

The following **Emit** constructor overload can use the **and** opcode:

- ILGenerator.Emit(OpCode)

Requirements

Platforms: Windows 98, Windows NT 4.0, Windows Millennium Edition, Windows 2000, Windows XP Home Edition, Windows XP Professional, Windows .NET Server family

OpCodes.Arglist Field

Returns an unmanaged pointer to the argument list of the current method.

```
[Visual Basic]
Public Shared ReadOnly Arglist As OpCode
```

```
[C#]
public static readonly OpCode Arglist;
[C++]
public: static OpCode Arglist;
[JScript]
public static var Arglist : OpCode;
```

Remarks

The following table lists the instruction's hexadecimal and Microsoft Intermediate Language (MSIL) assembly format, along with a brief reference summary:

Format	Assembly Format	Description
FE 00	arglist	Returns an argument list handle for the current method.

No evaluation stack behaviors are performed by this operation.

The **arglist** instruction returns an opaque handle (an unmanaged pointer, of type **natural int**) that represents the argument list of the current method. This handle is valid only during the lifetime of the current method. You can, however, pass the handle to other methods as long as the current method is on the thread of control. You can only execute the **arglist** instruction within a method that takes a variable number of arguments.

The following **Emit** constructor overload can use the **arglist** opcode:

• ILGenerator.Emit(OpCode)

Requirements

Platforms: Windows 98, Windows NT 4.0, Windows Millennium Edition, Windows 2000, Windows XP Home Edition, Windows XP Professional, Windows .NET Server family

OpCodes.Beq Field

Transfers control to a target instruction if two values are equal.

```
[Visual Basic]
Public Shared ReadOnly Beq As OpCode
[C#]
public static readonly OpCode Beq;
[C++]
public: static OpCode Beq;
[JScript]
public static var Beq : OpCode;
```

Remarks

The following table lists the instruction's hexadecimal and Microsoft Intermediate Language (MSIL) assembly format, along with a brief reference summary:

Format	Assembly Format	Description
3B < int32 >	beq target	Branch to the target instruction at offset *target* if the two values are equal.

The stack transitional behavior, in sequential order, is:

1. *value1* is pushed onto the stack.
2. *value2* is pushed onto the stack.
3. *value2* and *value1* are popped from the stack; if *value1* is equal to *value2*, the branch operation is performed.

The **beq** instruction transfers control to the specified target instruction if *value1* is equal to *value2*. The effect is the same as performing a **ceq** instruction followed by a **brtrue** branch to the specific target instruction. The target instruction is represented as a 4-byte signed offset from the beginning of the instruction following the current instruction.

The acceptable operand types are encapsulated below:

If the target instruction has one or more prefix codes, control can only be transferred to the first of these prefixes.

Control transfers into and out of **try, catch, filter,** and **finally** blocks cannot be performed by this instruction (such transfers are severely restricted and must use the **Leave** instruction instead).

The following **Emit** constructor overload can use the **beq** opcode:

• ILGenerator.Emit(OpCode, Label)

Requirements

Platforms: Windows 98, Windows NT 4.0, Windows Millennium Edition, Windows 2000, Windows XP Home Edition, Windows XP Professional, Windows .NET Server family

OpCodes.Beq_S Field

Transfers control to a target instruction (short form) if two values are equal.

```
[Visual Basic]
Public Shared ReadOnly Beq_S As OpCode
[C#]
public static readonly OpCode Beq_S;
[C++]
public: static OpCode Beq_S;
[JScript]
public static var Beq_S : OpCode;
```

Remarks

The following table lists the instruction's hexadecimal and Microsoft Intermediate Language (MSIL) assembly format, along with a brief reference summary:

Format	Assembly Format	Description
2E < int8 >	beq.s target	Branch to the target instruction at offset *target* if equal, short form

The stack transitional behavior, in sequential order, is:

1. *value1* is pushed onto the stack.
2. *value2* is pushed onto the stack.
3. *value2* and *value1* are popped from the stack; if *value1* is equal to *value2*, the branch operation is performed.

The **beq.s** instruction transfers control to to the specified target instruction if *value1* is equal to *value2*. The effect is the same as performing a **ceq** instruction followed by a **brtrue** branch to the specific target instruction. The target instruction is represented as a 1-byte signed offset from the beginning of the instruction following the current instruction.

The acceptable operand types are encapsulated below:

If the target instruction has one or more prefix codes, control can only be transferred to the first of these prefixes.

Control transfers into and out of **try**, **catch**, **filter**, and **finally** blocks cannot be performed by this instruction (such transfers are severely restricted and must use the **Leave** instruction instead).

The following **Emit** constructor overload can use the **beq.s** opcode:

• ILGenerator.Emit(OpCode, Label)

Requirements

Platforms: Windows 98, Windows NT 4.0, Windows Millennium Edition, Windows 2000, Windows XP Home Edition, Windows XP Professional, Windows .NET Server family

OpCodes.Bge Field

Transfers control to a target instruction if the first value is greater than or equal to the second value.

```
[Visual Basic]
Public Shared ReadOnly Bge As OpCode
[C#]
public static readonly OpCode Bge;
[C++]
public: static OpCode Bge;
[JScript]
public static var Bge : OpCode;
```

Remarks

The following table lists the instruction's hexadecimal and Microsoft Intermediate Language (MSIL) assembly format, along with a brief reference summary:

Format	Assembly Format	Description
3C <int32>	bge target	Branch to the target instruction at the specified offset if the first value is greater than or equal to the second value.

The stack transitional behavior, in sequential order, is:

1. *value1* is pushed onto the stack.
2. *value2* is pushed onto the stack.
3. *value2* and *value1* are popped from the stack; if *value1* is greater than or equal to *value2*, the branch operation is performed.

The **bge** instruction transfers control to the specified target instruction if *value1* is greater than or equal to *value2*. The effect is identical to performing a **clt.un** instruction followed by a **brfalse** branch to the specific target instruction. The target instruction is represented as a 4-byte signed offset from the beginning of the instruction following the current instruction.

Control can only be transferred to the first of these prefixes if the target instruction has one or more prefix codes. Control transfers into and out of **try**, **catch**, **filter**, and **finally** blocks cannot be performed by this instruction.

The following **Emit** constructor overload can use the **bge** opcode:

• ILGenerator.Emit(OpCode, Label)

Requirements

Platforms: Windows 98, Windows NT 4.0, Windows Millennium Edition, Windows 2000, Windows XP Home Edition, Windows XP Professional, Windows .NET Server family

OpCodes.Bge_S Field

Transfers control to a target instruction (short form) if the first value is greater than or equal to the second value.

```
[Visual Basic]
Public Shared ReadOnly Bge_S As OpCode
[C#]
public static readonly OpCode Bge_S;
[C++]
public: static OpCode Bge_S;
[JScript]
public static var Bge_S : OpCode;
```

Remarks

The following table lists the instruction's hexadecimal and Microsoft Intermediate Language (MSIL) assembly format, along with a brief reference summary:

Format	Assembly Format	Description
2F <int8>	bge.s target	Branch to the target instruction at the specified offset if the first value is greater than or equal to the second value, short form.

The stack transitional behavior, in sequential order, is:

1. *value1* is pushed onto the stack.
2. *value2* is pushed onto the stack.
3. *value2* and *value1* are popped from the stack; if *value1* is greater than or equal to *value2*, the branch operation is performed.

The **bge.s** instruction transfers control to the specified target instruction if *value1* is greater than or equal to *value2*. The effect is identical to performing a **clt.un** instruction followed by a **brfalse** branch to the specific target instruction. The target instruction is represented as a 1-byte signed offset from the beginning of the instruction following the current instruction.

Control can only be transferred to the first of these prefixes if the target instruction has one or more prefix codes. Control transfers into and out of **try**, **catch**, **filter**, and **finally** blocks cannot be performed by this instruction.

The following **Emit** constructor overload can use the **bge.s** opcode:

• ILGenerator.Emit(OpCode, Label)

Requirements

Platforms: Windows 98, Windows NT 4.0, Windows Millennium Edition, Windows 2000, Windows XP Home Edition, Windows XP Professional, Windows .NET Server family

OpCodes.Bge_Un Field

Transfers control to a target instruction if the the first value is greather than the second value, when comparing unsigned integer values or unordered float values.

```
[Visual Basic]
Public Shared ReadOnly Bge_Un As OpCode
[C#]
public static readonly OpCode Bge_Un;
[C++]
public: static OpCode Bge_Un;
[JScript]
public static var Bge_Un : OpCode;
```

Remarks

The following table lists the instruction's hexadecimal and Microsoft Intermediate Language (MSIL) assembly format, along with a brief reference summary:

Format	Assembly Format	Description
41 <int32>	bge.un *target*	Branch to the target instruction at the specified offset if the first value is greater than or equal to the second value (unsigned values).

The stack transitional behavior, in sequential order, is:

1. *value1* is pushed onto the stack.
2. *value2* is pushed onto the stack.
3. *value2* and *value1* are popped from the stack; if *value1* is greater than or equal to *value2*, the branch operation is performed.

The **bge.un** instruction transfers control to the specified target instruction if *value1* is greater than or equal to *value2*, when compared using unsigned integer or unordered float values. The effect is identical to performing a **clt** instruction followed by a **brfalse** branch to the specific target instruction. The target instruction is represented as a 4-byte signed offset from the beginning of the instruction following the current instruction.

Control can only be transferred to the first of these prefixes if the target instruction has one or more prefix codes. Control transfers into and out of **try**, **catch**, **filter**, and **finally** blocks cannot be performed by this instruction.

The following **Emit** constructor overload can use the **bge.un** opcode:

- ILGenerator.Emit(OpCode, Label)

Requirements

Platforms: Windows 98, Windows NT 4.0, Windows Millennium Edition, Windows 2000, Windows XP Home Edition, Windows XP Professional, Windows .NET Server family

OpCodes.Bge_Un_S Field

Transfers control to a target instruction (short form) if if the the first value is greather than the second value, when comparing unsigned integer values or unordered float values.

```
[Visual Basic]
Public Shared ReadOnly Bge_Un_S As OpCode
[C#]
public static readonly OpCode Bge_Un_S;
[C++]
public: static OpCode Bge_Un_S;
[JScript]
public static var Bge_Un_S : OpCode;
```

Remarks

The following table lists the instruction's hexadecimal and Microsoft Intermediate Language (MSIL) assembly format, along with a brief reference summary:

Format	Assembly Format	Description
34 < int8 >	bge.un.s *target*	Branch to the target instruction at the specified offset if the first value is greater than or equal to the second value (unsigned values), short form.

The stack transitional behavior, in sequential order, is:

1. *value1* is pushed onto the stack.
2. *value2* is pushed onto the stack.
3. *value2* and *value1* are popped from the stack; if *value1* is greater than or equal to *value2*, the branch operation is performed.

The **bge.un.s** instruction transfers control to the specified target instruction if *value1* is greater than or equal to *value2*, when compared using unsigned integer or unordered float values. The effect is identical to performing a **clt** instruction followed by a **brfalse** branch to the specific target instruction. The target instruction is represented as a 1-byte signed offset from the beginning of the instruction following the current instruction.

Control can only be transferred to the first of these prefixes if the target instruction has one or more prefix codes. Control transfers into and out of **try**, **catch**, **filter**, and **finally** blocks cannot be performed by this instruction.

The following **Emit** constructor overload can use the **bge.un.s** opcode:

- ILGenerator.Emit(OpCode, Label)

Requirements

Platforms: Windows 98, Windows NT 4.0, Windows Millennium Edition, Windows 2000, Windows XP Home Edition, Windows XP Professional, Windows .NET Server family

OpCodes.Bgt Field

Transfers control to a target instruction if the first value is greater than the second value.

```
[Visual Basic]
Public Shared ReadOnly Bgt As OpCode
[C#]
public static readonly OpCode Bgt;
[C++]
public: static OpCode Bgt;
[JScript]
public static var Bgt : OpCode;
```

Remarks

The following table lists the instruction's hexadecimal and Microsoft Intermediate Language (MSIL) assembly format, along with a brief reference summary:

Format	Assembly Format	Description
3D < int32 >	bgt *target*	Branch to the target instruction at the specified offset if the first value is greater than the second value.

The stack transitional behavior, in sequential order, is:

1. *value1* is pushed onto the stack.
2. *value2* is pushed onto the stack.
3. *value2* and *value1* are popped from the stack; if *value1* is greater than *value2*, the branch operation is performed.

The **bgt** instruction transfers control to the specified target instruction if *value1* is greater than *value2*. The effect is identical to performing a **cgt** instruction followed by a **brtrue** branch to the specific target instruction. The target instruction is represented as a 4-byte signed offset from the beginning of the instruction following the current instruction.

Control can only be transferred to the first of these prefixes if the target instruction has one or more prefix codes. Control transfers into and out of **try**, **catch**, **filter**, and **finally** blocks cannot be performed by this instruction.

The following **Emit** constructor overload can use the **bgt** opcode:

- ILGenerator.Emit(OpCode, Label)

Requirements

Platforms: Windows 98, Windows NT 4.0, Windows Millennium Edition, Windows 2000, Windows XP Home Edition, Windows XP Professional, Windows .NET Server family

OpCodes.Bgt_S Field

Transfers control to a target instruction (short form) if the first value is greater than the second value.

```
[Visual Basic]
Public Shared ReadOnly Bgt_S As OpCode
[C#]
public static readonly OpCode Bgt_S;
[C++]
public: static OpCode Bgt_S;
[JScript]
public static var Bgt_S : OpCode;
```

Remarks

The following table lists the instruction's hexadecimal and Microsoft Intermediate Language (MSIL) assembly format, along with a brief reference summary:

Format	Assembly Format	Description
30 < **int8** >	bgt.s *target*	Branch to the target instruction at the specified offset if the first value is greater than the second value, short form.

The stack transitional behavior, in sequential order, is:

1. *value1* is pushed onto the stack.
2. *value2* is pushed onto the stack.
3. *value2* and *value1* are popped from the stack; if *value1* is greater than *value2*, the branch operation is performed.

The **bgt.s** instruction transfers control to the specified target instruction if *value1* is greater than *value2*. The effect is identical to performing a **cgt** instruction followed by a **brtrue** branch to the specific target instruction. The target instruction is represented as a 1-byte signed offset from the beginning of the instruction following the current instruction.

Control can only be transferred to the first of these prefixes if the target instruction has one or more prefix codes. Control transfers into and out of **try**, **catch**, **filter**, and **finally** blocks cannot be performed by this instruction.

The following **Emit** constructor overload can use the **bgt.s** opcode:

- ILGenerator.Emit(OpCode, Label)

Requirements

Platforms: Windows 98, Windows NT 4.0, Windows Millennium Edition, Windows 2000, Windows XP Home Edition, Windows XP Professional, Windows .NET Server family

OpCodes.Bgt_Un Field

Transfers control to a target instruction if the first value is greater than the second value, when comparing unsigned integer values or unordered float values.

```
[Visual Basic]
Public Shared ReadOnly Bgt_Un As OpCode
[C#]
public static readonly OpCode Bgt_Un;
[C++]
public: static OpCode Bgt_Un;
[JScript]
public static var Bgt_Un : OpCode;
```

Remarks

The following table lists the instruction's hexadecimal and Microsoft Intermediate Language (MSIL) assembly format, along with a brief reference summary:

Format	Assembly Format	Description
42 < **int32** >	bgt.un *target*	Branch to the target instruction at the specified offset if the first value is greater than the second value (unsigned values).

The stack transitional behavior, in sequential order, is:

1. *value1* is pushed onto the stack.
2. *value2* is pushed onto the stack.
3. *value2* and *value1* are popped from the stack; if *value1* is greater than *value2*, the branch operation is performed.

The **bgt.un** instruction transfers control to the specified target instruction if *value1* is greater than *value2*, when compared using unsigned integer or unordered float values. The effect is identical to performing a **cgt.un** instruction followed by a **brtrue** branch to the specific target instruction. The target instruction is represented as a 4-byte signed offset from the beginning of the instruction following the current instruction.

Control can only be transferred to the first of these prefixes if the target instruction has one or more prefix codes. Control transfers into and out of **try**, **catch**, **filter**, and **finally** blocks cannot be performed by this instruction.

The following **Emit** constructor overload can use the **bgt.un** opcode:

- ILGenerator.Emit(OpCode, Label)

Requirements

Platforms: Windows 98, Windows NT 4.0,
Windows Millennium Edition, Windows 2000,
Windows XP Home Edition, Windows XP Professional,
Windows .NET Server family

OpCodes.Bgt_Un_S Field

Transfers control to a target instruction (short form) if the first value
is greater than the second value, when comparing unsigned integer
values or unordered float values.

```
[Visual Basic]
Public Shared ReadOnly Bgt_Un_S As OpCode
[C#]
public static readonly OpCode Bgt_Un_S;
[C++]
public: static OpCode Bgt_Un_S;
[JScript]
public static var Bgt_Un_S : OpCode;
```

Remarks

The following table lists the instruction's hexadecimal and Microsoft
Intermediate Language (MSIL) assembly format, along with a brief
reference summary:

Format	Assembly Format	Description
35 < int8 >	bgt.un.s *target*	Branch to the target instruction at the specified offset if the first value is greater than the second value (unsigned values), short form.

The stack transitional behavior, in sequential order, is:

1. *value1* is pushed onto the stack.
2. *value2* is pushed onto the stack.
3. *value2* and *value1* are popped from the stack; if *value1* is greater than *value2*, the branch operation is performed.

The **bgt.un.s** instruction transfers control to the specified target
instruction if *value1* is greater than *value2*, when compared using
unsigned integer or unordered float values. The effect is identical to
performing a **cgt.un** instruction followed by a **brtrue** branch to the
specific target instruction. The target instruction is represented as a
1-byte signed offset from the beginning of the instruction following
the current instruction.

Control can only be transferred to the first of these prefixes if the
target instruction has one or more prefix codes. Control transfers
into and out of **try**, **catch**, **filter**, and **finally** blocks cannot be
performed by this instruction.

The following **Emit** constructor overload can use the **bgt.un.s**
opcode:

- ILGenerator.Emit(OpCode, Label)

Requirements

Platforms: Windows 98, Windows NT 4.0,
Windows Millennium Edition, Windows 2000,
Windows XP Home Edition, Windows XP Professional,
Windows .NET Server family

OpCodes.Ble Field

Transfers control to a target instruction if the first value is less than
or equal to the second value.

```
[Visual Basic]
Public Shared ReadOnly Ble As OpCode
[C#]
public static readonly OpCode Ble;
[C++]
public: static OpCode Ble;
[JScript]
public static var Ble : OpCode;
```

Remarks

The following table lists the instruction's hexadecimal and Microsoft
Intermediate Language (MSIL) assembly format, along with a brief
reference summary:

Format	Assembly Format	Description
3E <int32>	ble *target*	Branch to the target instruction at the specified offset if the first value is less than or equal to the second value.

The stack transitional behavior, in sequential order, is:

1. *value1* is pushed onto the stack.
2. *value2* is pushed onto the stack.
3. *value2* and *value1* are popped from the stack; if *value1* is less than or equal to *value2*, the branch operation is performed.

The **ble** instruction transfers control to the specified target
instruction if *value1* is less than or equal to *value2*. The effect is
identical to performing a **cgt** instruction (**cgt.un** for floats) followed
by a **brfalse** branch to the specific target instruction. The target
instruction is represented as a 4-byte signed offset from the
beginning of the instruction following the current instruction.

Control can only be transferred to the first of these prefixes if the
target instruction has one or more prefix codes. Control transfers
into and out of **try**, **catch**, **filter**, and **finally** blocks cannot be
performed by this instruction.

The following **Emit** constructor overload can use the **ble** opcode:

- ILGenerator.Emit(OpCode, Label)

Requirements

Platforms: Windows 98, Windows NT 4.0,
Windows Millennium Edition, Windows 2000,
Windows XP Home Edition, Windows XP Professional,
Windows .NET Server family

OpCodes.Ble_S Field

Transfers control to a target instruction (short form) if the first value
is less than or equal to the second value.

```
[Visual Basic]
Public Shared ReadOnly Ble_S As OpCode
[C#]
public static readonly OpCode Ble_S;
[C++]
public: static OpCode Ble_S;
[JScript]
public static var Ble_S : OpCode;
```

Remarks

The following table lists the instruction's hexadecimal and Microsoft Intermediate Language (MSIL) assembly format, along with a brief reference summary:

Format	Assembly Format	Description
31 <int8>	ble.s *target*	Branch to the target instruction at the specified offset if the first value is less than or equal to the second value, short form.

The stack transitional behavior, in sequential order, is:

1. *value1* is pushed onto the stack.
2. *value2* is pushed onto the stack.
3. *value2* and *value1* are popped from the stack; if *value1* is less than or equal to *value2*, the branch operation is performed.

The **ble.s** instruction transfers control to the specified target instruction if *value1* is less than or equal to *value2*. The effect is identical to performing a **cgt** instruction (**cgt.un** for floats) instruction followed by a **brfalse** branch to the specific target instruction. The target instruction is represented as a 1-byte signed offset from the beginning of the instruction following the current instruction.

Control can only be transferred to the first of these prefixes if the target instruction has one or more prefix codes. Control transfers into and out of **try**, **catch**, **filter**, and **finally** blocks cannot be performed by this instruction.

The following **Emit** constructor overload can use the **ble.s** opcode:

• ILGenerator.Emit(OpCode, Label)

Requirements

Platforms: Windows 98, Windows NT 4.0, Windows Millennium Edition, Windows 2000, Windows XP Home Edition, Windows XP Professional, Windows .NET Server family

OpCodes.Ble_Un Field

Transfers control to a target instruction if the first value is less than or equal to the second value, when comparing unsigned integer values or unordered float values.

```
[Visual Basic]
Public Shared ReadOnly Ble_Un As OpCode
[C#]
public static readonly OpCode Ble_Un;
[C++]
public: static OpCode Ble_Un;
[JScript]
public static var Ble_Un : OpCode;
```

Remarks

The following table lists the instruction's hexadecimal and Microsoft Intermediate Language (MSIL) assembly format, along with a brief reference summary:

Format	Assembly Format	Description
43 <int32>	ble.un *target*	Branch to the target instruction at the specified offset if the first value is less than or equal to the second value (unsigned values).

The stack transitional behavior, in sequential order, is:

1. *value1* is pushed onto the stack.
2. *value2* is pushed onto the stack.
3. *value2* and *value1* are popped from the stack; if *value1* is less than or equal to *value2*, the branch operation is performed.

The **ble.un** instruction transfers control to the specified target instruction if *value1* is less than or equal to *value2*, when compared using unsigned integer or unordered float values. The effect is identical to performing a **cgt.un** instruction (**cgt** for floats) followed by a **brfalse** branch to the specific target instruction. The target instruction is represented as a 4-byte signed offset from the beginning of the instruction following the current instruction.

Control can only be transferred to the first of these prefixes if the target instruction has one or more prefix codes. Control transfers into and out of **try**, **catch**, **filter**, and **finally** blocks cannot be performed by this instruction.

The following **Emit** constructor overload can use the **ble.un** opcode:

• ILGenerator.Emit(OpCode, Label)

Requirements

Platforms: Windows 98, Windows NT 4.0, Windows Millennium Edition, Windows 2000, Windows XP Home Edition, Windows XP Professional, Windows .NET Server family

OpCodes.Ble_Un_S Field

Transfers control to a target instruction (short form) if the first value is less than or equal to the second value, when comparing unsigned integer values or unordered float values.

```
[Visual Basic]
Public Shared ReadOnly Ble_Un_S As OpCode
[C#]
public static readonly OpCode Ble_Un_S;
[C++]
public: static OpCode Ble_Un_S;
[JScript]
public static var Ble_Un_S : OpCode;
```

Remarks

The following table lists the instruction's hexadecimal and Microsoft Intermediate Language (MSIL) assembly format, along with a brief reference summary:

Format	Assembly Format	Description
36 <int8>	ble.un.s *target*	Branch to the target instruction at the specified offset if the first value is less than or equal to the second value (unsigned values), short form.

The stack transitional behavior, in sequential order, is:

1. *value1* is pushed onto the stack.
2. *value2* is pushed onto the stack.
3. *value2* and *value1* are popped from the stack; if *value1* is less than or equal to *value2*, the branch operation is performed.

The **ble.un.s** instruction transfers control to the specified target instruction if *value1* is less than or equal to *value2*, when compared using unsigned integer or unordered float values. The effect is identical to performing a **cgt.un** instruction (**cgt** for floats) followed by a **brfalse** branch to the specific target instruction. The target instruction is represented as a 1-byte signed offset from the beginning of the instruction following the current instruction.

Control can only be transferred to the first of these prefixes if the target instruction has one or more prefix codes. Control transfers into and out of **try**, **catch**, **filter**, and **finally** blocks cannot be performed by this instruction.

The following **Emit** constructor overload can use the **ble.un.s** opcode:

• ILGenerator.Emit(OpCode, Label)

Requirements

Platforms: Windows 98, Windows NT 4.0, Windows Millennium Edition, Windows 2000, Windows XP Home Edition, Windows XP Professional, Windows .NET Server family

OpCodes.Blt Field

Transfers control to a target instruction if the first value is less than the second value.

```
[Visual Basic]
Public Shared ReadOnly Blt As OpCode
[C#]
public static readonly OpCode Blt;
[C++]
public: static OpCode Blt;
[JScript]
public static var Blt : OpCode;
```

Remarks

The following table lists the instruction's hexadecimal and Microsoft Intermediate Language (MSIL) assembly format, along with a brief reference summary:

Format	Assembly Format	Description
3F < int32 >	blt *target*	Branch to the target instruction at the specified offset if the first value is less than the second value.

The stack transitional behavior, in sequential order, is:

1. *value1* is pushed onto the stack.
2. *value2* is pushed onto the stack.
3. *value2* and *value1* are popped from the stack; if *value1* is less than *value2*, the branch operation is performed.

The **blt** instruction transfers control to the specified target instruction if *value1* is less than or equal to *value2*. The effect is identical to performing a **clt** instruction followed by a **brtrue** branch to the specific target instruction. The target instruction is represented

as a 4-byte signed offset from the beginning of the instruction following the current instruction.

Control can only be transferred to the first of these prefixes if the target instruction has one or more prefix codes. Control transfers into and out of **try**, **catch**, **filter**, and **finally** blocks cannot be performed by this instruction.

The following **Emit** constructor overload can use the **blt** opcode:

• ILGenerator.Emit(OpCode, Label)

Requirements

Platforms: Windows 98, Windows NT 4.0, Windows Millennium Edition, Windows 2000, Windows XP Home Edition, Windows XP Professional, Windows .NET Server family

OpCodes.Blt_S Field

Transfers control to a target instruction (short form) if the first value is less than the second value.

```
[Visual Basic]
Public Shared ReadOnly Blt_S As OpCode
[C#]
public static readonly OpCode Blt_S;
[C++]
public: static OpCode Blt_S;
[JScript]
public static var Blt_S : OpCode;
```

Remarks

The following table lists the instruction's hexadecimal and Microsoft Intermediate Language (MSIL) assembly format, along with a brief reference summary:

Format	Assembly Format	Description
32 < int8 >	blt.s *target*	Branch to the target instruction at the specified offset if the first value is less than the second value, short form.

The stack transitional behavior, in sequential order, is:

1. *value1* is pushed onto the stack.
2. *value2* is pushed onto the stack.
3. *value2* and *value1* are popped from the stack; if *value1* is less than *value2*, the branch operation is performed.

The **blt.s** instruction transfers control to the specified target instruction if *value1* is less than *value2*. The effect is identical to performing a **clt** instruction followed by a **brtrue** branch to the specific target instruction. The target instruction is represented as a 1-byte signed offset from the beginning of the instruction following the current instruction.

Control can only be transferred to the first of these prefixes if the target instruction has one or more prefix codes. Control transfers into and out of **try**, **catch**, **filter**, and **finally** blocks cannot be performed by this instruction.

The following **Emit** constructor overload can use the **blt.s** opcode:

• ILGenerator.Emit(OpCode, Label)

Requirements

Platforms: Windows 98, Windows NT 4.0, Windows Millennium Edition, Windows 2000, Windows XP Home Edition, Windows XP Professional, Windows .NET Server family

OpCodes.Blt_Un Field

Transfers control to a target instruction if the first value is less than the second value, when comparing unsigned integer values or unordered float values.

```
[Visual Basic]
Public Shared ReadOnly Blt_Un As OpCode
[C#]
public static readonly OpCode Blt_Un;
[C++]
public: static OpCode Blt_Un;
[JScript]
public static var Blt_Un : OpCode;
```

Remarks

The following table lists the instruction's hexadecimal and Microsoft Intermediate Language (MSIL) assembly format, along with a brief reference summary:

Format	Assembly Format	Description
44 < int32 >	blt.un *target*	Branch to the target instruction at the specified offset if the first value is less than the second value (unsigned values).

The stack transitional behavior, in sequential order, is:

1. *value1* is pushed onto the stack.
2. *value2* is pushed onto the stack.
3. *value2* and *value1* are popped from the stack; if *value1* is less than *value2*, the branch operation is performed.

The **blt.un** instruction transfers control to the specified target instruction if *value1* is less than *value2*, when compared using unsigned integer or unordered float values. The effect is identical to performing a **clt.un** instruction followed by a **brtrue** branch to the specific target instruction. The target instruction is represented as a 4-byte signed offset from the beginning of the instruction following the current instruction.

Control can only be transferred to the first of these prefixes if the target instruction has one or more prefix codes. Control transfers into and out of **try**, **catch**, **filter**, and **finally** blocks cannot be performed by this instruction.

The following **Emit** constructor overload can use the **blt.un** opcode:

• ILGenerator.Emit(OpCode, Label)

Requirements

Platforms: Windows 98, Windows NT 4.0, Windows Millennium Edition, Windows 2000, Windows XP Home Edition, Windows XP Professional, Windows .NET Server family

OpCodes.Blt_Un_S Field

Transfers control to a target instruction (short form) if the first value is less than the second value, when comparing unsigned integer values or unordered float values.

```
[Visual Basic]
Public Shared ReadOnly Blt_Un_S As OpCode
[C#]
public static readonly OpCode Blt_Un_S;
[C++]
public: static OpCode Blt_Un_S;
[JScript]
public static var Blt_Un_S : OpCode;
```

Remarks

The following table lists the instruction's hexadecimal and Microsoft Intermediate Language (MSIL) assembly format, along with a brief reference summary:

Format	Assembly Format	Description
37 < int8 >	blt.un.s *target*	Branch to the target instruction at the specified offset if the first value is less than the second value (unsigned values), short form.

The stack transitional behavior, in sequential order, is:

1. *value1* is pushed onto the stack.
2. *value2* is pushed onto the stack.
3. *value2* and *value1* are popped from the stack; if *value1* is less than *value2*, the branch operation is performed.

The **blt.un** instruction transfers control to the specified target instruction if *value1* is less than *value2*, when compared using unsigned integer or unordered float values. The effect is identical to performing a **clt.un** instruction followed by a **brtrue** branch to the specific target instruction. The target instruction is represented as a 4-byte signed offset from the beginning of the instruction following the current instruction.

Control can only be transferred to the first of these prefixes if the target instruction has one or more prefix codes. Control transfers into and out of **try**, **catch**, **filter**, and **finally** blocks cannot be performed by this instruction.

The following **Emit** constructor overload can use the **blt.un.s** opcode:

• ILGenerator.Emit(OpCode, Label)

Requirements

Platforms: Windows 98, Windows NT 4.0, Windows Millennium Edition, Windows 2000, Windows XP Home Edition, Windows XP Professional, Windows .NET Server family

OpCodes.Bne_Un Field

Transfers control to a target instruction when two unsigned integer values or unordered float values are not equal.

```
[Visual Basic]
Public Shared ReadOnly Bne_Un As OpCode
[C#]
public static readonly OpCode Bne_Un;
```

```
[C++]
public: static OpCode Bne_Un;
[JScript]
public static var Bne_Un : OpCode;
```

Remarks

The following table lists the instruction's hexadecimal and Microsoft Intermediate Language (MSIL) assembly format, along with a brief reference summary:

Format	Assembly Format	Description
40 < **int32** >	bne.un *target*	Branch to the target instruction at the specified offset if two unsigned integer values are not equal (unsigned values).

The stack transitional behavior, in sequential order, is:

1. *value1* is pushed onto the stack.
2. *value2* is pushed onto the stack.
3. *value2* and *value1* are popped from the stack; if *value1* is not equal to *value2*, the branch operation is performed.

The **bne.un** instruction transfers control to the specified target instruction if *value1* is not equal to *value2*, when compared using unsigned integer or unordered float values. The effect is identical to performing a **ceq.un** instruction followed by a **brfalse** branch to the specific target instruction. The target instruction is represented as a 4-byte signed offset from the beginning of the instruction following the current instruction.

Control can only be transferred to the first of these prefixes if the target instruction has one or more prefix codes. Control transfers into and out of **try**, **catch**, **filter**, and **finally** blocks cannot be performed by this instruction.

The following **Emit** constructor overload can use the **bne.un** opcode:

- ILGenerator.Emit(OpCode, Label)

Requirements

Platforms: Windows 98, Windows NT 4.0, Windows Millennium Edition, Windows 2000, Windows XP Home Edition, Windows XP Professional, Windows .NET Server family

OpCodes.Bne_Un_S Field

Transfers control to a target instruction (short form) when two unsigned integer values or unordered float values are not equal.

```
[Visual Basic]
Public Shared ReadOnly Bne_Un_S As OpCode
[C#]
public static readonly OpCode Bne_Un_S;
[C++]
public: static OpCode Bne_Un_S;
[JScript]
public static var Bne_Un_S : OpCode;
```

Remarks

The following table lists the instruction's hexadecimal and Microsoft Intermediate Language (MSIL) assembly format, along with a brief reference summary:

Format	Assembly Format	Description
33 < **int8** >	bne.un.s *target*	Branch to the target instruction at the specified offset if two unsigned integer values are not equal (unsigned values), short form.

The stack transitional behavior, in sequential order, is:

1. *value1* is pushed onto the stack.
2. *value2* is pushed onto the stack.
3. *value2* and *value1* are popped from the stack; if *value1* is not equal to *value2*, the branch operation is performed.

The **bne.un** instruction transfers control to the specified target instruction if *value1* is not equal to *value2*, when compared using unsigned integer or unordered float values. The effect is identical to performing a **ceq.un** instruction followed by a **brfalse** branch to the specific target instruction. The target instruction is represented as a 4-byte signed offset from the beginning of the instruction following the current instruction.

Control can only be transferred to the first of these prefixes if the target instruction has one or more prefix codes. Control transfers into and out of **try**, **catch**, **filter**, and **finally** blocks cannot be performed by this instruction.

The following **Emit** constructor overload can use the **bne.un.s** opcode:

- ILGenerator.Emit(OpCode, Label)

Requirements

Platforms: Windows 98, Windows NT 4.0, Windows Millennium Edition, Windows 2000, Windows XP Home Edition, Windows XP Professional, Windows .NET Server family

OpCodes.Box Field

Converts a value type to an object reference (type **O**).

```
[Visual Basic]
Public Shared ReadOnly Box As OpCode
[C#]
public static readonly OpCode Box;
[C++]
public: static OpCode Box;
[JScript]
public static var Box : OpCode;
```

Remarks

The following table lists the instruction's hexadecimal and Microsoft Intermediate Language (MSIL) assembly format, along with a brief reference summary:

Format	Assembly Format	Description
8C < **T** >	box *valTypeToken*	Convert a value type (of the type specified in *valTypeToken*) to a true object reference.

The stack transitional behavior, in sequential order, is:

1. A value type is pushed onto the stack.
2. The value type is popped from the stack; the **box** operation is performed.
3. An object reference to the resulting "boxed" value type is pushed onto the stack.

A value type has two separate representations within the Common Language Infrastructure (CLI):

- A 'raw' form used when a value type is embedded within another object or on the stack.
- A 'boxed' form, where the data in the value type is wrapped (boxed) into an object so it can exist as an independent entity.

The **box** instruction converts the 'raw' (unboxed) value type into an object reference (type **O**). This is accomplished by creating a new object and copying the data from the value type into the newly allocated object. *valTypeToken* is a metadata token indicating the type of the value type on the stack.

OutOfMemoryException is thrown if there is insufficient memory to satisfy the request.

TypeLoadException is thrown if the class cannot be found. This is typically detected when Microsoft Intermediate Language (MSIL) is converted to native code, rather than at runtime.

The following **Emit** constructor overload can use the **box** opcode:

- ILGenerator.Emit(OpCode, Type)

Requirements

Platforms: Windows 98, Windows NT 4.0, Windows Millennium Edition, Windows 2000, Windows XP Home Edition, Windows XP Professional, Windows .NET Server family

OpCodes.Br Field

Unconditionally transfers control to a target instruction.

```
[Visual Basic]
Public Shared ReadOnly Br As OpCode
[C#]
public static readonly OpCode Br;
[C++]
public: static OpCode Br;
[JScript]
public static var Br : OpCode;
```

Remarks

The following table lists the instruction's hexadecimal and Microsoft Intermediate Language (MSIL) assembly format, along with a brief reference summary:

Format	Assembly Format	Description
38 < **int32** >	br *target*	Branches to a target instruction at the specified offset.

No evaluation stack behaviors are performed by this operation.

The **br** instruction unconditionally transfers control to a target instruction. The target instruction is represented as a 4-byte signed offset from the beginning of the instruction following the current instruction.

Control can only be transferred to the first of these prefixes if the target instruction has one or more prefix codes. Control transfers into and out of **try**, **catch**, **filter**, and **finally** blocks cannot be performed by this instruction.

The following **Emit** constructor overload can use the **br** opcode:

- ILGenerator.Emit(OpCode, Label)

Requirements

Platforms: Windows 98, Windows NT 4.0, Windows Millennium Edition, Windows 2000, Windows XP Home Edition, Windows XP Professional, Windows .NET Server family

OpCodes.Break Field

Signals the Common Language Infrastructure (CLI) to inform the debugger that a break point has been tripped.

```
[Visual Basic]
Public Shared ReadOnly Break As OpCode
[C#]
public static readonly OpCode Break;
[C++]
public: static OpCode Break;
[JScript]
public static var Break : OpCode;
```

Remarks

The following table lists the instruction's hexadecimal and Microsoft Intermediate Language (MSIL) assembly format, along with a brief reference summary:

Format	Assembly Format	Description
01	break	inform a debugger that a breakpoint has been reached.

No evaluation stack behaviors are performed by this operation.

The **break** instruction is for debugging support. It signals the CLI to inform the debugger that a break point has been tripped. It has no other effect on the interpreter state.

The **break** instruction has the smallest possible instruction size enabling code patching with a break point and generating minimal disturbance to the surrounding code.

The **break** instruction can trap to a debugger, do nothing, or raise a security exception. The exact behavior is implementation-defined.

The following **Emit** constructor overload can use the **break** opcode:

- ILGenerator.Emit(OpCode)

Requirements

Platforms: Windows 98, Windows NT 4.0, Windows Millennium Edition, Windows 2000, Windows XP Home Edition, Windows XP Professional, Windows .NET Server family

OpCodes.Brfalse Field

Transfers control to a target instruction if *value* is **false**, a null reference (**Nothing** in Visual Basic), or zero.

```
[Visual Basic]
Public Shared ReadOnly Brfalse As OpCode
[C#]
public static readonly OpCode Brfalse;
```

```
[C++]
public: static OpCode Brfalse;
[JScript]
public static var Brfalse : OpCode;
```

Remarks

The following table lists the instruction's hexadecimal and Microsoft Intermediate Language (MSIL) assembly format, along with a brief reference summary:

Format	Assembly Format	Description
39 < int32 >	brfalse *target* brnull *target* brzero *target*	Branches to a target instruction at the specified offset if **false**.

The stack transitional behavior, in sequential order, is:

1. *value* is pushed onto the stack by a previous operation.
2. *value* is popped from the stack; if *value* is **false**, branch to *target*.

The **brfalse** instruction (and its aliases **brnull** and **brzero**) transfers control to the specified target instruction if *value* (of type **int32**, **int64**, object reference **O**, managed pointer **&**, transient pointer *****, **natural int**) is zero (**false**). If *value* is non-zero (**true**) execution continues at the next instruction.

The target instruction is represented as a 4-byte signed offset from the beginning of the instruction following the current instruction.

Control can only be transferred to the first of these prefixes if the target instruction has one or more prefix codes. Control transfers into and out of **try**, **catch**, **filter**, and **finally** blocks cannot be performed by this instruction.

The following **Emit** constructor overload can use the **brfalse** opcode:

- ILGenerator.Emit(OpCode, Label)

Requirements

Platforms: Windows 98, Windows NT 4.0, Windows Millennium Edition, Windows 2000, Windows XP Home Edition, Windows XP Professional, Windows .NET Server family

OpCodes.Brfalse_S Field

Transfers control to a target instruction if *value* is **false**, a null reference, or zero.

```
[Visual Basic]
Public Shared ReadOnly Brfalse_S As OpCode
[C#]
public static readonly OpCode Brfalse_S;
[C++]
public: static OpCode Brfalse_S;
[JScript]
public static var Brfalse_S : OpCode;
```

Remarks

The following table lists the instruction's hexadecimal and Microsoft Intermediate Language (MSIL) assembly format, along with a brief reference summary:

Format	Assembly Format	Description
2C < int8 >	brfalse.s *target* brnull.s *target* brzero.s *target*	Branches to a target instruction at the specified offset if **false**, short form.

The stack transitional behavior, in sequential order, is:

1. *value* is pushed onto the stack by a previous operation.
2. *value* is popped from the stack; if *value* is **false**, branch to *target*.

The **brfalse.s** instruction (and its aliases **brnull** and **brzero**) transfers control to the specified target instruction if *value* (of type **int32**, **int64**, object reference **O**, managed pointer **&**, transient pointer *****, **natural int**) is zero (**false**). If *value* is non-zero (**true**) execution continues at the next instruction.

The target instruction is represented as a 1-byte signed offset from the beginning of the instruction following the current instruction.

Control can only be transferred to the first of these prefixes if the target instruction has one or more prefix codes. Control transfers into and out of **try**, **catch**, **filter**, and **finally** blocks cannot be performed by this instruction.

The following **Emit** constructor overload can use the **brfalse.s** opcode:

- ILGenerator.Emit(OpCode, Label)

Requirements

Platforms: Windows 98, Windows NT 4.0, Windows Millennium Edition, Windows 2000, Windows XP Home Edition, Windows XP Professional, Windows .NET Server family

OpCodes.Brtrue Field

Transfers control to a target instruction if *value* is **true**, not null, or non-zero.

```
[Visual Basic]
Public Shared ReadOnly Brtrue As OpCode
[C#]
public static readonly OpCode Brtrue;
[C++]
public: static OpCode Brtrue;
[JScript]
public static var Brtrue : OpCode;
```

Remarks

The following table lists the instruction's hexadecimal and Microsoft Intermediate Language (MSIL) assembly format, along with a brief reference summary:

Format	Assembly Format	Description
3A < int32 >	brtrue *target* brinst *target*	Branch to a target instruction at the specified offset if non-zero (**true**).

The stack transitional behavior, in sequential order, is:

1. *value* is pushed onto the stack by a previous operation.
2. *value* is popped from the stack; if *value* is **true**, branch to *target*.

The **brtrue** instruction transfers control to the specified target instruction if *value* (type **natural int**) is nonzero (**true**). If *value* is zero (**false**) execution continues at the next instruction.

If *value* is an object reference (type **O**) then **brinst** (an alias for **brtrue**) transfers control if it represents an instance of an object (for example, if it is not the null object reference; see **Ldnull**).

The target instruction is represented as a 4-byte signed offset from the beginning of the instruction following the current instruction.

Control can only be transferred to the first of these prefixes if the target instruction has one or more prefix codes. Control transfers into and out of **try**, **catch**, **filter**, and **finally** blocks cannot be performed by this instruction.

The following **Emit** constructor overload can use the **brtrue** opcode:

• ILGenerator.Emit(OpCode, Label)

Requirements

Platforms: Windows 98, Windows NT 4.0, Windows Millennium Edition, Windows 2000, Windows XP Home Edition, Windows XP Professional, Windows .NET Server family

OpCodes.Brtrue_S Field

Transfers control to a target instruction (short form) if *value* is **true**, not null, or non-zero.

```
[Visual Basic]
Public Shared ReadOnly Brtrue_S As OpCode
[C#]
public static readonly OpCode Brtrue_S;
[C++]
public: static OpCode Brtrue_S;
[JScript]
public static var Brtrue_S : OpCode;
```

Remarks

The following table lists the instruction's hexadecimal and Microsoft Intermediate Language (MSIL) assembly format, along with a brief reference summary:

Format	Assembly Format	Description
2D < **int8** >	brtrue.s *target* brinst.s *target*	Branch to a target instruction at the specified offset if non-zero (**true**), short form.

The stack transitional behavior, in sequential order, is:

1. *value* is pushed onto the stack by a previous operation.
2. *value* is popped from the stack; if *value* is **true**, branch to *target*.

The **brtrue.s** instruction transfers control to the specified target instruction if *value* (type **natural int**) is nonzero (**true**). If *value* is zero (**false**) execution continues at the next instruction.

If *value* is an object reference (type **O**) then **brinst** (an alias for **brtrue**) transfers control if it represents an instance of an object (for example, if it is not the null object reference; see **Ldnull**).

The target instruction is represented as a 1-byte signed offset from the beginning of the instruction following the current instruction.

Control can only be transferred to the first of these prefixes if the target instruction has one or more prefix codes. Control transfers into and out of **try**, **catch**, **filter**, and **finally** blocks cannot be performed by this instruction.

The following **Emit** constructor overload can use the **brtrue.s** opcode:

• ILGenerator.Emit(OpCode, Label)

Requirements

Platforms: Windows 98, Windows NT 4.0, Windows Millennium Edition, Windows 2000, Windows XP Home Edition, Windows XP Professional, Windows .NET Server family

OpCodes.Br_S Field

Unconditionally transfers control to a target instruction (short form).

```
[Visual Basic]
Public Shared ReadOnly Br_S As OpCode
[C#]
public static readonly OpCode Br_S;
[C++]
public: static OpCode Br_S;
[JScript]
public static var Br_S : OpCode;
```

Remarks

The following table lists the instruction's hexadecimal and Microsoft Intermediate Language (MSIL) assembly format, along with a brief reference summary:

Format	Assembly Format	Description
2B < **int8** >	br.s *target*	Branches to a target instruction at the specified offset, short form.

No evaluation stack behaviors are performed by this operation.

The **br.s** instruction unconditionally transfers control to a target instruction. The target instruction is represented as a 1-byte signed offset from the beginning of the instruction following the current instruction.

Control can only be transferred to the first of these prefixes if the target instruction has one or more prefix codes. Control transfers into and out of **try**, **catch**, **filter**, and **finally** blocks cannot be performed by this instruction.

The following **Emit** constructor overload can use the **br.s** opcode:

• ILGenerator.Emit(OpCode, Label)

Requirements

Platforms: Windows 98, Windows NT 4.0, Windows Millennium Edition, Windows 2000, Windows XP Home Edition, Windows XP Professional, Windows .NET Server family

OpCodes.Call Field

Calls the method indicated by the passed method descriptor.

```
[Visual Basic]
Public Shared ReadOnly Call As OpCode
[C#]
public static readonly OpCode Call;
[C++]
public: static OpCode Call;
[JScript]
public static var Call : OpCode;
```

Remarks

The following table lists the instruction's hexadecimal and Microsoft Intermediate Language (MSIL) assembly format, along with a brief reference summary:

Format	Assembly Format	Description
28 < **T** >	call *methodDesc*	Call the method described by *methodDesc*.

The stack transitional behavior, in sequential order, is:

1. Method arguments *arg1* through *argN* are pushed onto the stack.
2. Method arguments *arg1* through *argN* are popped from the stack; the method call is performed with these arguments and control is transferred to the method referred to by the method descriptor. When complete, a return value is generated by the callee method and sent to the caller.
3. The return value is pushed onto the stack.

The **call** instruction calls the method indicated by the method descriptor passed with the instruction. The method descriptor is a metadata token that indicates the method to call and the number, type, and order of the arguments that have been placed on the stack to be passed to that method as well as the calling convention to be used. The **call** instruction can be immediately preceded by a **tail** (**Tailcall**) prefix instruction to specify that the current method state should be released before transferring control. If the call transfers control to a method of higher trust than the origin method, the stack frame is not released. Instead, the execution continues silently as if the **tail** had not been supplied. The metadata token carries sufficient information to determine whether the call is to a static method, an instance method, a virtual method, or a global function. In all of these cases the destination address is determined entirely from the method descriptor (contrast this with the **Callvirt** instruction for calling virtual methods, where the destination address also depends upon the runtime type of the instance reference pushed before the **Callvirt**).

The arguments are placed on the stack in left-to-right order. That is, the first argument is computed and placed on the stack, then the second argument, then the third, until all necessary arguments are atop the stack in descending order. There are three important special cases:

1. Calls to an instance (or virtual) method must push that instance reference before any of the user-visible arguments. The instance reference must not be a null reference. The signature carried in the metadata does not contain an entry in the parameter list for the **this** pointer; instead, it uses a bit to indicate whether the method requires passing the **this** pointer.

2. It is valid to call a virtual method using **call** (rather than **callvirt**); this indicates that the method is to be resolved using the class specified by method rather than as specified dynamically from the object being invoked.

3. Note that a delegate's **Invoke** method can be called with either the **call** or **callvirt** instruction.

SecurityException may be thrown if system security does not grant the caller access to the called method. The security check may occur when the Microsoft Intermediate Language (MSIL) instructions are converted to native code rather than at runtime.

The following **Emit** constructor overload can use the **call** opcode:

- ILGenerator.Emit(OpCode, MethodInfo)
- ILGenerator.EmitCall(OpCode, MethodInfo, Type[])

Requirements

Platforms: Windows 98, Windows NT 4.0, Windows Millennium Edition, Windows 2000, Windows XP Home Edition, Windows XP Professional, Windows .NET Server family

OpCodes.Calli Field

Calls the method indicated on the evaluation stack (as a pointer to an entry point) with arguments described by a calling convention.

```
[Visual Basic]
Public Shared ReadOnly Calli As OpCode
[C#]
public static readonly OpCode Calli;
[C++]
public: static OpCode Calli;
[JScript]
public static var Calli : OpCode;
```

Remarks

The following table lists the instruction's hexadecimal and Microsoft Intermediate Language (MSIL) assembly format, along with a brief reference summary:

Format	Assembly Format	Description
29 < **T** >	calli *callSiteDescr*	Calls the method pointed to with arguments described by the calling convention.

The stack transitional behavior, in sequential order, is:

1. Method arguments *arg1* through *argN* are pushed onto the stack.
2. The method entry pointer is pushed onto the stack.
3. Method arguments *arg1* through *argN* and the method entry pointer are popped from the stack; the call to the method is performed. When complete, a return value is generated by the callee method and sent to the caller.
4. The return value is pushed onto the stack.

The **calli** instruction calls the method entry pointer with the arguments *arg1* through *argN*. The types of these arguments are described by the specific calling convention (*callSiteDesc*). The **calli** instruction may be immediately preceded by a **tail** prefix (**Tailcall**) to specify that the current method state should be released before transferring control. If the call would transfer control to a method of higher trust than the origin method the stack frame will not be released; instead, the execution will continue silently as if the **tail** had not been supplied.

The method entry pointer is assumed to be a specific pointer to native code (of the target machine) that can be legitimately called with the arguments described by the calling convention (a metadata token for a stand-alone signature). Such a pointer can be created using the **Ldftn** or **Ldvirtftn** instructions, or passed in from native code.

The calling convention is not checked dynamically, so code that uses a **calli** instruction does not work correctly if the destination does not actually use the specified calling convention.

The arguments are placed on the stack in left-to-right order. That is, the first argument is computed and placed on the stack, then the second argument, then the third, until all necessary arguments are atop the stack in descending order. The argument-building code sequence for an instance or virtual method must push that instance reference (which must not be a null reference) before any of the user-visible arguments.

SecurityException may be thrown if the system security does not grant the caller access to the called method. The security check can occur when the Microsoft Intermediate Language (MSIL) instructions are converted to native code rather than at runtime.

The following **EmitCalli** methods can be used to perform a **calli** instruction on the stack. Note that **calli** should be called through the below methods rather than using the **Emit** class to place the instruction directly on the stack.

- ILGenerator.EmitCalli(Opcode, CallingConventions, Type, Type[], Type[]) for calls using a managed calling convention.
- ILGenerator.EmitCalli(Opcode, CallingConvention, Type, Type[]) for calls using an unmanaged calling convention.

Requirements

Platforms: Windows 98, Windows NT 4.0, Windows Millennium Edition, Windows 2000, Windows XP Home Edition, Windows XP Professional, Windows .NET Server family

OpCodes.Callvirt Field

Calls a late-bound method on an object, pushing the return value onto the evaluation stack.

```
[Visual Basic]
Public Shared ReadOnly Callvirt As OpCode
[C#]
public static readonly OpCode Callvirt;
[C++]
public: static OpCode Callvirt;
[JScript]
public static var Callvirt : OpCode;
```

Remarks

The following table lists the instruction's hexadecimal and Microsoft Intermediate Language (MSIL) assembly format, along with a brief reference summary:

Format	Assembly Format	Description
6F < **T** >	callvirt *method*	Calls a specific method associated with *obj*.

The stack transitional behavior, in sequential order, is:

1. An object reference *obj* is pushed onto the stack.
2. Method arguments *arg1* through *argN* are pushed onto the stack.
3. Method arguments *arg1* through *argN* and the object reference *obj* are popped from the stack; the method call is performed with these arguments and control is transferred to the method in *obj* referred to by the method metadata token. When complete, a return value is generated by the callee method and sent to the caller.
4. The return value is pushed onto the stack.

The **callvirt** instruction calls a late-bound method on an object. That is, the method is chosen based on the runtime type of *obj* rather than the compile-time class visible in the method pointer. **Callvirt** can be used to call both virtual and instance methods. The **callvirt** instruction may be immediately preceded by a **tail** (**Tailcall**) prefix to specify that the current stack frame should be released before transferring control. If the call would transfer control to a method of higher trust than the original method the stack frame will not be released.

The method metadata token provides the name, class and signature of the method to call. The class associated with *obj* is the class of which it is an instance. If the class defines a non-static method that matches the indicated method name and signature, this method is called. Otherwise all classes in the base class chain of this class are checked in order. It is an error if no method is found.

Callvirt pops the object and the associated arguments off the evaluation stack before calling the method. If the method has a return value, it is pushed on the stack upon method completion. On the callee side, the *obj* parameter is accessed as argument 0, *arg1* as argument 1, and so on.

The arguments are placed on the stack in left-to-right order. That is, the first argument is computed and placed on the stack, then the second argument, then the third, until all necessary arguments are atop the stack in descending order. The instance reference *obj* (always required for **callvirt**) must be pushed before any of the user-visible arguments. The signature (carried in the metadata token) need not contain an entry in the parameter list for the this pointer.

Note that a virtual method can also be called using the **Call** instruction.

MissingMethodException is thrown if a non-static method with the indicated name and signature could not be found in the class associated with *obj* or any of its base classes. This is typically detected when Microsoft Intermediate Language (MSIL) instructions are converted to native code, rather than at runtime.

NullReferenceException is thrown if obj is null.

SecurityException is thrown if system security does not grant the caller access to the called method. The security check may occur when the CIL is converted to native code rather than at runtime.

The following **Emit** constructor overload can use the **callvirt** opcode:

- ILGenerator.Emit(OpCode, MethodInfo)
- ILGenerator.EmitCall(OpCode, MethodInfo, Type[])

Requirements

Platforms: Windows 98, Windows NT 4.0, Windows Millennium Edition, Windows 2000, Windows XP Home Edition, Windows XP Professional, Windows .NET Server family

OpCodes.Castclass Field

Attempts to cast an object passed by reference to the specified class.

```
[Visual Basic]
Public Shared ReadOnly Castclass As OpCode
[C#]
public static readonly OpCode Castclass;
[C++]
public: static OpCode Castclass;
[JScript]
public static var Castclass : OpCode;
```

Remarks

The following table lists the instruction's hexadecimal and Microsoft Intermediate Language (MSIL) assembly format, along with a brief reference summary:

Format	Assembly Format	Description
74 < **T** >	castclass *class*	Casts an object to a new object of type *class*.

The stack transitional behavior, in sequential order, is:

1. An object reference is pushed onto the stack.
2. The object reference is popped from the stack; the referenced object is cast as the specified *class*.
3. If successful, a new object reference is pushed onto the stack.

The **castclass** instruction attempts to cast the object reference (type **O**) atop the stack to a specified class. The new class is specified by a metadata token indicating the desired class. If the class of the object on the top of the stack does not implement the new class (assuming the new class is an interface) and is not a derived class of the new class then an **InvalidCastException** is thrown. If the object reference is a null reference, **castclass** succeeds and returns the new object as a null reference.

InvalidCastException is thrown if obj cannot be cast to class.

TypeLoadException is thrown if class cannot be found. This is typically detected when a Microsoft Intermediate Language (MSIL)instruction is converted to native code rather than at runtime.

The following **Emit** constructor overload can use the **castclass** opcode:

- ILGenerator.Emit(OpCode, Type)

Requirements

Platforms: Windows 98, Windows NT 4.0, Windows Millennium Edition, Windows 2000, Windows XP Home Edition, Windows XP Professional, Windows .NET Server family

OpCodes.Ceq Field

Compares two values. If they are equal, the integer value 1 (**int32**) is pushed onto the evaluation stack; otherwise 0 (**int32**) is pushed onto the evaluation stack.

```
[Visual Basic]
Public Shared ReadOnly Ceq As OpCode
[C#]
public static readonly OpCode Ceq;
[C++]
public: static OpCode Ceq;
[JScript]
public static var Ceq : OpCode;
```

Remarks

The following table lists the instruction's hexadecimal and Microsoft Intermediate Language (MSIL) assembly format, along with a brief reference summary:

Format	Assembly Format	Description
FE 01	ceq	Pushes 1 if *value1* equals *value2*; else pushes 0.

The stack transitional behavior, in sequential order, is:

1. *value1* is pushed onto the stack.
2. *value2* is pushed onto the stack.
3. *value2* and *value1* are popped from the stack; *value1* is added to *value2*.
4. The result is pushed onto the stack.

The **ceq** instruction compares *value1* and *value2*. If *value1* is equal to *value2*, then 1 (of type **int32**) is pushed on the stack. Otherwise 0 (of type **int32**) is pushed on the stack.

For floating-point number, **ceq** will return 0 if the numbers are unordered (either or both are NaN). The infinite values are equal to themselves.

The following **Emit** constructor overload can use the **ceq** opcode:

- ILGenerator.Emit(OpCode)

Requirements

Platforms: Windows 98, Windows NT 4.0, Windows Millennium Edition, Windows 2000, Windows XP Home Edition, Windows XP Professional, Windows .NET Server family

OpCodes.Cgt Field

Compares two values. If the first value is greater than the second, the integer value 1 (**int32**) is pushed onto the evaluation stack; otherwise 0 (**int32**) is pushed onto the evaluation stack.

```
[Visual Basic]
Public Shared ReadOnly Cgt As OpCode
[C#]
public static readonly OpCode Cgt;
[C++]
public: static OpCode Cgt;
[JScript]
public static var Cgt : OpCode;
```

Remarks

The following table lists the instruction's hexadecimal and Microsoft Intermediate Language (MSIL) assembly format, along with a brief reference summary:

Format	Assembly Format	Description
FE 02	cgt	Pushes 1 if *value1* is greater than *value2*; else pushes 0.

The stack transitional behavior, in sequential order, is:

1. *value1* is pushed onto the stack.
2. *value2* is pushed onto the stack.
3. *value2* and *value1* are popped from the stack; **cgt** tests if *value1* is greater than *value2*.
4. If *value1* is greater than *value2*, 1 is pushed onto the stack; otherwise 0 is pushed onto the stack.

The **cgt** instruction compares *value1* and *value2*. If *value1* is strictly greater than *value2*, then an **int32** value of 1 is pushed on the stack. Otherwise, an **int32** value of 0 is pushed on the stack.

- For floating-point numbers, **cgt** returns 0 if the numbers are unordered (that is, if one or both of the arguments are NaN).

The following **Emit** constructor overload can use the **cgt** opcode:

- ILGenerator.Emit(OpCode)

Requirements

Platforms: Windows 98, Windows NT 4.0, Windows Millennium Edition, Windows 2000, Windows XP Home Edition, Windows XP Professional, Windows .NET Server family

OpCodes.Cgt_Un Field

Compares two unsigned or unordered values. If the first value is greater than the second, the integer value 1 (**int32**) is pushed onto the evaluation stack; otherwise 0 (**int32**) is pushed onto the evaluation stack.

```
[Visual Basic]
Public Shared ReadOnly Cgt_Un As OpCode
[C#]
public static readonly OpCode Cgt_Un;
[C++]
public: static OpCode Cgt_Un;
[JScript]
public static var Cgt_Un : OpCode;
```

Remarks

The following table lists the instruction's hexadecimal and Microsoft Intermediate Language (MSIL) assembly format, along with a brief reference summary:

Format	Assembly Format	Description
FE 03	cgt.un	Pushes 1 if *value1* is greater than *value2*; else pushes 0 (unsigned values).

The stack transitional behavior, in sequential order, is:

1. *value1* is pushed onto the stack.
2. *value2* is pushed onto the stack.
3. *value2* and *value1* are popped from the stack; **cgt.un** tests if *value1* is greater than *value2*.
4. If *value1* is greater than *value2*, 1 is pushed onto the stack; otherwise 0 is pushed onto the stack.

An **int32** value of 1 is pushed on the stack if any of the following is **true**:For floating-point numbers, *value1* is not ordered with respect to *value2*.

For integer values, *value1* is strictly greater than *value2* when considered as unsigned numbers.

Otherwise an **int32** value of 0 is pushed on the stack.

The following **Emit** constructor overload can use the **cgt.un** opcode:

- ILGenerator.Emit(OpCode)

Requirements

Platforms: Windows 98, Windows NT 4.0, Windows Millennium Edition, Windows 2000, Windows XP Home Edition, Windows XP Professional, Windows .NET Server family

OpCodes.Ckfinite Field

Throws **ArithmeticException** if value is not a finite number.

```
[Visual Basic]
Public Shared ReadOnly Ckfinite As OpCode
[C#]
public static readonly OpCode Ckfinite;
[C++]
public: static OpCode Ckfinite;
[JScript]
public static var Ckfinite : OpCode;
```

Remarks

The following table lists the instruction's hexadecimal and Microsoft Intermediate Language (MSIL) assembly format, along with a brief reference summary:

Format	Assembly Format	Description
C3	ckfinite	throw **ArithmeticException** if value is not a finite number.

The stack transitional behavior, in sequential order, is:

1. *value* is pushed onto the stack..
2. *value* is popped from the stack and the **ckfinite** instruction is performed on it.
3. *value* is pushed back onto the stack if no exception is thrown.

The **ckfinite instruction** throws **ArithmeticException** if *value* (a floating-point number) is either a "not a number" value (NaN) or a **+-** infinity value. **Ckfinite** leaves the value on the stack if no exception is thrown. Execution is unspecified if *value* is not a floating-point number.

ArithmeticException is thrown if *value* is not a 'normal' number.

Note that a special exception or a derived class of **ArithmeticException** may be more appropriate, passing the incorrect value to the exception handler.

The following **Emit** constructor overload can use the **ckfinite** opcode:

- ILGenerator.Emit(OpCode)

Requirements

Platforms: Windows 98, Windows NT 4.0, Windows Millennium Edition, Windows 2000, Windows XP Home Edition, Windows XP Professional, Windows .NET Server family

OpCodes.Clt Field

Compares two values. If the first value is less than the second, the integer value 1 (**int32**) is pushed onto the evaluation stack; otherwise 0 (**int32**) is pushed onto the evaluation stack.

```
[Visual Basic]
Public Shared ReadOnly Clt As OpCode
[C#]
public static readonly OpCode Clt;
[C++]
public: static OpCode Clt;
[JScript]
public static var Clt : OpCode;
```

Remarks

The following table lists the instruction's hexadecimal and Microsoft Intermediate Language (MSIL) assembly format, along with a brief reference summary:

Format	Assembly Format	Description
FE 04	clt	Pushes 1 if *value1* is less than *value2*; else pushes 0.

The stack transitional behavior, in sequential order, is: *value1* is pushed onto the stack.

1. *value2* is pushed onto the stack.
2. *value2* and *value1* are popped from the stack; **clt** tests if *value1* is less than *value2*.

3. If *value1* is less than *value2*, 1 is pushed onto the stack; otherwise 0 is pushed onto the stack.

The **clt** instruction compares *value1* and *value2*. If *value1* is strictly less than *value2*, then an **int32** value of 1 is pushed on the stack. Otherwise, an **int32** value of 0 is pushed on the stack.

- For floating-point numbers, **clt** returns 0 if the numbers are unordered (that is, if one or both of the arguments are NaN).

The following **Emit** constructor overload can use the **clt** opcode:

- ILGenerator.Emit(OpCode)

Requirements

Platforms: Windows 98, Windows NT 4.0, Windows Millennium Edition, Windows 2000, Windows XP Home Edition, Windows XP Professional, Windows .NET Server family

OpCodes.Clt_Un Field

Compares the unsigned or unordered values *value1* and *value2*. If *value1* is less than *value2*, then the integer value 1 (**int32**) is pushed onto the evaluation stack; otherwise 0 (**int32**) is pushed onto the evaluation stack.

```
[Visual Basic]
Public Shared ReadOnly Clt_Un As OpCode
[C#]
public static readonly OpCode Clt_Un;
[C++]
public: static OpCode Clt_Un;
[JScript]
public static var Clt_Un : OpCode;
```

Remarks

The following table lists the instruction's hexadecimal and Microsoft Intermediate Language (MSIL) assembly format, along with a brief reference summary:

Format	Assembly Format	Description
FE 03	clt.un	Pushes 1 if *value1* is less than *value2*; else pushes 0 (unsigned values).

The stack transitional behavior, in sequential order, is:

1. *value1* is pushed onto the stack.
2. *value2* is pushed onto the stack.
3. *value2* and *value1* are popped from the stack; **clt.un** tests if *value1* is less than *value2*.
4. If *value1* is less than *value2*, 1 is pushed onto the stack; otherwise 0 is pushed onto the stack.

The **clt.un** instruction compares *value1* and *value2*. An **int32** value of 1 is pushed on the stack if any of the following is true:

- *value1* is strictly less than *value2* (as for **clt**).
- For floating-point numbers, *value1* is not ordered with respect to *value2*.
- For integer values, *value1* is strictly less than *value2* when considered as unsigned numbers.

Otherwise, an **int32** value of 0 is pushed on the stack.

The following **Emit** constructor overload can use the **clt.un** opcode:

- ILGenerator.Emit(OpCode)

Requirements

Platforms: Windows 98, Windows NT 4.0, Windows Millennium Edition, Windows 2000, Windows XP Home Edition, Windows XP Professional, Windows .NET Server family

OpCodes.Conv_I Field

Converts the value on top of the evaluation stack to **natural int**.

```
[Visual Basic]
Public Shared ReadOnly Conv_I As OpCode
[C#]
public static readonly OpCode Conv_I;
[C++]
public: static OpCode Conv_I;
[JScript]
public static var Conv_I : OpCode;
```

Remarks

The following table lists the instruction's hexadecimal and Microsoft Intermediate Language (MSIL) assembly format, along with a brief reference summary:

Format	Assembly Format	Description
D3	conv.i	Convert to **natural int**, pushing **natural int** on stack.

The stack transitional behavior, in sequential order, is:

1. *value* is pushed onto the stack.
2. *value* is popped from the stack and the conversion operation is attempted.
3. If the conversion is successful, the resulting value is pushed onto the stack.

The **conv.i** opcode converts the *value* on top of the stack to the type specified in the opcode, and leave that converted value on the top of the stack. Integer values of less than 4 bytes are extended to **int32** when they are loaded onto the evaluation stack (unless **conv.i** or **conv.u** is used, in which case the result is also **natural int**). Floating-point values are converted to the **F** type.

Conversion from floating-point numbers to integer values truncates the number toward zero. When converting from an **float64** to an **float32**, precision can be lost. If *value* is too large to fit in a **float32** (**F**), positive infinity (if *value* is positive) or negative infinity (if *value* is negative) is returned. If overflow occurs converting one integer type to another, the high order bits are truncated. If the result is smaller than an **int32**, the value is sign-extended to fill the slot.

If overflow occurs converting a floating-point type to an integer the value returned is unspecified.

No exceptions are ever thrown when using this field. See **Conv_Ovf_I** and **Conv_Ovf_I_Un** for equivalent instructions that will throw an exception when the result type can not properly represent the result value.

The following **Emit** constructor overload can use the **conv.i** opcode:

- ILGenerator.Emit(OpCode)

Requirements

Platforms: Windows 98, Windows NT 4.0, Windows Millennium Edition, Windows 2000, Windows XP Home Edition, Windows XP Professional, Windows .NET Server family

OpCodes.Conv_I1 Field

Converts the value on top of the evaluation stack to **int8**, then extends (pads) it to **int32**.

```
[Visual Basic]
Public Shared ReadOnly Conv_I1 As OpCode
[C#]
public static readonly OpCode Conv_I1;
[C++]
public: static OpCode Conv_I1;
[JScript]
public static var Conv_I1 : OpCode;
```

Remarks

The following table lists the instruction's hexadecimal and Microsoft Intermediate Language (MSIL) assembly format, along with a brief reference summary:

Format	Assembly Format	Description
67	conv.i1	Convert to **int8**, pushing **int32** on stack.

The stack transitional behavior, in sequential order, is:

1. *value* is pushed onto the stack.
2. *value* is popped from the stack and the conversion operation is attempted.
3. If the conversion is successful, the resulting value is pushed onto the stack.

The **conv.i1** opcode converts the *value* on top of the stack to the type specified in the opcode, and leave that converted value on the top of the stack. Integer values of less than 4 bytes are extended to **int32** when they are loaded onto the evaluation stack (unless **conv.i** or **conv.u** is used, in which case the result is also **natural int**). Floating-point values are converted to the **F** type.

Conversion from floating-point numbers to integer values truncates the number toward zero. When converting from an **float64** to an **float32**, precision can be lost. If *value* is too large to fit in a **float32** (**F**), positive infinity (if *value* is positive) or negative infinity (if *value* is negative) is returned. If overflow occurs converting one integer type to another, the high order bits are truncated. If the result is smaller than an **int32**, the value is sign-extended to fill the slot.

If overflow occurs converting a floating-point type to an integer the value returned is unspecified.

No exceptions are ever thrown when using this field. See **Conv_Ovf_I1** and **Conv_Ovf_I1_Un** for equivalent instructions that will throw an exception when the result type can not properly represent the result value.

The following **Emit** constructor overload can use the **conv.i1** opcode:

• ILGenerator.Emit(OpCode)

Requirements

Platforms: Windows 98, Windows NT 4.0, Windows Millennium Edition, Windows 2000, Windows XP Home Edition, Windows XP Professional, Windows .NET Server family

OpCodes.Conv_I2 Field

Converts the value on top of the evaluation stack to **int16**, then extends (pads) it to **int32**.

```
[Visual Basic]
Public Shared ReadOnly Conv_I2 As OpCode
[C#]
public static readonly OpCode Conv_I2;
[C++]
public: static OpCode Conv_I2;
[JScript]
public static var Conv_I2 : OpCode;
```

Remarks

The following table lists the instruction's hexadecimal and Microsoft Intermediate Language (MSIL) assembly format, along with a brief reference summary:

Format	Assembly Format	Description
68	conv.i2	Convert to **int16**, pushing **int32** on stack.

The stack transitional behavior, in sequential order, is:

1. *value* is pushed onto the stack.
2. *value* is popped from the stack and the conversion operation is attempted.
3. If the conversion is successful, the resulting value is pushed onto the stack.

The **conv.i2** opcode converts the *value* on top of the stack to the type specified in the opcode, and leave that converted value on the top of the stack. Integer values of less than 4 bytes are extended to **int32** when they are loaded onto the evaluation stack (unless **conv.i** or **conv.u** is used, in which case the result is also **natural int**). Floating-point values are converted to the **F** type.

Conversion from floating-point numbers to integer values truncates the number toward zero. When converting from an **float64** to an **float32**, precision can be lost. If *value* is too large to fit in a **float32** (**F**), positive infinity (if *value* is positive) or negative infinity (if *value* is negative) is returned. If overflow occurs converting one integer type to another, the high order bits are truncated. If the result is smaller than an **int32**, the value is sign-extended to fill the slot.

If overflow occurs converting a floating-point type to an integer the value returned is unspecified.

No exceptions are ever thrown when using this field. See **Conv_Ovf_I2** and **Conv_Ovf_I2_Un** for equivalent instructions that will throw an exception when the result type can not properly represent the result value.

The following **Emit** constructor overload can use the **conv.i2** opcode:

• ILGenerator.Emit(OpCode)

Requirements

Platforms: Windows 98, Windows NT 4.0, Windows Millennium Edition, Windows 2000, Windows XP Home Edition, Windows XP Professional, Windows .NET Server family

OpCodes.Conv_I4 Field

Converts the value on top of the evaluation stack to **int32**.

```
[Visual Basic]
Public Shared ReadOnly Conv_I4 As OpCode
[C#]
public static readonly OpCode Conv_I4;
[C++]
public: static OpCode Conv_I4;
[JScript]
public static var Conv_I4 : OpCode;
```

Remarks

The following table lists the instruction's hexadecimal and Microsoft Intermediate Language (MSIL) assembly format, along with a brief reference summary:

Format	Assembly Format	Description
69	conv.i4	Convert to **int32**, pushing **int32** on stack.

The stack transitional behavior, in sequential order, is:

1. *value* is pushed onto the stack.
2. *value* is popped from the stack and the conversion operation is attempted.
3. If the conversion is successful, the resulting value is pushed onto the stack.

The **conv.i4** opcode converts the *value* on top of the stack to the type specified in the opcode, and leave that converted value on the top of the stack. Integer values of less than 4 bytes are extended to **int32** when they are loaded onto the evaluation stack (unless **conv.i** or **conv.u** is used, in which case the result is also **natural int**). Floating-point values are converted to the **F** type.

Conversion from floating-point numbers to integer values truncates the number toward zero. When converting from an **float64** to an **float32**, precision can be lost. If *value* is too large to fit in a **float32** (**F**), positive infinity (if *value* is positive) or negative infinity (if *value* is negative) is returned. If overflow occurs converting one integer type to another, the high order bits are truncated. If the result is smaller than an **int32**, the value is sign-extended to fill the slot.

If overflow occurs converting a floating-point type to an integer the value returned is unspecified.

No exceptions are ever thrown when using this field. See **Conv_Ovf_I4** and **Conv_Ovf_I4_Un** for equivalent instructions that will throw an exception when the result type can not properly represent the result value.

The following **Emit** constructor overload can use the **conv.i4** opcode:

- ILGenerator.Emit(OpCode)

Requirements

Platforms: Windows 98, Windows NT 4.0, Windows Millennium Edition, Windows 2000, Windows XP Home Edition, Windows XP Professional, Windows .NET Server family

OpCodes.Conv_I8 Field

Converts the value on top of the evaluation stack to **int64**.

```
[Visual Basic]
Public Shared ReadOnly Conv_I8 As OpCode
[C#]
public static readonly OpCode Conv_I8;
[C++]
public: static OpCode Conv_I8;
[JScript]
public static var Conv_I8 : OpCode;
```

Remarks

The following table lists the instruction's hexadecimal and Microsoft Intermediate Language (MSIL) assembly format, along with a brief reference summary:

Format	Assembly Format	Description
6A	conv.i8	Convert to **int64**, pushing **int64** on stack.

The stack transitional behavior, in sequential order, is:

1. *value* is pushed onto the stack.
2. *value* is popped from the stack and the conversion operation is attempted.
3. If the conversion is successful, the resulting value is pushed onto the stack.

The **conv.i8** opcode converts the *value* on top of the stack to the type specified in the opcode, and leave that converted value on the top of the stack. Integer values of less than 4 bytes are extended to **int32** when they are loaded onto the evaluation stack (unless **conv.i** or **conv.u** is used, in which case the result is also **natural int**). Floating-point values are converted to the **F** type.

Conversion from floating-point numbers to integer values truncates the number toward zero. When converting from an **float64** to an **float32**, precision can be lost. If *value* is too large to fit in a **float32** (**F**), positive infinity (if *value* is positive) or negative infinity (if *value* is negative) is returned. If overflow occurs converting one integer type to another, the high order bits are truncated. If the result is smaller than an **int32**, the value is sign-extended to fill the slot.

If overflow occurs converting a floating-point type to an integer the value returned is unspecified.

No exceptions are ever thrown when using this field. See **Conv_Ovf_I8** and **Conv_Ovf_I8_Un** for equivalent instructions that will throw an exception when the result type can not properly represent the result value.

The following **Emit** constructor overload can use the **conv.i8** opcode:

- ILGenerator.Emit(OpCode)

Requirements

Platforms: Windows 98, Windows NT 4.0, Windows Millennium Edition, Windows 2000, Windows XP Home Edition, Windows XP Professional, Windows .NET Server family

OpCodes.Conv_Ovf_I Field

Converts the signed value on top of the evaluation stack to signed **natural int**, throwing **OverflowException** on overflow.

```
[Visual Basic]
Public Shared ReadOnly Conv_Ovf_I As OpCode
```

```
[C#]
public static readonly OpCode Conv_Ovf_I;
[C++]
public: static OpCode Conv_Ovf_I;
[JScript]
public static var Conv_Ovf_I : OpCode;
```

Remarks

The following table lists the instruction's hexadecimal and Microsoft Intermediate Language (MSIL) assembly format, along with a brief reference summary:

Format	Assembly Format	Description
D4	conv.ovf.i	Convert to a **natural int** (on the stack as **natural int**) and throw an exception on overflow.

The stack transitional behavior, in sequential order, is:

1. *value* is pushed onto the stack.
2. *value* is popped from the stack and the conversion operation is attempted. If overflow occurs, an exception is thrown.
3. If the conversion is successful, the resulting value is pushed onto the stack.

The **conv.ovf.i** opcode converts the *value* on top of the stack to the type specified in the opcode, and places that converted value on the top of the stack. If the value is too large or too small to be represented by the target type, an exception is thrown.

Conversions from floating-point numbers to integer values truncate the number toward zero. Note that integer values of less than 4 bytes are extended to **int32** when they are loaded onto the evaluation stack (unless **conv.ovf.i** or **conv.ovf.u** are used, in which case the result is also **natural int**).

OverflowException is thrown if the result can not be represented in the result type.

The following **Emit** constructor overload can use the **conv.ovf.i** opcode:

• ILGenerator.Emit(OpCode)

Requirements

Platforms: Windows 98, Windows NT 4.0, Windows Millennium Edition, Windows 2000, Windows XP Home Edition, Windows XP Professional, Windows .NET Server family

OpCodes.Conv_Ovf_I1 Field

Converts the signed value on top of the evaluation stack to signed **int8** and extends it to **int32**, throwing **OverflowException** on overflow.

```
[Visual Basic]
Public Shared ReadOnly Conv_Ovf_I1 As OpCode
[C#]
public static readonly OpCode Conv_Ovf_I1;
[C++]
public: static OpCode Conv_Ovf_I1;
[JScript]
public static var Conv_Ovf_I1 : OpCode;
```

Remarks

The following table lists the instruction's hexadecimal and Microsoft Intermediate Language (MSIL) assembly format, along with a brief reference summary:

Format	Assembly Format	Description
B3	conv.ovf.i1	Convert to an **int8** (on the stack as **int32**) and throw an exception on overflow.

The stack transitional behavior, in sequential order, is:

1. *value* is pushed onto the stack.
2. *value* is popped from the stack and the conversion operation is attempted. If overflow occurs, an exception is thrown.
3. If the conversion is successful, the resulting value is pushed onto the stack.

The **conv.ovf.i1** opcode converts the *value* on top of the stack to the type specified in the opcode, and places that converted value on the top of the stack. If the value is too large or too small to be represented by the target type, an exception is thrown.

Conversions from floating-point numbers to integer values truncate the number toward zero. Note that integer values of less than 4 bytes are extended to **int32** when they are loaded onto the evaluation stack (unless **conv.ovf.i** or **conv.ovf.u** are used, in which case the result is also **natural int**).

OverflowException is thrown if the result can not be represented in the result type.

The following **Emit** constructor overload can use the **conv.ovf.i1** opcode:

• ILGenerator.Emit(OpCode)

Requirements

Platforms: Windows 98, Windows NT 4.0, Windows Millennium Edition, Windows 2000, Windows XP Home Edition, Windows XP Professional, Windows .NET Server family

OpCodes.Conv_Ovf_I1_Un Field

Converts the unsigned value on top of the evaluation stack to signed **int8** and extends it to **int32**, throwing **OverflowException** on overflow.

```
[Visual Basic]
Public Shared ReadOnly Conv_Ovf_I1_Un As OpCode
[C#]
public static readonly OpCode Conv_Ovf_I1_Un;
[C++]
public: static OpCode Conv_Ovf_I1_Un;
[JScript]
public static var Conv_Ovf_I1_Un : OpCode;
```

Remarks

The following table lists the instruction's hexadecimal and Microsoft Intermediate Language (MSIL) assembly format, along with a brief reference summary:

Format	Assembly Format	Description
82	conv.ovf.i1.un	Converts an unsigned value to an **int8** (on the stack as **int32**) and throw an exception on overflow.

The stack transitional behavior, in sequential order, is:

1. *value* is pushed onto the stack.
2. *value* is popped from the stack and the conversion operation is attempted. If overflow occurs, an exception is thrown.
3. If the conversion is successful, the resulting value is pushed onto the stack.

The **conv.ovf.i1.un** opcode converts the *value* on top of the stack to the type specified in the opcode, and places that converted value on the top of the stack. If the value is too large or too small to be represented by the target type, an exception is thrown.

Conversions from floating-point numbers to integer values truncate the number toward zero. Note that integer values of less than 4 bytes are extended to **int32** when they are loaded onto the evaluation stack (unless **conv.ovf.i** or **conv.ovf.u** are used, in which case the result is also **natural int**).

OverflowException is thrown if the result can not be represented in the result type.

The following **Emit** constructor overload can use the **conv.ovf.i1.un** opcode:

- ILGenerator.Emit(OpCode)

Requirements

Platforms: Windows 98, Windows NT 4.0, Windows Millennium Edition, Windows 2000, Windows XP Home Edition, Windows XP Professional, Windows .NET Server family

OpCodes.Conv_Ovf_I2 Field

Converts the signed value on top of the evaluation stack to signed **int16** and extending it to **int32**, throwing **OverflowException** on overflow.

```
[Visual Basic]
Public Shared ReadOnly Conv_Ovf_I2 As OpCode
[C#]
public static readonly OpCode Conv_Ovf_I2;
[C++]
public: static OpCode Conv_Ovf_I2;
[JScript]
public static var Conv_Ovf_I2 : OpCode;
```

Remarks

The following table lists the instruction's hexadecimal and Microsoft Intermediate Language (MSIL) assembly format, along with a brief reference summary:

Format	Assembly Format	Description
B5	conv.ovf.i2	Convert to an **int16** (on the stack as **int32**) and throw an exception on overflow.

The stack transitional behavior, in sequential order, is:

1. *value* is pushed onto the stack.
2. *value* is popped from the stack and the conversion operation is attempted. If overflow occurs, an exception is thrown.
3. If the conversion is successful, the resulting value is pushed onto the stack.

The **conv.ovf.i2** opcode converts the *value* on top of the stack to the type specified in the opcode, and places that converted value on the top of the stack. If the value is too large or too small to be represented by the target type, an exception is thrown.

Conversions from floating-point numbers to integer values truncate the number toward zero. Note that integer values of less than 4 bytes are extended to **int32** when they are loaded onto the evaluation stack (unless **conv.ovf.i** or **conv.ovf.u** are used, in which case the result is also **natural int**).

OverflowException is thrown if the result can not be represented in the result type.

The following **Emit** constructor overload can use the **conv.ovf.i2** opcode:

- ILGenerator.Emit(OpCode)

Requirements

Platforms: Windows 98, Windows NT 4.0, Windows Millennium Edition, Windows 2000, Windows XP Home Edition, Windows XP Professional, Windows .NET Server family

OpCodes.Conv_Ovf_I2_Un Field

Converts the unsigned value on top of the evaluation stack to signed **int16** and extends it to **int32**, throwing **OverflowException** on overflow.

```
[Visual Basic]
Public Shared ReadOnly Conv_Ovf_I2_Un As OpCode
[C#]
public static readonly OpCode Conv_Ovf_I2_Un;
[C++]
public: static OpCode Conv_Ovf_I2_Un;
[JScript]
public static var Conv_Ovf_I2_Un : OpCode;
```

Remarks

The following table lists the instruction's hexadecimal and Microsoft Intermediate Language (MSIL) assembly format, along with a brief reference summary:

Format	Assembly Format	Description
83	conv.ovf.i2.un	Converts an unsigned value to an **int16** (on the stack as **int32**) and throw an exception on overflow.

The stack transitional behavior, in sequential order, is:

1. *value* is pushed onto the stack.
2. *value* is popped from the stack and the conversion operation is attempted. If overflow occurs, an exception is thrown.
3. If the conversion is successful, the resulting value is pushed onto the stack.

The **conv.ovf.i2.un** opcode converts the *value* on top of the stack to the type specified in the opcode, and places that converted value on the top of the stack. If the value is too large or too small to be represented by the target type, an exception is thrown.

Conversions from floating-point numbers to integer values truncate the number toward zero. Note that integer values of less than 4 bytes are extended to **int32** when they are loaded onto the evaluation stack (unless **conv.ovf.i** or **conv.ovf.u** are used, in which case the result is also **natural int**).

OverflowException is thrown if the result can not be represented in the result type.

The following **Emit** constructor overload can use the **conv.ovf.i2.un** opcode:

• ILGenerator.Emit(OpCode)

Requirements

Platforms: Windows 98, Windows NT 4.0, Windows Millennium Edition, Windows 2000, Windows XP Home Edition, Windows XP Professional, Windows .NET Server family

OpCodes.Conv_Ovf_I4 Field

Converts the signed value on top of the evaluation tack to signed **int32**, throwing **OverflowException** on overflow.

```
[Visual Basic]
Public Shared ReadOnly Conv_Ovf_I4 As OpCode
[C#]
public static readonly OpCode Conv_Ovf_I4;
[C++]
public: static OpCode Conv_Ovf_I4;
[JScript]
public static var Conv_Ovf_I4 : OpCode;
```

Remarks

The following table lists the instruction's hexadecimal and Microsoft Intermediate Language (MSIL) assembly format, along with a brief reference summary:

Format	Assembly Format	Description
B7	conv.ovf.i4	Convert to an **int32** (on the stack as **int32**) and throw an exception on overflow.

The stack transitional behavior, in sequential order, is:

1. *value* is pushed onto the stack.
2. *value* is popped from the stack and the conversion operation is attempted. If overflow occurs, an exception is thrown.
3. If the conversion is successful, the resulting value is pushed onto the stack.

The **conv.ovf.i4** opcode converts the *value* on top of the stack to the type specified in the opcode, and places that converted value on the top of the stack. If the value is too large or too small to be represented by the target type, an exception is thrown.

Conversions from floating-point numbers to integer values truncate the number toward zero. Note that integer values of less than 4 bytes are extended to **int32** when they are loaded onto the evaluation stack (unless **conv.ovf.i** or **conv.ovf.u** are used, in which case the result is also **natural int**).

OverflowException is thrown if the result can not be represented in the result type.

The following **Emit** constructor overload can use the **conv.ovf.i4** opcode:

• ILGenerator.Emit(OpCode)

Requirements

Platforms: Windows 98, Windows NT 4.0, Windows Millennium Edition, Windows 2000, Windows XP Home Edition, Windows XP Professional, Windows .NET Server family

OpCodes.Conv_Ovf_I4_Un Field

Converts the unsigned value on top of the evaluation stack to signed **int32**, throwing **OverflowException** on overflow.

```
[Visual Basic]
Public Shared ReadOnly Conv_Ovf_I4_Un As OpCode
[C#]
public static readonly OpCode Conv_Ovf_I4_Un;
[C++]
public: static OpCode Conv_Ovf_I4_Un;
[JScript]
public static var Conv_Ovf_I4_Un : OpCode;
```

Remarks

The following table lists the instruction's hexadecimal and Microsoft Intermediate Language (MSIL) assembly format, along with a brief reference summary:

Format	Assembly Format	Description
84	conv.ovf.i4.un	Converts an unsigned value to an **int32** (on the stack as **int32**) and throw an exception on overflow.

The stack transitional behavior, in sequential order, is:

1. *value* is pushed onto the stack.
2. *value* is popped from the stack and the conversion operation is attempted. If overflow occurs, an exception is thrown.
3. If the conversion is successful, the resulting value is pushed onto the stack.

The **conv.ovf.i4.un** opcode converts the *value* on top of the stack to the type specified in the opcode, and places that converted value on the top of the stack. If the value is too large or too small to be represented by the target type, an exception is thrown.

Conversions from floating-point numbers to integer values truncate the number toward zero. Note that integer values of less than 4 bytes are extended to **int32** when they are loaded onto the evaluation stack (unless **conv.ovf.i** or **conv.ovf.u** are used, in which case the result is also **natural int**).

OverflowException is thrown if the result can not be represented in the result type.

The following **Emit** constructor overload can use the **conv.ovf.i4.un** opcode:

• ILGenerator.Emit(OpCode)

Requirements

Platforms: Windows 98, Windows NT 4.0, Windows Millennium Edition, Windows 2000, Windows XP Home Edition, Windows XP Professional, Windows .NET Server family

OpCodes.Conv_Ovf_I8 Field

Converts the signed value on top of the evaluation stack to signed **int64**, throwing **OverflowException** on overflow.

```
[Visual Basic]
Public Shared ReadOnly Conv_Ovf_I8 As OpCode
[C#]
public static readonly OpCode Conv_Ovf_I8;
[C++]
public: static OpCode Conv_Ovf_I8;
```

[JScript]
```
public static var Conv_Ovf_I8 : OpCode;
```

Remarks

The following table lists the instruction's hexadecimal and Microsoft Intermediate Language (MSIL) assembly format, along with a brief reference summary:

Format	Assembly Format	Description
B9	conv.ovf.i8	Convert to an **int64** (on the stack as **int64**) and throw an exception on overflow.

The stack transitional behavior, in sequential order, is:

1. *value* is pushed onto the stack.
2. *value* is popped from the stack and the conversion operation is attempted. If overflow occurs, an exception is thrown.
3. If the conversion is successful, the resulting value is pushed onto the stack.

The **conv.ovf.i8** opcode converts the *value* on top of the stack to the type specified in the opcode, and places that converted value on the top of the stack. If the value is too large or too small to be represented by the target type, an exception is thrown.

Conversions from floating-point numbers to integer values truncate the number toward zero. Note that integer values of less than 4 bytes are extended to **int32** when they are loaded onto the evaluation stack (unless **conv.ovf.i** or **conv.ovf.u** are used, in which case the result is also **natural int**).

OverflowException is thrown if the result can not be represented in the result type.

The following **Emit** constructor overload can use the **conv.ovf.i8** opcode:

• ILGenerator.Emit(OpCode)

Requirements

Platforms: Windows 98, Windows NT 4.0, Windows Millennium Edition, Windows 2000, Windows XP Home Edition, Windows XP Professional, Windows .NET Server family

OpCodes.Conv_Ovf_I8_Un Field

Converts the unsigned value on top of the evaluation stack to signed **int64**, throwing **OverflowException** on overflow.

[Visual Basic]
```
Public Shared ReadOnly Conv_Ovf_I8_Un As OpCode
```
[C#]
```
public static readonly OpCode Conv_Ovf_I8_Un;
```
[C++]
```
public: static OpCode Conv_Ovf_I8_Un;
```
[JScript]
```
public static var Conv_Ovf_I8_Un : OpCode;
```

Remarks

The following table lists the instruction's hexadecimal and Microsoft Intermediate Language (MSIL) assembly format, along with a brief reference summary:

Format	Assembly Format	Description
85	conv.ovf.i8.un	Converts an unsigned value to an **int64** (on the stack as **int64**) and throw an exception on overflow.

The stack transitional behavior, in sequential order, is:

1. *value* is pushed onto the stack.
2. *value* is popped from the stack and the conversion operation is attempted. If overflow occurs, an exception is thrown.
3. If the conversion is successful, the resulting value is pushed onto the stack.

The **conv.ovf.i8.un** opcode converts the *value* on top of the stack to the type specified in the opcode, and places that converted value on the top of the stack. If the value is too large or too small to be represented by the target type, an exception is thrown.

Conversions from floating-point numbers to integer values truncate the number toward zero. Note that integer values of less than 4 bytes are extended to **int32** when they are loaded onto the evaluation stack (unless **conv.ovf.i** or **conv.ovf.u** are used, in which case the result is also **natural int**).

OverflowException is thrown if the result can not be represented in the result type.

The following **Emit** constructor overload can use the **conv.ovf.i8.un** opcode:

• ILGenerator.Emit(OpCode)

Requirements

Platforms: Windows 98, Windows NT 4.0, Windows Millennium Edition, Windows 2000, Windows XP Home Edition, Windows XP Professional, Windows .NET Server family

OpCodes.Conv_Ovf_I_Un Field

Converts the unsigned value on top of the evaluation stack to signed **natural int**, throwing **OverflowException** on overflow.

[Visual Basic]
```
Public Shared ReadOnly Conv_Ovf_I_Un As OpCode
```
[C#]
```
public static readonly OpCode Conv_Ovf_I_Un;
```
[C++]
```
public: static OpCode Conv_Ovf_I_Un;
```
[JScript]
```
public static var Conv_Ovf_I_Un : OpCode;
```

Remarks

The following table lists the instruction's hexadecimal and Microsoft Intermediate Language (MSIL) assembly format, along with a brief reference summary:

Format	Assembly Format	Description
8A	conv.ovf.i.un	Converts an unsigned value to a **natural int** (on the stack as **natural int**) and throw an exception on overflow.

The stack transitional behavior, in sequential order, is:

1. *value* is pushed onto the stack.

2. *value* is popped from the stack and the conversion operation is attempted. If overflow occurs, an exception is thrown.

3. If the conversion is successful, the resulting value is pushed onto the stack.

The **conv.ovf.i.un** opcode converts the *value* on top of the stack to the type specified in the opcode, and places that converted value on the top of the stack. If the value is too large or too small to be represented by the target type, an exception is thrown.

Conversions from floating-point numbers to integer values truncate the number toward zero. Note that integer values of less than 4 bytes are extended to **int32** when they are loaded onto the evaluation stack (unless **conv.ovf.i** or **conv.ovf.u** are used, in which case the result is also **natural int**).

OverflowException is thrown if the result can not be represented in the result type.

The following **Emit** constructor overload can use the **conv.ovf.i.un** opcode:

• ILGenerator.Emit(OpCode)

Requirements

Platforms: Windows 98, Windows NT 4.0, Windows Millennium Edition, Windows 2000, Windows XP Home Edition, Windows XP Professional, Windows .NET Server family

OpCodes.Conv_Ovf_U Field

Converts the signed value on top of the evaluation stack to **unsigned natural int**, throwing **OverflowException** on overflow.

```
[Visual Basic]
Public Shared ReadOnly Conv_Ovf_U As OpCode
[C#]
public static readonly OpCode Conv_Ovf_U;
[C++]
public: static OpCode Conv_Ovf_U;
[JScript]
public static var Conv_Ovf_U : OpCode;
```

Remarks

The following table lists the instruction's hexadecimal and Microsoft Intermediate Language (MSIL) assembly format, along with a brief reference summary:

Format	Assembly Format	Description
D5	conv.ovf.u	Convert to an **unsigned natural int** (on the stack as **natural int**) and throw an exception on overflow.

The stack transitional behavior, in sequential order, is:

1. *value* is pushed onto the stack.

2. *value* is popped from the stack and the conversion operation is attempted. If overflow occurs, an exception is thrown.

3. If the conversion is successful, the resulting value is pushed onto the stack.

The **conv.ovf.u** opcode converts the *value* on top of the stack to the type specified in the opcode, and places that converted value on the top of the stack. If the value is too large or too small to be represented by the target type, an exception is thrown.

Conversions from floating-point numbers to integer values truncate the number toward zero. Note that integer values of less than 4 bytes are extended to **int32** when they are loaded onto the evaluation stack (unless **conv.ovf.i** or **conv.ovf.u** are used, in which case the result is also **natural int**).

OverflowException is thrown if the result can not be represented in the result type.

The following **Emit** constructor overload can use the **conv.ovf.u** opcode:

• ILGenerator.Emit(OpCode)

Requirements

Platforms: Windows 98, Windows NT 4.0, Windows Millennium Edition, Windows 2000, Windows XP Home Edition, Windows XP Professional, Windows .NET Server family

OpCodes.Conv_Ovf_U1 Field

Converts the signed value on top of the evaluation stack to **unsigned int8** and extends it to **int32**, throwing **OverflowException** on overflow.

```
[Visual Basic]
Public Shared ReadOnly Conv_Ovf_U1 As OpCode
[C#]
public static readonly OpCode Conv_Ovf_U1;
[C++]
public: static OpCode Conv_Ovf_U1;
[JScript]
public static var Conv_Ovf_U1 : OpCode;
```

Remarks

The following table lists the instruction's hexadecimal and Microsoft Intermediate Language (MSIL) assembly format, along with a brief reference summary:

Format	Assembly Format	Description
B4	conv.ovf.u1	Convert to an **unsigned int8** (on the stack as **int32**) and throw an exception on overflow.

The stack transitional behavior, in sequential order, is:

1. *value* is pushed onto the stack.

2. *value* is popped from the stack and the conversion operation is attempted. If overflow occurs, an exception is thrown.

3. If the conversion is successful, the resulting value is pushed onto the stack.

The **conv.ovf.u1** opcode converts the *value* on top of the stack to the type specified in the opcode, and places that converted value on the top of the stack. If the value is too large or too small to be represented by the target type, an exception is thrown.

Conversions from floating-point numbers to integer values truncate the number toward zero. Note that integer values of less than 4 bytes are extended to **int32** when they are loaded onto the evaluation stack (unless **conv.ovf.i** or **conv.ovf.u** are used, in which case the result is also **natural int**).

OverflowException is thrown if the result can not be represented in the result type.

The following **Emit** constructor overload can use the **conv.ovf.u1** opcode:

• ILGenerator.Emit(OpCode)

Requirements

Platforms: Windows 98, Windows NT 4.0,
Windows Millennium Edition, Windows 2000,
Windows XP Home Edition, Windows XP Professional,
Windows .NET Server family

OpCodes.Conv_Ovf_U1_Un Field

Converts the unsigned value on top of the evaluation stack to **unsigned int8** and extends it to **int32**, throwing **OverflowException** on overflow.

```
[Visual Basic]
Public Shared ReadOnly Conv_Ovf_U1_Un As OpCode
[C#]
public static readonly OpCode Conv_Ovf_U1_Un;
[C++]
public: static OpCode Conv_Ovf_U1_Un;
[JScript]
public static var Conv_Ovf_U1_Un : OpCode;
```

Remarks

The following table lists the instruction's hexadecimal and Microsoft Intermediate Language (MSIL) assembly format, along with a brief reference summary:

Format	Assembly Format	Description
86	conv.ovf.u1.un	Converts an unsigned value to an **unsigned int8** (on the stack as **int32**) and throw an exception on overflow.

The stack transitional behavior, in sequential order, is:

1. *value* is pushed onto the stack.
2. *value* is popped from the stack and the conversion operation is attempted. If overflow occurs, an exception is thrown.
3. If the conversion is successful, the resulting value is pushed onto the stack.

The **conv.ovf.u1.un** opcode converts the *value* on top of the stack to the type specified in the opcode, and places that converted value on the top of the stack. If the value is too large or too small to be represented by the target type, an exception is thrown.

Conversions from floating-point numbers to integer values truncate the number toward zero. Note that integer values of less than 4 bytes are extended to **int32** when they are loaded onto the evaluation stack (unless **conv.ovf.i** or **conv.ovf.u** are used, in which case the result is also **natural int**).

OverflowException is thrown if the result can not be represented in the result type.

The following **Emit** constructor overload can use the **conv.ovf.u1.un** opcode:

• ILGenerator.Emit(OpCode)

Requirements

Platforms: Windows 98, Windows NT 4.0,
Windows Millennium Edition, Windows 2000,
Windows XP Home Edition, Windows XP Professional,
Windows .NET Server family

OpCodes.Conv_Ovf_U2 Field

Converts the signed value on top of the evaluation stack to **unsigned int16** and extends it to **int32**, throwing **OverflowException** on overflow.

```
[Visual Basic]
Public Shared ReadOnly Conv_Ovf_U2 As OpCode
[C#]
public static readonly OpCode Conv_Ovf_U2;
[C++]
public: static OpCode Conv_Ovf_U2;
[JScript]
public static var Conv_Ovf_U2 : OpCode;
```

Remarks

The following table lists the instruction's hexadecimal and Microsoft Intermediate Language (MSIL) assembly format, along with a brief reference summary:

Format	Assembly Format	Description
B6	conv.ovf.u2	Convert to an **unsigned int16** (on the stack as **int32**) and throw an exception on overflow.

The stack transitional behavior, in sequential order, is:

1. *value* is pushed onto the stack.
2. *value* is popped from the stack and the conversion operation is attempted. If overflow occurs, an exception is thrown.
3. If the conversion is successful, the resulting value is pushed onto the stack.

The **conv.ovf.u2** opcode converts the *value* on top of the stack to the type specified in the opcode, and places that converted value on the top of the stack. If the value is too large or too small to be represented by the target type, an exception is thrown.

Conversions from floating-point numbers to integer values truncate the number toward zero. Note that integer values of less than 4 bytes are extended to **int32** when they are loaded onto the evaluation stack (unless **conv.ovf.i** or **conv.ovf.u** are used, in which case the result is also **natural int**).

OverflowException is thrown if the result can not be represented in the result type.

The following **Emit** constructor overload can use the **conv.ovf.u2** opcode:

• ILGenerator.Emit(OpCode)

Requirements

Platforms: Windows 98, Windows NT 4.0,
Windows Millennium Edition, Windows 2000,
Windows XP Home Edition, Windows XP Professional,
Windows .NET Server family

OpCodes.Conv_Ovf_U2_Un Field

Converts the unsigned value on top of the evaluation stack to **unsigned int16** and extends it to **int32**, throwing **OverflowException** on overflow.

```
[Visual Basic]
Public Shared ReadOnly Conv_Ovf_U2_Un As OpCode
[C#]
public static readonly OpCode Conv_Ovf_U2_Un;
```

```
[C++]
public: static OpCode Conv_Ovf_U2_Un;
[JScript]
public static var Conv_Ovf_U2_Un : OpCode;
```

Remarks

The following table lists the instruction's hexadecimal and Microsoft Intermediate Language (MSIL) assembly format, along with a brief reference summary:

Format	Assembly Format	Description
87	conv.ovf.u2.un	Converts an unsigned value to an **unsigned int16** (on the stack as **int32**) and throw an exception on overflow.

The stack transitional behavior, in sequential order, is:

1. *value* is pushed onto the stack.
2. *value* is popped from the stack and the conversion operation is attempted. If overflow occurs, an exception is thrown.
3. If the conversion is successful, the resulting value is pushed onto the stack.

The **conv.ovf.u2.un** opcode converts the *value* on top of the stack to the type specified in the opcode, and places that converted value on the top of the stack. If the value is too large or too small to be represented by the target type, an exception is thrown.

Conversions from floating-point numbers to integer values truncate the number toward zero. Note that integer values of less than 4 bytes are extended to **int32** when they are loaded onto the evaluation stack (unless **conv.ovf.i** or **conv.ovf.u** are used, in which case the result is also **natural int**).

OverflowException is thrown if the result can not be represented in the result type.

The following **Emit** constructor overload can use the **conv.ovf.u2.un** opcode:

• ILGenerator.Emit(OpCode)

Requirements

Platforms: Windows 98, Windows NT 4.0, Windows Millennium Edition, Windows 2000, Windows XP Home Edition, Windows XP Professional, Windows .NET Server family

OpCodes.Conv_Ovf_U4 Field

Converts the signed value on top of the evaluation stack to **unsigned int32**, throwing **OverflowException** on overflow.

```
[Visual Basic]
Public Shared ReadOnly Conv_Ovf_U4 As OpCode
[C#]
public static readonly OpCode Conv_Ovf_U4;
[C++]
public: static OpCode Conv_Ovf_U4;
[JScript]
public static var Conv_Ovf_U4 : OpCode;
```

Remarks

The following table lists the instruction's hexadecimal and Microsoft Intermediate Language (MSIL) assembly format, along with a brief reference summary:

Format	Assembly Format	Description
B8	conv.ovf.u4	Convert to an **unsigned int32** (on the stack as **int32**) and throw an exception on overflow.

The stack transitional behavior, in sequential order, is:

1. *value* is pushed onto the stack.
2. *value* is popped from the stack and the conversion operation is attempted. If overflow occurs, an exception is thrown.
3. If the conversion is successful, the resulting value is pushed onto the stack.

The **conv.ovf.u4** opcode converts the *value* on top of the stack to the type specified in the opcode, and places that converted value on the top of the stack. If the value is too large or too small to be represented by the target type, an exception is thrown.

Conversions from floating-point numbers to integer values truncate the number toward zero. Note that integer values of less than 4 bytes are extended to **int32** when they are loaded onto the evaluation stack (unless **conv.ovf.i** or **conv.ovf.u** are used, in which case the result is also **natural int**).

OverflowException is thrown if the result can not be represented in the result type.

The following **Emit** constructor overload can use the **conv.ovf.u4** opcode:

• ILGenerator.Emit(OpCode)

Requirements

Platforms: Windows 98, Windows NT 4.0, Windows Millennium Edition, Windows 2000, Windows XP Home Edition, Windows XP Professional, Windows .NET Server family

OpCodes.Conv_Ovf_U4_Un Field

Converts the unsigned value on top of the evaluation stack to **unsigned int32**, throwing **OverflowException** on overflow.

```
[Visual Basic]
Public Shared ReadOnly Conv_Ovf_U4_Un As OpCode
[C#]
public static readonly OpCode Conv_Ovf_U4_Un;
[C++]
public: static OpCode Conv_Ovf_U4_Un;
[JScript]
public static var Conv_Ovf_U4_Un : OpCode;
```

Remarks

The following table lists the instruction's hexadecimal and Microsoft Intermediate Language (MSIL) assembly format, along with a brief reference summary:

Format	Assembly Format	Description
88	conv.ovf.u4.un	Converts an unsigned value to an **unsigned int32** (on the stack as **int32**) and throw an exception on overflow.

The stack transitional behavior, in sequential order, is:

1. *value* is pushed onto the stack.
2. *value* is popped from the stack and the conversion operation is attempted. If overflow occurs, an exception is thrown.

3. If the conversion is successful, the resulting value is pushed onto the stack.

The **conv.ovf.u4.un** opcode converts the *value* on top of the stack to the type specified in the opcode, and places that converted value on the top of the stack. If the value is too large or too small to be represented by the target type, an exception is thrown.

Conversions from floating-point numbers to integer values truncate the number toward zero. Note that integer values of less than 4 bytes are extended to **int32** when they are loaded onto the evaluation stack (unless **conv.ovf.i** or **conv.ovf.u** are used, in which case the result is also **natural int**).

OverflowException is thrown if the result can not be represented in the result type.

The following **Emit** constructor overload can use the **conv.ovf.u4.un** opcode:

- ILGenerator.Emit(OpCode)

Requirements

Platforms: Windows 98, Windows NT 4.0, Windows Millennium Edition, Windows 2000, Windows XP Home Edition, Windows XP Professional, Windows .NET Server family

OpCodes.Conv_Ovf_U8 Field

Converts the signed value on top of the evaluation stack to **unsigned int64**, throwing **OverflowException** on overflow.

```
[Visual Basic]
Public Shared ReadOnly Conv_Ovf_U8 As OpCode
[C#]
public static readonly OpCode Conv_Ovf_U8;
[C++]
public: static OpCode Conv_Ovf_U8;
[JScript]
public static var Conv_Ovf_U8 : OpCode;
```

Remarks

The following table lists the instruction's hexadecimal and Microsoft Intermediate Language (MSIL) assembly format, along with a brief reference summary:

Format	Assembly Format	Description
BA	conv.ovf.u8	Convert to an **unsigned int64** (on the stack as **int64**) and throw an exception on overflow.

The stack transitional behavior, in sequential order, is:

1. *value* is pushed onto the stack.
2. *value* is popped from the stack and the conversion operation is attempted. If overflow occurs, an exception is thrown.
3. If the conversion is successful, the resulting value is pushed onto the stack.

The **conv.ovf.u8** opcode converts the *value* on top of the stack to the type specified in the opcode, and places that converted value on the top of the stack. If the value is too large or too small to be represented by the target type, an exception is thrown.

Conversions from floating-point numbers to integer values truncate the number toward zero. Note that integer values of less than 4 bytes are extended to **int32** when they are loaded onto the evaluation stack

(unless **conv.ovf.i** or **conv.ovf.u** are used, in which case the result is also **natural int**).

OverflowException is thrown if the result can not be represented in the result type.

The following **Emit** constructor overload can use the **conv.ovf.u8** opcode:

- ILGenerator.Emit(OpCode)

Requirements

Platforms: Windows 98, Windows NT 4.0, Windows Millennium Edition, Windows 2000, Windows XP Home Edition, Windows XP Professional, Windows .NET Server family

OpCodes.Conv_Ovf_U8_Un Field

Converts the unsigned value on top of the evaluation stack to **unsigned int64**, throwing **OverflowException** on overflow.

```
[Visual Basic]
Public Shared ReadOnly Conv_Ovf_U8_Un As OpCode
[C#]
public static readonly OpCode Conv_Ovf_U8_Un;
[C++]
public: static OpCode Conv_Ovf_U8_Un;
[JScript]
public static var Conv_Ovf_U8_Un : OpCode;
```

Remarks

The following table lists the instruction's hexadecimal and Microsoft Intermediate Language (MSIL) assembly format, along with a brief reference summary:

Format	Assembly Format	Description
89	conv.ovf.u8.un	Converts an unsigned value to an **unsigned int64** (on the stack as **int64**) and throw an exception on overflow.

The stack transitional behavior, in sequential order, is:

1. *value* is pushed onto the stack.
2. *value* is popped from the stack and the conversion operation is attempted. If overflow occurs, an exception is thrown.
3. If the conversion is successful, the resulting value is pushed onto the stack.

The **conv.ovf.u8.un** opcode converts the *value* on top of the stack to the type specified in the opcode, and places that converted value on the top of the stack. If the value is too large or too small to be represented by the target type, an exception is thrown.

Conversions from floating-point numbers to integer values truncate the number toward zero. Note that integer values of less than 4 bytes are extended to **int32** when they are loaded onto the evaluation stack (unless **conv.ovf.i** or **conv.ovf.u** are used, in which case the result is also **natural int**).

OverflowException is thrown if the result can not be represented in the result type.

The following **Emit** constructor overload can use the **conv.ovf.u8.un** opcode:

- ILGenerator.Emit(OpCode)

Requirements

Platforms: Windows 98, Windows NT 4.0,
Windows Millennium Edition, Windows 2000,
Windows XP Home Edition, Windows XP Professional,
Windows .NET Server family

OpCodes.Conv_Ovf_U_Un Field

Converts the unsigned value on top of the evaluation stack to
unsigned natural int, throwing **OverflowException** on overflow.

```
[Visual Basic]
Public Shared ReadOnly Conv_Ovf_U_Un As OpCode
[C#]
public static readonly OpCode Conv_Ovf_U_Un;
[C++]
public: static OpCode Conv_Ovf_U_Un;
[JScript]
public static var Conv_Ovf_U_Un : OpCode;
```

Remarks

The following table lists the instruction's hexadecimal and Microsoft
Intermediate Language (MSIL) assembly format, along with a brief
reference summary:

Format	Assembly Format	Description
8B	conv.ovf.u.un	Converts un unsigned value to an **unsigned natural int** (on the stack as **natural int**) and throw an exception on overflow.

The stack transitional behavior, in sequential order, is:

1. *value* is pushed onto the stack.
2. *value* is popped from the stack and the conversion operation is attempted. If overflow occurs, an exception is thrown.
3. If the conversion is successful, the resulting value is pushed onto the stack.

The **conv.ovf.u.un** opcode converts the *value* on top of the stack to
the type specified in the opcode, and places that converted value on
the top of the stack. If the value is too large or too small to be
represented by the target type, an exception is thrown.

Conversions from floating-point numbers to integer values truncate
the number toward zero. Note that integer values of less than 4 bytes
are extended to **int32** when they are loaded onto the evaluation
stack (unless **conv.ovf.i** or **conv.ovf.u** are used, in which case the result is
also **natural int**).

OverflowException is thrown if the result can not be represented in
the result type.

The following **Emit** constructor overload can use the **conv.uvf.u.un**
opcode:

• ILGenerator.Emit(OpCode)

Requirements

Platforms: Windows 98, Windows NT 4.0,
Windows Millennium Edition, Windows 2000,
Windows XP Home Edition, Windows XP Professional,
Windows .NET Server family

OpCodes.Conv_R4 Field

Converts the value on top of the evaluation stack to **float32**.

```
[Visual Basic]
Public Shared ReadOnly Conv_R4 As OpCode
[C#]
public static readonly OpCode Conv_R4;
[C++]
public: static OpCode Conv_R4;
[JScript]
public static var Conv_R4 : OpCode;
```

Remarks

The following table lists the instruction's hexadecimal and Microsoft
Intermediate Language (MSIL) assembly format, along with a brief
reference summary:

Format	Assembly Format	Description
6B	conv.r4	Convert to **float32**, pushing **F** on stack.

The stack transitional behavior, in sequential order, is:

1. *value* is pushed onto the stack.
2. *value* is popped from the stack and the conversion operation is attempted.
3. If the conversion is successful, the resulting value is pushed onto the stack.

The **conv.r4** opcode converts the *value* on top of the stack to the type
specified in the opcode, and leave that converted value on the top of
the stack. Integer values of less than 4 bytes are extended to **int32**
when they are loaded onto the evaluation stack (unless **conv.i** or
conv.u is used, in which case the result is also **natural int**).
Floating-point values are converted to the **F** type.

Conversion from floating-point numbers to integer values truncates
the number toward zero. When converting from an **float64** to an
float32, precision can be lost. If *value* is too large to fit in a **float32**
(**F**), positive infinity (if *value* is positive) or negative infinity (if
value is negative) is returned. If overflow occurs converting
one integer type to another, the high order bits are truncated. If the result
is smaller than an **int32**, the value is sign-extended to fill the slot.

If overflow occurs converting a floating-point type to an integer the
value returned is unspecified.

No exceptions are ever thrown when using this field.

The following **Emit** constructor overload can use the **conv.r4**
opcode:

• ILGenerator.Emit(OpCode)

Requirements

Platforms: Windows 98, Windows NT 4.0,
Windows Millennium Edition, Windows 2000,
Windows XP Home Edition, Windows XP Professional,
Windows .NET Server family

OpCodes.Conv_R8 Field

Converts the value on top of the evaluation stack to **float64**.

```
[Visual Basic]
Public Shared ReadOnly Conv_R8 As OpCode
[C#]
public static readonly OpCode Conv_R8;
```

```
[C++]
public: static OpCode Conv_R8;
[JScript]
public static var Conv_R8 : OpCode;
```

Remarks

The following table lists the instruction's hexadecimal and Microsoft Intermediate Language (MSIL) assembly format, along with a brief reference summary:

Format	Assembly Format	Description
6C	conv.r8	Convert to **float64**, pushing **F** on stack.

The stack transitional behavior, in sequential order, is:

1. *value* is pushed onto the stack.
2. *value* is popped from the stack and the conversion operation is attempted.
3. If the conversion is successful, the resulting value is pushed onto the stack.

The **conv.r8** opcode converts the *value* on top of the stack to the type specified in the opcode, and leave that converted value on the top of the stack. Integer values of less than 4 bytes are extended to **int32** when they are loaded onto the evaluation stack (unless **conv.i** or **conv.u** is used, in which case the result is also **natural int**). Floating-point values are converted to the **F** type.

Conversion from floating-point numbers to integer values truncates the number toward zero. When converting from an **float64** to an **float32**, precision can be lost. If *value* is too large to fit in a **float32** (**F**), positive infinity (if *value* is positive) or negative infinity (if *value* is negative) is returned. If overflow occurs converting one integer type to another, the high order bits are truncated. If the result is smaller than an **int32**, the value is sign-extended to fill the slot.

If overflow occurs converting a floating-point type to an integer the value returned is unspecified.

No exceptions are ever thrown when using this field.

The following **Emit** constructor overload can use the **conv.r8** opcode:

- ILGenerator.Emit(OpCode)

Requirements

Platforms: Windows 98, Windows NT 4.0, Windows Millennium Edition, Windows 2000, Windows XP Home Edition, Windows XP Professional, Windows .NET Server family

OpCodes.Conv_R_Un Field

Converts the unsigned integer value on top of the evaluation stack to **float32**.

```
[Visual Basic]
Public Shared ReadOnly Conv_R_Un As OpCode
[C#]
public static readonly OpCode Conv_R_Un;
[C++]
public: static OpCode Conv_R_Un;
[JScript]
public static var Conv_R_Un : OpCode;
```

Remarks

The following table lists the instruction's hexadecimal and Microsoft Intermediate Language (MSIL) assembly format, along with a brief reference summary:

Format	Assembly Format	Description
76	conv.r.un	Convert unsigned integer to floating-point, pushing **F** on stack.

The stack transitional behavior, in sequential order, is:

1. *value* is pushed onto the stack.
2. *value* is popped from the stack and the conversion operation is attempted.
3. If the conversion is successful, the resulting value is pushed onto the stack.

The **conv.r.un** opcode converts the *value* on top of the stack to the type specified in the opcode, and leave that converted value on the top of the stack. Integer values of less than 4 bytes are extended to **int32** when they are loaded onto the evaluation stack (unless **conv.i** or **conv.u** is used, in which case the result is also **natural int**). Floating-point values are converted to the **F** type.

Conversion from floating-point numbers to integer values truncates the number toward zero. When converting from an **float64** to an **float32**, precision can be lost. If *value* is too large to fit in a **float32** (**F**), positive infinity (if *value* is positive) or negative infinity (if *value* is negative) is returned. If overflow occurs converting one integer type to another, the high order bits are truncated. If the result is smaller than an **int32**, the value is sign-extended to fill the slot.

If overflow occurs converting a floating-point type to an integer the *result* returned is unspecified. The **conv.r.un** operation takes an integer off the stack, interprets it as unsigned, and replaces it with a floating-point number to represent the integer: either a **float32**, if this is wide enough to represent the integer without loss of precision, or else a **float64**.

No exceptions are ever thrown when using this field.

The following **Emit** constructor overload can use the **conv.r.un** opcode:

- ILGenerator.Emit(OpCode)

Requirements

Platforms: Windows 98, Windows NT 4.0, Windows Millennium Edition, Windows 2000, Windows XP Home Edition, Windows XP Professional, Windows .NET Server family

OpCodes.Conv_U Field

Converts the value on top of the evaluation stack to **unsigned natural int**, and extends it to **natural int**.

```
[Visual Basic]
Public Shared ReadOnly Conv_U As OpCode
[C#]
public static readonly OpCode Conv_U;
[C++]
public: static OpCode Conv_U;
[JScript]
public static var Conv_U : OpCode;
```

Remarks

The following table lists the instruction's hexadecimal and Microsoft Intermediate Language (MSIL) assembly format, along with a brief reference summary:

Format	Assembly Format	Description
E0	conv.u	Convert to **unsigned natural int**, pushing **natural int** on stack.

The stack transitional behavior, in sequential order, is:

1. *value* is pushed onto the stack.
2. *value* is popped from the stack and the conversion operation is attempted.
3. If the conversion is successful, the resulting value is pushed onto the stack.

The **conv.u** opcode converts the *value* on top of the stack to the type specified in the opcode, and leave that converted value on the top of the stack. Integer values of less than 4 bytes are extended to **int32** when they are loaded onto the evaluation stack (unless **conv.i** or **conv.u** is used, in which case the result is also **natural int**). Floating-point values are converted to the **F** type.

Conversion from floating-point numbers to integer values truncates the number toward zero. When converting from an **float64** to an **float32**, precision can be lost. If *value* is too large to fit in a **float32** (**F**), positive infinity (if *value* is positive) or negative infinity (if *value* is negative) is returned. If overflow occurs converting one integer type to another, the high order bits are truncated. If the result is smaller than an **int32**, the value is sign-extended to fill the slot.

If overflow occurs converting a floating-point type to an integer the value returned is unspecified.

No exceptions are ever thrown when using this field. See **Conv_Ovf_I** and **Conv_Ovf_I_Un** for equivalent instructions that will throw an exception when the result type can not properly represent the result value.

The following **Emit** constructor overload can use the **conv.u** opcode:

- ILGenerator.Emit(OpCode)

Requirements

Platforms: Windows 98, Windows NT 4.0, Windows Millennium Edition, Windows 2000, Windows XP Home Edition, Windows XP Professional, Windows .NET Server family

Remarks

The following table lists the instruction's hexadecimal and Microsoft Intermediate Language (MSIL) assembly format, along with a brief reference summary:

Format	Assembly Format	Description
D2	conv.u1	Convert to **int8**, pushing **int32** on stack.

The stack transitional behavior, in sequential order, is:

1. *value* is pushed onto the stack.
2. *value* is popped from the stack and the conversion operation is attempted.
3. If the conversion is successful, the resulting value is pushed onto the stack.

The **conv.u1** opcode converts the *value* on top of the stack to the type specified in the opcode, and leave that converted value on the top of the stack. Integer values of less than 4 bytes are extended to **int32** when they are loaded onto the evaluation stack (unless **conv.i** or **conv.u** is used, in which case the result is also **natural int**). Floating-point values are converted to the **F** type.

Conversion from floating-point numbers to integer values truncates the number toward zero. When converting from an **float64** to an **float32**, precision can be lost. If *value* is too large to fit in a **float32** (**F**), positive infinity (if *value* is positive) or negative infinity (if *value* is negative) is returned. If overflow occurs converting one integer type to another, the high order bits are truncated. If the result is smaller than an **int32**, the value is sign-extended to fill the slot.

If overflow occurs converting a floating-point type to an integer the value returned is unspecified.

No exceptions are ever thrown when using this field. See **Conv_Ovf_I1** and **Conv_Ovf_I1_Un** for equivalent instructions that will throw an exception when the result type can not properly represent the result value.

The following **Emit** constructor overload can use the **conv.u1** opcode:

- ILGenerator.Emit(OpCode)

Requirements

Platforms: Windows 98, Windows NT 4.0, Windows Millennium Edition, Windows 2000, Windows XP Home Edition, Windows XP Professional, Windows .NET Server family

OpCodes.Conv_U1 Field

Converts the value on top of the evaluation stack to **unsigned int8**, and extends it to **int32**.

```
[Visual Basic]
Public Shared ReadOnly Conv_U1 As OpCode
[C#]
public static readonly OpCode Conv_U1;
[C++]
public: static OpCode Conv_U1;
[JScript]
public static var Conv_U1 : OpCode;
```

OpCodes.Conv_U2 Field

Converts the value on top of the evaluation stack to **unsigned int16**, and extends it to **int32**.

```
[Visual Basic]
Public Shared ReadOnly Conv_U2 As OpCode
[C#]
public static readonly OpCode Conv_U2;
[C++]
public: static OpCode Conv_U2;
[JScript]
public static var Conv_U2 : OpCode;
```

Remarks

The following table lists the instruction's hexadecimal and Microsoft Intermediate Language (MSIL) assembly format, along with a brief reference summary:

Format	Assembly Format	Description
D1	conv.u2	Convert to **int16**, pushing **int32** on stack.

The stack transitional behavior, in sequential order, is:

1. *value* is pushed onto the stack.
2. *value* is popped from the stack and the conversion operation is attempted.
3. If the conversion is successful, the resulting value is pushed onto the stack.

The **conv.u2** opcode converts the *value* on top of the stack to the type specified in the opcode, and leave that converted value on the top of the stack. Integer values of less than 4 bytes are extended to **int32** when they are loaded onto the evaluation stack (unless **conv.i** or **conv.u** is used, in which case the result is also **natural int**). Floating-point values are converted to the **F** type.

Conversion from floating-point numbers to integer values truncates the number toward zero. When converting from an **float64** to an **float32**, precision can be lost. If *value* is too large to fit in a **float32** (**F**), positive infinity (if *value* is positive) or negative infinity (if *value* is negative) is returned. If overflow occurs converting one integer type to another, the high order bits are truncated. If the result is smaller than an **int32**, the value is sign-extended to fill the slot.

If overflow occurs converting a floating-point type to an integer the value returned is unspecified.

No exceptions are ever thrown when using this field. See **Conv_Ovf_I2** and **Conv_Ovf_I2_Un** for equivalent instructions that will throw an exception when the result type can not properly represent the result value.

The following **Emit** constructor overload can use the **conv.u2** opcode:

- ILGenerator.Emit(OpCode)

Requirements

Platforms: Windows 98, Windows NT 4.0, Windows Millennium Edition, Windows 2000, Windows XP Home Edition, Windows XP Professional, Windows .NET Server family

OpCodes.Conv_U4 Field

Converts the value on top of the evaluation stack to **unsigned int32**, and extends it to **int32**.

```
[Visual Basic]
Public Shared ReadOnly Conv_U4 As OpCode
[C#]
public static readonly OpCode Conv_U4;
[C++]
public: static OpCode Conv_U4;
[JScript]
public static var Conv_U4 : OpCode;
```

Remarks

The following table lists the instruction's hexadecimal and Microsoft Intermediate Language (MSIL) assembly format, along with a brief reference summary:

Format	Assembly Format	Description
6D	conv.u4	Convert to **unsigned int32**, pushing **int32** on stack.

The stack transitional behavior, in sequential order, is:

1. *value* is pushed onto the stack.
2. *value* is popped from the stack and the conversion operation is attempted.
3. If the conversion is successful, the resulting value is pushed onto the stack.

The **conv.u4** opcode converts the *value* on top of the stack to the type specified in the opcode, and leave that converted value on the top of the stack. Integer values of less than 4 bytes are extended to **int32** when they are loaded onto the evaluation stack (unless **conv.i** or **conv.u** is used, in which case the result is also **natural int**). Floating-point values are converted to the **F** type.

Conversion from floating-point numbers to integer values truncates the number toward zero. When converting from an **float64** to an **float32**, precision can be lost. If *value* is too large to fit in a **float32** (**F**), positive infinity (if *value* is positive) or negative infinity (if *value* is negative) is returned. If overflow occurs converting one integer type to another, the high order bits are truncated. If the result is smaller than an **int32**, the value is sign-extended to fill the slot.

If overflow occurs converting a floating-point type to an integer the value returned is unspecified.

No exceptions are ever thrown when using this field. See **Conv_Ovf_I4** and **Conv_Ovf_I4_Un** for equivalent instructions that will throw an exception when the result type can not properly represent the result value.

The following **Emit** constructor overload can use the **conv.u4** opcode:

- ILGenerator.Emit(OpCode)

Requirements

Platforms: Windows 98, Windows NT 4.0, Windows Millennium Edition, Windows 2000, Windows XP Home Edition, Windows XP Professional, Windows .NET Server family

OpCodes.Conv_U8 Field

Converts the value on top of the evaluation stack to **unsigned int64**, and extends it to **int64**.

```
[Visual Basic]
Public Shared ReadOnly Conv_U8 As OpCode
[C#]
public static readonly OpCode Conv_U8;
[C++]
public: static OpCode Conv_U8;
[JScript]
public static var Conv_U8 : OpCode;
```

Remarks

The following table lists the instruction's hexadecimal and Microsoft Intermediate Language (MSIL) assembly format, along with a brief reference summary:

Format	Assembly Format	Description
6E	conv.u8	Convert to **int64**, pushing **int64** on stack.

The stack transitional behavior, in sequential order, is:

1. *value* is pushed onto the stack.
2. *value* is popped from the stack and the conversion operation is attempted.
3. If the conversion is successful, the resulting value is pushed onto the stack.

The **conv.u8** opcode converts the *value* on top of the stack to the type specified in the opcode, and leave that converted value on the top of the stack. Integer values of less than 4 bytes are extended to **int32** when they are loaded onto the evaluation stack (unless **conv.i** or **conv.u** is used, in which case the result is also **natural int**). Floating-point values are converted to the **F** type.

Conversion from floating-point numbers to integer values truncates the number toward zero. When converting from an **float64** to an **float32**, precision can be lost. If *value* is too large to fit in a **float32** (**F**), positive infinity (if *value* is positive) or negative infinity (if *value* is negative) is returned. If overflow occurs converting one integer type to another, the high order bits are truncated. If the result is smaller than an **int32**, the value is sign-extended to fill the slot.

If overflow occurs converting a floating-point type to an integer the value returned is unspecified.

No exceptions are ever thrown when using this field. See **Conv_Ovf_I8** and **Conv_Ovf_I8_Un** for equivalent instructions that will throw an exception when the result type can not properly represent the result value.

The following **Emit** constructor overload can use the **conv.u8** opcode:

• ILGenerator.Emit(OpCode)

Requirements

Platforms: Windows 98, Windows NT 4.0, Windows Millennium Edition, Windows 2000, Windows XP Home Edition, Windows XP Professional, Windows .NET Server family

OpCodes.Cpblk Field

Copies a specified number bytes from a source address to a destination address.

```
[Visual Basic]
Public Shared ReadOnly Cpblk As OpCode
[C#]
public static readonly OpCode Cpblk;
[C++]
public: static OpCode Cpblk;
[JScript]
public static var Cpblk : OpCode;
```

Remarks

The following table lists the instruction's hexadecimal and Microsoft Intermediate Language (MSIL) assembly format, along with a brief reference summary:

Format	Assembly Format	Description
FE 17	cpblk	Copy data from one memory block to another.

The stack transitional behavior, in sequential order, is:

1. The destination address is pushed onto the stack.
2. The source address is pushed onto the stack.
3. The number of bytes to copy is pushed onto the stack.
4. The number of bytes, the source address, and the destination address are popped from the stack; the specified number of bytes are copied from the source address to the destination address.

The **cpblk** instruction copies a number (type **unsigned int32**) of bytes from a source address (of type *, **natural int**, or **&**) to a destination address (of type *, **natural int**, or **&**). The behavior of **cpblk** is unspecified if the source and destination areas overlap.

cpblk assumes that both the source and destination addressed are aligned to the natural size of the machine. The **cpblk** instruction can be immediately preceded by the **unaligned.<prefix>** instruction to indicate that either the source or the destination is unaligned.

The operation of the **cpblk** instruction can be altered by an immediately preceding **Volatile** or **Unaligned** prefix instruction.

NullReferenceException may be thrown if an invalid address is detected.

The following **Emit** constructor overload can use the **cpblk** opcode:

• ILGenerator.Emit(OpCode)

Requirements

Platforms: Windows 98, Windows NT 4.0, Windows Millennium Edition, Windows 2000, Windows XP Home Edition, Windows XP Professional, Windows .NET Server family

OpCodes.Cpobj Field

Copies the value type located at the address of an object (type **&**, * or **natural int**) to the address of the destination object (type **&**, * or **natural int**).

```
[Visual Basic]
Public Shared ReadOnly Cpobj As OpCode
[C#]
public static readonly OpCode Cpobj;
[C++]
public: static OpCode Cpobj;
[JScript]
public static var Cpobj : OpCode;
```

Remarks

The following table lists the instruction's hexadecimal and Microsoft Intermediate Language (MSIL) assembly format, along with a brief reference summary:

Format	Assembly Format	Description
70 < **T** >	cpobj *classTok*	Copies a value type from a source object to a destination object.

The stack transitional behavior, in sequential order, is:

1. The destination object reference is pushed onto the stack.
2. The source object reference is pushed onto the stack.
3. The two object references are popped from the stack; the value type at the address of the source object is copied to the address of the destination object.

The behavior of **cpobj** is unspecified if the source and destination object references are not pointers to instances of the class represented by the class token *classTok* (a **typeref** or **typedef**), or if *classTok* does not represent a value type.

NullReferenceException may be thrown if an invalid address is detected.

The following **Emit** constructor overload can use the **cpobj** opcode:

• ILGenerator.Emit(OpCode, Type)

Requirements

Platforms: Windows 98, Windows NT 4.0, Windows Millennium Edition, Windows 2000, Windows XP Home Edition, Windows XP Professional, Windows .NET Server family

OpCodes.Div Field

Divides two values and pushes the result as a floating-point (type **F**) or quotient (type **int32**) onto the evaluation stack.

```
[Visual Basic]
Public Shared ReadOnly Div As OpCode
[C#]
public static readonly OpCode Div;
[C++]
public: static OpCode Div;
[JScript]
public static var Div : OpCode;
```

Remarks

The following table lists the instruction's hexadecimal and Microsoft Intermediate Language (MSIL) assembly format, along with a brief reference summary:

Format	Assembly Format	Description
5B	div	Divides two values to return a quotient or floating-point result.

The stack transitional behavior, in sequential order, is:

1. *value1* is pushed onto the stack.
2. *value2* is pushed onto the stack.
3. *value2* and *value1* are popped from the stack; *value1* is divided by *value2*.
4. The result is pushed onto the stack.

result = value1 div *value2* satisfies the following conditions:

| *result* | = | *value1* |/| *value2* |, and:

sign(*result*) = +, if sign(*value1*) = sign(*value2*), or -, if sign(*value1*) ~= sign(*value2*)

The **div** instruction computes the result and pushes it on the stack.

Integer division truncates towards zero.

Division of a finite number by zero produces the correctly signed infinite value.

Dividing zero by zero or infinity by infinity produces the NaN (Not-A-Number) value. Any number divided by infinity will produce a zero value.

Integral operations throw **ArithmeticException** if the result cannot be represented in the result type. This can happen if *value1* is the maximum negative value, and *value2* is -1.

Integral operations throw **DivideByZeroException** if *value2* is zero.

Note that on Intel-based platforms an **OverflowException** is thrown when computing (minint div -1). Floating-point operations never throw an exception (they produce NaNs or infinities instead).

The following **Emit** constructor overload can use the **div** opcode:

• ILGenerator.Emit(OpCode)

Requirements

Platforms: Windows 98, Windows NT 4.0, Windows Millennium Edition, Windows 2000, Windows XP Home Edition, Windows XP Professional, Windows .NET Server family

OpCodes.Div_Un Field

Divides two unsigned integer values and pushes the result (**int32**) onto the evaluation stack.

```
[Visual Basic]
Public Shared ReadOnly Div_Un As OpCode
[C#]
public static readonly OpCode Div_Un;
[C++]
public: static OpCode Div_Un;
[JScript]
public static var Div_Un : OpCode;
```

Remarks

The following table lists the instruction's hexadecimal and Microsoft Intermediate Language (MSIL) assembly format, along with a brief reference summary:

Format	Assembly Format	Description
5C	div.un	Divides two values, unsigned, returning a quotient.

The stack transitional behavior, in sequential order, is:

1. *value1* is pushed onto the stack.
2. *value2* is pushed onto the stack.
3. *value2* and *value1* are popped from the stack; *value1* is divided by *value2*.
4. The result is pushed onto the stack.

The **div.un** instruction computes *value1* divided by *value2*, both taken as unsigned integers, and pushes the *result* on the stack.

The following **Emit** constructor overload can use the **div.un** opcode:

• ILGenerator.Emit(OpCode)

Requirements

Platforms: Windows 98, Windows NT 4.0, Windows Millennium Edition, Windows 2000, Windows XP Home Edition, Windows XP Professional, Windows .NET Server family

OpCodes.Dup Field

Copies the current topmost value on the evaluation stack, and then pushes the copy onto the evaluation stack.

```
[Visual Basic]
Public Shared ReadOnly Dup As OpCode
```

```
[C#]
public static readonly OpCode Dup;
[C++]
public: static OpCode Dup;
[JScript]
public static var Dup : OpCode;
```

Remarks

The following table lists the instruction's hexadecimal and Microsoft Intermediate Language (MSIL) assembly format, along with a brief reference summary:

Format	Assembly Format	Description
25	dup	Duplicates the value on the top of the stack.

The stack transitional behavior, in sequential order, is:

1. *value* is pushed onto the stack.
2. *value* is popped off of the stack for duplication.
3. *value* is pushed back onto the stack.
4. A duplicate value is pushed onto the stack.

The **dup** instruction duplicates the top element of the stack, and leaves two identical values atop it.

The following **Emit** constructor overload can use the **dup** opcode:

• ILGenerator.Emit(OpCode)

Requirements

Platforms: Windows 98, Windows NT 4.0, Windows Millennium Edition, Windows 2000, Windows XP Home Edition, Windows XP Professional, Windows .NET Server family

OpCodes.Endfilter Field

Transfers control from the **filter** clause of an exception back to the Common Language Infrastructure (CLI) exception handler.

```
[Visual Basic]
Public Shared ReadOnly Endfilter As OpCode
[C#]
public static readonly OpCode Endfilter;
[C++]
public: static OpCode Endfilter;
[JScript]
public static var Endfilter : OpCode;
```

Remarks

The following table lists the instruction's hexadecimal and Microsoft Intermediate Language (MSIL) assembly format, along with a brief reference summary:

Format	Assembly Format	Description
FE 11	endfilter	End filter clause of SEH exception handling.

The stack transitional behavior, in sequential order, is:

1. *value* is pushed onto the stack.
2. *value* is popped from the stack; **endfilter** is executed and control is transferred to the exception handler.

Value (which must be of type **int32** and is one of a specific set of values) is returned from the filter clause. It should be one of:

• **exception_continue_search** (*value* = 0) to continue searching for an exception handler

• **exception_execute_handler** (*value* = 1) to start the second phase of exception handling where finally blocks are run until the handler associated with this filter clause is located. Upon discovery, the handler is executed.

Other integer values will produce unspecified results.

The entry point of a filter, as shown in the method's exception table, must be the first instruction in the filter's code block. The **endfilter** instruction must be the last instruction in the filter's code block (hence there can only be one **endfilter** for any single filter block). After executing the **endfilter** instruction, control logically flows back to the CLI exception handling mechanism.

Control cannot be transferred into a filter block except through the exception mechanism. Control cannot be transferred out of a filter block except through the use of a **throw** instruction or by executing the final **endfilter** instruction. You cannot embed a **try** block within a **filter** block. If an exception is thrown inside the **filter** block, it is intercepted and a value of 0 (**exception_continue_search**) is returned.

The following **Emit** constructor overload can use the **endfilter** opcode:

• ILGenerator.Emit(OpCode)

Requirements

Platforms: Windows 98, Windows NT 4.0, Windows Millennium Edition, Windows 2000, Windows XP Home Edition, Windows XP Professional, Windows .NET Server family

OpCodes.Endfinally Field

Transfers control from the **fault** or **finally** clause of an exception block back to the Common Language Infrastructure (CLI) exception handler.

```
[Visual Basic]
Public Shared ReadOnly Endfinally As OpCode
[C#]
public static readonly OpCode Endfinally;
[C++]
public: static OpCode Endfinally;
[JScript]
public static var Endfinally : OpCode;
```

Remarks

The following table lists the instruction's hexadecimal and Microsoft Intermediate Language (MSIL) assembly format, along with a brief reference summary:

Format	Assembly Format	Description
DC	endfinally endfault	Ends the **finally** or **fault** clause of an exception block.

There are no stack transition behaviors for this instruction.

Endfinally and **endfault** signal the end of the **finally** or **fault** clause so that stack unwinding can continue until the exception handler is invoked. The **endfinally** or **endfault** instruction transfers control back to the CLI exception mechanism. The mechanism then searches for the next **finally** clause in the chain if the protected block was exited with a leave instruction. If the protected block was exited with an exception, the CLI will search for the next **finally** or **fault**, or enter the exception handler chosen during the first pass of exception handling.

An **endfinally** instruction might only appear lexically within a **finally** block. Unlike the **endfilter** instruction, there is no requirement that the block end with an **endfinally** instruction, and there can be as many **endfinally** instructions within the block as required. These same restrictions apply to the **endfault** instruction and the **fault** block.

Control cannot be transferred into a **finally** (or **fault**) block except through the exception mechanism. Control cannot be transferred out of a **finally** (or **fault**) block except through the use of a **throw** instruction or executing the **endfinally** (or **endfault**) instruction. In particular, you cannot "fall out" of a **finally** (or **fault**) block or to execute a **Ret** or **Leave** instruction within a **finally** (or **fault**) block.

Note that the **endfault** and **endfinally** instructions are aliases - they correspond to the same opcode.

The following **Emit** constructor overload can use the **endfinally** (**endfault**) opcode, as well as the **ILGenerator** method **EndExceptionBlock**.

- ILGenerator.Emit(OpCode)
- ILGenerator.EndExceptionBlock()

Requirements

Platforms: Windows 98, Windows NT 4.0, Windows Millennium Edition, Windows 2000, Windows XP Home Edition, Windows XP Professional, Windows .NET Server family

OpCodes.Initblk Field

Initializes a specified block of memory at a specific address to a given size and initial value.

```
[Visual Basic]
Public Shared ReadOnly Initblk As OpCode
[C#]
public static readonly OpCode Initblk;
[C++]
public: static OpCode Initblk;
[JScript]
public static var Initblk : OpCode;
```

Remarks

The following table lists the instruction's hexadecimal and Microsoft Intermediate Language (MSIL) assembly format, along with a brief reference summary:

Format	Assembly Format	Description
FE 18	initblk	Set each location in a block of memory to a given value.

The stack transitional behavior, in sequential order, is:

1. A starting address is pushed onto the stack.
2. An initialization value is pushed onto the stack.
3. The number of bytes to initialize is pushed onto the stack.
4. The number of bytes, the initialization value, and the starting address are popped from the stack, and the initialization is performed as per their values.

The **initblk** instruction sets the number (**unsigned int32**) of bytes starting at the specified address (of type **natural int**, **&**, or *) to the

initialization value (of type **unsigned int8**). **initblk** assumes that the starting address is aligned to the natural size of the machine.

The operation of the **initblk** instructions can be altered by an immediately preceding **Volatile** or **Unaligned** prefix instruction.

NullReferenceException may be thrown if an invalid address is detected.

The following **Emit** constructor overload can use the **initblk** opcode:

- ILGenerator.Emit(OpCode)

Requirements

Platforms: Windows 98, Windows NT 4.0, Windows Millennium Edition, Windows 2000, Windows XP Home Edition, Windows XP Professional, Windows .NET Server family

OpCodes.Initobj Field

Initializes all the fields of the object at a specific address to a null reference or a 0 of the appropriate primitive type.

```
[Visual Basic]
Public Shared ReadOnly Initobj As OpCode
[C#]
public static readonly OpCode Initobj;
[C++]
public: static OpCode Initobj;
[JScript]
public static var Initobj : OpCode;
```

Remarks

The following table lists the instruction's hexadecimal and Microsoft Intermediate Language (MSIL) assembly format, along with a brief reference summary:

Format	Assembly Format	Description
FE 15 < **T** >	initobj *classTok*	Initializes a value type.

The stack transitional behavior, in sequential order, is:

1. The address of an object to initialize is pushed onto the stack.
2. The address is popped from the stack; the value type object at the specified address is initialized as type *classTok*.

The **initobj** instruction initializes all the fields of the object specified by the pushed address (of type **natural int**, **&**, or *) to a null reference or a 0 of the appropriate primitive type. After this method is called, the instance is ready for the constructor method to be called. Behavior is unspecified if either the address is not a pointer to an instance of the class represented by *classTok*, or if *classTok* does not represent a value type.

Unlike **Newobj**, the constructor method is not called by **initobj**. **Initobj** is intended for initializing value types, while **newobj** is used to allocate and initialize objects.

The following **Emit** constructor overloads can use the **initobj** opcode:

- ILGenerator.Emit(OpCode, Type)

Requirements

Platforms: Windows 98, Windows NT 4.0, Windows Millennium Edition, Windows 2000, Windows XP Home Edition, Windows XP Professional, Windows .NET Server family

OpCodes.Isinst Field

Tests whether an object reference (type **O**) is an instance of a particular class.

```
[Visual Basic]
Public Shared ReadOnly Isinst As OpCode
[C#]
public static readonly OpCode Isinst;
[C++]
public: static OpCode Isinst;
[JScript]
public static var Isinst : OpCode;
```

Remarks

The following table lists the instruction's hexadecimal and Microsoft Intermediate Language (MSIL) assembly format, along with a brief reference summary:

Format	Assembly Format	Description
75 < **T** >	isinst *class*	Tests if an object reference is an instance of *class*, returning either a null reference or an instance of that class or interface.

The stack transitional behavior, in sequential order, is:

1. An object reference is pushed onto the stack.
2. The object reference is popped from the stack and tested to see if it is an instance of the class passed in *class*.
3. The result (either an object reference or a null reference) is pushed onto the stack.

Class is a metadata token indicating the desired class. If the class of the object on the top of the stack implements *class* (if *class* is an interface) or is a derived class of *class* (if *class* is a regular class) then it is cast to type *class* and the result is pushed on the stack, exactly as though **Castclass** had been called. Otherwise, a null reference is pushed on the stack. If the object reference itself is a null reference, then **isinst** likewise returns a null reference.

TypeLoadException is thrown if class cannot be found. This is typically detected when the Microsoft Intermediate Language (MSIL) instructions are converted to native code rather than at runtime.

The following **Emit** constructor overload can use the **isinst** opcode:

• ILGenerator.Emit(OpCode, Type)

Requirements

Platforms: Windows 98, Windows NT 4.0, Windows Millennium Edition, Windows 2000, Windows XP Home Edition, Windows XP Professional, Windows .NET Server family

OpCodes.Jmp Field

Exits current method and jumps to specified method.

```
[Visual Basic]
Public Shared ReadOnly Jmp As OpCode
[C#]
public static readonly OpCode Jmp;
[C++]
public: static OpCode Jmp;
[JScript]
public static var Jmp : OpCode;
```

Remarks

The following table lists the instruction's hexadecimal and Microsoft Intermediate Language (MSIL) assembly format, along with a brief reference summary:

Format	Assembly Format	Description
27 < **T** >	jmp *method*	Exit current method and jump to specified method.

There are no stack transition behaviors for this instruction.

The **jmp** (jump) instruction transfers control to the method specified by *method*, which is a metadata token for a method reference. The current arguments are transferred to the destination method.

The evaluation stack must be empty when this instruction is executed. The calling convention, number and type of arguments at the destination address must match that of the current method.

The **jmp** instruction cannot be used to transferred control out of a **try**, **filter**, **catch**, or **finally** block.

The following **Emit** constructor overload can use the **jmp** opcode:

• ILGenerator.Emit(OpCode, MethodInfo)

Requirements

Platforms: Windows 98, Windows NT 4.0, Windows Millennium Edition, Windows 2000, Windows XP Home Edition, Windows XP Professional, Windows .NET Server family

OpCodes.Ldarg Field

Loads an argument (referenced by a specified index value) onto the stack.

```
[Visual Basic]
Public Shared ReadOnly Ldarg As OpCode
[C#]
public static readonly OpCode Ldarg;
[C++]
public: static OpCode Ldarg;
[JScript]
public static var Ldarg : OpCode;
```

Remarks

The following table lists the instruction's hexadecimal and Microsoft Intermediate Language (MSIL) assembly format, along with a brief reference summary:

Format	Assembly Format	Description
FE 09 < **unsigned int16** >	ldarg *index*	Load argument at *index* onto stack.

The stack transitional behavior, in sequential order, is:

1. The argument value at *index* is pushed onto the stack.

The **ldarg** instruction pushes the argument indexed at *index*, where arguments are indexed from 0 onwards, onto the evaluation stack. The **ldarg** instruction can be used to load a value type or a primitive value onto the stack by copying it from an incoming argument. The type of the argument value is the same as the type of the argument, as specified by the current method's signature.

For procedures that take a variable-length argument list, the **ldarg** instruction can be used only for the initial fixed arguments, not those in the variable part of the signature (see the **Arglist** instruction for more details).

Arguments that hold an integer value smaller than 4 bytes long are expanded to type **int32** when they are loaded onto the stack. Floating-point values are expanded to their native size (type **F**).

The following **Emit** constructor overload can use the **ldarg** opcode:

• ILGenerator.Emit(OpCode, short)

Requirements

Platforms: Windows 98, Windows NT 4.0, Windows Millennium Edition, Windows 2000, Windows XP Home Edition, Windows XP Professional, Windows .NET Server family

OpCodes.Ldarga Field

Load an argument address onto the evaluation stack.

```
[Visual Basic]
Public Shared ReadOnly Ldarga As OpCode
[C#]
public static readonly OpCode Ldarga;
[C++]
public: static OpCode Ldarga;
[JScript]
public static var Ldarga : OpCode;
```

Remarks

The following table lists the instruction's hexadecimal and Microsoft Intermediate Language (MSIL) assembly format, along with a brief reference summary:

Format	Assembly Format	Description
FE 0A < unsigned int16 >	ldarga *index*	Fetch the address of argument indexed by *index*.

The stack transitional behavior, in sequential order, is:

1. The address *addr* of the argument indexed by *index* is pushed onto the stack.

The **ldarga** instruction fetches the address (of type *****) of the argument indexed by *index*, where arguments are indexed from 0 onwards. The address *addr* is always aligned to a natural boundary on the target machine.

For procedures that take a variable-length argument list, the **ldarga** instruction can be used only for the initial fixed arguments, not those in the variable part of the signature.

ldarga is used for by-ref parameter passing. For other cases, **Ldarg** and **Starg** should be used.

The following **Emit** constructor overload can use the **ldarga** opcode:

• ILGenerator.Emit(OpCode, short)

Requirements

Platforms: Windows 98, Windows NT 4.0, Windows Millennium Edition, Windows 2000, Windows XP Home Edition, Windows XP Professional, Windows .NET Server family

OpCodes.Ldarga_S Field

Load an argument address, in short form, onto the evaluation stack.

```
[Visual Basic]
Public Shared ReadOnly Ldarga_S As OpCode
[C#]
public static readonly OpCode Ldarga_S;
[C++]
public: static OpCode Ldarga_S;
[JScript]
public static var Ldarga_S : OpCode;
```

Remarks

The following table lists the instruction's hexadecimal and Microsoft Intermediate Language (MSIL) assembly format, along with a brief reference summary:

Format	Assembly Format	Description
0F < unsigned int8 >	ldarga.s *index*	Fetch the address of argument indexed by *index*, short form.

The stack transitional behavior, in sequential order, is:

1. The address *addr* of the argument indexed by *index* is pushed onto the stack.

ldarga.s (the short form of **ldarga**) should be used for argument numbers 0 through 255, and is a more efficient encoding.

The **ldarga.s** instruction fetches the address (of type *****) of the argument indexed by *index*, where arguments are indexed from 0 onwards. The address *addr* is always aligned to a natural boundary on the target machine.

For procedures that take a variable-length argument list, the **ldarga.s** instruction can be used only for the initial fixed arguments, not those in the variable part of the signature.

ldarga.s is used for by-ref parameter passing. For other cases, **Ldarg_S** and **Starg_S** should be used.

The following **Emit** constructor overload can use the **ldarga.s** opcode:

• ILGenerator.Emit(OpCode, byte)

Requirements

Platforms: Windows 98, Windows NT 4.0, Windows Millennium Edition, Windows 2000, Windows XP Home Edition, Windows XP Professional, Windows .NET Server family

OpCodes.Ldarg_0 Field

Loads the argument at index 0 onto the evaluation stack.

```
[Visual Basic]
Public Shared ReadOnly Ldarg_0 As OpCode
[C#]
public static readonly OpCode Ldarg_0;
[C++]
public: static OpCode Ldarg_0;
[JScript]
public static var Ldarg_0 : OpCode;
```

Remarks

The following table lists the instruction's hexadecimal and Microsoft Intermediate Language (MSIL) assembly format, along with a brief reference summary:

Format	Assembly Format	Description
02	ldarg.0	Load argument 0 onto stack

The stack transitional behavior, in sequential order, is:

1. The argument value at index 0 is pushed onto the stack.

The **ldarg.0** instruction is an efficient encoding for loading the argument value at index 0.

The **ldarg.0** instruction pushes the argument indexed at 0 onto the evaluation stack. The **ldarg.0** instruction can be used to load a value type or a primitive value onto the stack by copying it from an incoming argument. The type of the argument value is the same as the type of the argument, as specified by the current method's signature.

Arguments that hold an integer value smaller than 4 bytes long are expanded to type **int32** when they are loaded onto the stack. Floating-point values are expanded to their native size (type **F**).

The following **Emit** constructor overload can use the **ldarg.0** opcode:

• ILGenerator.Emit(OpCode)

Requirements

Platforms: Windows 98, Windows NT 4.0, Windows Millennium Edition, Windows 2000, Windows XP Home Edition, Windows XP Professional, Windows .NET Server family

OpCodes.Ldarg_1 Field

Loads the argument at index 1 onto the evaluation stack.

```
[Visual Basic]
Public Shared ReadOnly Ldarg_1 As OpCode
[C#]
public static readonly OpCode Ldarg_1;
[C++]
public: static OpCode Ldarg_1;
[JScript]
public static var Ldarg_1 : OpCode;
```

Remarks

The following table lists the instruction's hexadecimal and Microsoft Intermediate Language (MSIL) assembly format, along with a brief reference summary:

Format	Assembly Format	Description
03	ldarg.1	Load argument 1 onto stack.

The stack transitional behavior, in sequential order, is:

1. The argument value at index 1 is pushed onto the stack.

The **ldarg.1** instruction is an efficient encoding for loading the argument value at index 1.

The **ldarg.1** instruction pushes the argument indexed at 1 onto the evaluation stack. The **ldarg.1** instruction can be used to load a value type or a primitive value onto the stack by copying it from an incoming argument. The type of the argument value is the same as

the type of the argument, as specified by the current method's signature.

Arguments that hold an integer value smaller than 4 bytes long are expanded to type **int32** when they are loaded onto the stack. Floating-point values are expanded to their native size (type **F**).

The following **Emit** constructor overload can use the **ldarg.1** opcode:

• ILGenerator.Emit(OpCode)

Requirements

Platforms: Windows 98, Windows NT 4.0, Windows Millennium Edition, Windows 2000, Windows XP Home Edition, Windows XP Professional, Windows .NET Server family

OpCodes.Ldarg_2 Field

Loads the argument at index 2 onto the evaluation stack.

```
[Visual Basic]
Public Shared ReadOnly Ldarg_2 As OpCode
[C#]
public static readonly OpCode Ldarg_2;
[C++]
public: static OpCode Ldarg_2;
[JScript]
public static var Ldarg_2 : OpCode;
```

Remarks

The following table lists the instruction's hexadecimal and Microsoft Intermediate Language (MSIL) assembly format, along with a brief reference summary:

Format	Assembly Format	Description
04	ldarg.2	Load argument 2 onto stack.

The stack transitional behavior, in sequential order, is:

1. The argument value at index 2 is pushed onto the stack.

The **ldarg.2** instruction is an efficient encoding for loading the argument value at index 2.

The **ldarg.2** instruction pushes the argument indexed at 2 onto the evaluation stack. The **ldarg.2** instruction can be used to load a value type or a primitive value onto the stack by copying it from an incoming argument. The type of the argument value is the same as the type of the argument, as specified by the current method's signature.

Arguments that hold an integer value smaller than 4 bytes long are expanded to type **int32** when they are loaded onto the stack. Floating-point values are expanded to their native size (type **F**).

The following **Emit** constructor overload can use the **ldarg.2** opcode:

• ILGenerator.Emit(OpCode)

Requirements

Platforms: Windows 98, Windows NT 4.0, Windows Millennium Edition, Windows 2000, Windows XP Home Edition, Windows XP Professional, Windows .NET Server family

OpCodes.Ldarg_3 Field

Loads the argument at index 3 onto the evaluation stack.

```
[Visual Basic]
Public Shared ReadOnly Ldarg_3 As OpCode
[C#]
public static readonly OpCode Ldarg_3;
[C++]
public: static OpCode Ldarg_3;
[JScript]
public static var Ldarg_3 : OpCode;
```

Remarks

The following table lists the instruction's hexadecimal and Microsoft Intermediate Language (MSIL) assembly format, along with a brief reference summary:

Format	Assembly Format	Description
05	ldarg.3	Load argument 3 onto stack.

The stack transitional behavior, in sequential order, is:

1. The argument value at index 3 is pushed onto the stack.

The **ldarg.3** instruction is an efficient encoding for loading the argument value at index 3.

The **ldarg.3** instruction pushes the argument indexed at 3 onto the evaluation stack. The **ldarg.3** instruction can be used to load a value type or a primitive value onto the stack by copying it from an incoming argument. The type of the argument value is the same as the type of the argument, as specified by the current method's signature.

Arguments that hold an integer value smaller than 4 bytes long are expanded to type **int32** when they are loaded onto the stack. Floating-point values are expanded to their native size (type **F**).

The following **Emit** constructor overload can use the **ldarg.3** opcode:

- ILGenerator.Emit(OpCode)

Requirements

Platforms: Windows 98, Windows NT 4.0, Windows Millennium Edition, Windows 2000, Windows XP Home Edition, Windows XP Professional, Windows .NET Server family

OpCodes.Ldarg_S Field

Loads the argument (referenced by a specified short form index) onto the evaluation stack.

```
[Visual Basic]
Public Shared ReadOnly Ldarg_S As OpCode
[C#]
public static readonly OpCode Ldarg_S;
[C++]
public: static OpCode Ldarg_S;
[JScript]
public static var Ldarg_S : OpCode;
```

Remarks

The following table lists the instruction's hexadecimal and Microsoft Intermediate Language (MSIL) assembly format, along with a brief reference summary:

Format	Assembly Format	Description
0E < unsigned int8 >	ldarg.s *index*	Load argument at *index* onto stack, short form.

The stack transitional behavior, in sequential order, is:

1. The argument value at *index* is pushed onto the stack.

The **ldarg.s** instruction is an efficient encoding for loading arguments indexed from 4 through 255.

The **ldarg.s** instruction pushes the argument indexed at *index*, where arguments are indexed from 0 onwards, onto the evaluation stack. The **ldarg.s** instruction can be used to load a value type or a primitive value onto the stack by copying it from an incoming argument. The type of the argument value is the same as the type of the argument, as specified by the current method's signature.

For procedures that take a variable-length argument list, the **ldarg.s** instruction can be used only for the initial fixed arguments, not those in the variable part of the signature (see the **Arglist** instruction for more details).

Arguments that hold an integer value smaller than 4 bytes long are expanded to type **int32** when they are loaded onto the stack. Floating-point values are expanded to their native size (type **F**).

The following **Emit** constructor overload can use the **ldarg.s** opcode:

- ILGenerator.Emit(OpCode, byte)

Requirements

Platforms: Windows 98, Windows NT 4.0, Windows Millennium Edition, Windows 2000, Windows XP Home Edition, Windows XP Professional, Windows .NET Server family

OpCodes.Ldc_I4 Field

Pushes a supplied value of type **int32** onto the evaluation stack as an **int32**.

```
[Visual Basic]
Public Shared ReadOnly Ldc_I4 As OpCode
[C#]
public static readonly OpCode Ldc_I4;
[C++]
public: static OpCode Ldc_I4;
[JScript]
public static var Ldc_I4 : OpCode;
```

Remarks

The following table lists the instruction's hexadecimal and Microsoft Intermediate Language (MSIL) assembly format, along with a brief reference summary:

Format	Assembly Format	Description
20 < int32 >	ldc.i4 *num*	Pushes the value *num* onto the stack.

The stack transitional behavior, in sequential order, is:

1. The value *num* is pushed onto the stack.

Note that there are special short (and hence more efficient) encodings for the integers -128 through 127, and especially short encodings for -1 through 8. All short encodings push 4 byte integers on the stack. Longer encodings are used for 8 byte integers and 4 and 8 byte floating-point numbers, as well as 4-byte values that do not fit in the short forms. There are three ways to push an 8 byte integer constant onto the stack

1. Use the **Ldc_I8** instruction for constants that must be expressed in more than 32 bits.

2. Use the **Ldc_I4** instruction followed by a **Conv_I8** for constants that require 9 to 32 bits.

3. Use a short form instruction followed by a **Conv_I8** for constants that can be expressed in 8 or fewer bits.

The following **Emit** constructor overload can use the **ldc.i4** opcode:

• ILGenerator.Emit(OpCode, int)

Requirements

Platforms: Windows 98, Windows NT 4.0, Windows Millennium Edition, Windows 2000, Windows XP Home Edition, Windows XP Professional, Windows .NET Server family

OpCodes.Ldc_I4_0 Field

Pushes the integer value of 0 onto the evaluation stack as an **int32**.

```
[Visual Basic]
Public Shared ReadOnly Ldc_I4_0 As OpCode
[C#]
public static readonly OpCode Ldc_I4_0;
[C++]
public: static OpCode Ldc_I4_0;
[JScript]
public static var Ldc_I4_0 : OpCode;
```

Remarks

The following table lists the instruction's hexadecimal and Microsoft Intermediate Language (MSIL) assembly format, along with a brief reference summary:

Format	Assembly Format	Description
16	ldc.i4.0	Pushes 0 onto the stack.

The stack transitional behavior, in sequential order, is:

1. The value 0 is pushed onto the stack.

This is a special short encoding for the push of the integer value 0. All special short encodings push 4 byte integers on the stack.

The following **Emit** constructor overload can use the **ldc.i4.0** opcode:

• ILGenerator.Emit(OpCode)

Requirements

Platforms: Windows 98, Windows NT 4.0, Windows Millennium Edition, Windows 2000, Windows XP Home Edition, Windows XP Professional, Windows .NET Server family

OpCodes.Ldc_I4_1 Field

Pushes the integer value of 1 onto the evaluation stack as an **int32**.

```
[Visual Basic]
Public Shared ReadOnly Ldc_I4_1 As OpCode
[C#]
public static readonly OpCode Ldc_I4_1;
[C++]
public: static OpCode Ldc_I4_1;
```

```
[JScript]
public static var Ldc_I4_1 : OpCode;
```

Remarks

The following table lists the instruction's hexadecimal and Microsoft Intermediate Language (MSIL) assembly format, along with a brief reference summary:

Format	Assembly Format	Description
17	ldc.i4.1	Pushes 1 onto the stack.

The stack transitional behavior, in sequential order, is:

1. The value 1 is pushed onto the stack.

This is a special short encoding for the push of the integer value 0. All special short encodings push 4 byte integers on the stack.

The following **Emit** constructor overload can use the **ldc.i4.1** opcode:

• ILGenerator.Emit(OpCode)

Requirements

Platforms: Windows 98, Windows NT 4.0, Windows Millennium Edition, Windows 2000, Windows XP Home Edition, Windows XP Professional, Windows .NET Server family

OpCodes.Ldc_I4_2 Field

Pushes the integer value of 2 onto the evaluation stack as an **int32**.

```
[Visual Basic]
Public Shared ReadOnly Ldc_I4_2 As OpCode
[C#]
public static readonly OpCode Ldc_I4_2;
[C++]
public: static OpCode Ldc_I4_2;
[JScript]
public static var Ldc_I4_2 : OpCode;
```

Remarks

The following table lists the instruction's hexadecimal and Microsoft Intermediate Language (MSIL) assembly format, along with a brief reference summary:

Format	Assembly Format	Description
18	ldc.i4.2	Pushes 2 onto the stack.

The stack transitional behavior, in sequential order, is:

1. The value 2 is pushed onto the stack.

This is a special short encoding for the push of the integer value 0. All special short encodings push 4 byte integers on the stack.

The following **Emit** constructor overload can use the **ldc.i4.2** opcode:

• ILGenerator.Emit(OpCode)

Requirements

Platforms: Windows 98, Windows NT 4.0, Windows Millennium Edition, Windows 2000, Windows XP Home Edition, Windows XP Professional, Windows .NET Server family

OpCodes.Ldc_I4_3 Field

Pushes the integer value of 3 onto the evaluation stack as an **int32**.

```
[Visual Basic]
Public Shared ReadOnly Ldc_I4_3 As OpCode
[C#]
public static readonly OpCode Ldc_I4_3;
[C++]
public: static OpCode Ldc_I4_3;
[JScript]
public static var Ldc_I4_3 : OpCode;
```

Remarks

The following table lists the instruction's hexadecimal and Microsoft Intermediate Language (MSIL) assembly format, along with a brief reference summary:

Format	Assembly Format	Description
19	ldc.i4.3	Pushes 3 onto the stack.

The stack transitional behavior, in sequential order, is:

1. The value 3 is pushed onto the stack.

This is a special short encoding for the push of the integer value 0. All special short encodings push 4 byte integers on the stack.

The following **Emit** constructor overload can use the **ldc.i4.3** opcode:

- ILGenerator.Emit(OpCode)

Requirements

Platforms: Windows 98, Windows NT 4.0, Windows Millennium Edition, Windows 2000, Windows XP Home Edition, Windows XP Professional, Windows .NET Server family

OpCodes.Ldc_I4_4 Field

Pushes the integer value of 4 onto the evaluation stack as an **int32**.

```
[Visual Basic]
Public Shared ReadOnly Ldc_I4_4 As OpCode
[C#]
public static readonly OpCode Ldc_I4_4;
[C++]
public: static OpCode Ldc_I4_4;
[JScript]
public static var Ldc_I4_4 : OpCode;
```

Remarks

The following table lists the instruction's hexadecimal and Microsoft Intermediate Language (MSIL) assembly format, along with a brief reference summary:

Format	Assembly Format	Description
1A	ldc.i4.4	Pushes 4 onto the stack.

The stack transitional behavior, in sequential order, is:

1. The value 4 is pushed onto the stack.

This is a special short encoding for the push of the integer value 0. All special short encodings push 4 byte integers on the stack.

The following **Emit** constructor overload can use the **ldc.i4.4** opcode:

- ILGenerator.Emit(OpCode)

Requirements

Platforms: Windows 98, Windows NT 4.0, Windows Millennium Edition, Windows 2000, Windows XP Home Edition, Windows XP Professional, Windows .NET Server family

OpCodes.Ldc_I4_5 Field

Pushes the integer value of 5 onto the evaluation stack as an **int32**.

```
[Visual Basic]
Public Shared ReadOnly Ldc_I4_5 As OpCode
[C#]
public static readonly OpCode Ldc_I4_5;
[C++]
public: static OpCode Ldc_I4_5;
[JScript]
public static var Ldc_I4_5 : OpCode;
```

Remarks

The following table lists the instruction's hexadecimal and Microsoft Intermediate Language (MSIL) assembly format, along with a brief reference summary:

Format	Assembly Format	Description
1B	ldc.i4.5	Pushes 5 onto the stack.

The stack transitional behavior, in sequential order, is:

1. The value 5 is pushed onto the stack.

This is a special short encoding for the push of the integer value 0. All special short encodings push 4 byte integers on the stack.

The following **Emit** constructor overload can use the **ldc.i4.5** opcode:

- ILGenerator.Emit(OpCode)

Requirements

Platforms: Windows 98, Windows NT 4.0, Windows Millennium Edition, Windows 2000, Windows XP Home Edition, Windows XP Professional, Windows .NET Server family

OpCodes.Ldc_I4_6 Field

Pushes the integer value of 6 onto the evaluation stack as an **int32**.

```
[Visual Basic]
Public Shared ReadOnly Ldc_I4_6 As OpCode
[C#]
public static readonly OpCode Ldc_I4_6;
[C++]
public: static OpCode Ldc_I4_6;
[JScript]
public static var Ldc_I4_6 : OpCode;
```

Remarks

The following table lists the instruction's hexadecimal and Microsoft Intermediate Language (MSIL) assembly format, along with a brief reference summary:

Format	Assembly Format	Description
1C	ldc.i4.6	Pushes 6 onto the stack.

The stack transitional behavior, in sequential order, is:

1. The value 6 is pushed onto the stack.

This is a special short encoding for the push of the integer value 0. All special short encodings push 4 byte integers on the stack.

The following **Emit** constructor overload can use the **ldc.i4.6** opcode:

- ILGenerator.Emit(OpCode)

Requirements

Platforms: Windows 98, Windows NT 4.0, Windows Millennium Edition, Windows 2000, Windows XP Home Edition, Windows XP Professional, Windows .NET Server family

OpCodes.Ldc_I4_7 Field

Pushes the integer value of 7 onto the evaluation stack as an **int32**.

```
[Visual Basic]
Public Shared ReadOnly Ldc_I4_7 As OpCode
[C#]
public static readonly OpCode Ldc_I4_7;
[C++]
public: static OpCode Ldc_I4_7;
[JScript]
public static var Ldc_I4_7 : OpCode;
```

Remarks

The following table lists the instruction's hexadecimal and Microsoft Intermediate Language (MSIL) assembly format, along with a brief reference summary:

Format	Assembly Format	Description
1D	ldc.i4.7	Pushes 7 onto the stack.

The stack transitional behavior, in sequential order, is:

1. The value 7 is pushed onto the stack.

This is a special short encoding for the push of the integer value 0. All special short encodings push 4 byte integers on the stack.

The following **Emit** constructor overload can use the **ldc.i4.7** opcode:

- ILGenerator.Emit(OpCode)

Requirements

Platforms: Windows 98, Windows NT 4.0, Windows Millennium Edition, Windows 2000, Windows XP Home Edition, Windows XP Professional, Windows .NET Server family

OpCodes.Ldc_I4_8 Field

Pushes the integer value of 8 onto the evaluation stack as an **int32**.

```
[Visual Basic]
Public Shared ReadOnly Ldc_I4_8 As OpCode
[C#]
public static readonly OpCode Ldc_I4_8;
[C++]
public: static OpCode Ldc_I4_8;
[JScript]
public static var Ldc_I4_8 : OpCode;
```

Remarks

The following table lists the instruction's hexadecimal and Microsoft Intermediate Language (MSIL) assembly format, along with a brief reference summary:

Format	Assembly Format	Description
1E	ldc.i4.8	Pushes 8 onto the stack.

The stack transitional behavior, in sequential order, is:

1. The value 8 is pushed onto the stack.

This is a special short encoding for the push of the integer value 0. All special short encodings push 4 byte integers on the stack.

The following **Emit** constructor overload can use the **ldc.i4.8** opcode:

- ILGenerator.Emit(OpCode)

Requirements

Platforms: Windows 98, Windows NT 4.0, Windows Millennium Edition, Windows 2000, Windows XP Home Edition, Windows XP Professional, Windows .NET Server family

OpCodes.Ldc_I4_M1 Field

Pushes the integer value of -1 onto the evaluation stack as an **int32**.

```
[Visual Basic]
Public Shared ReadOnly Ldc_I4_M1 As OpCode
[C#]
public static readonly OpCode Ldc_I4_M1;
[C++]
public: static OpCode Ldc_I4_M1;
[JScript]
public static var Ldc_I4_M1 : OpCode;
```

Remarks

The following table lists the instruction's hexadecimal and Microsoft Intermediate Language (MSIL) assembly format, along with a brief reference summary:

Format	Assembly Format	Description
15	ldc.i4.m1	Pushes -1 onto the stack.

The stack transitional behavior, in sequential order, is:

1. The value -1 is pushed onto the stack.

This is a special short encoding for the push of the integer value 0. All special short encodings push 4 byte integers on the stack.

The following **Emit** constructor overload can use the **ldc.i4.m1** opcode:

- ILGenerator.Emit(OpCode)

Requirements

Platforms: Windows 98, Windows NT 4.0, Windows Millennium Edition, Windows 2000, Windows XP Home Edition, Windows XP Professional, Windows .NET Server family

OpCodes.Ldc_I4_S Field

Pushes the supplied **int8** value onto the evaluation stack as an **int32**, short form.

```
[Visual Basic]
Public Shared ReadOnly Ldc_I4_S As OpCode
[C#]
public static readonly OpCode Ldc_I4_S;
[C++]
public: static OpCode Ldc_I4_S;
[JScript]
public static var Ldc_I4_S : OpCode;
```

Remarks

The following table lists the instruction's hexadecimal and Microsoft Intermediate Language (MSIL) assembly format, along with a brief reference summary:

Format	Assembly Format	Description
1F < int8 >	ldc.i4.s *num*	Pushes *num* onto the stack as **int32**, short form.

The stack transitional behavior, in sequential order, is:

1. The value *num* is pushed onto the stack.

ldc.i4.s is a more efficient encoding for pushing the integers from -127 to 128 onto the evaluation stack.

The following **Emit** constructor overload can use the **ldc.i4.s** opcode:

- ILGenerator.Emit(OpCode, byte)

Requirements

Platforms: Windows 98, Windows NT 4.0, Windows Millennium Edition, Windows 2000, Windows XP Home Edition, Windows XP Professional, Windows .NET Server family

OpCodes.Ldc_I8 Field

Pushes a supplied value of type **int64** onto the evaluation stack as an **int64**.

```
[Visual Basic]
Public Shared ReadOnly Ldc_I8 As OpCode
[C#]
public static readonly OpCode Ldc_I8;
[C++]
public: static OpCode Ldc_I8;
[JScript]
public static var Ldc_I8 : OpCode;
```

Remarks

The following table lists the instruction's hexadecimal and Microsoft Intermediate Language (MSIL) assembly format, along with a brief reference summary:

Format	Assembly Format	Description
21 < int64 >	ldc.i8 *num*	Pushes *num* onto the stack as **int64**.

The stack transitional behavior, in sequential order, is:

1. The value *num* is pushed onto the stack.

This encoding pushes an **int64** value onto the stack.

The following **Emit** constructor overload can use the **ldc.i8** opcode:

- ILGenerator.Emit(OpCode, long)

Requirements

Platforms: Windows 98, Windows NT 4.0, Windows Millennium Edition, Windows 2000, Windows XP Home Edition, Windows XP Professional, Windows .NET Server family

OpCodes.Ldc_R4 Field

Pushes a supplied value of type **float32** onto the evaluation stack as type **F** (float).

```
[Visual Basic]
Public Shared ReadOnly Ldc_R4 As OpCode
[C#]
public static readonly OpCode Ldc_R4;
[C++]
public: static OpCode Ldc_R4;
[JScript]
public static var Ldc_R4 : OpCode;
```

Remarks

The following table lists the instruction's hexadecimal and Microsoft Intermediate Language (MSIL) assembly format, along with a brief reference summary:

Format	Assembly Format	Description
22 < **float32** >	ldc.r4 *num*	Pushes *num* onto the stack as **F**.

The stack transitional behavior, in sequential order, is:

1. The value *num* is pushed onto the stack.

This encoding pushes a **float32** value onto the stack.

The following **Emit** constructor overload can use the **ldc.r4** opcode:

• ILGenerator.Emit(OpCode, single)

Requirements

Platforms: Windows 98, Windows NT 4.0, Windows Millennium Edition, Windows 2000, Windows XP Home Edition, Windows XP Professional, Windows .NET Server family

OpCodes.Ldc_R8 Field

Pushes a supplied value of type **float64** onto the evaluation stack as type **F** (float).

```
[Visual Basic]
Public Shared ReadOnly Ldc_R8 As OpCode
[C#]
public static readonly OpCode Ldc_R8;
[C++]
public: static OpCode Ldc_R8;
[JScript]
public static var Ldc_R8 : OpCode;
```

Remarks

The following table lists the instruction's hexadecimal and Microsoft Intermediate Language (MSIL) assembly format, along with a brief reference summary:

Format	Assembly Format	Description
23 < **float64** >	ldc.r8 *num*	Pushes *num* onto the stack as **F**.

The stack transitional behavior, in sequential order, is:

1. The value *num* is pushed onto the stack.

This encoding pushes a **float64** value onto the stack.

The following **Emit** constructor overload can use the **ldc.r8** opcode:

• ILGenerator.Emit(OpCode, double)

Requirements

Platforms: Windows 98, Windows NT 4.0, Windows Millennium Edition, Windows 2000, Windows XP Home Edition, Windows XP Professional, Windows .NET Server family

OpCodes.Ldelema Field

Loads the address of the array element at a specified array index onto the top of the evaluation stack as type **&** (managed pointer).

```
[Visual Basic]
Public Shared ReadOnly Ldelema As OpCode
[C#]
public static readonly OpCode Ldelema;
[C++]
public: static OpCode Ldelema;
[JScript]
public static var Ldelema : OpCode;
```

Remarks

The following table lists the instruction's hexadecimal and Microsoft Intermediate Language (MSIL) assembly format, along with a brief reference summary:

Format	Assembly Format	Description
8F < **T** >	ldelema *class*	Loads the address of the array element at *index* onto the top of the evaluation stack as type **&** (managed pointer).

The stack transitional behavior, in sequential order, is:

1. An object reference *array* is pushed onto the stack.
2. An index value *index* is pushed onto the stack.
3. *index* and *array* are popped from the stack; the address stored at position *index* in *array* is looked up.
4. The address is pushed onto the stack.

The **ldelema** is used to retrieve the address of an object at a particular index in an array of objects (of type *class*). The **ldelema** instruction loads the address of the value at index *index* (type **natural int**) in the zero-based one-dimensional array *array* and places it on the top of the stack. Arrays are objects and hence represented by a value of type **O**. The value must be of type *class* passed with the instruction.

The return value for **ldelema** is a managed pointer (type **&**).

Note that integer values of less than 4 bytes are extended to **int32** (not **natural int**) when they are loaded onto the evaluation stack.

NullReferenceException is thrown if *array* is a null reference.

ArrayTypeMismatchException is thrown if if *array* does not hold elements of the required type.

IndexOutOfRangeException is thrown if *index* is negative, or larger than the bound of *array*.

The following **Emit** constructor overload can use the **ldelema** opcode:

• ILGenerator.Emit(OpCode, Type)

Requirements

Platforms: Windows 98, Windows NT 4.0,
Windows Millennium Edition, Windows 2000,
Windows XP Home Edition, Windows XP Professional,
Windows .NET Server family

OpCodes.Ldelem_I Field

Loads the element with type **natural int** at a specified array index
onto the top of the evaluation stack as a **natural int**.

```
[Visual Basic]
Public Shared ReadOnly Ldelem_I As OpCode
[C#]
public static readonly OpCode Ldelem_I;
[C++]
public: static OpCode Ldelem_I;
[JScript]
public static var Ldelem_I : OpCode;
```

Remarks

The following table lists the instruction's hexadecimal and Microsoft
Intermediate Language (MSIL) assembly format, along with a brief
reference summary:

Format	Assembly Format	Description
97	ldelem.i	Loads the element with type **natural int** at *index* onto the top of the stack as a **natural int**.

The stack transitional behavior, in sequential order, is:

1. An object reference *array* is pushed onto the stack.
2. An index value *index* is pushed onto the stack.
3. *index* and *array* are popped from the stack; the value stored at
   position *index* in *array* is looked up.
4. The value is pushed onto the stack.

The **ldelem.i** instruction loads the value of the element with index
index (type **natural int**) in the zero-based one-dimensional array
array and places it on the top of the stack. Arrays are objects and
hence represented by a value of type **O**.

The return value for **ldelem.i** is **natural int**.

Note that integer values of less than 4 bytes are extended to **int32**
(not **natural int**) when they are loaded onto the evaluation stack.

NullReferenceException is thrown if *array* is a null reference.

ArrayTypeMismatchException is thrown if if *array* does not hold
elements of the required type.

IndexOutOfRangeException is thrown if *index* is negative, or
larger than the bound of *array*.

The following **Emit** constructor overload can use the **ldelem.i**
opcode:

• ILGenerator.Emit(OpCode)

Requirements

Platforms: Windows 98, Windows NT 4.0,
Windows Millennium Edition, Windows 2000,
Windows XP Home Edition, Windows XP Professional,
Windows .NET Server family

OpCodes.Ldelem_I1 Field

Loads the element with type **int8** at a specified array index onto the
top of the evaluation stack as an **int32**.

```
[Visual Basic]
Public Shared ReadOnly Ldelem_I1 As OpCode
[C#]
public static readonly OpCode Ldelem_I1;
[C++]
public: static OpCode Ldelem_I1;
[JScript]
public static var Ldelem_I1 : OpCode;
```

Remarks

The following table lists the instruction's hexadecimal and Microsoft
Intermediate Language (MSIL) assembly format, along with a brief
reference summary:

Format	Assembly Format	Description
90	ldelem.i1	Loads the element with type **int8** at *index* onto the top of the stack as an **int32**.

The stack transitional behavior, in sequential order, is:

1. An object reference *array* is pushed onto the stack.
2. An index value *index* is pushed onto the stack.
3. *index* and *array* are popped from the stack; the value stored at
   position *index* in *array* is looked up.
4. The value is pushed onto the stack.

The **ldelem.i1** instruction loads the value of the element with index
index (type **natural int**) in the zero-based one-dimensional array
array and places it on the top of the stack. Arrays are objects and
hence represented by a value of type **O**.

The return value for **ldelem.i1** is **int8**.

Note that integer values of less than 4 bytes are extended to **int32**
(not **natural int**) when they are loaded onto the evaluation stack.

NullReferenceException is thrown if *array* is a null reference.

ArrayTypeMismatchException is thrown if if *array* does not hold
elements of the required type.

IndexOutOfRangeException is thrown if *index* is negative, or
larger than the bound of *array*.

The following **Emit** constructor overload can use the **ldelem.i1**
opcode:

• ILGenerator.Emit(OpCode)

Requirements

Platforms: Windows 98, Windows NT 4.0,
Windows Millennium Edition, Windows 2000,
Windows XP Home Edition, Windows XP Professional,
Windows .NET Server family

OpCodes.Ldelem_I2 Field

Loads the element with type **int16** at a specified array index onto the
top of the evaluation stack as an **int32**.

```
[Visual Basic]
Public Shared ReadOnly Ldelem_I2 As OpCode
[C#]
public static readonly OpCode Ldelem_I2;
```

```
[C++]
public: static OpCode Ldelem_I2;
[JScript]
public static var Ldelem_I2 : OpCode;
```

Remarks

The following table lists the instruction's hexadecimal and Microsoft Intermediate Language (MSIL) assembly format, along with a brief reference summary:

Format	Assembly Format	Description
92	ldelem.i2	Loads the element with type **int16** at *index* onto the top of the stack as an **int32**.

The stack transitional behavior, in sequential order, is:
1. An object reference *array* is pushed onto the stack.
2. An index value *index* is pushed onto the stack.
3. *index* and *array* are popped from the stack; the value stored at position *index* in *array* is looked up.
4. The value is pushed onto the stack.

The **ldelem.i2** instruction loads the value of the element with index *index* (type **natural int**) in the zero-based one-dimensional array *array* and places it on the top of the stack. Arrays are objects and hence represented by a value of type **O**.

The return value for **ldelem.i2** is **int16**.

Note that integer values of less than 4 bytes are extended to **int32** (not natural int) when they are loaded onto the evaluation stack.

NullReferenceException is thrown if *array* is a null reference.

ArrayTypeMismatchException is thrown if *array* does not hold elements of the required type. **IndexOutOfRangeException** is thrown if *index* is negative, or larger than the bound of *array*.

The following **Emit** constructor overload can use the **ldelem.i2** opcode:
- ILGenerator.Emit(OpCode)

Requirements

Platforms: Windows 98, Windows NT 4.0, Windows Millennium Edition, Windows 2000, Windows XP Home Edition, Windows XP Professional, Windows .NET Server family

OpCodes.Ldelem_I4 Field

Loads the element with type **int32** at a specified array index onto the top of the evaluation stack as an **int32**.

```
[Visual Basic]
Public Shared ReadOnly Ldelem_I4 As OpCode
[C#]
public static readonly OpCode Ldelem_I4;
[C++]
public: static OpCode Ldelem_I4;
[JScript]
public static var Ldelem_I4 : OpCode;
```

Remarks

The following table lists the instruction's hexadecimal and Microsoft Intermediate Language (MSIL) assembly format, along with a brief reference summary:

Format	Assembly Format	Description
94	ldelem.i4	Loads the element with type **int32** at *index* onto the top of the stack as an **int32**.

The stack transitional behavior, in sequential order, is:
1. An object reference *array* is pushed onto the stack.
2. An index value *index* is pushed onto the stack.
3. *index* and *array* are popped from the stack; the value stored at position *index* in *array* is looked up.
4. The value is pushed onto the stack.

The **ldelem.i4** instruction loads the value of the element with index *index* (type **natural int**) in the zero-based one-dimensional array *array* and places it on the top of the stack. Arrays are objects and hence represented by a value of type **O**.

The return value for **ldelem.i4** is **int32**.

Note that integer values of less than 4 bytes are extended to int32 (not natural int) when they are loaded onto the evaluation stack.

NullReferenceException is thrown if *array* is a null reference.

ArrayTypeMismatchException is thrown if if *array* does not hold elements of the required type. **IndexOutOfRangeException** is thrown if *index* is negative, or larger than the bound of *array*.

The following **Emit** constructor overload can use the **ldelem.i4** opcode:
- ILGenerator.Emit(OpCode)

Requirements

Platforms: Windows 98, Windows NT 4.0, Windows Millennium Edition, Windows 2000, Windows XP Home Edition, Windows XP Professional, Windows .NET Server family

OpCodes.Ldelem_I8 Field

Loads the element with type **int64** at a specified array index onto the top of the evaluation stack as an **int64**.

```
[Visual Basic]
Public Shared ReadOnly Ldelem_I8 As OpCode
[C#]
public static readonly OpCode Ldelem_I8;
[C++]
public: static OpCode Ldelem_I8;
[JScript]
public static var Ldelem_I8 : OpCode;
```

Remarks

The following table lists the instruction's hexadecimal and Microsoft Intermediate Language (MSIL) assembly format, along with a brief reference summary:

Format	Assembly Format	Description
96	ldelem.i8	Loads the element with type **int64** at *index* onto the top of the stack as an **int64**.

The stack transitional behavior, in sequential order, is:
1. An object reference *array* is pushed onto the stack.
2. An index value *index* is pushed onto the stack.

3. *index* and *array* are popped from the stack; the value stored at position *index* in *array* is looked up.

4. The value is pushed onto the stack.

The **ldelem.i8** instruction loads the value of the element with index *index* (type **natural int**) in the zero-based one-dimensional array *array* and places it on the top of the stack. Arrays are objects and hence represented by a value of type **O**.

The return value for **ldelem.i8** is **int64**.

Note that integer values of less than 4 bytes are extended to **int32** (not **natural int**) when they are loaded onto the evaluation stack.

NullReferenceException is thrown if *array* is a null reference.

ArrayTypeMismatchException is thrown if if *array* does not hold elements of the required type. **IndexOutOfRangeException** is thrown if *index* is negative, or larger than the bound of *array*.

The following **Emit** constructor overload can use the **ldelem.i8** opcode:

• ILGenerator.Emit(OpCode)

Requirements

Platforms: Windows 98, Windows NT 4.0, Windows Millennium Edition, Windows 2000, Windows XP Home Edition, Windows XP Professional, Windows .NET Server family

OpCodes.Ldelem_R4 Field

Loads the element with type **float32** at a specified array index onto the top of the evaluation stack as type **F** (float).

```
[Visual Basic]
Public Shared ReadOnly Ldelem_R4 As OpCode
[C#]
public static readonly OpCode Ldelem_R4;
[C++]
public: static OpCode Ldelem_R4;
[JScript]
public static var Ldelem_R4 : OpCode;
```

Remarks

The following table lists the instruction's hexadecimal and Microsoft Intermediate Language (MSIL) assembly format, along with a brief reference summary:

Format	Assembly Format	Description
98	ldelem.r4	Loads the element with type **float32** at *index* onto the top of the stack as a type **F**.

The stack transitional behavior, in sequential order, is:

1. An object reference *array* is pushed onto the stack.
2. An index value *index* is pushed onto the stack.
3. *index* and *array* are popped from the stack; the value stored at position *index* in *array* is looked up.
4. The value is pushed onto the stack.

The **ldelem.r4** instruction loads the value of the element with index *index* (type **natural int**) in the zero-based one-dimensional array *array* and places it on the top of the stack. Arrays are objects and hence represented by a value of type **O**.

The return value for **ldelem.r4** is **float32**.

Floating-point values are converted to type **F** when loaded onto the evaluation stack.

NullReferenceException is thrown if *array* is a null reference.

ArrayTypeMismatchException is thrown if if *array* does not hold elements of the required type. **IndexOutOfRangeException** is thrown if *index* is negative, or larger than the bound of *array*.

The following **Emit** constructor overload can use the **ldelem.r4** opcode:

• ILGenerator.Emit(OpCode)

Requirements

Platforms: Windows 98, Windows NT 4.0, Windows Millennium Edition, Windows 2000, Windows XP Home Edition, Windows XP Professional, Windows .NET Server family

OpCodes.Ldelem_R8 Field

Loads the element with type **float64** at a specified array index onto the top of the evaluation stack as type **F** (float).

```
[Visual Basic]
Public Shared ReadOnly Ldelem_R8 As OpCode
[C#]
public static readonly OpCode Ldelem_R8;
[C++]
public: static OpCode Ldelem_R8;
[JScript]
public static var Ldelem_R8 : OpCode;
```

Remarks

The following table lists the instruction's hexadecimal and Microsoft Intermediate Language (MSIL) assembly format, along with a brief reference summary:

Format	Assembly Format	Description
99	ldelem.r8	Loads the element with type **float64** at *index* onto the top of the stack as type **F**.

The stack transitional behavior, in sequential order, is:

1. An object reference *array* is pushed onto the stack.
2. An index value *index* is pushed onto the stack.
3. *index* and *array* are popped from the stack; the value stored at position *index* in *array* is looked up.
4. The value is pushed onto the stack.

The **ldelem.r8** instruction loads the value of the element with index *index* (type **natural int**) in the zero-based one-dimensional array *array* and places it on the top of the stack. Arrays are objects and hence represented by a value of type **O**.

The return value for **ldelem.r8** is **float64**.

Floating-point values are converted to type **F** when loaded onto the evaluation stack.

NullReferenceException is thrown if *array* is a null reference.

ArrayTypeMismatchException is thrown if if *array* does not hold elements of the required type. **IndexOutOfRangeException** is thrown if *index* is negative, or larger than the bound of *array*.

The following **Emit** constructor overload can use the **ldelem.r8** opcode:

• ILGenerator.Emit(OpCode)

Requirements

Platforms: Windows 98, Windows NT 4.0,
Windows Millennium Edition, Windows 2000,
Windows XP Home Edition, Windows XP Professional,
Windows .NET Server family

OpCodes.Ldelem_Ref Field

Loads the element containing an object reference at a specified array index onto the top of the evaluation stack as type **O** (object reference).

```
[Visual Basic]
Public Shared ReadOnly Ldelem_Ref As OpCode
[C#]
public static readonly OpCode Ldelem_Ref;
[C++]
public: static OpCode Ldelem_Ref;
[JScript]
public static var Ldelem_Ref : OpCode;
```

Remarks

The following table lists the instruction's hexadecimal and Microsoft Intermediate Language (MSIL) assembly format, along with a brief reference summary:

Format	Assembly Format	Description
9A	ldelem.ref	Loads the element with an object reference at *index* onto the top of the stack as type **O**.

The stack transitional behavior, in sequential order, is:

1. An object reference *array* is pushed onto the stack.
2. An index value *index* is pushed onto the stack.
3. *index* and *array* are popped from the stack; the value stored at position *index* in *array* is looked up.
4. The value is pushed onto the stack.

The **ldelem.ref** instruction loads the value of the element with index *index* (type **natural int**) in the zero-based one-dimensional array *array* and places it on the top of the stack. Arrays are objects and hence represented by a value of type **O**.

The return value for **ldelem.ref** is type **O** (object reference).

NullReferenceException is thrown if *array* is a null reference.

ArrayTypeMismatchException is thrown if if *array* does not hold elements of the required type. **IndexOutOfRangeException** is thrown if *index* is negative, or larger than the bound of *array*.

The following **Emit** constructor overload can use the **ldelem.ref** opcode:

• ILGenerator.Emit(OpCode)

Requirements

Platforms: Windows 98, Windows NT 4.0,
Windows Millennium Edition, Windows 2000,
Windows XP Home Edition, Windows XP Professional,
Windows .NET Server family

OpCodes.Ldelem_U1 Field

Loads the element with type **unsigned int8** at a specified array index onto the top of the evaluation stack as an **int32**.

```
[Visual Basic]
Public Shared ReadOnly Ldelem_U1 As OpCode
[C#]
public static readonly OpCode Ldelem_U1;
[C++]
public: static OpCode Ldelem_U1;
[JScript]
public static var Ldelem_U1 : OpCode;
```

Remarks

The following table lists the instruction's hexadecimal and Microsoft Intermediate Language (MSIL) assembly format, along with a brief reference summary:

Format	Assembly Format	Description
91	ldelem.u1	Loads the element with type **unsigned int8** at *index* onto the top of the stack as an **int32**.

The stack transitional behavior, in sequential order, is:

1. An object reference *array* is pushed onto the stack.
2. An index value *index* is pushed onto the stack.
3. *index* and *array* are popped from the stack; the value stored at position *index* in *array* is looked up.
4. The value is pushed onto the stack.

The **ldelem.u1** instruction loads the value of the element with index *index* (type **natural int**) in the zero-based one-dimensional array *array* and places it on the top of the stack. Arrays are objects and hence represented by a value of type **O**.

The return value for **ldelem.u1** is **int8**.

Note that integer values of less than 4 bytes are extended to **int32** (not **natural int**) when they are loaded onto the evaluation stack.

NullReferenceException is thrown if *array* is a null reference.

ArrayTypeMismatchException is thrown if if *array* does not hold elements of the required type. **IndexOutOfRangeException** is thrown if *index* is negative, or larger than the bound of *array*.

The following **Emit** constructor overload can use the **ldelem.u1** opcode:

• ILGenerator.Emit(OpCode)

Requirements

Platforms: Windows 98, Windows NT 4.0,
Windows Millennium Edition, Windows 2000,
Windows XP Home Edition, Windows XP Professional,
Windows .NET Server family

OpCodes.Ldelem_U2 Field

Loads the element with type **unsigned int16** at a specified array index onto the top of the evaluation stack as an **int32**.

```
[Visual Basic]
Public Shared ReadOnly Ldelem_U2 As OpCode
[C#]
public static readonly OpCode Ldelem_U2;
```

```
[C++]
public: static OpCode Ldelem_U2;
[JScript]
public static var Ldelem_U2 : OpCode;
```

Remarks

The following table lists the instruction's hexadecimal and Microsoft Intermediate Language (MSIL) assembly format, along with a brief reference summary:

Format	Assembly Format	Description
93	ldelem.u2	Loads the element with type **unsigned int16** at index onto the top of the stack as an **int32**.

The stack transitional behavior, in sequential order, is:

1. An object reference *array* is pushed onto the stack.
2. An index value *index* is pushed onto the stack.
3. *index* and *array* are popped from the stack; the value stored at position *index* in *array* is looked up.
4. The value is pushed onto the stack.

The **ldelem.u2** instruction loads the value of the element with index *index* (type **natural int**) in the zero-based one-dimensional array *array* and places it on the top of the stack. Arrays are objects and hence represented by a value of type **O**.

The return value for **ldelem.u2** is **int16**.

Note that integer values of less than 4 bytes are extended to **int32** (not **natural int**) when they are loaded onto the evaluation stack.

NullReferenceException is thrown if *array* is a null reference.

ArrayTypeMismatchException is thrown if if *array* does not hold elements of the required type. **IndexOutOfRangeException** is thrown if *index* is negative, or larger than the bound of *array*.

The following **Emit** constructor overload can use the **ldelem.u2** opcode:

- ILGenerator.Emit(OpCode)

Requirements

Platforms: Windows 98, Windows NT 4.0, Windows Millennium Edition, Windows 2000, Windows XP Home Edition, Windows XP Professional, Windows .NET Server family

OpCodes.Ldelem_U4 Field

Loads the element with type **unsigned int32** at a specified array index onto the top of the evaluation stack as an **int32**.

```
[Visual Basic]
Public Shared ReadOnly Ldelem_U4 As OpCode
[C#]
public static readonly OpCode Ldelem_U4;
[C++]
public: static OpCode Ldelem_U4;
[JScript]
public static var Ldelem_U4 : OpCode;
```

Remarks

The following table lists the instruction's hexadecimal and Microsoft Intermediate Language (MSIL) assembly format, along with a brief reference summary:

Format	Assembly Format	Description
94	ldelem.u4	Loads the element with type **unsigned int32** at index onto the top of the stack as an **int32**.

The stack transitional behavior, in sequential order, is:

1. An object reference *array* is pushed onto the stack.
2. An index value *index* is pushed onto the stack.
3. *index* and *array* are popped from the stack; the value stored at position *index* in *array* is looked up.
4. The value is pushed onto the stack.

The **ldelem.u4** instruction loads the value of the element with index *index* (type **natural int**) in the zero-based one-dimensional array *array* and places it on the top of the stack. Arrays are objects and hence represented by a value of type **O**.

The return value for **ldelem.u4** is **int32**.

Note that integer values of less than 4 bytes are extended to **int32** (not **natural int**) when they are loaded onto the evaluation stack.

NullReferenceException is thrown if *array* is a null reference.

ArrayTypeMismatchException is thrown if array does not hold elements of the required type. **IndexOutOfRangeException** is thrown if *index* is negative, or larger than the bound of *array*.

The following **Emit** constructor overload can use the **ldelem.u4** opcode:

- ILGenerator.Emit(OpCode)

Requirements

Platforms: Windows 98, Windows NT 4.0, Windows Millennium Edition, Windows 2000, Windows XP Home Edition, Windows XP Professional, Windows .NET Server family

OpCodes.Ldfld Field

Finds the value of a field in the object whose reference is currently on the evaluation stack.

```
[Visual Basic]
Public Shared ReadOnly Ldfld As OpCode
[C#]
public static readonly OpCode Ldfld;
[C++]
public: static OpCode Ldfld;
[JScript]
public static var Ldfld : OpCode;
```

Remarks

The following table lists the instruction's hexadecimal and Microsoft Intermediate Language (MSIL) assembly format, along with a brief reference summary:

Format	Assembly Format	Description
7B < **T** >	ldfld *field*	Pushes the value of a field in a specified object onto the stack.

The stack transitional behavior, in sequential order, is:

1. An object reference (or pointer) is pushed onto the stack.
2. The object reference (or pointer) is popped from the stack; the value of the specified field in the object is found.
3. The value stored in the field is pushed onto the stack.

The **ldfld** instruction pushes the value of a field located in an object onto the stack. The object must be on the stack as an object reference (type **O**), a managed pointer (type **&**), an unmanaged pointer (type **natural int**), a transient pointer (type *), or an instance of a value type. The use of an unmanaged pointer is not permitted in verifiable code. The object's field is specified by a metadata token that must refer to a field member. The return type is the same as the one associated with the field. The field may be either an instance field (in which case the object must not be a null reference) or a static field.

The **ldfld** instruction can be preceded by either or both of the **Unaligned** and **Volatile** prefixes.

NullReferenceException is thrown if the object is null and the field is not static.

MissingFieldException is thrown if the specified field is not found in the metadata. This is typically checked when Microsoft Intermediate Language (MSIL) instructions are converted to native code, not at run time.

The following **Emit** constructor overload can use the **ldfld** opcode:

• ILGenerator.Emit(OpCode, FieldInfo)

Requirements

Platforms: Windows 98, Windows NT 4.0, Windows Millennium Edition, Windows 2000, Windows XP Home Edition, Windows XP Professional, Windows .NET Server family

OpCodes.Ldflda Field

Finds the address of a field in the object whose reference is currently on the evaluation stack.

```
[Visual Basic]
Public Shared ReadOnly Ldflda As OpCode
[C#]
public static readonly OpCode Ldflda;
[C++]
public: static OpCode Ldflda;
[JScript]
public static var Ldflda : OpCode;
```

Remarks

The following table lists the instruction's hexadecimal and Microsoft Intermediate Language (MSIL) assembly format, along with a brief reference summary:

Format	Assembly Format	Description
7C < **T** >	ldflda *field*	Pushes the address of *field* in a specified object onto the stack.

The stack transitional behavior, in sequential order, is:

1. An object reference (or pointer) is pushed onto the stack.
2. The object reference (or pointer) is popped from the stack; the address of the specified field in the object is found.
3. The address stored in the field is pushed onto the stack.

The **ldflda** instruction pushes the address of a field located in an object onto the stack. The object must be on the stack as an object reference (type **O**), a managed pointer (type **&**), an unmanaged pointer (type **natural int**), a transient pointer (type *), or an instance of a value type. The use of an unmanaged pointer is not permitted in verifiable code. The object's field is specified by a metadata token that must refer to a field member.

The value returned by **ldflda** is a managed pointer (type **&**) unless the object is pushed onto the stack as an unmanaged pointer, in which case the return address is also an unmanaged pointer (type **natural int**).

The **ldflda** instruction can be preceded by either or both of the **Unaligned** and **Volatile** prefixes.

InvalidOperationException is thrown if the object is not within the application domain from which it is being accessed. The address of a field that is not inside the accessing application domain cannot be loaded.

NullReferenceException is thrown if the object is null and the field is not static.

MissingFieldException is thrown if the specified field is not found in the metadata. This is typically checked when Microsoft Intermediate Language (MSIL) instructions are converted to native code, not at run time.

The following **Emit** constructor overload can use the **ldflda** opcode:

• ILGenerator.Emit(OpCode, FieldInfo)

Requirements

Platforms: Windows 98, Windows NT 4.0, Windows Millennium Edition, Windows 2000, Windows XP Home Edition, Windows XP Professional, Windows .NET Server family

OpCodes.Ldftn Field

Pushes an unmanaged pointer (type **natural int**) to the native code implementing a specific method onto the evaluation stack.

```
[Visual Basic]
Public Shared ReadOnly Ldftn As OpCode
[C#]
public static readonly OpCode Ldftn;
[C++]
public: static OpCode Ldftn;
[JScript]
public static var Ldftn : OpCode;
```

Remarks

The following table lists the instruction's hexadecimal and Microsoft Intermediate Language (MSIL) assembly format, along with a brief reference summary:

Format	Assembly Format	Description
FE 06 < **T** >	ldftn *method*	Pushes a pointer to a method referenced by *method* on the stack.

The stack transitional behavior, in sequential order, is:

1. The unmanaged pointer to a specific method is pushed onto the stack.

The specific method (*method*) can be called using the **Calli** instruction if it references a managed method (or a stub that transitions from managed to unmanaged code).

The value returned points to native code using the calling convention specified by the *method* metadata token. Thus, a method pointer can be easily passed to unmanaged native code (specifically, as a callback routine).

The following **Emit** constructor overload can use the **ldftn** opcode:

• ILGenerator.Emit(OpCode, MethodInfo)

Requirements

Platforms: Windows 98, Windows NT 4.0, Windows Millennium Edition, Windows 2000, Windows XP Home Edition, Windows XP Professional, Windows .NET Server family

OpCodes.Ldind_I Field

Loads a value of type **natural int** as a **natural int** onto the evaluation stack indirectly.

```
[Visual Basic]
Public Shared ReadOnly Ldind_I As OpCode
[C#]
public static readonly OpCode Ldind_I;
[C++]
public: static OpCode Ldind_I;
[JScript]
public static var Ldind_I : OpCode;
```

Remarks

The following table lists the instruction's hexadecimal and Microsoft Intermediate Language (MSIL) assembly format, along with a brief reference summary:

Format	Assembly Format	Description
4D	ldind.i	Loads the **natural int** value at address *addr* onto the stack as a **natural int**.

The stack transitional behavior, in sequential order, is:

1. An address is pushed onto the stack.
2. The address is popped from the stack; the value located at the address is fetched.
3. The fetched value is pushed onto the stack.

The **ldind.i** instruction indirectly loads a **natural int** value from the specified address (of type **natural int**, **&**, or *) onto the stack as a **natural int**.

All of the **ldind** instructions are shortcuts for a **Ldobj** instruction that specifies the corresponding built-in value class.

Note that integer values of less than 4 bytes are extended to **int32** (not **natural int**) when they are loaded onto the evaluation stack. Floating-point values are converted to **F** type when loaded onto the evaluation stack.

Correctly-formed Microsoft Intermediate Language (MSIL) ensures that the **ldind** instructions are used in a manner consistent with the type of the pointer.

The address initially pushed onto the stack must be aligned to the natural size of objects on the machine or a **NullReferenceException** can occur (see the **Unaligned** prefix instruction for preventative measures). The results of all MSIL instructions that return addresses (for example, **Ldloca** and **Ldarga**) are safely aligned. For datatypes larger than 1 byte, the byte ordering is dependent on the target CPU. Code that depends on byte ordering might not run on all platforms.

NullReferenceException can be thrown if an invalid address is detected.

The following **Emit** constructor overload can use the **ldind.i** opcode:

• ILGenerator.Emit(OpCode)

Requirements

Platforms: Windows 98, Windows NT 4.0, Windows Millennium Edition, Windows 2000, Windows XP Home Edition, Windows XP Professional, Windows .NET Server family

OpCodes.Ldind_I1 Field

Loads a value of type **int8** as an **int32** onto the evaluation stack indirectly.

```
[Visual Basic]
Public Shared ReadOnly Ldind_I1 As OpCode
[C#]
public static readonly OpCode Ldind_I1;
[C++]
public: static OpCode Ldind_I1;
[JScript]
public static var Ldind_I1 : OpCode;
```

Remarks

The following table lists the instruction's hexadecimal and Microsoft Intermediate Language (MSIL) assembly format, along with a brief reference summary:

Format	Assembly Format	Description
46	ldind.i1	Loads the **int8** value at address *addr* onto the stack as an **int32**.

The stack transitional behavior, in sequential order, is:

1. An address is pushed onto the stack.
2. The address is popped from the stack; the value located at the address is fetched.
3. The fetched value is pushed onto the stack..

The **ldind.i1** instruction indirectly loads an **int8** value from the specified address (of type **natural int**, **&**, or *) onto the stack as an **int32**.

All of the **ldind** instructions are shortcuts for a **Ldobj** instruction that specifies the corresponding built-in value class.

Note that integer values of less than 4 bytes are extended to **int32** (not **natural int**) when they are loaded onto the evaluation stack. Floating-point values are converted to **F** type when loaded onto the evaluation stack.

Correctly-formed Microsoft Intermediate Language (MSIL) ensures that the **ldind** instructions are used in a manner consistent with the type of the pointer.

The address initially pushed onto the stack must be aligned to the natural size of objects on the machine or a **NullReferenceException** can occur (see the **Unaligned** prefix instruction for preventative measures). The results of all MSIL instructions that return addresses (for example, **Ldloca** and **Ldarga**) are safely aligned. For datatypes larger than 1 byte, the byte ordering is dependent on the target CPU. Code that depends on byte ordering might not run on all platforms.

NullReferenceException can be thrown if an invalid address is detected.

The following **Emit** constructor overload can use the **ldind.i1** opcode:

*   ILGenerator.Emit(OpCode)

Requirements

Platforms: Windows 98, Windows NT 4.0, Windows Millennium Edition, Windows 2000, Windows XP Home Edition, Windows XP Professional, Windows .NET Server family

OpCodes.Ldind_I2 Field

Loads a value of type **int16** as an **int32** onto the evaluation stack indirectly.

```
[Visual Basic]
Public Shared ReadOnly Ldind_I2 As OpCode
[C#]
public static readonly OpCode Ldind_I2;
[C++]
public: static OpCode Ldind_I2;
[JScript]
public static var Ldind_I2 : OpCode;
```

Remarks

The following table lists the instruction's hexadecimal and Microsoft Intermediate Language (MSIL) assembly format, along with a brief reference summary:

Format	Assembly Format	Description
48	ldind.i2	Loads the **int16** value at address *addr* onto the stack as an **int32**.

The stack transitional behavior, in sequential order, is:

1. An address is pushed onto the stack.
2. The address is popped from the stack; the value located at the address is fetched.
3. The fetched value is pushed onto the stack.

The **ldind.i2** instruction indirectly loads an **int16** value from the specified address (of type **natural int**, **&**, or *) onto the stack as an **int32**.

All of the **ldind** instructions are shortcuts for a **Ldobj** instruction that specifies the corresponding built-in value class.

Note that integer values of less than 4 bytes are extended to **int32** (not **natural int**) when they are loaded onto the evaluation stack. Floating-point values are converted to **F** type when loaded onto the evaluation stack.

Correctly-formed Microsoft Intermediate Language (MSIL) ensures that the **ldind** instructions are used in a manner consistent with the type of the pointer.

The address initially pushed onto the stack must be aligned to the natural size of objects on the machine or a **NullReferenceException** can occur (see the **Unaligned** prefix instruction for preventative measures). The results of all MSIL instructions that return addresses (for example, **Ldloca** and **Ldarga**) are safely aligned. For datatypes larger than 1 byte, the byte ordering is dependent on the target CPU. Code that depends on byte ordering might not run on all platforms.

NullReferenceException can be thrown if an invalid address is detected.

The following **Emit** constructor overload can use the **ldind.i2** opcode:

*   ILGenerator.Emit(OpCode)

Requirements

Platforms: Windows 98, Windows NT 4.0, Windows Millennium Edition, Windows 2000, Windows XP Home Edition, Windows XP Professional, Windows .NET Server family

OpCodes.Ldind_I4 Field

Loads a value of type **int32** as an **int32** onto the evaluation stack indirectly.

```
[Visual Basic]
Public Shared ReadOnly Ldind_I4 As OpCode
[C#]
public static readonly OpCode Ldind_I4;
[C++]
public: static OpCode Ldind_I4;
[JScript]
public static var Ldind_I4 : OpCode;
```

Remarks

The following table lists the instruction's hexadecimal and Microsoft Intermediate Language (MSIL) assembly format, along with a brief reference summary:

Format	Assembly Format	Description
4A	ldind.i4	Loads the **int32** value at address *addr* onto the stack as an **int32**.

The stack transitional behavior, in sequential order, is:

1. An address is pushed onto the stack.
2. The address is popped from the stack; the value located at the address is fetched.
3. The fetched value is pushed onto the stack.

The **ldind.i4** instruction indirectly loads an **int32** value from the specified address (of type **natural int**, **&**, or *) onto the stack as a **int32**.

All of the **ldind** instructions are shortcuts for a **Ldobj** instruction that specifies the corresponding built-in value class.

Note that integer values of less than 4 bytes are extended to **int32** (not **natural int**) when they are loaded onto the evaluation stack. Floating-point values are converted to **F** type when loaded onto the evaluation stack.

Correctly-formed Microsoft Intermediate Language (MSIL) ensures that the **ldind** instructions are used in a manner consistent with the type of the pointer.

The address initially pushed onto the stack must be aligned to the natural size of objects on the machine or a **NullReferenceException** can occur (see the **Unaligned** prefix instruction for preventative measures). The results of all MSIL instructions that return addresses (for example, **Ldloca** and **Ldarga**) are safely aligned. For datatypes larger than 1 byte, the byte ordering is dependent on the target CPU. Code that depends on byte ordering might not run on all platforms.

NullReferenceException can be thrown if an invalid address is detected.

The following **Emit** constructor overload can use the **ldind.i4** opcode:

• ILGenerator.Emit(OpCode)

Requirements

Platforms: Windows 98, Windows NT 4.0, Windows Millennium Edition, Windows 2000, Windows XP Home Edition, Windows XP Professional, Windows .NET Server family

OpCodes.Ldind_I8 Field

Loads a value of type **int64** as an **int64** onto the evaluation stack indirectly.

```
[Visual Basic]
Public Shared ReadOnly Ldind_I8 As OpCode
[C#]
public static readonly OpCode Ldind_I8;
[C++]
public: static OpCode Ldind_I8;
[JScript]
public static var Ldind_I8 : OpCode;
```

Remarks

The following table lists the instruction's hexadecimal and Microsoft Intermediate Language (MSIL) assembly format, along with a brief reference summary:

Format	Assembly Format	Description
4C	ldind.i8	Loads the **int64** value at address *addr* onto the stack as an **int64**.

The stack transitional behavior, in sequential order, is:

1. An address is pushed onto the stack.
2. The address is popped from the stack; the value located at the address is fetched.
3. The fetched value is pushed onto the stack.

The **ldind.i8** instruction indirectly loads an **int64** value from the specified address (of type **natural int**, **&**, or *) onto the stack as an **int64**.

All of the **ldind** instructions are shortcuts for a **Ldobj** instruction that specifies the corresponding built-in value class.

Note that integer values of less than 4 bytes are extended to **int32** (not **natural int**) when they are loaded onto the evaluation stack. Floating-point values are converted to **F** type when loaded onto the evaluation stack.

Correctly-formed Microsoft Intermediate Language (MSIL) ensures that the **ldind** instructions are used in a manner consistent with the type of the pointer.

The address initially pushed onto the stack must be aligned to the natural size of objects on the machine or a **NullReferenceException** can occur (see the **Unaligned** prefix instruction for preventative measures). The results of all MSIL instructions that return addresses (for example, **Ldloca** and **Ldarga**) are safely aligned. For datatypes larger than 1 byte, the byte ordering is dependent on the target CPU. Code that depends on byte ordering might not run on all platforms.

NullReferenceException can be thrown if an invalid address is detected.

The following **Emit** constructor overload can use the **ldind.i8** opcode:

• ILGenerator.Emit(OpCode)

Requirements

Platforms: Windows 98, Windows NT 4.0, Windows Millennium Edition, Windows 2000, Windows XP Home Edition, Windows XP Professional, Windows .NET Server family

OpCodes.Ldind_R4 Field

Loads a value of type **float32** as a type **F** (float) onto the evaluation stack indirectly.

```
[Visual Basic]
Public Shared ReadOnly Ldind_R4 As OpCode
[C#]
public static readonly OpCode Ldind_R4;
[C++]
public: static OpCode Ldind_R4;
[JScript]
public static var Ldind_R4 : OpCode;
```

Remarks

The following table lists the instruction's hexadecimal and Microsoft Intermediate Language (MSIL) assembly format, along with a brief reference summary:

Format	Assembly Format	Description
4E	ldind.r4	Loads the **float32** value at address *addr* onto the stack as a type **F**.

The stack transitional behavior, in sequential order, is:

1. An address is pushed onto the stack.
2. The address is popped from the stack; the value located at the address is fetched.
3. The fetched value is pushed onto the stack.

The **ldind.r4** instruction indirectly loads a **float32** value from the specified address (of type **natural int**, **&**, or *) onto the stack as a type **F**.

All of the **ldind** instructions are shortcuts for a **Ldobj** instruction that specifies the corresponding built-in value class.

Note that integer values of less than 4 bytes are extended to **int32** (not **natural int**) when they are loaded onto the evaluation stack. Floating-point values are converted to **F** type when loaded onto the evaluation stack.

Correctly-formed Microsoft Intermediate Language (MSIL) ensures that the **ldind** instructions are used in a manner consistent with the type of the pointer.

The address initially pushed onto the stack must be aligned to the natural size of objects on the machine or a **NullReferenceException** can occur (see the **Unaligned** prefix instruction for preventative measures). The results of all MSIL instructions that return addresses (for example, **Ldloca** and **Ldarga**) are safely aligned. For datatypes larger than 1 byte, the byte ordering is dependent on the target CPU. Code that depends on byte ordering might not run on all platforms.

NullReferenceException can be thrown if an invalid address is detected.

The following **Emit** constructor overload can use the **ldind.r4** opcode:

* ILGenerator.Emit(OpCode)

Requirements

Platforms: Windows 98, Windows NT 4.0, Windows Millennium Edition, Windows 2000, Windows XP Home Edition, Windows XP Professional, Windows .NET Server family

OpCodes.Ldind_R8 Field

Loads a value of type **float64** as a type **F** (float) onto the evaluation stack indirectly.

```
[Visual Basic]
Public Shared ReadOnly Ldind_R8 As OpCode
[C#]
public static readonly OpCode Ldind_R8;
[C++]
public: static OpCode Ldind_R8;
[JScript]
public static var Ldind_R8 : OpCode;
```

Remarks

The following table lists the instruction's hexadecimal and Microsoft Intermediate Language (MSIL) assembly format, along with a brief reference summary:

Format	Assembly Format	Description
4F	ldind.r8	Loads the **float64** value at address *addr* onto the stack as a type **F**.

The stack transitional behavior, in sequential order, is:
1. An address is pushed onto the stack.
2. The address is popped from the stack; the value located at the address is fetched.
3. The fetched value is pushed onto the stack.

The **ldind.r8** instruction indirectly loads a **float64** value from the specified address (of type **natural int**, **&**, or *) onto the stack as a **float64**.

All of the **ldind** instructions are shortcuts for a **Ldobj** instruction that specifies the corresponding built-in value class.

Note that integer values of less than 4 bytes are extended to **int32** (not **natural int**) when they are loaded onto the evaluation stack. Floating-point values are converted to **F** type when loaded onto the evaluation stack.

Correctly-formed Microsoft Intermediate Language (MSIL) ensures that the **ldind** instructions are used in a manner consistent with the type of the pointer.

The address initially pushed onto the stack must be aligned to the natural size of objects on the machine or a **NullReferenceException** can occur (see the **Unaligned** prefix instruction for preventative measures). The results of all MSIL instructions that return addresses (for example, **Ldloca** and **Ldarga**) are safely aligned. For datatypes larger than 1 byte, the byte ordering is dependent on the target CPU. Code that depends on byte ordering might not run on all platforms.

NullReferenceException can be thrown if an invalid address is detected.

The following **Emit** constructor overload can use the **ldind.r8** opcode:

* ILGenerator.Emit(OpCode)

Requirements

Platforms: Windows 98, Windows NT 4.0, Windows Millennium Edition, Windows 2000, Windows XP Home Edition, Windows XP Professional, Windows .NET Server family

OpCodes.Ldind_Ref Field

Loads an object reference as a type **O** (object reference) onto the evaluation stack indirectly.

```
[Visual Basic]
Public Shared ReadOnly Ldind_Ref As OpCode
[C#]
public static readonly OpCode Ldind_Ref;
[C++]
public: static OpCode Ldind_Ref;
[JScript]
public static var Ldind_Ref : OpCode;
```

Remarks

The following table lists the instruction's hexadecimal and Microsoft Intermediate Language (MSIL) assembly format, along with a brief reference summary:

Format	Assembly Format	Description
50	ldind.ref	Loads the object reference at address *addr* onto the stack as a type **O**

The stack transitional behavior, in sequential order, is:
1. An address is pushed onto the stack.
2. The address is popped from the stack; the object reference located at the address is fetched.
3. The fetched reference is pushed onto the stack.

The **ldind.ref** instruction indirectly loads the object reference the specified address (of type **natural int**, **&**, or *) onto the stack as type **O**.

All of the **ldind** instructions are shortcuts for a **Ldobj** instruction that specifies the corresponding built-in value class.

Note that integer values of less than 4 bytes are extended to **int32** (not **natural int**) when they are loaded onto the evaluation stack. Floating-point values are converted to **F** type when loaded onto the evaluation stack.

Correctly-formed Microsoft Intermediate Language (MSIL) ensures that the **ldind** instructions are used in a manner consistent with the type of the pointer.

The address initially pushed onto the stack must be aligned to the natural size of objects on the machine or a **NullReferenceException** can occur (see the **Unaligned** prefix instruction for preventative measures). The results of all MSIL instructions that return addresses (for example, **Ldloca** and **Ldarga**) are safely aligned. For datatypes larger than 1 byte, the byte ordering is dependent on the target CPU. Code that depends on byte ordering might not run on all platforms.

NullReferenceException can be thrown if an invalid address is detected.

The following **Emit** constructor overload can use the **ldind.ref** opcode:

• ILGenerator.Emit(OpCode)

Requirements

Platforms: Windows 98, Windows NT 4.0, Windows Millennium Edition, Windows 2000, Windows XP Home Edition, Windows XP Professional, Windows .NET Server family

OpCodes.Ldind_U1 Field

Loads a value of type **unsigned int8** as an **int32** onto the evaluation stack indirectly.

```
[Visual Basic]
Public Shared ReadOnly Ldind_U1 As OpCode
[C#]
public static readonly OpCode Ldind_U1;
[C++]
public: static OpCode Ldind_U1;
[JScript]
public static var Ldind_U1 : OpCode;
```

Remarks

The following table lists the instruction's hexadecimal and Microsoft Intermediate Language (MSIL) assembly format, along with a brief reference summary:

Format	Assembly Format	Description
47	ldind.u1	Loads the u nsigned int8 value at address *addr* onto the stack as an **int32**.

The stack transitional behavior, in sequential order, is:

1. An address is pushed onto the stack.
2. The address is popped from the stack; the value located at the address is fetched.
3. The fetched value is pushed onto the stack.

The **ldind.u1** instruction indirectly loads an **unsigned int8** value from the specified address (of type **natural int**, **&**, or *) onto the stack as an **int32**.

All of the **ldind** instructions are shortcuts for a **Ldobj** instruction that specifies the corresponding built-in value class.

Note that integer values of less than 4 bytes are extended to **int32** (not **natural int**) when they are loaded onto the evaluation stack. Floating-point values are converted to **F** type when loaded onto the evaluation stack.

Correctly-formed Microsoft Intermediate Language (MSIL) ensures that the **ldind** instructions are used in a manner consistent with the type of the pointer.

The address initially pushed onto the stack must be aligned to the natural size of objects on the machine or a **NullReferenceException** can occur (see the **Unaligned** prefix instruction for preventative measures). The results of all MSIL instructions that return addresses (for example, **Ldloca** and **Ldarga**) are safely aligned. For datatypes larger than 1 byte, the byte ordering is dependent on the target CPU. Code that depends on byte ordering might not run on all platforms.

NullReferenceException can be thrown if an invalid address is detected.

The following **Emit** constructor overload can use the **ldind.u1** opcode:

• ILGenerator.Emit(OpCode)

Requirements

Platforms: Windows 98, Windows NT 4.0, Windows Millennium Edition, Windows 2000, Windows XP Home Edition, Windows XP Professional, Windows .NET Server family

OpCodes.Ldind_U2 Field

Loads a value of type **unsigned int16** as an **int32** onto the evaluation stack indirectly.

```
[Visual Basic]
Public Shared ReadOnly Ldind_U2 As OpCode
[C#]
public static readonly OpCode Ldind_U2;
[C++]
public: static OpCode Ldind_U2;
[JScript]
public static var Ldind_U2 : OpCode;
```

Remarks

The following table lists the instruction's hexadecimal and Microsoft Intermediate Language (MSIL) assembly format, along with a brief reference summary:

Format	Assembly Format	Description
49	ldind.u2	Loads the **unsigned int16** value at address *addr* onto the stack as an **int32**.

The stack transitional behavior, in sequential order, is:

1. An address is pushed onto the stack.
2. The address is popped from the stack; the value located at the address is fetched.
3. The fetched value is pushed onto the stack.

The **ldind.u2** instruction indirectly loads an **unsigned int16** value from the specified address (of type **natural int**, **&**, or *) onto the stack as an **int32**.

All of the **ldind** instructions are shortcuts for a **Ldobj** instruction that specifies the corresponding built-in value class.

Note that integer values of less than 4 bytes are extended to **int32** (not **natural int**) when they are loaded onto the evaluation stack. Floating-point values are converted to **F** type when loaded onto the evaluation stack.

Correctly-formed Microsoft Intermediate Language (MSIL) ensures that the **ldind** instructions are used in a manner consistent with the type of the pointer.

The address initially pushed onto the stack must be aligned to the natural size of objects on the machine or a **NullReferenceException** can occur (see the **Unaligned** prefix instruction for preventative measures). The results of all MSIL instructions that return addresses (for example, **Ldloca** and **Ldarga**) are safely aligned. For datatypes larger than 1 byte, the byte ordering is dependent on the target CPU. Code that depends on byte ordering might not run on all platforms.

NullReferenceException can be thrown if an invalid address is detected.

The following **Emit** constructor overload can use the **ldind.u2** opcode:

• ILGenerator.Emit(OpCode)

Requirements

Platforms: Windows 98, Windows NT 4.0, Windows Millennium Edition, Windows 2000, Windows XP Home Edition, Windows XP Professional, Windows .NET Server family

OpCodes.Ldind_U4 Field

Loads a value of type **unsigned int32** as an **int32** onto the evaluation stack indirectly.

```
[Visual Basic]
Public Shared ReadOnly Ldind_U4 As OpCode
[C#]
public static readonly OpCode Ldind_U4;
[C++]
public: static OpCode Ldind_U4;
[JScript]
public static var Ldind_U4 : OpCode;
```

Remarks

The following table lists the instruction's hexadecimal and Microsoft Intermediate Language (MSIL) assembly format, along with a brief reference summary:

Format	Assembly Format	Description
4B	ldind.u4	Loads the **unsigned int32** value at address *addr* onto the stack as an **int32**.

The stack transitional behavior, in sequential order, is:

1. An address is pushed onto the stack.
2. The address is popped from the stack; the value located at the address is fetched.
3. The fetched value is pushed onto the stack.

The **ldind.u4** instruction indirectly loads an **unsigned int32** value from the specified address (of type **natural int, &,** or *) onto the stack as an **int32**.

All of the **ldind** instructions are shortcuts for a **Ldobj** instruction that specifies the corresponding built-in value class.

Note that integer values of less than 4 bytes are extended to **int32** (not **natural int**) when they are loaded onto the evaluation stack. Floating-point values are converted to **F** type when loaded onto the evaluation stack.

Correctly-formed Microsoft Intermediate Language (MSIL) ensures that the **ldind** instructions are used in a manner consistent with the type of the pointer.

The address initially pushed onto the stack must be aligned to the natural size of objects on the machine or a **NullReferenceException** can occur (see the **Unaligned** prefix instruction for preventative measures). The results of all MSIL instructions that return addresses (for example, **Ldloca** and **Ldarga**) are safely aligned. For datatypes larger than 1 byte, the byte ordering is dependent on the target CPU. Code that depends on byte ordering might not run on all platforms.

NullReferenceException can be thrown if an invalid address is detected.

The following **Emit** constructor overload can use the **ldind.u4** opcode:

• ILGenerator.Emit(OpCode)

Requirements

Platforms: Windows 98, Windows NT 4.0, Windows Millennium Edition, Windows 2000, Windows XP Home Edition, Windows XP Professional, Windows .NET Server family

OpCodes.Ldlen Field

Pushes the number of elements of a zero-based, one-dimensional array onto the evaluation stack.

```
[Visual Basic]
Public Shared ReadOnly Ldlen As OpCode
[C#]
public static readonly OpCode Ldlen;
[C++]
public: static OpCode Ldlen;
[JScript]
public static var Ldlen : OpCode;
```

Remarks

The following table lists the instruction's hexadecimal and Microsoft Intermediate Language (MSIL) assembly format, along with a brief reference summary:

Format	Assembly Format	Description
8E	ldlen	Pushes the length (of type **natural unsigned int**) of an array on the stack.

The stack transitional behavior, in sequential order, is:

1. An object reference to an array is pushed onto the stack.
2. The array reference is popped from the stack and the length is computed.
3. The length is pushed onto the stack.

Arrays are objects and hence represented by a value of type **O**. The length is returned as a **natural unsigned int**.

NullReferenceException is thrown if the array reference is a null reference.

The following **Emit** constructor overload can use the **ldlen** opcode:

• ILGenerator.Emit(OpCode)

Requirements

Platforms: Windows 98, Windows NT 4.0, Windows Millennium Edition, Windows 2000, Windows XP Home Edition, Windows XP Professional, Windows .NET Server family

OpCodes.Ldloc Field

Loads the local variable at a specific index onto the evaluation stack.

```
[Visual Basic]
Public Shared ReadOnly Ldloc As OpCode
[C#]
public static readonly OpCode Ldloc;
[C++]
public: static OpCode Ldloc;
[JScript]
public static var Ldloc : OpCode;
```

Remarks

The following table lists the instruction's hexadecimal and Microsoft Intermediate Language (MSIL) assembly format, along with a brief reference summary:

Format	Assembly Format	Description
FE 06 < **unsigned int16** >	ldloc *index*	Loads the local variable at index *index* onto stack.

The stack transitional behavior, in sequential order, is:

1. The local variable value at the specified index is pushed onto the stack.

The **ldloc** instruction pushes the contents of the local variable number at the passed index onto the evaluation stack, where the local variables are numbered 0 onwards. Local variables are initialized to 0 before entering the method only if the initialize flag on the method is true. There are 65,535 (2^16-1) local variables possible (0-65,534). Index 65,535 is not valid since likely implementations will use a 2-byte integer to track both a local's index, along with the total number of locals for a given method. If an index of 65535 had been made valid, it would require a wider integer to track the number of locals in such a method.

The **ldloc.0**, **ldloc.1**, **ldloc.2**, and **ldloc.3** instructions provide an efficient encoding for accessing the first four local variables.

The type of the value is the same as the type of the local variable, which is specified in the method header. See Partition I. Local variables that are smaller than 4 bytes long are expanded to type **int32** when they are loaded onto the stack. Floating-point values are expanded to their native size (type **F**).

The following **Emit** constructor overloads can use the **ldloc** opcode:

- ILGenerator.Emit(OpCode, LocalBuilder)
- ILGenerator.Emit(OpCode, short)

Requirements

Platforms: Windows 98, Windows NT 4.0, Windows Millennium Edition, Windows 2000, Windows XP Home Edition, Windows XP Professional, Windows .NET Server family

OpCodes.Ldloca Field

Loads the address of the local variable at a specific index onto the evaluation stack.

```
[Visual Basic]
Public Shared ReadOnly Ldloca As OpCode
[C#]
public static readonly OpCode Ldloca;
```

```
[C++]
public: static OpCode Ldloca;
[JScript]
public static var Ldloca : OpCode;
```

Remarks

The following table lists the instruction's hexadecimal and Microsoft Intermediate Language (MSIL) assembly format, along with a brief reference summary:

Format	Assembly Format	Description
FE 0D < **unsigned int16** >	ldloca *index*	Loads the address of the local variable at *index* onto the evaluation stack.

The stack transitional behavior, in sequential order, is:

1. The address stored in the local variable at the specified index is pushed onto the stack.

The **ldloca** instruction pushes the address of the local variable number at the passed index onto the stack, where local variables are numbered 0 onwards. The value pushed on the stack is already aligned correctly for use with instructions like **Ldind_I** and **Stind_I**. The result is a transient pointer (type *).

The following **Emit** constructor overload can use the **ldloca** opcode:

- ILGenerator.Emit(OpCode, short)

Requirements

Platforms: Windows 98, Windows NT 4.0, Windows Millennium Edition, Windows 2000, Windows XP Home Edition, Windows XP Professional, Windows .NET Server family

OpCodes.Ldloca_S Field

Loads the address of the local variable at a specific index onto the evaluation stack, short form.

```
[Visual Basic]
Public Shared ReadOnly Ldloca_S As OpCode
[C#]
public static readonly OpCode Ldloca_S;
[C++]
public: static OpCode Ldloca_S;
[JScript]
public static var Ldloca_S : OpCode;
```

Remarks

The following table lists the instruction's hexadecimal and Microsoft Intermediate Language (MSIL) assembly format, along with a brief reference summary:

Format	Assembly Format	Description
12 < **unsigned int8** >	ldloca.s *index*	Loads the address of the local variable at *index* onto the evaluation stack, short form.

The stack transitional behavior, in sequential order, is:

1. The address stored in the local variable at the specified index is pushed onto the stack.

The **ldloca.s** instruction pushes the address of the local variable number at the passed index onto the stack, where local variables are numbered 0 onwards. The value pushed on the stack is already aligned correctly for use with instructions like **Ldind_I** and **Stind_I**. The result is a transient pointer (type *).

The **ldloca.s** instruction provides an efficient encoding for use with the local variables 0 through 255.

The following **Emit** constructor overload can use the **ldloca.s** opcode:

- ILGenerator.Emit(OpCode, byte)

Requirements

Platforms: Windows 98, Windows NT 4.0, Windows Millennium Edition, Windows 2000, Windows XP Home Edition, Windows XP Professional, Windows .NET Server family

OpCodes.Ldloc_0 Field

Loads the local variable at index 0 onto the evaluation stack.

```
[Visual Basic]
Public Shared ReadOnly Ldloc_0 As OpCode
[C#]
public static readonly OpCode Ldloc_0;
[C++]
public: static OpCode Ldloc_0;
[JScript]
public static var Ldloc_0 : OpCode;
```

Remarks

The following table lists the instruction's hexadecimal and Microsoft Intermediate Language (MSIL) assembly format, along with a brief reference summary:

Format	Assembly Format	Description
06	ldloc.0	Loads the local variable at index 0 onto the evaluation stack.

The stack transitional behavior, in sequential order, is:

1. The local variable value at the index 0 is pushed onto the stack.

ldloc.0 is an especially efficient encoding for **Ldloc**, allowing access to the local variable at index 0.

The type of the value is the same as the type of the local variable, which is specified in the method header. Local variables that are smaller than 4 bytes long are expanded to type **int32** when they are loaded onto the stack. Floating-point values are expanded to their native size (type **F**).

The following **Emit** constructor overload can use the **ldloc.0** opcode:

- ILGenerator.Emit(OpCode)

Requirements

Platforms: Windows 98, Windows NT 4.0, Windows Millennium Edition, Windows 2000, Windows XP Home Edition, Windows XP Professional, Windows .NET Server family

OpCodes.Ldloc_1 Field

Loads the local variable at index 1 onto the evaluation stack.

```
[Visual Basic]
Public Shared ReadOnly Ldloc_1 As OpCode
```

```
[C#]
public static readonly OpCode Ldloc_1;
[C++]
public: static OpCode Ldloc_1;
[JScript]
public static var Ldloc_1 : OpCode;
```

Remarks

The following table lists the instruction's hexadecimal and Microsoft Intermediate Language (MSIL) assembly format, along with a brief reference summary:

Format	Assembly Format	Description
07	ldloc.1	Loads the local variable at index 1 onto the evaluation stack.

The stack transitional behavior, in sequential order, is:

1. The local variable value at the index 1 is pushed onto the stack.

ldloc.1 is an especially efficient encoding for **Ldloc**, allowing access to the local variable at index 1.

The type of the value is the same as the type of the local variable, which is specified in the method header. Local variables that are smaller than 4 bytes long are expanded to type **int32** when they are loaded onto the stack. Floating-point values are expanded to their native size (type **F**).

The following **Emit** constructor overload can use the **ldloc.1** opcode:

- ILGenerator.Emit(OpCode)

Requirements

Platforms: Windows 98, Windows NT 4.0, Windows Millennium Edition, Windows 2000, Windows XP Home Edition, Windows XP Professional, Windows .NET Server family

OpCodes.Ldloc_2 Field

Loads the local variable at index 2 onto the evaluation stack.

```
[Visual Basic]
Public Shared ReadOnly Ldloc_2 As OpCode
[C#]
public static readonly OpCode Ldloc_2;
[C++]
public: static OpCode Ldloc_2;
[JScript]
public static var Ldloc_2 : OpCode;
```

Remarks

The following table lists the instruction's hexadecimal and Microsoft Intermediate Language (MSIL) assembly format, along with a brief reference summary:

Format	Assembly Format	Description
08	ldloc.2	Loads the local variable at index 2 onto the evaluation stack.

The stack transitional behavior, in sequential order, is:

1. The local variable value at the index 2 is pushed onto the stack.

ldloc.2 is an especially efficient encoding for **Ldloc**, allowing access to the local variable at index 2.

The type of the value is the same as the type of the local variable, which is specified in the method header. Local variables that are smaller than 4 bytes long are expanded to type **int32** when they are loaded onto the stack. Floating-point values are expanded to their native size (type **F**).

The following **Emit** constructor overload can use the **ldloc.2** opcode:

• ILGenerator.Emit(OpCode)

Requirements

Platforms: Windows 98, Windows NT 4.0, Windows Millennium Edition, Windows 2000, Windows XP Home Edition, Windows XP Professional, Windows .NET Server family

OpCodes.Ldloc_3 Field

Loads the local variable at index 3 onto the evaluation stack.

```
[Visual Basic]
Public Shared ReadOnly Ldloc_3 As OpCode
[C#]
public static readonly OpCode Ldloc_3;
[C++]
public: static OpCode Ldloc_3;
[JScript]
public static var Ldloc_3 : OpCode;
```

Remarks

The following table lists the instruction's hexadecimal and Microsoft Intermediate Language (MSIL) assembly format, along with a brief reference summary:

Format	Assembly Format	Description
09	ldloc.3	Loads the local variable at index 3 onto the evaluation stack.

The stack transitional behavior, in sequential order, is:

1. The local variable value at the index 3 is pushed onto the stack.

ldloc.3 is an especially efficient encoding for **Ldloc**, allowing access to the local variable at index 3.

The type of the value is the same as the type of the local variable, which is specified in the method header. Local variables that are smaller than 4 bytes long are expanded to type **int32** when they are loaded onto the stack. Floating-point values are expanded to their native size (type **F**).

The following **Emit** constructor overload can use the **ldloc.3** opcode:

• ILGenerator.Emit(OpCode)

Requirements

Platforms: Windows 98, Windows NT 4.0, Windows Millennium Edition, Windows 2000, Windows XP Home Edition, Windows XP Professional, Windows .NET Server family

OpCodes.Ldloc_S Field

Loads the local variable at a specific index onto the evaluation stack, short form.

```
[Visual Basic]
Public Shared ReadOnly Ldloc_S As OpCode
[C#]
public static readonly OpCode Ldloc_S;
[C++]
public: static OpCode Ldloc_S;
[JScript]
public static var Ldloc_S : OpCode;
```

Remarks

The following table lists the instruction's hexadecimal and Microsoft Intermediate Language (MSIL) assembly format, along with a brief reference summary:

Format	Assembly Format	Description
11 < unsigned int8 >	ldloc.s *index*	Loads the local variable at index *index* onto stack, short form.

The stack transitional behavior, in sequential order, is:

1. The local variable value at the specified index is pushed onto the stack.

The **ldloc.s** instruction pushes the contents of the local variable number at the passed index onto the evaluation stack, where the local variables are numbered 0 onwards. Local variables are initialized to 0 before entering the method if the initialize flag on the method is true. There are 256 (2^8) local variables possible (0-255) in the short form, which is a more efficient encoding than **ldloc**.

The type of the value is the same as the type of the local variable, which is specified in the method header. See Partition I. Local variables that are smaller than 4 bytes long are expanded to type **int32** when they are loaded onto the stack. Floating-point values are expanded to their native size (type **F**).

The following **Emit** constructor overloads can use the **ldloc.s** opcode:

• ILGenerator.Emit(OpCode, LocalBuilder)
• ILGenerator.Emit(OpCode, byte)

Requirements

Platforms: Windows 98, Windows NT 4.0, Windows Millennium Edition, Windows 2000, Windows XP Home Edition, Windows XP Professional, Windows .NET Server family

OpCodes.Ldnull Field

Pushes a null reference (type **O**) onto the evaluation stack.

```
[Visual Basic]
Public Shared ReadOnly Ldnull As OpCode
[C#]
public static readonly OpCode Ldnull;
[C++]
public: static OpCode Ldnull;
[JScript]
public static var Ldnull : OpCode;
```

Remarks

The following table lists the instruction's hexadecimal and Microsoft Intermediate Language (MSIL) assembly format, along with a brief reference summary:

Format	Assembly Format	Description
14	ldnull	push a null reference onto the stack

The stack transitional behavior, in sequential order, is:

1. A null object reference is pushed onto the stack.

ldnull pushes a null reference (type **O**) on the stack. This is used to initialize locations before they are populated with data, or when they become deprecated.

ldnull provides a null reference that is size-independent.

The following **Emit** constructor overload can use the **ldnull** opcode:

- ILGenerator.Emit(OpCode)

Requirements

Platforms: Windows 98, Windows NT 4.0, Windows Millennium Edition, Windows 2000, Windows XP Home Edition, Windows XP Professional, Windows .NET Server family

OpCodes.Ldobj Field

Copies the value type object pointed to by an address to the top of the evaluation stack.

```
[Visual Basic]
Public Shared ReadOnly Ldobj As OpCode
[C#]
public static readonly OpCode Ldobj;
[C++]
public: static OpCode Ldobj;
[JScript]
public static var Ldobj : OpCode;
```

Remarks

The following table lists the instruction's hexadecimal and Microsoft Intermediate Language (MSIL) assembly format, along with a brief reference summary:

Format	Assembly Format	Description
71 < **T** >	ldobj *class*	Copy instance of value type *class* to the stack.

The stack transitional behavior, in sequential order, is:

1. The address of a value type object is pushed onto the stack.
2. The address is popped from the stack and the instance at that particular address is looked up.
3. The value of the object stored at that address is pushed onto the stack.

The **ldobj** instruction is used to pass a value type as a parameter.

The **ldobj** instruction copies the value pointed to by *addrOfValObj* (of type **&**, *****, or **natural int**) to the top of the stack. The number of bytes copied depends on the size of the class (as specified by the *class* parameter). The *class* parameter is a metadata token representing the value type.

The operation of the **ldobj** instruction can be altered by an immediately preceding **Volatile** or **Unaligned** prefix instruction.

TypeLoadException is thrown if class cannot be found. This is typically detected when the Microsoft Intermediate Language (MSIL) instruction is converted to native code rather than at runtime.

The following **Emit** constructor overload can use the **ldobj** opcode:

- ILGenerator.Emit(OpCode, Type)

Requirements

Platforms: Windows 98, Windows NT 4.0, Windows Millennium Edition, Windows 2000, Windows XP Home Edition, Windows XP Professional, Windows .NET Server family

OpCodes.Ldsfld Field

Pushes the value of a static field onto the evaluation stack.

```
[Visual Basic]
Public Shared ReadOnly Ldsfld As OpCode
[C#]
public static readonly OpCode Ldsfld;
[C++]
public: static OpCode Ldsfld;
[JScript]
public static var Ldsfld : OpCode;
```

Remarks

The following table lists the instruction's hexadecimal and Microsoft Intermediate Language (MSIL) assembly format, along with a brief reference summary:

Format	Assembly Format	Description
7E < **T** >	ldsfld *field*	Push the value of *field* on the stack.

The stack transitional behavior, in sequential order, is:

1. The value of the specific field is pushed onto the stack.

The **ldsfld** instruction pushes the value of a static (shared among all instances of a class) field on the stack. The return type is that associated with the passed metadata token *field*.

The **ldsfld** instruction can have a **Volatile** prefix.

The following **Emit** constructor overload can use the **ldsfld** opcode:

- ILGenerator.Emit(OpCode, FieldInfo)

Requirements

Platforms: Windows 98, Windows NT 4.0, Windows Millennium Edition, Windows 2000, Windows XP Home Edition, Windows XP Professional, Windows .NET Server family

OpCodes.Ldsflda Field

Pushes the address of a static field onto the evaluation stack.

```
[Visual Basic]
Public Shared ReadOnly Ldsflda As OpCode
[C#]
public static readonly OpCode Ldsflda;
[C++]
public: static OpCode Ldsflda;
[JScript]
public static var Ldsflda : OpCode;
```

Remarks

The following table lists the instruction's hexadecimal and Microsoft Intermediate Language (MSIL) assembly format, along with a brief reference summary:

Format	Assembly Format	Description
7F < **T** >	ldsflda *field*	Push the address of *field* on the stack

The stack transitional behavior, in sequential order, is:

1. The address of a specific field is pushed onto the stack.

The **ldsflda** instruction pushes the address of a static (shared among all instances of a class) field on the stack. The address may be represented as a transient pointer (type *) if the metadata token *field* refers to a type whose memory is managed. Otherwise, it corresponds to an unmanaged pointer (type **natural int**). Note that *field* may be a static global with an assigned relative virtual address (the offset of the field from the base address at which its containing PE file is loaded into memory) where the memory is unmanaged.

The **ldsflda** instruction can have a **Volatile** prefix.

MissingFieldException is thrown if field is not found in the metadata. This is typically checked when Microsoft Intermediate Language (MSIL) instructions are converted to native code, not at runtime.

The following **Emit** constructor overload can use the **ldsflda** opcode:

- ILGenerator.Emit(OpCode, FieldInfo)

Requirements

Platforms: Windows 98, Windows NT 4.0, Windows Millennium Edition, Windows 2000, Windows XP Home Edition, Windows XP Professional, Windows .NET Server family

OpCodes.Ldstr Field

Pushes a new object reference to a string literal stored in the metadata.

```
[Visual Basic]
Public Shared ReadOnly Ldstr As OpCode
[C#]
public static readonly OpCode Ldstr;
[C++]
public: static OpCode Ldstr;
[JScript]
public static var Ldstr : OpCode;
```

Remarks

The following table lists the instruction's hexadecimal and Microsoft Intermediate Language (MSIL) assembly format, along with a brief reference summary:

Format	Assembly Format	Description
72 < **T** >	ldstr *mdToken*	Pushes a string object for the metadata string token *mdToken*.

The stack transitional behavior, in sequential order, is:

1. An object reference to a string is pushed onto the stack.

The **ldstr** instruction pushes an object reference (type **O**) to a new string object representing the specific string literal stored in the metadata. The **ldstr** instruction allocates the requisite amount of memory and performs any format conversion required to convert the string literal from the form used in the file to the string format required at runtime.

The Common Language Infrastructure (CLI) guarantees that the result of two **ldstr** instructions referring to two metadata tokens that have the same sequence of characters return precisely the same string object (a process known as "string interning").

The following **Emit** constructor overload can use the **ldstr** opcode:

- ILGenerator.Emit(OpCode, string)

Requirements

Platforms: Windows 98, Windows NT 4.0, Windows Millennium Edition, Windows 2000, Windows XP Home Edition, Windows XP Professional, Windows .NET Server family

OpCodes.Ldtoken Field

Converts a metadata token to its runtime representation, pushing it onto the evaluation stack.

```
[Visual Basic]
Public Shared ReadOnly Ldtoken As OpCode
[C#]
public static readonly OpCode Ldtoken;
[C++]
public: static OpCode Ldtoken;
[JScript]
public static var Ldtoken : OpCode;
```

Remarks

The following table lists the instruction's hexadecimal and Microsoft Intermediate Language (MSIL) assembly format, along with a brief reference summary:

Format	Assembly Format	Description
D0 < **T** >	ldtoken *token*	Converts a metadata token to its runtime representation.

The stack transitional behavior, in sequential order, is:

1. The passed token is converted to a **RuntimeHandle** and pushed onto the stack.

The **ldtoken** instruction pushes a **RuntimeHandle** for the specified metadata token. A **RuntimeHandle** can be a **fieldref/fielddef**, a **methodref/methoddef**, or a **typeref/typedef**.

The value pushed on the stack can be used in calls to **Reflection** methods in the system class library.

For information on runtime handles, see the following classes: **RuntimeFieldHandle**, **RuntimeTypeHandle**, and **RuntimeMethodHandle**.

The following **Emit** constructor overloads can use the **ldtoken** opcode:

- ILGenerator.Emit(OpCode, MethodInfo)
- ILGenerator.Emit(OpCode, FieldInfo)
- ILGenerator.Emit(OpCode, Type)

Requirements

Platforms: Windows 98, Windows NT 4.0, Windows Millennium Edition, Windows 2000, Windows XP Home Edition, Windows XP Professional, Windows .NET Server family

OpCodes.Ldvirtftn Field

Pushes an unmanaged pointer (type **natural int**) to the native code implementing a particular virtual method associated with a specified object onto the evaluation stack.

```
[Visual Basic]
Public Shared ReadOnly Ldvirtftn As OpCode
[C#]
public static readonly OpCode Ldvirtftn;
[C++]
public: static OpCode Ldvirtftn;
[JScript]
public static var Ldvirtftn : OpCode;
```

Remarks

The following table lists the instruction's hexadecimal and Microsoft Intermediate Language (MSIL) assembly format, along with a brief reference summary:

Format	Assembly Format	Description
FE 07 < **T** >	ldvirtftn *method*	Pushes the pointer to an object's virtual method *method* on the stack.

The stack transitional behavior, in sequential order, is:

1. An object reference is pushed onto the stack.
2. The object reference is popped from the stack and the address of the entry point to the method (as specified by the metadata token *method*) is looked up.
3. The pointer to *method* is pushed onto the stack.

The resulting unmanaged pointer pushed onto the stack by the **ldvirtftn** instruction can be called using the **Calli** instruction if it references a managed method (or a stub that transitions from managed to unmanaged code).

The unmanaged pointer points to native code using the calling convention specified by in the metadata token *method*. As a result, the method pointer can be passed to unmanaged native code (for example, as a callback routine) if that routine expects the corresponding calling convention.

The following **Emit** constructor overload can use the **ldvirtftn** opcode:

• ILGenerator.Emit(OpCode, MethodInfo)

Requirements

Platforms: Windows 98, Windows NT 4.0, Windows Millennium Edition, Windows 2000, Windows XP Home Edition, Windows XP Professional, Windows .NET Server family

OpCodes.Leave Field

Exits a protected region of code, unconditionally tranferring control to a specific target instruction.

```
[Visual Basic]
Public Shared ReadOnly Leave As OpCode
[C#]
public static readonly OpCode Leave;
[C++]
public: static OpCode Leave;
[JScript]
public static var Leave : OpCode;
```

Remarks

The following table lists the instruction's hexadecimal and Microsoft Intermediate Language (MSIL) assembly format, along with a brief reference summary:

Format	Assembly Format	Description
DD < **int32** >	leave *target*	Exits a protected region of code.

There is no stack transition behavior specified for this instruction.

The **leave** instruction unconditionally transfers control to the specific target instruction, represented as a 4-byte signed offset from the beginning of the instruction following the current instruction.

The **leave** instruction is similar to the **br** instruction, but it can be used to exit a **try**, **filter**, or **catch** block whereas the ordinary branch instructions can only be used in such a block to transfer control within it. The **leave** instruction empties the evaluation stack and ensures that the appropriate surrounding **finally** blocks are executed.

You cannot use a **leave** instruction to exit a **finally** block. To ease code generation for exception handlers it is valid from within a catch block to use a **leave** instruction to transfer control to any instruction within the associated **try** block.

If an instruction has one or more prefix codes, control can only be transferred to the first of these prefixes.

The following **Emit** constructor overloads can use the **leave** opcode:

• ILGenerator.Emit(OpCode, Label)

Requirements

Platforms: Windows 98, Windows NT 4.0, Windows Millennium Edition, Windows 2000, Windows XP Home Edition, Windows XP Professional, Windows .NET Server family

OpCodes.Leave_S Field

Exits a protected region of code, unconditionally tranferring control to a target instruction (short form).

```
[Visual Basic]
Public Shared ReadOnly Leave_S As OpCode
[C#]
public static readonly OpCode Leave_S;
[C++]
public: static OpCode Leave_S;
[JScript]
public static var Leave_S : OpCode;
```

Remarks

The following table lists the instruction's hexadecimal and Microsoft Intermediate Language (MSIL) assembly format, along with a brief reference summary:

Format	Assembly Format	Description
DE < **int8** >	leave.s *target*	Exit a protected region of code, short form.

There is no stack transition behavior specified for this instruction.

The **leave.s** instruction unconditionally transfers control to the passed target instruction, represented as a 1-byte signed offset from the beginning of the instruction following the current instruction.

The **leave.s** instruction is similar to the **br** instruction, but it can be used to exit a **try**, **filter**, or **catch** block whereas the ordinary branch instructions can only be used in such a block to transfer control within it. The **leave.s** instruction empties the evaluation stack and ensures that the appropriate surrounding **finally** blocks are executed.

You cannot use a **leave.s** instruction to exit a **finally** block. To ease code generation for exception handlers it is valid from within a catch block to use a **leave.s** instruction to transfer control to any instruction within the associated **try** block.

If an instruction has one or more prefix codes, control can only be transferred to the first of these prefixes.

The following **Emit** constructor overload can use the **leave.s** opcode:

• ILGenerator.Emit(OpCode, Label)

Requirements

Platforms: Windows 98, Windows NT 4.0, Windows Millennium Edition, Windows 2000, Windows XP Home Edition, Windows XP Professional, Windows .NET Server family

OpCodes.Localloc Field

Allocates a certain number of bytes from the local dynamic memory pool and pushes the address (a transient pointer, type *) of the first allocated byte onto the evaluation stack.

```
[Visual Basic]
Public Shared ReadOnly Localloc As OpCode
[C#]
public static readonly OpCode Localloc;
[C++]
public: static OpCode Localloc;
[JScript]
public static var Localloc : OpCode;
```

Remarks

The following table lists the instruction's hexadecimal and Microsoft Intermediate Language (MSIL) assembly format, along with a brief reference summary:

Format	Assembly Format	Description
FE 0F	localloc	Allocate space from the local heap.

The stack transitional behavior, in sequential order, is:

1. The number of bytes to be allocated is pushed onto the stack.
2. The number of bytes is popped from the stack; an amount of memory corresponding to the size is allocated from the local heap.
3. A pointer to the first byte of the allocated memory is pushed onto the stack.

The **localloc** instruction allocates *size* (type **natural unsigned int**) bytes from the local dynamic memory pool and returns the address (a transient pointer, type *) of the first allocated byte. The block of memory returned is initialized to 0 only if the initialize flag on the method is **true**. When the current method executes a **Ret**, the local memory pool is made available for reuse.

The resulting address is aligned so that any primitive data type can be stored there using the **stind** instructions (such as **Stind_I4**) and loaded using the **ldind** instructions (such as **Ldind_I4**).

The **localloc** instruction cannot occur within a **filter**, **catch**, **finally**, or **fault** block.

StackOverflowException is thrown if there is insufficient memory to service the request.

The following **Emit** constructor overload can use the **localloc** opcode:

• ILGenerator.Emit(OpCode)

Requirements

Platforms: Windows 98, Windows NT 4.0, Windows Millennium Edition, Windows 2000, Windows XP Home Edition, Windows XP Professional, Windows .NET Server family

OpCodes.Mkrefany Field

Pushes a typed reference to an instance of a specific type onto the evaluation stack.

```
[Visual Basic]
Public Shared ReadOnly Mkrefany As OpCode
[C#]
public static readonly OpCode Mkrefany;
[C++]
public: static OpCode Mkrefany;
[JScript]
public static var Mkrefany : OpCode;
```

Remarks

The following table lists the instruction's hexadecimal and Microsoft Intermediate Language (MSIL) assembly format, along with a brief reference summary:

Format	Assembly Format	Description
C6 < T >	mkrefany *class*	Pushes a typed reference of type *class* onto the stack.

The stack transitional behavior, in sequential order, is:

1. A pointer to piece of data is pushed onto the stack.
2. The pointer is popped and converted to a typed reference of type *class*.
3. The typed reference is pushed onto the stack.

The **mkrefany** instruction supports the passing of dynamically typed references. The pointer must be of type **&**, *****, or **natural int**, and hold the valid address of a piece of data. *Class* is the class token describing the type of the data referenced by the pointer. **Mkrefany** pushes a typed reference on the stack, providing an opaque descriptor of the pointer and the type *class*.

The only valid operation permitted upon a typed reference is to pass it to a method that requires a typed reference as a parameter. The callee can then use the **Refanytype** and **Refanyval** instructions to retrieve the type (class) and the address respectively.

TypeLoadException is thrown if *class* cannot be found. This is typically detected when Microsoft Intermediate Language (MSIL) instructions are converted to native code rather than at runtime.

The following **Emit** constructor overload can use the **mkrefany** opcode:

• ILGenerator.Emit(OpCode, Type)

Requirements

Platforms: Windows 98, Windows NT 4.0,
Windows Millennium Edition, Windows 2000,
Windows XP Home Edition, Windows XP Professional,
Windows .NET Server family

OpCodes.Mul Field

Multiplies two values and pushes the result on the evaluation stack.

```
[Visual Basic]
Public Shared ReadOnly Mul As OpCode
[C#]
public static readonly OpCode Mul;
[C++]
public: static OpCode Mul;
[JScript]
public static var Mul : OpCode;
```

Remarks

The following table lists the instruction's hexadecimal and Microsoft Intermediate Language (MSIL) assembly format, along with a brief reference summary:

Format	Assembly Format	Description
5A	mul	Multiplies two values on the stack.

The stack transitional behavior, in sequential order, is:

1. *value1* is pushed onto the stack.
2. *value2* is pushed onto the stack.
3. *value2* and *value1* are popped from the stack; *value1* is multiplied by *value2*.
4. The result is pushed onto the stack.

The **mul** instruction multiplies *value1* by *value2* and pushes the resulton the stack. Integer operations silently truncate the upper bits on overflow.

See **Mul_Ovf** for an integer-specific multiply operation with overflow handling.

For floating-point types, 0 * infinity = NaN.

The following **Emit** constructor overload can use the **mul** opcode:

• ILGenerator.Emit(OpCode)

Requirements

Platforms: Windows 98, Windows NT 4.0,
Windows Millennium Edition, Windows 2000,
Windows XP Home Edition, Windows XP Professional,
Windows .NET Server family

OpCodes.Mul_Ovf Field

Multiplies two integer values, performs an overflow check, and pushes the result onto the evaluation stack.

```
[Visual Basic]
Public Shared ReadOnly Mul_Ovf As OpCode
[C#]
public static readonly OpCode Mul_Ovf;
[C++]
public: static OpCode Mul_Ovf;
[JScript]
public static var Mul_Ovf : OpCode;
```

Remarks

The following table lists the instruction's hexadecimal and Microsoft Intermediate Language (MSIL) assembly format, along with a brief reference summary:

Format	Assembly Format	Description
D8	mul.ovf	Multiplies two integer values on the stack with an overflow check.

The stack transitional behavior, in sequential order, is:

1. *value1* is pushed onto the stack.
2. *value2* is pushed onto the stack.
3. *value2* and *value1* are popped from the stack; *value1* is multiplied by *value2*, with an overflow check.
4. The result is pushed onto the stack.

The **mul.ovf** instruction multiplies integer *value1* by integer *value2* and pushes the resulton the stack. An exception is thrown if the result will not fit in the result type.

OverflowException is thrown if the result can not be represented in the result type.

The following **Emit** constructor overload can use the **mul.ovf** opcode:

• ILGenerator.Emit(OpCode)

Requirements

Platforms: Windows 98, Windows NT 4.0,
Windows Millennium Edition, Windows 2000,
Windows XP Home Edition, Windows XP Professional,
Windows .NET Server family

OpCodes.Mul_Ovf_Un Field

Multiplies two unsigned integer values, performs an overflow check, and pushes the result onto the evaluation stack.

```
[Visual Basic]
Public Shared ReadOnly Mul_Ovf_Un As OpCode
[C#]
public static readonly OpCode Mul_Ovf_Un;
[C++]
public: static OpCode Mul_Ovf_Un;
[JScript]
public static var Mul_Ovf_Un : OpCode;
```

Remarks

The following table lists the instruction's hexadecimal and Microsoft Intermediate Language (MSIL) assembly format, along with a brief reference summary:

Format	Assembly Format	Description
D9	mul.ovf.un	Multiplies two unsigned values on the stack with an overflow check.

The stack transitional behavior, in sequential order, is:

1. *value1* is pushed onto the stack.
2. *value2* is pushed onto the stack.
3. *value2* and *value1* are popped from the stack; *value1* is multiplied by *value2*, with an overflow check.
4. The result is pushed onto the stack.

The **mul.ovf.un** instruction multiplies unsigned integer *value1* by unsigned integer *value2* and pushes the result on the stack. An exception is thrown if the result will not fit in the result type.

OverflowException is thrown if the result can not be represented in the result type.

The following **Emit** constructor overload can use the **mul.ovf.un** opcode:

• ILGenerator.Emit(OpCode)

Requirements

Platforms: Windows 98, Windows NT 4.0, Windows Millennium Edition, Windows 2000, Windows XP Home Edition, Windows XP Professional, Windows .NET Server family

OpCodes.Neg Field

Negates a value and pushes the result onto the evaluation stack.

```
[Visual Basic]
Public Shared ReadOnly Neg As OpCode
[C#]
public static readonly OpCode Neg;
[C++]
public: static OpCode Neg;
[JScript]
public static var Neg : OpCode;
```

Remarks

The following table lists the instruction's hexadecimal and Microsoft Intermediate Language (MSIL) assembly format, along with a brief reference summary:

Format	Assembly Format	Description
65	neg	Negates the value currently on top of the stack.

The stack transitional behavior, in sequential order, is:

1. A value is pushed onto the stack.
2. A value is popped from the stack and negated.
3. The result is pushed onto the stack.

The **neg** instruction negates value and pushes the result on top of the stack. The return type is the same as the operand type.

Negation of integral values is standard two's complement negation. In particular, negating the most negative number (which does not have a positive counterpart) yields the most negative number. To detect this overflow use the **Sub_Ovf** instruction instead (that is, subtract from 0).

Negating a floating-point number cannot overflow, and negating NaN returns NaN.

The following **Emit** constructor overload can use the **neg** opcode:

• ILGenerator.Emit(OpCode)

Requirements

Platforms: Windows 98, Windows NT 4.0, Windows Millennium Edition, Windows 2000, Windows XP Home Edition, Windows XP Professional, Windows .NET Server family

OpCodes.Newarr Field

Pushes an object reference to a new zero-based, one-dimensional array whose elements are of a specific type onto the evaluation stack.

```
[Visual Basic]
Public Shared ReadOnly Newarr As OpCode
[C#]
public static readonly OpCode Newarr;
[C++]
public: static OpCode Newarr;
[JScript]
public static var Newarr : OpCode;
```

Remarks

The following table lists the instruction's hexadecimal and Microsoft Intermediate Language (MSIL) assembly format, along with a brief reference summary:

Format	Assembly Format	Description
8D < T >	newarr *etype*	Createa a new array with elements of type *etype*.

The stack transitional behavior, in sequential order, is:

1. The number of elements in the array is pushed onto the stack.
2. The number of elementes is popped from the stack and the array is created.
3. An object reference to the new array is pushed onto the stack.

The **newarr** instruction pushes an object reference (type **O**) to a new zero-based, one-dimensional array whose elements are of type *etype* (a metadata token describing the type). The number of elements in the new array should be specified as a **natural int**. Valid array indexes range from zero to the maximum number of elements minus one.

The elements of an array can be any type, including value types.

Zero-based, one-dimensional arrays of numbers are created using a metadata token referencing the appropriate value type (**Int32**, and so on). Elements of the array are initialized to 0 of the appropriate type.

Nonzero-based one-dimensional arrays and multidimensional arrays are created using **Newobj** rather than **newarr**. More commonly, they are created using the methods of the **Array** class in the .NET Framework.

OutOfMemoryException is thrown if there is insufficient memory to satisfy the request.

OverflowException is thrown if *numElems* is less than 0.

The following **Emit** constructor overload can use the **newarr** opcode:

• ILGenerator.Emit(OpCode, Type)

Requirements

Platforms: Windows 98, Windows NT 4.0, Windows Millennium Edition, Windows 2000, Windows XP Home Edition, Windows XP Professional, Windows .NET Server family

OpCodes.Newobj Field

Creates a new object or a new instance of a value type, pushing an object reference (type **O**) onto the evaluation stack.

```
[Visual Basic]
Public Shared ReadOnly Newobj As OpCode
[C#]
public static readonly OpCode Newobj;
```

```
[C++]
public: static OpCode Newobj;
[JScript]
public static var Newobj : OpCode;
```

Remarks

The following table lists the instruction's hexadecimal and Microsoft Intermediate Language (MSIL) assembly format, along with a brief reference summary:

Format	Assembly Format	Description
73 < **T** >	newobj *ctor*	Allocates an uninitialized object or value type and calls the constructor method *ctor*.

The stack transitional behavior, in sequential order, is:

1. Arguments *arg1* through *argn* are pushed on the stack in sequence.
2. Arguments *argn* through *arg1* are popped from the stack and passed to *ctor* for object creation.
3. A reference to the new object is pushed onto the stack.

The **newobj** instruction creates a new object or a new instance of a value type. *Ctor* is a metadata token (a **methodref** or **methoddef** that must be marked as a constructor) that indicates the name, class and signature of the constructor to call.

The **newobj** instruction allocates a new instance of the class associated with *ctor* and initializes all the fields in the new instance to 0 (of the proper type) or null references as appropriate. It then calls the constructor *ctor* with the given arguments along with the newly created instance. After the constructor has been called, the now initialized object reference (type **O**) is pushed on the stack.

From the constructor's point of view, the uninitialized object is argument 0 and the other arguments passed to newobj follow in order.

All zero-based, one-dimensional arrays are created using **Newarr**, not **newobj**. On the other hand, all other arrays (more than one dimension, or one-dimensional but not zero-based) are created using **newobj**.

Value types are not usually created using **newobj**. They are usually allocated either as arguments or local variables, using **newarr** (for zero-based, one-dimensional arrays), or as fields of objects. Once allocated, they are initialized using **Initobj**. However, the **newobj** instruction can be used to create a new instance of a value type on the stack, that can then be passed as an argument, stored in a local, and so on.

OutOfMemoryException is thrown if there is insufficient memory to satisfy the request.

MissingMethodException is thrown if a constructor method *ctor* with the indicated name, class and signature could not be found. This is typically detected when Microsoft Intermediate Language (MSIL) instructions are converted to native code, rather than at runtime.

The following **Emit** constructor overload can use the **newobj** opcode:

- ILGenerator.Emit(OpCode, ConstructorInfo)

Requirements

Platforms: Windows 98, Windows NT 4.0, Windows Millennium Edition, Windows 2000, Windows XP Home Edition, Windows XP Professional, Windows .NET Server family

OpCodes.Nop Field

Fills space if opcodes are patched. No meaningful operation is performed although a processing cycle can be consumed.

```
[Visual Basic]
Public Shared ReadOnly Nop As OpCode
[C#]
public static readonly OpCode Nop;
[C++]
public: static OpCode Nop;
[JScript]
public static var Nop : OpCode;
```

Remarks

The following table lists the instruction's hexadecimal and Microsoft Intermediate Language (MSIL) assembly format, along with a brief reference summary:

Format	Assembly Format	Description
00	nop	Performs an operation without behavior.

There is no stack transitional behavior defined for this instruction.

The **nop** operation does nothing. It is intended to fill in space if opcodes are patched.

The following **Emit** constructor overload can use the **nop** opcode:

- ILGenerator.Emit(OpCode)

Requirements

Platforms: Windows 98, Windows NT 4.0, Windows Millennium Edition, Windows 2000, Windows XP Home Edition, Windows XP Professional, Windows .NET Server family

OpCodes.Not Field

Computes the bitwise complement of the integer value on top of the stack and pushes the result onto the evaluation stack as the same type.

```
[Visual Basic]
Public Shared ReadOnly Not As OpCode
[C#]
public static readonly OpCode Not;
[C++]
public: static OpCode Not;
[JScript]
public static var Not : OpCode;
```

Remarks

The following table lists the instruction's hexadecimal and Microsoft Intermediate Language (MSIL) assembly format, along with a brief reference summary:

Format	Assembly Format	Description
66	not	Computes the bitwise complement of a value.

The stack transitional behavior, in sequential order, is:

1. *value* is pushed onto the stack.
2. *value* is popped from the stack and its bitwise complement computed.
3. The result is pushed onto the stack.

The **not** instruction computes the bitwise complement of an integer value and pushes the result onto the stack. The return type is the same as the operand type.

The following **Emit** constructor overload can use the **not** opcode:

• ILGenerator.Emit(OpCode)

Requirements

Platforms: Windows 98, Windows NT 4.0, Windows Millennium Edition, Windows 2000, Windows XP Home Edition, Windows XP Professional, Windows .NET Server family

OpCodes.Or Field

Compute the bitwise complement of the two integer values on top of the stack and pushes the result onto the evaluation stack.

```
[Visual Basic]
Public Shared ReadOnly Or As OpCode
[C#]
public static readonly OpCode Or;
[C++]
public: static OpCode Or;
[JScript]
public static var Or : OpCode;
```

Remarks

The following table lists the instruction's hexadecimal and Microsoft Intermediate Language (MSIL) assembly format, along with a brief reference summary:

Format	Assembly Format	Description
60	or	Computes the bitwise OR of two integer values, returns an integer.

The stack transitional behavior, in sequential order, is:

1. *value1* is pushed onto the stack.
2. *value2* is pushed onto the stack.
3. *value2* and *value1* are popped from the stack and their bitwise OR computed.
4. The result is pushed onto the stack.

The **or** instruction computes the bitwise OR of two values atop the stack, pushing the result onto the stack.

Or is an integer-specific operation.

The following **Emit** constructor overload can use the **or** opcode:

• ILGenerator.Emit(OpCode)

Requirements

Platforms: Windows 98, Windows NT 4.0, Windows Millennium Edition, Windows 2000, Windows XP Home Edition, Windows XP Professional, Windows .NET Server family

OpCodes.Pop Field

Removes the value currently on top of the evaluation stack.

```
[Visual Basic]
Public Shared ReadOnly Pop As OpCode
[C#]
public static readonly OpCode Pop;
```

```
[C++]
public: static OpCode Pop;
[JScript]
public static var Pop : OpCode;
```

Remarks

The following table lists the instruction's hexadecimal and Microsoft Intermediate Language (MSIL) assembly format, along with a brief reference summary:

Format	Assembly Format	Description
26	pop	Pops the top value from the stack.

The stack transitional behavior, in sequential order, is:

1. The top value is popped from the stack.

The **pop** instruction removes the top element from the stack.

The following **Emit** constructor overload can use the **pop** opcode:

• ILGenerator.Emit(OpCode)

Requirements

Platforms: Windows 98, Windows NT 4.0, Windows Millennium Edition, Windows 2000, Windows XP Home Edition, Windows XP Professional, Windows .NET Server family

OpCodes.Prefix1 Field

This member supports the .NET Framework infrastructure and is not intended to be used directly from your code.

```
[Visual Basic]
Public Shared ReadOnly Prefix1 As OpCode
[C#]
public static readonly OpCode Prefix1;
[C++]
public: static OpCode Prefix1;
[JScript]
public static var Prefix1 : OpCode;
```

OpCodes.Prefix2 Field

This member supports the .NET Framework infrastructure and is not intended to be used directly from your code.

```
[Visual Basic]
Public Shared ReadOnly Prefix2 As OpCode
[C#]
public static readonly OpCode Prefix2;
[C++]
public: static OpCode Prefix2;
[JScript]
public static var Prefix2 : OpCode;
```

OpCodes.Prefix3 Field

This member supports the .NET Framework infrastructure and is not intended to be used directly from your code.

```
[Visual Basic]
Public Shared ReadOnly Prefix3 As OpCode
[C#]
public static readonly OpCode Prefix3;
```

```
[C++]
public: static OpCode Prefix3;
[JScript]
public static var Prefix3 : OpCode;
```

OpCodes.Prefix4 Field

This member supports the .NET Framework infrastructure and is not intended to be used directly from your code.

```
[Visual Basic]
Public Shared ReadOnly Prefix4 As OpCode
[C#]
public static readonly OpCode Prefix4;
[C++]
public: static OpCode Prefix4;
[JScript]
public static var Prefix4 : OpCode;
```

OpCodes.Prefix5 Field

This member supports the .NET Framework infrastructure and is not intended to be used directly from your code.

```
[Visual Basic]
Public Shared ReadOnly Prefix5 As OpCode
[C#]
public static readonly OpCode Prefix5;
[C++]
public: static OpCode Prefix5;
[JScript]
public static var Prefix5 : OpCode;
```

OpCodes.Prefix6 Field

This member supports the .NET Framework infrastructure and is not intended to be used directly from your code.

```
[Visual Basic]
Public Shared ReadOnly Prefix6 As OpCode
[C#]
public static readonly OpCode Prefix6;
[C++]
public: static OpCode Prefix6;
[JScript]
public static var Prefix6 : OpCode;
```

OpCodes.Prefix7 Field

This member supports the .NET Framework infrastructure and is not intended to be used directly from your code.

```
[Visual Basic]
Public Shared ReadOnly Prefix7 As OpCode
[C#]
public static readonly OpCode Prefix7;
[C++]
public: static OpCode Prefix7;
[JScript]
public static var Prefix7 : OpCode;
```

OpCodes.Prefixref Field

This member supports the .NET Framework infrastructure and is not intended to be used directly from your code.

```
[Visual Basic]
Public Shared ReadOnly Prefixref As OpCode
[C#]
public static readonly OpCode Prefixref;
[C++]
public: static OpCode Prefixref;
[JScript]
public static var Prefixref : OpCode;
```

OpCodes.Refanytype Field

Retrieves the type token embedded in a typed reference.

```
[Visual Basic]
Public Shared ReadOnly Refanytype As OpCode
[C#]
public static readonly OpCode Refanytype;
[C++]
public: static OpCode Refanytype;
[JScript]
public static var Refanytype : OpCode;
```

Remarks

The following table lists the instruction's hexadecimal and Microsoft Intermediate Language (MSIL) assembly format, along with a brief reference summary:

Format	Assembly Format	Description
FE 1D	refanytype	Pushes the type token stored in a typed reference.

The stack transitional behavior, in sequential order, is:

1. A value type reference is pushed onto the stack.
2. The typed reference is popped from the stack and its corresponding type token retrieved.
3. The type token is pushed onto the stack.

A typed reference contains a type token and an address to an object instance.

The **refanytype** instruction retrieves the type token embedded in the typed reference. See the **Mkrefany** instruction for information on creating typed references.

The following **Emit** constructor overload can use the **refanytype** opcode:

- ILGenerator.Emit(OpCode)

Requirements

Platforms: Windows 98, Windows NT 4.0, Windows Millennium Edition, Windows 2000, Windows XP Home Edition, Windows XP Professional, Windows .NET Server family

OpCodes.Refanyval Field

Retrieves the address (type **&**) embedded in a typed reference.

```
[Visual Basic]
Public Shared ReadOnly Refanyval As OpCode
[C#]
public static readonly OpCode Refanyval;
```

```
[C++]
public: static OpCode Refanyval;
[JScript]
public static var Refanyval : OpCode;
```

Remarks

The following table lists the instruction's hexadecimal and Microsoft Intermediate Language (MSIL) assembly format, along with a brief reference summary:

Format	Assembly Format	Description
C2 < T >	refanyval *type*	Pushes the address stored in a typed reference.

The stack transitional behavior, in sequential order, is:

1. A value type reference is pushed onto the stack.
2. The typed reference is popped from the stack and the corresponding address retrieved.
3. The address is pushed onto the stack.

A typed reference contains a type token and an address to an object instance.

The **refanyval** instruction retrieves the address embedded in the a typed reference. The type embedded in the typed reference supplied on the stack must match the type specified by *type* (a metadata token, either a **typedef** or a **typeref**). See the **Mkrefany** instruction for related content.

InvalidCastException is thrown if *type* is not identical to the type stored in the type reference (in this case, *type* is the class supplied to the **Mkrefany** instruction that constructed said typed reference).

TypeLoadException is thrown if *type* cannot be found.

The following **Emit** constructor overload can use the **refanyval** opcode:

- ILGenerator.Emit(OpCode, Type)

Requirements

Platforms: Windows 98, Windows NT 4.0, Windows Millennium Edition, Windows 2000, Windows XP Home Edition, Windows XP Professional, Windows .NET Server family

OpCodes.Rem Field

Divides two values and pushes the remainder onto the evaluation stack.

```
[Visual Basic]
Public Shared ReadOnly Rem As OpCode
[C#]
public static readonly OpCode Rem;
[C++]
public: static OpCode Rem;
[JScript]
public static var Rem : OpCode;
```

Remarks

The following table lists the instruction's hexadecimal and Microsoft Intermediate Language (MSIL) assembly format, along with a brief reference summary:

Format	Assembly Format	Description
5D	rem	Pushes the remainder of dividing *value1* by *value2* onto the stack.

The stack transitional behavior, in sequential order, is:

1. A *value1* is pushed onto the stack.
2. *value2* is pushed onto the stack.
3. *value2* and *value1* are popped from the stack and the remainder of *value1* div *value2* computed.
4. The result is pushed onto the stack.

result = *value1* **rem** *value2* satisfies the following conditions:

result = *value1* - *value2* × (*value1* **div** *value2*), and:

$0 = |result| < |value2|$, sign(*result*) = sign(*value1*), where **div** is the division instruction that truncates towards zero.

If *value2* is zero or *value1* is infinity the result is NaN. If *value2* is infinity, the result is *value1* (negated for **-infinity**).

Integral operations throw **DivideByZeroException** if *value2* is zero.

Note that on the Intel-based platforms an **OverflowException** is thrown when computing (minint **rem**-1).

The following **Emit** constructor overload can use the **rem** opcode:

- ILGenerator.Emit(OpCode)

Requirements

Platforms: Windows 98, Windows NT 4.0, Windows Millennium Edition, Windows 2000, Windows XP Home Edition, Windows XP Professional, Windows .NET Server family

OpCodes.Rem_Un Field

Divides two unsigned values and pushes the remainder onto the evaluation stack.

```
[Visual Basic]
Public Shared ReadOnly Rem_Un As OpCode
[C#]
public static readonly OpCode Rem_Un;
[C++]
public: static OpCode Rem_Un;
[JScript]
public static var Rem_Un : OpCode;
```

Remarks

The following table lists the instruction's hexadecimal and Microsoft Intermediate Language (MSIL) assembly format, along with a brief reference summary:

Format	Assembly Format	Description
5E	rem.un	Pushes the remainder of dividing unsigned *value1* by unsigned *value2* onto the stack.

The stack transitional behavior, in sequential order, is:

1. *value1* is pushed onto the stack.
2. *value2* is pushed onto the stack.
3. *value2* and *value1* are popped from the stack and the remainder of *value1* div *value2* computed.
4. The result is pushed onto the stack.

result = *value1* **rem.un** *value2* satisfies the following conditions:

result = *value1* - *value2* x(*value1* **div.un** *value2*), and:

0 = *result* < *value2*, where **div.un** is the unsigned division instruction.

The **rem.un** instruction computes *result* and pushes it on the stack. **Rem.un** treats its arguments as unsigned integers, while **Rem** treats them as signed integers.

Rem.un is unspecified for floating-point numbers.

Integral operations throw **DivideByZeroException** if *value2* is zero.

The following **Emit** constructor overload can use the **rem.un** opcode:

- ILGenerator.Emit(OpCode)

Requirements

Platforms: Windows 98, Windows NT 4.0, Windows Millennium Edition, Windows 2000, Windows XP Home Edition, Windows XP Professional, Windows .NET Server family

OpCodes.Ret Field

Returns from the current method, pushing a return value (if present) from the caller's evaluation stack onto the callee's evaluation stack.

```
[Visual Basic]
Public Shared ReadOnly Ret As OpCode
[C#]
public static readonly OpCode Ret;
[C++]
public: static OpCode Ret;
[JScript]
public static var Ret : OpCode;
```

Remarks

The following table lists the instruction's hexadecimal and Microsoft Intermediate Language (MSIL) assembly format, along with a brief reference summary:

Format	Assembly Format	Description
2A	ret	Returns from method, possibly returning a value.

The stack transitional behavior, in sequential order, is:

1. The return value is popped from the callee evaluation stack.
2. The return value obtained in step 1 is pushed onto the caller evaluation stack.

If the return value is not present on the callee evaluation stack, no value is returned (no stack transition behaviors for either the callee or caller method).

The type of the return value, if any, of the current method determines the type of value to be fetched from the top of the stack and copied onto the stack of the method that called the current method. The evaluation stack for the current method must be empty except for the value to be returned.

The **ret** instruction cannot be used to transfer control out of a **try**, **filter**, **catch**, or **finally** block. From within a **try** or **catch**, use the **Leave** instruction with a destination of a **ret** instruction that is outside all enclosing exception blocks. Because the **filter** and **finally** blocks are logically part of exception handling and not the method in which their code is embedded, correctly generated Microsoft

Intermediate Language (MSIL) instructions do not perform a method return from within a **filter** or **finally**.

The following **Emit** constructor overload can use the **ret** opcode:

- ILGenerator.Emit(OpCode)

Requirements

Platforms: Windows 98, Windows NT 4.0, Windows Millennium Edition, Windows 2000, Windows XP Home Edition, Windows XP Professional, Windows .NET Server family

OpCodes.Rethrow Field

Rethrows the current exception.

```
[Visual Basic]
Public Shared ReadOnly Rethrow As OpCode
[C#]
public static readonly OpCode Rethrow;
[C++]
public: static OpCode Rethrow;
[JScript]
public static var Rethrow : OpCode;
```

Remarks

The following table lists the instruction's hexadecimal and Microsoft Intermediate Language (MSIL) assembly format, along with a brief reference summary:

Format	Assembly Format	Description
FE 1A	rethrow	Rethrows the current exception

No stack transition behavior is defined for this instruction.

The *rethrow* instruction is only permitted within the body of a **catch** handler. It throws the same exception that was caught by this handler.

The following **Emit** constructor overload can use the **rethrow** opcode:

- ILGenerator.Emit(OpCode)

Requirements

Platforms: Windows 98, Windows NT 4.0, Windows Millennium Edition, Windows 2000, Windows XP Home Edition, Windows XP Professional, Windows .NET Server family

OpCodes.Shl Field

Shifts an integer value to the left (in zeroes) by a specified number of bits, pushing the result onto the evaluation stack.

```
[Visual Basic]
Public Shared ReadOnly Shl As OpCode
[C#]
public static readonly OpCode Shl;
[C++]
public: static OpCode Shl;
[JScript]
public static var Shl : OpCode;
```

Remarks

The following table lists the instruction's hexadecimal and Microsoft Intermediate Language (MSIL) assembly format, along with a brief reference summary:

Format	Assembly Format	Description
62	shl	Shifts an integer to the left (shifting in zeros).

The stack transitional behavior, in sequential order, is:

1. A value is pushed onto the stack.
2. The amount of bits to be shifted is pushed onto the stack.
3. The number of bits to be shifted and the value are popped from the stack; the value is shifted left by the specified number of bits.
4. The result is pushed onto the stack.

The **shl** instruction shifts the value (type **int32**, **int64** or **natural int**) left by the specified number of bits. The number of bits is a value of type **int32**, **int64** or **natural int**. The return value is unspecified if the number of bits to be shifted is greater than or equal to the width (in bits) of the supplied value.

Shl inserts a zero bit in the lowest position on each shift.

The following **Emit** constructor overload can use the **shl** opcode:

- ILGenerator.Emit(OpCode)

Requirements

Platforms: Windows 98, Windows NT 4.0, Windows Millennium Edition, Windows 2000, Windows XP Home Edition, Windows XP Professional, Windows .NET Server family

OpCodes.Shr Field

Shifts an integer value (in sign) to the right by a specified number of bits, pushing the result onto the evaluation stack.

```
[Visual Basic]
Public Shared ReadOnly Shr As OpCode
[C#]
public static readonly OpCode Shr;
[C++]
public: static OpCode Shr;
[JScript]
public static var Shr : OpCode;
```

Remarks

The following table lists the instruction's hexadecimal and Microsoft Intermediate Language (MSIL) assembly format, along with a brief reference summary:

Format	Assembly Format	Description
63	shr	Shifts an integer to the right (shifting in sign).

The stack transitional behavior, in sequential order, is:

1. A value is pushed onto the stack.
2. The amount of bits to be shifted is pushed onto the stack.
3. The number of bits to be shifted and the value are popped from the stack; the value is shifted right by the specified number of bits.
4. The result is pushed onto the stack.

The **shr.un** instruction shifts the value (type **int32**, **int64** or **natural int**) right by the specified number of bits. The number of bits is a value of type **int32**, **int64** or **natural int**. The return value is unspecified if the number of bits to be shifted is greater than or equal to the width (in bits) of the supplied value.

Shr replicates the high order bit on each shift, preserving the sign of the original value in the *result*.

The following **Emit** constructor overload can use the **shr** opcode:

- ILGenerator.Emit(OpCode)

Requirements

Platforms: Windows 98, Windows NT 4.0, Windows Millennium Edition, Windows 2000, Windows XP Home Edition, Windows XP Professional, Windows .NET Server family

OpCodes.Shr_Un Field

Shifts an unsigned integer value (in zeroes) to the right by a specified number of bits, pushing the result onto the evaluation stack.

```
[Visual Basic]
Public Shared ReadOnly Shr_Un As OpCode
[C#]
public static readonly OpCode Shr_Un;
[C++]
public: static OpCode Shr_Un;
[JScript]
public static var Shr_Un : OpCode;
```

Remarks

The following table lists the instruction's hexadecimal and Microsoft Intermediate Language (MSIL) assembly format, along with a brief reference summary:

Format	Assembly Format	Description
64	shr.un	Shifts an integer to the right (shifting in zeroes).

The stack transitional behavior, in sequential order, is:

1. A value is pushed onto the stack.
2. The amount of bits to be shifted is pushed onto the stack.
3. The number of bits to be shifted and the value are popped from the stack; the value is shifted right by the specified number of bits.
4. The result is pushed onto the stack.

The **shr.un** instruction shifts the value (type **int32**, **int64** or **natural int**) right by the specified number of bits. The number of bits is a value of type **int32**, **int64** or **natural int**. The return value is unspecified if the number of bits to be shifted is greater than or equal to the width (in bits) of the supplied value.

Shr.un inserts a zero bit in the highest position on each shift.

The following **Emit** constructor overload can use the **shr.un** opcode:

- ILGenerator.Emit(OpCode)

Requirements

Platforms: Windows 98, Windows NT 4.0, Windows Millennium Edition, Windows 2000, Windows XP Home Edition, Windows XP Professional, Windows .NET Server family

OpCodes.Sizeof Field

Pushes the size, in bytes, of a supplied value type onto the evaluation stack.

```
[Visual Basic]
Public Shared ReadOnly Sizeof As OpCode
[C#]
public static readonly OpCode Sizeof;
[C++]
public: static OpCode Sizeof;
[JScript]
public static var Sizeof : OpCode;
```

Remarks

The following table lists the instruction's hexadecimal and Microsoft Intermediate Language (MSIL) assembly format, along with a brief reference summary:

Format	Assembly Format	Description
FE 1C < **T** >	sizeof *valType*	Push the size, in bytes, of a value type as an **unsigned int32**.

The stack transitional behavior, in sequential order, is:

1. The size (in bytes) of the supplied value type (*valType*) is pushed onto the stack.

ValType must be a metadata token (a **typeref** or **typedef**) that specifies a value type.

The following **Emit** constructor overload can use the **sizeof** opcode:

• ILGenerator.Emit(OpCode, Type)

Requirements

Platforms: Windows 98, Windows NT 4.0, Windows Millennium Edition, Windows 2000, Windows XP Home Edition, Windows XP Professional, Windows .NET Server family

OpCodes.Starg Field

Stores the value on top of the evaluation stack in the argument slot at a specified index.

```
[Visual Basic]
Public Shared ReadOnly Starg As OpCode
[C#]
public static readonly OpCode Starg;
[C++]
public: static OpCode Starg;
[JScript]
public static var Starg : OpCode;
```

Remarks

The following table lists the instruction's hexadecimal and Microsoft Intermediate Language (MSIL) assembly format, along with a brief reference summary:

Format	Assembly Format	Description
FE OB < **unsigned int16** >	starg *num*	Pops the top value from the stack and stores it in argument slot *num*.

The stack transitional behavior, in sequential order, is:

1. The value currently on top of the stack is popped and placed in argument slot *num*.

The **starg** instruction pops a value from the stack and places it in argument slot *num*. The type of the value must match the type of the argument, as specified in the current method's signature.

For procedures that take a variable argument list, the **starg** instruction can be used only for the initial fixed arguments, not those in the variable part of the signature.

Performing a store into arguments that hold an integer value smaller than 4 bytes long truncates the value as it moves from the stack to the argument. Floating-point values are rounded from their native size (type **F**) to the size associated with the argument.

The following **Emit** constructor overload can use the **starg** opcode:

• ILGenerator.Emit(OpCode, short)

Requirements

Platforms: Windows 98, Windows NT 4.0, Windows Millennium Edition, Windows 2000, Windows XP Home Edition, Windows XP Professional, Windows .NET Server family

OpCodes.Starg_S Field

Stores the value on top of the evaluation stack in the argument slot at a specified index, short form.

```
[Visual Basic]
Public Shared ReadOnly Starg_S As OpCode
[C#]
public static readonly OpCode Starg_S;
[C++]
public: static OpCode Starg_S;
[JScript]
public static var Starg_S : OpCode;
```

Remarks

The following table lists the instruction's hexadecimal and Microsoft Intermediate Language (MSIL) assembly format, along with a brief reference summary:

Format	Assembly Format	Description
10 < **unsigned int8** >	starg.s *num*	Pops the top value from the stack and stores it in argument slot *num*, short form.

The stack transitional behavior, in sequential order, is:

1. The value currently on top of the stack is popped and placed in argument slot *num*.

The **starg.s** instruction pops a value from the stack and places it in argument slot *num*. The type of the value must match the type of the argument, as specified in the current method's signature.

The **starg.s** instruction provides an efficient encoding for use with the first 256 arguments.

For procedures that take a variable argument list, the **starg.s** instruction can be used only for the initial fixed arguments, not those in the variable part of the signature.

Performing a store into arguments that hold an integer value smaller than 4 bytes long truncates the value as it moves from the stack to the argument. Floating-point values are rounded from their native size (type **F**) to the size associated with the argument.

The following **Emit** constructor overload can use the **starg.s** opcode:

• ILGenerator.Emit(OpCode, byte)

Requirements

Platforms: Windows 98, Windows NT 4.0,
Windows Millennium Edition, Windows 2000,
Windows XP Home Edition, Windows XP Professional,
Windows .NET Server family

OpCodes.Stelem_I Field

Replaces the array element at a given index with the **natural int**
value on the evaluation stack.

```
[Visual Basic]
Public Shared ReadOnly Stelem_I As OpCode
[C#]
public static readonly OpCode Stelem_I;
[C++]
public: static OpCode Stelem_I;
[JScript]
public static var Stelem_I : OpCode;
```

Remarks

The following table lists the instruction's hexadecimal and Microsoft
Intermediate Language (MSIL) assembly format, along with a brief
reference summary:

Format	Assembly Format	Description
9B	stelem.i	Replaces an array element at the supplied index with the **natural int** value on the stack.

The stack transitional behavior, in sequential order, is:

1. An object reference to an array, *array*, is pushed onto the stack.
2. A valid index to an element in *array* is pushed onto the stack.
3. A value is pushed onto the stack.
4. The value, the index, and the array reference are popped from the stack; the value is put into the array element at the given index.

The **stelem.i** instruction replaces the value of the element *index* in
the one-dimensional array *array* with the **natural int** value pushed
onto the stack.

Arrays are objects and hence represented by a value of type **O**. The
index is type **natural int**.

NullReferenceException is thrown if *array* is a null reference.

IndexOutOfRangeException is thrown if *index* is negative, or
larger than the bound of *array*.

ArrayTypeMismatchException is thrown if *array* does not hold
elements of the required type.

The following **Emit** constructor overload can use the **stelem.i**
opcode:

• ILGenerator.Emit(OpCode)

Requirements

Platforms: Windows 98, Windows NT 4.0,
Windows Millennium Edition, Windows 2000,
Windows XP Home Edition, Windows XP Professional,
Windows .NET Server family

OpCodes.Stelem_I1 Field

Replaces the array element at a given index with the **int8** value on
the evaluation stack.

```
[Visual Basic]
Public Shared ReadOnly Stelem_I1 As OpCode
[C#]
public static readonly OpCode Stelem_I1;
[C++]
public: static OpCode Stelem_I1;
[JScript]
public static var Stelem_I1 : OpCode;
```

Remarks

The following table lists the instruction's hexadecimal and Microsoft
Intermediate Language (MSIL) assembly format, along with a brief
reference summary:

Format	Assembly Format	Description
9C	stelem.i1	Replaces an array element at the supplied index with the **int8** value on the stack.

The stack transitional behavior, in sequential order, is:

1. An object reference to an array, *array*, is pushed onto the stack.
2. A valid index to an element in *array* is pushed onto the stack.
3. A value is pushed onto the stack.
4. The value, the index, and the array reference are popped from the stack; the value is put into the array element at the given index.

The **stelem.i1** instruction replaces the value of the element *index* in
the one-dimensional array *array* with the **int8** value pushed onto the
stack.

Arrays are objects and hence represented by a value of type **O**. The
index is type **natural int**.

NullReferenceException is thrown if *array* is a null reference.

IndexOutOfRangeException is thrown if *index* is negative, or
larger than the bound of *array*.

ArrayTypeMismatchException is thrown if *array* does not hold
elements of the required type.

The following **Emit** constructor overload can use the **stelem.i1**
opcode:

• ILGenerator.Emit(OpCode)

Requirements

Platforms: Windows 98, Windows NT 4.0,
Windows Millennium Edition, Windows 2000,
Windows XP Home Edition, Windows XP Professional,
Windows .NET Server family

OpCodes.Stelem_I2 Field

Replaces the array element at a given index with the **int16** value on
the evaluation stack.

```
[Visual Basic]
Public Shared ReadOnly Stelem_I2 As OpCode
[C#]
public static readonly OpCode Stelem_I2;
[C++]
public: static OpCode Stelem_I2;
[JScript]
public static var Stelem_I2 : OpCode;
```

Remarks

The following table lists the instruction's hexadecimal and Microsoft Intermediate Language (MSIL) assembly format, along with a brief reference summary:

Format	Assembly Format	Description
9D	stelem.i2	Replaces an array element at the supplied index with the **int16** value on the stack.

The stack transitional behavior, in sequential order, is:

1. An object reference to an array, *array*, is pushed onto the stack.
2. A valid index to an element in *array* is pushed onto the stack.
3. A value is pushed onto the stack.
4. The value, the index, and the array reference are popped from the stack; the value is put into the array element at the given index.

The **stelem.i2** instruction replaces the value of the element *index* in the one-dimensional array *array* with the **int16** value pushed onto the stack.

Arrays are objects and hence represented by a value of type **O**. The index is type **natural int**.

NullReferenceException is thrown if *array* is a null reference.

IndexOutOfRangeException is thrown if *index* is negative, or larger than the bound of *array*.

ArrayTypeMismatchException is thrown if *array* does not hold elements of the required type.

The following **Emit** constructor overload can use the **stelem.i2** opcode:

* ILGenerator.Emit(OpCode)

Requirements

Platforms: Windows 98, Windows NT 4.0, Windows Millennium Edition, Windows 2000, Windows XP Home Edition, Windows XP Professional, Windows .NET Server family

OpCodes.Stelem_I4 Field

Replaces the array element at a given index with the **int32** value on the evaluation stack.

```
[Visual Basic]
Public Shared ReadOnly Stelem_I4 As OpCode
[C#]
public static readonly OpCode Stelem_I4;
[C++]
public: static OpCode Stelem_I4;
[JScript]
public static var Stelem_I4 : OpCode;
```

Remarks

The following table lists the instruction's hexadecimal and Microsoft Intermediate Language (MSIL) assembly format, along with a brief reference summary:

Format	Assembly Format	Description
9E	stelem.i4	Replaces an array element at the supplied index with the **int32** value on the stack.

The stack transitional behavior, in sequential order, is:

1. An object reference to an array, *array*, is pushed onto the stack.
2. A valid index to an element in *array* is pushed onto the stack.
3. A value is pushed onto the stack.
4. The value, the index, and the array reference are popped from the stack; the value is put into the array element at the given index.

The **stelem.i4** instruction replaces the value of the element *index* in the one-dimensional array *array* with the **int32** value pushed onto the stack.

Arrays are objects and hence represented by a value of type **O**. The index is type **natural int**.

NullReferenceException is thrown if *array* is a null reference.

IndexOutOfRangeException is thrown if *index* is negative, or larger than the bound of *array*.

ArrayTypeMismatchException is thrown if *array* does not hold elements of the required type.

The following **Emit** constructor overload can use the **stelem.i4** opcode:

* ILGenerator.Emit(OpCode)

Requirements

Platforms: Windows 98, Windows NT 4.0, Windows Millennium Edition, Windows 2000, Windows XP Home Edition, Windows XP Professional, Windows .NET Server family

OpCodes.Stelem_I8 Field

Replaces the array element at a given index with the **int64** value on the evaluation stack.

```
[Visual Basic]
Public Shared ReadOnly Stelem_I8 As OpCode
[C#]
public static readonly OpCode Stelem_I8;
[C++]
public: static OpCode Stelem_I8;
[JScript]
public static var Stelem_I8 : OpCode;
```

Remarks

The following table lists the instruction's hexadecimal and Microsoft Intermediate Language (MSIL) assembly format, along with a brief reference summary:

Format	Assembly Format	Description
9F	stelem.i8	Replaces an array element at the supplied index with the **int64** value on the stack.

The stack transitional behavior, in sequential order, is:

1. An object reference to an array, *array*, is pushed onto the stack.
2. A valid index to an element in *array* is pushed onto the stack.
3. A value is pushed onto the stack.
4. The value, the index, and the array reference are popped from the stack; the value is put into the array element at the given index.

The **stelem.i8** instruction replaces the value of the element *index* in the one-dimensional array *array* with the **int64** value pushed onto the stack.

Arrays are objects and hence represented by a value of type **O**. The index is type **natural int**.

NullReferenceException is thrown if *array* is a null reference.

IndexOutOfRangeException is thrown if *index* is negative, or larger than the bound of *array*.

ArrayTypeMismatchException is thrown if *array* does not hold elements of the required type.

The following **Emit** constructor overload can use the **stelem.i8** opcode:

* ILGenerator.Emit(OpCode)

Requirements

Platforms: Windows 98, Windows NT 4.0, Windows Millennium Edition, Windows 2000, Windows XP Home Edition, Windows XP Professional, Windows .NET Server family

OpCodes.Stelem_R4 Field

Replaces the array element at a given index with the **float32** value on the evaluation stack.

```
[Visual Basic]
Public Shared ReadOnly Stelem_R4 As OpCode
[C#]
public static readonly OpCode Stelem_R4;
[C++]
public: static OpCode Stelem_R4;
[JScript]
public static var Stelem_R4 : OpCode;
```

Remarks

The following table lists the instruction's hexadecimal and Microsoft Intermediate Language (MSIL) assembly format, along with a brief reference summary:

Format	Assembly Format	Description
A0	stelem.r4	Replaces an array element at the supplied index with the **float32** value on the stack.

The stack transitional behavior, in sequential order, is:

1. An object reference to an array, *array*, is pushed onto the stack.
2. A valid index to an element in *array* is pushed onto the stack.
3. A value is pushed onto the stack.
4. The value, the index, and the array reference are popped from the stack; the value is put into the array element at the given index.

The **stelem.r4** instruction replaces the value of the element *index* in the one-dimensional array *array* with the **float32** value pushed onto the stack.

Arrays are objects and hence represented by a value of type **O**. The index is type **natural int**.

NullReferenceException is thrown if *array* is a null reference.

IndexOutOfRangeException is thrown if *index* is negative, or larger than the bound of *array*.

ArrayTypeMismatchException is thrown if *array* does not hold elements of the required type.

The following **Emit** constructor overload can use the **stelem.r4** opcode:

* ILGenerator.Emit(OpCode)

Requirements

Platforms: Windows 98, Windows NT 4.0, Windows Millennium Edition, Windows 2000, Windows XP Home Edition, Windows XP Professional, Windows .NET Server family

OpCodes.Stelem_R8 Field

Replaces the array element at a given index with the **float64** value on the evaluation stack.

```
[Visual Basic]
Public Shared ReadOnly Stelem_R8 As OpCode
[C#]
public static readonly OpCode Stelem_R8;
[C++]
public: static OpCode Stelem_R8;
[JScript]
public static var Stelem_R8 : OpCode;
```

Remarks

The following table lists the instruction's hexadecimal and Microsoft Intermediate Language (MSIL) assembly format, along with a brief reference summary:

Format	Assembly Format	Description
A1	stelem.r8	Replaces an array element at the supplied index with the **float64** value on the stack.

The stack transitional behavior, in sequential order, is:

1. An object reference to an array, *array*, is pushed onto the stack.
2. A valid index to an element in *array* is pushed onto the stack.
3. A value is pushed onto the stack.
4. The value, the index, and the array reference are popped from the stack; the value is put into the array element at the given index.

The **stelem.r8** instruction replaces the value of the element *index* in the one-dimensional array *array* with the **float64** value pushed onto the stack.

Arrays are objects and hence represented by a value of type **O**. The index is type **natural int**.

NullReferenceException is thrown if *array* is a null reference.

IndexOutOfRangeException is thrown if *index* is negative, or larger than the bound of *array*.

ArrayTypeMismatchException is thrown if *array* does not hold elements of the required type.

The following **Emit** constructor overload can use the **stelem.r8** opcode:

* ILGenerator.Emit(OpCode)

Requirements

Platforms: Windows 98, Windows NT 4.0, Windows Millennium Edition, Windows 2000, Windows XP Home Edition, Windows XP Professional, Windows .NET Server family

OpCodes.Stelem_Ref Field

Replaces the array element at a given index with the object ref value (type **O**) on the evaluation stack.

```
[Visual Basic]
Public Shared ReadOnly Stelem_Ref As OpCode
[C#]
public static readonly OpCode Stelem_Ref;
[C++]
public: static OpCode Stelem_Ref;
[JScript]
public static var Stelem_Ref : OpCode;
```

Remarks

The following table lists the instruction's hexadecimal and Microsoft Intermediate Language (MSIL) assembly format, along with a brief reference summary:

Format	Assembly Format	Description
A2	stelem.ref	Replaces an array element at the supplied index with the **ref** value (type **O**) on the stack.

The stack transitional behavior, in sequential order, is:

1. An object reference to an array, *array*, is pushed onto the stack.
2. A valid index to an element in *array* is pushed onto the stack.
3. A value is pushed onto the stack.
4. The value, the index, and the array reference are popped from the stack; the value is put into the array element at the given index.

The **stelem.ref** instruction replaces the value of the element at the supplied index in the one-dimensional array *array* with the **ref** (type **O**) value pushed onto the stack.

Arrays are objects and hence represented by a value of type **O**. The index is type **natural int**.

Note that **stelem.ref** implicitly casts the supplied value to the element type of *array* before assigning the value to the array element. This cast can fail, even for verified code. Thus the **stelem.ref** instruction can throw **InvalidCastException**. For one-dimensional arrays that aren't zero-based and for multidimensional arrays, the **Array** class provides a **SetValue** method.

NullReferenceException is thrown if *array* is a null reference.

IndexOutOfRangeException is thrown if *index* is negative, or larger than the bound of *array*.

ArrayTypeMismatchException is thrown if *array* does not hold elements of the required type.

The following **Emit** constructor overload can use the **stelem.ref** opcode:

• ILGenerator.Emit(OpCode)

Requirements

Platforms: Windows 98, Windows NT 4.0, Windows Millennium Edition, Windows 2000, Windows XP Home Edition, Windows XP Professional, Windows .NET Server family

OpCodes.Stfld Field

Replaces the value stored in the field of an object reference or pointer with a new value.

```
[Visual Basic]
Public Shared ReadOnly Stfld As OpCode
[C#]
public static readonly OpCode Stfld;
```

```
[C++]
public: static OpCode Stfld;
[JScript]
public static var Stfld : OpCode;
```

Remarks

The following table lists the instruction's hexadecimal and Microsoft Intermediate Language (MSIL) assembly format, along with a brief reference summary:

Format	Assembly Format	Description
7D < **T** >	stfld *field*	Replaces the value of *field* of the object with a new value.

The stack transitional behavior, in sequential order, is:

1. An object reference or pointer is pushed onto the stack.
2. A value is pushed onto the stack.
3. The value and the object reference/pointer are popped from the stack; the value of *field* in the object is replaced with the supplied value.

The **stfld** instruction replaces the value of a field of an object (type **O**) or via a pointer (type **natural int**, **&**, or *****) with a givne value. *Field* is a metadata token that refers to a field member reference. The **stfld** instruction can have a prefix of either or both of **Unaligned** and **Volatile**.

NullReferenceException is thrown if the object reference or pointer is a null reference and the field isn't static.

MissingFieldException is thrown if *field* is not found in the metadata. This is typically checked when the Microsoft Intermediate Language (MSIL) instruction is converted to native code, not at runtime.

The following **Emit** constructor overload can use the **stfld** opcode:

• ILGenerator.Emit(OpCode, FieldInfo)

Requirements

Platforms: Windows 98, Windows NT 4.0, Windows Millennium Edition, Windows 2000, Windows XP Home Edition, Windows XP Professional, Windows .NET Server family

OpCodes.Stind_I Field

Stores a value of type **natural int** at a supplied address.

```
[Visual Basic]
Public Shared ReadOnly Stind_I As OpCode
[C#]
public static readonly OpCode Stind_I;
[C++]
public: static OpCode Stind_I;
[JScript]
public static var Stind_I : OpCode;
```

Remarks

The following table lists the instruction's hexadecimal and Microsoft Intermediate Language (MSIL) assembly format, along with a brief reference summary:

Format	Assembly Format	Description
DF	stind.i	Stores a **natural int** value at at a given address.

The stack transitional behavior, in sequential order, is:
1. An address is pushed onto the stack.
2. A value is pushed onto the stack.
3. The value and the address are popped from the stack; the value is stored at the address.

The **stind.i** instruction stores a **natural int** value at the supplied address (type **natural int**, *, or **&**).

Type safe operation requires that the **stind.i** instruction be used in a manner consistent with the type of the pointer. The operation of the **stind.i** instruction can be altered by an immediately preceding **Volatile** or **Unaligned** prefix instruction.

NullReferenceException is thrown if *addr* is not naturally aligned for the argument type implied by the instruction suffix.

The following **Emit** constructor overload can use the **stind.i** opcode:
- ILGenerator.Emit(OpCode)

Requirements

Platforms: Windows 98, Windows NT 4.0, Windows Millennium Edition, Windows 2000, Windows XP Home Edition, Windows XP Professional, Windows .NET Server family

OpCodes.Stind_I1 Field

Stores a value of type **int8** at a supplied address.

```
[Visual Basic]
Public Shared ReadOnly Stind_I1 As OpCode
[C#]
public static readonly OpCode Stind_I1;
[C++]
public: static OpCode Stind_I1;
[JScript]
public static var Stind_I1 : OpCode;
```

Remarks

The following table lists the instruction's hexadecimal and Microsoft Intermediate Language (MSIL) assembly format, along with a brief reference summary:

Format	Assembly Format	Description
52	stind.i1	Stores an **int8** value at at a given address.

The stack transitional behavior, in sequential order, is:
1. An address is pushed onto the stack.
2. A value is pushed onto the stack.
3. The value and the address are popped from the stack; the value is stored at the address.

The **stind.i1** instruction stores an **int8** value at the supplied address (type **natural int**, *, or **&**).

Type safe operation requires that the **stind.i1** instruction be used in a manner consistent with the type of the pointer. The operation of the **stind.i1** instruction can be altered by an immediately preceding **Volatile** or **Unaligned** prefix instruction.

NullReferenceException is thrown if *addr* is not naturally aligned for the argument type implied by the instruction suffix.

The following **Emit** constructor overload can use the **stind.i1** opcode:
- ILGenerator.Emit(OpCode)

Requirements

Platforms: Windows 98, Windows NT 4.0, Windows Millennium Edition, Windows 2000, Windows XP Home Edition, Windows XP Professional, Windows .NET Server family

OpCodes.Stind_I2 Field

Stores a value of type **int16** at a supplied address.

```
[Visual Basic]
Public Shared ReadOnly Stind_I2 As OpCode
[C#]
public static readonly OpCode Stind_I2;
[C++]
public: static OpCode Stind_I2;
[JScript]
public static var Stind_I2 : OpCode;
```

Remarks

The following table lists the instruction's hexadecimal and Microsoft Intermediate Language (MSIL) assembly format, along with a brief reference summary:

Format	Assembly Format	Description
53	stind.i2	Stores an **int16** value at at a given address.

The stack transitional behavior, in sequential order, is:
1. An address is pushed onto the stack.
2. A value is pushed onto the stack.
3. The value and the address are popped from the stack; the value is stored at the address.

The **stind.i2** instruction stores an **int16** value at the supplied address (type **natural int**, *, or **&**).

Type safe operation requires that the **stind.2i** instruction be used in a manner consistent with the type of the pointer. The operation of the **stind.i2** instruction can be altered by an immediately preceding **Volatile** or **Unaligned** prefix instruction.

NullReferenceException is thrown if *addr* is not naturally aligned for the argument type implied by the instruction suffix.

The following **Emit** constructor overload can use the **stind.i2** opcode:
- ILGenerator.Emit(OpCode)

Requirements

Platforms: Windows 98, Windows NT 4.0, Windows Millennium Edition, Windows 2000, Windows XP Home Edition, Windows XP Professional, Windows .NET Server family

OpCodes.Stind_I4 Field

Stores a value of type **int32** at a supplied address.

```
[Visual Basic]
Public Shared ReadOnly Stind_I4 As OpCode
[C#]
public static readonly OpCode Stind_I4;
[C++]
public: static OpCode Stind_I4;
[JScript]
public static var Stind_I4 : OpCode;
```

Remarks

The following table lists the instruction's hexadecimal and Microsoft Intermediate Language (MSIL) assembly format, along with a brief reference summary:

Format	Assembly Format	Description
54	stind.i4	Stores an **int32** value at at a given address.

The stack transitional behavior, in sequential order, is:

1. An address is pushed onto the stack.
2. A value is pushed onto the stack.
3. The value and the address are popped from the stack; the value is stored at the address.

The **stind.i4** instruction stores an **int32** value at the supplied address (type **natural int**, *, or **&**).

Type safe operation requires that the **stind.i4** instruction be used in a manner consistent with the type of the pointer. The operation of the **stind.i4** instruction can be altered by an immediately preceding **Volatile** or **Unaligned** prefix instruction.

NullReferenceException is thrown if *addr* is not naturally aligned for the argument type implied by the instruction suffix.

The following **Emit** constructor overload can use the **stind.i4** opcode:

• ILGenerator.Emit(OpCode)

Requirements

Platforms: Windows 98, Windows NT 4.0, Windows Millennium Edition, Windows 2000, Windows XP Home Edition, Windows XP Professional, Windows .NET Server family

OpCodes.Stind_I8 Field

Stores a value of type **int64** at a supplied address.

```
[Visual Basic]
Public Shared ReadOnly Stind_I8 As OpCode
[C#]
public static readonly OpCode Stind_I8;
[C++]
public: static OpCode Stind_I8;
[JScript]
public static var Stind_I8 : OpCode;
```

Remarks

The following table lists the instruction's hexadecimal and Microsoft Intermediate Language (MSIL) assembly format, along with a brief reference summary:

Format	Assembly Format	Description
55	stind.i8	Stores an **int64** value at at a given address.

The stack transitional behavior, in sequential order, is:

1. An address is pushed onto the stack.
2. A value is pushed onto the stack.
3. The value and the address are popped from the stack; the value is stored at the address.

The **stind.i8** instruction stores an **int64** value at the supplied address (type **natural int**, *, or **&**).

Type safe operation requires that the **stind.i8** instruction be used in a manner consistent with the type of the pointer. The operation of the **stind.i** instruction can be altered by an immediately preceding **Volatile** or **Unaligned** prefix instruction.

NullReferenceException is thrown if *addr* is not naturally aligned for the argument type implied by the instruction suffix.

The following **Emit** constructor overload can use the **stind.i8** opcode:

• ILGenerator.Emit(OpCode)

Requirements

Platforms: Windows 98, Windows NT 4.0, Windows Millennium Edition, Windows 2000, Windows XP Home Edition, Windows XP Professional, Windows .NET Server family

OpCodes.Stind_R4 Field

Stores a value of type **float32** at a supplied address.

```
[Visual Basic]
Public Shared ReadOnly Stind_R4 As OpCode
[C#]
public static readonly OpCode Stind_R4;
[C++]
public: static OpCode Stind_R4;
[JScript]
public static var Stind_R4 : OpCode;
```

Remarks

The following table lists the instruction's hexadecimal and Microsoft Intermediate Language (MSIL) assembly format, along with a brief reference summary:

Format	Assembly Format	Description
56	stind.r4	Stores a **float32** value at at a given address.

The stack transitional behavior, in sequential order, is:

1. An address is pushed onto the stack.
2. A value is pushed onto the stack.
3. The value and the address are popped from the stack; the value is stored at the address.

The **stind.r4** instruction stores a **float32** value at the supplied address (type **natural int**, *, or **&**).

Type safe operation requires that the **stind.r4** instruction be used in a manner consistent with the type of the pointer. The operation of the **stind.r4** instruction can be altered by an immediately preceding **Volatile** or **Unaligned** prefix instruction.

NullReferenceException is thrown if *addr* is not naturally aligned for the argument type implied by the instruction suffix.

The following **Emit** constructor overload can use the **stind.r4** opcode:

• ILGenerator.Emit(OpCode)

Requirements

Platforms: Windows 98, Windows NT 4.0, Windows Millennium Edition, Windows 2000, Windows XP Home Edition, Windows XP Professional, Windows .NET Server family

OpCodes.Stind_R8 Field

Stores a value of type **float64** at a supplied address.

```
[Visual Basic]
Public Shared ReadOnly Stind_R8 As OpCode
[C#]
public static readonly OpCode Stind_R8;
[C++]
public: static OpCode Stind_R8;
[JScript]
public static var Stind_R8 : OpCode;
```

Remarks

The following table lists the instruction's hexadecimal and Microsoft Intermediate Language (MSIL) assembly format, along with a brief reference summary:

Format	Assembly Format	Description
57	stind.r8	Stores a **float64** value at at a given address.

The stack transitional behavior, in sequential order, is:

1. An address is pushed onto the stack.
2. A value is pushed onto the stack.
3. The value and the address are popped from the stack; the value is stored at the address.

The **stind.r8** instruction stores a **float64** value at the supplied address (type **natural int**, *, or **&**).

Type safe operation requires that the **stind.r8** instruction be used in a manner consistent with the type of the pointer. The operation of the **stind.r8** instruction can be altered by an immediately preceding **Volatile** or **Unaligned** prefix instruction.

NullReferenceException is thrown if *addr* is not naturally aligned for the argument type implied by the instruction suffix.

The following **Emit** constructor overload can use the **stind.r8** opcode:

- ILGenerator.Emit(OpCode)

Requirements

Platforms: Windows 98, Windows NT 4.0, Windows Millennium Edition, Windows 2000, Windows XP Home Edition, Windows XP Professional, Windows .NET Server family

OpCodes.Stind_Ref Field

Stores a object reference value at a supplied address.

```
[Visual Basic]
Public Shared ReadOnly Stind_Ref As OpCode
[C#]
public static readonly OpCode Stind_Ref;
[C++]
public: static OpCode Stind_Ref;
[JScript]
public static var Stind_Ref : OpCode;
```

Remarks

The following table lists the instruction's hexadecimal and Microsoft Intermediate Language (MSIL) assembly format, along with a brief reference summary:

Format	Assembly Format	Description
51	stind.ref	Stores an object reference (type **O**) value at a given address.

The stack transitional behavior, in sequential order, is:

1. An address is pushed onto the stack.
2. A value is pushed onto the stack.
3. The value and the address are popped from the stack; the value is stored at the address.

The **stind.ref** instruction stores an object reference value at the supplied address (type **natural int**, *, or **&**).

Type safe operation requires that the **stind.ref** instruction be used in a manner consistent with the type of the pointer. The operation of the **stind.ref** instruction can be altered by an immediately preceding **Volatile** or **Unaligned** prefix instruction.

NullReferenceException is thrown if *addr* is not naturally aligned for the argument type implied by the instruction suffix.

The following **Emit** constructor overload can use the **stind.ref** opcode:

- ILGenerator.Emit(OpCode)

Requirements

Platforms: Windows 98, Windows NT 4.0, Windows Millennium Edition, Windows 2000, Windows XP Home Edition, Windows XP Professional, Windows .NET Server family

OpCodes.Stloc Field

Pops the current value from the top of the evaluation stack and stores it in a local variable list at a specified index.

```
[Visual Basic]
Public Shared ReadOnly Stloc As OpCode
[C#]
public static readonly OpCode Stloc;
[C++]
public: static OpCode Stloc;
[JScript]
public static var Stloc : OpCode;
```

Remarks

The following table lists the instruction's hexadecimal and Microsoft Intermediate Language (MSIL) assembly format, along with a brief reference summary:

Format	Assembly Format	Description
FE 0E < **unsigned int16** >	stloc *index*	Pops a value from the stack and stores it in local variable *index*.

The stack transitional behavior, in sequential order, is:

1. A value is popped off of the stack and placed in local variable *index*.

The **stloc** instruction pops the top value off the evaluation stack and moves it into local variable number *index*, where local variables are numbered 0 onwards. The type of the value must match the type of the local variable as specified in the current method's local signature.

Storing into locals that hold an integer value smaller than 4 bytes long truncates the value as it moves from the stack to the local variable. Floating-point values are rounded from their native size (type **F**) to the size associated with the argument.

Correct Microsoft Intermediate Language (MSIL) instructions require that *index* be a valid local index. For the **stloc** instruction, *index* must lie in the range 0 to 65534 inclusive (specifically, 65535 is not valid). The reason for excluding 65535 is pragmatic: likely implementations will use a 2-byte integer to track both a local's index, as well as the total number of locals for a given method. If an index of 65535 had been made valid, it would require a wider integer to track the number of locals in such a method.

The following **Emit** constructor overloads can use the **stloc** opcode:

- ILGenerator.Emit(OpCode, LocalBuilder)
- ILGenerator.Emit(OpCode, short)

Requirements

Platforms: Windows 98, Windows NT 4.0, Windows Millennium Edition, Windows 2000, Windows XP Home Edition, Windows XP Professional, Windows .NET Server family

OpCodes.Stloc_0 Field

Pops the current value from the top of the evaluation stack and stores it in a the local variable list at index 0.

```
[Visual Basic]
Public Shared ReadOnly Stloc_0 As OpCode
[C#]
public static readonly OpCode Stloc_0;
[C++]
public: static OpCode Stloc_0;
[JScript]
public static var Stloc_0 : OpCode;
```

Remarks

The following table lists the instruction's hexadecimal and Microsoft Intermediate Language (MSIL) assembly format, along with a brief reference summary:

Format	Assembly Format	Description
0A	stloc.0	Pops a value from the stack into local variable 0.

The stack transitional behavior, in sequential order, is:

1. A value is popped off of the stack and placed in the local variable indexed by 0.

The **stloc.0** instruction pops the top value off the evaluation stack and moves it into the local variable indexed by 0. The type of the value must match the type of the local variable as specified in the current method's local signature.

stloc.0 is an especially efficient encoding for storing values in local variable 0.

Storing into locals that hold an integer value smaller than 4 bytes long truncates the value as it moves from the stack to the local variable. Floating-point values are rounded from their native size (type **F**) to the size associated with the argument.

The following **Emit** constructor overload can use the **stloc.0** opcode:

- ILGenerator.Emit(OpCode)

Requirements

Platforms: Windows 98, Windows NT 4.0, Windows Millennium Edition, Windows 2000, Windows XP Home Edition, Windows XP Professional, Windows .NET Server family

OpCodes.Stloc_1 Field

Pops the current value from the top of the evaluation stack and stores it in a the local variable list at index 1.

```
[Visual Basic]
Public Shared ReadOnly Stloc_1 As OpCode
[C#]
public static readonly OpCode Stloc_1;
[C++]
public: static OpCode Stloc_1;
[JScript]
public static var Stloc_1 : OpCode;
```

Remarks

The following table lists the instruction's hexadecimal and Microsoft Intermediate Language (MSIL) assembly format, along with a brief reference summary:

Format	Assembly Format	Description
0B	stloc.1	Pops a value from the stack into local variable 1.

The stack transitional behavior, in sequential order, is:

1. A value is popped off of the stack and placed in the local variable indexed by 1.

The **stloc.1** instruction pops the top value off the evaluation stack and moves it into the local variable indexed by 1. The type of the value must match the type of the local variable as specified in the current method's local signature.

stloc.1 is an especially efficient encoding for storing values in local variable 1.

Storing into locals that hold an integer value smaller than 4 bytes long truncates the value as it moves from the stack to the local variable. Floating-point values are rounded from their native size (type **F**) to the size associated with the argument.

The following **Emit** constructor overload can use the **stloc.1** opcode:

- ILGenerator.Emit(OpCode)

Requirements

Platforms: Windows 98, Windows NT 4.0, Windows Millennium Edition, Windows 2000, Windows XP Home Edition, Windows XP Professional, Windows .NET Server family

OpCodes.Stloc_2 Field

Pops the current value from the top of the evaluation stack and stores it in a the local variable list at index 2.

```
[Visual Basic]
Public Shared ReadOnly Stloc_2 As OpCode
[C#]
public static readonly OpCode Stloc_2;
[C++]
public: static OpCode Stloc_2;
```

```
[JScript]
public static var Stloc_2 : OpCode;
```

Remarks

The following table lists the instruction's hexadecimal and Microsoft Intermediate Language (MSIL) assembly format, along with a brief reference summary:

Format	Assembly Format	Description
0C	stloc.2	Pops a value from the stack into local variable 2

The stack transitional behavior, in sequential order, is:

1. A value is popped off of the stack and placed in the local variable indexed by 2.

The **stloc.2** instruction pops the top value off the evaluation stack and moves it into the local variable indexed by 2. The type of the value must match the type of the local variable as specified in the current method's local signature.

stloc.2 is an especially efficient encoding for storing values in local variable 2.

Storing into locals that hold an integer value smaller than 4 bytes long truncates the value as it moves from the stack to the local variable. Floating-point values are rounded from their native size (type **F**) to the size associated with the argument.

The following **Emit** constructor overload can use the **stloc.2** opcode:

- ILGenerator.Emit(OpCode)

Requirements

Platforms: Windows 98, Windows NT 4.0, Windows Millennium Edition, Windows 2000, Windows XP Home Edition, Windows XP Professional, Windows .NET Server family

OpCodes.Stloc_3 Field

Pops the current value from the top of the evaluation stack and stores it in a the local variable list at index 3.

```
[Visual Basic]
Public Shared ReadOnly Stloc_3 As OpCode
[C#]
public static readonly OpCode Stloc_3;
[C++]
public: static OpCode Stloc_3;
[JScript]
public static var Stloc_3 : OpCode;
```

Remarks

The following table lists the instruction's hexadecimal and Microsoft Intermediate Language (MSIL) assembly format, along with a brief reference summary:

Format	Assembly Format	Description
0D	stloc.3	Pops a value from the stack into local variable 3

The stack transitional behavior, in sequential order, is:

1. A value is popped off of the stack and placed in the local variable indexed by 3.

The **stloc.3** instruction pops the top value off the evaluation stack and moves it into the local variable indexed by 3. The type of the value must match the type of the local variable as specified in the current method's local signature.

stloc.3 is an especially efficient encoding for storing values in local variable 3.

Storing into locals that hold an integer value smaller than 4 bytes long truncates the value as it moves from the stack to the local variable. Floating-point values are rounded from their native size (type **F**) to the size associated with the argument.

The following **Emit** constructor overload can use the **stloc.3** opcode:

- ILGenerator.Emit(OpCode)

Requirements

Platforms: Windows 98, Windows NT 4.0, Windows Millennium Edition, Windows 2000, Windows XP Home Edition, Windows XP Professional, Windows .NET Server family

OpCodes.Stloc_S Field

Pops the current value from the top of the evaluation stack and stores it in a the local variable list at *index* (short form).

```
[Visual Basic]
Public Shared ReadOnly Stloc_S As OpCode
[C#]
public static readonly OpCode Stloc_S;
[C++]
public: static OpCode Stloc_S;
[JScript]
public static var Stloc_S : OpCode;
```

Remarks

The following table lists the instruction's hexadecimal and Microsoft Intermediate Language (MSIL) assembly format, along with a brief reference summary:

Format	Assembly Format	Description
13 < unsigned int8 >	stloc.s *index*	Pops a value from the stack and stores it in local variable *index*, short form.

The stack transitional behavior, in sequential order, is:

1. A value is popped off of the stack and placed in local variable *index*.

The **stloc.s** instruction pops the top value off the evaluation stack and moves it into local variable number *index*, where local variables are numbered 0 onwards. The type of the value must match the type of the local variable as specified in the current method's local signature.

The **stloc.s** instruction provides an efficient encoding for local variables 0 through 255.

Storing into locals that hold an integer value smaller than 4 bytes long truncates the value as it moves from the stack to the local variable. Floating-point values are rounded from their native size (type **F**) to the size associated with the argument.

The following **Emit** constructor overloads can use the **stloc.s** opcode:

- ILGenerator.Emit(OpCode, LocalBuilder)
- ILGenerator.Emit(OpCode, byte)

Requirements

Platforms: Windows 98, Windows NT 4.0,
Windows Millennium Edition, Windows 2000,
Windows XP Home Edition, Windows XP Professional,
Windows .NET Server family

OpCodes.Stobj Field

Copies a value of a specified type from the evaluation stack into a
supplied memory address.

```
[Visual Basic]
Public Shared ReadOnly Stobj As OpCode
[C#]
public static readonly OpCode Stobj;
[C++]
public: static OpCode Stobj;
[JScript]
public static var Stobj : OpCode;
```

Remarks

The following table lists the instruction's hexadecimal and Microsoft
Intermediate Language (MSIL) assembly format, along with a brief
reference summary:

Format	Assembly Format	Description
81 < **T** >	stobj *class*	Stores a value of type *class* from the stack into memory.

The stack transitional behavior, in sequential order, is:

1. An address is pushed onto the stack.
2. A value type object of type *class* is pushed onto the stack.
3. The object and the address are popped from the stack; the value
    type object is stored at the address.

The **stobj** instruction copies the value type object into the address
specified by the address(a pointer of type **natural int**, *, or **&**). The
number of bytes copied depends on the size of the class represented
by *class*, a metadata token representing a value type.

The operation of the **stobj** instruction can be altered by an
immediately preceding **Volatile** or **Unaligned** prefix instruction.

TypeLoadException is thrown if class cannot be found. This is
typically detected when Microsoft Intermediate Language (MSIL)
instructions are converted to native code rather than at run time.

The following **Emit** constructor overload can use the **stobj** opcode:

*   ILGenerator.Emit(OpCode, Type)

Requirements

Platforms: Windows 98, Windows NT 4.0,
Windows Millennium Edition, Windows 2000,
Windows XP Home Edition, Windows XP Professional,
Windows .NET Server family

OpCodes.Stsfld Field

Replaces the value of a static field with a value from the evaluation
stack.

```
[Visual Basic]
Public Shared ReadOnly Stsfld As OpCode
[C#]
public static readonly OpCode Stsfld;
```

```
[C++]
public: static OpCode Stsfld;
[JScript]
public static var Stsfld : OpCode;
```

Remarks

The following table lists the instruction's hexadecimal and Microsoft
Intermediate Language (MSIL) assembly format, along with a brief
reference summary:

Format	Assembly Format	Description
80 < **T** >	stsfld *field*	Replaces the value in *field* with a supplied value.

The stack transitional behavior, in sequential order, is:

1. A value is pushed onto the stack.
2. A value is popped from the stack and stored in *field*.

The **stsfld** instruction replaces the value of a static field with a value
from the stack. *field* is a metadata token that must refer to a static
field member.

The **stsfld** instruction may be prefixed by **Volatile**.

MissingFieldException is thrown if field is not found in the
metadata. This is typically checked when Microsoft Intermediate
Language (MSIL) instructions are converted to native code, not at
run time.

The following **Emit** constructor overload can use the **stsfld** opcode:

*   ILGenerator.Emit(OpCode, FieldInfo)

Requirements

Platforms: Windows 98, Windows NT 4.0,
Windows Millennium Edition, Windows 2000,
Windows XP Home Edition, Windows XP Professional,
Windows .NET Server family

OpCodes.Sub Field

Subtracts one value from another and pushes the result onto the
evaluation stack.

```
[Visual Basic]
Public Shared ReadOnly Sub As OpCode
[C#]
public static readonly OpCode Sub;
[C++]
public: static OpCode Sub;
[JScript]
public static var Sub : OpCode;
```

Remarks

The following table lists the instruction's hexadecimal and Microsoft
Intermediate Language (MSIL) assembly format, along with a brief
reference summary:

Format	Assembly Format	Description
59	sub	Subtracts one value from another, returning a new numeric value.

The stack transitional behavior, in sequential order, is:

1. *value1* is pushed onto the stack.
2. *value2* is pushed onto the stack.

3. *value2* and *value1* are popped from the stack; *value2* is subtracted from *value1*.

4. The result is pushed onto the stack.

Overflow is not detected for integer operations (for proper overflow handling, see **Sub_Ovf**).

Integer subtraction wraps, rather than saturates. For example: assuming 8-bit integers, where *value1* is set to 255 and *value2* is set to 1, the "wrapped" result will be 0 rather than 256.

Floating-point overflow returns **+inf** (**PositiveInfinity**) or **-inf** (**NegativeInfinity**).

The following **Emit** constructor overload can use the **sub** opcode:

• ILGenerator.Emit(OpCode)

Requirements

Platforms: Windows 98, Windows NT 4.0, Windows Millennium Edition, Windows 2000, Windows XP Home Edition, Windows XP Professional, Windows .NET Server family

OpCodes.Sub_Ovf Field

Subtracts one integer value from another, performs an overflow check, and pushes the result onto the evaluation stack.

```
[Visual Basic]
Public Shared ReadOnly Sub_Ovf As OpCode
[C#]
public static readonly OpCode Sub_Ovf;
[C++]
public: static OpCode Sub_Ovf;
[JScript]
public static var Sub_Ovf : OpCode;
```

Remarks

The following table lists the instruction's hexadecimal and Microsoft Intermediate Language (MSIL) assembly format, along with a brief reference summary:

Format	Assembly Format	Description
DA	sub.ovf	Subtracts one integer value from another with an overflow check.

The stack transitional behavior, in sequential order, is:

1. *value1* is pushed onto the stack.
2. *value2* is pushed onto the stack.
3. *value2* and *value1* are popped from the stack; *value2* is subtracted from *value1* with a check for overflow.
4. The result is pushed onto the stack.

OverflowException is thrown if the result can not be represented in the result type.

This operation is performed on signed integers; for floating-point values, use **Sub**.

The following **Emit** constructor overload can use the **sub.ovf** opcode:

• ILGenerator.Emit(OpCode)

Requirements

Platforms: Windows 98, Windows NT 4.0, Windows Millennium Edition, Windows 2000, Windows XP Home Edition, Windows XP Professional, Windows .NET Server family

OpCodes.Sub_Ovf_Un Field

Subtracts one unsigned integer value from another, performs an overflow check, and pushes the result onto the evaluation stack.

```
[Visual Basic]
Public Shared ReadOnly Sub_Ovf_Un As OpCode
[C#]
public static readonly OpCode Sub_Ovf_Un;
[C++]
public: static OpCode Sub_Ovf_Un;
[JScript]
public static var Sub_Ovf_Un : OpCode;
```

Remarks

The following table lists the instruction's hexadecimal and Microsoft Intermediate Language (MSIL) assembly format, along with a brief reference summary:

Format	Assembly Format	Description
DB	sub.ovf.un	Subtracts one unsigned integer value from anotherwith an overflow check.

The stack transitional behavior, in sequential order, is:

1. *value1* is pushed onto the stack.
2. *value2* is pushed onto the stack.
3. *value2* and *value1* are popped from the stack; *value2* is subtracted from *value1* with a check for overflow.
4. The result is pushed onto the stack.

OverflowException is thrown if the result can not be represented in the result type.

This operation is performed on signed integers; for floating-point values, use **Sub**.

The following **Emit** constructor overload can use the **sub.ovf.un** opcode:

• ILGenerator.Emit(OpCode)

Requirements

Platforms: Windows 98, Windows NT 4.0, Windows Millennium Edition, Windows 2000, Windows XP Home Edition, Windows XP Professional, Windows .NET Server family

OpCodes.Switch Field

Implements a jump table.

```
[Visual Basic]
Public Shared ReadOnly Switch As OpCode
[C#]
public static readonly OpCode Switch;
[C++]
public: static OpCode Switch;
[JScript]
public static var Switch : OpCode;
```

Remarks

The following table lists the instruction's hexadecimal and Microsoft Intermediate Language (MSIL) assembly format, along with a brief reference summary:

Format	Assembly Format	Description
45 < **unsigned int32** > < **int32** > ... < **int32** >	switch (N, t1, t2 ... tN)	Jumps to one of N values.

The stack transitional behavior, in sequential order, is:

1. A value is pushed onto the stack.
2. The value is popped off the stack and execution is transferred to the instruction at the offset indexed by the value, where the value is less than N.

The **switch** instruction implements a jump table. The format of the instruction is an **unsigned int32** representing the number of targets N, followed by N int32 values specifying jump targets. These targets are represented as offsets (positive or negative) from the beginning of the instruction following this **switch** instruction.

The **switch** instruction pops a value off the stack and compares it, as an unsigned integer, to N. If value is less than N, execution is transferred to the target indexed by value, where targets are numbered from 0 (for example, a value of 0 takes the first target, a value of 1 takes the second target, and so on). If the value is greater than or equal to N, execution continues at the next instruction (fall through).

If the target instruction has one or more prefix codes, control can only be transferred to the first of these prefixes.

Control transfers into and out of **try**, **catch**, **filter**, and **finally** blocks cannot be performed by this instruction. (Such transfers are severely restricted and must use the leave instruction instead).

The following **Emit** constructor overload can use the **switch** opcode. The *Label[ ]* argument is an array of Labels representing 32-bit offsets.

- ILGenerator.Emit(OpCode, Label[])

Example

See related example in the **System.Reflection.Emit.OpCodes** class topic.

Requirements

Platforms: Windows 98, Windows NT 4.0, Windows Millennium Edition, Windows 2000, Windows XP Home Edition, Windows XP Professional, Windows .NET Server family

OpCodes.Tailcall Field

Performs a postfixed method call instruction such that the current method's stack frame is removed before the actual call instruction is executed.

```
[Visual Basic]
Public Shared ReadOnly Tailcall As OpCode
[C#]
public static readonly OpCode Tailcall;
[C++]
public: static OpCode Tailcall;
[JScript]
public static var Tailcall : OpCode;
```

Remarks

The following table lists the instruction's hexadecimal and Microsoft Intermediate Language (MSIL) assembly format, along with a brief reference summary:

Format	Assembly Format	Description
FE 14	tail.	Subsequent call terminates current methods

There is no stack transition behavior defined for this instruction.

The **tail** prefix instruction must immediately precede a **Call**, **Calli**, or **Callvirt** instruction. It indicates that the current method's stack frame should be removed before the call instruction is executed. It also implies that the value returned from the following call is also the value returned by the current method, and the call can therefore be converted into a cross-method jump.

The stack must be empty except for the arguments being transferred by the following call. The instruction following the call instruction must be a ret. Thus the only valid code sequence is **tail. call** (or **calli** or **callvirt**). Correct Microsoft Intermediate Language (MSIL) instructions must not branch to the **call** instruction, but they may branch to the subsequent **Ret**.

The current frame cannot be discarded when control is transferred from untrusted code to trusted code, since this would jeopardize code identity security. The .NET Framework security checks can therefore cause the **tail** to be ignored, leaving a standard **Call** instruction. Similarly, in order to allow the exit of a synchronized region to occur after the call returns, the **tail** prefix is ignored when used to exit a method that is marked synchronized.

The following **Emit** constructor overload can use the **tail** opcode:

- ILGenerator.Emit(OpCode)

Requirements

Platforms: Windows 98, Windows NT 4.0, Windows Millennium Edition, Windows 2000, Windows XP Home Edition, Windows XP Professional, Windows .NET Server family

OpCodes.Throw Field

Throws the exception object currently on the evaluation stack.

```
[Visual Basic]
Public Shared ReadOnly Throw As OpCode
[C#]
public static readonly OpCode Throw;
[C++]
public: static OpCode Throw;
[JScript]
public static var Throw : OpCode;
```

Remarks

The following table lists the instruction's hexadecimal and Microsoft Intermediate Language (MSIL) assembly format, along with a brief reference summary:

Format	Assembly Format	Description
7A	throw	Throws an exception.

The stack transitional behavior, in sequential order, is:

1. An object reference (to an exception) is pushed onto the stack.
2. The object reference is popped from the stack and the exception thrown.

The **throw** instruction throws the exception object (type **O**) currently on the stack.

NullReferenceException is thrown if the object reference is a null reference.

The following **Emit** constructor overload can use the **throw** opcode:
- ILGenerator.Emit(OpCode)

Requirements

Platforms: Windows 98, Windows NT 4.0, Windows Millennium Edition, Windows 2000, Windows XP Home Edition, Windows XP Professional, Windows .NET Server family

OpCodes.Unaligned Field

Indicates that an address currently atop the evaluation stack might not be aligned to the natural size of the immediately following **ldind**, **stind**, **ldfld**, **stfld**, **ldobj**, **stobj**, **initblk**, or **cpblk** instruction.

```
[Visual Basic]
Public Shared ReadOnly Unaligned As OpCode
[C#]
public static readonly OpCode Unaligned;
[C++]
public: static OpCode Unaligned;
[JScript]
public static var Unaligned : OpCode;
```

Remarks

The following table lists the instruction's hexadecimal and Microsoft Intermediate Language (MSIL) assembly format, along with a brief reference summary:

Format	Assembly Format	Description
FE 12 < **unsigned int8** >	unaligned. *alignment*	Indicates that the subsequent pointer instruction may be unaligned.

The stack transitional behavior, in sequential order, is:
1. An address is pushed onto the stack.

Unaligned specifies that the address (an unmanaged pointer, **natural int**) on the stack might not be aligned to the natural size of the immediately following **ldind**, **stind**, **ldfld**, **stfld**, **ldobj**, **stobj**, **initblk**, or **cpblk** instruction. That is, for a **Ldind_I4** instruction the alignment of the address may not be to a 4-byte boundary. For **initblk** and **cpblk** the default alignment is architecture dependent (4-byte on 32-bit CPUs, 8-byte on 64-bit CPUs). Code generators that do not restrict their output to a 32-bit word size must use **unaligned** if the alignment is not known at compile time to be 8-byte.

The value of alignment must be 1, 2, or 4 and means that the generated code should assume that the address is byte, double-byte, or quad-byte aligned, respectively. Note that transient pointers (type *) are always aligned.

While the alignment for a **cpblk** instruction would logically require two numbers (one for the source and one for the destination), there is no noticeable impact on performance if only the lower number is specified.

The **unaligned** and **volatile** prefixes can be combined in either order. They must immediately precede a **ldind**, **stind**, **ldfld**, **stfld**, **ldobj**, **stobj**, **initblk**, or **cpblk** instruction. Only the **Volatile** prefix is allowed for the **Ldsfld** and **Stsfld** instructions.

The following **Emit** constructor overloads can use the **unaligned** opcode:
- ILGenerator.Emit(OpCode, Label)
- ILGenerator.Emit(Opcode, long)

Requirements

Platforms: Windows 98, Windows NT 4.0, Windows Millennium Edition, Windows 2000, Windows XP Home Edition, Windows XP Professional, Windows .NET Server family

OpCodes.Unbox Field

Converts the boxed representation of a value type to its unboxed form.

```
[Visual Basic]
Public Shared ReadOnly Unbox As OpCode
[C#]
public static readonly OpCode Unbox;
[C++]
public: static OpCode Unbox;
[JScript]
public static var Unbox : OpCode;
```

Remarks

The following table lists the instruction's hexadecimal and Microsoft Intermediate Language (MSIL) assembly format, along with a brief reference summary:

Format	Assembly Format	Description
79 < **T** >	unbox *valType*	Extracts the value type data from *obj*, its boxed representation.

The stack transitional behavior, in sequential order, is:
1. An object reference is pushed onto the stack.
2. The object reference is popped from the stack and unboxed to a value type pointer.
3. The value type pointer is pushed onto the stack.

A value type has two separate representations within the the Common Language Infrastructre (CLI):
- A 'raw' form used when a value type is embedded within another object.
- A 'boxed' form, where the data in the value type is wrapped (boxed) into an object so it can exist as an independent entity.

The **unbox** instruction converts the object reference (type **O**), the boxed representation of a value type, to a value type pointer (a managed pointer, type **&**), its unboxed form. The supplied value type (*valType*) is a metadata token indicating the type of value type contained within the boxed object.

Unlike **Box**, which is required to make a copy of a value type for use in the object, **unbox** is not required to copy the value type from the object. Typically it simply computes the address of the value type that is already present inside of the boxed object.

InvalidCastException is thrown if the object is not boxed as *valType*.

NullReferenceException is thrown if the object reference is a null reference.

TypeLoadException is thrown if the value type *valType* cannot be found. This is typically detected when Microsoft Interenediate Language (MSIL) instructions are converted to native code, rather than at runtime.

The following **Emit** constructor overload can use the **unbox** opcode:

- ILGenerator.Emit(OpCode, Type)

Requirements

Platforms: Windows 98, Windows NT 4.0, Windows Millennium Edition, Windows 2000, Windows XP Home Edition, Windows XP Professional, Windows .NET Server family

OpCodes.Volatile Field

Specifies that an address currently atop the evaluation stack might be volatile, and the results of reading that location cannot be cached or that multiple stores to that location cannot be suppressed.

```
[Visual Basic]
Public Shared ReadOnly Volatile As OpCode
[C#]
public static readonly OpCode Volatile;
[C++]
public: static OpCode Volatile;
[JScript]
public static var Volatile : OpCode;
```

Remarks

The following table lists the instruction's hexadecimal and Microsoft Intermediate Language (MSIL) assembly format, along with a brief reference summary:

Format	Assembly Format	Description
FE 13	volatile.	Indicates that the subsequent pointer reference is volatile.

The stack transitional behavior, in sequential order, is:

1. An address is pushed onto the stack.

volatile. specifies that the address is a volatile address (that is, it can be referenced externally to the current thread of execution) and the results of reading that location cannot be cached or that multiple stores to that location cannot be suppressed. Marking an access as **volatile** affects only that single access; other accesses to the same location must be marked separately. Access to volatile locations need not be performed atomically.

The **Unaligned** and **volatile** prefixes can be combined in either order. They must immediately precede a **ldind**, **stind**, **ldfld**, **stfld**, **ldobj**, **stobj**, **initblk**, or **cpblk** instruction. Only the **volatile** prefix is allowed for the **Ldsfld** and **Stsfld** instructions.

The following **Emit** constructor overload can use the **volatile** opcode:

- ILGenerator.Emit(OpCode)

Requirements

Platforms: Windows 98, Windows NT 4.0, Windows Millennium Edition, Windows 2000, Windows XP Home Edition, Windows XP Professional, Windows .NET Server family

OpCodes.Xor Field

Computes the bitwise XOR of the top two values on the evaluation stack, pushing the result onto the evaluation stack.

```
[Visual Basic]
Public Shared ReadOnly Xor As OpCode
[C#]
public static readonly OpCode Xor;
[C++]
public: static OpCode Xor;
[JScript]
public static var Xor : OpCode;
```

Remarks

The following table lists the instruction's hexadecimal and Microsoft Intermediate Language (MSIL) assembly format, along with a brief reference summary:

Format	Assembly Format	Description
61	xor	Computes the bitwise XOR of two integer values and returns an integer.

The stack transitional behavior, in sequential order, is:

1. *value1* is pushed onto the stack.
2. *value2* is pushed onto the stack.
3. *value2* and *value1* are popped from the stack and their bitwise XOR computed.
4. *value2* and *value1* are popped from the stack and their bitwise XOR computed.

The **xor** instruction computes the bitwise XOR of the top two values on the stack and leaves the result on the stack.

Xor is an integer-specific operation.

The following **Emit** constructor overload can use the **xor** opcode:

- ILGenerator.Emit(OpCode)

Requirements

Platforms: Windows 98, Windows NT 4.0, Windows Millennium Edition, Windows 2000, Windows XP Home Edition, Windows XP Professional, Windows .NET Server family

OpCodes.TakesSingleByteArgument Method

Returns true or false if the supplied opcode takes a single byte argument.

```
[Visual Basic]
Public Shared Function TakesSingleByteArgument( _
   ByVal inst As OpCode _
) As Boolean
[C#]
public static bool TakesSingleByteArgument(
   OpCode inst
);
[C++]
public: static bool TakesSingleByteArgument(
   OpCode inst
);
```

```
[JScript]
public static function TakesSingleByteArgument(
    inst : OpCode
) : Boolean;
```

Parameters

inst

An instance of an Opcode object.

Return Value

True or **false**.

Remarks

This method can be used to find which MSIL opcodes are "short form", for use in optimized code.

TakesSingleByteArgument returns **true** if the **OpCode** instance takes a single byte argument in the following cases:

- The opcode performs a branch instruction to a byte-sized address (for example, **Br_S** and **Bgt_S**).
- The opcode pushes a byte value onto the stack (for example, **Ldc_I4_S**).
- The opcode references a variable or argument via the byte-sized "short form" (for example, **Ldloc_S** and **Stloc_S**).

Otherwise, it returns **false**.

Example

See the related example in the **System.Reflection.Emit.OpCodes** class topic.

Requirements

Platforms: Windows 98, Windows NT 4.0, Windows Millennium Edition, Windows 2000, Windows XP Home Edition, Windows XP Professional, Windows .NET Server family

OpCodeType Enumeration

Describes the types of the Microsoft intermediate language (MSIL) instructions.

```
[Visual Basic]
<Serializable>
Public Enum OpCodeType
[C#]
[Serializable]
public enum OpCodeType
[C++]
[Serializable]
__value public enum OpCodeType
[JScript]
public
    Serializable
enum OpCodeType
```

Members

Member name	Description
Annotation	This member supports the .NET Framework infrastructure and is not intended to be used directly from your code.
Macro	These are Microsoft intermediate language (MSIL) instructions that are used as a synonym for other MSIL instructions. For example, **ldarg.0** represents the **ldarg** *0* instruction.
Nternal	Describes a reserved Microsoft intermediate language (MSIL) instruction.
Objmodel	Describes a Microsoft intermediate language (MSIL) instruction that applies to objects.
Prefix	Describes a prefix instruction that modifies the behavior of the following instruction.
Primitive	Describes a built-in instruction.

Requirements

Namespace: System.Reflection.Emit

Platforms: Windows 98, Windows NT 4.0, Windows Millennium Edition, Windows 2000, Windows XP Home Edition, Windows XP Professional, Windows .NET Server family

Assembly: Mscorlib (in Mscorlib.dll)

OperandType Enumeration

Describes the operand type of Microsoft intermediate language (MSIL) instruction.

```
[Visual Basic]
<Serializable>
Public Enum OperandType
[C#]
[Serializable]
public enum OperandType
[C++]
[Serializable]
__value public enum OperandType
[JScript]
public
    Serializable
enum OperandType
```

Members

Member name	Description
InlineBrTarget	The operand is a 32-bit integer branch target.
InlineField	The operand is a 32-bit metadata token.
InlineI	The operand is a 32-bit integer.
InlineI8	The operand is a 64-bit integer.
InlineMethod	The operand is a 32-bit metadata token.
InlineNone	No operand.
InlinePhi	This member supports the .NET Framework infrastructure and is not intended to be used directly from your code.
InlineR	The operand is a 64-bit IEEE floating point number.
InlineSig	The operand is a 32-bit metadata signature token.
InlineString	The operand is a 32-bit metadata string token.
InlineSwitch	The operand is the 32-bit integer argument to a switch instruction.
InlineTok	The operand is a **FieldRef**, **MethodRef**, or **TypeRef** token.
InlineType	The operand is a 32-bit metadata token.
InlineVar	The operand is 16-bit integer containing the ordinal of a local variable or an argument.
ShortInlineBrTarget	The operand is an 8-bit integer branch target.
ShortInlineI	The operand is a 16-bit integer.
ShortInlineR	The operand is a 32-bit IEEE floating point number.
ShortInlineVar	The operand is an 8-bit integer containing the ordinal of a local variable or an argumenta .

Requirements

Namespace: System.Reflection.Emit

Platforms: Windows 98, Windows NT 4.0, Windows Millennium Edition, Windows 2000, Windows XP Home Edition, Windows XP Professional, Windows .NET Server family

Assembly: Mscorlib (in Mscorlib.dll)

PackingSize Enumeration

Specifies one of two factors that determine the memory alignment of fields when a type is marshaled.

This enumeration has a **FlagsAttribute** attribute that allows a bitwise combination of its member values.

```
[Visual Basic]
<Flags>
<Serializable>
Public Enum PackingSize
[C#]
[Flags]
[Serializable]
public enum PackingSize
[C++]
[Flags]
[Serializable]
__value public enum PackingSize
[JScript]
public
   Flags
   Serializable
enum PackingSize
```

Remarks

Packing size affects the alignment of fields in structures and classes whose organization is **LayoutKind.Sequential**. The packing size is one of two factors that determine the offset of a field when the structure or class is marshaled; the other factor is the effective size of the field. To determine the offset of a field:

1. Compute the minimum value for the offset by adding the size of the preceding field to the offset of the preceding field.

2. Compute the natural packing size for the field: If the field is a simple data type, use the size. If the field is an array, use the size of an array element. If the field is itself a structure, compare the packing size of that structure to the size of the largest field in that structure, and use the smaller of the two values.

3. Compute the effective packing size by comparing the packing size to the natural packing size of the field, computed in step 2. Use the smaller of the two numbers.

4. Compute the offset. The offset is the first memory location that is equal to or larger than the minimum, and a multiple of the effective packing size computed in step 3.

   > **Note** Once offsets have been computed for all the fields in the class or structure, padding is added so that the overall size is a multiple of the packing size.

For example, in a class containing a **byte** and a **long**, using packing size **Size1**, the offset of the **byte** field is zero (0) and the offset of the **long** field is one (1). If the packing size is **Size4**, the **long** field has offset four (4). In a class containing two **short** fields, using any packing size, the offset of the second **short** field is two (2).

   > **Note** Changing the packing size can affect performance if it causes fields to be aligned on offsets that are not multiples of their size.

Members

Member name	Description	Value
Size1	The packing size is 1 byte.	1
Size16	The packing size is 16 bytes.	16
Size2	The packing size is 2 bytes.	2
Size4	The packing size is 4 bytes.	4
Size8	The packing size is 8 bytes.	8
Unspecified	The packing size is not specified.	0

Requirements

Namespace: System.Reflection.Emit

Platforms: Windows 98, Windows NT 4.0, Windows Millennium Edition, Windows 2000, Windows XP Home Edition, Windows XP Professional, Windows .NET Server family

Assembly: Mscorlib (in Mscorlib.dll)

ParameterBuilder Class

Creates or associates parameter information.

System.Object
   System.Reflection.Emit.ParameterBuilder

```
[Visual Basic]
Public Class ParameterBuilder
[C#]
public class ParameterBuilder
[C++]
public __gc class ParameterBuilder
[JScript]
public class ParameterBuilder
```

Thread Safety

Reflection Emit is thread-safe when using assemblies that were
created with the **AppDomain.DefineDynamicAssembly** method
with the Boolean parameter *isSynchronized* set to **true**.

Remarks

Parameter attributes need to consistent with the method signature. If
you specify **Out** attributes for a parameter, you should ensure that
the type of that method parameter is a **ByRef** type.Some
ParameterBuilder attributes require that you call **DefineMethod**
with viable parameters in order for the Microsoft intermediate
language (MSIL) to work correctly at runtime. For example, if you
define a **ParameterBuilder** with ParameterAttributes.Out for
parameter 1 of a **MethodBuilder**, then parameter 1 of
MethodBuilder must be a reference such as
Type.GetType("System.String&"), rather than
Type.GetType("System.String").

Example

[Visual Basic, C#, C++] The following example demonstrates how
to create a dynamic method with a parameter passed by reference
using **ParameterBuilder**.

```
[Visual Basic]
Imports System
Imports System.Threading
Imports System.Reflection
Imports System.Reflection.Emit

_

Class ParamBuilderDemo

    Public Shared Function BuildCustomerDataType() As Type

        Dim myDomain As AppDomain = Thread.GetDomain()
        Dim myAsmName As New AssemblyName()
        myAsmName.Name = "MyDynamicAssembly"

        Dim myAsmBuilder As AssemblyBuilder = _
    myDomain.DefineDynamicAssembly(myAsmName, _
                    AssemblyBuilderAccess.Run)

        Dim myModBuilder As ModuleBuilder = _
    myAsmBuilder.DefineDynamicModule("MyMod")

        Dim myTypeBuilder As TypeBuilder = _
    myModBuilder.DefineType("CustomerData", TypeAttributes.Public)

        Dim customerNameBldr As FieldBuilder = _
    myTypeBuilder.DefineField("customerName", _
                    GetType(String), _
                    FieldAttributes.Private)

        Dim acctIDBldr As FieldBuilder = _
    myTypeBuilder.DefineField("acctID", _
                    GetType(String), _
                    FieldAttributes.Private)

        Dim balanceAmtBldr As FieldBuilder = _
    myTypeBuilder.DefineField("balanceAmt", _
                    GetType(Double), _
                    FieldAttributes.Private)

        Dim myCtorBuilder As ConstructorBuilder = _
    myTypeBuilder.DefineConstructor(MethodAttributes.Public, _
                    CallingConventions.HasThis, _
                    New Type() {GetType(String), _
                    GetType(String), _
                    GetType(Double)})

        Dim ctorIL As ILGenerator = myCtorBuilder.GetILGenerator()

        Dim objType As Type = Type.GetType("System.Object")
        Dim objCtor As ConstructorInfo = _
    objType.GetConstructor(New Type(){})

        ctorIL.Emit(OpCodes.Ldarg_0)
        ctorIL.Emit(OpCodes.Call, objCtor)

        ctorIL.Emit(OpCodes.Ldarg_0)
        ctorIL.Emit(OpCodes.Ldarg_1)
        ctorIL.Emit(OpCodes.Stfld, customerNameBldr)

        ctorIL.Emit(OpCodes.Ldarg_0)
        ctorIL.Emit(OpCodes.Ldarg_2)
        ctorIL.Emit(OpCodes.Stfld, acctIDBldr)

        ctorIL.Emit(OpCodes.Ldarg_0)
        ctorIL.Emit(OpCodes.Ldarg_3)
        ctorIL.Emit(OpCodes.Stfld, balanceAmtBldr)

        ctorIL.Emit(OpCodes.Ret)

        ' This method will take an amount from a static pool
    and add it to the balance.
        ' Note that we are passing the first parameter,
    fundsPool, by reference. Therefore,
        ' we need to inform the MethodBuilder to expect a
    ref, by declaring the first
        ' parameter's type to be System.Double& (a reference
    to a double).

        Dim myMthdBuilder As MethodBuilder = _
    myTypeBuilder.DefineMethod("AddFundsFromPool", _
                    MethodAttributes.Public, _
                    GetType(Double), _
                    New Type() _
    {Type.GetType("System.Double&"), _
                    GetType(Double)})

        Dim poolRefBuilder As ParameterBuilder = _
    myMthdBuilder.DefineParameter(1, _
                    ParameterAttributes.Out, "fundsPool")

        Dim amountFromPoolBuilder As ParameterBuilder = _
    myMthdBuilder.DefineParameter(2, _
                    ParameterAttributes.In, "amountFromPool")

        Dim mthdIL As ILGenerator = myMthdBuilder.GetILGenerator()

        mthdIL.Emit(OpCodes.Ldarg_1)
        mthdIL.Emit(OpCodes.Ldarg_1)
        mthdIL.Emit(OpCodes.Ldind_R8)
        mthdIL.Emit(OpCodes.Ldarg_2)
        mthdIL.Emit(OpCodes.Sub)

        mthdIL.Emit(OpCodes.Stind_R8)
```

```
        mthdIL.Emit(OpCodes.Ldarg_0)
        mthdIL.Emit(OpCodes.Ldarg_0)
        mthdIL.Emit(OpCodes.Ldfld, balanceAmtBldr)
        mthdIL.Emit(OpCodes.Ldarg_2)
        mthdIL.Emit(OpCodes.Add)

        mthdIL.Emit(OpCodes.Stfld, balanceAmtBldr)

        mthdIL.Emit(OpCodes.Ldarg_0)
        mthdIL.Emit(OpCodes.Ldfld, balanceAmtBldr)
        mthdIL.Emit(OpCodes.Ret)

        Return myTypeBuilder.CreateType()

    End Function 'BuildCustomerDataType

    Public Shared Sub Main()

        Dim custType As Type = Nothing
        Dim custObj As Object = Nothing

        Dim custArgTypes() As Type = {GetType(String), _
    GetType(String), GetType(Double)}

        ' Call the method to build our dynamic class.
        custType = BuildCustomerDataType()

        Console.WriteLine("---")

        Dim myCustCtor As ConstructorInfo = _
    custType.GetConstructor(custArgTypes)
        Dim initialBalance As Double = 100.0
        custObj = myCustCtor.Invoke(New Object() {"Joe Consumer", _
    "5678-XYZ", initialBalance})

        Dim myMemberInfo As MemberInfo() = _
    custType.GetMember("AddFundsFromPool")

        Dim thePool As Double = 1000.0
        Console.WriteLine("The pool is currently ${0}", thePool)
        Console.WriteLine("The original balance of the account _
    instance is ${0}", initialBalance)

        Dim amountFromPool As Double = 50.0
        Console.WriteLine("The amount to be subtracted from _
    the pool and added " & _
            "to the account is ${0}", amountFromPool)

        Console.WriteLine("---")
        Console.WriteLine("Calling {0} ...", myMemberInfo(0).ToString())
        Console.WriteLine("---")

        Dim passMe() As Object = {thePool, amountFromPool}
        Console.WriteLine("The new balance in the account _
    instance is ${0}", _
            custType.InvokeMember("AddFundsFromPool", _
            BindingFlags.InvokeMethod, Nothing, custObj, passMe))
        thePool = CDbl(passMe(0))
        Console.WriteLine("The new amount in the pool is ${0}", thePool)

    End Sub 'Main

End Class 'ParamBuilderDemo

[C#]
using System;
using System.Threading;
using System.Reflection;
using System.Reflection.Emit;

class ParamBuilderDemo

{
```

```
    public static Type BuildCustomerDataType()
    {

        AppDomain myDomain = Thread.GetDomain();
        AssemblyName myAsmName = new AssemblyName();
        myAsmName.Name = "MyDynamicAssembly";

        AssemblyBuilder myAsmBuilder =
    myDomain.DefineDynamicAssembly(myAsmName,
                        AssemblyBuilderAccess.Run);

        ModuleBuilder myModBuilder =
    myAsmBuilder.DefineDynamicModule("MyMod");

        TypeBuilder myTypeBuilder = myModBuilder.DefineType("CustomerData",
                    TypeAttributes.Public);

        FieldBuilder customerNameBldr =
    myTypeBuilder.DefineField("customerName",
                        typeof(string),
                        FieldAttributes.Private);
        FieldBuilder acctIDBldr = myTypeBuilder.DefineField("acctID",
                         typeof(string),
                         FieldAttributes.Private);
        FieldBuilder balanceAmtBldr =
    myTypeBuilder.DefineField("balanceAmt",
                        typeof(double),
                        FieldAttributes.Private);

        ConstructorBuilder myCtorBuilder = myTypeBuilder.DefineConstructor(
                    MethodAttributes.Public,
                    CallingConventions.HasThis,
                    new Type[] { typeof(string),
                            typeof(string),
                            typeof(double) });

        ILGenerator ctorIL = myCtorBuilder.GetILGenerator();

        Type objType = Type.GetType("System.Object");
        ConstructorInfo objCtor = objType.GetConstructor
    (new Type[] {});

        ctorIL.Emit(OpCodes.Ldarg_0);
        ctorIL.Emit(OpCodes.Call, objCtor);

        ctorIL.Emit(OpCodes.Ldarg_0);
        ctorIL.Emit(OpCodes.Ldarg_1);
        ctorIL.Emit(OpCodes.Stfld, customerNameBldr);

        ctorIL.Emit(OpCodes.Ldarg_0);
        ctorIL.Emit(OpCodes.Ldarg_2);
        ctorIL.Emit(OpCodes.Stfld, acctIDBldr);

        ctorIL.Emit(OpCodes.Ldarg_0);
        ctorIL.Emit(OpCodes.Ldarg_3);
        ctorIL.Emit(OpCodes.Stfld, balanceAmtBldr);

        ctorIL.Emit(OpCodes.Ret);

        // This method will take an amount from a static pool and
    add it to the balance.

        // Note that we are passing the first parameter, fundsPool,
    by reference. Therefore,
        // we need to inform the MethodBuilder to expect a ref, by
    declaring the first
        // parameter's type to be System.Double& (a reference to a double).

        MethodBuilder myMthdBuilder =
    myTypeBuilder.DefineMethod("AddFundsFromPool",
                    MethodAttributes.Public,
                    typeof(double),
                    new Type[] { Type.GetType("System.Double&"),
                            typeof(double) });
```

```csharp
    ParameterBuilder poolRefBuilder = myMthdBuilder.DefineParameter(1,
                    ParameterAttributes.Out,
                    "fundsPool");

    ParameterBuilder amountFromPoolBuilder =
myMthdBuilder.DefineParameter(2,
                    ParameterAttributes.In,
                    "amountFromPool");


    ILGenerator mthdIL = myMthdBuilder.GetILGenerator();

    mthdIL.Emit(OpCodes.Ldarg_1);
    mthdIL.Emit(OpCodes.Ldarg_1);
    mthdIL.Emit(OpCodes.Ldind_R8);
    mthdIL.Emit(OpCodes.Ldarg_2);
    mthdIL.Emit(OpCodes.Sub);

    mthdIL.Emit(OpCodes.Stind_R8);

    mthdIL.Emit(OpCodes.Ldarg_0);
    mthdIL.Emit(OpCodes.Ldarg_0);
    mthdIL.Emit(OpCodes.Ldfld, balanceAmtBldr);
    mthdIL.Emit(OpCodes.Ldarg_2);
    mthdIL.Emit(OpCodes.Add);

    mthdIL.Emit(OpCodes.Stfld, balanceAmtBldr);

    mthdIL.Emit(OpCodes.Ldarg_0);
    mthdIL.Emit(OpCodes.Ldfld, balanceAmtBldr);
    mthdIL.Emit(OpCodes.Ret);

    return myTypeBuilder.CreateType();

  }

  public static void Main()
  {
    Type custType = null;
    object custObj = null;

    Type[] custArgTypes = new Type[] {typeof(string),
typeof(string), typeof(double)};

    // Call the method to build our dynamic class.

    custType = BuildCustomerDataType();

    Console.WriteLine("---");

    ConstructorInfo myCustCtor = custType.GetConstructor(custArgTypes);
    double initialBalance = 100.00;
    custObj = myCustCtor.Invoke(new object[] { "Joe Consumer",
                    "5678-XYZ",
                    initialBalance });

    MemberInfo[] myMemberInfo = custType.GetMember("AddFundsFromPool");

    double thePool = 1000.00;
    Console.WriteLine("The pool is currently ${0}", thePool);
    Console.WriteLine("The original balance of the account
instance is ${0}",
                    initialBalance);

    double amountFromPool = 50.00;
    Console.WriteLine("The amount to be subtracted from the pool
and added " +
                "to the account is ${0}", amountFromPool);

    Console.WriteLine("---");
    Console.WriteLine("Calling {0} ...", myMemberInfo[0].ToString());
    Console.WriteLine("---");

    object[] passMe = new object[] { thePool, amountFromPool };
    Console.WriteLine("The new balance in the account instance
is ${0}",
```

```csharp
        custType.InvokeMember("AddFundsFromPool",
            BindingFlags.InvokeMethod,
            null, custObj, passMe));
    thePool = (double)passMe[0];
    Console.WriteLine("The new amount in the pool is ${0}", thePool);

  }

}
```

[C++]
```cpp
#using <mscorlib.dll>

using namespace System;
using namespace System::Threading;
using namespace System::Reflection;
using namespace System::Reflection::Emit;

Type* BuildCustomerDataType() {
    AppDomain*  myDomain = Thread::GetDomain();
    AssemblyName* myAsmName = new AssemblyName();
    myAsmName->Name = S"MyDynamicAssembly";

    AssemblyBuilder*  myAsmBuilder = myDomain->DefineDynamicAssembly(
        myAsmName,
        AssemblyBuilderAccess::Run);

    ModuleBuilder*  myModBuilder = myAsmBuilder-
>DefineDynamicModule(S"MyMod");

    TypeBuilder*  myTypeBuilder = myModBuilder->DefineType(
        S"CustomerData",
        TypeAttributes::Public);

    FieldBuilder*  customerNameBldr = myTypeBuilder->DefineField(
        S"customerName",
        __typeof(String),
        FieldAttributes::Private);
    FieldBuilder*  acctIDBldr = myTypeBuilder->DefineField(
        S"acctID",
        __typeof(String),
        FieldAttributes::Private);
    FieldBuilder*  balanceAmtBldr = myTypeBuilder->DefineField(
        S"balanceAmt",
        __typeof(double),
        FieldAttributes::Private);

    Type* temp0 [] = {__typeof(String), __typeof(String),
__typeof(double)};
    ConstructorBuilder*  myCtorBuilder = myTypeBuilder-
>DefineConstructor(
        MethodAttributes::Public,
        CallingConventions::HasThis,
        temp0);

    ILGenerator*  ctorIL = myCtorBuilder->GetILGenerator();

    Type*  objType = Type::GetType(S"System.Object");
    ConstructorInfo*  objCtor = objType->GetConstructor(new Type*[0]);

    ctorIL->Emit(OpCodes::Ldarg_0);
    ctorIL->Emit(OpCodes::Call, objCtor);

    ctorIL->Emit(OpCodes::Ldarg_0);
    ctorIL->Emit(OpCodes::Ldarg_1);
    ctorIL->Emit(OpCodes::Stfld, customerNameBldr);

    ctorIL->Emit(OpCodes::Ldarg_0);
    ctorIL->Emit(OpCodes::Ldarg_2);
    ctorIL->Emit(OpCodes::Stfld, acctIDBldr);

    ctorIL->Emit(OpCodes::Ldarg_0);
    ctorIL->Emit(OpCodes::Ldarg_3);
    ctorIL->Emit(OpCodes::Stfld, balanceAmtBldr);
```

```
    ctorIL->Emit(OpCodes::Ret);

    // This method will take an amount from a static pool and
    add it to the balance.

    // Note that we are passing the first parameter, fundsPool,
    by reference. Therefore,
    // we need to inform the MethodBuilder to expect a ref, by
    declaring the first
    // parameter's type to be System::Double& (a reference to a double).

    Type* temp4 [] = {Type::GetType(S"System.Double&"),
    __typeof(double)};
    MethodBuilder* myMthdBuilder = myTypeBuilder->DefineMethod(
        S"AddFundsFromPool",
        MethodAttributes::Public,
        __typeof(double),
        temp4);

    ParameterBuilder* poolRefBuilder = myMthdBuilder->DefineParameter(
        1,
        ParameterAttributes::Out,
        S"fundsPool");

    ParameterBuilder* amountFromPoolBuilder = myMthdBuilder-
    >DefineParameter(
        2,
        ParameterAttributes::In,
        S"amountFromPool");

    ILGenerator* mthdIL = myMthdBuilder->GetILGenerator();

    mthdIL->Emit(OpCodes::Ldarg_1);
    mthdIL->Emit(OpCodes::Ldarg_1);
    mthdIL->Emit(OpCodes::Ldind_R8);
    mthdIL->Emit(OpCodes::Ldarg_2);
    mthdIL->Emit(OpCodes::Sub);

    mthdIL->Emit(OpCodes::Stind_R8);

    mthdIL->Emit(OpCodes::Ldarg_0);
    mthdIL->Emit(OpCodes::Ldarg_0);
    mthdIL->Emit(OpCodes::Ldfld, balanceAmtBldr);
    mthdIL->Emit(OpCodes::Ldarg_2);
    mthdIL->Emit(OpCodes->Add);

    mthdIL->Emit(OpCodes::Stfld, balanceAmtBldr);

    mthdIL->Emit(OpCodes::Ldarg_0);
    mthdIL->Emit(OpCodes::Ldfld, balanceAmtBldr);
    mthdIL->Emit(OpCodes::Ret);

    return myTypeBuilder->CreateType();
}
int main() {
    Type* custType = 0;
    Object* custObj = 0;

    Type* custArgTypes[] = {__typeof(String), __typeof(String),
    __typeof(double)};

    // Call the method to build our dynamic class.

    custType = BuildCustomerDataType();

    Console::WriteLine(S"---");

    ConstructorInfo* myCustCtor = custType-
    >GetConstructor(custArgTypes);
    double initialBalance = 100.00;

    Object* temp5 [] = {S"Joe Consumer", S"5678-XYZ",
    __box(initialBalance)};
```

```
    custObj = myCustCtor->Invoke(temp5);

    MemberInfo* myMemberInfo[] = custType-
    >GetMember(S"AddFundsFromPool");

    double thePool = 1000.00;
    Console::WriteLine(S"The pool is currently ${0}", __box(thePool));
    Console::WriteLine(S"The original balance of the account
    instance is ${0}", __box(initialBalance));

    double amountFromPool = 50.00;
    Console::WriteLine(S"The amount to be subtracted from the pool
    and added to the account is ${0}", __box(amountFromPool));

    Console::WriteLine(S"---");
    Console::WriteLine(S"Calling {0} ...", myMemberInfo[0]);
    Console::WriteLine(S"---");

    Object* passMe[] = { __box(thePool), __box(amountFromPool) };
    Console::WriteLine(S"The new balance in the account
    instance is ${0}",
        custType->InvokeMember(S"AddFundsFromPool",
        BindingFlags::InvokeMethod,
        0, custObj, passMe));
    thePool = *dynamic_cast<double __gc *>(passMe[0]);
    Console::WriteLine(S"The new amount in the pool is ${0}",
    __box(thePool));
}
```

Requirements

Namespace: System.Reflection.Emit

Platforms: Windows 98, Windows NT 4.0,
Windows Millennium Edition, Windows 2000,
Windows XP Home Edition, Windows XP Professional,
Windows .NET Server family

Assembly: Mscorlib (in Mscorlib.dll)

ParameterBuilder.Attributes Property

Retrieves the attributes for this parameter.

```
[Visual Basic]
Public Overridable ReadOnly Property Attributes As Integer
[C#]
public virtual int Attributes {get;}
[C++]
public: __property virtual int get_Attributes();
[JScript]
public function get Attributes() : int;
```

Property Value

Read-only. Retrieves the attributes for this parameter.

Remarks

The values of the attribute correspond to the values of the
ParameterAttributes enumeration.

Requirements

Platforms: Windows 98, Windows NT 4.0,
Windows Millennium Edition, Windows 2000,
Windows XP Home Edition, Windows XP Professional,
Windows .NET Server family

ParameterBuilder.IsIn Property

Retrieves whether this is an input parameter.

```
[Visual Basic]
Public ReadOnly Property IsIn As Boolean
[C#]
public bool IsIn {get;}
[C++]
public: __property bool get_IsIn();
[JScript]
public function get IsIn() : Boolean;
```

Property Value

Read-only. Retrieves whether this is an input parameter.

Remarks

This method depends on an optional metadata flag. This flag can be inserted by compilers, but the compilers are not obligated to do so.

Requirements

Platforms: Windows 98, Windows NT 4.0, Windows Millennium Edition, Windows 2000, Windows XP Home Edition, Windows XP Professional, Windows .NET Server family

ParameterBuilder.IsOptional Property

Retrieves whether this parameter is optional.

```
[Visual Basic]
Public ReadOnly Property IsOptional As Boolean
[C#]
public bool IsOptional {get;}
[C++]
public: __property bool get_IsOptional();
[JScript]
public function get IsOptional() : Boolean;
```

Property Value

Read-only. Specifies whether this parameter is optional.

Requirements

Platforms: Windows 98, Windows NT 4.0, Windows Millennium Edition, Windows 2000, Windows XP Home Edition, Windows XP Professional, Windows .NET Server family

ParameterBuilder.IsOut Property

Retrieves whether this parameter is an output parameter.

```
[Visual Basic]
Public ReadOnly Property IsOut As Boolean
[C#]
public bool IsOut {get;}
[C++]
public: __property bool get_IsOut();
[JScript]
public function get IsOut() : Boolean;
```

Property Value

Read-only. Retrieves whether this parameter is an output parameter.

Requirements

Platforms: Windows 98, Windows NT 4.0, Windows Millennium Edition, Windows 2000, Windows XP Home Edition, Windows XP Professional, Windows .NET Server family

ParameterBuilder.Name Property

Retrieves the name of this parameter.

```
[Visual Basic]
Public Overridable ReadOnly Property Name As String
[C#]
public virtual string Name {get;}
[C++]
public: __property virtual String* get_Name();
[JScript]
public function get Name() : String;
```

Property Value

Read-only. Retrieves the name of this parameter.

Requirements

Platforms: Windows 98, Windows NT 4.0, Windows Millennium Edition, Windows 2000, Windows XP Home Edition, Windows XP Professional, Windows .NET Server family

ParameterBuilder.Position Property

Retrieves the signature position for this parameter.

```
[Visual Basic]
Public Overridable ReadOnly Property Position As Integer
[C#]
public virtual int Position {get;}
[C++]
public: __property virtual int get_Position();
[JScript]
public function get Position() : int;
```

Property Value

Read-only. Retrieves the signature position for this parameter.

Requirements

Platforms: Windows 98, Windows NT 4.0, Windows Millennium Edition, Windows 2000, Windows XP Home Edition, Windows XP Professional, Windows .NET Server family

ParameterBuilder.GetToken Method

Retrieves the token for this parameter.

```
[Visual Basic]
Public Overridable Function GetToken() As ParameterToken
[C#]
public virtual ParameterToken GetToken();
[C++]
public: virtual ParameterToken GetToken();
[JScript]
public function GetToken() : ParameterToken;
```

Return Value

Returns the token for this parameter.

Requirements

Platforms: Windows 98, Windows NT 4.0,
Windows Millennium Edition, Windows 2000,
Windows XP Home Edition, Windows XP Professional,
Windows .NET Server family

ParameterBuilder.SetConstant Method

Sets the default value of the parameter.

```
[Visual Basic]
Public Overridable Sub SetConstant( _
    ByVal defaultValue As Object _
)
[C#]
public virtual void SetConstant(
    object defaultValue
);
[C++]
public: virtual void SetConstant(
    Object* defaultValue
);
[JScript]
public function SetConstant(
    defaultValue : Object
);
```

Parameters

defaultValue
    The default value of this parameter.

Exceptions

Exception Type	Condition
ArgumentException	The type of *defaultValue* is not one of the types mentioned in the remarks section.

Remarks

defaultValue is restricted to the following types: **Boolean, SByte, Int16, Int32, Int64, Byte, UInt16, UInt32, UInt64, Single, Double, DateTime, Char, String,** and **Enum.** If the type of the parameter is **Decimal** or **Object,** *defaultValue* can only be null.

Requirements

Platforms: Windows 98, Windows NT 4.0,
Windows Millennium Edition, Windows 2000,
Windows XP Home Edition, Windows XP Professional,
Windows .NET Server family

ParameterBuilder.SetCustomAttribute Method

Sets a custom attribute.

Overload List

Set a custom attribute using a custom attribute builder.

[Visual Basic] **Overloads Public Sub SetCustomAttribute (CustomAttributeBuilder)**

[C#] **public void SetCustomAttribute (CustomAttributeBuilder);**

[C++] **public: void SetCustomAttribute (CustomAttributeBuilder*);**

[JScript] **public function SetCustomAttribute (CustomAttributeBuilder);**

Set a custom attribute using a specified custom attribute blob.

[Visual Basic] **Overloads Public Sub SetCustomAttribute(ConstructorInfo, Byte())**

[C#] **public void SetCustomAttribute(ConstructorInfo, byte[]);**

[C++] **public: void SetCustomAttribute(ConstructorInfo*, unsigned char __gc[]);**

[JScript] **public function SetCustomAttribute (ConstructorInfo, Byte[]);**

ParameterBuilder.SetCustomAttribute Method (CustomAttributeBuilder)

Set a custom attribute using a custom attribute builder.

```
[Visual Basic]
Overloads Public Sub SetCustomAttribute( _
    ByVal customBuilder As CustomAttributeBuilder _
)
[C#]
public void SetCustomAttribute(
    CustomAttributeBuilder customBuilder
);
[C++]
public: void SetCustomAttribute(
    CustomAttributeBuilder* customBuilder
);
[JScript]
public function SetCustomAttribute(
    customBuilder : CustomAttributeBuilder
);
```

Parameters

customBuilder
    An instance of a helper class to define the custom attribute.

Exceptions

Exception Type	Condition
ArgumentNullException	*con* is a null reference (**Nothing** in Visual Basic).

Requirements

Platforms: Windows 98, Windows NT 4.0,
Windows Millennium Edition, Windows 2000,
Windows XP Home Edition, Windows XP Professional,
Windows .NET Server family

ParameterBuilder.SetCustomAttribute Method (ConstructorInfo, Byte[])

Set a custom attribute using a specified custom attribute blob.

```
[Visual Basic]
Overloads Public Sub SetCustomAttribute( _
    ByVal con As ConstructorInfo, _
    ByVal binaryAttribute() As Byte _
)
```

```
[C#]
public void SetCustomAttribute(
    ConstructorInfo con,
    byte[] binaryAttribute
);
[C++]
public: void SetCustomAttribute(
    ConstructorInfo* con,
    unsigned char binaryAttribute __gc[]
);
[JScript]
public function SetCustomAttribute(
    con : ConstructorInfo,
    binaryAttribute : Byte[]
);
```

Parameters

con
> The constructor for the custom attribute.

binaryAttribute
> A byte blob representing the attributes.

Exceptions

Exception Type	Condition
ArgumentNullException	*con* or *binaryAttribute* is a null reference (**Nothing** in Visual Basic).

Remarks

See the metadata specification in the ECMA Partition II documentation for details on how to format *binaryAttribute*. The Partition II documentation is included with the .NET Framework SDK installation, and can be found in the %\Microsoft.NET\FrameworkSDK\Tool Developers Guide\docs directory.

Requirements

Platforms: Windows 98, Windows NT 4.0, Windows Millennium Edition, Windows 2000, Windows XP Home Edition, Windows XP Professional, Windows .NET Server family

ParameterBuilder.SetMarshal Method

Specifies the marshaling for this parameter.

```
[Visual Basic]
Public Overridable Sub SetMarshal( _
    ByVal unmanagedMarshal As UnmanagedMarshal _
)
[C#]
public virtual void SetMarshal(
    UnmanagedMarshal unmanagedMarshal
);
[C++]
public: virtual void SetMarshal(
    UnmanagedMarshal* unmanagedMarshal
);
[JScript]
public function SetMarshal(
    unmanagedMarshal : UnmanagedMarshal
);
```

Parameters

unmanagedMarshal
> The marshaling information for this parameter.

Exceptions

Exception Type	Condition
ArgumentNullException	*unmanagedMarshal* is a null reference (**Nothing** in Visual Basic).

Remarks

This method should throw the following exception but currently does not:

InvalidOperationException if the containing type has been created using TypeBuilder.CreateType().

Requirements

Platforms: Windows 98, Windows NT 4.0, Windows Millennium Edition, Windows 2000, Windows XP Home Edition, Windows XP Professional, Windows .NET Server family

ParameterToken Structure

The **ParameterToken** struct is an opaque representation of the token returned by the metadata to represent a parameter.

System.Object
 System.ValueType
  System.Reflection.Emit.ParameterToken

```
[Visual Basic]
<Serializable>
Public Structure ParameterToken
[C#]
[Serializable]
public struct ParameterToken
[C++]
[Serializable]
public __value struct ParameterToken
```

[JScript] In JScript, you can use the structures in the .NET Framework, but you cannot define your own.

Thread Safety

Reflection Emit is thread-safe when using assemblies that were created with the **AppDomain.DefineDynamicAssembly** method with the Boolean parameter *isSynchronized* set to **true**.

Requirements

Namespace: System.Reflection.Emit

Platforms: Windows 98, Windows NT 4.0, Windows Millennium Edition, Windows 2000, Windows XP Home Edition, Windows XP Professional, Windows .NET Server family

Assembly: Mscorlib (in Mscorlib.dll)

ParameterToken.Empty Field

The default **ParameterToken** with **Token** value 0.

```
[Visual Basic]
Public Shared ReadOnly Empty As ParameterToken
[C#]
public static readonly ParameterToken Empty;
[C++]
public: static ParameterToken Empty;
[JScript]
public static var Empty : ParameterToken;
```

Requirements

Platforms: Windows 98, Windows NT 4.0, Windows Millennium Edition, Windows 2000, Windows XP Home Edition, Windows XP Professional, Windows .NET Server family

ParameterToken.Token Property

Retrieves the metadata token for this parameter.

```
[Visual Basic]
Public ReadOnly Property Token As Integer
[C#]
public int Token {get;}
```

```
[C++]
public: __property int get_Token();
[JScript]
public function get Token() : int;
```

Property Value

Read-only. Retrieves the metadata token for this parameter.

Requirements

Platforms: Windows 98, Windows NT 4.0, Windows Millennium Edition, Windows 2000, Windows XP Home Edition, Windows XP Professional, Windows .NET Server family

ParameterToken.Equals Method

Checks if the given object is an instance of **ParameterToken** and is equal to this instance.

```
[Visual Basic]
Overrides Public Function Equals( _
   ByVal obj As Object _
) As Boolean
[C#]
public override bool Equals(
   object obj
);
[C++]
public: bool Equals(
   Object* obj
);
[JScript]
public override function Equals(
   obj : Object
) : Boolean;
```

Parameters

obj
   The object to compare to this object.

Return Value

true if *obj* is an instance of **ParameterToken** and equals the current instance; otherwise, **false**.

Requirements

Platforms: Windows 98, Windows NT 4.0, Windows Millennium Edition, Windows 2000, Windows XP Home Edition, Windows XP Professional, Windows .NET Server family

ParameterToken.GetHashCode Method

Generates the hash code for this parameter.

```
[Visual Basic]
Overrides Public Function GetHashCode() As Integer
[C#]
public override int GetHashCode();
[C++]
public: int GetHashCode();
[JScript]
public override function GetHashCode() : int;
```

Return Value

Returns the hash code for this parameter.

Requirements

Platforms: Windows 98, Windows NT 4.0, Windows Millennium Edition, Windows 2000, Windows XP Home Edition, Windows XP Professional, Windows .NET Server family

PEFileKinds Enumeration

Specifies the type of the portable executable (PE) file.

```
[Visual Basic]
<Serializable>
Public Enum PEFileKinds
[C#]
[Serializable]
public enum PEFileKinds
[C++]
[Serializable]
__value public enum PEFileKinds
[JScript]
public
   Serializable
enum PEFileKinds
```

Members

Member name	Description
ConsoleApplication	The application is a console (not a Windows-based) application.
Dll	The portable executable (PE) file is a DLL.
WindowApplication	The application is a Windows-based application.

Requirements

Namespace: System.Reflection.Emit

Platforms: Windows 98, Windows NT 4.0, Windows Millennium Edition, Windows 2000, Windows XP Home Edition, Windows XP Professional, Windows .NET Server family

Assembly: Mscorlib (in Mscorlib.dll)

PropertyBuilder Class

Defines the properties for a type.

System.Object
  System.Reflection.MemberInfo
    System.Reflection.PropertyInfo
      System.Reflection.Emit.PropertyBuilder

```
[Visual Basic]
NotInheritable Public Class PropertyBuilder
   Inherits PropertyInfo
[C#]
public sealed class PropertyBuilder : PropertyInfo
[C++]
public __gc __sealed class PropertyBuilder : public PropertyInfo
[JScript]
public class PropertyBuilder extends PropertyInfo
```

Thread Safety

Reflection Emit is thread-safe when using assemblies that were created with the **AppDomain.DefineDynamicAssembly** method with the Boolean parameter *isSynchronized* set to **true**.

Remarks

A **PropertyBuilder** is always associated with a **TypeBuilder**. The **TypeBuilder**. **DefineProperty** method will return a new **PropertyBuilder** to a client.

Example

[Visual Basic, C#, C++] The following code sample demonstrates how to implement properties in a dynamic type using a **PropertyBuilder** obtained via **TypeBuilder.DefineProperty** to create the property framework and an associated **MethodBuilder** to implement the IL logic within the property.

```
[Visual Basic]
Imports System
Imports System.Threading
Imports System.Reflection
Imports System.Reflection.Emit


Class PropertyBuilderDemo

   Public Shared Function BuildDynamicTypeWithProperties() As Type
      Dim myDomain As AppDomain = Thread.GetDomain()
      Dim myAsmName As New AssemblyName()
      myAsmName.Name = "MyDynamicAssembly"

      Dim myAsmBuilder As AssemblyBuilder = _
   myDomain.DefineDynamicAssembly(myAsmName, _
                        AssemblyBuilderAccess.Run)

      Dim myModBuilder As ModuleBuilder = _
   myAsmBuilder.DefineDynamicModule("MyModule")

      Dim myTypeBuilder As TypeBuilder = _
   myModBuilder.DefineType("CustomerData", TypeAttributes.Public)

      Dim customerNameBldr As FieldBuilder = _
   myTypeBuilder.DefineField("customerName", _
                     GetType(String), FieldAttributes.Private)

      Dim custNamePropBldr As PropertyBuilder = _
   myTypeBuilder.DefineProperty("CustomerName", _
                     PropertyAttributes.HasDefault, _
                     GetType(String), New Type() {GetType(String)})
```

```
      ' First, we'll define the behavior of the "get" property for
   CustomerName as a method.
      Dim custNameGetPropMthdBldr As MethodBuilder = _
   myTypeBuilder.DefineMethod("GetCustomerName", _
                        MethodAttributes.Public, _
   GetType(String), _
                     New Type() {})

      Dim custNameGetIL As ILGenerator = _
   custNameGetPropMthdBldr.GetILGenerator()

      custNameGetIL.Emit(OpCodes.Ldarg_0)
      custNameGetIL.Emit(OpCodes.Ldfld, customerNameBldr)
      custNameGetIL.Emit(OpCodes.Ret)

      ' Now, we'll define the behavior of the "set" property
   for CustomerName.
      Dim custNameSetPropMthdBldr As MethodBuilder = _
   myTypeBuilder.DefineMethod("SetCustomerName", _
                        MethodAttributes.Public, Nothing, _
                     New Type() {GetType(String)})

      Dim custNameSetIL As ILGenerator = _
   custNameSetPropMthdBldr.GetILGenerator()

      custNameSetIL.Emit(OpCodes.Ldarg_0)
      custNameSetIL.Emit(OpCodes.Ldarg_1)
      custNameSetIL.Emit(OpCodes.Stfld, customerNameBldr)
      custNameSetIL.Emit(OpCodes.Ret)

      ' Last, we must map the two methods created above to our
   PropertyBuilder to
      ' their corresponding behaviors, "get" and "set" respectively.
      custNamePropBldr.SetGetMethod(custNameGetPropMthdBldr)
      custNamePropBldr.SetSetMethod(custNameSetPropMthdBldr)

      Return myTypeBuilder.CreateType()
   End Function 'BuildDynamicTypeWithProperties

   Public Shared Sub Main()
      Dim custDataType As Type = BuildDynamicTypeWithProperties()

      Dim custDataPropInfo As PropertyInfo() = _
   custDataType.GetProperties()
      Dim pInfo As PropertyInfo
      For Each pInfo In  custDataPropInfo
         Console.WriteLine("Property '{0}' created!", pInfo.ToString())
      Next pInfo

      Console.WriteLine("---")
      ' Note that when invoking a property, you need to use
   the proper BindingFlags -
         ' BindingFlags.SetProperty when you invoke the "set"
   behavior, and
         ' BindingFlags.GetProperty when you invoke the "get"
   behavior. Also note that
         ' we invoke them based on the name we gave the property,
   as expected, and not
         ' the name of the methods we bound to the specific
   property behaviors.
      Dim custData As Object = Activator.CreateInstance(custDataType)
      custDataType.InvokeMember("CustomerName", _
   BindingFlags.SetProperty, Nothing, _
                     custData, New Object() {"Joe User"})

      Console.WriteLine("The customerName field of instance
   custData has been set to '{0}'.", _
                  custDataType.InvokeMember("CustomerName", _
   BindingFlags.GetProperty, _
                     Nothing, custData, New Object() {}))
   End Sub 'Main
End Class 'PropertyBuilderDemo

' --- O U T P U T ---
' The output should be as follows:
```

```
' --------------------
' Property 'System.String CustomerName [System.String]' created!
' ---
' The customerName field of instance custData has been set to
'Joe User'.
' --------------------
```

```
[C#]
using System;
using System.Threading;
using System.Reflection;
using System.Reflection.Emit;

class PropertyBuilderDemo

{

    public static Type BuildDynamicTypeWithProperties()
    {
        AppDomain myDomain = Thread.GetDomain();
        AssemblyName myAsmName = new AssemblyName();
        myAsmName.Name = "MyDynamicAssembly";

        AssemblyBuilder myAsmBuilder =
myDomain.DefineDynamicAssembly(myAsmName,
                            AssemblyBuilderAccess.Run);

        ModuleBuilder myModBuilder =
myAsmBuilder.DefineDynamicModule("MyModule");

        TypeBuilder myTypeBuilder = myModBuilder.DefineType("CustomerData",
                            TypeAttributes.Public);

        FieldBuilder customerNameBldr =
myTypeBuilder.DefineField("customerName",
                            typeof(string),
                            FieldAttributes.Private);

        PropertyBuilder custNamePropBldr =
myTypeBuilder.DefineProperty("CustomerName",
                            PropertyAttributes.HasDefault,
                            typeof(string),
                            new Type[] { typeof(string) });

        // First, we'll define the behavior of the "get"
property for CustomerName as a method.
        MethodBuilder custNameGetPropMthdBldr =
myTypeBuilder.DefineMethod("GetCustomerName",
                            MethodAttributes.Public,
                            typeof(string),
                            new Type[] { });

        ILGenerator custNameGetIL =
custNameGetPropMthdBldr.GetILGenerator();

        custNameGetIL.Emit(OpCodes.Ldarg_0);
        custNameGetIL.Emit(OpCodes.Ldfld, customerNameBldr);
        custNameGetIL.Emit(OpCodes.Ret);

        // Now, we'll define the behavior of the "set" property
for CustomerName.
        MethodBuilder custNameSetPropMthdBldr =
myTypeBuilder.DefineMethod("SetCustomerName",
                            MethodAttributes.Public,
                            null,
                            new Type[] { typeof(string) });

        ILGenerator custNameSetIL =
custNameSetPropMthdBldr.GetILGenerator();

        custNameSetIL.Emit(OpCodes.Ldarg_0);
        custNameSetIL.Emit(OpCodes.Ldarg_1);
        custNameSetIL.Emit(OpCodes.Stfld, customerNameBldr);
        custNameSetIL.Emit(OpCodes.Ret);
```

```
        // Last, we must map the two methods created above
to our PropertyBuilder to
        // their corresponding behaviors, "get" and "set" respectively.
        custNamePropBldr.SetGetMethod(custNameGetPropMthdBldr);
        custNamePropBldr.SetSetMethod(custNameSetPropMthdBldr);

        return myTypeBuilder.CreateType();

    }

    public static void Main()
    {
        Type custDataType = BuildDynamicTypeWithProperties();

        PropertyInfo[] custDataPropInfo = custDataType.GetProperties();
        foreach (PropertyInfo pInfo in custDataPropInfo) {
            Console.WriteLine("Property '{0}' created!", pInfo.ToString());
        }

        Console.WriteLine("---");
        // Note that when invoking a property, you need to use
the proper BindingFlags -
        // BindingFlags.SetProperty when you invoke the "set" behavior, and
        // BindingFlags.GetProperty when you invoke the "get"
behavior. Also note that
        // we invoke them based on the name we gave the property,
as expected, and not
        // the name of the methods we bound to the specific
property behaviors.

        object custData = Activator.CreateInstance(custDataType);
        custDataType.InvokeMember("CustomerName", BindingFlags.SetProperty,
                null, custData, new object[]{ "Joe User" });

        Console.WriteLine("The customerName field of instance
custData has been set to '{0}'.",
                custDataType.InvokeMember("CustomerName",
BindingFlags.GetProperty,
                        null, custData, new object[]{ }));
    }

}

// --- O U T P U T ---
// The output should be as follows:
// --------------------
// Property 'System.String CustomerName [System.String]' created!
// ---
// The customerName field of instance custData has been set to
'Joe User'.
// --------------------

[C++]
#using <mscorlib.dll>

using namespace System;
using namespace System::Threading;
using namespace System::Reflection;
using namespace System::Reflection::Emit;

Type* BuildDynamicTypeWithProperties() {
    AppDomain* myDomain = Thread::GetDomain();
    AssemblyName* myAsmName = new AssemblyName();
    myAsmName->Name = S"MyDynamicAssembly";

    AssemblyBuilder* myAsmBuilder = myDomain->DefineDynamicAssembly(
        myAsmName,
        AssemblyBuilderAccess::Run);

    ModuleBuilder* myModBuilder = myAsmBuilder-
>DefineDynamicModule(S"MyModule");

    TypeBuilder* myTypeBuilder = myModBuilder->DefineType(
        S"CustomerData",
        TypeAttributes::Public);
```

```
FieldBuilder*  customerNameBldr = myTypeBuilder->DefineField(
    S"customerName",
    __typeof(String),
    FieldAttributes::Private);

Type* temp0 [] = {__typeof(String)};
PropertyBuilder* custNamePropBldr = myTypeBuilder->DefineProperty(
    S"CustomerName",
    PropertyAttributes::HasDefault,
    __typeof(String),
    temp0);

// First, we'll define the behavior of the "get" property
for CustomerName as a method.
MethodBuilder*  custNameGetPropMthdBldr = myTypeBuilder-
>DefineMethod(
    S"GetCustomerName",
    MethodAttributes::Public,
    __typeof(String),
    new Type*[0]);

ILGenerator*  custNameGetIL = custNameGetPropMthdBldr-
>GetILGenerator();

custNameGetIL->Emit(OpCodes::Ldarg_0);
custNameGetIL->Emit(OpCodes::Ldfld, customerNameBldr);
custNameGetIL->Emit(OpCodes::Ret);

// Now, we'll define the behavior of the "set" property for
CustomerName.

Type* temp2 [] = {__typeof(String)};
MethodBuilder*  custNameSetPropMthdBldr = myTypeBuilder-
>DefineMethod(
    S"SetCustomerName",
    MethodAttributes::Public,
    0,
    temp2);

ILGenerator*  custNameSetIL = custNameSetPropMthdBldr-
>GetILGenerator();

custNameSetIL->Emit(OpCodes::Ldarg_0);
custNameSetIL->Emit(OpCodes::Ldarg_1);
custNameSetIL->Emit(OpCodes::Stfld, customerNameBldr);
custNameSetIL->Emit(OpCodes::Ret);

// Last, we must map the two methods created above to our
PropertyBuilder to
// their corresponding behaviors, "get" and "set" respectively.
custNamePropBldr->SetGetMethod(custNameGetPropMthdBldr);
custNamePropBldr->SetSetMethod(custNameSetPropMthdBldr);

return myTypeBuilder->CreateType();
}

int main() {
    Type*  custDataType = BuildDynamicTypeWithProperties();

    PropertyInfo* custDataPropInfo[] = custDataType->GetProperties();
    System::Collections::IEnumerator* myEnum = custDataPropInfo-
>GetEnumerator();
    while (myEnum->MoveNext()) {
        PropertyInfo* pInfo = __try_cast<PropertyInfo*>(myEnum->Current);
        Console::WriteLine(S"Property '{0}' created!", pInfo);
    }

    Console::WriteLine(S"---");
    // Note that when invoking a property, you need to use the
proper BindingFlags -
    // BindingFlags::SetProperty when you invoke the "set" behavior, and
    // BindingFlags::GetProperty when you invoke the "get"
behavior. Also note that
    // we invoke them based on the name we gave the property, as
expected, and not
```

```
    // the name of the methods we bound to the specific property
behaviors.

    Object* custData = Activator::CreateInstance(custDataType);

    Object* temp3 [] = {S"Joe User"};
    custDataType->InvokeMember(S"CustomerName",
BindingFlags::SetProperty,
        0, custData, temp3);

    Console::WriteLine(S"The customerName field of instance
custData has been set to '{0}'.",
        custDataType->InvokeMember(S"CustomerName",
BindingFlags::GetProperty,
        0, custData, new Object*[0]));
}
// --- O U T P U T ---
// The output should be as follows:
// ------------------
// Property 'System::String CustomerName [System::String]' created!
// ---
// The customerName field of instance custData has been set to
'Joe User'.
// ------------------
```

Requirements

Namespace: System.Reflection.Emit

Platforms: Windows 98, Windows NT 4.0,
Windows Millennium Edition, Windows 2000,
Windows XP Home Edition, Windows XP Professional,
Windows .NET Server family

Assembly: Mscorlib (in Mscorlib.dll)

PropertyBuilder.Attributes Property

Gets the attributes for this property.

```
[Visual Basic]
Overrides Public ReadOnly Property Attributes As PropertyAttributes
[C#]
public override PropertyAttributes Attributes {get;}
[C++]
public: __property PropertyAttributes get_Attributes();
[JScript]
public override function get Attributes() : PropertyAttributes;
```

Property Value

Attributes of this property.

Requirements

Platforms: Windows 98, Windows NT 4.0,
Windows Millennium Edition, Windows 2000,
Windows XP Home Edition, Windows XP Professional,
Windows .NET Server family

PropertyBuilder.CanRead Property

Gets a value indicating whether the property can be read.

```
[Visual Basic]
Overrides Public ReadOnly Property CanRead As Boolean
[C#]
public override bool CanRead {get;}
[C++]
public: __property bool get_CanRead();
[JScript]
public override function get CanRead() : Boolean;
```

Property Value

true if this property can be read; otherwise, **false**.

Remarks

Boolean property indicating if the property can be read. If the property does not have a get accessor, it cannot be read.

Requirements

Platforms: Windows 98, Windows NT 4.0, Windows Millennium Edition, Windows 2000, Windows XP Home Edition, Windows XP Professional, Windows .NET Server family

PropertyBuilder.CanWrite Property

Gets a value indicating whether the property can be written to.

```
[Visual Basic]
Overrides Public ReadOnly Property CanWrite As Boolean
[C#]
public override bool CanWrite {get;}
[C++]
public: __property bool get_CanWrite();
[JScript]
public override function get CanWrite() : Boolean;
```

Property Value

true if this property can be written to; otherwise, **false**.

Remarks

Boolean property indicating if the property can be written to. If the property does not have a set accessor, it cannot be written to.

Requirements

Platforms: Windows 98, Windows NT 4.0, Windows Millennium Edition, Windows 2000, Windows XP Home Edition, Windows XP Professional, Windows .NET Server family

PropertyBuilder.DeclaringType Property

Gets the class that declares this member.

```
[Visual Basic]
Overrides Public ReadOnly Property DeclaringType As Type
[C#]
public override Type DeclaringType {get;}
[C++]
public: __property Type* get_DeclaringType();
[JScript]
public override function get DeclaringType() : Type;
```

Property Value

The **Type** object for the class that declares this member.

Requirements

Platforms: Windows 98, Windows NT 4.0, Windows Millennium Edition, Windows 2000, Windows XP Home Edition, Windows XP Professional, Windows .NET Server family

PropertyBuilder.Name Property

Gets the name of this member.

```
[Visual Basic]
Overrides Public ReadOnly Property Name As String
[C#]
public override string Name {get;}
[C++]
public: __property String* get_Name();
[JScript]
public override function get Name() : String;
```

Property Value

A **String** containing the name of this member.

Requirements

Platforms: Windows 98, Windows NT 4.0, Windows Millennium Edition, Windows 2000, Windows XP Home Edition, Windows XP Professional, Windows .NET Server family

PropertyBuilder.PropertyToken Property

Retrieves the token for this property.

```
[Visual Basic]
Public ReadOnly Property PropertyToken As PropertyToken
[C#]
public PropertyToken PropertyToken {get;}
[C++]
public: __property PropertyToken get_PropertyToken();
[JScript]
public function get PropertyToken() : PropertyToken;
```

Property Value

Read-only. Retrieves the token for this property.

Requirements

Platforms: Windows 98, Windows NT 4.0, Windows Millennium Edition, Windows 2000, Windows XP Home Edition, Windows XP Professional, Windows .NET Server family

PropertyBuilder.PropertyType Property

Gets the type of the field of this property.

```
[Visual Basic]
Overrides Public ReadOnly Property PropertyType As Type
[C#]
public override Type PropertyType {get;}
[C++]
public: __property Type* get_PropertyType();
[JScript]
public override function get PropertyType() : Type;
```

Property Value

The type of this property.

Requirements

Platforms: Windows 98, Windows NT 4.0, Windows Millennium Edition, Windows 2000, Windows XP Home Edition, Windows XP Professional, Windows .NET Server family

PropertyBuilder.ReflectedType Property

Gets the class object that was used to obtain this instance of **MemberInfo**.

```
[Visual Basic]
Overrides Public ReadOnly Property ReflectedType As Type
[C#]
public override Type ReflectedType {get;}
[C++]
public: __property Type* get_ReflectedType();
[JScript]
public override function get ReflectedType() : Type;
```

Property Value

The **Type** object through which this **MemberInfo** object was obtained.

Requirements

Platforms: Windows 98, Windows NT 4.0, Windows Millennium Edition, Windows 2000, Windows XP Home Edition, Windows XP Professional, Windows .NET Server family

PropertyBuilder.AddOtherMethod Method

Adds one of the other methods associated with this property.

```
[Visual Basic]
Public Sub AddOtherMethod( _
   ByVal mdBuilder As MethodBuilder _
)
[C#]
public void AddOtherMethod(
   MethodBuilder mdBuilder
);
[C++]
public: void AddOtherMethod(
   MethodBuilder* mdBuilder
);
[JScript]
public function AddOtherMethod(
   mdBuilder : MethodBuilder
);
```

Parameters

mdBuilder
   A **MethodBuilder** object that represents the other method.

Exceptions

Exception Type	Condition
ArgumentNullException	*mdBuilder* is a null reference (**Nothing** in Visual Basic).
InvalidOperationException	**CreateType** has been called on the enclosing type.

Requirements

Platforms: Windows 98, Windows NT 4.0, Windows Millennium Edition, Windows 2000, Windows XP Home Edition, Windows XP Professional, Windows .NET Server family

PropertyBuilder.GetAccessors Method

Overload List

Returns an array of the public and non-public **get** and **set** accessors on this property.

   [Visual Basic] **Overloads Overrides Public Function GetAccessors(Boolean) As MethodInfo()**

   [C#] **public override MethodInfo[] GetAccessors(bool);**

   [C++] **public: MethodInfo* GetAccessors(bool) [];**

   [JScript] **public override function GetAccessors(Boolean) : MethodInfo[];**

Inherited from **PropertyInfo**.

   [Visual Basic] **Overloads Public Function GetAccessors() As MethodInfo()**

   [C#] **public MethodInfo[] GetAccessors();**

   [C++] **public: MethodInfo* GetAccessors() [];**

   [JScript] **public function GetAccessors() : MethodInfo[];**

PropertyBuilder.GetAccessors Method (Boolean)

Returns an array of the public and non-public **get** and **set** accessors on this property.

```
[Visual Basic]
Overrides Overloads Public Function GetAccessors( _
   ByVal nonOverloads Public As Boolean _
) As MethodInfo()
[C#]
public override MethodInfo[] GetAccessors(
   bool nonPublic
);
[C++]
public: MethodInfo* GetAccessors(
   bool nonPublic
) [];
[JScript]
public override function GetAccessors(
   nonPublic : Boolean
) : MethodInfo[];
```

Parameters

nonPublic
   Indicates whether non-public methods should be returned in the **MethodInfo** array. **true** if non-public methods are to be included; otherwise, **false**.

Return Value

An array of type **MethodInfo** containing the matching public or non-public accessors, or an empty array if matching accessors do not exist on this property.

Exceptions

Exception Type	Condition
NotSupportedException	This method is not supported.

Remarks

To get the accessors of a property, reflect on the property's parent type using Type.GetType or Assembly.GetType, retrieve the Reflection property object from the type, and call PropertyInfo.GetAccessors.

Requirements

Platforms: Windows 98, Windows NT 4.0,
Windows Millennium Edition, Windows 2000,
Windows XP Home Edition, Windows XP Professional,
Windows .NET Server family

PropertyBuilder.GetCustomAttributes Method

Returns all the custom attributes defined on this property.

Overload List

Returns an array of all the custom attributes for this property.

[Visual Basic] **Overloads Overrides Public Function
GetCustomAttributes(Boolean) As Object() Implements
ICustomAttributeProvider.GetCustomAttributes**

[C#] **public override object[] GetCustomAttributes(bool);**

[C++] **public: Object* GetCustomAttributes(bool) __gc[];**

[JScript] **public override function GetCustomAttributes
(Boolean) : Object[];**

Returns an array of custom attributes identified by **Type**.

[Visual Basic] **Overloads Overrides Public Function
GetCustomAttributes(Type, Boolean) As Object()
Implements
ICustomAttributeProvider.GetCustomAttributes**

[C#] **public override object[] GetCustomAttributes(Type,
bool);**

[C++] **public: Object* GetCustomAttributes(Type*, bool)
__gc[];**

[JScript] **public override function GetCustomAttributes
(Type, Boolean) : Object[];**

PropertyBuilder.GetCustomAttributes Method (Boolean)

Returns an array of all the custom attributes for this property.

```
[Visual Basic]
Overrides Overloads Public Function GetCustomAttributes( _
   ByVal inherit As Boolean _
) As Object() Implements ICustomAttributeProvider.GetCustomAttributes
[C#]
public override object[] GetCustomAttributes(
   bool inherit
);
[C++]
public: Object* GetCustomAttributes(
   bool inherit
) __gc[];
[JScript]
public override function GetCustomAttributes(
   inherit : Boolean
) : Object[];
```

Parameters

inherit

If **true**, walks up this property's inheritance chain to find the custom attributes

Return Value

An array of all the custom attributes.

Implements

ICustomAttributeProvider.GetCustomAttributes

Exceptions

Exception Type	Condition
NotSupportedException	This method is not supported.

Remarks

Reflect on the property's parent type using Type.GetType or Assembly.GetType, retrieve the Reflection property object from the type, and call PropertyInfo.GetCustomAttributes.

Requirements

Platforms: Windows 98, Windows NT 4.0,
Windows Millennium Edition, Windows 2000,
Windows XP Home Edition, Windows XP Professional,
Windows .NET Server family

PropertyBuilder.GetCustomAttributes Method (Type, Boolean)

Returns an array of custom attributes identified by **Type**.

```
[Visual Basic]
Overrides Overloads Public Function GetCustomAttributes( _
   ByVal attributeType As Type, _
   ByVal inherit As Boolean _
) As Object() Implements ICustomAttributeProvider.GetCustomAttributes
[C#]
public override object[] GetCustomAttributes(
   Type attributeType,
   bool inherit
);
[C++]
public: Object* GetCustomAttributes(
   Type* attributeType,
   bool inherit
) __gc[];
[JScript]
public override function GetCustomAttributes(
   attributeType : Type,
   inherit : Boolean
) : Object[];
```

Parameters

attributeType

An array of custom attributes identified by type.

inherit

If **true**, walks up this property's inheritance chain to find the custom attributes.

Return Value

An array of custom attributes defined on this reflected member, or a null reference (**Nothing** in Visual Basic) if no attributes are defined on this member.

Implements

ICustomAttributeProvider.GetCustomAttributes

Exceptions

Exception Type	Condition
NotSupportedException	This method is not supported.

Remarks

Reflect on the property's parent type using Type.GetType or Assembly.GetType, retrieve the Reflection property object from the type, and call PropertyInfo.GetCustomAttributes.

Requirements

Platforms: Windows 98, Windows NT 4.0, Windows Millennium Edition, Windows 2000, Windows XP Home Edition, Windows XP Professional, Windows .NET Server family

PropertyBuilder.GetGetMethod Method

Overload List

Returns the public and non-public get accessor for this property.

[Visual Basic] **Overloads Overrides Public Function GetGetMethod(Boolean) As MethodInfo**

[C#] **public override MethodInfo GetGetMethod(bool);**

[C++] **public: MethodInfo* GetGetMethod(bool);**

[JScript] **public override function GetGetMethod(Boolean) : MethodInfo;**

Inherited from **PropertyInfo**.

[Visual Basic] **Overloads Public Function GetGetMethod() As MethodInfo**

[C#] **public MethodInfo GetGetMethod();**

[C++] **public: MethodInfo* GetGetMethod();**

[JScript] **public function GetGetMethod() : MethodInfo;**

PropertyBuilder.GetGetMethod Method (Boolean)

Returns the public and non-public get accessor for this property.

```
[Visual Basic]
Overrides Overloads Public Function GetGetMethod( _
   ByVal nonOverloads Public As Boolean _
) As MethodInfo
[C#]
public override MethodInfo GetGetMethod(
   bool nonPublic
);
[C++]
public: MethodInfo* GetGetMethod(
   bool nonPublic
);
[JScript]
public override function GetGetMethod(
   nonPublic : Boolean
) : MethodInfo;
```

Parameters

nonPublic
Indicates whether non-public get accessors should be returned. **true** if non-public methods are to be included; otherwise, **false**.

Return Value

A **MethodInfo** object representing the get accessor for this property, if *nonPublic* is **true**. Returns a null reference (**Nothing** in Visual Basic) if *nonPublic* is **false** and the get accessor is non-public, or if *nonPublic* is **true** but no get accessors exist.

Remarks

To get the getter of a property, reflect on the property's parent type using Type.GetType or Assembly.GetType, retrieve the Reflection property object from the type, and call PropertyInfo.GetGetMethod.

Requirements

Platforms: Windows 98, Windows NT 4.0, Windows Millennium Edition, Windows 2000, Windows XP Home Edition, Windows XP Professional, Windows .NET Server family

PropertyBuilder.GetIndexParameters Method

Returns an array of all the index parameters for the property.

```
[Visual Basic]
Overrides Public Function GetIndexParameters() As ParameterInfo()
[C#]
public override ParameterInfo[] GetIndexParameters();
[C++]
public: ParameterInfo* GetIndexParameters() [];
[JScript]
public override function GetIndexParameters() : ParameterInfo[];
```

Return Value

An array of type **ParameterInfo** containing the parameters for the indexes.

Exceptions

Exception Type	Condition
NotSupportedException	This method is not supported.

Remarks

To get the index parameters of a property, reflect on the property's parent type using Type.GetType or Assembly.GetType, retrieve the Reflection property object from the type, and call PropertyInfo.GetIndexParameters.

Requirements

Platforms: Windows 98, Windows NT 4.0, Windows Millennium Edition, Windows 2000, Windows XP Home Edition, Windows XP Professional, Windows .NET Server family

PropertyBuilder.GetSetMethod Method

Overload List

Returns the set accessor for this property.

[Visual Basic] **Overloads Overrides Public Function GetSetMethod(Boolean) As MethodInfo**

[C#] **public override MethodInfo GetSetMethod(bool);**

[C++] **public: MethodInfo* GetSetMethod(bool);**

[JScript] **public override function GetSetMethod(Boolean) : MethodInfo;**

Inherited from **PropertyInfo**.

[Visual Basic] **Overloads Public Function GetSetMethod() As MethodInfo**

[C#] **public MethodInfo GetSetMethod();**

[C++] **public: MethodInfo* GetSetMethod();**

[JScript] **public function GetSetMethod() : MethodInfo;**

PropertyBuilder.GetSetMethod Method (Boolean)

Returns the set accessor for this property.

```
[Visual Basic]
Overrides Overloads Public Function GetSetMethod( _
   ByVal nonOverloads Public As Boolean _
) As MethodInfo
[C#]
public override MethodInfo GetSetMethod(
   bool nonPublic
);
[C++]
public: MethodInfo* GetSetMethod(
   bool nonPublic
);
[JScript]
public override function GetSetMethod(
   nonPublic : Boolean
) : MethodInfo;
```

Parameters

nonPublic

Indicates whether the accessor should be returned if it is non-public. **true** if non-public methods are to be included; otherwise, **false**.

Return Value

Value	Condition
A **MethodInfo** object representing the Set method for this property.	The set accessor is public.
	nonPublic is true and non-public methods can be returned.
null	*nonPublic* is true, but the property is read-only.
	nonPublic is false and the set accessor is non-public.

Remarks

To get the setter of a property, reflect on the property's parent type using Type.GetType or Assembly.GetType, retrieve the Reflection property object from the type, and call PropertyInfo.GetSetMethod.

Requirements

Platforms: Windows 98, Windows NT 4.0, Windows Millennium Edition, Windows 2000, Windows XP Home Edition, Windows XP Professional, Windows .NET Server family

PropertyBuilder.GetValue Method

Overload List

Gets the value of the indexed property by calling the property's getter method.

[Visual Basic] **Overloads Overrides Public Function GetValue(Object, Object()) As Object**

[C#] **public override object GetValue(object, object[]);**

[C++] **public: Object* GetValue(Object*, Object*[]);**

[JScript] **public override function GetValue(Object, Object[]) : Object;**

Gets the value of a property having the specified binding, index, and **CultureInfo**.

[Visual Basic] **Overloads Overrides Public Function GetValue(Object, BindingFlags, Binder, Object(), CultureInfo) As Object**

[C#] **public override object GetValue(object, BindingFlags, Binder, object[], CultureInfo);**

[C++] **public: Object* GetValue(Object*, BindingFlags, Binder*, Object*[], CultureInfo*);**

[JScript] **public override function GetValue(Object, BindingFlags, Binder, Object[], CultureInfo) : Object;**

PropertyBuilder.GetValue Method (Object, Object[])

Gets the value of the indexed property by calling the property's getter method.

```
[Visual Basic]
Overrides Overloads Public Function GetValue( _
   ByVal obj As Object, _
   ByVal index() As Object _
) As Object
[C#]
public override object GetValue(
   object obj,
   object[] index
);
[C++]
public: Object* GetValue(
   Object* obj,
   Object* index __gc[]
);
[JScript]
public override function GetValue(
   obj : Object,
   index : Object[]
) : Object;
```

Parameters

obj

The object whose property value will be returned.

index

Optional index values for indexed properties. This value should be a null reference (**Nothing** in Visual Basic) for non-indexed properties.

Return Value

The value of the specified indexed property.

Exceptions

Exception Type	Condition
NotSupportedException	This method is not supported.

Remarks

To get the value of a property, reflect on the property's parent type using Type.GetType or Assembly.GetType, retrieve the **Reflection** property object from the type, and call **PropertyInfo.GetValue**.

Requirements

Platforms: Windows 98, Windows NT 4.0, Windows Millennium Edition, Windows 2000, Windows XP Home Edition, Windows XP Professional, Windows .NET Server family

PropertyBuilder.GetValue Method (Object, BindingFlags, Binder, Object[], CultureInfo)

Gets the value of a property having the specified binding, index, and **CultureInfo**.

```
[Visual Basic]
Overrides Overloads Public Function GetValue( _
    ByVal obj As Object, _
    ByVal invokeAttr As BindingFlags, _
    ByVal binder As Binder, _
    ByVal index() As Object, _
    ByVal culture As CultureInfo _
) As Object
[C#]
public override object GetValue(
    object obj,
    BindingFlags invokeAttr,
    Binder binder,
    object[] index,
    CultureInfo culture
);
[C++]
public: Object* GetValue(
    Object* obj,
    BindingFlags invokeAttr,
    Binder* binder,
    Object* index __gc[],
    CultureInfo* culture
);
[JScript]
public override function GetValue(
    obj : Object,
    invokeAttr : BindingFlags,
    binder : Binder,
    index : Object[],
    culture : CultureInfo
) : Object;
```

Parameters

obj
    The object whose property value will be returned.
invokeAttr
    The invocation attribute. This must be a bit flag from **BindingFlags**: **InvokeMethod, CreateInstance, Static, GetField, SetField, GetProperty**, or **SetProperty**. A suitable invocation attribute must be specified. If a static member is to be invoked, the **Static** flag of **BindingFlags** must be set.
binder
    An object that enables the binding, coercion of argument types, invocation of members, and retrieval of **MemberInfo** objects using reflection. If *binder* is a null reference (**Nothing** in Visual Basic), the default binder is used.
index
    Optional index values for indexed properties. This value should be a null reference (**Nothing** in Visual Basic) for non-indexed properties.
culture
    The **CultureInfo** object that represents the culture for which the resource is to be localized. Note that if the resource is not localized for this culture, the **CultureInfo.Parent** method will be called successively in search of a match. If this value is a null reference (**Nothing** in Visual Basic), the **CultureInfo** is obtained from the **CultureInfo.CurrentUICulture** property.

Return Value

The property value for *obj*.

Exceptions

Exception Type	Condition
NotSupportedException	This method is not supported.

Remarks

To get the value of a property, reflect on the property's parent type using Type.GetType or Assembly.GetType, retrieve the Reflection property object from the type, and call PropertyInfo.GetValue.

Requirements

Platforms: Windows 98, Windows NT 4.0, Windows Millennium Edition, Windows 2000, Windows XP Home Edition, Windows XP Professional, Windows .NET Server family

PropertyBuilder.IsDefined Method

Indicates whether one or more instance of *attributeType* is defined on this property.

```
[Visual Basic]
Overrides Public Function IsDefined( _
    ByVal attributeType As Type, _
    ByVal inherit As Boolean _
) As Boolean Implements ICustomAttributeProvider.IsDefined
[C#]
public override bool IsDefined(
    Type attributeType,
    bool inherit
);
[C++]
public: bool IsDefined(
    Type* attributeType,
    bool inherit
);
[JScript]
public override function IsDefined(
    attributeType : Type,
    inherit : Boolean
) : Boolean;
```

Parameters

attributeType
    The **Type** object to which the custom attributes are applied.
inherit
    Specifies whether to walk up this property's inheritance chain to find the custom attributes.

Return Value

true if one or more instance of *attributeType* is defined on this property; otherwise **false**.

Implements

ICustomAttributeProvider.IsDefined

Exceptions

Exception Type	Condition
NotSupportedException	This method is not supported.

Remarks

Reflect on the property's parent type using Type.GetType or Assembly.GetType, retrieve the Reflection property object from the type, and call PropertyInfo.IsDefined.

Requirements

Platforms: Windows 98, Windows NT 4.0, Windows Millennium Edition, Windows 2000, Windows XP Home Edition, Windows XP Professional, Windows .NET Server family

PropertyBuilder.SetConstant Method

Sets the default value of this property.

```
[Visual Basic]
Public Sub SetConstant( _
   ByVal defaultValue As Object _
)
[C#]
public void SetConstant(
   object defaultValue
);
[C++]
public: void SetConstant(
   Object* defaultValue
);
[JScript]
public function SetConstant(
   defaultValue : Object
);
```

Parameters

defaultValue
    The default value of this property.

Exceptions

Exception Type	Condition
InvalidOperationException	CreateType has been called on the enclosing type.

Remarks

defaultValue is restricted to the following types: **Boolean, SByte, Int16, Int32, Int64, Byte, UInt16, UInt32, UInt64, Single, Double, DateTime, Char, String**, and **Enum**. If the type of the property is **Decimal** or **Object**, *defaultValue* can only be null.

Requirements

Platforms: Windows 98, Windows NT 4.0, Windows Millennium Edition, Windows 2000, Windows XP Home Edition, Windows XP Professional, Windows .NET Server family

PropertyBuilder.SetCustomAttribute Method

Sets a custom attribute.

Overload List

Set a custom attribute using a custom attribute builder.

    [Visual Basic] **Overloads Public Sub SetCustomAttribute (CustomAttributeBuilder)**

    [C#] **public void SetCustomAttribute (CustomAttributeBuilder);**

    [C++] **public: void SetCustomAttribute (CustomAttributeBuilder*);**

    [JScript] **public function SetCustomAttribute (CustomAttributeBuilder);**

Set a custom attribute using a specified custom attribute blob.

    [Visual Basic] **Overloads Public Sub SetCustomAttribute (ConstructorInfo, Byte())**

    [C#] **public void SetCustomAttribute(ConstructorInfo, byte[]);**

    [C++] **public: void SetCustomAttribute(ConstructorInfo*, unsigned char __gc[]);**

    [JScript] **public function SetCustomAttribute (ConstructorInfo, Byte[]);**

PropertyBuilder.SetCustomAttribute Method (CustomAttributeBuilder)

Set a custom attribute using a custom attribute builder.

```
[Visual Basic]
Overloads Public Sub SetCustomAttribute( _
   ByVal customBuilder As CustomAttributeBuilder _
)
[C#]
public void SetCustomAttribute(
   CustomAttributeBuilder customBuilder
);
[C++]
public: void SetCustomAttribute(
   CustomAttributeBuilder* customBuilder
);
[JScript]
public function SetCustomAttribute(
   customBuilder : CustomAttributeBuilder
);
```

Parameters

customBuilder
    An instance of a helper class to define the custom attribute.

Exceptions

Exception Type	Condition
ArgumentNullException	*customBuilder* is a null reference (**Nothing** in Visual Basic).
InvalidOperationException	if **CreateType** has been called on the enclosing type.

Requirements

Platforms: Windows 98, Windows NT 4.0, Windows Millennium Edition, Windows 2000, Windows XP Home Edition, Windows XP Professional, Windows .NET Server family

PropertyBuilder.SetCustomAttribute Method (ConstructorInfo, Byte[])

Set a custom attribute using a specified custom attribute blob.

```
[Visual Basic]
Overloads Public Sub SetCustomAttribute( _
   ByVal con As ConstructorInfo, _
   ByVal binaryAttribute() As Byte _
)
```

```
[C#]
public void SetCustomAttribute(
    ConstructorInfo con,
    byte[] binaryAttribute
);
[C++]
public: void SetCustomAttribute(
    ConstructorInfo* con,
    unsigned char binaryAttribute __gc[]
);
[JScript]
public function SetCustomAttribute(
    con : ConstructorInfo,
    binaryAttribute : Byte[]
);
```

Parameters

con

The constructor for the custom attribute.

binaryAttribute

A byte blob representing the attributes.

Exceptions

Exception Type	Condition
ArgumentNullException	*con* or *binaryAttribute* is a null reference (**Nothing** in Visual Basic).
InvalidOperationException	**CreateType** has been called on the enclosing type.

Remarks

See the metadata specification in the ECMA Partition II documentation for details on how to format *binaryAttribute*. The Partition II documentation is included with the .NET Framework SDK installation, and can be found in the %\Microsoft.NET\FrameworkSDK\Tool Developers Guide\docs directory.

Requirements

Platforms: Windows 98, Windows NT 4.0, Windows Millennium Edition, Windows 2000, Windows XP Home Edition, Windows XP Professional, Windows .NET Server family

PropertyBuilder.SetGetMethod Method

Sets the method that gets the property value.

```
[Visual Basic]
Public Sub SetGetMethod( _
    ByVal mdBuilder As MethodBuilder _
)
[C#]
public void SetGetMethod(
    MethodBuilder mdBuilder
);
[C++]
public: void SetGetMethod(
    MethodBuilder* mdBuilder
);
[JScript]
public function SetGetMethod(
    mdBuilder : MethodBuilder
);
```

Parameters

mdBuilder

A **MethodBuilder** object that represents the method that gets the property value.

Exceptions

Exception Type	Condition
ArgumentNullException	*mdBuilder* is a null reference (**Nothing** in Visual Basic).
InvalidOperationException	**CreateType** has been called on the enclosing type.

Example

See related example in the **System.Reflection.Emit.PropertyBuilder** class topic.

Requirements

Platforms: Windows 98, Windows NT 4.0, Windows Millennium Edition, Windows 2000, Windows XP Home Edition, Windows XP Professional, Windows .NET Server family

PropertyBuilder.SetSetMethod Method

Sets the method that sets the property value.

```
[Visual Basic]
Public Sub SetSetMethod( _
    ByVal mdBuilder As MethodBuilder _
)
[C#]
public void SetSetMethod(
    MethodBuilder mdBuilder
);
[C++]
public: void SetSetMethod(
    MethodBuilder* mdBuilder
);
[JScript]
public function SetSetMethod(
    mdBuilder : MethodBuilder
);
```

Parameters

mdBuilder

A **MethodBuilder** object that represents the method that sets the property value.

Exceptions

Exception Type	Condition
ArgumentNullException	*mdBuilder* is a null reference (**Nothing** in Visual Basic).
InvalidOperationException	**CreateType** has been called on the enclosing type.

Example

See related example in the **System.Reflection.Emit.PropertyBuilder** class topic.

Requirements

Platforms: Windows 98, Windows NT 4.0, Windows Millennium Edition, Windows 2000, Windows XP Home Edition, Windows XP Professional, Windows .NET Server family

PropertyBuilder.SetValue Method

Sets the property value for the given object to the given value.

Overload List

Sets the value of the property with optional index values for index properties.

[Visual Basic] **Overloads Overrides Public Sub SetValue(Object, Object, Object())**

[C#] **public override void SetValue(object, object, object[]);**

[C++] **public: void SetValue(Object*, Object*, Object*[]);**

[JScript] **public override function SetValue(Object, Object, Object[]);**

Sets the property value for the given object to the given value.

[Visual Basic] **Overloads Overrides Public Sub SetValue (Object, Object, BindingFlags, Binder, Object(), CultureInfo)**

[C#] **public override void SetValue(object, object, BindingFlags, Binder, object[], CultureInfo);**

[C++] **public: void SetValue(Object*, Object*, BindingFlags, Binder*, Object*[], CultureInfo*);**

[JScript] **public override function SetValue(Object, Object, BindingFlags, Binder, Object[], CultureInfo);**

PropertyBuilder.SetValue Method (Object, Object, Object[])

Sets the value of the property with optional index values for index properties.

```
[Visual Basic]
Overrides Overloads Public Sub SetValue( _
   ByVal obj As Object, _
   ByVal value As Object, _
   ByVal index() As Object _
)
[C#]
public override void SetValue(
   object obj,
   object value,
   object[] index
);
[C++]
public: void SetValue(
   Object* obj,
   Object* value,
   Object* index __gc[]
);
[JScript]
public override function SetValue(
   obj : Object,
   value : Object,
   index : Object[]
);
```

Parameters

obj
   The object whose property value will be set.
value
   The new value for this property.
index
   Optional index values for indexed properties. This value should be a null reference (**Nothing** in Visual Basic) for non-indexed properties.

Exceptions

Exception Type	Condition
NotSupportedException	This method is not supported.

Remarks

To set the value of a property, reflect on the property's parent type using Type.GetType or Assembly.GetType, retrieve the Reflection property object from the type, and call PropertyInfo.SetValue.

Requirements

Platforms: Windows 98, Windows NT 4.0, Windows Millennium Edition, Windows 2000, Windows XP Home Edition, Windows XP Professional, Windows .NET Server family

PropertyBuilder.SetValue Method (Object, Object, BindingFlags, Binder, Object[], CultureInfo)

Sets the property value for the given object to the given value.

```
[Visual Basic]
Overrides Overloads Public Sub SetValue( _
   ByVal obj As Object, _
   ByVal value As Object, _
   ByVal invokeAttr As BindingFlags, _
   ByVal binder As Binder, _
   ByVal index() As Object, _
   ByVal culture As CultureInfo _
)
[C#]
public override void SetValue(
   object obj,
   object value,
   BindingFlags invokeAttr,
   Binder binder,
   object[] index,
   CultureInfo culture
);
[C++]
public: void SetValue(
   Object* obj,
   Object* value,
   BindingFlags invokeAttr,
   Binder* binder,
   Object* index __gc[],
   CultureInfo* culture
);
[JScript]
public override function SetValue(
   obj : Object,
   value : Object,
   invokeAttr : BindingFlags,
   binder : Binder,
   index : Object[],
   culture : CultureInfo
);
```

Parameters

obj
   The object whose property value will be returned.
value
   The new value for this property.

invokeAttr

The invocation attribute. This must be a bit flag from
BindingFlags: **InvokeMethod**, **CreateInstance**, **Static**,
GetField, **SetField**, **GetProperty**, or **SetProperty**. A suitable
invocation attribute must be specified. If a static member is to be
invoked, the **Static** flag of **BindingFlags** must be set.

binder

An object that enables the binding, coercion of argument types,
invocation of members, and retrieval of **MemberInfo** objects
using reflection. If *binder* is a null reference (**Nothing** in Visual
Basic), the default binder is used.

index

Optional index values for indexed properties. This value should
be a null reference (**Nothing** in Visual Basic) for non-indexed
properties.

culture

The **CultureInfo** object that represents the culture for which the
resource is to be localized. Note that if the resource is not
localized for this culture, the **CultureInfo.Parent** method will be
called successively in search of a match. If this value is a null
reference (**Nothing** in Visual Basic), the **CultureInfo** is obtained
from the **CultureInfo.CurrentUICulture** property.

Exceptions

Exception Type	Condition
NotSupportedException	This method is not supported.

Remarks

To set the value of a property, reflect on the property's parent type
using Type.GetType or Assembly.GetType, retrieve the Reflection
property object from the type, and call PropertyInfo.SetValue.

Requirements

Platforms: Windows 98, Windows NT 4.0,
Windows Millennium Edition, Windows 2000,
Windows XP Home Edition, Windows XP Professional,
Windows .NET Server family

PropertyToken Structure

The **PropertyToken** struct is an opaque representation of the **Token** returned by the metadata to represent a property.

System.Object
   System.ValueType
      System.Reflection.Emit.PropertyToken

```
[Visual Basic]
<Serializable>
Public Structure PropertyToken
[C#]
[Serializable]
public struct PropertyToken
[C++]
[Serializable]
public __value struct PropertyToken
```

[JScript] In JScript, you can use the structures in the .NET Framework, but you cannot define your own.

Thread Safety

Reflection Emit is thread-safe when using assemblies that were created with the **AppDomain.DefineDynamicAssembly** method with the Boolean parameter *isSynchronized* set to **true**.

Requirements

Namespace: System.Reflection.Emit

Platforms: Windows 98, Windows NT 4.0, Windows Millennium Edition, Windows 2000, Windows XP Home Edition, Windows XP Professional, Windows .NET Server family

Assembly: Mscorlib (in Mscorlib.dll)

PropertyToken.Empty Field

The default **PropertyToken** with **Token** value 0.

```
[Visual Basic]
Public Shared ReadOnly Empty As PropertyToken
[C#]
public static readonly PropertyToken Empty;
[C++]
public: static PropertyToken Empty;
[JScript]
public static var Empty : PropertyToken;
```

Requirements

Platforms: Windows 98, Windows NT 4.0, Windows Millennium Edition, Windows 2000, Windows XP Home Edition, Windows XP Professional, Windows .NET Server family

PropertyToken.Token Property

Retrieves the metadata token for this property.

```
[Visual Basic]
Public ReadOnly Property Token As Integer
[C#]
public int Token {get;}
[C++]
public: __property int get_Token();
[JScript]
public function get Token() : int;
```

Property Value

Read-only. Retrieves the metadata token for this instance.

Requirements

Platforms: Windows 98, Windows NT 4.0, Windows Millennium Edition, Windows 2000, Windows XP Home Edition, Windows XP Professional, Windows .NET Server family

PropertyToken.Equals Method

Checks if the given object is an instance of **PropertyToken** and is equal to this instance.

```
[Visual Basic]
Overrides Public Function Equals( _
   ByVal obj As Object _
) As Boolean
[C#]
public override bool Equals(
   object obj
);
[C++]
public: bool Equals(
   Object* obj
);
[JScript]
public override function Equals(
   obj : Object
) : Boolean;
```

Parameters

obj
   The object to this object.

Return Value

true if *obj* is an instance of **PropertyToken** and equals the current instance; otherwise, **false**.

Requirements

Platforms: Windows 98, Windows NT 4.0, Windows Millennium Edition, Windows 2000, Windows XP Home Edition, Windows XP Professional, Windows .NET Server family

PropertyToken.GetHashCode Method

Generates the hash code for this property.

```
[Visual Basic]
Overrides Public Function GetHashCode() As Integer
[C#]
public override int GetHashCode();
[C++]
public: int GetHashCode();
[JScript]
public override function GetHashCode() : int;
```

Return Value

Returns the hash code for this property.

Requirements

Platforms: Windows 98, Windows NT 4.0, Windows Millennium Edition, Windows 2000, Windows XP Home Edition, Windows XP Professional, Windows .NET Server family

SignatureHelper Class

Provides methods for building signatures.

System.Object
  System.Reflection.Emit.SignatureHelper

```
[Visual Basic]
NotInheritable Public Class SignatureHelper
[C#]
public sealed class SignatureHelper
[C++]
public __gc __sealed class SignatureHelper
[JScript]
public class SignatureHelper
```

Thread Safety

Reflection Emit is thread-safe when using assemblies that were created with the **AppDomain.DefineDynamicAssembly** method with the Boolean parameter *isSynchronized* set to **true**.

Requirements

Namespace: System.Reflection.Emit

Platforms: Windows 98, Windows NT 4.0, Windows Millennium Edition, Windows 2000, Windows XP Home Edition, Windows XP Professional, Windows .NET Server family

Assembly: Mscorlib (in Mscorlib.dll)

SignatureHelper.AddArgument Method

Adds an argument to the signature.

```
[Visual Basic]
Public Sub AddArgument( _
   ByVal clsArgument As Type _
)
[C#]
public void AddArgument(
   Type clsArgument
);
[C++]
public: void AddArgument(
   Type* clsArgument
);
[JScript]
public function AddArgument(
   clsArgument : Type
);
```

Parameters

clsArgument
    The type of the argument.

Exceptions

Exception Type	Condition
ArgumentException	The signature has already been finished.

Remarks

Takes a type and determines whether it is one of the primitive types or a general class. In the former case, the method adds the appropriate shortcut encoding; otherwise, the method calculates and adds the proper description for the type.

Requirements

Platforms: Windows 98, Windows NT 4.0, Windows Millennium Edition, Windows 2000, Windows XP Home Edition, Windows XP Professional, Windows .NET Server family

SignatureHelper.AddSentinel Method

Marks the end of a vararg fixed part. This is only used if the caller is creating a vararg signature call site.

```
[Visual Basic]
Public Sub AddSentinel()
[C#]
public void AddSentinel();
[C++]
public: void AddSentinel();
[JScript]
public function AddSentinel();
```

Requirements

Platforms: Windows 98, Windows NT 4.0, Windows Millennium Edition, Windows 2000, Windows XP Home Edition, Windows XP Professional, Windows .NET Server family

SignatureHelper.Equals Method

Checks if this instance is equal to the given object.

```
[Visual Basic]
Overrides Public Function Equals( _
   ByVal obj As Object _
) As Boolean
[C#]
public override bool Equals(
   object obj
);
[C++]
public: bool Equals(
   Object* obj
);
[JScript]
public override function Equals(
   obj : Object
) : Boolean;
```

Parameters

obj
    The object with which this instance should be compared.

Return Value

true if the given object is a **SignatureHelper** and represents the same signature; otherwise, **false**.

Requirements

Platforms: Windows 98, Windows NT 4.0, Windows Millennium Edition, Windows 2000, Windows XP Home Edition, Windows XP Professional, Windows .NET Server family

SignatureHelper.GetFieldSigHelper Method

Returns a signature helper for a field.

```
[Visual Basic]
Public Shared Function GetFieldSigHelper( _
   ByVal mod As Module _
) As SignatureHelper
[C#]
public static SignatureHelper GetFieldSigHelper(
   Module mod
);
[C++]
public: static SignatureHelper* GetFieldSigHelper(
   Module* mod
);
[JScript]
public static function GetFieldSigHelper(
   mod : Module
) : SignatureHelper;
```

Parameters

mod

> The module that contains the field for which the **SignatureHelper** is requested.

Return Value

The **SignatureHelper** object for a field.

Requirements

Platforms: Windows 98, Windows NT 4.0, Windows Millennium Edition, Windows 2000, Windows XP Home Edition, Windows XP Professional, Windows .NET Server family

SignatureHelper.GetHashCode Method

Creates and returns a hash code for this instance.

```
[Visual Basic]
Overrides Public Function GetHashCode() As Integer
[C#]
public override int GetHashCode();
[C++]
public: int GetHashCode();
[JScript]
public override function GetHashCode() : int;
```

Return Value

Returns the hash code based on the name.

Remarks

The hash code is created from the name of this instance, so the return value is the same as if the **GetHashCode** method were called on the value of the **Name** property.

Requirements

Platforms: Windows 98, Windows NT 4.0, Windows Millennium Edition, Windows 2000, Windows XP Home Edition, Windows XP Professional, Windows .NET Server family

SignatureHelper.GetLocalVarSigHelper Method

Returns a signature helper for a local variable.

```
[Visual Basic]
Public Shared Function GetLocalVarSigHelper( _
   ByVal mod As Module _
) As SignatureHelper
[C#]
public static SignatureHelper GetLocalVarSigHelper(
   Module mod
);
[C++]
public: static SignatureHelper* GetLocalVarSigHelper(
   Module* mod
);
[JScript]
public static function GetLocalVarSigHelper(
   mod : Module
) : SignatureHelper;
```

Parameters

mod

> The module that contains the local variable for which the **SignatureHelper** is requested.

Return Value

The **SignatureHelper** object for a local variable.

Requirements

Platforms: Windows 98, Windows NT 4.0, Windows Millennium Edition, Windows 2000, Windows XP Home Edition, Windows XP Professional, Windows .NET Server family

SignatureHelper.GetMethodSigHelper Method

Returns a signature helper for a method.

Overload List

Returns a signature helper for a method given the method's module and an unmanaged calling convention.

> [Visual Basic] **Overloads Public Shared Function GetMethodSigHelper(Module, CallingConvention, Type) As SignatureHelper**
>
> [C#] **public static SignatureHelper GetMethodSigHelper (Module, CallingConvention, Type);**
>
> [C++] **public: static SignatureHelper* GetMethodSigHelper (Module*, CallingConvention, Type*);**
>
> [JScript] **public static function GetMethodSigHelper(Module, CallingConvention, Type) : SignatureHelper;**

Returns a signature helper for a method given the method's module, calling convention, and return type.

> [Visual Basic] **Overloads Public Shared Function GetMethodSigHelper(Module, CallingConventions, Type) As SignatureHelper**
>
> [C#] **public static SignatureHelper GetMethodSigHelper (Module, CallingConventions, Type);**
>
> [C++] **public: static SignatureHelper* GetMethodSigHelper (Module*, CallingConventions, Type*);**
>
> [JScript] **public static function GetMethodSigHelper(Module, CallingConventions, Type) : SignatureHelper;**

Returns a signature helper for a method, given the method's module, calling convention, return type, and parameter types.

> [Visual Basic] **Overloads Public Shared Function GetMethodSigHelper(Module, Type, Type()) As SignatureHelper**
>
> [C#] **public static SignatureHelper GetMethodSigHelper (Module, Type, Type[]);**
>
> [C++] **public: static SignatureHelper* GetMethodSigHelper (Module*, Type*, Type[]);**
>
> [JScript] **public static function GetMethodSigHelper(Module, Type, Type[]) : SignatureHelper;**

SignatureHelper.GetMethodSigHelper Method (Module, CallingConvention, Type)

Returns a signature helper for a method given the method's module and an unmanaged calling convention.

```
[Visual Basic]
Overloads Public Shared Function GetMethodSigHelper( _
   ByVal mod As Module, _
   ByVal unmanagedCallConv As CallingConvention, _
   ByVal returnType As Type _
) As SignatureHelper
[C#]
public static SignatureHelper GetMethodSigHelper(
   Module mod,
   CallingConvention unmanagedCallConv,
   Type returnType
);
[C++]
public: static SignatureHelper* GetMethodSigHelper(
   Module* mod,
   CallingConvention unmanagedCallConv,
   Type* returnType
);
[JScript]
public static function GetMethodSigHelper(
   mod : Module,
   unmanagedCallConv : CallingConvention,
   returnType : Type
) : SignatureHelper;
```

Parameters

mod
> The module that contains the method for which the **SignatureHelper** is requested.

unmanagedCallConv
> The unmanaged calling convention of the method.

returnType
> The return type of the method.

Return Value

The **SignatureHelper** object for a method.

Requirements

Platforms: Windows 98, Windows NT 4.0, Windows Millennium Edition, Windows 2000, Windows XP Home Edition, Windows XP Professional, Windows .NET Server family

SignatureHelper.GetMethodSigHelper Method (Module, CallingConventions, Type)

Returns a signature helper for a method given the method's module, calling convention, and return type.

```
[Visual Basic]
Overloads Public Shared Function GetMethodSigHelper( _
   ByVal mod As Module, _
   ByVal callingConvention As CallingConventions, _
   ByVal returnType As Type _
) As SignatureHelper
[C#]
public static SignatureHelper GetMethodSigHelper(
   Module mod,
   CallingConventions callingConvention,
   Type returnType
);
[C++]
public: static SignatureHelper* GetMethodSigHelper(
   Module* mod,
   CallingConventions callingConvention,
   Type* returnType
);
[JScript]
public static function GetMethodSigHelper(
   mod : Module,
   callingConvention : CallingConventions,
   returnType : Type
) : SignatureHelper;
```

Parameters

mod
> The module that contains the method for which the **SignatureHelper** is requested.

callingConvention
> The calling convention of the method.

returnType
> The return type of the method.

Return Value

The **SignatureHelper** object for a method.

Requirements

Platforms: Windows 98, Windows NT 4.0, Windows Millennium Edition, Windows 2000, Windows XP Home Edition, Windows XP Professional, Windows .NET Server family

SignatureHelper.GetMethodSigHelper Method (Module, Type, Type[])

Returns a signature helper for a method, given the method's module, calling convention, return type, and parameter types.

```
[Visual Basic]
Overloads Public Shared Function GetMethodSigHelper( _
   ByVal mod As Module, _
   ByVal returnType As Type, _
   ByVal parameterTypes() As Type _
) As SignatureHelper
[C#]
public static SignatureHelper GetMethodSigHelper(
   Module mod,
   Type returnType,
```

```
   Type[] parameterTypes
);
[C++]
public: static SignatureHelper* GetMethodSigHelper(
   Module* mod,
   Type* returnType,
   Type* parameterTypes[]
);
[JScript]
public static function GetMethodSigHelper(
   mod : Module,
   returnType : Type,
   parameterTypes : Type[]
) : SignatureHelper;
```

Parameters

mod

> The module that contains the method for which the **SignatureHelper** is requested.

returnType

> The return type of the method.

parameterTypes

> The types of the parameters of the method.

Return Value

The **SignatureHelper** object for a method.

Requirements

Platforms: Windows 98, Windows NT 4.0, Windows Millennium Edition, Windows 2000, Windows XP Home Edition, Windows XP Professional, Windows .NET Server family

SignatureHelper.GetPropertySigHelper Method

Returns a signature helper for a property given the property's module, return type, and parameter types.

```
[Visual Basic]
Public Shared Function GetPropertySigHelper( _
   ByVal mod As Module, _
   ByVal returnType As Type, _
   ByVal parameterTypes() As Type _
) As SignatureHelper
[C#]
public static SignatureHelper GetPropertySigHelper(
   Module mod,
   Type returnType,
   Type[] parameterTypes
);
[C++]
public: static SignatureHelper* GetPropertySigHelper(
   Module* mod,
   Type* returnType,
   Type* parameterTypes[]
);
[JScript]
public static function GetPropertySigHelper(
   mod : Module,
   returnType : Type,
   parameterTypes : Type[]
) : SignatureHelper;
```

Parameters

mod

> The module that contains the property for which the **SignatureHelper** is requested.

returnType

> The return type of the property.

parameterTypes

> The types of the parameters of the property.

Return Value

The **SignatureHelper** object for a property.

Requirements

Platforms: Windows 98, Windows NT 4.0, Windows Millennium Edition, Windows 2000, Windows XP Home Edition, Windows XP Professional, Windows .NET Server family

SignatureHelper.GetSignature Method

Adds the end token to the signature and marks the signature as finished, so no further tokens can be added.

```
[Visual Basic]
Public Function GetSignature() As Byte()
[C#]
public byte[] GetSignature();
[C++]
public: unsigned char GetSignature() __gc[];
[JScript]
public function GetSignature() : Byte[];
```

Return Value

Returns a byte array made up of the full signature.

Requirements

Platforms: Windows 98, Windows NT 4.0, Windows Millennium Edition, Windows 2000, Windows XP Home Edition, Windows XP Professional, Windows .NET Server family

SignatureHelper.ToString Method

Returns a string representing the signature parameters.

```
[Visual Basic]
Overrides Public Function ToString() As String
[C#]
public override string ToString();
[C++]
public: String* ToString();
[JScript]
public override function ToString() : String;
```

Return Value

Returns a string representing the parameters of this signature.

Requirements

Platforms: Windows 98, Windows NT 4.0, Windows Millennium Edition, Windows 2000, Windows XP Home Edition, Windows XP Professional, Windows .NET Server family

SignatureToken Structure

Represents the **Token** returned by the metadata to represent a signature.

System.Object
  System.ValueType
    System.Reflection.Emit.SignatureToken

```
[Visual Basic]
<Serializable>
Public Structure SignatureToken
[C#]
[Serializable]
public struct SignatureToken
[C++]
[Serializable]
public __value struct SignatureToken
```

[JScript] In JScript, you can use the structures in the .NET Framework, but you cannot define your own.

Thread Safety

Reflection Emit is thread-safe when using assemblies that were created with the **AppDomain.DefineDynamicAssembly** method with the Boolean parameter *isSynchronized* set to **true**.

Requirements

Namespace: System.Reflection.Emit

Platforms: Windows 98, Windows NT 4.0, Windows Millennium Edition, Windows 2000, Windows XP Home Edition, Windows XP Professional, Windows .NET Server family

Assembly: Mscorlib (in Mscorlib.dll)

SignatureToken.Empty Field

The default **SignatureToken** with **Token** value 0.

```
[Visual Basic]
Public Shared ReadOnly Empty As SignatureToken
[C#]
public static readonly SignatureToken Empty;
[C++]
public: static SignatureToken Empty;
[JScript]
public static var Empty : SignatureToken;
```

Requirements

Platforms: Windows 98, Windows NT 4.0, Windows Millennium Edition, Windows 2000, Windows XP Home Edition, Windows XP Professional, Windows .NET Server family

SignatureToken.Token Property

Retrieves the metadata token for the local variable signature for this method.

```
[Visual Basic]
Public ReadOnly Property Token As Integer
[C#]
public int Token {get;}
[C++]
public: __property int get_Token();
```

```
[JScript]
public function get Token() : int;
```

Property Value

Read-only. Retrieves the metadata token of this signature.

Remarks

This returns a numeric representation of the metadata token.

Requirements

Platforms: Windows 98, Windows NT 4.0, Windows Millennium Edition, Windows 2000, Windows XP Home Edition, Windows XP Professional, Windows .NET Server family

SignatureToken.Equals Method

Checks if the given object is an instance of **SignatureToken** and is equal to this instance.

```
[Visual Basic]
Overrides Public Function Equals( _
    ByVal obj As Object _
) As Boolean
[C#]
public override bool Equals(
    object obj
);
[C++]
public: bool Equals(
    Object* obj
);
[JScript]
public override function Equals(
    obj : Object
) : Boolean;
```

Parameters

obj
    The object to compare with this **SignatureToken**.

Return Value

true if *obj* is an instance of **SignatureToken** and is equal to this object; otherwise, **false**.

Requirements

Platforms: Windows 98, Windows NT 4.0, Windows Millennium Edition, Windows 2000, Windows XP Home Edition, Windows XP Professional, Windows .NET Server family

SignatureToken.GetHashCode Method

Generates the hash code for this signature.

```
[Visual Basic]
Overrides Public Function GetHashCode() As Integer
[C#]
public override int GetHashCode();
[C++]
public: int GetHashCode();
[JScript]
public override function GetHashCode() : int;
```

Return Value

Returns the hash code for this signature.

Requirements

Platforms: Windows 98, Windows NT 4.0,
Windows Millennium Edition, Windows 2000,
Windows XP Home Edition, Windows XP Professional,
Windows .NET Server family

StackBehaviour Enumeration

Describes how values are pushed onto a stack or popped off a stack.

```
[Visual Basic]
<Serializable>
Public Enum StackBehaviour
[C#]
[Serializable]
public enum StackBehaviour
[C++]
[Serializable]
__value public enum StackBehaviour
[JScript]
public
    Serializable
enum StackBehaviour
```

Members

Member name	Description
Pop0	No values are popped off the stack.
Pop1	Pops one value off the stack.
Pop1_pop1	Pops 1 value off the stack for the first operand, and 1 value of the stack for the second operand.
Popi	Pops a 32-bit integer off the stack.
Popi_pop1	Pops a 32-bit integer off the stack for the first operand, and a value off the stack for the second operand.
Popi_popi	Pops a 32-bit integer off the stack for the first operand, and a 32-bit integer off the stack for the second operand.
Popi_popi8	Pops a 32-bit integer off the stack for the first operand, and a 64-bit integer off the stack for the second operand.
Popi_popi_popi	Pops a 32-bit integer off the stack for the first operand, a 32-bit integer off the stack for the second operand, and a 32-bit integer off the stack for the third operand.
Popi_popr4	Pops a 32-bit integer off the stack for the first operand, and a 32-bit floating point number off the stack for the second operand.
Popi_popr8	Pops a 32-bit integer off the stack for the first operand, and a 64-bit floating point number off the stack for the second operand.
Popref	Pops a reference off the stack.
Popref_pop1	Pops a reference off the stack for the first operand, and a value off the stack for the second operand.
Popref_popi	Pops a reference off the stack for the first operand, and a 32-bit integer off the stack for the second operand.
Popref_popi_popi	Pops a reference off the stack for the first operand, a value off the stack for the second operand, and a value off the stack for the third operand.

Member name	Description
Popref_popi_popi8	Pops a reference off the stack for the first operand, a value off the stack for the second operand, and a 64-bit integer off the stack for the third operand.
Popref_popi_popr4	Pops a reference off the stack for the first operand, a value off the stack for the second operand, and a 32-bit integer off the stack for the third operand.
Popref_popi_popr8	Pops a reference off the stack for the first operand, a value off the stack for the second operand, and a 64-bit floating point number off the stack for the third operand.
Popref_popi_popref	Pops a reference off the stack for the first operand, a value off the stack for the second operand, and a reference off the stack for the third operand.
Push0	No values are pushed onto the stack.
Push1	Pushes one value onto the stack.
Push1_push1	Pushes 1 value onto the stack for the first operand, and 1 value onto the stack for the second operand.
Pushi	Pushes a 32-bit integer onto the stack.
Pushi8	Pushes a 64-bit integer onto the stack.
Pushr4	Pushes a 32-bit floating point number onto the stack.
Pushr8	Pushes a 64-bit floating point number onto the stack.
Pushref	Pushes a reference onto the stack.
Varpop	Pops a variable off the stack.
Varpush	Pushes a variable onto the stack.

Requirements

Namespace: System.Reflection.Emit

Platforms: Windows 98, Windows NT 4.0, Windows Millennium Edition, Windows 2000, Windows XP Home Edition, Windows XP Professional, Windows .NET Server family

Assembly: Mscorlib (in Mscorlib.dll)

StringToken Structure

Represents a token that represents a string.

System.Object
  System.ValueType
    System.Reflection.Emit.StringToken

```
[Visual Basic]
<Serializable>
Public Structure StringToken
[C#]
[Serializable]
public struct StringToken
[C++]
[Serializable]
public __value struct StringToken
```

[JScript] In JScript, you can use the structures in the .NET Framework, but you cannot define your own.

Thread Safety

Reflection Emit is thread-safe when using assemblies that were created with the **AppDomain.DefineDynamicAssembly** method with the Boolean parameter *isSynchronized* set to **true**.

Requirements

Namespace: System.Reflection.Emit

Platforms: Windows 98, Windows NT 4.0, Windows Millennium Edition, Windows 2000, Windows XP Home Edition, Windows XP Professional, Windows .NET Server family

Assembly: Mscorlib (in Mscorlib.dll)

StringToken.Token Property

Retrieves the metadata token for this string.

```
[Visual Basic]
Public ReadOnly Property Token As Integer
[C#]
public int Token {get;}
[C++]
public: __property int get_Token();
[JScript]
public function get Token() : int;
```

Property Value

Read-only. Retrieves the metadata token of this string.

Requirements

Platforms: Windows 98, Windows NT 4.0, Windows Millennium Edition, Windows 2000, Windows XP Home Edition, Windows XP Professional, Windows .NET Server family

StringToken.Equals Method

Checks if the given object is an instance of **StringToken** and is equal to this instance.

```
[Visual Basic]
Overrides Public Function Equals( _
   ByVal obj As Object _
) As Boolean
```

```
[C#]
public override bool Equals(
   object obj
);
[C++]
public: bool Equals(
   Object* obj
);
[JScript]
public override function Equals(
   obj : Object
) : Boolean;
```

Parameters

obj
    The object to compare with this **StringToken**.

Return Value

true if *obj* is an instance of **StringToken** and is equal to this object; otherwise, **false**.

Requirements

Platforms: Windows 98, Windows NT 4.0, Windows Millennium Edition, Windows 2000, Windows XP Home Edition, Windows XP Professional, Windows .NET Server family

StringToken.GetHashCode Method

Returns the hash code for this string.

```
[Visual Basic]
Overrides Public Function GetHashCode() As Integer
[C#]
public override int GetHashCode();
[C++]
public: int GetHashCode();
[JScript]
public override function GetHashCode() : int;
```

Return Value

Returns the underlying string token.

Requirements

Platforms: Windows 98, Windows NT 4.0, Windows Millennium Edition, Windows 2000, Windows XP Home Edition, Windows XP Professional, Windows .NET Server family

TypeBuilder Class

Defines and creates new instances of classes during runtime.

System.Object
  System.Reflection.MemberInfo
    System.Type
      System.Reflection.Emit.TypeBuilder

```
[Visual Basic]
NotInheritable Public Class TypeBuilder
   Inherits Type
[C#]
public sealed class TypeBuilder : Type
[C++]
public __gc __sealed class TypeBuilder : public Type
[JScript]
public class TypeBuilder extends Type
```

Thread Safety

Reflection Emit is thread-safe when using assemblies that were
created with the **AppDomain.DefineDynamicAssembly** method
with the Boolean parameter *isSynchronized* set to **true**.

Remarks

TypeBuilder is the root class used to control the creation of
dynamic classes in the runtime. **TypeBuilder** provides a set of
routines that are used to define classes, add methods and fields, and
create the class inside the runtime. A new **TypeBuilder** can be
created from a dynamic module.

To retrieve a **Type** object for an incomplete type, use
ModuleBuilder.GetType with a string representing the type name,
such as "MyType" or "MyType[]".

Example

[Visual Basic, C#, C++] The following code sample demonstrates
how to build a dynamic type using **TypeBuilder**.

```
[Visual Basic]
Imports System
Imports System.Threading
Imports System.Reflection
Imports System.Reflection.Emit

_

Class TestILGenerator

    Public Shared Function DynamicDotProductGen() As Type

        Dim ivType As Type = Nothing
        Dim ctorParams() As Type = {GetType(Integer), _
GetType(Integer), GetType(Integer)}

        Dim myDomain As AppDomain = Thread.GetDomain()
        Dim myAsmName As New AssemblyName()
        myAsmName.Name = "IntVectorAsm"

        Dim myAsmBuilder As AssemblyBuilder = _
myDomain.DefineDynamicAssembly( _
                    myAsmName, _
                    AssemblyBuilderAccess.RunAndSave)

        Dim IntVectorModule As ModuleBuilder = _
myAsmBuilder.DefineDynamicModule( _
                    "IntVectorModule", _
                    "Vector.dll")
```

```
        Dim ivTypeBld As TypeBuilder = _
IntVectorModule.DefineType("IntVector", TypeAttributes.Public)

        Dim xField As FieldBuilder = ivTypeBld.DefineField("x", _
                            GetType(Integer), _
                            FieldAttributes.Private)
        Dim yField As FieldBuilder = ivTypeBld.DefineField("y", _
                            GetType(Integer), _
                            FieldAttributes.Private)
        Dim zField As FieldBuilder = ivTypeBld.DefineField("z", _
                            GetType(Integer), _
                            FieldAttributes.Private)

        Dim objType As Type = Type.GetType("System.Object")
        Dim objCtor As ConstructorInfo = objType.GetConstructor _
(New Type() {})

        Dim ivCtor As ConstructorBuilder = ivTypeBld.DefineConstructor( _
                    MethodAttributes.Public, _
                    CallingConventions.Standard, _
                    ctorParams)
        Dim ctorIL As ILGenerator = ivCtor.GetILGenerator()
        ctorIL.Emit(OpCodes.Ldarg_0)
        ctorIL.Emit(OpCodes.Call, objCtor)
        ctorIL.Emit(OpCodes.Ldarg_0)
        ctorIL.Emit(OpCodes.Ldarg_1)
        ctorIL.Emit(OpCodes.Stfld, xField)
        ctorIL.Emit(OpCodes.Ldarg_0)
        ctorIL.Emit(OpCodes.Ldarg_2)
        ctorIL.Emit(OpCodes.Stfld, yField)
        ctorIL.Emit(OpCodes.Ldarg_0)
        ctorIL.Emit(OpCodes.Ldarg_3)
        ctorIL.Emit(OpCodes.Stfld, zField)
        ctorIL.Emit(OpCodes.Ret)

        ' Now, you'll construct the method find the dot product
of two vectors. First,
        ' let's define the parameters that will be accepted by
the method. In this case,
        ' it's an IntVector itself!

        Dim dpParams() As Type = {ivTypeBld}

        ' Here, you create a MethodBuilder containing the
        ' name, the attributes (public, static, private, and so on),
        ' the return type (int, in this case), and a array of Type
        ' indicating the type of each parameter. Since the sole parameter
        ' is a IntVector, the very class you're creating, you will
        ' pass in the TypeBuilder (which is derived from Type) instead of
        ' a Type object for IntVector, avoiding an exception.
        ' -- This method would be declared in VB.NET as:
        '     Public Function DotProduct(IntVector aVector) As Integer

        Dim dotProductMthd As MethodBuilder = _
ivTypeBld.DefineMethod("DotProduct", _
                    MethodAttributes.Public, GetType(Integer), _
                    dpParams)

        ' A ILGenerator can now be spawned, attached to the
MethodBuilder.
        Dim mthdIL As ILGenerator = dotProductMthd.GetILGenerator()

        ' Here's the body of our function, in MSIL form. We're
going to find the
        ' "dot product" of the current vector instance with the
passed vector
        ' instance. For reference purposes, the equation is:
        ' (x1 * x2) + (y1 * y2) + (z1 * z2) = the dot product
        ' First, you'll load the reference to the current instance "this"
        ' stored in argument 0 (ldarg.0) onto the stack. Ldfld,
the subsequent
        ' instruction, will pop the reference off the stack and
look up the
        ' field "x", specified by the FieldInfo token "xField".
```

```
        mthdIL.Emit(OpCodes.Ldarg_0)
        mthdIL.Emit(OpCodes.Ldfld, xField)

        ' That completed, the value stored at field "x" is now          ⏎
atop the stack.
        ' Now, you'll do the same for the object reference we passed as a
        ' parameter, stored in argument 1 (ldarg.1). After Ldfld        ⏎
executed,
        ' you'll have the value stored in field "x" for the             ⏎
passed instance
        ' atop the stack.
        mthdIL.Emit(OpCodes.Ldarg_1)
        mthdIL.Emit(OpCodes.Ldfld, xField)

        ' There will now be two values atop the stack - the "x"         ⏎
value for the
        ' current vector instance, and the "x" value for the           ⏎
passed instance.
        ' You'll now multiply them, and push the result onto the        ⏎
evaluation stack.
        mthdIL.Emit(OpCodes.Mul_Ovf_Un)

        ' Now, repeat this for the "y" fields of both vectors.
        mthdIL.Emit(OpCodes.Ldarg_0)
        mthdIL.Emit(OpCodes.Ldfld, yField)
        mthdIL.Emit(OpCodes.Ldarg_1)
        mthdIL.Emit(OpCodes.Ldfld, yField)
        mthdIL.Emit(OpCodes.Mul_Ovf_Un)

        ' At this time, the results of both multiplications             ⏎
should be atop
        ' the stack. You'll now add them and push the result            ⏎
onto the stack.
        mthdIL.Emit(OpCodes.Add_Ovf_Un)

        ' Multiply both "z" field and push the result onto the stack.
        mthdIL.Emit(OpCodes.Ldarg_0)
        mthdIL.Emit(OpCodes.Ldfld, zField)
        mthdIL.Emit(OpCodes.Ldarg_1)
        mthdIL.Emit(OpCodes.Ldfld, zField)
        mthdIL.Emit(OpCodes.Mul_Ovf_Un)

        ' Finally, add the result of multiplying the "z" fields with the
        ' result of the earlier addition, and push the result - the     ⏎
dot product -
        ' onto the stack.
        mthdIL.Emit(OpCodes.Add_Ovf_Un)

        ' The "ret" opcode will pop the last value from the stack       ⏎
and return it
        ' to the calling method. You're all done!
        mthdIL.Emit(OpCodes.Ret)

        ivType = ivTypeBld.CreateType()

        Return ivType
    End Function 'DynamicDotProductGen

    Public Shared Sub Main()

        Dim IVType As Type = Nothing
        Dim aVector1 As Object = Nothing
        Dim aVector2 As Object = Nothing
        Dim aVtypes() As Type = {GetType(Integer), GetType(Integer),
GetType(Integer)}
        Dim aVargs1() As Object = {10, 10, 10}
        Dim aVargs2() As Object = {20, 20, 20}

        ' Call the  method to build our dynamic class.
        IVType = DynamicDotProductGen()

        Dim myDTctor As ConstructorInfo = IVType.GetConstructor(aVtypes)
        aVector1 = myDTctor.Invoke(aVargs1)
        aVector2 = myDTctor.Invoke(aVargs2)
```

```
        Console.WriteLine("---")
        Dim passMe(0) As Object
        passMe(0) = CType(aVector2, Object)

        Console.WriteLine("(10, 10, 10) . (20, 20, 20) = {0}", _
                    IVType.InvokeMember("DotProduct",               ⏎
BindingFlags.InvokeMethod, _
                        Nothing, aVector1, passMe))
    End Sub 'Main
End Class 'TestILGenerator

' +++ OUTPUT +++
' ---
' (10, 10, 10) . (20, 20, 20) = 600
```

[C#]
```
using System;
using System.Threading;
using System.Reflection;
using System.Reflection.Emit;

class TestILGenerator {

    public static Type DynamicDotProductGen() {

        Type ivType = null;
        Type[] ctorParams = new Type[] { typeof(int),
                        typeof(int),
                    typeof(int)};

        AppDomain myDomain = Thread.GetDomain();
        AssemblyName myAsmName = new AssemblyName();
        myAsmName.Name = "IntVectorAsm";

        AssemblyBuilder myAsmBuilder = myDomain.DefineDynamicAssembly(
                    myAsmName,
                    AssemblyBuilderAccess.RunAndSave);

        ModuleBuilder IntVectorModule =                             ⏎
myAsmBuilder.DefineDynamicModule("IntVectorModule",
                            "Vector.dll");

        TypeBuilder ivTypeBld = IntVectorModule.DefineType("IntVector",
                        TypeAttributes.Public);

        FieldBuilder xField = ivTypeBld.DefineField("x", typeof(int),
FieldAttributes.Private);
        FieldBuilder yField = ivTypeBld.DefineField("y", typeof(int),
FieldAttributes.Private);
        FieldBuilder zField = ivTypeBld.DefineField("z", typeof(int),
FieldAttributes.Private);

        Type objType = Type.GetType("System.Object");
        ConstructorInfo objCtor = objType.GetConstructor(new        ⏎
Type[0]);

        ConstructorBuilder ivCtor = ivTypeBld.DefineConstructor(
                    MethodAttributes.Public,
                    CallingConventions.Standard,
                    ctorParams);
        ILGenerator ctorIL = ivCtor.GetILGenerator();
            ctorIL.Emit(OpCodes.Ldarg_0);
            ctorIL.Emit(OpCodes.Call, objCtor);
            ctorIL.Emit(OpCodes.Ldarg_0);
            ctorIL.Emit(OpCodes.Ldarg_1);
            ctorIL.Emit(OpCodes.Stfld, xField);
            ctorIL.Emit(OpCodes.Ldarg_0);
            ctorIL.Emit(OpCodes.Ldarg_2);
            ctorIL.Emit(OpCodes.Stfld, yField);
            ctorIL.Emit(OpCodes.Ldarg_0);
            ctorIL.Emit(OpCodes.Ldarg_3);
```

```
        ctorIL.Emit(OpCodes.Stfld, zField);
        ctorIL.Emit(OpCodes.Ret);

        // This method will find the dot product of the stored vector
        // with another.

        Type[] dpParams = new Type[] { ivTypeBld };

            // Here, you create a MethodBuilder containing the
            // name, the attributes (public, static, private, and so on),
            // the return type (int, in this case), and a array of Type
            // indicating the type of each parameter. Since the sole
parameter
            // is a IntVector, the very class you're creating, you will
            // pass in the TypeBuilder (which is derived from Type)
instead of
            // a Type object for IntVector, avoiding an exception.

            // -- This method would be declared in C# as:
            //    public int DotProduct(IntVector aVector)

            MethodBuilder dotProductMthd = ivTypeBld.DefineMethod(
                        "DotProduct",
                    MethodAttributes.Public,
                            typeof(int),
                            dpParams);

        // A ILGenerator can now be spawned, attached to
the MethodBuilder.

        ILGenerator mthdIL = dotProductMthd.GetILGenerator();

            // Here's the body of our function, in MSIL form. We're
going to find the
            // "dot product" of the current vector instance with the
passed vector
            // instance. For reference purposes, the equation is:
            // (x1 * x2) + (y1 * y2) + (z1 * z2) = the dot product

            // First, you'll load the reference to the current
instance "this"
            // stored in argument 0 (ldarg.0) onto the stack. Ldfld,
the subsequent
            // instruction, will pop the reference off the stack and
look up the
            // field "x", specified by the FieldInfo token "xField".

        mthdIL.Emit(OpCodes.Ldarg_0);
        mthdIL.Emit(OpCodes.Ldfld, xField);

            // That completed, the value stored at field "x" is now
atop the stack.
            // Now, you'll do the same for the object reference we
passed as a
            // parameter, stored in argument 1 (ldarg.1). After
Ldfld executed,
            // you'll have the value stored in field "x" for the
passed instance
            // atop the stack.

        mthdIL.Emit(OpCodes.Ldarg_1);
        mthdIL.Emit(OpCodes.Ldfld, xField);

            // There will now be two values atop the stack -
the "x" value for the
            // current vector instance, and the "x" value for the
passed instance.
            // You'll now multiply them, and push the result onto
the evaluation stack.

        mthdIL.Emit(OpCodes.Mul_Ovf_Un);

        // Now, repeat this for the "y" fields of both vectors.
```

```
        mthdIL.Emit(OpCodes.Ldarg_0);
        mthdIL.Emit(OpCodes.Ldfld, yField);
        mthdIL.Emit(OpCodes.Ldarg_1);
        mthdIL.Emit(OpCodes.Ldfld, yField);
        mthdIL.Emit(OpCodes.Mul_Ovf_Un);

            // At this time, the results of both multiplications
should be atop
            // the stack. You'll now add them and push the result
onto the stack.

        mthdIL.Emit(OpCodes.Add_Ovf_Un);

            // Multiply both "z" field and push the result onto the stack.
        mthdIL.Emit(OpCodes.Ldarg_0);
        mthdIL.Emit(OpCodes.Ldfld, zField);
        mthdIL.Emit(OpCodes.Ldarg_1);
        mthdIL.Emit(OpCodes.Ldfld, zField);
        mthdIL.Emit(OpCodes.Mul_Ovf_Un);

            // Finally, add the result of multiplying the "z" fields
with the
            // result of the earlier addition, and push the result -
the dot product -
            // onto the stack.
        mthdIL.Emit(OpCodes.Add_Ovf_Un);

            // The "ret" opcode will pop the last value from the
stack and return it
            // to the calling method. You're all done!

        mthdIL.Emit(OpCodes.Ret);

        ivType = ivTypeBld.CreateType();

        return ivType;

    }

    public static void Main() {

        Type IVType = null;
            object aVector1 = null;
            object aVector2 = null;
        Type[] aVtypes = new Type[] {typeof(int), typeof(int),
typeof(int)};
            object[] aVargs1 = new object[] {10, 10, 10};
            object[] aVargs2 = new object[] {20, 20, 20};

        // Call the  method to build our dynamic class.

        IVType = DynamicDotProductGen();

            Console.WriteLine("---");

        ConstructorInfo myDTctor = IVType.GetConstructor(aVtypes);
        aVector1 = myDTctor.Invoke(aVargs1);
        aVector2 = myDTctor.Invoke(aVargs2);

        object[] passMe = new object[1];
            passMe[0] = (object)aVector2;

        Console.WriteLine("(10, 10, 10) . (20, 20, 20) = {0}",
                    IVType.InvokeMember("DotProduct",
                            BindingFlags.InvokeMethod,
                            null,
                            aVector1,
                            passMe));

        // +++ OUTPUT +++
        // ---
        // (10, 10, 10) . (20, 20, 20) = 600

    }

}
```

```cpp
[C++]
#using <mscorlib.dll>

using namespace System;
using namespace System::Threading;
using namespace System::Reflection;
using namespace System::Reflection::Emit;

Type* DynamicDotProductGen() {

    Type* ivType = 0;

    Type* temp0 [] = {__typeof(int), __typeof(int), __typeof(int)};
    Type* ctorParams[] = temp0;

    AppDomain* myDomain = Thread::GetDomain();
    AssemblyName* myAsmName = new AssemblyName();
    myAsmName->Name = S"IntVectorAsm";

    AssemblyBuilder* myAsmBuilder = myDomain-
>DefineDynamicAssembly(myAsmName,
        AssemblyBuilderAccess::RunAndSave);

    ModuleBuilder* IntVectorModule = myAsmBuilder-
>DefineDynamicModule(S"IntVectorModule",
        S"Vector.dll");

    TypeBuilder* ivTypeBld = IntVectorModule->DefineType(S"IntVector",
        TypeAttributes::Public);

    FieldBuilder* xField = ivTypeBld->DefineField(S"x", __typeof(int),
        FieldAttributes::Private);
    FieldBuilder* yField = ivTypeBld->DefineField(S"y", __typeof(int),
        FieldAttributes::Private);
    FieldBuilder* zField = ivTypeBld->DefineField(S"z", __typeof(int),
        FieldAttributes::Private);

    Type* objType = Type::GetType(S"System.Object");
    ConstructorInfo* objCtor = objType->GetConstructor(new Type*[0]);

    ConstructorBuilder* ivCtor = ivTypeBld-
>DefineConstructor(MethodAttributes::Public,
        CallingConventions::Standard,
        ctorParams);
    ILGenerator* ctorIL = ivCtor->GetILGenerator();
    ctorIL->Emit(OpCodes::Ldarg_0);
    ctorIL->Emit(OpCodes::Call, objCtor);
    ctorIL->Emit(OpCodes::Ldarg_0);
    ctorIL->Emit(OpCodes::Ldarg_1);
    ctorIL->Emit(OpCodes::Stfld, xField);
    ctorIL->Emit(OpCodes::Ldarg_0);
    ctorIL->Emit(OpCodes::Ldarg_2);
    ctorIL->Emit(OpCodes::Stfld, yField);
    ctorIL->Emit(OpCodes::Ldarg_0);
    ctorIL->Emit(OpCodes::Ldarg_3);
    ctorIL->Emit(OpCodes::Stfld, zField);
    ctorIL->Emit(OpCodes::Ret);

    // This method will find the dot product of the stored vector
    // with another.

    Type* temp1 [] = {ivTypeBld};
    Type* dpParams[] = temp1;

    // Here, you create a MethodBuilder containing the
    // name, the attributes (public, static, private, and so on),
    // the return type (int, in this case), and a array of Type
    // indicating the type of each parameter. Since the sole parameter
    // is a IntVector, the very class you're creating, you will
    // pass in the TypeBuilder (which is derived from Type) instead of
    // a Type object for IntVector, avoiding an exception.

    // -- This method would be declared in C# as:
    //    public int DotProduct(IntVector aVector)
```

```cpp
    MethodBuilder* dotProductMthd = ivTypeBld-
>DefineMethod(S"DotProduct",
        MethodAttributes::Public,
        __typeof(int),
        dpParams);

    // A ILGenerator can now be spawned, attached to the MethodBuilder.

    ILGenerator* mthdIL = dotProductMthd->GetILGenerator();

    // Here's the body of our function, in MSIL form. We're going
    // to find the
    // "dot product" of the current vector instance with the
    // passed vector
    // instance. For reference purposes, the equation is:
    // (x1 * x2) + (y1 * y2) + (z1 * z2) = the dot product

    // First, you'll load the reference to the current instance "this"
    // stored in argument 0 (ldarg.0) onto the stack. Ldfld, the
    // subsequent
    // instruction, will pop the reference off the stack and look up the
    // field "x", specified by the FieldInfo token "xField".

    mthdIL->Emit(OpCodes::Ldarg_0);
    mthdIL->Emit(OpCodes::Ldfld, xField);

    // That completed, the value stored at field "x" is now atop
    // the stack.
    // Now, you'll do the same for the Object reference we passed as a
    // parameter, stored in argument 1 (ldarg.1). After Ldfld executed,
    // you'll have the value stored in field "x" for the passed instance
    // atop the stack.

    mthdIL->Emit(OpCodes::Ldarg_1);
    mthdIL->Emit(OpCodes::Ldfld, xField);

    // There will now be two values atop the stack - the "x" value
    // for the
    // current vector instance, and the "x" value for the passed
    // instance.
    // You'll now multiply them, and push the result onto the
    // evaluation stack.

    mthdIL->Emit(OpCodes::Mul_Ovf_Un);

    // Now, repeat this for the "y" fields of both vectors.

    mthdIL->Emit(OpCodes::Ldarg_0);
    mthdIL->Emit(OpCodes::Ldfld, yField);
    mthdIL->Emit(OpCodes::Ldarg_1);
    mthdIL->Emit(OpCodes::Ldfld, yField);
    mthdIL->Emit(OpCodes::Mul_Ovf_Un);

    // At this time, the results of both multiplications should be atop
    // the stack. You'll now add them and push the result onto
    // the stack.

    mthdIL->Emit(OpCodes->Add_Ovf_Un);

    // Multiply both "z" field and push the result onto the stack.
    mthdIL->Emit(OpCodes::Ldarg_0);
    mthdIL->Emit(OpCodes::Ldfld, zField);
    mthdIL->Emit(OpCodes::Ldarg_1);
    mthdIL->Emit(OpCodes::Ldfld, zField);
    mthdIL->Emit(OpCodes::Mul_Ovf_Un);

    // Finally, add the result of multiplying the "z" fields with the
    // result of the earlier addition, and push the result -
    // the dot product -
    // onto the stack.
    mthdIL->Emit(OpCodes->Add_Ovf_Un);

    // The "ret" opcode will pop the last value from the stack
    // and return it
    // to the calling method. You're all done!
```

```
    mthdIL->Emit(OpCodes::Ret);

    ivType = ivTypeBld->CreateType();

    return ivType;
}

int main() {

    Type* IVType = 0;
    Object* aVector1 = 0;
    Object* aVector2 = 0;

    Type* temp2 [] = {__typeof(int), __typeof(int), __typeof(int)};
    Type* aVtypes[] = temp2;

    Object* temp3 [] = {__box(10), __box(10), __box(10)};
    Object* aVargs1[] = temp3;

    Object* temp4 [] = {__box(20), __box(20), __box(20)};
    Object* aVargs2[] = temp4;

    // Call the  method to build our dynamic class.

    IVType = DynamicDotProductGen();

    Console::WriteLine(S"---");

    ConstructorInfo* myDTctor = IVType->GetConstructor(aVtypes);
    aVector1 = myDTctor->Invoke(aVargs1);
    aVector2 = myDTctor->Invoke(aVargs2);

    Object* passMe[] = new Object*[1];
    passMe->Item[0] = dynamic_cast<Object*>(aVector2);

    Console::WriteLine(S"(10, 10, 10) . (20, 20, 20) = {0}",
        IVType->InvokeMember(S"DotProduct",
        BindingFlags::InvokeMethod,
        0,
        aVector1,
        passMe));
}

    // +++ OUTPUT +++
    // ---
    // (10, 10, 10) . (20, 20, 20) = 600
```

Requirements

Namespace: System.Reflection.Emit

Platforms: Windows 98, Windows NT 4.0,
Windows Millennium Edition, Windows 2000,
Windows XP Home Edition, Windows XP Professional,
Windows .NET Server family

Assembly: Mscorlib (in Mscorlib.dll)

TypeBuilder.UnspecifiedTypeSize Field

Represents that total size for the type is not specified.

```
[Visual Basic]
Public Const UnspecifiedTypeSize As Integer
[C#]
public const int UnspecifiedTypeSize;
[C++]
public: const int UnspecifiedTypeSize;
[JScript]
public var UnspecifiedTypeSize : int;
```

Requirements

Platforms: Windows 98, Windows NT 4.0,
Windows Millennium Edition, Windows 2000,
Windows XP Home Edition, Windows XP Professional,
Windows .NET Server family

TypeBuilder.Assembly Property

Retrieves the dynamic assembly that contains this type definition.

```
[Visual Basic]
Overrides Public ReadOnly Property Assembly As Assembly
[C#]
public override Assembly Assembly {get;}
[C++]
public: __property Assembly* get_Assembly();
[JScript]
public override function get Assembly() : Assembly;
```

Property Value

Read-only. Retrieves the dynamic assembly that contains this type
definition.

Requirements

Platforms: Windows 98, Windows NT 4.0,
Windows Millennium Edition, Windows 2000,
Windows XP Home Edition, Windows XP Professional,
Windows .NET Server family

TypeBuilder.AssemblyQualifiedName Property

Returns the full name of this type qualified by the display name of
the assembly.

```
[Visual Basic]
Overrides Public ReadOnly Property AssemblyQualifiedName As String
[C#]
public override string AssemblyQualifiedName {get;}
[C++]
public: __property String* get_AssemblyQualifiedName();
[JScript]
public override function get AssemblyQualifiedName() : String;
```

Property Value

Read-only. The full name of this type qualified by the display name
of the assembly.

Remarks

The format of the returned string is:

<FullTypeName>, <AssemblyDisplayName>

See **AssemblyName** for a description of the format of the display
name of an assembly.

Example

Requirements

Platforms: Windows 98, Windows NT 4.0,
Windows Millennium Edition, Windows 2000,
Windows XP Home Edition, Windows XP Professional,
Windows .NET Server family

TypeBuilder.BaseType Property

Retrieves the base type of this type.

```
[Visual Basic]
Overrides Public ReadOnly Property BaseType As Type
[C#]
public override Type BaseType {get;}
[C++]
public: __property Type* get_BaseType();
[JScript]
public override function get BaseType() : Type;
```

Property Value

Read-only. Retrieves the base type of this type.

Requirements

Platforms: Windows 98, Windows NT 4.0,
Windows Millennium Edition, Windows 2000,
Windows XP Home Edition, Windows XP Professional,
Windows .NET Server family

TypeBuilder.DeclaringType Property

Returns the type that declared this type.

```
[Visual Basic]
Overrides Public ReadOnly Property DeclaringType As Type
[C#]
public override Type DeclaringType {get;}
[C++]
public: __property Type* get_DeclaringType();
[JScript]
public override function get DeclaringType() : Type;
```

Property Value

Read-only. The type that declared this type.

Requirements

Platforms: Windows 98, Windows NT 4.0,
Windows Millennium Edition, Windows 2000,
Windows XP Home Edition, Windows XP Professional,
Windows .NET Server family

TypeBuilder.FullName Property

Retrieves the full path of this type.

```
[Visual Basic]
Overrides Public ReadOnly Property FullName As String
[C#]
public override string FullName {get;}
[C++]
public: __property String* get_FullName();
[JScript]
public override function get FullName() : String;
```

Property Value

Read-only. Retrieves the full path of this type.

Remarks

The returned format is "enclosingTypeFullName+nestedTypeName"
for nested types and "typeName" for non-nested types.

Requirements

Platforms: Windows 98, Windows NT 4.0,
Windows Millennium Edition, Windows 2000,
Windows XP Home Edition, Windows XP Professional,
Windows .NET Server family

TypeBuilder.GUID Property

Retrieves the GUID of this type.

```
[Visual Basic]
Overrides Public ReadOnly Property GUID As Guid
[C#]
public override Guid GUID {get;}
[C++]
public: __property Guid get_GUID();
[JScript]
public override function get GUID() : Guid;
```

Property Value

Read-only. Retrieves the GUID of this type

Exceptions

Exception Type	Condition
NotSupportedException	This method is not currently supported for incomplete types.

Remarks

Retrieve the type using **GetType** or **GetType** and use reflection on
the retrieved type.

Requirements

Platforms: Windows 98, Windows NT 4.0,
Windows Millennium Edition, Windows 2000,
Windows XP Home Edition, Windows XP Professional,
Windows .NET Server family

TypeBuilder.Module Property

Retrieves the dynamic module that contains this type definition.

```
[Visual Basic]
Overrides Public ReadOnly Property Module As Module
[C#]
public override Module Module {get;}
[C++]
public: __property Module* get_Module();
[JScript]
public override function get Module() : Module;
```

Property Value

Read-only. Retrieves the dynamic module that contains this type
definition.

Requirements

Platforms: Windows 98, Windows NT 4.0,
Windows Millennium Edition, Windows 2000,
Windows XP Home Edition, Windows XP Professional,
Windows .NET Server family

TypeBuilder.Name Property

Retrieves the name of this type.

```
[Visual Basic]
Overrides Public ReadOnly Property Name As String
[C#]
public override string Name {get;}
[C++]
public: __property String* get_Name();
[JScript]
public override function get Name() : String;
```

Property Value

Read-only. Retrieves the **String** name of this type.

Requirements

Platforms: Windows 98, Windows NT 4.0,
Windows Millennium Edition, Windows 2000,
Windows XP Home Edition, Windows XP Professional,
Windows .NET Server family

TypeBuilder.Namespace Property

Retrieves the namespace where this **TypeBuilder** is defined.

```
[Visual Basic]
Overrides Public ReadOnly Property Namespace As String
[C#]
public override string Namespace {get;}
[C++]
public: __property String* get_Namespace();
[JScript]
public override function get Namespace() : String;
```

Property Value

Read-only. Retrieves the namespace where this **TypeBuilder** is defined.

Requirements

Platforms: Windows 98, Windows NT 4.0,
Windows Millennium Edition, Windows 2000,
Windows XP Home Edition, Windows XP Professional,
Windows .NET Server family

TypeBuilder.PackingSize Property

Retrieves the packing size of this type.

```
[Visual Basic]
Public ReadOnly Property PackingSize As PackingSize
[C#]
public PackingSize PackingSize {get;}
[C++]
public: __property PackingSize get_PackingSize();
[JScript]
public function get PackingSize() : PackingSize;
```

Property Value

Read-only. Retrieves the packing size of this type.

Requirements

Platforms: Windows 98, Windows NT 4.0,
Windows Millennium Edition, Windows 2000,
Windows XP Home Edition, Windows XP Professional,
Windows .NET Server family

TypeBuilder.ReflectedType Property

Returns the type that was used to obtain this type.

```
[Visual Basic]
Overrides Public ReadOnly Property ReflectedType As Type
[C#]
public override Type ReflectedType {get;}
[C++]
public: __property Type* get_ReflectedType();
[JScript]
public override function get ReflectedType() : Type;
```

Property Value

Read-only. The type that was used to obtain this type.

Requirements

Platforms: Windows 98, Windows NT 4.0,
Windows Millennium Edition, Windows 2000,
Windows XP Home Edition, Windows XP Professional,
Windows .NET Server family

TypeBuilder.Size Property

Retrieves the total size of a type.

```
[Visual Basic]
Public ReadOnly Property Size As Integer
[C#]
public int Size {get;}
[C++]
public: __property int get_Size();
[JScript]
public function get Size() : int;
```

Property Value

Read-only. Retrieves this type's total size.

Requirements

Platforms: Windows 98, Windows NT 4.0,
Windows Millennium Edition, Windows 2000,
Windows XP Home Edition, Windows XP Professional,
Windows .NET Server family

TypeBuilder.TypeHandle Property

Not supported in dynamic modules.

```
[Visual Basic]
Overrides Public ReadOnly Property TypeHandle As RuntimeTypeHandle
[C#]
public override RuntimeTypeHandle TypeHandle {get;}
[C++]
public: __property RuntimeTypeHandle get_TypeHandle();
[JScript]
public override function get TypeHandle() : RuntimeTypeHandle;
```

Property Value

Read-only.

Exceptions

Exception Type	Condition
NotSupportedException	Not supported in dynamic modules.

Remarks

Retrieve the type using **GetType** or **GetType** and use reflection on the retrieved type.

Requirements

Platforms: Windows 98, Windows NT 4.0, Windows Millennium Edition, Windows 2000, Windows XP Home Edition, Windows XP Professional, Windows .NET Server family

TypeBuilder.TypeToken Property

Returns the type token of this type.

```
[Visual Basic]
Public ReadOnly Property TypeToken As TypeToken
[C#]
public TypeToken TypeToken {get;}
[C++]
public: __property TypeToken get_TypeToken();
[JScript]
public function get TypeToken() : TypeToken;
```

Property Value

Read-only. Returns the **TypeToken** of this type.

Requirements

Platforms: Windows 98, Windows NT 4.0, Windows Millennium Edition, Windows 2000, Windows XP Home Edition, Windows XP Professional, Windows .NET Server family

TypeBuilder.UnderlyingSystemType Property

Returns the underlying system type for this **TypeBuilder**.

```
[Visual Basic]
Overrides Public ReadOnly Property UnderlyingSystemType As Type _
    Implements IReflect.UnderlyingSystemType
[C#]
public override Type UnderlyingSystemType {get;}
[C++]
public: __property Type* get_UnderlyingSystemType();
[JScript]
public override function get UnderlyingSystemType() : Type;
```

Property Value

Read-only. Returns the underlying system type.

Implements

IReflect.UnderlyingSystemType

Exceptions

Exception Type	Condition
InvalidOperationException	This type is an enum but there is no underlying system type.

Requirements

Platforms: Windows 98, Windows NT 4.0, Windows Millennium Edition, Windows 2000, Windows XP Home Edition, Windows XP Professional, Windows .NET Server family

TypeBuilder.AddDeclarativeSecurity Method

Adds declarative security to this type.

```
[Visual Basic]
Public Sub AddDeclarativeSecurity( _
    ByVal action As SecurityAction, _
    ByVal pset As PermissionSet _
)
[C#]
public void AddDeclarativeSecurity(
    SecurityAction action,
    PermissionSet pset
);
[C++]
public: void AddDeclarativeSecurity(
    SecurityAction action,
    PermissionSet* pset
);
[JScript]
public function AddDeclarativeSecurity(
    action : SecurityAction,
    pset : PermissionSet
);
```

Parameters

action
    The security action to be taken such as Demand, Assert, and so on.
pset
    The set of permissions the action applies to.

Exceptions

Exception Type	Condition
ArgumentOutOfRange-Exception	The *action* is invalid (**RequestMinimum, RequestOptional**, and **RequestRefuse** are invalid).
InvalidOperationException	The containing type has been created using **CreateType**. -or- The permission set *pset* contains an action that was added earlier by **AddDeclarativeSecurity**.
ArgumentNullException	*pset* is a null reference (**Nothing** in Visual Basic).

Remarks

AddDeclarativeSecurity may be called several times with each call specifying a security action (such as Demand, Assert, or Deny) and a set of permissions that apply to the action.

Example

See related example in the **System.Reflection.Emit.TypeBuilder** class topic.

Requirements

Platforms: Windows 98, Windows NT 4.0, Windows Millennium Edition, Windows 2000, Windows XP Home Edition, Windows XP Professional, Windows .NET Server family

TypeBuilder.AddInterfaceImplementation Method

Adds an interface that this type implements.

```
[Visual Basic]
Public Sub AddInterfaceImplementation( _
   ByVal interfaceType As Type _
)
[C#]
public void AddInterfaceImplementation(
   Type interfaceType
);
[C++]
public: void AddInterfaceImplementation(
   Type* interfaceType
);
[JScript]
public function AddInterfaceImplementation(
   interfaceType : Type
);
```

Parameters

interfaceType
    The interface that this type implements.

Exceptions

Exception Type	Condition
ArgumentNullException	*interfaceType* is a null reference (**Nothing** in Visual Basic).
InvalidOperationException	The type was previously created using **CreateType**.

Example

See related example in the **System.Reflection.Emit.TypeBuilder** class topic.

Requirements

Platforms: Windows 98, Windows NT 4.0, Windows Millennium Edition, Windows 2000, Windows XP Home Edition, Windows XP Professional, Windows .NET Server family

TypeBuilder.CreateType Method

Creates a **Type** object for the class. After defining fields and methods on the class, **CreateType** is called in order to load its **Type** object.

```
[Visual Basic]
Public Function CreateType() As Type
[C#]
public Type CreateType();
[C++]
public: Type* CreateType();
[JScript]
public function CreateType() : Type;
```

Return Value

Returns the new **Type** object for this class.

Exceptions

Exception Type	Condition
InvalidOperation-Exception	This type has been previously created.
	-or-
	The enclosing type has not been created.
	-or-
	This type is non-abstract and contains an abstract method.
	-or-
	This type is abstract and has a method with a method body.
	-or-
	This type is not an abstract class or an interface and has a method without a method body.
NotSupportedException	If the type contains invalid Microsoft Intermediate Language (MSIL) code.
	-or-
	The branch target is specified using a 1-byte offset but the target is at a distance greater than 127 bytes from the branch.

Remarks

If this type is a nested type, the **CreateType** must be called on the nesting (enclosing) type before calling the method on this type.

If the nesting type contains a field that is a value type defined as a nested type (for example, a field that is an enum defined as a nested type), calling **CreateType** on the nesting type will generate a **TypeResolve** event. This is because the loader cannot determine the size of the nesting type until the nested type has been completed. The caller should define a handler for the **TypeResolve** event to complete the definition of the nested type by calling **CreateType** on the nested type's **TypeBuilder**. The following example shows how to define the event handler.

Requirements

Platforms: Windows 98, Windows NT 4.0, Windows Millennium Edition, Windows 2000, Windows XP Home Edition, Windows XP Professional, Windows .NET Server family

TypeBuilder.DefineConstructor Method

Adds a new constructor to the class, with the given attributes and signature.

```
[Visual Basic]
Public Function DefineConstructor( _
   ByVal attributes As MethodAttributes, _
   ByVal callingConvention As CallingConventions, _
   ByVal parameterTypes() As Type _
) As ConstructorBuilder
[C#]
public ConstructorBuilder DefineConstructor(
   MethodAttributes attributes,
```

```
    CallingConventions callingConvention,
    Type[] parameterTypes
);
[C++]
public: ConstructorBuilder* DefineConstructor(
    MethodAttributes attributes,
    CallingConventions callingConvention,
    Type* parameterTypes[]
);
[JScript]
public function DefineConstructor(
    attributes : MethodAttributes,
    callingConvention : CallingConventions,
    parameterTypes : Type[]
) : ConstructorBuilder;
```

Parameters

attributes
> The attributes of the constructor.

callingConvention
> The calling convention of the constructor.

parameterTypes
> The types of the parameters of the constructor.

Return Value

The defined constructor.

Exceptions

Exception Type	Condition
InvalidOperationException	The type was previously created using **CreateType**.

Example

See related example in the **System.Reflection.Emit.TypeBuilder** class topic.

Requirements

Platforms: Windows 98, Windows NT 4.0, Windows Millennium Edition, Windows 2000, Windows XP Home Edition, Windows XP Professional, Windows .NET Server family

TypeBuilder.DefineDefaultConstructor Method

Defines the default constructor. The constructor defined here will simply call the default constructor of the parent.

```
[Visual Basic]
Public Function DefineDefaultConstructor( _
    ByVal attributes As MethodAttributes _
) As ConstructorBuilder
[C#]
public ConstructorBuilder DefineDefaultConstructor(
    MethodAttributes attributes
);
[C++]
public: ConstructorBuilder* DefineDefaultConstructor(
    MethodAttributes attributes
);
[JScript]
public function DefineDefaultConstructor(
    attributes : MethodAttributes
) : ConstructorBuilder;
```

Parameters

attributes
> A **MethodAttributes** object representing the attributes to be applied to the constructor.

Return Value

Returns the constructor.

Exceptions

Exception Type	Condition
NotSupportedException	The parent class does not have a default constructor

Remarks

Since the default constructor is automatically defined, it is only necessary to call this method if the attributes on the default constructor should be set to something other than MethodBase.Constructor. This method is provided here to make it easier to set the attributes.

Example

See related example in the **System.Reflection.Emit.TypeBuilder** class topic.

Requirements

Platforms: Windows 98, Windows NT 4.0, Windows Millennium Edition, Windows 2000, Windows XP Home Edition, Windows XP Professional, Windows .NET Server family

TypeBuilder.DefineEvent Method

Adds a new event to the class, with the given name, attributes and event type.

```
[Visual Basic]
Public Function DefineEvent( _
    ByVal name As String, _
    ByVal attributes As EventAttributes, _
    ByVal eventtype As Type _
) As EventBuilder
[C#]
public EventBuilder DefineEvent(
    string name,
    EventAttributes attributes,
    Type eventtype
);
[C++]
public: EventBuilder* DefineEvent(
    String* name,
    EventAttributes attributes,
    Type* eventtype
);
[JScript]
public function DefineEvent(
    name : String,
    attributes : EventAttributes,
    eventtype : Type
) : EventBuilder;
```

Parameters

name
> The name of the event. *name* cannot contain embedded nulls.

attributes
> The attributes of the event.

eventtype
    The type of the event.

Return Value

The defined event.

Exceptions

Exception Type	Condition
ArgumentException **ArgumentNullException**	The length of *name* is zero. *name* is a null reference (**Nothing** in Visual Basic). -or- *eventtype* is a null reference (**Nothing**).
InvalidOperationException	The type was previously created using **CreateType**

Requirements

Platforms: Windows 98, Windows NT 4.0, Windows Millennium Edition, Windows 2000, Windows XP Home Edition, Windows XP Professional, Windows .NET Server family

TypeBuilder.DefineField Method

Adds a new field to the class, with the given name, attributes and field type.

```
[Visual Basic]
Public Function DefineField( _
   ByVal fieldName As String, _
   ByVal type As Type, _
   ByVal attributes As FieldAttributes _
) As FieldBuilder
[C#]
public FieldBuilder DefineField(
   string fieldName,
   Type type,
   FieldAttributes attributes
);
[C++]
public: FieldBuilder* DefineField(
   String* fieldName,
   Type* type,
   FieldAttributes attributes
);
[JScript]
public function DefineField(
   fieldName : String,
   type : Type,
   attributes : FieldAttributes
) : FieldBuilder;
```

Parameters

fieldName
    The name of the field. *fieldName* cannot contain embedded nulls.
type
    The type of the field
attributes
    The attributes of the field.

Return Value

The defined field.

Exceptions

Exception Type	Condition
ArgumentException	The length of *fieldName* is zero. -or- *type* is System.Void. -or- A total size was specified for the parent class of this field.
ArgumentNullException	*fieldName* is a null reference (**Nothing** in Visual Basic).
InvalidOperationException	The type was previously created using **CreateType TypeBuilder**.

Requirements

Platforms: Windows 98, Windows NT 4.0, Windows Millennium Edition, Windows 2000, Windows XP Home Edition, Windows XP Professional, Windows .NET Server family

TypeBuilder.DefineInitializedData Method

Defines initialized data field in the .sdata section of the portable executable (PE) file.

```
[Visual Basic]
Public Function DefineInitializedData( _
   ByVal name As String, _
   ByVal data() As Byte, _
   ByVal attributes As FieldAttributes _
) As FieldBuilder
[C#]
public FieldBuilder DefineInitializedData(
   string name,
   byte[] data,
   FieldAttributes attributes
);
[C++]
public: FieldBuilder* DefineInitializedData(
   String* name,
   unsigned char data __gc[],
   FieldAttributes attributes
);
[JScript]
public function DefineInitializedData(
   name : String,
   data : Byte[],
   attributes : FieldAttributes
) : FieldBuilder;
```

Parameters

name
    The name used to refer to the data. *name* cannot contain embedded nulls.
data
    The blob of data.
attributes
    The attributes for the field.

Return Value

A field to reference the data.

Exceptions

Exception Type	Condition
ArgumentException	Length of *name* is zero.
	-or-
	The size of the data is less than or equal to zero or greater than or equal to 0x3f0000.
ArgumentNullException	*name* or *data* is a null reference (**Nothing** in Visual Basic).
InvalidOperationException	**CreateType** has been previously called.

Remarks

The field that you create with this method will be static (**Shared** in Visual Basic), even if you do not include **FieldAttributes.Static** in the *attributes* parameter.

Requirements

Platforms: Windows 98, Windows NT 4.0, Windows Millennium Edition, Windows 2000, Windows XP Home Edition, Windows XP Professional, Windows .NET Server family

TypeBuilder.DefineMethod Method

Defines a method.

Overload List

Adds a new method to the class, with the given name and method signature.

> [Visual Basic] **Overloads Public Function DefineMethod (String, MethodAttributes, Type, Type()) As MethodBuilder**
>
> [C#] **public MethodBuilder DefineMethod(string, MethodAttributes, Type, Type[]);**
>
> [C++] **public: MethodBuilder* DefineMethod(String*, MethodAttributes, Type*, Type[]);**
>
> [JScript] **public function DefineMethod(String, MethodAttributes, Type, Type[]) : MethodBuilder;**

Adds a new method to the class, with the given name and method signature.

> [Visual Basic] **Overloads Public Function DefineMethod (String, MethodAttributes, CallingConventions, Type, Type()) As MethodBuilder**
>
> [C#] **public MethodBuilder DefineMethod(string, MethodAttributes, CallingConventions, Type, Type[]);**
>
> [C++] **public: MethodBuilder* DefineMethod(String*, MethodAttributes, CallingConventions, Type*, Type[]);**
>
> [JScript] **public function DefineMethod(String, MethodAttributes, CallingConventions, Type, Type[]) : MethodBuilder;**

Example

See related example in the **System.Reflection.Emit.TypeBuilder** class topic.

TypeBuilder.DefineMethod Method (String, MethodAttributes, Type, Type[])

Adds a new method to the class, with the given name and method signature.

```
[Visual Basic]
Overloads Public Function DefineMethod( _
   ByVal name As String, _
   ByVal attributes As MethodAttributes, _
   ByVal returnType As Type, _
   ByVal parameterTypes() As Type _
) As MethodBuilder
[C#]
public MethodBuilder DefineMethod(
   string name,
   MethodAttributes attributes,
   Type returnType,
   Type[] parameterTypes
);
[C++]
public: MethodBuilder* DefineMethod(
   String* name,
   MethodAttributes attributes,
   Type* returnType,
   Type* parameterTypes[]
);
[JScript]
public function DefineMethod(
   name : String,
   attributes : MethodAttributes,
   returnType : Type,
   parameterTypes : Type[]
) : MethodBuilder;
```

Parameters

name
> The name of the method. *name* cannot contain embedded nulls.

attributes
> The attributes of the method.

returnType
> The return type of the method.

parameterTypes
> The types of the parameters of the method.

Return Value

The defined method.

Exceptions

Exception Type	Condition
ArgumentException	The length of *name* is zero.
	-or-
	The type of the parent of this method is an interface and this method is not virtual.
ArgumentNullException	*name* is a null reference (**Nothing** in Visual Basic).
InvalidOperationException	The type was previously created using **CreateType**

Example

See related example in the **System.Reflection.Emit.TypeBuilder** class topic.

Requirements

Platforms: Windows 98, Windows NT 4.0, Windows Millennium Edition, Windows 2000, Windows XP Home Edition, Windows XP Professional, Windows .NET Server family

TypeBuilder.DefineMethod Method (String, MethodAttributes, CallingConventions, Type, Type[])

Adds a new method to the class, with the given name and method signature.

```
[Visual Basic]
Overloads Public Function DefineMethod( _
    ByVal name As String, _
    ByVal attributes As MethodAttributes, _
    ByVal callingConvention As CallingConventions, _
    ByVal returnType As Type, _
    ByVal parameterTypes() As Type _
) As MethodBuilder
[C#]
public MethodBuilder DefineMethod(
    string name,
    MethodAttributes attributes,
    CallingConventions callingConvention,
    Type returnType,
    Type[] parameterTypes
);
[C++]
public: MethodBuilder* DefineMethod(
    String* name,
    MethodAttributes attributes,
    CallingConventions callingConvention,
    Type* returnType,
    Type* parameterTypes[]
);
[JScript]
public function DefineMethod(
    name : String,
    attributes : MethodAttributes,
    callingConvention : CallingConventions,
    returnType : Type,
    parameterTypes : Type[]
) : MethodBuilder;
```

Parameters

name
    The name of the method. *name* cannot contain embedded nulls.
attributes
    The attributes of the method.
callingConvention
    The calling convention of the method.
returnType
    The return type of the method.
parameterTypes
    The types of the parameters of the method.

Return Value

The defined method.

Exceptions

Exception Type	Condition
ArgumentException	The length of *name* is zero.
	-or-
	The type of the parent of this method is an interface and this method is not virtual.
ArgumentNullException	*name* is a null reference (**Nothing** in Visual Basic).
InvalidOperationException	The type was previously created using **CreateType**

Example

See related example in the **System.Reflection.Emit.TypeBuilder** class topic.

Requirements

Platforms: Windows 98, Windows NT 4.0, Windows Millennium Edition, Windows 2000, Windows XP Home Edition, Windows XP Professional, Windows .NET Server family

TypeBuilder.DefineMethodOverride Method

Specifies a given method body that implements a given method declaration.

```
[Visual Basic]
Public Sub DefineMethodOverride( _
    ByVal methodInfoBody As MethodInfo, _
    ByVal methodInfoDeclaration As MethodInfo _
)
[C#]
public void DefineMethodOverride(
    MethodInfo methodInfoBody,
    MethodInfo methodInfoDeclaration
);
[C++]
public: void DefineMethodOverride(
    MethodInfo* methodInfoBody,
    MethodInfo* methodInfoDeclaration
);
[JScript]
public function DefineMethodOverride(
    methodInfoBody : MethodInfo,
    methodInfoDeclaration : MethodInfo
);
```

Parameters

methodInfoBody
    The method body to be used. This should be a **MethodBuilder** object.
methodInfoDeclaration
    The method whose declaration is to be used.

Exceptions

Exception Type	Condition
ArgumentException	*methodInfoBody* does not belong to this class.

Exception Type	Condition
ArgumentNullException	*methodInfoBody* or *methodInfoDeclaration* is a null reference (**Nothing** in Visual Basic).
InvalidOperationException	The type was previously created using **CreateType**.
	-or-
	The method *methodInfoBody* 's declaring type is not this type.

Remarks

DefineMethodOverride defines a method impl. A method impl is a token point to an implementation and a token pointing to a declaration that the body will implement. The body must be defined on the type the method impl is defined and the body must be virtual. The declaration can be made to a method defined on an interface implemented by the type, a method on a derived class or a method defined in the type. If the declaration is on an interface only, the slot defined for the interface is altered. If the declaration is made to a method on a base type then the slot for the method is overridden and any duplicates for the overridden method are also replaced. The method overridden cannot be the actual method declared. If the method is on the same type then the slot is replaced and any duplicates for the replaced methods are overridden.

Example

See related example in the **System.Reflection.Emit.TypeBuilder** class topic.

Requirements

Platforms: Windows 98, Windows NT 4.0, Windows Millennium Edition, Windows 2000, Windows XP Home Edition, Windows XP Professional, Windows .NET Server family

TypeBuilder.DefineNestedType Method

Defines a nested type.

Overload List

Defines a nested type given its name.

[Visual Basic] **Overloads Public Function DefineNestedType (String) As TypeBuilder**

[C#] **public TypeBuilder DefineNestedType(string);**

[C++] **public: TypeBuilder* DefineNestedType(String*);**

[JScript] **public function DefineNestedType(String) : TypeBuilder;**

Defines a nested type given its name and attributes.

[Visual Basic] **Overloads Public Function DefineNestedType (String, TypeAttributes) As TypeBuilder**

[C#] **public TypeBuilder DefineNestedType(string, TypeAttributes);**

[C++] **public: TypeBuilder* DefineNestedType(String*, TypeAttributes);**

[JScript] **public function DefineNestedType(String, TypeAttributes) : TypeBuilder;**

Defines a nested type given its name, attributes, and the type that it extends.

[Visual Basic] **Overloads Public Function DefineNestedType (String, TypeAttributes, Type) As TypeBuilder**

[C#] **public TypeBuilder DefineNestedType(string, TypeAttributes, Type);**

[C++] **public: TypeBuilder* DefineNestedType(String*, TypeAttributes, Type*);**

[JScript] **public function DefineNestedType(String, TypeAttributes, Type) : TypeBuilder;**

Defines a nested type given its name, attributes, the total size of the type, and the type that it extends.

[Visual Basic] **Overloads Public Function DefineNestedType (String, TypeAttributes, Type, Integer) As TypeBuilder**

[C#] **public TypeBuilder DefineNestedType(string, TypeAttributes, Type, int);**

[C++] **public: TypeBuilder* DefineNestedType(String*, TypeAttributes, Type*, int);**

[JScript] **public function DefineNestedType(String, TypeAttributes, Type, int) : TypeBuilder;**

Defines a nested type given its name, attributes, the total size of the type, and the type that it extends.

[Visual Basic] **Overloads Public Function DefineNestedType (String, TypeAttributes, Type, PackingSize) As TypeBuilder**

[C#] **public TypeBuilder DefineNestedType(string, TypeAttributes, Type, PackingSize);**

[C++] **public: TypeBuilder* DefineNestedType(String*, TypeAttributes, Type*, PackingSize);**

[JScript] **public function DefineNestedType(String, TypeAttributes, Type, PackingSize) : TypeBuilder;**

Defines a nested type given its name, attributes, the type that it extends, and the interfaces that it implements.

[Visual Basic] **Overloads Public Function DefineNestedType (String, TypeAttributes, Type, Type()) As TypeBuilder**

[C#] **public TypeBuilder DefineNestedType(string, TypeAttributes, Type, Type[]);**

[C++] **public: TypeBuilder* DefineNestedType(String*, TypeAttributes, Type*, Type[]);**

[JScript] **public function DefineNestedType(String, TypeAttributes, Type, Type[]) : TypeBuilder;**

TypeBuilder.DefineNestedType Method (String)

Defines a nested type given its name.

```
[Visual Basic]
Overloads Public Function DefineNestedType( _
   ByVal name As String _
) As TypeBuilder
[C#]
public TypeBuilder DefineNestedType(
   string name
);
[C++]
public: TypeBuilder* DefineNestedType(
   String* name
);
[JScript]
public function DefineNestedType(
   name : String
) : TypeBuilder;
```

Parameters

name

The full path of the type. *name* cannot contain embedded nulls.

Return Value

The defined nested type.

Exceptions

Exception Type	Condition
ArgumentException	Length of *name* is zero.
ArgumentNullException	*name* is a null reference (**Nothing** in Visual Basic).
	-or-
	A null interface is specified in the *interfaces* array.
InvalidOperationException	The type was previously created using **CreateType**.

Remarks

The nested type needs to be complete before you can reflect on it using **GetMembers**, **GetNestedType**, or **GetNestedTypes**.

Requirements

Platforms: Windows 98, Windows NT 4.0, Windows Millennium Edition, Windows 2000, Windows XP Home Edition, Windows XP Professional, Windows .NET Server family

TypeBuilder.DefineNestedType Method (String, TypeAttributes)

Defines a nested type given its name and attributes.

```
[Visual Basic]
Overloads Public Function DefineNestedType( _
   ByVal name As String, _
   ByVal attr As TypeAttributes _
) As TypeBuilder
[C#]
public TypeBuilder DefineNestedType(
   string name,
   TypeAttributes attr
);
[C++]
public: TypeBuilder* DefineNestedType(
   String* name,
   TypeAttributes attr
);
[JScript]
public function DefineNestedType(
   name : String,
   attr : TypeAttributes
) : TypeBuilder;
```

Parameters

name

The full path of the type. *name* cannot contain embedded nulls.

attr

The attributes of the type.

Return Value

The defined nested type.

Exceptions

Exception Type	Condition
ArgumentException	The nested attribute is not specified.
	-or-
	This type is sealed.
	-or-
	This type is an array.
	-or-
	This type is an interface but the nested type is not an interface.
	-or-
	The length of *name* is zero.
ArgumentNullException	*name* is a null reference (**Nothing** in Visual Basic).
	- or-
	A null interface is specified in the *interfaces* array.
InvalidOperationException	The type was previously created using **CreateType**.

Remarks

The nested type needs to be complete before you can reflect on it using **GetMembers**, **GetNestedType**, or **GetNestedTypes**.

Requirements

Platforms: Windows 98, Windows NT 4.0, Windows Millennium Edition, Windows 2000, Windows XP Home Edition, Windows XP Professional, Windows .NET Server family

TypeBuilder.DefineNestedType Method (String, TypeAttributes, Type)

Defines a nested type given its name, attributes, and the type that it extends.

```
[Visual Basic]
Overloads Public Function DefineNestedType( _
   ByVal name As String, _
   ByVal attr As TypeAttributes, _
   ByVal parent As Type _
) As TypeBuilder
[C#]
public TypeBuilder DefineNestedType(
   string name,
   TypeAttributes attr,
   Type parent
);
[C++]
public: TypeBuilder* DefineNestedType(
   String* name,
   TypeAttributes attr,
   Type* parent
);
[JScript]
public function DefineNestedType(
   name : String,
   attr : TypeAttributes,
   parent : Type
) : TypeBuilder;
```

Parameters

name

The full path of the type. *name* cannot contain embedded nulls.

attr

The attributes of the type.

parent

The type that the nested type extends.

Return Value

The defined nested type.

Exceptions

Exception Type	Condition
ArgumentException	The nested attribute is not specified.
	-or-
	This type is sealed.
	-or-
	This type is an array.
	-or-
	This type is an interface but the nested type is not an interface.
	-or-
	The length of *name* is zero.
ArgumentNullException	*name* is a null reference (**Nothing** in Visual Basic).
	- or-
	A null interface is specified in the *interfaces* array.
InvalidOperationException	The type was previously created using **CreateType**.

Remarks

The nested type needs to be complete before you can reflect on it using **GetMembers**, **GetNestedType**, or **GetNestedTypes**.

Requirements

Platforms: Windows 98, Windows NT 4.0, Windows Millennium Edition, Windows 2000, Windows XP Home Edition, Windows XP Professional, Windows .NET Server family

TypeBuilder.DefineNestedType Method (String, TypeAttributes, Type, Int32)

Defines a nested type given its name, attributes, the total size of the type, and the type that it extends.

```
[Visual Basic]
Overloads Public Function DefineNestedType( _
    ByVal name As String, _
    ByVal attr As TypeAttributes, _
    ByVal parent As Type, _
    ByVal typeSize As Integer _
) As TypeBuilder
[C#]
public TypeBuilder DefineNestedType(
    string name,
    TypeAttributes attr,
    Type parent,
    int typeSize
);
```

```
[C++]
public: TypeBuilder* DefineNestedType(
    String* name,
    TypeAttributes attr,
    Type* parent,
    int typeSize
);
[JScript]
public function DefineNestedType(
    name : String,
    attr : TypeAttributes,
    parent : Type,
    typeSize : int
) : TypeBuilder;
```

Parameters

name

The full path of the type. *name* cannot contain embedded nulls.

attr

The attributes of the type.

parent

The type that the nested type extends.

typeSize

The total size of the type.

Return Value

The defined nested type.

Exceptions

Exception Type	Condition
ArgumentException	The nested attribute is not specified.
	-or-
	This type is sealed.
	-or-
	This type is an array.
	-or-
	This type is an interface but the nested type is not an interface.
	-or-
	The length of *name* is zero.
ArgumentNullException	*name* is a null reference (**Nothing** in Visual Basic).
	- or-
	A null interface is specified in the *interfaces* array.
InvalidOperationException	if the type was previously created using **CreateType**.

Remarks

The nested type needs to be complete before you can reflect on it using **GetMembers**, **GetNestedType**, or **GetNestedTypes**.

Requirements

Platforms: Windows 98, Windows NT 4.0, Windows Millennium Edition, Windows 2000, Windows XP Home Edition, Windows XP Professional, Windows .NET Server family

TypeBuilder.DefineNestedType Method (String, TypeAttributes, Type, PackingSize)

Defines a nested type given its name, attributes, the total size of the type, and the type that it extends.

```
[Visual Basic]
Overloads Public Function DefineNestedType( _
    ByVal name As String, _
    ByVal attr As TypeAttributes, _
    ByVal parent As Type, _
    ByVal packSize As PackingSize _
) As TypeBuilder
[C#]
public TypeBuilder DefineNestedType(
    string name,
    TypeAttributes attr,
    Type parent,
    PackingSize packSize
);
[C++]
public: TypeBuilder* DefineNestedType(
    String* name,
    TypeAttributes attr,
    Type* parent,
    PackingSize packSize
);
[JScript]
public function DefineNestedType(
    name : String,
    attr : TypeAttributes,
    parent : Type,
    packSize : PackingSize
) : TypeBuilder;
```

Parameters

name
> The full path of the type. *name* cannot contain embedded nulls.

attr
> The attributes of the type.

parent
> The type that the nested type extends.

packSize
> The packing size of the type.

Return Value

The defined nested type.

Exceptions

Exception Type	Condition
ArgumentException	The nested attribute is not specified.
	-or-
	This type is sealed.
	-or-
	This type is an array.
	-or-
	This type is an interface but the nested type is not an interface.
	-or-
	The length of *name* is zero.

Exception Type	Condition
ArgumentNullException	*name* is a null reference (**Nothing** in Visual Basic).
	- or-
	A null interface is specified in the *interfaces* array.
InvalidOperationException	The type was previously created using **CreateType**.

Remarks

The nested type needs to be complete before you can reflect on it using **GetMembers**, **GetNestedType**, or **GetNestedTypes**.

Requirements

Platforms: Windows 98, Windows NT 4.0, Windows Millennium Edition, Windows 2000, Windows XP Home Edition, Windows XP Professional, Windows .NET Server family

TypeBuilder.DefineNestedType Method (String, TypeAttributes, Type, Type[])

Defines a nested type given its name, attributes, the type that it extends, and the interfaces that it implements.

```
[Visual Basic]
Overloads Public Function DefineNestedType( _
    ByVal name As String, _
    ByVal attr As TypeAttributes, _
    ByVal parent As Type, _
    ByVal interfaces() As Type _
) As TypeBuilder
[C#]
public TypeBuilder DefineNestedType(
    string name,
    TypeAttributes attr,
    Type parent,
    Type[] interfaces
);
[C++]
public: TypeBuilder* DefineNestedType(
    String* name,
    TypeAttributes attr,
    Type* parent,
    Type* interfaces[]
);
[JScript]
public function DefineNestedType(
    name : String,
    attr : TypeAttributes,
    parent : Type,
    interfaces : Type[]
) : TypeBuilder;
```

Parameters

name
> The full path of the type. *name* cannot contain embedded nulls.

attr
> The attributes of the type.

parent
> The type that the nested type extends.

interfaces
> The interfaces that the nested type implements.

Return Value

The defined nested type.

Exceptions

Exception Type	Condition
ArgumentException	The nested attribute is not specified.
	-or-
	This type is sealed.
	-or-
	This type is an array.
	-or-
	This type is an interface but the nested type is not an interface.
	-or-
	The length of *name* is zero.
ArgumentNullException	*name* is a null reference (**Nothing** in Visual Basic) or a null interface is specified in the *interfaces* array.
InvalidOperationException	The type was previously created using **CreateType**.

Remarks

The nested type needs to be complete before you can reflect on it using **GetMembers**, **GetNestedType**, or **GetNestedTypes**.

Requirements

Platforms: Windows 98, Windows NT 4.0, Windows Millennium Edition, Windows 2000, Windows XP Home Edition, Windows XP Professional, Windows .NET Server family

TypeBuilder.DefinePInvokeMethod Method

Defines a **PInvoke** method.

Overload List

Defines a **PInvoke** method given its name, the name of the DLL in which the method is defined, the attributes of the method, the calling convention of the method, the return type of the method, the types of the parameters of the method, and the **PInvoke** flags.

[Visual Basic] **Overloads Public Function DefinePInvokeMethod(String, String, MethodAttributes, CallingConventions, Type, Type(), CallingConvention, CharSet) As MethodBuilder**

[C#] **public MethodBuilder DefinePInvokeMethod(string, string, MethodAttributes, CallingConventions, Type, Type[], CallingConvention, CharSet);**

[C++] **public: MethodBuilder* DefinePInvokeMethod (String*, String*, MethodAttributes, CallingConventions, Type*, Type[], CallingConvention, CharSet);**

[JScript] **public function DefinePInvokeMethod(String, String, MethodAttributes, CallingConventions, Type, Type[], CallingConvention, CharSet) : MethodBuilder;**

Defines a **PInvoke** method given its name, the name of the DLL in which the method is defined, the attributes of the method, the calling convention of the method, the return type of the method, the types of the parameters of the method, and the **PInvoke** flags.

[Visual Basic] **Overloads Public Function DefinePInvokeMethod(String, String, String, MethodAttributes, CallingConventions, Type, Type(), CallingConvention, CharSet) As MethodBuilder**

[C#] **public MethodBuilder DefinePInvokeMethod(string, string, string, MethodAttributes, CallingConventions, Type, Type[], CallingConvention, CharSet);**

[C++] **public: MethodBuilder* DefinePInvokeMethod (String*, String*, String*, MethodAttributes, CallingConventions, Type*, Type[], CallingConvention, CharSet);**

[JScript] **public function DefinePInvokeMethod(String, String, String, MethodAttributes, CallingConventions, Type, Type[], CallingConvention, CharSet) : MethodBuilder;**

Example

See related example in the **System.Reflection.Emit.TypeBuilder** class topic.

TypeBuilder.DefinePInvokeMethod Method (String, String, MethodAttributes, CallingConventions, Type, Type[], CallingConvention, CharSet)

Defines a **PInvoke** method given its name, the name of the DLL in which the method is defined, the attributes of the method, the calling convention of the method, the return type of the method, the types of the parameters of the method, and the **PInvoke** flags.

```
[Visual Basic]
Overloads Public Function DefinePInvokeMethod( _
   ByVal name As String, _
   ByVal dllName As String, _
   ByVal attributes As MethodAttributes, _
   ByVal callingConvention As CallingConventions, _
   ByVal returnType As Type, _
   ByVal parameterTypes() As Type, _
   ByVal nativeCallConv As CallingConvention, _
   ByVal nativeCharSet As CharSet _
) As MethodBuilder
[C#]
public MethodBuilder DefinePInvokeMethod(
   string name,
   string dllName,
   MethodAttributes attributes,
   CallingConventions callingConvention,
   Type returnType,
   Type[] parameterTypes,
   CallingConvention nativeCallConv,
   CharSet nativeCharSet
);
[C++]
public: MethodBuilder* DefinePInvokeMethod(
   String* name,
   String* dllName,
   MethodAttributes attributes,
   CallingConventions callingConvention,
   Type* returnType,
   Type* parameterTypes[],
   CallingConvention nativeCallConv,
   CharSet nativeCharSet
);
```

```
[JScript]
public function DefinePInvokeMethod(
   name : String,
   dllName : String,
   attributes : MethodAttributes,
   callingConvention : CallingConventions,
   returnType : Type,
   parameterTypes : Type[],
   nativeCallConv : CallingConvention,
   nativeCharSet : CharSet
) : MethodBuilder;
```

Parameters

name
   The name of the **PInvoke** method. *name* cannot contain
   embedded nulls.
dllName
   The name of the DLL in which the **PInvoke** method is defined.
attributes
   The attributes of the method.
callingConvention
   The method's calling convention.
returnType
   The method's return type.
parameterTypes
   The types of the method's parameters.
nativeCallConv
   The native calling convention.
nativeCharSet
   The method's native character set.

Return Value

The defined **PInvoke** method.

Exceptions

Exception Type	Condition
ArgumentException	The method is not static.
	-or-
	The parent type is an interface.
	-or-
	The method is abstract.
	-or-
	The method was previously defined.
	-or-
	The length of *name* or *dllName* is zero.
ArgumentNullException	*name* or *dllName* is a null reference (**Nothing** in Visual Basic).
InvalidOperationException	The containing type has been previously created using **CreateType**.

Remarks

Some DLL import attributes (see the description of
System.Runtime.InteropServices.DllImportAttribute) cannot be
specified as arguments to this method. Such attributes should be set
by emitting a custom attribute for the method. For example, the DLL
import attribute **PreserveSig** is set by emitting a custom attribute.

Example

See related example in the **System.Reflection.Emit.TypeBuilder**
class topic.

Requirements

Platforms: Windows 98, Windows NT 4.0,
Windows Millennium Edition, Windows 2000,
Windows XP Home Edition, Windows XP Professional,
Windows .NET Server family

TypeBuilder.DefinePInvokeMethod Method (String, String, String, MethodAttributes, CallingConventions, Type, Type[], CallingConvention, CharSet)

Defines a **PInvoke** method given its name, the name of the DLL in
which the method is defined, the attributes of the method, the calling
convention of the method, the return type of the method, the types of
the parameters of the method, and the **PInvoke** flags.

```
[Visual Basic]
Overloads Public Function DefinePInvokeMethod( _
   ByVal name As String, _
   ByVal dllName As String, _
   ByVal entryName As String, _
   ByVal attributes As MethodAttributes, _
   ByVal callingConvention As CallingConventions, _
   ByVal returnType As Type, _
   ByVal parameterTypes() As Type, _
   ByVal nativeCallConv As CallingConvention, _
   ByVal nativeCharSet As CharSet _
) As MethodBuilder
[C#]
public MethodBuilder DefinePInvokeMethod(
   string name,
   string dllName,
   string entryName,
   MethodAttributes attributes,
   CallingConventions callingConvention,
   Type returnType,
   Type[] parameterTypes,
   CallingConvention nativeCallConv,
   CharSet nativeCharSet
);
[C++]
public: MethodBuilder* DefinePInvokeMethod(
   String* name,
   String* dllName,
   String* entryName,
   MethodAttributes attributes,
   CallingConventions callingConvention,
   Type* returnType,
   Type* parameterTypes[],
   CallingConvention nativeCallConv,
   CharSet nativeCharSet
);
[JScript]
public function DefinePInvokeMethod(
   name : String,
   dllName : String,
   entryName : String,
   attributes : MethodAttributes,
   callingConvention : CallingConventions,
   returnType : Type,
```

```
    parameterTypes : Type[],
    nativeCallConv : CallingConvention,
    nativeCharSet : CharSet
) : MethodBuilder;
```

Parameters

name

> The name of the **PInvoke** method. *name* cannot contain embedded nulls.

dllName

> The name of the DLL in which the PInvoke method is defined.

entryName

> The name of the entry point in the DLL.

attributes

> The attributes of the method.

callingConvention

> The method's calling convention.

returnType

> The method's return type.

parameterTypes

> The types of the method's parameters.

nativeCallConv

> The native calling convention.

nativeCharSet

> The method's native character set.

Return Value

The defined PInvoke method.

Exceptions

Exception Type	Condition
ArgumentException	The method is not static.
	-or-
	The parent type is an interface.
	-or-
	The method is abstract.
	-or-
	The method was previously defined.
	-or-
	The length of *name*, *dllName,* or *entryName* is zero.
ArgumentNullException	*name, dllName*, or *entryName* is a null reference (**Nothing** in Visual Basic).
InvalidOperationException	The containing type has been previously created using **CreateType**.

Remarks

Some DLL import attributes (see the description of System.Runtime.InteropServices.DllImportAttribute) cannot be specified as arguments to this method. Such attributes should be set by emitting a custom attribute for the method. For example, the DLL import attribute **PreserveSig** is set by emitting a custom attribute.

Example

See related example in the **System.Reflection.Emit.TypeBuilder** class topic.

Requirements

Platforms: Windows 98, Windows NT 4.0, Windows Millennium Edition, Windows 2000, Windows XP Home Edition, Windows XP Professional, Windows .NET Server family

TypeBuilder.DefineProperty Method

Adds a new property to the class, with the given name and property signature.

```
[Visual Basic]
Public Function DefineProperty( _
   ByVal name As String, _
   ByVal attributes As PropertyAttributes, _
   ByVal returnType As Type, _
   ByVal parameterTypes() As Type _
) As PropertyBuilder
[C#]
public PropertyBuilder DefineProperty(
   string name,
   PropertyAttributes attributes,
   Type returnType,
   Type[] parameterTypes
);
[C++]
public: PropertyBuilder* DefineProperty(
   String* name,
   PropertyAttributes attributes,
   Type* returnType,
   Type* parameterTypes[]
);
[JScript]
public function DefineProperty(
   name : String,
   attributes : PropertyAttributes,
   returnType : Type,
   parameterTypes : Type[]
) : PropertyBuilder;
```

Parameters

name

> The name of the property. *name* cannot contain embedded nulls.

attributes

> The attributes of the property.

returnType

> The return type of the property.

parameterTypes

> The types of the parameters of the property.

Return Value

The defined property.

Exceptions

Exception Type	Condition
ArgumentException	The length of *name* is zero.
ArgumentNullException	*name* is a null reference (**Nothing** in Visual Basic)
	-or-
	if any of the elements of the *parameterTypes* array is a null reference (**Nothing**)

Exception Type	Condition
InvalidOperationException	The type was previously created using **CreateType**

Example

See related example in the **System.Reflection.Emit.TypeBuilder** class topic.

Requirements

Platforms: Windows 98, Windows NT 4.0, Windows Millennium Edition, Windows 2000, Windows XP Home Edition, Windows XP Professional, Windows .NET Server family

TypeBuilder.DefineTypeInitializer Method

Defines the initializer for this type.

```
[Visual Basic]
Public Function DefineTypeInitializer() As ConstructorBuilder
[C#]
public ConstructorBuilder DefineTypeInitializer();
[C++]
public: ConstructorBuilder* DefineTypeInitializer();
[JScript]
public function DefineTypeInitializer() : ConstructorBuilder;
```

Return Value

Returns a type initializer.

Exceptions

Exception Type	Condition
InvalidOperationException	The containing type has been previously created using **CreateType**.

Remarks

The initializer created is always public.

Example

See related example in the **System.Reflection.Emit.TypeBuilder** class topic.

Requirements

Platforms: Windows 98, Windows NT 4.0, Windows Millennium Edition, Windows 2000, Windows XP Home Edition, Windows XP Professional, Windows .NET Server family

TypeBuilder.DefineUninitializedData Method

Defines uninitialized data field in the .sdata section of the portable executable (PE) file.

```
[Visual Basic]
Public Function DefineUninitializedData( _
   ByVal name As String, _
   ByVal size As Integer, _
   ByVal attributes As FieldAttributes _
) As FieldBuilder
[C#]
public FieldBuilder DefineUninitializedData(
   string name,
   int size,
   FieldAttributes attributes
);
```

```
[C++]
public: FieldBuilder* DefineUninitializedData(
   String* name,
   int size,
   FieldAttributes attributes
);
[JScript]
public function DefineUninitializedData(
   name : String,
   size : int,
   attributes : FieldAttributes
) : FieldBuilder;
```

Parameters

name
   The name used to refer to the data. *name* cannot contain embedded nulls.
size
   The size of the data field.
attributes
   The attributes for the field.

Return Value

A field to reference the data.

Exceptions

Exception Type	Condition
ArgumentException	Length of *name* is zero.
	-or-
	size is less than or equal to zero or greater than or equal to 0x003f0000.
ArgumentNullException	*name* is a null reference (**Nothing** in Visual Basic).
InvalidOperationException	The type was previously created using **CreateType**.

Remarks

The field that you create with this method will be static (**Shared** in Visual Basic), even if you do not include **FieldAttributes.Static** in the *attributes* parameter.

Example

See related example in the **System.Reflection.Emit.TypeBuilder** class topic.

Requirements

Platforms: Windows 98, Windows NT 4.0, Windows Millennium Edition, Windows 2000, Windows XP Home Edition, Windows XP Professional, Windows .NET Server family

TypeBuilder.GetAttributeFlagsImpl Method

Returns the implementation attribute flags.

```
[Visual Basic]
Overrides Protected Function GetAttributeFlagsImpl() As _
   TypeAttributes
[C#]
protected override TypeAttributes GetAttributeFlagsImpl();
[C++]
protected: TypeAttributes GetAttributeFlagsImpl();
```

```
[JScript]
protected override function GetAttributeFlagsImpl() :
   TypeAttributes;
```

Return Value

Returns the implementation attribute flags.

Example

Requirements

Platforms: Windows 98, Windows NT 4.0,
Windows Millennium Edition, Windows 2000,
Windows XP Home Edition, Windows XP Professional,
Windows .NET Server family

TypeBuilder.GetConstructorImpl Method

Searches for a constructor whose parameters match the specified
argument types and modifiers, using the specified binding
constraints and the specified calling convention.

```
[Visual Basic]
Overrides Protected Function GetConstructorImpl( _
   ByVal bindingAttr As BindingFlags, _
   ByVal binder As Binder, _
   ByVal callConvention As CallingConventions, _
   ByVal types() As Type, _
   ByVal modifiers() As ParameterModifier _
) As ConstructorInfo
[C#]
protected override ConstructorInfo GetConstructorImpl(
   BindingFlags bindingAttr,
   Binder binder,
   CallingConventions callConvention,
   Type[] types,
   ParameterModifier[] modifiers
);
[C++]
protected: ConstructorInfo* GetConstructorImpl(
   BindingFlags bindingAttr,
   Binder* binder,
   CallingConventions callConvention,
   Type* types[],
   ParameterModifier modifiers[]
);
[JScript]
protected override function GetConstructorImpl(
   bindingAttr : BindingFlags,
   binder : Binder,
   callConvention : CallingConventions,
   types : Type[],
   modifiers : ParameterModifier[]
) : ConstructorInfo;
```

Parameters

bindingAttr

A bitmask comprised of one or more **BindingFlags** that specify
how the search is conducted.
-or-
Zero, to conduct a case-sensitive search for public methods.

binder

A **Binder** object that defines a set of properties and enables
binding, which can involve selection of an overloaded method,

coercion of argument types, and invocation of a member through
reflection.
-or-
A null reference (**Nothing** in Visual Basic), to use the
DefaultBinder.

callConvention

The **CallingConventions** object that specifies the set of rules to
use regarding the order and layout of arguments, how the return
value is passed, what registers are used for arguments, and the
stack is cleaned up.

types

An array of **Type** objects representing the number, order, and
type of the parameters for the constructor to get.
-or-
An empty array of the type **Type** (that is, Type[] types = new
Type[0]) to get a constructor that takes no parameters.

modifiers

An array of **ParameterModifier** objects representing the attributes associated with the corresponding element in the *types* array.

Return Value

A **ConstructorInfo** object representing the constructor that matches
the specified requirements, if found; otherwise, a null reference
(**Nothing** in Visual Basic).

Exceptions

Exception Type	Condition
NotSupportedException	This method is not implemented for incomplete type.

Remarks

Retrieve the type using **GetType** or **GetType** and use reflection on
the retrieved type.

Requirements

Platforms: Windows 98, Windows NT 4.0,
Windows Millennium Edition, Windows 2000,
Windows XP Home Edition, Windows XP Professional,
Windows .NET Server family

TypeBuilder.GetConstructors Method

Overload List

Returns an array of **ConstructorInfo** objects representing the public
and non-public constructors defined for this class, as specified.

   [Visual Basic] **Overloads Overrides Public Function
   GetConstructors(BindingFlags) As ConstructorInfo()**
   [C#] **public override ConstructorInfo[]
   GetConstructors(BindingFlags);**
   [C++] **public: ConstructorInfo*
   GetConstructors(BindingFlags) [];**
   [JScript] **public override function
   GetConstructors(BindingFlags) : ConstructorInfo[];**

Inherited from **Type.**

   [Visual Basic] **Overloads Public Function GetConstructors()
   As ConstructorInfo()**
   [C#] **public ConstructorInfo[] GetConstructors();**
   [C++] **public: ConstructorInfo* GetConstructors() [];**
   [JScript] **public function GetConstructors() :
   ConstructorInfo[];**

TypeBuilder.GetConstructors Method (BindingFlags)

Returns an array of **ConstructorInfo** objects representing the public and non-public constructors defined for this class, as specified.

```
[Visual Basic]
Overrides Overloads Public Function GetConstructors( _
    ByVal bindingAttr As BindingFlags _
) As ConstructorInfo()
[C#]
public override ConstructorInfo[] GetConstructors(
    BindingFlags bindingAttr
);
[C++]
public: ConstructorInfo* GetConstructors(
    BindingFlags bindingAttr
) [];
[JScript]
public override function GetConstructors(
    bindingAttr : BindingFlags
) : ConstructorInfo[];
```

Parameters

bindingAttr

This must be a bit flag from **BindingFlags** as in **InvokeMethod**, **NonPublic**, and so on.

Return Value

Returns an array of **ConstructorInfo** objects representing the specified constructors defined for this class. If no constructors are defined, an empty array is returned.

Exceptions

Exception Type	Condition
NotSupportedException	This method is not implemented for incomplete types.

Remarks

Retrieve the type using **GetType** or **GetType** and use reflection on the retrieved type.

Requirements

Platforms: Windows 98, Windows NT 4.0, Windows Millennium Edition, Windows 2000, Windows XP Home Edition, Windows XP Professional, Windows .NET Server family

.NET Framework Security:
- **ReflectionPermission TypeInformation** required for non-public members.

TypeBuilder.GetCustomAttributes Method

Returns the custom attributes defined for this type.

Overload List

Returns all the custom attributes defined for this type.

[Visual Basic] **Overloads Overrides Public Function GetCustomAttributes(Boolean) As Object() Implements ICustomAttributeProvider.GetCustomAttributes**

[C#] **public override object[] GetCustomAttributes(bool);**

[C++] **public: Object* GetCustomAttributes(bool) __gc[];**

[JScript] **public override function GetCustomAttributes(Boolean) : Object[];**

Checks if the specified custom attribute type is defined.

[Visual Basic] **Overloads Overrides Public Function GetCustomAttributes(Type, Boolean) As Object() Implements ICustomAttributeProvider.GetCustomAttributes**

[C#] **public override object[] GetCustomAttributes(Type, bool);**

[C++] **public: Object* GetCustomAttributes(Type*, bool) __gc[];**

[JScript] **public override function GetCustomAttributes (Type, Boolean) : Object[];**

TypeBuilder.GetCustomAttributes Method (Boolean)

Returns all the custom attributes defined for this type.

```
[Visual Basic]
Overrides Overloads Public Function GetCustomAttributes( _
    ByVal inherit As Boolean _
) As Object() Implements ICustomAttributeProvider.GetCustomAttributes
[C#]
public override object[] GetCustomAttributes(
    bool inherit
);
[C++]
public: Object* GetCustomAttributes(
    bool inherit
) __gc[];
[JScript]
public override function GetCustomAttributes(
    inherit : Boolean
) : Object[];
```

Parameters

inherit

Specifies whether to search this member's inheritance chain to find the attributes.

Return Value

Returns an array of objects representing all the custom attributes of this type.

Implements

ICustomAttributeProvider.GetCustomAttributes

Exceptions

Exception Type	Condition
NotSupportedException	This method is not currently supported for incomplete types. Retrieve the type using **GetType** and call **GetCustomAttributes** on the returned **Type**.

Requirements

Platforms: Windows 98, Windows NT 4.0, Windows Millennium Edition, Windows 2000, Windows XP Home Edition, Windows XP Professional, Windows .NET Server family

TypeBuilder.GetCustomAttributes Method (Type, Boolean)

Checks if the specified custom attribute type is defined.

[Visual Basic]
```
Overrides Overloads Public Function GetCustomAttributes( _
   ByVal attributeType As Type, _
   ByVal inherit As Boolean _
) As Object() Implements ICustomAttributeProvider.GetCustomAttributes
```
[C#]
```
public override object[] GetCustomAttributes(
   Type attributeType,
   bool inherit
);
```
[C++]
```
public: Object* GetCustomAttributes(
   Type* attributeType,
   bool inherit
) __gc[];
```
[JScript]
```
public override function GetCustomAttributes(
   attributeType : Type,
   inherit : Boolean
) : Object[];
```

Parameters
attributeType
   The **Type** object to which the custom attributes are applied.
inherit
   Specifies whether to search this member's inheritance chain to
   find the attributes.

Return Value
true if one or more instance of *attributeType* is defined on this
member; otherwise, **false**.

Implements
ICustomAttributeProvider.GetCustomAttributes

Exceptions

Exception Type	Condition
NotSupportedException	This method is not currently supported for incomplete types. Retrieve the type using **GetType** and call **GetCustomAttributes** on the returned **Type**.

Requirements
Platforms: Windows 98, Windows NT 4.0,
Windows Millennium Edition, Windows 2000,
Windows XP Home Edition, Windows XP Professional,
Windows .NET Server family

TypeBuilder.GetElementType Method

Calling this method always throws **NotSupportedException**.

[Visual Basic]
```
Overrides Public Function GetElementType() As Type
```
[C#]
```
public override Type GetElementType();
```
[C++]
```
public: Type* GetElementType();
```
[JScript]
```
public override function GetElementType() : Type;
```

Return Value
This method is not supported. No value is returned.

Exceptions

Exception Type	Condition
NotSupportedException	This method is not supported.

Remarks
Retrieve the type using **GetType** or **GetType** and use reflection on
the retrieved type.

Requirements
Platforms: Windows 98, Windows NT 4.0,
Windows Millennium Edition, Windows 2000,
Windows XP Home Edition, Windows XP Professional,
Windows .NET Server family

TypeBuilder.GetEvent Method
Overload List
Returns the event with the specified name.

   [Visual Basic] **Overloads Overrides Public Function
   GetEvent(String, BindingFlags) As EventInfo**
   [C#] **public override EventInfo GetEvent(string,
   BindingFlags);**
   [C++] **public: EventInfo* GetEvent(String*, BindingFlags);**
   [JScript] **public override function GetEvent(String,
   BindingFlags) : EventInfo;**

Inherited from **Type**.

   [Visual Basic] **Overloads Public Function GetEvent(String)
   As EventInfo**
   [C#] **public EventInfo GetEvent(string);**
   [C++] **public: EventInfo* GetEvent(String*);**
   [JScript] **public function GetEvent(String) : EventInfo;**

TypeBuilder.GetEvent Method (String, BindingFlags)
Returns the event with the specified name.

[Visual Basic]
```
Overrides Overloads Public Function GetEvent( _
   ByVal name As String, _
   ByVal bindingAttr As BindingFlags _
) As EventInfo
```
[C#]
```
public override EventInfo GetEvent(
   string name,
   BindingFlags bindingAttr
);
```
[C++]
```
public: EventInfo* GetEvent(
   String* name,
   BindingFlags bindingAttr
);
```
[JScript]
```
public override function GetEvent(
   name : String,
   bindingAttr : BindingFlags
) : EventInfo;
```

Parameters

name

The name of the event to get.

bindingAttr

This invocation attribute. This must be a bit flag from **BindingFlags**: **InvokeMethod**, **NonPublic**, and so on.

Return Value

Returns an **EventInfo** object representing the event declared or inherited by this type with the specified name. If there are no matches, then an empty array is returned.

Exceptions

Exception Type	Condition
NotSupportedException	This method is not implemented for incomplete types.

Remarks

Retrieve the type using **GetType** or **GetType** and use reflection on the retrieved type.

Requirements

Platforms: Windows 98, Windows NT 4.0, Windows Millennium Edition, Windows 2000, Windows XP Home Edition, Windows XP Professional, Windows .NET Server family

TypeBuilder.GetEvents Method

Overload List

Returns the events for the public events declared or inherited by this type.

[Visual Basic] **Overloads Overrides Public Function GetEvents() As EventInfo()**

[C#] **public override EventInfo[] GetEvents();**

[C++] **public: EventInfo* GetEvents() [];**

[JScript] **public override function GetEvents() : EventInfo[];**

Returns the public and non-public events that are declared by this type.

[Visual Basic] **Overloads Overrides Public Function GetEvents(BindingFlags) As EventInfo()**

[C#] **public override EventInfo[] GetEvents(BindingFlags);**

[C++] **public: EventInfo* GetEvents(BindingFlags) [];**

[JScript] **public override function GetEvents(BindingFlags) : EventInfo[];**

TypeBuilder.GetEvents Method ()

Returns the events for the public events declared or inherited by this type.

```
[Visual Basic]
Overrides Overloads Public Function GetEvents() As EventInfo()
[C#]
public override EventInfo[] GetEvents();
[C++]
public: EventInfo* GetEvents() [];
[JScript]
public override function GetEvents() : EventInfo[];
```

Return Value

Returns an array of **EventInfo** objects representing the public events declared or inherited by this type. An empty array is returned if there are no public events.

Exceptions

Exception Type	Condition
NotSupportedException	This method is not implemented for incomplete types.

Remarks

Retrieve the type using **GetType** or **GetType** and use reflection on the retrieved type.

Requirements

Platforms: Windows 98, Windows NT 4.0, Windows Millennium Edition, Windows 2000, Windows XP Home Edition, Windows XP Professional, Windows .NET Server family

TypeBuilder.GetEvents Method (BindingFlags)

Returns the public and non-public events that are declared by this type.

```
[Visual Basic]
Overrides Overloads Public Function GetEvents( _
   ByVal bindingAttr As BindingFlags _
) As EventInfo()
[C#]
public override EventInfo[] GetEvents(
   BindingFlags bindingAttr
);
[C++]
public: EventInfo* GetEvents(
   BindingFlags bindingAttr
) [];
[JScript]
public override function GetEvents(
   bindingAttr : BindingFlags
) : EventInfo[];
```

Parameters

bindingAttr

This must be a bit flag from **BindingFlags**, as in **InvokeMethod**, **NonPublic**, and so on.

Return Value

Returns an array of **EventInfo** objects representing the public and non-public events declared or inherited by this type. An empty array is returned if there are no events, as specified.

Exceptions

Exception Type	Condition
NotSupportedException	This method is not implemented for incomplete types.

Remarks

Retrieve the type using **GetType** or **GetType** and use reflection on the retrieved type.

Requirements

Platforms: Windows 98, Windows NT 4.0,
Windows Millennium Edition, Windows 2000,
Windows XP Home Edition, Windows XP Professional,
Windows .NET Server family

.NET Framework Security:

- **ReflectionPermission TypeInformation** required for non-public members

TypeBuilder.GetField Method

Overload List

Returns the field specified by the given name.

[Visual Basic] **Overloads Overrides Public Function
GetField(String, BindingFlags) As FieldInfo Implements
IReflect.GetField**

[C#] **public override FieldInfo GetField(string,
BindingFlags);**

[C++] **public: FieldInfo* GetField(String*, BindingFlags);**

[JScript] **public override function GetField(String,
BindingFlags) : FieldInfo;**

Inherited from **Type**.

[Visual Basic] **Overloads Public Function GetField(String) As
FieldInfo**

[C#] **public FieldInfo GetField(string);**

[C++] **public: FieldInfo* GetField(String*);**

[JScript] **public function GetField(String) : FieldInfo;**

TypeBuilder.GetField Method (String, BindingFlags)

Returns the field specified by the given name.

```
[Visual Basic]
Overrides Overloads Public Function GetField( _
   ByVal name As String, _
   ByVal bindingAttr As BindingFlags _
) As FieldInfo Implements IReflect.GetField
[C#]
public override FieldInfo GetField(
   string name,
   BindingFlags bindingAttr
);
[C++]
public: FieldInfo* GetField(
   String* name,
   BindingFlags bindingAttr
);
[JScript]
public override function GetField(
   name : String,
   bindingAttr : BindingFlags
) : FieldInfo;
```

Parameters

name

   The name of the field to get.

bindingAttr

   This must be a bit flag from **BindingFlags** as in **InvokeMethod**,
   NonPublic, and so on.

Return Value

Returns the **FieldInfo** object representing the field declared or
inherited by this type with the specified name and public or non-public modifier. If there are no matches then a null reference
(**Nothing** in Visual Basic) is returned.

Implements

IReflect.GetField

Exceptions

Exception Type	Condition
NotSupportedException	This method is not implemented for incomplete types.

Remarks

Retrieve the type using **GetType** or **GetType** and use reflection on
the retrieved type.

Requirements

Platforms: Windows 98, Windows NT 4.0,
Windows Millennium Edition, Windows 2000,
Windows XP Home Edition, Windows XP Professional,
Windows .NET Server family

.NET Framework Security:

- **ReflectionPermission TypeInformation** required for non-public members.

TypeBuilder.GetFields Method

Overload List

Returns the public and non-public fields that are declared by this
type.

[Visual Basic] **Overloads Overrides Public Function
GetFields(BindingFlags) As FieldInfo() Implements
IReflect.GetFields**

[C#] **public override FieldInfo[] GetFields(BindingFlags);**

[C++] **public: FieldInfo* GetFields(BindingFlags) [];**

[JScript] **public override function GetFields(BindingFlags) :
FieldInfo[];**

Inherited from **Type**.

[Visual Basic] **Overloads Public Function GetFields() As
FieldInfo()**

[C#] **public FieldInfo[] GetFields();**

[C++] **public: FieldInfo* GetFields() [];**

[JScript] **public function GetFields() : FieldInfo[];**

TypeBuilder.GetFields Method (BindingFlags)

Returns the public and non-public fields that are declared by this
type.

```
[Visual Basic]
Overrides Overloads Public Function GetFields( _
   ByVal bindingAttr As BindingFlags _
) As FieldInfo() Implements IReflect.GetFields
[C#]
public override FieldInfo[] GetFields(
   BindingFlags bindingAttr
);
```

```
[C++]
public: FieldInfo* GetFields(
    BindingFlags bindingAttr
) [];
[JScript]
public override function GetFields(
    bindingAttr : BindingFlags
) : FieldInfo[];
```

Parameters
bindingAttr
> This must be a bit flag from **BindingFlags**: **InvokeMethod**, **NonPublic**, and so on.

Return Value
Returns an array of **FieldInfo** objects representing the public and non-public fields declared or inherited by this type. An empty array is returned if there are no fields, as specified.

Implements
IReflect.GetFields

Exceptions

Exception Type	Condition
NotSupportedException	This method is not implemented for incomplete types.

Remarks
Retrieve the type using **GetType** or **GetType** and use reflection on the retrieved type.

Requirements
Platforms: Windows 98, Windows NT 4.0, Windows Millennium Edition, Windows 2000, Windows XP Home Edition, Windows XP Professional, Windows .NET Server family

.NET Framework Security:
- **ReflectionPermission TypeInformation** required for non-public members

TypeBuilder.GetInterface Method

Overload List
Returns the interface implemented (directly or indirectly) by this class with the fully-qualified name matching the given interface name.

> [Visual Basic] **Overloads Overrides Public Function GetInterface(String, Boolean) As Type**
> [C#] **public override Type GetInterface(string, bool);**
> [C++] **public: Type* GetInterface(String*, bool);**
> [JScript] **public override function GetInterface(String, Boolean) : Type;**

Inherited from **Type**.

> [Visual Basic] **Overloads Public Function GetInterface(String) As Type**
> [C#] **public Type GetInterface(string);**
> [C++] **public: Type* GetInterface(String*);**
> [JScript] **public function GetInterface(String) : Type;**

TypeBuilder.GetInterface Method (String, Boolean)
Returns the interface implemented (directly or indirectly) by this class with the fully-qualified name matching the given interface name.

```
[Visual Basic]
Overrides Overloads Public Function GetInterface( _
    ByVal name As String, _
    ByVal ignoreCase As Boolean _
) As Type
[C#]
public override Type GetInterface(
    string name,
    bool ignoreCase
);
[C++]
public: Type* GetInterface(
    String* name,
    bool ignoreCase
);
[JScript]
public override function GetInterface(
    name : String,
    ignoreCase : Boolean
) : Type;
```

Parameters
name
> The name of the interface.
ignoreCase
> If **true**, the search is case-insensitive. If **false**, the search is case-sensitive.

Return Value
Returns a **Type** object representing the implemented interface. Returns null if no interface matching name is found.

Exceptions

Exception Type	Condition
NotSupportedException	This method is not implemented for incomplete types.

Remarks
Retrieve the type using **GetType** or **GetType** and use reflection on the retrieved type.

Requirements
Platforms: Windows 98, Windows NT 4.0, Windows Millennium Edition, Windows 2000, Windows XP Home Edition, Windows XP Professional, Windows .NET Server family

TypeBuilder.GetInterfaceMap Method
Returns an interface mapping for the requested interface.

```
[Visual Basic]
Overrides Public Function GetInterfaceMap( _
    ByVal interfaceType As Type _
) As InterfaceMapping
[C#]
public override InterfaceMapping GetInterfaceMap(
    Type interfaceType
);
```

```
[C++]
public: InterfaceMapping GetInterfaceMap(
    Type* interfaceType
);
[JScript]
public override function GetInterfaceMap(
    interfaceType : Type
) : InterfaceMapping;
```

Parameters

interfaceType

The **Type** of the interface for which the mapping is to be retrieved.

Return Value

Returns the requested interface mapping.

Exceptions

Exception Type	Condition
NotSupportedException	This method is not implemented for incomplete types.

Remarks

Retrieve the type using **GetType** or **GetType** and use reflection on the retrieved type.

Requirements

Platforms: Windows 98, Windows NT 4.0, Windows Millennium Edition, Windows 2000, Windows XP Home Edition, Windows XP Professional, Windows .NET Server family

TypeBuilder.GetInterfaces Method

Returns an array of all the interfaces implemented on this a class and its base classes.

```
[Visual Basic]
Overrides Public Function GetInterfaces() As Type()
[C#]
public override Type[] GetInterfaces();
[C++]
public: Type* GetInterfaces() [];
[JScript]
public override function GetInterfaces() : Type[];
```

Return Value

Returns an array of **Type** objects representing the implemented interfaces. If none are defined, an empty array is returned.

Requirements

Platforms: Windows 98, Windows NT 4.0, Windows Millennium Edition, Windows 2000, Windows XP Home Edition, Windows XP Professional, Windows .NET Server family

TypeBuilder.GetMember Method

Overload List

Returns all the public and non-public members declared or inherited by this type, as specified.

[Visual Basic] **Overloads Overrides Public Function GetMember(String, MemberTypes, BindingFlags) As MemberInfo()**

[C#] **public override MemberInfo[] GetMember(string, MemberTypes, BindingFlags);**

[C++] **public: MemberInfo* GetMember(String*, MemberTypes, BindingFlags) [];**

[JScript] **public override function GetMember(String, MemberTypes, BindingFlags) : MemberInfo[];**

Inherited from **Type**.

[Visual Basic] **Overloads Public Function GetMember(String) As MemberInfo()**

[C#] **public MemberInfo[] GetMember(string);**

[C++] **public: MemberInfo* GetMember(String*) [];**

[JScript] **public function GetMember(String) : MemberInfo[];**

Inherited from **Type**.

[Visual Basic] **Overloads Public Overridable Function GetMember(String, BindingFlags) As MemberInfo() Implements IReflect.GetMember**

[C#] **public virtual MemberInfo[] GetMember(string, BindingFlags);**

[C++] **public: virtual MemberInfo* GetMember(String*, BindingFlags) [];**

[JScript] **public function GetMember(String, BindingFlags) : MemberInfo[];**

TypeBuilder.GetMember Method (String, MemberTypes, BindingFlags)

Returns all the public and non-public members declared or inherited by this type, as specified.

```
[Visual Basic]
Overrides Overloads Public Function GetMember( _
    ByVal name As String, _
    ByVal type As MemberTypes, _
    ByVal bindingAttr As BindingFlags _
) As MemberInfo()
[C#]
public override MemberInfo[] GetMember(
    string name,
    MemberTypes type,
    BindingFlags bindingAttr
);
[C++]
public: MemberInfo* GetMember(
    String* name,
    MemberTypes type,
    BindingFlags bindingAttr
) [];
[JScript]
public override function GetMember(
    name : String,
    type : MemberTypes,
    bindingAttr : BindingFlags
) : MemberInfo[];
```

Parameters

name

The name of the member.

type

The type of the member to return.

bindingAttr

This must be a bit flag from **BindingFlags**, as in **InvokeMethod**, **NonPublic**, and so on.

Return Value

Returns an array of **MemberInfo** objects representing the public and non-public members defined on this type if *nonPublic* is used; otherwise, only the public members are returned.

Exceptions

Exception Type	Condition
NotSupportedException	This method is not implemented for incomplete types.

Remarks

Retrieve the type using **GetType** or **GetType** and use reflection on the retrieved type.

Requirements

Platforms: Windows 98, Windows NT 4.0, Windows Millennium Edition, Windows 2000, Windows XP Home Edition, Windows XP Professional, Windows .NET Server family

TypeBuilder.GetMembers Method

Overload List

Returns the members for the public and non-public members declared or inherited by this type.

[Visual Basic] **Overloads Overrides Public Function GetMembers(BindingFlags) As MemberInfo() Implements IReflect.GetMembers**

[C#] **public override MemberInfo[] GetMembers(BindingFlags);**

[C++] **public: MemberInfo* GetMembers(BindingFlags) [];**

[JScript] **public override function GetMembers(BindingFlags) : MemberInfo[];**

Inherited from **Type**.

[Visual Basic] **Overloads Public Function GetMembers() As MemberInfo()**

[C#] **public MemberInfo[] GetMembers();**

[C++] **public: MemberInfo* GetMembers() [];**

[JScript] **public function GetMembers() : MemberInfo[];**

TypeBuilder.GetMembers Method (BindingFlags)

Returns the members for the public and non-public members declared or inherited by this type.

```
[Visual Basic]
Overrides Overloads Public Function GetMembers( _
   ByVal bindingAttr As BindingFlags _
) As MemberInfo() Implements IReflect.GetMembers
[C#]
public override MemberInfo[] GetMembers(
   BindingFlags bindingAttr
);
[C++]
public: MemberInfo* GetMembers(
   BindingFlags bindingAttr
) [];
```

```
[JScript]
public override function GetMembers(
   bindingAttr : BindingFlags
) : MemberInfo[];
```

Parameters

bindingAttr

This must be a bit flag from **BindingFlags**, such as **InvokeMethod**, **NonPublic**, and so on.

Return Value

Returns an array of **MemberInfo** objects representing the public and non-public members declared or inherited by this type. An empty array is returned if there are no matching members.

Implements

IReflect.GetMembers

Exceptions

Exception Type	Condition
NotSupportedException	This method is not implemented for incomplete types.

Remarks

Retrieve the type using **GetType** or **GetType** and use reflection on the retrieved type.

Requirements

Platforms: Windows 98, Windows NT 4.0, Windows Millennium Edition, Windows 2000, Windows XP Home Edition, Windows XP Professional, Windows .NET Server family

.NET Framework Security:

• **ReflectionPermission TypeInformation** required for non-public members

TypeBuilder.GetMethodImpl Method

Searches for the specified method whose parameters match the specified argument types and modifiers, using the specified binding constraints and the specified calling convention.

```
[Visual Basic]
Overrides Protected Function GetMethodImpl( _
   ByVal name As String, _
   ByVal bindingAttr As BindingFlags, _
   ByVal binder As Binder, _
   ByVal callConvention As CallingConventions, _
   ByVal types() As Type, _
   ByVal modifiers() As ParameterModifier _
) As MethodInfo
[C#]
protected override MethodInfo GetMethodImpl(
   string name,
   BindingFlags bindingAttr,
   Binder binder,
   CallingConventions callConvention,
   Type[] types,
   ParameterModifier[] modifiers
);
```

```
[C++]
protected: MethodInfo* GetMethodImpl(
   String* name,
   BindingFlags bindingAttr,
   Binder* binder,
   CallingConventions callConvention,
   Type* types[],
   ParameterModifier modifiers[]
);
[JScript]
protected override function GetMethodImpl(
   name : String,
   bindingAttr : BindingFlags,
   binder : Binder,
   callConvention : CallingConventions,
   types : Type[],
   modifiers : ParameterModifier[]
) : MethodInfo;
```

Parameters

name
> The **String** containing the name of the method to get.

bindingAttr
> A bitmask comprised of one or more **BindingFlags** that specify how the search is conducted.
>
> -or-
>
> Zero, to conduct a case-sensitive search for public methods.

binder
> A **Binder** object that defines a set of properties and enables binding, which can involve selection of an overloaded method, coercion of argument types, and invocation of a member through reflection.
>
> -or-
>
> A null reference (**Nothing** in Visual Basic), to use the **DefaultBinder**.

callConvention
> The **CallingConventions** object that specifies the set of rules to use regarding the order and layout of arguments, how the return value is passed, what registers are used for arguments, and what process cleans up the stack.

types
> An array of **Type** objects representing the number, order, and type of the parameters for the method to get.
>
> -or-
>
> An empty array of the type **Type** (that is, Type[] types = new Type[0]) to get a method that takes no parameters.

modifiers
> An array of **ParameterModifier** objects representing the attributes associated with the corresponding element in the *types* array.

Return Value

A **MethodInfo** object representing the method that matches the specified requirements, if found; otherwise, a null reference (**Nothing** in Visual Basic).

Exceptions

Exception Type	Condition
NotSupportedException	This method is not implemented for incomplete types.

Remarks

Retrieve the type using **GetType** or **GetType** and use reflection on the retrieved type.

Requirements

Platforms: Windows 98, Windows NT 4.0, Windows Millennium Edition, Windows 2000, Windows XP Home Edition, Windows XP Professional, Windows .NET Server family

TypeBuilder.GetMethods Method

Overload List

Returns all the public and non-public methods declared or inherited by this type, as specified.

> [Visual Basic] **Overloads Overrides Public Function GetMethods(BindingFlags) As MethodInfo() Implements IReflect.GetMethods**
>
> [C#] **public override MethodInfo[] GetMethods(BindingFlags);**
>
> [C++] **public: MethodInfo* GetMethods(BindingFlags) [];**
>
> [JScript] **public override function GetMethods(BindingFlags) : MethodInfo[];**

Inherited from **Type**.

> [Visual Basic] **Overloads Public Function GetMethods() As MethodInfo()**
>
> [C#] **public MethodInfo[] GetMethods();**
>
> [C++] **public: MethodInfo* GetMethods() [];**
>
> [JScript] **public function GetMethods() : MethodInfo[];**

TypeBuilder.GetMethods Method (BindingFlags)

Returns all the public and non-public methods declared or inherited by this type, as specified.

```
[Visual Basic]
Overrides Overloads Public Function GetMethods( _
   ByVal bindingAttr As BindingFlags _
) As MethodInfo() Implements IReflect.GetMethods
[C#]
public override MethodInfo[] GetMethods(
   BindingFlags bindingAttr
);
[C++]
public: MethodInfo* GetMethods(
   BindingFlags bindingAttr
) [];
[JScript]
public override function GetMethods(
   bindingAttr : BindingFlags
) : MethodInfo[];
```

Parameters

bindingAttr

This must be a bit flag from **BindingFlags** as in **InvokeMethod**, **NonPublic**, and so on.

Return Value

Returns an array of **MethodInfo** objects representing the public and non-public methods defined on this type if *nonPublic* is used; otherwise, only the public methods are returned.

Implements

IReflect.GetMethods

Exceptions

Exception Type	Condition
NotSupportedException	This method is not implemented for incomplete types.

Remarks

Retrieve the type using **GetType** or **GetType** and use reflection on the retrieved type.

Requirements

Platforms: Windows 98, Windows NT 4.0, Windows Millennium Edition, Windows 2000, Windows XP Home Edition, Windows XP Professional, Windows .NET Server family

.NET Framework Security:

- **ReflectionPermission TypeInformation** required for non-public members

TypeBuilder.GetNestedType Method

Overload List

Returns the public and non-public nested types that are declared by this type.

[Visual Basic] **Overloads Overrides Public Function GetNestedType(String, BindingFlags) As Type**

[C#] **public override Type GetNestedType(string, BindingFlags);**

[C++] **public: Type* GetNestedType(String*, BindingFlags);**

[JScript] **public override function GetNestedType(String, BindingFlags) : Type;**

Inherited from **Type**.

[Visual Basic] **Overloads Public Function GetNestedType(String) As Type**

[C#] **public Type GetNestedType(string);**

[C++] **public: Type* GetNestedType(String*);**

[JScript] **public function GetNestedType(String) : Type;**

TypeBuilder.GetNestedType Method (String, BindingFlags)

Returns the public and non-public nested types that are declared by this type.

```
[Visual Basic]
Overrides Overloads Public Function GetNestedType( _
    ByVal name As String, _
    ByVal bindingAttr As BindingFlags _
) As Type
```

```
[C#]
public override Type GetNestedType(
    string name,
    BindingFlags bindingAttr
);
```
```
[C++]
public: Type* GetNestedType(
    String* name,
    BindingFlags bindingAttr
);
```
```
[JScript]
public override function GetNestedType(
    name : String,
    bindingAttr : BindingFlags
) : Type;
```

Parameters

name

The **String** containing the name of the nested type to get.

bindingAttr

A bitmask comprised of one or more **BindingFlags** that specify how the search is conducted.

-or-

Zero, to conduct a case-sensitive search for public methods.

Return Value

A **Type** object representing the nested type that matches the specified requirements, if found; otherwise, a null reference (**Nothing** in Visual Basic).

Exceptions

Exception Type	Condition
NotSupportedException	This method is not implemented for incomplete types.

Remarks

Retrieve the type using **GetType** or **GetType** and use reflection on the retrieved type.

If this type is complete, for example, if **CreateType** has been called on this type, but there are nested types that are not complete, then **GetNestedTypes** will only return those nested types for which **CreateType** has been called.

Requirements

Platforms: Windows 98, Windows NT 4.0, Windows Millennium Edition, Windows 2000, Windows XP Home Edition, Windows XP Professional, Windows .NET Server family

TypeBuilder.GetNestedTypes Method

Overload List

Returns the public and non-public nested types that are declared or inherited by this type.

[Visual Basic] **Overloads Overrides Public Function GetNestedTypes(BindingFlags) As Type()**

[C#] **public override Type[] GetNestedTypes(BindingFlags);**

[C++] **public: Type* GetNestedTypes(BindingFlags) [];**

[JScript] **public override function GetNestedTypes(BindingFlags) : Type[];**

Inherited from **Type**.

[Visual Basic] **Overloads Public Function GetNestedTypes()
As Type()**

[C#] **public Type[] GetNestedTypes();**

[C++] **public: Type* GetNestedTypes() [];**

[JScript] **public function GetNestedTypes() : Type[];**

TypeBuilder.GetNestedTypes Method (BindingFlags)

Returns the public and non-public nested types that are declared or
inherited by this type.

```
[Visual Basic]
Overrides Overloads Public Function GetNestedTypes( _
   ByVal bindingAttr As BindingFlags _
) As Type()
[C#]
public override Type[] GetNestedTypes(
   BindingFlags bindingAttr
);
[C++]
public: Type* GetNestedTypes(
   BindingFlags bindingAttr
) [];
[JScript]
public override function GetNestedTypes(
   bindingAttr : BindingFlags
) : Type[];
```

Parameters

bindingAttr

> This must be a bit flag from **BindingFlags**, as in **InvokeMethod**,
> **NonPublic**, and so on.

Return Value

An array of **Type** objects representing all the types nested within the
current **Type** that match the specified binding constraints.

An empty array of type **Type**, if no types are nested within the
current **Type**, or if none of the nested types match the binding
constraints.

Exceptions

Exception Type	Condition
NotSupportedException	This method is not implemented for incomplete types.

Remarks

Retrieve the type using **GetType** or **GetType** and use reflection on
the retrieved type.

If this type is complete, for example, if **CreateType** has been called
on this type, but there are nested types that are not complete, then
GetNestedTypes will only return those nested types for which
CreateType has been called.

Requirements

Platforms: Windows 98, Windows NT 4.0,
Windows Millennium Edition, Windows 2000,
Windows XP Home Edition, Windows XP Professional,
Windows .NET Server family

TypeBuilder.GetProperties Method

Overload List

Returns all the public and non-public properties declared or
inherited by this type, as specified.

[Visual Basic] **Overloads Overrides Public Function
GetProperties(BindingFlags) As PropertyInfo() Implements
IReflect.GetProperties**

[C#] **public override PropertyInfo[]
GetProperties(BindingFlags);**

[C++] **public: PropertyInfo* GetProperties(BindingFlags) [];**

[JScript] **public override function
GetProperties(BindingFlags) : PropertyInfo[];**

Inherited from **Type**.

[Visual Basic] **Overloads Public Function GetProperties() As
PropertyInfo()**

[C#] **public PropertyInfo[] GetProperties();**

[C++] **public: PropertyInfo* GetProperties() [];**

[JScript] **public function GetProperties() : PropertyInfo[];**

TypeBuilder.GetProperties Method (BindingFlags)

Returns all the public and non-public properties declared or
inherited by this type, as specified.

```
[Visual Basic]
Overrides Overloads Public Function GetProperties( _
   ByVal bindingAttr As BindingFlags _
) As PropertyInfo() Implements IReflect.GetProperties
[C#]
public override PropertyInfo[] GetProperties(
   BindingFlags bindingAttr
);
[C++]
public: PropertyInfo* GetProperties(
   BindingFlags bindingAttr
) [];
[JScript]
public override function GetProperties(
   bindingAttr : BindingFlags
) : PropertyInfo[];
```

Parameters

bindingAttr

> This invocation attribute. This must be a bit flag from
> **BindingFlags**: **InvokeMethod**, **NonPublic**, and so on.

Return Value

Returns an array of **PropertyInfo** objects representing the public
and non-public properties defined on this type if *nonPublic* is used;
otherwise, only the public properties are returned.

Implements

IReflect.GetProperties

Exceptions

Exception Type	Condition
NotSupportedException	This method is not implemented for incomplete types.

Remarks

Retrieve the type using **GetType** or **GetType** and use reflection on the retrieved type.

Requirements

Platforms: Windows 98, Windows NT 4.0, Windows Millennium Edition, Windows 2000, Windows XP Home Edition, Windows XP Professional, Windows .NET Server family

TypeBuilder.GetPropertyImpl Method

Searches for the specified property whose parameters match the specified argument types and modifiers, using the specified binding constraints.

```
[Visual Basic]
Overrides Protected Function GetPropertyImpl( _
    ByVal name As String, _
    ByVal bindingAttr As BindingFlags, _
    ByVal binder As Binder, _
    ByVal returnType As Type, _
    ByVal types() As Type, _
    ByVal modifiers() As ParameterModifier _
) As PropertyInfo
[C#]
protected override PropertyInfo GetPropertyImpl(
    string name,
    BindingFlags bindingAttr,
    Binder binder,
    Type returnType,
    Type[] types,
    ParameterModifier[] modifiers
);
[C++]
protected: PropertyInfo* GetPropertyImpl(
    String* name,
    BindingFlags bindingAttr,
    Binder* binder,
    Type* returnType,
    Type* types[],
    ParameterModifier modifiers[]
);
[JScript]
protected override function GetPropertyImpl(
    name : String,
    bindingAttr : BindingFlags,
    binder : Binder,
    returnType : Type,
    types : Type[],
    modifiers : ParameterModifier[]
) : PropertyInfo;
```

Parameters

name
> The **String** containing the name of the property to get.

bindingAttr
> A bitmask comprised of one or more **BindingFlags** that specify how the search is conducted.
> -or-
> Zero, to conduct a case-sensitive search for public properties.

binder
> A **Binder** object that defines a set of properties and enables binding, which can involve selection of an overloaded member, coercion of argument types, and invocation of a member through reflection.
> -or-
> A null reference (**Nothing** in Visual Basic), to use the **DefaultBinder**.

returnType
> The return type of the property.

types
> An array of **Type** objects representing the number, order, and type of the parameters for the indexed property to get.
> -or-
> An empty array of the type **Type** (that is, Type[] types = new Type[0]) to get a property that is not indexed.

modifiers
> An array of **ParameterModifier** objects representing the attributes associated with the corresponding element in the *types* array.

Return Value

A **PropertyInfo** object representing the property that matches the specified requirements, if found; otherwise, a null reference (**Nothing** in Visual Basic).

Exceptions

Exception Type	Condition
NotSupportedException	This method is not implemented for incomplete types.

Remarks

Retrieve the type using **GetType** or **GetType** and use reflection on the retrieved type.

Requirements

Platforms: Windows 98, Windows NT 4.0, Windows Millennium Edition, Windows 2000, Windows XP Home Edition, Windows XP Professional, Windows .NET Server family

TypeBuilder.HasElementTypeImpl Method

Calling this method always throws **NotSupportedException**.

```
[Visual Basic]
Overrides Protected Function HasElementTypeImpl() As Boolean
[C#]
protected override bool HasElementTypeImpl();
[C++]
protected: bool HasElementTypeImpl();
[JScript]
protected override function HasElementTypeImpl() : Boolean;
```

Return Value

This method is not supported. No value is returned.

Exceptions

Exception Type	Condition
NotSupportedException	This method is not supported.

Remarks

Retrieve the type using **GetType** or **GetType** and use reflection on the retrieved type.

Requirements

Platforms: Windows 98, Windows NT 4.0, Windows Millennium Edition, Windows 2000, Windows XP Home Edition, Windows XP Professional, Windows .NET Server family

TypeBuilder.InvokeMember Method

Overload List

Invokes the specified member. The method that is to be invoked must be accessible and provide the most specific match with the specified argument list, under the contraints of the specified binder and invocation attributes.

[Visual Basic] **Overloads Overrides Public Function InvokeMember(String, BindingFlags, Binder, Object, Object(), ParameterModifier(), CultureInfo, String()) As Object Implements IReflect.InvokeMember**

[C#] **public override object InvokeMember(string, BindingFlags, Binder, object, object[], ParameterModifier[], CultureInfo, string[]);**

[C++] **public: Object* InvokeMember(String*, BindingFlags, Binder*, Object*, Object[], ParameterModifier[], CultureInfo*, String*[]);**

[JScript] **public override function InvokeMember(String, BindingFlags, Binder, Object, Object[], ParameterModifier[], CultureInfo, String[]) : Object;**

Inherited from **Type**.

[Visual Basic] **Overloads Public Function InvokeMember (String, BindingFlags, Binder, Object, Object()) As Object**

[C#] **public object InvokeMember(string, BindingFlags, Binder, object, object[]);**

[C++] **public: Object* InvokeMember(String*, BindingFlags, Binder*, Object*, Object[]);**

[JScript] **public function InvokeMember(String, BindingFlags, Binder, Object, Object[]) : Object;**

Inherited from **Type**.

[Visual Basic] **Overloads Public Function InvokeMember(String, BindingFlags, Binder, Object, Object(), CultureInfo) As Object**

[C#] **public object InvokeMember(string, BindingFlags, Binder, object, object[], CultureInfo);**

[C++] **public: Object* InvokeMember(String*, BindingFlags, Binder*, Object*, Object[], CultureInfo*);**

[JScript] **public function InvokeMember(String, BindingFlags, Binder, Object, Object[], CultureInfo) : Object;**

TypeBuilder.InvokeMember Method (String, BindingFlags, Binder, Object, Object[], ParameterModifier[], CultureInfo, String[])

Invokes the specified member. The method that is to be invoked must be accessible and provide the most specific match with the specified argument list, under the contraints of the specified binder and invocation attributes.

```
[Visual Basic]
Overrides Overloads Public Function InvokeMember( _
   ByVal name As String, _
   ByVal invokeAttr As BindingFlags, _
   ByVal binder As Binder, _
   ByVal target As Object, _
   ByVal args() As Object, _
   ByVal modifiers() As ParameterModifier, _
   ByVal culture As CultureInfo, _
   ByVal namedParameters() As String _
) As Object Implements IReflect.InvokeMember
[C#]
public override object InvokeMember(
   string name,
   BindingFlags invokeAttr,
   Binder binder,
   object target,
   object[] args,
   ParameterModifier[] modifiers,
   CultureInfo culture,
   string[] namedParameters
);
[C++]
public: Object* InvokeMember(
   String* name,
   BindingFlags invokeAttr,
   Binder* binder,
   Object* target,
   Object* args __gc[],
   ParameterModifier modifiers[],
   CultureInfo* culture,
   String* namedParameters __gc[]
);
[JScript]
public override function InvokeMember(
   name : String,
   invokeAttr : BindingFlags,
   binder : Binder,
   target : Object,
   args : Object[],
   modifiers : ParameterModifier[],
   culture : CultureInfo,
   namedParameters : String[]
) : Object;
```

Parameters

name
> The name of the member to invoke. This can be a constructor, method, property, or field. A suitable invocation attribute must be specified. Note that it is possible to invoke the default member of a class by passing an empty string as the name of the member.

invokeAttr
> The invocation attribute. This must be a bit flag from **BindingFlags**.

binder
> An object that enables the binding, coercion of argument types, invocation of members, and retrieval of **MemberInfo** objects using reflection. If binder is a null reference (**Nothing** in Visual Basic), the default binder is used. See **Binder**.

target
> The object on which to invoke the specified member. If the member is static, this parameter is ignored.

args

An argument list. This is an array of Objects that contains the number, order, and type of the parameters of the member to be invoked. If there are no parameters this should be null.

modifiers

An array of the same length as args with elements that represent the attributes associated with the arguments of the member to be invoked. A parameter has attributes associated with it in the metadata. They are used by various interoperability services. See the metadata specs for more details.

culture

An instance of **CultureInfo** used to govern the coercion of types. If this is null, the **CultureInfo** for the current thread is used. (Note that this is necessary to, for example, convert a String that represents 1000 to a Double value, since 1000 is represented differently by different cultures.)

namedParameters

Each parameter in the *namedParameters* array gets the value in the corresponding element in the *args* array. If the length of *args* is greater than the length of *namedParameters*, the remaining argument values are passed in order.

Return Value

Returns the return value of the invoked member.

Implements

IReflect.InvokeMember

Exceptions

Exception Type	Condition
NotSupportedException	This method is not currently supported for incomplete types.

Remarks

A method will be invoked if the number of parameters in the method declaration equals the number of arguments in the specified argument list, and the type of each argument can be converted by the binder to the type of the parameter.

The binder will find all of the matching methods. These methods are found based on the type of binding requested (BindingFlags.InvokeMethod, BindingFlags.GetProperties, and so on.). The set of methods is filtered by the name, number of arguments, and a set of search modifiers defined in the binder. After the method is selected, it will be invoked. Accessibility is checked at that point. The search can control which set of methods are searched based upon the accessibility attribute associated with the method. The **IBinder.BindToMethod** method is responsible for selecting the method to be invoked. The default binder selects the most specific match.

> **Note** Access restrictions are ignored for fully-trusted code. That is, private constructors, methods, fields, and properties can be accessed and invoked using Reflection whenever the code is fully-trusted.

This method is not currently supported. You can retrieve the type using **GetType** or **GetType** and use reflection on the retrieved type.

Requirements

Platforms: Windows 98, Windows NT 4.0, Windows Millennium Edition, Windows 2000, Windows XP Home Edition, Windows XP Professional, Windows .NET Server family

TypeBuilder.IsArrayImpl Method

Always returns **false**.

```
[Visual Basic]
Overrides Protected Function IsArrayImpl() As Boolean
[C#]
protected override bool IsArrayImpl();
[C++]
protected: bool IsArrayImpl();
[JScript]
protected override function IsArrayImpl() : Boolean;
```

Return Value

Returns **false**.

Requirements

Platforms: Windows 98, Windows NT 4.0, Windows Millennium Edition, Windows 2000, Windows XP Home Edition, Windows XP Professional, Windows .NET Server family

TypeBuilder.IsAssignableFrom Method

Determines whether an instance of the current **Type** can be assigned from an instance of the specified **Type**.

```
[Visual Basic]
Overrides Public Function IsAssignableFrom( _
   ByVal c As Type _
) As Boolean
[C#]
public override bool IsAssignableFrom(
   Type c
);
[C++]
public: bool IsAssignableFrom(
   Type* c
);
[JScript]
public override function IsAssignableFrom(
   c : Type
) : Boolean;
```

Parameters

c

The **Type** to compare with the current **Type**.

Return Value

true if the *c* parameter and the current **Type** represent the same type, or if the current **Type** is in the inheritance hierarchy of *c*, or if the current **Type** is an interface that *c* supports. **false** if none of these conditions are the case, or if *c* is a null reference (**Nothing** in Visual Basic).

Remarks

This method can be overridden by a derived class.

Requirements

Platforms: Windows 98, Windows NT 4.0, Windows Millennium Edition, Windows 2000, Windows XP Home Edition, Windows XP Professional, Windows .NET Server family

TypeBuilder.IsByRefImpl Method

Always returns **false**.

```
[Visual Basic]
Overrides Protected Function IsByRefImpl() As Boolean
[C#]
protected override bool IsByRefImpl();
[C++]
protected: bool IsByRefImpl();
[JScript]
protected override function IsByRefImpl() : Boolean;
```

Return Value

Always **false**.

Requirements

Platforms: Windows 98, Windows NT 4.0,
Windows Millennium Edition, Windows 2000,
Windows XP Home Edition, Windows XP Professional,
Windows .NET Server family

TypeBuilder.IsCOMObjectImpl Method

Checks if this type imports a COM type.

```
[Visual Basic]
Overrides Protected Function IsCOMObjectImpl() As Boolean
[C#]
protected override bool IsCOMObjectImpl();
[C++]
protected: bool IsCOMObjectImpl();
[JScript]
protected override function IsCOMObjectImpl() : Boolean;
```

Return Value

Returns **true** if this type imports a COM type; otherwise, **false**.

Requirements

Platforms: Windows 98, Windows NT 4.0,
Windows Millennium Edition, Windows 2000,
Windows XP Home Edition, Windows XP Professional,
Windows .NET Server family

TypeBuilder.IsDefined Method

Set a custom attribute using a custom attribute builder.

```
[Visual Basic]
Overrides Public Function IsDefined( _
   ByVal attributeType As Type, _
   ByVal inherit As Boolean _
) As Boolean Implements ICustomAttributeProvider.IsDefined
[C#]
public override bool IsDefined(
   Type attributeType,
   bool inherit
);
[C++]
public: bool IsDefined(
   Type* attributeType,
   bool inherit
);
```

```
[JScript]
public override function IsDefined(
   attributeType : Type,
   inherit : Boolean
) : Boolean;
```

Parameters

attributeType
   The **Type** object to which the custom attributes are applied.
inherit
   Specifies whether to search this member's inheritance chain to find the attributes.

Return Value

true if one or more instance of *attributeType* is defined on this member; otherwise **false**.

Implements

ICustomAttributeProvider.IsDefined

Exceptions

Exception Type	Condition
NotSupportedException	This method is not currently supported for incomplete types. Retrieve the type using **GetType** and call **IsDefined** on the returned **Type**.

Requirements

Platforms: Windows 98, Windows NT 4.0,
Windows Millennium Edition, Windows 2000,
Windows XP Home Edition, Windows XP Professional,
Windows .NET Server family

TypeBuilder.IsPointerImpl Method

Always returns **false**.

```
[Visual Basic]
Overrides Protected Function IsPointerImpl() As Boolean
[C#]
protected override bool IsPointerImpl();
[C++]
protected: bool IsPointerImpl();
[JScript]
protected override function IsPointerImpl() : Boolean;
```

Return Value

Always **false**.

Requirements

Platforms: Windows 98, Windows NT 4.0,
Windows Millennium Edition, Windows 2000,
Windows XP Home Edition, Windows XP Professional,
Windows .NET Server family

TypeBuilder.IsPrimitiveImpl Method

Always returns **false**.

```
[Visual Basic]
Overrides Protected Function IsPrimitiveImpl() As Boolean
[C#]
protected override bool IsPrimitiveImpl();
```

```
[C++]
protected: bool IsPrimitiveImpl();
[JScript]
protected override function IsPrimitiveImpl() : Boolean;
```

Return Value

Returns **false**.

Requirements

Platforms: Windows 98, Windows NT 4.0,
Windows Millennium Edition, Windows 2000,
Windows XP Home Edition, Windows XP Professional,
Windows .NET Server family

TypeBuilder.IsSubclassOf Method

Checks if this type is a derived class of the given type *c*.

```
[Visual Basic]
Overrides Public Function IsSubclassOf( _
    ByVal c As Type _
) As Boolean
[C#]
public override bool IsSubclassOf(
    Type c
);
[C++]
public: bool IsSubclassOf(
    Type* c
);
[JScript]
public override function IsSubclassOf(
    c : Type
) : Boolean;
```

Parameters

c
    A **Type** that is to be checked

Return Value

Read-only. Returns **true** if this type is the same as the type *c*, or is a
subtype of type *c*; otherwise, **false**.

Requirements

Platforms: Windows 98, Windows NT 4.0,
Windows Millennium Edition, Windows 2000,
Windows XP Home Edition, Windows XP Professional,
Windows .NET Server family

TypeBuilder.SetCustomAttribute Method

Sets a custom attribute.

Overload List

Set a custom attribute using a custom attribute builder.

    [Visual Basic] **Overloads Public Sub
SetCustomAttribute(CustomAttributeBuilder)**

    [C#] **public void SetCustomAttribute(CustomAttributeBuilder);**

    [C++] **public: void SetCustomAttribute(CustomAttributeBuilder*);**

    [JScript] **public function SetCustomAttribute(CustomAttributeBuilder);**

Sets a custom attribute using a specified custom attribute blob.

    [Visual Basic] **Overloads Public Sub
SetCustomAttribute(ConstructorInfo, Byte())**

    [C#] **public void SetCustomAttribute(ConstructorInfo,
byte[]);**

    [C++] **public: void SetCustomAttribute(ConstructorInfo*,
unsigned char __gc[]);**

    [JScript] **public function SetCustomAttribute(ConstructorInfo, Byte[]);**

TypeBuilder.SetCustomAttribute Method (CustomAttributeBuilder)

Set a custom attribute using a custom attribute builder.

```
[Visual Basic]
Overloads Public Sub SetCustomAttribute( _
    ByVal customBuilder As CustomAttributeBuilder _
)
[C#]
public void SetCustomAttribute(
    CustomAttributeBuilder customBuilder
);
[C++]
public: void SetCustomAttribute(
    CustomAttributeBuilder* customBuilder
);
[JScript]
public function SetCustomAttribute(
    customBuilder : CustomAttributeBuilder
);
```

Parameters

customBuilder
    An instance of a helper class to define the custom attribute.

Exceptions

Exception Type	Condition
ArgumentNullException	*con* is a null reference (**Nothing** in Visual Basic).

Requirements

Platforms: Windows 98, Windows NT 4.0,
Windows Millennium Edition, Windows 2000,
Windows XP Home Edition, Windows XP Professional,
Windows .NET Server family

.NET Framework Security:
• **ReflectionPermission** SecurityAction.Demand, ReflectionEmit

TypeBuilder.SetCustomAttribute Method (ConstructorInfo, Byte[])

Sets a custom attribute using a specified custom attribute blob.

```
[Visual Basic]
Overloads Public Sub SetCustomAttribute( _
    ByVal con As ConstructorInfo, _
    ByVal binaryAttribute() As Byte _
)
```

```
[C#]
public void SetCustomAttribute(
   ConstructorInfo con,
   byte[] binaryAttribute
);
[C++]
public: void SetCustomAttribute(
   ConstructorInfo* con,
   unsigned char binaryAttribute __gc[]
);
[JScript]
public function SetCustomAttribute(
   con : ConstructorInfo,
   binaryAttribute : Byte[]
);
```

Parameters

con
> The constructor for the custom attribute.

binaryAttribute
> A byte blob representing the attributes.

Exceptions

Exception Type	Condition
ArgumentNullException	*con* or *binaryAttribute* is a null reference (**Nothing** in Visual Basic).

Remarks

See the metadata specification in the ECMA Partition II documentation for details on how to format *binaryAttribute*. The Partition II documentation is included with the .NET Framework SDK installation, and can be found in the %\Microsoft.NET\FrameworkSDK\Tool Developers Guide\docs directory.

Requirements

Platforms: Windows 98, Windows NT 4.0, Windows Millennium Edition, Windows 2000, Windows XP Home Edition, Windows XP Professional, Windows .NET Server family

.NET Framework Security:
- **ReflectionPermission** SecurityAction.Demand, ReflectionEmit

TypeBuilder.SetParent Method

Sets the parent of this **Type**.

```
[Visual Basic]
Public Sub SetParent( _
   ByVal parent As Type _
)
[C#]
public void SetParent(
   Type parent
);
[C++]
public: void SetParent(
   Type* parent
);
[JScript]
public function SetParent(
   parent : Type
);
```

Parameters

parent
> The parent type.

Exceptions

Exception Type	Condition
ArgumentNullException	*parent* is a null reference (**Nothing** in Visual Basic).
InvalidOperationException	if the type was previously created using **CreateType**.

Requirements

Platforms: Windows 98, Windows NT 4.0, Windows Millennium Edition, Windows 2000, Windows XP Home Edition, Windows XP Professional, Windows .NET Server family

TypeBuilder.ToString Method

Returns the name of the type excluding the namespace.

```
[Visual Basic]
Overrides Public Function ToString() As String
[C#]
public override string ToString();
[C++]
public: String* ToString();
[JScript]
public override function ToString() : String;
```

Return Value

Read-only. The name of the type excluding the namespace.

Requirements

Platforms: Windows 98, Windows NT 4.0, Windows Millennium Edition, Windows 2000, Windows XP Home Edition, Windows XP Professional, Windows .NET Server family

TypeToken Structure

Represents the **Token** returned by the metadata to represent a type.

System.Object
  System.ValueType
    System.Reflection.Emit.TypeToken

```
[Visual Basic]
<Serializable>
Public Structure TypeToken
[C#]
[Serializable]
public struct TypeToken
[C++]
[Serializable]
public __value struct TypeToken
```

[JScript] In JScript, you can use the structures in the .NET Framework, but you cannot define your own.

Thread Safety

Reflection Emit is thread-safe when using assemblies that were created with the **AppDomain.DefineDynamicAssembly** method with the Boolean parameter *isSynchronized* set to **true**.

Remarks

The type of an object is also known as the class of an object.

Requirements

Namespace: System.Reflection.Emit

Platforms: Windows 98, Windows NT 4.0, Windows Millennium Edition, Windows 2000, Windows XP Home Edition, Windows XP Professional, Windows .NET Server family

Assembly: Mscorlib (in Mscorlib.dll)

TypeToken.Empty Field

The default **TypeToken** with **Token** value 0.

```
[Visual Basic]
Public Shared ReadOnly Empty As TypeToken
[C#]
public static readonly TypeToken Empty;
[C++]
public: static TypeToken Empty;
[JScript]
public static var Empty : TypeToken;
```

Requirements

Platforms: Windows 98, Windows NT 4.0, Windows Millennium Edition, Windows 2000, Windows XP Home Edition, Windows XP Professional, Windows .NET Server family

TypeToken.Token Property

Retrieves the metadata token for this class.

```
[Visual Basic]
Public ReadOnly Property Token As Integer
[C#]
public int Token {get;}
```

```
[C++]
public: __property int get_Token();
[JScript]
public function get Token() : int;
```

Property Value

Read-only. Retrieves the metadata token of this type.

Requirements

Platforms: Windows 98, Windows NT 4.0, Windows Millennium Edition, Windows 2000, Windows XP Home Edition, Windows XP Professional, Windows .NET Server family

TypeToken.Equals Method

Checks if the given object is an instance of **TypeToken** and is equal to this instance.

```
[Visual Basic]
Overrides Public Function Equals( _
   ByVal obj As Object _
) As Boolean
[C#]
public override bool Equals(
   object obj
);
[C++]
public: bool Equals(
   Object* obj
);
[JScript]
public override function Equals(
   obj : Object
) : Boolean;
```

Parameters

obj
    The object to compare with this TypeToken.

Return Value

true if *obj* is an instance of **TypeToken** and is equal to this object; otherwise, **false**.

Requirements

Platforms: Windows 98, Windows NT 4.0, Windows Millennium Edition, Windows 2000, Windows XP Home Edition, Windows XP Professional, Windows .NET Server family

TypeToken.GetHashCode Method

Generates the hash code for this type.

```
[Visual Basic]
Overrides Public Function GetHashCode() As Integer
[C#]
public override int GetHashCode();
[C++]
public: int GetHashCode();
[JScript]
public override function GetHashCode() : int;
```

Return Value

Returns the hash code for this type.

Requirements

Platforms: Windows 98, Windows NT 4.0,
Windows Millennium Edition, Windows 2000,
Windows XP Home Edition, Windows XP Professional,
Windows .NET Server family

UnmanagedMarshal Class

Represents the class that describes how to marshal a field from managed to unmanaged code. This class cannot be inherited.

System.Object
  System.Reflection.Emit.UnmanagedMarshal

```
[Visual Basic]
<Serializable>
NotInheritable Public Class UnmanagedMarshal
[C#]
[Serializable]
public sealed class UnmanagedMarshal
[C++]
[Serializable]
public __gc __sealed class UnmanagedMarshal
[JScript]
public
    Serializable
class UnmanagedMarshal
```

Thread Safety

Reflection Emit is thread-safe when using assemblies that were created with the **AppDomain.DefineDynamicAssembly** method with the Boolean parameter *isSynchronized* set to **true**.

Remarks

Marshaling is the process of packaging and unpackaging parameters so remote procedure calls can occur. During marshaling, a field might undergo a format conversion when the format of the managed type is different from the format of the corresponding unmanaged type. For example, you might want to marshal a **String** type as an unmanaged BSTR. Some format conversions are handled automatically by the runtime. To override the default behavior, you must use the **UnmanagedMarshal** class to define the format conversion.

Requirements

Namespace: System.Reflection.Emit

Platforms: Windows 98, Windows NT 4.0, Windows Millennium Edition, Windows 2000, Windows XP Home Edition, Windows XP Professional, Windows .NET Server family

Assembly: Mscorlib (in Mscorlib.dll)

UnmanagedMarshal.BaseType Property

Gets an unmanaged base type. This property is read-only.

```
[Visual Basic]
Public ReadOnly Property BaseType As UnmanagedType
[C#]
public UnmanagedType BaseType {get;}
[C++]
public: __property UnmanagedType get_BaseType();
[JScript]
public function get BaseType() : UnmanagedType;
```

Property Value

An **UnmanagedType** object.

Exceptions

Exception Type	Condition
ArgumentException	The unmanaged type is not an **LPArray** or a **SafeArray**.

Requirements

Platforms: Windows 98, Windows NT 4.0, Windows Millennium Edition, Windows 2000, Windows XP Home Edition, Windows XP Professional, Windows .NET Server family

UnmanagedMarshal.ElementCount Property

Gets a number element. This property is read-only.

```
[Visual Basic]
Public ReadOnly Property ElementCount As Integer
[C#]
public int ElementCount {get;}
[C++]
public: __property int get_ElementCount();
[JScript]
public function get ElementCount() : int;
```

Property Value

An integer indicating the element count.

Exceptions

Exception Type	Condition
ArgumentException	The argument is not an unmanaged element count.

Remarks

There is an **ElementCount** only if there is a **NativeTypeFixedArray**.

Requirements

Platforms: Windows 98, Windows NT 4.0, Windows Millennium Edition, Windows 2000, Windows XP Home Edition, Windows XP Professional, Windows .NET Server family

UnmanagedMarshal.GetUnmanagedType Property

Indicates an unmanaged type. This property is read-only.

```
[Visual Basic]
Public ReadOnly Property GetUnmanagedType As UnmanagedType
[C#]
public UnmanagedType GetUnmanagedType {get;}
[C++]
public: __property UnmanagedType get_GetUnmanagedType();
[JScript]
public function get GetUnmanagedType() : UnmanagedType;
```

Property Value

An **UnmanagedType** object.

Remarks

The **GetUnmanagedType** property is an accessor function for the native type.

Requirements

Platforms: Windows 98, Windows NT 4.0,
Windows Millennium Edition, Windows 2000,
Windows XP Home Edition, Windows XP Professional,
Windows .NET Server family

UnmanagedMarshal.IIDGuid Property

Gets a GUID. This property is read-only.

```
[Visual Basic]
Public ReadOnly Property IIDGuid As Guid
[C#]
public Guid IIDGuid {get;}
[C++]
public: __property Guid get_IIDGuid();
[JScript]
public function get IIDGuid() : Guid;
```

Property Value

A **Guid** object.

Exceptions

Exception Type	Condition
ArgumentException	The argument is not a custom marshaler.

Remarks

This property always returns Guid.Empty. This property might be
removed in a future release.

Requirements

Platforms: Windows 98, Windows NT 4.0,
Windows Millennium Edition, Windows 2000,
Windows XP Home Edition, Windows XP Professional,
Windows .NET Server family

UnmanagedMarshal.DefineByValArray Method

Specifies a fixed-length array (ByValArray) to marshal to
unmanaged code.

```
[Visual Basic]
Public Shared Function DefineByValArray( _
   ByVal elemCount As Integer _
) As UnmanagedMarshal
[C#]
public static UnmanagedMarshal DefineByValArray(
   int elemCount
);
[C++]
public: static UnmanagedMarshal* DefineByValArray(
   int elemCount
);
[JScript]
public static function DefineByValArray(
   elemCount : int
) : UnmanagedMarshal;
```

Parameters

elemCount
   The number of elements in the fixed-length array.

Return Value

An **UnmanagedMarshal** object.

Exceptions

Exception Type	Condition
ArgumentException	The argument is not a simple native type.

Remarks

The **DefineByValArray** method is not a simple native marshal.

Only unmanaged marshal constructs can be made using these static
constructors.

Marshaling an array is a more complex process than marshaling an
integer parameter. Array members are copied in a specific order so
that the other side can reconstruct the array exactly.

Requirements

Platforms: Windows 98, Windows NT 4.0,
Windows Millennium Edition, Windows 2000,
Windows XP Home Edition, Windows XP Professional,
Windows .NET Server family

UnmanagedMarshal.DefineByValTStr Method

Specifies a string in a fixed array buffer (ByValTStr) to marshal to
unmanaged code.

```
[Visual Basic]
Public Shared Function DefineByValTStr( _
   ByVal elemCount As Integer _
) As UnmanagedMarshal
[C#]
public static UnmanagedMarshal DefineByValTStr(
   int elemCount
);
[C++]
public: static UnmanagedMarshal* DefineByValTStr(
   int elemCount
);
[JScript]
public static function DefineByValTStr(
   elemCount : int
) : UnmanagedMarshal;
```

Parameters

elemCount
   The number of elements in the fixed array buffer.

Return Value

An **UnmanagedMarshal** object.

Exceptions

Exception Type	Condition
ArgumentException	The argument is not a simple native type.

Remarks

The **DefineByValStr** method is not a simple native marshal.

Only unmanaged marshal constructs can be made using these static
constructors.

Marshaling an array is a more complex process than marshaling an integer parameter. Array members are copied in a specific order so that the other side can reconstruct the array exactly.

Requirements

Platforms: Windows 98, Windows NT 4.0, Windows Millennium Edition, Windows 2000, Windows XP Home Edition, Windows XP Professional, Windows .NET Server family

UnmanagedMarshal.DefineLPArray Method

Specifies an **LPArray** to marshal to unmanaged code. The length of an **LPArray** is determined at runtime by the size of the actual marshaled array.

```
[Visual Basic]
Public Shared Function DefineLPArray( _
   ByVal elemType As UnmanagedType _
) As UnmanagedMarshal
[C#]
public static UnmanagedMarshal DefineLPArray(
   UnmanagedType elemType
);
[C++]
public: static UnmanagedMarshal* DefineLPArray(
   UnmanagedType elemType
);
[JScript]
public static function DefineLPArray(
   elemType : UnmanagedType
) : UnmanagedMarshal;
```

Parameters

elemType
   The unmanaged type to which to marshal the array.

Return Value

An **UnmanagedMarshal** object.

Exceptions

Exception Type	Condition
ArgumentException	The argument is not a simple native type.

Remarks

The **DefineLPArray** method is not a simple native marshal.

Only unmanaged marshal constructs can be made using these static constructors.

Marshaling an array is a more complex process than marshaling an integer parameter. Array members are copied in a specific order so that the other side can reconstruct the array exactly.

Requirements

Platforms: Windows 98, Windows NT 4.0, Windows Millennium Edition, Windows 2000, Windows XP Home Edition, Windows XP Professional, Windows .NET Server family

UnmanagedMarshal.DefineSafeArray Method

Specifies a **SafeArray** to marshal to unmanaged code.

```
[Visual Basic]
Public Shared Function DefineSafeArray( _
   ByVal elemType As UnmanagedType _
) As UnmanagedMarshal
[C#]
public static UnmanagedMarshal DefineSafeArray(
   UnmanagedType elemType
);
[C++]
public: static UnmanagedMarshal* DefineSafeArray(
   UnmanagedType elemType
);
[JScript]
public static function DefineSafeArray(
   elemType : UnmanagedType
) : UnmanagedMarshal;
```

Parameters

elemType
   The base type or the **UnmanagedType** of each element of the array.

Return Value

An **UnmanagedMarshal** object.

Exceptions

Exception Type	Condition
ArgumentException	The argument is not a simple native type.

Remarks

The **DefineSafeArray** method is not a simple native marshal.

Only unmanaged marshal constructs can be made using these static constructors.

Marshaling an array is a more complex process than marshaling an integer parameter. Array members are copied in a specific order so that the other side can reconstruct the array exactly.

Requirements

Platforms: Windows 98, Windows NT 4.0, Windows Millennium Edition, Windows 2000, Windows XP Home Edition, Windows XP Professional, Windows .NET Server family

UnmanagedMarshal.DefineUnmanagedMarshal Method

Specifies a given type that is to be marshaled to unmanaged code.

```
[Visual Basic]
Public Shared Function DefineUnmanagedMarshal( _
   ByVal unmanagedType As UnmanagedType _
) As UnmanagedMarshal
[C#]
public static UnmanagedMarshal DefineUnmanagedMarshal(
   UnmanagedType unmanagedType
);
[C++]
public: static UnmanagedMarshal* DefineUnmanagedMarshal(
   UnmanagedType unmanagedType
);
```

```
[JScript]
public static function DefineUnmanagedMarshal(
    unmanagedType : UnmanagedType
) : UnmanagedMarshal;
```

Parameters

unmanagedType

> The unmanaged type to which the type is to be marshaled.

Return Value

An **UnmanagedMarshal** object.

Exceptions

Exception Type	Condition
ArgumentException	The argument is not a simple native type.

Remarks

The **DefineUnmanagedMarshal** method is not a simple native marshal.Only unmanaged marshal constructs can be made using these static constructors.

Requirements

Platforms: Windows 98, Windows NT 4.0, Windows Millennium Edition, Windows 2000, Windows XP Home Edition, Windows XP Professional, Windows .NET Server family

System.Resources Namespace

The **System.Resources** namespace provides classes and interfaces that allow developers to create, store, and manage various culture-specific resources used in an application. One of the most important classes of the **System.Resources** namespace is the **ResourceManager** class.

The **ResourceManager** class allows the user to access and control resources stored in the main assembly or in resource satellite assemblies. Use the **ResourceManager.GetObject** and **ResourceManager.GetString** methods to retrieve culture-specific objects and strings.

IResourceReader Interface

Provides the base functionality to read data from resource files.

```
[Visual Basic]
Public Interface IResourceReader
   Inherits IEnumerable, IDisposable
[C#]
public interface IResourceReader : IEnumerable, IDisposable
[C++]
public __gc __interface IResourceReader : public IEnumerable,
   IDisposable
[JScript]
public interface IResourceReader implements IEnumerable,
   IDisposable
```

Classes that Implement IResourceReader

Class	Description
ResourceReader	Enumerates .resources files and streams, reading sequential resource name and value pairs.
ResXResourceReader	Enumerates XML resource (.resx) files and streams, and reads the sequential resource name and value pairs.

Remarks

Resource readers are used to read a stream of resource files in a particular file format. Implement this interface when you need to control the way in which a resource file is read (for example, if the resouce file was written using a customized **ResourceWriter**). Otherwise, use the default **ResourceReader** or **ResXResourceReader**.

Requirements

Namespace: System.Resources

Platforms: Windows 98, Windows NT 4.0, Windows Millennium Edition, Windows 2000, Windows XP Home Edition, Windows XP Professional, Windows .NET Server family, .NET Compact Framework - Windows CE .NET

Assembly: Mscorlib (in Mscorlib.dll)

IResourceReader.Close Method

Closes the resource reader after releasing any resources associated with it.

```
[Visual Basic]
Sub Close()
[C#]
void Close();
[C++]
void Close();
[JScript]
function Close();
```

Remarks

Use this function to close a network connection or a file, if necessary.

Requirements

Platforms: Windows 98, Windows NT 4.0, Windows Millennium Edition, Windows 2000, Windows XP Home Edition, Windows XP Professional, Windows .NET Server family, .NET Compact Framework - Windows CE .NET

IResourceReader.GetEnumerator Method

Returns an **IDictionaryEnumerator** of the resources for this reader.

```
[Visual Basic]
Function GetEnumerator() As IDictionaryEnumerator
[C#]
IDictionaryEnumerator GetEnumerator();
[C++]
IDictionaryEnumerator* GetEnumerator();
[JScript]
function GetEnumerator() : IDictionaryEnumerator;
```

Return Value

A dictionary enumerator for the resources for this reader.

Requirements

Platforms: Windows 98, Windows NT 4.0, Windows Millennium Edition, Windows 2000, Windows XP Home Edition, Windows XP Professional, Windows .NET Server family, .NET Compact Framework - Windows CE .NET

IResourceWriter Interface

Provides functionality to write resources to an output file or stream.

System.IDisposable
   System.Resources.IResourceWriter

```
[Visual Basic]
Public Interface IResourceWriter
   Inherits IDisposable
[C#]
public interface IResourceWriter : IDisposable
[C++]
public __gc __interface IResourceWriter : public IDisposable
[JScript]
public interface IResourceWriter implements IDisposable
```

Classes that Implement IResourceWriter

Class	Description
ResourceWriter	Writes resources in the system-default format to an output file or an output stream.
ResXResourceWriter	Writes resources in an XML resource (.resx) file or an output stream.

Remarks

Use resource writers to write resources in a particular file format. Generally, users will create a resource writer, call **AddResource** to add resources, and then call either **Generate** or **Close** to close the resource file.

Requirements

Namespace: System.Resources

Platforms: Windows 98, Windows NT 4.0, Windows Millennium Edition, Windows 2000, Windows XP Home Edition, Windows XP Professional, Windows .NET Server family

Assembly: Mscorlib (in Mscorlib.dll)

IResourceWriter.AddResource Method

Adds a resource to the list of resources to be written to an output file or output stream.

Overload List

Adds an 8-bit unsigned integer array as a named resource to the list of resources to be written.

   [Visual Basic] **Overloads Sub AddResource(String, Byte())**
   [C#] **void AddResource(string, byte[]);**
   [C++] **void AddResource(String*, unsigned char __gc[]);**
   [JScript] **function AddResource(String, Byte[]);**

Adds a named resource of type **Object** to the list of resources to be written.

   [Visual Basic] **Overloads Sub AddResource(String, Object)**
   [C#] **void AddResource(string, object);**
   [C++] **void AddResource(String*, Object*);**
   [JScript] **function AddResource(String, Object);**

Adds a named resource of type **String** to the list of resources to be written.

   [Visual Basic] **Overloads Sub AddResource(String, String)**
   [C#] **void AddResource(string, string);**
   [C++] **void AddResource(String*, String*);**
   [JScript] **function AddResource(String, String);**

IResourceWriter.AddResource Method (String, Byte[])

Adds an 8-bit unsigned integer array as a named resource to the list of resources to be written.

```
[Visual Basic]
Sub AddResource( _
   ByVal name As String, _
   ByVal value() As Byte _
)
[C#]
void AddResource(
   string name,
   byte[] value
);
[C++]
void AddResource(
   String* name,
   unsigned char value __gc[]
);
[JScript]
function AddResource(
   name : String,
   value : Byte[]
);
```

Parameters

name
   Name of a resource.
value
   Value of a resource as an 8-bit unsigned integer array.

Exceptions

Exception Type	Condition
ArgumentNullException	The *name* parameter is a null reference (**Nothing** in Visual Basic).

Remarks

The resources are not written until **Generate** is called.

Requirements

Platforms: Windows 98, Windows NT 4.0, Windows Millennium Edition, Windows 2000, Windows XP Home Edition, Windows XP Professional, Windows .NET Server family

IResourceWriter.AddResource Method (String, Object)

Adds a named resource of type **Object** to the list of resources to be written.

```
[Visual Basic]
Sub AddResource( _
   ByVal name As String, _
   ByVal value As Object _
)
```

```
[C#]
void AddResource(
    string name,
    object value
);
[C++]
void AddResource(
    String* name,
    Object* value
);
[JScript]
function AddResource(
    name : String,
    value : Object
);
```

Parameters

name
> The name of the resource.

value
> The value of the resource.

Exceptions

Exception Type	Condition
ArgumentNullException	The *name* parameter is a null reference (**Nothing** in Visual Basic).

Remarks

The resource is not written until **Generate** is called.

> **Note**   *value* might need to be serializable, so you might have to provide a type converter, depending on which resource writer is used.

Requirements

Platforms: Windows 98, Windows NT 4.0, Windows Millennium Edition, Windows 2000, Windows XP Home Edition, Windows XP Professional, Windows .NET Server family

IResourceWriter.AddResource Method (String, String)

Adds a named resource of type **String** to the list of resources to be written.

```
[Visual Basic]
Sub AddResource( _
    ByVal name As String, _
    ByVal value As String _
)
[C#]
void AddResource(
    string name,
    string value
);
[C++]
void AddResource(
    String* name,
    String* value
);
```

```
[JScript]
function AddResource(
    name : String,
    value : String
);
```

Parameters

name
> The name of the resource.

value
> The value of the resource.

Exceptions

Exception Type	Condition
ArgumentException	The *name* parameter is a null reference (**Nothing** in Visual Basic).

Remarks

The resource is not written until **Generate** is called.

Requirements

Platforms: Windows 98, Windows NT 4.0, Windows Millennium Edition, Windows 2000, Windows XP Home Edition, Windows XP Professional, Windows .NET Server family

IResourceWriter.Close Method

Closes the underlying resource file or stream, ensuring all the data has been written to the file.

```
[Visual Basic]
Sub Close()
[C#]
void Close();
[C++]
void Close();
[JScript]
function Close();
```

Remarks

If necessary, **Close** will call **Generate** to output the resources to the underlying file or stream before closing it.

Requirements

Platforms: Windows 98, Windows NT 4.0, Windows Millennium Edition, Windows 2000, Windows XP Home Edition, Windows XP Professional, Windows .NET Server family

IResourceWriter.Generate Method

Writes all the resources added by the **AddResource** method to the output file or stream.

```
[Visual Basic]
Sub Generate()
[C#]
void Generate();
[C++]
void Generate();
[JScript]
function Generate();
```

Remarks

Generate does not close the output file or output stream. Instead, consider calling **Close**. **Generate** is useful when you need to create a resource file but you don't want to close the output stream. **Generate** can only be called once. After calling **Generate**, all **IResourceWriter** methods other than **Close** will throw an exception.

Requirements

Platforms: Windows 98, Windows NT 4.0, Windows Millennium Edition, Windows 2000, Windows XP Home Edition, Windows XP Professional, Windows .NET Server family

MissingManifestResource-Exception Class

The exception thrown if the main assembly does not contain the resources for the neutral culture, and they are required because of a missing appropriate satellite assembly.

System.Object
  System.Exception
    System.SystemException
      System.Resources.MissingManifestResourceException

```
[Visual Basic]
<Serializable>
Public Class MissingManifestResourceException
   Inherits SystemException
[C#]
[Serializable]
public class MissingManifestResourceException : SystemException
[C++]
[Serializable]
public __gc class MissingManifestResourceException : public
   SystemException
[JScript]
public
   Serializable
class MissingManifestResourceException extends
   SystemException
```

Thread Safety

Any public static (**Shared** in Visual Basic) members of this type are safe for multithreaded operations. Any instance members are not guaranteed to be thread safe.

Remarks

MissingManifestResourceException uses the HRESULT COR_E_MISSINGMANIFESTRESOURCE which has the value 0x80131532.

MissingManifestResourceException uses the default **Equals** implementation, which supports reference equality.

For a list of initial property values for an instance of **MissingManifestResourceException**, see the **MissingManifestResourceException** constructors.

> **Note** It is strongly recommended that your main assembly contains a neutral set of resources, so if a satellite assembly is unavailable, your application will have some acceptable behavior.

Requirements

Namespace: System.Resources

Platforms: Windows 98, Windows NT 4.0, Windows Millennium Edition, Windows 2000, Windows XP Home Edition, Windows XP Professional, Windows .NET Server family, .NET Compact Framework - Windows CE .NET

Assembly: Mscorlib (in Mscorlib.dll)

MissingManifestResourceException Constructor

Constructs an instance of **MissingManifestResourceException**.

Overload List

Constructs an instance of **MissingManifestResourceException** with default properties.

Supported by the .NET Compact Framework.

[Visual Basic] **Public Sub New()**
[C#] **public MissingManifestResourceException();**
[C++] **public: MissingManifestResourceException();**
[JScript] **public function MissingManifestResourceException();**

Constructs an instance of **MissingManifestResourceException** with the specified error message.

Supported by the .NET Compact Framework.

[Visual Basic] **Public Sub New(String)**
[C#] **public MissingManifestResourceException(string);**
[C++] **public: MissingManifestResourceException(String*);**
[JScript] **public function MissingManifestResourceException(String);**

Initializes a new instance of the **MissingManifestResourceException** class from serialized data.

[Visual Basic] **Protected Sub New(SerializationInfo, StreamingContext)**
[C#] **protected MissingManifestResourceException(SerializationInfo, StreamingContext);**
[C++] **protected: MissingManifestResourceException(SerializationInfo*, StreamingContext);**
[JScript] **protected function MissingManifestResourceException(SerializationInfo, StreamingContext);**

Initializes a new instance of the **MissingManifestResourceException** class with a specified error message and a reference to the inner exception that is the cause of this exception.

Supported by the .NET Compact Framework.

[Visual Basic] **Public Sub New(String, Exception)**
[C#] **public MissingManifestResourceException(string, Exception);**
[C++] **public: MissingManifestResourceException(String*, Exception*);**
[JScript] **public function MissingManifestResourceException(String, Exception);**

MissingManifestResourceException Constructor ( )

Constructs an instance of **MissingManifestResourceException** with default properties.

```
[Visual Basic]
Public Sub New()
[C#]
public MissingManifestResourceException();
[C++]
public: MissingManifestResourceException();
```

```
[JScript]
public function MissingManifestResourceException();
```

Remarks

The following table shows the initial property values for an instance of **MissingManifestResourceException**.

Property	Value
InnerException	A null reference (**Nothing** in Visual Basic).
Message	The localized error message for **MissingManifestResourceException**.

Requirements

Platforms: Windows 98, Windows NT 4.0, Windows Millennium Edition, Windows 2000, Windows XP Home Edition, Windows XP Professional, Windows .NET Server family, .NET Compact Framework - Windows CE .NET

MissingManifestResourceException Constructor (String)

Constructs an instance of **MissingManifestResourceException** with the specified error message.

```
[Visual Basic]
Public Sub New( _
   ByVal message As String _
)
[C#]
public MissingManifestResourceException(
   string message
);
[C++]
public: MissingManifestResourceException(
   String* message
);
[JScript]
public function MissingManifestResourceException(
   message : String
);
```

Parameters

message
> The error message that explains the reason for the exception.

Remarks

The following table shows the initial property values for an instance of **MissingManifestResourceException**.

Property	Value
InnerException	A null reference (**Nothing** in Visual Basic).
Message	The *message* string.

Requirements

Platforms: Windows 98, Windows NT 4.0, Windows Millennium Edition, Windows 2000, Windows XP Home Edition, Windows XP Professional, Windows .NET Server family, .NET Compact Framework - Windows CE .NET

MissingManifestResourceException Constructor (SerializationInfo, StreamingContext)

Initializes a new instance of the **MissingManifestResourceException** class from serialized data.

```
[Visual Basic]
Protected Sub New( _
   ByVal info As SerializationInfo, _
   ByVal context As StreamingContext _
)
[C#]
protected MissingManifestResourceException(
   SerializationInfo info,
   StreamingContext context
);
[C++]
protected: MissingManifestResourceException(
   SerializationInfo* info,
   StreamingContext context
);
[JScript]
protected function MissingManifestResourceException(
   info : SerializationInfo,
   context : StreamingContext
);
```

Parameters

info
> The object that holds the serialized object data.

context
> The contextual information about the source or destination of the exception.

Exceptions

Exception Type	Condition
ArgumentNullException	The *info* parameter is a null reference (**Nothing** in Visual Basic).

Remarks

This constructor is called during deserialization to reconstitute the exception object transmitted over a stream. (For more information on serialization see **XML and SOAP Serialization**.)

Requirements

Platforms: Windows 98, Windows NT 4.0, Windows Millennium Edition, Windows 2000, Windows XP Home Edition, Windows XP Professional, Windows .NET Server family

MissingManifestResourceException Constructor (String, Exception)

Initializes a new instance of the **MissingManifestResourceException** class with a specified error message and a reference to the inner exception that is the cause of this exception.

```
[Visual Basic]
Public Sub New( _
   ByVal message As String, _
   ByVal inner As Exception _
)
```

```
[C#]
public MissingManifestResourceException(
   string message,
   Exception inner
);
[C++]
public: MissingManifestResourceException(
   String* message,
   Exception* inner
);
[JScript]
public function MissingManifestResourceException(
   message : String,
   inner : Exception
);
```

Parameters

message
> The error message that explains the reason for the exception.

inner
> The exception that is the cause of the current exception. If the
> *inner* parameter is not a null reference (**Nothing** in Visual Basic),
> the current exception is raised in a **catch** block that handles the
> inner exception.

Remarks

An exception that is thrown as a direct result of a previous exception
should include a reference to the previous exception in the
InnerException property. The **InnerException** property returns the
same value that is passed into the constructor, or a null reference
(**Nothing** in Visual Basic) if the **InnerException** property does not
supply the inner exception value to the constructor.

The following table shows the initial property values for an instance
of **MissingManifestResourceException**.

Property	Value
InnerException	The inner exception reference.
Message	The error message string.

Requirements

Platforms: Windows 98, Windows NT 4.0,
Windows Millennium Edition, Windows 2000,
Windows XP Home Edition, Windows XP Professional,
Windows .NET Server family,
.NET Compact Framework - Windows CE .NET

NeutralResourcesLanguage-Attribute Class

Informs the **ResourceManager** of the neutral culture of an assembly. This class cannot be inherited.

System.Object
  System.Attribute
    System.Resources.NeutralResourcesLanguageAttribute

```
[Visual Basic]
<AttributeUsage(AttributeTargets.Assembly)>
NotInheritable Public Class NeutralResourcesLanguageAttribute
    Inherits Attribute
[C#]
[AttributeUsage(AttributeTargets.Assembly)]
public sealed class NeutralResourcesLanguageAttribute : Attribute
[C++]
[AttributeUsage(AttributeTargets::Assembly)]
public __gc __sealed class NeutralResourcesLanguageAttribute :
    public Attribute
[JScript]
public
    AttributeUsage(AttributeTargets.Assembly)
class NeutralResourcesLanguageAttribute extends Attribute
```

Thread Safety

Any public static (**Shared** in Visual Basic) members of this type are safe for multithreaded operations. Any instance members are not guaranteed to be thread safe.

Remarks

The **NeutralResourcesLanguageAttribute** informs the **ResourceManager** of the language used to write the neutral culture's resources for an assembly. When looking up resources in the same culture as the neutral resources language, the **ResourceManager** will automatically use the resources located in the main assembly, instead of searching for a satellite assembly with the current user interface culture for the current thread. This will improve lookup performance for the first resource you load, and can reduce your working set.

> **Note** Apply this attribute to your main assembly, passing it the name of the neutral language that will work with your main assembly.

Requirements

Namespace: System.Resources

Platforms: Windows 98, Windows NT 4.0, Windows Millennium Edition, Windows 2000, Windows XP Home Edition, Windows XP Professional, Windows .NET Server family, .NET Compact Framework - Windows CE .NET

Assembly: Mscorlib (in Mscorlib.dll)

NeutralResourcesLanguageAttribute Constructor

Initializes a new instance of the **NeutralResourcesLanguageAttribute** class.

```
[Visual Basic]
Public Sub New( _
    ByVal cultureName As String _
)
[C#]
public NeutralResourcesLanguageAttribute(
    string cultureName
);
[C++]
public: NeutralResourcesLanguageAttribute(
    String* cultureName
);
[JScript]
public function NeutralResourcesLanguageAttribute(
    cultureName : String
);
```

Parameters

cultureName
    The name of the culture that the current assembly's neutral resources were written in.

Exceptions

Exception Type	Condition
ArgumentNullException	The *cultureName* parameter is a null reference (**Nothing** in Visual Basic).

Requirements

Platforms: Windows 98, Windows NT 4.0, Windows Millennium Edition, Windows 2000, Windows XP Home Edition, Windows XP Professional, Windows .NET Server family, .NET Compact Framework - Windows CE .NET

NeutralResourcesLanguageAttribute.Culture-Name Property

Gets the culture name.

```
[Visual Basic]
Public ReadOnly Property CultureName As String
[C#]
public string CultureName {get;}
[C++]
public: __property String* get_CultureName();
[JScript]
public function get CultureName() : String;
```

Property Value

A **String** with the name of the default culture for the main assembly.

Requirements

Platforms: Windows 98, Windows NT 4.0, Windows Millennium Edition, Windows 2000, Windows XP Home Edition, Windows XP Professional, Windows .NET Server family, .NET Compact Framework - Windows CE .NET

ResourceManager Class

Provides convenient access to culture-specific resources at runtime.

System.Object
  System.Resources.ResourceManager
    System.ComponentModel.ComponentResourceManager

```
[Visual Basic]
<Serializable>
Public Class ResourceManager
[C#]
[Serializable]
public class ResourceManager
[C++]
[Serializable]
public __gc class ResourceManager
[JScript]
public
   Serializable
class ResourceManager
```

Thread Safety

This type is safe for multithreaded operations.

Remarks

The **ResourceManager** class looks up culture-specific resources, provides resource fallback when a localized resource does not exist, and supports resource serialization.

Using the methods of **ResourceManager**, a caller can access the resources for a particular culture using the **GetObject** and **GetString** methods. By default, these methods return the resource for the culture determined by the current cultural settings of the thread that made the call. (See **Thread.CurrentUICulture** for more information.) A caller can use the **ResourceManager.GetResource-Set** method to obtain a **ResourceSet**, which represents the resources for a particular culture, ignoring culture fallback rules. You can then use the **ResourceSet** to access the resources, localized for that culture, by name.

Ideally, you should create resources for every language, or at least a meaningful subset of the language. The resource file names follow the naming convention basename.cultureName.resources, where basename is the name of the application or the name of a class, depending on the level of detail you want. The **CultureInfo** 's **Name** property is used to determine the cultureName. A resource for the neutral culture (returned by **InvariantCulture**) should be named basename.resources.

For example, suppose that an assembly has several resources in a resource file with the basename "MyResources". These resource files will have names such as "MyResources.ja-JP.resources", "MyResources.de.resources", "MyResources.zh-CHS.resources", or "MyResources.fr-BE.resources", which contain resources respectively for Japanese, German, simplified Chinese, and French (Belgium). The default resource file should be named MyResources.resources. The culture-specific resource files are commonly packaged in satellite assemblies for each culture. The default resource file should be in your main assembly.

Now suppose that a **ResourceManager** has been created to represent the resources with this basename. Using the **ResourceManager**, you can obtain a **ResourceSet** that encapsulates "MyResources.ja-JP.resources" by calling GetResourceSet(new CultureInfo ("ja-JP"), TRUE, FALSE). Or, if you know that "MyResources" contains a

resource named "TOOLBAR_ICON", you can obtain the value of that resource localized for Japan by calling GetObject("TOOLBAR_ICON", new CultureInfo("ja-JP")).

While not strictly necessary for the most basic uses of the **ResourceManager**, publicaly shipping assemblies should use the **SatelliteContractVersionAttribute** to support versioning your main assembly without redeploying your satellites, and the **NeutralResourcesLanguageAttribute** to avoid looking up a satellite assembly that might never exist.

> **CAUTION** Using standalone .resources files in an ASP.NET application will break XCOPY deployment, because the resources remain locked until they are explicitly released by the **ReleaseAllResources** method. If you want to deploy resources into ASP.NET applications, you should compile your .resources into satellite assemblies.

> **CAUTION** Resources marked as private are accessible only in the assembly in which they are placed. Because a satellite assembly contains no code, resources private to it become unavailable through any mechanism. Therefore, resources in satellite assemblies should always be public so that they are accessible from your main assembly. Resources embedded in your main assembly are accessible to your main assembly, whether private or public.

Requirements

Namespace: System.Resources

Platforms: Windows 98, Windows NT 4.0, Windows Millennium Edition, Windows 2000, Windows XP Home Edition, Windows XP Professional, Windows .NET Server family, .NET Compact Framework - Windows CE .NET

Assembly: Mscorlib (in Mscorlib.dll)

ResourceManager Constructor

Initializes a new instance of the **ResourceManager** class.

Overload List

Initializes a new instance of the **ResourceManager** class with default values.

Supported by the .NET Compact Framework.

  [Visual Basic] **Protected Sub New()**
  [C#] **protected ResourceManager();**
  [C++] **protected: ResourceManager();**
  [JScript] **protected function ResourceManager();**

Creates a **ResourceManager** that looks up resources in satellite assemblies based on information from the specified **Type**.

Supported by the .NET Compact Framework.

  [Visual Basic] **Public Sub New(Type)**
  [C#] **public ResourceManager(Type);**
  [C++] **public: ResourceManager(Type*);**
  [JScript] **public function ResourceManager(Type);**

Initializes a new instance of the **ResourceManager** class that looks up resources contained in files derived from the specified root name using the given **Assembly**.

Supported by the .NET Compact Framework.

[Visual Basic] **Public Sub New(String, Assembly)**

[C#] **public ResourceManager(string, Assembly);**

[C++] **public: ResourceManager(String*, Assembly*);**

[JScript] **public function ResourceManager(String, Assembly);**

Initializes a new instance of the **ResourceManager** class that looks up resources contained in files derived from the specified root name using the given **Assembly**.

Supported by the .NET Compact Framework.

[Visual Basic] **Public Sub New(String, Assembly, Type)**

[C#] **public ResourceManager(string, Assembly, Type);**

[C++] **public: ResourceManager(String*, Assembly*, Type*);**

[JScript] **public function ResourceManager(String, Assembly, Type);**

Example

See related example in the **System.Resources.ResourceManager** constructor topic.

ResourceManager Constructor ( )

Initializes a new instance of the **ResourceManager** class with default values.

```
[Visual Basic]
Protected Sub New()
[C#]
protected ResourceManager();
[C++]
protected: ResourceManager();
[JScript]
protected function ResourceManager();
```

Remarks

The current constructor is only useful for writing your own derived class of the **ResourceManager**.

Requirements

Platforms: Windows 98, Windows NT 4.0, Windows Millennium Edition, Windows 2000, Windows XP Home Edition, Windows XP Professional, Windows .NET Server family, .NET Compact Framework - Windows CE .NET

ResourceManager Constructor (Type)

Creates a **ResourceManager** that looks up resources in satellite assemblies based on information from the specified **Type**.

```
[Visual Basic]
Public Sub New( _
   ByVal resourceSource As Type _
)
[C#]
public ResourceManager(
   Type resourceSource
);
[C++]
public: ResourceManager(
   Type* resourceSource
);
```

```
[JScript]
public function ResourceManager(
   resourceSource : Type
);
```

Parameters

resourceSource

A **Type** from which the **ResourceManager** derives all information for finding .resources files.

Exceptions

Exception Type	Condition
ArgumentNullException	The *resourceSource* parameter is a null reference (**Nothing** in Visual Basic).

Remarks

The **ResourceManager** infers the assembly, the base name, and a namespace for .resources files from the **Type**. The **Resource-Manager** assumes you will be using satellite assemblies and want to use the default **ResourceSet** class. Given a type such as MyCompany.MyProduct.MyType, the **ResourceManager** will look for a .resources file (in the main assembly and satellite assemblies) named "MyCompany.MyProduct.MyType.[culture name.]resources" in the assembly that defines MyType.

Requirements

Platforms: Windows 98, Windows NT 4.0, Windows Millennium Edition, Windows 2000, Windows XP Home Edition, Windows XP Professional, Windows .NET Server family, .NET Compact Framework - Windows CE .NET

ResourceManager Constructor (String, Assembly)

Initializes a new instance of the **ResourceManager** class that looks up resources contained in files derived from the specified root name using the given **Assembly**.

```
[Visual Basic]
Public Sub New( _
   ByVal baseName As String, _
   ByVal assembly As Assembly _
)
[C#]
public ResourceManager(
   string baseName,
   Assembly assembly
);
[C++]
public: ResourceManager(
   String* baseName,
   Assembly* assembly
);
[JScript]
public function ResourceManager(
   baseName : String,
   assembly : Assembly
);
```

Parameters

baseName

> The root name of the resources. For example, the root name for the resource file named "MyResource.en-US.resources" is "MyResource".

assembly

> The main **Assembly** for the resources.

Exceptions

Exception Type	Condition
ArgumentNullException	The *baseName* or *assembly* parameter is a null reference (**Nothing** in Visual Basic).

Remarks

The individual resource files should be contained in satellite assemblies with the invariant culture's .resources file contained in the main assembly. A satellite assembly is assumed to contain resources for a single culture specified in that assembly's manifest, and are loaded as necessary.

This constructor uses the system provided **ResourceSet** implementation. To use a custom resource file format, you should derive from the **ResourceSet** class, override **GetDefaultReader** and **GetDefaultWriter**, and pass that type to the constructor that takes a **Type** as the third parameter. Using a custom **ResourceSet** can be useful for controlling resource caching policy or supporting your own resource file format, but is generally not necessary.

Example

See related example in the **System.Resources.ResourceManager** constructor topic.

Requirements

Platforms: Windows 98, Windows NT 4.0, Windows Millennium Edition, Windows 2000, Windows XP Home Edition, Windows XP Professional, Windows .NET Server family, .NET Compact Framework - Windows CE .NET

ResourceManager Constructor (String, Assembly, Type)

Initializes a new instance of the **ResourceManager** class that looks up resources contained in files derived from the specified root name using the given **Assembly**.

```
[Visual Basic]
Public Sub New( _
   ByVal baseName As String, _
   ByVal assembly As Assembly, _
   ByVal usingResourceSet As Type _
)
[C#]
public ResourceManager(
   string baseName,
   Assembly assembly,
   Type usingResourceSet
);
[C++]
public: ResourceManager(
   String* baseName,
   Assembly* assembly,
   Type* usingResourceSet
);
```

```
[JScript]
public function ResourceManager(
   baseName : String,
   assembly : Assembly,
   usingResourceSet : Type
);
```

Parameters

baseName

> The root name of the resources. For example, the root name for the resource file named "MyResource.en-US.resources" is "MyResource".

assembly

> The main **Assembly** for the resources.

usingResourceSet

> The **Type** of the custom **ResourceSet** to use. If a null reference (**Nothing** in Visual Basic), the default runtime **ResourceSet** is used.

Exceptions

Exception Type	Condition
ArgumentException	*usingResourceset* is not a derived class of **ResourceSet**.
ArgumentNullException	The *baseName* or *assembly* parameter is a null reference (**Nothing** in Visual Basic).

Remarks

The individual resource files should be contained in satellite assemblies with the invariant culture's .resources file contained in the main assembly. A satellite assembly is assumed to contain resources for a single culture specified in that assembly's manifest, and are loaded as necessary.

You can specify a **ResourceSet** implementation to be used. If you do not need a specific **ResourceSet** implementation but would like to use a custom resource file format, you should derive from the **ResourceSet** class, override **GetDefaultReader** and **GetDefaultWriter**, and pass that type to this constructor.

> **Note** The *usingResourceSet* parameter is used to support your own resource format, and will commonly be a null reference (**Nothing** in Visual Basic). This is different from the constructor that takes a **Type** only.

Requirements

Platforms: Windows 98, Windows NT 4.0, Windows Millennium Edition, Windows 2000, Windows XP Home Edition, Windows XP Professional, Windows .NET Server family, .NET Compact Framework - Windows CE .NET

ResourceManager.BaseNameField Field

Indicates the root name of the resource files that the **ResourceManager** searches for resources.

```
[Visual Basic]
Protected BaseNameField As String
[C#]
protected string BaseNameField;
[C++]
protected: String* BaseNameField;
```

```
[JScript]
protected var BaseNameField : String;
```

Requirements

Platforms: Windows 98, Windows NT 4.0,
Windows Millennium Edition, Windows 2000,
Windows XP Home Edition, Windows XP Professional,
Windows .NET Server family,
.NET Compact Framework - Windows CE .NET

ResourceManager.HeaderVersionNumber Field

A constant **readonly** value indicating the version of resource file
headers that the current implementation of **ResourceManager** can
interpret and produce.

```
[Visual Basic]
Public Shared ReadOnly HeaderVersionNumber As Integer
[C#]
public static readonly int HeaderVersionNumber;
[C++]
public: static int HeaderVersionNumber;
[JScript]
public static var HeaderVersionNumber : int;
```

Requirements

Platforms: Windows 98, Windows NT 4.0,
Windows Millennium Edition, Windows 2000,
Windows XP Home Edition, Windows XP Professional,
Windows .NET Server family,
.NET Compact Framework - Windows CE .NET

ResourceManager.MagicNumber Field

Holds the number used to identify resource files.

```
[Visual Basic]
Public Shared ReadOnly MagicNumber As Integer
[C#]
public static readonly int MagicNumber;
[C++]
public: static int MagicNumber;
[JScript]
public static var MagicNumber : int;
```

Remarks

The value is set to 0xBEEFCACE. The first four bytes of the system
default file format contain a 32-bit signed integer in little-endian
format.

If the **MagicNumber** is found, the bytes following it will be a version
number for a **ResourceManager** header, followed by a number
indicating how many bytes should be skipped to get past this header.
The next number indicates the version of the **ResourceManager** that
created the header, followed by version specific information.

The version number for the current implementation is one. The next
bytes are a length-prefixed string containing the name of an
IResourceReader, which can read this file.

Requirements

Platforms: Windows 98, Windows NT 4.0,
Windows Millennium Edition, Windows 2000,
Windows XP Home Edition, Windows XP Professional,
Windows .NET Server family,
.NET Compact Framework - Windows CE .NET

ResourceManager.MainAssembly Field

Indicates the main **Assembly** that contains the resources.

```
[Visual Basic]
Protected MainAssembly As Assembly
[C#]
protected Assembly MainAssembly;
[C++]
protected: Assembly* MainAssembly;
[JScript]
protected var MainAssembly : Assembly;
```

Requirements

Platforms: Windows 98, Windows NT 4.0,
Windows Millennium Edition, Windows 2000,
Windows XP Home Edition, Windows XP Professional,
Windows .NET Server family,
.NET Compact Framework - Windows CE .NET

ResourceManager.ResourceSets Field

Contains a **Hashtable** that returns a mapping from cultures to
ResourceSet objects.

```
[Visual Basic]
Protected ResourceSets As Hashtable
[C#]
protected Hashtable ResourceSets;
[C++]
protected: Hashtable* ResourceSets;
[JScript]
protected var ResourceSets : Hashtable;
```

Requirements

Platforms: Windows 98, Windows NT 4.0,
Windows Millennium Edition, Windows 2000,
Windows XP Home Edition, Windows XP Professional,
Windows .NET Server family,
.NET Compact Framework - Windows CE .NET

ResourceManager.BaseName Property

Gets the root name of the resource files that the **ResourceManager**
searches for resources.

```
[Visual Basic]
Public Overridable ReadOnly Property BaseName As String
[C#]
public virtual string BaseName {get;}
[C++]
public: __property virtual String* get_BaseName();
[JScript]
public function get BaseName() : String;
```

Property Value

The root name of the resource files that the **ResourceManager**
searches for resources.

Requirements

Platforms: Windows 98, Windows NT 4.0,
Windows Millennium Edition, Windows 2000,
Windows XP Home Edition, Windows XP Professional,
Windows .NET Server family,
.NET Compact Framework - Windows CE .NET

ResourceManager.IgnoreCase Property

Gets or sets a Boolean value indicating whether the current instance of ResourceManager allows case-insensitive resource lookups in the **GetString** and **GetObject** methods.

```
[Visual Basic]
Public Overridable Property IgnoreCase As Boolean
[C#]
public virtual bool IgnoreCase {get; set;}
[C++]
public: __property virtual bool get_IgnoreCase();
public: __property virtual void set_IgnoreCase(bool);
[JScript]
public function get IgnoreCase() : Boolean;
public function set IgnoreCase(Boolean);
```

Property Value

A Boolean value indicating whether the case of the resource names should be ignored.

Remarks

If the value of the **IgnoreCase** property is **false**, a resource with the name "Resource" is not equivalent to the resource with the name "resource". If **IgnoreCase** is **true**, a resource with the name "Resource" is equivalent to the resource with the name "resource". Note, however, that when **IgnoreCase** is **true**, the **ResourceManager.GetString** and **ResourceManager.GetObject** methods perform case-insensitive string comparisons using **CultureInfo.InvariantCulture**. The advantage is that results of case-insensitive string comparisons performed by these methods are the same on all computers regardless of culture. The disadvantage is that the results are not consistent with the casing rules of all cultures.

For example, the Turkish alphabet has two versions of the character I: one with a dot and one without a dot. In Turkish, the character I (Unicode 0049) is considered the uppercase version of a different character €(Unicode 0131). The character i (Unicode 0069) is considered the lowercase version of yet another character _ (Unicode 0130). According to these casing rules, a case-insensitive string comparison of the characters i (Unicode 0069) and I (Unicode 0049) should fail for the culture "tr-TR" (Turkish in Turkey). If **IgnoreCase** is **true**, this comparison succeeds.

> **Note** For performance reasons, it is best to always specify the correct case for your resource names. **IgnoreCase** can cause a significant workingset and performance hit.

Requirements

Platforms: Windows 98, Windows NT 4.0, Windows Millennium Edition, Windows 2000, Windows XP Home Edition, Windows XP Professional, Windows .NET Server family, .NET Compact Framework - Windows CE .NET

ResourceManager.ResourceSetType Property

Gets the **Type** of the **ResourceSet** the **ResourceManager** uses to construct a **ResourceSet** object.

```
[Visual Basic]
Public Overridable ReadOnly Property ResourceSetType As Type
[C#]
public virtual Type ResourceSetType {get;}
```

```
[C++]
public: __property virtual Type* get_ResourceSetType();
[JScript]
public function get ResourceSetType() : Type;
```

Property Value

The **Type** of the **ResourceSet** the **ResourceManager** uses to construct a **ResourceSet** object.

Requirements

Platforms: Windows 98, Windows NT 4.0, Windows Millennium Edition, Windows 2000, Windows XP Home Edition, Windows XP Professional, Windows .NET Server family, .NET Compact Framework - Windows CE .NET

ResourceManager.CreateFileBasedResource-Manager Method

Returns a **ResourceManager** that searches a specific directory for resources instead of in the assembly manifest.

```
[Visual Basic]
Public Shared Function CreateFileBasedResourceManager( _
    ByVal baseName As String, _
    ByVal resourceDir As String, _
    ByVal usingResourceSet As Type _
) As ResourceManager
[C#]
public static ResourceManager CreateFileBasedResourceManager(
    string baseName,
    string resourceDir,
    Type usingResourceSet
);
[C++]
public: static ResourceManager* CreateFileBasedResourceManager(
    String* baseName,
    String* resourceDir,
    Type* usingResourceSet
);
[JScript]
public static function CreateFileBasedResourceManager(
    baseName : String,
    resourceDir : String,
    usingResourceSet : Type
) : ResourceManager;
```

Parameters

baseName
   The root name of the resources. For example, the root name for the resource file named "MyResource.en-US.resources" is "MyResource".
resourceDir
   The name of the directory to search for the resources.
usingResourceSet
   The **Type** of the custom **ResourceSet** to use. If a null reference (**Nothing** in Visual Basic), the default runtime **ResourceSet** is used.

Return Value

The newly created **ResourceManager** that searches a specific directory for resources instead of in the assembly manifest.

Exceptions

Exception Type	Condition
ArgumentException	The *baseName* ends in .resources.
ArgumentNullException	The *baseName* parameter is a null reference (**Nothing** in Visual Basic).

Remarks

This method returns a **ResourceManager** that is not dependent on any particular assembly. The returned **ResourceManager** can be used to load resources for an ASP.NET page or for testing a **ResourceSet** implementation.

You can specify a **ResourceSet** implementation. If you do not need a specific **ResourceSet** implementation, but would like to use a custom resource file format, you should derive from the **ResourceSet** class, override **GetDefaultReader** and **GetDefaultWriter**, and pass that type to this constructor.

CAUTION   Using standalone .resources files in an ASP.NET application will break XCOPY deployment because the resources remain locked until they are explicitly released by the **ReleaseAllResources** method. If you want to deploy resources into ASP.NET applications, compile your .resources into satellite assemblies.

Requirements

Platforms: Windows 98, Windows NT 4.0, Windows Millennium Edition, Windows 2000, Windows XP Home Edition, Windows XP Professional, Windows .NET Server family, .NET Compact Framework - Windows CE .NET

.NET Framework Security:

- **ReflectionPermission** to enhance security and performance when invoked late-bound through mechanisms such as **Type.InvokeMember**. Associated enumeration: **ReflectionPermissionFlag.MemberAccess**.

ResourceManager.GetNeutralResourcesLanguage Method

Returns the **CultureInfo** for the main assembly's neutral resources by reading the value of the **NeutralResourcesLanguageAttribute** on a specified **Assembly**.

```
[Visual Basic]
Protected Shared Function GetNeutralResourcesLanguage( _
   ByVal a As Assembly _
) As CultureInfo
[C#]
protected static CultureInfo GetNeutralResourcesLanguage(
   Assembly a
);
[C++]
protected: static CultureInfo* GetNeutralResourcesLanguage(
   Assembly* a
);
[JScript]
protected static function GetNeutralResourcesLanguage(
   a : Assembly
) : CultureInfo;
```

Parameters

a
> The assembly for which to return a **CultureInfo**.

Return Value

The culture from the **NeutralResourcesLanguageAttribute**, if found; otherwise, **CultureInfo.InvariantCulture**.

Remarks

Use this method in derived classes of the **ResourceManager** to speed up lookups in one particular culture. For example, if this method returns "en-US" for the CultureInfo, then any U.S. English resource lookups will go straight to the main assembly and not look for the "en-US" nor "en" satellite assemblies.

Requirements

Platforms: Windows 98, Windows NT 4.0, Windows Millennium Edition, Windows 2000, Windows XP Home Edition, Windows XP Professional, Windows .NET Server family, .NET Compact Framework - Windows CE .NET

.NET Framework Security:

- **ReflectionPermission** to enhance security and performance when invoked late-bound through mechanisms such as **Type.InvokeMember**. Associated enumeration: **ReflectionPermissionFlag.MemberAccess**.

ResourceManager.GetObject Method

Gets the value of the specified **Object** resource for the current culture.

Overload List

Returns the value of the specified **Object** resource.

Supported by the .NET Compact Framework.

> [Visual Basic] **Overloads Public Overridable Function GetObject(String) As Object**
>
> [C#] **public virtual object GetObject(string);**
>
> [C++] **public: virtual Object* GetObject(String*);**
>
> [JScript] **public function GetObject(String) : Object;**

Gets the value of the **Object** resource localized for the specified culture.

Supported by the .NET Compact Framework.

> [Visual Basic] **Overloads Public Overridable Function GetObject(String, CultureInfo) As Object**
>
> [C#] **public virtual object GetObject(string, CultureInfo);**
>
> [C++] **public: virtual Object* GetObject(String*, CultureInfo*);**
>
> [JScript] **public function GetObject(String, CultureInfo) : Object;**

ResourceManager.GetObject Method (String)

Returns the value of the specified **Object** resource.

```
[Visual Basic]
Overloads Public Overridable Function GetObject( _
   ByVal name As String _
) As Object
```

```
[C#]
public virtual object GetObject(
    string name
);
[C++]
public: virtual Object* GetObject(
    String* name
);
[JScript]
public function GetObject(
    name : String
) : Object;
```

Parameters

name
> The name of the resource to get.

Return Value

The value of the resource localized for the caller's current culture settings. If a match is not possible, a null reference (**Nothing** in Visual Basic) is returned. The resource value can be a null reference (**Nothing**).

Exceptions

Exception Type	Condition
ArgumentNullException	The *name* parameter is a null reference (**Nothing** in Visual Basic).
MissingManifest-ResourceException	No usable set of resources has been found, and there are no neutral culture resources.

Remarks

The returned resource is localized for the culture determined by the current cultural settings of the current **Thread** (this is accomplished using the culture's **CurrentUICulture** property). If the resource has not been localized for that culture, the resource that is returned is localized for a best match (this is accomplished using the **Parent** property). Otherwise, a null reference (**Nothing** in Visual Basic) is returned.

If no usable set of resources has been found, the **ResourceManager** falls back on the neutral culture's resources, which are expected to be included in the main assembly. If an appropriate culture resource has not been found, a **MissingManifestResourceException** is thrown.

> **Note** The GetObject method is thread-safe.

Requirements

Platforms: Windows 98, Windows NT 4.0, Windows Millennium Edition, Windows 2000, Windows XP Home Edition, Windows XP Professional, Windows .NET Server family, .NET Compact Framework - Windows CE .NET

.NET Framework Security:

- **ReflectionPermission** to enhance security and performance when invoked late-bound through mechanisms such as **Type.InvokeMember**. Associated enumeration: **ReflectionPermissionFlag.MemberAccess**.

ResourceManager.GetObject Method (String, CultureInfo)

Gets the value of the **Object** resource localized for the specified culture.

```
[Visual Basic]
Overloads Public Overridable Function GetObject( _
    ByVal name As String, _
    ByVal culture As CultureInfo _
) As Object
[C#]
public virtual object GetObject(
    string name,
    CultureInfo culture
);
[C++]
public: virtual Object* GetObject(
    String* name,
    CultureInfo* culture
);
[JScript]
public function GetObject(
    name : String,
    culture : CultureInfo
) : Object;
```

Parameters

name
> The name of the resource to get.

culture
> The **CultureInfo** object that represents the culture for which the resource is localized. Note that if the resource is not localized for this culture, the lookup will fall back using the culture's **Parent** property, stopping after checking in the neutral culture.
>
> If this value is a null reference (**Nothing** in Visual Basic), the **CultureInfo** is obtained using the culture's **CurrentUICulture** property.

Return Value

The value of the resource, localized for the specified culture. If a "best match" is not possible, a null reference (**Nothing** in Visual Basic) is returned.

Exceptions

Exception Type	Condition
ArgumentNullException	The *name* parameter is a null reference (**Nothing** in Visual Basic).
MissingManifest-ResourceException	No usable set of resources have been found, and there are no neutral culture resources.

Remarks

If the resource has not been localized for the specified culture, the resource that is returned is localized for a best match (this is accomplished using the culture's **CurrentUICulture** property). Otherwise, a null reference (**Nothing** in Visual Basic) is returned.

If no usable set of resources has been found, the **ResourceManager** falls back on the neutral culture's resources, which are expected to be included in the main assembly. If an appropriate culture resource has not been found, a **MissingManifestResourceException** is thrown.

Note The **GetObject** method is thread-safe.

Requirements

Platforms: Windows 98, Windows NT 4.0,
Windows Millennium Edition, Windows 2000,
Windows XP Home Edition, Windows XP Professional,
Windows .NET Server family,
.NET Compact Framework - Windows CE .NET

.NET Framework Security:

- **ReflectionPermission** to enhance security and performance
  when invoked late-bound through mechanisms such as
  Type.InvokeMember. Associated enumeration:
  ReflectionPermissionFlag.MemberAccess.

ResourceManager.GetResourceFileName Method

Generates the name for the resource file for the given **CultureInfo**.

```
[Visual Basic]
Protected Overridable Function GetResourceFileName( _
   ByVal culture As CultureInfo _
) As String
[C#]
protected virtual string GetResourceFileName(
   CultureInfo culture
);
[C++]
protected: virtual String* GetResourceFileName(
   CultureInfo* culture
);
[JScript]
protected function GetResourceFileName(
   culture : CultureInfo
) : String;
```

Parameters

culture
    The **CultureInfo** for which a resource file name is constructed.

Return Value

The name that can be used for a resource file for the given
CultureInfo.

Remarks

This method uses **CultureInfo** 's **Name** property as part of the file
name for all cultures other than the invariant culture. This method
does not look in an assembly's manifest or touch the disk, and is
used only to construct what a resource file name (suitable for
passing to the **ResourceReader** constructor) or a manifest resource
blob name should be.

A derived class can override this method to look for a different
extension, such as ".ResX", or a completely different scheme for
naming files.

Requirements

Platforms: Windows 98, Windows NT 4.0,
Windows Millennium Edition, Windows 2000,
Windows XP Home Edition, Windows XP Professional,
Windows .NET Server family,
.NET Compact Framework - Windows CE .NET

.NET Framework Security:

- **ReflectionPermission** to enhance security and performance
  when invoked late-bound through mechanisms such as
  Type.InvokeMember. Associated enumeration:
  ReflectionPermissionFlag.MemberAccess.

ResourceManager.GetResourceSet Method

Gets the **ResourceSet** for a particular culture.

```
[Visual Basic]
Public Overridable Function GetResourceSet( _
   ByVal culture As CultureInfo, _
   ByVal createIfNotExists As Boolean, _
   ByVal tryParents As Boolean _
) As ResourceSet
[C#]
public virtual ResourceSet GetResourceSet(
   CultureInfo culture,
   bool createIfNotExists,
   bool tryParents
);
[C++]
public: virtual ResourceSet* GetResourceSet(
   CultureInfo* culture,
   bool createIfNotExists,
   bool tryParents
);
[JScript]
public function GetResourceSet(
   culture : CultureInfo,
   createIfNotExists : Boolean,
   tryParents : Boolean
) : ResourceSet;
```

Parameters

culture
    The **CultureInfo** to look for.
createIfNotExists
    If **true** and if the **ResourceSet** has not been loaded yet, load it.
tryParents
    If the **ResourceSet** cannot be loaded, try parent **CultureInfo**
    objects to see if they exist.

Return Value

The specified **ResourceSet**.

Exceptions

Exception Type	Condition
ArgumentNullException	The *culture* parameter is a null reference (**Nothing** in Visual Basic).

Remarks

The **ResourceSet** that is returned represents the resources localized
for the specified culture. If the resources have not been localized for
that culture and *tryParents* is **true**, **GetResourceSet** falls back to a
parent culture (this is accomplished using **CultureInfo** 's **Parent**
property), and the parent **ResourceSet** is returned. Otherwise, a null
reference (**Nothing** in Visual Basic) is returned.

The parameters let you control whether the **ResourceSet** is created
if it hasn't been loaded yet, and whether parent **CultureInfo** objects
should be loaded as well for resource inheritance.

Note The **GetResourceSet** method is thread-safe.

Requirements

Platforms: Windows 98, Windows NT 4.0,
Windows Millennium Edition, Windows 2000,
Windows XP Home Edition, Windows XP Professional,
Windows .NET Server family,
.NET Compact Framework - Windows CE .NET

.NET Framework Security:

- **ReflectionPermission** to enhance security and performance when invoked late-bound through mechanisms such as **Type.InvokeMember**. Associated enumeration: **ReflectionPermissionFlag.MemberAccess**.

ResourceManager.GetSatelliteContractVersion Method

Returns the **Version** specified by the **SatelliteContractVersionAttribute** in the given assembly.

```
[Visual Basic]
Protected Shared Function GetSatelliteContractVersion( _
    ByVal a As Assembly _
) As Version
[C#]
protected static Version GetSatelliteContractVersion(
    Assembly a
);
[C++]
protected: static Version* GetSatelliteContractVersion(
    Assembly* a
);
[JScript]
protected static function GetSatelliteContractVersion(
    a : Assembly
) : Version;
```

Parameters

a
    The **Assembly** for which to look up the **SatelliteContractVersionAttribute**.

Return Value

The satellite contract **Version** of the given assembly, or a null reference (**Nothing** in Visual Basic) if no version was found.

Exceptions

Exception Type	Condition
ArgumentException	The **Version** found in the assembly *a* is invalid.

Remarks

For more information about satellite assembly versioning, see **SatelliteContractVersionAttribute**.

Requirements

Platforms: Windows 98, Windows NT 4.0,
Windows Millennium Edition, Windows 2000,
Windows XP Home Edition, Windows XP Professional,
Windows .NET Server family,
.NET Compact Framework - Windows CE .NET

.NET Framework Security:

- **ReflectionPermission** to enhance security and performance when invoked late-bound through mechanisms such as **Type.InvokeMember**. Associated enumeration: **ReflectionPermissionFlag.MemberAccess**.

ResourceManager.GetString Method

Gets the value of the specified **String** resource for the current culture.

Overload List

Returns the value of the specified **String** resource.

Supported by the .NET Compact Framework.

    [Visual Basic] **Overloads Public Overridable Function GetString(String) As String**

    [C#] **public virtual string GetString(string);**

    [C++] **public: virtual String* GetString(String*);**

    [JScript] **public function GetString(String) : String;**

Gets the value of the **String** resource localized for the specified culture.

Supported by the .NET Compact Framework.

    [Visual Basic] **Overloads Public Overridable Function GetString(String, CultureInfo) As String**

    [C#] **public virtual string GetString(string, CultureInfo);**

    [C++] **public: virtual String* GetString(String*, CultureInfo*);**

    [JScript] **public function GetString(String, CultureInfo) : String;**

Example

See related example in the **System.Resources.ResourceManager** constructor topic.

ResourceManager.GetString Method (String)

Returns the value of the specified **String** resource.

```
[Visual Basic]
Overloads Public Overridable Function GetString( _
    ByVal name As String _
) As String
[C#]
public virtual string GetString(
    string name
);
[C++]
public: virtual String* GetString(
    String* name
);
[JScript]
public function GetString(
    name : String
) : String;
```

Parameters

name
    The name of the resource to get.

Return Value

The value of the resource localized for the caller's current culture settings. If a match is not possible, a null reference (**Nothing** in Visual Basic) is returned.

Exceptions

Exception Type	Condition
ArgumentNullException	The *name* parameter is a null reference (**Nothing** in Visual Basic).
InvalidOperation-Exception	The value of the specified resource is not a string.
MissingManifest-ResourceException	No usable set of resources has been found, and there are no neutral culture resources.

Remarks

The resource that is returned is localized for the culture determined by the cultural settings of the current **Thread** (this is accomplished using the culture's **CurrentUICulture** property). If the resource has not been localized for that culture, the resource that is returned is localized for a best match (this is accomplished using the **Parent** property). Otherwise, a null reference (**Nothing** in Visual Basic) is returned.

If no usable set of resources has been found, the **ResourceManager** falls back on the neutral culture's resources, which are expected to be in the main assembly. If an appropriate culture resource has not been found, a **MissingManifestResourceException** is thrown.

> **Note** The **GetString** method is thread-safe.

Example

See related example in the **System.Resources.ResourceManager** constructor topic.

Requirements

Platforms: Windows 98, Windows NT 4.0, Windows Millennium Edition, Windows 2000, Windows XP Home Edition, Windows XP Professional, Windows .NET Server family, .NET Compact Framework - Windows CE .NET

.NET Framework Security:

- **ReflectionPermission** to enhance security and performance when invoked late-bound through mechanisms such as **Type.InvokeMember**. Associated enumeration: **ReflectionPermissionFlag.MemberAccess**.

ResourceManager.GetString Method (String, CultureInfo)

Gets the value of the **String** resource localized for the specified culture.

```
[Visual Basic]
Overloads Public Overridable Function GetString( _
   ByVal name As String, _
   ByVal culture As CultureInfo _
) As String
[C#]
public virtual string GetString(
   string name,
   CultureInfo culture
);
```

```
[C++]
public: virtual String* GetString(
   String* name,
   CultureInfo* culture
);
[JScript]
public function GetString(
   name : String,
   culture : CultureInfo
) : String;
```

Parameters

name
>The name of the resource to get.

culture
>The **CultureInfo** object that represents the culture for which the resource is localized. Note that if the resource is not localized for this culture, the lookup will fall back using the culture's **Parent** property, stopping after looking in the neutral culture.
>
>If this value is a null reference (**Nothing** in Visual Basic), the **CultureInfo** is obtained using the culture's **CurrentUICulture** property.

Return Value

The value of the resource localized for the specified culture. If a best match is not possible, a null reference (**Nothing** in Visual Basic) is returned.

Exceptions

Exception Type	Condition
ArgumentNullException	The *name* parameter is a null reference (**Nothing** in Visual Basic).
InvalidOperation-Exception	The value of the specified resource is not a **String**.
MissingManifest-ResourceException	No usable set of resources has been found, and there are no neutral culture resources.

Remarks

If the resource has not been localized for that culture, the resource that is returned is localized for a best match (this is accomplished using the culture's **Parent** property). Otherwise, a null reference (**Nothing** in Visual Basic) is returned.

If no usable set of resources has been found, the **ResourceManager** falls back on the neutral culture's resources, which are expected to be in the main assembly. If an appropriate culture resource has not been found, a **MissingManifestResourceException** is thrown.

> **Note** The **GetString** method is thread-safe.

Example

See related example in the **System.Resources.ResourceManager** constructor topic.

Requirements

Platforms: Windows 98, Windows NT 4.0, Windows Millennium Edition, Windows 2000, Windows XP Home Edition, Windows XP Professional, Windows .NET Server family, .NET Compact Framework - Windows CE .NET

.NET Framework Security:

- **ReflectionPermission** to enhance security and performance when invoked late-bound through mechanisms such as **Type.InvokeMember**. Associated enumeration: **ReflectionPermissionFlag.MemberAccess**.

ResourceManager.InternalGetResourceSet Method

Provides the implementation for finding a **ResourceSet**.

```
[Visual Basic]
Protected Overridable Function InternalGetResourceSet( _
    ByVal culture As CultureInfo, _
    ByVal createIfNotExists As Boolean, _
    ByVal tryParents As Boolean _
) As ResourceSet
[C#]
protected virtual ResourceSet InternalGetResourceSet(
    CultureInfo culture,
    bool createIfNotExists,
    bool tryParents
);
[C++]
protected: virtual ResourceSet* InternalGetResourceSet(
    CultureInfo* culture,
    bool createIfNotExists,
    bool tryParents
);
[JScript]
protected function InternalGetResourceSet(
    culture : CultureInfo,
    createIfNotExists : Boolean,
    tryParents : Boolean
) : ResourceSet;
```

Parameters

culture
   The **CultureInfo** to look for.
createIfNotExists
   If **true** and if the **ResourceSet** has not been loaded yet, load it.
tryParents
   If the **ResourceSet** cannot be loaded, try parent **CultureInfo** objects to see if they exist.

Return Value

The specified **ResourceSet**.

Exceptions

Exception Type	Condition
MissingManifestResource Exception	The main assembly does not contain a .resources file and it is required to look up a resource.

Remarks

Notes to Inheritors: This method completes all the work necessary to find a **ResourceSet**, and can be recursive and reentrant. In other words, this method might load an assembly, triggering an **AssemblyLoad** event, which then calls back into the not-completely-initialized **ResourceManager**. To avoid taking extra locks, it is not thread safe. **GetResourceSet**, **GetString**, and **GetObject** do all the necessary synchronization.

Requirements

Platforms: Windows 98, Windows NT 4.0, Windows Millennium Edition, Windows 2000, Windows XP Home Edition, Windows XP Professional, Windows .NET Server family, .NET Compact Framework - Windows CE .NET

.NET Framework Security:

- **ReflectionPermission** to enhance security and performance when invoked late-bound through mechanisms such as **Type.InvokeMember**. Associated enumeration: **ReflectionPermissionFlag.MemberAccess**.

ResourceManager.ReleaseAllResources Method

Tells the **ResourceManager** to call **Close** on all **ResourceSet** objects and release all resources.

```
[Visual Basic]
Public Overridable Sub ReleaseAllResources()
[C#]
public virtual void ReleaseAllResources();
[C++]
public: virtual void ReleaseAllResources();
[JScript]
public function ReleaseAllResources();
```

Remarks

This method will shrink the working set in a running application. Any future resource lookups on this **ResourceManager** will be as extensive as the first lookup, since it will need to search and load resources again.

This can be useful in some complex threading scenarios, where creating a new **ResourceManager** is the appropriate behavior.

This method can also be used in situations where the .resources files opened by the current **ResourceManager** have to be released deterministically, without waiting for the **ResourceManager** to go completely out of scope and be garbage collected.

Requirements

Platforms: Windows 98, Windows NT 4.0, Windows Millennium Edition, Windows 2000, Windows XP Home Edition, Windows XP Professional, Windows .NET Server family, .NET Compact Framework - Windows CE .NET

.NET Framework Security:

- **ReflectionPermission** to enhance security and performance when invoked late-bound through mechanisms such as **Type.InvokeMember**. Associated enumeration: **ReflectionPermissionFlag.MemberAccess**.

ResourceReader Class

Enumerates .resources files and streams, reading sequential resource name and value pairs.

System.Object
  System.Resources.ResourceReader

[Visual Basic]
NotInheritable Public Class ResourceReader
   Implements IResourceReader, IEnumerable, IDisposable
[C#]
public sealed class ResourceReader : IResourceReader, IEnumerable,
   IDisposable
[C++]
public __gc __sealed class ResourceReader : public IResourceReader,
   IEnumerable, IDisposable
[JScript]
public class ResourceReader implements IResourceReader,
   IEnumerable, IDisposable

Thread Safety

Any public static (**Shared** in Visual Basic) members of this type are safe for multithreaded operations. Any instance members are not guaranteed to be thread safe.

Remarks

The **ResourceReader** provides a default implementation of the **IResourceReader** interface.

You can use resource readers to read resource name and resource value pairs from .resources files. The resources can be enumerated by traversing the **IDictionaryEnumerator** returned by the **GetEnumerator** method. The methods provided by the **IDictionaryEnumerator** are used to advance to the next resource and read the name and value of each resource in the .resources file.

> **Note** **IEnumerable.GetEnumerator** returns an **IEnumerator** not **IDictionaryEnumerator**.

Example

[Visual Basic, C#, C++] The following code sample displays the content of "myResources.resources" files on the console:

[Visual Basic]

```
Imports System
Imports System.Resources
Imports System.Collections

Public Class ReadResources

    Public Shared Sub Main()

        ' Opens a resource reader and get an enumerator from it.
        Dim reader As New ResourceReader("myResources.resources")
        Dim en As IDictionaryEnumerator = reader.GetEnumerator()

        ' Goes through the enumerator, printing out the key and
value pairs.
        While en.MoveNext()
            Console.WriteLine()
            Console.WriteLine("Name: {0}", en.Key)
            Console.WriteLine("Value: {0}", en.Value)
        End While
        reader.Close()

    End Sub
End Class
```

[C#]

```
using System;
using System.Resources;
using System.Collections;

public class ReadResources {

    public static void Main(string[] args) {

        // Opens a resource reader and gets an enumerator from it.
        IResourceReader reader = new
ResourceReader("myResources.resources");
        IDictionaryEnumerator en = reader.GetEnumerator();

        // Goes through the enumerator, printing out the key
and value pairs.
        while (en.MoveNext()) {
            Console.WriteLine();
            Console.WriteLine("Name: {0}", en.Key);
            Console.WriteLine("Value: {0}", en.Value);
        }
        reader.Close();
    }
}
```

[C++]

```
using namespace System;
using namespace System::Resources;
using namespace System::Collections;

void main(char** argv, int argc) {

    // Opens a resource reader and gets an enumerator from it.
    IResourceReader* reader = new
ResourceReader(S"myResources.resources");
    IDictionaryEnumerator* en = reader->GetEnumerator();

    // Goes through the enumerator, printing out the key
and value pairs.
    while (en->MoveNext()) {
        Console::WriteLine();
        Console::WriteLine(S"Name: {0}", en->Key);
        Console::WriteLine(S"Value: {0}", en->Value);
    }
    reader->Close();
}
```

Requirements

Namespace: System.Resources

Platforms: Windows 98, Windows NT 4.0, Windows Millennium Edition, Windows 2000, Windows XP Home Edition, Windows XP Professional, Windows .NET Server family, .NET Compact Framework - Windows CE .NET

Assembly: Mscorlib (in Mscorlib.dll)

ResourceReader Constructor

Initializes a new instance of the **ResourceReader** class.

Overload List

Initializes a new instance of the **ResourceReader** class for the specified stream.

Supported by the .NET Compact Framework.

   [Visual Basic] **Public Sub New(Stream)**

   [C#] **public ResourceReader(Stream);**

   [C++] **public: ResourceReader(Stream*);**

   [JScript] **public function ResourceReader(Stream);**

Initializes a new instance of the **ResourceReader** class for the specified resource file.

Supported by the .NET Compact Framework.

> [Visual Basic] **Public Sub New(String)**
> [C#] **public ResourceReader(string);**
> [C++] **public: ResourceReader(String*);**
> [JScript] **public function ResourceReader(String);**

Example

See related example in the **System.Resources.ResourceReader** class topic.

ResourceReader Constructor (Stream)

Initializes a new instance of the **ResourceReader** class for the specified stream.

```
[Visual Basic]
Public Sub New( _
   ByVal stream As Stream _
)
[C#]
public ResourceReader(
   Stream stream
);
[C++]
public: ResourceReader(
   Stream* stream
);
[JScript]
public function ResourceReader(
   stream : Stream
);
```

Parameters

stream
> The input stream for reading resources.

Exceptions

Exception Type	Condition
ArgumentException	The *stream* is not readable.
ArgumentNullException	The *stream* parameter is a null reference (**Nothing** in Visual Basic).
IOException	An I/O error has occured while accessing *stream*.

Example

See related example in the **System.Resources.ResourceReader** class topic.

Requirements

Platforms: Windows 98, Windows NT 4.0, Windows Millennium Edition, Windows 2000, Windows XP Home Edition, Windows XP Professional, Windows .NET Server family, .NET Compact Framework - Windows CE .NET

ResourceReader Constructor (String)

Initializes a new instance of the **ResourceReader** class for the specified resource file.

```
[Visual Basic]
Public Sub New( _
   ByVal fileName As String _
)
[C#]
public ResourceReader(
   string fileName
);
[C++]
public: ResourceReader(
   String* fileName
);
[JScript]
public function ResourceReader(
   fileName : String
);
```

Parameters

fileName
> The path of the resource file to be read.

Exceptions

Exception Type	Condition
ArgumentNullException	The *fileName* parameter is a null reference (**Nothing** in Visual Basic).
FileNotFoundException	The file cannot be found.
IOException	An I/O error has occured.

Example

See related example in the **System.Resources.ResourceReader** class topic.

Requirements

Platforms: Windows 98, Windows NT 4.0, Windows Millennium Edition, Windows 2000, Windows XP Home Edition, Windows XP Professional, Windows .NET Server family, .NET Compact Framework - Windows CE .NET

ResourceReader.Close Method

Releases all operating system resources associated with this **ResourceReader**.

```
[Visual Basic]
Public Overridable Sub Close() Implements IResourceReader.Close
[C#]
public virtual void Close();
[C++]
public: virtual void Close();
[JScript]
public function Close();
```

Implements

IResourceReader.Close

Remarks

Close can be safely called multiple times.

Example

See related example in the **System.Resources.ResourceReader** class topic.

Requirements

Platforms: Windows 98, Windows NT 4.0,
Windows Millennium Edition, Windows 2000,
Windows XP Home Edition, Windows XP Professional,
Windows .NET Server family,
.NET Compact Framework - Windows CE .NET

ResourceReader.GetEnumerator Method

Returns an enumerator for this **ResourceReader**.

```
[Visual Basic]
Public Overridable Function GetEnumerator() As IDictionaryEnumerator _
   Implements IResourceReader.GetEnumerator
[C#]
public virtual IDictionaryEnumerator GetEnumerator();
[C++]
public: virtual IDictionaryEnumerator* GetEnumerator();
[JScript]
public function GetEnumerator() : IDictionaryEnumerator;
```

Return Value

An **IDictionaryEnumerator** for this **ResourceReader**.

Implements

IResourceReader.GetEnumerator

Exceptions

Exception Type	Condition
InvalidOperation-Exception	The reader has already been closed, and thus cannot be accessed.

Example

See related example in the **System.Resources.ResourceReader**
class topic.

Requirements

Platforms: Windows 98, Windows NT 4.0,
Windows Millennium Edition, Windows 2000,
Windows XP Home Edition, Windows XP Professional,
Windows .NET Server family,
.NET Compact Framework - Windows CE .NET

ResourceReader.IDisposable.Dispose Method

Releases the resources used by the **ResourceReader**.

```
[Visual Basic]
Private Sub Dispose() Implements IDisposable.Dispose
[C#]
void IDisposable.Dispose();
[C++]
private: void IDisposable::Dispose();
[JScript]
private function IDisposable.Dispose();
```

Implements

IDisposable.Dispose

Remarks

Calling **Dispose** allows the resources used by the **ResourceReader**
to be reallocated for other purposes.

Example

See related example in the **System.Resources.ResourceReader**
class topic.

Requirements

Platforms: Windows 98, Windows NT 4.0,
Windows Millennium Edition, Windows 2000,
Windows XP Home Edition, Windows XP Professional,
Windows .NET Server family

ResourceReader.IEnumerable.GetEnumerator Method

Returns an enumerator for this **ResourceReader**.

```
[Visual Basic]
Private Function GetEnumerator() As IEnumerator Implements _
   IEnumerable.GetEnumerator
[C#]
IEnumerator IEnumerable.GetEnumerator();
[C++]
private: IEnumerator* IEnumerable::GetEnumerator();
[JScript]
private function IEnumerable.GetEnumerator() : IEnumerator;
```

Return Value

An **IEnumerator** for this **ResourceReader**.

Implements

IEnumerable.GetEnumerator

Exceptions

Exception Type	Condition
InvalidOperation-Exception	The reader has already been closed, and thus cannot be accessed.

Requirements

Platforms: Windows 98, Windows NT 4.0,
Windows Millennium Edition, Windows 2000,
Windows XP Home Edition, Windows XP Professional,
Windows .NET Server family

ResourceSet Class

Stores all the resources localized for one particular culture, ignoring all other cultures, including any fallback rules.

System.Object
  System.Resources.ResourceSet
    System.Resources.ResXResourceSet

```
[Visual Basic]
<Serializable>
Public Class ResourceSet
   Implements IDisposable, IEnumerable
[C#]
[Serializable]
public class ResourceSet : IDisposable, IEnumerable
[C++]
[Serializable]
public __gc class ResourceSet : public IDisposable, IEnumerable
[JScript]
public
   Serializable
class ResourceSet implements IDisposable, IEnumerable
```

Thread Safety

Any public static (**Shared** in Visual Basic) members of this type are safe for multithreaded operations. Any instance members are not guaranteed to be thread safe.

Remarks

The **ResourceSet** class enumerates over an **IResourceReader**, loading every name and value, and storing them in a **Hashtable**. A custom **IResourceReader** can be used.

Notes to Inheritors: Derived classes of **ResourceSet** using their own resource reader and writer should override **GetDefaultReader**, and **GetDefaultWriter**, to provide the appropriate functionality for interpreting the **ResourceSet**.

Requirements

Namespace: System.Resources

Platforms: Windows 98, Windows NT 4.0, Windows Millennium Edition, Windows 2000, Windows XP Home Edition, Windows XP Professional, Windows .NET Server family, .NET Compact Framework - Windows CE .NET

Assembly: Mscorlib (in Mscorlib.dll)

ResourceSet Constructor

Creates a new instance of the **ResourceSet** class.

Overload List

Initializes a new instance of the **ResourceSet** class with default properties.

Supported by the .NET Compact Framework.

  [Visual Basic] **Protected Sub New()**
  [C#] **protected ResourceSet();**
  [C++] **protected: ResourceSet();**
  [JScript] **protected function ResourceSet();**

Creates a new instance of the **ResourceSet** class using the specified resource reader.

Supported by the .NET Compact Framework.

  [Visual Basic] **Public Sub New(IResourceReader)**
  [C#] **public ResourceSet(IResourceReader);**
  [C++] **public: ResourceSet(IResourceReader*);**
  [JScript] **public function ResourceSet(IResourceReader);**

Creates a new instance of the **ResourceSet** class using the system default **ResourceReader** that reads resources from the given stream.

Supported by the .NET Compact Framework.

  [Visual Basic] **Public Sub New(Stream)**
  [C#] **public ResourceSet(Stream);**
  [C++] **public: ResourceSet(Stream*);**
  [JScript] **public function ResourceSet(Stream);**

Creates a new instance of the **ResourceSet** class using the system default **ResourceReader** that opens and reads resources from the given file.

Supported by the .NET Compact Framework.

  [Visual Basic] **Public Sub New(String)**
  [C#] **public ResourceSet(string);**
  [C++] **public: ResourceSet(String*);**
  [JScript] **public function ResourceSet(String);**

Example

[Visual Basic, C#, C++] **Note** This example shows how to use one of the overloaded versions of the **ResourceSet** constructor. For other examples that might be available, see the individual overload topics.

```
[Visual Basic]
Imports System
Imports System.Resources
Imports System.Collections
Imports Microsoft.VisualBasic

Class EnumerateResources

   Public Shared Sub Main()
      ' Create a ResourceSet for the file items.resources.
      Dim rs As New ResourceSet("items.resources")

      ' Create an IDictionaryEnumerator to read the data in   ⏎
the ResourceSet.
      Dim id As IDictionaryEnumerator = rs.GetEnumerator()

      ' Iterate through the ResourceSet and display the contents  ⏎
to the console.
      While id.MoveNext()
         Console.WriteLine(ControlChars.NewLine + "[{0}] " +   ⏎
ControlChars.Tab + "{1}", id.Key, id.Value)
      End While

      rs.Close()

   End Sub

End Class

[C#]
using System;
using System.Resources;
using System.Collections;
```

```
class EnumerateResources
{
    public static void Main()
    {
        // Create a ResourceSet for the file items.resources.
        ResourceSet rs = new ResourceSet("items.resources");

        // Create an IDictionaryEnumerator to read the data in
the ResourceSet.
        IDictionaryEnumerator id = rs.GetEnumerator();

        // Iterate through the ResourceSet and display the
contents to the console.
        while(id.MoveNext())
            Console.WriteLine("\n[{0}] \t{1}", id.Key, id.Value);

        rs.Close();

    }
}

[C++]
#using <mscorlib.dll>

using namespace System;
using namespace System::Resources;
using namespace System::Collections;

int main() {
    // Create a ResourceSet for the file items.resources.
    ResourceSet* rs = new ResourceSet(S"items.resources");

    // Create an IDictionaryEnumerator* to read the data
in the ResourceSet.
    IDictionaryEnumerator* id = rs->GetEnumerator();

    // Iterate through the ResourceSet and display the contents
to the console.
    while(id->MoveNext())
        Console::WriteLine(S"\n [{0}] \t {1}", id->Key, id->Value);

    rs->Close();

}
```

ResourceSet Constructor ()

Initializes a new instance of the **ResourceSet** class with default properties.

```
[Visual Basic]
Protected Sub New()
[C#]
protected ResourceSet();
[C++]
protected: ResourceSet();
[JScript]
protected function ResourceSet();
```

Requirements

Platforms: Windows 98, Windows NT 4.0,
Windows Millennium Edition, Windows 2000,
Windows XP Home Edition, Windows XP Professional,
Windows .NET Server family,
.NET Compact Framework - Windows CE .NET

ResourceSet Constructor (IResourceReader)

Creates a new instance of the **ResourceSet** class using the specified resource reader.

```
[Visual Basic]
Public Sub New( _
    ByVal reader As IResourceReader _
)
[C#]
public ResourceSet(
    IResourceReader reader
);
[C++]
public: ResourceSet(
    IResourceReader* reader
);
[JScript]
public function ResourceSet(
    reader : IResourceReader
);
```

Parameters

reader

> The reader that will be used.

Exceptions

Exception Type	Condition
ArgumentNullException	The *reader* parameter is a null reference (**Nothing** in Visual Basic).

Remarks

You can use this constructor to support custom resource formats using a user-provided **IResourceReader**.

Requirements

Platforms: Windows 98, Windows NT 4.0,
Windows Millennium Edition, Windows 2000,
Windows XP Home Edition, Windows XP Professional,
Windows .NET Server family,
.NET Compact Framework - Windows CE .NET

ResourceSet Constructor (Stream)

Creates a new instance of the **ResourceSet** class using the system default **ResourceReader** that reads resources from the given stream.

```
[Visual Basic]
Public Sub New( _
    ByVal stream As Stream _
)
[C#]
public ResourceSet(
    Stream stream
);
[C++]
public: ResourceSet(
    Stream* stream
);
[JScript]
public function ResourceSet(
    stream : Stream
);
```

Parameters

stream

The **Stream** of resources to be read. The stream should refer to an existing resources file.

Exceptions

Exception Type	Condition
ArgumentException	The *stream* is not readable.
ArgumentNullException	The *stream* parameter is a null reference (**Nothing** in Visual Basic).

Requirements

Platforms: Windows 98, Windows NT 4.0, Windows Millennium Edition, Windows 2000, Windows XP Home Edition, Windows XP Professional, Windows .NET Server family, .NET Compact Framework - Windows CE .NET

ResourceSet Constructor (String)

Creates a new instance of the **ResourceSet** class using the system default **ResourceReader** that opens and reads resources from the given file.

```
[Visual Basic]
Public Sub New( _
   ByVal fileName As String _
)
[C#]
public ResourceSet(
   string fileName
);
[C++]
public: ResourceSet(
   String* fileName
);
[JScript]
public function ResourceSet(
   fileName : String
);
```

Parameters

fileName

Resource file to read.

Exceptions

Exception Type	Condition
ArgumentNullException	The *fileName* parameter is a null reference (**Nothing** in Visual Basic).

Example

See related example in the **System.Resources.ResourceSet** constructor topic.

Requirements

Platforms: Windows 98, Windows NT 4.0, Windows Millennium Edition, Windows 2000, Windows XP Home Edition, Windows XP Professional, Windows .NET Server family, .NET Compact Framework - Windows CE .NET

ResourceSet.Reader Field

Indicates the **IResourceReader** used to read the resources.

```
[Visual Basic]
Protected Reader As IResourceReader
[C#]
protected IResourceReader Reader;
[C++]
protected: IResourceReader* Reader;
[JScript]
protected var Reader : IResourceReader;
```

Requirements

Platforms: Windows 98, Windows NT 4.0, Windows Millennium Edition, Windows 2000, Windows XP Home Edition, Windows XP Professional, Windows .NET Server family, .NET Compact Framework - Windows CE .NET

ResourceSet.Table Field

The **Hashtable** in which the resources are stored.

```
[Visual Basic]
Protected Table As Hashtable
[C#]
protected Hashtable Table;
[C++]
protected: Hashtable* Table;
[JScript]
protected var Table : Hashtable;
```

Requirements

Platforms: Windows 98, Windows NT 4.0, Windows Millennium Edition, Windows 2000, Windows XP Home Edition, Windows XP Professional, Windows .NET Server family, .NET Compact Framework - Windows CE .NET

ResourceSet.Close Method

Closes and releases any resources used by this **ResourceSet**.

```
[Visual Basic]
Public Overridable Sub Close()
[C#]
public virtual void Close();
[C++]
public: virtual void Close();
[JScript]
public function Close();
```

Remarks

All calls to methods on the **ResourceSet** after a call to this method might fail.

Close can be safely called multiple times.

> **Note** The current implementation of **Close** calls **Dispose** (**true**).

Example

See related example in the **System.Resources.ResourceSet** constructor topic.

Requirements

Platforms: Windows 98, Windows NT 4.0,
Windows Millennium Edition, Windows 2000,
Windows XP Home Edition, Windows XP Professional,
Windows .NET Server family,
.NET Compact Framework - Windows CE .NET

ResourceSet.Dispose Method

Releases resources used by the current **ResourceSet** instance.

Overload List

Disposes of the resources (other than memory) used by the current
instance of **ResourceSet**.

Supported by the .NET Compact Framework.

[Visual Basic] **Overloads Public Overridable Sub Dispose()**
Implements IDisposable.Dispose

[C#] **public virtual void Dispose();**

[C++] **public: virtual void Dispose();**

[JScript] **public function Dispose();**

Releases resources (other than memory) associated with the current
instance, closing internal managed objects if requested.

Supported by the .NET Compact Framework.

[Visual Basic] **Overloads Protected Overridable Sub**
Dispose(Boolean)

[C#] **protected virtual void Dispose(bool);**

[C++] **protected: virtual void Dispose(bool);**

[JScript] **protected function Dispose(Boolean);**

ResourceSet.Dispose Method ()

Disposes of the resources (other than memory) used by the current
instance of **ResourceSet**.

```
[Visual Basic]
Overloads Public Overridable Sub Dispose() Implements _
   IDisposable.Dispose
[C#]
public virtual void Dispose();
[C++]
public: virtual void Dispose();
[JScript]
public function Dispose();
```

Implements

IDisposable.Dispose

Remarks

Call **Dispose** when you are finished using the **ResourceSet**. The
Dispose method leaves the **ResourceSet** in an unusable state. After
calling **Dispose**, you must release all references to the **ResourceSet**
so the memory it was occupying can be reclaimed by garbage
collection.

> **Note** The current method is the implementation of
> **IDisposable.Dispose**. This implementation calls **Dispose**
> (**true**).

Requirements

Platforms: Windows 98, Windows NT 4.0,
Windows Millennium Edition, Windows 2000,
Windows XP Home Edition, Windows XP Professional,
Windows .NET Server family,
.NET Compact Framework - Windows CE .NET

ResourceSet.Dispose Method (Boolean)

Releases resources (other than memory) associated with the current
instance, closing internal managed objects if requested.

```
[Visual Basic]
Overloads Protected Overridable Sub Dispose( _
   ByVal disposing As Boolean _
)
[C#]
protected virtual void Dispose(
   bool disposing
);
[C++]
protected: virtual void Dispose(
   bool disposing
);
[JScript]
protected function Dispose(
   disposing : Boolean
);
```

Parameters

disposing
> Indicates whether the objects contained in the current instance
> should be explicitly closed.

Remarks

If the *dispose* parameter is **true**, the current method frees all the
resources associated with it as well as with all objects associated
with it. If *dispose* is **false**, the current method frees only the
resources allocated to it, and ignores any objects associated with it.

Requirements

Platforms: Windows 98, Windows NT 4.0,
Windows Millennium Edition, Windows 2000,
Windows XP Home Edition, Windows XP Professional,
Windows .NET Server family,
.NET Compact Framework - Windows CE .NET

ResourceSet.GetDefaultReader Method

Returns the preferred resource reader class for this kind of
ResourceSet.

```
[Visual Basic]
Public Overridable Function GetDefaultReader() As Type
[C#]
public virtual Type GetDefaultReader();
[C++]
public: virtual Type* GetDefaultReader();
[JScript]
public function GetDefaultReader() : Type;
```

Return Value

Returns the **Type** for the preferred resource reader for this kind of
ResourceSet.

Remarks

Notes to Inheritors: Derived classes of **ResourceSet** using their own resource reader should override **GetDefaultReader**, and **GetDefaultWriter**.

Requirements

Platforms: Windows 98, Windows NT 4.0, Windows Millennium Edition, Windows 2000, Windows XP Home Edition, Windows XP Professional, Windows .NET Server family, .NET Compact Framework - Windows CE .NET

ResourceSet.GetDefaultWriter Method

Returns the preferred resource writer class for this kind of **ResourceSet**.

```
[Visual Basic]
Public Overridable Function GetDefaultWriter() As Type
[C#]
public virtual Type GetDefaultWriter();
[C++]
public: virtual Type* GetDefaultWriter();
[JScript]
public function GetDefaultWriter() : Type;
```

Return Value

Returns the **Type** for the preferred resource writer for this kind of **ResourceSet**.

Remarks

Notes to Inheritors: Derived classes of **ResourceSet** using their own resource reader should override **GetDefaultReader**, and **GetDefaultWriter**.

Requirements

Platforms: Windows 98, Windows NT 4.0, Windows Millennium Edition, Windows 2000, Windows XP Home Edition, Windows XP Professional, Windows .NET Server family

ResourceSet.GetEnumerator Method

Note: This namespace, class, or member is supported only in version 1.1 of the .NET Framework.

Returns an **IDictionaryEnumerator** that can iterate through the **ResourceSet**.

```
[Visual Basic]
<ComVisible(False)>
Public Overridable Function GetEnumerator() As _
   IDictionaryEnumerator
[C#]
[ComVisible(false)]
public virtual IDictionaryEnumerator GetEnumerator();
[C++]
[ComVisible(false)]
public: virtual IDictionaryEnumerator* GetEnumerator();
[JScript]
public
   ComVisible(false)
function GetEnumerator() : IDictionaryEnumerator;
```

Return Value

An **IDictionaryEnumerator** for this **ResourceSet**.

Exceptions

Exception Type	Condition
InvalidOperation-Exception	This **ResourceSet** has been closed.

Remarks

Enumerators only allow reading the data in the collection. Enumerators cannot be used to modify the underlying collection.

Initially, the enumerator is positioned before the first element in the collection. **Reset** also brings the enumerator back to this position. At this position, calling **Current** throws an exception. Therefore, you must call **MoveNext** to advance the enumerator to the first element of the collection before reading the value of **Current**.

Current returns the same object until either **MoveNext** or **Reset** is called. **MoveNext** sets **Current** to the next element.

After the end of the collection is passed, the enumerator is positioned after the last element in the collection, and calling **MoveNext** returns **false**. If the last call to **MoveNext** returned **false**, calling **Current** throws an exception. To set **Current** to the first element of the collection again, you can call **Reset** followed by **MoveNext**.

An enumerator remains valid as long as the collection remains unchanged. If changes are made to the collection, such as adding, modifying or deleting elements, the enumerator is irrecoverably invalidated and the next call to **MoveNext** or **Reset** throws an **InvalidOperationException**. If the collection is modified between **MoveNext** and **Current**, **Current** will return the element that it is set to, even if the enumerator is already invalidated.

You can use the **IDictionaryEnumerator.Entry** property to access the value stored in the current element. Use the **IDictionary-Enumerator.Key** property to access the key of the current element. Use the **IDictionaryEnumerator.Value** property to access the value of the current element.

The enumerator does not have exclusive access to the collection; therefore, enumerating through a collection is intrinsically not a thread-safe procedure. Even when a collection is synchronized, other threads could still modify the collection, which causes the enumerator to throw an exception. To guarantee thread safety during enumeration, you can either lock the collection during the entire enumeration or catch the exceptions resulting from changes made by other threads.

Example

See related example in the **System.Resources.ResourceSet** constructor topic.

Requirements

Platforms: Windows 98, Windows NT 4.0, Windows Millennium Edition, Windows 2000, Windows XP Home Edition, Windows XP Professional, Windows .NET Server family

ResourceSet.GetObject Method

Returns a resource object with the specified name.

Overload List

Searches for a resource object with the specified name.

Supported by the .NET Compact Framework.

> [Visual Basic] **Overloads Public Overridable Function GetObject(String) As Object**
>
> [C#] **public virtual object GetObject(string);**
>
> [C++] **public: virtual Object* GetObject(String*);**
>
> [JScript] **public function GetObject(String) : Object;**

Searches for a resource object with the specified name in a case-insensitive manner, if requested.

Supported by the .NET Compact Framework.

> [Visual Basic] **Overloads Public Overridable Function GetObject(String, Boolean) As Object**
>
> [C#] **public virtual object GetObject(string, bool);**
>
> [C++] **public: virtual Object* GetObject(String*, bool);**
>
> [JScript] **public function GetObject(String, Boolean) : Object;**

ResourceSet.GetObject Method (String)

Searches for a resource object with the specified name.

```
[Visual Basic]
Overloads Public Overridable Function GetObject( _
   ByVal name As String _
) As Object
[C#]
public virtual object GetObject(
   string name
);
[C++]
public: virtual Object* GetObject(
   String* name
);
[JScript]
public function GetObject(
   name : String
) : Object;
```

Parameters

name
> Name of the resource to search for.

Return Value

The requested resource.

Exceptions

Exception Type	Condition
ArgumentNullException	The *name* parameter is a null reference (**Nothing** in Visual Basic).
InvalidOperation- Exception	This **ResourceSet** has been closed.

Requirements

Platforms: Windows 98, Windows NT 4.0, Windows Millennium Edition, Windows 2000, Windows XP Home Edition, Windows XP Professional, Windows .NET Server family, .NET Compact Framework - Windows CE .NET

ResourceSet.GetObject Method (String, Boolean)

Searches for a resource object with the specified name in a case-insensitive manner, if requested.

```
[Visual Basic]
Overloads Public Overridable Function GetObject( _
   ByVal name As String, _
   ByVal ignoreCase As Boolean _
) As Object
[C#]
public virtual object GetObject(
   string name,
   bool ignoreCase
);
[C++]
public: virtual Object* GetObject(
   String* name,
   bool ignoreCase
);
[JScript]
public function GetObject(
   name : String,
   ignoreCase : Boolean
) : Object;
```

Parameters

name
> Name of the resource to search for.

ignoreCase
> Indicates whether the case of the case of the specified name should be ignored.

Return Value

The requested resource.

Exceptions

Exception Type	Condition
ArgumentNullException	The *name* parameter is a null reference (**Nothing** in Visual Basic).
InvalidOperation- Exception	This **ResourceSet** has been closed.

Remarks

If the value of the *ignoreCase* parameter is **true**, a resource with the name "Resource" is equivalent to the resource with the name "resource". Note, however, that this method always performs case-insensitive string comparisons using **CultureInfo.InvariantCulture**. The advantage is that results of case-insensitive string comparisons performed by this method are the same on all computers regardless of culture. The disadvantage is that the results are not consistent with the casing rules of all cultures.

For example, the Turkish alphabet has two versions of the character I: one with a dot and one without a dot. In Turkish, the character I (Unicode 0049) is considered the uppercase version of a different character ı (Unicode 0131). The character i (Unicode 0069) is considered the lowercase version of yet another character İ (Unicode 0130). According to these casing rules, a case-insensitive string comparison of the characters i (Unicode 0069) and I (Unicode 0049) should fail for the culture "tr-TR" (Turkish in Turkey). Using the **GetObject** method with *ignoreCase* set to **true**, this comparison succeeds.

Requirements

Platforms: Windows 98, Windows NT 4.0,
Windows Millennium Edition, Windows 2000,
Windows XP Home Edition, Windows XP Professional,
Windows .NET Server family,
.NET Compact Framework - Windows CE .NET

ResourceSet.GetString Method

Returns a **String** resource with a specified name.

Overload List

Searches for a **String** resource with the specified name.

Supported by the .NET Compact Framework.

> [Visual Basic] **Overloads Public Overridable Function GetString(String) As String**
>
> [C#] **public virtual string GetString(string);**
>
> [C++] **public: virtual String* GetString(String*);**
>
> [JScript] **public function GetString(String) : String;**

Searches for a **String** resource with the specified name in a case-insensitive manner, if requested.

Supported by the .NET Compact Framework.

> [Visual Basic] **Overloads Public Overridable Function GetString(String, Boolean) As String**
>
> [C#] **public virtual string GetString(string, bool);**
>
> [C++] **public: virtual String* GetString(String*, bool);**
>
> [JScript] **public function GetString(String, Boolean) : String;**

ResourceSet.GetString Method (String)

Searches for a **String** resource with the specified name.

```
[Visual Basic]
Overloads Public Overridable Function GetString( _
  ByVal name As String _
) As String
[C#]
public virtual string GetString(
  string name
);
[C++]
public: virtual String* GetString(
  String* name
);
[JScript]
public function GetString(
  name : String
) : String;
```

Parameters

name
> Name of the resource to search for.

Return Value

The value of a resource, if the value is a **String**.

Exceptions

Exception Type	Condition
ArgumentNullException	The *name* parameter is a null reference (**Nothing** in Visual Basic).

Exception Type	Condition
InvalidOperation-Exception	The resource with the specified name is not a **String** or the current **ResourceSet** has been closed.

Requirements

Platforms: Windows 98, Windows NT 4.0,
Windows Millennium Edition, Windows 2000,
Windows XP Home Edition, Windows XP Professional,
Windows .NET Server family,
.NET Compact Framework - Windows CE .NET

ResourceSet.GetString Method (String, Boolean)

Searches for a **String** resource with the specified name in a case-insensitive manner, if requested.

```
[Visual Basic]
Overloads Public Overridable Function GetString( _
  ByVal name As String, _
  ByVal ignoreCase As Boolean _
) As String
[C#]
public virtual string GetString(
  string name,
  bool ignoreCase
);
[C++]
public: virtual String* GetString(
  String* name,
  bool ignoreCase
);
[JScript]
public function GetString(
  name : String,
  ignoreCase : Boolean
) : String;
```

Parameters

name
> Name of the resource to search for.

ignoreCase
> Indicates whether the case of the case of the specified name should be ignored.

Return Value

The value of a resource, if the value is a **String**.

Exceptions

Exception Type	Condition
ArgumentNullException	The *name* parameter is a null reference (**Nothing** in Visual Basic).
InvalidOperation-Exception	The resource with the specified name is not a **String** or the current **ResourceSet** has been closed.

Remarks

If the value of the *ignoreCase* parameter is **true**, a resource with the name "Resource" is equivalent to the resource with the name "resource". Note, however, that this method always performs case-insensitive string comparisons using **CultureInfo.Invariant-Culture**. The advantage is that results of case-insensitive string comparisons performed by this method are the same on all computers regardless of culture. The disadvantage is that the results are not consistent with the casing rules of all cultures.

For example, the Turkish alphabet has two versions of the character I: one with a dot and one without a dot. In Turkish, the character I (Unicode 0049) is considered the uppercase version of a different character ı (Unicode 0131). The character i (Unicode 0069) is considered the lowercase version of yet another character İ (Unicode 0130). According to these casing rules, a case-insensitive string comparison of the characters i (Unicode 0069) and I (Unicode 0049) should fail for the culture "tr-TR" (Turkish in Turkey). Using the **GetString** method with *ignoreCase* set to **true**, this comparison succeeds.

Requirements

Platforms: Windows 98, Windows NT 4.0, Windows Millennium Edition, Windows 2000, Windows XP Home Edition, Windows XP Professional, Windows .NET Server family, .NET Compact Framework - Windows CE .NET

Requirements

Platforms: Windows 98, Windows NT 4.0, Windows Millennium Edition, Windows 2000, Windows XP Home Edition, Windows XP Professional, Windows .NET Server family, .NET Compact Framework - Windows CE .NET

ResourceSet.IEnumerable.GetEnumerator Method

Note: This namespace, class, or member is supported only in version 1.1 of the .NET Framework.

This member supports the .NET Framework infrastructure and is not intended to be used directly from your code.

```
[Visual Basic]
Private Function GetEnumerator() As IEnumerator Implements _
   IEnumerable.GetEnumerator
[C#]
IEnumerator IEnumerable.GetEnumerator();
[C++]
private: IEnumerator* IEnumerable::GetEnumerator();
[JScript]
private function IEnumerable.GetEnumerator() : IEnumerator;
```

ResourceSet.ReadResources Method

Reads all the resources and stores them in a **Hashtable** indicated in the **Table** property.

```
[Visual Basic]
Protected Overridable Sub ReadResources()
[C#]
protected virtual void ReadResources();
[C++]
protected: virtual void ReadResources();
[JScript]
protected function ReadResources();
```

Remarks

Notes to Inheritors: Derived classes of **ResourceSet** should explicitly call **ReadResources** to load all the resources from the **IResourceReader** into **Table**, generally either in the constructor or lazily on the first call to either **GetString** or **GetObject**. However, if your resource set and IResourceReader already have information about each other and have a more efficient way to load just a few select resources, this step can be skipped. To minimize working set, write your resource set in such a way that it queries your IResourceReader for only the resource values requested by your application.

ResourceWriter Class

Writes resources in the system-default format to an output file or an output stream.

System.Object
   System.Resources.ResourceWriter

[Visual Basic]
```
NotInheritable Public Class ResourceWriter
   Implements IResourceWriter, IDisposable
```
[C#]
```
public sealed class ResourceWriter : IResourceWriter, IDisposable
```
[C++]
```
public __gc __sealed class ResourceWriter : public IResourceWriter,
   IDisposable
```
[JScript]
```
public class ResourceWriter implements IResourceWriter, IDisposable
```

Thread Safety

Any public static (**Shared** in Visual Basic) members of this type are safe for multithreaded operations. Any instance members are not guaranteed to be thread safe.

Remarks

ResourceWriter provides a default implementation of the **IResourceWriter** interface.

Resources are specified as name and value pairs using the **AddResource** method. Resource names are case-sensitive when used for lookups, but to more easily support authoring tools and help eliminate bugs, **ResourceWriter** will not allow a .resources file to have names that vary only by case.

To create a resources file, create a **ResourceWriter** with a unique file name, call **AddResource** at least once, call **Generate** to write the resources file to disk, and then call **Close** to close the file. Calling **Close** will implicitly **Generate** the file if required.

The resources will not necessarily be written in the same order they were added.

Example

[Visual Basic, C#, C++] The following example writes several strings into the myResources.resources file.

[Visual Basic]
```
Imports System
Imports System.Resources

Public Class WriteResources

    Public Shared Sub Main()

        ' Creates a resource writer.
        Dim writer As New ResourceWriter("myResources.resources")

        ' Adds resources to the resource writer.
        writer.AddResource("String 1", "First String")

        writer.AddResource("String 2", "Second String")

        writer.AddResource("String 3", "Third String")

        ' Writes the resources to the file or stream, and closes it.
        writer.Close()
    End Sub
End Class
```

[C#]
```
using System;
using System.Resources;

public class WriteResources {
    public static void Main(string[] args) {

        // Creates a resource writer.
        IResourceWriter writer = new
ResourceWriter("myResources.resources");

        // Adds resources to the resource writer.
        writer.AddResource("String 1", "First String");

        writer.AddResource("String 2", "Second String");

        writer.AddResource("String 3", "Third String");

        // Writes the resources to the file or stream, and closes it.
        writer.Close();
    }
}
```

[C++]
```
using namespace System;
using namespace System::Resources;

void main(char** argc, int argv) {

    // Creates a resource writer.
    IResourceWriter* writer = new
ResourceWriter(S"myResources.resources");

    // Adds resources to the resource writer.
    writer->AddResource(S"String 1", S"First String");

    writer->AddResource(S"String 2", S"Second String");

    writer->AddResource(S"String 3", S"Third String");

    // Writes the resources to the file or stream, and closes it.
    writer->Close();
}
```

Requirements

Namespace: System.Resources

Platforms: Windows 98, Windows NT 4.0, Windows Millennium Edition, Windows 2000, Windows XP Home Edition, Windows XP Professional, Windows .NET Server family

Assembly: Mscorlib (in Mscorlib.dll)

ResourceWriter Constructor

Initializes a new instance of the **ResourceWriter** class.

Overload List

Initializes a new instance of the **ResourceWriter** class that writes the resources to the provided stream.

    [Visual Basic] **Public Sub New(Stream)**

    [C#] **public ResourceWriter(Stream);**

    [C++] **public: ResourceWriter(Stream*);**

    [JScript] **public function ResourceWriter(Stream);**

Initializes a new instance of the **ResourceWriter** class that writes the resources to the specified file.

    [Visual Basic] **Public Sub New(String)**

    [C#] **public ResourceWriter(string);**

[C++] **public: ResourceWriter(String*);**

[JScript] **public function ResourceWriter(String);**

Example

See related example in the **System.Resources.ResourceWriter** class topic.

ResourceWriter Constructor (Stream)

Initializes a new instance of the **ResourceWriter** class that writes the resources to the provided stream.

```
[Visual Basic]
Public Sub New( _
   ByVal stream As Stream _
)
[C#]
public ResourceWriter(
   Stream stream
);
[C++]
public: ResourceWriter(
   Stream* stream
);
[JScript]
public function ResourceWriter(
   stream : Stream
);
```

Parameters

stream
    The output stream.

Exceptions

Exception Type	Condition
ArgumentException	The *stream* parameter is not writable.
ArgumentNullException	The *stream* parameter is a null reference (**Nothing** in Visual Basic).

Example

See related example in the **System.Resources.ResourceWriter** class topic.

Requirements

Platforms: Windows 98, Windows NT 4.0, Windows Millennium Edition, Windows 2000, Windows XP Home Edition, Windows XP Professional, Windows .NET Server family

ResourceWriter Constructor (String)

Initializes a new instance of the **ResourceWriter** class that writes the resources to the specified file.

```
[Visual Basic]
Public Sub New( _
   ByVal fileName As String _
)
[C#]
public ResourceWriter(
   string fileName
);
```

```
[C++]
public: ResourceWriter(
   String* fileName
);
[JScript]
public function ResourceWriter(
   fileName : String
);
```

Parameters

fileName
    The output file name.

Exceptions

Exception Type	Condition
ArgumentNullException	The *fileName* parameter is a null reference (**Nothing** in Visual Basic).

Example

See related example in the **System.Resources.ResourceWriter** class topic.

Requirements

Platforms: Windows 98, Windows NT 4.0, Windows Millennium Edition, Windows 2000, Windows XP Home Edition, Windows XP Professional, Windows .NET Server family

ResourceWriter.AddResource Method

Adds a resource to the list of resources to be written.

Overload List

Adds a named resource specified as a byte array to the list of resources to be written.

> [Visual Basic] **Overloads Public Overridable Sub AddResource(String, Byte()) Implements IResourceWriter.AddResource**
>
> [C#] **public virtual void AddResource(string, byte[]);**
>
> [C++] **public: virtual void AddResource(String*, unsigned char __gc[]);**
>
> [JScript] **public function AddResource(String, Byte[]);**

Adds a named resource specified as an object to the list of resources to be written.

> [Visual Basic] **Overloads Public Overridable Sub AddResource(String, Object) Implements IResourceWriter.AddResource**
>
> [C#] **public virtual void AddResource(string, object);**
>
> [C++] **public: virtual void AddResource(String*, Object*);**
>
> [JScript] **public function AddResource(String, Object);**

Adds a **String** resource to the list of resources to be written.

> [Visual Basic] **Overloads Public Overridable Sub AddResource(String, String) Implements IResourceWriter.AddResource**
>
> [C#] **public virtual void AddResource(string, string);**
>
> [C++] **public: virtual void AddResource(String*, String*);**
>
> [JScript] **public function AddResource(String, String);**

Example

See related example in the **System.Resources.ResourceWriter** class topic.

ResourceWriter.AddResource Method (String, Byte[])

Adds a named resource specified as a byte array to the list of resources to be written.

```
[Visual Basic]
Overloads Public Overridable Sub AddResource( _
   ByVal name As String, _
   ByVal value() As Byte _
) Implements IResourceWriter.AddResource
[C#]
public virtual void AddResource(
   string name,
   byte[] value
);
[C++]
public: virtual void AddResource(
   String* name,
   unsigned char value __gc[]
);
[JScript]
public function AddResource(
   name : String,
   value : Byte[]
);
```

Parameters

name
   The name of the resource.
value
   Value of the resource as an 8-bit unsigned integer array.

Implements

IResourceWriter.AddResource

Exceptions

Exception Type	Condition
ArgumentException	*name* (or a name that varies only by capitalization) has already been added to this **ResourceWriter**.
ArgumentNullException	The *name* or *value* parameter is a null reference (**Nothing** in Visual Basic).
InvalidOperation-Exception	This **ResourceWriter** has been closed and its **Hashtable** is unavailable.

Remarks

The resource is not written until **Generate** is called.

Requirements

Platforms: Windows 98, Windows NT 4.0, Windows Millennium Edition, Windows 2000, Windows XP Home Edition, Windows XP Professional, Windows .NET Server family

ResourceWriter.AddResource Method (String, Object)

Adds a named resource specified as an object to the list of resources to be written.

```
[Visual Basic]
Overloads Public Overridable Sub AddResource( _
   ByVal name As String, _
   ByVal value As Object _
) Implements IResourceWriter.AddResource
[C#]
public virtual void AddResource(
   string name,
   object value
);
[C++]
public: virtual void AddResource(
   String* name,
   Object* value
);
[JScript]
public function AddResource(
   name : String,
   value : Object
);
```

Parameters

name
   The name of the resource.
value
   The value of the resource.

Implements

IResourceWriter.AddResource

Exceptions

Exception Type	Condition
ArgumentException	*name* (or a name that varies only by capitalization) has already been added to this **ResourceWriter**.
ArgumentNullException	The *name* or *value* parameter is a null reference (**Nothing** in Visual Basic).
InvalidOperation-Exception	This **ResourceWriter** has been closed and its **Hashtable** is unavailable.

Remarks

The resource is not written until **Generate** is called. The resource that was added must be serializable.

Requirements

Platforms: Windows 98, Windows NT 4.0, Windows Millennium Edition, Windows 2000, Windows XP Home Edition, Windows XP Professional, Windows .NET Server family

ResourceWriter.AddResource Method (String, String)

Adds a **String** resource to the list of resources to be written.

```
[Visual Basic]
Overloads Public Overridable Sub AddResource( _
   ByVal name As String, _
   ByVal value As String _
) Implements IResourceWriter.AddResource
```

```
[C#]
public virtual void AddResource(
   string name,
   string value
);
[C++]
public: virtual void AddResource(
   String* name,
   String* value
);
[JScript]
public function AddResource(
   name : String,
   value : String
);
```

Parameters

name
    The name of the resource.
value
    The value of the resource.

Implements

IResourceWriter.AddResource

Exceptions

Exception Type	Condition
ArgumentException	*name* (or a name that varies only by capitalization) has already been added to this ResourceWriter.
ArgumentNullException	The *name* or *value* parameter is a null reference (**Nothing** in Visual Basic).
InvalidOperation-Exception	This **ResourceWriter** has been closed and its **Hashtable** is unavailable.

Remarks

The resource is not written until **Generate** is called.

Example

See related example in the **System.Resources.ResourceWriter** class topic.

Requirements

Platforms: Windows 98, Windows NT 4.0, Windows Millennium Edition, Windows 2000, Windows XP Home Edition, Windows XP Professional, Windows .NET Server family

ResourceWriter.Close Method

Saves the resources to the output stream and then closes it.

```
[Visual Basic]
Public Overridable Sub Close() Implements IResourceWriter.Close
[C#]
public virtual void Close();
[C++]
public: virtual void Close();
[JScript]
public function Close();
```

Implements

IResourceWriter.Close

Exceptions

Exception Type	Condition
IOException	An I/O error has occurred.
SerializationException	An error has occurred during serialization of the object.

Remarks

Generate is called implicitly by **Close**, if required.

Example

See related example in the **System.Resources.ResourceWriter** class topic.

Requirements

Platforms: Windows 98, Windows NT 4.0, Windows Millennium Edition, Windows 2000, Windows XP Home Edition, Windows XP Professional, Windows .NET Server family

ResourceWriter.Dispose Method

Allows users to close the resource file or stream, explicitly releasing resources.

```
[Visual Basic]
Public Overridable Sub Dispose() Implements IDisposable.Dispose
[C#]
public virtual void Dispose();
[C++]
public: virtual void Dispose();
[JScript]
public function Dispose();
```

Implements

IDisposable.Dispose

Exceptions

Exception Type	Condition
IOException	An I/O error has occurred.
SerializationException	An error has occurred during serialization of the object.

Remarks

The implementation of this method is the same as **Close**.

Example

See related example in the **System.Resources.ResourceWriter** class topic.

Requirements

Platforms: Windows 98, Windows NT 4.0, Windows Millennium Edition, Windows 2000, Windows XP Home Edition, Windows XP Professional, Windows .NET Server family

ResourceWriter.Generate Method

Saves all resources to the output stream in the system default format.

```
[Visual Basic]
Public Overridable Sub Generate() Implements _
   IResourceWriter.Generate
[C#]
public virtual void Generate();
[C++]
public: virtual void Generate();
[JScript]
public function Generate();
```

Implements

IResourceWriter.Generate

Exceptions

Exception Type	Condition
IOException	An I/O error occurred.
SerializationException	An error occurred during serialization of the object.
InvalidOperationException	This **ResourceWriter** has been closed and its **Hashtable** is unavailable.

Remarks

Generate can only be called once, after all calls to **AddResource** have been made. If an exception occurs while writing the resources, the output stream is closed since the information written is most likely invalid.

Generate does not close the output stream in normal cases. Unless you are combining extra data with your .resources file or need access to the stream afterwards, you should call **Close** after calling **Generate**, or simply call **Close**.

Example

See related example in the **System.Resources.ResourceWriter** class topic.

Requirements

Platforms: Windows 98, Windows NT 4.0, Windows Millennium Edition, Windows 2000, Windows XP Home Edition, Windows XP Professional, Windows .NET Server family

ResXFileRef Class

Represents a link to an external resource.

System.Object
   System.Resources.ResXFileRef

```
[Visual Basic]
<Serializable>
Public Class ResXFileRef
[C#]
[Serializable]
public class ResXFileRef
[C++]
[Serializable]
public __gc class ResXFileRef
[JScript]
public
   Serializable
class ResXFileRef
```

Thread Safety

Any public static (**Shared** in Visual Basic) members of this type are safe for multithreaded operations. Any instance members are not guaranteed to be thread safe.

Remarks

The **ResXFileRef** class is used to include references to files in an XML resource (.resx) file. A **ResXFileRef** object represents a link to an external resource. The resource manager loads the resource returned when the resource specified by the **ResXFileRef** object is queried.

In a data entry in a .resx file, the type is a **ResXFileRef**, and the value is the path location on disk. When the resource manager deserializes the object, the **ResXFileRef** performs the I/O to get the file.

When you compile a .resx file with ResGen.exe, the resources specified in the .resx file are embedded in the resulting document resource file.

The following example shows typical contents of a .resx file.

```
<data name="iconclip" type="System.Resources.ResXFileRef,
System.Windows.Forms">
 <value>lookout.bmp;System.Drawing.Bitmap, System.Drawing</value>
</data>
<data name="mailbackground" type="System.Resources.ResXFileRef,
System.Windows.Forms">
 <value>mailbackground.bmp;System.Drawing.Bitmap,
System.Drawing</value>
</data>
<data name="xplogo" type="System.Resources.ResXFileRef,
System.Windows.Forms">
 <value>xplogo.png;System.Drawing.Bitmap, System.Drawing</value>
</data>
```

Requirements

Namespace: System.Resources

Platforms: Windows 98, Windows NT 4.0, Windows Millennium Edition, Windows 2000, Windows XP Home Edition, Windows XP Professional, Windows .NET Server family

Assembly: System.Windows.Forms (in System.Windows.Forms.dll)

ResXFileRef Constructor

Creates a new instance of the **ResXFileRef** class that references the specified file.

```
[Visual Basic]
Public Sub New( _
   ByVal fileName As String, _
   ByVal typeName As String _
)
[C#]
public ResXFileRef(
   string fileName,
   string typeName
);
[C++]
public: ResXFileRef(
   String* fileName,
   String* typeName
);
[JScript]
public function ResXFileRef(
   fileName : String,
   typeName : String
);
```

Parameters

fileName
   The file to reference.
typeName
   The type of the resource that is referenced.

Remarks

The type referred to by the *typeName* parameter must support a public constructor that accepts a **Stream** as a parameter.

Requirements

Platforms: Windows 98, Windows NT 4.0, Windows Millennium Edition, Windows 2000, Windows XP Home Edition, Windows XP Professional, Windows .NET Server family

ResXFileRef.ToString Method

This member overrides **Object.ToString**.

```
[Visual Basic]
Overrides Public Function ToString() As String
[C#]
public override string ToString();
[C++]
public: String* ToString();
[JScript]
public override function ToString() : String;
```

Requirements

Platforms: Windows 98, Windows NT 4.0, Windows Millennium Edition, Windows 2000, Windows XP Home Edition, Windows XP Professional, Windows .NET Server family

ResXFileRef.Converter Class

Provides a type converter to convert data for a **ResXFileRef** to and from a string.

System.Object
  System.ComponentModel.TypeConverter
    System.Resources.ResXFileRef.Converter

```
[Visual Basic]
Public Class ResXFileRef.Converter
    Inherits TypeConverter
[C#]
public class ResXFileRef.Converter : TypeConverter
[C++]
public __gc class ResXFileRef.Converter : public TypeConverter
[JScript]
public class ResXFileRef.Converter extends TypeConverter
```

Thread Safety

Any public static (**Shared** in Visual Basic) members of this type are safe for multithreaded operations. Any instance members are not guaranteed to be thread safe.

Remarks

A **ResXFileRef.Converter** provides the object the **ResXFileRef** refers to. For example, if the **ResXFileRef** is "xplogo.bmp;System.Drawing.Bitmap, System.Drawing", then calling the **ConvertFrom** method of the converter will return a **Bitmap**, not a **ResXFileRef**.

> **Note** Typically, you do not directly create an instance of an **ImageIndexConverter**. Instead, call the **GetConverter** method of **TypeDescriptor**. For more information, see the examples in the **TypeConverter** base class.

Requirements

Namespace: System.Resources

Platforms: Windows 98, Windows NT 4.0, Windows Millennium Edition, Windows 2000, Windows XP Home Edition, Windows XP Professional, Windows .NET Server family

Assembly: System.Windows.Forms (in System.Windows.Forms.dll)

ResXFileRef.Converter Constructor

Initializes a new instance of the **ResXFileRef.Converter** class.

```
[Visual Basic]
Public Sub New()
[C#]
public ResXFileRef.Converter();
[C++]
public: Converter();
[JScript]
public function ResXFileRef.Converter();
```

Remarks

The default constructor initializes any fields to their default values.

Requirements

Platforms: Windows 98, Windows NT 4.0, Windows Millennium Edition, Windows 2000, Windows XP Home Edition, Windows XP Professional, Windows .NET Server family

ResXFileRef.Converter.CanConvertFrom Method

Overload List

This member supports the .NET Framework infrastructure and is not intended to be used directly from your code.

> [Visual Basic] **Overloads Overrides Public Function CanConvertFrom(ITypeDescriptorContext, Type) As Boolean**
> [C#] **public override bool CanConvertFrom(ITypeDescriptorContext, Type);**
> [C++] **public: bool CanConvertFrom(ITypeDescriptorContext*, Type*);**
> [JScript] **public override function CanConvertFrom(ITypeDescriptorContext, Type) : Boolean;**

Inherited from **TypeConverter**.

> [Visual Basic] **Overloads Public Function CanConvertFrom(Type) As Boolean**
> [C#] **public bool CanConvertFrom(Type);**
> [C++] **public: bool CanConvertFrom(Type*);**
> [JScript] **public function CanConvertFrom(Type) : Boolean;**

ResXFileRef.Converter.CanConvertFrom Method (ITypeDescriptorContext, Type)

This member overrides **TypeConverter.CanConvertFrom**.

```
[Visual Basic]
Overrides Overloads Public Function CanConvertFrom( _
    ByVal context As ITypeDescriptorContext, _
    ByVal sourceType As Type _
) As Boolean
[C#]
public override bool CanConvertFrom(
    ITypeDescriptorContext context,
    Type sourceType
);
[C++]
public: bool CanConvertFrom(
    ITypeDescriptorContext* context,
    Type* sourceType
);
[JScript]
public override function CanConvertFrom(
    context : ITypeDescriptorContext,
    sourceType : Type
) : Boolean;
```

Requirements

Platforms: Windows 98, Windows NT 4.0, Windows Millennium Edition, Windows 2000, Windows XP Home Edition, Windows XP Professional, Windows .NET Server family

ResXFileRef.Converter.CanConvertTo Method
Overload List

This member supports the .NET Framework infrastructure and is not intended to be used directly from your code.

[Visual Basic] **Overloads Overrides Public Function CanConvertTo(ITypeDescriptorContext, Type) As Boolean**

[C#] **public override bool CanConvertTo(ITypeDescriptorContext, Type);**

[C++] **public: bool CanConvertTo(ITypeDescriptorContext*, Type*);**

[JScript] **public override function CanConvertTo(ITypeDescriptorContext, Type) : Boolean;**

Inherited from **TypeConverter**.

[Visual Basic] **Overloads Public Function CanConvertTo(Type) As Boolean**

[C#] **public bool CanConvertTo(Type);**

[C++] **public: bool CanConvertTo(Type*);**

[JScript] **public function CanConvertTo(Type) : Boolean;**

ResXFileRef.Converter.CanConvertTo Method (ITypeDescriptorContext, Type)

This member overrides **TypeConverter.CanConvertTo**.

```
[Visual Basic]
Overrides Overloads Public Function CanConvertTo( _
   ByVal context As ITypeDescriptorContext, _
   ByVal destinationType As Type _
) As Boolean
[C#]
public override bool CanConvertTo(
   ITypeDescriptorContext context,
   Type destinationType
);
[C++]
public: bool CanConvertTo(
   ITypeDescriptorContext* context,
   Type* destinationType
);
[JScript]
public override function CanConvertTo(
   context : ITypeDescriptorContext,
   destinationType : Type
) : Boolean;
```

Requirements

Platforms: Windows 98, Windows NT 4.0, Windows Millennium Edition, Windows 2000, Windows XP Home Edition, Windows XP Professional, Windows .NET Server family

ResXFileRef.Converter.ConvertFrom Method
Overload List

This member supports the .NET Framework infrastructure and is not intended to be used directly from your code.

[Visual Basic] **Overloads Overrides Public Function ConvertFrom(ITypeDescriptorContext, CultureInfo, Object) As Object**

[C#] **public override object ConvertFrom(ITypeDescriptorContext, CultureInfo, object);**

[C++] **public: Object* ConvertFrom(ITypeDescriptorContext*, CultureInfo*, Object*);**

[JScript] **public override function ConvertFrom(ITypeDescriptorContext, CultureInfo, Object) : Object;**

Inherited from **TypeConverter**.

[Visual Basic] **Overloads Public Function ConvertFrom(Object) As Object**

[C#] **public object ConvertFrom(object);**

[C++] **public: Object* ConvertFrom(Object*);**

[JScript] **public function ConvertFrom(Object) : Object;**

ResXFileRef.Converter.ConvertFrom Method (ITypeDescriptorContext, CultureInfo, Object)

This member overrides **TypeConverter.ConvertFrom**.

```
[Visual Basic]
Overrides Overloads Public Function ConvertFrom( _
   ByVal context As ITypeDescriptorContext, _
   ByVal culture As CultureInfo, _
   ByVal value As Object _
) As Object
[C#]
public override object ConvertFrom(
   ITypeDescriptorContext context,
   CultureInfo culture,
   object value
);
[C++]
public: Object* ConvertFrom(
   ITypeDescriptorContext* context,
   CultureInfo* culture,
   Object* value
);
[JScript]
public override function ConvertFrom(
   context : ITypeDescriptorContext,
   culture : CultureInfo,
   value : Object
) : Object;
```

Requirements

Platforms: Windows 98, Windows NT 4.0, Windows Millennium Edition, Windows 2000, Windows XP Home Edition, Windows XP Professional, Windows .NET Server family

ResXFileRef.Converter.ConvertTo Method
Overload List

This member supports the .NET Framework infrastructure and is not intended to be used directly from your code.

[Visual Basic] **Overloads Overrides Public Function ConvertTo(ITypeDescriptorContext, CultureInfo, Object, Type) As Object**

[C#] **public override object ConvertTo(ITypeDescriptorContext, CultureInfo, object, Type);**

[C++] **public: Object* ConvertTo(ITypeDescriptorContext*, CultureInfo*, Object*, Type*);**

[JScript] **public override function ConvertTo(ITypeDescriptorContext, CultureInfo, Object, Type) : Object;**

Inherited from **TypeConverter**.

[Visual Basic] **Overloads Public Function ConvertTo(Object, Type) As Object**

[C#] **public object ConvertTo(object, Type);**

[C++] **public: Object* ConvertTo(Object*, Type*);**

[JScript] **public function ConvertTo(Object, Type) : Object;**

ResXFileRef.Converter.ConvertTo Method (ITypeDescriptorContext, CultureInfo, Object, Type)

This member overrides **TypeConverter.ConvertTo**.

```
[Visual Basic]
Overrides Overloads Public Function ConvertTo( _
    ByVal context As ITypeDescriptorContext, _
    ByVal culture As CultureInfo, _
    ByVal value As Object, _
    ByVal destinationType As Type _
) As Object
[C#]
public override object ConvertTo(
    ITypeDescriptorContext context,
    CultureInfo culture,
    object value,
    Type destinationType
);
[C++]
public: Object* ConvertTo(
    ITypeDescriptorContext* context,
    CultureInfo* culture,
    Object* value,
    Type* destinationType
);
[JScript]
public override function ConvertTo(
    context : ITypeDescriptorContext,
    culture : CultureInfo,
    value : Object,
    destinationType : Type
) : Object;
```

Requirements

Platforms: Windows 98, Windows NT 4.0,
Windows Millennium Edition, Windows 2000,
Windows XP Home Edition, Windows XP Professional,
Windows .NET Server family

ResXResourceReader Class

Enumerates XML resource (.resx) files and streams, and reads the sequential resource name and value pairs.

System.Object
  System.Resources.ResXResourceReader

```
[Visual Basic]
Public Class ResXResourceReader
   Implements IResourceReader, IEnumerable, IDisposable
[C#]
public class ResXResourceReader : IResourceReader, IEnumerable,
   IDisposable
[C++]
public __gc class ResXResourceReader : public IResourceReader,
   IEnumerable, IDisposable
[JScript]
public class ResXResourceReader implements IResourceReader,
   IEnumerable, IDisposable
```

Thread Safety

Any public static (**Shared** in Visual Basic) members of this type are safe for multithreaded operations. Any instance members are not guaranteed to be thread safe.

Remarks

The **ResXResourceReader** provides a default implementation of the **IResourceReader** interface that reads resource information in an XML format. To read resource information from a binary resource format, use **ResourceReader**.

You can use resource readers to read resource name and value pairs from .resx files. The resources can be enumerated by traversing the **IDictionaryEnumerator** returned by the **GetEnumerator** method. You can use the methods provided by the **IDictionaryEnumerator** to advance to the next resource and read the name and value of each resource in the .resx file.

> **Note**   **IEnumerable.GetEnumerator** returns an **IEnumerator** not **IDictionaryEnumerator**.

Example

[Visual Basic, C#, C++] The following example demonstrates how to use a **ResXResourceReader** to iterate through the resources in a .resx file. First, the **ResXResourceReader** rsxr is created for the file items.resx. Next, the **GetEnumerator** method is used to create an **IDictionaryEnumerator** to iterate through the resources and display the contents to the console.

```
[Visual Basic]
Imports System
Imports System.Resources
Imports System.Collections
Imports Microsoft.VisualBasic

Class ReadResXResources

   Public Shared Sub Main()

      ' Create a ResXResourceReader for the file items.resx.
      Dim rsxr As ResXResourceReader
      rsxr = New ResXResourceReader("items.resx")

      ' Create an IDictionaryEnumerator to iterate through the
resources.
      Dim id As IDictionaryEnumerator = rsxr.GetEnumerator()
```

```
      ' Iterate through the resources and display the contents
to the console.
      Dim d As DictionaryEntry
      For Each d In  rsxr
         Console.WriteLine(d.Key.ToString() + ":" +
ControlChars.Tab + d.Value.ToString())
      Next d

      'Close the reader.
      rsxr.Close()

   End Sub

End Class

[C#]
using System;
using System.Resources;
using System.Collections;

class ReadResXResources
{
   public static void Main()
   {

      // Create a ResXResourceReader for the file items.resx.
      ResXResourceReader rsxr = new ResXResourceReader("items.resx");

      // Create an IDictionaryEnumerator to iterate through the
resources.
      IDictionaryEnumerator id = rsxr.GetEnumerator();

      // Iterate through the resources and display the contents
to the console.
      foreach (DictionaryEntry d in rsxr)
      {
      Console.WriteLine(d.Key.ToString() + ":\t" + d.Value.ToString());
      }

      //Close the reader.
      rsxr.Close();
   }
}

[C++]
#using <mscorlib.dll>
#using <system.windows.forms.dll>

using namespace System;
using namespace System::Resources;
using namespace System::Collections;

void main()
{
   // Create a ResXResourceReader for the file items.resx.
   ResXResourceReader* rsxr = new ResXResourceReader(S"items.resx");

   // Create an IDictionaryEnumerator* to iterate through the
resources.
   IDictionaryEnumerator* id = rsxr->GetEnumerator();

   // Iterate through the resources and display the contents
to the console.
   IEnumerator* myEnum = rsxr->GetEnumerator();
   while (myEnum->MoveNext())
   {
      DictionaryEntry* d = __try_cast<DictionaryEntry*>(myEnum-
>Current);

      Console::WriteLine(S"{0}:\t {1}", d->Key, d->Value);
   }

   //Close the reader.
   rsxr->Close();
}
```

Requirements

Namespace: System.Resources

Platforms: Windows 98, Windows NT 4.0, Windows Millennium Edition, Windows 2000, Windows XP Home Edition, Windows XP Professional, Windows .NET Server family

Assembly: System.Windows.Forms (in System.Windows.Forms.dll)

ResXResourceReader Constructor

Initializes a new instance of the **ResXResourceReader** class.

Overload List

Initializes a new instance of the **ResXResourceReader** class for the specified stream.

> [Visual Basic] **Public Sub New(Stream)**
> [C#] **public ResXResourceReader(Stream);**
> [C++] **public: ResXResourceReader(Stream*);**
> [JScript] **public function ResXResourceReader(Stream);**

Initializes a new instance of the **ResXResourceReader** class for the specified resource file.

> [Visual Basic] **Public Sub New(String)**
> [C#] **public ResXResourceReader(string);**
> [C++] **public: ResXResourceReader(String*);**
> [JScript] **public function ResXResourceReader(String);**

Initializes a new instance of the **ResXResourceReader** class for the specified **TextReader**.

> [Visual Basic] **Public Sub New(TextReader)**
> [C#] **public ResXResourceReader(TextReader);**
> [C++] **public: ResXResourceReader(TextReader*);**
> [JScript] **public function ResXResourceReader(TextReader);**

This member supports the .NET Framework infrastructure and is not intended to be used directly from your code.

> [Visual Basic] **Public Sub New(Stream, ITypeResolutionService)**
> [C#] **public ResXResourceReader(Stream, ITypeResolutionService);**
> [C++] **public: ResXResourceReader(Stream*, ITypeResolutionService*);**
> [JScript] **public function ResXResourceReader(Stream, ITypeResolutionService);**

This member supports the .NET Framework infrastructure and is not intended to be used directly from your code.

> [Visual Basic] **Public Sub New(String, ITypeResolutionService)**
> [C#] **public ResXResourceReader(string, ITypeResolutionService);**
> [C++] **public: ResXResourceReader(String*, ITypeResolutionService*);**
> [JScript] **public function ResXResourceReader(String, ITypeResolutionService);**

This member supports the .NET Framework infrastructure and is not intended to be used directly from your code.

> [Visual Basic] **Public Sub New(TextReader, ITypeResolutionService)**
> [C#] **public ResXResourceReader(TextReader, ITypeResolutionService);**
> [C++] **public: ResXResourceReader(TextReader*, ITypeResolutionService*);**
> [JScript] **public function ResXResourceReader(TextReader, ITypeResolutionService);**

Example

See related example in the **System.Resources.ResXResourceReader** class topic.

ResXResourceReader Constructor (Stream)

Initializes a new instance of the **ResXResourceReader** class for the specified stream.

```
[Visual Basic]
Public Sub New( _
   ByVal stream As Stream _
)
[C#]
public ResXResourceReader(
   Stream stream
);
[C++]
public: ResXResourceReader(
   Stream* stream
);
[JScript]
public function ResXResourceReader(
   stream : Stream
);
```

Parameters

stream
>   The input stream for reading resources.

Remarks

> **Note** The **Dispose** and **Close** methods do not close the stream you specify in this constructor.

Requirements

Platforms: Windows 98, Windows NT 4.0, Windows Millennium Edition, Windows 2000, Windows XP Home Edition, Windows XP Professional, Windows .NET Server family

ResXResourceReader Constructor (String)

Initializes a new instance of the **ResXResourceReader** class for the specified resource file.

```
[Visual Basic]
Public Sub New( _
   ByVal fileName As String _
)
[C#]
public ResXResourceReader(
   string fileName
);
```

```
[C++]
public: ResXResourceReader(
   String* fileName
);
[JScript]
public function ResXResourceReader(
   fileName : String
);
```

Parameters

fileName

The path of the resource file to read.

Example

See related example in the
System.Resources.ResXResourceReader class topic.

Requirements

Platforms: Windows 98, Windows NT 4.0,
Windows Millennium Edition, Windows 2000,
Windows XP Home Edition, Windows XP Professional,
Windows .NET Server family

ResXResourceReader Constructor (TextReader)

Initializes a new instance of the **ResXResourceReader** class for the
specified **TextReader**.

```
[Visual Basic]
Public Sub New( _
   ByVal reader As TextReader _
)
[C#]
public ResXResourceReader(
   TextReader reader
);
[C++]
public: ResXResourceReader(
   TextReader* reader
);
[JScript]
public function ResXResourceReader(
   reader : TextReader
);
```

Parameters

reader

The character input stream for reading resources.

Requirements

Platforms: Windows 98, Windows NT 4.0,
Windows Millennium Edition, Windows 2000,
Windows XP Home Edition, Windows XP Professional,
Windows .NET Server family

ResXResourceReader Constructor (Stream, ITypeResolutionService)

This member supports the .NET Framework infrastructure and is not
intended to be used directly from your code.

```
[Visual Basic]
Public Sub New( _
   ByVal stream As Stream, _
   ByVal typeResolver As ITypeResolutionService _
)
[C#]
public ResXResourceReader(
   Stream stream,
   ITypeResolutionService typeResolver
);
[C++]
public: ResXResourceReader(
   Stream* stream,
   ITypeResolutionService* typeResolver
);
[JScript]
public function ResXResourceReader(
   stream : Stream,
   typeResolver : ITypeResolutionService
);
```

ResXResourceReader Constructor (String, ITypeResolutionService)

This member supports the .NET Framework infrastructure and is not
intended to be used directly from your code.

```
[Visual Basic]
Public Sub New( _
   ByVal fileName As String, _
   ByVal typeResolver As ITypeResolutionService _
)
[C#]
public ResXResourceReader(
   string fileName,
   ITypeResolutionService typeResolver
);
[C++]
public: ResXResourceReader(
   String* fileName,
   ITypeResolutionService* typeResolver
);
[JScript]
public function ResXResourceReader(
   fileName : String,
   typeResolver : ITypeResolutionService
);
```

ResXResourceReader Constructor (TextReader, ITypeResolutionService)

This member supports the .NET Framework infrastructure and is not
intended to be used directly from your code.

```
[Visual Basic]
Public Sub New( _
   ByVal reader As TextReader, _
   ByVal typeResolver As ITypeResolutionService _
)
```

```
[C#]
public ResXResourceReader(
   TextReader reader,
   ITypeResolutionService typeResolver
);
[C++]
public: ResXResourceReader(
   TextReader* reader,
   ITypeResolutionService* typeResolver
);
[JScript]
public function ResXResourceReader(
   reader : TextReader,
   typeResolver : ITypeResolutionService
);
```

ResXResourceReader.Close Method

Releases all resources used by the **ResXResourceReader**.

```
[Visual Basic]
Public Overridable Sub Close() Implements IResourceReader.Close
[C#]
public virtual void Close();
[C++]
public: virtual void Close();
[JScript]
public function Close();
```

Implements

IResourceReader.Close

Remarks

Calling **Close** enables the resources used by the **ResXResourceReader** to be reallocated for other purposes.

Example

See related example in the **System.Resources.ResXResourceReader** class topic.

Requirements

Platforms: Windows 98, Windows NT 4.0, Windows Millennium Edition, Windows 2000, Windows XP Home Edition, Windows XP Professional, Windows .NET Server family

ResXResourceReader.Dispose Method

Releases the unmanaged resources used by the **ResXResourceReader** and optionally releases the managed resources.

```
[Visual Basic]
Protected Overridable Sub Dispose( _
   ByVal disposing As Boolean _
)
[C#]
protected virtual void Dispose(
   bool disposing
);
[C++]
protected: virtual void Dispose(
   bool disposing
);
```

```
[JScript]
protected function Dispose(
   disposing : Boolean
);
```

Parameters

disposing
    true to release both managed and unmanaged resources; **false** to release only unmanaged resources.

Remarks

This method can be called by either the **System.Resources.ResXResourceReader.IDisposable.Dispose** method or the **Finalize** method. **System.Resources.ResXResourceReader.IDisposable.Dispose** invokes this method with the *disposing* parameter set to **true**. **Finalize** invokes this method with *disposing* set to **false**.

When the *disposing* parameter is **true**, this method releases all resources held by any managed objects that this **ResXResourceReader** references. This method invokes the **Dispose** method of each referenced object.

Notes to Inheritors: **Dispose** can be called multiple times by other objects. When overriding **Dispose(Boolean)**, be careful not to reference objects that have been previously disposed of in an earlier call to **Dispose**. For more information about how to implement **Dispose(Boolean)**, see **Implementing a Dispose Method**.

Requirements

Platforms: Windows 98, Windows NT 4.0, Windows Millennium Edition, Windows 2000, Windows XP Home Edition, Windows XP Professional, Windows .NET Server family

ResXResourceReader.Finalize Method

This member overrides **Object.Finalize**.

```
[Visual Basic]
Overrides Protected Sub Finalize()
[C#]
~ResXResourceReader();
[C++]
~ResXResourceReader();
[JScript]
protected override function Finalize();
```

Requirements

Platforms: Windows 98, Windows NT 4.0, Windows Millennium Edition, Windows 2000, Windows XP Home Edition, Windows XP Professional, Windows .NET Server family

ResXResourceReader.FromFileContents Method

Reads XML resources from the specified string.

Overload List

Reads XML resources from the specified string.

    [Visual Basic] **Overloads Public Shared Function FromFileContents(String) As ResXResourceReader**

    [C#] **public static ResXResourceReader FromFileContents(string);**

[C++] **public: static ResXResourceReader*** **FromFileContents(String*);**

[JScript] **public static function FromFileContents(String) :** **ResXResourceReader;**

This member supports the .NET Framework infrastructure and is not intended to be used directly from your code.

[Visual Basic] **Overloads Public Shared Function** **FromFileContents(String, ITypeResolutionService) As** **ResXResourceReader**

[C#] **public static ResXResourceReader** **FromFileContents(string, ITypeResolutionService);**

[C++] **public: static ResXResourceReader*** **FromFileContents(String*, ITypeResolutionService*);**

[JScript] **public static function FromFileContents(String,** **ITypeResolutionService) : ResXResourceReader;**

ResXResourceReader.FromFileContents Method (String)

Reads XML resources from the specified string.

```
[Visual Basic]
Overloads Public Shared Function FromFileContents( _
    ByVal fileContents As String _
) As ResXResourceReader
[C#]
public static ResXResourceReader FromFileContents(
    string fileContents
);
[C++]
public: static ResXResourceReader* FromFileContents(
    String* fileContents
);
[JScript]
public static function FromFileContents(
    fileContents : String
) : ResXResourceReader;
```

Parameters

fileContents
    A string containing XML resource-formatted information.

Return Value

A **ResXResourceReader** object.

Exceptions

Exception Type	Condition
XmlException	The *fileContents* string is incorrectly formatted or is not valid XML.

Remarks

You can use this method when you construct your own XML resource output. This method can construct a reader for that output.

Requirements

Platforms: Windows 98, Windows NT 4.0, Windows Millennium Edition, Windows 2000, Windows XP Home Edition, Windows XP Professional, Windows .NET Server family

ResXResourceReader.FromFileContents Method (String, ITypeResolutionService)

This member supports the .NET Framework infrastructure and is not intended to be used directly from your code.

```
[Visual Basic]
Overloads Public Shared Function FromFileContents( _
    ByVal fileContents As String, _
    ByVal typeResolver As ITypeResolutionService _
) As ResXResourceReader
[C#]
public static ResXResourceReader FromFileContents(
    string fileContents,
    ITypeResolutionService typeResolver
);
[C++]
public: static ResXResourceReader* FromFileContents(
    String* fileContents,
    ITypeResolutionService* typeResolver
);
[JScript]
public static function FromFileContents(
    fileContents : String,
    typeResolver : ITypeResolutionService
) : ResXResourceReader;
```

ResXResourceReader.GetEnumerator Method

Returns an enumerator for this **ResXResourceReader**.

```
[Visual Basic]
Public Overridable Function GetEnumerator() As IDictionaryEnumerator _
    Implements IResourceReader.GetEnumerator
[C#]
public virtual IDictionaryEnumerator GetEnumerator();
[C++]
public: virtual IDictionaryEnumerator* GetEnumerator();
[JScript]
public function GetEnumerator() : IDictionaryEnumerator;
```

Return Value

An **IDictionaryEnumerator** for this **ResourceReader**.

Implements

IResourceReader.GetEnumerator

Remarks

The **GetEnumerator** method steps though the name/value pairs stored in the XML resource (.resx) file.

Example

See related example in the **System.Resources.ResXResourceReader** class topic.

Requirements

Platforms: Windows 98, Windows NT 4.0, Windows Millennium Edition, Windows 2000, Windows XP Home Edition, Windows XP Professional, Windows .NET Server family

ResXResourceReader.IDisposable.Dispose Method

This member supports the .NET Framework infrastructure and is not intended to be used directly from your code.

```
[Visual Basic]
Private Sub Dispose() Implements IDisposable.Dispose
[C#]
void IDisposable.Dispose();
[C++]
private: void IDisposable::Dispose();
[JScript]
private function IDisposable.Dispose();
```

ResXResourceReader.IEnumerable.Get-Enumerator Method

This member supports the .NET Framework infrastructure and is not intended to be used directly from your code.

```
[Visual Basic]
Private Function GetEnumerator() As IEnumerator Implements _
    IEnumerable.GetEnumerator
[C#]
IEnumerator IEnumerable.GetEnumerator();
[C++]
private: IEnumerator* IEnumerable::GetEnumerator();
[JScript]
private function IEnumerable.GetEnumerator() : IEnumerator;
```

ResXResourceSet Class

Gathers all items that represent an XML resource (.resx) file into a single object.

System.Object
  System.Resources.ResourceSet
    System.Resources.ResXResourceSet

```
[Visual Basic]
Public Class ResXResourceSet
  Inherits ResourceSet
[C#]
public class ResXResourceSet : ResourceSet
[C++]
public __gc class ResXResourceSet : public ResourceSet
[JScript]
public class ResXResourceSet extends ResourceSet
```

Thread Safety

Any public static (**Shared** in Visual Basic) members of this type are safe for multithreaded operations. Any instance members are not guaranteed to be thread safe.

Remarks

The **ResXResourceSet** class enumerates over an **IResourceReader**, loading every name and value, and storing them in a hash table.

A **ResXResourceSet** provides a convenient way to read all the resources in a .resx file into memory. You can use the **GetObject** method to retrieve a particular resource once the .resx file has been read into a **ResXResourceSet**.

Notes to Inheritors: Derived classes of **ResXResourceSet** using their own resource reader and writer should override **GetDefaultReader** and **GetDefaultWriter** to provide the appropriate functionality for interpreting the **ResXResourceSet**.

Requirements

Namespace: System.Resources

Platforms: Windows 98, Windows NT 4.0, Windows Millennium Edition, Windows 2000, Windows XP Home Edition, Windows XP Professional, Windows .NET Server family

Assembly: System.Windows.Forms (in System.Windows.Forms.dll)

ResXResourceSet Constructor

Initializes a new instance of the **ResXResourceSet** class.

Overload List

Initializes a new instance of the **ResXResourceSet** class using the system default **ResXResourceReader** to read resources from the specified stream.

[Visual Basic] **Public Sub New(Stream)**
[C#] **public ResXResourceSet(Stream);**
[C++] **public: ResXResourceSet(Stream*);**
[JScript] **public function ResXResourceSet(Stream);**

Initializes a new instance of a **ResXResourceSet** class using the system default **ResXResourceReader** that opens and reads resources from the specified file.

[Visual Basic] **Public Sub New(String)**

[C#] **public ResXResourceSet(string);**
[C++] **public: ResXResourceSet(String*);**
[JScript] **public function ResXResourceSet(String);**

ResXResourceSet Constructor (Stream)

Initializes a new instance of the **ResXResourceSet** class using the system default **ResXResourceReader** to read resources from the specified stream.

```
[Visual Basic]
Public Sub New( _
  ByVal stream As Stream _
)
[C#]
public ResXResourceSet(
  Stream stream
);
[C++]
public: ResXResourceSet(
  Stream* stream
);
[JScript]
public function ResXResourceSet(
  stream : Stream
);
```

Parameters

stream

  The **Stream** of resources to be read. The stream should refer to an existing resource file.

Requirements

Platforms: Windows 98, Windows NT 4.0, Windows Millennium Edition, Windows 2000, Windows XP Home Edition, Windows XP Professional, Windows .NET Server family

ResXResourceSet Constructor (String)

Initializes a new instance of a **ResXResourceSet** class using the system default **ResXResourceReader** that opens and reads resources from the specified file.

```
[Visual Basic]
Public Sub New( _
  ByVal fileName As String _
)
[C#]
public ResXResourceSet(
  string fileName
);
[C++]
public: ResXResourceSet(
  String* fileName
);
[JScript]
public function ResXResourceSet(
  fileName : String
);
```

Parameters

fileName
> The name of the file to read resources from.

Requirements

Platforms: Windows 98, Windows NT 4.0,
Windows Millennium Edition, Windows 2000,
Windows XP Home Edition, Windows XP Professional,
Windows .NET Server family

Requirements

Platforms: Windows 98, Windows NT 4.0,
Windows Millennium Edition, Windows 2000,
Windows XP Home Edition, Windows XP Professional,
Windows .NET Server family

ResXResourceSet.GetDefaultReader Method

Returns the preferred resource reader class for this kind of
ResXResourceSet.

```
[Visual Basic]
Overrides Public Function GetDefaultReader() As Type
[C#]
public override Type GetDefaultReader();
[C++]
public: Type* GetDefaultReader();
[JScript]
public override function GetDefaultReader() : Type;
```

Return Value

The **Type** of the preferred resource reader for this kind of
ResXResourceSet.

Remarks

Notes to Inheritors: Derived classes of **ResXResourceSet** using
their own resource reader should override **GetDefaultReader** and
GetDefaultWriter.

Requirements

Platforms: Windows 98, Windows NT 4.0,
Windows Millennium Edition, Windows 2000,
Windows XP Home Edition, Windows XP Professional,
Windows .NET Server family

ResXResourceSet.GetDefaultWriter Method

Returns the preferred resource writer class for this kind of
ResXResourceSet.

```
[Visual Basic]
Overrides Public Function GetDefaultWriter() As Type
[C#]
public override Type GetDefaultWriter();
[C++]
public: Type* GetDefaultWriter();
[JScript]
public override function GetDefaultWriter() : Type;
```

Return Value

The **Type** of the preferred resource writer for this kind of
ResXResourceSet.

Remarks

Notes to Inheritors: Derived classes of **ResXResourceSet** using
their own resource reader should override **GetDefaultReader** and
GetDefaultWriter.

ResXResourceWriter Class

Writes resources in an XML resource (.resx) file or an output stream.

System.Object
  System.Resources.ResXResourceWriter

```
[Visual Basic]
Public Class ResXResourceWriter
  Implements IResourceWriter, IDisposable
[C#]
public class ResXResourceWriter : IResourceWriter, IDisposable
[C++]
public __gc class ResXResourceWriter : public IResourceWriter,
  IDisposable
[JScript]
public class ResXResourceWriter implements IResourceWriter,
  IDisposable
```

Thread Safety

Any public static (**Shared** in Visual Basic) members of this type are safe for multithreaded operations. Any instance members are not guaranteed to be thread safe.

Remarks

The **ResXResourceWriter** writes resources in XML format. To write a binary resource file, use **ResourceWriter**.

Resources are specified as name/value pairs using the **AddResource** method. Resource names are case-sensitive when used for lookups; but to more easily support authoring tools and help eliminate bugs, **ResXResourceWriter** does not allow a .resx file to have names that vary only by case.

To create a .resx file, create a **ResXResourceWriter** with a unique file name, call **AddResource** at least once, call **Generate** to write the resources file to disk, and then call **Close** to close the file. Calling **Close** will implicitly **Generate** the file if required.

The resources are not necessarily written in the same order they were added.

Requirements

Namespace: System.Resources

Platforms: Windows 98, Windows NT 4.0, Windows Millennium Edition, Windows 2000, Windows XP Home Edition, Windows XP Professional, Windows .NET Server family

Assembly: System.Windows.Forms (in System.Windows.Forms.dll)

ResXResourceWriter Constructor

Initializes a new instance of the **ResXResourceWriter** class.

Overload List

Initializes a new instance of the **ResXResourceWriter** class that writes the resources to the specified stream object.

[Visual Basic] **Public Sub New(Stream)**
[C#] **public ResXResourceWriter(Stream);**
[C++] **public: ResXResourceWriter(Stream*);**
[JScript] **public function ResXResourceWriter(Stream);**

Initializes a new instance of the **ResXResourceWriter** class that writes the resources to the specified file.

[Visual Basic] **Public Sub New(String)**
[C#] **public ResXResourceWriter(string);**
[C++] **public: ResXResourceWriter(String*);**
[JScript] **public function ResXResourceWriter(String);**

Initializes a new instance of the **ResXResourceWriter** class that writes to the specified **TextWriter** object.

[Visual Basic] **Public Sub New(TextWriter)**
[C#] **public ResXResourceWriter(TextWriter);**
[C++] **public: ResXResourceWriter(TextWriter*);**
[JScript] **public function ResXResourceWriter(TextWriter);**

ResXResourceWriter Constructor (Stream)

Initializes a new instance of the **ResXResourceWriter** class that writes the resources to the specified stream object.

```
[Visual Basic]
Public Sub New( _
  ByVal stream As Stream _
)
[C#]
public ResXResourceWriter(
  Stream stream
);
[C++]
public: ResXResourceWriter(
  Stream* stream
);
[JScript]
public function ResXResourceWriter(
  stream : Stream
);
```

Parameters

stream
  The output stream.

Remarks

> **Note** The **Close** method closes the stream you specify as a parameter. To write the resource to the stream without closing the stream, you must use the **Generate** method.

Requirements

Platforms: Windows 98, Windows NT 4.0, Windows Millennium Edition, Windows 2000, Windows XP Home Edition, Windows XP Professional, Windows .NET Server family

ResXResourceWriter Constructor (String)

Initializes a new instance of the **ResXResourceWriter** class that writes the resources to the specified file.

```
[Visual Basic]
Public Sub New( _
  ByVal fileName As String _
)
[C#]
public ResXResourceWriter(
  string fileName
);
```

```
[C++]
public: ResXResourceWriter(
    String* fileName
);
[JScript]
public function ResXResourceWriter(
    fileName : String
);
```

Parameters
fileName
> The output file name.

Requirements
Platforms: Windows 98, Windows NT 4.0,
Windows Millennium Edition, Windows 2000,
Windows XP Home Edition, Windows XP Professional,
Windows .NET Server family

ResXResourceWriter Constructor (TextWriter)

Initializes a new instance of the **ResXResourceWriter** class that
writes to the specified **TextWriter** object.

```
[Visual Basic]
Public Sub New( _
    ByVal textWriter As TextWriter _
)
[C#]
public ResXResourceWriter(
    TextWriter textWriter
);
[C++]
public: ResXResourceWriter(
    TextWriter* textWriter
);
[JScript]
public function ResXResourceWriter(
    textWriter : TextWriter
);
```

Parameters
textWriter
> The **TextWriter** object to send the output to.

Requirements
Platforms: Windows 98, Windows NT 4.0,
Windows Millennium Edition, Windows 2000,
Windows XP Home Edition, Windows XP Professional,
Windows .NET Server family

ResXResourceWriter.BinSerializedObjectMime-Type Field

This member supports the .NET Framework infrastructure and is not
intended to be used directly from your code.

```
[Visual Basic]
Public Shared ReadOnly BinSerializedObjectMimeType As String
[C#]
public static readonly string BinSerializedObjectMimeType;
[C++]
public: static String* BinSerializedObjectMimeType;
[JScript]
public static var BinSerializedObjectMimeType : String;
```

ResXResourceWriter.ByteArraySerializedObject-MimeType Field

This member supports the .NET Framework infrastructure and is not
intended to be used directly from your code.

```
[Visual Basic]
Public Shared ReadOnly ByteArraySerializedObjectMimeType As String
[C#]
public static readonly string ByteArraySerializedObjectMimeType;
[C++]
public: static String* ByteArraySerializedObjectMimeType;
[JScript]
public static var ByteArraySerializedObjectMimeType : String;
```

ResXResourceWriter.DefaultSerializedObject-MimeType Field

This member supports the .NET Framework infrastructure and is not
intended to be used directly from your code.

```
[Visual Basic]
Public Shared ReadOnly DefaultSerializedObjectMimeType As String
[C#]
public static readonly string DefaultSerializedObjectMimeType;
[C++]
public: static String* DefaultSerializedObjectMimeType;
[JScript]
public static var DefaultSerializedObjectMimeType : String;
```

ResXResourceWriter.ResMimeType Field

This member supports the .NET Framework infrastructure and is not
intended to be used directly from your code.

```
[Visual Basic]
Public Shared ReadOnly ResMimeType As String
[C#]
public static readonly string ResMimeType;
[C++]
public: static String* ResMimeType;
[JScript]
public static var ResMimeType : String;
```

ResXResourceWriter.ResourceSchema Field

This member supports the .NET Framework infrastructure and is not
intended to be used directly from your code.

```
[Visual Basic]
Public Shared ReadOnly ResourceSchema As String
[C#]
public static readonly string ResourceSchema;
[C++]
public: static String* ResourceSchema;
[JScript]
public static var ResourceSchema : String;
```

ResXResourceWriter.SoapSerializedObject-MimeType Field

This member supports the .NET Framework infrastructure and is not intended to be used directly from your code.

```
[Visual Basic]
Public Shared ReadOnly SoapSerializedObjectMimeType As String
[C#]
public static readonly string SoapSerializedObjectMimeType;
[C++]
public: static String* SoapSerializedObjectMimeType;
[JScript]
public static var SoapSerializedObjectMimeType : String;
```

ResXResourceWriter.Version Field

Specifies the version of the schema that the XML output conforms to. This field is read-only.

```
[Visual Basic]
Public Shared ReadOnly Version As String
[C#]
public static readonly string Version;
[C++]
public: static String* Version;
[JScript]
public static var Version : String;
```

Requirements

Platforms: Windows 98, Windows NT 4.0, Windows Millennium Edition, Windows 2000, Windows XP Home Edition, Windows XP Professional, Windows .NET Server family

ResXResourceWriter.AddResource Method

Adds a resource to the list of resources to write.

Overload List

Adds a named resource specified as a byte array to the list of resources to write.

[Visual Basic] **Overloads Public Overridable Sub AddResource (String, Byte()) Implements IResourceWriter.AddResource**

[C#] **public virtual void AddResource(string, byte[]);**

[C++] **public: virtual void AddResource(String*, unsigned char __gc[]);**

[JScript] **public function AddResource(String, Byte[]);**

Adds a named resource specified as an object to the list of resources to write.

[Visual Basic] **Overloads Public Overridable Sub AddResource (String, Object) Implements IResourceWriter.AddResource**

[C#] **public virtual void AddResource(string, object);**

[C++] **public: virtual void AddResource(String*, Object*);**

[JScript] **public function AddResource(String, Object);**

Adds a string resource to the resources.

[Visual Basic] **Overloads Public Overridable Sub AddResource (String, String) Implements IResourceWriter.AddResource**

[C#] **public virtual void AddResource(string, string);**

[C++] **public: virtual void AddResource(String*, String*);**

[JScript] **public function AddResource(String, String);**

ResXResourceWriter.AddResource Method (String, Byte[])

Adds a named resource specified as a byte array to the list of resources to write.

```
[Visual Basic]
Overloads Public Overridable Sub AddResource( _
    ByVal name As String, _
    ByVal value() As Byte _
) Implements IResourceWriter.AddResource
[C#]
public virtual void AddResource(
    string name,
    byte[] value
);
[C++]
public: virtual void AddResource(
    String* name,
    unsigned char value __gc[]
);
[JScript]
public function AddResource(
    name : String,
    value : Byte[]
);
```

Parameters

name
   The name of the resource.
value
   The value of the resource to add as an 8-bit unsigned integer array.

Implements

IResourceWriter.AddResource

Remarks

The resource is not written until **Generate** is called.

The resource is serialized and stored in a binary format.

Requirements

Platforms: Windows 98, Windows NT 4.0, Windows Millennium Edition, Windows 2000, Windows XP Home Edition, Windows XP Professional, Windows .NET Server family

ResXResourceWriter.AddResource Method (String, Object)

Adds a named resource specified as an object to the list of resources to write.

```
[Visual Basic]
Overloads Public Overridable Sub AddResource( _
    ByVal name As String, _
    ByVal value As Object _
) Implements IResourceWriter.AddResource
[C#]
public virtual void AddResource(
    string name,
    object value
);
[C++]
public: virtual void AddResource(
    String* name,
    Object* value
);
```

```
[JScript]
public function AddResource(
    name : String,
    value : Object
);
```

Parameters

name
    The name of the resource.
value
    The value of the resource.

Implements

IResourceWriter.AddResource

Remarks

The resource is not written until **Generate** is called. The resource that was added must be serializable.

If the resource being added is a string, it is written as a string; otherwise, the resource is serialized and stored in a binary format.

Requirements

Platforms: Windows 98, Windows NT 4.0, Windows Millennium Edition, Windows 2000, Windows XP Home Edition, Windows XP Professional, Windows .NET Server family

ResXResourceWriter.AddResource Method (String, String)

Adds a string resource to the resources.

```
[Visual Basic]
Overloads Public Overridable Sub AddResource( _
    ByVal name As String, _
    ByVal value As String _
) Implements IResourceWriter.AddResource
[C#]
public virtual void AddResource(
    string name,
    string value
);
[C++]
public: virtual void AddResource(
    String* name,
    String* value
);
[JScript]
public function AddResource(
    name : String,
    value : String
);
```

Parameters

name
    The name of the resource.
value
    The value of the resource.

Implements

IResourceWriter.AddResource

Remarks

The resource is not written until **Generate** is called.

Requirements

Platforms: Windows 98, Windows NT 4.0, Windows Millennium Edition, Windows 2000, Windows XP Home Edition, Windows XP Professional, Windows .NET Server family

ResXResourceWriter.Close Method

Releases all resources used by the **ResXResourceWriter**.

```
[Visual Basic]
Public Overridable Sub Close() Implements IResourceWriter.Close
[C#]
public virtual void Close();
[C++]
public: virtual void Close();
[JScript]
public function Close();
```

Implements

IResourceWriter.Close

Remarks

Calling this method is the equivalent of calling **Dispose**.

Requirements

Platforms: Windows 98, Windows NT 4.0, Windows Millennium Edition, Windows 2000, Windows XP Home Edition, Windows XP Professional, Windows .NET Server family

ResXResourceWriter.Dispose Method

Releases the resources used by the **ResXResourceWriter**.

Overload List

Releases all resources used by the **ResXResourceWriter**.

    [Visual Basic] **Overloads Public Overridable Sub Dispose() Implements IDisposable.Dispose**
    [C#] **public virtual void Dispose();**
    [C++] **public: virtual void Dispose();**
    [JScript] **public function Dispose();**

Releases the unmanaged resources used by the **ResXResourceWriter** and optionally releases the managed resources.

    [Visual Basic] **Overloads Protected Overridable Sub Dispose(Boolean)**
    [C#] **protected virtual void Dispose(bool);**
    [C++] **protected: virtual void Dispose(bool);**
    [JScript] **protected function Dispose(Boolean);**

ResXResourceWriter.Dispose Method ()

Releases all resources used by the **ResXResourceWriter**.

```
[Visual Basic]
Overloads Public Overridable Sub Dispose() Implements _
    IDisposable.Dispose
[C#]
public virtual void Dispose();
```

```
[C++]
public: virtual void Dispose();
[JScript]
public function Dispose();
```

Implements

IDisposable.Dispose

Remarks

Calling **Dispose** allows the resources used by the **ResXResourceWriter** to be reallocated for other purposes.

Requirements

Platforms: Windows 98, Windows NT 4.0, Windows Millennium Edition, Windows 2000, Windows XP Home Edition, Windows XP Professional, Windows .NET Server family

ResXResourceWriter.Dispose Method (Boolean)

Releases the unmanaged resources used by the **ResXResource-Writer** and optionally releases the managed resources.

```
[Visual Basic]
Overloads Protected Overridable Sub Dispose( _
    ByVal disposing As Boolean _
)
[C#]
protected virtual void Dispose(
    bool disposing
);
[C++]
protected: virtual void Dispose(
    bool disposing
);
[JScript]
protected function Dispose(
    disposing : Boolean
);
```

Parameters

disposing

> **true** to release both managed and unmanaged resources; **false** to release only unmanaged resources.

Remarks

This method is called by the public **Dispose()** method and the **Finalize** method. **Dispose()** invokes the protected **Dispose(Boolean)** method with the *disposing* parameter set to **true**. **Finalize** invokes **Dispose** with *disposing* set to **false**.

When the *disposing* parameter is **true**, this method releases all resources held by any managed objects that this **ResXResourceWriter** references. This method invokes the **Dispose()** method of each referenced object.

Notes to Inheritors: **Dispose** can be called multiple times by other objects. When overriding **Dispose(Boolean)**, be careful not to reference objects that have been previously disposed of in an earlier call to **Dispose**.

Requirements

Platforms: Windows 98, Windows NT 4.0, Windows Millennium Edition, Windows 2000, Windows XP Home Edition, Windows XP Professional, Windows .NET Server family

ResXResourceWriter.Finalize Method

This member overrides **Object.Finalize**.

```
[Visual Basic]
Overrides Protected Sub Finalize()
[C#]
~ResXResourceWriter();
[C++]
~ResXResourceWriter();
[JScript]
protected override function Finalize();
```

Requirements

Platforms: Windows 98, Windows NT 4.0, Windows Millennium Edition, Windows 2000, Windows XP Home Edition, Windows XP Professional, Windows .NET Server family

ResXResourceWriter.Generate Method

Writes all resources added by the **AddResource** method to the output file or stream.

```
[Visual Basic]
Public Overridable Sub Generate() Implements _
    IResourceWriter.Generate
[C#]
public virtual void Generate();
[C++]
public: virtual void Generate();
[JScript]
public function Generate();
```

Implements

IResourceWriter.Generate

Exceptions

Exception Type	Condition
InvalidOperation-Exception	The resource has already been saved.

Remarks

Writes the resources to the file or stream.

Generate does not close the output file or output stream. Instead, consider calling **Close**. **Generate** is useful when you need to create a resource file, but you do not want to close the output stream. **Generate** can only be called once. After calling **Generate**, all **IResourceWriter** methods other than **Close** will throw an exception.

Requirements

Platforms: Windows 98, Windows NT 4.0, Windows Millennium Edition, Windows 2000, Windows XP Home Edition, Windows XP Professional, Windows .NET Server family

SatelliteContractVersion-Attribute Class

Instructs the **ResourceManager** to ask for a particular version of a satellite assembly to simplify updates of the main assembly of an application.

System.Object
  System.Attribute
    System.Resources.SatelliteContractVersionAttribute

```
[Visual Basic]
<AttributeUsage(AttributeTargets.Assembly)>
NotInheritable Public Class SatelliteContractVersionAttribute
    Inherits Attribute
[C#]
[AttributeUsage(AttributeTargets.Assembly)]
public sealed class SatelliteContractVersionAttribute : Attribute
[C++]
[AttributeUsage(AttributeTargets::Assembly)]
public __gc __sealed class SatelliteContractVersionAttribute :
    public Attribute
[JScript]
public
    AttributeUsage(AttributeTargets.Assembly)
class SatelliteContractVersionAttribute extends Attribute
```

Thread Safety

Any public static (**Shared** in Visual Basic) members of this type are safe for multithreaded operations. Any instance members are not guaranteed to be thread safe.

Remarks

The **SatelliteContractVersionAttribute** establishes a contract between a main assembly and all its satellites. When the **ResourceManager** looks up resources, it explicitly loads the satellite version specified by this attribute on the main assembly, allowing a layer of indirection to facilitate versioning scenarios.

When the main assembly is updated, its assembly version number is incremented. However, you might not want to ship new copies of your satellite assemblies if the existing ones are sufficient and compatible with the newer version of your product. In this case, increment the main assembly's version number but leave the satellite contract version number the same. The **ResourceManager** will use your existing satellite assemblies.

If you need to revise a satellite assembly but not the main assembly, you must increment the version number on your satellite. In this case, ship a policy assembly along with your satellite assembly stating that your new satellite assembly has backward compatibility with your old satellite assembly. The **ResourceManager** will still use the old contract number written into your main assembly; however, the loader will bind to the satellite assembly version as specified by the policy assembly.

A publisher policy assembly is the way in which a vendor of a shared component makes a compatibility statement about a particular version of a released assembly. A publisher policy assembly is a strongly named assembly with a name in the format `policy.<major>.<minor>.<ComponentAssemblyName>`, and is registered in the **Global Assembly Cache** (GAC). The publisher policy is generated from an XML configuration file (see **<bindingRedirect> Element**) by using the **Assembly Linker (Al.exe)** tool. The assembly linker is used with the **/link** option to link the XML configuration file to a manifest assembly, that is then stored in the GAC. The publisher policy assemblies can be used when a vendor ships a maintenance release (Service Pack) that contains bug fixes.

> **Note** Apply this attribute to your main assembly, passing it the version number of the satellite assembly that will work with this version of the main assembly.

Requirements

Namespace: System.Resources

Platforms: Windows 98, Windows NT 4.0, Windows Millennium Edition, Windows 2000, Windows XP Home Edition, Windows XP Professional, Windows .NET Server family, .NET Compact Framework - Windows CE .NET

Assembly: Mscorlib (in Mscorlib.dll)

SatelliteContractVersionAttribute Constructor

Initializes a new instance of the **SatelliteContractVersionAttribute** class.

```
[Visual Basic]
Public Sub New( _
    ByVal version As String _
)
[C#]
public SatelliteContractVersionAttribute(
    string version
);
[C++]
public: SatelliteContractVersionAttribute(
    String* version
);
[JScript]
public function SatelliteContractVersionAttribute(
    version : String
);
```

Parameters

version
    A **String** with the version of the satellite assemblies to load.

Exceptions

Exception Type	Condition
ArgumentNullException	The *version* parameter is a null reference (**Nothing** in Visual Basic).

Remarks

The current constructor initializes the **Version** property with the *version* parameter.

Requirements

Platforms: Windows 98, Windows NT 4.0, Windows Millennium Edition, Windows 2000, Windows XP Home Edition, Windows XP Professional, Windows .NET Server family, .NET Compact Framework - Windows CE .NET

SatelliteContractVersionAttribute.Version Property

Gets the version of the satellite assemblies with the required resources.

```
[Visual Basic]
Public ReadOnly Property Version As String
[C#]
public string Version {get;}
[C++]
public: __property String* get_Version();
[JScript]
public function get Version() : String;
```

Property Value

A **String** containing the version of the satellite assemblies with the required resources.

Remarks

The current property indicates the version of the satellite assemblies that will be used with the main assembly marked with this attribute.

Requirements

Platforms: Windows 98, Windows NT 4.0, Windows Millennium Edition, Windows 2000, Windows XP Home Edition, Windows XP Professional, Windows .NET Server family, .NET Compact Framework - Windows CE .NET

System.Runtime.Compiler Services Namespace

The **System.Runtime.CompilerServices** namespace provides functionality for compiler writers using managed code to specify attributes in metadata that affect the run time behavior of the common language runtime.

This namespace is for compiler writers use only.

AccessedThroughProperty-Attribute Class

Specifies the name of the property that accesses the attributed field.

System.Object
  System.Attribute
    System.Runtime.CompilerServices.AccessedThrough-
    PropertyAttribute

```
[Visual Basic]
<AttributeUsage(AttributeTargets.Field)>
NotInheritable Public Class AccessedThroughPropertyAttribute
    Inherits Attribute
[C#]
[AttributeUsage(AttributeTargets.Field)]
public sealed class AccessedThroughPropertyAttribute : Attribute
[C++]
[AttributeUsage(AttributeTargets::Field)]
public __gc __sealed class AccessedThroughPropertyAttribute :
    public Attribute
[JScript]
public
    AttributeUsage(AttributeTargets.Field)
class AccessedThroughPropertyAttribute extends Attribute
```

Thread Safety

Any public static (**Shared** in Visual Basic) members of this type are safe for multithreaded operations. Any instance members are not guaranteed to be thread safe.

Remarks

You can apply this attribute to fields.

This attribute is for use by browsers or tools, and is ignored by the common language runtime.

The classes in System.Runtime.CompilerServices are for compiler writers use only.

Requirements

Namespace: System.Runtime.CompilerServices

Platforms: Windows 98, Windows NT 4.0,
Windows Millennium Edition, Windows 2000,
Windows XP Home Edition, Windows XP Professional,
Windows .NET Server family,
.NET Compact Framework - Windows CE .NET

Assembly: Mscorlib (in Mscorlib.dll)

AccessedThroughPropertyAttribute Constructor

Initializes a new instance of the
AccessedThroughPropertyAttribute class with the name of the property used to access the attributed field.

```
[Visual Basic]
Public Sub New( _
    ByVal propertyName As String _
)
[C#]
public AccessedThroughPropertyAttribute(
    string propertyName
);
[C++]
public: AccessedThroughPropertyAttribute(
    String* propertyName
);
[JScript]
public function AccessedThroughPropertyAttribute(
    propertyName : String
);
```

Parameters

propertyName
  The name of the property used to access the attributed field.

Requirements

Platforms: Windows 98, Windows NT 4.0,
Windows Millennium Edition, Windows 2000,
Windows XP Home Edition, Windows XP Professional,
Windows .NET Server family,
.NET Compact Framework - Windows CE .NET

AccessedThroughPropertyAttribute.Property-Name Property

Gets the name of the property used to access the attributed field.

```
[Visual Basic]
Public ReadOnly Property PropertyName As String
[C#]
public string PropertyName {get;}
[C++]
public: __property String* get_PropertyName();
[JScript]
public function get PropertyName() : String;
```

Property Value

The name of the property used to access the attributed field.

Requirements

Platforms: Windows 98, Windows NT 4.0,
Windows Millennium Edition, Windows 2000,
Windows XP Home Edition, Windows XP Professional,
Windows .NET Server family,
.NET Compact Framework - Windows CE .NET

CallConvCdecl Class

Indicates that the **Cdecl** calling convention should be used for a method.

System.Object
   System.Runtime.CompilerServices.CallConvCdecl

```
[Visual Basic]
Public Class CallConvCdecl
[C#]
public class CallConvCdecl
[C++]
public __gc class CallConvCdecl
[JScript]
public class CallConvCdecl
```

Thread Safety

Any public static (**Shared** in Visual Basic) members of this type are safe for multithreaded operations. Any instance members are not guaranteed to be thread safe.

Remarks

The caller cleans the stack. This enables calling functions with **varargs**.

This class is only used as a custom modifier of the metadata signature of a method.

The classes in System.Runtime.CompilerServices are for compiler writers use only.

Requirements

Namespace: System.Runtime.CompilerServices

Platforms: Windows 98, Windows NT 4.0, Windows Millennium Edition, Windows 2000, Windows XP Home Edition, Windows XP Professional, Windows .NET Server family

Assembly: Mscorlib (in Mscorlib.dll)

CallConvCdecl Constructor

Initializes a new instance of the **CallConvCdecl** class.

```
[Visual Basic]
Public Sub New()
[C#]
public CallConvCdecl();
[C++]
public: CallConvCdecl();
[JScript]
public function CallConvCdecl();
```

Remarks

The default constructor initializes any fields to their default values.

Requirements

Platforms: Windows 98, Windows NT 4.0, Windows Millennium Edition, Windows 2000, Windows XP Home Edition, Windows XP Professional, Windows .NET Server family

CallConvFastcall Class

This calling convention is not supported in this version of the .NET Framework.

System.Object
  System.Runtime.CompilerServices.CallConvFastcall

```
[Visual Basic]
Public Class CallConvFastcall
[C#]
public class CallConvFastcall
[C++]
public __gc class CallConvFastcall
[JScript]
public class CallConvFastcall
```

Thread Safety

Any public static (**Shared** in Visual Basic) members of this type are safe for multithreaded operations. Any instance members are not guaranteed to be thread safe.

Remarks

The **__fastcall** calling convention specifies that arguments to functions are to be passed in registers, when possible.

This class is only used as a custom modifier of the metadata signature of a method.

The classes in System.Runtime.CompilerServices are for compiler writers use only.

Requirements

Namespace: System.Runtime.CompilerServices

Platforms: Windows 98, Windows NT 4.0, Windows Millennium Edition, Windows 2000, Windows XP Home Edition, Windows XP Professional, Windows .NET Server family

Assembly: Mscorlib (in Mscorlib.dll)

CallConvFastcall Constructor

Initializes a new instance of the **CallConvFastcall** class.

```
[Visual Basic]
Public Sub New()
[C#]
public CallConvFastcall();
[C++]
public: CallConvFastcall();
[JScript]
public function CallConvFastcall();
```

Remarks

The default constructor initializes any fields to their default values.

Requirements

Platforms: Windows 98, Windows NT 4.0, Windows Millennium Edition, Windows 2000, Windows XP Home Edition, Windows XP Professional, Windows .NET Server family

CallConvStdcall Class

Indicates that the **StdCall** calling convention should be used for a method.

System.Object
  System.Runtime.CompilerServices.CallConvStdcall

```
[Visual Basic]
Public Class CallConvStdcall
[C#]
public class CallConvStdcall
[C++]
public __gc class CallConvStdcall
[JScript]
public class CallConvStdcall
```

Thread Safety

Any public static (**Shared** in Visual Basic) members of this type are safe for multithreaded operations. Any instance members are not guaranteed to be thread safe.

Remarks

The callee cleans the stack. This is the default convention for calling unmanaged functions from managed code.

This class is only used as a custom modifier of the metadata signature of a method.

The classes in System.Runtime.CompilerServices are for compiler writers use only.

Requirements

Namespace: System.Runtime.CompilerServices

Platforms: Windows 98, Windows NT 4.0, Windows Millennium Edition, Windows 2000, Windows XP Home Edition, Windows XP Professional, Windows .NET Server family

Assembly: Mscorlib (in Mscorlib.dll)

CallConvStdcall Constructor

Initializes a new instance of the **CallConvStdcall** class.

```
[Visual Basic]
Public Sub New()
[C#]
public CallConvStdcall();
[C++]
public: CallConvStdcall();
[JScript]
public function CallConvStdcall();
```

Remarks

The default constructor initializes any fields to their default values.

Requirements

Platforms: Windows 98, Windows NT 4.0, Windows Millennium Edition, Windows 2000, Windows XP Home Edition, Windows XP Professional, Windows .NET Server family

CallConvThiscall Class

Indicates that the **ThisCall** calling convention should be used for a method.

System.Object
   System.Runtime.CompilerServices.CallConvThiscall

```
[Visual Basic]
Public Class CallConvThiscall
[C#]
public class CallConvThiscall
[C++]
public __gc class CallConvThiscall
[JScript]
public class CallConvThiscall
```

Thread Safety

Any public static (**Shared** in Visual Basic) members of this type are safe for multithreaded operations. Any instance members are not guaranteed to be thread safe.

Remarks

The first parameter is the **this** pointer and is stored in register ECX. Other parameters are pushed on the stack. This calling convention is used to call methods on classes exported from an unmanaged DLL.

This class is only used as a custom modifier of the metadata signature of a method.

The classes in System.Runtime.CompilerServices are for compiler writers use only.

Requirements

Namespace: System.Runtime.CompilerServices

Platforms: Windows 98, Windows NT 4.0, Windows Millennium Edition, Windows 2000, Windows XP Home Edition, Windows XP Professional, Windows .NET Server family

Assembly: Mscorlib (in Mscorlib.dll)

CallConvThiscall Constructor

Initializes a new instance of the **CallConvThiscall** class.

```
[Visual Basic]
Public Sub New()
[C#]
public CallConvThiscall();
[C++]
public: CallConvThiscall();
[JScript]
public function CallConvThiscall();
```

Remarks

The default constructor initializes any fields to their default values.

Requirements

Platforms: Windows 98, Windows NT 4.0, Windows Millennium Edition, Windows 2000, Windows XP Home Edition, Windows XP Professional, Windows .NET Server family

CompilationRelaxations-Attribute Class

Controls the strictness of the code generated by the common language runtime's just-in-time (JIT) compiler.

System.Object
  System.Attribute
    System.Runtime.CompilerServices.Compilation-
    RelaxationsAttribute

```
[Visual Basic]
<AttributeUsage(AttributeTargets.Module)>
<Serializable>
Public Class CompilationRelaxationsAttribute
   Inherits Attribute
[C#]
[AttributeUsage(AttributeTargets.Module)]
[Serializable]
public class CompilationRelaxationsAttribute : Attribute
[C++]
[AttributeUsage(AttributeTargets::Module)]
[Serializable]
public __gc class CompilationRelaxationsAttribute : public
   Attribute
[JScript]
public
   AttributeUsage(AttributeTargets.Module)
   Serializable
class CompilationRelaxationsAttribute extends Attribute
```

Thread Safety

Any public static (**Shared** in Visual Basic) members of this type are safe for multithreaded operations. Any instance members are not guaranteed to be thread safe.

Remarks

This attribute is ignored in version 1.0 of the Microsoft .NET Framework.

The classes in System.Runtime.CompilerServices are for compiler writers use only.

Requirements

Namespace: System.Runtime.CompilerServices

Platforms: Windows 98, Windows NT 4.0, Windows Millennium Edition, Windows 2000, Windows XP Home Edition, Windows XP Professional, Windows .NET Server family

Assembly: Mscorlib (in Mscorlib.dll)

CompilationRelaxationsAttribute Constructor

Initializes a new instance of the **CompilationRelaxationsAttribute** class with the specified compilation relaxations.

```
[Visual Basic]
Public Sub New( _
   ByVal relaxations As Integer _
)
```

```
[C#]
public CompilationRelaxationsAttribute(
   int relaxations
);
[C++]
public: CompilationRelaxationsAttribute(
   int relaxations
);
[JScript]
public function CompilationRelaxationsAttribute(
   relaxations : int
);
```

Parameters

relaxations
    The specified compilation relaxations.

Requirements

Platforms: Windows 98, Windows NT 4.0, Windows Millennium Edition, Windows 2000, Windows XP Home Edition, Windows XP Professional, Windows .NET Server family

CompilationRelaxationsAttribute.Compilation-Relaxations Property

Gets the compilation relaxations specified when this instance was constructed.

```
[Visual Basic]
Public ReadOnly Property CompilationRelaxations As Integer
[C#]
public int CompilationRelaxations {get;}
[C++]
public: __property int get_CompilationRelaxations();
[JScript]
public function get CompilationRelaxations() : int;
```

Property Value

The compilation relaxations specified when this instance was constructed.

Requirements

Platforms: Windows 98, Windows NT 4.0, Windows Millennium Edition, Windows 2000, Windows XP Home Edition, Windows XP Professional, Windows .NET Server family

CompilerGlobalScopeAttribute Class

Indicates that a class should be treated as if it has global scope.

System.Object
  System.Attribute
    System.Runtime.CompilerServices.CompilerGlobalScope-
    Attribute

```
[Visual Basic]
<AttributeUsage(AttributeTargets.Class)>
<Serializable>
Public Class CompilerGlobalScopeAttribute
   Inherits Attribute
[C#]
[AttributeUsage(AttributeTargets.Class)]
[Serializable]
public class CompilerGlobalScopeAttribute : Attribute
[C++]
[AttributeUsage(AttributeTargets::Class)]
[Serializable]
public __gc class CompilerGlobalScopeAttribute : public Attribute
[JScript]
public
   AttributeUsage(AttributeTargets.Class)
   Serializable
class CompilerGlobalScopeAttribute extends Attribute
```

Thread Safety

Any public static (**Shared** in Visual Basic) members of this type are safe for multithreaded operations. Any instance members are not guaranteed to be thread safe.

Remarks

You can apply this attribute to classes.

This class is used only for communication with debugger tools.

The classes in System.Runtime.CompilerServices are for compiler writers use only.

Requirements

Namespace: System.Runtime.CompilerServices

Platforms: Windows 98, Windows NT 4.0, Windows Millennium Edition, Windows 2000, Windows XP Home Edition, Windows XP Professional, Windows .NET Server family

Assembly: Mscorlib (in Mscorlib.dll)

CompilerGlobalScopeAttribute Constructor

Initializes a new instance of the **CompilerGlobalScopeAttribute** class.

```
[Visual Basic]
Public Sub New()
[C#]
public CompilerGlobalScopeAttribute();
[C++]
public: CompilerGlobalScopeAttribute();
[JScript]
public function CompilerGlobalScopeAttribute();
```

Requirements

Platforms: Windows 98, Windows NT 4.0, Windows Millennium Edition, Windows 2000, Windows XP Home Edition, Windows XP Professional, Windows .NET Server family

CustomConstantAttribute Class

Defines a constant value that a compiler can persist for a field or method parameter.

System.Object
  System.Attribute
    System.Runtime.CompilerServices.CustomConstant-Attribute
      System.Runtime.CompilerServices.DateTimeConstant-Attribute
      System.Runtime.CompilerServices.IDispatchConstant-Attribute
      System.Runtime.CompilerServices.IUnknownConstant-Attribute

```
[Visual Basic]
<AttributeUsage(AttributeTargets.Field Or _
    AttributeTargets.Parameter)>
<Serializable>
MustInherit Public Class CustomConstantAttribute
    Inherits Attribute
[C#]
[AttributeUsage(AttributeTargets.Field |
    AttributeTargets.Parameter)]
[Serializable]
public abstract class CustomConstantAttribute : Attribute
[C++]
[AttributeUsage(AttributeTargets::Field |
    AttributeTargets::Parameter)]
[Serializable]
public __gc __abstract class CustomConstantAttribute : public
    Attribute
[JScript]
public
    AttributeUsage(AttributeTargets.Field | AttributeTargets.Parameter)
    Serializable
abstract class CustomConstantAttribute extends Attribute
```

Thread Safety

Any public static (**Shared** in Visual Basic) members of this type are safe for multithreaded operations. Any instance members are not guaranteed to be thread safe.

Remarks

You can apply this attribute to fields or parameters.

This class cannot be instantiated.

Compilers should create specific classes, derived from this class, that define the type of the constant value. If you are using **System.Reflection**, this pattern of deriving specific classes from **CustomConstantAttribute** enables you to find all occurances of custom constant attributes easily.

The classes in System.Runtime.CompilerServices are for compiler writers use only.

Requirements

Namespace: System.Runtime.CompilerServices

Platforms: Windows 98, Windows NT 4.0, Windows Millennium Edition, Windows 2000, Windows XP Home Edition, Windows XP Professional, Windows .NET Server family, .NET Compact Framework - Windows CE .NET

Assembly: Mscorlib (in Mscorlib.dll)

CustomConstantAttribute Constructor

Initializes a new instance of the **CustomConstantAttribute** class.

```
[Visual Basic]
Protected Sub New()
[C#]
protected CustomConstantAttribute();
[C++]
protected: CustomConstantAttribute();
[JScript]
protected function CustomConstantAttribute();
```

Remarks

This constructor is called by derived class constructors to initialize state in this type.

Requirements

Platforms: Windows 98, Windows NT 4.0, Windows Millennium Edition, Windows 2000, Windows XP Home Edition, Windows XP Professional, Windows .NET Server family, .NET Compact Framework - Windows CE .NET

CustomConstantAttribute.Value Property

Gets the constant value stored by this attribute.

```
[Visual Basic]
Public MustOverride ReadOnly Property Value As Object
[C#]
public abstract object Value {get;}
[C++]
public: __property virtual Object* get_Value() = 0;
[JScript]
public abstract function get Value() : Object;
```

Property Value

The constant value stored by this attribute.

Requirements

Platforms: Windows 98, Windows NT 4.0, Windows Millennium Edition, Windows 2000, Windows XP Home Edition, Windows XP Professional, Windows .NET Server family, .NET Compact Framework - Windows CE .NET

DateTimeConstantAttribute Class

Persists an 8-byte **DateTime** constant for a field or parameter.

System.Object
  System.Attribute
    System.Runtime.CompilerServices.CustomConstant-
    Attribute
      System.Runtime.CompilerServices.DateTimeConstant-
      Attribute

```
[Visual Basic]
<AttributeUsage(AttributeTargets.Field Or _
    AttributeTargets.Parameter)>
<Serializable>
NotInheritable Public Class DateTimeConstantAttribute
    Inherits CustomConstantAttribute
[C#]
[AttributeUsage(AttributeTargets.Field |
    AttributeTargets.Parameter)]
[Serializable]
public sealed class DateTimeConstantAttribute :
    CustomConstantAttribute
[C++]
[AttributeUsage(AttributeTargets::Field |
    AttributeTargets::Parameter)]
[Serializable]
public __gc __sealed class DateTimeConstantAttribute : public
    CustomConstantAttribute
[JScript]
public
    AttributeUsage(AttributeTargets.Field | AttributeTargets.Parameter)
    Serializable
class DateTimeConstantAttribute extends
    CustomConstantAttribute
```

Thread Safety

Any public static (**Shared** in Visual Basic) members of this type are safe for multithreaded operations. Any instance members are not guaranteed to be thread safe.

Remarks

You can apply this attribute to fields or parameters.

The classes in System.Runtime.CompilerServices are for compiler writers use only.

Requirements

Namespace: System.Runtime.CompilerServices

Platforms: Windows 98, Windows NT 4.0,
Windows Millennium Edition, Windows 2000,
Windows XP Home Edition, Windows XP Professional,
Windows .NET Server family,
.NET Compact Framework - Windows CE .NET

Assembly: Mscorlib (in Mscorlib.dll)

DateTimeConstantAttribute Constructor

Initializes a new instance of the **DateTimeConstantAttribute** class with the number of 100-nanosecond ticks that represent the date and time of this instance.

```
[Visual Basic]
Public Sub New( _
    ByVal ticks As Long _
)
[C#]
public DateTimeConstantAttribute(
    long ticks
);
[C++]
public: DateTimeConstantAttribute(
    __int64 ticks
);
[JScript]
public function DateTimeConstantAttribute(
    ticks : long
);
```

Parameters

ticks
    The number of 100-nanosecond ticks that represent the date and time of this instance.

Requirements

Platforms: Windows 98, Windows NT 4.0,
Windows Millennium Edition, Windows 2000,
Windows XP Home Edition, Windows XP Professional,
Windows .NET Server family,
.NET Compact Framework - Windows CE .NET

DateTimeConstantAttribute.Value Property

Gets the number of 100-nanosecond ticks that represent the date and time of this instance.

```
[Visual Basic]
Overrides Public ReadOnly Property Value As Object
[C#]
public override object Value {get;}
[C++]
public: __property Object* get_Value();
[JScript]
public override function get Value() : Object;
```

Property Value

The number of 100-nanosecond ticks that represent the date and time of this instance.

Requirements

Platforms: Windows 98, Windows NT 4.0,
Windows Millennium Edition, Windows 2000,
Windows XP Home Edition, Windows XP Professional,
Windows .NET Server family,
.NET Compact Framework - Windows CE .NET

DecimalConstantAttribute Class

Stores the value of a **System.Decimal** constant in metadata.

The **DecimalConstantAttribute** type is not CLS-compliant.

System.Object
  System.Attribute
    System.Runtime.CompilerServices.DecimalConstantAttribute

[Visual Basic]
```
<AttributeUsage(AttributeTargets.Field Or _
    AttributeTargets.Parameter)>
<CLSCompliant(False)>
<Serializable>
NotInheritable Public Class DecimalConstantAttribute
    Inherits Attribute
```
[C#]
```
[AttributeUsage(AttributeTargets.Field |
    AttributeTargets.Parameter)]
[CLSCompliant(false)]
[Serializable]
public sealed class DecimalConstantAttribute : Attribute
```
[C++]
```
[AttributeUsage(AttributeTargets::Field |
    AttributeTargets::Parameter)]
[CLSCompliant(false)]
[Serializable]
public __gc __sealed class DecimalConstantAttribute : public
    Attribute
```
[JScript]
```
public
    AttributeUsage(AttributeTargets.Field | AttributeTargets.Parameter)
    CLSCompliant(false)
    Serializable
class DecimalConstantAttribute extends Attribute
```

Thread Safety

Any public static (**Shared** in Visual Basic) members of this type are safe for multithreaded operations. Any instance members are not guaranteed to be thread safe.

Remarks

You can apply this attribute to fields or parameters.

For more information about constant attributes, see the **CustomConstantAttribute** class.

The classes in System.Runtime.CompilerServices are for compiler writers use only.

Requirements

Namespace: System.Runtime.CompilerServices

Platforms: Windows 98, Windows NT 4.0, Windows Millennium Edition, Windows 2000, Windows XP Home Edition, Windows XP Professional, Windows .NET Server family, .NET Compact Framework - Windows CE .NET

Assembly: Mscorlib (in Mscorlib.dll)

DecimalConstantAttribute Constructor

Initializes a new instance of the **DecimalConstantAttribute** class.

The **DecimalConstantAttribute** type is not CLS-compliant.

[Visual Basic]
```
Public Sub New( _
    ByVal scale As Byte, _
    ByVal sign As Byte, _
    ByVal hi As UInt32, _
    ByVal mid As UInt32, _
    ByVal low As UInt32 _
)
```
[C#]
```
public DecimalConstantAttribute(
    byte scale,
    byte sign,
    uint hi,
    uint mid,
    uint low
);
```
[C++]
```
public: DecimalConstantAttribute(
    unsigned char scale,
    unsigned char sign,
    unsigned int hi,
    unsigned int mid,
    unsigned int low
);
```
[JScript]
```
public function DecimalConstantAttribute(
    scale : Byte,
    sign : Byte,
    hi : UInt32,
    mid : UInt32,
    low : UInt32
);
```

Parameters

scale
  The power of 10 scaling factor that indicates the number of digits to the right of the decimal point. Valid values are 0 through 28 inclusive.

sign
  A value of 0 indicates a positive value, and a value of 1 indicates a negative value.

hi
  The high 32 bits of the 96-bit **Value**.

mid
  The middle 32 bits of the 96-bit **Value**.

low
  The low 32 bits of the 96-bit **Value**.

Exceptions

Exception Type	Condition
ArgumentOutOfRangeException	*scale* > 28.

Requirements

Platforms: Windows 98, Windows NT 4.0,
Windows Millennium Edition, Windows 2000,
Windows XP Home Edition, Windows XP Professional,
Windows .NET Server family,
.NET Compact Framework - Windows CE .NET,
Common Language Infrastructure (CLI) Standard

DecimalConstantAttribute.Value Property

Gets the decimal constant stored in this attribute.

The **DecimalConstantAttribute** type is not CLS-compliant.

```
[Visual Basic]
Public ReadOnly Property Value As Decimal
[C#]
public decimal Value {get;}
[C++]
public: __property Decimal get_Value();
[JScript]
public function get Value() : Decimal;
```

Property Value

The decimal constant stored in this attribute.

Requirements

Platforms: Windows 98, Windows NT 4.0,
Windows Millennium Edition, Windows 2000,
Windows XP Home Edition, Windows XP Professional,
Windows .NET Server family,
.NET Compact Framework - Windows CE .NET

DiscardableAttribute Class

Marks a type definition as discardable.

System.Object
  System.Attribute
    System.Runtime.CompilerServices.DiscardableAttribute

```
[Visual Basic]
Public Class DiscardableAttribute
   Inherits Attribute
[C#]
public class DiscardableAttribute : Attribute
[C++]
public __gc class DiscardableAttribute : public Attribute
[JScript]
public class DiscardableAttribute extends Attribute
```

Thread Safety

Any public static (**Shared** in Visual Basic) members of this type are
safe for multithreaded operations. Any instance members are not
guaranteed to be thread safe.

Remarks

A type definition might be marked discardable if it is not referenced
by any other code in its assembly. This might be useful for languages
that support separate compilation, where it is only at link phase that
it becomes known whether any type is actually referenced by other
code.

The classes in System.Runtime.CompilerServices are for compiler
writers use only.

Requirements

Namespace: System.Runtime.CompilerServices

Platforms: Windows 98, Windows NT 4.0,
Windows Millennium Edition, Windows 2000,
Windows XP Home Edition, Windows XP Professional,
Windows .NET Server family

Assembly: Mscorlib (in Mscorlib.dll)

DiscardableAttribute Constructor

Initializes a new instance of the **DiscardableAttribute** class with
default values.

```
[Visual Basic]
Public Sub New()
[C#]
public DiscardableAttribute();
[C++]
public: DiscardableAttribute();
[JScript]
public function DiscardableAttribute();
```

Requirements

Platforms: Windows 98, Windows NT 4.0,
Windows Millennium Edition, Windows 2000,
Windows XP Home Edition, Windows XP Professional,
Windows .NET Server family

IDispatchConstantAttribute Class

Indicates that the default value for the attributed field or parameter is an instance of **DispatchWrapper**, where the **WrappedObject** is a null reference (**Nothing** in Visual Basic).

System.Object
  System.Attribute
    System.Runtime.CompilerServices.CustomConstant-
    Attribute
      System.Runtime.CompilerServices.IDispatchConstant-
      Attribute

```
[Visual Basic]
<AttributeUsage(AttributeTargets.Field Or _
    AttributeTargets.Parameter)>
<Serializable>
NotInheritable Public Class IDispatchConstantAttribute
    Inherits CustomConstantAttribute
[C#]
[AttributeUsage(AttributeTargets.Field |
    AttributeTargets.Parameter)]
[Serializable]
public sealed class IDispatchConstantAttribute :
    CustomConstantAttribute
[C++]
[AttributeUsage(AttributeTargets::Field |
    AttributeTargets::Parameter)]
[Serializable]
public __gc __sealed class IDispatchConstantAttribute : public
    CustomConstantAttribute
[JScript]
public
    AttributeUsage(AttributeTargets.Field | AttributeTargets.Parameter)
    Serializable
class IDispatchConstantAttribute extends
    CustomConstantAttribute
```

Thread Safety

Any public static (**Shared** in Visual Basic) members of this type are safe for multithreaded operations. Any instance members are not guaranteed to be thread safe.

Remarks

You can apply this attribute to fields or parameters.

The type library importer uses this attribute to distinguish a default value of type **VT_DISPATCH** from a null reference (**Nothing** in Visual Basic).

The classes in System.Runtime.CompilerServices are for compiler writers use only.

Requirements

Namespace: System.Runtime.CompilerServices

Platforms: Windows 98, Windows NT 4.0, Windows Millennium Edition, Windows 2000, Windows XP Home Edition, Windows XP Professional, Windows .NET Server family

Assembly: Mscorlib (in Mscorlib.dll)

IDispatchConstantAttribute Constructor

Initializes a new instance of the **IDispatchConstantAttribute** class.

```
[Visual Basic]
Public Sub New()
[C#]
public IDispatchConstantAttribute();
[C++]
public: IDispatchConstantAttribute();
[JScript]
public function IDispatchConstantAttribute();
```

Requirements

Platforms: Windows 98, Windows NT 4.0, Windows Millennium Edition, Windows 2000, Windows XP Home Edition, Windows XP Professional, Windows .NET Server family

IDispatchConstantAttribute.Value Property

Gets the **IDispatch** constant stored in this attribute.

```
[Visual Basic]
Overrides Public ReadOnly Property Value As Object
[C#]
public override object Value {get;}
[C++]
public: __property Object* get_Value();
[JScript]
public override function get Value() : Object;
```

Property Value

The **IDispatch** constant stored in this attribute. Only a null reference (**Nothing** in Visual Basic) is allowed for an **IDispatch** constant value.

Requirements

Platforms: Windows 98, Windows NT 4.0, Windows Millennium Edition, Windows 2000, Windows XP Home Edition, Windows XP Professional, Windows .NET Server family

IndexerNameAttribute Class

Indicates the name by which an indexer is known in programming languages that do not support indexers directly.

System.Object
  System.Attribute
    System.Runtime.CompilerServices.IndexerNameAttribute

```
[Visual Basic]
<AttributeUsage(AttributeTargets.Property)>
<Serializable>
NotInheritable Public Class IndexerNameAttribute
    Inherits Attribute
[C#]
[AttributeUsage(AttributeTargets.Property)]
[Serializable]
public sealed class IndexerNameAttribute : Attribute
[C++]
[AttributeUsage(AttributeTargets::Property)]
[Serializable]
public __gc __sealed class IndexerNameAttribute : public
    Attribute
[JScript]
public
    AttributeUsage(AttributeTargets.Property)
    Serializable
class IndexerNameAttribute extends Attribute
```

Thread Safety

Any public static (**Shared** in Visual Basic) members of this type are safe for multithreaded operations. Any instance members are not guaranteed to be thread safe.

Remarks

You can apply this attribute to properties.

This attribute is directly processed by the compiler, and cannot be accessed after compilation through Reflection.

The classes in System.Runtime.CompilerServices are for compiler writers use only.

Requirements

Namespace: System.Runtime.CompilerServices

Platforms: Windows 98, Windows NT 4.0,
Windows Millennium Edition, Windows 2000,
Windows XP Home Edition, Windows XP Professional,
Windows .NET Server family,
.NET Compact Framework - Windows CE .NET

Assembly: Mscorlib (in Mscorlib.dll)

IndexerNameAttribute Constructor

Initializes a new instance of the **IndexerNameAttribute** class.

```
[Visual Basic]
Public Sub New( _
    ByVal indexerName As String _
)
[C#]
public IndexerNameAttribute(
    string indexerName
);
```

```
[C++]
public: IndexerNameAttribute(
    String* indexerName
);
[JScript]
public function IndexerNameAttribute(
    indexerName : String
);
```

Parameters

indexerName
    The name of the indexer, as shown to other languages.

Requirements

Platforms: Windows 98, Windows NT 4.0,
Windows Millennium Edition, Windows 2000,
Windows XP Home Edition, Windows XP Professional,
Windows .NET Server family,
.NET Compact Framework - Windows CE .NET

IsVolatile Class

Marks a field as volatile.

System.Object
    System.Runtime.CompilerServices.IsVolatile

```
[Visual Basic]
NotInheritable Public Class IsVolatile
[C#]
public sealed class IsVolatile
[C++]
public __gc __sealed class IsVolatile
[JScript]
public class IsVolatile
```

Thread Safety

Any public static (**Shared** in Visual Basic) members of this type are safe for multithreaded operations. Any instance members are not guaranteed to be thread safe.

Remarks

IsVolatile is used only in custom modifiers of method signatures to indicate that the field it marks is volatile. Any compiler that imports metadata with one or more fields marked as volatile must use instructions prefixed with "volatile." to access such fields.

The classes in System.Runtime.CompilerServices are for compiler writers use only.

Requirements

Namespace: System.Runtime.CompilerServices

Platforms: Windows 98, Windows NT 4.0, Windows Millennium Edition, Windows 2000, Windows XP Home Edition, Windows XP Professional, Windows .NET Server family

Assembly: Mscorlib (in Mscorlib.dll)

IUnknownConstantAttribute Class

Indicates that the default value for the attributed field or parameter is an instance of **UnknownWrapper**, where the **WrappedObject** is a null reference (**Nothing** in Visual Basic).

System.Object
  System.Attribute
    System.Runtime.CompilerServices.CustomConstant-Attribute
      System.Runtime.CompilerServices.IUnknownConstant-Attribute

```
[Visual Basic]
<AttributeUsage(AttributeTargets.Field Or _
    AttributeTargets.Parameter)>
<Serializable>
NotInheritable Public Class IUnknownConstantAttribute
    Inherits CustomConstantAttribute
[C#]
[AttributeUsage(AttributeTargets.Field |
    AttributeTargets.Parameter)]
[Serializable]
public sealed class IUnknownConstantAttribute :
    CustomConstantAttribute
[C++]
[AttributeUsage(AttributeTargets::Field |
    AttributeTargets::Parameter)]
[Serializable]
public __gc __sealed class IUnknownConstantAttribute : public
    CustomConstantAttribute
[JScript]
public
    AttributeUsage(AttributeTargets.Field | AttributeTargets.Parameter)
    Serializable
class IUnknownConstantAttribute extends
    CustomConstantAttribute
```

Thread Safety

Any public static (**Shared** in Visual Basic) members of this type are safe for multithreaded operations. Any instance members are not guaranteed to be thread safe.

Remarks

You can apply this attribute to fields or parameters.

The type library importer uses this attribute to distinguish a default value of type **VT_UNKNOWN** from a null reference (**Nothing** in Visual Basic).

The classes in System.Runtime.CompilerServices are for compiler writers use only.

Requirements

Namespace: System.Runtime.CompilerServices

Platforms: Windows 98, Windows NT 4.0, Windows Millennium Edition, Windows 2000, Windows XP Home Edition, Windows XP Professional, Windows .NET Server family

Assembly: Mscorlib (in Mscorlib.dll)

IUnknownConstantAttribute Constructor

Initializes a new instance of the **IUnknownConstantAttribute** class.

```
[Visual Basic]
Public Sub New()
[C#]
public IUnknownConstantAttribute();
[C++]
public: IUnknownConstantAttribute();
[JScript]
public function IUnknownConstantAttribute();
```

Requirements

Platforms: Windows 98, Windows NT 4.0, Windows Millennium Edition, Windows 2000, Windows XP Home Edition, Windows XP Professional, Windows .NET Server family

IUnknownConstantAttribute.Value Property

Gets the **IUnknown** constant stored in this attribute.

```
[Visual Basic]
Overrides Public ReadOnly Property Value As Object
[C#]
public override object Value {get;}
[C++]
public: __property Object* get_Value();
[JScript]
public override function get Value() : Object;
```

Property Value

The **IUnknown** constant stored in this attribute. Only a null reference (**Nothing** in Visual Basic) is allowed for an **IUnknown** constant value.

Requirements

Platforms: Windows 98, Windows NT 4.0, Windows Millennium Edition, Windows 2000, Windows XP Home Edition, Windows XP Professional, Windows .NET Server family

MethodCodeType Enumeration

Defines how a method is implemented.

This enumeration has a **FlagsAttribute** attribute that allows a bitwise combination of its member values.

```
[Visual Basic]
<Flags>
<Serializable>
Public Enum MethodCodeType
[C#]
[Flags]
[Serializable]
public enum MethodCodeType
[C++]
[Flags]
[Serializable]
__value public enum MethodCodeType
[JScript]
public
    Flags
    Serializable
enum MethodCodeType
```

Remarks

Used with **MethodImplAttribute**.

The classes in System.Runtime.CompilerServices are for compiler writers use only.

Members

Member name	Description	Value
IL Supported by the .NET Compact Framework.	Specifies that the method implementation is in Microsoft intermediate language (MSIL).	0
Native Supported by the .NET Compact Framework.	Specifies that the method is implemented in native code.	1
OPTIL Supported by the .NET Compact Framework.	This member supports the .NET Framework infrastructure and is not intended to be used directly from your code.	2
Runtime Supported by the .NET Compact Framework.	Specifies that the method implementation is provided by the runtime.	3

Requirements

Namespace: System.Runtime.CompilerServices

Platforms: Windows 98, Windows NT 4.0, Windows Millennium Edition, Windows 2000, Windows XP Home Edition, Windows XP Professional, Windows .NET Server family, .NET Compact Framework - Windows CE .NET

Assembly: Mscorlib (in Mscorlib.dll)

MethodImplAttribute Class

Specifies the details of how a method is implemented.

System.Object
  System.Attribute
    System.Runtime.CompilerServices.MethodImplAttribute

```
[Visual Basic]
<AttributeUsage(AttributeTargets.Constructor Or _
    AttributeTargets.Method)>
<Serializable>
NotInheritable Public Class MethodImplAttribute
    Inherits Attribute
[C#]
[AttributeUsage(AttributeTargets.Constructor |
    AttributeTargets.Method)]
[Serializable]
public sealed class MethodImplAttribute : Attribute
[C++]
[AttributeUsage(AttributeTargets::Constructor |
    AttributeTargets::Method)]
[Serializable]
public __gc __sealed class MethodImplAttribute : public Attribute
[JScript]
public
    AttributeUsage(AttributeTargets.Constructor |
    AttributeTargets.Method)
    Serializable
class MethodImplAttribute extends Attribute
```

Thread Safety

Any public static (**Shared** in Visual Basic) members of this type are safe for multithreaded operations. Any instance members are not guaranteed to be thread safe.

Remarks

You can apply this attribute to methods or constructors.

Requirements

Namespace: System.Runtime.CompilerServices

Platforms: Windows 98, Windows NT 4.0,
Windows Millennium Edition, Windows 2000,
Windows XP Home Edition, Windows XP Professional,
Windows .NET Server family,
.NET Compact Framework - Windows CE .NET

Assembly: Mscorlib (in Mscorlib.dll)

MethodImplAttribute Constructor

Initializes a new instance of the **MethodImplAttribute** class.

Overload List

Initializes a new instance of the **MethodImplAttribute** class.

Supported by the .NET Compact Framework.

  [Visual Basic] **Public Sub New()**
  [C#] **public MethodImplAttribute();**
  [C++] **public: MethodImplAttribute();**
  [JScript] **public function MethodImplAttribute();**

Initializes a new instance of the **MethodImplAttribute** class with the specified **MethodImplOptions** value.

Supported by the .NET Compact Framework.

  [Visual Basic] **Public Sub New(Short)**
  [C#] **public MethodImplAttribute(short);**
  [C++] **public: MethodImplAttribute(short);**
  [JScript] **public function MethodImplAttribute(Int16);**

Initializes a new instance of the **MethodImplAttribute** class with the specified **MethodImplOptions** value.

Supported by the .NET Compact Framework.

  [Visual Basic] **Public Sub New(MethodImplOptions)**
  [C#] **public MethodImplAttribute(MethodImplOptions);**
  [C++] **public: MethodImplAttribute(MethodImplOptions);**
  [JScript] **public function MethodImplAttribute(MethodImplOptions);**

MethodImplAttribute Constructor ()

Initializes a new instance of the **MethodImplAttribute** class.

```
[Visual Basic]
Public Sub New()
[C#]
public MethodImplAttribute();
[C++]
public: MethodImplAttribute();
[JScript]
public function MethodImplAttribute();
```

Requirements

Platforms: Windows 98, Windows NT 4.0,
Windows Millennium Edition, Windows 2000,
Windows XP Home Edition, Windows XP Professional,
Windows .NET Server family,
.NET Compact Framework - Windows CE .NET,
Common Language Infrastructure (CLI) Standard

MethodImplAttribute Constructor (Int16)

Initializes a new instance of the **MethodImplAttribute** class with the specified **MethodImplOptions** value.

```
[Visual Basic]
Public Sub New( _
    ByVal value As Short _
)
[C#]
public MethodImplAttribute(
    short value
);
[C++]
public: MethodImplAttribute(
    short value
);
[JScript]
public function MethodImplAttribute(
    value : Int16
);
```

Parameters

value
  A bitmask representing the desired **MethodImplOptions** value which specifies properties of the attributed method.

Requirements

Platforms: Windows 98, Windows NT 4.0,
Windows Millennium Edition, Windows 2000,
Windows XP Home Edition, Windows XP Professional,
Windows .NET Server family,
.NET Compact Framework - Windows CE .NET,
Common Language Infrastructure (CLI) Standard

MethodImplAttribute Constructor (MethodImplOptions)

Initializes a new instance of the **MethodImplAttribute** class with the specified **MethodImplOptions** value.

```
[Visual Basic]
Public Sub New( _
   ByVal methodImplOptions As MethodImplOptions _
)
[C#]
public MethodImplAttribute(
   MethodImplOptions methodImplOptions
);
[C++]
public: MethodImplAttribute(
   MethodImplOptions methodImplOptions
);
[JScript]
public function MethodImplAttribute(
   methodImplOptions : MethodImplOptions
);
```

Parameters

methodImplOptions
   A **MethodImplOptions** value specifying properties of the attributed method.

Requirements

Platforms: Windows 98, Windows NT 4.0,
Windows Millennium Edition, Windows 2000,
Windows XP Home Edition, Windows XP Professional,
Windows .NET Server family,
.NET Compact Framework - Windows CE .NET,
Common Language Infrastructure (CLI) Standard

MethodImplAttribute.MethodCodeType Field

A **MethodCodeType** value indicating what kind of implementation is provided for this method.

```
[Visual Basic]
Public MethodCodeType As MethodCodeType
[C#]
public MethodCodeType MethodCodeType;
[C++]
public: MethodCodeType MethodCodeType;
[JScript]
public var MethodCodeType : MethodCodeType;
```

Requirements

Platforms: Windows 98, Windows NT 4.0,
Windows Millennium Edition, Windows 2000,
Windows XP Home Edition, Windows XP Professional,
Windows .NET Server family,
.NET Compact Framework - Windows CE .NET

MethodImplAttribute.Value Property

Gets the **MethodImplOptions** value describing the attributed method.

```
[Visual Basic]
Public ReadOnly Property Value As MethodImplOptions
[C#]
public MethodImplOptions Value {get;}
[C++]
public: __property MethodImplOptions get_Value();
[JScript]
public function get Value() : MethodImplOptions;
```

Property Value

The **MethodImplOptions** value describing the attributed method.

Requirements

Platforms: Windows 98, Windows NT 4.0,
Windows Millennium Edition, Windows 2000,
Windows XP Home Edition, Windows XP Professional,
Windows .NET Server family,
.NET Compact Framework - Windows CE .NET,
Common Language Infrastructure (CLI) Standard

MethodImplOptions Enumeration

Defines the details of how a method is implemented.

This enumeration has a **FlagsAttribute** attribute that allows a bitwise combination of its member values.

```
[Visual Basic]
<Flags>
<Serializable>
Public Enum MethodImplOptions
[C#]
[Flags]
[Serializable]
public enum MethodImplOptions
[C++]
[Flags]
[Serializable]
__value public enum MethodImplOptions
[JScript]
public
   Flags
   Serializable
enum MethodImplOptions
```

Remarks

Used with **MethodImplAttribute**.

Specify multiple **MethodImplOptions** values using the bit-wise OR operator.

Members

Member name	Description	Value
ForwardRef Supported by the .NET Compact Framework.	Specifies that the method is declared, but its implementation is provided elsewhere.	16
InternalCall Supported by the .NET Compact Framework.	Specifies an internal call. An internal call is a call to a method implemented within the common language runtime itself.	4096
NoInlining Supported by the .NET Compact Framework.	Specifies that the method can not be inlined.	8
PreserveSig Supported by the .NET Compact Framework.	Specifies that the method signature is exported exactly as declared.	128
Synchronized Supported by the .NET Compact Framework.	Specifies the method can be executed by only one thread at a time.	32
Unmanaged Supported by the .NET Compact Framework.	Specifies that the method is implemented in unmanaged code.	4

Requirements

Namespace: System.Runtime.CompilerServices

Platforms: Windows 98, Windows NT 4.0, Windows Millennium Edition, Windows 2000, Windows XP Home Edition, Windows XP Professional, Windows .NET Server family, .NET Compact Framework - Windows CE .NET

Assembly: Mscorlib (in Mscorlib.dll)

RequiredAttributeAttribute Class

Specifies that an importing compiler must fully understand the symantics of a type definition, or refuse to use it.

System.Object
 System.Attribute
  System.Runtime.CompilerServices.RequiredAttribute-
  Attribute

```
[Visual Basic]
<AttributeUsage(AttributeTargets.Class Or AttributeTargets.Struct _
   Or AttributeTargets.Enum Or AttributeTargets.Interface)>
<Serializable>
NotInheritable Public Class RequiredAttributeAttribute
   Inherits Attribute
[C#]
[AttributeUsage(AttributeTargets.Class | AttributeTargets.Struct |
   AttributeTargets.Enum | AttributeTargets.Interface)]
[Serializable]
public sealed class RequiredAttributeAttribute : Attribute
[C++]
[AttributeUsage(AttributeTargets::Class | AttributeTargets::Struct
   | AttributeTargets::Enum | AttributeTargets::Interface)]
[Serializable]
public __gc __sealed class RequiredAttributeAttribute : public
   Attribute
[JScript]
public
   AttributeUsage(AttributeTargets.Class | AttributeTargets.Struct |
   AttributeTargets.Enum | AttributeTargets.Interface)
   Serializable
class RequiredAttributeAttribute extends Attribute
```

Thread Safety

Any public static (**Shared** in Visual Basic) members of this type are safe for multithreaded operations. Any instance members are not guaranteed to be thread safe.

Remarks

You can apply this attribute to classes, structures, enumerations, and interfaces.

For example, you can use this attribute to mark a C++ class that has a copy constructor. Any compiler that uses such a class must understand every constraint on its use, such as never create an object of said class in the garbage collected heap, because a relocation does not call its copy constructor.

The classes in System.Runtime.CompilerServices are for compiler writers use only.

Requirements

Namespace: System.Runtime.CompilerServices

Platforms: Windows 98, Windows NT 4.0, Windows Millennium Edition, Windows 2000, Windows XP Home Edition, Windows XP Professional, Windows .NET Server family

Assembly: Mscorlib (in Mscorlib.dll)

RequiredAttributeAttribute Constructor

Initializes a new instance of the **RequiredAttributeAttribute** class.

```
[Visual Basic]
Public Sub New( _
   ByVal requiredContract As Type _
)
[C#]
public RequiredAttributeAttribute(
   Type requiredContract
);
[C++]
public: RequiredAttributeAttribute(
   Type* requiredContract
);
[JScript]
public function RequiredAttributeAttribute(
   requiredContract : Type
);
```

Parameters

requiredContract
   This parameter is not supported in this version of the .NET Framework.

Requirements

Platforms: Windows 98, Windows NT 4.0, Windows Millennium Edition, Windows 2000, Windows XP Home Edition, Windows XP Professional, Windows .NET Server family

RequiredAttributeAttribute.RequiredContract Property

This property is not supported in this version of the .NET Framework.

```
[Visual Basic]
Public ReadOnly Property RequiredContract As Type
[C#]
public Type RequiredContract {get;}
[C++]
public: __property Type* get_RequiredContract();
[JScript]
public function get RequiredContract() : Type;
```

Property Value

This property is not supported in this version of the .NET Framework.

Requirements

Platforms: Windows 98, Windows NT 4.0, Windows Millennium Edition, Windows 2000, Windows XP Home Edition, Windows XP Professional, Windows .NET Server family

RuntimeHelpers Class

Provides a set of static methods and properties that provide support for compilers.

System.Object
　　System.Runtime.CompilerServices.RuntimeHelpers

```
[Visual Basic]
<Serializable>
NotInheritable Public Class RuntimeHelpers
[C#]
[Serializable]
public sealed class RuntimeHelpers
[C++]
[Serializable]
public _gc _sealed class RuntimeHelpers
[JScript]
public
   Serializable
class RuntimeHelpers
```

Thread Safety

Any public static (**Shared** in Visual Basic) members of this type are safe for multithreaded operations. Any instance members are not guaranteed to be thread safe.

Remarks

The classes in System.Runtime.CompilerServices are for compiler writers use only.

Requirements

Namespace: System.Runtime.CompilerServices

Platforms: Windows 98, Windows NT 4.0, Windows Millennium Edition, Windows 2000, Windows XP Home Edition, Windows XP Professional, Windows .NET Server family, .NET Compact Framework - Windows CE .NET

Assembly: Mscorlib (in Mscorlib.dll)

RuntimeHelpers.OffsetToStringData Property

Gets the offset in bytes to the data in the given string.

```
[Visual Basic]
Public Shared ReadOnly Property OffsetToStringData As Integer
[C#]
public static int OffsetToStringData {get;}
[C++]
public: _property static int get_OffsetToStringData();
[JScript]
public static function get OffsetToStringData() : int;
```

Property Value

The byte offset, from the start of the **String** object to the first character in the string.

Remarks

Compilers use this property for unsafe, but efficient, pointer operations on the characters in a managed string. Compilers should pin the string against movement by the garbage collector prior to use. Note that common language runtime strings are immutable, their contents can be read but not changed.

Requirements

Platforms: Windows 98, Windows NT 4.0, Windows Millennium Edition, Windows 2000, Windows XP Home Edition, Windows XP Professional, Windows .NET Server family, Common Language Infrastructure (CLI) Standard

RuntimeHelpers.Equals Method

Overload List

Determines whether the specified **Object** instances are considered equal.

> [Visual Basic] **Overloads Public Shared Shadows Function Equals(Object, Object) As Boolean**
>
> [C#] **public static new bool Equals(object, object);**
>
> [C++] **public: static bool Equals(Object*, Object*);**
>
> [JScript] **public static hide function Equals(Object, Object) : Boolean;**

Inherited from **Object**.

Supported by the .NET Compact Framework.

> [Visual Basic] **Overloads Public Overridable Function Equals(Object) As Boolean**
>
> [C#] **public virtual bool Equals(object);**
>
> [C++] **public: virtual bool Equals(Object*);**
>
> [JScript] **public function Equals(Object) : Boolean;**

RuntimeHelpers.Equals Method (Object, Object)

Note: This namespace, class, or member is supported only in version 1.1 of the .NET Framework.

Determines whether the specified **Object** instances are considered equal.

```
[Visual Basic]
Overloads Public Shared Shadows Function Equals( _
   ByVal o1 As Object, _
   ByVal o2 As Object _
) As Boolean
[C#]
public static new bool Equals(
   object o1,
   object o2
);
[C++]
public: static bool Equals(
   Object* o1,
   Object* o2
);
[JScript]
public static hide function Equals(
   o1 : Object,
   o2 : Object
) : Boolean;
```

Parameters

o1
　　The first **Object** to compare.
o2
　　The second **Object** to compare.

Return Value

true if the *o1* parameter is the same instance as the *o2* parameter or if both are a null reference (**Nothing** in Visual Basic) or if o1.Equals(o2) returns **true**; otherwise, **false**.

Requirements

Platforms: Windows 98, Windows NT 4.0, Windows Millennium Edition, Windows 2000, Windows XP Home Edition, Windows XP Professional, Windows .NET Server family

RuntimeHelpers.GetHashCode Method

Overload List

Serves as a hash function for a particular type, suitable for use in hashing algorithms and data structures such as a hash table.

[Visual Basic] **Overloads Public Shared Function GetHashCode(Object) As Integer**

[C#] **public static int GetHashCode(object);**

[C++] **public: static int GetHashCode(Object*);**

[JScript] **public static function GetHashCode(Object) : int;**

Inherited from **Object**.

Supported by the .NET Compact Framework.

[Visual Basic] **Overloads Public Overridable Function GetHashCode() As Integer**

[C#] **public virtual int GetHashCode();**

[C++] **public: virtual int GetHashCode();**

[JScript] **public function GetHashCode() : int;**

RuntimeHelpers.GetHashCode Method (Object)

Note: This namespace, class, or member is supported only in version 1.1 of the .NET Framework.

Serves as a hash function for a particular type, suitable for use in hashing algorithms and data structures such as a hash table.

```
[Visual Basic]
Overloads Public Shared Function GetHashCode( _
   ByVal o As Object _
) As Integer
[C#]
public static int GetHashCode(
   object o
);
[C++]
public: static int GetHashCode(
   Object* o
);
[JScript]
public static function GetHashCode(
   o : Object
) : int;
```

Parameters

o
   An **Object** to retrieve the hash code for.

Return Value

A hash code for the **Object** identified by the *o* parameter.

Requirements

Platforms: Windows 98, Windows NT 4.0, Windows Millennium Edition, Windows 2000, Windows XP Home Edition, Windows XP Professional, Windows .NET Server family

RuntimeHelpers.GetObjectValue Method

Boxes a value type.

```
[Visual Basic]
Public Shared Function GetObjectValue( _
   ByVal obj As Object _
) As Object
[C#]
public static object GetObjectValue(
   object obj
);
[C++]
public: static Object* GetObjectValue(
   Object* obj
);
[JScript]
public static function GetObjectValue(
   obj : Object
) : Object;
```

Parameters

obj
   The value type to be boxed.

Return Value

Returns a boxed copy of *obj* if it is a value class; otherwise *obj* itself is returned.

Remarks

Boxing a value type creates an object and performs a shallow copy of the fields of the specified value type into the new object.

Requirements

Platforms: Windows 98, Windows NT 4.0, Windows Millennium Edition, Windows 2000, Windows XP Home Edition, Windows XP Professional, Windows .NET Server family, .NET Compact Framework - Windows CE .NET

RuntimeHelpers.InitializeArray Method

Provides a fast way to initialize an array from data stored in a module.

```
[Visual Basic]
Public Shared Sub InitializeArray( _
   ByVal array As Array, _
   ByVal fldHandle As RuntimeFieldHandle _
)
[C#]
public static void InitializeArray(
   Array array,
   RuntimeFieldHandle fldHandle
);
```

```
[C++]
public: static void InitializeArray(
    Array* array,
    RuntimeFieldHandle fldHandle
);
[JScript]
public static function InitializeArray(
    array : Array,
    fldHandle : RuntimeFieldHandle
);
```

Parameters

array

> The array to be initialized.

fldHandle

> A **RuntimeFieldHandle** specifying the location of the data used to initialize the array.

Remarks

This method is for compiler use only.

Requirements

Platforms: Windows 98, Windows NT 4.0,
Windows Millennium Edition, Windows 2000,
Windows XP Home Edition, Windows XP Professional,
Windows .NET Server family,
.NET Compact Framework - Windows CE .NET,
Common Language Infrastructure (CLI) Standard

Requirements

Platforms: Windows 98, Windows NT 4.0,
Windows Millennium Edition, Windows 2000,
Windows XP Home Edition, Windows XP Professional,
Windows .NET Server family,
Common Language Infrastructure (CLI) Standard

RuntimeHelpers.RunClassConstructor Method

Runs a specified class constructor method.

```
[Visual Basic]
Public Shared Sub RunClassConstructor( _
    ByVal type As RuntimeTypeHandle _
)
[C#]
public static void RunClassConstructor(
    RuntimeTypeHandle type
);
[C++]
public: static void RunClassConstructor(
    RuntimeTypeHandle type
);
[JScript]
public static function RunClassConstructor(
    type : RuntimeTypeHandle
);
```

Parameters

type

> A **RuntimeTypeHandler** specifying the class constructor method to run.

Exceptions

Exception Type	Condition
TypeInitializationException	The class initializer threw an exception.

System.Runtime.Interop Services Namespace

The **System.Runtime.InteropServices** namespace provides a wide variety of members that support COM interop and platform invoke services.

Members of this namespace provide several categories of functionality, as shown in the following table. Attributes control marshaling behavior, such as how to arrange structures or how to represent strings. The most important attributes are **DllImportAttribute**, which you use to define platform invoke methods for accessing unmanaged APIs, and **MarshalAsAttribute**, which you use to specify how data is marshaled between managed and unmanaged memory.

ArrayWithOffset Structure

Encapsulates an array and an offset within the specified array.

System.Object
  System.ValueType
    System.Runtime.InteropServices.ArrayWithOffset

```
[Visual Basic]
Public Structure ArrayWithOffset
[C#]
public struct ArrayWithOffset
[C++]
public __value struct ArrayWithOffset
```

[JScript] In JScript, you can use the structures in the .NET Framework, but you cannot define your own.

Thread Safety

Any public static (**Shared** in Visual Basic) members of this type are safe for multithreaded operations. Any instance members are not guaranteed to be thread safe.

Remarks

Can be used as an argument to a native method reached through platform invoke. In this case, the platform invoke marshaler will retrieve the starting address of the array, add the offset, and pass the resulting pointer to the underlying native function. This structure only supports arrays containing no references, such as primitive type arrays and value type arrays containing only fields of primitive types.

Requirements

Namespace: System.Runtime.InteropServices

Platforms: Windows 98, Windows NT 4.0, Windows Millennium Edition, Windows 2000, Windows XP Home Edition, Windows XP Professional, Windows .NET Server family

Assembly: Mscorlib (in Mscorlib.dll)

ArrayWithOffset Constructor

Initializes a new instance of the **ArrayWithOffset** structure.

```
[Visual Basic]
Public Sub New( _
   ByVal array As Object, _
   ByVal offset As Integer _
)
[C#]
public ArrayWithOffset(
   object array,
   int offset
);
[C++]
public: ArrayWithOffset(
   Object* array,
   int offset
);
[JScript]
public function ArrayWithOffset(
   array : Object,
   offset : int
);
```

Parameters

array
  A managed array.

offset
  The offset in bytes, of the element to be passed through platform invoke.

Requirements

Platforms: Windows 98, Windows NT 4.0, Windows Millennium Edition, Windows 2000, Windows XP Home Edition, Windows XP Professional, Windows .NET Server family

ArrayWithOffset.Equals Method

Indicates whether the specified object matches the current **ArrayWithOffset**.

```
[Visual Basic]
Overrides Public Function Equals( _
   ByVal obj As Object _
) As Boolean
[C#]
public override bool Equals(
   object obj
);
[C++]
public: bool Equals(
   Object* obj
);
[JScript]
public override function Equals(
   obj : Object
) : Boolean;
```

Parameters

obj
  Object to compare with this instance.

Return Value

true if the object matches this **ArrayWithOffset**; otherwise, **false**.

Requirements

Platforms: Windows 98, Windows NT 4.0,
Windows Millennium Edition, Windows 2000,
Windows XP Home Edition, Windows XP Professional,
Windows .NET Server family

ArrayWithOffset.GetArray Method

Returns the managed array referenced by this **ArrayWithOffset**.

```
[Visual Basic]
Public Function GetArray() As Object
[C#]
public object GetArray();
[C++]
public: Object* GetArray();
[JScript]
public function GetArray() : Object;
```

Return Value

The managed array this instance references.

Requirements

Platforms: Windows 98, Windows NT 4.0,
Windows Millennium Edition, Windows 2000,
Windows XP Home Edition, Windows XP Professional,
Windows .NET Server family

ArrayWithOffset.GetHashCode Method

Returns a hash code for this value type.

```
[Visual Basic]
Overrides Public Function GetHashCode() As Integer
[C#]
public override int GetHashCode();
[C++]
public: int GetHashCode();
[JScript]
public override function GetHashCode() : int;
```

Return Value

The hash code for this instance.

Requirements

Platforms: Windows 98, Windows NT 4.0,
Windows Millennium Edition, Windows 2000,
Windows XP Home Edition, Windows XP Professional,
Windows .NET Server family

ArrayWithOffset.GetOffset Method

Returns the offset provided when this **ArrayWithOffset** was
constructed.

```
[Visual Basic]
Public Function GetOffset() As Integer
[C#]
public int GetOffset();
[C++]
public: int GetOffset();
```

```
[JScript]
public function GetOffset() : int;
```

Return Value

The offset for this instance.

Requirements

Platforms: Windows 98, Windows NT 4.0,
Windows Millennium Edition, Windows 2000,
Windows XP Home Edition, Windows XP Professional,
Windows .NET Server family

AssemblyRegistrationFlags Enumeration

Defines a set of flags used when registering assemblies.

This enumeration has a **FlagsAttribute** attribute that allows a bitwise combination of its member values.

```
[Visual Basic]
<Flags>
<Serializable>
Public Enum AssemblyRegistrationFlags
[C#]
[Flags]
[Serializable]
public enum AssemblyRegistrationFlags
[C++]
[Flags]
[Serializable]
__value public enum AssemblyRegistrationFlags
[JScript]
public
    Flags
    Serializable
enum AssemblyRegistrationFlags
```

Members

Member name	Description	Value
None	Indicates no special settings.	0
SetCodeBase	Indicates that the code base key for the assembly should be set in the registry.	1

Requirements

Namespace: System.Runtime.InteropServices

Platforms: Windows 98, Windows NT 4.0, Windows Millennium Edition, Windows 2000, Windows XP Home Edition, Windows XP Professional, Windows .NET Server family

Assembly: Mscorlib (in Mscorlib.dll)

AutomationProxyAttribute Class

Specifies whether the type should be marshaled using the Automation marshaler or a custom proxy and stub.

System.Object
  System.Attribute
    System.Runtime.InteropServices.AutomationProxyAttribute

```
[Visual Basic]
<AttributeUsage(AttributeTargets.Assembly Or AttributeTargets.Class _
   Or AttributeTargets.Interface)>
NotInheritable Public Class AutomationProxyAttribute
   Inherits Attribute
[C#]
[AttributeUsage(AttributeTargets.Assembly | AttributeTargets.Class
   | AttributeTargets.Interface)]
public sealed class AutomationProxyAttribute : Attribute
[C++]
[AttributeUsage(AttributeTargets::Assembly |
   AttributeTargets::Class | AttributeTargets::Interface)]
public __gc __sealed class AutomationProxyAttribute : public
   Attribute
[JScript]
public
   AttributeUsage(AttributeTargets.Assembly | AttributeTargets.Class |
   AttributeTargets.Interface)
class AutomationProxyAttribute extends Attribute
```

Thread Safety

Any public static (**Shared** in Visual Basic) members of this type are safe for multithreaded operations. Any instance members are not guaranteed to be thread safe.

Remarks

You can apply this attribute to assemblies, classes, or interfaces.

When applied to a class, it extends to the class interface for that class, if present.

Requirements

Namespace: System.Runtime.InteropServices

Platforms: Windows 98, Windows NT 4.0, Windows Millennium Edition, Windows 2000, Windows XP Home Edition, Windows XP Professional, Windows .NET Server family

Assembly: Mscorlib (in Mscorlib.dll)

AutomationProxyAttribute Constructor

Initializes a new instance of the **AutomationProxyAttribute** class.

```
[Visual Basic]
Public Sub New( _
   ByVal val As Boolean _
)
[C#]
public AutomationProxyAttribute(
   bool val
);
```

```
[C++]
public: AutomationProxyAttribute(
   bool val
);
[JScript]
public function AutomationProxyAttribute(
   val : Boolean
);
```

Parameters

val
    true if the class should be marshaled using the Automation Marshaler; **false** if a proxy stub marshaler should be used.

Requirements

Platforms: Windows 98, Windows NT 4.0, Windows Millennium Edition, Windows 2000, Windows XP Home Edition, Windows XP Professional, Windows .NET Server family

AutomationProxyAttribute.Value Property

Gets a value indicating the type of marshaler to use.

```
[Visual Basic]
Public ReadOnly Property Value As Boolean
[C#]
public bool Value {get;}
[C++]
public: __property bool get_Value();
[JScript]
public function get Value() : Boolean;
```

Property Value

true if the class should be marshaled using the Automation Marshaler; **false** if a proxy stub marshaler should be used.

Requirements

Platforms: Windows 98, Windows NT 4.0, Windows Millennium Edition, Windows 2000, Windows XP Home Edition, Windows XP Professional, Windows .NET Server family

BestFitMappingAttribute Class

Note: This namespace, class, or member is supported only in version 1.1 of the .NET Framework.

Controls whether Unicode characters are converted to the closest matching ANSI characters.

System.Object
  System.Attribute
    System.Runtime.InteropServices.BestFitMappingAttribute

```
[Visual Basic]
<AttributeUsage(AttributeTargets.Assembly Or AttributeTargets.Class _
    Or AttributeTargets.Struct Or AttributeTargets.Interface)>
NotInheritable Public Class BestFitMappingAttribute
    Inherits Attribute
[C#]
[AttributeUsage(AttributeTargets.Assembly | AttributeTargets.Class
    | AttributeTargets.Struct | AttributeTargets.Interface)]
public sealed class BestFitMappingAttribute : Attribute
[C++]
[AttributeUsage(AttributeTargets::Assembly |
    AttributeTargets::Class | AttributeTargets::Struct |
    AttributeTargets::Interface)]
public __gc __sealed class BestFitMappingAttribute : public
    Attribute
[JScript]
public
    AttributeUsage(AttributeTargets.Assembly | AttributeTargets.Class |
    AttributeTargets.Struct | AttributeTargets.Interface)
class BestFitMappingAttribute extends Attribute
```

Thread Safety

Any public static (**Shared** in Visual Basic) members of this type are safe for multithreaded operations. Any instance members are not guaranteed to be thread safe.

Remarks

You can apply this attribute to an assembly, interface, class, or structure.

By default, the common language runtime converts to ANSI characters any managed Unicode characters passed to an unmanaged method executing on Windows 98 or Windows Me. Best-fit mapping enables the **interop marshaler** to select a close-matching character when no exact match exists. For example, the marshaler converts the Unicode copyright character to 'c' for unmanaged methods that accept ANSI characters.

> **CAUTION** Some characters lack a best-fit representation; these characters are called unmappable. Unmappable characters are usually converted to the default '?' ANSI character. Certain Unicode characters are converted to dangerous characters, such as the backslash '\' character, which can inadvertently change a path.

BestFitMappingAttribute provides two parameters to control aspects of best-fit mapping. You use the first parameter to toggle best-fit mapping on and off. The default value is **true**, which enables best-fit mapping on the assembly, interface, and class levels. An attribute applied to an interface or class overrides an assembly-level attribute. You can likewise enable or disable best-fit mapping for

platform invoke calls by using the **DllImportAttribute.BestFitMapping** field. A value set by the platform invoke field overrides all levels of **BestFitMappingAttribute**.

You can use the second parameter to control throwing an exception on unmappable characters. The default value for the **ThrowOnUnmappableChar** field is **false**, which disables throwing an exception each time the runtime encounters a Unicode character that has to be converted to the '?' ANSI character. Even if best-fit mapping is **true**, unmappable characters generate an exception when the **ThrowOnUnmappableChar** field is **true**. To tighten security, you can toggle the first parameter to **false** and the second parameter to **true**. This combination of parameter settings turns best-fit mapping off, but enables the exception-throwing mechanism as a safety precaution.

> **CAUTION** You cannot change the default values provided by **BestFitMappingAttribute** when passing a managed array whose elements are ANSI Chars or LPSTRs to an unmanaged safe array. Best-fit mapping is always enabled and no exception can be thrown. Be aware that this combination can compromise your security model.

Example

[Visual Basic, C#] The following example shows how to disable best fit mapping and to throw an exception on the conversion of Unicode characters to the '?' ANSI character. Setting **BestFitMappingAttribute** parameters in this manner provides an added measure of security.

```
[Visual Basic]
<BestFitMapping(False, ThrowOnUnmappableChar := True)> _
Interface IMyInterface1
    'Insert code here.
End Interface

[C#]
[BestFitMapping(false, ThrowOnUnmappableChar = true)]
interface IMyInterface1
{
    //Insert code here.
}
```

Requirements

Namespace: System.Runtime.InteropServices

Platforms: Windows 98, Windows NT 4.0, Windows Millennium Edition, Windows 2000, Windows XP Home Edition, Windows XP Professional, Windows .NET Server family

Assembly: Mscorlib (in Mscorlib.dll)

BestFitMappingAttribute Constructor

Note: This namespace, class, or member is supported only in version 1.1 of the .NET Framework.

Initializes a new instance of the **BestFitMappingAttribute** class set to the value of the **BestFitMapping** property.

```
[Visual Basic]
Public Sub New( _
    ByVal BestFitMapping As Boolean _
)
```

```
[C#]
public BestFitMappingAttribute(
    bool BestFitMapping
);
[C++]
public: BestFitMappingAttribute(
    bool BestFitMapping
);
[JScript]
public function BestFitMappingAttribute(
    BestFitMapping : Boolean
);
```

Parameters

BestFitMapping

> **true** to indicate that best-fit mapping is enabled; otherwise, **false**. The default is **true**.

Requirements

Platforms: Windows 98, Windows NT 4.0, Windows Millennium Edition, Windows 2000, Windows XP Home Edition, Windows XP Professional, Windows .NET Server family

BestFitMappingAttribute.ThrowOnUnmappable Char Field

Note: This namespace, class, or member is supported only in version 1.1 of the .NET Framework.

Enables or disables the throwing of an exception on an unmappable Unicode character that is converted to an ANSI '?' character.

```
[Visual Basic]
Public ThrowOnUnmappableChar As Boolean
[C#]
public bool ThrowOnUnmappableChar;
[C++]
public: bool ThrowOnUnmappableChar;
[JScript]
public var ThrowOnUnmappableChar : Boolean;
```

Remarks

If **false**, the **ThrowOnUnmappableChar** field is disabled; otherwise, an exception is thrown each time the interop marshaler encounters an unmappable character. The default **false**.

Requirements

Platforms: Windows 98, Windows NT 4.0, Windows Millennium Edition, Windows 2000, Windows XP Home Edition, Windows XP Professional, Windows .NET Server family

BestFitMappingAttribute.BestFitMapping Property

Note: This namespace, class, or member is supported only in version 1.1 of the .NET Framework.

Gets the best-fit mapping behavior when converting Unicode characters to ANSI characters.

```
[Visual Basic]
Public ReadOnly Property BestFitMapping As Boolean
[C#]
public bool BestFitMapping {get;}
[C++]
public: __property bool get_BestFitMapping();
[JScript]
public function get BestFitMapping() : Boolean;
```

Property Value

true if best-fit mapping is enabled; otherwise, **false**. The default is **true**.

Remarks

If best-fit mapping is **false** and **ThrowOnUnmappableChar** is **true**, all Unicode characters that require conversion to ANSI format will generate an exception when passed to unmanaged code. Some characters are unmappable, even when best-fit mapping is **true**. Some characters lack a best-fit representation; these characters are called unmappable. Unmappable characters are usually converted to the default '?' ANSI character.

> **CAUTION**   Certain Unicode characters are converted to dangerous characters, such as the backslash '\' character, which can inadvertently change a path.

Requirements

Platforms: Windows 98, Windows NT 4.0, Windows Millennium Edition, Windows 2000, Windows XP Home Edition, Windows XP Professional, Windows .NET Server family

BIND_OPTS Structure

Stores the parameters that are used during a moniker-binding operation.

System.Object
  System.ValueType
    System.Runtime.InteropServices.BIND_OPTS

```
[Visual Basic]
<ComVisible(False)>
Public Structure BIND_OPTS
[C#]
[ComVisible(false)]
public struct BIND_OPTS
[C++]
[ComVisible(false)]
public __value struct BIND_OPTS
```

[JScript] In JScript, you can use the structures in the .NET Framework, but you cannot define your own.

Thread Safety

Any public static (**Shared** in Visual Basic) members of this type are safe for multithreaded operations. Any instance members are not guaranteed to be thread safe.

Remarks

For more information, please see the existing documentation for **BIND_OPTS** in the com subfolder of the MSDN library.

Requirements

Namespace: System.Runtime.InteropServices

Platforms: Windows 98, Windows NT 4.0, Windows Millennium Edition, Windows 2000, Windows XP Home Edition, Windows XP Professional, Windows .NET Server family

Assembly: Mscorlib (in Mscorlib.dll)

BIND_OPTS.cbStruct Field

Specifies the size of the **BIND_OPTS** structure in bytes.

```
[Visual Basic]
Public cbStruct As Integer
[C#]
public int cbStruct;
[C++]
public: int cbStruct;
[JScript]
public var cbStruct : int;
```

Remarks

For more information, please see the existing documentation for **BIND_OPTS** in the MSDN library.

Requirements

Platforms: Windows 98, Windows NT 4.0, Windows Millennium Edition, Windows 2000, Windows XP Home Edition, Windows XP Professional, Windows .NET Server family

BIND_OPTS.dwTickCountDeadline Field

Indicates the amount of time (clock time in milliseconds, as returned by the **GetTickCount** function) the caller specified to complete the binding operation.

```
[Visual Basic]
Public dwTickCountDeadline As Integer
[C#]
public int dwTickCountDeadline;
[C++]
public: int dwTickCountDeadline;
[JScript]
public var dwTickCountDeadline : int;
```

Remarks

This member lets the caller limit the execution time of an operation when speed is of primary importance.

For more information, please see the existing documentation for **BIND_OPTS** in the MSDN library.

Requirements

Platforms: Windows 98, Windows NT 4.0, Windows Millennium Edition, Windows 2000, Windows XP Home Edition, Windows XP Professional, Windows .NET Server family

BIND_OPTS.grfFlags Field

Controls aspects of moniker binding operations.

```
[Visual Basic]
Public grfFlags As Integer
[C#]
public int grfFlags;
[C++]
public: int grfFlags;
[JScript]
public var grfFlags : int;
```

Remarks

For more information, please see the existing documentation for **BIND_OPTS** in the MSDN library.

Requirements

Platforms: Windows 98, Windows NT 4.0, Windows Millennium Edition, Windows 2000, Windows XP Home Edition, Windows XP Professional, Windows .NET Server family

BIND_OPTS.grfMode Field

Flags that should be used when opening the file that contains the object identified by the moniker.

```
[Visual Basic]
Public grfMode As Integer
[C#]
public int grfMode;
[C++]
public: int grfMode;
[JScript]
public var grfMode : int;
```

Remarks

For more information, please see the existing documentation for
BIND_OPTS in the MSDN library.

Requirements

Platforms: Windows 98, Windows NT 4.0,
Windows Millennium Edition, Windows 2000,
Windows XP Home Edition, Windows XP Professional,
Windows .NET Server family

BINDPTR Structure

Contains a pointer to a bound-to **FUNCDESC**, **VARDESC**, or an **ITypeComp** interface.

System.Object
  System.ValueType
    System.Runtime.InteropServices.BINDPTR

```
[Visual Basic]
<ComVisible(False)>
Public Structure BINDPTR
[C#]
[ComVisible(false)]
public struct BINDPTR
[C++]
[ComVisible(false)]
public __value struct BINDPTR
```

[JScript] In JScript, you can use the structures in the .NET Framework, but you cannot define your own.

Thread Safety

Any public static (**Shared** in Visual Basic) members of this type are safe for multithreaded operations. Any instance members are not guaranteed to be thread safe.

Remarks

For more information about the **BINDPTR** type, see the MSDN Library.

Requirements

Namespace: System.Runtime.InteropServices

Platforms: Windows 98, Windows NT 4.0, Windows Millennium Edition, Windows 2000, Windows XP Home Edition, Windows XP Professional, Windows .NET Server family

Assembly: Mscorlib (in Mscorlib.dll)

BINDPTR.lpfuncdesc Field

Represents a pointer to a **FUNCDESC** structure.

```
[Visual Basic]
Public lpfuncdesc As IntPtr
[C#]
public IntPtr lpfuncdesc;
[C++]
public: IntPtr lpfuncdesc;
[JScript]
public var lpfuncdesc : IntPtr;
```

Requirements

Platforms: Windows 98, Windows NT 4.0, Windows Millennium Edition, Windows 2000, Windows XP Home Edition, Windows XP Professional, Windows .NET Server family

BINDPTR.lptcomp Field

Represents a pointer to a **UCOMITypeComp** interface.

```
[Visual Basic]
Public lptcomp As IntPtr
[C#]
public IntPtr lptcomp;
[C++]
public: IntPtr lptcomp;
[JScript]
public var lptcomp : IntPtr;
```

Requirements

Platforms: Windows 98, Windows NT 4.0, Windows Millennium Edition, Windows 2000, Windows XP Home Edition, Windows XP Professional, Windows .NET Server family

BINDPTR.lpvardesc Field

Represents a pointer to a **VARDESC** structure.

```
[Visual Basic]
Public lpvardesc As IntPtr
[C#]
public IntPtr lpvardesc;
[C++]
public: IntPtr lpvardesc;
[JScript]
public var lpvardesc : IntPtr;
```

Requirements

Platforms: Windows 98, Windows NT 4.0, Windows Millennium Edition, Windows 2000, Windows XP Home Edition, Windows XP Professional, Windows .NET Server family

CALLCONV Enumeration

Identifies the calling convention used by a method described in a **METHODDATA** structure.

```
[Visual Basic]
<Serializable>
<ComVisible(False)>
Public Enum CALLCONV
[C#]
[Serializable]
[ComVisible(false)]
public enum CALLCONV
[C++]
[Serializable]
[ComVisible(false)]
__value public enum CALLCONV
[JScript]
public
    Serializable
    ComVisible(false)
enum CALLCONV
```

Remarks

For additional information about **CALLCONV**, see the MSDN Library.

Members

Member name	Description
CC_CDECL	Indicates that the Cdecl calling convention is used for a method.
CC_MACPASCAL	Indicates that the Macpascal calling convention is used for a method.
CC_MAX	Indicates the end of the **CALLCONV** enumeration.
CC_MPWCDECL	Indicates that the Mpwcdecl calling convention is used for a method.
CC_MPWPASCAL	Indicates that the Mpwpascal calling convention is used for a method.
CC_MSCPASCAL	Indicates that the Mscpascal calling convention is used for a method.
CC_PASCAL	Indicates that the Pascal calling convention is used for a method.
CC_RESERVED	This value is reserved for future use.
CC_STDCALL	Indicates that the Stdcall calling convention is used for a method.
CC_SYSCALL	Indicates that the Syscall calling convention is used for a method.

Requirements

Namespace: System.Runtime.InteropServices

Platforms: Windows 98, Windows NT 4.0, Windows Millennium Edition, Windows 2000, Windows XP Home Edition, Windows XP Professional, Windows .NET Server family

Assembly: Mscorlib (in Mscorlib.dll)

CallingConvention Enumeration

Specifies the calling convention required to call methods implemented in unmanaged code.

```
[Visual Basic]
<Serializable>
Public Enum CallingConvention
[C#]
[Serializable]
public enum CallingConvention
[C++]
[Serializable]
__value public enum CallingConvention
[JScript]
public
    Serializable
enum CallingConvention
```

Remarks

Always use the **CallingConvention** enumeration rather than the **CALLCONV** enumeration to specify a calling convention in managed code. The latter exists only for the sake of COM definitions. The **CallingConvention** enumeration is used by **DllImportAttribute** and several classes in **System.Reflection.Emit** to dynamically emit platform invoke signatures.

Members

Member name	Description
Cdecl	The caller cleans the stack. This enables calling functions with **varargs**, which makes it appropriate to use for methods that accept a variable number of parameters, such as **Printf**.
FastCall	This calling convention is not supported.
StdCall	The callee cleans the stack. This is the default convention for calling unmanaged functions with platform invoke.
ThisCall	The first parameter is the **this** pointer and is stored in register ECX. Other parameters are pushed on the stack. This calling convention is used to call methods on classes exported from an unmanaged DLL.
Winapi Supported by the .NET Compact Framework.	This member is not actually a calling convention, but instead uses the default platform calling convention. For example, on Windows the default is **StdCall** and on Windows CE .NET it is **Cdecl**.

Example

[Visual Basic, C#] The following example demonstrates how to apply the **Cdecl** calling convention, which you must use because the stack is cleaned up by the caller.

```vb
[Visual Basic]
Imports System
Imports Microsoft.VisualBasic
Imports System.Runtime.InteropServices

Public Class LibWrap
' Visual Basic does not support varargs, so all arguments must be
' explicitly defined. CallingConvention.Cdecl must be used
ince the stack
' is cleaned up by the caller.
' int printf( const char *format [, argument]... )

<DllImport("msvcrt.dll", CallingConvention
:= CallingConvention.Cdecl)> _
Overloads Shared Function printf ( _
    format As String, i As Integer, d As Double) As Integer
End Function

<DllImport("msvcrt.dll", CallingConvention :=
CallingConvention.Cdecl)> _
Overloads Shared Function printf ( _
    format As String, i As Integer, s As String) As Integer
End Function
End Class 'LibWrap

Public Class App
    Public Shared Sub Main()
        LibWrap.printf(ControlChars.CrLf + "Print params: %i %f", 99, _
                99.99)
        LibWrap.printf(ControlChars.CrLf + "Print params: %i %s", 99, _
                "abcd")
    End Sub 'Main
End Class 'App
```

```csharp
[C#]
using System;
using System.Runtime.InteropServices;

public class LibWrap
{
// C# doesn't support varargs so all arguments must be
explicitly defined.
// CallingConvention.Cdecl must be used since the stack is
// cleaned up by the caller.

// int printf( const char *format [, argument]... )

[DllImport("msvcrt.dll", CharSet=CharSet.Ansi,
CallingConvention=CallingConvention.Cdecl)]
public static extern int printf(String format, int i, double d);

[DllImport("msvcrt.dll", CharSet=CharSet.Ansi,
CallingConvention=CallingConvention.Cdecl)]
public static extern int printf(String format, int i, String s);
}

public class App
{
    public static void Main()
    {
        LibWrap.printf("\nPrint params: %i %f", 99, 99.99);
        LibWrap.printf("\nPrint params: %i %s", 99, "abcd");
    }
}
```

Requirements

Namespace: System.Runtime.InteropServices

Platforms: Windows 98, Windows NT 4.0, Windows Millennium Edition, Windows 2000, Windows XP Home Edition, Windows XP Professional, Windows .NET Server family, .NET Compact Framework - Windows CE .NET

Assembly: Mscorlib (in Mscorlib.dll)

CharSet Enumeration

Dictates which character set marshaled strings should use.

```
[Visual Basic]
<Serializable>
Public Enum CharSet
[C#]
[Serializable]
public enum CharSet
[C++]
[Serializable]
__value public enum CharSet
[JScript]
public
   Serializable
enum CharSet
```

Remarks

Because there are several unmanaged string types and only one managed string type, you must use a character set to specify how managed strings should be marshaled to unmanaged code. This enumeration, which provides character set options, is used by **DllImportAttribute** and **StructLayoutAttribute**. For a detailed description of the string marshaling and name matching behavior associated with this enumeration, see **Specifying a Character Set**.

Members

Member name	Description
Ansi	Marshal strings as multiple-byte character strings.
Auto Supported by the .NET Compact Framework.	Automatically marshal strings appropriately for the target operating system. The default is **Unicode** on Windows NT, Windows 2000, Windows XP, and the Windows .NET Server family; the default is **Ansi** on Windows 98 and Windows Me.
None	This value is obsolete and has the same behavior as **CharSet.Ansi**.
Unicode Supported by the .NET Compact Framework.	Marshal strings as Unicode 2-byte characters.

Example

[Visual Basic, C#] The following code example shows how to specify a **CharSet** enumeration value when applying the **StructLayoutAttribute** to a managed definition.

```
[Visual Basic]
< StructLayout( LayoutKind.Sequential, CharSet := CharSet.Ansi )> _
Public Structure MyPerson
   Public first As String
   Public last As String
End Structure 'MyPerson
```

```
[C#]
[ StructLayout( LayoutKind.Sequential, CharSet=CharSet.Ansi )]
public struct MyPerson
{
   public String first;
   public String last;
}
```

Requirements

Namespace: System.Runtime.InteropServices

Platforms: Windows 98, Windows NT 4.0, Windows Millennium Edition, Windows 2000, Windows XP Home Edition, Windows XP Professional, Windows .NET Server family, .NET Compact Framework - Windows CE .NET

Assembly: Mscorlib (in Mscorlib.dll)

ClassInterfaceAttribute Class

Indicates the type of class interface to be generated for a class exposed to COM, if an interface is generated at all.

System.Object
  System.Attribute
    System.Runtime.InteropServices.ClassInterfaceAttribute

```
[Visual Basic]
<AttributeUsage(AttributeTargets.Assembly Or _
    AttributeTargets.Class)>
NotInheritable Public Class ClassInterfaceAttribute
    Inherits Attribute
[C#]
[AttributeUsage(AttributeTargets.Assembly |
    AttributeTargets.Class)]
public sealed class ClassInterfaceAttribute : Attribute
[C++]
[AttributeUsage(AttributeTargets::Assembly |
    AttributeTargets::Class)]
public __gc __sealed class ClassInterfaceAttribute : public
    Attribute
[JScript]
public
    AttributeUsage(AttributeTargets.Assembly | AttributeTargets.Class)
class ClassInterfaceAttribute extends Attribute
```

Thread Safety

Any public static (**Shared** in Visual Basic) members of this type are safe for multithreaded operations. Any instance members are not guaranteed to be thread safe.

Remarks

You can apply this attribute to assemblies or classes.

This attribute controls whether the **Type Library Exporter (Tlbexp.exe)** automatically generates a class interface for the attributed class. A class interface carries the same name as the class itself, but the name is prefixed with an underscore. When exposed, the class interface contains all the **public**, non- static (**Shared** in Visual Basic) members of the managed class, including members inherited from its base class. Managed classes cannot access a class interface and have no need to as they can access the class members directly. Tlbexp.exe generates a unique interface identifier (IID) for the class interface.

Class interfaces can be dual or dispatch-only interfaces. Optionally, you can suppress the generation of the class interface and provide a custom interface instead. You expose or suppress a class interface by specifying a **System.Runtime.InteropServices.ClassInterfaceType** enumeration member. When you apply **ClassInterfaceAttribute** to an assembly, the attribute pertains to all classes in the assembly unless the individual classes override the setting with their own attribute.

Although class interfaces eliminate the task of explicitly defining interfaces for each class, their use in production applications is strongly discouraged. Dual class interfaces allow clients to bind to a specific interface layout that is subject to change as the class evolves. For example, consider a managed class that exposes a class interface to COM clients. The first version of the class contains methods North and South. An unmanaged client can bind to the class interface, which provides North as the first method in the class interface and method South as the second method. Now consider the next version of the class, which has a new method, East, inserted between methods North and South. Unmanaged clients that try to bind to the new class through the old class interface end up calling method East when they intend to call method South, because the positioning of methods within the interface has changed. Moreover, any change to the layout of a base class also affects the layout of the class interface for all derived classes. Managed clients, which bind directly to classes, do not exhibit the same versioning problems. For specific guidelines on using a class interface, see **Introducing the Class Interface**.

The **Type Library Importer (Tlbimp.exe)** always applies to imported classes the **ClassInterfaceType.None** enumeration member to indicate that existing COM classes never expose managed interfaces.

Example

[Visual Basic, C#] The following example shows how to apply the **ClassInterfaceAttribute** with the **ClassInterfaceType** value **AutoDispatch**, which generates an **IDispatch** interface for MyClass.

```
[Visual Basic]
Imports System.Runtime.InteropServices

<ClassInterface(ClassInterfaceType.AutoDispatch)> _
Public Class SampleClass
    ' Insert class members here.
End Class
```

```
[C#]
using System.Runtime.InteropServices;

[ClassInterface(ClassInterfaceType.AutoDispatch)]
public class MyClass
{
    public MyClass() {}
}
```

Requirements

Namespace: System.Runtime.InteropServices

Platforms: Windows 98, Windows NT 4.0, Windows Millennium Edition, Windows 2000, Windows XP Home Edition, Windows XP Professional, Windows .NET Server family

Assembly: Mscorlib (in Mscorlib.dll)

ClassInterfaceAttribute Constructor

Initializes a new instance of the **ClassInterfaceAttribute** class.

Overload List

Initializes a new instance of the **ClassInterfaceAttribute** class with the specified **ClassInterfaceType** enumeration member.

  [Visual Basic] **Public Sub New(ClassInterfaceType)**

  [C#] **public ClassInterfaceAttribute(ClassInterfaceType);**

  [C++] **public: ClassInterfaceAttribute(ClassInterfaceType);**

  [JScript] **public function ClassInterfaceAttribute(ClassInterfaceType);**

Initializes a new instance of the **ClassInterfaceAttribute** class with the specified **ClassInterfaceType** enumeration value.

  [Visual Basic] **Public Sub New(Short)**

  [C#] **public ClassInterfaceAttribute(short);**

  [C++] **public: ClassInterfaceAttribute(short);**

  [JScript] **public function ClassInterfaceAttribute(Int16);**

ClassInterfaceAttribute Constructor (ClassInterfaceType)

Initializes a new instance of the **ClassInterfaceAttribute** class with the specified **ClassInterfaceType** enumeration member.

```
[Visual Basic]
Public Sub New( _
   ByVal classInterfaceType As ClassInterfaceType _
)
[C#]
public ClassInterfaceAttribute(
   ClassInterfaceType classInterfaceType
);
[C++]
public: ClassInterfaceAttribute(
   ClassInterfaceType classInterfaceType
);
[JScript]
public function ClassInterfaceAttribute(
   classInterfaceType : ClassInterfaceType
);
```

Parameters

classInterfaceType
> One of the **ClassInterfaceType** values that describes the type of interface that is generated for a class.

Remarks

For readable code that is less prone to error, always use this constructor.

Requirements

Platforms: Windows 98, Windows NT 4.0, Windows Millennium Edition, Windows 2000, Windows XP Home Edition, Windows XP Professional, Windows .NET Server family

ClassInterfaceAttribute Constructor (Int16)

Initializes a new instance of the **ClassInterfaceAttribute** class with the specified **ClassInterfaceType** enumeration value.

```
[Visual Basic]
Public Sub New( _
   ByVal classInterfaceType As Short _
)
[C#]
public ClassInterfaceAttribute(
   short classInterfaceType
);
[C++]
public: ClassInterfaceAttribute(
   short classInterfaceType
);
[JScript]
public function ClassInterfaceAttribute(
   classInterfaceType : Int16
);
```

Parameters

classInterfaceType
> Describes the type of interface that is generated for a class.

Remarks

This constructor takes an underlying 16-bit signed integer that represents each **ClassInterfaceType** enumeration member. The **Type Library Importer (Tlbimp.exe)** uses this constructor.

Requirements

Platforms: Windows 98, Windows NT 4.0, Windows Millennium Edition, Windows 2000, Windows XP Home Edition, Windows XP Professional, Windows .NET Server family

ClassInterfaceAttribute.Value Property

Gets the **ClassInterfaceType** value that describes which type of interface should be generated for the class.

```
[Visual Basic]
Public ReadOnly Property Value As ClassInterfaceType
[C#]
public ClassInterfaceType Value {get;}
[C++]
public: __property ClassInterfaceType get_Value();
[JScript]
public function get Value() : ClassInterfaceType;
```

Property Value

The **ClassInterfaceType** value that describes which type of interface should be generated for the class.

Requirements

Platforms: Windows 98, Windows NT 4.0, Windows Millennium Edition, Windows 2000, Windows XP Home Edition, Windows XP Professional, Windows .NET Server family

ClassInterfaceType Enumeration

Identifies the type of class interface that is generated for a class.

```
[Visual Basic]
<Serializable>
Public Enum ClassInterfaceType
[C#]
[Serializable]
public enum ClassInterfaceType
[C++]
[Serializable]
__value public enum ClassInterfaceType
[JScript]
public
   Serializable
enum ClassInterfaceType
```

Remarks

This enumeration is used in conjunction with the **ClassInterfaceAttribute**.

Members

Member name	Description
AutoDispatch	Indicates that the class only supports late binding for COM clients. A dispinterface for the class is automatically exposed to COM clients on request. The type library produced by the type **Type Library Exporter (Tlbexp.exe)** does not contain type information for the dispinterface in order to prevent clients from caching the DISPIDs of the interface. The dispinterface does not exhibit the versioning problems described in **ClassInterfaceAttribute** because clients can only late bind to the interface.
	This is the default setting for **ClassInterfaceAttribute**.
AutoDual	Indicates that a dual class interface is automatically generated for the class and exposed to COM. Type information is produced for the class interface and published in the type library. Using **AutoDual** is strongly discouraged because of the versioning limitations described in **ClassInterfaceAttribute**.

Member name	Description
None	Indicates that no class interface is generated for the class. If no interfaces are implemented explicitly, the class can only provide late bound access through the **IDispatch** interface. This is the recommended setting for **ClassInterfaceAttribute**. Using **ClassInterfaceType.None** is the only way to expose functionality through interfaces implemented explicitly by the class.
	The **Type Library Exporter (Tlbexp.exe)** exposes the first public, COM-visible interface implemented by the class as the default interface of the coclass. If the class implements no interfaces, the first public, COM-visible interface implemented by a base class becomes the default interface (starting with the most recently derived base class and working backward). Tlbexp.exe exposes **_Object** as the default interface if neither the class nor its base classes implement interfaces.

Requirements

Namespace: System.Runtime.InteropServices

Platforms: Windows 98, Windows NT 4.0, Windows Millennium Edition, Windows 2000, Windows XP Home Edition, Windows XP Professional, Windows .NET Server family

Assembly: Mscorlib (in Mscorlib.dll)

CoClassAttribute Class

Specifies the class identifier of a coclass imported from a type library.

System.Object
  System.Attribute
    System.Runtime.InteropServices.CoClassAttribute

[Visual Basic]
```
<AttributeUsage(AttributeTargets.Interface)>
NotInheritable Public Class CoClassAttribute
   Inherits Attribute
```
[C#]
```
[AttributeUsage(AttributeTargets.Interface)]
public sealed class CoClassAttribute : Attribute
```
[C++]
```
[AttributeUsage(AttributeTargets::Interface)]
public __gc __sealed class CoClassAttribute : public Attribute
```
[JScript]
```
public
   AttributeUsage(AttributeTargets.Interface)
class CoClassAttribute extends Attribute
```

Thread Safety

Any public static (**Shared** in Visual Basic) members of this type are safe for multithreaded operations. Any instance members are not guaranteed to be thread safe.

Remarks

You can apply this attribute to coclass interfaces, although the **Type Library Importer (Tlbimp.exe)** typically applies it for you when it imports a type library.

When Tlbimp.exe imports a coclass, it produces a managed class and an interface to represent the coclass. The coclass interface has the same interface identifier (IID) as the default interface of the original coclass. The imported coclass interface also retains the name of the coclass. Tlbimp.exe appends the original coclass name with "class" to identify the imported class.

You rarely apply this attribute. However, if plan to write source code that produces metadata that closely simulates metadata produced by Tlbimp.exe, you should create a coclass interface for each coclass. Use the name of the original coclass to name the coclass interface and derive it from the default interface. In addition to the **CoClassAttribute**, you must also apply the **System.Runtime.InteropServices.ComImportAttribute** and **System.Runtime.InteropServices.GuidAttribute** to the coclass interface.

Requirements

Namespace: System.Runtime.InteropServices

Platforms: Windows 98, Windows NT 4.0, Windows Millennium Edition, Windows 2000, Windows XP Home Edition, Windows XP Professional, Windows .NET Server family

Assembly: Mscorlib (in Mscorlib.dll)

CoClassAttribute Constructor

Initializes new instance of the **CoClassAttribute** with the class identifier of the original coclass.

[Visual Basic]
```
Public Sub New( _
   ByVal coClass As Type _
)
```
[C#]
```
public CoClassAttribute(
   Type coClass
);
```
[C++]
```
public: CoClassAttribute(
   Type* coClass
);
```
[JScript]
```
public function CoClassAttribute(
   coClass : Type
);
```

Parameters

coClass
    A **Type** that contains the class identifier of the original coclass.

Requirements

Platforms: Windows 98, Windows NT 4.0, Windows Millennium Edition, Windows 2000, Windows XP Home Edition, Windows XP Professional, Windows .NET Server family

CoClassAttribute.CoClass Property

Gets the class identifier of the original coclass.

[Visual Basic]
```
Public ReadOnly Property CoClass As Type
```
[C#]
```
public Type CoClass {get;}
```
[C++]
```
public: __property Type* get_CoClass();
```
[JScript]
```
public function get CoClass() : Type;
```

Property Value

A **Type** containing the class identifier of the original coclass.

Requirements

Platforms: Windows 98, Windows NT 4.0, Windows Millennium Edition, Windows 2000, Windows XP Home Edition, Windows XP Professional, Windows .NET Server family

ComAliasNameAttribute Class

Indicates the COM alias for a parameter or field type.

System.Object
  System.Attribute
    System.Runtime.InteropServices.ComAliasNameAttribute

```
[Visual Basic]
<AttributeUsage(AttributeTargets.Property Or AttributeTargets.Field _
   Or AttributeTargets.Parameter Or AttributeTargets.ReturnValue)>
NotInheritable Public Class ComAliasNameAttribute
   Inherits Attribute
[C#]
[AttributeUsage(AttributeTargets.Property | AttributeTargets.Field
   | AttributeTargets.Parameter | AttributeTargets.ReturnValue)]
public sealed class ComAliasNameAttribute : Attribute
[C++]
[AttributeUsage(AttributeTargets::Property |
   AttributeTargets::Field | AttributeTargets::Parameter |
   AttributeTargets::ReturnValue)]
public __gc __sealed class ComAliasNameAttribute : public
   Attribute
[JScript]
public
   AttributeUsage(AttributeTargets.Property | AttributeTargets.Field |
   AttributeTargets.Parameter | AttributeTargets.ReturnValue)
class ComAliasNameAttribute extends Attribute
```

Thread Safety

Any public static (**Shared** in Visual Basic) members of this type are
safe for multithreaded operations. Any instance members are not
guaranteed to be thread safe.

Remarks

You can apply this attribute to parameters, fields, properties, or
return values.

Example

[Visual Basic, C#] In the following type library, OLE_COLOR is an
alias for int. During import the arguments of the Color accessor are
marked with the **ComAliasNameAttribute** to indicate that type
library refers to them as OLE_COLOR.

```
typedef int OLE_COLOR;

interface Baz {
  HRESULT SetColor([in] OLE_COLOR cl);
  HRESULT GetColor([out, retval] OLE_COLOR *cl);
}
```

[Visual Basic, C#] imported as:

```
[Visual Basic]
Interface Baz
   Sub SetColor( <ComAliasName("stdole.OLE_COLOR")> cl As Integer)
   Function GetColor() As <ComAliasName("stdole.OLE_COLOR")> Integer
End Interface
```

```
[C#]
interface Baz {
  void SetColor([ComAliasName("stdole.OLE_COLOR")] int cl);
  [return: ComAliasName("stdole.OLE_COLOR")] int GetColor();
}
```

[C++, JScript] No example is available for C++ or JScript. To view a
Visual Basic or C# example, click the Language Filter button <IMG
SRC="filter1a.gif" ALT="Language Filter" BORDER=0> in the
upper-left corner of the page.

Requirements

Namespace: System.Runtime.InteropServices

Platforms: Windows 98, Windows NT 4.0,
Windows Millennium Edition, Windows 2000,
Windows XP Home Edition, Windows XP Professional,
Windows .NET Server family

Assembly: Mscorlib (in Mscorlib.dll)

ComAliasNameAttribute Constructor

Initializes a new instance of the **ComAliasNameAttribute** class
with the alias for the attributed field or parameter.

```
[Visual Basic]
Public Sub New( _
   ByVal alias As String _
)
[C#]
public ComAliasNameAttribute(
   string alias
);
[C++]
public: ComAliasNameAttribute(
   String* alias
);
[JScript]
public function ComAliasNameAttribute(
   alias : String
);
```

Parameters

alias
  The alias for the field or parameter as found in the type library
  when it was imported.

Requirements

Platforms: Windows 98, Windows NT 4.0,
Windows Millennium Edition, Windows 2000,
Windows XP Home Edition, Windows XP Professional,
Windows .NET Server family

ComAliasNameAttribute.Value Property

Gets the alias for the field or parameter as found in the type library
when it was imported.

```
[Visual Basic]
Public ReadOnly Property Value As String
[C#]
public string Value {get;}
[C++]
public: __property String* get_Value();
[JScript]
public function get Value() : String;
```

Property Value

The alias for the field or parameter as found in the type library when
it was imported.

Requirements

Platforms: Windows 98, Windows NT 4.0,
Windows Millennium Edition, Windows 2000,
Windows XP Home Edition, Windows XP Professional,
Windows .NET Server family

ComCompatibleVersion-Attribute Class

Note: This namespace, class, or member is supported only in version 1.1 of the .NET Framework

Indicates to a COM client that all classes in the current version of an assembly are compatible with classes in an earlier version of the assembly.

System.Object
  System.Attribute
    System.Runtime.InteropServices.ComCompatibleVersion-Attribute

[Visual Basic]
```
<AttributeUsage(AttributeTargets.Assembly)>
NotInheritable Public Class ComCompatibleVersionAttribute
   Inherits Attribute
```
[C#]
```
[AttributeUsage(AttributeTargets.Assembly)]
public sealed class ComCompatibleVersionAttribute : Attribute
```
[C++]
```
[AttributeUsage(AttributeTargets::Assembly)]
public __gc __sealed class ComCompatibleVersionAttribute : public
   Attribute
```
[JScript]
```
public
   AttributeUsage(AttributeTargets.Assembly)
class ComCompatibleVersionAttribute extends Attribute
```

Thread Safety

Any public static (**Shared** in Visual Basic) members of this type are safe for multithreaded operations. Any instance members are not guaranteed to be thread safe.

Remarks

You can apply this attribute to assemblies.

By default, the **Type Library Exporter (Tlbexp.exe)** uses an assembly's version number to calculate class identifiers (CLSIDs). All public, COM-visible classes receive new CLSIDs each time you export a new assembly version.

You can apply the **System.Runtime.InteropServices.ComCompatibleVersionAttribute.ComCompatibleVersionAttribute** attribute to force all CLSIDs for classes in the current version of an assembly to be the same as CLSIDs for classes in an earlier version of the assembly. As long as the CLSIDs remain the same, a legacy COM application can use the later version of a compatible assembly after you uninstall the original assembly. If you apply the **System.Runtime.InteropServices.GuidAttribute** to a class to explicitly set its CLSID, the **System.Runtime.InteropServices.ComCompatibleAttribute** has no effect.

The properties of this attribute combine to form the four parts of an assembly version. Always specify the lowest version that the current assembly is backward compatible with so that version is used to calculate all CLSIDs in the assembly.

Example

[Visual Basic, C#] The following example shows how to specify assembly version 1.0.0.0 in an assembly with a higher version number. Regardless of the new assembly version, all CLSIDs in the

assembly are generated using version 1.0.0.0 instead of using the current assembly version.

[Visual Basic]
```
Imports System
Imports System.Runtime.Interop
Assembly: AssemblyVersion ("3.0.0.0")
Assembly: ComCompatibleVersionAttribute(1,0,0,0)
Module MyNamespace
   Public Class MyClass
      ' Insert code.
   End Class
```

[C#]
```
using System;
using System.Runtime.InteropServices;
[Assembly: AssemblyVersion ("3.0.0.0")]
[Assembly: ComCompatibleVersion(1,0,0,0)]
namespace MyNamespace
{
   class MyClass
   {
      // Insert code.
   }
}
```

[C++, JScript] No example is available for C++ or JScript. To view a Visual Basic or C# example, click the Language Filter button <IMG SRC="filter1a.gif" ALT="Language Filter" BORDER=0> in the upper-left corner of the page.

Requirements

Namespace: System.Runtime.InteropServices

Platforms: Windows 98, Windows NT 4.0, Windows Millennium Edition, Windows 2000, Windows XP Home Edition, Windows XP Professional, Windows .NET Server family

Assembly: Mscorlib (in Mscorlib.dll)

ComCompatibleVersionAttribute Constructor

Note: This namespace, class, or member is supported only in version 1.1 of the .NET Framework

Initializes a new instance of the **ComCompatibleVersionAttribute** class with the major version, minor version, build, and revision numbers of the assembly.

[Visual Basic]
```
Public Sub New( _
   ByVal major As Integer, _
   ByVal minor As Integer, _
   ByVal build As Integer, _
   ByVal revision As Integer _
)
```
[C#]
```
public ComCompatibleVersionAttribute(
   int major,
   int minor,
   int build,
   int revision
);
```
[C++]
```
public: ComCompatibleVersionAttribute(
   int major,
   int minor,
```

```
    int build,
    int revision
);
[JScript]
public function ComCompatibleVersionAttribute(
    major : int,
    minor : int,
    build : int,
    revision : int
);
```

Parameters

major
  The major version number of the assembly.
minor
  The minor version number of the assembly.
build
  The build number of the assembly.
revision
  The revision number of the assembly.

Requirements

Platforms: Windows 98, Windows NT 4.0,
Windows Millennium Edition, Windows 2000,
Windows XP Home Edition, Windows XP Professional,
Windows .NET Server family

ComCompatibleVersionAttribute.BuildNumber Property

Note: This namespace, class, or member is supported only in
version 1.1 of the .NET Framework

Gets the build number of the assembly.

```
[Visual Basic]
Public ReadOnly Property BuildNumber As Integer
[C#]
public int BuildNumber {get;}
[C++]
public: __property int get_BuildNumber();
[JScript]
public function get BuildNumber() : int;
```

Property Value

The build number of the assembly.

Requirements

Platforms: Windows 98, Windows NT 4.0,
Windows Millennium Edition, Windows 2000,
Windows XP Home Edition, Windows XP Professional,
Windows .NET Server family

ComCompatibleVersionAttribute.MajorVersion Property

Note: This namespace, class, or member is supported only in
version 1.1 of the .NET Framework

Gets the major version number of the assembly.

```
[Visual Basic]
Public ReadOnly Property MajorVersion As Integer
[C#]
public int MajorVersion {get;}
```

```
[C++]
public: __property int get_MajorVersion();
[JScript]
public function get MajorVersion() : int;
```

Property Value

The major version number of the assembly.

Requirements

Platforms: Windows 98, Windows NT 4.0,
Windows Millennium Edition, Windows 2000,
Windows XP Home Edition, Windows XP Professional,
Windows .NET Server family

ComCompatibleVersionAttribute.MinorVersion Property

Note: This namespace, class, or member is supported only in
version 1.1 of the .NET Framework

Gets the minor version number of the assembly.

```
[Visual Basic]
Public ReadOnly Property MinorVersion As Integer
[C#]
public int MinorVersion {get;}
[C++]
public: __property int get_MinorVersion();
[JScript]
public function get MinorVersion() : int;
```

Property Value

The minor version number of the assembly.

Requirements

Platforms: Windows 98, Windows NT 4.0,
Windows Millennium Edition, Windows 2000,
Windows XP Home Edition, Windows XP Professional,
Windows .NET Server family

ComCompatibleVersionAttribute.RevisionNumber Property

Note: This namespace, class, or member is supported only in
version 1.1 of the .NET Framework

Gets the revision number of the assembly.

```
[Visual Basic]
Public ReadOnly Property RevisionNumber As Integer
[C#]
public int RevisionNumber {get;}
[C++]
public: __property int get_RevisionNumber();
[JScript]
public function get RevisionNumber() : int;
```

Property Value

The revision number of the assembly.

Requirements

Platforms: Windows 98, Windows NT 4.0,
Windows Millennium Edition, Windows 2000,
Windows XP Home Edition, Windows XP Professional,
Windows .NET Server family

ComConversionLossAttribute Class

Indicates that information was lost about a class or interface when it was imported from a type library to an assembly.

System.Object
  System.Attribute
    System.Runtime.InteropServices.ComConversionLoss-
    Attribute

```
[Visual Basic]
<AttributeUsage(AttributeTargets.All)>
NotInheritable Public Class ComConversionLossAttribute
   Inherits Attribute
[C#]
[AttributeUsage(AttributeTargets.All)]
public sealed class ComConversionLossAttribute : Attribute
[C++]
[AttributeUsage(AttributeTargets::All)]
public __gc __sealed class ComConversionLossAttribute : public
   Attribute
[JScript]
public
   AttributeUsage(AttributeTargets.All)
class ComConversionLossAttribute extends Attribute
```

Thread Safety

Any public static (**Shared** in Visual Basic) members of this type are safe for multithreaded operations. Any instance members are not guaranteed to be thread safe.

Remarks

The **Type Library Importer (Tlbimp.exe)** applies this attribute to classes or interfaces.

Methods that use **void** pointer arguments cause this attribute to be applied to the containing class or interface.

Requirements

Namespace: System.Runtime.InteropServices

Platforms: Windows 98, Windows NT 4.0, Windows Millennium Edition, Windows 2000, Windows XP Home Edition, Windows XP Professional, Windows .NET Server family

Assembly: Mscorlib (in Mscorlib.dll)

ComConversionLossAttribute Constructor

Initializes a new instance of the **ComConversionLossAttribute** class.

```
[Visual Basic]
Public Sub New()
[C#]
public ComConversionLossAttribute();
[C++]
public: ComConversionLossAttribute();
[JScript]
public function ComConversionLossAttribute();
```

Requirements

Platforms: Windows 98, Windows NT 4.0, Windows Millennium Edition, Windows 2000, Windows XP Home Edition, Windows XP Professional, Windows .NET Server family

ComEventInterfaceAttribute Class

Identifies the source interface and the class that implements the methods of the event interface that is generated when a coclass is imported from a COM type library.

System.Object
  System.Attribute
    System.Runtime.InteropServices.ComEventInterface-
    Attribute

```
[Visual Basic]
<AttributeUsage(AttributeTargets.Interface)>
NotInheritable Public Class ComEventInterfaceAttribute
    Inherits Attribute
[C#]
[AttributeUsage(AttributeTargets.Interface)]
public sealed class ComEventInterfaceAttribute : Attribute
[C++]
[AttributeUsage(AttributeTargets::Interface)]
public __gc __sealed class ComEventInterfaceAttribute : public
    Attribute
[JScript]
public
    AttributeUsage(AttributeTargets.Interface)
class ComEventInterfaceAttribute extends Attribute
```

Thread Safety

Any public static (**Shared** in Visual Basic) members of this type are safe for multithreaded operations. Any instance members are not guaranteed to be thread safe.

Remarks

You can apply this attribute to interfaces, although the **Type Library Importer (Tlbimp.exe)** typically applies it for you when it imports a type library.

When a source interface is imported from a type library, any methods it implements are added as events to a generated event interface. Tlbimp.exe applies **ComEventInterfaceAttribute** to the event interface to identify the managed class that implements the methods of the event interface and implements the original source interface. The common language runtime uses this attribute at run time to perform the following tasks:

- Associate events exposed by the interface to their implementation in the event provider class.
- Link the events to the original COM source interface.

You rarely apply this attribute. However, if you plan to write source code that produces metadata that closely simulates metadata produced by Tlbimp.exe, you should create a event interface for each original source interface.

Requirements

Namespace: System.Runtime.InteropServices

Platforms: Windows 98, Windows NT 4.0, Windows Millennium Edition, Windows 2000, Windows XP Home Edition, Windows XP Professional, Windows .NET Server family

Assembly: Mscorlib (in Mscorlib.dll)

ComEventInterfaceAttribute Constructor

Initializes a new instance of the **ComEventInterfaceAttribute** class with the source interface and event provider class.

```
[Visual Basic]
Public Sub New( _
    ByVal SourceInterface As Type, _
    ByVal EventProvider As Type _
)
[C#]
public ComEventInterfaceAttribute(
    Type SourceInterface,
    Type EventProvider
);
[C++]
public: ComEventInterfaceAttribute(
    Type* SourceInterface,
    Type* EventProvider
);
[JScript]
public function ComEventInterfaceAttribute(
    SourceInterface : Type,
    EventProvider : Type
);
```

Parameters

SourceInterface
  A **Type** that contains the original source interface from the type library. COM uses this interface to call back to the managed class.
EventProvider
  A **Type** that contains the class that implements the methods of the event interface.

Requirements

Platforms: Windows 98, Windows NT 4.0, Windows Millennium Edition, Windows 2000, Windows XP Home Edition, Windows XP Professional, Windows .NET Server family

ComEventInterfaceAttribute.EventProvider Property

Gets the class that implements the methods of the event interface.

```
[Visual Basic]
Public ReadOnly Property EventProvider As Type
[C#]
public Type EventProvider {get;}
[C++]
public: __property Type* get_EventProvider();
[JScript]
public function get EventProvider() : Type;
```

Property Value

A **Type** that contains the class that implements the methods of the event interface.

Remarks

This value is set to the type of the event provider class generated by the **Type Library Importer (Tlbimp.exe)**. Tlbimp.exe appends the source interface name with EventProvider. For example, IMyInterface becomes IMyInterfaceEventProvider.

Requirements

Platforms: Windows 98, Windows NT 4.0, Windows Millennium Edition, Windows 2000, Windows XP Home Edition, Windows XP Professional, Windows .NET Server family

ComEventInterfaceAttribute.SourceInterface Property

Gets the original source interface from the type library.

```
[Visual Basic]
Public ReadOnly Property SourceInterface As Type
[C#]
public Type SourceInterface {get;}
[C++]
public: __property Type* get_SourceInterface();
[JScript]
public function get SourceInterface() : Type;
```

Property Value

A **Type** containing the source interface.

Remarks

A source interface has at least one event member, and typically one for each method of the source interface. COM uses this interface to call back to the managed class.

Requirements

Platforms: Windows 98, Windows NT 4.0, Windows Millennium Edition, Windows 2000, Windows XP Home Edition, Windows XP Professional, Windows .NET Server family

COMException Class

The exception that is thrown when an unrecognized HRESULT is returned from a COM method call.

System.Object
  System.Exception
    System.SystemException
      System.Runtime.InteropServices.ExternalException
        System.Runtime.InteropServices.COMException

```
[Visual Basic]
<Serializable>
Public Class COMException
    Inherits ExternalException
[C#]
[Serializable]
public class COMException : ExternalException
[C++]
[Serializable]
public __gc class COMException : public ExternalException
[JScript]
public
    Serializable
class COMException extends ExternalException
```

Thread Safety

Any public static (**Shared** in Visual Basic) members of this type are safe for multithreaded operations. Any instance members are not guaranteed to be thread safe.

Remarks

The common language runtime transforms well-known HRESULTs to .NET exceptions, enabling COM objects to return meaningful error information to managed clients. The HRESULT to exception mapping also works in the other direction by returning specific HRESULTs to unmanaged clients. For mapping details, see **HRESULTs and Exceptions**.

When the runtime encounters an unfamiliar HRESULT (an HRESULT that lacks a specific, corresponding exception), it throws an instance of the **COMException** class. This all-purpose exception exposes the same members as any exception, and includes a public **ErrorCode** property that contains the HRESULT returned by the callee. If an error message is available to the runtime (obtained from the **IErrorInfo** interface or the **Err** object in Visual Basic, or in some cases from the operating system), the message is returned to the caller. However, if the COM component developer fails to include an error message, the runtime returns the eight-digit HRESULT in place of a message string. Having an HRESULT allows the caller to determine the cause of the generic exception.

Although you can use the **COMException** class to return specific HRESULTs to unmanaged clients, throwing a specific .NET exception is better than using a generic exception. Consider that managed clients as well as unmanaged clients can use your .NET object, and throwing an HRESULT to a managed caller is less comprehendible than throwing an exception.

Requirements

Namespace: System.Runtime.InteropServices

Platforms: Windows 98, Windows NT 4.0, Windows Millennium Edition, Windows 2000, Windows XP Home Edition, Windows XP Professional, Windows .NET Server family

Assembly: Mscorlib (in Mscorlib.dll)

COMException Constructor

Initializes a new instance of the **COMException** class.

Overload List

Initializes a new instance of the **COMException** class with default values.

> [Visual Basic] **Public Sub New()**
> [C#] **public COMException();**
> [C++] **public: COMException();**
> [JScript] **public function COMException();**

Initializes a new instance of the **COMException** class with a specified message.

> [Visual Basic] **Public Sub New(String)**
> [C#] **public COMException(string);**
> [C++] **public: COMException(String*);**
> [JScript] **public function COMException(String);**

Initializes a new instance of the **COMException** class from serialization data.

> [Visual Basic] **Protected Sub New(SerializationInfo, StreamingContext)**
> [C#] **protected COMException(SerializationInfo, StreamingContext);**
> [C++] **protected: COMException(SerializationInfo*, StreamingContext);**
> [JScript] **protected function COMException(Serialization-Info, StreamingContext);**

Initializes a new instance of the **COMException** class with a specified error message and a reference to the inner exception that is the cause of this exception.

> [Visual Basic] **Public Sub New(String, Exception)**
> [C#] **public COMException(string, Exception);**
> [C++] **public: COMException(String*, Exception*);**
> [JScript] **public function COMException(String, Exception);**

Initializes a new instance of the **COMException** class with a specified message and error code.

> [Visual Basic] **Public Sub New(String, Integer)**
> [C#] **public COMException(string, int);**
> [C++] **public: COMException(String*, int);**
> [JScript] **public function COMException(String, int);**

COMException Constructor ()

Initializes a new instance of the **COMException** class with default values.

```
[Visual Basic]
Public Sub New()
[C#]
public COMException();
[C++]
public: COMException();
[JScript]
public function COMException();
```

Remarks

COMException inherits from **ExternalException**. The following table shows how this constructor sets the properties of the **Exception** object.

Property	Value
InnerException	A null reference (**Nothing** in Visual Basic).
Message	A localized error message string.

Requirements

Platforms: Windows 98, Windows NT 4.0, Windows Millennium Edition, Windows 2000, Windows XP Home Edition, Windows XP Professional, Windows .NET Server family

COMException Constructor (String)

Initializes a new instance of the **COMException** class with a specified message.

```
[Visual Basic]
Public Sub New( _
   ByVal message As String _
)
[C#]
public COMException(
   string message
);
[C++]
public: COMException(
   String* message
);
[JScript]
public function COMException(
   message : String
);
```

Parameters

message
   The message that indicates the reason for the exception.

Remarks

COMException inherits from **ExternalException**. The following table shows how this constructor sets the properties of the **Exception** object.

Property	Value
InnerException	A null reference (**Nothing** in Visual Basic)
Message	*message*

Requirements

Platforms: Windows 98, Windows NT 4.0, Windows Millennium Edition, Windows 2000, Windows XP Home Edition, Windows XP Professional, Windows .NET Server family

COMException Constructor (SerializationInfo, StreamingContext)

Initializes a new instance of the **COMException** class from serialization data.

```
[Visual Basic]
Protected Sub New( _
   ByVal info As SerializationInfo, _
   ByVal context As StreamingContext _
)
[C#]
protected COMException(
   SerializationInfo info,
   StreamingContext context
);
[C++]
protected: COMException(
   SerializationInfo* info,
   StreamingContext context
);
[JScript]
protected function COMException(
   info : SerializationInfo,
   context : StreamingContext
);
```

Parameters

info
   The **SerializationInfo** object that holds the serialized object data.
context
   The **StreamingContext** object that supplies the contextual information about the source or destination.

Exceptions

Exception Type	Condition
ArgumentNullException	*info* is a null reference (**Nothing** in Visual Basic).

Remarks

This constructor is called during deserialization to reconstitute the exception object transmitted over a stream. For more information, see **XML and SOAP Serialization**.

COMException inherits from **ExternalException**.

Requirements

Platforms: Windows 98, Windows NT 4.0, Windows Millennium Edition, Windows 2000, Windows XP Home Edition, Windows XP Professional, Windows .NET Server family

COMException Constructor (String, Exception)

Initializes a new instance of the **COMException** class with a specified error message and a reference to the inner exception that is the cause of this exception.

```
[Visual Basic]
Public Sub New( _
   ByVal message As String, _
   ByVal inner As Exception _
)
```

```
[C#]
public COMException(
    string message,
    Exception inner
);
[C++]
public: COMException(
    String* message,
    Exception* inner
);
[JScript]
public function COMException(
    message : String,
    inner : Exception
);
```

Parameters

message
    The error message that explains the reason for the exception.
inner
    The exception that is the cause of the current exception. If the *inner* parameter is not a null reference (**Nothing** in Visual Basic), the current exception is raised in a **catch** block that handles the inner exception.

Remarks

An exception that is thrown as a direct result of a previous exception should include a reference to the previous exception in the **InnerException** property. The **InnerException** property returns the same value that is passed into the constructor, or a null reference (**Nothing** in Visual Basic) if the **InnerException** property does not supply the inner exception value to the constructor.

The following table shows how this constructor sets the properties of the **Exception** object.

Property	Value
InnerException	The inner exception reference.
Message	The error message string.

Requirements

Platforms: Windows 98, Windows NT 4.0, Windows Millennium Edition, Windows 2000, Windows XP Home Edition, Windows XP Professional, Windows .NET Server family

COMException Constructor (String, Int32)

Initializes a new instance of the **COMException** class with a specified message and error code.

```
[Visual Basic]
Public Sub New( _
    ByVal message As String, _
    ByVal errorCode As Integer _
)
[C#]
public COMException(
    string message,
    int errorCode
);
```

```
[C++]
public: COMException(
    String* message,
    int errorCode
);
[JScript]
public function COMException(
    message : String,
    errorCode : int
);
```

Parameters

message
    The message that indicates the reason the exception occurred.
errorCode
    The error code (HRESULT) value associated with this exception.

Remarks

This **COMException** constructor sets the base message with the error code. **COMException** inherits from **ExternalException**. The following table shows how this constructor sets the properties of the **Exception** object.

Property	Value
InnerException	A null reference (**Nothing** in Visual Basic)
Message	*message*

Requirements

Platforms: Windows 98, Windows NT 4.0, Windows Millennium Edition, Windows 2000, Windows XP Home Edition, Windows XP Professional, Windows .NET Server family

COMException.ToString Method

Converts the contents of the exception to a string.

```
[Visual Basic]
Overrides Public Function ToString() As String
[C#]
public override string ToString();
[C++]
public: String* ToString();
[JScript]
public override function ToString() : String;
```

Return Value

A string containing the **HResult**, **Message**, **InnerException**, and **StackTrace** properties of the exception.

Requirements

Platforms: Windows 98, Windows NT 4.0, Windows Millennium Edition, Windows 2000, Windows XP Home Edition, Windows XP Professional, Windows .NET Server family

ComImportAttribute Class

Indicates that the attributed type was previously defined in COM.

System.Object
  System.Attribute
    System.Runtime.InteropServices.ComImportAttribute

```
[Visual Basic]
<AttributeUsage(AttributeTargets.Class Or _
    AttributeTargets.Interface)>
NotInheritable Public Class ComImportAttribute
    Inherits Attribute
[C#]
[AttributeUsage(AttributeTargets.Class |
    AttributeTargets.Interface)]
public sealed class ComImportAttribute : Attribute
[C++]
[AttributeUsage(AttributeTargets::Class |
    AttributeTargets::Interface)]
public __gc __sealed class ComImportAttribute : public Attribute
[JScript]
public
    AttributeUsage(AttributeTargets.Class | AttributeTargets.Interface)
class ComImportAttribute extends Attribute
```

Thread Safety

Any public static (**Shared** in Visual Basic) members of this type are safe for multithreaded operations. Any instance members are not guaranteed to be thread safe.

Remarks

You can apply this attribute to classes or interfaces, although the **Type Library Importer (Tlbimp.exe)** typically applies it for you when it imports a type library.

ComImportAttribute is a pseudo-custom attribute that indicates that a type has been defined in a previously published type library. The common language runtime treats these types differently when activating, exporting, coercing, and so on.

A pseudo-custom attribute indicates that bits of the core metadata of a type need to be set when the attribute is present. Unlike a custom attribute that extends the metadata for a type and is saved along with the type, a pseudo-custom attribute modifies the metadata for the type and is discarded.

Requirements

Namespace: System.Runtime.InteropServices

Platforms: Windows 98, Windows NT 4.0, Windows Millennium Edition, Windows 2000, Windows XP Home Edition, Windows XP Professional, Windows .NET Server family

Assembly: Mscorlib (in Mscorlib.dll)

ComImportAttribute Constructor

Initializes a new instance of the **ComImportAttribute**.

```
[Visual Basic]
Public Sub New()
[C#]
public ComImportAttribute();
[C++]
public: ComImportAttribute();
[JScript]
public function ComImportAttribute();
```

Requirements

Platforms: Windows 98, Windows NT 4.0, Windows Millennium Edition, Windows 2000, Windows XP Home Edition, Windows XP Professional, Windows .NET Server family

ComInterfaceType Enumeration

Identifies how to expose an interface to COM.

```
[Visual Basic]
<Serializable>
Public Enum ComInterfaceType
[C#]
[Serializable]
public enum ComInterfaceType
[C++]
[Serializable]
__value public enum ComInterfaceType
[JScript]
public
   Serializable
enum ComInterfaceType
```

Remarks

This enumeration works in conjuction with
InterfaceTypeAttribute.

Members

Member name	Description
InterfaceIsDual	Indicates the interface is exposed to COM as a dual interface, which enables both early and late binding. **InterfaceIsDual** is the default value.
InterfaceIsIDispatch	Indicates an interface is exposed to COM as a dispinterface, which enables late binding only.
InterfaceIsIUnknown	Indicates an interface is exposed to COM as an **IUnknown**-derived interface, which enables only early binding.

Requirements

Namespace: System.Runtime.InteropServices

Platforms: Windows 98, Windows NT 4.0,
Windows Millennium Edition, Windows 2000,
Windows XP Home Edition, Windows XP Professional,
Windows .NET Server family

Assembly: Mscorlib (in Mscorlib.dll)

ComMemberType Enumeration

Describes the type of a COM member.

```
[Visual Basic]
<Serializable>
Public Enum ComMemberType
[C#]
[Serializable]
public enum ComMemberType
[C++]
[Serializable]
__value public enum ComMemberType
[JScript]
public
   Serializable
enum ComMemberType
```

Members

Member name	Description
Method	The member is a normal method.
PropGet	The member gets properties.
PropSet	The member sets properties.

Requirements

Namespace: System.Runtime.InteropServices

Platforms: Windows 98, Windows NT 4.0, Windows Millennium Edition, Windows 2000, Windows XP Home Edition, Windows XP Professional, Windows .NET Server family

Assembly: Mscorlib (in Mscorlib.dll)

ComRegisterFunctionAttribute Class

Specifies the method to call when you register an assembly for use from COM; this allows for the execution of user-written code during the registration process.

System.Object
  System.Attribute
    System.Runtime.InteropServices.ComRegisterFunction-
    Attribute

```
[Visual Basic]
<AttributeUsage(AttributeTargets.Method)>
NotInheritable Public Class ComRegisterFunctionAttribute
    Inherits Attribute
[C#]
[AttributeUsage(AttributeTargets.Method)]
public sealed class ComRegisterFunctionAttribute : Attribute
[C++]
[AttributeUsage(AttributeTargets::Method)]
public __gc __sealed class ComRegisterFunctionAttribute : public
    Attribute
[JScript]
public
    AttributeUsage(AttributeTargets.Method)
class ComRegisterFunctionAttribute extends Attribute
```

Thread Safety

Any public static (**Shared** in Visual Basic) members of this type are safe for multithreaded operations. Any instance members are not guaranteed to be thread safe.

Remarks

You can apply this attribute to methods.

ComRegisterFunctionAttribute enables you to add arbitrary registration code to accommodate the requirements of COM clients. For example, you can update the registry using registration functions from the **Microsoft.Win32** namespace. If you provide a registration method, you must also apply **System.Runtime.InteropServices.ComUnregisterFunctionAttribute** to an unregistration method, which reverses the operations done in the registration method.

The common language runtime calls the method with this attribute when its containing assembly is registered (directly or indirectly) with the **Assembly Registration Tool (Regasm.exe)** or through the **RegistrationServices.RegisterAssembly** API method. Methods with this attribute can have any visibility (public, private, and so on), but must be static (**Shared** in Visual Basic) and must take a single **Type** parameter for the type to register.

Example

[Visual Basic, C#, JScript] The following example demonstrates how to apply **ComRegisterFunctionAttribute** and **ComUnregisterFunctionAttribute** to methods with the appropriate signature.

```
[Visual Basic]
Imports System
Imports System.Runtime.InteropServices

Public Class MyClassThatNeedsToRegister

    <ComRegisterFunctionAttribute()> Public Shared Sub _
        RegisterFunction(t As Type)
        'Insert code here.
    End Sub

    <ComUnregisterFunctionAttribute()> Public Shared Sub _
        UnregisterFunction(t As Type)
        'Insert code here.
    End Sub
End Class

[C#]
using System;
using System.Runtime.InteropServices;

public class MyClassThatNeedsToRegister
{
    [ComRegisterFunctionAttribute]
    public static void RegisterFunction(Type t)
    {
        //Insert code here.
    }

    [ComUnregisterFunctionAttribute]
    public static void UnregisterFunction(Type t)
    {
        //Insert code here.
    }
}

[JScript]
import System;
import System.Runtime.InteropServices;

public class MyClassThatNeedsToRegister
{
    ComRegisterFunctionAttribute public static function
RegisterFunction(t : Type) : void
    {
        //Insert code here.
    }

    ComUnregisterFunctionAttribute public static function
UnregisterFunction(t : Type) : void
    {
        //Insert code here.
    }
}
```

Requirements

Namespace: System.Runtime.InteropServices

Platforms: Windows 98, Windows NT 4.0, Windows Millennium Edition, Windows 2000, Windows XP Home Edition, Windows XP Professional, Windows .NET Server family

Assembly: Mscorlib (in Mscorlib.dll)

ComRegisterFunctionAttribute Constructor

Initializes a new instance of the **ComRegisterFunctionAttribute** class.

```
[Visual Basic]
Public Sub New()
[C#]
public ComRegisterFunctionAttribute();
[C++]
public: ComRegisterFunctionAttribute();
[JScript]
public function ComRegisterFunctionAttribute();
```

Requirements

Platforms: Windows 98, Windows NT 4.0, Windows Millennium Edition, Windows 2000, Windows XP Home Edition, Windows XP Professional, Windows .NET Server family

ComSourceInterfacesAttribute Class

Identifies a list of interfaces that are exposed as COM event sources for the attributed class.

System.Object
  System.Attribute
    System.Runtime.InteropServices.ComSourceInterfaces-
    Attribute

```
[Visual Basic]
<AttributeUsage(AttributeTargets.Class)>
NotInheritable Public Class ComSourceInterfacesAttribute
   Inherits Attribute
[C#]
[AttributeUsage(AttributeTargets.Class)]
public sealed class ComSourceInterfacesAttribute : Attribute
[C++]
[AttributeUsage(AttributeTargets::Class)]
public __gc __sealed class ComSourceInterfacesAttribute : public
   Attribute
[JScript]
public
      AttributeUsage(AttributeTargets.Class)
   class ComSourceInterfacesAttribute extends Attribute
```

Thread Safety

Any public static (**Shared** in Visual Basic) members of this type are safe for multithreaded operations. Any instance members are not guaranteed to be thread safe.

Remarks

You can apply this attribute to classes.

You apply this attribute to a managed class to identify the event interfaces that the class exposes as COM connection points. An event interface contains methods that map to the event members of the class. The class event name and the interface method name must be the same. This attribute can accommodate up to four source interfaces for a class by passing the type of the source interface to the appropriate constructor, which take between one and four type arguments. For classes that want to expose more than four source interfaces, the string version of the constructor can be used

Example

[Visual Basic, C#, JScript] The following example shows how to apply the **ComSourceInterfacesAttribute** to connect the event sink interface to a class by passing the namespace and event sink interface.

```
[Visual Basic]
Imports System.Runtime.InteropServices

<ComSourceInterfacesAttribute("ButtonEventsLib.ButtonEvents,     ⌐
ButtonEventsLib")> _
public Class Baz
   'Insert code here.
End Class

[C#]
using System.Runtime.InteropServices;

[ComSourceInterfacesAttribute("ButtonEventsLib.ButtonEvents,     ⌐
ButtonEventsLib")]
public class Baz
{
```

```
   //Insert code here.
}
[JScript]
import System.Runtime.InteropServices;

ComSourceInterfacesAttribute("ButtonEventsLib.ButtonEvents,      ⌐
ButtonEventsLib") public class Baz
{
   //Insert code here.
}
```

Requirements

Namespace: System.Runtime.InteropServices

Platforms: Windows 98, Windows NT 4.0, Windows Millennium Edition, Windows 2000, Windows XP Home Edition, Windows XP Professional, Windows .NET Server family

Assembly: Mscorlib (in Mscorlib.dll)

ComSourceInterfacesAttribute Constructor

Initializes a new instance of the **ComSourceInterfacesAttribute** class.

Overload List

Initializes a new instance of the **ComSourceInterfacesAttribute** class with the name of the event source interface.

> [Visual Basic] **Public Sub New(String)**
>
> [C#] **public ComSourceInterfacesAttribute(string);**
>
> [C++] **public: ComSourceInterfacesAttribute(String*);**
>
> [JScript] **public function ComSourceInterfacesAttribute(String);**

Initializes a new instance of the **ComSourceInterfacesAttribute** class with the type to use as a source interface.

> [Visual Basic] **Public Sub New(Type)**
>
> [C#] **public ComSourceInterfacesAttribute(Type);**
>
> [C++] **public: ComSourceInterfacesAttribute(Type*);**
>
> [JScript] **public function ComSourceInterfacesAttribute(Type);**

Initializes a new instance of the **ComSourceInterfacesAttribute** class with the types to use as source interfaces.

> [Visual Basic] **Public Sub New(Type, Type)**
>
> [C#] **public ComSourceInterfacesAttribute(Type, Type);**
>
> [C++] **public: ComSourceInterfacesAttribute(Type*, Type*);**
>
> [JScript] **public function ComSourceInterfacesAttribute(Type, Type);**

Initializes a new instance of the **ComSourceInterfacesAttribute** class with the types to use as source interfaces.

> [Visual Basic] **Public Sub New(Type, Type, Type)**
>
> [C#] **public ComSourceInterfacesAttribute(Type, Type, Type);**
>
> [C++] **public: ComSourceInterfacesAttribute(Type*, Type*, Type*);**
>
> [JScript] **public function ComSourceInterfacesAttribute(Type, Type, Type);**

Initializes a new instance of the **ComSourceInterfacesAttribute** class with the types to use as source interfaces.

[Visual Basic] **Public Sub New(Type, Type, Type, Type)**

[C#] **public ComSourceInterfacesAttribute(Type, Type, Type, Type);**

[C++] **public: ComSourceInterfacesAttribute(Type*, Type*, Type*, Type*);**

[JScript] **public function ComSourceInterfacesAttribute(Type, Type, Type, Type);**

ComSourceInterfacesAttribute Constructor (String)

Initializes a new instance of the **ComSourceInterfacesAttribute** class with the name of the event source interface.

```
[Visual Basic]
Public Sub New( _
   ByVal sourceInterfaces As String _
)
[C#]
public ComSourceInterfacesAttribute(
   string sourceInterfaces
);
[C++]
public: ComSourceInterfacesAttribute(
   String* sourceInterfaces
);
[JScript]
public function ComSourceInterfacesAttribute(
   sourceInterfaces : String
);
```

Parameters

sourceInterfaces
   A a null reference (**Nothing** in Visual Basic)-delimited list of fully qualified event source interface names.

Remarks

Use this constructor to expose more than four event source interfaces to COM clients.

Requirements

Platforms: Windows 98, Windows NT 4.0, Windows Millennium Edition, Windows 2000, Windows XP Home Edition, Windows XP Professional, Windows .NET Server family

ComSourceInterfacesAttribute Constructor (Type)

Initializes a new instance of the **ComSourceInterfacesAttribute** class with the type to use as a source interface.

```
[Visual Basic]
Public Sub New( _
   ByVal sourceInterface As Type _
)
[C#]
public ComSourceInterfacesAttribute(
   Type sourceInterface
);
```

```
[C++]
public: ComSourceInterfacesAttribute(
   Type* sourceInterface
);
[JScript]
public function ComSourceInterfacesAttribute(
   sourceInterface : Type
);
```

Parameters

sourceInterface
   The **Type** of the source interface.

Remarks

Use this constructor to expose a single event source interface to COM clients.

Requirements

Platforms: Windows 98, Windows NT 4.0, Windows Millennium Edition, Windows 2000, Windows XP Home Edition, Windows XP Professional, Windows .NET Server family

ComSourceInterfacesAttribute Constructor (Type, Type)

Initializes a new instance of the **ComSourceInterfacesAttribute** class with the types to use as source interfaces.

```
[Visual Basic]
Public Sub New( _
   ByVal sourceInterface1 As Type, _
   ByVal sourceInterface2 As Type _
)
[C#]
public ComSourceInterfacesAttribute(
   Type sourceInterface1,
   Type sourceInterface2
);
[C++]
public: ComSourceInterfacesAttribute(
   Type* sourceInterface1,
   Type* sourceInterface2
);
[JScript]
public function ComSourceInterfacesAttribute(
   sourceInterface1 : Type,
   sourceInterface2 : Type
);
```

Parameters

sourceInterface1
   The **Type** of the default source interface.
sourceInterface2
   The **Type** of a source interface.

Remarks

Use this constructor to expose two event source interfaces to COM clients.

Requirements

Platforms: Windows 98, Windows NT 4.0, Windows Millennium Edition, Windows 2000, Windows XP Home Edition, Windows XP Professional, Windows .NET Server family

ComSourceInterfacesAttribute Constructor (Type, Type, Type)

Initializes a new instance of the **ComSourceInterfacesAttribute** class with the types to use as source interfaces.

```
[Visual Basic]
Public Sub New( _
    ByVal sourceInterface1 As Type, _
    ByVal sourceInterface2 As Type, _
    ByVal sourceInterface3 As Type _
)
[C#]
public ComSourceInterfacesAttribute(
    Type sourceInterface1,
    Type sourceInterface2,
    Type sourceInterface3
);
[C++]
public: ComSourceInterfacesAttribute(
    Type* sourceInterface1,
    Type* sourceInterface2,
    Type* sourceInterface3
);
[JScript]
public function ComSourceInterfacesAttribute(
    sourceInterface1 : Type,
    sourceInterface2 : Type,
    sourceInterface3 : Type
);
```

Parameters

sourceInterface1
　　The **Type** of the default source interface.
sourceInterface2
　　The **Type** of a source interface.
sourceInterface3
　　The **Type** of a source interface.

Remarks

Use this constructor to expose three event source interfaces to COM clients.

Requirements

Platforms: Windows 98, Windows NT 4.0, Windows Millennium Edition, Windows 2000, Windows XP Home Edition, Windows XP Professional, Windows .NET Server family

ComSourceInterfacesAttribute Constructor (Type, Type, Type, Type)

Initializes a new instance of the **ComSourceInterfacesAttribute** class with the types to use as source interfaces.

```
[Visual Basic]
Public Sub New( _
    ByVal sourceInterface1 As Type, _
    ByVal sourceInterface2 As Type, _
    ByVal sourceInterface3 As Type, _
    ByVal sourceInterface4 As Type _
)
[C#]
public ComSourceInterfacesAttribute(
    Type sourceInterface1,
```

```
    Type sourceInterface2,
    Type sourceInterface3,
    Type sourceInterface4
);
[C++]
public: ComSourceInterfacesAttribute(
    Type* sourceInterface1,
    Type* sourceInterface2,
    Type* sourceInterface3,
    Type* sourceInterface4
);
[JScript]
public function ComSourceInterfacesAttribute(
    sourceInterface1 : Type,
    sourceInterface2 : Type,
    sourceInterface3 : Type,
    sourceInterface4 : Type
);
```

Parameters

sourceInterface1
　　The **Type** of the default source interface.
sourceInterface2
　　The **Type** of a source interface.
sourceInterface3
　　The **Type** of a source interface.
sourceInterface4
　　The **Type** of a source interface.

Remarks

Use this constructor to expose four event source interfaces to COM clients.

Requirements

Platforms: Windows 98, Windows NT 4.0, Windows Millennium Edition, Windows 2000, Windows XP Home Edition, Windows XP Professional, Windows .NET Server family

ComSourceInterfacesAttribute.Value Property

Gets the fully qualified name of the event source interface.

```
[Visual Basic]
Public ReadOnly Property Value As String
[C#]
public string Value {get;}
[C++]
public: __property String* get_Value();
[JScript]
public function get Value() : String;
```

Property Value

The fully qualified name of the event source interface.

Remarks

If you specify more than one source interface, the value returned is a a null reference (**Nothing** in Visual Basic)-delimited list of fully qualified event source interface names.

Requirements

Platforms: Windows 98, Windows NT 4.0, Windows Millennium Edition, Windows 2000, Windows XP Home Edition, Windows XP Professional, Windows .NET Server family

ComUnregisterFunction-Attribute Class

Specifies the method to call when you unregister an assembly for use from COM; this allows for the execution of user-written code during the unregistration process.

System.Object
  System.Attribute
    System.Runtime.InteropServices.ComUnregisterFunction-Attribute

[Visual Basic]
```
<AttributeUsage(AttributeTargets.Method)>
NotInheritable Public Class ComUnregisterFunctionAttribute
   Inherits Attribute
```
[C#]
```
[AttributeUsage(AttributeTargets.Method)]
public sealed class ComUnregisterFunctionAttribute : Attribute
```
[C++]
```
[AttributeUsage(AttributeTargets::Method)]
public __gc __sealed class ComUnregisterFunctionAttribute : public
   Attribute
```
[JScript]
```
public
   AttributeUsage(AttributeTargets.Method)
class ComUnregisterFunctionAttribute extends Attribute
```

Thread Safety

Any public static (**Shared** in Visual Basic) members of this type are safe for multithreaded operations. Any instance members are not guaranteed to be thread safe.

Remarks

You can apply this attribute to methods.

ComUnregisterFunctionAttribute enables you to add code that reverses the operations performed by a registration method. If you apply the **ComRegisterFunctionAttribute** to provide a registration method, you must also provide an unregistration method to reverse the operations done in the registration method. You can have only one unregistration method for a class.

The common language runtime calls the method with this attribute when its containing assembly is unregistered (directly or indirectly) with the **Assembly Registration Tool (Regasm.exe)** or through the **RegistrationServices.UnregisterAssembly** API method. Methods with this attribute can have any visibility (public, private, and so on), but must be static (**Shared** in Visual Basic) and must take a single **Type** parameter for the **Type** to unregister.

Example

[Visual Basic, C#, JScript] The following example demonstrates applying **ComRegisterFunctionAttribute** and **ComUnregister-FunctionAttribute** to methods with the appropriate signature.

[Visual Basic]
```
Imports System
Imports System.Runtime.InteropServices

Public Class MyClassThatNeedsToRegister

   <ComRegisterFunctionAttribute()> Public Shared Sub _
      RegisterFunction(t As Type)
         'Insert code here.
   End Sub

   <ComUnregisterFunctionAttribute()> Public Shared Sub _
      UnregisterFunction(t As Type)
```
```
         'Insert code here.
   End Sub
End Class
```
[C#]
```
using System;
using System.Runtime.InteropServices;

public class MyClassThatNeedsToRegister
{
   [ComRegisterFunctionAttribute]
   public static void RegisterFunction(Type t)
   {
      //Insert code here.
   }

   [ComUnregisterFunctionAttribute]
   public static void UnregisterFunction(Type t)
   {
      //Insert code here.
   }
}
```
[JScript]
```
import System;
import System.Runtime.InteropServices;

public class MyClassThatNeedsToRegister
{
   ComRegisterFunctionAttribute public static function
RegisterFunction(t : Type) : void
   {
      //Insert code here.
   }

   ComUnregisterFunctionAttribute public static function
UnregisterFunction(t : Type) : void
   {
      //Insert code here.
   }
}
```

Requirements

Namespace: System.Runtime.InteropServices

Platforms: Windows 98, Windows NT 4.0, Windows Millennium Edition, Windows 2000, Windows XP Home Edition, Windows XP Professional, Windows .NET Server family

Assembly: Mscorlib (in Mscorlib.dll)

ComUnregisterFunctionAttribute Constructor

Initializes a new instance of the **ComUnregisterFunctionAttribute** class.

[Visual Basic]
```
Public Sub New()
```
[C#]
```
public ComUnregisterFunctionAttribute();
```
[C++]
```
public: ComUnregisterFunctionAttribute();
```
[JScript]
```
public function ComUnregisterFunctionAttribute();
```

Requirements

Platforms: Windows 98, Windows NT 4.0, Windows Millennium Edition, Windows 2000, Windows XP Home Edition, Windows XP Professional, Windows .NET Server family

ComVisibleAttribute Class

Controls accessibility of an individual managed type or member, or of all types within an assembly, to COM.

System.Object
  System.Attribute
    System.Runtime.InteropServices.ComVisibleAttribute

```
[Visual Basic]
<AttributeUsage(AttributeTargets.Assembly Or AttributeTargets.Class _
   Or AttributeTargets.Struct Or AttributeTargets.Enum Or _
   AttributeTargets.Method Or AttributeTargets.Property Or _
   AttributeTargets.Field Or AttributeTargets.Interface Or _
   AttributeTargets.Delegate)>
NotInheritable Public Class ComVisibleAttribute
   Inherits Attribute
[C#]
[AttributeUsage(AttributeTargets.Assembly | AttributeTargets.Class
   | AttributeTargets.Struct | AttributeTargets.Enum |
   AttributeTargets.Method | AttributeTargets.Property |
   AttributeTargets.Field | AttributeTargets.Interface |
   AttributeTargets.Delegate)]
public sealed class ComVisibleAttribute : Attribute
[C++]
[AttributeUsage(AttributeTargets::Assembly |
   AttributeTargets::Class | AttributeTargets::Struct |
   AttributeTargets::Enum | AttributeTargets::Method |
   AttributeTargets::Property | AttributeTargets::Field |
   AttributeTargets::Interface | AttributeTargets::Delegate)]
public __gc __sealed class ComVisibleAttribute : public Attribute
[JScript]
public
   AttributeUsage(AttributeTargets.Assembly | AttributeTargets.Class |
   AttributeTargets.Struct | AttributeTargets.Enum |
   AttributeTargets.Method | AttributeTargets.Property |
   AttributeTargets.Field | AttributeTargets.Interface |
   AttributeTargets.Delegate)
class ComVisibleAttribute extends Attribute
```

Thread Safety

Any public static (**Shared** in Visual Basic) members of this type are safe for multithreaded operations. Any instance members are not guaranteed to be thread safe.

Remarks

You can apply this attribute to assemblies, interfaces, classes, structures, delegates, enumerations, fields, methods, or properties.

The default is **true**, which indicates that the managed type is visible to COM. This attribute is not needed to make public managed assemblies and types visible; they are visible to COM by default. Only **public** types can be made visible. The attribute cannot be used to make an otherwise **internal** or **protected** type visible to COM or to make members of a nonvisible type visible.

Setting the attribute to **false** on the assembly hides all **public** types within the assembly. You can selectively make types within the assembly visible by setting the individual types to **true**. Setting the attribute to **false** on a specific type hides that type and its members. However, you cannot make members of a type visible if the type is invisible. Setting the attribute to **false** on a type prevents that type from being exported to a type library; classes are not registered; interfaces are never responsive to unmanaged **QueryInterface** calls.

Unless you explicitly set a class and its members to **false**, inherited classes can expose to COM base class members that are invisible in the original class. For example, if you set ClassA to **false** and do not apply the attribute to its members, the class and its members are invisible to COM. However, if you derive ClassB from ClassA and export ClassB to COM, ClassA members become visible base class members of ClassB.

Example

[Visual Basic, C#, JScript] The following example shows how you can control the visibility to COM of a class so that its members are invisible. By setting **ComVisibleAttribute** to false on MyClass, and **false** on MyMethod and MyProperty, you can avoid inadvertently exposing the members to COM through inheritance.

```
[Visual Basic]
Imports System.Runtime.InteropServices

<ComVisible(False)> _
Class SampleClass

    Public Sub New()
        'Insert code here.
    End Sub

    <ComVisible(False)> _
    Public Function MyMethod(param As String) As Integer
        Return 0
    End Function

    Public Function MyOtherMethod() As Boolean
        Return True
    End Function

    <ComVisible(False)> _
    Public ReadOnly Property MyProperty() As Integer
        Get
            Return MyProperty
        End Get
    End Property

End Class
```

```
[C#]
using System.Runtime.InteropServices;

[ComVisible(false)]
class MyClass
{
    public MyClass()
    {
        //Insert code here.
    }

    [ComVisible(false)]
    public int MyMethod(string param)
    {
        return 0;
    }

    public bool MyOtherMethod()
    {
        return true;
    }

    [ComVisible(false)]
    public int MyProperty
    {
        get
        {
            return MyProperty;
        }
    }
}
```

```
[JScript]
import System.Runtime.InteropServices;

ComVisible(false) class MyClass
{
   public function MyClass()
   {
      //Insert code here.
   }

   ComVisible(false) public function MyMethod(param : String) : int
   {
      return 0;
   }

   public function MyOtherMethod() : boolean
   {
      return true;
   }

   ComVisible(false) public function get MyProperty() : int
   {
      return MyProperty;
   }
}
```

Requirements

Namespace: System.Runtime.InteropServices

Platforms: Windows 98, Windows NT 4.0,
Windows Millennium Edition, Windows 2000,
Windows XP Home Edition, Windows XP Professional,
Windows .NET Server family,
.NET Compact Framework - Windows CE .NET

Assembly: Mscorlib (in Mscorlib.dll)

ComVisibleAttribute Constructor

Initializes a new instance of the **ComVisibleAttribute** class.

```
[Visual Basic]
Public Sub New( _
   ByVal visibility As Boolean _
)
[C#]
public ComVisibleAttribute(
   bool visibility
);
[C++]
public: ComVisibleAttribute(
   bool visibility
);
[JScript]
public function ComVisibleAttribute(
   visibility : Boolean
);
```

Parameters

visibility
   true to indicate that the type is visible to COM; otherwise, **false**.
   The default is **true**.

Remarks

To make types visible to COM, set the attribute to **true**. To hide
types from COM, set the attribute to **false**.

Requirements

Platforms: Windows 98, Windows NT 4.0,
Windows Millennium Edition, Windows 2000,
Windows XP Home Edition, Windows XP Professional,
Windows .NET Server family,
.NET Compact Framework - Windows CE .NET

ComVisibleAttribute.Value Property

Gets a value that indicates whether the COM type is visible.

```
[Visual Basic]
Public ReadOnly Property Value As Boolean
[C#]
public bool Value {get;}
[C++]
public: __property bool get_Value();
[JScript]
public function get Value() : Boolean;
```

Property Value

true if the type is visible; otherwise, **false**. The default value is **true**.

Requirements

Platforms: Windows 98, Windows NT 4.0,
Windows Millennium Edition, Windows 2000,
Windows XP Home Edition, Windows XP Professional,
Windows .NET Server family,
.NET Compact Framework - Windows CE .NET

CONNECTDATA Structure

Describes a connection that exists to a given connection point.

System.Object
  System.ValueType
    System.Runtime.InteropServices.CONNECTDATA

```
[Visual Basic]
<ComVisible(False)>
Public Structure CONNECTDATA
[C#]
[ComVisible(false)]
public struct CONNECTDATA
[C++]
[ComVisible(false)]
public __value struct CONNECTDATA
```

[JScript] In JScript, you can use the structures in the .NET Framework, but you cannot define your own.

Thread Safety

Any public static (**Shared** in Visual Basic) members of this type are safe for multithreaded operations. Any instance members are not guaranteed to be thread safe.

Remarks

The **CONNECTDATA** structure is the type enumerated through the **UCOMIEnumConnections.Next** method.

For more information about **CONNECTDATA**, see the MSDN Library.

Requirements

Namespace: System.Runtime.InteropServices

Platforms: Windows 98, Windows NT 4.0, Windows Millennium Edition, Windows 2000, Windows XP Home Edition, Windows XP Professional, Windows .NET Server family

Assembly: Mscorlib (in Mscorlib.dll)

CONNECTDATA.dwCookie Field

Represents a connection token that is returned from a call to **UCOMIConnectionPoint.Advise**.

```
[Visual Basic]
Public dwCookie As Integer
[C#]
public int dwCookie;
[C++]
public: int dwCookie;
[JScript]
public var dwCookie : int;
```

Requirements

Platforms: Windows 98, Windows NT 4.0, Windows Millennium Edition, Windows 2000, Windows XP Home Edition, Windows XP Professional, Windows .NET Server family

CONNECTDATA.pUnk Field

Represents a pointer to the **IUnknown** interface on a connected advisory sink. The caller must call **IUnknown::Release** on this pointer when the **CONNECTDATA** structure is no longer needed.

```
[Visual Basic]
Public pUnk As Object
[C#]
public object pUnk;
[C++]
public: Object* pUnk;
[JScript]
public var pUnk : Object;
```

Requirements

Platforms: Windows 98, Windows NT 4.0, Windows Millennium Edition, Windows 2000, Windows XP Home Edition, Windows XP Professional, Windows .NET Server family

CurrencyWrapper Class

Wraps objects the marshaler should marshal as a **VT_CY**.

System.Object
   System.Runtime.InteropServices.CurrencyWrapper

```
[Visual Basic]
NotInheritable Public Class CurrencyWrapper
[C#]
public sealed class CurrencyWrapper
[C++]
public __gc __sealed class CurrencyWrapper
[JScript]
public class CurrencyWrapper
```

Thread Safety

Any public static (**Shared** in Visual Basic) members of this type are safe for multithreaded operations. Any instance members are not guaranteed to be thread safe.

Remarks

Controls how the wrapped object is marshaled when passed as a Variant. Wrap a **Decimal** in a **CurrencyWrapper** to have it marshaled as a **VT_CY**.

Requirements

Namespace: System.Runtime.InteropServices

Platforms: Windows 98, Windows NT 4.0, Windows Millennium Edition, Windows 2000, Windows XP Home Edition, Windows XP Professional, Windows .NET Server family

Assembly: Mscorlib (in Mscorlib.dll)

CurrencyWrapper Constructor

Initializes a new instance of the **CurrencyWrapper** class.

Overload List

Initializes a new instance of the **CurrencyWrapper** class with the **Decimal** to be wrapped and marshaled as type **VT_CY**.

   [Visual Basic] **Public Sub New(Decimal)**
   [C#] **public CurrencyWrapper(decimal);**
   [C++] **public: CurrencyWrapper(Decimal);**
   [JScript] **public function CurrencyWrapper(Decimal);**

Initializes a new instance of the **CurrencyWrapper** class with the object containing the **Decimal** to be wrapped and marshaled as type **VT_CY**.

   [Visual Basic] **Public Sub New(Object)**
   [C#] **public CurrencyWrapper(object);**
   [C++] **public: CurrencyWrapper(Object*);**
   [JScript] **public function CurrencyWrapper(Object);**

CurrencyWrapper Constructor (Decimal)

Initializes a new instance of the **CurrencyWrapper** class with the **Decimal** to be wrapped and marshaled as type **VT_CY**.

```
[Visual Basic]
Public Sub New( _
    ByVal obj As Decimal _
)
[C#]
public CurrencyWrapper(
    decimal obj
);
[C++]
public: CurrencyWrapper(
    Decimal obj
);
[JScript]
public function CurrencyWrapper(
    obj : Decimal
);
```

Parameters

obj
   The **Decimal** to be wrapped and marshaled as **VT_CY**.

Requirements

Platforms: Windows 98, Windows NT 4.0, Windows Millennium Edition, Windows 2000, Windows XP Home Edition, Windows XP Professional, Windows .NET Server family

CurrencyWrapper Constructor (Object)

Initializes a new instance of the **CurrencyWrapper** class with the object containing the **Decimal** to be wrapped and marshaled as type **VT_CY**.

```
[Visual Basic]
Public Sub New( _
    ByVal obj As Object _
)
[C#]
public CurrencyWrapper(
    object obj
);
[C++]
public: CurrencyWrapper(
    Object* obj
);
[JScript]
public function CurrencyWrapper(
    obj : Object
);
```

Parameters

obj
   The object containing the **Decimal** to be wrapped and marshaled as **VT_CY**.

Requirements

Platforms: Windows 98, Windows NT 4.0, Windows Millennium Edition, Windows 2000, Windows XP Home Edition, Windows XP Professional, Windows .NET Server family

CurrencyWrapper.WrappedObject Property

Gets the wrapped object to be marshaled as type **VT_CY**.

```
[Visual Basic]
Public ReadOnly Property WrappedObject As Decimal
[C#]
public decimal WrappedObject {get;}
[C++]
public: __property Decimal get_WrappedObject();
[JScript]
public function get WrappedObject() : Decimal;
```

Property Value

The wrapped object to be marshaled as type **VT_CY**.

Requirements

Platforms: Windows 98, Windows NT 4.0,
Windows Millennium Edition, Windows 2000,
Windows XP Home Edition, Windows XP Professional,
Windows .NET Server family

DESCKIND Enumeration

Identifies the type description being bound to.

```
[Visual Basic]
<Serializable>
<ComVisible(False)>
Public Enum DESCKIND
[C#]
[Serializable]
[ComVisible(false)]
public enum DESCKIND
[C++]
[Serializable]
[ComVisible(false)]
__value public enum DESCKIND
[JScript]
public
   Serializable
   ComVisible(false)
enum DESCKIND
```

Remarks

For more information about the **DESCKIND** enumeration, see the MSDN Library.

Members

Member name	Description
DESCKIND_FUNCDESC	Indicates that a **FUNCDESC** was returned.
DESCKIND_IMPLICIT-APPOBJ	Indicates that an **IMPLICITAPPOBJ** was returned.
DESCKIND_MAX	Indicates an end of enumeration marker.
DESCKIND_NONE	Indicates that no match was found.
DESCKIND_TYPECOMP	Indicates that a **TYPECOMP** was returned.
DESCKIND_VARDESC	Indicates that a **VARDESC** was returned.

Requirements

Namespace: System.Runtime.InteropServices

Platforms: Windows 98, Windows NT 4.0, Windows Millennium Edition, Windows 2000, Windows XP Home Edition, Windows XP Professional, Windows .NET Server family

Assembly: Mscorlib (in Mscorlib.dll)

DispatchWrapper Class

Wraps objects the marshaler should marshal as a **VT_DISPATCH**.

System.Object
  System.Runtime.InteropServices.DispatchWrapper

```
[Visual Basic]
NotInheritable Public Class DispatchWrapper
[C#]
public sealed class DispatchWrapper
[C++]
public __gc __sealed class DispatchWrapper
[JScript]
public class DispatchWrapper
```

Thread Safety

Any public static (**Shared** in Visual Basic) members of this type are safe for multithreaded operations. Any instance members are not guaranteed to be thread safe.

Remarks

Use to wrap objects the marshaler should marshal as a **VT_DISPATCH**. This wrapper will force objects to be marshaled out as **VT_DISPATCH**. If the object does not support **IDispatch** then an exception will be thrown.

```
[C#]
void MyMethod(Object o);

Object o = new MyObject;

MyMethod(o); //passes o as VT_UNKNOWN

MyMethod(new DispatchWrapper(o)); //passes o as VT_DISPATCH
```

For more information on **VT_DISPATCH**, please see the existing documentation for **VARENUM::VT_DISPATCH** in the MSDN library.

Requirements

Namespace: System.Runtime.InteropServices

Platforms: Windows 98, Windows NT 4.0, Windows Millennium Edition, Windows 2000, Windows XP Home Edition, Windows XP Professional, Windows .NET Server family

Assembly: Mscorlib (in Mscorlib.dll)

DispatchWrapper Constructor

Initializes a new instance of the **DispatchWrapper** class with the object being wrapped.

```
[Visual Basic]
Public Sub New( _
    ByVal obj As Object _
)
[C#]
public DispatchWrapper(
    object obj
);
[C++]
public: DispatchWrapper(
    Object* obj
);
```

```
[JScript]
public function DispatchWrapper(
    obj : Object
);
```

Parameters

obj
    The object to be wrapped and converted to **VT_DISPATCH**.

Exceptions

Exception Type	Condition
ArgumentException	*obj* is not a class or an array. -or- *obj* does not support **IDispatch**.

Requirements

Platforms: Windows 98, Windows NT 4.0, Windows Millennium Edition, Windows 2000, Windows XP Home Edition, Windows XP Professional, Windows .NET Server family

DispatchWrapper.WrappedObject Property

Gets the object wrapped by the **DispatchWrapper**.

```
[Visual Basic]
Public ReadOnly Property WrappedObject As Object
[C#]
public object WrappedObject {get;}
[C++]
public: __property Object* get_WrappedObject();
[JScript]
public function get WrappedObject() : Object;
```

Property Value

The object wrapped by the **DispatchWrapper**.

Requirements

Platforms: Windows 98, Windows NT 4.0, Windows Millennium Edition, Windows 2000, Windows XP Home Edition, Windows XP Professional, Windows .NET Server family

DispIdAttribute Class

Specifies the COM dispatch identifier (DISPID) of a method, field, or property.

System.Object
  System.Attribute
    System.Runtime.InteropServices.DispIdAttribute

[Visual Basic]
```
<AttributeUsage(AttributeTargets.Method Or _
    AttributeTargets.Property Or AttributeTargets.Field Or _
    AttributeTargets.Event)>
NotInheritable Public Class DispIdAttribute
    Inherits Attribute
```
[C#]
```
[AttributeUsage(AttributeTargets.Method | AttributeTargets.Property
    | AttributeTargets.Field | AttributeTargets.Event)]
public sealed class DispIdAttribute : Attribute
```
[C++]
```
[AttributeUsage(AttributeTargets::Method |
    AttributeTargets::Property | AttributeTargets::Field |
    AttributeTargets::Event)]
public __gc __sealed class DispIdAttribute : public Attribute
```
[JScript]
```
public
    AttributeUsage(AttributeTargets.Method | AttributeTargets.Property
    | AttributeTargets.Field | AttributeTargets.Event)
class DispIdAttribute extends Attribute
```

Thread Safety

Any public static (**Shared** in Visual Basic) members of this type are safe for multithreaded operations. Any instance members are not guaranteed to be thread safe.

Remarks

You can apply this attribute to methods, fields, or properties.

This attribute contains the DISPID for the method, field, or property it describes. Unique DISPIDs are typically assigned by the common language runtime, but you can use this attribute to assign a specific DISPID to a method. When importing a type library, this attribute is applied to all methods with assigned DISPIDs. This ensures that any managed implementation of the same method retains the same DISPID if exposed to COM.

Example

[Visual Basic, C#] The following example demonstrates how explicit DISPIDs can be assigned to members of a class.

[Visual Basic]
```
Imports System.Runtime.InteropServices

Class SampleClass

    Public Sub New()
        'Insert code here.
    End Sub

    <DispIdAttribute(8)> _
    Public Sub MyMethod()
        'Insert code here.
    End Sub

    Public Function MyOtherMethod() As Integer
        'Insert code here.
        Return 0
    End Function
```

```
    <DispId(9)> _
    Public MyField As Boolean
End Class
```

[C#]
```
using System.Runtime.InteropServices;

public class MyClass
{
    public MyClass() {}

    [DispId(8)]
    public void MyMethod() {}

    public int MyOtherMethod() {
        return 0;
    }

    [DispId(9)]
    public bool MyField;
}
```

Requirements

Namespace: System.Runtime.InteropServices

Platforms: Windows 98, Windows NT 4.0, Windows Millennium Edition, Windows 2000, Windows XP Home Edition, Windows XP Professional, Windows .NET Server family, .NET Compact Framework - Windows CE .NET

Assembly: Mscorlib (in Mscorlib.dll)

DispIdAttribute Constructor

Initializes a new instance of the **DispIdAttribute** class with the specified DISPID.

[Visual Basic]
```
Public Sub New( _
    ByVal dispId As Integer _
)
```
[C#]
```
public DispIdAttribute(
    int dispId
);
```
[C++]
```
public: DispIdAttribute(
    int dispId
);
```
[JScript]
```
public function DispIdAttribute(
    dispId : int
);
```

Parameters

dispId
    The DISPID for the member.

Requirements

Platforms: Windows 98, Windows NT 4.0, Windows Millennium Edition, Windows 2000, Windows XP Home Edition, Windows XP Professional, Windows .NET Server family, .NET Compact Framework - Windows CE .NET

DispIdAttribute.Value Property

Gets the DISPID for the member.

```
[Visual Basic]
Public ReadOnly Property Value As Integer
[C#]
public int Value {get;}
[C++]
public: __property int get_Value();
[JScript]
public function get Value() : int;
```

Property Value

The DISPID for the member.

Requirements

Platforms: Windows 98, Windows NT 4.0,
Windows Millennium Edition, Windows 2000,
Windows XP Home Edition, Windows XP Professional,
Windows .NET Server family,
.NET Compact Framework - Windows CE .NET

DISPPARAMS Structure

Contains the arguments passed to a method or property by **IDispatch::Invoke**.

System.Object
    System.ValueType
        System.Runtime.InteropServices.DISPPARAMS

```
[Visual Basic]
<ComVisible(False)>
Public Structure DISPPARAMS
[C#]
[ComVisible(false)]
public struct DISPPARAMS
[C++]
[ComVisible(false)]
public __value struct DISPPARAMS
```

[JScript] In JScript, you can use the structures in the .NET Framework, but you cannot define your own.

Thread Safety

Any public static (**Shared** in Visual Basic) members of this type are safe for multithreaded operations. Any instance members are not guaranteed to be thread safe.

Remarks

For additional information about **DISPPARAMS**, see the MSDN Library.

Requirements

Namespace: System.Runtime.InteropServices

Platforms: Windows 98, Windows NT 4.0, Windows Millennium Edition, Windows 2000, Windows XP Home Edition, Windows XP Professional, Windows .NET Server family

Assembly: Mscorlib (in Mscorlib.dll)

DISPPARAMS.cArgs Field

Represents the count of arguments.

```
[Visual Basic]
Public cArgs As Integer
[C#]
public int cArgs;
[C++]
public: int cArgs;
[JScript]
public var cArgs : int;
```

Requirements

Platforms: Windows 98, Windows NT 4.0, Windows Millennium Edition, Windows 2000, Windows XP Home Edition, Windows XP Professional, Windows .NET Server family

DISPPARAMS.cNamedArgs Field

Represents the count of named arguments

```
[Visual Basic]
Public cNamedArgs As Integer
[C#]
public int cNamedArgs;
[C++]
public: int cNamedArgs;
[JScript]
public var cNamedArgs : int;
```

Requirements

Platforms: Windows 98, Windows NT 4.0, Windows Millennium Edition, Windows 2000, Windows XP Home Edition, Windows XP Professional, Windows .NET Server family

DISPPARAMS.rgdispidNamedArgs Field

Represents the dispatch IDs of named arguments.

```
[Visual Basic]
Public rgdispidNamedArgs As IntPtr
[C#]
public IntPtr rgdispidNamedArgs;
[C++]
public: IntPtr rgdispidNamedArgs;
[JScript]
public var rgdispidNamedArgs : IntPtr;
```

Requirements

Platforms: Windows 98, Windows NT 4.0, Windows Millennium Edition, Windows 2000, Windows XP Home Edition, Windows XP Professional, Windows .NET Server family

DISPPARAMS.rgvarg Field

Represents a reference to the array of arguments.

```
[Visual Basic]
Public rgvarg As IntPtr
[C#]
public IntPtr rgvarg;
[C++]
public: IntPtr rgvarg;
[JScript]
public var rgvarg : IntPtr;
```

Requirements

Platforms: Windows 98, Windows NT 4.0, Windows Millennium Edition, Windows 2000, Windows XP Home Edition, Windows XP Professional, Windows .NET Server family

DllImportAttribute Class

Indicates that the attributed method is exposed by an unmanaged dynamic-link library (DLL) as a static entry point.

System.Object
  System.Attribute
    System.Runtime.InteropServices.DllImportAttribute

```
[Visual Basic]
<AttributeUsage(AttributeTargets.Method)>
NotInheritable Public Class DllImportAttribute
   Inherits Attribute
[C#]
[AttributeUsage(AttributeTargets.Method)]
public sealed class DllImportAttribute : Attribute
[C++]
[AttributeUsage(AttributeTargets::Method)]
public __gc __sealed class DllImportAttribute : public Attribute
[JScript]
public
   AttributeUsage(AttributeTargets.Method)
class DllImportAttribute extends Attribute
```

Thread Safety

Any public static (**Shared** in Visual Basic) members of this type are safe for multithreaded operations. Any instance members are not guaranteed to be thread safe.

Remarks

You can apply this attribute to methods.

The **DllImportAttribute** attribute provides the information needed to call a function exported from an unmanaged DLL. As a minimum requirement, you must supply the name of the DLL containing the entry point.

You apply this attribute directly to C# and C++ method definitions; however, the Visual Basic compiler emits this attribute when you use the **Declare** statement. For complex method definitions that include **BestFitMapping**, **CallingConvention**, **ExactSpelling**, **PreserveSig**, **SetLastError**, or **ThrowOnUnmappableChar** fields, you apply this attribute directly to Visual Basic method definitions.

> **Note** JScript .NET does not support this attribute. You can use C# or Visual Basic wrapper classes to access unmanaged API methods from JScript .NET programs.

Example

[Visual Basic, C#] The following example shows how to apply the **DllImportAttribute** to a method.

```
[Visual Basic]
<DllImport("KERNEL32.DLL", EntryPoint := "MoveFileW", _
   SetLastError := True, CharSet := CharSet.Unicode, _
   ExactSpelling := True, _
   CallingConvention := CallingConvention.StdCall)> _
Public Shared Function MoveFile(src As String, dst As String) ⌐
 As Boolean
      ' Leave function empty - DLLImport attribute forwards calls ⌐
to MoveFile to
      ' MoveFileW in KERNEL32.DLL.
End Function

[C#]
[DllImport("KERNEL32.DLL", EntryPoint="MoveFileW", SetLastError=true,
CharSet=CharSet.Unicode, ExactSpelling=true,
CallingConvention=CallingConvention.StdCall)]
public static extern bool MoveFile(String src, String dst);
```

Requirements

Namespace: System.Runtime.InteropServices

Platforms: Windows 98, Windows NT 4.0, Windows Millennium Edition, Windows 2000, Windows XP Home Edition, Windows XP Professional, Windows .NET Server family, .NET Compact Framework - Windows CE .NET

Assembly: Mscorlib (in Mscorlib.dll)

DllImportAttribute Constructor

Initializes a new instance of the **DllImportAttribute** class with the name of the DLL containing the method to import.

```
[Visual Basic]
Public Sub New( _
   ByVal dllName As String _
)
[C#]
public DllImportAttribute(
   string dllName
);
[C++]
public: DllImportAttribute(
   String* dllName
);
[JScript]
public function DllImportAttribute(
   dllName : String
);
```

Parameters

dllName
  The name of the DLL that contains the unmanaged method.

Requirements

Platforms: Windows 98, Windows NT 4.0, Windows Millennium Edition, Windows 2000, Windows XP Home Edition, Windows XP Professional, Windows .NET Server family, .NET Compact Framework - Windows CE .NET, Common Language Infrastructure (CLI) Standard

DllImportAttribute.BestFitMapping Field

Note: This namespace, class, or member is supported only in version 1.1 of the .NET Framework.

Enables or disables best-fit mapping behavior when converting Unicode characters to ANSI characters.

```
[Visual Basic]
Public BestFitMapping As Boolean
[C#]
public bool BestFitMapping;
[C++]
public: bool BestFitMapping;
[JScript]
public var BestFitMapping : Boolean;
```

Remarks

If **true**, best-fit mapping behavior is enabled; otherwise, best-fit mapping is disabled. The **BestFitMapping** field is **true** by default.

Settings for this field override the any level settings for the **System.Runtime.InteropServices.BestFitMappingAttribute** attribute.

The common language runtime converts to ANSI characters any managed Unicode characters passed to an unmanaged method executing on Windows 98 or Windows Me. Best-fit mapping enables the **interop marshaler** to provide a close-matching character when no exact match exists. For example, the marshaler converts the Unicode copyright character to 'c' for unmanaged methods that accept ANSI characters. Some characters lack a best-fit representation; these characters are called unmappable. Unmappable characters are usually converted to the default '?' ANSI character.

> **CAUTION** Certain Unicode characters are converted to dangerous characters, such as the backslash '\' character, which can inadvertently change a path. By setting the **ThrowOnUnmappableChar** field to **true**, you can signal the presence of an unmappable character to the caller by throwing an exception.

> **CAUTION** You cannot change the default values provided by the **BestFitMapping** and **ThrowOnUnmappableChar** fields when passing a managed array whose elements are ANSI Chars or LPSTRs to an unmanaged safe array. Best-fit mapping is always enabled and no exception is thrown. Be aware that this combination can compromise your security model.

Example

[Visual Basic, C#] In some cases, Visual Basic developers use the **DllImportAttribute**, instead of the **Declare** statement, to define a DLL function in managed code. Setting the **BestFitMapping** field is one of those cases. The following example shows how to apply the strictest character mapping security to a platform invoke method definitions by specifying the ANSI character set, disabling best fit mapping behavior, and throwing an exception on unmapped Unicode characters.

[Visual Basic]
```
<DllImport( "My.dll", Charset := Charset.Ansi, _
                      BestfitMapping := False _
                      ThrowOnUnmappableChar := True )>
```

[C#]
```
[DllImport( "My.dll", Charset = Charset.Ansi,
                      BestfitMapping = false
                      ThrowOnUnmappableChar = true )]
```

Requirements

Platforms: Windows 98, Windows NT 4.0, Windows Millennium Edition, Windows 2000, Windows XP Home Edition, Windows XP Professional, Windows .NET Server family

DllImportAttribute.CallingConvention Field

Indicates the calling convention of an entry point.

```
[Visual Basic]
Public CallingConvention As CallingConvention
[C#]
public CallingConvention CallingConvention;
[C++]
public: CallingConvention CallingConvention;
[JScript]
public var CallingConvention : CallingConvention;
```

Remarks

You set this field to one of the **CallingConvention** enumeration members. The default value for the **CallingConvention** field is **WinAPI**, which in turn defaults to **StdCall** convention.

For more information, see Calling Convention in the MSDN library.

Example

[Visual Basic, C#] In some cases, Visual Basic developers use the **DllImportAttribute**, instead of the **Declare** statement, to define a DLL function in managed code. Setting the **CallingConvention** field is one of those cases.

```
[Visual Basic]
Imports System
Imports Microsoft.VisualBasic
Imports System.Runtime.InteropServices
Public Class LibWrap
' Visual Basic does not support varargs, so all arguments must be
' explicitly defined. CallingConvention.Cdecl must be used
since the stack
' is cleaned up by the caller.
' int printf( const char *format [, argument]... )
<DllImport("msvcrt.dll", CallingConvention :=
CallingConvention.Cdecl)> _
Overloads Shared Function printf ( _
    format As String, i As Integer, d As Double) As Integer
End Function
<DllImport("msvcrt.dll", CallingConvention :=
CallingConvention.Cdecl)> _
Overloads Shared Function printf ( _
    format As String, i As Integer, s As String) As Integer
End Function
End Class 'LibWrap
Public Class App
    Public Shared Sub Main()
        LibWrap.printf(ControlChars.CrLf + "Print params: %i %f", 99,
                       99.99)
        LibWrap.printf(ControlChars.CrLf + "Print params: %i %s", 99, _
                       "abcd")
    End Sub 'Main
End Class 'App

[C#]
using System;
using System.Runtime.InteropServices;
public class LibWrap
{
// C# doesn't support varargs so all arguments must be
  explicitly defined.
// CallingConvention.Cdecl must be used since the stack is
// cleaned up by the caller.
// int printf( const char *format [, argument]... )
[DllImport("msvcrt.dll", CharSet=CharSet.Ansi,
CallingConvention=CallingConvention.Cdecl)]
public static extern int printf(String format, int i, double d);
[DllImport("msvcrt.dll", CharSet=CharSet.Ansi,
CallingConvention=CallingConvention.Cdecl)]
public static extern int printf(String format, int i, String s);
}
public class App
{
    public static void Main()
    {
        LibWrap.printf("\nPrint params: %i %f", 99, 99.99);
        LibWrap.printf("\nPrint params: %i %s", 99, "abcd");
    }
}
```

Requirements

Platforms: Windows 98, Windows NT 4.0,
Windows Millennium Edition, Windows 2000,
Windows XP Home Edition, Windows XP Professional,
Windows .NET Server family,
.NET Compact Framework - Windows CE .NET,
Common Language Infrastructure (CLI) Standard

DllImportAttribute.CharSet Field

Indicates how to marshal string parameters to the method and
controls name mangling.

```
[Visual Basic]
Public CharSet As CharSet
[C#]
public CharSet CharSet;
[C++]
public: CharSet CharSet;
[JScript]
public var CharSet : CharSet;
```

Remarks

Use this field with a member of the **CharSet** enumeration to specify
the marshaling behavior of string parameters and to specify which
entry-point name to invoke (the exact name given or a name ending
with "A" or "W"). The default enumeration member for C# and Visual
Basic is **CharSet.Ansi** and the default enumeration member for C++
is **CharSet.None**, which is equivalent to **CharSet.Ansi**. In Visual
Basic, you use the **Declare** statement to specify the **CharSet** field.

The **ExactSpelling** field influences the behavior of the **CharSet**
field in determining which entry-point name to invoke.

Requirements

Platforms: Windows 98, Windows NT 4.0,
Windows Millennium Edition, Windows 2000,
Windows XP Home Edition, Windows XP Professional,
Windows .NET Server family,
.NET Compact Framework - Windows CE .NET,
Common Language Infrastructure (CLI) Standard

DllImportAttribute.EntryPoint Field

Indicates the name or ordinal of the DLL entry point to be called.

```
[Visual Basic]
Public EntryPoint As String
[C#]
public string EntryPoint;
[C++]
public: String* EntryPoint;
[JScript]
public var EntryPoint : String;
```

Remarks

You can specify the entry-point name by supplying a string
indicating the name of the DLL containing the entry point, or you
can identify the entry point by its ordinal. Ordinals are prefixed with
the # sign, for example, #1. If you omit this field, the common
language runtime uses the name of the .NET method marked with
the **DllImportAttribute**.

Requirements

Platforms: Windows 98, Windows NT 4.0,
Windows Millennium Edition, Windows 2000,
Windows XP Home Edition, Windows XP Professional,
Windows .NET Server family,
.NET Compact Framework - Windows CE .NET,
Common Language Infrastructure (CLI) Standard

DllImportAttribute.ExactSpelling Field

Controls whether the **DllImportAttribute.CharSet** field causes the
common language runtime to search an unmanaged DLL for entry-
point names other than the one specified.

```
[Visual Basic]
Public ExactSpelling As Boolean
[C#]
public bool ExactSpelling;
[C++]
public: bool ExactSpelling;
[JScript]
public var ExactSpelling : Boolean;
```

Remarks

If **false**, the entry point name appended with the letter A is invoked
when the **DllImportAttribute.CharSet** field is set to **CharSet.Ansi**,
and the entry-point name appended with the letter W is invoked when
the **DllImportAttribute.CharSet** field is set to the **CharSet.Uni-
code**. Typically, managed compilers set this field.The following table
shows the relationship between the **CharSet** and **ExactSpelling**
fields, based on default values imposed by the programming
language. You can override the default setting, but do so with caution.

Language	ANSI	Unicode	Auto
Visual Basic	ExactSpelling: =True	ExactSpelling: =True	ExactSpelling: =False
C#	ExactSpelling= false	ExactSpelling= false	ExactSpelling= false
C++	ExactSpelling= false	ExactSpelling= false	ExactSpelling= false

Example

[Visual Basic, C#, C++] In some cases, Visual Basic developers use
the **DllImportAttribute**, instead of using the **Declare** statement, to
define a DLL function in managed code. Setting the **ExactSpelling**
field is one of those cases.

```
[Visual Basic]
Imports System.Runtime.InteropServices
Public Class Win32
    <DllImport ("user32.dll", ExactSpelling := False)> _
    Public Shared Function MessageBox (ByVal hWnd As Integer, _
        ByVal txt As String, ByVal caption As String, _
        ByVal Typ As Integer) As Integer
    End Function
End Class
```

```
[C#]
using System.Runtime.InteropServices;
public class Win32 {
    [DllImport("user32.dll", CharSet=CharSet.Unicode,
            ExactSpelling=true)]
    public static extern int MessageBoxW(int hWnd, String text, String
                                    caption, uint type);
}
```

```
[C++]
using namespace System::Runtime::InteropServices;
typedef void* HWND;
[DllImport("user32", CharSet=CharSet::Ansi, ExactSpelling=true)]
extern "C" int MessageBoxA(HWND hWnd,
                           String* pText,
                           String* pCaption,
                           unsigned int uType);
```

Requirements

Platforms: Windows 98, Windows NT 4.0,
Windows Millennium Edition, Windows 2000,
Windows XP Home Edition, Windows XP Professional,
Windows .NET Server family,
Common Language Infrastructure (CLI) Standard

DllImportAttribute.PreserveSig Field

Indicates whether the signature is a direct translation of the
unmanaged entry point.

```
[Visual Basic]
Public PreserveSig As Boolean
[C#]
public bool PreserveSig;
[C++]
public: bool PreserveSig;
[JScript]
public var PreserveSig : Boolean;
```

Remarks

Most methods called with platform invoke do not return
HRESULTs, making the HRESULT/[out, retval] conversion
pointless. This is why the default behavior preserves the signature
exactly as defined. This field is **true** by default.

Occasionally, you do want to override the default behavior to
convert the signature. For example, the definition of a method such
as HRESULT

CoCreateInstance(...) should set this field to **false**.
When set to **false**, a call that returns an HRESULT of S_OK is
transformed such that the [out, retval] parameter is used as the
function return value. The S_OK HRESULT is discarded. For
HRESULTs other than S_OK, the runtime throws an exception and
discards the [out, retval] parameter. Only methods that return an
HRESULT can undergo a conversion.

This field is similar to the **PreserveSigAttribute**; however, in
contrast to the **PreserveSig** field, the default value for the attribute is
false.

Example

[Visual Basic, C#] In some cases, Visual Basic developers use the
DllImportAttribute, instead of using the **Declare** statement, to
define a DLL function in managed code. Setting the **PreserveSig**
field is one of those cases.

```
[Visual Basic]
Imports System.Runtime.InteropServices
Public Class Win32
    <DllImport ("user32.dll", PreserveSig := False)> _
    Public Shared Function MessageBoxA (ByVal hWnd As _
    Integer, ByVal txt As String, ByVal caption As String, _
    ByVal Typ As Integer) As Integer
    End Function
End Class
```

```
[C#]
using System.Runtime.InteropServices;
public class Win32 {
    [DllImport("user32.dll", PreserveSig=false)]
    public static extern int MessageBoxA(int hWnd, String text, String
        caption, uint type);
}
```

```
[C++]
using namespace System::Runtime::InteropServices;
typedef void* HWND;
[DllImport("user32", PreserveSig=true)]
extern "C" int MessageBoxA(HWND hWnd,
                           String* pText,
                           String* pCaption,
                           unsigned int uType);
```

Requirements

Platforms: Windows 98, Windows NT 4.0,
Windows Millennium Edition, Windows 2000,
Windows XP Home Edition, Windows XP Professional,
Windows .NET Server family

DllImportAttribute.SetLastError Field

Indicates whether the callee calls the **SetLastError** Win32 API
function before returning from the attributed method.

```
[Visual Basic]
Public SetLastError As Boolean
[C#]
public bool SetLastError;
[C++]
public: bool SetLastError;
[JScript]
public var SetLastError : Boolean;
```

Remarks

true to indicate that the callee will call **SetLastError**; otherwise,
false. The default is **false**, except in Visual Basic.

The runtime marshaler calls **GetLastError** and caches the value
returned to prevent it from being overwritten by other API calls. You
can retrieve the error code by calling **GetLastWin32Error**.

Example

[Visual Basic, C#, C++] In some cases, Visual Basic developers use
the **DllImportAttribute**, instead of using the **Declare** statement, to
define a DLL function in managed code. Setting the **SetLastError**
field is one of those cases.

```
[Visual Basic]
Imports System.Runtime.InteropServices
Public Class Win32
    <DllImport ("user32.dll", SetLastError := False)> _
    Public Shared Function MessageBoxA (ByVal hWnd As Integer, _
        ByVal txt As String, ByVal caption As String, _
        ByVal Typ As Integer) As Integer
    End Function
End Class
```

```
[C#]
using System.Runtime.InteropServices;
public class Win32 {
    [DllImport("user32.dll", SetLastError=true)]
    public static extern int MessageBoxA(int hWnd, String text,
                            String caption, uint type);
}
```

```
[C++]
using namespace System::Runtime::InteropServices;
typedef void* HWND;
[DllImport("user32", SetLastError=true)]
extern "C" int MessageBoxA(HWND hWnd,
                           String* pText,
                           String* pCaption,
                           unsigned int uType);
```

Requirements

Platforms: Windows 98, Windows NT 4.0,
Windows Millennium Edition, Windows 2000,
Windows XP Home Edition, Windows XP Professional,
Windows .NET Server family,
.NET Compact Framework - Windows CE .NET

DllImportAttribute.ThrowOnUnmappableChar Field

Note: This, class, or member is supported only in version 1.1 of namespace the .NET Framework.

Enables or disables the throwing of an exception on an unmappable Unicode character that is converted to an ANSI '?' character.

```
[Visual Basic]
Public ThrowOnUnmappableChar As Boolean
[C#]
public bool ThrowOnUnmappableChar;
[C++]
public: bool ThrowOnUnmappableChar;
[JScript]
public var ThrowOnUnmappableChar : Boolean;
```

Remarks

true to indicate that an exception is thrown each time the interop marshaler converts an unmappable character; **false** to indicate that the the **ThrowOnUnmappableChar** field is disabled. This field is **false** by default.

The common language runtime converts to ANSI characters any managed Unicode characters passed to an unmanaged method executing on Windows 98 or Windows Me. Best-fit mapping enables the **interop marshaler** to provide a close-matching character when no exact match exists. For example, the marshaler converts the Unicode copyright character to 'c' for unmanaged methods that accept ANSI characters. Some characters lack a best-fit representation; these characters are called unmappable. Unmappable characters are usually converted to the default '?' ANSI character.

> **CAUTION** Certain Unicode characters are converted to dangerous characters, such as the backslash '\' character, which can inadvertently change a path. By setting the **ThrowOnUnmappableChar** field to **true**, you can signal the presence of an unmappable character to the caller by throwing an exception.

> **CAUTION** You cannot change the default values provided by the **BestFitMapping** and **ThrowOnUnmappableChar** fields when passing a managed array whose elements are ANSI Chars or LPSTRs to an unmanaged safe array. Best-fit mapping is always enabled and no exception is thrown. Be aware that this combination can compromise your security model.

Example

[Visual Basic, C#] In some cases, Visual Basic developers use the **DllImportAttribute** to define a DLL function in managed code, instead of using the **Declare** statement. Setting the **ThrowOnUnmappableChar** field is one of those cases. The following example shows how to apply the strictest character mapping security to a platform invoke method definitions by specifying the ANSI character set, disabling best fit mapping behavior, and throwing an exception on unmapped Unicode characters.

```
[Visual Basic]
<DllImport( "My.dll", Charset := Charset.Ansi, _
            BestfitMapping := False _
            ThrowOnUnmappableChar := True )>
```

```
[C#]
[DllImport( "My.dll", Charset = Charset.Ansi,
            BestfitMapping = false
            ThrowOnUnmappableChar = true )]
```

Requirements

Platforms: Windows 98, Windows NT 4.0,
Windows Millennium Edition, Windows 2000,
Windows XP Home Edition, Windows XP Professional,
Windows .NET Server family

DllImportAttribute.Value Property

Gets the name of the DLL file that contains the entry point.

```
[Visual Basic]
Public ReadOnly Property Value As String
[C#]
public string Value {get;}
[C++]
public: __property String* get_Value();
[JScript]
public function get Value() : String;
```

Property Value

The name of the DLL file that contains the entry point.

Remarks

You can provide a full or relative path. If you provide no path, the DLL must be in the current path at run time, unless the DLL is loaded by some other means. Be aware, however, that using a fully qualified path can introduce inaccuracy if the DLL is moved.

Requirements

Platforms: Windows 98, Windows NT 4.0,
Windows Millennium Edition, Windows 2000,
Windows XP Home Edition, Windows XP Professional,
Windows .NET Server family,
.NET Compact Framework - Windows CE .NET,
Common Language Infrastructure (CLI) Standard

ELEMDESC Structure

Contains the type description and process transfer information for a variable, function, or a function parameter.

System.Object
    System.ValueType
        System.Runtime.InteropServices.ELEMDESC

```
[Visual Basic]
<ComVisible(False)>
Public Structure ELEMDESC
[C#]
[ComVisible(false)]
public struct ELEMDESC
[C++]
[ComVisible(false)]
public __value struct ELEMDESC
```

[JScript] In JScript, you can use the structures in the .NET Framework, but you cannot define your own.

Thread Safety

Any public static (**Shared** in Visual Basic) members of this type are safe for multithreaded operations. Any instance members are not guaranteed to be thread safe.

Remarks

For additional information about **ELEMDESC**, see the MSDN Library.

Requirements

Namespace: System.Runtime.InteropServices

Platforms: Windows 98, Windows NT 4.0, Windows Millennium Edition, Windows 2000, Windows XP Home Edition, Windows XP Professional, Windows .NET Server family

Assembly: Mscorlib (in Mscorlib.dll)

ELEMDESC.desc Field

Contains information about an element.

```
[Visual Basic]
Public desc As ELEMDESC.DESCUNION
[C#]
public ELEMDESC.DESCUNION desc;
[C++]
public: ELEMDESC.DESCUNION desc;
[JScript]
public var desc : ELEMDESC.DESCUNION;
```

Requirements

Platforms: Windows 98, Windows NT 4.0, Windows Millennium Edition, Windows 2000, Windows XP Home Edition, Windows XP Professional, Windows .NET Server family

ELEMDESC.tdesc Field

Identifies the type of the element.

```
[Visual Basic]
Public tdesc As TYPEDESC
[C#]
public TYPEDESC tdesc;
[C++]
public: TYPEDESC tdesc;
[JScript]
public var tdesc : TYPEDESC;
```

Remarks

For additional information about **ELEMDESC**, see the MSDN Library.

Requirements

Platforms: Windows 98, Windows NT 4.0, Windows Millennium Edition, Windows 2000, Windows XP Home Edition, Windows XP Professional, Windows .NET Server family

ELEMDESC.DESCUNION Structure

Contains information about an element.

System.Object
  System.ValueType
    System.Runtime.InteropServices.ELEMDESC.DESCUNION

```
[Visual Basic]
<ComVisible(False)>
Public Structure ELEMDESC.DESCUNION
[C#]
[ComVisible(false)]
public struct ELEMDESC.DESCUNION
[C++]
[ComVisible(false)]
public __value struct ELEMDESC.DESCUNION
```

[JScript] In JScript, you can use the structures in the .NET Framework, but you cannot define your own.

Thread Safety

Any public static (**Shared** in Visual Basic) members of this type are safe for multithreaded operations. Any instance members are not guaranteed to be thread safe.

Requirements

Namespace: System.Runtime.InteropServices

Platforms: Windows 98, Windows NT 4.0, Windows Millennium Edition, Windows 2000, Windows XP Home Edition, Windows XP Professional, Windows .NET Server family

Assembly: Mscorlib (in Mscorlib.dll)

ELEMDESC.DESCUNION.idldesc Field

Contains information for remoting the element.

```
[Visual Basic]
Public idldesc As IDLDESC
[C#]
public IDLDESC idldesc;
[C++]
public: IDLDESC idldesc;
[JScript]
public var idldesc : IDLDESC;
```

Requirements

Platforms: Windows 98, Windows NT 4.0, Windows Millennium Edition, Windows 2000, Windows XP Home Edition, Windows XP Professional, Windows .NET Server family

ELEMDESC.DESCUNION.paramdesc Field

Contains information about the parameter.

```
[Visual Basic]
Public paramdesc As PARAMDESC
[C#]
public PARAMDESC paramdesc;
[C++]
public: PARAMDESC paramdesc;
[JScript]
public var paramdesc : PARAMDESC;
```

Requirements

Platforms: Windows 98, Windows NT 4.0, Windows Millennium Edition, Windows 2000, Windows XP Home Edition, Windows XP Professional, Windows .NET Server family

ErrorWrapper Class

Wraps objects the marshaler should marshal as a **VT_ERROR**.

System.Object
   System.Runtime.InteropServices.ErrorWrapper

```
[Visual Basic]
NotInheritable Public Class ErrorWrapper
[C#]
public sealed class ErrorWrapper
[C++]
public __gc __sealed class ErrorWrapper
[JScript]
public class ErrorWrapper
```

Thread Safety

Any public static (**Shared** in Visual Basic) members of this type are safe for multithreaded operations. Any instance members are not guaranteed to be thread safe.

Remarks

By default, **Object** type arguments are marshaled as a **VARIANT** type, where the object type determines the **VARTYPE** value of the **VARIANT**. For example, an integer type passed as **Object** is marshaled as a **VT_I4**. In order to marshal the integer as a variant of type **VT_ERROR**, the integer can be wrapped in the **ErrorWrapper** before making the method call.

For more information on **VT_ERROR**, please see the existing documentation for **VARENUM::VT_ERROR** in the MSDN library.

Requirements

Namespace: System.Runtime.InteropServices

Platforms: Windows 98, Windows NT 4.0, Windows Millennium Edition, Windows 2000, Windows XP Home Edition, Windows XP Professional, Windows .NET Server family

Assembly: Mscorlib (in Mscorlib.dll)

ErrorWrapper Constructor

Initializes a new instance of the **ErrorWrapper** class.

Overload List

Initializes a new instance of the **ErrorWrapper** class with the HRESULT that corresponds to the exception supplied.

   [Visual Basic] **Public Sub New(Exception)**
   [C#] **public ErrorWrapper(Exception);**
   [C++] **public: ErrorWrapper(Exception*);**
   [JScript] **public function ErrorWrapper(Exception);**

Initializes a new instance of the **ErrorWrapper** class with the HRESULT of the error.

   [Visual Basic] **Public Sub New(Integer)**
   [C#] **public ErrorWrapper(int);**
   [C++] **public: ErrorWrapper(int);**
   [JScript] **public function ErrorWrapper(int);**

Initializes a new instance of the **ErrorWrapper** class with an object containing the HRESULT of the error.

   [Visual Basic] **Public Sub New(Object)**
   [C#] **public ErrorWrapper(object);**
   [C++] **public: ErrorWrapper(Object*);**
   [JScript] **public function ErrorWrapper(Object);**

ErrorWrapper Constructor (Exception)

Initializes a new instance of the **ErrorWrapper** class with the HRESULT that corresponds to the exception supplied.

```
[Visual Basic]
Public Sub New( _
   ByVal e As Exception _
)
[C#]
public ErrorWrapper(
   Exception e
);
[C++]
public: ErrorWrapper(
   Exception* e
);
[JScript]
public function ErrorWrapper(
   e : Exception
);
```

Parameters

e
   The exception to be converted to an error code.

Requirements

Platforms: Windows 98, Windows NT 4.0, Windows Millennium Edition, Windows 2000, Windows XP Home Edition, Windows XP Professional, Windows .NET Server family

ErrorWrapper Constructor (Int32)

Initializes a new instance of the **ErrorWrapper** class with the HRESULT of the error.

```
[Visual Basic]
Public Sub New( _
   ByVal errorCode As Integer _
)
[C#]
public ErrorWrapper(
   int errorCode
);
[C++]
public: ErrorWrapper(
   int errorCode
);
[JScript]
public function ErrorWrapper(
   errorCode : int
);
```

Parameters

errorCode
   The HRESULT of the error.

Requirements

Platforms: Windows 98, Windows NT 4.0,
Windows Millennium Edition, Windows 2000,
Windows XP Home Edition, Windows XP Professional,
Windows .NET Server family

ErrorWrapper Constructor (Object)

Initializes a new instance of the **ErrorWrapper** class with an object
containing the HRESULT of the error.

```
[Visual Basic]
Public Sub New( _
   ByVal errorCode As Object _
)
[C#]
public ErrorWrapper(
   object errorCode
);
[C++]
public: ErrorWrapper(
   Object* errorCode
);
[JScript]
public function ErrorWrapper(
   errorCode : Object
);
```

Parameters

errorCode
   The object containing the HRESULT of the error.

Requirements

Platforms: Windows 98, Windows NT 4.0,
Windows Millennium Edition, Windows 2000,
Windows XP Home Edition, Windows XP Professional,
Windows .NET Server family

ErrorWrapper.ErrorCode Property

Gets the error code of the wrapper.

```
[Visual Basic]
Public ReadOnly Property ErrorCode As Integer
[C#]
public int ErrorCode {get;}
[C++]
public: __property int get_ErrorCode();
[JScript]
public function get ErrorCode() : int;
```

Property Value

The HRESULT of the error.

Requirements

Platforms: Windows 98, Windows NT 4.0,
Windows Millennium Edition, Windows 2000,
Windows XP Home Edition, Windows XP Professional,
Windows .NET Server family

EXCEPINFO Structure

Describes the exceptions that occur during **IDispatch::Invoke**.

System.Object
  System.ValueType
    System.Runtime.InteropServices.EXCEPINFO

```
[Visual Basic]
<ComVisible(False)>
Public Structure EXCEPINFO
[C#]
[ComVisible(false)]
public struct EXCEPINFO
[C++]
[ComVisible(false)]
public __value struct EXCEPINFO
```

[JScript] In JScript, you can use the structures in the .NET Framework, but you cannot define your own.

Thread Safety

Any public static (**Shared** in Visual Basic) members of this type are safe for multithreaded operations. Any instance members are not guaranteed to be thread safe.

Remarks

For additional information about **EXCEPINFO**, see the MSDN Library.

Requirements

Namespace: System.Runtime.InteropServices

Platforms: Windows 98, Windows NT 4.0, Windows Millennium Edition, Windows 2000, Windows XP Home Edition, Windows XP Professional, Windows .NET Server family

Assembly: Mscorlib (in Mscorlib.dll)

EXCEPINFO.bstrDescription Field

Describes the error intended for the customer.

```
[Visual Basic]
Public bstrDescription As String
[C#]
public string bstrDescription;
[C++]
public: String* bstrDescription;
[JScript]
public var bstrDescription : String;
```

Requirements

Platforms: Windows 98, Windows NT 4.0, Windows Millennium Edition, Windows 2000, Windows XP Home Edition, Windows XP Professional, Windows .NET Server family

EXCEPINFO.bstrHelpFile Field

Contains the fully-qualified drive, path, and file name of a Help file with more information about the error.

```
[Visual Basic]
Public bstrHelpFile As String
```

```
[C#]
public string bstrHelpFile;
[C++]
public: String* bstrHelpFile;
[JScript]
public var bstrHelpFile : String;
```

Requirements

Platforms: Windows 98, Windows NT 4.0, Windows Millennium Edition, Windows 2000, Windows XP Home Edition, Windows XP Professional, Windows .NET Server family

EXCEPINFO.bstrSource Field

Indicates the name of the source of the exception. Typically, this is an application name.

```
[Visual Basic]
Public bstrSource As String
[C#]
public string bstrSource;
[C++]
public: String* bstrSource;
[JScript]
public var bstrSource : String;
```

Requirements

Platforms: Windows 98, Windows NT 4.0, Windows Millennium Edition, Windows 2000, Windows XP Home Edition, Windows XP Professional, Windows .NET Server family

EXCEPINFO.dwHelpContext Field

Indicates the Help context ID of the topic within the Help file.

```
[Visual Basic]
Public dwHelpContext As Integer
[C#]
public int dwHelpContext;
[C++]
public: int dwHelpContext;
[JScript]
public var dwHelpContext : int;
```

Requirements

Platforms: Windows 98, Windows NT 4.0, Windows Millennium Edition, Windows 2000, Windows XP Home Edition, Windows XP Professional, Windows .NET Server family

EXCEPINFO.pfnDeferredFillIn Field

Represents a pointer to a function that takes an **EXCEPINFO** structure as an argument and returns an HRESULT value. If deferred fill-in is not desired, this field is set to a null reference (**Nothing** in Visual Basic).

```
[Visual Basic]
Public pfnDeferredFillIn As IntPtr
[C#]
public IntPtr pfnDeferredFillIn;
```

```
[C++]
public: IntPtr pfnDeferredFillIn;
[JScript]
public var pfnDeferredFillIn : IntPtr;
```

Requirements

Platforms: Windows 98, Windows NT 4.0,
Windows Millennium Edition, Windows 2000,
Windows XP Home Edition, Windows XP Professional,
Windows .NET Server family

Requirements

Platforms: Windows 98, Windows NT 4.0,
Windows Millennium Edition, Windows 2000,
Windows XP Home Edition, Windows XP Professional,
Windows .NET Server family

EXCEPINFO.pvReserved Field

This field is reserved; must be set to a null reference (**Nothing** in
Visual Basic).

```
[Visual Basic]
Public pvReserved As IntPtr
[C#]
public IntPtr pvReserved;
[C++]
public: IntPtr pvReserved;
[JScript]
public var pvReserved : IntPtr;
```

Requirements

Platforms: Windows 98, Windows NT 4.0,
Windows Millennium Edition, Windows 2000,
Windows XP Home Edition, Windows XP Professional,
Windows .NET Server family

EXCEPINFO.wCode Field

Represents an error code identifying the error.

```
[Visual Basic]
Public wCode As Short
[C#]
public short wCode;
[C++]
public: short wCode;
[JScript]
public var wCode : Int16;
```

Requirements

Platforms: Windows 98, Windows NT 4.0,
Windows Millennium Edition, Windows 2000,
Windows XP Home Edition, Windows XP Professional,
Windows .NET Server family

EXCEPINFO.wReserved Field

This field is reserved; must be set to 0.

```
[Visual Basic]
Public wReserved As Short
[C#]
public short wReserved;
[C++]
public: short wReserved;
[JScript]
public var wReserved : Int16;
```

ExporterEventKind Enumeration

Describes the callbacks that the type library exporter makes when exporting a type library.

```
[Visual Basic]
<Serializable>
Public Enum ExporterEventKind
[C#]
[Serializable]
public enum ExporterEventKind
[C++]
[Serializable]
__value public enum ExporterEventKind
[JScript]
public
    Serializable
enum ExporterEventKind
```

Remarks

The type library exporter passes the values of this enumeration to the **ReportEvent** method of an object which implements the **ITypeLibExporterNotifySink** interface. The value passed identifies the specific kind of event being reported.

Members

Member name	Description
ERROR_REFTOIN-VALIDASSEMBLY	This value is not supported in this version of the .NET Framework.
NOTIF_CONVERT-WARNING	Specifies that the event is invoked when a warning occurs during conversion.
NOTIF_TYPE-CONVERTED	Specifies that the event is invoked when a type has been exported.

Requirements

Namespace: System.Runtime.InteropServices

Platforms: Windows 98, Windows NT 4.0, Windows Millennium Edition, Windows 2000, Windows XP Home Edition, Windows XP Professional, Windows .NET Server family

Assembly: Mscorlib (in Mscorlib.dll)

ExtensibleClassFactory Class

Enables customization of managed objects that extend from
unmanaged objects during creation.

System.Object
   System.Runtime.InteropServices.ExtensibleClassFactory

```
[Visual Basic]
NotInheritable Public Class ExtensibleClassFactory
[C#]
public sealed class ExtensibleClassFactory
[C++]
public _gc _sealed class ExtensibleClassFactory
[JScript]
public class ExtensibleClassFactory
```

Thread Safety

Any public static (**Shared** in Visual Basic) members of this type are
safe for multithreaded operations. Any instance members are not
guaranteed to be thread safe.

Remarks

The **ExtensibleClassFactory** allows users to specify a **delegate** that
is called during construction of a runtime callable wrapper (RCW)
that provides an instance of the underlying COM object. In effect,
the callback acts as the class factory for the COM object wrapped by
the RCW. Without the callback, the common language runtime
creates the underlying COM object by calling **CoCreateInstance**.
This callback provides an alternative way of activating the
underlying object, such as with a COM moniker or by providing a
singleton object. The **RegisterObjectCreationCallback** method
must be called in the static (**Shared** in Visual Basic) initializer of the
class that is extending the RCW. Only one object creation callback is
permitted per object type. When the extensible RCW is activated,
the callback is registered. When the underlying COM object needs to
be created, the callback is called to provide a reference to the object.
The callback must return an **IUnknown** interface pointer for the
base object.

Example

[Visual Basic, C#] Registers a **delegate** that will be called whenever
an instance of a managed type that extends from an unmanaged type
needs to allocate the aggregated unmanaged object. This **delegate** is
expected to allocate and aggregate the unmanaged object and is
called in place of a **CoCreateInstance**. This routine must be called
in the context of the static (**Shared** in Visual Basic) initializer for the
class for which the callbacks will be made.

```
[Visual Basic]
Imports System
Imports System.Runtime.InteropServices

Public Class CallBack

    Public Function Activate(Aggregator As IntPtr) As IntPtr
        Dim oCOM As New ECFSRV32Lib.ObjectActivator()
        Dim itf As ECFSRV32Lib.IObjectActivator = _
            CType(oCOM, ECFSRV32Lib.IObjectActivator)
        Return New
IntPtr(itf.CreateBaseComponent(Aggregator.ToInt32()))
    End Function
End Class

'
' The EcfInner class. First .NET class derived directly from COM class.
'
```

```
Public Class EcfInner
    Inherits ECFSRV32Lib.BaseComponent
    Private Shared callbackInner As CallBack

    Shared Sub RegisterInner()
        callbackInner = New CallBack()
        ExtensibleClassFactory.RegisterObjectCreationCallback( _
            New System.Runtime.InteropServices.ObjectCreationDelegate( _
            AddressOf callbackInner.Activate))
    End Sub

    'This is the static initializer.
    Shared Sub New()
        RegisterInner()
    End Sub
End Class

[C#]
using System;
using System.Runtime.InteropServices;

public class CallBack
{
    public IntPtr Activate(IntPtr Aggregator)
    {
        ECFSRV32Lib.ObjectActivator oCOM = new
ECFSRV32Lib.ObjectActivator();
        ECFSRV32Lib.IObjectActivator itf =
(ECFSRV32Lib.IObjectActivator)oCOM;
        return (IntPtr) itf.CreateBaseComponent((int)Aggregator);
    }
}

//
// The EcfInner class. First .NET class derived directly
// from COM class.
//
public class EcfInner : ECFSRV32Lib.BaseComponent
{
    static CallBack callbackInner;

    static void RegisterInner()
    {
        callbackInner = new CallBack();
        System.Runtime.InteropServices.ExtensibleClassFactory.
RegisterObjectCreationCallback(new
System.Runtime.InteropServices.ObjectCreationDelegate
(callbackInner.Activate));
    }

    //This is the static initializer.
    static EcfInner()
    {
        RegisterInner();
    }
}
```

Requirements

Namespace: System.Runtime.InteropServices

Platforms: Windows 98, Windows NT 4.0,
Windows Millennium Edition, Windows 2000,
Windows XP Home Edition, Windows XP Professional,
Windows .NET Server family

Assembly: Mscorlib (in Mscorlib.dll)

ExtensibleClassFactory.RegisterObjectCreation Callback Method

Registers a **delegate** that is called when an instance of a managed type, that extends from an unmanaged type, needs to allocate the aggregated unmanaged object.

```
[Visual Basic]
Public Shared Sub RegisterObjectCreationCallback( _
   ByVal callback As ObjectCreationDelegate _
)
[C#]
public static void RegisterObjectCreationCallback(
   ObjectCreationDelegate callback
);
[C++]
public: static void RegisterObjectCreationCallback(
   ObjectCreationDelegate* callback
);
[JScript]
public static function RegisterObjectCreationCallback(
   callback : ObjectCreationDelegate
);
```

Parameters

callback

A **delegate** that is called in place of **CoCreateInstance**.

Remarks

This **delegate** allocates and aggregates the unmanaged object and is called in place of **CoCreateInstance**. This **delegate** must be registered in the context of the static (**Shared** in Visual Basic) class initializer for which the callbacks will be made.

Only one class in an hierarchy should register a **delegate** callback.

Requirements

Platforms: Windows 98, Windows NT 4.0, Windows Millennium Edition, Windows 2000, Windows XP Home Edition, Windows XP Professional, Windows .NET Server family

ExternalException Class

The base exception type for all COM interop exceptions and structured exception handling (SEH) exceptions.

System.Object
  System.Exception
    System.SystemException
      System.Runtime.InteropServices.ExternalException
        Derived classes

```
[Visual Basic]
<Serializable>
Public Class ExternalException
   Inherits SystemException
[C#]
[Serializable]
public class ExternalException : SystemException
[C++]
[Serializable]
public __gc class ExternalException : public SystemException
[JScript]
public
   Serializable
class ExternalException extends SystemException
```

Thread Safety

Any public static (**Shared** in Visual Basic) members of this type are safe for multithreaded operations. Any instance members are not guaranteed to be thread safe.

Remarks

To enhance interoperability between legacy systems and the common language runtime, the **ErrorCode** property stores an integer value (HRESULT) that identifies the error. User defined exceptions should never derive from **ExternalException**, and an **ExternalException** should never be thrown by user code. Use the specific exceptions that derive from **ExternalException** instead.

ExternalException uses the HRESULT E_FAIL which has the value 0x80004005.

ExternalException uses the default **Equals** implementation, which supports reference equality.

For a list of initial values for an instance of **ExternalException**, see the **ExternalException** constructors.

Requirements

Namespace: System.Runtime.InteropServices

Platforms: Windows 98, Windows NT 4.0, Windows Millennium Edition, Windows 2000, Windows XP Home Edition, Windows XP Professional, Windows .NET Server family, .NET Compact Framework - Windows CE .NET

Assembly: Mscorlib (in Mscorlib.dll)

ExternalException Constructor

Initializes a new instance of the **ExternalException** class.

Overload List

Initializes a new instance of the **ExternalException** class with default properties.

Supported by the .NET Compact Framework.

  [Visual Basic] **Public Sub New()**
  [C#] **public ExternalException();**
  [C++] **public: ExternalException();**
  [JScript] **public function ExternalException();**

Initializes a new instance of the **ExternalException** class with a specified error message.

Supported by the .NET Compact Framework.

  [Visual Basic] **Public Sub New(String)**
  [C#] **public ExternalException(string);**
  [C++] **public: ExternalException(String*);**
  [JScript] **public function ExternalException(String);**

Initializes a new instance of the **ExternalException** class from serialization data.

  [Visual Basic] **Protected Sub New(SerializationInfo, StreamingContext)**
  [C#] **protected ExternalException(SerializationInfo, StreamingContext);**
  [C++] **protected: ExternalException(SerializationInfo*, StreamingContext);**
  [JScript] **protected function ExternalException(SerializationInfo, StreamingContext);**

Initializes a new instance of the **ExternalException** class with a specified error message and a reference to the inner exception that is the cause of this exception.

Supported by the .NET Compact Framework.

  [Visual Basic] **Public Sub New(String, Exception)**
  [C#] **public ExternalException(string, Exception);**
  [C++] **public: ExternalException(String*, Exception*);**
  [JScript] **public function ExternalException(String, Exception);**

Initializes a new instance of the **ExternalException** class with a specified error message and the HRESULT of the error.

  [Visual Basic] **Public Sub New(String, Integer)**
  [C#] **public ExternalException(string, int);**
  [C++] **public: ExternalException(String*, int);**
  [JScript] **public function ExternalException(String, int);**

ExternalException Constructor ( )

Initializes a new instance of the **ExternalException** class with default properties.

```
[Visual Basic]
Public Sub New()
[C#]
public ExternalException();
[C++]
public: ExternalException();
[JScript]
public function ExternalException();
```

Remarks

The following table shows the initial property values for an instance of **ExternalException**.

Property	Value
InnerException	A null reference (**Nothing** in Visual Basic).
Message	A localized error message string.

Requirements

Platforms: Windows 98, Windows NT 4.0, Windows Millennium Edition, Windows 2000, Windows XP Home Edition, Windows XP Professional, Windows .NET Server family, .NET Compact Framework - Windows CE .NET

ExternalException Constructor (String)

Initializes a new instance of the **ExternalException** class with a specified error message.

```
[Visual Basic]
Public Sub New( _
   ByVal message As String _
)
[C#]
public ExternalException(
   string message
);
[C++]
public: ExternalException(
   String* message
);
[JScript]
public function ExternalException(
   message : String
);
```

Parameters

message
    The error message that specifies the reason for the exception.

Remarks

The following table shows the initial property values for an instance of **ExternalException**.

Property	Value
InnerException	A null reference (**Nothing** in Visual Basic).
Message	*message*

Requirements

Platforms: Windows 98, Windows NT 4.0, Windows Millennium Edition, Windows 2000, Windows XP Home Edition, Windows XP Professional, Windows .NET Server family, .NET Compact Framework - Windows CE .NET

ExternalException Constructor (SerializationInfo, StreamingContext)

Initializes a new instance of the **ExternalException** class from serialization data.

```
[Visual Basic]
Protected Sub New( _
   ByVal info As SerializationInfo, _
   ByVal context As StreamingContext _
)
[C#]
protected ExternalException(
   SerializationInfo info,
   StreamingContext context
);
[C++]
protected: ExternalException(
   SerializationInfo* info,
   StreamingContext context
);
[JScript]
protected function ExternalException(
   info : SerializationInfo,
   context : StreamingContext
);
```

Parameters

info
    The object that holds the serialized object data.
context
    The contextual information about the source or destination.

Exceptions

Exception Type	Condition
ArgumentNullException	*info* is a null reference (**Nothing** in Visual Basic).

Remarks

This constructor is called during deserialization to reconstitute the exception object transmitted over a stream. For more information, see **XML and SOAP Serialization**.

Requirements

Platforms: Windows 98, Windows NT 4.0, Windows Millennium Edition, Windows 2000, Windows XP Home Edition, Windows XP Professional, Windows .NET Server family

ExternalException Constructor (String, Exception)

Initializes a new instance of the **ExternalException** class with a specified error message and a reference to the inner exception that is the cause of this exception.

```
[Visual Basic]
Public Sub New( _
   ByVal message As String, _
   ByVal inner As Exception _
)
[C#]
public ExternalException(
   string message,
   Exception inner
);
```

```
[C++]
public: ExternalException(
   String* message,
   Exception* inner
);
[JScript]
public function ExternalException(
   message : String,
   inner : Exception
);
```

Parameters

message
> The error message that explains the reason for the exception.

inner
> The exception that is the cause of the current exception. If the *inner* parameter is not a null reference (**Nothing** in Visual Basic), the current exception is raised in a **catch** block that handles the inner exception.

Remarks

An exception that is thrown as a direct result of a previous exception should include a reference to the previous exception in the **InnerException** property. The **InnerException** property returns the same value that is passed into the constructor, or a null reference (**Nothing** in Visual Basic) if the **InnerException** property does not supply the inner exception value to the constructor.

The following table shows the initial property values for an instance of **ExternalException**.

Property	Value
InnerException	The inner exception reference.
Message	The error message string.

Requirements

Platforms: Windows 98, Windows NT 4.0, Windows Millennium Edition, Windows 2000, Windows XP Home Edition, Windows XP Professional, Windows .NET Server family, .NET Compact Framework - Windows CE .NET

ExternalException Constructor (String, Int32)

Initializes a new instance of the **ExternalException** class with a specified error message and the HRESULT of the error.

```
[Visual Basic]
Public Sub New( _
   ByVal message As String, _
   ByVal errorCode As Integer _
)
[C#]
public ExternalException(
   string message,
   int errorCode
);
[C++]
public: ExternalException(
   String* message,
   int errorCode
);
```

```
[JScript]
public function ExternalException(
   message : String,
   errorCode : int
);
```

Parameters

message
> The error message that specifies the reason for the exception.

errorCode
> The HRESULT of the error.

Remarks

The following table shows the initial property values for an instance of **ExternalException**.

Property	Value
ErrorCode	The HRESULT of the error.
InnerException	A null reference (**Nothing** in Visual Basic)
Message	*message*

Requirements

Platforms: Windows 98, Windows NT 4.0, Windows Millennium Edition, Windows 2000, Windows XP Home Edition, Windows XP Professional, Windows .NET Server family

ExternalException.ErrorCode Property

Gets the HRESULT of the error.

```
[Visual Basic]
Public Overridable ReadOnly Property ErrorCode As Integer
[C#]
public virtual int ErrorCode {get;}
[C++]
public: __property virtual int get_ErrorCode();
[JScript]
public function get ErrorCode() : int;
```

Property Value

The HRESULT of the error.

Requirements

Platforms: Windows 98, Windows NT 4.0, Windows Millennium Edition, Windows 2000, Windows XP Home Edition, Windows XP Professional, Windows .NET Server family

FieldOffsetAttribute Class

Indicates the physical position of fields within the unmanaged representation of a class or structure.

System.Object
  System.Attribute
    System.Runtime.InteropServices.FieldOffsetAttribute

```
[Visual Basic]
<AttributeUsage(AttributeTargets.Field)>
NotInheritable Public Class FieldOffsetAttribute
    Inherits Attribute
[C#]
[AttributeUsage(AttributeTargets.Field)]
public sealed class FieldOffsetAttribute : Attribute
[C++]
[AttributeUsage(AttributeTargets::Field)]
public __gc __sealed class FieldOffsetAttribute : public Attribute
[JScript]
public
    AttributeUsage(AttributeTargets.Field)
class FieldOffsetAttribute extends Attribute
```

Thread Safety

Any public static (**Shared** in Visual Basic) members of this type are safe for multithreaded operations. Any instance members are not guaranteed to be thread safe.

Remarks

You can apply this attribute to fields.

This attribute is used when **System.Runtime.InteropServices.StructLayoutAttribute**, with **LayoutKind.Explicit** passed to its constructor, is applied to a class or structure to specify the offset of each non- static (**Shared** in Visual Basic) or constant member within the unmanaged representation of that class or structure. The attribute has no affect on the managed layout of the members of the type.

Example

[Visual Basic, C#] The following example demonstrates how to apply the **FieldOffsetAttribute** to members of a class with an explicit layout.

```
[Visual Basic]
<StructLayout(LayoutKind.Explicit)> _
Public Class SYSTEM_INFO
    <FieldOffset(0)> Private OemId As System.UInt64
    <FieldOffset(4)> Private PageSize As System.UInt64
    <FieldOffset(16)> Private ActiveProcessorMask As System.UInt64
    <FieldOffset(20)> Private NumberOfProcessors As System.UInt64
    <FieldOffset(24)> Private ProcessorType As System.UInt64
End Class

[C#]
[StructLayout(LayoutKind.Explicit)]
public class SYSTEM_INFO
{
[FieldOffset(0)] public ulong OemId;
[FieldOffset(4)] public ulong PageSize;
[FieldOffset(16)] public ulong ActiveProcessorMask;
[FieldOffset(20)] public ulong NumberOfProcessors;
[FieldOffset(24)] public ulong ProcessorType;
}
```

Requirements

Namespace: System.Runtime.InteropServices

Platforms: Windows 98, Windows NT 4.0, Windows Millennium Edition, Windows 2000, Windows XP Home Edition, Windows XP Professional, Windows .NET Server family

Assembly: Mscorlib (in Mscorlib.dll)

FieldOffsetAttribute Constructor

Initializes a new instance of the **FieldOffsetAttribute** class with the offset in the structure to the beginning of the field.

```
[Visual Basic]
Public Sub New( _
    ByVal offset As Integer _
)
[C#]
public FieldOffsetAttribute(
    int offset
);
[C++]
public: FieldOffsetAttribute(
    int offset
);
[JScript]
public function FieldOffsetAttribute(
    offset : int
);
```

Parameters

offset
    The offset in bytes from the beginning of the structure to the beginning of the field.

Requirements

Platforms: Windows 98, Windows NT 4.0, Windows Millennium Edition, Windows 2000, Windows XP Home Edition, Windows XP Professional, Windows .NET Server family, Common Language Infrastructure (CLI) Standard

FieldOffsetAttribute.Value Property

Gets the offset from the beginning of the structure to the beginning of the field.

```
[Visual Basic]
Public ReadOnly Property Value As Integer
[C#]
public int Value {get;}
[C++]
public: __property int get_Value();
[JScript]
public function get Value() : int;
```

Property Value

The offset from the beginning of the structure to the beginning of the field.

Requirements

Platforms: Windows 98, Windows NT 4.0, Windows Millennium Edition, Windows 2000, Windows XP Home Edition, Windows XP Professional, Windows .NET Server family, Common Language Infrastructure (CLI) Standard

FILETIME Structure

This structure is a 64-bit value representing the number of 100-nanosecond intervals since January 1, 1601.

System.Object
　System.ValueType
　　System.Runtime.InteropServices.FILETIME

```
[Visual Basic]
<ComVisible(False)>
Public Structure FILETIME
[C#]
[ComVisible(false)]
public struct FILETIME
[C++]
[ComVisible(false)]
public __value struct FILETIME
```

[JScript] In JScript, you can use the structures in the .NET Framework, but you cannot define your own.

Thread Safety

Any public static (**Shared** in Visual Basic) members of this type are safe for multithreaded operations. Any instance members are not guaranteed to be thread safe.

Remarks

For more information about the **FILETIME** structure, see the MSDN Library.

Requirements

Namespace: System.Runtime.InteropServices

Platforms: Windows 98, Windows NT 4.0, Windows Millennium Edition, Windows 2000, Windows XP Home Edition, Windows XP Professional, Windows .NET Server family

Assembly: Mscorlib (in Mscorlib.dll)

FILETIME.dwHighDateTime Field

Specifies the high 32 bits of the **FILETIME**.

```
[Visual Basic]
Public dwHighDateTime As Integer
[C#]
public int dwHighDateTime;
[C++]
public: int dwHighDateTime;
[JScript]
public var dwHighDateTime : int;
```

Requirements

Platforms: Windows 98, Windows NT 4.0, Windows Millennium Edition, Windows 2000, Windows XP Home Edition, Windows XP Professional, Windows .NET Server family

FILETIME.dwLowDateTime Field

Specifies the low 32 bits of the **FILETIME**.

```
[Visual Basic]
Public dwLowDateTime As Integer
[C#]
public int dwLowDateTime;
[C++]
public: int dwLowDateTime;
[JScript]
public var dwLowDateTime : int;
```

Requirements

Platforms: Windows 98, Windows NT 4.0, Windows Millennium Edition, Windows 2000, Windows XP Home Edition, Windows XP Professional, Windows .NET Server family

FUNCDESC Structure

Defines a function description.

System.Object
  System.ValueType
    System.Runtime.InteropServices.FUNCDESC

```
[Visual Basic]
<ComVisible(False)>
Public Structure FUNCDESC
[C#]
[ComVisible(false)]
public struct FUNCDESC
[C++]
[ComVisible(false)]
public __value struct FUNCDESC
```

[JScript] In JScript, you can use the structures in the .NET Framework, but you cannot define your own.

Thread Safety

Any public static (**Shared** in Visual Basic) members of this type are safe for multithreaded operations. Any instance members are not guaranteed to be thread safe.

Remarks

For additional information about **FUNCDESC**, see the MSDN Library.

Requirements

Namespace: System.Runtime.InteropServices

Platforms: Windows 98, Windows NT 4.0, Windows Millennium Edition, Windows 2000, Windows XP Home Edition, Windows XP Professional, Windows .NET Server family

Assembly: Mscorlib (in Mscorlib.dll)

FUNCDESC.callconv Field

Specifies the calling convention of a function.

```
[Visual Basic]
Public callconv As CALLCONV
[C#]
public CALLCONV callconv;
[C++]
public: CALLCONV callconv;
[JScript]
public var callconv : CALLCONV;
```

Remarks

For additional information about **FUNCDESC**, see the MSDN Library.

Requirements

Platforms: Windows 98, Windows NT 4.0, Windows Millennium Edition, Windows 2000, Windows XP Home Edition, Windows XP Professional, Windows .NET Server family

FUNCDESC.cParams Field

Counts the total number of parameters.

```
[Visual Basic]
Public cParams As Short
[C#]
public short cParams;
[C++]
public: short cParams;
[JScript]
public var cParams : Int16;
```

Remarks

For additional information about **FUNCDESC**, see the MSDN Library.

Requirements

Platforms: Windows 98, Windows NT 4.0, Windows Millennium Edition, Windows 2000, Windows XP Home Edition, Windows XP Professional, Windows .NET Server family

FUNCDESC.cParamsOpt Field

Counts the optional parameters.

```
[Visual Basic]
Public cParamsOpt As Short
[C#]
public short cParamsOpt;
[C++]
public: short cParamsOpt;
[JScript]
public var cParamsOpt : Int16;
```

Remarks

For additional information about **FUNCDESC**, see the MSDN Library.

Requirements

Platforms: Windows 98, Windows NT 4.0, Windows Millennium Edition, Windows 2000, Windows XP Home Edition, Windows XP Professional, Windows .NET Server family

FUNCDESC.cScodes Field

Counts the permitted return values.

```
[Visual Basic]
Public cScodes As Short
[C#]
public short cScodes;
[C++]
public: short cScodes;
[JScript]
public var cScodes : Int16;
```

Remarks

For additional information about **FUNCDESC**, see the MSDN Library.

Requirements

Platforms: Windows 98, Windows NT 4.0, Windows Millennium Edition, Windows 2000, Windows XP Home Edition, Windows XP Professional, Windows .NET Server family

FUNCDESC.elemdescFunc Field

Contains the return type of the function.

```
[Visual Basic]
Public elemdescFunc As ELEMDESC
[C#]
public ELEMDESC elemdescFunc;
[C++]
public: ELEMDESC elemdescFunc;
[JScript]
public var elemdescFunc : ELEMDESC;
```

Remarks

For additional information about **FUNCDESC**, see the MSDN Library.

Requirements

Platforms: Windows 98, Windows NT 4.0, Windows Millennium Edition, Windows 2000, Windows XP Home Edition, Windows XP Professional, Windows .NET Server family

FUNCDESC.funckind Field

Specifies whether the function is virtual, static, or dispatch-only.

```
[Visual Basic]
Public funckind As FUNCKIND
[C#]
public FUNCKIND funckind;
[C++]
public: FUNCKIND funckind;
[JScript]
public var funckind : FUNCKIND;
```

Remarks

For additional information about **FUNCDESC**, see the MSDN Library.

Requirements

Platforms: Windows 98, Windows NT 4.0, Windows Millennium Edition, Windows 2000, Windows XP Home Edition, Windows XP Professional, Windows .NET Server family

FUNCDESC.invkind Field

Specifies the type of a property function.

```
[Visual Basic]
Public invkind As INVOKEKIND
[C#]
public INVOKEKIND invkind;
[C++]
public: INVOKEKIND invkind;
[JScript]
public var invkind : INVOKEKIND;
```

Remarks

For additional information about **FUNCDESC**, see the MSDN Library.

Requirements

Platforms: Windows 98, Windows NT 4.0, Windows Millennium Edition, Windows 2000, Windows XP Home Edition, Windows XP Professional, Windows .NET Server family

FUNCDESC.lprgelemdescParam Field

Indicates the size of **cParams**.

```
[Visual Basic]
Public lprgelemdescParam As IntPtr
[C#]
public IntPtr lprgelemdescParam;
[C++]
public: IntPtr lprgelemdescParam;
[JScript]
public var lprgelemdescParam : IntPtr;
```

Remarks

For additional information about **FUNCDESC**, see the MSDN Library.

Requirements

Platforms: Windows 98, Windows NT 4.0, Windows Millennium Edition, Windows 2000, Windows XP Home Edition, Windows XP Professional, Windows .NET Server family

FUNCDESC.lprgscode Field

Stores the count of errors a function can return on a 16-bit system.

```
[Visual Basic]
Public lprgscode As IntPtr
[C#]
public IntPtr lprgscode;
[C++]
public: IntPtr lprgscode;
[JScript]
public var lprgscode : IntPtr;
```

Remarks

For additional information about **FUNCDESC**, see the MSDN Library.

Requirements

Platforms: Windows 98, Windows NT 4.0, Windows Millennium Edition, Windows 2000, Windows XP Home Edition, Windows XP Professional, Windows .NET Server family

FUNCDESC.memid Field

Identifies the function member ID.

```
[Visual Basic]
Public memid As Integer
[C#]
public int memid;
[C++]
public: int memid;
[JScript]
public var memid : int;
```

Remarks

For additional information about **FUNCDESC**, see the MSDN Library.

Requirements

Platforms: Windows 98, Windows NT 4.0, Windows Millennium Edition, Windows 2000, Windows XP Home Edition, Windows XP Professional, Windows .NET Server family

FUNCDESC.oVft Field

Specifies the offset in the VTBL for **FUNC_VIRTUAL**.

```
[Visual Basic]
Public oVft As Short
[C#]
public short oVft;
[C++]
public: short oVft;
[JScript]
public var oVft : Int16;
```

Remarks

For additional information about **FUNCDESC**, see the MSDN Library.

Requirements

Platforms: Windows 98, Windows NT 4.0, Windows Millennium Edition, Windows 2000, Windows XP Home Edition, Windows XP Professional, Windows .NET Server family

FUNCDESC.wFuncFlags Field

Indicates the **FUNCFLAGS** of a function.

```
[Visual Basic]
Public wFuncFlags As Short
[C#]
public short wFuncFlags;
[C++]
public: short wFuncFlags;
[JScript]
public var wFuncFlags : Int16;
```

Remarks

For additional information about **FUNCDESC**, see the MSDN Library.

Requirements

Platforms: Windows 98, Windows NT 4.0, Windows Millennium Edition, Windows 2000, Windows XP Home Edition, Windows XP Professional, Windows .NET Server family

FUNCFLAGS Enumeration

Identifies the constants that define the properties of a function.

This enumeration has a **FlagsAttribute** attribute that allows a bitwise combination of its member values.

```
[Visual Basic]
<Flags>
<Serializable>
<ComVisible(False)>
Public Enum FUNCFLAGS
[C#]
[Flags]
[Serializable]
[ComVisible(false)]
public enum FUNCFLAGS
[C++]
[Flags]
[Serializable]
[ComVisible(false)]
__value public enum FUNCFLAGS
[JScript]
public
    Flags
    Serializable
    ComVisible(false)
enum FUNCFLAGS
```

Remarks

For additional information about **FUNCFLAGS**, see the MSDN Library.

Members

Member name	Description	Value
FUNCFLAG_F-BINDABLE	The function that supports data binding.	4
FUNCFLAG_F-DEFAULTBIND	The function that best represents the object. Only one function in a type information can have this attribute.	32
FUNCFLAG_F-DEFAULT-COLLELEM	Permits an optimization in which the compiler looks for a member named "xyz" on the type of "abc". If such a member is found, and is flagged as an accessor function for an element of the default collection, a call is generated to that member function. Permitted on members in dispinterfaces and interfaces; not permitted on modules.	256
FUNCFLAG_F-DISPLAYBIND	The function that is displayed to the user as bindable. **FUNCFLAG_FBINDABLE** must also be set.	16
FUNCFLAG_F-HIDDEN	The function should not be displayed to the user, although it exists and is bindable.	64
FUNCFLAG_F-IMMEDIATEBIND	Mapped as individual bindable properties.	4096

Member name	Description	Value
FUNCFLAG_F-NONBROWSABLE	The property appears in an object browser, but not in a properties browser.	1024
FUNCFLAG_F-REPLACEABLE	Tags the interface as having default behaviors.	2048
FUNCFLAG_F-REQUESTEDIT	When set, any call to a method that sets the property results first in a call to **IPropertyNotify-Sink::OnRequestEdit**. The implementation of **OnRequest-Edit** determines if the call is allowed to set the property.	8
FUNCFLAG_F-RESTRICTED	The function should not be accessible from macro languages. This flag is intended for system-level functions or functions that type browsers should not display.	1
FUNCFLAG_F-SOURCE	The function returns an object that is a source of events.	2
FUNCFLAG_F-UIDEFAULT	The type information member is the default member for display in the user interface.	512
FUNCFLAG_F-USESGETLAST-ERROR	The function supports **GetLastError**. If an error occurs during the function, the caller can call **GetLastError** to retrieve the error code.	128

Requirements

Namespace: System.Runtime.InteropServices

Platforms: Windows 98, Windows NT 4.0, Windows Millennium Edition, Windows 2000, Windows XP Home Edition, Windows XP Professional, Windows .NET Server family

Assembly: Mscorlib (in Mscorlib.dll)

FUNCKIND Enumeration

Defines how to access a function.

```
[Visual Basic]
<Serializable>
<ComVisible(False)>
Public Enum FUNCKIND
[C#]
[Serializable]
[ComVisible(false)]
public enum FUNCKIND
[C++]
[Serializable]
[ComVisible(false)]
__value public enum FUNCKIND
[JScript]
public
   Serializable
   ComVisible(false)
enum FUNCKIND
```

Remarks

For additional information about **FUNCKIND**, see the MSDN Library.

Members

Member name	Description
FUNC_DISPATCH	The function can be accessed only through **IDispatch**.
FUNC_NONVIRTUAL	The function is accessed by static (**Shared** in Visual Basic) address and takes an implicit **this** pointer.
FUNC_PUREVIRTUAL	The function is accessed through the virtual function table (VTBL), and takes an implicit **this** pointer.
FUNC_STATIC	The function is accessed by static (**Shared** in Visual Basic) address and does not take an implicit **this** pointer.
FUNC_VIRTUAL	The function is accessed the same as **FUNC_PUREVIRTUAL**, except the function has an implementation.

Requirements

Namespace: System.Runtime.InteropServices

Platforms: Windows 98, Windows NT 4.0, Windows Millennium Edition, Windows 2000, Windows XP Home Edition, Windows XP Professional, Windows .NET Server family

Assembly: Mscorlib (in Mscorlib.dll)

GCHandle Structure

Provides a means for accessing a managed object from unmanaged memory.

System.Object
   System.ValueType
      System.Runtime.InteropServices.GCHandle

```
[Visual Basic]
Public Structure GCHandle
[C#]
public struct GCHandle
[C++]
public __value struct GCHandle
```

[JScript] In JScript, you can use the structures in the .NET Framework, but you cannot define your own.

Thread Safety

Any public static (**Shared** in Visual Basic) members of this type are safe for multithreaded operations. Any instance members are not guaranteed to be thread safe.

Remarks

The garbage collector handle, or **GCHandle** value type, is used in conjunction with the **GCHandleType** enumeration to create a handle corresponding to any managed object. This handle can be one of four types: **Weak**, **WeakTrackResurrection**, **Normal**, or **Pinned**. Once allocated, you can use a **GCHandle** to prevent the managed object from being collected by the garbage collector when an unmanaged client holds the only reference. Without such a handle, the object can be collected by the garbage collector before completing its work on behalf of the unmanaged client.

You can also use the **GCHandle** to create a pinned object that returns a memory address and prevents the garbage collector from moving the object in memory. From managed code, you can obtain a new object reference. For all but the **IsAllocated** property, you must apply unmanaged code permission by using **SecurityPermission** with the associated **SecurityPermissionFlag.UnmanagedCode** enumeration value.

Example

[Visual Basic, C#] The following example shows an App class that creates a handle to a managed object using the **GCHandle.Alloc** method, which prevents the managed object from being collected. A call to the **EnumWindows** method passes a delegate and a managed object (both declared as managed types, but not shown), and casts the handle to an **IntPtr**. The unmanaged function passes the type back to the caller as a parameter of the callback function.

```
[Visual Basic]
Public Class App
   Public Shared Sub Main()
      Dim tw As TextWriter = System.Console.Out
      Dim gch As GCHandle = GCHandle.Alloc( tw )

      ' Platform invoke prevents the delegate from being
garbage collected
      ' before the call ends.
      Dim cewp As CallBack
      cewp = AddressOf App.CaptureEnumWindowsProc
      LibWrap.EnumWindows( cewp, GCHandle.op_Explicit( gch ))
      gch.Free()
   End Sub 'Main

   Public Shared Function CaptureEnumWindowsProc( ByVal handle _
         As Integer, ByVal param As IntPtr ) As Boolean
```

```
      Dim gch As GCHandle = GCHandle.op_Explicit( param )
      Dim tw As TextWriter = CType( gch.Target, TextWriter )
      tw.WriteLine( handle )
      return True
   End Function 'CaptureEnumWindowsProc
End Class 'App
```

```
[C#]
public class App
{
   public static void Main()
   {
      TextWriter tw = System.Console.Out;
      GCHandle gch = GCHandle.Alloc( tw );
      CallBack cewp = new CallBack( CaptureEnumWindowsProc );

      // Platform invoke prevents the delegate from being garbage
      // collected before the call ends.
      LibWrap.EnumWindows( cewp, (IntPtr)gch );
      gch.Free();
   }

   private static bool CaptureEnumWindowsProc( int handle, IntPtr
param )
   {
      GCHandle gch = (GCHandle)param;
      TextWriter tw = (TextWriter)gch.Target;
      tw.WriteLine( handle );
      return true;
   }
}
```

Requirements

Namespace: System.Runtime.InteropServices

Platforms: Windows 98, Windows NT 4.0, Windows Millennium Edition, Windows 2000, Windows XP Home Edition, Windows XP Professional, Windows .NET Server family, .NET Compact Framework - Windows CE .NET

Assembly: Mscorlib (in Mscorlib.dll)

GCHandle.IsAllocated Property

Gets a value indicating whether the handle is allocated.

```
[Visual Basic]
Public ReadOnly Property IsAllocated As Boolean
[C#]
public bool IsAllocated {get;}
[C++]
public: __property bool get_IsAllocated();
[JScript]
public function get IsAllocated() : Boolean;
```

Property Value

true if the handle is allocated; otherwise, **false**.

Remarks

Use this property when using **Weak** handles to determine if the **GCHandle** is still available. When the garbage collector collects the object, the **Weak** handle can still be resurrected in the finalizer. In that case, the handle is not allocated (it is lost when the garbage collector attempts to collect the object), even though the target object is valid.

Requirements

Platforms: Windows 98, Windows NT 4.0,
Windows Millennium Edition, Windows 2000,
Windows XP Home Edition, Windows XP Professional,
Windows .NET Server family,
.NET Compact Framework - Windows CE .NET,
Common Language Infrastructure (CLI) Standard

GCHandle.Target Property

Gets or sets the object this handle represents.

```
[Visual Basic]
Public Property Target As Object
[C#]
public object Target {get; set;}
[C++]
public: __property Object* get_Target();
public: __property void set_Target(Object*);
[JScript]
public function get Target() : Object;
public function set Target(Object);
```

Property Value

The object this handle represents.

Exceptions

Exception Type	Condition
InvalidOperation-Exception	The handle was freed, or never initialized.

Requirements

Platforms: Windows 98, Windows NT 4.0,
Windows Millennium Edition, Windows 2000,
Windows XP Home Edition, Windows XP Professional,
Windows .NET Server family,
.NET Compact Framework - Windows CE .NET,
Common Language Infrastructure (CLI) Standard

.NET Framework Security:

- **SecurityPermission** for operating with unmanaged code. Associated enumeration: **SecurityPermissionFlag.UnmanagedCode**.

GCHandle.AddrOfPinnedObject Method

Retrieves the address of an object in a **Pinned** handle.

```
[Visual Basic]
Public Function AddrOfPinnedObject() As IntPtr
[C#]
public IntPtr AddrOfPinnedObject();
[C++]
public: IntPtr AddrOfPinnedObject();
[JScript]
public function AddrOfPinnedObject() : IntPtr;
```

Return Value

The address of the of the **Pinned** object as an **IntPtr**.

Exceptions

Exception Type	Condition
InvalidOperation-Exception	The handle is any type other than **Pinned**.

Remarks

This method is used to get a stable pointer to the object. Pinning an object prevents the garbage collector from moving it around in memory, thereby reducing the efficiency of the garbage collector.

Requirements

Platforms: Windows 98, Windows NT 4.0,
Windows Millennium Edition, Windows 2000,
Windows XP Home Edition, Windows XP Professional,
Windows .NET Server family,
.NET Compact Framework - Windows CE .NET,
Common Language Infrastructure (CLI) Standard

.NET Framework Security:

- **SecurityPermission** for operating with unmanaged code. Associated enumeration: **SecurityPermissionFlag.UnmanagedCode**.

GCHandle.Alloc Method

Allocates a handle for the specified object.

Overload List

Allocates a **Normal** handle for the specified object.

Supported by the .NET Compact Framework.

> [Visual Basic] **Overloads Public Shared Function Alloc(Object) As GCHandle**
>
> [C#] **public static GCHandle Alloc(object);**
>
> [C++] **public: static GCHandle Alloc(Object*);**
>
> [JScript] **public static function Alloc(Object) : GCHandle;**

Allocates a handle of the specified type for the specified object.

Supported by the .NET Compact Framework.

> [Visual Basic] **Overloads Public Shared Function Alloc(Object, GCHandleType) As GCHandle**
>
> [C#] **public static GCHandle Alloc(object, GCHandleType);**
>
> [C++] **public: static GCHandle Alloc(Object*, GCHandleType);**
>
> [JScript] **public static function Alloc(Object, GCHandleType) : GCHandle;**

GCHandle.Alloc Method (Object)

Allocates a **Normal** handle for the specified object.

```
[Visual Basic]
Overloads Public Shared Function Alloc( _
    ByVal value As Object _
) As GCHandle
[C#]
public static GCHandle Alloc(
    object value
);
[C++]
public: static GCHandle Alloc(
    Object* value
);
```

```
[JScript]
public static function Alloc(
    value : Object
) : GCHandle;
```

Parameters

value

The object that uses the **GCHandle**.

Return Value

A new **GCHandle** that protects the object from garbage collection. This **GCHandle** must be released with **Free** when it is no longer needed.

Exceptions

Exception Type	Condition
ArgumentException	An instance with nonprimitive (non-blittible) members cannot be pinned.

Remarks

Normal handles are opaque, which means that you cannot resolve the address of the object it contains through the handle.

Requirements

Platforms: Windows 98, Windows NT 4.0, Windows Millennium Edition, Windows 2000, Windows XP Home Edition, Windows XP Professional, Windows .NET Server family, .NET Compact Framework - Windows CE .NET, Common Language Infrastructure (CLI) Standard

.NET Framework Security:

- **SecurityPermission** for operating with unmanaged code. Associated enumeration: **SecurityPermissionFlag.UnmanagedCode**.

GCHandle.Alloc Method (Object, GCHandleType)

Allocates a handle of the specified type for the specified object.

```
[Visual Basic]
Overloads Public Shared Function Alloc( _
    ByVal value As Object, _
    ByVal type As GCHandleType _
) As GCHandle
[C#]
public static GCHandle Alloc(
    object value,
    GCHandleType type
);
[C++]
public: static GCHandle Alloc(
    Object* value,
    GCHandleType type
);
[JScript]
public static function Alloc(
    value : Object,
    type : GCHandleType
) : GCHandle;
```

Parameters

value

The object that uses the **GCHandle**.

type

One of the **GCHandleType** values, indicating the type of **GCHandle** to create.

Return Value

A new **GCHandle** of the specified type. This **GCHandle** must be released with **Free** when it is no longer needed.

Exceptions

Exception Type	Condition
ArgumentException	An instance with nonprimitive (non-blittible) members cannot be pinned.

Requirements

Platforms: Windows 98, Windows NT 4.0, Windows Millennium Edition, Windows 2000, Windows XP Home Edition, Windows XP Professional, Windows .NET Server family, .NET Compact Framework - Windows CE .NET, Common Language Infrastructure (CLI) Standard

.NET Framework Security:

- **SecurityPermission** for operating with unmanaged code. Associated enumeration: **SecurityPermissionFlag.UnmanagedCode**.

GCHandle.Free Method

Releases a **GCHandle**.

```
[Visual Basic]
Public Sub Free()
[C#]
public void Free();
[C++]
public: void Free();
[JScript]
public function Free();
```

Exceptions

Exception Type	Condition
InvalidOperation-Exception	The handle was freed or never initialized.

Remarks

The caller must ensure that for a given handle, **Free** is called only once.

Requirements

Platforms: Windows 98, Windows NT 4.0, Windows Millennium Edition, Windows 2000, Windows XP Home Edition, Windows XP Professional, Windows .NET Server family, .NET Compact Framework - Windows CE .NET, Common Language Infrastructure (CLI) Standard

.NET Framework Security:

- **SecurityPermission** for operating with unmanaged code. Associated enumeration: **SecurityPermissionFlag.UnmanagedCode**.

GCHandle to IntPtr Conversion

A **GCHandle** is stored using an internal integer representation.

```
[Visual Basic]
returnValue = GCHandle.op_Explicit(value)
[C#]
public static explicit operator IntPtr(
   GCHandle value
);
[C++]
public: static IntPtr op_Explicit();
[JScript]
returnValue = IntPtr(value);
```

[Visual Basic] In Visual Basic, you can use the conversion operators defined by a type, but you cannot define your own.

[JScript] In JScript, you can use the conversion operators defined by a type, but you cannot define your own.

Arguments [Visual Basic, JScript]

value

   The **GCHandle** for which the integer is required.

Parameters [C#]

value

   The **GCHandle** for which the integer is required.

Return Value

The integer value.

Remarks

This method can be used to retrieve the integer value from a **GCHandle**.

Requirements

Platforms: Windows 98, Windows NT 4.0, Windows Millennium Edition, Windows 2000, Windows XP Home Edition, Windows XP Professional, Windows .NET Server family, .NET Compact Framework - Windows CE .NET, Common Language Infrastructure (CLI) Standard

.NET Framework Security:

•   **SecurityPermission** for operating with unmanaged code. Associated enumeration: **SecurityPermissionFlag.UnmanagedCode.**

IntPtr to GCHandle Conversion

A **GCHandle** is stored using an internal integer representation.

```
[Visual Basic]
returnValue = GCHandle.op_Explicit(value)
[C#]
public static explicit operator GCHandle(
   IntPtr value
);
[C++]
public: static GCHandle op_Explicit(
   IntPtr value
);
[JScript]
returnValue = GCHandle(value);
```

[Visual Basic] In Visual Basic, you can use the conversion operators defined by a type, but you cannot define your own.

[JScript] In JScript, you can use the conversion operators defined by a type, but you cannot define your own.

Arguments [Visual Basic, JScript]

value

   An **IntPtr** that indicates the handle for which the conversion is required.

Parameters [C#, C++]

value

   An **IntPtr** that indicates the handle for which the conversion is required.

Return Value

The **GCHandle**.

Remarks

This method allows you to retrieve a **GCHandle** from an integer value.

Requirements

Platforms: Windows 98, Windows NT 4.0, Windows Millennium Edition, Windows 2000, Windows XP Home Edition, Windows XP Professional, Windows .NET Server family, .NET Compact Framework - Windows CE .NET, Common Language Infrastructure (CLI) Standard

.NET Framework Security:

•   **SecurityPermission** for operating with unmanaged code. Associated enumeration: **SecurityPermissionFlag.UnmanagedCode.**

GCHandleType Enumeration

Represents the types of handles the **GCHandle** class can allocate.

```
[Visual Basic]
<Serializable>
Public Enum GCHandleType
[C#]
[Serializable]
public enum GCHandleType
[C++]
[Serializable]
_value public enum GCHandleType
[JScript]
public
    Serializable
enum GCHandleType
```

Members

Member name	Description
Normal Supported by the .NET Compact Framework.	This handle type represents an opaque handle, meaning you cannot resolve the address of the pinned object through the handle. You can use this type to track an object and prevent its collection by the garbage collector. This enumeration member is useful when an unmanaged client holds the only reference, which is undetectable from the garbage collector, to a managed object.
Pinned Supported by the .NET Compact Framework.	This handle type is similar to **Normal**, but allows the address of the pinned object to be taken. This prevents the garbage collector from moving the object and hence undermines the efficiency of the garbage collector. Use the **Free** method to free the allocated handle as soon as possible.
Weak Supported by the .NET Compact Framework.	This handle type is used to track an object, but allow it to be collected. When an object is collected, the contents of the **GCHandle** are zeroed. **Weak** references are zeroed before the finalizer runs, so even if the finalizer resurrects the object, the **Weak** reference is still zeroed.
WeakTrackResurrection Supported by the .NET Compact Framework.	This handle type is similar to **Weak**, but the handle is not zeroed if the object is resurrected during finalization.

Requirements

Namespace: System.Runtime.InteropServices

Platforms: Windows 98, Windows NT 4.0, Windows Millennium Edition, Windows 2000, Windows XP Home Edition, Windows XP Professional, Windows .NET Server family, .NET Compact Framework - Windows CE .NET

Assembly: Mscorlib (in Mscorlib.dll)

GuidAttribute Class

Supplies an explicit **System.Guid** when an automatic GUID is undesirable.

System.Object
  System.Attribute
    System.Runtime.InteropServices.GuidAttribute

```
[Visual Basic]
<AttributeUsage(AttributeTargets.Assembly Or AttributeTargets.Class _
  Or AttributeTargets.Struct Or AttributeTargets.Enum Or _
  AttributeTargets.Interface Or AttributeTargets.Delegate)>
NotInheritable Public Class GuidAttribute
  Inherits Attribute
[C#]
[AttributeUsage(AttributeTargets.Assembly | AttributeTargets.Class
  | AttributeTargets.Struct | AttributeTargets.Enum |
  AttributeTargets.Interface | AttributeTargets.Delegate)]
public sealed class GuidAttribute : Attribute
[C++]
[AttributeUsage(AttributeTargets::Assembly |
  AttributeTargets::Class | AttributeTargets::Struct |
  AttributeTargets::Enum | AttributeTargets::Interface |
  AttributeTargets::Delegate)]
public __gc __sealed class GuidAttribute : public Attribute
[JScript]
public
  AttributeUsage(AttributeTargets.Assembly | AttributeTargets.Class |
  AttributeTargets.Struct | AttributeTargets.Enum |
  AttributeTargets.Interface | AttributeTargets.Delegate)
class GuidAttribute extends Attribute
```

Thread Safety

Any public static (**Shared** in Visual Basic) members of this type are safe for multithreaded operations. Any instance members are not guaranteed to be thread safe.

Remarks

You can apply this attribute to assemblies, interfaces, classes, enumerations, structures, or delegates, although the **Type Library Importer (Tlbimp.exe)** can apply it for you when it imports a type library.

The string passed to the attribute must be in a format that is an acceptable constructor argument for the type **Guid**. To avoid conflicts with the type **Guid**, use the long name **GuidAttribute** explicitly. Only use an explicit GUID when a type must have a specific GUID. If the attribute is omitted, a GUID is assigned automatically.

Example

[Visual Basic, C#, JScript] The following example demonstrates how to apply the **GuidAttribute** to a class that is exported to COM with a fixed GUID.

```
[Visual Basic]
<GuidAttribute("9ED54F84-A89D-4fcd-A854-44251E925F09")> _
Public Class SampleClass
    ' Insert class members here.
End Class

[C#]
[GuidAttribute("9ED54F84-A89D-4fcd-A854-44251E925F09")]

[JScript]
public GuidAttribute("9ED54F84-A89D-4fcd-A854-44251E925F09")
```

```
class SampleClass{
    // Insert class members here
}
```

Requirements

Namespace: System.Runtime.InteropServices

Platforms: Windows 98, Windows NT 4.0, Windows Millennium Edition, Windows 2000, Windows XP Home Edition, Windows XP Professional, Windows .NET Server family, .NET Compact Framework - Windows CE .NET

Assembly: Mscorlib (in Mscorlib.dll)

GuidAttribute Constructor

Initializes a new instance of the **GuidAttribute** class with the specified GUID.

```
[Visual Basic]
Public Sub New( _
   ByVal guid As String _
)
[C#]
public GuidAttribute(
   string guid
);
[C++]
public: GuidAttribute(
   String* guid
);
[JScript]
public function GuidAttribute(
   guid : String
);
```

Parameters

guid
    The **Guid** to be assigned.

Requirements

Platforms: Windows 98, Windows NT 4.0, Windows Millennium Edition, Windows 2000, Windows XP Home Edition, Windows XP Professional, Windows .NET Server family, .NET Compact Framework - Windows CE .NET

GuidAttribute.Value Property

Gets the **Guid** of the class.

```
[Visual Basic]
Public ReadOnly Property Value As String
[C#]
public string Value {get;}
[C++]
public: __property String* get_Value();
[JScript]
public function get Value() : String;
```

Property Value

The **Guid** of the class.

Requirements

Platforms: Windows 98, Windows NT 4.0,
Windows Millennium Edition, Windows 2000,
Windows XP Home Edition, Windows XP Professional,
Windows .NET Server family,
.NET Compact Framework - Windows CE .NET

HandleRef Structure

Wraps a managed object holding a handle to a resource that is passed to unmanaged code using platform invoke.

System.Object
  System.ValueType
    System.Runtime.InteropServices.HandleRef

```
[Visual Basic]
Public Structure HandleRef
[C#]
public struct HandleRef
[C++]
public __value struct HandleRef
```

[JScript] In JScript, you can use the structures in the .NET Framework, but you cannot define your own.

Thread Safety

Any public static (**Shared** in Visual Basic) members of this type are safe for multithreaded operations. Any instance members are not guaranteed to be thread safe.

Remarks

If you use platform invoke to call a managed object, and the object is not referenced elsewhere after the platform invoke call, it is possible for the garbage collector to finalize the managed object. This action releases the resource and invalidates the handle, causing the platform invoke call to fail. Wrapping a handle with **HandleRef** guarantees that the managed object is not garbage collected until the platform invoke call completes.

The **HandleRef** value type, like **GCHandle**, is a special type recognized by the interop marshaler. A normal, nonpinned **GCHandle** also prevents untimely garbage collection, yet **HandleRef** provides better performance. Although using **HandleRef** to keep an object alive for the duration of a platform invoke call is preferred, you can also use the **GC.KeepAlive** method for the same purpose.

The **HandleRef** constructor takes two parameters: an **Object** representing the wrapper, and an **IntPtr** representing the unmanaged handle. The interop marshaler passes only the handle to unmanaged code, and guarantees that the wrapper (passed as the first parameter to the constructor of the **HandleRef**) remains alive for the duration of the call.

Example

[Visual Basic, C#] The following example shows how to use **HandleRef** to keep alive an object passed as the first parameter. The interop marshaler passes only the handle to unmanaged code.

```
[Visual Basic]
Dim fs As New FileStream( "HandleRef.txt", FileMode.Open )
Dim hr As New HandleRef( fs, fs.Handle )
Dim buffer As New StringBuilder( 5 )
Dim read As Integer = 0

' platform invoke will hold reference to HandleRef until call ends

LibWrap.ReadFile( hr, buffer, 5, read, 0 )
Console.WriteLine( "Read with struct parameter: {0}", buffer )
```

```
[C#]
FileStream fs = new FileStream( "HandleRef.txt", FileMode.Open );
HandleRef hr = new HandleRef( fs, fs.Handle );
StringBuilder buffer = new StringBuilder( 5 );
int read = 0;
```

```
// platform invoke will hold reference to HandleRef until call ends
LibWrap.ReadFile( hr, buffer, 5, out read, 0 );
Console.WriteLine( "Read with struct parameter: {0}", buffer );
```

Requirements

Namespace: System.Runtime.InteropServices

Platforms: Windows 98, Windows NT 4.0, Windows Millennium Edition, Windows 2000, Windows XP Home Edition, Windows XP Professional, Windows .NET Server family

Assembly: Mscorlib (in Mscorlib.dll)

HandleRef Constructor

Initializes a new instance of the **HandleRef** class with the object to wrap and a handle to the resource used by unmanaged code.

```
[Visual Basic]
Public Sub New( _
    ByVal wrapper As Object, _
    ByVal handle As IntPtr _
)
[C#]
public HandleRef(
    object wrapper,
    IntPtr handle
);
[C++]
public: HandleRef(
    Object* wrapper,
    IntPtr handle
);
[JScript]
public function HandleRef(
    wrapper : Object,
    handle : IntPtr
);
```

Parameters

wrapper
    A managed object that should not be finalized until the platform invoke call returns.

handle
    An **IntPtr** that indicates a handle to a resource.

Requirements

Platforms: Windows 98, Windows NT 4.0, Windows Millennium Edition, Windows 2000, Windows XP Home Edition, Windows XP Professional, Windows .NET Server family

HandleRef.Handle Property

Gets the handle to a resource.

```
[Visual Basic]
Public ReadOnly Property Handle As IntPtr
[C#]
public IntPtr Handle {get;}
[C++]
public: __property IntPtr get_Handle();
```

```
[JScript]
public function get Handle() : IntPtr;
```

Property Value

The handle to a resource.

Requirements

Platforms: Windows 98, Windows NT 4.0,
Windows Millennium Edition, Windows 2000,
Windows XP Home Edition, Windows XP Professional,
Windows .NET Server family

HandleRef.Wrapper Property

Gets the object holding the handle to a resource.

```
[Visual Basic]
Public ReadOnly Property Wrapper As Object
[C#]
public object Wrapper {get;}
[C++]
public: __property Object* get_Wrapper();
[JScript]
public function get Wrapper() : Object;
```

Property Value

The object holding the handle to a resource.

Requirements

Platforms: Windows 98, Windows NT 4.0,
Windows Millennium Edition, Windows 2000,
Windows XP Home Edition, Windows XP Professional,
Windows .NET Server family

HandleRef to IntPtr Conversion

Returns the handle to a resource of the specified **HandleRef** object.

```
[Visual Basic]
returnValue = HandleRef.op_Explicit(value)
[C#]
public static explicit operator IntPtr(
   HandleRef value
);
[C++]
public: static IntPtr op_Explicit();
[JScript]
returnValue = IntPtr(value);
```

[Visual Basic] In Visual Basic, you can use the conversion operators defined by a type, but you cannot define your own. You can use the **Handle** method instead of the **HandleRef** to **IntPtr** conversion.

[JScript] In JScript, you can use the conversion operators defined by a type, but you cannot define your own.

Arguments [Visual Basic, JScript]

value
   The object that needs a handle.

Parameters [C#]

value
   The object that needs a handle.

Return Value

The handle to a resource of the specified **HandleRef** object.

Requirements

Platforms: Windows 98, Windows NT 4.0,
Windows Millennium Edition, Windows 2000,
Windows XP Home Edition, Windows XP Professional,
Windows .NET Server family

ICustomAdapter Interface

Provides a way for clients to access the actual object, rather than the adapter object handed out by a custom marshaler.

```
[Visual Basic]
Public Interface ICustomAdapter
[C#]
public interface ICustomAdapter
[C++]
public __gc __interface ICustomAdapter
[JScript]
public interface ICustomAdapter
```

Remarks

The objects that the built-in custom marshalers hand out to clients implement this interface.

Requirements

Namespace: System.Runtime.InteropServices

Platforms: Windows 98, Windows NT 4.0, Windows Millennium Edition, Windows 2000, Windows XP Home Edition, Windows XP Professional, Windows .NET Server family

Assembly: Mscorlib (in Mscorlib.dll)

ICustomAdapter.GetUnderlyingObject Method

Provides access to the underlying object wrapped by a custom marshaler.

```
[Visual Basic]
Function GetUnderlyingObject() As Object
[C#]
object GetUnderlyingObject();
[C++]
Object* GetUnderlyingObject();
[JScript]
function GetUnderlyingObject() : Object;
```

Return Value

The object contained by the adapter object.

Requirements

Platforms: Windows 98, Windows NT 4.0, Windows Millennium Edition, Windows 2000, Windows XP Home Edition, Windows XP Professional, Windows .NET Server family

ICustomFactory Interface

Enables users to write activation code for managed objects that extend **MarshalByRefObject**.

```
[Visual Basic]
Public Interface ICustomFactory
[C#]
public interface ICustomFactory
[C++]
public __gc __interface ICustomFactory
[JScript]
public interface ICustomFactory
```

Remarks

You can enable custom activation by providing a proxy class that implements **ICustomFactory** and attributing the **MarshalByRefObject** class with the **ProxyAttribute**. When the class is activated, the proxy's **CreateInstance** method is called by the common language runtime to activate the class.

Requirements

Namespace: System.Runtime.InteropServices

Platforms: Windows 98, Windows NT 4.0, Windows Millennium Edition, Windows 2000, Windows XP Home Edition, Windows XP Professional, Windows .NET Server family

Assembly: Mscorlib (in Mscorlib.dll)

ICustomFactory.CreateInstance Method

Creates a new instance of the specified type.

```
[Visual Basic]
Function CreateInstance( _
   ByVal serverType As Type _
) As MarshalByRefObject
[C#]
MarshalByRefObject CreateInstance(
   Type serverType
);
[C++]
MarshalByRefObject* CreateInstance(
   Type* serverType
);
[JScript]
function CreateInstance(
   serverType : Type
) : MarshalByRefObject;
```

Parameters

serverType
   The type to activate.

Return Value

A **MarshalByRefObject** associated with the specified type.

Remarks

CreateInstance is called by the common language runtime when a new object of the specified type needs to be created. Override this method to provide your own custom class factory.

Requirements

Platforms: Windows 98, Windows NT 4.0, Windows Millennium Edition, Windows 2000, Windows XP Home Edition, Windows XP Professional, Windows .NET Server family

ICustomMarshaler Interface

Designed to provide custom wrappers for handling method calls.

```
[Visual Basic]
Public Interface ICustomMarshaler
[C#]
public interface ICustomMarshaler
[C++]
public __gc __interface ICustomMarshaler
[JScript]
public interface ICustomMarshaler
```

Remarks

To use a custom marshaler, you must apply the **MarshalAsAttribute** to the parameter or field being marshaled. You must also pass **UnmanagedType.CustomMarshaler** to its constructor and specify the **MarshalType**. The attribute identifies the appropriate custom marshaler to activate the appropriate wrapper. The common language runtime's interop service then examines the attribute and creates the custom marshaler when the argument is marshaled. It calls on the custom marshaler's **MarshalNativeToManaged** and **MarshalManaged-ToNative** methods to activate the correct wrapper to handle the call.

In addition to implementing the **ICustomMarshaler** interface, custom marshalers must implement a static (**Shared** in Visual Basic) method called **GetInstance** that accepts a **String** as a parameter and has a return type of **ICustomMarshaler**. This static (**Shared** in Visual Basic) method is called by the common language runtime's COM interop layer to instantiate an instance of the custom marshaler. The **String** passed to **GetInstance** is a cookie that the method can use to customize the returned custom marshaler.

Requirements

Namespace: System.Runtime.InteropServices

Platforms: Windows 98, Windows NT 4.0, Windows Millennium Edition, Windows 2000, Windows XP Home Edition, Windows XP Professional, Windows .NET Server family

Assembly: Mscorlib (in Mscorlib.dll)

ICustomMarshaler.CleanUpManagedData Method

Performs necessary cleanup of the managed data when it is no longer needed.

```
[Visual Basic]
Sub CleanUpManagedData( _
   ByVal ManagedObj As Object _
)
[C#]
void CleanUpManagedData(
   object ManagedObj
);
[C++]
void CleanUpManagedData(
   Object* ManagedObj
);
[JScript]
function CleanUpManagedData(
   ManagedObj : Object
);
```

Parameters

ManagedObj
   The managed object to be destroyed.

Requirements

Platforms: Windows 98, Windows NT 4.0, Windows Millennium Edition, Windows 2000, Windows XP Home Edition, Windows XP Professional, Windows .NET Server family

ICustomMarshaler.CleanUpNativeData Method

Performs necessary cleanup of the unmanaged data when it is no longer needed.

```
[Visual Basic]
Sub CleanUpNativeData( _
   ByVal pNativeData As IntPtr _
)
[C#]
void CleanUpNativeData(
   IntPtr pNativeData
);
[C++]
void CleanUpNativeData(
   IntPtr pNativeData
);
[JScript]
function CleanUpNativeData(
   pNativeData : IntPtr
);
```

Parameters

pNativeData
   A pointer to the unmanaged data to be destroyed.

Requirements

Platforms: Windows 98, Windows NT 4.0, Windows Millennium Edition, Windows 2000, Windows XP Home Edition, Windows XP Professional, Windows .NET Server family

ICustomMarshaler.GetNativeDataSize Method

Returns the size of the native data to be marshaled.

```
[Visual Basic]
Function GetNativeDataSize() As Integer
[C#]
int GetNativeDataSize();
[C++]
int GetNativeDataSize();
[JScript]
function GetNativeDataSize() : int;
```

Return Value

The size in bytes of the native data.

Requirements

Platforms: Windows 98, Windows NT 4.0, Windows Millennium Edition, Windows 2000, Windows XP Home Edition, Windows XP Professional, Windows .NET Server family

ICustomMarshaler.MarshalManagedToNative Method

Converts the managed data to unmanaged data.

```
[Visual Basic]
Function MarshalManagedToNative( _
    ByVal ManagedObj As Object _
) As IntPtr
[C#]
IntPtr MarshalManagedToNative(
    object ManagedObj
);
[C++]
IntPtr MarshalManagedToNative(
    Object* ManagedObj
);
[JScript]
function MarshalManagedToNative(
    ManagedObj : Object
) : IntPtr;
```

Parameters

ManagedObj
> The managed object to be converted.

Return Value

Returns the COM view of the managed object.

Requirements

Platforms: Windows 98, Windows NT 4.0,
Windows Millennium Edition, Windows 2000,
Windows XP Home Edition, Windows XP Professional,
Windows .NET Server family

ICustomMarshaler.MarshalNativeToManaged Method

Converts the unmanaged data to managed data.

```
[Visual Basic]
Function MarshalNativeToManaged( _
    ByVal pNativeData As IntPtr _
) As Object
[C#]
object MarshalNativeToManaged(
    IntPtr pNativeData
);
[C++]
Object* MarshalNativeToManaged(
    IntPtr pNativeData
);
[JScript]
function MarshalNativeToManaged(
    pNativeData : IntPtr
) : Object;
```

Parameters

pNativeData
> A pointer to the unmanaged data to be wrapped.

Return Value

Returns the managed view of the COM data.

Requirements

Platforms: Windows 98, Windows NT 4.0,
Windows Millennium Edition, Windows 2000,
Windows XP Home Edition, Windows XP Professional,
Windows .NET Server family

IDispatchImplAttribute Class

Indicates which **IDispatch** implementation the common language runtime uses when exposing dual interfaces and dispinterfaces to COM.

System.Object
  System.Attribute
    System.Runtime.InteropServices.IDispatchImplAttribute

```
[Visual Basic]
<AttributeUsage(AttributeTargets.Assembly Or _
   AttributeTargets.Class)>
NotInheritable Public Class IDispatchImplAttribute
   Inherits Attribute
[C#]
[AttributeUsage(AttributeTargets.Assembly |
   AttributeTargets.Class)]
public sealed class IDispatchImplAttribute : Attribute
[C++]
[AttributeUsage(AttributeTargets::Assembly |
   AttributeTargets::Class)]
public __gc __sealed class IDispatchImplAttribute : public
   Attribute
[JScript]
public
   AttributeUsage(AttributeTargets.Assembly | AttributeTargets.Class)
class IDispatchImplAttribute extends Attribute
```

Thread Safety

Any public static (**Shared** in Visual Basic) members of this type are safe for multithreaded operations. Any instance members are not guaranteed to be thread safe.

Remarks

You can apply this attribute to classes or assemblies.

This attribute should only be set when an explicit implementation is required. When you set the attribute to **CompatibleImpl**, the **IDispatch** implementation is supplied by passing the type information for the object to COM's **CreateStdDispatch** API. When you set the attribute to **InternalImpl**, the **IDispatch** implementation is supplied by the common language runtime. Setting the attribute to **SystemDefinedImpl** allows the runtime to choose the appropriate implementation. When using the attribute on an assembly, the attribute applies to all classes defined within the assembly. When using the attribute on an individual class, the attribute applies only to the interfaces exposed by that class and overrides any assembly-level setting.

Requirements

Namespace: System.Runtime.InteropServices

Platforms: Windows 98, Windows NT 4.0, Windows Millennium Edition, Windows 2000, Windows XP Home Edition, Windows XP Professional, Windows .NET Server family

Assembly: Mscorlib (in Mscorlib.dll)

IDispatchImplAttribute Constructor

Initializes a new instance of the **IDispatchImplAttribute** class.

Overload List

Initializes a new instance of the **IDispatchImplAttribute** class with specified **IDispatchImplType** value.

  [Visual Basic] **Public Sub New(IDispatchImplType)**

  [C#] **public IDispatchImplAttribute(IDispatchImplType);**

  [C++] **public: IDispatchImplAttribute(IDispatchImplType);**

  [JScript] **public function IDispatchImplAttribute(IDispatchImplType);**

Initializes a new instance of the **IDispatchImplAttribute** class with specified **IDispatchImplType** value.

  [Visual Basic] **Public Sub New(Short)**

  [C#] **public IDispatchImplAttribute(short);**

  [C++] **public: IDispatchImplAttribute(short);**

  [JScript] **public function IDispatchImplAttribute(Int16);**

IDispatchImplAttribute Constructor (IDispatchImplType)

Initializes a new instance of the **IDispatchImplAttribute** class with specified **IDispatchImplType** value.

```
[Visual Basic]
Public Sub New( _
   ByVal implType As IDispatchImplType _
)
[C#]
public IDispatchImplAttribute(
   IDispatchImplType implType
);
[C++]
public: IDispatchImplAttribute(
   IDispatchImplType implType
);
[JScript]
public function IDispatchImplAttribute(
   implType : IDispatchImplType
);
```

Parameters

implType
  Indicates which **IDispatchImplType** enumeration will be used.

Remarks

For readable code that is less prone to error, always use this constructor.

Requirements

Platforms: Windows 98, Windows NT 4.0, Windows Millennium Edition, Windows 2000, Windows XP Home Edition, Windows XP Professional, Windows .NET Server family

IDispatchImplAttribute Constructor (Int16)

Initializes a new instance of the **IDispatchImplAttribute** class with specified **IDispatchImplType** value.

```
[Visual Basic]
Public Sub New( _
   ByVal implType As Short _
)
[C#]
public IDispatchImplAttribute(
   short implType
);
[C++]
public: IDispatchImplAttribute(
   short implType
);
[JScript]
public function IDispatchImplAttribute(
   implType : Int16
);
```

Parameters

implType
> Indicates which **IDispatchImplType** enumeration will be used.

Remarks

This constructor takes an underlying 16-bit signed integer that represents each **IDispatchImplType** enumeration member. The Type Library Importer (TlbImp.exe) uses this constructor to avoid generating a typeref to the **IDispatchImplType** value that *value* represents, and then builds the signature with that token.

Requirements

Platforms: Windows 98, Windows NT 4.0, Windows Millennium Edition, Windows 2000, Windows XP Home Edition, Windows XP Professional, Windows .NET Server family

IDispatchImplAttribute.Value Property

Gets the **IDispatchImplType** value used by the class.

```
[Visual Basic]
Public ReadOnly Property Value As IDispatchImplType
[C#]
public IDispatchImplType Value {get;}
[C++]
public: __property IDispatchImplType get_Value();
[JScript]
public function get Value() : IDispatchImplType;
```

Property Value

The **IDispatchImplType** value used by the class.

Requirements

Platforms: Windows 98, Windows NT 4.0, Windows Millennium Edition, Windows 2000, Windows XP Home Edition, Windows XP Professional, Windows .NET Server family

IDispatchImplType Enumeration

Indicates which **IDispatch** implementation to use for a particular class.

```
[Visual Basic]
<Serializable>
Public Enum IDispatchImplType
[C#]
[Serializable]
public enum IDispatchImplType
[C++]
[Serializable]
__value public enum IDispatchImplType
[JScript]
public
   Serializable
enum IDispatchImplType
```

Remarks

See **IDispatchImplAttribute** for more information.

Members

Member name	Description
CompatibleImpl	Specifies that the **IDispatch** implementation is supplied by passing the type information for the object to the COM **CreateStdDispatch** API method.
InternalImpl	Specifies that the **IDispatch** implemenation is supplied by the runtime.
SystemDefinedImpl	Specifies that the common language runtime decides which **IDispatch** implementation to use.

Requirements

Namespace: System.Runtime.InteropServices

Platforms: Windows 98, Windows NT 4.0, Windows Millennium Edition, Windows 2000, Windows XP Home Edition, Windows XP Professional, Windows .NET Server family

Assembly: Mscorlib (in Mscorlib.dll)

IDLDESC Structure

Contains information needed for transferring a structure element, parameter, or function return value between processes.

System.Object
  System.ValueType
    System.Runtime.InteropServices.IDLDESC

```
[Visual Basic]
<ComVisible(False)>
Public Structure IDLDESC
[C#]
[ComVisible(false)]
public struct IDLDESC
[C++]
[ComVisible(false)]
public __value struct IDLDESC
```

[JScript] In JScript, you can use the structures in the .NET Framework, but you cannot define your own.

Thread Safety

Any public static (**Shared** in Visual Basic) members of this type are safe for multithreaded operations. Any instance members are not guaranteed to be thread safe.

Remarks

For additional information about **IDLDESC**, see the MSDN Library.

Requirements

Namespace: System.Runtime.InteropServices

Platforms: Windows 98, Windows NT 4.0, Windows Millennium Edition, Windows 2000, Windows XP Home Edition, Windows XP Professional, Windows .NET Server family

Assembly: Mscorlib (in Mscorlib.dll)

IDLDESC.dwReserved Field

Reserved; set to a null reference (**Nothing** in Visual Basic).

```
[Visual Basic]
Public dwReserved As Integer
[C#]
public int dwReserved;
[C++]
public: int dwReserved;
[JScript]
public var dwReserved : int;
```

Remarks

For additional information about **IDLDESC**, see the MSDN Library.

Requirements

Platforms: Windows 98, Windows NT 4.0, Windows Millennium Edition, Windows 2000, Windows XP Home Edition, Windows XP Professional, Windows .NET Server family

IDLDESC.wIDLFlags Field

Indicates an **IDLFLAG** value describing the type.

```
[Visual Basic]
Public wIDLFlags As IDLFLAG
[C#]
public IDLFLAG wIDLFlags;
[C++]
public: IDLFLAG wIDLFlags;
[JScript]
public var wIDLFlags : IDLFLAG;
```

Remarks

For additional information about **IDLDESC**, see the MSDN Library.

Requirements

Platforms: Windows 98, Windows NT 4.0, Windows Millennium Edition, Windows 2000, Windows XP Home Edition, Windows XP Professional, Windows .NET Server family

IDLFLAG Enumeration

Describes how to transfer a structure element, parameter, or function return value between processes.

This enumeration has a **FlagsAttribute** attribute that allows a bitwise combination of its member values.

```
[Visual Basic]
<Flags>
<Serializable>
<ComVisible(False)>
Public Enum IDLFLAG
[C#]
[Flags]
[Serializable]
[ComVisible(false)]
public enum IDLFLAG
[C++]
[Flags]
[Serializable]
[ComVisible(false)]
__value public enum IDLFLAG
[JScript]
public
   Flags
   Serializable
   ComVisible(false)
enum IDLFLAG
```

Members

Member name	Description	Value
IDLFLAG_FIN	The parameter passes information from the caller to the callee.	1
IDLFLAG_FLCID	The parameter is the local identifier of a client application.	4
IDLFLAG_FOUT	The parameter returns information from the callee to the caller.	2
IDLFLAG_FRETVAL	The parameter is the return value of the member.	8
IDLFLAG_NONE	Whether the parameter passes or receives information is unspecified.	0

Requirements

Namespace: System.Runtime.InteropServices

Platforms: Windows 98, Windows NT 4.0, Windows Millennium Edition, Windows 2000, Windows XP Home Edition, Windows XP Professional, Windows .NET Server family

Assembly: Mscorlib (in Mscorlib.dll)

IMPLTYPEFLAGS Enumeration

Defines the attributes of an implemented or inherited interface of a type.

This enumeration has a **FlagsAttribute** attribute that allows a bitwise combination of its member values.

```
[Visual Basic]
<Flags>
<Serializable>
<ComVisible(False)>
Public Enum IMPLTYPEFLAGS
[C#]
[Flags]
[Serializable]
[ComVisible(false)]
public enum IMPLTYPEFLAGS
[C++]
[Flags]
[Serializable]
[ComVisible(false)]
__value public enum IMPLTYPEFLAGS
[JScript]
public
    Flags
    Serializable
    ComVisible(false)
enum IMPLTYPEFLAGS
```

Remarks

For additional information about **IMPLTYPEFLAGS**, see the MSDN Library.

Members

Member name	Description	Value
IMPLTYPE-FLAG_FDEFAULT	The interface or dispinterface represents the default for the source or sink.	1
IMPLTYPEFLAG_F-DEFAULTVTABLE	Sinks receive events through the virtual function table (VTBL).	8
IMPLTYPE-FLAG_FRESTRICTED	The member should not be displayed or programmable by users.	4
IMPLTYPE-FLAG_FSOURCE	This member of a coclass is called rather than implemented.	2

Requirements

Namespace: System.Runtime.InteropServices

Platforms: Windows 98, Windows NT 4.0, Windows Millennium Edition, Windows 2000, Windows XP Home Edition, Windows XP Professional, Windows .NET Server family

Assembly: Mscorlib (in Mscorlib.dll)

ImportedFromTypeLibAttribute Class

Indicates that the types defined within an assembly were originally defined in a type library.

System.Object
  System.Attribute
    System.Runtime.InteropServices.ImportedFromTypeLib-
    Attribute

```
[Visual Basic]
<AttributeUsage(AttributeTargets.Assembly)>
NotInheritable Public Class ImportedFromTypeLibAttribute
  Inherits Attribute
[C#]
[AttributeUsage(AttributeTargets.Assembly)]
public sealed class ImportedFromTypeLibAttribute : Attribute
[C++]
[AttributeUsage(AttributeTargets::Assembly)]
public __gc __sealed class ImportedFromTypeLibAttribute : public
  Attribute
[JScript]
public
  AttributeUsage(AttributeTargets.Assembly)
class ImportedFromTypeLibAttribute extends Attribute
```

Thread Safety

Any public static (**Shared** in Visual Basic) members of this type are safe for multithreaded operations. Any instance members are not guaranteed to be thread safe.

Remarks

You can apply this attribute to assemblies, although the **Type Library Importer (Tlbimp.exe)** typically applies it for you when it a type library.

The primary use of the attribute is to capture the original source of the type information. For example, you can import A.tlb as an interop assembly called A.dll and have assembly B.dll reference A.dll. When you export B.dll to B.tlb, this attribute causes the references in B.tlb that point to A.dll to point instead to A.tlb. This should not be confused with the **ComImportAttribute**, which specifies that an individual type is implemented in COM.

Requirements

Namespace: System.Runtime.InteropServices

Platforms: Windows 98, Windows NT 4.0, Windows Millennium Edition, Windows 2000, Windows XP Home Edition, Windows XP Professional, Windows .NET Server family

Assembly: Mscorlib (in Mscorlib.dll)

ImportedFromTypeLibAttribute Constructor

Initializes a new instance of the **ImportedFromTypeLibAttribute** class with the name of the original type library file.

```
[Visual Basic]
Public Sub New( _
  ByVal tlbFile As String _
)
[C#]
public ImportedFromTypeLibAttribute(
  string tlbFile
);
[C++]
public: ImportedFromTypeLibAttribute(
  String* tlbFile
);
[JScript]
public function ImportedFromTypeLibAttribute(
  tlbFile : String
);
```

Parameters

tlbFile
  The location of the original type library file.

Requirements

Platforms: Windows 98, Windows NT 4.0, Windows Millennium Edition, Windows 2000, Windows XP Home Edition, Windows XP Professional, Windows .NET Server family

ImportedFromTypeLibAttribute.Value Property

Gets the name of the original type library file.

```
[Visual Basic]
Public ReadOnly Property Value As String
[C#]
public string Value {get;}
[C++]
public: __property String* get_Value();
[JScript]
public function get Value() : String;
```

Property Value

The name of the original type library file.

Requirements

Platforms: Windows 98, Windows NT 4.0, Windows Millennium Edition, Windows 2000, Windows XP Home Edition, Windows XP Professional, Windows .NET Server family

ImporterEventKind Enumeration

Describes the callbacks that the type library importer makes when importing a type library.

```
[Visual Basic]
<Serializable>
Public Enum ImporterEventKind
[C#]
[Serializable]
public enum ImporterEventKind
[C++]
[Serializable]
__value public enum ImporterEventKind
[JScript]
public
    Serializable
enum ImporterEventKind
```

Remarks

The type library importer passes the values of this enumeration to the **ReportEvent** method of an object which implements the **ITypeLibExporterNotifySink** interface. The value passed identifies the specific kind of event being reported.

Members

Member name	Description
ERROR_REFTO-INVALIDTYPELIB	This property is not supported in this version of the .NET Framework.
NOTIF_CONVERT-WARNING	Specifies that the event is invoked when a warning occurs during conversion.
NOTIF_TYPE-CONVERTED	Specifies that the event is invoked when a type has been imported.

Requirements

Namespace: System.Runtime.InteropServices

Platforms: Windows 98, Windows NT 4.0, Windows Millennium Edition, Windows 2000, Windows XP Home Edition, Windows XP Professional, Windows .NET Server family

Assembly: Mscorlib (in Mscorlib.dll)

InAttribute Class

Indicates that data should be marshaled from the caller to the callee, but not back to the caller.

System.Object
  System.Attribute
    System.Runtime.InteropServices.InAttribute

```
[Visual Basic]
<AttributeUsage(AttributeTargets.Parameter)>
NotInheritable Public Class InAttribute
    Inherits Attribute
[C#]
[AttributeUsage(AttributeTargets.Parameter)]
public sealed class InAttribute : Attribute
[C++]
[AttributeUsage(AttributeTargets::Parameter)]
public __gc __sealed class InAttribute : public Attribute
[JScript]
public
    AttributeUsage(AttributeTargets.Parameter)
class InAttribute extends Attribute
```

Thread Safety

Any public static (**Shared** in Visual Basic) members of this type are safe for multithreaded operations. Any instance members are not guaranteed to be thread safe.

Remarks

You can apply this attribute to parameters.

The **InAttribute** is optional. The attribute is supported for COM interop and platform invoke only. In the absence of explicit settings, the interop marshaler assumes rules based on the parameter type, whether the parameter is passed by reference or by value, and whether the type is blittable or non-blittable. For example, the **StringBuilder** class is always assumed to be In/Out and an array of strings passed by value is assumed to be In.

You cannot apply the **InAttribute** to a parameter modified with the C#-styled **out** keyword. To avoid confusing the **In** keyword in Visual Basic with the **InAttribute**, minus Attribute, use the ⟨[In]⟩ form with brackets around the attribute.

Combining the **InAttribute** and **OutAttribute** is particularly useful when applied to arrays and formatted, non-blittable types. Callers see the changes a callee makes to these types only when you apply both attributes. Since these types require copying during marshaling, you can use **InAttribute** and **OutAttribute** to reduce unnecessary copies.

Requirements

Namespace: System.Runtime.InteropServices

Platforms: Windows 98, Windows NT 4.0, Windows Millennium Edition, Windows 2000, Windows XP Home Edition, Windows XP Professional, Windows .NET Server family, .NET Compact Framework - Windows CE .NET

Assembly: Mscorlib (in Mscorlib.dll)

InAttribute Constructor

Initializes a new instance of the **InAttribute** class.

```
[Visual Basic]
Public Sub New()
[C#]
public InAttribute();
[C++]
public: InAttribute();
[JScript]
public function InAttribute();
```

Requirements

Platforms: Windows 98, Windows NT 4.0, Windows Millennium Edition, Windows 2000, Windows XP Home Edition, Windows XP Professional, Windows .NET Server family, .NET Compact Framework - Windows CE .NET, Common Language Infrastructure (CLI) Standard

InterfaceTypeAttribute Class

Indicates whether a managed interface is dual, dispatch-only, or **IUnknown**-only when exposed to COM.

System.Object
  System.Attribute
    System.Runtime.InteropServices.InterfaceTypeAttribute

```
[Visual Basic]
<AttributeUsage(AttributeTargets.Interface)>
NotInheritable Public Class InterfaceTypeAttribute
   Inherits Attribute
[C#]
[AttributeUsage(AttributeTargets.Interface)]
public sealed class InterfaceTypeAttribute : Attribute
[C++]
[AttributeUsage(AttributeTargets::Interface)]
public __gc __sealed class InterfaceTypeAttribute : public
   Attribute
[JScript]
public
   AttributeUsage(AttributeTargets.Interface)
class InterfaceTypeAttribute extends Attribute
```

Thread Safety

Any public static (**Shared** in Visual Basic) members of this type are safe for multithreaded operations. Any instance members are not guaranteed to be thread safe.

Remarks

You can apply this attribute to interfaces.

By default, the **Type Library Exporter (Tlbexp.exe)** exposes a managed interface to COM as a dual interface, giving you the flexibility of late binding or the performance of early binding. The **ComInterfaceType** enumeration enables you to override the default behavior and specify late binding only or early binding only. For example, you can apply InterfaceType (ComInterfaceType.InterfaceIsIDispatch) to an interface to produce metadata to restrict callers to late binding only. Although interfaces that derive from the **IDispatch** interface are often dual, the **InterfaceIsIDispatch** enumeration member allows only late-bound calls to the interface methods. This attribute has no effect on the managed view of the interface. For additional information on how interfaces are exposed to COM, see **Exported Type Conversion**.

The **Type Library Importer (Tlbimp.exe)** also applies this attribute to imported, nondual interfaces; it applies the appropriate enumeration member to indicate that the interface is dispatch-only or **IUnknown**-only.

Example

[Visual Basic, C#, JScript] The following example shows how **InterfaceTypeAttribute** controls how the interface is exposed to COM.

```
[Visual Basic]
Imports System.Runtime.InteropServices

'Interface is exposed to COM as dual.
Interface IMyInterface1
     'Insert code here.
End Interface

'Interface is exposed to COM as IDispatch.
<InterfaceTypeAttribute(ComInterfaceType.InterfaceIsIDispatch)> _
```

```
Interface IMyInterface2
     'Insert code here.
End Interface

[C#]
using System.Runtime.InteropServices;

//Interface is exposed to COM as dual.
interface IMyInterface1
{
     //Insert code here.
}

//Interface is exposed to COM as IDispatch.
[InterfaceTypeAttribute(ComInterfaceType.InterfaceIsIDispatch)]
interface IMyInterface2
{
     //Insert code here.
}

[JScript]
import System.Runtime.InteropServices

//Interface will be exposed to COM as dual.
interface IMyInterface1{
     // ...
}

//Interface will be exposed to COM as IDispatch.
public InterfaceTypeAttribute(ComInterfaceType.InterfaceIsIDispatch)
interface IMyInterface2{
     // ...
}
```

Requirements

Namespace: System.Runtime.InteropServices

Platforms: Windows 98, Windows NT 4.0, Windows Millennium Edition, Windows 2000, Windows XP Home Edition, Windows XP Professional, Windows .NET Server family

Assembly: Mscorlib (in Mscorlib.dll)

InterfaceTypeAttribute Constructor

Initializes a new instance of the **InterfaceTypeAttribute** class.

Overload List

Initializes a new instance of the **InterfaceTypeAttribute** class with the specified **ComInterfaceType** enumeration member.

[Visual Basic] **Public Sub New(ComInterfaceType)**

[C#] **public InterfaceTypeAttribute(ComInterfaceType);**

[C++] **public: InterfaceTypeAttribute(ComInterfaceType);**

[JScript] **public function InterfaceTypeAttribute(ComInterfaceType);**

Initializes a new instance of the **InterfaceTypeAttribute** class with the specified **ComInterfaceType** enumeration member.

[Visual Basic] **Public Sub New(Short)**

[C#] **public InterfaceTypeAttribute(short);**

[C++] **public: InterfaceTypeAttribute(short);**

[JScript] **public function InterfaceTypeAttribute(Int16);**

InterfaceTypeAttribute Constructor (ComInterfaceType)

Initializes a new instance of the **InterfaceTypeAttribute** class with the specified **ComInterfaceType** enumeration member.

```
[Visual Basic]
Public Sub New( _
   ByVal interfaceType As ComInterfaceType _
)
[C#]
public InterfaceTypeAttribute(
   ComInterfaceType interfaceType
);
[C++]
public: InterfaceTypeAttribute(
   ComInterfaceType interfaceType
);
[JScript]
public function InterfaceTypeAttribute(
   interfaceType : ComInterfaceType
);
```

Parameters

interfaceType

One of the **ComInterfaceType** values that describes how the interface should be exposed to COM clients.

Remarks

For readable code that is less prone to error, always use this constructor.

Requirements

Platforms: Windows 98, Windows NT 4.0, Windows Millennium Edition, Windows 2000, Windows XP Home Edition, Windows XP Professional, Windows .NET Server family

InterfaceTypeAttribute Constructor (Int16)

Initializes a new instance of the **InterfaceTypeAttribute** class with the specified **ComInterfaceType** enumeration member.

```
[Visual Basic]
Public Sub New( _
   ByVal interfaceType As Short _
)
[C#]
public InterfaceTypeAttribute(
   short interfaceType
);
[C++]
public: InterfaceTypeAttribute(
   short interfaceType
);
[JScript]
public function InterfaceTypeAttribute(
   interfaceType : Int16
);
```

Parameters

interfaceType

Describes how the interface should be exposed to COM clients.

Remarks

This constructor takes an underlying 16-bit integer that represents each **ComInterfaceType** enumeration member. The **Type Library Importer (Tlbimp.exe)** uses this constructor.

Requirements

Platforms: Windows 98, Windows NT 4.0, Windows Millennium Edition, Windows 2000, Windows XP Home Edition, Windows XP Professional, Windows .NET Server family

InterfaceTypeAttribute.Value Property

Gets the **ComInterfaceType** value that describes how the interface should be exposed to COM.

```
[Visual Basic]
Public ReadOnly Property Value As ComInterfaceType
[C#]
public ComInterfaceType Value {get;}
[C++]
public: __property ComInterfaceType get_Value();
[JScript]
public function get Value() : ComInterfaceType;
```

Property Value

The **ComInterfaceType** value that describes how the interface should be exposed to COM.

Requirements

Platforms: Windows 98, Windows NT 4.0, Windows Millennium Edition, Windows 2000, Windows XP Home Edition, Windows XP Professional, Windows .NET Server family

InvalidComObjectException Class

The exception thrown when an invalid COM object is used.

System.Object
  System.Exception
    System.SystemException
      System.Runtime.InteropServices.InvalidComObjectException

```
[Visual Basic]
<Serializable>
Public Class InvalidComObjectException
   Inherits SystemException
[C#]
[Serializable]
public class InvalidComObjectException : SystemException
[C++]
[Serializable]
public __gc class InvalidComObjectException : public
   SystemException
[JScript]
public
   Serializable
class InvalidComObjectException extends SystemException
```

Thread Safety

Any public static (**Shared** in Visual Basic) members of this type are safe for multithreaded operations. Any instance members are not guaranteed to be thread safe.

Remarks

An **InvalidComObjectException** is thrown when an invalid COM object is used. This happens when the **__ComObject** type is used directly, without having a backing class factory. For more information, see **IsCOMObject**.

InvalidComObjectException uses the HRESULT COR_E_INVALIDCOMOBJECT which has the value 0x80131527.

Requirements

Namespace: System.Runtime.InteropServices

Platforms: Windows 98, Windows NT 4.0, Windows Millennium Edition, Windows 2000, Windows XP Home Edition, Windows XP Professional, Windows .NET Server family

Assembly: Mscorlib (in Mscorlib.dll)

InvalidComObjectException Constructor

Initializes an instance of the **InvalidComObjectException** class.

Overload List

Initializes an instance of the **InvalidComObjectException** with default properties.

  [Visual Basic] **Public Sub New()**
  [C#] **public InvalidComObjectException();**
  [C++] **public: InvalidComObjectException();**
  [JScript] **public function InvalidComObjectException();**

Initializes an instance of the **InvalidComObjectException** with a message.

  [Visual Basic] **Public Sub New(String)**
  [C#] **public InvalidComObjectException(string);**
  [C++] **public: InvalidComObjectException(String*);**
  [JScript] **public function InvalidComObjectException(String);**

Initializes a new instance of the **COMException** class from serialization data.

  [Visual Basic] **Protected Sub New(SerializationInfo, StreamingContext)**
  [C#] **protected InvalidComObjectException (SerializationInfo, StreamingContext);**
  [C++] **protected: InvalidComObjectException (SerializationInfo*, StreamingContext);**
  [JScript] **protected function InvalidComObjectException (SerializationInfo, StreamingContext);**

Initializes a new instance of the **InvalidComObjectException** class with a specified error message and a reference to the inner exception that is the cause of this exception.

  [Visual Basic] **Public Sub New(String, Exception)**
  [C#] **public InvalidComObjectException(string, Exception);**
  [C++] **public: InvalidComObjectException(String*, Exception*);**
  [JScript] **public function InvalidComObjectException(String, Exception);**

InvalidComObjectException Constructor ()

Initializes an instance of the **InvalidComObjectException** with default properties.

```
[Visual Basic]
Public Sub New()
[C#]
public InvalidComObjectException();
[C++]
public: InvalidComObjectException();
[JScript]
public function InvalidComObjectException();
```

Remarks

InvalidComObjectException inherits from **SystemException**. This constructor sets the properties of the **Exception** object as shown in the following table.

Property Type	Value
InnerException	A null reference (**Nothing** in Visual Basic).
Message	A localized error message string.

Requirements

Platforms: Windows 98, Windows NT 4.0, Windows Millennium Edition, Windows 2000, Windows XP Home Edition, Windows XP Professional, Windows .NET Server family

InvalidComObjectException Constructor (String)

Initializes an instance of the **InvalidComObjectException** with a message.

```
[Visual Basic]
Public Sub New( _
   ByVal message As String _
)
[C#]
public InvalidComObjectException(
   string message
);
[C++]
public: InvalidComObjectException(
   String* message
);
[JScript]
public function InvalidComObjectException(
   message : String
);
```

Parameters

message
> The message that indicates the reason for the exception.

Remarks

InvalidComObjectException inherits from **SystemException**. This constructor sets the properties of the **Exception** object as shown in the following table.

Property Type	Value
InnerException	A null reference (**Nothing** in Visual Basic).
Message	*message*

Requirements

Platforms: Windows 98, Windows NT 4.0, Windows Millennium Edition, Windows 2000, Windows XP Home Edition, Windows XP Professional, Windows .NET Server family

InvalidComObjectException Constructor (SerializationInfo, StreamingContext)

Initializes a new instance of the **COMException** class from serialization data.

```
[Visual Basic]
Protected Sub New( _
   ByVal info As SerializationInfo, _
   ByVal context As StreamingContext _
)
[C#]
protected InvalidComObjectException(
   SerializationInfo info,
   StreamingContext context
);
[C++]
protected: InvalidComObjectException(
   SerializationInfo* info,
   StreamingContext context
);
```

```
[JScript]
protected function InvalidComObjectException(
   info : SerializationInfo,
   context : StreamingContext
);
```

Parameters

info
> The object that holds the serialized object data.

context
> The contextual information about the source or destination.

Exceptions

Exception Type	Condition
ArgumentNullException	*info* is a null reference (**Nothing** in Visual Basic).

Remarks

This constructor is called during deserialization to reconstitute the exception object transmitted over a stream. For more information, see **System.Runtime.Serialization**.

InvalidComObjectException inherits from **SystemException**.

Requirements

Platforms: Windows 98, Windows NT 4.0, Windows Millennium Edition, Windows 2000, Windows XP Home Edition, Windows XP Professional, Windows .NET Server family

InvalidComObjectException Constructor (String, Exception)

Initializes a new instance of the **InvalidComObjectException** class with a specified error message and a reference to the inner exception that is the cause of this exception.

```
[Visual Basic]
Public Sub New( _
   ByVal message As String, _
   ByVal inner As Exception _
)
[C#]
public InvalidComObjectException(
   string message,
   Exception inner
);
[C++]
public: InvalidComObjectException(
   String* message,
   Exception* inner
);
[JScript]
public function InvalidComObjectException(
   message : String,
   inner : Exception
);
```

Parameters

message
> The error message that explains the reason for the exception.

inner

> The exception that is the cause of the current exception. If the *inner* parameter is not a null reference (**Nothing** in Visual Basic), the current exception is raised in a **catch** block that handles the inner exception.

Remarks

An exception that is thrown as a direct result of a previous exception should include a reference to the previous exception in the **InnerException** property. The **InnerException** property returns the same value that is passed into the constructor, or a null reference (**Nothing** in Visual Basic) if the **InnerException** property does not supply the inner exception value to the constructor.

The following table shows the initial property values for an instance of **InvalidComObjectException**.

Property	Value
InnerException	The inner exception reference.
Message	The error message string.

Requirements

Platforms: Windows 98, Windows NT 4.0, Windows Millennium Edition, Windows 2000, Windows XP Home Edition, Windows XP Professional, Windows .NET Server family

InvalidOleVariantTypeException Class

The exception thrown by the marshaler when it encounters an argument of a variant type that can not be marshaled to managed code.

System.Object
  System.Exception
    System.SystemException
      System.Runtime.InteropServices.InvalidOleVariantType-
      Exception

```
[Visual Basic]
<Serializable>
Public Class InvalidOleVariantTypeException
   Inherits SystemException
[C#]
[Serializable]
public class InvalidOleVariantTypeException : SystemException
[C++]
[Serializable]
public __gc class InvalidOleVariantTypeException : public
   SystemException
[JScript]
public
   Serializable
class InvalidOleVariantTypeException extends SystemException
```

Thread Safety

Any public static (**Shared** in Visual Basic) members of this type are safe for multithreaded operations. Any instance members are not guaranteed to be thread safe.

Remarks

InvalidOLEVariantTypeException uses the HRESULT COR_E_INVALIDOLEVARIANTTYPE which has the value 0x80131531.

Requirements

Namespace: System.Runtime.InteropServices

Platforms: Windows 98, Windows NT 4.0, Windows Millennium Edition, Windows 2000, Windows XP Home Edition, Windows XP Professional, Windows .NET Server family

Assembly: Mscorlib (in Mscorlib.dll)

InvalidOleVariantTypeException Constructor

Initializes a new instance of the **InvalidOleVariantTypeException** class.

Overload List

Initializes a new instance of the **InvalidOleVariantTypeException** class with default values.

  [Visual Basic] **Public Sub New()**

  [C#] **public InvalidOleVariantTypeException();**

  [C++] **public: InvalidOleVariantTypeException();**

  [JScript] **public function InvalidOleVariantTypeException();**

Initializes a new instance of the **InvalidOleVariantTypeException** class with a specified message.

  [Visual Basic] **Public Sub New(String)**

  [C#] **public InvalidOleVariantTypeException(string);**

  [C++] **public: InvalidOleVariantTypeException(String*);**

  [JScript] **public function InvalidOleVariantTypeException(String);**

Initializes a new instance of the **InvalidOleVariantTypeException** class from serialization data.

  [Visual Basic] **Protected Sub New(SerializationInfo, StreamingContext)**

  [C#] **protected InvalidOleVariantTypeException(SerializationInfo, StreamingContext);**

  [C++] **protected: InvalidOleVariantTypeException(SerializationInfo*, StreamingContext);**

  [JScript] **protected function InvalidOleVariantTypeException(SerializationInfo, StreamingContext);**

Initializes a new instance of the **InvalidOleVariantTypeException** class with a specified error message and a reference to the inner exception that is the cause of this exception.

  [Visual Basic] **Public Sub New(String, Exception)**

  [C#] **public InvalidOleVariantTypeException(string, Exception);**

  [C++] **public: InvalidOleVariantTypeException(String*, Exception*);**

  [JScript] **public function InvalidOleVariantTypeException(String, Exception);**

InvalidOleVariantTypeException Constructor ( )

Initializes a new instance of the **InvalidOleVariantTypeException** class with default values.

```
[Visual Basic]
Public Sub New()
[C#]
public InvalidOleVariantTypeException();
[C++]
public: InvalidOleVariantTypeException();
[JScript]
public function InvalidOleVariantTypeException();
```

Remarks

InvalidOleVariantTypeException inherits from **SystemException**. This constructor sets the properties of the **Exception** object as shown in the following table.

Property	Value
InnerException	A null reference (**Nothing** in Visual Basic).
Message	A localized error message string.

Requirements

Platforms: Windows 98, Windows NT 4.0, Windows Millennium Edition, Windows 2000, Windows XP Home Edition, Windows XP Professional, Windows .NET Server family

InvalidOleVariantTypeException Constructor (String)

Initializes a new instance of the **InvalidOleVariantTypeException** class with a specified message.

```
[Visual Basic]
Public Sub New( _
   ByVal message As String _
)
[C#]
public InvalidOleVariantTypeException(
   string message
);
[C++]
public: InvalidOleVariantTypeException(
   String* message
);
[JScript]
public function InvalidOleVariantTypeException(
   message : String
);
```

Parameters

message
   The message that indicates the reason for the exception.

Remarks

InvalidOleVariantTypeException inherits from **SystemException**. This constructor sets the properties of the **Exception** object as shown in the following table.

Property	Value
InnerException	A null reference (**Nothing** in Visual Basic).
Message	*message*

Requirements

Platforms: Windows 98, Windows NT 4.0, Windows Millennium Edition, Windows 2000, Windows XP Home Edition, Windows XP Professional, Windows .NET Server family

InvalidOleVariantTypeException Constructor (SerializationInfo, StreamingContext)

Initializes a new instance of the **InvalidOleVariantTypeException** class from serialization data.

```
[Visual Basic]
Protected Sub New( _
   ByVal info As SerializationInfo, _
   ByVal context As StreamingContext _
)
[C#]
protected InvalidOleVariantTypeException(
   SerializationInfo info,
   StreamingContext context
);
[C++]
protected: InvalidOleVariantTypeException(
   SerializationInfo* info,
   StreamingContext context
);
```

```
[JScript]
protected function InvalidOleVariantTypeException(
   info : SerializationInfo,
   context : StreamingContext
);
```

Parameters

info
   The object that holds the serialized object data.
context
   The contextual information about the source or destination.

Exceptions

Exception Type	Condition
ArgumentNullException	*info* is a null reference (**Nothing** in Visual Basic).

Remarks

This constructor is called during deserialization to reconstitute the exception object transmitted over a stream. For more information, see **System.Runtime.Serialization**.

InvalidOleVariantTypeException inherits from **SystemException**.

Requirements

Platforms: Windows 98, Windows NT 4.0, Windows Millennium Edition, Windows 2000, Windows XP Home Edition, Windows XP Professional, Windows .NET Server family

InvalidOleVariantTypeException Constructor (String, Exception)

Initializes a new instance of the **InvalidOleVariantTypeException** class with a specified error message and a reference to the inner exception that is the cause of this exception.

```
[Visual Basic]
Public Sub New( _
   ByVal message As String, _
   ByVal inner As Exception _
)
[C#]
public InvalidOleVariantTypeException(
   string message,
   Exception inner
);
[C++]
public: InvalidOleVariantTypeException(
   String* message,
   Exception* inner
);
[JScript]
public function InvalidOleVariantTypeException(
   message : String,
   inner : Exception
);
```

Parameters

message
   The error message that explains the reason for the exception.

inner

The exception that is the cause of the current exception. If the *inner* parameter is not a null reference (**Nothing** in Visual Basic), the current exception is raised in a **catch** block that handles the inner exception.

Remarks

An exception that is thrown as a direct result of a previous exception should include a reference to the previous exception in the **InnerException** property. The **InnerException** property returns the same value that is passed into the constructor, or a null reference (**Nothing** in Visual Basic) if the **InnerException** property does not supply the inner exception value to the constructor.

The following table shows the initial property values for an instance of **InvalidOleVariantTypeException**.

Property	Value
InnerException	The inner exception reference.
Message	The error message string.

Requirements

Platforms: Windows 98, Windows NT 4.0, Windows Millennium Edition, Windows 2000, Windows XP Home Edition, Windows XP Professional, Windows .NET Server family

INVOKEKIND Enumeration

Specifies how to invoke a function by **IDispatch::Invoke**.

```
[Visual Basic]
<Serializable>
<ComVisible(False)>
Public Enum INVOKEKIND
[C#]
[Serializable]
[ComVisible(false)]
public enum INVOKEKIND
[C++]
[Serializable]
[ComVisible(false)]
__value public enum INVOKEKIND
[JScript]
public
    Serializable
    ComVisible(false)
enum INVOKEKIND
```

Remarks

For additional information about **INVOKEKIND**, see the MSDN Library.

Members

Member name	Description
INVOKE_FUNC	The member is called using a normal function invocation syntax.
INVOKE_PROPERTY-GET	The function is invoked using a normal property-access syntax.
INVOKE_PROPERTY-PUT	The function is invoked using a property value assignment syntax.
INVOKE_PROPERTY-PUTREF	The function is invoked using a property reference assignment syntax.

Requirements

Namespace: System.Runtime.InteropServices

Platforms: Windows 98, Windows NT 4.0, Windows Millennium Edition, Windows 2000, Windows XP Home Edition, Windows XP Professional, Windows .NET Server family

Assembly: Mscorlib (in Mscorlib.dll)

IRegistrationServices Interface

Provides a set of services for registering and unregistering managed assemblies for use from COM.

```
[Visual Basic]
<Guid("CCBD682C-73A5-4568-B8B0-C7007E11ABA2")>
Public Interface IRegistrationServices
[C#]
[Guid("CCBD682C-73A5-4568-B8B0-C7007E11ABA2")]
public interface IRegistrationServices
[C++]
[Guid("CCBD682C-73A5-4568-B8B0-C7007E11ABA2")]
public __gc __interface IRegistrationServices
[JScript]
public
   Guid("CCBD682C-73A5-4568-B8B0-C7007E11ABA2")
interface IRegistrationServices
```

Classes that Implement IRegistrationServices

Class	Description
RegistrationServices	Provides a set of services for registering and unregistering managed assemblies for use from COM.

Remarks

Registration is needed when the objects within an assembly are being used by COM clients.

Requirements

Namespace: System.Runtime.InteropServices

Platforms: Windows 98, Windows NT 4.0, Windows Millennium Edition, Windows 2000, Windows XP Home Edition, Windows XP Professional, Windows .NET Server family

Assembly: Mscorlib (in Mscorlib.dll)

IRegistrationServices.GetManagedCategoryGuid Method

Returns the GUID of the COM category that contains the managed classes.

```
[Visual Basic]
Function GetManagedCategoryGuid() As Guid
[C#]
Guid GetManagedCategoryGuid();
[C++]
Guid GetManagedCategoryGuid();
[JScript]
function GetManagedCategoryGuid() : Guid;
```

Return Value

The GUID of the COM category that contains the managed classes.

Requirements

Platforms: Windows 98, Windows NT 4.0, Windows Millennium Edition, Windows 2000, Windows XP Home Edition, Windows XP Professional, Windows .NET Server family

IRegistrationServices.GetProgIdForType Method

Retrieves the COM ProgID for a specified type.

```
[Visual Basic]
Function GetProgIdForType( _
   ByVal type As Type _
) As String
[C#]
string GetProgIdForType(
   Type type
);
[C++]
String* GetProgIdForType(
   Type* type
);
[JScript]
function GetProgIdForType(
   type : Type
) : String;
```

Parameters

type
   The type whose ProgID is being requested.

Return Value

The ProgID for the specified type.

Requirements

Platforms: Windows 98, Windows NT 4.0, Windows Millennium Edition, Windows 2000, Windows XP Home Edition, Windows XP Professional, Windows .NET Server family

IRegistrationServices.GetRegistrableTypesIn-Assembly Method

Retrieves a list of classes in an assembly that would be registered by a call to **RegisterAssembly**.

```
[Visual Basic]
Function GetRegistrableTypesInAssembly( _
   ByVal assembly As Assembly _
) As Type()
[C#]
Type[] GetRegistrableTypesInAssembly(
   Assembly assembly
);
[C++]
Type* GetRegistrableTypesInAssembly(
   Assembly* assembly
) [];
[JScript]
function GetRegistrableTypesInAssembly(
   assembly : Assembly
) : Type[];
```

Parameters

assembly
   The assembly to search for classes.

Return Value

A **Type** array containing a list of classes in *assembly*.

Requirements

Platforms: Windows 98, Windows NT 4.0,
Windows Millennium Edition, Windows 2000,
Windows XP Home Edition, Windows XP Professional,
Windows .NET Server family

IRegistrationServices.RegisterAssembly Method

Registers the classes in a managed assembly to enable creation from
COM.

```
[Visual Basic]
Function RegisterAssembly( _
    ByVal assembly As Assembly, _
    ByVal flags As AssemblyRegistrationFlags _
) As Boolean
[C#]
bool RegisterAssembly(
    Assembly assembly,
    AssemblyRegistrationFlags flags
);
[C++]
bool RegisterAssembly(
    Assembly* assembly,
    AssemblyRegistrationFlags flags
);
[JScript]
function RegisterAssembly(
    assembly : Assembly,
    flags : AssemblyRegistrationFlags
) : Boolean;
```

Parameters

assembly
    The assembly to be registered.

flags
    An **AssemblyRegistrationFlags** value indicating any special
    settings needed when registering *assembly*.

Return Value

true if *assembly* contains types that were successfully registered;
otherwise **false** if the assembly contains no eligible types.

Exceptions

Exception Type	Condition
ArgumentNull-Exception	*assembly* is a null reference (**Nothing** in Visual Basic).
InvalidOperation-Exception	The full name of *assembly* is a null reference (**Nothing** in Visual Basic).
	-or-
	A method marked with **ComRegisterFunctionAttribute** is not static (**Shared** in Visual Basic) .
	-or-
	There is more than one method marked with **ComRegisterFunctionAttribute** at a given level of the hierarchy.
	-or-
	The signature of the method marked with **ComRegisterFunctionAttribute** is not valid.

Remarks

RegisterAssembly adds the appropriate registry entries for the types
in the specified assembly. This method also calls any registration
functions found in the assembly.

Use **Assembly.Load** to get an assembly.

Requirements

Platforms: Windows 98, Windows NT 4.0,
Windows Millennium Edition, Windows 2000,
Windows XP Home Edition, Windows XP Professional,
Windows .NET Server family

IRegistrationServices.RegisterTypeForComClients Method

Adds the appropriate registry entries for the specified type using the
specified GUID.

```
[Visual Basic]
Sub RegisterTypeForComClients( _
    ByVal type As Type, _
    ByRef g As Guid _
)
[C#]
void RegisterTypeForComClients(
    Type type,
    ref Guid g
);
[C++]
void RegisterTypeForComClients(
    Type* type,
    Guid* g
);
[JScript]
function RegisterTypeForComClients(
    type : Type,
    g : Guid
);
```

Parameters

type
    The type to be registered for use from COM.

g
    GUID used to register the specified type.

Remarks

This method is equivalent to calling **CoRegisterClassObject** in
COM.

Requirements

Platforms: Windows 98, Windows NT 4.0,
Windows Millennium Edition, Windows 2000,
Windows XP Home Edition, Windows XP Professional,
Windows .NET Server family

IRegistrationServices.TypeRepresentsComType Method

Determines whether the specified type is a COM type.

```
[Visual Basic]
Function TypeRepresentsComType( _
    ByVal type As Type _
) As Boolean
```

```
[C#]
bool TypeRepresentsComType(
    Type type
);
[C++]
bool TypeRepresentsComType(
    Type* type
);
[JScript]
function TypeRepresentsComType(
    type : Type
) : Boolean;
```

Parameters

type
    The type to determine if it is a COM type.

Return Value

true if the specified type is a COM type; otherwise **false**.

Requirements

Platforms: Windows 98, Windows NT 4.0,
Windows Millennium Edition, Windows 2000,
Windows XP Home Edition, Windows XP Professional,
Windows .NET Server family

IRegistrationServices.TypeRequiresRegistration Method

Determines whether the specified type requires registration.

```
[Visual Basic]
Function TypeRequiresRegistration( _
    ByVal type As Type _
) As Boolean
[C#]
bool TypeRequiresRegistration(
    Type type
);
[C++]
bool TypeRequiresRegistration(
    Type* type
);
[JScript]
function TypeRequiresRegistration(
    type : Type
) : Boolean;
```

Parameters

type
    The type to check for COM registration requirements.

Return Value

true if the type must be registered for use from COM; otherwise
false.

Requirements

Platforms: Windows 98, Windows NT 4.0,
Windows Millennium Edition, Windows 2000,
Windows XP Home Edition, Windows XP Professional,
Windows .NET Server family

IRegistrationServices.UnregisterAssembly Method

Unregisters the classes in a managed assembly.

```
[Visual Basic]
Function UnregisterAssembly( _
    ByVal assembly As Assembly _
) As Boolean
[C#]
bool UnregisterAssembly(
    Assembly assembly
);
[C++]
bool UnregisterAssembly(
    Assembly* assembly
);
[JScript]
function UnregisterAssembly(
    assembly : Assembly
) : Boolean;
```

Parameters

assembly
    The assembly to be unregistered.

Return Value

true if *assembly* contains types that were successfully unregistered;
otherwise **false** if the assembly contains no eligible types.

Exceptions

Exception Type	Condition
ArgumentNullException	*assembly* is a null reference (**Nothing** in Visual Basic).
InvalidOperation-Exception	The full name of *assembly* is a null reference (**Nothing** in Visual Basic).
	-or-
	A method marked with **ComUnregisterFunctionAttribute** is not static (**Shared** in Visual Basic).
	-or-
	There is more than one method marked with **ComUnregister-FunctionAttribute** at a given level of the hierarchy.
	-or-
	The signature of the method marked with **ComUnregister-FunctionAttribute** is not valid.

Remarks

UnregisterAssembly removes the registry entries for the types in
the specified assembly previously added by **RegisterAssembly**. This
method also calls any unregistration functions found in the
assembly.

Requirements

Platforms: Windows 98, Windows NT 4.0,
Windows Millennium Edition, Windows 2000,
Windows XP Home Edition, Windows XP Professional,
Windows .NET Server family

ITypeLibConverter Interface

Provides a set of services that convert a managed assembly to a COM type library and vice versa.

```
[Visual Basic]
<Guid("F1C3BF78-C3E4-11d3-88E7-00902754C43A")>
<InterfaceType(ComInterfaceType.InterfaceIsIUnknown)>
Public Interface ITypeLibConverter
[C#]
[Guid("F1C3BF78-C3E4-11d3-88E7-00902754C43A")]
[InterfaceType(ComInterfaceType.InterfaceIsIUnknown)]
public interface ITypeLibConverter
[C++]
[Guid("F1C3BF78-C3E4-11d3-88E7-00902754C43A")]
[InterfaceType(ComInterfaceType::InterfaceIsIUnknown)]
public __gc __interface ITypeLibConverter
[JScript]
public
   Guid("F1C3BF78-C3E4-11d3-88E7-00902754C43A")
   InterfaceType(ComInterfaceType.InterfaceIsIUnknown)
interface ITypeLibConverter
```

Classes that Implement ITypeLibConverter

Class	Description
TypeLibConverter	Provides a set of services that convert a managed assembly to a COM type library and vice versa.

Requirements

Namespace: System.Runtime.InteropServices

Platforms: Windows 98, Windows NT 4.0, Windows Millennium Edition, Windows 2000, Windows XP Home Edition, Windows XP Professional, Windows .NET Server family

Assembly: Mscorlib (in Mscorlib.dll)

ITypeLibConverter.ConvertAssemblyToTypeLib Method

Converts an assembly to a COM type library.

```
[Visual Basic]
Function ConvertAssemblyToTypeLib( _
   ByVal assembly As Assembly, _
   ByVal typeLibName As String, _
   ByVal flags As TypeLibExporterFlags, _
   ByVal notifySink As ITypeLibExporterNotifySink _
) As Object
[C#]
object ConvertAssemblyToTypeLib(
   Assembly assembly,
   string typeLibName,
   TypeLibExporterFlags flags,
   ITypeLibExporterNotifySink notifySink
);
[C++]
Object* ConvertAssemblyToTypeLib(
   Assembly* assembly,
   String* typeLibName,
```
```
   TypeLibExporterFlags flags,
   ITypeLibExporterNotifySink* notifySink
);
[JScript]
function ConvertAssemblyToTypeLib(
   assembly : Assembly,
   typeLibName : String,
   flags : TypeLibExporterFlags,
   notifySink : ITypeLibExporterNotifySink
) : Object;
```

Parameters

assembly
    The assembly to convert.

typeLibName
    The file name of the resulting type library.

flags
    A **TypeLibExporterFlags** value indicating any special settings.

notifySink
    The **ITypeLibExporterNotifySink** interface implemented by the caller.

Return Value

An object that implements the **ITypeLib** interface.

Remarks

For more information on **ITypeLib**, please see its existing documentation in the MSDN library.

Requirements

Platforms: Windows 98, Windows NT 4.0, Windows Millennium Edition, Windows 2000, Windows XP Home Edition, Windows XP Professional, Windows .NET Server family

ITypeLibConverter.ConvertTypeLibToAssembly Method

Converts a COM type library to an assembly.

Overload List

Converts a COM type library to an assembly.

    [Visual Basic] **Overloads Function ConvertTypeLibToAssembly(Object, String, Integer, ITypeLibImporterNotifySink, Byte(), StrongNameKeyPair, Boolean) As AssemblyBuilder**
    [C#] **AssemblyBuilder ConvertTypeLibToAssembly(object, string, int, ITypeLibImporterNotifySink, byte[], StrongNameKeyPair, bool);**
    [C++] **AssemblyBuilder* ConvertTypeLibToAssembly (Object*, String*, int, ITypeLibImporterNotifySink*, unsigned char __gc[], StrongNameKeyPair*, bool);**
    [JScript] **function ConvertTypeLibToAssembly(Object, String, int, ITypeLibImporterNotifySink, Byte[], StrongNameKeyPair, Boolean) : AssemblyBuilder;**

Converts a COM type library to an assembly.

    [Visual Basic] **Overloads Function ConvertTypeLibToAssembly(Object, String, TypeLibImporterFlags, ITypeLibImporterNotifySink, Byte(), StrongNameKeyPair, String, Version) As AssemblyBuilder**
    [C#] **AssemblyBuilder ConvertTypeLibToAssembly(object, string, TypeLibImporterFlags, ITypeLibImporterNotifySink, byte[], StrongNameKeyPair, string, Version);**

[C++] **AssemblyBuilder* ConvertTypeLibToAssembly(Object*, String*, TypeLibImporterFlags, ITypeLibImporterNotifySink*, unsigned char __gc[], StrongNameKeyPair*, String*, Version*);**

[JScript] **function ConvertTypeLibToAssembly(Object, String, TypeLibImporterFlags, ITypeLibImporterNotifySink, Byte[], StrongNameKeyPair, String, Version) : AssemblyBuilder;**

ITypeLibConverter.ConvertTypeLibToAssembly Method (Object, String, Int32, ITypeLibImporterNotifySink, Byte[], StrongNameKeyPair, Boolean)

Converts a COM type library to an assembly.

```
[Visual Basic]
Function ConvertTypeLibToAssembly( _
   ByVal typeLib As Object, _
   ByVal asmFileName As String, _
   ByVal flags As Integer, _
   ByVal notifySink As ITypeLibImporterNotifySink, _
   ByVal publicKey() As Byte, _
   ByVal keyPair As StrongNameKeyPair, _
   ByVal unsafeInterfaces As Boolean _
) As AssemblyBuilder
[C#]
AssemblyBuilder ConvertTypeLibToAssembly(
   object typeLib,
   string asmFileName,
   int flags,
   ITypeLibImporterNotifySink notifySink,
   byte[] publicKey,
   StrongNameKeyPair keyPair,
   bool unsafeInterfaces
);
[C++]
AssemblyBuilder* ConvertTypeLibToAssembly(
   Object* typeLib,
   String* asmFileName,
   int flags,
   ITypeLibImporterNotifySink* notifySink,
   unsigned char publicKey __gc[],
   StrongNameKeyPair* keyPair,
   bool unsafeInterfaces
);
[JScript]
function ConvertTypeLibToAssembly(
   typeLib : Object,
   asmFileName : String,
   flags : int,
   notifySink : ITypeLibImporterNotifySink,
   publicKey : Byte[],
   keyPair : StrongNameKeyPair,
   unsafeInterfaces : Boolean
) : AssemblyBuilder;
```

Parameters

typeLib
The object that implements the **ITypeLib** interface.
asmFileName
The file name of the resulting assembly.

flags
A **TypeLibImporterFlags** value indicating any special settings.
notifySink
ITypeLibImporterNotifySink interface implemented by the caller.
publicKey
A **byte** array containing the public key.
keyPair
A **StrongNameKeyPair** object containing the public and private cryptographic key pair.
unsafeInterfaces
If **true**, the interfaces require link time checks for **UnmanagedCode** permission. If **false**, the interfaces require run time checks that require a stack walk and are more expensive, but are more secure.

Return Value

An **AssemblyBuilder** object containing the converted type library.

Remarks

For more information on **ITypeLib**, please see its existing documentation in the MSDN library.

Requirements

Platforms: Windows 98, Windows NT 4.0, Windows Millennium Edition, Windows 2000, Windows XP Home Edition, Windows XP Professional, Windows .NET Server family

ITypeLibConverter.ConvertTypeLibToAssembly Method (Object, String, TypeLibImporterFlags, ITypeLibImporterNotifySink, Byte[], StrongNameKeyPair, String, Version)

Converts a COM type library to an assembly.

```
[Visual Basic]
Function ConvertTypeLibToAssembly( _
   ByVal typeLib As Object, _
   ByVal asmFileName As String, _
   ByVal flags As TypeLibImporterFlags, _
   ByVal notifySink As ITypeLibImporterNotifySink, _
   ByVal publicKey() As Byte, _
   ByVal keyPair As StrongNameKeyPair, _
   ByVal asmNamespace As String, _
   ByVal asmVersion As Version _
) As AssemblyBuilder
[C#]
AssemblyBuilder ConvertTypeLibToAssembly(
   object typeLib,
   string asmFileName,
   TypeLibImporterFlags flags,
   ITypeLibImporterNotifySink notifySink,
   byte[] publicKey,
   StrongNameKeyPair keyPair,
   string asmNamespace,
   Version asmVersion
);
[C++]
AssemblyBuilder* ConvertTypeLibToAssembly(
   Object* typeLib,
   String* asmFileName,
   TypeLibImporterFlags flags,
   ITypeLibImporterNotifySink* notifySink,
```

```
    unsigned char publicKey __gc[],
    StrongNameKeyPair* keyPair,
    String* asmNamespace,
    Version* asmVersion
);
[JScript]
function ConvertTypeLibToAssembly(
    typeLib : Object,
    asmFileName : String,
    flags : TypeLibImporterFlags,
    notifySink : ITypeLibImporterNotifySink,
    publicKey : Byte[],
    keyPair : StrongNameKeyPair,
    asmNamespace : String,
    asmVersion : Version
) : AssemblyBuilder;
```

Parameters

typeLib
> The object that implements the **ITypeLib** interface.

asmFileName
> The file name of the resulting assembly.

flags
> A **TypeLibImporterFlags** value indicating any special settings.

notifySink
> **ITypeLibImporterNotifySink** interface implemented by the caller.

publicKey
> A **byte** array containing the public key.

keyPair
> A **StrongNameKeyPair** object containing the public and private cryptographic key pair.

asmNamespace
> The namespace for the resulting assembly.

asmVersion
> The version of the resulting assembly. If a null reference (**Nothing** in Visual Basic), the version of the type library is used.

Return Value

An **AssemblyBuilder** object containing the converted type library.

Remarks

For more information on **ITypeLib**, please see its existing documentation in the MSDN library.

Requirements

Platforms: Windows 98, Windows NT 4.0, Windows Millennium Edition, Windows 2000, Windows XP Home Edition, Windows XP Professional, Windows .NET Server family

ITypeLibConverter.GetPrimaryInteropAssembly Method

Gets the name and code base of a primary interop assembly for a specified type library.

```
[Visual Basic]
Function GetPrimaryInteropAssembly( _
    ByVal g As Guid, _
    ByVal major As Integer, _
    ByVal minor As Integer, _
    ByVal lcid As Integer, _
    <Out()> ByRef asmName As String, _
    <Out()> ByRef asmCodeBase As String _
) As Boolean
[C#]
bool GetPrimaryInteropAssembly(
    Guid g,
    int major,
    int minor,
    int lcid,
    out string asmName,
    out string asmCodeBase
);
[C++]
bool GetPrimaryInteropAssembly(
    Guid g,
    int major,
    int minor,
    int lcid,
    [
    Out
] String** asmName,
    [
    Out
] String** asmCodeBase
);
[JScript]
function GetPrimaryInteropAssembly(
    g : Guid,
    major : int,
    minor : int,
    lcid : int,
    asmName : String,
    asmCodeBase : String
) : Boolean;
```

Parameters

g
> The GUID of the type library.

major
> The major version number of the type library.

minor
> The minor version number of the type library.

lcid
> The LCID of the type library.

asmName
> On successful return, the name of the primary interop assembly associated with *g*.

asmCodeBase
> On successful return, the code base of the primary interop assembly associated with *g*.

Return Value

true if the primary interop assembly was found in the registry; otherwise **false**.

Requirements

Platforms: Windows 98, Windows NT 4.0, Windows Millennium Edition, Windows 2000, Windows XP Home Edition, Windows XP Professional, Windows .NET Server family

ITypeLibExporterNameProvider Interface

Provides control over the casing of names when exported to a type library.

```
[Visual Basic]
<Guid("FA1F3615-ACB9-486d-9EAC-1BEF87E36B09")>
<InterfaceType(ComInterfaceType.InterfaceIsIUnknown)>
Public Interface ITypeLibExporterNameProvider
[C#]
[Guid("FA1F3615-ACB9-486d-9EAC-1BEF87E36B09")]
[InterfaceType(ComInterfaceType.InterfaceIsIUnknown)]
public interface ITypeLibExporterNameProvider
[C++]
[Guid("FA1F3615-ACB9-486d-9EAC-1BEF87E36B09")]
[InterfaceType(ComInterfaceType::InterfaceIsIUnknown)]
public __gc __interface ITypeLibExporterNameProvider
[JScript]
public
   Guid("FA1F3615-ACB9-486d-9EAC-1BEF87E36B09")
   InterfaceType(ComInterfaceType.InterfaceIsIUnknown)
interface ITypeLibExporterNameProvider
```

Remarks

In order to control how types are named when exported to a type library, an object must implement this interface, as well as **ITypeLibExporterNotifySink**. You then pass this object as the last parameter to **ConvertAssemblyToTypeLib**.

Requirements

Namespace: System.Runtime.InteropServices

Platforms: Windows 98, Windows NT 4.0, Windows Millennium Edition, Windows 2000, Windows XP Home Edition, Windows XP Professional, Windows .NET Server family

Assembly: Mscorlib (in Mscorlib.dll)

ITypeLibExporterNameProvider.GetNames Method

Returns a list of names to control the casing of.

```
[Visual Basic]
Function GetNames() As String()
[C#]
string[] GetNames();
[C++]
String* GetNames() __gc[];
[JScript]
function GetNames() : String[];
```

Return Value

An array of strings, where each element contains the name of a type to control casing for.

Remarks

Names in the array returned from this method must be unique. If a name appears twice in the array of names, even with different casing, the first occurance takes precedence.

Requirements

Platforms: Windows 98, Windows NT 4.0, Windows Millennium Edition, Windows 2000, Windows XP Home Edition, Windows XP Professional, Windows .NET Server family

ITypeLibExporterNotifySink Interface

Provides a callback mechanism for the assembly converter to inform the caller of the status of the conversion, and involve the caller in the conversion process itself.

```
[Visual Basic]
<Guid("F1C3BF77-C3E4-11d3-88E7-00902754C43A")>
<InterfaceType(ComInterfaceType.InterfaceIsIUnknown)>
Public Interface ITypeLibExporterNotifySink
[C#]
[Guid("F1C3BF77-C3E4-11d3-88E7-00902754C43A")]
[InterfaceType(ComInterfaceType.InterfaceIsIUnknown)]
public interface ITypeLibExporterNotifySink
[C++]
[Guid("F1C3BF77-C3E4-11d3-88E7-00902754C43A")]
[InterfaceType(ComInterfaceType::InterfaceIsIUnknown)]
public __gc __interface ITypeLibExporterNotifySink
[JScript]
public
    Guid("F1C3BF77-C3E4-11d3-88E7-00902754C43A")
    InterfaceType(ComInterfaceType.InterfaceIsIUnknown)
interface ITypeLibExporterNotifySink
```

Remarks

This interface is used in the process of converting a managed assembly to a COM type library.

Requirements

Namespace: System.Runtime.InteropServices

Platforms: Windows 98, Windows NT 4.0, Windows Millennium Edition, Windows 2000, Windows XP Home Edition, Windows XP Professional, Windows .NET Server family

Assembly: Mscorlib (in Mscorlib.dll)

ITypeLibExporterNotifySink.ReportEvent Method

Notifies the caller that an event occured during the conversion of an assembly.

```
[Visual Basic]
Sub ReportEvent( _
   ByVal eventKind As ExporterEventKind, _
   ByVal eventCode As Integer, _
   ByVal eventMsg As String _
)
[C#]
void ReportEvent(
   ExporterEventKind eventKind,
   int eventCode,
   string eventMsg
);
[C++]
void ReportEvent(
   ExporterEventKind eventKind,
   int eventCode,
   String* eventMsg
);
```

```
[JScript]
function ReportEvent(
   eventKind : ExporterEventKind,
   eventCode : int,
   eventMsg : String
);
```

Parameters

eventKind
An **ExporterEventKind** value indicating the type of event.
eventCode
Indicates extra information about the event.
eventMsg
A message generated by the event.

Remarks

If the event being reported is a warning or an error, *eventCode* will contain the HRESULT of the error. For any other event it will be 0.

Requirements

Platforms: Windows 98, Windows NT 4.0, Windows Millennium Edition, Windows 2000, Windows XP Home Edition, Windows XP Professional, Windows .NET Server family

ITypeLibExporterNotifySink.ResolveRef Method

Asks the user to resolve a reference to another assembly.

```
[Visual Basic]
Function ResolveRef( _
   ByVal assembly As Assembly _
) As Object
[C#]
object ResolveRef(
   Assembly assembly
);
[C++]
Object* ResolveRef(
   Assembly* assembly
);
[JScript]
function ResolveRef(
   assembly : Assembly
) : Object;
```

Parameters

assembly
The assembly to resolve.

Return Value

The type library for *assembly*.

Remarks

If a reference to another assembly is found during the conversion of an assembly, the caller is asked to return the correct type library (the object that implements **ITypeLib** interface) for that assembly.

Requirements

Platforms: Windows 98, Windows NT 4.0, Windows Millennium Edition, Windows 2000, Windows XP Home Edition, Windows XP Professional, Windows .NET Server family

ITypeLibImporterNotifySink Interface

Provides a callback mechanism for the type library converter to inform the caller of the status of the conversion, and involve the caller in the conversion process itself.

```
[Visual Basic]
<Guid("F1C3BF76-C3E4-11d3-88E7-00902754C43A")>
<InterfaceType(ComInterfaceType.InterfaceIsIUnknown)>
Public Interface ITypeLibImporterNotifySink
[C#]
[Guid("F1C3BF76-C3E4-11d3-88E7-00902754C43A")]
[InterfaceType(ComInterfaceType.InterfaceIsIUnknown)]
public interface ITypeLibImporterNotifySink
[C++]
[Guid("F1C3BF76-C3E4-11d3-88E7-00902754C43A")]
[InterfaceType(ComInterfaceType::InterfaceIsIUnknown)]
public __gc __interface ITypeLibImporterNotifySink
[JScript]
public
    Guid("F1C3BF76-C3E4-11d3-88E7-00902754C43A")
    InterfaceType(ComInterfaceType.InterfaceIsIUnknown)
interface ITypeLibImporterNotifySink
```

Remarks

This interface is used in the process of converting a COM type library to a managed assembly.

Requirements

Namespace: System.Runtime.InteropServices

Platforms: Windows 98, Windows NT 4.0, Windows Millennium Edition, Windows 2000, Windows XP Home Edition, Windows XP Professional, Windows .NET Server family

Assembly: Mscorlib (in Mscorlib.dll)

ITypeLibImporterNotifySink.ReportEvent Method

Notifies the caller that an event occured during the conversion of a type library.

```
[Visual Basic]
Sub ReportEvent( _
    ByVal eventKind As ImporterEventKind, _
    ByVal eventCode As Integer, _
    ByVal eventMsg As String _
)
[C#]
void ReportEvent(
    ImporterEventKind eventKind,
    int eventCode,
    string eventMsg
);
[C++]
void ReportEvent(
    ImporterEventKind eventKind,
    int eventCode,
    String* eventMsg
);
```

```
[JScript]
function ReportEvent(
    eventKind : ImporterEventKind,
    eventCode : int,
    eventMsg : String
);
```

Parameters

eventKind
> An **ImporterEventKind** value indicating the type of event.

eventCode
> Indicates extra information about the event.

eventMsg
> A message generated by the event.

Remarks

If the event being reported is a warning or an error, *eventCode* will contain the HRESULT of the error. For any other event it will be 0.

Requirements

Platforms: Windows 98, Windows NT 4.0, Windows Millennium Edition, Windows 2000, Windows XP Home Edition, Windows XP Professional, Windows .NET Server family

ITypeLibImporterNotifySink.ResolveRef Method

Asks the user to resolve a reference to another type library.

```
[Visual Basic]
Function ResolveRef( _
    ByVal typeLib As Object _
) As Assembly
[C#]
Assembly ResolveRef(
    object typeLib
);
[C++]
Assembly* ResolveRef(
    Object* typeLib
);
[JScript]
function ResolveRef(
    typeLib : Object
) : Assembly;
```

Parameters

typeLib
> The object implementing the **ITypeLib** interface that needs to be resolved.

Return Value

The assembly corresponding to *typeLib*.

Remarks

If a reference to another type library is found during the conversion of a type library, the caller is asked to return the correct assembly for that type library.

Requirements

Platforms: Windows 98, Windows NT 4.0, Windows Millennium Edition, Windows 2000, Windows XP Home Edition, Windows XP Professional, Windows .NET Server family

LayoutKind Enumeration

Controls the layout of an object when exported to unmanaged code.

```
[Visual Basic]
<Serializable>
Public Enum LayoutKind
[C#]
[Serializable]
public enum LayoutKind
[C++]
[Serializable]
__value public enum LayoutKind
[JScript]
public
    Serializable
enum LayoutKind
```

Remarks

This enumeration is used with **StructLayoutAttribute**. The common language runtime uses the **Auto** layout value by default. To reduce layout-related problems associated with the **Auto** value, C#, Visual Basic .NET, and C++ compilers specify **Sequential** layout for value types.

Members

Member name	Description
Auto Supported by the .NET Compact Framework.	The runtime automatically chooses an appropriate layout for the members of an object in unmanaged memory. Objects defined with this enumeration member cannot be exposed outside of managed code. Attempting to do so generates an exception.
Explicit Supported by the .NET Compact Framework.	The precise position of each member of an object in unmanaged memory is explicitly controlled. Each member must use the **FieldOffsetAttribute** to indicate the position of that field within the type.
Sequential Supported by the .NET Compact Framework.	The members of the object are laid out sequentially, in the order in which they appear when exported to unmanaged memory. The members are laid out according to the packing specified in **StructLayout-Attribute.Pack**, and can be noncontiguous.

Requirements

Namespace: System.Runtime.InteropServices

Platforms: Windows 98, Windows NT 4.0, Windows Millennium Edition, Windows 2000, Windows XP Home Edition, Windows XP Professional, Windows .NET Server family, .NET Compact Framework - Windows CE .NET

Assembly: Mscorlib (in Mscorlib.dll)

LCIDConversionAttribute Class

Indicates that a method's unmanaged signature expects a locale identifier (LCID) parameter.

System.Object
  System.Attribute
    System.Runtime.InteropServices.LCIDConversionAttribute

[Visual Basic]
```
<AttributeUsage(AttributeTargets.Method)>
NotInheritable Public Class LCIDConversionAttribute
    Inherits Attribute
```
[C#]
```
[AttributeUsage(AttributeTargets.Method)]
public sealed class LCIDConversionAttribute : Attribute
```
[C++]
```
[AttributeUsage(AttributeTargets::Method)]
public __gc __sealed class LCIDConversionAttribute : public
    Attribute
```
[JScript]
```
public
    AttributeUsage(AttributeTargets.Method)
class LCIDConversionAttribute extends Attribute
```

Thread Safety

Any public static (**Shared** in Visual Basic) members of this type are safe for multithreaded operations. Any instance members are not guaranteed to be thread safe.

Remarks

You can apply this attribute to methods.

This attribute indicates that the marshaler should expect an LCID to be passed after the designated method argument. When calls are made from managed to unmanaged code, the marshaler supplies the LCID argument automatically.

Example

[Visual Basic, C#, C++] The following example demonstrates different signature translations based on different values supplied to **LCIDConversionAttribute**.

[Visual Basic]
```
Imports System
Imports System.Runtime.InteropServices
Imports System.Reflection

Class LCIDAttrSampler

    Const LCID_INSTALLED As Integer = 1
    Const LCID_SUPPORTED As Integer = 2

    <DllImport("KERNEL32.DLL", EntryPoint:="IsValidLocale", _
    SetLastError:=True, CharSet:=CharSet.Unicode, _
    CallingConvention:=CallingConvention.StdCall), _
    LCIDConversionAttribute(0)> _
    Public Shared Function IsValidLocale(ByVal dwFlags As
Integer) As Boolean
    End Function

    Public Sub CheckCurrentLCID()
        Dim mthIfo As MethodInfo =
Me.GetType().GetMethod("IsValidLocale")
        Dim attr As Attribute = Attribute.GetCustomAttribute
(mthIfo, GetType(LCIDConversionAttribute))
```

```
        If Not(attr Is Nothing) Then
            Dim lcidAttr As LCIDConversionAttribute =
CType(attr, LCIDConversionAttribute)
            Console.WriteLine("Position of the LCID argument
in the unmanaged signature: " + lcidAttr.Value.ToString())
        End If

        Dim res As Boolean = IsValidLocale(LCID_INSTALLED)
        Console.WriteLine("Result LCID_INSTALLED " + res.ToString())
        res = IsValidLocale(LCID_SUPPORTED)
        Console.WriteLine("Result LCID_SUPPORTED " + res.ToString())
    End Sub

    Public Shared Sub Main()
        Dim smpl As LCIDAttrSampler = New LCIDAttrSampler()
        smpl.CheckCurrentLCID()
    End Sub

End Class
```

[C#]
```
using System;
using System.Runtime.InteropServices;
using System.Reflection;

class LCIDAttrSample
{
    private const int LCID_INSTALLED = 1;
    private const int LCID_SUPPORTED = 2;

    [DllImport("KERNEL32.DLL", EntryPoint="IsValidLocale",
SetLastError = true, CharSet = CharSet.Auto)]
    [LCIDConversionAttribute(0)] // Position of the LCID argument
    public static extern bool IsValidLocale(
                                        uint dwFlags
// options
                                        );

    public void CheckCurrentLCID()
    {
        MethodInfo mthIfo = this.GetType().GetMethod("IsValidLocale");
        Attribute attr =
Attribute.GetCustomAttribute(mthIfo,typeof(LCIDConversionAttribute));

        if( attr != null)
        {
            LCIDConversionAttribute lcidAttr =
(LCIDConversionAttribute)attr;
            Console.WriteLine("Position of the LCID
argument in the unmanaged signature: " + lcidAttr.Value.ToString());
        }

        bool res = IsValidLocale(LCID_INSTALLED);
        Console.WriteLine("Result LCID_INSTALLED " + res.ToString());
        res = IsValidLocale(LCID_SUPPORTED);
        Console.WriteLine("Result LCID_SUPPORTED " + res.ToString());
    }

    static void Main(string[] args)
    {
        LCIDAttrSample smpl = new LCIDAttrSample();
        smpl.CheckCurrentLCID();
    }
}
```

[C++]
```
using namespace System;
using namespace System::Runtime::InteropServices;
using namespace System::Reflection;

#define LCID_INSTALLED 1
#define LCID_SUPPORTED 2

__gc class LCIDAttrSample
    {

    public:
```

```
        [DllImport(S"KERNEL32.DLL", EntryPoint=S"IsValidLocale",
SetLastError = true, CharSet = CharSet::Auto)]
        [LCIDConversionAttribute(0)] // Position of the LCID argument
    static bool IsValidLocale(int dwFlags); // options

    void CheckCurrentLCID()
    {
            MethodInfo* mthIfo = this->GetType()-
>GetMethod(S"IsValidLocale");

            Attribute* attr = Attribute:
:GetCustomAttribute(mthIfo, __typeof(LCIDConversionAttribute));

            if (attr != 0) {
                LCIDConversionAttribute *lcidAttr =
dynamic_cast<LCIDConversionAttribute*>(attr);
                Console::WriteLine(S"Position of the
LCID argument in the unmanaged signature: {0}",__box(

lcidAttr->Value));
            }

            bool res = IsValidLocale(LCID_INSTALLED);
            Console::WriteLine(S"Result LCID_INSTALLED
{0}",__box( res));
            res = IsValidLocale(LCID_SUPPORTED);
            Console::WriteLine(S"Result LCID_SUPPORTED
{0}",__box( res));
        }
    };

    int main()
    {
            LCIDAttrSample *smpl = new LCIDAttrSample();
            smpl->CheckCurrentLCID();

    };
```

Requirements

Namespace: System.Runtime.InteropServices

Platforms: Windows 98, Windows NT 4.0,
Windows Millennium Edition, Windows 2000,
Windows XP Home Edition, Windows XP Professional,
Windows .NET Server family

Assembly: Mscorlib (in Mscorlib.dll)

LCIDConversionAttribute Constructor

Initializes a new instance of the **LCIDConversionAttribute** class
with the position of the LCID in the unmanaged signature.

```
[Visual Basic]
Public Sub New( _
   ByVal lcid As Integer _
)
[C#]
public LCIDConversionAttribute(
   int lcid
);
[C++]
public: LCIDConversionAttribute(
   int lcid
);
[JScript]
public function LCIDConversionAttribute(
   lcid : int
);
```

Parameters

lcid

Indicates the position of the LCID argument in the unmanaged
signature, where 0 is the first argument.

Requirements

Platforms: Windows 98, Windows NT 4.0,
Windows Millennium Edition, Windows 2000,
Windows XP Home Edition, Windows XP Professional,
Windows .NET Server family

LCIDConversionAttribute.Value Property

Gets the position of the LCID argument in the unmanaged signature.

```
[Visual Basic]
Public ReadOnly Property Value As Integer
[C#]
public int Value {get;}
[C++]
public: __property int get_Value();
[JScript]
public function get Value() : int;
```

Property Value

The position of the LCID argument in the unmanaged signature,
where 0 is the first argument.

Requirements

Platforms: Windows 98, Windows NT 4.0,
Windows Millennium Edition, Windows 2000,
Windows XP Home Edition, Windows XP Professional,
Windows .NET Server family

LIBFLAGS Enumeration

Defines flags that apply to type libraries.

This enumeration has a **FlagsAttribute** attribute that allows a bitwise combination of its member values.

```
[Visual Basic]
<Flags>
<Serializable>
<ComVisible(False)>
Public Enum LIBFLAGS
[C#]
[Flags]
[Serializable]
[ComVisible(false)]
public enum LIBFLAGS
[C++]
[Flags]
[Serializable]
[ComVisible(false)]
__value public enum LIBFLAGS
[JScript]
public
   Flags
   Serializable
   ComVisible(false)
enum LIBFLAGS
```

Remarks

For additional information about the **LIBFLAGS** enumeration, see the MSDN Library.

Members

Member name	Description	Value
LIBFLAG_FCONTROL	The type library describes controls, and should not be displayed in type browsers intended for nonvisual objects.	2
LIBFLAG_FHASDISK-IMAGE	The type library exists in a persisted form on disk.	8
LIBFLAG_FHIDDEN	The type library should not be displayed to users, although its use is not restricted. Should be used by controls. Hosts should create a new type library that wraps the control with extended properties.	4
LIBFLAG_F-RESTRICTED	The type library is restricted, and should not be displayed to users.	1

Requirements

Namespace: System.Runtime.InteropServices

Platforms: Windows 98, Windows NT 4.0, Windows Millennium Edition, Windows 2000, Windows XP Home Edition, Windows XP Professional, Windows .NET Server family

Assembly: Mscorlib (in Mscorlib.dll)

Marshal Class

Provides a collection of methods for allocating unmanaged memory, copying unmanaged memory blocks, and converting managed to unmanaged types, as well as other miscellaneous methods used when interacting with unmanaged code.

System.Object
   System.Runtime.InteropServices.Marshal

```
[Visual Basic]
NotInheritable Public Class Marshal
[C#]
public sealed class Marshal
[C++]
public __gc __sealed class Marshal
[JScript]
public class Marshal
```

Thread Safety

Any public static (**Shared** in Visual Basic) members of this type are safe for multithreaded operations. Any instance members are not guaranteed to be thread safe.

Remarks

The static (**Shared** in Visual Basic) methods defined on the **Marshal** class are essential to working with unmanaged code. Most methods defined here are typically used by advanced developers building custom marshalers who need to provide a bridge between the managed and unmanaged programming models. For example, the **StringToHGlobalAnsi** method copies the ANSI characters from a specified string (in the managed heap) to a buffer in the unmanaged heap. It also allocates the target heap of the right size, as the following C# code shows:

```
String s = "Hello";
    IntPtr p = Marshal.StringToHGlobalAnsi(s);
```

The common language runtime provides specific marshaling capabilities. For details on marshaling behavior, see **Interop Marshaling**.

The **Marshal** class comprises many diverse members. The following table assigns each member to the category that best describes its usage.

Category	Members
Advanced marshaling	**GetManagedThunkForUnmanagedMethodPtr, GetUnmanagedThunkForManagedMethodPtr, NumParamBytes**
COM library function	**BindToMoniker, GetActiveObject**
COM utilities	**ChangeWrapperHandleStrength, CreateWrapperOfType, GetComObjectData, GetComSlotForMethodInfo, GetEndComSlot, GetMethodInfoForComSlot, GetStartComSlot, ReleaseComObject, SetComObjectData**

Category	Members
Data transformation	Managed to unmanaged: **Copy, GetComInterfaceForObject, GetIDispatchForObject, GetIUnknownForObject, StringToBSTR, StringToCoTaskMemAnsi, StringToCoTaskMemAuto, StringToCoTaskMemUni, StringToHGlobalAnsi, StringToHGlobalAuto, StringToHGlobalUni, StructureToPtr, UnsafeAddrOfPinnedArrayElement**
	Unmanaged to managed: **Copy, GetObjectForIUnknown, GetObjectForNativeVariant, GetObjectsForNativeVariants, GetTypedObjectForIUnknown, GetTypeForITypeInfo, PtrToStringAnsi, PtrToStringAuto, PtrToStringBSTR, PtrToStringUni**
	Properties: **SystemDefaultCharSize, SystemMaxDBCSCharSize**
Direct reading and writing	**ReadByte, ReadInt16, ReadInt32, ReadInt64, ReadIntPtr, WriteByte, WriteInt16, WriteInt32, WriteInt64, WriteIntPtr**
Error handling	COM: **GetHRForException, ThrowExceptionForHR**
	Win32: **GetLastWin32Error, GetExceptionCode, GetExceptionPointers**
	Both: **GetHRForLastWin32Error**
Hosting utilities	**GetThreadFromFiberCookie**
IUnknown	**AddRef, QueryInterface, Release**
Memory management	COM: **AllocCoTaskMem, ReAllocCoTaskMem, FreeCoTaskMem, FreeBSTR**
	Win32: **AllocHGlobal, ReAllocHGlobal, FreeHGlobal**
	Both: **DestroyStructure**
Platform invoke utilities	**Prelink, PrelinkAll, GetHINSTANCE**
Structure inspection	**OffsetOf, SizeOf**
Type information	**GenerateGuidForType, GenerateProgIdForType, GetTypeInfoName, GetTypeLibGuid, GetTypeLibGuidForAssembly, GetTypeLibLcid, GetTypeLibName, IsComObject, IsTypeVisibleFromCom**

Requirements

Namespace: System.Runtime.InteropServices

Platforms: Windows 98, Windows NT 4.0, Windows Millennium Edition, Windows 2000, Windows XP Home Edition, Windows XP Professional, Windows .NET Server family, .NET Compact Framework - Windows CE .NET

Assembly: Mscorlib (in Mscorlib.dll)

Marshal.SystemDefaultCharSize Field

Represents the default character size on the system; the default is 2 for Unicode systems and 1 for ANSI systems. This field is read-only.

```
[Visual Basic]
Public Shared ReadOnly SystemDefaultCharSize As Integer
[C#]
public static readonly int SystemDefaultCharSize;
[C++]
public: static int SystemDefaultCharSize;
[JScript]
public static var SystemDefaultCharSize : int;
```

Requirements

Platforms: Windows 98, Windows NT 4.0, Windows Millennium Edition, Windows 2000, Windows XP Home Edition, Windows XP Professional, Windows .NET Server family, .NET Compact Framework - Windows CE .NET

Marshal.SystemMaxDBCSCharSize Field

Represents the maximum size of a double byte character set (DBCS) size, in bytes, for the current operating system. This field is read-only.

```
[Visual Basic]
Public Shared ReadOnly SystemMaxDBCSCharSize As Integer
[C#]
public static readonly int SystemMaxDBCSCharSize;
[C++]
public: static int SystemMaxDBCSCharSize;
[JScript]
public static var SystemMaxDBCSCharSize : int;
```

Requirements

Platforms: Windows 98, Windows NT 4.0, Windows Millennium Edition, Windows 2000, Windows XP Home Edition, Windows XP Professional, Windows .NET Server family

Marshal.AddRef Method

Increments the reference count on the specified interface.

```
[Visual Basic]
Public Shared Function AddRef( _
    ByVal pUnk As IntPtr _
) As Integer
[C#]
public static int AddRef(
    IntPtr pUnk
);
```

```
[C++]
public: static int AddRef(
    IntPtr pUnk
);
[JScript]
public static function AddRef(
    pUnk : IntPtr
) : int;
```

Parameters

pUnk
   The interface reference count to increment.

Return Value

The new value of the reference count on the *pUnk* parameter.

Remarks

The common language runtime manages the reference count of a COM object for you, making it unnecessary to use this method directly. In rare cases, such as testing a custom marshaler, you might find it necessary to manipulate an object's lifetime manually. After calling **AddRef**, you must decrement the reference count by using a method such as **Marshal.Release**. Do not rely on the return value of **AddRef**, as it can sometimes be unstable.

You can call **Marshal.GetComInterfaceForObject**, **Marshal.Get-IUnknownForObject**, or **Marshal.GetIDispatchForObject** to obtain an **IntPtr** value that represents an **IUnknown** interface pointer. You can also use these methods and the **AddRef** method on managed objects to obtain the COM interfaces represented by the managed object's COM callable wrapper. If you are not familiar with the details this wrapper type, see **COM Callable Wrapper**. For additional information about **IUnknown::AddRef**, see the MSDN Library.

> **Note** This method uses **SecurityAction.LinkDemand** to prevent it from being called from untrusted code; only the immediate caller is required to have **SecurityPermission-Attribute.UnmanagedCode** permission. If your code can be called from partially trusted code, do not pass user input to **Marshal** class methods without validation.

Requirements

Platforms: Windows 98, Windows NT 4.0, Windows Millennium Edition, Windows 2000, Windows XP Home Edition, Windows XP Professional, Windows .NET Server family

.NET Framework Security:

*   **SecurityPermission** for operating with unmanaged code. Associated enumeration: **SecurityPermissionFlag.UnmanagedCode**.

Marshal.AllocCoTaskMem Method

Allocates a block of memory of specified size from the COM task memory allocator.

```
[Visual Basic]
Public Shared Function AllocCoTaskMem( _
    ByVal cb As Integer _
) As IntPtr
[C#]
public static IntPtr AllocCoTaskMem(
    int cb
);
```

```
[C++]
public: static IntPtr AllocCoTaskMem(
    int cb
);
[JScript]
public static function AllocCoTaskMem(
    cb : int
) : IntPtr;
```

Parameters

cb

The size of the block of memory to be allocated.

Return Value

An integer representing the address of the block of memory allocated. This memory must be released with **Marshal.FreeCoTaskMem**.

Exceptions

Exception Type	Condition
OutOfMemoryException	There is insufficient memory to satisfy the request.

Remarks

AllocCoTaskMem is one of two memory allocation API methods in the **Marshal** class. (**Marshal.AllocHGlobal** is the other.) The initial memory content returned is undefined, and the allocated memory can be larger than the requested number of bytes. This method exposes the **CoTaskMemAlloc** COM API method, which is referred to as the COM task memory allocator. For additional information about **CoTaskMemAlloc**, see the MSDN Library.

> **Note** This method uses **SecurityAction.LinkDemand** to prevent it from being called from untrusted code; only the immediate caller is required to have **SecurityPermission-Attribute.UnmanagedCode** permission. If your code can be called from partially trusted code, do not pass user input to **Marshal** class methods without validation.

Requirements

Platforms: Windows 98, Windows NT 4.0, Windows Millennium Edition, Windows 2000, Windows XP Home Edition, Windows XP Professional, Windows .NET Server family

.NET Framework Security:

- **SecurityPermission** for operating with unmanaged code. Associated enumeration: **SecurityPermissionFlag.UnmanagedCode**.

Marshal.AllocHGlobal Method

Allocates a block of memory using **GlobalAlloc**.

Overload List

Allocates memory from the unmanaged memory of the process using **GlobalAlloc**.

> [Visual Basic] **Overloads Public Shared Function AllocHGlobal(Integer) As IntPtr**
>
> [C#] **public static IntPtr AllocHGlobal(int);**
>
> [C++] **public: static IntPtr AllocHGlobal(int);**
>
> [JScript] **public static function AllocHGlobal(int) : IntPtr;**

Allocates memory from the process's unmanaged memory.

> [Visual Basic] **Overloads Public Shared Function AllocHGlobal(IntPtr) As IntPtr**
>
> [C#] **public static IntPtr AllocHGlobal(IntPtr);**
>
> [C++] **public: static IntPtr AllocHGlobal(IntPtr);**
>
> [JScript] **public static function AllocHGlobal(IntPtr) : IntPtr;**

Marshal.AllocHGlobal Method (Int32)

Allocates memory from the unmanaged memory of the process using **GlobalAlloc**.

```
[Visual Basic]
Overloads Public Shared Function AllocHGlobal( _
    ByVal cb As Integer _
) As IntPtr
[C#]
public static IntPtr AllocHGlobal(
    int cb
);
[C++]
public: static IntPtr AllocHGlobal(
    int cb
);
[JScript]
public static function AllocHGlobal(
    cb : int
) : IntPtr;
```

Parameters

cb

The number of bytes in memory required.

Return Value

An **IntPtr** to the newly allocated memory. This memory must be released using the **Marshal.FreeHGlobal** method.

Exceptions

Exception Type	Condition
OutOfMemoryException	There is insufficient memory to satisfy the request.

Remarks

AllocHGlobal is one of two memory allocation API methods in the **Marshal** class. (**Marshal.AllocCoTaskMem** is the other.) This method exposes the **GlobalAlloc** Win32 API from Kernel32.dll. For additional information about **GlobalAlloc**, see the MSDN Library.

> **Note** This method uses **SecurityAction.LinkDemand** to prevent it from being called from untrusted code; only the immediate caller is required to have **SecurityPermission-Attribute.UnmanagedCode** permission. If your code can be called from partially trusted code, do not pass user input to **Marshal** class methods without validation.

Requirements

Platforms: Windows 98, Windows NT 4.0, Windows Millennium Edition, Windows 2000, Windows XP Home Edition, Windows XP Professional, Windows .NET Server family

.NET Framework Security:

- **SecurityPermission** for operating with unmanaged code. Associated enumeration: **SecurityPermissionFlag.UnmanagedCode**.

Marshal.AllocHGlobal Method (IntPtr)

Allocates memory from the process's unmanaged memory.

```
[Visual Basic]
Overloads Public Shared Function AllocHGlobal( _
   ByVal cb As IntPtr _
) As IntPtr
[C#]
public static IntPtr AllocHGlobal(
   IntPtr cb
);
[C++]
public: static IntPtr AllocHGlobal(
   IntPtr cb
);
[JScript]
public static function AllocHGlobal(
   cb : IntPtr
) : IntPtr;
```

Parameters

cb

The number of bytes in memory required.

Return Value

An **IntPtr** to the newly allocated memory. This memory must be released using the **Marshal.FreeHGlobal** method.

Exceptions

Exception Type	Condition
OutOfMemoryException	There is insufficient memory to satisfy the request.

Remarks

AllocHGlobal is one of two memory allocation API methods in the **Marshal** class. (**Marshal.AllocCoTaskMem** is the other.) This method exposes the **GlobalAlloc** Win32 API from Kernel32.dll. For additional information about **GlobalAlloc**, see the MSDN Library.

> **Note** This method uses **SecurityAction.LinkDemand** to prevent it from being called from untrusted code; only the immediate caller is required to have **SecurityPermission-Attribute.UnmanagedCode** permission. If your code can be called from partially trusted code, do not pass user input to **Marshal** class methods without validation.

Requirements

Platforms: Windows 98, Windows NT 4.0, Windows Millennium Edition, Windows 2000, Windows XP Home Edition, Windows XP Professional, Windows .NET Server family

.NET Framework Security:

- **SecurityPermission** for operating with unmanaged code. Associated enumeration: **SecurityPermissionFlag.UnmanagedCode**.

Marshal.BindToMoniker Method

Gets an interface pointer identified by the specified moniker.

```
[Visual Basic]
Public Shared Function BindToMoniker( _
   ByVal monikerName As String _
) As Object
```

```
[C#]
public static object BindToMoniker(
   string monikerName
);
[C++]
public: static Object* BindToMoniker(
   String* monikerName
);
[JScript]
public static function BindToMoniker(
   monikerName : String
) : Object;
```

Parameters

monikerName

The moniker corresponding to the desired interface pointer.

Return Value

An object containing a reference to the interface pointer identified by the *monikerName* parameter. A moniker is a name, and in this case, the moniker is defined by an interface.

Exceptions

Exception Type	Condition
COMException	An unrecognized HRESULT was returned by the unmanaged **BindToMoniker** method.

Remarks

Marshal.BindToMoniker exposes the **BindToMoniker** COM API method, which produces an object that you can cast to any COM interface you require. This method provides the same functionality as the **GetObject** method in Visual Basic 6.0 and Visual Basic .NET. For additional information about the **BindToMoniker** COM method, see the MSDN Library.

> **Note** This method uses **SecurityAction.LinkDemand** to prevent it from being called from untrusted code; only the immediate caller is required to have **SecurityPermission-Attribute.UnmanagedCode** permission. If your code can be called from partially trusted code, do not pass user input to **Marshal** class methods without validation.

Example

[Visual Basic, C#] The following example demonstrates how to use the **BindToMoniker** method with the SOAP moniker, provided by Microsoft Windows XP, to seamlessly access an XML Web service from managed code through COM interop:

```
[Visual Basic]
Dim translator As Object = Marshal.BindToMoniker( _
   "SOAP:wsdl=http://www.xmethods.net/sd/2001/BabelFishService.wsdl")
```

```
[C#]
object translator = Marshal.BindToMoniker(
   "SOAP:wsdl=http://www.xmethods.net/sd/2001/BabelFishService.wsdl");
```

Requirements

Platforms: Windows 98, Windows NT 4.0, Windows Millennium Edition, Windows 2000, Windows XP Home Edition, Windows XP Professional, Windows .NET Server family

.NET Framework Security:

- **SecurityPermission** for operating with unmanaged code. Associated enumeration: **SecurityPermissionFlag.UnmanagedCode**.

Marshal.ChangeWrapperHandleStrength Method

Changes the strength of a COM callable wrapper's (CCW) handle on the object it contains.

```
[Visual Basic]
Public Shared Sub ChangeWrapperHandleStrength( _
   ByVal otp As Object, _
   ByVal fIsWeak As Boolean _
)
[C#]
public static void ChangeWrapperHandleStrength(
   object otp,
   bool fIsWeak
);
[C++]
public: static void ChangeWrapperHandleStrength(
   Object* otp,
   bool fIsWeak
);
[JScript]
public static function ChangeWrapperHandleStrength(
   otp : Object,
   fIsWeak : Boolean
);
```

Parameters

otp
   The object whose COM callable wrapper (CCW) holds a reference counted handle. The handle is strong if the reference count on the CCW is greater than zero; otherwise it is weak.

fIsWeak
   true to change the strength of the handle on the *otp* parameter to weak, regardless of its reference count; **false** to reset the handle strength on *otp* to be reference counted.

Remarks

ChangeWrapperHandleStrength is used for object pooling functionality and should never be called by user code directly.

> **Note** This method uses **SecurityAction.LinkDemand** to prevent it from being called from untrusted code; only the immediate caller is required to have **SecurityPermission-Attribute.UnmanagedCode** permission. If your code can be called from partially trusted code, do not pass user input to **Marshal** class methods without validation.

Requirements

Platforms: Windows 98, Windows NT 4.0, Windows Millennium Edition, Windows 2000, Windows XP Home Edition, Windows XP Professional, Windows .NET Server family

.NET Framework Security:

- **SecurityPermission** for operating with unmanaged code. Associated enumeration: **SecurityPermissionFlag.UnmanagedCode**.

Marshal.Copy Method

Copies data from a managed array to an unmanaged memory pointer.

Overload List

Copies data from a one-dimensional, managed 8-bit unsigned integer array to an unmanaged memory pointer.

Supported by the .NET Compact Framework.

   [Visual Basic] **Overloads Public Shared Sub Copy(Byte(), Integer, IntPtr, Integer)**

   [C#] **public static void Copy(byte[], int, IntPtr, int);**

   [C++] **public: static void Copy(unsigned char __gc[], int, IntPtr, int);**

   [JScript] **public static function Copy(Byte[], int, IntPtr, int);**

Copies data from a one-dimensional, managed character array to an unmanaged memory pointer.

Supported by the .NET Compact Framework.

   [Visual Basic] **Overloads Public Shared Sub Copy(Char(), Integer, IntPtr, Integer)**

   [C#] **public static void Copy(char[], int, IntPtr, int);**

   [C++] **public: static void Copy(__wchar_t __gc[], int, IntPtr, int);**

   [JScript] **public static function Copy(Char[], int, IntPtr, int);**

Copies data from a one-dimensional, managed double-precision floating-point number array to an unmanaged memory pointer.

Supported by the .NET Compact Framework.

   [Visual Basic] **Overloads Public Shared Sub Copy(Double(), Integer, IntPtr, Integer)**

   [C#] **public static void Copy(double[], int, IntPtr, int);**

   [C++] **public: static void Copy(double __gc[], int, IntPtr, int);**

   [JScript] **public static function Copy(double[], int, IntPtr, int);**

Copies data from a one-dimensional, managed 16-bit signed integer array to an unmanaged memory pointer.

Supported by the .NET Compact Framework.

   [Visual Basic] **Overloads Public Shared Sub Copy(Short(), Integer, IntPtr, Integer)**

   [C#] **public static void Copy(short[], int, IntPtr, int);**

   [C++] **public: static void Copy(short __gc[], int, IntPtr, int);**

   [JScript] **public static function Copy(Int16[], int, IntPtr, int);**

Copies data from a one-dimensional, managed 32-bit signed integer array to an unmanaged memory pointer.

Supported by the .NET Compact Framework.

   [Visual Basic] **Overloads Public Shared Sub Copy(Integer(), Integer, IntPtr, Integer)**

   [C#] **public static void Copy(int[], int, IntPtr, int);**

   [C++] **public: static void Copy(int __gc[], int, IntPtr, int);**

   [JScript] **public static function Copy(int[], int, IntPtr, int);**

Copies data from a one-dimensional, managed 64-bit signed integer array to an unmanaged memory pointer.

Supported by the .NET Compact Framework.

   [Visual Basic] **Overloads Public Shared Sub Copy(Long(), Integer, IntPtr, Integer)**

   [C#] **public static void Copy(long[], int, IntPtr, int);**

   [C++] **public: static void Copy(__int64 __gc[], int, IntPtr, int);**

   [JScript] **public static function Copy(long[], int, IntPtr, int);**

Copies data from an unmanaged memory pointer to a managed 8-bit unsigned integer array.

Supported by the .NET Compact Framework.

[Visual Basic] **Overloads Public Shared Sub Copy(IntPtr, Byte(), Integer, Integer)**

[C#] **public static void Copy(IntPtr, byte[], int, int);**

[C++] **public: static void Copy(IntPtr, unsigned char __gc[], int, int);**

[JScript] **public static function Copy(IntPtr, Byte[], int, int);**

Copies data from an unmanaged memory pointer to a managed character array.

Supported by the .NET Compact Framework.

[Visual Basic] **Overloads Public Shared Sub Copy(IntPtr, Char(), Integer, Integer)**

[C#] **public static void Copy(IntPtr, char[], int, int);**

[C++] **public: static void Copy(IntPtr, __wchar_t __gc[], int, int);**

[JScript] **public static function Copy(IntPtr, Char[], int, int);**

Copies data from an unmanaged memory pointer to a managed double-precision floating-point number array.

Supported by the .NET Compact Framework.

[Visual Basic] **Overloads Public Shared Sub Copy(IntPtr, Double(), Integer, Integer)**

[C#] **public static void Copy(IntPtr, double[], int, int);**

[C++] **public: static void Copy(IntPtr, double __gc[], int, int);**

[JScript] **public static function Copy(IntPtr, double[], int, int);**

Copies data from an unmanaged memory pointer to a managed 16-bit signed integer array.

Supported by the .NET Compact Framework.

[Visual Basic] **Overloads Public Shared Sub Copy(IntPtr, Short(), Integer, Integer)**

[C#] **public static void Copy(IntPtr, short[], int, int);**

[C++] **public: static void Copy(IntPtr, short __gc[], int, int);**

[JScript] **public static function Copy(IntPtr, Int16[], int, int);**

Copies data from an unmanaged memory pointer to a managed 32-bit signed integer array.

Supported by the .NET Compact Framework.

[Visual Basic] **Overloads Public Shared Sub Copy(IntPtr, Integer(), Integer, Integer)**

[C#] **public static void Copy(IntPtr, int[], int, int);**

[C++] **public: static void Copy(IntPtr, int __gc[], int, int);**

[JScript] **public static function Copy(IntPtr, int[], int, int);**

Copies data from an unmanaged memory pointer to a managed 64-bit signed integer array.

Supported by the .NET Compact Framework.

[Visual Basic] **Overloads Public Shared Sub Copy(IntPtr, Long(), Integer, Integer)**

[C#] **public static void Copy(IntPtr, long[], int, int);**

[C++] **public: static void Copy(IntPtr, __int64 __gc[], int, int);**

[JScript] **public static function Copy(IntPtr, long[], int, int);**

Copies data from an unmanaged memory pointer to a managed single-precision floating-point number array.

Supported by the .NET Compact Framework.

[Visual Basic] **Overloads Public Shared Sub Copy(IntPtr, Single(), Integer, Integer)**

[C#] **public static void Copy(IntPtr, float[], int, int);**

[C++] **public: static void Copy(IntPtr, float __gc[], int, int);**

[JScript] **public static function Copy(IntPtr, float[], int, int);**

Copies data from a one-dimensional, managed single-precision floating-point number array to an unmanaged memory pointer.

Supported by the .NET Compact Framework.

[Visual Basic] **Overloads Public Shared Sub Copy(Single(), Integer, IntPtr, Integer)**

[C#] **public static void Copy(float[], int, IntPtr, int);**

[C++] **public: static void Copy(float __gc[], int, IntPtr, int);**

[JScript] **public static function Copy(float[], int, IntPtr, int);**

Example

[Visual Basic, C#] The following example demonstrates how to copy a one-dimensional array to an unmanaged memory pointer.

[Visual Basic, C#] **Note** This example shows how to use one of the overloaded versions of **Copy**. For other examples that might be available, see the individual overload topics.

[Visual Basic]
```
Public Overloads Shared Sub Copy(source As Single(), _
   startIndex As Integer, destination As IntPtr, length As Integer)
```

[C#]
```
public static void Copy(float[] source, int startIndex,
   IntPtr destination, int length);
```

Marshal.Copy Method (Byte[], Int32, IntPtr, Int32)

Copies data from a one-dimensional, managed 8-bit unsigned integer array to an unmanaged memory pointer.

[Visual Basic]
```
Overloads Public Shared Sub Copy( _
   ByVal source() As Byte, _
   ByVal startIndex As Integer, _
   ByVal destination As IntPtr, _
   ByVal length As Integer _
)
```
[C#]
```
public static void Copy(
   byte[] source,
   int startIndex,
   IntPtr destination,
   int length
);
```
[C++]
```
public: static void Copy(
   unsigned char source __gc[],
   int startIndex,
   IntPtr destination,
   int length
);
```
[JScript]
```
public static function Copy(
   source : Byte[],
   startIndex : int,
   destination : IntPtr,
   length : int
);
```

Parameters

source
    The one-dimensional array to copy from.

startIndex
    The zero-based index into the array where **Copy** should start.

destination
    The memory pointer to copy to.

length
    The number of array elements to copy.

Exceptions

Exception Type	Condition
ArgumentOutOfRange-Exception	*startIndex* and *length* are not valid.

Remarks

You can use this method to copy a subset of a one-dimensional, .NET-based array to an unmanaged C-style array.

> **Note** This method uses **SecurityAction.LinkDemand** to prevent it from being called from untrusted code; only the immediate caller is required to have **SecurityPermission-Attribute.UnmanagedCode** permission. If your code can be called from partially trusted code, do not pass user input to **Marshal** class methods without validation.

Example

[Visual Basic, C#] The following example demonstrates how to copy a one-dimensional array to an unmanaged memory pointer.

[Visual Basic]
```
Public Overloads Shared Sub Copy(source As Byte(), _
   startIndex As Integer, destination As IntPtr, length As Integer)
```

[C#]
```
public static void Copy(byte[] source, int startIndex,
   IntPtr destination, int length);
```

Requirements

Platforms: Windows 98, Windows NT 4.0, Windows Millennium Edition, Windows 2000, Windows XP Home Edition, Windows XP Professional, Windows .NET Server family, .NET Compact Framework - Windows CE .NET

.NET Framework Security:

- **SecurityPermission** for operating with unmanaged code. Associated enumeration: **SecurityPermissionFlag.UnmanagedCode**.

Marshal.Copy Method (Char[], Int32, IntPtr, Int32)

Copies data from a one-dimensional, managed character array to an unmanaged memory pointer.

[Visual Basic]
```
Overloads Public Shared Sub Copy( _
   ByVal source() As Char, _
   ByVal startIndex As Integer, _
   ByVal destination As IntPtr, _
   ByVal length As Integer _
)
```
[C#]
```
public static void Copy(
   char[] source,
```

```
   int startIndex,
   IntPtr destination,
   int length
);
```
[C++]
```
public: static void Copy(
   __wchar_t source __gc[],
   int startIndex,
   IntPtr destination,
   int length
);
```
[JScript]
```
public static function Copy(
   source : Char[],
   startIndex : int,
   destination : IntPtr,
   length : int
);
```

Parameters

source
    The one-dimensional array to copy from.

startIndex
    The zero-based index into the array where **Copy** should start.

destination
    The memory pointer to copy to.

length
    The number of array elements to copy.

Exceptions

Exception Type	Condition
ArgumentOutOfRange-Exception	*startIndex* and *length* are not valid.

Remarks

You can use this method to copy a subset of a one-dimensional, .NET-based array to an unmanaged C-style array.

> **Note** This method uses **SecurityAction.LinkDemand** to prevent it from being called from untrusted code; only the immediate caller is required to have **SecurityPermission-Attribute.UnmanagedCode** permission. If your code can be called from partially trusted code, do not pass user input to **Marshal** class methods without validation.

Example

[Visual Basic, C#] The following example demonstrates how to copy a one-dimensional array to an unmanaged memory pointer.

[Visual Basic]
```
Public Overloads Shared Sub Copy(source As Char(), _
   startIndex As Integer, destination As IntPtr, length As Integer)
```

[C#]
```
public static void Copy(char[] source, int startIndex,
   IntPtr destination, int length);
```

Requirements

Platforms: Windows 98, Windows NT 4.0, Windows Millennium Edition, Windows 2000, Windows XP Home Edition, Windows XP Professional, Windows .NET Server family, .NET Compact Framework - Windows CE .NET

.NET Framework Security:
- **SecurityPermission** for operating with unmanaged code. Associated enumeration: **SecurityPermissionFlag.UnmanagedCode**.

Marshal.Copy Method (Double[], Int32, IntPtr, Int32)

Copies data from a one-dimensional, managed double-precision floating-point number array to an unmanaged memory pointer.

[Visual Basic]
```
Overloads Public Shared Sub Copy( _
   ByVal source() As Double, _
   ByVal startIndex As Integer, _
   ByVal destination As IntPtr, _
   ByVal length As Integer _
)
```
[C#]
```
public static void Copy(
   double[] source,
   int startIndex,
   IntPtr destination,
   int length
);
```
[C++]
```
public: static void Copy(
   double source __gc[],
   int startIndex,
   IntPtr destination,
   int length
);
```
[JScript]
```
public static function Copy(
   source : double[],
   startIndex : int,
   destination : IntPtr,
   length : int
);
```

Parameters
source
   The one-dimensional array to copy from.
startIndex
   The zero-based index into the array where **Copy** should start.
destination
   The memory pointer to copy to.
length
   The number of array elements to copy.

Exceptions

Exception Type	Condition
ArgumentOutOfRange-Exception	*startIndex* and *length* are not valid.

Remarks
You can use this method to copy a subset of a one-dimensional, .NET-based array to an unmanaged C-style array.

> **Note** This method uses **SecurityAction.LinkDemand** to prevent it from being called from untrusted code; only the immediate caller is required to have **SecurityPermission-Attribute.UnmanagedCode** permission. If your code can be called from partially trusted code, do not pass user input to **Marshal** class methods without validation.

Example
[Visual Basic, C#] The following example demonstrates how to copy a one-dimensional array to an unmanaged memory pointer.

[Visual Basic]
```
Public Overloads Shared Sub Copy(source As Double(), _
   startIndex As Integer, destination As IntPtr, length As Integer)
```

[C#]
```
public static void Copy(double[] source, int startIndex,
   IntPtr destination, int length);
```

Requirements
Platforms: Windows 98, Windows NT 4.0, Windows Millennium Edition, Windows 2000, Windows XP Home Edition, Windows XP Professional, Windows .NET Server family, .NET Compact Framework - Windows CE .NET

.NET Framework Security:
- **SecurityPermission** for operating with unmanaged code. Associated enumeration: **SecurityPermissionFlag.UnmanagedCode**.

Marshal.Copy Method (Int16[], Int32, IntPtr, Int32)

Copies data from a one-dimensional, managed 16-bit signed integer array to an unmanaged memory pointer.

[Visual Basic]
```
Overloads Public Shared Sub Copy( _
   ByVal source() As Short, _
   ByVal startIndex As Integer, _
   ByVal destination As IntPtr, _
   ByVal length As Integer _
)
```
[C#]
```
public static void Copy(
   short[] source,
   int startIndex,
   IntPtr destination,
   int length
);
```
[C++]
```
public: static void Copy(
   short source __gc[],
   int startIndex,
   IntPtr destination,
   int length
);
```
[JScript]
```
public static function Copy(
   source : Int16[],
   startIndex : int,
   destination : IntPtr,
   length : int
);
```

Parameters
source
   The one-dimensional array to copy from.
startIndex
   The zero-based index into the array where **Copy** should start.

destination
>   The memory pointer to copy to.

length
>   The number of array elements to copy.

Exceptions

Exception Type	Condition
ArgumentOutOfRange-Exception	*startIndex* and *length* are not valid.

Remarks

You can use this method to copy a subset of a one-dimensional, .NET-based array to an unmanaged C-style array.

> **Note** This method uses **SecurityAction.LinkDemand** to prevent it from being called from untrusted code; only the immediate caller is required to have **SecurityPermission-Attribute.UnmanagedCode** permission. If your code can be called from partially trusted code, do not pass user input to **Marshal** class methods without validation.

Example

[Visual Basic, C#] The following example demonstrates how to copy a one-dimensional array to an unmanaged memory pointer.

[Visual Basic]
```
Public Overloads Shared Sub Copy(source As Short(), _
    startIndex As Integer, destination As IntPtr, length As Integer)
```

[C#]
```
public static void Copy(short[] source, int startIndex,
    IntPtr destination, int length);
```

Requirements

Platforms: Windows 98, Windows NT 4.0, Windows Millennium Edition, Windows 2000, Windows XP Home Edition, Windows XP Professional, Windows .NET Server family, .NET Compact Framework - Windows CE .NET

.NET Framework Security:
- **SecurityPermission** for operating with unmanaged code. Associated enumeration: **SecurityPermissionFlag.UnmanagedCode**.

Marshal.Copy Method (Int32[], Int32, IntPtr, Int32)

Copies data from a one-dimensional, managed 32-bit signed integer array to an unmanaged memory pointer.

[Visual Basic]
```
Overloads Public Shared Sub Copy( _
    ByVal source() As Integer, _
    ByVal startIndex As Integer, _
    ByVal destination As IntPtr, _
    ByVal length As Integer _
)
```
[C#]
```
public static void Copy(
    int[] source,
    int startIndex,
    IntPtr destination,
    int length
);
```

[C++]
```
public: static void Copy(
    int source __gc[],
    int startIndex,
    IntPtr destination,
    int length
);
```
[JScript]
```
public static function Copy(
    source : int[],
    startIndex : int,
    destination : IntPtr,
    length : int
);
```

Parameters

source
>   The one-dimensional array to copy from.

startIndex
>   The zero-based index into the array where **Copy** should start.

destination
>   The memory pointer to copy to.

length
>   The number of array elements to copy.

Exceptions

Exception Type	Condition
ArgumentOutOfRange-Exception	*startIndex* and *length* are not valid.

Remarks

You can use this method to copy a subset of a one-dimensional, .NET-based array to an unmanaged C-style array.

> **Note** This method uses **SecurityAction.LinkDemand** to prevent it from being called from untrusted code; only the immediate caller is required to have **SecurityPermission-Attribute.UnmanagedCode** permission. If your code can be called from partially trusted code, do not pass user input to **Marshal** class methods without validation.

Example

[Visual Basic, C#] The following example demonstrates how to copy a one-dimensional array to an unmanaged memory pointer.

[Visual Basic]
```
Public Overloads Shared Sub Copy(source As IntPrt(), _
    startIndex As Integer, destination As IntPtr, length As Integer)
```

[C#]
```
public static void Copy(IntPtr[] source, int startIndex,
    IntPtr destination, int length);
```

Requirements

Platforms: Windows 98, Windows NT 4.0, Windows Millennium Edition, Windows 2000, Windows XP Home Edition, Windows XP Professional, Windows .NET Server family, .NET Compact Framework - Windows CE .NET

.NET Framework Security:
- **SecurityPermission** for operating with unmanaged code. Associated enumeration: **SecurityPermissionFlag.UnmanagedCode**.

Marshal.Copy Method (Int64[], Int32, IntPtr, Int32)

Copies data from a one-dimensional, managed 64-bit signed integer array to an unmanaged memory pointer.

```
[Visual Basic]
Overloads Public Shared Sub Copy( _
   ByVal source() As Long, _
   ByVal startIndex As Integer, _
   ByVal destination As IntPtr, _
   ByVal length As Integer _
)
[C#]
public static void Copy(
   long[] source,
   int startIndex,
   IntPtr destination,
   int length
);
[C++]
public: static void Copy(
   __int64 source __gc[],
   int startIndex,
   IntPtr destination,
   int length
);
[JScript]
public static function Copy(
   source : long[],
   startIndex : int,
   destination : IntPtr,
   length : int
);
```

Parameters

source
   The one-dimensional array to copy from.
startIndex
   The zero-based index into the array where **Copy** should start.
destination
   The memory pointer to copy to.
length
   The number of array elements to copy.

Exceptions

Exception Type	Condition
ArgumentOutOfRange-Exception	*startIndex* and *length* are not valid.

Remarks

You can use this method to copy a subset of a one-dimensional, .NET-based array to an unmanaged C-style array.

> **Note** This method uses **SecurityAction.LinkDemand** to prevent it from being called from untrusted code; only the immediate caller is required to have **SecurityPermission-Attribute.UnmanagedCode** permission. If your code can be called from partially trusted code, do not pass user input to **Marshal** class methods without validation.

Example

[Visual Basic, C#] The following example demonstrates how to copy a one-dimensional array to an unmanaged memory pointer.

```
[Visual Basic]
Public Overloads Shared Sub Copy(source As Long(), _
   startIndex As Integer, destination As IntPtr, length As Integer)

[C#]
public static void Copy(long[] source, int startIndex,
   IntPtr destination, int length);
```

Requirements

Platforms: Windows 98, Windows NT 4.0, Windows Millennium Edition, Windows 2000, Windows XP Home Edition, Windows XP Professional, Windows .NET Server family, .NET Compact Framework - Windows CE .NET

.NET Framework Security:

- **SecurityPermission** for operating with unmanaged code. Associated enumeration: **SecurityPermissionFlag.UnmanagedCode**.

Marshal.Copy Method (IntPtr, Byte[], Int32, Int32)

Copies data from an unmanaged memory pointer to a managed 8-bit unsigned integer array.

```
[Visual Basic]
Overloads Public Shared Sub Copy( _
   ByVal source As IntPtr, _
   ByVal destination() As Byte, _
   ByVal startIndex As Integer, _
   ByVal length As Integer _
)
[C#]
public static void Copy(
   IntPtr source,
   byte[] destination,
   int startIndex,
   int length
);
[C++]
public: static void Copy(
   IntPtr source,
   unsigned char destination __gc[],
   int startIndex,
   int length
);
[JScript]
public static function Copy(
   source : IntPtr,
   destination : Byte[],
   startIndex : int,
   length : int
);
```

Parameters

source
   The memory pointer to copy from.
destination
   The array to copy to.
startIndex
   The zero-based index into the array where **Copy** should start.
length
   The number of array elements to copy.

Remarks

Unmanaged, C-style arrays do not contain bounds information, which prevents the *startIndex* and *length* parameters from being validated. Thus, the unmanaged data corresponding to the *source* parameter populates the managed array regardless of its usefulness. You must initalize the managed array with the appropriate size before calling the **Marshal.Copy** method.

> **Note** This method uses **SecurityAction.LinkDemand** to prevent it from being called from untrusted code; only the immediate caller is required to have **SecurityPermission-Attribute.UnmanagedCode** permission. If your code can be called from partially trusted code, do not pass user input to **Marshal** class methods without validation.

Example

[Visual Basic, C#] The following example demonstrates how to copy data from an unmanaged memory pointer into a managed array.

[Visual Basic]
```
Public Overloads Shared Sub Copy(source As IntPtr, _
    destination As Byte(), startIndex As Integer, length As Integer)
```

[C#]
```
public static void Copy(IntPtr source, byte[] destination,
    int startIndex, int length);
```

Requirements

Platforms: Windows 98, Windows NT 4.0, Windows Millennium Edition, Windows 2000, Windows XP Home Edition, Windows XP Professional, Windows .NET Server family, .NET Compact Framework - Windows CE .NET

.NET Framework Security:
- **SecurityPermission** for operating with unmanaged code. Associated enumeration: **SecurityPermissionFlag.UnmanagedCode**.

Marshal.Copy Method (IntPtr, Char[], Int32, Int32)

Copies data from an unmanaged memory pointer to a managed character array.

[Visual Basic]
```
Overloads Public Shared Sub Copy( _
    ByVal source As IntPtr, _
    ByVal destination() As Char, _
    ByVal startIndex As Integer, _
    ByVal length As Integer _
)
```
[C#]
```
public static void Copy(
    IntPtr source,
    char[] destination,
    int startIndex,
    int length
);
```
[C++]
```
public: static void Copy(
    IntPtr source,
    __wchar_t destination __gc[],
    int startIndex,
    int length
);
```

[JScript]
```
public static function Copy(
    source : IntPtr,
    destination : Char[],
    startIndex : int,
    length : int
);
```

Parameters

source
> The memory pointer to copy from.

destination
> The array to copy to.

startIndex
> The zero-based index into the array where **Copy** should start.

length
> The number of array elements to copy.

Remarks

Unmanaged, C-style arrays do not contain bounds information, which prevents the *startIndex* and *length* parameters from being validated. Thus, the unmanaged data corresponding to the *source* parameter populates the managed array regardless of its usefulness. You must initalize the managed array with the appropriate size before calling the **Marshal.Copy** method.

> **Note** This method uses **SecurityAction.LinkDemand** to prevent it from being called from untrusted code; only the immediate caller is required to have **SecurityPermission-Attribute.UnmanagedCode** permission. If your code can be called from partially trusted code, do not pass user input to **Marshal** class methods without validation.

Example

[Visual Basic, C#] The following example demonstrates how to copy data from an unmanaged memory pointer into a managed array.

[Visual Basic]
```
Public Overloads Shared Sub Copy(source As IntPtr, _
    destination As Char(), startIndex As Integer, length As Integer)
```

[C#]
```
public static void Copy(IntPtr source, char[] destination,
    int startIndex, int length);
```

Requirements

Platforms: Windows 98, Windows NT 4.0, Windows Millennium Edition, Windows 2000, Windows XP Home Edition, Windows XP Professional, Windows .NET Server family, .NET Compact Framework - Windows CE .NET

.NET Framework Security:

- **SecurityPermission** for operating with unmanaged code. Associated enumeration: **SecurityPermissionFlag.UnmanagedCode**.

Marshal.Copy Method (IntPtr, Double[], Int32, Int32)

Copies data from an unmanaged memory pointer to a managed double-precision floating-point number array.

```
[Visual Basic]
Overloads Public Shared Sub Copy( _
   ByVal source As IntPtr, _
   ByVal destination() As Double, _
   ByVal startIndex As Integer, _
   ByVal length As Integer _
)
[C#]
public static void Copy(
   IntPtr source,
   double[] destination,
   int startIndex,
   int length
);
[C++]
public: static void Copy(
   IntPtr source,
   double destination __gc[],
   int startIndex,
   int length
);
[JScript]
public static function Copy(
   source : IntPtr,
   destination : double[],
   startIndex : int,
   length : int
);
```

Parameters

source
   The memory pointer to copy from.
destination
   The array to copy to.
startIndex
   The zero-based index into the array where **Copy** should start.
length
   The number of array elements to copy.

Remarks

Unmanaged, C-style arrays do not contain bounds information, which prevents the *startIndex* and *length* parameters from being validated. Thus, the unmanaged data corresponding to the *source* parameter populates the managed array regardless of its usefulness. You must initalize the managed array with the appropriate size before calling the **Marshal.Copy** method.

> **Note** This method uses **SecurityAction.LinkDemand** to prevent it from being called from untrusted code; only the immediate caller is required to have **SecurityPermission-Attribute.UnmanagedCode** permission. If your code can be called from partially trusted code, do not pass user input to **Marshal** class methods without validation.

Example

[Visual Basic, C#] The following example demonstrates how to copy data from an unmanaged memory pointer into a managed array.

```
[Visual Basic]
Public Overloads Shared Sub Copy(source As IntPtr, _
   destination As Double(), startIndex As Integer, length As Integer)
[C#]
public static void Copy(IntPtr source, double[] destination,
   int startIndex, int length);
```

Requirements

Platforms: Windows 98, Windows NT 4.0, Windows Millennium Edition, Windows 2000, Windows XP Home Edition, Windows XP Professional, Windows .NET Server family, .NET Compact Framework - Windows CE .NET

.NET Framework Security:

- **SecurityPermission** for operating with unmanaged code. Associated enumeration: **SecurityPermissionFlag.UnmanagedCode**.

Marshal.Copy Method (IntPtr, Int16[], Int32, Int32)

Copies data from an unmanaged memory pointer to a managed 16-bit signed integer array.

```
[Visual Basic]
Overloads Public Shared Sub Copy( _
   ByVal source As IntPtr, _
   ByVal destination() As Short, _
   ByVal startIndex As Integer, _
   ByVal length As Integer _
)
[C#]
public static void Copy(
   IntPtr source,
   short[] destination,
   int startIndex,
   int length
);
[C++]
public: static void Copy(
   IntPtr source,
   short destination __gc[],
   int startIndex,
   int length
);
[JScript]
public static function Copy(
   source : IntPtr,
   destination : Int16[],
   startIndex : int,
   length : int
);
```

Parameters

source
   The memory pointer to copy from.
destination
   The array to copy to.

startIndex

    The zero-based index into the array where **Copy** should start.

length

    The number of array elements to copy.

Remarks

Unmanaged, C-style arrays do not contain bounds information, which prevents the *startIndex* and *length* parameters from being validated. Thus, the unmanaged data corresponding to the *source* parameter populates the managed array regardless of its usefulness. You must initalize the managed array with the appropriate size before calling the **Marshal.Copy** method.

> **Note** This method uses **SecurityAction.LinkDemand** to prevent it from being called from untrusted code; only the immediate caller is required to have **SecurityPermission-Attribute.UnmanagedCode** permission. If your code can be called from partially trusted code, do not pass user input to **Marshal** class methods without validation.

Example

[Visual Basic, C#] The following example demonstrates how to copy data from an unmanaged memory pointer into a managed array.

[Visual Basic]
```
Public Overloads Shared Sub Copy(source As IntPtr, _
   destination As Short(), startIndex As Integer, length As Integer)
```

[C#]
```
public static void Copy(IntPtr source, short[] destination,
   int startIndex, int length);
```

Requirements

Platforms: Windows 98, Windows NT 4.0, Windows Millennium Edition, Windows 2000, Windows XP Home Edition, Windows XP Professional, Windows .NET Server family, .NET Compact Framework - Windows CE .NET

.NET Framework Security:

- **SecurityPermission** for operating with unmanaged code. Associated enumeration: **SecurityPermissionFlag.UnmanagedCode**.

Marshal.Copy Method (IntPtr, Int32[], Int32, Int32)

Copies data from an unmanaged memory pointer to a managed 32-bit signed integer array.

[Visual Basic]
```
Overloads Public Shared Sub Copy( _
   ByVal source As IntPtr, _
   ByVal destination() As Integer, _
   ByVal startIndex As Integer, _
   ByVal length As Integer _
)
```
[C#]
```
public static void Copy(
   IntPtr source,
   int[] destination,
   int startIndex,
   int length
);
```

[C++]
```
public: static void Copy(
   IntPtr source,
   int destination __gc[],
   int startIndex,
   int length
);
```
[JScript]
```
public static function Copy(
   source : IntPtr,
   destination : int[],
   startIndex : int,
   length : int
);
```

Parameters

source

    The memory pointer to copy from.

destination

    The array to copy to.

startIndex

    The zero-based index into the array where **Copy** should start.

length

    The number of array elements to copy.

Remarks

Unmanaged, C-style arrays do not contain bounds information, which prevents the *startIndex* and *length* parameters from being validated. Thus, the unmanaged data corresponding to the *source* parameter populates the managed array regardless of its usefulness. You must initalize the managed array with the appropriate size before calling the **Marshal.Copy** method.

> **Note** This method uses **SecurityAction.LinkDemand** to prevent it from being called from untrusted code; only the immediate caller is required to have **SecurityPermission-Attribute.UnmanagedCode** permission. If your code can be called from partially trusted code, do not pass user input to **Marshal** class methods without validation.

Example

[Visual Basic, C#] The following example demonstrates how to copy data from an unmanaged memory pointer into a managed array.

[Visual Basic]
```
Public Overloads Shared Sub Copy(source As IntPtr, _
   destination As Integer(), startIndex As Integer, length As Integer)
```

[C#]
```
public static void Copy(IntPtr source, int[] destination,
   int startIndex, int length);
```

Requirements

Platforms: Windows 98, Windows NT 4.0, Windows Millennium Edition, Windows 2000, Windows XP Home Edition, Windows XP Professional, Windows .NET Server family, .NET Compact Framework - Windows CE .NET

.NET Framework Security:

- **SecurityPermission** for operating with unmanaged code. Associated enumeration: **SecurityPermissionFlag.UnmanagedCode**.

Marshal.Copy Method (IntPtr, Int64[], Int32, Int32)

Copies data from an unmanaged memory pointer to a managed 64-bit signed integer array.

```
[Visual Basic]
Overloads Public Shared Sub Copy( _
   ByVal source As IntPtr, _
   ByVal destination() As Long, _
   ByVal startIndex As Integer, _
   ByVal length As Integer _
)
[C#]
public static void Copy(
   IntPtr source,
   long[] destination,
   int startIndex,
   int length
);
[C++]
public: static void Copy(
   IntPtr source,
   __int64 destination __gc[],
   int startIndex,
   int length
);
[JScript]
public static function Copy(
   source : IntPtr,
   destination : long[],
   startIndex : int,
   length : int
);
```

Parameters

source
   The memory pointer to copy from.
destination
   The array to copy to.
startIndex
   The zero-based index into the array where **Copy** should start.
length
   The number of array elements to copy.

Remarks

Unmanaged, C-style arrays do not contain bounds information, which prevents the *startIndex* and *length* parameters from being validated. Thus, the unmanaged data corresponding to the *source* parameter populates the managed array regardless of its usefulness. You must initalize the managed array with the appropriate size before calling the **Marshal.Copy** method.

> **Note** This method uses **SecurityAction.LinkDemand** to prevent it from being called from untrusted code; only the immediate caller is required to have **SecurityPermission-Attribute.UnmanagedCode** permission. If your code can be called from partially trusted code, do not pass user input to **Marshal** class methods without validation.

Example

[Visual Basic, C#] The following example demonstrates how to copy data from an unmanaged memory pointer into a managed array.

```
[Visual Basic]
Public Overloads Shared Sub Copy(source As IntPtr, _
   destination As Long(), startIndex As Integer, length As Integer)
[C#]
public static void Copy(IntPtr source, long[] destination,
   int startIndex, int length);
```

Requirements

Platforms: Windows 98, Windows NT 4.0, Windows Millennium Edition, Windows 2000, Windows XP Home Edition, Windows XP Professional, Windows .NET Server family, .NET Compact Framework - Windows CE .NET

.NET Framework Security:

• **SecurityPermission** for operating with unmanaged code. Associated enumeration: **SecurityPermissionFlag.UnmanagedCode**.

Marshal.Copy Method (IntPtr, Single[], Int32, Int32)

Copies data from an unmanaged memory pointer to a managed single-precision floating-point number array.

```
[Visual Basic]
Overloads Public Shared Sub Copy( _
   ByVal source As IntPtr, _
   ByVal destination() As Single, _
   ByVal startIndex As Integer, _
   ByVal length As Integer _
)
[C#]
public static void Copy(
   IntPtr source,
   float[] destination,
   int startIndex,
   int length
);
[C++]
public: static void Copy(
   IntPtr source,
   float destination __gc[],
   int startIndex,
   int length
);
[JScript]
public static function Copy(
   source : IntPtr,
   destination : float[],
   startIndex : int,
   length : int
);
```

Parameters

source
   The memory pointer to copy from.
destination
   The array to copy to.
startIndex
   The zero-based index into the array where **Copy** should start.
length
   The number of array elements to copy.

Remarks

Unmanaged, C-style arrays do not contain bounds information, which prevents the *startIndex* and *length* parameters from being validated. Thus, the unmanaged data corresponding to the *source* parameter populates the managed array regardless of its usefulness. You must initalize the managed array with the appropriate size before calling the **Marshal.Copy** method.

> **Note** This method uses **SecurityAction.LinkDemand** to prevent it from being called from untrusted code; only the immediate caller is required to have **SecurityPermission-Attribute.UnmanagedCode** permission. If your code can be called from partially trusted code, do not pass user input to **Marshal** class methods without validation.

Example

[Visual Basic, C#] The following example demonstrates how to copy data from an unmanaged memory pointer into a managed array.

[Visual Basic]
```
Public Overloads Shared Sub Copy(source As IntPtr, _
   destination As Single(), startIndex As Integer, length As Integer)
```

[C#]
```
public static void Copy(IntPtr source, float[] destination,
   int startIndex, int length);
```

Requirements

Platforms: Windows 98, Windows NT 4.0, Windows Millennium Edition, Windows 2000, Windows XP Home Edition, Windows XP Professional, Windows .NET Server family, .NET Compact Framework - Windows CE .NET

.NET Framework Security:

- **SecurityPermission** for operating with unmanaged code. Associated enumeration: **SecurityPermissionFlag.UnmanagedCode**.

Marshal.Copy Method (Single[], Int32, IntPtr, Int32)

Copies data from a one-dimensional, managed single-precision floating-point number array to an unmanaged memory pointer.

[Visual Basic]
```
Overloads Public Shared Sub Copy( _
   ByVal source() As Single, _
   ByVal startIndex As Integer, _
   ByVal destination As IntPtr, _
   ByVal length As Integer _
)
```
[C#]
```
public static void Copy(
   float[] source,
   int startIndex,
   IntPtr destination,
   int length
);
```
[C++]
```
public: static void Copy(
   float source __gc[],
   int startIndex,
   IntPtr destination,
   int length
);
```

[JScript]
```
public static function Copy(
   source : float[],
   startIndex : int,
   destination : IntPtr,
   length : int
);
```

Parameters

source
> The one-dimensional array to copy from.

startIndex
> The zero-based index into the array where **Copy** should start.

destination
> The memory pointer to copy to.

length
> The number of array elements to copy.

Exceptions

Exception Type	Condition
ArgumentOutOfRange-Exception	*startIndex* and *length* are not valid.

Remarks

You can use this method to copy a subset of a one-dimensional, .NET-based array to an unmanaged C-style array.

> **Note** This method uses **SecurityAction.LinkDemand** to prevent it from being called from untrusted code; only the immediate caller is required to have **SecurityPermission-Attribute.UnmanagedCode** permission. If your code can be called from partially trusted code, do not pass user input to **Marshal** class methods without validation.

Example

[Visual Basic, C#] The following example demonstrates how to copy a one-dimensional array to an unmanaged memory pointer.

[Visual Basic]
```
Public Overloads Shared Sub Copy(source As Single(), _
   startIndex As Integer, destination As IntPtr, length As Integer)
```

[C#]
```
public static void Copy(float[] source, int startIndex,
   IntPtr destination, int length);
```

Requirements

Platforms: Windows 98, Windows NT 4.0, Windows Millennium Edition, Windows 2000, Windows XP Home Edition, Windows XP Professional, Windows .NET Server family, .NET Compact Framework - Windows CE .NET

.NET Framework Security:

- **SecurityPermission** for operating with unmanaged code. Associated enumeration: **SecurityPermissionFlag.UnmanagedCode**.

Marshal.CreateWrapperOfType Method

Wraps the specified COM object in an object of the specified type.

```
[Visual Basic]
Public Shared Function CreateWrapperOfType( _
  ByVal o As Object, _
  ByVal t As Type _
) As Object
[C#]
public static object CreateWrapperOfType(
  object o,
  Type t
);
[C++]
public: static Object* CreateWrapperOfType(
  Object* o,
  Type* t
);
[JScript]
public static function CreateWrapperOfType(
  o : Object,
  t : Type
) : Object;
```

Parameters

o

The object to be wrapped.

t

The **Type** of wrapper to create.

Return Value

The newly wrapped object that is an instance of the desired type.

Exceptions

Exception Type	Condition
ArgumentException	*t* must derive from **__ComObject**.
InvalidCastException	*o* cannot be converted to the destination type since it does not support all required interfaces.

Remarks

CreateWrapperOfType converts one COM class type, typically the generic **__ComObject** type, to another COM class type. The input COM object, represented by parameter *o*, is a runtime callable wrapper.

Both the *t* and *o* parameters must be classes whose signatures are attributed with **System.Runtime.InteropServices.ComImportAttribute**. The Type Library Importer (Tlbimp.exe) applies this attribute for you when it imports a type library. If you create the runtime callable wrapper manually in source code, you should apply this attribute to the managed signature representing the original coclass to signify its COM origins.

Tlbimp.exe imports a COM coclass as a managed class and an interface. The coclass interface has the same name as the original coclass and the managed class has the original coclass name appended with Class. For example, a coclass called MyCoclass becomes a coclass interface called MyCoclass and a managed class called MyCoclassClass. Since *t* must be a class, not an interface, be sure to specify the managed class (MyCoclassClass) and not the coclass interface.

> **Note** You lose the identity of the input COM object because a new runtime callable wrapper instance wraps the **IUnknown** pointer exposed by the original runtime callable wrapper.

> **Note** This method uses **SecurityAction.LinkDemand** to prevent it from being called from untrusted code; only the immediate caller is required to have **SecurityPermission-Attribute.UnmanagedCode** permission. If your code can be called from partially trusted code, do not pass user input to **Marshal** class methods without validation.

Requirements

Platforms: Windows 98, Windows NT 4.0, Windows Millennium Edition, Windows 2000, Windows XP Home Edition, Windows XP Professional, Windows .NET Server family

.NET Framework Security:

- **SecurityPermission** for operating with unmanaged code. Associated enumeration: **SecurityPermissionFlag.UnmanagedCode**.

Marshal.DestroyStructure Method

Frees all substructures pointed to by the specified unmanaged memory block.

```
[Visual Basic]
Public Shared Sub DestroyStructure( _
  ByVal ptr As IntPtr, _
  ByVal structuretype As Type _
)
[C#]
public static void DestroyStructure(
  IntPtr ptr,
  Type structuretype
);
[C++]
public: static void DestroyStructure(
  IntPtr ptr,
  Type* structuretype
);
[JScript]
public static function DestroyStructure(
  ptr : IntPtr,
  structuretype : Type
);
```

Parameters

ptr

A pointer to an unmanaged block of memory.

structuretype

Type of a formatted class. This provides the layout information necessary to delete the buffer in the *ptr* parameter.

Exceptions

Exception Type	Condition
ArgumentException	*structureType* has an automatic layout. Use sequential or explicit instead.

Remarks

You can use this method to free reference-type fields, such as strings, of an unmanaged structure. Unlike its fields, a structure can be a value type or reference type. Value-type structures containing value-type fields (all blittable) have no references whose memory must be freed. **StructureToPtr** uses this method to prevent memory leaks when reusing memory occupied by a structure.

DestroyStructure calls the **SysFreeString** COM API method, which in turn frees an allocated string. For additional information about **SysFreeString**, see the MSDN Library.

In addition to **DestroyStructure**, the **Marshal** class provides two other memory-deallocation methods: **Marshal.FreeCoTaskMem** and **Marshal.FreeHGlobal**.

> **Note** This method uses **SecurityAction.LinkDemand** to prevent it from being called from untrusted code; only the immediate caller is required to have **SecurityPermission-Attribute.UnmanagedCode** permission. If your code can be called from partially trusted code, do not pass user input to **Marshal** class methods without validation.

Requirements

Platforms: Windows 98, Windows NT 4.0, Windows Millennium Edition, Windows 2000, Windows XP Home Edition, Windows XP Professional, Windows .NET Server family

.NET Framework Security:

- **SecurityPermission** for operating with unmanaged code. Associated enumeration: **SecurityPermissionFlag.UnmanagedCode**.

Marshal.FreeBSTR Method

Frees a BSTR using **SysFreeString**.

```
[Visual Basic]
Public Shared Sub FreeBSTR( _
   ByVal ptr As IntPtr _
)
[C#]
public static void FreeBSTR(
   IntPtr ptr
);
[C++]
public: static void FreeBSTR(
   IntPtr ptr
);
[JScript]
public static function FreeBSTR(
   ptr : IntPtr
);
```

Parameters

ptr
   The address of the BSTR to be freed.

Exceptions

Exception Type	Condition
ArgumentNullException	*ptr* is a null reference (**Nothing** in Visual Basic).

Remarks

Like **Marshal.FreeCoTaskMem** and **Marshal.FreeHGlobal**, you can use this method to deallocate memory. **FreeBSTR** calls **SysFreeString**, a COM API method, which frees memory allocated by any of the following unmanaged methods: **SysAllocString**, **SysAllocStringByteLen**, **SysAllocStringLen**, **SysReAllocString**, **SysReAllocStringLen**. You can call unmanaged methods such as these with platform invoke.

> **Note** This method uses **SecurityAction.LinkDemand** to prevent it from being called from untrusted code; only the immediate caller is required to have **SecurityPermission-Attribute.UnmanagedCode** permission. If your code can be called from partially trusted code, do not pass user input to **Marshal** class methods without validation.

Requirements

Platforms: Windows 98, Windows NT 4.0, Windows Millennium Edition, Windows 2000, Windows XP Home Edition, Windows XP Professional, Windows .NET Server family

.NET Framework Security:

- **SecurityPermission** for operating with unmanaged code. Associated enumeration: **SecurityPermissionFlag.UnmanagedCode**.

Marshal.FreeCoTaskMem Method

Frees a block of memory allocated by the unmanaged COM task memory allocator with **Marshal.AllocCoTaskMem**.

```
[Visual Basic]
Public Shared Sub FreeCoTaskMem( _
   ByVal ptr As IntPtr _
)
[C#]
public static void FreeCoTaskMem(
   IntPtr ptr
);
[C++]
public: static void FreeCoTaskMem(
   IntPtr ptr
);
[JScript]
public static function FreeCoTaskMem(
   ptr : IntPtr
);
```

Parameters

ptr
   The address of the memory to be freed.

Exceptions

Exception Type	Condition
ArgumentNullException	*ptr* is a null reference (**Nothing** in Visual Basic).

Remarks

You can use **FreeCoTaskMem** to free any memory allocated by **AllocCoTaskMem**, **ReAllocCoTaskMem**, or any equivalent unmanaged API. If the *ptr* parameter is a null reference (**Nothing** in Visual Basic), the method does nothing.

FreeCoTaskMem exposes the **CoTaskMemFree** COM API function, which frees all bytes so that you can no longer use the memory pointed to by the *ptr* parameter. For additional information about **CoTaskMemFree**, see the MSDN library.

In addition to **FreeCoTaskMem**, the **Marshal** class provides two other memory-deallocation methods: **Marshal.DestroyStructure** and **Marshal.FreeHGlobal**.

> **Note** This method uses **SecurityAction.LinkDemand** to prevent it from being called from untrusted code; only the immediate caller is required to have **SecurityPermission-Attribute.UnmanagedCode** permission. If your code can be called from partially trusted code, do not pass user input to **Marshal** class methods without validation.

Requirements

Platforms: Windows 98, Windows NT 4.0, Windows Millennium Edition, Windows 2000, Windows XP Home Edition, Windows XP Professional, Windows .NET Server family

.NET Framework Security:

- **SecurityPermission** for operating with unmanaged code. Associated enumeration: **SecurityPermissionFlag.UnmanagedCode**.

Marshal.FreeHGlobal Method

Frees memory previously allocated from the unmanaged memory of the process with **AllocHGlobal**.

```
[Visual Basic]
Public Shared Sub FreeHGlobal( _
   ByVal hglobal As IntPtr _
)
[C#]
public static void FreeHGlobal(
   IntPtr hglobal
);
[C++]
public: static void FreeHGlobal(
   IntPtr hglobal
);
[JScript]
public static function FreeHGlobal(
   hglobal : IntPtr
);
```

Parameters

hglobal
   The handle returned by the original matching call to **AllocHGlobal**.

Remarks

You can use **FreeHGlobal** to free any memory from the global heap allocated by **AllocHGlobal**, **ReAllocHGlobal**, or any equivalent unmanaged API method. If the *hglobal* parameter is a null reference (**Nothing** in Visual Basic), the method does nothing.

FreeHGlobal exposes the **GlobalFree** function from Kernel32.DLL, which frees all bytes so that you can no longer use the memory pointed to by *hglobal*. For additional information about **GlobalFree**, see the MSDN Library.

In addition to **FreeHGlobal**, the **Marshal** class provides two other memory-deallocation API methods: **DestroyStructure** and **FreeCoTaskMem**.

> **Note** This method uses **SecurityAction.LinkDemand** to prevent it from being called from untrusted code; only the immediate caller is required to have **SecurityPermission-Attribute.UnmanagedCode** permission. If your code can be called from partially trusted code, do not pass user input to **Marshal** class methods without validation.

Requirements

Platforms: Windows 98, Windows NT 4.0, Windows Millennium Edition, Windows 2000, Windows XP Home Edition, Windows XP Professional, Windows .NET Server family

.NET Framework Security:

- **SecurityPermission** for operating with unmanaged code. Associated enumeration: **SecurityPermissionFlag.UnmanagedCode**.

Marshal.GenerateGuidForType Method

Returns the globally unique identifier (GUID) for the specified type, or generates a GUID using the algorithm used by the Type Library Exporter (Tlbexp.exe).

```
[Visual Basic]
Public Shared Function GenerateGuidForType( _
   ByVal type As Type _
) As Guid
[C#]
public static Guid GenerateGuidForType(
   Type type
);
[C++]
public: static Guid GenerateGuidForType(
   Type* type
);
[JScript]
public static function GenerateGuidForType(
   type : Type
) : Guid;
```

Parameters

type
   The **Type** to generate a GUID for.

Return Value

A **Guid** for the specified type.

Remarks

If the type has a GUID in the metadata, it is returned. Otherwise, a GUID is automatically generated. You can use this method to programmatically determine the COM GUID for any managed type, including COM-invisible types. Class interfaces are the only exception since they do not correspond to a managed type. **GenerateGuidForType** provides the same functionality as the **Type.GUID** property.

Note This method uses **SecurityAction.LinkDemand** to prevent it from being called from untrusted code; only the immediate caller is required to have **SecurityPermission-Attribute.UnmanagedCode** permission. If your code can be called from partially trusted code, do not pass user input to **Marshal** class methods without validation.

Requirements

Platforms: Windows 98, Windows NT 4.0, Windows Millennium Edition, Windows 2000, Windows XP Home Edition, Windows XP Professional, Windows .NET Server family

.NET Framework Security:

- **SecurityPermission** for operating with unmanaged code. Associated enumeration: **SecurityPermissionFlag.UnmanagedCode**.

Marshal.GenerateProgIdForType Method

Returns a programmatic identifier (ProgID) for the specified type.

```
[Visual Basic]
Public Shared Function GenerateProgIdForType( _
   ByVal type As Type _
) As String
[C#]
public static string GenerateProgIdForType(
   Type type
);
[C++]
public: static String* GenerateProgIdForType(
   Type* type
);
[JScript]
public static function GenerateProgIdForType(
   type : Type
) : String;
```

Parameters

type
  The **Type** to get a ProgID for.

Return Value

The ProgID of the specified type.

Exceptions

Exception Type	Condition
ArgumentException	*type* is not a class that can be create by COM. The class must be public, have a public default constructor, and be COM visible.

Remarks

If the type has a ProgID in the metadata, then it is returned. Otherwise a ProgID is generated based on the fully qualified name of the type.

Note This method uses **SecurityAction.LinkDemand** to prevent it from being called from untrusted code; only the immediate caller is required to have **SecurityPermission-Attribute.UnmanagedCode** permission. If your code can be called from partially trusted code, do not pass user input to **Marshal** class methods without validation.

Requirements

Platforms: Windows 98, Windows NT 4.0, Windows Millennium Edition, Windows 2000, Windows XP Home Edition, Windows XP Professional, Windows .NET Server family

.NET Framework Security:

- **SecurityPermission** for operating with unmanaged code. Associated enumeration: **SecurityPermissionFlag.UnmanagedCode**.

Marshal.GetActiveObject Method

Obtains a running instance of the specified object from the Running Object Table (ROT).

```
[Visual Basic]
Public Shared Function GetActiveObject( _
   ByVal progID As String _
) As Object
[C#]
public static object GetActiveObject(
   string progID
);
[C++]
public: static Object* GetActiveObject(
   String* progID
);
[JScript]
public static function GetActiveObject(
   progID : String
) : Object;
```

Parameters

progID
  The ProgID of the object being requested.

Return Value

The object requested. You can cast this object to any COM interface that it supports.

Remarks

Marshal.GetActiveObject exposes the **GetActiveObject** COM API method from OLEAUT32.DLL; however, the latter expects a class identifier (CLSID) instead of the programmatic identifier (ProgID) expected by this method. To obtain a running instance of a COM object without a registered ProgID, use platform invoke to define the **GetActivateObject** COM method. For a description of platform invoke, see **Consuming Unmanaged DLL Functions**. For additional information about the **GetActiveObject** COM method, see the MSDN Library.

Note This method uses **SecurityAction.LinkDemand** to prevent it from being called from untrusted code; only the immediate caller is required to have **SecurityPermission-Attribute.UnmanagedCode** permission. If your code can be called from partially trusted code, do not pass user input to **Marshal** class methods without validation.

Requirements

Platforms: Windows 98, Windows NT 4.0, Windows Millennium Edition, Windows 2000, Windows XP Home Edition, Windows XP Professional, Windows .NET Server family

.NET Framework Security:

- **SecurityPermission** for operating with unmanaged code. Associated enumeration: **SecurityPermissionFlag.UnmanagedCode**.

Marshal.GetComInterfaceForObject Method

Returns an **IUnknown** pointer representing the specified interface for an object.

```
[Visual Basic]
Public Shared Function GetComInterfaceForObject( _
   ByVal o As Object, _
   ByVal T As Type _
) As IntPtr
[C#]
public static IntPtr GetComInterfaceForObject(
   object o,
   Type T
);
[C++]
public: static IntPtr GetComInterfaceForObject(
   Object* o,
   Type* T
);
[JScript]
public static function GetComInterfaceForObject(
   o : Object,
   T : Type
) : IntPtr;
```

Parameters

o

The object providing the interface.

T

The **Type** of interface that is requested.

Return Value

The **IUnknown** pointer representing the interface for the object.

Exceptions

Exception Type	Condition
ArgumentException	*t* is not an interface.
	-or-
	The type is not visible to COM.
InvalidCastException	*o* does not support the requested interface.

Remarks

This method returns an **IUnknown** pointer that represents the requested interface on the specified object. Calling an object with this method causes the reference count to increment on the interface pointer before the pointer is returned. Always use **Marshal.Release** to decrement the reference count once you have finished with the pointer. You must adhere to the rules defined by COM when using raw COM interface pointers.

GetComInterfaceForObject is useful when calling a method that exposes a COM object parameter as an **IntPtr** type, or with custom marshaling. Although less common, you can use this method on a managed object to obtain a pointer to the object's COM callable wrapper. For example, you can use **GetComInterfaceForObject** on a managed object that is exported to COM to obtain an interface

pointer for **System.Runtime.InteropServices.UCOMIConnectionPointContainer**. You cannot obtain a pointer to a class interface since a class interface lacks the corresponding type to pass to the second parameter (*t*). Instead, use **Marshal.GetIDispatchForObject** to invoke the members on the default interface of the COM callable wrapper, which is usually an auto-dispatch class interface.

For additional information on runtime callable wrappers and COM callable wrappers, see **COM Wrappers**.

> **Note** This method uses **SecurityAction.LinkDemand** to prevent it from being called from untrusted code; only the immediate caller is required to have **SecurityPermissionAttribute.UnmanagedCode** permission. If your code can be called from partially trusted code, do not pass user input to **Marshal** class methods without validation.

Requirements

Platforms: Windows 98, Windows NT 4.0, Windows Millennium Edition, Windows 2000, Windows XP Home Edition, Windows XP Professional, Windows .NET Server family

.NET Framework Security:

- **SecurityPermission** for operating with unmanaged code. Associated enumeration: **SecurityPermissionFlag.UnmanagedCode**.

Marshal.GetComObjectData Method

Gets data referenced by the specified key from the specified COM object.

```
[Visual Basic]
Public Shared Function GetComObjectData( _
   ByVal obj As Object, _
   ByVal key As Object _
) As Object
[C#]
public static object GetComObjectData(
   object obj,
   object key
);
[C++]
public: static Object* GetComObjectData(
   Object* obj,
   Object* key
);
[JScript]
public static function GetComObjectData(
   obj : Object,
   key : Object
) : Object;
```

Parameters

obj

The COM object containing the desired data.

key

The key in the internal hash table of *obj* to retrieve the data from.

Return Value

The data represented by the *key* parameter in the internal hash table of the *obj* parameter.

Exceptions

Exception Type	Condition
ArgumentNullException	*obj* is a null reference (**Nothing** in Visual Basic).
	-or-
	key is a null reference (**Nothing**).
ArgumentException	*obj* is not a COM object.

Remarks

All COM objects wrapped in a runtime callable wrapper have an associated hash table, which **GetComObjectData** retrieves. **Marshal.SetComObjectData** adds data to the hash table. You should never have to call either method from your code.

> **Note** This method uses **SecurityAction.LinkDemand** to prevent it from being called from untrusted code; only the immediate caller is required to have **SecurityPermission-Attribute.UnmanagedCode** permission. If your code can be called from partially trusted code, do not pass user input to **Marshal** class methods without validation.

Requirements

Platforms: Windows 98, Windows NT 4.0, Windows Millennium Edition, Windows 2000, Windows XP Home Edition, Windows XP Professional, Windows .NET Server family

.NET Framework Security:

- **SecurityPermission** for operating with unmanaged code. Associated enumeration: **SecurityPermissionFlag.UnmanagedCode**.

Marshal.GetComSlotForMethodInfo Method

Gets the virtual function table (VTBL) slot for a specified **System.Reflection.MemberInfo** when exposed to COM.

```
[Visual Basic]
Public Shared Function GetComSlotForMethodInfo( _
   ByVal m As MemberInfo _
) As Integer
[C#]
public static int GetComSlotForMethodInfo(
   MemberInfo m
);
[C++]
public: static int GetComSlotForMethodInfo(
   MemberInfo* m
);
[JScript]
public static function GetComSlotForMethodInfo(
   m : MemberInfo
) : int;
```

Parameters

m
   A **MemberInfo** that represents an interface method.

Return Value

The VTBL (also called v-table) slot *m* identifier when it is exposed to COM.

Remarks

The zero-based slot number returned by this method accounts for three **IUnknown** and possibly four **IDispatch** methods, making the value of the first available slot either 3 or 7. **GetComSlotForMethodInfo** provides the opposite functionality of **Marshal.GetMethodInfoForComSlot**.

You can use this method to retrieve slot numbers for members of interfaces not visible from COM and for members of private interfaces. The slot numbers returned correspond to the v-table numbers that would be reserved if the type was exposed to COM. COM-invisible members actually occupy a slot in an exposed v-table, even though the COM client cannot use the slot. You cannot use **GetComSlotForMethodInfo** on a class interface by passing **MemberInfo** from a class.

> **Note** This method uses **SecurityAction.LinkDemand** to prevent it from being called from untrusted code; only the immediate caller is required to have **SecurityPermission-Attribute.UnmanagedCode** permission. If your code can be called from partially trusted code, do not pass user input to **Marshal** class methods without validation.

Requirements

Platforms: Windows 98, Windows NT 4.0, Windows Millennium Edition, Windows 2000, Windows XP Home Edition, Windows XP Professional, Windows .NET Server family

.NET Framework Security:

- **SecurityPermission** for operating with unmanaged code. Associated enumeration: **SecurityPermissionFlag.UnmanagedCode**.

Marshal.GetEndComSlot Method

Gets the last slot in the virtual function table (VTBL) of a type when exposed to COM.

```
[Visual Basic]
Public Shared Function GetEndComSlot( _
   ByVal t As Type _
) As Integer
[C#]
public static int GetEndComSlot(
   Type t
);
[C++]
public: static int GetEndComSlot(
   Type* t
);
[JScript]
public static function GetEndComSlot(
   t : Type
) : int;
```

Parameters

t
   A **Type** representing an interface or class.

Return Value

The last VTBL (also called v-table) slot of the interface when exposed to COM. If the *t* parameter is a class, the returned VTBL slot is the last slot in the interface that is generated from the class.

Remarks

This method returns the zero-based, v-table number for an interface or a class. When used on a class, the slot number returned refers to the class interface for the class. If the class interface is auto-dual, this method always returns -1 to indicate that the dispatch-only interface does not expose a v-table to managed clients. You can use **GetEndComSlot** and **Marshal.GetStartComSlot** in conjunction with **Marshal.GetMethodInfoForComSlot** to pass slots within a specified range.

> **Note** This method uses **SecurityAction.LinkDemand** to prevent it from being called from untrusted code; only the immediate caller is required to have **SecurityPermission-Attribute.UnmanagedCode** permission. If your code can be called from partially trusted code, do not pass user input to **Marshal** class methods without validation.

Requirements

Platforms: Windows 98, Windows NT 4.0, Windows Millennium Edition, Windows 2000, Windows XP Home Edition, Windows XP Professional, Windows .NET Server family

.NET Framework Security:

- **SecurityPermission** for operating with unmanaged code. Associated enumeration: **SecurityPermissionFlag.UnmanagedCode**.

Marshal.GetExceptionCode Method

Retrieves a code that identifies the type of the exception that occurred.

```
[Visual Basic]
Public Shared Function GetExceptionCode() As Integer
[C#]
public static int GetExceptionCode();
[C++]
public: static int GetExceptionCode();
[JScript]
public static function GetExceptionCode() : int;
```

Return Value

The type of the exception.

Remarks

GetExceptionCode is exposed for complier support of structured exception handling (SEH) only. If called before an exception is thrown, this method returns 0xCCCCCCCC.

> **Note** This method uses **SecurityAction.LinkDemand** to prevent it from being called from untrusted code; only the immediate caller is required to have **SecurityPermission-Attribute.UnmanagedCode** permission. If your code can be called from partially trusted code, do not pass user input to **Marshal** class methods without validation.

Requirements

Platforms: Windows 98, Windows NT 4.0, Windows Millennium Edition, Windows 2000, Windows XP Home Edition, Windows XP Professional, Windows .NET Server family

.NET Framework Security:

- **SecurityPermission** for operating with unmanaged code. Associated enumeration: **SecurityPermissionFlag.UnmanagedCode**.

Marshal.GetExceptionPointers Method

Retrieves a computer-independent description of an exception, and information about the state that existed for the thread when the exception occurred.

```
[Visual Basic]
Public Shared Function GetExceptionPointers() As IntPtr
[C#]
public static IntPtr GetExceptionPointers();
[C++]
public: static IntPtr GetExceptionPointers();
[JScript]
public static function GetExceptionPointers() : IntPtr;
```

Return Value

An **IntPtr** to an **EXCEPTION_POINTERS** structure.

Remarks

GetExceptionPointers is exposed for complier support of structured exception handling (SEH) only.

> **Note** This method uses **SecurityAction.LinkDemand** to prevent it from being called from untrusted code; only the immediate caller is required to have **SecurityPermission-Attribute.UnmanagedCode** permission. If your code can be called from partially trusted code, do not pass user input to **Marshal** class methods without validation.

Requirements

Platforms: Windows 98, Windows NT 4.0, Windows Millennium Edition, Windows 2000, Windows XP Home Edition, Windows XP Professional, Windows .NET Server family

.NET Framework Security:

- **SecurityPermission** for operating with unmanaged code. Associated enumeration: **SecurityPermissionFlag.UnmanagedCode**.

Marshal.GetHINSTANCE Method

Returns the instance handle (HINSTANCE) for the specified module.

```
[Visual Basic]
Public Shared Function GetHINSTANCE( _
    ByVal m As Module _
) As IntPtr
[C#]
public static IntPtr GetHINSTANCE(
    Module m
);
[C++]
public: static IntPtr GetHINSTANCE(
    Module* m
);
```

```
[JScript]
public static function GetHINSTANCE(
    m : Module
) : IntPtr;
```

Parameters

m

The **Module** whose HINSTANCE is desired.

Return Value

The HINSTANCE for *m*; -1 if the module does not have an HINSTANCE.

Remarks

When dynamic or in-memory, modules do not have an HINSTANCE.

> **Note** This method uses **SecurityAction.LinkDemand** to prevent it from being called from untrusted code; only the immediate caller is required to have **SecurityPermission-Attribute.UnmanagedCode** permission. If your code can be called from partially trusted code, do not pass user input to **Marshal** class methods without validation.

Requirements

Platforms: Windows 98, Windows NT 4.0, Windows Millennium Edition, Windows 2000, Windows XP Home Edition, Windows XP Professional, Windows .NET Server family

.NET Framework Security:

- **SecurityPermission** for operating with unmanaged code. Associated enumeration: **SecurityPermissionFlag.UnmanagedCode**.

Marshal.GetHRForException Method

Converts the specified exception to an HRESULT.

```
[Visual Basic]
Public Shared Function GetHRForException( _
    ByVal e As Exception _
) As Integer
[C#]
public static int GetHRForException(
    Exception e
);
[C++]
public: static int GetHRForException(
    Exception* e
);
[JScript]
public static function GetHRForException(
    e : Exception
) : int;
```

Parameters

e

The **Exception** to convert to an HRESULT.

Return Value

The HRESULT mapped to the supplied exception.

Remarks

GetHRForException also sets up an **IErrorInfo** interface for the exception that can be obtained by calling the **GetErrorInfo** COM API method. You can use this method to return an HRESULT value on a managed class implementation of a COM interface where you apply the **System.Runtime.InteropServices.PreserveSigAttribute**. Have the attributed method catch all exceptions and use **GetHRForException** to return the appropriate HRESULT value. Allowing an exception to propagate outside the method produces incorrect behavior. (In fact, the common language runtime fails to pass an exception to a COM client calling such a method through a v-table.) For additional information about the **IErrorInfo** interface and **GetErrorInfo** COM methods, see the MSDN Library.

> **Note** This method uses **SecurityAction.LinkDemand** to prevent it from being called from untrusted code; only the immediate caller is required to have **SecurityPermission-Attribute.UnmanagedCode** permission. If your code can be called from partially trusted code, do not pass user input to **Marshal** class methods without validation.

Requirements

Platforms: Windows 98, Windows NT 4.0, Windows Millennium Edition, Windows 2000, Windows XP Home Edition, Windows XP Professional, Windows .NET Server family

.NET Framework Security:

- **SecurityPermission** for operating with unmanaged code. Associated enumeration: **SecurityPermissionFlag.UnmanagedCode**.

Marshal.GetHRForLastWin32Error Method

Returns the HRESULT corresponding to the last error incurred by Win32 code executed using **Marshal**.

```
[Visual Basic]
Public Shared Function GetHRForLastWin32Error() As Integer
[C#]
public static int GetHRForLastWin32Error();
[C++]
public: static int GetHRForLastWin32Error();
[JScript]
public static function GetHRForLastWin32Error() : int;
```

Return Value

The HRESULT corresponding to the last Win32 error code.

Remarks

The target function must have had the **setLastError** metadata flag set. For example, the **SetLastError** field of the **System.Runtime.InteropServices.DllImportAttribute** must be **true**. The process for this varies depending upon the source language used: C# and C++ are **false** by default, but the **Declare** statement in Visual Basic is **true**.

> **Note** This method uses **SecurityAction.LinkDemand** to prevent it from being called from untrusted code; only the immediate caller is required to have **SecurityPermission-Attribute.UnmanagedCode** permission. If your code can be called from partially trusted code, do not pass user input to **Marshal** class methods without validation.

Requirements

Platforms: Windows 98, Windows NT 4.0,
Windows Millennium Edition, Windows 2000,
Windows XP Home Edition, Windows XP Professional,
Windows .NET Server family

.NET Framework Security:

*   **SecurityPermission** for operating with unmanaged code.
    Associated enumeration:
    SecurityPermissionFlag.UnmanagedCode.

Marshal.GetIDispatchForObject Method

Returns an **IDispatch** interface from a managed object.

```
[Visual Basic]
Public Shared Function GetIDispatchForObject( _
   ByVal o As Object _
) As IntPtr
[C#]
public static IntPtr GetIDispatchForObject(
   object o
);
[C++]
public: static IntPtr GetIDispatchForObject(
   Object* o
);
[JScript]
public static function GetIDispatchForObject(
   o : Object
) : IntPtr;
```

Parameters

o

   The object whose **IDispatch** interface is requested.

Return Value

The **IDispatch** pointer for the *o* parameter.

Exceptions

Exception Type	Condition
InvalidCastException	*o* does not support the requested interface.

Remarks

In managed code, you seldom work directly with the **IDispatch**
interface. However, **GetIDispatchForObject** is useful when calling
a method that exposes a COM object parameter as an **IntPtr** type, or
with custom marshaling. Calling an object with this method causes
the reference count to increment on the interface pointer before the
pointer is returned. Always use **Marshal.Release** to decrement the
reference count once you have finished with the pointer.

You can also use this method on a managed object to obtain an
interface pointer to the COM callable wrapper for the object.

> **Note** This method uses **SecurityAction.LinkDemand** to
> prevent it from being called from untrusted code; only the
> immediate caller is required to have **SecurityPermission-**
> **Attribute.UnmanagedCode** permission. If your code can be
> called from partially trusted code, do not pass user input to
> **Marshal** class methods without validation.

Requirements

Platforms: Windows 98, Windows NT 4.0,
Windows Millennium Edition, Windows 2000,
Windows XP Home Edition, Windows XP Professional,
Windows .NET Server family

.NET Framework Security:

*   **SecurityPermission** for operating with unmanaged code.
    Associated enumeration:
    SecurityPermissionFlag.UnmanagedCode.

Marshal.GetITypeInfoForType Method

Returns an **ITypeInfo** interface from a managed type.

```
[Visual Basic]
Public Shared Function GetITypeInfoForType( _
   ByVal t As Type _
) As IntPtr
[C#]
public static IntPtr GetITypeInfoForType(
   Type t
);
[C++]
public: static IntPtr GetITypeInfoForType(
   Type* t
);
[JScript]
public static function GetITypeInfoForType(
   t : Type
) : IntPtr;
```

Parameters

t

   The **Type** whose **ITypeInfo** interface is being requested.

Return Value

The **ITypeInfo** pointer for the *t* parameter.

Exceptions

Exception Type	Condition
ArgumentException	*t* is not a visible type to COM.
COMException	A type library is registered for the assembly that contains the type, but the type definition cannot be found.

Remarks

This method returns a pointer to an **ITypeInfo** implementation that
is based on the original type. Calling an object with
GetITypeInfoForType causes the reference count to increment on
the interface pointer before the pointer is returned. Always use
Marshal.Release to decrement the reference count once you have
finished with the pointer. You can apply the
System.Runtime.InteropServices.MarshalAsAttribute to replace
standard interop marshaling behavior with this custom marshaler.
For additional information about **ITypeInfo**, see the MSDN library.

> **Note** This method uses **SecurityAction.LinkDemand** to
> prevent it from being called from untrusted code; only the
> immediate caller is required to have **SecurityPermission-**
> **Attribute.UnmanagedCode** permission. If your code can be
> called from partially trusted code, do not pass user input to
> **Marshal** class methods without validation.

Requirements

Platforms: Windows 98, Windows NT 4.0,
Windows Millennium Edition, Windows 2000,
Windows XP Home Edition, Windows XP Professional,
Windows .NET Server family

.NET Framework Security:

- **SecurityPermission** for operating with unmanaged code.
  Associated enumeration:
  SecurityPermissionFlag.UnmanagedCode.

Marshal.GetIUnknownForObject Method

Returns an **IUnknown** interface from a managed object.

```
[Visual Basic]
Public Shared Function GetIUnknownForObject( _
   ByVal o As Object _
) As IntPtr
[C#]
public static IntPtr GetIUnknownForObject(
   object o
);
[C++]
public: static IntPtr GetIUnknownForObject(
   Object* o
);
[JScript]
public static function GetIUnknownForObject(
   o : Object
) : IntPtr;
```

Parameters

o
   The object whose **IUnknown** interface is requested.

Return Value

The **IUnknown** pointer for the *o* parameter.

Remarks

In managed code, you seldom work directly with the **IUnknown** interface. However, **GetIUnknownForObject** is useful when calling a method that exposes a COM object parameter as an **IntPtr** type, or with custom marshaling. Calling an object with this method causes the reference count to increment on the interface pointer before the pointer is returned. Always use **Marshal.Release** to decrement the reference count once you have finished with the pointer. This method provides the opposite functionality of the **Marshal.GetObjectForIUnknown** method.

You can also use this method on a managed object to obtain an interface pointer to the COM callable wrapper for the object.

> **Note** This method uses **SecurityAction.LinkDemand** to prevent it from being called from untrusted code; only the immediate caller is required to have **SecurityPermission-Attribute.UnmanagedCode** permission. If your code can be called from partially trusted code, do not pass user input to **Marshal** class methods without validation.

Requirements

Platforms: Windows 98, Windows NT 4.0,
Windows Millennium Edition, Windows 2000,
Windows XP Home Edition, Windows XP Professional,
Windows .NET Server family

.NET Framework Security:

- **SecurityPermission** for operating with unmanaged code.
  Associated enumeration:
  SecurityPermissionFlag.UnmanagedCode.

Marshal.GetLastWin32Error Method

Returns the error code returned by the last unmanaged function called using platform invoke that has the **DllImportAttribute.SetLastError** flag set.

```
[Visual Basic]
Public Shared Function GetLastWin32Error() As Integer
[C#]
public static int GetLastWin32Error();
[C++]
public: static int GetLastWin32Error();
[JScript]
public static function GetLastWin32Error() : int;
```

Return Value

The last error code set by a call to the Win32 **SetLastError** API method.

Remarks

GetLastWin32Error exposes the Win32 **GetLastError** API method from Kernel32.DLL. This method exists because it is not safe to make a direct platform invoke call to **GetLastError** to obtain this information. If you want to access this error code, you must call **GetLastWin32Error** rather than writing your own platform invoke definition for **GetLastError** and calling it. The common language runtime can make internal calls to APIs that overwrite the operating system maintained **GetLastError**.

You can only use this method to obtain error codes if you apply the **System.Runtime.InteropServices.DllImportAttribute** to the method signature and set the **SetLastError** field to **true**. The process for this varies depending upon the source language used: C# and C++ are **false** by default, but the **Declare** statement in Visual Basic is **true**. For additional information about the **GetLastError** and **SetLastError** Win32 API methods, see the MSDN Library.

> **Note** This method uses **SecurityAction.LinkDemand** to prevent it from being called from untrusted code; only the immediate caller is required to have **SecurityPermission-Attribute.UnmanagedCode** permission. If your code can be called from partially trusted code, do not pass user input to **Marshal** class methods without validation.

Requirements

Platforms: Windows 98, Windows NT 4.0,
Windows Millennium Edition, Windows 2000,
Windows XP Home Edition, Windows XP Professional,
Windows .NET Server family,
.NET Compact Framework - Windows CE .NET

.NET Framework Security:

- **SecurityPermission** for operating with unmanaged code.
  Associated enumeration:
  SecurityPermissionFlag.UnmanagedCode.

Marshal.GetManagedThunkForUnmanaged-MethodPtr Method

Gets a pointer to a thunk that marshals a call from managed to unmanaged code.

```
[Visual Basic]
Public Shared Function GetManagedThunkForUnmanagedMethodPtr( _
    ByVal pfnMethodToWrap As IntPtr, _
    ByVal pbSignature As IntPtr, _
    ByVal cbSignature As Integer _
) As IntPtr
[C#]
public static IntPtr GetManagedThunkForUnmanagedMethodPtr(
    IntPtr pfnMethodToWrap,
    IntPtr pbSignature,
    int cbSignature
);
[C++]
public: static IntPtr GetManagedThunkForUnmanagedMethodPtr(
    IntPtr pfnMethodToWrap,
    IntPtr pbSignature,
    int cbSignature
);
[JScript]
public static function GetManagedThunkForUnmanagedMethodPtr(
    pfnMethodToWrap : IntPtr,
    pbSignature : IntPtr,
    cbSignature : int
) : IntPtr;
```

Parameters

pfnMethodToWrap
    A pointer to the method to marshal.
pbSignature
    A pointer to the method signature.
cbSignature
    The number of bytes in *pbSignature*.

Return Value

A pointer to the thunk that will marshal a call from the *pfnMethodToWrap* parameter.

Remarks

GetManagedThunkForUnmanagedMethodPtr is exposed for compiler support only.

> **Note** This method uses **SecurityAction.LinkDemand** to prevent it from being called from untrusted code; only the immediate caller is required to have **SecurityPermission-Attribute.UnmanagedCode** permission. If your code can be called from partially trusted code, do not pass user input to **Marshal** class methods without validation.

Requirements

Platforms: Windows 98, Windows NT 4.0, Windows Millennium Edition, Windows 2000, Windows XP Home Edition, Windows XP Professional, Windows .NET Server family

.NET Framework Security:

• **SecurityPermission** for operating with unmanaged code. Associated enumeration: **SecurityPermissionFlag.UnmanagedCode**.

Marshal.GetMethodInfoForComSlot Method

Retrieves **MethodInfo** for the specified virtual function table (VTBL) slot.

```
[Visual Basic]
Public Shared Function GetMethodInfoForComSlot( _
    ByVal t As Type, _
    ByVal slot As Integer, _
    ByRef memberType As ComMemberType _
) As MemberInfo
[C#]
public static MemberInfo GetMethodInfoForComSlot(
    Type t,
    int slot,
    ref ComMemberType memberType
);
[C++]
public: static MemberInfo* GetMethodInfoForComSlot(
    Type* t,
    int slot,
    ComMemberType* memberType
);
[JScript]
public static function GetMethodInfoForComSlot(
    t : Type,
    slot : int,
    memberType : ComMemberType
) : MemberInfo;
```

Parameters

t
    The type for which the **MethodInfo** is to be retrieved.
slot
    The VTBL slot.
memberType
    On successful return, the type of the member. This is one of the **ComMemberType** enumeration members.

Return Value

The **MemberInfo** that represents the member at the specified VTBL (also called v-table) slot.

Exceptions

Exception Type	Condition
ArgumentException	*t* is not visible from COM.

Remarks

The zero-based slot number returned by this method accounts for three **IUnknown** and possibly four **IDispatch** methods, making the value of the first available slot either 3 or 7. **GetMethodInfoForComSlot** provides the opposite functionality of **Marshal.GetComSlotForMethodInfo**. You can use **Marshal.GetEndComSlot** and **Marshal.GetStartComSlot** in conjunction with **GetMethodInfoForComSlot** to pass slots within a specified range.

The *memberType* parameter is only important on return. It contains the type of the COM member that corresponds to the returned **MemberInfo**: a regular method or a property accessor (get, set, or other).

Note This method uses **SecurityAction.LinkDemand** to prevent it from being called from untrusted code; only the immediate caller is required to have **SecurityPermission-Attribute.UnmanagedCode** permission. If your code can be called from partially trusted code, do not pass user input to **Marshal** class methods without validation.

Requirements

Platforms: Windows 98, Windows NT 4.0, Windows Millennium Edition, Windows 2000, Windows XP Home Edition, Windows XP Professional, Windows .NET Server family

.NET Framework Security:

- **SecurityPermission** for operating with unmanaged code. Associated enumeration: **SecurityPermissionFlag.UnmanagedCode**.

Marshal.GetNativeVariantForObject Method

Converts an object to a COM VARIANT.

```
[Visual Basic]
Public Shared Sub GetNativeVariantForObject( _
   ByVal obj As Object, _
   ByVal pDstNativeVariant As IntPtr _
)
[C#]
public static void GetNativeVariantForObject(
   object obj,
   IntPtr pDstNativeVariant
);
[C++]
public: static void GetNativeVariantForObject(
   Object* obj,
   IntPtr pDstNativeVariant
);
[JScript]
public static function GetNativeVariantForObject(
   obj : Object,
   pDstNativeVariant : IntPtr
);
```

Parameters

obj
    The object for which to get a COM VARIANT.
pDstNativeVariant
    An **IntPtr** to receive the VARIANT corresponding to the *obj* parameter.

Remarks

The *pDstNativeVariant* parameter must point to sufficient memory to store the resulting VARIANT.

Note This method uses **SecurityAction.LinkDemand** to prevent it from being called from untrusted code; only the immediate caller is required to have **SecurityPermission-Attribute.UnmanagedCode** permission. If your code can be called from partially trusted code, do not pass user input to **Marshal** class methods without validation.

Requirements

Platforms: Windows 98, Windows NT 4.0, Windows Millennium Edition, Windows 2000, Windows XP Home Edition, Windows XP Professional, Windows .NET Server family

.NET Framework Security:

- **SecurityPermission** for operating with unmanaged code. Associated enumeration: **SecurityPermissionFlag.UnmanagedCode**.

Marshal.GetObjectForIUnknown Method

Returns an instance of a type that represents a COM object by a pointer to its **IUnknown** interface.

```
[Visual Basic]
Public Shared Function GetObjectForIUnknown( _
   ByVal pUnk As IntPtr _
) As Object
[C#]
public static object GetObjectForIUnknown(
   IntPtr pUnk
);
[C++]
public: static Object* GetObjectForIUnknown(
   IntPtr pUnk
);
[JScript]
public static function GetObjectForIUnknown(
   pUnk : IntPtr
) : Object;
```

Parameters

pUnk
    A pointer to the **IUnknown** interface.

Return Value

An object representing the specified unmanaged COM object.

Remarks

This method calls **Marshal.AddRef** before the pointer is returned. Always use **Marshal.Release** to decrement the reference count once you have finished with the pointer.

The first parameter, *pUnk*, represents an **IUnknown** interface pointer; however, because all COM interfaces derive directly or indirectly from **IUnknown**, you can pass any COM interface to this method. The object returned by **GetObjectForIUnknown** is a runtime callable wrapper, which the common language runtime manages as it does any other managed object. The type of this wrapper is often a generic **System.__ComObject** type, which is a hidden type used when the wrapper type is ambiguous. You can still make late-bound calls to such a generic type as long as the COM object implements the **IDispatch** interface. Likewise, you can cast the returned object to an appropriate COM interface. For additional information, see **Runtime Callable Wrapper**.

For an object to be wrapped with a specific managed class type (and not a generic wrapper type), you must adhere to the following requirements:

- Implement the **IProvideClassInfo** interface for the COM object.
- Register the containing assembly with the Assembly Registration Tool (Regasm.exe).

Alternatively, you can avoid these requirements and still get an object that is wrapped with a specific managed class type by using the **Marshal.GetTypedObjectForIUnknown** method.

> **Note** This method uses **SecurityAction.LinkDemand** to prevent it from being called from untrusted code; only the immediate caller is required to have **SecurityPermission-Attribute.UnmanagedCode** permission. If your code can be called from partially trusted code, do not pass user input to **Marshal** class methods without validation.

Requirements

Platforms: Windows 98, Windows NT 4.0, Windows Millennium Edition, Windows 2000, Windows XP Home Edition, Windows XP Professional, Windows .NET Server family

.NET Framework Security:

- **SecurityPermission** for operating with unmanaged code. Associated enumeration: **SecurityPermissionFlag.UnmanagedCode**.

Marshal.GetObjectForNativeVariant Method

Converts a COM VARIANT to an object.

```
[Visual Basic]
Public Shared Function GetObjectForNativeVariant( _
   ByVal pSrcNativeVariant As IntPtr _
) As Object
[C#]
public static object GetObjectForNativeVariant(
   IntPtr pSrcNativeVariant
);
[C++]
public: static Object* GetObjectForNativeVariant(
   IntPtr pSrcNativeVariant
);
[JScript]
public static function GetObjectForNativeVariant(
   pSrcNativeVariant : IntPtr
) : Object;
```

Parameters

pSrcNativeVariant
   An **IntPtr** containing a COM VARIANT.

Return Value

An object corresponding to the *pSrcNativeVaraint* parameter.

Exceptions

Exception Type	Condition
InvalidOleVariantType-Exception	*pSrcNativeVaraint* is not a valid VARIANT type.
NotSupportedException	*pSrcNativeVaraint* has an unsupported type.

Remarks

GetObjectForNativeVariant returns a managed object corresponding to a raw pointer to an unmanaged VARIANT type. The interop marshaler performs the identical transformation when exposing a VARIANT type to managed code. **GetObjectForNativeVariant** provides the opposite functionality of **Marshal.GetNativeVariantForObject**.

> **Note** This method uses **SecurityAction.LinkDemand** to prevent it from being called from untrusted code; only the immediate caller is required to have **SecurityPermission-Attribute.UnmanagedCode** permission. If your code can be called from partially trusted code, do not pass user input to **Marshal** class methods without validation.

Requirements

Platforms: Windows 98, Windows NT 4.0, Windows Millennium Edition, Windows 2000, Windows XP Home Edition, Windows XP Professional, Windows .NET Server family

.NET Framework Security:

- **SecurityPermission** for operating with unmanaged code. Associated enumeration: **SecurityPermissionFlag.UnmanagedCode**.

Marshal.GetObjectsForNativeVariants Method

Converts an array of COM VARIANTs to an array of objects.

```
[Visual Basic]
Public Shared Function GetObjectsForNativeVariants( _
   ByVal aSrcNativeVariant As IntPtr, _
   ByVal cVars As Integer _
) As Object()
[C#]
public static object[] GetObjectsForNativeVariants(
   IntPtr aSrcNativeVariant,
   int cVars
);
[C++]
public: static Object* GetObjectsForNativeVariants(
   IntPtr aSrcNativeVariant,
   int cVars
) __gc[];
[JScript]
public static function GetObjectsForNativeVariants(
   aSrcNativeVariant : IntPtr,
   cVars : int
) : Object[];
```

Parameters

aSrcNativeVariant
   An **IntPtr** containing the first element of an array of COM VARIANTs.
cVars
   The count of COM VARIANTs in *aSrcNativeVariant*.

Return Value

An object array corresponding to *aSrcNativeVariant*.

Exceptions

Exception Type	Condition
ArgumentOutOfRange-Exception	*cVars* cannot be a negative number.

Remarks

GetObjectsForNativeVariants returns an array of managed objects corresponding to a raw pointer to a C-style array of unmanaged VARIANT types. The interop marshaler performs the identical transformation when exposing a VARIANT type to managed code. The method returns an empty array when the *cVars* parameter is 0.

> **Note** This method uses **SecurityAction.LinkDemand** to prevent it from being called from untrusted code; only the immediate caller is required to have **SecurityPermission-Attribute.UnmanagedCode** permission. If your code can be called from partially trusted code, do not pass user input to **Marshal** class methods without validation.

Requirements

Platforms: Windows 98, Windows NT 4.0, Windows Millennium Edition, Windows 2000, Windows XP Home Edition, Windows XP Professional, Windows .NET Server family

.NET Framework Security:

- **SecurityPermission** for operating with unmanaged code. Associated enumeration: **SecurityPermissionFlag.UnmanagedCode**.

Marshal.GetStartComSlot Method

Gets the first slot in the virtual function table (VTBL) that contains user defined methods.

```
[Visual Basic]
Public Shared Function GetStartComSlot( _
   ByVal t As Type _
) As Integer
[C#]
public static int GetStartComSlot(
   Type t
);
[C++]
public: static int GetStartComSlot(
   Type* t
);
[JScript]
public static function GetStartComSlot(
   t : Type
) : int;
```

Parameters

t

A **Type** representing an interface.

Return Value

The first VTBL (also called v-table) slot that contains user defined methods. The first slot is 3 if the interface is **IUnknown** based, and 7 if the interface is **IDispatch** based.

Exceptions

Exception Type	Condition
ArgumentException	*t* is not visible from COM.

Remarks

This method returns the zero-based v-table number for an interface or a class. When used on a class, the slot number returned refers to the class interface for the class. If the class interface is auto-dispatch, this method always returns -1 to indicate that the dispatch-only interface does not expose a v-table to managed clients. You can use **GetStartComSlot** and **Marshal.GetEndComSlot** in conjunction

with **Marshal.GetMethodInfoForComSlot** to pass slots within a specified range.

> **Note** This method uses **SecurityAction.LinkDemand** to prevent it from being called from untrusted code; only the immediate caller is required to have **SecurityPermission-Attribute.UnmanagedCode** permission. If your code can be called from partially trusted code, do not pass user input to **Marshal** class methods without validation.

Requirements

Platforms: Windows 98, Windows NT 4.0, Windows Millennium Edition, Windows 2000, Windows XP Home Edition, Windows XP Professional, Windows .NET Server family

.NET Framework Security:

- **SecurityPermission** for operating with unmanaged code. Associated enumeration: **SecurityPermissionFlag.UnmanagedCode**.

Marshal.GetThreadFromFiberCookie Method

Converts a fiber cookie into the corresponding **System.Threading.Thread** instance.

```
[Visual Basic]
Public Shared Function GetThreadFromFiberCookie( _
   ByVal cookie As Integer _
) As Thread
[C#]
public static Thread GetThreadFromFiberCookie(
   int cookie
);
[C++]
public: static Thread* GetThreadFromFiberCookie(
   int cookie
);
[JScript]
public static function GetThreadFromFiberCookie(
   cookie : int
) : Thread;
```

Parameters

cookie

An integer representing a fiber cookie.

Return Value

A **Thread** corresponding to the *cookie* parameter.

Remarks

Fiber cookies are opaque tokens that are used by the host when alerting the common language runtime to its fiber-scheduling decisions. They consist of a stack and register context.

> **Note** This method uses **SecurityAction.LinkDemand** to prevent it from being called from untrusted code; only the immediate caller is required to have **SecurityPermission-Attribute.UnmanagedCode** permission. If your code can be called from partially trusted code, do not pass user input to **Marshal** class methods without validation.

Requirements

Platforms: Windows 98, Windows NT 4.0,
Windows Millennium Edition, Windows 2000,
Windows XP Home Edition, Windows XP Professional,
Windows .NET Server family

.NET Framework Security:

- **SecurityPermission** for operating with unmanaged code.
  Associated enumeration:
  SecurityPermissionFlag.UnmanagedCode.

Marshal.GetTypedObjectForIUnknown Method

Returns a managed object of a specified type that represents a COM
object.

```
[Visual Basic]
Public Shared Function GetTypedObjectForIUnknown( _
   ByVal pUnk As IntPtr, _
   ByVal t As Type _
) As Object
[C#]
public static object GetTypedObjectForIUnknown(
   IntPtr pUnk,
   Type t
);
[C++]
public: static Object* GetTypedObjectForIUnknown(
   IntPtr pUnk,
   Type* t
);
[JScript]
public static function GetTypedObjectForIUnknown(
   pUnk : IntPtr,
   t : Type
) : Object;
```

Parameters

pUnk
   A pointer to the **IUnknown** interface of the unmanaged object.

t
   The **Type** of the requested managed class.

Return Value

An instance of the class corresponding to the **Type** object that
represents the requested unmanaged COM object.

Exceptions

Exception Type	Condition
ArgumentException	*t* is not attributed with **System.Runtime.InteropServices. ComImportAttribute**.

Remarks

The *t* parameter must be either a COM-imported type or a subtype of
a COM-imported type. In addition, *t* must be a type whose metadata
was imported by the Type Library Importer (Tlbimp.exe). This type
must be a class and not an associated coclass interface, which carries
the name of the COM class. For example, suppose Tlbimp.exe
imports Myclass as a class called MyclassClass and a coclass
interface called Myclass. Be sure to use MyclassClass, not Myclass
with this method.

If an object has already been obtained for the *pUnk* parameter, then *t*
is ignored and the existing object is returned. *pUnk* represents an
IUnknown interface pointer; however, because all COM interfaces
derive directly or indirectly from **IUnknown**, you can pass any
COM interface to this method. The object returned by
GetTypedObjectForIUnknown is a runtime callable wrapper,
which the common language runtime manages as it does any other
managed object. For additional information, see **Runtime Callable
Wrapper**.

> **Note** This method uses **SecurityAction.LinkDemand** to
> prevent it from being called from untrusted code; only the
> immediate caller is required to have **SecurityPermission-
> Attribute.UnmanagedCode** permission. If your code can be
> called from partially trusted code, do not pass user input to
> **Marshal** class methods without validation.

Requirements

Platforms: Windows 98, Windows NT 4.0,
Windows Millennium Edition, Windows 2000,
Windows XP Home Edition, Windows XP Professional,
Windows .NET Server family

.NET Framework Security:

- **SecurityPermission** for operating with unmanaged code.
  Associated enumeration:
  SecurityPermissionFlag.UnmanagedCode.

Marshal.GetTypeForITypeInfo Method

Converts an **ITypeInfo** into a managed **Type** object.

```
[Visual Basic]
Public Shared Function GetTypeForITypeInfo( _
   ByVal piTypeInfo As IntPtr _
) As Type
[C#]
public static Type GetTypeForITypeInfo(
   IntPtr piTypeInfo
);
[C++]
public: static Type* GetTypeForITypeInfo(
   IntPtr piTypeInfo
);
[JScript]
public static function GetTypeForITypeInfo(
   piTypeInfo : IntPtr
) : Type;
```

Parameters

piTypeInfo
   The **ITypeInfo** interface to marshal.

Return Value

A managed **Type** that represents the unmanaged **ITypeInfo**.

Remarks

GetTypeForITypeInfo returns a **System.Type** instance that is based
on the original type. You can apply the
System.Runtime.InteropServices.MarshalAsAttribute to replace
standard interop marshaling behavior with this custom marshaler.
The Type Library Importer (Tlbimp.exe) uses the custom marshaler
to translate **ITypeInfo** parameters to **Type** parameters. However, if
you obtain an **ITypeInfo** interface by some means other than

Tlbimp.exe, you can use **GetTypeForITypeInfo** to manually perform the same translation. For additional information about **ITypeInfo**, see the MSDN Library.

> **Note** This method uses **SecurityAction.LinkDemand** to prevent it from being called from untrusted code; only the immediate caller is required to have **SecurityPermission-Attribute.UnmanagedCode** permission. If your code can be called from partially trusted code, do not pass user input to **Marshal** class methods without validation.

Requirements

Platforms: Windows 98, Windows NT 4.0, Windows Millennium Edition, Windows 2000, Windows XP Home Edition, Windows XP Professional, Windows .NET Server family

.NET Framework Security:

- **SecurityPermission** for operating with unmanaged code. Associated enumeration: **SecurityPermissionFlag.UnmanagedCode**.

Marshal.GetTypeInfoName Method

Retrieves the name of the type represented by an **ITypeInfo**.

```
[Visual Basic]
Public Shared Function GetTypeInfoName( _
   ByVal pTI As UCOMITypeInfo _
) As String
[C#]
public static string GetTypeInfoName(
   UCOMITypeInfo pTI
);
[C++]
public: static String* GetTypeInfoName(
   UCOMITypeInfo* pTI
);
[JScript]
public static function GetTypeInfoName(
   pTI : UCOMITypeInfo
) : String;
```

Parameters

pTI
   A **UCOMITypeInfo** that represents an **ITypeInfo** pointer.

Return Value

The name of the type pointed to by the *pTI* parameter.

Remarks

You can also retrieve the name of the type represented by an **ITypeInfo** by calling the **UCOMITypeInfo.GetDocumentation** method and passing a -1 for its first parameter. For additional information about **ITypeInfo**, see the MSDN Library.

> **Note** This method uses **SecurityAction.LinkDemand** to prevent it from being called from untrusted code; only the immediate caller is required to have **SecurityPermission-Attribute.UnmanagedCode** permission. If your code can be called from partially trusted code, do not pass user input to **Marshal** class methods without validation.

Requirements

Platforms: Windows 98, Windows NT 4.0, Windows Millennium Edition, Windows 2000, Windows XP Home Edition, Windows XP Professional, Windows .NET Server family

.NET Framework Security:

- **SecurityPermission** for operating with unmanaged code. Associated enumeration: **SecurityPermissionFlag.UnmanagedCode**.

Marshal.GetTypeLibGuid Method

Retrieves the library identifier (LIBID) of a type library.

```
[Visual Basic]
Public Shared Function GetTypeLibGuid( _
   ByVal pTLB As UCOMITypeLib _
) As Guid
[C#]
public static Guid GetTypeLibGuid(
   UCOMITypeLib pTLB
);
[C++]
public: static Guid GetTypeLibGuid(
   UCOMITypeLib* pTLB
);
[JScript]
public static function GetTypeLibGuid(
   pTLB : UCOMITypeLib
) : Guid;
```

Parameters

pTLB
   A **UCOMITypeLib** that represents an **ITypeLib** pointer.

Return Value

The LIBID (that is, the **Guid**) of the type library pointed to by the *pTLB* parameter.

Remarks

GetTypeLibGuid extracts the LIBID directly from an existing type library. This action differs from that of the **Marshal.GetTypeLibGuidForAssembly** method, which calculates what the LIBID should be based on the current assembly. For additional information about **ITypeLib**, see the MSDN Library.

> **Note** This method uses **SecurityAction.LinkDemand** to prevent it from being called from untrusted code; only the immediate caller is required to have **SecurityPermission-Attribute.UnmanagedCode** permission. If your code can be called from partially trusted code, do not pass user input to **Marshal** class methods without validation.

Requirements

Platforms: Windows 98, Windows NT 4.0, Windows Millennium Edition, Windows 2000, Windows XP Home Edition, Windows XP Professional, Windows .NET Server family

.NET Framework Security:

- **SecurityPermission** for operating with unmanaged code. Associated enumeration: **SecurityPermissionFlag.UnmanagedCode**.

Marshal.GetTypeLibGuidForAssembly Method

Retrieves the library identifier (LIBID) that is assigned to a type library when it was exported from the specified assembly.

```
[Visual Basic]
Public Shared Function GetTypeLibGuidForAssembly( _
   ByVal asm As Assembly _
) As Guid
[C#]
public static Guid GetTypeLibGuidForAssembly(
   Assembly asm
);
[C++]
public: static Guid GetTypeLibGuidForAssembly(
   Assembly* asm
);
[JScript]
public static function GetTypeLibGuidForAssembly(
   asm : Assembly
) : Guid;
```

Parameters

asm

A managed **Assembly**.

Return Value

The LIBID (that is, the **Guid**) that is assigned to a type library when it is exported from the *asm* parameter.

Remarks

When assemblies are exported to type libraries, the type library is assigned a LIBID. You can set the LIBID explicitly by applying the **System.Runtime.InteropServices.GuidAttribute** at the assembly level, or it can be generated automatically. The Type Library Exporter (Tlbexp.exe) calculates a LIBID value based on the identity of the assembly. **GetTypeLibGuid** returns the LIBID associated with the **GuidAttribute**, if the attribute is applied. Otherwise, **GetTypeLibGuidForAssembly** returns the calculated value. Alternatively, you can use the **Marshal.GetTypeLibGuid** method to extract the actual LIBID from an existing type library.

> **Note** This method uses **SecurityAction.LinkDemand** to prevent it from being called from untrusted code; only the immediate caller is required to have **SecurityPermission-Attribute.UnmanagedCode** permission. If your code can be called from partially trusted code, do not pass user input to **Marshal** class methods without validation.

Requirements

Platforms: Windows 98, Windows NT 4.0, Windows Millennium Edition, Windows 2000, Windows XP Home Edition, Windows XP Professional, Windows .NET Server family

.NET Framework Security:

- **SecurityPermission** for operating with unmanaged code. Associated enumeration: **SecurityPermissionFlag.UnmanagedCode**.

Marshal.GetTypeLibLcid Method

Retrieves the LCID of a type library.

```
[Visual Basic]
Public Shared Function GetTypeLibLcid( _
   ByVal pTLB As UCOMITypeLib _
) As Integer
[C#]
public static int GetTypeLibLcid(
   UCOMITypeLib pTLB
);
[C++]
public: static int GetTypeLibLcid(
   UCOMITypeLib* pTLB
);
[JScript]
public static function GetTypeLibLcid(
   pTLB : UCOMITypeLib
) : int;
```

Parameters

pTLB

A **UCOMITypeLib** that represents an **ITypeLib** pointer.

Return Value

The LCID of the type library pointed to by the *pTLB* parameter.

Remarks

> **Note** This method uses **SecurityAction.LinkDemand** to prevent it from being called from untrusted code; only the immediate caller is required to have **SecurityPermission-Attribute.UnmanagedCode** permission. If your code can be called from partially trusted code, do not pass user input to **Marshal** class methods without validation.

Requirements

Platforms: Windows 98, Windows NT 4.0, Windows Millennium Edition, Windows 2000, Windows XP Home Edition, Windows XP Professional, Windows .NET Server family

.NET Framework Security:

- **SecurityPermission** for operating with unmanaged code. Associated enumeration: **SecurityPermissionFlag.UnmanagedCode**.

Marshal.GetTypeLibName Method

Retrieves the name of a type library.

```
[Visual Basic]
Public Shared Function GetTypeLibName( _
   ByVal pTLB As UCOMITypeLib _
) As String
[C#]
public static string GetTypeLibName(
   UCOMITypeLib pTLB
);
[C++]
public: static String* GetTypeLibName(
   UCOMITypeLib* pTLB
);
[JScript]
public static function GetTypeLibName(
   pTLB : UCOMITypeLib
) : String;
```

Parameters

pTLB

A **UCOMITypeLib** that represents an **ITypeLib** pointer.

Return Value

The name of the type library pointed to by the *pTLB* parameter.

Remarks

The name returned by this method is the identifier used with the library statement, such as ADODB for the Microsoft ADO type library. The name is not a file name.

You can also retrieve the type library name by calling the **UCOMITypeInfo.GetDocumentation** method and passing a -1 for its first parameter.

> **Note** This method uses **SecurityAction.LinkDemand** to prevent it from being called from untrusted code; only the immediate caller is required to have **SecurityPermission-Attribute.UnmanagedCode** permission. If your code can be called from partially trusted code, do not pass user input to **Marshal** class methods without validation.

Requirements

Platforms: Windows 98, Windows NT 4.0, Windows Millennium Edition, Windows 2000, Windows XP Home Edition, Windows XP Professional, Windows .NET Server family

.NET Framework Security:

- **SecurityPermission** for operating with unmanaged code. Associated enumeration: **SecurityPermissionFlag.UnmanagedCode**.

Marshal.GetUnmanagedThunkForManagedMethodPtr Method

Gets a pointer to a thunk that marshals a call from unmanaged to managed code.

```
[Visual Basic]
Public Shared Function GetUnmanagedThunkForManagedMethodPtr( _
  ByVal pfnMethodToWrap As IntPtr, _
  ByVal pbSignature As IntPtr, _
  ByVal cbSignature As Integer _
) As IntPtr
[C#]
public static IntPtr GetUnmanagedThunkForManagedMethodPtr(
  IntPtr pfnMethodToWrap,
  IntPtr pbSignature,
  int cbSignature
);
[C++]
public: static IntPtr GetUnmanagedThunkForManagedMethodPtr(
  IntPtr pfnMethodToWrap,
  IntPtr pbSignature,
  int cbSignature
);
[JScript]
public static function GetUnmanagedThunkForManagedMethodPtr(
  pfnMethodToWrap : IntPtr,
  pbSignature : IntPtr,
  cbSignature : int
) : IntPtr;
```

Parameters

pfnMethodToWrap

A pointer to the method to marshal.

pbSignature

A pointer to the method signature.

cbSignature

The number of bytes in *pbSignature*.

Return Value

A pointer to the thunk that will marshal a call from *pfnMethodToWrap*.

Remarks

GetUnmanagedThunkForManagedMethodPtr is exposed for complier support only.

> **Note** This method uses **SecurityAction.LinkDemand** to prevent it from being called from untrusted code; only the immediate caller is required to have **SecurityPermission-Attribute.UnmanagedCode** permission. If your code can be called from partially trusted code, do not pass user input to **Marshal** class methods without validation.

Requirements

Platforms: Windows 98, Windows NT 4.0, Windows Millennium Edition, Windows 2000, Windows XP Home Edition, Windows XP Professional, Windows .NET Server family

.NET Framework Security:

- **SecurityPermission** for operating with unmanaged code. Associated enumeration: **SecurityPermissionFlag.UnmanagedCode**.

Marshal.IsComObject Method

Indicates whether a specified object represents a COM object.

```
[Visual Basic]
Public Shared Function IsComObject( _
  ByVal o As Object _
) As Boolean
[C#]
public static bool IsComObject(
  object o
);
[C++]
public: static bool IsComObject(
  Object* o
);
[JScript]
public static function IsComObject(
  o : Object
) : Boolean;
```

Parameters

o

The object to check.

Return Value

true if the *o* parameter is a COM type; otherwise, **false**.

Remarks

IsComObject returns **true** if the class type of the instance is attributed with **System.Runtime.InteropServices.ComImportAttribute** or if it derives directly or indirectly from a class attributed with **ComImportAttribute**. The Type Library Importer (Tlbimp.exe) applies this attribute for you when it imports a type library.

Two other methods also determine whether a specified object represents a COM object, but the requirements for returning **true** differ from this method's requirements. **Type.IsImport** returns **true** if the class (or interface) is attributed with **ComImportAttribute** directly; it does not return **true** for derived types. **RegistrationServices.TypeRepresentsComType** returns **true** if the type is attributed with **ComImportAttribute** or derives from a type with the same GUID.

> **Note** This method uses **SecurityAction.LinkDemand** to prevent it from being called from untrusted code; only the immediate caller is required to have **SecurityPermission-Attribute.UnmanagedCode** permission. If your code can be called from partially trusted code, do not pass user input to **Marshal** class methods without validation.

Requirements

Platforms: Windows 98, Windows NT 4.0, Windows Millennium Edition, Windows 2000, Windows XP Home Edition, Windows XP Professional, Windows .NET Server family, .NET Compact Framework - Windows CE .NET

.NET Framework Security:
- **SecurityPermission** for operating with unmanaged code. Associated enumeration: **SecurityPermissionFlag.UnmanagedCode**.

Marshal.IsTypeVisibleFromCom Method

Indicates whether a type is visible to COM clients.

```
[Visual Basic]
Public Shared Function IsTypeVisibleFromCom( _
   ByVal t As Type _
) As Boolean
[C#]
public static bool IsTypeVisibleFromCom(
   Type t
);
[C++]
public: static bool IsTypeVisibleFromCom(
   Type* t
);
[JScript]
public static function IsTypeVisibleFromCom(
   t : Type
) : Boolean;
```

Parameters

t

    The **Type** to check for COM visibility.

Return Value

true if the type is visible to COM; otherwise, **false**.

Remarks

IsTypeVisibleFromCom is useful because it enables you to check for COM visibility in one step. Types that are not visible cannot be used from COM. A type is visible if the type is **public** and is not otherwise hidden with the **System.Runtime.InteropServices.ComVisibleAttribute**.

> **Note** This method uses **SecurityAction.LinkDemand** to prevent it from being called from untrusted code; only the immediate caller is required to have **SecurityPermission-Attribute.UnmanagedCode** permission. If your code can be called from partially trusted code, do not pass user input to **Marshal** class methods without validation.

Requirements

Platforms: Windows 98, Windows NT 4.0, Windows Millennium Edition, Windows 2000, Windows XP Home Edition, Windows XP Professional, Windows .NET Server family

.NET Framework Security:
- **SecurityPermission** for operating with unmanaged code. Associated enumeration: **SecurityPermissionFlag.UnmanagedCode**.

Marshal.NumParamBytes Method

Calculates the number of bytes required to hold the parameters for the specified method.

```
[Visual Basic]
Public Shared Function NumParamBytes( _
   ByVal m As MethodInfo _
) As Integer
[C#]
public static int NumParamBytes(
   MethodInfo m
);
[C++]
public: static int NumParamBytes(
   MethodInfo* m
);
[JScript]
public static function NumParamBytes(
   m : MethodInfo
) : int;
```

Parameters

m

    A **MethodInfo** that identifies the method to be checked.

Return Value

The number of bytes required.

Remarks

NumParamBytes is exposed for complier support only.

> **Note** This method uses **SecurityAction.LinkDemand** to prevent it from being called from untrusted code; only the immediate caller is required to have **SecurityPermission-Attribute.UnmanagedCode** permission. If your code can be called from partially trusted code, do not pass user input to **Marshal** class methods without validation.

Requirements

Platforms: Windows 98, Windows NT 4.0,
Windows Millennium Edition, Windows 2000,
Windows XP Home Edition, Windows XP Professional,
Windows .NET Server family

.NET Framework Security:

- **SecurityPermission** for operating with unmanaged code.
  Associated enumeration:
  SecurityPermissionFlag.UnmanagedCode.

Marshal.OffsetOf Method

Returns the field offset of the unmanaged form of the managed class.

```
[Visual Basic]
Public Shared Function OffsetOf( _
   ByVal t As Type, _
   ByVal fieldName As String _
) As IntPtr
[C#]
public static IntPtr OffsetOf(
   Type t,
   string fieldName
);
[C++]
public: static IntPtr OffsetOf(
   Type* t,
   String* fieldName
);
[JScript]
public static function OffsetOf(
   t : Type,
   fieldName : String
) : IntPtr;
```

Parameters

t

A **Type**, specifying the specified class. You must apply the
StructLayoutAttribute to the class.

fieldName

The field within the *t* parameter.

Return Value

The offset, in bytes, for the *fieldName* parameter within the platform
invoke declared class *t*.

Exceptions

Exception Type	Condition
ArgumentException	The class cannot be exported as a structure or the field is nonpublic.

Remarks

OffsetOf provides the offset in terms of the unmanaged structure
layout, which does not necessarily correspond to the offset of the
managed structure layout. Marshaling the can transform the layout
and alter the offset. The *t* parameter can be a value type or a
formatted reference type (with either a sequential or explicit layout).
You can obtain the size of the entire layout by using the
Marshal.SizeOf method. For additional information, see **Default
Marshaling for Value Types**.

Note This method uses **SecurityAction.LinkDemand** to
prevent it from being called from untrusted code; only the
immediate caller is required to have **SecurityPermission-
Attribute.UnmanagedCode** permission. If your code can be
called from partially trusted code, do not pass user input to
Marshal class methods without validation.

Requirements

Platforms: Windows 98, Windows NT 4.0,
Windows Millennium Edition, Windows 2000,
Windows XP Home Edition, Windows XP Professional,
Windows .NET Server family

.NET Framework Security:

- **SecurityPermission** for operating with unmanaged code.
  Associated enumeration:
  SecurityPermissionFlag.UnmanagedCode.

Marshal.Prelink Method

Executes one-time method setup tasks without calling the method.

```
[Visual Basic]
Public Shared Sub Prelink( _
   ByVal m As MethodInfo _
)
[C#]
public static void Prelink(
   MethodInfo m
);
[C++]
public: static void Prelink(
   MethodInfo* m
);
[JScript]
public static function Prelink(
   m : MethodInfo
);
```

Parameters

m

A **System.Reflection.MethodInfo** that identifies the method to
be checked.

Remarks

Setup tasks provide early initialization and are performed
automatically when the target method is invoked. First-time tasks
include:

- Verifying that the platform invoke metadata is correctly
  formatted.
- Verifying that all the managed types are valid parameters of
  platform invoke functions.
- Locating and loading the unmanaged DLL into the process.
- Locating the entry point in the process.

Calling **Prelink** on a method outside of platform invoke has no
effect. To execute setup tasks on all platform invoke methods in a
type, use **Marshal.PrelinkAll**.

> **Note** This method uses **SecurityAction.LinkDemand** to prevent it from being called from untrusted code; only the immediate caller is required to have **SecurityPermission-Attribute.UnmanagedCode** permission. If your code can be called from partially trusted code, do not pass user input to **Marshal** class methods without validation.

Example

[Visual Basic, C#] The following example demonstrates using **Prelink** on an instance with a private static platform invoke signature for the **MessageBox** function from USER32.DLL.

```
[Visual Basic]
' Get a MethodInfo for the Private Shared Sub
Dim mi As MethodInfo = obj.GetType().GetMethod("MessageBox", _
  BindingFlags.Static Or BindingFlags.NonPublic)
' Call Prelink using the MethodInfo instance
Marshal.Prelink(mi)
```

```
[C#]
// Get a MethodInfo for the private static method
MethodInfo mi = obj.GetType().GetMethod("MessageBox",
  BindingFlags.Static | BindingFlags.NonPublic);
// Call Prelink using the MethodInfo instance
Marshal.Prelink(mi);
```

Requirements

Platforms: Windows 98, Windows NT 4.0, Windows Millennium Edition, Windows 2000, Windows XP Home Edition, Windows XP Professional, Windows .NET Server family

.NET Framework Security:

- **SecurityPermission** for operating with unmanaged code. Associated enumeration: **SecurityPermissionFlag.UnmanagedCode**.

Marshal.PrelinkAll Method

Performs a pre-link check for all methods on a class.

```
[Visual Basic]
Public Shared Sub PrelinkAll( _
  ByVal c As Type _
)
[C#]
public static void PrelinkAll(
  Type c
);
[C++]
public: static void PrelinkAll(
  Type* c
);
[JScript]
public static function PrelinkAll(
  c : Type
);
```

Parameters

c
    A **Type** that identifies the class whose methods are to be checked.

Exceptions

Exception Type	Condition
ArgumentNullException	*c* is not a valid type.

Remarks

The **PrelinkAll** method invokes **Marshal.Prelink** on every method for a given type. **Prelink** executes one-time method setup tasks without calling each method. You can only use **PrelinkAll** for platform invoke calls.

> **Note** This method uses **SecurityAction.LinkDemand** to prevent it from being called from untrusted code; only the immediate caller is required to have **SecurityPermission-Attribute.UnmanagedCode** permission. If your code can be called from partially trusted code, do not pass user input to **Marshal** class methods without validation.

Example

[Visual Basic, C#] The following example demonstrates how to use **PrelinkAll**.

```
[Visual Basic]
Marshal.PrelinkAll(obj.GetType())
```

```
[C#]
Marshal.PrelinkAll(obj.GetType());
```

[Visual Basic, C#]

Requirements

Platforms: Windows 98, Windows NT 4.0, Windows Millennium Edition, Windows 2000, Windows XP Home Edition, Windows XP Professional, Windows .NET Server family

.NET Framework Security:

- **SecurityPermission** for operating with unmanaged code. Associated enumeration: **SecurityPermissionFlag.UnmanagedCode**.

Marshal.PtrToStringAnsi Method

Allocates a managed **String** and copies all or part of an unmanaged ANSI string into it.

Overload List

Copies all characters up to the first null from an unmanaged ANSI string to a managed **String**. Widens each ANSI character to Unicode.

> [Visual Basic] **Overloads Public Shared Function PtrToStringAnsi(IntPtr) As String**
>
> [C#] **public static string PtrToStringAnsi(IntPtr);**
>
> [C++] **public: static String* PtrToStringAnsi(IntPtr);**
>
> [JScript] **public static function PtrToStringAnsi(IntPtr) : String;**

Allocates a managed **String**, copies a specified number of characters from an unmanaged ANSI string into it, and widens each ANSI character to Unicode.

> [Visual Basic] **Overloads Public Shared Function PtrToStringAnsi(IntPtr, Integer) As String**
>
> [C#] **public static string PtrToStringAnsi(IntPtr, int);**
>
> [C++] **public: static String* PtrToStringAnsi(IntPtr, int);**
>
> [JScript] **public static function PtrToStringAnsi(IntPtr, int) : String;**

Marshal.PtrToStringAnsi Method (IntPtr)

Copies all characters up to the first null from an unmanaged ANSI string to a managed **String**. Widens each ANSI character to Unicode.

```
[Visual Basic]
Overloads Public Shared Function PtrToStringAnsi( _
   ByVal ptr As IntPtr _
) As String
[C#]
public static string PtrToStringAnsi(
   IntPtr ptr
);
[C++]
public: static String* PtrToStringAnsi(
   IntPtr ptr
);
[JScript]
public static function PtrToStringAnsi(
   ptr : IntPtr
) : String;
```

Parameters

ptr
   The address of the first character of the unmanaged string.

Return Value

A managed **String** object that holds a copy of the unmanaged ANSI string.

Exceptions

Exception Type	Condition
ArgumentNullException	*ptr* is a null reference (**Nothing** in Visual Basic).

Remarks

PtrToStringAnsi is useful for custom marshaling or when mixing managed and unmanaged code. Since this method creates a copy of the unmanaged string's contents, you must free the original string as appropriate. This method provides the opposite functionality of **Marshal.StringToCoTaskMemAnsi** and **Marshal.StringToHGlobalAnsi**.

> **Note** This method uses **SecurityAction.LinkDemand** to prevent it from being called from untrusted code; only the immediate caller is required to have **SecurityPermission-Attribute.UnmanagedCode** permission. If your code can be called from partially trusted code, do not pass user input to **Marshal** class methods without validation.

Requirements

Platforms: Windows 98, Windows NT 4.0, Windows Millennium Edition, Windows 2000, Windows XP Home Edition, Windows XP Professional, Windows .NET Server family

.NET Framework Security:
- **SecurityPermission** for operating with unmanaged code. Associated enumeration: **SecurityPermissionFlag.UnmanagedCode**.

Marshal.PtrToStringAnsi Method (IntPtr, Int32)

Allocates a managed **String**, copies a specified number of characters from an unmanaged ANSI string into it, and widens each ANSI character to Unicode.

```
[Visual Basic]
Overloads Public Shared Function PtrToStringAnsi( _
   ByVal ptr As IntPtr, _
   ByVal len As Integer _
) As String
[C#]
public static string PtrToStringAnsi(
   IntPtr ptr,
   int len
);
[C++]
public: static String* PtrToStringAnsi(
   IntPtr ptr,
   int len
);
[JScript]
public static function PtrToStringAnsi(
   ptr : IntPtr,
   len : int
) : String;
```

Parameters

ptr
   The address of the first character of the unmanaged string.
len
   The byte count of the input string to copy.

Return Value

A managed **String** that holds a copy of the native ANSI string.

Exceptions

Exception Type	Condition
ArgumentException	*len* is less than zero.
ArgumentNullException	*ptr* is a null reference (**Nothing** in Visual Basic).

Remarks

PtrToStringAnsi is useful for custom marshaling or when mixing managed and unmanaged code. Since this method creates a copy of the unmanaged string's contents, you must free the original string as appropriate. This method provides the opposite functionality of **Marshal.StringToCoTaskMemAnsi** and **Marshal.StringToHGlobalAnsi**.

> **Note** This method uses **SecurityAction.LinkDemand** to prevent it from being called from untrusted code; only the immediate caller is required to have **SecurityPermission-Attribute.UnmanagedCode** permission. If your code can be called from partially trusted code, do not pass user input to **Marshal** class methods without validation.

Requirements

Platforms: Windows 98, Windows NT 4.0, Windows Millennium Edition, Windows 2000, Windows XP Home Edition, Windows XP Professional, Windows .NET Server family

.NET Framework Security:
- **SecurityPermission** for operating with unmanaged code. Associated enumeration: **SecurityPermissionFlag.UnmanagedCode.**

Marshal.PtrToStringAuto Method

Allocates a managed **String** and copies a specified number of characters from an unmanaged string into it.

Overload List

Allocates a managed **String** and copies all characters up to the first null character from a string stored in unmanaged memory into it.

[Visual Basic] **Overloads Public Shared Function PtrToStringAuto(IntPtr) As String**

[C#] **public static string PtrToStringAuto(IntPtr);**

[C++] **public: static String* PtrToStringAuto(IntPtr);**

[JScript] **public static function PtrToStringAuto(IntPtr) : String;**

Copies a specified number of characters from a string stored in unmanaged memory to a managed **String**.

[Visual Basic] **Overloads Public Shared Function PtrToStringAuto(IntPtr, Integer) As String**

[C#] **public static string PtrToStringAuto(IntPtr, int);**

[C++] **public: static String* PtrToStringAuto(IntPtr, int);**

[JScript] **public static function PtrToStringAuto(IntPtr, int) : String;**

Marshal.PtrToStringAuto Method (IntPtr)

Allocates a managed **String** and copies all characters up to the first null character from a string stored in unmanaged memory into it.

```
[Visual Basic]
Overloads Public Shared Function PtrToStringAuto( _
   ByVal ptr As IntPtr _
) As String
[C#]
public static string PtrToStringAuto(
   IntPtr ptr
);
[C++]
public: static String* PtrToStringAuto(
   IntPtr ptr
);
[JScript]
public static function PtrToStringAuto(
   ptr : IntPtr
) : String;
```

Parameters

ptr

For Unicode platforms, the address of the first Unicode character.

-or-

For ANSI platforms, the address of the first ANSI character.

Return Value

A managed string that holds a copy of the unmanaged string.

Exceptions

Exception Type	Condition
ArgumentNullException	*ptr* is a null reference (**Nothing** in Visual Basic).

Remarks

If the current platform is Unicode, each ANSI character is widened to a Unicode character and this method calls **PtrToStringUni**. Otherwise this method calls **PtrToStringAnsi**.

PtrToStringAuto is useful for custom marshaling or when mixing managed and unmanaged code. Since this method creates a copy of the unmanaged string's contents, you must free the original string as appropriate. **PtrToStringAnsi** provides the opposite functionality of **Marshal.StringToCoTaskMemAuto** and **Marshal.StringToHGlobalAuto.**

> **Note** This method uses **SecurityAction.LinkDemand** to prevent it from being called from untrusted code; only the immediate caller is required to have **SecurityPermission-Attribute.UnmanagedCode** permission. If your code can be called from partially trusted code, do not pass user input to **Marshal** class methods without validation.

Requirements

Platforms: Windows 98, Windows NT 4.0, Windows Millennium Edition, Windows 2000, Windows XP Home Edition, Windows XP Professional, Windows .NET Server family

.NET Framework Security:
- **SecurityPermission** for operating with unmanaged code. Associated enumeration: **SecurityPermissionFlag.UnmanagedCode.**

Marshal.PtrToStringAuto Method (IntPtr, Int32)

Copies a specified number of characters from a string stored in unmanaged memory to a managed **String**.

```
[Visual Basic]
Overloads Public Shared Function PtrToStringAuto( _
   ByVal ptr As IntPtr, _
   ByVal len As Integer _
) As String
[C#]
public static string PtrToStringAuto(
   IntPtr ptr,
   int len
);
[C++]
public: static String* PtrToStringAuto(
   IntPtr ptr,
   int len
);
[JScript]
public static function PtrToStringAuto(
   ptr : IntPtr,
   len : int
) : String;
```

Parameters

ptr

For Unicode platforms, the address of the first Unicode character.
-or-
For ANSI platforms, the address of the first ANSI character.

len

The number of characters to copy.

Return Value

A managed string that holds a copy of the native string.

Exceptions

Exception Type	Condition
ArgumentException	*len* is less than zero.
ArgumentNullException	*ptr* is a null reference (**Nothing** in Visual Basic).

Remarks

On Unicode platforms, this method calls **PtrToStringUni**; on ANSI platforms, it calls **PtrToStringAnsi**. No transformations are done before these methods are called.

PtrToStringAuto is useful for custom marshaling or when mixing managed and unmanaged code. Since this method creates a copy of the unmanaged string's contents, you must free the original string as appropriate. **PtrToStringAnsi** provides the opposite functionality of **Marshal.StringToCoTaskMemAuto** and **Marshal.StringToHGlobalAuto**.

> **Note** This method uses **SecurityAction.LinkDemand** to prevent it from being called from untrusted code; only the immediate caller is required to have **SecurityPermission-Attribute.UnmanagedCode** permission. If your code can be called from partially trusted code, do not pass user input to **Marshal** class methods without validation.

Requirements

Platforms: Windows 98, Windows NT 4.0, Windows Millennium Edition, Windows 2000, Windows XP Home Edition, Windows XP Professional, Windows .NET Server family

.NET Framework Security:

- **SecurityPermission** for operating with unmanaged code. Associated enumeration: **SecurityPermissionFlag.UnmanagedCode**.

Marshal.PtrToStringBSTR Method

Allocates a managed **String** and copies a BSTR string stored in unmanaged memory into it.

```
[Visual Basic]
Public Shared Function PtrToStringBSTR( _
   ByVal ptr As IntPtr _
) As String
[C#]
public static string PtrToStringBSTR(
   IntPtr ptr
);
```

```
[C++]
public: static String* PtrToStringBSTR(
   IntPtr ptr
);
[JScript]
public static function PtrToStringBSTR(
   ptr : IntPtr
) : String;
```

Parameters

ptr

The address of the first character of the unmanaged string.

Return Value

A managed string that holds a copy of the native string.

Exceptions

Exception Type	Condition
ArgumentNullException	*ptr* is a null reference (**Nothing** in Visual Basic).

Remarks

Only call this method on strings allocated with the unmanaged **SysAllocString** and **SysAllocStringLen** functions.

PtrToStringBSTR is useful for custom marshaling or when mixing managed and unmanaged code. Since this method creates a copy of the unmanaged string's contents, you must free the original string as appropriate. This method provides the opposite functionality of **Marshal.StringToBSTR**.

> **Note** This method uses **SecurityAction.LinkDemand** to prevent it from being called from untrusted code; only the immediate caller is required to have **SecurityPermission-Attribute.UnmanagedCode** permission. If your code can be called from partially trusted code, do not pass user input to **Marshal** class methods without validation.

Requirements

Platforms: Windows 98, Windows NT 4.0, Windows Millennium Edition, Windows 2000, Windows XP Home Edition, Windows XP Professional, Windows .NET Server family

.NET Framework Security:

- **SecurityPermission** for operating with unmanaged code. Associated enumeration: **SecurityPermissionFlag.UnmanagedCode**.

Marshal.PtrToStringUni Method

Allocates a managed **String** and copies a specified number of characters from an unmanaged Unicode string into it.

Overload List

Allocates a managed **String** and copies all characters up to the first null character from an unmanaged Unicode string into it.

Supported by the .NET Compact Framework.

[Visual Basic] **Overloads Public Shared Function PtrToStringUni(IntPtr) As String**

[C#] **public static string PtrToStringUni(IntPtr);**

[C++] **public: static String* PtrToStringUni(IntPtr);**

[JScript] **public static function PtrToStringUni(IntPtr) : String;**

Copies a specified number of characters from a Unicode string stored in native heap to a managed **String**.

Supported by the .NET Compact Framework.

> [Visual Basic] **Overloads Public Shared Function PtrToStringUni(IntPtr, Integer) As String**
>
> [C#] **public static string PtrToStringUni(IntPtr, int);**
>
> [C++] **public: static String* PtrToStringUni(IntPtr, int);**
>
> [JScript] **public static function PtrToStringUni(IntPtr, int) : String;**

Marshal.PtrToStringUni Method (IntPtr)

Allocates a managed **String** and copies all characters up to the first null character from an unmanaged Unicode string into it.

```
[Visual Basic]
Overloads Public Shared Function PtrToStringUni( _
   ByVal ptr As IntPtr _
) As String
[C#]
public static string PtrToStringUni(
   IntPtr ptr
);
[C++]
public: static String* PtrToStringUni(
   IntPtr ptr
);
[JScript]
public static function PtrToStringUni(
   ptr : IntPtr
) : String;
```

Parameters

ptr

> The address of the first character of the unmanaged string.

Return Value

A managed string holding a copy of the native string.

Exceptions

Exception Type	Condition
ArgumentNullException	*ptr* is a null reference (**Nothing** in Visual Basic).

Remarks

PtrToStringUni is useful for custom marshaling or for use when mixing managed and unmanaged code. Since this method creates a copy of the unmanaged string's contents, you must free the original string as appropriate. This method provides the opposite functionality of **Marshal.StringToCoTaskMemUni** and **Marshal.StringToHGlobalUni**.

> **Note** This method uses **SecurityAction.LinkDemand** to prevent it from being called from untrusted code; only the immediate caller is required to have **SecurityPermission-Attribute.UnmanagedCode** permission. If your code can be called from partially trusted code, do not pass user input to **Marshal** class methods without validation.

Requirements

Platforms: Windows 98, Windows NT 4.0, Windows Millennium Edition, Windows 2000, Windows XP Home Edition, Windows XP Professional, Windows .NET Server family, .NET Compact Framework - Windows CE .NET

.NET Framework Security:

* **SecurityPermission** for operating with unmanaged code. Associated enumeration: **SecurityPermissionFlag.UnmanagedCode**.

Marshal.PtrToStringUni Method (IntPtr, Int32)

Copies a specified number of characters from a Unicode string stored in native heap to a managed **String**.

```
[Visual Basic]
Overloads Public Shared Function PtrToStringUni( _
   ByVal ptr As IntPtr, _
   ByVal len As Integer _
) As String
[C#]
public static string PtrToStringUni(
   IntPtr ptr,
   int len
);
[C++]
public: static String* PtrToStringUni(
   IntPtr ptr,
   int len
);
[JScript]
public static function PtrToStringUni(
   ptr : IntPtr,
   len : int
) : String;
```

Parameters

ptr

> The address of the first character of the unmanaged string.

len

> The number of Unicode characters to copy.

Return Value

A managed string that holds a copy of the native string.

Exceptions

Exception Type	Condition
ArgumentException	*len* is less than zero.
ArgumentNullException	*ptr* is a null reference (**Nothing** in Visual Basic).

Remarks

PtrToStringUni is useful for custom marshaling or when mixing managed and unmanaged code. Since this method creates a copy of the unmanaged string's contents, you must free the original string as appropriate. This method provides the opposite functionality of **Marshal.StringToCoTaskMemUni** and **Marshal.StringToHGlobalUni**.

> **Note** This method uses **SecurityAction.LinkDemand** to prevent it from being called from untrusted code; only the immediate caller is required to have **SecurityPermission-Attribute.UnmanagedCode** permission. If your code can be called from partially trusted code, do not pass user input to **Marshal** class methods without validation.

Requirements

Platforms: Windows 98, Windows NT 4.0,
Windows Millennium Edition, Windows 2000,
Windows XP Home Edition, Windows XP Professional,
Windows .NET Server family,
.NET Compact Framework - Windows CE .NET

.NET Framework Security:

• **SecurityPermission** for operating with unmanaged code.
Associated enumeration:
SecurityPermissionFlag.UnmanagedCode.

Marshal.PtrToStructure Method

Marshals data from an unmanaged block of memory to a managed object.

Overload List

Marshals data from an unmanaged block of memory to a managed object.

Supported by the .NET Compact Framework.

[Visual Basic] **Overloads Public Shared Sub PtrToStructure(IntPtr, Object)**

[C#] **public static void PtrToStructure(IntPtr, object);**

[C++] **public: static void PtrToStructure(IntPtr, Object*);**

[JScript] **public static function PtrToStructure(IntPtr, Object);**

Marshals data from an unmanaged block of memory to a newly allocated managed object of the specified type.

Supported by the .NET Compact Framework.

[Visual Basic] **Overloads Public Shared Function PtrToStructure(IntPtr, Type) As Object**

[C#] **public static object PtrToStructure(IntPtr, Type);**

[C++] **public: static Object* PtrToStructure(IntPtr, Type*);**

[JScript] **public static function PtrToStructure(IntPtr, Type) : Object;**

Example

[Visual Basic, C#] The following example demonstrates using **PtrToStructure** after calling **UCOMITypeInfo.GetTypeAttr** to obtain a **TYPEATTR** structure. **GetTypeAttr** is defined with a by-reference **IntPtr** parameter because the unmanaged signature's **TYPEATTR**** parameter is not supported by the interop marshaler.

> [Visual Basic, C#] **Note** This example shows how to use one of the overloaded versions of **PtrToStructure**. For other examples that might be available, see the individual overload topics.

```
[Visual Basic]
Dim typeInfo As UCOMITypeInfo = ...
Dim ptr As IntPtr = IntPtr.Zero
typeInfo.GetTypeAttr(ptr)
Dim attr As TYPEATTR = _
  CType(Marshal.PtrToStructure(ptr, GetType(TYPEATTR)), TYPEATTR)
```

```
[C#]
UCOMITypeInfo typeInfo = ...;
IntPtr ptr = IntPtr.Zero;
typeInfo.GetTypeAttr(ref ptr);
TYPEATTR attr = (TYPEATTR)Marshal.PtrToStructure(ptr,
    typeof(TYPEATTR));
```

Marshal.PtrToStructure Method (IntPtr, Object)

Marshals data from an unmanaged block of memory to a managed object.

```
[Visual Basic]
Overloads Public Shared Sub PtrToStructure( _
   ByVal ptr As IntPtr, _
   ByVal structure As Object _
)
[C#]
public static void PtrToStructure(
   IntPtr ptr,
   object structure
);
[C++]
public: static void PtrToStructure(
   IntPtr ptr,
   Object* structure
);
[JScript]
public static function PtrToStructure(
   ptr : IntPtr,
   structure : Object
);
```

Parameters

ptr
> A pointer to an unmanaged block of memory.

structure
> The object to which the data is to be copied. This must be an instance of a formatted class.

Exceptions

Exception Type	Condition
ArgumentException	Structure layout is not sequential or explicit. -or- Structure is a boxed value type.

Remarks

PtrToStructure is often necessary in COM interop and platform invoke when structure parameters are represented as an **System.IntPtr** value. You cannot use this overload method with value types.

> **Note** This method uses **SecurityAction.LinkDemand** to prevent it from being called from untrusted code; only the immediate caller is required to have **SecurityPermission-Attribute.UnmanagedCode** permission. If your code can be called from partially trusted code, do not pass user input to **Marshal** class methods without validation.

Requirements

Platforms: Windows 98, Windows NT 4.0,
Windows Millennium Edition, Windows 2000,
Windows XP Home Edition, Windows XP Professional,
Windows .NET Server family,
.NET Compact Framework - Windows CE .NET

.NET Framework Security:

• **SecurityPermission** for operating with unmanaged code.
Associated enumeration:
SecurityPermissionFlag.UnmanagedCode.

Marshal.PtrToStructure Method (IntPtr, Type)

Marshals data from an unmanaged block of memory to a newly allocated managed object of the specified type.

```
[Visual Basic]
Overloads Public Shared Function PtrToStructure( _
   ByVal ptr As IntPtr, _
   ByVal structureType As Type _
) As Object
[C#]
public static object PtrToStructure(
   IntPtr ptr,
   Type structureType
);
[C++]
public: static Object* PtrToStructure(
   IntPtr ptr,
   Type* structureType
);
[JScript]
public static function PtrToStructure(
   ptr : IntPtr,
   structureType : Type
) : Object;
```

Parameters

ptr

A pointer to an unmanaged block of memory.

structureType

The **Type** of object to be created. This type object must represent a formatted class or a structure.

Return Value

A managed object containing the data pointed to by the *ptr* parameter.

Exceptions

Exception Type	Condition
ArgumentException	*structureType* layout is not sequential or explicit.

Remarks

PtrToStructure is often necessary in COM interop and platform invoke when structure parameters are represented as an **System.IntPtr** value. You can pass a value type to this overload method. In this case, the returned object is a boxed instance.

> **Note** This method uses **SecurityAction.LinkDemand** to prevent it from being called from untrusted code; only the immediate caller is required to have **SecurityPermission-Attribute.UnmanagedCode** permission. If your code can be called from partially trusted code, do not pass user input to **Marshal** class methods without validation.

Example

[Visual Basic, C#] The following example demonstrates using **PtrToStructure** after calling **UCOMITypeInfo.GetTypeAttr** to obtain a **TYPEATTR** structure. **GetTypeAttr** is defined with a by-reference **IntPtr** parameter because the unmanaged signature's **TYPEATTR**** parameter is not supported by the interop marshaler.

```
[Visual Basic]
Dim typeInfo As UCOMITypeInfo = ...
Dim ptr As IntPtr = IntPtr.Zero
typeInfo.GetTypeAttr(ptr)
Dim attr As TYPEATTR = _
   CType(Marshal.PtrToStructure(ptr, GetType(TYPEATTR)), TYPEATTR)

[C#]
UCOMITypeInfo typeInfo = ...;
IntPtr ptr = IntPtr.Zero;
typeInfo.GetTypeAttr(ref ptr);
TYPEATTR attr = (TYPEATTR)Marshal.PtrToStructure(ptr,
   typeof(TYPEATTR));
```

Requirements

Platforms: Windows 98, Windows NT 4.0, Windows Millennium Edition, Windows 2000, Windows XP Home Edition, Windows XP Professional, Windows .NET Server family, .NET Compact Framework - Windows CE .NET

.NET Framework Security:

- **SecurityPermission** for operating with unmanaged code. Associated enumeration: **SecurityPermissionFlag.UnmanagedCode**.

Marshal.QueryInterface Method

Requests a pointer to a specified interface from a COM object.

```
[Visual Basic]
Public Shared Function QueryInterface( _
   ByVal pUnk As IntPtr, _
   ByRef iid As Guid, _
   <Out()> ByRef ppv As IntPtr _
) As Integer
[C#]
public static int QueryInterface(
   IntPtr pUnk,
   ref Guid iid,
   out IntPtr ppv
);
[C++]
public: static int QueryInterface(
   IntPtr pUnk,
   Guid* iid,
   [
   Out
] IntPtr* ppv
);
[JScript]
public static function QueryInterface(
   pUnk : IntPtr,
   iid : Guid,
   ppv : IntPtr
) : int;
```

Parameters

pUnk

The interface to be queried.

iid

A **Guid**, passed by reference, that is the interface identifier (IID) of the requested interface.

ppv

When this method returns, contains a reference to the returned interface.

Return Value

The returned interface.

Remarks

The **QueryInterface** method exposes the
IUnknown::QueryInterface of a COM object, which attempts to
obtain a specific interface pointer. Using **QueryInterface** on a COM
object is the same as performing a cast operation in managed code.
Calling an object with this method causes the reference count to
increment on the interface pointer before the pointer is returned.
Always use **Marshal.Release** to decrement the reference count once
you have finished with the pointer. To obtain an **IntPtr** value that
represents a **IUnknown** interface pointer, you can call **Marshal.Get-
ComInterfaceForObject**, **Marshal.GetIUnknownForObject**, or
Marshal.GetIDispatchForObject.

> **Note** This method uses **SecurityAction.LinkDemand** to
> prevent it from being called from untrusted code; only the
> immediate caller is required to have **SecurityPermission-
> Attribute.UnmanagedCode** permission. If your code can be
> called from partially trusted code, do not pass user input to
> **Marshal** class methods without validation.

Requirements

Platforms: Windows 98, Windows NT 4.0,
Windows Millennium Edition, Windows 2000,
Windows XP Home Edition, Windows XP Professional,
Windows .NET Server family

.NET Framework Security:

- **SecurityPermission** for operating with unmanaged code.
  Associated enumeration:
  SecurityPermissionFlag.UnmanagedCode.

Marshal.ReadByte Method

Reads a single byte from an unmanaged pointer.

Overload List

Reads a single byte from an unmanaged pointer.

Supported by the .NET Compact Framework.

[Visual Basic] **Overloads Public Shared Function
ReadByte(IntPtr) As Byte**

[C#] **public static byte ReadByte(IntPtr);**

[C++] **public: static unsigned char ReadByte(IntPtr);**

[JScript] **public static function ReadByte(IntPtr) : Byte;**

Reads a single byte at a given offset (or index) from an unmanaged
pointer.

Supported by the .NET Compact Framework.

[Visual Basic] **Overloads Public Shared Function
ReadByte(IntPtr, Integer) As Byte**

[C#] **public static byte ReadByte(IntPtr, int);**

[C++] **public: static unsigned char ReadByte(IntPtr, int);**

[JScript] **public static function ReadByte(IntPtr, int) : Byte;**

Reads a single byte from an unmanaged pointer.

[Visual Basic] **Overloads Public Shared Function
ReadByte(Object, Integer) As Byte**

[C#] **public static byte ReadByte(object, int);**

[C++] **public: static unsigned char ReadByte(Object, int);**

[JScript] **public static function ReadByte(Object, int) : Byte;**

Example

[Visual Basic, C#] The following example compares two ways of
interacting with an unmanaged C-style byte array. The **ReadByte**
method provides direct access to the element values of the array.

> [Visual Basic, C#] **Note** This example shows how to use one of
> the overloaded versions of **ReadByte**. For other examples that
> might be available, see the individual overload topics.

```
[Visual Basic]
Dim unmanagedArray As IntPtr = ...
Dim i As Integer
' One way to print the 10 elements of the C-style unmanagedArray
Dim newArray As Byte(9)
Marshal.Copy(unmanagedArray, newArray, 0, 10)
For i = 0 To newArray.Length
  Console.WriteLine(newArray(i))
Next i
' Another way to print the 10 elements of the C-style unmanagedArray
For i = 0 To 10
  Console.WriteLine(Marshal.ReadByte(unmanagedArray, i))
Next i
```

```
[C#]
IntPtr unmanagedArray = ...;
// One way to print the 10 elements of the C-style unmanagedArray
byte [] newArray = new byte[10];
Marshal.Copy(unmanagedArray, newArray, 0, 10);
for (int i = 0; i < newArray.Length; i++)
  Console.WriteLine(newArray[i]);
// Another way to print the 10 elements of the C-style unmanagedArray
for (int i = 0; i < 10; i++)
  Console.WriteLine(Marshal.ReadByte(unmanagedArray, i));
```

Marshal.ReadByte Method (IntPtr)

Reads a single byte from an unmanaged pointer.

```
[Visual Basic]
Overloads Public Shared Function ReadByte( _
   ByVal ptr As IntPtr _
) As Byte
[C#]
public static byte ReadByte(
   IntPtr ptr
);
[C++]
public: static unsigned char ReadByte(
   IntPtr ptr
);
[JScript]
public static function ReadByte(
   ptr : IntPtr
) : Byte;
```

Parameters

ptr
   The address in unmanaged memory from which to read.

Return Value

The byte read from the *ptr* parameter.

Exceptions

Exception Type	Condition
ArgumentException	*ptr* is not a recognized format.

Remarks

ReadByte has an implied offset of 0. This method enables direct interaction with an unmanaged C-style byte array, eliminating the expense of copying an entire unmanaged array (using **Marshal.Copy**) to a separate managed array before reading its element values.

> **Note** This method uses **SecurityAction.LinkDemand** to prevent it from being called from untrusted code; only the immediate caller is required to have **SecurityPermission-Attribute.UnmanagedCode** permission. If your code can be called from partially trusted code, do not pass user input to **Marshal** class methods without validation.

Requirements

Platforms: Windows 98, Windows NT 4.0, Windows Millennium Edition, Windows 2000, Windows XP Home Edition, Windows XP Professional, Windows .NET Server family, .NET Compact Framework - Windows CE .NET

.NET Framework Security:

- **SecurityPermission** for operating with unmanaged code. Associated enumeration: **SecurityPermissionFlag.UnmanagedCode**.

Marshal.ReadByte Method (IntPtr, Int32)

Reads a single byte at a given offset (or index) from an unmanaged pointer.

```
[Visual Basic]
Overloads Public Shared Function ReadByte( _
   ByVal ptr As IntPtr, _
   ByVal ofs As Integer _
) As Byte
[C#]
public static byte ReadByte(
   IntPtr ptr,
   int ofs
);
[C++]
public: static unsigned char ReadByte(
   IntPtr ptr,
   int ofs
);
[JScript]
public static function ReadByte(
   ptr : IntPtr,
   ofs : int
) : Byte;
```

Parameters

ptr

  The base address in unmanaged memory from which to read.

ofs

  An additional byte offset, added to the *ptr* parameter before reading.

Return Value

The byte read from the *ptr* parameter.

Exceptions

Exception Type	Condition
ArgumentException	*ptr* is not a recognized format.

Remarks

ReadByte enables direct interaction with an unmanaged C-style byte array, eliminating the expense of copying an entire unmanaged array (using **Marshal.Copy**) to a separate managed array before reading its element values.

> **Note** This method uses **SecurityAction.LinkDemand** to prevent it from being called from untrusted code; only the immediate caller is required to have **SecurityPermission-Attribute.UnmanagedCode** permission. If your code can be called from partially trusted code, do not pass user input to **Marshal** class methods without validation.

Example

[Visual Basic, C#] The following example compares two ways of interacting with an unmanaged C-style byte array. The **ReadByte** method provides direct access to the element values of the array.

```
[Visual Basic]
Dim unmanagedArray As IntPtr = ...
Dim i As Integer
' One way to print the 10 elements of the C-style unmanagedArray
Dim newArray As Byte(9)
Marshal.Copy(unmanagedArray, newArray, 0, 10)
For i = 0 To newArray.Length
   Console.WriteLine(newArray(i))
Next i
' Another way to print the 10 elements of the C-style unmanagedArray
For i = 0 To 10
   Console.WriteLine(Marshal.ReadByte(unmanagedArray, i))
Next i
```

```
[C#]
IntPtr unmanagedArray = ...;
// One way to print the 10 elements of the C-style unmanagedArray
byte [] newArray = new byte[10];
Marshal.Copy(unmanagedArray, newArray, 0, 10);
for (int i = 0; i < newArray.Length; i++)
   Console.WriteLine(newArray[i]);
// Another way to print the 10 elements of the C-style unmanagedArray
for (int i = 0; i < 10; i++)
   Console.WriteLine(Marshal.ReadByte(unmanagedArray, i));
```

Requirements

Platforms: Windows 98, Windows NT 4.0, Windows Millennium Edition, Windows 2000, Windows XP Home Edition, Windows XP Professional, Windows .NET Server family, .NET Compact Framework - Windows CE .NET

Marshal.ReadByte Method (Object, Int32)

Reads a single byte from an unmanaged pointer.

```
[Visual Basic]
Overloads Public Shared Function ReadByte( _
   <InteropServices.In()> ByVal ptr As Object, _
   ByVal ofs As Integer _
) As Byte
[C#]
public static byte ReadByte(
   [
   In
] object ptr,
   int ofs
);
```

```
[C++]
public: static unsigned char ReadByte(
   [
    In
] Object* ptr,
    int ofs
);
[JScript]
public static function ReadByte(
    ptr : Object,
    ofs : int
) : Byte;
```

Parameters

ptr
   The base address in unmanaged memory of the source object.

ofs
   An additional byte offset, added to the *ptr* parameter before reading.

Return Value

The byte read from the *ptr* parameter.

Exceptions

Exception Type	Condition
ArgumentException	*ptr* is not a recognized format.

Remarks

ReadByte enables direct interaction with an unmanaged C-style byte array, eliminating the expense of copying an entire unmanaged array (using **Marshal.Copy**) to a separate managed array before reading its element values.

> **Note** This method uses **SecurityAction.LinkDemand** to prevent it from being called from untrusted code; only the immediate caller is required to have **SecurityPermission-Attribute.UnmanagedCode** permission. If your code can be called from partially trusted code, do not pass user input to **Marshal** class methods without validation.

Requirements

Platforms: Windows 98, Windows NT 4.0, Windows Millennium Edition, Windows 2000, Windows XP Home Edition, Windows XP Professional, Windows .NET Server family

Marshal.ReadInt16 Method

Reads a 16-bit signed integer from unmanaged memory.

Overload List

Reads a 16-bit signed integer from the unmanaged memory.

Supported by the .NET Compact Framework.

[Visual Basic] **Overloads Public Shared Function ReadInt16(IntPtr) As Short**
[C#] **public static short ReadInt16(IntPtr);**
[C++] **public: static short ReadInt16(IntPtr);**
[JScript] **public static function ReadInt16(IntPtr) : Int16;**

Reads a 16-bit signed integer from unmanaged memory.

Supported by the .NET Compact Framework.

[Visual Basic] **Overloads Public Shared Function ReadInt16(IntPtr, Integer) As Short**

[C#] **public static short ReadInt16(IntPtr, int);**
[C++] **public: static short ReadInt16(IntPtr, int);**
[JScript] **public static function ReadInt16(IntPtr, int) : Int16;**

Reads a 16-bit signed integer from unmanaged memory.

[Visual Basic] **Overloads Public Shared Function ReadInt16(Object, Integer) As Short**
[C#] **public static short ReadInt16(object, int);**
[C++] **public: static short ReadInt16(Object, int);**
[JScript] **public static function ReadInt16(Object, int) : Int16;**

Example

[Visual Basic, C#] The following example compares two ways of interacting with an unmanaged C-style Int16 array. The **ReadInt16** method provides direct access to the array's element values.

> [Visual Basic, C#] **Note** This example shows how to use one of the overloaded versions of **ReadInt16**. For other examples that might be available, see the individual overload topics.

```
[Visual Basic]
Dim unmanagedArray As IntPtr = ...
Dim i As Integer
' One way to print the 10 elements of the C-style unmanagedArray
Dim newArray As Int16(9)
Marshal.Copy(unmanagedArray, newArray, 0, 10)
For i = 0 To newArray.Length
   Console.WriteLine(newArray(i))
Next i
' Another way to print the 10 elements of the C-style unmanagedArray
For i = 0 To 10
   Console.WriteLine(Marshal.ReadInt16(unmanagedArray, i))
Next i
```

```
[C#]
IntPtr unmanagedArray = ...;
// One way to print the 10 elements of the C-style unmanagedArray
byte [] newArray = new Int16[10];
Marshal.Copy(unmanagedArray, newArray, 0, 10);
for (int i = 0; i < newArray.Length; i++)
   Console.WriteLine(newArray[i]);
// Another way to print the 10 elements of the C-style unmanagedArray
for (int i = 0; i < 10; i++)
   Console.WriteLine(Marshal.ReadInt16(unmanagedArray, i));
```

Marshal.ReadInt16 Method (IntPtr)

Reads a 16-bit signed integer from the unmanaged memory.

```
[Visual Basic]
Overloads Public Shared Function ReadInt16( _
   ByVal ptr As IntPtr _
) As Short
[C#]
public static short ReadInt16(
   IntPtr ptr
);
[C++]
public: static short ReadInt16(
   IntPtr ptr
);
[JScript]
public static function ReadInt16(
   ptr : IntPtr
) : Int16;
```

Parameters

ptr

The address in unmanaged memory from which to read.

Return Value

The 16-bit signed integer read from the *ptr* parameter.

Exceptions

Exception Type	Condition
ArgumentException	*ptr* is not a recognized format.

Remarks

ReadInt16 has an implied offset of 0. This method enables direct interaction with an unmanaged C-style Int16 array, eliminating the expense of copying an entire unmanaged array (using **Marshal.Copy**) to a separate managed array before reading its element values.

> **Note** This method uses **SecurityAction.LinkDemand** to prevent it from being called from untrusted code; only the immediate caller is required to have **SecurityPermission-Attribute.UnmanagedCode** permission. If your code can be called from partially trusted code, do not pass user input to **Marshal** class methods without validation.

Requirements

Platforms: Windows 98, Windows NT 4.0, Windows Millennium Edition, Windows 2000, Windows XP Home Edition, Windows XP Professional, Windows .NET Server family, .NET Compact Framework - Windows CE .NET

.NET Framework Security:

- **SecurityPermission** for operating with unmanaged code. Associated enumeration: **SecurityPermissionFlag.UnmanagedCode**.

Marshal.ReadInt16 Method (IntPtr, Int32)

Reads a 16-bit signed integer from unmanaged memory.

```
[Visual Basic]
Overloads Public Shared Function ReadInt16( _
   ByVal ptr As IntPtr, _
   ByVal ofs As Integer _
) As Short
[C#]
public static short ReadInt16(
   IntPtr ptr,
   int ofs
);
[C++]
public: static short ReadInt16(
   IntPtr ptr,
   int ofs
);
[JScript]
public static function ReadInt16(
   ptr : IntPtr,
   ofs : int
) : Int16;
```

Parameters

ptr

The base address in unmanaged memory from which to read.

ofs

An additional byte offset, added to the *ptr* parameter before reading.

Return Value

The 16-bit signed integer read from *ptr*.

Exceptions

Exception Type	Condition
ArgumentException	*ptr* is not a recognized format.

Remarks

ReadInt16 enables direct interaction with an unmanaged 16-bit signed array, eliminating the expense of copying an entire unmanaged array (using **Marshal.Copy**) to a separate managed array before reading its element values.

> **Note** This method uses **SecurityAction.LinkDemand** to prevent it from being called from untrusted code; only the immediate caller is required to have **SecurityPermission-Attribute.UnmanagedCode** permission. If your code can be called from partially trusted code, do not pass user input to **Marshal** class methods without validation.

Example

[Visual Basic, C#] The following example compares two ways of interacting with an unmanaged C-style Int16 array. The **ReadInt16** method provides direct access to the array's element values.

```
[Visual Basic]
Dim unmanagedArray As IntPtr = ...
Dim i As Integer
' One way to print the 10 elements of the C-style unmanagedArray
Dim newArray As Int16(9)
Marshal.Copy(unmanagedArray, newArray, 0, 10)
For i = 0 To newArray.Length
  Console.WriteLine(newArray(i))
Next i
' Another way to print the 10 elements of the C-style unmanagedArray
For i = 0 To 10
  Console.WriteLine(Marshal.ReadInt16(unmanagedArray, i))
Next i

[C#]
IntPtr unmanagedArray = ...;
// One way to print the 10 elements of the C-style unmanagedArray
byte [] newArray = new Int16[10];
Marshal.Copy(unmanagedArray, newArray, 0, 10);
for (int i = 0; i < newArray.Length; i++)
  Console.WriteLine(newArray[i]);
// Another way to print the 10 elements of the C-style unmanagedArray
for (int i = 0; i < 10; i++)
  Console.WriteLine(Marshal.ReadInt16(unmanagedArray, i));
```

Requirements

Platforms: Windows 98, Windows NT 4.0, Windows Millennium Edition, Windows 2000, Windows XP Home Edition, Windows XP Professional, Windows .NET Server family, .NET Compact Framework - Windows CE .NET

Marshal.ReadInt16 Method (Object, Int32)

Reads a 16-bit signed integer from unmanaged memory.

```
[Visual Basic]
Overloads Public Shared Function ReadInt16( _
    <InteropServices.In()> ByVal ptr As Object, _
    ByVal ofs As Integer _
) As Short
[C#]
public static short ReadInt16(
    [
    In
    ] object ptr,
    int ofs
);
[C++]
public: static short ReadInt16(
    [
    In
    ] Object* ptr,
    int ofs
);
[JScript]
public static function ReadInt16(
    ptr : Object,
    ofs : int
) : Int16;
```

Parameters

ptr
> The base address in unmanaged memory of the source object.

ofs
> An additional byte offset, added to the *ptr* parameter before reading.

Return Value

The 16-bit signed integer read from the *ptr* parameter.

Exceptions

Exception Type	Condition
ArgumentException	*ptr* is not a recognized format.

Remarks

ReadInt16 enables direct interaction with an unmanaged 16-bit signed array, eliminating the expense of copying an entire unmanaged array (using **Marshal.Copy**) to a separate managed array before reading its element values.

> **Note** This method uses **SecurityAction.LinkDemand** to prevent it from being called from untrusted code; only the immediate caller is required to have **SecurityPermission-Attribute.UnmanagedCode** permission. If your code can be called from partially trusted code, do not pass user input to **Marshal** class methods without validation.

Requirements

Platforms: Windows 98, Windows NT 4.0, Windows Millennium Edition, Windows 2000, Windows XP Home Edition, Windows XP Professional, Windows .NET Server family

Marshal.ReadInt32 Method

Reads a 32-bit signed integer from unmanaged memory.

Overload List

Reads a 32-bit signed integer from unmanaged memory.

Supported by the .NET Compact Framework.

> [Visual Basic] **Overloads Public Shared Function ReadInt32(IntPtr) As Integer**
>
> [C#] **public static int ReadInt32(IntPtr);**
>
> [C++] **public: static int ReadInt32(IntPtr);**
>
> [JScript] **public static function ReadInt32(IntPtr) : int;**

Reads a 32-bit signed integer from unmanaged memory.

Supported by the .NET Compact Framework.

> [Visual Basic] **Overloads Public Shared Function ReadInt32(IntPtr, Integer) As Integer**
>
> [C#] **public static int ReadInt32(IntPtr, int);**
>
> [C++] **public: static int ReadInt32(IntPtr, int);**
>
> [JScript] **public static function ReadInt32(IntPtr, int) : int;**

Reads a 32-bit signed integer from unmanaged memory.

> [Visual Basic] **Overloads Public Shared Function ReadInt32(Object, Integer) As Integer**
>
> [C#] **public static int ReadInt32(object, int);**
>
> [C++] **public: static int ReadInt32(Object, int);**
>
> [JScript] **public static function ReadInt32(Object, int) : int;**

Example

[Visual Basic, C#] The following example compares two ways of interacting with an unmanaged C-style Int32 array. The **ReadInt32** method provides direct access to the array's element values.

> [Visual Basic, C#] **Note** This example shows how to use one of the overloaded versions of **ReadInt32**. For other examples that might be available, see the individual overload topics.

```
[Visual Basic]
Dim unmanagedArray As IntPtr = ...
Dim i As Integer
' One way to print the 10 elements of the C-style unmanagedArray
Dim newArray As Int32(9)
Marshal.Copy(unmanagedArray, newArray, 0, 10)
For i = 0 To newArray.Length
    Console.WriteLine(newArray(i))
Next i
' Another way to print the 10 elements of the C-style unmanagedArray
For i = 0 To 10
    Console.WriteLine(Marshal.ReadInt32(unmanagedArray, i))
Next i

[C#]
IntPtr unmanagedArray = ...;
// One way to print the 10 elements of the C-style unmanagedArray
byte [] newArray = new Int32[10];
Marshal.Copy(unmanagedArray, newArray, 0, 10);
for (int i = 0; i < newArray.Length; i++)
    Console.WriteLine(newArray[i]);
// Another way to print the 10 elements of the C-style unmanagedArray
for (int i = 0; i < 10; i++)
    Console.WriteLine(Marshal.ReadInt32(unmanagedArray, i));
```

Marshal.ReadInt32 Method (IntPtr)

Reads a 32-bit signed integer from unmanaged memory.

```
[Visual Basic]
Overloads Public Shared Function ReadInt32( _
   ByVal ptr As IntPtr _
) As Integer
[C#]
public static int ReadInt32(
   IntPtr ptr
);
[C++]
public: static int ReadInt32(
   IntPtr ptr
);
[JScript]
public static function ReadInt32(
   ptr : IntPtr
) : int;
```

Parameters

ptr

   The address in unmanaged from which to read.

Return Value

The 32-bit signed integer read from the *ptr* parameter.

Exceptions

Exception Type	Condition
ArgumentException	*ptr* is not a recognized format.

Remarks

ReadInt32 has an implied offset of 0. This method enables direct interaction with an unmanaged C-style Int32 array, eliminating the expense of copying an entire unmanaged array (using **Marshal.Copy**) to a separate managed array before reading its element values.

> **Note** This method uses **SecurityAction.LinkDemand** to prevent it from being called from untrusted code; only the immediate caller is required to have **SecurityPermission-Attribute.UnmanagedCode** permission. If your code can be called from partially trusted code, do not pass user input to **Marshal** class methods without validation.

Requirements

Platforms: Windows 98, Windows NT 4.0, Windows Millennium Edition, Windows 2000, Windows XP Home Edition, Windows XP Professional, Windows .NET Server family, .NET Compact Framework - Windows CE .NET

.NET Framework Security:

*   **SecurityPermission** for operating with unmanaged code. Associated enumeration: **SecurityPermissionFlag.UnmanagedCode**.

Marshal.ReadInt32 Method (IntPtr, Int32)

Reads a 32-bit signed integer from unmanaged memory.

```
[Visual Basic]
Overloads Public Shared Function ReadInt32( _
   ByVal ptr As IntPtr, _
   ByVal ofs As Integer _
) As Integer
```

```
[C#]
public static int ReadInt32(
   IntPtr ptr,
   int ofs
);
[C++]
public: static int ReadInt32(
   IntPtr ptr,
   int ofs
);
[JScript]
public static function ReadInt32(
   ptr : IntPtr,
   ofs : int
) : int;
```

Parameters

ptr

   The base address in unmanaged memory from which to read.

ofs

   An additional byte offset, added to the *ptr* parameter before reading.

Return Value

The 32-bit signed integer read from the *ptr* parameter.

Exceptions

Exception Type	Condition
ArgumentException	*ptr* is not a recognized format.

Remarks

ReadInt32 enables direct interaction with an unmanaged 32-bit signed array, eliminating the expense of copying an entire unmanaged array (using **Marshal.Copy**) to a separate managed array before reading its element values.

> **Note** This method uses **SecurityAction.LinkDemand** to prevent it from being called from untrusted code; only the immediate caller is required to have **SecurityPermission-Attribute.UnmanagedCode** permission. If your code can be called from partially trusted code, do not pass user input to **Marshal** class methods without validation.

Example

[Visual Basic, C#] The following example compares two ways of interacting with an unmanaged C-style Int32 array. The **ReadInt32** method provides direct access to the array's element values.

```
[Visual Basic]
Dim unmanagedArray As IntPtr = ...
Dim i As Integer
' One way to print the 10 elements of the C-style unmanagedArray
Dim newArray As Int32(9)
Marshal.Copy(unmanagedArray, newArray, 0, 10)
For i = 0 To newArray.Length
   Console.WriteLine(newArray(i))
Next i
' Another way to print the 10 elements of the C-style unmanagedArray
For i = 0 To 10
   Console.WriteLine(Marshal.ReadInt32(unmanagedArray, i))
Next i

[C#]
IntPtr unmanagedArray = ...;
// One way to print the 10 elements of the C-style unmanagedArray
byte [] newArray = new Int32[10];
```

```
Marshal.Copy(unmanagedArray, newArray, 0, 10);
for (int i = 0; i < newArray.Length; i++)
  Console.WriteLine(newArray[i]);
// Another way to print the 10 elements of the C-style unmanagedArray
for (int i = 0; i < 10; i++)
  Console.WriteLine(Marshal.ReadInt32(unmanagedArray, i));
```

Requirements

Platforms: Windows 98, Windows NT 4.0,
Windows Millennium Edition, Windows 2000,
Windows XP Home Edition, Windows XP Professional,
Windows .NET Server family,
.NET Compact Framework - Windows CE .NET

Marshal.ReadInt32 Method (Object, Int32)

Reads a 32-bit signed integer from unmanaged memory.

```
[Visual Basic]
Overloads Public Shared Function ReadInt32( _
  <InteropServices.In()> ByVal ptr As Object, _
  ByVal ofs As Integer _
) As Integer
[C#]
public static int ReadInt32(
  [
  In
  ] object ptr,
  int ofs
);
[C++]
public: static int ReadInt32(
  [
  In
  ] Object* ptr,
  int ofs
);
[JScript]
public static function ReadInt32(
  ptr : Object,
  ofs : int
) : int;
```

Parameters

ptr
> The base address in unmanaged memory of the source object.

ofs
> An additional byte offset, added to the *ptr* parameter before reading.

Return Value

The 32-bit signed integer read from the *ptr* parameter.

Exceptions

Exception Type	Condition
ArgumentException	*ptr* is not a recognized format.

Remarks

ReadInt32 enables direct interaction with an unmanaged 32-bit signed array, eliminating the expense of copying an entire unmanaged array (using **Marshal.Copy**) to a separate managed array before reading its element values.

> **Note** This method uses **SecurityAction.LinkDemand** to prevent it from being called from untrusted code; only the immediate caller is required to have **SecurityPermission-Attribute.UnmanagedCode** permission. If your code can be called from partially trusted code, do not pass user input to **Marshal** class methods without validation.

Requirements

Platforms: Windows 98, Windows NT 4.0,
Windows Millennium Edition, Windows 2000,
Windows XP Home Edition, Windows XP Professional,
Windows .NET Server family

Marshal.ReadInt64 Method

Reads a 64-bit signed integer from unmanaged memory.

Overload List

Reads a 64-bit signed integer from unmanaged memory.

> [Visual Basic] **Overloads Public Shared Function ReadInt64(IntPtr) As Long**
>
> [C#] **public static long ReadInt64(IntPtr);**
>
> [C++] **public: static __int64 ReadInt64(IntPtr);**
>
> [JScript] **public static function ReadInt64(IntPtr) : long;**

Reads a 64-bit signed integer from unmanaged memory.

> [Visual Basic] **Overloads Public Shared Function ReadInt64(IntPtr, Integer) As Long**
>
> [C#] **public static long ReadInt64(IntPtr, int);**
>
> [C++] **public: static __int64 ReadInt64(IntPtr, int);**
>
> [JScript] **public static function ReadInt64(IntPtr, int) : long;**

Reads a 64-bit signed integer from unmanaged memory.

> [Visual Basic] **Overloads Public Shared Function ReadInt64(Object, Integer) As Long**
>
> [C#] **public static long ReadInt64(object, int);**
>
> [C++] **public: static __int64 ReadInt64(Object, int);**
>
> [JScript] **public static function ReadInt64(Object, int) : long;**

Example

[Visual Basic, C#] The following example compares two ways of interacting with an unmanaged C-style Int64 array. The **ReadInt64** method provides direct access to the array's element values.

> [Visual Basic, C#] **Note** This example shows how to use one of the overloaded versions of **ReadInt64**. For other examples that might be available, see the individual overload topics.

```
[Visual Basic]
Dim unmanagedArray As IntPtr = ...
Dim i As Integer
' One way to print the 10 elements of the C-style unmanagedArray
Dim newArray As Int64(9)
Marshal.Copy(unmanagedArray, newArray, 0, 10)
For i = 0 To newArray.Length
  Console.WriteLine(newArray(i))
Next i
' Another way to print the 10 elements of the C-style unmanagedArray
For i = 0 To 10
  Console.WriteLine(Marshal.ReadInt64(unmanagedArray, i))
Next i
```

```
[C#]
IntPtr unmanagedArray = ...;
// One way to print the 10 elements of the C-style unmanagedArray
byte [] newArray = new Int64[10];
Marshal.Copy(unmanagedArray, newArray, 0, 10);
for (int i = 0; i < newArray.Length; i++)
  Console.WriteLine(newArray[i]);
// Another way to print the 10 elements of the C-style unmanagedArray
for (int i = 0; i < 10; i++)
  Console.WriteLine(Marshal.ReadInt64(unmanagedArray, i));
```

Marshal.ReadInt64 Method (IntPtr)

Reads a 64-bit signed integer from unmanaged memory.

```
[Visual Basic]
Overloads Public Shared Function ReadInt64( _
   ByVal ptr As IntPtr _
) As Long
[C#]
public static long ReadInt64(
   IntPtr ptr
);
[C++]
public: static __int64 ReadInt64(
   IntPtr ptr
);
[JScript]
public static function ReadInt64(
   ptr : IntPtr
) : long;
```

Parameters

ptr

The address in unmanaged memory from which to read.

Return Value

The 64-bit signed integer read from the *ptr* parameter.

Exceptions

Exception Type	Condition
ArgumentException	*ptr* is not a recognized format.

Remarks

ReadInt64 has an implied offset of 0. This method enables direct interaction with an unmanaged C-style Int64 array, eliminating the expense of copying an entire unmanaged array (using **Marshal.Copy**) to a separate managed array before reading its element values.

> **Note** This method uses **SecurityAction.LinkDemand** to prevent it from being called from untrusted code; only the immediate caller is required to have **SecurityPermission-Attribute.UnmanagedCode** permission. If your code can be called from partially trusted code, do not pass user input to **Marshal** class methods without validation.

Requirements

Platforms: Windows 98, Windows NT 4.0, Windows Millennium Edition, Windows 2000, Windows XP Home Edition, Windows XP Professional, Windows .NET Server family

.NET Framework Security:

- **SecurityPermission** for operating with unmanaged code. Associated enumeration: **SecurityPermissionFlag.UnmanagedCode**.

Marshal.ReadInt64 Method (IntPtr, Int32)

Reads a 64-bit signed integer from unmanaged memory.

```
[Visual Basic]
Overloads Public Shared Function ReadInt64( _
   ByVal ptr As IntPtr, _
   ByVal ofs As Integer _
) As Long
[C#]
public static long ReadInt64(
   IntPtr ptr,
   int ofs
);
[C++]
public: static __int64 ReadInt64(
   IntPtr ptr,
   int ofs
);
[JScript]
public static function ReadInt64(
   ptr : IntPtr,
   ofs : int
) : long;
```

Parameters

ptr

The base address in unmanaged memory from which to read.

ofs

An additional byte offset, added to the *ptr* parameter before reading.

Return Value

The 64-bit signed integer read from the *ptr* parameter.

Exceptions

Exception Type	Condition
ArgumentException	*ptr* is not a recognized format.

Remarks

ReadInt64 enables direct interaction with an unmanaged 64-bit signed array, eliminating the expense of copying an entire unmanaged array (using **Marshal.Copy**) to a separate managed array before reading its element values.

> **Note** This method uses **SecurityAction.LinkDemand** to prevent it from being called from untrusted code; only the immediate caller is required to have **SecurityPermission-Attribute.UnmanagedCode** permission. If your code can be called from partially trusted code, do not pass user input to **Marshal** class methods without validation.

Example

[Visual Basic, C#] The following example compares two ways of interacting with an unmanaged C-style Int64 array. The **ReadInt64** method provides direct access to the array's element values.

```
[Visual Basic]
Dim unmanagedArray As IntPtr = ...
Dim i As Integer
' One way to print the 10 elements of the C-style unmanagedArray
Dim newArray As Int64(9)
Marshal.Copy(unmanagedArray, newArray, 0, 10)
For i = 0 To newArray.Length
  Console.WriteLine(newArray(i))
Next i
```

```
' Another way to print the 10 elements of the C-style unmanagedArray
For i = 0 To 10
   Console.WriteLine(Marshal.ReadInt64(unmanagedArray, i))
Next i

[C#]
IntPtr unmanagedArray = ...;
// One way to print the 10 elements of the C-style unmanagedArray
byte [] newArray = new Int64[10];
Marshal.Copy(unmanagedArray, newArray, 0, 10);
for (int i = 0; i < newArray.Length; i++)
   Console.WriteLine(newArray[i]);
// Another way to print the 10 elements of the C-style unmanagedArray
for (int i = 0; i < 10; i++)
   Console.WriteLine(Marshal.ReadInt64(unmanagedArray, i));
```

Requirements

Platforms: Windows 98, Windows NT 4.0,
Windows Millennium Edition, Windows 2000,
Windows XP Home Edition, Windows XP Professional,
Windows .NET Server family

Marshal.ReadInt64 Method (Object, Int32)

Reads a 64-bit signed integer from unmanaged memory.

```
[Visual Basic]
Overloads Public Shared Function ReadInt64( _
   <InteropServices.In()> ByVal ptr As Object, _
   ByVal ofs As Integer _
) As Long
[C#]
public static long ReadInt64(
   [
   In
   ] object ptr,
   int ofs
);
[C++]
public: static __int64 ReadInt64(
   [
   In
   ] Object* ptr,
   int ofs
);
[JScript]
public static function ReadInt64(
   ptr : Object,
   ofs : int
) : long;
```

Parameters

ptr
   The base address in unmanaged memory of the source object.

ofs
   An additional byte offset, added to the *ptr* parameter before reading.

Return Value

The 64-bit signed integer read from the *ptr* parameter.

Exceptions

Exception Type	Condition
ArgumentException	*ptr* is not a recognized format.

Remarks

ReadInt64 enables direct interaction with an unmanaged 64-bit signed array, eliminating the expense of copying an entire unmanaged array (using **Marshal.Copy**) to a separate managed array before reading its element values.

> **Note** This method uses **SecurityAction.LinkDemand** to prevent it from being called from untrusted code; only the immediate caller is required to have **SecurityPermission-Attribute.UnmanagedCode** permission. If your code can be called from partially trusted code, do not pass user input to **Marshal** class methods without validation.

Requirements

Platforms: Windows 98, Windows NT 4.0,
Windows Millennium Edition, Windows 2000,
Windows XP Home Edition, Windows XP Professional,
Windows .NET Server family

Marshal.ReadIntPtr Method

Reads a processor native sized integer from unmanaged memory.

Overload List

Reads a processor native sized integer from unmanaged memory.

[Visual Basic] **Overloads Public Shared Function ReadIntPtr(IntPtr) As IntPtr**

[C#] **public static IntPtr ReadIntPtr(IntPtr);**

[C++] **public: static IntPtr ReadIntPtr(IntPtr);**

[JScript] **public static function ReadIntPtr(IntPtr) : IntPtr;**

Reads a processor native sized integer from unmanaged memory.

[Visual Basic] **Overloads Public Shared Function ReadIntPtr(IntPtr, Integer) As IntPtr**

[C#] **public static IntPtr ReadIntPtr(IntPtr, int);**

[C++] **public: static IntPtr ReadIntPtr(IntPtr, int);**

[JScript] **public static function ReadIntPtr(IntPtr, int) : IntPtr;**

Reads a processor native sized integer from unmanaged memory.

[Visual Basic] **Overloads Public Shared Function ReadIntPtr(Object, Integer) As IntPtr**

[C#] **public static IntPtr ReadIntPtr(object, int);**

[C++] **public: static IntPtr ReadIntPtr(Object, int);**

[JScript] **public static function ReadIntPtr(Object, int) : IntPtr;**

Example

[Visual Basic, C#] The following example compares two ways of interacting with an unmanaged C-style IntPtr array. The **ReadIntPtr** method provides direct access to the array's element values.

> [Visual Basic, C#] **Note** This example shows how to use one of the overloaded versions of **ReadIntPtr**. For other examples that might be available, see the individual overload topics.

```
[Visual Basic]
Dim unmanagedArray As IntPtr = ...
Dim i As Integer
' One way to print the 10 elements of the C-style unmanagedArray
Dim newArray As IntPtr(9)
Marshal.Copy(unmanagedArray, newArray, 0, 10)
```

```
For i = 0 To newArray.Length
  Console.WriteLine(newArray(i))
Next i
' Another way to print the 10 elements of the C-style unmanagedArray
For i = 0 To 10
  Console.WriteLine(Marshal.ReadIntPtr(unmanagedArray, i))
Next i

[C#]
IntPtr unmanagedArray = ...;
// One way to print the 10 elements of the C-style unmanagedArray
byte [] newArray = new IntPtr[10];
Marshal.Copy(unmanagedArray, newArray, 0, 10);
for (int i = 0; i < newArray.Length; i++)
  Console.WriteLine(newArray[i]);
// Another way to print the 10 elements of the C-style unmanagedArray
for (int i = 0; i < 10; i++)
  Console.WriteLine(Marshal.ReadIntPtr(unmanagedArray, i));
```

Marshal.ReadIntPtr Method (IntPtr)

Reads a processor native sized integer from unmanaged memory.

```
[Visual Basic]
Overloads Public Shared Function ReadIntPtr( _
  ByVal ptr As IntPtr _
) As IntPtr
[C#]
public static IntPtr ReadIntPtr(
  IntPtr ptr
);
[C++]
public: static IntPtr ReadIntPtr(
  IntPtr ptr
);
[JScript]
public static function ReadIntPtr(
  ptr : IntPtr
) : IntPtr;
```

Parameters

ptr

The address in unmanaged memory from which to read.

Return Value

The **IntPtr** read from the *ptr* parameter.

Exceptions

Exception Type	Condition
ArgumentException	*ptr* is not a recognized format.

Remarks

ReadIntPtr has an implied offset of 0. This method enables direct interaction with an unmanaged C-style IntPtr array, eliminating the expense of copying an entire unmanaged array (using **Marshal.Copy**) to a separate managed array before reading its element values.

> **Note** This method uses **SecurityAction.LinkDemand** to prevent it from being called from untrusted code; only the immediate caller is required to have **SecurityPermissionAttribute.UnmanagedCode** permission. If your code can be called from partially trusted code, do not pass user input to **Marshal** class methods without validation.

Requirements

Platforms: Windows 98, Windows NT 4.0, Windows Millennium Edition, Windows 2000,

Windows XP Home Edition, Windows XP Professional, Windows .NET Server family

.NET Framework Security:

- **SecurityPermission** for operating with unmanaged code. Associated enumeration: **SecurityPermissionFlag.UnmanagedCode**.

Marshal.ReadIntPtr Method (IntPtr, Int32)

Reads a processor native sized integer from unmanaged memory.

```
[Visual Basic]
Overloads Public Shared Function ReadIntPtr( _
  ByVal ptr As IntPtr, _
  ByVal ofs As Integer _
) As IntPtr
[C#]
public static IntPtr ReadIntPtr(
  IntPtr ptr,
  int ofs
);
[C++]
public: static IntPtr ReadIntPtr(
  IntPtr ptr,
  int ofs
);
[JScript]
public static function ReadIntPtr(
  ptr : IntPtr,
  ofs : int
) : IntPtr;
```

Parameters

ptr

The base address in unmanaged memory from which to read.

ofs

An additional byte offset, added to the *ptr* parameter before reading.

Return Value

The **IntPtr** read from the *ptr* parameter.

Exceptions

Exception Type	Condition
ArgumentException	*ptr* is not a recognized format.

Remarks

ReadIntPtr enables direct interaction with an unmanaged C-style IntPtr array, eliminating the expense of copying an entire unmanaged array (using **Marshal.Copy**) to a separate managed array before reading its element values.

> **Note** This method uses **SecurityAction.LinkDemand** to prevent it from being called from untrusted code; only the immediate caller is required to have **SecurityPermissionAttribute.UnmanagedCode** permission. If your code can be called from partially trusted code, do not pass user input to **Marshal** class methods without validation.

Example

[Visual Basic, C#] The following example compares two ways of interacting with an unmanaged C-style IntPtr array. The **ReadIntPtr** method provides direct access to the array's element values.

```
[Visual Basic]
Dim unmanagedArray As IntPtr = ...
Dim i As Integer
' One way to print the 10 elements of the C-style unmanagedArray
Dim newArray As IntPtr(9)
Marshal.Copy(unmanagedArray, newArray, 0, 10)
For i = 0 To newArray.Length
  Console.WriteLine(newArray(i))
Next i
' Another way to print the 10 elements of the C-style unmanagedArray
For i = 0 To 10
  Console.WriteLine(Marshal.ReadIntPtr(unmanagedArray, i))
Next i

[C#]
IntPtr unmanagedArray = ...;
// One way to print the 10 elements of the C-style unmanagedArray
byte [] newArray = new IntPtr[10];
Marshal.Copy(unmanagedArray, newArray, 0, 10);
for (int i = 0; i < newArray.Length; i++)
  Console.WriteLine(newArray[i]);
// Another way to print the 10 elements of the C-style unmanagedArray
for (int i = 0; i < 10; i++)
  Console.WriteLine(Marshal.ReadIntPtr(unmanagedArray, i));
```

Requirements

Platforms: Windows 98, Windows NT 4.0, Windows Millennium Edition, Windows 2000, Windows XP Home Edition, Windows XP Professional, Windows .NET Server family

.NET Framework Security:
- **SecurityPermission** for operating with unmanaged code. Associated enumeration: **SecurityPermissionFlag.UnmanagedCode**.

Marshal.ReadIntPtr Method (Object, Int32)

Reads a processor native sized integer from unmanaged memory.

```
[Visual Basic]
Overloads Public Shared Function ReadIntPtr( _
  <InteropServices.In()> ByVal ptr As Object, _
  ByVal ofs As Integer _
) As IntPtr
[C#]
public static IntPtr ReadIntPtr(
  [
  In
  ] object ptr,
  int ofs
);
[C++]
public: static IntPtr ReadIntPtr(
  [
  In
  ] Object* ptr,
  int ofs
);
[JScript]
public static function ReadIntPtr(
  ptr : Object,
  ofs : int
) : IntPtr;
```

Parameters

ptr
   The base address in unmanaged memory of the source object.
ofs
   An additional byte offset, added to the *ptr* parameter before reading.

Return Value

The **IntPtr** read from the *ptr* parameter.

Exceptions

Exception Type	Condition
ArgumentException	*ptr* is not a recognized format.

Remarks

ReadIntPtr enables direct interaction with an unmanaged C-style IntPtr array, eliminating the expense of copying an entire unmanaged array (using **Marshal.Copy**) to a separate managed array before reading its element values.

> **Note** This method uses **SecurityAction.LinkDemand** to prevent it from being called from untrusted code; only the immediate caller is required to have **SecurityPermission-Attribute.UnmanagedCode** permission. If your code can be called from partially trusted code, do not pass user input to **Marshal** class methods without validation.

Requirements

Platforms: Windows 98, Windows NT 4.0, Windows Millennium Edition, Windows 2000, Windows XP Home Edition, Windows XP Professional, Windows .NET Server family

.NET Framework Security:
- **SecurityPermission** for operating with unmanaged code. Associated enumeration: **SecurityPermissionFlag.UnmanagedCode**.

Marshal.ReAllocCoTaskMem Method

Resizes a block of memory previously allocated with **AllocCoTaskMem**.

```
[Visual Basic]
Public Shared Function ReAllocCoTaskMem( _
  ByVal pv As IntPtr, _
  ByVal cb As Integer _
) As IntPtr
[C#]
public static IntPtr ReAllocCoTaskMem(
  IntPtr pv,
  int cb
);
[C++]
public: static IntPtr ReAllocCoTaskMem(
  IntPtr pv,
  int cb
);
[JScript]
public static function ReAllocCoTaskMem(
  pv : IntPtr,
  cb : int
) : IntPtr;
```

Parameters

pv

A pointer to memory allocated with **AllocCoTaskMem**.

cb

The new size of the allocated block.

Return Value

An integer representing the address of the block of memory reallocated. This memory must be released with **FreeCoTaskMem**.

Exceptions

Exception Type	Condition
OutOfMemoryException	There is insufficient memory to satisfy the request.

Remarks

ReAllocCoTaskMem is one of two memory reallocation API methods in the **Marshal** class. (**ReAllocHGlobal** is the other.) The beginning of the reallocated memory content is the same as the original content; however, the entire memory block can be in a different location. This method exposes the **CoTaskMemRealloc** COM API method, which is referred to as the COM task memory allocator. For additional information about **CoTaskMemRealloc**, see the MSDN Library.

> **Note** This method uses **SecurityAction.LinkDemand** to prevent it from being called from untrusted code; only the immediate caller is required to have **SecurityPermission-Attribute.UnmanagedCode** permission. If your code can be called from partially trusted code, do not pass user input to **Marshal** class methods without validation.

Requirements

Platforms: Windows 98, Windows NT 4.0, Windows Millennium Edition, Windows 2000, Windows XP Home Edition, Windows XP Professional, Windows .NET Server family

.NET Framework Security:

• **SecurityPermission** for operating with unmanaged code. Associated enumeration: **SecurityPermissionFlag.UnmanagedCode**.

Marshal.ReAllocHGlobal Method

Resizes a block of memory previously allocated with **AllocHGlobal**.

```
[Visual Basic]
Public Shared Function ReAllocHGlobal( _
   ByVal pv As IntPtr, _
   ByVal cb As IntPtr _
) As IntPtr
[C#]
public static IntPtr ReAllocHGlobal(
   IntPtr pv,
   IntPtr cb
);
[C++]
public: static IntPtr ReAllocHGlobal(
   IntPtr pv,
   IntPtr cb
);
```

```
[JScript]
public static function ReAllocHGlobal(
   pv : IntPtr,
   cb : IntPtr
) : IntPtr;
```

Parameters

pv

A pointer to memory allocated with **AllocHGlobal**.

cb

The new size of the allocated block.

Return Value

An **IntPtr** to the reallocated memory. This memory must be released using **Marshal.FreeHGlobal**.

Exceptions

Exception Type	Condition
OutOfMemoryException	There is insufficient memory to satisfy the request.

Remarks

ReAllocHGlobal is one of two memory allocation API methods in the **Marshal** class. (**Marshal.ReAllocCoTaskMem** is the other.) This method exposes the **GlobalRealloc** Win32 API method from Kernel32.dll. The returned pointer can differ from the original. For additional information about **GlobalAlloc**, see the MSDN Library.

> **Note** This method uses **SecurityAction.LinkDemand** to prevent it from being called from untrusted code; only the immediate caller is required to have **SecurityPermission-Attribute.UnmanagedCode** permission. If your code can be called from partially trusted code, do not pass user input to **Marshal** class methods without validation.

Requirements

Platforms: Windows 98, Windows NT 4.0, Windows Millennium Edition, Windows 2000, Windows XP Home Edition, Windows XP Professional, Windows .NET Server family

.NET Framework Security:

• **SecurityPermission** for operating with unmanaged code. Associated enumeration: **SecurityPermissionFlag.UnmanagedCode**.

Marshal.Release Method

Decrements the reference count on the specified interface.

```
[Visual Basic]
Public Shared Function Release( _
   ByVal pUnk As IntPtr _
) As Integer
[C#]
public static int Release(
   IntPtr pUnk
);
[C++]
public: static int Release(
   IntPtr pUnk
);
```

```
[JScript]
public static function Release(
    pUnk : IntPtr
) : int;
```

Parameters

pUnk

The interface to release.

Return Value

The new value of the reference count on the interface specified by the *pUnk* parameter.

Remarks

The common language runtime manages the reference count of a COM object for you, making it unnecessary to use this method directly. Use this value only for testing purposes. In rare cases, such as testing a custom marshaler, you might find it necessary to manipulate an object's lifetime manually. Only programs that call **Marshal.AddRef** should call **Release**. Calling **Release** after the reference count has reached zero causes undefined behavior.

You can call **Marshal.GetComInterfaceForObject**, **Marshal.GetIUnknownForObject**, or **Marshal.GetIDispatchForObject** to obtain an **IntPtr** value that represents a **IUnknown** interface pointer to release. You can also use these methods and the **Release** method on managed objects to release the COM interfaces represented by the managed object's COM callable wrapper. If you are not familiar with the details of this wrapper type, see **COM Callable Wrapper**.

> **Note** This method uses **SecurityAction.LinkDemand** to prevent it from being called from untrusted code; only the immediate caller is required to have **SecurityPermissionAttribute.UnmanagedCode** permission. If your code can be called from partially trusted code, do not pass user input to **Marshal** class methods without validation.

Example

[Visual Basic, C#] The following code example demonstrates the use of the **Release** method. This example uses **GetIUnknownForObject** to obtain an **IntPtr** value representing the COM object's **IUnknown** interface pointer.

```
[Visual Basic]
Dim pUnk As IntPtr = Marshal.GetIUnknownForObject(myComObject)
Dim refCount As Integer = Marshal.Release(pUnk)
```

```
[C#]
IntPtr pUnk = Marshal.GetIUnknownForObject(myComObject);
int refCount = Marshal.Release(pUnk);
```

Requirements

Platforms: Windows 98, Windows NT 4.0, Windows Millennium Edition, Windows 2000, Windows XP Home Edition, Windows XP Professional, Windows .NET Server family

.NET Framework Security:

- **SecurityPermission** for operating with unmanaged code. Associated enumeration: **SecurityPermissionFlag.UnmanagedCode**.

Marshal.ReleaseComObject Method

Decrements the reference count of the supplied runtime callable wrapper.

```
[Visual Basic]
Public Shared Function ReleaseComObject( _
    ByVal o As Object _
) As Integer
[C#]
public static int ReleaseComObject(
    object o
);
[C++]
public: static int ReleaseComObject(
    Object* o
);
[JScript]
public static function ReleaseComObject(
    o : Object
) : int;
```

Parameters

o

The COM object to release.

Return Value

The new value of the reference count of the runtime callable wrapper associated with *o*. This value is typically zero since the runtime callable wrapper keeps just one reference to the wrapped COM object regardless of the number of managed clients calling it.

Exceptions

Exception Type	Condition
ArgumentException	*o* is not a COM object.

Remarks

Every time a COM interface pointer enters the common language runtime, it is wrapped in an runtime callable wrapper.

This method is used to explicitly control the lifetime of a COM object used from managed code. You should use this method to free the underlying COM object that holds references to resources in a timely manner or when objects must be freed in a specific order.

The runtime callable wrapper has a reference count that is incremented every time a COM interface pointer is mapped to it. The **ReleaseComObject** method decrements the reference count of a runtime callable wrapper. When the reference count reached zero, the runtime releases all its references on the unmanaged COM object, and throws a **System.NullReferenceException** if you attempt to use the object further. If the same COM interface is passed more than once from unmanaged to managed code, the reference count on the wrapper is incremented every time and calling **ReleaseComObject** returns the number of remaining references.

> **Note** To ensure that the runtime callable wrapper and the original COM object are released, construct a loop from which you call this method until the returned reference count reaches zero.

> **Note** This method uses **SecurityAction.LinkDemand** to prevent it from being called from untrusted code; only the immediate caller is required to have **SecurityPermissionAttribute.UnmanagedCode** permission. If your code can be called from partially trusted code, do not pass user input to **Marshal** class methods without validation.

Requirements

Platforms: Windows 98, Windows NT 4.0,
Windows Millennium Edition, Windows 2000,
Windows XP Home Edition, Windows XP Professional,
Windows .NET Server family

.NET Framework Security:

*   **SecurityPermission** for operating with unmanaged code.
    Associated enumeration:
    SecurityPermissionFlag.UnmanagedCode.

Marshal.ReleaseThreadCache Method

This member supports the .NET Framework infrastructure and is not
intended to be used directly from your code.

```
[Visual Basic]
Public Shared Sub ReleaseThreadCache()
[C#]
public static void ReleaseThreadCache();
[C++]
public: static void ReleaseThreadCache();
[JScript]
public static function ReleaseThreadCache();
```

Requirements

Platforms: Windows 98, Windows NT 4.0,
Windows Millennium Edition, Windows 2000,
Windows XP Home Edition, Windows XP Professional,
Windows .NET Server family

Marshal.SetComObjectData Method

Sets data referenced by the specified key in the specified COM
object.

```
[Visual Basic]
Public Shared Function SetComObjectData( _
   ByVal obj As Object, _
   ByVal key As Object, _
   ByVal data As Object _
) As Boolean
[C#]
public static bool SetComObjectData(
   object obj,
   object key,
   object data
);
[C++]
public: static bool SetComObjectData(
   Object* obj,
   Object* key,
   Object* data
);
[JScript]
public static function SetComObjectData(
   obj : Object,
   key : Object,
   data : Object
) : Boolean;
```

Parameters

obj
    The COM object in which to store the data.

key
    The key in the internal hash table of the COM object in which to
    store the data.
data
    The data to set.

Return Value

true if the data was set successfully; otherwise, **false**.

Exceptions

Exception Type	Condition
ArgumentNullException	*obj* is a null reference (**Nothing** in Visual Basic).
	-or-
	key is a null reference (**Nothing**).
ArgumentException	*obj* is not a COM object.

Remarks

All COM objects wrapped in a runtime callable wrapper have an
associated hash table, to which **SetComObjectData** adds data.
Marshal.GetComObjectData retrieves data from the hash table.
You should never have to call either method from your code.

> **Note** This method uses **SecurityAction.LinkDemand** to
> prevent it from being called from untrusted code; only the
> immediate caller is required to have **SecurityPermission-
> Attribute.UnmanagedCode** permission. If your code can be
> called from partially trusted code, do not pass user input to
> **Marshal** class methods without validation.

Requirements

Platforms: Windows 98, Windows NT 4.0,
Windows Millennium Edition, Windows 2000,
Windows XP Home Edition, Windows XP Professional,
Windows .NET Server family

.NET Framework Security:

*   **SecurityPermission** for operating with unmanaged code.
    Associated enumeration:
    SecurityPermissionFlag.UnmanagedCode.

Marshal.SizeOf Method

Returns the unmanaged size, in bytes, of a class using **Marshal**.

Overload List

Returns the unmanaged size of an object in bytes.

Supported by the .NET Compact Framework.

> [Visual Basic] **Overloads Public Shared Function
> SizeOf(Object) As Integer**
>
> [C#] **public static int SizeOf(object);**
>
> [C++] **public: static int SizeOf(Object*);**
>
> [JScript] **public static function SizeOf(Object) : int;**

Returns the size of an unmanaged type in bytes.

Supported by the .NET Compact Framework.

> [Visual Basic] **Overloads Public Shared Function
> SizeOf(Type) As Integer**
>
> [C#] **public static int SizeOf(Type);**
>
> [C++] **public: static int SizeOf(Type*);**
>
> [JScript] **public static function SizeOf(Type) : int;**

Marshal.SizeOf Method (Object)

Returns the unmanaged size of an object in bytes.

```
[Visual Basic]
Overloads Public Shared Function SizeOf( _
   ByVal structure As Object _
) As Integer
[C#]
public static int SizeOf(
   object structure
);
[C++]
public: static int SizeOf(
   Object* structure
);
[JScript]
public static function SizeOf(
   structure : Object
) : int;
```

Parameters

structure
   The object whose size is to be returned.

Return Value

The size of the *structure* parameter in unmanaged code.

Exceptions

Exception Type	Condition
ArgumentException	*structure* is not a **Marshal** class.
	-or-
	structure is an array type.
NullReferenceException	*structure* is a null reference (**Nothing** in Visual Basic).

Remarks

This method accepts an instance of a structure, which can be a reference type or a boxed value type. The layout must be sequential or explicit.

The size returned is the size of the unmanaged object. The unmanaged and managed sizes of an object can differ. For character types, the size is affected by the **CharSet** value applied to that class.

> **Note** This method uses **SecurityAction.LinkDemand** to prevent it from being called from untrusted code; only the immediate caller is required to have **SecurityPermission-Attribute.UnmanagedCode** permission. If your code can be called from partially trusted code, do not pass user input to **Marshal** class methods without validation.

Requirements

Platforms: Windows 98, Windows NT 4.0, Windows Millennium Edition, Windows 2000, Windows XP Home Edition, Windows XP Professional, Windows .NET Server family, .NET Compact Framework - Windows CE .NET

.NET Framework Security:

- **SecurityPermission** for operating with unmanaged code. Associated enumeration: **SecurityPermissionFlag.UnmanagedCode**.

Marshal.SizeOf Method (Type)

Returns the size of an unmanaged type in bytes.

```
[Visual Basic]
Overloads Public Shared Function SizeOf( _
   ByVal t As Type _
) As Integer
[C#]
public static int SizeOf(
   Type t
);
[C++]
public: static int SizeOf(
   Type* t
);
[JScript]
public static function SizeOf(
   t : Type
) : int;
```

Parameters

t
   The **Type** whose size is to be returned.

Return Value

The size of the *structure* parameter in unmanaged code.

Exceptions

Exception Type	Condition
ArgumentException	*structure* is not a **Marshal** class object.
	-or-
	structure is an array type.
NullReferenceException	*structure* is a null reference (**Nothing** in Visual Basic).

Remarks

You can use this method when you do not have a structure. The layout must be sequential or explicit.

The size returned is the actually the size of the unmanaged type. The unmanaged and managed sizes of an object can differ. For character types, the size is affected by the **CharSet** value applied to that class.

> **Note** This method uses **SecurityAction.LinkDemand** to prevent it from being called from untrusted code; only the immediate caller is required to have **SecurityPermission-Attribute.UnmanagedCode** permission. If your code can be called from partially trusted code, do not pass user input to **Marshal** class methods without validation.

Requirements

Platforms: Windows 98, Windows NT 4.0, Windows Millennium Edition, Windows 2000, Windows XP Home Edition, Windows XP Professional, Windows .NET Server family, .NET Compact Framework - Windows CE .NET

.NET Framework Security:

- **SecurityPermission** for operating with unmanaged code. Associated enumeration: **SecurityPermissionFlag.UnmanagedCode**.

Marshal.StringToBSTR Method

Allocates a BSTR and copies the contents of a managed **String** into it.

```
[Visual Basic]
Public Shared Function StringToBSTR( _
   ByVal s As String _
) As IntPtr
[C#]
public static IntPtr StringToBSTR(
   string s
);
[C++]
public: static IntPtr StringToBSTR(
   String* s
);
[JScript]
public static function StringToBSTR(
   s : String
) : IntPtr;
```

Parameters

s

   The managed string to be copied.

Return Value

An unmanaged pointer to the BSTR, or 0 if a null reference (**Nothing** in Visual Basic) string was supplied.

Exceptions

Exception Type	Condition
OutOfMemoryException	There is insufficient memory available.

Remarks

StringToBSTR is useful for custom marshaling or when mixing managed and unmanaged code. Since this method allocates the unmanaged memory required for a string, always free the BSTR when finished by calling **Marshal.FreeBSTR**. This method provides the opposite functionality of **Marshal.PtrToStringBSTR**.

> **Note** This method uses **SecurityAction.LinkDemand** to prevent it from being called from untrusted code; only the immediate caller is required to have **SecurityPermission-Attribute.UnmanagedCode** permission. If your code can be called from partially trusted code, do not pass user input to **Marshal** class methods without validation.

Requirements

Platforms: Windows 98, Windows NT 4.0, Windows Millennium Edition, Windows 2000, Windows XP Home Edition, Windows XP Professional, Windows .NET Server family

.NET Framework Security:

- **SecurityPermission** for operating with unmanaged code. Associated enumeration: **SecurityPermissionFlag.UnmanagedCode**.

Marshal.StringToCoTaskMemAnsi Method

Copies the contents of a managed **String** to a block of memory allocated from the unmanaged COM task allocator.

```
[Visual Basic]
Public Shared Function StringToCoTaskMemAnsi( _
   ByVal s As String _
) As IntPtr
[C#]
public static IntPtr StringToCoTaskMemAnsi(
   string s
);
[C++]
public: static IntPtr StringToCoTaskMemAnsi(
   String* s
);
[JScript]
public static function StringToCoTaskMemAnsi(
   s : String
) : IntPtr;
```

Parameters

s

   A managed string to be copied.

Return Value

An integer representing a pointer to the block of memory allocated for the string, or 0 if a null reference (**Nothing** in Visual Basic) string was supplied.

Exceptions

Exception Type	Condition
OutOfMemoryException	There is insufficient memory available.

Remarks

StringToCoTaskMemAnsi is useful for custom marshaling or when mixing managed and unmanaged code. Since this method allocates the unmanaged memory required for a string, always free the memory by calling **FreeCoTaskMem**. This method provides the opposite functionality of **Marshal.PtrToStringAnsi**. The characters of the string are copied as ANSI characters.

> **Note** This method uses **SecurityAction.LinkDemand** to prevent it from being called from untrusted code; only the immediate caller is required to have **SecurityPermission-Attribute.UnmanagedCode** permission. If your code can be called from partially trusted code, do not pass user input to **Marshal** class methods without validation.

Requirements

Platforms: Windows 98, Windows NT 4.0, Windows Millennium Edition, Windows 2000, Windows XP Home Edition, Windows XP Professional, Windows .NET Server family

.NET Framework Security:

- **SecurityPermission** for operating with unmanaged code. Associated enumeration: **SecurityPermissionFlag.UnmanagedCode**.

Marshal.StringToCoTaskMemAuto Method

Copies the contents of a managed **String** to a block of memory allocated from the unmanaged COM task allocator.

```
[Visual Basic]
Public Shared Function StringToCoTaskMemAuto( _
   ByVal s As String _
) As IntPtr
[C#]
public static IntPtr StringToCoTaskMemAuto(
   string s
);
[C++]
public: static IntPtr StringToCoTaskMemAuto(
   String* s
);
[JScript]
public static function StringToCoTaskMemAuto(
   s : String
) : IntPtr;
```

Parameters

s

   A managed string to be copied.

Return Value

The allocated memory block, or 0 if a null reference (**Nothing** in Visual Basic) string was supplied.

Exceptions

Exception Type	Condition
OutOfMemoryException	There is insufficient memory available.

Remarks

StringToCoTaskMemAuto is useful for custom marshaling or for use when mixing managed and unmanaged code. Since this method allocates the unmanaged memory required for a string, always free the memory by calling **FreeCoTaskMem**. This method provides the opposite functionality of **Marshal.PtrToStringAuto**.

The characters of the string are copied as either ANSI or Unicode characters, depending on the operating system where the code is executing. On Windows 98, the characters are copied as ANSI characters. On Windows NT 4.0, Windows 2000, Windows XP, and the Windows .NET Server family, the characters are copied as Unicode characters.

> **Note** This method uses **SecurityAction.LinkDemand** to prevent it from being called from untrusted code; only the immediate caller is required to have **SecurityPermission-Attribute.UnmanagedCode** permission. If your code can be called from partially trusted code, do not pass user input to **Marshal** class methods without validation.

Requirements

Platforms: Windows 98, Windows NT 4.0, Windows Millennium Edition, Windows 2000, Windows XP Home Edition, Windows XP Professional, Windows .NET Server family

.NET Framework Security:

- **SecurityPermission** for operating with unmanaged code. Associated enumeration: **SecurityPermissionFlag.UnmanagedCode**.

Marshal.StringToCoTaskMemUni Method

Copies the contents of a managed **String** to a block of memory allocated from the unmanaged COM task allocator.

```
[Visual Basic]
Public Shared Function StringToCoTaskMemUni( _
   ByVal s As String _
) As IntPtr
[C#]
public static IntPtr StringToCoTaskMemUni(
   string s
);
[C++]
public: static IntPtr StringToCoTaskMemUni(
   String* s
);
[JScript]
public static function StringToCoTaskMemUni(
   s : String
) : IntPtr;
```

Parameters

s

   A managed string to be copied.

Return Value

An integer representing a pointer to the block of memory allocated for the string, or 0 if a null reference (**Nothing** in Visual Basic) string was supplied.

Exceptions

Exception Type	Condition
OutOfMemoryException	There is insufficient memory available.

Remarks

StringToCoTaskMemUni is useful for custom marshaling or for use when mixing managed and unmanaged code. Since this method allocates the unmanaged memory required for a string, always free the memory by calling **Marshal.FreeCoTaskMem**. This method provides the opposite functionality of **Marshal.PtrToStringUni**. The characters of the string are copied as Unicode characters.

> **Note** This method uses **SecurityAction.LinkDemand** to prevent it from being called from untrusted code; only the immediate caller is required to have **SecurityPermission-Attribute.UnmanagedCode** permission. If your code can be called from partially trusted code, do not pass user input to **Marshal** class methods without validation.

Requirements

Platforms: Windows 98, Windows NT 4.0, Windows Millennium Edition, Windows 2000, Windows XP Home Edition, Windows XP Professional, Windows .NET Server family

.NET Framework Security:

- **SecurityPermission** for operating with unmanaged code. Associated enumeration: **SecurityPermissionFlag.UnmanagedCode**.

Marshal.StringToHGlobalAnsi Method

Copies the contents of a managed **String** into unmanaged memory, converting into ANSI format as it copies.

```
[Visual Basic]
Public Shared Function StringToHGlobalAnsi( _
   ByVal s As String _
) As IntPtr
[C#]
public static IntPtr StringToHGlobalAnsi(
   string s
);
[C++]
public: static IntPtr StringToHGlobalAnsi(
   String* s
);
[JScript]
public static function StringToHGlobalAnsi(
   s : String
) : IntPtr;
```

Parameters

s
   A managed string to be copied.

Return Value

The address, in unmanaged memory, to where *s* was copied, or 0 if a null reference (**Nothing** in Visual Basic) string was supplied.

Exceptions

Exception Type	Condition
OutOfMemoryException	There is insufficient memory available.
ArgumentException	*s* is a null reference (**Nothing** in Visual Basic).

Remarks

StringToHGlobalAnsi is useful for custom marshaling or when mixing managed and unmanaged code. Since this method allocates the unmanaged memory required for a string, always free the memory by calling **FreeCoTaskMem**. **StringToHGlobalAnsi** provides the opposite functionality of **Marshal.PtrToStringAnsi**.

> **Note** This method uses **SecurityAction.LinkDemand** to prevent it from being called from untrusted code; only the immediate caller is required to have **SecurityPermission-Attribute.UnmanagedCode** permission. If your code can be called from partially trusted code, do not pass user input to **Marshal** class methods without validation.

Requirements

Platforms: Windows 98, Windows NT 4.0, Windows Millennium Edition, Windows 2000, Windows XP Home Edition, Windows XP Professional, Windows .NET Server family

.NET Framework Security:
- **SecurityPermission** for operating with unmanaged code. Associated enumeration: **SecurityPermissionFlag.UnmanagedCode**.

Marshal.StringToHGlobalAuto Method

Copies the contents of a managed **String** into unmanaged memory, converting into ANSI format if required.

```
[Visual Basic]
Public Shared Function StringToHGlobalAuto( _
   ByVal s As String _
) As IntPtr
[C#]
public static IntPtr StringToHGlobalAuto(
   string s
);
[C++]
public: static IntPtr StringToHGlobalAuto(
   String* s
);
[JScript]
public static function StringToHGlobalAuto(
   s : String
) : IntPtr;
```

Parameters

s
   A managed string to be copied.

Return Value

The address, in unmanaged memory, to where the string was copied, or 0 if a null reference (**Nothing** in Visual Basic) string was supplied.

Exceptions

Exception Type	Condition
OutOfMemoryException	There is insufficient memory available.

Remarks

StringToHGlobalAuto is useful for custom marshaling or for use when mixing managed and unmanaged code. Since this method allocates the unmanaged memory required for a string, always free the memory by calling **FreeCoTaskMem**. This method provides the opposite functionality of **Marshal.PtrToStringAuto**.

> **Note** This method uses **SecurityAction.LinkDemand** to prevent it from being called from untrusted code; only the immediate caller is required to have **SecurityPermission-Attribute.UnmanagedCode** permission. If your code can be called from partially trusted code, do not pass user input to **Marshal** class methods without validation.

Requirements

Platforms: Windows 98, Windows NT 4.0, Windows Millennium Edition, Windows 2000, Windows XP Home Edition, Windows XP Professional, Windows .NET Server family

.NET Framework Security:
- **SecurityPermission** for operating with unmanaged code. Associated enumeration: **SecurityPermissionFlag.UnmanagedCode**.

Marshal.StringToHGlobalUni Method

Copies the contents of a managed **String** into unmanaged memory.

```
[Visual Basic]
Public Shared Function StringToHGlobalUni( _
   ByVal s As String _
) As IntPtr
[C#]
public static IntPtr StringToHGlobalUni(
   string s
);
[C++]
public: static IntPtr StringToHGlobalUni(
   String* s
);
[JScript]
public static function StringToHGlobalUni(
   s : String
) : IntPtr;
```

Parameters

s

A managed string to be copied.

Return Value

The address, in unmanaged memory, to where the *s* was copied, or 0 if a null reference (**Nothing** in Visual Basic) string was supplied.

Exceptions

Exception Type	Condition
OutOfMemoryException	The method could not allocate enough native heap memory.

Remarks

StringToHGlobalUni is useful for custom marshaling or for use when mixing managed and unmanaged code. Since this method allocates the unmanaged memory required for a string, always free the memory by calling **FreeCoTaskMem**. This method provides the opposite functionality of **Marshal.PtrToStringUni**.

> **Note** This method uses **SecurityAction.LinkDemand** to prevent it from being called from untrusted code; only the immediate caller is required to have **SecurityPermission-Attribute.UnmanagedCode** permission. If your code can be called from partially trusted code, do not pass user input to **Marshal** class methods without validation.

Note[note] This method uses **SecurityAction.LinkDemand** to prevent it from being called from untrusted code; only the immediate caller is required to have **SecurityPermissionAttribute.Un-managedCode** permission. If your code can be called from partially trusted code, do not pass user input to **Marshal** class methods without validation. For important limitations on using the **LinkDemand** member, see "Secure Coding Guidelines for the .NET Framework" in the MSDN Library.

Requirements

Platforms: Windows 98, Windows NT 4.0, Windows Millennium Edition, Windows 2000, Windows XP Home Edition, Windows XP Professional, Windows .NET Server family

.NET Framework Security:

- **SecurityPermission** for operating with unmanaged code. Associated enumeration: **SecurityPermissionFlag.UnmanagedCode**.

Marshal.StructureToPtr Method

Marshals data from a managed object to an unmanaged block of memory.

```
[Visual Basic]
Public Shared Sub StructureToPtr( _
   ByVal structure As Object, _
   ByVal ptr As IntPtr, _
   ByVal fDeleteOld As Boolean _
)
[C#]
public static void StructureToPtr(
   object structure,
   IntPtr ptr,
   bool fDeleteOld
);
[C++]
public: static void StructureToPtr(
   Object* structure,
   IntPtr ptr,
   bool fDeleteOld
);
[JScript]
public static function StructureToPtr(
   structure : Object,
   ptr : IntPtr,
   fDeleteOld : Boolean
);
```

Parameters

structure

A managed object holding the data to be marshaled. This object must be an instance of a formatted class.

ptr

A pointer to an unmanaged block of memory, which must be allocated before this method is called.

fDeleteOld

true to have the **Marshal.DestroyStructure** method called on the *ptr* parameter before this method executes. Note that passing **false** can lead to a memory leak.

Remarks

StructureToPtr copies the contents of structure to the pre-allocated block of memory pointed to by the *ptr* parameter. If the *fDeleteOld* parameter is **true**, the buffer originally pointed to by *ptr* is deleted with the appropriate delete API on the embedded pointer. This method cleans up every reference field specified in the mirrored managed class.

Suppose your unmanaged block of memory is pointed to by *ptr*. The layout of this block is described by a corresponding managed class, *structure*. **StructureToPtr** marshals field values from a structure to a pointer. Suppose the *ptr* block includes a reference field, pointing to a string buffer currently holding "abc". Suppose the corresponding field on the managed side is a string holding "vwxyz". If you do not tell it otherwise, **StructureToPtr** allocates a new unmanaged buffer to hold "vwxyz", and hooks it up to the *ptr* block. This action casts the old buffer "abc" adrift without freeing it back to the unmanaged heap. You end up with an orphan buffer that represents a memory leak in your code. If you set the *fDeleteOld* parameter true, **StructureToPtr** frees the buffer holding "abc" before going on to allocate a new buffer for "vwxyz".

> **Note** To pin an existing structure, instead of copying it, use the **System.Runtime.InteropServices.GCHandle** type to create a pinned handle for the structure. For details on how to pin, see **Copying and Pinning**.

> **Note** This method uses **SecurityAction.LinkDemand** to prevent it from being called from untrusted code; only the immediate caller is required to have **SecurityPermission-Attribute.UnmanagedCode** permission. If your code can be called from partially trusted code, do not pass user input to **Marshal** class methods without validation.

Example

[Visual Basic, C#] As the following example demonstrates, **StructureToPtr** is useful for swapping one structure with another in the same memory location.

```
[Visual Basic]
Dim IntPtr addressOfStructure1 As IntPtr = ...
Dim structure2 As TYPEATTR = ...
Marshal.StructureToPtr(structure2, addressOfStructure1, True)
```

```
[C#]
IntPtr addressOfStructure1 = ...;
TYPEATTR structure2 = ...;
Marshal.StructureToPtr(structure2, addressOfStructure1, true);
```

Requirements

Platforms: Windows 98, Windows NT 4.0, Windows Millennium Edition, Windows 2000, Windows XP Home Edition, Windows XP Professional, Windows .NET Server family, .NET Compact Framework - Windows CE .NET

.NET Framework Security:
- **SecurityPermission** for operating with unmanaged code. Associated enumeration: **SecurityPermissionFlag.UnmanagedCode**.

Marshal.ThrowExceptionForHR Method

Throws an exception with a specific failure HRESULT value.

Overload List

Throws an exception with a specific failure HRESULT value.

[Visual Basic] **Overloads Public Shared Sub ThrowExceptionForHR(Integer)**

[C#] **public static void ThrowExceptionForHR(int);**

[C++] **public: static void ThrowExceptionForHR(int);**

[JScript] **public static function ThrowExceptionForHR(int);**

Throws an exception with a specific failure HRESULT.

[Visual Basic] **Overloads Public Shared Sub ThrowExceptionForHR(Integer, IntPtr)**

[C#] **public static void ThrowExceptionForHR(int, IntPtr);**

[C++] **public: static void ThrowExceptionForHR(int, IntPtr);**

[JScript] **public static function ThrowExceptionForHR(int, IntPtr);**

Marshal.ThrowExceptionForHR Method (Int32)

Throws an exception with a specific failure HRESULT value.

```
[Visual Basic]
Overloads Public Shared Sub ThrowExceptionForHR( _
    ByVal errorCode As Integer _
)
[C#]
public static void ThrowExceptionForHR(
    int errorCode
);
[C++]
public: static void ThrowExceptionForHR(
    int errorCode
);
[JScript]
public static function ThrowExceptionForHR(
    errorCode : int
);
```

Parameters

errorCode
> The HRESULT corresponding to the desired exception.

Remarks

This method creates an exception object for the specified failure HRESULT. If the HRESULT is 0 or positive (a success code), the method returns without creating or throwing an exception.

Some failure HRESULTs map to well-defined exceptions, while others do not map to a defined exception. If the HRESULT maps to a defined exception, **ThrowExceptionForHR** creates an instance of the exception and throws it. Otherwise, it creates an instance of **System.Runtime.InteropServices.COMException**, initializes the error code field with the HRESULT, and throws that exception. When this method is invoked, it attemps to retrieve extra information regarding the error by using the unmanaged **GetErrorInfo** function.

> **Note** This method uses **SecurityAction.LinkDemand** to prevent it from being called from untrusted code; only the immediate caller is required to have **SecurityPermission-Attribute.UnmanagedCode** permission. If your code can be called from partially trusted code, do not pass user input to **Marshal** class methods without validation.

Requirements

Platforms: Windows 98, Windows NT 4.0, Windows Millennium Edition, Windows 2000, Windows XP Home Edition, Windows XP Professional, Windows .NET Server family

.NET Framework Security:
- **SecurityPermission** for operating with unmanaged code. Associated enumeration: **SecurityPermissionFlag.UnmanagedCode**.

Marshal.ThrowExceptionForHR Method (Int32, IntPtr)

Throws an exception with a specific failure HRESULT.

```
[Visual Basic]
Overloads Public Shared Sub ThrowExceptionForHR( _
    ByVal errorCode As Integer, _
    ByVal errorInfo As IntPtr _
)
```

```
[C#]
public static void ThrowExceptionForHR(
    int errorCode,
    IntPtr errorInfo
);
[C++]
public: static void ThrowExceptionForHR(
    int errorCode,
    IntPtr errorInfo
);
[JScript]
public static function ThrowExceptionForHR(
    errorCode : int,
    errorInfo : IntPtr
);
```

Parameters

errorCode
  The HRESULT corresponding to the desired exception.

errorInfo
  A pointer to the **IErrorInfo** interface provided by the COM object.

Remarks

This method creates an exception object for the specified failure HRESULT. If the HRESULT is 0 or positive (a success code), the method returns without creating or throwing an exception.

Some failure HRESULTs map to well-defined exceptions, while others do not map to a defined exception. If the HRESULT maps to a defined exception, **ThrowExceptionForHR** creates an instance of the exception and throws it. Otherwise, it creates an instance of **System.Runtime.InteropServices.COMException**, initializes the error code field with the HRESULT, and throws that exception. The *errorInfo* parameter is used to retrieve extra information regarding the error.

> **Note** This method uses **SecurityAction.LinkDemand** to prevent it from being called from untrusted code; only the immediate caller is required to have **SecurityPermissionAttribute.UnmanagedCode** permission. If your code can be called from partially trusted code, do not pass user input to **Marshal** class methods without validation.

Requirements

Platforms: Windows 98, Windows NT 4.0, Windows Millennium Edition, Windows 2000, Windows XP Home Edition, Windows XP Professional, Windows .NET Server family

.NET Framework Security:
* **SecurityPermission** for operating with unmanaged code. Associated enumeration: **SecurityPermissionFlag.UnmanagedCode**.

Marshal.UnsafeAddrOfPinnedArrayElement Method

Gets the address of the element at the specified index inside the specified array.

```
[Visual Basic]
Public Shared Function UnsafeAddrOfPinnedArrayElement( _
    ByVal arr As Array, _
    ByVal index As Integer _
) As IntPtr
```

```
[C#]
public static IntPtr UnsafeAddrOfPinnedArrayElement(
    Array arr,
    int index
);
[C++]
public: static IntPtr UnsafeAddrOfPinnedArrayElement(
    Array* arr,
    int index
);
[JScript]
public static function UnsafeAddrOfPinnedArrayElement(
    arr : Array,
    index : int
) : IntPtr;
```

Parameters

arr
  The **Array** containing the desired element.

index
  The index in the *arr* parameter of the desired element.

Return Value

The address of *index* inside *arr*.

Remarks

The array must be pinned using a **GCHandle** before it is passed to this method. For maximum performance, this method does no validation on the array passed to it; this can result in unexpected behavior.

> **Note** This method uses **SecurityAction.LinkDemand** to prevent it from being called from untrusted code; only the immediate caller is required to have **SecurityPermissionAttribute.UnmanagedCode** permission. If your code can be called from partially trusted code, do not pass user input to **Marshal** class methods without validation.

Requirements

Platforms: Windows 98, Windows NT 4.0, Windows Millennium Edition, Windows 2000, Windows XP Home Edition, Windows XP Professional, Windows .NET Server family

.NET Framework Security:
* **SecurityPermission** for operating with unmanaged code. Associated enumeration: **SecurityPermissionFlag.UnmanagedCode**.

Marshal.WriteByte Method

Writes a single byte value to unmanaged memory.

Overload List

Writes a single byte value to unmanaged memory.

Supported by the .NET Compact Framework.

> [Visual Basic] **Overloads Public Shared Sub WriteByte(IntPtr, Byte)**
> [C#] **public static void WriteByte(IntPtr, byte);**
> [C++] **public: static void WriteByte(IntPtr, unsigned char);**
> [JScript] **public static function WriteByte(IntPtr, Byte);**

Writes a single byte value to unmanaged memory.

Supported by the .NET Compact Framework.

[Visual Basic] **Overloads Public Shared Sub WriteByte(IntPtr, Integer, Byte)**

[C#] **public static void WriteByte(IntPtr, int, byte);**

[C++] **public: static void WriteByte(IntPtr, int, unsigned char);**

[JScript] **public static function WriteByte(IntPtr, int, Byte);**

Writes a single byte value to unmanaged memory.

[Visual Basic] **Overloads Public Shared Sub WriteByte(Object, Integer, Byte)**

[C#] **public static void WriteByte(object, int, byte);**

[C++] **public: static void WriteByte(Object, int, unsigned char);**

[JScript] **public static function WriteByte(Object, int, Byte);**

Example

[Visual Basic, C#] The following example compares two ways of interacting with an unmanaged C-style byte array. The **WriteByte** method provides direct access to the element values of the array, setting its ten elements to the values 1 through 10.

[Visual Basic, C#] **Note** This example shows how to use one of the overloaded versions of **WriteByte**. For other examples that might be available, see the individual overload topics.

```
[Visual Basic]
Dim unmanagedArray As IntPtr = ...
Dim i As Integer
' One way to set the 10 elements of the C-style unmanagedArray
Dim newArray As Byte(9)
Marshal.Copy(unmanagedArray, newArray, 0, 10)
For i = 0 To newArray.Length
  newArray(i) = i+1
Next i
Marshal.Copy(newArray, 0, unmanagedArray, 10)
' Another way to set the 10 elements of the C-style unmanagedArray
For i = 0 To 10
  Marshal.WriteByte(unmanagedArray, i, i+1)
Next i
```

```
[C#]
IntPtr unmanagedArray = ...;
// One way to set the 10 elements of the C-style unmanagedArray
byte [] newArray = new byte[10];
Marshal.Copy(unmanagedArray, newArray, 0, 10);
for (int i = 0; i < newArray.Length; i++)
  newArray[i] = i+1;
Marshal.Copy(newArray, 0, unmanagedArray, 10);
// Another way to set the 10 elements of the C-style unmanagedArray
for (int i = 0; i < 10; i++)
  Marshal.WriteByte(unmanagedArray, i, i+1);
```

Marshal.WriteByte Method (IntPtr, Byte)

Writes a single byte value to unmanaged memory.

```
[Visual Basic]
Overloads Public Shared Sub WriteByte( _
   ByVal ptr As IntPtr, _
   ByVal val As Byte _
)
[C#]
public static void WriteByte(
   IntPtr ptr,
   byte val
);
```

```
[C++]
public: static void WriteByte(
   IntPtr ptr,
   unsigned char val
);
[JScript]
public static function WriteByte(
   ptr : IntPtr,
   val : Byte
);
```

Parameters

ptr
   The address in unmanaged memory from which to write.
val
   The value to write.

Exceptions

Exception Type	Condition
ArgumentException	*ptr* is not a recognized format.

Remarks

WriteByte enables direct interaction with an unmanaged C-style byte array, eliminating the expense of copying an entire unmanaged array (using **Marshal.Copy**) to a separate managed array before setting its element values.

Note This method uses **SecurityAction.LinkDemand** to prevent it from being called from untrusted code; only the immediate caller is required to have **SecurityPermission-Attribute.UnmanagedCode** permission. If your code can be called from partially trusted code, do not pass user input to **Marshal** class methods without validation.

Requirements

Platforms: Windows 98, Windows NT 4.0, Windows Millennium Edition, Windows 2000, Windows XP Home Edition, Windows XP Professional, Windows .NET Server family, .NET Compact Framework - Windows CE .NET

.NET Framework Security:
- **SecurityPermission** for operating with unmanaged code. Associated enumeration: **SecurityPermissionFlag.UnmanagedCode**.

Marshal.WriteByte Method (IntPtr, Int32, Byte)

Writes a single byte value to unmanaged memory.

```
[Visual Basic]
Overloads Public Shared Sub WriteByte( _
   ByVal ptr As IntPtr, _
   ByVal ofs As Integer, _
   ByVal val As Byte _
)
[C#]
public static void WriteByte(
   IntPtr ptr,
   int ofs,
   byte val
);
```

```
[C++]
public: static void WriteByte(
   IntPtr ptr,
   int ofs,
   unsigned char val
);
[JScript]
public static function WriteByte(
   ptr : IntPtr,
   ofs : int,
   val : Byte
);
```

Parameters

ptr

   The base address in unmanaged memory from which to write.

ofs

   An additional byte offset, added to the *ptr* parameter before writing.

val

   The value to write.

Exceptions

Exception Type	Condition
ArgumentException	*ptr* is not a recognized format.

Remarks

WriteByte enables direct interaction with an unmanaged C-style byte array, eliminating the expense of copying an entire unmanaged array (using **Marshal.Copy**) to a separate managed array before setting its element values.

> **Note** This method uses **SecurityAction.LinkDemand** to prevent it from being called from untrusted code; only the immediate caller is required to have **SecurityPermission-Attribute.UnmanagedCode** permission. If your code can be called from partially trusted code, do not pass user input to **Marshal** class methods without validation.

Example

[Visual Basic, C#] The following example compares two ways of interacting with an unmanaged C-style byte array. The **WriteByte** method provides direct access to the element values of the array, setting its ten elements to the values 1 through 10.

```
[Visual Basic]
Dim unmanagedArray As IntPtr = ...
Dim i As Integer
' One way to set the 10 elements of the C-style unmanagedArray
Dim newArray As Byte(9)
Marshal.Copy(unmanagedArray, newArray, 0, 10)
For i = 0 To newArray.Length
  newArray(i) = i+1
Next i
Marshal.Copy(newArray, 0, unmanagedArray, 10)
' Another way to set the 10 elements of the C-style unmanagedArray
For i = 0 To 10
  Marshal.WriteByte(unmanagedArray, i, i+1)
Next i
```

```
[C#]
IntPtr unmanagedArray = ...;
// One way to set the 10 elements of the C-style unmanagedArray
byte [] newArray = new byte[10];
Marshal.Copy(unmanagedArray, newArray, 0, 10);
for (int i = 0; i < newArray.Length; i++)
  newArray[i] = i+1;
```

```
Marshal.Copy(newArray, 0, unmanagedArray, 10);
// Another way to set the 10 elements of the C-style unmanagedArray
for (int i = 0; i < 10; i++)
  Marshal.WriteByte(unmanagedArray, i, i+1);
```

Requirements

Platforms: Windows 98, Windows NT 4.0, Windows Millennium Edition, Windows 2000, Windows XP Home Edition, Windows XP Professional, Windows .NET Server family, .NET Compact Framework - Windows CE .NET

Marshal.WriteByte Method (Object, Int32, Byte)

Writes a single byte value to unmanaged memory.

```
[Visual Basic]
Overloads Public Shared Sub WriteByte( _
   <InteropServices.In(), _
   Out()> ByVal ptr As Object, _
   ByVal ofs As Integer, _
   ByVal val As Byte _
)
[C#]
public static void WriteByte(
   [
   In,
   Out
   ] object ptr,
   int ofs,
   byte val
);
[C++]
public: static void WriteByte(
   [
   In,
   Out
   ] Object** ptr,
   int ofs,
   unsigned char val
);
[JScript]
public static function WriteByte(
   ptr : Object,
   ofs : int,
   val : Byte
);
```

Parameters

ptr

   The base address in unmanaged memory of the target object.

ofs

   An additional byte offset, added to the *ptr* parameter before writing.

val

   The value to write.

Exceptions

Exception Type	Condition
ArgumentException	*ptr* is not a recognized format.

Remarks

WriteByte enables direct interaction with an unmanaged C-style byte array, eliminating the expense of copying an entire unmanaged array (using **Marshal.Copy**) to a separate managed array before setting its element values.

> **Note** This method uses **SecurityAction.LinkDemand** to prevent it from being called from untrusted code; only the immediate caller is required to have **SecurityPermission-Attribute.UnmanagedCode** permission. If your code can be called from partially trusted code, do not pass user input to **Marshal** class methods without validation.

Requirements

Platforms: Windows 98, Windows NT 4.0, Windows Millennium Edition, Windows 2000, Windows XP Home Edition, Windows XP Professional, Windows .NET Server family

Marshal.WriteInt16 Method

Writes a 16-bit signed integer value to unmanaged memory.

Overload List

Writes a 16-bit signed integer value to unmanaged memory.

[Visual Basic] **Overloads Public Shared Sub WriteInt16(IntPtr, Char)**

[C#] **public static void WriteInt16(IntPtr, char);**

[C++] **public: static void WriteInt16(IntPtr, __wchar_t);**

[JScript] **public static function WriteInt16(IntPtr, Char);**

Writes a 16-bit integer value to unmanaged memory.

Supported by the .NET Compact Framework.

[Visual Basic] **Overloads Public Shared Sub WriteInt16(IntPtr, Short)**

[C#] **public static void WriteInt16(IntPtr, short);**

[C++] **public: static void WriteInt16(IntPtr, short);**

[JScript] **public static function WriteInt16(IntPtr, Int16);**

Writes a 16-bit signed integer value to unmanaged memory.

[Visual Basic] **Overloads Public Shared Sub WriteInt16(IntPtr, Integer, Char)**

[C#] **public static void WriteInt16(IntPtr, int, char);**

[C++] **public: static void WriteInt16(IntPtr, int, __wchar_t);**

[JScript] **public static function WriteInt16(IntPtr, int, Char);**

Writes a 16-bit signed integer value into unmanaged memory.

Supported by the .NET Compact Framework.

[Visual Basic] **Overloads Public Shared Sub WriteInt16(IntPtr, Integer, Short)**

[C#] **public static void WriteInt16(IntPtr, int, short);**

[C++] **public: static void WriteInt16(IntPtr, int, short);**

[JScript] **public static function WriteInt16(IntPtr, int, Int16);**

Writes a 16-bit signed integer value to unmanaged memory.

[Visual Basic] **Overloads Public Shared Sub WriteInt16(Object, Integer, Char)**

[C#] **public static void WriteInt16(object, int, char);**

[C++] **public: static void WriteInt16(Object, int, __wchar_t);**

[JScript] **public static function WriteInt16(Object, int, Char);**

Writes a 16-bit signed integer value to unmanaged memory.

[Visual Basic] **Overloads Public Shared Sub WriteInt16(Object, Integer, Short)**

[C#] **public static void WriteInt16(object, int, short);**

[C++] **public: static void WriteInt16(Object, int, short);**

[JScript] **public static function WriteInt16(Object, int, Int16);**

Example

[Visual Basic, C#] The following example compares two ways of interacting with an unmanaged C-style Int16 array. The **WriteInt16** method provides direct access to the element values of the array, setting its ten elements to the values 1 through 10.

> [Visual Basic, C#] **Note** This example shows how to use one of the overloaded versions of **WriteInt16**. For other examples that might be available, see the individual overload topics.

```
[Visual Basic]
Dim unmanagedArray As IntPtr = ...
Dim i As Integer
' One way to set the 10 elements of the C-style unmanagedArray
Dim newArray As Short(9)
Marshal.Copy(unmanagedArray, newArray, 0, 10)
For i = 0 To newArray.Length
  newArray(i) = i+1
Next i
Marshal.Copy(newArray, 0, unmanagedArray, 10)
' Another way to set the 10 elements of the C-style unmanagedArray
For i = 0 To 10
  Marshal.WriteInt16(unmanagedArray, i, i+1)
Next i
```

```
[C#]
IntPtr unmanagedArray = ...;
// One way to set the 10 elements of the C-style unmanagedArray
byte [] newArray = new short[10];
Marshal.Copy(unmanagedArray, newArray, 0, 10);
for (int i = 0; i < newArray.Length; i++)
  newArray[i] = i+1;
Marshal.Copy(newArray, 0, unmanagedArray, 10);
// Another way to set the 10 elements of the C-style unmanagedArray
for (int i = 0; i < 10; i++)
  Marshal.WriteInt16(unmanagedArray, i, i+1);
```

Marshal.WriteInt16 Method (IntPtr, Char)

Writes a 16-bit signed integer value to unmanaged memory.

```
[Visual Basic]
Overloads Public Shared Sub WriteInt16( _
   ByVal ptr As IntPtr, _
   ByVal val As Char _
)
[C#]
public static void WriteInt16(
   IntPtr ptr,
   char val
);
[C++]
public: static void WriteInt16(
   IntPtr ptr,
   __wchar_t val
);
[JScript]
public static function WriteInt16(
   ptr : IntPtr,
   val : Char
);
```

Parameters

ptr
   The address in unmanaged memory from which to write.
val
   The value to write.

Exceptions

Exception Type	Condition
ArgumentException	*ptr* is not a recognized format.

Remarks

WriteInt16 enables direct interaction with an unmanaged 16-bit signed array, eliminating the expense of copying an entire unmanaged array (using **Marshal.Copy**) to a separate managed array before setting its element values.

> **Note** This method uses **SecurityAction.LinkDemand** to prevent it from being called from untrusted code; only the immediate caller is required to have **SecurityPermission-Attribute.UnmanagedCode** permission. If your code can be called from partially trusted code, do not pass user input to **Marshal** class methods without validation.

Requirements

Platforms: Windows 98, Windows NT 4.0, Windows Millennium Edition, Windows 2000, Windows XP Home Edition, Windows XP Professional, Windows .NET Server family

.NET Framework Security:

*   **SecurityPermission** for operating with unmanaged code. Associated enumeration: **SecurityPermissionFlag.UnmanagedCode**.

Marshal.WriteInt16 Method (IntPtr, Int16)

Writes a 16-bit integer value to unmanaged memory.

```
[Visual Basic]
Overloads Public Shared Sub WriteInt16( _
   ByVal ptr As IntPtr, _
   ByVal val As Short _
)
[C#]
public static void WriteInt16(
   IntPtr ptr,
   short val
);
[C++]
public: static void WriteInt16(
   IntPtr ptr,
   short val
);
[JScript]
public static function WriteInt16(
   ptr : IntPtr,
   val : Int16
);
```

Parameters

ptr
   The address in unmanaged memory from which to write.

val
   The value to write.

Exceptions

Exception Type	Condition
ArgumentException	*ptr* is not a recognized format.

Remarks

WriteInt16 enables direct interaction with an unmanaged 16-bit signed array, eliminating the expense of copying an entire unmanaged array (using **Marshal.Copy**) to a separate managed array before setting its element values.

> **Note** This method uses **SecurityAction.LinkDemand** to prevent it from being called from untrusted code; only the immediate caller is required to have **SecurityPermission-Attribute.UnmanagedCode** permission. If your code can be called from partially trusted code, do not pass user input to **Marshal** class methods without validation.

Requirements

Platforms: Windows 98, Windows NT 4.0, Windows Millennium Edition, Windows 2000, Windows XP Home Edition, Windows XP Professional, Windows .NET Server family, .NET Compact Framework - Windows CE .NET

.NET Framework Security:

*   **SecurityPermission** for operating with unmanaged code. Associated enumeration: **SecurityPermissionFlag.UnmanagedCode**.

Marshal.WriteInt16 Method (IntPtr, Int32, Char)

Writes a 16-bit signed integer value to unmanaged memory.

```
[Visual Basic]
Overloads Public Shared Sub WriteInt16( _
   ByVal ptr As IntPtr, _
   ByVal ofs As Integer, _
   ByVal val As Char _
)
[C#]
public static void WriteInt16(
   IntPtr ptr,
   int ofs,
   char val
);
[C++]
public: static void WriteInt16(
   IntPtr ptr,
   int ofs,
   __wchar_t val
);
[JScript]
public static function WriteInt16(
   ptr : IntPtr,
   ofs : int,
   val : Char
);
```

Parameters

ptr

The base address in the native heap from which to write.

ofs

An additional byte offset, added to the *ptr* parameter before writing.

val

The value to write.

Exceptions

Exception Type	Condition
ArgumentException	*ptr* is not a recognized format.

Remarks

WriteInt16 enables direct interaction with an unmanaged 16-bit signed array, eliminating the expense of copying an entire unmanaged array (using **Marshal.Copy**) to a separate managed array before setting its element values.

> **Note** This method uses **SecurityAction.LinkDemand** to prevent it from being called from untrusted code; only the immediate caller is required to have **SecurityPermission-Attribute.UnmanagedCode** permission. If your code can be called from partially trusted code, do not pass user input to **Marshal** class methods without validation.

Example

[Visual Basic, C#] The following example compares two ways of interacting with an unmanaged C-style Int16 array. The **WriteInt16** method provides direct access to the element values of the array, setting its ten elements to the values 1 through 10.

```
[Visual Basic]
Dim unmanagedArray As IntPtr = ...
Dim i As Integer
' One way to set the 10 elements of the C-style unmanagedArray
Dim newArray As Char(9)
Marshal.Copy(unmanagedArray, newArray, 0, 10)
For i = 0 To newArray.Length
  newArray(i) = i+1
Next i
Marshal.Copy(newArray, 0, unmanagedArray, 10)
' Another way to set the 10 elements of the C-style unmanagedArray
For i = 0 To 10
  Marshal.WriteInt16(unmanagedArray, i, i+1)
Next i
```

```
[C#]
IntPtr unmanagedArray = ...;
// One way to set the 10 elements of the C-style unmanagedArray
byte [] newArray = new char[10];
Marshal.Copy(unmanagedArray, newArray, 0, 10);
for (int i = 0; i < newArray.Length; i++)
  newArray[i] = i+1;
Marshal.Copy(newArray, 0, unmanagedArray, 10);
// Another way to set the 10 elements of the C-style unmanagedArray
for (int i = 0; i < 10; i++)
  Marshal.WriteInt16(unmanagedArray, i, i+1);
```

Requirements

Platforms: Windows 98, Windows NT 4.0, Windows Millennium Edition, Windows 2000, Windows XP Home Edition, Windows XP Professional, Windows .NET Server family

Marshal.WriteInt16 Method (IntPtr, Int32, Int16)

Writes a 16-bit signed integer value into unmanaged memory.

```
[Visual Basic]
Overloads Public Shared Sub WriteInt16( _
  ByVal ptr As IntPtr, _
  ByVal ofs As Integer, _
  ByVal val As Short _
)
[C#]
public static void WriteInt16(
  IntPtr ptr,
  int ofs,
  short val
);
[C++]
public: static void WriteInt16(
  IntPtr ptr,
  int ofs,
  short val
);
[JScript]
public static function WriteInt16(
  ptr : IntPtr,
  ofs : int,
  val : Int16
);
```

Parameters

ptr

The base address in unmanaged memory from which to write.

ofs

An additional byte offset, added to the *ptr* parameter before writing.

val

The value to write.

Exceptions

Exception Type	Condition
ArgumentException	*ptr* is not a recognized format.

Remarks

WriteInt16 enables direct interaction with an unmanaged 16-bit signed array, eliminating the expense of copying an entire unmanaged array (using **Marshal.Copy**) to a separate managed array before setting its element values.

> **Note** This method uses **SecurityAction.LinkDemand** to prevent it from being called from untrusted code; only the immediate caller is required to have **SecurityPermission-Attribute.UnmanagedCode** permission. If your code can be called from partially trusted code, do not pass user input to **Marshal** class methods without validation.

Example

[Visual Basic, C#] The following example compares two ways of interacting with an unmanaged C-style Int16 array. The **WriteInt16** method provides direct access to the element values of the array, setting its ten elements to the values 1 through 10.

```
[Visual Basic]
Dim unmanagedArray As IntPtr = ...
Dim i As Integer
```

```
' One way to set the 10 elements of the C-style unmanagedArray
Dim newArray As Short(9)
Marshal.Copy(unmanagedArray, newArray, 0, 10)
For i = 0 To newArray.Length
  newArray(i) = i+1
Next i
Marshal.Copy(newArray, 0, unmanagedArray, 10)
' Another way to set the 10 elements of the C-style unmanagedArray
For i = 0 To 10
  Marshal.WriteInt16(unmanagedArray, i, i+1)
Next i

[C#]
IntPtr unmanagedArray = ...;
// One way to set the 10 elements of the C-style unmanagedArray
byte [] newArray = new short[10];
Marshal.Copy(unmanagedArray, newArray, 0, 10);
for (int i = 0; i < newArray.Length; i++)
  newArray[i] = i+1;
Marshal.Copy(newArray, 0, unmanagedArray, 10);
// Another way to set the 10 elements of the C-style unmanagedArray
for (int i = 0; i < 10; i++)
  Marshal.WriteInt16(unmanagedArray, i, i+1);
```

Requirements

Platforms: Windows 98, Windows NT 4.0,
Windows Millennium Edition, Windows 2000,
Windows XP Home Edition, Windows XP Professional,
Windows .NET Server family,
.NET Compact Framework - Windows CE .NET

Marshal.WriteInt16 Method (Object, Int32, Char)

Writes a 16-bit signed integer value to unmanaged memory.

```
[Visual Basic]
Overloads Public Shared Sub WriteInt16( _
   <InteropServices.In(), _
   Out()> ByVal ptr As Object, _
   ByVal ofs As Integer, _
   ByVal val As Char _
)
[C#]
public static void WriteInt16(
   [
   In,
   Out
] object ptr,
   int ofs,
   char val
);
[C++]
public: static void WriteInt16(
   [
   In,
   Out
] Object** ptr,
   int ofs,
   __wchar_t val
);
[JScript]
public static function WriteInt16(
   ptr : Object,
   ofs : int,
   val : Char
);
```

Parameters

ptr

The base address in unmanaged memory of the target object.

ofs

An additional byte offset, added to the *ptr* parameter before writing.

val

The value to write.

Exceptions

Exception Type	Condition
ArgumentException	*ptr* must be a recognized format.

Remarks

WriteInt16 enables direct interaction with an unmanaged 16-bit signed array, eliminating the expense of copying an entire unmanaged array (using **Marshal.Copy**) to a separate managed array before setting its element values.

> **Note** This method uses **SecurityAction.LinkDemand** to prevent it from being called from untrusted code; only the immediate caller is required to have **SecurityPermission-Attribute.UnmanagedCode** permission. If your code can be called from partially trusted code, do not pass user input to **Marshal** class methods without validation.

Requirements

Platforms: Windows 98, Windows NT 4.0,
Windows Millennium Edition, Windows 2000,
Windows XP Home Edition, Windows XP Professional,
Windows .NET Server family

Marshal.WriteInt16 Method (Object, Int32, Int16)

Writes a 16-bit signed integer value to unmanaged memory.

```
[Visual Basic]
Overloads Public Shared Sub WriteInt16( _
   <InteropServices.In(), _
   Out()> ByVal ptr As Object, _
   ByVal ofs As Integer, _
   ByVal val As Short _
)
[C#]
public static void WriteInt16(
   [
   In,
   Out
] object ptr,
   int ofs,
   short val
);
[C++]
public: static void WriteInt16(
   [
   In,
   Out
] Object** ptr,
   int ofs,
   short val
);
```

```
[JScript]
public static function WriteInt16(
   ptr : Object,
   ofs : int,
   val : Int16
);
```

Parameters

ptr

   The base address in unmanaged memory of the target object.

ofs

   An additional byte offset, added to the *ptr* parameter before writing.

val

   The value to write.

Exceptions

Exception Type	Condition
ArgumentException	*ptr* is not a recognized format.

Remarks

WriteInt16 enables direct interaction with an unmanaged 16-bit signed array, eliminating the expense of copying an entire unmanaged array (using **Marshal.Copy**) to a separate managed array before setting its element values.

> **Note** This method uses **SecurityAction.LinkDemand** to prevent it from being called from untrusted code; only the immediate caller is required to have **SecurityPermission-Attribute.UnmanagedCode** permission. If your code can be called from partially trusted code, do not pass user input to **Marshal** class methods without validation.

Requirements

Platforms: Windows 98, Windows NT 4.0, Windows Millennium Edition, Windows 2000, Windows XP Home Edition, Windows XP Professional, Windows .NET Server family

.NET Framework Security:

* **ArgumentException**

Marshal.WriteInt32 Method

Writes a 32-bit signed integer value to unmanaged memory.

Overload List

Writes a 32-bit signed integer value to unmanaged memory.

Supported by the .NET Compact Framework.

   [Visual Basic] **Overloads Public Shared Sub WriteInt32(IntPtr, Integer)**

   [C#] **public static void WriteInt32(IntPtr, int);**

   [C++] **public: static void WriteInt32(IntPtr, int);**

   [JScript] **public static function WriteInt32(IntPtr, int);**

Writes a 32-bit signed integer value into unmanaged memory.

Supported by the .NET Compact Framework.

   [Visual Basic] **Overloads Public Shared Sub WriteInt32(IntPtr, Integer, Integer)**

   [C#] **public static void WriteInt32(IntPtr, int, int);**

   [C++] **public: static void WriteInt32(IntPtr, int, int);**

   [JScript] **public static function WriteInt32(IntPtr, int, int);**

Writes a 32-bit signed integer value to unmanaged memory.

   [Visual Basic] **Overloads Public Shared Sub WriteInt32(Object, Integer, Integer)**

   [C#] **public static void WriteInt32(object, int, int);**

   [C++] **public: static void WriteInt32(Object, int, int);**

   [JScript] **public static function WriteInt32(Object, int, int);**

Example

[Visual Basic, C#] The following example compares two ways of interacting with an unmanaged C-style Int32 array. The **WriteInt32** method provides direct access to the element values of the array, setting its ten elements to the values 1 through 10.

> [Visual Basic, C#] **Note** This example shows how to use one of the overloaded versions of **WriteInt32**. For other examples that might be available, see the individual overload topics.

```
[Visual Basic]
Dim unmanagedArray As IntPtr = ...
Dim i As Integer
' One way to set the 10 elements of the C-style unmanagedArray
Dim newArray As Integer(9)
Marshal.Copy(unmanagedArray, newArray, 0, 10)
For i = 0 To newArray.Length
   newArray(i) = i+1
Next i
Marshal.Copy(newArray, 0, unmanagedArray, 10)
' Another way to set the 10 elements of the C-style unmanagedArray
For i = 0 To 10
   Marshal.WriteInt32(unmanagedArray, i, i+1)
Next i
```

```
[C#]
IntPtr unmanagedArray = ...;
// One way to set the 10 elements of the C-style unmanagedArray
byte [] newArray = new int[10];
Marshal.Copy(unmanagedArray, newArray, 0, 10);
for (int i = 0; i < newArray.Length; i++)
   newArray[i] = i+1;
Marshal.Copy(newArray, 0, unmanagedArray, 10);
// Another way to set the 10 elements of the C-style unmanagedArray
for (int i = 0; i < 10; i++)
   Marshal.WriteInt32(unmanagedArray, i, i+1);
```

Marshal.WriteInt32 Method (IntPtr, Int32)

Writes a 32-bit signed integer value to unmanaged memory.

```
[Visual Basic]
Overloads Public Shared Sub WriteInt32( _
   ByVal ptr As IntPtr, _
   ByVal val As Integer _
)
[C#]
public static void WriteInt32(
   IntPtr ptr,
   int val
);
[C++]
public: static void WriteInt32(
   IntPtr ptr,
   int val
);
[JScript]
public static function WriteInt32(
   ptr : IntPtr,
   val : int
);
```

Parameters

ptr
  The address in unmanaged memory from which to write.

val
  The value to write.

Exceptions

Exception Type	Condition
ArgumentException	*ptr* is not a recognized format.

Remarks

WriteInt32 enables direct interaction with an unmanaged 32-bit signed array, eliminating the expense of copying an entire unmanaged array (using **Marshal.Copy**) to a separate managed array before setting its element values.

> **Note** This method uses **SecurityAction.LinkDemand** to prevent it from being called from untrusted code; only the immediate caller is required to have **SecurityPermission-Attribute.UnmanagedCode** permission. If your code can be called from partially trusted code, do not pass user input to **Marshal** class methods without validation.

Requirements

Platforms: Windows 98, Windows NT 4.0, Windows Millennium Edition, Windows 2000, Windows XP Home Edition, Windows XP Professional, Windows .NET Server family, .NET Compact Framework - Windows CE .NET

.NET Framework Security:

- **SecurityPermission** for operating with unmanaged code. Associated enumeration: **SecurityPermissionFlag.UnmanagedCode**.

Marshal.WriteInt32 Method (IntPtr, Int32, Int32)

Writes a 32-bit signed integer value into unmanaged memory.

```
[Visual Basic]
Overloads Public Shared Sub WriteInt32( _
    ByVal ptr As IntPtr, _
    ByVal ofs As Integer, _
    ByVal val As Integer _
)
[C#]
public static void WriteInt32(
    IntPtr ptr,
    int ofs,
    int val
);
[C++]
public: static void WriteInt32(
    IntPtr ptr,
    int ofs,
    int val
);
[JScript]
public static function WriteInt32(
    ptr : IntPtr,
    ofs : int,
    val : int
);
```

Parameters

ptr
  The base address in unmanaged memory from which to write.

ofs
  An additional byte offset, added to the *ptr* parameter before writing.

val
  The value to write.

Exceptions

Exception Type	Condition
ArgumentException	*ptr* is not a recognized format.

Remarks

WriteInt32 enables direct interaction with an unmanaged 32-bit signed array, eliminating the expense of copying an entire unmanaged array (using **Marshal.Copy**) to a separate managed array before setting its element values.

> **Note** This method uses **SecurityAction.LinkDemand** to prevent it from being called from untrusted code; only the immediate caller is required to have **SecurityPermission-Attribute.UnmanagedCode** permission. If your code can be called from partially trusted code, do not pass user input to **Marshal** class methods without validation.

Example

[Visual Basic, C#] The following example compares two ways of interacting with an unmanaged C-style Int32 array. The **WriteInt32** method provides direct access to the element values of the array, setting its ten elements to the values 1 through 10.

```
[Visual Basic]
Dim unmanagedArray As IntPtr = ...
Dim i As Integer
' One way to set the 10 elements of the C-style unmanagedArray
Dim newArray As Integer(9)
Marshal.Copy(unmanagedArray, newArray, 0, 10)
For i = 0 To newArray.Length
    newArray(i) = i+1
Next i
Marshal.Copy(newArray, 0, unmanagedArray, 10)
' Another way to set the 10 elements of the C-style unmanagedArray
For i = 0 To 10
    Marshal.WriteInt32(unmanagedArray, i, i+1)
Next i
```

```
[C#]
IntPtr unmanagedArray = ...;
// One way to set the 10 elements of the C-style unmanagedArray
byte [] newArray = new int[10];
Marshal.Copy(unmanagedArray, newArray, 0, 10);
for (int i = 0; i < newArray.Length; i++)
    newArray[i] = i+1;
Marshal.Copy(newArray, 0, unmanagedArray, 10);
// Another way to set the 10 elements of the C-style unmanagedArray
for (int i = 0; i < 10; i++)
    Marshal.WriteInt32(unmanagedArray, i, i+1);
```

Requirements

Platforms: Windows 98, Windows NT 4.0, Windows Millennium Edition, Windows 2000, Windows XP Home Edition, Windows XP Professional, Windows .NET Server family, .NET Compact Framework - Windows CE .NET

Marshal.WriteInt32 Method (Object, Int32, Int32)

Writes a 32-bit signed integer value to unmanaged memory.

```
[Visual Basic]
Overloads Public Shared Sub WriteInt32( _
   <InteropServices.In(), _
   Out()> ByVal ptr As Object, _
   ByVal ofs As Integer, _
   ByVal val As Integer _
)
[C#]
public static void WriteInt32(
   [
   In,
   Out
] object ptr,
   int ofs,
   int val
);
[C++]
public: static void WriteInt32(
   [
   In,
   Out
] Object** ptr,
   int ofs,
   int val
);
[JScript]
public static function WriteInt32(
   ptr : Object,
   ofs : int,
   val : int
);
```

Parameters

ptr

   The base address in unmanaged memory of the target object.

ofs

   An additional byte offset, added to the *ptr* parameter before writing.

val

   The value to write.

Exceptions

Exception Type	Condition
ArgumentException	*ptr* is not a recognized format.

Remarks

WriteInt32 enables direct interaction with an unmanaged 32-bit signed array, eliminating the expense of copying an entire unmanaged array (using **Marshal.Copy**) to a separate managed array before setting its element values.

> **Note** This method uses **SecurityAction.LinkDemand** to prevent it from being called from untrusted code; only the immediate caller is required to have **SecurityPermissionAttribute.UnmanagedCode** permission. If your code can be called from partially trusted code, do not pass user input to **Marshal** class methods without validation.

Requirements

Platforms: Windows 98, Windows NT 4.0, Windows Millennium Edition, Windows 2000, Windows XP Home Edition, Windows XP Professional, Windows .NET Server family

Marshal.WriteInt64 Method

Writes a 64-bit signed integer value to unmanaged memory.

Overload List

Writes a 64-bit signed integer value to unmanaged memory.

   [Visual Basic] **Overloads Public Shared Sub WriteInt64(IntPtr, Long)**

   [C#] **public static void WriteInt64(IntPtr, long);**

   [C++] **public: static void WriteInt64(IntPtr, __int64);**

   [JScript] **public static function WriteInt64(IntPtr, long);**

Writes a 64-bit signed integer value to unmanaged memory.

   [Visual Basic] **Overloads Public Shared Sub WriteInt64(IntPtr, Integer, Long)**

   [C#] **public static void WriteInt64(IntPtr, int, long);**

   [C++] **public: static void WriteInt64(IntPtr, int, __int64);**

   [JScript] **public static function WriteInt64(IntPtr, int, long);**

Writes a 64-bit signed integer value to unmanaged memory.

   [Visual Basic] **Overloads Public Shared Sub WriteInt64(Object, Integer, Long)**

   [C#] **public static void WriteInt64(object, int, long);**

   [C++] **public: static void WriteInt64(Object, int, __int64);**

   [JScript] **public static function WriteInt64(Object, int, long);**

Example

[Visual Basic, C#] The following example compares two ways of interacting with an unmanaged C-style Int64 array. The **WriteInt64** method provides direct access to the element values of the array, setting its ten elements to the values 1 through 10.

> [Visual Basic, C#] **Note** This example shows how to use one of the overloaded versions of **WriteInt64**. For other examples that might be available, see the individual overload topics.

```
[Visual Basic]
Dim unmanagedArray As IntPtr = ...
Dim i As Integer
' One way to set the 10 elements of the C-style unmanagedArray
Dim newArray As Long(9)
Marshal.Copy(unmanagedArray, newArray, 0, 10)
For i = 0 To newArray.Length
   newArray(i) = i+1
Next i
Marshal.Copy(newArray, 0, unmanagedArray, 10)
' Another way to set the 10 elements of the C-style unmanagedArray
For i = 0 To 10
   Marshal.WriteInt64(unmanagedArray, i, i+1)
Next i

[C#]
IntPtr unmanagedArray = ...;
// One way to set the 10 elements of the C-style unmanagedArray
byte [] newArray = new long[10];
Marshal.Copy(unmanagedArray, newArray, 0, 10);
for (int i = 0; i < newArray.Length; i++)
   newArray[i] = i+1;
Marshal.Copy(newArray, 0, unmanagedArray, 10);
```

```
// Another way to set the 10 elements of the C-style unmanagedArray
for (int i = 0; i < 10; i++)
  Marshal.WriteInt64(unmanagedArray, i, i+1);
```

Marshal.WriteInt64 Method (IntPtr, Int64)

Writes a 64-bit signed integer value to unmanaged memory.

```
[Visual Basic]
Overloads Public Shared Sub WriteInt64( _
  ByVal ptr As IntPtr, _
  ByVal val As Long _
)
[C#]
public static void WriteInt64(
  IntPtr ptr,
  long val
);
[C++]
public: static void WriteInt64(
  IntPtr ptr,
  __int64 val
);
[JScript]
public static function WriteInt64(
  ptr : IntPtr,
  val : long
);
```

Parameters

ptr
    The address in unmanaged memory from which to write.
val
    The value to write.

Exceptions

Exception Type	Condition
ArgumentException	*ptr* is not a recognized format.

Remarks

WriteInt64 enables direct interaction with an unmanaged 64-bit signed array, eliminating the expense of copying an entire unmanaged array (using **Marshal.Copy**) to a separate managed array before setting its element values.

> **Note** This method uses **SecurityAction.LinkDemand** to prevent it from being called from untrusted code; only the immediate caller is required to have **SecurityPermission-Attribute.UnmanagedCode** permission. If your code can be called from partially trusted code, do not pass user input to **Marshal** class methods without validation.

Requirements

Platforms: Windows 98, Windows NT 4.0, Windows Millennium Edition, Windows 2000, Windows XP Home Edition, Windows XP Professional, Windows .NET Server family

.NET Framework Security:
- **SecurityPermission** for operating with unmanaged code. Associated enumeration: **SecurityPermissionFlag.UnmanagedCode**.

Marshal.WriteInt64 Method (IntPtr, Int32, Int64)

Writes a 64-bit signed integer value to unmanaged memory.

```
[Visual Basic]
Overloads Public Shared Sub WriteInt64( _
  ByVal ptr As IntPtr, _
  ByVal ofs As Integer, _
  ByVal val As Long _
)
[C#]
public static void WriteInt64(
  IntPtr ptr,
  int ofs,
  long val
);
[C++]
public: static void WriteInt64(
  IntPtr ptr,
  int ofs,
  __int64 val
);
[JScript]
public static function WriteInt64(
  ptr : IntPtr,
  ofs : int,
  val : long
);
```

Parameters

ptr
    The base address in unmanaged memory from which to write.
ofs
    An additional byte offset, added to the *ptr* parameter before writing.
val
    The value to write.

Exceptions

Exception Type	Condition
ArgumentException	*ptr* is not a recognized format.

Remarks

WriteInt64 enables direct interaction with an unmanaged 64-bit signed array, eliminating the expense of copying an entire unmanaged array (using **Marshal.Copy**) to a separate managed array before setting its element values.

> **Note** This method uses **SecurityAction.LinkDemand** to prevent it from being called from untrusted code; only the immediate caller is required to have **SecurityPermission-Attribute.UnmanagedCode** permission. If your code can be called from partially trusted code, do not pass user input to **Marshal** class methods without validation.

Example

[Visual Basic, C#] The following example compares two ways of interacting with an unmanaged C-style Int64 array. The **WriteInt64** method provides direct access to the element values of the array, setting its ten elements to the values 1 through 10.

```
[Visual Basic]
Dim unmanagedArray As IntPtr = ...
Dim i As Integer
' One way to set the 10 elements of the C-style unmanagedArray
Dim newArray As Long(9)
Marshal.Copy(unmanagedArray, newArray, 0, 10)
For i = 0 To newArray.Length
  newArray(i) = i+1
Next i
Marshal.Copy(newArray, 0, unmanagedArray, 10)
' Another way to set the 10 elements of the C-style unmanagedArray
For i = 0 To 10
  Marshal.WriteInt64(unmanagedArray, i, i+1)
Next i
```

```
[C#]
IntPtr unmanagedArray = ...;
// One way to set the 10 elements of the C-style unmanagedArray
byte [] newArray = new long[10];
Marshal.Copy(unmanagedArray, newArray, 0, 10);
for (int i = 0; i < newArray.Length; i++)
  newArray[i] = i+1;
Marshal.Copy(newArray, 0, unmanagedArray, 10);
// Another way to set the 10 elements of the C-style unmanagedArray
for (int i = 0; i < 10; i++)
  Marshal.WriteInt64(unmanagedArray, i, i+1);
```

Requirements

Platforms: Windows 98, Windows NT 4.0,
Windows Millennium Edition, Windows 2000,
Windows XP Home Edition, Windows XP Professional,
Windows .NET Server family

Marshal.WriteInt64 Method (Object, Int32, Int64)

Writes a 64-bit signed integer value to unmanaged memory.

```
[Visual Basic]
Overloads Public Shared Sub WriteInt64( _
   <InteropServices.In(), _
   Out()> ByVal ptr As Object, _
   ByVal ofs As Integer, _
   ByVal val As Long _
)
[C#]
public static void WriteInt64(
   [
   In,
   Out
] object ptr,
   int ofs,
   long val
);
[C++]
public: static void WriteInt64(
   [
   In,
   Out
] Object** ptr,
   int ofs,
   __int64 val
);
[JScript]
public static function WriteInt64(
   ptr : Object,
   ofs : int,
   val : long
);
```

Parameters

ptr
> The base address in unmanaged memory of the target object.

ofs
> An additional byte offset, added to the *ptr* parameter before writing.

val
> The value to write.

Exceptions

Exception Type	Condition
ArgumentException	*ptr* is not a recognized format.

Remarks

WriteInt64 enables direct interaction with an unmanaged 64-bit signed array, eliminating the expense of copying an entire unmanaged array (using **Marshal.Copy**) to a separate managed array before setting its element values.

> **Note** This method uses **SecurityAction.LinkDemand** to prevent it from being called from untrusted code; only the immediate caller is required to have **SecurityPermission-Attribute.UnmanagedCode** permission. If your code can be called from partially trusted code, do not pass user input to **Marshal** class methods without validation.

Requirements

Platforms: Windows 98, Windows NT 4.0,
Windows Millennium Edition, Windows 2000,
Windows XP Home Edition, Windows XP Professional,
Windows .NET Server family

Marshal.WriteIntPtr Method

Writes a processor native sized integer value to unmanaged memory.

Overload List

Writes a processor native sized integer value into unmanaged memory.

> [Visual Basic] **Overloads Public Shared Sub WriteIntPtr(IntPtr, IntPtr)**
>
> [C#] **public static void WriteIntPtr(IntPtr, IntPtr);**
>
> [C++] **public: static void WriteIntPtr(IntPtr, IntPtr);**
>
> [JScript] **public static function WriteIntPtr(IntPtr, IntPtr);**

Writes a processor native sized integer value to unmanaged memory.

> [Visual Basic] **Overloads Public Shared Sub WriteIntPtr(IntPtr, Integer, IntPtr)**
>
> [C#] **public static void WriteIntPtr(IntPtr, int, IntPtr);**
>
> [C++] **public: static void WriteIntPtr(IntPtr, int, IntPtr);**
>
> [JScript] **public static function WriteIntPtr(IntPtr, int, IntPtr);**

Writes a processor native sized integer value to unmanaged memory.

> [Visual Basic] **Overloads Public Shared Sub WriteIntPtr(Object, Integer, IntPtr)**
>
> [C#] **public static void WriteIntPtr(object, int, IntPtr);**
>
> [C++] **public: static void WriteIntPtr(Object, int, IntPtr);**
>
> [JScript] **public static function WriteIntPtr(Object, int, IntPtr);**

Example

[Visual Basic, C#] The following example compares two ways of interacting with an unmanaged C-style IntPtr array. The

WriteIntPtr method provides direct access to the element values of the array, setting its ten elements to the values 1 through 10.

> [Visual Basic, C#] **Note** This example shows how to use one of the overloaded versions of **WriteIntPtr**. For other examples that might be available, see the individual overload topics.

[Visual Basic]
```
Dim unmanagedArray As IntPtr = ...
Dim i As Integer
' One way to set the 10 elements of the C-style unmanagedArray
Dim newArray As IntPtr(9)
Marshal.Copy(unmanagedArray, newArray, 0, 10)
For i = 0 To newArray.Length
  newArray(i) = i+1
Next i
Marshal.Copy(newArray, 0, unmanagedArray, 10)
' Another way to set the 10 elements of the C-style unmanagedArray
For i = 0 To 10
  Marshal.WriteIntPtr(unmanagedArray, i, i+1)
Next i
```

[C#]
```
IntPtr unmanagedArray = ...;
// One way to set the 10 elements of the C-style unmanagedArray
byte [] newArray = new IntPtr[10];
Marshal.Copy(unmanagedArray, newArray, 0, 10);
for (int i = 0; i < newArray.Length; i++)
  newArray[i] = i+1;
Marshal.Copy(newArray, 0, unmanagedArray, 10);
// Another way to set the 10 elements of the C-style unmanagedArray
for (int i = 0; i < 10; i++)
  Marshal.WriteIntPtr(unmanagedArray, i, i+1);
```

Marshal.WriteIntPtr Method (IntPtr, IntPtr)

Writes a processor native sized integer value into unmanaged memory.

[Visual Basic]
```
Overloads Public Shared Sub WriteIntPtr( _
  ByVal ptr As IntPtr, _
  ByVal val As IntPtr _
)
```
[C#]
```
public static void WriteIntPtr(
  IntPtr ptr,
  IntPtr val
);
```
[C++]
```
public: static void WriteIntPtr(
  IntPtr ptr,
  IntPtr val
);
```
[JScript]
```
public static function WriteIntPtr(
  ptr : IntPtr,
  val : IntPtr
);
```

Parameters

ptr
> The address in unmanaged memory from which to write.

val
> The value to write.

Exceptions

Exception Type	Condition
ArgumentException	*ptr* is not a recognized format.

Remarks

WriteIntPtr enables direct interaction with an unmanaged C-style IntPtr array, eliminating the expense of copying an entire unmanaged array (using **Marshal.Copy**) to a separate managed array before setting its element values.

> **Note** This method uses **SecurityAction.LinkDemand** to prevent it from being called from untrusted code; only the immediate caller is required to have **SecurityPermission-Attribute.UnmanagedCode** permission. If your code can be called from partially trusted code, do not pass user input to **Marshal** class methods without validation.

Requirements

Platforms: Windows 98, Windows NT 4.0, Windows Millennium Edition, Windows 2000, Windows XP Home Edition, Windows XP Professional, Windows .NET Server family

.NET Framework Security:
- **SecurityPermission** for operating with unmanaged code. Associated enumeration: **SecurityPermissionFlag.UnmanagedCode.**

Marshal.WriteIntPtr Method (IntPtr, Int32, IntPtr)

Writes a processor native sized integer value to unmanaged memory.

[Visual Basic]
```
Overloads Public Shared Sub WriteIntPtr( _
  ByVal ptr As IntPtr, _
  ByVal ofs As Integer, _
  ByVal val As IntPtr _
)
```
[C#]
```
public static void WriteIntPtr(
  IntPtr ptr,
  int ofs,
  IntPtr val
);
```
[C++]
```
public: static void WriteIntPtr(
  IntPtr ptr,
  int ofs,
  IntPtr val
);
```
[JScript]
```
public static function WriteIntPtr(
  ptr : IntPtr,
  ofs : int,
  val : IntPtr
);
```

Parameters

ptr
> The base address in unmanaged memory from which to write.

ofs
> An additional byte offset, added to the *ptr* parameter before writing.

val
> The value to write.

Exceptions

Exception Type	Condition
ArgumentException	*ptr* is not a recognized format.

Remarks

WriteIntPtr enables direct interaction with an unmanaged C-style IntPtr array, eliminating the expense of copying an entire unmanaged array (using **Marshal.Copy**) to a separate managed array before setting its element values.

> **Note** This method uses **SecurityAction.LinkDemand** to prevent it from being called from untrusted code; only the immediate caller is required to have **SecurityPermission-Attribute.UnmanagedCode** permission. If your code can be called from partially trusted code, do not pass user input to **Marshal** class methods without validation.

Example

[Visual Basic, C#] The following example compares two ways of interacting with an unmanaged C-style IntPtr array. The **WriteIntPtr** method provides direct access to the element values of the array, setting its ten elements to the values 1 through 10.

```
[Visual Basic]
Dim unmanagedArray As IntPtr = ...
Dim i As Integer
' One way to set the 10 elements of the C-style unmanagedArray
Dim newArray As IntPtr(9)
Marshal.Copy(unmanagedArray, newArray, 0, 10)
For i = 0 To newArray.Length
  newArray(i) = i+1
Next i
Marshal.Copy(newArray, 0, unmanagedArray, 10)
' Another way to set the 10 elements of the C-style unmanagedArray
For i = 0 To 10
  Marshal.WriteIntPtr(unmanagedArray, i, i+1)
Next i
```

```
[C#]
IntPtr unmanagedArray = ...;
// One way to set the 10 elements of the C-style unmanagedArray
byte [] newArray = new IntPtr[10];
Marshal.Copy(unmanagedArray, newArray, 0, 10);
for (int i = 0; i < newArray.Length; i++)
  newArray[i] = i+1;
Marshal.Copy(newArray, 0, unmanagedArray, 10);
// Another way to set the 10 elements of the C-style unmanagedArray
for (int i = 0; i < 10; i++)
  Marshal.WriteIntPtr(unmanagedArray, i, i+1);
```

Requirements

Platforms: Windows 98, Windows NT 4.0, Windows Millennium Edition, Windows 2000, Windows XP Home Edition, Windows XP Professional, Windows .NET Server family

.NET Framework Security:

- **SecurityPermission** for operating with unmanaged code. Associated enumeration: **SecurityPermissionFlag.UnmanagedCode**.

Marshal.WriteIntPtr Method (Object, Int32, IntPtr)

Writes a processor native sized integer value to unmanaged memory.

```
[Visual Basic]
Overloads Public Shared Sub WriteIntPtr( _
   <InteropServices.In(), _
   Out()> ByVal ptr As Object, _
   ByVal ofs As Integer, _
   ByVal val As IntPtr _
)
```

```
[C#]
public static void WriteIntPtr(
   [
   In,
   Out
   ] object ptr,
   int ofs,
   IntPtr val
);
```

```
[C++]
public: static void WriteIntPtr(
   [
   In,
   Out
   ] Object** ptr,
   int ofs,
   IntPtr val
);
```

```
[JScript]
public static function WriteIntPtr(
   ptr : Object,
   ofs : int,
   val : IntPtr
);
```

Parameters

ptr
  The base address in unmanaged memory of the target object.
ofs
  An additional byte offset, added to the *ptr* parameter before writing.
val
  The value to write.

Exceptions

Exception Type	Condition
ArgumentException	*ptr* is not a recognized format.

Remarks

WriteIntPtr enables direct interaction with an unmanaged C-style byte array, eliminating the expense of copying an entire unmanaged array (using **Marshal.Copy**) to a separate managed array before setting its element values.

> **Note** This method uses **SecurityAction.LinkDemand** to prevent it from being called from untrusted code; only the immediate caller is required to have **SecurityPermission-Attribute.UnmanagedCode** permission. If your code can be called from partially trusted code, do not pass user input to **Marshal** class methods without validation.

Requirements

Platforms: Windows 98, Windows NT 4.0, Windows Millennium Edition, Windows 2000, Windows XP Home Edition, Windows XP Professional, Windows .NET Server family

.NET Framework Security:

- **SecurityPermission** for operating with unmanaged code. Associated enumeration: **SecurityPermissionFlag.UnmanagedCode**.

MarshalAsAttribute Class

Indicates how to marshal the data between managed and unmanaged code.

System.Object
  System.Attribute
    System.Runtime.InteropServices.MarshalAsAttribute

```
[Visual Basic]
<AttributeUsage(AttributeTargets.Field Or _
    AttributeTargets.Parameter Or AttributeTargets.ReturnValue)>
NotInheritable Public Class MarshalAsAttribute
    Inherits Attribute
[C#]
[AttributeUsage(AttributeTargets.Field | AttributeTargets.Parameter
    | AttributeTargets.ReturnValue)]
public sealed class MarshalAsAttribute : Attribute
[C++]
[AttributeUsage(AttributeTargets::Field |
    AttributeTargets::Parameter | AttributeTargets::ReturnValue)]
public __gc __sealed class MarshalAsAttribute : public Attribute
[JScript]
public
    AttributeUsage(AttributeTargets.Field | AttributeTargets.Parameter
    | AttributeTargets.ReturnValue)
class MarshalAsAttribute extends Attribute
```

Thread Safety

Any public static (**Shared** in Visual Basic) members of this type are safe for multithreaded operations. Any instance members are not guaranteed to be thread safe.

Remarks

You can apply this attribute to parameters, fields, or return values.

This attribute is optional, as each data type has a default marshaling behavior. This attribute is only necessary when a given type can be marshaled to multiple types. For example, you can marshal a string to unmanaged code as either a **LPStr**, a **LPWStr**, a **LPTStr**, or a **BStr**. By default, the common language runtime marshals a string parameter as a **BStr** to COM methods. You can apply the **MarshalAsAttribute** attribute to an individual field or parameter to cause that particular string to be marshaled as a **LPStr** instead of a **BStr**. The **Type Library Exporter (Tlbexp.exe)** passes your marshaling preferences to the common language runtime.

Some parameters and return values have different default marshaling behavior when used with COM interop or platform invoke. By default, the runtime marshals a string parameter (and fields in a value type) as a **LPStr** to a platform invoke method or function.

In most cases, the attribute simply identifies the format of the unmanaged data using the **UnmanagedType** enumeration, as shown in the following C# signature:

```
void
    MyMethod([MarshalAs(LPStr)] String s);
```

Some **UnmanagedType** enumeration members require additional information. For example, additional information is needed when the **UnmanagedType** is **LPArray**.

The **Type Library Importer (Tlbimp.exe)** also applies this attribute to parameters, fields, and return values to indicate that the data type in the input type library is not the default type for the corresponding managed data type. Tlbimp.exe always applies the **MarshalAsAttribute** to **String** and **Object** types for clarity, regardless of the type specified in the input type library.

Example

[Visual Basic, C#] The following examples show the placement of the **MarshalAsAttribute** in managed source code as applied to parameters, field, and return values.

```
[Visual Basic]
'Applied to a parameter.
  Public Sub M1 (<MarshalAs(UnmanagedType.LPWStr)> msg As String)
'Applied to a field within a class.
  Class MsgText
    <MarshalAs(UnmanagedType.LPWStr)> Public msg As String
  End Class
'Applied to a a return value.
  Public Function M2() As <MarshalAs(UnmanagedType.LPWStr)> String

[C#]
//Applied to a parameter.
  public void M1 ([MarshalAs(UnmanagedType.LPWStr)]String msg);
//Applied to a field within a class.
  class MsgText {
    [MarshalAs(UnmanagedType.LPWStr)] Public String msg;
  }
//Applied to a return value.
[return: MarshalAs(UnmanagedType.LPWStr)]
public String GetMessage();
```

Requirements

Namespace: System.Runtime.InteropServices

Platforms: Windows 98, Windows NT 4.0, Windows Millennium Edition, Windows 2000, Windows XP Home Edition, Windows XP Professional, Windows .NET Server family

Assembly: Mscorlib (in Mscorlib.dll)

MarshalAsAttribute Constructor

Initializes a new instance of the **MarshalAsAttribute** class.

Overload List

Initializes a new instance of the **MarshalAsAttribute** class with the specified **UnmanagedType** value.

  [Visual Basic] **Public Sub New(Short)**

  [C#] **public MarshalAsAttribute(short);**

  [C++] **public: MarshalAsAttribute(short);**

  [JScript] **public function MarshalAsAttribute(Int16);**

Initializes a new instance of the **MarshalAsAttribute** class with the specified **UnmanagedType** enumeration member.

  [Visual Basic] **Public Sub New(UnmanagedType)**

  [C#] **public MarshalAsAttribute(UnmanagedType);**

  [C++] **public: MarshalAsAttribute(UnmanagedType);**

  [JScript] **public function MarshalAsAttribute(UnmanagedType);**

MarshalAsAttribute Constructor (Int16)

Initializes a new instance of the **MarshalAsAttribute** class with the specified **UnmanagedType** value.

```
[Visual Basic]
Public Sub New( _
   ByVal unmanagedType As Short _
)
[C#]
public MarshalAsAttribute(
   short unmanagedType
);
[C++]
public: MarshalAsAttribute(
   short unmanagedType
);
[JScript]
public function MarshalAsAttribute(
   unmanagedType : Int16
);
```

Parameters

unmanagedType
   The **UnmanagedType** value the data is to be marshaled as.

Remarks

This constructor takes an underlying 16-bit signed integer that represents each **UnmanagedType** enumeration member. The **Type Library Importer (Tlbimp.exe)** uses this constructor.

Requirements

Platforms: Windows 98, Windows NT 4.0, Windows Millennium Edition, Windows 2000, Windows XP Home Edition, Windows XP Professional, Windows .NET Server family, Common Language Infrastructure (CLI) Standard

MarshalAsAttribute Constructor (UnmanagedType)

Initializes a new instance of the **MarshalAsAttribute** class with the specified **UnmanagedType** enumeration member.

```
[Visual Basic]
Public Sub New( _
   ByVal unmanagedType As UnmanagedType _
)
[C#]
public MarshalAsAttribute(
   UnmanagedType unmanagedType
);
[C++]
public: MarshalAsAttribute(
   UnmanagedType unmanagedType
);
[JScript]
public function MarshalAsAttribute(
   unmanagedType : UnmanagedType
);
```

Parameters

unmanagedType
   The **UnmanagedType** value the data is to be marshaled as.

Remarks

For readable code that is less prone to error, always use this constructor.

Requirements

Platforms: Windows 98, Windows NT 4.0, Windows Millennium Edition, Windows 2000, Windows XP Home Edition, Windows XP Professional, Windows .NET Server family, Common Language Infrastructure (CLI) Standard

MarshalAsAttribute.ArraySubType Field

Specifies the element type of the unmanaged **UnmanagedType.LPArray** or **UnmanagedType.ByValArray**.

```
[Visual Basic]
Public ArraySubType As UnmanagedType
[C#]
public UnmanagedType ArraySubType;
[C++]
public: UnmanagedType ArraySubType;
[JScript]
public var ArraySubType : UnmanagedType;
```

Remarks

You can set this parameter to a value from the **System.Runtime.InteropServices.UnmanagedType** enumeration to specify the type of the array's elements. If a type is not specified, the default unmanaged type corresponding to the managed array's element type is used. For example, the **ArraySubType** for a **LPWStr** array in COM is **UnmanagedType.LPWStr**.

Requirements

Platforms: Windows 98, Windows NT 4.0, Windows Millennium Edition, Windows 2000, Windows XP Home Edition, Windows XP Professional, Windows .NET Server family, Common Language Infrastructure (CLI) Standard

MarshalAsAttribute.MarshalCookie Field

Provides additional information to a custom marshaler.

```
[Visual Basic]
Public MarshalCookie As String
[C#]
public string MarshalCookie;
[C++]
public: String* MarshalCookie;
[JScript]
public var MarshalCookie : String;
```

Remarks

This field is optional when using a custom marshaler.

You can set this field to a string that supplies additional information to a custom marshaler. For example, the same marshaler can be used to provide a number of wrappers, where the cookie is used to indicate the specific wrapper.

Requirements

Platforms: Windows 98, Windows NT 4.0, Windows Millennium Edition, Windows 2000, Windows XP Home Edition, Windows XP Professional, Windows .NET Server family, Common Language Infrastructure (CLI) Standard

MarshalAsAttribute.MarshalType Field

Specifies the fully qualified name of a custom marshaler.

```
[Visual Basic]
Public MarshalType As String
[C#]
public string MarshalType;
[C++]
public: String* MarshalType;
[JScript]
public var MarshalType : String;
```

Remarks

You can use either the **MarshalType** or
MarshalAsAttribute.MarshalTypeRef field specify a custom
marshaler type for the attributed parameter, field, or return type. The
MarshalType field enables you to specify a string representing the
fully qualified name of a custom marshaler. It is useful for late-
bound references, but is less preferred than **MarshalTypeRef** for
specifying a custom marshaler.

Requirements

Platforms: Windows 98, Windows NT 4.0,
Windows Millennium Edition, Windows 2000,
Windows XP Home Edition, Windows XP Professional,
Windows .NET Server family,
Common Language Infrastructure (CLI) Standard

MarshalAsAttribute.MarshalTypeRef Field

Implements **MarshalAsAttribute.MarshalType** as a type.

```
[Visual Basic]
Public MarshalTypeRef As Type
[C#]
public Type MarshalTypeRef;
[C++]
public: Type* MarshalTypeRef;
[JScript]
public var MarshalTypeRef : Type;
```

Remarks

You can use either the **MarshalTypeRef** or **MarshalType** field to
specify a custom marshaler type for the attributed parameter, field,
or return type. The **MarshalTypeRef** field allows easier usage of
MarshalType by shortening the syntax. In the following example,
the first line represents syntax using **MarshalType** and the second
line represents syntax using **MarshalTypeRef**.

```
[MarshalAs(UnmanagedType.CustomMarshaler, MarshalType = "Assembly,
NameSpace.TypeName"]

[MarshalAs(UnmanagedType.CustomMarshaler, MarshalTypeRef =
typeof(NameSpace.TypeName)]
```

You can set a **Type** object using **typeof** in C#, **GetType** in Visual
Basic, or **__typeof** in C++.

Requirements

Platforms: Windows 98, Windows NT 4.0,
Windows Millennium Edition, Windows 2000,
Windows XP Home Edition, Windows XP Professional,
Windows .NET Server family,
Common Language Infrastructure (CLI) Standard

MarshalAsAttribute.SafeArraySubType Field

Indicates the element type of the **UnmanagedType.SafeArray**.

```
[Visual Basic]
Public SafeArraySubType As VarEnum
[C#]
public VarEnum SafeArraySubType;
[C++]
public: VarEnum SafeArraySubType;
[JScript]
public var SafeArraySubType : VarEnum;
```

Remarks

You can set this field to a value from the
System.Runtime.InteropServices.VarEnum enumeration to
specify the type of the safe array's elements. If a type is not
specified, the managed element type's default type (if passed as a
VARIANT) is used. For example, the **SafeArraySubType** for an **int**
array in COM is **VT_I4**.

Requirements

Platforms: Windows 98, Windows NT 4.0,
Windows Millennium Edition, Windows 2000,
Windows XP Home Edition, Windows XP Professional,
Windows .NET Server family

MarshalAsAttribute.SafeArrayUserDefinedSub-Type Field

Indicates the user-defined element type of the
UnmanagedType.SafeArray.

```
[Visual Basic]
Public SafeArrayUserDefinedSubType As Type
[C#]
public Type SafeArrayUserDefinedSubType;
[C++]
public: Type* SafeArrayUserDefinedSubType;
[JScript]
public var SafeArrayUserDefinedSubType : Type;
```

Remarks

Initialize this field with your custom type to enable the elements of
the **SAFEARRAY** to be marshaled successfully. This field is only
needed when the **MarshalAsAttribute.SafeArraySubType** is
either **VarEnum.VT_UNKNOWN**, **VarEnum.VT_DISPATCH**, or
VarEnum.VT_RECORD.

Requirements

Platforms: Windows 98, Windows NT 4.0,
Windows Millennium Edition, Windows 2000,
Windows XP Home Edition, Windows XP Professional,
Windows .NET Server family

MarshalAsAttribute.SizeConst Field

Indicates the number of elements in the fixed-length array or the
number of characters (not bytes) in a string to import.

```
[Visual Basic]
Public SizeConst As Integer
[C#]
public int SizeConst;
```

```
[C++]
public: int SizeConst;
[JScript]
public var SizeConst : int;
```

Remarks

This field is required for the **ByValArray** and **ByValTStr** members of the **System.Runtime.InteropServices.UnmanagedType** enumeration.

Requirements

Platforms: Windows 98, Windows NT 4.0,
Windows Millennium Edition, Windows 2000,
Windows XP Home Edition, Windows XP Professional,
Windows .NET Server family,
Common Language Infrastructure (CLI) Standard

MarshalAsAttribute.SizeParamIndex Field

Indicates which parameter contains the count of array elements, much like **size_is** in COM, and is zero-based.

```
[Visual Basic]
Public SizeParamIndex As Short
[C#]
public short SizeParamIndex;
[C++]
public: short SizeParamIndex;
[JScript]
public var SizeParamIndex : Int16;
```

Remarks

This field is used when building managed objects that work with COM. **SizeParamIndex** is only valid on managed methods that are called from COM clients, where one of the parameters is an array. Since the marshaler cannot determine the size of an unmanaged array, this information is passed in a separate parameter.

The parameter containing the size must be an integer that is passed by value. If you specify both the **SizeParamIndex** and **MarshalAsAttribute.SizeConst** with a **UnmanagedType.LPArray**, the sum of their values produces a size total. This field does not have any effect on managed code that calls COM objects.

Example

```
[Visual Basic]
Option Strict Off

Imports System.Runtime.InteropServices
Imports SomeNamespace

Namespace SomeNamespace
    ' Force the layout of your fields to the C style struct layout.
    ' Without this, the .NET Framework will reorder your fields.

    <StructLayout(LayoutKind.Sequential)> _
    Structure Vertex
        Dim x As Decimal
        Dim y As Decimal
        Dim z As Decimal
    End Structure

    Class SomeClass
        ' Add [In] or [In, Out] attributes as appropriate.
        ' Marshal as a C style array of Vertex, where the
```

```
    second (SizeParamIndex is zero-based)
        ' parameter (size) contains the count of array elements.

        Declare Auto Sub SomeUnsafeMethod Lib "somelib.dll" ( _
                <MarshalAs(UnmanagedType.LPArray, _
    SizeParamIndex:=1)> data() As Vertex, _
                                size As Long )

        Public Sub SomeMethod()
            Dim verts(3) As Vertex
            SomeUnsafeMethod( verts, verts.Length )
        End Sub

    End Class

End Namespace

Module Test
    Sub Main
        Dim AClass As New SomeClass

        AClass.SomeMethod
    End Sub
End Module
```

```
[C#]
using System.Runtime.InteropServices;
using SomeNamespace;

namespace SomeNamespace
{
    // Force the layout of your fields to the C style struct layout.
    // Without this, the .NET Framework will reorder your fields.
    [StructLayout(LayoutKind.Sequential)]
    public struct Vertex
    {
        float   x;
        float   y;
        float   z;
    }

    class SomeClass
    {
        // Add [In] or [In, Out] attributes as appropriate.
        // Marshal as a C style array of Vertex, where the
    second (SizeParamIndex is zero-based)
        //  parameter (size) contains the count of array elements.
        [DllImport ("SomeDll.dll")]
        public static extern void SomeUnsafeMethod(
                [MarshalAs
    (UnmanagedType.LPArray, SizeParamIndex=1)] Vertex[] data,
                                long size );

        public void SomeMethod()
        {
            Vertex[] verts = new Vertex[3];
            SomeUnsafeMethod( verts, verts.Length );
        }

    }
}

class Test
{
    public static void Main()
    {
        SomeClass AClass = new SomeClass();

        AClass.SomeMethod();
    }
}
```

```
[C++]
#using <mscorlib.dll>

using namespace System;
//using namespace System::Reflection;
//using namespace System::Reflection::Emit;
using namespace System::Runtime::InteropServices;

   // Force the layout of your fields to the C style struct layout.
   // Without this, the .NET Framework will reorder your fields.
   // [StructLayoutAttribute(Sequential)]
   __value struct Vertex
     {
        float   x;
     float   y;
        float   z;
     };

        // Add [In] or [In, Out] attributes as approppriate.
        // Marshal as a C style array of Vertex, where the              ⌐
second (SizeParamIndex is zero-based)
        //  parameter (size) contains the count of array elements.
        [DllImport ("SomeDLL.dll")]
        //extern void SomeUnsafeMethod(long data, long size );
     extern void SomeUnsafeMethod( [MarshalAs(UnmanagedType:       ⌐
:LPArray, SizeParamIndex=1)] Vertex data __gc[], long size );

   int main()
     {
        Vertex verts[] = new Vertex[3];

        SomeUnsafeMethod(verts, verts->Length );
     }
```

Requirements

Platforms: Windows 98, Windows NT 4.0,
Windows Millennium Edition, Windows 2000,
Windows XP Home Edition, Windows XP Professional,
Windows .NET Server family,
Common Language Infrastructure (CLI) Standard

MarshalAsAttribute.Value Property

Gets the **UnmanagedType** value the data is to be marshaled as.

```
[Visual Basic]
Public ReadOnly Property Value As UnmanagedType
[C#]
public UnmanagedType Value {get;}
[C++]
public: __property UnmanagedType get_Value();
[JScript]
public function get Value() : UnmanagedType;
```

Property Value

The **UnmanagedType** value the data is to be marshaled as.

Remarks

This value is used with **MarshalAsAttribute** to indicate how types
should be marshaled between managed and unmanaged code. In
some cases, you can use this field with certain **UnmanagedType**
enumeration members. For **CustomMarshaler** and **ByValArray**,
you must use additional named parameters.

Requirements

Platforms: Windows 98, Windows NT 4.0,
Windows Millennium Edition, Windows 2000,
Windows XP Home Edition, Windows XP Professional,
Windows .NET Server family,
Common Language Infrastructure (CLI) Standard

MarshalDirectiveException Class

The exception that is thrown by the marshaler when it encounters a **MarshalAsAttribute** it does not support.

System.Object
  System.Exception
    System.SystemException
      System.Runtime.InteropServices.MarshalDirective-Exception

```
[Visual Basic]
<Serializable>
Public Class MarshalDirectiveException
   Inherits SystemException
[C#]
[Serializable]
public class MarshalDirectiveException : SystemException
[C++]
[Serializable]
public __gc class MarshalDirectiveException : public
   SystemException
[JScript]
public
   Serializable
class MarshalDirectiveException extends SystemException
```

Thread Safety

Any public static (**Shared** in Visual Basic) members of this type are safe for multithreaded operations. Any instance members are not guaranteed to be thread safe.

Remarks

MarshalDirectiveException uses the HRESULT COR_E_MARSHALDIRECTIVE which has the value 0x80131535.

Requirements

Namespace: System.Runtime.InteropServices

Platforms: Windows 98, Windows NT 4.0, Windows Millennium Edition, Windows 2000, Windows XP Home Edition, Windows XP Professional, Windows .NET Server family

Assembly: Mscorlib (in Mscorlib.dll)

MarshalDirectiveException Constructor

Initializes a new instance of the **MarshalDirectiveException** class.

Overload List

Initializes a new instance of the **MarshalDirectiveException** class with default properties.

> [Visual Basic] **Public Sub New()**
> [C#] **public MarshalDirectiveException();**
> [C++] **public: MarshalDirectiveException();**
> [JScript] **public function MarshalDirectiveException();**

Initializes a new instance of the **MarshalDirectiveException** class with a specified error message.

> [Visual Basic] **Public Sub New(String)**
> [C#] **public MarshalDirectiveException(string);**
> [C++] **public: MarshalDirectiveException(String*);**
> [JScript] **public function MarshalDirectiveException(String);**

Initializes a new instance of the **MarshalDirectiveException** class from serialization data.

> [Visual Basic] **Protected Sub New(SerializationInfo, StreamingContext)**
> [C#] **protected MarshalDirectiveException(SerializationInfo, StreamingContext);**
> [C++] **protected: MarshalDirectiveException(SerializationInfo*, StreamingContext);**
> [JScript] **protected function MarshalDirectiveException(SerializationInfo, StreamingContext);**

Initializes a new instance of the **MarshalDirectiveException** class with a specified error message and a reference to the inner exception that is the cause of this exception.

> [Visual Basic] **Public Sub New(String, Exception)**
> [C#] **public MarshalDirectiveException(string, Exception);**
> [C++] **public: MarshalDirectiveException(String*, Exception*);**
> [JScript] **public function MarshalDirectiveException(String, Exception);**

MarshalDirectiveException Constructor ( )

Initializes a new instance of the **MarshalDirectiveException** class with default properties.

```
[Visual Basic]
Public Sub New()
[C#]
public MarshalDirectiveException();
[C++]
public: MarshalDirectiveException();
[JScript]
public function MarshalDirectiveException();
```

Remarks

The following table shows the initial property values for an instance of **MarshalDirectiveException**.

Property	Value
InnerException	A null reference (**Nothing** in Visual Basic).
Message	A localized error message string.

Requirements

Platforms: Windows 98, Windows NT 4.0, Windows Millennium Edition, Windows 2000, Windows XP Home Edition, Windows XP Professional, Windows .NET Server family

MarshalDirectiveException Constructor (String)

Initializes a new instance of the **MarshalDirectiveException** class with a specified error message.

```
[Visual Basic]
Public Sub New( _
    ByVal message As String _
)
[C#]
public MarshalDirectiveException(
    string message
);
[C++]
public: MarshalDirectiveException(
    String* message
);
[JScript]
public function MarshalDirectiveException(
    message : String
);
```

Parameters

message
> The error message that specifies the reason for the exception.

Remarks

The following table shows the initial property values for an instance of **MarshalDirectiveException**.

Property	Value
InnerException	A null reference (**Nothing** in Visual Basic).
Message	*message*

Requirements

Platforms: Windows 98, Windows NT 4.0, Windows Millennium Edition, Windows 2000, Windows XP Home Edition, Windows XP Professional, Windows .NET Server family

MarshalDirectiveException Constructor (SerializationInfo, StreamingContext)

Initializes a new instance of the **MarshalDirectiveException** class from serialization data.

```
[Visual Basic]
Protected Sub New( _
    ByVal info As SerializationInfo, _
    ByVal context As StreamingContext _
)
[C#]
protected MarshalDirectiveException(
    SerializationInfo info,
    StreamingContext context
);
[C++]
protected: MarshalDirectiveException(
    SerializationInfo* info,
    StreamingContext context
);
[JScript]
protected function MarshalDirectiveException(
    info : SerializationInfo,
    context : StreamingContext
);
```

Parameters

info
> The object that holds the serialized object data.

context
> The contextual information about the source or destination.

Exceptions

Exception Type	Condition
ArgumentNullException	*info* is a null reference (**Nothing** in Visual Basic).

Remarks

This constructor is called during deserialization to reconstitute the exception object transmitted over a stream. For more information, see **XML and SOAP Serialization**.

Requirements

Platforms: Windows 98, Windows NT 4.0, Windows Millennium Edition, Windows 2000, Windows XP Home Edition, Windows XP Professional, Windows .NET Server family

MarshalDirectiveException Constructor (String, Exception)

Initializes a new instance of the **MarshalDirectiveException** class with a specified error message and a reference to the inner exception that is the cause of this exception.

```
[Visual Basic]
Public Sub New( _
    ByVal message As String, _
    ByVal inner As Exception _
)
[C#]
public MarshalDirectiveException(
    string message,
    Exception inner
);
[C++]
public: MarshalDirectiveException(
    String* message,
    Exception* inner
);
[JScript]
public function MarshalDirectiveException(
    message : String,
    inner : Exception
);
```

Parameters

message
> The error message that explains the reason for the exception.

inner
> The exception that is the cause of the current exception. If the *inner* parameter is not a null reference (**Nothing** in Visual Basic), the current exception is raised in a **catch** block that handles the inner exception.

Remarks

An exception that is thrown as a direct result of a previous exception should include a reference to the previous exception in the **InnerException** property. The **InnerException** property returns the same value that is passed into the constructor, or a null reference (**Nothing** in Visual Basic) if the **InnerException** property does not supply the inner exception value to the constructor.

The following table shows the initial property values for an instance of **MarshalDirectiveException**.

Property	Value
InnerException	The inner exception reference.
Message	The error message string.

Requirements

Platforms: Windows 98, Windows NT 4.0, Windows Millennium Edition, Windows 2000, Windows XP Home Edition, Windows XP Professional, Windows .NET Server family

ObjectCreationDelegate Delegate

Creates a COM object.

```
[Visual Basic]
<Serializable>
Public Delegate Function Sub ObjectCreationDelegate( _
   ByVal aggregator As IntPtr _
) As IntPtr
[C#]
[Serializable]
public delegate IntPtr ObjectCreationDelegate(
   IntPtr aggregator
);
[C++]
[Serializable]
public __gc __delegate IntPtr ObjectCreationDelegate(
   IntPtr aggregator
);
```

[JScript] In JScript, you can use the delegates in the .NET
Framework, but you cannot define your own.

Parameters [Visual Basic, C#, C++]

The declaration of your callback method must have the same
parameters as the **ObjectCreationDelegate** delegate declaration.

aggregator
   A pointer to the managed object's **IUnknown** interface.

Remarks

This delegate is called to create a COM object as an alternative to
CoCreateInstance when a managed object needs to create a new
instance of its unmanaged portion. The **IUnknown** of the managed
object is passed as a parameter and the delegate should return the
IUnknown of the unmanaged object. Both interfaces are passed as
type **IntPtr** to avoid marshaling.

Every derived class of **Delegate** and **MulticastDelegate** have a
constructor and an **Invoke** method.

Requirements

Namespace: System.Runtime.InteropServices

Platforms: Windows 98, Windows NT 4.0,
Windows Millennium Edition, Windows 2000,
Windows XP Home Edition, Windows XP Professional,
Windows .NET Server family

Assembly: Mscorlib (in Mscorlib.dll)

OptionalAttribute Class

Indicates that a parameter is optional.

System.Object
  System.Attribute
    System.Runtime.InteropServices.OptionalAttribute

```
[Visual Basic]
<AttributeUsage(AttributeTargets.Parameter)>
NotInheritable Public Class OptionalAttribute
   Inherits Attribute
[C#]
[AttributeUsage(AttributeTargets.Parameter)]
public sealed class OptionalAttribute : Attribute
[C++]
[AttributeUsage(AttributeTargets::Parameter)]
public __gc __sealed class OptionalAttribute : public Attribute
[JScript]
public
   AttributeUsage(AttributeTargets.Parameter)
class OptionalAttribute extends Attribute
```

Thread Safety

Any public static (**Shared** in Visual Basic) members of this type are
safe for multithreaded operations. Any instance members are not
guaranteed to be thread safe.

Remarks

You can apply this attribute to parameters.

Optional parameters are not supported by all languages.

Requirements

Namespace: System.Runtime.InteropServices

Platforms: Windows 98, Windows NT 4.0,
Windows Millennium Edition, Windows 2000,
Windows XP Home Edition, Windows XP Professional,
Windows .NET Server family

Assembly: Mscorlib (in Mscorlib.dll)

OptionalAttribute Constructor

Initializes a new instance of the **OptionalAttribute** class with
default values.

```
[Visual Basic]
Public Sub New()
[C#]
public OptionalAttribute();
[C++]
public: OptionalAttribute();
[JScript]
public function OptionalAttribute();
```

Requirements

Platforms: Windows 98, Windows NT 4.0,
Windows Millennium Edition, Windows 2000,
Windows XP Home Edition, Windows XP Professional,
Windows .NET Server family

OutAttribute Class

Indicates that data should be marshaled from callee back to caller.

System.Object
  System.Attribute
    System.Runtime.InteropServices.OutAttribute

```
[Visual Basic]
<AttributeUsage(AttributeTargets.Parameter)>
NotInheritable Public Class OutAttribute
    Inherits Attribute
[C#]
[AttributeUsage(AttributeTargets.Parameter)]
public sealed class OutAttribute : Attribute
[C++]
[AttributeUsage(AttributeTargets::Parameter)]
public __gc __sealed class OutAttribute : public Attribute
[JScript]
public
    AttributeUsage(AttributeTargets.Parameter)
class OutAttribute extends Attribute
```

Thread Safety

Any public static (**Shared** in Visual Basic) members of this type are safe for multithreaded operations. Any instance members are not guaranteed to be thread safe.

Remarks

You can apply this attribute to parameters.

The **OutAttribute** is optional. The attribute is supported for COM interop and platform invoke only. In the absence of explicit settings, the interop marshaler assumes rules based on the parameter type, whether the parameter is passed by reference or by value, and whether the type is blittable or non-blittable. For example, the **StringBuilder** class is always assumed to be In/Out and an array of strings passed by value is assumed to be In.

Out-only behavior is never a default marshaling behavior for parameters. You can apply the **OutAttribute** to value and reference types passed by reference to change In/Out behavior to Out-only behavior, which is equivalent to using the **out** keyword in C#. For example, arrays passed by value, marshaled as In-only parameters by default, can be changed to Out-only. However, the behavior does not always provide expected semantics when the types include all-blittable elements or fields because the interop marshaler uses pinning. If you do not care about passing data into the callee, Out-only marshaling can provide better performance for non-blittable types.

Combining the **InAttribute** and **OutAttribute** is particularly useful when applied to arrays and formatted, non-blittable types. Callers see the changes a callee makes to these types only when you apply both attributes. Since these types require copying during marshaling, you can use **InAttribute** and **OutAttribute** to reduce unnecessary copies.

Requirements

Namespace: System.Runtime.InteropServices

Platforms: Windows 98, Windows NT 4.0, Windows Millennium Edition, Windows 2000, Windows XP Home Edition, Windows XP Professional, Windows .NET Server family, .NET Compact Framework - Windows CE .NET

Assembly: Mscorlib (in Mscorlib.dll)

OutAttribute Constructor

Initializes a new instance of the **OutAttribute** class.

```
[Visual Basic]
Public Sub New()
[C#]
public OutAttribute();
[C++]
public: OutAttribute();
[JScript]
public function OutAttribute();
```

Requirements

Platforms: Windows 98, Windows NT 4.0, Windows Millennium Edition, Windows 2000, Windows XP Home Edition, Windows XP Professional, Windows .NET Server family, .NET Compact Framework - Windows CE .NET, Common Language Infrastructure (CLI) Standard

PARAMDESC Structure

Contains information about how to transfer a structure element, parameter, or function return value between processes.

System.Object
  System.ValueType
    System.Runtime.InteropServices.PARAMDESC

```
[Visual Basic]
<ComVisible(False)>
Public Structure PARAMDESC
[C#]
[ComVisible(false)]
public struct PARAMDESC
[C++]
[ComVisible(false)]
public __value struct PARAMDESC
```

[JScript] In JScript, you can use the structures in the .NET Framework, but you cannot define your own.

Thread Safety

Any public static (**Shared** in Visual Basic) members of this type are safe for multithreaded operations. Any instance members are not guaranteed to be thread safe.

Remarks

For additional information about **PARAMDESC**, see the MSDN Library.

Requirements

Namespace: System.Runtime.InteropServices

Platforms: Windows 98, Windows NT 4.0, Windows Millennium Edition, Windows 2000, Windows XP Home Edition, Windows XP Professional, Windows .NET Server family

Assembly: Mscorlib (in Mscorlib.dll)

PARAMDESC.lpVarValue Field

Represents a pointer to a value that is being passed between processes.

```
[Visual Basic]
Public lpVarValue As IntPtr
[C#]
public IntPtr lpVarValue;
[C++]
public: IntPtr lpVarValue;
[JScript]
public var lpVarValue : IntPtr;
```

Remarks

For additional information about **PARAMDESC**, see the MSDN Library.

Requirements

Platforms: Windows 98, Windows NT 4.0, Windows Millennium Edition, Windows 2000, Windows XP Home Edition, Windows XP Professional, Windows .NET Server family

PARAMDESC.wParamFlags Field

Represents bitmask values that describe the structure element, parameter, or return value.

```
[Visual Basic]
Public wParamFlags As PARAMFLAG
[C#]
public PARAMFLAG wParamFlags;
[C++]
public: PARAMFLAG wParamFlags;
[JScript]
public var wParamFlags : PARAMFLAG;
```

Remarks

For additional information about **PARAMDESC**, see the MSDN Library.

Requirements

Platforms: Windows 98, Windows NT 4.0, Windows Millennium Edition, Windows 2000, Windows XP Home Edition, Windows XP Professional, Windows .NET Server family

PARAMFLAG Enumeration

Describes how to transfer a structure element, parameter, or function return value between processes.

This enumeration has a **FlagsAttribute** attribute that allows a bitwise combination of its member values.

```
[Visual Basic]
<Flags>
<Serializable>
<ComVisible(False)>
Public Enum PARAMFLAG
[C#]
[Flags]
[Serializable]
[ComVisible(false)]
public enum PARAMFLAG
[C++]
[Flags]
[Serializable]
[ComVisible(false)]
__value public enum PARAMFLAG
[JScript]
public
    Flags
    Serializable
    ComVisible(false)
enum PARAMFLAG
```

Members

Member name	Description	Value
PARAMFLAG_FHAS-CUSTDATA	The parameter has custom data.	64
PARAMFLAG_FHAS-DEFAULT	The parameter has default behaviors defined.	32
PARAMFLAG_FIN	The parameter passes information from the caller to the callee.	1
PARAMFLAG_FLCID	The parameter is the local identifier of a client application.	4
PARAMFLAG_FOPT	The parameter is optional.	16
PARAMFLAG_FOUT	The parameter returns information from the callee to the caller.	2
PARAMFLAG_FRET-VAL	The parameter is the return value of the member.	8
PARAMFLAG_NONE	Whether the parameter passes or receives information is unspecified.	0

Requirements

Namespace: System.Runtime.InteropServices

Platforms: Windows 98, Windows NT 4.0, Windows Millennium Edition, Windows 2000, Windows XP Home Edition, Windows XP Professional, Windows .NET Server family

Assembly: Mscorlib (in Mscorlib.dll)

PreserveSigAttribute Class

Indicates that the HRESULT or **retval** signature transformation that takes place during COM interop calls should be suppressed.

System.Object
  System.Attribute
    System.Runtime.InteropServices.PreserveSigAttribute

```
[Visual Basic]
<AttributeUsage(AttributeTargets.Method)>
NotInheritable Public Class PreserveSigAttribute
   Inherits Attribute
[C#]
[AttributeUsage(AttributeTargets.Method)]
public sealed class PreserveSigAttribute : Attribute
[C++]
[AttributeUsage(AttributeTargets::Method)]
public __gc __sealed class PreserveSigAttribute : public Attribute
[JScript]
public
   AttributeUsage(AttributeTargets.Method)
class PreserveSigAttribute extends Attribute
```

Thread Safety

Any public static (**Shared** in Visual Basic) members of this type are safe for multithreaded operations. Any instance members are not guaranteed to be thread safe.

Remarks

You can apply this attribute to methods.

By default, the **Type Library Exporter (Tlbexp.exe)** ensures that a call that returns an HRESULT of S_OK is transformed such that the [out, retval] parameter is used as the function return value. The S_OK HRESULT is discarded. For HRESULTs other than S_OK, the runtime throws an exception and discards the [out, retval] parameter. When you apply the **PreserveSigAttribute** to a managed method signature, the managed and unmanaged signatures of the attributed method are identical.

Preserving the original method signature is necessary if the member returns more than one success HRESULT value and you want to detect the different values. Since most COM member return an HRESULT, by applying the **PreserveSigAttribute**, you can retrieve an integer representing the success or failure HRESULT. Tlbexp.exe preserves any [out, retavl] parameters as out parameters in the managed signature.

The **Type Library Importer (Tlbimp.exe)** also applies this attribute; it applies the attribute to dispinterfaces when it imports a type library.

Example

The following example shows how Tlbexp.exe converts a C# method without **PreserveSigAttribute** when exporting an assembly to a COM type library.

Managed signature:

```
int DoSomething (long l);
```

Unmanaged signature:

```
HRESULT DoSomething ([in] long l, [out, retval] int * i);
```

When you apply **PreserveSigAttribute** to the same C# method and export the assembly, the method conversion differs from the previous example. Notice that Tlbexp.exe removes the HRESULT and the [out, retval] parameter modifier.

Managed signature:

```
[PreserveSig] int DoSomething (long l);
```

Unmanaged signature:

```
int DoSomething ([in] long l);
```

Requirements

Namespace: System.Runtime.InteropServices

Platforms: Windows 98, Windows NT 4.0, Windows Millennium Edition, Windows 2000, Windows XP Home Edition, Windows XP Professional, Windows .NET Server family

Assembly: Mscorlib (in Mscorlib.dll)

PreserveSigAttribute Constructor

Initializes a new instance of the **PreserveSigAttribute** class.

```
[Visual Basic]
Public Sub New()
[C#]
public PreserveSigAttribute();
[C++]
public: PreserveSigAttribute();
[JScript]
public function PreserveSigAttribute();
```

Requirements

Platforms: Windows 98, Windows NT 4.0, Windows Millennium Edition, Windows 2000, Windows XP Home Edition, Windows XP Professional, Windows .NET Server family

PrimaryInteropAssembly-Attribute Class

Indicates that the attributed assembly is a primary interop assembly.

System.Object
  System.Attribute
    System.Runtime.InteropServices.PrimaryInteropAssembly-
    Attribute

```
[Visual Basic]
<AttributeUsage(AttributeTargets.Assembly)>
NotInheritable Public Class PrimaryInteropAssemblyAttribute
   Inherits Attribute
[C#]
[AttributeUsage(AttributeTargets.Assembly)]
public sealed class PrimaryInteropAssemblyAttribute : Attribute
[C++]
[AttributeUsage(AttributeTargets::Assembly)]
public __gc __sealed class PrimaryInteropAssemblyAttribute :
   public Attribute
[JScript]
public
   AttributeUsage(AttributeTargets.Assembly)
class PrimaryInteropAssemblyAttribute extends Attribute
```

Thread Safety

Any public static (**Shared** in Visual Basic) members of this type are safe for multithreaded operations. Any instance members are not guaranteed to be thread safe.

Remarks

You can apply this attribute to assemblies, although the **Type Library Importer (Tlbimp.exe)** typically applies it for you when it imports a type library.

An interop assembly contains metadata that describes exiting COM types, which are often already described in a COM type library. Tlbimp.exe produces interop assemblies from COM type libraries. Interop assemblies typically only contain metadata (no code). Primary interop assemblies are provided by the same publisher as the type library they describe, and provide the official definitions of the types defined with that type library. Primary interop assemblies are always signed by their publisher to ensure uniqueness.

You can generate a primary interop assembly from a type library in the following ways:

- Run TlbImp.exe with the **/primary** option from the command line.
- Apply the **PrimaryInteropAssemblyAttribute** at design time.

To specify a primary interop assembly in managed source code, you must apply the **System.Runtime.InteropServices.GuidAttribute** and **PrimaryInteropAssemblyAttribute** to the assembly at design time. The **GuidAttribute** on the primary interop assembly identifies the LIBID of the type library and the **PrimaryInteropAssemblyAttribute** identifies the version of the particular type library for which this assembly is the primary interop assembly. The **PrimaryInteropAssemblyAttribute** can appear multiple times if the assembly is the primary interop assembly for multiple versions of the same type library.

When using the types defined in a type library, always reference the primary interop assembly for that type library, rather than reimporting or redefining the types themselves. For guidelines and procedures on how to produce or use primary interop assemblies, see **Primary Interop Assemblies**.

Requirements

Namespace: System.Runtime.InteropServices

Platforms: Windows 98, Windows NT 4.0, Windows Millennium Edition, Windows 2000, Windows XP Home Edition, Windows XP Professional, Windows .NET Server family

Assembly: Mscorlib (in Mscorlib.dll)

PrimaryInteropAssemblyAttribute Constructor

Initializes a new instance of the **PrimaryInteropAssemblyAttribute** class with the major and minor version numbers of the type library for which this assembly is the primary interop assembly.

```
[Visual Basic]
Public Sub New( _
   ByVal major As Integer, _
   ByVal minor As Integer _
)
[C#]
public PrimaryInteropAssemblyAttribute(
   int major,
   int minor
);
[C++]
public: PrimaryInteropAssemblyAttribute(
   int major,
   int minor
);
[JScript]
public function PrimaryInteropAssemblyAttribute(
   major : int,
   minor : int
);
```

Parameters

major
    The major version of the type library for which this assembly is the primary interop assembly.
minor
    The minor version of the type library for which this assembly is the primary interop assembly.

Remarks

The **PrimaryInteropAssemblyAttribute** can appear multiple times if the assembly is the primary interop assembly for multiple versions of the same type library.

Requirements

Platforms: Windows 98, Windows NT 4.0, Windows Millennium Edition, Windows 2000, Windows XP Home Edition, Windows XP Professional, Windows .NET Server family

PrimaryInteropAssemblyAttribute.MajorVersion Property

Gets the major version number of the type library for which this assembly is the primary interop assembly.

```
[Visual Basic]
Public ReadOnly Property MajorVersion As Integer
[C#]
public int MajorVersion {get;}
[C++]
public: __property int get_MajorVersion();
[JScript]
public function get MajorVersion() : int;
```

Property Value

The major version number of the type library for which this assembly is the primary interop assembly.

Requirements

Platforms: Windows 98, Windows NT 4.0, Windows Millennium Edition, Windows 2000, Windows XP Home Edition, Windows XP Professional, Windows .NET Server family

PrimaryInteropAssemblyAttribute.MinorVersion Property

Gets the minor version number of the type library for which this assembly is the primary interop assembly.

```
[Visual Basic]
Public ReadOnly Property MinorVersion As Integer
[C#]
public int MinorVersion {get;}
[C++]
public: __property int get_MinorVersion();
[JScript]
public function get MinorVersion() : int;
```

Property Value

The minor version number of the type library for which this assembly is the primary interop assembly.

Requirements

Platforms: Windows 98, Windows NT 4.0, Windows Millennium Edition, Windows 2000, Windows XP Home Edition, Windows XP Professional, Windows .NET Server family

ProgIdAttribute Class

Allows the user to specify the ProgID of a class.

System.Object
  System.Attribute
    System.Runtime.InteropServices.ProgIdAttribute

```
[Visual Basic]
<AttributeUsage(AttributeTargets.Class)>
NotInheritable Public Class ProgIdAttribute
    Inherits Attribute
[C#]
[AttributeUsage(AttributeTargets.Class)]
public sealed class ProgIdAttribute : Attribute
[C++]
[AttributeUsage(AttributeTargets::Class)]
public __gc __sealed class ProgIdAttribute : public Attribute
[JScript]
public
    AttributeUsage(AttributeTargets.Class)
class ProgIdAttribute extends Attribute
```

Thread Safety

Any public static (**Shared** in Visual Basic) members of this type are safe for multithreaded operations. Any instance members are not guaranteed to be thread safe.

Remarks

You can apply this attribute to classes.

ProgIDs are automatically generated for a class by combining the namespace with the type name. This can produce an invalid ProgID however, as ProgIDs are limited to 39 characters and can contain no punctuation other than a period. In such case, a ProgID can be manually assigned to the class using **ProgIdAttribute**.

Requirements

Namespace: System.Runtime.InteropServices

Platforms: Windows 98, Windows NT 4.0, Windows Millennium Edition, Windows 2000, Windows XP Home Edition, Windows XP Professional, Windows .NET Server family

Assembly: Mscorlib (in Mscorlib.dll)

ProgIdAttribute Constructor

Initializes a new instance of the **ProgIdAttribute** with the specified ProgID.

```
[Visual Basic]
Public Sub New( _
    ByVal progId As String _
)
[C#]
public ProgIdAttribute(
    string progId
);
[C++]
public: ProgIdAttribute(
    String* progId
);
```

```
[JScript]
public function ProgIdAttribute(
    progId : String
);
```

Parameters

progId
  The ProgID to be assigned to the class.

Requirements

Platforms: Windows 98, Windows NT 4.0, Windows Millennium Edition, Windows 2000, Windows XP Home Edition, Windows XP Professional, Windows .NET Server family

ProgIdAttribute.Value Property

Gets the ProgID of the class.

```
[Visual Basic]
Public ReadOnly Property Value As String
[C#]
public string Value {get;}
[C++]
public: __property String* get_Value();
[JScript]
public function get Value() : String;
```

Property Value

The ProgID of the class.

Requirements

Platforms: Windows 98, Windows NT 4.0, Windows Millennium Edition, Windows 2000, Windows XP Home Edition, Windows XP Professional, Windows .NET Server family

RegistrationServices Class

Provides a set of services for registering and unregistering managed assemblies for use from COM.

System.Object
  System.Runtime.InteropServices.RegistrationServices

```
[Visual Basic]
<ClassInterface(ClassInterfaceType.None)>
<Guid("475E398F-8AFA-43a7-A3BE-F4EF8D6787C9")>
Public Class RegistrationServices
   Implements IRegistrationServices
[C#]
[ClassInterface(ClassInterfaceType.None)]
[Guid("475E398F-8AFA-43a7-A3BE-F4EF8D6787C9")]
public class RegistrationServices : IRegistrationServices
[C++]
[ClassInterface(ClassInterfaceType::None)]
[Guid("475E398F-8AFA-43a7-A3BE-F4EF8D6787C9")]
public __gc class RegistrationServices : public
   IRegistrationServices
[JScript]
public
   ClassInterface(ClassInterfaceType.None)
   Guid("475E398F-8AFA-43a7-A3BE-F4EF8D6787C9")
class RegistrationServices implements IRegistrationServices
```

Thread Safety

Any public static (**Shared** in Visual Basic) members of this type are safe for multithreaded operations. Any instance members are not guaranteed to be thread safe.

Remarks

Registration is needed when the objects within an assembly are being used by COM clients. The **Assembly Registration Tool (Regasm.exe)** and Microsoft Visual Studio .NET use methods exposed by the **RegistrationServices** class to add or remove COM-enabling registry entries for managed assemblies.

You can use the following methods to assist you in preparing a registration file:

- **GetManagedCategoryGuid**
- **GetProgIdForType**
- **GetRegistrableTypesInAssembly**
- **TypeRepresentsComType**

Although these methods help in gathering information to be used in a registration file, they do not actually produce a registration file. Instead, you can use **Regasm.exe** with the **/regfile** option for perform this task. **RegistrationServices** methods also cannot export and register a type library. You can use **Regasm.exe /tlb** for this.

Requirements

Namespace: System.Runtime.InteropServices

Platforms: Windows 98, Windows NT 4.0, Windows Millennium Edition, Windows 2000, Windows XP Home Edition, Windows XP Professional, Windows .NET Server family

Assembly: Mscorlib (in Mscorlib.dll)

RegistrationServices Constructor

Initializes a new instance of the **RegistrationServices** class.

```
[Visual Basic]
Public Sub New()
[C#]
public RegistrationServices();
[C++]
public: RegistrationServices();
[JScript]
public function RegistrationServices();
```

Remarks

The default constructor initializes any fields to their default values.

Requirements

Platforms: Windows 98, Windows NT 4.0, Windows Millennium Edition, Windows 2000, Windows XP Home Edition, Windows XP Professional, Windows .NET Server family

RegistrationServices.GetManagedCategoryGuid Method

Returns the GUID of the COM category that contains the managed classes.

```
[Visual Basic]
Public Overridable Function GetManagedCategoryGuid() As Guid _
   Implements IRegistrationServices.GetManagedCategoryGuid
[C#]
public virtual Guid GetManagedCategoryGuid();
[C++]
public: virtual Guid GetManagedCategoryGuid();
[JScript]
public function GetManagedCategoryGuid() : Guid;
```

Return Value

The GUID of the COM category that contains the managed classes.

Implements

IRegistrationServices.GetManagedCategoryGuid

Requirements

Platforms: Windows 98, Windows NT 4.0, Windows Millennium Edition, Windows 2000, Windows XP Home Edition, Windows XP Professional, Windows .NET Server family

RegistrationServices.GetProgIdForType Method

Retrieves the COM ProgID for the specified type.

```
[Visual Basic]
Public Overridable Function GetProgIdForType( _
   ByVal type As Type _
) As String Implements IRegistrationServices.GetProgIdForType
[C#]
public virtual string GetProgIdForType(
   Type type
);
```

```
[C++]
public: virtual String* GetProgIdForType(
    Type* type
);
[JScript]
public function GetProgIdForType(
    type : Type
) : String;
```

Parameters

type
> The type corresponding to the ProgID that is being requested.

Return Value

The ProgID for the specified type.

Implements

IRegistrationServices.GetProgIdForType

Requirements

Platforms: Windows 98, Windows NT 4.0,
Windows Millennium Edition, Windows 2000,
Windows XP Home Edition, Windows XP Professional,
Windows .NET Server family

RegistrationServices.GetRegistrableTypesIn-Assembly Method

Retrieves a list of classes in an assembly that would be registered by a call to **RegisterAssembly**.

```
[Visual Basic]
Public Overridable Function GetRegistrableTypesInAssembly( _
    ByVal assembly As Assembly _
) As Type() Implements
IRegistrationServices.GetRegistrableTypesInAssembly
[C#]
public virtual Type[] GetRegistrableTypesInAssembly(
    Assembly assembly
);
[C++]
public: virtual Type* GetRegistrableTypesInAssembly(
    Assembly* assembly
) [];
[JScript]
public function GetRegistrableTypesInAssembly(
    assembly : Assembly
) : Type[];
```

Parameters

assembly
> The assembly to search for classes.

Return Value

A **Type** array containing a list of classes in *assembly*.

Implements

IRegistrationServices.GetRegistrableTypesInAssembly

Requirements

Platforms: Windows 98, Windows NT 4.0,
Windows Millennium Edition, Windows 2000,
Windows XP Home Edition, Windows XP Professional,
Windows .NET Server family

RegistrationServices.RegisterAssembly Method

Registers the classes in a managed assembly to enable creation from COM.

```
[Visual Basic]
Public Overridable Function RegisterAssembly( _
    ByVal assembly As Assembly, _
    ByVal flags As AssemblyRegistrationFlags _
) As Boolean Implements IRegistrationServices.RegisterAssembly
[C#]
public virtual bool RegisterAssembly(
    Assembly assembly,
    AssemblyRegistrationFlags flags
);
[C++]
public: virtual bool RegisterAssembly(
    Assembly* assembly,
    AssemblyRegistrationFlags flags
);
[JScript]
public function RegisterAssembly(
    assembly : Assembly,
    flags : AssemblyRegistrationFlags
) : Boolean;
```

Parameters

assembly
> The assembly to be registered.

flags
> An **AssemblyRegistrationFlags** value indicating any special settings used when registering *assembly*.

Return Value

true if *assembly* contains types that were successfully registered; otherwise **false** if the assembly contains no eligible types.

Implements

IRegistrationServices.RegisterAssembly

Exceptions

Exception Type	Condition
ArgumentNullException	*assembly* is a null reference (**Nothing** in Visual Basic).
InvalidOperation-Exception	The full name of *assembly* is a null reference (**Nothing** in Visual Basic).
	-or-
	A method marked with **ComRegisterFunctionAttribute** is not static (**Shared** in Visual Basic) .
	-or-
	There is more than one method marked with **ComRegisterFunctionAttribute** at a given level of the hierarchy.
	-or-
	The signature of the method marked with **ComRegisterFunctionAttribute** is not valid.

Remarks

RegisterAssembly adds the appropriate registry entries for the types in the specified assembly. This method also calls any registration functions found in the assembly.

Use **Assembly.Load** to get an assembly.

Example

The following entries are added to your registry.

```
HKEY_CLASSES_ROOT\progid
   (default) = progId
HKEY_CLASSES_ROOT\progid\CLSID
   (default) = clsid
HKEY_CLASSES_ROOT\CLSID\{clsid}
   (default) = progid
HKEY_CLASSES_ROOT\CLSID\{clsid}\InProcServer32
   (default) = mscoree.dll
   Class = ClassName
   ThreadingModel = Both
   Assembly = Stringized_assembly_reference
   Codebase = path_of_private_assembly
   RuntimeVersion = version_of_the_runtime
HKEY_CLASSES_ROOT\CLSID\{clsid}\Implemented Categories\
{62C8FE65-4EBB-45e7-B440-6E39B2CDBF29}
HKEY_CLASSES_ROOT\CLSID\{clsid}\ProgId
   (default) = progid
```

If the **/codebase** switch is used, the following additional entry is created in the registry. The assembly must be strong named when using the **/codebase** switch.

```
HKEY_CLASSES_ROOT\CLSID\{clsid}\InProcServer32
   Codebase = path_of_private_assembly
```

If the **/tlb** switch is used, a type library is generated and the following additional entries are created in the registry.

```
HKEY_CLASSES_ROOT\{clsid}\TypeLib
   (default) = tlbid
HKEY_CLASSES_ROOT\Typelib\{tlbid}\x.y\lcid\win32
   (default) = location of type library file
HKEY_CLASSES_ROOT\Typelib\{tlbid}\x.y\FLAGS
   (default) = 0
```

Where:

progid is the programmatic identifier assigned to the class.

clsid is the guid assigned to the class.

tlbid is the guid that identifies the type library.

x.y is the major and minor versions of the type library.

lcid is the locale id of the type library.

The *stringized_assembly_reference* found under the InProcServer32 key is the string form of the name of the assembly containing the class. The string is obtained from **AssemblyName.FullName** and is used to locate and load the assembly when the class is being created. An example of a stringized assembly name is "FunnyFarm.BarnYard.Mammal, Ver=1.2.5.1".

The *path_of_private_assembly* field should only be used for private assemblies that are not installed in the Global Assembly Cache. The path should be the full path, including the file name, where the assembly is located.

The *version_of_the_runtime* field identifies which version of the runtime to use when more than one runtime version is installed on a system.

The component category identified by the guid 62C8FE65-4EBB-45e7-B440-6E39B2CDBF29 identifies all .NET components.

Requirements

Platforms: Windows 98, Windows NT 4.0, Windows Millennium Edition, Windows 2000, Windows XP Home Edition, Windows XP Professional, Windows .NET Server family

RegistrationServices.RegisterTypeForComClients Method

Adds the appropriate registry entries for the specified type using the specified GUID. This method is not intended to be used directly from your code.

```
[Visual Basic]
Public Overridable Sub RegisterTypeForComClients( _
   ByVal type As Type, _
   ByRef g As Guid _
) Implements IRegistrationServices.RegisterTypeForComClients
[C#]
public virtual void RegisterTypeForComClients(
   Type type,
   ref Guid g
);
[C++]
public: virtual void RegisterTypeForComClients(
   Type* type,
   Guid* g
);
[JScript]
public function RegisterTypeForComClients(
   type : Type,
   g : Guid
);
```

Parameters

type
   The **Type** to be registered for use from COM.

g
   The **Guid** used to register the specified type.

Implements

IRegistrationServices.RegisterTypeForComClients

Remarks

This method, which is equivalent to calling **CoRegisterClassObject** in COM, is not intended to be used directly from your code. It registers a type but there is no equivalent unregistration method in the **RegistrationServices** class. Using the **RegisterTypeForComClients** method can cause unpredictable results, particularly if the application is multithreaded. Instead, to register the assembly containing the type, use the **RegistrationServices.RegisterAssembly** method.

Requirements

Platforms: Windows 98, Windows NT 4.0, Windows Millennium Edition, Windows 2000, Windows XP Home Edition, Windows XP Professional, Windows .NET Server family

.NET Framework Security:

• **SecurityPermission** for operating with unmanaged code. Associated enumeration: **SecurityPermissionFlag.UnmanagedCode**.

RegistrationServices.TypeRepresentsComType Method

Determines whether the specified type is a COM type.

```
[Visual Basic]
Public Overridable Function TypeRepresentsComType( _
   ByVal type As Type _
) As Boolean Implements IRegistrationServices.TypeRepresentsComType
[C#]
public virtual bool TypeRepresentsComType(
   Type type
);
[C++]
public: virtual bool TypeRepresentsComType(
   Type* type
);
[JScript]
public function TypeRepresentsComType(
    type : Type
) : Boolean;
```

Parameters

type
   The type to check for being a COM type.

Return Value

true if the specified type is a COM type; otherwise **false**.

Implements

IRegistrationServices.TypeRepresentsComType

Requirements

Platforms: Windows 98, Windows NT 4.0,
Windows Millennium Edition, Windows 2000,
Windows XP Home Edition, Windows XP Professional,
Windows .NET Server family

RegistrationServices.TypeRequiresRegistration Method

Determines whether the specified type requires registration.

```
[Visual Basic]
Public Overridable Function TypeRequiresRegistration( _
   ByVal type As Type _
) As Boolean Implements IRegistrationServices.TypeRequiresRegistration
[C#]
public virtual bool TypeRequiresRegistration(
   Type type
);
[C++]
public: virtual bool TypeRequiresRegistration(
   Type* type
);
[JScript]
public function TypeRequiresRegistration(
    type : Type
) : Boolean;
```

Parameters

type
   The type to check for COM registration requirements.

Return Value

true if the type must be registered for use from COM; otherwise **false**.

Implements

IRegistrationServices.TypeRequiresRegistration

Requirements

Platforms: Windows 98, Windows NT 4.0,
Windows Millennium Edition, Windows 2000,
Windows XP Home Edition, Windows XP Professional,
Windows .NET Server family

RegistrationServices.UnregisterAssembly Method

Unregisters the classes in a managed assembly.

```
[Visual Basic]
Public Overridable Function UnregisterAssembly( _
   ByVal assembly As Assembly _
) As Boolean Implements IRegistrationServices.UnregisterAssembly
[C#]
public virtual bool UnregisterAssembly(
   Assembly assembly
);
[C++]
public: virtual bool UnregisterAssembly(
   Assembly* assembly
);
[JScript]
public function UnregisterAssembly(
    assembly : Assembly
) : Boolean;
```

Parameters

assembly
   The assembly to be unregistered.

Return Value

true if *assembly* contains types that were successfully unregistered;
otherwise **false** if the assembly contains no eligible types.

Implements

IRegistrationServices.UnregisterAssembly

Exceptions

Exception Type	Condition
ArgumentNull-Exception	*assembly* is a null reference (**Nothing** in Visual Basic).
InvalidOperation-Exception	The full name of *assembly* is a null reference (**Nothing** in Visual Basic).
	-or-
	A method marked with **ComUnregisterFunctionAttribute** is not static (**Shared** in Visual Basic) .
	-or-
	There is more than one method marked with **ComUnregisterFunctionAttribute** at a given level of the hierarchy.
	-or-
	The signature of the method marked with **ComUnregisterFunctionAttribute** is not valid.

Remarks

UnregisterAssembly removes the registry entries for the types in
the specified assembly previously added by **RegisterAssembly**. This
method also calls any unregistration functions found in the
assembly.

Requirements

Platforms: Windows 98, Windows NT 4.0,
Windows Millennium Edition, Windows 2000,
Windows XP Home Edition, Windows XP Professional,
Windows .NET Server family

RuntimeEnvironment Class

Provides a collection of static (**Shared** in Visual Basic) methods that return information about the common language runtime environment.

System.Object
    System.Runtime.InteropServices.RuntimeEnvironment

```
[Visual Basic]
Public Class RuntimeEnvironment
[C#]
public class RuntimeEnvironment
[C++]
public __gc class RuntimeEnvironment
[JScript]
public class RuntimeEnvironment
```

Thread Safety

Any public static (**Shared** in Visual Basic) members of this type are safe for multithreaded operations. Any instance members are not guaranteed to be thread safe.

Requirements

Namespace: System.Runtime.InteropServices

Platforms: Windows 98, Windows NT 4.0, Windows Millennium Edition, Windows 2000, Windows XP Home Edition, Windows XP Professional, Windows .NET Server family

Assembly: Mscorlib (in Mscorlib.dll)

RuntimeEnvironment Constructor

Initializes a new instance of the **RuntimeEnvironment** class.

```
[Visual Basic]
Public Sub New()
[C#]
public RuntimeEnvironment();
[C++]
public: RuntimeEnvironment();
[JScript]
public function RuntimeEnvironment();
```

Remarks

The default constructor initializes any fields to their default values.

Requirements

Platforms: Windows 98, Windows NT 4.0, Windows Millennium Edition, Windows 2000, Windows XP Home Edition, Windows XP Professional, Windows .NET Server family

RuntimeEnvironment.SystemConfigurationFile Property

Gets the path to the system configuration file.

```
[Visual Basic]
Public Shared ReadOnly Property SystemConfigurationFile As String
[C#]
public static string SystemConfigurationFile {get;}
```

```
[C++]
public: __property static String* get_SystemConfigurationFile();
[JScript]
public static function get SystemConfigurationFile() : String;
```

Property Value

The path to the system configuration file.

Requirements

Platforms: Windows 98, Windows NT 4.0, Windows Millennium Edition, Windows 2000, Windows XP Home Edition, Windows XP Professional, Windows .NET Server family

.NET Framework Security:

- **FileIOPermission** for accessing files and folders. Associated enumeration: **FileIOPermissionAccess.PathDiscovery**.

RuntimeEnvironment.FromGlobalAccessCache Method

Tests whether the specified assembly is loaded in the global assembly cache (GAC).

```
[Visual Basic]
Public Shared Function FromGlobalAccessCache( _
    ByVal a As Assembly _
) As Boolean
[C#]
public static bool FromGlobalAccessCache(
    Assembly a
);
[C++]
public: static bool FromGlobalAccessCache(
    Assembly* a
);
[JScript]
public static function FromGlobalAccessCache(
    a : Assembly
) : Boolean;
```

Parameters

a
    The assembly to determine if it is loaded in the GAC.

Return Value

true if the assembly is loaded in the GAC; otherwise, **false**.

Requirements

Platforms: Windows 98, Windows NT 4.0, Windows Millennium Edition, Windows 2000, Windows XP Home Edition, Windows XP Professional, Windows .NET Server family

RuntimeEnvironment.GetRuntimeDirectory Method

Gets the directory where the common language runtime is installed.

```
[Visual Basic]
Public Shared Function GetRuntimeDirectory() As String
[C#]
public static string GetRuntimeDirectory();
```

```
[C++]
public: static String* GetRuntimeDirectory();
[JScript]
public static function GetRuntimeDirectory() : String;
```

Return Value

A string containing the path to the directory where the common
language runtime is installed.

Requirements

Platforms: Windows 98, Windows NT 4.0,
Windows Millennium Edition, Windows 2000,
Windows XP Home Edition, Windows XP Professional,
Windows .NET Server family

.NET Framework Security:

*   **FileIOPermission** for accessing files and folders. Associated
    enumeration: **FileIOPermissionAccess.PathDiscovery**.

RuntimeEnvironment.GetSystemVersion Method

Gets the version number of the common language runtime that is
running the current process.

```
[Visual Basic]
Public Shared Function GetSystemVersion() As String
[C#]
public static string GetSystemVersion();
[C++]
public: static String* GetSystemVersion();
[JScript]
public static function GetSystemVersion() : String;
```

Return Value

A string containing the version number of the common language
runtime.

Requirements

Platforms: Windows 98, Windows NT 4.0,
Windows Millennium Edition, Windows 2000,
Windows XP Home Edition, Windows XP Professional,
Windows .NET Server family

SafeArrayRankMismatch-Exception Class

The exception thrown when the rank of an incoming **SAFEARRAY** does not match the rank specified in the managed signature.

System.Object
  System.Exception
    System.SystemException
      System.Runtime.InteropServices.SafeArrayRank-
      MismatchException

```
[Visual Basic]
<Serializable>
Public Class SafeArrayRankMismatchException
   Inherits SystemException
[C#]
[Serializable]
public class SafeArrayRankMismatchException : SystemException
[C++]
[Serializable]
public __gc class SafeArrayRankMismatchException : public
   SystemException
[JScript]
public
   Serializable
class SafeArrayRankMismatchException extends SystemException
```

Thread Safety

Any public static (**Shared** in Visual Basic) members of this type are safe for multithreaded operations. Any instance members are not guaranteed to be thread safe.

Remarks

SafeArrayRankMismatchException uses the HRESULT COR_E_SAFEARRAYRANKMISMATCH which has the value 0x80131538.

The rank of a **SAFEARRAY** is the number of dimensions in that array.

Requirements

Namespace: System.Runtime.InteropServices

Platforms: Windows 98, Windows NT 4.0, Windows Millennium Edition, Windows 2000, Windows XP Home Edition, Windows XP Professional, Windows .NET Server family

Assembly: Mscorlib (in Mscorlib.dll)

SafeArrayRankMismatchException Constructor

Initializes a new instance of the **SafeArrayRankMismatchException** class.

Overload List

Initializes a new instance of the **SafeArrayTypeMismatchException** class with default values.

> [Visual Basic] **Public Sub New()**
> [C#] **public SafeArrayRankMismatchException();**
> [C++] **public: SafeArrayRankMismatchException();**

[JScript] **public function SafeArrayRankMismatchException();**

Initializes a new instance of the **SafeArrayRankMismatch-Exception** class with the specified message.

> [Visual Basic] **Public Sub New(String)**
> [C#] **public SafeArrayRankMismatchException(string);**
> [C++] **public: SafeArrayRankMismatchException(String*);**
> [JScript] **public function SafeArrayRankMismatchException(String);**

Initializes a new instance of the **SafeArrayTypeMismatch-Exception** class from serialization data.

> [Visual Basic] **Protected Sub New(SerializationInfo, StreamingContext)**
> [C#] **protected SafeArrayRankMismatchException (SerializationInfo, StreamingContext);**
> [C++] **protected: SafeArrayRankMismatchException (SerializationInfo*, StreamingContext);**
> [JScript] **protected function SafeArrayRankMismatch-Exception(SerializationInfo, StreamingContext);**

Initializes a new instance of the **SafeArrayRankMismatch-Exception** class with a specified error message and a reference to the inner exception that is the cause of this exception.

> [Visual Basic] **Public Sub New(String, Exception)**
> [C#] **public SafeArrayRankMismatchException(string, Exception);**
> [C++] **public: SafeArrayRankMismatchException(String*, Exception*);**
> [JScript] **public function SafeArrayRankMismatchException(String, Exception);**

SafeArrayRankMismatchException Constructor ( )

Initializes a new instance of the **SafeArrayTypeMismatchException** class with default values.

```
[Visual Basic]
Public Sub New()
[C#]
public SafeArrayRankMismatchException();
[C++]
public: SafeArrayRankMismatchException();
[JScript]
public function SafeArrayRankMismatchException();
```

Remarks

SafeArrayRankMismatchException inherits from **SystemException**. This constructor sets the properties of the **Exception** object as shown in the following table.

Property	Value
InnerException	A null reference (**Nothing** in Visual Basic).
Message	A localized error message string.

Requirements

Platforms: Windows 98, Windows NT 4.0, Windows Millennium Edition, Windows 2000, Windows XP Home Edition, Windows XP Professional, Windows .NET Server family

SafeArrayRankMismatchException Constructor (String)

Initializes a new instance of the **SafeArrayRankMismatch-Exception** class with the specified message.

```
[Visual Basic]
Public Sub New( _
   ByVal message As String _
)
[C#]
public SafeArrayRankMismatchException(
   string message
);
[C++]
public: SafeArrayRankMismatchException(
   String* message
);
[JScript]
public function SafeArrayRankMismatchException(
   message : String
);
```

Parameters
message
    The message that indicates the reason for the exception.

Remarks
SafeArrayRankMismatchException inherits from **SystemException**. This constructor sets the properties of the **Exception** object as shown in the following table.

Property	Value
InnerException	A null reference (**Nothing** in Visual Basic).
Message	*message*

Requirements
Platforms: Windows 98, Windows NT 4.0, Windows Millennium Edition, Windows 2000, Windows XP Home Edition, Windows XP Professional, Windows .NET Server family

SafeArrayRankMismatchException Constructor (SerializationInfo, StreamingContext)

Initializes a new instance of the **SafeArrayTypeMismatchException** class from serialization data.

```
[Visual Basic]
Protected Sub New( _
   ByVal info As SerializationInfo, _
   ByVal context As StreamingContext _
)
[C#]
protected SafeArrayRankMismatchException(
   SerializationInfo info,
   StreamingContext context
);
[C++]
protected: SafeArrayRankMismatchException(
   SerializationInfo* info,
   StreamingContext context
);
```

```
[JScript]
protected function SafeArrayRankMismatchException(
   info : SerializationInfo,
   context : StreamingContext
);
```

Parameters
info
    The object that holds the serialized object data.
context
    The contextual information about the source or destination.

Exceptions

Exception Type	Condition
ArgumentNullException	*info* is a null reference (**Nothing** in Visual Basic).

Remarks
This constructor is called during deserialization to reconstitute the exception object transmitted over a stream. For more information, see **System.Runtime.Serialization**.

SafeArrayRankMismatchException inherits from **SystemException**.

Requirements
Platforms: Windows 98, Windows NT 4.0, Windows Millennium Edition, Windows 2000, Windows XP Home Edition, Windows XP Professional, Windows .NET Server family

SafeArrayRankMismatchException Constructor (String, Exception)

Initializes a new instance of the **SafeArrayRankMismatch-Exception** class with a specified error message and a reference to the inner exception that is the cause of this exception.

```
[Visual Basic]
Public Sub New( _
   ByVal message As String, _
   ByVal inner As Exception _
)
[C#]
public SafeArrayRankMismatchException(
   string message,
   Exception inner
);
[C++]
public: SafeArrayRankMismatchException(
   String* message,
   Exception* inner
);
[JScript]
public function SafeArrayRankMismatchException(
   message : String,
   inner : Exception
);
```

Parameters
message
    The error message that explains the reason for the exception.

inner

The exception that is the cause of the current exception. If the *inner* parameter is not a null reference (**Nothing** in Visual Basic), the current exception is raised in a **catch** block that handles the inner exception.

Remarks

An exception that is thrown as a direct result of a previous exception should include a reference to the previous exception in the **InnerException** property. The **InnerException** property returns the same value that is passed into the constructor, or a null reference (**Nothing** in Visual Basic) if the **InnerException** property does not supply the inner exception value to the constructor.

The following table shows the initial property values for an instance of **SafeArrayRankMismatchException**.

Property	Value
InnerException	The inner exception reference.
Message	The error message string.

Requirements

Platforms: Windows 98, Windows NT 4.0, Windows Millennium Edition, Windows 2000, Windows XP Home Edition, Windows XP Professional, Windows .NET Server family

SafeArrayTypeMismatch-Exception Class

The exception thrown when the type of the incoming **SAFEARRAY** does not match the type specified in the managed signature.

System.Object
  System.Exception
    System.SystemException
      System.Runtime.InteropServices.SafeArrayType-
      MismatchException

```
[Visual Basic]
<Serializable>
Public Class SafeArrayTypeMismatchException
   Inherits SystemException
[C#]
[Serializable]
public class SafeArrayTypeMismatchException : SystemException
[C++]
[Serializable]
public __gc class SafeArrayTypeMismatchException : public
   SystemException
[JScript]
public
   Serializable
class SafeArrayTypeMismatchException extends SystemException
```

Thread Safety

Any public static (**Shared** in Visual Basic) members of this type are safe for multithreaded operations. Any instance members are not guaranteed to be thread safe.

Remarks

SafeArrayTypeMismatchException uses the HRESULT COR_E_SAFEARRAYTYPEMISMATCH which has the value 0x80131533.

Requirements

Namespace: System.Runtime.InteropServices

Platforms: Windows 98, Windows NT 4.0, Windows Millennium Edition, Windows 2000, Windows XP Home Edition, Windows XP Professional, Windows .NET Server family

Assembly: Mscorlib (in Mscorlib.dll)

SafeArrayTypeMismatchException Constructor

Initializes a new instance of the **SafeArrayTypeMismatchException** class.

Overload List

Initializes a new instance of the **SafeArrayTypeMismatchException** class with default values.

  [Visual Basic] **Public Sub New()**
  [C#] **public SafeArrayTypeMismatchException();**
  [C++] **public: SafeArrayTypeMismatchException();**
  [JScript] **public function SafeArrayTypeMis-matchException();**

Initializes a new instance of the **SafeArrayTypeMismatch-Exception** class with the specified message.

  [Visual Basic] **Public Sub New(String)**
  [C#] **public SafeArrayTypeMismatchException(string);**
  [C++] **public: SafeArrayTypeMismatchException(String*);**
  [JScript] **public function SafeArrayTypeMismatchException(String);**

Initializes a new instance of the **SafeArrayTypeMismatchException** class from serialization data.

  [Visual Basic] **Protected Sub New(SerializationInfo, StreamingContext)**
  [C#] **protected SafeArrayTypeMismatchException(SerializationInfo, StreamingContext);**
  [C++] **protected: SafeArrayTypeMismatchException(SerializationInfo*, StreamingContext);**
  [JScript] **protected function SafeArrayTypeMismatchException(SerializationInfo, StreamingContext);**

Initializes a new instance of the **SafeArrayTypeMismatch-Exception** class with a specified error message and a reference to the inner exception that is the cause of this exception.

  [Visual Basic] **Public Sub New(String, Exception)**
  [C#] **public SafeArrayTypeMismatchException(string, Exception);**
  [C++] **public: SafeArrayTypeMismatchException(String*, Exception*);**
  [JScript] **public function SafeArrayTypeMismatchException(String, Exception);**

SafeArrayTypeMismatchException Constructor ()

Initializes a new instance of the **SafeArrayTypeMismatchException** class with default values.

```
[Visual Basic]
Public Sub New()
[C#]
public SafeArrayTypeMismatchException();
[C++]
public: SafeArrayTypeMismatchException();
[JScript]
public function SafeArrayTypeMismatchException();
```

Remarks

SafeArrayTypeMismatchException inherits from **SystemException**. This constructor sets the properties of the **Exception** object as shown in the following table.

Property	Value
InnerException	A null reference (**Nothing** in Visual Basic).
Message	A localized error message string.

Requirements

Platforms: Windows 98, Windows NT 4.0, Windows Millennium Edition, Windows 2000, Windows XP Home Edition, Windows XP Professional, Windows .NET Server family

SafeArrayTypeMismatchException Constructor (String)

Initializes a new instance of the **SafeArrayTypeMismatch-Exception** class with the specified message.

```
[Visual Basic]
Public Sub New( _
   ByVal message As String _
)
[C#]
public SafeArrayTypeMismatchException(
   string message
);
[C++]
public: SafeArrayTypeMismatchException(
   String* message
);
[JScript]
public function SafeArrayTypeMismatchException(
   message : String
);
```

Parameters

message
   The message that indicates the reason for the exception.

Remarks

SafeArrayTypeMismatchException inherits from **SystemException**. This constructor sets the properties of the **Exception** object as shown in the following table.

Property	Value
InnerException	A null reference (**Nothing** in Visual Basic).
Message	*message*

Requirements

Platforms: Windows 98, Windows NT 4.0, Windows Millennium Edition, Windows 2000, Windows XP Home Edition, Windows XP Professional, Windows .NET Server family

SafeArrayTypeMismatchException Constructor (SerializationInfo, StreamingContext)

Initializes a new instance of the **SafeArrayTypeMismatchException** class from serialization data.

```
[Visual Basic]
Protected Sub New( _
   ByVal info As SerializationInfo, _
   ByVal context As StreamingContext _
)
[C#]
protected SafeArrayTypeMismatchException(
   SerializationInfo info,
   StreamingContext context
);
[C++]
protected: SafeArrayTypeMismatchException(
   SerializationInfo* info,
   StreamingContext context
);
```

```
[JScript]
protected function SafeArrayTypeMismatchException(
   info : SerializationInfo,
   context : StreamingContext
);
```

Parameters

info
   The object that holds the serialized object data.
context
   The contextual information about the source or destination.

Exceptions

Exception Type	Condition
ArgumentNullException	*info* is a null reference (**Nothing** in Visual Basic).

Remarks

This constructor is called during deserialization to reconstitute the exception object transmitted over a stream.

SafeArrayTypeMismatchException inherits from **SystemException**.

Requirements

Platforms: Windows 98, Windows NT 4.0, Windows Millennium Edition, Windows 2000, Windows XP Home Edition, Windows XP Professional, Windows .NET Server family

SafeArrayTypeMismatchException Constructor (String, Exception)

Initializes a new instance of the **SafeArrayTypeMismatchException** class with a specified error message and a reference to the inner exception that is the cause of this exception.

```
[Visual Basic]
Public Sub New( _
   ByVal message As String, _
   ByVal inner As Exception _
)
[C#]
public SafeArrayTypeMismatchException(
   string message,
   Exception inner
);
[C++]
public: SafeArrayTypeMismatchException(
   String* message,
   Exception* inner
);
[JScript]
public function SafeArrayTypeMismatchException(
   message : String,
   inner : Exception
);
```

Parameters

message
   The error message that explains the reason for the exception.

inner

> The exception that is the cause of the current exception. If the *inner* parameter is not a null reference (**Nothing** in Visual Basic), the current exception is raised in a **catch** block that handles the inner exception.

Remarks

An exception that is thrown as a direct result of a previous exception should include a reference to the previous exception in the **InnerException** property. The **InnerException** property returns the same value that is passed into the constructor, or a null reference (**Nothing** in Visual Basic) if the **InnerException** property does not supply the inner exception value to the constructor.

The following table shows the initial property values for an instance of **SafeArrayTypeMismatchException**.

Property	Value
InnerException	The inner exception reference.
Message	The error message string.

Requirements

Platforms: Windows 98, Windows NT 4.0, Windows Millennium Edition, Windows 2000, Windows XP Home Edition, Windows XP Professional, Windows .NET Server family

SEHException Class

Represents Structured Exception Handler (SEH) errors.

System.Object
  System.Exception
    System.SystemException
      System.Runtime.InteropServices.ExternalException
        System.Runtime.InteropServices.SEHException

```
[Visual Basic]
<Serializable>
Public Class SEHException
    Inherits ExternalException
[C#]
[Serializable]
public class SEHException : ExternalException
[C++]
[Serializable]
public __gc class SEHException : public ExternalException
[JScript]
public
    Serializable
class SEHException extends ExternalException
```

Thread Safety

Any public static (**Shared** in Visual Basic) members of this type are safe for multithreaded operations. Any instance members are not guaranteed to be thread safe.

Remarks

The **SEHException** class handles errors from the SEH code.

SEHException uses the HRESULT E_FAIL which has the value 0x80004005.

Requirements

Namespace: System.Runtime.InteropServices

Platforms: Windows 98, Windows NT 4.0, Windows Millennium Edition, Windows 2000, Windows XP Home Edition, Windows XP Professional, Windows .NET Server family

Assembly: Mscorlib (in Mscorlib.dll)

SEHException Constructor

Initializes an instance of the **SEHException** class.

Overload List

Initializes an instance of the **SEHException** with default properties.

  [Visual Basic] **Public Sub New()**
  [C#] **public SEHException();**
  [C++] **public: SEHException();**
  [JScript] **public function SEHException();**

Initializes a new instance of the **SEHException** class with a specified message.

  [Visual Basic] **Public Sub New(String)**
  [C#] **public SEHException(string);**
  [C++] **public: SEHException(String*);**
  [JScript] **public function SEHException(String);**

Initializes a new instance of the **SEHException** class from serialization data.

  [Visual Basic] **Protected Sub New(SerializationInfo, StreamingContext)**
  [C#] **protected SEHException(SerializationInfo, StreamingContext);**
  [C++] **protected: SEHException(SerializationInfo*, StreamingContext);**
  [JScript] **protected function SEHException(SerializationInfo, StreamingContext);**

Initializes a new instance of the **SEHException** class with a specified error message and a reference to the inner exception that is the cause of this exception.

  [Visual Basic] **Public Sub New(String, Exception)**
  [C#] **public SEHException(string, Exception);**
  [C++] **public: SEHException(String*, Exception*);**
  [JScript] **public function SEHException(String, Exception);**

SEHException Constructor ()

Initializes an instance of the **SEHException** with default properties.

```
[Visual Basic]
Public Sub New()
[C#]
public SEHException();
[C++]
public: SEHException();
[JScript]
public function SEHException();
```

Remarks

SEHException inherits from **ExternalException**. This constructor sets the properties of the **Exception** object as shown in the following table.

Property Type	Condition
InnerException	A null reference (**Nothing** in Visual Basic).
Message	A localized error message string.

Requirements

Platforms: Windows 98, Windows NT 4.0, Windows Millennium Edition, Windows 2000, Windows XP Home Edition, Windows XP Professional, Windows .NET Server family

SEHException Constructor (String)

Initializes a new instance of the **SEHException** class with a specified message.

```
[Visual Basic]
Public Sub New( _
    ByVal message As String _
)
[C#]
public SEHException(
    string message
);
```

```
[C++]
public: SEHException(
    String* message
);
[JScript]
public function SEHException(
    message : String
);
```

Parameters

message
> The message that indicates the reason for the exception.

Remarks

SEHException inherits from **ExternalException**. This constructor sets the properties of the **Exception** object as shown in the following table.

Property Type	Condition
InnerException	A null reference (**Nothing** in Visual Basic).
Message	*message*

Requirements

Platforms: Windows 98, Windows NT 4.0, Windows Millennium Edition, Windows 2000, Windows XP Home Edition, Windows XP Professional, Windows .NET Server family

SEHException Constructor (SerializationInfo, StreamingContext)

Initializes a new instance of the **SEHException** class from serialization data.

```
[Visual Basic]
Protected Sub New( _
    ByVal info As SerializationInfo, _
    ByVal context As StreamingContext _
)
[C#]
protected SEHException(
    SerializationInfo info,
    StreamingContext context
);
[C++]
protected: SEHException(
    SerializationInfo* info,
    StreamingContext context
);
[JScript]
protected function SEHException(
    info : SerializationInfo,
    context : StreamingContext
);
```

Parameters

info
> The object that holds the serialized object data.

context
> The contextual information about the source or destination.

Exceptions

Exception Type	Condition
ArgumentNullException	*info* is a null reference (**Nothing** in Visual Basic).

Remarks

This constructor is called during deserialization to reconstitute the exception object transmitted over a stream. For more information, see **System.Runtime.Serialization**.

SEHException inherits from **ExternalException**.

Requirements

Platforms: Windows 98, Windows NT 4.0, Windows Millennium Edition, Windows 2000, Windows XP Home Edition, Windows XP Professional, Windows .NET Server family

SEHException Constructor (String, Exception)

Initializes a new instance of the **SEHException** class with a specified error message and a reference to the inner exception that is the cause of this exception.

```
[Visual Basic]
Public Sub New( _
    ByVal message As String, _
    ByVal inner As Exception _
)
[C#]
public SEHException(
    string message,
    Exception inner
);
[C++]
public: SEHException(
    String* message,
    Exception* inner
);
[JScript]
public function SEHException(
    message : String,
    inner : Exception
);
```

Parameters

message
> The error message that explains the reason for the exception.

inner
> The exception that is the cause of the current exception. If the *inner* parameter is not a null reference (**Nothing** in Visual Basic), the current exception is raised in a **catch** block that handles the inner exception.

Remarks

An exception that is thrown as a direct result of a previous exception should include a reference to the previous exception in the **InnerException** property. The **InnerException** property returns the same value that is passed into the constructor, or a null reference (**Nothing** in Visual Basic) if the **InnerException** property does not supply the inner exception value to the constructor.

The following table shows the initial property values for an instance of **SEHException**.

Property	Value
InnerException	The inner exception reference.
Message	The error message string.

Requirements

Platforms: Windows 98, Windows NT 4.0,
Windows Millennium Edition, Windows 2000,
Windows XP Home Edition, Windows XP Professional,
Windows .NET Server family

SEHException.CanResume Method

Indicates whether the exception can be recovered from or not, and if
the code can continue from the point where the exception was
thrown.

```
[Visual Basic]
Public Overridable Function CanResume() As Boolean
[C#]
public virtual bool CanResume();
[C++]
public: virtual bool CanResume();
[JScript]
public function CanResume() : Boolean;
```

Return Value

Resumable exceptions are not yet implemented, so this method
always returns **false**.

Remarks

CanResume can be resumable, which means a filtered exception
handler can correct the problem that caused the exception, and the
code will continue from the point that threw the exception.

Requirements

Platforms: Windows 98, Windows NT 4.0,
Windows Millennium Edition, Windows 2000,
Windows XP Home Edition, Windows XP Professional,
Windows .NET Server family

STATSTG Structure

Contains statistical information about an open storage, stream, or byte-array object.

System.Object
  System.ValueType
    System.Runtime.InteropServices.STATSTG

```
[Visual Basic]
<ComVisible(False)>
Public Structure STATSTG
[C#]
[ComVisible(false)]
public struct STATSTG
[C++]
[ComVisible(false)]
public __value struct STATSTG
```

[JScript] In JScript, you can use the structures in the .NET Framework, but you cannot define your own.

Thread Safety

Any public static (**Shared** in Visual Basic) members of this type are safe for multithreaded operations. Any instance members are not guaranteed to be thread safe.

Remarks

For more information, please see the existing documentation for **STATSTG** in the com subfolder of the MSDN library.

Requirements

Namespace: System.Runtime.InteropServices

Platforms: Windows 98, Windows NT 4.0, Windows Millennium Edition, Windows 2000, Windows XP Home Edition, Windows XP Professional, Windows .NET Server family

Assembly: Mscorlib (in Mscorlib.dll)

STATSTG.atime Field

Indicates the last access time for this storage, stream or byte array

```
[Visual Basic]
Public atime As FILETIME
[C#]
public FILETIME atime;
[C++]
public: FILETIME atime;
[JScript]
public var atime : FILETIME;
```

Remarks

For more information, please see the existing documentation for **STATSTG** in the MSDN library.

Requirements

Platforms: Windows 98, Windows NT 4.0, Windows Millennium Edition, Windows 2000, Windows XP Home Edition, Windows XP Professional, Windows .NET Server family

STATSTG.cbSize Field

Specifies the size in bytes of the stream or byte array.

```
[Visual Basic]
Public cbSize As Long
[C#]
public long cbSize;
[C++]
public: __int64 cbSize;
[JScript]
public var cbSize : long;
```

Remarks

For more information, please see the existing documentation for **STATSTG** in the MSDN library.

Requirements

Platforms: Windows 98, Windows NT 4.0, Windows Millennium Edition, Windows 2000, Windows XP Home Edition, Windows XP Professional, Windows .NET Server family

STATSTG.clsid Field

Indicates the class identifier for the storage object.

```
[Visual Basic]
Public clsid As Guid
[C#]
public Guid clsid;
[C++]
public: Guid clsid;
[JScript]
public var clsid : Guid;
```

Remarks

Initialized to **CLSID_NULL** for new storage objects.

For more information, please see the existing documentation for **STATSTG** in the MSDN library.

Requirements

Platforms: Windows 98, Windows NT 4.0, Windows Millennium Edition, Windows 2000, Windows XP Home Edition, Windows XP Professional, Windows .NET Server family

STATSTG.ctime Field

Indicates the creation time for this storage, stream, or byte array.

```
[Visual Basic]
Public ctime As FILETIME
[C#]
public FILETIME ctime;
[C++]
public: FILETIME ctime;
[JScript]
public var ctime : FILETIME;
```

Remarks

For more information, please see the existing documentation for **STATSTG** in the MSDN library.

Requirements

Platforms: Windows 98, Windows NT 4.0,
Windows Millennium Edition, Windows 2000,
Windows XP Home Edition, Windows XP Professional,
Windows .NET Server family

STATSTG.grfLocksSupported Field

Indicates the types of region locking supported by the stream or byte array.

```
[Visual Basic]
Public grfLocksSupported As Integer
[C#]
public int grfLocksSupported;
[C++]
public: int grfLocksSupported;
[JScript]
public var grfLocksSupported : int;
```

Remarks

For more information, please see the existing documentation for **STATSTG** in the MSDN library.

Requirements

Platforms: Windows 98, Windows NT 4.0,
Windows Millennium Edition, Windows 2000,
Windows XP Home Edition, Windows XP Professional,
Windows .NET Server family

STATSTG.grfMode Field

Indicates the access mode that was specified when the object was opened.

```
[Visual Basic]
Public grfMode As Integer
[C#]
public int grfMode;
[C++]
public: int grfMode;
[JScript]
public var grfMode : int;
```

Remarks

For more information, please see the existing documentation for **STATSTG** in the MSDN library.

Requirements

Platforms: Windows 98, Windows NT 4.0,
Windows Millennium Edition, Windows 2000,
Windows XP Home Edition, Windows XP Professional,
Windows .NET Server family

STATSTG.grfStateBits Field

Indicates the current state bits of the storage object (the value most recently set by the **IStorage::SetStateBits** method).

```
[Visual Basic]
Public grfStateBits As Integer
[C#]
public int grfStateBits;
```

```
[C++]
public: int grfStateBits;
[JScript]
public var grfStateBits : int;
```

Remarks

For more information, please see the existing documentation for **STATSTG** in the MSDN library.

Requirements

Platforms: Windows 98, Windows NT 4.0,
Windows Millennium Edition, Windows 2000,
Windows XP Home Edition, Windows XP Professional,
Windows .NET Server family

STATSTG.mtime Field

Indicates the last modification time for this storage, stream, or byte array.

```
[Visual Basic]
Public mtime As FILETIME
[C#]
public FILETIME mtime;
[C++]
public: FILETIME mtime;
[JScript]
public var mtime : FILETIME;
```

Remarks

For more information, please see the existing documentation for **STATSTG** in the MSDN library.

Requirements

Platforms: Windows 98, Windows NT 4.0,
Windows Millennium Edition, Windows 2000,
Windows XP Home Edition, Windows XP Professional,
Windows .NET Server family

STATSTG.pwcsName Field

Pointer to a null-terminated string containing the name of the object described by this structure.

```
[Visual Basic]
Public pwcsName As String
[C#]
public string pwcsName;
[C++]
public: String* pwcsName;
[JScript]
public var pwcsName : String;
```

Remarks

For more information, please see the existing documentation for **STATSTG** in the MSDN library.

Requirements

Platforms: Windows 98, Windows NT 4.0,
Windows Millennium Edition, Windows 2000,
Windows XP Home Edition, Windows XP Professional,
Windows .NET Server family

STATSTG.reserved Field

Reserved for future use.

```
[Visual Basic]
Public reserved As Integer
[C#]
public int reserved;
[C++]
public: int reserved;
[JScript]
public var reserved : int;
```

Remarks

For more information, please see the existing documentation for
STATSTG in the MSDN library.

Requirements

Platforms: Windows 98, Windows NT 4.0,
Windows Millennium Edition, Windows 2000,
Windows XP Home Edition, Windows XP Professional,
Windows .NET Server family

STATSTG.type Field

Indicates the type of storage object which is one of the values from
the **STGTY** enumeration.

```
[Visual Basic]
Public type As Integer
[C#]
public int type;
[C++]
public: int type;
[JScript]
public var type : int;
```

Remarks

For more information, please see the existing documentation for
STATSTG in the MSDN library.

Requirements

Platforms: Windows 98, Windows NT 4.0,
Windows Millennium Edition, Windows 2000,
Windows XP Home Edition, Windows XP Professional,
Windows .NET Server family

StructLayoutAttribute Class

The **StructLayoutAttribute** class allows the user to control the physical layout of the data fields of a class or structure.

System.Object
  System.Attribute
    System.Runtime.InteropServices.StructLayoutAttribute

```
[Visual Basic]
<AttributeUsage(AttributeTargets.Class Or AttributeTargets.Struct)>
NotInheritable Public Class StructLayoutAttribute
   Inherits Attribute
[C#]
[AttributeUsage(AttributeTargets.Class | AttributeTargets.Struct)]
public sealed class StructLayoutAttribute : Attribute
[C++]
[AttributeUsage(AttributeTargets::Class |
   AttributeTargets::Struct)]
public __gc __sealed class StructLayoutAttribute : public
   Attribute
[JScript]
public
   AttributeUsage(AttributeTargets.Class | AttributeTargets.Struct)
class StructLayoutAttribute extends Attribute
```

Thread Safety

Any public static (**Shared** in Visual Basic) members of this type are safe for multithreaded operations. Any instance members are not guaranteed to be thread safe.

Remarks

You can apply this attribute to classes or structures.

Typically, the common language runtime controls the physical layout of the data fields of a class or structure in managed memory. If the class or structure needs to be arranged a certain way, you can use **StructLayoutAttribute**. Explicit control of a class layout is important if the class is to be passed to unmanaged code that expects a specific layout. The **LayoutKind** value **Sequential** is used to force the members to be laid out sequentially in the order they appear. **Explicit** controls the precise position of each data member. With **Explicit**, each member must use the **FieldOffsetAttribute** to indicate the position of that field within the type.

C#, Visual Basic. NET, and C++ compilers apply the **Sequential** layout value to classes and structures by default. The **Type Library Importer (Tlbimp.exe)** also applies this attribute; it always applies the **Sequential** value when it imports a type library.

Requirements

Namespace: System.Runtime.InteropServices

Platforms: Windows 98, Windows NT 4.0, Windows Millennium Edition, Windows 2000, Windows XP Home Edition, Windows XP Professional, Windows .NET Server family, .NET Compact Framework - Windows CE .NET

Assembly: Mscorlib (in Mscorlib.dll)

StructLayoutAttribute Constructor

Initalizes a new instance of the **StructLayoutAttribute** class.

Overload List

Initalizes a new instance of the **StructLayoutAttribute** class with the specified **System.Runtime.InteropServices.LayoutKind** enumeration member.

> [Visual Basic] **Public Sub New(Short)**
> [C#] **public StructLayoutAttribute(short);**
> [C++] **public: StructLayoutAttribute(short);**
> [JScript] **public function StructLayoutAttribute(Int16);**

Initalizes a new instance of the **StructLayoutAttribute** class with the specified **System.Runtime.InteropServices.LayoutKind** enumeration member.

Supported by the .NET Compact Framework.

> [Visual Basic] **Public Sub New(LayoutKind)**
> [C#] **public StructLayoutAttribute(LayoutKind);**
> [C++] **public: StructLayoutAttribute(LayoutKind);**
> [JScript] **public function StructLayoutAttribute(LayoutKind);**

StructLayoutAttribute Constructor (Int16)

Initalizes a new instance of the **StructLayoutAttribute** class with the specified **System.Runtime.InteropServices.LayoutKind** enumeration member.

```
[Visual Basic]
Public Sub New( _
   ByVal layoutKind As Short _
)
[C#]
public StructLayoutAttribute(
   short layoutKind
);
[C++]
public: StructLayoutAttribute(
   short layoutKind
);
[JScript]
public function StructLayoutAttribute(
   layoutKind : Int16
);
```

Parameters

layoutKind
> One of the **LayoutKind** values that specifes how the class or structure should be arranged.

Remarks

This constructor takes an underlying 16-bit integer that represents each **LayoutKind** enumeration member. The **Type Library Importer (Tlbimp.exe)** uses this constructor.

Requirements

Platforms: Windows 98, Windows NT 4.0, Windows Millennium Edition, Windows 2000, Windows XP Home Edition, Windows XP Professional, Windows .NET Server family, Common Language Infrastructure (CLI) Standard

StructLayoutAttribute Constructor (LayoutKind)

Initalizes a new instance of the **StructLayoutAttribute** class with the specified **System.Runtime.InteropServices.LayoutKind** enumeration member.

```
[Visual Basic]
Public Sub New( _
   ByVal layoutKind As LayoutKind _
)
[C#]
public StructLayoutAttribute(
   LayoutKind layoutKind
);
[C++]
public: StructLayoutAttribute(
   LayoutKind layoutKind
);
[JScript]
public function StructLayoutAttribute(
   layoutKind : LayoutKind
);
```

Parameters

layoutKind

One of the **LayoutKind** values that specifes how the class or structure should be arranged.

Remarks

For readable code that is less prone to error, always use this constructor.

Requirements

Platforms: Windows 98, Windows NT 4.0, Windows Millennium Edition, Windows 2000, Windows XP Home Edition, Windows XP Professional, Windows .NET Server family, .NET Compact Framework - Windows CE .NET, Common Language Infrastructure (CLI) Standard

StructLayoutAttribute.CharSet Field

Indicates how string data fields within the class should be marshaled as **LPWSTR** or **LPSTR** by default.

```
[Visual Basic]
Public CharSet As CharSet
[C#]
public CharSet CharSet;
[C++]
public: CharSet CharSet;
[JScript]
public var CharSet : CharSet;
```

Remarks

If the **CharSet** field is set to **CharSet.Unicode**, all string arguments are converted to Unicode characters (**LPWSTR**) before being passed to the unmanaged implementation. If the field is set to **CharSet.Ansi**, the strings are converted to ANSI strings (**LPSTR**). If the **CharSet** field is set to **CharSet.Auto**, the conversion is platform dependent (Unicode on Windows NT, Windows 2000, Windows XP, and Windows .NET Server family; ANSI on Windows 98 and Windows Me).

Requirements

Platforms: Windows 98, Windows NT 4.0, Windows Millennium Edition, Windows 2000, Windows XP Home Edition, Windows XP Professional, Windows .NET Server family, Common Language Infrastructure (CLI) Standard

StructLayoutAttribute.Pack Field

Controls the alignment of data fields of a class or structure in memory.

```
[Visual Basic]
Public Pack As Integer
[C#]
public int Pack;
[C++]
public: int Pack;
[JScript]
public var Pack : int;
```

Remarks

This field indicates the packing size that should be used when the **LayoutKind.Sequential** value is specified. The value of **Pack** must be 0, 1, 2, 4, 8, 16, 32, 64, or 128. A value of 0 indicates that the packing alignment is set to the default for the current platform.

The default packing size is 8, except for unmanaged structures that typically have a default packing size of 4.

Requirements

Platforms: Windows 98, Windows NT 4.0, Windows Millennium Edition, Windows 2000, Windows XP Home Edition, Windows XP Professional, Windows .NET Server family, Common Language Infrastructure (CLI) Standard

StructLayoutAttribute.Size Field

Indicates the absolute size of the class or structure.

```
[Visual Basic]
Public Size As Integer
[C#]
public int Size;
[C++]
public: int Size;
[JScript]
public var Size : int;
```

Remarks

Must be greater or equal to the sum of all members. This field is primarily for compiler writers to specify the total size (in bytes) of the class or structure, and is useful for extending memory occupied by a structure for direct, unmanaged access. For example, you can use this field when working with unions that are not represented in metadata directly.

Requirements

Platforms: Windows 98, Windows NT 4.0, Windows Millennium Edition, Windows 2000, Windows XP Home Edition, Windows XP Professional, Windows .NET Server family, .NET Compact Framework - Windows CE .NET, Common Language Infrastructure (CLI) Standard

StructLayoutAttribute.Value Property

Gets the **LayoutKind** value that specifies how the class or structure is arranged.

```
[Visual Basic]
Public ReadOnly Property Value As LayoutKind
[C#]
public LayoutKind Value {get;}
[C++]
public: __property LayoutKind get_Value();
[JScript]
public function get Value() : LayoutKind;
```

Property Value

The **LayoutKind** value that specifies how the class or structure is arranged.

Requirements

Platforms: Windows 98, Windows NT 4.0,
Windows Millennium Edition, Windows 2000,
Windows XP Home Edition, Windows XP Professional,
Windows .NET Server family,
Common Language Infrastructure (CLI) Standard

SYSKIND Enumeration

Identifies the target operating system platform.

```
[Visual Basic]
<Serializable>
<ComVisible(False)>
Public Enum SYSKIND
[C#]
[Serializable]
[ComVisible(false)]
public enum SYSKIND
[C++]
[Serializable]
[ComVisible(false)]
__value public enum SYSKIND
[JScript]
public
   Serializable
   ComVisible(false)
enum SYSKIND
```

Remarks

For additional information about the **SYSKIND** enumeration, see
the MSDN Library.

Members

Member name	Description
SYS_MAC	The target operating system for the type library is Apple Macintosh. By default, all data fields are aligned on even-byte boundaries.
SYS_WIN16	The target operating system for the type library is 16-bit Windows systems. By default, data fields are packed.
SYS_WIN32	The target operating system for the type library is 32-bit Windows systems. By default, data fields are naturally aligned (for example, 2-byte integers are aligned on even-byte boundaries; 4-byte integers are aligned on quad-word boundaries, and so on).

Requirements

Namespace: System.Runtime.InteropServices

Platforms: Windows 98, Windows NT 4.0,
Windows Millennium Edition, Windows 2000,
Windows XP Home Edition, Windows XP Professional,
Windows .NET Server family

Assembly: Mscorlib (in Mscorlib.dll)

TYPEATTR Structure

Contains attributes of a **UCOMITypeInfo**.

System.Object
   System.ValueType
      System.Runtime.InteropServices.TYPEATTR

```
[Visual Basic]
<ComVisible(False)>
Public Structure TYPEATTR
[C#]
[ComVisible(false)]
public struct TYPEATTR
[C++]
[ComVisible(false)]
public __value struct TYPEATTR
```

[JScript] In JScript, you can use the structures in the .NET Framework, but you cannot define your own.

Thread Safety

Any public static (**Shared** in Visual Basic) members of this type are safe for multithreaded operations. Any instance members are not guaranteed to be thread safe.

Remarks

For additional information about **TYPEATTR**, see the MSDN Library.

Requirements

Namespace: System.Runtime.InteropServices

Platforms: Windows 98, Windows NT 4.0, Windows Millennium Edition, Windows 2000, Windows XP Home Edition, Windows XP Professional, Windows .NET Server family

Assembly: Mscorlib (in Mscorlib.dll)

TYPEATTR.cbAlignment Field

Specifies the byte alignment for an instance of this type.

```
[Visual Basic]
Public cbAlignment As Short
[C#]
public short cbAlignment;
[C++]
public: short cbAlignment;
[JScript]
public var cbAlignment : Int16;
```

Remarks

For additional information about **TYPEATTR**, see the MSDN Library.

Requirements

Platforms: Windows 98, Windows NT 4.0, Windows Millennium Edition, Windows 2000, Windows XP Home Edition, Windows XP Professional, Windows .NET Server family

TYPEATTR.cbSizeInstance Field

The size of an instance of this type.

```
[Visual Basic]
Public cbSizeInstance As Integer
[C#]
public int cbSizeInstance;
[C++]
public: int cbSizeInstance;
[JScript]
public var cbSizeInstance : int;
```

Remarks

For additional information about **TYPEATTR**, see the MSDN Library.

Requirements

Platforms: Windows 98, Windows NT 4.0, Windows Millennium Edition, Windows 2000, Windows XP Home Edition, Windows XP Professional, Windows .NET Server family

TYPEATTR.cbSizeVft Field

The size of this type's virtual method table (VTBL).

```
[Visual Basic]
Public cbSizeVft As Short
[C#]
public short cbSizeVft;
[C++]
public: short cbSizeVft;
[JScript]
public var cbSizeVft : Int16;
```

Remarks

For additional information about **TYPEATTR**, see the MSDN Library.

Requirements

Platforms: Windows 98, Windows NT 4.0, Windows Millennium Edition, Windows 2000, Windows XP Home Edition, Windows XP Professional, Windows .NET Server family

TYPEATTR.cFuncs Field

Indicates the number of functions on the interface this structure describes.

```
[Visual Basic]
Public cFuncs As Short
[C#]
public short cFuncs;
[C++]
public: short cFuncs;
[JScript]
public var cFuncs : Int16;
```

Remarks

For additional information about **TYPEATTR**, see the MSDN Library.

Requirements

Platforms: Windows 98, Windows NT 4.0, Windows Millennium Edition, Windows 2000, Windows XP Home Edition, Windows XP Professional, Windows .NET Server family

TYPEATTR.cImplTypes Field

Indicates the number of implemented interfaces on the interface this structure describes.

```
[Visual Basic]
Public cImplTypes As Short
[C#]
public short cImplTypes;
[C++]
public: short cImplTypes;
[JScript]
public var cImplTypes : Int16;
```

Remarks

For additional information about **TYPEATTR**, see the MSDN Library.

Requirements

Platforms: Windows 98, Windows NT 4.0, Windows Millennium Edition, Windows 2000, Windows XP Home Edition, Windows XP Professional, Windows .NET Server family

TYPEATTR.cVars Field

Indicates the number of variables and data fields on the interface described by this structure.

```
[Visual Basic]
Public cVars As Short
[C#]
public short cVars;
[C++]
public: short cVars;
[JScript]
public var cVars : Int16;
```

Remarks

For additional information about **TYPEATTR**, see the MSDN Library.

Requirements

Platforms: Windows 98, Windows NT 4.0, Windows Millennium Edition, Windows 2000, Windows XP Home Edition, Windows XP Professional, Windows .NET Server family

TYPEATTR.dwReserved Field

Reserved for future use.

```
[Visual Basic]
Public dwReserved As Integer
[C#]
public int dwReserved;
[C++]
public: int dwReserved;
[JScript]
public var dwReserved : int;
```

Remarks

For additional information about **TYPEATTR**, see the MSDN Library.

Requirements

Platforms: Windows 98, Windows NT 4.0, Windows Millennium Edition, Windows 2000, Windows XP Home Edition, Windows XP Professional, Windows .NET Server family

TYPEATTR.guid Field

The GUID of the type information.

```
[Visual Basic]
Public guid As Guid
[C#]
public Guid guid;
[C++]
public: Guid guid;
[JScript]
public var guid : Guid;
```

Remarks

For additional information about **TYPEATTR**, see the MSDN Library.

Requirements

Platforms: Windows 98, Windows NT 4.0, Windows Millennium Edition, Windows 2000, Windows XP Home Edition, Windows XP Professional, Windows .NET Server family

TYPEATTR.idldescType Field

IDL attributes of the described type.

```
[Visual Basic]
Public idldescType As IDLDESC
[C#]
public IDLDESC idldescType;
[C++]
public: IDLDESC idldescType;
[JScript]
public var idldescType : IDLDESC;
```

Remarks

For additional information about **TYPEATTR**, see the MSDN Library.

Requirements

Platforms: Windows 98, Windows NT 4.0, Windows Millennium Edition, Windows 2000, Windows XP Home Edition, Windows XP Professional, Windows .NET Server family

TYPEATTR.lcid Field

Locale of member names and documentation strings.

```
[Visual Basic]
Public lcid As Integer
[C#]
public int lcid;
[C++]
public: int lcid;
[JScript]
public var lcid : int;
```

Remarks

For additional information about **TYPEATTR**, see the MSDN Library.

Requirements

Platforms: Windows 98, Windows NT 4.0, Windows Millennium Edition, Windows 2000, Windows XP Home Edition, Windows XP Professional, Windows .NET Server family

TYPEATTR.lpstrSchema Field

Reserved for future use.

```
[Visual Basic]
Public lpstrSchema As IntPtr
[C#]
public IntPtr lpstrSchema;
[C++]
public: IntPtr lpstrSchema;
[JScript]
public var lpstrSchema : IntPtr;
```

Remarks

For additional information about **TYPEATTR**, see the MSDN Library.

Requirements

Platforms: Windows 98, Windows NT 4.0, Windows Millennium Edition, Windows 2000, Windows XP Home Edition, Windows XP Professional, Windows .NET Server family

TYPEATTR.MEMBER_ID_NIL Field

A constant used with the **memidConstructor** and **memidDestructor** fields.

```
[Visual Basic]
Public Const MEMBER_ID_NIL As Integer
[C#]
public const int MEMBER_ID_NIL;
[C++]
public: const int MEMBER_ID_NIL;
[JScript]
public var MEMBER_ID_NIL : int;
```

Remarks

For additional information about **TYPEATTR**, see the MSDN Library.

Requirements

Platforms: Windows 98, Windows NT 4.0, Windows Millennium Edition, Windows 2000, Windows XP Home Edition, Windows XP Professional, Windows .NET Server family

TYPEATTR.memidConstructor Field

ID of constructor, or **MEMBER_ID_NIL** if none.

```
[Visual Basic]
Public memidConstructor As Integer
```

```
[C#]
public int memidConstructor;
[C++]
public: int memidConstructor;
[JScript]
public var memidConstructor : int;
```

Remarks

For additional information about **TYPEATTR**, see the MSDN Library.

Requirements

Platforms: Windows 98, Windows NT 4.0, Windows Millennium Edition, Windows 2000, Windows XP Home Edition, Windows XP Professional, Windows .NET Server family

TYPEATTR.memidDestructor Field

ID of destructor, or **MEMBER_ID_NIL** if none.

```
[Visual Basic]
Public memidDestructor As Integer
[C#]
public int memidDestructor;
[C++]
public: int memidDestructor;
[JScript]
public var memidDestructor : int;
```

Remarks

For additional information about **TYPEATTR**, see the MSDN Library.

Requirements

Platforms: Windows 98, Windows NT 4.0, Windows Millennium Edition, Windows 2000, Windows XP Home Edition, Windows XP Professional, Windows .NET Server family

TYPEATTR.tdescAlias Field

If **typekind == TKIND_ALIAS**, specifies the type for which this type is an alias.

```
[Visual Basic]
Public tdescAlias As TYPEDESC
[C#]
public TYPEDESC tdescAlias;
[C++]
public: TYPEDESC tdescAlias;
[JScript]
public var tdescAlias : TYPEDESC;
```

Remarks

For additional information about **TYPEATTR**, see the MSDN Library.

Requirements

Platforms: Windows 98, Windows NT 4.0, Windows Millennium Edition, Windows 2000, Windows XP Home Edition, Windows XP Professional, Windows .NET Server family

TYPEATTR.typekind Field

A **TYPEKIND** value describing the type this information describes.

```
[Visual Basic]
Public typekind As TYPEKIND
[C#]
public TYPEKIND typekind;
[C++]
public: TYPEKIND typekind;
[JScript]
public var typekind : TYPEKIND;
```

Remarks

For additional information about **TYPEATTR**, see the MSDN Library.

Requirements

Platforms: Windows 98, Windows NT 4.0, Windows Millennium Edition, Windows 2000, Windows XP Home Edition, Windows XP Professional, Windows .NET Server family

TYPEATTR.wMajorVerNum Field

Major version number.

```
[Visual Basic]
Public wMajorVerNum As Short
[C#]
public short wMajorVerNum;
[C++]
public: short wMajorVerNum;
[JScript]
public var wMajorVerNum : Int16;
```

Remarks

For additional information about **TYPEATTR**, see the MSDN Library.

Requirements

Platforms: Windows 98, Windows NT 4.0, Windows Millennium Edition, Windows 2000, Windows XP Home Edition, Windows XP Professional, Windows .NET Server family

TYPEATTR.wMinorVerNum Field

Minor version number.

```
[Visual Basic]
Public wMinorVerNum As Short
[C#]
public short wMinorVerNum;
[C++]
public: short wMinorVerNum;
[JScript]
public var wMinorVerNum : Int16;
```

Remarks

For additional information about **TYPEATTR**, see the MSDN Library.

Requirements

Platforms: Windows 98, Windows NT 4.0, Windows Millennium Edition, Windows 2000, Windows XP Home Edition, Windows XP Professional, Windows .NET Server family

TYPEATTR.wTypeFlags Field

A **TYPEFLAGS** value describing this information.

```
[Visual Basic]
Public wTypeFlags As TYPEFLAGS
[C#]
public TYPEFLAGS wTypeFlags;
[C++]
public: TYPEFLAGS wTypeFlags;
[JScript]
public var wTypeFlags : TYPEFLAGS;
```

Remarks

For additional information about **TYPEATTR**, see the MSDN Library.

Requirements

Platforms: Windows 98, Windows NT 4.0, Windows Millennium Edition, Windows 2000, Windows XP Home Edition, Windows XP Professional, Windows .NET Server family

TYPEDESC Structure

Describes the type of a variable, return type of a function, or the type of a function parameter.

System.Object
  System.ValueType
    System.Runtime.InteropServices.TYPEDESC

```
[Visual Basic]
<ComVisible(False)>
Public Structure TYPEDESC
[C#]
[ComVisible(false)]
public struct TYPEDESC
[C++]
[ComVisible(false)]
public __value struct TYPEDESC
```

[JScript] In JScript, you can use the structures in the .NET Framework, but you cannot define your own.

Thread Safety

Any public static (**Shared** in Visual Basic) members of this type are safe for multithreaded operations. Any instance members are not guaranteed to be thread safe.

Remarks

For additional information about **TYPEDESC**, see the MSDN Library.

Requirements

Namespace: System.Runtime.InteropServices

Platforms: Windows 98, Windows NT 4.0, Windows Millennium Edition, Windows 2000, Windows XP Home Edition, Windows XP Professional, Windows .NET Server family

Assembly: Mscorlib (in Mscorlib.dll)

TYPEDESC.lpValue Field

Indicates the variant type for the item described by this **TYPEDESC**.

```
[Visual Basic]
Public lpValue As IntPtr
[C#]
public IntPtr lpValue;
[C++]
public: IntPtr lpValue;
[JScript]
public var lpValue : IntPtr;
```

Remarks

For additional information about **TYPEDESC**, see the MSDN Library.

Requirements

Platforms: Windows 98, Windows NT 4.0, Windows Millennium Edition, Windows 2000, Windows XP Home Edition, Windows XP Professional, Windows .NET Server family

TYPEDESC.vt Field

If the variable is **VT_SAFEARRAY** or **VT_PTR**, the **lpValue** field contains a pointer to a **TYPEDESC** that specifies the element type.

```
[Visual Basic]
Public vt As Short
[C#]
public short vt;
[C++]
public: short vt;
[JScript]
public var vt : Int16;
```

Remarks

For additional information about **TYPEDESC**, see the MSDN Library.

Requirements

Platforms: Windows 98, Windows NT 4.0, Windows Millennium Edition, Windows 2000, Windows XP Home Edition, Windows XP Professional, Windows .NET Server family

TYPEFLAGS Enumeration

Defines the properties and attributes of a type description.

This enumeration has a **FlagsAttribute** attribute that allows a bitwise combination of its member values.

```
[Visual Basic]
<Flags>
<Serializable>
<ComVisible(False)>
Public Enum TYPEFLAGS
[C#]
[Flags]
[Serializable]
[ComVisible(false)]
public enum TYPEFLAGS
[C++]
[Flags]
[Serializable]
[ComVisible(false)]
__value public enum TYPEFLAGS
[JScript]
public
   Flags
   Serializable
   ComVisible(false)
enum TYPEFLAGS
```

Remarks

For additional information about **TYPEFLAGS**, see the MSDN Library.

Members

Member name	Description	Value
TYPEFLAG_F-AGGREGATABLE	The class supports aggregation.	1024
TYPEFLAG_F-APPOBJECT	A type description that describes an Application object.	1
TYPEFLAG_F-CANCREATE	Instances of the type can be created by **ITypeInfo::CreateInstance**.	2
TYPEFLAG_F-CONTROL	The type is a control from which other types will be derived, and should not be displayed to users.	32
TYPEFLAG_F-DISPATCHABLE	Indicates that the interface derives from **IDispatch**, either directly or indirectly. This flag is computed, there is no Object Description Language for the flag.	4096
TYPEFLAG_FDUAL	The interface supplies both **IDispatch** and VTBL binding.	64
TYPEFLAG_F-HIDDEN	The type should not be displayed to browsers.	16
TYPEFLAG_F-LICENSED	The type is licensed.	4
TYPEFLAG_F-NONEXTENSIBLE	The interface cannot add members at run time.	128

Member name	Description	Value
TYPEFLAG_F-OLEAUTOMATION	The types used in the interface are fully compatible with Automation, including VTBL binding support. Setting dual on an interface sets this flag in addition to **TYPEFLAG_FDUAL**. Not allowed on dispinterfaces.	256
TYPEFLAG_F-PREDECLID	The type is predefined. The client application should automatically create a single instance of the object that has this attribute. The name of the variable that points to the object is the same as the class name of the object.	8
TYPEFLAG_F-PROXY	Indicates that the interface will be using a proxy/stub dynamic link library. This flag specifies that the type library proxy should not be unregistered when the type library is unregistered.	16384
TYPEFLAG_F-REPLACEABLE	The object supports **IConnectionPointWithDefault**, and has default behaviors.	2048
TYPEFLAG_F-RESTRICTED	Should not be accessible from macro languages. This flag is intended for system-level types or types that type browsers should not display.	512
TYPEFLAG_F-REVERSEBIND	Indicates base interfaces should be checked for name resolution before checking children, the reverse of the default behavior.	8192

Requirements

Namespace: System.Runtime.InteropServices

Platforms: Windows 98, Windows NT 4.0, Windows Millennium Edition, Windows 2000, Windows XP Home Edition, Windows XP Professional, Windows .NET Server family

Assembly: Mscorlib (in Mscorlib.dll)

TYPEKIND Enumeration

Specifies various types of data and functions.

```
[Visual Basic]
<Serializable>
<ComVisible(False)>
Public Enum TYPEKIND
[C#]
[Serializable]
[ComVisible(false)]
public enum TYPEKIND
[C++]
[Serializable]
[ComVisible(false)]
__value public enum TYPEKIND
[JScript]
public
    Serializable
    ComVisible(false)
enum TYPEKIND
```

Remarks

For additional information about **TYPEKIND**, see the MSDN Library.

Members

Member name	Description
TKIND_ALIAS	A type that is an alias for another type.
TKIND_COCLASS	A set of implemented components interfaces.
TKIND_DISPATCH	A set of methods and properties that are accessible through **IDispatch::Invoke**. By default, dual interfaces return **TKIND_DISPATCH**.
TKIND_ENUM	A set of enumerators.
TKIND_INTERFACE	A type that has virtual functions, all of which are pure.
TKIND_MAX	End of enumeration marker.
TKIND_MODULE	A module that can only have static functions and data (for example, a DLL).
TKIND_RECORD	A structure with no methods.
TKIND_UNION	A union of all members that have an offset of zero.

Requirements

Namespace: System.Runtime.InteropServices

Platforms: Windows 98, Windows NT 4.0, Windows Millennium Edition, Windows 2000, Windows XP Home Edition, Windows XP Professional, Windows .NET Server family

Assembly: Mscorlib (in Mscorlib.dll)

TYPELIBATTR Structure

Identifies a particular type library and provides localization support for member names.

System.Object
  System.ValueType
    System.Runtime.InteropServices.TYPELIBATTR

```
[Visual Basic]
<ComVisible(False)>
Public Structure TYPELIBATTR
[C#]
[ComVisible(false)]
public struct TYPELIBATTR
[C++]
[ComVisible(false)]
public __value struct TYPELIBATTR
```

[JScript] In JScript, you can use the structures in the .NET Framework, but you cannot define your own.

Thread Safety

Any public static (**Shared** in Visual Basic) members of this type are safe for multithreaded operations. Any instance members are not guaranteed to be thread safe.

Remarks

For additional information about the **TLIBATTR** structure, see the MSDN Library.

Requirements

Namespace: System.Runtime.InteropServices

Platforms: Windows 98, Windows NT 4.0, Windows Millennium Edition, Windows 2000, Windows XP Home Edition, Windows XP Professional, Windows .NET Server family

Assembly: Mscorlib (in Mscorlib.dll)

TYPELIBATTR.guid Field

Represents a globally unique library ID of a type library.

```
[Visual Basic]
Public guid As Guid
[C#]
public Guid guid;
[C++]
public: Guid guid;
[JScript]
public var guid : Guid;
```

Remarks

For additional information about the **TLIBATTR** structure, see the MSDN Library.

Requirements

Platforms: Windows 98, Windows NT 4.0, Windows Millennium Edition, Windows 2000, Windows XP Home Edition, Windows XP Professional, Windows .NET Server family

TYPELIBATTR.lcid Field

Represents a locale ID of a type library.

```
[Visual Basic]
Public lcid As Integer
[C#]
public int lcid;
[C++]
public: int lcid;
[JScript]
public var lcid : int;
```

Remarks

For additional information about the **TLIBATTR** structure, see the MSDN Library.

Requirements

Platforms: Windows 98, Windows NT 4.0, Windows Millennium Edition, Windows 2000, Windows XP Home Edition, Windows XP Professional, Windows .NET Server family

TYPELIBATTR.syskind Field

Represents the target hardware platform of a type library.

```
[Visual Basic]
Public syskind As SYSKIND
[C#]
public SYSKIND syskind;
[C++]
public: SYSKIND syskind;
[JScript]
public var syskind : SYSKIND;
```

Remarks

For additional information about the **TLIBATTR** structure, see the MSDN Library.

Requirements

Platforms: Windows 98, Windows NT 4.0, Windows Millennium Edition, Windows 2000, Windows XP Home Edition, Windows XP Professional, Windows .NET Server family

TYPELIBATTR.wLibFlags Field

Represents library flags.

```
[Visual Basic]
Public wLibFlags As LIBFLAGS
[C#]
public LIBFLAGS wLibFlags;
[C++]
public: LIBFLAGS wLibFlags;
[JScript]
public var wLibFlags : LIBFLAGS;
```

Remarks

For additional information about the **TLIBATTR** structure, see the MSDN Library.

Requirements

Platforms: Windows 98, Windows NT 4.0,
Windows Millennium Edition, Windows 2000,
Windows XP Home Edition, Windows XP Professional,
Windows .NET Server family

TYPELIBATTR.wMajorVerNum Field

Represents the major version number of a type library.

```
[Visual Basic]
Public wMajorVerNum As Short
[C#]
public short wMajorVerNum;
[C++]
public: short wMajorVerNum;
[JScript]
public var wMajorVerNum : Int16;
```

Remarks

For additional information about the **TLIBATTR** structure, see the
MSDN Library.

Requirements

Platforms: Windows 98, Windows NT 4.0,
Windows Millennium Edition, Windows 2000,
Windows XP Home Edition, Windows XP Professional,
Windows .NET Server family

TYPELIBATTR.wMinorVerNum Field

Represents the minor version number of a type library.

```
[Visual Basic]
Public wMinorVerNum As Short
[C#]
public short wMinorVerNum;
[C++]
public: short wMinorVerNum;
[JScript]
public var wMinorVerNum : Int16;
```

Remarks

For additional information about the **TLIBATTR** structure, see the
MSDN Library.

Requirements

Platforms: Windows 98, Windows NT 4.0,
Windows Millennium Edition, Windows 2000,
Windows XP Home Edition, Windows XP Professional,
Windows .NET Server family

TypeLibConverter Class

Provides a set of services that convert a managed assembly to a COM type library and vice versa.

System.Object
  System.Runtime.InteropServices.TypeLibConverter

```
[Visual Basic]
<ClassInterface(ClassInterfaceType.None)>
<Guid("F1C3BF79-C3E4-11d3-88E7-00902754C43A")>
NotInheritable Public Class TypeLibConverter
    Implements ITypeLibConverter
[C#]
[ClassInterface(ClassInterfaceType.None)]
[Guid("F1C3BF79-C3E4-11d3-88E7-00902754C43A")]
public sealed class TypeLibConverter : ITypeLibConverter
[C++]
[ClassInterface(ClassInterfaceType::None)]
[Guid("F1C3BF79-C3E4-11d3-88E7-00902754C43A")]
public __gc __sealed class TypeLibConverter : public
    ITypeLibConverter
[JScript]
public
    ClassInterface(ClassInterfaceType.None)
    Guid("F1C3BF79-C3E4-11d3-88E7-00902754C43A")
class TypeLibConverter implements ITypeLibConverter
```

Thread Safety

Any public static (**Shared** in Visual Basic) members of this type are safe for multithreaded operations. Any instance members are not guaranteed to be thread safe.

Requirements

Namespace: System.Runtime.InteropServices

Platforms: Windows 98, Windows NT 4.0, Windows Millennium Edition, Windows 2000, Windows XP Home Edition, Windows XP Professional, Windows .NET Server family

Assembly: Mscorlib (in Mscorlib.dll)

TypeLibConverter Constructor

Initializes a new instance of the **TypeLibConverter** class.

```
[Visual Basic]
Public Sub New()
[C#]
public TypeLibConverter();
[C++]
public: TypeLibConverter();
[JScript]
public function TypeLibConverter();
```

Remarks

The default constructor initializes any fields to their default values.

Requirements

Platforms: Windows 98, Windows NT 4.0, Windows Millennium Edition, Windows 2000, Windows XP Home Edition, Windows XP Professional, Windows .NET Server family

TypeLibConverter.ConvertAssemblyToTypeLib Method

Converts an assembly to a COM type library.

```
[Visual Basic]
Public Overridable Function ConvertAssemblyToTypeLib( _
    ByVal assembly As Assembly, _
    ByVal strTypeLibName As String, _
    ByVal flags As TypeLibExporterFlags, _
    ByVal notifySink As ITypeLibExporterNotifySink _
) As Object Implements ITypeLibConverter.ConvertAssemblyToTypeLib
[C#]
public virtual object ConvertAssemblyToTypeLib(
    Assembly assembly,
    string strTypeLibName,
    TypeLibExporterFlags flags,
    ITypeLibExporterNotifySink notifySink
);
[C++]
public: virtual Object* ConvertAssemblyToTypeLib(
    Assembly* assembly,
    String* strTypeLibName,
    TypeLibExporterFlags flags,
    ITypeLibExporterNotifySink* notifySink
);
[JScript]
public function ConvertAssemblyToTypeLib(
    assembly : Assembly,
    strTypeLibName : String,
    flags : TypeLibExporterFlags,
    notifySink : ITypeLibExporterNotifySink
) : Object;
```

Parameters

assembly
  The assembly to convert.
strTypeLibName
  The file name of the resulting type library.
flags
  A **TypeLibExporterFlags** value indicating any special settings.
notifySink
  The **ITypeLibExporterNotifySink** interface implemented by the caller.

Return Value

An object that implements the **ITypeLib** interface.

Implements

ITypeLibConverter.ConvertAssemblyToTypeLib

Remarks

For more information on **ITypeLib**, please see its existing documentation in the MSDN library.

Example

```
[Visual Basic]
Imports System
Imports System.Reflection
Imports System.Reflection.Emit
Imports System.Runtime.InteropServices

<ComImport(), GuidAttribute
  ("00020406-0000-0000-C000-000000000046"),
InterfaceTypeAttribute(ComInterfaceType.InterfaceIsIUnknown),
ComVisible(False)> _
```

```vb
Public Interface UCOMICreateITypeLib
    Sub CreateTypeInfo()
    Sub SetName()
    Sub SetVersion()
    Sub SetGuid()
    Sub SetDocString()
    Sub SetHelpFileName()
    Sub SetHelpContext()
    Sub SetLcid()
    Sub SetLibFlags()
    Sub SaveAllChanges()
End Interface 'UCOMICreateITypeLib

Public Class App

    Public Shared Sub Main()
        Dim asm As [Assembly] = [Assembly].LoadFrom("MyAssembly.dll")
        Dim converter As New TypeLibConverter()
        Dim eventHandler As New ConversionEventHandler()

        Dim typeLib As UCOMICreateITypeLib =
CType(converter.ConvertAssemblyToTypeLib(asm, "MyTypeLib.dll"
, 0, eventHandler), UCOMICreateITypeLib)
        typeLib.SaveAllChanges()
    End Sub 'Main
End Class 'App

Public Class ConversionEventHandler
    Implements ITypeLibExporterNotifySink

    Public Sub ReportEvent(ByVal eventKind As
ExporterEventKind, ByVal eventCode As Integer, ByVal eventMsg
As String) Implements ITypeLibExporterNotifySink.ReportEvent
        ' Handle the warning event here.
    End Sub 'ReportEvent

    Public Function ResolveRef(ByVal asm As [Assembly]) As
[Object] Implements ITypeLibExporterNotifySink.ResolveRef
        ' Resolve the reference here and return a correct type library.
        Return Nothing
    End Function 'ResolveRef

End Class 'ConversionEventHandler
```

```csharp
[C#]
using System;
using System.Reflection;
using System.Reflection.Emit;
using System.Runtime.InteropServices;

[ComImport,
GuidAttribute( "00020406-0000-0000-C000-000000000046" ),
InterfaceTypeAttribute( ComInterfaceType.InterfaceIsIUnknown ),
ComVisible( false )]
public interface UCOMICreateITypeLib
{
    void CreateTypeInfo();
    void SetName();
    void SetVersion();
    void SetGuid();
    void SetDocString();
    void SetHelpFileName();
    void SetHelpContext();
    void SetLcid();
    void SetLibFlags();
    void SaveAllChanges();
}

public class App
{
    public static void Main()
    {
        Assembly asm = Assembly.LoadFrom( "MyAssembly.dll" );
        TypeLibConverter converter = new TypeLibConverter();
        ConversionEventHandler eventHandler = new
ConversionEventHandler();
```

```csharp
        UCOMICreateITypeLib typeLib =
(UCOMICreateITypeLib)converter.ConvertAssemblyToTypeLib
( asm, "MyTypeLib.dll", 0, eventHandler );
        typeLib.SaveAllChanges();
    }
}

public class ConversionEventHandler : ITypeLibExporterNotifySink
{
    public void ReportEvent( ExporterEventKind eventKind,
int eventCode, string eventMsg )
    {
        // Handle the warning event here.
    }

    public Object ResolveRef( Assembly asm )
    {
        // Resolve the reference here and return a correct
type library.
        return null;
    }
}
```

Requirements

Platforms: Windows 98, Windows NT 4.0,
Windows Millennium Edition, Windows 2000,
Windows XP Home Edition, Windows XP Professional,
Windows .NET Server family

TypeLibConverter.ConvertTypeLibToAssembly Method

Converts a COM type library to an assembly.

Overload List

Converts a COM type library to an assembly.

[Visual Basic] **Overloads Public Overridable Function
ConvertTypeLibToAssembly(Object, String, Integer,
ITypeLibImporterNotifySink, Byte(),
StrongNameKeyPair,
Boolean) As AssemblyBuilder Implements
ITypeLibConverter.ConvertTypeLibToAssembly**

[C#] **public virtual AssemblyBuilder ConvertTypeLibTo-
Assembly(object, string, int, ITypeLibImporterNotifySink,
byte[], StrongNameKeyPair, bool);**

[C++] **public: virtual AssemblyBuilder* ConvertTypeLib-
ToAssembly(Object*, String*, int, ITypeLibImporterNotify-
Sink*, unsigned char __gc[], StrongNameKeyPair*, bool);**

[JScript] **public function ConvertTypeLibToAssembly
(Object, String, int, ITypeLibImporterNotifySink, Byte[],
StrongNameKeyPair, Boolean) : AssemblyBuilder;**

Converts a COM type library to an assembly.

[Visual Basic] **Overloads Public Overridable Function Con-
vertTypeLibToAssembly(Object, String, TypeLibImporter-
Flags, ITypeLibImporterNotifySink, Byte(), StrongName-
KeyPair, String, Version) As AssemblyBuilder Implements
ITypeLibConverter.ConvertTypeLibToAssembly**

[C#] **public virtual AssemblyBuilder ConvertTypeLibTo-
Assembly(object, string, TypeLibImporterFlags, ITypeLib-
ImporterNotifySink, byte[], StrongNameKeyPair, string,
Version);**

[C++] **public: virtual AssemblyBuilder* ConvertTypeLib-
ToAssembly(Object*, String*, TypeLibImporterFlags,
ITypeLibImporterNotifySink*, unsigned char __gc[],
StrongNameKeyPair*, String*, Version*);**

[JScript] **public function ConvertTypeLibToAssembly (Object, String, TypeLibImporterFlags, ITypeLibImporter-NotifySink, Byte[], StrongNameKeyPair, String, Version) : AssemblyBuilder;**

Example

[Visual Basic, C#, C++] **Note** This example shows how to use one of the overloaded versions of **ConvertTypeLibTo-Assembly**. For other examples that might be available, see the individual overload topics.

[Visual Basic]
```
Imports System
Imports System.Reflection
Imports System.Reflection.Emit
Imports System.Runtime.InteropServices

Public Class App
    Private Enum RegKind
        RegKind_Default = 0
        RegKind_Register = 1
        RegKind_None = 2
    End Enum 'RegKind

    <DllImport("oleaut32.dll", CharSet:=CharSet.Unicode, _
PreserveSig:=False)> _
    Private Shared Sub LoadTypeLibEx(ByVal strTypeLibName As _
[String], ByVal regKind As RegKind, _
<MarshalAs(UnmanagedType.Interface)> ByRef typeLib As [Object])
    End Sub

    Public Shared Sub Main()
        Dim typeLib As [Object]
        LoadTypeLibEx("SHDocVw.dll", RegKind.RegKind_None, typeLib)

        If typeLib Is Nothing Then
            Console.WriteLine("LoadTypeLibEx failed.")
            Return
        End If

        Dim converter As New TypeLibConverter()
        Dim eventHandler As New ConversionEventHandler()
        Dim asm As AssemblyBuilder = _
converter.ConvertTypeLibToAssembly(typeLib, "ExplorerLib.dll", _
0, eventHandler, Nothing, Nothing, Nothing, Nothing)
        asm.Save("ExplorerLib.dll")
    End Sub 'Main
End Class 'App
-
Public Class ConversionEventHandler
    Implements ITypeLibImporterNotifySink

    Public Sub ReportEvent(ByVal eventKind As ImporterEventKind, _
ByVal eventCode As Integer, ByVal eventMsg As String) _
Implements ITypeLibImporterNotifySink.ReportEvent
        ' handle warning event here...
    End Sub 'ReportEvent

    Public Function ResolveRef(ByVal typeLib As Object) As [Assembly] _
Implements ITypeLibImporterNotifySink.ResolveRef
        ' resolve reference here and return a correct assembly...
        Return Nothing
    End Function 'ResolveRef
End Class 'ConversionEventHandler
```

[C#]
```
using System;
using System.Reflection;
using System.Reflection.Emit;
using System.Runtime.InteropServices;

public class App
{
```

```
    private enum RegKind
    {
        RegKind_Default = 0,
        RegKind_Register = 1,
        RegKind_None = 2
    }

    [ DllImport( "oleout32.dll", CharSet = CharSet.Unicode,
PreserveSig = false )]
    private static extern void LoadTypeLibEx( String
strTypeLibName, RegKind regKind,
        [ MarshalAs( UnmanagedType.Interface )] out Object typeLib );

    public static void Main()
    {
        Object typeLib;
        LoadTypeLibEx( "SHDocVw.dll", RegKind.RegKind_None, out
typeLib );

        if( typeLib == null )
        {
            Console.WriteLine( "LoadTypeLibEx failed." );
            return;
        }

        TypeLibConverter converter = new TypeLibConverter();
        ConversionEventHandler eventHandler = new
ConversionEventHandler();
        AssemblyBuilder asm = converter.ConvertTypeLibToAssembly(
typeLib, "ExplorerLib.dll", 0, eventHandler, null, null, null, null );
        asm.Save( "ExplorerLib.dll" );
    }
}

public class ConversionEventHandler : ITypeLibImporterNotifySink
{
    public void ReportEvent( ImporterEventKind eventKind, int
eventCode, string eventMsg )
    {
        // handle warning event here...
    }

    public Assembly ResolveRef( object typeLib )
    {
        // resolve reference here and return a correct assembly...
        return null;
    }
}
```

[C++]
```
#using <mscorlib.dll>

using namespace System;
using namespace System::Reflection;
using namespace System::Reflection::Emit;
using namespace System::Runtime::InteropServices;

typedef enum tagREGKIND
    {
        REGKIND_DEFAULT,
        REGKIND_REGISTER,
        REGKIND_NONE
    } REGKIND;


__gc class ConversionEventHandler : public ITypeLibImporterNotifySink {
public:
    void ReportEvent(ImporterEventKind eventKind, int eventCode,
String* eventMsg) {
        // handle warning event here...
    }

    Assembly* ResolveRef(Object* typeLib) {
        // resolve reference here and return a correct assembly...
        return 0;
    }
};
```

```
    [ DllImport(S"oleaut32.dll", CharSet = CharSet::Unicode,
PreserveSig = false)]
    extern void LoadTypeLibEx(String *strTypeLibName,REGKIND regkind,
        [ MarshalAs(UnmanagedType::Interface)] [out]
Object ** typeLib);

    int main() {

        Object* typeLib = new Object();


LoadTypeLibEx(S"SHDocVw.dll", REGKIND_NONE, & typeLib);

        if (typeLib == 0) {
            Console::WriteLine(S"LoadTypeLibEx failed.");
            return 0;
        }

        TypeLibConverter* converter = new TypeLibConverter();
        ConversionEventHandler* eventHandler = new
ConversionEventHandler();
        AssemblyBuilder* asmb =
converter->ConvertTypeLibToAssembly(typeLib,
 S"ExplorerLib.dll",
(System::Runtime::InteropServices::TypeLibImporterFlags)0,
eventHandler, 0, 0, 0, 0);
        asmb->Save(S"ExplorerLib.dll");
    }
```

TypeLibConverter.ConvertTypeLibToAssembly Method (Object, String, Int32, ITypeLibImporterNotifySink, Byte[], StrongNameKeyPair, Boolean)

Converts a COM type library to an assembly.

```
[Visual Basic]
Overloads Public Overridable Function ConvertTypeLibToAssembly( _
    ByVal typeLib As Object, _
    ByVal asmFileName As String, _
    ByVal flags As Integer, _
    ByVal notifySink As ITypeLibImporterNotifySink, _
    ByVal publicKey() As Byte, _
    ByVal keyPair As StrongNameKeyPair, _
    ByVal unsafeInterfaces As Boolean _
) As AssemblyBuilder Implements
ITypeLibConverter.ConvertTypeLibToAssembly
[C#]
public virtual AssemblyBuilder ConvertTypeLibToAssembly(
    object typeLib,
    string asmFileName,
    int flags,
    ITypeLibImporterNotifySink notifySink,
    byte[] publicKey,
    StrongNameKeyPair keyPair,
    bool unsafeInterfaces
);
[C++]
public: virtual AssemblyBuilder* ConvertTypeLibToAssembly(
    Object* typeLib,
    String* asmFileName,
    int flags,
    ITypeLibImporterNotifySink* notifySink,
    unsigned char publicKey __gc[],
    StrongNameKeyPair* keyPair,
    bool unsafeInterfaces
);
```

```
[JScript]
public function ConvertTypeLibToAssembly(
    typeLib : Object,
    asmFileName : String,
    flags : int,
    notifySink : ITypeLibImporterNotifySink,
    publicKey : Byte[],
    keyPair : StrongNameKeyPair,
    unsafeInterfaces : Boolean
) : AssemblyBuilder;
```

Parameters

typeLib
    The object that implements the **ITypeLib** interface.

asmFileName
    The file name of the resulting assembly.

flags
    A **TypeLibImporterFlags** value indicating any special settings.

notifySink
    ITypeLibImporterNotifySink interface implemented by the caller.

publicKey
    A **byte** array containing the public key.

keyPair
    A **StrongNameKeyPair** object containing the public and private cryptographic key pair.

unsafeInterfaces
    If **true**, the interfaces require link time checks for **Unmanaged-Code** permission. If **false**, the interfaces require run time checks that require a stack walk and are more expensive, but are more secure.

Return Value

An **AssemblyBuilder** object containing the converted type library.

Implements

ITypeLibConverter.ConvertTypeLibToAssembly

Exceptions

Exception Type	Condition
ArgumentNullException	*typeLib* is a null reference (**Nothing** in Visual Basic).
	-or-
	asmFileName is a null reference (**Nothing**).
	-or-
	notifySink is a null reference (**Nothing**).
ArgumentException	*asmFileName* is an empty string.
	-or-
	asmFileName is longer than MAX_PATH.
InvalidOperation-Exception	*flags* is not **PrimaryInteropAssembly**.
	-or-
	publicKey and *keyPair* are a null reference (**Nothing** in Visual Basic).
ReflectionTypeLoad-Exception	The metadata produced has errors preventing any types from loading.

Remarks

If you do not want to generate a strong name for your assembly, it is valid for *publicKey* and *keyPair* to be a null reference (**Nothing** in Visual Basic), as long as *flags* does not equal **TypeLibImporterFlags.PrimaryInteropAssembly**. Otherwise, atleast one of these parameters must be specified. If *publicKey* is a null reference (**Nothing**), the public key in *keyPair* will be set in the target assembly's manifest metadata and a signature will be generated based on the contents of the assembly. If *keyPair* is a null reference (**Nothing**), *publicKey* will be set in the target assembly's manifest metadata and no signature will be generated. Specifying both parameters is valid, but is not generally useful, and can result in an invalid signature.

For more information on **ITypeLib**, please see its existing documentation in the MSDN library.

Requirements

Platforms: Windows 98, Windows NT 4.0, Windows Millennium Edition, Windows 2000, Windows XP Home Edition, Windows XP Professional, Windows .NET Server family

TypeLibConverter.ConvertTypeLibToAssembly Method (Object, String, TypeLibImporterFlags, ITypeLibImporterNotifySink, Byte[], StrongNameKeyPair, String, Version)

Converts a COM type library to an assembly.

```
[Visual Basic]
Overloads Public Overridable Function ConvertTypeLibToAssembly( _
   ByVal typeLib As Object, _
   ByVal asmFileName As String, _
   ByVal flags As TypeLibImporterFlags, _
   ByVal notifySink As ITypeLibImporterNotifySink, _
   ByVal publicKey() As Byte, _
   ByVal keyPair As StrongNameKeyPair, _
   ByVal asmNamespace As String, _
   ByVal asmVersion As Version _
) As AssemblyBuilder Implements
ITypeLibConverter.ConvertTypeLibToAssembly
[C#]
public virtual AssemblyBuilder ConvertTypeLibToAssembly(
   object typeLib,
   string asmFileName,
   TypeLibImporterFlags flags,
   ITypeLibImporterNotifySink notifySink,
   byte[] publicKey,
   StrongNameKeyPair keyPair,
   string asmNamespace,
   Version asmVersion
);
[C++]
public: virtual AssemblyBuilder* ConvertTypeLibToAssembly(
   Object* typeLib,
   String* asmFileName,
   TypeLibImporterFlags flags,
   ITypeLibImporterNotifySink* notifySink,
   unsigned char publicKey __gc[],
   StrongNameKeyPair* keyPair,
   String* asmNamespace,
   Version* asmVersion
);
```

```
[JScript]
public function ConvertTypeLibToAssembly(
   typeLib : Object,
   asmFileName : String,
   flags : TypeLibImporterFlags,
   notifySink : ITypeLibImporterNotifySink,
   publicKey : Byte[],
   keyPair : StrongNameKeyPair,
   asmNamespace : String,
   asmVersion : Version
) : AssemblyBuilder;
```

Parameters

typeLib
> The object that implements the **ITypeLib** interface.

asmFileName
> The file name of the resulting assembly.

flags
> A **TypeLibImporterFlags** value indicating any special settings.

notifySink
> **ITypeLibImporterNotifySink** interface implemented by the caller.

publicKey
> A **byte** array containing the public key.

keyPair
> A **StrongNameKeyPair** object containing the public and private cryptographic key pair.

asmNamespace
> The namespace for the resulting assembly.

asmVersion
> The version of the resulting assembly. If a null reference (**Nothing** in Visual Basic), the version of the type library is used.

Return Value

An **AssemblyBuilder** object containing the converted type library.

Implements

ITypeLibConverter.ConvertTypeLibToAssembly

Exceptions

Exception Type	Condition
ArgumentNullException	*typeLib* is a null reference (**Nothing** in Visual Basic).
	-or-
	asmFileName is a null reference (**Nothing**).
	-or-
	notifySink is a null reference (**Nothing**).
ArgumentException	*asmFileName* is an empty string.
	-or-
	asmFileName is longer than MAX_PATH.
InvalidOperationException	*flags* is not **PrimaryInteropAssembly**.
	-or-
	publicKey and *keyPair* are a null reference (**Nothing** in Visual Basic).
ReflectionTypeLoadException	The metadata produced has errors preventing any types from loading.

Remarks

If you do not want to generate a strong name for your assembly, it is valid for *publicKey* and *keyPair* to be a null reference (**Nothing** in Visual Basic), as long as *flags* does not equal **TypeLibImporterFlags.PrimaryInteropAssembly**. Otherwise, atleast one of these parameters must be specified. If *publicKey* is a null reference (**Nothing**), the public key in *keyPair* will be set in the target assembly's manifest metadata and a signature will be generated based on the contents of the assembly. If *keyPair* is a null reference (**Nothing**), *publicKey* will be set in the target assembly's manifest metadata and no signature will be generated. Specifying both parameters is valid, but is not generally useful, and can result in an invalid signature.

For more information on **ITypeLib**, please see its existing documentation in the MSDN library.

Example

```
[Visual Basic]
Imports System
Imports System.Reflection
Imports System.Reflection.Emit
Imports System.Runtime.InteropServices

Public Class App
    Private Enum RegKind
        RegKind_Default = 0
        RegKind_Register = 1
        RegKind_None = 2
    End Enum 'RegKind

    <DllImport("oleaut32.dll", CharSet:=CharSet.Unicode,
PreserveSig:=False)> _
    Private Shared Sub LoadTypeLibEx(ByVal strTypeLibName As
[String], ByVal regKind As RegKind,
<MarshalAs(UnmanagedType.Interface)> ByRef typeLib As [Object])
    End Sub

    Public Shared Sub Main()
        Dim typeLib As [Object]
        LoadTypeLibEx("SHDocVw.dll", RegKind.RegKind_None, typeLib)

        If typeLib Is Nothing Then
            Console.WriteLine("LoadTypeLibEx failed.")
            Return
        End If

        Dim converter As New TypeLibConverter()
        Dim eventHandler As New ConversionEventHandler()
        Dim asm As AssemblyBuilder =
converter.ConvertTypeLibToAssembly(typeLib, "ExplorerLib.dll",
0, eventHandler, Nothing, Nothing, Nothing, Nothing)
            asm.Save("ExplorerLib.dll")
    End Sub 'Main
End Class 'App


Public Class ConversionEventHandler
    Implements ITypeLibImporterNotifySink

    Public Sub ReportEvent(ByVal eventKind As ImporterEventKind,
ByVal eventCode As Integer, ByVal eventMsg As String) Implements
ITypeLibImporterNotifySink.ReportEvent
        ' handle warning event here...
    End Sub 'ReportEvent

    Public Function ResolveRef(ByVal typeLib As Object) As [Assembly]
Implements ITypeLibImporterNotifySink.ResolveRef
        ' resolve reference here and return a correct assembly...
        Return Nothing
    End Function 'ResolveRef
End Class 'ConversionEventHandler
```

```
[C#]
using System;
using System.Reflection;
using System.Reflection.Emit;
using System.Runtime.InteropServices;

public class App
{
    private enum RegKind
    {
        RegKind_Default = 0,
        RegKind_Register = 1,
        RegKind_None = 2
    }

    [ DllImport( "oleaut32.dll", CharSet = CharSet.Unicode,
PreserveSig = false )]
    private static extern void LoadTypeLibEx(
String strTypeLibName, RegKind regKind,
        [ MarshalAs( UnmanagedType.Interface )] out Object typeLib );

    public static void Main()
    {
        Object typeLib;
        LoadTypeLibEx( "SHDocVw.dll", RegKind.RegKind_None, out
typeLib );

        if( typeLib == null )
        {
            Console.WriteLine( "LoadTypeLibEx failed." );
            return;
        }

        TypeLibConverter converter = new TypeLibConverter();
        ConversionEventHandler eventHandler = new
ConversionEventHandler();
        AssemblyBuilder asm = converter.ConvertTypeLibToAssembly(
typeLib, "ExplorerLib.dll", 0, eventHandler, null, null, null, null );
        asm.Save( "ExplorerLib.dll" );
    }
}

public class ConversionEventHandler : ITypeLibImporterNotifySink
{
    public void ReportEvent( ImporterEventKind eventKind, int
eventCode, string eventMsg )
    {
        // handle warning event here...
    }

    public Assembly ResolveRef( object typeLib )
    {
        // resolve reference here and return a correct assembly...
        return null;
    }
}
```

```
[C++]
#using <mscorlib.dll>

using namespace System;
using namespace System::Reflection;
using namespace System::Reflection::Emit;
using namespace System::Runtime::InteropServices;

typedef enum tagREGKIND
    {
        REGKIND_DEFAULT,
        REGKIND_REGISTER,
        REGKIND_NONE
    } REGKIND;

__gc class ConversionEventHandler : public ITypeLibImporterNotifySink {
public:
```

```
    void ReportEvent(ImporterEventKind eventKind, int eventCode,
String* eventMsg) {
        // handle warning event here...
    }

    Assembly* ResolveRef(Object* typeLib) {
        // resolve reference here and return a correct assembly...
        return 0;
    }
};


    [ DllImport(S"oleaut32.dll", CharSet = CharSet::Unicode,
PreserveSig = false)]
    extern void LoadTypeLibEx(String *strTypeLibName,REGKIND regkind,
        [ MarshalAs(UnmanagedType::Interface)] [out] Object **
typeLib);

    int main() {

        Object* typeLib = new Object();


LoadTypeLibEx(S"SHDocVw.dll", REGKIND_NONE, & typeLib);

        if (typeLib == 0) {
            Console::WriteLine(S"LoadTypeLibEx failed.");
            return 0;
        }

        TypeLibConverter* converter = new TypeLibConverter();
        ConversionEventHandler* eventHandler = new
ConversionEventHandler();
        AssemblyBuilder*  asmb =
converter->ConvertTypeLibToAssembly(typeLib,
S"ExplorerLib.dll",
        (System::Runtime::InteropServices::TypeLibImporterFlags)0,
eventHandler, 0, 0, 0, 0);
        asmb->Save(S"ExplorerLib.dll");
    }
```

Requirements

Platforms: Windows 98, Windows NT 4.0,
Windows Millennium Edition, Windows 2000,
Windows XP Home Edition, Windows XP Professional,
Windows .NET Server family

TypeLibConverter.GetPrimaryInteropAssembly Method

Gets the name and code base of a primary interop assembly for a
specified type library.

```
[Visual Basic]
Public Overridable Function GetPrimaryInteropAssembly( _
    ByVal g As Guid, _
    ByVal major As Integer, _
    ByVal minor As Integer, _
    ByVal lcid As Integer, _
    <Out()> ByRef asmName As String, _
    <Out()> ByRef asmCodeBase As String _
) As Boolean Implements ITypeLibConverter.GetPrimaryInteropAssembly
[C#]
public virtual bool GetPrimaryInteropAssembly(
    Guid g,
    int major,
    int minor,
    int lcid,
```

```
    out string asmName,
    out string asmCodeBase
);
[C++]
public: virtual bool GetPrimaryInteropAssembly(
    Guid g,
    int major,
    int minor,
    int lcid,
    [
    Out
] String** asmName,
    [
    Out
] String** asmCodeBase
);
[JScript]
public function GetPrimaryInteropAssembly(
    g : Guid,
    major : int,
    minor : int,
    lcid : int,
    asmName : String,
    asmCodeBase : String
) : Boolean;
```

Parameters

g
    The GUID of the type library.
major
    The major version number of the type library.
minor
    The minor version number of the type library.
lcid
    The LCID of the type library.
asmName
    On successful return, the name of the primary interop assembly associated with *g*.
asmCodeBase
    On successful return, the code base of the primary interop assembly associated with *g*.

Return Value

true if the primary interop assembly was found in the registry; otherwise **false**.

Implements

ITypeLibConverter.GetPrimaryInteropAssembly

Requirements

Platforms: Windows 98, Windows NT 4.0,
Windows Millennium Edition, Windows 2000,
Windows XP Home Edition, Windows XP Professional,
Windows .NET Server family

TypeLibExporterFlags Enumeration

Indicates how a type library should be produced.

This enumeration has a **FlagsAttribute** attribute that allows a bitwise combination of its member values.

```
[Visual Basic]
<Flags>
<Serializable>
Public Enum TypeLibExporterFlags
[C#]
[Flags]
[Serializable]
public enum TypeLibExporterFlags
[C++]
[Flags]
[Serializable]
__value public enum TypeLibExporterFlags
[JScript]
public
    Flags
    Serializable
enum TypeLibExporterFlags
```

Remarks

Used with **ConvertAssemblyToTypeLib**.

Members

Member name	Description	Value
OnlyReference-Registered	Export references to types that were imported from COM as **IUnknown** if the type does not have a registered type library.	1

Requirements

Namespace: System.Runtime.InteropServices

Platforms: Windows 98, Windows NT 4.0, Windows Millennium Edition, Windows 2000, Windows XP Home Edition, Windows XP Professional, Windows .NET Server family

Assembly: Mscorlib (in Mscorlib.dll)

TypeLibFuncAttribute Class

Contains the **FUNCFLAGS** that were originally imported for this method from the COM type library.

System.Object
  System.Attribute
    System.Runtime.InteropServices.TypeLibFuncAttribute

```
[Visual Basic]
<AttributeUsage(AttributeTargets.Method)>
NotInheritable Public Class TypeLibFuncAttribute
    Inherits Attribute
[C#]
[AttributeUsage(AttributeTargets.Method)]
public sealed class TypeLibFuncAttribute : Attribute
[C++]
[AttributeUsage(AttributeTargets::Method)]
public __gc __sealed class TypeLibFuncAttribute : public Attribute
[JScript]
public
    AttributeUsage(AttributeTargets.Method)
class TypeLibFuncAttribute extends Attribute
```

Thread Safety

Any public static (**Shared** in Visual Basic) members of this type are safe for multithreaded operations. Any instance members are not guaranteed to be thread safe.

Remarks

The **Type Library Importer (Tlbimp.exe)** applies this attribute to methods.

This attribute is applied when a type library is imported and should never be changed. It is only applied when the method's **FUNCFLAGS** evaluate to non zero. The attribute is designed to be used by tools that need to know how the original **FUNCFLAGS** were set. The common language runtime does not use this attribute.

Requirements

Namespace: System.Runtime.InteropServices

Platforms: Windows 98, Windows NT 4.0, Windows Millennium Edition, Windows 2000, Windows XP Home Edition, Windows XP Professional, Windows .NET Server family

Assembly: Mscorlib (in Mscorlib.dll)

TypeLibFuncAttribute Constructor

Initializes a new instance of the **TypeLibFuncAttribute** class.

Overload List

Initializes a new instance of the **TypeLibFuncAttribute** class with the specified **System.Runtime.InteropServices.TypeLibFuncFlags** value.

  [Visual Basic] **Public Sub New(Short)**
  [C#] **public TypeLibFuncAttribute(short);**
  [C++] **public: TypeLibFuncAttribute(short);**
  [JScript] **public function TypeLibFuncAttribute(Int16);**

Initializes a new instance of the **TypeLibFuncAttribute** class with the specified **System.Runtime.InteropServices.TypeLibFunc-Flags** value.

```
[Visual Basic] Public Sub New(TypeLibFuncFlags)
[C#] public TypeLibFuncAttribute(TypeLibFuncFlags);
[C++] public: TypeLibFuncAttribute(TypeLibFuncFlags);
[JScript] public function
TypeLibFuncAttribute(TypeLibFuncFlags);
```

TypeLibFuncAttribute Constructor (Int16)

Initializes a new instance of the **TypeLibFuncAttribute** class with the specified **System.Runtime.InteropServices.TypeLibFuncFlags** value.

```
[Visual Basic]
Public Sub New( _
    ByVal flags As Short _
)
[C#]
public TypeLibFuncAttribute(
    short flags
);
[C++]
public: TypeLibFuncAttribute(
    short flags
);
[JScript]
public function TypeLibFuncAttribute(
    flags : Int16
);
```

Parameters

flags
  The **TypeLibFuncFlags** value for the attributed method as found in the type library it was imported from.

Requirements

Platforms: Windows 98, Windows NT 4.0, Windows Millennium Edition, Windows 2000, Windows XP Home Edition, Windows XP Professional, Windows .NET Server family

TypeLibFuncAttribute Constructor (TypeLibFuncFlags)

Initializes a new instance of the **TypeLibFuncAttribute** class with the specified **System.Runtime.InteropServices.TypeLibFuncFlags** value.

```
[Visual Basic]
Public Sub New( _
    ByVal flags As TypeLibFuncFlags _
)
[C#]
public TypeLibFuncAttribute(
    TypeLibFuncFlags flags
);
[C++]
public: TypeLibFuncAttribute(
    TypeLibFuncFlags flags
);
[JScript]
public function TypeLibFuncAttribute(
    flags : TypeLibFuncFlags
);
```

Parameters

flags

The **TypeLibFuncFlags** value for the attributed method as found in the type library it was imported from.

Requirements

Platforms: Windows 98, Windows NT 4.0,
Windows Millennium Edition, Windows 2000,
Windows XP Home Edition, Windows XP Professional,
Windows .NET Server family

TypeLibFuncAttribute.Value Property

Gets the **System.Runtime.InteropServices.TypeLibFuncFlags** value for this method.

```
[Visual Basic]
Public ReadOnly Property Value As TypeLibFuncFlags
[C#]
public TypeLibFuncFlags Value {get;}
[C++]
public: __property TypeLibFuncFlags get_Value();
[JScript]
public function get Value() : TypeLibFuncFlags;
```

Property Value

The **TypeLibFuncFlags** value for this method.

Requirements

Platforms: Windows 98, Windows NT 4.0,
Windows Millennium Edition, Windows 2000,
Windows XP Home Edition, Windows XP Professional,
Windows .NET Server family

TypeLibFuncFlags Enumeration

Describes the original settings of the **FUNCFLAGS** in the COM type library from where this method was imported.

This enumeration has a **FlagsAttribute** attribute that allows a bitwise combination of its member values.

```
[Visual Basic]
<Flags>
<Serializable>
Public Enum TypeLibFuncFlags
[C#]
[Flags]
[Serializable]
public enum TypeLibFuncFlags
[C++]
[Flags]
[Serializable]
__value public enum TypeLibFuncFlags
[JScript]
public
   Flags
   Serializable
enum TypeLibFuncFlags
```

Remarks

TypeLibFuncFlags is used with the **TypeLibFuncAttribute**. The flags are retained for reference only. They are not used by the common language runtime.

For more information about **FUNCFLAGS**, see the MSDN library.

Members

Member name	Description	Value
FBindable	The function that supports data binding.	4
FDefaultBind	The function that best represents the object. Only one function in a type information can have this attribute.	32
FDefaultCollelem	Permits an optimization in which the compiler looks for a member named "xyz" on the type "abc". If such a member is found and is flagged as an accessor function for an element of the default collection, then a call is generated to that member function.	256
FDisplayBind	The function that is displayed to the user as bindable. **FBindable** must also be set.	16
FHidden	The function should not be displayed to the user, although it exists and is bindable.	64
FImmediateBind	The function is mapped as individual bindable properties.	4096
FNonBrowsable	The property appears in an object browser, but not in a properties browser.	1024

Member name	Description	Value
FReplaceable	Tags the interface as having default behaviors.	2048
FRequestEdit	When set, any call to a method that sets the property results first in a call to **IPropertyNotifySink::OnRequestEdit**.	8
FRestricted	This flag is intended for system-level functions or functions that type browsers should not display.	1
FSource	The function returns an object that is a source of events.	2
FUiDefault	The type information member is the default member for display in the user interface.	512
FUsesGetLast-Error	The function supports **GetLastError**.	128

Requirements

Namespace: System.Runtime.InteropServices

Platforms: Windows 98, Windows NT 4.0, Windows Millennium Edition, Windows 2000, Windows XP Home Edition, Windows XP Professional, Windows .NET Server family

Assembly: Mscorlib (in Mscorlib.dll)

TypeLibTypeAttribute Class

Contains the **TYPEFLAGS** that were originally imported for this type from the COM type library.

System.Object
  System.Attribute
    System.Runtime.InteropServices.TypeLibTypeAttribute

```
[Visual Basic]
<AttributeUsage(AttributeTargets.Class Or AttributeTargets.Struct _
    Or AttributeTargets.Enum Or AttributeTargets.Interface)>
NotInheritable Public Class TypeLibTypeAttribute
    Inherits Attribute
[C#]
[AttributeUsage(AttributeTargets.Class | AttributeTargets.Struct |
    AttributeTargets.Enum | AttributeTargets.Interface)]
public sealed class TypeLibTypeAttribute : Attribute
[C++]
[AttributeUsage(AttributeTargets::Class | AttributeTargets::Struct
    | AttributeTargets::Enum | AttributeTargets::Interface)]
public __gc __sealed class TypeLibTypeAttribute : public Attribute
[JScript]
public
    AttributeUsage(AttributeTargets.Class | AttributeTargets.Struct |
    AttributeTargets.Enum | AttributeTargets.Interface)
class TypeLibTypeAttribute extends Attribute
```

Thread Safety

Any public static (**Shared** in Visual Basic) members of this type are safe for multithreaded operations. Any instance members are not guaranteed to be thread safe.

Remarks

The **Type Library Importer (Tlbimp.exe)** applies this attribute to classes or interfaces.

This attribute is applied when a type library is imported and should never be changed. It is only applied when the method's **TYPEFLAGS** evaluate to non-zero. The attribute is designed to be used by tools that need to know how the original **TYPEFLAGS** were set. The common language runtime does not use this attribute.

Requirements

Namespace: System.Runtime.InteropServices

Platforms: Windows 98, Windows NT 4.0, Windows Millennium Edition, Windows 2000, Windows XP Home Edition, Windows XP Professional, Windows .NET Server family

Assembly: Mscorlib (in Mscorlib.dll)

TypeLibTypeAttribute Constructor

Initializes a new instance of the **TypeLibTypeAttribute** class.

Overload List

Initializes a new instance of the **TypeLibTypeAttribute** class with the specified **TypeLibTypeFlags** value.

  [Visual Basic] **Public Sub New(Short)**

  [C#] **public TypeLibTypeAttribute(short);**

  [C++] **public: TypeLibTypeAttribute(short);**

  [JScript] **public function TypeLibTypeAttribute(Int16);**

Initializes a new instance of the **TypeLibTypeAttribute** class with the specified **System.Runtime.InteropServices.TypeLibTypeFlags** value.

  [Visual Basic] **Public Sub New(TypeLibTypeFlags)**

  [C#] **public TypeLibTypeAttribute(TypeLibTypeFlags);**

  [C++] **public: TypeLibTypeAttribute(TypeLibTypeFlags);**

  [JScript] **public function TypeLibTypeAttribute(TypeLibTypeFlags);**

TypeLibTypeAttribute Constructor (Int16)

Initializes a new instance of the **TypeLibTypeAttribute** class with the specified **TypeLibTypeFlags** value.

```
[Visual Basic]
Public Sub New( _
    ByVal flags As Short _
)
[C#]
public TypeLibTypeAttribute(
    short flags
);
[C++]
public: TypeLibTypeAttribute(
    short flags
);
[JScript]
public function TypeLibTypeAttribute(
    flags : Int16
);
```

Parameters

flags
  The **TypeLibTypeFlags** value for the attributed type as found in the type library it was imported from.

Requirements

Platforms: Windows 98, Windows NT 4.0, Windows Millennium Edition, Windows 2000, Windows XP Home Edition, Windows XP Professional, Windows .NET Server family

TypeLibTypeAttribute Constructor (TypeLibTypeFlags)

Initializes a new instance of the **TypeLibTypeAttribute** class with the specified **System.Runtime.InteropServices.TypeLibTypeFlags** value.

```
[Visual Basic]
Public Sub New( _
    ByVal flags As TypeLibTypeFlags _
)
[C#]
public TypeLibTypeAttribute(
    TypeLibTypeFlags flags
);
[C++]
public: TypeLibTypeAttribute(
    TypeLibTypeFlags flags
);
```

```
[JScript]
public function TypeLibTypeAttribute(
    flags : TypeLibTypeFlags
);
```

Parameters

flags

> The **TypeLibTypeFlags** value for the attributed type as found in
> the type library it was imported from.

Requirements

Platforms: Windows 98, Windows NT 4.0,
Windows Millennium Edition, Windows 2000,
Windows XP Home Edition, Windows XP Professional,
Windows .NET Server family

TypeLibTypeAttribute.Value Property

Gets the **System.Runtime.InteropServices.TypeLibTypeFlags**
value for this type.

```
[Visual Basic]
Public ReadOnly Property Value As TypeLibTypeFlags
[C#]
public TypeLibTypeFlags Value {get;}
[C++]
public: __property TypeLibTypeFlags get_Value();
[JScript]
public function get Value() : TypeLibTypeFlags;
```

Property Value

The **TypeLibTypeFlags** value for this type.

Requirements

Platforms: Windows 98, Windows NT 4.0,
Windows Millennium Edition, Windows 2000,
Windows XP Home Edition, Windows XP Professional,
Windows .NET Server family

TypeLibTypeFlags Enumeration

Describes the original settings of the **TYPEFLAGS** in the COM type library from which the type was imported.

This enumeration has a **FlagsAttribute** attribute that allows a bitwise combination of its member values.

```
[Visual Basic]
<Flags>
<Serializable>
Public Enum TypeLibTypeFlags
[C#]
[Flags]
[Serializable]
public enum TypeLibTypeFlags
[C++]
[Flags]
[Serializable]
__value public enum TypeLibTypeFlags
[JScript]
public
    Flags
    Serializable
enum TypeLibTypeFlags
```

Remarks

TypeLibTypeFlags is used along with the **TypeLibTypeAttribute**. The flags are retained for reference only. They are not used by the common language runtime.

For more information, see **TYPEFLAGS** in the MSDN library.

Members

Member name	Description	Value
FAggregatable	The class supports aggregation.	1024
FAppObject	A type description that describes an **Application** object.	1
FCanCreate	Instances of the type can be created by **ITypeInfo::CreateInstance**.	2
FControl	The type is a control from which other types will be derived, and should not be displayed to users.	32
FDispatchable	Indicates that the interface derives from **IDispatch**, either directly or indirectly.	4096
FDual	The interface supplies both **IDispatch** and V-table binding.	64
FHidden	The type should not be displayed to browsers.	16
FLicensed	The type is licensed.	4
FNonExtensible	The interface cannot add members at run time.	128
FOleAutomation	The types used in the interface are fully compatible with Automation, including vtable binding support.	256

Member name	Description	Value
FPreDeclId	The type is predefined. The client application should automatically create a single instance of the object that has this attribute. The name of the variable that points to the object is the same as the class name of the object.	8
FReplaceable	The object supports **IConnectionPointWithDefault**, and has default behaviors.	2048
FRestricted	This flag is intended for system-level types or types that type browsers should not display.	512
FReverseBind	Indicates base interfaces should be checked for name resolution before checking child interfaces. This is the reverse of the default behavior.	8192

Requirements

Namespace: System.Runtime.InteropServices

Platforms: Windows 98, Windows NT 4.0, Windows Millennium Edition, Windows 2000, Windows XP Home Edition, Windows XP Professional, Windows .NET Server family

Assembly: Mscorlib (in Mscorlib.dll)

TypeLibVarAttribute Class

Contains the **VARFLAGS** that were originally imported for this field from the COM type library.

System.Object
  System.Attribute
    System.Runtime.InteropServices.TypeLibVarAttribute

```
[Visual Basic]
<AttributeUsage(AttributeTargets.Field)>
NotInheritable Public Class TypeLibVarAttribute
    Inherits Attribute
[C#]
[AttributeUsage(AttributeTargets.Field)]
public sealed class TypeLibVarAttribute : Attribute
[C++]
[AttributeUsage(AttributeTargets::Field)]
public __gc __sealed class TypeLibVarAttribute : public Attribute
[JScript]
public
    AttributeUsage(AttributeTargets.Field)
class TypeLibVarAttribute extends Attribute
```

Thread Safety

Any public static (**Shared** in Visual Basic) members of this type are safe for multithreaded operations. Any instance members are not guaranteed to be thread safe.

Remarks

The **Type Library Importer (Tlbimp.exe)** applies this attribute to fields.

This attribute is applied when a type library is imported and should never be changed. It is only applied when the method's **VARFLAGS** evaluate to non-zero. The attribute is designed to be used by tools that need to know how the original **VARFLAGS** were set. The common language runtime does not use this attribute.

Example

[Visual Basic, C#] The following example demonstrates how to get the **TypeLibVarAttribute** value of a field.

```
[Visual Basic]
Imports System
Imports System.Reflection
Imports System.Runtime.InteropServices

Module D
    Public Function IsHiddenField(ByVal fi As FieldInfo) As Boolean
        Dim FieldAttributes As Object() =
fi.GetCustomAttributes(GetType(TypeLibVarAttribute), True)

        If FieldAttributes.Length > 0 Then
            Dim tlv As TypeLibVarAttribute = FieldAttributes(0)
            Dim flags As TypeLibVarFlags = tlv.Value
            Return (flags & TypeLibVarFlags.FHidden) > 0
        End If
        Return False
    End Function
End Module

[C#]
using System;
using System.Reflection;
using System.Runtime.InteropServices;

namespace D
{
```

```
class ClassD
{
    public static bool IsHiddenField( FieldInfo fi )
    {
        object[] FieldAttributes = fi.GetCustomAttributes
( typeof( TypeLibVarAttribute ), true);

        if( FieldAttributes.Length > 0 )
        {
            TypeLibVarAttribute tlv = ( TypeLibVarAttribute
)FieldAttributes[0];
            TypeLibVarFlags  flags = tlv.Value;
            return ( flags & TypeLibVarFlags.FHidden ) != 0;
        }
        return false;
    }
}
}
```

Requirements

Namespace: System.Runtime.InteropServices

Platforms: Windows 98, Windows NT 4.0, Windows Millennium Edition, Windows 2000, Windows XP Home Edition, Windows XP Professional, Windows .NET Server family

Assembly: Mscorlib (in Mscorlib.dll)

TypeLibVarAttribute Constructor

Initializes a new instance of the **TypeLibVarAttribute** class.

Overload List

Initializes a new instance of the **TypeLibVarAttribute** class with the specified **System.Runtime.InteropServices.TypeLibVarFlags** value.

> [Visual Basic] **Public Sub New(Short)**
> [C#] **public TypeLibVarAttribute(short);**
> [C++] **public: TypeLibVarAttribute(short);**
> [JScript] **public function TypeLibVarAttribute(Int16);**

Initializes a new instance of the **TypeLibVarAttribute** class with the specified **System.Runtime.InteropServices.TypeLibVarFlags** value.

> [Visual Basic] **Public Sub New(TypeLibVarFlags)**
> [C#] **public TypeLibVarAttribute(TypeLibVarFlags);**
> [C++] **public: TypeLibVarAttribute(TypeLibVarFlags);**
> [JScript] **public function TypeLibVarAttribute(TypeLibVarFlags);**

TypeLibVarAttribute Constructor (Int16)

Initializes a new instance of the **TypeLibVarAttribute** class with the specified **System.Runtime.InteropServices.TypeLibVarFlags** value.

```
[Visual Basic]
Public Sub New( _
    ByVal flags As Short _
)
[C#]
public TypeLibVarAttribute(
    short flags
);
```

```
[C++]
public: TypeLibVarAttribute(
    short flags
);
[JScript]
public function TypeLibVarAttribute(
    flags : Int16
);
```

Parameters

flags

> The **TypeLibVarFlags** value for the attributed field as found in the type library it was imported from.

Requirements

Platforms: Windows 98, Windows NT 4.0,
Windows Millennium Edition, Windows 2000,
Windows XP Home Edition, Windows XP Professional,
Windows .NET Server family

TypeLibVarAttribute Constructor (TypeLibVarFlags)

Initializes a new instance of the **TypeLibVarAttribute** class with the specified **System.Runtime.InteropServices.TypeLibVarFlags** value.

```
[Visual Basic]
Public Sub New( _
    ByVal flags As TypeLibVarFlags _
)
[C#]
public TypeLibVarAttribute(
    TypeLibVarFlags flags
);
[C++]
public: TypeLibVarAttribute(
    TypeLibVarFlags flags
);
[JScript]
public function TypeLibVarAttribute(
    flags : TypeLibVarFlags
);
```

Parameters

flags

> The **TypeLibVarFlags** value for the attributed field as found in the type library it was imported from.

Requirements

Platforms: Windows 98, Windows NT 4.0,
Windows Millennium Edition, Windows 2000,
Windows XP Home Edition, Windows XP Professional,
Windows .NET Server family

TypeLibVarAttribute.Value Property

Gets the **TypeLibVarFlags** value for this field.

```
[Visual Basic]
Public ReadOnly Property Value As TypeLibVarFlags
[C#]
public TypeLibVarFlags Value {get;}
```

```
[C++]
public: __property TypeLibVarFlags get_Value();
[JScript]
public function get Value() : TypeLibVarFlags;
```

Property Value

The **TypeLibVarFlags** value for this field.

Requirements

Platforms: Windows 98, Windows NT 4.0,
Windows Millennium Edition, Windows 2000,
Windows XP Home Edition, Windows XP Professional,
Windows .NET Server family

TypeLibVarFlags Enumeration

Describes the original settings of the **VARFLAGS** in the COM type library from which the variable was imported.

This enumeration has a **FlagsAttribute** attribute that allows a bitwise combination of its member values.

```
[Visual Basic]
<Flags>
<Serializable>
Public Enum TypeLibVarFlags
[C#]
[Flags]
[Serializable]
public enum TypeLibVarFlags
[C++]
[Flags]
[Serializable]
__value public enum TypeLibVarFlags
[JScript]
public
    Flags
    Serializable
enum TypeLibVarFlags
```

Remarks

TypeLibVarFlags is used in conjunction with the **TypeLibVarAttribute**. The flags are retained for reference only. They are not used by the common language runtime.

Members

Member name	Description	Value
FBindable	The variable supports data binding.	4
FDefaultBind	The variable is the single property that best represents the object. Only one variable in a type info can have this value.	32
FDefaultCollelem	Permits an optimization in which the compiler looks for a member named "xyz" on the type "abc". If such a member is found and is flagged as an accessor function for an element of the default collection, then a call is generated to that member function.	256
FDisplayBind	The variable is displayed as bindable. **FBindable** must also be set.	16
FHidden	The variable should not be displayed in a browser, though it exists and is bindable.	64
FImmediateBind	The variable is mapped as individual bindable properties.	4096
FNonBrowsable	The variable appears in an object browser, but not in a properties browser.	1024
FReadOnly	Assignment to the variable should not be allowed.	1
FReplaceable	Tags the interface as having default behaviors.	2048

Member name	Description	Value
FRequestEdit	Indicates that the property supports the COM **OnRequestEdit** notification.	8
FRestricted	This flag is intended for system-level functions or functions that type browsers should not display.	128
FSource	The variable returns an object that is a source of events.	2
FUiDefault	The default display in the user interface.	512

Requirements

Namespace: System.Runtime.InteropServices

Platforms: Windows 98, Windows NT 4.0, Windows Millennium Edition, Windows 2000, Windows XP Home Edition, Windows XP Professional, Windows .NET Server family

Assembly: Mscorlib (in Mscorlib.dll)

TypeLibVersionAttribute Class

Note: This namespace, class, or member is supported only in version 1.1 of the .NET Framework.

Specifies the version number of an exported type library.

System.Object
  System.Attribute
    System.Runtime.InteropServices.TypeLibVersionAttribute

[Visual Basic]
```
<AttributeUsage(AttributeTargets.Assembly)>
NotInheritable Public Class TypeLibVersionAttribute
   Inherits Attribute
```
[C#]
```
[AttributeUsage(AttributeTargets.Assembly)]
public sealed class TypeLibVersionAttribute : Attribute
```
[C++]
```
[AttributeUsage(AttributeTargets::Assembly)]
public __gc __sealed class TypeLibVersionAttribute : public
   Attribute
```
[JScript]
```
public
   AttributeUsage(AttributeTargets.Assembly)
class TypeLibVersionAttribute extends Attribute
```

Thread Safety

Any public static (**Shared** in Visual Basic) members of this type are safe for multithreaded operations. Any instance members are not guaranteed to be thread safe.

Remarks

You can apply this attribute to assemblies.

By default, the **Type Library Exporter (Tlbexp.exe)** generates a type library version from the first two numbers of an assembly version. For example, Tlb.exe exports assembly version 1.2.5000.0 as a type library version 1.2, eliminating the build and revision numbers of the assembly. If this behavior is undesirable, you can control the generation of the type library number explicitly by applying the **TypeLibVersionAttribute**.

It is useful to control the generation of a type library version explicitly when two assembly versions produce the same type library version. For example, assembly version 1.2.0.0 and assembly version 1.2.500.0 both produce a type library version of 1.2, which can cause problems when you uninstall one of the assemblies. To differentiate the type library versions, you can force the second assembly (version 1.2.500.0) to produce a type library version of 1.25.

Example

[Visual Basic, C#] The following example shows how to apply the **System.Runtime.InteropServices.TypelibVersionAttribute** to explicitly set the type library version to 1.25.

[Visual Basic]
```
Imports System
Imports System.Runtime.Interop
<Assembly: AssemblyVersion ("1.2.500.0")>
<Assembly: TypeLibVersionAttribute(1,25)>
Module MyNamespace
   Public Class c
      ' Insert code.
   End Class
```

[C#]
```
using System;
using System.Runtime.InteropServices;
[Assembly: AssemblyVersion ("1.2.500.0")>
[Assembly: TypeLibVersion(1,25)]
namespace MyNamespace
{
   class MyClass
   {
      // Insert code.
   }
}
```

Requirements

Namespace: System.Runtime.InteropServices

Platforms: Windows 98, Windows NT 4.0, Windows Millennium Edition, Windows 2000, Windows XP Home Edition, Windows XP Professional, Windows .NET Server family

Assembly: Mscorlib (in Mscorlib.dll)

TypeLibVersionAttribute Constructor

Note: This namespace, class, or member is supported only in version 1.1 of the .NET Framework.

Initializes a new instance of the **TypeLibVersionAttribute** class with the major and minor version numbers of the type library.

[Visual Basic]
```
Public Sub New( _
   ByVal major As Integer, _
   ByVal minor As Integer _
)
```
[C#]
```
public TypeLibVersionAttribute(
   int major,
   int minor
);
```
[C++]
```
public: TypeLibVersionAttribute(
   int major,
   int minor
);
```
[JScript]
```
public function TypeLibVersionAttribute(
   major : int,
   minor : int
);
```

Parameters

major
   The major version number of the type library.
minor
   The minor version number of the type library.

Requirements

Platforms: Windows 98, Windows NT 4.0, Windows Millennium Edition, Windows 2000, Windows XP Home Edition, Windows XP Professional, Windows .NET Server family

TypeLibVersionAttribute.MajorVersion Property

Note: This namespace, class, or member is supported only in version 1.1 of the .NET Framework.

Gets the major version number of the type library.

```
[Visual Basic]
Public ReadOnly Property MajorVersion As Integer
[C#]
public int MajorVersion {get;}
[C++]
public: __property int get_MajorVersion();
[JScript]
public function get MajorVersion() : int;
```

Property Value

The major version number of the type library.

Requirements

Platforms: Windows 98, Windows NT 4.0, Windows Millennium Edition, Windows 2000, Windows XP Home Edition, Windows XP Professional, Windows .NET Server family

TypeLibVersionAttribute.MinorVersion Property

Note: This namespace, class, or member is supported only in version 1.1 of the .NET Framework.

Gets the minor version number of the type library.

```
[Visual Basic]
Public ReadOnly Property MinorVersion As Integer
[C#]
public int MinorVersion {get;}
[C++]
public: __property int get_MinorVersion();
[JScript]
public function get MinorVersion() : int;
```

Property Value

The minor version number of the type library.

Requirements

Platforms: Windows 98, Windows NT 4.0, Windows Millennium Edition, Windows 2000, Windows XP Home Edition, Windows XP Professional, Windows .NET Server family

UCOMIBindCtx Interface

Managed definition of the **IBindCtx** interface.

```
[Visual Basic]
<Guid("0000000e-0000-0000-C000-000000000046")>
<InterfaceType(ComInterfaceType.InterfaceIsIUnknown)>
Public Interface UCOMIBindCtx
[C#]
[Guid("0000000e-0000-0000-C000-000000000046")]
[InterfaceType(ComInterfaceType.InterfaceIsIUnknown)]
public interface UCOMIBindCtx
[C++]
[Guid("0000000e-0000-0000-C000-000000000046")]
[InterfaceType(ComInterfaceType::InterfaceIsIUnknown)]
public __gc __interface UCOMIBindCtx
[JScript]
public
   Guid("0000000e-0000-0000-C000-000000000046")
   InterfaceType(ComInterfaceType.InterfaceIsIUnknown)
interface UCOMIBindCtx
```

Remarks

For more information, please see the existing documentation for **IBindCtx** in the com subfolder of the MSDN library.

Requirements

Namespace: System.Runtime.InteropServices

Platforms: Windows 98, Windows NT 4.0, Windows Millennium Edition, Windows 2000, Windows XP Home Edition, Windows XP Professional, Windows .NET Server family

Assembly: Mscorlib (in Mscorlib.dll)

UCOMIBindCtx.EnumObjectParam Method

Enumerate the strings which are the keys of the internally-maintained table of contextual object parameters.

```
[Visual Basic]
Sub EnumObjectParam( _
   <Out()> ByRef ppenum As UCOMIEnumString _
)
[C#]
void EnumObjectParam(
   out UCOMIEnumString ppenum
);
[C++]
void EnumObjectParam(
   [
   Out
] UCOMIEnumString** ppenum
);
[JScript]
function EnumObjectParam(
   ppenum : UCOMIEnumString
);
```

Parameters

ppenum
    On successful return, a reference to the object parameter enumerator.

Remarks

For more information, please see the existing documentation for **IBindCtx::EnumObjectParam** in the MSDN library.

Requirements

Platforms: Windows 98, Windows NT 4.0, Windows Millennium Edition, Windows 2000, Windows XP Home Edition, Windows XP Professional, Windows .NET Server family

UCOMIBindCtx.GetBindOptions Method

Return the current binding options stored in this bind context.

```
[Visual Basic]
Sub GetBindOptions( _
   ByRef pbindopts As BIND_OPTS _
)
[C#]
void GetBindOptions(
   ref BIND_OPTS pbindopts
);
[C++]
void GetBindOptions(
   BIND_OPTS* pbindopts
);
[JScript]
function GetBindOptions(
   pbindopts : BIND_OPTS
);
```

Parameters

pbindopts
    A pointer to the structure to receive the binding options.

Remarks

For more information, please see the existing documentation for **IBindCtx::GetBindOptions** in the MSDN library.

Requirements

Platforms: Windows 98, Windows NT 4.0, Windows Millennium Edition, Windows 2000, Windows XP Home Edition, Windows XP Professional, Windows .NET Server family

UCOMIBindCtx.GetObjectParam Method

Lookup the given key in the internally-maintained table of contextual object parameters and return the corresponding object, if one exists.

```
[Visual Basic]
Sub GetObjectParam( _
   ByVal pszKey As String, _
   <Out()> ByRef ppunk As Object _
)
[C#]
void GetObjectParam(
   string pszKey,
   out object ppunk
);
[C++]
void GetObjectParam(
   String* pszKey,
```

```
    [
    Out
] Object** ppunk
);
[JScript]
function GetObjectParam(
    pszKey : String,
    ppunk : Object
);
```

Parameters

pszKey

> The name of the object to search for.

ppunk

> On successful return, the object interface pointer.

Remarks

For more information, please see the existing documentation for **IBindCtx::GetObjectParam** in the MSDN library.

Requirements

Platforms: Windows 98, Windows NT 4.0, Windows Millennium Edition, Windows 2000, Windows XP Home Edition, Windows XP Professional, Windows .NET Server family

UCOMIBindCtx.GetRunningObjectTable Method

Return access to the Running Object Table (ROT) relevant to this binding process.

```
[Visual Basic]
Sub GetRunningObjectTable( _
    <Out()> ByRef pprot As UCOMIRunningObjectTable _
)
[C#]
void GetRunningObjectTable(
    out UCOMIRunningObjectTable pprot
);
[C++]
void GetRunningObjectTable(
    [
    Out
] UCOMIRunningObjectTable** pprot
);
[JScript]
function GetRunningObjectTable(
    pprot : UCOMIRunningObjectTable
);
```

Parameters

pprot

> On successful return, a reference to the ROT.

Remarks

For more information, please see the existing documentation for **IBindCtx::GetRunningObjectTable** in the MSDN library.

Requirements

Platforms: Windows 98, Windows NT 4.0, Windows Millennium Edition, Windows 2000, Windows XP Home Edition, Windows XP Professional, Windows .NET Server family

UCOMIBindCtx.RegisterObjectBound Method

Register the passed object as one of the objects that has been bound during a moniker operation and which should be released when it is complete.

```
[Visual Basic]
Sub RegisterObjectBound( _
    ByVal punk As Object _
)
[C#]
void RegisterObjectBound(
    object punk
);
[C++]
void RegisterObjectBound(
    Object* punk
);
[JScript]
function RegisterObjectBound(
    punk : Object
);
```

Parameters

punk

> The object to register for release.

Remarks

For more information, please see the existing documentation for **IBindCtx::RegisterObjectBound** in the MSDN library.

Requirements

Platforms: Windows 98, Windows NT 4.0, Windows Millennium Edition, Windows 2000, Windows XP Home Edition, Windows XP Professional, Windows .NET Server family

UCOMIBindCtx.RegisterObjectParam Method

Register the given object pointer under the specified name in the internally-maintained table of object pointers.

```
[Visual Basic]
Sub RegisterObjectParam( _
    ByVal pszKey As String, _
    ByVal punk As Object _
)
[C#]
void RegisterObjectParam(
    string pszKey,
    object punk
);
[C++]
void RegisterObjectParam(
    String* pszKey,
    Object* punk
);
[JScript]
function RegisterObjectParam(
    pszKey : String,
    punk : Object
);
```

Parameters

pszKey

The name to register *punk* with.

punk

The object to register.

Remarks

For more information, please see the existing documentation for **IBindCtx::RegisterObjectParam** in the MSDN library.

Requirements

Platforms: Windows 98, Windows NT 4.0, Windows Millennium Edition, Windows 2000, Windows XP Home Edition, Windows XP Professional, Windows .NET Server family

UCOMIBindCtx.ReleaseBoundObjects Method

Releases all the objects currently registered with the bind context by **RegisterObjectBound**.

```
[Visual Basic]
Sub ReleaseBoundObjects()
[C#]
void ReleaseBoundObjects();
[C++]
void ReleaseBoundObjects();
[JScript]
function ReleaseBoundObjects();
```

Remarks

For more information, please see the existing documentation for **IBindCtx::ReleaseBoundObjects** in the MSDN library.

Requirements

Platforms: Windows 98, Windows NT 4.0, Windows Millennium Edition, Windows 2000, Windows XP Home Edition, Windows XP Professional, Windows .NET Server family

UCOMIBindCtx.RevokeObjectBound Method

Removes the object from the set of registered objects that need to be released.

```
[Visual Basic]
Sub RevokeObjectBound( _
   ByVal punk As Object _
)
[C#]
void RevokeObjectBound(
   object punk
);
[C++]
void RevokeObjectBound(
   Object* punk
);
[JScript]
function RevokeObjectBound(
   punk : Object
);
```

Parameters

punk

The object to unregister for release.

Remarks

For more information, please see the existing documentation for **IBindCtx::RevokeObjectBound** in the MSDN library.

Requirements

Platforms: Windows 98, Windows NT 4.0, Windows Millennium Edition, Windows 2000, Windows XP Home Edition, Windows XP Professional, Windows .NET Server family

UCOMIBindCtx.RevokeObjectParam Method

Revoke the registration of the object currently found under this key in the internally-maintained table of contextual object parameters, if any such key is currently registered.

```
[Visual Basic]
Sub RevokeObjectParam( _
   ByVal pszKey As String _
)
[C#]
void RevokeObjectParam(
   string pszKey
);
[C++]
void RevokeObjectParam(
   String* pszKey
);
[JScript]
function RevokeObjectParam(
   pszKey : String
);
```

Parameters

pszKey

The key to unregister.

Remarks

For more information, please see the existing documentation for **IBindCtx::RevokeObjectParam** in the MSDN library.

Requirements

Platforms: Windows 98, Windows NT 4.0, Windows Millennium Edition, Windows 2000, Windows XP Home Edition, Windows XP Professional, Windows .NET Server family

UCOMIBindCtx.SetBindOptions Method

Store in the bind context a block of parameters that will apply to later **UCOMIMoniker** operations using this bind context.

```
[Visual Basic]
Sub SetBindOptions( _
   <InteropServices.In()> ByRef pbindopts As BIND_OPTS _
)
```

```
[C#]
void SetBindOptions(
   [
   In
] ref BIND_OPTS pbindopts
);
[C++]
void SetBindOptions(
   [
   In
] BIND_OPTS* pbindopts
);
[JScript]
function SetBindOptions(
   pbindopts : BIND_OPTS
);
```

Parameters

pbindopts

    The structure containing the binding options to set.

Remarks

For more information, please see the existing documentation for
IBindCtx::SetBindOptions in the MSDN library.

Requirements

Platforms: Windows 98, Windows NT 4.0,
Windows Millennium Edition, Windows 2000,
Windows XP Home Edition, Windows XP Professional,
Windows .NET Server family

UCOMIConnectionPoint Interface

Managed definition of the **IConnectionPoint** interface.

```
[Visual Basic]
<Guid("B196B286-BAB4-101A-B69C-00AA00341D07")>
<InterfaceType(ComInterfaceType.InterfaceIsIUnknown)>
Public Interface UCOMIConnectionPoint
[C#]
[Guid("B196B286-BAB4-101A-B69C-00AA00341D07")]
[InterfaceType(ComInterfaceType.InterfaceIsIUnknown)]
public interface UCOMIConnectionPoint
[C++]
[Guid("B196B286-BAB4-101A-B69C-00AA00341D07")]
[InterfaceType(ComInterfaceType::InterfaceIsIUnknown)]
public __gc __interface UCOMIConnectionPoint
[JScript]
public
    Guid("B196B286-BAB4-101A-B69C-00AA00341D07")
    InterfaceType(ComInterfaceType.InterfaceIsIUnknown)
interface UCOMIConnectionPoint
```

Remarks

For more information, please see the existing documentation for **IConnectionPoint** in the com subfolder of the MSDN library.

Requirements

Namespace: System.Runtime.InteropServices

Platforms: Windows 98, Windows NT 4.0, Windows Millennium Edition, Windows 2000, Windows XP Home Edition, Windows XP Professional, Windows .NET Server family

Assembly: Mscorlib (in Mscorlib.dll)

UCOMIConnectionPoint.Advise Method

Establishes an advisory connection between the connection point and the caller's sink object.

```
[Visual Basic]
Sub Advise( _
   ByVal pUnkSink As Object, _
   <Out()> ByRef pdwCookie As Integer _
)
[C#]
void Advise(
   object pUnkSink,
   out int pdwCookie
);
[C++]
void Advise(
   Object* pUnkSink,
   [
   Out
] int* pdwCookie
);
[JScript]
function Advise(
   pUnkSink : Object,
   pdwCookie : int
);
```

Parameters

pUnkSink
> Reference to the sink to receive calls for the outgoing interface managed by this connection point.

pdwCookie
> On successful return, contains the connection cookie.

Remarks

For more information, please see the existing documentation for **IConnectionPoint::Advise** in the MSDN library.

Requirements

Platforms: Windows 98, Windows NT 4.0, Windows Millennium Edition, Windows 2000, Windows XP Home Edition, Windows XP Professional, Windows .NET Server family

UCOMIConnectionPoint.EnumConnections Method

Creates an enumerator object for iteration through the connections that exist to this connection point.

```
[Visual Basic]
Sub EnumConnections( _
   <Out()> ByRef ppEnum As UCOMIEnumConnections _
)
[C#]
void EnumConnections(
   out UCOMIEnumConnections ppEnum
);
[C++]
void EnumConnections(
   [
   Out
] UCOMIEnumConnections** ppEnum
);
[JScript]
function EnumConnections(
   ppEnum : UCOMIEnumConnections
);
```

Parameters

ppEnum
> On successful return, contains the newly created enumerator.

Remarks

For more information, please see the existing documentation for **IConnectionPoint::EnumConnections** in the MSDN library.

Requirements

Platforms: Windows 98, Windows NT 4.0, Windows Millennium Edition, Windows 2000, Windows XP Home Edition, Windows XP Professional, Windows .NET Server family

UCOMIConnectionPoint.GetConnectionInterface Method

Returns the IID of the outgoing interface managed by this connection point.

```
[Visual Basic]
Sub GetConnectionInterface( _
    <Out()> ByRef pIID As Guid _
)
[C#]
void GetConnectionInterface(
    out Guid pIID
);
[C++]
void GetConnectionInterface(
    [
    Out
] Guid* pIID
);
[JScript]
function GetConnectionInterface(
    pIID : Guid
);
```

Parameters

pIID

On successful return, contains the IID of the outgoing interface managed by this connection point.

Remarks

For more information, please see the existing documentation for **IConnectionPoint::GetConnectionInterface** in the MSDN library.

Requirements

Platforms: Windows 98, Windows NT 4.0, Windows Millennium Edition, Windows 2000, Windows XP Home Edition, Windows XP Professional, Windows .NET Server family

UCOMIConnectionPoint.GetConnectionPoint-Container Method

Retrieves the **IConnectionPointContainer** interface pointer to the connectable object that conceptually owns this connection point.

```
[Visual Basic]
Sub GetConnectionPointContainer( _
    <Out()> ByRef ppCPC As UCOMIConnectionPointContainer _
)
[C#]
void GetConnectionPointContainer(
    out UCOMIConnectionPointContainer ppCPC
);
[C++]
void GetConnectionPointContainer(
    [
    Out
] UCOMIConnectionPointContainer** ppCPC
);
[JScript]
function GetConnectionPointContainer(
    ppCPC : UCOMIConnectionPointContainer
);
```

Parameters

ppCPC

On successful return, contains the connectable object's **IConnectionPointContainer** interface.

Remarks

For more information, please see the existing documentation for **IConnectionPoint::GetConnectionPointContainer** in the MSDN library.

Requirements

Platforms: Windows 98, Windows NT 4.0, Windows Millennium Edition, Windows 2000, Windows XP Home Edition, Windows XP Professional, Windows .NET Server family

UCOMIConnectionPoint.Unadvise Method

Terminates an advisory connection previously established through **Advise**.

```
[Visual Basic]
Sub Unadvise( _
    ByVal dwCookie As Integer _
)
[C#]
void Unadvise(
    int dwCookie
);
[C++]
void Unadvise(
    int dwCookie
);
[JScript]
function Unadvise(
    dwCookie : int
);
```

Parameters

dwCookie

The connection cookie previously returned from **Advise**.

Remarks

For more information, please see the existing documentation for **IConnectionPoint::Unadvise** in the MSDN library.

Requirements

Platforms: Windows 98, Windows NT 4.0, Windows Millennium Edition, Windows 2000, Windows XP Home Edition, Windows XP Professional, Windows .NET Server family

UCOMIConnectionPointContainer Interface

Managed definition of the **IConnectionPointContainer** interface.

```
[Visual Basic]
<Guid("B196B284-BAB4-101A-B69C-00AA00341D07")>
<InterfaceType(ComInterfaceType.InterfaceIsIUnknown)>
Public Interface UCOMIConnectionPointContainer
[C#]
[Guid("B196B284-BAB4-101A-B69C-00AA00341D07")]
[InterfaceType(ComInterfaceType.InterfaceIsIUnknown)]
public interface UCOMIConnectionPointContainer
[C++]
[Guid("B196B284-BAB4-101A-B69C-00AA00341D07")]
[InterfaceType(ComInterfaceType::InterfaceIsIUnknown)]
public __gc __interface UCOMIConnectionPointContainer
[JScript]
public
    Guid("B196B284-BAB4-101A-B69C-00AA00341D07")
    InterfaceType(ComInterfaceType.InterfaceIsIUnknown)
interface UCOMIConnectionPointContainer
```

Remarks

For more information, please see the existing documentation for **IConnectionPointContainer** in the com subfolder of the MSDN library.

Requirements

Namespace: System.Runtime.InteropServices

Platforms: Windows 98, Windows NT 4.0, Windows Millennium Edition, Windows 2000, Windows XP Home Edition, Windows XP Professional, Windows .NET Server family

Assembly: Mscorlib (in Mscorlib.dll)

UCOMIConnectionPointContainer.EnumConnectionPoints Method

Creates an enumerator of all the connection points supported in the connectable object, one connection point per IID.

```
[Visual Basic]
Sub EnumConnectionPoints( _
    <Out()> ByRef ppEnum As UCOMIEnumConnectionPoints _
)
[C#]
void EnumConnectionPoints(
    out UCOMIEnumConnectionPoints ppEnum
);
[C++]
void EnumConnectionPoints(
    [
    Out
    ] UCOMIEnumConnectionPoints** ppEnum
);
[JScript]
function EnumConnectionPoints(
    ppEnum : UCOMIEnumConnectionPoints
);
```

Parameters

ppEnum
> On successful return, contains the interface pointer of the enumerator.

Remarks

For more information, please see the existing documentation for **IConnectionPointContainer::EnumConnectionPoints** in the MSDN library.

Requirements

Platforms: Windows 98, Windows NT 4.0, Windows Millennium Edition, Windows 2000, Windows XP Home Edition, Windows XP Professional, Windows .NET Server family

UCOMIConnectionPointContainer.FindConnectionPoint Method

Asks the connectable object if it has a connection point for a particular IID, and if so, returns the **IConnectionPoint** interface pointer to that connection point.

```
[Visual Basic]
Sub FindConnectionPoint( _
    ByRef riid As Guid, _
    <Out()> ByRef ppCP As UCOMIConnectionPoint _
)
[C#]
void FindConnectionPoint(
    ref Guid riid,
    out UCOMIConnectionPoint ppCP
);
[C++]
void FindConnectionPoint(
    Guid* riid,
    [
    Out
    ] UCOMIConnectionPoint** ppCP
);
[JScript]
function FindConnectionPoint(
    riid : Guid,
    ppCP : UCOMIConnectionPoint
);
```

Parameters

riid
> A reference to the outgoing interface IID whose connection point is being requested.

ppCP
> On successful return, contains the connection point that manages the outgoing interface *riid*.

Remarks

For more information, please see the existing documentation for **IConnectionPointContainer::FindConnectionPoint** in the MSDN library.

Requirements

Platforms: Windows 98, Windows NT 4.0, Windows Millennium Edition, Windows 2000, Windows XP Home Edition, Windows XP Professional, Windows .NET Server family

UCOMIEnumConnectionPoints Interface

Manages the definition of the **IEnumConnectionPoints** interface.

```
[Visual Basic]
<Guid("B196B285-BAB4-101A-B69C-00AA00341D07")>
<InterfaceType(ComInterfaceType.InterfaceIsIUnknown)>
Public Interface UCOMIEnumConnectionPoints
[C#]
[Guid("B196B285-BAB4-101A-B69C-00AA00341D07")]
[InterfaceType(ComInterfaceType.InterfaceIsIUnknown)]
public interface UCOMIEnumConnectionPoints
[C++]
[Guid("B196B285-BAB4-101A-B69C-00AA00341D07")]
[InterfaceType(ComInterfaceType::InterfaceIsIUnknown)]
public __gc __interface UCOMIEnumConnectionPoints
[JScript]
public
    Guid("B196B285-BAB4-101A-B69C-00AA00341D07")
    InterfaceType(ComInterfaceType.InterfaceIsIUnknown)
interface UCOMIEnumConnectionPoints
```

Remarks

For more information about the **IEnumConnectionPoints** interface, see the MSDN Library.

Requirements

Namespace: System.Runtime.InteropServices

Platforms: Windows 98, Windows NT 4.0, Windows Millennium Edition, Windows 2000, Windows XP Home Edition, Windows XP Professional, Windows .NET Server family

Assembly: Mscorlib (in Mscorlib.dll)

UCOMIEnumConnectionPoints.Clone Method

Creates another enumerator that contains the same enumeration state as the current one.

```
[Visual Basic]
Sub Clone( _
    <Out()> ByRef ppenum As UCOMIEnumConnectionPoints _
)
[C#]
void Clone(
    out UCOMIEnumConnectionPoints ppenum
);
[C++]
void Clone(
    [
    Out
] UCOMIEnumConnectionPoints** ppenum
);
[JScript]
function Clone(
    ppenum : UCOMIEnumConnectionPoints
);
```

Parameters

ppenum

    On successful return, a reference to the newly created enumerator.

Remarks

For more information about **IEnumConnectionPoints::Clone**, see the MSDN Library.

Requirements

Platforms: Windows 98, Windows NT 4.0, Windows Millennium Edition, Windows 2000, Windows XP Home Edition, Windows XP Professional, Windows .NET Server family

UCOMIEnumConnectionPoints.Next Method

Retrieves a specified number of items in the enumeration sequence.

```
[Visual Basic]
Function Next( _
    ByVal celt As Integer, _
    <Out()> ByVal rgelt() As UCOMIConnectionPoint, _
    <Out()> ByRef pceltFetched As Integer _
) As Integer
[C#]
int Next(
    int celt,
    [
    Out
] UCOMIConnectionPoint[] rgelt,
    out int pceltFetched
);
[C++]
int Next(
    int celt,
    [
    Out
] UCOMIConnectionPoint** rgelt[],
    [
    Out
] int* pceltFetched
);
[JScript]
function Next(
    celt : int,
    rgelt : UCOMIConnectionPoint[],
    pceltFetched : int
) : int;
```

Parameters

celt

    The number of **IConnectionPoint** references to return in *rgelt*.

rgelt

    On successful return, a reference to the enumerated connections.

pceltFetched

    On successful return, a reference to the actual number of connections enumerated in *rgelt*.

Return Value

S_OK if the *pceltFetched* parameter equals the *celt* parameter; otherwise, **S_FALSE**.

Remarks

For more information about **IEnumConnectionPoints::Next**, see the MSDN Library.

Requirements

Platforms: Windows 98, Windows NT 4.0, Windows Millennium Edition, Windows 2000, Windows XP Home Edition, Windows XP Professional, Windows .NET Server family

UCOMIEnumConnectionPoints.Reset Method

Resets the enumeration sequence to the beginning.

```
[Visual Basic]
Function Reset() As Integer
[C#]
int Reset();
[C++]
int Reset();
[JScript]
function Reset() : int;
```

Return Value

An HRESULT with the value **S_OK**.

Remarks

For more information about **IEnumConnectionPoints::Reset**, see the MSDN Library.

Requirements

Platforms: Windows 98, Windows NT 4.0, Windows Millennium Edition, Windows 2000, Windows XP Home Edition, Windows XP Professional, Windows .NET Server family

UCOMIEnumConnectionPoints.Skip Method

Skips over a specified number of items in the enumeration sequence.

```
[Visual Basic]
Function Skip( _
   ByVal celt As Integer _
) As Integer
[C#]
int Skip(
   int celt
);
[C++]
int Skip(
   int celt
);
[JScript]
function Skip(
   celt : int
) : int;
```

Parameters

celt
    The number of elements to skip in the enumeration.

Return Value

S_OK if the number of elements skipped equals the *celt* parameter; otherwise, **S_FALSE**.

Remarks

For more information about **IEnumConnectionPoints::Skip**, see the MSDN Library.

Requirements

Platforms: Windows 98, Windows NT 4.0, Windows Millennium Edition, Windows 2000, Windows XP Home Edition, Windows XP Professional, Windows .NET Server family

UCOMIEnumConnections Interface

Manages the definition of the **IEnumConnections** interface.

```
[Visual Basic]
<Guid("B196B2B7-BAB4-101A-B69C-00AA00341D07")>
<InterfaceType(ComInterfaceType.InterfaceIsIUnknown)>
Public Interface UCOMIEnumConnections
[C#]
[Guid("B196B2B7-BAB4-101A-B69C-00AA00341D07")]
[InterfaceType(ComInterfaceType.InterfaceIsIUnknown)]
public interface UCOMIEnumConnections
[C++]
[Guid("B196B2B7-BAB4-101A-B69C-00AA00341D07")]
[InterfaceType(ComInterfaceType::InterfaceIsIUnknown)]
public __gc __interface UCOMIEnumConnections
[JScript]
public
    Guid("B196B2B7-BAB4-101A-B69C-00AA00341D07")
    InterfaceType(ComInterfaceType.InterfaceIsIUnknown)
interface UCOMIEnumConnections
```

Remarks

For more information about the **IEnumConnections** interface, see the MSDN Library.

Requirements

Namespace: System.Runtime.InteropServices

Platforms: Windows 98, Windows NT 4.0, Windows Millennium Edition, Windows 2000, Windows XP Home Edition, Windows XP Professional, Windows .NET Server family

Assembly: Mscorlib (in Mscorlib.dll)

UCOMIEnumConnections.Clone Method

Creates another enumerator that contains the same enumeration state as the current one.

```
[Visual Basic]
Sub Clone( _
    <Out()> ByRef ppenum As UCOMIEnumConnections _
)
[C#]
void Clone(
    out UCOMIEnumConnections ppenum
);
[C++]
void Clone(
    [
    Out
] UCOMIEnumConnections** ppenum
);
[JScript]
function Clone(
    ppenum : UCOMIEnumConnections
);
```

Parameters

ppenum

    On successful return, a reference to the newly created enumerator.

Remarks

For more information about **IEnumConnections::Clone**, see the MSDN Library.

Requirements

Platforms: Windows 98, Windows NT 4.0, Windows Millennium Edition, Windows 2000, Windows XP Home Edition, Windows XP Professional, Windows .NET Server family

UCOMIEnumConnections.Next Method

Retrieves a specified number of items in the enumeration sequence.

```
[Visual Basic]
Function Next( _
    ByVal celt As Integer, _
    <Out()> ByVal rgelt() As CONNECTDATA, _
    <Out()> ByRef pceltFetched As Integer _
) As Integer
[C#]
int Next(
    int celt,
    [
    Out
] CONNECTDATA[] rgelt,
    out int pceltFetched
);
[C++]
int Next(
    int celt,
    [
    Out
] CONNECTDATA* rgelt[],
    [
    Out
] int* pceltFetched
);
[JScript]
function Next(
    celt : int,
    rgelt : CONNECTDATA[],
    pceltFetched : int
) : int;
```

Parameters

celt

    The number of **CONNECTDATA** structures to return in *rgelt*.

rgelt

    On successful return, a reference to the enumerated connections.

pceltFetched

    On successful return, a reference to the actual number of connections enumerated in *rgelt*.

Return Value

S_OK if the *pceltFetched* parameter equals the *celt* parameter; otherwise, **S_FALSE**.

Remarks

For more information about **IEnumConnections::Next**, see the MSDN Library.

Requirements

Platforms: Windows 98, Windows NT 4.0, Windows Millennium Edition, Windows 2000, Windows XP Home Edition, Windows XP Professional, Windows .NET Server family

Remarks

For more information about **IEnumConnections::Skip**, see the MSDN Library.

Requirements

Platforms: Windows 98, Windows NT 4.0, Windows Millennium Edition, Windows 2000, Windows XP Home Edition, Windows XP Professional, Windows .NET Server family

UCOMIEnumConnections.Reset Method

Resets the enumeration sequence to the beginning.

```
[Visual Basic]
Sub Reset()
[C#]
void Reset();
[C++]
void Reset();
[JScript]
function Reset();
```

Return Value

An HRESULT with the value **S_OK**.

Remarks

For more information about **IEnumConnections::Reset**, see the MSDN Library.

Requirements

Platforms: Windows 98, Windows NT 4.0, Windows Millennium Edition, Windows 2000, Windows XP Home Edition, Windows XP Professional, Windows .NET Server family

UCOMIEnumConnections.Skip Method

Skips over a specified number of items in the enumeration sequence.

```
[Visual Basic]
Function Skip( _
    ByVal celt As Integer _
) As Integer
[C#]
int Skip(
    int celt
);
[C++]
int Skip(
    int celt
);
[JScript]
function Skip(
    celt : int
) : int;
```

Parameters

celt
    The number of elements to skip in the enumeration.

Return Value

S_OK if the number of elements skipped equals the *celt* parameter; otherwise, **S_FALSE**.

UCOMIEnumMoniker Interface

Manages the definition of the **IEnumMoniker** interface.

```
[Visual Basic]
<Guid("00000102-0000-0000-C000-000000000046")>
<InterfaceType(ComInterfaceType.InterfaceIsIUnknown)>
Public Interface UCOMIEnumMoniker
[C#]
[Guid("00000102-0000-0000-C000-000000000046")]
[InterfaceType(ComInterfaceType.InterfaceIsIUnknown)]
public interface UCOMIEnumMoniker
[C++]
[Guid("00000102-0000-0000-C000-000000000046")]
[InterfaceType(ComInterfaceType::InterfaceIsIUnknown)]
public __gc __interface UCOMIEnumMoniker
[JScript]
public
    Guid("00000102-0000-0000-C000-000000000046")
    InterfaceType(ComInterfaceType.InterfaceIsIUnknown)
interface UCOMIEnumMoniker
```

Remarks

For more information about the **IEnumMoniker** interface, see the
MSDN Library.

Requirements

Namespace: System.Runtime.InteropServices

Platforms: Windows 98, Windows NT 4.0,
Windows Millennium Edition, Windows 2000,
Windows XP Home Edition, Windows XP Professional,
Windows .NET Server family

Assembly: Mscorlib (in Mscorlib.dll)

UCOMIEnumMoniker.Clone Method

Creates another enumerator that contains the same enumeration state
as the current one.

```
[Visual Basic]
Sub Clone( _
    <Out()> ByRef ppenum As UCOMIEnumMoniker _
)
[C#]
void Clone(
    out UCOMIEnumMoniker ppenum
);
[C++]
void Clone(
    [
    Out
] UCOMIEnumMoniker** ppenum
);
[JScript]
function Clone(
    ppenum : UCOMIEnumMoniker
);
```

Parameters

ppenum
>On successful return, a reference to the newly created
enumerator.

Remarks

For more information about **IEnumMoniker::Clone**, see the
MSDN Library.

Requirements

Platforms: Windows 98, Windows NT 4.0,
Windows Millennium Edition, Windows 2000,
Windows XP Home Edition, Windows XP Professional,
Windows .NET Server family

UCOMIEnumMoniker.Next Method

Retrieves a specified number of items in the enumeration sequence.

```
[Visual Basic]
Function Next( _
    ByVal celt As Integer, _
    <Out()> ByVal rgelt() As UCOMIMoniker, _
    <Out()> ByRef pceltFetched As Integer _
) As Integer
[C#]
int Next(
    int celt,
    [
    Out
] UCOMIMoniker[] rgelt,
    out int pceltFetched
);
[C++]
int Next(
    int celt,
    [
    Out
] UCOMIMoniker** rgelt[],
    [
    Out
] int* pceltFetched
);
[JScript]
function Next(
    celt : int,
    rgelt : UCOMIMoniker[],
    pceltFetched : int
) : int;
```

Parameters

celt
>The number of monikers to return in *rgelt*.

rgelt
>On successful return, a reference to the enumerated monikers.

pceltFetched
>On successful return, a reference to the actual number of
monikers enumerated in *rgelt*.

Return Value

S_OK if the *pceltFetched* parameter equals the *celt* parameter;
otherwise, **S_FALSE**.

Remarks

For more information about **IEnumMoniker::Next**, see the MSDN Library.

Requirements

Platforms: Windows 98, Windows NT 4.0, Windows Millennium Edition, Windows 2000, Windows XP Home Edition, Windows XP Professional, Windows .NET Server family

UCOMIEnumMoniker.Reset Method

Resets the enumeration sequence to the beginning.

```
[Visual Basic]
Function Reset() As Integer
[C#]
int Reset();
[C++]
int Reset();
[JScript]
function Reset() : int;
```

Return Value

An HRESULT with the value **S_OK**.

Remarks

For more information about **IEnumMoniker::Reset**, see the MSDN Library.

Requirements

Platforms: Windows 98, Windows NT 4.0, Windows Millennium Edition, Windows 2000, Windows XP Home Edition, Windows XP Professional, Windows .NET Server family

UCOMIEnumMoniker.Skip Method

Skips over a specified number of items in the enumeration sequence.

```
[Visual Basic]
Function Skip( _
    ByVal celt As Integer _
) As Integer
[C#]
int Skip(
    int celt
);
[C++]
int Skip(
    int celt
);
[JScript]
function Skip(
    celt : int
) : int;
```

Parameters

celt
    The number of elements to skip in the enumeration.

Return Value

S_OK if the number of elements skipped equals the *celt* parameter; otherwise, **S_FALSE**.

Remarks

For more information about **IEnumMoniker::Skip**, see the MSDN Library.

Requirements

Platforms: Windows 98, Windows NT 4.0, Windows Millennium Edition, Windows 2000, Windows XP Home Edition, Windows XP Professional, Windows .NET Server family

UCOMIEnumString Interface

Manages the definition of the **IEnumString** interface.

```
[Visual Basic]
<Guid("00000101-0000-0000-C000-000000000046")>
<InterfaceType(ComInterfaceType.InterfaceIsIUnknown)>
Public Interface UCOMIEnumString
[C#]
[Guid("00000101-0000-0000-C000-000000000046")]
[InterfaceType(ComInterfaceType.InterfaceIsIUnknown)]
public interface UCOMIEnumString
[C++]
[Guid("00000101-0000-0000-C000-000000000046")]
[InterfaceType(ComInterfaceType::InterfaceIsIUnknown)]
public __gc __interface UCOMIEnumString
[JScript]
public
   Guid("00000101-0000-0000-C000-000000000046")
   InterfaceType(ComInterfaceType.InterfaceIsIUnknown)
interface UCOMIEnumString
```

Remarks

For more information about the **IEnumString** interface, see the MSDN Library.

Requirements

Namespace: System.Runtime.InteropServices

Platforms: Windows 98, Windows NT 4.0, Windows Millennium Edition, Windows 2000, Windows XP Home Edition, Windows XP Professional, Windows .NET Server family

Assembly: Mscorlib (in Mscorlib.dll)

UCOMIEnumString.Clone Method

Creates another enumerator that contains the same enumeration state as the current one.

```
[Visual Basic]
Sub Clone( _
   <Out()> ByRef ppenum As UCOMIEnumString _
)
[C#]
void Clone(
   out UCOMIEnumString ppenum
);
[C++]
void Clone(
   [
   Out
] UCOMIEnumString** ppenum
);
[JScript]
function Clone(
   ppenum : UCOMIEnumString
);
```

Parameters

ppenum
   On successful return, a reference to the newly created enumerator.

Remarks

For more information about **IEnumString::Clone**, see the MSDN Library.

Requirements

Platforms: Windows 98, Windows NT 4.0, Windows Millennium Edition, Windows 2000, Windows XP Home Edition, Windows XP Professional, Windows .NET Server family

UCOMIEnumString.Next Method

Retrieves a specified number of items in the enumeration sequence.

```
[Visual Basic]
Function Next( _
   ByVal celt As Integer, _
   <Out()> ByVal rgelt() As String, _
   <Out()> ByRef pceltFetched As Integer _
) As Integer
[C#]
int Next(
   int celt,
   [
   Out
] string[] rgelt,
   out int pceltFetched
);
[C++]
int Next(
   int celt,
   [
   Out
] String* rgelt __gc[],
   [
   Out
] int* pceltFetched
);
[JScript]
function Next(
   celt : int,
   rgelt : String[],
   pceltFetched : int
) : int;
```

Parameters

celt
   The number of strings to return in *rgelt*.
rgelt
   On successful return, a reference to the enumerated strings.
pceltFetched
   On successful return, a reference to the actual number of strings enumerated in *rgelt*.

Return Value

S_OK if the *pceltFetched* parameter equals the *celt* parameter; otherwise, **S_FALSE**.

Remarks

For more information about **IEnumString::Next**, see the MSDN Library.

Requirements

Platforms: Windows 98, Windows NT 4.0,
Windows Millennium Edition, Windows 2000,
Windows XP Home Edition, Windows XP Professional,
Windows .NET Server family

Requirements

Platforms: Windows 98, Windows NT 4.0,
Windows Millennium Edition, Windows 2000,
Windows XP Home Edition, Windows XP Professional,
Windows .NET Server family

UCOMIEnumString.Reset Method

Resets the enumeration sequence to the beginning.

```
[Visual Basic]
Function Reset() As Integer
[C#]
int Reset();
[C++]
int Reset();
[JScript]
function Reset() : int;
```

Return Value

An HRESULT with the value **S_OK**.

Remarks

For more information about **IEnumString::Reset**, see the MSDN
Library.

Requirements

Platforms: Windows 98, Windows NT 4.0,
Windows Millennium Edition, Windows 2000,
Windows XP Home Edition, Windows XP Professional,
Windows .NET Server family

UCOMIEnumString.Skip Method

Skips over a specified number of items in the enumeration sequence.

```
[Visual Basic]
Function Skip( _
   ByVal celt As Integer _
) As Integer
[C#]
int Skip(
   int celt
);
[C++]
int Skip(
   int celt
);
[JScript]
function Skip(
   celt : int
) : int;
```

Parameters

celt
    The number of elements to skip in the enumeration.

Return Value

S_OK if the number of elements skipped equals the *celt* parameter;
otherwise, **S_FALSE**.

Remarks

For more information about **IEnumString::Skip**, see the MSDN
Library.

UCOMIEnumVARIANT Interface

Manages the definition of the **IEnumVARIANT** interface.

```
[Visual Basic]
<Guid("00020404-0000-0000-C000-000000000046")>
<InterfaceType(ComInterfaceType.InterfaceIsIUnknown)>
Public Interface UCOMIEnumVARIANT
[C#]
[Guid("00020404-0000-0000-C000-000000000046")]
[InterfaceType(ComInterfaceType.InterfaceIsIUnknown)]
public interface UCOMIEnumVARIANT
[C++]
[Guid("00020404-0000-0000-C000-000000000046")]
[InterfaceType(ComInterfaceType::InterfaceIsIUnknown)]
public __gc __interface UCOMIEnumVARIANT
[JScript]
public
   Guid("00020404-0000-0000-C000-000000000046")
   InterfaceType(ComInterfaceType.InterfaceIsIUnknown)
interface UCOMIEnumVARIANT
```

Remarks

For more information about the **IEnumVARIANT** interface, see the MSDN Library.

Requirements

Namespace: System.Runtime.InteropServices

Platforms: Windows 98, Windows NT 4.0, Windows Millennium Edition, Windows 2000, Windows XP Home Edition, Windows XP Professional, Windows .NET Server family

Assembly: Mscorlib (in Mscorlib.dll)

UCOMIEnumVARIANT.Clone Method

Creates another enumerator that contains the same enumeration state as the current one.

```
[Visual Basic]
Sub Clone( _
   ByVal ppenum As Integer _
)
[C#]
void Clone(
   int ppenum
);
[C++]
void Clone(
   int ppenum
);
[JScript]
function Clone(
   ppenum : int
);
```

Parameters

ppenum
    On successful return, a reference to the newly created enumerator.

Remarks

For more information about **IEnumVARIANT::Clone**, see the MSDN Library.

Requirements

Platforms: Windows 98, Windows NT 4.0, Windows Millennium Edition, Windows 2000, Windows XP Home Edition, Windows XP Professional, Windows .NET Server family

UCOMIEnumVARIANT.Next Method

Retrieves a specified number of items in the enumeration sequence.

```
[Visual Basic]
Function Next( _
   ByVal celt As Integer, _
   ByVal rgvar As Integer, _
   ByVal pceltFetched As Integer _
) As Integer
[C#]
int Next(
   int celt,
   int rgvar,
   int pceltFetched
);
[C++]
int Next(
   int celt,
   int rgvar,
   int pceltFetched
);
[JScript]
function Next(
   celt : int,
   rgvar : int,
   pceltFetched : int
) : int;
```

Parameters

celt
    The number of elements to return in *rgelt*.
rgvar
    On successful return, a reference to the enumerated elements.
pceltFetched
    On successful return, a reference to the actual number of elements enumerated in *rgelt*.

Return Value

S_OK if the *pceltFetched* parameter equals the *celt* parameter; otherwise, **S_FALSE**.

Remarks

For more information about **IEnumVARIANT::Next**, see the MSDN Library.

Requirements

Platforms: Windows 98, Windows NT 4.0, Windows Millennium Edition, Windows 2000, Windows XP Home Edition, Windows XP Professional, Windows .NET Server family

UCOMIEnumVARIANT.Reset Method

Resets the enumeration sequence to the beginning.

```
[Visual Basic]
Function Reset() As Integer
[C#]
int Reset();
[C++]
int Reset();
[JScript]
function Reset() : int;
```

Return Value

An HRESULT with the value **S_OK**.

Remarks

For more information about **IEnumVARIANT::Reset**, see the MSDN Library.

Requirements

Platforms: Windows 98, Windows NT 4.0, Windows Millennium Edition, Windows 2000, Windows XP Home Edition, Windows XP Professional, Windows .NET Server family

UCOMIEnumVARIANT.Skip Method

Skips over a specified number of items in the enumeration sequence.

```
[Visual Basic]
Function Skip( _
    ByVal celt As Integer _
) As Integer
[C#]
int Skip(
    int celt
);
[C++]
int Skip(
    int celt
);
[JScript]
function Skip(
    celt : int
) : int;
```

Parameters

celt
    The number of elements to skip in the enumeration.

Return Value

S_OK if the number of elements skipped equals *celt* parameter; otherwise, **S_FALSE**.

Remarks

For more information about **IEnumVARIANT::Skip**, see the MSDN Library.

Requirements

Platforms: Windows 98, Windows NT 4.0, Windows Millennium Edition, Windows 2000, Windows XP Home Edition, Windows XP Professional, Windows .NET Server family

UCOMIMoniker Interface

Managed definition of the **IMoniker** interface, with COM functionality from **IPersist** and **IPersistStream**.

```
[Visual Basic]
<Guid("0000000f-0000-0000-C000-000000000046")>
<InterfaceType(ComInterfaceType.InterfaceIsIUnknown)>
Public Interface UCOMIMoniker
[C#]
[Guid("0000000f-0000-0000-C000-000000000046")]
[InterfaceType(ComInterfaceType.InterfaceIsIUnknown)]
public interface UCOMIMoniker
[C++]
[Guid("0000000f-0000-0000-C000-000000000046")]
[InterfaceType(ComInterfaceType::InterfaceIsIUnknown)]
public __gc __interface UCOMIMoniker
[JScript]
public
    Guid("0000000f-0000-0000-C000-000000000046")
    InterfaceType(ComInterfaceType.InterfaceIsIUnknown)
interface UCOMIMoniker
```

Remarks

For more information about the **IMoniker**, **IPersist**, and **IPersistStream** interfaces, see the MSDN Library.

Requirements

Namespace: System.Runtime.InteropServices

Platforms: Windows 98, Windows NT 4.0, Windows Millennium Edition, Windows 2000, Windows XP Home Edition, Windows XP Professional, Windows .NET Server family

Assembly: Mscorlib (in Mscorlib.dll)

UCOMIMoniker.BindToObject Method

Uses the moniker to bind to the object it identifies.

```
[Visual Basic]
Sub BindToObject( _
    ByVal pbc As UCOMIBindCtx, _
    ByVal pmkToLeft As UCOMIMoniker, _
    <InteropServices.In()> ByRef riidResult As Guid, _
    <Out()> ByRef ppvResult As Object _
)
[C#]
void BindToObject(
    UCOMIBindCtx pbc,
    UCOMIMoniker pmkToLeft,
    [
    In
    ] ref Guid riidResult,
    out object ppvResult
);
[C++]
void BindToObject(
    UCOMIBindCtx* pbc,
    UCOMIMoniker* pmkToLeft,
    [
    In
    ] Guid* riidResult,
```

```
    [
    Out
    ] Object** ppvResult
);
[JScript]
function BindToObject(
    pbc : UCOMIBindCtx,
    pmkToLeft : UCOMIMoniker,
    riidResult : Guid,
    ppvResult : Object
);
```

Parameters

pbc
A reference to the **IBindCtx** interface on the bind context object used in this binding operation.

pmkToLeft
A reference to the moniker to the left of this moniker, if the moniker is part of a composite moniker.

riidResult
The interface identifier (IID) of the interface the client intends to use to communicate with the object that the moniker identifies.

ppvResult
On successful return, reference to the interface requested by *riidResult*.

Remarks

For more information about **IMoniker::BindToObject**, see the MSDN Library.

Requirements

Platforms: Windows 98, Windows NT 4.0, Windows Millennium Edition, Windows 2000, Windows XP Home Edition, Windows XP Professional, Windows .NET Server family

UCOMIMoniker.BindToStorage Method

Retrieves an interface pointer to the storage that contains the object identified by the moniker.

```
[Visual Basic]
Sub BindToStorage( _
    ByVal pbc As UCOMIBindCtx, _
    ByVal pmkToLeft As UCOMIMoniker, _
    <InteropServices.In()> ByRef riid As Guid, _
    <Out()> ByRef ppvObj As Object _
)
[C#]
void BindToStorage(
    UCOMIBindCtx pbc,
    UCOMIMoniker pmkToLeft,
    [
    In
    ] ref Guid riid,
    out object ppvObj
);
[C++]
void BindToStorage(
    UCOMIBindCtx* pbc,
    UCOMIMoniker* pmkToLeft,
    [
    In
```

```
] Guid* riid,
  [
  Out
] Object** ppvObj
);
[JScript]
function BindToStorage(
  pbc : UCOMIBindCtx,
  pmkToLeft : UCOMIMoniker,
  riid : Guid,
  ppvObj : Object
);
```

Parameters

pbc

A reference to the **IBindCtx** interface on the bind context object used during this binding operation.

pmkToLeft

A reference to the moniker to the left of this moniker, if the moniker is part of a composite moniker.

riid

The interface identifier (IID) of the storage interface requested.

ppvObj

On successful return, a reference to the interface requested by *riid*.

Remarks

For more information about **IMoniker::BindToStorage**, see the MSDN Library.

Requirements

Platforms: Windows 98, Windows NT 4.0, Windows Millennium Edition, Windows 2000, Windows XP Home Edition, Windows XP Professional, Windows .NET Server family

UCOMIMoniker.CommonPrefixWith Method

Creates a new moniker based on the common prefix that this moniker shares with another moniker.

```
[Visual Basic]
Sub CommonPrefixWith( _
  ByVal pmkOther As UCOMIMoniker, _
  <Out()> ByRef ppmkPrefix As UCOMIMoniker _
)
[C#]
void CommonPrefixWith(
  UCOMIMoniker pmkOther,
  out UCOMIMoniker ppmkPrefix
);
[C++]
void CommonPrefixWith(
  UCOMIMoniker* pmkOther,
  [
  Out
] UCOMIMoniker** ppmkPrefix
);
[JScript]
function CommonPrefixWith(
  pmkOther : UCOMIMoniker,
  ppmkPrefix : UCOMIMoniker
);
```

Parameters

pmkOther

A reference to the **IMoniker** interface on another moniker to compare with this for a common prefix.

ppmkPrefix

On successful return, contains the moniker that is the common prefix of this moniker and *pmkOther*.

Remarks

For more information about **IMoniker::CommonPrefixWith**, see the MSDN Library.

Requirements

Platforms: Windows 98, Windows NT 4.0, Windows Millennium Edition, Windows 2000, Windows XP Home Edition, Windows XP Professional, Windows .NET Server family

UCOMIMoniker.ComposeWith Method

Combines the current moniker with another moniker, creating a new composite moniker.

```
[Visual Basic]
Sub ComposeWith( _
  ByVal pmkRight As UCOMIMoniker, _
  ByVal fOnlyIfNotGeneric As Boolean, _
  <Out()> ByRef ppmkComposite As UCOMIMoniker _
)
[C#]
void ComposeWith(
  UCOMIMoniker pmkRight,
  bool fOnlyIfNotGeneric,
  out UCOMIMoniker ppmkComposite
);
[C++]
void ComposeWith(
  UCOMIMoniker* pmkRight,
  bool fOnlyIfNotGeneric,
  [
  Out
] UCOMIMoniker** ppmkComposite
);
[JScript]
function ComposeWith(
  pmkRight : UCOMIMoniker,
  fOnlyIfNotGeneric : Boolean,
  ppmkComposite : UCOMIMoniker
);
```

Parameters

pmkRight

A reference to the **IMoniker** interface on the moniker to compose onto the end of this moniker.

fOnlyIfNotGeneric

If **true**, the caller requires a nongeneric composition, so the operation proceeds only if *pmkRight* is a moniker class that this moniker can compose with in some way other than forming a generic composite. If **false**, the method can create a generic composite if necessary.

ppmkComposite

On successful return, a reference to the resulting composite moniker.

Remarks

For more information about **IMoniker::ComposeWith**, see the MSDN Library.

Requirements

Platforms: Windows 98, Windows NT 4.0, Windows Millennium Edition, Windows 2000, Windows XP Home Edition, Windows XP Professional, Windows .NET Server family

UCOMIMoniker.Enum Method

Supplies a pointer to an enumerator that can enumerate the components of a composite moniker.

```
[Visual Basic]
Sub Enum( _
    ByVal fForward As Boolean, _
    <Out()> ByRef ppenumMoniker As UCOMIEnumMoniker _
)
[C#]
void Enum(
    bool fForward,
    out UCOMIEnumMoniker ppenumMoniker
);
[C++]
void Enum(
    bool fForward,
    [
    Out
] UCOMIEnumMoniker** ppenumMoniker
);
[JScript]
function Enum(
    fForward : Boolean,
    ppenumMoniker : UCOMIEnumMoniker
);
```

Parameters

fForward
> If **true**, enumerates the monikers from left to right. If **false**, enumerates from right to left.

ppenumMoniker
> On successful return, references the enumerator object for the moniker.

Remarks

For more information about **IMoniker::Enum**, see the MSDN Library.

Requirements

Platforms: Windows 98, Windows NT 4.0, Windows Millennium Edition, Windows 2000, Windows XP Home Edition, Windows XP Professional, Windows .NET Server family

UCOMIMoniker.GetClassID Method

Retrieves the class identifier (CLSID) of an object.

```
[Visual Basic]
Sub GetClassID( _
    <Out()> ByRef pClassID As Guid _
)
```

```
[C#]
void GetClassID(
    out Guid pClassID
);
[C++]
void GetClassID(
    [
    Out
] Guid* pClassID
);
[JScript]
function GetClassID(
    pClassID : Guid
);
```

Parameters

pClassID
> On successful return, contains the CLSID.

Remarks

For more information about **IPersist::GetClassID**, see the MSDN Library.

Requirements

Platforms: Windows 98, Windows NT 4.0, Windows Millennium Edition, Windows 2000, Windows XP Home Edition, Windows XP Professional, Windows .NET Server family

UCOMIMoniker.GetDisplayName Method

Gets the display name, which is a user-readable representation of this moniker.

```
[Visual Basic]
Sub GetDisplayName( _
    ByVal pbc As UCOMIBindCtx, _
    ByVal pmkToLeft As UCOMIMoniker, _
    <Out()> ByRef ppszDisplayName As String _
)
[C#]
void GetDisplayName(
    UCOMIBindCtx pbc,
    UCOMIMoniker pmkToLeft,
    out string ppszDisplayName
);
[C++]
void GetDisplayName(
    UCOMIBindCtx* pbc,
    UCOMIMoniker* pmkToLeft,
    [
    Out
] String** ppszDisplayName
);
[JScript]
function GetDisplayName(
    pbc : UCOMIBindCtx,
    pmkToLeft : UCOMIMoniker,
    ppszDisplayName : String
);
```

Parameters

pbc
> A reference to the bind context to use in this operation.

pmkToLeft
> A reference to the moniker to the left of this moniker, if the moniker is part of a composite moniker.

ppszDisplayName
> On successful return, contains the display name string.

Remarks

For more information about **IMoniker::GetDisplayName**, see the MSDN Library.

Requirements

Platforms: Windows 98, Windows NT 4.0, Windows Millennium Edition, Windows 2000, Windows XP Home Edition, Windows XP Professional, Windows .NET Server family

UCOMIMoniker.GetSizeMax Method

Returns the size in bytes of the stream needed to save the object.

```
[Visual Basic]
Sub GetSizeMax( _
    <Out()> ByRef pcbSize As Long _
)
[C#]
void GetSizeMax(
    out long pcbSize
);
[C++]
void GetSizeMax(
    [
    Out
    ] __int64* pcbSize
);
[JScript]
function GetSizeMax(
    pcbSize : long
);
```

Parameters

pcbSize
> On successful return, contains a **long** value indicating the size in bytes of the stream needed to save this object.

Remarks

For more information about **IPersistStream::GetSizeMax**, see the MSDN Library.

Requirements

Platforms: Windows 98, Windows NT 4.0, Windows Millennium Edition, Windows 2000, Windows XP Home Edition, Windows XP Professional, Windows .NET Server family

UCOMIMoniker.GetTimeOfLastChange Method

Provides a number representing the time the object identified by this moniker was last changed.

```
[Visual Basic]
Sub GetTimeOfLastChange( _
    ByVal pbc As UCOMIBindCtx, _
    ByVal pmkToLeft As UCOMIMoniker, _
    <Out()> ByRef pFileTime As FILETIME _
)
[C#]
void GetTimeOfLastChange(
    UCOMIBindCtx pbc,
    UCOMIMoniker pmkToLeft,
    out FILETIME pFileTime
);
[C++]
void GetTimeOfLastChange(
    UCOMIBindCtx* pbc,
    UCOMIMoniker* pmkToLeft,
    [
    Out
    ] FILETIME* pFileTime
);
[JScript]
function GetTimeOfLastChange(
    pbc : UCOMIBindCtx,
    pmkToLeft : UCOMIMoniker,
    pFileTime : FILETIME
);
```

Parameters

pbc
> A reference to the bind context to be used in this binding operation.

pmkToLeft
> A reference to the moniker to the left of this moniker, if the moniker is part of a composite moniker.

pFileTime
> On successful return, contains the time of last change.

Remarks

For more information about **IMoniker::GetTimeOfLastChange**, see the MSDN Library.

Requirements

Platforms: Windows 98, Windows NT 4.0, Windows Millennium Edition, Windows 2000, Windows XP Home Edition, Windows XP Professional, Windows .NET Server family

UCOMIMoniker.Hash Method

Calculates a 32-bit integer using the internal state of the moniker.

```
[Visual Basic]
Sub Hash( _
    <Out()> ByRef pdwHash As Integer _
)
[C#]
void Hash(
    out int pdwHash
);
```

```
[C++]
void Hash(
    [
    Out
] int* pdwHash
);
[JScript]
function Hash(
    pdwHash : int
);
```

Parameters
pdwHash
    On successful return, contains the hash value for this moniker.

Remarks
For more information about **IMoniker::Hash**, see the MSDN Library.

Requirements
Platforms: Windows 98, Windows NT 4.0, Windows Millennium Edition, Windows 2000, Windows XP Home Edition, Windows XP Professional, Windows .NET Server family

UCOMIMoniker.Inverse Method

Provides a moniker that, when composed to the right of this moniker or one of similar structure, composes to nothing.

```
[Visual Basic]
Sub Inverse( _
    <Out()> ByRef ppmk As UCOMIMoniker _
)
[C#]
void Inverse(
    out UCOMIMoniker ppmk
);
[C++]
void Inverse(
    [
    Out
] UCOMIMoniker** ppmk
);
[JScript]
function Inverse(
    ppmk : UCOMIMoniker
);
```

Parameters
ppmk
    On successful return, contains a moniker that is the inverse of this moniker.

Remarks
For more information about **IMoniker::Inverse**, see the MSDN Library.

Requirements
Platforms: Windows 98, Windows NT 4.0, Windows Millennium Edition, Windows 2000, Windows XP Home Edition, Windows XP Professional, Windows .NET Server family

UCOMIMoniker.IsDirty Method

Checks the object for changes since it was last saved.

```
[Visual Basic]
Function IsDirty() As Integer
[C#]
int IsDirty();
[C++]
int IsDirty();
[JScript]
function IsDirty() : int;
```

Remarks
For more information about **IPersistStream::IsDirty**, see the MSDN Library.

Requirements
Platforms: Windows 98, Windows NT 4.0, Windows Millennium Edition, Windows 2000, Windows XP Home Edition, Windows XP Professional, Windows .NET Server family

UCOMIMoniker.IsEqual Method

Compares this moniker with a specified moniker and indicates whether they are identical.

```
[Visual Basic]
Sub IsEqual( _
    ByVal pmkOtherMoniker As UCOMIMoniker _
)
[C#]
void IsEqual(
    UCOMIMoniker pmkOtherMoniker
);
[C++]
void IsEqual(
    UCOMIMoniker* pmkOtherMoniker
);
[JScript]
function IsEqual(
    pmkOtherMoniker : UCOMIMoniker
);
```

Parameters
pmkOtherMoniker
    A reference to the moniker to be used for comparison.

Remarks
For more information about **IMoniker::IsEqual**, see the MSDN Library.

Requirements
Platforms: Windows 98, Windows NT 4.0, Windows Millennium Edition, Windows 2000, Windows XP Home Edition, Windows XP Professional, Windows .NET Server family

UCOMIMoniker.IsRunning Method

Determines whether the object that is identified by this moniker is currently loaded and running.

```vb
[Visual Basic]
Sub IsRunning( _
    ByVal pbc As UCOMIBindCtx, _
    ByVal pmkToLeft As UCOMIMoniker, _
    ByVal pmkNewlyRunning As UCOMIMoniker _
)
```

```csharp
[C#]
void IsRunning(
    UCOMIBindCtx pbc,
    UCOMIMoniker pmkToLeft,
    UCOMIMoniker pmkNewlyRunning
);
```

```cpp
[C++]
void IsRunning(
    UCOMIBindCtx* pbc,
    UCOMIMoniker* pmkToLeft,
    UCOMIMoniker* pmkNewlyRunning
);
```

```jscript
[JScript]
function IsRunning(
    pbc : UCOMIBindCtx,
    pmkToLeft : UCOMIMoniker,
    pmkNewlyRunning : UCOMIMoniker
);
```

Parameters

pbc

A reference to the bind context to be used in this binding operation.

pmkToLeft

A reference to the moniker to the left of this moniker if this moniker is part of a composite.

pmkNewlyRunning

A reference to the moniker most recently added to the Running Object Table.

Remarks

For more information about **IMoniker::IsRunning**, see the MSDN Library.

Requirements

Platforms: Windows 98, Windows NT 4.0, Windows Millennium Edition, Windows 2000, Windows XP Home Edition, Windows XP Professional, Windows .NET Server family

UCOMIMoniker.IsSystemMoniker Method

Indicates whether this moniker is of one of the system-supplied moniker classes.

```vb
[Visual Basic]
Sub IsSystemMoniker( _
    <Out()> ByRef pdwMksys As Integer _
)
```

```csharp
[C#]
void IsSystemMoniker(
    out int pdwMksys
);
```

```cpp
[C++]
void IsSystemMoniker(
    [
    Out
] int* pdwMksys
);
```

```jscript
[JScript]
function IsSystemMoniker(
    pdwMksys : int
);
```

Parameters

pdwMksys

A pointer to an integer that is one of the values from the **MKSYS** enumeration, and refers to one of the COM moniker classes.

Remarks

For details on the values of the **MKSYS** enumeration and for information about **IMoniker::IsSystemMoniker**, see the MSDN Library.

Requirements

Platforms: Windows 98, Windows NT 4.0, Windows Millennium Edition, Windows 2000, Windows XP Home Edition, Windows XP Professional, Windows .NET Server family

UCOMIMoniker.Load Method

Initializes an object from the stream where it was previously saved.

```vb
[Visual Basic]
Sub Load( _
    ByVal pStm As UCOMIStream _
)
```

```csharp
[C#]
void Load(
    UCOMIStream pStm
);
```

```cpp
[C++]
void Load(
    UCOMIStream* pStm
);
```

```jscript
[JScript]
function Load(
    pStm : UCOMIStream
);
```

Parameters

pStm

Stream from which the object is loaded.

Remarks

For more information about **IPersistStream::Load**, see the MSDN Library.

Requirements

Platforms: Windows 98, Windows NT 4.0, Windows Millennium Edition, Windows 2000, Windows XP Home Edition, Windows XP Professional, Windows .NET Server family

UCOMIMoniker.ParseDisplayName Method

Reads as many characters of the specified display name as it
understands and builds a moniker corresponding to the portion read.

```
[Visual Basic]
Sub ParseDisplayName( _
   ByVal pbc As UCOMIBindCtx, _
   ByVal pmkToLeft As UCOMIMoniker, _
   ByVal pszDisplayName As String, _
   <Out()> ByRef pchEaten As Integer, _
   <Out()> ByRef ppmkOut As UCOMIMoniker _
)
[C#]
void ParseDisplayName(
   UCOMIBindCtx pbc,
   UCOMIMoniker pmkToLeft,
   string pszDisplayName,
   out int pchEaten,
   out UCOMIMoniker ppmkOut
);
[C++]
void ParseDisplayName(
   UCOMIBindCtx* pbc,
   UCOMIMoniker* pmkToLeft,
   String* pszDisplayName,
   [
   Out
   ] int* pchEaten,
   [
   Out
   ] UCOMIMoniker** ppmkOut
);
[JScript]
function ParseDisplayName(
   pbc : UCOMIBindCtx,
   pmkToLeft : UCOMIMoniker,
   pszDisplayName : String,
   pchEaten : int,
   ppmkOut : UCOMIMoniker
);
```

Parameters

pbc
   A reference to the bind context to be used in this binding
   operation.
pmkToLeft
   A reference to the moniker that has been built out of the display
   name up to this point.
pszDisplayName
   A reference to the string containing the remaining display name
   to parse.
pchEaten
   On successful return, contains the number of characters in
   pszDisplayName that were consumed in this step.
ppmkOut
   Reference to the moniker that was built from *pszDisplayName*.

Remarks

For more information about **IMoniker::ParseDisplayName**, see the
MSDN Library.

Requirements

Platforms: Windows 98, Windows NT 4.0,
Windows Millennium Edition, Windows 2000,
Windows XP Home Edition, Windows XP Professional,
Windows .NET Server family

UCOMIMoniker.Reduce Method

Returns a reduced moniker which is another moniker that refers to
the same object as this moniker but can be bound with equal or
greater efficiency.

```
[Visual Basic]
Sub Reduce( _
   ByVal pbc As UCOMIBindCtx, _
   ByVal dwReduceHowFar As Integer, _
   ByRef ppmkToLeft As UCOMIMoniker, _
   <Out()> ByRef ppmkReduced As UCOMIMoniker _
)
[C#]
void Reduce(
   UCOMIBindCtx pbc,
   int dwReduceHowFar,
   ref UCOMIMoniker ppmkToLeft,
   out UCOMIMoniker ppmkReduced
);
[C++]
void Reduce(
   UCOMIBindCtx* pbc,
   int dwReduceHowFar,
   UCOMIMoniker** ppmkToLeft,
   [
   Out
   ] UCOMIMoniker** ppmkReduced
);
[JScript]
function Reduce(
   pbc : UCOMIBindCtx,
   dwReduceHowFar : int,
   ppmkToLeft : UCOMIMoniker,
   ppmkReduced : UCOMIMoniker
);
```

Parameters

pbc
   A reference to the **IBindCtx** interface on the bind context to be
   used in this binding operation.
dwReduceHowFar
   Specifies how far this moniker should be reduced.
ppmkToLeft
   A reference to the moniker to the left of this moniker.
ppmkReduced
   On successful return, a reference to the reduced form of this
   moniker, which can be a null reference (**Nothing** in Visual Basic)
   if an error occurs or if this moniker is reduced to nothing.

Remarks

For more information about **IMoniker::Reduce**, see the MSDN
Library.

Requirements

Platforms: Windows 98, Windows NT 4.0,
Windows Millennium Edition, Windows 2000,
Windows XP Home Edition, Windows XP Professional,
Windows .NET Server family

UCOMIMoniker.RelativePathTo Method

Supplies a moniker that, when appended to this moniker (or one with
a similar structure), yields the specified moniker.

```
[Visual Basic]
Sub RelativePathTo( _
    ByVal pmkOther As UCOMIMoniker, _
    <Out()> ByRef ppmkRelPath As UCOMIMoniker _
)
[C#]
void RelativePathTo(
    UCOMIMoniker pmkOther,
    out UCOMIMoniker ppmkRelPath
);
[C++]
void RelativePathTo(
    UCOMIMoniker* pmkOther,
    [
    Out
] UCOMIMoniker** ppmkRelPath
);
[JScript]
function RelativePathTo(
    pmkOther : UCOMIMoniker,
    ppmkRelPath : UCOMIMoniker
);
```

Parameters

pmkOther
> A reference to the moniker to which a relative path should be
> taken.

ppmkRelPath
> On successful return, reference to the relative moniker.

Remarks

For more information about **IMoniker::RelativePath**, see the
MSDN Library.

Requirements

Platforms: Windows 98, Windows NT 4.0,
Windows Millennium Edition, Windows 2000,
Windows XP Home Edition, Windows XP Professional,
Windows .NET Server family

UCOMIMoniker.Save Method

Saves an object to the specified stream.

```
[Visual Basic]
Sub Save( _
    ByVal pStm As UCOMIStream, _
    ByVal fClearDirty As Boolean _
)
```

```
[C#]
void Save(
    UCOMIStream pStm,
    bool fClearDirty
);
[C++]
void Save(
    UCOMIStream* pStm,
    bool fClearDirty
);
[JScript]
function Save(
    pStm : UCOMIStream,
    fClearDirty : Boolean
);
```

Parameters

pStm
> The stream into which the object is saved.

fClearDirty
> Indicates whether to clear the modified flag after the save is
> complete.

Remarks

For more information about **IPersistStream::Save**, see the MSDN
Library.

Requirements

Platforms: Windows 98, Windows NT 4.0,
Windows Millennium Edition, Windows 2000,
Windows XP Home Edition, Windows XP Professional,
Windows .NET Server family

UCOMIPersistFile Interface

Managed definition of the **IPersistFile** interface, with functionality from **IPersist**.

```
[Visual Basic]
<Guid("0000010b-0000-0000-C000-000000000046")>
<InterfaceType(ComInterfaceType.InterfaceIsIUnknown)>
Public Interface UCOMIPersistFile
[C#]
[Guid("0000010b-0000-0000-C000-000000000046")]
[InterfaceType(ComInterfaceType.InterfaceIsIUnknown)]
public interface UCOMIPersistFile
[C++]
[Guid("0000010b-0000-0000-C000-000000000046")]
[InterfaceType(ComInterfaceType::InterfaceIsIUnknown)]
public __gc __interface UCOMIPersistFile
[JScript]
public
    Guid("0000010b-0000-0000-C000-000000000046")
    InterfaceType(ComInterfaceType.InterfaceIsIUnknown)
interface UCOMIPersistFile
```

Remarks

For more information, please see the existing documentation for **IPersistFile** and **IPersist** in the com subfolder of the MSDN library.

Requirements

Namespace: System.Runtime.InteropServices

Platforms: Windows 98, Windows NT 4.0, Windows Millennium Edition, Windows 2000, Windows XP Home Edition, Windows XP Professional, Windows .NET Server family

Assembly: Mscorlib (in Mscorlib.dll)

UCOMIPersistFile.GetClassID Method

Retrieves the class identifier (CLSID) of an object.

```
[Visual Basic]
Sub GetClassID( _
    <Out()> ByRef pClassID As Guid _
)
[C#]
void GetClassID(
    out Guid pClassID
);
[C++]
void GetClassID(
    [
    Out
    ] Guid* pClassID
);
[JScript]
function GetClassID(
    pClassID : Guid
);
```

Parameters

pClassID
   On successful return, a reference to the CLSID.

Remarks

For more information, please see the existing documentation for **IPersist::GetClassID** in the MSDN library.

Requirements

Platforms: Windows 98, Windows NT 4.0, Windows Millennium Edition, Windows 2000, Windows XP Home Edition, Windows XP Professional, Windows .NET Server family

UCOMIPersistFile.GetCurFile Method

Retrieves either the absolute path to current working file of the object, or if there is no current working file, the default filename prompt of the object.

```
[Visual Basic]
Sub GetCurFile( _
    <Out()> ByRef ppszFileName As String _
)
[C#]
void GetCurFile(
    out string ppszFileName
);
[C++]
void GetCurFile(
    [
    Out
    ] String** ppszFileName
);
[JScript]
function GetCurFile(
    ppszFileName : String
);
```

Parameters

ppszFileName
   The address of a pointer to a zero-terminated string containing the path for the current file, or the default filename prompt (such as *.txt).

Remarks

For more information, please see the existing documentation for **IPersistFile::GetCurFile** in the MSDN library.

Requirements

Platforms: Windows 98, Windows NT 4.0, Windows Millennium Edition, Windows 2000, Windows XP Home Edition, Windows XP Professional, Windows .NET Server family

UCOMIPersistFile.IsDirty Method

Checks an object for changes since it was last saved to its current file.

```
[Visual Basic]
Function IsDirty() As Integer
[C#]
int IsDirty();
[C++]
int IsDirty();
[JScript]
function IsDirty() : int;
```

Return Value

S_OK if the file has changed since it was last saved; **S_FALSE** if the file has not changed since it was last saved.

Remarks

For more information, please see the existing documentation for **IPersistFile::IsDirty** in the MSDN library.

Requirements

Platforms: Windows 98, Windows NT 4.0, Windows Millennium Edition, Windows 2000, Windows XP Home Edition, Windows XP Professional, Windows .NET Server family

UCOMIPersistFile.Load Method

Opens the specified file and initializes an object from the file contents.

```
[Visual Basic]
Sub Load( _
   ByVal pszFileName As String, _
   ByVal dwMode As Integer _
)
[C#]
void Load(
   string pszFileName,
   int dwMode
);
[C++]
void Load(
   String* pszFileName,
   int dwMode
);
[JScript]
function Load(
   pszFileName : String,
   dwMode : int
);
```

Parameters

pszFileName
   A zero-terminated string containing the absolute path of the file to open.
dwMode
   A combination of values from the **STGM** enumeration to indicate the access mode in which to open *pszFileName*.

Remarks

The **STGM** enumeration is not part of the .NET Framework, but is documented in the MSDN library.

For more information, please see the existing documentation for **IPersistFile::Load** in the MSDN library.

Requirements

Platforms: Windows 98, Windows NT 4.0, Windows Millennium Edition, Windows 2000, Windows XP Home Edition, Windows XP Professional, Windows .NET Server family

UCOMIPersistFile.Save Method

Saves a copy of the object into the specified file.

```
[Visual Basic]
Sub Save( _
   ByVal pszFileName As String, _
   ByVal fRemember As Boolean _
)
[C#]
void Save(
   string pszFileName,
   bool fRemember
);
[C++]
void Save(
   String* pszFileName,
   bool fRemember
);
[JScript]
function Save(
   pszFileName : String,
   fRemember : Boolean
);
```

Parameters

pszFileName
   A zero-terminated string containing the absolute path of the file to which the object is saved.
fRemember
   Indicates whether *pszFileName* is to be used as the current working file.

Remarks

For more information, please see the existing documentation for **IPersistFile::Save** in the MSDN library.

Requirements

Platforms: Windows 98, Windows NT 4.0, Windows Millennium Edition, Windows 2000, Windows XP Home Edition, Windows XP Professional, Windows .NET Server family

UCOMIPersistFile.SaveCompleted Method

Notifies the object that it can write to its file.

```
[Visual Basic]
Sub SaveCompleted( _
   ByVal pszFileName As String _
)
[C#]
void SaveCompleted(
   string pszFileName
);
[C++]
void SaveCompleted(
   String* pszFileName
);
[JScript]
function SaveCompleted(
   pszFileName : String
);
```

Parameters

pszFileName

>   The absolute path of the file where the object was previously saved.

Remarks

For more information, please see the existing documentation for **IPersistFile::SaveCompleted** in the MSDN library.

Requirements

Platforms: Windows 98, Windows NT 4.0, Windows Millennium Edition, Windows 2000, Windows XP Home Edition, Windows XP Professional, Windows .NET Server family

UCOMIRunningObjectTable Interface

Managed definition of the **IRunningObjectTable** interface.

```
[Visual Basic]
<Guid("00000010-0000-0000-C000-000000000046")>
<InterfaceType(ComInterfaceType.InterfaceIsIUnknown)>
Public Interface UCOMIRunningObjectTable
[C#]
[Guid("00000010-0000-0000-C000-000000000046")]
[InterfaceType(ComInterfaceType.InterfaceIsIUnknown)]
public interface UCOMIRunningObjectTable
[C++]
[Guid("00000010-0000-0000-C000-000000000046")]
[InterfaceType(ComInterfaceType::InterfaceIsIUnknown)]
public __gc __interface UCOMIRunningObjectTable
[JScript]
public
    Guid("00000010-0000-0000-C000-000000000046")
    InterfaceType(ComInterfaceType.InterfaceIsIUnknown)
interface UCOMIRunningObjectTable
```

Remarks

For more information, please see the existing documentation for
IRunningObjectTable in the com subfolder of the MSDN library.

Requirements

Namespace: System.Runtime.InteropServices

Platforms: Windows 98, Windows NT 4.0,
Windows Millennium Edition, Windows 2000,
Windows XP Home Edition, Windows XP Professional,
Windows .NET Server family

Assembly: Mscorlib (in Mscorlib.dll)

UCOMIRunningObjectTable.EnumRunning Method

Enumerates the objects currently registered as running.

```
[Visual Basic]
Sub EnumRunning( _
    <Out()> ByRef ppenumMoniker As UCOMIEnumMoniker _
)
[C#]
void EnumRunning(
    out UCOMIEnumMoniker ppenumMoniker
);
[C++]
void EnumRunning(
    [
    Out
] UCOMIEnumMoniker** ppenumMoniker
);
[JScript]
function EnumRunning(
    ppenumMoniker : UCOMIEnumMoniker
);
```

Parameters

ppenumMoniker
> On successful return, the new enumerator for the ROT.

Remarks

For more information, please see the existing documentation for
IRunningObjectTable::EnumRunning in the MSDN library.

Requirements

Platforms: Windows 98, Windows NT 4.0,
Windows Millennium Edition, Windows 2000,
Windows XP Home Edition, Windows XP Professional,
Windows .NET Server family

UCOMIRunningObjectTable.GetObject Method

Returns the registered object if the supplied object name is registered
as running.

```
[Visual Basic]
Sub GetObject( _
    ByVal pmkObjectName As UCOMIMoniker, _
    <Out()> ByRef ppunkObject As Object _
)
[C#]
void GetObject(
    UCOMIMoniker pmkObjectName,
    out object ppunkObject
);
[C++]
void GetObject(
    UCOMIMoniker* pmkObjectName,
    [
    Out
] Object** ppunkObject
);
[JScript]
function GetObject(
    pmkObjectName : UCOMIMoniker,
    ppunkObject : Object
);
```

Parameters

pmkObjectName
> Reference to the moniker to search for in the ROT.

ppunkObject
> On successful return, contains the requested running object.

Remarks

For more information, please see the existing documentation for
IRunningObjectTable::GetObject in the MSDN library.

Requirements

Platforms: Windows 98, Windows NT 4.0,
Windows Millennium Edition, Windows 2000,
Windows XP Home Edition, Windows XP Professional,
Windows .NET Server family

UCOMIRunningObjectTable.GetTimeOfLast-Change Method

Searches for this moniker in the ROT and reports the recorded time of change, if present.

```
[Visual Basic]
Sub GetTimeOfLastChange( _
   ByVal pmkObjectName As UCOMIMoniker, _
   <Out()> ByRef pfiletime As FILETIME _
)
[C#]
void GetTimeOfLastChange(
   UCOMIMoniker pmkObjectName,
   out FILETIME pfiletime
);
[C++]
void GetTimeOfLastChange(
   UCOMIMoniker* pmkObjectName,
   [
   Out
] FILETIME* pfiletime
);
[JScript]
function GetTimeOfLastChange(
   pmkObjectName : UCOMIMoniker,
   pfiletime : FILETIME
);
```

Parameters

pmkObjectName
   Reference to the moniker to search for in the ROT.
pfiletime
   On successful return, contains the objects last change time.

Remarks

For more information, please see the existing documentation for **IRunningObjectTable::GetTimeOfLastChange** in the MSDN library.

Requirements

Platforms: Windows 98, Windows NT 4.0, Windows Millennium Edition, Windows 2000, Windows XP Home Edition, Windows XP Professional, Windows .NET Server family

UCOMIRunningObjectTable.IsRunning Method

Determines if the specified moniker is currently registered in the Running Object Table.

```
[Visual Basic]
Sub IsRunning( _
   ByVal pmkObjectName As UCOMIMoniker _
)
[C#]
void IsRunning(
   UCOMIMoniker pmkObjectName
);
[C++]
void IsRunning(
   UCOMIMoniker* pmkObjectName
);
```

```
[JScript]
function IsRunning(
   pmkObjectName : UCOMIMoniker
);
```

Parameters

pmkObjectName
   Reference to the moniker to search for in the Running Object Table.

Remarks

For more information, please see the existing documentation for **IRunningObjectTable::IsRunning** in the MSDN library.

Requirements

Platforms: Windows 98, Windows NT 4.0, Windows Millennium Edition, Windows 2000, Windows XP Home Edition, Windows XP Professional, Windows .NET Server family

UCOMIRunningObjectTable.NoteChangeTime Method

Makes a note of the time that a particular object has changed so **IMoniker::GetTimeOfLastChange** can report an appropriate change time.

```
[Visual Basic]
Sub NoteChangeTime( _
   ByVal dwRegister As Integer, _
   ByRef pfiletime As FILETIME _
)
[C#]
void NoteChangeTime(
   int dwRegister,
   ref FILETIME pfiletime
);
[C++]
void NoteChangeTime(
   int dwRegister,
   FILETIME* pfiletime
);
[JScript]
function NoteChangeTime(
   dwRegister : int,
   pfiletime : FILETIME
);
```

Parameters

dwRegister
   The ROT entry of the changed object.
pfiletime
   Reference to the object's last change time.

Remarks

For more information, please see the existing documentation for **IRunningObjectTable::NoteChangeTime** in the MSDN library.

Requirements

Platforms: Windows 98, Windows NT 4.0, Windows Millennium Edition, Windows 2000, Windows XP Home Edition, Windows XP Professional, Windows .NET Server family

UCOMIRunningObjectTable.Register Method

Registers that the supplied object has entered the running state.

```
[Visual Basic]
Sub Register( _
    ByVal grfFlags As Integer, _
    ByVal punkObject As Object, _
    ByVal pmkObjectName As UCOMIMoniker, _
    <Out()> ByRef pdwRegister As Integer _
)
[C#]
void Register(
    int grfFlags,
    object punkObject,
    UCOMIMoniker pmkObjectName,
    out int pdwRegister
);
[C++]
void Register(
    int grfFlags,
    Object* punkObject,
    UCOMIMoniker* pmkObjectName,
    [
    Out
] int* pdwRegister
);
[JScript]
function Register(
    grfFlags : int,
    punkObject : Object,
    pmkObjectName : UCOMIMoniker,
    pdwRegister : int
);
```

Parameters

grfFlags
Specifies whether the Running Object Table's (ROT) reference to *punkObject* is weak or strong, and controls access to the object through its entry in the ROT.

punkObject
Reference to the object being registered as running.

pmkObjectName
Reference to the moniker that identifies *punkObject*.

pdwRegister
Reference to a 32-bit value that can be used to identify this ROT entry in subsequent calls to **Revoke** or **NoteChangeTime**.

Remarks

For more information, please see the existing documentation for **IRunningObjectTable::Register** in the MSDN library.

Requirements

Platforms: Windows 98, Windows NT 4.0, Windows Millennium Edition, Windows 2000, Windows XP Home Edition, Windows XP Professional, Windows .NET Server family

UCOMIRunningObjectTable.Revoke Method

Unregisters the specified object from the ROT.

```
[Visual Basic]
Sub Revoke( _
    ByVal dwRegister As Integer _
)
[C#]
void Revoke(
    int dwRegister
);
[C++]
void Revoke(
    int dwRegister
);
[JScript]
function Revoke(
    dwRegister : int
);
```

Parameters

dwRegister
The ROT entry to revoke.

Remarks

For more information, please see the existing documentation for **IRunningObjectTable::Revoke** in the MSDN library.

Requirements

Platforms: Windows 98, Windows NT 4.0, Windows Millennium Edition, Windows 2000, Windows XP Home Edition, Windows XP Professional, Windows .NET Server family

UCOMIStream Interface

Managed definition of the **IStream** interface, with **ISequentialStream** functionality.

```
[Visual Basic]
<Guid("0000000c-0000-0000-C000-000000000046")>
<InterfaceType(ComInterfaceType.InterfaceIsIUnknown)>
Public Interface UCOMIStream
[C#]
[Guid("0000000c-0000-0000-C000-000000000046")]
[InterfaceType(ComInterfaceType.InterfaceIsIUnknown)]
public interface UCOMIStream
[C++]
[Guid("0000000c-0000-0000-C000-000000000046")]
[InterfaceType(ComInterfaceType::InterfaceIsIUnknown)]
public __gc __interface UCOMIStream
[JScript]
public
    Guid("0000000c-0000-0000-C000-000000000046")
    InterfaceType(ComInterfaceType.InterfaceIsIUnknown)
interface UCOMIStream
```

Remarks

For more information, please see the existing documentation for **IStream** and **ISequentialStream** in the com subfolder of the MSDN library.

Requirements

Namespace: System.Runtime.InteropServices

Platforms: Windows 98, Windows NT 4.0, Windows Millennium Edition, Windows 2000, Windows XP Home Edition, Windows XP Professional, Windows .NET Server family

Assembly: Mscorlib (in Mscorlib.dll)

UCOMIStream.Clone Method

Creates a new stream object with its own seek pointer that references the same bytes as the original stream.

```
[Visual Basic]
Sub Clone( _
    <Out()> ByRef ppstm As UCOMIStream _
)
[C#]
void Clone(
    out UCOMIStream ppstm
);
[C++]
void Clone(
    [
    Out
] UCOMIStream** ppstm
);
[JScript]
function Clone(
    ppstm : UCOMIStream
);
```

Parameters

ppstm
    On successful return, contains the new stream object.

Remarks

For more information, please see the existing documentation for **IStream::Clone** in the MSDN library.

Requirements

Platforms: Windows 98, Windows NT 4.0, Windows Millennium Edition, Windows 2000, Windows XP Home Edition, Windows XP Professional, Windows .NET Server family

UCOMIStream.Commit Method

Ensures that any changes made to a stream object open in transacted mode are reflected in the parent storage.

```
[Visual Basic]
Sub Commit( _
    ByVal grfCommitFlags As Integer _
)
[C#]
void Commit(
    int grfCommitFlags
);
[C++]
void Commit(
    int grfCommitFlags
);
[JScript]
function Commit(
    grfCommitFlags : int
);
```

Parameters

grfCommitFlags
    Controls how the changes for the stream object are committed.

Remarks

For more information, please see the existing documentation for **IStream::Commit** in the MSDN library.

Requirements

Platforms: Windows 98, Windows NT 4.0, Windows Millennium Edition, Windows 2000, Windows XP Home Edition, Windows XP Professional, Windows .NET Server family

UCOMIStream.CopyTo Method

Copies a specified number of bytes from the current seek pointer in the stream to the current seek pointer in another stream.

```
[Visual Basic]
Sub CopyTo( _
    ByVal pstm As UCOMIStream, _
    ByVal cb As Long, _
    ByVal pcbRead As IntPtr, _
    ByVal pcbWritten As IntPtr _
)
[C#]
void CopyTo(
    UCOMIStream pstm,
    long cb,
    IntPtr pcbRead,
    IntPtr pcbWritten
);
```

```
[C++]
void CopyTo(
    UCOMIStream* pstm,
    __int64 cb,
    IntPtr pcbRead,
    IntPtr pcbWritten
);
[JScript]
function CopyTo(
    pstm : UCOMIStream,
    cb : long,
    pcbRead : IntPtr,
    pcbWritten : IntPtr
);
```

Parameters

pstm

Reference to the destination stream.

cb

The number of bytes to copy from the source stream.

pcbRead

On successful return, contains the actual number of bytes read from the source.

pcbWritten

On successful return, contains the actual number of bytes written to the destination.

Remarks

For more information, please see the existing documentation for **IStream::CopyTo** in the MSDN library.

Requirements

Platforms: Windows 98, Windows NT 4.0, Windows Millennium Edition, Windows 2000, Windows XP Home Edition, Windows XP Professional, Windows .NET Server family

UCOMIStream.LockRegion Method

Restricts access to a specified range of bytes in the stream.

```
[Visual Basic]
Sub LockRegion( _
    ByVal libOffset As Long, _
    ByVal cb As Long, _
    ByVal dwLockType As Integer _
)
[C#]
void LockRegion(
    long libOffset,
    long cb,
    int dwLockType
);
[C++]
void LockRegion(
    __int64 libOffset,
    __int64 cb,
    int dwLockType
);
```

```
[JScript]
function LockRegion(
    libOffset : long,
    cb : long,
    dwLockType : int
);
```

Parameters

libOffset

The byte offset for the beginning of the range.

cb

The length of the range, in bytes, to restrict.

dwLockType

The requested restrictions on accessing the range.

Remarks

For more information, please see the existing documentation for **IStream::LockRegion** in the MSDN library.

Requirements

Platforms: Windows 98, Windows NT 4.0, Windows Millennium Edition, Windows 2000, Windows XP Home Edition, Windows XP Professional, Windows .NET Server family

UCOMIStream.Read Method

Reads a specified number of bytes from the stream object into memory starting at the current seek pointer.

```
[Visual Basic]
Sub Read( _
    <Out()> ByVal pv() As Byte, _
    ByVal cb As Integer, _
    ByVal pcbRead As IntPtr _
)
[C#]
void Read(
    [
    Out
    ] byte[] pv,
    int cb,
    IntPtr pcbRead
);
[C++]
void Read(
    [
    Out
    ] unsigned char pv __gc[],
    int cb,
    IntPtr pcbRead
);
[JScript]
function Read(
    pv : Byte[],
    cb : int,
    pcbRead : IntPtr
);
```

Parameters

pv

On successful return, contains the data read frtom the stream.

cb

The number of bytes to read from the stream object.

pcbRead

Pointer to a **ULONG** variable that receives the actual number of bytes read from the stream object.

Remarks

For more information, please see the existing documentation for **ISequentialStream::Read** in the MSDN library.

Requirements

Platforms: Windows 98, Windows NT 4.0, Windows Millennium Edition, Windows 2000, Windows XP Home Edition, Windows XP Professional, Windows .NET Server family

UCOMIStream.Revert Method

Discards all changes that have been made to a transacted stream since the last **Commit** call.

```
[Visual Basic]
Sub Revert()
[C#]
void Revert();
[C++]
void Revert();
[JScript]
function Revert();
```

Remarks

For more information, please see the existing documentation for **IStream::Revert** in the MSDN library.

Requirements

Platforms: Windows 98, Windows NT 4.0, Windows Millennium Edition, Windows 2000, Windows XP Home Edition, Windows XP Professional, Windows .NET Server family

UCOMIStream.Seek Method

Changes the seek pointer to a new location relative to the beginning of the stream, to the end of the stream, or to the current seek pointer.

```
[Visual Basic]
Sub Seek( _
   ByVal dlibMove As Long, _
   ByVal dwOrigin As Integer, _
   ByVal plibNewPosition As IntPtr _
)
[C#]
void Seek(
   long dlibMove,
   int dwOrigin,
   IntPtr plibNewPosition
);
[C++]
void Seek(
   __int64 dlibMove,
   int dwOrigin,
   IntPtr plibNewPosition
);
```

```
[JScript]
function Seek(
   dlibMove : long,
   dwOrigin : int,
   plibNewPosition : IntPtr
);
```

Parameters

dlibMove

Displacement to add to *dwOrigin*.

dwOrigin

Specifies the origin of the seek. The origin can be the beginning of the file, the current seek pointer, or the end of the file.

plibNewPosition

On successful return, contains the offset of the seek pointer from the beginning of the stream.

Remarks

For more information, please see the existing documentation for **IStream::Seek** in the MSDN library.

Requirements

Platforms: Windows 98, Windows NT 4.0, Windows Millennium Edition, Windows 2000, Windows XP Home Edition, Windows XP Professional, Windows .NET Server family

UCOMIStream.SetSize Method

Changes the size of the stream object.

```
[Visual Basic]
Sub SetSize( _
   ByVal libNewSize As Long _
)
[C#]
void SetSize(
   long libNewSize
);
[C++]
void SetSize(
   __int64 libNewSize
);
[JScript]
function SetSize(
   libNewSize : long
);
```

Parameters

libNewSize

Specifies the new size of the stream as a number of bytes.

Remarks

For more information, please see the existing documentation for **IStream::SetSize** in the MSDN library.

Requirements

Platforms: Windows 98, Windows NT 4.0, Windows Millennium Edition, Windows 2000, Windows XP Home Edition, Windows XP Professional, Windows .NET Server family

UCOMIStream.Stat Method

Retrieves the **STATSTG** structure for this stream.

```
[Visual Basic]
Sub Stat( _
   <Out()> ByRef pstatstg As STATSTG, _
   ByVal grfStatFlag As Integer _
)
[C#]
void Stat(
   out STATSTG pstatstg,
   int grfStatFlag
);
[C++]
void Stat(
   [
   Out
] STATSTG* pstatstg,
   int grfStatFlag
);
[JScript]
function Stat(
   pstatstg : STATSTG,
   grfStatFlag : int
);
```

Parameters

pstatstg

On successful return, contains a **STATSTG** structure which describes this stream object.

grfStatFlag

Specifies some of the members in the **STATSTG** structure that this method does not return, thus saving some memory allocation operations.

Remarks

For more information, please see the existing documentation for **IStream::Stat** in the MSDN library.

Requirements

Platforms: Windows 98, Windows NT 4.0, Windows Millennium Edition, Windows 2000, Windows XP Home Edition, Windows XP Professional, Windows .NET Server family

UCOMIStream.UnlockRegion Method

Removes the access restriction on a range of bytes previously restricted with **LockRegion**.

```
[Visual Basic]
Sub UnlockRegion( _
   ByVal libOffset As Long, _
   ByVal cb As Long, _
   ByVal dwLockType As Integer _
)
[C#]
void UnlockRegion(
   long libOffset,
   long cb,
   int dwLockType
);
[C++]
```

```
void UnlockRegion(
   __int64 libOffset,
   __int64 cb,
   int dwLockType
);
[JScript]
function UnlockRegion(
   libOffset : long,
   cb : long,
   dwLockType : int
);
```

Parameters

libOffset

The byte offset for the beginning of the range.

cb

The length, in bytes, of the range to restrict.

dwLockType

The access restrictions previously placed on the range.

Remarks

For more information, please see the existing documentation for **IStream::UnlockRegion** in the MSDN library.

Requirements

Platforms: Windows 98, Windows NT 4.0, Windows Millennium Edition, Windows 2000, Windows XP Home Edition, Windows XP Professional, Windows .NET Server family

UCOMIStream.Write Method

Writes a specified number of bytes into the stream object starting at the current seek pointer.

```
[Visual Basic]
Sub Write( _
   ByVal pv() As Byte, _
   ByVal cb As Integer, _
   ByVal pcbWritten As IntPtr _
)
[C#]
void Write(
   byte[] pv,
   int cb,
   IntPtr pcbWritten
);
[C++]
void Write(
   unsigned char pv __gc[],
   int cb,
   IntPtr pcbWritten
);
[JScript]
function Write(
   pv : Byte[],
   cb : int,
   pcbWritten : IntPtr
);
```

Parameters

pv

>   Buffer to write this stream to.

cb

>   The number of bytes to write into the stream.

pcbWritten

>   On successful return, contains the actual number of bytes written
>   to the stream object. The caller can set this pointer to a null
>   reference (**Nothing** in Visual Basic), in which case this method
>   does not provide the actual number of bytes written.

Remarks

For more information, please see the existing documentation for
ISequentialStream::Write in the MSDN library.

Requirements

Platforms: Windows 98, Windows NT 4.0,
Windows Millennium Edition, Windows 2000,
Windows XP Home Edition, Windows XP Professional,
Windows .NET Server family

UCOMITypeComp Interface

Managed definition of the **ITypeComp** interface.

```
[Visual Basic]
<Guid("00020403-0000-0000-C000-000000000046")>
<InterfaceType(ComInterfaceType.InterfaceIsIUnknown)>
Public Interface UCOMITypeComp
[C#]
[Guid("00020403-0000-0000-C000-000000000046")]
[InterfaceType(ComInterfaceType.InterfaceIsIUnknown)]
public interface UCOMITypeComp
[C++]
[Guid("00020403-0000-0000-C000-000000000046")]
[InterfaceType(ComInterfaceType::InterfaceIsIUnknown)]
public __gc __interface UCOMITypeComp
[JScript]
public
    Guid("00020403-0000-0000-C000-000000000046")
    InterfaceType(ComInterfaceType.InterfaceIsIUnknown)
interface UCOMITypeComp
```

Remarks

For more information about the **ITypeComp** interface, see the MSDN Library.

Requirements

Namespace: System.Runtime.InteropServices

Platforms: Windows 98, Windows NT 4.0, Windows Millennium Edition, Windows 2000, Windows XP Home Edition, Windows XP Professional, Windows .NET Server family

Assembly: Mscorlib (in Mscorlib.dll)

UCOMITypeComp.Bind Method

Maps a name to a member of a type, or binds global variables and functions contained in a type library.

```
[Visual Basic]
Sub Bind( _
    ByVal szName As String, _
    ByVal lHashVal As Integer, _
    ByVal wFlags As Short, _
    <Out()> ByRef ppTInfo As UCOMITypeInfo, _
    <Out()> ByRef pDescKind As DESCKIND, _
    <Out()> ByRef pBindPtr As BINDPTR _
)
[C#]
void Bind(
    string szName,
    int lHashVal,
    short wFlags,
    out UCOMITypeInfo ppTInfo,
    out DESCKIND pDescKind,
    out BINDPTR pBindPtr
);
[C++]
void Bind(
    String* szName,
    int lHashVal,
    short wFlags,
```

```
    [
    Out
    ] UCOMITypeInfo** ppTInfo,
    [
    Out
    ] DESCKIND* pDescKind,
    [
    Out
    ] BINDPTR* pBindPtr
);
[JScript]
function Bind(
    szName : String,
    lHashVal : int,
    wFlags : Int16,
    ppTInfo : UCOMITypeInfo,
    pDescKind : DESCKIND,
    pBindPtr : BINDPTR
);
```

Parameters

szName
: The name to bind.

lHashVal
: A hash value for *szName* computed by **LHashValOfNameSys**.

wFlags
: A flags word containing one or more of the invoke flags defined in the **INVOKEKIND** enumeration.

ppTInfo
: On successful return, a reference to the type description that contains the item to which it is bound, if a **FUNCDESC** or **VARDESC** was returned.

pDescKind
: A reference to a **DESCKIND** enumerator that indicates whether the name bound to is a **VARDESC**, **FUNCDESC**, or **TYPECOMP**.

pBindPtr
: A reference to the bound-to **VARDESC**, **FUNCDESC**, or **ITypeComp** interface.

Remarks

For more information, please see the existing documentation for **ITypeComp::Bind** in the MSDN library.

Requirements

Platforms: Windows 98, Windows NT 4.0, Windows Millennium Edition, Windows 2000, Windows XP Home Edition, Windows XP Professional, Windows .NET Server family

UCOMITypeComp.BindType Method

Binds to the type descriptions contained within a type library.

```
[Visual Basic]
Sub BindType( _
    ByVal szName As String, _
    ByVal lHashVal As Integer, _
    <Out()> ByRef ppTInfo As UCOMITypeInfo, _
    <Out()> ByRef ppTComp As UCOMITypeComp _
)
```

```
[C#]
void BindType(
   string szName,
   int lHashVal,
   out UCOMITypeInfo ppTInfo,
   out UCOMITypeComp ppTComp
);
[C++]
void BindType(
   String* szName,
   int lHashVal,
   [
   Out
] UCOMITypeInfo** ppTInfo,
   [
   Out
] UCOMITypeComp** ppTComp
);
[JScript]
function BindType(
   szName : String,
   lHashVal : int,
   ppTInfo : UCOMITypeInfo,
   ppTComp : UCOMITypeComp
);
```

Parameters

szName

    The name to bind.

lHashVal

    A hash value for *szName* determined by **LHashValOfNameSys**.

ppTInfo

    On successful return, a reference to an **ITypeInfo** of the type to which *szName* was bound.

ppTComp

    On successful return, a reference to an **ITypeComp** variable.

Remarks

For more information, please see the existing documentation for **ITypeComp::BindType** in the MSDN library.

Requirements

Platforms: Windows 98, Windows NT 4.0, Windows Millennium Edition, Windows 2000, Windows XP Home Edition, Windows XP Professional, Windows .NET Server family

UCOMITypeInfo Interface

Managed definition of the **ITypeInfo** interface.

```
[Visual Basic]
<Guid("00020401-0000-0000-C000-000000000046")>
<InterfaceType(ComInterfaceType.InterfaceIsIUnknown)>
Public Interface UCOMITypeInfo
[C#]
[Guid("00020401-0000-0000-C000-000000000046")]
[InterfaceType(ComInterfaceType.InterfaceIsIUnknown)]
public interface UCOMITypeInfo
[C++]
[Guid("00020401-0000-0000-C000-000000000046")]
[InterfaceType(ComInterfaceType::InterfaceIsIUnknown)]
public __gc __interface UCOMITypeInfo
[JScript]
public
    Guid("00020401-0000-0000-C000-000000000046")
    InterfaceType(ComInterfaceType.InterfaceIsIUnknown)
interface UCOMITypeInfo
```

Remarks

For additional information about **ITypeInfo**, see the MSDN Library.

Requirements

Namespace: System.Runtime.InteropServices

Platforms: Windows 98, Windows NT 4.0,
Windows Millennium Edition, Windows 2000,
Windows XP Home Edition, Windows XP Professional,
Windows .NET Server family

Assembly: Mscorlib (in Mscorlib.dll)

UCOMITypeInfo.AddressOfMember Method

Retrieves the addresses of static functions or variables, such as those
defined in a DLL.

```
[Visual Basic]
Sub AddressOfMember( _
    ByVal memid As Integer, _
    ByVal invKind As INVOKEKIND, _
    <Out()> ByRef ppv As IntPtr _
)
[C#]
void AddressOfMember(
    int memid,
    INVOKEKIND invKind,
    out IntPtr ppv
);
[C++]
void AddressOfMember(
    int memid,
    INVOKEKIND invKind,
    [
    Out
    ] IntPtr* ppv
);
[JScript]
function AddressOfMember(
    memid : int,
    invKind : INVOKEKIND,
```

```
    ppv : IntPtr
);
```

Parameters

memid

Member ID of the static (**Shared** in Visual Basic) member's
address to retrieve.

invKind

Specifies whether the member is a property, and if so, what kind.

ppv

On successful return, a reference to the static (**Shared** in Visual
Basic) member.

Remarks

For additional information about **ITypeInfo::AddressOfMember**,
see the MSDN Library.

Requirements

Platforms: Windows 98, Windows NT 4.0,
Windows Millennium Edition, Windows 2000,
Windows XP Home Edition, Windows XP Professional,
Windows .NET Server family

UCOMITypeInfo.CreateInstance Method

Creates a new instance of a type that describes a component class
(coclass).

```
[Visual Basic]
Sub CreateInstance( _
    ByVal pUnkOuter As Object, _
    ByRef riid As Guid, _
    <Out()> ByRef ppvObj As Object _
)
[C#]
void CreateInstance(
    object pUnkOuter,
    ref Guid riid,
    out object ppvObj
);
[C++]
void CreateInstance(
    Object* pUnkOuter,
    Guid* riid,
    [
    Out
    ] Object** ppvObj
);
[JScript]
function CreateInstance(
    pUnkOuter : Object,
    riid : Guid,
    ppvObj : Object
);
```

Parameters

pUnkOuter

Object which acts as the controlling **IUnknown**.

riid

The IID of the interface that the caller will use to communicate
with the resulting object.

ppvObj

On successful return, a reference to the created object.

Remarks

For additional information about **ITypeInfo::CreateInstance**, see the MSDN Library.

Requirements

Platforms: Windows 98, Windows NT 4.0, Windows Millennium Edition, Windows 2000, Windows XP Home Edition, Windows XP Professional, Windows .NET Server family

UCOMITypeInfo.GetContainingTypeLib Method

Retrieves the type library that contains this type description and its index within that type library.

```
[Visual Basic]
Sub GetContainingTypeLib( _
   <Out()> ByRef ppTLB As UCOMITypeLib, _
   <Out()> ByRef pIndex As Integer _
)
[C#]
void GetContainingTypeLib(
   out UCOMITypeLib ppTLB,
   out int pIndex
);
[C++]
void GetContainingTypeLib(
   [
   Out
] UCOMITypeLib** ppTLB,
   [
   Out
] int* pIndex
);
[JScript]
function GetContainingTypeLib(
   ppTLB : UCOMITypeLib,
   pIndex : int
);
```

Parameters

ppTLB
    On successful return, a reference to the containing type library.
pIndex
    On successful return, a reference to the index of the type description within the containing type library.

Remarks

For additional information about **ITypeInfo::GetContainingTypeLib**, see the MSDN Library.

Requirements

Platforms: Windows 98, Windows NT 4.0, Windows Millennium Edition, Windows 2000, Windows XP Home Edition, Windows XP Professional, Windows .NET Server family

UCOMITypeInfo.GetDllEntry Method

Retrieves a description or specification of an entry point for a function in a DLL.

```
[Visual Basic]
Sub GetDllEntry( _
   ByVal memid As Integer, _
   ByVal invKind As INVOKEKIND, _
   <Out()> ByRef pBstrDllName As String, _
   <Out()> ByRef pBstrName As String, _
   <Out()> ByRef pwOrdinal As Short _
)
[C#]
void GetDllEntry(
   int memid,
   INVOKEKIND invKind,
   out string pBstrDllName,
   out string pBstrName,
   out short pwOrdinal
);
[C++]
void GetDllEntry(
   int memid,
   INVOKEKIND invKind,
   [
   Out
] String** pBstrDllName,
   [
   Out
] String** pBstrName,
   [
   Out
] short* pwOrdinal
);
[JScript]
function GetDllEntry(
   memid : int,
   invKind : INVOKEKIND,
   pBstrDllName : String,
   pBstrName : String,
   pwOrdinal : Int16
);
```

Parameters

memid
    ID of the member function whose DLL entry description is to be returned.
invKind
    Specifies the kind of member identified by *memid*.
pBstrDllName
    If not a null reference (**Nothing** in Visual Basic), the function sets *pBstrDllName* to a **BSTR** that contains the name of the DLL.
pBstrName
    If not a null reference (**Nothing** in Visual Basic), the function sets *lpbstrName* to a **BSTR** that contains the name of the entry point.
pwOrdinal
    If not a null reference (**Nothing** in Visual Basic), and the function is defined by an ordinal, then *lpwOrdinal* is set to point to the ordinal.

Remarks

For additional information about **ITypeInfo::GetDllEntry**, see the MSDN Library.

Requirements

Platforms: Windows 98, Windows NT 4.0,
Windows Millennium Edition, Windows 2000,
Windows XP Home Edition, Windows XP Professional,
Windows .NET Server family

UCOMITypeInfo.GetDocumentation Method

Retrieves the documentation string, the complete Help file name and
path, and the context ID for the Help topic for a specified type
description.

```
[Visual Basic]
Sub GetDocumentation( _
    ByVal index As Integer, _
    <Out()> ByRef strName As String, _
    <Out()> ByRef strDocString As String, _
    <Out()> ByRef dwHelpContext As Integer, _
    <Out()> ByRef strHelpFile As String _
)
[C#]
void GetDocumentation(
    int index,
    out string strName,
    out string strDocString,
    out int dwHelpContext,
    out string strHelpFile
);
[C++]
void GetDocumentation(
    int index,
    [
    Out
] String** strName,
    [
    Out
] String** strDocString,
    [
    Out
] int* dwHelpContext,
    [
    Out
] String** strHelpFile
);
[JScript]
function GetDocumentation(
    index : int,
    strName : String,
    strDocString : String,
    dwHelpContext : int,
    strHelpFile : String
);
```

Parameters

index
    ID of the member whose documentation is to be returned.
strName
    On successful return, the name of the item method.
strDocString
    On successful return, the documentation string for the specified
    item.

dwHelpContext
    On successful return, a reference to the Help context associated
    with the specified item.
strHelpFile
    On successful return, the fully qualified name of the Help file.

Remarks

For additional information about **ITypeInfo::GetDocumentation**,
see the MSDN Library.

Requirements

Platforms: Windows 98, Windows NT 4.0,
Windows Millennium Edition, Windows 2000,
Windows XP Home Edition, Windows XP Professional,
Windows .NET Server family

UCOMITypeInfo.GetFuncDesc Method

Retrieves the **FUNCDESC** structure that contains information about
a specified function.

```
[Visual Basic]
Sub GetFuncDesc( _
    ByVal index As Integer, _
    <Out()> ByRef ppFuncDesc As IntPtr _
)
[C#]
void GetFuncDesc(
    int index,
    out IntPtr ppFuncDesc
);
[C++]
void GetFuncDesc(
    int index,
    [
    Out
] IntPtr* ppFuncDesc
);
[JScript]
function GetFuncDesc(
    index : int,
    ppFuncDesc : IntPtr
);
```

Parameters

index
    Index of the function description to return.
ppFuncDesc
    Reference to a **FUNCDESC** that describes the specified
    function.

Remarks

The values of *ppFuncDesc* can be accessed through
PtrToStructure.

For additional information about **ITypeInfo::GetFuncDesc**, see the
MSDN Library.

Requirements

Platforms: Windows 98, Windows NT 4.0,
Windows Millennium Edition, Windows 2000,
Windows XP Home Edition, Windows XP Professional,
Windows .NET Server family

UCOMITypeInfo.GetIDsOfNames Method

Maps between member names and member IDs, and parameter names and parameter IDs.

```
[Visual Basic]
Sub GetIDsOfNames( _
    <InteropServices.In()> ByVal rgszNames() As String, _
    ByVal cNames As Integer, _
    <Out()> ByVal pMemId() As Integer _
)
[C#]
void GetIDsOfNames(
    [
    In
] string[] rgszNames,
    int cNames,
    [
    Out
] int[] pMemId
);
[C++]
void GetIDsOfNames(
    [
    In
] String* rgszNames __gc[],
    int cNames,
    [
    Out
] int pMemId __gc[]
);
[JScript]
function GetIDsOfNames(
    rgszNames : String[],
    cNames : int,
    pMemId : int[]
);
```

Parameters

rgszNames
    On succesful return, an array of names to map.
cNames
    Count of names to map.
pMemId
    Reference to an array in which name mappings are placed.

Remarks

For additional information about **ITypeInfo::GetIDsOfNames**, see the MSDN Library.

Requirements

Platforms: Windows 98, Windows NT 4.0,
Windows Millennium Edition, Windows 2000,
Windows XP Home Edition, Windows XP Professional,
Windows .NET Server family

UCOMITypeInfo.GetImplTypeFlags Method

Retrieves the **IMPLTYPEFLAGS** value for one implemented interface or base interface in a type description.

```
[Visual Basic]
Sub GetImplTypeFlags( _
    ByVal index As Integer, _
```

```
    <Out()> ByRef pImplTypeFlags As Integer _
)
[C#]
void GetImplTypeFlags(
    int index,
    out int pImplTypeFlags
);
[C++]
void GetImplTypeFlags(
    int index,
    [
    Out
] int* pImplTypeFlags
);
[JScript]
function GetImplTypeFlags(
    index : int,
    pImplTypeFlags : int
);
```

Parameters

index
    Index of the implemented interface or base interface.
pImplTypeFlags
    On successful return, a reference to the **IMPLTYPEFLAGS** enumeration.

Remarks

For additional information about **ITypeInfo::GetImplTypeFlags**, see the MSDN Library.

Requirements

Platforms: Windows 98, Windows NT 4.0,
Windows Millennium Edition, Windows 2000,
Windows XP Home Edition, Windows XP Professional,
Windows .NET Server family

UCOMITypeInfo.GetMops Method

Retrieves marshaling information.

```
[Visual Basic]
Sub GetMops( _
    ByVal memid As Integer, _
    <Out()> ByRef pBstrMops As String _
)
[C#]
void GetMops(
    int memid,
    out string pBstrMops
);
[C++]
void GetMops(
    int memid,
    [
    Out
] String** pBstrMops
);
[JScript]
function GetMops(
    memid : int,
    pBstrMops : String
);
```

Parameters

memid

The member ID that indicates which marshaling information is needed.

pBstrMops

A reference to the opcode string used in marshaling the fields of the structure described by the referenced type description, or returns a null reference (**Nothing** in Visual Basic) if there is no information to return.

Remarks

For additional information about **ITypeInfo::GetMops**, see the MSDN Library.

Requirements

Platforms: Windows 98, Windows NT 4.0, Windows Millennium Edition, Windows 2000, Windows XP Home Edition, Windows XP Professional, Windows .NET Server family

UCOMITypeInfo.GetNames Method

Retrieves the variable with the specified member ID (or the name of the property or method and its parameters) that correspond to the specified function ID.

```
[Visual Basic]
Sub GetNames( _
    ByVal memid As Integer, _
    <Out()> ByVal rgbstrNames() As String, _
    ByVal cMaxNames As Integer, _
    <Out()> ByRef pcNames As Integer _
)
[C#]
void GetNames(
    int memid,
    [
    Out
    ] string[] rgbstrNames,
    int cMaxNames,
    out int pcNames
);
[C++]
void GetNames(
    int memid,
    [
    Out
    ] String* rgbstrNames __gc[],
    int cMaxNames,
    [
    Out
    ] int* pcNames
);
[JScript]
function GetNames(
    memid : int,
    rgbstrNames : String[],
    cMaxNames : int,
    pcNames : int
);
```

Parameters

memid

The ID of the member whose name (or names) is to be returned.

rgBstrNames

On succesful return, contains the name (or names) associated with the member.

cMaxNames

Length of the *rgBstrNames* array.

pcNames

On succesful return, the number of names in the *rgBstrNames* array.

Remarks

For additional information about **ITypeInfo::GetNames**, see the MSDN Library.

Requirements

Platforms: Windows 98, Windows NT 4.0, Windows Millennium Edition, Windows 2000, Windows XP Home Edition, Windows XP Professional, Windows .NET Server family

UCOMITypeInfo.GetRefTypeInfo Method

If a type description references other type descriptions, it retrieves the referenced type descriptions.

```
[Visual Basic]
Sub GetRefTypeInfo( _
    ByVal hRef As Integer, _
    <Out()> ByRef ppTI As UCOMITypeInfo _
)
[C#]
void GetRefTypeInfo(
    int hRef,
    out UCOMITypeInfo ppTI
);
[C++]
void GetRefTypeInfo(
    int hRef,
    [
    Out
    ] UCOMITypeInfo** ppTI
);
[JScript]
function GetRefTypeInfo(
    hRef : int,
    ppTI : UCOMITypeInfo
);
```

Parameters

hRef

Handle to the referenced type description to return.

ppTI

On successful return, the referenced type description.

Remarks

For additional information about **ITypeInfo::GetRefTypeInfo**, see the MSDN Library.

Requirements

Platforms: Windows 98, Windows NT 4.0, Windows Millennium Edition, Windows 2000, Windows XP Home Edition, Windows XP Professional, Windows .NET Server family

UCOMITypeInfo.GetRefTypeOfImplType Method

If a type description describes a COM class, it retrieves the type description of the implemented interface types.

```
[Visual Basic]
Sub GetRefTypeOfImplType( _
   ByVal index As Integer, _
   <Out()> ByRef href As Integer _
)
[C#]
void GetRefTypeOfImplType(
   int index,
   out int href
);
[C++]
void GetRefTypeOfImplType(
   int index,
   [
   Out
] int* href
);
[JScript]
function GetRefTypeOfImplType(
   index : int,
   href : int
);
```

Parameters

index
   Index of the implemented type whose handle is returned.
href
   Reference to a handle for the implemented interface.

Remarks

For additional information about **ITypeInfo::GetRefTypeOfImplType**, see the MSDN Library.

Requirements

Platforms: Windows 98, Windows NT 4.0, Windows Millennium Edition, Windows 2000, Windows XP Home Edition, Windows XP Professional, Windows .NET Server family

UCOMITypeInfo.GetTypeAttr Method

Retrieves a **TYPEATTR** structure that contains the attributes of the type description.

```
[Visual Basic]
Sub GetTypeAttr( _
   <Out()> ByRef ppTypeAttr As IntPtr _
)
[C#]
void GetTypeAttr(
   out IntPtr ppTypeAttr
);
[C++]
void GetTypeAttr(
   [
   Out
] IntPtr* ppTypeAttr
);
```

```
[JScript]
function GetTypeAttr(
   ppTypeAttr : IntPtr
);
```

Parameters

ppTypeAttr
   On successful return, a reference to the structure that contains the attributes of this type description.

Remarks

The values of *ppTypeAttr* can be accessed through **PtrToStructure**.

For additional information about **ITypeInfo::GetTypeAttr**, see the MSDN Library.

Requirements

Platforms: Windows 98, Windows NT 4.0, Windows Millennium Edition, Windows 2000, Windows XP Home Edition, Windows XP Professional, Windows .NET Server family

UCOMITypeInfo.GetTypeComp Method

Retrieves the **ITypeComp** interface for the type description, which enables a client compiler to bind to the type description's members.

```
[Visual Basic]
Sub GetTypeComp( _
   <Out()> ByRef ppTComp As UCOMITypeComp _
)
[C#]
void GetTypeComp(
   out UCOMITypeComp ppTComp
);
[C++]
void GetTypeComp(
   [
   Out
] UCOMITypeComp** ppTComp
);
[JScript]
function GetTypeComp(
   ppTComp : UCOMITypeComp
);
```

Parameters

ppTComp
   On successful return, a reference to the **UCOMITypeComp** of the containing type library.

Remarks

For additional information about **ITypeInfo::GetTypeComp**, see the MSDN Library.

Requirements

Platforms: Windows 98, Windows NT 4.0, Windows Millennium Edition, Windows 2000, Windows XP Home Edition, Windows XP Professional, Windows .NET Server family

UCOMITypeInfo.GetVarDesc Method

Retrieves a **VARDESC** structure that describes the specified variable.

```
[Visual Basic]
Sub GetVarDesc( _
    ByVal index As Integer, _
    <Out()> ByRef ppVarDesc As IntPtr _
)
[C#]
void GetVarDesc(
    int index,
    out IntPtr ppVarDesc
);
[C++]
void GetVarDesc(
    int index,
    [
    Out
] IntPtr* ppVarDesc
);
[JScript]
function GetVarDesc(
    index : int,
    ppVarDesc : IntPtr
);
```

Parameters

index

Index of the variable description to return.

ppVarDesc

On successful return, a reference to the **VARDESC** that describes the specified variable.

Remarks

The values of *ppVarDesc* can be accessed through **PtrToStructure**.

For additional information about **ITypeInfo::GetVarDesc**, see the MSDN Library.

Requirements

Platforms: Windows 98, Windows NT 4.0, Windows Millennium Edition, Windows 2000, Windows XP Home Edition, Windows XP Professional, Windows .NET Server family

UCOMITypeInfo.Invoke Method

Invokes a method, or accesses a property of an object, that implements the interface described by the type description.

```
[Visual Basic]
Sub Invoke( _
    ByVal pvInstance As Object, _
    ByVal memid As Integer, _
    ByVal wFlags As Short, _
    ByRef pDispParams As DISPPARAMS, _
    <Out()> ByRef pVarResult As Object, _
    <Out()> ByRef pExcepInfo As EXCEPINFO, _
    <Out()> ByRef puArgErr As Integer _
)
[C#]
void Invoke(
    object pvInstance,
    int memid,
    short wFlags,
    ref DISPPARAMS pDispParams,
```

```
    out object pVarResult,
    out EXCEPINFO pExcepInfo,
    out int puArgErr
);
[C++]
void Invoke(
    Object* pvInstance,
    int memid,
    short wFlags,
    DISPPARAMS* pDispParams,
    [
    Out
] Object** pVarResult,
    [
    Out
] EXCEPINFO* pExcepInfo,
    [
    Out
] int* puArgErr
);
[JScript]
function Invoke(
    pvInstance : Object,
    memid : int,
    wFlags : Int16,
    pDispParams : DISPPARAMS,
    pVarResult : Object,
    pExcepInfo : EXCEPINFO,
    puArgErr : int
);
```

Parameters

pvInstance

Reference to the interface described by this type description.

memid

Identifies the interface member.

wFlags

Flags describing the context of the invoke call.

pDispParams

Reference to a structure that contains an array of arguments, an array of DISPIDs for named arguments, and counts of the number of elements in each array.

pVarResult

Reference to the location at which the result is to be stored. If *wFlags* specifies **DISPATCH_PROPERTYPUT** or **DISPATCH_PROPERTYPUTREF**, *pVarResult* is ignored. Set to a null reference (**Nothing** in Visual Basic) if no result is desired.

pExcepInfo

Points to an exception information structure, which is filled in only if **DISP_E_EXCEPTION** is returned.

puArgErr

If **Invoke** returns **DISP_E_TYPEMISMATCH**, *puArgErr* indicates the index within *rgvarg* of the argument with incorrect type. If more than one argument returns an error, *puArgErr* indicates only the first argument with an error.

Remarks

The values of *pDispParams* can be accessed through **PtrToStructure**.

Valid values for *wFlags* are:

Value	Description
DISPATCH_METHOD	The member is accessed as a method. If there is ambiguity, both this and the **DISPATCH_PROPERTYGET** flag can be set.
DISPATCH_PROPERTY-GET	The member is retrieved as a property or data member.
DISPATCH_PROPERTY-PUT	The member is changed as a property or data member.
DISPATCH_PROPERTY-PUTREF	The member is changed by using a reference assignment, rather than a value assignment. This value is only valid when the property accepts a reference to an object.

For additional information about **ITypeInfo::Invoke**, see the MSDN Library.

Requirements

Platforms: Windows 98, Windows NT 4.0, Windows Millennium Edition, Windows 2000, Windows XP Home Edition, Windows XP Professional, Windows .NET Server family

UCOMITypeInfo.ReleaseFuncDesc Method

Releases a **FUNCDESC** previously returned by **GetFuncDesc**.

```
[Visual Basic]
Sub ReleaseFuncDesc( _
   ByVal pFuncDesc As IntPtr _
)
[C#]
void ReleaseFuncDesc(
   IntPtr pFuncDesc
);
[C++]
void ReleaseFuncDesc(
   IntPtr pFuncDesc
);
[JScript]
function ReleaseFuncDesc(
   pFuncDesc : IntPtr
);
```

Parameters

pFuncDesc
    Reference to the **FUNCDESC** to release.

Remarks

For additional information about **ITypeInfo::ReleaseFuncDesc**, see the MSDN Library.

Requirements

Platforms: Windows 98, Windows NT 4.0, Windows Millennium Edition, Windows 2000, Windows XP Home Edition, Windows XP Professional, Windows .NET Server family

UCOMITypeInfo.ReleaseTypeAttr Method

Releases a **TYPEATTR** previously returned by **GetTypeAttr**.

```
[Visual Basic]
Sub ReleaseTypeAttr( _
   ByVal pTypeAttr As IntPtr _
)
[C#]
void ReleaseTypeAttr(
   IntPtr pTypeAttr
);
[C++]
void ReleaseTypeAttr(
   IntPtr pTypeAttr
);
[JScript]
function ReleaseTypeAttr(
   pTypeAttr : IntPtr
);
```

Parameters

pTypeAttr
    Reference to the **TYPEATTR** to release.

Remarks

For additional information about **ITypeInfo::ReleaseTypeAttr**, see the MSDN Library.

Requirements

Platforms: Windows 98, Windows NT 4.0, Windows Millennium Edition, Windows 2000, Windows XP Home Edition, Windows XP Professional, Windows .NET Server family

UCOMITypeInfo.ReleaseVarDesc Method

Releases a **VARDESC** previously returned by **GetVarDesc**.

```
[Visual Basic]
Sub ReleaseVarDesc( _
   ByVal pVarDesc As IntPtr _
)
[C#]
void ReleaseVarDesc(
   IntPtr pVarDesc
);
[C++]
void ReleaseVarDesc(
   IntPtr pVarDesc
);
[JScript]
function ReleaseVarDesc(
   pVarDesc : IntPtr
);
```

Parameters

pVarDesc
    Reference to the **VARDESC** to release.

Remarks

For additional information about **ITypeInfo::ReleaseVarDesc**, see the MSDN Library.

Requirements

Platforms: Windows 98, Windows NT 4.0, Windows Millennium Edition, Windows 2000, Windows XP Home Edition, Windows XP Professional, Windows .NET Server family

UCOMITypeLib Interface

Managed definition of the **ITypeLib** interface.

```
[Visual Basic]
<Guid("00020402-0000-0000-C000-000000000046")>
<InterfaceType(ComInterfaceType.InterfaceIsIUnknown)>
Public Interface UCOMITypeLib
[C#]
[Guid("00020402-0000-0000-C000-000000000046")]
[InterfaceType(ComInterfaceType.InterfaceIsIUnknown)]
public interface UCOMITypeLib
[C++]
[Guid("00020402-0000-0000-C000-000000000046")]
[InterfaceType(ComInterfaceType::InterfaceIsIUnknown)]
public __gc __interface UCOMITypeLib
[JScript]
public
    Guid("00020402-0000-0000-C000-000000000046")
    InterfaceType(ComInterfaceType.InterfaceIsIUnknown)
interface UCOMITypeLib
```

Remarks

For additional information about the **ITypeLib** interface, see the MSDN Library.

Requirements

Namespace: System.Runtime.InteropServices

Platforms: Windows 98, Windows NT 4.0, Windows Millennium Edition, Windows 2000, Windows XP Home Edition, Windows XP Professional, Windows .NET Server family

Assembly: Mscorlib (in Mscorlib.dll)

UCOMITypeLib.FindName Method

Finds occurrences of a type description in a type library.

```
[Visual Basic]
Sub FindName( _
    ByVal szNameBuf As String, _
    ByVal lHashVal As Integer, _
    <Out()> ByVal ppTInfo() As UCOMITypeInfo, _
    <Out()> ByVal rgMemId() As Integer, _
    ByRef pcFound As Short _
)
[C#]
void FindName(
    string szNameBuf,
    int lHashVal,
    [
    Out
] UCOMITypeInfo[] ppTInfo,
    [
    Out
] int[] rgMemId,
    ref short pcFound
);
[C++]
void FindName(
    String* szNameBuf,
    int lHashVal,
    [
```

```
    Out
] UCOMITypeInfo** ppTInfo[],
    [
    Out
] int rgMemId __gc[],
    short* pcFound
);
[JScript]
function FindName(
    szNameBuf : String,
    lHashVal : int,
    ppTInfo : UCOMITypeInfo[],
    rgMemId : int[],
    pcFound : Int16
);
```

Parameters

szNameBuf
  The name to search for.

lHashVal
  A hash value to speed up the search, computed by the **LHashValOfNameSys** function. If *lHashVal* is 0, a value is computed.

ppTInfo
  On successful return, an array of pointers to the type descriptions that contain the name specified in *szNameBuf*.

rgMemId
  An array of the **MEMBERID** 's of the found items; *rgMemId* [i] is the **MEMBERID** that indexes into the type description specified by *ppTInfo* [i]. Cannot be a null reference (**Nothing** in Visual Basic).

pcFound
  On entry, indicates how many instances to look for. For example, *pcFound* = 1 can be called to find the first occurrence. The search stops when one instance is found.

  On exit, indicates the number of instances that were found. If the **in** and **out** values of *pcFound* are identical, there might be more type descriptions that contain the name.

Remarks

There must be enough room in *rgMemId* to hold *pcFound* entries.

For additional information about **ITypeLib::FindName**, see the MSDN Library.

Requirements

Platforms: Windows 98, Windows NT 4.0, Windows Millennium Edition, Windows 2000, Windows XP Home Edition, Windows XP Professional, Windows .NET Server family

UCOMITypeLib.GetDocumentation Method

Retrieves the library's documentation string, the complete Help file name and path, and the context identifier for the library Help topic in the Help file.

```
[Visual Basic]
Sub GetDocumentation( _
    ByVal index As Integer, _
    <Out()> ByRef strName As String, _
    <Out()> ByRef strDocString As String, _
    <Out()> ByRef dwHelpContext As Integer, _
    <Out()> ByRef strHelpFile As String _
)
```

```
[C#]
void GetDocumentation(
    int index,
    out string strName,
    out string strDocString,
    out int dwHelpContext,
    out string strHelpFile
);
[C++]
void GetDocumentation(
    int index,
    [
    Out
    ] String** strName,
    [
    Out
    ] String** strDocString,
    [
    Out
    ] int* dwHelpContext,
    [
    Out
    ] String** strHelpFile
);
[JScript]
function GetDocumentation(
    index : int,
    strName : String,
    strDocString : String,
    dwHelpContext : int,
    strHelpFile : String
);
```

Parameters

index
> Index of the type description whose documentation is to be returned.

strName
> Returns a string that contains the name of the specified item.

strDocString
> Returns a string that contains the documentation string for the specified item.

dwHelpContext
> Returns the Help context identifier associated with the specified item.

strHelpFile
> Returns a string that contains the fully qualified name of the Help file.

Remarks

For additional information about **ITypeLib::GetDocumentation**, see the MSDN Library.

Requirements

Platforms: Windows 98, Windows NT 4.0, Windows Millennium Edition, Windows 2000, Windows XP Home Edition, Windows XP Professional, Windows .NET Server family

UCOMITypeLib.GetLibAttr Method

Retrieves the structure that contains the library's attributes.

```
[Visual Basic]
Sub GetLibAttr( _
    <Out()> ByRef ppTLibAttr As IntPtr _
)
[C#]
void GetLibAttr(
    out IntPtr ppTLibAttr
);
[C++]
void GetLibAttr(
    [
    Out
    ] IntPtr* ppTLibAttr
);
[JScript]
function GetLibAttr(
    ppTLibAttr : IntPtr
);
```

Parameters

ppTLibAttr
> On successful return, a structure that contains the library's attributes.

Remarks

The values of the structure referenced by *ppTLibAttr* can be obtained by **PtrToStructure**.

For additional information about **ITypeLib::GetTypeLibAttr**, see the MSDN Library.

Requirements

Platforms: Windows 98, Windows NT 4.0, Windows Millennium Edition, Windows 2000, Windows XP Home Edition, Windows XP Professional, Windows .NET Server family

UCOMITypeLib.GetTypeComp Method

Enables a client compiler to bind to a library's types, variables, constants, and global functions.

```
[Visual Basic]
Sub GetTypeComp( _
    <Out()> ByRef ppTComp As UCOMITypeComp _
)
[C#]
void GetTypeComp(
    out UCOMITypeComp ppTComp
);
[C++]
void GetTypeComp(
    [
    Out
    ] UCOMITypeComp** ppTComp
);
[JScript]
function GetTypeComp(
    ppTComp : UCOMITypeComp
);
```

Parameters

ppTComp

    On successful return, an instance of a **UCOMITypeComp** instance for this **ITypeLib**.

Remarks

For additional information about **ITypeLib::GetTypeComp**, see the MSDN Library.

Requirements

Platforms: Windows 98, Windows NT 4.0, Windows Millennium Edition, Windows 2000, Windows XP Home Edition, Windows XP Professional, Windows .NET Server family

UCOMITypeLib.GetTypeInfo Method

Retrieves the specified type description in the library.

```
[Visual Basic]
Sub GetTypeInfo( _
   ByVal index As Integer, _
   <Out()> ByRef ppTI As UCOMITypeInfo _
)
[C#]
void GetTypeInfo(
   int index,
   out UCOMITypeInfo ppTI
);
[C++]
void GetTypeInfo(
   int index,
   [
   Out
] UCOMITypeInfo** ppTI
);
[JScript]
function GetTypeInfo(
   index : int,
   ppTI : UCOMITypeInfo
);
```

Parameters

index

    Index of the **UCOMITypeInfo** interface to return.

ppTI

    On successful return, a **UCOMITypeInfo** describing the type referenced by *index*.

Remarks

For additional information about **ITypeLib::GetTypeInfo**, see the MSDN Library.

Requirements

Platforms: Windows 98, Windows NT 4.0, Windows Millennium Edition, Windows 2000, Windows XP Home Edition, Windows XP Professional, Windows .NET Server family

UCOMITypeLib.GetTypeInfoCount Method

Returns the number of type descriptions in the type library.

```
[Visual Basic]
Function GetTypeInfoCount() As Integer
```

```
[C#]
int GetTypeInfoCount();
[C++]
int GetTypeInfoCount();
[JScript]
function GetTypeInfoCount() : int;
```

Return Value

The number of type descriptions in the type library.

Remarks

For additional information about **ITypeLib::GetTypeInfoCount**, see the MSDN Library.

Requirements

Platforms: Windows 98, Windows NT 4.0, Windows Millennium Edition, Windows 2000, Windows XP Home Edition, Windows XP Professional, Windows .NET Server family

UCOMITypeLib.GetTypeInfoOfGuid Method

Retrieves the type description that corresponds to the specified GUID.

```
[Visual Basic]
Sub GetTypeInfoOfGuid( _
   ByRef guid As Guid, _
   <Out()> ByRef ppTInfo As UCOMITypeInfo _
)
[C#]
void GetTypeInfoOfGuid(
   ref Guid guid,
   out UCOMITypeInfo ppTInfo
);
[C++]
void GetTypeInfoOfGuid(
   Guid* guid,
   [
   Out
] UCOMITypeInfo** ppTInfo
);
[JScript]
function GetTypeInfoOfGuid(
   guid : Guid,
   ppTInfo : UCOMITypeInfo
);
```

Parameters

guid

    IID of the interface of CLSID of the class whose type info is requested.

ppTInfo

    On successful return, the requested **ITypeInfo** interface.

Remarks

For additional information about **ITypeLib::GetTypeInfoOfGuid**, see the MSDN Library.

Requirements

Platforms: Windows 98, Windows NT 4.0, Windows Millennium Edition, Windows 2000, Windows XP Home Edition, Windows XP Professional, Windows .NET Server family

UCOMITypeLib.GetTypeInfoType Method

Retrieves the type of a type description.

```
[Visual Basic]
Sub GetTypeInfoType( _
   ByVal index As Integer, _
   <Out()> ByRef pTKind As TYPEKIND _
)
[C#]
void GetTypeInfoType(
   int index,
   out TYPEKIND pTKind
);
[C++]
void GetTypeInfoType(
   int index,
   [
   Out
] TYPEKIND* pTKind
);
[JScript]
function GetTypeInfoType(
   index : int,
   pTKind : TYPEKIND
);
```

Parameters

index
   The index of the type description within the type library.
pTKind
   Reference to the **TYPEKIND** enumeration for the type description.

Remarks

For additional information about **ITypeLib::GetTypeInfoOfType**, see the MSDN Library.

Requirements

Platforms: Windows 98, Windows NT 4.0, Windows Millennium Edition, Windows 2000, Windows XP Home Edition, Windows XP Professional, Windows .NET Server family

UCOMITypeLib.IsName Method

Indicates whether a passed-in string contains the name of a type or member described in the library.

```
[Visual Basic]
Function IsName( _
   ByVal szNameBuf As String, _
   ByVal lHashVal As Integer _
) As Boolean
[C#]
bool IsName(
   string szNameBuf,
   int lHashVal
);
[C++]
bool IsName(
   String* szNameBuf,
   int lHashVal
);
```

```
[JScript]
function IsName(
   szNameBuf : String,
   lHashVal : int
) : Boolean;
```

Parameters

szNameBuf
   The string to test.
lHashVal
   The hash value of *szNameBuf*.

Return Value

true if *szNameBuf* was found in the type library; otherwise **false**.

Remarks

For additional information about **ITypeLib::IsName**, see the MSDN Library.

Requirements

Platforms: Windows 98, Windows NT 4.0, Windows Millennium Edition, Windows 2000, Windows XP Home Edition, Windows XP Professional, Windows .NET Server family

UCOMITypeLib.ReleaseTLibAttr Method

Releases the **TYPELIBATTR** originally obtained from **GetLibAttr**.

```
[Visual Basic]
Sub ReleaseTLibAttr( _
   ByVal pTLibAttr As IntPtr _
)
[C#]
void ReleaseTLibAttr(
   IntPtr pTLibAttr
);
[C++]
void ReleaseTLibAttr(
   IntPtr pTLibAttr
);
[JScript]
function ReleaseTLibAttr(
   pTLibAttr : IntPtr
);
```

Parameters

pTLibAttr
   The **TLIBATTR** to release.

Remarks

For additional information about **ITypeLib::ReleaseTLibAttr**, see the MSDN Library.

Requirements

Platforms: Windows 98, Windows NT 4.0, Windows Millennium Edition, Windows 2000, Windows XP Home Edition, Windows XP Professional, Windows .NET Server family

UnknownWrapper Class

Wraps objects the marshaler should marshal as a **VT_UNKNOWN**.

System.Object
   System.Runtime.InteropServices.UnknownWrapper

```
[Visual Basic]
NotInheritable Public Class UnknownWrapper
[C#]
public sealed class UnknownWrapper
[C++]
public __gc __sealed class UnknownWrapper
[JScript]
public class UnknownWrapper
```

Thread Safety

Any public static (**Shared** in Visual Basic) members of this type are safe for multithreaded operations. Any instance members are not guaranteed to be thread safe.

Remarks

Only applies when the managed signature of a method takes an object.

```
int MyMethod(Object o); //Managed signature
   HRESULT MyMethod(VARIANT o); //COM signature
   MyObject o = new MyObject();
   MyMethod(o); //o gets passed as VARIANT VT_DISPATCH
   MyMethod(new UnknownWrapper(o)); //o gets passed as
VARIANT VT_UNKNOWN
```

Requirements

Namespace: System.Runtime.InteropServices

Platforms: Windows 98, Windows NT 4.0, Windows Millennium Edition, Windows 2000, Windows XP Home Edition, Windows XP Professional, Windows .NET Server family

Assembly: Mscorlib (in Mscorlib.dll)

UnknownWrapper Constructor

Initializes a new instance of the **UnknownWrapper** class with the object to be wrapped.

```
[Visual Basic]
Public Sub New( _
   ByVal obj As Object _
)
[C#]
public UnknownWrapper(
   object obj
);
[C++]
public: UnknownWrapper(
   Object* obj
);
[JScript]
public function UnknownWrapper(
   obj : Object
);
```

Parameters

obj
   The object being wrapped.

Requirements

Platforms: Windows 98, Windows NT 4.0, Windows Millennium Edition, Windows 2000, Windows XP Home Edition, Windows XP Professional, Windows .NET Server family

UnknownWrapper.WrappedObject Property

Gets the object contained by this wrapper.

```
[Visual Basic]
Public ReadOnly Property WrappedObject As Object
[C#]
public object WrappedObject {get;}
[C++]
public: __property Object* get_WrappedObject();
[JScript]
public function get WrappedObject() : Object;
```

Property Value

The wrapped object.

Requirements

Platforms: Windows 98, Windows NT 4.0, Windows Millennium Edition, Windows 2000, Windows XP Home Edition, Windows XP Professional, Windows .NET Server family

UnmanagedType Enumeration

Identifies how to marshal parameters or fields to unmanaged code.

```
[Visual Basic]
<Serializable>
Public Enum UnmanagedType
[C#]
[Serializable]
public enum UnmanagedType
[C++]
[Serializable]
__value public enum UnmanagedType
[JScript]
public
    Serializable
enum UnmanagedType
```

Remarks

This enumeration is used by **System.Runtime.InteropServices.MarshalAsAttribute** to specify nondefault values for **Array**, **Boolean**, and **String** data types or to make the default behavior explicit. You can also use the enumeration members to specify simple value types (I1, I2, I4, I8, R4, R8, U2, U4, and U8), unmanaged types that are unavailable in the .NET Framework, and various miscellaneous types. Some members represent types to be use with platform invoke methods only.

Members

Member name	Description
AnsiBStr Supported by the .NET Compact Framework.	An ANSI character string that is a length prefixed, single byte. You can use this member on the **String** data type.
AsAny Supported by the .NET Compact Framework.	A dynamic type that determines the type of an object at run time and marshals the object as that type. Valid for platform invoke methods only.
Bool Supported by the .NET Compact Framework.	A 4-byte Boolean value (**true** != 0, **false** = 0). This is the Win32 BOOL type.
BStr Supported by the .NET Compact Framework.	A Unicode character string that is a length-prefixed double byte. You can use this member, which is the default string in COM, on the **String** data type.
ByValArray Supported by the .NET Compact Framework.	When **MarshalAsAttribute.Value** is set to **ByValArray**, the **SizeConst** must be set to indicate the number of elements in the array. The **ArraySubType** field can optionally contain the **UnmanagedType** of the array elements when it is necessary to differentiate among string types. You can only use this **UnmanagedType** on an array that appear as fields in a structure.

Member name	Description
ByValTStr Supported by the .NET Compact Framework.	Used for in-line, fixed-length character arrays that appear within a structure. The character type used with **ByValTStr** is determined by the **System.Runtime.InteropServices. CharSet** argument of the **System.- Runtime.InteropServices.Struct- LayoutAttribute** applied to the containing structure. Always use the **MarshalAsAttribute.SizeConst** field to indicate the size of the array. .NET Framework **ByValTStr** types behave like C-style, fixed-size strings inside a structure (for example, char s[5]). The behavior in managed code differs from the Microsoft Visual Basic 6.0 behavior, which is not null terminated (for example, MyString As String * 5).
Currency	Used on a **System.Decimal** to marshal the decimal value as a COM currency type instead of as a **Decimal**.
CustomMarshaler Supported by the .NET Compact Framework.	Specifies the custom marshaler class when used with **MarshalAsAttri- bute.MarshalType** or **MarshalAs- Attribute.MarshalTypeRef**. The **MarshalAsAttribute.MarshalCook ie** field can be used to pass additional information to the custom marshaler. You can use this member on any reference type.
Error Supported by the .NET Compact Framework.	This native type associated with an **I4** or a **U4** causes the parameter to be exported as a HRESULT in the exported type library.
FunctionPtr Supported by the .NET Compact Framework.	An integer that can be used as a C- style function pointer. You can use this member on a **Delegate** data type or a type that inherits from a **Delegate**.
I1 Supported by the .NET Compact Framework.	A 1-byte signed integer. You can use this member to transform a Boolean value into a 1-byte, C-style **bool** (**true** = 1, **false** = 0).
I2 Supported by the .NET Compact Framework.	A 2-byte signed integer.
I4 Supported by the .NET Compact Framework.	A 4-byte signed integer.
I8 Supported by the .NET Compact Framework.	An 8-byte signed integer.
IDispatch Supported by the .NET Compact Framework.	A COM **IDispatch** pointer (**Object** in Microsoft Visual Basic 6.0).

Member name	Description
Interface Supported by the .NET Compact Framework.	A COM interface pointer. The **Guid** of the interface is obtained from the class metadata. Use this member to specify the exact interface type or the default interface type if you apply it to a class. This member produces **UnmanagedType.IUnknown** behavior when you apply it to the **Object** data type.
IUnknown Supported by the .NET Compact Framework.	A COM **IUnknown** pointer. You can use this member on the **Object** data type.
LPArray Supported by the .NET Compact Framework.	A pointer to the first element of a C-style array. When marshaling from managed to unmanaged, the length of the array is determined by the length of the managed array. When marshaling from unmanaged to managed, the length of the array is determined from the **MarshalAsAttribute.SizeConst** and the **MarshalAsAttribute.SizeParamIndex** fields, optionally followed by the unmanaged type of the elements within the array when it is necessary to differentiate among string types.
LPStr Supported by the .NET Compact Framework.	A single byte, null-terminated ANSI character string. You can use this member on the **System.String** or **System.Text.StringBuilder** data types
LPStruct Supported by the .NET Compact Framework.	A pointer to a C-style structure that you use to marshal managed formatted classes. Valid for platform invoke methods only.
LPTStr Supported by the .NET Compact Framework.	A platform-dependent character string: ANSI on Windows 98 and Unicode on Windows NT and Windows XP. This value is only supported for platform invoke, and not COM interop, because exporting a string of type **LPTStr** is not supported.
LPWStr Supported by the .NET Compact Framework.	A 2-byte, null-terminated Unicode character string.
R4 Supported by the .NET Compact Framework.	A 4-byte floating point number.
R8 Supported by the .NET Compact Framework.	An 8-byte floating point number.

Member name	Description
SafeArray Supported by the .NET Compact Framework.	A **SafeArray** is a self-describing array that carries the type, rank, and bounds of the associated array data. You can use this member with the **MarshalAsAttribute.SafeArraySubType** field to override the default element type.
Struct Supported by the .NET Compact Framework.	A VARIANT, which is used to marshal managed formatted classes and value types.
SysInt Supported by the .NET Compact Framework.	A platform-dependent, signed integer. 4-bytes on 32 bit Windows, 8-bytes on 64 bit Windows.
SysUInt Supported by the .NET Compact Framework.	A platform-dependent, unsigned integer. 4-bytes on 32 bit Windows, 8-bytes on 64 bit Windows.
TBStr Supported by the .NET Compact Framework.	A length-prefixed, platform-dependent **char** string. ANSI on Windows 98, Unicode on Windows NT. You rarely use this BSTR-like member.
U1 Supported by the .NET Compact Framework.	A 1-byte unsigned integer.
U2 Supported by the .NET Compact Framework.	A 2-byte unsigned integer.
U4 Supported by the .NET Compact Framework.	A 4-byte unsigned integer.
U8 Supported by the .NET Compact Framework.	An 8-byte unsigned integer.
VariantBool Supported by the .NET Compact Framework.	A 2-byte, OLE-defined VARIANT_BOOL type (**true** = -1, **false** = 0).
VBByRefStr Supported by the .NET Compact Framework.	Allows Visual Basic .NET to change a string in unmanaged code, and have the results reflected in managed code. This value is only supported for platform invoke.

Requirements

Namespace: System.Runtime.InteropServices

Platforms: Windows 98, Windows NT 4.0, Windows Millennium Edition, Windows 2000, Windows XP Home Edition, Windows XP Professional, Windows .NET Server family, .NET Compact Framework - Windows CE .NET

Assembly: Mscorlib (in Mscorlib.dll)

VARDESC Structure

Describes a variable, constant, or data member.

System.Object
  System.ValueType
    System.Runtime.InteropServices.VARDESC

```
[Visual Basic]
<ComVisible(False)>
Public Structure VARDESC
[C#]
[ComVisible(false)]
public struct VARDESC
[C++]
[ComVisible(false)]
public __value struct VARDESC
```

[JScript] In JScript, you can use the structures in the .NET Framework, but you cannot define your own.

Thread Safety

Any public static (**Shared** in Visual Basic) members of this type are safe for multithreaded operations. Any instance members are not guaranteed to be thread safe.

Remarks

For additional information about **VARDESC**, see the MSDN Library.

Requirements

Namespace: System.Runtime.InteropServices

Platforms: Windows 98, Windows NT 4.0, Windows Millennium Edition, Windows 2000, Windows XP Home Edition, Windows XP Professional, Windows .NET Server family

Assembly: Mscorlib (in Mscorlib.dll)

VARDESC.elemdescVar Field

Contains the variable type.

```
[Visual Basic]
Public elemdescVar As ELEMDESC
[C#]
public ELEMDESC elemdescVar;
[C++]
public: ELEMDESC elemdescVar;
[JScript]
public var elemdescVar : ELEMDESC;
```

Requirements

Platforms: Windows 98, Windows NT 4.0, Windows Millennium Edition, Windows 2000, Windows XP Home Edition, Windows XP Professional, Windows .NET Server family

VARDESC.lpstrSchema Field

This field is reserved for future use.

```
[Visual Basic]
Public lpstrSchema As String
[C#]
public string lpstrSchema;
```

```
[C++]
public: String* lpstrSchema;
[JScript]
public var lpstrSchema : String;
```

Remarks

For additional information about **VARDESC**, see the MSDN Library.

Requirements

Platforms: Windows 98, Windows NT 4.0, Windows Millennium Edition, Windows 2000, Windows XP Home Edition, Windows XP Professional, Windows .NET Server family

VARDESC.memid Field

Indicates the member ID of a variable.

```
[Visual Basic]
Public memid As Integer
[C#]
public int memid;
[C++]
public: int memid;
[JScript]
public var memid : int;
```

Remarks

For additional information about **VARDESC**, see the MSDN Library.

Requirements

Platforms: Windows 98, Windows NT 4.0, Windows Millennium Edition, Windows 2000, Windows XP Home Edition, Windows XP Professional, Windows .NET Server family

VARDESC.varkind Field

Defines how a variable should be marshaled.

```
[Visual Basic]
Public varkind As VarEnum
[C#]
public VarEnum varkind;
[C++]
public: VarEnum varkind;
[JScript]
public var varkind : VarEnum;
```

Requirements

Platforms: Windows 98, Windows NT 4.0, Windows Millennium Edition, Windows 2000, Windows XP Home Edition, Windows XP Professional, Windows .NET Server family

VARDESC.wVarFlags Field

Defines the properties of a variable.

```
[Visual Basic]
Public wVarFlags As Short
```

```
[C#]
public short wVarFlags;
[C++]
public: short wVarFlags;
[JScript]
public var wVarFlags : Int16;
```

Requirements

Platforms: Windows 98, Windows NT 4.0,
Windows Millennium Edition, Windows 2000,
Windows XP Home Edition, Windows XP Professional,
Windows .NET Server family

VARDESC.DESCUNION Structure

Contains information about a variable.

System.Object
  System.ValueType
    System.Runtime.InteropServices.VARDESC.DESCUNION

```
[Visual Basic]
<ComVisible(False)>
Public Structure VARDESC.DESCUNION
[C#]
[ComVisible(false)]
public struct VARDESC.DESCUNION
[C++]
[ComVisible(false)]
public __value struct VARDESC.DESCUNION
```

[JScript] In JScript, you can use the structures in the .NET Framework, but you cannot define your own.

Thread Safety

Any public static (**Shared** in Visual Basic) members of this type are safe for multithreaded operations. Any instance members are not guaranteed to be thread safe.

Requirements

Namespace: System.Runtime.InteropServices

Platforms: Windows 98, Windows NT 4.0, Windows Millennium Edition, Windows 2000, Windows XP Home Edition, Windows XP Professional, Windows .NET Server family

Assembly: Mscorlib (in Mscorlib.dll)

VARDESC.DESCUNION.lpvarValue Field

Describes a symbolic constant.

```
[Visual Basic]
Public lpvarValue As IntPtr
[C#]
public IntPtr lpvarValue;
[C++]
public: IntPtr lpvarValue;
[JScript]
public var lpvarValue : IntPtr;
```

Requirements

Platforms: Windows 98, Windows NT 4.0, Windows Millennium Edition, Windows 2000, Windows XP Home Edition, Windows XP Professional, Windows .NET Server family

VARDESC.DESCUNION.oInst Field

Indicates the offset of this variable within the instance.

```
[Visual Basic]
Public oInst As Integer
[C#]
public int oInst;
```

```
[C++]
public: int oInst;
[JScript]
public var oInst : int;
```

Requirements

Platforms: Windows 98, Windows NT 4.0, Windows Millennium Edition, Windows 2000, Windows XP Home Edition, Windows XP Professional, Windows .NET Server family

VarEnum Enumeration

Indicates how to marshal the array elements when an array is marshaled from managed to unmanaged code as a **UnmanagedType.SafeArray**.

```
[Visual Basic]
<Serializable>
Public Enum VarEnum
[C#]
[Serializable]
public enum VarEnum
[C++]
[Serializable]
__value public enum VarEnum
[JScript]
public
    Serializable
enum VarEnum
```

Remarks

Used with **System.Runtime.InteropServices.MarshalAsAttribute** to explicitly control the element type of the **SafeArray**.

Members

Member name	Description
VT_ARRAY	Indicates a **SAFEARRAY** pointer.
VT_BLOB	Indicates length prefixed bytes.
VT_BLOB_OBJECT	Indicates that a blob contains an object.
VT_BOOL	Indicates a Boolean value.
VT_BSTR	Indicates a BSTR string.
VT_BYREF	Indicates that a value is a reference.
VT_CARRAY	Indicates a C style array.
VT_CF	Indicates the clipboard format.
VT_CLSID	Indicates a class ID.
VT_CY	Indicates a currency value.
VT_DATE	Indicates a DATE value.
VT_DECIMAL	Indicates a **decimal** value.
VT_DISPATCH	Indicates an **IDispatch** pointer.
VT_EMPTY	Indicates that a value was not specified.
VT_ERROR	Indicates an SCODE.
VT_FILETIME	Indicates a FILETIME value.
VT_HRESULT	Indicates an HRESULT.
VT_I1	Indicates a **char** value.
VT_I2	Indicates a **short** integer.
VT_I4	Indicates a **long** integer.
VT_I8	Indicates a 64-bit integer.
VT_INT	Indicates an integer value.
VT_LPSTR	Indicates a a null reference (**Nothing** in Visual Basic) terminated string.
VT_LPWSTR	Indicates a wide string terminated by a null reference (**Nothing** in Visual Basic).

Member name	Description
VT_NULL	Indicates a a null reference (**Nothing** in Visual Basic) value, similar to a null value in SQL.
VT_PTR	Indicates a pointer type.
VT_R4	Indicates a **float** value.
VT_R8	Indicates a **double** value.
VT_RECORD	Indicates a user defined type.
VT_SAFEARRAY	Indicates a SAFEARRAY. Not valid in a VARIANT.
VT_STORAGE	Indicates that the name of a storage follows.
VT_STORED_OBJECT	Indicates that a storage contains an object.
VT_STREAM	Indicates that the name of a stream follows.
VT_STREAMED_-OBJECT	Indicates that a stream contains an object.
VT_UI1	Indicates a **byte**.
VT_UI2	Indicates an **unsigned short**.
VT_UI4	Indicates an **unsigned long**.
VT_UI8	Indicates an 64-bit unsigned integer.
VT_UINT	Indicates an **unsigned** integer value.
VT_UNKNOWN	Indicates an **IUnknown** pointer.
VT_USERDEFINED	Indicates a user defined type.
VT_VARIANT	Indicates a VARIANT **far** pointer.
VT_VECTOR	Indicates a simple, counted array.
VT_VOID	Indicates a C style **void**.

Requirements

Namespace: System.Runtime.InteropServices

Platforms: Windows 98, Windows NT 4.0, Windows Millennium Edition, Windows 2000, Windows XP Home Edition, Windows XP Professional, Windows .NET Server family

Assembly: Mscorlib (in Mscorlib.dll)

VARFLAGS Enumeration

Identifies the constants that define the properties of a variable.

This enumeration has a **FlagsAttribute** attribute that allows a bitwise combination of its member values.

```
[Visual Basic]
<Flags>
<Serializable>
<ComVisible(False)>
Public Enum VARFLAGS
[C#]
[Flags]
[Serializable]
[ComVisible(false)]
public enum VARFLAGS
[C++]
[Flags]
[Serializable]
[ComVisible(false)]
__value public enum VARFLAGS
[JScript]
public
   Flags
   Serializable
   ComVisible(false)
enum VARFLAGS
```

Remarks

For additional information about **VARFLAGS**, see the MSDN Library.

Members

Member name	Description	Value
VARFLAG_F-BINDABLE	The variable supports data binding.	4
VARFLAG_F-DEFAULTBIND	The variable is the single property that best represents the object. Only one variable in type information can have this attribute.	32
VARFLAG_F-DEFAULT-COLLELEM	Permits an optimization in which the compiler looks for a member named "xyz" on the type of "abc". If such a member is found and is flagged as an accessor function for an element of the default collection, then a call is generated to that member function. Permitted on members in dispinterfaces and interfaces; not permitted on modules.	256
VARFLAG_F-DISPLAYBIND	The variable is displayed to the user as bindable. **VARFLAG_FBINDABLE** must also be set.	16
VARFLAG_F-HIDDEN	The variable should not be displayed to the user in a browser, although it exists and is bindable.	64
VARFLAG_F-IMMEDIATE-BIND	The variable is mapped as individual bindable properties.	4096

Member name	Description	Value
VARFLAG_F-NON-BROWSABLE	The variable appears in an object browser, but not in a properties browser.	1024
VARFLAG_F-READONLY	Assignment to the variable should not be allowed.	1
VARFLAG_F-REPLACEABLE	Tags the interface as having default behaviors.	2048
VARFLAG_F-REQUESTEDIT	When set, any attempt to directly change the property results in a call to **IPropertyNotifySink::OnRequest Edit**. The implementation of **OnRequestEdit** determines if the change is accepted.	8
VARFLAG_F-RESTRICTED	The variable should not be accessible from macro languages. This flag is intended for system-level variables or variables that you do not want type browsers to display.	128
VARFLAG_F-SOURCE	The variable returns an object that is a source of events.	2
VARFLAG_F-UIDEFAULT	The variable is the default display in the user interface.	512

Requirements

Namespace: System.Runtime.InteropServices

Platforms: Windows 98, Windows NT 4.0, Windows Millennium Edition, Windows 2000, Windows XP Home Edition, Windows XP Professional, Windows .NET Server family

Assembly: Mscorlib (in Mscorlib.dll)

System.Runtime. InteropServices.Custom- Marshalers Namespace

This namespace supports the .NET Framework infrastructure and is not intended to be used directly from your code.

EnumerableToDispatch- Marshaler Class

This type supports the .NET Framework infrastructure and is not intended to be used directly from your code.

```
[Visual Basic]
Public Class EnumerableToDispatchMarshaler
   Implements ICustomMarshaler
[C#]
public class EnumerableToDispatchMarshaler : ICustomMarshaler
[C++]
public __gc class EnumerableToDispatchMarshaler : public
   ICustomMarshaler
[JScript]
public class EnumerableToDispatchMarshaler implements
   ICustomMarshaler
```

EnumerableToDispatchMarshaler.CleanUp-ManagedData Method

This member overrides **EnumerableToDispatchMarshaler. CleanUpManagedData**.

```
[Visual Basic]
Overrides Public Sub CleanUpManagedData( _
   ByVal pManagedObj As Object _
) Implements ICustomMarshaler.CleanUpManagedData
[C#]
public override void CleanUpManagedData(
   object pManagedObj
);
[C++]
public: void CleanUpManagedData(
   Object* pManagedObj
);
[JScript]
public override function CleanUpManagedData(
   pManagedObj : Object
);
```

Requirements

Platforms: Windows 98, Windows NT 4.0, Windows Millennium Edition, Windows 2000, Windows XP Home Edition, Windows XP Professional, Windows .NET Server family

.NET Framework Security:
- Full trust for the immediate caller. This member cannot be used by partially trusted code.

EnumerableToDispatchMarshaler. CleanUpNativeData Method

This member overrides **EnumerableToDispatchMarshaler. CleanUpNativeData**.

```
[Visual Basic]
Overrides Public Sub CleanUpNativeData( _
   ByVal pNativeData As IntPtr _
) Implements ICustomMarshaler.CleanUpNativeData
[C#]
public override void CleanUpNativeData(
   IntPtr pNativeData
);
[C++]
public: void CleanUpNativeData(
   IntPtr pNativeData
);
[JScript]
public override function CleanUpNativeData(
   pNativeData : IntPtr
);
```

Requirements

Platforms: Windows 98, Windows NT 4.0, Windows Millennium Edition, Windows 2000, Windows XP Home Edition, Windows XP Professional, Windows .NET Server family

.NET Framework Security:
- Full trust for the immediate caller. This member cannot be used by partially trusted code.

EnumerableToDispatchMarshaler.GetInstance Method

This member supports the .NET Framework infrastructure and is not intended to be used directly from your code.

```
[Visual Basic]
Public Shared Function GetInstance( _
   ByVal pstrCookie As String _
) As ICustomMarshaler
[C#]
public static ICustomMarshaler GetInstance(
   string pstrCookie
);
[C++]
public: static ICustomMarshaler* GetInstance(
   String* pstrCookie
);
[JScript]
public static function GetInstance(
   pstrCookie : String
) : ICustomMarshaler;
```

EnumerableToDispatchMarshaler.GetNative-DataSize Method

This member overrides **EnumerableToDispatchMarshaler. GetNativeDataSize**.

```
[Visual Basic]
Overrides Public Function GetNativeDataSize() As Integer Implements _
  ICustomMarshaler.GetNativeDataSize
[C#]
public override int GetNativeDataSize();
[C++]
public: int GetNativeDataSize();
[JScript]
public override function GetNativeDataSize() : int;
```

Requirements

Platforms: Windows 98, Windows NT 4.0, Windows Millennium Edition, Windows 2000, Windows XP Home Edition, Windows XP Professional, Windows .NET Server family

.NET Framework Security:
- Full trust for the immediate caller. This member cannot be used by partially trusted code.

EnumerableToDispatchMarshaler.Marshal-ManagedToNative Method

This member overrides **EnumerableToDispatchMarshaler. MarshalManagedToNative**.

```
[Visual Basic]
Overrides Public Function MarshalManagedToNative( _
  ByVal pManagedObj As Object _
) As IntPtr Implements ICustomMarshaler.MarshalManagedToNative
[C#]
public override IntPtr MarshalManagedToNative(
  object pManagedObj
);
[C++]
public: IntPtr MarshalManagedToNative(
  Object* pManagedObj
);
[JScript]
public override function MarshalManagedToNative(
  pManagedObj : Object
) : IntPtr;
```

Requirements

Platforms: Windows 98, Windows NT 4.0, Windows Millennium Edition, Windows 2000, Windows XP Home Edition, Windows XP Professional, Windows .NET Server family

.NET Framework Security:
- Full trust for the immediate caller. This member cannot be used by partially trusted code.

EnumerableToDispatchMarshaler.Marshal-NativeToManaged Method

This member overrides **EnumerableToDispatchMarshaler. MarshalNativeToManaged**.

```
[Visual Basic]
Overrides Public Function MarshalNativeToManaged( _
  ByVal pNativeData As IntPtr _
) As Object Implements ICustomMarshaler.MarshalNativeToManaged
[C#]
public override object MarshalNativeToManaged(
  IntPtr pNativeData
);
[C++]
public: Object* MarshalNativeToManaged(
  IntPtr pNativeData
);
[JScript]
public override function MarshalNativeToManaged(
  pNativeData : IntPtr
) : Object;
```

Requirements

Platforms: Windows 98, Windows NT 4.0, Windows Millennium Edition, Windows 2000, Windows XP Home Edition, Windows XP Professional, Windows .NET Server family

.NET Framework Security:
- Full trust for the immediate caller. This member cannot be used by partially trusted code.

EnumeratorToEnumVariant-
Marshaler Class

This type supports the .NET Framework infrastructure and is not intended to be used directly from your code.

```
[Visual Basic]
Public Class EnumeratorToEnumVariantMarshaler
   Implements ICustomMarshaler
[C#]
public class EnumeratorToEnumVariantMarshaler : ICustomMarshaler
[C++]
public __gc class EnumeratorToEnumVariantMarshaler : public
   ICustomMarshaler
[JScript]
public class EnumeratorToEnumVariantMarshaler implements
   ICustomMarshaler
```

EnumeratorToEnumVariantMarshaler.
CleanUpManagedData Method

This member overrides **EnumeratorToEnumVariantMarshaler. CleanUpManagedData**.

```
[Visual Basic]
Overrides Public Sub CleanUpManagedData( _
   ByVal pManagedObj As Object _
) Implements ICustomMarshaler.CleanUpManagedData
[C#]
public override void CleanUpManagedData(
   object pManagedObj
);
[C++]
public: void CleanUpManagedData(
   Object* pManagedObj
);
[JScript]
public override function CleanUpManagedData(
   pManagedObj : Object
);
```

Requirements

Platforms: Windows 98, Windows NT 4.0, Windows Millennium Edition, Windows 2000, Windows XP Home Edition, Windows XP Professional, Windows .NET Server family

.NET Framework Security:
- Full trust for the immediate caller. This member cannot be used by partially trusted code.

EnumeratorToEnumVariantMarshaler.CleanUp-
NativeData Method

This member overrides **EnumeratorToEnumVariantMarshaler. CleanUpNativeData**.

```
[Visual Basic]
Overrides Public Sub CleanUpNativeData( _
   ByVal pNativeData As IntPtr _
) Implements ICustomMarshaler.CleanUpNativeData
```

```
[C#]
public override void CleanUpNativeData(
   IntPtr pNativeData
);
[C++]
public: void CleanUpNativeData(
   IntPtr pNativeData
);
[JScript]
public override function CleanUpNativeData(
   pNativeData : IntPtr
);
```

Requirements

Platforms: Windows 98, Windows NT 4.0, Windows Millennium Edition, Windows 2000, Windows XP Home Edition, Windows XP Professional, Windows .NET Server family

.NET Framework Security:
- Full trust for the immediate caller. This member cannot be used by partially trusted code.

EnumeratorToEnumVariantMarshaler.Get-
Instance Method

This member supports the .NET Framework infrastructure and is not intended to be used directly from your code.

```
[Visual Basic]
Public Shared Function GetInstance( _
   ByVal pstrCookie As String _
) As ICustomMarshaler
[C#]
public static ICustomMarshaler GetInstance(
   string pstrCookie
);
[C++]
public: static ICustomMarshaler* GetInstance(
   String* pstrCookie
);
[JScript]
public static function GetInstance(
   pstrCookie : String
) : ICustomMarshaler;
```

EnumeratorToEnumVariantMarshaler.
GetNativeDataSize Method

This member overrides **EnumeratorToEnumVariantMarshaler. GetNativeDataSize**.

```
[Visual Basic]
Overrides Public Function GetNativeDataSize() As Integer Implements _
   ICustomMarshaler.GetNativeDataSize
[C#]
public override int GetNativeDataSize();
[C++]
public: int GetNativeDataSize();
[JScript]
public override function GetNativeDataSize() : int;
```

Requirements

Platforms: Windows 98, Windows NT 4.0,
Windows Millennium Edition, Windows 2000,
Windows XP Home Edition, Windows XP Professional,
Windows .NET Server family

.NET Framework Security:

- Full trust for the immediate caller. This member cannot be used
  by partially trusted code.

EnumeratorToEnumVariantMarshaler.Marshal-ManagedToNative Method

This member overrides **EnumeratorToEnumVariantMarshaler. MarshalManagedToNative**.

```
[Visual Basic]
Overrides Public Function MarshalManagedToNative( _
   ByVal pManagedObj As Object _
) As IntPtr Implements ICustomMarshaler.MarshalManagedToNative
[C#]
public override IntPtr MarshalManagedToNative(
   object pManagedObj
);
[C++]
public: IntPtr MarshalManagedToNative(
   Object* pManagedObj
);
[JScript]
public override function MarshalManagedToNative(
   pManagedObj : Object
) : IntPtr;
```

Requirements

Platforms: Windows 98, Windows NT 4.0,
Windows Millennium Edition, Windows 2000,
Windows XP Home Edition, Windows XP Professional,
Windows .NET Server family

.NET Framework Security:

- Full trust for the immediate caller. This member cannot be used
  by partially trusted code.

EnumeratorToEnumVariantMarshaler. MarshalNativeToManaged Method

This member overrides **EnumeratorToEnumVariantMarshaler. MarshalNativeToManaged**.

```
[Visual Basic]
Overrides Public Function MarshalNativeToManaged( _
   ByVal pNativeData As IntPtr _
) As Object Implements ICustomMarshaler.MarshalNativeToManaged
[C#]
public override object MarshalNativeToManaged(
   IntPtr pNativeData
);
[C++]
public: Object* MarshalNativeToManaged(
   IntPtr pNativeData
);
```

```
[JScript]
public override function MarshalNativeToManaged(
   pNativeData : IntPtr
) : Object;
```

Requirements

Platforms: Windows 98, Windows NT 4.0,
Windows Millennium Edition, Windows 2000,
Windows XP Home Edition, Windows XP Professional,
Windows .NET Server family

.NET Framework Security:

- Full trust for the immediate caller. This member cannot be used
  by partially trusted code.

ExpandoToDispatchEx-Marshaler Class

This type supports the .NET Framework infrastructure and is not intended to be used directly from your code.

```
[Visual Basic]
Public Class ExpandoToDispatchExMarshaler
    Implements ICustomMarshaler
[C#]
public class ExpandoToDispatchExMarshaler : ICustomMarshaler
[C++]
public __gc class ExpandoToDispatchExMarshaler : public
    ICustomMarshaler
[JScript]
public class ExpandoToDispatchExMarshaler implements
    ICustomMarshaler
```

ExpandoToDispatchExMarshaler.CleanUp-ManagedData Method

This member overrides **ExpandoToDispatchExMarshaler. CleanUpManagedData**.

```
[Visual Basic]
Overrides Public Sub CleanUpManagedData( _
    ByVal pManagedObj As Object _
) Implements ICustomMarshaler.CleanUpManagedData
[C#]
public override void CleanUpManagedData(
    object pManagedObj
);
[C++]
public: void CleanUpManagedData(
    Object* pManagedObj
);
[JScript]
public override function CleanUpManagedData(
    pManagedObj : Object
);
```

Requirements

Platforms: Windows 98, Windows NT 4.0, Windows Millennium Edition, Windows 2000, Windows XP Home Edition, Windows XP Professional, Windows .NET Server family

.NET Framework Security:
- Full trust for the immediate caller. This member cannot be used by partially trusted code.

ExpandoToDispatchExMarshaler. CleanUpNativeData Method

This member overrides **ExpandoToDispatchExMarshaler. CleanUpNativeData**.

```
[Visual Basic]
Overrides Public Sub CleanUpNativeData( _
    ByVal pNativeData As IntPtr _
) Implements ICustomMarshaler.CleanUpNativeData
```

```
[C#]
public override void CleanUpNativeData(
    IntPtr pNativeData
);
[C++]
public: void CleanUpNativeData(
    IntPtr pNativeData
);
[JScript]
public override function CleanUpNativeData(
    pNativeData : IntPtr
);
```

Requirements

Platforms: Windows 98, Windows NT 4.0, Windows Millennium Edition, Windows 2000, Windows XP Home Edition, Windows XP Professional, Windows .NET Server family

.NET Framework Security:
- Full trust for the immediate caller. This member cannot be used by partially trusted code.

ExpandoToDispatchExMarshaler.GetInstance Method

This member supports the .NET Framework infrastructure and is not intended to be used directly from your code.

```
[Visual Basic]
Public Shared Function GetInstance( _
    ByVal pstrCookie As String _
) As ICustomMarshaler
[C#]
public static ICustomMarshaler GetInstance(
    string pstrCookie
);
[C++]
public: static ICustomMarshaler* GetInstance(
    String* pstrCookie
);
[JScript]
public static function GetInstance(
    pstrCookie : String
) : ICustomMarshaler;
```

ExpandoToDispatchExMarshaler. GetNativeDataSize Method

This member overrides **ExpandoToDispatchExMarshaler. GetNativeDataSize**.

```
[Visual Basic]
Overrides Public Function GetNativeDataSize() As Integer Implements _
    ICustomMarshaler.GetNativeDataSize
[C#]
public override int GetNativeDataSize();
[C++]
public: int GetNativeDataSize();
[JScript]
public override function GetNativeDataSize() : int;
```

Requirements

Platforms: Windows 98, Windows NT 4.0, Windows Millennium Edition, Windows 2000, Windows XP Home Edition, Windows XP Professional, Windows .NET Server family

.NET Framework Security:

- Full trust for the immediate caller. This member cannot be used by partially trusted code.

ExpandoToDispatchExMarshaler.MarshalManagedToNative Method

This member overrides **ExpandoToDispatchExMarshaler. MarshalManagedToNative**.

```
[Visual Basic]
Overrides Public Function MarshalManagedToNative( _
   ByVal pManagedObj As Object _
) As IntPtr Implements ICustomMarshaler.MarshalManagedToNative
[C#]
public override IntPtr MarshalManagedToNative(
   object pManagedObj
);
[C++]
public: IntPtr MarshalManagedToNative(
   Object* pManagedObj
);
[JScript]
public override function MarshalManagedToNative(
   pManagedObj : Object
) : IntPtr;
```

Requirements

Platforms: Windows 98, Windows NT 4.0, Windows Millennium Edition, Windows 2000, Windows XP Home Edition, Windows XP Professional, Windows .NET Server family

.NET Framework Security:

- Full trust for the immediate caller. This member cannot be used by partially trusted code.

ExpandoToDispatchExMarshaler. MarshalNativeToManaged Method

This member overrides **ExpandoToDispatchExMarshaler. MarshalNativeToManaged**.

```
[Visual Basic]
Overrides Public Function MarshalNativeToManaged( _
   ByVal pNativeData As IntPtr _
) As Object Implements ICustomMarshaler.MarshalNativeToManaged
[C#]
public override object MarshalNativeToManaged(
   IntPtr pNativeData
);
[C++]
public: Object* MarshalNativeToManaged(
   IntPtr pNativeData
);
```

```
[JScript]
public override function MarshalNativeToManaged(
   pNativeData : IntPtr
) : Object;
```

Requirements

Platforms: Windows 98, Windows NT 4.0, Windows Millennium Edition, Windows 2000, Windows XP Home Edition, Windows XP Professional, Windows .NET Server family

.NET Framework Security:

- Full trust for the immediate caller. This member cannot be used by partially trusted code.

TypeToTypeInfoMarshaler Class

This type supports the .NET Framework infrastructure and is not intended to be used directly from your code.

```
[Visual Basic]
Public Class TypeToTypeInfoMarshaler
    Implements ICustomMarshaler
[C#]
public class TypeToTypeInfoMarshaler : ICustomMarshaler
[C++]
public __gc class TypeToTypeInfoMarshaler : public ICustomMarshaler
[JScript]
public class TypeToTypeInfoMarshaler implements ICustomMarshaler
```

TypeToTypeInfoMarshaler.CleanUpManagedData Method

This member overrides **TypeToTypeInfoMarshaler. CleanUpManagedData**.

```
[Visual Basic]
Overrides Public Sub CleanUpManagedData( _
    ByVal pManagedObj As Object _
) Implements ICustomMarshaler.CleanUpManagedData
[C#]
public override void CleanUpManagedData(
    object pManagedObj
);
[C++]
public: void CleanUpManagedData(
    Object* pManagedObj
);
[JScript]
public override function CleanUpManagedData(
    pManagedObj : Object
);
```

Requirements

Platforms: Windows 98, Windows NT 4.0, Windows Millennium Edition, Windows 2000, Windows XP Home Edition, Windows XP Professional, Windows .NET Server family

.NET Framework Security:
- Full trust for the immediate caller. This member cannot be used by partially trusted code.

TypeToTypeInfoMarshaler.CleanUpNativeData Method

This member overrides **TypeToTypeInfoMarshaler. CleanUpNativeData**.

```
[Visual Basic]
Overrides Public Sub CleanUpNativeData( _
    ByVal pNativeData As IntPtr _
) Implements ICustomMarshaler.CleanUpNativeData
```

```
[C#]
public override void CleanUpNativeData(
    IntPtr pNativeData
);
[C++]
public: void CleanUpNativeData(
    IntPtr pNativeData
);
[JScript]
public override function CleanUpNativeData(
    pNativeData : IntPtr
);
```

Requirements

Platforms: Windows 98, Windows NT 4.0, Windows Millennium Edition, Windows 2000, Windows XP Home Edition, Windows XP Professional, Windows .NET Server family

.NET Framework Security:
- Full trust for the immediate caller. This member cannot be used by partially trusted code.

TypeToTypeInfoMarshaler.GetInstance Method

This member supports the .NET Framework infrastructure and is not intended to be used directly from your code.

```
[Visual Basic]
Public Shared Function GetInstance( _
    ByVal pstrCookie As String _
) As ICustomMarshaler
[C#]
public static ICustomMarshaler GetInstance(
    string pstrCookie
);
[C++]
public: static ICustomMarshaler* GetInstance(
    String* pstrCookie
);
[JScript]
public static function GetInstance(
    pstrCookie : String
) : ICustomMarshaler;
```

TypeToTypeInfoMarshaler.GetNativeDataSize Method

This member overrides **TypeToTypeInfoMarshaler. GetNativeDataSize**.

```
[Visual Basic]
Overrides Public Function GetNativeDataSize() As Integer Implements _
    ICustomMarshaler.GetNativeDataSize
[C#]
public override int GetNativeDataSize();
[C++]
public: int GetNativeDataSize();
[JScript]
public override function GetNativeDataSize() : int;
```

Requirements

Platforms: Windows 98, Windows NT 4.0,
Windows Millennium Edition, Windows 2000,
Windows XP Home Edition, Windows XP Professional,
Windows .NET Server family

.NET Framework Security:

- Full trust for the immediate caller. This member cannot be used by partially trusted code.

TypeToTypeInfoMarshaler.MarshalManagedTo-Native Method

This member overrides **TypeToTypeInfoMarshaler.
MarshalManagedToNative**.

```
[Visual Basic]
Overrides Public Function MarshalManagedToNative( _
   ByVal pManagedObj As Object _
) As IntPtr Implements ICustomMarshaler.MarshalManagedToNative
[C#]
public override IntPtr MarshalManagedToNative(
   object pManagedObj
);
[C++]
public: IntPtr MarshalManagedToNative(
   Object* pManagedObj
);
[JScript]
public override function MarshalManagedToNative(
   pManagedObj : Object
) : IntPtr;
```

Requirements

Platforms: Windows 98, Windows NT 4.0,
Windows Millennium Edition, Windows 2000,
Windows XP Home Edition, Windows XP Professional,
Windows .NET Server family

.NET Framework Security:

- Full trust for the immediate caller. This member cannot be used by partially trusted code.

TypeToTypeInfoMarshaler.MarshalNativeTo-Managed Method

This member overrides **TypeToTypeInfoMarshaler.
MarshalNativeToManaged**.

```
[Visual Basic]
Overrides Public Function MarshalNativeToManaged( _
   ByVal pNativeData As IntPtr _
) As Object Implements ICustomMarshaler.MarshalNativeToManaged
[C#]
public override object MarshalNativeToManaged(
   IntPtr pNativeData
);
[C++]
public: Object* MarshalNativeToManaged(
   IntPtr pNativeData
);
```

```
[JScript]
public override function MarshalNativeToManaged(
   pNativeData : IntPtr
) : Object;
```

Requirements

Platforms: Windows 98, Windows NT 4.0,
Windows Millennium Edition, Windows 2000,
Windows XP Home Edition, Windows XP Professional,
Windows .NET Server family

.NET Framework Security:

- Full trust for the immediate caller. This member cannot be used by partially trusted code.

System.Runtime.Interop-Services.Expando Namespace

The **System.Runtime.InteropServices.Expando** namespace contains the **IExpando** interface which allows modification of an object by adding or removing its members.

IExpando Interface

Enables modification of objects by adding and removing members, represented by **MemberInfo** objects.

System.Reflection.IReflect
  System.Runtime.InteropServices.Expando.IExpando

```
[Visual Basic]
<Guid("AFBF15E6-C37C-11d2-B88E-00A0C9B471B8")>
Public Interface IExpando
    Inherits IReflect
[C#]
[Guid("AFBF15E6-C37C-11d2-B88E-00A0C9B471B8")]
public interface IExpando : IReflect
[C++]
[Guid("AFBF15E6-C37C-11d2-B88E-00A0C9B471B8")]
public __gc __interface IExpando : public IReflect
[JScript]
public
    Guid("AFBF15E6-C37C-11d2-B88E-00A0C9B471B8")
interface IExpando implements IReflect
```

Requirements

Namespace: System.Runtime.InteropServices.Expando

Platforms: Windows 98, Windows NT 4.0, Windows Millennium Edition, Windows 2000, Windows XP Home Edition, Windows XP Professional, Windows .NET Server family

Assembly: Mscorlib (in Mscorlib.dll)

IExpando.AddField Method

Adds the named field to the Reflection object.
```
[Visual Basic]
Function AddField( _
    ByVal name As String _
) As FieldInfo
[C#]
FieldInfo AddField(
    string name
);
[C++]
FieldInfo* AddField(
    String* name
);
```

```
[JScript]
function AddField(
    name : String
) : FieldInfo;
```

Parameters

name
    The name of the field.

Return Value

A **FieldInfo** object representing the added field.

Exceptions

Exception Type	Condition
NotSupportedException	The **IExpando** object does not support this method.

Requirements

Platforms: Windows 98, Windows NT 4.0, Windows Millennium Edition, Windows 2000, Windows XP Home Edition, Windows XP Professional, Windows .NET Server family

IExpando.AddMethod Method

Adds the named method to the Reflection object.
```
[Visual Basic]
Function AddMethod( _
    ByVal name As String, _
    ByVal method As Delegate _
) As MethodInfo
[C#]
MethodInfo AddMethod(
    string name,
    Delegate method
);
[C++]
MethodInfo* AddMethod(
    String* name,
    Delegate* method
);
[JScript]
function AddMethod(
    name : String,
    method : Delegate
) : MethodInfo;
```

Parameters

name
    The name of the method.
method
    The delegate to the method.

Return Value

A **MethodInfo** object representing the added method.

Exceptions

Exception Type	Condition
NotSupportedException	The **IExpando** object does not support this method.

Requirements

Platforms: Windows 98, Windows NT 4.0,
Windows Millennium Edition, Windows 2000,
Windows XP Home Edition, Windows XP Professional,
Windows .NET Server family

IExpando.AddProperty Method

Adds the named property to the Reflection object.

```
[Visual Basic]
Function AddProperty( _
    ByVal name As String _
) As PropertyInfo
[C#]
PropertyInfo AddProperty(
    string name
);
[C++]
PropertyInfo* AddProperty(
    String* name
);
[JScript]
function AddProperty(
    name : String
) : PropertyInfo;
```

Parameters

name
    The name of the property.

Return Value

A **PropertyInfo** object representing the added property.

Exceptions

Exception Type	Condition
NotSupportedException	The **IExpando** object does not support this method.

Requirements

Platforms: Windows 98, Windows NT 4.0,
Windows Millennium Edition, Windows 2000,
Windows XP Home Edition, Windows XP Professional,
Windows .NET Server family

IExpando.RemoveMember Method

Removes the specified member.

```
[Visual Basic]
Sub RemoveMember( _
    ByVal m As MemberInfo _
)
[C#]
void RemoveMember(
    MemberInfo m
);
[C++]
void RemoveMember(
    MemberInfo* m
);
```

```
[JScript]
function RemoveMember(
    m : MemberInfo
);
```

Parameters

m
    The member to remove.

Exceptions

Exception Type	Condition
NotSupportedException	The **IExpando** object does not support this method.

Requirements

Platforms: Windows 98, Windows NT 4.0,
Windows Millennium Edition, Windows 2000,
Windows XP Home Edition, Windows XP Professional,
Windows .NET Server family